THE EUROPA
WORLD
YEAR BOOK
2004

THE EUROPA WORLD YEAR BOOK 2004

VOLUME II

KAZAKHSTAN–ZIMBABWE

Europa Publications
Taylor & Francis Group

LONDON AND NEW YORK

First published 1926

© Europa Publications 2004
11 New Fetter Lane, London, EC4P 4EE, England
(A member of the Taylor & Francis Group)

ISBN 1-85743-253-3 (The Set)
1-85743-255-X (Vol. II)
ISSN 0071-2302
Library of Congress Catalog Card Number 59-2942

Typeset in New Century Schoolbook

Typeset by Unwin Brothers Limited, The Gresham Press, Old Woking, Surrey

Printed and bound by William Clowes Limited, Beccles, Suffolk

FOREWORD

THE EUROPA WORLD YEAR BOOK (formerly THE EUROPA YEAR BOOK: A WORLD SURVEY) was first published in 1926. Since 1960 it has appeared in annual two-volume editions, and has become established as an authoritative reference work, providing a wealth of detailed information on the political, economic and commercial institutions of the world.

Volume I contains a comprehensive listing of more than 1,650 international organizations and the first part of the alphabetical survey of countries of the world, from Afghanistan to Jordan. Volume II contains countries from Kazakhstan to Zimbabwe. An Index of Territories covered in both volumes can be found at the end of Volume II.

Each country is covered by an individual chapter, containing: an introductory survey including recent history, economic affairs, government, defence, education, and public holidays; an economic and demographic survey using the latest available statistics on area and population, health and welfare, agriculture, forestry, fishing, industry, finance, trade, transport, tourism, the media, and education; and a directory section containing names, addresses and other useful facts about government, political parties, diplomatic representation, judiciary, religious groups, the media, telecommunications, banks, insurance, trade and industry, development organizations, chambers of commerce, industrial and trade associations, utilities, trade unions, transport and tourism.

The entire content of the print edition of THE EUROPA WORLD YEAR BOOK is now available online as EUROPA WORLD, incorporating sophisticated search and browse functions as well as specially commissioned visual and statistical content. An ongoing programme of updates of key areas of information ensures currency of content, and enhances the richness of the information for which THE EUROPA WORLD YEAR BOOK is renowned. This prestigious resource is available at www.europaworld.com.

Readers are referred to our annual regional surveys, AFRICA SOUTH OF THE SAHARA, CENTRAL AND SOUTH-EASTERN EUROPE, EASTERN EUROPE, RUSSIA AND CENTRAL ASIA, THE FAR EAST AND AUSTRALASIA, THE MIDDLE EAST AND NORTH AFRICA, SOUTH AMERICA, CENTRAL AMERICA AND THE CARIBBEAN, SOUTH ASIA, THE USA AND CANADA and WESTERN EUROPE, for additional analysis of the geography, history and economy of these areas. More detailed coverage of international organizations may be found in THE EUROPA DIRECTORY OF INTERNATIONAL ORGANIZATIONS.

The information is extensively revised and updated annually by a variety of methods, including direct mailing to all the institutions listed. Many other sources are used, such as national statistical offices, government departments and diplomatic missions. The editors thank the innumerable individuals and organizations throughout the world whose generous co-operation in providing current information for this edition is invaluable in presenting the most accurate and up-to-date material available.

May 2004.

ACKNOWLEDGEMENTS

The editors gratefully acknowledge particular indebtedness for permission to reproduce material from the following publications: the United Nations' *Demographic Yearbook, Statistical Yearbook, Monthly Bulletin of Statistics, Industrial Commodity Statistics Yearbook* and *International Trade Statistics Yearbook*; the United Nations Educational, Scientific and Cultural Organization's *Statistical Yearbook*; the Food and Agriculture Organization of the United Nations' Statistical Database and *Yearbook of Fishery Statistics*; the International Labour Office's Statistical Database and *Yearbook of Labour Statistics*; the World Bank's *World Bank Atlas, Global Development Finance, World Development Report* and *World Development Indicators*; the International Monetary Fund's Statistical Database and *International Financial Statistics* and *Government Finance Statistics Yearbook*; the World Tourism Organization's *Yearbook of Tourism Statistics*; and *The Military Balance 2003–2004*, a publication of the International Institute for Strategic Studies, Arundel House, 13–15 Arundel Street, London WC2R 3DX.

HEALTH AND WELFARE STATISTICS: SOURCES AND DEFINITIONS

Total fertility rate Source: WHO, *The World Health Report* (2003). The number of children that would be born per woman, assuming no female mortality at child-bearing ages and the age-specific fertility rates of a specified country and reference period.

Under-5 mortality rate Source: UNICEF, *The State of the World's Children* (2003). The ratio of registered deaths of children under 5 years to the total number of registered live births over the same period.

HIV/AIDS Source: UNAIDS. Estimated percentage of adults aged 15 to 49 years living with HIV/AIDS. < indicates 'fewer than'.

Health expenditure Source: WHO, *The World Health Report* (2003).
US $ per head (PPP)
International dollar estimates, derived by dividing local currency units by an estimate of their purchasing-power parity (PPP) compared with the US dollar. PPPs are the rates of currency conversion that equalize the purchasing power of different currencies by eliminating the differences in price levels between countries.
% of GDP
GDP levels for OECD countries follow the most recent UN System of National Accounts. For non-OECD countries a value was estimated by utilizing existing UN, IMF and World Bank data.
Public expenditure
Government health-related outlays plus expenditure by social schemes compulsorily affiliated with a sizeable share of the population, and extrabudgetary funds allocated to health services. Figures include grants or loans provided by international agencies, other national authorities, and sometimes commercial banks.

Access to water and sanitation Source: WHO, *Global Water Supply and Sanitation Assessment* (2000 Report). Defined in terms of the type of technology and levels of service afforded. For water, this includes house connections, public standpipes, boreholes with handpumps, protected dug wells, protected spring and rainwater collection; allowance is also made for other locally defined technologies. 'Access' is broadly defined as the availability of at least 20 litres per person per day from a source within 1 km of the user's dwelling. Sanitation is defined to include connection to a sewer or septic tank system, pour-flush latrine, simple pit or ventilated improved pit latrine, again with allowance for acceptable local technologies. Access to water and sanitation does not imply that the level of service or quality of water is 'adequate' or 'safe'.

Human Development Index (HDI) Source: UNDP, *Human Development Report* (2003). A summary of human development measured by three basic dimensions: prospects for a long and healthy life, measured by life expectancy at birth; knowledge, measured by adult literacy rate (two-thirds' weight) and the combined gross enrolment ratio in primary, secondary and tertiary education (one-third weight); and standard of living, measured by GDP per head (PPP US $). The index value obtained lies between zero and one. A value above 0.8 indicates high human development, between 0.5 and 0.8 medium human development, and below 0.5 low human development. A centralized data source for all three dimensions was not available for all countries. In some such cases other data sources were used to calculate a substitute value; however, this was excluded from the ranking. Other countries, including non-UNDP members, were excluded from the HDI altogether. In total, 175 countries were ranked for 2001.

CONTENTS

CONTENTS

ABBREVIATIONS

AB	Aktiebolag (Joint-Stock Company); Alberta
Abog.	Abogado (Lawyer)
Acad.	Academician; Academy
ACP	African, Caribbean and Pacific (countries)
ACT	Australian Capital Territory
AD	anno Domini
ADB	African Development Bank; Asian Development Bank
ADC	aide-de-camp
Adm.	Admiral
admin.	administration
AfDB	African Development Bank
AG	Aktiengesellschaft (Joint-Stock Company)
AH	anno Hegirae
a.i.	ad interim
AID	(US) Agency for International Development
AIDS	acquired immunodeficiency syndrome
AK	Alaska
Al.	Aleja (Alley, Avenue)
AL	Alabama
ALADI	Asociación Latinoamericana de Integración
Alt.	Alternate
AM	Amplitude Modulation
a.m.	ante meridiem (before noon)
amalg.	amalgamated
Apdo	Apartado (Post Box)
APEC	Asia-Pacific Economic Co-operation
approx.	approximately
Apt	Apartment
AR	Arkansas
AŞ	Anonim Şrketi (Joint-Stock Company)
A/S	Aktieselskab (Joint-Stock Company)
ASEAN	Association of South East Asian Nations
asscn	association
assoc.	associate
ASSR	Autonomous Soviet Socialist Republic
asst	assistant
AU	African Union
Aug.	August
auth.	authorized
av., Ave	Avenue
Avda	Avenida (Avenue)
Avv.	Avvocato (Lawyer)
AZ	Arizona
BC	British Columbia
BC	before Christ
Bd	Board
Bd, Bld, Blv., Blvd	Boulevard
b/d	barrels per day
BFPO	British Forces' Post Office
Bhd	Berhad (Public Limited Company)
Bldg	Building
blk	block
Blvr	Bulevar
BP	Boîte postale (Post Box)
br.(s)	branch(es)
Brig.	Brigadier
BSE	Bovine spongiform encephalopathy
BSEC	(Organization of) Black Sea Economic Co-operation
bte	boîte (box)
BTN	Brussels Tariff Nomenclature
Bul.	Bulvar (boulevard)
bulv.	bulvaris (boulevard)
C	Centigrade
c.	circa; cuadra(s) (block(s))
CA	California
CACM	Central American Common Market
Cad.	Caddesi (Street)
CAP	Common Agricultural Policy
cap.	capital
Capt.	Captain
CARICOM	Caribbean Community and Common Market
CBSS	Council of Baltic Sea States
CCL	Caribbean Congress of Labour
Cdre	Commodore
CEMAC	Communauté économique et monétaire de l'Afrique centrale
Cen.	Central
CEO	Chief Executive Officer
CFA	Communauté Financière Africaine; Coopération Financière en Afrique centrale
CFP	Common Fisheries Policy; Communauté française du Pacifique; Comptoirs français du Pacifique
Chair.	Chairman/person/woman
Chih.	Chihuahua
CI	Channel Islands
Cia	Companhia
Cía	Compañía
Cie	Compagnie
c.i.f.	cost, insurance and freight
C-in-C	Commander-in-Chief
circ.	circulation
CIS	Commonwealth of Independent States
CJD	Creutzfeldt-Jakob disease
cm	centimetre(s)
cnr	corner
CO	Colorado
Co	Company; County
c/o	care of
Coah.	Coahuila
Col	Colonel
Col.	Colima; Colonia
COMESA	Common Market for Eastern and Southern Africa
Comm.	Commission; Commendatore
Commdr	Commander
Commdt	Commandant
Commr	Commissioner
Cond.	Condiminio
Confed.	Confederation
Cont.	Contador (Accountant)
COO	Chief Operating Officer
Corp.	Corporate
Corpn	Corporation
CP	Case Postale, Caixa Postal, Casella Postale (Post Box); Communist Party
CPSU	Communist Party of the Soviet Union
Cres.	Crescent
CSCE	Conference on Security and Co-operation in Europe
CSTAL	Confederación Sindical de los Trabajadores de América Latina
CT	Connecticut
CTCA	Confederación de Trabajadores Centro-americanos
Cttee	Committee
cu	cubic
cwt	hundredweight
DC	District of Columbia; Distrito Capital; Distrito Central
DE	Departamento Estatal; Delaware
Dec.	December
Del.	Delegación
Dem.	Democratic; Democrat
Dep.	Deputy
dep.	deposits
Dept	Department
devt	development
DF	Distrito Federal
Dgo	Durango
Diag.	Diagonal
Dir	Director
Div.	Division(al)
DM	Deutsche Mark
DMZ	demilitarized zone
DN	Distrito Nacional
Doc.	Docent
Dott.	Dottore/essa
Dr	Doctor
Dr.	Drive
Dra	Doctora
Dr Hab.	Doktor Habilitowany (Assistant Professor)
dr.(e)	drachma(e)
Drs	Doctorandus
DU	depleted uranium
dwt	dead weight tons
E	East; Eastern
EBRD	European Bank for Reconstruction and Development
EC	European Community
ECA	(United Nations) Economic Commission for Africa
ECE	(United Nations) Economic Commission for Europe
ECLAC	(United Nations) Economic Commission for Latin America and the Caribbean
ECO	Economic Co-operation Organization
Econ.	Economist; Economics
ECOSOC	(United Nations) Economic and Social Council
ECOWAS	Economic Community of West African States
ECU	European Currency Unit
Edif.	Edificio (Building)
edn	edition
EEA	European Economic Area
EFTA	European Free Trade Association
e.g.	exempli gratia (for example)
EIB	European Investment Bank
eKv	electron kilovolt
EMS	European Monetary System
EMU	economic and monetary union
eMv	electron megavolt
Eng.	Engineer; Engineering
EP	Empresa Pública
ERM	exchange rate mechanism
ESACA	Emisora de Capital Abierto Sociedad Anónima
Esc.	Escuela; Escudos; Escritorio
ESCAP	(United Nations) Economic and Social Commission for Asia and the Pacific
ESCWA	(United Nations) Economic and Social Commission for Western Asia
esq.	esquina (corner)
est.	established; estimate; estimated
etc.	et cetera
EU	European Union
eV	eingetragener Verein

excl.	excluding
exec.	executive
Ext.	Extension
F	Fahrenheit
f.	founded
FAO	Food and Agriculture Organization
f.a.s.	free alongside ship
Feb.	February
Fed.	Federation; Federal
FL	Florida
FM	frequency modulation
fmr(ly)	former(ly)
f.o.b.	free on board
Fr	Father
Fr.	Franc
Fri.	Friday
FRY	Federal Republic of Yugoslavia
ft	foot (feet)
FYRM	former Yugoslav republic of Macedonia
g	gram(s)
GA	Georgia
GATT	General Agreement on Tariffs and Trade
GCC	Gulf Co-operation Council
Gdns	Gardens
GDP	gross domestic product
Gen.	General
GeV	giga electron volts
GM	genetically modified
GmbH	Gesellschaft mit beschränkter Haftung (Limited Liability Company)
GMT	Greenwich Mean Time
GNI	gross national income
GNP	gross national product
Gov.	Governor
Govt	Government
Gro	Guerrero
grt	gross registered tons
Gto	Guanajuato
GWh	gigawatt hours
ha	hectares
HE	His/Her Eminence; His/Her Excellency
hf	hlutafelag (Limited Company)
HI	Hawaii
HIPC	heavily indebted poor country
HIV	human immunodeficiency virus
hl	hectolitre(s)
HM	His/Her Majesty
Hon.	Honorary, Honourable
hp	horsepower
HQ	Headquarters
HRH	His/Her Royal Highness
HSH	His/Her Serene Highness
IA	Iowa
IBRD	International Bank for Reconstruction and Development (World Bank)
ICC	International Chamber of Commerce; International Criminal Court
ICFTU	International Confederation of Free Trade Unions
ICRC	International Committee of the Red Cross
ICTR	International Criminal Tribunal for Rwanda
ICTY	International Criminal Tribunal for the former Yugoslavia
ID	Idaho
IDA	International Development Association
IDB	Inter-American Development Bank
IDPs	Internally Displaced Persons
i.e.	id est (that is to say)

IFC	International Finance Corporation
IGAD	Intergovernmental Authority on Development
IL	Illinois
ILO	International Labour Organization/Office
IMF	International Monetary Fund
in (ins)	inch (inches)
IN	Indiana
Inc, Incorp.	
Incd	Incorporated
incl.	including
Ind.	Independent
INF	Intermediate-Range Nuclear Forces
Ing.	Engineer
Insp.	Inspector
Int.	International
Inzå.	Engineer
IPU	Inter-Parliamentary Union
Ir	Engineer
IRF	International Road Federation
irreg.	irregular
Is	Islands
ISIC	International Standard Industrial Classification
IT	information technology
ITU	International Telecommunication Union
Iur.	Lawyer
Jal.	Jalisco
Jan.	January
Jnr	Junior
Jr	Jonkheer (Esquire); Junior
Jt	Joint
kg	kilogram(s)
KG	Kommandit Gesellschaft (Limited Partnership)
kHz	kilohertz
KK	Kaien Kaisha (Limited Company)
km	kilometre(s)
kom.	komnata (room)
kor.	korpus (block)
KS	Kansas
kv.	kvartal (apartment block); kvartira (apartment)
kW	kilowatt(s)
kWh	kilowatt hours
KY	Kentucky
LA	Louisiana
lauk	laukums (square)
lb	pound(s)
LDCs	Least Developed Countries
Lic.	Licenciado
Licda	Licenciada
LNG	liquefied natural gas
LPG	liquefied petroleum gas
Lt, Lieut	Lieutenant
Ltd	Limited
m	metre(s)
m.	million
MA	Massachusetts
Maj.	Major
Man.	Manager; managing
MB	Manitoba
mbH	mit beschränkter Haftung (with limited liability)
MD	Maryland
ME	Maine
Me	Maître
mem.(s)	member(s)
MEP	Member of the European Parliament
Mercosul	Mercado Comum do Sul (Southern Common Market)
Mercosur	Mercado Común del Sur (Southern Common Market)

Méx.	México
MFN	most favoured nation
mfrs	manufacturers
Mgr	Monseigneur; Monsignor
MHz	megahertz
MI	Michigan
MIA	missing in action
Mich.	Michoacán
MIGA	Multilateral Investment Guarantee Agency
Mil.	Military
Mlle	Mademoiselle
mm	millimetre(s)
Mme	Madame
MN	Minnesota
MO	Missouri
Mon.	Monday
Mor.	Morelos
MOU	memorandum of understanding
MP	Member of Parliament
MS	Mississippi
MSS	Manuscripts
MT	Montana
MW	megawatt(s); medium wave
MWh	megawatt hour(s)
N	North; Northern
n.a.	not available
nab.	naberezhnaya (embankment, quai)
NAFTA	North American Free Trade Agreement
nám.	náměstí (square)
Nat.	National
NATO	North Atlantic Treaty Organization
Nay.	Nayarit
NB	New Brunswick
NC	North Carolina
NCO	non-commissioned officer
ND	North Dakota
NE	Nebraska; North-East
NEPAD	New Partnership for Africa's Development
NF	Newfoundland
NGO	non-governmental organization
NH	New Hampshire
NJ	New Jersey
NL	Nuevo León
NM	New Mexico
NMP	net material product
no	numéro, número (number)
no.	number
Nov.	November
nr	near
nrt	net registered tons
NS	Nova Scotia
NSW	New South Wales
NV	Naamloze Vennootschap (Limited Company); Nevada
NW	North-West
NY	New York
NZ	New Zealand
OAPEC	Organization of Arab Petroleum Exporting Countries
OAS	Organization of American States
OAU	Organization of African Unity
Oax.	Oaxaca
Oct.	October
OECD	Organisation for Economic Co-operation and Development
OECS	Organisation of Eastern Caribbean States
Of.	Oficina (Office)
OH	Ohio
OIC	Organization of the Islamic Conference
OK	Oklahoma
ON	Ontario
OPEC	Organization of the Petroleum Exporting Countries
opp.	opposite

ABBREVIATIONS

OR	Oregon
Org.	Organization
ORIT	Organización Regional Interamericana de Trabajadores
OSCE	Organization for Security and Co-operation in Europe
p.	page
p.a.	per annum
PA	Palestinian Authority; Pennsylvania
Parl.	Parliament(ary)
per.	pereulok (lane, alley)
PE	Prince Edward Island
Perm. Rep.	Permanent Representative
PF	Postfach (Post Box)
PK	Post Box (Turkish)
Pl.	Plac, Plads (square)
pl.	platz; place; ploshchad (square)
PLC	Public Limited Company
PLO	Palestine Liberation Organization
p.m.	post meridiem (after noon)
PMB	Private Mail Bag
PNA	Palestinian National Authority
POB	Post Office Box
pp.	pages
PPP	purchasing-power parity
PQ	Québec
PR	Puerto Rico
pr.	prospekt (avenue)
Pres.	President
PRGF	Poverty Reduction and Growth Facility
Prin.	Principal
Prof.	Professor
Propr	Proprietor
Prov.	Province; Provincial; Provinciale (Dutch)
prov.	provulok (lane)
PT	Perseroan Terbatas (Limited Company)
Pte	Private; Puente (Bridge)
Pty	Proprietary
p.u.	paid up
publ.	publication; published
Publr	Publisher
Pue.	Puebla
Pvt.	Private
QC	Québec
QIP	Quick Impact Project
Qld	Queensland
Qro	Querétaro
Q. Roo	Quintana Roo
q.v.	quod vide (to which refer)
Rag.	Ragioniere (Accountant)
Rd	Road
R(s)	rand; rupee(s)
reg., regd	register; registered
reorg.	reorganized
Rep.	Republic; Republican; Representative
Repub.	Republic
res	reserve(s)
retd	retired
Rev.	Reverend
RI	Rhode Island
RJ	Rio de Janeiro
Rm	Room
RN	Royal Navy
ro-ro	roll-on roll-off
RP	Recette principale
Rp.(s)	rupiah(s)
RSFSR	Russian Soviet Federative Socialist Republic
Rt	Right
S	South; Southern; San
SA	Société Anonyme, Sociedad Anónima (Limited Company); South Australia
SAARC	South Asian Association for Regional Co-operation
SAECA	Sociedad Anónima Emisora de Capital Abierto
SADC	Southern African Development Community
SAR	Special Administrative Region
SARL	Sociedade Anônima de Responsabilidade Limitada (Joint-Stock Company of Limited Liability)
SARS	Severe Acute Respiratory Syndrome
Sat.	Saturday
SC	South Carolina
SD	South Dakota
Sdn Bhd	Sendirian Berhad (Private Limited Company)
SDR(s)	Special Drawing Right(s)
SE	South-East
Sec.	Secretary
Secr.	Secretariat
Sen.	Senior; Senator
Sept.	September
SER	Sua Eccellenza Reverendissima (His Eminence)
SFRY	Socialist Federal Republic of Yugoslavia
Sin.	Sinaloa
SITC	Standard International Trade Classification
SJ	Society of Jesus
SK	Saskatchewan
SLP	San Luis Potosí
SMEs	small and medium-sized enterprises
s/n	sin número (without number)
Soc.	Society
Sok.	Sokak (Street)
Son.	Sonora
Şos.	Şosea (Road)
SP	São Paulo
SpA	Società per Azioni (Joint-Stock Company)
Sq.	Square
sq	square (in measurements)
Sr	Senior; Señor
Sra	Señora
Srl	Società a Responsabilità Limitata (Limited Company)
SSR	Soviet Socialist Republic
St	Saint, Sint; Street
Sta	Santa
Ste	Sainte
str.	strada, stradă (street)
str-la	stradelă (street)
subs.	subscriptions; subscribed
Sun.	Sunday
Supt	Superintendent
sv.	Saint
SW	South-West
Tab.	Tabasco
Tamps	Tamaulipas
TAŞ	Turkiye Anonim Şirketi (Turkish Joint-Stock Company)
Tas	Tasmania
TD	Teachta Dàla (Member of Parliament)
tech., techn.	technical
tel.	telephone
TEU	20-ft equivalent unit
Thur.	Thursday
TN	Tennessee
Treas.	Treasurer
Tue.	Tuesday
TV	television
TX	Texas
u.	utca (street)
u/a	unit of account
UAE	United Arab Emirates
UEE	Unidade Económica Estatal
UEMOA	Union économique et monetaire ouest-africaine
UK	United Kingdom
ul.	ulica, ulitsa (street)
UM	ouguiya
UN	United Nations
UNAIDS	United Nations Joint Programme on HIV/AIDS
UNCTAD	United Nations Conference on Trade and Development
UNDP	United Nations Development Programme
UNEP	United Nations Environment Programme
UNESCO	United Nations Educational, Scientific and Cultural Organization
UNHCHR	UN High Commissioner for Human Rights
UNHCR	United Nations High Commissioner for Refugees
UNICEF	United Nations Children's Fund
Univ.	University
UNODC	United Nations Office on Drugs and Crime
UNRWA	United Nations Relief and Works Agency for Palestine Refugees in the Near East
Urb.	Urbanización (District)
USA	United States of America
USAID	United States Agency for International Development
USSR	Union of Soviet Socialist Republics
UT	Utah
VA	Virginia
VAT	value-added tax
VEB	Volkseigener Betrieb (Public Company)
v-CJD	variant Creutzfeldt-Jakob disease
Ven.	Venerable
Ver.	Veracruz
VHF	Very High Frequency
VI	(US) Virgin Islands
Vic	Victoria
Vn	Veien (Street)
vol.(s)	volume(s)
VT	Vermont
vul.	vulitsa, vulytsa (street)
W	West; Western
WA	Western Australia; Washington (State)
WCL	World Confederation of Labour
Wed.	Wednesday
WEU	Western European Union
WFP	World Food Programme
WFTU	World Federation of Trade Unions
WHO	World Health Organization
WI	Wisconsin
WSSD	World Summit on Sustainable Development
WTO	World Tourism Organization; World Trade Organization
WV	West Virginia
WY	Wyoming
yr	year
YT	Yukon Territory
Yuc.	Yucatán

INTERNATIONAL TELEPHONE CODES

To make international calls to telephone and fax numbers listed in *The Europa World Year Book*, dial the international code of the country from which you are calling, followed by the appropriate country code for the organization you wish to call (listed below), followed by the area code (if applicable) and telephone or fax number listed in the entry.

	Country code	+ or – GMT*		Country code	+ or – GMT*
Afghanistan	93	+4½	Djibouti	253	+3
Albania	355	+1	Dominica	1 767	–4
Algeria	213	+1	Dominican Republic	1 809	–4
Andorra	376	+1	Ecuador	593	–5
Angola	244	+1	Egypt	20	+2
Antigua and Barbuda	1 268	–4	El Salvador	503	–6
Argentina	54	–3	Equatorial Guinea	240	+1
Armenia	374	+4	Eritrea	291	+3
Australia	61	+8 to +10	Estonia	372	+2
Australian External Territories:			Ethiopia	251	+3
Australian Antarctic Territory	672	+3 to +10	Fiji	679	+12
Christmas Island	61	+7	Finland	358	+2
Cocos (Keeling) Islands	61	+6½	Finnish External Territory:		
Norfolk Island	672	+11½	Åland Islands	358	+2
Austria	43	+1	France	33	+1
Azerbaijan	994	+5	French Overseas Departments:		
The Bahamas	1 242	–5	French Guiana	594	–3
Bahrain	973	+3	Guadeloupe	590	–4
Bangladesh	880	+6	Martinique	596	–4
Barbados	1 246	–4	Réunion	262	+4
Belarus	375	+2	French Overseas Collectivité Territoriale:		
Belgium	32	+1	Saint Pierre and Miquelon	508	–3
Belize	501	–6	French Overseas Collectivité Départementale:		
Benin	229	+1	Mayotte	269	+3
Bhutan	975	+6	French Overseas Territory:		
Bolivia	591	–4	Wallis and Futuna Islands	681	+12
Bosnia and Herzegovina	387	+1	French Overseas Countries:		
Botswana	267	+2	French Polynesia	689	–9 to –10
Brazil	55	–3 to –4	New Caledonia	687	+11
Brunei	673	+8	Gabon	241	+1
Bulgaria	359	+2	Gambia	220	0
Burkina Faso	226	0	Georgia	995	+4
Burundi	257	+2	Germany	49	+1
Cambodia	855	+7	Ghana	233	0
Cameroon	237	+1	Greece	30	+2
Canada	1	–3 to –8	Grenada	1 473	–4
Cape Verde	238	–1	Guatemala	502	–6
The Central African Republic	236	+1	Guinea	224	0
Chad	235	+1	Guinea-Bissau	245	0
Chile	56	–4	Guyana	592	–4
China, People's Republic	86	+8	Haiti	509	–5
Special Administrative Regions:			Honduras	504	–6
Hong Kong	852	+8	Hungary	36	+1
Macao	853	+8	Iceland	354	0
China (Taiwan)	886	+8	India	91	+5½
Colombia	57	–5	Indonesia	62	+7 to +9
The Comoros	269	+3	Iran	98	+3½
Congo, Democratic Republic	243	+1	Iraq	964	+3
Congo, Republic	242	+1	Ireland	353	0
Costa Rica	506	–6	Israel	972	+2
Côte d'Ivoire	225	0	Italy	39	+1
Croatia	385	+1	Jamaica	1 876	–5
Cuba	53	–5	Japan	81	+9
Cyprus	357	+2	Jordan	962	+2
'Turkish Republic of Northern			Kazakhstan	7	+6
Cyprus'	90 392	+2	Kenya	254	+3
Czech Republic	420	+1	Kiribati	686	+12 to +13
Denmark	45	+1	Korea, Democratic People's		
Danish External Territories:			Republic (North Korea)	850	+9
Faroe Islands	298	0	Korea, Republic (South Korea)	82	+9
Greenland	299	–1 to –4	Kuwait	965	+3

	Country code	+ or – GMT*
Kyrgyzstan	996	+5
Laos	856	+7
Latvia	371	+2
Lebanon	961	+2
Lesotho	266	+2
Liberia	231	0
Libya	218	+1
Liechtenstein	423	+1
Lithuania	370	+2
Luxembourg	352	+1
Macedonia, former Yugoslav republic	389	+1
Madagascar	261	+3
Malawi	265	+2
Malaysia	60	+8
Maldives	960	+5
Mali	223	0
Malta	356	+1
Marshall Islands	692	+12
Mauritania	222	0
Mauritius	230	+4
Mexico	52	–6 to –7
Micronesia, Federated States	691	+10 to +11
Moldova	373	+2
Monaco	377	+1
Mongolia	976	+7 to +9
Morocco	212	0
Mozambique	258	+2
Myanmar	95	+6½
Namibia	264	+2
Nauru	674	+12
Nepal	977	+5¾
Netherlands	31	+1
Netherlands Dependencies:		
Aruba	297	–4
Netherlands Antilles	599	–4
New Zealand	64	+12
New Zealand's Dependent and Associated Territories:		
Tokelau	690	–10
Cook Islands	682	–10
Niue	683	–11
Nicaragua	505	–6
Niger	227	+1
Nigeria	234	+1
Norway	47	+1
Norwegian External Territory:		
Svalbard	47	+1
Oman	968	+4
Pakistan	92	+5
Palau	680	+9
Palestinian Autonomous Areas	970	+2
Panama	507	–5
Papua New Guinea	675	+10
Paraguay	595	–4
Peru	51	–5
The Philippines	63	+8
Poland	48	+1
Portugal	351	0
Qatar	974	+3
Romania	40	+2
Russian Federation	7	+2 to +12
Rwanda	250	+2
Saint Christopher and Nevis	1 869	–4
Saint Lucia	1 758	–4
Saint Vincent and the Grenadines	1 784	–4
Samoa	685	–11
San Marino	378	+1
São Tomé and Príncipe	239	0
Saudi Arabia	966	+3
Senegal	221	0
Serbia and Montenegro	381	+1

	Country code	+ or – GMT*
Seychelles	248	+4
Sierra Leone	232	0
Singapore	65	+8
Slovakia	421	+1
Slovenia	386	+1
Solomon Islands	677	+11
Somalia	252	+3
South Africa	27	+2
Spain	34	+1
Sri Lanka	94	+6
Sudan	249	+2
Suriname	597	–3
Swaziland	268	+2
Sweden	46	+1
Switzerland	41	+1
Syria	963	+2
Tajikistan	992	+5
Tanzania	255	+3
Thailand	66	+7
Timor-Leste	670	+9
Togo	228	0
Tonga	676	+13
Trinidad and Tobago	1 868	–4
Tunisia	216	+1
Turkey	90	+2
Turkmenistan	993	+5
Tuvalu	688	+12
Uganda	256	+3
Ukraine	380	+2
United Arab Emirates	971	+4
United Kingdom	44	0
United Kingdom Crown Dependencies	44	0
United Kingdom Overseas Territories:		
Anguilla	1 264	–4
Ascension Island	247	0
Bermuda	1 441	–4
British Virgin Islands	1 284	–4
Cayman Islands	1 345	–5
Diego Garcia (British Indian Ocean Territory)	246	+5
Falkland Islands	500	–4
Gibraltar	350	+1
Montserrat	1 664	–4
Pitcairn Islands	872	–8
Saint Helena	290	0
Tristan da Cunha	2 897	0
Turks and Caicos Islands	1 649	–5
United States of America	1	–5 to –10
United States Commonwealth Territories:		
Northern Mariana Islands	1 670	+10
Puerto Rico	1 787	–4
United States External Territories:		
American Samoa	1 684	–11
Guam	1 671	+10
United States Virgin Islands	1 340	–4
Uruguay	598	–3
Uzbekistan	998	+5
Vanuatu	678	+11
Vatican City	39	+1
Venezuela	58	–4
Viet Nam	84	+7
Yemen	967	+3
Zambia	260	+2
Zimbabwe	263	+2

* Time difference in hours + or – Greenwich Mean Time (GMT). The times listed compare the standard (winter) times. Some countries adopt Summer (Daylight Saving) Time — i.e. + 1 hour — for part of the year.

KAZAKHSTAN

Introductory Survey

Location, Climate, Language, Religion, Flag, Capital

The Republic of Kazakhstan (until December 1991 the Kazakh Soviet Socialist Republic) is the second largest of the former Soviet republics, extending some 1,900 km (1,200 miles) from the Volga river in the west to the Altai mountains in the east, and about 1,300 km from the Siberian plain in the north to the Central Asian deserts in the south. To the south it borders Turkmenistan, Uzbekistan and Kyrgyzstan. To the east the border is with the People's Republic of China. There is a long border in the north with Russia and a coastline of 2,320 km on the Caspian Sea in the south-west. The climate is of a strongly continental type, but there are wide variations throughout the territory. Average temperatures in January range from –18°C (0°F) in the north to –3°C (27°F) in the south. In July average temperatures are 19°C (66°F) in the north and 28°C–30°C (82°F–86°F) in the south. Similarly, average annual rainfall in mountainous regions reaches 1,600 mm (63 ins), whereas in the central desert areas it is less than 100 mm (4 ins). The official language is Kazakh. The predominant religion is Islam, most ethnic Kazakhs being Sunni Muslims of the Hanafi school. Other ethnic groups have their own religious communities, notably the (Christian) Eastern Orthodox Church, which is attended mainly by Slavs. The national flag (proportions 1 by 2) consists of a light blue field, at the centre of which is a yellow sun (a disc surrounded by 32 rays), framed by the wings of a flying eagle, also in yellow, with a vertical stripe of national ornamentation in yellow near the hoist. In November 1997 the capital was moved from Almaty to Akmola (formerly Tselinograd), now known as Astana.

Recent History

After the February Revolution and the Bolshevik *coup d'état* in Russia in 1917, there was civil war throughout Kazakhstan, which had come under Russian control in the first half of the 18th century. Bolshevik forces finally overcame those of the anti-Bolshevik White Army, foreign interventionists and local nationalists. In 1920 the Kyrgyz Autonomous Soviet Socialist Republic (ASSR) was created within the Russian Soviet Federative Socialist Republic (the Russian Federation): the Kazakhs were known to the Russians as Kyrgyz, to distinguish them from the unrelated Cossacks. In 1925 the Kyrgyz ASSR was renamed the Kazakh ASSR; the Karakalpak region (now in Uzbekistan) was detached in 1930, and became an autonomous republic within the Uzbek Soviet Socialist Republic (SSR) in 1936. In December 1936 the Kazakh ASSR became a full Union Republic of the USSR, the Kazakh SSR.

Under Soviet rule parts of Kazakhstan were heavily industrialized. However, Kazakhstan was one of the worst-affected regions during the campaign in the early 1930s to collectivize agriculture and settle nomadic peoples, and more than 1m. people were estimated to have died as a result of starvation. There was severe repression from the 1930s, and Russian immigration was greatly increased. Many of those deported from parts of the USSR during the Second World War (including Germans, Crimean Tatars and Caucasian peoples) were sent to Kazakhstan, causing considerable local resentment. During Nikita Khrushchev's period in office as Soviet leader (1953–64) large areas of previously uncultivated land in Kazakhstan were transformed into arable land under the 'Virgin Lands' programme. This and other schemes, including nuclear-testing sites in eastern Kazakhstan, the Baikonur space centre at Leninsk (now Turatam) and the huge industrial complexes in the north and east, brought large numbers of ethnic Russians to Kazakhstan; the proportion of Russians increased from 19.7% of the population in 1926 to 42.7% in 1959.

Mikhail Gorbachev's accession to power in 1985 and his subsequent anti-corruption campaign, as well as the new policy of *glasnost* (openness), had important consequences in Kazakhstan. In December 1986 some 3,000 people took part in protests in the capital, Almaty (Alma-Ata), after Gennadii Kolbin, an ethnic Russian, was appointed First Secretary of the Communist Party of Kazakhstan (CPK), in place of the populist, but corrupt Dinmukhamed Kunayev, an ethnic Kazakh. Four people

died when the protesters were dispersed by police. Kolbin subsequently dismissed many of Kunayev's former associates.

In June 1989 Kolbin was transferred to the Soviet and Russian capital, Moscow, and Nursultan Nazarbayev, a prominent ethnic Kazakh, who had been Chairman of the republic's Council of Ministers since March 1984, was appointed First Secretary of the CPK. Nazarbayev advocated economic reform, while emphasizing the need for political stability. Political and administrative changes were instituted in September 1989: a permanent Supreme Soviet (parliament) was to be established, and elections were to be conducted on a multi-candidate basis. In addition, the state duties that had hitherto been the responsibility of the First Secretary of the CPK were transferred to the office of the Chairman of the Kazakh Supreme Soviet, to which post Nazarbayev was elected in February 1990. Many candidates stood unopposed at elections to the Supreme Soviet in March, and the system of reserved seats for CPK-affiliated organizations was retained, resulting in a substantial communist majority. In April the new body elected Nazarbayev to the newly established post of President of Kazakhstan.

Meanwhile, in September 1989 the Kazakh Supreme Soviet adopted legislation establishing Kazakh as the official language of the republic, while Russian remained a language of inter-ethnic communication. However, the new law was opposed by many non-Kazakh residents. A local branch of the Russian nationalist organization Yedinstvo (Unity) was established, and some members campaigned for annexation of Kazakhstan's northern regions by Russia. Many of the unofficial, quasi-political groups established in Kazakhstan in the late 1980s were concerned with environmental issues, such as the harmful effects of nuclear testing near Semipalatinsk. In September 1990 an explosion in a factory producing nuclear fuel at Ulba, in eastern Kazakhstan, led to the contamination by toxic gases of a large area, including the nearby city of Ust-Kamenogorsk.

On 25 October 1990 the Kazakh Supreme Soviet declared its sovereignty, asserting republican control over natural resources and the economy. Although the declaration emphasized ethnic equality, there were protests in the predominantly Slav-populated city of Ust-Kamenogorsk; Kazakh nationalist groups, meanwhile, judged the declaration too weak. Nazarbayev strongly supported a redefinition of the respective all-Union (Soviet) and republican powers, and the Kazakh Government participated in discussions on the new Union Treaty in early 1991. However, Nazarbayev also sought economic sovereignty for Kazakhstan, where some 90% of enterprises were under all-Union control.

In the referendum on the future of the USSR conducted in nine Soviet republics in March 1991, almost 90% of the electorate voted in Kazakhstan, of whom 94% endorsed the proposal to preserve the USSR as a 'union of sovereign states with equal rights'. In June the Kazakh Supreme Soviet voted, in principle, to adopt a draft union treaty, although Nazarbayev expressed reservations about certain aspects of the proposed federation. Kazakhstan was to sign the treaty in August, but the event was forestalled by the attempted *coup d'état* in Moscow. Nazarbayev did not initially condemn the coup, but subsequently denounced the group leading the *putsch* as illegal and harmful to economic and political progress. As the coup attempt collapsed, Nazarbayev resigned from the Politburo and Central Committee of the Communist Party of the Soviet Union (CPSU), in protest at the open support granted to the putschists by the CPSU leadership. The CPK was ordered to cease activities in state and government organs, and in September the party withdrew from the CPSU; it was re-formed as the independent Socialist Party of Kazakhstan (SPK).

In October 1991 Kazakhstan signed, with seven other republics, a treaty to establish an economic community, and in November agreed to the draft treaty of the new Union of Sovereign States. These accords were largely nullified by the Commonwealth of Independent States (CIS, see p. 180), agreed by the leaders of the three Slavic republics (Russia, Ukraine and Belarus) in December. Kazakhstan (despite initial reluctance) and the other Central Asian republics agreed to join the new

Commonwealth. Nazarbayev was re-elected President of Kazakhstan, with 98.8% of the votes cast, on 1 December. On 16 December Kazakhstan became the last of the republics to declare independence from the USSR, and was redesignated the Republic of Kazakhstan. The country was formally recognized as a co-founder of the CIS at the Almaty meeting on 21 December.

Although Kazakhstan did not experience the inter-ethnic violence that affected several other former Soviet republics, some racial unrest was reported during 1992, particularly among Kazakhstan's ethnic Russian community (which constituted an estimated 38% of the total population, while ethnic Kazakhs comprised 40%). The Constitution, adopted in January 1993, invoked the law of 1989 (denoting Kazakh as the state language, with Russian as a language of inter-ethnic communication). The document also required that the President of the Republic be a fluent speaker of Kazakh. Meanwhile, increased emigration from the country, particularly by ethnic Germans (more than 300,000 of whom left Kazakhstan in the early 1990s) and Russians, was accompanied by the return of ethnic Kazakhs from, most notably, Kyrgyzstan, Mongolia, Tajikistan and Turkmenistan. According to official figures released by the Kazakh authorities in early 1998, a total of 1,652,700 emigrants left Kazakhstan in 1992–97; in May 1998 the number of ethnic Kazakhs who had returned in 1991–97 was officially said to exceed 100,000.

Opposition to Nazarbayev's administration became more pronounced during 1992. In June some 5,000 people demonstrated in Almaty against continued communist predominance in the Government and Supreme Kenges (as the legislature was now styled), demanding the formation of a new, coalition administration. In October the three most prominent nationalist opposition parties (the Azat movement, the Republican Party and the Dzheltoqsan National Democratic Party) united to form the Republican Party—Azat (RP—A). The Union of National Unity of Kazakhstan was established in February 1993, with a declared aim of promoting social harmony and countering radical nationalism. Nazarbayev (who had held no party affiliation since August 1991) became Chairman of the Union, which was reorganized as a political party, the People's Unity Party (PUP), later in 1993.

In December 1993 the Supreme Kenges voted to dissolve itself and to grant Nazarbayev the power to rule by decree pending elections to a new standing legislature, which was to be reduced in size from 360 to 177 seats. Kazakhstan's first multi-party elections were duly held on 7 March 1994, with the participation of 74% of the electorate. A number of irregularities were reported by international observers, with many prospective candidates allegedly being prevented from registering, and there were also complaints of discrimination against the Russian community. The final composition of the new Kenges was 59% Kazakh and 28% Russian. The PUP obtained 33 seats, which, when combined with the 42 seats won by candidates from the so-called 'President's List' (candidates nominated by Nazarbayev) and those of pro-Nazarbayev independents, ensured that Nazarbayev's supporters emerged as the strongest force in the assembly. Other parties and groups achieved a significantly lower representation: the Confederation of Kazakh Trade Unions (CKTU) won 11 seats, the People's Congress Party of Kazakhstan (PCPK) nine and the SPK eight. After several unsuccessful attempts at re-establishment, the CPK was granted legal status in March. In May the CPK (claiming a membership of some 50,000) and other opposition parties, including the SPK, the PCPK and the RP—A, together with the CKTU, formed an opposition bloc in the Supreme Kenges, with the stated aim of acting as a guarantor against 'dictatorship by executive bodies'.

In May 1994 96 members of the Supreme Kenges endorsed a motion expressing 'no confidence' in the Government's economic, social and legal policies, and in June Nazarbayev announced a major government reorganization, in an attempt to stimulate economic reform. The Government of Sergei Tereshchenko (the Prime Minister since 1991) resigned in October 1994, admitting its failure to reform the economy. Akezhan Kazhegeldin, an economist and First Deputy Prime Minister in the outgoing Council of Ministers, was appointed premier.

A crisis arose in February 1995, when the Constitutional Court declared the result of the 1994 general election to be null and void, owing to procedural irregularities. Following an unsuccessful attempt by the Supreme Kenges to amend the Constitution in order to overrule the Court's decision, in March 1995 the legislature was forced to tender its resignation (and

likewise the Government), on the grounds that it had been approved by an unconstitutional parliament (although it was subsequently reinstated virtually unchanged). Nazarbayev was thus effectively empowered to rule by decree pending further legislative elections, prompting opposition parties to allege that the situation had been orchestrated by him in order to remove an obstructionist parliament. At a national referendum on 29 April more than 95% of voters endorsed the extension of Nazarbayev's five-year mandate until 1 December 2000: the President had asserted that the measure was necessary to ensure political stability.

In May 1995 Nazarbayev ordered the establishment of a special council to prepare (under his guidance) a new constitution. Opposition activists denounced provisions whereby, they considered, the President would be guaranteed 'unchecked rule'. A final draft was approved by 89.1% of the electorate in a referendum on 30 August. The new Constitution preserved the extensive executive powers of the President, and abolished the post of Vice-President. The Supreme Kenges was replaced by a bicameral Parliament, comprising a 47-member Senate (the upper chamber—with 40 members elected by Kazakhstan's regional administrative bodies and seven appointed by the President) and a directly elected, 67-member Majlis (Assembly). The Constitutional Court was replaced by a Constitutional Council, the rulings of which were to be subject to a presidential right of veto.

At elections to the Senate held on 5 December 1995, 38 of the 40 regionally elected seats were filled; Nazarbayev duly appointed seven senators. Direct elections were held to the Majlis on 9 December, with the participation of 80.7% of the electorate. However, the necessary two-thirds' quorum was not attained, as candidates succeeded in obtaining the requisite 50% of the votes in only 41 of the 67 constituencies. Further rounds of voting (contested by the two leading candidates from the first round) were held in the remaining 26 constituencies on 23 December and 4 February 1996, with 13 seats being filled at each round. A number of procedural violations in the elections to the Majlis were reported by foreign observers.

Popular dissatisfaction with the Government's economic and social policies became more pronounced in 1996. In April a new opposition movement, Azamat (Citizen), was established by a group of scientists, writers and public figures. (It was finally registered as a political party, the Azamat Democratic Party of Kazakhstan, in 1999.) Social tensions were exacerbated in late 1996 by widespread energy shortages. In October the leaders of Kazakhstan's two main trade union federations organized rallies to protest against declining standards of living. Negotiations between political groups and parliamentary deputies followed, but requests for permission to organize a further rally in Almaty in November were refused by the city authorities. A silent demonstration proceeded, none the less, following which the organizers, including Petr Svoik (one of Azamat's leaders) and the Chairman of the Confederation of Free Trade Unions, Leonid Solomin, were briefly arrested. Prolonged delays in payments of wages, owing to the insolvency of numerous state-owned enterprises, were a principal cause of strikes and unauthorized demonstrations throughout 1997 and early 1998.

The ongoing reform of pensions legislation also continued to provoke protests. Draft legislation regulating the pensions system was approved by the Majlis in May 1997 and by Nazarbayev in June. Opponents of the new legislation (effective from January 1998) claimed that it would lead to the curtailment of many social guarantees. Meanwhile, demonstrations were held, in protest at the level of non-payment of pensions (amounting to some to US $500m. in May 1997). Payment of pensions arrears commenced in August, apparently funded by revenue from the privatization of two Kazakh petroleum companies; in February 1998 it was announced that all such arrears had been cleared.

Meanwhile, in late 1996 the relocation of civil servants from Almaty to the northern city of Akmola (formerly Tselinograd) marked the beginning of the transfer of the capital city (in July 1994 the Supreme Kenges had approved a proposal by Nazarbayev to transfer the capital to Akmola by 2000). In November 1997 the new capital was officially inaugurated by Nazarbayev, and a joint session of both chambers of Parliament was held for the first time in Akmola in the following month. However, the costly transfer attracted widespread criticism, and it was reported that the initial stages had been poorly managed: in particular, an acute housing shortage in Akmola had not been adequately addressed. None the less, a ceremony was held in early June 1998 to mark the official opening of the capital under the new name of Astana (a presidential decree changing the name of the capital had been issued in May).

Nazarbayev undertook several far-reaching measures to re-structure and rationalize the state administration in March 1997. The number of ministries and other government agencies was reduced from 48 to 25. The Ministry of Petroleum and Natural Gas, headed by Nurlan Balgymbayev, was abolished and replaced by a new state company, KazakhOil, which was also led by Balgymbayev. The State Committee for Investment became the sole body governing foreign investment, and the State Property Committee was dissolved. Seven government institutions—including the Ministries of Defence and of Internal Affairs and the newly established Agency for Control of Strategic Resources—became directly subordinate to the President. Nazarbayev continued the reform process by reducing the number of administrative regions from 19 to 14.

That the restructuring had been effected by Nazarbayev while Kazhegeldin was out of the country led to speculation that the President's confidence in the Prime Minister had begun to decline. Kazhegeldin's position appeared more precarious in August 1997, owing to an investigation by the National Security Committee (KNB) into alleged financial malpractice (although he was exonerated of corruption charges). The Prime Minister's position was further undermined when, in the following month, a Russian newspaper published an admission by Kazhegeldin of his involvement, in the late 1980s, with the former Soviet state security service (KGB). In September 1997 it was announced that Kazhegeldin had resigned, ostensibly for health reasons. He was temporarily replaced by Akhmetzan Yesimov, and in October Balgymbayev was named Prime Minister.

In January 1998, in an apparent attempt to counter increasing opposition to Nazarbayev, 17 political parties and movements signed a 'memorandum on mutual understanding and co-operation', pledging their support for the President's policies and reforms. However, political tensions were revived in April, when one of the leaders of the Workers' Movement of Kazakhstan, Madel Ismailov, was sentenced to one year's imprisonment, having been convicted of insulting the President during an unauthorized rally in November 1997.

In September 1998, in his annual address to Parliament, Nazarbayev outlined proposals for political reforms, including amendments to electoral procedures and enhanced legislative powers. In October, however, a joint session of Parliament rejected Nazarbayev's proposed constitutional reforms, amid apparent concerns that the President was attempting to miti-gate his personal responsibility in the event of any future economic or political crisis. The session subsequently voted in favour of a parliamentary amendment whereby a presidential election would take place before the expiry of Nazarbayev's extended mandate in 2000. Other amendments included an increase in the minimum age for presidential candidates from 35 to 40 years and the abolition of the upper age limit (of 65 years); parties were, henceforth, required to win at least 7% of the votes cast in legislative elections, in order to secure representation (previously, the minimum requirement was 10%).

During November 1998 several opposition figures were deemed ineligible to contest the presidency by the Central Electoral Commission, in accordance with a presidential decree, enacted in May, which prevented those convicted of an admin-istrative offence in the 12 months prior to an election from registering as a candidate. The most prominent disqualification was that of former Prime Minister Kazhegeldin, on the grounds of attending a meeting of an unauthorized political organization, the Movement for Honest Elections; he had been widely regarded as Nazarbayev's principal rival. Kazhegeldin sub-sequently established a new political party, the Republican People's Party of Kazakhstan (RPPK), which was inaugurated in mid-December. A number of other opposition parties were formed in late 1998 and early 1999, although applications for registration by many of these were rejected by the Ministry of Justice. Among those to be accorded official status was a new pro-presidential party, Otan (Fatherland).

The Organization for Security and Co-operation in Europe (OSCE, see p. 302) was among international bodies to express serious concern at the conduct of the election, which took place on 10 January 1999, despite appeals for a postponement, and resulted in victory for the incumbent, with 81.0% of the votes cast. The rate of participation was 88.3% of the registered electorate. Nazarbayev was sworn in on 20 January, and a new Government, under Balgymbayev, was appointed two days later.

In August 1999 the President of KazakhOil, Nurlan Kaparov, was dismissed, accused by Nazarbayev of having exceeded his powers. Earlier that month both the Minister of Defence, Gen. Mukhtar Altynbayev, and the Chairman of the KNB, Nurtai Abykayev, had been dismissed, after admitting responsibility for the attempted illegal sale of MiG-21 fighter aircraft to the Democratic People's Republic of Korea. Although Bakhytzhan Yertayev was subsequently appointed acting Minister of Defence he, too, was accused of involvement in the scandal; despite his acquittal in early February 2000, he was dismissed from his position as Chief of the General Staff in May.

Meanwhile, in early September 1999 Kazhegeldin, who had been charged with tax evasion in April, was arrested at Moscow airport, but released following criticism of his detention by the OSCE. None the less, owing to the outstanding charges against him, Kazhegeldin, together with two other leading members of the RPPK, was barred from registering as a candidate for the parliamentary elections in October. (Further charges were brought against him in late February 2000.)

On 17 September 1999, in an election criticized by OSCE, 29 candidates contested 16 seats in the Senate, representing 14 oblasts and the cities of Astana and Almaty. In late September the RPPK announced that it would boycott the elections to the Majlis, in protest at the severe restrictions imposed on opposi-tion parties by the President, although some of the party's members were to stand as independents. In early October, prior to the parliamentary elections, Balgymbayev resigned the pre-miership and returned to his former position as President of KazakhOil. He was replaced as Prime Minister by Kasymzho-mart Tokayev, a former Minister of Foreign Affairs. A govern-ment reorganization followed. Elections to the Majlis (as well as to municipal and local councils) were held on 10 October. According to official reports, 65 candidates from nine political parties contested 10 seats allocated, for the first time, according to a party list system, and almost 500 candidates competed for the remaining 67 seats in single-mandate constituencies. Although all of the 10 party list seats were filled at the first round (with the pro-presidential Otan winning four seats and the CPK, the Agrarian Party of Kazakhstan and the Civic Party of Kazakhstan each taking two), only 20 of the 67 directly elected seats were filled, and a second round of voting was held on 24 October. (In three of the 47 'run-off' elections, voting was declared invalid and was repeated on 26 December.) Final results indicated that Otan was to be the largest political grouping in the new Majlis, with a total of 23 seats, with the Civic Party holding 13. Three other parties achieved representa-tion, and 34 seats were taken by independent candidates. The rate of participation by voters was reported to be 62.6%. Observers from the OSCE cited numerous breaches of electoral law and claimed that its officials had been denied access to several key locations during the vote-counting.

In May 2000 a new opposition party, the Party of Patriots of Kazakhstan (PPK), was formed by Gani Kasymov, a presi-dential candidate in January 1999. In late June 2000 a law was passed awarding President Nazarbayev certain guarantees and rights, as the first President of Kazakhstan, which were to remain in place even after the expiry of his term of office. Despite opposition protests, the Constitutional Court upheld the legislation in the following month. In September the President signed a decree, which authorized greater independence for the judiciary. In December Nazarbayev carried out a government reorganization, including the abolition of a number of ministries and state agencies. A further, minor government reorganization was carried out in May 2001.

In mid-June 2001 a month-long amnesty was declared, to allow the return of capital that had been transferred abroad in violation of tax laws and other financial legislation; the Chairman of the National Bank of Kazakhstan (NBK) con-sequently announced that US $480m. had been returned to domestic banks. However, the amnesty attracted criticism from Kazhegeldin, who claimed that the sale of petroleum alone had accounted for some $2,000m. in illegal transfers to Caribbean banks in 2000. In September 2001 Kazhegeldin, who had been tried *in absentia* on charges of abuse of power, tax evasion and the illegal possession of weapons, was sentenced to 10 years' imprisonment, amid allegations that his trial had been politi-cally motivated.

In mid-November 2001 Nazarbayev approved the resignation of Rakhat Aliyev as Deputy Chairman of the National Security Committee, amid accusations of abuse of power. Persistent reports that Aliyev, the husband of Nazarbayev's daughter,

Darigha Nazarbayeva, controlled the majority of Kazakhstan's media outlets, and influenced their output, prompted the Akim (Governor) of Pavlodar Oblast, Galymzhan Zhakiyanov, and a number of other prominent political and business figures, including the Deputy Prime Minister, Uraz Dzhandosov, to announce the formation of a new political movement, the Democratic Choice of Kazakhstan (DCK), in late November. The DCK, which aimed to revive democratic reform, decentralize political power and ensure the freedom of the mass media, criticized the concentration of power among members of Nazarbayev's family and a small group of leading entrepreneurs. Prime Minister Tokayev subsequently announced that two attempts to assassinate the President had recently been averted, and threatened to tender his resignation unless the President dismissed ministers whom he denounced as disloyal, owing to their involvement in the formation of the DCK. Dzhandosov, Alikhan Baymenov (the Minister of Labour and Social Security) and two deputy ministers resigned shortly afterwards, announcing that they were unable to work with the Prime Minister; Nazarbayev dismissed Zhakiyanov on the same day. In December the Azamat Democratic Party, the PCPK and Akezhan Kazhegeldin's RPPK announced their intention to merge to form the United Democratic Party (UDP). The UDP, which was established in early 2002, declared its main aim to be the creation of a parliamentary republic, with a unicameral legislature and a new constitution, to be adopted by means of a referendum.

Meanwhile, in early December 2001 Gen. Mukhtar Altynbayev was reappointed Minister of Defence (he had been dismissed from the post in 1999—see above), replacing Lt-Gen. Sat Tokpakbayev. In January 2002 amendments to media legislation came into effect, which required 50% of all radio and television programmes to be broadcast in Kazakh, restricted the rebroadcast of foreign (mainly Russian) television programmes, and subjected internet sites to the same controls as print media. In mid-January a further assassination attempt against the President, attributed to international terrorist organizations, was reported to have been thwarted by the security services. In late January Tokayev announced his resignation; the entire Government duly resigned, in accordance with the Constitution. Some observers believed Tokayev's resignation to have been prompted by divisions within the political élite, and others agreed that the high-profile ministerial resignations of November 2001 had discredited the Prime Minister. Divisions also emerged within the DCK in late January 2002, when a number of its founding members, including Dzhandosov and Zhakiyanov, announced their intention to found a new opposition party, Ak Zhol (Light Road), which held its founding congress in mid-March. On 31 January a new Government was sworn in, led by a former Deputy Prime Minister, Imangali Tasmagambetov; Tokayev was appointed State Secretary and Minister of Foreign Affairs.

In March 2002 a warrant was issued for the arrest of Zhakiyanov, on charges of abuse of power during his tenure as Governor of Pavlodar oblast. He subsequently sought refuge in the French embassy until early April, when agreement was reached between the Government and the ambassadors of France, Germany, the United Kingdom and the USA that Zhakiyanov would be permitted to go free until an investigation into the allegations had been carried out. However, less than one week later he was arrested and flown from Almaty to Pavlodar, in contravention of the agreement, to assist the police there with their enquiries. In mid-May it was reported that Zhakiyanov had been admitted to hospital following interrogation by security officials. Zhakiyanov's trial commenced in July, and he was sentenced to a seven-year term in early August, prompting expressions of concern from human rights groups.

Meanwhile, in early April 2002 Tasmagambetov admitted that a clandestine foreign bank account, funded by the sale of a 20% stake in the large Tengiz oilfield, had been established in 1996, in an attempt to avoid sudden large increases in consumer-price inflation. The Prime Minister stated that the account's foundation had been authorized by Kazhegeldin, and that money from the account had been used to settle pensions arrears in 1997–98. The remaining funds had subsequently been transferred to the National Fund, which was officially established in 2001. In response to the revelations, opposition leaders from the oil-producing regions of western Kazakhstan announced their intention to establish a People's Oil Fund, to monitor the Government's economic activities and to promote transparency in its financial affairs.

At the end of April 2002 a new National Council was established by presidential decree, to function as an advisory and consultative body. In late May the Minister of Agriculture, Akhmetzhan Yesimov, was appointed to the additional position of Deputy Prime Minister. In the following month the former Minister of Transport and Communications, Abylai Myrzhakhmetov, was arrested; he had been dismissed in April, owing to allegations of embezzlement during his previous role as General Director of Kazakhstan Railways. In mid-July Nazarbayev signed into law controversial new legislation on political parties, which required a party to demonstrate that it had at least 50,000 members (rather than the previous 3,000), representing every region of the country, in order to qualify for registration. All parties were required to re-register. In the same month a former Minister of Energy, Industry and Trade and founding member of the DCK, Mukhtar Ablyazov, was sentenced to six years' imprisonment, having been found guilty of abuse of office. In late August Nazarbayev carried out a major reorganization of the Government, abolishing the Ministry of State Revenues, and establishing a new Ministry of Industry and Trade. Aleksandr Pavlov was appointed First Deputy Prime Minister. On 8 October partial elections to fill 16 seats in the Senate took place. Otan retained the largest representation in the Senate of any party, accounting for 18 of the upper chamber's 47 members. By-elections took place in late December, to fill three empty seats in the Majlis.

In early January 2003 it was reported that the leader of the reformist party Ak Zhol, Uraz Dzhandosov, had been appointed as an aide to President Nazarbayev, suggesting to many observers that the party was in fact supportive of the incumbent leadership. In the same month the DCK's party registration was annulled by the Ministry of Justice, and in mid-January the establishment of a new opposition bloc, Democracy-Elections-Kazakhstan, was announced, with the aim of uniting those parties prevented from re-registering by the new legislation on political parties. By the end of the re-registration period in April, only seven parties had successfully satisfied the registration criteria.

In late January 2003 Sergei Duvanov, an independent journalist, was convicted of rape and sentenced to more than three years' imprisonment. He had been arrested in October 2002, shortly before he was due to travel to the USA to speak about press freedoms and human rights issues. Duvanov's conviction prompted the US embassy to express concern about judicial procedure during his trial, and in mid-February 2003 the European Parliament adopted a resolution condemning the sentences awarded to Duvanov and the opposition politicians Ablyazov and Zhakiyanov, and demanding that an independent investigation into their trials be carried out. Ablyazov was pardoned in May, and subsequently announced his withdrawal from politics, but an appeal by Duvanov against his conviction was rejected by the Supreme Court in November. Meanwhile, in March Nazarbayev's links with US petroleum companies came under scrutiny, when a US businessman was indicted in the USA for allegedly offering financial incentives to Kazakhstani officials, in an attempt to influence the award of important contracts (see below).

In mid-May 2003 the Government won a parliamentary vote of 'no confidence', prompted by plans to introduce legislation on land reform, providing for the private ownership of land. However, on 9 June Tasmagambetov tendered his resignation, after it emerged that the results of the confidence vote had been falsified (it was later claimed that the Prime Minister had not been implicated in the fraud). The entire Government duly resigned, in accordance with the Constitution, and on 13 June Daniyal Akhmetov, a former Governor of Pavlodar oblast, was approved as the new premier. Subsequently, more than two-thirds of the ministers in the previous administration were reappointed to the Government. The controversial land reform bill was approved by Parliament on 20 June.

A limited reorganization of the Government took place in mid-September 2003. Zautbek Turisbekov was appointed as Minister of Internal Affairs, replacing Col-Gen. Kairbek Suleimonov, after Nazarbayev reportedly decreed that the heads of the law-enforcement and security bodies should be civilian appointments. The Ministry of Culture, Information and Public Accord was replaced by separate Ministries of Culture and of Information, to which new ministers were appointed. Elections to local councils took place on 20 September, with further rounds of voting in October–November. The OSCE was again critical of the conduct of the electoral process, noting that in almost one-half of the districts only one candidate stood for election.

In late October 2003 a new party, Asar (All Together), led by Darigha Nazarbayeva, was registered with the Ministry of Justice. Some observers speculated that the establishment of the party by Nazarbayev's daughter was part of a long-term strategy to prepare for the succession. However, at the end of January it was reported that Nazarbayev had stated his intention to stand for re-election in 2006. Meanwhile, in early January 2004 Nazarbayev had appointed Grigorii Marchenko, hitherto Chairman of the NBK, to the post of First Deputy Prime Minister, replacing Aleksandr Pavlov; however, Marchenko resigned in mid-April. In March Nurtai Abykayev, a former Chairman of the KNB (who had been dismissed in August 1999—see above), was appointed as Chairman of the Senate. In early April 2004 Arman Dunayev was appointed as the country's new Minister of Finance and Yerbolat Dosayev became Minister of Public Health.

Relations between Kazakhstan and neighbouring Russia, the most influential CIS member, have periodically been strained by the issue of Kazakhstan's large Russian minority (comprising some 35.8% of the total population at the beginning of 1994). In early 1997 draft legislation to enhance the status of the Kazakh language attracted criticism from ethnic Russians resident in Kazakhstan. In July Parliament reconfirmed Kazakh as the state language, although Russian was to retain its parity with Kazakh in state organizations and as a language of inter-ethnic communication. According to official statistics, 72.4% of emigrants from Kazakhstan in 1997 departed for Russia.

The issue of the legal status of the Caspian Sea—and the division of the substantial mineral resources believed to be located in the seabed—was a further source of tension between Kazakhstan and Russia, as well as the other littoral states (Azerbaijan, Turkmenistan and Iran). Nevertheless, in July 1998 Nazarbayev and the Russian President, Boris Yeltsin, signed a bilateral agreement on the delineation of their respective boundaries of the Caspian seabed, by which Russia for the first time formally recognized Kazakhstan's claim to, and right to exploit, its offshore petroleum resources. The arrangement attracted particular criticism from Iran, which continued to assert that partitioning of the seabed required the consensus of all five littoral states. In October 2000 the Presidents of Kazakhstan and Russia signed an additional agreement, on the definition of the legal status of the Caspian Sea, and the 1998 agreement was further augmented in May 2002, when an accord was signed on the equal division of three oilfields in the northern Caspian, prompting condemnation by Iran. Russia and Kazakhstan have also signed a Treaty of Eternal Friendship and Co-operation, which provides for mutual military assistance in the event of aggression by a third party. In November 2001 Kazakhstan concluded a bilateral agreement with Azerbaijan on the two countries' respective mineral rights in the Caspian Sea, which also prompted protests from Iran. In mid-May 2003 Azerbaijan, Kazakhstan and Russia signed a further, trilateral agreement. In November representatives of Azerbaijan, Iran, Kazakhstan, Russia and Turkmenistan, meeting in Tehran, Iran, signed a UN-sponsored framework Convention for the Protection of the Marine Environment of the Caspian Sea, which sought to alleviate environmental damage in the Caspian Sea region.

As the largest and most influential of the five Central Asian republics of the former USSR, Kazakhstan has been regarded as a potential guarantor of peace in the region. However, the issue of the formerly Soviet, subsequently Russian-controlled, nuclear warheads deployed in Kazakhstan (effectively making the country the fourth largest nuclear power in the world) was the focus of international concern. Following the dissolution of the USSR, Kazakhstan asserted its commitment to rid itself of its nuclear weapons, either by their destruction or transfer to Russia. In September 1992 the Kazakh legislature ratified the first Strategic Arms Reduction Treaty, signed by the USA and the USSR in July 1991, the provisions of which affected Kazakhstan as a (nuclear) successor state to the USSR. In December 1993 the Kazakh legislature ratified the Treaty on the Non-Proliferation of Nuclear Weapons (International Atomic Energy Agency, see p. 88). The USA provided Kazakhstan with substantial technical and financial aid for the dismantling of its nuclear arsenal. By April 1995 all nuclear warheads had been transferred to Russia, and in September 1996 Russia and Kazakhstan signed a final protocol governing the withdrawal of military units linked to the Russian nuclear weapons facilities in Kazakhstan. In November 2001 the Kazakh legislature ratified the Comprehensive Nuclear Test Ban Treaty. In late 2000, as a result of escalating conflict in Kyrgyzstan and Uzbekistan, Kazakhstan assumed a peace-making role, offering to provide military assistance to the two countries.

In April 2001, at a meeting of leaders of the Turkic-speaking countries, the Presidents of Azerbaijan, Kazakhstan, Kyrgyzstan, Turkey and Turkmenistan, and the Chairman of the Uzbek legislature signed an agreement on regional co-operation to combat terrorism and drugs-trafficking, to revive the old 'Silk Road' trade route between the People's Republic of China and Europe, and to ensure further protection of the environment. One month later the signatories of the CIS Collective Security Treaty—Armenia, Belarus, Kazakhstan, Kyrgyzstan, Russia and Tajikistan—agreed to form a Collective Rapid Reaction Force in Bishkek, Kyrgyzstan, to combat Islamist militancy in Central Asia; in January 2002 it was announced that the force was ready to undertake combat missions. An anti-terrorism centre became operational in Bishkek in August 2001. In late April 2003 a successor organization to the Collective Security Treaty was formed, when Armenia, Belarus, Kazakhstan, Kyrgyzstan, Russia and Tajikistan inaugurated the Collective Security Treaty Organization (CSTO).

In July and October 1999 Russian craft exploded following their launch from the Baikonur space centre at Turatam, causing considerable damage to the surrounding area. The accidents provoked anger among local residents, environmentalists and the Kazakh Government, which responded by suspending launches of Russian-made rockets from Baikonur. In November Russia agreed to pay outstanding rental fees of US $115m. and an undisclosed sum in compensation for the damage incurred, and to improve facilities at Baikonur. The restriction on Russian launches was lifted in February 2000. In January 2004 President Nazarbayev and the Russian President, Vladimir Putin, signed an agreement permitting Russia's continued use of the Baikonur space centre until 2050.

In 1992 Kazakhstan, together with other Central Asian states, joined the Economic Co-operation Organization (ECO, see p. 201), founded originally by Iran, Pakistan and Turkey. The Government, eager to establish good relations with the international community, explained that its intention was to facilitate economic activity, rather than to create an Islamist bloc. In early 1994 Kazakhstan and the neighbouring CIS states of Kyrgyzstan and Uzbekistan formed a trilateral economic area, and in February 1995 an Interstate Council was established to supervise its implementation. Several agreements to expand economic co-operation were signed by the three countries in 1996, and in December 1997 the Council met in Akmola (now Astana) to discuss the possibility of full economic integration. In March 1998 Tajikistan joined the alliance, which was renamed the Central Asian Co-operation Organization in March 2002. Meanwhile, in January 1995 Kazakhstan established a customs union with Russia and Belarus, and in March 1996 the three members of the customs union were joined by Kyrgyzstan in signing a treaty aimed at creating a 'community of integrated states'. The treaty provided for the closer integration of the signatories' economies, as well as of their cultural and social affairs; Tajikistan joined the union in April 1998. In October 2000 a new economic body, the Eurasian Economic Community (EAEC), was established to supersede the customs union. The EAEC was to have its own institutions, staff and budget, and had as its objective the creation of common policies on currencies, customs tariffs, employment and tax. In September 2002 President Nazarbayev and the President of Uzbekistan, Islam Karimov, signed a bilateral agreement on the delimitation of remaining sectors of their common border (another border agreement had been signed in the previous year). A border agreement with Turkmenistan, which had been signed in July 2001, was ratified by the Kazakhstani Senate in June 2003, and in July President Nazarbayev signed a number of laws confirming the delimitation of Kazakhstan's borders with Kyrgyzstan, Turkmenistan and Uzbekistan.

Kazakhstan expressed concern at the underground nuclear tests carried out in the early 1990s by the People's Republic of China at Lop Nor in the Xinjiang Uygur Autonomous Region, which borders eastern Kazakhstan. In 1995 Nazarbayev made an official visit to China, where an agreement was signed to improve long-term stability between the two countries. Bilateral relations were further strengthened by two accords concluded in 1997, whereby China was granted permission to exploit two of the largest oilfields in Kazakhstan. The agreements, worth an estimated US $9,500m., provided, *inter alia*, for the construction of a petroleum pipeline connecting the two countries, on which work was expected to commence in 2004. In July 1998 Nazarbayev and President Jiang Zemin of China signed an agreement concerning disputed areas of their joint border, and agreed to a 15-year programme of bilateral economic co-operation. In late November Nazarbayev made another state visit to China, which resulted in the signing of a communiqué on the full settlement of outstanding border issues, and of an agreement outlining future bilateral relations. In addition, China and Kazakhstan attended annual summit meetings of the heads of state of the so-called Shanghai Five (also comprising Kyrgyzstan, Russia and Tajikistan), which aimed to promote economic co-operation and regional co-ordination on border and security issues. Members of the alliance, later known as the Shanghai Forum, and renamed the Shanghai Co-operation Organization (see p. 371) upon the accession of Uzbekistan in mid-2001, signed the Shanghai Convention on Combating Terrorism, Separatism and Extremism in mid-June 2001. In August 2003 Kazakhstan and China jointly hosted military manoeuvres involving the member states of the Organization.

Following the large-scale suicide attacks on the USA on 11 September 2001, President Nazarbayev expressed his support for US-led retaliatory attacks against the al-Qa'ida (Base) organization of the Saudi-born militant Islamist, Osama bin Laden, and the regime of its hosts, the Taliban, in Afghanistan (see the chapters on Afghanistan and the USA). The military action drew international attention to Central Asia, and the USA, in particular, acknowledged Kazakhstan's strategic importance; Kazakhstan offered the USA the use of airports, airspace and military bases. Nazarbayev's links with US petroleum companies were subject to legal scrutiny from late March 2003, when James H. Giffen, a US businessman and former adviser to Nazarbayev, was indicted in the USA under the 1977 Foreign Corrupt Practices Act (which prohibits US companies or individuals from offering financial inducements to foreign officials in order to secure an agreement). He was accused of offering bribes to prominent Kazakhstani politicians, including Nazarbayev and former Prime Minister Nurlan Balgymbayev, in return for securing valuable contracts for US petroleum companies. Giffen's trial was due to commence in 2004.

Government

Under the terms of the 1995 Constitution (to which a number of amendments were made in October 1998), the President of the Republic is Head of State and commander-in-chief of the armed forces, and holds broad executive powers. The President is directly elected by universal adult suffrage for a seven-year term (and may serve a maximum of two consecutive terms). The Government, headed by the Prime Minister, is responsible to the President. The supreme legislative organ is the bicameral Parliament, comprising the 39-member Senate (upper chamber) and the 77-member Majlis (Assembly, lower chamber). Seven Senators are appointed by the President of the Republic, while the remaining 32 are elected for six years by regional assemblies. The deputies of the Majlis are directly elected every six years. One-half of the elected deputies in the Senate are subject to election every three years. The seven-member Constitutional Council is empowered to ensure the correct implementation of the Constitution; its rulings are subject to a presidential right of veto.

For administrative purposes, Kazakhstan is divided into 16 local governments (14 regions and the cities of Almaty and Astana). (The city of Leninsk—now Turatam—serving the Baikonur space centre, and formerly one of Kazakhstan's administrative units, was transferred to Russian jurisdiction in August 1995.)

Defence

In May 1992 President Nursultan Nazarbayev issued a decree on the establishment of Kazakhstan's armed forces (until independence, Kazakhstan had no armed forces separate from those of the USSR). By August 2003 the estimated strength of the national armed forces was 65,800 (army 46,800 and air force 19,000). In addition, there were 34,500 paramilitary troops (including an estimated 20,000 troops attached to the Ministry of Internal Affairs, and an estimated 12,000 border guards). In March 1998 the Kazakh Ministry of Defence reportedly announced that the strength of the armed forces was to be halved by reducing the period of military service for junior ranks from two years to one. Kazakhstan participates, with Russia, Azerbaijan and Turkmenistan, in the operation of the Caspian Sea Flotilla, a former Soviet force based, under Russian command, at Astrakhan (Russia). In mid-1992 Kazakhstan signed a Collective Security Treaty with five other members of the Commonwealth of Independent States (CIS, see p. 180); in May 2001 it was announced that the signatory countries were to form a Collective Rapid Reaction Force to combat Islamist militancy in Central Asia. In April 2003 the Collective Security Treaty Organization (CSTO) was inaugurated as the successor to the CIS collective security system, with the participation of Armenia, Belarus, Kazakhstan, Kyrgyzstan, Russia and Tajikistan. A nuclear successor state to the USSR, Kazakhstan undertook to dismantle its nuclear capabilities, ratifying the first Strategic Arms Reduction Treaty in 1992 and the Treaty on the Non-Proliferation of Nuclear Weapons in 1993. All nuclear warheads had been transferred to Russia by mid-1995, and a final protocol for the withdrawal of the Russian strategic-missile troops was signed in September 1996. In July 2000 the Semipalatinsk nuclear facility, once the world's largest nuclear-testing ground, was finally closed. In late 2001 Kazakhstan ratified the Comprehensive Nuclear Test Ban Treaty. In May 1994 Kazakhstan joined the North Atlantic Treaty Organization's (NATO) 'Partnership for Peace' (see p. 291) programme of military co-operation. Kazakhstan also became a full member of the UN Conference on Disarmament in August 1999. The defence budget for 2003 was an estimated 41,400m. tenge.

Economic Affairs

In 2002, according to estimates by the World Bank, Kazakhstan's gross national income (GNI), measured at average 2000–02 prices, was US $22,268m., equivalent to $1,510 per head (or $5,480 per head on an international purchasing-power parity basis). During 1990–2002, it was estimated, the population decreased at an average annual rate of 0.8%, while gross domestic product (GDP) per head decreased, in real terms, by an average of 0.4% per year. Overall GDP declined, in real terms, at an average annual rate of 1.2% in 1990–2002. However, real GDP increased by 13.5% in 2001 and by 9.6% in 2002.

Agriculture (including forestry and fishing) contributed an estimated 7.9% of GDP in 2002, when the sector provided 35.5% of total employment. There are large areas of land suitable for agriculture, and Kazakhstan is a major producer and exporter of agricultural products. The principal crops include fruit, sugar beet, vegetables, potatoes, cotton and, most importantly, cereals. Livestock-breeding is also important, and Kazakhstan is a significant producer of karakul and astrakhan wools. The GDP of the agricultural sector decreased, in real terms, by an average of 4.9% per year in 1990–2002. Agricultural GDP increased by 16.9% in 2001, but declined by 6.0% in 2002.

Industry (including mining, manufacturing, construction, and power) contributed an estimated 35.5% of GDP in 2002, when the sector provided 16.3% of total employment. Measured by the gross value of output, the principal branches of industry in 1997 were the fuel industry (accounting for 27.7% of the total), metal-processing (23.9%), food-processing (15.4%) and electrical power generation (14.1%). Industrial GDP declined, in real terms, at an average annual rate of 4.3% in 1990–2002. However, the GDP of the sector increased by 15.1% in 2001, and there was growth of 10.7% in 2002.

Mining and quarrying provided 2.0% of employment in 1998. Kazakhstan possesses immense mineral wealth, and large-scale mining and processing industries have been developed. There are major coalfields (in the Karaganda, Turgai, Ekibastuz and Maikuben basins), as well as substantial deposits of iron ore, lead, zinc ore, titanium, magnesium, chromium, tungsten, molybdenum, gold, silver, copper and manganese. Petroleum is extracted, and Kazakhstan possesses what are believed to be among the world's largest unexploited oilfields (in the Caspian depression) and substantial reserves of natural gas. The discovery of major petroleum reserves at the offshore Kashagan oilfield was announced in mid-2000. At the end of 2002 Kazakhstan's proven total reserves (onshore and offshore) of petroleum and natural gas were estimated at 1,200m. metric tons and 1,840,000m. cu m, respectively.

Manufacturing provided 10.2% of employment in 1998, and an estimated 17.4% of GDP in 2002. The GDP of the manufacturing sector declined at an average annual rate of 23.2% in 1990–95.

In 2000 coal-fired thermal power stations provided about 69.9% of annual domestic electricity production, while hydroelectric power stations accounted for 14.6% of production and natural gas for 10.6%. In 2002 mineral fuels accounted for approximately 12.7% of total imports.

In 2002 the services sector contributed some 56.6% of GDP, and provided 48.2% of employment. During 1990–2002 the GDP of the services sector increased, in real terms, at an average annual rate of 3.2%. Services GDP increased by 10.8% in 2001 and by 8.6% in 2002.

In 2001 Kazakhstan recorded a visible trade surplus of US $2,301.2m., and there was a deficit of $695.8m. on the current account of the balance of payments. In 2002 the principal source of imports was Russia (accounting for 39.1% of total imports). Other major suppliers were the USA and Germany. The principal market for exports in that year was Bermuda (accounting for 20.7% of total exports). Other important purchasers of exports were Russia, the People's Republic of China, Italy and Switzerland. The main exports in 2002 were petroleum and gas condensate and base metals. The principal imports in that year were machinery and electrical equipment, mineral products, vehicles, base metals and chemicals.

In 2002 Kazakhstan recorded a budgetary deficit of some 13,000m. tenge (equivalent to approximately 0.3% of GDP). At the end of 2001 Kazakhstan's external debt amounted to US $14,372m. of which $3,446m. was long-term public debt. In that year the cost of debt-servicing was equivalent to 31.4% of the value of exports of goods and services. The annual rate of inflation averaged 79.9% during 1992–2002. Inflation slowed in the latter half of the 1990s, and consumer prices increased by 8.4% in 2001 and by 5.8% in 2002. In 2002 9.3% of the labour force were unemployed.

In addition to its membership of the economic bodies of the Commonwealth of Independent States (CIS, see p. 180), Kazakhstan has joined the Asian Development Bank (ADB, see p. 151), is a 'Country of Operations' of the European Bank for Reconstruction and Development (EBRD, see p. 203) and is a member of the Economic Co-operation Organization (ECO, see p. 201).

After independence in 1991, contraction in all sectors was recorded annually until 1995, when signs of an economic recovery emerged, following the initiation in 1993 of a comprehensive stabilization and reform programme, with support from the international financial community. A large-scale programme of privatization was extended in 1996 to include the strategic hydrocarbons and metallurgical sectors, thereby increasing foreign direct investment (already the highest per head among the CIS countries). In 1998 the economy was severely affected by the economic crises in Russia and Asia, and the subsequent decline in world prices of Kazakhstan's principal exports. However, by mid-2000 Kazakhstan announced that it had been able to repay fully all debts owed to the IMF, seven years ahead of schedule, as the result of improved regional demand, increased world petroleum prices and prudent macroeconomic policies. Strong economic growth was recorded in 2001–02, and Kazakhstan's long-term economic prospects were considered to be highly favourable, owing to the country's immense, and largely unexploited, hydrocarbons and other mineral resources. The discovery, announced in July 2000, of substantial petroleum deposits at the offshore Kashagan oilfield (thought to be the world's second largest) was expected to be of enormous benefit to the economy, although delays in the development of the field were announced in 2003, and the commercial extraction of petroleum was not expected to commence before 2007. However, petroleum exports had increased significantly following the official opening, in November 2001, of a new, 1,500-km petroleum pipeline, connecting the onshore Tengiz field in western Kazakhstan with Novorossiisk, on the Russian Black Sea coast. In addition, the extraction of petroleum and natural gas was expected to expand significantly as a result of a trilateral agreement, signed with Azerbaijan and Russia in May 2003, on the division of mineral resources in the Caspian seabed, and work was expected to commence in 2004 on the construction of a long-delayed, 3,000-km petroleum export pipeline between Kazakhstan and the People's Republic of China. Meanwhile, the Government hoped to use its mineral wealth to implement a programme for the diversification of the economy. To this end, a National Fund had been established in 2001, although its management was criticized for a lack of transparency. Moreover, growth in the non-petroleum sector remained highly dependent on the implementation of further structural reforms, the liberalization of trade and an improved business environment.

Education

General education (primary and secondary) is compulsory, and is fully funded by the state. Primary education begins at seven years of age and lasts for four years. Secondary education, beginning at 11 years of age, lasts for a further seven years, comprising a first cycle of five years and a second of two years. In 2000/01 total enrolment at primary schools was equivalent to 89% of the relevant age-group (females 88%), and the comparable ratio for secondary enrolment was 83% (females 82%). After completing general education, pupils may continue their studies at specialized secondary schools. In 2002/03 there was a total of 177 higher schools (including universities), with a total enrolment of 597,500 students. Ethnic Kazakhs form a greater proportion (64% in 1995/96) of students in higher education than in general education, since many ethnic Russians choose to study at universities outside Kazakhstan. None the less, the majority of higher education students (approximately 75% in 1997) are instructed in Russian. The number of private general schools in Kazakhstan increased from 18 in 1994/95 to 199 in 1999, as part of a government programme to encourage the private provision of education, although this figure had declined to 153 by 2000. In that year there were 117 private specialized secondary schools and 112 private higher schools (including universities). Government expenditure on education in 2001 was 105,024m. tenge (14.7% of total spending).

Public Holidays

2004: 1–2 January (New Year), 8 March (International Women's Day), 21 March (Nauryz Meyramy, Spring Holiday), 1 May (Day of Unity of Nationalities of Kazakhstan), 9 May (Victory Day, Day of Remembrance), 30 August (Constitution Day), 25 October (Republic Day), 16 December (Independence Day).

2005: 1–2 January (New Year), 8 March (International Women's Day), 21 March (Nauryz Meyramy, Spring Holiday), 1 May (Day of Unity of Nationalities of Kazakhstan), 9 May (Victory Day, Day of Remembrance), 30 August (Constitution Day), 25 October (Republic Day), 16 December (Independence Day).

Weights and Measures

The metric system is in force.

Statistical Survey

Source (unless otherwise stated): Agency on Statistics of the Republic of Kazakhstan, 480008 Almaty, pr. Abaya 125; tel. (3272) 62-66-45; fax (3272) 42-08-24; e-mail kazstat@mail.banknet.kz; internet www.stat.kz.

Area and Population

AREA, POPULATION AND DENSITY

Area (sq km)	2,717,300*
Population (census results)	
12 January 1989†	16,464,464
25 February–4 March 1999	
Males	7,201,785
Females.	7,751,341
Total	14,953,126
Population (official estimates at 31 December)	
2000	14,862,700
2001	14,846,000
2002	14,862,500
Density (per sq km) at 31 December 2002	5.5

* 1,049,150 sq miles.
† Figure refers to the *de jure* population. The *de facto* total was 16,536,511.

PRINCIPAL ETHNIC GROUPS
(permanent inhabitants, at 1999 census)

	Number*	%
Kazakh	7,985,000	53.4
Russian	4,479,600	30.0
Ukrainian	547,100	3.7
Uzbek	370,700	2.5
German	353,400	2.4
Tatar	249,000	1.7
Uigur	210,400	1.4
Belarusian	111,900	0.7
Korean	99,700	0.7
Azeri	78,300	0.5
Turkish	75,900	0.5
Others.	392,100	2.6
Total	14,953,100	100.0

* Figures are rounded to the nearest 100 persons.

PRINCIPAL TOWNS
(population at 1999 census)

Astana* (capital). .	313,000	Petropavlovsk . .	203,500
Almaty (Alma-Ata) .	1,129,400	Uralsk. . . .	195,500
Karaganda . . .	436,900	Temirtau . . .	170,500
Shymkent			
(Chimkent). . .	360,100	Kzyl-Orda . .	157,400
Taraz†	330,100	Aktau§ . . .	143,400
Ust-Kamenogorsk .	311,000	Atyrau‖ . . .	142,500
Pavlodar . . .	300,500	Ekibastuz . . .	127,200
Semipalatinsk . .	269,600	Kokchetau . .	123,400
Aktobe‡ . . .	253,100	Rudniy . . .	109,500
Kustanai . . .	221,400		

* Formerly Akmola.
† Formerly Dzhambul.
‡ Formerly Aktyubinsk.
§ Formerly Shevchenko.
‖ Formerly Guriyev.

Mid-2000 (UN estimate, incl. suburbs): Almaty (Alma-Ata) 1,127,000 (Source: UN, *World Urbanization Prospects: The 2001 Revision*).

Mid-2001 (UN estimate, incl. suburbs): Astana 328,000 (Source: UN, *World Urbanization Prospects: The 2001 Revision*).

BIRTHS, MARRIAGES AND DEATHS

	Registered live births		Registered marriages		Registered deaths	
	Number	Rate (per 1,000)	Number	Rate (per 1,000)	Number	Rate (per 1,000)
1995 . . .	277,006	17.2	116,380	7.2	168,885	10.5
1996 . . .	253,175	16.3	102,558	6.6	166,028	10.7
1997 . . .	232,356	15.2	101,874	6.6	160,138	10.4
1998 . . .	222,380	14.8	96,048	6.4	154,314	10.2
1999 . . .	209,039	14.0	85,872	5.8	144,450	9.7
2000 . . .	217,379	14.6	90,873	6.1	148,834	10.0
2001* . .	220,748	14.8	92,852	6.3	147,587	10.0
2002 . . .	227,169	15.3	98,986	6.7	148,706	10.0

* Provisional figures.

Source: partly UN, *Demographic Yearbook* and *Population and Vital Statistics Report*.

Expectation of life (years at birth): 63.6 (males 58.7; females 68.9) in 2002 (Source: WHO, *World Health Report*).

ECONOMICALLY ACTIVE POPULATION
(annual averages, '000 persons)

	1997	1998	1999
Agriculture, forestry and fishing	1,542	1,360	1,342
Industry*	921	903	904
Construction	261	223	211
Trade, restaurants and hotels . .	1,382	1,405	1,398
Transport, storage and communications	646	560	576
Financing and insurance . .	37	38	36
Community, social and personal services	1,387	1,639	1,638
Activities not adequately defined	296	—	—
Total employed.	6,472	6,128	6,105
Unemployed	968	925	950
Total labour force	7,440	7,053	7,055

Source: UN, *Statistical Yearbook for Asia and the Pacific*.

2000 (annual average, '000 persons aged 15 years and over): Total employed 6,201.0; Unemployed 906.4; Total labour force 7,107.4.

2001 (annual average, '000 persons aged 15 years and over): Total employed 6,698.8; Unemployed 780.3; Total labour force 7,479.1.

2002 ('000 persons aged 15 years and over): Agriculture, hunting and forestry 2,366.7; Fishing 13.5; Industry* 824.0; Construction 268.4; Wholesale and retail trade, repair of cars and household appliances 1,007.2; Restaurants and hotels 56.5; Transport, storage and communications 503.7; Financial intermediation 50.1; Real estate, renting and business activities 203.4; Public administration 280.4; Education 589.0; Health and social work 292.6; Other community, social and personal service activities 186.3; Private households with employed persons 66.8; Extra-territorial organizations and bodies 0.3; Total employed 6,708.9; Unemployed 690.7; Total labour force 7,399.7.

* Including mining and quarrying, manufacturing, and electricity, gas and water.

Health and Welfare

KEY INDICATORS

Total fertility rate (children per woman, 2002)	2.0
Under-5 mortality rate (per 1,000 live births, 2001)	76
HIV/AIDS (% of persons aged 15–49, 2001)	0.1
Physicians (per 1,000 head, 2001)	3.46
Hospital beds (per 1,000 head, 2001)	7.44
Health expenditure (2001): US $ per head (PPP)	204
Health expenditure (2001): % of GDP	3.1
Health expenditure (2001): public (% of total)	60.4
Access to water (% of persons, 2000)	91
Access to sanitation (% of persons, 2000)	99
Human Development Index (2001): ranking	76
Human Development Index (2001): value	0.765

For sources and definitions, see explanatory note on p. vi.

Agriculture

PRINCIPAL CROPS
('000 metric tons)

	2000	2001	2002
Wheat	9,073.5	12,706.8	12,670.0
Rice (paddy)	214.3	198.7	199.1
Barley	1,663.6	2,243.8	2,208.9
Maize	248.8	320.4	435.2
Rye	48.3	43.4	106.5
Oats	181.8	220.2	183.2
Millet	62.3	65.3	39.2
Buckwheat	28.7	44.9	29.6
Other cereals	25.8	28.8*	24.8*
Potatoes	1,692.6	2,185.0	2,268.8
Sugar beet	272.7	282.5	372.2
Dry peas	9.2	13.6	26.7
Soybeans	4.0	7.0	25.1
Sunflower seed	104.6	149.0	189.8
Safflower seed	25.4	25.0	37.9
Cottonseed	172.3*	240.0	189.0*
Cabbages	262.7	303.5	321.8
Tomatoes	387.0	447.2	448.9
Cucumbers and gherkins*	190.6	218.1	257.4
Aubergines (Eggplants)*	21.5	24.8	28.0
Chillies and green peppers	34.0*	47.4*	51.7
Dry onions	302.0*	348.9	309.9
Leeks and other alliacious vegetables*	12.0	13.9	15.0
Green beans*	8.5	9.8	11.0
Carrots	163.6	189.1	214.5
Other vegetables*	165.6	190.4	203.2
Apples	144.6	132.4	110.5
Pears	10.2	9.4	9.6
Cherries	12.0	6.4*	14.0
Plums	7.4	5.7*	12.5
Strawberries	5.3	5.7*	12.5
Grapes	61.6	43.0	26.3
Watermelons	421.6	519.0	628.8
Other fruits*	22.5	12.2	26.9
Tobacco (leaves)	16.2	15.0†	15.8
Cotton (lint)	95.5	112.7	90.4

* Unofficial figure(s).
† FAO estimate.

Source: FAO.

LIVESTOCK
('000 head, year ending September)

	2000	2001	2002
Horses	970	976	986
Asses*	30	30	30
Cattle	3,998	4,107	4,282
Buffaloes*	9	9	9
Camels	96	99†	98*
Pigs	984	1,076	1,124
Sheep	8,725	8,939	9,208
Goats	931	1,042	1,271
Chickens	18,023	19,706	21,279
Turkeys	69†	70†	70*
Rabbits*	60,000	61,500	62,000

* FAO estimate(s).
† Unofficial figure.

Source: FAO.

LIVESTOCK PRODUCTS
('000 metric tons)

	2000	2001	2002
Beef and veal	306.3	287.6	297.1
Mutton and lamb	91.2	91.7	93.9
Goat meat	3.9*	5.0*	7.2
Horse meat	57.9	54.3*	50.0*
Pig meat	133.4	181.3	186.9
Poultry meat	33.3	33.8	36.1
Cows' milk	3,730.2	3,922.9	4,068.2
Sheeps' milk	34.8*	35.0†	40.7*
Goats' milk	9.7	10.5	11.0†
Cheese	10.8	10.2	11.2
Butter	4.4	3.9	4.0†
Hen eggs*	93.8	103.0	116.6
Wool: greasy	22.9	23.6	23.8
Wool: scoured	13.7	14.2	14.3
Cattle hides (fresh)†	34.8	34.5	36.1
Sheepskins (fresh)†	9.9	10.3	10.4

* Unofficial figure(s).
† FAO estimate(s).

Source: FAO.

Forestry

ROUNDWOOD REMOVALS
('000 cubic metres, excl. bark)

	1995	1996	1997
Total (all fuel wood)	339	315	315

1998–2002: No production recorded.

Source: FAO.

SAWNWOOD PRODUCTION
('000 cubic metres, incl. railway sleepers)

	2000*	2001	2002
Coniferous (softwood)	261	227	222
Broadleaved (hardwood)	199	3	2
Total	460	230	224

* Unofficial figures.

Source: FAO.

Fishing

('000 metric tons, live weight)

	1999	2000	2001
Capture	36.2	36.6	30.7
Freshwater bream .	11.0*	12.0*	12.6
Crucian carp	1.9*	1.8*	1.7
Roaches .	1.0*	0.9*	0.6
Wels (Som) catfish.	0.8*	0.8*	0.8
Pike-perch	2.5*	2.0*	1.6
Azov sea sprat .	6.1	3.0	n.a.
Aquaculture .	1.2	0.8*	0.4
Silver carp .	1.1	0.8	0.4
Total catch .	37.4	37.4	31.1

* FAO estimate.

Source: FAO, *Yearbook of Fishery Statistics*.

Mining

('000 metric tons, unless otherwise indicated)

	1998	1999	2000
Hard coal .	68,058 }	58,378	74,872
Brown coal (incl. lignite) .	1,715 }		
Crude petroleum* .	25,945	26,736	30,648
Natural gas (million cu m) .	7,948	9,946	11,542
Iron ore (gross weight) .	8,693	9,617	13,829
Copper ore (metal content) .	339	374	430
Nickel ore (metal content, metric tons)† .	6,000	n.a.	3,000
Bauxite .	3,437	3,607	3,730
Lead ore (metal content) .	30	34	39
Zinc ore (metal content) .	224	270	322
Manganese ore .	399	563	720
Chromite .	1,603	2,406	2,607
Titanium (metric tons) .	12,000	8,767	8,280
Vanadium (metal content, metric tons)† .	1,000	1,000	1,000
Silver ore (metal content, metric tons) .	726	905	927
Uranium (metal content, metric tons) .	1,074	1,367	1,740
Gold (metal content, kg) .	18,100	20,236	28,171
Asbestos .	155	139	233

* Including gas condensate.
† Estimates.

Source: mainly US Geological Survey.

2001 ('000 metric tons, unless otherwise indicated): Coal 76,455; Crude petroleum 36,060; Natural gas (million cu m) 11,610; Iron ore 29,637; Copper ore 34,872; Lead and zinc ore 5,740.

2002 ('000 metric tons, unless otherwise indicated): Coal 70,603; Crude petroleum 42,037; Natural gas (million cu m) 13,137; Iron ore 33,520; Copper ore 36,668; Lead and zinc ore 6,214.

Industry

SELECTED PRODUCTS

('000 metric tons, unless otherwise indicated)

	1998	1999	2000
Wheat flour .	1,546	1,262	1,741
Raw sugar.	230	228	280
Wine ('000 hectolitres) .	163	218	n.a.
Beer ('000 hectolitres) .	8,503	8,244	13,568
Mineral water ('000 hectolitres) .	475	549	n.a.
Cigarettes (million) .	21,747	18,773	19,293
Cotton yarn .	1.9	1.8	1.0
Woven cotton fabrics (million sq metres) .	10	9	5
Sulphuric acid .	605	685	635
Motor spirit (petrol) .	1,732	1,298	1,255
Kerosene .	229	71	63
Gas-diesel (distillate fuel) oils .	2,495	1,830	1,954
Residual fuel oils.	3,052	2,133	2,391
Cement .	622	838	1,175
Pig-iron .	2,594	3,438	4,010
Crude steel .	3,116	4,105	4,799
Copper (unrefined) .	335.0	384.2	n.a.
Electric energy (million kWh) .	49,145	47,498	51,635

Sources: mainly UN, *Statistical Yearbook for Asia and the Pacific* and *Industrial Commodity Statistics Yearbook*.

2001 ('000 metric tons, unless otherwise indicated): Raw sugar 347; Wine ('000 litres) 41,032; Cotton (carded and combed) 113; Woven cotton fabrics (million sq metres) 8; Motor spirit (petrol) 1,582; Cement 2,029; Pig-iron 3,907; Steel 4,691; Copper (refined) 426; Electric energy (million kWh) 55,384.

2002 ('000 metric tons, unless otherwise indicated): Raw sugar 395; Wine ('000 litres) 37,955; Cotton (carded and combed) 146; Woven cotton fabrics (million sq metres) 14; Motor spirit (petrol) 1,691; Cement 2,129; Pig-iron 4,089; Steel 4,868; Copper (refined) 453; Electric energy (million kWh) 58,475.

Finance

CURRENCY AND EXCHANGE RATES

Monetary Units
100 tein = 1 tenge.

Sterling, Dollar and Euro Equivalents (31 December 2003)
£1 sterling = 257.39 tenge;
US $1 = 144.22 tenge;
€1 = 182.15 tenge;
1,000 tenge = £3.885 = $6.934 = €5.490.

Average Exchange Rate (tenge per US $)
2001   146.74
2002   153.28
2003   149.58

Note: The tenge was introduced on 15 November 1993, replacing the old Russian (formerly Soviet) rouble at an exchange rate of 1 tenge = 500 roubles. On 18 November the rate was adjusted to 250 roubles per tenge. In April 1999 the tenge was allowed to 'float' on foreign exchange markets.

STATE BUDGET

(million tenge)

Revenue	1999	2000	2001*
Tax revenue .	330,267	524,058	635,792
Other current revenue .	26,896	38,602	70,539
Capital revenue .	35,787	24,378	24,267
Official transfers .	2,629	3,169	233
Repayment of debt principal .	3,013	8,511	12,719
Total .	398,592	598,746	743,550†

Expenditure‡	1999	2000	2001
General public services . . .	28,856	35,114	47,771
Defence	17,198	20,379	32,347
Public order and security . . .	32,507	47,738	63,681
Education	78,491	84,668	105,024
Health care	44,825	54,323	62,238
Social security and social assistance	159,064	171,065	186,641
Recreation and cultural activities .	12,237	17,487	18,076
Housing and communal services .	6,012	22,106	30,396
Economic affairs and services . .	48,794	87,761	132,188
Agriculture, forestry, water management, fishing and environmental protection. . .	6,944	11,441	23,113
Mining and minerals (excl. fuel), manufacturing and construction	2,867	7,191	4,558
Transport and communications .	12,865	37,804	41,651
Other purposes	19,442	35,541	37,764
Debt interest	19,442	35,541	37,764
Total	**447,426**	**576,182**	**716,126**

* Provisional figures.
† Including adjustment (28 million tenge).
‡ Excluding lending minus repayments (million tenge): 20,997 in 1999; 25,842 in 2000; 32,966 in 2001.

Revised totals (million tenge, rounded figures): *Revenue:* 598,700 in 2000; 746,600 in 2001; *Expenditure (excluding lending minus repayments):* 602,000 in 2000; 759,600 in 2001.

2002 (million tenge, rounded figures): Total revenue 821,200; Total expenditure (excluding lending minus repayments) 834,200.

INTERNATIONAL RESERVES
(US $ million at 31 December)

	2001	2002	2003
Gold	510.7	585.6	725.9
IMF special drawing rights. . .	—	1.0	1.2
Reserve position in IMF. . .	0.01	0.01	0.01
Foreign exchange.	1,997.2	2,549.7	4,235.0
Total	**2,507.9**	**3,136.3**	**4,962.1**

Source: IMF, *International Financial Statistics.*

MONEY SUPPLY
(million tenge at 31 December)

	2000	2001	2002
Currency outside banks. . . .	106,428	131,175	161,701
Demand deposits at commercial banks	126,124	137,014	219,423
Total money (incl. others). . .	**236,163**	**270,009**	**381,975**

Source: IMF, *International Financial Statistics.*

COST OF LIVING
(Consumer Price Index; base: 1992 = 100)

	1997	1998	1999
Food	50,946.3	53,208.3	57,161.7
Clothing	27,476.1	28,174.6	30,263.2
Rent	49,590.9	54,922.6	57,014.6
All items (incl. others) . . .	**62,775.9**	**67,245.5**	**72,833.6**

2000: Food 66,302.0; All items 82,419.0.

2001: Food 73,894.0; All items 89,309.0.

Source: ILO.

NATIONAL ACCOUNTS
('000 million tenge at current prices)
Expenditure on the Gross Domestic Product

	2000	2001	2002
Government final consumption expenditure	314.0	436.0	435.9
Private final consumption expenditure	1,595.4	1,875.6	2,094.9
Increase in stocks	21.3	102.3	117.3
Gross fixed capital formation. .	450.3	771.4	847.2
Total domestic expenditure .	**2,381.0**	**3,185.3**	**3,495.3**
Exports of goods and services . } Less Imports of goods and services . . . . . . }	222.9	−53.6	42.3
Sub-total	**2,603.9**	**3,131.7**	**3,537.6**
Statistical discrepancy* . . .	−4.0	118.9	209.6
GDP in purchasers' values .	**2,599.9**	**3,250.6**	**3,747.2**
GDP at constant 1993 prices .	**26.7**	**30.3**	**33.2**

* Referring to the difference between the sum of the expenditure components and official estimates of GDP, compiled from the production approach.

Source: Asian Development Bank, *Key Indicators of Developing Asian and Pacific Countries.*

Gross Domestic Product by Economic Activity

	2000	2001	2002
Agriculture, forestry and fishing.	210.9	283.6	297.5
Industry*	864.7	997.1	1,099.0
Construction	134.6	117.7	229.8
Trade, restaurants and hotels .	323.5	392.9	449.9
Transport, storage and communications	298.5	362.6	429.6
Other services . . . . . } Import duties . . . . . } Less Imputed bank service charges . . . . . . }	767.7	1,096.7	1,241.4
GDP in purchasers' values .	**2,599.9**	**3,250.6**	**3,747.2**

* Including mining and quarrying, manufacturing, and electricity, gas and water.

Source: Asian Development Bank, *Key Indicators of Developing Asian and Pacific Countries.*

BALANCE OF PAYMENTS
(US $ million)

	2000	2001	2002
Exports of goods f.o.b.	9,288.1	8,927.8	10,027.6
Imports of goods f.o.b.	−6,848.2	−7,607.3	−7,726.3
Trade balance	**2,439.9**	**1,320.5**	**2,301.2**
Exports of services	1,133.3	1,306.8	1,587.5
Imports of services	−2,004.3	−2,824.6	−3,667.2
Balance on goods and services	**1,568.9**	**−197.3**	**221.5**
Other income received	138.8	224.8	233.8
Other income paid	−1,281.2	−1,368.4	−1,264.6
Balance on goods, services and income	**426.5**	**−1,340.9**	**−809.3**
Current transfers received . .	352.2	394.4	425.6
Current transfers paid . . .	−103.2	−162.4	−312.2
Current balance	**675.5**	**−1,108.9**	**−695.8**
Capital account (net)	−290.6	−194.0	−119.9
Direct investment abroad . . .	−4.4	25.6	−426.3
Direct investment from abroad. .	1,282.5	2,835.0	2,583.3
Portfolio investment assets . .	−85.5	−1,348.9	−1,077.6
Portfolio investment liabilities . .	30.7	31.4	−182.9
Other investment assets . . .	43.6	464.8	−1,098.0
Other investment liabilities . .	41.2	605.7	1,558.7
Net errors and omissions . . .	−1,122.7	−926.1	−6.5
Overall balance	**570.3**	**384.7**	**535.1**

Source: IMF, *International Financial Statistics.*

External Trade

PRINCIPAL COMMODITIES
(US $ million)

Imports c.i.f.	2000	2001	2002
Prepared foodstuffs	289.9	331.0	320.9
Mineral products	657.6	904.4	826.3
Chemical products	545.8	667.1	706.1
Plastics and rubber	193.2	239.8	265.9
Base metals and articles thereof	562.9	889.5	735.5
Machinery, mechanical appliances and electrical equipment	1,402.2	1,852.2	1,846.6
Transportation equipment	563.0	625.0	793.3
Total (incl. others)	5,040.0	6,443.0	6,490.5

Exports f.o.b.	2000	2001	2002
Vegetable products	559.7	392.7	412.5
Mineral products	4,790.6	5,028.8	5,951.2
Chemical products	378.2	405.9	418.9
Pearls, precious and semi-precious stones, and metals	387.6	264.6	267.2
Base metals and articles thereof	2,279.7	2,109.9	2,237.9
Total (incl. others)	8,812.2	8,636.9	9,709.1

Source: Asian Development Bank, *Key Indicators of Developing Asian and Pacific Countries.*

PRINCIPAL TRADING PARTNERS
(US $ million)

Imports c.i.f.	2000*	2001	2002
Belarus	39.9	46.1	54.4
China, People's Repub.	154.0	169.2	304.8
Finland	57.4	69.1	68.3
France	75.4	138.4	107.5
Germany	333.7	471.4	565.3
Italy	155.0	266.1	212.6
Japan	105.5	140.2	161.6
Korea, Repub.	82.5	106.5	107.2
Netherlands	64.7	82.4	85.6
Poland	58.8	59.3	72.2
Russia	2,459.8	2,890.9	2,540.4
Switzerland	54.3	65.8	57.1
Turkey	142.6	131.3	166.8
Ukraine	79.8	154.9	215.6
United Kingdom	219.4	246.3	255.7
USA	276.9	341.6	637.7
Uzbekistan	73.3	80.2	84.9
Total (incl. others)	5,051.7	6,363.0	6,490.5

Exports f.o.b.	2000*	2001	2002
Bermuda	1,358.1	1,221.2	2,011.3
China, People's Repub.	670.3	655.5	1,020.2
Finland	n.a	56.1	48.6
Germany	566.6	509.7	218.6
Italy	891.9	970.9	921.6
Korea, Repub.	n.a	45.4	49.3
Kyrgyzstan	58.5	87.1	107.6
Netherlands	240.0	145.0	123.2
Poland	71.2	164.2	320.4
Russia	1,783.9	1,748.4	1,524.2
Switzerland	497.6	407.3	786.8
Tajikistan	n.a	61.3	46.0
Turkey	n.a	74.4	98.0
Ukraine	268.5	490.5	291.8
United Kingdom	231.0	295.0	132.9
USA	211.0	159.1	118.8
Uzbekistan	139.2	148.8	103.6
Total (incl. others)	9,138.0	8,646.9	9,709.1

* Source: Asian Development Bank, *Key Indicators of Developing Asian and Pacific Countries.*

Transport

RAILWAYS
(estimated traffic)

	1999	2000	2001
Passenger-km (million)	8,859	10,215	10,384
Freight net ton-km (million)	91,700	124,983	135,653

ROAD TRAFFIC
(motor vehicles in use at 31 December)

	1998	1999	2000
Passenger cars	971,170	987,724	1,000,298
Buses and coaches	44,295	43,421	45,666
Lorries and vans	270,198	247,693	233,045
Motorcycles and mopeds	200,637	155,850	112,742

Source: International Road Federation, *World Road Statistics.*

SHIPPING

Merchant Fleet
(registered at 31 December)

	2000	2001	2002
Number of vessels	20	21	20
Total displacement (grt)	11,476	13,096	11,845

Source: Lloyd's Register-Fairplay, *World Fleet Statistics.*

CIVIL AVIATION
(traffic on scheduled services)

	1999	2000	2001
Passengers carried ('000)	800	800	900
Passenger-km (million)	2,136	1,797	1,901
Total ton-km (million)	64	118	44

Kilometres flown (million): 20 in 1996; 20 in 1997; 35 in 1998 (Source: UN, *Statistical Yearbook*).

Passengers carried ('000): 1,904 in 2002.

Communications Media

	1999	2000	2001
Television receivers ('000 in use) .	3,900	4,670	5,440
Telephones ('000 main lines in use)	1,759.8	1,834.2	1,939.6
Facsimile machines (number in use)	2,045	n.a.	n.a.
Mobile cellular telephones ('000 subscribers).	49.5	197.3	582.0
Internet users ('000)	70.0	100.0	150.0

Book production (incl. pamphlets, 1996): Titles 1,226; Copies 21,014,000.

Daily newspapers (1996): Titles 3; Average circulation 500,000.

Radio receivers ('000 in use, 1997): 6,470.

2002: Mobile cellular telephones ('000 subscribers) 582.0; Internet users ('000) 150.0.

Sources: UNESCO, *Statistical Yearbook*; UN, *Statistical Yearbook*; International Telecommunication Union.

Education

(1999/2000, unless otherwise indicated)

	Institutions	Teachers	Students
Pre-primary	1,102	12,600	124,400
Primary	1,447	62,700	1,208,300
Secondary: general . . .	8,309*	176,900	1,913,100
Secondary: vocational . .	293*	n.a.	89,900
Higher: universities, etc. . .}	170* {	27,189†	440,700*
Higher: other . . . . . .}		11,998‡}	

* 2000/01.

† 1994/95.

‡ 1995/96.

Sources: partly Ministry of Education; UNESCO, *Statistical Yearbook*; UN, *Statistical Yearbook for Asia and the Pacific*.

2002/03: *Secondary (general):* Institutions 8,334; Students 3,115,000; *Secondary (vocational):* Institutions 335; Students 211,300; *Higher (universities and other):* Institutions 177, Students 597,500.

Adult literacy rate (census results): 99.4% (males 99.7%; females 99.2%) in 2001 (Source: UNDP, *Human Development Report*).

Directory

The Constitution

The Constitution of the Republic of Kazakhstan was endorsed by 89% of the electorate voting in a national referendum on 30 August 1995, and was officially adopted on 6 September, replacing the Constitution of January 1993. A number of constitutional amendments were adopted on 8 October 1998. The following is a summary of the Constitution's main provisions:

GENERAL PROVISIONS

The Republic of Kazakhstan is a democratic, secular, law-based, unitary state with a presidential system of rule. The state ensures the integrity, inviolability and inalienability of its territory. State power belongs to the people, who exercise it directly through referendums and free elections, and also delegate the exercise of their power to state bodies. State power is separated into legislative, executive and judicial branches; these interact, with a system of checks and balances being applied.

Ideological and political diversity are recognized. State and private property are recognized and afforded equal protection. The state language is Kazakh. Russian is employed officially in state bodies and local government bodies on a par with Kazakh. The state creates the conditions necessary for the study and development of the languages of the peoples of Kazakhstan.

HUMAN AND CIVIL RIGHTS AND LIBERTIES

Citizenship of the Republic of Kazakhstan is acquired and terminated in accordance with the law. Citizenship of another state is not recognized for any citizen of Kazakhstan. The rights and liberties of the individual are recognized and guaranteed. No one may be subjected to discrimination on grounds of origin, sex, race, language, religious or other beliefs, or place of residence. No one may be subjected to torture, violence or other treatment or punishment that is cruel or degrading. All are entitled to use their native language and culture. Freedom of speech and creativity are guaranteed. Censorship is prohibited. Citizens are entitled to assemble and to hold meetings, rallies, demonstrations, marches and picket-lines peacefully and without weapons. Defence of the republic is the sacred duty and obligation of every citizen. Human and civil rights and liberties may be restricted only by law and only to the extent that is necessary to defend the constitutional system and to safeguard public order, and human rights and liberties. Any action capable of disrupting inter-ethnic accord is deemed unconstitutional. Restriction of civil rights and liberties on political grounds is not permitted in any form.

THE PRESIDENT OF THE REPUBLIC

The President of the Republic is the Head of State and highest official of Kazakhstan, who determines the main directions of the state's domestic and foreign policy and represents Kazakhstan within the country and in international relations. The President is symbol and guarantor of the unity of people and state power, the permanency of the Constitution and of human and civil rights and liberties. The President is elected for a seven-year term by secret ballot on the basis of general, equal and direct suffrage. No person may be elected to the office for more than two consecutive terms. A citizen of the republic by birth, who is at least 40 years of age, has a fluent command of the state language, and has lived in Kazakhstan for no less than 15 years, may be elected President.

The President addresses an annual message to the people; schedules regular and extraordinary elections to Parliament; signs and promulgates laws submitted by the Senate, or returns draft legislation for further discussion; with the consent of Parliament, appoints the Prime Minister and relieves him of office; on the recommendation of the Prime Minister, determines the structure of the Government, appoints its members to office and relieves them of office; presides at sessions of the Government on matters of particular importance; may cancel or suspend acts of the Government and of the akims (heads of regional administrative bodies); with the consent of Parliament, appoints to and relieves of office the Chairman of the National Bank; with the consent of the Senate, appoints to and relieves of office the Prosecutor-General and the Chairman of the National Security Committee; appoints and recalls the heads of diplomatic missions of the republic; decides on the holding of referendums; negotiates and signs international treaties; is supreme Commander-in-Chief of the armed forces; bestows state awards and confers honours; resolves matters of citizenship and of granting political asylum; in the event of aggression against the republic, imposes martial law or announces a partial or general mobilization; forms the Security Council, the Supreme Judicial Council and other consultative and advisory bodies.

The President may be relieved of office only in the event of his having committed an act of treason or if he exhibits a consistent incapacity to carry out his duties owing to illness. A decision on the President's early dismissal is adopted at a joint sitting of the chambers of Parliament by a majority of no less than three-quarters of the total number of deputies of each chamber. Dismissal of a treason indictment against the President at any stage shall result in the early termination of the powers of the Majlis members who initiated the consideration of the matter. The question of dismissal of the President may not be raised at the same time as he is considering early termination of the authority of Parliament.

PARLIAMENT

Parliament is the supreme representative body of the republic, exercising legislative functions. It consists of two chambers, the Senate (upper chamber) and the Majlis (assembly, lower chamber). The Senate comprises 39 members, of whom 32 are elected at joint sittings of the deputies of all representative bodies of the regions and the capital, while the remaining seven deputies are appointed by the President. The Majlis consists of 67 deputies elected from single-mandate constituencies by secret ballot on the basis of general, equal and direct suffrage and 10 elected by party lists. The Senate's term is six years, and that of the Majlis is five years. One-half of the elected deputies in the Senate are subject to election every three years.

THE GOVERNMENT

The Government exercises the executive power of the republic and is responsible to the President. The Government drafts the main areas of the state's socio-economic policy, defence capability, security and public order, and orders their implementation; presents to Parliament the republican budget and the report of its implementation, and ensures that the budget is implemented; submits draft legislation to the Majlis and provides for the implementation of laws; organizes the management of state property; formulates measures for the pursuit of Kazakhstan's foreign policy; directs the activity of Ministries, State Committees and other central and local executive bodies. The Prime Minister organizes and directs the activity of the Government and is personally responsible for its work.

THE CONSTITUTIONAL COUNCIL

The Constitutional Council consists of seven members whose term of office is six years. Former Presidents of the Republic are by right life members of the Constitutional Council. The Chairman and two members of the Council are appointed by the President of the Republic, two members are appointed by the Chairman of the Senate and two by the Chairman of the Majlis. One-half of the members of the Council are replaced every three years. The Council decides whether to hold a presidential or parliamentary election, or a republican referendum; prior to signature by the President, examines laws passed by Parliament for compliance with the Constitution; prior to ratification, examines international treaties.

LOCAL STATE ADMINISTRATION AND GOVERNMENT

Local state administration is exercised by local representative and executive bodies, which are responsible for the state of affairs on their own territory. The local representative bodies—the councils (maslikhat)—express the will of the population of the corresponding administrative-territorial units and, bearing in mind the overall state interest, define the measures necessary to realize this will and monitor the ways in which these are implemented. Councils are elected for a four-year term by a secret ballot of the public on the basis of general, equal and direct suffrage. The local executive bodies are part of the unified system of executive bodies of Kazakhstan, and ensure that the general state policy of the executive authority is implemented in co-ordination with the interests and development needs of the corresponding territory. Each local executive body is headed by the akim of the corresponding administrative-territorial unit, who is the representative of the President and the Government of the Republic.

The Government

HEAD OF STATE

President of the Republic of Kazakhstan: NURSULTAN A. NAZARBAYEV (elected 1 December 1991; re-elected 10 January 1999).

GOVERNMENT
(April 2004)

Prime Minister: DANIYAL AKHMETOV.

First Deputy Prime Minister: (vacant).

Deputy Prime Ministers: SAUAT MYNBAYEV, KARIM MASIMOV.

Deputy Prime Minister and Minister of Agriculture: AKHMETZHAN YESIMOV.

Minister of Finance: ARMAN DUNAYEV.

State Secretary and Minister of Foreign Affairs: KASYMZHOMART K. TOKAYEV.

Minister of Internal Affairs: ZAUTBEK TURISBEKOV.

Ministry of Economy and Budget Planning: KEYRAT NEMATOVICH KELIMBETOV.

Minister of Energy and Mineral Resources: VLADIMIR S. SHKOLNIK.

Minister of Defence: Gen. MUKHTAR ALTYNBAYEV.

Minister of Industry and Trade: ADILBEK DZHAKSYBEKOV.

Minister of Labour and Social Security: GULZHANA KARAGUSOVA.

Minister of Education and Science: ZHAKSYBEK KULEKEYEV.

Minister of Environmental Protection: AITKUL B. SAMAKOVA.

Minister of Justice: GEORGI KIM.

Minister of Culture: DYUSEN KASEINOV.

Minister of Information: SAUTBEK ABDRAKHMANOV.

Minister of Transport and Communications: KAZHMURAT NAGMANOV.

Minister of Public Health: YERBOLAT DOSAYEV.

Mayor of Astana: TEMIRKHAN DOSMUHAMBETOV.

HEADS OF GOVERNMENT BODIES

National Bank: ANVAR SAIDENOV.

National Commission on Family and Women's Affairs: AITKUL B. SAMAKOVA.

National Security Council: BULAT UTEMURATOV.

State Committee for Affairs of the Commonwealth of Independent States: ASAN KOZHAKOV.

State Committee for Aviation and Space: ALMAS KOSUNOV.

State Agency for Emergency Situations: (vacant).

State Committee for Energy Supervision: MURAT RAMAZANOV.

State Agency for Financial Police: SARYBAY KALMURZAYEV.

State Agency for Management of Land Resources: BAKYT OSPANOV.

State Agency for Material Reserves: KABIDOLLA SAREKENOV.

State Agency for Migration and Demography: ALTYNSHASH DZHAGANOVA.

State Agency for the Protection of State Secrets: SERIK AKHMETOV.

State Committee for State Property and Privatization: MAKSUTBEK RAKHANOV.

State Agency for Statistics: ALIKHAN SMAILOV.

State Agency for Tourism and Sports: DAULET TURLYKHANOV.

MINISTRIES

Office of the President: 473000 Astana, Beibitshilik 11; tel. (3172) 32-13-99; fax (3172) 32-61-72; internet www.president.kz.

Office of the Prime Minister: 473000 Astana, Beibitshilik 11; tel. (3172) 32-31-04; fax (3172) 32-40-89.

Ministry of Agriculture: 473000 Astana, pr. Abaya 49; tel. (3172) 32-37-63; fax (3172) 32-62-99; e-mail mailbox@minagri.kz; internet www.minagri.kz.

Ministry of Culture: Astana.

Ministry of Defence: 473000 Astana, Beibitshilik 51A; tel. and fax (3172) 33-78-89.

Ministry of Economy and Budget Planning: 473000 Astana, Popeda 33; tel. (3172) 71-77-70; fax (3172) 71-77-12; e-mail mineconom@nursat.kz; internet www.minplan.kz.

Ministry of Education and Science: 473000 Astana, Kenesary 83; tel. (3172) 32-25-40; fax (3172) 32-64-82.

Ministry of Energy and Mineral Resources: 473000 Astana, Beibitshilik 37; tel. (3172) 31-71-33; fax (3172) 31-71-64; e-mail ministr@minenergo.kegoc.kz; internet www.minenergo.kz.

Ministry of Environmental Protection: 473000 Astana, Pobeda 31; tel. (3172) 59-19-44; fax (3172) 59-19-73; internet www.nature.kz.

Ministry of Finance: 473000 Astana, pl. Respubliki 60; tel. (3172) 28-00-65; fax (3172) 32-40-89; internet www.minfin.kz.

Ministry of Foreign Affairs: 473000 Astana, Beibitshilik 11; tel. (3172) 32-76-69; fax (3172) 32-76-67; internet www.mfa.kz.

Ministry of Industry and Trade: 473000 Astana.

Ministry of Information: Astana.

Ministry of Internal Affairs: 473000 Astana, Manasa 4; tel. (3172) 34-36-01; fax (3172) 34-17-38; internet www.mvd.kz.

Ministry of Justice: 473000 Astana, Pobeda 45; tel. (3172) 39-12-13; fax (3172) 32-15-54; internet www.minjust.kz.

Ministry of Labour and Social Security: 473000 Astana, Manasa 2; tel. (3172) 15-36-02; internet www.enbek.banknet.kz.

Ministry of Public Health: Astana.

Ministry of Transport and Communications: 473000 Astana, pr. Abaya 49; tel. (3172) 32-62-77; fax (3172) 32-16-96.

President and Legislature

Presidential Election, 10 January 1999

Candidate	% of votes
Nursultan A. Nazarbayev	80.97
Serikbolsyn A. Abdildin	11.87
Gani Kasymov	4.68
Engels Gabbasov	0.77
Against all candidates	1.71
Total	**100.00**

PARLIAMENT

Parliament is a bicameral legislative body, comprising the Senate and the Majlis (Assembly). Elections to Parliament were held for the first time in December 1995.

Parliament: e-mail www@parlam.kz; internet www.parlam.kz.

Senate

Chairman: NURTAI ABYKAYEV.

The Senate is the upper chamber of Parliament. It comprises 39 members: 32 elected by special electoral colleges (comprising members of local councils) in Kazakhstan's 14 regions and two cities (the country's third city, Turatam, is effectively governed by Russia), and seven appointed by the President of the Republic. At the first elections to the Senate, held on 5 December 1995, only 38 of the then 40 regionally elected seats were filled, necessitating further voting at a later date for the remaining two seats. The remaining seven Senators were appointed by President Nazarbayev. Elections are held every three years for one-half of the elected seats. Partial elections to the Senate were held on 17 September 1999 and 8 October 2002.

Majlis

Chairman: ZHARMAKHAN A. TUYAKBAYEV.

The Majlis is the 77-seat lower chamber of Parliament. The first direct elections to a 67-seat Majlis were held on 9 December 1995. Further direct elections to the Majlis were held on 10 October 1999, with the participation of 62.6% of the electorate. For the first time, an additional 10 seats were elected by party lists, bringing the total number of seats to 77. However, the required two-thirds' quorum was not achieved, as candidates succeeded in obtaining the requisite 50% of the votes in only 20 of the 67 single-mandate constituencies. A further round of voting took place in the remaining 47 constituencies on 24 October. Three of these results were subsequently declared to be invalid, thus necessitating a third round of voting in the three constituencies on 26 December.

General Election, 10 and 24 October and 26 December 1999

Party	Number of seats		
	Single-mandate constituencies	Party lists	Total
Independents and others	34	—	34
Otan	19	4	23
Civic Party of Kazakhstan	11	2	13
Communist Party of Kazakhstan	1	2	3
Agrarian Party of Kazakhstan	1	2	3
National Co-operative Party of Kazakhstan	1	—	1
Total	**67**	**10**	**77**

Political Organizations

A new law was introduced in July 2002, which required all parties to have a minimum of 50,000 members from among all the country's regions in order to qualify for official registration. By the end of 2003 the following parties were registered with the Ministry of Justice.

Agrarian Party of Kazakhstan: Astana, Pobedy 104; tel. (3172) 32-48-06 (Astana); e-mail agro@mail.kz; f. 1999 to support farmers and campaign for the introduction of private land ownership; centrist; Leader ROMIN MADINOV; 95,000 mems.

Ak Zhol (Light Road) (Democratic Party of Kazakhstan): 480004 Almaty, Gogol 111A; tel. (3272) 50-46-25; fax (3272) 50-46-27; e-mail ca@dpkakzhol.kz; internet www.dpkakzhol.kz; f. 2002 by former members of the Democratic Choice of Kazakhstan; Co-Chair. ALTYNBEK SARSENBAYEV; c. 65,000 mems.

Asar (All Together): Almaty; f. 2003; centrist; Leader DARIGHA NAZARBAYEVA; 77,000 mems.

Aul (Village) Peasant and Social Democratic Party: Almaty; f. 2000; Leader GANI KALIYEV.

Civic Party of Kazakhstan: Almaty, Zheltoksan 115, pav. 50; tel. (3272) 62-19-16; e-mail civicparty@mail.kz; f. 1998; seeks strengthening of state system and improvements in the provision of social welfare; Leaders AZAT PERUASHEV, DYUSEMBAY DUYSENOV; over 50,000 mems.

Communist Party of Kazakhstan (CPK): Almaty, Karasai batyr 85/312; tel. (3272) 65-11-19; suspended Aug. 1991, re-registered March 1994 and March 2003; Chair. SERIKBOLSYN A. ABDILDIN.

Otan (Fatherland): Almaty, Furmanov 174B; tel. (3272) 63-29-79; e-mail party_otan@nursat.kz; internet www.otan.nursat.kz; f. 1999 by the People's Unity Party, the Kazakhstan–2030 Movement, the Liberal Movement of Kazakhstan and the Democratic Party of Kazakhstan; pro-presidential republican party; seeks to strengthen the state system and preserve political stability; mergers with the People's Co-operative Party of Kazakhstan and the Republican Labour Party reported in Sept. and Nov. 2002, respectively; Chair. SERGEI TERESHCHENKO; Deputy Chair. KAZBEK KAZKENOV; 126,000 mems.

Party of Patriots of Kazakhstan (PPK): Almaty; f. 2000; Leader GANI KASYMOV.

Rukhaniyat (Spirituality): f. 2003; aims to tackle social issues through morality and spirituality; improve the economy; and promote political stability; Leader ALTYNSHASH DZHAGANOVA.

Diplomatic Representation

EMBASSIES IN KAZAKHSTAN

Afghanistan: Almaty, Mira 12; tel. and fax (3272) 55-27-92; Chargé d'affaires SAYD ZAHER SHAH AKHBARI.

Armenia: 480075 Almaty, Seifullina 579, 7th Floor; tel. (3272) 67-46-00; fax (3272) 72-52-68; e-mail akod100@hotmail.com; Ambassador Dr EDUARD SH. KHURSHUDIAN.

Azerbaijan: Astana; Ambassador LYATIF QANDILOV.

Belarus: 473000 Astana, pr. Respubliki 17; tel. (3172) 32-18-70; fax (3172) 32-06-65; e-mail kazakhstan@belembassy.org; Ambassador PAKUSH LARISA VLADIMIROVNA.

Bulgaria: 480002 Almaty, Makatayeva 13A; tel. (3272) 33-27-55; fax (3272) 30-27-55; e-mail dekov@itte.kz; Chargé d'affaires a.i. DIMITAR DEKOV.

Canada: 480100 Almaty, Karasai Batyr 34; tel. (3272) 50-11-51; fax (3272) 58-24-93; e-mail almat@dfait-maeci.gc.ca; internet www.canada.nursat.kz; Ambassador HECTOR COWAN.

China, People's Republic: Almaty, Furmanova 137; tel. (3272) 63-49-66; fax (3272) 63-82-09; e-mail chinaemb_kz@mfa.gov.cn; Ambassador ZHOU XIAOPEI.

Cuba: 473005 Astana, Samal 10, kv. 1; tel. and fax (3172) 22-14-19; e-mail embacuba@cubakaz.com; internet www.cubakaz.com; Chargé d'affaires a.i. BLÁS NABEL PÉREZ CAMEJO.

Czech Republic: 480002 Almaty, Dostyk 212, POB 5; tel. (3272) 64-16-06; fax (3272) 64-49-97; e-mail amaata@embassy.mzv.cz; Ambassador MILAN SEDLÁČEK.

Egypt: 480100 Almaty, Zenkova 59; tel. (3272) 60-16-22; fax (3272) 61-10-22; e-mail sphinx_emb@nursat.kz; Ambassador (vacant).

France: 480110 Almaty, Furmanova 173; tel. (3272) 50-62-36; fax (3272) 50-61-59; e-mail ambafrance@mail.kz; Ambassador GÉRARD PERROLET.

Georgia: Almaty, Bayan Aul 7; tel. (3272) 31-09-09; Ambassador NUGZAR DUCHIDZE.

Germany: 480091 Almaty, Furmanova 173; tel. (3272) 50-61-55; fax (3272) 50-62-76; e-mail german_embassy_almaty@nursat.kz; internet www.deutschebotschaft-almaty.org; Ambassador ANDREAS R. KÖRTING.

Greece: 480051 Almaty, pr. Dostyka 216/1, Zavodskaya; tel. (3272) 50-39-61; fax (3272) 50-39-38; e-mail gr_embassy@kaznet.kz; Ambassador NIKOLAS HATOUPIS.

Holy See: 473000 Astana, Zelyonaya Alleya 20; tel. (3172) 24-16-03; fax (3172) 24-16-04; Apostolic Nuncio JÓZEF WESOŁOWSKI.

Hungary: 480000 Almaty, ul. Muszabajeva 4; tel. (3272) 55-12-08; fax (3272) 58-18-37; e-mail titkarsagala@mail.online.kz; Ambassador MIKLÓS JACZKOVITS.

India: 480091 Almaty, Maulenova 71; tel. (3272) 92-14-11; fax (3272) 92-67-67; e-mail ambind@netel.kz; Ambassador Dr VIDYA SAGAR VERMA.

Iran: Almaty, Kabanbai Batyr 119; tel. (3272) 67-78-46; fax (3272) 54-27-54; Ambassador MURTAZA SAFFARI.

Israel: Almaty, Zheltoksan 87; tel. (3272) 50-72-15; fax (3272) 50-62-83; e-mail emb_isr_almaty@kaznet.kz; Ambassador MOSHE KIMCHE.

Italy: 480100 Almaty, Kazybek bi 20A, 3rd Floor; tel. (3272) 91-00-07; fax (3272) 91-00-53; e-mail ambalma@nursat.kz; Ambassador DIEGO LORENZO LONGO.

Japan: Almaty, Kazybek bi 41, 3rd Floor; tel. (3272) 60-86-00; fax (3272) 60-86-01; e-mail taishikz@nursat.kz; internet www.kz .emb-japan.go.jp; Ambassador TOSHIO TSUNOZAKI.

Korea, Democratic People's Republic: Almaty, Voronezhskaya 58; tel. (3272) 61-89-98; fax (3272) 25-27-66; Ambassador PAK UI CHUN.

Korea, Republic: Almaty, Jarkentskaya 2/77; tel. (3272) 53-26-60; fax (3272) 50-70-59; e-mail swtae76@mofat.go.kr; Ambassador TAE SUK-WON.

Kyrgyzstan: Almaty, Amangeldy 68A; tel. (3272) 63-33-09; fax (3272) 63-33-62; Ambassador DZHUMAGUL SAADANBEKOVICH SAADANBEKOV.

Lebanon: Almaty, Sovkhoz 'Alatau', Naberezhnaya 20; tel. (3272) 48-71-51; Ambassador ASSIF NASSER.

Libya: Almaty, Satpaeva 10, kv. 2; tel. (3272) 62-67-17; fax (3272) 62-22-23; e-mail libya@nursat.kz; Chargé d'affaires a.i. OMAR ALI GEIT.

Lithuania: 480099 Almaty, Iskanderova 15; tel. (3272) 65-61-23; fax (3272) 65-14-60; e-mail lrambkaz@nursat.kz; Chargé d'affaires a.i. JONAS VORONAVIČIUS.

Malaysia: 480099 Almaty, pr. Al Farabi 36/2; tel. (3272) 53-35-03; fax (3272) 53-35-06; e-mail mwalmaty@nursat.kz; Ambassador TAN SEN SUNG.

Mongolia: Almaty, Kazybek bi 18; tel. (3272) 20-08-65; fax (3272) 60-17-23; e-mail monkazel@kazmail.asdc.kz; Ambassador DANDIMZHAVYN DASHNYAM.

Netherlands: 480072 Almaty, Nauryzbai Batyr 103; tel. (3272) 50-37-73; fax (3272) 50-37-72; e-mail alm@minbuza.nl; internet www .nlembassy-almaty.org; Ambassador PETER VAN LEEUWEN.

Pakistan: 480004 Almaty, Tulebayeva 25; tel. (3272) 73-35-48; fax (3272) 73-13-00; e-mail parepalmaty@hotmail.com; Ambassador DURRAY SHAHWAR KURESHI.

Poland: 480099 Almaty, Dzharkentskaya 9–11, POB 228; tel. (3272) 58-15-51; fax (3272) 58-15-50; e-mail ambpol@mail.kz; Ambassador ZDZISŁAW NOWICKI.

Romania: 480100 Almaty, Pushkina 97; tel. (3272) 63-57-72; fax (3272) 58-83-17; e-mail ambro@nursat.kz; Ambassador VASILE SOARE.

Russia: Almaty, Dzhandosova 4; tel. (3272) 44-64-91; fax (3272) 44-83-23; e-mail rfe@nursat.kz; Ambassador VLADIMIR BABICHEV.

Saudi Arabia: Almaty, Gornaya 137; tel. (3272) 65-77-91; fax (3272) 50-28-11; e-mail emb_kz@hotmail.com; Ambassador ALI AL-HAMDAN.

Spain: Almaty, Baitursinova 102; tel. (3272) 50-09-06; fax (3272) 50-35-30; e-mail embespkz@mail.mae.es; Ambassador FRANCISCO PASCUAL DE LA PARTE.

Tajikistan: Almaty, Al Farabi 96; tel. (3272) 93-51-65; fax (3272) 93-51-80; e-mail tajemb-kaz@vitelco.kz; Chargé d'affaires DAVLAT SIPINEROV.

Turkey: 480100 Almaty, Tole bi 29; tel. (3272) 61-81-53; fax (3272) 50-62-08; e-mail almatyturk@kaznet.kz; Ambassador HAKKI TANER SEBEN.

Turkmenistan: 473000 Astana, Otyrar 64; tel. and fax (3172) 28-08-82; e-mail tm_emb@at.kz; Ambassador MUHAMMAD ABALAKOV.

Ukraine: Astana, Aezova 57; tel. (3172) 32-60-42; fax (3172) 32-68-11; e-mail embassy_ua@kepter.kz; internet ukrembassy.kepter.kz; Ambassador VASILIY G. TSUBENKO.

United Kingdom: 480110 Almaty, Furmanova 173; tel. (3272) 50-61-91; fax (3272) 50-62-60; e-mail british-embassy@nursat.kz; internet www.britishembassy.gov.uk/kazakhstan; Ambassador JAMES LYALL SHARP.

USA: 480091 Almaty, Furmanova 97–99A; tel. (3272) 63-39-21; fax (3272) 63-38-83; e-mail usembassy-almaty@freenet.kz; internet www.usembassy-kazakhstan.freenet.kz; Ambassador LARRY NAPPER.

Uzbekistan: 480100 Almaty, Baribayeva 36; tel. (3272) 61-02-35; fax (3272) 61-10-55; Ambassador TURDIKUL BUTAYAROV.

Judicial System

Chairman of the Constitutional Council: YURII KHITRIN.

Chairman of the Supreme Court: IGOR I. ROGOV.

Prosecutor-General: RASHID T. TUSUPBEKOV.

Religion

The major religion of the Kazakhs is Islam. They are almost exclusively Sunni Muslims of the Hanafi school. The Russian Orthodox Church is the dominant Christian denomination; it is attended mainly by Slavs. There are also Protestant Churches (mainly Baptists), as well as a Roman Catholic (Latin Rite) presence.

ISLAM

The Kazakhs were converted to Islam only in the early 19th century, and for many years elements of animist practices remained. Over the period 1985–90 the number of mosques in Kazakhstan increased from 25 to 60, 12 of which were newly built. By 1991 there were an estimated 230 Muslim religious communities functioning in Kazakhstan and an Islamic institute had been opened in Almaty. The Islamic revival intensified following Kazakhstan's independence from the USSR, and during 1991–94 some 4,000 mosques were reported to have been opened.

Mufti of Kazakhstan: ABSATTAR B. DERBISALIYEV, Almaty.

CHRISTIANITY

The Roman Catholic Church

In May 2003 the hierarchy of the Roman Catholic Church in Kazakhstan was restructured. The former apostolic administration of Astana was elevated to the status of archdiocese, with authority over the dioceses of Almaty (formerly an apostolic administration) and Karaganda, and the apostolic administration of Atyrau. Adherents to the Roman Catholic Church totalled an estimated 182,600 at 31 December 2002.

Archbishop of the Most Holy Virgin Mary in Astana: Rt Rev. TOMASZ PETA, 473033 Astana, Tashenova 3, POB 622; tel. (3172) 34-29-35; fax (3172) 34-29-27.

The Russian Orthodox Church (Moscow Patriarchate)

Metropolitanate of Astana and Alma-Ata: Almaty; internet www.svet.orthodoxy.ru/epr/epr.htm; f. 2003; three dioceses; Metropolitan MEFODII.

The Press

At July 2001 an estimated 950 newspaper and 342 periodical titles were published in Kazakhstan. In addition, 15 news agencies were operating in the country.

PRINCIPAL DAILY NEWSPAPERS

Almaty Asia Times: Almaty, Dzhandosova 60/412; tel. (3272) 44-74-54; fax (3272) 44-78-40.

Almaty Herald: Almaty, pr. Dostyk 85A; tel. and fax (3272) 63-36-55; internet www.herald.asdc.kz.

Ekspress-K: 480044 Almaty, Abdullinykh 6; tel. (3272) 59-60-00; fax (3272) 59-60-39; e-mail daily@express-k.kz; internet www .express-k.kz; f. 1922; 5 a week; in Russian; Editor-in-Chief IGOR SHAKHNOVICH; circ. 18,500.

Kazakhstanskaya Pravda (Truth of Kazakhstan): 480044 Almaty, Gogolya 39; Astana; tel. (3272) 63-65-65; fax (3272) 50-18-73; tel. (3172) 32-19-44; e-mail kpam@kaznet.kz; internet www .kazpravda.kz; f. 1920; 5 a week; publ. by the Government; in Russian; Editor-in-Chief V. MIKHAILOV; circ. 34,115.

Khalyk Kenesi (Councils of the People): Almaty; tel. (3272) 33-10-85; f. 1990; 5 a week; publ. by Parliament; in Kazakh; Editor-in-Chief ZH. KENZHALIN.

Vecherniy Almaty (Evening Almaty): Almaty, Ablai Khan 2; tel. (3272) 33-34-87; fax (3272) 39-64-24.

Yegemen Kazakhstan (Sovereign Kazakhstan): 480044 Almaty, Gogolya 39; Astana; tel. and fax (3272) 63-25-46; tel. (3172) 34-16-41; e-mail astegemen@nursat.kz; f. 1919; 6 a week; organ of the Government; in Kazakh; Editor-in-Chief M. SERKHANOV; circ. 31,840.

OTHER PUBLICATIONS

Akikat (Justice): 480044 Almaty, Gogolya 39; tel. (3272) 63-94-33; fax (3272) 63-94-19; f. 1921; monthly; social and political; circ. 1,484.

Aktsionerny (Stock Business Guide): 480004 Almaty, Chaikovskogo 11; tel. (3272) 32-96-09; fax (3272) 39-98-95; f. 1990; in Russian; twice a week; Editor-in-Chief VIKTOR SHATSKY.

Ana Tili (Native Language): 484044 Almaty, pr. Dostyk 7; tel. (3272) 33-22-21; fax (3272) 33-34-73; f. 1990; weekly; publ. by the Kazakh Tili society; in Kazakh; Editor-in-Chief ZH. BEISENBAY-ULY; circ. 11,073.

Ara-Shmel (Bumble-bee): 480044 Almaty, Gogolya 39; tel. (3272) 63-59-46; f. 1956; monthly; satirical; in Kazakh and Russian; Editor-in-Chief S. ZHUMABEKOV; circ. 53,799.

Arai (Dawn): Almaty, Furmanova 53; tel. (3272) 32-29-45; f. 1987; every two months; socio-political; Editor-in-Chief S. KUTTYKADAMOV; circ. 7,500.

Atameken (Fatherland): 484100 Almaty, pr. Dostyk 85; tel. (3272) 63-58-43; f. 1991; ecological; publ. by Ministry of Environmental Protection; circ. 25,063.

Aziya Kino (Asian Cinema): 480100 Almaty, Tole bi 23A; tel. (3272) 61-86-55; f. 1994; monthly; in Russian and Kazakh; Editor-in-Chief G. ABIKEYEVA.

Baldyrgan (Sprout): 480044 Almaty, pr. Zhibek zholy 50; tel. (3272) 33-16-73; f. 1958; monthly; illustrated; for pre-school and first grades of school; in Kazakh; Editor-in-Chief T. MOLDAGALIYEV; circ. 150,000.

Budem: 480004 Almaty, Chaikovskogo 11; tel. (3272) 39-97-04; f. 1997; monthly; in Russian; Editor-in-Chief R. GARIPOV.

Business World: Astana, Pushkina 166; tel. and fax (3172) 75-19-34; e-mail areket-kz@hotmail.com; f. 1999; weekly; circ. 10,000.

Continent: 480000 Almaty, General Post Office, POB 271; tel. (3272) 50-10-39; fax (3272) 50-10-41; e-mail bzchyt@kaznet.kz; f. 1999; policy and society journal; Editor-in-Chief ANDREI KUKUSHKIN; circ. 10,000.

Delovaya Nedelya (Business Week): 484044 Almaty, pr. Zhibek zholy 64; tel. (3272) 50-62-72; fax (3272) 33-91-48; e-mail rikki@kazmail.asdc.kz; internet www.dn.kz; f. 1992; weekly; in Russian; Editor-in-Chief O. CHERVINSKII; circ. 16,066.

Deutsche Allgemeine Zeitung: 480044 Almaty, pr. Zhibek zholy 50, Office 418; tel. (3272) 73-42-69; fax (3272) 73-92-91; e-mail daz@ok.kz; f. 1966; weekly; political, economic, cultural, social; in German; Editor-in-Chief IRINA ZIRENTSCHIKOWA; circ. 1,700.

Ekonomika i Zhizn (Economics and Life): Almaty; tel. (3272) 63-96-86; f. 1926; monthly; publ. by the Government; in Russian; Editor-in-Chief MURAT T. SARSENOV; circ. 4,800.

Globe: 480009 Almaty, pr. Abaya 155, Rms 13/14; tel. (3272) 50-76-39; fax (3272) 50-63-62; e-mail ipa@mailonline.kz; internet www.globe.kz; f. 1995; twice a week; in English and Russian; Editor-in-Chief NURLAN ABLYAZOV; circ. 5,550.

Golos Kazakha (Voice of Kazakhstan): Almaty, Zenkov 75; tel. (3272) 61-79-09; fax (3272) 61-94-47; f. 1989; weekly; organ of the Federation of Trade Unions of Kazakhstan; circ. 30,000.

Islam Nury (The Light of Islam): Semipalatinsk; f. 2000; every two weeks; Islamic.

Kakadu: 480004 Almaty, Chaikovskogo 11; tel. (3272) 39-97-04; f. 1995; monthly; in Russian; Editor-in-Chief L. GERTZY.

Karavan: 480004 Almaty, Chaikovskogo 11; tel. (3272) 32-08-39; fax (3272) 32-97-57; e-mail advertising@caravan.kz; internet www.caravan.kz; f. 1991; 20% of shares were reported to have been sold to a US investment co in 2001; weekly; in Russian; Editor-in-Chief ANDREI SHUKHOV; circ. 250,000.

Kazakh Adebiety (Kazakh Literature): 484091 Almaty, pr. Ablai-khana 105; tel. and fax (3272) 69-54-62; f. 1934; weekly; organ of the Union of Writers of Kazakhstan; in Kazakh; Editor-in-Chief A. ZHAKSYBAYEV; circ. 7,874.

Kazakhstan: 480044 Almaty, pr. Zhibek zholy 50; tel. (3272) 33-13-56; f. 1992; weekly; economic reform; in English; Editor-in-Chief N. ORAZBEKOV.

Kazakhstan Aielderi (Women of Kazakhstan): 480044 Almaty, pr. Zhibek zholy 50; tel. (3272) 33-06-23; fax (3272) 46-15-53; f. 1925; monthly; literary, artistic, social and political; in Kazakh; Editor-in-Chief ALTYNSHASH K. JAGANOVA; circ. 15,200.

Kazakhstan Business: 480044 Almaty, pr. Zhibek zholy 50; tel. (3272) 33-42-56; f. 1991; weekly; in Russian; Editor-in-Chief B. SUKHARBEKOV.

Kazakhstan Mektebi (Kazakh School): 480004 Almaty, pr. Ablaikhana 34; tel. (3272) 39-76-65; f. 1925; monthly; in Kazakh; Editor-in-Chief S. ABISHEVA; circ. 10,000.

Kazakhstan Mugalimi (Kazakh Teacher): 484100 Almaty, Dzhambula 25; tel. (3272) 61-60-58; f. 1935; weekly; in Kazakh; Editor-in-Chief ZH. TEMIRBEKOV; circ. 6,673.

Kazakhstan Zaman (Kazakh Time): 480002 Almaty, pr. Dostyk 106G; tel. (3272) 65-07-39; e-mail kazakistanzaman@mail.ru; f. 1992; in Kazakh and Turkish; weekly; publ. by the al-Farabi Foundation; circ. 15,000; Gen. Dir ERSIN DEMIRCI.

Korye Ilbo: 480044 Almaty, pr. Zhibek zholy 50; tel. (3272) 33-90-10; fax (3272) 63-25-46; f. 1923; weekly; in Korean and Russian; Editor-in-Chief YAN WON SIK.

Medicina (Medicine): Almaty, pr. Ablaikhana 63; tel. (3272) 33-48-01; fax (3272) 33-16-90; e-mail zdrav_kz@nursat.kz; f. 2000 (fmrly appeared as *Densaulik*); monthly; in Kazakh; Editor-in-Chief A. SH. SEYSENBAYEV.

Novoye Pokoleniye (New Generation): 484044 Almaty, pl. Republiki 13; tel. (3272) 63-53-17; fax (3272) 63-45-69; e-mail kazakhstantoday@astelmail.kz; f. 1993; weekly; in Russian; Editor-in-Chief OLEG C. CHERVINSKY; circ. 52,830.

Panorama: 480013 Almaty, pl. Respubliki 15, Office 647; tel. (3272) 63-28-34; fax (3272) 63-66-16; e-mail panorama@kazmail.asdc.kz; internet www.panorama.kz; f. 1992; weekly; in Russian; Editor-in-Chief LERA TSOY; circ. 18,500.

Parasat (Intellect): 480044 Almaty, pr. Zhibek zholy 50; tel. (3272) 33-49-29; fax (3272) 33-64-58; f. 1958; socio-political, literary, illustrated; in Kazakh; Editor-in-Chief BAKKOZHA S. MUKAY; circ. 20,000.

Petroleum of Kazakhstan: 480091 Almaty, Bogenbai Batyr 139; tel. (3272) 63-96-45; fax (3272) 50-95-46; e-mail office@petroleumjournal.kz; internet www.petroleumjournal.kz; every two months; in Russian and English; Editor-in-Chief OLEG C. CHERVINSKY; circ. 2,000.

Prostor (Expanse): 480091 Almaty, pr. Ablaikhana 105; tel. (3272) 69-61-87; e-mail info@prstr.samal.kz; internet prostor.samal.kz; f. 1933; monthly; literary and artistic; in Russian; Editor-in-Chief R. V. PETROV; circ. 1,800.

Russkii Yazyk i Literatura (Russian Language and Literature): 480091 Almaty, pr. Ablaikhana 34; tel. (3272) 39-76-68; f. 1962; monthly; in Russian; Editor-in-Chief B. S. MUKANOV; circ. 17,465.

Shalkar: 480044 Almaty, pr. Zhibek zholy 50; tel. (3272) 33-86-85; f. 1976; twice a month; in Kazakh (in the Arabic script); Editor-in-Chief A. KAIYRBEKOV; circ. 2,500.

Soviety Kazakhstana (Councils of Kazakhstan): 480002 Almaty, pr. Zhibek zholy 15; tel. (3272) 34-92-19; f. 1990; weekly; publ. by Parliament; in Russian; Editor-in-Chief YU. GURSKII; circ. 30,000.

Sport and ks: 480044 Almaty, pr. Zhibek zholy 50; tel. (3272) 33-92-90; f. 1959; weekly; in Kazakh and Russian; Editor-in-Chief (vacant); circ. 20,000.

Turkistan: 484012 Almaty, Bogenbai Batyr 150; tel. (3272) 69-61-54; fax (3272) 62-08-98; f. 1994; weekly; political; in Kazakh; circ. 4,883.

Uigur Avazi (The Voice of Uigur): 480044 Almaty, pr. Zhibek zholy 50; tel. (3272) 33-84-59; f. 1957; 2 a week; publ. by the Government; socio-political; in Uigur; Editor-in-Chief I. AZAMATOV; circ. 9,179.

Ukrainski Novyny (Ukrainian News): 473000 Astana, pr. Respubliki 17; tel. (3172) 21-74-62; e-mail un_astana@mail.kz; internet ukrnovini.host.kz; f. 1994; weekly; in Ukrainian; Editor-in-Chief TARAS CHERNEGA; circ. 1,200.

Ulan: 480044 Almaty, pr. Zhibek zholy 50; tel. (3272) 33-80-03; f. 1930; weekly; in Kazakh; Editor-in-Chief S. KALIYEV; circ. 183,014.

Vremya (Time): 480060 Almaty, Dzhandosova 60A; tel. (3272) 44-49-03; fax (3272) 45-51-44; internet www.time.kz; f. 1999; weekly; in Russian; Editor-in-Chief IGOR MELTSER; circ. 250,000.

Zerde (Intellect): 480044 Almaty, pr. Zhibek zholy 50; tel. (3272) 33-83-81; f. 1960; monthly; popular, scientific, technical; in Kazakh; Editor-in-Chief E. RAUSHAN-ULY; circ. 68,629.

Zhalyn (Flame): Almaty; tel. (3272) 33-22-21; f. 1969; monthly; literary, artistic, social and political; in Kazakh; Editor-in-Chief M. KULKENOV; circ. 2,196.

Zhas Alash (Young Generation): 480044 Almaty, Makatayeva 22; tel. (3272) 30-60-90; fax (3272) 30-24-69; internet www.zhasalash.kz; f. 1921; publ. by the Kazakhstan Youth Union; in Kazakh; Editor-in-Chief ZHUSIP NURTORE; circ. 133,000.

Zhuldyz (Star): 480091 Almaty, pr. Ablai-Khan 105; tel. (3272) 62-51-37; f. 1922; monthly; journal of the Union of Writers of Kazakhstan; literary, artistic, socio-political; in Kazakh; Editor-in-Chief MUKHTAR MAGAUIN; circ. 1,539.

NEWS AGENCY

National Information Agency (Kazinform): 473000 Astana, Dzhambul 32A; tel. (3172) 23-83-58; e-mail info@inform.kz; internet www.inform.kz; f. 1997; 100% state-owned open joint-stock company; provides information on government activities in Kazakhstan and abroad; Pres. GADILBEK M. SHALAKHMETOV.

Foreign Bureaux

Agence France-Presse (AFP): 480100 Almaty, Dostyk 29/31; tel. (3272) 91-06-58; fax (3272) 91-06-58.

Anadolu Ajansı (Turkey): Almaty, Panfilova 83, kv. 55; tel. (3272) 33-15-64; fax (3272) 50-79-49; e-mail almati@anadoluajansi.com.tr.

Informatsionnoye Telegrafnoye Agentstvo Rossii—Telegrafnoye Agentstvo Suverennykh Stran (ITAR—TASS) (Russia): Almaty; Astana; tel. (3272) 33-96-81; tel. (3172) 32-42-02; Correspondent IGOR CHEREPANOV; Correspondent ORAL KAPISHEV.

Internews Network Agency (USA): 480091 Almaty, Nauryzbai Batyr 58, 1st Floor; tel. (3272) 50-89-50; fax (3272) 50-89-59; e-mail oleg@internews.kz; internet www.internews.kz.

Islamic Republic News Agency (IRNA) (Iran): Almaty; tel. (3272) 68-10-05; e-mail irna@irna.com; internet www.irna.com; Correspondent BAHARVAND ALI RAHMAD.

Reuters (United Kingdom): Astana; tel. (3172) 50-94-10.

Rossiiskoye Informatsionnoye Agentstvo—Novosti (RIA—Novosti) (Russia): Almaty; tel. (3272) 33-99-50; Correspondent REVMIRA VOSHENKO.

Xinhua (New China) News Agency (People's Republic of China): Almaty; tel. (3272) 24-68-68.

Publishers

Green Movement Centre (GMC): 484006 Taraz, Lunacharskii 42–2; tel. and fax (32622) 3-27-93; e-mail alex@zagribelny.jambyl.kz; f. 1988; education; environment; Chair. ALEX ZAGRIBELNYI.

Gylym (Science): 480100 Almaty, Pushkina 111–113; tel. (3272) 91-18-77; fax (3272) 61-88-45; f. 1946; books on natural sciences, humanities and scientific research journals; Dir S. G. BAIMENOV.

Izdatelstvo Kazakhstan (Kazakhstan Publishing House): 480124 Almaty, pr. Abaya 143; tel. and fax (3272) 42-29-29; f. 1920; political science, economics, medicine, general and social sciences; Dir E. KH. SYZDYKOV; Editors-in-Chief M. D. SITKO, M. A. RASHEV.

Kainar (Spring): 480124 Almaty, pr. Abaya 143; tel. (3272) 42-27-96; f. 1962; agriculture, history, culture; Dir ORAZBEK S. SARSENBAYEV; Editor-in-Chief I. I. ISKUZHIN.

Kazakhskaya Entsiklopediya (Kazakh Encyclopedia): Almaty; tel. (3272) 62-55-66; f. 1968; Editor-in-Chief R. N. NURGALIYEV.

Mektep: 480009 Almaty, pr. Abaya 143; tel. (3272) 42-26-24; fax (3272) 77-85-44; e-mail oao_mektep@nursat.kz; f. 1947; dictionaries, children's textbooks; fiction by young writers; Pres. E. SATYBALDIYEV; Editor-in-Chief SH. GUSAKOVA.

Oner (Art): 480124 Almaty, pr. Abaya 143; tel. (3272) 42-08-88; f. 1980; Dir S. S. ORAZALINOV; Editor-in-Chief A. A. ASKAROV.

Zhazushy (Writer): 480124 Almaty, pr. Abaya 143; tel. (3272) 42-28-49; f. 1934; literature, literary criticism, essays and poetry; Dir D. I. ISABEKOV; Editor-in-Chief A. T. SARAYEV.

Broadcasting and Communications

TELECOMMUNICATIONS

Beket: 480002 Almaty, Zhurgeneva 9; tel. (3272) 30-16-33; fax (3272) 30-01-43; mobile telecommunications services.

Kazakhtelekom: 480091 Almaty, pr. Abylai Khan 86; tel. (3272) 62-05-41; fax (3272) 63-93-95; internet www.itte.kz; f. 1994; national telecommunications corpn; 60% state-owned, 40% owned by Daewoo Corpn (Republic of Korea); Pres. SERIK BURKITBAYEV.

  Satel: 480100 Almaty, Zenkov 22; tel. (3272) 63-64-32; fax (3272) 63-87-69; telecommunications services; joint venture between Telstra Corpn Ltd (Australia) and Kazakhtelecom; Man. Dir JERRY KOLETH.

BROADCASTING

Private radio and television stations began operating in Kazakhstan in the 1990s. In mid-2001 there were an estimated 124 radio and television stations.

Kazakh State Television and Radio Broadcasting Corporation: 480013 Almaty, Zheltoksan 175A; tel. (3272) 63-37-16; f. 1920; Pres. YERMEK TURSUNOV.

Radio

Kazakh Radio: 480013 Almaty, Zheltoksan 175A; tel. (3272) 63-19-68; fax (3272) 65-03-87; e-mail kazradio@astel.kz; internet www.radio.kz; f. 1921; broadcasts in Kazakh, Russian, Uigur, German and other minority languages; Gen. Dir TOREKHAN DANIYAR.

Television

Khabar News Agency: 480013 Almaty, pl. Respubliki 13; tel. (3272) 63-83-69; fax (3272) 50-63-45; e-mail naz@khabar.almaty.kz; internet www.khabar.kz; f. 1959; international broadcasts in Kazakh, Uigur, Russian and German; two television channels; Dir DARIGHA NAZARBAYEVA.

KTK (Kazakh Commercial Television): Almaty, pl. Respubliki 13; tel. (3272) 63-44-28; fax (3272) 50-66-25; e-mail ktkao@kzaira.com; f. 1990; independent; 20% of shares were reported to have been sold to a US investment co in 2001; Gen. Dir ANDREI SHUKHOV; Pres. SHOKAN LAUULIN.

NTK (Association of TV and Radio Broadcasters of Kazakhstan): 480013 Almaty, pl. Respubliki 13, 6th Floor; tel. (3272) 70-01-83; fax (3272) 70-01-85; e-mail kaztvradio@nursat.kz; f. 2000; privately owned; Pres. AIDAR ZHUMABAYEV.

Finance

(cap. = capital; res = reserves; dep. = deposits; m. = million; brs = branches; amounts in tenge, unless otherwise indicated)

BANKING

From 1994 the National Bank of Kazakhstan (NBK) effected a series of measures aimed at rationalizing the banking sector, in order to ensure a sound financial infrastructure. Numerous banks had their licences revoked: between 1995 and 1998 the number of commercial banks declined by almost one-half, and it continued to decline thereafter. By July 2003 the banking system comprised 35 banks, including two state banks and 16 with foreign participation. At 1 July 2003 commercial banks in Kazakhstan had aggregate equity of 183,900m. tenge, and aggregate assets of 1,378,600m. tenge.

Central Bank

National Bank of Kazakhstan (NBK): 480090 Almaty, Koktem-3 21; tel. (3272) 50-46-25; fax (3272) 50-60-90; e-mail hq@nationalbank.kz; internet www.nationalbank.kz; f. 1990; cap. 20,000m., res 148,937m., dep. 172,575m. (Dec. 2002); Chair. ANVAR SAIDENOV; 19 brs.

Major Commercial Banks

Abidbank: 480100 Almaty, pr. Dostyka 85A; tel. and fax (3272) 41-60-67; e-mail herald@mailbox.kz; f. 1993; Chair. ANATOLII P. NEDELIN.

ABN AMRO Bank Kazakhstan CJSC: 480099 Almaty, Khadji Mukana 45; tel. (3272) 50-73-00; fax (3272) 50-72-98; e-mail aabk@kz.abnamro.com; internet www.abnamro.kz; f. 1994; 51% owned by ABN AMRO Bank NV (Netherlands); cap. 1,800.0m., res 121m., dep. 26,963m. (Oct. 2001); Chair. DOUGLAS KENNEDY; 3 brs.

Alashbank: 480012 Almaty, Sharipova 84; tel. (3272) 92-60-08; fax (3272) 67-01-44; e-mail alashbnk@online.ru; f. 1992; Pres. MADZHED M. K. ALBSURIY; 1 br.

Alfa Bank Kazakhstan: 480012 Almaty, ul. Masanchi 57A, Room 202; tel. (3272) 67-00-12; fax (3272) 50-78-03; e-mail elerkh@alfabank.ru; f. 1994; Chair. A. I. ARTISHKO; 3 brs.

Almaty Commercial Bank: 480002 Almaty, Nauryzbay Batyr 19; tel. (3272) 58-82-26; fax (3272) 58-82-24; e-mail acb1@kaznet.kz; f. 1993; Chair. YERLAN U. BAYMURATOV.

Astana Bank: 487010 Turkestan, Aiteke bi 31; tel. (3252) 57-24-39; e-mail astanabnk@shym.kz.

ATF Bank: 480091 Almaty, Furmanova 100; tel. (3272) 50-30-40; fax (3272) 50-19-95; e-mail info@amb.kz; internet www.amb.kz; f. 1995 as Almaty Merchant Bank, name changed as above in June 2002; cap. 3,100.0m., res 465.3m., dep. 31,422.0m. (Dec. 2002); Chair. TIMUR ISSATAYEV; 10 brs.

Bank Caspiyskiy OJSC: 480012 Almaty, Adi Sharipova 90; tel. (3272) 50-85-92; fax (3272) 50-95-96; e-mail office@bankcaspian.kz; internet www.bankcaspian.kz; f. 1997 by merger of Kazdorbank with Caspiyskiy; cap. 1,756.8m., res 426.3m., dep. 24,597.3m. (Dec. 2002); Chair. IGOR KIM; 17 brs.

Bank Centercredit OJSC: 480072 Almaty, Shevchenko 100; tel. (3272) 59-85-46; fax (3272) 50-78-13; e-mail info@centercredit.kz; internet www.centercredit.kz; f. 1988 as Co-op Bank of the Almaty Union of Co-operatives; name changed to Centerbank 1991, to Centercredit 1996, to JS Centercredit 1998 (following merger with Zhilstroi Bank); cap. 3,167m., res 978m., dep. 21,523m. (Oct. 2003); Chair. of Council BAKHYTBEK R. BAYSEITOV; Chair. of Bd VLADISLAV S. LI; 19 brs.

Bank of Development of Kazakhstan: 473000 Astana, Samal 12; tel. (3172) 58-02-60; e-mail info@kdb.kz.

Bank Turan Alem: 480099 Almaty, Samal 2, Zholdasbekov 97; tel. (3272) 50-40-70; fax (3272) 50-02-24; e-mail post@bta.kz; internet www.bta.kz; f. 1997 by merger of Turanbank—Kazakh Corpn Bank and Alembank; privatized in 1998; cap. 16,091m., res 687m., dep. 195,696m. (Dec. 2002); Chair. YERZHAN N. TATISHEV; 23 brs.

Central Asian Bank of Co-operation and Development: 480008 Almaty, pr. Abaya 115A; tel. (3272) 33-01-12; fax (3272) 50-62-38; e-mail cab@asdc.kz; f. 1994; Chair. GAMAL K. SOODANBEKOV; 1 br.

Citibank Kazakhstan: 480100 Almaty, Kazybek bi 41A; tel. (3272) 60-84-00; fax (3272) 60-83-99; e-mail citibank.kazakhstan@citicorp .com; internet www.citibank.com/kazakhstan; f. 1995; cap. US $25m. (1998); Chair. REZA GAFFARI.

DanaBank: 637000 Pavlodar, Lenina 119; tel. (3182) 32-01-20; e-mail dana@kaznet.kz; 4 brs.

Demir Kazakhstan Bank: 480091 Almaty, Kurmangazy 61A; tel. (3272) 50-85-50; fax (3272) 50-85-25; e-mail demirbank@demirbank .kz; internet www.demirbank.kz; f. 1997; cap. 1,000.0m., res 212.4m., dep. 992.4m.. (Dec. 2002); Chair. IHSAN UGUR.

Eurasian Bank: 480002 Almaty, Kunayeva 56; tel. (3272) 50-86-07; fax (3272) 50-86-50; e-mail info@eurasian-bank.kz; internet www .eurasian-bank.kz; f. 1994; cap. 2,925.3m. (Oct. 2003), res 1,377.1m., dep. 13,225.0m. (Dec. 2002); Chair. KIM INESSA; 5 brs.

Eximbank Kazakhstan (Eximbank): 480100 Almaty, Pushkina 118; tel. (3272) 63-43-00; fax (3272) 50-75-49; e-mail post_mail@ eximbank.kz; f. 1994; fmrly Export–Import Bank of Kazakhstan; state-owned; cap. 6,091m. (March 2000); Chair. BEISENBAY IZTELEUOV.

Industrial Bank of Kazakhstan: 480020 Almaty, pr. Dostyka 264; tel. (3272) 93-51-99; fax (3272) 42-96-03; e-mail info@ibk.kz.

OJSC Kazakhstan International Bank: 480072 Almaty, Seifullina 597; tel. (3272) 92-99-62; fax (3272) 92-90-74; e-mail kib@kib .almaty.kz; f. 1993; cap. 887.8m., res 8.2m.; Chair. ASKAR B. NASENOV.

Kazakhstan-Ziraat International Bank (KZI Bank): 480057 Almaty, Klochkova 132, POB 34; tel. (3272) 50-60-80; fax (3272) 50-60-82; e-mail kzibank@kzibank.com; f. 1993 as Kazkommerts Ziraat International Bank; name changed as above in 1999; cap. 1,058.3m., res 55.6m., dep. 957.6m. (Dec. 2001); Chair. SALIH CANGA; Gen. Man. HALIL TEKPINAR.

Kazkommertsbank: 480060 Almaty, Zh. Gagarina 135; tel. (3272) 58-52-81; fax (3272) 58-52-81; e-mail mailbox@kkb.kz; internet www .kkb.kz; f. 1990; assets US $2,462.2m., cap. $248.0m., dep. $729.7m. (June 2003); Chair. NINA A. ZHUSSUPOVA; Man. Dirs ANDRIY TIM-CHENKO, DENIS FEDOSENKO; 23 brs.

Lariba-Bank: 480060 Almaty, Rozibakiyeva 181A; tel. (3272) 49-14-32; fax (3272) 49-64-21; e-mail lariba@kazmail.asdc.kz; f. 1992; Chair. ALEKSANDR G. BOYCHENKO; 1 br.

Neftebank: 466200 Aktau, Microraion 9/23A; tel. (3292) 43-61-61; fax (3292) 43-61-45; e-mail nb@neftebank.kz; 5 brs.

OJSC Nurbank: 465050 Atyrau, Seifullina 5; tel. (3122) 25-41-75; fax (3122) 21-02-49; e-mail bank@nurbank.kz; internet www .nurbank.kz; f. 1992; cap. 3,000.0m., dep. 29,608.8m. (Dec. 2002); Chair. ABILMAZHEN KUANYSHEVICH GILIMOV.

OJSC Temirbank: 480008 Almaty, pr. Abaya 68/74; tel. (3272) 58-78-88; fax (3272) 50-67-72; e-mail board@temirbank.kz; internet www.temirbank.kz; f. 1992; cap. 2,825m., res 555m. (Oct. 2003); Chair. OLEG KONONENKO; 17 brs.

Tsesnabank: 473000 Astana, Beibitshilik 43; tel. (3172) 31-81-92; fax (3172) 31-82-58; e-mail tsesnabank_uavt@kepter.kz; internet www.tsesnabank.kz; f. 1992; cap. 531.1m., res 566.5m., dep. 7,424.3m. (Dec. 2002); Chair. SERIK JAKSYBEKOV; 4 brs.

Savings Bank

Halyk (People's) Savings Bank of Kazakhstan: 480046 Almaty, Rozybakiyeva 97; tel. (3272) 59-00-00; fax (3272) 59-02-71; e-mail hsbk@halykbank.kz; internet www.halykbank.kz; f. 1936 as br. of Savings Bank of USSR, reorganized as joint-stock savings bank in 1994; fully privatized in Nov. 2001; cap. 9,683.8m., res 2,615.7m., dep. 172,408.0m. (Dec. 2002); Chair. KAIRAT SATYLGANOV; Man. Dir KAIRAT RAKHMANOV; 611 brs.

Bankers' Organization

Kazakhstan Bank Association: Almaty, Panfilova 98; tel. (3272) 73-16-89; fax (3272) 73-90-85; Pres. BAKHYTBEK BAISEITOV.

STOCK AND COMMODITY EXCHANGES

Kazakhstan Stock Exchange (KASE): 480091 Almaty, Aiteke bi 67; tel. (3272) 63-98-98; fax (3272) 63-89-80; e-mail info@kase.kz; internet www.kase.kz; f. 1993; Pres. and Chief Exec. AZAMAT M. DZHOLDASBEKOV.

Ken Dala Central Kazakhstan Commodity Exchange: 470074 Karaganda, pr. Stroitelei 28; tel. (3212) 74-27-80; fax (3212) 74-43-35; f. 1991; auth. cap. 6m.; Pres. MADEGDA PAK.

Kazakhstan also has a Metal Exchange (f. 1992).

INSURANCE

At August 2000 there were 41 licensed insurance companies in Kazakhstan.

Almaty International Insurance Group: 480091 Almaty, ul. Kabanbay Batyr 112; tel. and fax (3272) 50-12-31; e-mail aiig@ world2.almaty.kz; internet www.aiig.escort.kz; f. 1994; Chair. SUREN AMBARTSUMIAN.

Dynasty Life Insurance Co: Almaty, Seifullina 410; tel. (3272) 50-73-95; e-mail dynasty@bta.nursat.kz; Chair. SERIK TEMIRGALEYEV.

Industrial Insurance Group (IIG): 480046 Almaty, Nauryzbai Batyr 65–69; tel. (3272) 50-96-95; fax (3272) 50-96-98; e-mail iig@ kaznet.kz; internet www.iig.kz; f. 1998; Pres. IVAN MIKHAILOV.

KazAgroPolicy: 480091 Almaty, Nauryzbai Batyr 49–61; tel. (3272) 32-13-24; fax (3272) 32-13-26; e-mail kazagropolise@mail .banknet.kz; Chair. YERMEK USPANOV.

Kazakhinstrakh: Almaty; tel. (3272) 33-73-49; fax (3272) 50-74-37; e-mail kiscentr@nursat.kz; Chair. NURLAN MOLDAKHMETOV.

Kazkommerts-Policy: 480013 Almaty, Satpayeva 24; tel. (3272) 58-48-08; fax (3272) 92-73-97; e-mail kkp@mail.kz; internet www .kkp.kz; Chair. SERGEI G. SUKHAREV; Dir TALGAT K. USSENOV.

MSCA Interteach: 480091 Almaty, Kabanbai Batyr 122A; tel. and fax (3272) 58-23-32; e-mail interteach@kaznet.kaz; internet www .interteachmsca.com; f. 1989; medical and travel insurance, health care, accident and employee liability insurance; 290 employees; 48 brs; Gen. Dir ERNST M. KURLEUTOV.

Interteach Assistance: 480091 Almaty, Furmanova 111/48; tel. and fax (3272) 58-23-32; e-mail interteach@kaznet.kz; internet www.interteachmsca.com; f. 2001; medical and travel insurance, health care; 196 employees; 26 brs; Gen. Dir SAULE DZHUNDUBAYEVA.

West-Kazakhstan Insurance Firm: Uralsk, pr. Lenina 203; tel. (31122) 50-62-94; Chair. BOLAT DJUMAGALIYEV.

Trade and Industry

GOVERNMENT AGENCY

State Committee for Investment: Astana.

CHAMBERS OF COMMERCE

Union of Chambers of Commerce and Industry of Kazakhstan: 480091 Almaty, Masanchi 26; tel. (3272) 67-78-23; fax (3272) 50-70-29; e-mail tpprkaz@online.ru; internet www.ccikaz.kz; f. 1959; Chair. KHAMIT RAKISHEV.

Akmola Chamber of Commerce and Industry: 475000 Kokshatau, Marks 107; tel. (3162) 25-76-68; e-mail tpp@kokc.kz; Chair. TURSUNHAN T. KALIASKAROVA.

Aktobe Chamber of Commerce and Industry: 463000 Aktobe, Zhubanova 289/1; tel. (3132) 51-02-20; e-mail akbtpp@nursat.kz; Chair. ELENA A. RUDENKO.

Almaty Chamber of Commerce: 488000 Taldykorgan, Taulsizdik 101/37; tel. (3282) 7-20-40; Chair. EMMA V. KIM.

Almaty City Chamber of Commerce and Industry: 480091 Almaty, Tole bi 45; tel. (3272) 62-03-01; e-mail alcci@nursat.kz; internet www.atpp.marketcenter.ru; Chair. ZULFIYA K. AKHMETZHA-NOVA.

Astana City Chamber of Commerce and Industry: 473000 Astana, Auezov 66, POB 1966; tel. (3172) 32-38-33; e-mail akmcci@ dan.kz; internet www.chamber.kz; Chair. TATYANA I. KONONOVA.

Atyrau Chamber of Commerce and Industry: 465050 Atyrau, Satpayev 36/79; tel. (3122) 23-19-97; e-mail torgpal_atr@asdc.kz; Chair. NURZHAMAL ZH. SULTANOVA.

East Kazakhstan Chamber of Commerce and Industry: 492000 Ust-Kamenogorsk, Novatorova 3, POB 177; tel. (3232) 26-53-10; fax (3232) 26-72-47; e-mail cci@ustk.kz; Chair. KAJRAT M. MUKEYEV.

Karaganda Chamber of Commerce and Industry: 470061 Karaganda, Mir Bulvar 31; tel. (3212) 56-32-32; e-mail ccikr@nursat.kz; f. 1994; Chair. NESIP SEITOVA.

Kostanai Chamber of Commerce and Industry: 458000 Kostanai, Taran 165; tel. (3142) 54-66-72; e-mail ko_tpp@mail.kz; Chair. VALENTINA N. TRIBUSHNAYA.

Kyzylorda Chamber of Commerce and Industry: 467014 Kyzylorda, Aiteke bi 24; tel. (3242) 26-24-36; Chair. TAMARA V. HRAMTSOVA.

Mangistau Chamber of Commerce and Industry: 466200 Aktau, Skr. 6, 26/131; tel. (3292) 51-19-52; e-mail akt_cci@nursat.kz; Chair. NATELLA D. OTELEPKO.

North Kazakhstan Chamber of Commerce and Industry: 642015 Petropavlovsk, Mir 112; tel. (3152) 46-05-68; e-mail tpp@petropavl.kz; internet www.tppsko.freenet.kz; Chair. NELLI F. KUKUSHKINA.

Pavlodar Chamber of Commerce and Industry: 637002 Pavlodar, Toraigyrova 95/1; tel. (3182) 75-79-69; e-mail pav-cci@kaznet.kz; Chair. RAJHANGUL SATABAYEVA.

Semipalatinsk Chamber of Commerce and Industry: 490050 Semipalatinsk, Abaya 92/22; tel. (3222) 62-78-87; e-mail tpp@relcom.kz; Chair. TAMARA SOPOLEVA.

South Kazakhstan Chamber of Commerce and Industry: 486050 Shymkent, Tauke Khan 31; tel. (3252) 21-14-05; Chair. SYRLYBAJ ORDABEKOV.

West Kazakhstan Chamber of Commerce and Industry: 417000 Uralsk, Kuibyshev 67; tel. (3112) 50-44-40; e-mail zktpp@kaznet.kz; Chair. KAIR A. SYUNTIYEV.

Zhambyl Chamber of Commerce and Industry: 484039 Taraz, Karakhana 2; tel. (3262) 43-05-98; Chair. ADILKHAN ZHAPARBEKOV.

EMPLOYERS' ORGANIZATIONS

Confederation of Employers of the Republic of Kazakhstan (KRRK): 480072 Almaty, Abai 42/44; tel. (3272) 93-07-42; fax (3272) 92-27-68; e-mail krrk@krrk.kz; internet www.krrk.kz; Pres. KADYR BAYIKENOV.

Kazakhstan Petroleum Association: 480100 Almaty, pr. Dostyk 38, Office 517; tel. (3272) 50-18-16; fax (3272) 50-18-17; e-mail kpa@arna.kz; internet www.kpa.kz; f. 1998; Chair. Dr SAGINDYK K. NURALIYEV; 49 mem. cos.

UTILITIES

Electricity

Privatization of the electric power sector was undertaken from 1996. Many power stations were withdrawn from the national electricity company and transformed into independent joint-stock companies; several power-supply network companies were established in the region. The state had completed the privatization of virtually all electricity producers and local distribution companies by the end of 2001.

State Committee for Energy Supervision: Chair. MURAT RAMAZANOV.

Kazakstan Electric Grid Operational Company (KEGOC): Almaty; internet www.kegoc.kz; f. 1997; technical electricity network operator; Vice-Pres. ESBERGEN ABITAYEV (Operations), ALMASADAM SATKALIYEV (Finance).

Kazakhstan Energy and Power Market Operating Company (KEPMOC): Almaty; f. 2000 under a government resolution; electricity broker.

Water

Almaty Vodocanal: 480057 Almaty, Jarokova 196; tel. (3272) 44-00-17; fax (3272) 44-84-02; f. 1937; state-owned co; responsible for water supply and sewerage in Almaty and surrounding villages; Gen. Dir SHARIPBEK SHARDARBEKOV.

STATE HYDROCARBONS COMPANIES

Aktobemunaigaz: Aktyubinsk; 25.1% state-owned; 60.3% owned by China National Petroleum Co (CNPC).

KazMunaiGaz National Co: Almaty; e-mail g.nauryzbekova@kmg.kz; internet www.kmg.kz; f. 2002 by merger of KazakhOil and Transneftegas; Chair. UZAKBAI KARABALIN; Vice-Chair. TIMUR KULIBAYEV; Exec. Dir KAIRGELDY KABILDIN.

KazTransOil: Astana, pr. Kabanbay Batyr 20B; tel. (3172) 55-56-53; fax (3172) 55-56-52; internet www.kaztransoil.kz; transportation of petroleum; Dir-Gen. ASKAR SMANKULOV.

KazTransGas: e-mail info@intergas.kz; internet www.kaztransgas.kz; transportation of natural gas; Dir-Gen. ABAY SADYKOV.

Munaigaz: Almaty; tel. (3272) 69-58-00; fax (3272) 69-52-72; f. 1991; petroleum and gas prospecting and producing; Pres. T. A. KHAZANOV.

Aktyubinskneft: 463022 Aktobe, Atynsarin 8; tel. (3132) 22-47-82; fax (3132) 22-93-21; f. 1993; produces petroleum and natural gas; Pres. S. P. ZIMIN; 10,500 employees.

JSC Mangistaumunaigaz: 466200 Mangistauskaya, Aktau, Mikrorayon 1; tel. (3292) 51-45-57; fax (3292) 43-39-19; 60% owned by Central Asian Petroleum (Indonesia), 10% owned by employees; production and transportation of petroleum and natural gas; Gen. Dir V. MIROSHNIKOV.

Pavlodar Petrochemical Joint Stock Co: 637043 Pavlodar, Khimkombinatovskaya 1; tel. (3182) 39-65-20; fax (3182) 39-60-98; e-mail bekturov@pnhz.kz; f. 1978; 51% owned by JSC Mangistaumunaigaz; processes petroleum from western Siberia (Russia); produces unleaded petroleum, diesel fuel, petroleum chemical gases, bitumen and petroleum coke; Gen. Dir YURII GINATULIN; Exec. Dir RUSTEM BEKTUROV.

Tengizchevroil (TCO): 466440 Atyrau, Atyrau Airport, TCO Interim Office; tel. (312) 30-26-818; fax (312) 30-26-729; e-mail tiny@tengizchevroil.com; f. 1993; joint venture between the Govt (20%), Chevron Corpn (USA—with 50%), ExxonMobil (USA—25%) and LUKArco (a joint venture between LUKoil of the Russian Federation and Atlantic Richfield of the USA—5%); Gen. Dir KEN GODARD.

TRADE UNIONS

Confederation of Free Trade Unions: f. 1991; fmrly Independent Trade Union Centre of Kazakhstan; 9 regional brs with 2,200 mems; Chair. SERGEI BELKIN.

Confederation of Free Trade Unions of Coal and Mining Industries: Almaty; Chair. V. GAIPOV.

Federation of Trade Unions of Kazakhstan: 473000 Astana, pr. Abaya 94; tel. (3172) 216-68-14; fax (3172) 21-68-35; e-mail fprkastana@nursat.kz; internet www.trud.org/kazakhstan; 30 affiliated unions with 2,300,000 mems (2001); Chair. SIYAZBEK MUKASHEV.

National Trade Union of Journalists of Kazakhstan: Pres. MADRID RYSBEKOV.

Union of Manufacturers and Businessmen: Almaty; tel. (3272) 62-23-07; fax (3272) 66-54-90.

Transport

RAILWAYS

In 2000 the total length of rail track in use was 13,615 km (3,725 km of which were electrified). The rail network is most concentrated in the north of the country, where it joins the rail lines of Russia. From the former capital, Almaty, lines run north-eastward, to join the Trans-Siberian Railway, and west, to Shymkent, and then north-west along the Syr-Dar'ya river, to Orenburg in European Russia. In mid-2003 Kazakhstan and Kyrgyzstan announced that a 100-km railway link was to be built between Almaty and lake Issyk-Kul in Kyrgyzstan. Construction work was expected to be completed by 2008. From Chu lines run to central and northern regions of Kazakhstan, while a main line runs from Shymkent south to Uzbekistan. There is an international line between Druzhba, on the eastern border of Kazakhstan, and Alataw Shankou, in the People's Republic of China.

In the late 1990s construction was under way of the first line of a new underground railway (metro) in Almaty. It was envisaged that the metro system, when completed, would comprise three lines (35.4 km in length).

Department of Railways (Ministry of Transport and Communications): 480091 Almaty, Vinogradova 56; tel. (3272) 60-49-06; fax (3272) 39-52-55; Dir-Gen. BAURZHAN BAYMUKHANOV.

Kazakhstan Temir Zholy CJSC (Kazakhstan Railways): 473000 Astana, pr. Pobedy 98; tel. (3172) 14-44-00; fax (3172) 32-82-30; e-mail temirzholy@railways.kz; internet www.railways.kz; f. 1991 following break-up of former Soviet Railways (SZD); Gen. Dir A. I. MYRZAKHMETOV.

ROADS

In 2001 Kazakhstan's total road network was 82,638 km, including 22,758 km of main roads and 59,880 km of secondary roads. Some

93.9% of the network was hard-surfaced. Kazakhstan is linked by road with Russia (46 border crossings), Kyrgyzstan (seven), Uzbekistan (seven) and, via Uzbekistan and Turkmenistan, with Iran. There are six road connections with the People's Republic of China (including two international crossings, at Korgas and Bakhty). In 2000 the Islamic Development Bank agreed to donate $200m. towards the rehabilitation of the Karaganda–Astana road.

Department of Roads (Ministry of Transport and Communications): 473000 Astana, pr. Abaya 49; tel. (3172) 32-02-08; fax (3172) 32-16-96; Dir S. LARICHEV.

INLAND WATERWAYS

Kazakhstan has an inland waterway network extending over some 4,000 km. The main navigable river is the Irtysh, accounting for approximately 80% of cargo transported by river. The Kazakhstan River Fleet Industrial Association (Kazrechmorflot), comprising 11 water companies, administers river traffic.

Department of Water Transport (Ministry of Transport and Communications): 473000 Astana, pr. Abaya 49; tel. (3172) 32-03-58; fax (3172) 32-10-58; Dir JENYS M. KASYMBEK.

SHIPPING

Kazakhstan's ports of Atyrau and Aktau are situated on the eastern shores of the Caspian Sea. The first stage of a project to upgrade the port of Aktau was scheduled for completion in 1999, and it was forecast that by 2000 Aktau would handle more than 7.5m. metric tons of petroleum and up to 1m. tons of dry freight annually. A ferry port was inaugurated at Aktau in September 2001 as part of the Transport Corridor Europa—Caucasus—Asia (TRACECA) programme, with lines to Azerbaijan, Iran and Russia; the port was capable of processing some 10m. tons of petroleum and up to 30m. tons of dry goods per year. At 31 December 2002 Kazakhstan's merchant fleet comprised 20 vessels, with a combined total displacement of 11,845 grt.

Aktau Commercial Sea Port: Aktau, Umirzak; tel. (3292) 44-51-26; fax (3292) 44-51-01; e-mail seaport_akt@kaznet.kz; internet www.portaktau.kz; f. 1963; Dir TALGAT B. ABYLGAZIN; 407 employees.

Atyrauozenporty (Atyrau Port): tel. (3122) 25-45-63; fax (3122) 25-45-16; e-mail atr_info@asdc.kz.

CIVIL AVIATION

There are 18 domestic airports and three airports with international services (at Almaty, Aktau and Atyrau). In 2002 plans were announced for the reconstruction of Atyrau airport, with the help of financial assistance from the European Bank for Reconstruction and Development. In that year 19 of the country's 56 air companies had their activities suspended and their licences revoked, in the interests of safety; it was envisaged that many of these companies would merge by the end of the year. Almaty airport has scheduled links with cities in Russia and other former Soviet republics, as well as with destinations in Europe, other parts of Asia and the Middle East.

Department of Aviation (Ministry of Transport and Communications): 473000 Astana, pr. Abaya 49; tel. (3172) 32-63-16; fax (3172) 32-16-96; Dir S. BURANBAYEV.

Aeroservice Kazakhstan Aviakompania: 480028 Almaty, Alga basskaya 2A; tel. (3272) 36-69-26; fax (3272) 52-93-45; f. 1991; provides charter services to Europe, the Middle East, Pakistan and the Republic of Korea.

Air Astana: 473000 Astana, POB 1416, Samal Microdistrict 12, Astana Towers Business Centre, 12th Floor; tel. (3172) 58-09-50; fax (3172) 58-09-80; e-mail astana@air-astana.kz; internet www.air-astana.kz; f. 2001 jointly by the Government and BAE Systems (United Kingdom); domestic flights; Pres. LLOYD PAXTON.

Air Kazakhstan CJSC (Kazakhstan Airlines): 480079 Almaty, Ogareva 14; tel. (3272) 57-29-82; fax (3272) 57-25-03; e-mail office@airkaz.com; internet www.airkaz.com; f. 1997, in succession to Kazakhstan Aue Zholy; all domestic and international flights were suspended in Feb. 2004; state-owned; Pres. YERKIN KALIYEV.

Asiya Servis Aue Zholy (Asia Service Airlines): Almaty, Zheltoksan 59; tel. (3272) 33-63-49; operates services to Atyrau and Aktau.

Jana-Arka Air: 480012 Almaty, Ninogradova 85; tel. (3272) 63-28-74; fax (3272) 63-19-09; privately owned; provides both domestic and regional flights; Pres. YALKEN VALIN.

Sayakhat Air: 480091 Almaty, Bogenbai Batyr 124; tel. (3272) 62-26-28; fax (3272) 62-28-70; e-mail sayakhat@ducatmail.kz; internet www.sayakhat.com; f. 1989 as the country's first privately owned airline; commenced operations in 1991; passenger and cargo services to Africa, Asia and Europe; Pres. and Dir VLADIMIR KOUROPATENKO.

Tourism

Tourism is not widely developed in Kazakhstan, owing to its Soviet legacy and infrastructural limitations. However, the country possesses mountain ranges, lakes and a number of historical sites. Chimbulak, above Almaty, is a popular local skiing resort.

State Agency for Tourism and Sport: 473000 Astana, Mukhtar Auezov 126; tel. (3172) 39-66-38; fax (3172) 39-64-68; e-mail turlykhanov@kazsport.kz; internet www.kazsport.kz; f. 2000; Chair. DAULET TURLYKHANOV.

KENYA
Introductory Survey

Location, Climate, Language, Religion, Flag, Capital

The Republic of Kenya lies astride the equator on the east coast of Africa, with Somalia to the north-east, Ethiopia and Sudan to the north, Uganda to the west and Tanzania to the south. The climate varies with altitude: the coastal region is hot and humid, with temperatures averaging between 20°C and 32°C (69°F–90°F), while inland, at more than 1,500 m (5,000 ft) above sea-level, temperatures average 7°C–27°C (45°F–80°F). The highlands and western areas receive ample rainfall (an annual average of 1,000 mm–1,250 mm) but most of northern Kenya is very dry (about 250 mm). Kiswahili is the official language, while English is widely spoken and 22% and 13% of the population, respectively, speak Kikuyu and Luo as their mother tongue. Most of the country's inhabitants follow traditional beliefs. There is a sizeable Christian community, while Muslims form a smaller proportion of the population. The national flag (proportions 2 by 3) has three broad horizontal stripes, of black, red and green, separated by two narrow white stripes. Superimposed in the centre is a red shield, with black and white markings, upon crossed white spears. The capital is Nairobi.

Recent History

Kenya was formerly a British colony (inland) and protectorate (along the coast). The first significant African nationalist organization was the Kenya African Union (KAU), founded in 1944, which was supported mainly by the Kikuyu, the largest ethnic group in Kenya. In 1947 Jomo Kenyatta, a Kikuyu, became President of the KAU. During 1952 a campaign of terrorism was launched by Mau Mau, a predominantly Kikuyu secret society that aimed to expel European (mainly British) settlers from Kenya. The British authorities declared a state of emergency in October 1952 and banned the KAU in 1953, when Kenyatta was imprisoned for alleged involvement with Mau Mau activities. The terrorist campaign ceased in 1956, and the state of emergency was revoked in January 1960.

Kenyatta was released from prison in 1961 and elected to the Legislative Council in 1962. Following general elections in May 1963, Kenya was granted internal self-government in June. The country became independent, within the Commonwealth, on 12 December 1963, and a republic exactly one year later. Kenyatta, then leader of the Kenya African National Union (KANU), was appointed Prime Minister in June 1963 and became the country's first President in December 1964. (He was subsequently re-elected to the presidency, unopposed, in 1969 and 1974.) In December 1966 Kenya's two parliamentary chambers, the Senate and the House of Representatives, were merged to form a unicameral National Assembly. The assassination in 1969 of Tom Mboya, a cabinet minister and the Secretary-General of KANU, led to civil unrest and the banning of the opposition Kenya People's Union. KANU was the only party to contest elections to the National Assembly in 1969 and 1974.

Kenyatta died in August 1978; the Vice-President, Daniel arap Moi, was proclaimed President in October, and was the sole candidate at a presidential election held (concurrently with a KANU-only general election) in November 1979. In June 1982 the National Assembly officially declared Kenya a one-party state. A series of political detentions and increasing press censorship were followed by an attempted coup in August, in which several hundred people were killed. Several cabinet ministers lost their seats at legislative elections in September 1983. Nevertheless, at a simultaneous presidential election Moi was returned unopposed. In August 1986 KANU approved an open 'queue-voting' system to replace the secret ballot in the preliminary stage of a general election. In December the National Assembly adopted constitutional amendments that increased the power of the President. In June 1987 it was announced that only members of the ruling party were to be entitled to vote during the preliminary stages of a general election.

In February 1988 Moi was nominated unopposed to serve a third term as President. In the same month preliminary elections under the 'queue-voting' system produced a KANU-approved list to contest 123 of the 188 elective seats in the National Assembly at a general election held in March (54 candidates

received more than 70% of votes cast at the preliminary stage, and were thus deemed to have been elected, while 11 were elected unopposed). In an extensive cabinet reshuffle following the election, the Vice-President, Mwai Kibaki, was replaced by Josephat Karanja. In July the National Assembly adopted constitutional amendments allowing the President to dismiss senior judges at will, and increasing from 24 hours to 14 days the legally permissible period of detention without trial for people suspected of capital offences. In December Kenneth Matiba, the Minister of Transport and Communications, resigned and was expelled from KANU, after criticizing the conduct of the party elections.

In April 1989 the National Assembly unanimously approved a motion of 'no confidence' in Karanja, following allegations that he had abused his position as Vice-President to further his own personal and tribal interests. Karanja, while denying the charges against him, resigned shortly afterwards, and was replaced by the Minister of Finance, Prof. George Saitoti. In June Moi released all political prisoners being held without trial, and offered an amnesty to exiled dissidents.

In February 1990 the Minister of Foreign Affairs and International Co-operation, Dr Robert Ouko, died in suspicious circumstances. Allegations that the Moi administration was implicated in his death led to anti-Government riots. In response, Moi banned all demonstrations and requested an investigation by British police into Ouko's death; the results of this were presented to the Kenyan authorities in September, and in October Moi ordered a judicial inquiry into the affair. In May a broad alliance of intellectuals, lawyers and clergy, under the leadership of Matiba, began to exert pressure on the Government to legalize political opposition to KANU. In July Moi ordered the arrests of Matiba and other prominent members of the alliance. Serious rioting ensued in Nairobi and its environs; more than 1,000 protesters were reportedly arrested.

In December 1990 KANU abolished the system of 'queue-voting' and resolved to cease expelling party members, readmitting 31 expelled members in the following month. In June Matiba was released from prison, apparently on grounds of ill health. In the following month four of those who had been arrested during the July 1990 riots were found guilty of sedition and each sentenced to seven years' imprisonment. In August six opposition leaders, including Oginga Odinga (Kenya's Vice-President in 1964–66), formed a new political movement, the Forum for the Restoration of Democracy (FORD); the Government outlawed the grouping, but it continued to operate.

In September 1991 the judicial inquiry into the death of Ouko was presented with evidence that he had been murdered; in November Moi dismissed the Minister of Industry, Nicholas Biwott, in response to widespread suspicion that the latter was implicated in the alleged assassination. Shortly afterwards Moi ordered the dissolution of the judicial inquiry. A suspect was eventually charged with the murder, but was acquitted in July 1994. (Biwott was reappointed to the Cabinet in 1997. In December 2000 Biwott won a libel case against the British authors of a book that implicated him in the murder of Ouko.)

In November 1991 several members of FORD were arrested prior to a planned pro-democracy rally in Nairobi; protesters at the rally (which had been banned by the Government) were dispersed by the security forces. The Kenyan authorities were condemned internationally for suppressing the demonstration, and most of the opposition activists who had been detained were subsequently released. Bilateral and multilateral creditors suspended aid to Kenya indefinitely, pending the acceleration of both economic and political reforms. In December a special conference of KANU delegates acceded to the pressure for reform, resolving to introduce a multi-party political system. The National Assembly subsequently endorsed appropriate amendments to the Constitution. Former Vice-President Kibaki resigned as Minister of Health later in the month, in protest against alleged electoral malpractice by KANU and against the unsatisfactory outcome of the judicial inquiry into the death of Ouko, and founded the Democratic Party (DP). Five other ministers and deputy ministers resigned their posts in subsequent weeks.

During the first half of 1992 some 2,000 people were reportedly killed in tribal clashes in western Kenya. In March the Government banned all political rallies, and restrictions were placed on the activities of the press. Following a two-day general strike in April, organized by FORD, the Government ended the ban on political rallies. In August FORD split into two opposing factions, which were registered in October as separate political parties, FORD—Asili and FORD—Kenya, respectively led by Matiba and Odinga.

Multi-party presidential and legislative elections took place in December 1992. Prior to the elections opposition parties had protested that administrative and legal obstacles were effectively disenfranchising some sectors of the electorate. Moi was elected for a fourth term of office as President, winning 36.3% of the votes cast, ahead of Matiba (26.0%), Kibaki (19.5%) and Odinga (17.5%). Of the 188 elective seats in the National Assembly, KANU won 100 (including 16 uncontested); FORD—Asili and FORD—Kenya secured 31 seats each, and the DP took 23. Some 15 former cabinet ministers lost their seats. Votes were cast predominantly in accordance with ethnic affiliations, with the two largest tribes, the Kikuyu and Luo, overwhelmingly rejecting KANU. The leaders of FORD—Asili, FORD—Kenya and the DP initially campaigned to have the results declared invalid, alleging that there had been gross electoral irregularities. In January 1993, however, a Commonwealth monitoring group concluded that the outcome of the elections reflected 'the will of the people'. An extensive reshuffle of cabinet posts was effected.

Tribal clashes in western regions continued during 1993, escalating significantly in October. In November the human rights organization Africa Watch reiterated persistent accusations by the opposition that the Government was covertly inciting ethnic violence in order to discredit political pluralism in Kenya. During that month several people were arrested and charged with co-ordinating the unrest. Meanwhile, the international donor community agreed to resume the provision of aid to Kenya, in response to what it recognized as the Government's progress in implementing political and economic reforms.

In January 1994 Odinga died; he was succeeded as the Chairman of FORD—Kenya by Michael Wamalwa Kijana, hitherto the party's Vice-President. In June main opposition groups, excluding FORD—Asili, formed a loose coalition, the United National Democratic Alliance, which was, however, subsequently divided by disagreements. Disunity was also becoming apparent within individual opposition parties, with vying factions evident within both FORD—Kenya and FORD—Asili.

In May 1995 leading opposition activists formed a new political organization, Safina. Dr Richard Leakey, a prominent white Kenyan and former Director of the Kenya Wildlife Service (KWS), was appointed as Safina's Secretary-General. The party (which was refused registration) aimed to combat corruption and human rights abuses by the Kenyan authorities and to campaign for the introduction of an electoral system of proportional representation. During August several Safina officials were attacked by members of KANU's youth wing. In October Koigi wa Wamwere, a founding member of Safina, was found guilty of attempted robbery and sentenced to four years' imprisonment. Opposition members of the National Assembly subsequently denounced the conduct of Wamwere's trial. Wamwere's conviction was eventually overturned in November 1997.

During the mid-1990s Kenya's human rights record came under intense domestic and international scrutiny. In April 1995 the country's Roman Catholic bishops accused the Government of eroding judicial independence and of condoning police brutality and endemic corruption. In December the human rights organization Amnesty International alleged that the security forces were systematically torturing criminal suspects and opposition activists. In response to its critics, the Moi administration provisionally withdrew controversial draft legislation in January 1996 that would have severely restricted the freedom of the press and, in July, inaugurated a human rights committee to investigate alleged humanitarian abuses.

Divisions within opposition parties continued to undermine efforts to present a cohesive challenge to Moi and KANU prior to the 1997 elections. A renewed attempt to establish a coalition of opposition organizations, initiated in November 1995, was short-lived. Meanwhile, following an unsuccessful attempt to oust Wamalwa as Chairman of FORD—Kenya, Raila Odinga (the son of Oginga Odinga and a prominent opposition activist)

left that party and subsequently became leader of the National Development Party (NDP). In October 1997 Matiba's faction of FORD—Asili registered as an independent party, the Forum for the Restoration of Democracy for the People (FORD—People). During the mid-1990s several opposition deputies, disaffected by these internal rivalries, defected to KANU. Within KANU itself rivalries also began to emerge, not least because the Constitution permitted Moi to stand for only one further term as President.

In January 1997 Amnesty International accused the Moi administration of failing to halt the widespread torture of detainees. In the same month the reappointment to the Cabinet of Biwott (a principal suspect in the inquiry into the assassination of Robert Ouko in 1990) provoked considerable disquiet. In February 1997 Kenya became a signatory to the UN Convention Against Torture and Other Cruel, Inhuman and Degrading Treatment or Punishment.

During the first half of 1997 Moi repeatedly refused to accede to opposition demands for a review of the Constitution prior to the forthcoming elections. Opposition organizations protested that constitutional reforms and a reorganization of the supervisory Electoral Commission were essential in order to eliminate an in-built electoral advantage for the Moi administration. In April the National Convention Executive Council (NCEC) was established as a forum embracing representatives of non-governmental organizations, religious groups and opposition parties (excluding, however, supporters of Matiba and Odinga). In June opposition parliamentarians disrupted the budget speech, in protest at the Moi administration's perceived intransigence, and anti-Government activists demonstrated in Nairobi. Illegal protest rallies in early July were brutally suppressed by the security forces, resulting in several fatalities and provoking strong condemnation from abroad. Eventually, in mid-July, Moi agreed to meet with opposition and religious leaders to discuss constitutional reform. It was subsequently announced that the opposition would henceforth be permitted to organize registered public meetings, and that a constitutional review commission would be established.

At the beginning of August 1997 the IMF suspended assistance to Kenya, pending the implementation of decisive action to eliminate official corruption and to improve the system of revenue collection; the Government consequently announced the inauguration of an anti-corruption body. The NCEC organized a one-day general strike in early August, in support of its demands for constitutional reform. In late August serious unrest erupted in and around Mombasa. While the Government blamed the NCEC for orchestrating the attacks, the NCEC alleged that the Government was inciting inter-ethnic conflict with the aim of depriving opposition supporters from the predominantly Luo region of the opportunity to vote in the forthcoming elections by forcing them to flee their homes. In the following month the National Assembly approved legislation that amended the Constitution with the stated aim of ensuring free and fair democratic elections. All political parties were granted equal access to the media, and detention without trial was prohibited. In addition, the new legislation enabled the opposition to participate in selecting the 12 nominated members of the National Assembly and 10 of the 12 members of the supervisory Electoral Commission.

The presidential and legislative elections, which took place concurrently on 29 December 1997, were undermined by allegations of widespread fraud, as well as by logistical difficulties. Moi was re-elected President, winning 40.6% of the valid votes cast. Mwai Kibaki, the leader of the DP and former Vice-President, came second, with 31.5% of the votes cast. KANU secured 107 of the 210 elected seats in the enlarged National Assembly, while the remainder were divided between nine opposition parties, with the DP taking 39 seats, the NDP 21, FORD—Kenya 17 and the Social Democratic Party 15. Safina (which had finally been registered in November) won five seats. Moi was inaugurated for a fifth (and final) term as President in January 1998. Shortly afterwards Moi appointed a new Cabinet. However, he postponed the designation of a new Vice-President, evidently in order not to give an indication of his preferred successor to the presidency. No Kikuyu or Luo were appointed as ministers. Following the elections, Kibaki petitioned the High Court to declare Moi's re-election invalid. A group of independent Kenyan observers had, none the less, pronounced the electoral process 'satisfactory'.

In early 1998 inter-ethnic violence erupted once again in the volatile Rift Valley. The Moi administration blamed the conflict on bitterness in the Kikuyu and Luo communities at the outcome of the elections, while the latter alleged persecution both by the security forces and by smaller tribal groups that had voted predominantly for Moi and KANU. During January and February about 100 people were reported to have been killed in the unrest, while more than 300,000 were believed to have been displaced. Government troops reportedly embarked on a programme of disarmament in the Rift Valley in May. In July the authorities organized a judicial inquiry into the causes of the ethnic disturbances of both 1992 and 1998. In August 2000 Fr John Kaiser, a US missionary known for his outspoken criticism of human rights abuses and government misconduct, was found shot dead. Amid fears that his killing had been politically motivated, agents from the US Federal Bureau of Investigation (FBI) travelled to Kenya to assist with the investigation into the death. It was reported that Fr Kaiser had documents linking two cabinet ministers to the ethnic disturbances of 1992 and 1998, which he had intended to present to a commission of inquiry into land issues established in November 1999. In April 2001, however, the FBI investigation concluded that Kaiser had committed suicide. This verdict was rejected by the Roman Catholic Church and Kenyan human rights groups, which subsequently demanded a public inquest into Kaiser's death. Tension between the Kikuyu and Kalenjin communities in the Rift valley remained, especially over disputed land vacated by the Kikuyu during the clashes.

In early August 1998 a car-bomb exploded at the US embassy in central Nairobi, concurrently with a similar attack on the US mission in Dar es Salaam, Tanzania. Some 254 people were killed in Nairobi, and more than 5,000 suffered injuries. The attacks were believed to have been co-ordinated by international Islamic fundamentalist terrorists, and, in mid-August, the USA retaliated by launching air strikes against targets in Afghanistan and Sudan. In the aftermath of the bomb attacks, Kenyan investigators and US federal agents made extensive nation-wide inquiries, concentrating their search for the perpetrators particularly on the Muslim community in Mombasa and the surrounding coastal region. Evidence emerged during October that young Kenyan Muslims had been systematically recruited for military training by international Islamist guerrilla groups. Meanwhile, the Government banned five local Islamic aid organizations, provoking strong resentment in the Muslim community. Four men were convicted of involvement in the bombings by a court in New York, USA, in May 2001 and were later sentenced to life imprisonment. A total of 22 people had been charged in connection with the bomb attacks; two were to be tried separately and three awaited extradition from the United Kingdom, while a further 13, including Osama bin Laden, the fugitive Saudi-born Islamist activist whom the US authorities held ultimately responsible for the bombings, were still at large.

During early 1998 an apparent *rapprochement* between Odinga and Moi caused considerable disquiet in both the NDP and KANU. A consultative forum on the constitutional review process was inaugurated in April, with the aim of organizing the long-anticipated constitutional review commission. In February 1999 the Cabinet was reorganized. Most significantly the Minister of Finance, Simeon Nyachae, exchanged portfolios with the Minister of Industrial Development, Yekokanda Francis Masakhalia; this effectively represented a demotion for Nyachae, who had played a leading role in ongoing attempts to eliminate corruption and financial mismanagement from the public sector. Nyachae, claiming to have been victimized by senior government figures allegedly involved in corrupt activities, immediately resigned from his new post. In April Saitoti was reappointed to the position of Vice-President (vacant since January 1998). In July Moi appointed Dr Leakey as head of the civil service and Secretary to the Cabinet, with responsibility for combating corruption in the public services. In September Moi effected a major reorganization of the Cabinet, merging several ministries and reducing the number of government ministers from 27 to 15.

During early 2000 Moi appealed for international aid to combat a severe drought and resultant famine. Aid was pledged by various donors, including the World Bank and the IMF. However, in September the World Bank suspended its support for public-sector water projects, reportedly citing large-scale misappropriation of funds. The German Government pledged Ks. 150m. to assist famine victims, but insisted that it be channelled through international charitable organizations, stating that Germany would no longer support relief operations controlled by politicians.

In December 1999 the KANU-NDP majority in the National Assembly voted in favour of appointing a parliamentary select committee on constitutional review. However, a rival commission was established by an alliance of opposition and religious groups, known as Ufungamano, which intended to propose its own recommendations for constitutional change. Moi opposed the Ufungamano commission, although many Kenyans appeared to support it. In April 2000 the parliamentary committee, headed by Raila Odinga of the NDP, completed its review, proposing the establishment of a constitutional review commission, comprising 15 members, to be nominated by the National Assembly prior to their appointment by Moi. However, in November, following months of recriminations between the two rival commissions, Prof. Yash Pal Ghai, appointed by Moi to head the parliamentary commission, refused to be sworn into office. Ghai declared that he first wanted to negotiate with Ufungamano in an attempt to unite the two groups. The merger went ahead in May 2001; the new commission comprised 27 members, 12 of whom were drawn from Ufungamano. The commission was to complete its review of the Constitution in time for the 2002 elections, although there were fears that it might be delayed in its task by political infighting.

In July 2000 the civil service commenced the reduction of its work-force by some 25,000 in the first three-month phase of a programme of reforms to be effected over three years. Meanwhile, a parliamentary anti-graft committee was seeking the adoption by the National Assembly of a report in which the alleged perpetrators of corruption were named. (The Government later deleted the addendum containing the list of names, causing widespread outrage.) The committee also proposed legislation on economic crimes that would allow the anti-corruption authority (which had been established in 1997 at the insistence of the IMF) to prosecute alleged perpetrators of corruption without seeking permission from the Attorney-General. As a result of these measures, the IMF announced that it was to resume lending to Kenya. The Government agreed to a number of conditions, including the introduction of a law binding public officials to declare their wealth and liabilities and the enactment of the legislation on economic crimes. However, less than one month after the resumption of aid the High Court temporarily halted the retrenchment of civil servants, pending the final determination of a lawsuit on the issue, and ruled that all civil servants who had already been retrenched should be reinstated. The revelation in October that Leakey and his staff were earning approximately 50 times the basic civil-service wage, and that their salaries were being paid with loans from international donors, caused controversy. In January 2001 the IMF and the World Bank expressed concern over the set-backs in the reforms, particularly the failure to approve legislation on public-service ethics and economic crimes, and suspended aid to Kenya until the situation could be resolved. In August Kenyan deputies again refused to approve anti-corruption legislation, and the IMF suspended aid to Kenya indefinitely. Moi subsequently created a new police body to combat corruption. Meanwhile, in March Leakey resigned as head of the civil service and Secretary to the Cabinet (two months before the expiry of his contract) and was replaced by Dr Sally Kosgei, an ally of Moi. Leakey's departure, along with the dismissal of most of his colleagues, prompted a major reshuffle within the senior civil service. Many observers believed that Moi was now intent on gathering loyal followers around him in preparation for the 2002 elections.

In January 2001 Raila Odinga of the Luo-dominated NDP signed a memorandum of understanding with KANU, which allowed Moi to appoint ministers from the NDP. In June 2001 Moi reshuffled the Cabinet and appointed Odinga as Minister of Energy, thereby creating the first coalition Government in Kenya's history. Moi reshuffled the Cabinet again in November, introducing younger KANU ministers in an apparent attempt to provide suitable candidates for his succession; most notably Uhuru Kenyatta (son of the late President Jomo Kenyatta) and Cyrus Jirongo were appointed as Minister for Local Government and Minister for Rural Development, respectively. Saitoti remained Vice-President, while the Secretary-General of KANU, Joseph Kamotho, hitherto Minister of Local Government, was named Minister of the Environment. Furthermore, Moi appointed Chrisanthus Okemo, previously Minister of Finance, as co-Minister of Energy, which, effectively, amounted to a demotion for both Okemo and Odinga.

The NDP was dissolved and absorbed into KANU in mid-March 2002, despite opposition from elements within both parties; Moi was elected as party Chairman, while Odinga was elected as Secretary-General, when the incumbent, Kamotho, withdrew from the contest. In June it emerged that the Government was considering using its parliamentary majority to extend the life of the National Assembly by one year, thereby delaying the elections. However, in response to fierce domestic and international criticism, KANU abandoned the proposal in the following month. In July some 12 opposition parties, including the DP, FORD—Kenya and the National Party of Kenya, formed an electoral alliance, the National Alliance Party of Kenya (NAK).

In August 2002 Moi publicly announced that he favoured Uhuru Kenyatta as KANU's presidential candidate. However, several senior KANU members, including Vice-President Saitoti and Odinga, subsequently announced their intention to seek the party's presidential nomination and formed the Rainbow Alliance to campaign within KANU for a democratic vote to select its candidate. Moi responded by dismissing the Vice-President. In mid-October, in protest at Moi's attempts to impose his preferred successor, members of the Rainbow Alliance resigned from their posts in the Government and from KANU, together with some 30 KANU deputies. The Rainbow Alliance subsequently boycotted the KANU conference, at which Kenyatta's presidential candidacy was endorsed. It was widely believed that Moi was hoping to extend his rule through Kenyatta, a close family friend of Moi, who was likely to protect Moi's wealth and shield him from prosecution. Later in October the Rainbow Alliance established a new party, the Liberal Democratic Party (LDP), and joined with the NAK to form the National Rainbow Coalition (NARC), with Mwai Kibaki as its presidential candidate. Shortly afterwards, and with nine more ex-KANU members in their ranks, the NARC proposed a vote of no confidence in Moi's Government, stating that the Government was illegally attempting to block the introduction of a new constitution, and citing Moi's failure to appoint a new Vice-President. However, Moi forestalled the tabling of the motion by dissolving the National Assembly on 25 October, thereby ensuring that the elections would be held under the current Constitution.

At the presidential and legislative elections, held concurrently on 27 December 2002, the opposition secured an emphatic victory, with Kibaki winning 62.3% of the votes cast in the presidential election, and the NARC securing 125 of the 210 elected seats in the National Assembly, while Kenyatta received 31.2% of the votes cast for the presidency, and KANU won 64 seats in the legislature. The NARC were allocated a further seven appointed seats, increasing their representation to 132, and KANU a further four seats, bringing their total to 68. The electoral turn-out was 56.1%. Moi stepped down, as promised; he resigned as Chairman of KANU in September 2003.

Following his inauguration as President on 30 December 2002, Kibaki promised reforms, including the adoption of a new constitution, under which certain powers would be transferred from the President to the legislature and the full independence of the judiciary guaranteed, the adoption of anti-corruption legislation, the privatization of state-owned companies and the dismissal of corrupt civil servants. In January 2003 Kibaki appointed a new Cabinet, which included Michael Kijana Wamalwa as Vice-President, Odinga as Minister of Roads, Public Works and Housing, and Saitoti as Minister of Education. One of the new Government's first acts was to abolish fees for primary education with immediate effect. However, divisions within the ruling coalition soon became apparent, as a group of 25 LDP deputies accused Kibaki of breaching a power-sharing agreement signed by the constituent parties of the NARC prior to the elections. Furthermore, the Government suffered a setback in late January, when a charter aircraft crashed near the Ugandan border, killing Ahmed Mohamed Khalif, the new Minister of Labour and Human Resources Development, and injuring three other ministers who were also on board. Meanwhile, Kibaki himself was hospitalized to receive further treatment for injuries he sustained in a car crash during campaigning. In May the Anti-Corruption and Economic Crimes Act, which provided for the establishment of the Kenya Anti-Corruption Commission, and the Public Service (Code of Conduct and Ethics) Act, which required elected officials and senior civil servants to declare their wealth, came into effect.

In February 2003 Kibaki appointed a commission of inquiry into the Goldenberg financial scandal, in which public funds had been paid to the company Goldenberg International in 1990–93 as subsidies for non-existent exports of gold and diamonds. Evidence presented at the inquiry indicated that Goldenberg

had initially received some Ks. 13,500m. (around US $180m.) under the Government's export compensation scheme. After thousands of transfers, including dubious foreign-exchange transactions, made with the alleged complicity of officials at the central bank, the payments to Goldenberg increased to Ks. 25,000m. ($600m.), equivalent to more than 10% of Kenya's annual GDP, although it was estimated that the total amount misappropriated could reach $4,000m. The scandal had also contributed to an IMF decision to suspend the disbursement to Kenya of loans worth some $500m. in 1997. The inquiry was halted temporarily in October 2003, when its Vice-Chairman was one of 23 appeals court and high court judges suspended, in response to the publication of a report into corruption in the judiciary; tribunals were established to examine the allegations against the judges, and some 82 magistrates were also placed under investigation. Proceedings in the Goldenberg inquiry were again disrupted for one week in January 2004, following allegations linking senior investigators with corruption. It was reported that bribes were being offered to investigators by people anxious to influence the outcome of the inquiry. Former President Moi was questioned in connection with the scandal in June 2003; he denied any involvement, but promised to co-operate fully with the inquiry.

In March 2003 a parliamentary select committee was established to reinvestigate the murder of Robert Ouko in 1990 (see above). Moi and Biwott, who both denied any involvement in the murder, were both summoned to give evidence, as was Ouko's maid and Ouko's widow and brother, Eston Barrack Mbajah. In his evidence, Mbajah claimed that Moi had attempted to bribe him to make a public statement calling for the initial investigation into Ouko's death to be halted, and that after he had refused the offer, he had been detained by the police and tortured. A British detective who had participated in an earlier inquiry into the case stated that Ouko was probably killed because he was about to expose corruption by ministers, and named one of Ouko's fellow ministers and a senior civil servant, both close allies of Moi, as key suspects. The investigation was ongoing in April 2004.

Meanwhile, the constitutional review conference opened in April 2003, but divisions over the proposed post of Prime Minister led to an impasse. The LDP advocated an executive Prime Minister with powers to appoint the Cabinet, but Kibaki and his supporters sought to maintain a strong presidency. The ensuing tensions between the NAK and LDP factions of the NARC threatened to split the ruling coalition. In August the death of Vice-President Wamalwa, who had been regarded as a moderating influence within the Government, led to an intensification of the power struggle. President Kibaki faced demands for a successor both from Wamalwa's Luhya ethnic group and from the Luo, who proposed the appointment of Odinga to the vice-presidency. In late September Kibaki named the Minister of Home Affairs, Moody Awori (a Luhya), as Vice-President and effected a minor government reshuffle. In March 2004 most of the 629 delegates at the constitutional review conference, including three cabinet ministers, voted to reduce the powers vested in the presidency and to create the new post of executive Prime Minister following the next elections, which were due in 2007. Under the recommendations adopted by the conference, more power was to be accorded to the National Assembly. The Government withdrew from the conference in protest and attempted to block the process, but the draft constitution was successfully presented to the Attorney-General, after which it was to be considered by the National Assembly. The High Court subsequently ruled that before the draft constitution could enter into force it had also to be approved in a referendum. However, the Government introduced two bills to the National Assembly that, if adopted, would allow the legislature to amend the draft constitution, contrary to the Constitutional Review Act.

Security in Kenya was a major concern in 2002–03. In November 2002 two simultaneous terrorist attacks were carried out in Mombasa. Two surface-to-air missiles narrowly missed an Israeli charter aircraft as it took off from Mombasa airport, while in a nearby tourist resort suicide bombers attacked an Israeli-owned hotel, killing 18 people and injuring many more. The militant Islamist al-Qa'ida (Base) organization later claimed responsibility for the attacks. Agents from the US and Israeli intelligence services arrived in Kenya soon afterwards to assist the authorities with their investigations, and by the end of the month 12 people had been arrested. Four Kenyan men were charged with murder in connection with the attacks in June 2003, and their trial began in Nairobi in February 2004. A further three Kenyans were being tried separately, on charges of conspiracy, for their alleged involvement in the Mombasa attacks, the 1998 bombing of the US embassy and an alleged plot to target the new US embassy between November 2002 and June 2003. The USA had closed its embassy in Nairobi in June 2003, in response to intelligence reports regarding a suspected imminent attack, and British and Israeli flights to Kenya had been temporarily suspended in the previous month. The Kenyan Government subsequently suspended flights to and from Somalia, and announced draft anti-terrorism legislation, although this had yet to be enacted by early 2004. In December 2003 the British and US authorities warned their citizens against travelling to Kenya; the Kenyan Government claimed that these warnings were unnecessary and severely damaging to its tourism industry.

Kenya's relations with Tanzania were strained during the late 1970s. However, the Kenya–Tanzania border, which had been closed prior to the dissolution of the East African Community (EAC) in 1977, was reopened in November 1983, following an agreement on the distribution of EAC assets and liabilities between the three former members (Kenya, Tanzania and Uganda), and in December Kenya and Tanzania agreed to establish full diplomatic relations. Following the seizure of power by the National Resistance Army in Uganda in January 1986, Moi offered full co-operation to the new Ugandan President, Yoweri Museveni. After visits to Kenya by Museveni and President Ali Hassan Mwinyi of Tanzania in June, it was announced that joint commissions were to be formed to enhance co-operation between the three countries. In September, however, Ugandan authorities claimed that Kenya was harbouring anti-Museveni rebels, and stationed troops at the two countries' common border. These claims were denied, and in December, when Ugandan troops allegedly entered Kenya in pursuit of rebels, Ugandan and Kenyan armed forces exchanged fire across the border for several days; at least 15 people were reported to have been killed. Later in December Moi and Museveni agreed to withdraw troops from either side of the border. In July 1988 the Ugandan Government accused Kenya of complicity in smuggling weapons to rebels in Uganda. During 1988–89 the Kenyan authorities repeatedly accused the Ugandan armed forces of making incursions into Kenya. Moi visited Museveni in August 1990, indicating a renewed *détente* between Kenya and Uganda. In November 1994 Moi, Museveni and Mwinyi met in Arusha, Tanzania, and established a commission for co-operation; in March 1996 the Secretariat of the Permanent Tripartite Commission for East African Co-operation was formally inaugurated, with a view to reviving the EAC. A treaty for the re-establishment of the EAC, providing for the promotion of free trade between the member states, the development of the region's infrastructure and economy and the creation of a regional legislative assembly and court, was ratified by the Kenyan, Tanzanian and Ugandan Heads of State in November 1999. The new EAC (see p. 359) was officially inaugurated in Arusha in January 2001. Talks on integrating the economies of the three EAC members followed, and in March 2004 Kibaki, Museveni and President Benjamin Mkapa of Tanzania signed a protocol on the creation of a customs union, eliminating most duties on goods traded within the EAC, which was scheduled for September.

Relations between Kenya and Sudan deteriorated in mid-1988, as the two countries made mutual accusations of aiding rebel factions. In early 1989 Sudan renewed a long-standing dispute with Kenya over the sovereignty of territory on the Kenyan side of the two countries' common border, known as the 'Elemi triangle'. During the late 1990s Kenya hosted a series of peace talks between the Sudanese Government and opposition leaders, under the auspices of the Intergovernmental Authority on Development (see p. 259), in an attempt to resolve the conflict in southern Sudan. Further negotiations were held in Nairobi in September 2000 and June 2001, and in July 2002 the Sudanese Government and the opposition Sudan People's Liberation Army (SPLA) signed an accord in Machakos, Kenya, which provided for the holding of a referendum on self-determination for southern Sudan after a transitional period of six years. In September 2003 Kenya and Sudan agreed to form a joint border committee. Talks aimed at achieving a final peace settlement between the Sudanese Government and the SPLA continued in Kenya throughout 2003 and early 2004 (see the chapter on Sudan).

Somalia has traditionally laid claim to part of north-eastern Kenya. During 1989 tension developed between the Kenyan

authorities and ethnic Somalis from both sides of the Kenya–Somalia border, when Somalis were alleged to be largely responsible for wildlife-poaching and banditry in north-eastern Kenya. In September Moi protested strongly to the Somali Government, following an incursion into Kenya by Somali troops (reportedly pursuing Somali rebels), which resulted in the deaths of four Kenyans. The Kenyan Government closed the two countries' common border in mid-1999, in response to rising insecurity in the area. The border was reopened in April 2000. In September the Kenyan Minister of Foreign Affairs and International Co-operation, Dr Bonaya Godana, stated that, while the Government supported the peace process in Somalia, it had not, as had been reported, officially declared recognition of the interim Somali President, Abdulkasim Hasan, or his Government. Moi later agreed to mediate between the interim Government and opposing rebel factions in Somalia. In July 2001 Kenya again closed the border after numerous clashes were reported on the Somali side, which threatened to spill over into Kenya. However, Moi agreed to reopen the border in November. An IGAD-sponsored Somali reconciliation conference opened in the Kenyan town of Eldoret in October 2002 and was moved to Nairobi in February 2003; the talks continued throughout 2003 and early 2004, despite various disruptions, and in January 2004 representatives from more than 20 factions in attendance reached agreement on the establishment of a new Somali parliament (see the chapter on Somalia). In July 2003 President Kibaki had appointed Mohamed Affey as Kenya's first ambassador to Somalia for 13 years.

Relations between the Kenyan and Ethiopian Governments became strained in 1997, owing to an increased incidence of cross-border cattle-rustling, including an attack in March during which 16 members of the Kenyan security forces were killed. A number of communiqués were subsequently signed by representatives of the two countries, agreeing to reinforce border security, to take measures to prevent the smuggling of arms and drugs, and to enhance trade. In November 1998 some 189 people (mainly Somalis) were found to have been massacred in north-eastern Kenya; Ethiopian guerrillas were widely believed to be responsible. In January 1999 the Kenyan Government protested to the Ethiopian authorities, following an incursion into Kenya by Ethiopian security forces, who were alleged to be in pursuit of Ethiopian rebels. Kenya deployed additional troops at the two countries' common frontier in May, following a series of landmine explosions in the region, which had resulted in several fatalities. Ethiopian troops allegedly made a further infiltration into Kenyan territory in July. Bilateral relations deteriorated further during late 2000 after it was reported that some 50 Kenyans had been killed, allegedly by Ethiopian militia forces, in cross-border clashes. In January 2001 representatives from both countries met in Nairobi and agreed to initiate measures aimed at ending border disputes.

In October 1995, despite strong condemnation from foreign Governments, the Kenyan authorities refused to permit the international tribunal that was investigating war crimes committed in Rwanda during 1994 access to alleged Rwandan perpetrators of genocide who had fled to Kenya. In June 1996 the Moi Government closed the Rwandan embassy in Nairobi in protest at the Rwandan Government's refusal to waive diplomatic immunity for an embassy official who was suspected of plotting a murder in Kenya; the diplomat was deported. In September, however, the first arrest in Kenya was made of a Rwandan Hutu suspected of involvement in genocide. Kenya strongly denied accusations, in November, of supplying arms to Rwandan Hutu rebels operating from within Zaire (now the Democratic Republic of the Congo). Following the *coup d'état* in Burundi in July 1996, Kenya, along with other countries of the region, imposed full economic sanctions on the administration of Maj. Pierre Buyoya; these sanctions were subsequently relaxed, and eventually withdrawn in January 1999. In November and December 1996 regional summit meetings were held in Nairobi to discuss the crisis in the Great Lakes region. Relations between the Kenyan and Rwandan Governments improved during 1997, when further Rwandan Hutus were arrested by the Kenyan security forces to stand trial on charges of genocide at the UN tribunal in Arusha, Tanzania. During a visit by Moi to Rwanda in May 2000 the two countries agreed to reopen the Kenyan embassy in Kigali and to establish a joint commission for bilateral relations.

In 1995 Kenya was reportedly sheltering about 200,000 refugees from the conflict in Somalia. The Moi Government, which claims that the refugees place an intolerable burden on the country's resources, has repeatedly requested the UN to repatriate the total refugee population. By mid-1998 an estimated 155,000 Somalis had been repatriated from Kenya, with assistance from the office of the UN High Commissioner for Refugees. However, continuing instability in Somalia resulted in further influxes of refugees to Kenya. Kenya's total refugee population stood at 233,671 at the end of 2002, including 155,767 from Somalia and 57,779 from Sudan.

Government

Legislative power is vested in the unicameral National Assembly, with 224 members (210 elected by universal adult suffrage, the Attorney-General, the Speaker and 12 nominated members), who serve a term of five years, subject to dissolution. Executive power is held by the President, also directly elected for five years, who is assisted by an appointed Vice-President and Cabinet.

Defence

In August 2003 Kenya's active armed forces numbered 24,120, comprising an army of 20,000, an air force of 2,500 and a navy of 1,620, and the paramilitary Police General Service Unit had a membership of 5,000. Military service is voluntary. Defence was allocated Ks. 16,268m. in the budget for the financial year to 30 June 2002 (equivalent to 7.6% of total budgetary expenditure by the central Government). Military assistance is received from the United Kingdom and from the USA, whose Rapid Deployment Force uses port and onshore facilities in Kenya.

Economic Affairs

In 2002, according to estimates by the World Bank, Kenya's gross national income (GNI), measured at average 2000–02 prices, was US $11,296m., equivalent to $360 per head (or $990 per head on an international purchasing-power parity basis). During 1990–2002, it was estimated, the population increased at an average annual rate of 2.5%, while gross domestic product (GDP) per head declined, in real terms, by an average of 0.8% per year. Overall GDP increased, in real terms, at an average annual rate of 1.6% in 1990–2002. Real GDP increased by 1.8% in 2002.

Agriculture (including forestry and fishing) contributed 19.1% of GDP and employed about 74.6% of the labour force in 2002. The principal cash crops are tea (which contributed 29.3% of total export earnings in 2000) and coffee (accounting for 9.8% of export earnings in 2000). Horticultural produce (Kenya is the world's fourth largest exporter of cut flowers), pyrethrum, sisal, sugar cane and cotton are also important. Maize is the principal subsistence crop. There is a significant dairy industry for domestic consumption and export. During 1990–2002, according to the World Bank, agricultural GDP increased at an average annual rate of 0.7%. Agricultural GDP increased by 1.0% in 2002.

Industry (including mining, manufacturing, construction and power) contributed 18.3% of GDP in 2002, and employed an estimated 19.8% of the total labour force in 1995. During 1990–2002, according to the World Bank, industrial GDP increased at an average annual rate of 1.4%. Industrial GDP increased by 1.4% in 2002.

Mining contributed 0.2% of GDP (at factor cost) in 2001. Soda ash is the principal mineral export. Fluorspar, iron ore, salt, limestone, gold, gemstones (including rubies and sapphires), vermiculite and lead are also mined. Kenya has substantial reserves of titanium.

Manufacturing contributed 12.7% of GDP in 2002. During 1990–2002, according to the World Bank, manufacturing GDP increased at an average annual rate of 1.9%. Manufacturing GDP increased by 3.5% in 2002.

Owing to severe drought, hydroelectric power accounted for only 34.1% of total electricity generated in 2000 (compared with 56.6% in 1999 and 72.8% in 1998), while a further 54.8% was derived from petroleum (34.5% in 1999 and 18.5% in 1998). Energy for domestic use is derived principally from fuel wood and charcoal. The prolonged drought led to severe power shortages in 2000. In February 2004 it was announced that the Kenyan and Tanzanian national grids were to be connected to that of Zambia under a cross-border energy project; the first phase of the project, which was to cost some US $300m., was to be commissioned in 2007, followed by a second phase in 2012. In 2000 imports of mineral fuels and lubricants (including crude petroleum intended for refining) comprised 26.2% of the value of total imports.

The services sector contributed 62.6% of GDP in 2002, and engaged 15.5% of the total labour force in 1991. Tourism makes an important contribution to Kenya's economy, and has been the country's principal source of foreign exchange since 1987. In 1998, however, a decline of 10.6% in tourist arrivals, to 894,300, was attributed partly to the effects of civil unrest in coastal areas during 1997. In 1999–2000 there was some recovery in tourism, with arrivals increasing to 1,036,628 in 2000. The GDP of the services sector increased at an average annual rate of 2.9% in 1990–2002, according to the World Bank. Services GDP increased by 3.6% in 2002.

In 2001 Kenya recorded a visible trade deficit of US $1,282.1m., and there was a deficit of $317.8m. on the current account of the balance of payments. In 2000 the principal source of imports was the United Arab Emirates (which supplied 19.5% of total imports in that year); other major suppliers were the United Kingdom, South Africa, Saudi Arabia and Japan. Uganda was the principal market for Kenya's exports (purchasing 18.0%) in that year; other important purchasers were the United Kingdom, Tanzania, Pakistan and the Netherlands. The principal exports in 2000 were tea, vegetables and fruit, coffee and refined petroleum products. The principal imports in that year were petroleum and petroleum products, aircraft and parts, cereals and cereal preparations, and road vehicles and parts.

In the financial year ending 30 June 2003 there was a budgetary deficit of Ks. 32,814m., equivalent to 3.2% of GDP. The country's external debt was US $5,833m. at the end of 2001, of which $4,930m. was long-term public debt. In that year the cost of debt-servicing was equivalent to 15.4% of the value of exports of goods and services. The annual rate of inflation averaged 13.8% in 1990–2002; consumer prices increased by an average of 4.3% in 2002. Some 23% of the labour force were estimated to be unemployed in late 2000, and the rate of unemployment was reported to be approaching 30% by October 2001.

Kenya is a member of the Common Market for Eastern and Southern Africa (see p. 171) and, with Tanzania and Uganda, of the East African Community (see p. 359). The International Tea Promotion Association (see p. 357) is based in Kenya.

Kenya's economy is reasonably diversified, although most employment is dependent on agriculture. Agricultural development has been intermittently hindered by adverse weather conditions (generally low rainfall, although severe flooding occurred in 1997–98), resulting in sporadic food shortages, and also by rural ethnic unrest. Moreover, the country is highly vulnerable to fluctuations in international prices for its cash crops, most notably tea and coffee. Poverty is widespread, with population growth considerably higher than growth in GNI per head, which actually declined every year between 1997 and 2002. Hopes that the change in Government in December 2002 would lead to a rapid recovery were disappointed to a large extent, and economic performance remained weak in 2003, as the expected resumption of IMF lending, which had been suspended in 2001, was delayed. A new agreement with the IMF was eventually reached in November 2003, when a three-year Poverty Reduction and Growth Facility (PRGF) arrangement, worth some US $252.8m., was approved. In addition, at a meeting of the World Bank's Consultative Group held later that month, donors pledged some $4,100m. in grants and concessionary loans for Kenya, to be disbursed over a three-year period. The IMF and donor funding was to support the Government's ambitious Economic Recovery Strategy for Wealth and Employment Creation, which aimed to achieve a return to the higher growth rates of the 1980s, with an average annual increase in GDP of 4.7% forecast for 2003–07, and the fostering of an economic environment that could support the creation of some 500,000 jobs per year. The Government also planned to improve conditions for business by reducing bureaucracy and high energy and communications costs; however, although there were signs of increased investment in the first part of 2004, Kenya's record of attracting and retaining private-sector finance had been described by the World Bank as 'dismal' in the previous year. There was some increase in private-sector borrowing, but this remained below expectations, despite low interest rates. Moreover, the competitiveness of Kenyan companies was hampered by the Government's decision to issue fewer work permits for foreign workers (see Recent History). Also of concern was the Government's reluctance to reduce the state's interest in strategic sectors; there was some movement towards restructuring and privatization (of companies involved in telecommunications, electricity generation and banking), but there appeared to be little real political impetus behind the divestiture programme. Public-sector salaries, which accounted for more than 9% of GDP, remained a source of contention with the IMF, which advocated a reduction in the wage bill, although the Government was also under pressure from elsewhere to raise low state pay, which was regarded by many as an incentive for the endemic corruption which the Government had promised to eradicate.

Education

The Government provides, or assists in the provision of, schools. Primary education, which is compulsory, is provided free of charge. The education system involves eight years of primary education (beginning at six years of age), four years at secondary school and four years of university education. Primary enrolment in 2000/01 included 69% of children in the relevant age-group (males 68%; females 69%), according to UNESCO estimates. In the same year, however, secondary enrolment included only 23% of the appropriate age-group (males 23%; females 23%), according to UNESCO estimates. There are five state universities and five chartered private universities. In 1998/99 there were 61,526 students enrolled at institutes of higher education. The education sector was allocated Ks.

54,653m. in the budget for 2001/02 (equivalent to 25.6% of total budgetary expenditure by the central Government).

Public Holidays

2004: 1 January (New Year's Day), 1 February* (Id al Adha, Feast of the Sacrifice), 9–12 April (Easter), 1 May (Labour Day, anniversary of self-government), 1 June (Madaraka Day, anniversary of self-government), 10 October (Moi Day), 20 October (Kenyatta Day), 14 November* (Id al Fitr, end of Ramadan), 12 December (Independence Day), 25–26 December (Christmas).

2005: 1 January (New Year's Day), 21 January* (Id al Adha, Feast of the Sacrifice), 25–28 March (Easter), 1 May (Labour Day, anniversary of self-government), 1 June (Madaraka Day, anniversary of self-government), 10 October (Moi Day), 20 October (Kenyatta Day), 4 November* (Id al Fitr, end of Ramadan), 12 December (Independence Day), 25–26 December (Christmas).

*These holidays are determined by the Islamic lunar calendar and may vary by one or two days from the dates given.

Weights and Measures

The metric system is in use.

Statistical Survey

Source (unless otherwise stated): Central Bureau of Statistics, Ministry of Finance and Planning, POB 30266, Nairobi; tel. (20) 333971; fax (20) 333030; internet www.cbs.go.ke.

Area and Population

AREA, POPULATION AND DENSITY

Area (sq km)	580,367*
Population (census results)†	
24 August 1989	21,443,636
24 August 1999	
Males	14,205,589
Females.	14,481,018
Total	28,686,607
Population (official estimates at mid-year)	
2000	29,573,434
2001	30,493,792
Density (per sq km) at mid-2001	52.5

* 224,081 sq miles. Total includes 11,230 sq km (4,336 sq miles) of inland water.
† Excluding adjustment for underenumeration.

PRINCIPAL ETHNIC GROUPS
(census of August 1989)

African . . .	21,163,076	European . . .		34,560
Arab . . .	41,595	Other* . . .		115,220
Asian . . .	89,185	**Total** . . .		21,443,636

* Includes persons who did not state 'tribe' or 'race'.

POPULATION BY PROVINCE
(census of August 1999)

Nairobi . . .	2,143,254	Nyanza . . .		4,392,196
Central . . .	3,724,159	Rift Valley . . .		6,987,036
Coast . . .	2,487,264	Western . . .		3,358,776
Eastern . . .	4,631,779			
North-Eastern . .	962,143	**Total** . . .		28,686,607

PRINCIPAL TOWNS
(estimated population at census of August 1999)

Nairobi (capital) . .	2,143,020	Meru . . .		78,100
Mombasa . . .	660,800	Kitale . . .		63,245
Nakuru . . .	219,366	Malindi* . . .		53,805
Kisumu* . . .	194,390	Nyeri* . . .		46,969
Eldoret* . . .	167,016	Kericho . . .		30,023
Thika . . .	82,665	Kisii . . .		29,634

* Boundaries extended between 1979 and 1989.

BIRTHS AND DEATHS
(UN estimates, annual averages)

	1985–90	1990–95	1995–2000
Birth rate (per 1,000)	46.2	38.2	34.9
Death rate (per 1,000)	10.9	10.1	13.0

Source: UN, *World Population Prospects: The 2002 Revision*.

Expectation of life (WHO estimates, years at birth): 50.9 (males 49.8; females 51.9) in 2002 (Source: WHO, *World Health Report*).

ECONOMICALLY ACTIVE POPULATION

	1999	2000	2001*
Agriculture and forestry . . .	311,257	312,200	312,500
Mining and quarrying . . .	5,162	5,300	5,200
Manufacturing	219,604	218,700	216,600
Electricity and water . . .	22,713	22,700	21,400
Construction	78,647	78,600	76,800
Wholesale and retail trade . .	153,629	155,500	156,900
Transport and communications .	83,805	84,200	84,300
Finance, insurance, real estate and business services	84,528	85,000	70,300
Community, social and personal services	714,205	733,100	719,600
Total	1,673,550	1,695,300	1,663,600

* Provisional figures.

Source: IMF, *Kenya: Statistical Appendix* (July 2003).

Health and Welfare

KEY INDICATORS

Total fertility rate (children per woman, 2002).	4.1
Under-5 mortality rate (per 1,000 live births, 2001) . . .	122
HIV/AIDS (% of persons aged 15–49, 2001).	15.01
Physicians (per 1,000 head, 1995)	0.13
Hospital beds (per 1,000 head, 1990)	1.65
Health expenditure (2001): US $ per head (PPP) . . .	114
Health expenditure (2001): % of GDP	7.8
Health expenditure (2001): public (% of total)	21.4
Access to water (% of persons, 2000).	49
Access to sanitation (% of persons, 2000)	86
Human Development Index (2001): ranking	146
Human Development Index (2001): value	0.489

For sources and definitions, see explanatory note on p. vi.

Agriculture

PRINCIPAL CROPS
('000 metric tons)

	2000	2001	2002
Wheat	204	252	234
Rice (paddy)	52	45	50
Barley	45	47	45
Maize	2,160	2,776	2,340
Millet	45	45	45
Sorghum	82	117	72
Potatoes	670	1,113	900
Sweet potatoes	528	552	520
Cassava (Manioc)	418	608	600
Sugar cane	3,941	3,551	4,502
Pulses	453	387	415
Groundnuts (in shell)*	30	30	30
Coconuts	63*	63*	60
Sesame seed*	10	10	10
Cottonseed*	13	13	13
Tomatoes	257	271	259
Dry onions	57	57	58
Green beans	21*	23*	23
Other vegetables*	570	570	570
Bananas†	206	271	208
Plantains†	822	867	830
Oranges*	26	26	26
Grapefruits*	13	13	13
Mangoes	113	180	118
Pineapples	607	612	600*
Other fruits (excl. melons)	77	91	90*
Coffee (green)	101	51	48
Tea (made)	236	295	287
Tobacco (leaves)	18	20†	20
Sisal	17	17	20

* FAO estimate(s).
† Unofficial figure(s).

Source: FAO.

LIVESTOCK
('000 head, year ending September)

	2000	2001	2002
Cattle	11,706	11,745	11,500*
Sheep	7,940	7,609	7,700*
Goats	10,004	10,980	10,960
Pigs	311	333	332
Camels	825	830*	830*
Chickens	26	23	28

* FAO estimate.

Source: FAO.

LIVESTOCK PRODUCTS
('000 metric tons)

	2000	2001	2002
Beef and veal	287	295	295
Mutton and lamb*	26	26	26
Goats' meat	31*	34*	31
Pig meat	11	14*	11
Poultry meat	54	54*	54
Game meat*	14	14	14
Camel meat*	20	20	20
Cows' milk	2,672	2,442	2,689
Sheeps' milk*	31	31	31
Goats' milk	116	97	96*
Hen eggs*	60	61	61
Honey	25	25*	22
Wool: greasy	2	2*	2
Cattle hides*	55	47	39
Goatskins*	10	11	11

* FAO estimate(s).

Source: FAO.

Forestry

ROUNDWOOD REMOVALS
(FAO estimates, '000 cubic metres, excluding bark)

	2000	2001	2002
Sawlogs, veneer logs and logs for sleepers*	460	460	460
Pulpwood*	357	357	357
Other industrial wood	1,160	1,160	1,160
Fuel wood	19,658	19,827	20,002
Total	21,635	21,804	21,979

* Annual output is assumed to be unchanged since 1989.

Source: FAO.

SAWNWOOD PRODUCTION
('000 cubic metres, including railway sleepers)

	1987	1988	1989
Total	195	188	185

1990–2002: Production as in 1989 (FAO estimates).

Source: FAO.

Fishing

('000 metric tons, live weight)

	1999	2000	2001
Capture	205.3	215.1	164.2
Silver cyprinid	48.8	49.6	41.4
Nile tilapia	17.5	19.3	7.3
Other tilapias	18.2	19.9	19.1
Nile perch	103.0	109.8	78.5
Other freshwater fishes	4.2	4.9	5.2
Aquaculture	0.3	0.5	1.0
Total catch	205.6	215.6	165.2

Note: Figures exclude crocodiles, recorded by number rather than by weight. The number of Nile crocodiles caught was: 3,350 in 1999; 3,460 in 2000; 4,250 in 2001.

Source: FAO, *Yearbook of Fishery Statistics*.

Mining

('000 metric tons)

	2000	2001	2002
Soda ash	238.2	297.8	304.1
Fluorspar	100.1	118.9	85.0
Salt	16.4	5.7	18.8
Limestone flux	32	32	32

Industry

SELECTED PRODUCTS
('000 metric tons, unless otherwise indicated)

	2000	2001	2002
Wheat flour	189	181	188
Raw sugar	402	377	494
Beer ('000 hectolitres)	2,029	1,843	1,919
Cigarettes (million)	6,009	5,850	5,950
Cement	1,366	1,319	1,495
Kerosene and jet fuels	400	320	273
Motor spirit (petrol)	335	273	253
Gas-diesel (distillate fuel) oils	511	436	405
Residual fuel oil	616	535	533
Electric energy (million kWh)	3,958	4,338	4,447

Finance

CURRENCY AND EXCHANGE RATES

Monetary Units

100 cents = 1 Kenya shilling (Ks.).

Ks. 20 = 1 Kenya pound (K£).

Sterling, Dollar and Euro Equivalents (31 December 2003)

£1 sterling = Ks. 135.89;

US $1 = Ks. 76.14;

€1 = Ks. 96.16;

Ks. 1,000 = £7.36 sterling = $13.13 = €10.40.

Average Exchange Rate (Ks. per US $)

2001   78.563

2002   78.749

2003   75.936

Note: The foregoing information refers to the Central Bank's mid-point exchange rate. However, with the introduction of a foreign exchange bearer certificate (FEBC) scheme in October 1991, a dual exchange rate system is in effect. In May 1994 foreign exchange transactions were liberalized and the Kenya shilling became fully convertible against other currencies.

BUDGET
(Ks. million, year ending 30 June)

Revenue	1999/2000	2000/01	2001/02*
Tax revenue	151,359.5	160,771.6	160,394.2
Taxes on income and profits . .	53,317.0	53,428.9	55,861.9
Taxes on goods and services . .	69,437.3	78,538.9	82,948.6
Value-added tax. . . .	40,944.2	50,220.9	50,871.7
Excise duties	28,493.1	28,317.9	32,076.9
Taxes on international trade. .	28,605.2	28,803.7	21,583.7
Import duties	28,605.2	28,803.7	21,583.7
Non-tax revenue	27,585.1	26,306.1	25,399.4
Property income	6,482.4	4,786.1	4,105.5
Administrative fees and charges	21,538.1	21,538.1	21,293.9
Total (incl. others)	184,550.9	192,221.0	187,863.8

Expenditure	1999/2000	2000/01	2001/02*
General administration	44,080.7	62,943.3	57,584.5
Defence	10,427.2	14,202.8	16,268.2
Social services	59,670.4	67,611.1	71,953.1
Education	47,726.8	49,611.3	54,653.0
Health	9,188.6	15,629.3	14,336.5
Economic services	28,481.1	39,362.3	38,069.4
General administration . . .	5,101.3	14,085.6	12,696.2
Agriculture, forestry and fishing	8,115.4	8,269.6	7,850.1
Roads	8,848.5	9,458.4	8,856.7
Interest on public debt	28,917.8	24,425.5	29,850.9
Total	171,577.2	208,545.7	213,726.2

* Forecasts.

INTERNATIONAL RESERVES
(US $ million at 31 December)

	2000	2001	2002
IMF special drawing rights. . .	0.3	1.0	0.8
Reserve position in IMF. . . .	16.2	15.8	17.1
Foreign exchange.	881.2	1,048.1	1,050.0
Total	897.7	1,064.9	1,067.9

Source: IMF, *International Financial Statistics*.

MONEY SUPPLY
(Ks. million at 31 December)

	2000	2001	2002
Currency outside banks	43,466	45,349	53,895
Demand deposits at commercial banks	65,206	76,220	86,651
Total money (incl. others) . . .	118,968	126,332	140,546

Source: IMF, *International Financial Statistics*.

COST OF LIVING
(Consumer Price Index at December; base: October 1997 = 100)

	2000	2001	2002
Food and non-alcoholic beverages .	136.3	134.8	142.5
Alcohol and tobacco	120.8	136.3	137.1
Clothing and footwear . . .	109.9	109.8	110.7
Housing	121.6	129.3	133.9
Fuel and power	143.1	154.1	165.8
Household goods and services . .	117.6	119.0	120.8
Medical goods and services . . .	134.1	152.6	158.8
Transport and communnications .	128.4	127.7	130.8
Recreation and education . .	120.2	129.6	132.8
Personal goods and services .	118.2	120.5	122.8
All items (incl. others)	129.0	131.1	136.7

Source: IMF, *Kenya: Statistical Appendix* (July 2003).

NATIONAL ACCOUNTS
(Ks. million at current prices)

Expenditure on the Gross Domestic Product

	1999	2000	2001*
Government final consumption expenditure.	125,943	139,159	150,430
Private final consumption expenditure.	539,058	609,938	695,472
Increase in stocks	7,142	6,142	5,282
Gross fixed capital formation . .	112,961	116,369	124,259
Total domestic expenditure. .	785,103	871,607	975,443
Exports of goods and services . .	189,265	211,433	234,213
Less Imports of goods and services	232,233	287,067	314,377
GDP in purchasers' values . .	742,136	795,972	895,278
GDP at constant 1982 prices .	117,742.	117,548	118,845

Gross Domestic Product by Economic Activity
(at factor cost)

	1999	2000	2001*
Agriculture, forestry and fishing .	149,507	135,269	146,639
Mining and quarrying	994	1,143	1,260
Manufacturing	79,121	88,715	96,969
Electricity, gas and water . . .	7,434	8,162	8,937
Construction	27,070	29,134	33,161
Trade, restaurants and hotels . .	138,031	162,391	194,611
Transport, storage and communication.	45,617	50,339	53,107
Finance, insurance, real estate and business services	76,078	69,750	75,731
Other services	115,206	141,258	162,478
Total	639,056	686,159	772,893

* Provisional figures.

Source: IMF, *Kenya: Statistical Appendix* (July 2003).

BALANCE OF PAYMENTS
(US $ million)

	1999	2000	2001
Exports of goods f.o.b.	1,756.7	1,782.2	1,894.0
Imports of goods f.o.b.	−2,731.8	−3,044.0	−3,176.1
Trade balance	−975.1	−1,261.7	−1,282.1
Exports of services	934.5	993.4	1,087.2
Imports of services	−570.4	−724.5	−825.5
Balance on goods and services	−611.0	−992.9	−1,020.4
Other income received	31.7	45.0	42.8
Other income paid	−190.9	−178.1	−190.3
Balance on goods, services and income	−770.2	−1,126.0	−1,167.8
Current transfers received	685.3	926.6	850.0
Current transfers paid	−4.7	−4.2	—
Current balance	−89.6	−203.7	−317.8
Capital account	55.4	49.6	69.0
Direct investment from abroad	13.8	110.9	5.3
Portfolio investment assets	—	−10.9	−7.3
Portfolio investment liabilities	−8.0	−6.0	2.4
Other investment assets	−89.9	−55.7	−86.4
Other investment liabilities	249.7	116.5	167.2
Net errors and omissions	−165.5	−10.0	117.0
Overall balance	−34.0	−6.8	−47.5

Source: IMF, *International Financial Statistics*.

External Trade

PRINCIPAL COMMODITIES
(distribution by SITC, Ks. million)

Imports c.i.f.	1998	1999	2000
Food and live animals	18,905.4	13,132.9	21,332.6
Cereals and cereal preparations	11,071.7	85,114.0	14,353.3
Crude materials (inedible) except fuels	6,299.3	5,791.0	6,364.0
Mineral fuels, lubricants, etc	32,189.1	30,745.6	64,855.9
Petroleum, petroleum products, etc.	31,828.5	30,224.1	64,358.0
Crude petroleum oils	15,036.6	11,087.0	41,907.2
Refined petroleum products	16,317.9	18,593.0	21,882.6
Animal and vegetable oils, fats and waxes	8,750.1	9,087.8	8,015.8
Chemicals and related products	30,018.1	31,918.4	32,796.7
Medicinal and pharmaceutical products	6,559.4	6,378.6	5,975.8
Artificial resins, plastic materials, etc	6,108.2	6,006.5	7,134.8
Basic manufactures	25,307.2	28,169.1	27,562.4
Iron and steel	7,899.7	9,136.9	8,603.8
Machinery and transport equipment	63,341.0	59,519.1	72,131.3
Power-generating machinery and equipment	5,160.0	6,011.9	12,142.8
Machinery specialized for particular industries	7,564.8	5,914.4	4,817.6
General industrial machinery, equipment and parts	8,735.8	8,530.4	8,831.9
Electrical machinery, apparatus, etc.	6,310.7	6,390.4	6,685.3
Road vehicles and parts*	17,737.0	14,992.4	12,546.1
Passenger motor cars (excl. buses)	6,458.8	5,290.3	4,763.2
Motor vehicles for goods transport and special purposes	6,062.5	4,805.1	2,798.1
Aircraft, associated equipment and parts*	8,545.7	8,838.5	14,972.7
Miscellaneous manufactured articles	12,002.4	15,193.0	13,353.8
Total (incl. others)	197,788.7	195,003.7	247,803.9

* Data on parts exclude tyres, engines and electrical parts.

Exports f.o.b.*	1998	1999	2000
Food and live animals	62,850.0	63,471.2	66,953.7
Vegetables and fruit	9,384.0	11,147.8	13,420.8
Fresh or simply preseved vegetables	3,714.6	4,327.0	7,812.7
Coffee, tea, cocoa and spices	46,393.9	45,749.1	47,519.5
Coffee (green and roasted)	12,875.0	12,104.9	11,759.2
Tea	32,970.7	33,065.1	35,149.9
Crude materials (inedible) except fuels	10,196.7	11,578.9	13,575.9
Cut flowers and foliage	5,155.4	5,965.5	6,896.7
Mineral fuels, lubricants, etc.	9,915.1	9,603.1	9,705.4
Petroleum, petroleum products, etc.	9,865.4	9,555.1	9,641.9
Refined petroleum products	9,671.5	9,392.4	9,441.3
Chemicals and related products	7,336.5	7,406.2	6,712.8
Basic manufactures	13,269.4	12,113.7	12,357.3
Iron and steel	3,823.7	2,757.5	2,605.1
Miscellaneous manufactured articles	4,868.4	5,637.6	5,736.1
Total (incl. others)	114,445.3	115,405.5	119,763.7

* Excluding re-exports.

PRINCIPAL TRADING PARTNERS
(Ks. million)

Imports c.i.f.	1998	1999	2000
Australia	1,724.7	2,692.3	2,611.4
Belgium-Luxembourg	3,277.4	3,152.8	5,580.6
China, People's Repub.	4,139.0	4,785.7	7,755.5
France	8,031.9	6,735.4	8,297.1
Germany	11,138.6	11,210.0	8,713.8
India	8,648.5	8,995.2	10,139.0
Indonesia	3,060.0	1,650.8	2,706.4
Italy	5,103.4	4,814.9	7,205.7
Japan	15,675.0	15,366.0	12,514.4
Netherlands	5,369.3	5,030.0	8,673.6
Saudi Arabia	12,384.4	10,872.7	15,004.5
Singapore	1,331.2	4,278.5	4,775.8
South Africa	14,197.6	17,134.1	16,585.6
Switzerland	2,386.5	2,945.9	2,671.0
United Arab Emirates	17,810.3	25,529.1	48,211.8
United Kingdom	24,354.5	23,122.8	25,135.8
USA	16,509.3	13,189.7	10,083.7
Total (incl. others)	197,788.7	206,400.6	247,803.9

Exports f.o.b.	1998	1999	2000
Belgium-Luxembourg	1,717.3	1,590.4	1,911.5
Congo, Democratic Republic	2,014.8	2,031.0	3,042.5
Egypt	5,693.6	6,739.2	7,107.4
Ethiopia	1,535.0	1,412.4	2,056.9
France	1,889.9	2,290.1	2,143.4
Germany	5,550.2	5,773.0	5,577.4
Italy	1,747.6	1,650.3	1,518.7
Netherlands	5,284.4	6,152.0	7,292.6
Pakistan	8,276.0	9,019.9	9,986.2
Rwanda	3,037.2	3,110.3	3,504.1
Somalia	1,842.3	2,051.5	2,940.3
Sudan	2,989.5	2,705.4	2,191.4
Sweden	1,427.9	1,338.0	915.5
Tanzania	16,116.4	13,766.6	11,092.1
Uganda	19,466.3	21,189.1	24,186.1
United Kingdom	16,227.6	17,013.9	18,655.2
USA	3,053.4	2,761.2	2,803.8
Total (incl. others)	121,180.5	122,559.0	134,527.1

Transport

RAILWAYS
(traffic)

	2000	2001	2002*
Passenger-km (million)	302	216	288
Freight ton-km (million)	1,557	1,603	1,538

* Provisional figures.

ROAD TRAFFIC
(estimates, motor vehicles in use)

	2000	2001	2002*
Motor cars	244,836	255,379	269,925
Light vans	159,450	162,603	166,811
Lorries, trucks and heavy vans	57,796	58,501	59,835
Buses and mini-buses	38,930	42,629	46,606
Motorcycles and autocycles	44,894	46,004	47,451
Other motor vehicles	31,820	32,255	32,724

* Provisional figures.

SHIPPING

Merchant Fleet
(registered at 31 December)

	2000	2001	2002
Number of vessels	38	36	36
Total displacement ('000 grt)	20.6	19.1	19.1

Source: Lloyd's Register-Fairplay, *World Fleet Statistics*.

International Sea-borne Freight Traffic
(estimates, '000 metric tons)

	1999	2000	2001*
Goods loaded	1,845	1,722	1,998
Goods unloaded	6,200	7,209	8,299

* Provisional figures.

CIVIL AVIATION
(traffic on scheduled services)

	1997	1998	1999
Kilometres flown (million)	19	21	24
Passengers carried ('000)	836	1,138	1,358
Passenger-km (million)	1,824	2,091	2,513
Total ton-km (million)	216	243	292

Source: UN, *Statistical Yearbook*.

Tourism

FOREIGN TOURIST ARRIVALS
(number of visitors by country of origin)

	1998	1999	2000
Austria	17,411	19,441	20,789
France	41,764	46,633	49,866
Germany	136,658	152,589	163,168
India	20,844	23,274	24,889
Italy	48,592	52,024	55,631
Sweden	32,034	33,535	35,860
Switzerland	34,145	38,126	40,769
Tanzania	108,310	109,016	116,574
Uganda	60,974	68,083	72,803
United Kingdom	132,811	148,293	158,574
USA	61,944	63,604	68,014
Total (incl. others)	894,300	969,419	1,036,628

Source: World Tourism Organization, *Yearbook of Tourism Statistics*.

Tourism receipts (Ks. million): 17,500 in 1998; 21,400 in 1999.

Communications Media

	1999	2000	2001
Television receivers ('000 in use)	660	768	n.a.
Telephones ('000 main lines in use)	305	322	313
Mobile cellular telephones ('000 subscribers)	24	127	500
Personal computers ('000 in use)	125	150	175
Internet users ('000)	35	200	500

2002: Telephones ('000 main lines in use) 328; Mobile cellular telephones ('000 subscribers) 1,352.

Source: International Telecommunication Union.

Radio receivers ('000 in use, 1999): 6,383.

Facsimile machines (number in use, year ending 30 June 1995): 3,800.

Daily newspapers (2000): 4 titles (average circulation 310,000 copies).

Book production (titles, 1994): 300 first editions (excl. pamphlets).

Sources: UNESCO, *Statistical Yearbook*; UN, *Statistical Yearbook*.

Education
(1998/99, unless otherwise indicated)

	Institutions	Teachers	Pupils
Pre-primary	23,977	37,752	1,016,606
Primary	17,611	192,306	5,480,689
Secondary:			
general secondary	3,057	43,694	1,139,569
technical*	36	1,147	11,700
teacher training	26†	808‡	18,992§
Higher	n.a.‖	n.a.‖	61,526

* 1988 figures.
† 1995 figure.
‡ 1985 figure.
§ 1992 figure.
‖ In 1990 there were four universities, with 4,392 teachers.

Sources: Ministry of Education, Nairobi; UNESCO Institute for Statistics.

Adult literacy rate (UNESCO estimates): 88.3% (males 89.5%; females 77.3%) in 2001 (Source: UN Development Programme, *Human Development Report*).

Directory

The Constitution

The Constitution was introduced at independence on 12 December 1963. Subsequent amendments, including the adoption of republican status on 12 December 1964, were consolidated in 1969. A further amendment in December 1991 permitted the establishment of a multi-party system. In September 1997 the National Assembly approved legislation which amended the Constitution with a view to ensuring free and fair democratic elections. All political parties were granted equal access to the media, and detention without trial was prohibited. In addition, the opposition was to participate in selecting the 12 nominated members of the National Assembly and 10 of the 12 members of the supervisory Electoral Commission. An amendment to the Constitution, approved by the National Assembly in November 1999, reduced the level of presidential control over the legislative process. The Constitution can be amended by the affirmative vote on Second and Third Reading of 65% of the membership of the National Assembly (excluding the Speaker and Attorney-General).

The central legislative authority is the unicameral National Assembly, in which there are 210 directly elected Representatives, 12 nominated members and two *ex-officio* members, the Attorney-General and the Speaker. The maximum term of the National Assembly is five years from its first meeting (except in wartime). It can be dissolved by the President at any time, and the National Assembly may force its own dissolution by a vote of 'no confidence', whereupon presidential and Assembly elections have to be held within 90 days.

Executive power is vested in the President, Vice-President and Cabinet. Both the Vice-President and the Cabinet are appointed by the President, who must be a member of the Assembly and at least 35 years of age. Election of the President, for a five-year term, is by direct popular vote; the winning candidate at a presidential election must receive no less than 25% of the votes in at least five of Kenya's eight provinces. If a President dies, or a vacancy otherwise occurs during a President's period of office, the Vice-President becomes interim President for up to 90 days while a successor is elected.

The Government

HEAD OF STATE

President: MWAI KIBAKI (took office 30 December 2002).

CABINET
(April 2004)

Vice-President and Minister of Home Affairs: ARTHUR MOODY AWORI.

Minister of Finance: DAVID MWIRARIA.

Minister of Foreign Affairs: STEPHEN KALONZO MUSYOKA.

Minister of Roads, Public Works and Housing: RAILA AMOLO ODINGA.

Minister of Education, Science and Technology: Prof. GEORGE SAITOTI.

Minister of Labour and Human Resources Development: CHIRAU ALI MWAKWERE.

Minister of Transport and Communication: JOHN NJOROGE MICHUKI.

Minister of Energy: GEORGE OCHILO MBOGO AYACKO.

Minister of the Environment, Natural Resources and Wildlife: Dr NEWTON W. KULUNDU.

Minister of Agriculture: KIPRUTO RONO ARAP KIRWA.

Minister of Trade and Industry: Dr MUKHISA KITUYI.

Minister of Tourism and Information: RAPHAEL TUJU.

Minister of Health: CHARITY KALUKI NGILU.

Minister of Local Government: EMMANUEL KARISA MAITHA.

Minister of Lands and Settlement: AMOS M. KIMUNYA.

Minister of Planning and National Development: Prof. PETER ANYANG' NYONGO.

Minister of Justice and Constitutional Affairs: KIRAITU MURUNGI.

Minister of Water Resources Management and Development: MARTHA WANGARI KARUA.

Minister of Co-operative Development: PETER NJERU NDWIGA.

Minister of Gender, Sports, Culture and Social Services: NAJIB M. BALALA.

Ministry of Livestock and Fisheries Development: JOSEPH KONZOLO MUNYAO.

Minister of Regional Development: MUSIKARI KOMBO.

Minister of State for Provincial Administration and National Security in the Office of the President: CHRISTOPHER N. MURUNGARU.

Minister of State for Public Service in the Office of the President: (vacant).

Minister of State in the Vice-President's Office: LINAH JEBII KILIMO.

MINISTRIES

Office of the President: Harambee House, Harambee Ave, POB 30510, Nairobi; tel. (20) 227411; internet www.officeofthepresident.go.ke.

Office of the Vice-President and Ministry of Home Affairs: Jogoo House 'A', Taifa Rd, POB 30520, Nairobi; tel. (20) 228411.

Ministry of Agriculture: Kilimo House, Cathedral Rd, POB 30028, Nairobi; tel. (20) 718870; fax (20) 720586; internet www.agriculture.go.ke.

Ministry of Co-operative Development: Reinsurance Plaza, Taifa Rd, POB 30547, 00100 Nairobi; tel. (20) 339650; internet www.kenya.go.ke/cooperative.

Ministry of Education, Science and Technology: Jogoo House 'B', Harambee Ave, POB 30040, Nairobi; tel. (20) 334411; e-mail elimul@africaonline.co.ke; internet www.education.go.ke.

Ministry of Energy: Nyayo House, Kenyatta Ave, POB 30582, Nairobi; tel. (20) 333551; internet www.energy.go.ke.

Ministry of the Environment, Natural Resources and Wildlife: Maji House, Ngong Rd, POB 49720, Nairobi; tel. (20) 716103; e-mail mec@nbnet.co.ke; internet www.environment.go.ke.

Ministry of Finance: Treasury Bldg, Harambee Ave, POB 30007, Nairobi; tel. (20) 338111; fax (20) 330426; e-mail info@treasury.go.ke; internet www.treasury.go.ke.

Ministry of Foreign Affairs: Treasury Bldg, Harambee Ave, POB 30551, Nairobi; tel. (20) 334433; e-mail mfapress@nbnet.co.ke; internet www.mfa.go.ke.

Ministry of Gender, Sports, Culture and Social Services: Jogoo House 'A', Taifa Rd, POB 30520, Nairobi; tel. (20) 228411; internet www.kenya.go.ke/gender.

Ministry of Health: Medical HQ, Afya House, Cathedral Rd, POB 30016, Nairobi; tel. (20) 717077; fax (20) 725902; internet www.health.go.ke.

Ministry of Justice and Constitutional Affairs: State Law Office, Harambee Ave, POB 40112, Nairobi; tel. (20) 227461; internet www.kenya.go.ke/justice.

Ministry of Labour and Human Resources Development: Social Security House, Block 'C', Bishop Rd, POB 40326, Nairobi; tel. (20) 729800; fax (20) 726497; internet www.labour.go.ke.

Ministry of Lands and Settlement: Ardhi House, Ngong Rd, POB 30450, Nairobi; tel. (20) 718050; internet www.landsandsettlement.go.ke.

Ministry of Livestock and Fisheries Development: Kilimo House, Cathedral Rd, POB 30028, Nairobi; tel. (20) 718870; fax (20) 2711149.

Ministry of Local Government: Jogoo House 'A', Taifa Rd, POB 30004, Nairobi; tel. (20) 217475; e-mail mlog@form-net.com; internet www.localgovernment.go.ke.

Ministry of Planning and National Development: Treasury Bldg, Harambee Ave, POB 30007, Nairobi; tel. (20) 338111; internet www.planning.go.ke.

Ministry of Regional Development: Harambee Ave, POB 62345, Nairobi; tel. (20) 227411.

Ministry of Roads, Public Works and Housing: Ministry of Works Bldg, Ngong Rd, POB 30260, Nairobi; tel. (20) 723101; fax

(20) 720044; e-mail ps@roadsnet.go.ke; internet www.publicworks.go.ke.

Ministry of Tourism and Information: Utalii House, 5th Floor, off Uhuru Highway, POB 30027, Nairobi; tel. (20) 333555; fax (20) 318045; internet www.tourism.go.ke.

Ministry of Trade and Industry: Teleposta Towers, Kenyatta Ave, POB 30430, Nairobi; tel. (20) 331030; internet www.tradeandindustry.go.ke.

Ministry of Transport and Communication: Transcom House, Ngong Rd, POB 52692, Nairobi; tel. (20) 729200; fax (20) 726362; internet www.transport.go.ke.

Ministry of Water Resources Management and Development: Maji House, Ngong Rd, POB 49720, Nairobi; tel. (20) 716103; internet www.kenya.go.ke/water.

President and Legislature

PRESIDENT

Election, 27 December 2002

Candidates	Votes	%
Mwai Kibaki (NARC)	3,646,409	62.3
Uhuru Kenyatta (KANU)	1,828,914	31.2
Simeon Nyachae (Ford—People)	345,378	5.9
James Orengo (SDP)	24,537	0.4
David Ng'ethe (CCU)	10,038	0.2
Total	**5,855,276**	**100.0**

NATIONAL ASSEMBLY

Speaker: FRANCIS XAVIER OLE KAPARO.

General Election, 27 December 2002

Party	Seats
NARC	125
KANU	64
FORD—People	14
FORD—Asili	2
Safina	2
SKS	2
SPK	1
Total	**210***

*In addition to the 210 directly elected seats, 12 are held by nominees (NARC 7; KANU 4; FORD—People 1). The Attorney-General and the Speaker are, *ex officio*, members of the National Assembly.

Political Organizations

Chama Cha Uma (CCU): Nairobi; DAVID NG'ETHE.

Democratic Party of Kenya (DP): Continental House, POB 56396, Nairobi; ; tel. (20) 340044; f. 1991; Chair. MWAI KIBAKI; Sec. JOSEPH MUNYAO; rival faction led by NGENGI MUIGAI.

Forum for the Restoration of Democracy—Asili (FORD—Asili): Anyany Estate, POB 72595, Nairobi; f. 1992; Chair. GEORGE NTHENGE; Sec. MARTIN J. SHIKUKU.

Forum for the Restoration of Democracy—Kenya (FORD—Kenya): Odinga House, POB 57449, Nairobi; tel. (20) 570361; f. 1992; predominantly Luo support; Chair. MICHAEL CHRISTOPHER KIJANA WAMALWA; Sec. GITOBU IMANYARA.

Forum for the Restoration of Democracy for the People (FORD—People): Nairobi; f. 1997 by fmr mems of FORD—Asili; Chair. KIMANI WA NYOIKE; Sec.-Gen. (vacant).

Kenya African National Union (KANU): KICC POB 72394, Nairobi; tel. (20) 332383; f. 1960; sole legal party 1982–91; absorbed the National Development Party (f. 1994) in 2002; Pres. UHURU KENYATTA (acting); Sec.-Gen. JULIUS SUNKULI.

Kenya National Congress (KNC): POB 9474, Nairobi; f. 1992; Chair. Prof. KATANA MKANGI; Sec.-Gen. ONESMUS MUSYOKA MBALI.

Kenya National Democratic Alliance (KENDA): Wetithe House, Nkrumah St, POB 1851, Thika; tel. (151) 562304; f. 1991; Chair. JORAM GAINYE KARIUKI; Sec. PATRICK OUMA KANG'ETHE.

Kenya Social Congress (KSC): POB 55318, Nairobi; f. 1992; Chair. GEORGE MOSETI ANYONA; Sec.-Gen. KASHINI MALOBA FAFNA.

Labour Party Democracy: POB 7905, Nairobi; Chair. GEOFFREY MBURU; Sec. DAVID MBURI NGACHURA.

Liberal Party: Chair. WANGARI MAATHAI.

National Party of Kenya (NPK): f. 2001; Chair. CHARITY KALUKI NGILU; Sec.-Gen. FIDELIS MWEKE.

National Rainbow Coalition (NARC): Mwenge House, Ole Odume Rd, off Gitanga Rd and near Methodist Guest House, Nairobi; tel. (20) 571506; internet www.narc-kenya.org; f. 2002; electoral alliance of the LDP and the NAK; Chair. TITUS MBATHI; Sec. BURUDI NABWERA.

> **Liberal Democratic Party (LDP):** Nairobi; f. 2002 by fmr mems of KANU.

> **National Alliance Party of Kenya (NAPK):** Nairobi; f. 2002; alliance of some 12 parties, including the DP, FORD—Kenya and the NPK.

Party of Independent Candidates of Kenya (PICK): Plot No 299/096 Kenyatta Ave, POB 21821, Nairobi; Chair. G. N. MUSYIMI; Sec. F. NGUGI.

Patriotic Pastoralist Alliance of Kenya: f. 1997; represents the interests of northern Kenyan pastoralist communities; Leaders KHALIF ABDULLAHI, IBRAHIM WOCHE, JACKSON LAISAGOR.

People's Alliance for Change in Kenya (PACK): Nairobi; f. 1999; aims to unite diverse ethnic groups; Sec.-Gen. OLANG SANA.

People's Union of Justice and New Order: Kisumu; Islamic support; Leader WILSON OWILI.

Safina ('Noah's Ark'): POB 135, Nairobi; f. 1995; aims to combat corruption and human rights abuses and to introduce proportional representation; Chair. CLEMENT MUTURI KIGANO; Sec.-Gen. MWANDAWIRO MGHANGA.

Shirikisho Party of Kenya (SPK): POB 70421, Nairobi; Chair. HAMISI SAIDI JEFFAH; Sec. OMARA ABAE KALASINGHA.

Sisi Kwa Sisi (SKS): Nairobi; f. 2001; Leader JOHN RUKENYA KABUGUA.

Social Democratic Party of Kenya (SDP): POB 55845, Nairobi; tel. (20) 260309; f. 1992; Chair. JUSTUS NYAGAYA; Sec.-Gen. Dr APOLLO LUGANO NJONJO.

United Agri Party of Kenya: f. 2001; Chair. GEORGE KINYUA; Sec.-Gen. SIMON MITOBIO.

United Democratic Movement: Nairobi; Chair. KIPRUTO RONO ARAP KIRWA; Sec.-Gen. STEPHEN TARUS.

United Patriotic Party of Kenya: POB 115, Athi River; Chair. JOSEPHAT GATHUA GATHIGA; Sec. MICHAEL NJUGUNA KIGANYA.

The following organizations are banned:

February Eighteen Resistance Army: believed to operate from Uganda; Leader Brig. JOHN ODONGO (also known as STEPHEN AMOKE).

Islamic Party of Kenya (IPK): Mombasa; f. 1992; Islamic fundamentalist; Chair. Sheikh KHALIFA MUHAMMAD (acting); Sec.-Gen. ABDULRAHMAN WANDATI.

Diplomatic Representation

EMBASSIES AND HIGH COMMISSIONS IN KENYA

Algeria: 37 Muthaiga Rd, POB 53902, Nairobi; tel. (20) 310430; fax (20) 310450; e-mail algerianembassy@mitsuminett.com.

Argentina: Posta Sacco, 6th Floor, University Way, POB 30283, Nairobi; tel. (20) 335242; fax (20) 217693; e-mail argentina@form-net.com; Ambassador JOSÉ MARÍA CANTILO.

Australia: ICIPE House, River Side Drive, off Chiromo Rd, POB 39341, Nairobi; tel. (20) 445034; fax (20) 444718; High Commissioner PAUL COMFORT.

Austria: City House, 2nd Floor, Wabera St, POB 30560, Nairobi; tel. and fax (20) 331792; e-mail austria@africaonline.co.ke; Ambassador FRANZ HÖRLBERGER.

Bangladesh: Lenana Rd, POB 41645, Nairobi; tel. (20) 583354; fax (20) 562817; High Commissioner Dr M. AFSARUL QADER.

Belgium: Muthaiga, Limuru Rd, POB 30461, Nairobi; tel. (20) 741564; fax (20) 442701; e-mail belgianembke@form-net.com; Ambassador LEO WILLEMS.

Brazil: Jeevan Bharati Bldg, 4th Floor, Harambee Ave, POB 30754, Nairobi; tel. (20) 332649; fax (20) 336245; Ambassador MÁRIO AGUSTO SANTOS.

Burundi: Development House, 14th Floor, Moi Ave, POB 44439, Nairobi; tel. (20) 575113; fax (20) 219005; Ambassador GERMAIN NKESHIMANA.

Canada: Comcraft House, 6th Floor, Haile Selassie Ave, POB 30481, Nairobi; tel. (20) 214804; fax (20) 226987; High Commissioner GERRY CAMPBELL.

Chile: International House, 5th Floor, Mama Ngina St, POB 45554, Nairobi; tel. (20) 331320; fax (20) 215648; e-mail echileke@form-net.com; Ambassador Dr VICENTE SÁNCHEZ.

China, People's Republic: Nairobi; tel. (20) 722559; fax (20) 746402; Ambassador AN YONGYU.

Colombia: International House, 8th Floor, POB 48494, Nairobi; tel. (20) 246770; fax (20) 246771; e-mail embcol@form-net.com; Ambassador Dr GERMÁN GARCÍA-DURÁN.

Congo, Democratic Republic: Electricity House, Harambee Ave, POB 48106, Nairobi; tel. (20) 229771; fax (20) 334539; Ambassador (vacant).

Cyprus: Eagle House, 5th Floor, Kimathi St, POB 30739, 00100 Nairobi; tel. (20) 220881; fax (20) 331232; e-mail cyphc@nbnet.co.ke; High Commissioner CONSTANTINOS ELIADES.

Czech Republic: Embassy House, Harambee Ave, POB 48785, Nairobi; tel. (20) 210494; fax (20) 223447; e-mail zamini.cz@africaonline.co.ke; Ambassador VÁCLAV HUBINGER.

Denmark: HFCK Bldg, 11th Floor, Kenyatta Ave, POB 40412, Nairobi; tel. (20) 331088; fax (20) 331492; e-mail dkembnbo@africaonline.co.ke; Ambassador KLAUS DAHLGAARD.

Djibouti: Comcraft House, 2nd Floor, Haile Selassie Ave, POB 59528, Nairobi; tel. (20) 339640; Ambassador SALEH HAJI FARAH.

Egypt: Harambee Plaza, 7th Floor, Haile Selassie Ave, POB 30285, Nairobi; tel. (20) 570360; fax (20) 570383; Ambassador MOHAMMED ASIM IBRAHIM.

Eritrea: New Rehema House, 2nd Floor, Westlands, POB 38651, Nairobi; tel. (20) 443164; fax (20) 443165; e-mail eriembk@africaonline.co.ke; Ambassador MOHAMED ALI OMARO.

Ethiopia: State House Ave, POB 45198, Nairobi; tel. (20) 723027; fax (20) 723401; e-mail ethembnb@africaonline.co.ke; Ambassador TOSHOME TOGA.

Finland: International House, 2nd Floor, Mama Ngina St, POB 30379, Nairobi; tel. (20) 334777; fax (20) 335986; e-mail finland@form-net.com; Ambassador LAURI KANGAS.

France: Barclays Plaza, 9th Floor, Loita St, POB 41784, Nairobi; tel. (20) 339783; fax (20) 339421; e-mail ienkenya@form-net.com; Ambassador JACQUES DEPAIGNE.

Germany: Williamson House, 8th Floor, 4th Ngong Ave, POB 30180, Nairobi; tel. (20) 712527; fax (20) 714886; e-mail ger-emb@form-net.com; Ambassador JÜRGEN WEERTH.

Greece: Nation Centre, 13th Floor, Kimathi St, POB 30543, Nairobi; tel. (20) 228465; fax (20) 216044; Ambassador (vacant).

Holy See: Apostolic Nunciature, Manyani Rd West, Waiyaki Way, POB 14326, 00800 Nairobi; tel. (20) 4442975; fax (20) 4446789; e-mail nunciokenya@kenyaweb.com; Apostolic Nuncio Most Rev. GIOVANNI TONUCCI (Titular Archbishop of Torcello).

Hungary: Ole Odume Rd, POB 61146, Nairobi; tel. (20) 560060; fax (20) 560114; e-mail huembnai@africaonline.co.ke; Ambassador ANDRÁS TÓTH.

India: Jeevan Bharati Bldg, 2nd Floor, Harambee Ave, POB 30074, Nairobi; tel. (20) 225104; fax (20) 334167; e-mail hcindia@form-net.com; High Commissioner T. P. SREENIVASAN.

Indonesia: Menengai House, Upper Hill, POB 48868, Nairobi; tel. (20) 714196; fax (20) 713475; e-mail indonbi@arcc.or.ke; Ambassador TUPUCK SUTRISNO.

Iran: Dennis Pritt Rd, POB 49170, Nairobi; tel. (20) 720343; fax (20) 339936; Ambassador HAMID MOAYYER.

Israel: Bishop's Rd, POB 30354, Nairobi; tel. (20) 722182; fax (20) 715966; Ambassador MENASHE ZIPORI.

Italy: International House, 9th Floor, Mama Ngina St, POB 30107, Nairobi; tel. (20) 337356; fax (20) 337056; e-mail afra@form-net.com; Ambassador Dr ALBERTO BALBONI.

Japan: ICEA Bldg, 15th Floor, Kenyatta Ave, POB 60202, Nairobi; tel. and fax (20) 332955; Ambassador MORIHISA AOKI.

Korea, Republic: Anniversary Towers, 15th Floor, University Way, POB 30455, Nairobi; tel. (20) 333581; fax (20) 217772; e-mail emb-ke@mofat.go.kr; Ambassador KWON JONG RAK.

Kuwait: Muthaiga Rd, POB 42353, Nairobi; tel. (20) 761614; fax (20) 762837; e-mail kuwaitembassy@form-net.com; Chargé d'affaires a.i. JABER SALEM HUSSAIN EBRAHEEM.

Lesotho: Nairobi; tel. (20) 224876; fax (20) 337493; High Commissioner (vacant).

Malawi: Waiyaki Way (between Mvuli and Church Rds), POB 30453, 00100 Nairobi; tel. (20) 440569; fax 440568; e-mail malawihi@clubinternetk.com; High Commissioner Pastor KENN D. B. BILIMA (acting).

Mexico: Kibagare Way, off Loresho Ridge, POB 14145, Nairobi; tel. (20) 582850; fax (20) 581500; e-mail mexico@embamexken.co.ke; Ambassador LEANDRO ARELLANO.

Morocco: Diamond Trust House, 3rd Floor, Moi Ave, POB 61093, Nairobi; tel. (20) 222361; fax (20) 222364; e-mail embassymorocco@form-net.com; Chargé d'affaires a.i. DRISS KASSIMI.

Mozambique: Bruce House, 3rd Floor, Standard St, POB 66923, Nairobi; tel. (20) 221979; fax (20) 222446; High Commissioner PAULO ELIAS CIGARRO.

Netherlands: Uchumi House, 6th Floor, Nkrumah Ave, POB 41537, Nairobi; tel. (20) 227111; fax (20) 339155; e-mail holland@form-net.com; Ambassador RUUD J. TREFFERS.

Nigeria: Lenana Rd, Hurlingham, POB 30516, Nairobi; tel. (20) 564116; fax (20) 564117; High Commissioner CLARKSON N. UMELO.

Norway: International House, 1st Floor, Mama Ngina St, POB 46363, Nairobi; tel. (20) 341415; fax (20) 216009; e-mail emb.nairobi@mfa.no; Chargé d'affaires a.i. OVE DANBOLDT.

Pakistan: St Michel Rd, Westlands Ave, POB 30045, Nairobi; tel. (20) 443911; fax (20) 446507; High Commissioner (vacant).

Poland: Kabarnet Rd, off Ngong Rd, Woodley, POB 30086, 00100 Nairobi; tel. (20) 566288; fax (20) 727701; e-mail polambnairobi@form-net.com; Ambassador WOJCIECH JASINSKI.

Portugal: Reinsurance Plaza, 10th Floor, Aga Khan Walk, POB 34020, Nairobi; tel. (20) 338990; fax (20) 214711; Ambassador JOSÉ LAMEIRAS.

Romania: POB 63240, Nairobi; tel. (20) 743209; fax (20) 741696; e-mail roembken@wananchi.com; Chargé d'affaires a.i. PAUL FINANTU.

Russia: Lenana Rd, POB 30049, Nairobi; tel. (20) 728700; fax (20) 721888; e-mail russemb@swiftkenya.com; Ambassador BORIS SEPTOV.

Rwanda: International House, 12th Floor, Mama Ngina St, POB 48579, Nairobi; tel. (20) 560178; fax (20) 561932.

Saudi Arabia: Muthaiga Rd, POB 58297, Nairobi; tel. (20) 762781; fax (20) 760939; Chargé d'affaires IBRAHIM AMMAR.

Serbia and Montenegro: State House Ave, Nairobi; tel. (20) 720670.

Slovakia: Milimani Rd, POB 30204, Nairobi; tel. (20) 721896; fax (20) 721898.

Somalia: POB 30769, Nairobi; tel. (20) 580165; fax (20) 581683.

South Africa: Lonhro House, 14th Floor, Standard St, POB 42441, Nairobi; tel. (20) 32063100; fax (20) 32063236; e-mail sahc@africaonline.co.ke; High Commissioner L. M. MAKHUBELA.

Spain: Bruce House, 5th Floor, Standard St, POB 45503, Nairobi; tel. (20) 335711; fax (20) 332858; Ambassador ANIBAL JULIO JIMÉNEZ ABASCAL.

Sri Lanka: Lenana Rd, POB 48145 GPO, Nairobi; tel. (20) 572627; fax (20) 572141; e-mail slhckeny@africaonline.co.ke; internet www.lk/dipmissionf.html; High Commissioner HABEEB MOHAMMED FAROOK.

Sudan: Minet-ICDC Bldg, 7th Floor, Mamlaka Rd, POB 48784, Nairobi; tel. (20) 720853; fax (20) 721015; Ambassador OMER EL-SHEIKH.

Swaziland: Transnational Plaza, 3rd Floor, Mama Ngina St, POB 41887, Nairobi; tel. (20) 339231; fax (20) 330540; High Commissioner Prince MBILINI DLAMINI.

Sweden: Lion Place, 3rd Floor, Waiyaki Way, Westlands, POB 30600, 00100 Nairobi; tel. (20) 4234000; fax (20) 4234070; e-mail ambassaden.nairobi@sida.se; Ambassador Bo GÖRANSSON.

Switzerland: International House, 7th Floor, Mama Ngina St, POB 30752, Nairobi; tel. (20) 228735; fax (20) 217388; e-mail vertretung@nai.rep.admin.ch; Ambassador Dr ARMIN KAMER.

Tanzania: Continental House, Uhuru Highway, POB 47790, Nairobi; tel. (20) 721742; fax (20) 218269; High Commissioner MIRISHO SAM HAGGAI SARAKIKYA.

Thailand: Ambassador House, Rose Ave, POB 58349, Nairobi; tel. (20) 715800; fax (20) 715801; e-mail thainbi@form-net.com; Ambassador PONGSAK DISYATAT.

Turkey: Gigiri Rd, off Limuru Rd, POB 64748, Nairobi; tel. (20) 522562; fax (20) 522778; e-mail tcbenair@wananchi.com; Ambassador VAROL ÖZKOÇAK.

Uganda: Uganda House, 5th Floor, Kenyatta Ave, POB 60853, Nairobi; tel. (20) 330801; fax (20) 330970; High Commissioner J. TOMUSANGE.

United Kingdom: Upper Hill Rd, POB 30465, Nairobi; tel. (20) 714699; fax (20) 719486; e-mail bhcinfo@iconnect.co.ke; internet www.britain.or.ke; High Commissioner Sir JEFFREY JAMES.

USA: Mombasa Rd, POB 30137, Nairobi; tel. (20) 537800; fax (20) 537810; e-mail irc@pd.state.gov; internet us.state.gov/nairobi; Ambassador JOHNNIE CARSON.

Venezuela: Ngong/Kabarnet Rd, POB 34477, Nairobi; tel. (20) 574646; fax (20) 337487; e-mail embavene@africaonline.co.ke; Chargé d'affaires a.i. NOEL D. QUINTERO.

Yemen: cnr Ngong and Kabarnet Rds, POB 44642, Nairobi; tel. (20) 564379; fax (20) 564394; Ambassador AHMAD MAYSARI.

Zambia: Nyerere Rd, POB 48741, Nairobi; tel. (20) 724850; fax (20) 718494; High Commissioner ENESS CHISHALA CHIYENGE.

Zimbabwe: Minet-ICDC Bldg, 6th Floor, Mamlaka Rd, POB 30806, Nairobi; tel. (20) 721071; fax (20) 726503; Ambassador LUCAS PANDE TAVAYA.

Judicial System

The Kenya Court of Appeal
POB 30187, Nairobi.

The final court of appeal for Kenya in civil and criminal process; sits at Nairobi, Mombasa, Kisumu, Nakuru and Nyeri.

Chief Justice: EVANS GICHERU.

Justices of Appeal: MATHEW MULI, J. M. GACHUHI, J. R. O. MASIME, SAMUEL BOSIRE, R. O. KWACH, EFFIE OWUOR.

The High Court of Kenya: Harambee Ave, POB 30041, Nairobi; tel. (20) 221221; e-mail hck-lib@nbnet.co.ke; has unlimited criminal and civil jurisdiction at first instance, and sits as a court of appeal from subordinate courts in both criminal and civil cases. The High Court is also a court of admiralty. There are two resident puisne judges at Mombasa and at Nakuru, and one resident puisne judge at Eldoret, Kakamega, Kisumu, Nyeri, Kisii and Meru.

Resident Magistrates' Courts: have country-wide jurisdiction, with powers of punishment by imprisonment up to five years or by fine up to K£500. If presided over by a chief magistrate or senior resident magistrate the court is empowered to pass any sentence authorized by law. For certain offences, a resident magistrate may pass minimum sentences authorized by law.

District Magistrates' Courts: of first, second and third class; have jurisdiction within districts and powers of punishment by imprisonment for up to five years, or by fines of up to K£500.

Kadhi's Courts: have jurisdiction within districts, to determine questions of Islamic law.

Religion

Most of the population hold traditional African beliefs, although there are significant numbers of African Christians. The Arab inhabitants are Muslims, and the Indian population is partly Muslim and partly Hindu. The Europeans and Goans are predominantly Christian. Muslims are found mainly along the coastline; however, the Islamic faith has also established itself among Africans around Nairobi and among some ethnic groups in the northern districts. East Africa is also an important centre for the Bahá'í faith.

CHRISTIANITY

National Council of Churches of Kenya: Church House, Moi Ave, POB 45009, Nairobi; tel. (20) 242278; fax (20) 224463; f. 1943 as Christian Council of Kenya; 35 full mems and eight assoc. mems; Chair. Rev. JOSEPH WAITHONGA; Sec.-Gen. Rev. MUTAVA MUSYIMI.

The Anglican Communion

Anglicans are adherents of the Church of the Province of Kenya, which was established in 1970. It comprises 28 dioceses, and has about 2.5m. members.

Archbishop of Kenya and Bishop of Nairobi: Most Rev. Dr DAVID M. GITARI, POB 40502, Nairobi; tel. (20) 2714755; fax (20) 2718442; e-mail davidgitari@insightkenya.com.

Greek Orthodox Church

Archbishop of East Africa: NICADEMUS OF IRINOUPOULIS, Nairobi; jurisdiction covers Kenya, Tanzania and Uganda.

The Roman Catholic Church
Kenya comprises four archdioceses, 19 dioceses and one Apostolic Vicariate. At 31 December 2002 an estimated 24.5% of the total population were adherents of the Roman Catholic Church.

Kenya Episcopal Conference
Kenya Catholic Secretariat, POB 13475, Nairobi; tel. (20) 443133; fax (20) 442910; e-mail csk@users.africaonline.co.ke.
f. 1976; Pres. Rt Rev. JOHN NJUE (Bishop of Embu).

Archbishop of Kisumu: Most Rev. ZACCHAEUS OKOTH, POB 1728, Kisumu; tel. (35) 41765; fax (35) 62247; e-mail archdiocese-ksm@net2000ke.com.

Archbishop of Mombasa: Most Rev. JOHN NJENGA, Catholic Secretariat, Nyerere Ave, POB 83131, Mombasa; tel. (11) 471320; fax (11) 473166; e-mail msadio@africaonline.co.ke.

Archbishop of Nairobi: Most Rev. RAPHAEL NDINGI MWANA'A NZEKI, Archbishop's House, POB 14231, 00800 Nairobi; tel. (20) 4441919; fax 4447027; e-mail arch-nbo@wananchi.com.

Archbishop of Nyeri: Most Rev. NICODEMUS KIRIMA, POB 288, Nyeri; tel. (17) 30446; fax (17) 30435.

Other Christian Churches
Africa Inland Church in Kenya: Bishop Rev. Dr TITUS M. KIVUNZI.

African Christian Church and Schools: POB 1365, Thika; tel. (15) 47; f. 1948; Moderator Rt Rev. JOHN NJUNGUNA; Gen. Sec. Rev. SAMUEL MWANGI; 50,000 mems.

African Church of the Holy Spirit: POB 183, Kakamega; f. 1927; 20,000 mems.

African Israel Nineveh Church: Nineveh HQ, POB 701, Kisumu; f. 1942; High Priest Rt Rev. JOHN KIVULI, II; Gen. Sec. Rev. JOHN ARAP TONUI; 350,000 mems.

Baptist Convention of Kenya: POB 14907, Nairobi; Pres. Rev. ELIUD MUNGAI.

Church of God in East Africa: Pres. Rev. Dr BYRUM MAKOKHA.

Evangelical Fellowship of Kenya: Co-ordinator Rt Rev. ARTHUR GITONGA; Sec.-Gen. Dr WASHINGTON NG'ENG'I.

Evangelical Lutheran Church in Kenya: POB 874, Kisii; tel. (40) 31231; fax (40) 30475; e-mail elok@africaonline.co.ke; Bishop Rev. FRANCIS NYAMWARO ONDERI; 65,000 mems.

Methodist Church in Kenya: POB 47633, Nairobi; tel. (20) 724841; f. 1862; autonomous since 1967; Presiding Bishop Rev. Dr ZABLON NTHAMBURI; 854,000 mems (2000).

Presbyterian Church of East Africa: POB 48268, Nairobi; tel. (20) 504417; fax (20) 504442; e-mail pcea@africaonline.co.ke; Moderator Rt Rev. Dr JESSE KAMAU; Sec.-Gen. Rev. Dr PATRICK RUKENYA.

Other denominations active in Kenya include the Africa Gospel Church, the African Brotherhood Church, the African Independent Pentecostal Church, the African Interior Church, the Episcopal Church of Kenya, the Free Pentecostal Fellowship of Kenya, the Full Gospel Churches of Kenya, the Lutheran Church in Kenya, the National Independent Church of Africa, the Pentecostal Assemblies of God, the Pentecostal Evangelistic Fellowship of God and the Reformed Church of East Africa.

BAHÁ'Í FAITH

National Spiritual Assembly: POB 47562, Nairobi; tel. (20) 725447; mems resident in 9,654 localities.

ISLAM

Supreme Council of Kenyan Muslims (SUPKEM)
POB 45163, Nairobi; tel. and fax (20) 243109.

Nat. Chair. Prof. ABD AL-GHAFUR AL-BUSAIDY; Sec.-Gen. MOHAMMED KHALIF.

Chief Kadhi: NASSOR NAHDI.

The Press

PRINCIPAL DAILIES

Daily Nation: POB 49010, Nairobi; tel. and fax (20) 337710; e-mail nation@insightkenya.com; internet www.nationaudio.com; f. 1960; English; owned by Nation Media Group; Editor-in-Chief WANGETHI MWANGI; Man. Editor JOSEPH ODINDO; circ. 170,000.

East African Standard: POB 30080, Nairobi; tel. (20) 540280; fax (20) 553939; e-mail online@eastandard.net; internet www

.eastandard.net; f. 1902; Group Man. Editor WARURU WACHIRO; circ. 60,000.

Kenya Leo: POB 30958, Nairobi; tel. (20) 332390; f. 1983; Kiswahili; KANU party newspaper; Group Editor-in-Chief AMBOKA ANDERE; circ. 6,000.

Kenya Times: POB 30958, Nairobi; tel. (20) 24251; f. 1983; English; KANU party newspaper; Group Editor-in-Chief AMBOKA ANDERE; circ. 10,000.

The People: POB 10296, 00100 Nairobi; tel. (20) 249686; fax (20) 253344; e-mail info@people.co.ke; f. 1993; Editor-in-Chief BEDAU MOUGUA; circ. 40,000.

Taifa Leo: POB 49010, Nairobi; tel. (20) 337691; Kiswahili; f. 1960; daily and weekly edns; owned by Nation Media Group; Editor ROBERT MWANGI; circ. 57,000.

Kenya has a thriving vernacular press, but titles are often short-lived. Newspapers in African languages include:

Kihooto (The Truth): Kikuyu; satirical.

Mwaria Ma (Honest Speaker): Nyeri; f. 1997; Publr Canon JAMLICK M. MIANO.

Mwihoko (Hope): POB 734, Muranga; f. 1997; Roman Catholic.

Nam Dar: Luo.

Otit Mach (Firefly): Luo.

SELECTED PERIODICALS

Weeklies and Fortnightlies

The Business Chronicle: POB 53328, Nairobi; tel. (20) 544283; fax (20) 532736; f. 1994; weekly; Man. Editor MUSYOKA KYENDO.

Coastweek: Oriental Bldg, 2nd Floor, Nkrumah Rd, POB 87270, Mombasa; tel. (11) 313767; fax (11) 225003; e-mail coastwk@africaonline.co.ke; internet www.coastweek.com; f. 1978; English; weekly; Editor ADRIAN GRIMWOOD; circ. 40,000.

The East African: POB 49010 Nairobi; tel. (20) 337710; fax (20) 213946; e-mail nation@insightkenya.com; internet www.nationaudio.com/news/eastafrican/current; f. 1994; weekly; English; owned by Nation Media Group; Editor-in-Chief WANGETHI MWANGI; Man. Editor MBATAU WA NGAI.

The Herald: POB 30958, Nairobi; tel. (20) 332390; English; sponsored by KANU; Editor JOB MUTUNGI; circ. 8,000.

Kenrail: POB 30121, Nairobi; tel. (20) 221211; fax (20) 340049; English and Kiswahili; publ. by Kenya Railways Corpn; Editor J. N. LUSENO; circ. 20,000.

Kenya Gazette: POB 30746, Nairobi; tel. (20) 334075; f. 1898; official notices; weekly; circ. 8,000.

Post on Sunday: Nairobi; weekly; independent; Editor-in-Chief TONY GACHOKA.

The Standard on Sunday: POB 30080, Nairobi; tel. (20) 540280; fax (20) 553939; English; Man. Editor FRED MUTISO; circ. 90,000.

Sunday Nation: POB 49010, Nairobi; f. 1960; English; owned by Nation Media Group; Man. Editor BERNARD NDERITU; circ. 170,000.

Sunday Times: POB 30958, Nairobi; tel. (20) 337798; Group Editor AMBOKA ANDERE.

Taifa Jumapili: POB 49010, Nairobi; f. 1987; Kiswahili; owned by Nation Media Group; Editor ROBERT K. MWANGI; circ. 56,000.

Taifa Weekly: POB 49010, Nairobi; tel. (20) 337691; f. 1960; Kiswahili; Editor ROBERT K. MWANGI; circ. 68,000.

Trans Nzoia Post: POB 34, Kitale; weekly.

The Weekly Review: POB 42271, Nairobi; tel. (20) 251473; fax (20) 222555; f. 1975; English; Man. Dir JAINDI KISERO; circ. 16,000.

What's On: Rehema House, Nairobi; tel. (20) 27651; Editor NANCY KAIRO; circ. 10,000.

Monthlies

Africa Law Review: Tumaini House, 4th Floor, Nkrumah Ave, POB 53234, Nairobi; tel. (20) 330480; fax (20) 230173; e-mail alr@africalaw.org; f. 1987; English; Editor-in-Chief GITOBU IMANYARA.

East African Medical Journal: POB 41632, 00100 Nairobi; tel. (20) 712010; fax (20) 724617; e-mail eamj@wananchi.com; English; f. 1923; Editor-in-Chief Prof. WILLIAM LORE; circ. 4,500.

East African Report on Trade and Industry: POB 30339, Nairobi; journal of Kenya Asscn of Mfrs; Editor GORDON BOY; circ. 3,000.

Executive: POB 47186, Nairobi; tel. (20) 530598; fax (20) 557815; e-mail spacesellers@wanachi.com; f. 1980; business; Publr SYLVIA KING; circ. 25,000.

Kenya Export News: POB 30339, Nairobi; tel. (20) 340010; fax (20) 218845; English; publ. for Kenya External Trade Authority, Ministry of Trade and Industry; Editor Prof. SAMUEL NJOROGE; circ. 5,000.

Kenya Farmer (Journal of the Agricultural Society of Kenya): c/o English Press, POB 30127, Nairobi; tel. (20) 20377; f. 1954; English and Kiswahili; Editor ROBERT IRUNGU; circ. 20,000.

Kenya Yetu: POB 8053, Nairobi; tel. (20) 250083; fax (20) 340659; f. 1965; Kiswahili; publ. by Ministry of Tourism and Information; Editor M. NDAVI; circ. 10,000.

Nairobi Handbook: POB 30127, Accra Rd, Nairobi; Editor R. OUMA; circ. 20,000.

News from Kenya: POB 8053, Nairobi; tel. (20) 253083; fax (20) 340659; publ. by Ministry of Tourism and Information.

PC World (East Africa): Gilgil House, Monrovia St, Nairobi; tel. (20) 246808; fax (20) 215643; f. 1996; Editor ANDREW KARANJA.

Presence: POB 10988, Nairobi; tel. (20) 568043; fax (20) 560420; e-mail emme-ken@africaonline.co.ke; f. 1984; economics, law, women's issues, fiction.

Sparkle: POB 47186, Nairobi; tel. (20) 530598; fax (20) 557815; e-mail spacesellers@wanachi.com; f. 1990; children's; Editor ANNA NDILA NDUTO.

Today in Africa: POB 60, Kijabe; tel. (25) 64210; English; Man. Editor MWAURA NJOROGE; circ. 13,000.

Other Periodicals

African Ecclesiastical Review: POB 4002, Eldoret; tel. (32) 61218; fax (32) 62570; e-mail gabapubs@net2000ke.com; f. 1969; scripture, religion and development; 6 a year; Editor AGATHA RADOLI; circ. 2,500.

Afya: POB 30125, Nairobi; tel. (20) 501301; fax (20) 506112; e-mail amrefkco@africaonline.co.ke; journal for medical and health workers; quarterly.

Busara: Nairobi; literary; 2 a year; Editor KIMANI GECAU; circ. 3,000.

East African Agricultural and Forestry Journal: POB 30148, Nairobi; f. 1935; English; quarterly; Editor J. O. MUGAH; circ. 1,000.

Eastern African Economic Review: POB 30022, Nairobi; f. 1954; 2 a year; Editor J. K. MAITHA.

Economic Review of Agriculture: POB 30028, Nairobi; tel. (20) 728370; f. 1968; publ. by Ministry of Agriculture; quarterly; Editor OKIYA OKOITI.

Education in Eastern Africa: Nairobi; f. 1970; 2 a year; Editor JOHN C. B. BIGALA; circ. 2,000.

Finance: Nairobi; monthly; Editor-in-Chief NJEHU GATABAKI.

Inside Kenya Today: POB 8053, Nairobi; tel. (20) 340010; fax (20) 340659; English; publ. by Ministry of Tourism; quarterly; Editor M. NDAVI; circ. 10,000.

Kenya Education Journal: Nairobi; f. 1958; English; 3 a year; Editor W. G. BOWMAN; circ. 5,500.

Kenya Statistical Digest: POB 30007, Nairobi; tel. (20) 338111; fax (20) 330426; publ. by Ministry of Finance; quarterly.

Target: POB 72839, Nairobi; f. 1964; English; 6 a year; religious; Editor FRANCIS MWANIKI; circ. 17,000.

NEWS AGENCIES

Kenya News Agency (KNA): Information House, POB 8053, Nairobi; tel. (20) 223201; f. 1963; Dir S. MUSANDU.

Foreign Bureaux

Agence France-Presse (AFP): International Life House, Mama Ngina St, POB 30671, 00100 Nairobi; tel. (20) 230613; fax (20) 230649; e-mail afpnai@swiftkenya.com; Bureau Chief GERARD VANDENBERGHE.

Agenzia Nazionale Stampa Associata (ANSA) (Italy): 12 Kyuna Rd, Spring Valley, Morningside, POB 20444, 00220 Nairobi; tel. (20) 583565; fax (20) 229383; e-mail ansake@africaonline.co.ke; Rep. Dr LUCIANO CAUSA.

Associated Press (AP) (USA): Chester House, Koinange St, POB 47590, Nairobi; tel. (20) 250168; fax (20) 221449; e-mail naiburo@ap.org; Bureau Chief SUSAN LINNÉE.

Deutsche Presse-Agentur (dpa) (Germany): Chester House, 1st Floor, Koinange St, POB 48546, 00100 Nairobi; tel. (20) 633379; fax (20) 330274; e-mail dpa@swiftkenya.com; Bureau Chief Dr ULRIKE KOLTERMANN.

Informatsionnoye Telegrafnoye Agentstvo Rossii—Telegrafnoye Agentstvo Suverennykh Stran (ITAR—TASS) (Russia): Likoni Lane, POB 49602, Nairobi; tel. and fax (20) 721978;

e-mail itartass@swiftkenya.com; Correspondent ANDREI K. POLY-AKOV.

Inter Press Service (IPS) (Italy): POB 54386, Nairobi; tel. (20) 335418; Correspondent HORACE AWORI.

Kyodo Tsushin (Japan): Koinange St, POB 58281, Nairobi; tel. (20) 243250; fax (20) 230448; e-mail kyodonew@africaonline.co.ke; Bureau Chief OHNO KEIICHIRO.

Newslink Africa (UK): POB 3325, Nairobi; tel. (20) 241339; Correspondent PAMPHIL KWEYUH.

Reuters (UK): Finance House, 12th Floor, Loita St, POB 34043, Nairobi; tel. (20) 330261; fax (20) 338860; e-mail nairobi.newsroom@reuters.com; Bureau Chief DAVID FOX.

United Press International (UPI) (USA): POB 76282, Nairobi; tel. (20) 337349; fax (20) 213625; Correspondent JOE KHAMISI.

Xinhua (New China) News Agency (People's Republic of China): Ngong Rd at Rose Ave, POB 30728, Nairobi; tel. and fax (20) 711685; Pres. and Editor-in-Chief Prof. FLAMINGO Q. M. CHEN.

Publishers

Academy Science Publishers: POB 24916, Nairobi; tel. (20) 884401; fax (20) 884406; e-mail asp@africaonline.co.ke; f. 1989; part of the African Academy of Sciences; Editor-in-Chief Prof. KETO E. MSHIGENI.

Amecea Gaba Publications: Amecea Pastoral Institute, POB 4002, Eldoret; tel. (32) 61218; fax (32) 62570; e-mail gabapubs@net2000ke.com; f. 1989; anthropology, religious; Dir Sister AGATHA RADOLI.

Camerapix Publishers International: POB 45048, Nairobi; tel. (20) 4448923; fax (20) 4448926; e-mail info@camerapix.com; internet www.camerapix.com; f. 1960; travel, topography, natural history; Man. Dir RUKHSANA HAQ.

East African Educational Publishers: cnr Mpaka Rd and Woodvale Grove, Westlands, POB 45314, Nairobi; tel. (20) 222057; fax (20) 448753; e-mail eaep@africaonline.co.ke; internet www.eastafricanpublishers.com; f. 1965 as Heinemann Kenya Ltd, present name adopted 1992; academic, educational, creative writing; some books in Kenyan languages; Man. Dir and Chief Exec. HENRY CHAKAVA.

Evangel Publishing House: Lumumba Drive, Roysambu, off Thika Rd, POB 28963, 00200 Nairobi; tel. (20) 802033; fax (20) 802034; e-mail evanglit@maf.or.ke; f. 1954; religious; Man. BARINE A. KIRIMI.

Foundation Books: Nairobi; tel. (20) 765485; f. 1974; biography, poetry; Man. Dir F. O. OKWANYA.

Kenway Publications Ltd: POB 45314, Nairobi; tel. (20) 444700; fax (20) 448753; e-mail eaep@africaonline.co.ke; f. 1981; general, regional interests; Chair. HENRY CHAKAVA.

Kenya Literature Bureau: Bellevue Area, off Mombasa Rd, POB 30022, 00100 Nairobi; tel. (20) 605598; fax (20) 601474; e-mail klb@onlinekenya.com; f. 1977; parastatal body under Ministry of Education, Science and Technolgy; literary, educational, cultural and scientific books and journals; Man. Dir M. A. KARAURI.

Jomo Kenyatta Foundation: Industrial Area, Enterprise Rd, POB 30533, Nairobi; tel. (20) 557222; fax (20) 531966; e-mail publish@jomokenyattaf.com; f. 1966; primary, secondary, university textbooks; Man. Dir F. Z. K. MENJO.

Longman Kenya Ltd: Banda School, Magadi Rd, POB 24722, Nairobi; tel. (20) 891458; fax (20) 891307; f. 1966; textbooks and educational materials; Gen. Man. JANET NJOROGE.

Macmillan Kenya Publishers Ltd: Kijabe St, POB 30797, Nairobi; tel. (20) 220012; fax (20) 212179; e-mail dmuita@macken.co.ke; f. 1970; atlases, children's educational, guide books, literature; Man. Dir DAVID MUITA.

Newspread International: POB 46854, Nairobi; tel. (20) 331402; fax (20) 607252; f. 1971; reference, economic development; Exec. Editor KUL BHUSHAN.

Oxford University Press (Eastern Africa): Waiyaki Way, ABC Place, POB 72532, Nairobi; tel. (20) 440555; fax (20) 443972; f. 1954; children's, educational and general; Regional Man. ABDULLAH ISMAILY.

Paulines Publications-Africa: POB 49026, Nairobi; tel. (20) 447202; fax (20) 442097; e-mail paulines@iconnect.co.ke; f. 1985; children's, educational; religious; Pres. Sister MARIA PEZZINI; Dir Sister TERESA MARCAZZAN.

Transafrica Press: Kenwood House, Kimathi St, POB 48239, Nairobi; tel. (20) 331762; f. 1976; general, educational and children's; Man. Dir JOHN NOTTINGHAM.

Government Publishing House

Government Printing Press: POB 30128, Nairobi; tel. (20) 334075.

PUBLISHERS' ORGANIZATION

Kenya Publishers' Association: POB 42767, 00100 Nairobi; tel. (20) 3752344; fax (20) 3754076; e-mail kenyapublishers@wananchi.com; internet www.kenyabooks.org; f. 1971; organizes Nairobi International Book Fair each September; Chair. JANET NJOROGE.

Broadcasting and Communications

TELECOMMUNICATIONS

KenCell Communications Ltd: Parkside Towers, City Sq., Mombasa Rd, POB 73146, 00200 Nairobi; e-mail info@kencell.co.ke; internet www.kencell.co.ke; f. 2000; operates a national mobile cellular telephone network; Man. Dir and CEO PHILLIPE VANDEBROUCK.

Telkom Kenya Ltd: Telposta Towers, Kenyatta Ave, POB 30301, Nairobi; tel. (20) 227401; fax (20) 251071; e-mail mdtelkom@kenyaeafix.net; f. 1999; operates a national fixed telephone network; privatization pending; Man. Dir AUGUSTINE CHESEREM.

Safaricom Ltd: Safaricom House, Waiyaki Way, Westlands, POB 46350, Nairobi; e-mail info@safaricom.co.ke; internet www.safaricom.co.ke; f. 1999; owned by Telkom Kenya Ltd and Vodafone Airtouch (UK); operates a national mobile telephone network; Gen. Man. and CEO MICHAEL JOSEPH.

Regulatory Authority

Communications Commission of Kenya (CCK): Kijabe St, Longonot Place, POB 14448, Nairobi; tel. (20) 240165; fax (20) 252547; e-mail info@cck.go.ke; internet www.cck.go.ke; f. 1999; Dir-Gen. and Chief Exec. SAMUEL K. CHEPKONG'A.

BROADCASTING

Radio

Kenya Broadcasting Corpn (KBC): Broadcasting House, Harry Thuku Rd, POB 30456, Nairobi; tel. (20) 334567; fax (20) 220675; e-mail kbc@swiftkenya.com; internet www.kbc.co.ke; f. 1989; state corpn responsible for radio and television services; Chair. Dr JULIUS KIANO; Man. Dir JOE M. KHAMISI.

   Radio: National service (Kiswahili); General service (English); Vernacular services (Borana, Burji, Hindustani, Kalenjin, Kikamba, Kikuyu, Kimasai, Kimeru, Kisii, Kuria, Luo, Luhya, Rendile, Somali, Suba, Teso and Turkana).

Capital FM: Lonrho House, Standard St, POB 74933, Nairobi; tel. (20) 210020; fax (20) 332349; e-mail info@capitalfm.co.ke; internet www.capitalfm.co.ke; f. 1999; commercial station broadcasting to Nairobi and environs; Man. Dir LYNDA HOLT.

Citizen Radio: Ambank House, University Way, POB 45897, Nairobi; tel. (20) 249122; fax (20) 249126; commercial radio station broadcasting in Nairobi and its environs; Man. Dir S. K. MACHARIA.

IQRA Broadcasting Network: Bandari Plaza, 7th Floor, Woodvale Grove, Westlands, POB 45163 GPO, Nairobi; tel. (20) 4447624; fax (20) 4443978; e-mail iqrafm@swiftkenya.com; Islamic radio station broadcasting religious programmes in Nairobi; Man. Dir SHARIF HUSSEIN OMAR.

Kameme FM: Longonot Pl., Kijabe St, POB 49640, Nairobi; tel. (20) 217963; fax (20) 33129; e-mail rreach@form-net.com; commercial radio station broadcasting in Kikuyu in Nairobi and its environs; Man. Dir ROSE KIMOTHO.

Kitambo Communications Ltd: NSSF Bldg, POB 56155, Nairobi; tel. (20) 331770; fax (20) 212847; commercial radio and television station broadcasting Christian programmes in Mombasa and Nairobi; Man. Dir Dr R. AYAH.

Nation FM: Nation Centre, POB 49010, Nairobi; tel. (20) 337710; fax (20) 217112; internet www.nationalaudio.com; commercial radio station broadcasting in Nairobi and its environs; owned by Nation Media Group; Man. Dir CYRILLE NABUTOLA.

Radio Africa Ltd (KISS FM): Safina Towers, 16th Floor, University of Nairobi, POB 45897, Nairobi; tel. (20) 245368; fax (20) 245565; Man. Dir KIPRONO KITTONY.

Sauti ya Raheme RTV Network: Eldoret; POB 4139, Eldoret; Christian, broadcasts in Eldoret and its environs; Man. Dir Rev. ELI ROP.

Television

Kenya Broadcasting Corpn (KBC): see Radio.

Television: KBC–TV, financed by licence fees and commercial advertisements; services in Kiswahili and English; operates on five channels for *c.* 50 hours per week. KBC–II: private subscription service.

Citizen TV: POB 45897, Nairobi; tel. (20) 249122; fax (20) 249126; commercial station broadcasting in Nairobi and its environs.

Family TV: NSSF Bldg, POB 56155, Nairobi; tel. (20) 331770; fax (20) 212847.

Kenya Television Network (KTN–TV): Nyayo House, 22nd Floor, POB 56985, Nairobi; tel. (20) 227122; fax (20) 214467; e-mail ktn@form-net.com; f. 1990; commercial station operating in Nairobi and Mombasa; Man. Dir D. J. DAVIES.

Nation TV: POB 49010, Nairobi; e-mail nation@users.co.ke; f. 1999; commercial station; owned by Nation Media Group; Man. Dir CYRILLE NABUTOLA.

Stellagraphics TV (STV): NSSF Bldg, 22nd Floor, POB 42271, Nairobi; tel. (20) 218043; fax (20) 222555; f. 1998; commercial station broadcasting in Nairobi; Man. Dir HILLARY NGWENO.

Finance

(cap. = capital; res = reserves; dep. = deposits; m. = million; brs = branches; amounts in Kenya shillings)

BANKING

Central Bank

Central Bank of Kenya (Banki Kuu Ya Kenya): Haile Selassie Ave, POB 60000, Nairobi; tel. (20) 226431; fax (20) 217940; e-mail info@centralbank.go.ke; internet www.centralbank.go.ke; f. 1966; bank of issue; cap. 1,500m., res 4,248m., dep. 79,776m. (June 2002); Gov. Dr ANDREW KAVULYA MULLEI.

Commercial Banks

African Banking Corpn Ltd: ABC-Bank House, Koinange St, POB 46452, Nairobi; tel. (20) 223922; fax (20) 222437; e-mail ho@abcthebank.co.ke; f. 1995; cap. 350m., dep. 2,869m. (Dec. 2002); Exec. Chair. ASHRAF SAVANI; Gen. Man. GHULAM HUSSAIN SHEIKH; 7 brs.

Akiba Bank Ltd: Fedha Towers, 2nd Floor, Muindi Mbingu St, POB 49584, Nairobi; tel. (20) 249633; fax (20) 225694; e-mail akiba .ho@akibabank.com; internet www.akibabank.com; cap. 500m., res 75m., dep. 1,800m. (Dec. 2000); Exec. Chair. L. J. PANDIT; Exec. Dir D. L. PANDIT; 3 brs.

Barclays Bank of Kenya Ltd: Barclays Plaza, Loita St, POB 30120, Nairobi; tel. (20) 332230; fax (20) 213915; e-mail barclays .kenya@barclays.com; f. 1978; cap. 1,852m., dep. 57,617m. (Dec. 2001); Chair. SAMUEL O. J. AMBUNDO; Man. Dir ADAN MOHAMMED; 87 brs.

CFC Bank Ltd: CFC Centre, Chiromo Rd, POB 72833, Nairobi; tel. (20) 340091; fax (20) 223032; cap. 500m. (Dec. 1998); Chair. P. K. JANI; Man. Dir N. MAJMUDAR.

Chase Bank (Kenya) Ltd: Prudential Assurance Bldg, Wabera St, POB 28987, Nairobi; tel. (20) 244035; fax (20) 246334; e-mail info@chasebank.co.ke; cap. 300m. (Dec. 2001); Chair. WILFRIED STROTHMANN; Man. Dir ZAFRULLAH KHAN.

Commercial Bank of Africa Ltd: Commercial Bank Bldg, cnr Wabera and Standard Sts, POB 30437, Nairobi; tel. (20) 228881; fax (20) 335827; e-mail cba@cba.co.ke; internet www.cba.co.ke; f. 1962; owned by Kenyan shareholders; cap. 1,000m., res 683m., dep. 14,216m. (Dec. 2002); Chair. M. H. DA GAMA-ROSE; Pres and Man. Dir ISAAC O. AWUONDO; 9 brs.

Consolidated Bank of Kenya Ltd: Consolidated Bank House, Koinange St, POB 51133, Nairobi; tel. (20) 340551; fax (20) 340213; e-mail consobank@iconnect.co.ke; f. 1989; state-owned; cap. 1,120m., res –271m., dep. 817m. (Dec. 1999); Chair. ANDREW N. LIGALE; Man. Dir E. K. MATHIU.

Delphis Bank Ltd: Finance House, Koinange St, POB 44080, Nairobi; tel. (20) 228461; fax (20) 219469; e-mail delphiskenya@iconnect.co.ke; internet www.delphisbank.com; f. 1991; cap. 250m., res 836m., dep. 247m. (Dec. 2002); Chair. G. V. SHAH; Man. Dir Y. M. SHUKLA.

Dubai Bank Kenya Ltd: ICEA Bldg, Kenyatta Ave, POB 11129, Nairobi; tel. (20) 330562; fax (20) 245242; e-mail info@dubaibank.co .ke; internet www.dubaibank.co.ke; 25% owned by World of Marble and Granite, Dubai (United Arab Emirates); cap. 293m., res 3m.,

dep. 491m. (Dec. 2001); Chair. ABDULLAH S. DAHIR; Man. Dir AHMED HASSAN ZUBEIDI.

Equatorial Commercial Bank Ltd: Sasini House, Loita St, POB 52467, Nairobi; tel. (20) 331122; fax (20) 331606; e-mail ecb@saamnet.com; internet www.sameer-group.com; cap. 306m. (Dec. 2001); Chair. EDGAR I. MANASSEH; Man. Dir TAHIR N. KHWAJA.

Fidelity Commercial Bank Ltd: IPS Bldg, 7th Floor, Kimathi St, POB 34886, Nairobi; tel. (20) 242348; fax (20) 243389; e-mail customerservice@fidelitybankkenya.com; f. 1993 as Fidelity Finance; present name adopted 1996; CEO SULTAN KHIMJI.

Kenya Commercial Bank Ltd: Kencom House, Moi Ave, POB 48400, Nairobi; tel. (20) 223846; fax (20) 215565; e-mail kcbhq@kcb .co.ke; internet www.kcb.co.ke; f. 1970; 35% state-owned; cap. 1,496m., res 474m., dep. 50,376m. (Dec. 2002); CEO and Man. Dir TERRY DAVIDSON; 105 brs and sub-brs.

Middle East Bank Kenya Ltd: Mebank Tower, Milimani Rd, POB 47387, Nairobi; tel. (20) 723120; fax (20) 335168; e-mail info@mebkenya.com; internet www.mebkenya.com; f. 1981; 25% owned by Banque Belgolaise SA (Belgium), 75% owned by Kenyan shareholders; cap. 507m., res 38m., dep. 3,212m. (Dec. 2001); Chair. A. A. K. ESMAIL; Man. Dir DEB GHOSH; 3 brs.

National Bank of Kenya Ltd (Banki ya Taifa La Kenya Ltd): National Bank Bldg, Harambee Ave, POB 72866, Nairobi; tel. (20) 339690; fax (20) 330784; e-mail nbkops@nbnet.co.ke; internet www .nationalbank.co.ke; f. 1968; 64.5% state-owned; cap. 1,000m., res 1,457m., dep. 19,840m. (Dec. 2001); Exec. Chair. JOHN P. N. SIMBA; Gen. Man. A. H. AHMED; 25 brs.

Stanbic Bank Kenya Ltd: Stanbic Bank Bldg, Kenyatta Ave, POB 30550, Nairobi; tel. (20) 335888; fax (20) 330227; e-mail stanbickenya@stanbic.com; internet www.stanbic.co.ke; f. 1992; 93% owned by Standard Bank Investment Corpn Ltd (Botswana), 7% state-owned; cap. 1,260m., res 128m., dep. 5,526m. (Dec. 2001); Chair. J. B. WANJUI; Man. Dir P. R. SOUTHEY; 3 brs.

Standard Chartered Bank Kenya Ltd: Stanbank House, Moi Ave, POB 30003, Nairobi; tel. (20) 330200; fax (20) 214086; e-mail mds.office@ke.standardchartered.com; internet www .standardchartered.com/ke; f. 1987; owned by Standard Chartered Holdings (Africa) BV (Netherlands); cap. 824m., res 3,698m., dep. 34,939m. (Dec. 1999); Chair. HARRINGTON AWORI; CEO LES GIBSON; 43 brs.

Trans-National Bank Ltd: Transnational Plaza, 2nd Floor, Mama Ngina St, POB 34352, 00100 Nairobi; tel. (20) 224234; fax (20) 339227; e-mail tnbl@form-net.com; f. 1985; cap. 504m., res 324m., dep. 753m. (Dec. 2001); Chair. MWAKAI SIO; Man. Dir PATRICK NOBLE; 5 brs.

Trust Bank Ltd: Trustforte Bldg, Moi Ave, POB 46342, Nairobi; tel. (20) 226413; fax (20) 243538; e-mail gmupcountry@trustbnk.com; f. 1988; placed under statutory management Sept. 1998; cap. 10,821m. (Dec. 1999); Chair. TARLOK S. NANDHRA; Man. Dir BHARAT JANI; 21 brs.

Victoria Commercial Bank Ltd: Victor House, Kimathi St, POB 41114, Nairobi; tel. (20) 228732; fax (20) 220548; e-mail atul@vicbank.com; f. 1987 as Victoria Finance Co Ltd, name changed 1996; cap. 399m. (Dec. 2001), res 76m., dep. 3,097.8m. (Dec. 1998); Chair. KANJI D. PATTNI; Gen. Man. YOGESH KANJI PATTNI.

Merchant Banks

Barclays Merchant Finance Ltd: Barclays Plaza, Loita St, POB 46661, Nairobi; tel. (20) 331324; fax (20) 331396; Man. Dir GARETH A. GEORGE.

Diamond Trust Bank of Kenya Ltd: Nation Centre, 8th Floor, Kimathi St, POB 61711, Nairobi; tel. (20) 210988; fax (20) 336836; e-mail user@dtbkenya.co.ke; f. 1945; cap. 318m., res 131m., dep. 4,766m. (Dec. 2002); Chair. ROBERT A. BIRD; Man. Dir NASIM DEVJI.

Kenya Commercial Finance Co Ltd: Kenyan House, 6th Floor, Moi Ave, POB 21984, Nairobi; tel. (20) 339074; fax (20) 215881; e-mail kcfc@kcb.co.ke; internet www.kcb.co.ke; f. 1971; cap. 300m. (Dec. 1999), dep. 4,042m. (1998); Chair. PETER C. J. O. NYAKIAMO; Man. Dir JAMES G. CHEGE.

Kenya National Capital Corpn Ltd: POB 73469, Nairobi; tel. (20) 336077; fax (20) 338217; f. 1977; 60% owned by National Bank of Kenya, 40% by Kenya National Assurance Co; cap. 80m., dep. 1,024m. (1996); Chair. R. GITAU; Gen. Man. C. M. KIBUNJA.

National Industrial Credit Bank Ltd (NIC): NIC House, Masaba Rd, POB 44599, Nairobi; tel. (20) 718200; fax (20) 718232; e-mail nic@iconnect.co.ke; cap. 412m. (Dec. 2001); Chair. N. MURIUKI MUGWANDIA; Man. Dir M. N. DAVIDSON.

Standard Chartered Financial Services Ltd: International House, 1st Floor, Mama Ngina St, POB 40310, Nairobi; tel. (20) 336333; fax (20) 334934; owned by Standard Chartered Bank Kenya, cap. and res 161.7m., dep. 1,700m. (Dec. 1992); Chair. A. CLEARY; Man. Dir W. VON ISENBURG.

Foreign Banks

ABN AMRO Bank NV (Netherlands): Triad House, 83 Muthaiga Rd, POB 30262, Nairobi; tel. (20) 3749632; fax (20) 3749654; e-mail info@abnamro.co.ke; internet www.abnamro.com/kenya; Country Man. ADRIAN VAN DER POL; 2 brs.

Bank of Baroda (Kenya) Ltd (India): Bank of Baroda Bldg, cnr Mondlane St and Tom Mboya St, POB 30033, Nairobi; tel. (20) 228405; fax (20) 333089; e-mail barodabk_ho@form-net.com; Exec. Chair. C. K. DAIYA; Man. Dir T. K. KRISHMAN; 6 brs.

Bank of India: Kenyatta Ave, POB 30246, Nairobi; tel. (20) 221414; fax (20) 229462; e-mail boi10@calva.com; internet www.bankofindia.co.ke; CEO G. L. N. SASTRY.

Citibank NA (USA): Citibank House, Upperhill Rd, POB 30711, 00100 Nairobi; tel. (20) 2711221; fax (20) 2714811; internet www.citibank.co.ke; f. 1974; Gen. Man. SRIDHAR SRINIVASAN.

Crédit Agricole Indosuez (France): Reinsurance Plaza, Taifa Rd, POB 69562, Nairobi; tel. (20) 211175; fax (20) 214166; e-mail user@ke.ca-indosuez.com; Regional Man. BENOÎT DESTOPPELAIRE.

First American Bank of Kenya Ltd (USA): First American Bank Centre, Nyerere Rd, POB 30691, 00100 Nairobi; tel. (20) 2710455; fax (20) 2714511; e-mail fabk@fabk.com; internet www.fabk.com; f. 1987; 20.5% owned by Sameer Investments Ltd; cap. 1,200m., res 43m., dep. 5,309m. (Dec. 2003); Chair. D. G. M. HUTCHINSON; Man. Dir MANLIO BLASETTI; 3 brs.

Habib Bank AG Zurich (Switzerland): Nagina House, Koinange St, POB 30584, Nairobi; tel. (20) 334984; fax (20) 218699; e-mail habibbanks@form-net.com; Country Man. IQBAL A. ALLAWALA.

MashreqBank PSC (UAE): ICEA Bldg, Ground Floor, Kenyatta Ave, POB 11129, Nairobi; tel. (20) 212166; fax (20) 330792; e-mail m6cbd@gsm.net.com; Gen. Man. SYED AKHTAR IMAN.

Co-operative Bank

Co-operative Bank of Kenya Ltd: Co-operative Bank House, POB 48231, Nairobi; tel. (20) 32076000; fax (20) 249474; e-mail md@co-opbank.co.ke; internet www.co-opbank.co.ke; f. 1968; cap. 1,211m., res 589m., dep. 25,084m. (Dec. 2002); Chair. STANLEY C. MUCHIRI; Man. Dir GIDEON MURIUKI; 30 brs.

Development Banks

Development Bank of Kenya Ltd: Finance House, Loita St, POB 30483, Nairobi; tel. (20) 340401; fax (20) 338426; e-mail dbk@africaonline.co.ke; f. 1963 as Development Finance Co of Kenya, current name adopted 1996; owned by Industrial and Commercial Devt Corpn (30.5%), govt agencies of Germany and the Netherlands (28.8% and 22.8% respectively), the Commonwealth Development Corpn (10.7%) and the International Finance Corpn (7.2%); cap. 348m., res 479m., dep. 769m. (Dec. 2002); Chair. Prof. HAROUN NGENY KIPKEMBOI MENGECH; Man. Dir SAJAL RAKHIT.

East African Development Bank: Lonrho House, 12th Floor, Standard St, Nairobi; tel. (20) 340642; fax (20) 216651; Man. G. RUHURIRA.

Industrial Development Bank Ltd (IDB): National Bank Bldg, 18th Floor, Harambee Ave, POB 44036, Nairobi; tel. (20) 337079; fax (20) 334594; e-mail bizcare@idbkenya.com; f. 1973; 49% state-owned; cap. 258m., res 267m., dep. 142m. (Dec. 2001); Chair. DAVID LANGAT; Man. Dir L. A. MASAVIRU.

STOCK EXCHANGE

Nairobi Stock Exchange (NSE): Nation Centre, 1st Floor, Kimathi St, POB 43633, Nairobi; tel. (20) 230692; fax (20) 224200; e-mail info@nse.co.ke; internet www.nse.co.ke; f. 1954; Chair. BETHUEL A. KIPLAGAT; CEO KIBBY KARRITHI.

INSURANCE

American Life Insurance Co (Kenya) Ltd: POB 30364, 00100 Nairobi; tel. (20) 2711242; fax (20) 2711378; e-mail alicolife@alico-kenya.com; internet www.alico-kenya.com; f. 1964; life and general; Man. Dir ERWIN BREWSTER.

Apollo Insurance Co Ltd: POB 30389, Nairobi; tel. (20) 223562; fax (20) 339260; e-mail insurance@apollo.co.ke; f. 1977; life and general; Chief Exec. ASHOK K. M. SHAH.

Blue Shield Insurance Co Ltd: POB 49610, Nairobi; tel. (20) 219592; fax (20) 337808; f. 1983; life and general.

Cannon Assurance (Kenya) Ltd: Haile Selassie Ave, POB 30216, Nairobi; tel. (20) 335478; fax (20) 331235; e-mail info@cannon.co.ke;

internet www.cannon.co.ke; f. 1964; life and general; Man. Dir I. J. TALWAR.

Fidelity Shield Insurance Ltd: POB 47435, Nairobi; tel. (20) 430635; fax (20) 445699.

Heritage AII Insurance Co Ltd: CFC Centre, Chiromo Rd, POB 30390, Nairobi; tel. (20) 3749118; fax (20) 3752621; e-mail info@heriaii.com; f. 1976; general; Man. Dir J. H. D. MILNE.

Insurance Co of East Africa Ltd (ICEA): ICEA Bldg, Kenyatta Ave, POB 46143, Nairobi; tel. (20) 221652; fax (20) 338089; e-mail hof@icea.co.ke; internet www.icea.co.ke; life and general; Man. Dir J. K. NDUNGU.

Jubilee Insurance Co Ltd: POB 30376, Nairobi; tel. (20) 340343; fax (20) 216882; f. 1937; life and general; Chair. ABDUL JAFFER.

Kenindia Assurance Co Ltd: Kenindia House, Loita St, POB 44372, Nairobi; tel. (20) 333100; fax (20) 218380; e-mail kenindia@users.africaonline.co.ke; f. 1978; life and general; Exec. Dir R. S. BEDI.

Kenya Reinsurance Corpn Ltd (KenyaRe): Reinsurance Plaza, Taifa Rd, POB 30271, Nairobi; tel. (20) 240188; fax (20) 339161; e-mail kenyare@kenyare.co.ke; internet www.kenyare.co.ke; f. 1970; Man. Dir JOHNSON GITHAKA.

Lion of Kenya Insurance Co Ltd: POB 30190, Nairobi; tel. (20) 710400; fax (20) 711177; e-mail insurance@lionofkenya.com; f. 1978; general; CEO J. P. M. NDEGWA.

Mercantile Life and General Assurance Co Ltd: Nairobi; tel. (20) 218244; fax (20) 215528; e-mail mercantile@form-net.com; Gen. Man. SUPRIYO SEN.

Monarch Insurance Co Ltd: Chester House, 2nd Floor, Koinange St, POB 44003, Nairobi; tel. (20) 330042; fax (20) 340691; e-mail monarch@form-net.com; f. 1975; general; Exec. Dir R. A. VADGAMA.

Pan Africa Insurance Co Ltd: POB 30065, Nairobi; tel. (20) 252168; fax (20) 217675; e-mail insure@pan-africa.com; f. 1946; life and general; Man. Dir WILLIAM OLOTCH.

Phoenix of East Africa Assurance Co Ltd: Ambank House, University Way, POB 30129, Nairobi; tel. (20) 338784; fax (20) 211848; general; Man. Dir D. K. SHARMA.

Prudential Assurance Co of Kenya Ltd: Yaya Centre, Argwings Kodhek Rd, POB 76190, Nairobi; tel. (20) 567374; fax (20) 567433; f. 1979; general; Man. Dir JOSEPH MURAGE.

PTA Reinsurance Co (ZEP-RE): Anniversary Towers, 13th Floor, University Way, POB 42769, Nairobi; tel. (20) 212792; fax (20) 224102; e-mail mail@zep-re.com; internet www.zep-re.com; f. 1992; Man. Dir S. M. LUBASI.

Royal Insurance Co of East Africa Ltd: Mama Ngina St, POB 40001, Nairobi; tel. (20) 717888; fax (20) 712620; f. 1979; general; CEO S. K. KAMAU.

Standard Assurance (Kenya) Ltd: POB 42996, Nairobi; tel. (20) 224721; fax (20) 224862; Man. Dir WILSON K. KAPKOTI.

UAP Provincial Insurance Co of East Africa Ltd: Old Mutual Bldg, Kimathi St, POB 43013, Nairobi; tel. (20) 330173; fax (20) 340483; f. 1980; general; CEO E. C. BATES.

United Insurance Co Ltd: POB 30961, Nairobi; tel. (20) 227345; fax (20) 215609; Man. Dir G. KARRUIKI.

Trade and Industry

GOVERNMENT AGENCIES

Export Processing Zones Authority: POB 50563, Nairobi; tel. (20) 712800; fax (20) 713704; e-mail epzahq@africaonline.co.ke; established by the Govt to promote investment in Export Processing Zones; CEO SILAS ITA.

Export Promotion Council: POB 40247, Nairobi; tel. (20) 228534; fax (20) 218013; f. 1992; promotes exports; CEO PETER MUTHOKA.

Investment Promotion Centre: National Bank Bldg, 8th Floor, Harambee Ave, POB 55704, 00200 Nairobi; tel. (20) 221401; fax (20) 336663; e-mail info@investmentkenya.com; internet www.investmentkenya.com; f. 1986; promotes and facilitates local and foreign investment; CEO LUKA E. OBBANDA.

Kenya National Trading Corpn Ltd: Yarrow Rd, off Nanyuki Rd, POB 30587, Nairobi; tel. (20) 543121; fax (20) 532800; f. 1965; promotes national control of trade in both locally produced and imported items; exports coffee and sugar; CEO S. W. O. OGESSA.

Settlement Fund Trustees: POB 30449, Nairobi; administers a land purchase programme involving over 1.2m. ha for resettlement of African farmers.

DEVELOPMENT ORGANIZATIONS

Agricultural Development Corpn: POB 47101, Nairobi; tel. (20) 338530; fax (20) 336524; f. 1965 to promote agricultural development and reconstruction; CEO Dr WALTER KILELE.

Agricultural Finance Corpn: POB 30367, Nairobi; tel. (20) 333733; a statutory organization providing agricultural loans; Gen. Man. G. K. TOROITICH.

Horticultural Crops Development Authority: POB 42601, Nairobi; tel. (20) 8272601; fax (20) 827264; e-mail hcdamd@wananchi.com; internet www.hcda.or.ke; f. 1968; invests in production, dehydration, processing and freezing of fruit and vegetables; exports of fresh fruit and vegetables; Chair. Prof. ROSALIND W. MUTUA; Man. Dir S. P. GACHANJA.

Housing Finance Co of Kenya Ltd: Rehani House, cnr Kenyatta Ave and Koinange St, POB 30088, 00100 Nairobi; tel. (20) 333910; fax (20) 334670; e-mail hfck@hfck.co.ke; internet www.hfck.co.ke; f. 1965; Chair. RICHARD KEMOLI; Man. Dir PETER LEWIS-JONES.

Industrial and Commercial Development Corpn: Uchumi House, Aga Khan Walk, POB 45519, Nairobi; tel. (20) 229213; fax (20) 333880; e-mail icdcexe@africaonline.co.ke; f. 1954; govt-financed; assists industrial and commercial development; Chair. JOHN NGUTHU MUTIO; Exec. Dir K. ETICH ARAP BETT.

Kenya Fishing Industries Ltd: Nairobi; Man. Dir ABDALLA MBWANA.

Kenya Industrial Estates Ltd: Nairobi Industrial Estate, Likoni Rd, POB 78029, Nairobi; tel. (20) 530551; fax (20) 534625; f. 1967 to finance and develop small-scale industries.

Kenya Industrial Research and Development Institute: POB 30650, Nairobi; tel. (20) 557762; f. 1942; reorg. 1979; restructured 1995; research and development in industrial and allied technologies including engineering, commodity technologies, mining and power resources; Dir Dr H. L. KAANE.

Kenya Tea Development Agency: POB 30213, Nairobi; tel. (20) 221441; fax (20) 211240; e-mail info@ktdateas.com; internet www.ktdateas.com; f. 1964 as Kenya Tea Development Authority to develop tea growing, manufacturing and marketing among African smallholders; operates 51 factories; privatized in 2000; Chair. STEPHEN M. IMANYARA; Man. Dir ERIC KIMANI.

CHAMBER OF COMMERCE

Kenya National Chamber of Commerce and Industry: Ufanisi House, Haile Selassie Ave, POB 47024, Nairobi; tel. (20) 220867; fax (20) 334293; f. 1965; 69 brs; Nat. Chair. DAVID M. GITHERE; Chief Exec. TITUS G. RUHIU.

INDUSTRIAL AND TRADE ASSOCIATIONS

Central Province Marketing Board: POB 189, Nyeri.

Coffee Board of Kenya: POB 30566, Nairobi; tel. (20) 332896; fax (20) 330546; f. 1947; Chair. JOHN NGARI ZACHARIAH; Gen. Man. AGGREY MURUNGA.

East African Tea Trade Association: Tea Trade Centre, Nyerere Ave, POB 85174, Mombasa; tel. (11) 315687; fax (11) 225823; e-mail info@eatta.co.ke; internet www.eatta.co.ke; f. 1957; organizes Mombasa weekly tea auctions; Exec. Sec. LUCY MICHENI; 264 mems.

Fresh Produce Exporters' Association of Kenya: Nairobi; Chair. JAMES MATHENGE.

Kenya Association of Manufacturers: POB 30225, Nairobi; tel. (20) 746005; fax (20) 746028; e-mail kam@users.africaonline.co.ke; Chair. MANU CHANDARIA; Exec. Sec. LUCY MICHENI; 200 mems.

Kenya Dairy Board: POB 30406, Nairobi.

Kenya Flower Council: POB 24856, Nairobi; tel. and fax (20) 883041; e-mail kfc@africaonline.co.ke; internet www.kenyaflowers.co.ke; regulates production of cut flowers; Exec. Dir MICHAEL MORLAND.

Kenya Meat Corpn: POB 30414, Nairobi; tel. (20) 340750; f. 1953; purchasing, processing and marketing of beef livestock; Chair. H. P. BARCLAY.

Kenya Planters' Co-operative Union Ltd: Nairobi; e-mail gm@kpcu.co.ke; coffee processing and marketing; Chair. J. M. MACHARIA; Gen. Man. RUTH MWANIKI.

Kenya Sisal Board: Mutual Bldg, Kimathi St, POB 41179, Nairobi; tel. (20) 223457; f. 1946; CEO J. H. WAIRAGU; Man. Dir KENNETH MUKUMA.

Kenya Sugar Authority: NSSF Complex, 9th Floor, Bishops Rd, POB 51500, Nairobi; tel. (20) 710600; fax (20) 723903; e-mail ksa@users.africaonline.co.ke; Chair. LUKE R. OBOK; CEO F. M. CHAHONYO.

Mild Coffee Trade Association of Eastern Africa (MCTA): Nairobi; F. J. MWANGI.

National Cereals and Produce Board: POB 30586, Nairobi; tel. (20) 536028; fax (20) 542024; e-mail cereals@africaonline.co.ke; f. 1995; grain marketing and handling, provides drying, weighing, storage and fumigation services to farmers and traders, stores and manages strategic national food reserves, distributes famine relief; Chair. JAMES MUTUA; Man. Dir Maj. W. K. KOITABA.

Pyrethrum Board of Kenya: POB 420, Nakuru; tel. (37) 211567; fax (37) 45274; e-mail pbk@pyrethrum.co.ke; internet www.kenya-pyrethrum.com; f. 1935; 14 mems; Chair. J. O. MARIARIA; CEO J. C. KIPTOON.

Tea Board of Kenya: POB 20064, Nairobi; tel. (20) 572421; fax (20) 562120; internet www.teaboard.or.ke; f. 1950; regulates tea industry on all matters of policy, licenses tea planting and processing, combats pests and diseases, controls the export of tea, finances research on tea, promotes Kenyan tea internationally; 17 mems; Chair. JOHNSTONE O. MORONGE; CEO STEPHEN NKANATA.

EMPLOYERS' ORGANIZATIONS

Federation of Kenya Employers: Waajiri House, Argwings Kodhek Rd, POB 48311, Nairobi; tel. (20) 721929; fax (20) 721990; Chair. J. P. N. SIMBA; Exec. Dir TOM DIJU OWUOR.

    Association of Local Government Employers: POB 52, Muranga; Chair. S. K. ITONGU.

    Distributive and Allied Industries Employers' Association: POB 30587, Nairobi; Chair. P. J. MWAURA.

    Engineering and Allied Industries Employers' Association: POB 48311, Nairobi; tel. (20) 721929; Chair. D. M. NJOROGE.

    Kenya Association of Building and Civil Engineering Contractors: Nairobi; Chair. G. S. HIRANI.

    Kenya Association of Hotelkeepers and Caterers: POB 46406, Nairobi; tel. (20) 726642; fax (20) 714401; f. 1944; Chair. P. MURIUKI.

    Kenya Bankers' Association: POB 73100, Nairobi; tel. (20) 221792; e-mail kba@kenyaweb.com; Chair. (vacant).

    Kenya Sugar Employers' Union: Kisumu; Chair. L. OKECH.

    Kenya Tea Growers' Association: POB 320, Kericho; tel. (20) 21010; fax (20) 32172; Chair. M. K. A. SANG.

    Kenya Vehicle Manufacturers' Association: POB 1436, Thika; Chair. C. PETERSON.

    Motor Trade and Allied Industries Employers' Association: POB 48311, Nairobi; tel. (20) 721929; fax (20) 721990; Exec. Sec. G. N. KONDITI.

    Sisal Growers' and Employers' Association: POB 47523, Nairobi; tel. (20) 720170; fax (20) 721990; Chair. A. G. COMBOS.

    Timber Industries Employers' Association: POB 18070, Nairobi; Chair. H. S. BAMBRAH.

UTILITIES

Electricity

Kenya Electricity Generating Co Ltd (KenGen): Stima Plaza, Phase 3, Kolobot Rd, Parklands, POB 47936, Nairobi; tel. (20) 3666000; fax (20) 248848; e-mail comms@kengen.co.ke; internet www.kengen.co.ke; f. 1997 as Kenya Power Co, present name adopted 1998; generates 82% of Kenya's electricity requirements; Man. Dir EDWARD NJOROGE.

Kenya Power and Lighting Co (KPLC): Stima Plaza, Kolobot Rd, POB 30099, Nairobi; tel. (20) 243366; fax (20) 337351; e-mail isd@form-net.com; state-owned; co-ordinates electricity transmission and distribution; Man. Dir SAMUEL GICHURU.

TRADE UNIONS

Central Organization of Trade Unions (Kenya) (COTU): Solidarity Bldg, Digo Rd, POB 13000, Nairobi; tel. (20) 761375; fax (20) 762695; f. 1965 as the sole trade union fed.; Chair. PETER G. MUTHEE; Sec.-Gen. JOSEPH J. MUGALLA.

    Amalgamated Union of Kenya Metalworkers: POB 73651, Nairobi; tel. (20) 211060; Gen. Sec. F. E. OMIDO.

    Bakers', Confectionary Manufacturing and Allied Workers' Union (Kenya): POB 57751, 00200 Nairobi; Lengo House, 3rd Floor, Room 20, Tom Mboya St, opposite Gill House, Nairobi; tel. (20) 330275; fax (20) 222735; e-mail bakers@form-net.com.

    Communication Workers' Union of Kenya: POB 48155, Nairobi; tel. (20) 219345; e-mail cowuk@clubinternet.com.

    Dockworkers' Union: POB 98207, Mombasa; tel. (11) 491427; f. 1954; Gen. Sec. J. KHAMIS.

Kenya Airline Pilots' Association: POB 57505, Nairobi; tel. (20) 716986.

Kenya Building, Construction, Timber, Furniture and Allied Industries Employees' Union: POB 49628, Nairobi; tel. (20) 336414; Gen. Sec. FRANCIS KARIMI MURAGE.

Kenya Chemical and Allied Workers' Union: POB 73820, Nairobi; tel. (20) 338815; Gen. Sec. WERE DIBI OGUTO.

Kenya Electrical Trades Allied Workers' Union: POB 47060, Nairobi; tel. (20) 334655.

Kenya Engineering Workers' Union: POB 73987, Nairobi; tel. (20) 333745; Gen. Sec. JUSTUS MULEI.

Kenya Game Hunting and Safari Workers' Union: Nairobi; tel. (20) 25049; Gen. Sec. J. M. NDOLO.

Kenya Jockey and Betting Workers' Union: POB 55094, Nairobi; tel. (20) 332120.

Kenya Local Government Workers' Union: POB 55827, Nairobi; tel. (20) 217213; Gen. Sec. WASIKE NDOMBI.

Kenya National Union of Fishermen: POB 83322, Nairobi; tel. (20) 227899.

Kenya Petroleum Oil Workers' Union: POB 48125, Nairobi; tel. (20) 338756; Gen. Sec. JACOB OCHINO.

Kenya Plantation and Agricultural Workers' Union: POB 1161, Nakuru; tel. and fax (37) 212310; e-mail kpawu@africaonline.co.ke; Gen. Sec. FRANCIS ATWOLI.

Kenya Quarry and Mine Workers' Union: POB 332120, Nairobi; f. 1961; Gen. Sec. WAFULA WA MUSAMIA.

Kenya Railway Workers' Union: RAHU House, Mfangano St, POB 72029, Nairobi; tel. (20) 340302; f. 1952; Nat. Chair. FRANCIS O'LORE; Sec.-Gen. RICHARD A. KANANI.

Kenya Scientific Research, International Technical and Allied Institutions Workers' Union: Ngumba House, Tom Mboya St, POB 55094, Nairobi; tel. (20) 215713; Sec.-Gen. FRANCIS D. KIRUBI.

Kenya Shipping, Clearing and Warehouse Workers' Union: POB 84067, Mombasa; tel. (11) 312000.

Kenya Shoe and Leather Workers' Union: POB 49629, Nairobi; tel. (20) 533827; Gen. Sec. JAMES AWICH.

Kenya Union of Commercial, Food and Allied Workers: POB 46818, Nairobi; tel. (20) 212545.

Kenya Union of Domestic, Hotel, Educational Institutions, Hospitals and Allied Workers: POB 41763, 00100 Nairobi; tel. (20) 211840.

Kenyan Union of Entertainment and Music Industry Employees: Nairobi; tel. (20) 333745.

Kenya Union of Journalists: POB 47035, 00100 Nairobi; tel. (20) 250888; fax (20) 250880; e-mail info@kujkenya.org; f. 1962; Gen. Sec. and CEO EZEKIEL MUTUA; Chair. TERVIL OKOKO.

Kenya Union of Printing, Publishing, Paper Manufacturers and Allied Workers: POB 72358, Nairobi; tel. (20) 331387; Gen. Sec. JOHN BOSCO.

Kenya Union of Sugar Plantation Workers: POB 36, Kisumu; tel. (35) 22221; Gen. Sec. ONYANGO MIDIKA.

National Seamen's Union of Kenya: Mombasa; tel. (11) 312106; Gen. Sec. I. S. ABDALLAH MWARUA.

Tailors' and Textile Workers' Union: POB 72076, Nairobi; tel. (20) 338836.

Transport and Allied Workers' Union: POB 45171, Nairobi; tel. (20) 545317; Gen. Sec. JULIAS MALII.

Independent Unions

Academic Staff Association: Nairobi; e-mail dorata@uonbi.ac.ke; Interim Chair. Dr KORWA ADAR.

Kenya Medical Practitioners' and Dentists' Union: not officially registered; Nat. Chair. GIBBON ATEKA.

Kenya National Union of Teachers: POB 30407, Nairobi; f. 1957; Sec.-Gen. AMBROSE ADEYA ADONGO.

Transport

RAILWAYS

In 1999 there were some 2,700 km of track open for traffic.

Kenya Railways Corpn: POB 30121, Nairobi; tel. (20) 221211; fax (20) 224156; f. 1977; privatization pending; Man. Dir A. HARIZ.

ROADS

At the end of 1996 there were an estimated 63,800 km of classified roads, of which 6,360 km were main roads and 19,600 km were secondary roads. Only an estimated 13.9% of road surfaces were paved. An all-weather road links Nairobi to Addis Ababa, in Ethiopia, and there is a 590-km road link between Kitale (Kenya) and Juba (Sudan). The rehabilitation of the important internal road link between Nairobi and Mombasa (funded by a US $165m. loan from the World Bank) was undertaken during the late 1990s.

Abamba Public Road Services: POB 40322, Nairobi; tel. (20) 556062; fax (20) 559884; operates bus services from Nairobi to all major towns in Kenya and to Kampala in Uganda.

East African Road Services Ltd: Nairobi; tel. (20) 764622; f. 1947; operates bus services from Nairobi to all major towns in Kenya; Chair. S. H. NATHOO.

Kenya Roads Board: Nairobi; tel. (20) 722865; f. 2000 to co-ordinate maintenance, rehabilitation and development of the road network; Chair. SHEM ODUOR NOAH.

Nyayo Bus Service Corpn: Nairobi; tel. (20) 803588; f. 1986; operates bus services within and between major towns in Kenya.

Speedways Trans-Africa Freighters: POB 75755, Nairobi; tel. (20) 544267; private road haulier; CEO HASSAN KANYARE.

SHIPPING

The major international seaport of Mombasa has 16 deep-water berths, with a total length of 3,044 m, and facilities for the off-loading of bulk carriers, tankers and container vessels. Mombasa port handled more than 8.5m. metric tons of cargo in 1998. In August 2000 it was announced that the container terminal at Mombasa port was to be privatized by 2003 . An inland container depot with a potential full capacity of 120,000 20-ft (6-m) equivalent units was opened in Nairobi in 1984. Two further inland depots were scheduled to begin operating in the mid-1990s at Eldoret and Kisumu.

Kenya Ports Authority: POB 95009, Mombasa; tel. (11) 312211; fax (11) 311867; e-mail kpa_md@africaonline.co.ke; internet www.kenya.ports.com; f. 1978; sole operator of coastal port facilities, and operates two inland container depots; Chair. JONATHAN MTURI; Man. Dir BROWN M. M. ONDEGO.

Kenya Cargo Handling Services Ltd: POB 95187, Mombasa; tel. (11) 25955; division of Kenya Ports Authority; Man. Dir JOSHUA KEGODE.

Inchcape Shipping Services Kenya Ltd: POB 90194, Mombasa; tel. (11) 314245; fax (11) 314224; Man. Dir DAVID MACKAY.

Kenya Shipping Agency Ltd: POB 84831, Mombasa; tel. (11) 220501; fax (11) 314494; e-mail ksamba@africaonline.co.ke; f. 1967; 60% govt-owned, 40% owned by Southern Shield Group; dry cargo, container, bulk carrier and tanker agents; Chair. RAY KESTER; Man. Dir JONATHAN MTURI.

Mackenzie Maritime Ltd: Maritime Centre, Archbishop Makarios Close, POB 90120, Mombasa; tel. (11) 221273; fax (11) 316260; e-mail mml@africaonline.co.ke; shipping agents; Man. Dir M. M. BROWN.

Marship Ltd: Mombasa; tel. (11) 314705; fax (11) 316654; f. 1986; shipbrokers, ship management and chartering agents; Man. Dir MICHELE ESPOSITO.

Mitchell Cotts Kenya Ltd: Cotts House, Wabera St, POB 30182, Nairobi; tel. (20) 221273; fax (20) 214228.

Motaku Shipping Agencies Ltd: Motaku House, Tangana Rd, POB 80419, 80100 Mombasa; tel. (11) 312562; fax (11) 220777; e-mail motaku@motakushipping.com; f. 1977; ship managers and shipping agents; Man. Dir KARIM KUDRATI.

PIL (Kenya) Ltd: POB 43050, Mombasa; tel. (11) 225361; fax (11) 312296.

Shipmarc Ltd: POB 99553, Mombasa; tel. (11) 229241; fax (11) 315673; e-mail shipmarc@form-net.com.

Southern Line Ltd: POB 90102, Mombasa 80107; tel. (11) 229241; fax (11) 221390; e-mail shipmarc@africaonline.co.ke; operating dry cargo and tanker vessels between East African ports, Red Sea ports, the Persian (Arabian) Gulf and Indian Ocean islands.

Spanfreight Shipping Ltd: Cannon Towers, Moi Ave, POB 99760, Mombasa; tel. (11) 315623; fax (11) 312092; e-mail a23ke464@gncomtext.com; Exec. Dir DILIPKUMAR AMRITLAL SHAH.

Star East Africa Co: POB 86725, Mombasa; tel. (11) 314060; fax (11) 312818; shipping agents and brokers; Man. Dir YEUDA FISHER.

CIVIL AVIATION

Jomo Kenyatta International Airport (JKIA), in south-eastern Nairobi, Moi International Airport, at Mombasa, and Eldoret International Airport (which opened in 1997) all service international flights. Wilson Airport, in south-western Nairobi, and airports at Malindi and Kisumu handle internal flights. Kenya has about 150 smaller airfields. The rehabilitation and expansion of JKIA and Moi International Airport was undertaken during the late 1990s. A new cargo handling facility, The Nairobi Cargo Centre, opened at JKIA in June 1999, increasing the airport's capacity for storing horticultural exports.

Kenya Airports Authority: Jomo Kenyatta International Airport, POB 19001, Nairobi; tel. (20) 825400; fax (20) 822078; e-mail info@ kenyaairports.co.ke; f. 1991; state-owned; responsible for the provision, management and operation of all airports and private airstrips; Man. Dir GEORGE MUHOHO.

African Airlines International: POB 74772, Nairobi; tel. (20) 824333; fax (20) 823999; placed under receivership mid-1999; CEO Capt. MUSA BULHAN.

Airkenya Aviation: Wilson Airport, POB 30357, Nairobi; tel. (20) 605730; fax (20) 500845; e-mail info@airkenya.com; internet www .airkenya.com; f. 1985; operates internal scheduled and charter passenger services; Man. Dir JOHN BUCKLEY.

Blue Bird Aviation Ltd: Wilson Airport, Langata Rd, POB 52382, Nairobi; tel. (20) 506004; fax (20) 602337; e-mail bbal@form-net.com.

Eagle Aviation (African Eagle): POB 93926, Mombasa; tel. (11) 434502; fax (11) 434249; e-mail eaglemsa@africaonline.co.ke; f. 1986; scheduled regional and domestic passenger and cargo services; Chair. RAJA TANUJ; CEO Capt. KIRAN PATEL.

East African Safari Air: Mombasa; operates charter service.

Kenya Airways Ltd: Jomo Kenyatta International Airport, POB 19002, Nairobi; tel. (20) 823000; fax (20) 823757; e-mail gmurira@ kenya-airways.com; internet www.kenyaairways.co.uk; f. 1977; in private-sector ownership since 1996; passenger services to Africa, Asia, Europe and Middle East; freight services to Europe; internal services from Nairobi to Kisumu, Mombasa and Malindi; also oper-

ates a freight subsidiary; Chair. ISAAC OMOLO OKERO; CEO RICHARD NYAGA.

Civil Aviation Authority

Kenya Directorate of Civil Aviation: Jomo Kenyatta International Airport, POB 30163, Nairobi; tel. (20) 822950; f. 1948; under Kenya govt control since 1977; responsible for the conduct of civil aviation; advises the Govt on civil aviation policy; Dir J. P. AYUGA.

Kenya Civil Aviation Authority: POB 30163, 00100 Nairobi; tel. (20) 824557; fax (20) 824716; e-mail cav@insightkenya.com; f. 2002; regulatory and advisory services for air navigation; Dir Gen. C. A. KUTO.

Tourism

Kenya's main attractions for visitors are its wildlife, with 25 National Parks and 23 game reserves, the Indian Ocean coast and an equable year-round climate. A decline in the number of visitors in 1996–98 was attributed both to competition from other countries of the region, and to perceptions of high rates of crime and shortcomings in security within Kenya. There was a modest recovery in 1999–2000, with an estimated 1,036,628 foreign tourist arrivals recorded in 2000. Earnings from the sector totalled Ks. 21,400m. in 1999.

Kenya Tourism Board: Nairobi; internet www.kenyatourism.com; f. 1996; promotes Kenya as a tourist destination, monitors the standard of tourist facilities; Chair. UHURU KENYATTA.

Kenya Tourist Development Corpn: Utalii House, 11th Floor, Uhuru Highway, POB 42013, Nairobi; tel. (20) 330820; fax (20) 227815; e-mail info@ktdc.co.uk; internet www.ktdc.co.uk; f. 1965; Chair. PAUL KITOLOLO; Man. Dir JOHN A. M. MALITI.

KIRIBATI

Introductory Survey

Location, Climate, Language, Religion, Flag, Capital

The Republic of Kiribati (pronounced 'Kir-a-bas') comprises 33 atolls, in three principal groups, scattered within an area of about 5m. sq km (2m. sq miles) in the mid-Pacific Ocean. The country extends about 3,870 km (2,400 miles) from east to west and about 2,050 km (1,275 miles) from north to south. Its nearest neighbours are Nauru, to the west, and Tuvalu and Tokelau, to the south. The climate varies between maritime equatorial in the central islands and tropical in the north and south, with daytime temperatures varying between 26°C (79°F) and 32°C (90°F). There is a season of north-westerly trade winds from March to October and a season of rains and gales from October to March. Average annual rainfall, however, varies greatly, from 3,000 mm (118 ins) in the northern islands to 1,500 mm (59 ins) in Tarawa and 700 mm (28 ins) in the Line Islands. Droughts often occur in the central and southern islands. The principal languages are I-Kiribati (Gilbertese) and English, and the islands' inhabitants are mostly Christians. The national flag (proportions 1 by 2) depicts a golden frigate bird in flight, on a red background, above a rising sun and six alternating wavy horizontal lines of blue and white, representing the sea. The capital is the island of Bairiki, in Tarawa Atoll.

Recent History

In 1892 the United Kingdom established a protectorate over the 16 atolls of the Gilbert Islands and the nine Ellice Islands (now Tuvalu). The two groups were administered together by the Western Pacific High Commission (WPHC), which was based in Fiji until its removal to the British Solomon Islands (now Solomon Islands) in 1953. The phosphate-rich Ocean Island (now Banaba), west of the Gilberts, was annexed by the United Kingdom in 1900. The Gilbert and Ellice Islands were annexed in 1915, effective from January 1916, when the protectorate became a colony. The local representative of the WPHC was the Resident Commissioner, based on Tarawa Atoll in the Gilbert group. Later in 1916 the new Gilbert and Ellice Islands Colony (GEIC) was extended to include Ocean Island and two of the Line Islands, far to the east. Christmas Island (now Kiritimati), another of the Line Islands, was added in 1919, and the eight Phoenix Islands (then uninhabited) in 1937. The Line and Phoenix Islands, south of Hawaii, were also claimed by the USA. A joint British-US administration for two of the Phoenix group, Canton (now Kanton) and Enderbury, was agreed in April 1939. During the Second World War the GEIC was invaded by Japanese forces, who occupied the Gilbert Islands in 1942–43. Tarawa Atoll was the scene of some of the fiercest fighting in the Pacific between Japan and the USA.

As part of the British Government's programme to develop its own nuclear weapons, the first test of a British hydrogen bomb was conducted near Christmas Island in May 1957. Two further tests in the same vicinity followed later that year.

In 1963, to prepare the GEIC for self-government, the first of a series of legislative and executive bodies were established. In 1972 a Governor of the GEIC was appointed to assume almost all the functions previously exercised in the colony by the High Commissioner. The five uninhabited Central and Southern Line Islands, previously administered directly by the High Commissioner, became part of the GEIC at this time. In 1974 the Legislative Council was replaced by a House of Assembly, with 28 elected members and three official members. The House elected Naboua Ratieta as Chief Minister.

In October 1975 the Ellice Islands were allowed to secede from the GEIC to form a separate territory, Tuvalu (q.v.). The remainder of the GEIC was renamed the Gilbert Islands, and the House of Assembly's membership was reduced.

In 1975 the British Government refused to recognize as legitimate a demand for independence by the people of Ocean Island (Banaba), who had been in litigation with the British Government since 1971 over revenues derived from exports of phosphate. Open-cast mining had so adversely affected the island's environment that most Banabans had been resettled on Rabi Island, 2,600 km (1,600 miles) away in the Fiji group. The Banabans rejected the British Government's argument that phosphate revenues should be distributed over the whole territory of the Gilbert Islands. In 1976 the British High Court dismissed the Banabans' claim for unpaid royalties but upheld that for damages. An offer made by the British Government in 1977 of an *ex gratia* payment of $A10m., without admission of liability and on condition that no further judicial appeal would be made, was rejected.

The Gilbert Islands obtained internal self-government on 1 January 1977. Later in that year the number of elected members in the House of Assembly was increased to 36, and provision was subsequently made for a member appointed by the Rabi Council of Leaders. Following a general election in 1978, Ieremia Tabai, Leader of the Opposition in the previous House, was elected Chief Minister. On 12 July 1979 the Gilbert Islands became an independent republic within the Commonwealth, under the name of Kiribati. The House of Assembly was renamed the Maneaba ni Maungatabu, and Ieremia Tabai became the country's first President (Beretitenti). In September Kiribati signed a treaty of friendship with the USA, which relinquished its claim to the Line and Phoenix Islands, including Kanton and Enderbury. Kiribati did not become a member of the UN until September 1999, although it had previously joined some of the organization's agencies.

In 1981 the Banaban community on Rabi accepted the British Government's earlier *ex gratia* offer of compensation, but they continued to seek self-government. The 1979 Constitution provided for the establishment of an independent commission of inquiry to review the political status of the Banabans three years after Kiribati had achieved independence, but the inquiry was not commissioned until 1985.

The first general election since independence took place in March–April 1982. The members of the new Maneaba all sat as independents. In accordance with the 1979 Constitution, the legislature nominated from among its members candidates for the country's first presidential election, to be held on the basis of direct popular vote. President Tabai was confirmed in office at the election in May. The Government resigned in December, after the Maneaba had twice rejected proposals to increase salaries for civil servants. The legislature was dissolved, and a general election took place in January 1983. The formation of the new Maneaba necessitated a further presidential election in February, at which Tabai was re-elected for a third term of office. He was returned to office in May 1987 (following a general election in March). The May 1991 legislative election was followed by a presidential election in July, at which the former Vice-President, Teatao Teannaki, narrowly defeated Roniti Teiwaki to replace Tabai, who had served the maximum number of presidential terms permitted by the Constitution.

In 1992 the Maneaba approved an opposition motion urging the Government to seek compensation from Japan for damage caused during the Second World War. The intention to seek compensation was reiterated by President Teburoro Tito (see below) in late 1994.

In May 1994 the Government was defeated on a motion of confidence, following opposition allegations that government ministers had misused travel allowances. The Maneaba was dissolved, and at legislative elections in July five cabinet ministers lost their seats. Of the newly elected members, 13 were supporters of the Maneaban Te Mauri, while only eight were known to support the previously dominant National Progressive Party grouping. At the presidential election in September Teburoro Tito, of the Maneaban Te Mauri, was elected, receiving 51.1% of the total votes. The new President declared that reducing Kiribati's dependence on foreign aid would be a major objective for his Government. He also announced his intention to pursue civil and criminal action against members of the previous administration for alleged misuse of public funds while in office.

In 1995 a committee was created with the aim of assessing public opinion regarding possible amendments to the Constitution. In March 1998 more than 200 delegates attended a Constitutional Review Convention in Bairiki to consider the recommendations of a report presented to the Government in 1996, which included equalizing the status of men and women regarding the citizenship rights of foreigners marrying I-Kiribati and changes to the structure of the Council of State. Leaders of the Banaban community in Rabi, Fiji, were also consulted during 1998 as part of the review process.

A general election, held on 23 September 1998 and contested by a record 191 candidates, failed to produce a conclusive result, necessitating a second round of voting one week later, at which the Government and opposition each lost seven seats. The new Maneaba convened in October, when it selected three presidential candidates. At a presidential election on 27 November Tito was re-elected with 52.3% of total votes cast, defeating Dr Harry Tong, who obtained 45.8% of votes, and Ambreroti Nikora, with 1.8%.

In mid-1999 John Kum Kee, a member of the Maneaba, was sentenced to four years' imprisonment, having been convicted of bribing a customs official and evasion of customs duty. Controversy continued in 1999 regarding the renamed Millennium Island (previously Caroline Island). The island had been renamed in 1997 in an attempt to promote it as a tourist destination for the year 2000. In 1994 Kiribati had moved the international date-line to incorporate the Line and Phoenix Islands groups (including Millennium Island) in the same time zone as the Gilbert group, thus creating a large eastward anomaly in the date-line. Millennium Island's position as the first place to celebrate the New Year, however, was subsequently confirmed. In early 2000, however, opposition politicians severely criticized the Government for failing to attract the predicted numbers of tourists to the islands' millennium celebrations, despite expenditure of more than $A1m. Meanwhile, in April 1999 the Kiribati Government reiterated its desire to acquire Baker, Howland and Jarvis Islands (see US External Territories—Other Territories) from the USA, citing the potential economic value of their fishing resources.

In late 1999 concerns were expressed by a Pacific media organization after a New Zealand journalist working for Agence France-Presse was banned from entering Kiribati. The Kiribati Government claimed that a series of articles by the correspondent, unfavourable to Kiribati, which had been published in a regional magazine, were biased and sensationalist. In December former President Ieremia Tabai and a former member of the Maneaba, Atiera Tetoa, were fined, having been convicted of importing telecommunications equipment without a permit. They had launched Newair FM, an independent commercial radio station, 12 months previously; it had been immediately suspended and a criminal investigation was instigated by the police. Tabai subsequently established Kiribati's first private newspaper, the *Kiribati Newstar*, in an attempt to reduce the Government's control over the media in the islands. Its first published edition coincided with Media Freedom Week in May 2000.

In November 2000 the Vice-President and Minister for Home Affairs and Rural Development, Tewarika Tentoa, collapsed while addressing the Maneaba and died. The post of Vice-President was subsequently combined with the cabinet portfolio of finance and economic planning.

In mid-October 2002 Tito's administration suffered a rare defeat when a government bill aimed at amending the Constitution was rejected, after failing to gain the two-thirds support necessary. The proposed legislation, which received 20 parliamentary votes in favour and 13 against, included measures to replace the Chief Justice with the Attorney-General on the Council of State and amendments to the number of members of Parliament from each island. Opposition members criticized the proposals, which they claimed would favour the Government in the forthcoming general election.

Campaigning for the general election during November 2002 was characterized by numerous allegations of improper conduct. Observers noted that officials from the Chinese embassy in Tarawa, accompanied by government candidates, had been donating gifts to the local community in the weeks preceding the election. (The Government had recently amended the Elections Act to allow gifts to be distributed to the public by candidates during their electoral campaigns, a practice that had been banned hitherto.) The opposition, which had stated its intention to close the Chinese satellite-tracking station (based on South Tarawa—see below) if elected, claimed that this action constituted a clear attempt to influence voters. Moreover, under a newly amended Newspaper Registration Act, Tito ordered police to seize opposition election pamphlets in November. Further allegations that the Government was attempting to stifle

freedom of expression were made by former President Iremia Tabai, whose private radio station was finally granted a licence to broadcast in December, following delays totalling almost four years in issuing the permit.

A total of 176 candidates contested the general election on 29 November 2002. The Government suffered significant losses with 14 of its members (including seven ministers) failing to retain their seats. The presidential election was postponed from its original date and finally took place on 25 February 2003. At the poll Tito received 14,160 votes, while the opposition candidate Taberannang Timeon secured 13,613. Tito was sworn in for his third term as President on 28 February and many of his former opponents in the legislature were expected to cross the floor to support him. However, in late March Tito was narrowly defeated on a motion of 'no confidence' and his Government was replaced by an interim administration, the Council of State (comprising the Speaker, the Chief Justice and the Public Service Commissioner). In accordance with the Constitution, another general election took place on 9 and 14 May, at which supporters of Tito secured a majority of seats. A presidential election took place in early July at which the opposition candidate, Anote Tong, narrowly defeated his brother, Harry Tong. Anote Tong's electoral campaign, which had focused on his pledge to review the lease of the Chinese satellite-tracking station on South Tarawa, had been characterized by a series of personal attacks on his brother.

In early November 2003 President Anote Tong announced the establishment of diplomatic relations with Taiwan. The Government's decision to switch its allegiance from the People's Republic of China to Taiwan caused considerable controversy within Kiribati and the region. Several hundred people staged a protest in Tarawa against the Government's decision, claiming that it had been made in return for Taiwanese funding of Anote Tong's electoral campaign. The President strongly refuted this allegation, but did, however, state that Taiwan had offered extensive development funds to Kiribati for adopting its position. By late November it was reported that Chinese technicians were dismantling the satellite-tracking station, which had played an important role in China's recent first manned space flight. The Chinese embassy, however, remained open while China requested that Kiribati reconsider its decision. Despite its efforts, which, according to many commentators, were motivated largely by the islands' strategic importance to China, in late November that country suspended diplomatic relations with Kiribati. In the same week the police in Kiribati announced the launch of an investigation into the death threats received by President Tong, believed to be from a Chinese source. A Taiwanese embassy was opened in Tarawa in January 2004.

As a result of discussions held at the Pacific Islands Forum summit meeting in Kiribati in October 2000, Japan announced that it was willing to negotiate compensation claims with the islanders for damage caused during the Second World War. Furthermore, a six-day visit by President Tito to Japan in February 2001 resulted in a number of informal agreements aimed at enhancing relations between the two countries. These included a decision to try to resolve a dispute over tuna fishing, caused by Japan's refusal to sign a convention aimed at protecting tuna stocks in the central and western Pacific Ocean and agreements to address their differences over whaling and nuclear-fuel shipments. Tito also appeared to modify his position on nuclear energy following the visit to Japan, stating that emissions of harmful 'greenhouse gases' could be reduced by replacing fossil with nuclear fuel.

In September 1995 Kiribati severed relations with France, in protest at the French Government's decision to renew nuclear-weapons testing at Mururoa Atoll in French Polynesia.

Reports that Palmyra Atoll (a privately owned uninhabited US territory some 200 km north of Kiribati's northern Line Islands) was to be sold and used by a US company for the storage of nuclear waste prompted a unanimous resolution of the Maneaba, in May 1996, urging the Government to convey to the US Government the islanders' concerns over the proposals. The islanders' anxieties centred largely on Palmyra's proximity to Kiribati, coupled with the belief that the atoll's fragility and porous structure make it an unstable environment for the storage of highly toxic materials. In November 2000, however, Palmyra was purchased by The Nature Conservancy, a conservation group that planned to preserve the natural state of the atoll.

Owing to the high rate of population growth within the territory (about 2% per year) and, in particular, the situation of over-population on South Tarawa and its associated social and economic problems, it was announced in 1988 that nearly 5,000 inhabitants were to be resettled on outlying atolls, mainly in the Line Islands. A further programme of resettlement from South Tarawa to five islands in the Phoenix group was initiated in 1995.

A Chinese satellite-tracking station was opened on South Tarawa in late 1997 but was dismantled in late 2003 following the suspension of diplomatic relations between the two countries (see above). Sea Launch, an international consortium led by the US Boeing Commercial Space Company, also announced plans to undertake a rocket-launching project from a converted oil-rig near the islands. A prototype satellite was launched in March 1999, and commercial operations began in late 1999. Kiribati, which, together with the South Pacific Regional Environmental Programme (SPREP, see p. 368), had expressed concerns regarding the potential negative environmental impact of the site, was not expected to benefit financially from the project, as the consortium had sought to carry out its activities in international waters near the outer limits of the islands' exclusive economic zone. The US authorities dismissed environmental concerns about the negative impact of the site (particularly the dumping of large quantities of waste fuel in the islands' waters), which were expressed by both the Government of Kiribati and SPREP in 1998. These fears were compounded in March 2000 after a rocket launched from the site crashed, and, furthermore, Sea Launch refused to disclose where it had landed. In November 1999 it was announced that the Government of Kiribati and the National Space Development Agency of Japan had reached agreement on the proposed establishment of a space-vehicle launching and landing facility on Kiritimati. In the following year the Japanese organization was also given permission by the Kiribati Government to use land and runway facilities on the island, free of charge, until 2020 and to construct a 100–150-room hotel.

In 1989 a UN report on the 'greenhouse effect' (the heating of the earth's atmosphere, and a resultant rise in sea-level as a result of pollution) listed Kiribati as one of the countries that would completely disappear beneath the sea in the 21st century, unless drastic action were taken. None of the land on the islands is more than two metres above sea-level, making the country extremely vulnerable to the effects of climate change. A rise in sea-level would not only cause flooding, but would also upset the balance between sea and fresh water (below the coral sands), rendering water supplies undrinkable. In late 1997 President Tito strongly criticized the Australian Government's refusal, at the Conference of the Parties to the Framework Convention on Climate Change (under the auspices of the UN Environment Programme, see p. 53) in Kyoto, Japan, to reduce its emission of gases known to contribute to the 'greenhouse effect'. In mid-1999 it was announced that two of Kiribati's uninhabited coral reefs had been submerged as a result of the 'greenhouse effect'. Meanwhile, a state of emergency was declared in early 1999, owing to one of the worst droughts ever recorded in the islands. Concern among the islanders intensified in early 2001 when many of the causeways linking villages on Tarawa atoll were flooded by high tides. A report released by the World Bank in 2000 listed the flooding and loss of low-lying areas, more intense cyclones and droughts, the failure of subsistence crops and coastal fisheries, the death of coral reefs and the spread of mosquito-borne diseases such as malaria and dengue fever as consequences of the 'greenhouse effect' on Pacific island nations. In April 2001 the USA's decision to reject the Kyoto Protocol to the UN's Framework Convention on Climate Change was widely criticized. In March 2002 Kiribati, Tuvalu and the Maldives announced their decision to take legal action against the USA for its refusal to sign the Kyoto Protocol.

Government

Legislative power is vested in the unicameral Maneaba ni Maungatabu. It has 39 members elected by universal adult suffrage for four years (subject to dissolution), one nominated representative of the Banaban community and, if he is not an elected member, the Attorney-General as an *ex-officio* member. The Head of State is the Beretitenti (President), who is also Head of Government. The President is elected by direct popular vote. The President governs with the assistance of the Vice-President and Cabinet, whom he appoints from among members of the Maneaba. Executive authority is vested in the Cabinet, which is responsible to the Maneaba.

Economic Affairs

In 2002, according to estimates by the World Bank, Kiribati's gross national income (GNI), measured at average 2000–2002 prices, was US $77m., equivalent to US $810 per head. During 1990–2002, it was estimated, the population increased by an average of 2.3% per year, while gross domestic product (GDP) per head increased, in real terms, by an estimated average of 0.3% per year. Overall GDP, according to revised estimates by the Asian Development Bank (ADB), expanded, in real terms, by 1.8% in 2001, by 1.0% in 2002 and by 2.5% in 2003. The ADB forecast an increase of 1.8% in real GDP for 2004.

According to official figures, agriculture (including fishing), contributed an estimated 14.2% of monetary GDP in 2002. In 2002, according to FAO, agriculture engaged 26% of the economically active population. The principal cash crop is coconut, yielding copra—which accounted for an estimated 23.4% of domestic export earnings in 2000 (compared with 63.9% in the previous year). Construction of a new copra mill, near Betio port, began in March 2002. Bananas, screw-pine (*Pandanus*), breadfruit and papaya are cultivated as food crops. The cultivation of seaweed began on Tabuaeran in the mid-1980s: seaweed provided an estimated 15.9% of domestic export earnings in 2000. Pigs and chickens are kept. Fish provided only 1.8% of export earnings in 2000 (compared with 46.2% in 1990); however, pet fish are a significant export commodity, contributing 13.6% of export earnings in 1999 (although this figure declined to 1.9% in 2000). The sale of fishing licences to foreign fleets (notably from South Korea, Japan, the People's Republic of China, Taiwan and the USA) provides an important source of income: revenue from the sale of fishing licences reached a record $A52m. in 2001 but declined to $A32m. in 2002. The GDP of the agriculture, fishing and seaweed sectors increased at an average annual rate of 0.8% in 1991–2000. According to the ADB, agricultural GDP rose by 0.2% in 2001 but decreased by 4.5% in 2002.

Industry (including manufacturing, construction and power) contributed an estimated 10.9% of monetary GDP in 2002. Industrial GDP increased by an average of 0.5% per year in 1991–2000. Compared with the previous year, industrial GDP was estimated by the ADB to have expanded by 21.6% in 2001, but to have contracted by 7.8% in 2002.

Mining of phosphate rock on the island of Banaba, which ceased in 1979, formerly provided some 80% of export earnings. Interest from a phosphate reserve fund (the Revenue Equalization Reserve Fund—RERF), established in 1956, continues to be an important source of income (see below). The production of solar-evaporated salt for export to other islands of the Pacific (for use on fishing vessels with brine refrigeration systems) began on Kiritimati in 1985.

Manufacturing, which contributed an estimated 0.8% of monetary GDP in 2002, is confined to the small-scale production of coconut-based products, soap, foods, handicrafts, furniture, leather goods and garments. Manufacturing GDP increased by an annual average of 5.6% in 1991–2000. In 2002, compared with the previous year, the GDP of the manufacturing sector contracted by an estimated 3.0%, in contrast to the 18.6% increase recorded in 2001.

Production of electrical energy declined from 14.5m. kWh in 2000 to 12.5m. kWh in 2001. Mineral fuels accounted for an estimated 8.8% of total import costs in 2000. In August 2001 the European Union (EU) announced that it planned to fund the introduction of 1,500 new solar energy systems, valued at more than $A6m., to Kiribati. Moreover, in May 2003 the Government announced the completion of a Japanese-funded programme to construct a new power station, to install two new generating units and to upgrade 16 km of power lines. The project, which cost a total of US $11m. to implement, was expected to ensure a power supply sufficient to meet Kiribati's increasing demand.

Services provided 75.0% of monetary GDP in 2002. Tourism makes a significant contribution to the economy: the trade and hotels sector provided an estimated 16.6% of GDP in 2000. Tourist arrivals at Tarawa and Kiritimati rose from 3,112 in 1999 to 4,829 in 2000, in which year receipts from tourism reached $A2.2m. Arrivals for 2003 totalled 4,288. The GDP of the services sector increased at an annual average rate of 5.1% in 1991–2000. According to revised estimates from the ADB, the services sector's GDP decreased by 0.5% in 2001 but increased by 3.2% in 2002.

In 2001 Kiribati recorded a trade deficit of an estimated US $27.6m., and a surplus of US $1.7m. on the current account of the balance of payments. In that year Kiribati's trade deficit decreased to the equivalent of 58.5% of GDP, as a decline in income from copra exports was more than offset by a fall in imports. By 2003 the ADB estimated that the deficit on the current account was equivalent to 21.5% of GDP. In 2002 the principal sources of imports were France (29.1%), Australia (26.6%) and Fiji (12.7%). The principal recipients of exports in that year were Japan (55.9%) and Thailand (16.9%). The major imports in 2000 were food and live animals, machinery and transport equipment, manufactures, mineral fuels, beverages and tobacco, and chemicals. The major domestic exports were copra, seaweed and shark fins.

Budgetary expenditure for 2002, announced in December 2001, was projected at $A77.9m., 15% less than the revised estimates for 2001, and required a drawdown of $A16.7m. from the RERF. In 2002, according to the ADB, the government surplus increased to reach the equivalent of 21.4% of GDP, but a deficit of 12.9% of GDP was projected for 2003. In April 2003 the interim administration enacted a budget providing for expenditure of $A32m. over the next five months. Kiribati's total external debt was estimated by the ADB to have risen from US $8m. in 2001 to $14m. In 2002 In 2001 the cost of debt-servicing was equivalent to 7.9% of revenue from exports of goods and services. The annual rate of inflation averaged 3.1% in 1990–2000. Consumer prices increased by an annual average of 6.0% in 2001 and by 3.2% in 2002. About 2.8% of the labour force were unemployed in 1990. Only around 8,600 people, equivalent to less than 20% of the working-age population, were formally employed in 2001.

Kiribati is a member of the Pacific Community (see p. 323), the Pacific Islands Forum (see p. 325) and the Asian Development Bank (ADB, see p. 151); it is an associate member of the UN Economic and Social Commission for Asia and the Pacific (ESCAP, see p. 31), and is a signatory to the South Pacific Regional Trade and Economic Co-operation Agreement (SPARTECA, see p. 328) and to the Lomé Conventions and successor Cotonou Agreement (see p. 251) with the EU. The Council of Micronesian Government Executives, of which Kiribati was a founder member in 1996, aims to facilitate discussion of economic developments in the region and to examine possibilities for reducing the considerable cost of shipping essential goods between the islands.

According to UN criteria, Kiribati is one of the world's least-developed nations. The islands' vulnerability to adverse climatic conditions was illustrated in early 1999 when a state of national emergency was declared following a prolonged period of severe drought. Kiribati's extremely limited export base and dependence on imports of almost all essential commodities result in a permanent trade deficit, which in most years is only partially offset by revenue from fishing licence fees, interest earned on the RERF and remittances from I-Kiribati working overseas. The RERF usually provides the Government with investment income equivalent to around 33% of GDP per year. In 2001 the ADB estimated that the value of the RERF was such that Kiribati had sufficient foreign reserves to cover the costs of 10 years of imports. By the end of 2001 the value of the fund was put at US $329m. Although the value of the RERF had trebled within 10 years, the fund declined in value in 2001 as a result of the downturn in world stock markets (its assets being invested in offshore markets). By the end of 2003, however, international stocks had begun to recover. The country is reliant on foreign assistance for its development budget. Official development assistance declined from a total of US $20.9m. in 1999 to US $17.9m. in 2000. In 2003/04 Australia provided $A11.4m. in development assistance, with emphasis on the management of human resources, governance, health, education and improved customs procedures, within the framework of a new co-operation strategy. New Zealand provided $NZ3.14m. in bilateral aid for 2003/04. In early 2003 Kiribati established a non-government body to secure US $840,000 in EU funding under the Cotonou Agreement, which would be spent on projects over the next five years. Development finance was expected to be received from Taiwan following the establishment of diplomatic relations in late 2003. Dependence on external finance, however, is widely regarded as having left Kiribati vulnerable to foreign exploitation. Moreover, concern has been expressed that, although foreign companies specializing in advanced technology (particularly telecommunications and satellite systems) are seeking to establish operations in the islands, Kiribati will not benefit significantly from the major investment involved in such projects. In 2000 the Government generated some US $400,000 of revenue through the sale of I-Kiribati passports to investors in the islands. Further passport sales in 2001 were worth US $375,000 and, combined with sales of Kiribati Residential Permits, produced more than $A2.5m. in revenue. The Government's policy of subsidizing copra producers following a sharp fall in world prices of the commodity, however, had a negative impact on the economy; in 2001 these subsidies totalled $A2m. The economy recovered somewhat in 2001, largely as a result of a substantial increase in recurrent government expenditure, an improvement in copra production and the implementation of various development projects. Modest rates of economic growth were maintained in 2002–03. The Government's National Development Strategy for 2000–03 sought to reform the public sector and promote private-sector development. Investors have in the past been deterred by the country's weak banking system and shortage of investment opportunities. It was estimated in 2001 that around 75% of capital belonging to Kiribati's companies and private citizens was invested abroad. The new proposals were intended to encourage greater investment in the country's private sector, which would allow the creation of jobs and the broadening of the islands' narrow base of exports.

Education

Education is compulsory for nine years between the ages of six and 15 years, comprising six years of primary school and three years of junior secondary school, an initiative introduced in 1998. Students may then continue at secondary school for a further three years. Every atoll is provided with at least one primary and junior secondary school. An estimated 92% of children aged six to 12 receive primary education. The Government administers a technical college and training colleges for teachers, nurses and seamen (the last, the Marine Training Centre, trains about 200 seamen each year for employment by overseas shipping companies). An extra-mural centre of the University of the South Pacific (based in Fiji) is located on South Tarawa. In 2000 the Government allocated $A12.8m. (equivalent to 19.9% of total budgetary expenditure) to expenditure.

Public Holidays

2004: 1 January (New Year), 9–12 April (Easter), 18 May (National Health Day), 11 July (National Church Day), 12–16 July (National Day Celebrations), 3 August (Youth Day), 10 December (Human Rights and Peace Day), 25–26 December (Christmas).

2005: 1 January (New Year), 25–28 March (Easter), 18 May (National Health Day), 11 July (National Church Day), 12–16 July (National Day Celebrations), 3 August (Youth Day), 10 December (Human Rights and Peace Day), 25–26 December (Christmas).

Statistical Survey

Source (unless otherwise stated): Statistics Office, Ministry of Finance and Economic Planning, POB 67, Bairiki, Tarawa; tel. 21082; fax 21307.

AREA AND POPULATION

Area: 810.5 sq km (312.9 sq miles). *Principal Atolls* (sq km): Banaba (island) 6.29 Tarawa 31.02 (North 15.26, South 15.76); Abemama 27.37; Tabiteuea 37.63 (North 25.78, South 11.85); Total Gilbert group (incl. others) 285.52; Kanton (Phoenix Is) 9.15; Teraina (Fanning) 33.73; Kiritimati (Christmas—Line Is) 388.39.

Population: 77,658 at census of 7 November 1995; 84,494 (males 41,646, females 42,848) at census of 7 November 2000; 87,400 (estimate) at mid-2002. *Principal Atolls* (2000): Banaba (island) 276; Abaiang 5,794; Tarawa 41,194 (North 4,477, South—including Bairiki, the capital—36,717); Tabiteuea 4,582 (North 3,365, South 1,217); Total Gilbert group (incl. others) 78,158; Kanton (Phoenix Is) 61; Kiritimati 3,431; Total Line and Phoenix Is (incl. others) 6,336.

Density (November 2000): 104.2 per sq km.

Ethnic Groups (census of 2000): Micronesians 83,452; Polynesians 641; Europeans 154; Others 247; Total 84,494.

Principal Towns: (population in '000, 1990): Bairiki (capital) 18.1; Bikenibeu 5.1; Taburao 3.5; Butaritari 3.2. Source: Stefan Helders, *World Gazetteer* (internet www.world-gazetteer.com).

Births, Marriages and Deaths: Registered live births (1996) 2,299 (birth rate 29.5 per 1,000); Marriages (registrations, 1988) 352 (marriage rate 5.2 per 1,000); Death rate (estimate, 1995) 7 per 1,000.

Expectation of Life (WHO estimates, years at birth): 64.1 (males 61.8; females 66.7) in 2002. Source: WHO, *World Health Report*.

Employment (paid employees, 1995, provisional): Agriculture, hunting, forestry and fishing 487; Manufacturing 104; Electricity, gas and water 182; Construction 215; Trade, restaurants and hotels 1,026; Transport, storage and communications 710; Financing, insurance real estate and business services 349; Community, social and personal services 4,778; *Total employed* 7,848. Source: UN, *Statistical Yearbook for Asia and the Pacific*.

HEALTH AND WELFARE

Key Indicators

Total Fertility Rate (children per woman, 2002): 4.1.

Under-5 Mortality Rate (per 1,000 live births, 2001): 69.

Physicians (per 1,000 head, 1998): 0.30.

Hospital Beds (per 1,000 head, 1990): 4.27.

Health Expenditure (2001): US $ per head (PPP): 143.

Health Expenditure (2001): % of GDP: 8.6.

Health Expenditure (2001): public (% of total): 98.8.

Access to Water (% of persons, 2000): 47.

Access to Sanitation (% of persons, 2000): 48.
For sources and definitions, see explanatory note on p. vi.

AGRICULTURE, ETC.

Principal Crops (FAO estimates, '000 metric tons, 2002): Taro (Coco yam) 1.7; Other roots and tubers 7.2; Coconuts 96; Vegetables 5.6; Bananas 4.6; Other fruits 1.2.

Livestock (FAO estimates, '000 head, year ending September 2002): Pigs 12; Chickens 450. Source: FAO.

Livestock Products (FAO estimates, metric tons, 2002): Pig meat 892; Poultry meat 450; Hen eggs 230. Source: FAO.

Fishing ('000 metric tons, live weight, 2001): Capture 32.4 (Snappers 2.8, Flyingfishes 1.6, Jacks and crevalles 2.9, Skipjack tuna 3.3, Emperors 3.9, Clupeoids 2.1, Marine molluscs 3.3); Aquaculture 0.0; Total catch 32.4. Figures exclude aquatic plants ('000 metric tons): 1.2 (all aquaculture). Source: FAO, *Yearbook of Fishery Statistics*.

INDUSTRY

Copra Production (metric tons): 5,853 in 2000; 6,741 in 2001; 5,903 in 2002.

Electric Energy (million kWh): 12.86 in 1999; 14.48 in 2000; 12.46 in 2001.
Source: Asian Development Bank, *Key Indicators of Developing Asian and Pacific Countries*.

FINANCE

Currency and Exchange Rates: Australian currency: 100 cents = 1 Australian dollar ($A). *Sterling, US Dollar and Euro Equivalents* (31 December 2003): £1 sterling = $A2.3796; US $1 = $A1.3333; €1 = $A1.6840; $A100 = £42.02 = US $75.00 = €59.38. *Average Exchange Rate* (US $ per Australian dollar): 1.9334 in 2001; 1.8406 in 2002; 1.5419 in 2003.

Budget ($A million, 2000): *Revenue*: Tax revenue 18.7 (Corporate tax 4.7, Import duties 13.9); Other current revenue 42.6 (Fishing licence fees 31.2, Fees and incidental sales 5.8); Capital revenue 0.0; Total 61.3. *Expenditure*: General public services 7.0; Public order and safety 4.7; Education 12.8; Health 8.8; Welfare and environment 1.1; Community amenities 1.5; Agriculture and fishing 2.3; Construction 1.9; Communication 1.7; Commerce 0.7; Labour affairs 1.7; Others 20.0; Total 64.3 (Current 53.9, Capital 10.4).

Cost of Living (Consumer Price Index for Tarawa; base: 1996 = 100): 107.9 in 2000; 114.3 in 2001; 118.0 in 2002.

Expenditure on the Gross Domestic Product ($A '000 at current prices, 1992): Government final consumption expenditure 25,039; Private final consumption expenditure 31,592; Increase in stocks 250; Gross fixed capital formation 25,750; *Total domestic expenditure* 82,631; Exports of goods and services 5,798; *Less* Imports of goods and services 52,625; Statistical discrepancy 10,456; *GDP in purchasers' values* 46,260. Source: UN, *Statistical Yearbook for Asia and the Pacific*.

Gross Domestic Product by Economic Activity ($A '000 at current factor cost, 2002): Agriculture (incl. fishing) 11,605; Manufacturing 695; Electricity, gas and water 1,000; Construction 7,224; Trade, hotels and bars 11,632; Transport and communications 9,834; Finance (incl. imputed bank charges) 680; Public administration 34,640; Others (incl. owner-occupied dwelling) 4,680; *Subtotal* 81,990; Indirect taxes, *less* subsidies 16,223; *GDP in market prices* 98,213. Source: Asian Development Bank, *Key Indicators of Developing Asian and Pacific Countries* .

Balance of Payments (estimates, US $ million, 2001): *Trade balance* −27.6; Exports of services and income 39.3; Imports of services and income −21.5; *Balance on goods, services and income* −9.8; Current transfers received 13.0; Current transfers paid −1.4; *Current balance* 1.7; *Capital account* (net) 3.6; *Direct investment* (net) −0.5; *Portfolio investment* −5.7; *Overall balance* −0.9. Source: Asian Development Bank, *Key Indicators of Developing Asian and Pacific Countries*.

EXTERNAL TRADE

Principal Commodities (estimates, $A million, 2000): *Imports f.o.b.*: Food and live animals 19.5; Beverages and tobacco 4.6; Mineral fuels, lubricants, etc. 6.0; Chemicals 3.1; Basic manufactures 11.1; Machinery and transport equipment 15.9; Miscellaneous manufactured articles 5.4; Total (incl. others) 67.9. *Exports f.o.b.*: Copra 2.5; Seaweed 1.7; Pet fish 0.2; Shark fins 0.4; Total (incl. others) 10.7 .

Principal Trading Partners (US $ million, 2002): *Imports*: Australia 23.2; Fiji 11.0; France 25.3; Japan 8.3; Latvia 4.8; New Zealand 3.1; Poland 10.8; USA 4.1; Total (incl. others) 87.2. *Exports* (incl. re-exports): Bangladesh 0.9; Japan 18.8; Korea, Republic 4.5; Thailand 5.7; USA 1.2; Total (incl. others) 33.5. Source: Asian Development Bank, *Key Indicators of Developing Asian and Pacific Countries*.

TRANSPORT

Road Traffic (motor vehicles registered on South Tarawa, 2000): Motor cycles 702; Passenger cars 477; Buses 10; Trucks 267; Minibuses 392; Others 13; Total 1,861.

Shipping: *Merchant Fleet* (registered, at 31 December 2002): 8 vessels; total displacement 4,198 grt. (Source: Lloyd's Register-Fairplay, *World Fleet Statistics*). *International Sea-borne Freight Traffic* ('000 metric tons, 1990): Goods loaded 15; Goods unloaded 26 (Source: UN, *Monthly Bulletin of Statistics*).

Civil Aviation (traffic on scheduled services, 1998): Passengers carried 28,000; Passenger-km 11 million; Total ton-km 2 million. Source: UN, *Statistical Yearbook*.

TOURISM

Foreign Tourist Arrivals (at Tarawa and Kiritimati): 4,842 in 2001; 4,831 in 2002; 4,288 in 2003.

Tourism Receipts ($A million): 2.0 in 1998; 2.1 in 1999; 2.2 in 2000.

COMMUNICATIONS MEDIA

Radio Receivers (1997): 17,000 in use.

Television Receivers (1997): 1,000 in use.

Telephones (main lines in use, 2001): 3,600.

Facsimile Machines (1996): 200 in use.

Mobile Cellular Telephones (subscribers, 2001): 500.

Personal Computers ('000 in use, 2001): 2.

Internet Users ('000, 2001): 2.

Non-daily Newspapers (2002): 2; estimated combined circulation 3,600.
Sources: UNESCO, *Statistical Yearbook*; UN, *Statistical Yearbook*; International Telecommunication Union; Australian Press Council.

EDUCATION

Primary (2001): 88 schools; 16,096 students; 627 teachers.

Junior Secondary (2001): 19 schools; 5,743 students; 324 teachers.

Secondary (2001): 14 schools; 5,743 students; 324 teachers.

Teacher-training (2001): 198 students; 22 teachers.

Vocational (2001): 1,303 students; 17 teachers.

Adult Literacy Rate (UNESCO estimates): 92.5% (males 93%; females 92%) in 2001. Source: UNESCO, *Assessment of Resources, Best Practices and Gaps in Gender, Science and Technology in Kiribati*.

Directory

The Constitution

A new Constitution was promulgated at independence on 12 July 1979. The main provisions are as follows:

The Constitution states that Kiribati is a sovereign democratic Republic and that the Constitution is the supreme law. It guarantees protection of all fundamental rights and freedoms of the individual and provides for the determination of citizenship.

The President, known as the Beretitenti, is Head of State and Head of the Government and presides over the Cabinet which consists of the Beretitenti, the Kauoman-ni-Beretitenti (Vice-President), the Attorney-General and not more than eight other ministers appointed by the Beretitenti from an elected parliament known as the Maneaba ni Maungatabu. The Constitution provided that the pre-independence Chief Minister became the first Beretitenti, but that in future the Beretitenti would be elected. After each general election for the Maneaba, the chamber nominates, from among its members, three or four candidates from whom the Beretitenti is elected by universal adult suffrage. Executive authority is vested in the Cabinet, which is directly responsible to the Maneaba ni Maungatabu. The Constitution also provides for a Council of State consisting of the Chairman of the Public Services Commission, the Chief Justice and the Speaker of the Maneaba.

Legislative power resides with the single-chamber Maneaba ni Maungatabu, composed of 40 members elected by universal adult suffrage for four years (subject to dissolution), one nominated member (see below) and the Attorney-General as an *ex-officio* member if he is not elected. The Maneaba is presided over by the Speaker, who is elected by the Maneaba from among persons who are not members of the Maneaba.

One chapter makes special provision for Banaba and the Banabans, stating that one seat in the Maneaba is reserved for a nominated member of the Banaban community. The Banabans' inalienable right to enter and reside in Banaba is guaranteed and, where any right over or interest in land there has been acquired by the Republic of Kiribati or by the Crown before independence, the Republic is required to hand back the land on completion of phosphate extraction. A Banaba Island Council is provided for, as is an independent commission of inquiry to review the provisions relating to Banaba.

The Constitution also makes provision for finance, for a Public Service and for an independent judiciary (see Judicial System).

The Government

HEAD OF STATE

President (Beretitenti): ANOTE TONG (elected 4 July 2003).

Vice-President (Kauoman-ni-Beretitenti): TEIMA ONORIO.

THE CABINET
(April 2004)

President and Minister for Foreign Affairs: ANOTE TONG.

Vice-President and Minister for Education, Youth and Sport Development: TEIMA ONORIO.

Minister for Commerce, Industry and Co-operatives: IOTEBA REDFERN.

Minister for Communications, Transport and Tourism Development: NAATAN TEEWE.

Minister for Environment, Lands and Agricultural Development: MARTIN TOFINGA.

Minister for Finance and Economic Development: NABUTI MWEMWENIKARAWA.

Minister for Health and Medical Services: NATANERA KIRATA.

Minister for Human Resources Development: BAURO TONGAAI.

Minister for Internal Affairs and Social Development: AMBEROTI NIKORA.

Minister for the Line and Phoenix Islands: TAWITA TEMOKU.

Minister for Natural Resources Development: TETABO NAKARA.

Minister for Public Works and Utilities: JAMES TAOM.

MINISTRIES

Office of the President (Beretitenti): POB 68, Bairiki, Tarawa; tel. 21183; fax 21145.

Ministry of Commerce, Industry and Co-operatives: POB 510, Betio, Tarawa; tel. 26158/26157; fax 26233; e-mail commerce@tskl.net.ki.

Ministry of Communications, Transport and Tourism Development: POB 487, Betio, Tarawa; tel. 26003/26435; fax 26193.

Ministry of Education, Youth and Sport Development: POB 263, Bikenibeu, Tarawa; tel. 28091/28033; fax 28222.

Ministry of the Environment, Lands and Agricultural Development: POB 234, Bikenibeu, Tarawa; tel. 28211/28071; fax 28334.

Ministry of Finance and Economic Development: POB 67, Bairiki, Tarawa; tel. 21802/21805; fax 21307.

Ministry of Foreign Affairs: POB 68, Bairiki, Tarawa; tel. 21342; fax 21466; e-mail mfa@tskl.net.ki.

Ministry of Health and Medical Services: POB 268, Bikenibeu, Tarawa; tel. 28100; fax 28152.

Ministry of Human Resources and Development: POB 69, Bairiki, Tarawa; tel. 21068/21071; fax 21452.

Ministry of Internal Affairs and Social Development: POB 75, Bairiki, Tarawa; tel. 21092; fax 21133; e-mail homeaffairs@tskl.net.ki.

Ministry of Line and Phoenix Islands: Kiritimati Island; tel. 21449/81213; fax 81278.

Ministry of Natural Resources Development: POB 64, Bairiki, Tarawa; tel. 21099; fax 21120.

Ministry of Public Works and Utilities: POB 498, Betio, Tarawa; tel. 26192; fax 26172.

President and Legislature

PRESIDENT

Election, 4 July 2003

Candidate	Votes
Anote Tong	13,556
Harry Tong	12,457

A third candidate, Banuera Berina, secured a small number of votes in the election.

MANEABA NI MAUNGATABU
(House of Assembly)

This is a unicameral body comprising 40 elected members (most of whom formally present themselves for election as independent candidates), and one nominated representative of the Banaban community. A general election was held on 29 November 2002. However, in late March 2003, following its defeat on a motion of 'no confidence', the Government was replaced by an interim authority. A further general election was held on 9 and 14 May 2003, at which supporters of former President Teburoro Tito secured a majority of seats.

Speaker: TAOMATI IUTA.

Political Organizations

There are no organized political parties in Kiribati. However, loose groupings of individuals supporting similar policies do exist, the most prominent being the Maneaban Te Mauri (Protect the Maneaba), led by Teburoro Tito, the National Progressive Party, led by Teatao Teannaki, the Liberal Party, led by Tewareka Tentoa, and the Boutokan Te Koaua (Pillars of Truth), led by Dr Harry Tong.

Diplomatic Representation

EMBASSY AND HIGH COMMISSIONS IN KIRIBATI

Australia: POB 77, Bairiki, Tarawa; tel. 21184; fax 21904; e-mail AHC_Tarawa@dfat.gov.au; High Commissioner JUREK JUSZCZYK.

China (Taiwan): Bairiki, Tarawa; Ambassador SAMUEL CHEN.

New Zealand: POB 53, Bairiki, Tarawa; tel. 21400; fax 21402; e-mail nzhc.tar@mfat.govt.nz; High Commissioner JOHN GOODMAN.

United Kingdom: POB 5, Bairiki, Tarawa; tel. 22501; fax 22505; e-mail ukrep@tskl.net.ki; internet www.ukinthepacific.bhc.org.fj; High Commissioner CHARLES F. MOCHAN (resident in Suva, Fiji).

Judicial System

There are 24 Magistrates' Courts (each consisting of one presiding magistrate and up to eight other magistrates) hearing civil, criminal and land cases. When hearing civil or criminal cases, the presiding magistrate sits with two other magistrates, and when hearing land cases with four other magistrates. A single magistrate has national jurisdiction in civil and criminal matters. Appeal from the Magistrates' Courts lies, in civil and criminal matters, to a single judge of the High Court, and, in matters concerning land, divorce and inheritance, to the High Court's Land Division, which consists of a judge and two Land Appeal Magistrates.

The High Court of Kiribati is a superior court of record and has unlimited jurisdiction. It consists of the Chief Justice and a Puisne Judge. Appeal from a single judge of the High Court, both as a Court of the First Instance and in its appellate capacity, lies to the Kiribati Court of Appeal, which is also a court of record and consists of a panel of three judges.

All judicial appointments are made by the Beretitenti (President).

High Court

POB 501, Betio, Tarawa; tel. 26007; fax 26149; e-mail highcourt@tskl.net.ki.

Chief Justice: ROBIN MILLHOUSE.

Judges of the Kiribati Court of Appeal: ROBIN MILLHOUSE (President), Sir MAURICE CASEY, Sir MICHAEL HARDIE-BOYS, Sir DAVID TOMPKINS, PETER PENLINGTON.

Religion

CHRISTIANITY

Most of the population are Christians: 53.4% Roman Catholic and 39.2% members of the Kiribati Protestant Church, according to the 1990 census.

The Roman Catholic Church

Kiribati forms part of the diocese of Tarawa and Nauru, suffragan to the archdiocese of Suva (Fiji). At 31 December 2002 the diocese contained an estimated 48,908 adherents. The Bishop participates in the Catholic Bishops' Conference of the Pacific, based in Suva (Fiji).

Bishop of Tarawa and Nauru: Most Rev. PAUL EUSEBIUS MEA KAIUEA, Bishop's House, POB 79, Bairiki, Tarawa; fax 21401; e-mail cathchurch@tskl.net.ki.

The Anglican Communion

Kiribati is within the diocese of Polynesia, part of the Anglican Church in Aotearoa, New Zealand and Polynesia. The Bishop in Polynesia is resident in Fiji.

Protestant Church

Kiribati Protestant Church: POB 80, Bairiki, Tarawa; tel. 21195; fax 21453; f. 1988; Moderator Rev. BAITEKE NABETARI; Gen. Sec. Rev. TIAONTIN ARUE; 29,432 mems in 1998.

Other Churches

Seventh-day Adventist, Church of God and Assembly of God communities are also represented, as is the Church of Jesus Christ of Latter-day Saints (Mormon).

BAHÁ'Í FAITH

National Spiritual Assembly: POB 269, Bikenibeu, Tarawa; tel. and fax 28074; e-mail emi@tskl.net.ki; 2,400 mems resident in 100 localities in 1995.

The Press

Butim'aea Manin te Euangkerio: POB 80, Bairiki, Tarawa; tel. 21195; e-mail kpc@tskl.net.ki; f. 1913; Protestant Church newspaper; weekly; a monthly publication Te Kaotan te Ota is also produced; Editor Rev. TOOM TOAKAI.

Kiribati Business Link: Bairiki, Tarawa; English.

Kiribati Newstar: POB 10, Bairiki, Tarawa; tel. 21652; fax 21671; e-mail newstar@tskl.net.ki; internet www.users.bigpond.com/kiribati_newstar; f. 2000; independent; weekly; English and I-Kiribati; Editor-in-Chief NGAUEA UATIOA.

Te Itoi ni Kiribati: POB 231, Bikenibeu, Tarawa; tel. 28138; fax 21341; f. 1914; Roman Catholic Church newsletter; monthly; circ. 2,300.

Te Uekera: Broadcasting and Publications Authority, POB 78, Bairiki, Tarawa; tel. 21162; fax 21096; f. 1945; weekly; English and I-Kiribati; Editor TIBWERE BOBO; circ. 5,000.

Broadcasting and Communications

TELECOMMUNICATIONS

Telecom Kiribati Ltd: Bairiki, Tarawa; Gen. Man. ENOTA INGINTAU.

Telecom Services Kiribati Ltd: POB 72, Bairiki, Tarawa; tel. 21446; fax 21424; e-mail ceo@tskl.net.ki; internet www.tski.net.ki; owned by Govt of Kiribati; Gen. Man. STUART EASTWARD; CEO CLIFF MACALPINE.

BROADCASTING

Regulatory Authority

Broadcasting and Publications Authority: POB 78, Bairiki, Tarawa; tel. 21187; fax 21096.

Radio

Radio Kiribati: Broadcasting and Publications Authority, POB 78, Bairiki, Tarawa; tel. 21187; fax 21096; f. 1954; statutory body; station Radio Kiribati broadcasting on SW and MW transmitters; programmes in I-Kiribati (90%) and English (10%); some advertising; Man. BILL REIHER.

Television

Television Kiribati: Broadcasting and Publications Authority, POB 78, Bairiki, Tarawa; tel. 21187; fax 21096; in process of establishing services.

Finance

(cap. = capital; dep. = deposits; res = reserves)

BANKING

The Bank of Kiribati Ltd: POB 66, Bairiki, Tarawa; tel. 21095; fax 21200; e-mail bankofkiribati@tskl.net.ki; f. 1984; 75% owned by ANZ Bank, 25% by Govt of Kiribati; dep. $A42.8m., res $A1.3m., total assets $A46.3m. (Sept. 1999); Chair. ALAN WALTER; Gen. Man. BOB COWLEY; 3 brs.

Development Bank of Kiribati: POB 33, Bairiki, Tarawa; tel. 21345; fax 21297; e-mail dbk@tskl.net.ki; f. 1986; took over the assets of the National Loans Board; identifies, promotes and finances small-scale projects; auth. cap. $A2m.; Gen. Man. KIETAU TABWEBWEITI; 5 brs.

A network of lending entities known as 'village banks' operates throughout the islands, as do a number of credit unions under the management of the Credit Union League. In August 1995 there were 26 credit unions operating in Tarawa and seven in the outer islands with a total membership of 1,808 people.

INSURANCE

Kiribati Insurance Corpn: POB 38, Bairiki, Tarawa; tel. 21260; fax 21426; e-mail kirins@tskl.net.ki; f. 1981; govt-owned; only insurance co; reinsures overseas; Gen. Man. TEAIRO TOOMA.

Trade and Industry

GOVERNMENT AGENCIES

Kiribati Housing Corporation: Bairiki, Tarawa; tel. 21092; operates the Housing Loan and Advice Centre; Chair. TOKOREAUA KAIRORO.

Kiribati Provident Fund: POB 76, Bairiki, Tarawa; tel. 21300; fax 21186; f. 1977; total equity $A56.8m. (Dec. 1998); Gen. Man. TOKAATA NIATA.

CHAMBER OF COMMERCE

Kiribati Chamber of Commerce: POB 550, Betio, Tarawa; tel. 26351; fax 26351; Pres. WAYSANG KUM KEE; Sec.-Gen. TIARITE KWONG.

UTILITIES

Public Utilities Board: POB 443, Betio, Tarawa; tel. 26292; fax 26106; e-mail pub@tskl.net.ki; f. 1977; govt-owned; provides electricity, water and sewerage services in Tarawa; CEO TOKIA GREIG.

Solar Energy Company: Tarawa; e-mail sec@tskl.net.ki; a co-operative administering and implementing solar-generated electricity projects in North Tarawa and the outer islands.

CO-OPERATIVE SOCIETIES

Co-operative societies dominate trading in Tarawa and enjoy a virtual monopoly outside the capital, except for Banaba and Kiritimati.

The Kiribati Copra Co-operative Society Ltd: POB 489, Betio, Tarawa; tel. 26534; fax 26391; f. 1976; the sole exporter of copra; seven cttee mems; 29 mem. socs; Chair. RAIMON TAAKE; CEO RUTIANO BENETITO.

Bobotin Kiribati Ltd: POB 485, Betio, Tarawa; tel. 26092; fax 26224; replaced Kiribati Co-operative Wholesale Society; govt-owned; Gen. Man. AKAU TIARE.

TRADE UNIONS

Kiribati Trades Union Congress (KTUC): POB 502, Betio, Tarawa; tel. 26277; fax 26257; f. 1982; unions and asscns affiliated to the KTUC include the Fishermen's Union, the Co-operative Workers' Union, the Seamen's Union, the Teachers' Union, the Nurses' Asscn, the Public Employees' Asscn, the Bankers' Union, Butaritari Rural Workers' Union, Christmas Island Union of Federated Workers, the Pre-School Teachers' Asscn, Makim Island Rural Workers' Org., Nanolelei Retailers' Union, the Plantation Workers' Union of Fanning Island and the Overseas Fishermen's Union (formed in 1998); 2,500 mems; Pres. TATOA KAITEIE; Gen. Sec. TAMARETI TAAU.

Transport

ROADS

Wherever practicable, roads are built on all atolls, and connecting causeways between islets are also being built as funds and labour permit. A programme to construct causeways between North and South Tarawa was completed in the mid-1990s. Kiribati has about 670 km of roads that are suitable for motor vehicles; all-weather roads exist in Tarawa and Kiritimati. In 2000 there were about 1,468 motor vehicles registered in the islands, of which some 48% were motorcycles.

SHIPPING

A major project to rehabilitate the port terminal and facilities at Betio, with finance totalling some US $22m. from Japan, was completed in May 2000. There are other port facilities at Banaba, Kanton and English Harbour.

Kiribati Shipping Services Ltd: POB 495, Betio, Tarawa; tel. 26195; fax 26204; e-mail kssl@tskl.net.ki; operates three passenger/freight vessels on inter-island services and one landing craft; govt-owned; Gen. Man. Capt. ITIBWINNANG AIAIMOA.

MATS Shipping and Transport: POB 413, Betio, Tarawa; tel. 26355; operates a fortnightly passenger and cargo service to the outer islands and occasional longer journeys.

CIVIL AVIATION

There are five international airports (Bonriki on South Tarawa, Cassidy on Kiritimati, Antekana on Butaritari, as well as others on Kanton and Tabuaeran) and several other airfields in Kiribati. The airport at Bonriki was enlarged in the early 1990s, using a loan from the Bank of China. Air Nauru and Air Marshall Islands also operate international services to Tarawa, and Aloha Airlines operates a charter flight service between Kiritimati Island and Honolulu, Hawaii. In December 2001 the Government announced its decision to lease a prop-jet, which it intended to operate from Tarawa to the Marshall Islands, Tuvalu and Fiji.

Air Kiribati Ltd: POB 274, Bonriki, Tarawa; tel. 28088; fax 28216; e-mail airkiribati.admin@tsklnet.ki; f. 1977; fmrly Air Tungaru; national airline; operates scheduled services to 15 outer islands; Chair. TAKEI TAOABA; CEO TANIERA TEIBUAKO.

Tourism

Previous attempts to establish tourism have been largely unsuccessful, owing mainly to the remoteness of the islands. There were 14,211 visitor arrivals in 1998 (of whom fewer than 40% were tourists). Of total tourist arrivals in 1998, some 58.3% came from Asia and Oceania, and 26.9% came from the Americas. The number of tourist arrivals at Tarawa and Kiritimati airports rose from 3,112 in 1999 to 4,829 in 2000 and totalled 4,288 in 2003. In 2000 the industry earned some $A2.2m. In 1996 there were 201 hotel rooms in the islands. In 1989 the Government adopted a plan to develop hotels in the Line Islands and to exploit sites of Second World War battles. A further Tourism Development Action Plan was introduced in 1997. Game-fishing and 'eco-tourism', particularly bird-watching, were promoted in the late 1990s in an attempt to increase tourist arrivals to Kiritimati. Kiribati also exploited the location of some of its islands in the Line and Phoenix group by marketing the area as a destination for tourists wishing to celebrate the year 2000. In 1997 Caroline Island, situated close to the recently realigned international date-line, was renamed Millennium Island in an attempt to maximize its potential for attracting visitors. In late 2000 an agreement was signed with the Norwegian Shipping Line company allowing large cruise ships to make weekly calls to the Line Islands from the end of 2001.

Kiribati Visitors Bureau: Ministry of Communications Transport and Tourism Development, POB 487, Betio, Tarawa; tel. 26003; fax 26193; e-mail tourism@mict; internet www.spto.com; Sec. TINIAN REIHER; Senior Tourist Officer TARATAAKE TEANNAKI.

THE DEMOCRATIC PEOPLE'S REPUBLIC OF KOREA

Introductory Survey

Location, Climate, Language, Religion, Flag, Capital

The Democratic People's Republic of Korea (North Korea) occupies the northern part of the Korean peninsula, bordered to the north by the People's Republic of China and, for a very short section to the north-east, by the Russian Federation, and to the south by the Republic of Korea. The climate is continental, with cold, dry winters and hot, humid summers; temperatures range from −6°C to 25°C (21°F to 77°F). The language is Korean. Buddhism, Christianity and Chundo Kyo are officially cited as the principal religions. The national flag (proportions 33 by 65) is red, with blue stripes on the upper and lower edges, each separated from the red by a narrow white stripe. Left of centre is a white disc containing a five-pointed red star. The capital is Pyongyang.

Recent History

Korea was formerly an independent monarchy. It was occupied by Japanese forces in 1905 and annexed by Japan in 1910, when the Emperor was deposed. Following Japan's surrender in August 1945, ending the Second World War, Korea was divided at latitude 38°N into military occupation zones, with Soviet forces in the North and US forces in the South. A Provisional People's Committee, led by Kim Il Sung of the Korean Communist Party (KCP), was established in the North in February 1946 and accorded government status by the Soviet occupation forces. In July the KCP merged with another group to form the North Korean Workers' Party. In 1947 a legislative body, the Choe Ko In Min Hoe Ui (Supreme People's Assembly—SPA), was established, and Kim Il Sung became Premier. A new Assembly was elected in August 1948, and the Democratic People's Republic of Korea (DPRK) was proclaimed on 9 September. In the same year the Republic of Korea (q.v.) was proclaimed in the South. Initially, the DPRK was recognized only by the USSR and other communist countries. Soviet forces withdrew from North Korea in December 1948. In the following year, as a result of a merger between communists in the North and South, the Korean Workers' Party (KWP) was formed, under the leadership of Kim Il Sung; it has held power in North Korea ever since.

The two republics each claimed to have legitimate jurisdiction over the whole Korean peninsula. North Korean forces crossed the 38th parallel in June 1950, precipitating a three-year war between North and South. The UN mounted a collective defence action in support of South Korea, and the invasion was repelled. North Korean forces were supported by the People's Republic of China from October 1950. Peace talks began in July 1951 and an armistice agreement was concluded in July 1953. The cease-fire line, which approximately follows the 38th parallel, remains the frontier between North and South Korea. A demilitarized zone (DMZ), supervised by UN forces, separates the two countries.

Through the 'personality cult' of Kim Il Sung (the 'Great Leader') and of his son Kim Jong Il (the 'Dear Leader'), and a policy of strict surveillance of the entire population, overt opposition to the KWP has effectively been eliminated. The only organized opposition to the regime (albeit in exile) appears to be the Salvation Front for the Democratic Unification of Chosun, established by former military and other officials of the DPRK in the early 1990s, which has branches in Russia, Japan and the People's Republic of China. International human rights organizations have indicated that they believe there to be a number of concentration camps in North Korea, in which as many as 200,000 political prisoners may be held.

A new Constitution, adopted in December 1972, created the office of President, and Kim Il Sung was duly elected to the post. Kim Jong Il was appointed to several key positions within the KWP in 1980. In July 1984 Radio Pyongyang referred to Kim Jong Il, for the first time, as the 'sole successor' to his father, but there were reports of opposition to the President's heir, particularly among older members of the KWP.

Following elections to the eighth SPA, in November 1986 (when the 655 members were returned unopposed), Kim Il Sung was re-elected President, and a new Administration Council (cabinet) was formed. In March 1990 Kim Il Sung was returned to the post of President, and Kim Jong Il was appointed to his first state (as distinct from party) post, as First Vice-Chairman of the National Defence Commission. In February 1991 it was rumoured that there had been an unsuccessful military coup against Kim Jong Il. In December he was appointed Supreme Commander of the Korean People's Army (KPA), in place of his father, and in January 1992 he was reported to have been given control of foreign policy. In April Kim Jong Il was appointed to the rank of Marshal, while his father assumed the title of Grand Marshal.

In what was interpreted as a partial attempt to adapt to the change in international conditions following the collapse of communist regimes world-wide, the SPA (according to South Korean reports) made several amendments to the DPRK's Constitution in April 1992. Principal among these were the deletion of all references to Marxism-Leninism, and the promotion of 'economic openness' to allow limited foreign investment in the DPRK (although the KWP's guiding principle of *Juche*, or self-reliance, was strongly emphasized). In September measures to address the deteriorating economic situation included a drastic devaluation of the national currency. In December changes were made to the hierarchy of the KWP, and a reshuffle of the Administration Council was effected. The extent of the DPRK's economic difficulties was indicated by the budget proposals for 1993, which envisaged substantial reductions in expenditure, and by persistent reports of food riots. At the fifth session of the ninth SPA in April 1993 Kim Jong Il was elected Chairman of the National Defence Commission. In July Kim Il Sung's younger brother, Kim Yong Ju, unexpectedly returned to political life after a 17-year absence, and was subsequently elevated to the position of Vice-President and to membership of the Central Committee of the KWP's Politburo.

Kim Il Sung died of heart failure on 8 July 1994. One hundred days of national mourning were observed, but, contrary to expectations, Kim Jong Il was not appointed to the three leading post of President of the DPRK. Although the official media now referred to Kim Jong Il as the 'Great Leader', he did not appear in public during this period, reviving earlier speculation that he was either in poor health or that a struggle for power was taking place. It was thought that Kim Il Sung's widow, Kim Song Ae, who was the stepmother of Kim Jong Il, favoured her eldest son Kim Pyong Il for the presidency. In February 1995 the Minister of the People's Armed Forces, Marshal O Jin U died; O had been a significant supporter within the military of Kim Jong Il's succession, and his death was seen as a potential set-back for Kim. Scheduled elections to the SPA did not take place in April 1995, and no session of the assembly was convened in 1996. Meanwhile, from the mid-1990s, the influence of the KPA expanded significantly, as Kim Jong Il increasingly relied upon the military to maintain his power. The 50th anniversary of the establishment of the KWP in October 1995 was dominated by the military rather than the party, and several generals were promoted. Kim Jong Il, however, failed to assume any new posts. In February 1996 Sung Hye Rim, a former wife of Kim Jong Il and mother of his eldest son, defected to a western European country. In February 1997 Premier Kang Song San, who had made no public appearance since early 1996, was dismissed, and replaced on an acting basis by Hong Song Nam. Deepening social unrest was indicated by an increase in the rate of defections. In February Hwang Jang Yop, a close adviser to Kim Jong Il, sought political asylum in the South Korean embassy in the People's Republic of China while returning from an official visit to Japan, and warned that the DPRK was preparing to launch a military assault on South Korea. Hwang's defection appeared to precipitate significant changes in the KWP and military high command, as did the deaths of the Minister of the People's Armed Forces, Marshal Choe Kwang, and also of his deputy, Kim Kwang Jin. Many senior figures in the formal hierarchy were replaced, and some 123 generals, including many allies of Kim Jong Il, were promoted in rank in April. In August two senior North Korean diplomats, including the ambassador to Egypt, defected to the USA. There were also rumours of unrest and coup attempts, and several senior figures disappeared from public view without explanation. The official mourning period for Kim Il Sung was formally declared to be at an end in July 1997, on the third anniversary of his death. It was announced that, henceforth, the country was to use the *Juche* calendar, with 1912, the year of Kim Il Sung's birth, designated the first year of the new calendar. On 8 October 1997, in accordance with the recommendations of recent municipal and provincial conferences of the KWP (including KPA delegates) Kim Jong Il was elected General Secretary of the KWP.

Elections to the SPA finally took place in July 1998, at which the single list of candidates received 100% of the votes cast. Some two-thirds of the 687 deputies were newcomers to the Assembly, while the military reportedly doubled its representation. The first session of the 10th SPA was convened in September, shortly before the 50th anniversary of the establishment of North Korea. However, the anticipated appointment of Kim Jong Il as President of the DPRK did not occur, as the post was effectively abolished under major amendments to the Constitution that extensively revised the structure of government. The deceased Kim Il Sung was designated 'Eternal President', thus remaining *de jure* Head of State, while Kim Jong Il, who had been re-elected to the Chairmanship of the National Defence Commission (now apparently the highest office in the state hierarchy), assumed the role of *de facto* Head of State. Vice-Marshal Jo Myong Rok, the Director of the General Political Bureau of the KPA, was appointed First Vice-Chairman of the Commission, becoming the *de facto* second-ranking official in the DPRK. The Cabinet, as the Administration Council was redesignated, assumed many of the functions of the Central People's Committee, which was abolished. A new Presidium of the SPA was established, the President of which was to represent the State in diplomatic affairs; Kim Yong Nam, hitherto Minister of Foreign Affairs, was appointed to this position. Hong Song Nam was formally appointed Premier of the new Cabinet. Two technocrats, Jo Chang Dok and Kwak Pom Gi, were appointed Vice-Premiers.

By late 1998 Kim Jong Il had come to rely on an informal group of senior military leaders, party technocrats, former classmates and members of his extended family (including his sister, Kim Kyong Hui, and her husband, Jang Song Taek) as his power base. His succession had been facilitated by the fact that many younger technocrats were themselves the sons and daughters of revolutionary leaders.

Elections to the Local People's Assemblies were held in March 1999; it was reported that all candidates were fully endorsed. In October 2000 the Minister of Finance, Rim Kyong Suk, and the President of the central bank, Jong Song Taek, were dismissed. They were replaced, respectively, by Mun Il Bong and Kim Wan Su. No reasons were given for their dismissal. The replacement of the Minister of Foreign Trade, Kang Chong Mo, in December, by Ri Kwang Gun, was also unexplained. The Minister of Agriculture was replaced in March 2001. Meanwhile, in October 2000 the 55th anniversary of the founding of the KWP was marked by a military parade, attended, *inter alia*, by an invited delegation from South Korea.

In January 2001 the Government urged a 'new way of thinking' to solve the country's economic and domestic problems and to complement the *Kangsong Taeguk* ('prosperous and powerful nation') philosophy adopted in the late 1990s. In April the fourth session of the 10th SPA was held, but lasted only a single day; the meeting approved the budget for the coming year. Meanwhile, the number of people defecting from the North to the South continued to increase, with nearly 650 such persons having settled in the latter since 1996.

During 2001 several senior officials died or were replaced. In February the Chairman of the General Association of Korean Residents in Japan (*Chongryon*), Han Dok Su, passed away, and was replaced by So Man Sul in May. Also in February, Pak Song Bong, a senior figure in the munitions industry, died. In May the Secretary-General of the Party Central Committee, Ri Song Bok, a senior aide to Kim Jong Il, died of cancer. In August Vice Marshal Jo Myong Rok, the First Vice-Chairman of the National Defence Commission, returned to Pyongyang after a kidney

transplant operation in Beijing. He subsequently received medical treatment in France in late September. At this time, South Korean intelligence reported a reshuffle in economy-related agencies in which younger technocrats assumed principal posts. In October Kim Gyong Ho replaced Ri Il Hwan as head of the Kim Il Sung Socialist Youth League.

In January 2002 official media urged that the *Kangsong Taeguk* principle be strengthened. In mid-February Kim Jong Il duly celebrated his 60th birthday, but the commemoration was less grandiose than expected, possibly so as not to overshadow the 90th anniversary of the birth of Kim Il Sung in mid-April. In late March the fifth session of the 10th SPA was held. In addition to announcing a new budget, the SPA also adopted a new land planning law, aimed at improving and intensifying land work. Prime Minister Hong Song Nam also urged improved trade and economic co-operation, including joint ventures with other countries and international organizations. In mid-April Kim Jong Il promoted some 55 military leaders, including Jang Song U, brother of Jang Song Taek. At the same time Shin Il Nam, hitherto a Vice-Minister of Public Security, was appointed Vice-Premier in charge of the Commission for Capital Construction.

At the end of April 2002 the authorities opened the long-awaited two-month *Arirang* festival held across the country, mainly to attract foreign visitors while the Republic of Korea co-hosted the 2002 football World Cup (see below).

The question of the succession of the next generation leadership became increasingly important during 2002–03, following Kim Jong Il's 60th birthday. Kim was initially believed to have been preparing his eldest son, Kim Jong Nam, eventually to succeed him. Kim Jong Nam had served in the Ministry of Public Security and as head of the country's information technology (IT) industry since the late 1990s; however, in May 2001 he was detained in Tokyo, Japan, on charges of entering the country with a false passport, and subsequently deported to China. The incident discredited Kim Jong Nam, and thenceforth it was reported that Kim Jong Il was preparing Kim Jong Chol, the elder son of his current wife, Ko Yong Hui. Kim Jong Nam spent much of 2002 in Russia, where his mother, Sung Hye Rim, died in July. Meanwhile, in August Japanese sources reported that one of Kim Jong Il's sons, Kim Hyon (also known as Kim Hyon Nam) had been appointed head of the KWP's propaganda and agitation department, a post that Kim Jong Il himself had held in the 1960s when chosen as his father's successor.

In late September 2002 the Government designated the city of Sinuiju a 'Special Administrative Region' designed to attract foreign investment, and appointed Yang Bin, a Chinese-born Dutch citizen, as its first governor. However, within days of his appointment, Yang was arrested by the Chinese authorities on corruption charges, and he was unable to assume his post. None the less, the creation of the region was a significant development in the country's efforts to open up the economy. Under the 'Basic Law' establishing the region, Sinuiju would have its own government and legal system for a 50-year period, without interference from Pyongyang. In late 2002 the Government also established a special industrial zone in Kaesong, and a special tourist zone in the region of Mount Kumgang, although these did not have the same special status as Sinuiju. Despite these developments, a meeting of senior law enforcement officials was held in Pyongyang in early December during which Premier Hong urged the elimination of 'non-socialist elements'. In early 2003 it was reported that travel restrictions within the country had been reintroduced, in order to improve security.

The sixth session of the 10th SPA was held in late March 2003. Unlike previous sessions, Kim Jong Il did not attend the meeting, and South Korean observers noted that Kim had disappeared from public view for 50 days between February and early April. Furthermore, Vice-Marshal Jo Myong Rok received treatment for kidney disease in Beijing—although his visit was believed to be linked to discussions with China over the situation on the Korean Peninsula (see below). Kim reappeared in early April to make an inspection of a military medical university, and later in that month celebrations took place in Pyongyang to mark the 10th anniversary of Kim's election as Chairman of the National Defence Commission. Further celebrations took place in July to mark the 50th anniversary of the Korean War truce (celebrated as a triumph for the DPRK by the country's media), as well as in September on the occasion of the 55th anniversary of the establishment of the DPRK. In August 2003 elections were held to form the 11th SPA. Voter turn-out was reported to be have been 99.9%, and all 687 candidates were elected unopposed. At the first session of the 11th SPA in September, Kim Jong Il was re-elected as Chairman of the National Defence Commission. In October Kim Yong Sun, a member of the KWP Secretariat and Chairman of the Korea Asia-Pacific Peace Committee, died, reportedly as a result of a traffic accident. Kim Yong Sun had been an important figure in inter-Korean relations (see below). Also in October, it was reported that Kim's wife, Ko Yong Hui, was critically ill; however, her condition remained unknown. Vice-Marshal Jo Myong Rok was hospitalized in China again in December 2003.

In early 2004 reports from defectors, as well as some documentary evidence, indicated that mistreatment of political prisoners in the DPRK had included human experimentation for the purposes of chemical weapons development. On the occasion of Kim's 62nd birthday in February 2004, there was renewed speculation on the question of his successor. It was rumoured that Kim Jong Un, younger son of Ko Yong Hui, might have emerged as the most likely candidate, having been referred to by some sources as the 'Morning Star King'.

In April 2004 more than 150 people were killed and 1,300 injured by a massive explosion on a railway line at Ryongchon, a town near the border with China. Many children were among the victims of the accident, apparently caused when electric cables ignited chemical and other materials being transported by rail, only hours after a train carrying Kim Jong Il had travelled through the area. Overwhelmed by the scale of the disaster, the North Korean authorities withheld information on the accident for two days, but subsequently accepted international humanitarian aid, including a donation (made through the Red Cross) from the USA.

Meanwhile, the DPRK's economic difficulties and widespread food shortages were exacerbated by unusually serious flooding in 1995 and 1996, forcing the country to appeal to the UN and other international organizations for emergency food aid and flood relief. Assistance was provided by the USA, the Republic of Korea and Japan in 1995, but in early 1996 further shipments of cereals were halted, pending a positive response by North Korea to US proposals for peace negotiations (see below). Renewed appeals for emergency aid were issued by the UN in mid-1996, to which the USA, South Korea and Japan responded on humanitarian grounds. In January 1997 it was reported that the People's Republic of China had agreed to provide 500,000 metric tons of rice annually for five years. This was followed, in February, by an unprecedented admission from the DPRK that the country was experiencing 'temporary food problems' and that it had only one-half of the cereals necessary to feed its people.

In April and July 1997 the UN World Food Programme (WFP) issued two further appeals for food and medical supplies. UN representatives sent to the DPRK to assess the extent of the crisis confirmed that chronic malnutrition was widespread, particularly among infants, and that the medical system was no longer able to provide even basic health care. The situation deteriorated in mid-1997, when severe drought devastated most of North Korea's maize crop; further damage was caused by a tidal wave on the western coast, which left many people homeless. In January 1998 WFP issued the largest appeal in the organization's history, requesting emergency aid valued at some US $380m. Agreement was reached with the DPRK whereby additional UN staff were to be permitted to enter the country in order to monitor the distribution of aid, following allegations that supplies had been diverted to the army. Despite the provision of aid, severe food shortages persisted during 1998 and malnutrition was widespread among children. In December the UN issued an appeal for humanitarian aid. In January 1999 WFP announced that substantial food aid would be required for the DPRK in that year. By mid-1999 WFP announced that increased aid had prevented starvation in the country for the time being, although poor infrastructure continued to hamper food distribution, and entry to 49 of the country's 211 counties was still forbidden. In August serious flooding destroyed large areas of farm land and caused severe damage to the communications network.

Severe weather conditions during 2000 exacerbated food shortages in North Korea, leaving it in increased need of international aid. In November 2000 the UN estimated North Korea's food shortage for 2001 at some 1.2m. metric tons. In December 2000 the organization appealed to the international community for aid worth some US $390m., including 810,000 tons of food. The total international assistance received by the DPRK in 2000 was US $220.4m., of which the Republic of Korea provided 52%,

including 500,000 tons of rice and corn, and 300,000 tons of fertilizer.

In February 2001 WFP agreed to provide 810,000 tons of food and US $93m. in aid. The UN subsequently urged members to provide $383m. in humanitarian aid in 2002. In April 2001 the head of WFP in the country stated that the most recent winter had been especially severe and could thus result in food shortages comparable to those of 1996–97. In May the South began deliveries of 200,000 tons of agricultural fertilizer, and in June WFP stated that the North had received 389,775 tons of food aid between January and May, but would require an additional 250,000 tons to prevent starvation later in the year. The official state media announced in June, meanwhile, that the country had experienced 100 days of continuous drought since March; WFP subsequently estimated that the 2001 grain harvest would fall to 2.57m. tons as a result, far less than the 4.8m. tons needed overall. The worst-affected drought areas were South Hwanghae, Kangwon, and South Pyongan Provinces. In October WFP delivered emergency food supplies to flood-stricken Kangwon Province, and the Government began land rezoning programmes aimed at modernizing agricultural production in South Hwanghae Province. In November the head of the World Health Organization (WHO), Gro Harlem Brundtland, visited the DPRK and opened a permanent WHO office in Pyongyang. In December 2001 the Government launched an intensive campaign for potato and double-crop growing, in order to ease the famine.

In September–October 2002 representatives of FAO and WFP visited the DPRK and released a special report on the food situation. According to this report, in 2002 the harvest was believed to have improved somewhat, with cereal production 4.9% higher than in the previous year. Overall food production was 49% higher than in 2001, but 6% below the levels of 1995/96. Total cereal production, including potato equivalents, for 2002/03 was expected to reach 3.8m. tons, whereas food requirements were forecast at 4.9m. tons, thus leaving a deficit of 1.1m. tons. Urban residents remained more vulnerable to food shortages than rural residents, and food consumption per caput per day was projected at 270g of cereal in cities, compared with 600g in rural areas. Thus, urban residents were forced to spend 75%–85% of income on food purchases. The introduction in July 2002 of a quasi-market pricing system caused a significant inflation of food prices, despite the concurrent increase in salaries. The FAO-WFP mission therefore recommended concentrating resources on assisting urban areas and vulnerable groups, such as children and pregnant women.

In November 2003 the UN made a new appeal for humanitarian assistance to North Korea, stating that aid of more than US $200m. would be required in order to resolve the 'chronic emergency' in the DPRK. UNICEF's representative in the DPRK stated that 40% of North Korean children were malnourished. It was believed that international concerns over the North Korean nuclear weapons programme, as well as aid demands from Afghanistan and Iraq, had led to a decline in donations during 2003. By February 2004 the aid crisis had deepened, with WFP stating that in early 2004 it would be able to give food rations to only 100,000 people, leaving the remainder of the 6.5m. people hitherto supported by WFP vulnerable to food shortages.

In 1971, meanwhile, talks took place for the first time between the Red Cross Societies of North and South Korea. Negotiations were, however, suspended in 1973, and hopes for better relations were undermined by a series of clashes between North and South Korean vessels in disputed waters during 1974. Propaganda campaigns, suspended by agreement in 1972, were resumed by both sides, and minor border incidents continued. In October 1978 the UN Command (UNC—under which troops were stationed in South Korea) accused North Korea of threatening the 1953 truce, after the discovery of an underground tunnel (the third since 1974) beneath the DMZ. During the 1980s the increasing prominence of Kim Jong Il, who advocated an uncompromising policy towards the South, appeared to aggravate the situation. In 1983 some 17 South Koreans, including four government ministers, were killed in a bomb explosion in Burma (now Myanmar), in what appeared to be an assassination attempt on the South Korean President, Chun Doo-Hwan. The DPRK was held responsible for the attack, and Burma severed relations with Pyongyang. In January 1984, none the less, the DPRK suggested tripartite talks on reunification, involving North and South Korea and the USA; however the proposal was rejected by South Korea, which favoured bilateral talks. During 1984 the DPRK's propaganda campaign was moderated, and in September North Korea provided emergency relief to flood-stricken areas of the South. In November the first talks, on possible economic co-operation, were held, and negotiations continued in 1985. However, in February 1986, during the annual South Korean-US 'Team Spirit' military manoeuvres, North Korea suspended all negotiations with the South. The DPRK denied accusations by the South of North Korean involvement in the explosion of a South Korean airliner over Burma in November 1987, despite the subsequent confession of an alleged North Korean agent. In his 1988 New Year message, none the less, Kim Il Sung reiterated proposals for the convening of a joint conference. In August three sessions of talks were held at the 'peace village' of Panmunjom (in the DMZ) between delegates of the legislatures of North and South Korea, although the discussions (the first formal contact between the two countries since 1986) produced no conclusive results. Further negotiations in 1989 were suspended by the DPRK.

Inter-Korean talks resumed in mid-1990, and in September the DPRK Premier visited the South Korean capital, Seoul, for discussions with his counterpart, the highest-level bilateral contact since the end of the Korean War. Subsequent discussions culminated in the signing of an 'Agreement on Reconciliation, Non-aggression and Exchanges and Co-operation between the South and the North', in Seoul in December 1991. Both states pledged, *inter alia*, to desist from mutual slander, vilification and sabotage, to promote economic and other co-operation and the reunion of families separated by the war, and to work towards a full peace treaty to replace the 1953 armistice agreement. In November 1992, however, the DPRK threatened a complete suspension of contacts with the South, in protest at the latter's decision to resume the 'Team Spirit' military exercises in March 1993. (The 1992 exercises had been cancelled, owing to the improvement in relations between the two states.) Relations had also been seriously impaired by the South's announcement, in October 1992, that an extensive North Korean espionage network had been discovered in South Korea, and by the North's repeated refusals to agree to simultaneous nuclear inspections in both countries (see below).

The controversy surrounding the DPRK's suspected nuclear programme prevented any improvement in inter-Korean relations during 1993 and the first half of 1994, and contacts were also strained by the DPRK's withdrawal, in May 1994, of its mission to the Military Armistice Commission (the Panmunjom-based body overseeing the maintenance of the 1953 truce). Following talks between Kim Il Sung and former US President Jimmy Carter, who visited the DPRK (on a private initiative) in June 1994, it was announced that the first summit meeting at presidential level between the two Korean states would be held in Pyongyang in July. However, the death of Kim Il Sung led to the indefinite postponement of the summit meeting. The DPRK was, furthermore, angered by the Republic of Korea's failure to express official condolences at Kim's demise. The signature of the US-DPRK nuclear accord in October (see below) caused South Korea to make renewed efforts to resume the inter-Korean negotiations, and in February 1995 the South announced the cancellation of the annual 'Team Spirit' manoeuvres (for the second consecutive year), as a gesture of goodwill.

Tension increased markedly in April 1996, when the DPRK announced its decision to abandon the 1953 armistice. North Korean troops subsequently made a number of incursions into the DMZ, thereby violating the provisions of the agreement. Later in the month, in an attempt to revitalize the peace process and replace the armistice agreement with a formal peace treaty, President Bill Clinton of the USA and President Kim Young-Sam of the Republic of Korea proposed four-way talks, involving the two Koreas, the USA and the People's Republic of China. China responded positively, but the DPRK declared its willingness to hold discussions only with the USA. Following severe flooding in the DPRK in mid-1996, the USA, the Republic of Korea and Japan agreed to provide additional food aid to North Korea as an inducement to participate in the proposed quadripartite talks. North Korea, however, imposed conditions for its participation. Relations between the two Koreas deteriorated considerably in September, when a submarine from North Korea was discovered abandoned in South Korean waters. One of the two surviving crew members claimed that this was the fourth such mission undertaken by armed North Koreans. South Korea suspended all contact with the DPRK, including the provision of food aid, and the UN Security Council subsequently expressed 'serious concern' at the incident. Following protracted

mediation by the USA, an unprecedented apology was broadcast in South Korea by the (North) Korean Central News Agency.

In March 1997 explanatory talks between delegates from the DPRK, the Republic of Korea and the USA were held in New York to discuss the proposed quadripartite negotiations. Following the talks, the DPRK announced that its participation in full quadripartite negotiations was conditional upon the receipt of substantial food aid. In May representatives of the Red Cross organizations of North and South Korea (in the first such meeting for five years) reached agreement on the provision of grain to the DPRK, the distribution of which was to be monitored by South Korean Red Cross officials. Further supplies were pledged following meetings in July. Negotiations were concluded in October to allow foreign airlines, including those from South Korea, to use North Korean airspace. This was regarded as a significant breakthrough in bilateral relations.

Exploratory discussions on the proposed quadripartite negotiations were held at intervals throughout the first half of 1997. In July a military confrontation between North and South Korean troops in the DMZ jeopardized the progress of the discussions. Full quadripartite negotiations, aimed at concluding a peace treaty between North and South Korea, finally opened in Geneva, Switzerland, in December 1997. A second round of full discussions was held in March 1998, but proved unsuccessful, since the DPRK continued to insist on the inclusion on the agenda of the withdrawal of US troops from the Korean peninsula. In December 1997, meanwhile, negotiations in Beijing between the South and North Korean Red Cross organizations foundered, owing to North Korea's reluctance to allow South Korean officials access to the DPRK to monitor the distribution of food aid. At a subsequent meeting, in March 1998, the provision of additional food aid was agreed.

Following the inauguration of the new South Korean President, Kim Dae-Jung, in February 1998, the DPRK urged 'dialogue and negotiation' with the South Korean administration. Nevertheless, a ministerial-level meeting held in Beijing, People's Republic of China, in April, to discuss the provision of fertilizer to North Korea (the first such direct contact for four years), broke down amid mutual accusations of inflexibility, when the South Koreans insisted that the DPRK enter into negotiations on the reunion of families. In that month, however, as part of Kim Dae-Jung's 'sunshine' policy of co-operation with the DPRK, the South Korean Government announced measures to encourage inter-Korean economic contacts, allowing the transfer of private funds to the North and relaxing legislation on investment. In June, in an historic development, Chung Ju-Yung, the founder of the South Korean conglomerate Hyundai, was permitted to cross the DMZ to deliver a gift of cattle to his home town; proposals for several other joint ventures were also discussed, including a plan to operate tour boats to Mount Kumgang, just north of the border. This improvement in relations seemed to be in jeopardy when, during the visit, a North Korean submarine was caught in the nets of a southern fishing boat; all nine crew members were found dead inside the vessel. The UNC condemned the incursion during a meeting with North Korean army officers in Panmunjom, the first such talks to be held in seven years. (The DPRK had suspended direct contacts with UNC officers in 1991, in protest at the appointment of a South Korean general to command the force.) A further delivery of cattle was made by Chung Ju-Yung in October 1998, when he also met with Kim Jong Il, and in November some 800 tourists from South Korea participated in the first visit to Mount Kumgang. In December, during Chung's third visit to North Korea, a proposal for the construction of an industrial complex at Haeju was approved. Following further visits in early 1999, it was announced that these would continue on a monthly basis. Private and business-related inter-Korean contacts increased substantially during 1998. In December 1998 South Korean naval forces sank a suspected North Korean spy boat, after pursuing it into international waters.

Meanwhile, at a third session of quadripartite talks, held in Geneva in October 1998, agreement was reached on the creation of two sub-committees—one with a view to the establishment of a permanent peace mechanism for the Korean peninsula, and one to seek ways of easing tension. The sub-committees were formally inaugurated during the next round of negotiations in January 1999, although little substantive progress was reported. Proceedings were somewhat overshadowed by the reported defection of a North Korean diplomat in Germany, who was said to be seeking asylum in the USA, and by claims by the DPRK that the envoy had, in fact, been abducted by South

Korean intelligence agents. In early February the North Korean authorities proposed senior-level political talks with South Korea, but attached a series of conditions that were unacceptable to the South, including the cessation of joint military exercises with foreign troops and the abrogation of South Korea's national security law. Later that month 17 North Korean political detainees, who had been imprisoned in South Korea for up to 41 years, were among more than 8,000 prisoners released in a special amnesty. In March South Korea announced that it would provide, via the Red Cross, humanitarian assistance in the form of fertilizers.

In June 1999 a week-long confrontation between North and South Korean naval forces in the Yellow Sea resulted in a brief gun battle, during which one North Korean torpedo boat was sunk and five other vessels were damaged. Two rounds of bilateral talks in Beijing in late June and early July ended in failure, after North Korean representatives demanded an apology for the sinking of the boat, and refused to discuss the issue of reunion of families until further fertilizer aid was delivered by the South. (South Korea had recently sent 100,000 metric tons of fertilizer, and had promised a second delivery if some agreement was reached at the talks.) Furthermore, Hyundai was forced to suspend tours to Mount Kumgang for more than a month, after a South Korean tourist was detained in late June for allegedly encouraging northern tour guides to defect. In September the DPRK declared invalid the Northern Limit Line (the maritime border that has separated the two Koreas since 1953), in protest at the UNC's refusal to renegotiate its demarcation. Meanwhile, no discernible progress had been achieved at sessions of the quadripartite talks held in April and August 1999. None the less, Hyundai proceeded with its plans for a number of projects in North Korea: in October the company concluded an agreement with the DPRK on the construction of the proposed industrial complex, which, it was envisaged, would comprise some 850 businesses, employing some 220,000 people, and would be capable of producing export goods worth an estimated US $3,000m. annually. In February 2000 foreign residents in South Korea were permitted to visit Mount Kumgang for the first time. In December 1999 another major South Korean company, Samsung Electronics, announced that it had signed a contract with the DPRK for the joint development of computer software and the manufacture of electronic products. In February 2000 the construction of a motor vehicle assembly plant, in a joint venture with the Pyonghwa Motor Company of South Korea, began in Nampo, south-west of Pyongyang. According to South Korean estimates, inter-Korean trade increased by 50.2% in 1999. A number of joint North-South cultural and sporting events took place in 1999. In March 2000 Kim Dae-Jung urged North Korea to develop economic contacts with the South at governmental level. In April, following a series of high-level bilateral contacts in Beijing, North and South Korea jointly announced that an historic summit meeting would take place between Kim Dae-Jung and Kim Jong Il in Pyongyang in June.

Following the presidential summit meeting on 13–15 June 2000, detailed agreements were signed pledging economic co-operation, the building of mutual trust and the resolution of reunification issues. In July ministerial-level delegations from both countries met in Seoul. This was the first visit to the South by North Korean officials since 1991. Although the two sides failed to reach an agreement on military matters, a joint communiqué was issued allowing for, *inter alia*, the reopening of liaison offices at Panmunjom which had been closed in 1996, and the reconnection of the inter-Korean Kyongui railway line. The construction of a highway to run alongside the railway from North to South was subsequently agreed. In September Kim Dae-Jung formally inaugurated the project to remove thousands of landmines (to be undertaken by soldiers from each side respectively) and rebuild the railway line and adjacent highway. Meanwhile, benefiting from the progress made at the summit meeting in June, in August 100 North Korean families travelled to Seoul and 100 South Korean families visited Pyongyang simultaneously to meet with relatives from whom they had been separated by the Korean War. The second ministerial meeting between the two sides was held in Pyongyang later that month. Negotiations were extended for one day because of an inability to agree on terms for beginning a dialogue between the two countries' military establishments. A compromise was reached after consultation with Kim Jong Il. It was agreed to hold two more cross-border family reunions by the end of 2000 and to commence talks on economic co-operation. In a symbolic display

of unity, in September the two countries marched under the same flag in the opening ceremony of the Olympic Games in Sydney, Australia. In late September the DPRK's Minister of the People's Armed Forces, Vice-Marshal Kim Il Chol, visited the South and met his counterpart, Cho Seong-Tae, the first such ministerial meeting ever held. In October Kim Dae-Jung was awarded the Nobel Peace Prize in recognition of his reunification efforts. Further rounds of inter-ministerial, military and economic talks took place during 2000 and early 2001. In an indication of the improvement in relations, in December 2000 a meeting was also held between trade union representatives from the two countries.

Despite the increased level of dialogue and co-operation between the two countries, however, in December 2000 South Korea published its annual defence policy document, which described the North as its main enemy and alleged that it had expanded its military capacity along the DMZ. The DPRK was antagonized by its continued status as South Korea's most likely adversary. International analysts, however, felt that hostility was not imminent. North Korea was also angered in that month by the approval of a resolution by the South Korean legislature to demand the repatriation of prisoners of war who, it alleged, continued to be held by the North, despite the DPRK's denial of the existence of these prisoners.

In early 2001 the uncompromising attitude displayed by the new US administration towards North Korea threatened to undermine the reconciliation process. In March the DPRK unilaterally postponed scheduled cabinet-level talks following a visit to the USA by Kim Dae-Jung, raising speculation that Pyongyang wanted time to formulate a response to US criticism of its regime (see below), and in April North Korea denounced joint US-South Korean military exercises as a betrayal of the goodwill surrounding the June 2000 summit meeting. Ministerial discussions resumed in Seoul in mid-September, the sixth round of which was concluded in mid-November (having been postponed from late October) without any agreement—the first unsuccessful such round since the presidential summit meeting. The North blamed the South, in particular the Minister of Unification, Hong Soon-Young, for the failure of the talks.

Meanwhile, during 2001 Kim Jong Il's long-awaited visit to Seoul for a second presidential summit meeting failed to materialize, and there was continued uncertainty as to when such a visit would take place. US President George W. Bush's reference in January 2002 to North Korea as part of an 'axis of evil' threatened to damage inter-Korean relations.

A stalemate in inter-Korean relations was broken in early April 2002, however, when the North received Kim Dae-Jung's special envoy, Lim Dong-Won. Following the visit, during which Lim met Kim Jong Il, the two sides agreed to further reunions for separated families (see below) and to continuing discussions on economic co-operation. The DPRK also agreed to Lim's request that it renew dialogue with the USA and Japan. In mid-May Park Geun-Hye, a South Korean legislator and the daughter of former President Park Chung-Hee, visited the North and met Kim Jong Il. The visit was unusual because Northern agents had killed Park's mother in 1974 in a bid to assassinate her father. Despite the cordial visit, North Korea cancelled economic co-operation discussions with the South in May.

In May 2002 the increasing number of defectors from the North received international attention as several groups sought asylum at Canadian, Japanese and South Korean diplomatic buildings in China. They were eventually allowed to travel to the South, albeit via the Philippines. The South Korean Ministry of Unification reported in January 2003 that during 2002 some 1,141 North Koreans had defected to the South, compared with 583 in 2001.

At the end of June 2002 a gun battle between North and South Korean vessels in the Yellow Sea resulted in the sinking of a Southern patrol boat and the deaths of six crew members. South Korean military sources estimated that 30 Northern crewmen were also killed in the confrontation, which had started when two North Korean vessels accompanying a fishing boat reportedly crossed the Northern Limit Line. Following the incident, in July South Korea suspended rice shipments to the North and economic co-operation projects, reflecting widespread public anger there. None the less, Kim Dae-Jung maintained his 'sunshine' policy towards the North, and later expressed regret for the incident. Meanwhile, North Korean state television showed selected highlights of matches played by the South Korean football team in the 2002 football World Cup—although refrained from transmitting extensive coverage of the event, which was being co-hosted by Japan.

In mid-August 2002 North and South Korea held a seventh round of ministerial talks in Seoul, aimed at improving relations in the aftermath of the latest naval confrontation, and focusing on the issue of future family reunions, railway links (see below) and cultural exchanges. Regarding the latter, more than 300 North Korean athletes travelled to the South and participated in the Asian Games held in Busan during October. In late September the first inter-Korean military 'hotline' was inaugurated to allow for improved communications during sensitive occasions. Meanwhile, Pyongyang's revelation that it had abducted 12 Japanese citizens in the 1970s and 1980s (see below) highlighted the outstanding issue of several hundred missing South Korean citizens believed to have been abducted by the North.

The eighth round of ministerial talks was held in Pyongyang in late October 2002 and mainly focused on economic co-operation issues, despite the fact that the USA had earlier revealed the existence of a secret nuclear weapons programme in the North (see below). At the end of that month a North Korean economic delegation began a nine-day tour of the South, including several major industrial facilities in the itinerary. Noteworthy was the fact that the delegation included Jang Song Taek, Kim Jong Il's brother-in-law and one of his most trusted advisers, and also Kim Hi Taek, the first deputy head of the KWP's Central Committee. At the end of December 2002 the South Korean Ministry of National Defence published a 'white paper' which, for the first time, excluded any reference to the North as its main enemy.

By late 2002 some of the goodwill generated by the historic inter-Korean summit meeting in June 2000 had been undermined by the revelation that Kim Dae-Jung had arranged for the Korea Development Bank to give a Hyundai affiliate substantial funds. to transfer to the North in order to finance the meeting. However, the election in December of Roh Moo-Hyun, the candidate of Kim's Millennium Democratic Party (MDP), as President of the Republic of Korea heralded a continuation of Kim's 'sunshine' policy. In early January 2003 representatives of Roh secretly met Northern officials in Beijing, and later in that month a ninth round of ministerial talks was held in Seoul. Kim also dispatched Lim Dong-Won to Pyongyang at the end of the month, but Lim failed to secure a meeting with Kim Jong Il, instead relaying a goodwill message through one of the latter's aides.

North and South Korea continued their efforts to improve bilateral relations during 2003, despite a severe deterioration in relations between the North and the USA over the issue of the former's nuclear weapons programme (see below). In early 2003 Roh was exploring a long-standing idea of developing gas pipelines between Sakhalin, Russia, and North Korea that would supply the latter with energy in return for an abandonment of its nuclear programme. The DPRK hosted the 10th round of ministerial talks at the end of April. In mid-May, however, Pyongyang announced that it no longer recognized a joint declaration on the 'denuclearization' of the Korean peninsula, signed with the South in 1992 (see below). Also in May, at talks between the two Koreas on economic matters, North Korea warned that the South would risk 'unspeakable disaster' if it became too confrontational in co-operating with the USA on the nuclear issue (the threat followed a summit meeting between Roh and US President George W. Bush). Attempts to develop inter-Korean relations were also complicated by confirmation in June by South Korean investigators that former President Kim Dae-Jung had paid US $100m. to arrange the historic inter-Korean summit meeting of 2000 (see above). In August the suicide of Hyundai official Chung Mong-Hun, who had been indicted in connection with the illegal payments to the North, further undermined the credibility of the 'sunshine' policy. Meanwhile, the 50th anniversary in July of the *de facto* end of the Korean War, celebrated as a triumph in North Korea, was commemorated in a sombre fashion in South Korea. Also in July, cross-border gunfire was exchanged between North and South Korean soldiers. In October North Korean official Kim Yong Sun, an important figure in inter-Korean affairs who had attended the presidential summit meeting in 2000, died, reportedly as a result of a traffic accident. In November two well-known North Korean defectors, Hwang Jang Yop (see above) and former North Korean official Kim Dok Hong, left their posts at the South Korean Institute of National Unification Policy. There was a suggestion that their resignations might have been due to fears that their criticism of the North Korean regime

might be damaging to South Korean attempts to negotiate with North Korea. The resignation in January 2004 of the South Korean Minister of Foreign Affairs, Yoon Young-Kwan, was believed to have been related to tensions within the South Korean Government over the country's co-operation with the USA on the issue of North Korean weapons.

The arrangements for further family reunions came under the auspices of the North and South Korean Red Cross organizations, which held several rounds of talks on the subject and co-ordinated the exchange of lists of potential candidates for reunion. In October 2000 South Korea accepted a North Korean proposal that the second exchange of family members should take place in late November–early December. Relations between the two sides subsequently deteriorated, casting doubt on the likelihood of the meetings taking place, when North Korea accused the head of the South Korean Red Cross of defaming the former's political system. The official was replaced in January 2001. The DPRK continued to dictate terms for reunions, asking the Republic of Korea to limit the amount of money and gifts transferred during the events, which took place in November–December 2000 and at the end of February 2001. It was subsequently reported that North Korean officials had confiscated money given to delegates for use as state funds. Meanwhile, in January 2001 an historic accord between the two sides allowed 300 separated families from the North and South each to exchange letters in mid-March. A fourth round of family reunions was initially scheduled for mid-October, but was cancelled owing to the heightened security situation following the terrorist attacks in the USA on 11 September. They were subsequently held at Mount Kumgang in late April 2002. A fifth round was held in mid-September 2002, again at Mount Kumgang, where officials from the two sides planned to build a centre for such meetings. A further three rounds of reunions took place at Mount Kumgang in 2003. The eighth round of reunions in September 2003 involved 604 South Koreans and 365 North Koreans.

As the DPRK's financial situation worsened, economic issues played an important part in inter-Korean relations from 2000. There was speculation that Pyongyang's new openness was motivated by the necessity of securing increased assistance. In January 2001, however, a South Korean vessel carrying aid was refused permission to dock in North Korea. Also in that month, it was reported that the DPRK's energy shortages had reached crisis point, and that the country was desperately researching alternative power sources. A summit meeting took place between the two Koreas in February, at which the DPRK requested immediate and substantial electricity supplies to alleviate its pressing needs. Frustration resulted from South Korean insistence on the necessity of on-site investigations prior to the commencement of deliveries. Meanwhile, in August 2000 Hyundai agreed to establish a technologically-advanced electronic industrial compound in Kaesong in the DPRK. Hyundai's financial problems, however, were likely to delay the implementation of the project. The company was also obliged to reduce its royalty payments to Pyongyang for the Mount Kumgang tourist initiative in 2000, owing to the attraction's failure to make a profit. In March 2001 the future of the initiative was jeopardized by its lack of profitability, and Hyundai appealed to the South Korean Government for assistance; the Government subsequently pledged 90,000m. won to maintain the tourist cruises. Hyundai founder Chung Ju-Yung died in late March, meanwhile, and his funeral was attended by a delegation sent by Kim Jong Il. On May Day workers from trade unions from the North and South attended a rally at Mount Kumgang. Progress on economic co-operation in Kaesong was made from 2002, with Kaesong being declared a special industrial zone in November of that year (see also Economic Affairs). In June 2003 the DPRK announced regulations for the development of the zone, as well as plans to develop an area of 3.3 sq km in a first phase of development extending to 2007. A South Korean company, Korea Land, was to invest around US $184m. in the project. These plans were finalized at a meeting of North and South Korean economic officials in November 2003. Although inter-Korean trade increased steadily, reportedly amounting to US $700m. in 2003, South Korea shared international concerns over North Korea's suspected illicit trade in weapons and narcotics. In June 2003 South Korean customs officials in the port of Pusan seized 40 kg of methamphetamines believed to have originated in North Korea. There were also fears of very serious economic consequences for South Korea if reunification of the two Koreas were to become an imminent prospect.

Negotiations to re-establish the inter-Korean rail link continued during 2001. It was hoped that such a link would create a new Eurasian transport corridor that would reduce the cost and time involved in the transit of goods from North-East Asia to European markets from 25 days to about 15 days, bringing economic benefits to all participants. In February 2001 a meeting was held at the DMZ to arrange regulations for troops and workers employed to rebuild the line, and a parallel highway. However, the DPRK failed to attend a UN regional transport meeting held in Seoul in mid-November, following the failure of the sixth round of ministerial talks. A New Year's editorial in January 2002 described the upgrading of the railway as a priority during that year, and both Koreas agreed to accelerate the reconnection following bilateral talks in April 2002. Ground-breaking ceremonies for the reconnection of the railway and road links were held on both sides of the DMZ in late September 2002, and South Korea released a loan to the North to assist the funding of the work. In early February 2003 the first road reconnecting the North with the South was completed, on the eastern coast of the Korean peninsula. In June 2003 rail links between the two Koreas were officially opened. However, the connections remained largely symbolic, as construction on the North Korean side to link the new railways with wider networks was yet to be completed in early 2004.

In the early 1990s there was growing international concern that the DPRK had intensified its clandestine nuclear programme at Yongbyon, north of Pyongyang, and would soon be capable of manufacturing a nuclear weapon. During 1991 pressure was increasingly applied, by the USA and Japan in particular, for the DPRK to sign the Nuclear Safeguards Agreement (NSA) with the International Atomic Energy Agency (IAEA, see p. 86). This was required by the DPRK's signature, in 1985, of the Treaty on the Non-Proliferation of Nuclear Weapons (the Non-Proliferation Treaty—NPT), in order that IAEA representatives might be permitted to inspect the country's nuclear facilities. However, the DPRK consistently refused to allow such inspections to take place unless there was to be a simultaneous inspection (or withdrawal) of US nuclear weapons sited in South Korea. Tension was eased considerably by the USA's decision, in October 1991, to remove all its tactical nuclear weapons from South Korea, and by South Korea's subsequent declaration that it would not manufacture, deploy or use nuclear, chemical or biological weapons. In December the South Korean Government stated that all US nuclear weapons had been withdrawn, and proposed that simultaneous inspections of military bases in the South and nuclear facilities in the North be conducted. Later in the month the two Korean states concluded an agreement 'to create a non-nuclear Korean peninsula', and in January 1992 the DPRK signed the NSA. In March delegates of North and South, meeting at Panmunjom, agreed to form a Joint Nuclear Control Commission (JNCC) to permit inter-Korean nuclear inspections to take place.

In May 1992 the DPRK submitted to the IAEA an unexpectedly detailed report on its nuclear facilities, describing, *inter alia*, the Yongbyon installation as a research laboratory. In the same month IAEA inspectors were permitted to visit North Korean nuclear facilities (the first in a series of official visits during that year). Despite the findings of the inspectors (who concluded that the Yongbyon plant was 'primitive' and far from completion, although potentially capable of producing plutonium), suspicions persisted regarding North Korean nuclear ambitions. Moreover, the DPRK repeatedly failed to agree to separate nuclear inspections by the JNCC, finally announcing in January 1993 its intention to boycott all future inter-Korean nuclear talks (in protest at the imminent resumption of the 'Team Spirit' manoeuvres). The situation became critical in February, when the DPRK refused to allow IAEA inspections of two 'undeclared' sites near Yongbyon, claiming that these were military installations unrelated to nuclear activities. In an unprecedented move, the DPRK announced in March that it was to withdraw from the NPT. In May the UN Security Council adopted a resolution urging the DPRK to reconsider its decision to withdraw from the NPT and calling on the country to allow an inspection by the IAEA of its nuclear facilities. Following negotiations with the USA in May and June, the DPRK agreed to suspend its withdrawal from the NPT; in return, the USA agreed to assist the DPRK in the development of its non-military nuclear programme. International concern regarding the North Korean weapons programme was, meanwhile, heightened by the successful testing of a medium-range missile, the *Rodong-1*, in May. In response to US pressure, the DPRK subsequently

agreed to further negotiations with the IAEA. Talks at the organization's headquarters in Vienna, Austria, in September were, however, inconclusive, and further meetings were cancelled.

In February 1994, following further discussions between the DPRK and the USA, an agreement was reached whereby the IAEA would be allowed to visit all the country's declared nuclear facilities. In March, however, the inspectors were impeded in their efforts to remove samples from nuclear installations, and it was discovered that seals placed on nuclear materials by IAEA representatives during previous visits had been broken, leading the IAEA to conclude that the DPRK had, in all probability, produced more plutonium than had been admitted. In June the DPRK again threatened to withdraw from the NPT, and also to declare war against the Republic of Korea, if economic sanctions were imposed by the UN. In August the USA and the DPRK reached an agreement on the replacement of the latter's existing nuclear reactors by two light-water reactors, which were considered to be less easily adapted to the production of nuclear weaponry. The agreement also recommended the establishment of a restricted form of diplomatic representation between the two countries. However, the DPRK discounted the possibility of an inspection by the IAEA of the two contentious sites at Yongbyon. Further negotiations in October led to the signing of an Agreed Framework whereby the USA undertook to establish an international consortium to finance and supply the light-water reactors, while the DPRK agreed to suspend operation of its existing reactors and halt construction at two further sites. To compensate for the DPRK's consequent shortfall in energy production until the new reactors were fully operational, the USA agreed to donate to the DPRK 500,000 metric tons annually of heavy fuel oil. IAEA inspectors subsequently travelled to Pyongyang to oversee the suspension of the country's nuclear programme.

In March 1995 several countries, led by the USA, the Republic of Korea and Japan, created the Korean Peninsula Energy Development Organization (KEDO), which insisted that the DPRK accept a South Korean-designed reactor. This demand was opposed by the DPRK at renewed negotiations with the USA. However, in August the North permitted a KEDO delegation (including South Korean engineers) to visit Sinpo, on the east coast of the DPRK, in order to assess its suitability as the site of the proposed nuclear power station. Finally, in December the DPRK and KEDO reached agreement on the details of implementing the October 1994 accord; this implied acceptance by the DPRK of South Korean light-water reactors. In January 1996 the DPRK announced its willingness to permit routine inspections of its nuclear installations by the IAEA. In March the Korea Electric Power Corporation (KEPCO), of South Korea, was commissioned by KEDO as the principal contractor for the construction of the light-water reactors. Discussions between KEDO and the DPRK to negotiate the terms of repayment by the latter of the construction costs of the light-water reactors were successfully concluded in April 1997, with the DPRK agreeing to reimburse KEDO over a 17-year period.

Meanwhile, US energy experts began the sealing of spent fuel rods at the DPRK's nuclear facilities. However, North Korea's continued refusal to grant IAEA inspectors access to several contentious laboratories, despite meetings to negotiate the implementation of the provisions of the NSA, again provoked concern that the DPRK was developing its nuclear programme. Preparation of the nuclear-reactor site at Sinpo formally began in August 1997: the initial project involved the construction of facilities to house the estimated 2,000 site employees. Negotiations held in early 1998 between the participants in KEDO (which the European Union—EU—had joined in mid-1997) concerning the financing of the light-water reactors (estimated at US \$5,170m.) proved difficult, and were further complicated by South Korea's financial problems, raising fears that progress on the project would be hindered. In June 1998 the North Korean Government admitted to having sold nuclear missiles abroad, claiming that such exports were necessary, given ongoing US economic sanctions against the DPRK, in order to earn foreign currency. Some progress was made at talks between the USA and the DPRK in New York, USA, in September, when the DPRK agreed to resume sealing of spent fuel rods (which had been suspended earlier that year), while the USA promised to deliver the delayed shipment of heavy fuel oil. The US Congress was, however, increasingly reluctant to approve financing for the purchase of fuel oil, obliging President Clinton personally to authorize the disbursement of the necessary funds in October, in order to safeguard the 1994 nuclear accord.

Concerns regarding a suspected nuclear-related underground facility at Kumchang-ri, some 40 km north-west of Yongbyon, dominated a series of senior-level talks between the USA and the DPRK in late 1998 and early 1999. US attempts to gain access to the site, which the DPRK insisted was non-nuclear, were unsuccessful, with the USA rejecting North Korean demands for compensation in return for an inspection of the site. The North Korean authorities were angered by reports that KEDO had decided, in January 1999, to delay commencing the basic construction of the light-water reactors until mid-1999. In March, following protracted negotiations in New York, agreement was finally reached permitting US access to the suspected nuclear facility. The USA announced that it would donate substantial food aid to the DPRK, in addition to agricultural assistance, although it was emphasized that the aid was being granted on purely humanitarian grounds and did not constitute compensation. The US officials who inspected the Kumchang-ri site in May found it to be incomplete and largely empty. (The facility was reinspected in May 2000, and this finding was confirmed.) At the same time the USA announced the provision of an additional 400,000 metric tons of food aid for 1999.

In May 1999 William Perry, a former US Secretary of Defense who had been appointed to review policy towards the DPRK, visited Pyongyang, where he reportedly advised the North Korean Government to abandon its nuclear ambitions in exchange for substantial economic and political benefits. Talks held during mid-1999 between the USA and the DPRK to discuss the latter's missile development programme culminated in September in a decision by the USA to ease several long-standing economic sanctions (principally on non-military trade, travel and banking) against the DPRK. In return, the country agreed to suspend missile test-firing for the duration of negotiations with the USA. Earlier in the month Perry had presented a report recommending a comprehensive, long-term approach to the establishment of normal relations with the DPRK to the US President and Congress. Discussions aimed at improving US-North Korean relations were held in Beijing in November 1999 and January 2000. In March preparatory talks took place in New York for a proposed higher-level meeting, scheduled to be held in Washington, DC, in April. It was reported, however, that disagreement had arisen over the DPRK's insistence on its removal from the US list of countries supporting terrorism prior to the Washington talks.

Meanwhile, in November 1999 it was reported that the IAEA was supervising the final stage of the sealing of spent fuel rods at Yongbyon. After several months of delays caused by disputes over the division of the costs of the project, in December KEDO and KEPCO finally signed the contract for the construction of the two light-water reactors; in February 2000 it was reported that construction of the reactors was unlikely to be completed before 2007, some four years later than scheduled. In November 2000 North Korea, frustrated by the delay, threatened to restart missile testing unless construction of the reactors was accelerated. The DPRK refuted the IAEA's claim that delays were due to the former's refusal to allow nuclear inspections. Also in that month, the EU agreed to provide US $130m. for the construction of the reactors.

In June 2000 Pyongyang confirmed its moratorium on test flights of ballistic missiles. Various rounds of discussion on the missile issue took place throughout 2000, although no substantive progress had been achieved by the end of the year. In July the USA rejected the DPRK's demand for annual payments from the USA of US $1,000m. in return for the curtailment of weapons exports. The fundamental issues of missile development and export remained unresolved. A planned visit to Pyongyang by the outgoing US President, Bill Clinton, was cancelled in December when the DPRK rejected a US proposal that the two sides prepare a draft missile accord to form a basis for talks. In early 2001 the new administration of George W. Bush adopted a less conciliatory stance towards the DPRK, officials reportedly referring to Kim Jong Il as a 'dictator', and refusing to grant economic aid unless transparency in North Korea's missile production and export was assured and verified. Since the late 1990s elements in Bush's Republican Party had been strongly arguing in favour of a planned 'national missile defence' (NMD) system to protect the USA from attack, and had frequently cited North Korea as a developer and exporter of such missiles. US officials feared that the DPRK had developed an intercontinental ballistic missile, the *Taepo Dong 2*, capable of striking the west coast of the USA. Bush's commitment to develop NMD was denounced by the DPRK, which responded by threatening to abandon the 1994 framework, and to resume ballistic missile testing. In March the USA appointed Charles Kartman, a former special envoy to the DPRK under the Clinton administration, as the new head of KEDO, and US Secretary of State Colin Powell suggested that revisions to the 1994 framework might be required. In May 2001 an EU delegation travelled to North Korea, in an effort to renew diplomatic initiatives aimed at advancing the process of détente. Discussions focused on North Korea's missile programme and on humanitarian issues. Kim Jong Il reportedly agreed to maintain the moratorium on the testing of missiles until at least 2003 and declared his willingness to attend another meeting with President Kim Dae-Jung. In June 2001 President Bush sought to broaden discussions with North Korea about its missile programme to include nuclear technology and a reduction of the country's conventional forces. The North responded that discussions on the latter would take place only following the withdrawal of the 37,000 US troops from the South, and that it was also seeking financial compensation for the delay in building KEDO's two light-water reactors, which were not expected to be completed until 2008 at the earliest. In October the North rejected suggestions by the head of the IAEA and later by US officials that inspections of its nuclear facilities were necessary; however, in December it agreed to limited international access to certain laboratories. Meanwhile, in November, a team of North Korean nuclear engineers visited power plants in the South, indicating their commitment to acquire southern-style reactors. (See relations with the USA, below, for subsequent developments on the DPRK's nuclear weapons programme.)

The DPRK's relations with Japan have long been dominated by continuing hostility towards the latter as a result of the atrocities committed in Korea during the Japanese occupation (1910–45). Pyongyang had demanded thousands of millions of dollars in compensation from Japan, before normal relations could be restored. In the 1980s, following the testimony of defectors, Japan began to suspect that North Korean agents had kidnapped a number of Japanese citizens during the late 1970s and early 1980s. Japan imposed sanctions on the DPRK after its agents were accused of attempting to assassinate the South Korean President in Burma 1983. Following the destruction of a South Korean aircraft in 1987, allegedly by North Korean agents posing as Japanese citizens (see above) Japan reimposed sanctions during 1988; the DPRK then severed diplomatic contacts with Japan, although mutual trade continued. From late 1990 there was a significant *rapprochement* between the DPRK and Japan, and in January 1991 a Japanese government delegation visited Pyongyang for discussions concerning the possible normalization of diplomatic relations. The Japanese delegation offered apologies, on behalf of its Government, for Japanese colonial aggression on the Korean peninsula between 1910 and 1945. Moreover, the Japanese Government expressed its willingness to make reparations for Japanese abuses of human rights in Korea during this period. Subsequent negotiations in 1991 foundered, however, owing to the DPRK's demand for reparations for damage inflicted after 1945 (which the Japanese Government denied) and to Japan's insistence that North Korea's nuclear installations be opened to outside inspection; normalization talks collapsed in November 1992, as the North Korean delegation abandoned the proceedings. Relations with Japan were further strained after the DPRK's testing of the *Rodong-1* missile in the Sea of Japan in May 1993. The missile, according to US intelligence reports, would be capable of reaching most of Japan's major cities (and possibly of carrying either a conventional or a nuclear warhead). None the less, Japan, like the Republic of Korea, opposed the possible imposition of international economic sanctions on the DPRK in response to North Korea's refusal to allow inspections of its nuclear facilities. Attempts failed to resume normalization talks in 1994, but in March 1995 a Japanese parliamentary group visited the DPRK and reached an agreement for the resumption of talks later that year. In May Japan agreed to North Korea's request for emergency rice aid, and later in the year Japan provided aid to help the DPRK overcome the effects of serious flooding (see above). In early 1996 Japan provided a shipment of fuel oil to alleviate the DPRK's energy shortfall.

Relations were complicated in 1997 by Japanese allegations that North Korea had abducted several Japanese citizens during the 1970s. However, in August 1997, for the first time since

1992, negotiations opened on the restoration of normal bilateral relations. The main focus of discussions was the issue of some 1,800 Japanese women married to North Koreans, who had never been permitted to leave the DPRK. An agreement was signed whereby the women were to be allowed to visit their relatives in Japan for short periods; the first such visits took place in November 1997 and January 1998. Moreover, in October 1997 the Japanese Government resumed the provision of aid to North Korea, suspended since mid-1996, donating food and medical supplies in response to the renewed appeals issued by the UN. Relations deteriorated in mid-1998, however, when the North Korean Government cancelled a third visit of the Japanese women to their homeland, following Japan's rejection of a North Korean investigation into the alleged abduction of Japanese nationals. The testing by the DPRK of a suspected *Taepo Dong-1* missile over Japanese territory, in August, further exacerbated tensions, prompting Japan to break off normalization talks, suspend food aid and postpone its contribution to the KEDO project. The DPRK subsequently claimed that the object launched was in fact a satellite. Tension between the two countries increased in March 1999, when Japanese naval forces pursued and opened fire on suspected North Korean spy ships that had infiltrated Japanese waters. Relations improved, however, following the DPRK's agreement with the USA, in September, to suspend its reported plans to test a new long-range missile. In October unofficial talks between North Korean and Japanese government officials were held in Singapore, and two weeks later Japan decided to allow the resumption of charter flights to the DPRK. In December, following a successful visit to the DPRK by a group of Japanese parliamentarians, Japan announced an end to its ban on food aid. Later in that month intergovernmental preparatory talks on re-establishing diplomatic relations were held in Beijing, and Japanese and North Korean Red Cross officials reached some agreement on humanitarian issues. Further progress was achieved by the two countries' Red Cross Societies at a meeting in March 2000. It was reported that the DPRK had agreed to co-operate in a further investigation into the fate of some 10 missing Japanese nationals, while Japan had agreed to a search for Korean citizens who had disappeared prior to 1945. In addition, visits to their homeland by Japanese women married to North Koreans were to resume shortly, and Japan was to provide some 100,000 metric tons of rice to the DPRK through WFP. In late April Japanese charter flights to North Korea resumed. Meanwhile, following further informal contacts between the North Korean and Japanese Governments, full normalization talks commenced in April 2000; further rounds of discussions took place during the year, despite an announcement by Japan in September that relations between the two countries would not be normalized until the cases of Japanese citizens allegedly abducted by North Korean agents had been solved. In October, however, a further round of negotiations took place in Beijing, China. The two sides agreed to meet again, but no date was set. In November the DPRK rejected an offer by Japan to extend economic aid rather than grant wartime compensation. Meanwhile, in September the long-delayed third visits home by the Japanese wives of North Korean men took place. In October Japan decided, on humanitarian grounds, to provide 500,000 metric tons of rice to North Korea. Later that month meetings held with the USA and Japan focused on obtaining the extradition from the DPRK, in return for economic aid, of terrorist Japanese Red Army members, who had hijacked a Japanese aircraft and forced it to fly to Pyongyang in 1970 (later being granted political asylum in North Korea). No agreement was reached.

In December 2000 the DPRK reiterated that normal relations with Japan could be restored only after the latter delivered an apology and compensation for its earlier colonial rule. However, at the same time former Japanese Prime Minister Tomiichi Murayama led a non-governmental delegation to Pyongyang, in an attempt to improve relations. In May 2001 Japan deported Kim Jong Nam, son of Kim Jong Il, for entering the country on a false passport (see above). In June the DPRK condemned Japan's refusal to issue visas to North Koreans planning to attend a conference on Japanese compensation for Korea, held in Japan. In August the DPRK demanded compensation for Korean victims of the atomic bombs dropped on Hiroshima and Nagasaki in 1945, and also for the collision of cargo ships from the two countries in July 2001.

The DPRK was one of several Asian countries that strongly condemned Japanese Prime Minister Junichiro Koizumi's visit to the Yasukuni Shrine in August 2001. During late 2001 the DPRK denounced Japan's military support for the USA's 'war on terrorism', stating that such support was aimed entirely at expanding Japan's military sphere of activities. In November Japanese police arrested Kan Young Kwan, an executive of the Japan-based, pro-North Korean organization, *Chongryon*, on charges of diverting funds through the use of local credit unions. The incident highlighted the sometimes-illegal activities of the North Korean community in Japan.

In mid-December 2001 the DPRK announced that it was abandoning efforts to locate missing Japanese nationals thought to have been abducted by North Korean agents. At the end of the month a suspected North Korean spy vessel was sunk by Japanese coastguard forces after it had been expelled from Japan's exclusive economic zone. The DPRK condemned the incident, but denied any involvement, accusing Japan of seeking to mislead world opinion. Japanese coastguard forces searched the sunken vessel in May 2002, and raised it in September of that year. In February 2002 the DPRK released a Japanese journalist who had been detained on spying charges since December 1999.

In an unexpected diplomatic move, Junichiro Koizumi visited Pyongyang in mid-September 2002, becoming the first incumbent Japanese Prime Minister to do so. His one-day visit, during which he held discussions with Kim Jong Il, was dominated by the latter's admission that North Korean agents had abducted 12 Japanese citizens in the 1970s and 1980s, of whom five were still alive. The remainder were said to have died of natural causes, although suspicions remained that they might have been executed, after Pyongyang failed to locate their graves. Kim apologized for the incidents, but attributed them to rogue elements within the security services. The admission led some sources to indicate that the total number of Japanese abductees might be as high as 100. The surviving captives were temporarily allowed to return to Japan in mid-October, although they had to leave behind any spouses or children. The Japanese authorities, however, refused to allow them to return to the DPRK after the visit. Despite this, representatives from the two countries held the first round of resumed discussions on the restoration of normal diplomatic relations in Malaysia at the end of October, but failed to make any progress.

In October 2002 the alleged admission by North Korean officials to their visiting US counterparts that Pyongyang was pursuing a secret nuclear weapons programme, alarmed Japan. Koizumi announced that Japan would halt further economic co-operation with the DPRK until the issues of the abducted Japanese citizens and the nuclear programme were resolved. Pyongyang warned Japan that it would abandon its moratorium on missile testing if normalization talks failed to make any progress. In separate incidents in late February and early March 2003 the DPRK test-launched two short-range ground-to-ship missiles in the Sea of Japan, and in early April tested a third missile in the Yellow Sea. However, it refrained from testing longer-range ballistic missiles, which Tokyo considered a threat to its security. In late March the DPRK was angered by Japan's launching of two spy satellites, believed to be part of a programme of intelligence-gathering on the DPRK initiated following the testing of the North Korean *Taepo Dong* missile over Japan in 1998 (see above). The Director-General of Japan's Defence Agency warned the DPRK that Japan could conduct a pre-emptive strike on North Korean missile facilities if necessary.

In May 2003 a North Korean vessel which had been sunk by Japanese coastguard forces in 2001 was put on display in a Tokyo museum. Some evidence found aboard the ship suggested links between North Korean drug manufacturers and criminal gangs in Japan. In June the DPRK cancelled a voyage of the *Man Gyong Bong* passenger ferry, used by ethnic Korean residents in Japan to visit relatives in North Korea, apparently owing to more stringent inspections of North Korean ships by Japan amid speculation of illegal goods transport. In August a group of 10 North Korean refugees claimed asylum at the Japanese embassy in the Thai capital of Bangkok, in what was believed to be the first incident of this kind outside China. At the end of the month Japan was one of six nations taking part in talks on the North Korean nuclear weapons programme held in Beijing. At the talks, Japan reportedly attempted to raise the issue of Japanese citizens abducted by the DPRK (see above). In the same month, Japanese authorities seized premises owned by the General Association of Korean Residents in Japan (*Chongryon*), reportedly owing to tax evasion. Also in August, the *Man Gyong Bong* ferry arrived in the Japanese port of Niigata on its first trip to Japan in seven months. Departure of the ship from Niigata was subsequently delayed after the vessel failed safety inspections carried out by the Japanese authorities. Relatives of Japanese nationals abducted by North Korea, as well as Japanese right-wing groups, held anti-North Korean protests at the port. In October the DPRK announced that it did not wish Japan to participate in future negotiations on its nuclear weapons programme, claiming that Japan was 'an obstacle to the peaceful settlement' of the nuclear issue, and citing Japanese attempts to 'blockade' North Korea. In January 2004 the Japanese House of Representatives approved legislation to permit the imposition of economic sanctions on the DPRK.

The DPRK has considered the USA to be its main enemy since the time of the Korean War and repeatedly accused the Republic of Korea of being a US 'puppet' state. Relations deteriorated after the DPRK seized a US naval vessel, the *USS Pueblo*, in 1968 and detained its crew for several months. In 1969 the DPRK shot down a US reconnaissance aircraft which had apparently violated North Korean airspace, resulting in the deaths of 31 US servicemen. In 1987, in response to alleged North Korean involvement in the bombing of a South Korean airliner, the USA placed the DPRK on its list of countries supporting terrorism, and restricted contacts between US and North Korean diplomats. Relations with the USA in the 1990s were largely dominated by the DPRK's suspected nuclear ambitions (see above). In December 1994 it was announced that agreement had been reached to establish liaison offices in Washington, DC, and Pyongyang in 1995, in preparation for an eventual resumption of full diplomatic relations. The USA insisted, however, that normal relations would be restored only when the DPRK ceased to export ballistic missiles and withdrew its troops from the border with South Korea; the DPRK, in turn, stated that liaison offices could only be opened when light-water nuclear reactors, in accordance with the October 1994 agreement between the DPRK and the USA, had been supplied. Relations faltered following the shooting-down of a US army helicopter which had apparently entered North Korean airspace; the DPRK initially refused to negotiate, but, after direct bilateral talks in December, the pilot was repatriated. In January 1995 the DPRK opened its ports to US commercial shipping and removed restrictions on the import of goods from the USA. Following the severe flooding in the DPRK in 1995 and 1996, the USA provided food aid and other flood relief.

The issue of four-way talks (see above) dominated relations between the USA and the DPRK in 1996, but parallel negotiations were conducted concerning the estimated 8,100 US soldiers who were listed as 'missing in action' following the Korean war. The USA agreed to provide funds to assist in locating the bodies, and it was reported that the DPRK had requested additional food aid in return for its co-operation. In December, following the issuing of a (US-brokered) apology by the DPRK for the submarine incursion in September, it was reported that the USA was prepared partially to revoke its economic sanctions against North Korea, and to allow the gradual expansion of bilateral trade. In early 1997 the USA responded to a renewed appeal issued by the UN for food aid and humanitarian assistance for North Korea, as a result of which the DPRK announced its intention to take part in exploratory discussions about the proposed quadripartite talks. Bilateral discussions with the USA during 1997 focused on the establishment of liaison offices, missile non-proliferation and procedures for the exhumation of the US servicemen listed as 'missing in action'. In August, however, the defection to the USA of two North Korean diplomats (the most senior officials yet to seek asylum in North America) resulted in the suspension of the third round of missile non-proliferation talks. The DPRK was unsuccessful in attempting to make its participation in full quadripartite talks conditional upon the withdrawal of US forces from the Korean peninsula and upon the provision of food aid. None the less, the USA responded positively, on humanitarian grounds, to two further UN appeals for food aid during the year. Relations with the USA were dominated by nuclear issues and other concerns regarding the DPRK's missile development programme in 1998 and 1999 (see above). The exhumation of US soldiers listed as 'missing in action' proceeded, with 22 sets of remains returned to the USA in 1998. In October 1999 US officials visited Pyongyang to receive the remains of four soldiers, in the first such transfer to take place on North Korean territory without the involvement of the UNC. A further 15 sets of remains were returned in

November 2000. Trade between the USA and the DPRK increased significantly following the partial revocation of economic sanctions against the latter in September 1999 (see above); US exports to the DPRK increased massively in 1999. Meanwhile, the USA continued to provide emergency food aid to the DPRK.

Relations between the DPRK and the USA were variable during 2000. In June the USA announced the partial easing of economic sanctions against the country. In August a round of talks with the USA in Washington on the DPRK's removal from the list of terrorist sponsors ended without agreement, although the meeting was described as productive. In September, however, officials from the DPRK declined to attend the UN Millennium summit meeting in New York, following a confrontation between the delegation and US security officials, who suspected the North Koreans of terrorism, at Frankfurt airport in Germany. The USA subsequently apologized, describing the incident as an 'innocent mistake' and refuting the DPRK's claim of a 'brazen plot'. In October Kim Jong Il's special envoy, Vice-Marshal Jo Myong Rok, paid a state visit to the USA, the most senior North Korean official ever to do so. Later that month the US Secretary of State, Madeleine Albright, reciprocated the visit and in Pyongyang met Kim Jong Il, who agreed in principle to halt his country's long-range missile-testing programme. Talks were described as 'serious and constructive'. Shortly afterwards, however, tension arose when two US fighter aircraft participating in a US-South Korean joint manoeuvre briefly crossed the military demarcation line into North Korean airspace. The DPRK protested to the UN, demanding a formal apology and the implementation of measures to prevent a recurrence of the incident.

Relations between the DPRK and the USA deteriorated during 2001 following the inauguration of George W. Bush as President of the latter. Bush adopted a tougher position towards the DPRK compared with his predecessor, and this also adversely affected inter-Korean relations (see above). The DPRK condemned the joint US-South Korean military exercises held in April. In May a non-governmental delegation from the USA visited the DPRK to examine evidence of atrocities committed by US troops during the Korean War. In June Bush stated that he was willing to resume negotiations with the DPRK, albeit linking these to a reduction in North Korea's missile programme and military deployments—terms rejected by the North. In July the North Korean Minister of Foreign Affairs, Paek Nam Sun, failed to attend the Association of South East Asian Nations (ASEAN) forum in Viet Nam, also attended by the US Secretary of State. During his visit to Moscow in August, Kim Jong Il reiterated North Korea's long-standing demand for the withdrawal of US troops from the South.

Following the terrorist attacks on the USA in September 2001, the USA paid increasing attention to North Korea's biological, chemical and nuclear weapons programmes. Although the DPRK had condemned those attacks, it subsequently opposed the US bombing of Afghanistan, and failed to provide any intelligence on terrorist networks to the USA. By late 2001 the DPRK was drawing increasing criticism from the USA, and in October the US State Department released its annual report on religious freedom, which included the DPRK on a list of countries suppressing such beliefs. In November Bush warned the DPRK not to take advantage of the war in Afghanistan to increase tensions on the Korean peninsula. Despite signing two UN treaties against terrorism in November, the DPRK remained on the USA's list of states sponsoring terrorism.

In late January 2002 the DPRK's relations with the USA deteriorated further following President Bush's reference to North Korea as forming an 'axis of evil' with Iran and Iraq. Bush's comments were believed to reflect concern that the DPRK was exporting weapons technology to countries the USA considered to be 'rogue states'. (During the 1990s the DPRK had exported missiles and related technology to countries such as Egypt, Iran, Libya, Pakistan and Syria, allegedly earning up to US $1,000m. a year.) However, when Bush visited the DMZ on a visit to the South, he urged the North to open up to the outside world. Although the USA ruled out any military action against the DPRK, in March 2002 it was revealed that the DPRK was one of seven nations considered a potential target for a US nuclear first strike, in the event of emergency circumstances. The DPRK responded by threatening to withdraw from existing agreements with the USA (see above). However, in April the North accepted a South Korean request to reopen dialogue with the USA, and invited a US envoy, Jack Pritchard, to discuss outstanding issues. At the same time the USA announced that it would release US \$95m. to the DPRK in order to accelerate the building of the replacement nuclear reactors—construction of which finally began in August 2002, with a view to completion in 2008. Pritchard himself attended the ground-breaking ceremony, but stated that the DPRK must accept international inspection of its nuclear facilities, a demand that Pyongyang stated was not mandatory until 2005.

Meanwhile, in July 2002 the Minister of Foreign Affairs, Paek Nam Sun, held an informal meeting with the US Secretary of State, Colin Powell, on the sidelines of the ASEAN Regional Forum (ARF) in Brunei—the highest-level contact between Pyongyang and the Bush Administration. In August the DPRK rejected US demands for a significant reduction of its conventional military forces along its border with the South. The USA had long-feared that these could be used to attack the 15,000 US troops deployed between Seoul and the DMZ in the event of hostilities.

Relations between the DPRK and the USA deteriorated significantly from October 2002 after the USA announced that senior North Korean officials had admitted to the visiting US Assistant Secretary of State for East Asian and Pacific Affairs, James Kelly, that the DPRK was pursuing a secret nuclear weapons programme in violation of the 1994 agreement. The clandestine programme was allegedly based on uranium extraction, whereas the suspended programme had been based on plutonium extraction. The admission reportedly came after Kelly presented his Northern hosts with credible US intelligence reports about the programme, although Pyongyang later denied that it had made such an admission. Within days the USA declared the 1994 framework null and void and placed renewed pressure on the DPRK to halt its nuclear activities. The DPRK responded by stating that it would consider halting its nuclear programme if the USA would sign a non-aggression treaty guaranteeing the DPRK's sovereignty with Pyongyang—a demand rejected by Washington. Pyongyang subsequently warned the USA of severe military measures if it continued to reject such a treaty. In the middle of November, however, the USA finally halted petroleum shipments to North Korea, citing the latter's violation of the 1994 framework. Further confusion over Pyongyang's nuclear programme emerged on 17 November 2002 when North Korean radio reportedly admitted that the country already possessed nuclear weapons. However, the exact translation of the statement was in doubt, and most analysts concluded that the broadcast had stated that the DPRK was entitled to possess such weapons. At the same time it was widely reported that Pakistan had provided the technical expertise of North Korea's nuclear programme in exchange for ballistic missiles. Attention focused on the north-western city of Kusong, some 30 km north west of Yongbyon, as the centre of the secret programme.

The diplomatic crisis between the DPRK and the USA worsened in December 2002 when Pyongyang announced that it would restart its nuclear reactor at Yongbyon, and the USA accused the DPRK of narcotics trafficking in order to raise money to support its declining economy. Amid increasingly strong rhetoric from both sides, former US President Bill Clinton revealed that he had come close to ordering airstrikes on the DPRK's nuclear facilities in 1994, and Spanish commandos, acting on intelligence supplied by the USA, seized a North Korean cargo vessel, the *So San*, carrying Scud missiles to Yemen, in the Arabian Sea. However, the vessel was allowed to deliver its cargo after Yemen confirmed the legitimacy of the order. The incident was widely seen as a US warning to Pyongyang regarding its weapons proliferation. Later in that month the DPRK removed the IAEA's monitoring and surveillance equipment from the Yongbyon facility. The US Secretary of Defense, Donald Rumsfeld, warned Pyongyang not to take advantage of the USA's planned attack on Iraq (see the chapter on Iraq) to raise regional tensions, stating that the USA could fight against both countries simultaneously. Rumsfeld had earlier stated that the DPRK possessed nuclear weapons, and security analysts concluded that Pyongyang already possessed between two and five nuclear devices.

In late December 2002 the IAEA reported that North Korean technicians had transferred 1,000 fuel rods (out of 8,000 necessary to reactivate it) to the Yongbyon reactor, ostensibly for the production of electricity, but probably for the production of plutonium required to manufacture nuclear devices. The DPRK expelled the two remaining IAEA inspectors at the end of that year.

In early January 2003 the DPRK announced its withdrawal from the NPT, and the IAEA responded by adopting a resolution condemning Pyongyang's recent behaviour. However, President Bush indicated that the USA would resume petroleum deliveries if the DPRK abandoned its nuclear weapons programme. Meanwhile, North Korean diplomats in January held unofficial discussions with the Governor of New Mexico, Bill Richardson, who had negotiated with Pyongyang in the past. In February Pyongyang stated that the Yongbyon reactor was operating normally, and that any US military build-up in the region could lead the North to launch a pre-emptive strike on US forces anywhere in the world. Pyongyang also threatened to withdraw from the 1953 armistice if the USA imposed a blockade on the DPRK. Despite these threats, the USA deployed long-range bombers to its bases on the Pacific island of Guam as a precautionary measure, and warned that although it favoured a peaceful resolution of the crisis, it had not ruled out any options—including military action.

In early March 2003 the USA and South Korea began their annual joint military exercises amid condemnation by the North, which announced at the end of the month that it was severing military contacts with the USA at the liaison office at the DMZ. Also in early March four North Korean fighter aircraft intercepted a US reconnaissance aircraft in international airspace and closely pursued its flight, the first such incident in 32 years. Between late February and the beginning of April 2003 the DPRK also test-fired three short-range missiles, although refrained from testing its longer-range ballistic missiles. The commencement of the US-led campaign in Iraq in late March 2003 alarmed Pyongyang, which reportedly believed that the USA would target itself at some future date. By early April the USA had imposed new sanctions on the DPRK's Government and its Changgwang Sinyong Corporation, for exporting ballistic missiles to Pakistan. However, the sanctions were largely symbolic, since the USA had minimal economic links with the DPRK. Japanese sources reported that North Korean and US diplomats were quietly seeking a peaceful solution to the crisis. Later in the month, the seizure by Australian authorities of the *Pong Su*, a North Korean ship carrying 50 kg of heroin confirmed US claims that the DPRK was involved in drugs trafficking. Also in April, the UN Security Council held discussions on the North Korean crisis for the first time. The DPRK stated prior to the talks that the imposition of economic sanctions through the Security Council would amount to a declaration of war.

Tensions between the DPRK and the USA increased in late April 2003 after ambiguous statements by the North's official media in which it indicated it was preparing to reprocess, or was actually reprocessing, 8,000 spent fuel rods, a move that would enable it rapidly to produce nuclear weapons. Officials from North Korea, the USA and China held high-level discussions in Beijing during 23–24 April over Pyongyang's nuclear weapons programme. No agreements were reached, however, and US sources stated that the DPRK had, for the first time, admitted to possessing nuclear weapons and had threatened to carry out a nuclear test. Whilst the DPRK insisted on a guarantee of non-aggression from the USA before it would consider dismantling its nuclear programme, the latter remained adamant that North Korea should not be permitted to make demands for complying with its international obligations. In mid-May Pyongyang cited US behaviour against it as a reason for abandoning the Joint Declaration of the Denuclearization of the Korean Peninsula, a 1992 commitment with the South on a nuclear-free peninsula.

In June 2003 the DPRK for the first time publicly defended its nuclear weapons strategy, declaring through the state news agency that the development of nuclear weapons was a 'deterrent', and that the programme' was not aimed at threatening or blackmailing'. In July there were new indications from US and Asian intelligence sources that the DPRK was operating a second secret nuclear facility, in addition to the plant at Yongbyon. At the end of July it was announced that the DPRK had agreed to take part in multilateral talks on its nuclear weapons programme with the USA, the Republic of Korea, Japan, China and Russia. Prior to the talks, tensions were exacerbated by comments of US Under-Secretary of State John Bolton, who launched a virulent attack on Kim Jong Il in the course of a speech given in Seoul. Pyongyang responded by describing Bolton as 'human scum' and refusing to negotiate with him at the talks. Furthermore, immediately in advance of the negotiations, Jack Pritchard resigned as US special envoy to North Korea. The six-party talks duly took place in Beijing in late August, but little progress was achieved. US Assistant Secretary of State James Kelly demanded that the DPRK unconditionally abandon its nuclear weapons programme in a 'complete, verifiable and irreversible manner'. The North Korean Vice-Minister of Foreign Affairs, Kim Yong Il, however, warned that unless the USA provided a guarantee of non-aggression, Pyongyang would continue to develop its nuclear self-defence capacity.

Following the six-party talks in Beijing, it was reported in September 2003 that President George W. Bush had authorized James Kelly to abandon the USA's insistence on the full dismantling of the North Korean weapons programme before any concessions could be made. It was indicated that verifiable progress on dismantling might be sufficient. In October President Bush said in Bangkok that the USA would be prepared to offer security assurances to the DPRK in exchange for verifiable dismantling. However, he said that a bilateral non-aggression treaty, as desired by Pyongyang, was not a possibility, and that any guarantee would involve China, Russia, the Republic of Korea and Japan, as well as the USA. Also in October, the North Korean state news agency claimed that the DPRK had successfully completed the reprocessing of 8,000 spent fuel rods, thus generating sufficient plutonium to build a nuclear bomb. The USA, however, dismissed the claim. It was reported in the same month that neither the USA or IAEA possessed certainty as to whether the DPRK was capable of producing a nuclear bomb. However, in November the Central Intelligence Agency (CIA) reported to the US Congress that it believed the DPRK had the technology to turn its nuclear fuel into functioning weapons. In early December KEDO (an international consortium established in 1995 following a 1994 agreement with the USA on assistance for energy development in the DPRK in return for nuclear non-proliferation, see above) announced that it would be suspending for one year its construction in the DPRK of two non-military nuclear reactors. Also in December, the USA rejected an offer from the DPRK to 'freeze' its nuclear programme in return for concessions on security and energy aid. The USA maintained that the suspension of the nuclear programme was insufficient, and that verifiable dismantling of North Korean nuclear capacity remained necessary.

In January 2004 a group of US nuclear scientists, including Siegfried Hecker, the former director of the Los Alamos nuclear research centre, was permitted to visit the Yongbyon plant in an unofficial capacity. Hecker subsequently stated that although he had seen no proof that the DPRK had produced a nuclear bomb, he had been shown radioactive plutonium metal. Also in January, the influential International Institute for Strategic Studies, based in the United Kingdom, predicted that the DPRK could be producing as many as 13 nuclear bombs a year in the near future and warned that deadlock in negotiations was giving the country time to develop its capacities. There was further speculation on the existence of a second nuclear programme for enriching uranium (in addition to the plutonium-reprocessing activities at Yongbyon). The DPRK continued to deny the existence of such a programme. In February a fresh round of six-party talks took place in Beijing, but no significant resolutions were reached. The DPRK continued to reject US demands for 'complete, verifiable and irreversible dismantling' of its nuclear capabilities.

During the years of the so-called Sino-Soviet dispute the DPRK fluctuated in its allegiance to each of its powerful northern neighbours, the People's Republic of China and the USSR. Kim Il Sung made several official visits to China in the late 1980s, which were interpreted by some Western observers as an attempt to establish closer relations in view of the erosion of communist power in many Eastern European countries. However, the DPRK was aggrieved at China's establishment of full diplomatic relations with the Republic of Korea in August 1992. China appeared largely conciliatory with regard to North Korea's nuclear programme, and during 1993 and the first months of 1994 indicated that it would veto any attempt by the UN Security Council to impose economic sanctions on the DPRK. In 1997 China agreed to provide substantial food aid to the DPRK to alleviate the effects of flooding. Later in that year China accepted US and South Korean proposals for quadri-partite negotiations with North Korea to conclude a new peace agreement with the South, and between December 1997 and August 1999 it participated in all six rounds of these negotiations. Relations between the DPRK and China remained close in 1998, with the latter donating grain, fertilizers and crude petroleum to Pyongyang over the course of the year. A high-level

North Korean delegation visited China in June 1999. During the visit China announced that it would provide the country with 150,000 metric tons of food aid and 400,000 tons of coke over the following months. In October 1999 the Chinese Minister of Foreign Affairs, Tang Jiaxuan, participated in celebrations held in Pyongyang to commemorate the 50th anniversary of the establishment of diplomatic relations between the two countries.

In late 1999 international attention was focused on the uncertain situation of the large number of North Koreans (estimated at some 30,000 by South Korean sources and at 200,000 by the voluntary organization Médecins Sans Frontières) who had crossed the border into the People's Republic of China in recent years. In early 2000 it was reported that China had returned some 10,000 escapees to the DPRK during 1999. The number of migrants was thought to fluctuate, according to the season.

In February 2000 China permitted the DPRK to open a consulate-general in Hong Kong. In the following month Kim Jong Il attended a function at the People's Republic of China's embassy in Pyongyang. This was his first visit to the mission for 15 years. In May Kim Jong Il visited China, his first official trip abroad for 17 years, in advance of the historic inter-Korean summit meeting. In late October Kim Jong Il met the visiting Chinese Minister of Defence, Chi Haotian. In mid-January 2001 the North Korean leader paid a second visit to the People's Republic. During this visit, Kim held extensive talks with Chinese leaders in Beijing, and also toured the new business zones of Shanghai and Shenzhen, where he observed joint-venture projects with foreign multinational corporations, telecommunications projects and the Shanghai Stock Exchange. It was widely believed that he was seeking inspiration for the revival of the DPRK's crisis-ridden economy and advice from Chinese leaders on developing Pyongyang's role within the international community.

In early September 2001 Chinese President Jiang Zemin paid an official visit to North Korea, his first such visit since 1990. Jiang promised an additional 200,000 tons of food aid and 30,000 tons of diesel oil as a gesture of goodwill to alleviate North Korea's economic crisis. Jiang also reportedly urged North Korea to resume discussions with the South. By early 2002 it was thought that the DPRK was placing a renewed emphasis on relations with China in order to deflect criticism from the USA.

During 2002 the DPRK and China continued to seek the reconnection of the inter-Korean railway lines and their subsequent linking to China's own railway system. In May 2002, however, China's forcible removal of North Korean refugees from South Korean embassies in the People's Republic again brought the issue of the refugees to international attention. Several groups of North Korean refugees had, in 2002, fled to Western, Japanese and South Korean diplomatic offices in China, embarrassing the latter, since Beijing had signed a treaty with Pyongyang providing for the repatriation of refugees. In late June Beijing allowed 24 northern refugees who had been concealed in the embassy of the Republic of Korea to leave for that country. After that incident, Beijing began an operation against South Korean activists and missionaries who had been helping northerners to flee via China. It was estimated that as many as 300,000 North Korean refugees were already residing in China, with US sources stating that as many as 50,000 had fled to China in 2001 alone.

In October 2002 the DPRK appointed a Chinese entrepreneur of Dutch citizenship, Yang Bin, as the new governor of its recently created Sinuiju Special Administrative Region; however, the Beijing authorities arrested him on charges of bribery and fraud (see above). By early 2003 China was becoming increasingly concerned about the growing diplomatic crisis between the DPRK and the USA over the former's decision formally to restart its nuclear programme. In late February 2003 the President of the DPRK's SPA Presidium, Kim Yong Nam, visited Beijing and pledged to maintain strong bilateral relations. Beijing was expected to use its influence with Pyongyang to resolve the situation, albeit warning the UN Security Council not to involve itself in the matter. In March China cut its oil supply to the DPRK via a pipeline from Liaoning Province for three days, following North Korean missile tests in the Sea of Japan (see above).

In late April 2003 China hosted and participated in senior-level meetings between the DPRK and the USA over Pyongyang's nuclear weapons programme (see above). Immediately prior to the talks, Vice-Marshal Jo Myong Rok, Pyongyang's second-highest ranking official, led a military delegation to

China, and held meetings with President Hu Jintao and senior military leaders. Chinese diplomatic efforts played a major role in ensuring North Korean participation in the six-party talks on the nuclear issue that were held in Beijing in August 2003. In late October Wu Bangguo, Chairman of the Standing Committee of China's National People's Congress, made an official visit to Pyongyang. In April 2004 Kim Jong Il made a secretive visit to China, where he held talks with President Hu Jintao and other officials. Topics under discussion included the nuclear issue, with China reportedly urging the DPRK to modify its stance, and economic matters.

In the mid-1980s the DPRK placed increased emphasis on its relations with the USSR, culminating in a new arrangement for the supply of Soviet aircraft and an exchange visit by senior government officials. The DPRK's diplomatic isolation became more pronounced in the early 1990s, as former communist bloc countries moved to foster relations with the Republic of Korea. Furthermore, the USSR announced that, from January 1991, its barter trading system with the DPRK would be abolished in favour of trade in convertible currencies at world market prices. However, an agreement was reported to have been signed in May 1993 by the DPRK and the Russian Federation (which, following the dissolution of the USSR, had assumed responsibility for many of the USSR's international undertakings) on technological and scientific co-operation. Negotiations on the renewal of the 1961 bilateral treaty of friendship, co-operation and assistance, which expired in 1996 (but remained valid in the interim), opened in January 1997. Discussions on the rescheduling of the terms of repayment of North Korea's debt to Russia took place in October. In March 1999 a new bilateral treaty of friendship, good neighbourliness and co-operation was initialled in Pyongyang; a formal signing followed in February 2000, during a visit to Pyongyang by the Russian Minister of Foreign Affairs, Igor Ivanov. The treaty was ratified by the DPRK in April. In July President Vladimir Putin became the first Russian (or Soviet leader) to visit North Korea. During the trip Kim Jong Il declared himself willing to halt missile development in exchange for access to space rocket technology funded by other countries, although he subsequently seemed to renege on this offer. Following Putin's visit, co-operation between Russia and the DPRK placed a strong emphasis on connecting the latter's rail system to the Trans-Siberian railway, with a view to creating a long-awaited Eurasian transport corridor, and in March 2001 the two countries signed a railway co-operation agreement.

In late April 2001 the DPRK's Minister of the People's Armed Forces, Vice-Marshal Kim Il Chol, visited Moscow and reportedly negotiated the acquisition of defensive weapons such as SU-27 aircraft, anti-aircraft systems and intelligence-gathering equipment, in addition to signing a military co-operation protocol.

In August 2001 Kim Jong Il paid a 24-day visit across Russia to Moscow, where he and President Putin signed a new declaration of co-operation in politics, the economy, military, science and technology, and culture. However, Russia also urged the DPRK to settle the latter's outstanding bilateral debt of as much as US $5,500m. The DPRK had repaid some of this amount by sending hundreds of forced-labour woodcutters to work in Khabarovsk Krai (territory)—although such labour camps were reportedly closed down by late 2002. During his visit, Kim also toured industrial plants, including those manufacturing power equipment and tanks, a pig farm, beer brewery and the Krunichev Space Centre, outside Moscow. Kim reaffirmed the DPRK's moratorium on missile-testing until 2003, and urged the withdrawal of US troops from South Korea. Kim's visit suggested that the DPRK was seeking closer relations with Russia, in addition to China, to strengthen its international standing. In late October 2001 the new Russian ambassador in Pyongyang, Andrei Karlov, held a banquet at which he spoke of strengthening bilateral ties. In December Kim had a meeting with Karlov.

The DPRK continued to maintain strong relations with Russia in 2002. In April two separate Russian delegations, one led by the Mayor of St Petersburg, Vladimir Yakovlev, the other by the Russian Presidential Representative in the Far Eastern Federal Okrug (district), Konstantin Pulikovskii, visited Pyongyang to discuss co-operation in all fields, particularly business. In May the Minister of Foreign Affairs, Paek Nam Sun, visited Moscow, in the first such visit in 15 years. In late July the Russian Minister of Foreign Affairs, Igor Ivanov, visited Pyongyang, and in late August Kim Jong Il visited the Russian city of Vladivostok, where he held discussions with Putin, mainly

focusing on the reconnection of railway links across the Korean peninsula. At the same time the DPRK and the Russian Oblast of Amur signed a co-operation agreement on agriculture and forestry. In October 2002 two North Korean military delegations visited Russia, and in December the Mayor of Moscow, Yurii Luzhkov, visited Pyongyang.

As the diplomatic crisis over the DPRK's nuclear weapons programme deteriorated in January 2003, Russia sought to defuse the situation by sending the Deputy Minister of Foreign Affairs, Aleksandr Losyukov, to Pyongyang, where he held discussions with Kim Jong Il. Losyukov, who had earlier visited China and subsequently the USA, urged a three-stage formula whereby the international community would accept a nuclear-free Korean peninsula, guarantees for the regime's security, and a resumption of humanitarian and economic aid. Pyongyang reiterated that the crisis could be resolved only through discussions with the USA. In February Kim Jong Il again visited the Russian embassy in Pyongyang, where a banquet was held on the occasion of his 61st birthday.

In late March 2003 a hitherto unrealized Russian proposal to supply the DPRK with natural gas from the island of Sakhalin in return for Pyongyang's abandonment of its nuclear programme was raised by the South Korean Government. Russia's Deputy Minister of Foreign Affairs, Alexandr Losyukov, attended the six-party talks held in Beijing in August 2003 to discuss the North Korean nuclear weapons programme. At the talks Losyukov urged both the USA and the DPRK to show flexibility. In late 2003 Russia appeared to be expanding its economic links with the DPRK, with a team of Russian engineers inspecting a cargo port and petroleum refinery at Raijin, as well as assessing a stretch of railway linking the two countries across the Tumen river. In March 2004 Kim Jong Il sent a congratulatory message to Vladimir Putin upon his re-election as Russia's President.

The DPRK's unilateral application for UN membership, first announced in May 1991, represented a radical departure from its earlier insistence that the two Koreas should occupy a single UN seat. This development was welcomed by the Republic of Korea, and both countries were admitted separately to the UN in September of that year. In September 1999, for the first time in seven years, the North Korean Minister of Foreign Affairs attended and addressed the annual session of the UN General Assembly, in what was perceived as an attempt to end the DPRK's diplomatic isolation. Furthermore, in January 2000 Italy became the first of the G-7 group of Western industrialized nations (and the sixth member of the EU) to establish diplomatic relations with the DPRK, and in May Australia restored diplomatic ties with Pyongyang. Diplomatic relations were established with the Philippines in July and with the United Kingdom in December. During 2001 the DPRK further expanded its range of diplomatic partners, opening relations with the Netherlands, Belgium, Canada, Spain, Germany, Luxembourg, Greece, Brazil, New Zealand, Kuwait, the European Union, Bahrain, Turkey, and Liechtenstein. A number of these countries appointed chargés d'affaires to serve in Seoul prior to the foundation of embassies in Pyongyang. Relations with Timor-Leste were established in late 2002. In May 2003 the DPRK opened its first embassy in London, amid protests from human rights protesters. Relations with Ireland were established in December. In March 2004 the Australian ambassador to Beijing, Alan Thomas, was instructed to present his credentials in Pyongyang.

In April 2000 the DPRK formally applied to join ASEAN (see p. 154). Following the DPRK's admittance to the ASEAN Regional Forum (ARF), a meeting in Thailand in July was attended for the first time by the North Korean Minister of Foreign Affairs, Paek Nam Sun, who held unprecedented meetings with his South Korean, Japanese and US counterparts. In November the Asia-Pacific Economic Co-operation (APEC, see p. 147) forum supported the DPRK's guest status of that organization. Full membership was expected to follow in 2007, upon the expiry of a 10-year moratorium on new members. In late July 2001 the President of the Presidium of the SPA, Kim Yong Nam, visited Viet Nam, Laos and Cambodia. In early March 2002 Kim visited Thailand and Malaysia, where he discussed mainly trade issues. Prime Minister Mahathir bin Mohamad of Malaysia accepted an invitation to visit the DPRK, and Indonesian President Megawati Sukarnoputri visited the country at the end of March 2002. Kim Yong Nam reciprocated Megawati's visit in July of that year. The President of Viet Nam, Tran Duc Luong, visited the DPRK in May 2002 and signed several economic and legal co-operation agreements. In late 2002 the DPRK and Taiwan were exploring the possibility of establishing mutual liaison offices. In 2003 there were reports that the DPRK was selling military equipment to Pakistan, and also that military relations with Myanmar were being developed. In early 2004 Pakistani nuclear scientist Abdul Qadeer Khan confessed that he had sold nuclear secrets to the DPRK.

Pyongyang maintained close links with a number of Arab and Middle Eastern countries, including Egypt, Libya, Syria and Iran. The President of the Presidium of the SPA, Kim Yong Nam, visited Libya and Syria in July 2002. The DPRK retained long-standing ties with many African countries, and had military advisers working in 12 of them. In January 2004 the Vice-President of the Presidium of the SPA, Yang Hyong Sop, visited Nigeria to discuss an agreement on military technology.

Government

The highest organ of state power is the unicameral Supreme People's Assembly (SPA), with 687 members, elected (unopposed) for five years by universal adult suffrage. The SPA elects, for its duration, the Chairman of the National Defence Commission, who, since the effective abolition of the presidency in September 1998, holds the most senior accessible office of state (although this is not formally stated in the Constitution). The SPA elects the Premier and, on the latter's recommendation, appoints other Ministers to form the Cabinet. The President of the SPA Presidium, whose members are elected by the SPA, represents the State in its relations with foreign countries.

Political power is held by the communist Korean Workers' Party (KWP), which is the most influential party in the Democratic Front for the Reunification of the Fatherland (comprising the KWP and two minor parties). The Front presents an approved list of candidates for elections to representative bodies. The KWP's highest authority is the Party Congress, which elects a Central Committee to supervise party work. The Committee elects a Political Bureau (Politburo) to direct policy. The Presidium of the Politburo is the KWP's most powerful policy-making body.

The DPRK comprises nine provinces and two cities, each with an elected Local People's Assembly.

Defence

Military service is selective: army five to eight years, navy five to 10 years, and air force three to four years. The estimated total strength of the armed forces in August 2003 was 1,082,000: army 950,000, air force 86,000, and navy 46,000. Security and border troops numbered 189,000, and there was a workers' and peasants' militia ('Red Guards') numbering about 3.5m. In late 2002 it was reported that the DPRK was planning to make substantial reductions to its armed forces. The ratio of North Korea's armed forces to total population is believed to be the highest in the world. Defence expenditure for 2003 was budgeted at 15.4% of total spending, up from 14.9% (3,200m. won) in 2002. South Korean intelligence sources estimated the real level of defence expenditure at 43.5% of total spending in 2003.

Economic Affairs

In 2002, according to South Korean estimates, the DPRK's gross national income (GNI) was about US $17,045m., equivalent to some $762 per head. It was estimated that in 1998 the North Korean economy declined for the ninth successive year, contracting by 1.1%, in real terms. In 1999, however, it was estimated that the economy grew by 6.2%, and in 2000 by 1.3%. Growth was estimated at 3.7% in 2001 and at 1.2% in 2002. During 1990–2002, according to estimates by the World Bank, the population increased by an annual average of 1.0%.

Agriculture (including forestry and fishing) contributed an estimated 30.2% of gross domestic product (GDP) in 2002, according to South Korean sources. In 2002, according to FAO estimates, 28.7% of the economically active population were employed in agriculture. The principal crops are rice, maize, potatoes, sweet potatoes and soybeans. The DPRK is not self-sufficient in food, and imports substantial amounts of wheat, rice and maize annually. Food shortages became a severe problem from the mid-1990s. By 1999 the food situation had improved to some extent, owing to fertilizer aid from international donors, agrarian reform and increased potato production, although shortages continued and were exacerbated by severe drought in 2000 and 2001, and subsequent typhoons and floods.

According to the World Food Programme, cereal shortfalls of some 40,000 tons affected 2.2m. people in December 2003. In December 2000 the Government launched an intensive campaign for potato growing and double-crop farming, and in November 2001 construction began on a 7,000-ha goat farm near Pyongyang. According to South Korean estimates, grain production was 3.9m. tons in 2001 and 4.1m. tons in 2002. Potato production was 2.3m. tons in 2001 and 1.9m. tons in 2002, according to FAO. The raising of livestock (principally cattle and pigs), forestry and fishing are important. During 1991–2002, according to FAO, agricultural production decreased by an annual average of 1.8%. In 2002, according to South Korean estimates, agricultural GDP rose by 4.2%, following an increase of 6.8% in 2001 and a decline of 1.9% in 2000.

In 2002, according to South Korean estimates, industry (including mining, manufacturing, construction and power) contributed 38.2% of GDP. In 1990 the industrial sector employed 31.6% of the labour force. In 2002 the GDP of the mining and manufacturing sector declined by an estimated 2.5%, compared with 2001 (when an increase of 3.9% was estimated), but that of the construction sector increased by an estimated 10.4%, compared with a rise of 7.0% in 2001.

Mining contributed 7.8% of GDP in 2002, according to South Korean estimates. The DPRK possesses considerable mineral wealth, with large deposits of coal, iron, lead, copper, zinc, tin, silver and gold. The country was formerly the second largest producer of magnesia products in the world, but output is believed to have declined significantly. There are unexploited offshore deposits of petroleum and natural gas. South Korean sources estimated that in 2002 output in the mining sector declined by 3.8%—compared with growth rates of 5.8% in 2000 and 4.8% in 2001.

In 2002, according to South Korean estimates, the manufacturing sector contributed 18.0% of GDP (light industries 7.0% and heavy industries 11.0%). In the 1990s industrial development concentrated on heavy industry (metallurgy—notably steel production—machine-building, cement and chemicals). The textiles industry has provided significant exports. South Korean sources estimated that the GDP of the manufacturing sector declined by 2.0% in 2002, following an increase of 3.5% in 2001.

In 2000 it was estimated that 86% of the DPRK's energy supply was derived from coal, followed in importance by hydroelectricity and petroleum (6%). A 30-MW nuclear reactor was believed to have been inaugurated in 1987. Light-water nuclear reactors were being constructed, for the purpose of electricity generation, in accordance with an agreement concluded with the USA in 1994 (see Recent History). However, in December 2003 construction of the reactors was suspended for one year, following North Korea's resumption of its nuclear weapons programme. In 2000, according to South Korean sources, some 67% of the DPRK's electricity was generated by hydroelectric power stations, with the remaining 33% of the country's requirements being provided by thermal power stations. During the 1990s the DPRK experienced increasing power shortages, as generation and transmission infrastructure deteriorated. Although South Korean sources estimated that electricity production increased by some 30% between 1986 and 1994, output is insufficient for the DPRK's needs, and there have been frequent reports of rationing in an effort to conserve fuel and energy. The DPRK's total electricity consumption in 1998 was only 61% of that in 1991. Severe drought in the late 1990s and 2000 adversely affected the production of hydroelectric power. In early 2003 the DPRK was attempting to increase its electricity output through the construction of new hydroelectric power plants in various provinces. In May 2003 the DPRK also reportedly signed a memorandum concerning a high-voltage grid project with a Swiss company. Petroleum imports totalled only around 0.6m. metric tons in 2001 and 2002. The USA suspended fuel oil shipments in late 2002, following Pyongyang's alleged admission that it was pursuing a secret nuclear programme. From the 1990s, and especially in early 2002, the DPRK sought greater foreign assistance in developing its offshore oilfields, located to the west in the Bohai Sea, and also in the north-east, near Chongjin city. A limited number of joint ventures were established with foreign oil companies. In 1999 the DPRK succeeded in producing 300,000 tons of petroleum from a well located off Sukchon County, equivalent to about half the amount of petroleum imported in that year, although falling far short of the amount needed to meet the country's acute energy needs. In 2001, according to South Korean sources, per caput energy consumption in North Korea in 2001 was 0.73 tons of oil equivalent, around six times less that the figure for South Korea.

The services sector employed an estimated 30.4% of the labour force in 1990. South Korean sources estimated that in 2002 the DPRK's services sector accounted for 31.6% of GDP. In 2002 output in the sector was estimated to have declined by 0.2%, having decreased by 0.3% in 2001, and increased by 1.2% in 2000.

The trade deficit, including exchanges with South Korea, totalled US $889.0m. in 2002. In 2002 total exports, excluding trade with South Korea, reached $735.0m. and imports totalled $1,525.4m., thus giving a trade deficit of $790.4m. (compared with a deficit of $970.1m. in the previous year). The DPRK's principal source of imports in 2002 was the People's Republic of China (accounting for 24.7% of total imports), followed by the Republic of Korea (19.5%) and Thailand (7.1%). The principal market for exports was the Republic of Korea, which purchased 27.0% of total exports, followed by China (26.9%), and then Japan (23.3%). China was a source of crude petroleum, food and vehicles, while Japan was a destination for industrial and agricultural goods. Inter-Korean trade increased by 28% in 2000, to reach US $425.2m., rising to $403.0m. in 2001. In 2002 inter-Korean trade increased by 59% to $641.7m. Total trade (excluding exchanges with the Republic of Korea) increased by 15.1% to reach $2,270m. in 2001, but decreased slightly, by 0.4%, to $2,260.4m. in 2002. The principal exports in that year were live animals (35.5% of the value of total exports, excluding trade with the Republic of Korea), textiles (16.7%) and machinery and electrical equipment (11.6%). Other export commodities in the late 1990s included tobacco and silk. The principal imports in 2002 were mineral products (15.5% of the value of total imports, excluding trade with the Republic of Korea), machinery and electrical equipment (15.4%), and textiles (10.4%). Other import items included road vehicles, chemicals and groceries. The 2002 budget envisaged revenue and expenditure balancing at 22,174m. won, compared with 21,571m. won in 2001. A budgetary deficit of 38.7m. won was recorded in 2001. The DPRK's total external debt was estimated to be US $12,460m. in 2000. The average annual rate of inflation in 1993 was estimated at 5%. However, following the introduction of market-orientated reforms in 2002, the inflation rate was said to have reached 4,000% in that year.

It is difficult to present an accurate economic profile of the DPRK, owing to the lack of reliable statistical data. North Korea's economic situation deteriorated sharply in the early 1990s, following the abandonment, in 1991 and 1992, respectively, of the barter trading system between the DPRK and the USSR (then its major trading partner) and China in favour of trade conducted exclusively in convertible currencies. The USSR also substantially reduced deliveries of crude petroleum and cereals, resulting in a severe decline in industrial production. The years 1994–97 were designated 'a period of adjustment in socialist economic construction', during which emphasis was to be transferred from traditional heavy industries to agriculture, light industry and trade. The Rajin-Sonbong Free Economic and Trade Zone was established in 1991 in the north-east of the country; however, attempts to attract foreign capital into the Zone were largely unsuccessful. The severe food shortages in the mid-1990s prompted Pyongyang to appeal for international food aid and humanitarian assistance. From the late 1990s the DPRK slowly began to open up its economy, developing trading relations with various European and Asian countries and increasing the number of limited joint ventures with foreign firms. In October 2000 the DPRK reportedly established a research institute on capitalism, and it was believed that Kim Jong Il was seeking to introduce Chinese-style economic reforms following his visit to China in January 2001 (see above). The DPRK also began developing its information technology (IT) industry, and by 2001 was operating six official websites. Joint IT ventures were established with institutes in the South, and in October the DPRK launched its first e-mail service provider in co-operation with a company based in China. In May the DPRK joined Intelsat (an international commercial satellite telecommunications organization), and in November the country agreed to adopt the global system for mobile communications (GSM) in the Rajin-Sonbong enterprise zone. During 2002 there were signs of a significant change in economic policy. In July the Government abandoned rationing, allowing farmers to sell produce at market prices, and wages were raised by a factor of 10–17, to take into account the concomitant price rises caused by the reforms. State assistance was reduced, and the value of the won decreased to as little as one-fiftieth of its previous value in relation to the US dollar. (In 2003 academics at Kim Il Sung University in Pyongyang reportedly revised economics textbooks to reflect changes in the DPRK's economic system.) Also in 2002, a new 150-km waterway linking Pyongyang and Nampo was completed in October; and from December, in apparent displeasure with US policy towards the DPRK, the North Korean Government prohibited the use of the US dollar and adopted the euro as its official currency of foreign exchange. A further major reform of 2002 was the creation in September of a 'Special Administrative Region' in the city of Sinuiju, followed later in the year by the establishment of a special industrial zone at Kaesong and a new tourist zone at Mount Kumgang. Whilst prospects for the special zone in Sinuiju were inauspicious following the arrest of its governor, Yang Bin (see Recent History), it was hoped that the special zone at Kaesong, on the border with South Korea, would attract investment from South Korean small- and medium-sized enterprises. In 2003 South Korean companies Hyundai and Korean Land were developing an international business park in Kaesong. In March 2003 the Minister of Finance announced that the state budget's revenue would be 13.6% higher than in 2002, while expenditure would be 14.4% higher than in the previous year. Defence spending amounted to 15.4% of total projected expenditure, an increase of 0.5% in comparison with the previous year. The Government would also issue bonds for the first time in 50 years. However, analysts remained doubtful about Kim Jong Il's ability to restructure the economy without destabilizing the foundations of the ruling regime, and prospects for economic development remained uncertain in the context of international tension over the DPRK's nuclear weapons programme. Suspected state-sponsored trade in weapons and narcotics was believed to account for a significant proportion of government income. The economic reforms of 2002 (see above) seemed in 2003 to have improved availability of commodities to some extent; however, price increases as a result of the reforms were believed to have brought further hardship to some sectors of the population. The South Korean Ministry of Unification believed that the North Korean economy had shown modest growth in 2003. There were concerns in early 2004 that the introduction of new legislation in Japan in January allowing the Japanese Government to impose economic sanctions on countries considered to be a threat to national security might be damaging to the North Korean economy, were such measures to be taken against the DPRK.

Education

Universal compulsory primary and secondary education were introduced in 1956 and 1958, respectively, and are provided at state expense. Free and compulsory 11-year education in state schools was introduced in 1975. Children enter kindergarten at five years of age, and people's school at the age of six. After four years, they advance to senior middle school for six years. In 1986 there were 519 university-level institutions and colleges; in the following year 325,000 students were enrolled in such institutions. In 1988 the Government announced the creation of new educational establishments, including one university, eight colleges, three factory colleges, two farmers' colleges and five special schools. English is compulsory as a second language at the age of 14. A report submitted to UNESCO by the North Korean Government in 2000 stated that there were 27,017 nurseries for 1,575,000 pupils, 14,167 kindergartens for 748,416 pupils, 4,886 primary schools for 1,609,865 pupils, 4,772 senior middle schools for 2,181,524 pupils, and more that 300 universities and colleges with 1.89m. students and academics. The adult literacy rate was reported by the Korean-American Educational Commission in 2001 to be more than 90%.

Public Holidays

The *Juche* calendar was introduced in the DPRK in 1997; 1912, the year of the late Kim Il Sung's birth, was designated the first year of the new calendar.

2004: 1 January (New Year), 16–17 February (Kim Jong Il's Birthday), 8 March (International Women's Day), 15 April (Day of the Sun, Kim Il Sung's birthday), 1 May (May Day), 15 August (Anniversary of Liberation), 9 September (Independence Day),

LIVESTOCK
('000 head)

	2000	2001	2002
Horses*	46	47	48
Cattle	579	570	575
Pigs	3,120	3,137	3,152
Sheep	185	189	170
Goats	2,276	2,566	2,693
Chickens	15,733	16,894	18,506
Ducks	2,078	3,158	4,189
Rabbits	11,475	19,455	19,482

* FAO estimates.

Source: FAO.

LIVESTOCK PRODUCTS
(FAO estimates, '000 metric tons)

	2000	2001	2002
Beef and veal	20.0	21.5	21.8
Goat meat	10.2	10.5	11.0
Pig meat	140.0	145.0	145.7
Poultry meat	26.8	30.8	33.7
Cows' milk	90.0	92.0	92.0
Poultry eggs	110.0	120.0	130.0
Cattle hides (fresh)	2.8	3.0	3.0

Source: FAO.

Forestry

ROUNDWOOD REMOVALS
(FAO estimates, '000 cubic metres, excl. bark)

	2000	2001	2002
Sawlogs, veneer logs and logs for sleepers	1,000	1,000	1,000
Other industrial wood	500	500	500
Fuel wood	5,503	5,561	5,620
Total	7,003	7,061	7,120

Sawnwood production ('000 cubic metres, incl. railway sleepers): 280 (coniferous 185, broadleaved 95) per year in 1970–2002 (FAO estimates).

Source: FAO.

Fishing

(FAO estimates, '000 metric tons, live weight)

	1999	2000	2001
Capture	210.0	200.9	200.0
Freshwater fishes	20.0	20.0	20.0
Alaska pollock	55.0	52.0	52.0
Other marine fishes	109.9	104.8	104.1
Marine crustaceans	15.0	14.3	14.3
Squids	10.0	9.5	9.5
Aquaculture	68.5	66.7	63.7
Molluscs	65.0	63.0	60.0
Total catch	278.5	267.6	263.7

Note: Figures exclude aquatic plants (FAO estimates, '000 metric tons, aquaculture only): 413.0 in 1999; 401.0 in 2000; 391.0 in 2001.
Source: FAO, *Yearbook of Fishery Statistics*.

Mining

(estimates, '000 metric tons, unless otherwise indicated)

	1999	2000	2001
Hard coal	30,000	27,000	24,000
Brown coal and lignite	10,000	9,000	7,000
Iron ore: gross weight	700	700	700
Iron ore: metal content	300	300	300
Copper ore*	14	13	13
Lead ore*	60	60	60
Zinc ore*	100	100	100
Tungsten concentrates (metric tons)*	700	700	700
Silver (metric tons)*	40	40	40
Gold (kg)*	2,500	2,000	2,000
Magnesite (crude)	1,000	1,000	1,000
Phosphate rock†	350	350	350
Fluorspar‡	25	25	25
Barite (Barytes)	70	70	70
Salt (unrefined)	500	500	500
Graphite (natural)	33	30	25
Talc, soapstone and pyrophyllite	120	120	120

Note: No recent data are available for the production of molybdenum ore and asbestos.
* Figures refer to the metal content of ores and concentrates.
† Figures refer to gross weight. The phosphoric acid content (estimates, '000 metric tons) was: 105 in 1999; 105 in 2000; n.a. in 2001.
‡ Metallurgical grade.

Source: US Geological Survey.

Industry

SELECTED PRODUCTS
('000 metric tons, unless otherwise indicated)

	1999	2000	2001
Nitrogenous fertilizers *	72	72	n.a.
Motor spirit (petrol)	848†	902	n.a.
Kerosene	168†	185	n.a.
Gas-diesel (Distillate fuel) oils	925†	994	n.a.
Residual fuel oils	539†	573	n.a.
Coke-oven coke (excl. breeze)	3,098†	3,098†	n.a.
Cement‡	6,000	6,000	5,160
Pig-iron†‡	250	250	250
Crude steel†‡	1,000	1,000	1,000
Refined copper (unwrought)†‡	16	14	14
Lead (primary metal)†‡	75	75	75
Zinc (primary metal)†‡	180	200	180
Electric energy (million kWh)§	n.a.	n.a.	20,200

* Output is measured in terms of nitrogen.
† Provisional or estimated figure(s).
‡ Data from the US Geological Survey.
§ Data from the Bank of Korea (Republic of Korea).

Source: UN, *Industrial Commodity Statistics Yearbook*.

Finance

CURRENCY AND EXCHANGE RATES
Monetary Units
    100 chon (jun) = 1 won.
Sterling, Dollar and Euro Equivalents (30 May 2003)
    £1 sterling = 244.389 won;
    US $1 = 148.330 won;
    €1 = 175.356 won;
    100 won = £0.41 = $0.67 = €0.57.

Note: In August 2002 it was reported that a currency reform had been introduced, whereby the exchange rate was adjusted from US $1 = 2.15 won to $1 = 150 won: a devaluation of 98.6%.

10 October (Anniversary of the foundation of the Korean Workers' Party), 27 December (Anniversary of the Constitution).

2005: 1 January (New Year), 16–17 February (Kim Jong Il's Birthday), 8 March (International Women's Day), 15 April (Day of the Sun, Kim Il Sung's birthday), 1 May (May Day), 15 August (Anniversary of Liberation), 9 September (Independence Day), 10 October (Anniversary of the foundation of the Korean Workers' Party), 27 December (Anniversary of the Constitution).

Weights and Measures

The metric system is in force.

Statistical Survey

Area and Population

AREA, POPULATION AND DENSITY*

Area (sq km)	122,762†
Population (census results)	
31 December 1993	
Males	10,329,699
Females.	10,883,679
Total	21,213,378
Population (UN estimates at mid-year)‡	
2000	22,268,000
2001	22,409,000
2002	22,541,000
Density (per sq km) at mid-2002	183.6

* Excluding the demilitarized zone between North and South Korea, with an area of 1,262 sq km (487 sq miles).
† 47,399 sq miles.
‡ Source: UN, *World Population Prospects: The 2002 Revision.*

PRINCIPAL TOWNS
(population at 1993 census)

Pyongyang (capital) .	2,741,260	Wonsan	300,148
Nampo	731,448	Pyongsong . . .	272,934
Hamhung	709,730	Sariwon . . .	254,146
Chongjin . . .	582,480	Haeju	229,172
Kaesong	334,433	Kanggye . . .	223,410
Sinuiju	326,011	Hyesan . . .	178,020

Source: UN, *Demographic Yearbook.*

BIRTHS AND DEATHS
(UN estimates, annual averages)

	1985–90	1990–95	1995–2000
Birth rate (per 1,000)	20.6	20.8	18.6
Death rate (per 1,000)	5.8	7.0	10.4

Expectation of life (years at birth): 65.8 (males 64.4; females 67.1) in 2002 (Source: WHO *World Health Report*).

ECONOMICALLY ACTIVE POPULATION
(ILO estimates, '000 persons at mid-1990)

	Males	Females	Total
Agriculture, etc.	2,027	1,877	3,904
Industry	2,206	1,043	3,249
Services	1,577	1,549	3,126
Total labour force	5,810	4,469	10,279

Source: ILO, *Economically Active Population Estimates and Projections, 1950–2010.*

Mid-2001 (estimates in '000): Agriculture, etc. 3,382; Total labour force 11,511 (Source: FAO).

Health and Welfare

KEY INDICATORS

Total fertility rate (children per woman, 2002).	2.0
Under-5 mortality rate (per 1,000 live births, 2001)	55
HIV/AIDS (% of persons aged 15–49, 1994).	<0.01
Health expenditure (2001): US $ per head (PPP) . . .	44
Health expenditure (2001): % of GDP	2.5
Health expenditure (2001): public (% of total)	73.4
Access to water (% of persons, 2000).	100
Access to sanitation (% of persons, 2000)	99

For sources and definitions, see explanatory note on p. vi.

Agriculture

PRINCIPAL CROPS
('000 metric tons)

	2000	2001	2002
Wheat	50*	124	130
Rice (paddy)	1,690	2,060	2,190
Barley	29*	70	69
Maize	1,041	1,483	1,651
Rye†	75	75	75
Oats†	11	11	11
Millet†	45	45	45
Sorghum†	10	10	10
Potatoes	1,870	2,268	1,884
Sweet potatoes	290*	320†	340†
Pulses†	290	300	300
Soybeans (Soya beans)* . . .	350	350	360
Cottonseed†	23	23	24
Cabbages†	630	650	680
Tomatoes†	62	70	70
Pumpkins, squash and gourds† .	85	88	88
Cucumbers and gherkins† . .	64	65	65
Aubergines (Eggplants)† . .	43	45	45
Chillies and green peppers† . .	55	57	57
Green onions and shallots† . .	90	95	95
Dry onions†	82	84	84
Garlic†	80	85	85
Other vegetables†	2,406	2,406	2,406
Apples†	650	660	660
Pears†	130	130	130
Peaches and nectarines† . . .	110	115	115
Watermelons†	104	105	105
Cantaloupes and other melons† .	110	112	112
Other fruits and berries† . . .	460	480	480
Tobacco (leaves)†	63	63	63
Hemp fibre†	13	13	13
Cotton (lint)†	12	12	12

* Unofficial figure(s).
† FAO estimate(s).

Source: FAO.

amount needed to meet the country's acute energy needs. In 2001, according to South Korean sources, per caput energy consumption in North Korea in 2001 was 0.73 tons of oil equivalent, around six times less that the figure for South Korea.

The services sector employed an estimated 30.4% of the labour force in 1990. South Korean sources estimated that in 2002 the DPRK's services sector accounted for 31.6% of GDP. In 2002 output in the sector was estimated to have declined by 0.2%, having decreased by 0.3% in 2001, and increased by 1.2% in 2000.

The trade deficit, including exchanges with South Korea, totalled US $889.0m. in 2002. In 2002 total exports, excluding trade with South Korea, reached $735.0m. and imports totalled $1,525.4m., thus giving a trade deficit of $790.4m. (compared with a deficit of $970.1m. in the previous year). The DPRK's principal source of imports in 2002 was the People's Republic of China (accounting for 24.7% of total imports), followed by the Republic of Korea (19.5%) and Thailand (7.1%). The principal market for exports was the Republic of Korea, which purchased 27.0% of total exports, followed by China (26.9%), and then Japan (23.3%). China was a source of crude petroleum, food and vehicles, while Japan was a destination for industrial and agricultural goods. Inter-Korean trade increased by 28% in 2000, to reach US $425.2m., rising to $403.0m. in 2001. In 2002 inter-Korean trade increased by 59% to $641.7m. Total trade (excluding exchanges with the Republic of Korea) increased by 15.1% to reach $2,270m. in 2001, but decreased slightly, by 0.4%, to $2,260.4m. in 2002. The principal exports in that year were live animals (35.5% of the value of total exports, excluding trade with the Republic of Korea), textiles (16.7%) and machinery and electrical equipment (11.6%). Other export commodities in the late 1990s included tobacco and silk. The principal imports in 2002 were mineral products (15.5% of the value of total imports, excluding trade with the Republic of Korea), machinery and electrical equipment (15.4%), and textiles (10.4%). Other import items included road vehicles, chemicals and groceries. The 2002 budget envisaged revenue and expenditure balancing at 22,174m. won, compared with 21,571m. won in 2001. A budgetary deficit of 38.7m. won was recorded in 2001. The DPRK's total external debt was estimated to be US $12,460m. in 2000. The average annual rate of inflation in 1993 was estimated at 5%. However, following the introduction of market-orientated reforms in 2002, the inflation rate was said to have reached 4,000% in that year.

It is difficult to present an accurate economic profile of the DPRK, owing to the lack of reliable statistical data. North Korea's economic situation deteriorated sharply in the early 1990s, following the abandonment, in 1991 and 1992, respectively, of the barter trading system between the DPRK and the USSR (then its major trading partner) and China in favour of trade conducted exclusively in convertible currencies. The USSR also substantially reduced deliveries of crude petroleum and cereals, resulting in a severe decline in industrial production. The years 1994–97 were designated 'a period of adjustment in socialist economic construction', during which emphasis was to be transferred from traditional heavy industries to agriculture, light industry and trade. The Rajin-Sonbong Free Economic and Trade Zone was established in 1991 in the north-east of the country; however, attempts to attract foreign capital into the Zone were largely unsuccessful. The severe food shortages in the mid-1990s prompted Pyongyang to appeal for international food aid and humanitarian assistance. From the late 1990s the DPRK slowly began to open up its economy, developing trading relations with various European and Asian countries and increasing the number of limited joint ventures with foreign firms. In October 2000 the DPRK reportedly established a research institute on capitalism, and it was believed that Kim Jong Il was seeking to introduce Chinese-style economic reforms following his visit to China in January 2001 (see above). The DPRK also began developing its information technology (IT) industry, and by 2001 was operating six official websites. Joint IT ventures were established with institutes in the South, and in October the DPRK launched its first e-mail service provider in co-operation with a company based in China. In May the DPRK joined Intelsat (an international commercial satellite telecommunications organization), and in November the country agreed to adopt the global system for mobile communications (GSM) in the Rajin-Sonbong enterprise zone. During 2002 there were signs of a significant change in economic policy. In July the Government abandoned rationing, allowing farmers to sell produce at market prices, and wages were raised by a factor of 10–17, to take into account the concomitant price rises caused by the reforms. State assistance was reduced, and the value of the won decreased to as little as one-fiftieth of its previous value in relation to the US dollar. (In 2003 academics at Kim Il Sung University in Pyongyang reportedly revised economics textbooks to reflect changes in the DPRK's economic system.) Also in 2002, a new 150-km waterway linking Pyongyang and Nampo was completed in October; and from December, in apparent displeasure with US policy towards the DPRK, the North Korean Government prohibited the use of the US dollar and adopted the euro as its official currency of foreign exchange. A further major reform of 2002 was the creation in September of a 'Special Administrative Region' in the city of Sinuiju, followed later in the year by the establishment of a special industrial zone at Kaesong and a new tourist zone at Mount Kumgang. Whilst prospects for the special zone in Sinuiju were inauspicious following the arrest of its governor, Yang Bin (see Recent History), it was hoped that the special zone at Kaesong, on the border with South Korea, would attract investment from South Korean small- and medium-sized enterprises. In 2003 South Korean companies Hyundai and Korean Land were developing an international business park in Kaesong. In March 2003 the Minister of Finance announced that the state budget's revenue would be 13.6% higher than in 2002, while expenditure would be 14.4% higher than in the previous year. Defence spending amounted to 15.4% of total projected expenditure, an increase of 0.5% in comparison with the previous year. The Government would also issue bonds for the first time in 50 years. However, analysts remained doubtful about Kim Jong Il's ability to restructure the economy without destabilizing the foundations of the ruling regime, and prospects for economic development remained uncertain in the context of international tension over the DPRK's nuclear weapons programme. Suspected state-sponsored trade in weapons and narcotics was believed to account for a significant proportion of government income. The economic reforms of 2002 (see above) seemed in 2003 to have improved availability of commodities to some extent; however, price increases as a result of the reforms were believed to have brought further hardship to some sectors of the population. The South Korean Ministry of Unification believed that the North Korean economy had shown modest growth in 2003. There were concerns in early 2004 that the introduction of new legislation in Japan in January allowing the Japanese Government to impose economic sanctions on countries considered to be a threat to national security might be damaging to the North Korean economy, were such measures to be taken against the DPRK.

Education

Universal compulsory primary and secondary education were introduced in 1956 and 1958, respectively, and are provided at state expense. Free and compulsory 11-year education in state schools was introduced in 1975. Children enter kindergarten at five years of age, and people's school at the age of six. After four years, they advance to senior middle school for six years. In 1986 there were 519 university-level institutions and colleges; in the following year 325,000 students were enrolled in such institutions. In 1988 the Government announced the creation of new educational establishments, including one university, eight colleges, three factory colleges, two farmers' colleges and five special schools. English is compulsory as a second language at the age of 14. A report submitted to UNESCO by the North Korean Government in 2000 stated that there were 27,017 nurseries for 1,575,000 pupils, 14,167 kindergartens for 748,416 pupils, 4,886 primary schools for 1,609,865 pupils, 4,772 senior middle schools for 2,181,524 pupils, and more that 300 universities and colleges with 1.89m. students and academics. The adult literacy rate was reported by the Korean-American Educational Commission in 2001 to be more than 90%.

Public Holidays

The *Juche* calendar was introduced in the DPRK in 1997; 1912, the year of the late Kim Il Sung's birth, was designated the first year of the new calendar.
2004: 1 January (New Year), 16–17 February (Kim Jong Il's Birthday), 8 March (International Women's Day), 15 April (Day of the Sun, Kim Il Sung's birthday), 1 May (May Day), 15 August (Anniversary of Liberation), 9 September (Independence Day),

legal co-operation agreements. In late 2002 the DPRK and Taiwan were exploring the possibility of establishing mutual liaison offices. In 2003 there were reports that the DPRK was selling military equipment to Pakistan, and also that military relations with Myanmar were being developed. In early 2004 Pakistani nuclear scientist Abdul Qadeer Khan confessed that he had sold nuclear secrets to the DPRK.

Pyongyang maintained close links with a number of Arab and Middle Eastern countries, including Egypt, Libya, Syria and Iran. The President of the Presidium of the SPA, Kim Yong Nam, visited Libya and Syria in July 2002. The DPRK retained long-standing ties with many African countries, and had military advisers working in 12 of them. In January 2004 the Vice-President of the Presidium of the SPA, Yang Hyong Sop, visited Nigeria to discuss an agreement on military technology.

Government

The highest organ of state power is the unicameral Supreme People's Assembly (SPA), with 687 members, elected (unopposed) for five years by universal adult suffrage. The SPA elects, for its duration, the Chairman of the National Defence Commission, who, since the effective abolition of the presidency in September 1998, holds the most senior accessible office of state (although this is not formally stated in the Constitution). The SPA elects the Premier and, on the latter's recommendation, appoints other Ministers to form the Cabinet. The President of the SPA Presidium, whose members are elected by the SPA, represents the State in its relations with foreign countries.

Political power is held by the communist Korean Workers' Party (KWP), which is the most influential party in the Democratic Front for the Reunification of the Fatherland (comprising the KWP and two minor parties). The Front presents an approved list of candidates for elections to representative bodies. The KWP's highest authority is the Party Congress, which elects a Central Committee to supervise party work. The Committee elects a Political Bureau (Politburo) to direct policy. The Presidium of the Politburo is the KWP's most powerful policy-making body.

The DPRK comprises nine provinces and two cities, each with an elected Local People's Assembly.

Defence

Military service is selective: army five to eight years, navy five to 10 years, and air force three to four years. The estimated total strength of the armed forces in August 2003 was 1,082,000: army 950,000, air force 86,000, and navy 46,000. Security and border troops numbered 189,000, and there was a workers' and peasants' militia ('Red Guards') numbering about 3.5m. In late 2002 it was reported that the DPRK was planning to make substantial reductions to its armed forces. The ratio of North Korea's armed forces to total population is believed to be the highest in the world. Defence expenditure for 2003 was budgeted at 15.4% of total spending, up from 14.9% (3,200m. won) in 2002. South Korean intelligence sources estimated the real level of defence expenditure at 43.5% of total spending in 2003.

Economic Affairs

In 2002, according to South Korean estimates, the DPRK's gross national income (GNI) was about US $17,045m., equivalent to some $762 per head. It was estimated that in 1998 the North Korean economy declined for the ninth successive year, contracting by 1.1%, in real terms. In 1999, however, it was estimated that the economy grew by 6.2%, and in 2000 by 1.3%. Growth was estimated at 3.7% in 2001 and at 1.2% in 2002. During 1990–2002, according to estimates by the World Bank, the population increased by an annual average of 1.0%.

Agriculture (including forestry and fishing) contributed an estimated 30.2% of gross domestic product (GDP) in 2002, according to South Korean sources. In 2002, according to FAO estimates, 28.7% of the economically active population were employed in agriculture. The principal crops are rice, maize, potatoes, sweet potatoes and soybeans. The DPRK is not self-sufficient in food, and imports substantial amounts of wheat, rice and maize annually. Food shortages became a severe problem from the mid-1990s. By 1999 the food situation had improved to some extent, owing to fertilizer aid from international donors, agrarian reform and increased potato production, although shortages continued and were exacerbated by severe drought in 2000 and 2001, and subsequent typhoons and floods.

According to the World Food Programme, cereal shortfalls of some 40,000 tons affected 2.2m. people in December 2003. In December 2000 the Government launched an intensive campaign for potato growing and double-crop farming, and in November 2001 construction began on a 7,000-ha goat farm near Pyongyang. According to South Korean estimates, grain production was 3.9m. tons in 2001 and 4.1m. tons in 2002. Potato production was 2.3m. tons in 2001 and 1.9m. tons in 2002, according to FAO. The raising of livestock (principally cattle and pigs), forestry and fishing are important. During 1991–2002, according to FAO, agricultural production decreased by an annual average of 1.8%. In 2002, according to South Korean estimates, agricultural GDP rose by 4.2%, following an increase of 6.8% in 2001 and a decline of 1.9% in 2000.

In 2002, according to South Korean estimates, industry (including mining, manufacturing, construction and power) contributed 38.2% of GDP. In 1990 the industrial sector employed 31.6% of the labour force. In 2002 the GDP of the mining and manufacturing sector declined by an estimated 2.5%, compared with 2001 (when an increase of 3.9% was estimated), but that of the construction sector increased by an estimated 10.4%, compared with a rise of 7.0% in 2001.

Mining contributed 7.8% of GDP in 2002, according to South Korean estimates. The DPRK possesses considerable mineral wealth, with large deposits of coal, iron, lead, copper, zinc, tin, silver and gold. The country was formerly the second largest producer of magnesia products in the world, but output is believed to have declined significantly. There are unexploited offshore deposits of petroleum and natural gas. South Korean sources estimated that in 2002 output in the mining sector declined by 3.8%—compared with growth rates of 5.8% in 2000 and 4.8% in 2001.

In 2002, according to South Korean estimates, the manufacturing sector contributed 18.0% of GDP (light industries 7.0% and heavy industries 11.0%). In the 1990s industrial development concentrated on heavy industry (metallurgy—notably steel production—machine-building, cement and chemicals). The textiles industry has provided significant exports. South Korean sources estimated that the GDP of the manufacturing sector declined by 2.0% in 2002, following an increase of 3.5% in 2001.

In 2000 it was estimated that 86% of the DPRK's energy supply was derived from coal, followed in importance by hydro-electricity and petroleum (6%). A 30-MW nuclear reactor was believed to have been inaugurated in 1987. Light-water nuclear reactors were being constructed, for the purpose of electricity generation, in accordance with an agreement concluded with the USA in 1994 (see Recent History). However, in December 2003 construction of the reactors was suspended for one year, following North Korea's resumption of its nuclear weapons programme. In 2000, according to South Korean sources, some 67% of the DPRK's electricity was generated by hydroelectric power stations, with the remaining 33% of the country's requirements being provided by thermal power stations. During the 1990s the DPRK experienced increasing power shortages, as generation and transmission infrastructure deteriorated. Although South Korean sources estimated that electricity production increased by some 30% between 1986 and 1994, output is insufficient for the DPRK's needs, and there have been frequent reports of rationing in an effort to conserve fuel and energy. The DPRK's total electricity consumption in 1998 was only 61% of that in 1991. Severe drought in the late 1990s and 2000 adversely affected the production of hydroelectric power. In early 2003 the DPRK was attempting to increase its electricity output through the construction of new hydroelectric power plants in various provinces. In May 2003 the DPRK also reportedly signed a memorandum concerning a high-voltage grid project with a Swiss company. Petroleum imports totalled only around 0.6m. metric tons in 2001 and 2002. The USA suspended fuel oil shipments in late 2002, following Pyongyang's alleged admission that it was pursuing a secret nuclear programme. From the 1990s, and especially in early 2002, the DPRK sought greater foreign assistance in developing its offshore oilfields, located to the west in the Bohai Sea, and also in the north-east, near Chongjin city. A limited number of joint ventures were established with foreign oil companies. In 1999 the DPRK succeeded in producing 300,000 tons of petroleum from a well located off Sukchon County, equivalent to about half the amount of petroleum imported in that year, although falling far short of the

BUDGET
(projected, million won)

	1992	1993	1994
Revenue	39,500.9	40,449.9	41,525.2
Expenditure	39,500.9	40,449.9	41,525.2
Economic development	26,675.1	27,423.8	28,164.0
Socio-cultural sector	7,730.6	7,751.5	8,218.3
Defence	4,582.1	4,692.2	4,816.9
Administration and management	513.1	582.4	326.0

1998 (estimates, million won): Total revenue 19,790.8; Total expenditure 20,015.2.

1999 (estimates, million won): Total revenue 19,801.0; Total expenditure 20,018.2.

2000 (estimates, million won): Total revenue 20,955.0; Total expenditure 20,903.0.

2001 (projected, million won): Total revenue 21,571.0; Total expenditure 21,571.0.

2002 (projected, million won): Total revenue 22,174.0; Total expenditure 22,174.0.

NATIONAL ACCOUNTS

Gross Domestic Product by Economic Activity
(% of total)

	2000	2001	2002
Agriculture, forestry and fishing	30.4	30.4	30.2
Mining	7.7	8.0	7.8
Manufacturing	17.7	18.1	18.0
Electricity, gas and water	4.8	4.8	4.4
Construction	6.9	7.0	8.0
Government services	22.6	22.2	22.0
Other services	9.8	9.7	9.6
Total	100.0	100.0	100.0

Source: Bank of Korea (Republic of Korea).

External Trade

PRINCIPAL COMMODITIES
(US $ million)*

Imports	2000	2001	2002
Live animals and animal products	20.3	73.9	103.4
Vegetable products	159.0	221.0	118.4
Animal or vegetable fats and oils; prepared edible fats; animal or vegetable waxes; Prepared foodstuffs; beverages, spirits and vinegar; tobacco and manufactured substitutes	89.1	89.9	72.3
Mineral products	171.2	231.1	235.9
Products of chemical or allied industries	108.4	123.4	122.1
Plastics, rubber and articles thereof	67.5	66.0	66.0
Textiles and textile articles	171.9	203.9	158.5
Base metals and articles thereof	85.2	100.4	88.2
Machinery and mechanical appliances; electrical equipment; sound and television apparatus	205.1	243.8	234.7
Vehicles, aircraft, vessels and associated transport equipment	146.2	88.4	76.1
Total (incl. others)	1,406.5	1,620.3	1,525.4

Exports	2000	2001	2002
Live animals and animal products	97.9	158.4	261.1
Vegetable products	30.3	42.0	27.5
Mineral products	43.2	50.5	69.8
Products of chemical or allied industries; Plastics, rubber and articles thereof	44.9	44.6	42.4
Wood, cork and articles thereof; wood charcoal; manufactures of straw, esparto, etc.	10.9	5.6	10.2
Textiles and textile articles	140.0	140.5	123.1
Natural or cultured pearls, precious or semi-precious stones, precious metals and articles thereof; imitation jewellery; coin	9.8	14.1	14.6
Base metals and articles thereof	43.9	60.2	57.4
Machinery and mechanical appliances; electrical equipment, sound and television apparatus	105.2	97.9	85.6
Total (incl. others)	565.8	650.2	735.0

* Excluding trade with the Republic of Korea (US $ million): Imports 272.8 in 2000, 226.8 in 2001, 370.2 in 2002; Exports 152.4 in 2000, 176.2 in 2001, 271.6 in 2002.

Source: Korea Trade-Investment Promotion Agency (KOTRA), Republic of Korea.

PRINCIPAL TRADING PARTNERS
(US $ million)*

Imports	2000	2001	2002
China, People's Republic	450.8	570.7	467.3
Germany	53.6	82.1	140.4
Hong Kong	68.5	42.6	29.2
India	142.9	154.8	186.6
Japan	206.8	249.1	135.2
Netherlands	n.a.	9.1	27.6
Russia	42.9	63.8	77.0
Singapore	46.2	112.3	83.0
Spain	15.3	31.6	n.a.
Thailand	188.3	106.0	172.0
United Kingdom	25.3	40.7	n.a.
Total (incl. others)	1,406.5	1,620.3	1,525.4

Exports	2000	2001	2002
Bangladesh	n.a.	38.0	32.3
China, People's Republic	37.2	166.8	270.9
Germany	25.6	22.8	27.8
Hong Kong	46.4	38.0	21.9
India	25.5	3.1	4.8
Japan	256.9	225.6	234.4
Netherlands	n.a.	10.4	6.4
Spain	12.7	12.6	n.a.
Thailand	19.5	24.9	44.6
Total (incl. others)	565.8	650.2	735.0

* Excluding trade with the Republic of Korea (US $ million): Imports 272.8 in 2000, 226.8 in 2001, 370.2 in 2002; Exports 152.4 in 2000, 176.2 in 2001, 271.6 in 2002.

Source: Korea Trade-Investment Promotion Agency (KOTRA), Republic of Korea.

Transport

SHIPPING

Merchant Fleet
(registered at 31 December)

	2000	2001	2002
Number of vessels	176	176	225
Total displacement ('000 grt)	652.6	697.8	870.5

Source: Lloyd's Register-Fairplay, *World Fleet Statistics*.

International Sea-borne Freight Traffic
(estimates, '000 metric tons)

	1988	1989	1990
Goods loaded	630	640	635
Goods unloaded	5,386	5,500	5,520

Source: UN, *Monthly Bulletin of Statistics.*

CIVIL AVIATION
(traffic on scheduled services)

	1995	1996	1997
Kilometres flown (million) . . .	3	3	5
Passengers carried ('000) . . .	254	254	280
Passenger-km (million)	207	207	286
Total ton-km (million)	22	22	30

Source: UN, *Statistical Yearbook.*

Tourism

	1996	1997	1998
Tourist arrivals ('000)	127	128	130

Source: World Tourism Organization, mainly *Yearbook of Tourism Statistics.*

Communications Media

	1994	1995	1996
Radio receivers ('000 in use) . .	2,950	3,000	3,300
Television receivers ('000 in use) .	1,000	1,050	1,090
Telephones ('000 main lines in use)*	1,100	1,100	1,100
Telefax stations (number in use) .	3,000*	n.a.	n.a.
Daily newspapers:			
number	11	11*	3
average circulation ('000 copies)*	5,000	5,000	4,500

* Estimate(s).

1997 ('000 in use): Radio receivers 3,360; Television receivers 1,200.

Sources: UNESCO, *Statistical Yearbook*; UN, *Statistical Yearbook.*

Education

(2000)

	Institutions	Students
Kindergartens	14,167	748,416
Primary	4,886	1,609,865
Senior middle schools	4,772	2,181,524

Source: mainly Government of the Democratic People's Republic of Korea, *UNESCO Education for All Assessment Report 2000.*

Universities and Colleges: The *UNESCO Education for All Assessment Report 2000* identified more than 300 universities and colleges with 1.89m. students and academics.

Teachers (1987/88, UNESCO, *Statistical Yearbook*): Pre-primary 35,000, Primary 59,000, Secondary 111,000, Universities and colleges 23,000, Other tertiary 4,000.

Directory

The Constitution

A new Constitution was adopted on 27 December 1972. According to South Korean sources, several amendments were made in April 1992, including the deletion of references to Marxism-Leninism, the extension of the term of the Supreme People's Assembly from four to five years, and the promotion of limited 'economic openness'. Extensive amendments to the Constitution were approved on 5 September 1998. The main provisions of the revised Constitution are summarized below:

The Democratic People's Republic of Korea is an independent socialist state; the revolutionary traditions of the State are stressed (its ideological basis being the *Juche* idea of the Korean Workers' Party), as is the desire to achieve national reunification by peaceful means on the basis of national independence. The Late President Kim Il Sung is the Eternal President of the Republic.

National sovereignty rests with the working people, who exercise power through the Supreme People's Assembly and Local People's Assemblies at lower levels, which are elected by universal, equal and direct suffrage by secret ballot.

The foundation of an independent national economy, based on socialist and *Juche* principles, is stressed. The means of production are owned solely by the State and socialist co-operative organizations.

Culture and education provide the working people with knowledge to advance a socialist way of life. Education is free, universal and compulsory for 11 years.

Defence is emphasized, as well as the rights of overseas nationals, the principles of friendly relations between nations based on equality, mutual respect and non-interference, proletarian internationalism, support for national liberation struggles and due observance of law.

The basic rights and duties of citizens are laid down and guaranteed. These include the right to vote and to be elected (for citizens who are more than 17 years of age), to work (the working day being eight hours), to free medical care and material assistance for the old, infirm or disabled, and to political asylum. National defence is the supreme duty of citizens.

THE STRUCTURE OF STATE

The Supreme People's Assembly

The Supreme People's Assembly is the highest organ of state power, exercises legislative power and is elected by direct, equal, universal and secret ballot for a term of five years. Its chief functions are: (i) to adopt, amend or supplement legal or constitutional enactments; (ii) to determine state policy; (iii) to elect the Chairman of the National Defence Commission; (iv) to elect the Vice-Chairmen and other members of the National Defence Commission (on the recommendation of the Chairman of the National Defence Commission); (v) to elect the President and other members of the Presidium of the Supreme People's Assembly, the Premier of the Cabinet, the President of the Central Court and other legal officials; (vi) to appoint the Vice-Premiers and other members of the Cabinet (on the recommendation of the Premier of the Cabinet); (vii) to approve the State Plan and Budget; (viii) to receive a report on the work of the Cabinet and adopt measures, if necessary; (ix) to decide on the ratification or abrogation of treaties. It holds regular and extraordinary sessions, the former being once or twice a year, the latter as necessary at the request of at least one-third of the deputies. Legislative enactments are adopted when approved by more than one-half of those deputies present. The Constitution is amended and supplemented when approved by more than two-thirds of the total number of deputies.

The National Defence Commission

The National Defence Commission, which consists of a Chairman, first Vice-Chairman, other Vice-Chairmen and members, is the highest military organ of state power, and is accountable to the Supreme People's Assembly. The National Defence Commission directs and commands the armed forces and guides defence affairs. The Chairman of the National Defence Commission serves a five-year term of office and has the most senior post in the state hierarchy.

The Presidium of the Supreme People's Assembly

The Presidium of the Supreme People's Assembly, which consists of a President, Vice-Presidents, secretaries and members, is the highest organ of power in the intervals between sessions of the Supreme People's Assembly, to which it is accountable. It exercises the following chief functions: (i) to convene sessions of the Supreme People's Assembly; (ii) to examine and approve new legislation, the State Plan and the State Budget, when the Supreme People's Assembly is in recess; (iii) to interpret the Constitution and legislative enactments; (iv) to supervise the observance of laws of State organs; (v) to organize elections to the Supreme People's Assembly and Local People's Assemblies; (vi) to form or abolish ministries or commissions of the Cabinet; (vii) to appoint or remove Vice-Premiers and other cabinet or ministry members, on the recommendation of the Premier, when the Supreme People's Assembly is not in session; (viii) to elect or transfer judges of the Central Court; (ix) to ratify or abrogate treaties concluded with other countries; (x) to appoint or recall diplomatic envoys; (xi) to confer decorations, medals, honorary titles and diplomatic ranks; (xii) to grant general amnesties or special pardon. The President of the Presidium represents the State and receives credentials and letters of recall of diplomatic representatives accredited by a foreign state.

The Cabinet

The Cabinet is the administrative and executive body of the Supreme People's Assembly and a general state management organ. It serves a five-year term and comprises the Premier, Vice-Premiers, Chairmen of Commissions and other necessary members. Its major functions are the following: (i) to adopt measures to execute state policy; (ii) to guide the work of ministries and other organs responsible to it; (iii) to establish and remove direct organs of the Cabinet and main administrative economic organizations; (iv) to draft the State Plan and adopt measures to make it effective; (v) to compile the State Budget and to implement its provisions; (vi) to organize and execute the work of all sectors of the economy, as well as education, science, culture, health and environmental protection; (vii) to adopt measures to strengthen the monetary and banking system; (viii) to adopt measures to maintain social order, protect State interests and guarantee citizens' rights; (ix) to conclude treaties; (x) to abolish decisions and directives of economic administrative organs which run counter to those of the Cabinet. The Cabinet is accountable to the Supreme People's Assembly.

Local People's Assemblies

The Local People's Assemblies and Committees of the province (or municipality directly under central authority), city (or district) and county are local organs of power. The Local People's Assemblies consist of deputies elected by direct, equal, universal and secret ballot. The Local People's Committees consist of a Chairman, Vice-Chairmen, secretaries and members. The Local People's Assemblies and Committees serve a four-year term and exercise local budgetary functions, elect local administrative and judicial personnel and carry out the decisions at local level of higher executive and administrative organs.

THE JUDICIARY

Justice is administered by the Central Court (the highest judicial organ of the State), local courts and the Special Court. Judges and other legal officials are elected by the Supreme People's Assembly. The Central Court protects state property, constitutional rights, guarantees that all state bodies and citizens observe state laws, and executes judgments. Justice is administered by the court comprising one judge and two people's assessors. The court is independent and judicially impartial. Judicial affairs are conducted by the Central Procurator's Office, which exposes and institutes criminal proceedings against accused persons. The Office of the Central Procurator is responsible to the Chairman of the National Defence Commission, the Supreme People's Assembly and the Central People's Committee.

The Government

HEAD OF STATE

President: President KIM IL SUNG died on 8 July 1994 and was declared 'Eternal President' in September 1998.

Chairman of the National Defence Commission: Marshal KIM JONG IL.

First Vice-Chairman: Vice-Marshal JO MYONG ROK.

Vice-Chairmen: YON HYONG MUK, Vice-Marshal RI YONG MU.

Other members: Vice-Marshal KIM YONG CHUN, KIM IL CHOL, CHOE RYONG SU, PAEK SE BONG, JON BYONG HO.

CABINET
(April 2004)

Premier: PAK PONG JU.

Vice-Premiers: RO TU CHOL, KWAK POM GI, JON SUNG HUN.

Minister of Foreign Affairs: PAEK NAM SUN.

Minister of People's Security: CHOE RYONG SU.

Minister of the People's Armed Forces: Vice-Marshal KIM IL CHOL.

Chairman of the State Planning Commission: KIM KWANG RIM.

Minister of Power and Coal Industry: JU TONG IL.

Minister of Extractive Industries: RI KWANG NAM.

Minister of Metal and Machine-Building Industries: KIM SUNG HYON.

Minister of Construction and Building Materials Industries: JO YUN HUI.

Minister of the Electronics Industry: O SU YONG.

Minister of Railways: KIM YONG SAM.

Minister of Land and Marine Transport: KIM YONG IL.

Minister of Agriculture: RI KYONG SIK.

Minister of Chemical Industry: RI MU YONG.

Minister of Light Industry: RI JU O.

Minister of Foreign Trade: RI KWANG GUN.

Minister of Forestry: RI SANG MU.

Minister of Fisheries: RI SONG UNG.

Minister of City Management: CHOE JONG GON.

Minister of Land and Environmental Protection: JANG IL SON.

Minister of State Construction Control: PAE TAL JUN.

Minister of Commerce: RI YONG SON.

Minister of Procurement and Food Administration: CHOE NAM GYUN.

Minister of Education: KIM YONG JIN.

Minister of Post and Telecommunications: RI KUM BOM.

Minister of Culture: CHOE IK GYU.

Minister of Finance: MUN IL BONG.

Minister of Labour: RI WON IL.

Minister of Public Health: KIM SU HAK.

Minister of State Inspection: KIM UI SUN.

Chairman of the Physical Culture and Sports Guidance Committee: PAK MYONG CHOL.

President of the National Academy of Sciences: PYON YONG RIP.

President of the Central Bank: KIM WAN SU.

Director of the Central Statistics Bureau: KIM CHANG SU.

Chief Secretary of the Cabinet: JONG MUN SAN.

MINISTRIES

All Ministries and Commissions are in Pyongyang.

Legislature

CHOE KO IN MIN HOE UI
(Supreme People's Assembly)

The 687 members of the 11th Supreme People's Assembly (SPA) were elected unopposed for a five-year term on 3 August 2003. The SPA's permanent body is the Presidium.

Chairman: CHOE TAE BOK.

President of the Presidium: KIM YONG NAM.

Vice-Presidents of the Presidium: YANG HYONG SOP, KIM YONG DAE.

Political Organizations

Democratic Front for the Reunification of the Fatherland: Pyongyang; f. 1946; a vanguard organization comprising political parties and mass working people's organizations seeking the unification of North and South Korea; Mems of Presidium PAK SONG CHOL, RYOM TAE JUN, YANG HYONG SOP, JONG TU HWAN, RI YONG SU, JONG SHIN HYOK, KIM PONG JU, PYON CHANG BOK, RYU MI YONG, RYO WON GU, KANG RYON HAK.

The component parties are:

Chondoist Chongu Party: Pyongyang; tel. (2) 334241; f. 1946; supports policies of Korean Workers' Party; follows the guiding principle of *Innaechon* (the realization of 'heaven on earth'); Chair. RYU MI YONG.

Korean Social Democratic Party (KSDP) (Joson Sahoeminju-dang): Pyongyang; tel. (2) 5211981; fax (2) 3814410; f. 1945; advocates national independence and a democratic socialist society; supports policies of Korean Workers' Party; Chair. KIM YONG DAE; First Vice-Chair. KANG PYONG HAK.

Korean Workers' Party (KWP): Pyongyang; f. 1945; merged with the South Korean Workers' Party in 1949; the guiding principle is the *Juche* idea, based on the concept that man is the master and arbiter of all things; 3m. mems; Gen. Sec. Marshal KIM JONG IL.

Sixth Central Committee

General Secretary: Marshal KIM JONG IL.

Politburo

Presidium: Marshal KIM JONG IL.

Full Members: KIM YONG NAM, PAK SONG CHOL, KIM YONG JU, KYE UNG TAE, JON BYONG HO, HAN SONG RYONG.

Alternate Members: HONG SONG NAM, YON HYONG MUK, YANG HYONG SOP, CHOE TAE BOK, KIM CHOL MAN, CHOE YONG RIM, RI SON SHIL.

Secretariat: Marshal KIM JONG IL, KYE UNG TAE, JON BYONG HO, HAN SONG RYONG, CHOE TAE BOK, KIM KI NAM, KIM KUK TAE, KIM JUNG RIN, (vacant), JONG HA CHOL.

The component mass working people's organizations (see under Trade Unions) are:

General Federation of Trade Unions of Korea (GFTUK).

Kim Il Sung Socialist Youth League.

Korean Democratic Women's Union (KDWU).

Union of Agricultural Working People of Korea.

There is one opposition organization in exile, with branches in Tokyo (Japan), Moscow (Russia) and Beijing (People's Republic of China):

Salvation Front for the Democratic Unification of Chosun: f. early 1990s; seeks the overthrow of the Kim dynasty, the establishment of democracy in the DPRK and Korean reunification; Chair. PAK KAP DONG.

Diplomatic Representation

EMBASSIES IN THE DEMOCRATIC PEOPLE'S REPUBLIC OF KOREA

Algeria: Munsudong, Taedongkang District, Pyongyang; tel. (2) 90372; Ambassador MOKHTAR REGUIEG.

Benin: Pyongyang; Ambassador A. OGIST.

Bulgaria: Munsudong, Taedongkang District, Pyongyang; tel. (2) 3827343; fax (2) 3817342; Ambassador YORDAN MUTAFCHIYEV.

Cambodia: Munsudong, Taedongkang District, Pyongyang; tel. (2) 3817283; fax (2) 3817625.

China, People's Republic: Kinmauldong, Moranbong District, Pyongyang; tel. (2) 3823316; fax (2) 3813425; Ambassador WU DONGHE.

Cuba: Munsudong, taedongkang District, Pyongyang; tel. (2) 3827380; fax (2) 3817703; Ambassador ESTEBAN LOBAINA ROMERO.

Czech Republic: Munsudong, Taedongkang District, Pyongyang.

Egypt: Pyongyang; tel. (2) 3817414; fax (2) 3817611; Ambassador AHMED RAMY AWAD ALHOSAINY.

Ethiopia: POB 55, Munsudong, Taedongkang District, Pyongyang; tel. (2) 3827554; fax (2) 3827550; Chargé d'affaires FEKADE S.G. MESKEL.

Germany: Munsudong, Taedongkang District, Pyongyang; tel. (2) 3827490; fax (2) 3817397.

India: Block 53, Munsudong, Taehak St, Taedongkang District, Pyongyang; tel. (2) 3817274; fax (2) 3817619; Ambassador R. P. SINGH.

Indonesia: 5 Foreigners' Bldg, Munsudong, Taedongkang District, Pyongyang; tel. (2) 3827439; fax (2) 3817620; e-mail kbripyg@public .east.cn.net; Ambassador BUCHARI EFFENDI.

Iran: Munhungdong, Monsu St, Taedongkang District, Pyongyang; tel. (2) 3817492; fax (2) 3817612; Ambassador MUHAMMAD GANJI-DOOST.

Laos: Munhungdong, Taedongkang District, Pyongyang; tel. (2) 3827363; fax (2) 3817722; Ambassador KHAMKENG SAYAKEO.

Libya: Munsudong, Taedongkang District, Pyongyang; tel. (2) 3827544; fax (2) 3817267; Secretary of People's Bureau AHMED AMER AL-MUAKKAF.

Mali: Pyongyang; Ambassador NAKOUNTE DIAKITÉ.

Mongolia: Munsudong, Taedongkang District, Pyongyang; tel. (2) 3827322; fax (2) 3817321; Ambassador J. LOMBO.

Nigeria: Munsudong, Taedongkang District, Pyongyang; tel. (2) 3827558; fax (2) 3817293; Ambassador ADOGA ONAH.

Pakistan: Munsudong, Taedongkang District, Pyongyang; tel. (2) 3827478; fax 3817622; Ambassador SULTAN HABIB.

Poland: Munsudong, Taedongkang District, Pyongyang; tel. (2) 3817327; fax (2) 3817634; Ambassador WOJCIECH KALUZA.

Romania: Munhungdong, Taedongkang District, Pyongyang; tel. (2) 3827336; fax (2) 3817336; e-mail ambrophe@di.chesin.com; Chargé d'affaires a.i. EUGEN POPA.

Russia: Sinyangdong, Central District, Pyongyang; tel. (2) 3823102; fax (2) 3813427; e-mail rusembdprk@yahoo.com; Ambassador ANDREI KARLOV.

Sweden: Munsudung, Taedongkang District, Pyongyang; tel. (2) 3817908; fax (2) 3817258; e-mail ambassaden.pyongyang@foreign .ministry.se; Ambassador PAUL BEIJER.

Syria: Munsudong, Taedongkang District, Pyongyang; tel. (2) 3827473; fax (2) 3817635; Ambassador YASSER AL-FARRA.

Thailand: Pyongyang; Ambassador NIKHOM TANTEMSAPYA.

United Kingdom: Munsudong, Taedongkang District, Pyongyang; tel. (2) 3817980; fax (2) 3817985; Ambassador DAVID SLINN.

Viet Nam: Munsudong, Taedongkang District, Pyongyang; tel. (2) 3817353; fax (2) 3817632; Ambassador LE XUAN VINH.

Judicial System

The judicial organs include the Central Court, the Court of the Province (or city under central authority) and the People's Court. Each court is composed of judges and people's assessors.

Procurators supervise the ordinances and regulations of all ministries and the decisions and directives of local organs of state power to ensure that they conform to the Constitution, laws and decrees, as well as to the decisions and other measures of the Cabinet. Procurators bring suits against criminals in the name of the State, and participate in civil cases to protect the interests of the State and citizens.

Central Court

Pyongyang.

The highest judicial organ; supervises the work of all courts.

President: KIM BYONG RYUL.

First Vice-President: YUN MYONG GUK.

Central Procurator's Office

Supervises work of procurator's offices in provinces, cities and counties.

Procurator-General: RI KIL SONG.

Religion

The religions that are officially reported to be practised in the DPRK are Buddhism, Christianity and Chundo Kyo, a religion peculiar to Korea combining elements of Buddhism and Christianity. Religious co-ordinating bodies are believed to be under strict state control.

Korean Religious Believers Council: Pyongyang; f. 1989; brings together members of religious organizations in North Korea; Chair. JANG JAE ON.

BUDDHISM

In 1995, according to North Korean sources, there were some 60 Buddhist temples and an estimated 300 monks in the DPRK; the number of believers was about 10,000.

Korean Buddhists Federation: POB 77, Pyongyang; tel. (2) 43698; fax (2) 3812100; f. 1945; Chair. Cen. Cttee PAK TAE HWA; Sec. SHIM SANG RYON.

CHRISTIANITY

In 1995, according to North Korean sources, there were approximately 13,000 Christians (including 3,000 Roman Catholics) in the country, many of whom worshipped in house churches (of which there were about 500).

Korean Christians Federation: Pyongyang; f. 1946; Chair. Cen. Cttee KANG YONG SOP; Sec. O KYONG U.

The Roman Catholic Church

For ecclesiastical purposes, North and South Korea are nominally under a unified jurisdiction. North Korea contains two dioceses (Hamhung and Pyongyang), both suffragan to the archdiocese of Seoul (in South Korea), and the territorial abbacy of Tokwon (Tokugen), directly responsible to the Holy See.

Korean Roman Catholics Association: Changchung 1-dong, Songyo District, Pyongyang; tel. (2) 23492; f. 1988; Chair. Cen. Cttee JANG JAE ON; Vice-Chair. MUN CHANG HAK.

Diocese of Hamhung: Catholic Mission, Hamhung; 134-1 Waekwan-dong Kwan Eub, Chil kok kun, Gyeongbuk 718-800, Republic of Korea; tel. (545) 970-2000; Bishop (vacant); Apostolic Administrator of Hamhung and of the Abbacy of Tokwon Fr PLACIDUS DONG-HO RI.

Diocese of Pyongyang: Catholic Mission, Pyongyang; Bishop Rt Rev. FRANCIS HONG YONG HO (absent); Apostolic Administrator Most Rev. NICHOLAS CHEONG JIN-SUK (Archbishop of Seoul).

CHUNDO KYO

Korean Chundoists Association: Pyongyang; tel. (2) 334241; f. 1946; Chair. of Central Guidance Cttee RYU MI YONG.

The Press

PRINCIPAL NEWSPAPERS

Choldo Sinmun: Pyongyang; f. 1947; every two days.

Joson Inmingun (Korean People's Army Daily): Pyongyang; f. 1948; daily; Editor-in-Chief RI TAE BONG.

Kyowon Sinmun: Pyongyang; f. 1948; publ. by the Education Commission; weekly.

Minju Choson (Democratic Korea): Pyongyang; f. 1946; govt organ; 6 a week; Editor-in-Chief KIM JONG SUK; circ. 200,000.

Nongup Kunroja: Pyongyang; publ. of Cen. Cttee of the Union of Agricultural Working People of Korea.

Pyongyang Sinmun: Pyongyang; f. 1957; general news; 6 a week; Editor-in-Chief SONG RAK GYUN.

Rodong Chongnyon (Working Youth): Pyongyang; f. 1946; organ of the Cen. Cttee of the Kim Il Sung Socialist Youth League; 6 a week; Editor-in-Chief RI JONG GI.

Rodong Sinmun (Labour Daily): Pyongyang; f. 1946; organ of the Cen. Cttee of the Korean Workers' Party; daily; Editor-in-Chief CHOE CHIL NAM; circ. 1.5m.

Rodongja Sinmun (Workers' Newspaper): Pyongyang; f. 1945; organ of the Gen. Fed. of Trade Unions of Korea; Editor-in-Chief RI SONG JU.

Saenal (New Day): Pyongyang; f. 1971; publ. by the Kim Il Sung Socialist Youth League; 2 a week; Deputy Editor CHOE SANG IN.

Sonyon Sinmun: Pyongyang; f. 1946; publ. by the Kim Il Sung Socialist Youth League; 2 a week; circ. 120,000.

Tongil Sinbo: Kangan 1-dong, Youth Ave, Songyo District, Pyongyang; f. 1972; non-affiliated; weekly; Chief Editor JO HYON YONG; circ. 300,000.

PRINCIPAL PERIODICALS

Chollima: Pyongyang; popular magazine; monthly.

Choson (Korea): Pyongyang; social, economic, political and cultural; bi-monthly.

Choson Minju Juuiinmin Gonghwaguk Palmyonggongbo (Official Report of Inventions in the DPRK): Pyongyang; 6 a year.

Choson Munhak (Korean Literature): Pyongyang; organ of the Cen. Cttee of the Korean Writers' Union; monthly.

Choson Yesul (Korean Arts): Pyongyang; organ of the Cen. Cttee of the Gen. Fed. of Unions of Literature and Arts of Korea; monthly.

Economics: POB 73, Pyongyang; fax (2) 3814410; quarterly.

History: POB 73, Pyongyang; fax (2) 3814410; quarterly.

Hwahakgwa Hwahakgoneop: Pyongyang; organ of the Hamhung br. of the Korean Acad. of Sciences; chemistry and chemical engineering; 6 a year.

Jokook Tongil: Kangan 1-dong, Youth Ave, Songyo District, Pyongyang; organ of the Cttee for the Peaceful Unification of Korea; f. 1961; monthly; Chief Editor LI MYONG GYU; circ. 70,000.

Korean Medicine: POB 73, Pyongyang; fax (2) 3814410; quarterly.

Kunroja (Workers): 1 Munshindong, Tongdaewon, Pyongyang; f. 1946; organ of the Cen. Cttee of the Korean Workers' Party; monthly; Editor-in-Chief RYANG KYONG BOK; circ. 300,000.

Kwahakwon Tongbo (Bulletins of the Academy of Science): POB 73, Pyongyang; fax (2) 3814410; organ of the Standing Cttee of the Korean Acad. of Sciences; 6 a year.

Mulri (Physics): POB 73, Pyongyang; fax (2) 3814410; quarterly.

Munhwao Haksup (Study of Korean Language): POB 73, Pyongyang; fax (2) 3814410; publ. by the Publishing House of the Acad. of Social Sciences; quarterly.

Philosophy: PO Box 73, Pyongyang; fax (2) 3814410; quarterly.

Punsok Hwahak (Analysis): POB 73, Pyongyang; fax (2) 3814410; organ of the Cen. Analytical Inst. of the Korean Acad. of Sciences; quarterly.

Ryoksagwahak (Historical Science): Pyongyang; publ. by the Acad. of Social Sciences; quarterly.

Saengmulhak (Biology): POB, Pyongyang; fax (2) 3814410; publ. by the Korea Science and Encyclopedia Publishing House; quarterly.

Sahoekwahak (Social Science): Pyongyang; publ. by the Acad. of Social Sciences; 6 a year.

Suhakkwa Mulli: Pyongyang; organ of the Physics and Mathematics Cttee of the Korean Acad. of Sciences; quarterly.

FOREIGN LANGUAGE PUBLICATIONS

The Democratic People's Republic of Korea: Korea Pictorial, Pyongyang; f. 1956; illustrated news; Korean, Russian, Chinese, English, French, Arabic and Spanish edns; monthly; Editor-in-Chief HAN POM CHIK.

Foreign Trade of the DPRK: Foreign Trade Publishing House, Potonggang District, Pyongyang; economic developments and export promotion; English, French, Japanese, Russian and Spanish edns; monthly.

Korea: Pyongyang; f. 1956; illustrated; Korean, Arabic, Chinese, English, French, Spanish and Russian edns; monthly.

Korea Today: Foreign Languages Publishing House, Pyongyang; current affairs; Chinese, English, French, Russian and Spanish edns; monthly; Vice-Dir and Editor-in-Chief HAN PONG CHAN.

Korean Women: Pyongyang; English and French edns; quarterly.

Korean Youth and Students: Pyongyang; English and French edns; monthly.

The Pyongyang Times: Sochondong, Sosong District, Pyongyang; tel. (2) 51951; English, Spanish and French edns; weekly.

NEWS AGENCIES

Korean Central News Agency (KCNA): Potonggangdong 1, Potonggang District, Pyongyang; internet www.kcna.co.jp; f. 1946; sole distributing agency for news in the DPRK; publs daily bulletins in English, Russian, French and Spanish; Dir-Gen. KIM KI RYONG.

Foreign Bureaux

Informatsionnoye Telegrafnoye Agentstvo Rossii—Telegrafnoye Agentstvo Suverennykh Stran (ITAR—TASS) (Russia): Munsudong, Bldg 4, Flat 30, Taedongkang District, Pyongyang; tel. (2) 3817318; Correspondent ALEKSANDR VALIYEV.

The Xinhua (New China) News Agency (People's Republic of China) is also represented in the DPRK.

Press Association

Korean Journalists Union: Pyongyang; tel. (2) 36897; f. 1946; assists in the ideological work of the Korean Workers' Party; Chair. Cen. Cttee KIM SONG GUK.

Publishers

Academy of Sciences Publishing House: Nammundong, Central District, Pyongyang; tel. (2) 51956; f. 1953.

Academy of Social Sciences Publishing House: Pyongyang; Dir CHOE KWAN SHIK.

Agricultural Press: Pyongyang; labour, industrial relations; Pres. HO KYONG PIL.

Central Science and Technology Information Agency: Pyongyang; f. 1963; Dir JU SONG RYONG.

Education Publishing House: Pyongyang; f. 1945; Pres. KIM CHANG SON.

Foreign Language Press Group: Sochondong, Sosong District, Pyongyang; tel. (2) 841342; fax (2) 812100; f. 1949; Dir CHOE KYONG GUK.

Foreign Language Publishing House: Oesong District, Pyongyang; Dir SONG KI HYON.

Higher Educational Books Publishing House: Pyongyang; f. 1960; Pres. JU IL JUNG.

Industrial Publishing House: Pyongyang; f. 1948; technical and economic; Dir KIM TONG SU.

Kim Il Sung University Publishing House: Pyongyang; f. 1965.

Korea Science and Encyclopedia Publishing House: POB 73, Pyongyang; tel. (2) 18111; fax (2) 3814410; publishes numerous periodicals and monographs; f. 1952; Dir Gen. KIM YONG IL; Dir of International Co-operation JEAN BAHNG.

Korean People's Army Publishing House: Pyongyang; Pres. YUN MYONG DO.

Korean Social Democratic Party Publishing House: Pyongyang; tel. (2) 3818038; fax (2) 3814410; f. 1946; publishes quarterly journal *Joson Sahoemingjudang* (in Korean) and *KSDP Says* (in English); Dir KIM SOK JUN.

Korean Workers' Party Publishing House: Pyongyang; f. 1945; fiction, politics; Dir RYANG KYONG BOK.

Kumsong Youth Publishing House: Pyongyang; f. 1946; Dir HAN JONG SOP.

Literature and Art Publishing House: Pyongyang; f. by merger of Mass Culture Publishing House and Publishing House of the Gen. Fed. of Literary and Art Unions; Dir Gen. YUN KYONG NAM.

Transportation Publishing House: Namgyodong, Hyongjaesan District, Pyongyang; f. 1952; travel; Editor PAEK JONG HAN.

Working People's Organizations Publishing House: Pyongyang; f. 1946; fiction, government, political science; Dir PAK SE HYOK.

WRITERS' UNION

Korean Writers' Union: Pyongyang; Chair. Cen. Cttee KIM PYONG HUN.

Broadcasting and Communications

North Korea established a satellite communications station in Pyongyang, through an agreement with France in 1986, which enabled North Korea to communicate by satellite with Western countries. In 1990 an agreement was reached on satellite communications for the operation of telephone, telex and telegram services between North Korea and Japan. In October 2001 North Korea launched its first e-mail service provider in co-operation with China-based company Silibank.com, which was used for business and trade purposes. However, access to the internet remained severely limited, with information flow within North Korea still being conducted mainly via a closed intranet system (Kwangmyong).

TELECOMMUNICATIONS

Korea Post and Telecommunications Co: Pyongyang; Dir KIM HYON JONG.

BROADCASTING

Regulatory Authorities

DPRK Radio and Television Broadcasting Committee: see Radio, below.

Pyongyang Municipal Broadcasting Committee: Pyongyang; Chair. KANG CHUN SHIK.

Radio

DPRK Radio and Television Broadcasting Committee: Jonsungdong, Moranbong District, Pyongyang; tel. (2) 3816035; fax (2) 3812100; programmes relayed nationally with local programmes supplied by local radio cttees; loudspeakers are installed in factories and in open spaces in all towns; home broadcasting 22 hours daily; foreign broadcasts in Russian, Chinese, English, French, German, Japanese, Spanish and Arabic; Chair. CHA SUNG SU.

Television

General Bureau of Television: Gen. Dir CHA SUNG SU.

DPRK Radio and Television Broadcasting Committee: see Radio.

Kaesong Television: Kaesong; broadcasts five hours on weekdays, 11 hours at weekends.

Korean Central Television Station: Ministry of Post and Telecommunications, Pyongyang; broadcasts five hours daily; satellite broadcasts commenced Oct. 1999.

Mansudae Television Station: Mansudae, Pyongyang; f. 1983; broadcasts nine hours of cultural programmes, music and dance, foreign films and news reports at weekends.

Finance

(cap. = capital; res = reserves; dep. = deposits; m. = million; brs = branches)

BANKING

During 1946–47 all banking institutions in North Korea, apart from the Central Bank and the Farmers Bank, were abolished. The Farmers Bank was merged with the Central Bank in 1959. The Foreign Trade Bank (f. 1959) conducts the international business of the Central Bank. Other banks, established in the late 1970s, are responsible for the foreign-exchange and external payment business of North Korean foreign trade enterprises.

The entry into force of the Joint-Venture Act in 1984 permitted the establishment of joint-venture banks, designed to attract investment into North Korea by Koreans resident overseas. The Foreign Investment Banking Act was approved in 1993.

Central Bank

Central Bank of the DPRK: Munsudong, Seungri St 58-1, Central District, Pyongyang; tel. (2) 3338196; fax (2) 3814624; f. 1946; bank of issue; supervisory and control bank; Pres. KIM WAN SU; 227 brs.

State Banks

Changgwang Credit Bank: Saemaeul 1-dong, Pyongchon District, Pyongyang; tel. (2) 18111; fax (2) 3814793; f. 1983; commercial, joint-stock and state bank; cap. 601.0m. won, res 1,194.2m. won, dep. 10,765.8m. won (Dec. 1997); Chair. KIM CHOL HWAN; Pres. KYE CHANG HO; 172 brs.

Credit Bank of Korea: Chongryu 1-dong, Munsu St, Otandong, Central District, Pyongyang; tel. (2) 3818285; fax (2) 3817806; f. 1986 as International Credit Bank, name changed 1989; Pres. LI SUN BOK; Vice-Pres. SON YONG SUN.

Foreign Trade Bank of the DPRK: FTB Bldg, Jungsongdong, Seungri St, Central District, Pyongyang; tel. (2) 3815270; fax (2) 3814467; f. 1959; deals in international settlements and all banking business; Pres. KIM JUN CHOL; 11 brs.

International Industrial Development Bank: Jongpyong-dong, Pyongchon District, Pyongyang; tel. (2) 3818610; fax (2) 3814427; f. 2001; Pres. SHIN DOK SONG.

Korea Daesong Bank: Segoridong, Gyongheung St, Potonggang District, Pyongyang; tel. (2) 3818221; fax (2) 3814576; f. 1978; Pres. RI HONG.

Koryo Bank: Ponghwadong, Potonggang District, Pyongyang; tel. (2) 3818168; fax (2) 3814033; f. 1989 as Koryo Finance Joint Venture Co, name changed 1994; co-operative, development, regional, savings and universal bank; Pres. RI CHANG HWAN; 10 brs.

Kumgang Bank: Jungsongdong, Central District, Pyongyang; tel. (2) 3818532; fax (2) 3814467; f. 1979; Chair. KIM JANG HO.

Joint-Venture Banks

Korea Commercial Bank: f. 1988; joint venture with Koreans resident in the USA.

Korea Joint Financial Co: f. 1988; joint venture with Koreans resident in the USA.

Korea Joint Venture Bank: Ryugyongdong, Potonggang District, Pyongyang; tel. (2) 3818151; fax (2) 3814410; f. 1989; with co-operation of the Federation of Korean Traders and Industrialists in Japan; cap. US $1,932.5m. (1994); Chair PAK IL RAK; Vice-Pres. KIM SONG HWAN; 6 brs.

Korea Nagwon Joint Financial Co: f. 1987 by Nagwon Trade Co and a Japanese co.

Korea Rakwon Joint Banking Co: Pyongyang; Man. Dir HO POK DOK.

Korea United Development Bank: Central District, Pyongyang; tel. (2) 3814165; fax (2) 3814497; f. 1991; 51% owned by Zhongce Investment Corpn (Hong Kong), 49% owned by Osandok General Bureau; cap. US $60m.; Pres. KIM SE HO.

Koryo Joint Finance Co: Pyongyang; Dir KIM YONG GU.

Foreign-Investment Banks

Golden Triangle Bank: Rajin-Sonbong Free Economic and Trade Zone; f. 1995.

Daesong Credit Development Bank: Potonggang Hotel, 301 Ansan-dong, Pyongchon District, Pyongyang; tel. (2) 3814866; fax (2) 3814723; f. 1996 as Peregrine-Daesong Development Bank; jt venture between Oriental Commercial Holdings Ltd (Hong Kong) and Korea Daesong Bank; Man. NIGEL COWIE.

INSURANCE

State Insurance Bureau: Central District, Pyongyang; tel. (2) 38196; handles all life, fire, accident, marine, hull insurance and reinsurance.

Korea Foreign Insurance Co (Chosunbohom): Central District, Pyongyang; tel. (2) 3818024; fax (2) 3814464; f. 1974; conducts marine, motor, aviation and fire insurance, reinsurance of all classes, and all foreign insurance; brs in Chongjin, Hungnam and Nampo, and agencies in foreign ports; overseas representative offices in Chile, France, Germany, Pakistan, Singapore; Pres. RI JANG SU.

Korea International Insurance Co: Pyongyang; Dir (vacant).

Korea Mannyon Insurance Co: Pyongyang; Pres. PAK IL HYONG.

Trade and Industry

GOVERNMENT AGENCIES

DPRK Committee for the Promotion of External Economic Co-operation: Jungsongdong, Central District, Pyongyang; tel. (2) 333974; fax (2) 3814498; Chair. KIM YONG SUL.

DPRK Committee for the Promotion of International Trade: Central District, Pyongyang; Pres. RI SONG ROK; Chair. KIM JONG GI.

Economic Co-operation Management Bureau: Ministry of Foreign Trade, Pyongyang; f. 1998; Dir KIM YONG SUL.

Korea International Joint Venture Promotion Committee: Pyongyang; Chair. CHAE HUI JONG.

Korean Association for the Promotion of Asian Trade: Pyongyang; Pres. RI SONG ROK.

Korean International General Joint Venture Co: Pyongyang; f. 1986; promotes joint economic ventures with foreign countries; Man. Dir RI KWANG GUN.

Korean General Merchandise Export and Import Corpn: Pyongyang.

INDUSTRIAL AND TRADE ASSOCIATIONS

Korea Building Materials Trading Co: Tongdaewon District, Pyongyang; tel. (2) 18111–3818085; fax (2) 38145555; chemical building materials, woods, timbers, cement, sheet glass, etc; Dir SHIN TONG BOM.

Korea Cement Export Corpn: Central District, Pyongyang; f. 1982; cement and building materials.

Korea Cereals Export and Import Corpn: Central District, Pyongyang; high-quality vegetable starches, etc.

Korea Chemicals Export and Import Corpn: Central District, Pyongyang; petroleum and petroleum products, raw materials for the chemical industry, rubber and rubber products, fertilizers, etc.

Korea Daesong Jei Trading Corpn: Pulgungori 1–dong, Potonggang District, Pyongyang; tel. (2) 18111-3818213; fax (2) 3814431; machinery and equipment, chemical products, textiles, agricultural products, etc.

Korea Daesong Jesam Trading Corpn: Pulgungori 1-dong, Potonggang District, Pyongyang; tel. (2) 18111–3818562; fax (2) 3814431; remedies for diabetes, tonics, etc.

Korea Ferrous Metals Export and Import Corpn: Potonggang 2–dong, Potonggang District, Pyongyang; tel. (2) 18111-3818078; fax (2) 381-4581; steel products.

Korea Film Export and Import Corpn: Daedongmundong, Central District, POB 113, Pyongyang; tel. (2) 180008034; fax (2) 3814410; f. 1956; feature films, cartoons, scientific and documentary films; Dir-Gen. CHOE HYOK U.

Korea First Equipment Export and Import Co: Central District, Pyongyang; tel. (2) 334825; f. 1960; export and import of ferrous and non-ferrous metallurgical plants, geological exploration and mining equipment, communication equipment, machine-building plant, etc.; construction of public facilities such as airports, hotels, tourist facilities, etc.; joint-venture business in similar projects; Pres. CHAE WON CHOL.

Korea Foodstuffs Export and Import Corpn: Kangan 2–dong, Songyo District, Pyongyang; tel. (2) 18111-3818289; fax (2) 3814417; cereals, wines, meat, canned foods, fruits, cigarettes, etc.

Korea Fruit and Vegetables Export Corpn: Central District, Pyongyang; tel. (2) 35117; vegetables, fruit and their products.

Korea General Corpn for External Construction (GENCO): Sungri St 25, Jungsong-dong, Central District, Pyongyang; tel. (2) 18111-3818090 ; fax (2) 3814611; e-mail gen122@co.chesin.com; f. 1961; construction of dwelling houses, public establishments, factories, hydroelectric and thermal power stations, irrigation systems, ports, bridges, and transport services, technical services; Gen. Dir CHOE BONG SU.

Korea General Export and Import Corpn: Central District, Pyongyang; plate glass, tiles, granite, locks, medicinal herbs, foodstuffs and light industrial products.

Korea General Machine Co: Tongsin 3-dong, Tongdaewon, Pyongyang; tel. (2) 18555-3818102; fax (2) 381-4495; Dir RA IN GYUN.

Korea Hyopdong Trading Corpn: Othan-dong, Kangan St, Central District, Pyongyang; tel. (2) 18111-3818011; fax (2) 3814454; fabrics, glass products, ceramics, chemical goods, building materials, foodstuffs, machinery, etc.

Korea Industrial Technology Co: Junsongdong, Central District, Pyongyang; tel. (2) 18111-3818025; fax (2) 3814537; Pres. KWON YONG SON.

Korea International Chemical Joint Venture Co: Pyongyang; Chair. RYO SONG GUN.

Korea International Joint Venture Co: Pyongyang; Man. Dir HONG SONG NAM.

Korea Jangsu Trading Co: Kyogudong, Central District, Pyongyang; tel. (2) 18111-3818834; fax (2) 3814410; medicinal products and clinical equipment.

Korea Jeil Equipment Export and Import Corpn: Jungsongdong, Central District, Pyongyang; tel. (2) 334825; f. 1960; ferrous and non-ferrous metallurgical plant, geological exploration and mining equipment, power plant, communications and broadcasting equipment, machine-building equipment, railway equipment, construction of public facilities; Pres. CHO JANG DOK.

Korea Jesam Equipment Export and Import Corpn: Central District, Pyongyang; chemical, textile, pharmaceutical and light industry plant.

Korea Koryo Trading Corpn: Jongpyongdong, Pyongchon District, Pyongyang; tel. (2) 18111-3818104; fax (2) 3814646; Dir KIM HUI DUK.

Korea Kwangmyong Trading Corpn: Jungsongdong, Central District, Pyongyang; tel. (2) 18111-3818111; fax (2) 3814410; dried herbs, dried and pickled vegetables; Dir CHOE JONG HUN.

Korea Light Industry Import-Export Co: Juchetab St, Tongdaewon District, Pyongyang; tel. (2) 37661; exports silk, cigarettes, canned goods, drinking glasses, ceramics, handbags, pens, plastic flowers, musical instruments, etc.; imports chemicals, dyestuffs, machinery, etc.; Dir CHOE PYONG HYON.

Korea Machine Tool Trading Corpn: Tongdaewon District, Pyongyang; tel. (2) 18555-381810; fax (2) 3814495; Dir KIM KWANG RYOP.

Korea Machinery and Equipment Export and Import Corpn: Potonggang District, Pyongyang; tel. (2) 333449; f. 1948; metallurgical machinery and equipment, electric machines, building machinery, farm machinery, diesel engines, etc.

Korea Maibong Trading Corpn: Central District, Pyongyang; non-ferrous metal ingots and allied products, non-metallic minerals, agricultural and marine products.

Korea Manpung Trading Corpn: Central District, Pyongyang; chemical and agricultural products, machinery and equipment.

Korea Mansu Trading Corpn: Chollima St, Central District, POB 250, Pyongyang; tel. (2) 43075; fax (2) 812100; f. 1974; antibiotics, pharmaceuticals, vitamin compounds, drugs, medicinal herbs; Dir KIM JANG HUN.

Korea Marine Products Export and Import Corpn: Central District, Pyongyang; canned, frozen, dried, salted and smoked fish, fishing equipment and supplies.

Korea Minerals Export and Import Corpn: Central District, Pyongyang; minerals, solid fuel, graphite, precious stones, etc.

Korea Namheung Trading Co: Sinri-dong, Tongdaewon District, Pyongyang; tel. (2) 18111-3818974; fax (2) 3814623; high-purity reagents, synthetic resins, vinyl films, essential oils, menthol and peppermint oil.

Korea Non-ferrous Metals Export and Import Corpn: Potonggang 2-dong, Potonggang District, Pyongyang; tel. (2) 18111-3818247; fax (2) 3814569.

Korea Okyru Trading Corpn: Kansongdong, Pyongchon District, Pyongyang; tel. (2) 18111-3818110; fax (2) 3814618; agricultural and marine products, household goods, clothing, chemical and light industrial products.

Korea Ponghwa Contractual Joint Venture Co: Pyongyang; Dir RIM TONG CHON.

Korea Ponghwa General Trading Corpn: Jungsong-dong, Central District, Pyongyang; tel. (2) 18111-3818023; fax (2) 3814444; machinery, metal products, minerals and chemicals.

Korea Publications Export and Import Corpn: Yokjondong, Yonggwang St, Central District, Pyongyang; tel. (2) 3818536; fax (2) 3814404; f. 1948; export of books, periodicals, postcards, paintings, cassettes, videos, CDs, CD-ROMs, postage stamps and records; import of books; Pres. RI YONG.

Korea Pyongyang Trading Co Ltd: Central District, POB 550, Pyongyang; pig iron, steel, magnesia clinker, textiles, etc.

Korea Rungra Co: Sinwondong, Potonggang District, Pyongyang; tel. (2) 18111-3818112; fax (2) 3814608; Dir CHOE HENG UNG.

Korea Rungrado Trading Corpn: Segori-dong, Potonggang District, Pyongyang; tel. (2) 18111-3818022; fax (2) 3814507; food and animal products; Gen. Dir PAK KYU HONG.

Korea Ryongaksan General Trading Corpn: Pyongyang; Gen. Dir HAN YU RO.

Korea Samcholli General Corpn: Pyongyang; Dir JONG UN OP.

Korea Senbong Trading Corpn: Central District, Pyongyang; ferrous and non-ferrous metals, rolled steels, mineral ores, chemicals, etc.

Korea Somyu Hyopdong Trading Corpn: Oesong District, Pyongyang; clothing and textiles.

Korea Songhwa Trading Corpn: Oesong District, Pyongyang; ceramics, glass, hardware, leaf tobaccos, fruit and wines.

Korea Technology Corpn: Jungsongdong, Central District, Pyongyang; tel. (2) 18111-3818090; fax (2) 3814410; scientific and technical co-operation.

Korea Unha Trading Corpn: Rungra 1-dong, Taedonggang District, Pyongyang; tel. (2) 18111-3818236; fax (2) 3814506; clothing and fibres.

Korea Yonghung Trading Co: Tongan-dong, Central District, Pyongyang; tel. (2) 18111-3818223; fax (2) 3814527; e-mail greenlam@co.chesin.com; f. 1979; export of freight cars, vehicle parts, marine products, electronic goods, import of steel, chemical products; Pres. CHOE YONG DOK.

TRADE UNIONS

General Federation of Trade Unions of Korea (GFTUK): POB 333, Dongmun-dong, Daedonggang District, Pyongyang; fax (2) 3814427; f. 1945; 1.6m. mems (2003); seven affiliated unions (2003); Pres. RYOM SUN GIL.

Trade Union of Metal and Engineering Industries of Korea: Pyongyang; f. 1945; 332,800 mems (2003); Pres. CHOE GWANG HYON.

Trade Union of Mining and Power Industries of Korea: Pyongyang; f. 1945; 221,000 mems (2003); Pres. SON YONG JUN.

Trade Union of Light and Chemical Industries of Korea: Pyongyang; f. 1945; 372,500 mems (2003); Pres. RI JIN HAK.

Trade Union of Public Employees and Service Workers of Korea: Pyongyang; f. 1945; 305,900 mems (2003); Pres. KIM GANG HO.

Trade Union of Construction and Forestry Workers of Korea: Pyongyang; f. 1945; 160,000 mems (2003); Pres. WON HYONG GUK.

Trade Union of Educational and Cultural Workers: Pyongyang; f. 1946; 89,800 mems (2003); Pres. KIM SONG CHOL.

Trade Union of Transport and Fisheries Workers of Korea: Pyongyang; f. 1945; 119,800 mems (2003); Pres. CHOE RYONG SU.

General Federation of Agricultural and Forestry Technique of Korea: Chung Kuyuck Nammundong, Pyongyang; f. 1946; 523,000 mems.

General Federation of Unions of Literature and Arts of Korea: Pyongyang; f. 1946; seven br. unions; Chair. Cen. Cttee CHANG CHOL.

Kim Il Sung Socialist Youth League: Pyongyang; fmrly League of Socialist Working Youth of Korea; First Sec. KIM GYONG HO.

Korean Architects' Union: Pyongyang; f. 1954; 500 mems; Chair. Cen. Cttee PAE TAL JUN.

Korean Democratic Lawyers' Association: Ryonhwa 1, Central District, Pyongyang; fax (2) 3814644; f. 1954; Chair. HAM HAK SONG.

Korean Democratic Scientists' Association: Pyongyang; f. 1956.

Korean Democratic Women's Union: Jungsongdong, Central District, Pyongyang; fax (2) 3814416; f. 1945; Chief Officer PAK SUN HUI.

Korean General Federation of Science and Technology: Jungsongdong, Seungri St, Central District, Pyongyang; tel. (2) 3224389; fax (2) 3814410; f. 1946; 550,000 mems; Chair. Cen. Cttee CHOE HUI JONG.

Korean Medical Association: Pyongyang; f. 1970; Chair. CHOE CHANG SHIK.

Union of Agricultural Working People of Korea: Pyongyang; f. 1965 to replace fmr Korean Peasants' Union; 2.4m. mems; Chair. Cen. Cttee SUNG SANG SOP.

Transport

RAILWAYS

Railways were responsible for some 62% of passenger journeys in 1991 and for some 74% of the volume of freight transported in 1997. In 2002 the total length of track was estimated at 5,235 km, of which some 70% was electrified. There are international train services to Moscow (Russia) and Beijing (People's Republic of China). Construction work on the reconnection of the Kyongui (West coast, Sinuiju–Seoul) and East Coast Line (Wonsan–Seoul) began in September 2002. The two lines were officially opened in June 2003, but were not yet open to traffic, as construction work on the Northern side remained to be completed. Reconnection work was subject to disruption by the changing political situation. Eventually the two would be linked to the Trans-China and Trans-Siberian railways respectively, greatly enhancing the region's transportation links.

There is an underground railway system in Pyongyang, with two public lines. Unspecified plans to expand the system were announced in February 2002.

ROADS

In 2000, according to South Korean estimates, the road network totalled 23,407 km (of which only about 8% was paved), including 682 km of multi-lane highways.

INLAND WATERWAYS

The Yalu (Amnok-gang) and Taedong, Tumen and Ryesong are the most important commercial rivers. Regular passenger and freight services: Nampo–Chosan–Supung; Chungsu–Sinuiju–Dasado; Nampo–Jeudo; Pyongyang–Nampo.

SHIPPING

The principal ports are Nampo, Wonsan, Chongjin, Rajin, Hungnam, Songnim and Haeju. In 1997 North Korean ports had a combined capacity for handling 35m. tons of cargo. At 31 December 2002 North Korea's merchant fleet comprised 225 vessels, with a combined displacement of 870,458 grt.

Korea Chartering Corpn: Central District, Pyongyang; arranges cargo transportation and chartering.

Korea Daehung Shipping Co: Ansan 1–dong, Pyongchon District, Pyongyang; tel. (2) 18111 ext 8695; fax (2) 3814508; f. 1994; owns 6 reefers, 3 oil tankers, 1 cargo ship.

Korea East Sea Shipping Co: Pyongyang; Dir RI TUK HYON.

Korea Foreign Transportation Corpn: Central District, Pyongyang; arranges transportation of export and import cargoes (transit goods and charters).

Korean-Polish Shipping Co Ltd: Moranbong District, Pyongyang; tel. (2) 3814384; fax (2) 3814607; f. 1967; maritime trade mainly with Polish, Far East and DPRK ports.

Korea Tonghae Shipping Co: Changgwang St, Central District, POB 120, Pyongyang; tel. (2) 345805; fax (2) 3814583; arranges transportation by Korean vessels.

Ocean Maritime Management Co Ltd: Tonghungdong, Central District, Pyongyang.

Ocean Shipping Agency of the DPRK: Moranbong District, POB 21, Pyongyang; tel. (2) 3818100; fax (2) 3814531; Pres. O JONG HO.

CIVIL AVIATION

The international airport is at Sunan, 24 km from Pyongyang. In September 2003 the first tourist flight from Seoul to Pyongyang was completed by an Air Koryo plane, representing the first commercial flight between North and South Korea in more than 50 years. In January 2004 plans were announced for an aviation agreement between North and South Korea, which would allow regular inter-Korean flight routes to be opened.

Chosonminhang/General Civil Aviation Bureau of the DPRK: Sunan Airport, Sunan District, Pyongyang; tel. (2) 37917; fax (2) 3814625; f. 1954; internal services and external flights by Air Koryo to Beijing and Shenyang (People's Republic of China), Bangkok (Thailand), Macao, Nagoya (Japan), Moscow, Khabarovsk and Vladivostok (Russia), Sofia (Bulgaria) and Berlin (Germany); charter services are operated to Asia, Africa and Europe; Pres. KIM YO UNG.

Tourism

The DPRK was formally admitted to the World Tourism Organization in 1987. Tourism is permitted only in officially accompanied parties. In 1999 there were more than 60 international hotels (including nine in Pyongyang) with 7,500 beds. Tourist arrivals totalled 130,000 in 1998. A feasibility study was undertaken in 1992 regarding the development of Mount Kumgang as a tourist attraction. The study proposed the construction of an international airport at Kumnan and of a number of hotels and leisure facilities in the Wonsan area. Local ports were also to be upgraded. It was hoped that the development, scheduled to cost some US $20,000m. and to be completed by 2004, would attract 3m. tourists to the area each year. In November 1998 some 800 South Korean tourists visited Mount Kumgang, as part of a joint venture mounted by the North Korean authorities and Hyundai, the South Korean conglomerate. By November 2000 only 350,000 South Korean tourists had visited the attraction. In November 2002, in an effort to increase profit-

ability, Mount Kumgang was designated a special tax-free economic zone. In 1996 it was reported that proposals had been made to create a tourist resort in the Rajin-Sonbong Free Economic and Trade Zone, in the north-east of the country. It was announced that hotels to accommodate some 5,000 people were to be constructed, as well as an airport to service the area. There were reports in 1998 that a heliport had been opened in the Zone, and in 1999 the resort was completed. Mount Chilbo, Mount Kuwol, Mount Jongbang and the Ryongmum Cave were transformed into new tourist destinations in that year. In August 2000 plans were announced for the development, jointly with China, of the western part of Mount Paektu, Korea's highest mountain, as a tourist resort. In September 2003 South Korean tourists were able to visit Pyongyang for the first time. In 2003 it was also estimated that around 1,500 Western tourists visited North Korea annually.

Korea International Tourist Bureau: Pyongyang; Pres. HAN PYONG UN.

Korean International Youth Tourist Co: Mankyongdae District, Pyongyang; tel. (2) 73406; f. 1985; Dir HWANG CHUN YONG.

Kumgangsan International Tourist Co: Central District, Pyongyang; tel. (2) 31562; fax (2) 3812100; f. 1988.

National Tourism Administration of the DPRK: Central District, Pyongyang; tel. (2) 3818901; fax (2) 3814547; e-mail nta@silibank.com; f. 1953; state-run tourism promotion organization; Dir RYO SUNG CHOL.

Ryohaengsa (Korea International Travel Company): Central District, Pyongyang; tel. (2) 3817201; fax (2) 3817607; f. 1953; has relations with more than 200 tourist companies throughout the world; Pres. CHO SONG HUN.

State General Bureau of Tourism: Pyongyang; Pres. RYO SUNG CHOL.

THE REPUBLIC OF KOREA

Introductory Survey

Location, Climate, Language, Religion, Flag, Capital

The Republic of Korea (South Korea) forms the southern part of the Korean peninsula, in eastern Asia. To the north, separated by a frontier which roughly follows the 38th parallel, is the country's only neighbour, the Democratic People's Republic of Korea (North Korea). To the west is the Yellow Sea, to the south is the East China Sea, and to the east is the Sea of Japan. The climate is marked by cold, dry winters, with an average temperature of –6°C (21°F), and hot, humid summers, with an average temperature of 25°C (77°F). The language is Korean. Confucianism, Mahayana Buddhism, and Chundo Kyo are the principal traditional religions. Chundo Kyo is peculiar to Korea, and combines elements of Shaman, Buddhist and Christian doctrines. There are some 17.5m. Christians, of whom about 83% are Protestants. The national flag (proportions 2 by 3) comprises, in the centre of a white field, a disc divided horizontally by an S-shaped line, red above and blue below, surrounded by four configurations of parallel, broken and unbroken black bars. The capital is Seoul.

Recent History

(For more details of the history of Korea up to 1953, including the Korean War, see the chapter on the Democratic People's Republic of Korea—DPRK, (see p. 2462).)

UN-supervised elections to a new legislature, the National Assembly (Kuk Hoe), took place in May 1948. The Assembly adopted a democratic Constitution, and South Korea became the independent Republic of Korea on 15 August 1948, with Dr Syngman Rhee, leader of the Liberal Party, as the country's first President. He remained in the post until his resignation in April 1960. Elections in July were won by the Democratic Party, led by Chang Myon, but his Government was deposed in May 1961 by a military coup, led by Gen. Park Chung-Hee. Power was assumed by the Supreme Council for National Reconstruction, which dissolved the National Assembly, suspended the Constitution and disbanded all existing political parties. In January 1963 the military leadership formed the Democratic Republican Party (DRP). Under a new Constitution, Gen. Park became President of the Third Republic in December.

Opposition to Park's regime led to the imposition of martial law in October 1972. A Constitution for the Fourth Republic, giving the President greatly increased powers, was approved by national referendum in November. A new body, the National Conference for Unification (NCU), was elected in December. The NCU re-elected President Park for a six-year term, and the DRP obtained a decisive majority in elections to the new National Assembly. In May 1975 opposition to the Government was effectively banned, and political trials followed. Elections to the NCU were held in May 1978, and the President was re-elected for a further six-year term in July. In October 1979 serious rioting erupted when Kim Young-Sam, the leader of the opposition New Democratic Party (NDP), was accused of subversive activities and expelled from the National Assembly. On 26 October Park was assassinated in an alleged coup attempt, led by the head of the Korean Central Intelligence Agency. Martial law was reintroduced (except on the island of Jeju), and in December the Prime Minister, Choi Kyu-Hah, was elected President by the NCU. Instability in the DRP and the army resulted in a military coup in December, led by the head of the Defence Security Command, Lt-Gen. Chun Doo-Hwan, who arrested the Army Chief of Staff and effectively took power. Nevertheless, President Choi was inaugurated on 21 December to complete his predecessor's term of office (to 1984).

Choi promised liberalizing reforms, but in May 1980 demonstrations by students and confrontation with the army led to the arrest of about 30 political leaders, including Kim Dae-Jung, former head of the NDP. Martial law was extended throughout the country, the National Assembly was suspended, and all political activity was banned. Almost 200 people were killed when troops stormed the southern city of Gwangju, which had been occupied by students and dissidents. In August Choi resigned, and Gen. Chun was elected President. Acting Prime Minister Nam Duck-Woo formed a new State Council (cabinet)

in September. In the same month the sentencing to death of Kim Dae-Jung for plotting rebellion was condemned internationally. (This sentence was subsequently suspended.) In October a new Constitution was overwhelmingly approved by referendum.

Martial law was ended in January 1981, and new political parties were formed. In the following month President Chun was re-elected: the start of his new term, in March, inaugurated the Fifth Republic. Chun's Democratic Justice Party (DJP) became the majority party in the new National Assembly, which was elected shortly afterwards. Amid opposition demands for liberalization, Chun pledged that he would retire at the end of his term in 1988, thus becoming the country's first Head of State to transfer power constitutionally.

During 1984, following an escalation of student unrest, the Government adopted a more flexible attitude towards dissidents. Several thousand prisoners were released, and the political 'blacklist' was finally abolished in March 1985. In January 1985 the New Korea Democratic Party (NKDP) was established by supporters of Kim Young-Sam and Kim Dae-Jung. At the general election to the National Assembly held in February, the DJP retained its majority, but the NKDP emerged as the major opposition force, boosted by the return from exile of Kim Dae-Jung. The new party secured 67 of the Assembly's 276 seats, while the DJP won 148 seats. Chun appointed a new State Council, with Lho Shin-Yong as Prime Minister. Before the opening session of the new National Assembly many deputies defected to the NKDP, increasing the party's strength to 102 seats.

In April 1987 internal divisions within the NKDP led to the formation of a new opposition party, the Reunification Democratic Party (RDP); Kim Young-Sam was elected to its presidency in May. In April Chun unexpectedly announced the suspension of the process of reform until after the Olympic Games (due to be held in Seoul in September 1988). While confirming that he would leave office in February 1988, Chun indicated that his successor would be elected by the existing electoral college system, precipitating violent clashes between anti-Government demonstrators and riot police.

In June 1987 Roh Tae-Woo was nominated as the DJP's presidential candidate. However, Roh subsequently informed Chun that he would relinquish both the DJP chairmanship and his presidential candidature if the principal demands of the opposition for constitutional and electoral reform were not satisfied. Under international pressure, Chun acceded, and negotiations on constitutional amendments were announced. In August the DJP and the RDP announced that a bipartisan committee had agreed a draft Constitution. Among its provisions were the reintroduction of direct presidential elections by universal suffrage, and the restriction of the presidential mandate to a single five-year term; the President's emergency powers were also to be reduced, and serving military officers were to be prohibited from taking government office. Having been approved by the National Assembly, the amendments were endorsed in a national referendum in October, and the amended Constitution was promulgated shortly thereafter.

Kim Dae-Jung joined the RDP in August 1987; in November, however, he became President of a new Peace and Democracy Party (PDP), and declared himself a rival presidential candidate. At the election, in December, Roh Tae-Woo won some 36% of the votes, while Kim Dae-Jung and Kim Young-Sam each achieved about 27%. Roh Tae-Woo was inaugurated as President on 25 February 1988, whereupon the Sixth Republic was established. At the general election to the National Assembly, in April, the DJP failed to achieve an overall majority, securing 125 of the 299 seats. The PDP achieved 70 seats, thus becoming the main opposition party; the remainder went to the RDP and the New Democratic Republican Party (NDRP—the revived and renamed DRP), led by Kim Jong-Pil.

During 1988 the Government granted greater autonomy to universities, permitted the formation of student associations, and eased restrictions on the press. The number of trade unions increased, and greater freedom to undertake foreign travel was granted to South Korean citizens.

In February 1990 the DJP merged with the RDP and the NDRP to form the Democratic Liberal Party (DLP). Roh was subsequently elected President of the DLP, while Kim Young-Sam and Kim Jong-Pil were elected as two of the party's three Chairmen. The DLP thus controlled more than two-thirds of the seats in the National Assembly. The PDP, effectively isolated as the sole opposition party, condemned the merger and demanded new elections. In March a new opposition group, the Democratic Party (DP), was formed, largely comprising members of the RDP who had opposed the merger.

In July 1990 a large rally was held in Seoul to denounce the adoption by the National Assembly of several items of controversial legislation, including proposals to restructure the military leadership and to reorganize the broadcasting media. Shortly afterwards all the opposition members of the National Assembly tendered their resignation, in protest at the legislation. Although the Assembly's Speaker refused to accept the resignations, the PDP deputies returned to the National Assembly only in November, following an agreement with the DLP that local council elections would take place in the first half of 1991, to be followed by gubernatorial and mayoral elections in 1992. The DLP also agreed to abandon plans for the transfer, by constitutional amendment, of executive powers to the State Council. The local elections (the first to be held in the Republic of Korea for 30 years) took place in March and June 1991, and resulted in a decisive victory for the DLP.

Meanwhile, in April 1991 the PDP merged with the smaller opposition Party for New Democratic Alliance to form the New Democratic Party (NDP). In September the NDP and the DP agreed to merge (under the latter's name) to form a stronger opposition front. A further opposition group, the Unification National Party (UNP), was established in January 1992 by Chung Ju-Yung, the founder and honorary chairman of the powerful Hyundai industrial conglomerate.

At elections to the National Assembly in March 1992 the DLP unexpectedly failed to secure an absolute majority, obtaining a total of 149 of the 299 seats. The remainder of the seats were won by the DP (97), the UNP (31) and independent candidates (21). In May Kim Young-Sam was chosen as the DLP's candidate for the presidential election, scheduled for December, and in August he replaced Roh as the party's President. Roh's decision to resign from the DLP altogether, in order to create a neutral government in anticipation of the election, was welcomed by opposition deputies. Serious divisions within the DLP led to defections from the party by opponents of Kim Young-Sam.

The presidential election, on 18 December 1992, was won by Kim Young-Sam, with some 42% of the votes cast. Kim (who was inaugurated on 25 February 1993) was the first South Korean President since 1960 without military connections. The defeated Kim Dae-Jung subsequently retired from political life. In February 1993 Chung Ju-Yung resigned as President of the United People's Party (UPP—as the UNP had been renamed), following allegations that he had embezzled Hyundai finances to fund his election campaign. Kim Young-Sam appointed Hwang In-Sung as Prime Minister, and a new State Council was formed.

Kim Young-Sam acted swiftly to honour his campaign pledge to eliminate corruption in business and political life; in all, during 1993, Kim's anti-corruption measures were reported to have resulted in the dismissal of, or disciplinary action against, some 3,000 business, government and military figures. One of Roh Tae-Woo's former Ministers of National Defence, Lee Jong-Koo, was sentenced in November 1993 to three years' imprisonment, after having been convicted of accepting bribes from defence contractors. At the same time the announcement of measures to restrict the activities of the country's industrial conglomerates (*chaebol*) was accompanied by corruption proceedings against several prominent business executives. In November Chung Ju-Yung was sentenced to three years' imprisonment, although the sentence was suspended on account of his age (78) and past contribution South Korean economic development. Meanwhile, in August a presidential decree outlawed the opening of bank accounts under false names (a practice believed to have been used to conceal large-scale financial irregularities). In September the disclosure of the assets of some 1,500 public officials and the submission of these accounts for scrutiny by a government ethics committee prompted the resignation of several senior figures.

Hwang In-Sung resigned as Prime Minister in December 1993 and was succeeded by Lee Hoi-Chang, hitherto Chairman of the Board of Audit and Inspection (BAI). However, he resigned in April 1994 and was replaced by Lee Yung-Duk, latterly the Deputy Prime Minister responsible for national unification.

In July 1994 the UPP and a smaller opposition party, the New Political Reform Party, merged to form the New People's Party (NPP). In October the Government announced that its inquiry into the role played by former Presidents Chun and Roh in the 1979 coup had found that both had participated in a 'premeditated military rebellion'. Prosecution proceedings were not initiated at this stage. In December 1994 Lee Hong-Koo (hitherto the Deputy Prime Minister responsible for national unification) was appointed Prime Minister, as part of a major restructuring of the State Council. Kim Deok, the new Deputy Prime Minister responsible for national unification, was obliged to resign in February 1995, following accusations that, in his former position as Director of the Agency for National Security Planning (the South Korean intelligence service), he had considered postponing the forthcoming local elections to allow for the revision of boundaries to the advantage of the DLP.

The DLP fared badly at elections for gubernatorial, mayoral and other municipal and provincial posts in May 1995 (the first full local elections to be held in the Republic of Korea for 34 years). A contributory factor to the DLP's poor performance was the success of a new party, the United Liberal Democrats (ULD), established in March by defectors from the DLP and led by Kim Jong-Pil (who had resigned as DLP Chairman earlier in the year). In September Kim Dae-Jung returned to political life, establishing his own party, the National Congress for New Politics (NCNP). The DP was severely undermined when many of its members left to join the NCNP.

A major scandal erupted in October 1995, when Roh Tae-Woo admitted in a televised address that he had amassed a large sum of money during his term of office. He was arrested in the following month; at his trial, which opened in December, Roh admitted to having received donations from South Korean businesses, but denied that these constituted bribes. Many senior political figures and business leaders were also detained and interrogated in connection with the affair. Kim Dae-Jung, meanwhile, unexpectedly admitted that his campaign for the 1992 presidential election had been supported by a donation of money from Roh's 'slush fund'. Kim Young-Sam denied opposition allegations that he too had benefited from a similar donation. In December 1995, in an effort to distance his party from the deepening scandal, Kim changed the DLP's name to the New Korea Party (NKP). A major reorganization of the State Council was effected, in which Lee Hong-Koo was replaced as Prime Minister by Lee Soo-Sung, the President of Seoul National University.

In late 1995 it was announced that Roh Tae-Woo and Chun Doo-Hwan were to be prosecuted for their involvement in the 1979 coup and 1980 Gwangju massacre. Chun was arrested in December 1995, and in the following month he was additionally accused of accumulating a huge political 'slush fund'. At the opening of his trial for corruption in February 1996 Chun denied charges that the fund had been amassed as a result of bribe-taking. Legal proceedings in connection with the events of 1979 and 1980 opened in March 1996: Chun was charged with mutiny for his organization of the 1979 coup, and with sedition in connection with the Gwangju massacre, while Roh was charged with aiding Chun. Meanwhile, also in March 1996, one of Kim Young-Sam's personal aides was arrested on bribery charges. Roh and Chun were convicted as charged in August. For their role in the *coup d'état* and Gwangju massacre, Chun was sentenced to death and Roh to 22½ years' imprisonment; each was heavily fined in the corruption cases. Several others were also convicted for their part in the events of 1979 and 1980. Following an appeal, in which their contribution to the country's impressive economic growth and to the establishment of democratic government were cited as mitigating factors, Chun's sentence was commuted to one of life imprisonment, while Roh's term of imprisonment was reduced to 17 years.

Elections to the National Assembly took place in April 1996. Contrary to widespread predictions, the NKP only narrowly failed to retain its parliamentary majority, winning a total of 139 of the 299 seats. One factor contributing to the NKP's success was believed to have been the recent incursions into the demilitarized zone (DMZ) by North Korean troops, which, although apparently intended to destabilize the electoral proceedings, in fact caused many voters to favour the ruling party out of concern for national security. The NCNP performed less well than had been expected, taking 79 seats; moreover, the party's leader, Kim Dae-Jung, failed to win a seat. The ULD obtained 50 seats and the DP only 15 (compared with 97 at the previous election); independent candidates won the remaining 16 seats. By the time the National Assembly convened in June, the NKP had secured a working majority with the support of several opposition and independent members. The opening of the Assembly was disrupted by opposition deputies, alleging electoral malpractice, but the boycott of the legislature was ended in July, following an agreement by the NKP to investigate the allegations.

The revision of the Republic of Korea's labour laws, with the aim of introducing greater flexibility into the labour market—a condition of the country's impending membership of the Organisation for Economic Co-operation and Development (OECD, see p. 295)—was initiated in May 1996. Disagreements over the extent of the labour reforms led to widespread strikes in the manufacturing industries in June. Reforms proposed by the Government in early December were severely criticized by trade unions and opposition parties. South Korea's principal workers' confederation, the Federation of Korean Trade Unions (FKTU), hitherto regarded as generally acquiescent to the Government, called a general strike in late December, after the Government convened a dawn session of the National Assembly, which approved the labour reform bill in the absence of opposition deputies. Controversial legislation was also passed to extend the powers of the Agency for National Security Planning. Many thousands of workers from key manufacturing industries, as well as public-sector employees, participated in the strike, which lasted for three weeks. Anti-Government demonstrators in Seoul and other major cities frequently clashed with riot police, and warrants were issued for the arrest of several leaders of the Korean Confederation of Trade Unions (KCTU), who were barricaded in the Roman Catholic Cathedral in Seoul. Concern was expressed that President Kim might be resorting to a more authoritarian style of leadership, particularly when it was alleged that the DPRK was lending its support to the striking workers (a tactic used by the South Korean authorities in the past to justify the suppression of domestic dissent); furthermore, foreign labour officials, including a representative of OECD, were threatened with deportation for encouraging union action. By mid-January 1997 support for the strikes was abating; the KCTU proposed weekly one-day stoppages, in order to minimize financial losses, and suggested that it might accept a modification of the labour law, having previously insisted on its complete annulment. OECD issued a severe rebuke to the Government for failing to honour its pledges on the issue of labour reform, and, in a significant concession, Kim agreed to meet the leaders of the opposition parties to discuss amendments to the law; warrants for the arrest of union leaders were also suspended. In March the National Assembly approved a revised version of the legislation, whereby the implementation of certain proposals was delayed for two years, while the KCTU was granted immediate official recognition.

Meanwhile, political and economic scandals persisted throughout 1996, particularly concerning allegations of bribery, which resulted in several government resignations. The infiltration of a North Korean submarine into South Korean waters in September (see below) resulted in the dismissal of the Minister of Defence, Lee Yang-Ho. He was subsequently charged with divulging classified information and with receiving bribes in connection with the procurement of helicopters for the army, and in December was sentenced to four years' imprisonment.

In January 1997 a further major scandal erupted when Hanbo, one of the country's largest steel and construction conglomerates, was declared bankrupt. Allegations were made that Hanbo had bribed the Government to exert pressure on banks to provide substantial loans to the conglomerate. The chief executives of several large Korean banks were arrested on charges of receiving bribes, and in February the Minister of Home Affairs, Kim Woo-Suk, resigned following allegations that he too had accepted payments from the company. President Kim issued an official apology for the loan scandal, and in March Lee Soo-Sung resigned as Prime Minister in a gesture of contrition. He was replaced by Goh Kun, hitherto President of Myongju University. In May the President's son, Kim Hyun-Chul, was arrested on charges of tax evasion and accepting bribes in return for influencing official appointments. The repercussions of the Hanbo affair widened further, implicating, among others, Kim Soo-Han, the Speaker of the National Assembly, and President Kim himself, whose 1992 election campaign was alleged to have been funded partially by the conglomerate. Kim Hyun-Chul was, however, formally cleared of any involvement. In June 1997 the former Chairman of Hanbo and several senior banking officials and politicians, including Kim Woo-Suk, were convicted on charges relating to the scandal.

In July 1997 Lee Hoi-Chang, former Prime Minister and Chairman of the NKP, was nominated as the ruling party's candidate for the presidential election, scheduled for December. Lee's candidacy was severely affected by various scandals surrounding the NKP and his family. Moreover, Rhee In-Je, the defeated challenger in the contest for the NKP nomination, decided to contest the presidency, subsequently forming his own political organization, the New Party by the People. In September Lee was elected President of the NKP, replacing Kim Young-Sam, who subsequently resigned from the party in order to ensure his neutrality in the forthcoming election. In October the NCNP and the ULD established an alliance, formulating a joint programme of proposed constitutional amendments and uniting behind the NCNP presidential nominee, Kim Dae-Jung, with the ULD to propose the Prime Minister in the event of victory. The conviction of Kim Hyun-Chul in October on charges of bribery and tax evasion was a further reverse for the NKP, which, in November, announced its merger with the DP, to form the Grand National Party (GNP).

Internal party politics were, however, overshadowed by the crisis experienced by the Korean economy in the latter half of 1997. Many of the conglomerates (*chaebol*) reported serious financial difficulties, having amassed huge debts which they were subsequently unable to service. Measures aimed at stabilizing the financial markets, announced in October, were unsuccessful. Moreover, in an unexpected reversal of its non-interventionist policy, the Government declared that part of the Kia Group, which was close to collapse, was to be nationalized, in an attempt to prevent further bankruptcies. Following the rejection by the legislature of the Government's financial liberalization measures, President Kim dismissed Kang Kyung-Shik, the Deputy Prime Minister and Minister of Finance and the Economy, in November, replacing him with Lim Chang-Yul, latterly Minister of Trade, Industry and Energy. An extensive economic stabilization programme, announced shortly afterwards, had little effect in curbing the depreciation of the national currency, the won, and the Government was forced to request the assistance of the IMF. This recourse to the IMF was condemned by opposition politicians and the media as a 'national shame'. The true extent of the country's economic crisis, described as the most serious in the South Korean history, became apparent upon the conclusion of negotiations with the IMF in early December 1997. In the IMF's largest ever rescue programme, worth US $57,000m., funds were to be allocated to prevent the Republic of Korea from defaulting on its repayments of external debt. Provision of the loans remained conditional upon the implementation of a programme of extensive financial and economic reforms.

The presidential election, held on 18 December 1997, was narrowly won by Kim Dae-Jung. Supporters of the ruling NKP were divided between Lee Hoi-Chang and Rhee In-Je, thus assuring victory for the NCNP-ULD alliance and the first peaceful transfer of power to an opposition politician in the Republic of Korea's history. Four other candidates contested the election. In a gesture to promote a sense of national unity, former Presidents Chun Doo-Hwan and Roh Tae-Woo were granted a presidential pardon and released from prison.

Legislation for financial reforms, to comply with the terms of the IMF agreement, was approved by the National Assembly in late December 1997. Discussions held throughout January 1998 with South Korea's overseas creditors to renegotiate the terms of the country's debt repayments were successfully concluded at the end of the month. An agreement was reached with labour leaders and business executives in early February to legalize redundancies (in return for which social welfare provisions would be improved); to permit unions to engage in political activities; and to allow state-employed teachers to form trade unions. Compulsory reform of the *chaebol*, which had been widely criticized for contributing to the debt-repayment crisis through their extensive borrowing, and legislation to allow foreign investors to acquire majority shareholdings in South Korean companies, were among reform measures promulgated in early 1998.

In addition to economic reform proposals, procedures to implement wide-ranging administrative reforms, including a reduction in government bureaucracy, were under discussion by the incoming leadership in early 1998. Constitutional amendments, including the replacement of the President by the Prime Minister as head of the Government, were also under consideration. Kim Dae-Jung was formally inaugurated as President in late February 1998. Despite resistance from the opposition, Kim Dae-Jung designated Kim Jong-Pil, the leader of the ULD, as acting Prime Minister, and a Cabinet was formed in early March, with the ministries divided equally between the NCNP and the ULD. Various administrative reforms were implemented, including the abolition of the two posts of Deputy Prime Minister, the merger of the Ministries for Home Affairs and Government Administration and a reduction in the powers of the Ministry of Finance and the Economy. The number of cabinet ministers was reduced to 17 (excluding the Prime Minister).

At the beginning of May 1998 a large rally organized by the KCTU in protest at job losses ended in violent clashes with riot police. Later that month a two-day strike was called to demand that the Government fully honour its pledge to improve unemployment benefits and to reform the *chaebol*; according to the KCTU, some 120,000 workers supported the first day of the strike. The NCNP and the ULD performed well in local elections in June, although the turn-out was low. As the economic recession deepened, with the unemployment rate rising above 7%, labour unrest increased. Tens of thousands participated in strikes in July to protest against unemployment, the Government's privatization proposals and plans from Hyundai Motor and Daewoo Motor for mass redundancies.

In August 1998 the National Assembly formally confirmed Kim Jong-Pil as Prime Minister, following months of legislative inactivity, during which the GNP had refused to support his nomination. The GNP, however, boycotted parliamentary sessions throughout September and into October, further delaying the consideration of urgent economic reforms, in protest at a government anti-corruption campaign, which it claimed was partisan and aimed at dividing the opposition. Several GNP members were placed under investigation on suspicion of illegally raising electoral campaign funds. In late October three former aides to Lee Hoi-Chang were charged in connection with an alleged attempt to bribe North Korean officials to organize a border incursion into the DMZ in December 1997, with the aim of aiding Lee's campaign for the presidency. The dispute escalated in December 1998, when a number of opposition deputies entered a room in the assembly buildings, which was being used by the intelligence agency, and removed confidential documents on 44 political figures. The GNP claimed that the agency had been carrying out surveillance of opposition deputies and subsequently boycotted legislative proceedings. In early January 1999, as the boycott continued, the ruling parties unilaterally passed 130 bills without debate, including legislation on banking reform and the endorsement of a controversial fishing agreement with Japan (see below). In mid-January, however, the ruling and opposition parties agreed that all issues relating to the affair be referred to the National Assembly's steering committee.

Tension arose within the ruling coalition in January 1999, when NCNP leaders proposed the postponement of plans for the introduction of a parliamentary, rather than presidential, system of government, with the Prime Minister assuming more power, as favoured by the ULD. Kim Young-Sam, who had refused to testify, was held responsible for the 1997 financial crisis in a report that was issued on the findings of parliamentary hearings held throughout February 1999. Meanwhile, the KCTU withdrew from a tripartite committee on management, labour and government (which had been established in early 1998), demanding an end to mass redundancies, a reduction in working hours and an improvement in the welfare system for the unemployed.

In late May 1999 a major reshuffle of the State Council was effected; an additional ministry was also created by the elevation to ministerial status of the Planning and Budget Commission. Kang Bong-Kyun, regarded as a strong advocate of reform, was appointed to the post of Minister of Finance and the Economy. In June, however, corruption scandals led to the replacement of two of the new ministers, and were believed to have contributed to the ruling coalition's failure to retain two parliamentary seats in by-elections held that month. Kim Tae-Joung, the Minister of Justice, was dismissed over allegations that, during his tenure as Prosecutor-General, a subordinate had encouraged a strike at a state-managed corporation. (An accusation that the minister's wife had accepted a gift from the wife of an insurance tycoon being investigated on allegations of fraud had also prompted demands for his dismissal.) Later that

month the new Minister of the Environment, Son Suk, an actress, resigned amid controversy over her acceptance of a gift of money during a recent theatre performance. In July Kim Dae-Jung and Kim Jong-Pil agreed not to seek a constitutional amendment on the adoption of a parliamentary system of government in 1999, despite protests from several senior ULD members.

Preparations for legislative elections (scheduled for April) dominated internal politics in early 2000. In January Kim Jong-Pil resigned as Prime Minister to chair the ULD, nominating Park Tae-Joon, the founder of Pohang Iron and Steel Company (the world's largest steel producer), as his successor. Kim Dae-Jung reshuffled the State Council, as a number of ministers resigned to concentrate on campaigning for parliamentary seats. Lee Hun-Jai, hitherto the Chairman of the Financial Supervisory Commission, was appointed as Minister of Finance and the Economy. There was speculation that by the appointments of Park and Lee, shortly before the elections, the ruling parties hoped to remind voters of the Government's relative success in overcoming the severe economic problems experienced by the Republic of Korea in 1997–98. Later in January 2000 Kim Dae-Jung established a new party, the Millennium Democratic Party (MDP), to succeed the ruling NCNP, having reportedly failed in attempts to effect a merger with the ULD. Meanwhile, civic groups exerting pressure on the main political parties to reform were receiving considerable popular support, in what was perceived as a reflection of increasing public discontent with South Korean party politics, following months of legislative inactivity. A grouping of some 470 civic organizations, styled the Citizens' Alliance for the 2000 General Elections, published a list of politicians whom it considered unfit to stand in the elections, largely on grounds of alleged corruption and incompetence. The ULD condemned the inclusion of Kim Jong-Pil on the list, accusing the MDP of involvement in its compilation. In February the National Assembly approved revisions to the election law, which reduced the number of legislative seats from 299 to 273 (227 directly elected and 46 allocated by proportional representation), and reversed a ban on campaigning by civic groups against candidates. A proposal by the MDP for the introduction of a two-ballot system was rejected by the National Assembly; the ULD was believed to have voted with the opposition GNP against its coalition partner. Lee Han-Dong, recently elected as President of the ULD, subsequently announced the party's withdrawal from the ruling coalition, claiming that the MDP had failed to fulfil its electoral pledges, although Prime Minister Park was to remain in the Government.

The elections to the National Assembly were held on 13 April 2000. The GNP, which won 133 of the 273 seats, retained its position as the largest party in the Assembly, but remained four seats short of a majority. The ruling MDP secured 115 seats, while the ULD suffered a serious reverse, taking only 17 seats (compared with 50 in the 1996 elections). Only two seats were won by the Democratic People's Party, which had been formed in February by defectors from the GNP who had failed to be nominated as parliamentary candidates by their former party. The New Korea Party of Hope won one seat, and independents five. In mid-May Park resigned as Prime Minister, amid increasing controversy over allegations of tax evasion. The designation of Lee Han-Dong as Park's successor indicated a restoration of MDP-ULD co-operation. Furthermore, the MDP's Lee Man-Sup was elected as Speaker of the National Assembly in early June, with the support of the ULD, the two smallest parliamentary parties and independents.

Amid criticism that reform of the *chaebol* was proceeding too slowly, Kim Dae-Jung effected a major government reorganization in August 2000, which primarily concerned the economic portfolios. Notably, Lee Hun-Jai was dismissed as Minister of Finance and was replaced by Jin Nyum, hitherto Minister of Planning and Budget. Later that month Song Ha resigned as Minister of Education following allegations of serious irregularities in his financial affairs.

While President Kim enjoyed increasing admiration and respect within the international community, in October 2000 being awarded the Nobel Peace Prize for his contribution to democracy and human rights (and particularly for his successful attempts at reconciliation with the Democratic People's Republic of Korea), his pursuit of reunification was criticized domestically by those who felt that the Republic of Korea, confronted by its own economic problems, could ill afford assistance to its northern neighbour, which was not perceived to be reciprocating in a magnanimous manner.

In November 2000 Kim Yong-Kap, a GNP member of the National Assembly, described the ruling MDP as a 'subsidiary of the North Korean KWP (Korean Workers' Party)'. The comments shocked and embarrassed both the MDP and the GNP, and the National Assembly was suspended. On the following day talks between the two parties were held, and it was agreed that the National Assembly would reconvene that evening, when the GNP would make a public apology for Kim's remarks and would strike them from the parliamentary record. Shortly after the legislature reconvened, however, the GNP walked out in protest at an MDP motion to dismiss Kim from his seat. A few days later there was renewed tension in the National Assembly as the GNP walked out again, this time prompted by the MDP's obstruction of a motion to impeach the Prosecutor-General, Park Soon-Yong, for alleged bias in the investigation of irregularities during the April elections. The GNP returned to the session one week later, citing the need for the Assembly to work to resolve the increasing economic difficulties and social instability. In December Kim Dae-Jung effected leadership changes in the MDP. Kim Joong-Kwon, Secretary to the President, was appointed Chairman in place of Suh Young-Hoon, who had resigned, and Park Sang-Kyu assumed the role of Secretary-General. Kim Dae-Jung rejected suggestions, both within and outside the party, that as Head of State he should relinquish the post of MDP President.

During 2000 and early 2001 dissatisfaction with the Government manifested itself on numerous occasions in the form of industrial and agricultural unrest. In late June 2000 doctors throughout the country participated in a strike to demonstrate their opposition to legislation depriving physicians of the right to prescribe drugs (which had been intended to restrict excessive prescription of medication and alleged profiteering by doctors). Several deaths were linked to the strike, which ended five days later following an offer by the Government to revise the legislation in July. Further action took place, however, in October, as a satisfactory compromise had not been reached. Mounting public anger obliged the abandonment of the renewed strike. In the following month farmers held a strike to demand that their debts be cancelled and that the Government intervene on their behalf at the World Trade Organization (WTO, see p. 343). Meanwhile, as the Daewoo Motor Company had been declared bankrupt, compounding anxieties for the future of other *chaebol*, some 15,000 workers protested in November 2000 in Seoul against government-led corporate restructuring which would result, it was feared, in large-scale retrenchment. Several more strikes in various sectors took place in late 2000, arising from fears of mass unemployment.

In January 2001 the State Council approved legislation providing for debt-relief loans to farmers and fishermen. At the end of that month a minor reorganization of the State Council was effected, when changes included Jin Nyum's elevation to the post of Deputy Prime Minister for Finance and the Economy. It was believed that the promotion would give Jin increased power to revitalize economic reform. Simultaneously, a government organization law came into effect that conferred the status of Deputy Prime Minister on the portfolios of Finance and Economy and of Education and Human Resources. Han Wang-Sang assumed the latter position. A Ministry of Gender Equality was also created, for which Han Myong-Sook was allocated responsibility. In late March there was a major reorganization of the State Council, following the resignation of the Minister of Foreign Affairs and Trade, Lee Joung-Binn, who had caused controversy by signing a joint statement with Russia criticizing the USA's planned 'national missile defence' (NMD) system. Han Seung-Soo, a member of the Democratic People's Party, replaced him. Lim Dong-Won, hitherto Chairman of the National Intelligence Service, was appointed Minister of Unification. He was widely recognized as having played a major role in Korean reunification efforts. Other changes included the replacement of the Ministers of National Defence and of Construction and Transportation. It was thought that the reshuffle was an attempt by President Kim to improve the public image of the Government, in the face of widespread dissatisfaction over its handling of economic and health reforms. The former Minister of Culture, Park Jie-Won, who had resigned in September 2000 following allegations of corruption, was appointed chief presidential policy adviser. Park had organized the historic inter-Korean summit in June 2000 (see below), and his appoint-

ment to this post reaffirmed Kim Dae-Jung's commitment to his 'sunshine' policy.

In early April 2001 the minor opposition Democratic People's Party joined the ruling MDP-led coalition, despite protests from within the MDP. Later that month the MDP suffered a defeat in local by-elections, and by May Kim Dae-Jung's popularity had fallen sharply, as voters grew disillusioned by his failure to implement political reforms. President Kim had also received criticism for his appointment of ministers and advisers from his home region of Jeolla, in the south-west, thereby antagonizing the south-eastern Gyeongsang region. In late May the newly appointed Minister of Justice, Ahn Dong-Soo, was forced to resign after having apparently pledged to support the MDP's forthcoming presidential election campaign. The pledge was embarrassing because it suggested that the leading investigative agencies were being manipulated against political opponents. Ahn was replaced by Choi Kyung-Won.

In June 2001 the KCTU organized a national strike involving 55,000 workers from 125 trade unions, who were protesting against decreasing wages and worsening working conditions. The strikes were joined by thousands of nurses and also airline pilots and ground staff, but denounced by President Kim as illegal. At the same time the country experienced its worst drought since 1904, adversely affecting agriculture and necessitating the mobilization of 130,000 troops to the most badly-stricken areas. The drought was followed by the worst floods in 37 years.

In July 2001 the Government's campaign against the alleged tax evasion and other financial dealings of the country's 23 news organizations (including major newspapers) led to accusations that President Kim was trying to stifle the media; one newspaper in particular, *Chosun Ilbo*, had been highly critical of Kim and his 'sunshine' policy. The National Tax Service had imposed fines totalling US $388m. in late June following a four-month investigation, which Kim defended as being part of ongoing anti-corruption campaigns but which opposition parties attributed to attempts by the MDP to boost its chances of winning the 2002 presidential election. Opinion polls showed the public to be generally supportive of the investigations and sceptical about the media, itself perceived as corrupt. In late August the owners of three newspapers, including *Chosun Ilbo*, were arrested for tax evasion.

Also in August 2001 the Minister of Construction and Transportation, Oh Jang-Seop, resigned after the US Federal Aviation Administration (FAA) downgraded the safety rating of the Republic of Korea's two main airlines and prevented them from flying to the USA. At the same time, Minister of Unification Lim Dong-Won came under heavy criticism from the opposition after delegates from several South Korean non-governmental organizations (NGOs) travelled to the North to mark the anniversary of Korean liberation from Japanese rule, on 15 August. In early September Lim was forced to resign after the National Assembly approved a motion of no-confidence in him, organized by the GNP and supported by the MDP's coalition partner, the ULD. The latter's actions effectively dissolved the ruling coalition, and President Kim appointed four new ministers: of Labour; Agriculture and Forestry; Construction and Transportation; and Maritime Affairs and Fisheries. In addition, Hong Soon-Young, hitherto ambassador to China, was appointed Minister of Unification. Lim was immediately appointed presidential adviser on reunification, national security and foreign affairs, reaffirming Kim's confidence in him. At the end of the month the new Minister of Construction and Transportation, Ahn Jung-Nam, resigned citing health reasons, and was replaced by Lim In-Taik. However, Ahn had been accused of corruption by the opposition.

In late October 2001 the GNP won three by-elections, increasing its seats in the National Assembly to 136—just one short of a majority. The opposition victory created new rifts within the ruling MDP between younger reformers and party veterans, and President Kim subsequently resigned from the party presidency in early November, ostensibly in order to administer state affairs without being involved in party disputes. He was succeeded, on an interim basis, by Han Kwang-Ok. Further infighting in the MDP ensued as senior party officials sought to strengthen their positions with a view to securing the party presidential nomination for the 2002 election. At the same time Park Jie-Won, the senior secretary for policy planning and a close aide of the president, also resigned. By early December some eight presidential candidates had emerged within the MDP and were forming political support networks.

In early January 2002 the MDP announced that it would hold a primary election in April to select its presidential candidate. Also at this time, President Kim's reputation suffered a set-back when his nominee for the head of the newly created Presidential Commission for Anti-corruption, Kim Sung-Nam, was himself linked to a spy scandal in the 1980s.

In late January 2002 President Kim again reorganized the State Council , dismissing Minister of Unification Hong Soon-Young and reallocating seven other posts, as well as the positions of six of the eight senior presidential secretaries and his chief of staff. Hong was succeeded by Jeong Se-Hyun, hitherto a special assistant to the director of the National Intelligence Service (NIS), while Jeon Yun-Churl, hitherto Minister of Planning and Budget was appointed chief presidential secretary (chief of staff). Jeon was succeeded in his previous post by Chang Seung-Woo. Park Jie-Won returned as Kim's special aide for policy, emphasizing his close relationship with the President. The changes were intended to strengthen Kim's authority during his final year in office. Within days, the Minister of Foreign Affairs and Trade, Han Seung-Soo, was also dismissed, owing to Seoul's strained relations with the USA, and replaced by Choi Sung-Hong, hitherto Vice-Minister.

The contest for the MDP's presidential nomination intensified during February 2002 as putative reformist candidates sought to present a joint candidate, and opponents of the leading contender, Rhee In-Je, moved against him. The opposition GNP also experienced a power struggle, resulting in the party Vice-President, Park Geun-Hye (daughter of former military ruler Park Chung-Hee), leaving the party later in the month, initially with the intention of standing for the presidency as an independent candidate. Her decision undermined the chances of Lee Hoi-Chang, who had been leading in the opinion polls, and threatened to precipitate a political realignment. In May Park established a new party, the Korean Coalition for the Future (KCF), serving as its chairwoman.

Meanwhile, in late February 2002 the country suffered another general strike, by thousands of railway and energy workers, who were protesting against privatization plans and shortened working hours. In early April the KCTU cancelled a major strike after reaching a settlement with the Government. The KCTU leadership subsequently resigned *en masse*, following criticism that it had made too many concessions to the Government. However, limited strike action continued in May.

By late April 2002 Roh Moo-Hyun had secured the MDP presidential nomination, while the GNP remained mired in internal disputes; the party's eight vice-presidents all resigned on 24 March in order to 'renew the face of the party', and were succeeded by a collective leadership. Meanwhile, Lee Hoi-Chang had secured the GNP's nomination for the national presidency. Also in mid-April President Kim replaced the Deputy Prime Minister for Finance and the Economy, Jin Nyum, with Jeon Yun-Churl, hitherto the chief of staff to the President. Jeon was succeeded by Park Jie-Won.

In early May 2002 President Kim and six of his ministers resigned from the MDP in order to focus on state affairs during the final months of Kim's presidency. By that time, Kim had become increasingly embarrassed by the corruption scandals involving his second and third sons, Kim Hong-Up and Kim Hong-Gul respectively, and he publicly apologized for their behaviour. In early June Kim Hong-Gul was charged with bribery and tax evasion, and subsequently went on trial. Kim Hong-Up was arrested later that month, accused of receiving bribes from businessmen. A nephew of the President's wife, Lee Hyung-Taek, was also sentenced for receiving bribes. The scandals adversely affected the MDP's performance in local elections held in mid-June, in which the party secured only four posts (three of which were in Jeolla, its traditional support base), while the GNP won 11 posts and the ULD one post.

In early July 2002 President Kim reorganized the cabinet, appointing Chang Sang, hitherto President of Ewha Woman's University, as the country's first female Prime Minister. At the same time, six ministers were replaced. Notable new appointments were Lee Jun, a retired general, as Minister of National Defence, Kim Jung-Kil as Minister of Justice, and Kim Jin-Pyo as Minister of Government Policy Co-ordination. However, at the end of that month the National Assembly rejected Chang's appointment on the grounds of questionable property dealings and the fact that her son had adopted US citizenship. In her place, President Kim nominated Chang Dae-Whan, a former newspaper proprietor, but he too was rejected by the National Assembly in late August on the grounds of questionable finan-

cial practices. In September Kim nominated Kim Suk-Soo, a former Supreme Court judge and former Head of the National Election Commission, as his candidate for the post of Prime Minister, and he was accepted by the National Assembly in early October, thus ending months of political paralysis.

Meanwhile, the popularity of Roh Moo-Hyun deteriorated so significantly after his nomination for the presidency that members of the MDP considered replacing him altogether. The MDP also suffered further set-backs in by-elections held in early August 2002 when the GNP won 11 out of 13 seats contested, giving it an overall majority in the National Assembly. In September Chung Mong-Joon, the sixth son of Hyundai founder Chung Ju-Yung, and who was also an independent legislator, President of the Korean Football Association and Vice-President of FIFA (the international football federation), announced that he was standing for the country's presidency. Chung's popularity had risen sharply following the Republic of Korea's successful co-hosting of the 2002 football World Cup and had surpassed that of Roh. In early November Chung formally launched his 'National Unity 21' party, receiving support from a broad political spectrum, including defectors from the MDP. However, later in that month Chung moved closer to Roh, and the two agreed to present a joint candidate for the presidency, namely Roh, in order to prevent Lee Hoi-Chang's election as President in December. Under the terms of the Roh-Chung partnership, there was to be a constitutional amendment whereby the powers of the presidency would be reduced in favour of those of the Prime Minister. A similar arrangement had been agreed between Kim Dae-Jung and Kim Jong-Pil in 1997 but never implemented.

The final months of 2002 witnessed the ruling MDP mired in further scandals. In October it emerged that President Kim and Chung Mong-Joon had arranged for a Hyundai subsidiary to transfer US $200m. to North Korea via the (Southern) state-owned Korea Development Bank prior to the historic inter-Korean summit of June 2000 (see below), effectively 'buying' the meeting. Furthermore, Kim Hong-Up was sentenced to three-and-a-half years' imprisonment in early November for accepting bribes. Kim Hong-Gul was also sentenced, separately, to two years' imprisonment (with three years' suspension) for bribery and tax evasion. Both received heavy fines, and their convictions further undermined President Kim and the MDP. In November Park Geun-Hye, who had left the opposition GNP earlier in the year to form the new KCF (see above), agreed with Lee Hoi-Chang to merge her party with the GNP, thus lending support to Lee's election campaign.

None the less, the presidential election, held on 19 December 2002, was narrowly won by Roh Moo-Hyun, who received 48.9% of the votes cast, against Lee Hoi-Chang's 46.6%. Roh's victory came despite the last-minute withdrawal of Chung Mong-Joon's support, for which the latter subsequently apologized. It was generally acknowledged that Roh's victory was due to his uncompromising stance in favour of a foreign policy more independent from the USA, whereas Lee was widely seen as having very close relations with Washington, DC. The MDP in early December accused the USA of supporting Lee in the election, citing a meeting between him and the US ambassador. Relations with the USA (see below) had become a major election issue, as anti-American sentiment increased following several incidents involving US servicemen, and differences between the two countries emerged over how to resolve tensions with the North. As with past presidential elections, regionalism was manifested strongly in voting patterns, with some pro-Roh regions (Jeolla) voting 92% in his favour, while some pro-Lee regions (Gyeongsang) voted 78% in his favour. Support for the two main candidates also indicated the emergence of a generational gap, with younger voters favouring Roh, while older voters supported Lee. Kwon Young-Gil of the Democratic Labour Party came a distant third, with 3.9% of the votes cast. The level of participation was estimated at 70.8%. Following his defeat, Lee Hoi-Chang retired from politics.

In January 2003 President-elect Roh began making appointments to his new Government. Goh Kun, hitherto the president of Transparency International Korea, an anti-corruption agency, and himself a former Prime Minister, was reappointed to that post. Moon Hee-Sang, an MDP legislator, was appointed chief of staff, and concurrently Chairman of the Civil Service Commission, while Ryu In-Tae, a former legislator, was named presidential secretary for political affairs. Ra Jong-Yil, hitherto ambassador to the United Kingdom, was appointed national security adviser. President Kim meanwhile dissolved his

Donggyo-dong faction of MDP loyalists in preparation for the transfer of power. Roh himself was inaugurated on 25 February 2003 and promptly appointed a new cabinet. Notable appointments included Kim Jin-Pyo as Deputy Prime Minister for Finance and Economy, Yoon Deok-Hong, hitherto President of Daegu University, as Deputy Prime Minister for Education and Human Resources Development, and Kang Gum-Sil as Minister of Justice. Yoon Young-Kwan, hitherto professor of International Relations at Seoul National University, was appointed Minister of Foreign Affairs and Trade, while Gen. (retd) Cho Young-Kil became Minister of National Defence. Jeong Se-Hyun was retained as Minister of National Unification, indicating continuity of Kim Dae-Jung's 'sunshine' policy towards the North. The new cabinet contained four women, a record number thus far. President Roh also reorganized the military and intelligence services, appointing Gen. Kim Jong-Hwan as Chairman of the Joint Chiefs of Staff, and Ko Young-Koo, a human rights lawyer, as director of the National Intelligence Service (NIS). The latter appointment reflected Roh's determination to depoliticize the agency, which had been responsible for surveillance of political figures even after the transition to democracy.

Roh faced immediate challenges on assuming office, most notably the diplomatic crisis between the DPRK and the USA, which had strained Seoul's relations with the latter. Other problems included the ongoing scandal surrounding Hyundai and the inter-Korean summit meeting of 2000, and a subway fire in Daegu in February 2003, which killed more than 200 people and highlighted the inadequacy of safety measures in public infrastructure. In March Roh appointed a special counsel to investigate the alleged transfer of funds by Hyundai to the DPRK in connection with the 2000 presidential summit meeting (see below). In the longer term Roh aimed to address regional imbalances and the disparity between rich and poor, to reduce corruption in business and the economy and to improve living standards and labour management.

In late April 2003 the GNP won two out of three seats in by-elections to the National Assembly, raising its total representation to 153. However, the victory of a reformist ally of the MDP, Rhyu Si-Min, was welcomed by the Government as an indication of support for the reform process. Also in April, the National Assembly voted in favour of the dispatch of South Korean troops to support US military action in Iraq in a non-combat capacity. Despite his independent stance on relations with the USA (see above), President Roh justified the deployment in terms of strengthening Korean-US relations. There was widespread public opposition to the Iraq deployment, with opinion polls showing that around 80% of the South Korean population disapproved of the US military action in Iraq.

In June 2003 two aides of former President Kim Dae-Jung, former Minister of Unification Lim Dong-Won and former Minister of Culture and Tourism Park Jie-Won, were charged in connection with illegal payments made through the Hyundai group to the DPRK to arrange the 2000 presidential summit meeting (Lim Dong-Won received an 18-month prison sentence in September, and Park Jie-Won was sentenced to 12 years' imprisonment in December). Also implicated in the scandal was Hyundai heir Chung Mong-Hun, who committed suicide in August. In July, meanwhile, a strike by railway workers protesting against privatization in the industry was cancelled by the KCTU, representing an acknowledgement that previous strikes had not prevented the approval of legislation on privatization by the National Assembly. Also in July, the Minister of Agriculture and Forestry, Kim Young-Jin, resigned in protest at a decision to suspend work on a coastal reclamation project, which had been criticized on environmental grounds.

In September 2003 a faction of the MDP announced its intention to form a new party owing to internal divisions over corruption and other issues within the MDP. President Roh subsequently relinquished his membership of the MDP, although he did not commit himself to joining the new organization. The new group was initially referred to as the New Party for Participatory Citizens, but in October the new name of Uri (meaning 'our') Party was adopted. A large number of MDP legislators, including MDP Chairman Chyung Dai-Chul, joined the Uri Party, thus leaving the MDP with only 62 seats in the National Assembly. The Uri Party was officially launched in November under a temporary leadership (Chung Dong-Young was elected Uri Party Chairman in early 2004). Another development in September, meanwhile, was the resignation of the Minister of Home Affairs, Kim Doo-Kwan, following an incident in which protesters had infiltrated a US base in Pocheon. The National Assembly had approved Kim Doo-Kwan's dismissal, despite President Roh's policy of increased independence in relations with the USA. In October there were renewed public protests over a proposal to send additional troops to Iraq.

President Roh's declining popularity was further undermined in October 2003 by the investigation and subsequent arrest of his former aide Choi Do-Sul, who was accused of having received illegal funds from the SK group following the 2002 presidential election. In an attempt to restore his popularity, President Roh announced proposals for a referendum to be held on the issue of his presidency later in the year. However, the proposed referendum prompted further political instability, with Prime Minister Goh Kun and other government ministers offering their resignations (which were rejected by President Roh). Both the GNP and the MDP dismissed the referendum proposal as unconstitutional.

Official investigations into illegal campaign funding from leading *chaebol* during the 2002 presidential election, involving both the MDP and the GNP, were instigated at the end of October 2003. Initially focusing on donations from the SK Group, the investigation widened in November, with forcible searches taking place at the offices of other *chaebol*, including Hyundai, LG Group and Samsung. At the end of November President Roh vetoed a bill, already approved by the National Assembly, which urged an independent investigation into the funding allegations. GNP leader Choe Byung-Yul commenced a hunger strike in protest at the veto. In early December the National Assembly voted to rescind the veto on an independent investigation, in the country's first reversal of a presidential decision since 1954. An independent investigator was subsequently appointed. In the same month President Roh announced that he would step down if the MDP were found by the investigation to have received one-tenth of the illegal funding taken by the GNP. In a further development in December, the GNP's Lee Hoi-Chang, Roh's rival in the 2002 election, publicly admitted that his party had accepted US $42m. in illegal donations.

Meanwhile, there was further public opposition in early December 2003 to the Republic of Korea's involvement in Iraq, following the killing of two South Korean engineers engaged in reconstruction work in the country. However, the Government announced that there would be no change in its policy on Iraq as a result of the deaths. Also in December, the Minister for Commerce, Energy and Industry, Yoon Jin-Shik, resigned as a result of controversy over radioactive waste disposal, and the Deputy Prime Minister for Education and Human Resources Development, Yoon Deok-Hong, also resigned over the issue of management of personal information on students.

In January 2004 the Minister of Foreign Affairs and Trade, Yoon Young-Kwan, relinquished his post, reportedly following criticism of presidential policy by his advisers. The dispute was widely reported to have been related to President Roh's policy on independence from the USA over issues such as the North Korean nuclear weapons programme. However, there was also a suggestion that Yoon Young-Kwan's departure was due to internal divisions and was only incidentally connected to the Republic of Korea's relations with the USA. Yoon Young-Kwan was replaced by Ban Ki-Moon. There were further government changes in February, following the resignation of Kim Jin-Pyo, the Deputy Prime Minister for Finance and the Economy, in order to stand as a Uri Party candidate in the legislative elections scheduled for April. Also in February, the National Assembly approved the deployment of an additional 3,000 non-combat troops to Iraq (the deployment was delayed in March owing to security concerns).

Meanwhile, investigations into political corruption continued in early 2004. In January former MDP Chairman Chyung Dai-Chul (now of the Uri Party) was arrested, amid allegations that he had accepted bribes from various business groups. The former Secretary-General of the GNP, Kim Young-Iel, was also arrested in connection with allegations of illegal fund-raising during the 2002 election. In February there was also speculation that Park Geun-Hye, who had returned to the GNP in advance of the 2002 elections (see above), had received undeclared funds from the GNP for the purposes of a merger with her Korean Coalition for the Future. In March 2004 it was reported that President Roh's MDP election campaign had received 12,500m. won in illicit funds, amounting to one-seventh of the 84,000m. allegedly received by the GNP and thus to more than the proportion of one-tenth that Roh had previously stated would prompt his resignation. At the end of March it was confirmed that Roh's former aide Choi Do-Sul (see above) had received US $530,000 in illegal funding.

As the legislative election of April 2004 approached, there were dramatic developments in mid-March with the impeachment of President Roh over the issue of his support for the pro-Government Uri Party, whereby he had allegedly violated electoral law. A total of 193 legislators, mostly from the GNP and Roh's former party, the MDP, voted in favour of the impeachment. There were vehement protests from supporters of President Roh in the National Assembly following the vote, as well as widespread public protests in support of the President, with opinion polls indicating that around 70% of the population did not support the impeachment. President Roh's position was to be reviewed by the Constitutional Court within six months, with Prime Minister Goh Kun becoming acting head of state for this period. Also in March, Park Geun-Hye, daughter of former President Park Chung-Hee, was appointed Chairwoman of the GNP following party leadership elections.

At the elections to the National Assembly on 15 April 2004, the Uri Party won a narrow majority in the legislature, securing 152 seats of the total of 299 in the newly expanded chamber. The main opposition party, the GNP, now under the leadership of Park Geun-Hye, secured 121 seats. Roh's former party, the MDP, won only nine seats. The success of the Uri Party was seen as victory for Roh and an expression of public disapproval of his impeachment. It was expected that the election result would influence the ongoing trial by the Constitutional Court of the impeached President Roh.

The South Korean Constitution, meanwhile, stipulates that the Republic of Korea shall seek the peaceful unification of the Korean peninsula. During the 1980s relations with the DPRK were characterized by mutual suspicion, aggravated by various incidents—including the discovery of several pro-North Korean spy rings, and the death in October 1983 of four South Korean government ministers in a bomb explosion in Burma (now Myanmar), for which President Chun held the DPRK responsible. During 1985 representatives of the two states conferred on economic and humanitarian issues, but discussions were suspended in early 1986 when Kim Il Sung denounced the annual 'Team Spirit' military manoeuvres, held jointly with US troops in South Korea. Subsequent inter-Korean negotiations were likewise regularly suspended, owing to North Korean objections to the 'Team Spirit' exercises. In November 1987 the destruction of a South Korean airliner in flight over Burma, by a bomb that had allegedly been concealed aboard the aircraft by North Korean agents, caused a new outbreak of verbal hostility between the two countries.

However, with the appointment of Roh Tae-Woo as South Korean President in 1988, there appeared to be a greater willingness by the South to foster closer relations with the DPRK. Roh's announcement in early 1990 that the forthcoming 'Team Spirit' manoeuvres would be reduced in size and duration also contributed to an improvement in inter-Korean relations. In September of that year the North Korean Premier travelled to Seoul for discussions with his South Korean counterpart. The meeting represented the most senior-level contact between the two countries since the end of the Korean War in 1953. Further talks between the two premiers took place in late 1990. The DPRK's abandonment, announced in May 1991, of its long-standing position that the two Koreas should occupy a single seat at the UN was regarded as a significant concession. Accordingly, North and South Korea were admitted separately to the UN in September.

Prime-ministerial negotiations resumed in late 1991, and resulted in the signature of an 'Agreement on Reconciliation, Non-aggression and Exchanges and Co-operation between the South and the North'. At the end of December 1991 both states pledged to ban nuclear weapons from the Korean peninsula, and in early 1992 they agreed to form a joint commission to facilitate the simultaneous inspection of nuclear installations in the North and US military bases in the South. In recognition of the recent inter-Korean *rapprochement*, the Republic of Korea cancelled the 1992 'Team Spirit' exercises, and in the latter half of the year the DPRK permitted the inspection of its nuclear facilities by the International Atomic Energy Agency (IAEA, see p. 86). This apparent progress on military and nuclear issues was, however, reversed by the North's decision, in January 1993, to boycott all future inter-Korean nuclear talks, followed in March by its threatened withdrawal from the Treaty on the Non-Proliferation of Nuclear Weapons. Inter-Korean relations deteriorated further in early 1994, following the UN's announce-

ment that it was considering the imposition of economic sanctions on North Korea: the DPRK, in turn, threatened to declare war on South Korea. The North Korean leadership was also incensed by South Korea's decision not to send a representative to the funeral, in July, of Kim Il Sung, and by its refusal to permit public mourning within South Korea. None the less, following the signing in October of the nuclear accord between the USA and the DPRK, the South Korean Government agreed to finance, in part, the construction and supply to the DPRK of light-water nuclear reactors, which are less easily adapted to the production of nuclear weapons (a key element of the accord), provided that reactors of a South Korean design were used.

The DPRK's announcement, in April 1996, that it was abandoning the 1953 armistice agreement was followed by a series of incursions by North Korean troops into the DMZ. The USA and South Korea proposed the holding of quadripartite negotiations with the People's Republic of China and North Korea; China subsequently agreed to the proposal, but the North Korean administration refused to commit itself to discussions. In September 1996 tension increased when a North Korean submarine was found abandoned near the South Korean coast; armed crew members in South Korean military uniforms were found dead near the submarine, others were killed by South Korean troops, and one was captured and interrogated. The South Korean Government denounced the incident and, demanding an apology, suspended all contacts with the North, including the provision of emergency food aid. In an unprecedented move, in December the DPRK issued an apology for the incident and agreed to participate in preliminary talks about the proposed negotiations.

Exploratory discussions took place in New York, USA, in March 1997. Attempts by the DPRK to link the progress of negotiations with the provision of food aid were unsuccessful. However, in May, in the first such meeting for five years, representatives of the Red Cross organizations of North and South Korea reached agreement on the provision of 50,000 metric tons of grain to the DPRK. In October negotiations to allow foreign airlines, including those from South Korea, to enter North Korean airspace reached a successful conclusion.

Despite a military confrontation between North and South Korean troops in the DMZ in July 1997 full quadripartite negotiations (with the USA and China), aimed at concluding a peace treaty between North and South Korea, opened in Geneva, Switzerland, in early December. Agreement was reached on procedural arrangements for future sessions, and a second round of full discussions was held in March 1998. A meeting held in Beijing, in April, between North and South Korean government ministers, the first such direct contact for four years, broke down following mutual accusations of inflexibility.

A further improvement in relations between North and South Korea followed Kim Dae-Jung's inauguration in February 1998. Private and business-related inter-Korean contacts increased substantially during 1998, following the South Korean Government's introduction, in April, of measures designed to facilitate such activity, as part of Kim's new 'sunshine' policy of engagement with the North. Chung Ju-Yung, the founder of the Hyundai Group, initiated a number of historic joint-ventures, including, in June and October, the delivery of cattle across the DMZ to his home town in North Korea and the organization, in November, of a visit of some 800 South Korean tourists to Mount Kumgang, just north of the border. Despite fears that this improvement in relations would be jeopardized by evidence of continued North Korean incursions, South Korea affirmed that it would continue to pursue a policy of conciliation.

At a third session of quadripartite talks, held in Geneva in late October 1998, agreement was reached on the creation of two sub-committees on the establishment of a permanent peace mechanism on the Korean peninsula and on ways of easing tension. The sub-committees were formally inaugurated during a further round of negotiations in January 1999. In February, as part of an amnesty, the South Korean Government released 17 North Korean long-term political detainees, who had refused to renounce their communist beliefs. In March the South Korean Government announced its provision of fertilizer to the DPRK, through the Red Cross. In June 1999 a brief gun battle took place between vessels from the two Koreas in the Yellow Sea following a week-long confrontation. Subsequent bilateral talks on family reunification issues made little progress in Beijing. Meanwhile, no discernible progress was made at sessions of the quadripartite talks in April and August 1999.

None the less, private-level economic co-operation continued throughout 1999 and early 2000, and a number of joint cultural and sporting events also took place. In October 1999 Hyundai concluded an agreement with the DPRK on the construction of an industrial complex, and in December Samsung Electronics announced it had signed a contract with the DPRK for the joint development of computer software and the manufacture of electronic products. Inter-Korean trade increased by some 50.2% in 1999. In March 2000, during a visit to Germany, Kim Dae-Jung urged the DPRK to agree to government-level talks, and proposed the development of public-sector economic co-operation in areas such as agriculture, communications and the construction of infrastructure in the North. In April, following a series of high-level contacts in Beijing between officials of both countries, North and South Korea jointly announced that an historic summit meeting would take place between Kim Dae-Jung and Kim Jong Il in June 2000, during a three-day visit by the former to Pyongyang.

Following a delay of one day requested by the DPRK for 'technical reasons' the presidential summit meeting took place on 13–15 June 2000. Detailed agreements were then signed pledging economic co-operation, the development of mutual trust and the resolution of reunification issues. In July ministerial-level delegations from both countries met in Seoul. This was the first visit to South Korea by Northern officials since 1991. Although the two sides failed to reach an agreement on military matters, a joint communiqué was issued allowing for, *inter alia*, the reopening of liaison offices at Panmunjom, which had been closed in 1996, and the reconnection of the inter-Korean Kyongui railway line. The construction of a highway to run alongside the railway from North to South was subsequently agreed. In September Kim Dae-Jung formally inaugurated the project to remove thousands of landmines (to be undertaken by soldiers from each side respectively) and rebuild the railway line and adjacent highway. (Final details for the restoration of the rail link were agreed in February 2001.) Meanwhile, benefiting from the progress made at the summit meeting in June, in August 100 South Korean families visited Pyongyang and 100 North Korean families travelled to Seoul simultaneously to meet with relatives from whom they had been separated by the Korean War. The second ministerial meeting between the two sides was held in Pyongyang later that month. Negotiations were extended for one day because of an inability to agree on terms for beginning a dialogue between the two countries' military establishments. A compromise was reached after consultation with Kim Jong Il. It was agreed to hold two more cross-border family reunions by the end of 2000 and to commence talks on economic co-operation. In a symbolic display of unity, in September the two countries marched under the same flag in the opening ceremony of the Olympic Games in Sydney, Australia. In late September the South Korean Minister of National Defence, Cho Seong-Tae, received his northern counterpart, Vice-Marshal Kim Il Chol, for discussions held on Jeju Island, the first such ministerial meeting ever conducted. Further rounds of inter-ministerial, military and economic talks took place during 2000 and early 2001. In an indication of the improvement in relations, in December 2000 a meeting was also held between trade union representatives from the two countries.

Despite this progress, in December 2000 the Republic of Korea published its annual defence policy document, which classified the DPRK as its main enemy, and alleged that it had expanded its military capacity along the DMZ, an accusation that angered the DPRK. International analysts, however, felt that hostility was not imminent. Also in that month a resolution was passed by the South Korean legislature to demand the repatriation of prisoners of war who it alleged continued to be held by the North, despite the DPRK's denial of the existence of these prisoners. The two incidents seemed to demonstrate the growing reluctance of many South Koreans to continue with the process of reunification as it stood, which they regarded as having become increasingly unbalanced to the detriment of the South.

In early 2001 the uncompromising attitude adopted by the new US Administration towards the DPRK threatened to undermine severely the reconciliation process. In March the DPRK unilaterally postponed scheduled cabinet-level talks following Kim Dae-Jung's visit to the USA (see below), during which the latter had criticized Pyongyang's regime. Later that month, however, a member of the North Korean football team was permitted to join a South Korean squad. In April the DPRK denounced joint US-South Korean military exercises as a

betrayal of the goodwill surrounding the June 2000 summit meeting. Ministerial talks resumed in Seoul in mid-September, the sixth round of which was concluded in mid-November (having been postponed from late October) without any agreement—the first unsuccessful such round since the presidential summit meeting. North Korea blamed the South, particularly Unification Minister Hong Soon-Young, for the failure of the talks.

Meanwhile, Kim Jong Il's long-awaited visit to Seoul for a second presidential summit meeting failed to materialize during 2001, and there was continued uncertainty as to when such a visit would occur. US President George W. Bush's reference in January 2002 to North Korea as being part of an 'axis of evil' further jeopardized inter-Korean relations.

A stalemate in inter-Korean relations was broken in late March 2002, however, when the North agreed to receive Kim Dae-Jung's special envoy, Lim Dong-Won, in early April. Following the visit, during which Lim met Kim Jong Il, the two sides agreed to further reunions for separated families (see below), and to continuing talks on economic co-operation. The DPRK also agreed to Lim's request that it renew dialogue with the USA and Japan. In mid-May Park Geun-Hye visited the North and met Kim Jong Il. The visit was notable because Northern agents had killed Park's mother in 1974 in a failed bid to assassinate her father. Despite the cordial visit, North Korea cancelled economic co-operation discussions with the South in May.

In May 2002 the increasing number of defectors from the North to the South received international attention as several groups sought asylum at Canadian, Japanese and South Korean diplomatic buildings in China. They were eventually allowed to travel to the South, albeit via the Philippines. The South Korean Ministry of Unification reported in January 2003 that during 2002 some 1,141 North Koreans had defected to the South, compared with 583 in 2001.

At the end of June 2002 a gun battle between North and South Korean vessels in the Yellow Sea resulted in the sinking of a Southern patrol boat and the deaths of six crew members. South Korean military sources estimated that 30 Northern crewmen had also been killed in the confrontation, which had started when two North Korean vessels accompanying a fishing boat reportedly crossed the Northern Limit Line (the maritime border separating the two Koreas). Following the incident, in July South Korea suspended rice shipments to the North and economic co-operation projects, reflecting widespread public anger. None the less, Kim Dae-Jung maintained his 'sunshine' policy towards the North, which later expressed regret for the incident. Meanwhile, North Korean state television showed selected highlights of football matches played by the South Korean team in the 2002 World Cup, although it refrained from transmitting extensive coverage of the event, which was being co-hosted by Japan.

In mid-August 2002 North and South Korea held a seventh round of ministerial talks in Seoul, aimed at improving relations in the aftermath of the latest naval confrontation and focusing on the issue of future family reunions, railway links (see below) and cultural exchanges. Regarding the latter, more than 300 North Korean athletes travelled to the South and participated in the Asian Games held in Busan during October. In late September the first inter-Korean military 'hotline' was inaugurated to allow for improved communications during sensitive occasions. Meanwhile, Pyongyang's revelation that it had abducted 12 Japanese citizens in the 1970s and 1980s highlighted the outstanding issue of the whereabouts of several hundred missing South Korean citizens believed to have been abducted by the North.

The eighth round of ministerial talks was held in Pyongyang in late October 2002 and focused mainly on economic co-operation issues, despite the fact that the USA had earlier revealed the existence of a secret nuclear weapons programme in the North (see the chapter on the Democratic People's Republic of Korea). At the end of that month a North Korean economic delegation began a nine-day tour of the South, including several major industrial facilities. Noteworthy was the fact that the delegation included Jang Song Taek, Kim Jong Il's brother-in-law and one of his most trusted advisers, and also Kim Hi Taek, the first deputy head of the KWP's Central Committee. At the end of December 2002 the South Korean Ministry of National Defence published a 'white paper' which, for the first time, excluded any reference to the North as its main enemy.

By late 2002 some of the goodwill generated by the historic inter-Korean summit meeting in June 2000 had been undermined by the revelation that Kim Dae-Jung had arranged for the Korea Development Bank to give a Hyundai affiliate US $200m. to transfer to the North in order to arrange the summit. However, the election in December of Roh Moo-Hyun as President of the Republic of Korea heralded a continuation of Kim's 'sunshine' policy. In early January 2003 representatives of Roh secretly met Northern officials in Beijing, and later in that month a ninth round of ministerial talks was held in Seoul. Kim also dispatched Lim Dong-Won to Pyongyang at the end of January, but Lim failed to secure a meeting with Kim Jong Il, instead relaying a goodwill message through one of the latter's aides.

North and South Korea continued their efforts to improve bilateral relations during 2003, despite a severe deterioration in relations between the North and the USA over the issue of the North Korean nuclear weapons programme (see chapter on the Democratic People's Republic of Korea). In March 2003 Roh was exploring a long-standing idea of developing gas pipelines between Sakhalin, Russia, and the DPRK that would supply the latter with energy in return for an abandonment of its nuclear programme. The DPRK hosted the 10th round of ministerial talks at the end of April. In mid-May, however, Pyongyang announced that it no longer recognized the Joint Declaration of the Denuclearization of the Korean Peninsula, signed with the South in 1992. Also in May, at talks between the two Koreas on economic matters, North Korea warned that the South would risk 'unspeakable disaster' if it became too confrontational in co-operating with the USA on the nuclear issue (the threat followed a summit meeting between Roh and US President George W. Bush). Attempts to develop inter-Korean relations were also complicated by confirmation in June by South Korean investigators that former President Kim Dae-Jung had paid US $100m. to arrange the historic inter-Korean summit meeting of 2000 (see above). In August the suicide of Hyundai official Chung Mong-Hun, who had been indicted in connection with the illegal payments to the North, further undermined the credibility of the 'sunshine' policy. Meanwhile, the 50th anniversary in July of the *de facto* end of the Korean War, celebrated as a triumph in North Korea, was commemorated in a sombre fashion in South Korea. Also in July, cross-border gunfire was exchanged between North and South Korean soldiers. In October North Korean official Kim Yong Sun, an important figure in inter-Korean affairs who had attended the presidential summit meeting in 2000, died, reportedly as a result of a traffic accident. In November two well-known North Korean defectors, Hwang Jang Yop and Kim Dok Hong, left their posts at the South Korean Institute of National Unification Policy. There was a suggestion that their resignations might have been due to fears that their criticism of the North Korean regime might be damaging to South Korean attempts to negotiate with the North. The resignation in January 2004 of the South Korean Minister of Foreign Affairs, Yoon Young-Kwan, was believed to have been related to tensions within the Government over South Korea's co-operation with the USA on the issue of North Korean weapons (see above).

The arrangements for further family reunions came under the auspices of the North and South Korean Red Cross organizations, which held several rounds of talks on the subject and co-ordinated the exchange of lists of potential candidates for reunion. In October 2000 the Republic of Korea accepted a North Korean proposal that the second exchange of family members should take place in late November–early December. Relations between the two sides subsequently deteriorated, when North Korea accused the head of the South Korean Red Cross of defaming the former's political system. The official was replaced in January 2001. The DPRK continued to dictate terms for reunions, asking the Republic of Korea to limit the amount of money and gifts transferred during the events, which took place in November–December 2000 and at the end of February 2001. It was subsequently reported that North Korean officials had confiscated money given to delegates for use as state funds. There was a notable decline in the level of enthusiasm for the reunions, which were proceeding slowly and on a small scale, among the South Korean populace (other than those who were directly involved). Meanwhile, in January 2001 an historic accord between the two sides allowed 300 separated families from the North and South each to exchange letters in mid-March. A fourth round of family reunions was initially scheduled for mid-October, but was cancelled owing to the heightened

security situation following the terrorist attacks in the USA on 11 September. They were subsequently held at Mount Kumgang in late April 2002. A fifth round was held in mid-September 2002, again at Mount Kumgang, where officials from the two sides planned to build a centre for such meetings. A further three rounds of reunions took place at Mount Kumgang in 2003. The eighth round of reunions in September 2003 involved 604 South Koreans and 365 North Koreans.

Of particular concern to those South Koreans who had begun to question the wisdom of extensive aid without firm preconditions was the fact that, as the DPRK's financial situation worsened, economic issues played an increasingly important part in inter-Korean relations during 2000 and 2001. There was speculation that Pyongyang's new openness was motivated by the necessity to secure greater assistance. South Korea provided 52% of the total international aid to North Korea in 2000. In January 2001, however, a South Korean vessel carrying aid was refused permission to dock in the DPRK. Also in that month, it was reported that North Korea's energy shortages had reached crisis point, and that it was desperately researching alternative power sources. A summit meeting took place between the two Koreas in February, at which the DPRK requested immediate and substantial electricity supplies to alleviate its pressing needs. The Republic of Korea, however, insisted that on-site investigations be conducted prior to the commencement of deliveries. Meanwhile, in August 2000 Hyundai agreed to establish a technologically-advanced electronic industrial compound in Kaesong in the DPRK. Hyundai's financial problems, however, were likely to delay the implementation of the project. The company was also obliged to reduce its royalty payments to Pyongyang for the Mount Kumgang tourist initiative in 2000, owing to the attraction's failure to make a profit. In March 2001 the future of the initiative was jeopardized by its lack of profitability, and Hyundai appealed to the South Korean Government for assistance; the Government subsequently pledged 90,000m. won to maintain the tourist cruises. Hyundai founder Chung Ju-Yung died in late March 2001, meanwhile, and his funeral was attended by a delegation sent by Kim Jong Il. On May Day workers from trade unions from the North and South attended a rally at Mount Kumgang. Progress on economic co-operation in Kaesong was made from 2002, with Kaesong being declared a special industrial zone in November of that year. In June 2003 the DPRK announced regulations for development of the zone, as well as plans to develop an area of 3.3 sq km in a first phase of development extending to 2007. A South Korean company, Korea Land, was to invest around US $184m. in the project. These plans were finalized at a meeting of South and North Korean economic officials in November 2003. Although inter-Korean trade increased steadily, reportedly amounting to US $700m. in 2003, South Korea shared international concerns over North Korea's suspected illicit trade in weapons and narcotics. In June 2003 South Korean customs officials in the port of Pusan seized 40 kg of methamphetamines believed to have originated in North Korea. There were also fears of very serious economic consequences for South Korea if reunification of the Koreas were to become an imminent prospect.

Negotiations to reconnect the inter-Korean rail link continued during 2001. It was hoped that such a link would create a new Eurasian transport corridor that would reduce the cost and time of the transit of goods from North-East Asia to European markets from 25 days to about 15 days, bringing economic benefits to all participants. In February 2001 a meeting was held at the DMZ to arrange regulations for troops and workers employed to rebuild the line, and a parallel highway. However, the DPRK failed to attend a UN Asian transport meeting held in Seoul in mid-November, following the breakdown of the sixth round of ministerial discussions. A New Year's editorial in the North in January 2002 described upgrading the railway as a priority during that year, and both Koreas agreed to accelerate the reconnection following bilateral talks in April 2002. Groundbreaking ceremonies for the reconnection of the railway and road links were held on both sides of the DMZ in late September 2002, and South Korea released a loan to the North to assist the funding of the work. In late 2002 South Korean officials attended the ground-breaking ceremony for the North's new industrial zone at Kaesong. In early February 2003 the first road reconnecting the North with the South was completed, on the eastern coast of the Korean peninsula. In June 2003 rail links between the two Koreas were officially opened. However, the connections remained largely symbolic, as construction on the North Korean side to link the new railways with wider networks was still to be completed in early 2004.

Owing to its geographical position, Korea's foreign relations have long been dominated by its relations with the 'great powers' in the region—Russia, China, the USA and Japan. Following President Roh Tae-Woo's inauguration in 1988, relations with the communist bloc showed signs of improvement. Trade with the USSR and the People's Republic of China expanded, and in 1990 full diplomatic relations were established with the USSR. These developments were denounced by the DPRK, its diplomatic isolation being compounded by the Republic of Korea's establishment of full diplomatic relations with the People's Republic of China (hitherto the North's principal ally) in August 1992. In August 1993 the Russian authorities published a new report into the shooting down, by Soviet forces, of a South Korean passenger aircraft in 1983, concluding that the airliner, which had been following an incorrect course, had been mistaken for a US aircraft engaged in espionage; previously, the Soviet authorities had maintained that the Korean aircraft was itself on a spying mission. In September 1993 it was announced that the Republic of Korea and Russia were to participate in joint naval exercises, and in 1994 it was reported that Russia was to supply 'defensive missiles' in order to repay a part of its debt to the Republic of Korea. Further arrangements were made concerning the settlement of Russia's debt, through the provision of commodities, in July 1997. There was speculation, however, that the Republic of Korea was no longer to receive the Russian defence systems, following pressure from the USA, hitherto the Republic of Korea's principal supplier of weaponry.

Relations were severely tested in mid-1998 by a diplomatic dispute, provoked by Russia's expulsion of a South Korean diplomat following allegations of espionage and bribery, which culminated in the resignation of the South Korean Minister of Foreign Affairs and Trade, Park Chung-Soo. During a state visit to Russia in May 1999, Kim Dae-Jung held a summit meeting with President Boris Yeltsin. Issues discussed included South Korea's engagement policy with North Korea, a proposed expansion of Moscow's role in regional affairs and bilateral economic co-operation. The Russian Minister of Defence visited Seoul in September 1999, and the two countries conducted their first joint naval exercises in April 2000. President Vladimir Putin of Russia paid a three-day state visit to the Republic of Korea in February 2001, during which the two nations confirmed their commitment to improving bilateral relations, and Putin agreed to proceed with a tripartite framework of co-operation between Russia and both Koreas. Arrangements were made for Russia to supply weapons to the Republic of Korea, which were to be partially paid for by the cancellation of some Soviet-era debt. The Republic of Korea and Russia also issued a joint statement supporting the 1972 Anti-Ballistic Missile (ABM) treaty; however, US displeasure with this led to the resignation of the Minister of Foreign Affairs and Trade, Lee Joung-Binn.

In mid-August 2001 a Russian diplomat, Valentin Moiseyev, was imprisoned for four-and-a-half years for passing secrets to South Korea; however, the incident did not adversely affect bilateral relations.

A key area of co-operation between the Republic of Korea and Russia during 2001–02 remained the reconnection of the North–South Korea rail network, and its planned connection with the Trans-Siberian railway, thereby creating a Eurasian transport corridor. This would allow South Korea to become a major trading hub, linking Europe and Asia with the Americas. Meanwhile, in December 2002 the Republic of Korea agreed to receive US $534m. worth of military equipment from Russia as part of a 1995 agreement aimed at repaying Moscow's $2,000m. debt to the Republic of Korea. The transaction, the last of its kind, was to be completed by 2006.

In September 2002 in response to growing labour shortages in South Korea, the Government extended working visas for ethnic Korean residents of Russia and the former Soviet Union from three months to one year. It was expected that many of the estimated 40,000 ethnic Koreans in Sakhalin, Russia, would take advantage of the changes.

There were indications that Roh Moo-Hyun would seek to improve relations with Russia during his presidency, as part of a broader policy of reducing dependency on the USA. In March 2003 Roh revived the idea of building a 4,000-km pipeline that would provide the DPRK with Russian natural gas from Sakhalin in exchange for the abandonment of its nuclear weapons programme. At a summit meeting in Bangkok in October 2003 Roh and Russian President Putin agreed to co-operate on the North Korean nuclear issue. Progress on the connection of the North–South Korea rail network to the Trans-Siberian railway (see above) was delayed in 2003 by tensions over North Korea's nuclear ambitions. However, in late 2003 a team of Russian engineers were assessing a stretch of railway linking Russia with the Korean peninsula across the Tumen river. Following President Roh's impeachment in March 2004 a planned visit by Roh to Russia was postponed.

Relations with China were strengthened in November 1998, when President Kim Dae-Jung paid an official visit to Beijing, meeting with Chinese President Jiang Zemin and Premier Zhu Rongji. Several accords were initialled during the visit. In August 1999 co-operative ties with China were further consolidated by the first visit of a South Korean defence minister to Beijing; a reciprocal visit to the Republic of Korea by the Chinese Minister of National Defence, Chi Haotian, took place in January 2000. The South Korean Government requested Chi's assistance in resolving the issue of seven North Korean defectors, who had recently been repatriated by China, despite South Korean protests. In October 2000 relations improved further when, during a visit to Seoul by Zhu Rongji, agreement was reached on the resumption of the quadripartite conference, incorporating the two Koreas, China and the USA, with the aim of establishing a peace mechanism for the Korean Peninsula. Later in the month, following strong opposition from Beijing, the Republic of Korea refused to grant a visa to the Dalai Lama, Tibet's spiritual leader, on the grounds that it would be 'inappropriate'.

During 2001 China continued to seek stability on the Korean peninsula. A diplomatic dispute arose between Seoul and Beijing in October, however, following the execution in China of a South Korean national and the alleged torture of another Korean prisoner, both convicted of drug-trafficking. In early November the ministers of economics, finance and foreign affairs from China, the Republic of Korea and Japan agreed to hold regular meetings to foster closer co-operation. In late 2001 there were concerns in South Korean business circles that China's admission to the WTO would divert investment and labour to the People's Republic and undercut the competitiveness of Korean goods. Nevertheless, the South Korean Minister of National Defence, Kim Dong-Shin, paid a week-long visit to China in December, where he sought closer military co-operation with his Chinese counterparts.

By 2002 economic and trade links were increasingly leading to closer relations between the Republic of Korea and China. During 2001 South Koreans invested more funding in China than in the USA, and in 2002 China displaced the USA as the Republic of Korea's largest trading partner. However, there was concern among domestic manufacturers that lower labour costs in China would undermine their competitiveness, and there were occasional trade disputes between the two countries.

In January 2002 China reacted with concern following the proposal to the South Korean National Assembly of legislation that would give special rights to ethnic Koreans living in China and elsewhere. In March the two countries announced the introduction of a new extradition pact, to take effect from April, and at the same time Wang Jiarui, the deputy head of the international liaison department of the Chinese Communist Party, visited Seoul.

Tensions between South Korea and China temporarily increased in mid-2002 when the Chinese authorities sought to prevent North Korean refugees from seeking asylum in various diplomatic buildings in China, including the South Korean embassy in Beijing, where a group of 23 had hidden. The members of the group, and others like them, were later permitted to travel to South Korea, but only via a third country—often the Philippines or Singapore. In response, the Chinese authorities increased efforts to combat South Korean NGOs and religious groups that were seeking to increase the number of North Korean refugees in China. In July and September Chinese military delegations visited Seoul to discuss bilateral military co-operation, and in August the Minister of Foreign Affairs and Trade received his Chinese counterpart in Seoul. In September Lee Hoi-Chang visited China and met President Jiang Zemin. In October the Minister of Finance proposed a three-way alliance comprising the Republic of Korea, China and Japan to manage the region's development. Also in that month the Government decided to extend working visas for ethnic Koreans in China to two years, with unlimited extensions. The move was designed to reduce the illegal trafficking of ethnic Koreans from China and its associated problems.

The growing diplomatic crisis over North Korea's nuclear programme in late 2002 and early 2003 led South Korea to seek China's assistance in persuading the North to work towards a peaceful solution. Roh made a four-day state visit to Beijing in July. Chinese diplomatic efforts played a major role in ensuring North Korean participation in talks on the DPRK's nuclear weapons programme attended by six nations, including the Republic of Korea, in Beijing in August (see chapter on the Democratic People's Republic of Korea).

Relations between the Republic of Korea and the USA were frequently strained in the late 1970s, in particular by the proposal to withdraw US ground troops from South Korea (which was abandoned in 1979) and by the trial of Kim Dae-Jung (see above). Disputes between the Republic of Korea and the USA in the late 1980s over trade issues had subsided by mid-1991. President George Bush of the USA visited the country in January 1992, and the two leaders agreed to cancel that year's 'Team Spirit' exercises. In December 1991 it had been announced that all US nuclear weapons had been withdrawn from South Korean territory. The 'Team Spirit' exercises were resumed in 1993. In July, during a visit to Seoul, President Clinton affirmed his country's continuing commitment to the defence of the Republic of Korea; he subsequently stated that an attack by the DPRK on the Republic of Korea would be tantamount to an act of aggression against the USA. In January 1994 it was announced that the USA was to deploy air-defence missiles on the Republic of Korean territory. In April 1996, during a visit to Seoul, Clinton issued a joint US-the Republic of Korean proposal for quadripartite negotiations with the DPRK and the People's Republic of China (see above). In October 1997 the US Government asked the South Korean administration to reconsider its decision to order an air-defence missile system from France. The Republic of Korea, however, was seeking to reduce its dependence on the USA for military technology. Later in that year the USA pledged financial support for the Republic of Korea, following the conclusion of the agreement with the IMF.

President Kim Dae-Jung was warmly received on a state visit to the USA in June 1998, during which he outlined his 'sunshine' policy of engagement towards North Korea. A reciprocal visit was made by Clinton to Seoul in November. Meanwhile, occasional differences over trade issues persisted in 1998. In October agreement was reached on US access to the South Korean vehicle market, after a protracted dispute during which the USA had threatened to impose sanctions on imports from South Korea. In February 1999 the USA filed a complaint with the WTO over the Republic of Korea's refusal to allow foreign companies to tender for contracts for the construction of a new airport near Seoul. In March the South Korean Government welcomed a breakthrough in negotiations between the DPRK and the USA on US access to a suspected nuclear site in North Korea (for further details, see the chapter on the DPRK). During a second visit by Kim Dae-Jung to the USA in July 1999, the US administration reaffirmed its support for the 'sunshine' policy. US-South Korean talks were held in late 1999 and early 2000 regarding the Republic of Korea's proposed extension of its missile range, from 180 km to 300 km for military purposes, and to 500 km for research and development. (In January 2001 a revised missile accord was signed between the Republic of Korea and the USA, permitting the former to develop missiles with greatly increased ranges and payloads.) In October 1999 the US and South Korean Governments began investigations into the alleged massacre of as many as 300 Korean refugees by US troops near Nogun-ri, in the South Korean province of North Chungcheong, shortly after the beginning of the Korean War. Revelations surrounding the use of defoliants in the DMZ in the late 1960s created further controversy in November 1999. The herbicides, which had apparently been provided by the USA but applied by South Korean troops, included Agent Orange, which had later been found to be highly toxic. The South Korean Government announced that it was prepared to compensate both soldiers and civilians adversely affected by the defoliants, but the USA reportedly refused to accept any liability. In December a lawsuit was filed against seven US chemical companies by a group of Koreans demanding compensation for damage they claimed to have suffered as a consequence of the herbicides.

In May 2000 there was further tension between the two countries when a US aircraft accidentally released several bombs close to a village south-west of Seoul, causing minor injuries and damage to property. Violent protests were held outside the US embassy in Seoul, and the USA subsequently agreed to cease using the Koon-ni range for such training missions. (Operations subsequently resumed, the USA citing a lack of suitable alternative facilities.) Following the incident, opposition politicians demanded a review of the Status of Forces Agreement (SOFA), which governed the 37,000 US troops stationed in South Korea. In August negotiations were held on the issue, and resulted in partial agreement. Further talks held in December successfully revised the agreement, which was signed in January 2001. South Korean civic groups, however, protested that the partnership between the two countries remained biased in favour of the USA. Also in December 2000, the WTO ruled that the USA had breached its rules in imposing 'anti-dumping' duties on South Korean exports of stainless steel, but did not recommend that the duties be revoked. In January 2001 outgoing US President Bill Clinton made an unprecedented statement of regret for the massacre near Nogun-ri. Many South Koreans, however, were angry that no apology was forthcoming. Later, in January 2002, a British Broadcasting Corporation (BBC) investigation revealed that US commanders had repeatedly ordered troops to fire on refugees at Nogun-ri and elsewhere during the opening months of the Korean War. Some South Korean historians were, in late 2001, also investigating the USA's possible role in the massacre by South Korean troops of 30,000 people on Jeju Island in a suppression of communist elements in late 1948 and early 1949. Meanwhile, the USA welcomed the improvement in inter-Korean relations during 2000. US Secretary of State Madeleine Albright visited Seoul in June and in October of that year to discuss developments. In March 2001 Kim Dae-Jung paid a visit to the new Bush administration in Washington, DC, hoping to secure support for his 'sunshine' policy. US President George W. Bush, however, took a firmer stance than his predecessor and declared that North Korea must prove its abandonment of its missile testing and development programme prior to any improvement in relations or release of aid.

In April 2001 a Seoul court ruled that the US air force's firing and bombing ranges near the village of Maehyang-ri caused damage and duress to inhabitants, and ordered the central Government to pay them compensation. In early May the US Deputy Secretary of State, Richard Armitage, visited the Republic of Korea, seeking Seoul's support for the USA's planned NMD system and urging the continuation of negotiations between North and South.

Disagreements between South Korea and the USA on how to deal with North Korea, however, continued to strain bilateral relations during 2001. In July Seoul refused to allow Hwang Jang Yop, the highest-ranking North Korean defector, to visit the USA and testify before Congress, fearing that such a move would exacerbate the already strained inter-Korean relations.

The Republic of Korea immediately pledged support to the USA following the terrorist attacks on the latter in September 2001, and in early December the National Assembly endorsed the deployment of non-combat troops to assist the US-led campaign in Afghanistan, mainly in a logistical capacity. Meanwhile, in November the USA and the Republic of Korea agreed to a major 'land-swap' whereby existing US bases would relocate to other areas within the country, allowing a consolidation of bases and training facilities over the next 10 years.

In January 2002 South Korea reacted with concern to President Bush's reference to North Korea as being part of an 'axis of evil', a remark that further undermined Kim Dae-Jung's 'sunshine' policy. None the less the South Korean military planned to purchase US $800m. worth of surface-to-surface missiles capable of attacking most of North Korea, from US manufacturers. At the same time GNP leader Lee Hoi-Chang visited the USA and met senior US officials, his attitude to the DPRK generally being closer to that of Bush than of Kim. Lee favoured a policy of 'strategic engagement' based on reciprocity and transparency. Bush himself visited South Korea in late February and urged the North to change its ways, while ruling out any US invasion. South Korea feared that any US-induced stalemate might lead to a major crisis on the peninsula.

In March 2002 the USA announced plans to deploy a new mobile military force unit to South Korea by 2007. Some South Korean officials had previously indicated that US troops might remain in Korea even after any unification, possibly serving as peace-keepers in the North. Later in the month the USA agreed to sell a combat-radar system to the Republic of Korea, and the two countries held their biggest-ever joint military exercises, which antagonized the North. Also in that month the Republic of Korea reacted angrily to Bush's imposition of new tariffs on imported steel, since the country was a major steel exporter. At the end of the month the Ministry of National Defence announced that the Boeing Company of the USA had secured a US $4,500m. contract to supply the Republic of Korea with 40 F-15K fighter planes, having beaten rivals Dassault of France, the Eurofighter consortium and Sukhoi of Russia. Critics of the deal said that Daussault's *Rafale* aicraft offered greater technology transfer and value, as well as local manufacturing opportunities. The Republic of Korea hoped to develop an indigenous fighter aircraft by 2015.

Relations between the Republic of Korea and the USA deteriorated noticeably after an accident in June 2002 in which a US army vehicle killed two teenaged Korean girls. The US military charged two US soldiers with negligent homicide, and the South Korean authorities subsequently requested their submission for trial at a local court, but this was rejected by the US army. In November the two soldiers were acquitted by a US military court, leading to a significant increase in anti-US sentiment among the public. Although President Bush apologized for the incident, in mid-December hundreds of thousands of people attended anti-US rallies in Seoul and across the country, and there were several incidents of assaults on and hostility towards US troops and businesses. Although precipitated by the issue of the acquittals, the rallies became a forum of protest against the country's dependency on the USA and that country's policy towards North Korea. Meanwhile, in October a new joint base pact came into force whereby the US military would reduce the number of bases from 41 to 23 and return 50% of the land it used to South Korea. However, there had yet to be changes to the SOFA that governed the conduct of US troops in Korea—amendments to which had long been demanded by South Koreans. Public anger towards the USA was further raised by the crash of a U2 reconnaissance plane in January, causing destruction of property.

The election of Roh Moo-Hyun as President raised fears that the Republic of Korea's relations with the USA would be further undermined, since Roh had once called for the removal of US troops from South Korea (although he had subsequently rescinded such demands) and had campaigned for a foreign policy more independent from the USA. However, in January 2003 he indicated a more conciliatory stance, but nevertheless warned the USA against attacking North Korea, instead urging the USA to resume dialogue with Pyongyang. He also instructed the military to prepare contingency plans for the possible withdrawal of US troops, and the US Secretary of Defense, Donald Rumsfeld, in March stated that the troops could be reduced or withdrawn completely. The USA announced that it planned to remove its 15,000 troops stationed between Seoul and the DMZ and deploy them in the south of the country. Kim Dae-Jung had previously criticized the USA's policy of 'tailored containment' to isolate Pyongyang, warning that it would be ineffective.

In late February 2003 the commander of the United States Forces Korea, Gen. Leon LaPorte, stated that the USA and South Korea would review their 1953 Mutual Defense Treaty, with the possibility of ending provisions under the 'Combined Forces Command' for the transfer of control over South Korea's military to the USA in wartime. However, it was noted that South Korea still remained dependent on the USA for military intelligence. Despite disagreements, South Korea and the USA held their annual joint military exercises during March. In early April the US military announced that it would move its main base away from Seoul as part of a global redeployment of forces, and the two countries began major discussions on the long-term future of their alliance. The USA envisioned eventually consolidating its forces in two major hubs: the Osan-Pyeongtaek, and Daegu-Busan regions. Meanwhile, Roh arranged to send 700 non-combatant troops to Iraq in support of the USA, despite domestic protests. Roh visited President Bush in Washington, DC, in mid-May, and the two leaders agreed to work towards a peaceful solution to the crisis over North Korea's nuclear programme, although differences remained between US and South Korean policies towards Pyongyang. In July South Korea rejected US calls for UN intervention in the North Korean nuclear crisis.

In March 2003, meanwhile, US Secretary of Defense Donald Rumsfeld stated that the USA was considering withdrawing troops from the North–South Korean border, and in June plans were confirmed to withdraw US troops to locations 120 km south of the DMZ, as part of a wider reorganization of US forces in South Korea. There were some concern in South Korea that these developments were in preparation for an attack by the USA on North Korean nuclear facilities. Also in June, some 20,000 people protested at the US embassy in Seoul to mark the anniversary of the killing of two Korean girls by a US army vehicle (see above). In November Donald Rumsfeld visited the Republic of Korea to discuss the US military presence as well as the deployment of South Korean troops to Iraq.

Relations between the Republic of Korea and Japan, which had long been strained, were eased by President Chun's official visit to Japan in September 1984 (the first such visit undertaken by a South Korean Head of State), during which Emperor Hirohito and Prime Minister Nakasone formally expressed their regret for Japanese aggression in Korea in the past. In May 1990, during President Roh's visit to Japan, Emperor Akihito offered official apologies for the cruelties of Japanese colonial rule in Korea. In January 1992 the Japanese Prime Minister, Kiichi Miyazawa, visited the Republic of Korea, where he publicly expressed regret at the enslavement during the Second World War of an estimated 100,000 Korean women, who were used by the Japanese military for sexual purposes ('comfort women'), but declined to state whether the Japanese Government would consider financial compensation. In late 1994 the Japanese Government announced that it would not make compensation payments directly to individuals, but would finance a programme to construct vocational training centres for the women concerned. In August 1995, on the 50th anniversary of the end of the Second World War, the Japanese Prime Minister, Tomiichi Murayama, issued a statement expressing 'deep reflection and sincere apologies' for Japanese colonial aggression. At the end of a summit meeting with President Kim in June 1996, the Japanese Prime Minister, Ryutaro Hashimoto, issued a public apology to the 'comfort women'. However, the South Korean Government regarded Japanese proposals to provide compensation through private sources of funding, rather than government money, as amounting to a denial of moral responsibility. The conclusion of new defence co-operation guide-lines between Japan and the USA in September 1997 was of concern for the Republic of Korea, which feared an expansion in Japanese military capability. Negotiations for a new fisheries agreement, under way since mid-1996, were unilaterally terminated by Japan in January 1998, following the continuing disagreement regarding sovereignty of a group of islets in the Sea of Japan, to which both countries laid claim. In April 1998 the South Korean Government announced its intention to make payments itself to surviving 'comfort women', apparently abandoning its attempts to gain compensation for the women from the Japanese Government. Later that month, however, a Japanese district court ordered the Government to pay compensation to three former 'comfort women' from the Republic of Korea. Another group of South Korean 'comfort women' was refused the right to recompense by the Japanese High Court in November 2000, and in March 2001 the 1998 compensation ruling was overturned by a regional High Court.

Relations with Japan improved considerably in October 1998, meanwhile, during a four-day state visit to Tokyo by President Kim Dae-Jung. A joint declaration was signed, in which Japan apologized for the suffering inflicted on the Korean people during Japanese colonial rule. In addition, the Republic of Korea agreed to revoke a ban on the import of various Japanese goods, while Japan promised financial aid to the Republic of Korea in support of its efforts to stimulate economic recovery. In November the two countries concluded negotiations on the renewal of their bilateral fisheries agreement, which came into effect in January 1999, despite the objections of the main South Korean opposition party, which protested that it failed positively to affirm the Republic of Korea's claim to sovereignty over the disputed islets. Differences over the accord and its implementation continued to create tension in early 1999, however, particularly in the Republic of Korea, where protests from fishermen, who were apparently suffering heavy losses because of the revised agreement, forced the resignation of the Minister for Maritime Affairs and Fisheries. In March increasing co-operation between the two countries was highlighted during a visit to the Republic of Korea by the Japanese Prime Minister, Keizo Obuchi, despite protests against Japan's military ties with the USA and failure fully to compensate the 'comfort women'. Both countries agreed to strengthen bilateral economic relations, and Japan pledged a further US $1,000m. in aid to the Republic of Korea. The Japanese Prime Minister, Yoshiro Mori, visited Seoul in May 2000 and met with Kim Dae-Jung. In November of that year the South Korean Minister of Foreign Affairs and Trade paid a visit to Tokyo to discuss ways of improving bilateral relations.

Relations with Japan deteriorated during 2001 following the publication in February of new Japanese history textbooks which sought to justify Japan's aggression towards its Asian neighbours during the Second World War, and neglected to mention the forced prostitution of Asian (mainly Korean) 'comfort women' by the Japanese army and the forcible transfer and use of Koreans as slave labour in Japan. Large-scale protests were held in Seoul, and the Japanese ambassador was summoned to the Ministry of Foreign Affairs and Trade. In April the Republic of Korea temporarily withdrew its ambassador from Japan. President Kim Dae-Jung urged Japan to adopt 'a correct understanding of history', and the South Korean National Assembly pressed the Government to reconsider any further opening of its markets to Japanese cultural products unless the books were abandoned. The South Korean Ministry of Foreign Affairs and Trade demanded 35 major revisions to the books, but in July Japan's Ministry of Education ruled out any further significant changes, prompting Kim Dae-Jung to refuse to receive a visiting Japanese delegation and the suspension of bilateral military co-operation. Protests also took place outside the Japanese embassy in Seoul. In mid-August the Republic of Korea was further outraged by the visit of the Japanese Prime Minister, Junichiro Koizumi, to the controversial Yasukuni Shrine in Tokyo honouring Japan's war dead. Koizumi's visit was seen as a sign of resurgent Japanese nationalism and was denounced by the Republic of Korea, as well as by Japan's other Asian neighbours. Koizumi visited Seoul in mid-October and delivered an apology for the suffering of Koreans under Japanese rule, but his visit was greeted by protests and he was forced to cancel a visit to the National Assembly owing to the hostile sentiment held by some legislators. However, both sides recognized the need to improve relations prior to co-hosting the football World Cup in 2002. In early January 2002, meanwhile, the Republic of Korea and Japan resolved a fishing dispute over access to waters claimed by Japan.

Along with China and North Korea, South Korea condemned Koizumi's visits to the Yasukuni Shrine in late April 2002 and mid-January 2003. However, Koizumi and Kim Dae-Jung in late March 2002 agreed to begin discussions on a possible bilateral free-trade agreement, and at the end of May Koizumi attended the opening ceremony of the 2002 football World Cup in Seoul. Also in attendance was Prince Takamado and his wife, who were making the first official visit to the Republic of Korea by a member of the Imperial family. The football tournament, a major source of prestige for both countries, passed off without incident. Any remaining mutual hostility between the two countries was overshadowed in 2002 by the need for co-operation in engaging with the North. In December 2002 Koizumi and South Korean President-elect Roh Moo-Hyun agreed to forge a united front when dealing with the North. Koizumi subsequently attended Roh's inauguration in late February 2003. In June Roh made his first state visit to Japan and had discussions with Koizumi on the issue of North Korea's nuclear weapons programme. Although both leaders opposed any development of nuclear weapons in North Korea, Roh urged dialogue with the DPRK, whereas Koizumi favoured stricter measures towards Pyongyang. Japan and the Republic of Korea continued efforts towards reaching a free-trade agreement in 2003.

In November 2000, after eight years' suspension, the 25th Joint Conference of Korea-Taiwan Business Councils took place in Seoul. It was agreed that henceforth conferences would be held annually alternately in Seoul and Taipei. In the same month a Korean passenger aircraft flew from Seoul to Taipei for the first time since 1992, when diplomatic relations had been severed. The Republic of Korea also maintained close relations with South-East Asian countries, and Minister of Defence Kim Dong-Shin and Prime Minister Lee Han-Dong visited Viet Nam in December 2001 and April 2002 respectively. Security, economic and trade issues were the main topics of discussions. Viet Nam had already become the principal recipient of South Korean aid. In early 2003 a South Korean newspaper funded the opening of a peace park in southern Viet Nam, as a gesture of atonement for atrocities committed by South Korean soldiers, some 300,000 of whom had fought on behalf of South Viet Nam, during the Viet Nam war. In early 2004 terrorist threats were made towards South Korean organizations in a number of South-East Asian countries, including Malaysia, Indonesia,

Laos and Viet Nam. It was believed that the threats might be related to immigration issues concerning Thai nationals in South Korea.

In February 2003 the Republic of Korea signed its first-ever free-trade agreement, with Chile, that would reduce tariffs on two-thirds of South Korean goods. The agreement was approved by the National Assembly in February 2004. In early 2004 Seoul was also negotiating on a free-trade agreement with Singapore.

Government

Under the Constitution of the Sixth Republic (adopted in October 1987), executive power is held by the President, who is directly elected for one term of five years by universal suffrage. The President appoints and governs with the assistance of the State Council (Cabinet), led by the Prime Minister. Legislative power is vested in the unicameral National Assembly (Kuk Hoe), popularly elected for a four-year term. The Assembly has 273 members.

Defence

Protection of the frontier separating North and South Korea is the responsibility of the UN. Military service lasts for 26 months in the South Korean army, and for 30 months in the navy and in the air force. In August 2003 the strength of the active armed forces was 686,000 (including an estimated 159,000 conscripts): army 560,000, navy 63,000, air force 63,000. Paramilitary forces included a 3.5m.-strong civilian defence corps. In August 2003 38,500 US troops were stationed in South Korea. Expenditure on defence was budgeted at 17,900,000m. won for 2003.

Economic Affairs

In 2002, according to estimates by the World Bank, the Republic of Korea's gross national income (GNI), measured at average 2000–02 prices, was US $473,050m., equivalent to $9,930 per head (or $16,480 per head on an international purchasing-power parity basis). During 1990–2002, it was estimated, the population increased at an average annual rate of 0.9%, while gross domestic product (GDP) per head increased, in real terms, by an average of 5.0% per year. Overall GDP increased, in real terms, at an average annual rate of 5.9% in 1990–2002. GDP increased by 6.3% in 2002 compared with the previous year.

Agriculture (including forestry and fishing) contributed 3.9% of GDP in 2002, and engaged 10.4% of the employed labour force in 2003. The principal crop is rice, but maize, barley, potatoes, sweet potatoes and fruit are also important, as is the raising of livestock (principally pigs and cattle). Fishing provides food for domestic consumption, as well as a surplus for export. In the late 1990s the Republic of Korea was one of the world's leading ocean-fishing nations. During 1990–2002, according to figures from the World Bank, agricultural GDP increased by an average of 1.7% per year. Agricultural GDP increased by 1.9% in 2001. There was a decrease in agricultural GDP of 4.1% in 2002.

Industry (including mining and quarrying, manufacturing, power and construction) contributed 40.3% of GDP in 2002, and engaged 28.1% of the employed labour force in 2000. Industry is dominated by large conglomerate companies (*chaebol*), with greatly diversified interests, especially in construction and manufacturing. According to figures from the World Bank, during 1990–2002 industrial GDP increased at an average annual rate of 6.5%. Industrial GDP increased by 2.9% in 2001 and by 6.1% in 2002.

South Korea is not richly endowed with natural resources, and mining and quarrying contributed only 0.3% of GDP in 2002. In 2001 less than 0.1% of the employed labour force were engaged in the sector. There are deposits of coal (mainly anthracite).Other minerals include iron ore, lead, zinc, silver, gold and limestone, and sizeable offshore reserves of natural gas have been discovered. According to figures from the Asian Development Bank (ADB, see p. 151), mining GDP declined at an average annual rate of 0.8% in 1990–2002.

Manufacturing contributed 28.8% of GDP in 2002, and engaged 19.7% of the employed labour force in 2001. The most important branches of manufacturing include electrical machinery, transport equipment—mainly road motor vehicles and ship-building, non-electrical machinery, chemicals, food products, iron and steel, and textiles. During 1990–2002, manufacturing GDP increased by an average of 7.6% per year. The sector's GDP increased by 2.1% in 2001. Manufacturing GDP expanded by an estimated 6.3% in 2002.

Energy is derived principally from nuclear power, coal and petroleum. In 2003 40.2% of total electricity output was generated by nuclear power, while thermal and hydroelectric power

Introductory Survey

provided 57.6% and 2.1%, respectively. A total of 14 nuclear power plants were to be constructed between 1993 and 2006. The Republic of Korea also produces liquefied natural gas for domestic and industrial consumption. Imports of petroleum and its products comprised an estimated 15.8% of the value of merchandise imports in 2003.

The services sector contributed 55.8% of GDP in 2002, and engaged 61.0% of the employed labour force in 2000. An important source of 'invisible' export earnings has been overseas construction work, mostly in the Middle East. Receipts from tourism are also significant (totalling an estimated US $5,276.9m. in 2002). During 1990–2002, according to figures from the World Bank, the GDP of the services sector increased at an average annual rate of 6.0%. The GDP of the sector increased by 3.4% in 2001. Growth was estimated at 7.6% in 2002.

In 2002 the Republic of Korea recorded a visible trade surplus of US $14,180m., and there was a surplus of $6,092m. on the current account of the balance of payments. Japan and the USA were the principal sources of imports in 2003 (accounting for, respectively, 20.3% and 13.9% of total imports in that year); another important supplier was the People's Republic of China. The People's Republic of China emerged as the principal market for exports in 2003 (purchasing 18.1%), followed by the USA (17.7%). The main exports in 2003 were electrical machinery, miscellaneous manufactured articles, road vehicles, textiles and chemical products. The principal imports in that year were machinery and transport equipment (especially electrical machinery), petroleum and petroleum products, basic manufactures and chemical products.

The Republic of Korea's budget surplus for 2003 was projected at the equivalent of 2.7% of GDP—the third consecutive year of surplus. The budget for 2004 envisaged expenditure of 168,272,000m. won (including capital expenditure of 24,647,000m. won). At the end of 2001 the Republic of Korea's total external debt was US $117,652m., of which $33,742m. was long-term public debt. In that year the cost of debt-servicing was equivalent to 13.8% of the value of exports of goods and services. The average annual rate of inflation was 4.8% in 1990–2002. Consumer prices increased by an average of 2.7% in 2002 and by 3.6% in 2003. The rate of unemployment increased from 3.1% of the labour force in 2002 to 3.4% in 2003.

The Republic of Korea is a member of the UN Economic and Social Commission for Asia and the Pacific (ESCAP, see p. 31), the ADB, Asia-Pacific Economic Co-operation (APEC, see p. 147), the Colombo Plan (see p. 359) and the Organisation for Economic Co-operation and Development (OECD, see p. 295).

In 1997 the Republic of Korea experienced its most serious economic crisis in 50 years. Several major *chaebol* collapsed, the won depreciated substantially against the US dollar and foreign-exchange reserves were almost depleted. The country was forced to seek extensive assistance from the IMF. President Kim Dae-Jung assumed office in February 1998, promising widespread economic reform, and accepted a three-year programme formulated by the IMF, which stipulated the implementation of stringent economic and financial liberalization measures. By the end of 1999 the economy appeared to have made a remarkable recovery, and in December 2000 the IMF ended its rescue programme, which it declared to have been a success. Economic difficulties however, mainly resulting from incomplete reform of the banking sector and *chaebol*, persisted. Official intervention was much in evidence from 2001, reversing previous IMF-led policy, with many heavily-indebted companies receiving government aid. Vested interest groups with links to the *chaebol* continued to resist reform, and restructuring of the *chaebol* seemed to have stalled. In early 2003 the Fair Trade Commission launched a large-scale investigation of *chaebol* business practices. In October the Commission imposed fines totalling 31,500m. won in connection with illegal transactions at six companies, which included Samsung, LG Group and Hyundai companies as well as SK Group. Economic difficulties in the banking sector continued in 2003, with an ongoing financial crisis at credit card lender LG Card. Meanwhile, organized labour movements continued to arrange industrial action by workers fearing unemployment and seeking better working conditions, and strikes were held during 2001 and 2002. There was further industrial unrest in 2003 in connection with railway privatization and lawsuits filed against union leaders. Although the overall rate of average unemployment in 2003 was 3.4%, the rate of unemployment amongst young people was believed to be much higher. Decreased demand from the USA, the country's

principal export market, and the deceleration in the world economy substantially reduced the Republic of Korea's trade surplus and rate of growth in 2001. Sales of semiconductors, computers and other such goods were particularly badly affected. Strong GDP resumed in 2002, however, in part aided by a recovery in exports. The corporate and financial sectors reported record profits in 2002, reflecting the success of reforms introduced during the preceding years. Although the Republic of Korea co-hosted the football World Cup with Japan in mid-2002, the overall economic benefits were limited, with much of the financing for infrastructure having been spent during the previous three years, and many businesses closing during major matches. Furthermore, far fewer foreign visitors attended the event than expected. In 2003, according to the Bank of Korea, GDP growth decreased to around 3.1%, owing largely to weak domestic consumption and low corporate investment, with the economy having entered recession in the first half of the year, for the first time since 1998. In July 2003 the Government announced a supplementary budget of 4,500,000m. won, aimed at halting the economic decline. However, recovery was evident in the second half of the year, driven by strong growth in the export sector. Total exports increased by 19.3% in 2003, with exports to China having increased by 47.8%, compared with the previous year. Also in 2003, the country experienced its worst typhoon for 100 years, which caused more than 100 deaths and damage to property estimated at US $3,600m. Another dramatic incident in 2003 was the suicide of a South Korean farmer in September during the course of a summit meeting of the World Trade Organization (WTO) in Cancún, Mexico, in protest at the Organization's policies. Meanwhile, continued uncertainty over the North Korean nuclear programme was likely to reduce business confidence, especially among foreign investors. Increased tension with North Korea was reflected in the draft budget for 2004, announced in August 2003, which outlined plans to increase spending on defence by 8%. In February 2004 the Republic of Korea approved its first free-trade agreement, with Chile. The agreement prompted protests by South Korean farmers fearing the effect of increased competition in the agricultural sector. GDP growth in 2004 was forecast at 5.2% by the Bank of Korea in late 2003; however, the IMF stated a lower estimate, of 4.75%. Economic prospects were adversely affected by internal political instability in early 2004, with the impeachment of President Roh in March prompting a sharp decrease in the value of the South Korean currency and a decline in stock market prices.

Education

Education, available free of charge, is compulsory between the ages of six and 15. Primary education begins at six years of age and lasts for six years. In 1997 enrolment at primary schools included 93% of children in the appropriate age-group (males 92%; females 93%). Secondary education begins at 12 years of age and lasts for up to six years, comprising two cycles of three years each, the first of which is compulsory. Enrolment at secondary schools in 1996 included 97% of children in the appropriate age-group (males 97%; females 98%). In 2002 there were 163 university-level institutions, with a student enrolment of 1,771,738. In that year there were 945 graduate schools, with a student enrolment of 262,867. Expenditure on education by the central Government totalled 17,779,200m. won in 1998 (representing 15.8% of total spending).

Public Holidays

2004: 1 January (New Year), 21–23 January (Lunar New Year), 1 March (Sam Il Jol, Independence Movement Day), 5 April (Arbor Day), 5 May (Children's Day), 26 May (Buddha's Birthday), 6 June (Memorial Day), 17 July (Constitution Day), 15 August (Liberation Day), 27–29 September (Juseok, Korean Thanksgiving Day), 3 October (National Foundation Day), 25 December (Christmas Day).

2005: 1 January (New Year), 8–10 February (Lunar New Year), 1 March (Sam Il Jol, Independence Movement Day), 5 April (Arbor Day), 5 May (Children's Day), 15 May (Buddha's Birthday), 6 June (Memorial Day), 17 July (Constitution Day), 15 August (Liberation Day), 17–19 September (Juseok, Korean Thanksgiving Day), 3 October (National Foundation Day), 25 December (Christmas Day).

Weights and Measures

The metric system is in force, although a number of traditional measures are also used.

Statistical Survey

Source (unless otherwise stated): National Statistical Office, Bldg III, Government Complex-Daejeon 920, Dunsan-dong, Seo-gu, Daejeon 302-701; tel. (42) 481-4114; fax (42) 481-2460; internet www.nso.go.kr.

Area and Population

AREA, POPULATION AND DENSITY*

Area (sq km)	99,313†
Population (census results)‡	
1 November 1995	44,608,726
1 November 2000	
Males	23,068,181
Females	22,917,108
Total	45,985,289
Population (official estimates at mid-year)	
2001	47,342,828
2002	47,639,618
2003	47,925,318
Density (per sq km) at mid-2003	482.6

* Excluding the demilitarized zone between North and South Korea, with an area of 1,262 sq km (487 sq miles).
† 38,345 sq miles. The figure indicates territory under the jurisdiction of the Republic of Korea, surveyed on the basis of land register.
‡ Excluding adjustment for underenumeration, estimated at 1.4% in 1995.

PRINCIPAL TOWNS
(population at 1995 census)

Seoul (capital) . .	10,231,217		Jeonju (Chonju) . .	563,153
Busan (Pusan) . .	3,814,325		Jeongju (Chongju) .	531,376
Daegu (Taegu) . .	2,449,420		Masan	441,242
Incheon (Inchon). .	2,308,188		Jinju (Chinju) . .	329,886
Daejeon (Taejon). .	1,272,121		Kunsan	266,559
Gwangju (Kwangju)	1,257,636		Jeju (Cheju) . . .	258,511
Ulsan	967,429		Mokpo	247,452
Seongnam				
(Songnam) . . .	869,094		Chuncheon	
			(Chunchon). . .	234,528
Suwon	755,550			

2000 census: 9,853,972; Busan 3,655,437; Daegu 2,473,990; Incheon 2,466,338; Daejeon 1,365,961; Gwangju 1,350,948; Ulsan 1,012,110.

BIRTHS, MARRIAGES AND DEATHS*

	Registered live births		Registered marriages		Registered deaths	
	Number	Rate (per 1,000)	Number	Rate (per 1,000)	Number	Rate (per 1,000)
1994 . . .	728,515	16.3	393,121	8.7	248,377	5.5
1995 . . .	721,074	16.0	398,484	8.7	248,089	5.4
1996 . . .	695,825	15.3	434,911	9.4	245,588	5.3
1997 . . .	678,402	14.8	388,591	8.4	247,938	5.3
1998 . . .	642,972	13.8	375,616	8.0	248,443	5.3
1999 . . .	616,322	13.2	362,673	7.7	246,539	5.2
2000 . . .	636,780	13.4	334,030	7.0	247,346	5.2
2001 . . .	557,228	11.6	320,063	6.7	242,730	5.1

* Owing to late registration, figures are subject to continuous revision. The foregoing data refer to events registered by the end of 2000, tabulated by year of occurrence.

Expectation of life (WHO estimates, years at birth): 75.5 (males 71.8; females 79.4) in 2002 (Source: WHO, *World Health Report*).

ECONOMICALLY ACTIVE POPULATION*
(annual averages, '000 persons aged 15 years and over)

	1998	1999	2000
Agriculture, forestry and fishing .	2,480	2,349	2,288
Mining and quarrying	21	20	18
Manufacturing	3,898	4,006	4,244
Electricity, gas and water . . .	61	61	63
Construction	1,578	1,476	1,583
Trade, restaurants and hotels . .	5,571	5,724	5,943
Transport, storage and communications	1,169	1,202	1,260
Financing, insurance, real estate and business services	1,856	1,925	2,089
Community, social and personal services	3,339	3,499	3,551
Total employed (incl. others) . .	19,994	20,281	21,061
Unemployed	1,461	1,353	889
Total labour force	21,456	21,634	21,950
Males	12,893	12,889	12,950
Females	8,562	8,745	9,000

2001 ('000 persons aged 15 years and over): Total employed 21,572; Unemployed 845; Total labour force 22,417 (Males 13,142; Females 9,275).
2002 ('000 persons aged 15 years and over): Total employed 22,169; Unemployed 708; Total labour force 22,877 (Males 13,411; Females 9,466).
2003 ('000 persons aged 15 years and over): Total employed 22,139; Unemployed 777; Total labour force 22,916 (Males 13,518; Females 9,397).

* Excluding armed forces.

Health and Welfare

KEY INDICATORS

Total fertility rate (children per woman, 2002)	1.4
Under-5 mortality rate (per 1,000 live births, 2001) . . .	5
HIV/AIDS (% of persons aged 15–49, 2001)	<0.10
Physicians (per 1,000 head, 2000)	1.3
Hospital beds (per 1,000 head, 2000)	6.1
Health expenditure (2001): US $ per head (PPP)	948
Health expenditure (2001): % of GDP	6.0
Health expenditure (2001): public (% of total)	44.4
Access to water (% of persons, 2000)	92
Access to sanitation (% of persons, 2000)	63
Human Development Index (2001): ranking	30
Human Development Index (2001): value	0.879

For sources and definitions, see explanatory note on p. vi.

Agriculture

PRINCIPAL CROPS
('000 metric tons)

	2000	2001	2002
Rice (paddy)	7,124.8	7,453.0	6,650.0*
Barley	226.6	382.8	382.8†
Maize	64.2	57.0	60.0*
Potatoes	704.6	605.0	750.0†
Sweet potatoes . . .	344.9	273.1	250.0†
Dry beans	21.0	24.0*	24.0†
Chestnuts	92.8	94.1	94.1†
Soybeans (Soya beans) . . .	113.2	117.7	110.0*
Sesame seed	31.7	31.0	31.0†
Other oilseeds	25.7	25.0*	27.5†
Cabbages	3,420.2	3,420.2	3,420.2†
Lettuce	203.5	200.0†	200.0†
Spinach	120.8	122.0†	122.0†
Tomatoes	276.7	200.0†	200.0†
Pumpkins, squash and gourds .	240.5	240.0†	240.0†
Cucumbers and gherkins . .	453.5	450.0†	450.0†
Chillies and green peppers . .	391.3	380.0†	380.0†
Green onions and shallots . .	657.9	636.0	636.0†
Dry onions	877.5	1,073.7	1,073.7†
Garlic	474.4	406.4	406.4†
Carrots	155.2	150.0†	150.0†
Mushrooms	21.8	21.3†	21.3†
Other vegetables	3,694.8*	3,765.8*	3,765.8†
Tangerines, mandarins, clementines and satsumas .	563.5	645.0	780.0*
Apples	489.0	403.6	403.6†
Pears	324.2	417.2	417.2†
Peaches and nectarines . . .	170.0	166.0	166.0†
Plums	51.7	55.0†	55.0†
Strawberries	180.2	185.0†	185.0†
Grapes	475.6	454.0	454.0†
Watermelons	922.7	850.0†	850.0†
Cantaloupes and other melons .	332.8	320.0†	320.0†
Persimmons	287.8	270.0	270.0†
Other fruits	82.1	82.8†	82.8†
Tobacco (leaves)	68.2	55.6	55.6†

* Unofficial figure.
† FAO estimate.

Source: FAO.

LIVESTOCK
('000 head)

	2000	2001	2002
Cattle	2,134	1,954	1,951*
Pigs	8,214	8,720	8,811*
Goats	445	440	435†
Rabbits	436	600†	600†
Chickens	102,547	102,393	107,000†
Ducks	5,405	6,716	8,000†

* Unofficial figure.
† FAO estimate.

Source: FAO.

LIVESTOCK PRODUCTS
('000 metric tons)

	2000	2001	2002
Beef and veal	305.9	226.0	180.0*
Pig meat	915.9	927.7	1,030.0*
Chicken meat	373.6	377.1	395.0*
Duck meat	44.7*	56.0†	56.0†
Other meat†	8.9	10.1	10.1
Cows' milk	2,252.8	2,338.9	2,390.0
Goats' milk†	4.6	4.4	4.4
Butter†	54.9	57.1	57.1
Hen eggs	478.8	522.0*	510.0†
Other poultry eggs . . .	21.3	23.5†	23.5†
Honey	17.7	19.0†	20.5†
Cattle hides (fresh)† . . .	50.9	37.6	37.6

* Unofficial figure.
† FAO estimate(s).

Source: FAO.

Forestry

ROUNDWOOD REMOVALS
(FAO estimates, '000 cubic metres, excl. bark)

	2000	2001	2002
Sawlogs, veneer logs and logs for sleepers	420	575	646
Pulpwood	552	376	373
Other industrial wood	620	582	586
Fuel wood	2,449	2,454	2,458
Total	**4,041**	**3,987**	**4,063**

Source: FAO.

SAWNWOOD PRODUCTION
('000 cubic metres, incl. sleepers)

	2000	2001	2002
Coniferous (softwood) . . .	4,044	4,330	5,045
Broadleaved (hardwood) . . .	500	90	149
Total	**4,544**	**4,420**	**5,194**

Source: FAO.

Fishing

('000 metric tons, live weight)

	1999	2000	2001
Capture	2,119.7	1,823.2	1,988.0
Alaska (walleye) pollock . .	146.2	86.1	197.4
Croakers and drums . .	114.2	67.6	50.8
Japanese anchovy . . .	238.5	201.2	273.9
Skipjack tuna . . .	109.8	137.0	137.6
Chub mackerel . . .	177.6	145.9	203.7
Largehead hairtail . . .	64.4	81.1	79.9
Argentine shortfin squid . .	271.7	150.1	142.6
Japanese flying squid . . .	249.3	226.3	225.6
Aquaculture	303.1	323.2	294.5
Pacific cupped oyster . . .	177.3	177.1	174.1
Total catch	**2,422.8**	**2,146.4**	**2,282.5**

Note: Figures exclude aquatic plants ('000 metric tons): 486.6 (capture 12.9, aquaculture 473.7) in 1999; 387.7 (capture 13.0, aquaculture 374.6) in 2000; 388.5 (capture 14.9, aquaculture 373.5) in 2001. Also excluded are aquatic mammals, recorded by number rather than by weight. The number of whales and dolphins caught was: 105 in 1999; 174 in 2000; 376 in 2001.

Source: FAO, *Yearbook of Fishery Statistics*.

Mining

('000 metric tons, unless otherwise indicated)

	2000	2001	2002
Hard coal (Anthracite) . . .	4,174	3,817	3,318
Iron ore: gross weight . . .	336	195	157
Iron ore: metal content . . .	188	109	88
Lead ore (metric tons)* . . .	2,724	988	28
Zinc ore (metric tons)* . . .	11,474	5,129	99
Kaolin	2,098.5	2,384.0	2,831
Feldspar	330.4	389.4	415.6
Salt (unrefined)†	800	800	800
Mica (metric tons) . . .	65,249	109,339	29,870
Talc (metric tons)	11,344	47,712	37,863
Pyrophyllite	918.0	1,101.8	890.0

* Figures refer to the metal content of ores.
† Estimated production.

Source: US Geological Survey.

Industry

SELECTED PRODUCTS
('000 metric tons, unless otherwise indicated)

	1999	2000	2001
Wheat flour	1,834	1,871	1,843
Refined sugar	1,182	1,257	1,264
Beer (million litres)	1,487	1,654	1,777
Cigarettes (million)	95,995	94,531	94,116
Cotton yarn—pure and mixed	282.6	294.1	303.5
Plywood ('000 cu m)	774	817	801
Newsprint	1,718	1,770	1,585
Rubber tyres ('000)*	67,120	71,348	68,728
Caustic soda (metric tons)	1,163	1,203	1,309
Liquefied petroleum gas	2,595	2,997	n.a.
Naphtha	18,815	19,109	n.a.
Kerosene	11,648	11,299	n.a.
Distillate fuel oil	30,245	31,535	n.a.
Bunker C oil (million litres)	36,509	n.a.	n.a.
Residual fuel oil	36,341	34,813	n.a.
Cement	48,579	51,417	53,062
Pig-iron	23,328	24,943	26,182
Crude steel	41,502	43,423	44,199
Television receivers ('000)	15,556	10,054	9,321
Passenger cars—produced ('000 units)	2,158	2,626	2,477
Lorries and trucks—produced (number)	264,212	265,448	254,233
Electric energy (million kWh)	266,818	295,156	n.a.

* Tyres for passenger cars and commercial vehicles.

Shipbuilding (merchant ships launched, '000 grt): 8,977 in 1999; 11,211 in 2000; 8,385 in 2001 (Source: UN, *Industrial Commodity Statistics Yearbook*).

Finance

CURRENCY AND EXCHANGE RATES

Monetary Units
100 chun (jeon) = 10 hwan = 1 won.

Sterling, Dollar and Euro Equivalents (31 December 2003)
£1 sterling = 2,128.43 won;
US $1 = 1,192.60 won;
€1 = 1,506.25 won;
10,000 won = £4.698 = $8.385 = €6.639.

Average Exchange Rate (won per US $)
2001   1,290.99
2002   1,251.09
2003   1,191.61

BUDGET
('000 million won)*

Revenue	1996	1997	1998
Taxation	72,385	78,434	78,310
Taxes on income, profits and capital gains	24,137	24,292	27,975
Income tax	14,767	14,868	17,194
Corporation tax	9,356	9,425	10,776
Social security contributions	7,425	8,506	10,512
Employees	2,804	3,433	n.a.
Employers	4,261	4,864	n.a.
Taxes on property	1,473	1,590	1,379
Domestic taxes on goods and services	27,478	30,650	27,159
Value-added tax	16,790	19,488	15,707
Excises	10,027	10,373	10,530
Import duties	5,309	5,798	3,836
Other current revenue	11,791	13,639	17,480
Entrepreneurial and property income	4,600	5,634	9,854
Administrative fees and charges, non-industrial and incidental sales	1,518	1,394	1,530
Fines and forfeits	3,502	5,032	4,646
Capital revenue	1,352	1,295	883
Total	85,528	93,368	96,673

Expenditure	1996	1997	1998
General public services	7,847	9,039	10,841
Defence	12,553	13,159	13,621
Education	14,435	16,249	17,779
Health	682	777	957
Social security and welfare	7,884	9,632	12,252
Housing and community amenities	7,077	6,677	7,336
Recreational, cultural and religious affairs and services	534	679	788
Economic affairs and services	21,965	24,334	28,453
Interest expenditures	2,241	2,258	3,399
Other	9,211	18,084	20,263
Total	84,429	100,888	115,689
Current	n.a.	62,812	70,631
Capital	n.a.	18,791	20,359
Net lending	n.a.	19,285	23,375
Other expenditures	n.a.	0	1,324

Source: IMF, *Republic of Korea: Statistical Appendix* (February 2000).

1999 ('000 million won)* Total revenue 107,923 (current 106,523; capital 1,386); Total expenditure (excl. net lending and other expenditures) 101,236 (current 76,798; capital 24,438) (Source: Bank of Korea, Ministry of Planning and Budget).

2000 ('000 million won)* Total revenue 133,584 (current 132,366; capital 1,218); Total expenditure (excl. net lending and other expenditures) 108,259 (current 82,667; capital 25,592) (Source: Bank of Korea, Ministry of Planning and Budget).

2001 ('000 million won)* Total revenue 139,890 (current 138,203; capital 1,697); Total expenditure (excl. net lending and other expenditures) 122,275 (current 99,755; capital 22,520) (Source: Bank of Korea, Ministry of Planning and Budget).

2002 ('000 million won)* Total revenue 151,873 (current 150,239; capital 1,633); Total expenditure (excl. net lending and other expenditures) 131,993 (current 109,123; capital 22,870) (Source: Bank of Korea, Ministry of Planning and Budget).

2003 ('000 million won): Total revenue 169,563 (current 168,159; capital 1,404); Total expenditure (excl. net lending and other expenditures) 144,785 (current 120,741; capital 24,044).

2004 ('000 million won): Total revenue 183,077 (current 181,724; capital 1,353); Total expenditure (excl. net lending and other expenditures) 168,272 (current 143,625; capital 24,647).

* Figures refer to the consolidated operations of the central Government, including extrabudgetary accounts, but excluding enterprise special accounts. Figures refer to the fiscal year.

INTERNATIONAL RESERVES
(US $ million at 31 December)

	2000	2001	2002
Gold*	67.6	68.3	69.2
IMF special drawing rights	3.5	3.3	11.8
Reserve position in IMF	271.8	262.4	522.0
Foreign exchange	95,855.1	102,487.5	120,811.4
Total	96,198.1	102,821.6	121,414.4

* National valuation.

Source: IMF, *International Financial Statistics*.

MONEY SUPPLY
('000 million won at 31 December)

	2000	2001	2002
Currency outside banks	17,636	18,702	19,863
Demand deposits at deposit money banks	29,193	34,918	43,265

Source: IMF, *International Financial Statistics*.

COST OF LIVING
(Consumer Price Index; base: 2000 = 100)

	2001	2002	2003
Food	103.5	107.7	112.4
Housing	103.9	109.2	113.2
Fuel, light and water	111.1	107.1	113.1
Furniture and utensils	102.4	104.0	106.7
Clothing and footwear	103.1	106.3	110.1
Medical treatment	112.3	111.4	114.1
Education	104.4	110.3	116.8
Culture and recreation	99.7	100.0	100.0
Transport and communications	102.0	101.4	102.7
All items (incl. others)	104.1	106.9	110.7

NATIONAL ACCOUNTS
('000 million won at current prices)

National Income and Product

	2000	2001	2002
Compensation of employees	229,605.2	250,979.1	268,311.8
Operating surplus	160,338.7	156,338.5	172,442.9
Domestic factor incomes	389,943.9	407,317.6	440,754.7
Consumption of fixed capital	61,655.9	65,732.9	67,295.7
Gross domestic product (GDP) at factor cost	451,599.8	473,050.5	508,050.4
Indirect taxes	71,811.8	80,487.7	90,604.9
Less Subsidies	1,452.4	1,980.6	2,274.1
GDP in purchasers' values	521,959.2	551,557.6	596,381.2
Net factor income from abroad	−2,731.8	−1,543.1	500.0
Gross national product	519,227.4	550,014.5	596,881.2
Less Consumption of fixed capital	61,655.9	65,732.9	67,295.7
National income in market prices	457,571.5	484,281.6	529,585.5
Other current transfers from abroad (net)	644.3	−467.2	−1,491.6
National disposable income	458,215.8	483,814.3	528,093.8

Expenditure on the Gross Domestic Product

	2000	2001	2002
Government final consumption expenditure	52,480	57,180	62,968
Private final consumption expenditure	299,122	326,210	358,835
Increase in stocks	−1,034	−506	−4,159
Gross fixed capital formation	148,203	148,717	159,482
Statistical discrepancy	7,242	7,391	10,677
Total domestic expenditure	506,012	538,992	587,803
Exports of goods and services	233,792	233,007	238,634
Less Imports of goods and services	217,845	220,442	230,056
GDP in purchasers' values	521,959	551,558	596,381
GDP at constant 1995 prices	478,533	493,380	524,689

Source: IMF, *International Financial Statistics*.

Gross Domestic Product by Economic Activity

	2000	2001	2002*
Agriculture, forestry and fishing	24,517.6	23,935.2	23,593.5
Mining and quarrying	1,802.2	1,893.5	2,069.7
Manufacturing	163,283.2	168,160.4	174,247.1
Electricity, gas and water	14,374.4	15,591.2	17,401.5
Construction	41,788.0	45,918.4	50,463.0
Trade, restaurants and hotels	63,201.6	67,577.9	71,454.7
Transport, storage and communications	34,901.1	36,745.7	39,280.4
Finance, insurance, real estate and business services	98,977.1	105,546.3	127,538.5
Government services	39,018.5	43,476.7	47,765.8
Other community, social and personal services	27,484.8	32,375.0	36,820.8
Private non-profit services to households	12,320.7	13,410.5	14,659.7
Sub-total	521,669.2	554,630.8	605,294.7
Import duties	19,446.6	21,028.0	22,391.7
Less Imputed bank service charge	19,156.5	24,101.4	31,305.2
GDP in purchasers' values	521,959.2	551,557.5	596,381.2

* Figures are provisional.

BALANCE OF PAYMENTS
(US $ million)

	2000	2001	2002
Exports of goods f.o.b.	175,948	151,262	162,554
Imports of goods f.o.b.	−159,076	−137,770	−148,374
Trade balance	16,872	13,492	14,180
Exports of services	30,534	29,055	28,143
Imports of services	−33,423	−32,883	−35,603
Balance on goods and services	13,982	9,664	6,719
Other income received	6,375	6,650	6,807
Other income paid	−8,797	−7,848	−6,356
Balance on goods, services and income	11,561	8,466	7,171
Current transfers received	6,500	6,687	7,293
Current transfers paid	−5,820	−6,914	−8,372
Current balance	12,241	8,239	6,092
Capital account (net)	−615	−731	−1,091
Direct investment abroad	−4,999	−2,420	−2,674
Direct investment from abroad	9,283	3,528	1,972
Portfolio investment assets	−520	−5,521	−5,036
Portfolio investment liabilities	12,697	12,227	4,940
Financial derivatives assets	532	463	1,308
Financial derivatives liabilities	−711	−586	−1,029
Other investment assets	−2,289	7,099	−2,404
Other investment liabilities	−1,268	−11,650	5,538
Net errors and omissions	−561	2,629	4,155
Overall balance	23,790	13,278	11,770

Source: IMF, *International Financial Statistics*.

External Trade

PRINCIPAL COMMODITIES
(distribution by SITC, US $ million)*

Imports c.i.f.	2001	2002	2003
Food and live animals . . .	6,789.3	7,620.7	8,330.9
Crude materials (inedible) except fuels	9,052.3	9,178.9	10,146.5
Mineral fuels, lubricants, etc. .	34,069.3	31,052.6	37,213.5
Petroleum, petroleum products, etc. .	26,485.6	23,183.1	28,192.4
Crude petroleum oils, etc. . .	21,367.8	n.a.	n.a.
Refined petroleum products . .	4,650.3	n.a.	n.a.
Gas (natural and manufactured)	5,236.6	5,394.3	6,468.7
Chemicals and related products	12,941.6	14,133.3	16,459.0
Organic chemicals	4,329.6	4,604.8	5,408.0
Basic manufactures	16,683.8	19,192.3	22,312.1
Iron and steel.	4,420.0	5,533.3	7,355.0
Machinery and transport equipment.	47,911.0	53,314.2	62,655.2
Machinery specialized for particular industries . . .	3,713.1	4,110.5	5,080.6
General industrial machinery, equipment and parts . . .	4,594.2	5,232.9	6,100.4
Office machines and automatic data-processing machines .	5,640.8	5,486.7	5,433.6
Telecommunications and sound equipment	4,821.5	4,910.2	5,486.1
Other electrical machinery, apparatus, etc..	22,616.5	25,581.6	31,296.8
Thermionic valves and tubes, microprocessors, transistors, etc.	15,865.2	n.a.	n.a.
Electronic integrated circuits and microassemblies. . .	13,356.8	n.a.	n.a.
Miscellaneous manufactured articles.	11,166.6	13,358.9	16,234.0
Total (incl. others)	141,097.8	152,126.2	178,826.7

Exports f.o.b.	2001	2002	2003
Mineral fuels, lubricants, etc. .	8,009.1	1,949.8	1,915.0
Petroleum, petroleum products, etc.	7,892.7	1,884.2	1,812.3
Refined petroleum products .	7,736.3	n.a.	n.a.
Chemicals and related products	12,523.8	13,756.9	16,928.6
Plastics in primary forms . .	4,633.2	5,080.6	6,447.0
Basic manufactures	26,789.5	26,986.3	30,125.9
Textile yarn, fabrics, etc. . .	10,940.8	10,940.5	10,776.2
Iron and steel.	5,825.8	5,704.1	7,782.6
Machinery and transport equipment.	86,694.8	99,597.8	121,142.2
Office machines and automatic data-processing machines .	13,498.7	16,445.1	18,069.3
Automatic data-processing machines and units, etc. .	7,484.9	n.a.	n.a.
Parts and accessories for automatic data-processing equipment	5,640.2	n.a.	n.a.

Exports f.o.b.— *continued*	2001	2002	2003
Telecommunications and sound equipment	15,943.6	20,150.1	26,634.3
Transmission apparatus for radio or television . . .	7,483.6	n.a.	n.a.
Other electrical machinery, apparatus, etc. . . .	21,694.0	23,694.4	28,604.0
Thermionic valves and tubes, microprocessors, transistors, etc.	14,741.9	n.a.	n.a.
Electronic integrated circuits and microassemblies . . .	11,142.3	n.a.	n.a.
Road vehicles and parts† . . .	15,363.1	17,198.0	22,900.5
Passenger motor cars (excl. buses).	12,029.4	n.a.	n.a.
Other transport equipment and parts†	10,229.9	11,041.9	11,645.3
Ships, boats and floating structures	9,699.2	n.a.	n.a.
Miscellaneous manufactured articles.	11,247.0	10,466.0	12,063.4
Total (incl. others)	150,439.1	162,470.5	193,817.4

* Figures exclude trade with the Democratic People's Republic of Korea (US $ million): Total imports 152.4 in 2000, 176.2 in 2001, 271.6 in 2002; Total exports 272.8 in 2000, 226.8 in 2001, 370.2 in 2002.

† Data on parts exclude tyres, engines and electrical parts.

Source: Korea Trade Information Services.

PRINCIPAL TRADING PARTNERS
(US $ million)*

Imports c.i.f.	2001	2002	2003
Australia.	5,534.1	5,973.4	5,915.7
Canada	1,821.3	1,845.5	1,860.2
China, People's Republic . . .	13,302.7	17,399.8	21,909.1
France	2,092.3	2,116.2	2,220.3
Germany.	4,473.4	5,472.4	6,821.7
Hong Kong	1,227.6	1,695.0	2,735.4
Indonesia	4,473.5	4,723.4	5,212.3
Iran	2,099.3	1,335.4	1,844.7
Italy	1,787.5	2,274.2	2,382.2
Japan.	26,633.4	29,856.2	36,313.1
Kuwait	2,250.7	2,230.4	3,191.1
Malaysia	4,125.0	4,041.4	4,249.1
Oman.	2,310.9	1,895.9	2,322.8
Philippines	1,819.0	1,867.4	1,964.0
Qatar	2,572.1	2,173.0	3,139.8
Russia	1,929.5	2,217.6	2,521.8
Saudi Arabia	8,058.0	7,550.8	9,267.8
Singapore	3,011.5	3,430.1	4,089.8
Taiwan	4,301.4	4,832.0	5,879.6
Thailand	1,589.2	1,702.5	1,897.7
United Arab Emirates . . .	4,633.0	4,210.2	5,756.5
United Kingdom	2,353.5	2,437.4	2,703.3
USA	22,376.2	23,008.6	24,814.1
Total (incl. others)	141,097.8	152,126.2	178,826.7

Exports f.o.b.	2001	2002	2003
Australia	2,173.2	2,339.6	3,272.1
Brazil	1,611.2	1,247.2	1,137.4
Canada	2,035.7	2,340.6	2,682.1
China, People's Republic	18,190.2	23,753.6	35,109.7
France	1,541.2	1,629.0	1,755.4
Germany	4,321.8	4,287.2	5,603.3
Greece	1,222.4	1,653.6	1,765.0
Hong Kong	9,451.7	10,145.5	14,653.7
India	1,407.7	1,384.1	2,853.0
Indonesia	3,279.8	3,144.8	3,377.6
Italy	2,063.3	2,217.3	2,560.6
Japan	16,505.8	15,143.2	17,276.1
Malaysia	2,628.0	3,218.3	3,851.8
Mexico	2,148.9	2,230.8	2,455.0
Netherlands	2,532.1	2,567.2	2,535.0
Panama	1,719.0	1,184.4	1,252.3
Philippines	2,535.4	2,950.0	2,975.0
Singapore	4,079.6	4,221.6	4,636.0
Spain	1,518.2	1,552.5	2,015.8
Taiwan	5,835.3	6,631.6	7,044.6
Thailand	1,848.2	2,335.4	2,523.8
United Arab Emirates	2,169.1	2,268.8	2,207.6
United Kingdom	3,490.0	4,255.5	4,094.3
USA	31,210.8	32,780.2	34,219.4
Viet Nam	1,731.7	2,240.2	2,561.2
Total (incl. others)	150,439.1	162,470.5	193,817.4

* Excluding trade with the Democratic People's Republic of Korea.

Source: Korea Trade Information Services.

Transport

RAILWAYS
(traffic)

	2000	2001	2002
Passengers carried ('000)	814,472	912,149	983,266
Passenger-km (million)	27,787	29,172	28,743
Freight ('000 metric tons)	45,240	45,122	45,733
Freight ton-km (million)	10,803	10,492	10,784

ROAD TRAFFIC
(motor vehicles in use at 31 December)

	2001	2002	2003
Passenger cars	8,889,327	9,737,428	10,278,923
Goods vehicles	2,728,405	2,894,412	3,016,407
Buses and coaches	1,257,008	1,275,319	1,246,629
Motorcycles and mopeds	1,700,600	1,708,457	1,730,193

SHIPPING

Merchant Fleet
(registered at 31 December)

	2000	2001	2002
Number of vessels	2,502	2,426	2,532
Total displacement ('000 grt)	6,199.8	6,395.0	7,049.7

Source: Lloyd's Register-Fairplay, *World Fleet Statistics*.

Sea-borne Freight Traffic
('000 metric tons)*

	2000	2001	2002
Goods loaded	282,768	315,297	290,951
Goods unloaded	550,811	571,076	575,209

* Including coastwise traffic loaded and unloaded.

CIVIL AVIATION

	2000	2001	2002
Passengers ('000)	41,967	42,162	43,965
Passenger-km (million)	83,955	84,544	92,175
Freight ('000 metric tons)	2,383	2,295	2,510
Freight ton-km (million)	12,430	11,327	12,606

Tourism

FOREIGN VISITOR ARRIVALS*†

Country of nationality	2000	2001	2002
China, People's Republic	442,794	482,227	539,466
Hong Kong	200,874	204,959	179,299
Japan	2,472,054	2,377,321	2,320,837
Philippines	248,737	210,975	215,848
Russia	155,392	134,727	165,341
Taiwan	127,120	129,410	136,921
USA	458,617	426,817	459,362
Total (incl. others)	5,321,792	5,147,204	5,347,468

* Including same-day visitors (excursionists) and crew members from ships.

† Including Korean nationals resident abroad.

Source: Korean National Tourism Organization.

Receipts from tourism (US $ million): 6,811.3 in 2000; 6,373.2 in 2001; 5,276.9 (estimate) in 2002 (Source: Bank of Korea).

Communications Media

	2000	2001	2002
Television receivers ('000 in use)	17,229	n.a.	n.a.
Telephones ('000 main lines in use)	21,931.7	22,724.7	23,257.0
Mobile cellular telephones ('000 subscribers)	26,816.4	29,045.6	32,342.0
Personal computers ('000 in use)	11,255	12,000	26,458
Internet users ('000)	19,040	24,380	26,270
Book production:			
titles	25,632	25,146	27,113
copies ('000)	68,408	74,914	81,513

1996: Facsimile machines (estimate, '000 in use): 400; Daily newspapers: Number 60, Circulation ('000 copies) 17,700 (estimate).

1997: Radio receivers ('000 in use) 47,500.

Sources: mainly UNESCO, *Statistical Yearbook*; UN, *Statistical Yearbook*; International Telecommunication Union.

Education

(2002)

	Institutions	Teachers	Pupils
Kindergarten	8,343	29,673	550,256
Primary schools	5,384	147,497	4,138,366
Middle schools	2,809	95,283	1,841,030
High schools	1,995	114,304	1,795,509
Junior vocational colleges	159	12,156	963,129
Teachers' colleges	11	721	23,259
Universities and colleges	163	44,177	1,771,738
Graduate schools	945	n.a.	262,867

Adult literacy rate (UNESCO estimates): 97.9% (males 99.2%; females 96.6%) in 2001 (Source: UN Development Programme, *Human Development Report*).

Directory

Note: from 2001 the romanization of place-names in South Korea was in the process of change, to be completed by 2005. Transliteration of names of people and corporations was to remain unchanged for the time being.

The Constitution

The Constitution of the Sixth Republic (Ninth Amendment) was approved by national referendum on 29 October 1987. It came into effect on 25 February 1988. The main provisions are summarized below:

THE EXECUTIVE

The President

The President shall be elected by universal, equal, direct and secret ballot of the people for one term of five years. Re-election of the President is prohibited. In times of national emergency and under certain conditions the President may issue emergency orders and take emergency action with regard to budgetary and economic matters. The President shall notify the National Assembly of these measures and obtain its concurrence, or they shall lose effect. He may, in times of war, armed conflict or similar national emergency, declare martial law in accordance with the provisions of law. He shall lift the emergency measures and martial law when the National Assembly so requests with the concurrence of a majority of the members. The President may not dissolve the National Assembly. He is authorized to take directly to the people important issues through national referendums. The President shall appoint the Prime Minister (with the consent of the National Assembly) and other public officials.

The State Council

The State Council shall be composed of the President, the Prime Minister and no more than 30 and no fewer than 15 others appointed by the President (on the recommendation of the Prime Minister), and shall deliberate on policies that fall within the power of the executive. No member of the armed forces shall be a member of the Council, unless retired from active duty.

The Board of Audit and Inspection

The Board of Audit and Inspection shall be established under the President to inspect the closing of accounts of revenue and expenditures, the accounts of the State and other organizations as prescribed by law, and to inspect the administrative functions of the executive agencies and public officials. It shall be composed of no fewer than five and no more than 11 members, including the Chairman. The Chairman shall be appointed by the President with the consent of the National Assembly, and the members by the President on the recommendation of the Chairman. Appointments shall be for four years and members may be reappointed only once.

THE NATIONAL ASSEMBLY

Legislative power shall be vested in the National Assembly. The Assembly shall be composed of not fewer than 200 members, a number determined by law, elected for four years by universal, equal, direct and secret ballot. The constituencies of members of the Assembly, proportional representation and other matters pertaining to the Assembly elections shall be determined by law. A regular session shall be held once a year and extraordinary sessions shall be convened upon requests of the President or one-quarter of the Assembly's members. The period of regular sessions shall not exceed 100 days and of extraordinary sessions 30 days. The Assembly has the power to recommend to the President the removal of the Prime Minister or any other Minister. The Assembly shall have the authority to pass a motion for the impeachment of the President or any other public official, and may inspect or investigate state affairs, under procedures to be established by law.

THE CONSTITUTIONAL COURT

The Constitutional Court shall be composed of nine members appointed by the President, three of whom shall be appointed from persons selected by the National Assembly and three from persons nominated by the Chief Justice. The term of office shall be six years. It shall pass judgment upon the constitutionality of laws upon the request of the courts, matters of impeachment and the dissolution of political parties. In these judgments the concurrence of six members or more shall be required.

THE JUDICIARY

The courts shall be composed of the Supreme Court, which is the highest court of the State, and other courts at specified levels (for further details, see section on Judicial System). The Chief Justice and justices of the Supreme Court are appointed by the President, subject to the consent of the National Assembly. When the constitutionality of a law is a prerequisite to a trial, the Court shall request a decision of the Constitutional Court. The Supreme Court shall have the power to pass judgment upon the constitutionality or legality of administrative decrees, and shall have final appellate jurisdiction over military tribunals. No judge shall be removed from office except following impeachment or a sentence of imprisonment.

ELECTION MANAGEMENT

Election Commissions shall be established for the purpose of fair management of elections and national referendums. The National Election Commission shall be composed of three members appointed by the President, three appointed by the National Assembly and three appointed by the Chief Justice of the Supreme Court. Their term of office is six years, and they may not be expelled from office except following impeachment or a sentence of imprisonment.

POLITICAL PARTIES

The establishment of political parties shall be free and the plural party system guaranteed. However, a political party whose aims or activities are contrary to the basic democratic order may be dissolved by the Constitutional Court.

AMENDMENTS

A motion to amend the Constitution shall be proposed by the President or by a majority of the total number of members of the National Assembly. Amendments extending the President's term of office or permitting the re-election of the President shall not be effective for the President in office at the time of the proposal. Proposed amendments to the Constitution shall be put before the public by the President for 20 days or more. Within 60 days of the public announcement, the National Assembly shall decide upon the proposed amendments, which require a two-thirds majority of the National Assembly. They shall then be submitted to a national referendum not later than 30 days after passage by the National Assembly and shall be determined by more than one-half of votes cast by more than one-half of voters eligible to vote in elections for members of the National Assembly. If these conditions are fulfilled, the proposed amendments shall be finalized and the President shall promulgate them without delay.

FUNDAMENTAL RIGHTS

Under the Constitution all citizens are equal before the law. The right of habeas corpus is guaranteed. Freedom of speech, press, assembly and association are guaranteed, as are freedom of choice of residence and occupation. No state religion is to be recognized and freedom of conscience and religion is guaranteed. Citizens are protected against retrospective legislation, and may not be punished without due process of law.

Rights and freedoms may be restricted by law when this is deemed necessary for the maintenance of national security, order or public welfare. When such restrictions are imposed, no essential aspect of the right or freedom in question may be violated.

GENERAL PROVISIONS

Peaceful unification of the Korean peninsula, on the principles of liberal democracy, is the prime national aspiration. The Constitution mandates the State to establish and implement a policy of unification. The Constitution expressly stipulates that the armed forces must maintain political neutrality at all times.

The Government

HEAD OF STATE

President: ROH MOO-HYUN (took office 25 February 2003; suspended 12 March 2004).

STATE COUNCIL
(April 2004)

Prime Minister: GOH KUN (appointed acting Head of State 12 March 2004).

Deputy Prime Minister for Finance and the Economy: LEE HUN-JAI.

Deputy Prime Minister for Education and Human Resources Development: AHN BYUNG-YOUNG.

Minister of Unification: JEONG SE-HYUN.

Minister of Foreign Affairs and Trade: BAN KI-MOON.

Minister of Justice: KANG GUM-SIL.

Minister of National Defence: Gen. (retd) CHO YOUNG-KIL.

Minister of Government Administration and Home Affairs: HUH SUNG-KWAN.

Minister of Science and Technology: OH MYUNG.

Minister of Culture and Tourism: LEE CHANG-DONG.

Minister of Agriculture and Forestry: HUH SANG-MAN.

Minister of Commerce, Industry and Energy: LEE HEE-BEOM.

Minister of Information and Communication: CHIN DAE-JAE.

Minister of Health and Welfare: KIM HWA-JOONG.

Minister of the Environment: KWAK KYUL-HO.

Minister of Labour: KIM DAE-HWAN.

Minister of Gender Equality: JI EUN-HEE.

Minister of Construction and Transportation: KANG DONG-SUK.

Minister of Maritime Affairs and Fisheries: CHANG SEUNG-WOO.

Minister of Planning and Budget: KIM BYUNG-IL.

Chairman of the Civil Service Commission: Dr CHO CHANG-HYUN.

Chairman of the Financial Supervisory Commission: LEE JUNG-JAE.

Minister of Government Policy Co-ordination: HAN DUCK-SOO.

Minister of the Government Information Agency: JOUNG SOON-KYUN.

Chairman of the Korea Independent Commission Against Corruption: LEE NAM-JOO.

MINISTRIES

Office of the President: Chong Wa Dae (The Blue House), 1, Sejong-no, Jongno-gu, Seoul; tel. (2) 770-0055; fax (2) 770-0344; e-mail president@cwd.go.kr; internet www.bluehouse.go.kr.

Office of the Prime Minister: 77, Sejong-no, Jongno-gu, Seoul; tel. (2) 737-0094; fax (2) 739-5830; internet www.opm.go.kr.

Ministry of Agriculture and Forestry: 1, Jungang-dong, Gwacheon City, Gyeonggi Prov.; tel. (2) 503-7200; fax (2) 503-7238; internet www.maf.go.kr.

Ministry of Commerce, Industry and Energy: 1, Jungang-dong, Gwacheon City, Gyeonggi Prov.; tel. (2) 503-7171; fax (2) 503-3142; internet www.mocie.go.kr.

Ministry of Construction and Transportation: 1, Jungang-dong, Gwacheon City, Gyeonggi Prov. 427–712; tel. (2) 503-9405; fax (2) 503-9408; e-mail webmaster@moct.go.kr; internet www.moct.go.kr.

Ministry of Culture and Tourism: 82-1, Sejong-no, Jongno-gu, Seoul 110-050; tel. (2) 7704-9114; fax (2) 3704-9119; internet www.mct.go.kr.

Ministry of Education and Human Resources Development: 77, 1-ga, Sejong-no, Jongno-gu, Seoul 110-760; tel. (2) 720-3404; fax (2) 720-1501; internet www.moe.go.kr.

Ministry of Environment: 1, Jungang-dong, Gwacheon City, Gyeonggi Prov.; tel. (2) 2110-6576; fax (2) 504-9277; internet www.moenv.go.kr.

Ministry of Finance and the Economy: 1, Jungang-dong, Gwacheon City, Gyeonggi Prov.; tel. (2) 503-9032; fax (2) 503-9033; internet www.mofe.go.kr.

Ministry of Foreign Affairs and Trade: 77, 1-ga, Sejong-no, Jongno-gu, Seoul; tel. (2) 3703-2555; fax (2) 720-2686; internet www.mofat.go.kr.

Ministry of Gender Equality: 520-3, Banpo-dong, Seocho-gu, Seoul 137-756; tel. (2) 2106-5000; fax (2) 2106-5145; internet www.moge.go.kr.

Ministry of Government Administration and Home Affairs: 77-6, Sejong-no, Jongno-gu, Seoul; tel. (2) 3703-4110; fax (2) 3703-5501; internet www.mogaha.go.kr.

Ministry of Health and Welfare: 1, Jungang-dong, Gwacheon City, Gyeonggi Prov. 427-760; tel. (2) 503-7505; fax (2) 503-7568; internet www.mohw.go.kr.

Ministry of Information and Communication: 100, Sejong-no, Jongno-gu, Seoul 110-777; tel. (2) 750-2000; fax (2) 750-2915; internet www.mic.go.kr.

Ministry of Justice: 1, Jungang-dong, Gwacheon City, Gyeonggi Prov.; tel. (2) 503-7012; fax (2) 504-3337; internet www.moj.go.kr.

Ministry of Labour: 1, Jungang-dong, Gwacheon City, Gyeonggi Prov.; tel. (2) 503-9713; fax (2) 503-8862; internet www.molab.go.kr.

Ministry of Maritime Affairs and Fisheries: 139 Chungjeong-no 3, Seodaemun-gu, Seoul 120-715; tel. (2) 3148-6040; fax (2) 3148-6044; internet www.momaf.go.kr.

Ministry of National Defence: 1, 3-ga, Yonsan-dong, Yeongsan-gu, Seoul; tel. (2) 795-0071; fax (2) 796-0369; internet www.mnd.go.kr.

Ministry of Planning and Budget: 520-3, Banpo-dong, Seocho-gu, Seoul 137-756; tel. (2) 3480-7716; fax (2) 3480-7600; internet www.mpb.go.kr.

Ministry of Science and Technology: 1, Jungang-dong, Gwacheon City, Gyeonggi Prov.; tel. (2) 503-7619; fax (2) 503-7673; internet www.most.go.kr.

Ministry of Unification: 77-6, Sejong-no, Jongno-gu, Seoul 110-760; tel. (2) 720-2424; fax (2) 720-2149; internet www.unikorea.go.kr.

Civil Service Commission: Kolon Bldg, 35-34, Dongui-dong, Jongno-gu, Seoul 110-040; tel. (2) 3703-3633; fax (2) 3771-5027; internet www.csc.go.kr.

Financial Supervisory Commission: 27 Yoido-dong, Yeongdeungpo-gu, Seoul 150-743; tel. (2) 3771-5000; fax (2) 3771-5027; e-mail webmaster@fsc.go.kr; internet www.fsc.go.kr.

Korea Independent Commission Against Corruption: Seoul City Tower, 581, 5-ga, Namdaemun-no, Jung-gu, Seoul 100-095; tel. (2) 2126-0114; fax (2) 2126-0310; internet www.kicac.go.kr.

President and Legislature

PRESIDENT

Election, 19 December 2002

Candidate	Votes	% of total
Roh Moo-Hyun	12,014,277	48.9
Lee Hoi-Chang	11,443,297	46.6
Kwon Young-Gil	957,148	3.9
Lee Han-Dong.	74,027	0.3
Kim Gil-Su.	51,104	0.2
Kim Yeong-Kyu	22,063	0.1
Total	**24,561,916**	**100.0**

KUK HOE
(National Assembly)

1 Yeouido-dong, Yeongdeungpo-gu, Seoul; tel. (2) 788-2786; fax (2) 788-3375; internet www.assembly.go.kr.

Speaker: to be appointed.

General Election, 15 April 2004

Party	Elected representatives	Proportional representatives	Total seats
Uri Party	129	23	152
Grand National Party	100	21	121
Democratic Labour Party	2	8	10
Millennium Democratic Party	5	4	9
United Liberal Democrats	4	—	4
Others	3	—	3
Total	**243**	**56**	**299**

Political Organizations

Democratic Labour Party (DLP): Hanyang Bldg, 14-31 Yoido-dong, Yeongdeungpo-gu, Seoul 150-748; tel. (2) 761-1333; fax (2) 761-4115; e-mail inter@kdlp.org; internet www.kdlp.org; f. 2000; Pres. KWON YOUNG-GIL.

Grand National Party (GNP) (Hannara Party): 17-7, Yeouido-dong, Yeongdeungpo-gu, Seoul 150-010; tel. (2) 3786-3373; fax (2)

3786-3610; internet www.hannara.or.kr; f. 1997 by merger of Democratic Party and New Korea Party; Chair. PARK GEUN-HYE.

Millennium Democratic Party (MDP): 15, Gisan Bldg, Yeongdeungpo-gu, Seoul; tel. (2) 784-7007; fax (2) 784-6070; internet www.minjoo.or.kr; f. 2000 following dissolution of National Congress for New Politics (f. 1995); Chair. CHOUGH SOON-HYUNG; Rep. CHOO MI-AE.

United Liberal Democrats (ULD): Insan Bldg, 103-4, Shinsu-dong, Mapo-gu, Seoul 121-110; tel. (2) 701-3355; fax (2) 707-1637; internet www.jamin.or.kr; f. 1995 by fmr mems of the Democratic Liberal Party; Pres. (vacant).

Uri Party: c/o National Assembly, 1 Yeouido-dong, Yeongdeungpo-gu, Seoul; Chair. CHUNG DONG-YOUNG ; party founded Nov. 2003 by defectors from the MDP.

Civic groups play an increasingly significant role in South Korean politics. These include: the People's Solidarity for Participatory Democracy (Dir Jang Hasung); the Citizens' Coalition for Economic Justice; and the Citizens' Alliance for Political Reform (Leader Kim Sok-Su).

Diplomatic Representation

EMBASSIES IN THE REPUBLIC OF KOREA

Algeria: 2-6, Itaewon 2-dong, Yeongsan-gu, Seoul 140-202; tel. (2) 794-5034; fax (2) 792-7845; e-mail sifdja01@kornet.net; internet www.algerianemb.or.kr; Ambassador AHMED BOUTACHE.

Argentina: Chun Woo Bldg, 5th Floor, 534 Itaewon-dong, Yeongsan-gu, Seoul 140-861; tel. (2) 793-4062; fax (2) 792-5820; Ambassador RODOLFO IGNACIO RODRÍGUEZ.

Australia: Kyobo Bldg, 11th Floor, 1, 1-ga, Jongno-gu, Seoul 110-714; tel. (2) 2003-0100; fax (2) 722-9264; internet www.australia.or.kr; Ambassador COLIN STUART HESELTINE.

Austria: Kyobo Bldg, Rm 1913, 1-1, 1-ga, Jongno, Jongno-gu, Seoul 110-714; tel. (2) 732-9071; fax (2) 739-9486; e-mail seoul-ob@bmaa.gv.at; internet www.austria.or.kr; Ambassador Dr HELMUT BOECK.

Bangladesh: 7-18, Woo Sung Bldg, Dongbinggo-dong, Yeongsan-gu, Seoul; tel. (2) 796-4056; fax (2) 790-5313; e-mail dootrok@soback.kornet21.net; Ambassador HUMAYUN A. KAMAL.

Belarus: 432-1636 Sindang 2-dong, Jung-gu, Seoul; tel. (2) 2237-8171; fax (2) 2237-8174; e-mail consul_korea@belembassy.org; Ambassador ALYAKSANDR VIKTOROVICH SEMESHKO.

Belgium: 1-94, Dongbinggo-dong, Yeongsan-gu, Seoul 140-230; tel. (2) 749-0381; fax (2) 797-1688; e-mail seoul@diplobel.org; Ambassador KOENRAAD ROUVROY.

Brazil: Ihn Gallery Bldg, 4th and 5th Floors, 141 Palpan-dong, Jongno-gu, Seoul; tel. (2) 738-4970; fax (2) 738-4974; e-mail braseul@soback.kornet21.net; Ambassador PEDRO PAULO PINTO ASSUMPÇÃO.

Brunei: Gwanghwamun Bldg, 7th Floor, 211, Sejong-no, Jongnogu, Seoul 110-050; tel. (2) 399-3707; fax (2) 399-3709; e-mail kbnbd_seoul@yahoo.com; Ambassador Dato' ABD. RAHMAN HAMID.

Bulgaria: 723-42, Hannam 2-dong, Yeongsan-gu, Seoul 140-894; tel. (2) 794-8626; fax (2) 794-8627; e-mail ebdy1990@unitel.co.kr; Chargé d'affaires a.i. VALERY ARZHENTINSKI.

Cambodia: 657-162, Hannam-dong, Yeongsan-gu, Seoul 140–910; tel. (2) 3785-1041; fax (2) 3785-1040; e-mail camboemb@korea.com; Ambassador CHHEANG VUN.

Canada: Kolon Bldg, 10-11th Floors, 45, Mugyo-dong, Jung-gu, Seoul 100-662; tel. (2) 3455-6000; fax (2) 3455-6123; e-mail canada@cec.or.kr; internet www.korea.gc.ca; Ambassador DENIS COMEAU.

Chile: Heungkuk Life Insurance Bldg, 14th Floor, 226 Sinmun-no 1-ga, Jongno-gu, Seoul; tel. (2) 2122-2600; fax (2) 2122-2601; e-mail echilekr@unitelkr; Ambassador FERNANDO SCHMIDT.

China, People's Republic: 54, Hyoja-dong, Jongno-gu, Seoul; tel. (2) 738-1038; fax (2) 738-1077; Ambassador LI BIN.

Colombia: Kyobo Bldg, 13th Floor, 1-ga, Jongno, Jongno-gu, Seoul; tel. (2) 720-1369; fax (2) 725-6959; Ambassador Dr MIGUEL DURÁN ORDÓÑEZ.

Congo, Democratic Republic: 702, Daewoo Complex Bldg, 167 Naesu-dong, Jongno-gu, Seoul; tel. (2) 6722-7958; fax (2) 6722-7998; e-mail congokrembassy@yahoo.com; Ambassador N. CHRISTOPHE NGWEY.

Côte d'Ivoire: Chungam Bldg, 2nd Floor, 794-4, Hannam-dong, Yeongsan-gu, Seoul; tel. (2) 3785-0561; fax (2) 3785-0564; e-mail abenikof@hotmail.com; Ambassador HONORAT ABENI KOFFI.

Czech Republic: 1-121, 2-ga, Sinmun-no, Jongno-gu, Seoul 110-062; tel. (2) 725-6765; fax (2) 734-6452; e-mail seoul@embassy.mzv.cz; internet www.mzv.cz/seoul; Ambassador IVAN HOTĚK.

Denmark: Namsong Bldg, 5th Floor, 260-199, Itaewon-dong, Yeongsan-gu, Seoul 140-200; tel. (2) 795-4187; fax (2) 796-0986; e-mail selamb@um.dk; Ambassador LEIF DONDE.

Dominican Republic: Taepyeong-no Bldg, 19th Floor, 2-ga, 310 Taepyeong-no, Jung-gu, Seoul; tel. (2) 756-3513; fax (2) 756-3514; Ambassador JOSÉ M. NUNEZ.

Ecuador: Korea First Bldg, 19th Floor, 100 Gongpyeong-dong, Jongno-gu, Seoul; tel. (2) 739-2401; fax (2) 739-2355; e-mail mecuadorcor1@kornet.net; Ambassador FRANKLIN ESPINOSA.

Egypt: 46-1, Hannam-dong, Yeongsan-gu, Seoul; tel. (2) 749-0787; fax (2) 795-2588; internet www.mfg.gov.eg; Ambassador AMR HELMY.

El Salvador: Samsung Life Insurance Bldg, 20th Floor, Taepyeong-no 2-ga, Jung-gu, Seoul 100-716; tel. (2) 753-3432; fax (2) 753-3456; e-mail koembsal@hananet.net; Ambassador ALFREDO FRANCISCO UNGO.

Finland: Kyobo Bldg, Suite 1602, 1-1, 1-ga, Jongno, Jongno-gu, Seoul 110-714; tel. (2) 732-6737; fax (2) 723-4969; e-mail sanomat.seo@formin.fi; internet www.finlandembassy.or.kr; Ambassador LAURI KORPINEN.

France: 30, Hap-dong, Seodaemun-gu, Seoul 120-030; tel. (2) 3149–4300; fax (2) 3149–4328; e-mail ambfraco@elim.net; internet www.ambafrance-kr.org; Ambassador FRANÇOIS DESCOUEYTE.

Gabon: Yoosung Bldg, 4th Floor, 738-20, Hannam-dong, Yeongsan-gu, Seoul; tel. (2) 793-9575; fax (2) 793-9574; e-mail amgabsel@unitel.co.kr; Ambassador EMMANUEL ISSOZE-NGONDET.

Germany: 308-5, Dongbinggo-dong, Yeongsan-gu, Seoul 140-816; tel. (2) 748-4114; fax (2) 748-4161; e-mail dboseoul@kornet.net; internet www.gembassy.or.kr; Ambassador MICHAEL GEIER.

Ghana: 5-4, Hannam-dong, Yeongsan-gu, Seoul (CPOB 3887); tel. (2) 3785-1427; fax (2) 3785-1428; e-mail ghana3@kornet.net; Ambassador EDWARD OBENG KUFUOR.

Greece: Hanwha Bldg, 27th Floor, 1, Janggyo-dong, Jung-gu, Seoul 100-797; tel. (2) 729-1401; fax (2) 729-1402; Ambassador GEORGE ASSIMACOPOULOS.

Guatemala: 614, Lotte Hotel, 1, Sogong-dong, Jung-gu, Seoul 100-635; tel. (2) 771-7582; fax (2) 771-7584; e-mail embcorea@minex.gob.gt; Ambassador EMILIO R. MALDONADO.

Holy See: 2, Gungjeong-dong, Jongno-gu, Seoul (Apostolic Nunciature); tel. (2) 736-5725; fax (2) 739-2310; e-mail nunseoul@kornet.net; Apostolic Nuncio Most Rev. GIOVANNI BATTISTA MORANDINI (Titular Archbishop of Numida).

Honduras: Jongno Tower Bldg, 2nd Floor, 6, Jongno 2-ga, Jongno-gu, Seoul 110-160; tel. (2) 738-8402; fax (2) 738-8403; e-mail hondseul@kornet.net; Ambassador RENE FRANCISCO UMANA CHINCHILLA.

Hungary: 1-103, Dongbinggo-dong, Yeongsan-gu, Seoul 140-230; tel. (2) 792-2105; fax (2) 792-2109; e-mail huembsel@kornet.net; Ambassador Dr ISTVÁN TORZSA.

India: 37-3, Hannam-dong, Yeongsan-gu, CPOB 3466, Seoul 140-210; tel. (2) 798-4257; fax (2) 796-9534; e-mail eoiseoul@soback.kornet.nm.kr; Chargé d'affaires MOHINDER SINGH GROVER.

Indonesia: 55, Yeouido-dong, Yeongdeungpo-gu, Seoul 150-010; tel. (2) 783-5675; fax (2) 780-4280; e-mail bidpen@soback.kornet21.net; Ambassador ABDUL GHANI.

Iran: 726-126, Hannam-dong, Yeongsan-gu, Seoul; tel. (2) 793-7751; fax (2) 792-7052; e-mail iranssy@chollian.net; internet www.mfa.gov.ir; Ambassador MOHSEN TALAE'I.

Ireland: Daehan Fire and Marine Insurance Bldg, 15th Floor, 51-1, Namchang-dong, Jung-gu, Seoul; tel. (2) 774-6455; fax (2) 774-6458; e-mail hibernia@bora.dacom.co.kr; Ambassador PAUL MURRAY.

Israel: Dae-kong Bldg, 15th Floor, 823-21, Yeoksam-dong, Gangnam-gu, Seoul 135-080; tel. (2) 564-3448; fax (2) 564-3449; e-mail israeli@chollian.net; internet www.israelemb.or.kr; Ambassador UZI MANOR.

Italy: 1-398, Hannam-dong, Yeongsan-gu, Seoul 140-210; tel. (2) 796-0491; fax (2) 797-5560; e-mail ambseoul@italyemb.or.kr; Ambassador FRANCESCO RAUSI.

Japan: 18-11, Junghak-dong, Jongno-gu, Seoul; tel. (2) 2170-5200; fax (2) 734-4528; Ambassador TOSHIYUKI TAKANO.

Kazakhstan: 13-10, Seongbuk-dong, Seongbuk-gu, Seoul; tel. (2) 744-9714; fax (2) 744-9760; e-mail kazkor@chollian.net; Ambassador BORLAT K. NURGALIEV.

Kuwait: 309-15, Dongbinggo-dong, Yeongsan-gu, Seoul; tel. (2) 749-3688; fax (2) 749-3687; Ambassador FAWZI AL-JASEM.

Laos: 657-93, Hannam-dong, Yeongsan-gu, Seoul; tel. (2) 796-1713; fax (2) 796-1771; e-mail laoseoul@korea.com; Ambassador THONGSAVATH PRASEUTH.

Lebanon: 1-48, Dongbinggo-dong, Yeongsan-gu, Seoul 140-230; tel. (2) 794-6482; fax (2) 794-6485; e-mail emleb@nuri.net; Ambassador MOHAMAD NASRAT EL-ASSAAD.

Libya: 4-5, Hannam-dong, Yeongsan-gu, Seoul; tel. (2) 797-6001; fax (2) 797-6007; e-mail libyaemb@kornet.net; Sec. of People's Bureau AHMED MOHAMED TABULI.

Malaysia: 4-1, Hannam-dong, Yeongsan-gu, Seoul 140-210; tel. (2) 794-0349; fax (2) 794-5488; e-mail mwseoul@kornet.net; Ambassador Dato' VYRAMUTTU YOOGALINGAM.

Mexico: 33-6, Hannam 1-dong, Yeongsan-gu, Seoul 140-885; tel. (2) 798-1694; fax (2) 790-0939; Ambassador ROGELIO GRANGUILLHOME.

Mongolia: 33-5, Hannam-dong, Yeongsan-gu, Seoul; tel. (2) 794-1350; fax (2) 794-7605; e-mail monemb@uriel.net; internet www.mongoliaemb.or.kr; Ambassador URJINLHUNDEV PERENLEYN.

Morocco: S-15, UN Village, 270-3, Hannam-dong, Yeongsan-gu, Seoul; tel. (2) 793-6249; fax (2) 792-8178; e-mail sifamase@bora.dacom.co.kr; internet www.moroccoemb.or.kr; Ambassador JAAFAR ALJ HAKIM.

Myanmar: 724-1, Hannam-dong, Yeongsan-gu, Seoul 140-210; tel. (2) 792-3341; fax (2) 796-5570; e-mail myanmare@ppp.kornet.net; Ambassador U NYO WIN.

Netherlands: Kyobo Bldg, 14th Floor, 1-ga, Jongno, Jongno-gu, Seoul 110-714; tel. (2) 737-9514; fax (2) 735-1321; e-mail seo@minbuza.nl; Ambassador RADINCK J. VAN VOLLENHOVEN.

New Zealand: Kyobo Bldg, 18th Floor, 1, 1-ga, Jongno, Jongno-gu, CPOB 1059, Seoul 100-610; tel. (2) 730-7794; fax (2) 737-4861; e-mail nzembsel@kornet.net; internet www.nzembassy.com/korea; Ambassador DAVID TAYLOR.

Nigeria: 310-19, Dongbinggo-dong, Yeongsan-gu, Seoul; tel. (2) 797-2370; fax (2) 796-1848; e-mail chancery@nigeriaembassy.or.kr; Ambassador ABBA A. JIJANI.

Norway: 258-8, Itaewon-dong, Yeongsan-gu, CPOB 355, Seoul 100-603; tel. (2) 795-6850; fax (2) 798-6072; e-mail emb.seoul@mfa.no; internet www.norway.or.kr; Ambassador ARILD BRAASTAD.

Oman: 309-3, Dongbinggo-dong, Yeongsan-gu, Seoul; tel. (2) 790-2431; fax (2) 790-2430; e-mail omanembs@ppp.kornet.nm.kr; Ambassador MOOSA HAMDAN AL-TAEE.

Pakistan: 124-13, Itaewon-dong, Yeongsan-gu, Seoul 140-200; tel. (2) 796-8252; fax (2) 796-0313; e-mail heamb@pakistan-korea-trade.org; internet www.pakistan-korea-trade.org; Ambassador SYED PERVEZ HUSSAIN.

Panama: Northgate Bldg, 6th Floor, 66, Jeokseon-dong, Jongno-gu, Seoul; tel. (2) 734-8610; fax (2) 734-8613; e-mail panaemba@kornet.net; Ambassador FÉLIX PÉREZ ESPINOSA.

Papua New Guinea: 36-1, Hannam 1-dong, Yeongsan-gu, Seoul; tel. (2) 798-9854; fax (2) 798-9856; e-mail pngembsl@ppp.kornet.nm.kr; Ambassador DAVID ANGGO.

Paraguay: SK Bldg, 2nd Floor, 99 Seorin-dong, Jongno-gu, Seoul 110-728; tel. (2) 730-8335; fax (2) 730-8336; e-mail pyemc2@hananet.net; Ambassador LUIS FERNANDO AVALOS GIMÉNEZ.

Peru: Namhan Bldg, 6th Floor, 76-42, Hannam-dong, Yeongsan-gu, Seoul 140-210; tel. (2) 793-5810; fax (2) 797-3736; e-mail ipruseul@uriel.net; Chargé d'affaires GUSTAVO LEMBCKE.

Philippines: Diplomatic Center, 9th Floor, 1376-1, Seocho 2-dong, Seocho-gu, Seoul; tel. (2) 577-6147; fax (2) 574-4286; e-mail phsk@soback.kornet.net; Ambassador JUANITO P. JARASA.

Poland: 70 Sagan-dong, Jongno-gu, Seoul; tel. (2) 723-9681; fax (2) 723-9680; e-mail embassy@polandseoul.org; internet www.polandseoul.org; Ambassador TADEUSZ CHOMICKI.

Portugal: Wonseo Bldg, 2nd Floor, 171, Wonseo-dong, Jongno-gu, Seoul; tel. (2) 3675-2251; fax (2) 3675-2250; e-mail ambport@chollian.net; Ambassador FERNANDO MACHADO.

Qatar: 309-5, Dongbinggo-dong, Yeongsan-gu, Seoul; tel. (2) 790-1308; fax (2) 790-1027; Ambassador ABDUL RAZZAK AL-ABDULKGHANI.

Romania: 1-42, UN Village, Hannam-dong, Yeongsan-gu, Seoul 140-210; tel. (2) 797-4924; fax (2) 794-3114; e-mail romemb@uriel.net; internet www.uriel.net/~romemb; Ambassador VALERIU ARTENI.

Russia: 34-16, Jeong-dong, Jung-gu, Seoul 100–120; tel. (2) 318-2116; fax (2) 754-0417; e-mail rusemb@uriel.net; internet www.russian-embassy.org; Ambassador TEYMURAZ. O. RAMISHVILI.

Saudi Arabia: 1-112, 2-ga, Sinmun-no, Jongno-gu, Seoul; tel. (2) 739-0631; fax (2) 732-3110; Ambassador SALEH BIN MANSOUR AL-RAJHY.

Singapore: Seoul Finance Bldg, 28th Floor, 84, 1-ga, Taepyeong-no, Jung-gu, Seoul 100-102; tel. (2) 774-2464; fax (2) 773-2465; e-mail singemb@unitel.co.kr; Ambassador CALVIN EU MUN HOO.

Slovakia: 802, Hyundai Liberty House, 258, Hannam-dong, Yeongsan-gu, Seoul 140-210; tel. (2) 794-3981; fax (2) 794-3982; e-mail slovakemb@yahoo.com; Chargé d'affaires a.i. JÁN CHLÁDEK.

South Africa: 1-37, Hannam-dong, Yeongsan-gu, Seoul 140-210; tel. (2) 792-4855; fax (2) 792-4856; e-mail sae@saembasy.dacom.net; internet saembassy.dacom.net; Ambassador SYDNEY BAFANA KUBHEKA.

Spain: 726-52 Hannam-dong, Yeongsan-gu, Seoul; tel. (2) 794-3581; fax (2) 796-8207; Ambassador ENRIQUE PANES CALPE.

Sri Lanka: Kyobo Bldg, Rm 2002, 1-1, 1-ga, Jongno, Jongno-gu, Seoul 110-714; tel. (2) 735-2966; fax (2) 737-9577; e-mail lankaemb@chollian.net; Ambassador K. C. LOGESWARAN.

Sudan: 653-24, Hannam-dong, Yeongsan-gu, Seoul; tel. (2) 793-8692; fax (2) 793-8693; Ambassador BABIKER A. KHALIFA.

Sweden: Seoul Central Bldg, 12th Floor, 136, Seorin-dong, Jongno-gu, KPO Box 1154, Seoul 110-110; tel. (2) 738-0846; fax (2) 733-1317; e-mail swedemb@swedemb.or.kr; internet www.swedemb.or.kr; Ambassador HARALD SANDBERG.

Switzerland: 32-10, Songwol-dong, Jongno-gu, Seoul 110-101; tel. (2) 739-9511; fax (2) 737-9392; e-mail swissemb@elim.net; internet www.elim.net/~swissemb/; Ambassador CHRISTIAN MUEHLETHALER.

Thailand: 653-7, Hannam-dong, Yeongsan-gu, Seoul; tel. (2) 795-3098; fax (2) 798-3448; e-mail rteseoul@elim.net; Ambassador SOMBOON SANGIAMBUT.

Tunisia: 1-17, Dongbinggo-dong, Yeongsan-gu, Seoul 140-809; tel. (2) 790-4334; fax (2) 790-4333; e-mail ambtnkor@kornet.net; Ambassador OTHMAN JERANDI.

Turkey: Vivien Corpn Bldg, 4th Floor, 4-52, Seobinggo-dong, Yeongsan-gu, Seoul; tel. (2) 794-0255; fax (2) 797-8546; e-mail tcseulbe@kornet.net; Ambassador SELIM KUNERALP.

Ukraine: 1-97, Dongbinggo-dong, Yeongsan-gu, Seoul; tel. (2) 790-5696; fax (2) 790-5697; e-mail secretary@ukrembrk.com; internet www.ukrembrk.com; Ambassador VOLODYMYR V. FURKALO.

United Arab Emirates: 5-5, Hannam-dong, Yeongsan-gu, Seoul; tel. (2) 790-3235; fax (2) 790-3238; Ambassador ABDULLA MOHAMED ALI AL-SHURAFA AL-HAMMADY.

United Kingdom: Taepyeongno 40, 4, Jeong-dong, Jung-gu, Seoul 100-120; tel. (2) 3210-5500; fax (2) 725-1738; e-mail bembassy@britain.or.kr; internet www.britain.or.kr; Ambassador WARWICK MORRIS.

USA: 32, Sejong-no, Jongno-gu, Seoul 110-710; tel. (2) 397-4114; fax (2) 735-3903; internet usembassy.state.gov/seoul/; Ambassador THOMAS C. HUBBARD.

Uruguay: Daewoo Bldg, 1025, 541, 5-ga, Namdaemun, Jung-gu, Seoul; tel. (2) 753-7893; fax (2) 777-4129; e-mail uruseul@kornet.net; Ambassador JULIO GIAMBRUNO.

Uzbekistan: Diplomatic Center, Rm. 701, 1376-1, Seocho 2-dong, Seocho-gu, Seoul; tel. (2) 574-6554; fax (2) 578-0576; Ambassador VITALI V. FEN.

Venezuela: 16th Floor, Korea First Bank Bldg, 100 Gongpyeong-dong, Jongno-gu, 110-702 Seoul; tel. (2) 732-1546; fax (2) 732-1548; e-mail emvesel@soback.kornet.net; internet www.venezuelaemb.or.kr; Ambassador GUILLERMO QUINTERO.

Viet Nam: 28-58, Samcheong-dong, Jongno-gu, Seoul 140-210; tel. (2) 738-2318; fax (2) 739-2064; e-mail vietnam@elim.net; Ambassador DUONG CHINH THUC.

Yemen: 11-444, Hannam-dong, Yeongsan-gu, Seoul 140-210; tel. (2) 792-9883; fax (2) 792-9885; e-mail yemensel@ppp.kornet21.net; internet www.gpc.org.ye; Chargé d'affaires YAHYA AHMED AL-WAZIR.

Judicial System

SUPREME COURT

The Supreme Court is the highest court, consisting of 14 Justices, including the Chief Justice. The Chief Justice is appointed by the President, with the consent of the National Assembly, for a term of six years. Other Justices of the Supreme Court are appointed for six years by the President on the recommendation of the Chief Justice. The appointment of the Justices of the Supreme Court, however, requires the consent of the National Assembly. The Chief Justice may not be reappointed. The court is empowered to receive and decide on appeals against decisions of the High Courts, the Patent Court, and the appellate panels of the District Courts or the Family Court in civil, criminal, administrative, patent and domestic relations cases. It is also authorized to act as the final tribunal to review decisions of courts-martial and to consider cases arising from presidential and parliamentary elections.

Chief Justice: CHOI JONG-YOUNG, 967, Seocho-dong, Seocho-gu, Seoul; tel. (2) 3480-1002; fax (2) 533-1911; internet www.scourt.go.kr.

Justices: KOH HYUN-CHUL, KIM YONG-DAM, CHO MOO-JEH, BYUN JAE-SEUNG, YOO JI-DAM, YOON JAE-SIK, LEE YONG-WOO, BAE KI-WON, KANG SHIN-WOOK, LEE KYU-HONG, LEE KANG-KOOK, SON JI-YOL, PARK JAE-YOON.

CONSTITUTIONAL COURT

The Constitutional Court is composed of nine adjudicators appointed by the President, of whom three are chosen from among persons selected by the National Assembly and three from persons nominated by the Chief Justice. The Court adjudicates the following matters: constitutionality of a law (when requested by the other courts); impeachment; dissolution of a political party; disputes between state agencies, or between state agencies and local governments; and petitions relating to the Constitution.

President: YUN YOUNG-CHUL, 83 Jae-dong, Jongno-gu, Seoul 110-250; tel. (2) 708-3456; fax (2) 708-3566; internet www.ccourt.go.kr.

HIGH COURTS

There are five courts, situated in Seoul, Daegu, Busan, Gwangju and Daejeon, with five chief, 78 presiding and 145 other judges. The courts have appellate jurisdiction in civil and criminal cases and can also pass judgment on administrative litigation against government decisions.

PATENT COURT

The Patent Court opened in Daejeon in March 1998, to deal with cases in which the decisions of the Intellectual Property Tribunal are challenged. The examination of the case is conducted by a judge, with the assistance of technical examiners.

DISTRICT COURTS

District Courts are established in 13 major cities; there are 13 chief, 241 presiding and 966 other judges. They exercise jurisdiction over all civil and criminal cases in the first instance.

MUNICIPAL COURTS

There are 103 Municipal Courts within the District Court system, dealing with small claims, minor criminal offences, and settlement cases.

FAMILY COURT

There is one Family Court, in Seoul, with a chief judge, four presiding judges and 16 other judges. The court has jurisdiction in domestic matters and juvenile delinquency.

ADMINISTRATIVE COURT

An Administrative Court opened in Seoul in March 1998, to deal with cases that are specified in the Administrative Litigation Act. The Court has jurisdiction over cities and counties adjacent to Seoul, and deals with administrative matters, including taxes, expropriations of land, labour and other general administrative matters. District Courts deal with administrative matters within their districts until the establishment of regional administrative courts is complete.

COURTS-MARTIAL

These exercise jurisdiction over all offences committed by armed forces personnel and civilian employees. They are also authorized to try civilians accused of military espionage or interference with the execution of military duties.

Religion

The traditional religions are Mahayana Buddhism, Confucianism and Chundo Kyo, a religion peculiar to Korea and combining elements of Shaman, Buddhist and Christian doctrines.

BUDDHISM

Korean Mahayana Buddhism has about 80 denominations. The Chogye-jong is the largest Buddhist order in Korea, having been introduced from China in AD 372. The Chogye Order accounts for almost two-thirds of all Korean Buddhists. In 1995 it had 2,426 out of 19,059 Buddhist temples and there were 12,470 monks.

Korean United Buddhist Association (KUBA): 46-19, Soosong-dong, Jongno-gu, Seoul 110-140; tel. (2) 732-4885; 28 mem. Buddhist orders; Pres. SONG WOL-JOO.

Won Buddhism

Won Buddhism combines elements of Buddhism and Confucianism. In 1995 there were 404 temples, 9,815 priests, and 86,823 believers.

CHRISTIANITY

National Council of Churches in Korea: Christian Bldg, Rm 706, 136-46, Yeonchi-dong, Jongno-gu, Seoul 110-736; tel. (2) 763-8427; fax (2) 744-6189; e-mail kncc@kncc.or.kr; internet www.kncc.or.kr; f. 1924 as National Christian Council; present name adopted 1946; eight mem. churches; Gen. Sec. Rev. PAIK DO-WOONG.

The Anglican Communion

South Korea has three Anglican dioceses, collectively forming the Anglican Church of Korea (founded as a separate province in April 1993), under its own Primate, the Most Rev. Matthew Chung Chul-Bum.

Bishop of Pusan (Busan): Rt Rev. JOSEPH DAE-YONG LEE, 455-2, Oncheon-1-dong, Dongnae-gu, Busan 607-061; tel. (51) 554-5742; fax (51) 553-9643; e-mail bpjoseph@hanmail.net.

Bishop of Seoul: Most Rev. MATTHEW CHUNG CHUL-BUM, 3, Jeong-dong, Jung-gu, Seoul 100-120; tel. (2) 738-6597; fax (2) 723-2640; e-mail bishop100@hosanna.net.

Bishop of Taejon (Daejeon): Rt Rev. PAUL YOON HWAN, 88-1, Sonhwa 2-dong, POB 22, Daejeon 300-600; tel. (42) 256-9987; fax (42) 255-8918.

The Roman Catholic Church

For ecclesiastical purposes, North and South Korea are nominally under a unified jurisdiction. South Korea comprises three archdioceses, 11 dioceses, and one military ordinate. At 31 December 2002 some 4,262,263 people were adherents of the Roman Catholic Church.

Bishops' Conference

Catholic Bishops' Conference of Korea, 643-1, Junggok-dong, Gwangjin-gu, Seoul 143-912; tel. (2) 460-7500; fax (2) 460-7505; e-mail cbck@cbck.or.kr; internet www.cbck.or.kr.

f. 1857; Pres. Most Rev. ANDREAS CHOI CHANG-MOU (Archbishop of Gwangju).

Archbishop of Kwangju (Gwangju): Most Rev. ANDREAS CHOI CHANG-MOU, Archdiocesan Office, 5-32, Im-dong, Buk-gu, Gwangju 500-868; tel. (62) 510-2838; fax (62) 525-6873; e-mail biseo@kjcatholic.or.kr.

Archbishop of Seoul: Most Rev. NICHOLAS CHEONG JIN-SUK, Archdiocesan Office, 1, 2-ga, Myeong-dong, Jung-gu, Seoul 100-022; tel. (2) 727-2114; fax (2) 773-1947; e-mail ao@seoul.catholic.or.kr.

Archbishop of Taegu (Daegu): Most Rev. PAUL RI MOON-HI, Archdiocesan Office, 225-1, Namsan 3-dong, Jung-gu, Daegu 700-804; tel. (53) 253-7011; fax (53) 253-9441; e-mail taegu@tgcatholic.or.kr.

Protestant Churches

Korean Methodist Church: 64-8, 1-ga, Taepyeong-no, Jung-gu, Seoul 100-101; KPO Box 285, Seoul 110-602; tel. (2) 399-4300; fax (2) 399-4307; e-mail bishop@kmcweb.or.kr; internet www.kmcweb.or.kr; f. 1885; 1,470,042 mems (2001); Bishop CHANG KWANG-YOUNG.

Presbyterian Church in the Republic of Korea (PROK): 1501, Ecumenical Bldg, 136-56, Yeonchi-dong, Jongno-gu, Seoul 110-470; tel. (2) 708-4021; fax (2) 708-4027; e-mail prok3000@chollian.net; internet www.prok.org; f. 1953; 332,915 mems (2001); Gen. Sec. Rev. Dr KIM JONG-MOO.

Presbyterian Church of Korea (PCK): Korean Church Centennial Memorial Bldg; 135, Yeochi-dong, Jongno-gu, Seoul 110-470; tel. (2) 741-4350; fax (2) 766-2427; e-mail thepck@pck.or.kr; internet www.pck.or.kr; 2,328,413 mems (2001); Moderator Rev. CHOI BYUNG-GON; Gen. Sec. Rev. Dr. KIM SANG-HAK.

There are some 160 other Protestant denominations in the country, including the Korea Baptist Convention and the Korea Evangelical Church.

CHUNDO KYO

A religion indigenous and unique to Korea, Chundo Kyo combines elements of Shaman, Buddhist, and Christian doctrines. In 1995 there were 274 temples, 5,597 priests, and 28,184 believers.

CONFUCIANISM

In 1995 there were 730 temples, 31,833 priests, and 210,927 believers.

TAEJONG GYO

Taejong Gyo is Korea's oldest religion, dating back 4,000 years, and comprising beliefs in the national foundation myth, and the triune god, Hanul. By the 15th century the religion had largely disappeared, but began a revival in the late 19th century. In 1995 there were 103 temples, 346 priests, and 7,603 believers.

The Press

NATIONAL DAILIES
(In Korean, unless otherwise indicated)

Chosun Ilbo: 61, 1-ga, Taepyeong-no, Jung-gu, Seoul 100-756; tel. (2) 724-5114; fax (2) 724-5059; internet www.chosun.com; f. 1920; morning, weekly and children's edns; independent; Pres. BANG SANG-HOON; Editor-in-Chief KIM DAE-JUNG; circ. 2,470,000.

Daily Sports Seoul: 25, 1-ga, Taepyeong-no, Jung-gu, Seoul; tel. (2) 721-5114; fax (2) 721-5396; internet www.seoul.co.kr; f. 1985; morning; sports and leisure; Pres. LEE HAN-SOO; Man. Editor SON CHU-WHAN.

Dong-A Ilbo: 139-1, 3-ga, Sejong-no, Jongno-gu, Seoul 100-715; tel. (2) 2020-0114; fax (2) 2020-1239; e-mail newsroom@donga.com; internet www.donga.com; f. 1920; morning; independent; Pres. KIM HAK-JOON; Editor-in-Chief LEE HYUN-NAK; circ. 2,150,000.

Han-Joong Daily News: 91-1, 2-ga, Myeong-dong, Jung-gu, Seoul; tel. (2) 776-2801; fax (2) 778-2803; Chinese.

Hankook Ilbo: 14, Junghak-dong, Jongno-gu, Seoul; tel. (2) 724-2114; fax (2) 724-2244; internet www.hankooki.com; f. 1954; morning; independent; Pres. CHANG CHAE-KEUN; Editor-in-Chief YOON KOOK-BYUNG; circ. 2,000,000.

Hankyoreh Shinmun (One Nation): 116-25, Gongdeok-dong, Mapo-gu, Seoul 121-020; tel. (2) 710-0114; fax (2) 710-0210; internet www.hani.co.kr; f. 1988; centre-left; Chair. KIM DOO-SHIK; Editor-in-Chief SUNG HAN-PYO; circ. 500,000.

Ilgan Sports (The Daily Sports): 14, Junghak-dong, Jongno-gu, Seoul 110-792; tel. (2) 724-2114; fax (2) 724-2299; internet www .dailysports.co.kr; morning; f. 1969; Pres. CHANG CHAE-KEUN; Editor KIM JIN-DONG; circ. 600,000.

Jeil Economic Daily: 24-5 Yeouido-dong, Yeongdeungpo-gu, Seoul; tel. (2) 792-1131; fax (2) 792-1130; f. 1988; morning; Pres. HWANG MYUNG-SOON; Editor LEE SOO-SAM.

JoongAng Ilbo (JoongAng Daily News): 7, Soonhwa-dong, Jung-gu, Seoul; tel. (2) 751-5114; fax (2) 751-9709; internet www.joins .com; f. 1965; morning; Pres. LEE JE-HOON; Man. Editor LEE CHANG-KYU; circ. 2,300,000.

Kookmin Ilbo: 12, Yeouido-dong, Yeongdeungpo-gu, Seoul; tel. (2) 781-9114; fax (2) 781-9781; internet www.kukminilbo.co.kr; Pres. CHA IL-SUK.

Korea Daily News: 25, 1-ga, Taepyeong-no, Jung-gu, Seoul; tel. (2) 2000-9000; fax (2) 2000-9659; internet www.kdaily.com; f. 1945; morning; independent; Publr and Pres. SON CHU-HWAN; Man. Editor LEE DONG-HWA; circ. 700,000.

Korea Economic Daily: 441, Junglim-dong, Jung-gu, Seoul 100-791; tel. (2) 360-4114; fax (2) 779-4447; internet www.ked.co.kr; f. 1964; morning; Pres. PARK YONG-JUNG; Man. Dir and Editor-in-Chief CHOI KYU-YOUNG.

The Korea Herald: 1-12, 3-ga, Hoehyeon-dong, Jung-gu, Seoul; tel. (2) 727-0114; fax (2) 727-0670; internet www.koreaherald.co.kr; f. 1953; morning; English; independent; Pres. KIM CHIN-OUK; Man. Editor MIN BYUNG-IL; circ. 150,000.

The Korea Times: 14, Junghak-dong, Jongno-gu, Seoul 110-792; tel. (2) 724-2114; fax (2) 732-4125; e-mail kt@koreatimes.co.kr; internet www.koreatimes.co.kr; f. 1950; morning; English; independent; Pres. YOON KOOK-BYUNG; Man. Ed. LEE SANG-SEOK; circ. 100,000.

Kyung-hyang Shinmun: 22, Jeong-dong, Jung-gu, Seoul; tel. (2) 3701-1114; fax (2) 737-6362; internet www.khan.co.kr; f. 1946; evening; independent; Pres. HONG SUNG-MAN; Editor KIM HI-JUNG; circ. 733,000.

Maeil Business Newspaper: 51-9, 1-ga, Bil-dong, Jung-gu, Seoul 100-728; tel. (2) 2000-2114; fax (2) 2269-6200; internet www.mk.co .kr; f. 1966; evening; economics and business; Pres. CHANG DAE-WHAN; Editor JANG BYUNG-CHANG; circ. 235,000.

Munhwa Ilbo: 68, 1-ga, Chungjeong-no, Jung-gu, Seoul 110-170; tel. (2) 3701-5114; fax (2) 722-8328; internet www.munhwa.co.kr; f. 1991; evening; Pres. NAM SI-UK; Editor-in-Chief KANG SIN-KU.

Naeway Economic Daily: 1-12, 3-ga, Hoehyon-dong, Jung-gu, Seoul 100; tel. (2) 727-0114; fax (2) 727-0661; internet www.naeway

.co.kr; f. 1973; morning; Pres. KIM CHIN-OUK; Man. Editor HAN DONG-HEE; circ. 300,000.

Segye Times: 63-1, 3-ga, Hangang-no, Yeongsan-gu, Seoul; tel. (2) 799-4114; fax (2) 799-4520; internet www.segyetimes.co.kr; f. 1989; morning; Pres. HWANG HWAN-CHAI; Editor MOK JUNG-GYUM.

Seoul Kyungje Shinmun: 19, Junghak-dong, Jongno-gu, Seoul 100; tel. (2) 724-2114; fax (2) 732-2140; internet www.sed.co.kr; f. 1960; morning; Pres. KIM YOUNG-LOUL; Man. Editor KIM SEO-WOONG; circ. 500,000.

Sports Chosun: 61, 1-ga, Taepyeong-no, Jung-gu, Seoul; tel. (2) 724-6114; fax (2) 724-6979; internet www.sportschosun.com; f. 1964; Publr BANG SANG-HOON; circ. 400,000.

LOCAL DAILIES

Cheju Daily News: 2324-6, Yeon-dong, Jeju; tel. (64) 740-6114; fax (64) 740-6500; internet www.chejunews.co.kr; f. 1945; evening; Pres. KIM DAE-SUNG; Man. Editor KANG BYUNG-HEE.

Chonbuk Domin Ilbo: 207-10, 2-ga, Deokjin-dong, Deokjin-dong, Jeonju, N Jeolla Prov.; tel. (63) 251-7114; fax (63) 251-7127; internet www.domin.co.kr; f. 1988; morning; Pres. LIM BYOUNG-CHAN; Man. Editor YANG CHAE-SUK.

Chonju Ilbo: 568-132, Sonosong-dong, Deokjin-gu, Jeonju, N. Jeolla Prov.; tel. (63) 285-0114; fax (63) 285-2060; f. 1991; morning; Chair. KANG DAE-SOON; Man. Editor SO CHAE-CHOL.

Chonnam Ilbo: 700-5, Jungheung-dong, Buk-gu, Gwangju, 500-758; tel. (62) 527-0015; fax (62) 510-0436; internet www .chonnamilbo.co.kr; f. 1989; morning; Pres. LIM WON-SIK; Editor-in-Chief KIM YONG-OK.

Chunbuk Ilbo: 710-5, Kumam-dong, Deokjin-gu, Jeonju, N. Jeolla Prov.; tel. (63) 250-5500; fax (63) 250-5550; f. 1950; evening; Pres. SUH JUNG-SANG; Man. Editor LEE KON-WOONG.

Chungchong Daily News: 304, Sachang-dong, Hungduk-gu, Cheongju, N. Chungcheong Prov.; tel. (43) 279-5114; fax (43) 262-2000; internet www.ccnews.co.kr; f. 1946; morning; Pres. SEO JEONG-OK; Editor IM BAIK-SOO.

Halla Ilbo: 568-1, Samdo 1-dong, Jeju; tel. (64) 750-2114; fax (64) 750-2520; internet www.hallailbo.com; f. 1989; evening; Chair. KANG YONG-SOK; Man. Editor HONG SONG-MOK.

Incheon Ilbo: 18-1, 4-ga, Hang-dong, Jung-gu, Incheon; tel. (32) 763-8811; fax (32) 763-7711; internet www.inchonnews.co.kr; f. 1988; evening; Chair. MUN PYONG-HA; Man. Editor LEE JAE-HO.

Jungdo Daily Newspaper: 274-7, Galma-dong, Seo-gu, Daejeon; tel. (42) 530-4114; fax (42) 535-5334; internet www.joongdo.com; f. 1951; morning; Chair. KI-CHANG; Man. Editor SONG HYOUNG-SOP.

Kangwon Ilbo: 53, 1-ga, Jungang-no, Chuncheon, Gangwon Prov.; tel. (33) 252-7228; fax (33) 252-5884; internet www.kwnews.co.kr; f. 1945; evening; Pres. CHO NAM-JIN; Man. Editor KIM KEUN-TAE.

Kookje Daily News: 76-2, Goje-dong, Yeonje-gu, Busan 611-702; tel. (51) 500-5114; fax (51) 500-4274; e-mail jahwang@ms.kookje.co .kr; internet www.kookje.co.kr; f. 1947; morning; Pres. LEE JONG-DEOK; Editor-in-Chief JEONG WON-YOUNG.

Kwangju Ilbo: 1, 1-ga, Geumnam-no, Dong-gu, Gwangju; tel. (62) 222-8111; fax (62) 227-9500; internet www.kwangju.co.kr; f. 1952; evening; Chair. KIM CHONG-TAE; Man. Editor CHO DONG-SU.

Kyeonggi Ilbo: 452-1, Songjuk-dong, Changan-gu, Suwon, Gyeonggi Prov.; tel. (31) 247-3333; fax (31) 247-3349; internet www .kgib.co.kr; f. 1988; evening; Chair. SHIN SON-CHOL; Man. Editor LEE CHIN-YONG.

Kyeongin Ilbo: 1121-11, Ingye-dong, Paldal-gu, Suwon, Gyeonggi Prov.; tel. (31) 231-5114; fax (31) 232-1231; internet www.kyeongin .com; f. 1960; evening; Chair. SUNG BAEK-EUNG; Man. Editor KIM HWA-YANG.

Kyungnam Shinmun: 100-5, Sinwol-dong, Changwon, S. Gyeong-sang Prov.; tel. (55) 283-2211; fax (55) 283-2227; internet www .knnews.co.kr; f. 1946; evening; Pres. KIM DONG-KYU; Editor PARK SUNG-KWAN.

Maeil Shinmun: 71, 2-ga, Gyesan-dong, Jung-gu, Daegu; tel. (53) 255-5001; fax (53) 255-8902; internet www.m2000.co.kr; f. 1946; evening; Chair. KIM BOO-KI; Editor LEE YONG-KEUN; circ. 300,000.

Pusan Daily News: 1-10, Sujeong-dong, Dong-gu, Busan 601-738; tel. (51) 461-4114; fax (51) 463-8880; internet www.pusanilbo.co.kr; f. 1946; Pres. JEONG HAN-SANG; Man. Editor AHN KI-HO; circ. 427,000.

Taegu Ilbo: 81-2, Sincheon 3-dong, Dong-gu, Daegu; tel. (53) 757-4500; fax (53) 751-8086; internet www.tgnews.go.kr; f. 1953; morning; Pres. PARK GWON-HEUM; Editor KIM KYUNG-PAL.

Taejon Ilbo: 1-135, Munhwa 1-dong, Jung-gu, Daejeon; tel. (42) 251-3311; fax (42) 253-3320; internet www.taejontimes.co.kr; f. 1950; evening; Chair. SUH CHOON-WON; Editor KWAK DAE-YEON.

Yeongnam Ilbo: 111, Sincheon-dong, Dong-gu, Daegu; tel. (53) 757-5114; fax (53) 756-9009; internet www.yeongnam.co.kr; f. 1945; morning; Chair. PARK CHANG-HO; Man. Editor KIM SANG-TAE.

SELECTED PERIODICALS

Academy News: 50, Unjung-dong, Bundang-gu, Seongnam, Gyeonggi Prov. 463-791; tel. (31) 709-8111; fax (31) 709-9945; organ of the Acad. of Korean Studies; Pres. HAN SANG-JIN.

Business Korea: 26-3, Yeouido-dong, Yeongdeungpo-gu, Seoul 150-010; tel. (2) 784-4010; fax (2) 784-1915; f. 1983; monthly; Pres. KIM KYUNG-HAE; circ. 35,000.

Eumak Dong-A: 139, Sejong-no, Jongno-gu, Seoul 110-715; tel. (2) 781-0640; fax (2) 705-4547; f. 1984; monthly; music; Publr KIM BYUNG-KWAN; Editor KWON O-KIE; circ. 85,000.

Han Kuk No Chong (FKTU News): Federation of Korean Trade Unions, FKTU Bldg, 35, Yeouido-dong, Yeongdeungpo-gu, Seoul; tel. (2) 786-3970; fax (2) 786-2864; e-mail fktuintl@nownuri.net; internet www.fktu.or.kr; f. 1961; labour news; circ. 20,000.

Hyundae Munhak: Mokjung Bldg, 1st Floor, 1361-5, Seocho-dong, Seocho-gu, Seoul; tel. (2) 3472-8151; fax (2) 563-9319; f. 1955; literature; Publr KIM SUNG-SIK; circ. 200,000.

Korea Business World: Yeouido, POB 720, Seoul 150-607; tel. (2) 532-1364; fax (2) 594-7663; f. 1985; monthly; English; Publr and Pres. LEE KIE-HONG; circ. 40,200.

Korea Buyers Guide: Rm 2301, Korea World Trade Center, 159, Samseong-dong, Gangnam-gu, Seoul; tel. (2) 551-2376; fax (2) 551-2377; e-mail info@buyersguide.co.kr; internet www.buykorea21.com; f. 1973; monthly; consumer goods; quarterly, hardware; Pres. YOU YOUNG-PYO; circ. 30,000.

Korea Journal: CPOB 54, Seoul 100-022; tel. (2) 776-2804; organ of the UNESCO Korean Commission; Gen. Dir CHUNG HEE-CHAE.

Korea Newsreview: 1-12, 3-ga, Hoehyeon-dong, Jung-gu, Seoul 100-771; tel. (2) 756-7711; weekly; English; Publr and Editor PARK CHUNG-WOONG.

Korean Business Review: FKI Bldg, 28-1, Yeouido-dong, Yeongdeungpo-gu, Seoul 150-756; tel. (2) 3771-0114; fax (2) 3771-0138; monthly; publ. by Fed. of Korean Industries; Publr KIM KAK-CHOONG; Editor SOHN BYUNG-DOO.

Korea and World Affairs: Rm 1723, Daewoo Center Bldg, 5-541, Namdaemun-no, Jung-gu, Seoul 100-714; tel. (2) 777-2628; fax (2) 319-9591; organ of the Research Center for Peace and Unification of Korea; Pres. CHANG DONG-HOON.

Literature and Thought: Seoul; tel. (2) 738-0542; fax (2) 738-2997; f. 1972; monthly; Pres. LIM HONG-BIN; circ. 10,000.

Monthly Travel: Cross Bldg, 2nd Floor, 46-6, 2-ga, Namsan-dong, Jung-gu, Seoul 100-042; tel. (2) 757-6161; fax (2) 757-6089; e-mail kotfa@unitel.co.kr; Pres. SHIN JOONG-MOK; circ. 50,000.

News Maker: 22, Jung-dong, Jung-gu, Seoul 110-702; tel. (2) 3701-1114; fax (2) 739-6190; e-mail hudy@kyunghyang.com; internet www.kyunghyang.com/newsmaker; f. 1992; Pres. JANG JUN-BONG; Editor PARK MYUNG-HUN.

Reader's Digest: 295-15, Deoksan 1-dong, Geumcheon-gu, Seoul 153-011; tel. (2) 866-8800; fax (2) 839-4545; f. 1978; monthly; general; Pres. YANG SUNG-MO; Editor PARK SOON-HWANG; circ. 115,000.

Shin Dong-A (New East Asia): 139, Chungjeong-no, Seodaemun-gu, Seoul 120–715; tel. (2) 361-0974; fax (2) 361-0988; f. 1931; monthly; general; Publr KIM HAK-JUN; Editor YOU YOUNG-EUL; circ. 170,000.

Taekwondo: Sinmun-no Bldg, 5th Floor, 238 Sinmun-no, 1-ga, Jongno-gu, Seoul 110-061; tel. (2) 566-2505; fax (2) 553-4728; e-mail wtf@unitel.co.kr; internet www.wtf.org; f. 1973; organ of the World Taekwondo Fed.; Pres. Dr KIM UN-YONG.

Vantage Point: 85-1 Susong-dong, Jongno-gu, Seoul, 110-140; tel. (2) 398-3519; fax (2) 398-3539; e-mail kseungji@yna.co.kr; internet www.yna.co.kr; f. 1978; monthly; developments in North Korea; Editor KWAK SEUNG-JI.

Weekly Chosun: 61, Taepyeong-no 1, Jung-gu, Seoul; tel. (2) 724-5114; fax (2) 724-6199; weekly; Publr BANG SANG-HOON; Editor CHOI JOON-MYONG; circ. 350,000.

The Weekly Hankook: 14, Junghak-dong, Jongno-gu, Seoul; tel. (2) 732-4151; fax (2) 724-2444; f. 1964; Publr CHANG CHAE-KUK; circ. 400,000.

Wolgan Mot: 139, Sejong-no, Jongno-gu, Seoul 110; tel. (2) 733-5221; f. 1984; monthly; fashion; Publr KIM SEUNG-YUL; Editor KWON O-KIE; circ. 120,000.

Women's Weekly: 14, Junghak-dong, Jongno-gu, Seoul; tel. (2) 735-9216; fax (2) 732-4125.

Yosong Dong-A (Women's Far East): 139, Sejong-no, Jongno-gu, Seoul 110-715; tel. (2) 721-7621; fax (2) 721-7676; f. 1933; monthly; women's magazine; Publr KIM BYUNG-KWAN; Editor KWON O-KIE; circ. 237,000.

NEWS AGENCIES

Yonhap News Agency: 85-1, Susong-dong, Jongno-gu, Seoul; tel. (2) 398-3114; fax (2) 398-3257; internet www.yonhapnews.co.kr; f. 1980; Pres. KIM KUN.

Foreign Bureaux

Agence France-Presse (AFP): Yonhap News Agency Bldg, 3rd Floor, 85-1, Susong-dong, Jongno-gu, Seoul; tel. (2) 737-7353; fax (2) 737-6598; e-mail seoul@afp.com; Bureau Chief TIM WITCHER.

Associated Press (AP) (USA): Yonhap News Agency Bldg, 85-1, Susong-dong, Jongno-gu, Seoul; tel. (2) 739-0692; fax (2) 737-0650; Bureau Chief REID MILLER.

Central News Agency (Taiwan): 33-1, 2-ga, Myeong-dong, Jung-gu, Seoul; tel. (2) 753-0195; fax (2) 753-0197; Bureau Chief CHIANG YUAN-CHEN.

Deutsche Presse-Agentur (Germany): 148, Anguk-dong, Jongno-gu, Seoul; tel. (2) 738-3808; fax (2) 738-6040; Correspondent NIKO-LAUS PREDE.

Informatsionnoye Telegrafnoye Agentstvo Rossii—Telegrafnoye Agentstvo Suverennykh Stran (ITAR—TASS) (Russia): 1-302, Chonghwa, 22-2, Itaewon-dong, Yeongsan-gu, Seoul; tel. (2) 796-9193; fax (2) 796-9194.

Jiji Tsushin (Jiji Press) (Japan): Joong-ang Ilbo Bldg, 7, Soonhwa-dong, Jung-gu, Seoul; tel. (2) 753-4525; fax (2) 753-8067; Chief Correspondent KENJIRO TSUJITA.

Kyodo News Service (Japan): Yonhap News Agency Bldg, 85-1, Susong-dong, Jongno-gu, Seoul; tel. (2) 739-2791; fax (2) 737-1776; Bureau Chief HISASHI HIRAI.

Reuters (UK): Byuck San Bldg, 7th Floor, 12-5, Dongja-dong, Yeongsan-gu, Seoul 140-170; tel. (2) 727-5151; fax (2) 727-5666; Bureau Chief ANDREW BROWNE.

Rossiiskoye Informatsionnoye Agentstvo—Novosti (RIA—Novosti) (Russia): 14, Junghak-dong, Jongno-gu, Seoul; tel. (2) 737-2829; fax (2) 798-0010; Correspondent SERGEI KUDASOV.

United Press International (UPI) (USA): Yonhap News Agency Bldg, Rm 603, 85-1, Susong-dong, Jongno-gu, Seoul; tel. (2) 737-9054; fax (2) 738-8206; Correspondent JASON NEELY.

Xinhua News Agency (People's Republic of China): B-1, Hillside Villa, 726-111, Hannam-dong, Yeongsan-gu, Seoul; tel. (2) 795-8258; fax (2) 796-7459.

PRESS ASSOCIATIONS

Korean Newspaper Editors' Association: Korea Press Center, 13th Floor, 25, 1-ga, Taepyeong-no, Jung-gu, Seoul; tel. (2) 732-1726; fax (2) 739-1985; f. 1957; 416 mems; Pres. SEONG BYONG-WUK.

Korean Newspapers Association: Korea Press Center, 13th Floor, 25, 1-ga, Taepyeong-no, Jung-gu, Seoul 100-745; tel. (2) 733-2251; fax (2) 720-3291; e-mail ccy73_2000@yahoo.co.kr; f. 1962; 49 mems; Pres. CHOE HAK-RAE.

Seoul Foreign Correspondents' Club: Korea Press Center, 18th Floor, 25, 1-ga, Taepyeong-no, Jung-gu, Seoul; tel. (2) 734-3272; fax (2) 734-7712; f. 1956; Pres. PARK HAN-CHUN.

Publishers

Ahn Graphics Ltd: 260-88, Seongbuk 2-dong, Seongbuk-gu, Seoul 136-012; tel. (2) 763-2320; fax (2) 743-3352; e-mail lbr@ag.co.kr; f. 1985; computer graphics; Pres. KIM OK-CHUL.

Bak-Young Publishing Co: 13-31, Pyeong-dong, Jongno-gu, Seoul; tel. (2) 733-6771; fax (2) 736-4818; f. 1952; sociology, philosophy, literature, linguistics, social science; Pres. AHN JONG-MAN.

BIR Publishing Co Ltd: 506, Sinsa-dong, Gangnam-gu, Seoul 135-120; tel. (2) 515-2000; fax (2) 514-3249.

Bobmun Sa Publishing Co: Hanchung Bldg, 4th Floor, 161-7, Yomni-dong, Mapo-gu, Seoul 121-090; tel. (2) 703-6541; fax (2) 703-6594; f. 1954; law, politics, philosophy, history; Pres. BAE HYO-SEON.

Bumwoo Publishing Co: 21-1, Kusu-dong, Mapo-gu, Seoul 121-130; tel. (2) 717-2121; fax (2) 717-0429; f. 1966; philosophy, religion, social science, technology, art, literature, history; Pres. YOON HYUNG-DOO.

Cheong Moon Gak Publishing Co Ltd: 486-9, Kirum 3-dong, Seongbuk-gu, Seoul 136-800; tel. (2) 985-1451; fax (2) 988-1456;

e-mail cmgbook@cmgbook.co.kr; internet www.cmgbook.co.kr; f. 1974; science, technology, business; subsidiaries HanSeung Publishers, Lux Media; Pres. KIM HONG-SEOK; Man. Dir HANS KIM.

Design House Publishing Co: Paradise Bldg, 186-210, Jangchung-dong, 2-ga, Jung-gu, Seoul 100-392; tel. (2) 2275-6151; fax (2) 2275-7884; f. 1987; social science, art, literature, languages, children's periodicals; Pres. LEE YOUNG-HEE.

Dong-Hwa Publishing Co: 130-4, 1-ga, Wonhyoro, Yeongsan-gu, Seoul 140-111; tel. (2) 713-5411; fax (2) 701-7041; f. 1968; language, literature, fine arts, history, religion, philosophy; Pres. LIM IN-KYU.

Doosan Co-operation Publishing BG: 18-12, Ulchi-ro, 6-ga, Jeong-gu, Seoul 100-196; tel. (2) 3398-880; fax (2) 3398-2670; f. 1951; general works, school reference, social science, periodicals; Pres. CHOI TAE-KYUNG.

Eulyoo Publishing Co Ltd: 46-1, Susong-dong, Jongno-gu, Seoul 110-603; tel. (2) 733-8151; fax (2) 732-9154; e-mail eulyoo@chollian.net; internet www.eulyoo.co.kr; f. 1945; linguistics, literature, social science, history, philosophy; Pres. CHUNG CHIN-SOOK.

Hainaim Publishing Co Ltd: Minjin Bldg, 5th Floor, 464-41, Seokyo-dong, Mapo-gu, Seoul 121-210; tel. (2) 326-1600; fax (2) 333-7543; e-mail hainaim@chollian.net; f. 1983; philosophy, literature, children's; Pres. SONG YOUNG-SUK.

Hakwon Publishing Co Ltd: Seocho Plaza, 4th Floor, 1573-1, Seocho-dong, Seocho-gu, Seoul; tel. (2) 587-2396; fax (2) 584-9306; f. 1945; general, languages, literature, periodicals; Pres. KIM YOUNG-SU.

Hangil Publishing Co: 506, Sinsa-dong, Gangnam-gu, Seoul 135-120; tel. (2) 515-4811; fax (2) 515-4816; f. 1976; social science, history, literature; Pres. KIM EOUN-HO.

Hanul Publishing Company: 201, Hyuam Bldg, 503-24, Changcheon-dong, Seodaemun-gu, Seoul 120-180; tel. (2) 336-6183; fax (2) 333-7543; e-mail newhanul@nuri.net; f. 1980; general, philosophy, university books, periodicals; Pres. KIM CHONG-SU.

Hollym Corporation: 13-13, Gwancheol-dong, Jongno-gu, Seoul 110-111; tel. (2) 735-7551-4; fax (2) 730-5149; e-mail hollym@chollian.net; internet www.hollym.co.kr; f. 1963; academic and general books on Korea in English; Pres. HAM KI-MAN.

Hyang Mun Sa Publishing Co: 645-20, Yeoksam-dong, Gangnam-gu, Seoul 135-081; tel. (2) 538-5672; fax (2) 538-5673; f. 1950; science, agriculture, history, engineering, home economics; Pres. NAH JOONG-RYOL.

Hyonam Publishing Co Ltd: 627-5, Ahyun 3-dong, Mapo-gu, Seoul 121-013; tel. (2) 365-5056; fax (2) 365-5251; e-mail lawhyun@chollian.net; f. 1951; general, children's, literature, periodicals; Pres. CHO KEUN-TAE.

Il Ji Sa Publishing Co: 46-1, Junghak-dong, Jongno-gu, Seoul 110-150; tel. (2) 732-3980; fax (2) 722-2807; f. 1956; literature, social sciences, juvenile, fine arts, philosophy, linguistics, history; Pres. KIM SUNG-JAE.

Ilchokak Publishing Co Ltd: 9, Gongpyeong-dong, Jongno-gu, Seoul 110-160; tel. (2) 733-5430; fax (2) 738-5857; f. 1953; history, literature, sociology, linguistics, medicine, law, engineering; Pres. HAN MAN-NYUN.

Jigyungsa Publishers Ltd: 790-14, Yeoksam-dong, Gangnam-gu, Seoul 135-080; tel. (2) 557-6351; fax (2) 557-6352; e-mail jigyung@uriel.net; internet www.jigyung.co.kr; f. 1979; children's, periodicals; Pres. KIM BYUNG-JOON.

Jihak Publishing Co Ltd: 180-20, Dongkyo-dong, Mapo-gu, Seoul 121-200; tel. (2) 330-5220; fax (2) 325-5835; f. 1965; philosophy, language, literature; Pres. KWON BYONG-IL.

Jipmoondang: 95, Waryon-dong, Jongno-gu, Seoul 110-360; tel. (2) 743-3098; fax (2) 743-3192; philosophy, social science, Korean studies, history, Korean folklore; Pres. LIM KYOUNG-HWAN.

Jisik Sanup Publications Co Ltd: 35-18, Dongui-dong, Jongno-gu, Seoul 110-040; tel. (2) 738-1978; fax (2) 720-7900; f. 1969; religion, social science, art, literature, history, children's; Pres. KIM KYUNG-HEE.

Jung-Ang Publishing Co Ltd: 172-11, Yomni-dong, Mapo-gu, Seoul 121-090; tel. (2) 717-2111; fax (2) 716-1369; f. 1972; study books, children's; Pres. KIM DUCK-KI.

Kemongsa Publishing Co Ltd: 772, Yeoksam-dong, Gangnam-gu, Seoul 135-080; tel. (2) 531-5335; fax (2) 531-5520; f. 1946; picture books, juvenile, encyclopaedias, history, fiction; Pres. RHU SEUNG-HEE.

Ki Moon Dang: 286-20, Haengdang-dong, Seongdong-gu, Seoul 133-070; tel. (2) 2295-6171; fax (2) 2296-8188; f. 1976; engineering, fine arts, dictionaries; Pres. KANG HAE-JAK.

Korea Britannica Corpn: 117, 1-ga, Jungchung-dong, Seoul 100-391; tel. (2) 272-2151; fax (2) 278-9983; f. 1968; encyclopaedias, dictionaries; Pres. JANG HO-SANG, SUJAN ELEN TAPANI.

Korea University Press: 5-1, Anam-dong, 5-ga, Seongbuk-gu, Seoul 136-701; tel. (2) 3290-4231; fax (2) 923-6311; e-mail kupress@korea.ac.uk; internet www.korea.ac.kr/~kupress; f. 1956; philosophy, history, language, literature, Korean studies, education, psychology, social science, natural science, engineering, agriculture, medicine; Pres. EUH YOON-DAE.

Kum Sung Publishing Co: 242-63, Gongdeok-dong, Mapo-gu, Seoul 121-022; tel. (2) 713-9651; fax (2) 718-4362; f. 1965; literature, juvenile, social sciences, history, fine arts; Pres. KIM NAK-JOON.

Kyohak-sa Publishing Co Ltd: 105-67, Gongdeok-dong, Mapo-gu, Seoul 121-020; tel. (2) 717-4561; fax (2) 718-3976; f. 1952; dictionaries, educational, children's; Pres. YANG CHEOL-WOO.

Kyung Hee University Press: 1, Hoeki-dong, Dongdaemun-gu, Seoul 130-701; tel. (2) 961-0106; fax (2) 962-8840; f. 1960; general, social science, technology, language, literature; Pres. CHOE YOUNG-SEEK.

Kyungnam University Press: 28-42, Samchung-dong, Jongno-gu, Seoul 110-230; tel. (2) 370-0700; fax (2) 735-4359; Pres. PARK JAE-KYU.

Minumsa Publishing Co Ltd: 5/F Kangnam Publishing Culture Centre, 506, Sinsa-dong, Gangnam-gu, Seoul 135-120; tel. (2) 515-2000; fax (2) 515-2007; e-mail michell@bora.dacom.co.kr; f. 1966; literature, philosophy, linguistics, pure science; Pres. PARK MAENG-HO.

Munhakdongne Publishing Co Ltd: 6/F Dongsomun B/D 260, Dongsomundong 4-ga, Seongbuk-gu, Seoul 136-034; tel. (2) 927-6790; fax (2) 927-6793; e-mail etepluie@hotmail.com; internet www.munhak.com; f. 1993; art, literature, science, philosophy, non-fiction, children's, periodicals; Pres. KANG BYUNG-SUN.

Panmun Book Co Ltd: 923-11, Mok 1-dong, Yangcheon-gu, Seoul 158-051; tel. (2) 653-5131; fax (2) 653-2454; e-mail skliu@panmun.co.kr; internet www.medicalplus.co.kr; f. 1955; social science, pure science, technology, medicine, linguistics; Pres. LIU SUNG-KWON.

Sakyejul Publishing Ltd: 1-181, Sinmun-no-2-ga, Jongno-gu, Seoul 110-062; tel. (2) 736-9380; fax (2) 737-8595; e-mail sakyejul@soback.kornet.nm.kr; f. 1982; social sciences, art, literature, history, children's; Pres. KANG MAR-XILL.

Sam Joong Dang Publishing Co: 261-23, Soke-dong, Yeongsan-gu, Seoul 140-140; tel. (2) 704-6816; fax (2) 704-6819; f. 1931; literature, history, philosophy, social sciences, dictionaries; Pres. LEE MIN-CHUL.

Sam Seong Dang Publishing Co: 101-14, Non Hyun-dong, Gangnam-gu, Seoul 135-010; tel. (2) 3442-6767; fax (2) 3442-6768; e-mail kyk@ssdp.co.kr; f. 1968; literature, fine arts, history, philosophy; Pres. KANG MYUNG-CHAE.

Sam Seong Publishing Co Ltd: 1516-2, Seocho-dong, Seocho-gu, Seoul 137-070; tel. (2) 3470-6900; fax (2) 597-1507; internet www.howpc.com; f. 1951; literature, history, juvenile, philosophy, arts, religion, science, encyclopaedias; Pres. KIM JIN-YONG.

Samsung Publishing Co Ltd: Seocho-dong, Seocho-gu, Seoul 137-871; tel. (2) 3470-6900; fax (2) 521-8534; e-mail lisababy@ssbooks.com; internet www.ssbooks.com; www.samsungbooks.com; children's books, comics, cooking, parenting, health, travel; f. 1951; Chief Editor BOSUNG KONG.

Segyesa Publishing Co Ltd: Dasan Bldg 102, 494-85, Yeongkan-dong, Mapo-gu, Seoul 121-070; tel. (2) 715-1542; fax (2) 715-1544; f. 1988; general, philosophy, literature, periodicals; Pres. CHOI SUN-HO.

Se-Kwang Music Publishing Co: 232-32, Seogye-dong, Yeongsan-gu, Seoul 140-140; tel. (2) 719-2652; fax (2) 719-2656; f. 1953; music, art; Pres. PARK SEI-WON; Chair. PARK SHIN-JOON.

Seong An Dang Publishing Co: 4579, Singil-6-dong, Yeongdeungpo-gu, Seoul 150-056; tel. (2) 3142-4151; fax (2) 323-5324; f. 1972; technology, text books, university books, periodicals; Pres. LEE JONG-CHOON.

Seoul National University Press: 56-1, Sinrim-dong, Gwanak-gu, Seoul 151-742; tel. (2) 889-0434; fax (2) 888-4148; e-mail snubook@chollian.net; f. 1961; philosophy, engineering, social science, art, literature; Pres. LEE KI-JUN.

Si-sa-young-o-sa, Inc: 55-1, 2-ga, Jongno, Jongno-gu, Seoul 110-122; tel. (2) 274-0509; fax (2) 271-3980; internet www.ybmsisa.co.kr; f. 1959; language, literature; Pres. CHUNG YOUNG-SAM.

Sogang University Press: 1, Sinsu-dong, Mapo-gu, Seoul 121-742; tel. (2) 705-8212; fax (2) 705-8612; f. 1978; philosophy, religion, science, art, history; Pres. LEE HAN-TAEK.

Sookmyung Women's University Press: 53-12, 2-ga, Jongpa-dong, Yeongsan-gu, Seoul 140-742; tel. (2) 710-9162; fax (2) 710-9090; f. 1968; general; Pres. LEE KYUNG-SOOK.

Tam Gu Dang Publishing Co: 158, 1-ga, Hanggangno, Yeongsan-gu, Seoul 140-011; tel. (2) 3785-2271; fax (2) 3785-2272; f. 1950; linguistics, literature, social sciences, history, fine arts; Pres. HONG SUK-WOO.

Tong Moon Gwan: 147, Gwanhoon-dong, Jongno-gu, Seoul 110-300; tel. (2) 732-4355; f. 1954; literature, art, philosophy, religion, history; Pres. LEE KYUM-NO.

Woongjin.com Co. Ltd: Woongjin Bldg, 112-2, Inui-dong, Jongno-gu, Seoul; tel. (2) 3670-1832; fax (2) 766-2722; e-mail lois.kim@email .woongjin.com; internet www.woongjin.com; children's; Pres. YOON SUCK-KEUM.

Yearimdang Publishing Co Ltd: Yearim Bldg, 153-3, Samseong-dong, Gangnam-gu, Seoul 135-090; tel. (2) 566-1004; fax (2) 567-9610; e-mail yearim@yearim.co.kr; internet www.yearim.co.kr; f. 1973; children's; Pres. NA CHOON-HO.

Yonsei University Press: 134, Sincheon-dong, Seodaemun-gu, Seoul 120-749; tel. (2) 361-3380; fax (2) 393-1421; e-mail ysup@ yonsei.ac.kr; f. 1955; philosophy, religion, literature, history, art, social science, pure science; Pres. KIM BYUNG-SOO.

Youl Hwa Dang: 506, Sinsa-dong, Gangnam-gu, Seoul 135-120; tel. (2) 515-3141; fax (2) 515-3144; e-mail horang2@unitel.co.kr; f. 1971; art; Pres. YI KI-UNG.

PUBLISHERS' ASSOCIATION

Korean Publishers Association: 105-2, Sagan-dong, Jongno-gu, Seoul 110-190; tel. (2) 735-2702; fax (2) 738-5414; e-mail kpa@kpa21 .or.kr; internet www.kpa21.or.kr; f. 1947; Pres. LEE JUNG-IL; Sec.-Gen. JUNG JONG-JIN.

Broadcasting and Communications

TELECOMMUNICATIONS

Dacom Corpn: Dacom Bldg, 706-1, Yeoksam-dong, Gangnam-gu, Seoul 135-610; tel. (2) 6220-0220; fax (2) 6220-0702; internet www .dacom.net; f. 1982; domestic and international long-distance telecommunications services and broadband internet services; CEO. PARK UN-SUH.

Daewoo Telecom Co Ltd: 14-34, Yeouido-dong, Yeongdeungpo-gu, Seoul; tel. (2) 3779-7114; fax (2) 3779-7500; internet www.dwt.co.kr; Pres. (vacant).

Hanaro Telecom: Kukje Electronics Center Bldg, 24th Floor, 1445-3, Seocho-dong, Seocho-gu, Seoul 137-728; tel. (2) 6266-4114; fax (2) 6266-4379; internet www.hanaro.com; local telecommunications and broadband internet services; Pres. and CEO YOON CHANG-BUN.

Korea Mobile Telecommunications Corpn: 267, 5-ga, Namdae-mun-no, Jung-gu, Seoul; tel. (2) 3709-1114; fax (2) 3709-0499; f. 1984; Pres. SEO JUNG-UK.

Korea Telecom: 206 Jungja-dong, Bundang-gu, Seongnam-si, Gyeonggi Prov. 463-711-; tel. (2) 727-0114; fax (2) 750-3994; internet www.kt.co.kr; domestic and international telecommunications services and broadband internet services; privatized in June 2002; Pres. LEE YONG-KYUNG.

Korea Telecom (KT) Freetel: Seoul; 33% owned by Korea Telecom; 3.17m. subscribers (1999); Pres. LEE SANG-CHUL.

KTF: KTF Tower, 890-20, Daechi-dong, Gangnam-gu, Seoul 135-280; tel. (2) 2016-1114; fax (2) 2016-0032; internet www.ktf.com; mobile telecommunications and wireless internet services; merged with KTm.com in May 2001; commenced (code division multiple access) commercial CDMA2000 1x services in May 2001, and (evolution data only) 1x EV-DO services in May 2002; 10m. subscribers (2002); CEO LEE KYUNG-JOON.

LG Telecom: LG Gangnam Tower, 19th Floor, 679 Yeoksam-dong, Gangnam-gu, Seoul 135-985; tel. (2) 2005-7114; fax (2) 2005-7505; internet www.lg019.co.kr; mobile telecommunications and wireless internet services; commenced commercial CDMA2000 1x service in May 2001; 4m. subscribers (2002); CEO NAM YONG.

Onse Telecom: 192-2, Gumi-dong, Bundang-gu, Seongnam-si, Gyeonggi Prov. 463-500; tel. and fax (31) 738-6000; internet www .onse.net; domestic and international telecommunications services; Pres. and CEO HWANG KEE-YEON.

SK Telecom Co Ltd: 99, Seorin-dong, Jongno-gu, Seoul 110-110; tel. (2) 2121-2114; fax (2) 2121-3999; internet www.sktelecom.com; cellular mobile telecommunications and wireless internet services; merged with Shinsegi Telecom in Jan. 2002; 16m. subscribers (2002); Chair. and CEO (vacant).

BROADCASTING

Regulatory Authority

Korean Broadcasting Commission: KBS Bldg, 923-5, Mok-dong, Yangcheon-gu, Seoul 158-715; tel. (2) 3219-5117; fax (2) 3219-5371; Chair. KANG DAE-IN.

Radio

Korean Broadcasting System (KBS): 18, Yeouido-dong, Yeong-deungpo-gu, Seoul 150-010; tel. (2) 781-1000; fax (2) 781-4179; internet www.kbs.co.kr; f. 1926; publicly-owned corpn with 26 local broadcasting and 855 relay stations; overseas service in Korean, English, German, Indonesian, Chinese, Japanese, French, Spanish, Russian and Arabic; Pres. JUNG YUN-JOO.

Buddhist Broadcasting System (BBS): 140, Mapo-dong, Mapo-gu, Seoul 121-050; tel. (2) 705-5114; fax (2) 705-5229; internet www .bbsfm.ko.kr; f. 1990; Pres. CHO HAE-HYONG.

Christian Broadcasting System (CBS): 917-1, Mok-dong, Yang-cheon-gu, Seoul 158-701; tel. (2) 650-7000; fax (2) 654-2456; internet www.cbs.co.kr; f. 1954; independent religious network with seven network stations in Seoul, Daegu, Busan, Gwangju, Chonbuk, Jeonju and Chuncheon; programmes in Korean; Pres. Rev. KWON HO-KYUNG.

Educational Broadcasting System (EBS): 92-6, Umyeon-dong, Seocho-gu, Seoul 137-791; tel. (2) 526-2000; fax (2) 526-2179; internet www.ebs.co.kr; f. 1990; Pres. Dr PARK HEUNG-SOO.

Far East Broadcasting Co (FEBC): 89, Sangsu-dong, Mapo-gu, MPO Box 88, Seoul 121-707; tel. (2) 320-0114; fax (2) 320-0129; e-mail febcadm@febc.or.kr; internet www.febc.net; Dir Dr BILLY KIM.

Radio Station HLAZ: MPO Box 88, Seoul 121-707; tel. (2) 320-0114; fax (2) 320-0129; e-mail febcadm@febc.net; internet www .febc.net; f. 1973; religious, educational service operated by Far East Broadcasting Co; programmes in Korean, Chinese, Russian and Japanese; Dir Dr BILLY KIM.

Radio Station HLKX: MPO Box 88, Seoul 121-707; tel. (2) 320-0114; fax (2) 320-0129; e-mail febcadm@febc.net; internet www .febc.net; f. 1956; religious, educational service operated by Far East Broadcasting Co; programmes in Korean, Chinese and English; Dir Dr BILLY KIM.

Munhwa Broadcasting Corpn (MBC): 31, Yeouido-dong, Yeong-deungpo-gu, Seoul 150-728; tel. (2) 784-2000; fax (2) 784-0880; e-mail mbcir@imbc.com; internet www.imbc.com; f. 1961; public; Pres. KIM JOONG-BAE.

Pyong Hwa Broadcasting Corpn (PBC): 2-3, 1-ga, Jeo-dong, Jung-gu, Seoul 100-031; tel. (2) 270-2114; fax (2) 270-2210; internet www.pbc.co.kr; f. 1990; religious and educational programmes; Pres. Rev. PARK SHIN-EON.

Seoul Broadcasting System (SBS): 10-2, Yeouido-dong, Yeong-deungpo-gu, Seoul 150-010; tel. (2) 786-0792; fax (2) 780-2530; internet www.sbs.co.kr; f. 1991; Pres. SONG DO-KYUN.

US Forces Network Korea (AFN Korea): Seoul; tel. (2) 7914-6495; fax (2) 7914-5870; e-mail info@afnkorea.com; internet afnkorea.com; f. 1950; six originating stations and 19 relay stations; 24 hours a day.

Television

In late 1997 almost 40 domestic television channels were in operation.

Educational Broadcasting System (EBS): see Radio.

Inchon Television Ltd (ITV): 587-46, Hakik-dong, Nam-gu, Incheon; tel. (32) 830-1000; fax (32) 865-6300; internet www.itv.co .kr; f. 1997.

Jeonju Television Corpn (JTV): 656-3, Sonosong-dong, Deokjin-gu, Jeonju, N. Jeolla Prov.; tel. (63) 250-5231; fax (63) 250-5249; e-mail jtv@jtv.co.kr; f. 1997.

Korean Broadcasting System (KBS): 18, Yeouido-dong, Yeong-deungpo-gu, Seoul 150-790; tel. (2) 781-1000; fax (2) 781-4179; f. 1961; publicly-owned corpn with 25 local broadcasting and 770 relay stations; Pres. JUNG YUN-JOO.

Munhwa Broadcasting Corpn (MBC-R/TV): 31, Yeouido-dong, Yeongdeungpo-gu, Seoul 150-728; tel. (2) 789-2851; fax (2) 782-3094; e-mail song@mbc.co.kr; internet www.imbc.com; f. 1961; public; 19 TV networks; Pres. LEE KEUNG-HEE.

Seoul Broadcasting System (SBS): see Radio.

US Forces Network Korea (AFN Korea): Seoul; tel. (2) 7914-2711; fax (2) 7914-5870; f. 1950; main transmitting station in Seoul; 19 rebroadcast transmitters and translators; 168 hours weekly.

Finance

(cap. = capital; res = reserves; dep. = deposits; m. = million;
brs = branches; amounts in won, unless otherwise indicated)

BANKING

The modern financial system in South Korea was established in 1950 with the foundation of the central bank, the Bank of Korea. Under financial liberalization legislation, adopted in the late 1980s, banks were accorded greater freedom to engage in securities or insurance operations. In March 1999 there were 87 commercial banks in South Korea, comprising 11 nation-wide banks, eight provincial banks and 68 branches of foreign banks. The Financial Supervisory Service oversees the operations of commercial banks and the financial services sector.

Specialized banks were created in the 1960s to provide funds for sectors of the economy not covered by commercial banks. There are also two development banks: the Korea Development Bank and the Export-Import Bank of Korea.

In late 1997 many merchant banks were forced to cease operations, after incurring heavy losses through corporate bankruptcies. In June 1998 five commercial banks were also required to cease operations.

Regulatory Authority

Financial Supervisory Service: 27, Yeouido-dong, Yeongdeungpo-gu, Seoul 150-743; tel. (2) 3771-5000; fax (2) 785-3475; internet www.fss.or.kr; Gov. LEE JUNG-JAE.

Central Bank

Bank of Korea: 110, 3-ga, Namdaemun-no, Jung-gu, Seoul 100-794; tel. (2) 759-4114; fax (2) 759-4139; e-mail bokdiri@bok.or.kr; internet www.bok.or.kr; f. 1950; bank of issue; res 5,456,500m., dep. 139,210,300m. (Dec. 2002); Gov. PARK SEUNG; Dep. Gov. LEE SEONG-TAE; 16 domestic brs, 7 overseas offices.

Commercial Banks

Chohung Bank: 14, 1-ga, Namdaemun-no, Jung-gu, Seoul 100-757; tel. (2) 733-2000; fax (2) 723-6473; internet www.chb.co.kr; f. 1897; merged with Chungbuk Bank in May 1999 and Kangwon Bank in Sept. 1999; 80.4% owned by Shinhan Financial Group; cap. 3,395,592m., dep. 45,125,839m. (Dec. 2002); Chair. SUNG BOK-WEE; Dir HONG CHIL-SUN; 446 domestic brs, 11 overseas brs.

Hana Bank: 101-1, 1-ga, Ulchi-no, Jung-gu, Seoul 100-191; tel. (2) 2002-1111; fax (2) 775-7472; e-mail webmaster@hanabank.com; internet www.hanabank.co.kr; f. 1991; merged with Boram Bank in Jan. 1999; merged with Seoulbank in Dec. 2002; cap. 987,161m., res 877,633m., dep. 60,814,076m. (Dec. 2002); Chair. and CEO KIM SEUNG-YU; 303 brs.

Kookmin Bank: 9-1, 2-ga, Namdaemun-no, Jung-gu, CPOB 815, Seoul 100-703; tel. (2) 317-2891; fax (2) 317-2885; e-mail corres@kookminbank.com; internet www.kookminbank.com; f. 1963 as Citizen's National Bank, renamed 1995; re-established Jan. 1999, following merger with Korea Long Term Credit Bank; merged with H&CB in November 2001; cap. 1,641,293m., res 6,251,573m., dep. 150,341.3m. (Dec. 2002); Chair. KIM SANG-HOON; Pres. and CEO KIM JUNG-TAE; 1,122 domestic brs, 6 overseas brs.

KorAm Bank: 39, Da-dong, Jung-gu, Seoul 100-180; tel. (2) 3455-2114; fax (2) 3455-2966; e-mail shk@goodbank.com; internet www.goodbank.com; f. 1983; jt venture with Bank of America; cap. 1,093,334m., res 227,185m., dep. 25,760,831m. (Dec. 2002); CEO and Chair. HA YUNG-KU; 227 domestic brs, 4 overseas brs.

Korea Exchange Bank: 181, 2-ga, Ulchi-no, Jung-gu, Seoul 100-793; tel. (2) 729-0114; fax (2) 775-2565; internet www.keb.co.kr; f. 1967; merged with Korea International Merchant Bank in Jan. 1999; cap. 1,850,875m., res 92,637m.m., dep. 42,545,293m. (Dec. 2002); Chair. CHUNG MOON-SOO; Pres. LEE KANG-WON; 269 domestic brs.

Korea First Bank: 100, Gongpyeong-dong, Jongno-gu, Seoul 110-702; tel. (2) 3702-3114; fax (2) 3702-4934; e-mail master@kfb.co.kr; internet www.kfb.co.kr; f. 1929; 49% owned by Newbridge Capital Ltd (USA), 51% govt-owned; cap. 980,584m., res 149,838m., dep. 25,427,255m. (Dec. 2002); Pres. and CEO ROBERT COHEN; 389 domestic brs, 2 overseas brs.

Shinhan Bank: 120, 2-ga, Taepyeong-no, Jung-gu, Seoul 100-102; tel. (2) 756-0505; fax (2) 774-7013; internet www.shinhan.com; f. 1982; cap. 1,223,153m., res 846,104m., dep. 41,252,363m. (Dec. 2002); Pres. and CEO LEE IN-HO; 347 domestic brs, 7 overseas brs.

Woori Bank: 203, 1-ga, Hoehyeon-dong, Jung-gu, Seoul; tel. (2) 2002-3000; fax (2) 2002-5687; internet www.wooribank.com; f. 2002; following the merger of Hanvit Bank and Peace Bank of Korea; 100% government-owned; cap. 2,764,400m., res 1,378,457m., dep. 68,126,751m. (Dec. 2002); Pres. LEE DUK-HOON; 668 domestic brs.

Development Banks

Export-Import Bank of Korea: 16-1, Yeouido-dong, Yeongdeungpo-gu, Seoul 150-873; tel. (2) 3779-6114; fax (2) 3779-6732; e-mail kexim@koreaexim.go.kr; internet www.koreaexim.go.kr; f. 1976; cap. 2,675,755m., res 132,001m. (Dec. 2001); Chair. and Pres. SHIN DONG-KYU; 8 brs.

Korea Development Bank: 16-3, Yeouido-dong, Yeongdeungpo-gu, Seoul 150-793; tel. (2) 787-4000; fax (2) 787-6191; internet www.kdb.co.kr; f. 1954; cap. 7,161,861m., dep. 42,345,324m. (Dec. 2002); Gov. JUNG KEUN-YONG; 32 domestic brs, 5 overseas brs.

Specialized Banks

Industrial Bank of Korea: 50, 2-ga, Ulchi-no, Jung-gu, Seoul 100-758; tel. (2) 729-6114; fax (2) 729-6402; e-mail ifd@ibk.co.kr; internet www.ibk.co.kr; f. 1961 as the Small and Medium Industry Bank; 85.5% govt-owned; cap. 2,291,385m., res 1,090,736m., dep. 42,737,135m. (Dec. 2002); Chair. and Pres. KIM JONG-CHANG; 387 domestic brs, 6 overseas brs.

Korean-French Banking Corpn (SogeKo): Marine Center, 118, 2-ga, Namdaemun-no, Jung-gu, CPOB 8572, Seoul 100-092; tel. (2) 777-7711; fax (2) 756-0464; f. 1977; cap. 130,000m., res 6,631m., dep. 255,359m. (Dec. 2002); Pres. KIM DOO-BAE.

National Agricultural Co-operative Federation (NACF): 75, 1-ga, Chungjeong-no, Jung-gu, Seoul 100-707; tel. (2) 397-5114; fax (2) 397-5140; e-mail nacfico@nuri.net; internet www.nonghyup.com; f. 1961; merged with National Livestock Co-operatives Federation in July 2000; cap. 2,564,400m., res 1,395,800m., dep. 64,063,500m. (2002); Chair. and Pres. CHUNG DAE-KUN; 2,025 brs and member co-operatives.

National Federation of Fisheries Co-operatives: 11-6, Sincheon-dong, Songpa-gu, Seoul 138-730; tel. (2) 2240-2114; fax (2) 2240-3049; internet www.suhyup.co.kr; f. 1962; cap. 1,158,100m., res 301,900m., dep. 4,371,000m. (2002); Chair. and Pres. CHANG BYUNG-KOO; 120 brs.

Provincial Banks

Cheju Bank: 1349, Ido-1-dong, Jeju 690-021, Jeju Prov.; tel. (64) 734-1711; fax (64) 720-0183; f. 1969; cap. 55,500m., res. 30,700m., dep. 1,044,100m. (2002); merged with Central Banking Co in 2000; Chair. and Pres. KANG JOON-HONG; 29 brs.

Daegu Bank Ltd: 118, 2-ga, Susong-dong, Susong-gu, Daegu 706-712; tel. (53) 756-2001; fax (53) 740-6902; internet www.daegubank.co.kr; f. 1967; cap. 660,625m., res 7,482m., dep. 12,064,956m. (Dec. 2002); Chair. and Pres. KIM KUK-NYON; 183 brs.

Jeonbuk Bank Ltd: 669-2, Geumam-dong, Deokjin-gu, Jeonju 561-711, N Jeolla Prov.; tel. (63) 250-7114; fax (63) 250-7078; internet www.jbbank.co.kr; f. 1969; cap. 165,300m., res 30,200m., dep. 2,784,100m. (2002); Chair. and Pres. HONG SUNG-JOO; 68 brs.

Kwangju Bank Ltd: 7-12, Daein-dong, Dong-gu, Gwangju 501-719; tel. (62) 239-5000; fax (62) 239-5199; e-mail kbjintl@nuri.net; internet www.kjbank.com; f. 1968; cap. 170,403m., res 598m., dep. 6,277,745m. (Dec. 2002); Chair. and Pres. UM JONG-DAE; 135 brs.

Kyongnam Bank: 246-1, Sokjeon-dong, Hoewon-gu, Masan 630-010, Gyeongsang Prov.; tel. (551) 290-8000; fax (551) 294-9426; internet www.knbank.co.kr; f. 1970 as Gyeongnam Bank Ltd, name changed 1987; cap. 259,000m., res 22,851m., dep. 7,847,571m. (Dec. 2002); Chair. and Pres. KANG SHIN-CHUL; 110 brs.

Samyang Merchant Bank: 38-3, 3-ga, Gyongwon-dong, Wansan-gu, Jeonju 560-020; tel. (63) 83-7111; fax (63) 84-3056; f. 1979; cap. 30,254m., res 43,487m., dep. 400,426m. (March 1996); Pres. and CEO KIM PAIK-JOON.

Foreign Banks

ABN-AMRO Bank NV (Netherlands): Seoul City Tower Bldg, 11–12th Floors, 581, 5-ga, Namdaemun-no, Jung-gu, Seoul; tel. (2) 2131-6000; fax (2) 399-6554; f. 1979; Gen. Man. CHUNG DUCK-MO.

American Express Bank Ltd (USA): Gwanghwamun Bldg, 15th Floor, 64-8, 1-ga, Taepyeong-no, Jung-gu, CPOB 1390, Seoul 100-101; tel. (2) 399-2929; fax (2) 399-2966; f. 1977; Gen. Man. CHOE JAE-ICK.

Arab Bank PLC (Jordan): Daewoo Center Bldg, 22nd Floor, 541, 5-ga, Namdaemun-no, Jung-gu, CPOB 1331, Seoul 100-714; tel. (2) 317-9000; fax (2) 757-0124; Gen. Man. JO SEUNG-SHIK.

Australia and New Zealand Banking Group Ltd (Australia): Kyobo Bldg, 18th Floor, 1, 1-ga, Jongno, Jongno-gu, CPOB 1065, Seoul 110-714; tel. (2) 730-3151; fax (2) 737-6325; f. 1987; Gen. Man. PHIL MICHELL.

Bank Mellat (Iran): Bon Sol Bldg, 14th Floor, 144-27, Samseong-dong, Gangnam-gu, Seoul; tel. (2) 558-4448; fax (2) 557-4448; e-mail info@bankmellat.co.kr; internet www.bankmellat.co.kr; f. 2001; Gen. Man. ALI AFZALI.

Bank of America (USA): Hanwha Bldg, 9th Floor, 1, Janggyo-dong, Jung-gu, Seoul 100-797; tel. (2) 729-4500; fax (2) 729-4400; Gen. Man. BANG CHOON-HO.

Bank of Hawaii (USA): Daeyonkak Bldg, 14th Floor, 25-5, 1-ga, Jungmu-no, Jung-gu, Seoul 100-011; tel. (2) 757-0831; fax (2) 757-3516; Man. PARK YONG-SOO.

Bank of Nova Scotia (Canada): KCCI Bldg, 9th Floor, 45, 4-ga, Namdaemun-no, Jung-gu, Seoul 100-094; tel. (2) 757-7171; fax (2) 752-7189; e-mail bns.seoul@scotiabank.com; Gen. Man. HENRY YONG.

Bank of Tokyo-Mitsubishi Ltd (Japan): Young Poong Bldg, 4th Floor, 33, Seorin-dong, Jongno-gu, Seoul; tel. (2) 399-6474; fax (2) 735-4897; f. 1967; Gen. Man. KAZUMASA KOGA.

Bankers Trust Co (USA): Center Bldg, 10th Floor, 111-5, Sokong-dong, Jung-gu, Seoul; tel. (2) 3788-6000; fax (2) 756-2648; f. 1978; Man. Dir LEE KEUN-SAM.

BNP Paribas (France): Dong Yang Chemical Bldg, 8th Floor, 50, Sogong-dong, Jung-gu, Seoul 100-070; tel. (2) 317-1700; fax (2) 757-2530; e-mail bnppseoul@asia.bnparibas.com; f. 1976; Gen. Man. ALAIN PÉNICAUT.

Citibank NA (USA): Citicorp Center Bldg, 89-29, 2-ga, Sinmun-no, Jongno-gu, CPOB 749, Seoul 110-062; tel. (2) 2004-1114; fax (2) 722-3644; f. 1967; Gen. Man. SAJJAD RAZVI.

Crédit Agricole Indosuez (France): Kyobo Bldg, 19th Floor, 1, 1-ga, Jongno, Jongno-gu, CPOB 158, Seoul 110-714; tel. (2) 3700-9500; fax (2) 738-0325; f. 1974; Gen. Man. PATRICE COUVEGNES.

Crédit Lyonnais SA (France): You One Bldg, 8th–10th Floors, 75-95, Seosomun-dong, Jung-gu, Seoul 100-110; tel. (2) 772-8000; fax (2) 755-5379; f. 1978; Gen. Man. GEOFFROY DE LASSUS.

DBS Bank Ltd (Development Bank of Singapore Ltd): Gwanghwamun Bldg, 20th Floor, 64-8, 1-ga, Taepyeong-no, Jung-gu, CPOB 9896, Seoul; tel. (2) 399-2660; fax (2) 732-7953; e-mail jeefun@dbs.com; f. 1981; Gen. Man. LOW JEE FUN.

Deutsche Bank AG (Germany): Sei An Bldg, 20th–22nd Floor, 116, 1-ga, Sinmun-no, Jongno-gu, Seoul 110-700; tel. (2) 724-4500; fax (2) 724-4645; f. 1978; Gen. Man. KIM JIN-IL.

First National Bank of Chicago (USA): Oriental Chemical Bldg, 15th Floor, 50, Sokong-dong, Jung-gu, Seoul 100-070; tel. (2) 316-9700; fax (2) 753-7917; f. 1976; Vice-Pres. and Gen. Man. MICHAEL S. BROWN.

Fuji Bank Ltd (Japan): Doosan Bldg, 15th Floor, 101-1, 1-ga, Ulchi-no, Jung-gu, Seoul 100-191; tel. (2) 311-2000; fax (2) 754-8177; f. 1972; Gen. Man. IKUO YAMAMOTO.

Hongkong and Shanghai Banking Corpn Ltd (Hong Kong): HSBC Bldg, 1-ga, Bongrae-dong, Jung-gu, CPOB 6910, Seoul 110-161; tel. (2) 2004-0000; fax (2) 381-9100; Gen. Man. G. P. S. CALVERT.

Indian Overseas Bank: Daeyungak Bldg, 3rd Floor, 25-5, 1-ga, Jungmu-no, Jung-gu, CPOB 3332, Seoul 100-011; tel. (2) 753-0741; fax (2) 756-0279; e-mail iobseoul@chollian.net; f. 1977; Gen. Man. K. P. MUNIRATHMAN.

Industrial and Commercial Bank of China (China): Taepyeong Bldg, 17th Floor, 310, 2-ga, Taepyeong-no, Seoul; tel. (2) 755-5688; fax (2) 779-2750; f. 1997; Gen. Man. ZHANG KEXIN.

ING Bank NV (Netherlands): Hungkuk Life Insurance Bldg, 15th Floor, 226, 1-ga, Sinmun-no, Jongno-gu, Seoul 110-061; tel. (2) 317-1800; fax (2) 317-1883; Man. YIM SANG-KYUN.

JP Morgan Chase Bank (USA): Chase Plaza, 34-35, Jeong-dong, Jung-gu, Seoul 100-120; tel. (2) 758-5114; fax (2) 758-5420; f. 1978; Gen. Man. KIM MYUNG-HAN.

Mizuho Bank Ltd (Japan): Nae Wei Bldg, 14th Floor, 6, 2-ga, Ulchi-no, Jung-gu, Seoul 100-192; tel. (2) 756-8181; fax (2) 754-6844; f. 1972; Gen. Man. TSUNEO KIKUCHI.

National Australia Bank Ltd: KDIC Bldg, 16th Floor, 33, Da-dong, Jung-gu, Seoul; tel. (2) 3705-4600; fax (2) 3705-4602; Gen. Man. MARK EDMONDS.

National Bank of Canada: Leema Bldg, 6th Floor, 146-1, Susong-dong, Jongno-gu, Seoul 110-140; tel. (2) 733-5012; fax (2) 736-1508; Vice-Pres. and Country Man. C. N. KIM.

National Bank of Pakistan: Kyobo Bldg, 12th Floor, 1, 1-ga, Jongno, Jongno-gu, CPOB 1633, Seoul 110-121; tel. (2) 732-0277; fax (2) 734-5817; f. 1987; Gen. Man. ABDUL GHAFOOR.

Overseas Union Bank Ltd (Singapore): Kyobo Bldg, 8th Floor, Suite 806, 1, 1-ga, Jongno, Jongno-gu, Seoul 110-714; tel. (2) 739-3441; fax (2) 732-9004; Vice-Pres. and Gen. Man. OOI KOOI KEAT.

Royal Bank of Canada: Kyobo Bldg, 22nd Floor, 1, 1-ga, Jongno, Jongno-gu, Seoul 110-714; tel. (2) 730-7791; fax (2) 736-2995; f. 1982; Gen. Man. THOMAS P. FEHLNER, Jr.

Société Générale (France): Sean Bldg, 10th Floor, 1-ga, Sinmun-no, Jongno-gu, Seoul 110-700; tel. (2) 2195-7777; fax (2) 2195-7700; f. 1984; CEO ERIC BERTHÉLEMY.

Standard Chartered Bank (UK): Seoul Finance Center, 22nd Floor, 84, 1-ga, Taepyeong-no, Jung-gu, Seoul; tel. (2) 750-6114; fax (2) 757-7444; Gen. Man. WILLIAM GEMMEL.

UBS AG (Switzerland): Young Poong Bldg, 10th Floor, 33, Seorin-dong, Jongno-gu, Seoul 110-752; tel. (2) 3702-8888; fax (2) 3708-8714; f. 1999; Gen. Man. LEE JAE-HONG.

UFJ Bank Ltd (Japan): Lotte Bldg, 22nd Floor, 1, 1-ga, Sogong-dong, Jung-gu, Seoul; tel. (2) 752-7321; fax (2) 754-3870; Gen. Man. HIDEKI YAMAUCHI.

Union Bank of California NA (USA): Kyobo Bldg, 12th Floor, 1, 1-ga, Jongno, Jongno-gu, CPOB 329, Seoul 110; tel. (2) 721-1700; fax (2) 732-9526; Gen. Man. KIM TAEK-JOONG.

Union de Banques Arabes et Françaises (France): ACE Tower, 3rd Floor, 1-170, Sunhwa-dong, Jung-gu, CPOB 1224, Seoul 100-742; tel. (2) 3455-5300; fax (2) 3455-5354; f. 1979; Gen. Man. PATRICK OBERREINER.

United Overseas Bank Ltd (Singapore): Kyobo Bldg, 20th Floor, 1, 1-ga, Jongno, Jongno-gu, Seoul 110-714; tel. (2) 739-3916; fax (2) 730-9570; Gen. Man. LIEW CHAN HARN.

Banking Association

Korea Federation of Banks: 4-1, 1-ga, Myeong-dong, Jung-gu, Seoul 100-021; tel. (2) 3705-5000; fax (2) 3705-5337; internet www.kfb.or.kr; f. 1928; Chair. SHIN DONG-HYUCK; Vice-Chair. KIM KONG-JIN.

STOCK EXCHANGE

Korea Stock Exchange: 33, Yeouido-dong, Yeongdeungpo-gu, Seoul 150-977; tel. (2) 3774-9000; fax (2) 786-0263; e-mail world@kse.or.kr; internet www.kse.or.kr; f. 1956; Chair. and CEO KANG YUNG-JOO.

Kosdaq Stock Market, Inc: 45-2, Yeouido-dong, Yeongdeungpo-gu, Seoul 150-974; tel. (2) 2001-5700; fax (2) 784-4505; e-mail webmaster@kosdaq.or.kr; internet www.kosdaq.or.kr; f. 1996; stock market for knowledge-based venture cos; 828 listed cos (Aug. 2002) with a market capitalization of US $39,945m.; Pres. and CEO SHIN HO-JOO.

INSURANCE

Principal Life Companies

Allianz Jeil Life Insurance Co Ltd: 1303-35, Seocho 4-dong, Seocho-gu, Seoul 137-074; tel. (2) 3481-3111; fax (2) 3481-0960; f. 1954; Pres. LEE TAE-SIK.

Choson Life Insurance Co Ltd: 111, Sincheon-dong, Dong-gu, Daegu 701-620; tel. (53) 743-3600; fax (53) 742-9263; f. 1988; cap. 12,000m.; Pres. LEE YOUNG-TAEK.

Daishin Life Insurance Co Ltd: 395-68, Sindaebang-dong, Dongjak-gu, Seoul 156-010; tel. (2) 3284-7000; fax (2) 3284-7451; internet www.dslife.co.kr; f. 1989; cap. 144,200m. (2002); Pres. PARK BYUNG-MYUNG.

Dong-Ah Life Insurance Co Ltd: Dong-Ah Life Insurance Bldg, 33, Da-dong, Jung-gu, Seoul; tel. (2) 317-5114; fax (2) 771-7561; f. 1973; cap. 10,000m.; Pres. KIM CHANG-LAK; 900 brs.

Dongbu Life Insurance Co Ltd: Dongbu Bldg, 7th Floor, 891-10, Daechi-dong, Gangnam-gu, Seoul 135-820; tel. (2) 1588-3131; fax (2) 3011-4100; internet www.dongbulife.co.kr; f. 1989; cap. 85,200m. (2002); Pres. CHANG KI-JE.

Dongyang Life Insurance Co Ltd: 185, Ulchi-no 2-ga, Jung-gu, Seoul 100-192; tel. (2) 728-9114; fax (2) 771-1347; internet www.myangel.co.kr; f. 1989; cap. 340,325m. (2002); Pres. KU JA-HONG.

Doowon Life Insurance Co Ltd: 259-6, Sokjon-dong, Hoewon-gu, Masan 630-500; tel. (55) 52-3100; fax (55) 52-3119; f. 1990; cap. 10,000m.; Pres. CHOI IN-YONG.

Han Deuk Life Insurance Co Ltd: 878-1, Bumchyun 1-dong, Busanjin-gu, Busan 641-021; tel. (51) 631-8700; fax (51) 631-8809; f. 1989; cap. 10,000m.; Pres. SUH WOO-SHICK.

Hanil Life Insurance Co Ltd: 118, 2-ga, Namdaemun-no, Jung-gu, Seoul 100-770; tel. (2) 2126-7777; fax (2) 2126-7631; internet www.hanillife.co.kr; f. 1993; cap. 115,000m. (2002); Pres. LEE MYUNG-HYUN.

Hankuk Life Insurance Co Ltd: Daehan Fire Bldg, 51-1, Namchang-dong, Jung-gu, Seoul 100-060; tel. (2) 773-3355; fax (2) 773-1778; f. 1989; cap. 10,000m.; Pres. PARK HYUN-KOOK.

Hansung Life Insurance Co Ltd: 3, Sujung-dong, Dong-gu, Busan 601-030; tel. (51) 461-7700; fax (51) 465-0581; f. 1988; Pres. CHO YONG-KEUN.

Hungkuk Life Insurance Co Ltd: 226, Sinmun-no 1-ga, Jongno-gu, Seoul 100-061; tel. (2) 2002-7000; fax (2) 2002-7804; internet www.hungkuk.co.kr; f. 1958; cap. 12,221m. (2002); Pres. RYU SEOK-KEE.

ING Life Insurance Co Korea Ltd: Sean Bldg, 116, Sinmun-no, Jongno-gu, Seoul 110-700; tel. (2) 3703-9500; fax (2) 734-3309; f. 1991; cap. 64,820m. (2002); Pres. JOOST KENEMANS.

Korea Life Insurance Co Ltd: 60, Yeouido-dong, Yeongdeungpo-gu, Seoul 150-603; tel. (2) 789-5114; fax (2) 789-8173; internet www .korealife.com; f. 1946; cap. 3,550,000m. (2002); Pres. LEE KANG-HWAN.

Korean Reinsurance Company: 80, Susong-dong, Jongno-gu, Seoul 110-733; tel. (2) 3702-6000; fax (2) 739-3754; internet www .koreanre.co.kr; f. 1963; Pres. PARK JONG-WON.

Kumho Life Insurance Co Ltd: 57, 1-ga, Sinmun-no, Jongno-gu, Seoul 110-061; tel. (2) 6303-5000; fax (2) 771-7561; internet www .kumholife.co.kr; f. 1988; cap. 211,249m. (2002); Pres. SONG KEY-HYUCK.

Kyobo Life Insurance Co Ltd: 1, 1-ga, Jongno, Jongno-gu, Seoul 110-714; tel. (2) 721-2121; fax (2) 737-9970; internet www.kyobo.co .kr; f. 1958; cap. 92,500m.; Pres. and CEO CHANG HYUNG-DUK; 84 main brs.

Lucky Life Insurance Co Ltd: 3, Sujung-dong, Dong-gu, Busan 601-716; tel. (51) 461-7700; fax (51) 465-0581; internet www .luckylife.co.kr; f. 1988; cap. 139,054m. (2002); Pres. CHANG NAM-SIK.

MetLife Insurance Co of Korea Ltd: Sungwon Bldg, 8th Floor, 141, Samseong-dong, Gangnam-gu, Seoul 135-716; tel. (2) 3469-9600; fax (2) 3469-9700; internet www.metlifekorea.co.kr; f. 1989; cap. 97,700m. (2002); Pres. STUART B. SOLOMON.

Pacific Life Insurance Co Ltd: 705-9, Yeoksam-dong, Gangnam-gu, Seoul 135-080; tel. (2) 3458-0114; fax (2) 3458-0392; internet www.pli.co.kr; f. 1989; cap. 10,000m.; Pres. KIM SUNG-MOO.

PCA Life Insurance Co Ltd: 142, Nonhyun-dong, Gangnam-gu, Seoul 135-749; tel. (2) 515-5300; fax (2) 514-3844; f. 1990; cap. 52,100m. (2002); Pres. MIKE BISHOP.

Prudential Life Insurance Co of Korea Ltd: Prudential Bldg, Yeoksam-dong, Gangnam-gu, Seoul; tel. (2) 2144-2000; fax (2) 2144-2100; internet www.prudential.or.kr; f. 1989; cap. 26,400m.; Pres. JAMES C. SPACKMAN.

Samshin All State Life Insurance Co Ltd: Samwhan Bldg, 5th Floor, 98-5, Unni-dong, Jongno-gu, Seoul 110-742; tel. (2) 3670-5000; fax (2) 742-8197; Pres. KIM KYUNG-YOP.

Samsung Life Insurance Co Ltd: 150, 2-ga, Taepyeong-no, Jung-gu, Seoul 100-716; tel. (2) 751-8000; fax (2) 751-8100; internet www .samsunglife.com; f. 1957; cap. 100,000m. (2002); Pres. BAE JUNG-CHOONG; 1,300 brs.

Shinhan Life Insurance Co Ltd: 120, 2-ga, Taepyeong-no, Jung-gu, Seoul 100-102; tel. (2) 3455-4000; fax (2) 753-9351; internet www .shinhanlife.co.kr; f. 1990; Pres. HAN DONG-WOO.

SK Life Insurance Co Ltd: 168, Gongduk-dong, Mapo-gu, Seoul 121-705; tel. (2) 3271-4114; fax (2) 3271-4400; internet www.sklife .com; f. 1988; cap. 246,275m. (2002); Pres. KANG HONG-SIN.

Non-Life Companies

Daehan Fire and Marine Insurance Co Ltd: 51-1, Namchang-dong, Jung-gu, Seoul 100-778; tel. (2) 3455-3114; fax (2) 756-9194; e-mail dhplane@daeins.co.kr; internet www.daeins.co.kr; f. 1946; cap. 19,500m.; Pres. LEE YOUNG-DONG.

Dongbu Insurance Co Ltd: Dongbu Financial Center, 891-10, Daechi-dong, Gangnam-gu, Seoul 135-840; tel. (2) 2262-3450; fax (2) 2273-6785; e-mail dongbu@dongbuinsurance.co.kr; internet www .idongbu.com; f. 1962; cap. 30,000m.; Pres. LEE SU-KWANG.

First Fire and Marine Insurance Co Ltd: 12-1, Seosomun-dong, Jung-gu, CPOB 530, Seoul 100-110; tel. (2) 316-8114; fax (2) 771-7319; internet www.insumall.co.kr; f. 1949; cap. 17,200m.; Pres. KIM WOO-HOANG.

Green Fire and Marine Insurance Co Ltd: Seoul City Tower, 581, 5-ga, Namdaemun-no, Jung-gu, Seoul 100-803; tel. (2) 1588-5959; fax (2) 773-1214; internet www.greenfire.co.kr; KIM JONG-CHEN.

Haedong Insurance Co Ltd: 1424-2, Seocho-dong, Seocho-gu, Seoul; tel. (2) 520-2114; e-mail webmaster@haedong.co.kr; internet

www.haedong.co.kr; f. 1953; cap. p.u. 12,000m.; Chair. KIM DONG-MAN; CEO NAH BOO-WHAN.

Hankuk Fidelity and Surety Co Ltd: 51-1, Namchang-dong, Jung-gu, Seoul; tel. (2) 773-3355; fax (2) 773-1778; e-mail hfs025@ unitel.co.kr; f. 1989; cap. 103,000m.; Pres. CHO AM-DAE.

Hyundai Marine and Fire Insurance Co Ltd: 8th Floor, 140-2, Kye-dong, Jongno-gu, Seoul 110-793; tel. (2) 3701-8000; fax (2) 732-5687; e-mail webpd@hdinsurance.co.kr; internet www.hi.co.kr; f. 1955; cap. 30,000m.; Pres. KIM HO-IL.

Korean Reinsurance Co: 80, Susong-dong, Jongno-gu, Seoul 100-733; tel. (2) 3702-6000; fax (2) 739-3754; e-mail service@koreanre.co .kr; internet www.koreanre.co.kr; f. 1963; cap. 34,030m.; Pres. PARK JONG-WON.

Kukje Hwajae Insurance Co Ltd: 120, 5-ga, Namdaemun-no, Jung-gu, Seoul 100-704; tel. (2) 753-1101; fax (2) 773-1214; internet www.directins.co.kr; f. 1947; cap. 10,784m.; Chair. LEE BONG-SUH.

Kyobo Auto Insurance Co Ltd: 76-4, Jamwon-dong, Seocho-gu, Seoul 137-909; tel. (2) 3479-4900; fax (2) 3479-4800; internet www .kyobodirect.com; Pres. SHIN YONG-KIL.

LG Insurance Co Ltd: LG Da-dong Bldg, 85, Da-dong, Jung-gu, Seoul 100-180; tel. (2) 310-2391; fax (2) 753-1002; e-mail webmaster@lginsure.com; internet www.lginsure.com; f. 1959; Pres. KOO CHA-HOON.

Oriental Fire and Marine Insurance Co Ltd: 25-1, Yeouido-dong, Yeongdeungpo-gu, Seoul 150-010; tel. (2) 3786-1910; fax (2) 3886-1940; e-mail webmaster@ofmi.co.kr; internet www.insuworld .co.kr; f. 1922; cap. 42,900m.; Pres. CHUNG KUN-SUB.

Samsung Fire and Marine Insurance Co Ltd: Samsung Insurance Bldg, 87, 1-ga, Ulchi-no, Jung-gu, Seoul 100-191; tel. (2) 758-7948; fax (2) 758-7831; internet www.samsungfire.com; f. 1952; cap. 6,566m.; Pres. LEE SOO-CHANG.

Seoul Guarantee Insurance Co: 136-74, Yeonchi-dong, Jongno-gu, Seoul 110-470; tel. (2) 3671-7459; fax (2) 3671-7480; internet www.sgic.co.kr; Pres. PARK HAE-CHOON.

Shindongah Fire and Marine Insurance Co Ltd: 43, 2-ga, Taepyeong-no, Jung-gu, Seoul; tel. (2) 6366-7000; fax (2) 755-8006; internet www.sdafire.com; f. 1946; cap. 60,220m.; Pres. JEON HWA-SOO.

Ssangyong Fire and Marine Insurance Co Ltd: 60, Doryeom-dong, Jongno-gu, Seoul 110-716; tel. (2) 724-9000; fax (2) 730-1628; e-mail sfmi@ssy.insurance.co.kr; internet www.insurance.co.kr; f. 1948; cap. 27,400m.; Pres. LEE JIN-MYUNG.

Insurance Associations

Korea Life Insurance Association: Kukdong Bldg, 16th Floor, 60-1, 3-ga, Jungmu-no, Jung-gu, Seoul 100-705; tel. (2) 2262-6600; fax (2) 2262-6580; internet www.klia.or.kr; f. 1950; Chair. BAE CHAN-BYUNG.

Korea Non-Life Insurance Association: KRIC Bldg, 6th Floor, 80, Susong-dong, Jongno-gu, Seoul; tel. (2) 3702-8539; fax (2) 3702-8549; internet www.knia.or.kr; f. 1946; 13 corporate mems; Chair. PARK JONG-IK.

Trade and Industry

GOVERNMENT AGENCIES

Fair Trade Commission: 1, Jungang-dong, Gwacheon-si, Gyeonggi Prov. 427-760; internet www.ftc.go.kr; Chair. LEE NAM-KEE.

Federation of Korean Industries: FKI Bldg, 2nd Floor, 28-1, Yeouido-dong, Yeongdeungpo-gu, Seoul 150-756; tel. (2) 3771-0114; fax (2) 3771-0110; e-mail webmaster@fki.or.kr; internet www.fki.or .kr; f. 1961; conducts research and survey work on domestic and overseas economic conditions and trends; advises the Govt and other interested parties on economic matters; exchanges economic and trade missions with other countries; sponsors business conferences; 380 corporate mems and 65 business asscns; Chair. KANG SHIN-HO.

Korea Appraisal Board: 171-2, Samseong-dong, Gangnam-gu, Seoul; tel. (2) 555-1174; Chair. KANG KIL-BOO.

Korea Asset Management Corpn (KAMCO): 814, Yeoksam-dong, Gangnam-gu, Seoul; tel. (2) 3420-5049; fax (2) 3420-5100; internet www.kamco.co.kr; f. 1963; collection and foreclosure agency; appointed following Asian financial crisis as sole institution to manage and dispose of non-performing loans for financial institutions; Pres. CHUNG JAE-RYONG.

Korea Export Industrial Corpn: 33, Seorin-dong, Jongno-gu, Seoul; tel. (2) 853-5573; f. 1964; encourages industrial exports, provides assistance and operating capital, conducts market surveys; Pres. KIM KI-BAE.

Korea Export Insurance Corpn: 136, Seorin-dong, Jongno-gu, Seoul 110-729; tel. (2) 399-6800; fax (2) 399-6679; internet www.keic .or.kr; f. 1992; and official export credit agency of Korea; Pres. LIM TAE-JIN.

Korea Institute for Industrial Economics and Trade (KIET): 206-9, Cheongnyangni-dong, Dongdaemun-gu, Seoul; tel. (2) 3299-3114; fax (2) 963-8540; internet www.kiet.re.kr; f. 1976; economic and industrial research; Pres. PAI KWANG-SUN.

Korean Intellectual Property Office: Government Complex-Daejeon, Dunsan-dong, Seo-gu, Daejeon; tel. (42) 481-5027; fax (42) 481-3455; internet www.kipo.go.kr; Commissioner KIM GWANG-LIM.

Korea Industrial Research Institutes: FKI Bldg, 28-1, Yeouido-dong, Yeongdeungpo-gu, Seoul; tel. (2) 780-7601; fax (2) 785-5771; f. 1979; analyses industrial and technological information from abroad; Pres. KIM CHAE-KYUM.

Korea Trade-Investment Promotion Agency (KOTRA): 300-9, Yeomgok-dong, Seocho-gu, Seoul; tel. (2) 3460-7114; fax (2) 3460-7777; e-mail net-mgr@kotra.or.kr; internet www.kotra.or.kr; f. 1962; various trade promotion activities, market research, cross-border investment promotion, etc.; 98 overseas brs; Pres. OH YOUNG-KYO.

CHAMBER OF COMMERCE

Korea Chamber of Commerce and Industry: 45, 4-ga, Namdaemun-no, Jung-gu, Seoul 100-743; tel. (2) 316-3114; fax (2) 757-9475; internet www.korcham.net; f. 1884; over 80,000m. mems; 63 local chambers; promotes development of the economy and of international economic co-operation; Pres. PARK YONG-SUNG.

INDUSTRIAL AND TRADE ASSOCIATIONS

Agricultural and Fishery Marketing Corpn: 191, 2-ga, Hangang-no, Yeongsan-gu, CPOB 3212, Seoul 140; tel. (2) 790-8010; fax (2) 798-7513; internet www.afmc.co.kr; f. 1967; integrated development for secondary processing and marketing distribution for agricultural products and fisheries products; Pres. AHN KYO-DUCK; Exec. Vice-Pres. KIM JIN-KYU.

Construction Association of Korea: Construction Bldg, 8th Floor, 71-2, Nonhyon-dong, Gangnam-gu, Seoul 135-701; tel. (2) 547-6101; fax (2) 542-6264; f. 1947; national licensed contractors' asscn; 2,700 mem. firms (1995); Pres. CHOI WON-SUK; Vice-Pres. PARK KU-YEOL.

Electronic Industries Association of Korea: 648, Yeoksam-dong, Gangnam-gu, CPOB 5650, Seoul 135-080; tel. (2) 553-0941; fax (2) 555-6195; e-mail eiak@soback.kornet.nm.kr; internet www.eiak .org; f. 1976; 328 mems; Chair. JOHN KOO.

Korea Automobile Manufacturers Association: 658-4. Deungchon-dong, Gangseo-gu, Seoul; tel. (2) 3660-1800; fax (2) 3660-1900; e-mail cwkim@kama.or.kr; internet www.kama.or.kr; f. 1988; Chair. KIM NOI-MYUNG.

Korea Coal Association: 80-6, Susong-dong, Jongno-gu, Seoul; tel. (2) 734-8891; fax (2) 734-7959; f. 1949; 49 corporate mems; Chair. JANG BYEONG-DUCK.

Korea Consumer Goods Exporters Association: KWTC Bldg, Rm 1802, 159, Samseong-dong, Gangnam-gu, Seoul; tel. (2) 551-1865; fax (2) 551-1870; f. 1986; 230 corporate mems; Pres. YONG WOONG-SHIN.

Korea Federation of Textile Industries: 944-31, Daechi-dong, Gangnam-gu, Seoul; tel. (2) 528-4001; fax (2) 528-4069; e-mail kofoti@kofoti.or.kr; internet www.kofoti.or.kr; f. 1980; 50 corporate mems; Pres. PARK SANG-CHUL.

Korea Foods Industry Association: 1002-6, Bangbae-dong, Seocho-gu, Seoul; tel. (2) 585-5052; fax (2) 586-4906; internet www .kfia.or.kr; f. 1969; 104 corporate mems; Pres. CHUN MYUNG-KE.

Korea Importers Association (KOIMA): 218, Hangang-no, 2-ga, Yeongsan-gu, Seoul 140-875; tel. (2) 792-1581; fax (2) 785-4373; e-mail info@aftak.com; internet www.koima.or.kr; f. 1970; 11,903 mems; Chair. CHIN CHUL-PYUNG.

Korea International Trade Association: 159-1, Samseong-dong, Gangnam-gu, Seoul; tel. (2) 6000-5114; fax (2) 6000-5115; internet www.kita.org; f. 1946; private, non-profitmaking business org. representing all licensed traders in South Korea; provides foreign businessmen with information, contacts and advice; 80,000 corporate mems; Pres. KIM JAE-CHUL.

Korea Iron and Steel Association: 824, Yeoksam-dong, Gangnam-gu, Seoul; tel. (2) 559-3500; fax (2) 559-3508; internet www.kosa.or.kr; f. 1975; 39 corporate mems; Chair. YOO SANG-BOO.

Korea Oil Association: 28-1, Yeouido-dong, Yeongdeungpo-gu, Seoul; tel. (2) 3775-0520; fax (2) 761-9573; f. 1980; Pres. CHOI DOO-HWAN.

Korea Productivity Center: 122-1, Jeokseon-dong, Jongno-gu, Seoul 110-052; tel. (2) 724-1114; fax (2) 736-0322; internet www.kpc .or.kr; f. 1957; services to increase productivity of the industries, consulting services, education and training of specialized personnel; Chair. and CEO LEE HEE-BEOM.

Korea Sericultural Association: 17-9, Yeouido-dong, Yeongdeungpo-gu, Seoul; tel. (2) 783-6072; fax (2) 780-0706; f. 1946; improvement and promotion of silk production; 50,227 corporate mems; Pres. CHOI YON-HONG.

Korea Shipbuilders' Association: 65-1, Unni-dong, Jongno-gu, Seoul; tel. (2) 766-4631; fax (2) 766-4307; internet www.koshipa.or .kr; f. 1977; 9 mems; Chair. KIM HYUNG-BYUK.

Korea Textiles Trade Association: Textile Center, 16th Floor, 944-31, Daechi-dong, Gangnam-gu, Seoul; tel. (2) 528-5158; fax (2) 528-5188; f. 1981; 947 corporate mems; Pres. KANG TAE-SEUNG.

Korean Apparel Industry Association: KWTC Bldg, Rm 801, 159, Samseong-dong, Gangnam-gu, Seoul 135-729; tel. (2) 551-1454; fax (2) 551-1467; f. 1993; 741 corporate mems; Pres. PARK SEI-YOUNG.

Korean Development Associates: Seoul; tel. (2) 392-3854; fax (2) 312-3856; f. 1965; economic research; 25 corporate mems; Pres. KIM DONG-KYU.

Mining Association of Korea: 35-24, Dongui-dong, Jongno-gu, Seoul 110; tel. (2) 737-7748; fax (2) 720-5592; f. 1918; 128 corporate mems; Pres. KIM SANG-BONG.

Spinners and Weavers Association of Korea: 43-8, Gwancheol-dong, Jongno-gu, Seoul 110; tel. (2) 735-5741; fax (2) 735-5749; internet www.swak.org; f. 1947; 20 corporate mems; Pres. SUH MIN-SOK.

EMPLOYERS' ORGANIZATION

Korea Employers' Federation: KEF Bldg, 276-1 Daeheung-dong, Mapo-gu, Seoul 121-726; tel. (2) 3270-7336; fax (2) 701-2495; e-mail delee@kef.or.kr; internet www.kef.or.kr; f. 1970; advocates employers' interests with regard to labour and social affairs; 13 regional employers' asscns, 20 economic and trade asscns, and 4,000 major enterprises; Chair. LEE SOO-YOUNG.

UTILITIES

Electricity

Korea Electric Power Corpn (KEPCO): 167, Samseong-dong, Gangnam-gu, Seoul; tel. (2) 3456-3630; fax (2) 3456-3699; internet www.kepco.co.kr; f. 1961; transmission and distribution of electric power, and development of electric power sources; privatization pending; Pres. KANG DONG-SUK.

Gas

Korea Gas Corpn: 215, Jeongja-dong, Bundang-gu, Seongnam, Gyeonggi Prov.; tel. (31) 710-0114; fax (31) 710-0117; internet www .kogas.or.kr; state-owned; proposed transfer to private-sector ownership announced in July 1998; Pres. KIM MYUNG-KYU.

Samchully Co Ltd: 35-6, Yeouido-dong, Yeongdeungpo-gu, Seoul; tel. (2) 368-3300; fax (2) 783-1206; internet www.samchully.co.kr; f. 1966; gas supply co for Seoul metropolitan area and Gyeonggi Prov.; Chair. JIN JU-HWA.

Water

Korea Water Resources Corpn: 6-2, Yeonchuk-dong, Daedeok-gu, Daejeon; tel. (42) 629-3114; fax (42) 623-0963; internet www .kowaco.or.kr.

Office of Waterworks, Seoul Metropolitan Govt: 27-1 Hapdong, Seodaemun-gu, Seoul; tel. (2) 390-7332; fax (2) 362-3653; f. 1908; responsible for water supply in Seoul; Head SON JANG-HO.

Ulsan City Water and Sewerage Board: 646-4, Sin-Jung 1-dong, Nam-gu, Ulsan; tel. (52) 743-020; fax (52) 746-928; f. 1979; responsible for water supply and sewerage in Ulsan; Dir HO KUN-SONG.

CO-OPERATIVES

Korea Computers Co-operative: Seoul; tel. (2) 780-0511; fax (2) 780-7509; f. 1981; Pres. MIN KYUNG-HYUN.

Korea Federation of Knitting Industry Co-operatives: 586-1, Sinsa-dong, Gangnam-gu, Seoul; tel. (2) 548-2131; fax (2) 3444-9929; internet www.knit.or.kr; f. 1962; Chair. JOUNG MAN-SUB.

Korea Federation of Non-ferrous Metal Industry Co-operatives: Backsang Bldg, Rm 715, 35-2, Yeouido-dong, Yeongdeungpo-gu, Seoul; tel. (2) 780-8551; fax (2) 784-9473; f. 1962; Chair. Park Won-Sik.

Korea Federation of Small and Medium Business (KFSB): 16-2, Yeouido-dong, Yeongdeungpo-gu, Seoul 150-010; tel. (2) 2124-3114; fax (2) 782-0247; f. 1962; Chair. Kim Young-Soo.

Korea Mining Industry Co-operative: 35-24, Dongui-dong, Jongno-gu, Seoul; tel. (2) 735-3490; fax (2) 735-4658; f. 1966; Chair. Jeon Hyang-Sik.

Korea Steel Industry Co-operative: 915-14, Bangbae-dong, Seocho-gu, Seoul; tel. (2) 587-3121; fax (2) 588-3671; internet www.kosic.or.kr; f. 1962; Pres. Kim Duk-Nam.

Korea Woollen Spinners and Weavers Co-operatives: Rm 503, Seawha Bldg, 36, 6-ga, Jongno-gu, Seoul; tel. (2) 747-3871; fax (2) 747-3874; e-mail woollen@woolspd.or.kr; internet www.woolspd.or.kr; f. 1964; Pres. Kim Young-Sik.

National Agricultural Co-operative Federation (NACF): 1, 1-ga, Chungjeong-no, Jung-gu, Seoul; tel. (2) 397-5114; fax (2) 397-5380; internet www.nacf.co.kr; f. 1961; international banking, marketing, co-operative trade, utilization and processing, supply, co-operative insurance, banking and credit services, education and research; Pres. Won Chul-Hee.

National Federation of Fisheries Co-operatives: 11-6, Sincheon-dong, Songpa-gu, Seoul; tel. (2) 2240-3114; fax (2) 2240-3024; internet www.suhyup.co.kr; f. 1962; Pres. Hong Jong-Moon.

TRADE UNIONS

Federation of Korean Trade Unions (FKTU): FKTU Bldg, 35, Yeouido-dong, Yeongdeungpo-gu, Seoul; tel. (2) 782-3884; fax (2) 784-2864; e-mail fktuintl@nownuri.net; internet www.fktu.org; f. 1941; Pres. (vacant); affiliated to ICFTU; 29 union federations are affiliated with a membership of some 960,000.

Federation of Foreign Organization Employees' Unions: 5-1, 3-ga, Dangsan-dong, Yeongdeungpo-gu, Seoul; tel. (2) 2068-1645; fax (2) 2068-1644; f. 1961; Pres. Kang In-Sik; 22,450 mems.

Federation of Korean Apartment Workers' Unions: 922-1, Bangbae-dong, Seocho-gu, Seoul; tel. (2) 522-6860; fax (2) 522-4624; f. 1997; Pres. Lee Dae-Hyung; 3,670 mems.

Federation of Korean Chemical Workers' Unions: Sukchun Bldg, 2nd Floor, 32-100, 4-ga, Dangsan-dong, Yeongdeungpo-gu, Seoul; tel. (2) 761-8251; fax (2) 761-8255; e-mail fkcu@chollian.net; internet www.fkcu.or.kr; f. 1961; Pres. Park Hun-Soo; 116,286 mems.

Federation of Korean Metalworkers' Unions: 1570-2, Sinrim-dong, Gwanak-gu, Seoul; tel. (2) 864-2901; fax (2) 864-0457; e-mail fkmtu@chollian.net; internet www.metall.or.kr; f. 1961; Pres. Lee Byung-Kyun; 130,000 mems.

Federation of Korean Mine Workers' Unions: Guangno Bldg, 2nd Floor, 10-4, Karak-dong, Songpa-gu, Seoul; tel. (2) 403-0973; fax (2) 400-1877; f. 1961; Pres. Kim Dong-Chul; 6,930 mems.

Federation of Korean Printing Workers' Unions: 201, 792-155, 3-ga, Guro-dong, Guro-gu, Seoul; tel. (2) 780-7969; fax (2) 780-6097; f. 1961; Pres. Lee Kwang-Joo; 5,609 mems.

Federation of Korean Public Construction Unions: 293-1, Kumdo-dong, Sujong-gu, Seongnam-si, Gyeonggi-do; tel. (2) 2304-7016; fax (2) 230-4602; f. 1998; Pres. Hong Sang-Ki (acting); 9,185 mems.

Federation of Korean Public Service Unions: Sukchun Bldg, 3rd Floor, 32-100, 4-ga, Dangsan-dong, Yeongdeungpo-gu, Seoul; tel. (2) 769-1330; fax (2) 769-1332; internet www.fkpu.or.kr; f. 1997; Pres. Lee Kwan-Boo; 15,641 mems.

Federation of Korean Rubber Workers' Unions: 830-240, 2-ga, Bumil-dong, Dong-gu, Busan; tel. (51) 637-2101; fax (51) 637-2103; f. 1988; Pres. Cho Yung-Soo; 6,600 mems.

Federation of Korean Seafarers' Unions: 544, Donhwa-dong, Mapo-gu, Seoul; tel. (2) 716-2764; fax (2) 702-2271; e-mail fksu@chollian.net; internet www.fksu.or.kr; f. 1961; Pres. Kim Pil-Jae; 60,037 mems.

Federation of Korean State-invested Corporation Unions: Sunwoo Bldg, 501, 350-8, Yangjae-dong, Seocho-gu, Seoul; tel. (2) 529-2268; fax (2) 529-2270; internet www.publicunion.or.kr; f. 1998; Pres. Jang Dae-Ik; 19,375 mems.

Federation of Korean Taxi & Transport Workers' Unions: 415-7, Janan 1-dong, Dongdaemun-gu, Seoul; tel. (2) 2210-8500; fax (2) 2247-7890; internet www.ktaxi.or.kr; f. 1988; Pres. Kwan Oh-Man; 105,118 mems.

Federation of Korean Textile Workers' Unions: 274-8, Yeomchang-dong, Gangseo-gu, Seoul; tel. (2) 3665-3117; fax (2) 3662-4373; f. 1954; Pres. Oh Young-Bong; 6,930 mems.

Federation of Korean United Workers' Unions: Sukchun Bldg, 32-100, 4-ga, Dangsan-dong, Yeongdeungpo-gu, Seoul; internet www.fkuwu.or.kr; f. 1961; 51,802 mems.

Federation of Korean Urban Railway Unions: Urban Railway Station, 3-ga, Yeouido-dong, Yeongdeungpo-gu, Seoul; tel. (2) 786-5163; fax (2) 786-5165; f. 1996; Pres. Ha Won-Joon; 9,628 mems.

Korea Automobile & Transport Workers' Federation: 678-27, Yeoksam-dong, Gangnam-gu, Seoul; tel. (2) 554-0890; fax (2) 554-1558; f. 1963; Pres. Kang Sung-Chun; 84,343 mems.

Korea Federation of Bank & Financial Workers' Unions: 88, Da-dong, Jung-gu, Seoul; tel. (2) 756-2389; fax (2) 754-4893; internet www.kfiu.org; f. 1961; Pres. Lee Yung-Duk; 113,994 mems.

Korea Federation of Communication Trade Unions: 10th Floor, 106-6, Guro 5-dong, Guro-gu, Seoul; tel. (2) 864-0055; fax (2) 864-5519; internet www.ictu.co.kr; f. 1961; Pres. Oh Dong-In; 18,810 mems.

Korea Federation of Food Industry Workers' Unions: 106-2, 1-ga, Yanpyeong-dong, Yeongdeungpo-gu, Seoul; tel. (2) 679-6441; fax (2) 679-6444; f. 2000; Pres. Baek Young-Gil; 19,146 mems.

Korea Federation of Port & Transport Workers' Unions: Bauksan Bldg, 19th Floor, 12-5, Dongja-dong, Yeongsan-gu, Seoul; tel. (2) 727-4741; fax (2) 727-4749; f. 1980; Pres. Choi Bong-Hong; 33,347 mems.

Korea National Electrical Workers' Union: 167, Samseong-dong, Gangnam-gu, Seoul; tel. (2) 3456-6017; fax (2) 3456-6004; internet www.knewu.or.kr; f. 1961; Pres. Kim Ju-Young; 16,741 mems.

Korea Professional Artist Federation: Hanil Bldg, 43-4, Donui-dong, Jongno-gu, Seoul; tel. (2) 764-5310; fax (2) 3675-5314; f. 1999; Pres. Park Il-Nam; 2,395 mems.

Korea Tobacco & Ginseng Workers' Unions: 100, Pyeongchon-dong, Daedeok-gu, Daejeon; tel. (42) 932-7118; fax (42) 931-1812; f. 1960; Pres. Kang Tae-Heung; 6,008 mems.

Korea Unions of Teaching and Educational Workers: Dongin Bldg, 7th Floor, 65-33, Singil 1-dong, Yeongdeungpo-gu, Seoul; tel. (2) 849-1281; fax (2) 835-0556; internet www.kute.or.kr; f. 1999; Pres. Son Kyung-Soon; 18,337 mems.

Korean Postal Workers' Union: 154-1, Seorin-dong, Jongno-gu, Seoul 110-110; tel. (2) 2195-1773; fax (2) 2195-1761; e-mail cheshin@chol.com; internet www.kpwu.or.kr; f. 1958; Pres. Jung Hyun-Young; 23,500 mems.

Korean Railway Workers' Union: 40, 3-ga, Hangang-no, Yeongsan-gu, Seoul; tel. (2) 795-6174; f. 1947; Pres. Kim Jong-Wook; 31,041 mems.

Korean Tourist Industry Workers' Federation: 749, 5-ga, Namdaemun-no, Jung-gu, Seoul 100-095; tel. (2) 779-1297; fax (2) 779-1298; f. 1970; Pres. Jeong Young-Ki; 27,273 mems.

National Medical Industry Workers' Federation of Korea: 134, Sincheon-dong, Seodaemun-gu, Seoul; tel. (2) 313-3900; fax (2) 393-6877; f. 1999; Pres. Lee Yong-Moo; 5,610 mems.

Korean Confederation of Trade Unions: 139, 2-ga, Yeouido-dong, Yeongdeungpo-gu, Seoul; tel. (2) 635-1133; fax (2) 635-1134; internet www.kctu.org; f. 1995; legalized 1999; Chair. Lee Soo-Ho; c. 600,000 mems.

Transport

RAILWAYS

At the end of 2001 there were 6,819 km (including freight routes) of railways in operation. Construction of a new high-speed rail system connecting Seoul to Busan (412 km) via Cheonan, Daejeon, Daegu, and Gyungju, was under way in 2003. The first phase, Seoul–Daejeon, was scheduled for completion in 2004. The second phase, Daejeon–Busan, was scheduled for completion in 2010. Construction work on the reconnection of the Kyongui (West coast, Sinuiju (North Korea)–Seoul) and East Coast Line (Wonsan (North Korea)–Seoul) began in September 2002. The two lines were officially opened in June 2003, but were not yet open to traffic, as construction work on the Northern side remained to be completed. Reconnection work was subject to disruption by the changing political situation. Eventually the two would be linked to the Trans-China and Trans-Siberian railways respectively, greatly enhancing the region's transportation links.

Korean National Railroad: 920, Dunsan-dong, Seo-gu, Daejeon 302-701; tel. (42) 1544-7788; fax (42) 481-373; internet www.korail.go.kr; f. 1963; operates all railways under the supervision of the

Ministry of Construction and Transportation; total track length of 6,819 km (2001); Admin. Son Hak-Lae.

City Underground Railways

Busan Subway: Busan Urban Transit Authority, 861-1, Bumchun-dong, Busan 614-021; tel. (51) 633-8783; e-mail ipsubway@buta.or.kr; internet subway.busan.kr; f. 1988; length of 71.6 km (2 lines, with a further 3rd line under construction); Pres. Lee Hyang-Yeul.

Daegu Metropolitan Subway Corpn: 1500 Sangin 1-dong, Dalseo-gu, Daegu; tel. (53) 640-2114; fax (53) 640-2229; e-mail webmaster@daegusubway.co.kr; internet www.daegusubway.co.kr; length of 28.3 km (1 line, with a further five routes totalling 125.4 km planned or under construction); Pres. Yoon Jin-Tae.

Incheon Rapid Transit Corpn: 67-2, Gansok-dong, Namdong-gu, Incheon 405-233; tel. (32) 451-2114; fax (32) 451-2160; internet www.irtc.co.kr; length of 24.6 km (22 stations, 1 line), with two further lines planned; Pres. Choung In-Soung.

Seoul Metropolitan Rapid Transit Corporation: Seoul; internet www.smrt.co.kr; operates lines 5-8.

Seoul Metropolitan Subway Corpn: 447-7, Bangbae-dong, Seocho-gu, Seoul; tel. (2) 520-5020; fax (2) 520-5039; internet www.seoulsubway.co.kr; f. 1981; length of 134.9 km (115 stations, lines 1-4); Pres. Kim Jung-Gook.

Underground railways were also under construction in Daejeon and Gwangju.

ROADS

At the end of 2001 there were 91,396 km of roads, of which 76.7% were paved. A network of motorways (2,637 km) links all the principal towns, the most important being the 428-km Seoul–Busan motorway. Improvements in relations with North Korea resulted in the commencement of work on a four-lane highway to link Seoul and the North Korean capital, Pyongyang, in September 2000. In February 2003 a road link between the two countries was reportedly opened.

Korea Highway Corpn: 293-1, Kumto-dong, Sujong-gu, Seongnam, Gyeonggi Prov.; tel. (822) 2230-4114; fax (822) 2230-4308; internet www.freeway.co.kr; f. 1969; responsible for construction, maintenance and management of toll roads; Pres. Oh Jum-Lock.

SHIPPING

In December 2002 South Korea's merchant fleet (2,532 vessels) had a total displacement of 7,049,734 grt. Major ports include Busan, Incheon, Donghae, Masan, Yeosu, Gunsan, Mokpo, Pohang, Ulsan, Jeju and Gwangyang.

Korea Maritime and Port Authority: 112-2, Inui-dong, Jongno-gu, Seoul 110; tel. (2) 3466-2214; f. 1976; operates under the Ministry of Maritime Affairs and Fisheries; supervises all aspects of shipping and port-related affairs; Admin. Ahn Kong-Hyuk.

Korea Shipowners' Association: Sejong Bldg, 10th Floor, 100, Dangju-dong, Jongno-gu, Seoul 110-071; tel. (2) 739-1551; fax (2) 739-1565; e-mail korea@shipowners.or.kr; internet www.shipowners.co.kr; f. 1960; 40 shipping co mems; Chair. Hyun Yung-Won.

Korea Shipping Association: 66010, Dungchon 3-dong, Gangseo-gu, Seoul 157-033; tel. (2) 6096-2024; fax (2) 6096-2029; e-mail kimny@haewoon.co.kr; internet www.haewoon.co.kr; f. 1962; management consulting and investigation, mutual insurance; 1,189 mems; Chair. Park Hong-Jin.

Principal Companies

Cho Yang Shipping Co Ltd: Chongam Bldg, 85-3, Seosomun-dong, Jung-gu, CPOB 1163, Seoul 100; tel. (2) 3708-6000; fax (2) 3708-6926; internet www.choyang.co.kr; f. 1961; Korea–Japan, Korea–China, Korea–Australia–Japan, Asia–Mediterranean–America liner services and world-wide tramping; Chair. N. K. Park; Pres. J. W. Park.

DooYang Line Co Ltd: 166-4, Samseong-dong, Gangnam-gu, Seoul 135-091; tel. (2) 550-1700; fax (2) 550-1777; internet www.dooyang.co.kr; f. 1984; world-wide tramping and conventional liner trade; Pres. Cho Dong-Hyun.

Hanjin Shipping Ltd: 25-11, Yeouido-dong, Yeongdeungpo-gu, Seoul; tel. (2) 3770-6114; fax (2) 3770-6740; internet www.hanjin.com; f. 1977; marine transportation, harbour service, warehousing, shipping and repair, vessel sales, harbour department and cargo service; Pres. Choi Won-Pyo.

Hyundai Merchant Marine Co Ltd: 66, Jeokseon-dong, Jongno-gu, Seoul 110-052; tel. (2) 3706-5114; fax (2) 723-2193; internet www.hmm.co.kr; f. 1976; Chair. Hyun Yung-Won.

Korea Line Corpn: Dae Il Bldg, 43, Insa-dong, Jongno-gu, Seoul 110-290; tel. (2) 3701-0114; fax (2) 733-1610; f. 1968; world-wide transportation service and shipping agency service in Korea; Pres. Jang Hak-Se.

Pan Ocean Shipping Co Ltd: 51-1, Namchang-dong, Jung-gu, CPOB 3051, Seoul 100-060; tel. (2) 316-5114; fax (2) 316-5296; f. 1966; transportation of passenger cars and trucks, chemical and petroleum products, dry bulk cargo; Pres. Chiang Jin-Won.

CIVIL AVIATION

There are seven international airports in Korea; at Incheon (Seoul), Gimpo (Seoul), Busan, Cheongju, Daegu, Gwangju, Jeju and Yangyang. The main gateway into Seoul is Incheon International Airport, which opened for service in March 2001. It is used by 30m. passengers annually, and has a capacity for 240,000 aircraft movements annually. The second phase began construction in 2002, with completion due by 2008. When complete, the airport will handle 44m. passengers and 4.5m. tons of cargo annually. The airport is located 52 km from Seoul. A new airport, Yangyang International Airport, opened in Gangwon province in April 2002.

Asiana Airlines Inc: 47, Osae-dong, Gangseo-gu, Seoul; tel. (2) 758-8114; fax (2) 758-8008; e-mail asianacr@asiana.co.kr; internet www.asiana.co.kr; f. 1988; serves 14 domestic cities and 36 destinations in 16 countries; CEO Park Sam-Koo.

Korean Air: 1370, Gonghang-dong, Gangseo-gu, Seoul; tel. (2) 656-7092; fax (2) 656-7289; internet www.koreanair.com; f. 1962 by the Govt, privately owned since 1969; fmrly Korean Air Lines (KAL); operates domestic and regional services and routes to the Americas, Europe, the Far East and the Middle East, serving 73 cities in 26 countries; Pres. and CEO Shim Yi-Taek.

Seoul Air International: CPOB 10352, Seoul 100-699; tel. (2) 699-0991; fax (2) 699-0954; operates domestic flights and routes throughout Asia.

Tourism

South Korea's mountain scenery and historic sites are the principal attractions for tourists. Jeju Island, located some 100 km off the southern coast, is a popular resort. In 2001 there were 5,147,204 visitors to South Korea, of whom about 46% came from Japan. Receipts from tourism in 2001 amounted to US $6,282.5m.

Korea National Tourism Organization: KNTO Bldg, 10, Da-dong, Jung-gu, CPOB 903, Seoul 100; tel. (2) 729-9600; fax (2) 757-5997; internet www.knto.or.kr; f. 1962 as Korea Tourist Service; Pres. Lee Deuk-Ryul.

Korea Tourism Association: Saman Bldg, 11th Floor, 945, Daechi-dong, Gangnam-gu, Seoul; tel. (2) 556-2356; fax (2) 556-3818; f. 1963; Pres. Cho Hang-Kyu, Kim Jae-Gi.

KUWAIT

Introductory Survey

Location, Climate, Language, Religion, Flag, Capital

The State of Kuwait lies at the north-west extreme of the Persian (Arabian) Gulf, bordered to the north-west by Iraq and to the south by Saudi Arabia. The State comprises a mainland region and nine small islands, of which the largest is Bubiyan and the most populous is Failaka. Immediately to the south of Kuwait, along the Gulf, lies a Neutral (Partitioned) Zone of 5,700 sq km, which is shared between Kuwait and Saudi Arabia. Much of Kuwait is arid desert, and the climate is generally hot and humid. Temperatures in July and August often exceed 45°C (113°F), and in the winter months are frequently above 20°C (68°F)—although there is often frost at night. Average annual rainfall is only 111 mm. The official language is Arabic, which is spoken by the majority of Kuwaiti nationals (estimated, by official definition, to have comprised 41.2% of Kuwait's population at mid-2000) and by many of the country's non-Kuwaiti residents. Apart from other Arabs, the non-Kuwaitis are mainly Iranians, Indians and Pakistanis. At the 1975 census 95.0% of the population were Muslims (of whom about 70% are now thought to belong to the Sunni sect), while 4.5% were Christians, Hindus or adherents of other faiths. The national flag (proportions 1 by 2) has three equal horizontal stripes, of green, white and red, with a superimposed black trapezoid at the hoist. The capital is Kuwait City.

Recent History

Kuwait became part of Turkey's Ottoman Empire in the 16th century. During the later years of Ottoman rule Kuwait became a semi-autonomous Arab monarchy, with local administration controlled by a Sheikh of the Sabah family, which is still the ruling dynasty. In 1899, fearing an extension of Turkish control, the ruler of Kuwait made a treaty with the United Kingdom, accepting British protection while surrendering control over external relations. Nominal Turkish suzerainty over Kuwait ended in 1918, with the dissolution of the Ottoman Empire.

Petroleum was first discovered in Kuwait in 1938, but exploration was interrupted by the Second World War. After 1945 drilling resumed on a large scale, and extensive deposits of petroleum were found. Sheikh Ahmad (ruler since 1921) was succeeded in 1950 by his cousin, Sheikh Abdullah as-Salim as-Sabah, who inaugurated a programme of public works and educational development, funded by petroleum revenues, which transformed Kuwait's infrastructure and introduced a comprehensive system of welfare services.

Kuwait became fully independent on 19 June 1961, when the United Kingdom and Kuwait agreed to terminate the 1899 treaty. The ruler took the title of Amir and assumed full executive power. Kuwait was admitted to the League of Arab States (the Arab League, see p. 278) despite opposition from Iraq, which claimed that Kuwait was historically part of Iraqi territory. Kuwait's first election took place in December 1961, when voters chose 20 members of a Constituent Assembly (the other members being cabinet ministers appointed by the Amir). The Assembly drafted a new Constitution, which was adopted in December 1962. A 50-member Majlis al-Umma (National Assembly) was elected, under a limited franchise (see Government, below), in January 1963. In the absence of formal political parties (which remain illegal), candidates contested the poll as independents, although some known opponents of the Government were elected. In the same month the Amir appointed his brother, Sheikh Sabah as-Salem as-Sabah (the heir apparent), to be Prime Minister. Iraq renounced its claim to Kuwait in October, and diplomatic relations were established.

In January 1965, following conflict between the paternalistic ruling family and the democratically inclined Majlis, the powers of the Council of Ministers were strengthened. The Amir died in November 1965, and Sheikh Sabah succeeded to the throne. He was replaced as Prime Minister by his cousin, Sheikh Jaber al-Ahmad as-Sabah, who was named heir apparent in May 1966. The Neutral (Partitioned) Zone between Kuwait and Saudi Arabia was formally divided between the two countries in 1969: revenues from oil production in the area are shared equally.

As Kuwait's petroleum sector expanded during the 1960s, the country became increasingly wealthy. The Government effected an extensive redistribution of income, through public expenditure and a land compensation scheme, but there was some popular discontent concerning corruption and official manipulation of the media and the Majlis. A more representative legislature was elected in January 1971 (again under a limited franchise). A further general election took place in January 1975, but in August 1976 the Amir dissolved the Majlis, on the grounds that it was acting against the best interests of the State. Sheikh Sabah died on 31 December 1977 and was succeeded by Crown Prince Jaber. In January 1978 the new Amir appointed Sheikh Saad al-Abdullah as-Salim as-Sabah to be his heir apparent. The new Crown Prince, hitherto Minister of Defence and the Interior, became Prime Minister in the following month. In accordance with an Amiri decree of August 1980, a new Majlis was elected in February 1981, although only one-half of the eligible 6% of the population registered to vote.

The collapse of Kuwait's unofficial stock exchange, the Souk al-Manakh, in September 1982 caused a prolonged financial crisis, and eventually led to the resignations of the Ministers of Finance (in 1983) and of Justice (in 1985). The Majlis subsequently opposed several government measures, including proposed price increases for public services, educational reforms and legislation to restrict the press, and questioned the competence of certain ministers. In July 1986 the Council of Ministers submitted its resignation to the Amir, who then dissolved the Majlis and suspended some articles of the Constitution, declaring his intention to rule by decree. The Crown Prince was immediately reappointed Prime Minister. An Amiri decree accorded the Council of Ministers greater powers of censorship, including the right to suspend publication of newspapers for up to two years.

In late 1989 the Amir refused to accept a petition, signed by more than 20,000 Kuwaiti citizens, seeking the restoration of the Majlis. In January 1990 police dispersed two pro-democracy demonstrations, although later in the month the Government agreed to relax press censorship. In June 62% of eligible voters participated in a general election for 50 members of a 'provisional' National Council; a further 25 members were appointed by the Amir. The election was boycotted by pro-democracy activists, who continued to demand the full restoration of the Majlis.

Of all the Gulf states, Kuwait has been most vulnerable to regional disruption. Immediately after independence British troops (soon replaced by an Arab League force) were dispatched to support the country against the territorial claim by Iraq. The force remained until 1963, and relations between Kuwait and Iraq were stable until 1973, when Iraqi troops occupied a Kuwaiti outpost on their joint border. Kuwait none the less supplied aid to Iraq from the outbreak of the Iran–Iraq war in 1980. As a result, Kuwaiti petroleum installations and shipping in the Persian (Arabian) Gulf were targeted intermittently by Iranian forces, and by pro-Iranian groups within Kuwait, for much of the 1980s. A large number of Iranians were among 27,000 expatriates deported in 1985–86, and in 1987 the Government initiated a five-year plan to reduce the number of expatriates in the Kuwaiti work-force. Kuwait resumed diplomatic relations with Iran following the 1988 cease-fire between Iran and Iraq.

In July 1990 the Iraqi Government implicitly criticized Kuwait (among other states) for disregarding the petroleum production quotas stipulated by the Organization of the Petroleum Exporting Countries (OPEC, see p. 317). It also declared that Kuwait should cancel Iraq's war debt and compensate it for losses of revenue incurred during the war with Iran, and as a result of Kuwait's overproduction of petroleum—to which Iraq attributed a decline in international oil prices. In addition, Iraq alleged that Kuwait had established military posts and drilled oil wells on Iraqi territory. Despite regional mediation efforts, Iraq subsequently began to deploy armed forces on the Kuwait–Iraq border. Direct negotiations in Jeddah, Saudi Arabia, at the end of the month between Kuwaiti and Iraqi officials collapsed, and on 2 August some 100,000 Iraqi troops invaded Kuwait (whose total military strength was about 20,000): Iraq stated that it had entered at the invitation of insurgents who had overthrown the Kuwaiti Government. The Amir and other government members fled to Saudi Arabia, where they established a 'Government-in-exile', while Iraq declared that a provisional Government had been formed in Kuwait comprising Iraqi-sponsored Kuwaiti dissidents. The UN Security Council immediately adopted a series of resolutions, of which the first (Resolution 660) condemned the invasion, demanded the immediate and unconditional withdrawal of Iraqi forces from Kuwait, and appealed for a negotiated settlement of the conflict. A trade embargo was then imposed on Iraq and Kuwait. Meanwhile, the USA and member states of the European Community (now European Union—EU, see p. 208) froze all Kuwait's overseas assets to prevent their repatriation. Five days after the invasion US troops and aircraft were deployed in Saudi Arabia, with the stated aim of securing that country's borders with Kuwait in the event of further Iraqi territorial expansion. A number of European Governments, together with some Arab League states, agreed to provide military support for the US forces. The Iraqi Government subsequently announced the formal annexation of Kuwait, and ordered the closure of foreign diplomatic missions there. At the end of August most of Kuwait was officially declared to be the 19th Governorate of Iraq, while a northern strip was incorporated into the Basra Governorate.

In the months following the invasion apparent attempts at demographic manipulation—by settling Iraqis and Palestinians in Kuwait and by forcing Kuwaitis to assume Iraqi citizenship—were documented. The population was estimated to have decreased from approximately 2m. prior to the invasion to some 700,000, of whom Kuwaitis constituted about 300,000, Palestinians 200,000, and the remainder comprised other Arab and Asian expatriates. Many Kuwaitis, and Arab and Asian expatriates, had fled Iraq and Kuwait into Jordan, while most European and US expatriates were detained as hostages; by the end of 1990 it was claimed that all hostages had been released.

UN Security Council Resolution 678, adopted in November 1990, authorized the multinational force by now stationed in Saudi Arabia and the Gulf region to use 'all necessary means' to liberate Kuwait. It was implied that should Iraq not begin, by 15 January 1991, to implement the terms of 10 resolutions hitherto adopted regarding the invasion, military action would ensue. Renewed international diplomatic attempts failed to avert a military confrontation. On the night of 16–17 January the US-led multinational force launched an intensive aerial bombardment of Iraq. Ground forces entered Kuwait during the night of 23–24 February, encountering relatively little effective Iraqi opposition. Within three days the Iraqi Government had agreed to comply with the terms of all Security Council resolutions concerning Kuwait, and on 28 February the USA announced a suspension of military operations. Resolutions 686 and 687, adopted by the UN Security Council in March and April respectively, dictated the terms to Iraq for a permanent cease-fire: Iraq was required to release all allied prisoners of war and Kuwaitis detained as hostages, repeal all laws and decrees concerning the annexation of Kuwait, and recognize the inviolability of the Iraq–Kuwait border. Iraq promptly announced its compliance with both resolutions. Resolution 689, adopted in April, provided for the establishment of a demilitarized zone, to be supervised by a UN Iraq-Kuwait Observer Mission (UNIKOM).

Meanwhile, in October 1990, at a conference in Jeddah of some 1,000 prominent Kuwaitis, the exiled Crown Prince Saad agreed to establish government advisory committees on political, social and financial matters, and pledged to restore the country's Constitution and legislature and to organize free elections after Kuwait's eventual liberation. In February 1991, however, the Government-in-exile excluded the possibility of early elections, maintaining that the need to rebuild and repopulate the country took precedence over that for political reform. Immediately following liberation an Amiri decree imposed martial law in Kuwait, and in March the formation of a state security committee was announced: its objectives included the investigation of individuals suspected of collaboration with the Iraqi authorities in Kuwait, the prevention of unofficial acts of reprisal and the identification of those civilians relocated to Kuwait by Iraq. Palestinians in Kuwait were a particular target of reprisals, and it was alleged by several human rights organizations that they were subject to torture by Kuwaiti security forces. Kuwait's Palestinian population, which had totalled around 400,000 prior to the Iraqi invasion, was estimated to have declined to less than 50,000 by early 1992.

The Amir, the Prime Minister and other members of the exiled regime returned to Kuwait in March 1991. The Council of Ministers resigned later that month, apparently in response to public discontent at the Government's failure to restore essential services. Although several specialists were appointed to strategic posts within the new Government named by Sheikh Saad in April (most notably to the finance, planning and oil portfolios), other important positions (including the foreign affairs, interior and defence ministries) were allocated to members of the as-Sabah family.

In May 1991 it was revealed that some 900 people were under investigation in Kuwait in connection with crimes committed during the Iraqi occupation; about 200 of these were accused of collaboration. The human rights organization Amnesty International expressed concern that trials were being conducted without the provision of adequate defence counsel, and alleged that torture had in some cases been used to extract confessions. The Government undertook to investigate such abuses. Martial law was ended in June, and 29 death sentences hitherto imposed on convicted collaborators were commuted to custodial terms. Outstanding trials relating to the occupation were to be referred to civilian courts, and in August a tribunal, said to guarantee defendants the right to greater legal protection as well as a right of appeal, was established to replace the martial law courts. Amid continuing international criticism of Kuwait's record on human rights, measures were subsequently taken to prevent clandestine deportations of alleged collaborators and to permit international supervision of the expulsion of foreign nationals. However, it was widely believed that Kuwait had been motivated to curb human rights abuses primarily in an attempt to procure international support for its efforts to secure the release of Kuwaiti nationals detained in Iraq.

It was announced in May 1991 that a US military presence would remain in Kuwait until September, by which time, it was envisaged, a regional defence force would be established. However, little progress was achieved in negotiations for such a force, and in August the USA announced that it would maintain 1,500 troops in Kuwait for several more months. In September the US and Kuwaiti Governments signed a 10-year military co-operation agreement, permitting the storage of US supplies and equipment in Kuwait, and providing for joint military training and exercises. (The agreement was renewed for a further 10 years in February 2001.) Defence accords were signed with both the United Kingdom and France in 1992.

In June 1993 the State Security Court was reported to have issued death sentences against 17 people who had been found guilty of collaborating with Iraq in 1990–91; Alaa Hussein Ali, the leader of the provisional Government installed by Iraq in August 1990, was convicted *in absentia*. In February 1994 Amnesty International again alleged serious violations of human rights in Kuwait, asserting that at least 120 alleged collaborators had been convicted by trials that failed to satisfy international minimum standards. Human rights organizations welcomed the endorsement by the Majlis, in August 1995, of government proposals to abolish the State Security Court. In January 1997 the Government announced the creation of a new human rights committee within the Ministry of the Interior.

Press censorship was partially relaxed in January 1992. Elections to the new Majlis, on 5 October, were contested by some 280 candidates, many of whom (although nominally independent) were affiliated to one of several quasi-political organizations. The franchise was again restricted, with only about 81,400 men eligible to vote. Anti-Government candidates, notably those representing Islamist groups, were unexpectedly successful, securing 31 of the Assembly's 50 seats. The Prime Minister subsequently formed a new Government, including six members of the Majlis, who were allocated, *inter alia*, the oil and justice portfolios; members of the ruling family retained control of foreign affairs, the interior and defence.

The Majlis voted in December 1992 to establish a commission of inquiry into the circumstances surrounding the 1990 invasion. The commission's report, published in May 1995, revealed profound negligence on the part of government and military officials, who had apparently ignored warnings of an imminent invasion. The report also claimed that the immediate flight of members of the royal family and the Council of Ministers had deprived the country of political leadership and military organization.

Meanwhile, in January 1993 legislation was enacted whereby the Majlis would have automatic access to the financial accounts of all state-owned companies and investment organizations, and stricter penalties would be imposed in cases of abuse of public funds. Demands for greater parliamentary scrutiny of the State's investments were largely prompted by revelations of the misappropriation of funds by the London-based Kuwait Investment Office (KIO), responsible for much of Kuwait's overseas investment portfolio (22 former KIO executives, including Sheikh Fahd Muhammad as-Sabah—its Chairman at the time of the Iraqi invasion—were reportedly implicated in the allegations), and also by emerging evidence of financial misconduct at the state-owned Kuwait Oil Tanker Co (KOTC). In July 1996 three former executives received prison sentences of between 15 and 40 years, having been convicted of corruption by the criminal court; they were ordered to repay embezzled funds, together with fines totalling more than US $100m. In June 1999 the High Court in London ruled that Sheikh Fahd and two other former KIO senior executives were guilty, in absentia, of conspiracy and fraud involving some $460m. against the KIO's Spanish subsidiary during 1988–92.

The ruling family retained control of the foreign affairs, interior and defence portfolios following a reorganization of the Council of Ministers in April 1994. In June the Majlis approved legislation extending the franchise to sons of naturalized Kuwaitis. In July 1995 the Assembly approved a bill reducing from 30 years to 20 the minimum period after which naturalized Kuwaitis would become eligible to vote. In July 1996 the Ministry of the Interior announced that an electorate of just over 107,000 men was entitled to vote in the forthcoming elections to the Majlis, scheduled for 7 October. Pro-Government candidates were the most successful, securing the majority of the 50 seats. Sheikh Saad was reappointed Prime Minister; his new Council of Ministers included four newly elected deputies.

In March 1998 Sheikh Saad submitted his Government's resignation, after members of the Majlis proposed a motion of 'no confidence' in the Minister of Information, Sheikh Sa'ud Nasir as-Sa'ud as-Sabah, who had allowed what were deemed 'un-Islamic' publications to be exhibited at a book fair in Kuwait. The Amir immediately reappointed the Crown Prince as Prime Minister, and a new Government was named at the end of the month. The promotion of Sheikh Sa'ud to the post of Minister of Oil was controversial not only because of the recent action by the Majlis against him, but also because the oil portfolio was not customarily allocated to a member of the ruling family. An institutional crisis appeared imminent in June, when the Majlis sought to cross-examine the Minister of the Interior, Sheikh Muhammad Khalid al-Hamad as-Sabah, on issues including corruption, illicit drugs and human rights. However, the ministry in question was deemed by the Government to be 'sovereign' and therefore exempt from examination by the Majlis. Relations between the Government and the Majlis deteriorated further, necessitating intervention by the Amir to dispel rumours that the Assembly would be dissolved and a general election called. Tensions were swiftly revived in July, when the Government introduced amendments to legislation enacted in 1993 (and previously amended in 1995) regarding repayment of debts arising from the collapse of the Souk al-Manakh in 1982. Many deputies regarded new arrangements for the discharge of liabilities to be unduly favourable to debtors, many of whom were members of the ruling family, and boycotted an initial vote before reluctantly approving the amendments in August 1998. The Deputy Prime Minister and Minister of State for Cabinet Affairs, Nasir Abdullah ar-Rodhan, resigned in November. He was replaced in the following month by Abd al-Aziz ad-Dakhil, hitherto Minister of Commerce and Industry, whose former post was allocated to Hisham al-Otaibi, President of the Kuwait Stock Exchange.

Confrontation persisted between the Government and the Majlis, which in February 1999 refused to refer to its finance committee government proposals for economic reform. In May the Amir dissolved the legislature and called fresh elections, after deputies had in the previous month questioned the Minister of Justice, Awqaf (Religious Endowments) and Islamic Affairs over errors that had appeared in copies of the Koran printed and distributed by his ministry. Some 80% of an eligible electorate of 113,000 Kuwaiti men voted in the election, which took place on 3 July. Pro-Government candidates recorded the greatest losses, taking only 12 seats; Islamist candidates won 20 seats, and liberals 14 seats, with the remaining four won by independents. Sheikh Saad was immediately reappointed Prime

Minister, and a new Council of Ministers was inaugurated in mid-July. The ruling family retained control of the strategic foreign affairs, oil, interior and defence portfolios, although a number of liberal deputies joined the Government. Meanwhile, during the period between the dissolution of the Majlis and the election, the Government promulgated some 60 decrees (subject to legislative approval), most notably one proposing that women should be allowed to contest and to vote in elections from 2003. However, the law on female suffrage was defeated by a considerable majority when subjected to a vote in the new Majlis in November 1999, as liberal deputies, who supported women's enfranchisement, registered their protest at what they considered to be the unconstitutionality of legislation by decree by joining Islamist and conservative deputies in voting against the measure. Liberal deputies immediately submitted identical legislation regarding women's suffrage, but this was narrowly defeated in a vote at the end of the month. Kuwaiti women suffered a further reverse in their attempts to secure the right to contest and vote in elections in January 2001, when the Constitutional Court rejected a lawsuit brought by a male citizen against the State's election department for having failed to register the names of five women on electoral lists in his constituency. In March the Majlis rejected, on procedural grounds, draft legislation that would increase women's political rights.

In January 2000 Alaa Hussein Ali, leader of the provisional Government installed by Iraq in August 1990, who had been in self-imposed exile since Kuwait's liberation, returned to Kuwait in order to appeal against the death sentence pronounced in June 1993 (see above); the appeal hearing began at the Court of First Instance in February 2000. In May it was announced that Hussein had lost his appeal, and that he planned a further challenge to his sentence. The Court of Appeal upheld the previous ruling in July, but in March 2001 commuted Hussein's death sentence to one of life imprisonment.

In July 2000 unrest was reported in the Al-Jahra region, where a community of *bidoon* ('stateless' Arabs) form the majority of the population. (About 100,000 *bidoon* reside in Kuwait, but the authorities refuse to recognize their claims to Kuwaiti nationality.) The unrest followed the approval, in May, of a draft amendment to the Citizenship Law that would grant only a small number of *bidoon* the right to Kuwaiti citizenship. Some 1,000 *bidoon* obtained Kuwaiti citizenship in early 2001, leading to protests by those whose applications had been refused.

The issue of press freedom caused a renewed deterioration in relations between the Government and the Majlis in February 2000, when deputies criticized government efforts to suspend publication of two Kuwaiti newspapers, *Al-Watan* and *As-Seyassah*, for publishing reports of salary increases for the security forces. The Amir subsequently ordered that any planned action against the publications be abandoned. Later in the month a joint statement issued by several newspaper editors accused the Minister of Information of allowing actions that impeded press freedom. Amnesty International expressed concern in March that freedom of expression remained under threat in Kuwait, and urged the Government to end its practice of punishing journalists and authors for using what it deemed to be 'un-Islamic' language.

In November 2000 the Amir accepted the resignation of the Minister of Information, Dr Saad Muhammad bin Teflah al-Ajmi. Sheikh Saad tendered his Government's resignation in January 2001. The Crown Prince denied that this constituted an attempt to prevent parliamentary scrutiny of the Minister of Justice and of Awqaf and Islamic Affairs, Saad Jasem Yousuf al-Hashil, relating to allegations of inefficiency and corruption in his ministry. The Amir immediately reappointed Sheikh Saad as Prime Minister, and a new 15-member Government was named in mid-February. The new administration included five younger members of the ruling family, as well as four members of the Majlis. The outgoing Deputy Prime Minister and Minister of Defence, Sheikh Salim Sabah as-Salim as-Sabah, left the Government, although the defence, foreign affairs and interior portfolios remained in the hands of the as-Sabah family. A new minister, Ahmad Yaqub Bakir al-Abdullah, was named as Minister of Justice and of Awqaf and Islamic Affairs, while some controversy was caused by the allocation of the oil portfolio to Dr Adil Khalid as-Sabih, the minister previously responsible for the electricity, water and housing portfolios who had recently survived a parliamentary vote of 'no confidence' in respect of his business interests.

Meanwhile, during November 2000, as the crisis in Israeli–Palestinian relations deepened, 16 suspected Islamist militants (Kuwaitis and other Arab nationals) were arrested in Kuwait, accused of involvement in plotting bomb attacks on US military installations in the Gulf region in retaliation for perceived US support for Israel. The arrests of the alleged saboteurs followed reports that a Moroccan aide to the Saudi-born leader of the militant Islamist al-Qa'ida (Base) organization, Osama bin Laden, had entered Kuwait from Afghanistan; however, the aide subsequently fled to Iran. In June 2001 a senior Kuwaiti military official was convicted of concealing weapons to be used for terrorist purposes; he received a 10-year prison sentence, but in December this was reduced to seven years. (Eight of the suspected militants were given suspended sentences and ordered to pay fines; the remainder were acquitted.)

At the end of January 2002 four people died and about 19 were injured following a major explosion at Raudhatain, Kuwait's second largest oilfield, to the north of Kuwait City. Adil Khalid as-Sabih immediately submitted his resignation as Minister of Oil, stating that he accepted responsibility for the incident; he also ordered an investigation into the cause of the explosion. The Minister of Information, Sheikh Ahmad al-Fahd al-Ahmad as-Sabah, was subsequently named as acting Minister of Oil. However, a political crisis ensued after it proved impossible to find a permanent replacement for Dr as-Sabih, and Sheikh Ahmad was asked to remain in charge of the oil portfolio until the general election (scheduled for mid-2003). Meanwhile, several members of the Majlis demanded the resignation of the entire Government, alleging that the explosion at Raudhatain was the result of state corruption and mismanagement. In January 2003 the Amir accepted the resignation of the Minister of Finance, of Planning and Minister of State for Administrative Development Affairs, Dr Yousuf Hamad al-Ibrahim, who had been the object of severe parliamentary criticism. Dr al-Ibrahim, a leading reformist, had in July 2002 survived a vote of 'no confidence' instigated by Islamist Majlis deputies who accused him of poor management of the Government's fiscal affairs. The finance and planning portfolios were provisionally passed to the Minister of State for Foreign Affairs, Sheikh Muhammad Sabah as-Salim as-Sabah, and the Minister of Education and Higher Education, Dr Musaad Rashid al-Haroun, was given the additional position of Acting Minister of State for Administrative Development Affairs.

After a campaign that was overshadowed by the US-led military intervention in Iraq (which was largely conducted from Kuwaiti territory), parliamentary elections were held, as scheduled, on 5 July 2003. Islamist candidates secured 21 of the 50 seats in the Majlis, while pro-Government candidates won 14 seats, independents (regarded as being aligned with the Government) 12 and liberals three. The rate of voter participation was reported to be only 45% of the 6% of the total population who form the electorate. The results were viewed as a major setback for those seeking political reform, and were widely interpreted as signalling popular dissatisfaction with the entire political process.

Following the elections, in July 2003 the Crown Prince relinquished the position of Prime Minister. The appointment of Sheikh Sabah as his replacement represented an unprecedented separation between the post of Prime Minister and the position of Crown Prince, and provided some encouragement to reformists after their heavy electoral losses. A new Council of Ministers, including six new appointments, was also announced in mid-July. The most significant change was the merger of the oil portfolio with the Ministry of Electricity and Water to form the Ministry of Energy, to be headed by Sheikh Ahmad al-Fahd al-Ahmad as-Sabah. In late July Faisal al-Hajji was appointed as Minister of Social Affairs and Labour, a position that had been filled on an interim basis by the Minister of Foreign Affairs, Sheikh Muhammad Sabah as-Salim as-Sabah. In October the Council of Ministers approved a new law that would henceforth give women the right to vote in and contest municipal elections. However, the new policy would not alter the exclusion of women from parliamentary elections.

In March 2004 the Minister of Finance, Mahmud Abd al-Khaliq an-Nuri, narrowly survived a vote of 'no confidence', having been heavily criticized by the Majlis for mismanagement during the sale of state property.

Friction between Kuwait and Iraq in the aftermath of the Gulf War was exacerbated by the issue of the demarcation of their joint border. The UN commission with responsibility for delineating the frontier formalized the land border as it had been defined by British administrators in 1932 (and officially agreed by Kuwait and Iraq in 1963). The boundary, the validity of which was now rejected by Iraq, was established some 570 m north of its pre-war position, dividing the Iraqi port of Umm Qasr, with the effect that Iraq retained the town and much of the harbour while Kuwait was awarded hinterland which included an abandoned Iraqi naval base; the border also situated several Iraqi oil wells on Kuwaiti territory. In January 1993 the USA led air attacks on Iraq, and more than 1,000 US troops were dispatched to Kuwait, in response to a series of incursions by Iraqi forces into Kuwaiti territory in the days immediately preceding the designated entry into force of the new border; its formal delineation was completed in March, when the UN commission defined the maritime border along the median line of the Khawr Abd Allah waterway. Allegations made by Kuwait of Iraqi violations of the border, and of attempts to impede construction of a trench along the land border, intensified during the second half of 1993, and there were sporadic reports of exchanges of fire in the border region. In November a 775-strong armed UNIKOM reinforcement was deployed in northern Kuwait, with authorization (under specific circumstances) to use its weapons to assist the unarmed force already in the demilitarized zone.

In October 1994 Iraq deployed some 70,000 troops and 700 tanks near the border with Kuwait, in an apparent attempt to force an easing of UN economic sanctions. Kuwait immediately mobilized its army reserves, and dispatched some 20,000 troops to the border region. The USA committed almost 40,000 land, naval and air forces to the region; France and the United Kingdom deployed naval vessels, and the United Kingdom dispatched about 1,200 troops. Following Russian mediation, Iraq announced its willingness to recognize Kuwait's sovereignty and borders on condition that the UN ease sanctions against Iraq after six months. However, the UN Security Council adopted a resolution (No. 949) requiring Iraq's unconditional recognition of Kuwait's sovereignty and borders and restricting the movement of Iraqi troops in the border area. In November Iraq officially recognized Kuwait's sovereignty, territorial integrity and political independence, as well as its UN-defined borders. Most of the US and British reinforcements deployed in the region in October had been withdrawn by the end of the year. Kuwait's relations with Iraq deteriorated sharply in September 1996, after the Kuwaiti Government agreed to the deployment in Kuwait of US military aircraft and troops in support of a US operation to force the withdrawal of Iraqi armed forces from the Kurdish 'safe haven' in northern Iraq. In December the USA announced that some 4,200 US troops deployed in Kuwait during 1996 would be withdrawn by the end of the year, although the deployment of US F-117 *Stealth* fighter aircraft was to be extended.

Kuwait and Iraq made mutual accusations of territorial violations and attacks on shipping during 1997. Meanwhile, Kuwait continued to support the maintenance of international sanctions against Iraq, and to demand adherence by Iraq to all relevant UN resolutions adopted since the Gulf crisis. Furthermore, statements by the Iraqi Government that it was holding no Kuwaiti prisoners of war were refuted by Kuwait: the Kuwaiti authorities, asserting that some 600 Kuwaitis remained captive in Iraq, claimed in late 1997 to be in possession of documentation, passed by Iraq to the International Committee of the Red Cross (ICRC), relating to 126 Kuwaiti prisoners of war. As the crisis involving weapons inspections in Iraq by the UN Special Commission (see the Recent History of Iraq) deepened in February 1998, fears were expressed for Kuwait's security—in particular that an attack on Iraq might result in the use of chemical or other weapons of mass destruction against Kuwait. Although Kuwait was the only country in the region to announce its approval of the use of force against Iraq should diplomatic efforts fail, it emphasized that any military action would exacerbate hardship suffered by the Iraqi people and increase regional instability. The USA, supported by the United Kingdom, undertook a military deployment in the Gulf region at this time: by the end of the month, when the UN Secretary-General and the Iraqi Government reached a compromise agreement regarding weapons inspections, some 6,000 US ground troops had been dispatched to Kuwait. A series of air-strikes against targets in Iraq by US and British forces from December 1998 again increased tensions between Kuwait and Iraq. Iraq accused Kuwait of collaborating in the air attacks, and frequently reiterated claims to Kuwaiti territory. In September 1999 Kuwait lodged an official protest over changes made to the final draft of an Arab League report to which, Kuwait asserted, references to the formation of a 'mechanism' to resolve the issue of Kuwaiti and other prisoners of war in Iraq had been added; Kuwait maintained that the ICRC was the only body empowered to deal with the issue. In November the Majlis established a committee to examine future relations with Iraq, and in December the Kuwaiti Government welcomed UN Security Council Resolution 1284 (establishing a new weapons inspectorate for Iraq, q.v.), which incorporated demands for the repatriation of Kuwaiti and other prisoners from Iraq, for Iraq's co-operation with the ICRC, and for the return of Kuwaiti property seized during the occupation.

In September 2000 ministers responsible for foreign affairs of the Co-operation Council for the Arab States of the Gulf (Gulf Co-operation Council—GCC, see p. 184) expressed concerns after the Iraqi leadership had repeatedly denounced both Kuwait and Saudi Arabia for allowing US and British military aircraft to use their airspace in order to conduct military attacks on Iraq, and had vowed to launch a new invasion of Kuwait. Iraq also renewed its long-standing accusation that Kuwait was drilling oil wells on Iraqi territory, and accused Kuwait and Saudi Arabia of inflicting suffering on the Iraqi population through the maintenance of UN sanctions. At the same time a number of small commercial vessels found to be entering or leaving Iraqi ports, allegedly in violation of the sanctions regime, were intercepted by Kuwaiti military units. In September and again in October Kuwait reinforced security along its border with Iraq, in the latter month to prevent a possible influx of *bidoon*, who had reportedly entered the demilitarized zone from Iraq and who were demanding the right of return to Kuwait (from where they had been excluded since the Gulf crisis).

In March 2001 a summit meeting of Arab League heads of state, held in Amman, Jordan, was considered as having made the most comprehensive effort hitherto in addressing divisions arising from the Gulf conflict. None the less, a draft resolution presented by the Iraqi delegation urging an end to UN sanctions and a resumption of civilian flights failed to secure adoption, owing to Iraq's unwillingness—on the grounds that it had already done sufficient to make clear its recognition of Kuwait's territorial integrity—to accede to a requirement of a specific guarantee that Iraq would not repeat the invasion of 1990. In November 2001 Kuwait issued a formal complaint to the UN following an alleged violation of its territory by Iraq. The incident occurred shortly after a senior Iraqi official had reiterated claims of sovereignty over Kuwait. In January 2002 the Kuwaiti leadership was reported to have rejected attempts by the Arab League to persuade it to accept Iraqi proposals apparently aimed at improving bilateral relations: as part of Iraq's diplomatic offensive to secure the support of the Arab world in view of the threat of US-led military action against Saddam Hussain's regime, the Iraqi leader had conveyed an appeal to Arab states to set aside their differences, referring specifically to the need to improve relations with Kuwait and Saudi Arabia. Later in the month it was reported that Iraq had announced its preparedness to allow a delegation from Kuwait to visit Iraq to verify that no Kuwaiti prisoners of war were being held. (Kuwait continued to assert that Iraq was detaining at least 90 Kuwaiti nationals.) At the Arab League summit held in Beirut, Lebanon, in late March 2002, however, it was announced that Kuwait and Iraq had reached agreement on the resolution of outstanding differences. The summit's final communiqué welcomed Iraq's assurances that it would respect the 'independence, sovereignty and security' of Kuwait, and safeguard its 'territorial integrity'; Iraq was urged to co-operate in seeking a 'definitive solution' to issues of Kuwaiti prisoners and detainees, and of the return of property, while Kuwait was called upon to 'co-operate with what Iraq offers with respect to its nationals' reported as missing through the ICRC. Kuwait's First Deputy Prime Minister and Minister of Foreign Affairs was subsequently reported as having expressed his complete satisfaction with the agreement.

Relations with Iraq were profoundly affected by the political repercussions of the September 2001 suicide attacks against the mainland USA. Kuwait, which strongly condemned the attacks, thereafter assumed an important role in persuading other Gulf states to join the US-led 'coalition against terror'. US bases in Kuwait were subsequently used to provide logistical support to the US-led campaign against al-Qa'ida (held by the USA to be principally responsible for the attacks on New York and Washington, DC) and its Taliban hosts in Afghanistan during late 2001. Meanwhile, in October 2001 the Kuwaiti authorities revoked the citizenship of the official spokesman of al-Qa'ida,

Sulayman Abu Ghaith, after remarks he had made via the Qatar-based Al-Jazeera television station. In late 2001 the Central Bank of Kuwait implemented measures designed to prevent Islamic charitable organizations from using Kuwait's financial institutions to channel funds to al-Qa'ida.

During the course of 2002 increased speculation that the US Administration of George W. Bush intended to extend the 'war against terror' to target the regime of Saddam Hussain in Iraq, exemplified not least by a series of visits to Kuwait by prominent US officials, threatened to fuel opposition to a continued US presence in the region and exacerbate an increasingly tense political situation in Kuwait. At the end of December some 12,000 US troops were stationed in Kuwait, and in early 2003 Kuwait's Ministry of Defence declared that the entire northern half of Kuwait would be designated a closed military zone from 15 February. Several US soldiers and civilians were killed in late 2002 and early 2003 in attacks by Kuwaitis, some of whom, it was alleged, had links to al-Qa'ida. In March an emergency meeting of the Arab League, hosted by Qatar, to discuss the deepening crisis descended into a bitter exchange of insults between, primarily, a senior Iraqi official and the Kuwaiti Minister of Information. Kuwait subsequently supported a proposal made by the President of the United Arab Emirates (UAE) for Saddam Hussain to go into exile in order to prevent a US-led war to remove his regime. At the outset of military action, which commenced on 20 March, US-led troops in Kuwait, the base for the main ground assault on Iraq, numbered some 140,000. Iraqi armed forces launched several missiles at Kuwaiti territory, although little damage was caused in the emirate during the course of the conflict. In mid-April, following the removal from power of Saddam Hussain, Kuwait announced that it had established a reward fund of US $1m. for information to help uncover the fate of persons missing since the 1990–91 Gulf crisis, who were estimated to number more than 600. In the aftermath of the most intense period of fighting, which President Bush declared to have ended by early May 2003, Kuwait renewed its financial demands against Iraq, while a number of Kuwaiti firms entered into agreements with the US-led occupying powers. In early October the demilitarized zone between Iraq and Kuwait was ended and, having fulfilled its mandate, UNIKOM's operations were terminated.

Meanwhile, in May 1994 the governing body of the UN Compensation Commission (UNCC), responsible for considering claims for compensation arising from the Gulf crisis, approved the first disbursements (to 670 families or individuals in 16 countries), totalling US $2.7m. By late 1996 payments amounting to $3,000m. (to be partly financed by Iraqi oil revenues) had been endorsed by the UN, which had yet to consider claims for a further $190,000m. In December international arbitrators recommended that a payment of $610m. should be made to the Kuwait Oil Company (KOC), in compensation for the cost of extinguishing oil wells set alight by retreating Iraqi troops in early 1991. In March 1997 the Kuwaiti general committee responsible for evaluating war damages stated that it was to begin compensation payments, initially to some 4,500 citizens who had incurred losses valued at less than $100,000. The disbursement of a further $84m. to some 33,800 individuals was authorized by the UN in February 1999. In September 2000 the UN Security Council approved the payment to the Kuwait Petroleum Corporation (which controls the KOC) of $15,900m. in compensation for lost petroleum revenues arising from the Iraqi occupation; this was the largest claim to have been considered by the UNCC hitherto. However, the Security Council decided at the same time to reduce the share of Iraqi oil revenues to be paid into the compensation fund from 30% to 25%: France and Russia, which increasingly opposed the maintenance of sanctions against Iraq, had delayed a decision by the UNCC on the payment, and Russia had warned of its inclination to oppose Kuwaiti claims to reparations unless the levy on Iraqi oil revenues was reduced. By mid-2003 the majority of individual claimants (Kuwaitis and expatriates in Kuwait and Iraq during the Gulf war) had received compensation, with total disbursements being valued at some $17,600m. Meanwhile, the UNCC was considering a claim of $86,000m. by the Kuwait Investment Agency, principally in recompense for lost earnings during the conflict. However, in a deposition issued in June 2003, the UNCC rejected all but $1,500m. of the claim. In late May 2003 UN Security Council Resolution 1483 had reduced the share of Iraqi petroleum revenues to be used for compensation payments from 25% to 5%, which was expected to result in outstanding compensation payments believed to total more than

$30,000m. remaining unpaid for several decades. In January 2004, after a meeting with US envoy James Baker and following similar announcements by the Governments of the UAE and Qatar, Sheikh Sabah stated that Kuwait was prepared to waive a 'significant proportion' of the estimated $16,000m. owed by Iraq. This did not, however, include any war reparations still claimed by the Government.

Relations with Jordan, which had deteriorated following that country's failure openly to denounce the Iraqi invasion, gradually eased in the mid-1990s. Flights between Kuwait and Jordan by both countries' national airlines, which had been suspended in 1990, resumed in July 1997, and the normalization of relations generally continued thereafter. Ministerial visits, which had not been undertaken since the Gulf crisis, were made by the Jordanian Minister of Planning and the Kuwaiti Deputy Prime Minister and Minister of State for Cabinet Affairs in June 1998 and January 1999, respectively, and in March 1999 the Jordanian embassy in Kuwait, which had been closed in 1990, was reopened. In September 1999 the new King Abdullah of Jordan made his first visit to Kuwait (his father, King Hussein, had not visited after 1990), where he held talks with the Amir. Jordan and Kuwait signed a bilateral free-trade agreement in December.

In July 2000 Kuwait and Saudi Arabia signed an agreement finalizing the delineation of their maritime borders. Kuwait subsequently commenced negotiations with Iran on the demarcation of respective rights to the continental shelf, following complaints by the Kuwaiti and Saudi authorities over Iran's decision to begin drilling for gas in a disputed offshore area. Iraq asserted that, as a concerned party, it should be included in the Kuwaiti-Iranian discussions. In December a defence agreement was signed by the six member states of the GCC.

Government

Under the 1962 Constitution, executive power is vested in the Amir, the Head of State (who is chosen by and from members of the ruling family), and is exercised through the Council of Ministers. The Amir appoints the Prime Minister and, on the latter's recommendation, other ministers. Legislative power is vested in the unicameral Majlis al-Umma (National Assembly), with 50 elected members who serve for four years (subject to dissolution). Only literate adult male Kuwaiti citizens, excluding members of the armed forces, may vote. The country is divided administratively into six governorates.

Defence

In August 2003 Kuwait's active armed forces numbered 15,500—a land army of 11,000 (including 1,600 foreign personnel), an air force of an estimated 2,500 and a navy of around 2,000—and there were reserve forces of 23,700. Paramilitary forces comprised a 6,600-strong national guard and a coastguard. There is a two-year period of compulsory military service (one year for university students). The defence budget for 2003 was estimated at KD 1,100m. Capital expenditure on defence procurement in 1992–2002 was to total some KD 3,500m.

A US force numbering an estimated 38,160 (34,000 army, 1,150 air force, 10 navy and some 3,000 marines), a British force of an estimated 3,000 and, as part of Operation Enduring Freedom (the US-led mission in Afghanistan which commenced in late 2001), a German force of 50 were stationed in Kuwait in August 2003.

Economic Affairs

In 2001, according to estimates by the World Bank, Kuwait's gross national income (GNI), measured at average 1999–2001 prices, was US $37,352m., equivalent to $18,270 per head (or $18,800 on an international purchasing-power parity basis). During 1990–2002, it was estimated, the population decreased at an average annual rate of 0.1%, while gross domestic product (GDP) per head increased, in real terms, by an average of 0.8% per year during 1992–2001. Overall GDP was estimated to have declined, in real terms, by some 10% annually in 1990–92. Following reconstruction, the gradual increase in oil production contributed to a renewed period of economic advance after 1992, with average annual GDP growth, in real terms, for the period 1992–2001 estimated at 5.1%. However, real GDP declined by 1.0% in 2001.

Agriculture (including hunting, forestry and fishing) contributed 0.4% of GDP in 2002. About 1.1% of the labour force were employed in the sector in mid-2002. The principal crops are tomatoes, cucumbers, potatoes, aubergines, cauliflower and dates. Owing to scarcity of water, little grain is produced, and the bulk of food requirements is imported. (Imports of food and live animals accounted for 14.0% of merchandise imports in 2002.) Livestock, poultry and fishing are also important. During 1992–97 agricultural GDP increased, in real terms, by an average of 30.3% per year. Agricultural production, which fell by some 84% in 1991, had recovered to pre-occupation levels by the mid-1990s; output increased at an average annual rate of 1.4% in 1995–2001.

Industry (including mining, manufacturing, construction and power) provided 51.0% of GDP in 2002, and employed 23.1% of the labour force in 1995. During 1993–2001 industrial GDP increased, in real terms, at an average annual rate of 0.9%.

Mining and quarrying contributed 39.5% of GDP in 2002, although the sector engaged only 2.1% of the labour force in 1995. The production of petroleum and its derivatives is the most important industry in Kuwait, providing 91.6% of export revenue in 2002. At the end of 2002 the country's proven recoverable reserves of petroleum were 96,500m. barrels, representing about 9.2% of world reserves. According to oil industry figures, Kuwait's petroleum production averaged 1.87m. barrels per day (b/d) in 2002. With effect from 1 April 2004, Kuwait's production quota, as agreed by Organization of the Petroleum Exporting Countries (OPEC, see p. 317), was 1.89m. b/d. Kuwait aimed to increase its production capacity from 2.5m. b/d in 2000 to 4.0m. b/d by 2020. There are significant reserves of natural gas (1,490,000m. cu m at the end of 2002) associated with the petroleum deposits. During 1993–2001 the GDP of the mining sector increased, in real terms, at an average rate of 0.8% per year.

Manufacturing provided 6.6% of GDP in 2002, and employed 5.4% of the labour force in 1995. Petroleum refineries accounted for 75.9% of manufacturing activity, measured by gross value of output, in 1997. Of the other branches of manufacturing, the most important are the production of building materials (and related activities such as aluminium extrusion), fertilizer production, food processing and the extraction of salt and chlorine. During 1993–2001 manufacturing GDP increased, in real terms, at an average annual rate of 1.5%.

Electrical energy is derived from Kuwait's own resources of petroleum (providing 75.6% of total electricity production in 2000) and both local and imported natural gas (24.4%). (The value of fuel imports in 2001 was equivalent to 0.5% of the value of total merchandise imports.) Total installed electricity-generating capacity increased from 6,898 MW in 1996 to 9,298 MW in 2000, following the completion of a 2,400-MW plant at Subiya; however, the proposed 2,500-MW az-Zour North plant was not scheduled for completion until 2006. Under the terms of an accord signed in early 2002, Qatar is to supply natural gas to the az-Zour plant from the end of 2005.

Services contributed 48.6% of GDP in 2002, and employed 74.8% of the labour force in 1995. Kuwait's second most important source of revenue is investment abroad (the total value of which was estimated to be in excess of US $45,000m. in the late 1990s), both in petroleum-related ventures and in other industries, chiefly in the USA, Western Europe and Japan; many such investments are held by the Reserve Fund for Future Generations (RFFG—to which 10% of petroleum revenues must by law be contributed each year, and which is intended to provide an income after hydrocarbon resources have been exhausted) and managed by the Kuwait Investment Authority. Prior to the Iraqi invasion the value of the RFFG was believed to have been some $100,000m. As part of its efforts to diversify the economy, the Government planned to develop the islands of Bubiyan and Failaka into major tourist resorts. In January 2004 a US company was selected as project manager for the Bubiyan island project, the first phase of which—the construction of a new port—was expected to cost about $800m. The combined GDP of the service sectors increased, in real terms, at an average rate of 2.9% per year during 1993–2001.

In 2002 Kuwait recorded a visible trade surplus of US $7,249m., and there was a surplus of $4,192m. on the current account of the balance of payments. In 2002 the principal sources of imports were the USA and Japan, which provided, respectively, 11.0% and 10.7% of total imports; other important suppliers in that year were Germany, Saudi Arabia, Italy and the People's Republic of China. Details concerning the destination of Kuwait's petroleum exports are not available for recent years; however, the major markets for non-petroleum exports in 2002 included Saudi Arabia (13.3%), the UAE, Indonesia and India. The principal exports are petroleum and petroleum products. The principal imports are machinery and transport equipment, which accounted for 39.8% of total imports in 2002, basic manufactures and other manufactured goods, food and live animals, and chemicals and related products.

A budget surplus of KD 791m. was recorded for the financial year ending 30 June 2004. Kuwait's total external debt in mid-1996 was estimated to be equivalent to 8.5% of GDP. The average annual rate of inflation in 1995–2002 was 1.7%; consumer prices increased by an annual average of 1.4% in 2002. National unemployment was estimated at only 1.4% in the mid-1990s and reported to be only 1% in 2001, the lowest rate in the region; however, underemployment was unofficially reported to be in excess of 50%.

Kuwait is a member of the GCC; the six GCC states established a unified regional customs tariff in January 2003, and it has been agreed to create a single market and currency no later than January 2010. Kuwait also belongs to the Organization of Arab Petroleum Exporting Countries (OAPEC, see p. 311) and to OPEC. Kuwait is a major aid donor, disbursing loans to developing countries through the Kuwait Fund for Arab Economic Development (KFAED) and the Arab Fund for Economic and Social Development (AFESD, see p. 144).

Despite its significant, oil-based wealth, Kuwait has a number of fundamental weaknesses in its economic structure: instability in its relations with Iraq have necessitated a high level of defence expenditure; reliance on oil revenues has impeded diversification into other industries; and its constitutional commitment to provide employment for all Kuwaitis has resulted in a heavy burden on government spending (an estimated 84% of the annual budget is allocated to salaries and subsidies). In 1999 the Government attempted to address this problem by proposing new taxes for companies and expatriate workers that would be used to create an employment fund to facilitate private-sector work for Kuwaitis. The value of shares quoted on the Kuwait Stock Exchange (KSE) declined during 1999–2001, apparently demonstrating a lack of investor confidence in the Government's economic reforms despite new legislation, enacted in May 2000, which allowed non-GCC investors to enter the market. However, since then shares have traded strongly and by February 2004 the KSE share value was reported to be at its highest level ever recorded. During the early years of this century plans by the Kuwait Petroleum Corporation to allow foreign participation in a development project (known as 'Project Kuwait'), valued at US $7,000m., for the northern oilfields made slow progress; the project aimed to increase production from 400,000 b/d to 900,000 b/d by its completion date of 2005. Approval by the Majlis was still required in April 2004, and, despite assurances that all reserves would remain Kuwaiti-owned, many Kuwaitis remained opposed to any foreign involvement in the petroleum sector. Nevertheless, in 2001 the Kuwaiti Government pursued legislation that would increase foreign investment in the economy, including the limited participation of international oil companies in the petroleum sector and measures that would permit foreign banks to operate in Kuwait; the legislation was eventually passed by the Majlis in 2003. Moreover, in November 2003 the legislature approved plans to deregulate the aviation sector—a decision that brought to an end the monopoly of the state-owned Kuwait Airways Corporation and opened the industry to international competition. The recovery in world petroleum prices from late 1999, despite being interrupted in the period following the September 2001 suicide attacks in the USA, was the principal factor contributing to budget surpluses during 1999/2000–2002/03. (An increase in expenditure in 2003/04 led to a deficit in that year.) Petroleum prices reached particularly high levels in early 2003, reflecting uncertainty regarding oil supplies in the event of a US-led military campaign against the Iraqi regime of Saddam Hussain. The removal of the threat from Saddam Hussain's Baathist regime provided a special impetus to construction in areas other than the hydrocarbons sector. In particular, huge infrastructure and tourism projects provided grounds for optimism that the economy could be successfully diversified. It was hoped that another increase in government expenditure in the 2004/05 budget, which was expected to lead to a 15% increase in the fiscal deficit, would further stimulate growth in the non-petroleum sector. On 1 January 2003 Kuwait pegged the dinar to the US dollar, as part of the GCC plan to create a single currency by 2010. Real GDP was estimated to have declined by 0.5% in the 2002/03 fiscal year, although non-oil GDP increased by some 5%. Economic growth was expected to benefit strongly from the reconstruction of Iraq.

Education

Education is compulsory for eight years between the ages of six and 14. Although private schools exist, state education is free, and is graded into pre-primary (for children between four and six years of age), primary (for children aged six to 10), intermediate (10 to 14) and secondary (14 to 18). In 1996 enrolment at primary schools included 62% of children in the relevant age-group (males 62%; females 61%), while secondary enrolment included 61% of children in the relevant age-group (males 62%; females 61%). There is a teacher-training college, a technical college, and a university (where some 18,000 students were enrolled in 1998/99). In addition, more than 4,500 Kuwaiti students receive education abroad. Expenditure on education by the central Government in 2003/04 was budgeted at KD 517.9m. (8.9% of total expenditure).

Public Holidays

2004: 1 January (New Year's Day), 1 February* (Id al-Adha, Feast of the Sacrifice), 22 February* (Islamic New Year), 25 February (Kuwaiti National Day), 26 February (Liberation Day), 2 May* (Birth of the Prophet), 12 September* (Leilat al-Meiraj, Ascension of the Prophet), 14 November* (Id al-Fitr, end of Ramadan).

2005: 1 January (New Year's Day), 21 January* (Id al-Adha, Feast of the Sacrifice), 10 February* (Islamic New Year), 25 February (Kuwaiti National Day), 26 February (Liberation Day), 21 April* (Birth of the Prophet), 2 September* (Leilat al-Meiraj, Ascension of the Prophet), 4 November* (Id al-Fitr, end of Ramadan).

* These holidays are dependent on the Islamic lunar calendar and may vary by one or two days from the dates given.

Weights and Measures

The metric system is in force.

Statistical Survey

Sources (unless otherwise stated): Economic Research Department, Central Bank of Kuwait, POB 526, 13006 Safat, Kuwait City; tel. 2403257; fax 2440887; e-mail cbk@cbk.gov.kw; internet www.cbk.gov.kw; Central Statistical Office, Ministry of Transport and Planning, POB 26188, 13122 Safat, Kuwait City; tel. 2454968; fax 2430464; e-mail salah@mop.gov.kw; internet www.mop.gov.kw.
Note: Unless otherwise indicated, data refer to the State of Kuwait as constituted at 1 August 1990, prior to the Iraqi invasion and annexation of the territory and its subsequent liberation. Furthermore, no account has been taken of the increase in the area of Kuwait as a result of the adjustment to the border with Iraq that came into force on 15 January 1993.

Area and Population

AREA, POPULATION AND DENSITY

Area (sq km)	17,818*
Population (census results)†‡	
21 April 1985	1,697,301
20 April 1995	
Males	913,402
Females.	662,168
Total	1,575,570
Population (official estimates)†	
2000	2,217,300
2001	2,309,100
2002	2,419,900
Density (per sq km) at mid-2002	135.8

* 6,880 sq miles.
† Figures include Kuwaiti nationals abroad. The total population at the 1995 census comprised 653,616 Kuwaiti nationals (326,301 males; 327,315 females) and 921,954 non-Kuwaitis (587,101 males; 334,853 females).
‡ Excluding adjustment for underenumeration.

GOVERNORATES
(estimated population at mid-2001)

Governorate	Area (sq km)*	Population	Density (per sq km)	Capital
Capital . . .	199.8	388,532	1,944.6	Kuwait City
Hawalli . . .	}	488,294	}	Hawalli
Great Mubarak .	368.4	144,981	3,272.3	n.a.
Farwaniya . .	}	572,252	}	Farwaniya
Al-Jahra . .	11,230.2	282,353	25.1	Jahra
Al-Ahmadi . .	5,119.6	364,484	71.2	Ahmadi City
Total† . .	16,918.0	2,243,080	132.6	

* Excluding the islands of Bubiyan and Warba (combined area 900 sq km).
† Including 2,184 unallocated.

PRINCIPAL TOWNS
(population at 1995 census)

Kuwait City (capital)	28,747	Subbah as-Salem .	54,608
Salmiya	129,775	Sulaibiah . . .	53,639
Jaleeb ash-Shuyukh.	102,169	Farwaniya . . .	52,928
Hawalli . . .	82,154	Al-Kreen . . .	50,689
South Kheetan . .	62,241	Subahiya . . .	50,644

BIRTHS, MARRIAGES AND DEATHS

	Registered live births		Registered marriages		Registered deaths	
	Number	Rate (per 1,000)	Number	Rate (per 1,000)	Number	Rate (per 1,000)
1993 . .	37,379	25.6	10,077	6.9	3,441	2.4
1994 . .	38,868	24.0	9,550	5.9	3,464	2.1
1995 . .	41,169	22.8	9,515	5.3	3,781	2.1
1996 . .	44,620	23.6	9,022	4.8	3,812	2.0
1997 . .	42,817	21.6	9,610	4.9	4,017	2.0
1998 . .	41,424	20.4	10,335	5.1	4,216	2.1
1999 . .	41,135	19.5	10,847	5.1	4,187	2.0
2000 . .	41,843	19.1	10,785	4.9	4,227	1.9

Expectation of life (WHO estimates, years at birth): 76.2 (males 75.8; females 76.9) in 2002 (Source: WHO, *World Health Report*).

ECONOMICALLY ACTIVE POPULATION
(persons aged 15 years and over, census of April 1995)*

	Kuwaitis	Non-Kuwaitis	Total
Agriculture, hunting and fishing .	216	15,140	15,356
Mining and quarrying	7,168	8,306	15,474
Manufacturing	997	39,107	40,104
Electricity, gas and water . . .	32	137	169
Construction.	1,415	113,804	115,219
Trade, restaurants and hotels. .	3,852	115,493	119,345
Transport, storage and communications	4,865	20,637	25,502
Finance, insurance, real estate and business services . . .	4,139	53,077	57,216
Community, social and personal services	117,093	234,236	351,329
Activities not adequately defined	2,982	4,838	7,820
Total	142,759	604,775	747,534

* Figures exclude persons seeking work for the first time, totalling 14,086 (5,009 Kuwaitis; 9,077 non-Kuwaitis), but include other unemployed persons, totalling 15,919 (5,564 Kuwaitis; 10,355 non-Kuwaitis).

Mid-2001 (official estimates, persons aged 15 years and over): Total employed 1,204,717 (Kuwaitis 235,757; non-Kuwaitis 968,960); Unemployed 9,464 (Kuwaitis 2,463; non-Kuwaitis 7,001); *Total labour force* 1,214,181 (Kuwaitis 238,220; non-Kuwaitis 975,961).

Health and Welfare

KEY INDICATORS

Total fertility rate (children per woman, 2002).	2.7
Under-5 mortality rate (per 1,000 live births, 2001) . . .	10
HIV/AIDS (% of persons aged 15–49, 1994).	0.12
Physicians (per 1,000 head, 1997)	1.9
Hospital beds (per 1,000 head, 1997)	2.76
Health expenditure (2001): US $ per head (PPP)	612
Health expenditure (2001): % of GDP	3.9
Health expenditure (2001): public (% of total)	78.8
Human Development Index (2001): ranking	46
Human Development Index (2001): value	0.820

For sources and definitions, see explanatory note on p. vi.

Agriculture

PRINCIPAL CROPS
('000 metric tons)

	2000	2001	2002
Potatoes	18.0	31.9	32.6
Cabbages	5.3	6.5	8.9
Lettuce.	7.9	6.6	6.3
Tomatoes	36.7	41.1	35.1
Cauliflower	6.6	7.7	11.4
Pumpkins, squash and gourds .	4.9	4.9*	4.9*
Cucumbers and gherkins . . .	33.0	33.0*	33.0*
Aubergines (Eggplants)	12.0	12.0*	12.0*
Chillies and green peppers . . .	5.5	6.8	6.8
Dry onions	6.6	4.9	3.7
Other vegetables	25.0†	25.3*	23.5*
Dates	10.2	10.4	10.4

* FAO estimate.
† Unofficial figure.

Source: FAO.

LIVESTOCK
('000 head, year ending September)

	2000	2001	2002
Cattle	21	22*	18*
Camels*	9	9	9
Sheep	616	630	800
Goats	153	130	130*
Poultry	26,314	32,463	32,500*

* FAO estimate(s).

Source: FAO.

LIVESTOCK PRODUCTS
('000 metric tons)

	2000	2001	2002
Beef and veal*	1.6	1.8	1.6
Mutton and lamb*	35.7	32.0	34.0
Poultry meat	33.0	42.2	42.8*
Cows' milk	30.8	39.6	36.0*
Goats' milk	4.5	4.8	4.8*
Hen eggs	21.3	22.5*	23.5*
Sheepskins (fresh)*	11.9	10.8	12.0

* FAO estimate(s).

Source: FAO.

Fishing

(metric tons, live weight)

	1999	2000	2001
Capture	6,271	6,000*	5,846
Hilsha shad	970	650*	337
Mullets	1,054	760*	456
Groupers	237	250*	268
Grunts and sweetlips	245	210*	191
Croakers and drums	1,385	1,100*	853
Yellowfin seabream	464	350*	271
Indo-Pacific king mackerel	211	210*	204
Silver pomfret	259	200*	133
Natantian decapods	720	1,300*	1,977
Aquaculture	264	376	195
Total catch	6,535	6,376*	6,041

* FAO estimate.

Source: FAO, *Yearbook of Fishery Statistics*.

Mining*

	1999	2000	2001
Crude petroleum (million barrels)	708	766	755
Natural gas (million cu metres)†	8,688	9,600	9,500

* Estimates, including an equal share of production with Saudi Arabia from the Neutral/Partitioned Zone.

† On a dry basis.

Source: US Geological Survey.

Industry

SELECTED PRODUCTS
('000 metric tons, unless otherwise stated)

	1998	1999	2000
Wheat flour	155	159	162
Sulphur (by-product)*†	650	639	512
Chlorine	19	18	15
Caustic soda (Sodium hydroxide)	22	21	19
Nitrogenous fertilizers‡	361	331	288
Motor spirit (petrol) ('000 barrels)*†§	17,520	17,000	10,000
Kerosene and jet fuels ('000 barrels)§	51,571	57,012	45,049
Gas-diesel (Distillate fuel) oils ('000 barrels)§	91,830	97,142	83,981
Residual fuel oils ('000 barrels)§	71,591	73,598	57,116
Petroleum bitumen (asphalt)*§	252	297	331
Liquefied petroleum gas§	3,124	3,228	2,997
Quicklime*†	40	40	40
Cement	2,310	947	n.a.
Electric energy (million kWh)§	29,988	31,576	32,323

2001†: Sulphur (by-product) 524; Motor spirit (petrol) ('000 barrels) 10,000§; Quicklime 40*.

* Provisional or estimated figure(s).

† Source: US Geological Survey.

‡ Production in terms of nitrogen.

§ Including an equal share of production with Saudi Arabia from the Neutral/Partitioned Zone.

Finance

CURRENCY AND EXCHANGE RATES

Monetary Units

1,000 fils = 10 dirhams = 1 Kuwaiti dinar (KD).

Sterling, Dollar and Euro Equivalents (31 December 2003)

£1 sterling = 525.95 fils;
US $1 = 294.70 fils;
€1 = 372.21 fils;
100 Kuwaiti dinars = £190.13 = $339.33 = €268.67.

Average Exchange Rate (US $ per KD)

2001   3.2481
2002   3.3382
2003   3.3933

Since 1 January 2003 the official exchange rate has been fixed within the range of US $1 = 289 fils to $1 = 310 fils (KD 1 = $3.4602 to KD 1 = $3.2258).

GENERAL BUDGET
(KD million, year ending 30 June)

Revenue	2001/02	2002/03	2003/04*
Tax revenue	110.6	136.5	117.7
International trade and transactions	85.8	100.6	84.2
Non-tax revenue	5,266.0	6,082.5	3,437.3
Oil revenue	4,525.0	5,498.5	2,970.5
Total operating revenue of government enterprises	329.0	346.2	584.5
Total	5,376.6	6,219.0	3,554.9

Expenditure	2000/01	2002/03	2003/04*
Current expenditure.	3,655.0	3,538.4	3,858.7
Defence, security and justice.	1,001.2	1,082.2	1,176.3
Education	453.0	500.3	517.9
Health	305.5	317.0	335.2
Social and labour affairs	122.8	134.9	138.4
Electricity and water	377.7	401.5	454.3
Land acquisitions	—	48.0	48.0
Capital expenditure	35.0	38.0	57.0
Development expenditure	583.0	622.0	674.0
Public works	100.0	113.0	187.0
Electricity and water	288.6	311.0	312.0
Transfers to attached and public institutions	1,000.9	1,181.6	1,186.3
Total	**5,273.9**	**5,428.0**	**5,824.0**

* Projections.

INTERNATIONAL RESERVES
(US $ million at 31 December)

	2000	2001	2002
Gold*	103.9	103.1	106.0
IMF special drawing rights	90.9	108.0	132.9
Reserve position in IMF	487.0	598.3	718.2
Foreign exchange.	6,504.4	9,191.1	8,357.0
Total	**7,186.3**	**10,000.5**	**9,314.1**

* National valuation of gold reserves (2,539,000 troy ounces in each year).

Source: IMF, *International Financial Statistics.*

MONEY SUPPLY
(KD million at 31 December)

	2000	2001	2002
Currency outside banks	416.6	401.2	442.2
Demand deposits at deposit money banks	1,051.1	1,240.2	1,624.6
Total money	**1,467.7**	**1,641.4**	**2,066.8**

Source: IMF, *International Financial Statistics.*

COST OF LIVING
(Consumer Price Index; base: 1978 = 100)

	2000	2001	2002
Food	172.9	172.9	175.1
Beverages and tobacco	305.8	313.8	345.1
Clothing and footwear	259.4	269.3	270.1
Housing services	204.3	206.6	208.4
All items (incl. others)	**209.2**	**212.7**	**215.6**

NATIONAL ACCOUNTS
(KD million at current prices)

Expenditure on the Gross Domestic Product

	2000	2001	2002
Government final consumption expenditure	2,485	2,521	2,838
Private final consumption expenditure	4,958	5,377	5,986
Increase in stocks } Gross fixed capital formation. }	868	910	979
Total domestic expenditure	**8,311**	**8,808**	**9,803**
Exports of goods and services	6,534	5,490	5,184
Less Imports of goods and services	3,488	3,803	4,250
GDP in purchasers' values	**11,357**	**10,495**	**10,737**

Source: IMF, *International Financial Statistics.*

Gross Domestic Product by Economic Activity

	2000	2001	2002
Agriculture, hunting, forestry and fishing	42.0	47.7	48.1
Mining and quarrying	5,544.6	4,587.2	4,406.2
Manufacturing	801.3	666.7	736.6
Electricity, gas and water	245.5	250.8	276.0
Construction	248.5	255.3	258.7
Trade, restaurants and hotels	676.7	712.8	764.2
Transport, storage and communications	506.4	552.4	563.9
Finance, insurance, real estate and business services	1,326.8	1,405.8	1,456.0
Community, social and personal services	2,363.5	2,422.2	2,633.4
Sub-total	**11,755.3**	**10,900.9**	**11,143.1**
Import duties } *Less* Imputed bank service charges }	−398.6	−405.4	−405.6
GDP in purchasers' values	**11,356.7**	**10,495.5**	**10,737.5**

BALANCE OF PAYMENTS
(US $ million)

	2000	2001	2002
Exports of goods f.o.b.	19,478	16,238	15,366
Imports of goods f.o.b.	−6,451	−7,046	−8,117
Trade balance	**13,027**	**9,192**	**7,249**
Exports of services	1,822	1,663	1,648
Imports of services	−4,920	−5,354	−5,919
Balance on goods and services	**9,929**	**5,500**	**2,978**
Other income received	7,315	5,426	3,725
Other income paid	−616	−525	−365
Balance on goods, services and income	**16,628**	**10,401**	**6,337**
Current transfers received	85	52	49
Current transfers paid	−2,041	−2,129	−2,195
Current balance	**14,672**	**8,324**	**4,192**
Capital account (net)	2,217	2,931	1,668
Direct investment abroad	303	−365	158
Direct investment from abroad.	16	−147	7
Portfolio investment assets	−12,923	−7,366	−3,425
Portfolio investment liabilities	254	−78	161
Other investment assets	−1,108	505	−3,751
Other investment liabilities	−316	1,138	1,695
Net errors and omissions	−847	−2,038	−1,677
Overall balance	**2,268**	**2,905**	**−973**

Source: IMF, *International Financial Statistics.*

External Trade

PRINCIPAL COMMODITIES
(distribution by SITC, KD million)

Imports c.i.f.	2000	2001	2002
Food and live animals	349.0	355.3	382.9
Chemicals and related products	207.9	221.9	238.6
Basic manufactures	395.2	451.9	510.5
Machinery and transport equipment	820.1	912.2	1,089.5
Miscellaneous manufactured articles	304.3	348.9	378.1
Total (incl. others)	**2,195.4**	**2,413.3**	**2,735.8**

Exports f.o.b.	2000	2001	2002
Mineral fuels, lubricants, etc.	5,581.3	4,594.0	4,275.8
Petroleum, petroleum products, etc.*	5,578.3	4,590.8	4,272.8
Chemicals and related products	255.0	246.5	248.2
Total (incl. others)*	5,962.7	4,969.7	4,666.2

* Estimate(s) by the Central Bank of Kuwait.

PRINCIPAL TRADING PARTNERS
(KD million)*

Imports c.i.f.	2000	2001	2002
Australia	64.9	83.4	103.3
Brazil	18.1	27.2	25.0
Canada	52.6	54.3	41.3
China, People's Repub.	85.8	105.5	142.4
France (incl. Monaco)	70.8	86.7	88.0
Germany	178.4	238.8	255.1
India	82.8	90.2	106.4
Iran	35.3	39.0	43.8
Italy	117.1	141.3	153.0
Japan	214.1	230.7	292.4
Korea, Repub.	87.4	66.0	70.0
Malaysia	32.6	32.4	36.8
Netherlands	39.9	38.6	44.1
Saudi Arabia	154.4	156.0	176.5
Spain	36.6	40.2	43.3
Switzerland-Liechtenstein	37.0	37.4	39.5
Taiwan	26.7	27.9	31.2
Thailand	27.4	30.7	33.6
Turkey	35.5	41.8	56.3
United Arab Emirates	79.5	86.5	96.5
United Kingdom	123.3	120.0	122.0
USA	239.3	255.9	299.7
Total (incl. others)	2,195.4	2,413.3	2,735.8

Exports f.o.b.†	2000	2001	2002
Bahrain	6.8	8.0	7.7
Belgium-Luxembourg	9.9	6.1	5.7
China, People's Repub.	23.3	25.7	23.9
Egypt	11.8	13.1	10.6
India	26.9	19.0	25.1
Indonesia	30.9	30.0	39.5
Iran	4.5	6.6	7.8
Japan	5.7	2.8	5.8
Jordan	7.7	8.0	9.1
Korea, Repub.	2.9	6.3	0.7
Lebanon	5.1	6.0	5.5
Malaysia	2.9	10.9	7.0
Oman	5.4	6.9	6.5
Pakistan	18.4	20.7	17.6
Philippines	7.0	6.2	8.7
Qatar	7.5	6.9	11.1
Saudi Arabia	46.7	50.3	52.4
Singapore	8.0	2.7	2.8
Spain	24.0	15.5	15.7
Syria	8.0	9.3	8.3
Taiwan	4.3	3.3	4.0
Turkey	4.9	3.4	8.0
United Arab Emirates	27.7	39.8	41.9
United Kingdom	4.2	3.0	3.2
USA	14.3	6.5	2.9
Total (incl. others)	384.4	378.9	393.4

* Imports by country of production; exports by country of last consignment.
† Excluding petroleum exports.

Transport

ROAD TRAFFIC
(motor vehicles in use at 31 December)

	1995	1996	1997
Passenger cars	662,946	701,172	747,042
Buses and coaches	11,937	12,322	13,094
Goods vehicles	116,813	121,753	127,386

1999: Buses and coaches 12,775; Goods vehicles 97,706.

2000: Buses and coaches 10,974; Goods vehicles 80,378.

SHIPPING

Merchant Fleet
(registered at 31 December)

	2000	2001	2002
Number of vessels	205	200	201
Displacement ('000 grt)	2,415.3	2,291.7	2,256.0

Source: Lloyd's Register-Fairplay, *World Fleet Statistics*.

International Sea-borne Freight Traffic
('000 metric tons)*

	1988	1989	1990
Goods loaded	61,778	69,097	51,400
Goods unloaded	7,123	7,015	4,522

* Including Kuwait's share of traffic in the Neutral/Partitioned Zone.

Source: UN, *Monthly Bulletin of Statistics*.

Goods loaded ('000 metric tons): 89,945 in 1997.

Goods unloaded ('000 metric tons): 746 in 1991 (July–December only); 2,537 in 1992; 4,228 in 1993; 5,120 in 1994; 5,854 in 1995; 6,497 in 1996; 6,049 in 1997.

CIVIL AVIATION
(traffic on scheduled services)

	1997	1998	1999
Kilometres flown (million)	43	45	36
Passengers carried ('000)	2,114	2,190	2,130
Passenger-km (million)	5,997	6,207	6,158
Total ton-km (million)	912	932	829

Source: UN, *Statistical Yearbook*.

Tourism

VISITOR ARRIVALS BY COUNTRY OF ORIGIN
(incl. excursionists)

	1999	2000	2001
Bahrain	49,658	50,024	61,726
Bangladesh	79,731	54,466	61,027
Egypt	226,262	219,553	238,308
India	226,629	225,642	270,619
Iran	93,801	100,328	101,604
Lebanon	48,001	48,642	50,695
Pakistan	78,206	74,429	75,854
Philippines	37,357	43,310	47,969
Saudi Arabia	574,924	641,691	660,916
Sri Lanka	54,816	54,804	56,204
Syria	146,084	143,020	165,097
Total (incl. others)	1,883,633	1,944,233	2,069,051

Tourism receipts (US $ million): 207 in 1998; 243 in 1999.

Source: World Tourism Organization, *Yearbook of Tourism Statistics*.

Communications Media

	1999	2000	2001
Radio receivers ('000 in use) . .	1,200	n.a.	n.a.
Television receivers ('000 in use) .	910	930	n.a.
Telephones ('000 main lines in use)	455.6	467.1	472.4
Facsimile machines ('000 in use)	60	n.a.	n.a.
Mobile cellular telephones ('000 subscribers).	300.0	476.0	489.2
Personal computers ('000 in use)	230	250	272
Internet users ('000)	100	150	200
Book titles published	219	n.a.	n.a.

1996: Daily newspapers 8 (average circulation 635,000 copies); Non-daily newspapers 78.

Sources: UNESCO, *Statistical Yearbook*; UN, *Statistical Yearbook*; International Telecommunication Union.

Education

(state-controlled schools, 2000/01)

	Schools	Teachers	Students		
			Males	Females	Total
Kindergarten . .	153	3,379	22,142	22,128	44,270
Primary	184	8,151	48,796	49,322	98,118
Intermediate . .	165	9,073	47,955	47,509	95,464
Secondary . . .	117	9,234	34,868	41,353	76,221
Religious institutes	7	351	n.a.	n.a.	2,454
Special training institutes . .	33	756	n.a.	n.a.	543

Private education (1996/97): 63 kindergarten schools (598 teachers, 12,172 students); 80 primary schools (2,341 teachers, 47,111 students); 82 intermediate schools (1,860 teachers, 36,254 students); 66 secondary schools (1,576 teachers, 20,932 students).

2000/01 (private education): 112 schools; 7,324 teachers; 128,204 students.

Adult literacy rate (UNESCO estimates): 82.4% (males 84.3%; females 80.3%) in 2001 (Source: UNDP, *Human Development Report*).

Directory

The Constitution

The principal provisions of the Constitution, promulgated on 16 November 1962, are set out below. On 29 August 1976 the Amir suspended four articles of the Constitution dealing with the National Assembly, the Majlis al-Umma. On 24 August 1980 the Amir issued a decree ordering the establishment of an elected legislature before the end of February 1981. The new Majlis was elected on 23 February 1981, and fresh legislative elections followed on 20 February 1985. The Majlis was dissolved by Amiri decree in July 1986, and some sections of the Constitution, including the stipulation that new elections should be held within two months of dissolving the legislature (see below), were suspended. A new Majlis was elected on 5 October 1992 and convened on 20 October.

SOVEREIGNTY

Kuwait is an independent sovereign Arab State; its sovereignty may not be surrendered, and no part of its territory may be relinquished. Offensive war is prohibited by the Constitution.

Succession as Amir is restricted to heirs of the late Mubarak as-Sabah, and an Heir Apparent must be appointed within one year of the accession of a new Amir.

EXECUTIVE AUTHORITY

Executive power is vested in the Amir, who exercises it through the Council of Ministers. The Amir will appoint the Prime Minister 'after the traditional consultations', and will appoint and dismiss ministers on the recommendation of the Prime Minister. Ministers need not be members of the Majlis al-Umma, although all ministers who are not members of parliament assume membership *ex officio* in the legislature for the duration of office. The Amir also formulates laws, which shall not be effective unless published in the *Official Gazette*. The Amir establishes public institutions. All decrees issued in these respects shall be conveyed to the Majlis. No law is issued unless it is approved by the Majlis.

LEGISLATURE

A National Assembly, the Majlis al-Umma, of 50 members will be elected for a four-year term by all natural-born Kuwaiti males over the age of 21 years, except servicemen and police, who may not vote. Candidates for election must possess the franchise, be over 30 years of age and literate. The Majlis will convene for at least eight months in any year, and new elections shall be held within two months of the last dissolution of the outgoing legislature.

Restrictions on the commercial activities of ministers include an injunction forbidding them to sell property to the Government.

The Amir may ask for reconsideration of a bill that has been approved by the Majlis and sent to him for ratification, but the bill would automatically become law if it were subsequently adopted by a two-thirds' majority at the next sitting, or by a simple majority at a subsequent sitting. The Amir may declare martial law, but only with the approval of the legislature.

The Majlis may adopt a vote of 'no confidence' in a minister, in which case the minister must resign. Such a vote is not permissible in the case of the Prime Minister, but the legislature may approach the Amir on the matter, and the Amir shall then either dismiss the Prime Minister or dissolve the Majlis.

CIVIL SERVICE

Entry to the civil service is confined to Kuwaiti citizens.

PUBLIC LIBERTIES

Kuwaitis are equal before the law in prestige, rights and duties. Individual freedom is guaranteed. No one shall be seized, arrested or exiled except within the rules of law.

No punishment shall be administered except for an act or abstaining from an act considered a crime in accordance with a law applicable at the time of committing it, and no penalty shall be imposed more severe than that which could have been imposed at the time of committing the crime.

Freedom of opinion is guaranteed to everyone, and each has the right to express himself through speech, writing or other means within the limits of the law.

The press is free within the limits of the law, and it should not be suppressed except in accordance with the dictates of law.

Freedom of performing religious rites is protected by the State according to prevailing customs, provided it does not violate the public order and morality.

Trade unions will be permitted and property must be respected. An owner is not banned from managing his property except within the boundaries of law. No property should be taken from anyone, except within the prerogatives of law, unless a just compensation be given.

Houses may not be entered, except in cases provided by law. Every Kuwaiti has freedom of movement and choice of place of residence within the State. This right shall not be controlled except in cases stipulated by law.

Every person has the right to education and freedom to choose his type of work. Freedom to form peaceful societies is guaranteed within the limits of law.

The Government

HEAD OF STATE

Amir of Kuwait: His Highness Sheikh JABER AL-AHMAD AS-SABAH (acceded 31 December 1977).

COUNCIL OF MINISTERS
(April 2004)

Prime Minister: Sheikh SABAH AL-AHMAD AL-JABER AS-SABAH.

Deputy Prime Minister and Minister of Defence: Sheikh JABER MUBARAK AL-HAMAD AS-SABAH.

Deputy Prime Minister and Minister of the Interior: Sheikh NAWWAF AL-AHMAD AL-JABER AS-SABAH.

Deputy Prime Minister, Minister of State for Cabinet Affairs and for National Assembly Affairs: MUHAMMAD DHAIFALLAH SHARAR.

Minister of Foreign Affairs: Sheikh MUHAMMAD SABAH AS-SALIM AS-SABAH.

Minister of Justice: AHMAD YA'QUB BAQIR AL-ABDULLAH.

Minister of Information: MUHAMMAD ABDULLAH ABU-AL-HASSAN.

Minister of Commerce and Industry: ABD AR-RAHMAN AT-TAWIL.

Minister of Public Works and Minister of State for Housing Affairs: BADIR NASIR AL-HUMAYDI.

Minister of Health: MUHAMMAD AHMAD AL-JARALLAH.

Minister of Education and Higher Education: RASHID HAMAD MUHAMMAD AL-HAMAD.

Minister of Awqaf (Religious Endowments) and Islamic Affairs: ABDULLAH MA'TUQ AL-MA'TUQ.

Minister of Transport and Planning and Minister of State for Administrative Development Affairs: Sheikh AHMAD ABDULLAH AL-AHMAD AS-SABAH.

Minister of Finance: MAHMUD ABD AL-KHALIQ AN-NURI.

Minister of Energy: Sheikh AHMAD AL-FAHD AL-AHMAD AS-SABAH.

Minister of Social Affairs and Labour: FAISAL AL-HAJJI.

PROVINCIAL GOVERNORS

Al-Ahmadi: Sheikh ALI ABDULLAH AS-SALIM AS-SABAH.

Farwaniya: Dr IBRAHIM DUAIJ AL-IBRAHIM AS-SABAH.

Great Mubarak: MUBARAK HUMUD AL-JABER AS-SABAH.

Hawalli: IBRAHIM JASEM AL-MUDHAF.

Al-Jahra: ALI JABER AL-AHMAD AS-SABAH.

Kuwait (Capital): Dr DAUD MUSAED AS-SALIH.

MINISTRIES

Ministry of Awqaf (Religious Endowments) and Islamic Affairs: POB 13, 13001 Safat, Kuwait City; tel. 2466300; fax 2449943; internet www.awkaf.net.

Ministry of Commerce and Industry: POB 2944, 13030 Safat, Kuwait City; tel. 2463600; fax 2424411.

Ministry of Defence: POB 1170, 13012 Safat, Kuwait City; tel. 4819277; fax 4846059.

Ministry of Education and Higher Education: POB 7, 13001 Safat, Hilali St, Kuwait City; tel. 4836800; fax 2423676; e-mail webmaster@moe.edu.kw; internet www.moe.edu.kw.

Ministry of Energy: POB 12, 13001 Safat, Kuwait City; tel. 4896000; fax 4897484.

Ministry of Finance: POB 9, 13001 Safat, al-Morkab St, Ministries Complex, Kuwait City; tel. 2468200; fax 2404025; e-mail webmaster@mof.gov.kw; internet www.mof.gov.kw.

Ministry of Foreign Affairs: POB 3, 13001 Safat, Gulf St, Kuwait City; tel. 2425141; fax 2430559; e-mail info@mofa.org; internet www.mofa.gov.kw.

Ministry of Health: POB 5, 13001 Safat, Arabian Gulf St, Kuwait City; tel. 4877422; fax 4865414.

Ministry of Information: POB 193, 13002 Safat, as-Sour St, Kuwait City; tel. 2415300; fax 2419642; e-mail info@moinfo.gov.kw; internet www.moinfo.gov.kw.

Ministry of the Interior: POB 11, 13001 Safat, Kuwait City; tel. 2524199; fax 2561268.

Ministry of Justice: POB 6, 13001 Safat, al-Morkab St, Ministries Complex, Kuwait City; tel. 2467300; fax 2466957; e-mail qht@moj.gov.kw; internet www.moj.gov.kw.

Ministry of Public Works: POB 8, 13001 Safat, Kuwait City; tel. 5385520; fax 5380829.

Ministry of Social Affairs and Labour: POB 563, 13006 Safat, Kuwait City; tel. 2464500; fax 2419877.

Ministry of Transport and Planning: POB 15, 13001 Safat, Kuwait City; tel. 2428100; fax 2414734; e-mail info@mop.gov.kw; internet www.mop.gov.kw.

Legislature

MAJLIS AL-UMMA
(National Assembly)

Speaker: JASEM AL-KHARAFI.

Elections to the 50-seat Majlis took place on 5 July 2003: 21 seats were secured by Islamist candidates, 14 were won by pro-Government candidates, three by liberals and 12 by independents.

Political Organizations

Political parties are not permitted in Kuwait. However, several quasi-political organizations are in existence. Among those that have been represented in the Majlis since 1992 are:

Constitutional Group: supported by merchants.

Islamic Constitutional Movement: Sunni Muslim. moderate.

Kuwait Democratic Forum: internet www.kuwaitdf.org/df; f. 1991; secular, liberal.

National Democratic Rally (NDR): f. 1997; secular, liberal; Sec.-Gen. Dr AHMAD BISHARA.

National Islamic Coalition: Shi'a Muslim.

Salafeen (Islamic Popular Movement): Sunni Muslim.

Diplomatic Representation

EMBASSIES IN KUWAIT

Afghanistan: Mishref, Block 6, St 42, Villa 57, Kuwait City; tel. 5379211; fax 5379212; e-mail ekuwa@mrecic.gov.ar; Chargé d'affaires RICARDO E. INSUA.

Algeria: POB 578, 13006 Safat, Istiqlal St, Kuwait City; tel. 2519987; fax 2563052; Ambassador MUHAMMAD BURUBA.

Argentina: POB 1125, 45712 Surra, Kuwait City; tel. 5323014; fax 5323053; e-mail embargkuwait@hotmail.com; Chargé d'affaires a.i. ARMANDO MAURICIO BECHER.

Austria: POB 15013, Daiya, 35451 Kuwait City; tel. 2552532; fax 2563052; e-mail kuwait-ob@bnaa.gv.at; Ambassador ROLAND HAUSER.

Bahrain: POB 196, 13002 Safat, Area 6, Surra Rd, Villa 35, Kuwait City; tel. 5318530; fax 5330882; e-mail 61116@kems.net; Ambassador ABD AR-RAHMAN M. AL-FADHEL.

Bangladesh: POB 22344, 13084 Safat, Khaldya, Block 6, Ali bin Abi Taleb St, House 361, Kuwait City; tel. 5316042; fax 5316041; e-mail bdoot@ncc.moc.kw; internet www.bdsociety.com/embassy; Ambassador AMINUL HOSSAIN SARKER.

Belgium: POB 3280, 13033 Safat, Salmiya, Baghdad St, House 15, Kuwait City; tel. 5722014; fax 5748389; Ambassador PHILIPPE-HENRI ARCQ.

Bhutan: POB 1510, 13016 Safat, Jabriya, Block 9, St 20, Villa 7, Kuwait City; tel. 5331506; fax 5338959; e-mail bhutankuwait@hotmail.com; Ambassador TSHERING WANGDI.

Bosnia and Herzegovina: POB 6131, 32036 Hawalli, Kuwait City; tel. 5392637; fax 5392106; Ambassador EDHEM PASIĆ.

Brazil: POB 39761, 73058 Nuzha, Block 2, St 1, Jadah 1, Villa 8, Kuwait City; tel. 5328610; fax 5328613; e-mail brasemb@ncc.moc.kw; Ambassador (vacant).

Bulgaria: POB 12090, 71651 Shamiya, Jabriya, Block 11, St 107, Kuwait City; tel. 5314459; fax 5321453; e-mail bgembkw@qualitynet.com; Ambassador ANGEL N. MANTCHEV.

Canada: POB 25281, 13113 Safat, Diiya, Block 4, 24 al-Motawakell St, Plot 121, Villa 24, Kuwait City; tel. 2563025; fax 2563023; e-mail kwait@dfait-maeci.gc.ca; Ambassador RICHARD MANN.

China, People's Republic: POB 2346, 13024 Safat, Dasmah, Sheikh Ahmad al-Jaber Bldgs 4 & 5, Kuwait City; tel. 5333340; fax 5333341; Ambassador WU JIUHONG.

Czech Republic: POB 1151, 13012 Safat, Kuwait City; tel. 2529018; fax 2529021; e-mail kuwait@embassy.mzv; internet www.mzv.cz/kuwait; Chargé d'affaires a.i. Dr PETR KORBEL.

Egypt: POB 11252, 35153 Dasmah, Istiqlal St, Kuwait City; tel. 2519955; fax 2553877; Ambassador MAHMOUD WAJDI ABU ZEID.

Eritrea: POB 53016, 73015 Nuzha, Jabriya, Block 9, St 21, House 9, Kuwait City; tel. 5317426; fax 5317429; Ambassador MOUSA YASSIEN SHEIKH AD-DIN.

Ethiopia: POB 939, Surra, 45710 Safat, Kuwait City; tel. 5334276; fax 5331179; Ambassador RAZENE ARAYA.

Finland: POB 26699, 13127 Safat, Surra, Block 4, St 1, Villa 8, Kuwait City; tel. 5312890; fax 5324198; Ambassador MARKKU NII-NIOJA.

France: POB 1037, 13011 Safat, Mansouriah, Block 1, St 13, No. 24, Kuwait City; tel. 2571061; fax 2571058; Ambassador PATRICE PAOLI.

Germany: POB 805, 13009 Safat, Dahiya Abdullah as-Salem, Area 1, Ave 14, Villa 13, Kuwait City; tel. 2520857; fax 2520763; e-mail reg1@kuwa.diplo.de; Ambassador Dr WERNER DAUM.

Greece: POB 23812, 13099 Safat, Khaldiya, Block 4, St 44, House 4, Kuwait City; tel. 4817101; fax 4817103; e-mail grembkw@hotmail .com; Ambassador STAVROS LYKIDIS.

Hungary: POB 23955, 13100 Safat, Qortuba, Area 2, Al-Baha'a bin Zuheir St 776, Kuwait City; tel. 5323901; fax 5323904; e-mail huembkwi@quality.net; Ambassador JENŐ FÖLDESI.

India: POB 1450, 13015 Safat, 34 Istiqlal St, Kuwait City; tel. 2530600; fax 2525811; e-mail indemb@ncc.moc.kw; Ambassador B. M. C. MYER.

Indonesia: POB 21560, 13076 Safat, Keifan, Block 5, As-Sebhani St, House 21, Kuwait City; tel. 4839927; fax 4819250; e-mail batik@ ncc.moc.kw; Ambassador D. SOESJONO.

Iran: POB 4686, 13047 Safat, Daiyah, Embassies Area, Block B, Kuwait City; tel. 2560694; fax 2529868; Ambassador ALI JANNATI.

Italy: POB 4453, 13045 Safat, Shuwaikh 'B', Block 5, Villa 1, Kuwait City; tel. 4817400; fax 4817244; e-mail ambkuwa@ncc.moc.kw; Ambassador FRANCESCO CAPECE GALEOTA.

Japan: POB 2304, 13024 Safat, Jabriya, Area 9, Plot 496, Kuwait City; tel. 5312870; fax 5326168; Ambassador SHIGERU TSUMORI.

Jordan: POB 15314, 35305 Diiyah, Istiqlal St, Embassies Area, Kuwait City; tel. 2533500; Ambassador MUHAMMAD AL-QURAAN.

Korea, Republic: POB 20771, 13068 Safat, Rawda, Block 1, St 10, House 17, Kuwait City; tel. 2554206; fax 2526874; Ambassador PARK IN-KOOK.

Lebanon: POB 253, 13003 Safat, 31 Istiqlal St, Kuwait City; tel. 2562103; fax 2571682; Ambassador KHALED AL-KILANI.

Libya: POB 21460, 13075 Safat, 27 Istiqlal St, Kuwait City; tel. 2562103; fax 2571682; Chargé d'affaires IDRIS DAHMANI BU DIB.

Malaysia: POB 4105, 13042 Safat, Daiya, Diplomatic Enclave, Area 5, Istiqlal St, Plot 5, Kuwait City; tel. 2550394; fax 2550384; e-mail mwkuwait@qualitynet.net; Ambassador HUSNI ZAI BIN YAACOL.

Morocco: POB 784, 13008 Safat, Jabriya, Block 12, Villa 24, St 101, Kuwait City; tel. 4813912; fax 4814156; Ambassador DRISS KETTANI.

Netherlands: POB 21822, 13079 Safat, Jabriya, Area 9, St 1, Plot 40A, Kuwait City; tel. 5312650; fax 5326334; e-mail kwe@minbuza .nl; Ambassador HENK REVIS.

Niger: POB 44451, 32059 Hawalli, Salwa, Block 12, St 6, Villa 183, Kuwait City; tel. 5652943; fax 5640478; Ambassador ASSOUMANE GUIAOURI.

Nigeria: POB 6432, 32039 Hawalli, Surra, Area 1, St 14, House 25, Kuwait City; tel. 5320794; fax 5320834; Ambassador MUHAMMAD ADAMU JUMBA.

Oman: POB 21975, 13080 Safat, Istiqlal St, Villa 3, Kuwait City; tel. 2561962; fax 2561963; Ambassador NASSER BIN KHALSAN AL-KHAROSSI.

Pakistan: POB 988, 13010 Safat, Jabriya, Plot 5, Block 11, Villa 7, Kuwait City; tel. 5327649; fax 5327648; Ambassador MUSHTAQ MEHR.

Philippines: POB 26288, 13123 Safat, Jabriya, Police Station St, Area 10, House 363, Kuwait City; tel. 5329316; fax 5329319; e-mail phembkt@ncc.moc.kw; Ambassador SUKARNO D. TANGGOL.

Poland: POB 5066, 13051 Safat, Jabriya, Plot 8, St 20, House 377, Kuwait City; tel. 5311571; fax 5311576; e-mail polamba@qualitynet .net; Ambassador WOJCIECH BOŻEK.

Qatar: POB 1825, 13019 Safat, Diiyah, Istiqlal St, Kuwait City; tel. 2513606; fax 2513604; Ambassador MUHAMMAD ALI AL-ANSARI.

Romania: 13574 Khaitan, Kuwait City; tel. 4843419; fax 4848929; e-mail ambsaat@ncc.moc.kw; Ambassador PATRA POPESCU.

Russia: POB 1765, Daya Diplomatic Area, Block 17, Kuwait City; tel. 2560427; fax 2524969; e-mail ruspos@qualitynet.net; Ambassador AZAMAT R. KULMUKHAMETOV.

Saudi Arabia: POB 20498, 13065 Safat, Istiqlal St, Kuwait City; tel. 2400250; fax 2426541; Ambassador AHMAD AL-HAMAD AL-YAHYA.

Senegal: POB 23892, 13099 Safat, Rawdah, Parcel 3, St 35, House 9, Kuwait City; tel. 2510823; fax 2542044; e-mail senegal_embassy@ yahoo.com; Ambassador ABDOU LAHAD MBACKE.

Serbia and Montenegro: POB 20511, 13066 Safat, Jabriya, Block 7, St 12, Plot 382, Kuwait City; tel. 5327548; fax 5327568; e-mail embscgkw@qualitynet.net; Ambassador ZORAN VEJNOVIĆ.

Somalia: POB 22766, 13088 Safat, Bayan, St 4, Block 4, Villa 4, Kuwait City; tel. 5394795; fax 5394829; e-mail som.emb@usa.net; Ambassador ABDUL KHADIR AMIN ABUBAKER.

South Africa: POB 2262, 40173 Mishref, Kuwait City; tel. 5617988; fax 5617917; e-mail mslabber@southafricaq8.com; internet www .southafricaq8.com; Ambassador M. N. SLABBER.

Spain: POB 22207, 13083 Safat, Surra, Block 3, St 14, Villa 19, Kuwait City; tel. 5325827; fax 5325826; Ambassador ALVARO ALABERT FERNÁNDEZ-CAVADA.

Sri Lanka: POB 13212, 71952 Keifan, House 381, St 9, Block 5, Salwa; tel. 5612261; fax 5612264; e-mail lankemb@kuwait.net; Ambassador DARSIN SERASINGHE.

Sweden: POB 21448, 13075 Safat, Faiha, Area 7, ash-Shahba St, Kuwait City; tel. 2523588; fax 2572157; Ambassador THOMAS GANS-LANDT.

Switzerland: POB 23954, 13100 Safat, Qortuba, Block 2, St 1, Villa 122, Kuwait City; tel. 5340175; fax 5340176; e-mail vertretung@kow .rep.admin.ch; Ambassador JEAN-PHILIPPE TISSIÈRES.

Syria: POB 25600, 13116 Safat, Kuwait City; tel. 5396560; fax 5396509; Ambassador MUSTAFA HAJ ALI.

Thailand: POB 66647, 43757 Bayan, Plot 1, St No. 8, Bldg No. 6, Jabiyra, Kuwait City; tel. 5317531; fax 5317532; e-mail thaiemkw@ qualitynet.net; Ambassador (vacant).

Tunisia: POB 5976, 13060 Safat, Nuzha, Plot 2, Nuzha St, Villa 45, Kuwait City; tel. 2542144; fax 2528995; e-mail tunemrku@ncc.moc .kw; Ambassador MUHAMMAD SAAD.

Turkey: POB 20627, 13067 Safat, Block 16, Plot 10, Istiqlal St, Kuwait City; tel. 2531785; fax 2560653; e-mail trkemb@ncc.moc.kw; internet www.turkish-embassy.org.kw; Ambassador AHMET ERTAY.

United Arab Emirates: POB 1828, 13019 Safat, Plot 70, Istiqlal St, Kuwait City; tel. 2528544; fax 2526382; Ambassador YOUSUF A. AL-ANSARI.

United Kingdom: POB 2, 13001 Safat, Arabian Gulf St, Kuwait City; tel. 2403336; fax 2426799; e-mail general@ britishembassy-kuwait.org; internet www.britishembassy-kuwait .org; Ambassador RICHARD MUIR.

USA: POB 77, 13001 Safat, Bayan, Al-Masjed Al-Aqsa St, Plot 14, Block 14, Kuwait City; tel. 5395307; fax 5380282; e-mail usisirc@ qualitynet.net; internet www.usembassy.gov.kw; Ambassador RICHARD LE BARON.

Venezuela: POB 24440, 13105 Safat, Block 5, St 7, Area 356, Surra, Kuwait City; tel. 5324367; fax 5324368; Chargé d'affaires ALBERTO ARMAS.

Zimbabwe: POB 36484, 24755 Salmiya, Kuwait City; tel. 5621517; fax 5621491; e-mail ZimKuwait@hotmail.com; Ambassador S. C. CHIKETA.

Judicial System

SPECIAL JUDICIARY

Constitutional Court: Comprises five judges. Interprets the provisions of the Constitution; considers disputes regarding the constitutionality of legislation, decrees and rules; has jurisdiction in challenges relating to the election of members, or eligibility for election, to the Majlis al-Umma.

ORDINARY JUDICIARY

Court of Cassation: Comprises five judges. Is competent to consider the legality of verdicts of the Court of Appeal and State Security Court; Chief Justice MUHAMMAD YOUSUF AR-RIFA'I.

Court of Appeal: Comprises three judges. Considers verdicts of the Court of First Instance; Chief Justice RASHED AL-HAMMAD.

Court of First Instance: Comprises the following divisions: Civil and Commercial (one judge), Personal Status Affairs (one judge), Lease (three judges), Labour (one judge), Crime (three judges), Administrative Disputes (three judges), Appeal (three judges), Challenged Misdemeanours (three judges); Chief Justice MUHAMMAD AS-SAKHOBY.

Summary Courts: Each governorate has a Summary Court, comprising one or more divisions. The courts have jurisdiction in the following areas: Civil and Commercial, Urgent Cases, Lease, Misdemeanours. The verdict in each case is delivered by one judge. There is also a **Traffic Court**, with one presiding judge.

Attorney-General: Muhammad Abd al-Haih al-Bannaiy.

Advocate-General: Hamed al-Uthman.

Religion

ISLAM

The majority of Kuwaitis are Muslims of the Sunni or Shi'a sects. The Shi'ite community comprises about 30% of the total.

CHRISTIANITY

The Roman Catholic Church

Latin Rite

For ecclesiastical purposes, Kuwait forms an Apostolic Vicariate. At 31 December 2002 there were an estimated 156,000 adherents in the country.

Vicar Apostolic: Mgr Francis Adeodatus Micallef (Titular Bishop of Tinisa in Proconsulari), Bishop's House, POB 266, 13003 Safat, Kuwait City; tel. 2431561; fax 2409981; e-mail kuwaitbishop@hotmail.com.

Melkite Rite

The Greek-Melkite Patriarch of Antioch is resident in Damascus, Syria. The Patriarchal Exarchate of Kuwait had an estimated 600 adherents at 31 December 2002.

Exarch Patriarchal: Archimandrite Basilios Kanakry, Vicariat Patriarcal Greek-Melkite, POB 1205, Salwa Block 12, St No. 6, House 58, 22013 Salmiya, Kuwait City; tel. 6016691.

Syrian Rite

The Syrian Catholic Patriarch of Antioch is resident in Beirut, Lebanon. The Patriarchal Exarchate of Basra and Kuwait, with an estimated 1,200 adherents at 31 December 2000, is based in Basra, Iraq.

The Anglican Communion

Within the Episcopal Church in Jerusalem and the Middle East, Kuwait forms part of the diocese of Cyprus and the Gulf. The Anglican congregation in Kuwait is entirely expatriate. The Bishop in Cyprus and the Gulf is resident in Cyprus, while the Archdeacon in the Gulf is resident in Qatar.

Other Christian Churches

National Evangelical Church in Kuwait: POB 80, 13001 Safat, Kuwait City; tel. 2407195; fax 2431087; e-mail elc@ncc.moc.kw; Rev. Nabil Attallah (pastor of the Arabic-language congregation), Rev. Jerry A. Zandstra (senior pastor of the English-speaking congregation); an independent Protestant Church founded by the Reformed Church in America; services in Arabic, English, Korean, Malayalam and other Indian languages; combined weekly congregation of some 20,000.

The Armenian, Greek, Coptic and Syrian Orthodox Churches are also represented in Kuwait.

The Press

Freedom of the press and publishing is guaranteed in the Constitution, although press censorship was in force between mid-1986 and early 1992 (when journalists adopted a voluntary code of practice); in February 1995 a ruling by the Constitutional Court effectively endorsed the Government's right to suspend publication of newspapers (see History). The Government provides financial support to newspapers and magazines. In 1999 there were eight daily and 20 weekly newspapers, and 196 periodicals.

DAILIES

Al-Anbaa (The News): POB 23915, 13100 Safat, Kuwait City; tel. 4831168; fax 4837914; f. 1976; Arabic; general; Editor-in-Chief Bibi Khalid al-Marzooq; circ. 85,000.

Arab Times: POB 2270, 13023 Safat, Kuwait City; tel. 4813566; fax 4833628; f. 1977; English; political and financial; no Friday edition; Editor-in-Chief Ahmad Abd al-Aziz al-Jarallah; Man. Editor Mishal al-Jarallah; circ. 41,922.

Kuwait Times: POB 1301, 13014 Safat, Kuwait City; tel. 4833199; fax 4835621; e-mail info@kuwaittimes.net; internet www

.kuwaittimes.net; f. 1961; weekend edition also published; English, Malayalam and Urdu; political; Owner and Editor-in-Chief Yousuf Alyyan; Gen. Man. Badrya Darwish; circ. 32,000.

Al-Qabas (Firebrand): POB 21800, 13078 Safat, Kuwait City; tel. 4812822; fax 4834355; e-mail alqabas@ncc.moc.kw; internet www .moc.kw/alqabas; f. 1972; Arabic; independent; Gen. Man. Fouzan al-Fares; Editor-in-Chief Waleed Abd al-Latif an-Nisf; circ. 60,000.

Ar-Ra'i al-'Aam (Public Opinion): POB 761, 13008 Safat, Kuwait City; tel. 4817777; fax 4838352; f. 1961; Arabic; political, social and cultural; Editor-in-Chief Yousuf al-Jalahma; circ. 101,500.

As-Seyassah (Policy): POB 2270, Shuwaikh, Kuwait City; tel. 4816326; fax 4833628; e-mail alsyasah@qualitynet.net; f. 1965; Arabic; political and financial; Editor-in-Chief Ahmad Abd al-Aziz al-Jarallah; circ. 70,000.

Al-Watan (The Homeland): POB 1142, 13012 Safat, Kuwait City; tel. 4840950; fax 4818481; e-mail webmaster@alwatan.com.kw; internet www.alwatan.com.kw; f. 1962; Arabic; political; Editor-in-Chief Muhammad Abd al-Qader al-Jasem; Gen. Man. Yousuf bin Jasem; circ. 91,726.

WEEKLIES AND PERIODICALS

Al-Balagh (Communiqué): POB 4558, 13046 Safat, Kuwait City; tel. 4818606; fax 4819008; f. 1969; weekly; Arabic; general, political and Islamic; Editor-in-Chief Abd ar-Rahman Rashid al-Walayati; circ. 29,000.

Ad-Dakhiliya (The Interior): POB 71655, 12500 Shamiah, Kuwait City; tel. 2410091; fax 2410609; e-mail moipr@qualitynet.net; monthly; Arabic; official reports, transactions and proceedings; publ. by Public Relations Dept, Ministry of the Interior; Editor-in-Chief Lt-Col Ahmad A. ash-Sharqawi.

Dalal Magazine: POB 6000, 13060 Safat, Kuwait City; tel. 4832098; fax 4840630; internet www.alyaqza.com; f. 1997; monthly; Arabic; family affairs, beauty, fashion; Editor-in-Chief Ahmad Yousuf Behbehani.

Al-Hadaf (The Objective): POB 2270, 13023 Safat, Kuwait City; tel. 4813566; fax 4833628; f. 1964; weekly; Arabic; social and cultural; Editor-in-Chief Ahmad Abd al-Aziz al-Jarallah; circ. 268,904.

Hayatuna (Our Life): POB 26733, 13128 Safat, Kuwait City; tel. 2530120; fax 2530736; f. 1968; fortnightly; Arabic; medicine and hygiene; publ. by Al-Awadi Press Corpn; Editor-in-Chief Abd ar-Rahman al-Awadi; circ. 6,000.

Al-Iqtisadi al-Kuwaiti (Kuwaiti Economist): POB 775, 13008 Safat, Kuwait City; tel. 805580; fax 2412927; e-mail kcci@kcci.org .kw; internet www.kcci.org.kw; f. 1960; monthly; Arabic; commerce, trade and economics; publ. by Kuwait Chamber of Commerce and Industry; Editor Majed Jamal ad-Din; circ. 6,000.

Journal of the Gulf and Arabian Peninsula Studies: POB 17073, 72451 Khaldiya, Kuwait University, Kuwait City; tel. 4833215; fax 4833705; e-mail jotgaaps@kuc01.kuniv.edu.kw; f. 1974; quarterly; Arabic; English; Editor-in-Chief Prof. Salem Marzouk at-Tuhaieh.

Al-Khaleej Business Magazine: POB 25725, 13118 Safat, Kuwait City; tel. 2433765; e-mail aljabriya@gulfweb.com; Editor-in-Chief Ahmad Ismail Behbehani.

Kuwait al-Youm (Kuwait Today): POB 193, 13002 Safat, Kuwait City; tel. 4842167; fax 4831044; f. 1954; weekly; Arabic; statistics, Amiri decrees, laws, govt announcements, decisions, invitations for tenders, etc.; publ. by the Ministry of Information; circ. 5,000.

Al-Kuwaiti (The Kuwaiti): Information Dept, POB 9758, 61008 Ahmadi, Kuwait City; tel. 3989111; fax 3983661; e-mail kocinfo@kockw.com; f. 1961; monthly journal of the Kuwait Oil Co; Arabic; Editor-in-Chief Ali H. Murad; circ. 6,500.

The Kuwaiti Digest: Information Dept, POB 9758, 61008 Ahmadi, Kuwait City; tel. 3980651; fax 3983661; e-mail kocinfo@kockw.com; f. 1972; quarterly journal of Kuwait Oil Co; English; Editor-in-Chief Ra'ad Salem al-Jandal; circ. 7,000.

Kuwait Medical Journal (KMJ): POB 1202, 13013 Safat, Kuwait City; tel. 5317972; fax 5312630; e-mail kmj@kma.org.kw; internet www.kma.org.kw/kmj; f. 1967; quarterly; English; case reports, articles, reviews; Editor-in-Chief Dr Nael an-Naqeeb; circ. 10,000.

Al-Majaless (Meetings): POB 5605, 13057 Safat, Kuwait City; tel. 4841178; fax 4847126; weekly; Arabic; current affairs; Editor-in-Chief (vacant); circ. 60,206.

Mejallat al-Kuwait (Kuwait Magazine): POB 193, 13002 Safat, Kuwait City; tel. 2415300; fax 2419642; f. 1961; monthly; Arabic; illustrated magazine; science, arts and literature; publ. by the Ministry of Information.

Mirat al-Umma (Mirror of the Nation): POB 1142, 13012 Safat, Kuwait City; tel. 4837212; fax 4838671; weekly; Arabic; Editor-in-Chief MUHAMMAD AL-JASSEM; circ. 79,500.

An-Nahdha (The Renaissance): POB 695, 13007 Safat, Kuwait City; tel. 4813133; fax 4849298; f. 1967; weekly; Arabic; social and political; Editor-in-Chief THAMER AS-SALAH; circ. 170,000.

Osrati (My Family): POB 2995, 13030 Safat, Kuwait City; tel. 4813233; fax 4838933; f. 1978; weekly; Arabic; women's magazine; publ. by Fahad al-Marzouk Establishment; Editor GHANIMA F. AL-MARZOUK; circ. 10,500.

Sawt al-Khaleej (Voice of the Gulf): POB 659, Safat, Kuwait City; tel. 4815590; fax 4839261; f. 1962; politics and literature; Arabic; Editor-in-Chief CHRISTINE KHRAIBET; Owner BAKER ALI KHRAIBET; circ. 20,000.

At-Talia (The Ascendant): POB 1082, 13011 Safat, Kuwait City; tel. 4831200; fax 4840471; f. 1962; weekly; Arabic; politics and literature; Editor AHMAD YOUSUF AN-NAFISI; circ. 10,000.

Al-Yaqza (The Awakening): POB 6000, 13060 Safat, Kuwait City; tel. 4831318; fax 4840630; f. 1966; weekly; Arabic; political, economic, social and general; Editor-in-Chief AHMAD YOUSUF BEHBEHANI; circ. 91,340.

Az-Zamed: POB 42181, 13150 Safat, Kuwait City; tel. 4848279; fax 4819985; f. 1961; weekly; Arabic; political, social and cultural; Editor SHAWQI RAFA'E.

NEWS AGENCIES

Kuwait News Agency (KUNA): POB 24063, 13101 Safat, Kuwait City; tel. 4834546; fax 4813424; e-mail kuna@kuna.net.kw; internet www.kuna.net.kw; f. 1976; public corporate body; independent; also publishes research digests on topics of common and special interest; Chair. and Dir-Gen. MUHAMMAD AHMAD AL-AJEERI.

Foreign Bureaux

Informatsionnoye Telegrafnoye Agentstvo Rossii—Telegrafnoye Agentstvo Suverennykh Stran (ITAR—TASS) (Russia): POB 1765, 13018 Safat, Kuwait City; tel. and fax 5639260; Correspondent CONSTANTINE MATHULSKI.

Middle East News Agency (MENA) (Egypt): POB 1927, Safat, Fahd as-Salem St, Kuwait City; Dir REDA SOLIMAN.

Reuters Middle East Ltd (UK): POB 5616, 13057 Safat, Mubarak al-Kabir St, Kuwait Stock Exchange Bldg, 4th Floor, Kuwait City; tel. 2431920; fax 2460340; internet www.reuters.com/gulf; Country Man. ISSAM MAKKI.

Xinhua (New China) News Agency (People's Republic of China): POB 22168, Safat, Sheikh Ahmad al-Jaber Bldg, 10 Dasman St, Kuwait City; tel. 4809423; fax 4809396; Correspondent HUANG JIANMING.

AFP (France), **Anadolu Ajansı** (Turkey), **AP** (USA), **dpa** (Germany), **JANA** (Libya), **QNA** (Qatar), **RIA—Novosti** (Russia) and **SANA** (Syria) are also represented.

PRESS ASSOCIATION

Kuwait Journalist Association: POB 5454, Safat, Kuwait City; tel. 4843351; fax 4842874; Chair. AHMAD BAHBEHANI.

Publishers

Al-Abraj Translation and Publishing Co WLL: POB 26177, 13122 Safat, Kuwait City; tel. 2444665; fax 2436889; Man. Dir Dr TARIQ ABDULLAH.

Dar as-Seyassah Publishing, Printing and Distribution Co: POB 2270, 13023 Safat, Kuwait City; tel. 4813566; fax 4833628; internet www.contactkuwait.com/dar-alseyasa; publ. *Arab Times*, *As-Seyassah* and *Al-Hadaf*.

Gulf Centre Publishing and Publicity: POB 2722, 13028 Safat, Kuwait City; tel. 2402760; fax 2458833; Propr HAMZA ISMAIL ESSLAH.

Kuwait Publishing House: POB 29126, 13150 Safat, Kuwait City; tel. 2417810; Dir ESAM AS'AD ABU AL-FARAJ.

Kuwait United Advertising, Publishing and Distribution Co WLL: POB 29359, 13153 Safat, Kuwait City; tel. 4817111; fax 4817797.

At-Talia Printing and Publishing Co: POB 1082, Airport Rd, Shuwaikh, 13011 Safat, Kuwait City; tel. 4840470; fax 4815611; Man. AHMAD YOUSUF AN-NAFISI.

Government Publishing House

Ministry of Information: POB 193, 13002 Safat, as-Sour St, Kuwait City; tel. 2433038; fax 2434715; e-mail info@moinfo.gov.kw; internet www.moinfo.gov.kw.

Broadcasting and Communications

TELECOMMUNICATIONS

Plans to privatize the state telecommunications sector, and to reorganize the Ministry of Communications as a company, designated the Kuwaiti Communications Corporation, initiated in 1998, were completed in 2000. In 2001 the Government commenced the sale of up to one-half of its 48% share of the National Mobile Telcommunications Co.

Mobile Telecommunications Co (MTC): POB 22244, 1308 Safat, Kuwait City; tel. 4842000; fax 4837755; e-mail mtcweb@mtc.com.kw; internet www.mtc.com.kw; f. 1983; Chair. and Man. Dir SALMAN YOUSUF AR-ROUMI.

National Mobile Telecommunications Co KSC (Wataniya Telecom): POB 613, 13007 Safat, Kuwait City; tel. 2435500; fax 2436600; internet www.wataniya.com; f. 1998; Chair. and Man. Dir FAISAL HAMAD AL-AYYAR; CEO and Gen. Man. DAVID MURRAY.

BROADCASTING

Radio

Radio of the State of Kuwait: POB 397, 13004 Safat, Kuwait City; tel. 2423774; fax 2456660; e-mail radiokuwait@radiokuwait.org; internet www.radiokuwait.org; f. 1951; broadcasts daily in Arabic, Farsi, English and Urdu, some in stereo; Dir of Radio Dr ABD AL-AZIZ ALI MANSOUR; Dir of Radio Programmes ABD AR-RAHMAN HADI.

Television

Kuwait Television: POB 193, 13002 Safat, Kuwait City; tel. 2413501; fax 2438403; internet www.moinfo.gov.kw/KTV/index.html; f. 1961; transmission began privately in Kuwait in 1957; transmits in Arabic; colour television service began in 1973; has a total of five channels; Head of News Broadcasting MUHAMMAD AL-KAHTANI.

Plans were announced in early 1998 for the establishment of a private satellite broadcasting television channel, with administrative offices in Kuwait and transmission facilities in Dubai, United Arab Emirates.

Finance

(cap. = capital; res = reserves; dep. = deposits; m. = million; brs = branches; amounts in Kuwaiti dinars unless otherwise stated)

BANKING

Central Bank

Central Bank of Kuwait: POB 526, 13006 Safat, Abdullah as-Salem St, Kuwait City; tel. 2449200; fax 2464887; e-mail cbk@cbk.gov.kw; internet www.cbk.gov.kw; f. 1969; cap. 5.0m., res 340.3m., dep. 1,224.4m. (March 2003); Governor Sheikh SALEM ABD AL-AZIZ SA'UD AS-SABAH.

National Banks

Al-Ahli Bank of Kuwait KSC: POB 1387, 13014 Safat, Ahmad al-Jaber St, Safat Sq., Kuwait City; tel. 2400900; fax 2424557; e-mail headoffice@abkuwait.com; internet www.abk-kuwait.com; f. 1967; wholly owned by private Kuwaiti interests; cap. 87.9m., res 81.7m., dep. 1,117.9m. (Dec. 2002); Chair. MORAD YOUSUF BEHBEHANI; Gen. Man. and CEO ERVIN B. KNOX; 14 brs.

Bank of Bahrain and Kuwait: POB 24396, 13104 Safat, Ahmad al-Jaber St, Kuwait City; tel. 2417140; fax 2440937; e-mail bbkp@bbkonline.com.bh; internet www.bbkonline.com.bh; f. 1971; owned equally by the Govts of Bahrain and Kuwait; cap. BD 56.9m., res BD 35.3m., dep. BD 1,069.4m. (Dec. 2002); Gen. Man. IAN JOHNSTON (acting).

Bank of Kuwait and the Middle East KSC (BKME): POB 71, 13001 Safat, Joint Banking Centre, East Tower, Darwazat Abd ar-Razzak, Kuwait City; tel. 2459771; fax 2461430; e-mail bkmekw@bkme.com.kw; internet www.bkme.com; f. 1971; 43% owned by Ahli United Bank (Bahrain); cap. 70.4m., res 61.0m., dep. 1,242.2m. (Dec. 2002); Chair. and Man. Dir HAMAD ABD AL-MOHSEN ALMARZOUQ; 16 brs.

Burgan Bank SAK: POB 5389, 12170 Safat, Ahmad al-Jaber St, Kuwait City; tel. 2439000; fax 2461148; e-mail mainbr@burgan.com.kw; internet www.burgan.com; f. 1975; cap. 78.1m., res 102.8m., dep. 1,459.9m. (Dec. 2002); Chair. and Man. Dir ABD AL-AZIZ IBRAHIM AN-NABHAN; Gen. Man. FAISAL AR-RAWDAN; 17 brs.

Commercial Bank of Kuwait SAK: POB 2861, 13029 Safat, Mubarak al-Kabir St, Kuwait City; tel. 2411001; fax 2450150; e-mail cbkinq@banktijari.com; internet www.cbk.com; f. 1960 by Amiri decree; cap. 72.2m., res 138.9m., dep. 1,259.9m. (Dec. 2002); Chair. and Man. Dir Sheikh MUHAMMAD JARRAH AS-SABAH; Gen. Man. and CEO JAMAL AL-MUTAWA; 28 brs.

Gulf Bank KSC: POB 3200, 13032 Safat, Mubarak al-Kabir St, Kuwait City; tel. 2449501; fax 2445212; e-mail customerservice@gulfbank.com.kw; internet www.gulfbank.com.kw; f. 1960; cap. 82.1m., res 99.7m., dep. 1,710.1m. (Dec. 2002); Chair. and Man. Dir BASSAM Y. ALGHANIM; 29 brs.

Industrial Bank of Kuwait KSC: POB 3146, 13032 Safat, Joint Banking Centre, Commercial Area 9, Kuwait City; tel. 2457661; fax 2462057; e-mail em.ibk@ncc.moc.kw; internet www.ibkuwt.com; 31.4% state-owned; f. 1973; cap. 20.0m., res 120.8m., dep. 54.6m. (Dec. 2002); Chair. and Man. Dir SALEH MUHAMMAD AL-YOUSUF; Gen. Man. ALI ABD AN-NABI KHAJAH.

Kuwait Finance House KSC (KFH): POB 24989, 13110 Safat, Abdullah al-Mubarak St, Kuwait City; tel. 2445050; fax 2455135; e-mail kfh@kfh.com.kw; internet www.kfh.com; f. 1977; Islamic banking and investment company; 45% state-owned; cap. 68.3m., res 193.7m., dep. 1,989.5m. (Dec. 2002); Chair. and Man. Dir BADER ABD AL-MOHSEN AL-MUKHAISEEM; Gen. Man. JASSAR D. AL-JASSAR; 27 brs.

Kuwait Real Estate Bank KSC: POB 22822, 13089 Safat, West Tower—Joint Banking Centre, Darwazat Abd ar-Razzak, Kuwait City; tel. 2458177; fax 2462516; e-mail kreb@yahoo.com; internet www.akaribank.com; f. 1973; wholly owned by private Kuwaiti interests; cap. 43.5m., res 61.6m., dep. 421.9m. (Dec. 2002); Chair. TEWFIK ABDULLAH AL-GHARABALLY; Man. Dir MOAYAD HAMAD AS-SALEH; Gen. Man. AHMAD ABD AL-QADER MUHAMMAD (acting); 6 brs.

National Bank of Kuwait SAK (NBK): POB 95, 13001 Safat, Abdullah al-Ahmad St, Kuwait City; tel. 2422011; fax 2431888; e-mail webmaster@nbk.com; internet www.nbk.com; f. 1952; cap. 147.4m., res 225.3m., dep. 4,638.7m. (Dec. 2002); Chair. MUHAMMAD ABD AR-RAHMAN AL-BAHAR; CEO IBRAHIM S. DABDOUB; 41 brs.

INSURANCE

Al-Ahleia Insurance Co SAK: POB 1602, Ahmad al-Jaber St, 13017 Safat, Kuwait City; tel. 2448870; fax 2430308; f. 1962; all forms of insurance; cap. 11.7m.; Chair. and Man. Dir SULAYMAN HAMAD AD-DALALI.

Al-Ittihad al-Watani Insurance Co for the Near East SAL: POB 781, 13008 Safat, Kuwait City; tel. 4843988; fax 4847244; Man. JOSEPH ZACCOUR.

Arab Commercial Enterprises WLL (Kuwait): POB 2474, 13025 Safat, Kuwait City; tel. 2425995; fax 2409450; e-mail acekwt@ace-ins.com; f. 1952.

Gulf Insurance Co KSC: POB 1040, 13011 Safat, Kuwait City; tel. 2423384; fax 2422320; f. 1962; cap. 11.3m.; all forms of insurance; Chair. FAISAL HAMAD AL-AYYAR.

Kuwait Insurance Co SAK (KIC): POB 769, 13008 Safat, Abdullah as-Salem St, Kuwait City; tel. 2420135; fax 2428530; e-mail info@kic-kw.com; internet www.kic-kw.com; f. 1960; cap. US $64.6m.; all life and non-life insurance; Chair. MUHAMMAD SALEH BEHBEHANI; Gen. Man. ALI HAMAD AL-BAHAR.

Kuwait Reinsurance Company: POB 21929, Munther Tower, Salhiya, 13080 Safat, Kuwait City; tel. 2432011; fax 2427823; e-mail kuwaitre@kuwaitre.com; f. 1972; cap. 10.0m. (March 2003); Gen. Man. AMIR AL-MUHANNA.

Kuwait Technical Insurance Office: POB 25349, 13114 Safat, Kuwait City; tel. 2413986; fax 2413986.

Mohd Saleh Behbehani & Co: POB 370, 13004 Safat, Kuwait City; tel. 2412085; fax 2412089.

New India Assurance Co: POB 370, 13004 Safat, Kuwait City; tel. 2412085; fax 2412089.

The Northern Insurance Co Ltd: POB 579, 13006 Safat, Kuwait City; tel. 2427930; fax 2462739.

The Oriental Insurance Co Ltd: POB 22431, 13085 Safat, Kuwait City; tel. 2424016; fax 2424017; Man. JUGAL KISHORE MADAAN.

Sumitomo Marine & Fire Insurance Co (Kuwait Agency): POB 3458, 13055 Safat, Kuwait City; tel. 2433087; fax 2430853.

Warba Insurance Co SAK: POB 24282, 13103 Safat, Kuwait City; tel. 2445140; fax 2466131; internet www.kuwait.net/~warba; f. 1976; Chair. ABDULLAH HASSAN JARALLAH; 1 br.

Some 20 Arab and other foreign insurance companies are active in Kuwait.

STOCK EXCHANGE

Kuwait Stock Exchange: POB 22235, 13083 Safat, Mubarak al-Kabir St, Kuwait City; tel. 2423130; fax 2429771; e-mail borse@qualitynet.net; internet www.kuwaitse.com; f. 1983; 96 companies and five mutual funds listed in March 2003; Dir Dr SAFAAQ ABDULLAH AR-RUKAIBI.

Markets Association

Kuwait Financial Markets Association (KFMA): POB 25228, 13113 Safat, Kuwait City; internet www.kfma.org.kw; f. 1977; represents treasury, financial and capital markets and their members; Pres. THUNAYAN AL-GHANIM; Sec.-Gen. ZUHAIR AL-JUMA.

Trade and Industry

GOVERNMENT AGENCY

Kuwait Investment Authority (KIA): POB 64, 13001 Safat, Kuwait City; tel. 2439595; fax 2454059; e-mail webmaster@kia.gov.kw; internet www.kia.gov.kw; oversees the Kuwait Investment Office (London); responsible for the Kuwaiti General Reserve; Chair. Minister of Finance; Man. Dir SALEH MUBARAK AL-FALAH.

DEVELOPMENT ORGANIZATIONS

Arab Planning Institute (API): POB 5834, 13059 Safat, Kuwait City; tel. 4843130; fax 4842935; e-mail api@api.org.kw; internet www.arab-api.org; f. 1966; 15 mem. states; publishes annual directory, *Journal of Development and Economic Policies* and proceedings of seminars and discussion group meetings, offers research, training programmes and advisory services; Dir ESSA ALGHAZALI.

Industrial Investments Company (IIC): POB 26019, 13121 Safat, Kuwait City; tel. 2429073; fax 2448850; f. 1983; invests directly in industry; partly owned by the Kuwait Investment Authority; privatization initiated in April 1996; Man. Dir TALEB A. ALI.

Kuwait Fund for Arab Economic Development (KFAED): POB 2921, 13030 Safat, cnr Mubarak al-Kabir St and al-Hilali St, Kuwait City; tel. 2468800; fax 2436289; e-mail info@kuwait-fund.org; internet www.kuwait-fund.org; f. 1961; cap. KD 2,000m.; state-owned; provides and administers financial and technical assistance to the countries of the developing world; Chair. Minister of Finance; Dir-Gen. BADER M. AL-HUMAIDHI.

Kuwait International Investment Co SAK (KIIC): POB 22792, 13088 Safat, as-Salhiya Commercial Complex, Kuwait City; tel. 2438273; fax 2454931; 30% state-owned; cap. p.u. KD 31.9m., total assets KD 146.9m. (1988); domestic real estate and share markets; Chair. and Man. Dir JASEM MUHAMMAD AL-BAHAR.

Kuwait Investment Co SAK (KIC): POB 1005, 13011 Safat, 5th Floor, al-Manakh Bldg, Mubarak al-Kabir St, Kuwait City; tel. 2438111; fax 2444896; e-mail info@kic.com.kw; f. 1981; 88% state-owned, 12% owned by private Kuwaiti interests; total resources KD 50.1m. (1996); international banking and investment; Chair. and Man. Dir BADER A. AR-RUSHAID AL-BADER.

Kuwait Planning Board: c/o Ministry of Planning, POB 21688, 13122 Safat, Kuwait City; tel. 2428200; fax 2414734; f. 1962; supervises long-term development plans; through its Central Statistical Office publishes information on Kuwait's economic activity; Dir-Gen. AHMAD ALI AD-DUAIJ.

National Industries Co SAK (NIC): POB 417, 13005 Safat, Kuwait City; tel. 4815466; fax 4839582; f. 1960; 22.7% owned by KIA; cap. p.u. KD 34.9m.; has controlling interest in various construction enterprises; privatization initiated in March 1995; Chair. and Man. Dir SAUD M. AL-OSMANI.

Shuaiba Area Authority SAA: POB 4690, 13047 Safat, Kuwait City; POB 10033, Shuaiba; tel. 3260903; f. 1964; an independent governmental authority to supervise and run the industrial area and Port of Shuaiba; has powers and duties to develop the area and its industries which include an oil refinery, cement factory, fishing plant, power stations and distillation plants, chemical fertilizer and petrochemical industries, sanitary ware factory, asbestos plant and sand lime bricks plant; Dir-Gen. SULAYMAN K. AL-HAMAD.

CHAMBER OF COMMERCE

Kuwait Chamber of Commerce and Industry: POB 775, 13008 Safat, Chamber's Bldg, ash-Shuhada St, Kuwait City; tel. 805580; fax 2404110; e-mail kcci@kcci.org.kw; internet www.kcci.org.kw; f. 1959; 50,000 mems; Chair. ABD AR-RAZZAK KHALID ZAID AL-KHALID; Dir-Gen. AHMAD RASHED AL-HAROUN.

STATE HYDROCARBONS COMPANIES

Kuwait Petroleum Corpn (KPC): POB 26565, 13126 Safat, as-Salhiya Commercial Complex, Fahed as-Salem St, Kuwait City; tel. 2455455; fax 2467159; e-mail webmaster@kpc.com.kw; internet www.kpc.com.kw; f. 1980; co-ordinating organization to manage the petroleum industry; controls Kuwait Aviation Fuelling Co (KAFCO), Kuwait Foreign Petroleum Exploration Co (KUFPEC), Kuwait National Petroleum Co (KNPC), Kuwait Oil Co (KOC), Kuwait Oil Tanker Co (KOTC), Kuwait Petroleum International Ltd (KPI), Petrochemical Industries Co (PIC), Santa Fe International Corpn (SFIC); Chair. Minister of Oil; Deputy Chair. and CEO NADER HAMAD SULTAN.

Kuwait Aviation Fuelling Co KSC: POB 1654, 13017 Safat, Kuwait City; tel. 4330482; fax 4330475; Gen. Man. ABD AL-AZIZ AS-SERRI.

Kuwait Foreign Petroleum Exploration Co KSC (KUFPEC): POB 5291, 13053 Safat, Kuwait City; tel. 2421677; fax 2420405; f. 1981; state-owned; overseas oil and gas exploration and development; Chair. and Man. Dir BADER AL-KHASHTI.

Kuwait National Petroleum Co KSC (KNPC): POB 70, 13001 Safat, Ali as-Salem St, Kuwait City; tel. 2420121; fax 2433839; f. 1960; oil refining, production of liquefied petroleum gas, and domestic marketing and distribution of petroleum by-products; output of 855,000 b/d of refined petroleum in 1996/97; Chair. and Man. Dir HANI ABD AL-AZIZ HUSSEIN.

Kuwait Oil Co KSC (KOC): POB 9758, 61008 Ahmadi; tel. 3989111; fax 3983661; e-mail kocinfo@kockw.com; internet www.kockw.com; f. 1934; state-owned; Chair. and Man. Dir AHMAD AL-ARBEED.

Kuwait Petroleum International Ltd (Q8) (KPI): POB 1819, 13019 Safat, Chamber of Commerce and Industry Bldg, Al-Murgab, Mubarak al-Kabir St, Kuwait City; tel. 2404087; fax 2407523; internet www.q8.com; marketing division of KPC; controls 6,500 petrol retail stations in Europe, and European refineries with capacity of 235,000 b/d; Pres. KAMEL HARAMI.

UTILITIES

In 1998 there were plans to create regulatory bodies for each of Kuwait's utilities, with a view to facilitating their privatization.

Ministry of Energy: see Ministries (above); provides subsidized services throughout Kuwait.

TRADE UNIONS

Kuwait Trade Union Federation (KTUF): POB 5185, 13052 Safat, Kuwait City; tel. 5616053; fax 5627159; e-mail ktuf@hotmail.com; f. 1967; central authority to which all trade unions are affiliated.

KOC Workers Union: Kuwait City; f. 1964; Chair. HAMAD SAWYAN.

Federation of Petroleum and Petrochemical Workers: Kuwait City; f. 1965; Chair. JASEM ABD AL-WAHAB AT-TOURA.

Transport

RAILWAYS

There are no railways in Kuwait.

ROADS

Roads in the towns are metalled, and the most important are motorways or dual carriageways. There are metalled roads linking Kuwait City to Ahmadi, Mina al-Ahmadi and other centres of population in Kuwait, and to the Iraqi and Saudi Arabian borders, amounting to a total road network of 4,273 km in 1989 (280 km of motorways, 1,232 km of other major roads and 2,761 km of secondary roads). The total road network was estimated at 4,450 km in 1999.

Kuwait Public Transport Co SAK (KPTC): POB 375, 13004 Safat, Murghab, Safat Sq., Kuwait City; tel. 2469420; fax 2401265; e-mail info@kptc.com.kw; f. 1962; state-owned; provides internal bus service; regular service to Mecca, Saudi Arabia; Chair. and Man. Dir MAHMOUD A. AN-NOURI.

SHIPPING

Kuwait has three commercial seaports. The largest, Shuwaikh, situated about 3 km from Kuwait City, was built in 1960. By 1987 it comprised 21 deep-water berths, with a total length of 4 km, three shallow-water berths and three basins for small craft, each with a depth of 3.35 m. In 1988 3.6m. metric tons of cargo were imported and 133,185 tons were exported through the port. A total of 1,189 vessels passed through Shuwaikh in 1988.

Shuaiba Commercial Port, 56 km south of Kuwait City, was built in 1967 to facilitate the import of primary materials and heavy equipment, necessary for the construction of the Shuaiba Industrial Area. By 1987 the port comprised a total of 20 berths, plus two docks for small wooden boats. Four of the berths constitute a station for unloading containers. Shuaiba handled a total of 3,457,871 metric tons of dry cargo, barge cargo and containers in 1988.

Doha, the smallest port, was equipped in 1981 to receive small coastal ships carrying light goods between the Gulf states. It has 20 small berths, each 100 m long. Doha handled a total of 20,283 metric tons of dry cargo, barge cargo and containers in 1988.

The oil port at Mina al-Ahmadi, 40 km south of Kuwait City, is capable of handling the largest oil tankers afloat, and the loading of over 2m. barrels of oil per day. By 1987 the port comprised 12 tanker berths, one bitumen-carrier berth, two LPG export berths and bunkering facilities.

At 31 December 2002 Kuwait's merchant fleet numbered 201 vessels, with a total displacement of 2,255,972 grt.

Kuwait Ports Authority: POB 3874, 13039 Safat, Kuwait City; tel. 4812774; fax 4819714; f. 1977; Dir-Gen. ABD AR-RAHMAN AN-NAIBARI.

Principal Shipping Companies

Arab Maritime Petroleum Transport Co (AMPTC): POB 22525, 13086 Safat, OAPEC Bldg, Shuwaikh, Airport St, Kuwait City; tel. 4844500; fax 4842996; e-mail amptc@ncc.moc.kw; f. 1973; seven tankers and four LPG carriers; sponsored by OAPEC and financed by Algeria, Bahrain, Egypt, Iraq, Kuwait, Libya, Qatar, Saudi Arabia and the UAE; Chair. Dr RAMADAN AS-SANUSSI BELHAG (Libya); Gen. Man. SULAYMAN I. AL-BASSAM.

Kuwait Maritime Transport Co KSC (KMTC): POB 25344, 13086 Safat, Nafisi and Khatrash Bldg, Jaber al-Mubarak St, Kuwait City; tel. 2449974; fax 2420513; f. 1981; Chair. FOUAD M. T. AL-GHANIM.

Kuwait Oil Tanker Co SAK (KOTC): POB 810, 13009 Safat, as-Salhiya Commercial Complex, Blocks 3, 5, 7 and 9, Kuwait City; tel. 2455455; fax 2445907; e-mail ysm@kotc.com.kw; internet www.kotc.com.kw; f. 1957; state-owned; operates six crude oil tankers, 16 product tankers and six LPG vessels; sole tanker agents for Mina al-Ahmadi, Shuaiba and Mina Abdullah and agents for other ports; LPG filling and distribution; Chair. and Man. Dir ABDULLAH HAMAD AR-ROUMI.

Kuwait Shipbuilding and Repairyard Co SAK (KSRC): POB 21998, 13080 Safat, Kuwait City; tel. 4830308; fax 4815947; e-mail mahmoud@ksrc.com.kw; internet www.ksrc.com.kw; ship repairs and engineering services, underwater services, maintenance of refineries, power stations and storage tanks; maintains floating dock for vessels up to 35,000 dwt; synchrolift for vessels up to 5,000 dwt with transfer yard; seven repair jetties up to 550 m in length and floating workshop for vessels lying at anchor; Chair. and Man. Dir MOUSA J. MARAFI; Commercial Man. MAHMOUD ASAD.

United Arab Shipping Co SAG (UASC): POB 3636, 13037 Safat, Shuwaikh, Airport Rd, Kuwait City; tel. 4843150; fax 4845388; e-mail gencom@uasc.com.kw; internet www.uasc.com.kw; f. 1976; national shipping company of six Arabian Gulf countries; services between Europe, Far East, Mediterranean ports, Japan and east coast of USA and South America, and ports of participant states on Persian (Arabian) Gulf and Red Sea; operates 24 container carriers and 27 general cargo vessels; subsidiary cos: Kuwait Shipping Agencies, Arab Transport Co (Aratrans), United Arab Chartering Ltd (United Kingdom), Middle East Container Repair Co (Dubai), Arabian Chemicals Carriers (Saudi Arabia), United Arab Agencies Inc. (USA) and United Arab Shipping Agencies Co (Saudi Arabia); Pres. and CEO ABDULLAH MAHDI AL-MAHDI.

CIVIL AVIATION

Kuwait International Airport opened in 1980, and is designed to receive up to 5.0m. passengers per year; in 2001 3.82m. arrivals and departures were recorded. The airport is undergoing a major programme of expansion, at a cost of some US $300m.

Directorate-General of Civil Aviation (DGCA): POB 17, 13001 Safat, Kuwait City; tel. 4335599; fax 4713504; e-mail isc@kuwait-airport.com.kw; internet www.kuwait-airport.com.kw; Pres. Sheikh JABER AL-MUBARAK AS-SABAH; Dir-Gen. YACOUB Y. AS-SAQER.

Kuwait Airways Corpn (KAC): POB 394, Kuwait International Airport, 13004 Safat, Kuwait City; tel. 4345555; fax 4314118; e-mail info@kuwait-airways.com; internet www.kuwait-airways.com; f. 1954; scheduled and charter passenger and cargo services to the Arabian peninsula, Asia, Africa, the USA and Europe; scheduled for privatization; Chair. and Man. Dir AHMAD FAISAL AZ-ZABIN.

Tourism

Attractions for visitors include the Kuwait Towers leisure and reservoir complex, the Entertainment City theme park, the Kuwait Zoological Garden in Omariya and the Khiran Resort tourist village near the border with Saudi Arabia, as well as extensive facilities for

sailing and other water sports. In 2000 there were 20 hotels with a total of 2,857 beds for visitors. Foreign tourist arrivals totalled some 2.1m. in 2001.

Department of Tourism: Ministry of Information, Tourism Affairs, POB 193, 18th Floor, Fahad as-Salem Tower, Fahad as-Salem St, 13002 Safat, Kuwait City; tel. 2457591; fax 2401540; e-mail tourism_kw@media.gov.kw.

Touristic Enterprises Co (TEC): POB 23310, 13094 Safat, Kuwait City; tel. 5652775; fax 5657594; f. 1976; 92% state-owned; manages 23 tourist facilities; Chair. BADER AL-BAHAR; Vice-Chair. SHAKER AL-OTHMAN.

KYRGYZSTAN

Introductory Survey

Location, Climate, Language, Religion, Flag, Capital

The Kyrgyz Republic (formerly the Kyrgyz Soviet Socialist Republic and, between December 1990 and May 1993, the Republic of Kyrgyzstan) is a small, land-locked state situated in eastern Central Asia. The country has also been known as Kyrgyzia (or Kirghizia). It borders Kazakhstan to the north, Uzbekistan to the west, Tajikistan to the south and west, and the People's Republic of China to the east. There are distinct variations in climate between low-lying and high-altitude areas. In the valleys the mean July temperature is 28°C (82°F), whereas in January it falls to an average of –18°C (–0.5°F). Annual rainfall ranges from 180 mm (7 ins) in the eastern Tien Shan mountains to 750 mm–1,000 mm (30 ins–39 ins) in the Fergana mountain range. In the settled valleys the annual average varies between 100 mm and 500 mm (4 ins–20 ins). The state language is Kyrgyz; Russian additionally has the status of an official language. The major religion is Islam, with the majority of ethnic Kyrgyz being Sunni Muslims of the Hanafi school. The national flag (proportions 3 by 5) consists of a red field, at the centre of which is a yellow sun, with 40 counter-clockwise rays surrounding a red-bordered yellow disc, on which are superimposed two intersecting sets of three red, curved, narrow bands. The capital is Bishkek (called Frunze between 1926 and 1991).

Recent History

Following the October Revolution of 1917 in Russia, Kyrgyzia (which had been formally incorporated into the Russian Empire in 1876) experienced a period of civil war, with anti-Bolshevik forces, including the Russian 'White' Army and local armed groups (basmachi), fighting against the Bolshevik Red Army. Soviet power was established in the region by 1919. In 1918 the Turkestan Autonomous Soviet Socialist Republic (ASSR) was established within the Russian Soviet Federative Socialist Republic (the Russian Federation) and included Kyrgyzia until 1924, when the Kara-Kyrgyz Autonomous Oblast (Region) was created. (At this time the Russians used the term Kara-Kyrgyz to distinguish the Kyrgyz from the Kazakhs, then also known as Kyrgyz by the Russians.) In 1925 the region was renamed the Kyrgyz Autonomous Oblast, and it became the Kyrgyz ASSR in February 1926. On 5 December 1936 the Kyrgyz Soviet Socialist Republic (SSR) was established as a full union republic of the USSR.

During the 1920s considerable economic and social developments were made in Kyrgyzia, when land reforms resulted in the settlement of many of the nomadic Kyrgyz. The agricultural collectivization programme of the early 1930s was strongly opposed in the republic and prompted a partial revival of the basmachi movement. Despite the suppression of nationalism under Stalin (Iosif V. Dzhugashvili—Soviet leader in 1924–53), many aspects of Kyrgyz national culture were retained. Leading members of the Kyrgyz Communist Party (KCP) attempted to increase the role of ethnic Kyrgyz in the government of the republic, but these so-called 'national communists' were expelled from the KCP and often imprisoned or exiled, particularly during the late 1930s. Tensions with the all-Union (Soviet) authorities continued following the death of Stalin in 1953. There were, notably, allegations that the murder in December 1980 of Sultan Ibraimov, the Chairman of the Kyrgyz Council of Ministers, was a result of his support for greater republican autonomy.

The election of Mikhail Gorbachev as Soviet leader in 1985, and his introduction of the policies of perestroika (restructuring) and glasnost (openness), led to the resignation of Turdakan Usubaliyev as First Secretary of the KCP. His successor, Absamat Masaliyev, accused Usubaliyev of corruption and nepotism, and dismissed many of his closest allies from office. However, Masaliyev's commitment to Gorbachev's reforms did not extend much beyond correcting the excesses of his predecessor. None the less, the republic's Supreme Soviet adopted Kyrgyz as the official language, and Russian was retained as a language of inter-ethnic communication. The conservative Kyrgyz leadership opposed the development of unofficial quasi-political groups, several of which were established with the aim of alleviating the republic's acute housing shortage by seizing vacant land. One such group, Ashar, was partially tolerated by the authorities and soon developed a wider political role.

Osh Aymaghi, a similar organization to Ashar, based in Osh Oblast, attempted to obtain land and housing provision for ethnic Kyrgyz in the region. (Osh had been incorporated into Kyrgyzia in 1924, although Uzbeks formed the majority of the population, and these had recently begun to demand the establishment of an Uzbek autonomous region there.) Disputes over land and homes in the crowded Fergana valley region of Osh precipitated violent confrontation between Kyrgyz and Uzbeks in 1990, in which, according to official reports, more than 300 people died (although other sources cited as many as 1,000 deaths). A state of emergency (which remained in force until 1995) and a curfew were introduced in the region, and the Uzbek–Kyrgyz border was closed.

Despite the growing influence of the nascent democratic movement, elections to the 350-member Kyrgyz Supreme Soviet (legislature) in February 1990 were conducted along Soviet lines, with KCP candidates winning most seats unopposed. In April Masaliyev was elected to the new office of Chairman of the Supreme Soviet. He favoured the introduction of an executive presidency, election to which was to be by the Supreme Soviet. The strong KCP majority in the legislature appeared to guarantee Masaliyev's election. However, by October, when an extraordinary session of the Supreme Soviet was convened to elect the President, Masaliyev had been seriously discredited by the conflict in Osh; moreover, the opposition, which had united as the Democratic Movement of Kyrgyzstan (DMK), had become a significant political force. In the first round of voting Masaliyev failed to achieve the requisite proportion of votes to be elected, and in a further round Askar Akayev, the President of the Kyrgyz Academy of Sciences, was elected to the executive presidency. Akayev rapidly allied himself with reformist politicians and economists, including leaders of the DMK. A State Committee for Economic Reform was appointed and plans were announced for an extensive programme of privatization. In December Masaliyev resigned as Chairman of the Supreme Soviet, and was replaced by Medetkan Sherimkulov. In that month, despite opposition from the KCP (and Masaliyev, in particular), the Kyrgyz Supreme Soviet voted to change the name of the republic from the Kyrgyz SSR to the Republic of Kyrgyzstan. In February 1991, moreover, the capital, Frunze (named after the Red Army commander who had conquered much of Central Asia in the Civil War), reverted to its pre-1926 name of Bishkek. However, economic realities appeared to prevail against secession. In the referendum on the preservation of the USSR, held in nine republics in March, an overwhelming majority (87.7%) of eligible voters in Kyrgyzstan approved the proposal to retain the USSR as a 'renewed federation'.

In January 1991 Akayev replaced the unwieldy Council of Ministers with a smaller cabinet, comprising mainly reformist politicians. However, his programme of political and economic reform had many opponents within the KCP and the security forces. In April, apparently owing to differences with Akayev, Masaliyev resigned as First Secretary of the KCP; he was replaced by Jumgalbek Amanbayev. Although Amanbayev appeared more sympathetic to Akayev's reform programme, there was much opposition within the KCP leadership to controversial plans for the 'departyization' (removal of KCP cells from workplaces) of government and the security forces.

In August 1991, when the State Committee for the State of Emergency (SCSE) announced that it had assumed power in the Russian and Soviet capital, Moscow, there was an attempt to depose Akayev in Kyrgyzstan. The KCP declared its support for the coup leaders, and the commander of the Turkestan Military District (which comprised the five Central Asian republics) threatened to dispatch troops and tanks to the republic. Akayev dismissed the Chairman of the republican KGB (state security service), and ordered troops of the Ministry of Internal Affairs to guard strategic buildings in Bishkek. He publicly denounced the coup and issued a decree prohibiting activity by any political party in government or state bodies. After the coup had collapsed in Moscow, Akayev and Vice-President German Kuznetsov renounced their membership of the Communist Party of the Soviet Union (CPSU), and the entire politburo and secretariat of the KCP resigned. On 31 August the Kyrgyz Supreme Soviet voted to declare independence from the USSR. Akayev (the sole candidate) was re-elected President of Kyrgyzstan by direct popular vote on 12 October, receiving 95% of the votes cast.

In October 1991 Akayev signed, with representatives of seven other republics, a treaty to establish a new economic community, and when Russia, Belarus and Ukraine proposed the creation of the Commonwealth of Independent States (CIS, see p. 180), Akayev was quick to announce his approval. On 21 December Kyrgyzstan was among the 11 signatories to the Almaty (Alma-Ata) Declaration, which formally established the CIS.

Discussions were held throughout 1992 to draft a new constitution, during which opposition forces demanded the restriction of the President's powers and a stronger role for the legislature. The Constitution, which was finally promulgated on 5 May 1993, provided for a parliamentary system of government, with the Prime Minister as head of the executive (the Government had hitherto been subordinate to the President). Legislative power was to be vested in a smaller (105-member) Zhogorku Kenesh, following a general election, which was due to be held by 1995; in the mean time, the existing assembly would continue to act as the republic's parliament. The new Constitution included provisions aimed at mitigating the concerns of Kyrgyzstan's Slavic community and other ethnic groups; most notably Russian was accorded the constitutional status of a language of inter-ethnic communication. None the less, the country's official name was changed from the Republic of Kyrgyzstan to the less ethnically neutral Kyrgyz Republic, and in July Akayev's attempts to encourage non-Kyrgyz to remain in the republic suffered a serious reverse when Kuznetsov, by this time the First Deputy Prime Minister and the most prominent Slav in government, announced his decision to return to Russia. At mid-1993 it was estimated that some 145,000 Russians had left the republic since 1989.

Akayev's presidency was further destabilized during 1993 by a series of corruption scandals, which his reformist supporters claimed were orchestrated by communist and nationalist forces. In March a commission of inquiry was appointed to investigate the business dealings of the Vice-President, Feliks Kulov. A second commission was established by the legislature later in the year to examine allegations that senior politicians—including the Prime Minister since February 1992, Tursunbek Chyngyshev—had been involved in unauthorized gold exports. In December 1993 Kulov resigned as Vice-President for 'ethical reasons', urging the Government to do likewise. The legislature subsequently held a vote of confidence in Chyngyshev and his Government: the motion failed to secure the required two-thirds' majority and Akayev dismissed the entire cabinet. Later in the month the legislature approved a new Government, headed by Apas Dzhumagulov (Chairman of the Council of Ministers in 1986–91). The Government's composition was largely ethnic Kyrgyz, although it included one representative each of the Russian, German, Uzbek and Jewish communities. Amanbayev was appointed one of the six Deputy Prime Ministers and, following a parliamentary decree that government ministers could not remain members of the legislature, he resigned his seat in the Kenesh, and also the leadership of the KCP. A referendum of confidence in the presidency was held (on Akayev's initiative) in January 1994, at which 96.2% of voters endorsed Akayev's leadership.

In June 1994, in an attempt to curb the rate of emigration from Kyrgyzstan (more than 100,000 people—mainly Russians—were reported to have left the country in that year), Akayev announced that Russian was to become an official language in regions predominantly populated by Russian-speakers, as well as in areas of economic importance. The procedure of application for dual citizenship was to be simplified and the equitable representation of ethnic Russians in the state administration was to be guaranteed. Akayev further requested that the Government delay the final date for the full establishment of Kyrgyz as the official state language from 1995 to 2000 (subsequently extended until 2005). A resolution based on Akayev's decree was adopted by the Zhogorku Kenesh in March 1996. This measure, together with the opening of a Slavonic university in Bishkek in 1993, probably contributed to the decline in the number of Russians emigrating from the republic, estimated at 20,000 in 1996.

Divisions within the legislature evolved into a parliamentary crisis in September 1994, when more than 180 pro-reform deputies announced their intention to boycott the next session of the Zhogorku Kenesh, in protest at the continuing obstruction by former communists of the economic reform process; they also demanded the dissolution of the Kenesh and the holding of fresh elections. The entire Government tendered its resignation, and Akayev announced that parliamentary elections would be held forthwith. The Government was promptly reinstated by Akayev, who announced the holding of a referendum in October on constitutional amendments. Of the 87% of the electorate who participated, more than 70% endorsed proposals for a restructured Zhogorku Kenesh comprising a 70-member People's Assembly (upper chamber) to represent regional interests at twice-yearly sessions and a permanent 35-member Legislative Assembly (lower chamber) representing the population as a whole.

Elections to the two chambers of the new Zhogorku Kenesh were held on 5 February 1995, with the participation of some 62% of the electorate. However, only 16 seats were filled, since in many constituencies the large number of candidates prevented any individual from receiving the requisite minimum proportion of the votes cast. A second round was held on 19 February (again with a participation rate of 62%); however, as voting did not take place in some constituencies, only 73 of the remaining 89 seats were filled. The Zhogorku Kenesh was, none the less, quorate, and its two chambers held their inaugural sessions on 28 March; Mukar Cholponbayev, a former Minister of Justice, was elected Chairman (Speaker) of the Legislative Assembly, while Almambet Matubraimov, a former First Deputy Prime Minister, was elected Speaker of the People's Assembly. The vacant seats in the lower chamber were subsequently filled. A new Government, again led by Dzhumagulov, was appointed in April.

In August 1995 an estimated 1.2m. signatures were collected by supporters of Akayev, in favour of a proposal to hold a referendum on extending the President's term of office until 2001. The campaign appeared to have been inspired by similar votes held in 1994–95 in the neighbouring Central Asian republics of Kazakhstan, Turkmenistan and Uzbekistan, as a result of which the respective Presidents had their mandates extended without seeking re-election. In Kyrgyzstan, however, the Legislative Assembly vetoed the referendum proposal and a direct presidential election was scheduled for 24 December 1995. Akayev emerged as the victor, receiving a reported 71.6% of the votes cast by some 82% of the electorate; Masaliyev (who had recently been reinstated as the leader of the revived KCP) won 24.4% of the votes. Akayev was inaugurated on 30 December. One of his first acts was to decree that a referendum be held on increasing the powers of the President's office, while limiting those of the legislature. A reported 96.6% of the electorate participated in the referendum, on 10 February 1996, of whom 94.3% endorsed the proposed amendments to the Constitution. The Government resigned later that month; Dzhumagulov was reinstated as Prime Minister in March and a new Government was appointed by Akayev shortly afterwards.

In September 1996, following an investigation into claims of government corruption, several leading officials were dismissed for serious financial impropriety, and senior members of the Government were severely reprimanded. The First Deputy Prime Minister was relieved of his duties in a government reorganization effected in December, amid speculation that he had been implicated in the scandal. Meanwhile, in November Cholponbayev was replaced as Speaker of the Legislative Assembly by Usup Mukambayev, after the Constitutional Court declared his election to have been invalid.

Protests held in Bishkek in June 1997, against the imprisonment of two journalists of an independent opposition newspaper, who had been found guilty of libel against the Director of the state gold concern, Kyrgyzaltyn, resulted in clashes with security forces; the journalists' sentences were subsequently reduced. Legislation imposing reporting restrictions on the media, approved by the Zhogorku Kenesh in November, was criticized by the Kyrgyz Committee for Human Rights as a violation of press freedom. In January 1998 a new criminal code was promulgated, which effectively abolished the death penalty by imposing a moratorium on its implementation, in what was described by the Government as a measure to comply with international legal standards. In February, however, the adoption by the Zhogorku Kenesh of draft legislation concerning the organization of public gatherings, whereby permission to hold a rally was to be sought from the local authorities at least 20 days prior to the event, appeared further to restrict civil rights.

In March 1998 Dzhumagulov announced his retirement. The Zhogorku Kenesh endorsed the appointment of Kuvachbek Dzhumaliyev as the new Prime Minister, and a cabinet reorganization was effected. A further, extensive cabinet reshuffle was undertaken in early April, with the aim of accelerating economic and political reform. In July a ruling by the Constitutional Court allowed Akayev to seek a third term in the presidential election due to be held in 2000 (a number of deputies had argued that, although the 1993 Constitution allowed a President to serve a maximum of two terms, Akayev's election in 1991 had taken place under the previous Soviet Constitution). In early September 1998 Akayev announced a referendum to seek approval for several proposed constitutional amendments, prompting strong criticism from members of the Zhogorku Kenesh, which had not been consulted. Early the following month the Ministry of Justice banned the Kyrgyz Committee for Human Rights, citing irregularities in the adoption of its 1996 charter. (However, the Chairman of the organization, Ramazan Dyryldayev, alleged that the ban had been imposed as a result of the group's anti-Government stance, and to prevent it from acting as an observer at the referendum.) The referendum took place on 17 October 1998, with the participation of about 96% of the electorate, and some 90% of voters approved the following amendments: the number of deputies in the Legislative Assembly was to increase to 60, and representation in the People's Assembly was to be reduced to 45; the electoral system was to be reformed; restrictions on parliamentary immunity were to be introduced; private land ownership was to be legalized; the presentation of unbalanced or unattainable budgets was to be banned; and the adoption of any legislation restricting freedom of speech or of the press was to be prohibited. The Zhogorku Kenesh and the majority of political parties declared their opposition to the constitutional changes and, in particular, to the introduction of private land ownership, which they feared would result in the transfer of land to foreign ownership. In August 1999 the Kyrgyz Committee for Human Rights was re-registered, following pressure from the international community. Facing arrest in July 2000, however, Dyryldayev fled to Vienna, Austria, from where he continued to oversee the work of the Committee.

Akayev's declared campaign against financial crime and corruption intensified in mid-December 1998, when a number of senior government officials, including three deputy ministers, were arrested on charges of corruption and abuse of office, bringing to 383 the number dismissed on similar grounds since 1993. In late December 1998 the President dissolved the Government for its failure to address the country's economic problems. Dzhumabek Ibraimov, hitherto the Chairman of the State Property Committee, was appointed Prime Minister and a new Government was formed, although 10 ministers from the previous administration retained their portfolios. Akayev also issued a decree extending the Prime Minister's mandate, giving him the right to appoint and dismiss ministers and heads of departments (which had previously been the exclusive right of the President). In early April 1999 Ibraimov died; the nomination of Amangeldy Muraliyev, a former regional governor, as Prime Minister was approved by the Zhogorku Kenesh later in the month.

A new electoral law was introduced at the end of May 1999 whereby, henceforth, 15 seats in the Legislative Assembly were to be allocated on a proportional basis for those parties that secured a minimum of 5% of the votes; the legislation also banned the use of foreign and private funds in electoral campaigns. In mid-June new legislation came into effect, which banned political organizations considered a threat to Kyrgyzstan's stability and ethnic harmony. In July two new opposition parties were established: the Ar-Namys (Dignity) Party, led by the former Vice-President and Mayor of Bishkek, Feliks Kulov, and the Adilettuuluk (Justice) Party. In mid-August a group of communists, under the leadership of Klara Ajibekova, broke away from the KCP to form a rival organization, the Communist Party of Kyrgyzstan (CPK). Ajibekova stated that the KCP leader, Absamat Masaliyev, had betrayed the ideology of the party by defending several deputies found guilty of corruption. Another opposition party, the Republican Party of Kyrgyzstan (RPK), was established in mid-October and officially registered with the Ministry of Justice. In the following month Akayev

announced that parliamentary elections would be held on 20 February 2000.

At the elections to both chambers of the restructured Zhogorku Kenesh, held on 20 February 2000, a total of six parties passed the 5% threshold required to secure party-list seats in the Legislative Assembly. (The elections were the first to take place since constitutional amendments had been approved in October 1998.) Although the Central Election Commission declared the elections to have been 'free and fair', a number of electoral violations were reported by the Organization for Security and Co-operation in Europe (OSCE, see p. 302), which expressed particular concern regarding infringements of the freedom of the media and the election administration, as well as the alleged intimidation of opposition leaders. In a second round of voting on 12 March, the KCP secured 27.7% of the votes cast, the Union of Democratic Forces 18.6%, the Democratic Women's Party of Kyrgyzstan 12.7%, the Party of Veterans of the War in Afghanistan and of Participation in other Local Conflicts 8.0%, the Ata-Meken (Fatherland) Socialist Party 6.5% and the My Country Party of Action 5.0%. In terms of seats, the Union of Democratic Forces achieved the greatest representation of any party or bloc in the combined Zhogorku Kenesh, once single-mandate constituency seats had been included, securing 12 seats, compared with the KCP's six. Independent candidates took 73 of the total 105 seats in the two chambers. Kulov, who stood as an independent after his Ar-Namys Party was prohibited from participating, failed to win a seat, prompting opposition protests and allegations of official corruption. Later in March Kulov was arrested on charges of abuse of office while serving as Minister of National Security in 1997–98. Although Kulov was acquitted in August 2000, the Bishkek military court subsequently ordered a retrial, and he was sentenced to seven years' imprisonment in January 2001. An appeal was rejected in March, prompting members of Ar-Namys to denounce the sentence as politically motivated. (In May 2002 Kulov was found guilty of further charges, of embezzlement.)

Meanwhile, at the presidential election, held on 29 October 2000, Akayev secured 74.5% of the votes cast. Tekebayev won 13.9% of the votes and Almazbek Atambayev 6.0%. According to the Central Election Commission, 74% of the electorate participated. However, on the day of the election a criminal case opened in Bishkek following the discovery, by international observers, of several hundred ballot papers, marked in favour of Akayev, before polling had officially begun. In addition, opposition parties claimed that they had been prevented from taking part in media broadcasts during their election campaigns. The Chairman of the Central Election Commission was forced to concede that electoral violations had, indeed, taken place, leading to international condemnation. Mass protests took place, and demands were made for the election to be repeated. None the less, on 10 November the Constitutional Court formally endorsed the results of the election.

Akayev was inaugurated for a third term on 9 December 2000. On 21 December Kurmanbek Bakiyev, hitherto the Governor of Chui Oblast, was appointed Prime Minister. At the end of the month a proposal for a revised structure of government was submitted to the Legislative Assembly, which aimed to reduce the number of ministries and state institutions in order to limit both bureaucracy and expenditure. A new Government was announced at the beginning of January 2001.

In April 2001, in an apparent attempt to combat Islamist extremism, the Government banned religious education in state schools and decreed that specialist religious schools would henceforth require a licence. In the same month the leaders of nine opposition parties formally announced the establishment of an alliance known as the People's Patriotic Movement, which stated its objectives to be the safeguarding of democracy and of human and constitutional rights. The movement organized demonstrations against the erosion of the independent media and against the imprisonment of Feliks Kulov and another opposition leader, the Chairman of the Erkindik (Liberty) Party, Topchubek Turgunaliyev, who had been convicted in September 2000 of conspiring to assassinate the President. (Turgunaliyev was pardoned in August 2001.) In early November opposition parties including the Ar-Namys Party, the Ata-Meken Socialist Party and Erkindik announced the formation of a new People's Congress, and elected Kulov as Chairman of the alliance. In the following month the President signed into law a constitutional amendment granting Russian the status of official language, in what was considered a further attempt to halt the emigration of ethnic Russians from Kyrgyzstan.

In January 2002 the arrest of Azimbek Beknazarov, an opposition deputy and a former Chairman of the parliamentary committee on court reforms and legality, was denounced as politically motivated (Beknazarov had publicly criticized President Akayev's signature of the 1999 Sino-Kyrgyz border treaty—see below). International human rights organizations also expressed concern at this apparent suppression of political dissent, and members of the People's Congress initiated a hunger strike in protest at the detention of both Kulov and Beknazarov. Nevertheless, Beknazarov's trial commenced in February 2002 (although it was adjourned until the following month). On 17–18 March large-scale protests took place in Jalal-Abad against the ongoing trial; six people were reported to have died, following clashes with security forces. Although the trial was subsequently suspended and Beknazarov was temporarily released, the Government accused the opposition of instigating the riots in an attempt to stage a *coup d'état* and maintained that the security forces had acted in self-defence. On 10 May the Legislative Assembly ratified the controversial Sino-Kyrgyz treaty, prompting two weeks of anti-Government demonstrations, hunger strikes and acts of civil disobedience. Protesters demanded that the Government accept responsibility for the violence of mid-March; rescind the ratification of the border treaty (which they claimed was signed illegally by President Akayev, since he had agreed to cede land to the People's Republic of China without the consent of the legislature); and close the criminal case against Beknazarov. Nevertheless, the treaty was ratified by the People's Assembly in mid-May, and subsequently signed into law by the President. Also in mid-May a state commission established to investigate the protests in Jalal-Abad issued its report to the President, in which it criticized all levels of government and the law-enforcement bodies for failing to recognize the instability of the political situation and the rising levels of popular discontent in the region during Beknazarov's trial. The commission also stated the security forces' use of weapons to control the demonstrators to have been illegal.

On 22 May 2002 Prime Minister Bakiyev tendered his resignation, and the entire Government duly resigned, in accordance with the Constitution. The Chief of the Presidential Administration also resigned, together with a senior prosecutor, and several senior police-officers were dismissed. The First Deputy Prime Minister, Nikolai Tanayev, was appointed Prime Minister (initially on an acting basis) and a new Government was announced on 19 June. Meanwhile, in late May Beknazarov received a one-year, suspended prison sentence. An appeal against the sentence, heard in late June, was preceded by further large-scale demonstrations in Jalal-Abad, Kerben and Osh. Although the initial guilty verdict was upheld by the court of appeal, Beknazorov's sentence was annulled, enabling him to retain his parliamentary seat. In the same month Tanayev proposed an amnesty (approved by the Legislative Assembly on 28 June) for those involved in the disturbances of mid-March. The amnesty applied to both protesters and law-enforcement officials, and Tanayev stated that he would release the remaining detainees provided that the organizers of the rallies agreed to a number of conditions, including the cessation of protests against the Sino-Kyrgyz treaty.

In mid-January 2003 President Akayev announced that a referendum on several proposed constitutional amendments was to be held on 2 February. Despite opposition demands for the referendum's postponement, the amendments, providing, *inter alia*, for the introduction of a unicameral legislature from 2005, were duly approved by 76.6% of the electorate, and 78.7% of voters supported Akayev's remaining in office until 2005; the reported rate of participation was 86.7%. The hasty scheduling of the referendum attracted criticism from international human rights organizations, and there were also allegations of procedural violations. Nevertheless, the constitutional amendments were endorsed by the President, who insisted that they would serve to reinforce democracy in the country, on 18 February 2003. In December the Legislative Assembly adopted legislation eliminating the party-list system of election, in compliance with the constitutional amendments.

Meanwhile, in November 2003 Satyvaldy Chyrmashev, the Minister of Ecology and Emergency Situations, was elected Mayor of Osh City; Temirbek Akmataliyev, hitherto the Deputy Chief of the Presidential Administration and Minister of Internal Affairs during the unrest of March 2002, assumed the vacated portfolio in December. A major government reorganization took place in early February 2004, as part of which Ku-

banychbek Dzhumaliyev was elevated to the post of First Deputy Prime Minister (he retained the transport and communications portfolio) and Ularbek Mateyev was appointed to the new position of Deputy Prime Minister and Minister of Social Mobilization. The Ministries of Foreign Trade and Industry and of Economic Development and Investments were incorporated into a new Ministry of Economic Development, Industry and Trade. A number of state bodies were abolished or reconstituted, while new state bodies included a National Commission for State Service and a State Commission for Culture. The reorganization was widely interpreted as an attempt by Akayev to reduce the cost of government bureaucracy.

Kyrgyzstan has sought to establish close relations with Arab and other Muslim states, in particular Turkey, with which it shares ethnic, cultural and linguistic ties. President Akayev has also stressed that, despite Islam being the dominant religion, Kyrgyzstan will remain a secular state, and the country opposes Islamist extremism. In 1992 the Kyrgyz Government participated in negotiations aimed at ending the civil conflict in neighbouring Tajikistan between forces of the Tajik Government and rebel Islamist groups. In January 1993, however, it was reported that groups of armed Tajiks had crossed into Kyrgyzstan, seeking to incite an Islamist insurrection among the local population. The Kyrgyz Government subsequently intensified controls along the border with Tajikistan and contributed troops to a CIS peace-keeping mission on the Tajik–Afghan border. Border tensions increased in mid-1996, and requests were made by the Kyrgyz Government for assistance from Tajikistan in the rehabilitation of an estimated 15,000 Tajik refugees who had fled to Kyrgyzstan. The peace agreement concluded in Tajikistan in June 1997 was welcomed by the Kyrgyz authorities, and in late 1999 Kyrgyzstan began to withdraw its peace-keeping troops from the Tajik–Afghan border. The Kyrgyz leadership remained concerned at the increase in drugs-trafficking across the Tajik–Kyrgyz border, and a customs accord was signed by Kyrgyzstan and Tajikistan in September 1998, with the aim of combating arms- and drugs-trafficking. (However, in 2003 it was reported that drugs-trafficking from Afghanistan was increasing.) Border negotiations with Tajikistan, which had commenced in 1997, before being suspended, owing to the unstable political situation in that country, recommenced in December 2002.

Relations with Kyrgyzstan's other neighbouring Central Asian republics, Uzbekistan and Kazakhstan, deteriorated sharply in May 1993, following Kyrgyzstan's sudden introduction of its own currency, the som. The Uzbek Government, fearing a massive influx of roubles into Uzbekistan, closed its border with Kyrgyzstan, suspending trade and telecommunications links for several days. However, relations between the two states improved following talks in June. In January 1994 Kyrgyzstan joined the economic zone newly established by Kazakhstan and Uzbekistan, and in February 1995 an Interstate Council was formed to co-ordinate economic activity in the zone. Following the admission of Tajikistan in March 1998, in May the four countries were formally constituted as the Central Asian Economic Union (known as the Central Asian Co-operation Organization from March 2002). Meanwhile, in March 1996 Kyrgyzstan signed a treaty with Russia, Belarus and Kazakhstan to create a 'community of integrated states', in an attempt to achieve closer economic, cultural and social integration, and joined a customs union established by the three other countries. In April 1998 Tajikistan joined the union, and in October 2000 it was superseded by a new economic body, the Eurasian Economic Community (EAEC).

Kyrgyzstan's campaign against Islamist extremism intensified in mid-1999, when Islamist groups believed to be based in Uzbekistan and Tajikistan held a number of people hostage in separate events in the southern region of Osh. In mid-August Kyrgyz and Uzbek forces launched air-strikes against Tajik militants in the Osh region, in an attempt to prevent further acts of insurgency. However, later that month a senior Kyrgyz military commander was among more than 25 people kidnapped by a group of rebels, which captured three villages near the Tajik border. The rebels appeared to be members of the Islamic Movement of Uzbekistan (IMU), which demanded the release of Islamists imprisoned in that country. The hostage crisis intensified, with Kyrgyz government troops engaging in a large-scale military operation in order to defeat the rebels and free the hostages; fighting continued throughout September. It was announced in late October that all of the hostages had been released, following negotiations between Kyrgyz officials and members of the Islamist organization. (However, it was reported in mid-November that the body of a police-officer, taken hostage in late August, had been discovered.) From mid-August Islamist militants made a further series of incursions into Kyrgyzstan from Tajikistan, leading to armed conflict with government forces. The number of insurgents amassing on the Kyrgyz–Tajik border increased, despite intensive shelling and aerial bombardment by Kyrgyz troops. By the end of October, however, the Government claimed that all the rebels had left Kyrgyzstan and that it had regained full control of the regions bordering Tajikistan.

In April 2001 a local government official accused the Uzbek authorities of laying landmines along the Kyrgyz border, and demanded the removal of Uzbek troops, deployed in an effort to combat the incursions of Islamist militants and drugs-traffickers, from Kyrgyz border territories. Following claims in September that the laying of mines was continuing, the Kyrgyz Legislative Assembly refused to ratify an agreement with Uzbekistan on arms' supplies. Meanwhile, reports in May indicated that Islamist rebels were increasingly recruiting from southern Kyrgyzstan. One month later two members of the IMU (subsequently known as the Islamic Party of Turkestan), arrested during fighting in the Kyrgyz border territories in mid-2000, on charges that included murder and terrorism, were sentenced to death. The severity of the sentences was expected to act as a warning to other militants. In July 2003 it was reported that Kyrgyzstan was to commence the unilateral removal of landmines along the border with Uzbekistan. Negotiations on the final delimitation of the Kyrgyz–Uzbek border were ongoing in 2004.

In April 2001, at a meeting of leaders of the Turkic-speaking countries, the Presidents of Azerbaijan, Kazakhstan, Kyrgyzstan, Turkey and Turkmenistan, and the Chairman of the Uzbek legislature signed an agreement on regional co-operation to combat terrorism and drugs-trafficking, to revive the old 'Silk Road' trade route between the People's Republic of China and Europe, and to ensure further protection of the environment. One month later the signatories of the CIS Collective Security Treaty—Armenia, Belarus, Kazakhstan, Kyrgyzstan, Russia and Tajikistan—agreed to form a Collective Rapid Reaction Force in Bishkek to combat Islamist militancy in Central Asia; in January 2002 it was announced that the force was ready to undertake combat missions. In late April 2003 a successor organization to the Collective Security Treaty was formed, when its six signatories inaugurated the Collective Security Treaty Organization (CSTO). In 2003 the Islamic Party of Turkestan and the Uzbek fundamentalist Hizb-ut-Tahrir al-Islami (Party of Islamic Liberation) continued to be regarded as threats to stability in Kyrgyzstan. The latter, which aimed to unite Muslim countries and establish Islamic law through peaceful means, had become the most widespread illegal movement in Kyrgyzstan, despite government attempts to suppress it.

President Akayev has endeavoured to maintain good relations with the largest and most influential CIS member, Russia, and the issue of ethnic Russians in Kyrgyzstan (numbering some 603,000 in 1999) has been at the centre of discussions between the two countries. In June 1992 Akayev and the Russian President, Boris Yeltsin, signed a treaty of friendship, co-operation and mutual assistance, and the two countries signed a further declaration on friendship, alliance and partnership in July 2000. Military agreements, including a treaty of non-aggression, have also been concluded. An agreement concerning the expansion of Russian-Kyrgyz military co-operation was concluded in October 1997, whereby Russia was to lease four military installations in Kyrgyzstan in return for training Kyrgyz army recruits. In October 2003 a Russian airbase became operational at Kant, some 30 km from an airbase at Manas, occupied by the US-led anti-terrorism coalition (see below); the new base was the first Russian military installation to be established outside Russia since the collapse of the USSR.

Kyrgyzstan reached a series of bilateral co-operation agreements with the People's Republic of China during 1996, the terms of which provided for the partial demarcation of their shared border, which was undertaken from mid-2001. Another border treaty was signed in August 1999, which ceded almost 95,000 ha of disputed territory to China. Akayev signed the agreement without the consent of the legislature, causing widespread protests upon its ratification in 2002 (see above). Meanwhile, an agreement signed in April 1997 with China, Russia, Kazakhstan and Tajikistan (which, together with Kyrgyzstan, constituted the so-called Shanghai Five, later known as the

Shanghai Forum) aimed to improve joint border security. The alliance, renamed the Shanghai Co-operation Organization upon the accession of Uzbekistan, signed the Shanghai Convention on Combating Terrorism, Separatism and Extremism in mid-2001. In August an associated anti-terrorism centre became operational in Bishkek. The Presidents of Kazakhstan and Kyrgyzstan signed a border agreement in December. In March 2002 China agreed to provide Kyrgyzstan with military assistance worth some US $1.2m. In August 2003 Kyrgyz forces participated in major anti-terrorist manoeuvres, hosted by China and Kazakhstan.

From early 1997 Kyrgyzstan was concerned by unrest on the country's border with the People's Republic of China, caused by members of an organization called For a Free Eastern Turkestan, which was seeking to create an Islamic state on the territory of China's Xinjiang Uygur (Uigur) Autonomous Region. Akayev assumed personal control of policies to prevent the proliferation of Islamist extremism and particularly Wahhabism, a conservative group within Sunni Islam. In May a group of Uigur separatists were arrested in Kyrgyzstan on charges including terrorism and the dissemination of Wahhabi propaganda; two of the activists were sentenced to terms of imprisonment in December. A draft law on religious freedom was adopted in March 1999, purportedly to prevent abuses by religious organizations attempting to 'destabilize' society under the original legislation, which had been in force since October 1991.

Following the large-scale suicide attacks on the US cities of New York and Washington, DC, on 11 September 2001, President Akayev announced that he was prepared to allow US military aircraft to have access to Kyrgyz airspace for the aerial bombardment of militants of the al-Qa'ida (Base) organization (held principally responsible by the USA for having co-ordinated the attacks), and its Taliban hosts in Afghanistan. In late November the Government agreed to give the US-led anti-terrorism coalition access to its military bases and, later, its main airport. Kyrgyzstan undertook joint exercises with US troops in February 2002, which aimed to facilitate attempts to counter insurgency in the country's mountainous regions (see below). In September Akayev met the US President, George W. Bush, and the US Secretary of State, Colin Powell, in Washington, where they discussed Kyrgyzstan's human rights record, the USA's declared 'war against terrorism' and economic issues.

Government

According to constitutional amendments approved at a referendum on 17 October 1998, supreme legislative power in the Kyrgyz Republic is vested in the bicameral, 105-member Zhogorku Kenesh (Supreme Council), comprising a permanent 45-member Legislative Assembly (lower chamber) and a 60-member People's Assembly (upper chamber); the latter meets twice yearly to debate regional issues. The Zhogorku Kenesh is elected by universal suffrage for a term of five years. Further constitutional amendments were approved in February 2003, according to which the Zhogorku Kenesh was to be transformed into a unicameral assembly. The President of the Republic, who is directly elected for a five-year term, is Head of State and Commander-in-Chief of the Armed Forces, and also holds extensive executive powers. The Prime Minister is appointed by the President, subject to the approval of the Zhogorku Kenesh; the remaining members of the Government are appointed by the President. The Prime Minister was also empowered to appoint and dismiss ministers and heads of departments. For administrative purposes, Kyrgyzstan is divided into seven regions (oblasts or dubans) and the municipality of Bishkek (the capital).

Defence

Kyrgyzstan began to raise a national army in 1992. In August 2003 Kyrgyzstan's total armed forces numbered 10,900 (army 8,500, air force 2,400). There are also an estimated 5,000 personnel in paramilitary forces. Military service is compulsory and lasts for 18 months. Kyrgyzstan joined the defence structures of the Commonwealth of Independent States (CIS, see p. 180) by signing, with five other member states, a collective security agreement in May 1992; in May 2001 it was announced that the signatory countries were to form a Collective Rapid Reaction Force to combat Islamist militancy in Central Asia. In April 2003 the Collective Security Treaty Organization (CSTO) was inaugurated as the successor to the CIS collective security system, with the participation of Armenia, Belarus, Kazakhstan, Kyrgyzstan, Russia and Tajikistan. In June 1994 Kyrgyzstan joined the North Atlantic Treaty Organization's (NATO) 'Partnership for Peace' (see p. 291) programme of military co-operation. The country's defence budget for 2003 was some 1,100m. soms (US $24.0m.).

Economic Affairs

In 2002, according to estimates by the World Bank, Kyrgyzstan's gross national product (GNI), measured at average 2000–02 prices, was US $1,454m., equivalent to $290 per head (or $1,520 per head on an international purchasing-power parity basis). During 1990–2002, it was estimated, the population increased by an annual average of 1.0%, while gross domestic product (GDP) per head declined, in real terms, at an average annual rate of 3.9%. Overall GDP declined, in real terms, at an estimated average annual rate of 2.9% in 1990–2002. Real GDP increased by 5.3% in 2001, but decreased by 0.5% in 2002.

Agriculture (including forestry and fishing) contributed an estimated 38.7% of GDP in 2003, according to preliminary official figures. In 1999 52.4% of the labour force were employed in the sector. By tradition, the Kyrgyz are a pastoral nomadic people, and the majority of the population (some 65.2% in 1999) reside in rural areas. Livestock-rearing, once the mainstay of agricultural activity, is declining in importance. Only about 7% of the country's land area is arable; of this, some 70% depends on irrigation. The principal crops are grain, potatoes, vegetables and sugar beet. By 2002, according to government figures, collective farms accounted for only around 6% of agricultural production, while state farms accounted for just under 2%. The GDP of the agricultural sector increased, in real terms, by an average of 1.6% per year in 1990–2002; real agricultural GDP increased by 7.3% in 2001 and by 3.3% in 2002.

Industry (comprising manufacturing, mining, utilities and construction) contributed an estimated 22.9% of GDP in 2003, according to preliminary official data. The industrial sector provided 11.6% of employment in 1999. Real industrial GDP declined at an average annual rate of 8.5% in 1990–2002; the GDP of the sector increased, in real terms, by 5.2% in 2001, but contracted by 11.2% in 2002.

In 1999 the mining and quarrying sector employed just 0.5% of the work-force. Kyrgyzstan has considerable mineral deposits, including coal, gold, tin, mercury, antimony, zinc, tungsten and uranium. In May 2001 the Government announced the discovery of new deposits of petroleum, estimated to total 70m. barrels, in an oilfield in the west. Production of gold from the Kumtor mine, which is believed to contain the eighth largest deposit of gold in the world, began in January 1997. As a result, Kyrgyzstan had become the 10th largest extractor and seller of gold in the world by 2001.

According to World Bank estimates, manufacturing contributed 10.5% of GDP in 2002. The manufacturing sector employed 7.2% of the work-force in 1999. In 2002 the principal branches of manufacturing, measured by gross value of output, were food products, beverages and tobacco (accounting for 34.0% of the total) and metallurgy (29.9%). Real manufacturing GDP declined by an average of 12.3% per year in 1990–2002; according to the World Bank, the GDP of the sector declined by 3.0% in 2001, but registered an increase of 3.1% in 2002.

Kyrgyzstan's principal source of domestic energy production (and also a major export) is hydroelectricity (generated by the country's mountain rivers), which provided 91.7% of the country's total energy requirements in 2000. Kyrgyzstan has insufficient petroleum and natural gas to meet its needs, and substantial imports of hydrocarbons are thus required; Kyrgyzstan exports electricity to Kazakhstan and Uzbekistan in return for coal and natural gas, respectively. Imports of mineral fuels comprised 27.8% of the value of total recorded imports in 2002. Exports of electricity contributed some 15.8% of the value of total exports in 2000.

In 2003, according to preliminary official figures, the services sector contributed an estimated 38.4% of GDP. Services provided 36.1% of employment in 1999. In 1990–2002 the GDP of the sector declined, in real terms, by an average of 2.9% per year; services GDP increased by 3.3% in 2001 and by 4.2% in 2002.

In 2002 Kyrgyzstan recorded a visible trade deficit of US $54.0m., and a deficit of $34.7m. on the current account of the balance of payments. In 2003 the principal source of recorded imports (24.6%) was Russia; other major suppliers were Kazakhstan, the People's Republic of China, the USA, Uzbekistan and Germany. The main market for exports in that year was the United Arab Emirates (24.8%). Other principal markets were Switzerland, Russia and Kazakhstan. The main exports in 2002 were precious and semi-precious stones and

metals, mineral products, textiles, foodstuffs, beverages and tobacco, machinery and chemicals. The principal recorded imports in that year were mineral products (mostly petroleum and natural gas), machinery and electrical equipment, chemicals, foodstuffs, beverages and tobacco, textiles and metals.

In 2002 Kyrgyzstan recorded an overall budgetary deficit of 776.9m. soms (equivalent to 1.0% of GDP). Kyrgyzstan's total external debt was US $1,717m. at the end of 2001, of which $1,256m. was long-term public debt. In that year the cost of debt-servicing was equivalent to 29.8% of the value of exports of goods and services. Annual inflation averaged 65.7% in 1992–2002. Consumer prices increased by 18.7% in 2000, by 6.9% in 2001 and by 2.2% in 2002. The average rate of unemployment was 12.5% in 2002.

Kyrgyzstan participates in the economic bodies of the Commonwealth of Independent States (CIS, see p. 180), and has also joined the European Bank for Reconstruction and Development (EBRD, see p. 203), as a 'Country of Operations', and the Economic Co-operation Organization (ECO, see p. 201). In addition, Kyrgyzstan is a member of the Asian Development Bank (ADB, see p. 151). In February 1995 Kyrgyzstan signed a 10-year 'partnership and co-operation' agreement with the European Union. In October 1998 Kyrgyzstan became the first CIS country to join the World Trade Organization (WTO, see p. 343).

Following independence in 1991, the Kyrgyz Government embarked on an ambitious programme of economic reforms to establish a market-based economy and achieve macroeconomic stabilization. Although significant growth was registered in 1996–97, the economy slowed considerably from mid-1998, owing to reduced growth in gold and agricultural production and the financial crisis in Russia. The privatization programme was relaunched in 1998, and in 2000 the Government approved a further two-year privatization programme to facilitate the sale of strategic enterprises; by the end of 2003 official figures revealed that 7,060 state enterprises had been privatized since 1991. There was rapid growth in GDP in 2000–01, and in 2001 an annual rate of inflation of less than 10% was recorded for the first time since independence. In November 2001 it was reported that the IMF had agreed to cancel or restructure a proportion of the country's external debt, and in March 2002 the 'Paris Club' of creditor countries agreed to reschedule, over a period of 20 years, the repayment of some US $95m., which had been due to be serviced in 2002–04. In October 2002 a conference was held in Bishkek, at which international donors pledged some $700m. for 2003–05, a significant proportion of which was to be used in support of the country's poverty reduction programme. However, in 2002 GDP registered its first decline since 1995, largely owing to reduced industrial output after a landslide at the Kumtor gold mine. Although growth resumed in 2003, reaching some 5.2%, in the medium term it was likely to be severely affected by the economy's reliance on the output of the mine, the closure of which was anticipated in 2010; new gold projects were not expected to be able to compensate for the consequent decline in production. The introduction of value-added tax on agricultural products and the adoption of a new property tax was expected to be of substantial benefit to the economy in 2004, and additional large-scale privatization commenced in 2003. In October of that year the Government announced plans to divest Kairat Bank, the country's fifth largest, and in February 2004 Gazprom of Russia agreed to acquire a majority stake in Kyrgyzneftegaz, the state-owned petroleum and natural gas company. Ultimately, however, sustained economic growth was dependent on the greater diversification of both exports (trade in which was already constrained by regional restrictions on commerce, as well as Kyrgyzstan's lack of access to the sea) and industry.

Education

Education is officially compulsory for nine years, comprising four years of primary school (between the ages of seven and 10), followed by five years of lower secondary school (ages 11 to 15). Pupils may then continue their studies in upper secondary schools (two years' duration), specialized secondary schools (two to four years) or technical and vocational schools (from 15 years of age). In 2000/01 total enrolment at primary schools was equivalent to 89% of the relevant age group; enrolment at secondary-school level was equivalent to 83%. A decree signed in December 2001 abolished free schooling. At April 2002 there were 44 institutes of higher education in Kyrgyzstan (compared with the 10 in place at independence), providing courses lasting between four and six years. These include the Kyrgyz State University, which has 12 faculties, the Kyrgyz Technical University and the Kyrgyz-Russian Slavonic University, which opened in Bishkek in 1993. In 1995/96 enrolment at tertiary level was equivalent to 12.2% of those in the relevant age-group (males 11.6%; females 12.8%). In 1993/94 63.6% of pupils in primary and secondary schools were taught in Kyrgyz, 23.4% were taught in Russian, 12.7% in Uzbek and 0.3% in Tajik. However, Russian was the principal language of instruction in higher educational establishments. Budgetary expenditure on education in 2002 amounted to 3,350.4m. soms (22.1% of total spending).

Public Holidays

2004: 1 January (New Year's Day), 7 January (Christmas), 1 February* (Kurban Ait, Feast of the Sacrifice), 8 March (International Women's Day), 21 March (Nooruz, Kyrgyz New Year),

1 May (International Labour Day), 5 May (Constitution Day), 9 May (Victory Day), 31 August (Independence Day), 14 November* (Orozo Ait, end of Ramadan).

2005: 1 January (New Year's Day), 7 January (Christmas), 21 January* (Kurban Ait, Feast of the Sacrifice), 8 March (International Women's Day), 21 March (Nooruz, Kyrgyz New Year), 1 May (International Labour Day), 5 May (Constitution Day), 9 May (Victory Day), 31 August (Independence Day), 4 November* (Orozo Ait, end of Ramadan).

* These holidays are dependent on the Islamic lunar calendar and may vary by one or two days from the dates given.

Weights and Measures

The metric system is in force.

Statistical Survey

Source (unless otherwise stated): National Statistical Committee, 720033 Bishkek, Frunze 374; tel. (312) 22-63-63; fax (312) 22-07-59; e-mail zkudabaev@ nsc.bishkek.su; internet nsc.bishkek.su.

Area and Population

AREA, POPULATION AND DENSITY

Area (sq km)	199,900*
Population (census results)†	
12 January 1989	4,257,755
24 March 1999	
Males	2,380,465
Females	2,442,473
Total	4,822,938
Population (UN estimates at mid-year)‡	
2000	4,921,000
2001	4,995,000
2002	5,067,000
Density (per sq km) at mid-2002	25.3

* 77,182 sq miles.
† The figures refer to *de jure* population. The *de facto* total was 4,290,442 at the 1989 census and 4,850,700 at the 1999 census.
‡ Source: UN, *World Population Prospects: The 2002 Revision*.

PRINCIPAL ETHNIC GROUPS
(permanent inhabitants, 1999 census)

	Number	%
Kyrgyz	3,128,147	64.9
Uzbek	664,950	13.8
Russian	603,201	12.5
Dungan	51,766	1.1
Ukrainian	50,442	1.0
Uigur	46,944	1.0
Tatar	45,438	0.9
Kazakh	42,657	0.9
Tajik	42,636	0.9
Turkish	33,327	0.7
German	21,471	0.4
Korean	19,784	0.4
Others	72,175	1.5
Total	**4,822,938**	**100.0**

ADMINISTRATIVE DIVISIONS
(1999 census)

Oblast	Area (sq km)	Population
Batken	17,000	382,426
Chui	20,200	770,811
Issyk-Kul	43,100	413,149
Jalal-Abad	33,700	869,259
Naryn	45,200	249,115
Osh	29,200	1,175,998
Talas	11,400	199,872
Bishkek City	100	762,308
Total	**199,900**	**4,822,938**

PRINCIPAL TOWNS
(population at census of March 1999)

Bishkek (capital)* .	750,327	Karakol†	64,322
Osh	208,520	Tokmok	59,409
Jalal-Abad . . .	70,401	Kara-Balta . . .	53,887

* Known as Frunze between 1926 and 1991.
† Formerly Przhevalsk.

Mid-2001 (UN estimate, incl. suburbs): Bishkek 736,000 (Source: UN, *World Urbanization Prospects: The 2001 Revision*).

BIRTHS, MARRIAGES AND DEATHS*

	Registered live births		Registered marriages		Registered deaths	
	Number	Rate (per 1,000)	Number	Rate (per 1,000)	Number	Rate (per 1,000)
1993 . .	116,795	26.1	36,874	8.2	34,513	7.7
1994 . .	110,113	24.6	26,097	5.8	37,109	8.3
1995 . .	117,340	26.0	26,866	6.0	36,915	8.2
1996 . .	108,007	23.4	26,188	5.7	34,562	7.6
1997 . .	102,050	21.8	26,588	5.7	34,540	7.4
1998 . .	104,183	21.9	25,726	5.4	34,596	7.2
1999 . .	104,068	21.5	26,033	5.4	32,850	6.8
2000 . .	96,770	19.8	n.a.	n.a.	34,111	7.0

* Rates have not been revised to take account of the results of the 1999 census.

Source: UN, *Demographic Yearbook* and *Population and Vital Statistics Report*.

Expectation of life (WHO estimates, years at birth): 64.5 (males 60.4; females 68.9) in 2002 (Source: WHO, *World Health Report*).

ECONOMICALLY ACTIVE POPULATION
(annual averages, '000 persons)

	1997	1998	1999
Agriculture, hunting and forestry	815.6	835.4	923.8
Fishing	n.a.	n.a.	0.5
Mining and quarrying	8.9	8.2	9.5
Manufacturing	143.7	143.3	127.0
Electricity, gas and water supply	19.0	20.3	22.1
Construction	57.0	50.7	45.2
Wholesale and retail trade; repair of motor vehicles, motor cycles and personal and household goods	174.7	180.2	183.7
Hotels and restaurants	12.1	13.9	11.5
Transport, storage and communications	79.3	75.2	65.8
Financial intermediation	7.2	8.1	7.1
Real estate, renting and business activities	41.3	38.9	28.7
Public administration and defence; compulsory social security	60.4	63.0	65.7
Education	139.4	139.3	140.7
Health and social work	88.6	84.5	85.2
Other services	42.1	43.9	47.8
Total employed	1,689.3	1,704.9	1,764.3
Males	907.9	918.7	971.6
Females	781.4	786.2	792.7

Registered unemployed ('000 persons): 54.6 in 1997; 55.9 in 1998; 54.7 in 1999.

Source: ILO, *Yearbook of Labour Statistics*.

Total unemployed (estimates, '000 persons, incl. unregistered): 103.0 in 1997; 106.4 in 1998; 136.8 in 1999.

2000 ('000 persons): Total employed 1,768.4; Total unemployed 144.3.

2001 ('000 persons): Total employed 1,787.0; Total unemployed 152.0.

2002 ('000 persons): Total employed 1,850.1; Total unemployed 265.5.

Health and Welfare

KEY INDICATORS

Total fertility rate (children per woman, 2002)	2.7
Under-5 mortality rate (per 1,000 live births, 2001)	61
HIV/AIDS (% of persons aged 15–49, 2001)	<0.10
Physicians (per 1,000 head, 2000)	2.92
Hospital beds (per 1,000 head, 1999)	7.9
Health expenditure (2001): US $ per head (PPP)	108
Health expenditure (2001): % of GDP	4.0
Health expenditure (2001): public (% of total)	48.7
Access to water (% of persons, 2000)	77
Access to sanitation (% of persons, 2000)	100
Human Development Index (2001): ranking	102
Human Development Index (2001): value	0.727

For sources and definitions, see explanatory note on p. vi.

Agriculture

PRINCIPAL CROPS
('000 metric tons)

	2000	2001	2002
Wheat	1,039.1	1,190.6	1,163.0
Rice (paddy)	19.0	16.6	19.0
Barley	150.2	139.9	165.9
Maize	338.3	442.8	428.2
Potatoes	1,045.6	1,168.4	1,244.0
Sugar beet	449.8	286.6	524.5
Sunflower seed*	40.0	47.0	57.8
Cabbages	100.5	119.1	130.1
Tomatoes	155.6	165.5	183.5
Cucumbers and gherkins*	124.0	162.1	170.0
Dry onions	147.4	149.2	131.9
Carrots	109.4	112.5	126.7
Other vegetables*	109.9	105.0	76.3
Apples*	127.9	126.3	115.2
Apricots*	16.7	16.5	14.9
Peaches and nectarines*	6.4	8.0	10.0
Grapes	26.5	27.4	17.7
Watermelons†	67.1	85.5	83.0
Cotton (lint)	28.7	33.7*	46.0*
Cottonseed	55.0	64.3	63.2
Tobacco (leaves)	34.6	24.0	8.2

* Unofficial figure(s).
† Including melons, pumpkins and squash.

Source: FAO.

LIVESTOCK
('000 head at 1 January)

	2000	2001	2002
Horses	350	354	354
Asses*	8	7	7
Cattle	932	947	970
Camels*	47	46	46
Pigs	105	101	87
Sheep	3,264	3,198	3,104
Goats	543	601	640
Chickens	2,980	3,064	3,254
Turkeys	140†	125*	130*

* FAO estimate(s).
† Unofficial figure.

Source: FAO.

LIVESTOCK PRODUCTS
('000 metric tons)

	2000	2001	2002
Beef and veal	100.6	100.1	98.1
Mutton and lamb	39.4	40.0	41.5
Goat meat	3.7	3.8	3.8
Pig meat	23.8	25.7	25.7
Horse meat	23.7	24.8	27.1
Poultry meat	4.6	4.9	4.5
Cows' milk	1,078.7	1,110.4	1,140.3
Cheese	3.3	4.0	4.0
Butter	1.4	1.9	1.4
Hen eggs	11.4	12.7	13.4
Honey	1.3	1.4	1.3
Wool: greasy	11.3	11.1	10.9
Wool: scoured	6.8	6.7	6.5
Cattle hides*	10.0	9.8	9.7
Sheepskins*	5.9	6.2	6.4

* FAO estimates.

Source: FAO.

Forestry

ROUNDWOOD REMOVALS
('000 cubic metres, excl. bark)

	2000*	2001*	2002†
Sawlogs, veneer logs and logs for sleepers	4	5	5
Other industrial wood	1	1	1
Fuel wood	20	16	16
Total	25	22	22

* Unofficial figures.
† FAO estimates.
Source: FAO.

SAWNWOOD PRODUCTION
('000 cubic metres, incl. railway sleepers, unofficial figures)

	1999	2000	2001
Coniferous (softwood)	9	2	2
Broadleaved (hardwood)	14	4	4
Total	23	6	6

2002: Production as in 2001 (FAO estimates).
Source: FAO.

Fishing

(metric tons, live weight)

	1999	2000	2001
Capture	48*	52*	57
Freshwater bream	3*	3*	4
Common carp	9*	10*	11
Silver carp	7*	8*	19
Other cyprinids	11*	12*	8
Pike-perch	2*	2*	1
Whitefishes	15*	16*	12
Aquaculture	71	58	144
Common carp	31	10	27
Grass carp	5	5	43
Silver carp	35	43	74
Total catch	119	110	201

* FAO estimate.
Source: FAO, *Yearbook of Fishery Statistics*.

Mining

	2001	2002	2003
Coal ('000 metric tons)	475.0	459.0	411.3
Crude petroleum ('000 metric tons)	75.5	75.5	68.5
Natural gas (million cu metres)	32.8	30.1	27.1
Cement ('000 metric tons)	468.9	757.5	532.8

Gold (metric tons): 20.0 in 1999; 22.0 in 2000; 24.6 in 2001 (Source: Gold Fields Mineral Services, *Gold Survey 2002*).

Industry

SELECTED PRODUCTS
('000 metric tons, unless otherwise indicated)

	2001	2002	2003
Vegetable oil	6.9	9.2	10.7
Refined sugar	30.5	75.5	51.2
Vodka ('000 hectolitres)	18.2	23.6	24.1
Beer ('000 hectolitres)	n.a.	7.7	n.a.
Cigarettes (million)	3,013.4	3,102.0	2,927.3
Textile fabrics ('000 sq metres)	7,260.8	1,809.7	5,545.5
Footwear ('000 pairs)	188.7	237.1	171.0
Motor spirit (petrol)	47.8	27.1	40.1
Gas-diesel (distillate fuel) oil	43.4	23.0	26.8
Cement	468.9	757.5	532.8
Electric energy (million kWh)	13,666.9	13,978.1	11,921.9

Finance

CURRENCY AND EXCHANGE RATES

Monetary Units
100 tyiyns = 1 som.

Sterling, Dollar and Euro Equivalents (31 December 2003)
£1 sterling = 78.87 soms;
US $1 = 44.19 soms;
€1 = 55.81 soms;
1,000 soms = £12.68 = $22.63 = €17.92.

Average Exchange Rate (soms per US $)
2001   48.378
2002   46.937
2003   43.648

Note: In May 1993 Kyrgyzstan introduced its own currency, the som, replacing the Russian (former Soviet) rouble at an exchange rate of 1 som = 200 roubles.

BUDGET
(million soms)*

Revenue†	2000	2001	2002
Taxation	7,675.5	9,187.9	10,474.7
Personal income taxes	753.8	960.9	1,083.3
Profit taxes	572.8	993.7	967.6
Value-added tax	2,976.2	4,221.4	4,793.7
Excises	1,518.4	1,102.6	1,082.0
Taxes on international trade and transactions	275.1	301.4	418.9
Other current revenue	1,581.0	2,672.6	2,983.9
Capital revenue	23.5	57.1	129.5
Total	9,280.1	11,917.7	13,588.1

Expenditure‡	2000	2001	2002
Administration, defence and internal security	3,637.1	3,837.5	4,310.6
Education	2,293.0	2,847.6	3,350.4
Health care	1,295.9	1,379.0	1,527.2
Social insurance and security	1,113.9	1,417.1	2,340.5
Housing and public utilities	666.5	800.9	1,131.2
Subsidies to economic sectors	1,342.7	1,423.0	1,894.7
Total (incl. others)	11,308.2	12,255.7	15,188.6

* Figures represent a consolidation of the budgetary transactions of the central Government and local governments. The operations of extra-budgetary accounts, including the Social Fund (formed in 1994 by an amalgamation of the Pension Fund, the Unemployment Fund and the Social Insurance Fund), are excluded.
† Excluding grants received (million soms): 608.2 in 2000; 622.0 in 2001; 823.6 in 2002.
‡ Including lending minus repayments.

INTERNATIONAL RESERVES
(US $ million at 31 December)

	2001	2002	2003
Gold	23.0	28.5	34.7
IMF special drawing rights	1.3	0.6	10.3
Foreign exchange	262.2	288.2	354.3
Total	286.5	317.3	399.3

Source: IMF, *International Financial Statistics*.

MONEY SUPPLY
(million soms at 31 December)

	2001	2002	2003
Currency outside banks	5,016	6,866	9,302
Demand deposits at banking institutions	542	811	1,314
Total money	5,558	7,677	10,616

Source: IMF, *International Financial Statistics*.

COST OF LIVING
(Retail price index; base: 1992 = 100)

	1999	2000	2001
Food	10,604.7	12,679.3	13,407.1
Fuel and light	6,040.1	8,018.7	10,285.1
Clothing	4,748.3	5,121.8	5,064.4
Rent	278,485.7	255,000.0	389,892.9
All items (incl. others)	11,678.3	13,862.4	14,821.9

Food (base: 2000=100): 105.7 in 2001; 106.1 in 2002.

All items (base: 2000=100): 106.9 in 2001; 109.2 in 2002.

Source: ILO.

NATIONAL ACCOUNTS
(million soms at current prices)

Expenditure on the Gross Domestic Product

	2000	2001	2002
Government final consumption expenditure	13,098.6	12,911.7	14,032.7
Private final consumption expenditure	42,929.6	47,893.1	50,896.7
Increase in stocks	1,136.0	724.3	852.1
Gross fixed capital formation	11,942.1	12,574.2	12,417.5
Total domestic expenditure	69,106.3	74,103.3	78,199.0
Exports of goods and services	27,350.8	27,133.4	29,831.2
Less Imports of goods and services	31,099.2	27,353.4	32,663.5
GDP in purchasers' values	65,357.9	73,883.3	75,366.7

Gross Domestic Product by Economic Activity

	2001	2002	2003*
Agriculture, forestry and fishing	25,520.1	25,929.8	29,380.3
Mining	377.4	362.9	376.6
Manufacturing	13,033.5	9,834.2	11,384.5
Electricity, gas and water supply	3,633.1	3,287.2	3,267.0
Construction	2,780.8	2,579.2	2,383.4
Trade, repair of motor vehicles, household appliances and articles of personal use	9,008.7	10,752.9	12,319.7
Hotels and restaurants	589.5	839.1	1,047.3
Transport and communications	3,095.1	3,845.3	4,225.0
Housing, social and personal services	961.9	801.6	880.2
Health care and social services	1,181.7	1,298.7	1,222.4
Education	2,329.4	2,535.1	2,695.8
Financial activities	819.9	1,131.2	519.3
Real estate, rent and rendering services	1,971.1	2,307.3	2,224.9
Government administration	3,741.3	3,947.3	3,989.5
Sub-total	69,043.5	69,451.8	75,915.9
Less Imputed bank service charge	516.5	641.4	—
GDP at basic prices	68,527.0	68,810.4	75,915.9
Taxes on products *Less* Subsidies on products	5,356.3	6,556.3	7,504.9
GDP in purchasers' values	73,883.3	75,366.7	83,420.8

* Preliminary data.

BALANCE OF PAYMENTS
(US $ million)

	2000	2001	2002
Exports of goods f.o.b.	510.9	480.3	498.1
Imports of goods f.o.b.	−506.9	−440.4	−552.1
Trade balance	4.0	39.9	−54.0
Exports of services	61.8	80.3	138.4
Imports of services	−148.8	−124.7	−145.5
Balance on goods and services	−83	−4.5	−61.1
Income (net)	−83.9	−65.5	−59.7
Balance on goods, services and income	−166.9	−70.0	−120.8
Current transfers (net)	87.4	51.1	86.1
Current balance	−79.5	−18.9	−34.7
Capital account (net)	−11.3	−32.0	−27.9
Direct investment (net)	−6.9	−1.1	4.8
Portfolio investment (net)	−1.3	1.2	−12.0
Financial derivatives assets	25.8	17.6	−5.1
Other investment (net)	46.7	14.0	83.3
Statistical discrepancy	10.3	18.6	20.8
Overall balance	−16.2	−0.6	29.2

External Trade

PRINCIPAL COMMODITIES
(US $ million)

Imports c.i.f.	2000	2001	2002
Vegetable products	42.3	15.5	21.7
Prepared foodstuffs, beverages and tobacco	31.0	35.8	47.4
Mineral products	133.3	129.5	163.4
Products of chemical or allied industries	59.3	67.3	78.4
Plastics, rubber and articles thereof	22.8	22.0	24.9
Textiles and fabrics	35.2	28.8	38.9
Metals and articles thereof	27.6	27.3	29.7
Machinery, electrical equipment and parts	98.2	56.5	89.6
Vehicles and transport equipment	41.8	31.8	32.1
Total (incl. others)	554.1	467.2	586.8

Exports f.o.b.	2000	2001	2002
Vegetable products	14.4	13.3	19.9
Prepared foodstuffs, beverages and tobacco	37.3	32.7	30.1
Mineral products	86.8	58.4	62.4
Products of chemical or allied industries	14.5	18.0	25.2
Raw hides and skins, leather, fur, travel articles and bags . .	7.6	10.3	24.2
Textiles and fabrics	42.8	29.5	59.8
Natural and cultured pearls, precious and semi-precious stones, precious metals and products, and coins . . .	196.9	226.7	164.8
Metals and articles thereof . .	34.8	15.3	23.4
Machinery, electrical equipment and parts	33.4	28.5	26.9
Vehicles and transport equipment.	14.9	26.5	21.2
Total (incl. others) . . .	**504.5**	**476.2**	**485.5**

PRINCIPAL TRADING PARTNERS
(US $ million)

Imports c.i.f.	2001	2002	2003
Belarus	6.0	5.1	5.9
Belgium	8.4	1.6	3.3
Canada	1.9	9.0	8.3
China, People's Republic . .	48.5	59.1	77.7
Germany	24.3	31.4	38.2
Iran	6.7	4.3	5.9
Japan	5.8	6.4	11.8
Kazakhstan	81.8	123.9	170.9
Korea, Republic . . .	7.8	7.0	11.7
Netherlands	4.0	16.1	12.3
Poland	4.9	3.9	6.1
Russia	85.1	116.7	176.1
Sweden	0.9	7.4	2.0
Turkey	15.8	17.0	26.0
Turkmenistan	9.0	1.7	0.4
Ukraine	6.2	7.8	12.6
United Arab Emirates . . .	6.8	7.3	7.8
United Kingdom	4.8	2.8	2.5
USA	26.8	47.4	47.9
Uzbekistan	66.7	60.1	39.2
Total (incl. others) . . .	**467.2**	**586.8**	**717.0**

Exports f.o.b.	2001	2002	2003
Afghanistan	1.6	4.4	6.1
Azerbaijan. . . .	2.1	5.6	2.0
China, People's Republic . .	19.4	41.1	23.3
France	1.8	5.6	0.2
Germany	94.4	1.8	3.0
India	1.4	6.1	0.7
Iran	8.2	4.7	2.1
Kazakhstan	39.0	36.8	57.1
Latvia	3.4	8.7	9.4
Russia	64.5	80.0	97.0
Switzerland	124.2	96.4	117.9
Tajikistan	6.7	10.2	18.9
Turkey	13.8	16.4	11.0
United Arab Emirates . . .	0.5	68.8	144.3
United Kingdom	14.1	0.9	0.1
USA	7.1	36.1	6.5
Uzbekistan	48.0	27.8	16.3
Total (incl. others) . . .	**476.2**	**485.5**	**581.7**

Transport

RAILWAYS
(traffic)

	1998	1999	2000
Passenger-km (million) . . .	59	31	44
Freight net ton-km (million) . .	466	354	348

Source: UN, *Statistical Yearbook*.

ROAD TRAFFIC
(vehicles in use at 31 December)

	1997	1998	1999
Passenger cars	176,075	187,734	187,322
Motorcycles and mopeds . . .	26,634	23,909	20,789

Source: International Road Federation, *World Road Statistics*.

CIVIL AVIATION
(traffic on scheduled services)

	1997	1998	1999
Kilometres flown (million) . . .	8	9	9
Passengers carried ('000) . . .	423	427	312
Passenger-km (million) . . .	531	519	532
Total ton-km (million) . . .	52	60	56

Source: UN, *Statistical Yearbook*.

Tourism

FOREIGN TOURIST ARRIVALS

Country of Residence	1998	1999
China, People's Republic	6,088	6,237
CIS countries*	42,027	31,158
Germany	822	1,695
India	1,360	1,870
Turkey	2,467	2,882
USA	696	2,868
Total (incl. others)	**59,363**	**68,863**

* Comprising Armenia, Azerbaijan, Belarus, Georgia, Kazakhstan, Moldova, the Russian Federation, Tajikistan, Turkmenistan, Ukraine and Uzbekistan.

2001 (total arrivals): 69,000.

Tourism receipts (US $ million): 8 in 1998; 14 in 1999; 15 in 2000; 15 in 2001.

Sources: World Tourism Organization, *Yearbook of Tourism Statistics*; World Bank, *World Development Indicators*.

Communications Media

	2000	2001	2002
Television receivers ('000 in use) . . .	240	242	n.a.
Telephones ('000 main lines in use) . .	376.1	376.1	394.8
Mobile cellular telephones ('000 subscribers)	9.0	27.0	53.1
Internet users ('000)	51.6	51.6	152.0

Radio receivers ('000 in use): 520 in 1997.

Daily newspapers: 3 (average circulation 67,000) in 1996.

Non-daily newspapers: 146 (average circulation 896,000) in 1996.

Book production: 351 titles (1,980,000 copies) in 1996.

Sources: International Telecommunication Union; UNESCO, *Statistical Yearbook*.

Education
(1999/2000)

	Institutions	Teachers	Students
Pre-primary	420	2,500	45,000
Primary	1,985	19,200	466,200
Secondary: general	n.a.	36,600	633,900
Secondary: vocational	n.a.	5,100	52,200
Higher (all institutions)	n.a.	8,400	159,200

Source: UN, *Statistical Yearbook for Asia and the Pacific*.

Adult literacy rate (UNESCO estimate): 97.0% in 2001 (Source: UNDP, *Human Development Report*).

Directory

The Constitution

A new Constitution was proclaimed on 5 May 1993. The following is a summary of its main provisions (including amendments endorsed in referendums held on 22 October 1994, 10 February 1996, 17 October 1998 and 2 February 2003, and other modifications approved by the Constitutional Court):

GENERAL PROVISIONS

The Kyrgyz Republic (Kyrgyzstan) is a sovereign, unitary, democratic republic founded on the principle of lawful, secular government. All state power belongs to the people, who exercise this power through the state bodies, on the basis of the Constitution and laws of the republic, and through the bodies of self-governance. Matters of legislation and other issues pertaining to the state may be decided by the people by referendum. The President of the Republic, the deputies of the Zhogorku Kenesh (Supreme Council), and representatives of local administrative bodies are all elected directly by the people. Elections are held on the basis of universal, equal and direct suffrage by secret ballot. All citizens of 18 years and over are eligible to vote.

The territory of the Kyrgyz Republic is integral and inviolable. The state languages are Kyrgyz and Russian. The equality and free use of other languages are guaranteed. The rights and freedoms of citizens may not be restricted on account of ignorance of the state language.

THE PRESIDENT

The President of the Kyrgyz Republic is Head of State and Commander-in-Chief of the Armed Forces, and represents Kyrgyzstan both within the country and internationally. Any citizen of the republic between the ages of 35 and 65, who has a fluent command of the state language, may stand for election. The President's term of office is five years; he/she may not serve more than two consecutive terms. The President is directly elected by the people.

The President appoints and dismisses (subject to approval by the legislature) the Prime Minister; appoints the other members of the Government, as well as heads of administrative offices and other leading state posts; presents draft legislation to the Zhogorku Kenesh on his/her own initiative; signs legislation approved by the Zhogorku Kenesh or returns it for further scrutiny; signs international agreements; may call referendums on issues of state; may dissolve the legislature (should a referendum demand this) and call fresh elections; announces a general or partial mobilization; and declares a state of war in the event of an invasion by a foreign power.

ZHOGORKU KENESH
(SUPREME COUNCIL)

Supreme legislative power is vested in the 105-member Zhogorku Kenesh, which comprises two chambers: the 45-member Legislative Assembly (lower chamber), which is a permanent chamber, and the 60-member People's Assembly (upper chamber), which sits twice yearly and represents regional interests. Members of both chambers are elected for a term of five years on the basis of universal, equal and direct suffrage by secret ballot.

The Zhogorku Kenesh approves amendments and additions to the Constitution; enacts legislation; confirms the republican budget and supervises its execution; determines questions pertaining to the administrative and territorial structure of the republic; designates presidential elections; approves the appointment of the Prime Minister, as nominated by the President; approves the appointment of the Procurator-General, the Chairman of the Supreme Court and the Chairman of the National Bank, as nominated by the President; ratifies or abrogates international agreements, and decides questions of war and peace; and organizes referendums on issues of state.

In 2005 the Zhogorku Kenesh was to be transformed into a unicameral assembly, with one member (rather than two) from each electoral district.

THE GOVERNMENT

The Government of the Kyrgyz Republic is the highest organ of executive power in Kyrgyzstan. The Prime Minister heads the Government, which also comprises Deputy Prime Ministers and Ministers. The members of the Government are appointed by the President; however, the President's appointment of the Prime Minister depends upon approval by the Zhogorku Kenesh. The President supervises the work of the Government and has the right to chair its sessions. The Prime Minister must deliver an annual report to the Zhogorku Kenesh on the work of the Government.

The Government determines all questions of state administration, other than those ascribed to the Constitution or to the competence of the President and the Zhogorku Kenesh; drafts the republican budget and submits it to the Zhogorku Kenesh for approval; co-ordinates budgetary, financial, fiscal and monetary policy; administers state property; takes measures to defend the country and state security; executes foreign policy; and strives to guarantee the rights and freedoms of the citizens and to protect property and social order.

JUDICIAL SYSTEM

The judicial system comprises the Constitutional Court, the Supreme Court, the Higher Court of Arbitration and regional courts. Judges of the Constitutional Court are appointed by the Zhogorku Kenesh, on the recommendation of the President, for a term of 15 years, while those of the Supreme Court and the Higher Court of Arbitration are appointed by the Zhogorku Kenesh, on the recommendation of the President, for ten years. The Constitutional Court is the supreme judicial body protecting constitutionality. It comprises the Chairman/woman, his/her deputies and seven judges. The Supreme Court is the highest organ of judicial power in the sphere of civil, criminal and administrative justice.

The Government

HEAD OF STATE

President of the Kyrgyz Republic: ASKAR AKAYEV (elected 28 October 1990; re-elected, by direct popular vote, 12 October 1991, 24 December 1995 and 29 October 2000).

GOVERNMENT
(April 2004)

Prime Minister: NIKOLAI TANAYEV.

First Deputy Prime Minister and Minister of Transport and Communications: KUBANYCHBEK DZHUMALIYEV.

Deputy Prime Minister: BAZARBAI MAMBETOV.

Deputy Prime Minister and Minister of Social Mobilization: ULARBEK MATEYEV.

Minister of Economic Development, Industry and Trade: AMANGELDY MURALIYEV (acting).

Minister of Agriculture, Water Resources and Processing Industry: ALEKSANDR KOSTYUK.

Minister of Foreign Affairs: ASKAR AITMATOV.

Minister of Education: MUSTAFA KIDIBAYEV.

Minister of Health: MITALIP MAMYTOV.

Minister of Finance: BOLOT ABILDAYEV.

Minister of Justice: NELYA BEYSHENALIYEVA.

Minister of Labour and Social Welfare: ROZA AKNAZAROVA.

Minister of Internal Affairs: BAKIRDIN SUBANBEKOV.

Minister of Defence: Maj.-Gen. ESEN TOPOYEV.

Minister of Local Self-Government and Regional Development Affairs: TOLOBEK OMURALIYEV.

Minister of Ecology and Emergency Situations: TEMIRBEK AKMATALIYEV.

Chief of Presidential Administration: TOYCHUBEK KASIMOV.

HEADS OF GOVERNMENT BODIES

National Bank: ULAN SARBANOV.

National Commission for State Service: (vacant).

National Institute of Standards and Metrology: BATYRBEK DAVLESOV.

National Security Service: KALYK IMANKULOV.

State Secretary: OSMONAKUN IBRAIMOV.

State Agency for Geology and Mineral Resources: SHEISHENALY MURZAGAZIYEV.

State Agency for Power Engineering: EMILBEK UZAKBAYEV.

State Agency for Registration of Real Estate Rights: KENESHBEK KARACHALOV.

State Agency for Science and Intellectual Property: ROMAN OMOROV.

State Border Service: KALMURAT SADIYEV.

State Commission for Architecture and Construction: ANVAR TURSONOV.

State Commission for Culture: BOLOT OSMONOV.

State Commission for Drugs Control: KURMANBEK KUBATBEKOV.

State Commission for Religious Affairs: OMURZAK MAMAYUSUPOV.

State Commission for Standards, Financial Accounts and Auditing: KANATBEK SAGYNOV.

State Committee for Attraction of Direct Investment: SADRIDDIN DZHIYENBEKOV (acting).

State Committee for Management of State Property: RAVSHAN DZHEYENBEKOV (acting).

State Comittee for Tourism, Sport and Youth Policy: OKMOTBEK ALMAKUCHUKOV.

State Communications Agency: ANDREI TITOV.

State Securities Commission: URAN ABDYNASYROV.

MINISTRIES

Office of the President: 720003 Bishkek, Govt House, Dom Pravitelstva; tel. (312) 21-24-66; fax (312) 21-86-27; e-mail office@mail.gov.kg; internet www.president.kg.

Office of the Prime Minister: 720003 Bishkek, Govt House; tel. (312) 22-56-56; fax (312) 21-86-27; internet www.gov.kg/prime.htm.

Office of the First Deputy Prime Minister: 720003 Bishkek, Govt House; tel. (312) 21-89-35 (Economic Policy Dept); tel. 21-16-52 (Social Policy Dept); fax (312) 21-86-27 (Agriculture Dept); internet www.gov.kg/vicep.htm.

Ministry of Agriculture, Water Resources and Processing Industry: 720040 Bishkek, Kievskaya 96A; tel. (312) 62-36-33; fax (312) 62-36-32; e-mail mawr@bishkek.gov.kg.

Ministry of Defence: 720001 Bishkek, Logvinenko 26; tel. (312) 22-78-79; e-mail ud@bishkek.gov.kg.

Ministry of Ecology and Emergency Situations: 720055 Bishkek, Aliyaskara Toktonaliyeva 2/1; e-mail admin@mecd.bishkek.gov.kg.

Ministry of Economic Development, Industry and Trade: Bishkek.

Ministry of Education: 720040 Bishkek, Tynystanova 257; tel. (312) 26-31-52; fax (312) 22-86-04; e-mail monk@monk.bishkek.gov.kg.

Ministry of Finance: 720040 Bishkek, pr. Erkindik 58; tel. (312) 66-45-80; fax (312) 66-26-45; e-mail postmaster@mf.gov.kg; internet www.minfin.kg.

Ministry of Foreign Affairs: 720050 Bishkek, Razzakova 59; tel. (312) 22-05-45; fax (312) 26-36-39; e-mail postmaster@mfa.bishkek.gov.kg.

Ministry of Health: 720040 Bishkek, Moskovskaya 148; tel. (312) 22-86-97; fax (312) 22-84-24; e-mail minzdrav@minzdrav.bishkek.gov.kg; internet www.med.kg.

Ministry of Internal Affairs: 720040 Bishkek, Frunze 469; tel. (312) 22-38-66; fax (312) 22-32-78; e-mail mail@mvd.bishkek.gov.kg.

Ministry of Justice: 720321 Bishkek, Orozbekova 37; tel. (312) 22-84-89; fax (312) 26-11-15; e-mail minjust@bishkek.gov.kg; internet www.minjust.bishkek.gov.kg.

Ministry of Labour and Social Welfare: 720041 Bishkek, Tynystanova 215; tel. (312) 26-42-50; e-mail mlsp@mlsp.kg; internet mlsp.bishkek.gov.kg.

Ministry of Local Self-Government and Regional Development Affairs: 720040 Bishkek, Orozbekova 44; e-mail gosreg@bishkek.gov.kg.

Ministry of Social Mobilization: Bishkek.

Ministry of Transport and Communications: 720017 Bishkek, Isanova 42; tel. (312) 61-04-72; fax (312) 66-47-81; e-mail mtk@mtk.bishkek.gov.kg; internet www.mtk.bishkek.gov.kg.

President and Legislature

PRESIDENT

Presidential Election, 29 October 2000

Candidates	% of votes
Askar Akayev	74.5
Omurbek Tekebayev	13.9
Almazbek Atambayev	6.0
Melis Eshimkanov	1.1
Bakir Ulu Tursunbay	1.0
Tursunbek Akunov	0.4
Blank or spoiled	3.1
Total	**100.0**

ZHOGORKU KENESH
(SUPREME COUNCIL)

The Zhogorku Kenesh is a bicameral legislative body, comprising the People's Assembly and the Legislative Assembly.

People's Assembly and Legislative Assembly: 720003 Bishkek, Kirova 205; tel. (312) 22-55-23; fax (312) 22-24-04; e-mail postmaster@kenesh.gov.kg; internet kenesh.bishkek.gov.kg.

Chairman (Speaker) of People's Assembly: ALTAI BORUBAYEV.

Chairman (Speaker) of Legislative Assembly: ABDYGANY ERKEBAYEV.

Elections were held to both chambers of the Zhogorku Kenesh on 20 February 2000, with a second round of voting ('run-off' elections) held on 12 March.

General Election, 20 February and 12 March 2000*

Parties and blocs	Party-list seats	Single-mandate constituency seats	Total seats
Union of Democratic Forces	4	8	12
Party of Communists of Kyrgyzstan	5	1	6
My Country Party of Action	1	3	4
Ata-Meken Socialist Party	1	1	2
Democratic Women's Party of Kyrgyzstan†	2	—	2
Party of Veterans of the War in Afghanistan	2	—	2
Poor and Unprotected People's Party	—	2	2
Agrarian Labour Party of Kyrgyzstan	—	1	1
Erkin Kyrgyzstan Progressive and Democratic Party	—	1	1
Independents	—	73	73
Total	**15**	**90**	**105**

* Election results include both the People's Assembly (the 45-member upper chamber) and the Legislative Assembly (the 60-member lower chamber).

† In August 2000 it was reported that the two seats gained by representatives of the Democratic Women's Party of Kyrgyzstan had been withdrawn, owing to the violation of regulations during the nomination process.

Political Organizations

Adilettuuluk (Justice): Cholpon-Ata; f. 1999 to campaign for the rights of national minorities; Leader MARAT SULTANOV; Deputy Leader BOLOT KARABALAYEV.

Agrarian Labour Party of Kyrgyzstan: Bishkek, Kievskaya 120; tel. (312) 26-58-13; f. 1994; Chair. U. S. SYDYKOV.

Agrarian Party of Kyrgyzstan: Bishkek, Kievskaya 96; tel. (312) 22-68-52; f. 1993; represents farmers' interests; Chair. E. ALIYEV.

Ar-Namys (Dignity) Party: Bishkek, Isanova 60; e-mail info@ar-namys.org; internet www.ar-namys.org; f. 1999; moderate opposition party; Chair. FELIKS KULOV (imprisoned); Leader EMIL ALIYEV (acting).

Asaba (Banner) Party of National Revival: Bishkek, pr. Chui 26; tel. (312) 43-04-45; fax (312) 28-53-64; f. 1991; nationalist party;

forms part of the For People Power electoral alliance; Chair. CHAP-RASHTY BAZARBAYEV.

Ashar: Bishkek, pr. Molodoi Gvardii 132; tel. (312) 25-71-88; f. 1989; socio-political movement concerned with development of a parliamentary state and with the revival of national architecture; Chair. ZHUMAGAZY USUP-CHONAIU.

Ata-Meken (Fatherland) Socialist Party: Bishkek, bul. Erkindik 38; tel. (312) 27-17-79; f. 1992; nationalist; Leader ONURBEK TEKE-BAYEV.

Birimdik Party: 720040 Bishkek, Tynystanova 249; tel. (312) 66-38-12; fax (312) 66-29-50; e-mail birimdik_party@mail.ru; f. 1994; seeks to unite people within a democratic movement; Chair. KARYPBEK ALYMKULOV.

Communist Party of Kyrgyzstan (CPK): Bishkek, Panfilov 242/12; tel. (312) 22-25-80; f. 1999, following split from the Party of Communists of Kyrgyzstan; Chair. KLARA ADZHIBEKOVA.

Democratic Movement of Kyrgyzstan (DMK): Bishkek, Abdymomunova 205; tel. (312) 27-14-95; f. 1990; registered as a political party in 1993; campaigns for civil liberties; forms part of the For People Power electoral alliance; Pres. DZHYPAR DZHEKSHEYEV.

Democratic Party of Economic Unity: Bishkek, Popova 4; f. 1994; Chair. A. D. TASHTANBEKOV.

Economic Revival Party: Chui Duban, Sokuluk raion, vil. Voenno-Antonovka; f. 1998; Leader VALERII KHON.

El (Beibecharalai) Partiyasy: Bishkek, Moskovskaya 172; tel. (312) 21-59-64; f. 1995; Chair. DANIYAR USENOV.

Emgekchil (Working People) el Partiyasy: Bishkek, Microdistrict 5/43; tel. (312) 66-56-95; f. 1997; supports the democratic movement and private ownership; Chair. E. O. OMURAKUNOV.

Erkin (Free) Kyrgyzstan Progressive-Democratic Party (ERK): Bishkek, Abdymomunova 207; tel. (312) 22-49-57; fax (312) 22-60-35; f. 1991; social-democratic party; forms part of the For People Power electoral alliance; Chair. BAKIR ULU TURSUNBAY.

Erkindik (Liberty): Bishkek; f. 2000 following a split from the ERK; forms part of the For People Power electoral alliance; Chair. TOPCHUBEK TURGUNALIYEV.

Islamic Democratic Party: Bishkek; f. 2002; Leader NARKAS MULLADZHANOV.

Kayran El (Poor Nation) Party: Bishkek, 8 Microdistrict 29/12; registered in 1999; nationalist; forms part of the For People Power electoral alliance; Leader TOKTOBAY MULKUBATOV.

Kok-Zhar Sociopolitical Organization: Bishkek, Mikroraion 7-34-64; f. 1992; seeks to provide housing for the underprivileged; Chair. ZH. ISAYEV.

Kyrgyz Committee for Human Rights: Bishkek, Kievskaya 96; e-mail chrights@imfiko.bishkek.su; internet www.kchr.elcat.kg; banned by the Ministry of Justice in Oct. 1998, re-registered in Aug. 1999 following international pressure; Chair. BOLOT TYNALIYEV.

Local Communities', Peasants' and Farmers' Party of Kyrgyzstan: Bishkek, Ivanitsyn 117; f. 1999 as Socio-Political Peasants' (Farmers') Party of Kyrgyzstan; renamed as above in 2004; Chair. ESENGUL ISAKOV; 38,000 mems.

Manas: Bishkek; f. 2000; electoral bloc formed prior to Feb. 2000 parliamentary election; composed of the Republican Popular Party and the Party for the Protection of the Interests of Industrial Workers, Farmers and Poor Families.

Manas El Party of Spiritual Revival: Bishkek, Balyk Kumar 44, Orto Sai; tel. (312) 47-01-84; registered 1995; Leader ALI SULTAN ISHIMOV.

My Country Party of Action: 720040 Bishkek, Tynystanova 110; tel. (312) 22-75-81; e-mail mstrana@hotmail.com; internet www.strana.kg; f. 1998; 670 mems; Chair. DZHOOMART OTARBAYEV; Leader ALMAZBEK ISMANKULOV.

National Unity Democratic Movement: Bishkek, bul. Erkindik 41-17; tel. (312) 22-50-84; f. 1991; seeks to unite different ethnic groups; Chair. YU. RAZGULYAYEV.

New Force: Bishkek, Abdymomunova 207; tel. (312) 27-16-81; f. 1994 as the Democratic Party of Women, to encourage the participation of women in politics; membership open to both men and women; pro-presidential; Chair. TOKON ASANOVNA SHAILIYEVA.

Party of Communists of Kyrgyzstan (KCP): Bishkek, bul. Erkindik 31/6; tel. (312) 62-48-07; fax (312) 67-17-77; e-mail absamat@kenesh.gov.kg; formerly known as the Communist Party; disbanded 1991, re-established 1992; 25,000 mems; Chair. ABSAMAT M. MASALIYEV.

Party for the Protection of the Interests of Industrial Workers, Farmers and Poor Families: Bishkek, pr. Mira 1; tel. (312)

21-58-42; f. 1996; promotes social and economic reforms; Chair. AKBARALY AITIKEYEV.

Party for Destitute People: Bishkek, Turusbekov 172, 4th Floor; tel. (312) 21-59-64; registered in 1995; reform of government and the judiciary; Leader DANIYAR USENOV.

Party of Veterans of the War in Afghanistan and of Participants in Other Local Conflicts: Bishkek, bul. Chui A; tel. (312) 53-02-15; registered in 1994; Leader AKBOKON TASHTANBEKOV.

Patriotic Party of Kyrgyzstan: Bishkek; f. 1998; not registered with the Ministry of Justice; Leader NAZARBEK NYSHANOV.

People's Congress: Bishkek; f. 2001 as an opposition alliance; Chair. FELIKS KULOV (imprisoned).

People's Mother: Bishkek; f. 2000 to encourage women from all social backgrounds to take part in politics.

People's Patriotic Movement: Bishkek; f. 2001; alliance of the Agrarian Labour Party, the Ar-Namys (Dignity) Party, the Ata-Meken (Fatherland) Socialist Party, the Communist Party of Kyrgyzstan, Erkindik, Kairan-El, the Party of Communists of Kyrgyzstan, the People's Party and the Republican Party; aims to defend democracy and human rights.

Republican Movement for the Union and Brotherhood of Nations: Bishkek, pr. Chui 114; tel. (312) 22-16-49; Chair. K. AJIBEKOVA.

Republican Party of Kyrgyzstan (RPK): tel. (312) 22-14-16; registered in 1999; advocates parliamentary republicanism; forms part of the For People Power electoral alliance; Chair. GIYAZ TOKOMBAYEV; Leader ZAMIRA SIDIKOVA.

Republican Party of Kyrgystan (Adilet): Bishkek, Bokonbayev 109; tel. (312) 66-48-17; fax (312) 66-50-84; f. 1999; campaigns for economic reform, modernization and investment; Chair. CHINGIZ T. AITMATOV.

Republican People's Party: Bishkek, Kievskaya 77; tel. (312) 22-25-65; f. 1992 by prominent scientists and academics; centrist; Chair. ZH. TENTIYEV.

Slavic Association Soglasiye (Accord): Bishkek; f. 1994 to eliminate causes of Russian emigration and to preserve Russian community in Kyrgyzstan; Vice-Pres. ANATOLII BULGAKOV.

Social Democratic Party of Kyrgyzstan: Bishkek, Alma-Atinskaya 4B/203; tel. (312) 43-15-07; f. 1994; Leader ABDYGANY ERKEBAYEV.

Union of Democratic Forces: Bishkek; f. 1999; pro-Government electoral alliance formed prior to Feb. 2000 parliamentary election; composed of the Social Democratic Party of Kyrgyzstan, the Economic Revival Party and the Birimdik Party.

Unity Party of Kyrgyzstan: Bishkek, Tynystanova 249; tel. (312) 22-88-62; fax (312) 22-87-65; f. 1994; centrist; pro-presidential; planned merger with Alga, Kyrgyzstan (Forward, Kyrgyzstan—f. 2003) announced in Jan. 2004; Leader AMANGELDY MURALIYEV.

Youth Party of Kyrgyzstan: Bishkek; Leader AIDAR BAKIYEV.

The following Islamist groups were banned by the Supreme Court in November 2003: Hizb-ut-Tahrir al-Islami (Party of Islamic Liberation), the Islamic Party of Turkestan, Sharq azzat Turkestan (East Turkestan Liberation Organization) and Sharq Turkestan Islam Partiyasy (East Turkestan Islamic Party).

Diplomatic Representation

EMBASSIES IN KYRGYZSTAN

Afghanistan: Bishkek, Aini 4; tel. (312) 42-63-72; fax (312) 54-34-28; Ambassador SHAHJAHAN AHMADI.

Belarus: 720040 Bishkek, Moskovskaya 210; tel. (312) 24-29-43; fax (312) 65-11-77; e-mail kyrgyzstan@belembassy.org; Ambassador ALYAKSANDR KOZYR.

China, People's Republic: 720001 Bishkek, Toktogula 196; tel. (312) 61-08-58; fax (312) 66-30-14; e-mail chinaemb_kg@mfa.gov.cn; Ambassador ZHANG YANNIAN.

Germany: 720040 Bishkek, Razzakova 28; tel. (312) 66-66-24; fax (312) 66-66-30; e-mail gerembi@elcat.kg; internet www.deutschebotschaft.bishkek.kg; Ambassador KLAUS ACHENBACH.

India: Bishkek, pr. Chui 164A, Hotel Bishkek; tel. (312) 21-08-63; fax (312) 66-07-08; e-mail india@elcat.kg; Ambassador APPUNNI RAMESH.

Iran: Bishkek, Razzakova 36; tel. (312) 22-69-64; fax (312) 66-02-09; e-mail sefabish@amil.elcat.gg; Ambassador GHOLAMREZA BAGHERI MOGHADAM.

Japan: 720040 Bishkek, pr. Chui 245, Demir Kyrgyz International Bank bldg, 2nd Floor; tel. (312) 61-18-75; fax (312) 61-18-82; Ambassador TOSHIO TSUNOZAKI.

Kazakhstan: Bishkek, Togolok Moldo 10; tel. (312) 22-54-63; fax (312) 22-54-63; e-mail kaz_emb@imfico.bishkek.su; Ambassador UMARZAK UZBEKOV.

Kuwait: Bishkek; Ambassador FAISAL RASHID AL-GAISA.

Morocco: Bishkek; Ambassador ABDELLAH ZAGUR.

Pakistan: Bishkek, Serova-Bailonova 37; tel. (312) 22-72-09; fax (312) 66-15-50; e-mail parepbishkek@exnet.kg; internet www .pakemb.com.kg; Ambassador MOHAMMAD ALAM BRAHIM.

Russia: Bishkek, Razzakova 17; tel. (312) 22-16-91; fax (312) 22-18-23; e-mail rusemb@imfiko.bishkek.su; Ambassador YEVGENII SHMAGIN.

Syria: Bishkek; Ambassador VAHIB FADEL.

Turkey: 720001 Bishkek, Moskovskaya 89; tel. (312) 22-78-82; fax (312) 66-05-19; e-mail biskbe@infotel.kg; Ambassador MUSTAFA EROKTEM.

Ukraine: 720040 Bishkek, Panfilova 150; tel. (312) 66-55-90; fax (312) 66-20-12; e-mail emb_kg@mfa.gov.ua; internet www .ukraine-emb.elcat.kg; Ambassador PETRO SHAPOVAL.

USA: 720016 Bishkek, pr. Mira 171; tel. (312) 55-12-41; fax (312) 55-12-64; e-mail mukambaevaibx@state.gov; internet bishkek .usembassy.gov; Ambassador STEPHEN YOUNG.

Uzbekistan: 720040 Bishkek, Tynystanova 213; tel. (312) 66-20-65; fax (312) 66-44-03; e-mail uzbembish@infotel.kg; Ambassador ALISHER SALAHITDINOV.

Viet Nam: Bishkek; Ambassador FAM ZUI SHON.

Judicial System

(see under Constitution, above)

Chairman of the Constitutional Court: CHOLPON BAYEKOVA.

Chairman of the Supreme Court: KURMANBEK OSMONOV.

Prosecutor-General: MYKTYBEK ABDYLDAYEV.

Religion

State Commission for Religious Affairs: 720040 Bishkek, Kievskaya 90; e-mail mail@religion.bishkek.gov.kg; Chair. OMURZAK MAMAYUSUPOV.

ISLAM

The majority of Kyrgyz are Sunni Muslims (Hanafi school), as are some other groups living in the republic, such as Uzbeks and Tajiks. Muslims in Kyrgyzstan are officially under the jurisdiction of the Muslim Board of Central Asia, based in Uzbekistan. The Board is represented in the country by a kazi.

Kazi of Muslims of Kyrgyzstan: Mullah ABDYSATAR.

Mufti of the Spiritual Directorate of Kyrgyzstan Muslims: Haji MURTALY AJI JUMANOV.

Islamic Centre of Kyrgyzstan: Osh; Pres. Haji SADYKZHAN KAMALOV.

CHRISTIANITY

Roman Catholic Church

The Church is represented in Kyrgyzstan by a Mission, established in December 1997. There were an estimated 300 adherents at 31 December 2002.

Superior: Rev. Fr ALEKSANDR KAN, 720072 Bishkek, Vasilyeva 203; tel. and fax (312) 21-78-32; e-mail church@freenet.kg.

The Russian Orthodox Church (Moscow Patriarchate)

The Russian Orthodox Church in Kyrgyzstan comes under the jurisdiction of the Eparchy of Tashkent and Central Asia (Metropolitan of Tashkent and Central Asia, VLADIMIR (IKIM)), in Uzbekistan.

The Press

In 1996 there were 146 non-daily newspapers published in Kyrgyzstan, and the average circulation per issue was 896,000 copies. There were three daily newspapers published in that year, with an average circulation of 67,000 copies.

PRINCIPAL NEWSPAPERS

Asaba (The Standard): Bishkek; tel. (312) 26-47-39; weekly; Kyrgyz; publication resumed in Oct. 2001, after having been suspended for seven months; supplement in Russian *Asaba-Bishkek*; Editors JUMABEK MEDERALIYEV; *Asaba*, BERMET BUKASHEVA; *Asaba-Bishkek*; circ. 10,000.

Bishkek Observer: 720040 Bishkek, Ibraimora 105; tel. (312) 29-28-21; e-mail observer@elcat.kg; independent; Russian and English; Editor AVTAR SINGH.

Bishkek Shamy (Bishkek Evening Newspaper): Bishkek, Pravdi 24; tel. (312) 72-57-80; f. 1989; daily; official organ of the Bishkek City Council; Kyrgyz; Editor ABDIDJAPAR SOOTBEKOV; circ. 10,000.

Char Tarap (Echo of Events): Bishkek; tel. (312) 28-94-63; f. 1994; weekly; Kyrgyz; Editor KALEN SYDYKOVA; circ. 5,000; parallel edition in Russian, *Ekho Sobytii*; Editor MURSURKUL KABYLBEKOV.

Chui Baayni (Chui Story): Bishkek, Ibraimova 24; tel. (312) 42-83-31; weekly; organ of Chui Duban; Kyrgyz; Editor KURMANBEK RAMATOV.

Chuskye Izvestiya (Chui News): 720040 Bishkek, Ibraimova 24; tel. (312) 42-69-26; weekly; organ of Chui Duban; Russian; Editor-in-Chief A. BLINDINA; circ. 10,000.

Delo No (Case Number): Bishkek; tel. (312) 22-84-62; fax (312) 66-36-03; e-mail delo@transfer.kg; internet delo.to.kg; f. 1991; weekly; Russian; opposition; Editor VIKTOR ZAPOLSKII; circ. 50,000.

Erkin Too (Free Mountain): 720040 Bishkek, Ibraimova 24; tel. (312) 42-03-15; 3 a week; organ of the Government; Kyrgyz; Editor-in-Chief T. TEMIROV; circ. 10,000.

Kyrgyz Madaniyaty (Kyrgyz Culture): 720301 Bishkek, Bokonbayeva 99; tel. (312) 26-14-58; f. 1967; weekly; organ of the Union of Writers; Editor NURALY KAPAROV; circ. 15,940.

Kyrgyz Tuusu (Flag of Kyrgyzstan): 720040 Bishkek, Abdymomunova 193; tel. (312) 22-45-09; fax (312) 22-24-59; f. 1924; daily; organ of the Government; Kyrgyz; Editor A. MATISAKOV; circ. 17,000–20,000.

Kyrgyzstan Chronicle: Bishkek; tel. (312) 22-48-32; f. 1993; weekly; independent; English; Editor BAYAN SARYGULOV; circ. 5,000.

Limon: Bishkek, ul. Moskovskaya 189; tel. (312) 65-03-03; fax (312) 65-02-04; e-mail limon@akipress.org; internet www.akipress.org; f. 1994; Russian; independent; Editor-in-Chief MARAT TAZABEKOV.

Moya Stolitsa—Novosti (My Capital—News): Bishkek; tel. (312) 21-29-79; e-mail city@infotel.kg; internet www.msn.kg; f. 2001; independent; Russian; Editor-in-Chief A. KIM.

Res Publica (Republic): 720017 Bishkek, Isanova 8; tel. (312) 21-77-57; fax (312) 21-84-12; e-mail repub@kyrnet.kg; internet gazeta .respublica.kg/; f. 1992; 2 a week; independent; Russian and English; publication suspended Jan.–May 2002; Editor ZAMIRA SIDIKOVA; circ. 10,000.

Slovo Kyrgyzstana (Word of Kyrgyzstan): 720004 Bishkek, Abdymomunova 193; tel. (312) 22-53-92; e-mail slovo@infotel.kg; internet www.sk.kg; f. 1925; daily; organ of the Government; Russian; Editor ALEKSANDR I. MALEVANY.

Svobodniye Gori (The Free Mountains): Bishkek, Razzakova 63, POB 1450; tel. (312) 26-34-22; 3 a week; Russian; Editor L. DJOLMY-KHAMEDOVA.

The Times of Central Asia: 720000 Bishkek, pr. Chui 155; tel. (312) 68-05-67; fax (312) 68-07-69; e-mail edittimes@infotel.kg; internet www.times.kg; f. 1995; weekly; English; also distributed in Kazakhstan, Turkmenistan and Uzbekistan; subscribers in Canada, Europe, Malaysia, Turkey and the USA; Editor LYDIA SAVINA.

Vechernii Bishkek (Bishkek Evening Newspaper): Bishkek, pr. Usenbayev 2; tel. (312) 28-45-97; fax (312) 68-02-68; e-mail webmaster@vb.kg; internet www.vb.kg; f. 1974; daily; independent; Russian; Editor KHASAN YA. MUSTAFAYEV; circ. (Mon.–Thur.) 20,000, (Fri.) 50,000.

Yuzhnyi Kurier (Southern Courier): Bishkek; tel. (312) 26-10-53; f. 1993; weekly; independent; Russian; Editor ALEKSANDR KNYAZYEV; circ. 10,000.

Zaman Kyrgyzstan (Kyrgyzstan Herald): 720040 Bishkek, Ibraimova 24; tel. (312) 42-62-35; e-mail zamantur@elcat.kg; f. 1992; weekly; independent; Kyrgyz, Turkish and English; Editor-in-Chief A. KUSH; circ. 15,000.

PRINCIPAL PERIODICALS

Monthly, unless otherwise indicated.

Ala Too (Ala Too Mountains): Bishkek; tel. (312) 26-55-12; f. 1931; organ of the Union of Writers; politics, novels, short stories, plays, poems of Kyrgyz authors and translations into Kyrgyz; Kyrgyz; Editor KENESH JUSUPOV; circ. 3,000.

Chalkan (Stinging Nettle): Bishkek; tel. (312) 42-16-38; f. 1955; satirical; Kyrgyz; Editor B. Azizov; circ. 7,600.

Den-sooluk (Health): Bishkek; tel. (312) 22-46-37; f. 1960; weekly; journal of the Ministry of Health; popular science; Kyrgyz; Editor Mar Aliyev; circ. 20,000.

Korporativnyi Vestnik (Corporate Bulletin): Bishkek, pr. Chui 106; tel. (312) 22-45-07; fax (312) 66-16-64; e-mail kv@cdc.kg; bulletin of the govt-controlled Corporate Development Centre; Dir B. Kartanbayev.

Kyrgyz Analytical Magazine: Bishkek, ul. Moskovskaya 189; tel. (312) 65-02-02; fax (312) 65-02-04; e-mail aki@inftel.kg; internet www.akipress.kg; f. 1993; Russian; independent; Dir Marat Tazabekov.

Kyrgyzstan Ayaldary (Women of Kyrgyzstan): Bishkek; tel. (312) 42-12-26; f. 1951; popular; Kyrgyz; Editor S. Akmatbekova; circ. 500.

Literaturnyi Kyrgyzstan (Literary Kyrgyzstan): 720301 Bishkek, Pushkina 70; tel. (312) 26-14-63; e-mail lk@users.kyrnet.kg; internet lk.kyrnet.kg; f. 1955; journal of the Union of Writers; fiction, literary criticism, journalism; Russian; Editor-in-Chief A. I. Ivanov; circ. 3,000.

Zdravookhraneniye Kyrgyzstana (Public Health System of Kyrgyzstan): 720005 Bishkek, Sovetskaya 34; tel. (312) 44-41-39; f. 1938; 4 a year; publ. by the Ministry of Health; experimental medical work; Russian; Editor-in-Chief N. K. Kasiyev; circ. 3,000.

NEWS AGENCIES

AKIpress: Bishkek, ul. Moskovskaya 189; tel. (312) 61-03-96; fax (312) 65-02-04; e-mail post@akipress.org; internet www.akipress.org; f. 2000; Russian and English; independent; Dir Marat Tazabekov.

Belyi Parokhod: 720011 Bishkek, Pushkina 50; tel. (312) 26-45-23; e-mail parokhod@infotel.kg; internet www.kg/parokhod; f. 1997; independent.

KABAR (Kyrgyz News Agency): 720337 Bishkek, Sovetskaya 175; tel. (312) 62-05-74; fax (312) 66-11-68; e-mail s1@kabar.gov.kg; internet www.kabar.kg; fmrly KyrgyzTag until 1992, and Kyrgyzkabar until 1995; Pres. Koubanychbek Taabaldiyev; Editor-in-Chief Djumakan Sariyev.

Foreign Bureaux

Interfax (Russia): Bishkek, Toktogula 97, Rm 6; tel. and fax (312) 26-72-87; Bureau Chief Bermet Malikova.

ITAR—TASS (Information Telegraphic Agency of Russia—Telegraphic Agency of the Sovereign Countries) (Russia): Bishkek, pr. Erkindik 43/4; tel. (312) 58-24-22; fax (312) 66-09-97; Correspondent Vladimir Neshkumai.

Reuters (United Kingdom): Bishkek; tel. (312) 54-52-01.

Publishers

Akyl: 720000 Bishkek, Sovetskaya 170; tel. (312) 22-47-57; f. 1994; science, politics, economics, culture, literature; Chair. Amanbek Karypkulov.

Ilim (Science): 720071 Bishkek, pr. Chui 265A; tel. (312) 25-53-60; e-mail ilimph@hotmail.kg; internet ilim.aknet.kg; scientific and science fiction; Dir L. V. Tarasova.

Kyrgyzskaya Entsiklopediya (Kyrgyz Encyclopedia): 720040 Bishkek, bul. Erkindik 56; tel. (312) 22-77-57; dictionaries and encyclopedias; Dir Baktygul Kaldybayeva; Editor-in-Chief Amanbek Karypkulov.

Kyrgyzstan (Kyrgyzstan Publishing House): Bishkek; tel. (312) 26-48-54; politics, science, economics, literature; Dir Berik N. Chalagyzov.

Uchkun: Bishkek, Ibraimova 24; tel. (312) 42-22-98; e-mail reception@uchkun.kg; internet www.uchkun.kg; state-owned; Pres. Kanybek K. Imanaliyev.

Broadcasting and Communications

State Communications Agency: 720005 Bishkek, Sovetskaya 76; e-mail nta@infotel.kg; Dir Andrei Titov.

TELECOMMUNICATIONS

Kyrgyztelekom: 720000 Bishkek, pr. Chui 96; tel. (312) 68-16-16; fax (312) 66-24-24; e-mail info@kt.kg; internet www.kt.kg; f. 1994, transformed into public co in 1997; state telecommunications co;

77.84% state-owned; scheduled for privatization; Pres. Nasirdin Turdaliyev; Vice-Pres. Burkan Jumabayev, Iskender Kolbayev.

BROADCASTING

Radio

State National Television and Radio Broadcasting Corpn: 720010 Bishkek, Molodoi Gvardii 59; tel. (312) 65-56-77; internet www.ktr.kg; Pres. Aytikeyeva T. Dzhekshenovna.

Kyrgyz Radio: 720010 Bishkek, Molodoi Gvardii 59; tel. (312) 25-79-36; fax (312) 65-10-64; internet www.ktr.kg; f. 1931; broadcasts in Kyrgyz, Russian, English, German, Ukrainian, Uzbek, Dungan and Uigur; Vice-Pres. M. Mambetaliyev.

Dom Radio: 720885 Bishkek, Molodoi Gvardii 63.

Radio Azattyk: Bishkek; tel. (312) 66-88-17; fax (312) 66-68-14; e-mail kiyas@liberty.elcat.kg; internet www.azattyk.org; Kyrgyz language news broadcasts by Radio Free Europe/Radio Liberty (USA—based in the Czech Republic); Dir Tyntchtykbek Tchoroev; Bureau Chief Kyias Moldokasymov.

Radio Pyramid: 720300 Bishkek, Molodoi Gvardii 59; tel. (312) 28-28-28; fax (312) 52-61-65; e-mail pyramid@mail.elcat.kg; internet www.pyramid.elcat.kg; f. 1992; privately owned; broadcasts to Bishkek and neighbouring regions.

Sodruzhestvo: Osh; f. 1996; broadcasts to Kazakhstan, Kyrgyzstan, Tajikistan and Uzbekistan; established by ethnic Russian groups.

There are several other private radio stations operating in Kyrgyzstan.

Television

State National Television and Radio Broadcasting Corpn (see above):

Kyrgyz Television: 720300 Bishkek, pr. Molodoi Gvardii 63; tel. (312) 25-79-36; fax (312) 25-79-30; internet www.ktr.kg; Vice-Pres. Moldoseit Mambetakunov.

TV Pyramid: 720005 Bishkek; tel. and fax (312) 41-01-31; e-mail pyramid@ss5-22.kyrnet.kg; internet www.pyramid.elcat.kg/tv; f. 1991; privately owned; broadcasts to Bishkek and neighbouring regions.

Finance

(cap. = capital; res = reserves; m. = million; brs = branches; amounts in soms, unless otherwise indicated)

BANKING

Central Bank

National Bank of the Kyrgyz Republic: 720040 Bishkek, Umetaliyeva 101; tel. (312) 66-90-11; fax (312) 61-07-30; e-mail mail@nbkr.kg; internet www.nbkr.kg; f. 1991, name changed in 1992, and as above in 1993; cap. 50m., res 660.3m., dep. 4,933.7m. (Dec. 2001); Chair. Ulan K. Sarbanov.

Other Banks

In early 2001 there were 22 commercial banks in operation in Kyrgyzstan.

Amanbank: 720400 Bishkek, Tynystanova 249; tel. (312) 62-20-77; fax (312) 90-04-97; e-mail bank@amanbank.kg; internet www.amanbank.kg; f. 1995; cap. 55m., dep. 65.8m. (Aug. 2003); Chair. Shatkul I. Kudabayeva; 6 brs.

AsiaUniversalBank JSC: 720001 Bishkek, Toktogula 187; tel. (312) 62-02-52; fax (312) 62-02-50; e-mail reception@aub.bg; internet www.aub.kg; f. 1997 as International Business Bank, changed name as above 2000; cap. 200.0m., dep. 4,012.0m. (Oct. 2003); Pres. Nurdin Abdrazakov; 2 brs.

Bank Bakai: 720001 Bishkek, Isanov 75; tel. (312) 66-06-10; fax (312) 66-06-12; e-mail bank@bakai.kg; internet www.bakai.kg; f. 1998; cap. 47.0m., dep. 158.4m. (Oct. 2003); Chair. Marat Alapayev; Pres. Muhammad Ibragimov; 3 brs.

Energobank JSC: 720070 Bishkek, Jibek-Jolu 493; tel. and fax (312) 67-04-71; e-mail energkg@elcat.kg; internet www.energobank.kg; f. 1992 as Kyrgyzenergobank, changed name as above 2000; cap. US $1.7m., dep. $9.4m. (Oct. 2003); Pres. Bakirdin E. Sartkaziyev; Chair. Maksat Ishenbayev; 6 brs.

Investment Export-Import Bank: 720001 Bishkek, K. Akiyev 57; tel. (312) 65-06-10; fax (312) 62-06-54; e-mail ineximbank@infotel.kg; internet www.ineximbank.com; f. 1996 as Eridan Bank, name changed 2001; cap. 100.0m., res 4.1m., dep. 44.8m. (Aug. 2002); Chair. Petros Shaginyan; 1 br.

JSCB Kyrgyzstan Bank: 720001 Bishkek, Togolok Moldo 54; tel. (312) 21-95-98; fax (312) 61-02-20; e-mail akb@bankkg.kg; internet www.bankkg.kg; f. 1991; cap. 127.0m., res 36.4m., dep. 280.7m. (Jan. 2002); Pres. Sharipa S. Sadybakasova; 29 brs.

JSCB Tolubay Bank: 720010 Bishkek, Toktogula 247; tel. (312) 24-02-46; fax (312) 25-63-14; e-mail tolubay@infotel.kg; f. 1996; cap. 26m., res 1.5m., dep. 69.0m. (Dec. 2002); Pres. Jenishbek S. Baiguttiyev; 1 br.

Kairat Bank: 720033 Bishkek, Frunze 390; tel. (312) 21-89-32; fax (312) 21-89-55; e-mail kairat@kairatbank.kg; internet www .kairatbank.kg; f. 1999 to replace Maksat Bank (f. 1991); state-owned; scheduled for privatization; cap. 38.1m., total assets 454.4m.; Chair. Mamytova Kastoru Kasymbekovna; 5 brs.

Kazkommertsbank Kyrgyzstan: 720017 Bishkek, Isanova 42; tel. (312) 66-46-46; fax (312) 66-07-04; e-mail bishkek@kkb.kz; internet kg.kkb.kz; f. 1991, changed name as above in 2002; cap. 25.6m., dep. 101.2m. (Dec. 2001); Chair. Kanat Mamakeyev; 6 brs.

OJSC Kyrgyzpromstroibank: 720040 Bishkek, pr. Chui 168; tel. (312) 61-07-43; fax (312) 21-84-45; e-mail kirgpasb@transfer.kz; f. 1991; cap. 100m. (Jan. 2001), dep. 43.3m. (Jan. 2000); Pres. Muratbek O. Mukashev; 26 brs.

Foreign Banks

Demir Kyrgyz International Bank (DKIB): 720001 Bishkek, pr. Chui 245; tel. (312) 61-06-10; fax (312) 61-04-45; e-mail dkib@ demirbank.kg; internet www.demirbank.kg; f. 1997; cap. 54.1m., dep. 524.1m. (Dec. 2002); Chair. Halit Cingillioglu; Gen. Man. Ahmet Kamil Parmaksiz.

Ecobank: 720031 Bishkek, Geologicheskii per. 17; tel. (312) 54-35-82; fax (312) 54-35-80; e-mail office@ecobank; internet www.ecobank .kg; f. 1996 as Bank Rossiiskii Kredit; name changed 1998; joint-stock commercial bank; cap. 78.0m., dep. 181.5m. (Oct. 2003); Chair. Askar A. Abdyvasiyev; Deputy Chair. Galina V. Hohlova, Aleksandr A. Stelkin; 5 brs.

National Bank of Pakistan: 720017 Bishkek, pr. Manas 9; tel. (312) 66-15-60; fax (312) 60-06-01; e-mail npb.bishkek@transfer.kg; internet nbp.com.pk; Gen. Man. Shuja ul-Mulk.

COMMODITY EXCHANGE

Kyrgyzstan Commodity and Raw Materials Exchange: 720001 Bishkek, Belinskaya 40; tel. (312) 22-13-75; fax (312) 22-27-44; f. 1990; Gen. Dir Temir Sariyev.

STOCK EXCHANGE

Kyrgyz Stock Exchange: 720010 Bishkek, Moskovskaya 172; tel. (312) 66-50-59; fax (312) 66-15-95; e-mail kse@kse.kg; internet www .kse.kg; Pres. (vacant); Chair. Chinarbek Otunchiyev.

INSURANCE

Kyrgyzinstrakh: 72001 Bishkek, pr. Chui 219; tel. (312) 21-95-54; fax (312) 61-00-98; e-mail kinstrakh@infotel.kg; internet kyrgyzinstrakh.online.kg; f. 1996 by the Russian joint-stock insurance company Investstrakh, Kyrgyz insurance companies and the Kyrgyz Government to insure foreign investors.

Trade and Industry

GOVERNMENT AGENCIES

National Institute of Standards and Metrology: 720040 Bishkek, Panfilova 197; tel. (312) 22-78-84; fax (312) 66-13-67; e-mail gost@kmc.bishkek.gov.kg; internet www.kmc.bishkek.gov .kg; f. 1927; certification, control and testing of products and services; Dir Batyrbek Davlesov.

State Agency for Geology and Mineral Resources: 720739 Bishkek, pr. Erkindik 2; tel. (312) 66-49-01; fax (312) 66-03-91; e-mail mail@geoagency.bishkek.gov.kg; internet www.kgs.bishkek .gov.kg; Chair. Sheishenaly Murzagaziyev.

State Agency for Power Engineering: 720055 Bishkek, Akhunbayeva 119; e-mail postmaster@gae.bishkek.gov.kg; Dir Emilbek Uzakbayev.

State Agency for Registration of Real Estate Rights: 720040 Bishkek, Orozbekova 44; e-mail gosreg@bishkek.gov.kg; Chair. Keneshbek Karachalov.

State Agency for Science and Intellectual Property: 720021 Bishkek, Moskovskaya 62; tel. (312) 68-08-19; fax (312) 68-17-03;

e-mail kyrgyzpatent@infotel.kg; internet www.kyrgyzpatent.kg; Dir Roman Omorov.

State Commission for Architecture and Construction: 720026 Bishkek, pr. Manasa 28; e-mail mail@gosstroy.bishkek.gov.kg; Chair. Anvar Tursunov.

State Commission for Drugs Control: 720010 Bishkek, Razzakova 63; e-mail gkkn@bishkek.gov.kg; Chair. Kurmanbek Kubatbekov.

State Commission for Standards, Financial Accounts and Auditing: 720040 Bishkek, pr. Chui 106; e-mail scaas@intranet.kg; Chair. Kanatbek Sagynov.

State Committee for Management of State Property: 720002 Bishkek, pr. Erkindik 57; tel. (312) 22-77-06; fax (312) 66-02-36; e-mail spf@intranet.kg; internet spf.gov.kg; f. 1991; responsible for the privatization of state-owned enterprises and deals with bankruptcies; Chair. Ravshan Dzheyenbekov.

State Securities Commission: 720040 Bishkek, pr. Chui 114; tel. (312) 62-44-60; fax (312) 66-26-53; e-mail nsc@nsc.kg; internet www .nsc.kg; Chair. Jurii N. Svistov.

CHAMBER OF COMMERCE

Chamber of Commerce and Industry of the Kyrgyz Republic: 720001 Bishkek, Kievskaya 107; tel. (312) 21-05-65; fax (312) 21-05-75; e-mail cci-kr@totel.kg; f. 1959; supports foreign economic relations and the development of small and medium-sized enterprises; Pres. Boris V. Perfiliyev.

TRADE ASSOCIATION

Kyrgyzvneshtorg Ltd: 720033 Bishkek, Abdymomunova 276; tel. (312) 21-39-78; fax (312) 66-08-36; e-mail kvt@infotel.kg; f. 1992; export-import org.; Gen. Dir K. K. Kaliyev.

UTILITIES

Electricity

JSC National Electric Grid of Kyrgyzstan: 720070 Bishkek, Jibek Jolu 326; tel. (312) 66-10-00; fax (312) 66-06-56; e-mail aoke@ infotel.kg; divided into seven companies in 2001; privatization commenced in 2003; Gen. Dir Bakirgin Saratkaziyev.

Gas

Kyrgyzazmunayzat: 720000 Bishkek, L. Tolstogo 114; tel. (312) 24-53-80; fax (312) 24-53-93; state-owned joint-stock co; f. 1997 through merger; Dir-Gen. Bakirdin Subanbekov.

Kyrgyzgaz: 720661 Bishkek, Gorkogo 22; tel. (312) 53-00-45; fax (312) 43-09-80; state-owned joint-stock co; scheduled for privatization; Dir-Gen. Avtandil Sydykov.

Kyrgyzneftegaz JSC: 715622 Kochkor-Ata, Lenina 44; tel. (312) 66-12-66; fax (312) 52-60-21; internet www.kyrgysneftegaz.narod .ru; state-owned petroleum and natural gas co; scheduled for privatization; Gazprom (Russia) agreed to acquire majority shareholding in 2004; Pres. Kasim Ismanov.

TRADE UNIONS

Kyrgyzstan Federation of Trade Unions: 720032 Bishkek, Chui 207; tel. (312) 21-49-30; fax (312) 21-76-87; Chair. S. Bozbunbayev.

Transport

RAILWAYS

Owing to the country's mountainous terrain, the railway network consists of only one main line (340 km) in northern Kyrgyzstan, which connects the republic, via Kazakhstan, with the railway system of Russia. Osh, Jalal-Abad and four other towns in regions of Kyrgyzstan bordering Uzbekistan are linked to that country by short lengths of railway track. In mid-1998 work began on a US $2,500m. project to construct a railway line connecting eastern Uzbekistan with southern Kyrgyzstan. In June 2001 the Governments of Kyrgyzstan and the People's Republic of China signed a memorandum on the construction of a rail link from Kashgar (China) to Bishkek. In mid-2003 Kyrgyzstan and Kazakhstan announced that a 100-km railway link was to be built between the lake of Issyk-Kul and Almaty, Kazakhstan. Construction work was expected to be completed by 2008.

Kyrgyzian Railways: 720009 Bishkek, L. Tolstogo 83; tel. (312) 25-30-54; fax (312) 25-30-34; f. 1992 following break-up of former Soviet Railways; Pres. I. S. Omurkulov.

ROADS

In 1999 Kyrgyzstan's road network totalled an estimated 18,500 km, including 140 km of motorway; in 1996 there were 3,200 km of main roads and 6,380 km of secondary roads. About 91% of roads were paved. Many of the best road links are with neighbouring countries—mainly with Kazakhstan in the north, with Uzbekistan in the west and with the People's Republic of China in the south-east. In March 2003 it was announced that work had begun on the third and final phase of a project to reconstruct the main Bishkek—Osh highway.

CIVIL AVIATION

There are three international airports at Bishkek (Manas Airport), Osh and Tamchy (in the Issyk-Kul region—inaugurated in August 2003). At early 2001 there were 13 privately owned airlines in Kyrgyzstan.

Asian Star: 720000 Bishkek, Tynystanova 120; tel. (312) 26-34-55; fax (312) 64-04-05; regional charter passenger services; Pres. BORIS ROLNIK.

Kyrgyz Air: 720021 Bishkek, Abdrahmanova 129; tel. (312) 62-21-23; e-mail kyrgyzair@aviareps.co.ru; internet www.kyrgyzair.com; f. 2003; regional charter passenger services.

Kyrgyzstan Airlines (Kyrgyzstan Aba Zholdoru): 720026 Bishkek, Manas Airport; tel. and fax (312) 31-30-84; e-mail office@ kyrgyzstanairlines.kg; internet www.minartravels.com/kyrgyzair; f. 1992; operates scheduled and charter flights to destinations in Azerbaijan, the People's Republic of China, Germany, India, Kazakhstan, Pakistan, Russia and Uzbekistan; scheduled for privatization; Pres. ORUSKUL KUTTUBAYEV.

Tourism

There was little tourism in Kyrgyzstan during the Soviet period. In the first years of independence tourist facilities remained very limited, and foreign visitors tended to be mountaineers. However, the Government hoped that the country's spectacular and largely unspoilt mountain scenery, as well as the great crater lake of Issyk-Kul, might attract foreign tourists and investment. By the late 1990s the number of tourists visiting Kyrgyzstan was increasing, and there were some 69,000 tourist arrivals in 2001, compared with around 59,000 in 1998. The Government's promotion strategy centred on the country's position on the ancient 'Silk Road' trade route, and its potential as a destination for nature tourism and adventure holidays. There were also plans to develop Kyrgyzstan's ski resorts.

State Committee for Tourism, Sport and Youth Policy: 720033 Bishkek, Togolok Moldo 17; tel. (312) 62-24-99; fax (312) 21-28-45; e-mail gktsm@gks.gov.kg; Chair. OKMOTBEK ALMAKUCHUKOV.

LAOS

Introductory Survey

Location, Climate, Language, Religion, Flag, Capital

The Lao People's Democratic Republic is a land-locked country in South-East Asia, bordered by the People's Republic of China to the north, by Viet Nam to the east, by Cambodia to the south, by Thailand to the west and by Myanmar (formerly Burma) to the north-west. The climate is tropical, with a rainy monsoon season lasting from May to September. The temperature in the capital ranges between 23°C and 38°C in the hottest month, April, and between 14°C and 28°C in the coolest month, January. Laos comprises 47 ethnic groups. The official language, Lao or Laotian, is spoken by about two-thirds of the population. French is also spoken, and there are numerous tribal languages, including Meo. The principal religion is Buddhism. There are also some Christians and followers of animist beliefs. The national flag (proportions 2 by 3) has three horizontal stripes, of red, blue (half the total depth) and red, with a white disc in the centre. The capital is Vientiane (Viangchan).

Recent History

Laos was formerly a part of French Indo-China and comprised the three principalities of Luang Prabang, Vientiane and Champasak. These were merged in 1946, when France recognized Sisavang Vong, ruler of Luang Prabang since 1904, as King of Laos. In May 1947 the King promulgated a democratic constitution (although women were not allowed to vote until 1957). The Kingdom of Laos became independent, within the French Union, in July 1949, and full sovereignty was recognized by France in October 1953. The leading royalist politician was Prince Souvanna Phouma, who was Prime Minister in 1951–54, 1956–58, 1960 and in 1962–75. King Sisavang Vong died in October 1959, and was succeeded by his son, Savang Vatthana.

From 1950 the Royal Government was opposed by the Neo Lao Haksat (Lao Patriotic Front—LPF), an insurgent movement formed by a group of former anti-French activists. The LPF's Chairman was Prince Souphanouvong, a half-brother of Prince Souvanna Phouma, but its dominant element was the communist People's Party of Laos (PPL), led by Kaysone Phomvihane. During the 1950s the LPF's armed forces, the Pathet Lao, gradually secured control of the north-east of the country with the assistance of the Vietnamese communists, the Viet Minh, who were engaged in war with the French (until 1954). Several agreements between the Royal Government and the LPF, attempting to end the guerrilla war and reunite the country, failed during the 1950s and early 1960s. By 1965 the *de facto* partition of Laos was established, with the LPF refusing to participate in national elections and consolidating its power over the north-eastern provinces.

During the 1960s, as the 'Ho Chi Minh Trail' (the communist supply route to South Viet Nam) ran through Pathet Lao-controlled areas, Laos remained closely involved with the war between communist forces and anti-communist troops (supported by the USA) in Viet Nam. In 1973 the Viet Nam peace negotiations included provisions for a cease-fire in Laos. A new Government was formed in April 1974 under Prince Souvanna Phouma, with royalist, neutralist and LPF participation; Prince Souphanouvong was appointed Chairman of the Joint National Political Council. However, the LPF increased its power and eventually gained effective control of the country. This was confirmed by election victories in October and November 1975. In November King Savang Vatthana abdicated, and Prince Souvanna Phouma resigned.

In December 1975 the National Congress of People's Representatives (264 delegates elected by local authorities) abolished the monarchy and elected a 45-member legislative body, the Supreme People's Council (now the Supreme People's Assembly). Souphanouvong was appointed President of the renamed Lao People's Democratic Republic and President of the Supreme People's Council. Kaysone Phomvihane, who had become Secretary-General of the Phak Pasason Pativat Lao (Lao People's Revolutionary Party—LPRP, a successor to the PPL), was appointed Prime Minister. The former King, Savang Vatthana, was designated Supreme Counsellor to the President, but he refused to co-operate with the new regime and was arrested

in March 1977. (He was subsequently stated to have died in a 're-education camp'.) The LPF was replaced in February 1979 by the Lao Front for National Construction (LFNC), under the leadership of the LPRP.

In October 1986 the ailing Souphanouvong announced his resignation from his duties as President of the Republic (while retaining the title) and of the Supreme People's Assembly. Phoumi Vongvichit, formerly a Vice-Chairman in the Council of Ministers, became acting President of the Republic, while Sisomphon Lovansai, a Vice-President of the Supreme People's Assembly and a member of the LPRP Politburo, became acting President of the Assembly. In November Kaysone Phomvihane was re-elected Secretary-General of the LPRP. In September 1987 it was announced that Phoumi Vongvichit had also replaced Souphanouvong as Chairman of the LFNC.

In June 1988 elections (the first since the formation of the Lao People's Democratic Republic) took place to determine the members of 113 district-level People's Councils. The LFNC approved 4,462 candidates to contest 2,410 seats. Provincial prefectural elections took place in November, when 898 candidates contested 651 seats. At a general election in March 1989, 121 candidates contested 79 seats in the enlarged Supreme People's Assembly. At its inaugural session in May, Nouhak Phoumsavanh (a Vice-Chairman of the Council of Ministers) was elected President of the Assembly.

Armed opposition to the Government persisted during the 1980s, particularly among hill tribes. In October 1982 Gen. Phoumi Nosavan, a 'conservative' who had been living in exile since 1965, formed the anti-communist Royal Lao Democratic Government, led by former Laotian military officers. However, many prominent exiles and resistance fighters in the United Front for the National Liberation of the Lao People (UFNLLP—formed in September 1980, and reportedly led by Gen. Phoumi since mid-1981) dissociated themselves from the Royal Government, which had established itself in southern Laos. In October 1988 the Government announced the capture of the Chief of Staff of the UFNLLP.

In December 1989 the right-wing United Lao National Liberation Front (ULNLF) proclaimed the 'Revolutionary Provisional Government' of Laos. The self-styled Government, which was headed by Outhong Souvannavong (the former President of the Royal Council of King Savang Vatthana), claimed to have used military force to 'liberate' one-third of Laotian territory. Although there were reports of attacks by insurgent guerrillas in northern Laos at this time, it was widely assumed that the ULNLF's claims were exaggerated and that its proclamation was an attempt to elicit popular support. Responsibility for defence was reportedly allocated to Gen. Vang Pao, a leader of the Hmong tribe who in the 1970s had been a commander of the Royalist army (and who had lived in exile in the USA since 1975); Somphorn Wang (also formerly a prominent Royalist) was described as secretary of state in the 'Revolutionary Provisional Government'. In late 1992 Gen. Vang Pao reportedly travelled to Singapore to direct an unsuccessful military operation from Thailand. In October Gen. Vang Pao's brother, Vang Fung, and another Hmong rebel, Moua Yee Julan (who were allegedly preparing an incursion into Laos under Gen. Vang Pao's command), were arrested in Thailand. In September 1993 Thai troops launched an offensive against Gen. Vang Pao's forces, expelling 320 rebels from Thai territory.

In June 1990 a draft constitution, enshrining free-market principles, was published in the LPRP newspaper, *Pasason*. Later in the same month the Supreme People's Assembly approved legislation that included provision for the ownership of property, for inheritance rights and contractual obligations. In October three former government officials were arrested in connection with what were termed 'activities aimed at overthrowing the regime'. It was reported in Thailand that they had formed part of a 'Social Democrat Group', which was actively seeking the introduction of multi-party democracy. In November 1992 all three were sentenced to 14 years' imprisonment. In March 1991, at the Fifth Congress of the LPRP, Souphanouvong retired from all his party posts. Phoumi Vongvichit and

Sisomphon Lovansai also retired, and the three were appointed to a newly created advisory board to the LPRP Central Committee. Kaysone Phomvihane's title was altered from General Secretary to President of the LPRP, and his power was slightly enhanced following the abolition of the party Secretariat. A new Politburo and (younger) Party Central Committee were elected. Gen. Sisavat Keobounphan, the military Chief of the General Staff, was not re-elected to the Politburo. The leadership pledged a continuance of free-market economic reforms, but denied the need for political pluralism. However, the national motto ('peace, independence, unity, socialism') was changed to 'peace, independence, democracy, unity, prosperity'.

On 14 August 1991 the Supreme People's Assembly adopted a new constitution, which provided for a National Assembly, confirmed the leading role of the LPRP, enshrined the right to private ownership, and endowed the presidency with executive powers; new electoral legislation was also promulgated. Kaysone Phomvihane was appointed President of Laos. Gen. Khamtay Siphandone, a Vice-Chairman of the Council of Ministers, Minister of National Defence and Supreme Commander of the Lao People's Army, replaced Kaysone Phomvihane as Chairman of the Council of Ministers, restyled Prime Minister.

Kaysone Phomvihane died in November 1992. He was replaced as President of the LPRP by Gen. Khamtay Siphandone, and on 25 November a specially convened meeting of the Supreme People's Assembly elected Nouhak Phoumsavanh as President of State. Elections to the new National Assembly took place on 20 December; 99.33% of eligible voters participated in the election, in which 154 LFNC-approved candidates contested 85 seats. On 22 February 1993 the new National Assembly re-elected Nouhak Phoumsavanh as President, confirmed Khamtay Siphandone as Prime Minister, and implemented the most extensive reorganization of the Council of Ministers since the LPRP's accession to power in 1975. Phoumi Vongvichit died in January 1994, and Souphanouvong in January 1995.

Although the 20th anniversary of the beginning of communist rule was celebrated in 1995, the Laotian Government was gradually attempting to replace communist ideology with Lao nationalism, as Laos developed as a market economy with increasing foreign participation. In July senior Buddhist monks were assembled in Vientiane (as Buddhism was deemed central to Laotian cultural identity) and were encouraged by the Government to lead a 'cultural renaissance'. Meanwhile, the Government urged the security forces to suppress social problems, particularly corruption and prostitution, perceived as arising from increasing external influences.

The results of the elections at the LPRP congress at the end of March 1996 consolidated the country's apparent progress towards a form of military-dominated authoritarian government. The armed forces gained a majority of seats on the new nine-member Politburo; Khamtay Siphandone was elected as its President (replacing Nouhak Phoumsavanh, who retired from this post), and the Minister of National Defence and Commander-in-Chief of the armed forces, Lt-Gen. Choummali Saignason, was promoted to third position, after the Chairman of the National Assembly, Lt-Gen. Saman Vignaket. The most significant development was the failure of Khamphoui Keoboualapha, a Deputy Prime Minister responsible for many of Laos's reforms, to be re-elected either to the Politburo or to the Central Committee. Lts-Gen. Choummali Saignason and Saman Vignaket were widely reported to be opposed to rapid economic and political reform.

At the opening session of the National Assembly in April 1996 Nouhak Phoumsavanh was, despite his retirement from the Politburo, confirmed as Head of State until the end of his term of office in February 1998. Sisavat Keobounphan (who had been restored to the Politburo at the previous month's elections) was elected to the new office of Vice-President, in order to relieve Nouhak Phoumsavanh of a number of presidential duties. Boungnang Volachit was approved by the National Assembly as a Deputy Prime Minister, although, contrary to expectation, Khamphoui Keoboualapha also retained his posts as Deputy Prime Minister and Chairman of the State Committee for Planning and Co-operation. However, it was expected that the latter's influence would be diminished by his exclusion from the Politburo and also by the establishment of a new State Planning Committee, which was to assume some of the responsibilities hitherto exercised by Khamphoui's Committee.

Elections to the National Assembly took place on 21 December 1997, at which 159 LFNC-approved candidates, including 41 members of the outgoing legislature, contested 99 seats. The three members of the LPRP Politburo and 10 Central Committee members who stood for election were all successful; one of the four 'independent' candidates without affiliation to the LPRP was elected. The level of participation by voters was officially registered to have been 99.37%. The first session of the new National Assembly was held on 23–26 February 1998, during which the Assembly elected Gen. Khamtay to succeed Phoumsavanh as President of State. The Assembly also endorsed the appointment of Sisavat Keobounphan as Prime Minister and of Oudom Khattigna in his place as Vice-President, re-elected Saman Vignaket as President of the National Assembly, and approved a redistribution of ministerial posts.

As part of another reorganization of the Council of Ministers in March 2001, Oudom was replaced as Vice-President by Lt-Gen. Choummali Saignason, who had relinquished his bid for the premiership owing to ill health. Prime Minister Sisavat Keobounphan became another scapegoat of the Asian financial crisis, when he was forced to resign after only three years in office, in order to take responsibility for the mismanagement of the economy. His successor, the former Deputy Prime Minister and Minister of Finance, Boungnang Volachit, provided a civilian balance to the entirely military executive branch. The appointment of Thongloun Sisolit to the post of Deputy Prime Minister further enhanced the greater civilian representation on the Council of Ministers.

From the mid-1990s uprisings against the Government became more frequent. In July 1995 an army unit based near Luang Prabang mutinied after its commander, a Hmong general, was passed over for promotion. Five members of the armed forces died in the rebellion, which was believed to be symptomatic of the resentment felt by hill tribes over the political and military dominance of the lowland Lao. About 2,000 troops were dispatched to Luang Prabang to restore order. In November several people were killed in an armed assault on a bus near Luang Prabang. The attack was attributed to disaffected Hmong tribesmen who had pledged to disrupt that year's 20th anniversary celebrations of the beginning of communist rule. In October a shipment of explosives, allegedly destined for Hmong insurgents, had been intercepted on the Mekong River. Several incidents in the Luang Prabang region during 1996 were ascribed to Hmong rebels. Meanwhile, fund-raising by the Hmong community in the USA was reportedly a cause for concern within the Laotian Government.

In October 1999 an anti-Government demonstration by students and teachers was held in Vientiane. The protest, which constituted an extremely rare overt demonstration of public dissatisfaction, was reportedly swiftly dispersed by police. The Government subsequently refuted claims that about 50 people who were involved or suspected to have been involved in the protest had been arrested, and, furthermore, denied that the demonstration had taken place; in late March 2000, however, it was reported that the whereabouts of one professor and at least five students arrested during the protest remained unknown.

Civil unrest intensified throughout 2000, with a spate of bomb attacks. The first occurred in a restaurant in March, immediately drawing international attention to the event, as several tourists were injured in the blast. Two further attacks took place in Vientiane in May, coinciding with the separate visits of the Thai Prime Minister, Chuan Leekpai, and his Minister of Foreign Affairs, Surin Pitsuwan. Two more strikes followed within a week of each other, bringing the total to five explosions within three months, more than 20 people having been injured and at least two killed. Under pressure, the Government, blaming the campaign on Hmong insurgents, claimed to have arrested two men (one Lao and one Hmong) carrying explosive devices in mid-June. Despite the arrests, the bombing operation continued unabated. A bomb was defused near the Vietnamese embassy in Vientiane at the end of July, lending credence to the suspicion that the action was part of an internal power struggle between pro-Chinese and pro-Vietnamese governmental factions. In total, at least nine bombs exploded between March 2000 and January 2001, with the penultimate detonation occurring on the eve of the meeting of the European Union and Association of South East Asian Nations (EU-ASEAN summit) in December 2000.

Although no group admitted responsibility for the bombings, a pre-dawn raid in July 2000 on immigration and customs offices in Vang Tao, opposite the Chong Mek checkpoint, indicated the involvement of royalist rebels. The Government claimed that the attack was merely a robbery, but during the incursion the former royal flag was raised over the immigration office. In mid-

November 2000 about 200 workers and students were reported to have staged a demonstration in the southern province of Champasak, calling for democracy. The protest was swiftly quelled, with 15 people being arrested. The timing of the demonstration, however, exacerbated the increasing sense of instability, as less than two weeks previously, Helen Clark, the Prime Minister of New Zealand, had confirmed that her Government had granted political asylum to Khamsay Souphanouvong, a minister attached to the Prime Minister's office and son of the first President of the Lao People's Democratic Republic.

In December 2000 Kerry and Kay Danes, an Australian couple, were arrested on suspicion of involvement in the theft of over US $6m. worth of sapphires. Following the conclusion of an investigation into the case in April 2001, a Laotian court finally convicted the couple of embezzlement, tax evasion and destruction of evidence in June. They were sentenced to prison terms of seven years each. However, the couple were provisionally released in October 2001, having spent 10 months in custody. Following protracted diplomatic negotiations, and in large part due to Laos's strong ties with Australia, the pair received a formal presidential pardon in November.

In October 2001 five European activists, including Olivier Dupuis, a Belgian member of the European Parliament, were arrested for handing out pro-democracy leaflets at a peaceful protest in Vientiane. The protest was held to commemorate the second anniversary of the disappearance of five students who had participated in the demonstration of October 1999. In November 2001, following expressions of concern at the conditions the detainees were being forced to endure, Romani Prodi, President of the European Commission, warned the Laotian authorities that the continued detention of the activists would threaten diplomatic relations with the EU. In the same month, following a swift trial, the prisoners were convicted of attempting to spread unrest and ordered to be deported. They were also fined and given two-year suspended prison terms.

On 24 February 2002 elections took place from among 166 LFNC-approved candidates to the 109 seats available in the National Assembly. Only one of the elected members was not affiliated to the LPRP, ensuring that the ruling party secured a comprehensive victory. In April, at the opening session of the National Assembly, the existing Cabinet was almost wholly re-elected. The former Minister of the Interior, Maj.-Gen. Asang Laoli, became Deputy Prime Minister and Maj.-Gen. Soudchai Thammasith subsequently assumed the interior portfolio. In January 2003 a cabinet reorganization was announced in an apparent attempt to strengthen the national economy. The former Governor of the Central Bank, Chansy Phosikham, was appointed Minister of Finance, Onneua Phommachanh became Minister of Industry and Handicrafts and Soulivong Daravong was placed in charge of the Ministry of Commerce and Tourism.

In September 2002 a bomb exploded at the Si Muang temple in Vientiane, injuring two children; it was unclear whether the attack was linked to the bombings that had occurred in 2000. In January 2003, for the first time, national celebrations were held to commemorate the anniversary of the birth of King Fa Ngoum, accredited with founding the Kingdom of Lane Xang in 1353; a statue was erected and a public holiday declared. In the following month a group of armed men ambushed a bus near the town of Vang Vieng; the attack resulted in the deaths of 13 people, including three foreign nationals, two of whom were tourists. Several arrests were later made in connection with the ambush, which was thought to have been carried out by bandits rather than terrorists. It was feared that the incident might discourage tourists from visiting the country. Such fears were intensified in April by a further attack on a bus travelling between Luang Prabang and Vientiane; at least 12 people died as a result of the incident, which was thought to have been perpetrated by Hmong rebels. In August 2003 an attack on a bus in the north of the country killed five people. In October three bombs exploded in Vientiane. A previously unknown group, the Free Democratic People's Government of Laos (FDPGL), claimed responsibility for the bombings, as well as for the spate of bomb attacks that had occurred in the capital since 2000. It was believed that the group consisted of disaffected former members of the armed forces. However, a German-based organization, the Committee for Independence and Democracy in Laos, later claimed responsibility for all the bombings, including two further attacks that occurred in early 2004, one in Savannakhet and one in Vientiane.

In June 2003 it was reported that two European journalists, together with their Lao-US interpreter, had been arrested owing to their suspected involvement in the murder of a Lao national and for reporting from the country in contravention of the terms of their tourist visas. The journalists had allegedly been researching the Hmong insurgency in the country, which they had found to be almost exhausted and desperate for assistance. Following a summary trial, the three were sentenced to 15-year prison terms. Three Hmong defendants were given 20-year prison sentences. However, following intense diplomatic pressure from their respective Governments, the three foreign nationals were released in the following month. In October Politburo member Bousone Boupavanh was appointed fourth Deputy Prime Minister, with responsibility for home affairs. His appointment was believed to be, in part, a governmental response to the deteriorating security situation in the country.

From 1975 Laos was dependent on Vietnamese economic and military assistance, permitting the stationing of Vietnamese troops (estimated in 1987 to number between 30,000 and 50,000) on its territory. In 1977 a 25-year treaty of friendship between the two countries was signed, and Laos supported the Vietnamese-led overthrow of the Khmer Rouge regime in Kampuchea (Cambodia) in January 1979. Following the outbreak of hostilities between Viet Nam and the People's Republic of China in that year, Laos allied itself with the former. Viet Nam withdrew its military presence from Laos during 1988. The two countries signed a protocol governing military co-operation in March 1994. In July 2001 Prime Minister Boungnang Volachit visited Viet Nam on his first overseas trip since assuming office in March. In May 2002 President Gen. Khamtai Siphandone paid an official friendship visit to Viet Nam, which was reciprocated in October by the Chairman of the Vietnamese National Assembly, Nguyen Van An. The visits affirmed the strength of ties between the two countries.

In February 1993 Laos, Thailand, Viet Nam and Cambodia signed a joint communiqué providing for the resumption of co-operation in the development of the Mekong River. In April 1995 in Chiang Rai, Thailand, representatives of the four countries signed an agreement on the joint exploitation and development of the lower Mekong. The accord provided for the establishment of the Mekong River Commission (see p. 361) as a successor to the Committee for Co-ordination of Investigations of the Lower Mekong Basin.

In July 1992 Laos strengthened ties with members of the Association of South East Asian Nations (ASEAN, see p. 154) by signing the ASEAN Treaty of Amity and Co-operation, which provided for wider regional co-operation and was regarded as a preliminary step to full membership of the Association. Laos attended ASEAN meetings with observer status from this time, and applied for membership of the organization in March 1996. The country was formally admitted as a full member at the organization's meeting of ministers responsible for foreign affairs in July 1997.

Relations with the People's Republic of China improved in December 1986, when a Chinese delegation, led by the Deputy Minister of Foreign Affairs, made the first official Chinese visit to Laos since 1978. In December 1987, after an assurance from the People's Republic of China that support would be withdrawn from Laotian resistance groups operating from within China, the two countries agreed to restore full diplomatic relations and to encourage bilateral trade. Relations between the LPRP and the Chinese Communist Party were fully restored in August 1989. In October 1991 the Laotian and Chinese Prime Ministers signed a border treaty, which established a framework for meetings of a Laotian-Chinese joint border committee. In January 1992 the committee adopted a resolution providing for the demarcation of the common border, and in June an agreement on the delineation of boundaries was signed. In November 1994 Laos and China signed a reciprocal agreement on the transport of passengers and goods on each other's sections of the Mekong River. In February 1996 Laos and China opened a section of their border to highway traffic. In October 1997 Chinese Vice-Premier Wu Bangguo made a three-day visit to Laos, and in early 1999 Prime Minister Sisavat Keobounphan made an eight-day official visit to China. The first visit ever made by a Chinese head of state to Laos was by President Jiang Zemin in November 2000.

Relations with Thailand from 1975 were characterized by mutual suspicion. Thailand intermittently closed its border to Laotian imports and exports, causing considerable hardship. Disputed sovereignty claims in border areas were a cause of friction, and led to clashes between Laotian and Thai troops in 1984. Further hostilities began in December 1987, resulting in hundreds of casualties. In February 1988 the two sides agreed to declare a cease-fire, to withdraw their troops from the combat area, and to attempt to negotiate a peaceful solution. In March 1991 (following the recent military coup in Thailand) representatives of the two countries signed an agreement providing for the immediate withdrawal of troops from disputed areas. The Thai Government also undertook to suppress the activities of Laotian insurgents operating from Thai territory. In December Thailand and Laos signed a border co-operation agreement.

In June 1992 the Thai Crown Prince, Maha Vajiralongkorn, visited Vientiane for the first time. On the following day, however, about 300 guerrillas from a Thai-based rebel group, the Free Democratic Lao National Salvation Force, attacked three Laotian government posts, killing two people and causing significant damage. In the same month Laos refuted allegations made by a senior Thai military officer that a Laotian government unit was receiving training in chemical warfare from Cuban and Vietnamese experts, and also dismissed previous accusations by Laotian resistance fighters and Western aid agencies of its use of chemical warfare to suppress the activities of rebel groups. Bilateral relations improved in July, when the Thai authorities announced the arrest of 11 Laotian citizens accused of planning subversive activities against the Government in Vientiane. The first bridge (over the Mekong River) linking Laos and Thailand was opened in April 1994. In September 1996 the countries' Joint Co-operation Commission agreed to establish a boundary commission, in an effort to resolve demarcation problems. Despite various diplomatic moves to stimulate further co-operation between the two countries, such as the signing of an extradition treaty in January 2001, the relationship was strained by the July 2000 incursion launched from Thai territory by suspected royalist rebels. The situation deteriorated further after Laotian troops occupied two islands in the Mekong River, evicting 65 Thai farming families. Laos claimed that under a 1926 treaty it had sovereignty over all the islands in the Mekong, while Thailand merely requested the withdrawal of the troops. Nevertheless, there were plans for the building of another Mekong Friendship Bridge. Construction was scheduled to begin in 2004 and to be completed in 2007. In April 2001 the Thai Minister of Foreign Affairs, Surakiart Sathirathai, visited Laos, affirming the beginning of a new era of friendly Lao-Thai relations based on shared cultural values. In June Thai Prime Minister Thaksin Shinawatra arrived in Vientiane on a two-day official visit intended further to consolidate co-operative ties between the two countries. In late 2003, following a meeting of the Joint Co-operation Commission, the two countries pledged to resolve all outstanding border demarcation issues, as well as agreeing to work together on a variety of social development initiatives.

During the 1970s and 1980s thousands of Laotian refugees fled to Thailand to escape from civil war and food shortages. In January 1989 an estimated 90,000 Laotian refugees remained in border camps in Thailand. The office of the UN High Commissioner for Refugees (UNHCR) began a programme of voluntary repatriation in 1980. By late 1990 fewer than 6,000 refugees had been repatriated under UNHCR supervision, while some 15,000 had returned independently, and others had been resettled abroad. In June 1991 UNHCR, Laos and Thailand signed an agreement guaranteeing the repatriation or resettlement in a third country of the remaining 60,000 Laotian refugees in Thailand by the end of 1994. In July 1994, however, UNHCR, Laos and Thailand revised their agreement to the effect that the repatriation programme would be completed by early 1995, and this deadline was subsequently revised on several occasions. In December 1996, according to UNHCR figures, 3,293 Laotian refugees remained in Thailand. In December 1997 UNHCR announced that a final review of the status of the last remaining refugees at Ban Napho camp in Thailand would be completed by January 1998, whereupon they would be repatriated or resettled in a third country. Among the camp's 1,344 refugees were reportedly 964 Hmong, most of whom were unwilling to return to Laos. In December 2003 it was reported that the USA had agreed to accept around 14,000 Laotian Hmong refugees living in refugee camps in Thailand.

Laos's uneasy political relationship with Thailand, in conjunction with Thailand's economic superiority in the region, is widely regarded as having prompted the Laotian Government during the 1990s to forge closer links with Myanmar and, more recently, with Cambodia. In February 1992 Khamtay Siphandone was the first foreign head of government to visit Myanmar since the military coup in that country in 1988, and in June 1994

Senior Gen. Than Shwe visited Laos, his first foreign visit as Myanmar's Head of State. Bilateral contacts continued on a frequent basis. Laos signed a treaty of friendship and assistance with Cambodia in December 1995, further to which Joint Co-operation Committees were established. In November 2001 Prince Norodom Ranariddh headed a Cambodian delegation on an official goodwill visit to Laos, confirming the continued strength of bilateral ties.

From 1989 the Laotian Government sought to improve relations with non-communist countries, in order to reduce its (especially economic) dependence on the USSR and Viet Nam. Following a visit to Japan in that year by Kaysone Phomvihane (his first official visit to a non-communist country), the Japanese Government agreed to increase grant aid to Laos. In December 1995 Japan announced that it would resume the provision of official loans to Laos in 1996. In January 2000 the Japanese Prime Minister, Keizo Obuchi, made an official visit to Laos, and in August 2000 a bridge over the Mekong, built with a 5,460m.-yen grant from the Japanese Government, was officially opened in Paksé. In mid-2001 Prince Akishino of Japan made a 10-day unofficial visit to Laos and, in September, Japan agreed a further loan to fund the construction of the second Mekong Friendship Bridge.

In November 2002 the Prime Minister of India, Atal Bihari Vajpayee, paid the first visit to Laos by an Indian head of government in more than 45 years. During his stay the two countries signed agreements on co-operation in defence issues and control of drug-trafficking. The Indian Government also agreed to provide US $10m. of credit to Laos at low interest rates.

During the Viet Nam war US aircraft completed almost 600,000 bombing missions over Laos, leaving large amounts of undetonated explosives, which were estimated to cause 50–100 fatalities per year in the 1990s. The National Unexploded Ordnance Awareness and Clearance Programme was established in Laos in May 1995, with support from the UN.

In 1985 Laos agreed to co-operate with the USA in recovering the remains of US soldiers 'missing in action' in Laos since the war in Viet Nam. In August 1987 a US delegation visited Vientiane to discuss 'humanitarian co-operation' by Laos in tracing missing US soldiers, and agreed to provide Laos with aid. The first remains of US soldiers were passed to the US Government in February 1988. Laos postponed further searching for a short period in 1989, when the USA, alleging that Laos was failing to assist in the suppression of drugs-trafficking, suspended aid and preferential treatment. The USA restored aid to Laos in early 1990, following a visit to Vientiane by the Chairman of the US House of Representatives Committee on Narcotics and Drug Control. (In March 1992 Laos, Myanmar and Thailand signed a draft co-operation treaty on narcotics suppression.) In November 1991, in response to continued Laotian co-operation and the implementation of limited political and economic reforms, the US Government announced that diplomatic relations with Laos were to be upgraded to ambassadorial level. Further progress was achieved in tracing the remains of US soldiers during 1992, and in January 1993 a joint recovery operation was undertaken. In the same month, following 17 months of hearings, a special US Senate panel concluded that (despite considerable public speculation to the contrary) there was 'no compelling evidence' of the survival of US servicemen in the region. During 1993–98 Laos and the USA co-operated in further operations to locate the remains of US soldiers. In May 1995 the USA announced the ending of a 20-year embargo on aid to Laos. In November 1997 the US Deputy Secretary of State, Strobe Talbott, led the highest-level US delegation to Laos since the mid-1970s. During the visit further US support was pledged for a programme to clear unexploded ordnance from the Viet Nam war, which had been supported by the USA since 1996. In mid-1998 US officials agreed to extend financial and logistical support for the programme until September 1999. Further co-operation between the two nations occurred in March–April 2000, when a joint operation in search of US soldiers' remains was resumed. The search operation continued from 2001.

Government

Under the terms of the 1991 Constitution, executive power is vested in the President of State, while legislative power resides with the National Assembly. The President is elected for five years by the National Assembly. Members of the National Assembly are elected for a period of five years by universal adult suffrage. The Lao People's Revolutionary Party remains the sole legal political party. With the approval of the National Assembly, the President appoints the Prime Minister and members of the Council of Ministers, who conduct the government of the country. The President also appoints provincial governors and mayors of municipalities, who are responsible for local administration.

Defence

In August 2003, according to Western estimates, the strength of the armed forces was 29,100 (Lao People's Army 25,600, navy 600, air force 3,500). Military service is compulsory for a minimum of 18 months. There is a paramilitary self-defence force numbering more than 100,000. In 2003 defence expenditure was budgeted at an estimated 115,000m. kips.

Economic Affairs

In 2002, according to estimates by the World Bank, Laos's gross national income (GNI), measured at average 2000–02 prices, was US $1,709m., equivalent to $310 per head (or $1,610 per head on an international purchasing-power parity basis). During 1990–2002, it was estimated, the population increased by an annual average of 2.5%, while gross domestic product (GDP) per head increased, in real terms, by an average of 3.6% per year. Overall GDP increased, in real terms, at an average annual rate of 6.1% in 1990–2002. According to the Asian Development Bank (ADB), GDP increased by 5.8% in 2001 and by 5.9% in 2002.

Agriculture (including forestry and fishing) contributed an estimated 50.4% of GDP in 2002. An estimated 76.3% of the working population were employed in the sector in 2001. Rice is the staple crop. Other crops include sweet potatoes, maize, cassava and sugar cane; coffee is grown for export. In 2000 forest covered about 55.4% of the country's total land area. Wood products were the third largest export commodity in 2001, accounting for an estimated 23.2% of total export revenue. The cultivation and illicit export of narcotic drugs is believed to be widespread. Despite having been outlawed in 1997, opium production was estimated to total 120 metric tons in 2003. According to the UN Office on Drugs and Crime (formerly the UN Office of Drug Control and Crime Prevention), Laos was the third largest source of illicit opium in the world in that year, behind Afghanistan and Myanmar. However, the Government was achieving some success in its efforts to eliminate opium production; the area under cultivation was steadily decreasing. During 1990–2002, according to the ADB, agricultural GDP increased by an average of 4.5% per year. Compared with the previous year, the rate of growth was estimated at 3.8% in 2001 and at 4.0% in 2002.

Industry (including mining, manufacturing, construction and utilities) contributed an estimated 24.7% of GDP in 2002. The sector employed about 6.3% of the working population in 1990. During 1990–2002, according to the ADB, industrial GDP increased at an average annual rate of 11.0%. Growth in the sector was estimated at 10.1% in 2001 and at 10.3% in 2002.

Mining contributed only an estimated 0.5% of GDP in 2002. Laos has, however, considerable mineral resources: iron ore (the country's principal mineral resource), coal, tin and gypsum are among the minerals that are exploited. Other known mineral deposits include zinc, copper, nickel, potash, lead, limestone and small quantities of gold, silver and precious stones. During 1990–2002, according to the ADB, the GDP of the mining sector increased by an average of 17.4% per year. Growth was estimated at 1.2% in 2001 and at 10.1% in 2002.

Manufacturing contributed an estimated 19.1% of GDP in 2002, although the sector employed less than 1% of the working population in the mid-1980s. It is mainly confined to the processing of raw materials (chiefly sawmilling) and agricultural produce, the production of textiles and garments (a principal export commodity), and the manufacture of handicrafts and basic consumer goods for the domestic market. According to the ADB, manufacturing GDP increased at an average annual rate of 12.1% in 1990–2002; manufacturing GDP increased by 12.1% in 2001 and by 13.0% in 2002.

Electrical energy is principally derived from hydroelectric power. Electricity is exported to Thailand and Viet Nam, and is one of Laos's principal sources of foreign exchange. In 2001 the country's total electricity generation reached an estimated 3,590m. kWh. Laos's total hydroelectric power potential was estimated at 25,000 MW in 2000. In 2002 the Government granted a concession to the Nam Theun 2 Power Company (NTPC), enabling it to assume control of the construction of a US $1,100m. hydroelectric dam—Nam Theun 2. In November 2003 the Electricity Generating Authority of Thailand signed an agreement with the NTPC to buy 995 MW of electricity over 25 years, at an estimated cost of US $5,000m. Nam Theun 2 was scheduled for completion in 2009. Also in 2002, Laos signed an agreement with Cambodia, China, Myanmar, Thailand and Viet Nam concerning the establishment of a regional power distribution system, which would form the basis for a programme of hydropower development in the Mekong region. Laos is totally dependent on imports, mainly from Thailand, for supplies of mineral fuels.

The services sector contributed an estimated 25.0% of GDP in 2002, and engaged 17.2% of the total labour force in 1980. Receipts from tourism increased from US $43.6m. in 1996 to $114m. in 2000, but decreased to $104m. in 2001. Tourist arrivals declined from 737,208 in 2000 to 673,823 in 2001. According to the ADB, the GDP of the services sector increased at an average annual rate of 6.5% in 1990–2002. Annual increases were estimated at 5.7% in 2001 and again at 5.7% in 2002.

In 2001 Laos recorded a visible trade deficit of US $216.8m., and there was a deficit of $82.4m. on the current account of the balance of payments. Remittances from relatives residing overseas are a significant source of income for many Lao. In 2002 Thailand was the principal source of imports, supplying an estimated 58.2% of the total. Viet Nam was also an important source of imports (12.2%) in that year, along with China, Singapore and Japan. The principal destination of exports from Laos in 2002 was Viet Nam, purchasing 25.9% of the total. Other significant purchasers in that year were Thailand (an estimated 19.2%), France (7.5%) and Germany (5.4%). It was estimated that the main exports in 2001 were electricity (32.6% of the total), garments (28.6%), wood products (23.2%) and motorcycles (6.7%). The principal imports in that year were consumer goods (49.4%), investment goods (29.3%), materials for the garments industry (11.8%) and motorcycle parts for assembly (5.3%).

In the financial year ending 30 September 2002 Laos projected an overall budget deficit of 1,133,000m. kips. At the end of 2001 the country's external debt totalled US $2,495m., of which $2,456m. was long-term public debt. In that year the cost of debt-servicing was equivalent to 9.0% of revenue from export of goods and services. Consumer prices increased by an annual average of 37.7% in 1995–2002. According to the ADB, the annual rate of inflation averaged 7.8% in 2001, before increasing to 10.6% in 2002 and to an estimated 14.0% in 2003. The unemployment rate totalled 2.4% in 1995, according to the census conducted in that year.

Laos is a member of the UN Economic and Social Commission for Asia and the Pacific (ESCAP, see p. 31), of the Asian Development Bank (ADB, see p. 151), of the Association of South East Asian Nations (ASEAN, see p. 154), of the Colombo Plan (see p. 359), which promotes economic and social development in Asia and the Pacific, and of the Mekong River Commission (see p. 361).

From 1986 the Government undertook a radical programme of economic liberalization, known as the New Economic Mechanism, with the aim of transforming the hitherto centrally planned economy into a market-orientated system. Various reforms were introduced, including the enactment of a liberal foreign investment law in 1988 and the implementation of a privatization programme. Laos has remained extremely underdeveloped, however, and, as one of the poorest countries in Asia, is heavily reliant on external aid. The regional economic crisis of 1997 resulted in a significant loss of foreign capital for Laos, as Thailand and other countries affected by the crisis had been among the most important investors in the country. Having reached US $159.8m. in 1996, according to the ADB, foreign direct investment subsequently declined to only $33.9m. in 2000, before rising to $83.3m. in 2001. By early 2001 the economy had begun to recover. The Fifth Five-Year Plan (2001–05), announced at the Seventh Congress of the Lao People's Revolutionary Party (LPRP) in March 2001, envisaged an average annual GDP growth rate of between 7.0% and 7.5%. The Plan emphasized the eradication of poverty, the restriction of opium cultivation and integrated rural development through the strengthening of basic political units. Other targets included a reduction in the annual level of inflation to a single-digit rate, the maintenance of a stable exchange rate and the restriction of the budget deficit to the equivalent of 5% of GDP. International donors, however, were disappointed at the Plan's failure to incorporate development of the private sector, while corruption among Lao officials and the lack of skilled personnel to manage the financial sector remained causes for concern. Having declined sharply in value in 1997 and fluctuated thereafter, the national currency suffered another significant depreciation in mid-2002. This weakening of the kip was accompanied by a rise in inflation, which reached a high of 18% in May 2003 (according to the IMF). In 2003 the country's increasing security problems (see Recent History), together with a decrease in the amount of foreign aid to the country, threatened economic stability. In that year, according to the ADB, GDP growth was an estimated 5.5%. In early 2004 it was feared that a regional epidemic of avian influenza would have a negative impact upon economic growth, owing to the enforced destruction of some of the country's poultry stock. None the less, GDP was expected to record strong growth in that year, benefiting from improvements in the global economy which, it was hoped, would lead to increasing inflows of foreign direct investment. However, further reforms remained essential if an environment were to be created in which sustained economic growth might be achieved. The reduction of state involvement in the country's commercial sector and increased access to the resources necessary to reduce the country's high level of poverty remained priorities.

Education

Education, which is officially compulsory for five years between the ages of six and 15, was greatly disrupted by the civil war, causing a high illiteracy rate, but educational facilities have since improved significantly. Lao is the medium of instruction. A comprehensive education system is in force. In 1990 the Government issued a decree permitting the establishment of private schools, in an effort to accommodate the increasing number of students.

Primary education begins at six years of age and lasts for five years. Secondary education, beginning at the age of 11, lasts for six years, comprising two three-year cycles. In 1996 enrolment in secondary education was equivalent to 28% of the relevant age-group (males 34%; females 23%). The total enrolment at primary and secondary schools was equivalent to 72% of the school-age population (males 80%; females 63%). Government expenditure on education for 1997/98 was forecast at 37,400m. kips, representing 6.9% of total projected expenditure.

Public Holidays

2004: 1 January (New Year's Day), 5 January (Anniversary of Birth of King Fa Ngoum), 6 January (Pathet Lao Day), 20 January (Army Day), 8 March (Women's Day), 22 March (People's Party Day), 13–15 April (Lao New Year), 1 May (Labour Day), 1 June (Children's Day), 13 August (Free Laos Day), 23 August (Liberation Day), 12 October (Liberation from the French Day, Vientiane only), 2 December (Independence Day).

2005: 1 January (New Year's Day), 5 January (Anniversary of Birth of King Fa Ngoum), 6 January (Pathet Lao Day), 20 January (Army Day), 8 March (Women's Day), 22 March (People's Party Day), 13–15 April (Lao New Year), 1 May (Labour Day), 1 June (Children's Day), 13 August (Free Laos Day), 23 August (Liberation Day), 12 October (Liberation from the French Day, Vientiane only), 2 December (Independence Day).

Weights and Measures

The metric system is in force.

Statistical Survey

Source (unless otherwise stated): Service National de la Statistique, Vientiane.

Area and Population

AREA, POPULATION AND DENSITY

Area (sq km)	236,800*
Population (census results)	
1 March 1985.	3,584,803
1 March 1995	
Males	2,265,867
Females.	2,315,391
Total	4,581,258
Population (UN estimates at mid-year)†	
2000	5,279,000
2001	5,403,000
2002	5,529,000
Density (per sq km) at mid-2002	23.3

* 91,400 sq miles.

† Source: UN, *World Population Prospects: The 2002 Revision.*

PROVINCES
(official estimates, mid-1995)

	Area (sq km)	Population	Density (per sq km)
Vientiane (municipality) . . .	3,920	531,800	135.6
Phongsali	16,270	153,400	9.4
Luang Namtha	9,325	115,200	12.4
Oudomxay.	15,370	211,300	13.7
Bokeo	6,196	114,900	18.5
Luang Prabang	16,875	367,200	21.8
Houaphanh	16,500	247,300	15.0
Sayabouri	16,389	293,300	17.9
Xiangkhouang	15,880	201,200	12.7
Vientiane	15,927	286,800	18.0
Bolikhamsai	14,863	164,900	11.1
Khammouane.	16,315	275,400	16.9
Savannakhet	21,774	674,900	31.0
Saravan	10,691	258,300	24.2
Sekong.	7,665	64,200	8.4
Champasak	15,415	503,300	32.7
Attopu	10,320	87,700	8.5
Special region.	7,105	54,200	7.6
Total	**236,800**	**4,605,300**	**19.4**

PRINCIPAL TOWNS
(population at 1995 census)

Viangchan (Vientiane— capital) . . .	160,000	Xam Nua (Sam Neua) . . .	33,500
Savannakhet (Khanthaboury) .	58,500	Luang Prabang . .	25,500
Pakxe (Paksé) . .	47,000	Thakek (Khammouan) . .	22,500

Source: Stefan Helders, *World Gazetteer* (internet www.world-gazetteer.com).

Mid-2001 (UN estimate, incl. suburbs): Vientiane 663,000 (Source: UN, *World Urbanization Prospects: The 2001 Revision*).

BIRTHS AND DEATHS
(UN estimates, annual averages)

	1985–90	1990–95	1995–2000
Birth rate (per 1,000) . . .	44.6	41.3	38.2
Death rate (per 1,000) . . .	18.2	15.8	14.1

Source: UN, *World Population Prospects: The 2002 Revision.*

Birth rate (1999): 38.8 per 1,000.

Death rate (1999): 13.0 per 1,000.

Source: UN, *Statistical Yearbook for Asia and the Pacific.*

Expectation of life (WHO estimates, years at birth): 55.1 (males 54.1; females 56.2) in 2002 (Source: WHO, *World Health Report*).

ECONOMICALLY ACTIVE POPULATION
(ILO estimates, '000 persons at mid-1980)

	Males	Females	Total
Agriculture, etc.	717	675	1,393
Industry	79	51	130
Services	193	123	316
Total labour force	990	849	1,839

Source: ILO, *Economically Active Population Estimates and Projections, 1950–2025.*

Mid-2001 (estimates in '000): Agriculture, etc. 2,059; Total labour force 2,699 (Source: FAO).

Health and Welfare

KEY INDICATORS

Total fertility rate (children per woman, 2002)	4.8
Under-5 mortality rate (per 1,000 live births, 2001) . . .	100
HIV/AIDS (% of persons aged 15–49, 2001)	<0.10
Physicians (per 1,000 head, 1996)	0.24
Hospital beds (per 1,000 head, 1990)	2.57
Health expenditure (2001): US $ per head (PPP) . . .	51
Health expenditure (2001): % of GDP	3.1
Health expenditure (2001): public (% of total)	55.5
Access to adequate water (% of persons, 2000)	90
Access to adequate sanitation (% of persons, 2000) . . .	46
Human Development Index (2001): ranking	135
Human Development Index (2001): value	0.525

For sources and definitions, see explanatory note on p. vi.

Agriculture

PRINCIPAL CROPS
('000 metric tons)

	2000	2001	2002
Rice (paddy)	2,202	2,335	2,417
Maize	117	112	124
Potatoes	33†	35†	35*
Sweet potatoes	118	101	194
Cassava (Manioc)	100	7	83
Sugar cane	297	209	222
Pulses*	14	14	14
Soybeans	5	3	3
Groundnuts (in shell) . . .	13	17	16
Sesame seed	5*	3	4
Vegetables*	671	664	796
Watermelons	n.a.	4	83
Bananas*	37	46	53
Oranges*	29	28	29
Pineapples*	35	35	36
Other fruit (excl. melons)* . . .	93	93	95
Coffee (green)	24	26	32
Tobacco (leaves)	40	30	27

* FAO estimate(s).
† Unofficial figure.
Source: FAO.

LIVESTOCK
('000 head, year ending September)

	2000	2001	2002
Horses*	29	29	30
Cattle	1,100	1,217	1,208
Buffaloes	1,028	1,051	1,089
Pigs	1,425	1,426	1,416
Goats	121	124	128
Chickens	13,095	14,063	15,274
Ducks*	1,630	1,700	1,900

* FAO estimates.
Source: FAO.

LIVESTOCK PRODUCTS
('000 metric tons)

	2000	2001	2002
Beef and veal	16	17	20
Buffalo meat	17	17	17
Pig meat	28	32	32
Poultry meat	12	13	13
Cows' milk*	6	6	6
Hen eggs	10	12	13
Cattle and buffalo hides (fresh)*	4	4	4

* FAO estimates.
Source: FAO.

Forestry

ROUNDWOOD REMOVALS
('000 cubic metres, excl. bark)

	2000	2001	2002
Sawlogs, veneer logs and logs for sleepers	435	438	260
Other industrial wood*	132	132	132
Fuel wood*	5,872	5,885	5,899
Total	6,439	6,455	6,291

* FAO estimates.
Source: FAO.

SAWNWOOD PRODUCTION
('000 cubic metres, incl. railway sleepers)

	2000	2001	2002
Total (all broadleaved)	208	227	182

Source: FAO.

Fishing

(FAO estimates, '000 metric tons, live weight)

	1999	2000	2001
Capture	30.0	29.3	30.0
Cyprinids	4.5	4.4	4.5
Other freshwater fishes . . .	25.5	24.9	25.5
Aquaculture	30.4	42.1	50.0
Common carp	3.9	5.4	6.4
Roho labeo	3.8	5.2	6.2
Mrigal carp	3.8	5.2	6.2
Bighead carp	3.8	5.2	6.2
Catla	3.8	5.2	6.2
Grass carp (White amur) . . .	3.8	5.2	6.2
Silver carp	3.8	5.2	6.2
Nile tilapia	3.8	5.2	6.2
Total catch	60.4	71.3	80.0

Source: FAO, *Yearbook of Fishery Statistics.*

Mining

('000 metric tons, unless otherwise indicated)

	2000	2001	2002*
Coal (all grades)	126.3	103.2	110.0
Gemstones ('000 carats). . . .	189.3	n.a.	200.0
Gypsum	131.5	107.7	130.0
Salt.	1.8	2.3	2.3
Tin (metric tons)†	408	343	350

* Estimated production.
† Figures refer to metal content.

Source: US Geological Survey.

Industry

SELECTED PRODUCTS

	1999	2000	2001*
Beer ('000 hectolitres) . . .	480	508	577
Soft drinks ('000 hectolitres) . .	123	143	142
Cigarettes (million packs) . .	38	41	41
Garments ('000 pieces) . . .	21	24	32
Wood furniture (million kips) .	12,725	12,700	15,240
Plastic products (metric tons) .	3,900	3,850	4,350
Detergent (metric tons) . . .	879	900	700
Agricultural tools ('000) . . .	4	4	4
Nails (metric tons)	691	650	740
Bricks (million)	65	66	87
Electric energy (million kWh) .	2,436	3,678	3,590
Tobacco (metric tons) . . .	757	1,277	358
Plywood ('000 sheets) . . .	2,086	2,150	2,200

* Estimates.

Source: IMF, *Lao People's Democratic Republic: Selected Issues and Statistical Appendix* (September 2002).

Finance

CURRENCY AND EXCHANGE RATES

Monetary Units
  100 at (cents) = 1 new kip.

Sterling, Dollar and Euro Equivalents (29 August 2003)
  £1 sterling = 16,795.4 new kips;
  US $1 = 10,630.0 new kips;
  €1 = 11,615.4 new kips;
  100,000 new kips = £5.954 = $9.407 = €8.609.

Average Exchange Rate (new kips per US $)
  2000   7,887.64
  2001   8,954.58
  2002   10,056.33

Note: In September 1995 a policy of 'floating' exchange rates was adopted, with commercial banks permitted to set their rates.

GENERAL BUDGET

('000 million new kips, year ending 30 September)*

Revenue†	1999/2000	2000/01‡	2001/02§
Tax revenue	1,367	1,629	2,043
Profits tax	187	205	362
Income tax	117	153	190
Turnover tax	290	318	452
Taxes on foreign trade . .	176	236	291
Import duties	135	179	229
Export duties	41	57	62
Excise tax	226	371	362
Timber royalties	273	182	165
Hydro royalties	22	51	55
Other revenue	324	372	438
Payment for depreciation or dividend transfers . . .	42	67	89
Leasing income	15	39	57
Administrative fees . . .	17	41	62
Overflight	123	114	153
Interest or amortization . .	79	76	42
Total	**1,691**	**2,000**	**2,481**

Expenditure	1999/2000‡	2000/01‡	2001/02§
Current expenditure.	1,050	1,229	1,449
Wages and salaries . . .	335	410	517
Transfers	130	243	292
Materials and supplies . .	174	330	370
Interest	103	134	145
Timber royalty-financed expenditure	242	—	—
Capital expenditure and net lending	1,704	1,911	2,165
Domestically-financed. . .	481	872	1,017
Foreign-financed	1,302	1,200	1,256
Loan-funded projects . .	827	724	826
Grant-funded projects . .	475	476	430
Onlending (net)	−78	−160	−108
Total (incl. others)	**2,754**	**3,140**	**3,614**

* Since 1992 there has been a unified budget covering the operations of the central Government, provincial administrations and state enterprises.
† Excluding grants received ('000 million new kips): 475 in 1999/2000; 476 in 2000/01‡; 549 in 2001/02§.
‡ Estimates.
§ Budget forecasts.

Source: IMF, *Lao People's Democratic Republic: Selected Issues and Statistical Appendix* (September 2002).

INTERNATIONAL RESERVES

(US $ million at 31 December)

	2000	2001	2002
Gold*	0.59	2.53	2.53
IMF special drawing rights. . .	0.10	3.42	6.07
Foreign exchange.	138.87	127.51	185.51
Total	**139.56**	**133.46**	**194.14**

* National valuation.

Source: IMF, *International Financial Statistics*.

MONEY SUPPLY

(million new kips at 31 December)

	2000	2001	2002
Currency outside banks	67,830	113,080	228,810
Demand deposits at commercial banks	272,230	256,880	358,150
Total (incl. others)	**344,351**	**371,840**	**587,000**

Source: IMF, *International Financial Statistics*.

COST OF LIVING

(Consumer Price Index for Vientiane; base: 1995 = 100)

	2000	2001	2002
All items	786.4	847.8	937.9

Source: IMF, *International Financial Statistics*.

NATIONAL ACCOUNTS

Expenditure on the Gross Domestic Product
(million new kips at current prices)

	1989	1990	1991
Government final consumption expenditure	34,929	61,754	69,499
Private final consumption expenditure	414,639	558,437	647,826
Increase in stocks . . . . } Gross fixed capital formation. . }	55,560	75,572	91,435
Total domestic expenditure .	505,128	695,763	808,760
Exports of goods and services .	49,421	69,411	73,359
Less Imports of goods and services	128,613	150,154	156,550
GDP in purchasers' values .	**425,936**	**615,020**	**725,569**
GDP at constant 1987 prices .	**213,769**	**228,105**	**237,098**

Source: World Bank, *Historically Planned Economies: A Guide to the Data.*

Gross Domestic Product by Economic Activity
(million new kips at current prices)

	2000	2001	2002
Agriculture, hunting, forestry and fishing	7,127,372	7,974,629	9,173,517
Mining and quarrying	67,033	73,150	89,114
Manufacturing	2,305,848	2,786,838	3,483,192
Electricity, gas and water	423,331	450,414	536,315
Construction	309,341	376,985	389,893
Wholesale and retail trade, restaurants and hotels	1,283,970	1,506,869	1,792,015
Transport, storage and communications	794,024	929,724	1,114,964
Finance, insurance, real estate and business services	105,170	127,836	75,979
Public administration	392,690	517,137	633,063
Other services	756,786	820,391	930,824
GDP at factor cost	13,565,564	15,563,971	18,218,874
Indirect taxes *less* subsidies	106,772	140,899	171,501
GDP in purchasers' values	13,672,336	15,704,870	18,390,375

Source: Asian Development Bank, *Key Indicators of Developing Asian and Pacific Countries.*

BALANCE OF PAYMENTS
(US $ million)

	1999	2000	2001
Exports of goods f.o.b.	338.2	330.3	311.1
Imports of goods f.o.b.	−527.7	−535.3	−527.9
Trade balance	−189.5	−205.0	−216.8
Exports of services	130.0	175.7	166.1
Imports of services	−51.8	−43.1	−31.6
Balance on goods and services	−111.3	−72.4	−82.3
Other income received	10.5	7.3	5.8
Other income paid	−49.9	−59.7	−39.6
Balance on goods, services and income	−150.7	−124.7	−116.1
Current transfers received	80.2	116.3	33.7
Current transfers paid	−50.6	—	—
Current balance	−121.1	−8.5	−82.4
Other investment assets	−43.2	18.8	25.2
Other investment liabilities	−3.7	73.3	86.6
Net errors and omissions	−165.1	−74.2	−57.2
Overall balance	−333.1	43.4	−3.9

Source: IMF, *International Financial Statistics.*

External Trade

PRINCIPAL COMMODITIES
(US $ million)

Imports c.i.f.	1999	2000	2001*
Investment goods	184.0	161.8	166.4
Machinery and equipment	21.0	16.2	—
Vehicles†	35.8	23.3	—
Fuel†	36.7	79.1	—
Construction/electrical equipment	90.5	43.2	—
Consumption goods	252.7	288.0	280.1
Materials for garments industry	66.5	60.4	67.2
Motorcycle parts for assembly	38.4	22.6	30.0
Unrecorded imports	—	27.0‡	9.4
Total	554.3	569.4	567.4

* Estimates.
† Estimates based on the assumption that 50% of total are consumption goods.
‡ Estimate included due to weaknesses in customs data.

Exports f.o.b.	1999	2000	2001*
Wood products	84.9	87.1	81.0
Logs	20.0	26.0	n.a.
Timber	26.9	37.7	n.a.
Other and unrecorded	38.0	23.4	n.a.
Coffee	15.2	12.1	7.8
Other agricultural products	8.3	15.4	12.6
Manufactures†	27.9	9.6	9.7
Garments	72.0	91.6	100.0
Motorcycles	38.4	22.1	23.4
Electricity	90.5	112.2	114.2
Total (incl. others)	342.1	351.0	349.8

* Estimates.
† Excluding garments and wood products.

Source: IMF, *Lao People's Democratic Republic: Selected Issues and Statistical Appendix* (September 2002).

PRINCIPAL TRADING PARTNERS
(US $ million)

Imports	2000	2001	2002
China, People's Republic	37.9	59.9	71.5
France	27.5	8.5	9.2
Germany	3.6	7.4	8.7
Hong Kong	7.9	10.1	10.9
Japan	23.6	13.0	17.4
Korea, Republic	4.9	6.9	7.5
Singapore	32.9	28.9	29.1
Thailand*	419.0	451.7	444.0
United Kingdom	6.1	3.7	2.6
Viet Nam	77.7	85.8	93.1
Total (incl. others)	689.7	733.1	763.1

Exports	2000	2001	2002
Belgium	13.6	10.4	9.1
France	27.1	33.7	33.4
Germany	20.8	25.5	24.1
Italy	9.2	10.9	9.6
Japan	10.9	6.3	6.0
Netherlands	10.0	9.7	9.8
Thailand*	68.9	81.0	85.0
United Kingdom	7.2	9.3	13.4
USA	8.8	3.6	2.6
Viet Nam	96.1	106.1	115.0
Total (incl. others)	392.1	422.3	443.2

* Trade with Thailand may be overestimated, as it may include goods in transit to and from other countries.

Source: Asian Development Bank, *Key Indicators of Developing Asian and Pacific Countries.*

Transport

ROAD TRAFFIC
(motor vehicles in use at 31 December, estimates)

	1994	1995	1996
Passenger cars	18,240	17,280	16,320
Buses and coaches	440	n.a.	n.a.
Lorries and vans	7,920	6,020	4,200
Motorcycles and mopeds	169,000	200,000	231,000

Source: International Road Federation, *World Road Statistics.*

SHIPPING

Inland Waterways
(traffic)

	1993	1994	1995
Freight ('000 metric tons)	290	876	898
Freight ton-kilometres (million)	18.7	40.8	98.8
Passengers ('000)	703	898	652
Passenger-kilometres (million)	110.2	60.6	24.3

Source: Ministry of Communications, Transport, Post and Construction.

Merchant Fleet
(registered at 31 December)

	2000	2001	2002
Number of vessels	1	1	1
Displacement ('000 grt)	2.4	2.4	2.4

Source: Lloyd's Register-Fairplay, *World Fleet Statistics*.

CIVIL AVIATION
(traffic on scheduled services)

	1997	1998	1999
Kilometres flown (million) . .	1	1	1
Passengers carried ('000) . . .	125	124	197
Passenger-kilometres (million). .	48	48	78
Total ton-kilometres (million) . .	5	5	8

Source: UN, *Statistical Yearbook*.

Tourism

FOREIGN VISITOR ARRIVALS
(incl. excursionists)

Country of Nationality	1999	2000	2001
China, People's Republic . . .	20,269	28,215	40,644
France	19,960	24,534	21,662
Japan	14,860	20,687	15,547
Thailand	356,105	442,564	376,685
United Kingdom	12,298	15,204	15,722
USA	24,672	32,869	25,779
Viet Nam	71,748	68,751	82,411
Total (incl. others)	614,278	737,208	673,823

Source: World Tourism Organization, *Yearbook of Tourism Statistics*.

Tourism receipts (US $ million): 97 in 1999; 114 in 2000; 104 in 2001 (Source: World Bank).

Communications Media

	2000	2001	2002
Television receivers ('000 in use) .	52	n.a.	n.a.
Telephones ('000 main lines in use)	40.9	52.6	61.9
Mobile cellular telephones ('000 subscribers).	12.7	29.5	55.2
Personal computers ('000 in use)	14	16	18
Internet users ('000)	6.0	10.0	15.0

Radio receivers ('000 in use): 730 in 1997.

Facsimile machines (estimated number in use): 500 in 1994 (Source: UN, *Statistical Yearbook*).

Book production (1995): Titles 88; copies ('000) 995.

Daily newspapers (1996): 3 (average circulation 18,000).

Non-daily newspapers (1988, estimates): 4 (average circulation 20,000).

Sources (unless otherwise specified): International Telecommunication Union; UNESCO, *Statistical Yearbook*.

Education

(1996/97)

	Institu-tions	Teachers	Students		
			Males	Females	Total
Pre-primary . . .	695	2,173	18,502	19,349	37,851
Primary	7,896	25,831	438,241	348,094	786,335
Secondary:					
general	n.a.	10,717	108,996	71,164	180,160
vocational* . . .	n.a.	808	3,731	1,928	5,659
teacher training .	n.a.	197	960	780	1,740
University level . .	n.a.	456	3,509	1,764	5,273
Other higher . . .	n.a.	913	5,378	2,081	7,459

* Data for 1995/96.

Source: UNESCO, *Statistical Yearbook*.

Adult literacy rate (UNESCO estimates): 65.6% (males 76.8%; females 54.4%) in 2001 (Source: UN Development Programme, *Human Development Report*).

Directory

The Constitution

The new Constitution was unanimously endorsed by the Supreme People's Assembly on 14 August 1991. Its main provisions are summarized below:

POLITICAL SYSTEM

The Lao People's Democratic Republic (Lao PDR) is an independent, sovereign and united country and is indivisible.

The Lao PDR is a people's democratic state. The people's rights are exercised and ensured through the functioning of the political system, with the Lao People's Revolutionary Party as its leading organ. The people exercise power through the National Assembly, which functions in accordance with the principle of democratic centralism.

The State respects and protects all lawful activities of Buddhism and the followers of other religious faiths.

The Lao PDR pursues a foreign policy of peace, independence, friendship and co-operation. It adheres to the principles of peaceful co-existence with other countries, based on mutual respect for independence, sovereignty and territorial integrity.

SOCIO-ECONOMIC SYSTEM

The economy is market-orientated, with intervention by the State. The State encourages all economic sectors to compete and co-operate in the expansion of production and trade.

Private ownership of property and rights of inheritance are protected by the State.

The State authorizes the operation of private schools and medical services, while promoting the expansion of public education and health services.

FUNDAMENTAL RIGHTS AND OBLIGATIONS OF CITIZENS

Lao citizens, irrespective of their sex, social status, education, faith and ethnic group, are equal before the law.

Lao citizens aged 18 years and above have the right to vote, and those over 21 years to be candidates, in elections.

Lao citizens have freedom of religion, speech, press and assembly, and freedom to establish associations and to participate in demonstrations which do not contradict the law.

THE NATIONAL ASSEMBLY

The National Assembly is the legislative organ, which also oversees the activities of the administration and the judiciary. Members of the National Assembly are elected for a period of five years by universal adult suffrage. The National Assembly elects its own Standing Committee, which consists of the Chairman and Vice-Chairman of the National Assembly (and thus also of the National Assembly Standing Committee) and a number of other members. The National Assembly convenes its ordinary session twice annually. The National Assembly Standing Committee may convene an extraordinary session of the National Assembly if it deems this necessary. The National Assembly is empowered to amend the Constitution; to endorse, amend or abrogate laws; to elect or remove the President of State and Vice-Presidents of State, as proposed by the Standing Committee of the National Assembly; to adopt motions expressing 'no confidence' in the Government; to elect or remove the

President of the People's Supreme Court, on the recommendation of the National Assembly Standing Committee.

THE PRESIDENT OF STATE

The President of State, who is also Head of the Armed Forces, is elected by the National Assembly for a five-year tenure. Laws adopted by the National Assembly must be promulgated by the President of State not later than 30 days after their enactment. The President is empowered to appoint or dismiss the Prime Minister and members of the Government, with the approval of the National Assembly; to appoint government officials at provincial and municipal levels; and to promote military personnel, on the recommendation of the Prime Minister.

THE GOVERNMENT

The Government is the administrative organ of the State. It is composed of the Prime Minister, Deputy Prime Ministers and Ministers or Chairmen of Committees (which are equivalent to Ministries), who are appointed by the President, with the approval of the National Assembly, for a term of five years. The Government implements the Constitution, laws and resolutions adopted by the National Assembly and state decrees and acts of the President of State. The Prime Minister is empowered to appoint Deputy Ministers and Vice-Chairmen of Committees, and lower-level government officials.

LOCAL ADMINISTRATION

The Lao PDR is divided into provinces, municipalities, districts and villages. Provincial governors and mayors of municipalities are appointed by the President of State. Deputy provincial governors, deputy mayors and district chiefs are appointed by the Prime Minister. Administration at village level is conducted by village heads.

THE JUDICIARY

The people's courts comprise the People's Supreme Court, the people's provincial and municipal courts, the people's district courts and military courts. The President of the People's Supreme Court and the Public Prosecutor-General are elected by the National Assembly, on the recommendation of the National Assembly Standing Committee. The Vice-President of the People's Supreme Court and the judges of the people's courts at all levels are appointed by the National Assembly Standing Committee.

The Government

HEAD OF STATE

President of State: Gen. KHAMTAY SIPHANDONE (took office February 1998).

Vice-President: Lt-Gen. CHOUMMALI SAIGNASON.

COUNCIL OF MINISTERS
(April 2004)

Prime Minister: BOUNGNANG VOLACHIT.

Deputy Prime Minister and President of the State Planning Committee: THONGLOUN SISOLIT.

Deputy Prime Minister and Minister of Foreign Affairs: SOMSAVAT LENGSAVAT.

Deputy Prime Ministers: Maj.-Gen. ASANG LAOLI, BOUSONE BOUPAVANH.

Minister of Defence: Maj.-Gen. DOUANGCHAI PHICHIT.

Minister of Finance: CHANSY PHOSIKHAM.

Minister of Security: Maj.-Gen. SOUDCHAI THAMMASITH.

Minister of Justice: KHAMOUANE BOUPHA.

Minister of Agriculture and Forestry: SIANE SAPHANTHONG.

Minister of Communications, Transport, Post and Construction: BOUATHONG VONGLOKHAM.

Minister of Industry and Handicrafts: ONNEUA PHOMMACHANH.

Minister of Commerce and Tourism: SOULIVONG DARAVONG.

Minister of Information and Culture: PHANDOUANGCHIT VONGSA.

Minister of Labour and Social Welfare: SOMPHAN PHENGKHAMMI.

Minister of Education: PHIMMASONE LEUANGKHAMMA.

Minister of Public Health: Dr PONEMEKH DARALOY.

Minister to the Office of the President: SOUBANH SRITHIRATH.

Ministers to the Prime Minister's Office: BOUNTIEM PHITSAMAI, SOULI NANTHAVONG, SAISENGLI TENGBIACHU, SOMPHUNG MONGKHUNVILAI.

MINISTRIES

Office of the President: rue Lane Xang, Vientiane; tel. (21) 214200; fax (21) 214208.

Office of the Prime Minister: Ban Sisavat, Vientiane; tel. (21) 213653; fax (21) 213560.

Ministry of Agriculture and Forestry: Ban Phonxay, Vientiane; tel. (21) 412359; fax (21) 412344.

Ministry of Commerce and Tourism: Ban Phonxay, Muang Saysettha, Vientiane; tel. (21) 412436; fax (21) 412434; internet www.moc.gov.la.

Ministry of Communications, Transport, Post and Construction: ave Lane Xang, Vientiane; tel. (21) 412251; fax (21) 414123.

Ministry of Education: BP 67, Vientiane; tel. (21) 216004; fax (21) 212108.

Ministry of Finance: rue That Luang, Ban Phonxay, Vientiane; tel. (21) 412401; fax (21) 412415.

Ministry of Foreign Affairs: rue That Luang 01004, Ban Phonxay, Vientiane; tel. (21) 413148; fax (21) 414009; e-mail sphimmas@laonet.net; internet www.mfa.laogov.net.

Ministry of Industry and Handicrafts: rue Nongbone, Ban Phai, BP 4708, Vientiane; tel. (21) 416718; fax (21) 413005; e-mail mihplan@laotel.com.

Ministry of Information and Culture: rue Sethathirath, Ban Xiengnheun, Vientiane; tel. (21) 210409; fax (21) 212408.

Ministry of Justice: Ban Phonxay, Vientiane; tel. (21) 414105.

Ministry of Labour and Social Welfare: rue Pangkham, Ban Sisaket, Vientiane; tel. (21) 213003.

Ministry of National Defence: rue Phone Kheng, Ban Phone Kheng, Vientiane; tel. (21) 412803.

Ministry of Public Health: Ban Simeuang, Vientiane; tel. (21) 214002; fax (21) 214001; e-mail cabinet.fr@moh.gov.la.

Ministry of Security: rue Nongbone, Ban Hatsady, Vientiane; tel. (21) 212500.

Legislature

At the election held on 24 February 2002 166 candidates, approved by the Lao Front for National Construction, contested the 109 seats in the National Assembly.

President of the National Assembly: Lt-Gen. SAMAN VIGNAKET.

Vice-President: PANY YATHOTU.

Political Organizations

Lao Front for National Construction (LFNC): BP 1828, Vientiane; f. 1979 to replace the Lao Patriotic Front; comprises representatives of various political and social groups, of which the LPRP (see below) is the dominant force; fosters national solidarity; Pres. Gen. SISAVAT KEOBOUNPHAN; Vice-Chair. SIHO BANNAVONG, KHAMPHOUI CHANTHASOUK, TONG YEUTHOR.

Phak Pasason Pativat Lao (Lao People's Revolutionary Party—LPRP): Vientiane; f. 1955 as the People's Party of Laos; reorg. under present name in 1972; Cen. Cttee of 53 full mems elected March 2001; Pres. Gen. KHAMTAY SIPHANDONE.

Political Bureau (Politburo)

Full members: Gen. KHAMTAY SIPHANDONE, Lt-Gen. SAMAN VIGNAKET, Lt-Gen. CHOUMMALI SAIGNASON, THONGSIN THAMMAVONG, BOUNGNANG VOLACHIT, Gen. SISAVAT KEOBOUNPHAN, Maj.-Gen. ASANG LAOLI, THOUNGLONG SISOLIT, Maj.-Gen. DOUANGCHAI PHICHIT, BOUSONE BOUPAVANH.

Numerous factions are in armed opposition to the Government. The principal groups are:

Ethnics' Liberation Organization of Laos: Leader PA KAO HER.

Free Democratic Lao National Salvation Force: based in Thailand.

United Front for the Liberation of Laos: Leader PHOUNGPHET PHANARETH.

United Front for the National Liberation of the Lao People: f. 1980; led by Gen. PHOUMI NOSAVAN until his death in 1985.

United Lao National Liberation Front: Sayabouri Province; comprises an estimated 8,000 members, mostly Hmong (Meo) tribesmen; Sec.-Gen. VANG SHUR.

Diplomatic Representation

EMBASSIES IN LAOS

Australia: rue Pandit J. Nehru, quartier Phonxay, BP 292, Vientiane; tel. (21) 413600; fax (21) 413601; internet www.laos.embassy.gov.au; Ambassador MICHAEL JONATHAN THWAITES.

Brunei: Unit 12, Ban Thoungkang, rue Lao-Thai Friendship, Muang Sisattanak, Xaysettha District, Vientiane; tel. (21) 352294; fax (21) 352291; e-mail embdlaos@laonet.com; Ambassador Pengiran Haji HAMDAN bin Haji ISMAIL.

Cambodia: rue Thadeua, Km 2, BP 34, Vientiane; tel. (21) 314952; fax (21) 314951; e-mail recamlao@laotel.com; Ambassador HUOT PHAL.

China, People's Republic: rue Wat Nak, Muang Sisattanak, BP 898, Vientiane; tel. (21) 315100; fax (21) 315104; e-mail embassyprc@laonet.net; Ambassador LIU YONGXING.

Cuba: Ban Saphanthong Neua 128, BP 1017, Vientiane; tel. (21) 314902; fax (21) 314901; e-mail embacuba@laonet.net; Ambassador EDUARDO VALIDO GARCÍA.

France: rue Sethathirath, BP 06, Vientiane; tel. (21) 215253; fax (21) 215250; e-mail contact@ambafrance-laos.org; internet www.ambafrance-laos.org; Ambassador BERNARD POTTIER.

Germany: rue Sok Paluang 26, BP 314, Vientiane; tel. (21) 312110; fax (21) 351152; e-mail zreg@vien.diplo.de; Ambassador CHRISTIAN K. G. BERGER.

India: 2 Ban Wat Nak, rue Thadeua, Km 3, Sisattanak District, Vientiane; tel. (21) 352301; fax (21) 352300; e-mail indiaemb@laotel.com; internet www.indianembassylao.com; Ambassador TSEWANG TOPDEN.

Indonesia: ave Phone Keng, BP 277, Vientiane; tel. (21) 413909; fax (21) 214828; e-mail kbrivte@laotel.com; Ambassador ZAINUDDIN NASUTION.

Japan: rue Sisangvone, Vientiane; tel. (21) 414401; fax (21) 414406; Ambassador ITSUO HASHIMOTO.

Korea, Democratic People's Republic: quartier Wat Nak, Vientiane; tel. (21) 315261; fax (21) 315260; Ambassador CHOE PYONG KWAN.

Korea, Republic: rue Lao-Thai Friendship, Ban Watnak, Sisattanak District, BP 7567, Vientiane; tel. (21) 415833; fax (21) 415831; e-mail koramb@laotel.com; Ambassador CHANG CHUL-KYOON.

Malaysia: rue That Luang, quartier Pholxay, BP 789, Vientiane; tel. (21) 414205; fax (21) 414201; e-mail mwvntian@laopdr.com; Ambassador MOHAMMED DAUD MOHAMMED YUSOF.

Mongolia: rue Wat Nak, Km 3, BP 370, Vientiane; tel. (21) 315220; fax (21) 315221; e-mail embmong@laotel.com; Ambassador N. ALIASUREN.

Myanmar: Ban Thong Kang, rue Sok Palaung, BP 11, Vientiane; tel. (21) 314910; fax (21) 314913; e-mail mev@loxinfo.co.th; Ambassador U TIN OO.

Philippines: Ban Phonsinuane, Sisattanak, BP 2415, Vientiane; tel. (21) 452490; fax (21) 452493; e-mail pelaopdr@laotel.com; Ambassador ANTONIO CABANGON CHUA.

Poland: 39 Ban Thadeua, Km 3, quartier Wat Nak, BP 1106, Vientiane; tel. (21) 312940; fax (21) 312085; e-mail vieampol@laotel.com; Chargé d'affaires Dr TOMASZ GERLACH.

Russia: Ban Thadeua, quartier Thaphalanxay, BP 490, Vientiane; tel. (21) 312222; fax (21) 312210; e-mail rusemb@laotel.com; Ambassador YURI RAIKOV.

Singapore: Unit 12, Ban Naxay, rue Nong Bong, Muang Sat Settha, Vientiane; tel. (21) 416860; fax (21) 416855; e-mail sinemvte@laotel.com; internet www.mfa.gov.sg/vientiane; Ambassador KAREN TAN.

Thailand: ave Phone Keng, Vientiane; tel. (21) 214581; fax (21) 214580; e-mail thaivtn@mfa.go.th; Ambassador RATHAKIT MANATHAT.

USA: 19 rue Bartholonie, BP 114, Vientiane; tel. (21) 212581; fax (21) 212584; e-mail khammanpx@state.gov; internet usembassy.state.gov/laos; Ambassador DOUGLAS A. HARTWICK.

Viet Nam: 85 rue That Luang, Vientiane; tel. (21) 413409; fax (21) 413379; e-mail dsqvn@laotel.com; Ambassador HUYNH ANH DUNG.

Judicial System

President of the People's Supreme Court: KHAMMY SAYAVONG.

Vice-President: DAVON VANGVICHIT.

People's Supreme Court Judges: NOUANTHONG VONGSA, NHOTSENG LITTHIDETH, PHOUKHONG CHANTHALATH, SENGSOUVANH CHANTHALOUNNAVONG, KESON PHANLACK, KONGCHI YANGCHY, KHAMPON PHASAIGNAVONG.

Public Prosecutor-General: KHAMPANE PHILAVONG.

Religion

The 1991 Constitution guarantees freedom of religious belief. The principal religion of Laos is Buddhism.

BUDDHISM

Lao Unified Buddhists' Association: Maha Kudy, Wat That Luang, Vientiane; f. 1964; Pres. (vacant); Sec.-Gen. Rev. SIHO SIHAVONG.

CHRISTIANITY

The Roman Catholic Church

For ecclesiastical purposes, Laos comprises four Apostolic Vicariates. At 31 December 2002 an estimated 0.7% of the population were adherents.

Episcopal Conference of Laos and Cambodia

c/o Mgr Pierre Bach, Paris Foreign Missions, 254 Silom Rd, Bangkok 10500, Thailand.

f. 1971; Pres. Mgr JEAN KHAMSÉ VITHAVONG (Titular Bishop of Moglaena, Vicar Apostolic of Vientiane).

Vicar Apostolic of Luang Prabang: (vacant), Evêché, BP 74, Luang Prabang.

Vicar Apostolic of Paksé: Mgr LOUIS-MARIE LING MANGKHANEKHOUN (Titular Bishop of Proconsulari), Centre Catholique, BP 77, Paksé, Champasak; tel. (31) 212879.

Vicar Apostolic of Savannakhet: Mgr JEAN SOMMENG VORACHAK (Titular Bishop of Muzuca in Proconsulari), Centre Catholique, BP 12, Thakhek, Khammouane; tel. (51) 212184; fax (51) 213070.

Vicar Apostolic of Vientiane: Mgr JEAN KHAMSÉ VITHAVONG (Titular Bishop of Moglaena), Centre Catholique, BP 113, Vientiane; tel. (21) 216219; fax (21) 215085.

The Anglican Communion

Laos is within the jurisdiction of the Anglican Bishop of Singapore.

The Protestant Church

Lao Evangelical Church: BP 4200, Vientiane; tel. (21) 169136; fax.

BAHÁ'Í FAITH

National Spiritual Assembly: BP 189, Vientiane; tel. and fax (21) 216996; e-mail usme@laotel.com; f. 1956; Sec. SUSADA SENCHANTHISAY.

The Press

Aloun Mai (New Dawn): Vientiane; f. 1985; theoretical and political organ of the LPRP.

Finance: Vientiane; organ of Ministry of Finance.

Heng Ngan: 87 ave Lane Xang, BP 780, Vientiane; tel. (21) 212750; fortnightly; organ of the Federation of Lao Trade Unions; Editor BOUAPHENG BOUNSOULINH.

Lao Dong (Labour): 87 ave Lane Xang, Vientiane; f. 1986; fortnightly; organ of the Federation of Lao Trade Unions; circ. 46,000.

Laos: 80 rue Setthathirath, BP 3770, Vientiane; tel. (21) 21447; fax (21) 21445; internet www.laolink.com; quarterly; published in Lao and English; illustrated; Editor V. PHOMCHANHEUANG; English Editor O. PHRAKHAMSAY.

Meying Lao: rue Manthatoarath, BP 59, Vientiane; e-mail chansoda@hotmail.com; f. 1980; monthly; women's magazine; organ of the Lao Women's Union; Editor-in-Chief VATSADY KHUTNGOTHA; Editor CHANSODA PHONETHIP; circ. 7,000.

Noum Lao (Lao Youth): Vientiane; f. 1979; fortnightly; organ of the Lao People's Revolutionary Youth Union; Editor DOUANGDY INTHAVONG; circ. 6,000.

Pasason (The People): 80 rue Setthathirath, BP 110, Vientiane; f. 1940; daily; Lao; organ of the Cen. Cttee of the LPRP; Editor BOUABAN VOLAKHOUN; circ. 28,000.

Pasason Van Athit: Vientiane; weekly; circ. 2,000.

Pathet Lao: 80 rue Setthathirath, Vientiane; tel. (21) 215402; fax (21) 212446; f. 1979; monthly; Lao and English; organ of Khao San Pathet Lao (KPL); Dep. Dir SOUNTHONE KHANTHAVONG.

Sciences and Technics: Dept of Science and Technology, Science, Technology and the Environment Agency (STEA), BP 2279, Vientiane; f. 1991 as Technical Science Magazine; quarterly; organ of the Dept of Science and Technology; scientific research and development.

Siang Khong Gnaovason Song Thanva (Voice of the 2nd December Youths): Vientiane; monthly; youth journal.

Sieng Khene Lao: Vientiane; monthly; organ of the Lao Writers' Association.

Suksa Mai: Vientiane; monthly; organ of the Ministry of Education.

Valasan Khosana (Propaganda Journal): Vientiane; f. 1987; organ of the Cen. Cttee of the LPRP.

Vannasinh: Vientiane; monthly; literature magazine.

Vientiane Mai (New Vientiane): rue Setthathirath, BP 989, Vientiane; tel. (21) 2623; fax (21) 5989; f. 1975; morning daily; organ of the LPRP Cttee of Vientiane province and city; Editor SICHANE (acting); circ. 2,500.

Vientiane Times: BP 5723, Vientiane; tel. (21) 216364; fax (21) 216365; internet www.vientianetimes.com; f. 1994; 2 a week; English; emphasis on investment opportunities; Editor SOMSANOUK MIXAY; circ. 3,000.

Vientiane Tulakit (Vientiane Business-Social): rue Setthathirath, Vientiane; tel. (21) 2623; fax (21) 6365; weekly; circ. 2,000.

There is also a newspaper published by the Lao People's Army, and several provinces have their own newsletters.

NEWS AGENCIES

Khao San Pathet Lao (KPL): 80 rue Setthathirath, Vientiane; tel. (21) 215402; fax (21) 212446; e-mail kpl@laonet.net; internet www.kplnet.net; f. 1968; organ of the Cttee of Information, Press, Radio and Television Broadcasting; news service; daily bulletins in Lao, English and French; teletype transmission in English; Gen. Dir KHAMSÈNE PHONGSA.

Foreign Bureaux

Rossiiskoye Informatsionnoye Agentstvo—Novosti (RIA—Novosti) (Russia): Vientiane; tel. (21) 213510; f. 1963.

Viet Nam News Agency (VNA): Vientiane; Chief DO VAN PHUONG.

Reuters (UK) is also represented in Laos.

PRESS ASSOCIATION

The Journalists' Association of the Lao PDR: BP 122, Vientiane; tel. (21) 212420; fax (21) 212408; Pres. BOUABANE VORAKHOUNE; Sec.-Gen. KHAM KHONG KONGVONGSA.

Publishers

Khoualuang Kanphim: 2–6 Khoualuang Market, Vientiane.

Lao-phanit: Ministry of Education, Bureau des Manuels Scolaires, rue Lane Xang, Ban Sisavat, Vientiane; educational, cookery, art, music, fiction.

Pakpassak Kanphin: 9–11 quai Fa-Hguun, Vientiane.

State Printing: 314/C rue Samsemthai, BP 2160, Vientiane; tel. (21) 213273; fax (21) 215901; Dir NOUPHAY KOUNLAVONG.

Broadcasting and Communications

TELECOMMUNICATIONS

Entreprises des Postes et Télécommunications de Laos: ave Lane Xang, 01000 Vientiane; tel. (21) 215767; fax (21) 212779; e-mail laoposts@laotel.com; state enterprise, responsible for the postal service and telecommunications; Dir-Gen. KIENG KHAMKETH.

Lao Télécommunications Co Ltd: ave Lane Xang, BP 5607, 0100 Vientiane; tel. (21) 216465; fax (21) 216156; e-mail marketin@laotel.com; internet www.laotel.com; f. 1996; a jt venture between a subsidiary of the Shinawatra Group of Thailand and Entreprises des Postes et Télécommunications de Laos; awarded a 25-year contract

by the Government in 1996 to undertake all telecommunications projects in the country; Dir-Gen. HOUMPHANH INTHARATH.

BROADCASTING

Radio

In addition to the national radio service, there are several local stations.

Lao National Radio: rue Phangkham, Km 6, BP 310, Vientiane; tel. (21) 212428; fax (21) 212432; e-mail natradio@laonet.net; f. 1960; state-owned; programmes in Lao, French, English, Thai, Khmer and Vietnamese; domestic and international services; Dir-Gen. BOUNTHANH INTHAXAY.

In 1990 resistance forces in Laos established an illegal radio station, broadcasting anti-Government propaganda: **Satthani Vithayou Kachai Siang Latthaban Potpoi Sat Lao** (Radio Station of the Government for the Liberation of the Lao Nation): programmes in Lao and Hmong languages; broadcasts four hours daily.

Television

A domestic television service began in December 1983. In May 1988 a second national television station commenced transmissions from Savannakhet. In December 1993 the Ministry of Information and Culture signed a 15-year joint-venture contract with a Thai firm on the development of broadcasting services in Laos. Under the resultant International Broadcasting Corporation Lao Co Ltd, IBC Channel 3 was inaugurated in 1994 (see below).

Lao National Television (TVNL): rue Chommany Neua, Km 6, BP 5635, Vientiane; tel. (21) 412183; fax (21) 412182; f. 1983; colour television service; Dir-Gen. BOUASONE PHONGPHAVANH.

Laos Television 3: BP 860, Vientiane; tel. (21) 315449; fax (21) 215628; operated by the International Broadcasting Corpn Lao Co Ltd; f. 1994 as IBC Channel 3; 30% govt-owned, 70% owned by the International Broadcasting Corpn Co Ltd of Thailand; programmes in Lao.

Finance

(cap. = capital; dep. = deposits; br.(s) = branch(es); m. = million)

BANKING

The banking system was reorganized in 1988–89, ending the state monopoly of banking. Some commercial banking functions were transferred from the central bank and the state commercial bank to a new network of autonomous banks. The establishment of joint ventures with foreign financial institutions was permitted. Foreign banks have been permitted to open branches in Laos since 1992. In 1998 there were nine private commercial banks in Laos, most of them Thai. In March 1999 the Government consolidated six state-owned banks into two new institutions—Lane Xang Bank Ltd and Lao May Bank Ltd; these merged in 2001.

Central Bank

Banque de la RDP Lao: rue Yonnet, BP 19, Vientiane; tel. (21) 213109; fax (21) 213108; e-mail bol@pan-laos.net.la; internet www.bol.gov.la; f. 1959 as the bank of issue, became Banque Pathetlao 1968, took over the operations of Banque Nationale du Laos 1975; known as Banque d'Etat de la RDP Lao from 1982 until adoption of present name; Gov. PHOUMI THIPPHAVONE.

Commercial Banks

Agriculture Promotion Bank: 58 rue Hengboun, Ban Haysok, BP 5456, Vientiane; tel. (21) 212024; fax (21) 213957; e-mail apblaopdr@laonet.net; Man. Dir BOUNSONG SOMMALAVONG.

Banque pour le Commerce Extérieur Lao (BCEL): 1 rue Pangkham, BP 2925, Vientiane; tel. (21) 213200; fax (21) 213202; e-mail bcelhovt@hotmail.com; f. 1975; 100% state-owned; Chair. AKSONE BOUPHAKONEKHAM; Gen. Dir SONOXAY SITHPHAXAY.

Joint Development Bank: 82 ave Lane Xang, BP 3187, Vientiane; e-mail jdb@jdbbank.com; internet www.jdbbank.com; f. 1989; the first joint-venture bank between Laos and a foreign partner; 30% owned by Banque de la RDP Lao, 70% owned by Thai company, Phrom Suwan Silo and Drying Co Ltd; cap. US $4m.

Lao May Bank Ltd: 39 rue Pangkam, BP 2700, Vientiane; tel. (21) 213300; fax (21) 213304; f. 1999 as a result of the consolidation by the Government of ParkTai Bank, Lao May Bank and NakornLuang Bank; merged with Lane Xang Bank Ltd in 2001.

Lao-Viet Bank (LVB): 5 ave Lane Xang, Vientiane; tel. (21) 216316; fax (21) 212197; e-mail lvbho@laotel.com; internet www.laovietbank.com; f. 1999; joint venture between BCEL and the Bank for Investment and Development of Vietnam.

Vientiane Commercial Bank Ltd: 33 ave Lane Xang, Ban Hatsady, Chanthaboury, Vientiane; tel. (21) 222700; fax (21) 213513; f. 1993; privately-owned joint venture by Laotian, Thai, Taiwanese and Australian investors; Man. Dir SOP SISOMPHOU.

Foreign Banks

Bangkok Bank Public Co Ltd (Thailand): 38/13–15 rue Hatsady, BP 5400, Vientiane; tel. (21) 213560; fax (21) 213561; f. 1993; Man. TOSSATIS RODPRASERT.

Bank of Ayudhya Public Co Ltd (Thailand): 79/6 Unit 17, ave Lane Xang, BP 5072, Vientiane; tel. (21) 213521; fax (21) 213520; e-mail baylaos@laotel.com; internet www.bay.co.th; f. 1994; Man. SUWAT TANTIPATANASAKUL.

Krung Thai Bank Public Co Ltd (Thailand): Unit 21, 80 ave Lane Xang, Ban Xiengngeuanthong, Chanthaboury, Vientiane; tel. (21) 213480; fax (21) 222762; e-mail ktblao@laotel.com; internet www .ktb.co.th; f. 1993; Gen. Man. SOMCHAI KANOKPETCH.

Public Bank Berhad (Malaysia): 100/1–4 rue Talat Sao, BP 6614, Vientiane; tel. (21) 216614; fax (21) 222743; e-mail pbbvte@laotel .com; Gen. Man. TAY HONG HENG.

Siam Commercial Bank Public Co Ltd (Thailand): 117 ave Lane Xang-Samsenethai, BP 4809, Ban Sisaket Mouang, Chanthaboury, Vientiane; tel. (21) 213500; fax (21) 213502; Gen. Man. CHARANYA DISSAMARN.

Thai Military Bank Public Co Ltd: 69 rue Khoun Boulom, Chanthaboury, BP 2423, Vientiane; tel. (21) 217174; fax (21) 216486; the first foreign bank to be represented in Laos; Man. AMNAT KOSKTPON.

INSURANCE

Assurances Générales du Laos (AGL): Vientiane Commercial Bank Bldg, ave Lane Xang, BP 4223, Vientiane; tel. (21) 215903; fax (21) 215904; e-mail agl@agl-allianz.com; internet www.agl-allianz .com; Man. Dir PHILIPPE ROBINEAU.

Trade and Industry

GOVERNMENT AGENCY

National Economic Research Institute: rue Luang Prabang, Sithanneua, Vientiane; tel. (21) 216653; fax (21) 216660; e-mail neri@pan-laos.net; govt policy development unit; Dir SOUPHAN KEOMISAY.

DEVELOPMENT ORGANIZATIONS

Department of Livestock and Fisheries: Ministry of Agriculture and Forestry, Ban Phonxay, BP 811, Vientiane; tel. (21) 416932; fax (21) 415674; e-mail eulaodlf@laotel.com; public enterprise; imports and markets agricultural commodities; produces and distributes feed and animals; Dir-Gen. SINGKHAM PHONVISAY.

State Committee for State Planning: Office of the Prime Minister, Ban Sisavat, Vientiane; tel. (21) 213653; fax (21) 213560; Pres. THOUNGLONG SISOLIT.

CHAMBER OF COMMERCE

Lao National Chamber of Commerce and Industry: rue Sihom, Ban Haisok, BP 4596, Vientiane; tel. and fax (21) 219223; e-mail ccilcciv@laotel.com; internet www.lncci.laotel.com; f. 1989; 470 mems; Pres. KISSANA VONGSAY; Sec. Gen. KHAMPANH SENGTHONGKHAM.

INDUSTRIAL AND TRADE ASSOCIATION

Société Lao Import-Export (SOLIMPEX): 43–47 ave Lane Xang, BP 278, Vientiane; tel. (21) 213818; fax (21) 217054; Dir KANHKEO SAYCOCIE; Dep. Dir PHONGSAMOUTH VONGKOT.

UTILITIES

Electricity

Electricité du Laos: rue Nongbone, BP 309, Vientiane; tel. (21) 451519; fax (21) 416381; e-mail edlgmo@laotel.com; responsible for production and distribution of electricity; Gen. Man. VIRAPHONH VIRAVONG.

Lao National Grid Co: Vientiane; responsible for Mekong hydro-electricity exports.

Water

In 1998 the Government adopted a policy of decentralization with regard to water supply and sanitation in Laos. As a result, the national water supply authority, Nam Papa Lao, was divided into

Nam Papa Vientiane, with jurisdiction over the capital, and a number of provincial authorities. Activities within the sector were to be co-ordinated by a newly established body, the Water Supply Authority.

Nam Papa Vientiane (Lao Water Supply Authority): rue Phone Kheng, Thatluang Neua Village, Sat Settha District, Vientiane; tel. (21) 412880; fax (21) 414378; f. 1962; fmrly Nam Papa Lao; authority responsible for the water supply of Vientiane; Gen. Man. Dr SOMPHON DETHOUDON; Dep. Man. KHAMPINH VORACHAKDAOVY.

Water Supply Authority (WASA): Dept of Housing and Urban Planning, Ministry of Communications, Transport, Post and Construction, ave Lane Xang, Vientiane; tel. (21) 415764; fax (21) 451826; e-mail mctpcwwa@laotel.com; f. 1998; Dir NOUPHEUAK VIRABOUTH.

STATE ENTERPRISES

Agricultural Forestry Development Import-Export and General Service Co: trading co of the armed forces.

Bolisat Phatthana Khet Phoudoi Import-Export Co: Lak Sao; f. 1984; trading co of the armed forces.

Dao-Heuang Import-Export Co: Ban Thaluang, Champasak Province; tel. (31) 212250; fax (31) 212438; e-mail info@dao-heuang .com; internet www.dao-heuang.com; f. 1990; imports and distributes whisky, beer, mineral water and foodstuffs.

Luen Fat Hong Lao Plywood Industry Co: BP 83, Vientiane; tel. (21) 314990; fax (21) 314992; e-mail lfhsdsj@laotel.com; internet www.luenfathongyada.laopdr.com; development and management of forests, logging and timber production.

CO-OPERATIVES

Central Leading Committee to Guide Agricultural Co-operatives: Vientiane; f. 1978 to help organize and plan regulations and policies for co-operatives; by the end of 1986 there were some 4,000 co-operatives, employing about 74% of the agricultural labour force; Chair. (vacant).

TRADE UNION ORGANIZATION

Federation of Lao Trade Unions: 87 ave Lane Xang, BP 780, Vientiane; tel. (21) 313682; e-mail kammabanlao@pan-laos.net.la; f. 1956; 21-mem. Cen. Cttee and five-mem. Control Cttee; Pres. BOSAIKHAM VONGDALA (acting); 70,000 mems.

Transport

RAILWAYS

The construction of a 30-km rail link between Vientiane and the Thai border town of Nong Khai began in January 1996 but was indefinitely postponed in February 1998 as an indirect consequence of a severe downturn in the Thai economy. In 1997 the Government announced plans to develop a comprehensive railway network, and awarded a contract to a Thai company, although no timetable for the implementation of the scheme was announced. In 2003 the Thai Government agreed to finance a 3.5-km rail link from Tha Naleng (near Vientiane) to Nong Khai.

ROADS

The road network provides the country's main method of transport, accounting for about 90% of freight traffic and 95% of passenger traffic in 1993 (according to the Asian Development Bank—ADB). In 1999 there were an estimated 21,716 km of roads, of which 9,664 km were paved. The main routes link Vientiane and Luang Prabang with Ho Chi Minh City in southern Viet Nam and with northern Viet Nam and the Cambodian border, Vientiane with Savannakhet, Phongsali to the Chinese border, Vientiane with Luang Prabang and the port of Ha Tinh (northern Viet Nam), and Savannakhet with the port of Da Nang (Viet Nam). In 2002 Laos, Thailand and China agreed to a US $45m. road project intended to link the three countries; most of the road construction would be carried out in Laos. The project was to be completed by 2006.

The Friendship Bridge across the Mekong River, linking Laos and Thailand between Tha Naleng and Nong Khai, was opened in April 1994. In early 1998 construction work began in Paksé on another bridge across the Mekong River. The project was granted substantial funding from the Japanese Government, and was completed in August 2000. Construction was scheduled to commence in early 2004 on a second Friendship Bridge, linking Savannakhet and Mukdahan.

INLAND WATERWAYS

The Mekong River, which forms the western frontier of Laos for much of its length, is the country's greatest transport artery. However, the size of river vessels is limited by rapids, and traffic is seasonal. In April 1995 Laos, Cambodia, Thailand and Viet Nam signed an agreement regarding the joint development of the lower Mekong, and established a Mekong River Commission. There are about 4,600 km of navigable waterways.

CIVIL AVIATION

Wattai airport, Vientiane, is the principal airport. Following the signing of an agreement in 1995, the airport was to be upgraded by Japan; renovation work commenced in 1997, and a new passenger terminal was opened in 1998. The development of Luang Prabang airport by Thailand, at a cost of 50m. baht, began in May 1994 and the first phase of the development programme was completed in 1996; the second phase was completed in 1998. In April 1998 Luang Prabang airport gained formal approval for international flights. The airports at Paksé and Savannakhet were also scheduled to be upgraded to enable them to accommodate wide-bodied civilian aircraft; renovation work on the airport at Savannakhet was completed in April 2000. Construction of a new airport in Oudomxay Province was completed in the late 1990s.

Lao Civil Aviation Department: BP 119, Vientiane; tel. and fax (21) 512163; e-mail laodca@laotel.com; Dir-Gen. YAKUA LOPANGKAO.

Lao Airlines: National Air Transport Co, 2 rue Pangkham, BP 6441, Vientiane; tel. (21) 212057; fax (21) 212056; e-mail laoairlines@laoairlines.com; internet www.laoairlines.com; f. 1975; state airline, fmrly Lao Aviation; operates internal and international passenger and cargo transport services within South-East Asia; Gen. Man. Dir POTHONG NGONPHACHANH.

Tourism

Laos boasts spectacular scenery, ancient pagodas and abundant wildlife. However, the development of tourism remains constrained by the poor infrastructure in much of the country. Western tourists were first permitted to enter Laos in 1989. In 1994, in order to stimulate the tourist industry, Vientiane ended restrictions on the movement of foreigners in Laos. Also in 1994 Laos, Viet Nam and Thailand agreed measures for the joint development of tourism. Luang Prabang was approved by UNESCO as a World Heritage site in February 1998. The years 1999–2000 were designated as Visit Laos Years. The number of visitors reached 737,208 in 2000, when receipts from tourism totalled an estimated US $114m. Visitor arrivals decreased to 673,823 in 2001, however, and receipts declined to $104m. in that year.

National Tourism Authority of Lao PDR: ave Lane Xang, BP 3556, Hadsady, Chanthaboury, Vientiane; tel. (21) 212251; fax (21) 212769; e-mail mtsc@mekongcenter.com; internet www .mekongcenter.com; 17 provincial offices; Dir CHENG SAYAVONG.

LATVIA

Introductory Survey

Location, Climate, Language, Religion, Flag, Capital

The Republic of Latvia (formerly the Latvian Soviet Socialist Republic) is situated in north-eastern Europe, on the east coast of the Baltic Sea. The country is bounded by Estonia to the north and by Lithuania to the south and south-west. To the east it borders Russia, and to the south-east Belarus. Owing to the influence of maritime factors, the climate is relatively temperate, but changeable. Average temperatures in January range from −2.8°C (26.6°F) in the western coastal town of Liepāja to −6.6°C (20.1°F) in the inland town of Daugavpils. Mean temperatures for July range from 16.7°C (62.1°F) in Liepāja to 17.6°C (63.7°F) in Daugavpils. Average annual rainfall in Rīga is 617 mm (24 ins). The official language is Latvian. The major religion is Christianity: most ethnic Latvians are traditionally Lutherans or Roman Catholics, whereas ethnic Russians are mainly adherents of the Russian Orthodox Church or Old Believers. The national flag (proportions 1 by 2) has a maroon background, with a narrow white horizontal stripe superimposed across the central part. The capital is Rīga (Riga).

Recent History

In November 1917 representatives of Latvian nationalist groups elected a provisional national council, which informed the Russian Government of its intention to establish a sovereign, independent Latvian state. On 18 November 1918 the Latvian National Council, which had been constituted on the previous day, proclaimed the independent Republic of Latvia, with Jānis Čakste as President. Independence, under the nationalist Government of Kārlis Ulmanis, was fully achieved after the expulsion of the Bolsheviks from Rīga in May 1919, with the aid of German troops, and from the eastern province of Latgale, with Polish and Estonian assistance, in January 1920. A Latvian-Soviet peace treaty was finally signed in August 1920. Latvia's first Constitution was adopted in 1922. An electoral system based on proportional representation permitted a large number of small parties to be represented in the Saeima (Parliament). As a result, there was little administrative stability, with 18 changes of government in 1922–34. None the less, under the dominant party, the Latvian Farmers' Union (LFU), led by Ulmanis), agrarian reforms were successfully introduced and agricultural exports flourished. The world-wide economic decline of the early 1930s, together with domestic political fragmentation, prompted a (bloodless) *coup d'état* in May 1934, led by Ulmanis. Martial law was introduced, the Saeima was dissolved and all political parties, including the LFU, were banned. A Government of National Unity, with Ulmanis as Prime Minister, assumed the legislative functions of the Saeima. Ulmanis became President in 1936.

Under the Treaty of Non-Aggression (the 'Molotov-Ribbentrop Pact'), signed by Germany and the USSR in August 1939, the incorporation of Latvia into the USSR was agreed by the two powers. A Treaty of Mutual Aid between the USSR and Latvia allowed the establishment of Soviet military bases in Latvia, and in June 1940 it was occupied by Soviet forces. In common with the neighbouring Baltic states of Estonia and Lithuania, Latvia did not offer military resistance, being greatly outnumbered by the Soviet forces. A new 'puppet' administration, under Augusts Kirhenšteins, was installed, and the election to the Saeima of Soviet-approved candidates took place in July. In that month the legislature proclaimed the Latvian Soviet Socialist Republic, which in the following month was formally incorporated into the USSR as a constituent union republic.

In the first year of Soviet rule almost 33,000 Latvians were deported to Siberia and other areas of the Russian Federation, and a further 1,350 were killed. Latvian language, traditions and culture were also suppressed. In July 1941 Soviet rule in Latvia was interrupted by German occupation. Most German troops had withdrawn by 1944, although the Kurzeme region, in south-western Latvia, was retained by Germany until the end of the Second World War. Soviet Latvia was re-established in 1944–45 and the process of 'sovietization' was resumed. There were further mass deportations of Latvians to Russia and Central Asia. Independent political activities were prohibited and

exclusive political power was exercised by the Communist Party of Latvia (CPL). A process of industrialization encouraged significant and sustained Russian and other Soviet immigration into the republic. The problem of agricultural stagnation (a consequence of Latvia's industrialization) was not addressed until the mid-1950s, when the Latvian authorities were accorded greater powers as a result of the policy of economic decentralization introduced in the USSR. This coincided with a movement within the CPL for greater cultural, especially linguistic, autonomy. However, under CPL First Secretary Arvīds Pelše (appointed in 1959) and his successor, Augusts Voss (First Secretary, 1966–84), the limited autonomy gained in the 1950s was reversed, and repression of Latvian cultural and literary life was increased.

There was a significant revival in traditional Latvian culture from the late 1970s. Political groups began to be established, including the Environmental Protection Club and Helsinki-86, established to monitor Soviet observance of the Helsinki Final Act adopted in 1975 by the Conference on (now Organization for) Security and Co-operation in Europe (CSCE—now OSCE, see p. 302). In June and August 1986 anti-Soviet demonstrations, organized by Helsinki-86, were suppressed by the police. In 1987 there were further demonstrations on the anniversaries of significant events in Latvian history. Such movements, fostered by the greater freedom of expression permitted under the new Soviet policy of *glasnost* (openness), were strongly opposed by the CPL, headed from 1984 by Boris Pugo. In 1988 opposition movements in Latvia began to unite, forging a significant political force. Prominent intellectuals, led by Jānis Peters (the Chairman of the Latvian Writers' Union), criticized the CPL for its reactionary attitude to the new Soviet policy of *perestroika* (restructuring) and advocated more radical political and economic change. In October representatives of the leading opposition movements, together with CPL radicals, organized the inaugural congress of the Popular Front of Latvia (PFL), at which delegates resolved to seek sovereignty for Latvia within a renewed Soviet federation. The PFL, chaired by Dainis Ivāns, rapidly became the largest and most influential political force in Latvia, with an estimated membership of 250,000 by the end of 1988.

In September 1988 Boris Pugo was transferred to the Russian and Soviet capital, Moscow, and replaced as First Secretary of the CPL by Jānis Vagris. The new CPL leadership came increasingly under the influence of members of the PFL. At the end of September Latvian was designated the state language. In March 1989 candidates supported by the PFL won 26 of the 34 contested seats in elections to the USSR's Congress of People's Deputies. On 28 July, following similar moves by Lithuania and Estonia, the Latvian Supreme Soviet (legislature) adopted a declaration of sovereignty and economic independence. However, there was growing support within the republic for full independence from the USSR, as advocated by the Latvian National Independence Movement (LNIM), formed in 1988. In December 1989, despite the establishment of political groups opposed to the PFL, candidates supported by the PFL won some 75% of seats contested in local elections.

In January 1990 the Latvian Supreme Soviet voted to abolish the constitutional provisions that guaranteed the CPL's political predominance. In the following month the Supreme Soviet adopted a declaration condemning the Latvian legislature's decision to request admission to the USSR in 1940, and the flag, state emblems and anthem of pre-1940 Latvia were restored to official use. At elections to the Supreme Soviet held in March and April 1990, pro-independence candidates endorsed by the PFL won 131 of the 201 seats; the CPL and the anti-independence Interfront (dominated by members of the Russian-speaking population) together won 59 seats. The CPL subsequently split into two parties: the majority of delegates at an extraordinary congress rejected a motion to leave the Communist Party of the Soviet Union (CPSU), and elected Alfrēds Rubiks, an opponent of independence, as First Secretary. Meanwhile, a pro-independence faction established the Independent Communist Party of Latvia, under the chairmanship of Ivars Kezbers.

The new Supreme Council (the former Supreme Soviet) was convened in early May 1990, and elected Anatolijs Gorbunovs, a member of the CPSU-affiliated CPL, as its Chairman (*de facto* President of the Republic). On 4 May the Supreme Council adopted a resolution that declared the incorporation of Latvia into the USSR in 1940 as unlawful, and announced the beginning of a transitional period that was to lead to full political and economic independence. Four articles of the 1922 Constitution, defining Latvia as an independent democratic state and asserting the sovereignty of the Latvian people, were restored, and were to form the basis of the newly declared Republic of Latvia's legitimacy. Ivars Godmanis, the Deputy Chairman of the PFL, was elected Prime Minister in a new, PFL-dominated Government. Meanwhile, a rival body to the Supreme Soviet had been convened at the end of April 1990. This Congress of Latvia had been elected in an unofficial poll, in which some 700,000 people were reported to have participated: only citizens of the pre-1940 republic and their descendants had been entitled to vote. The Congress, in which members of the radical LNIM predominated, declared Latvia to be an occupied country and adopted resolutions on independence and the withdrawal of Soviet troops.

The Supreme Council's resolutions, although more cautious than independence declarations adopted in Lithuania and Estonia, severely strained relations with the Soviet authorities. On 14 May 1990 the Soviet President, Mikhail Gorbachev, issued a decree that annulled the Latvian declaration of independence, condemning it as a violation of the USSR Constitution. The declaration was also opposed within the republic by some non-Latvians, who organized protest strikes and demonstrations. In subsequent months local anti-Government movements (allied with Soviet troops stationed in Latvia) conducted a campaign of propaganda and harassment against the Government. In December the Latvian Government claimed that special units (OMON) of the Soviet Ministry of Internal Affairs had been responsible for a series of explosions in Rīga, and in January 1991 OMON troops seized the Rīga Press House, previously the property of the CPL. Later in January a 'Committee of Public Salvation', headed by Alfrēds Rubiks, declared itself as a rival Government to the Godmanis administration; on the same day five people died when OMON troops attacked the Ministry of the Interior in Rīga. (In November 1999 10 former Soviet officers were convicted of attempting to overthrow the Latvian Government in 1991: seven received suspended prison sentences of up to four years' duration.)

The attempted seizure of power by Rubiks' Committee reinforced opposition in Latvia to inclusion in the new union treaty being prepared by nine Soviet republics. Latvia refused to conduct the all-Union referendum on the future of the USSR, which was scheduled for 17 March 1991 (although some 680,000 people, mostly Russians and Ukrainians, did participate, on an unofficial basis). Instead, a referendum on Latvian independence took place on 3 March. Of those eligible to vote, 87.6% participated, of whom, according to official results, 73.7% endorsed proposals for a democratic, independent Latvian republic.

At the time of the attempted overthrow of the Gorbachev administration in Moscow in August 1991, immediate Soviet military intervention in Latvia was widely anticipated. However, an emergency session of the Supreme Council was convened and the full independence of Latvia was proclaimed. As the coup collapsed, the Godmanis Government took prompt action to assert control in Latvia, banning the CPL and detaining Rubiks. (In July 1995 Rubiks was found guilty of the coup attempt. He was released in November 1997.) On 6 September 1991 the USSR State Council formally recognized the independent Republic of Latvia, and the country was admitted to the UN later that month. In late 1991 the Supreme Council adopted legislation guaranteeing the right of citizenship to all citizens of the pre-1940 republic (including non-ethnic Latvians) and their descendants. Remaining residents of Latvia (mainly Russians and other Slavs) were to be required to apply for naturalization after final legislation governing citizenship was determined by a restored Saeima.

The first legislative elections since the restoration of independence took place in June 1993, with the participation of about 90% of the electorate. Only citizens of pre-1940 Latvia and their descendants were entitled to vote; consequently, some 27% of the population (mainly ethnic Russians) were excluded from the election. A total of 23 parties, movements and alliances contested the poll, of which eight secured representation in the

100-seat Saeima. The Latvian Way, a broadly-based movement established earlier in the year, emerged as the strongest party, with more than 32% of the votes and 36 seats in the assembly. Only 11 of the elected deputies were non-ethnic Latvians (six of whom were ethnic Russians). The results of the elections demonstrated strong popular support for the more moderate nationalist parties, and socialist-orientated parties (including the successor of the CPL, the Latvian Socialist Party—LSP) failed to win representation. The PFL also failed to secure any seats.

At the first session of the Saeima on 6 July 1993 Anatolijs Gorbunovs was elected Chairman (speaker). The Saeima also voted to restore the Constitution of 1922, and undertook to elect the President of the Republic from among three prominent deputies. At a third round of voting on 7 July 1993 Guntis Ulmanis (the great-nephew of Kārlis Ulmanis) of the revived LFU succeeded in winning a majority of 53 votes. He was inaugurated as President the following day, whereupon he appointed Valdis Birkavs (formerly a Deputy Chairman of the Supreme Council and a leading member of the Latvian Way) as Prime Minister. Birkavs' Cabinet of Ministers represented a coalition agreement between the Latvian Way (the majority partner) and the LFU.

The requirements for naturalization proposed by the Government's draft citizenship law included a minimum of 10 years' permanent residence, a knowledge of Latvian to conversational level and an oath of loyalty to the republic. In March 1994 the Saeima approved the establishment of the new post of State Minister for Human Rights, in an attempt to counter accusations of violations of minority rights. Although final legislation on citizenship and naturalization was adopted by the Saeima in June, following international criticism, and amid concern that the new law would jeopardize Latvia's application for membership of the Council of Europe (see p. 190), the Cabinet of Ministers persuaded President Ulmanis to reject it. The Saeima adopted an amended citizenship law in July. Latvia was admitted to the Council of Europe in February 1995.

Meanwhile, in July 1994 the LFU announced its withdrawal from the governing coalition, following disagreements with the Latvian Way over economic and agricultural policy. A new Cabinet was appointed in September. It, too, was dominated by Latvian Way members, including the Prime Minister, Māris Gailis (hitherto Deputy Prime Minister and Minister of State Reform); Birkavs became Deputy Prime Minister and Minister of Foreign Affairs. Four opposition factions within the Saeima—including the Latvian National Conservative Party (LNCP), as the LNIM had been renamed, and the LFU—announced their union as a 'national bloc' to co-ordinate opposition activities in the legislature.

A general election was held on 30 September–1 October 1995. Nine parties and coalitions succeeded in obtaining the 5% of the votes required for representation in the Saeima; as a result, the assembly was highly fragmented. The Latvian Way's share of the 100 seats was more than halved, to 17, while the largest number of seats (18) was won by the newly established, leftist Democratic Party Saimnieks (The Master—DPS). The People's Movement for Latvia (Zigerists' Party—PML) won 16 seats. The party, established by Joahims Zigerists, had campaigned on a platform of nationalist and anti-Russian policies; moreover, Zigerists was linked to an extremist right-wing organization in Germany, and in 1994 had been convicted in that country for inciting racial hatred. Negotiations among parties to form a coalition government capable of commanding a parliamentary majority proved to be protracted. In December 1995 the Saeima finally endorsed a Cabinet of Ministers led by Andris Šķēle (an entrepreneur with no party affiliation). The new Government was a broad coalition of the DPS, the Latvian Way, the Union 'For Fatherland and Freedom' (UFF), the LNCP, the LFU and the Latvian Unity Party (LUP). The PML was, notably, excluded from the coalition. Former Prime Ministers Gailis and Birkavs were appointed to the new Cabinet, the former as Deputy Prime Minister and Minister of Environmental Protection and Regional Development, and the latter as Minister of Foreign Affairs. The stability of the coalition was tested in May 1996, when the Deputy Prime Minister and Minister of Agriculture, Alberīs Kauls, was dismissed, after criticizing the Prime Minister's agricultural policies. The LUP (of which Kauls was the leader) temporarily withdrew its support from the coalition, but shortly afterwards rejoined the Government, having secured approval for a new candidate as Minister of Agriculture.

On 18 June 1996 the Saeima re-elected Guntis Ulmanis as President for a second three-year term. The presidential election revealed disagreements among the coalition members over the choice of candidate, and in July Šķēle conducted a cabinet reshuffle in an attempt to create a more cohesive Government. In the same month it was announced that the LUP was to merge with the DPS, reinforcing the latter as the dominant party in the coalition. None the less, instability in both the Government and the legislature continued. In October Aivars Kreituss tendered his resignation as Minister of Finance, having in the previous month been expelled from the DPS for his perceived failure to promote the party's interests. Meanwhile, Alfrēds Čepānis was elected to the post of Chairman of the Saeima, following the removal from office of Ilga Kreituse. In the same month the Deputy Prime Minister, Ziedonis Čevers (also leader of the DPS) submitted his resignation, citing differences of opinion with Šķēle. The collapse of the coalition appeared inevitable in January 1997, when Šķēle resigned as Prime Minister, in what was interpreted as a response to criticism from President Ulmanis over Šķēle's approval of Vasilijs Melniks as the new Minister of Finance. Negotiations began for the formation of a new Government, but Šķēle was swiftly reappointed by Ulmanis, who indicated his support for the continuation of the Prime Minister's economic and structural reforms. A new, largely unaltered Cabinet was appointed in February; Roberts Zīle replaced Melniks as Minister of Finance. Local elections conducted in March demonstrated a considerable increase in support for the LFU, which won 168 seats, compared with 83 for the DPS and 44 for the UFF.

By July 1997 the governing coalition had begun to disintegrate, not least because a series of corruption scandals had, since May, prompted the resignation of several ministers, and at the end of the month Šķēle announced the resignation of the Government. Ulmanis invited Guntars Krasts, the outgoing Minister of the Economy, to form a new administration. In early August the Saeima approved Krasts' proposals for a new, five-party coalition, comprising the Conservative Union 'For Fatherland and Freedom'/LNNK (his own party, formed in the previous month by the merger of the UFF and the Latvian National Independence Movement—LNNK), the DPS, the Latvian Way, the LFU and the Christian Democratic Union of Latvia (CDUL). Krasts' leadership was tested in early 1998 following suggestions by an investigative parliamentary committee that he had been guilty of negligence with regard to a privatization proposal for the state power utility, Latvenergo, as Minister of the Economy. In March Krasts formally requested that the Saeima conduct a vote of confidence in his personal integrity, in order to confirm his mandate. The refusal of any parliamentary faction to organize such a vote was interpreted by the Prime Minister as an endorsement of his leadership. In that month former Prime Minister Šķēle announced the formation of a new political party, later named the People's Party, to contest the forthcoming elections.

In April 1998 the Minister of the Economy, Atis Sausnītis, was dismissed, following a well-publicized attempt to draw attention to the possible adverse economic consequences of sustained diplomatic tensions with Russia (see below). Sensing that Krasts' Government might be on the point of collapse, the DPS announced its withdrawal from the coalition. At the end of the month, however, Krasts survived a parliamentary vote of 'no confidence' proposed by the LFU and the Latvian Way. At the same session the Saeima approved appointments to a new coalition Government, with members of the Cabinet of Ministers drawn from the LFU, the Latvian Way and an alliance of the Latvian National Reform Party and the Latvian Green Party.

The question of citizenship returned to prominence in April 1998, following the adoption, in response to long-standing recommendations made by the OSCE, of draft amendments to the strict legislation regulating rights to citizenship. The amendments, which removed the age-related system of naturalization that allocated dates for application by age-group, granted citizenship to stateless children (permanently resident in Latvia) born after the 1991 declaration of independence and relaxed the citizenship requirements for Russian-speakers, were approved by the Saeima in June 1998. Although widely welcomed elsewhere in Europe, the amendments were deemed inadequate by the Russian authorities, and nationalist groups within the Latvian legislature rallied sufficient support inside and outside the Saeima to force a delay to the enactment of the new legislation and the organization of a referendum on the subject. The referendum was duly conducted concurrently with the 3 October general election; the results demonstrated a 52.5% majority in favour of the amendments, which were promulgated later in the month.

At the general election, Šķēle's People's Party was the most successful single party, taking 21.2% of the votes (and 24 seats), ahead of the Latvian Way with 18.1% (21 seats) and the Conservative Union 'For Fatherland and Freedom'/LNNK with 14.7% (17 seats). Only six of the 21 participating political parties secured the minimum 5% of the votes necessary for representation in the Saeima. It was not until the end of November that the Saeima approved a new, three-party, minority coalition Government, to be headed by Vilis Krištopans of the Latvian Way. The coalition, comprising the Latvian Way, the Conservative Union 'For Fatherland and Freedom'/LNNK and the New Party (which held eight legislative seats), also drew support from the Latvian Social Democratic Alliance, which controlled 14 seats in the Saeima. In early February 1999 the Social Democrats formally joined the coalition with the appointment of one of their members to the agriculture portfolio in the Cabinet of Ministers.

On 17 June 1999 Vaira Viķe-Freiberga was elected President at a seventh round of voting in the Saeima, with the support of 53 deputies (compared with 20 for Valdis Birkavs of the Latvian Way and nine for Ingrīda Udre of the New Party). Born in Latvia, but resident in Canada from the end of the Second World War until 1998, Viķe-Freiberga thus became the first female President in central and eastern Europe. At her inauguration on 8 July 1999 Viķe-Freiberga identified as priorities for her presidency Latvia's entry into the European Union (EU, see p. 208) and the North Atlantic Treaty Organization (NATO, see p. 289). Three days before her inauguration, Kristopans announced his Government's resignation, apparently in response to the recent signing by the Conservative Union 'For Fatherland and Freedom'/LNNK of a co-operation accord with the opposition People's Party. President Viķe-Freiberga subsequently asked Andris Šķēle to form a new government. Šķēle thus became Prime Minister for the third time, leading a coalition of his People's Party, the Conservative Union 'For Fatherland and Freedom'/LNNK and the Latvian Way; the coalition controlled 62 of the 100 seats in the Saeima.

In early July 1999 the Saeima adopted controversial new language legislation, which, notably, required that all business and all state- and municipally-organized gatherings be conducted in Latvian. Russia immediately denounced the legislation as discriminatory against Latvia's national minorities, and it was also condemned by the OSCE, the Council of Europe and the European Commission. Within Latvia, the legislation attracted criticism from groups representing non-ethnic Latvians. Viķe-Freiberga swiftly returned the legislation to the Saeima for further consideration, and revised legislation was approved in early December. The new law, which incorporated amendments urged by the OSCE, was said by its proponents to allow the preservation and strengthening of the Latvian language, while ensuring compliance with international standards: Latvian was to be used for all business in the state sector, and for certain private-sector activities. In August 2000 implementation regulations were adopted, concerning issues such as transliteration, and the revised language law came into effect at the beginning of September, prompting protests from both the parliamentary opposition and the ethnic Russian community. Meanwhile, amendments to the pensions law were approved by the Saeima in early August 1999, whereby the statutory retirement age was to be increased, and payments reduced for those of pensionable age who continued to work. The changes were condemned by trade unions and groups representing the elderly.

A much-publicized paedophilia scandal assumed wider political significance in February 2000, when Jānis Ādamsons, the Chairman of a parliamentary commission established to investigate the affair, alleged that witnesses had implicated Prime Minister Šķēle, former Prime Minister Birkavs (by this time Minister of Justice) and the head of the State Revenue Service. The Office of the Prosecutor-General immediately instigated slander proceedings, and Šķēle denounced the assertions as politically motivated. The charges against Birkavs and Sonciks were dismissed on 31 July, and on the following day the Prosecutor-General's office announced that it had closed the case against Šķēle.

In the mean time, Šķēle had resigned the premiership in mid-April 2000, after the Latvian Way withdrew from the governing coalition, owing to a dispute over the running of the Latvian Privatization Agency. President Viķe-Freiberga asked Andris Bērziņš, hitherto the Mayor of Rīga, to form a new government; his cabinet (a coalition of the People's Party, the Latvian Way, the Conservative Union 'For Fatherland and Freedom'/LNNK and the New Party) was approved by the Saeima in early May. In mid-January 2001 the New Party was renamed the New Christian Party; the New Faction was formed by disenchanted former New Party members. In late January the Prime Minister asked the New Faction to leave the Government, after parliamentary deputies from the party supported an opposition tax proposal. The party resigned from the Government early in the following month, and in late February it signed a co-operation agreement with the Latvian Social Democratic Workers' Party. Local elections held in March demonstrated a considerable increase in support for the latter party in the capital and in surrounding areas.

In November 2001 Einārs Repše resigned as Governor of the Bank of Latvia, in order to found a new political party, New Era. The rightist party attracted immediate popular support, and Repše was elected Chairman of New Era at its founding congress in early February 2002. In May the Saeima adopted amendments to national electoral legislation, abolishing the controversial requirement that candidates be fluent in the Latvian language, which had been perceived as an obstacle to NATO membership; however, the Saeima had passed legislation reinforcing Latvian as the official working language of parliament at the end of the preceding month. Also in May the new Christian, centrist First Party of Latvia (LPP) was formed.

In legislative elections held, as scheduled, on 5 October 2002, Einars Repše's New Era won 23.9% of the votes cast (26 seats); the leftist, pro-Russian electoral bloc For Human Rights in a United Latvia, which included the National Harmony Party and the Latvian Socialist Party, obtained 18.9% of the votes (25 seats); and the People's Party received 16.7% (20 seats). Other parties to achieve representation in the Saeima were the Greens' and Farmers' Union (an alliance of the Centre Party: Latvian Farmers' Union and the Latvian Green Party), with 12 seats, the LPP (10 seats) and the Conservative Union 'For Fatherland and Freedom'/LNNK (seven); the Latvian Way failed to secure the 5% of the votes required to obtain a seat in the Saeima. The rate of participation by the electorate was some 72.5%. Following the collapse of talks with the People's Party, Repše formed a coalition government with the LPP, the Greens' and Farmers' Union and the Conservative Union 'For Fatherland and Freedom'/LNNK. The new Government, led by Repše, was approved by the Saeima on 7 November; New Era assumed nine posts in the Cabinet of Ministers, the LPP took responsibility for four, the Greens' and Farmers' Union took three portfolios (as well as the position of parliamentary Chairman), and the Conservative Union 'For Fatherland and Freedom'/LNNK controlled two ministries. The Minister of Defence, Ģirts Kristovskis, was the only member of the Cabinet of Ministers to have retained his previous portfolio; a new post of Deputy Prime Minister was established, to which Ainārs Šlesers was appointed. At the end of November Atis Slakteris replaced Andris Šķēle as Chairman of the People's Party; in January 2003 Šķēle announced his intention to withdraw from politics.

In early January 2003 the Cabinet of Ministers approved measures that increased ministers' salaries three-fold, with the reported aim of discouraging corruption. In February the National Harmony Party withdrew from the For Human Rights in a United Latvia alliance, apparently in a desire to pursue more moderate policies. In late March the Minister of Health, Aris Auders, was dismissed, despite having survived a parliamentary vote of 'no confidence' in January, following allegations of corruption in his former post; he was replaced by Ingrīda Circene. In mid-May Jānis Naglis was elected as Chairman of the Latvian Way, in succession to former Prime Minister Andris Bērziņš. In early June the Latvian Socialist Party withdrew from the For Human Rights in a United Latvia alliance, effectively dissolving the coalition.

In mid-June 2003 Prime Minister Repše survived a vote of 'no confidence' in the Saeima, proposed by the People's Party. On 20 June Vaira Viķe-Freiberga was re-elected unopposed (by 88 votes to six) to serve a second term of office; she was inaugurated as President on 8 July. In late September tensions emerged within the Government, when its constituent parties (with the exception of New Era) issued a statement expressing support for the coalition, but a lack of confidence in the Prime Minister, accusing him of authoritarianism. A compromise agreement was reached, following inter-party discussions, and in mid-November the Chairmen of the four ruling parties signed a memorandum of understanding, which emphasized the equality of

coalition members; the importance of unanimity; the need for member parties to refrain from public criticism, in the absence of substantiating evidence; and the need for the Prime Minister to inform party leaders in a timely manner should he wish to dismiss a minister. On 26 January 2004 Repše dismissed Deputy Prime Minister Ainārs Šlesers of the LPP, apparently owing to a failure to perform his duties, although Šlesers alleged that his dismissal had been prompted by a proposal to establish a special investigative committee to examine some of the premier's property dealings. Two days later the LPP withdrew from the Government, and on 5 February Repše announced the resignation of his administration, declaring that a minority Government was unworkable.

Following the collapse of the Government, President Viķe-Freiberga emphasized the need to maintain a stable political course in preparation for NATO and EU membership, and on 20 February 2004 she nominated the co-Chairman of the Latvian Green Party (part of the Greens' and Farmers' Union), Indulis Emsis, as premier. Following negotiations, in early March Emsis secured the support of the Greens' and Farmers' Union, the LPP and the People's Party, and a new right-of-centre coalition Government was approved by the Saeima on 9 March, with the parliamentary support of the left-wing National Harmony Party; Emsis also received the support of New Era member Andrejs Radzevičs, who was appointed Minister of Regional Development and Local Governments. Šlesers was re-appointed Deputy Prime Minister.

Latvia's post-independence relations with its eastern neighbour, Russia, were troubled by two issues. The first concerned the citizenship and linguistic rights of Latvia's large Russian community (see above). Of comparable importance was the issue of the 100,000 former Soviet troops still stationed in Latvia (jurisdiction over whom had been transferred, following the dissolution of the USSR, to Russia). Following negotiations, which commenced in 1992, withdrawal of the troops began early in that year. The process was hampered by a series of disagreements, in particular over the issue of a Russian military radar station at Skrunda, in western Latvia, that the Russians wished to retain. However, in February 1994 Latvia and Russia accepted a US-sponsored compromise, and in April agreements were concluded on the complete withdrawal of the remaining 10,000 Russian troops by the end of August, as well as on social guarantees for the estimated 22,000 Russian military pensioners residing in Latvia. Installations at the Skrunda base were subsequently dismantled.

Negotiations regarding the demarcation of the Latvian–Russian border, and Latvia's claim to some 1,640 sq km of land transferred from Latvia to Russia during the Soviet era, commenced in April 1996. Latvia initially insisted (as Estonia had done) that any future border agreement should include a reference to the 1920 treaty in which Russia recognized Latvia's independence. However, in February 1997 the Latvian administration abandoned this demand, and agreed that claims to property in the disputed territory should be discussed separately from the main border agreement. In March a draft treaty on the demarcation of the border was agreed by the two countries, and full agreement on a border treaty was reached in October. However, the Russian Government subsequently signalled its intention to link its acceptance of the treaty to an improvement in the civil rights of ethnic Russians in Latvia. Relations became strained in March 1998, following the use of force by the Latvian police in order to disperse a demonstration of about 1,000 protesters—mostly ethnic-Russian pensioners—who were demonstrating in Rīga against price increases. Relations deteriorated further later in the month, following the organization, in Rīga, of a rally of Latvian veterans of Nazi German *Waffen SS* units, who had fought Soviet forces during the Second World War; the participation of senior Latvian politicians and military personnel attracted particular criticism from the Russian authorities. When the rally was repeated in March 2000 government officials and serving military officers were not permitted to take part. Meanwhile, the Government had been criticized by Russia for what it perceived as anti-Soviet bias in the pursuit of criminal cases against individuals accused of war crimes. The Russian authorities asserted that Latvia's concern to expedite the prosecution of those suspected of crimes under the Soviet occupation contrasted with its apparent tardiness in investigating and bringing to justice alleged perpetrators of war crimes during the Nazi era. Tensions arising from repeated Russian threats to impose economic sanctions against Latvia, if the Government did not promptly address the perceived infringement of minority rights, were exacerbated by Latvia's new state language law (see above). In November 1999 the Russian State Duma voted to impose economic sanctions against Latvia, although this decision was never enforced. The revised language law, as approved by the Saeima in December, was again denounced by Russia. The OSCE's announcement, in December 2001, that its mandate in Latvia had been fulfilled, and the subsequent closure of its office there, also prompted criticism from Russia, which maintained that insufficient measures had been taken to protect the ethnic Russian population in Latvia from discrimination. Economic issues threatened to raise further tensions between the two countries in early 2003, following Russia's decision to cease using the port of Ventspils for its petroleum exports, primarily owing to the opening of a new Russian petroleum terminal at Primorsk. Russia also condemned proposed amendments to legislation on education, according to which 60% of lessons in minority schools were to be taught in the Latvian language from September 2004; in February 2004 thousands of ethnic Russians protested in Rīga against the reforms.

Latvia enjoys close political, economic and cultural relations with Estonia and Lithuania, and the three countries have established a number of institutions to promote co-operation, including the interparliamentary Baltic Assembly and the Baltic Council of Ministers (which meets twice yearly). In 1992 Latvia became a founder member, with Estonia, Lithuania and other countries of the region, of the Council of Baltic Sea States (see p. 188), a principal aim of which was to assist the political and economic development of its three former communist member states. Differences arose in the mid-1990s between Latvia and its two closest Baltic neighbours, in particular concerning the demarcation of maritime borders. However, agreement on the delimitation of the sea border with Estonia was reached in May 1996, and the document was ratified by both countries' legislatures in August. A further agreement on fishing rights was concluded in early 1997. The demarcation of the land border between the two countries was completed in December 1997. Negotiations between Latvia and Lithuania on their maritime border were complicated in October 1996 by the Saeima's ratification of an agreement with two foreign petroleum companies to explore and develop offshore oilfields in disputed areas of the Baltic Sea. Although the two countries signed an agreement on the delimitation of their territorial waters in July 1999, protests from the Latvian fishing industry prevented the agreement from being ratified by the Saeima. In December 2000 a protocol was signed on the re-demarcation of the land border between the two countries.

A priority of Latvian foreign policy has been attaining full membership of the EU. Latvia became an associate member of the EU in June 1995, and in October it applied for full membership. A number of political and economic agreements concluded between the EU and the Baltic states in 1995, with the aim of facilitating their membership of the EU, came into force on 1 February 1998. In May, in contravention of the European Convention on Human Rights and Fundamental Freedoms, the Saeima voted to retain the death penalty for certain criminal acts, frustrating the attempts of President Ulmanis to fulfil a commitment to abolish capital punishment made by Latvia on its accession to the Council of Europe in 1995. The Saeima finally abolished the death penalty in April 1999. In December a summit meeting of EU Heads of State and Government, held in Helsinki, Finland, endorsed proposals to begin accession talks with six countries, including Latvia; formal negotiations commenced in February 2000, and in December 2002 Latvia, together with nine other countries, was formally invited to become a full member of the EU from May 2004. A referendum on EU membership was held in Latvia on 20 September 2003. Of the 72.5% of the electorate who participated in the plebiscite, 66.8% voted in support of Latvia's accession to the EU. The country became a full member on 1 May 2004.

Latvia also sought membership of NATO, as the principal guarantor of its security. In February 2002 the Secretary-General of NATO warned the Latvian Government that its existing language requirements, which demanded that candidates standing in regional and national elections be fluent in Latvian, threatened to affect adversely the likelihood of the country being admitted to the Alliance; amendments to the electoral law were duly passed in May, mitigating the language requirements. At a summit meeting held in Prague, Czech Republic, in November, Latvia was one of seven countries (including Estonia and Lithuania) invited to join NATO in 2004. Latvia became a full member of the Alliance on 29 March 2004.

Government

Under the terms of the 1922 Constitution, which was restored in July 1993 (and amended in December 1997), Latvia is an independent democratic parliamentary republic. The supreme legislative body is the Saeima (Parliament), the 100 members of which are elected by universal adult suffrage for a four-year term. The President of the Republic, who is Head of State, is elected by a secret ballot of the Saeima, also for a period of four years. The President, who is also Head of the Armed Forces, may not serve for more than two consecutive terms. Executive power is held by the Cabinet of Ministers, which is headed by the Prime Minister. The Prime Minister is appointed by the President; the remaining members of the Cabinet are nominated by the Prime Minister. For administrative purposes, Latvia is divided into 26 districts and seven towns (including the capital, Rīga).

Defence

Until independence in August 1991, Latvia had no armed forces separate from those of the USSR. A Ministry of Defence was established in November, and by August 2003 Latvia's total armed forces numbered 4,880, comprising an army of 4,000, a navy of 620 and an air force of 250. In addition, there was a paramilitary force numbering 3,200. There were also reserve forces in the national guard (of an estimated 13,050). Military service is compulsory from 19 years of age and lasts for 12 months. In August 1994 the withdrawal from Latvia of all former Soviet forces was completed. In January 1998 it was announced that an additional 742-strong professional military unit (the Latvian Battalion—LATBAT) was to be created over the next four years. In 1998 the Baltic states agreed to establish a joint airspace observation system (BALTNET), a defence college (BALTDEFCOL) and a peace-keeping battalion (BALTBAT). A Baltic naval unit (BALTRON) was established in mid-1998. Latvia joined the North Atlantic Treaty Organization's (NATO) 'Partnership for Peace' (see p. 291) programme in February 1994, and became a full member of the Alliance on 29 March 2004. In early April BALTNET was formally absorbed into the NATO Integrated Air Defence System. The budget for 2003 allocated 111m. LVL to defence, compared with defence expenditure of 91m. LVL in 2002.

Economic Affairs

In 2002, according to estimates by the World Bank, Latvia's gross national income (GNI), measured at average 2000–02 prices, was US $8,134m., equivalent to $3,480 per head (or $8,940 per head on an international purchasing-power parity basis). During 1990–2002, it was estimated, the population decreased by an annual average of 1.1%, while gross domestic product (GDP) per head decreased at an average annual rate of 1.5%, in real terms. Overall GDP decreased, in real terms, by an annual average of 2.6% in 1990–2002; however, according to official figures, real GDP increased by 6.1% in 2002 and by 7.5% in 2003.

Agriculture (including hunting, forestry and fishing) contributed 4.5% of GDP in 2003, and provided 15.5% of employment in 2002. The principal sectors are dairy farming and pig-breeding. Cereals, sugar beet, potatoes and fodder crops are the main crops grown. As part of the process of land reform and privatization, the liquidation of collective and state farms was undertaken in the early 1990s (some 38% of all arable land had been privatized by 1995). In 2003 Latvia approved a seven-year ban on the sale of rural land to foreign purchasers. Fishing makes an important contribution to the economy (an estimated 70% of the total annual catch is exported). There was considerable growth potential in the forestry industry (43.9% of Latvia's land area is classified as forest), and output increased rapidly from 1996. Agricultural GDP decreased, in real terms, by an average of 5.2% per year in 1990–2002; however, according to official figures, the real GDP of the sector (excluding fishing) increased by 4.2% in 2002 and by 2.6% in 2003.

Industry (comprising mining and quarrying, manufacturing, construction and utilities) contributed 24.5% of GDP in 2003, and provided 25.5% of employment in 2002. Industrial GDP declined, in real terms, at an average annual rate of 7.4% in 1990–2002. However, real sectoral GDP increased by 6.9% in 2001 and by 5.8% in 2002.

Mining and quarrying contributed just 0.2% of GDP in 2003, and employed only 0.3% of workers in 2002. Latvia has limited mineral resources, the most important being peat, dolomite, limestone, gypsum, amber, gravel and sand. Offshore and onshore petroleum reserves have been located. The GDP of the mining sector decreased at an average annual rate of 14.5% in 1990–98; however, real mining GDP increased by 5.7% in 1999, by 8.1% in 2000, by 16.7% in 2001, by 7.7% in 2002 and by 7.2% in 2003.

The manufacturing sector contributed 14.9% of GDP in 2003, and provided 16.9% of employment in 2002. In 2001 the principal branches of manufacturing, measured by value of output, were food products (31.6%), wood products, light industry and machinery and equipment. Real manufacturing GDP decreased by an average of 6.4% per year in 1990–2002. However, according to official figures, the GDP of the sector increased, in real terms, by 7.2% in 2002 and by 9.1% in 2003.

Latvia is highly dependent on imported fuels to provide energy. In 2002 imports of mineral products represented 9.7% of the total value of Latvia's imports. Electric energy is supplied primarily by Estonia and Lithuania, and petroleum products are supplied by Russia and Lithuania. In 2000 hydroelectric plants provided some 68.2% of annual domestic electricity production in Latvia; a further 27.3% was derived from natural gas, and the remainder from petroleum and coal.

The services sector has increased in importance, and in 2003 it contributed 70.9% of GDP; the sector accounted for 59.0% of employment in 2002. The sector's GDP increased, in real terms, by an average of 2.6% annually during 1990–2002; according to official figures, real services GDP increased by 5.9% in 2002 and by 7.0% in 2003.

In 2002 Latvia recorded a visible trade deficit of US $1,444m., and there was a deficit of $647m. on the current account of the balance of payments. The principal source of imports in 2002 was Germany, which accounted for 17.2% of total imports; other major sources were Lithuania, Russia, Finland, Sweden, Estonia and Poland. The main market for exports in that year was also Germany, accounting for 15.5% of total exports; other significant purchasers were the United Kingdom, Sweden, Lithuania, Estonia and Denmark. The principal exports in 2002 were wood and wood products, followed by base metals and manufactures, textiles, prepared foodstuffs, beverages and tobacco, machinery and electrical equipment, miscellaneous manufactured items, and chemicals. The principal imports in that year were machinery and electrical equipment, chemicals, vehicles and transport equipment, mineral products, base metals and manufactures, textiles, and foodstuffs, beverages and tobacco.

In 2001 the consolidated state budget recorded a deficit of 64.6m. LVL (equivalent to 1.4% of GDP). Latvia's total external debt at the end of 2001 was US $5,710m., of which $978m. was long-term public debt. In that year the cost of debt-servicing was equivalent to 13.7% of the value of exports of goods and services. Annual inflation averaged 43.9% in 1991–2002; the rate of increase in consumer prices had slowed to an average of 17.6% by 1996, and it continued to decline in subsequent years. Consumer prices increased by 1.9% in 2002 and by 2.9% in 2003. At 1 March 2004 some 94,900 people were registered as unemployed (representing 9.0% of the economically active population).

Latvia is a member (as a 'country of operations') of the European Bank for Reconstruction and Development (EBRD, see p. 203). An agreement on a free-trade area between Latvia, Lithuania and Estonia entered into effect in April 1994, and in July of that year Latvia signed an agreement on free trade with the European Union (EU, see p. 208); Latvia became an associate member of the EU in June 1995, and a full member on 1 May 2004. Latvia became a member of the World Trade Organization (WTO, see p. 343) in February 1999.

The Government's programme of stabilization, initiated in 1992, achieved considerable success. A crisis in the banking sector in 1995 undermined economic recovery, but following the introduction of new legal requirements and stricter bank licensing regulations the situation was stabilized by 1996. Growth slowed in 1999, largely as a consequence of the Russian economic crisis of 1998. However, there were signs of economic recovery in 2000, and in 2001 Latvia demonstrated one of the best economic performances of all the candidate countries for EU membership. The rate of inflation in 2002 was the lowest to be recorded since independence, and strong growth was recorded in both 2002 and 2003. However, there was concern at the sizeable budgetary deficit, particularly since the EU stipulated that the public-finance deficit of member states be restrained to less than 3% of GDP. In anticipation of the increased financial commitments associated with membership of the EU and NATO from 2004 and in order to conform with EU practices, in December 2003 the Saeima adopted legislative amendments increasing the rate of value-added tax (VAT) from 9% to 18%, and imposing VAT of 5% on a number of previously untaxed goods from 1 May 2004 (the rate of corporate income tax, however, was to be reduced from 19% to 15%, in an effort to encourage increased foreign direct investment). None the less, international concerns focused on Latvia's role as a regional financial centre and the difficulties in eliminating the associated practice of money 'laundering' (the processing of illicitly obtained funds into legitimate holdings). Although Latvia was the poorest of the EU accession countries, its economy was expected to continue to expand rapidly. The budget for 2004 envisaged GDP growth of 6.1%, in real terms, and an annual rate of consumer-price inflation of around 3%, together with a budgetary deficit equivalent to some 2% of GDP.

Education

Primary education begins at seven years of age and lasts for four years. Secondary education, beginning at the age of 11, lasts for up to eight years, comprising a first cycle of five years and a second of three years. The first nine years of education are officially compulsory. In 1998 primary enrolment included 94% of children in the relevant age-group. The comparable ratio in secondary enrolment was 83%. In the 2002/03 academic year some 63% of school-age pupils were taught in Latvian-language schools and some 26% were taught in Russian-language schools; 11% were taught in schools offering instruction in both Latvian and Russian. In 2002/03 there were 158 Russian schools, five Polish schools, one Ukrainian school and one Belarusian school. Latvian was due to become the main language of instruction in all secondary schools from September 2004. In 2002/03 higher education was offered at 37 institutions, with a total enrolment of 118,944 students. According to the IMF, in 2001 consolidated central Government expenditure on education amounted to 87.8m. LVL (representing 6.3% of expenditure).

Public Holidays

2004: 1 January (New Year's Day), 9–12 April (Easter), 1 May (Labour Day), 23–24 June (Midsummer Festival), 18 November (National Day, proclamation of the Republic), 25–26 December (Christmas), 31 December (New Year's Eve).

2005: 1 January (New Year's Day), 25–28 March (Easter), 1 May (Labour Day), 23–24 June (Midsummer Festival), 18 November (National Day, proclamation of the Republic), 25–26 December (Christmas), 31 December (New Year's Eve).

Weights and Measures

The metric system is in force.

Statistical Survey

Source (unless otherwise stated): Central Statistical Bureau of Latvia, Lāčplēša iela 1, Rīga 1301; tel. 736-6850; fax 783-0137; e-mail csb@csb.lv; internet www.csb.lv.

Area and Population

AREA, POPULATION AND DENSITY

Area (sq km)	64,589*
Population (census results)†	
12 January 1989	2,666,567
31 March 2000	
Males	1,094,964
Females	1,282,419
Total	2,377,383
Population (official estimates at 1 January)	
2001	2,364,254
2002	2,345,768
2003	2,311,480
Density (per sq km) at 1 January 2003	35.8

* 24,938 sq miles.
† Figure refers to the resident population.

POPULATION BY ETHNIC GROUP
(permanent inhabitants)

	1989 census		2000 census	
	Number	%	Number	%
Latvian	1,387,757	52.0	1,370,703	57.7
Russian	905,515	34.0	703,243	29.6
Belarusian	119,702	4.5	97,150	4.1
Ukrainian	92,101	3.5	63,644	2.7
Polish	60,416	2.3	59,505	2.5
Lithuanian	34,630	1.3	33,430	1.4
Jewish	22,897	0.9	10,385	0.4
Total (incl. others) . . .	2,666,567	100.0	2,377,383	100.0

PRINCIPAL TOWNS
(population at 1 January 2003)

Rīga (Riga, the capital) . . .	739,232	Jūrmala	55,156
Daugavpils . . .	112,609	Ventspils	44,010
Liepāja . . .	86,983	Rēzekne	37,777
Jelgava . . .	65,754		

BIRTHS, MARRIAGES AND DEATHS

	Registered live births		Registered marriages		Registered deaths	
	Number	Rate (per 1,000)	Number	Rate (per 1,000)	Number	Rate (per 1,000)
1996 . . .	19,782	8.1	9,634	3.9	34,320	14.0
1997 . . .	18,830	7.7	9,680	4.0	33,533	13.8
1998 . .	18,410	7.6	9,641	4.0	34,200	14.2
1999 . .	19,396	8.1	9,399	3.9	32,844	13.7
2000 . .	20,248	8.5	9,211	3.9	32,205	13.6
2001 . .	19,664	8.3	9,258	3.9	32,991	14.0
2002 . .	20,044	8.6	9,738	4.2	32,498	13.9
2003 . .	21,070	9.1	9,989	4.3	32,630	14.0

Expectation of life (WHO estimates, years at birth): 70.3 (males 64.6; females 75.8) in 2002 (Source: WHO, *World Health Report*).

IMMIGRATION AND EMIGRATION

	2001	2002	2003
Immigrants	1,443	1,428	1,364
Emigrants	6,602	3,262	2,209

EMPLOYMENT
(annual averages, '000 persons)

	2000	2001	2002
Agriculture, hunting and forestry	134	143	147
Fishing	2	2	6
Mining and quarrying . . .	2	1	3
Manufacturing	170	156	167
Electricity, gas and water . . .	12	19	22
Construction	56	68	60
Wholesale and retail trade; repair of motor vehicles, motorcycles and personal and household goods	145	160	148
Hotels and restaurants	22	22	24
Transport, storage and communications . . .	79	78	86
Financial intermediation . . .	12	14	13
Real estate, renting and business activities	45	41	39
Public administration and defence, compulsory social security . .	71	68	68
Education	87	88	88
Health and social work . . .	48	50	60
Other community, social and personal service activities . .	44	49	53
Total (incl. others)	941	962	989
Males	n.a.	n.a.	505
Females	n.a.	n.a.	484

Registered unemployed (annual averages, '000 persons): 101.2 in 2000; 93.3 in 2001; 93.6 in 2002.

Health and Welfare

KEY INDICATORS

Total fertility rate (children per woman, 2002)	1.1
Under-5 mortality rate (per 1,000 live births, 2001) . . .	21
HIV/AIDS (% of persons aged 15–49, 2001)	0.40
Physicians (per 1,000 head, 1998)	2.82
Hospital beds (per 1,000 head, 1996)	10.3
Health expenditure (2001): US $ per head (PPP) . . .	509
Health expenditure (2001): % of GDP	6.4
Health expenditure (2001): public (% of total)	52.5
Human Development Index (2000): ranking	53
Human Development Index (2000): value	0.800

For sources and definitions, see explanatory note on p. vi.

Agriculture

PRINCIPAL CROPS
('000 metric tons)

	2000	2001	2002
Wheat	427.4	451.7	519.5
Barley	261.1	231.1	262.4
Rye	110.7	107.2	101.5
Oats	79.6	82.4	79.7
Triticale (wheat-rye hybrid) . .	13.5	28.9	40.9
Other cereals*	48.4	37.8	40.0
Potatoes	747.1	615.3	768.4
Sugar beet	407.7	491.2	622.3
Dry peas	3.0	2.6	3.3
Other pulses	1.1	1.4	1.4
Rapeseed	10.0	13.0	32.7
Cabbages	50.4	61.8	61.7
Cucumbers and gherkins . . .	10.4	17.4*	14.0*

— *continued*	2000	2001	2002
Dry onions	8.3	7.1	14.1
Carrots	21.1	42.8	23.0
Other vegetables*	15.7	30.6	30.3
Apples	35.4	36.1	50.3
Currants	3.4	4.1	3.5
Cranberries	8	8†	8†

* Unofficial figure(s).
† FAO estimate.
Source: FAO.

LIVESTOCK
('000 head at 1 January)

	2000	2001	2002
Cattle	378	367	388
Pigs	405	394	453
Sheep	27	29	32
Goats	8	10	13
Horses	19	20	20
Chickens	3,237	3,105	3,882

Source: FAO.

LIVESTOCK PRODUCTS
('000 metric tons, unless otherwise indicated)

	2000	2001	2002
Beef and veal	22.3	19.0	16.0
Pig meat	31.5	31.6	35.9
Chickenmeat	7.2	8.9	10.6
Cows' milk	823.0	846.0	811.4
Cheese	11.1	13.2	11.9
Butter	7.2	7.1	7.3
Hen eggs	24.4	27.1	30.3
Cattle hides*	3.5	2.7	2.0
Sheepskins*	13.9	12.6	12.8

* FAO estimates.
Source: FAO.

Forestry

ROUNDWOOD REMOVALS
('000 cubic metres, excl. bark)

	2000	2001	2002
Sawlogs, veneer logs and logs for sleepers	8,642	7,359	9,861
Pulpwood	3,517	3,330	1,861
Other industrial wood	465	572	547
Fuel wood	1,680	1,580	1,198
Total	14,304	12,841	13,467

Source: FAO.

SAWNWOOD PRODUCTION
('000 cubic metres, incl. railway sleepers)

	2000	2001	2002
Coniferous (softwood)	3,320	3,195	3,100
Broadleaved (hardwood)	580	645	848
Total	3,900	3,840	3,948

Source: FAO.

Fishing
('000 metric tons, live weight)

	1999	2000	2001
Capture	125.4	136.4	125.4
Atlantic cod	6.9	6.3	6.3
Jack and horse mackerels	14.3	22.6	17.6
Atlantic herring	27.2	26.8	26.6
Sardinellas	15.0	7.9	7.3
European sprat	42.8	46.2	42.8
Chub mackerel	3.1	7.2	9.2
European anchovy	4.9	10.1	8.6
Aquaculture	0.5	0.3	0.5
Total catch	125.9	136.7	125.9

Source: FAO, *Yearbook of Fishery Statistics*.

Mining
('000 metric tons)

	1997	1998	1999
Peat	554.7	171.7	956.4
for fuel	362.1	45.6	315.4
for agriculture	163.9	111.1	567.1
Gypsum	116.9	119.1	96.6
Limestone	372.7	363.3	436.8

Peat for fuel ('000 metric tons): 61.8 in 2000; 68.3 in 2001.

Peat for agriculture ('000 metric tons): 323.6 in 2000; 430.8 in 2001.

2002 ('000 metric tons, selected enterprises): Peat for fuel 114.2; Peat for agriculture 575.4.

Industry

SELECTED PRODUCTS
('000 metric tons, unless otherwise indicated)

	1997	1998	1999*
Sausages	32.2	33.1	26.4
Preserved fish	89.9	76.6	62.8
Whole milk	61.2	67.3	14.6†
Yoghurt	5.0	4.8	4.4
Ice-cream	6.2	4.7	9.8†
Preserved milk	15.1	17.5	6.1
Chocolate and sugar confectionery containing cocoa	10.1	7.1	10.8
Mayonnaise	5.5	4.4	4.5
Refined sugar	88.5	85.6	66.5
Beer ('000 hectolitres)	714.9	721.0	953.2
Cigarettes (million)	1,775	2,018	1,916
Woven cotton fabrics (million sq metres)	3.1	7.4	11.8
Linen fabrics (million sq metres)	0.6	0.4	3.7
Leather footwear ('000 pairs)	577	620	350
Rubber footwear ('000 pairs)	499	605	186
Plywood ('000 cu metres)	121.4	150.5	202.8
Paper	4.4	3.8	2.4
Synthetic resins	31.4	39.6	25.9
Cement	246	366	301
Crude steel	465.0	471.0	483.7
Washing machines ('000)	3.0	1.5	—
Chain drives	6.3‡	6.6‡	3.6
Milking machines ('000)	0.1	0.3	0.3
Radio receivers ('000)	9.9	2.3	1.7
Buses (number)	102		
Electric energy (million kWh)	4,503	5,797	4,101

* From 1999 data on industrial production are compiled according to EU classification methods.
† Million litres.
‡ Million metres.

2000 ('000 metric tons, unless otherwise indicated): Sausages 28.3; Preserved fish 72.4; Whole milk 14.5; Yoghurt 5.5; Ice-cream 9.3; Mayonnaise 6.8; Beer ('000 hectolitres) 945.1; Woven cotton fabrics (million sq metres) 13.0; Leather footwear ('000 pairs) 288; Plywood (million cu metres) 245.5; Electric energy (million kWh) 4,134.

2001 ('000 metric tons, unless otherwise indicated): Sausages 28.6; Preserved fish 92.8; Whole milk 22.7; Yoghurt 5.4; Ice-cream 10.0; Mayonnaise 6.4; Beer ('000 hectolitres) 996.6; Woven cotton fabrics (million sq metres) 15.1; Leather footwear ('000 pairs) 282; Plywood (million cu metres) 266.9; Electric energy (million kWh) 4,287.

2002 (selected enterprises, '000 metric tons, unless otherwise indicated): Sausages 27.5; Preserved fish 97.5; Whole milk 17.5; Yoghurt 5.4; Ice-cream 12.6; Mayonnaise 5.4; Beer ('000 hectolitres) 1,179.0; Woven cotton fabrics (million sq metres) 18.7; Leather footwear ('000 pairs) 325; Plywood (million cu metres) 410.7; Electric energy (million kWh) 3,885.

Finance

CURRENCY AND EXCHANGE RATES

Monetary Units
100 santimi = 1 lats (LVL).

Sterling, Dollar and Euro Equivalents (31 December 2003)
£1 sterling = 96.6 santimi;
US $1 = 54.1 santimi;
€1 = 68.3 santimi;
100 LVL = £103.57 = $184.84 = €146.35.

Average Exchange Rate (LVL per US $)
2001 0.628
2002 0.618
2003 0.571

Note: Between March and June 1993 Latvia reintroduced its national currency, the lats, replacing the Latvian rouble (Latvijas rublis), at a conversion rate of 1 lats = 200 Latvian roubles. The Latvian rouble had been introduced in May 1992, replacing (and initially at par with) the Russian (formerly Soviet) rouble.

BUDGET
(million LVL*)

Revenue†	1999	2000	2001
Tax revenue	1,072.9	1,096.9	1,156.5
Taxes on income, profits and capital gains	161.0	147.9	178.2
Individual	68.8	74.2	79.8
Corporate	92.2	73.7	98.4
Social security contributions	411.3	424.5	439.2
Domestic taxes on goods and services	483.8	509.9	524.2
General sales, turnover or value-added taxes	316.2	337.9	350.6
Excises	155.1	164.0	161.0
Import duties	16.1	14.4	15.3
Other current revenue	147.9	141.6	87.2
Administrative fees and charges, non-industrial and incidental sales	99.4	95.9	39.2
Capital revenue	12.0	0.4	0.5
Total	1,232.8	1,238.9	1,244.1

Expenditure‡	1999	2000	2001
General public services	77.0	74.7	77.4
Defence	34.5	36.6	43.4
Public order and safety	99.3	93.6	97.7
Education	66.9	77.1	87.8
Health	150.8	146.4	154.4
Social security and welfare	591.4	577.4	570.6
Housing and community amenities	12.2	18.9	16.8
Recreational, cultural and religious affairs and services	25.5	29.1	25.6
Economic affairs and services	190.8	165.1	161.5
Agriculture, forestry, fishing and hunting	76.7	62.4	61.3
Transport and communications	90.6	77.8	75.6

Expenditure— *continued*‡	1999	2000	2001
Other purposes	131.6	152.2	164.7
Interest payments	28.0	45.2	48.6
Total	1,379.9	1,371.1	1,399.8
Current	1,267.7	1,275.7	1,310.2
Capital	112.2	95.4	89.7

* Figures refer to the consolidated accounts of the central Government, comprising the operations of the general budget, the Social Security Fund, the State Property Privatization Fund and other extrabudgetary special funds. In 1997 there were changes to education and health functions within the components of central Government and between the Government and local authorities.
† Excluding grants received (million LVL): 16.7 in 1999; 25.9 in 2000; 96.8 in 2001. Data on grants provided through some foreign assistance programmes are not included.
‡ Excluding lending minus repayments (million LVL): 3.3 in 1999; 5.4 in 2000; 5.7 in 2001.
Source: IMF, *Government Finance Statistics Yearbook*.

INTERNATIONAL RESERVES
(US $ million at 31 December)

	2000	2001	2002
Gold*	68.38	69.66	85.90
IMF special drawing rights	0.01	0.09	0.07
Reserve position in IMF	0.07	0.07	0.08
Foreign exchange	850.83	1,148.59	1,241.27
Total	919.29	1,218.40	1,327.32

* Valued at market prices.
Source: IMF, *International Financial Statistics*.

MONEY SUPPLY
(million LVL at 31 December)

	2000	2001	2002
Currency outside banks	427.66	485.19	543.13
Demand deposits at banking institutions	332.97	374.97	501.36
Total money (incl. others)	764.57	863.59	1,047.50

Source: IMF, *International Financial Statistics*.

COST OF LIVING
(Consumer price index; base: 1993 = 100)

	2000	2001	2002
Food and non-alcoholic beverages	180.0	188.7	195.2
Fuel and light	202.8	206.0	206.5
Clothing (incl. footwear)	301.0	303.6	301.1
Rent	470.4	482.9	485.2
All items (incl. others)	238.2	244.2	248.9

NATIONAL ACCOUNTS
(million LVL at current prices)

Expenditure on the Gross Domestic Product

	2000	2001	2002
Government final consumption expenditure	857.0	928.9	1,038.0
Private final consumption expenditure	2,693.5	2,988.9	3,259.3
Increase in stocks	22.5	135.0	112.8
Gross fixed capital formation	1,151.5	1,297.5	1,335.6
Total domestic expenditure	4,724.5	5,350.3	5,745.7
Exports of goods and services	1,983.8	2,138.3	2,361.5
Less Imports of goods and services	2,360.0	2,676.0	2,912.5
GDP in purchasers' values	4,348.3	4,812.6	5,194.7
GDP at constant 2000 prices	4,348.3	4,693.4	4,978.1

Gross Domestic Product by Economic Activity

	2001	2002	2003
Agriculture and hunting . . .	126.2	133.2	137.8
Forestry, logging and related services	66.2	72.2	84.5
Fishing	13.3	11.2	13.0
Mining and quarrying	6.0	6.9	7.9
Manufacturing	633.6	686.1	773.5
Electricity, gas and water supply .	159.7	167.2	175.1
Construction	259.9	283.1	316.7
Wholesale and retail trade; repair of motor vehicles, motorcycles and personal and household goods	790.4	920.5	1,056.7
Hotels and restaurants	54.8	56.3	68.0
Transport, storage and communications	661.3	672.6	752.6
Financial intermediation . . .	204.6	211.3	253.7
Real estate, renting and business activities	478.8	513.3	541.3
Public administration and defence; compulsory social security . .	279.0	303.7	337.0
Education	223.2	249.0	283.0
Health and social work	129.7	136.7	156.0
Other community, social and personal service activities . .	178.8	197.9	232.3
GDP at basic prices	4,265.5	4,621.2	5,189.2
Taxes *less* subsidies on products	547.1	573.5	683.0
GDP in purchasers' values . .	4,812.6	5,194.7	5,872.2

BALANCE OF PAYMENTS
(US $ million)

	2000	2001	2002
Exports of goods f.o.b.	2,058	2,216	2,576
Imports of goods f.o.b.	−3,116	−3,566	−4,020
Trade balance	−1,058	−1,351	−1,444
Exports of services	1,212	1,189	1,252
Imports of services	−770	−693	−708
Balance on goods and services	−616	−854	−900
Other income received	215	278	289
Other income paid	−191	−234	−296
Balance on goods, services and income	−592	−810	−907
Current transfers received . . .	203	221	537
Current transfers paid	−105	−143	−278
Current balance	−495	−732	−647
Capital account (net)	30.0	45	18
Direct investment abroad . . .	−9	−12	−8
Direct investment from abroad . .	410	164	382
Portfolio investment assets . . .	−346	−57	−220
Portfolio investment liabilities . .	25	184	−10
Financial derivatives assets . .	2	3	−7
Financial derivatives liabilities .	−0	−3	20
Other investment assets . . .	−361	−67	−476
Other investment liabilities . .	773	741	1,017
Net errors and omissions . . .	−26	47	−57
Overall balance	3	314	12

Source: IMF, *International Financial Statistics*.

External Trade

PRINCIPAL COMMODITIES
(million LVL)

Imports c.i.f.	2000	2001	2002
Vegetable products	77.1	73.4	82.2
Prepared foodstuffs; beverages spirits and vinegar; tobacco and manufactured substitutes . .	115.2	135.6	165.3
Mineral products	249.4	245.1	243.2
Products of chemical or allied industries	205.5	230.4	261.1
Plastics, rubber and articles thereof	89.0	104.2	124.0
Paper-making material; paper and paperboard and articles thereof	82.4	92.0	107.7
Textiles and textile articles . . .	147.8	163.4	171.5
Base metals and articles thereof .	162.7	182.4	210.8
Machinery and mechanical appliances; electrical equipment; sound and television apparatus .	400.8	465.0	530.8
Vehicles, aircraft, vessels and associated transport equipment	150.2	206.6	244.5
Total (incl. others)	1,933.9	2,201.6	2,497.4

Exports f.o.b.	2000	2001	2002
Prepared foodstuffs; beverages spirits and vinegar; tobacco and manufactured substitutes . . .	40.1	72.5	100.8
Mineral products	30.7	21.2	24.1
Products of chemical or allied industries	72.0	79.5	81.5
Wood, cork and articles thereof; wood charcoal; manufactures of straw, esparto, etc. . . .	423.3	427.3	472.8
Textiles and textile articles . . .	158.7	177.5	180.1
Base metals and artices thereof .	151.2	159.8	185.4
Machinery and mechanical appliances; electrical equipment; sound and television apparatus .	62.2	80.0	91.0
Miscellaneous manufactured articles	60.4	71.2	83.0
Total (incl. others)	1,131.3	1,256.4	1,408.8

PRINCIPAL TRADING PARTNERS
(million LVL)*

Imports c.i.f.	2000	2001	2002
Austria	20.7	25.3	34.8
Belarus	66.5	85.3	68.2
Belgium	34.6	40.4	48.9
Czech Republic	24.3	31.2	34.4
Denmark	69.8	81.9	84.8
Estonia	120.5	139.1	153.9
Finland	167.1	176.5	200.2
France	58.7	53.3	65.4
Germany	302.6	374.9	429.5
Italy	70.5	90.6	104.4
Lithuania	146.4	186.4	245.8
Netherlands	66.6	71.5	84.4
Norway	21.6	27.7	31.4
Poland	91.9	110.2	125.8
Russia	224.5	202.2	218.8
Sweden	130.4	143.1	159.5
Switzerland	34.0	38.3	47.8
Ukraine	26.0	31.2	34.0
United Kingdom	51.3	53.1	57.9
USA	38.4	40.6	39.3
Total (incl. others)	1,933.9	2,201.6	2,497.4

Exports f.o.b.	2000	2001	2002
Belarus	13.7	22.5	21.2
Belgium	14.7	15.9	15.3
Denmark	65.9	72.6	80.4
Estonia	60.1	72.1	84.5
Finland	21.7	28.7	32.8
France	20.4	24.3	28.7
Germany	194.3	209.5	218.3
Italy	17.4	23.0	30.4
Lithuania	85.7	102.0	117.7
Netherlands	45.1	46.3	53.8
Poland	18.2	24.1	22.0
Russia	47.3	73.5	82.5
Sweden	122.5	120.1	148.6
Ukraine	26.8	20.9	25.8
United Kingdom	196.5	196.8	205.4
USA	37.7	32.6	59.6
Total (incl. others)	1,131.3	1,256.4	1,408.8

* Imports by country of origin; exports by country of destination.

Transport

RAILWAYS
(traffic)*

	2001	2002	2003
Passenger journeys (million)	20.1	22.0	23.0
Passenger-kilometres (million)	706	744	n.a.
Freight transported (million metric tons)	37.9	40.1	48.4
Freight ton-kilometres (million)	14,179	15,020	17,604

* Data relating to passengers include railway personnel, and data on freight include passengers' baggage, parcel post and mail.

ROAD TRAFFIC
(motor vehicles in use at 31 December)

	2000	2001	2002
Passenger cars	556,771	586,209	619,081
Buses and coaches	11,501	11,294	11,164
Lorries and vans	97,081	99,708	102,734
Motorcycles and mopeds	20,732	21,366	22,157

SHIPPING

Merchant Fleet
(registered at 31 December)

	2000	2001	2002
Number of vessels	163	160	158
Total displacement ('000 grt)	97.9	68.3	88.7

Source: Lloyd's Register-Fairplay, *World Fleet Statistics*.

International Sea-borne Freight Traffic
('000 metric tons)

	2001	2002	2003
Goods loaded	54,372	48,735	50,918
Goods unloaded	2,546	3,420	3,837

CIVIL AVIATION
(traffic)

	2000	2001	2002
Passengers carried ('000)	271.0	298.7	325.9
Passenger-kilometres (million)	288.8	276.0	338.1
Cargo ton-kilometres ('000)	6,645	6,544	10,491

Tourism

FOREIGN TOURIST ARRIVALS*

Country of residence	2000	2001	2002
Belarus	6,918	7,806	8,364
Denmark	10,212	11,307	10,202
Estonia	23,840	31,272	35,187
Finland	41,561	50,455	55,702
Germany	31,679	47,674	48,544
Lithuania	19,484	23,949	28,382
Norway	8,859	10,386	11,516
Russia	21,755	28,690	36,403
Sweden	22,408	19,363	20,735
United Kingdom	14,644	15,889	15,657
USA	9,965	11,425	12,805
Total (incl. others)	268,083	322,916	360,927

* Figures refer to arrivals at accommodation establishments. Including excursionists, the total number of visitor arrivals (in '000) was: 1,914 in 2000; 2,039 in 2001; 2,273 in 2002.

Tourism receipts (US $ million): 131 in 2000; 120 in 2001; 161 in 2002.

Communications Media

	2000	2001	2002
Telephones ('000 main lines in use)*	735	722	701
Mobile cellular telephones (subscribers)	401,263	625,197	n.a.
Personal computers ('000 in use)	340	360	n.a.
Internet users ('000)	150	170	n.a.
Book production: titles	2,546	2,530	2,326
Book production: copies ('000)	7,033	6,181	4,599
Daily newspapers: number	9	9	8
Daily newspapers: average circulation ('000 copies)	196	212	183
Non-daily newspapers: number	218	213	211
Non-daily newspapers: average circulation ('000 copies)	1,885	2,041	2,112
Other periodicals: number	325	355	365
Other periodicals: average circulation ('000 copies)	1,856	1,952	1,952

* At 31 December.

Radio receivers ('000 in use): 1,760 in 1997.

Television receivers ('000 in use): 1,220 in 1997.

Facsimile machines (number in use): 900 in 1996.

Sources: mostly UNESCO, *Statistical Yearbook*; UN, *Statistical Yearbook* and International Telecommunication Union.

Education

(2002/03)

	Institutions	Students
Schools*	953	315,448
Latvian	683	199,211
Russian	158	81,715
Latvian-Russian†	105	33,125
Polish	5	1,003
Ukrainian	1	307
Belarusian	1	87
Vocational schools	124	46,533
Higher education institutions	37	118,944
Special schools (for the physically and mentally handicapped)	64	10,055

* Including primary (Grades 1–4), basic schools (Grades 1–9) and secondary schools (Grades 1–12).
† Mixed schools with two languages of instruction.

Teachers: Pre-primary 1,178; Primary (including basic schools) 9,252; Secondary 16,495; Special schools 1,837; Vocational 5,639.

Adult literacy rate (UNESCO estimates): 99.8% (males 99.8%; females 99.8%) in 2001 (Source: UN Development Programme, *Human Development Report*).

Directory

The Constitution

The Constitution of the Republic of Latvia, which had been adopted on 15 February 1922, was annulled at the time of the Soviet annexation in 1940. Latvia became a Union Republic of the USSR and a new Soviet-style Constitution became the legal basis for the governmental system of the republic. The constitutional authority for Latvian membership of the USSR, the Resolution on Latvian Entry into the USSR of 21 July 1940, was declared null and void on 4 May 1990. In the same declaration the Latvian Supreme Council announced the restoration of Articles 1, 2 and 3 of the 1922 Constitution, which describe Latvia as an independent and sovereign state, and Article 6, which states that the legislature (the Saeima) is elected by universal, equal, direct and secret vote, on the basis of proportional representation. On 6 July 1993 the 1922 Constitution was fully restored by the Saeima, following its election on 5 and 6 June. A summary of the Constitution's main provisions (including amendments adopted since its restoration) is given below.

BASIC PROVISIONS

Latvia is an independent, democratic republic, in which the sovereign power of the State belongs to the people. The territory of the Republic of Latvia comprises the provinces of Vidzeme, Latgale, Kurzeme and Zemgale, within the boundaries stipulated by international treaties.

THE SAEIMA

The Saeima (Parliament) comprises 100 representatives of the people and, according to a constitutional amendment adopted in December 1997, is elected by universal, equal, direct and secret vote, on the basis of proportional representation, for a period of four years. All Latvian citizens who have attained 18 years of age are entitled to vote and are eligible for election to the Saeima.

The Saeima elects a Board, which consists of the Chairperson, two Deputies, and Secretaries. The Board convenes the sessions of the Saeima and decrees regular and extraordinary sittings. The sessions of the Saeima are public (sittings in camera are held only by special request).

The right of legislation belongs to both the Saeima and the people. Draft laws may be presented to the Saeima by the President of the Republic, the Cabinet of Ministers, the Committees of the Saeima, no fewer than five members of the Saeima, or, in special cases, by one-tenth of the electorate. Before the commencement of each financial year, the Saeima approves the state budget, the draft of which is submitted by the Cabinet of Ministers. The Saeima decides on the strength of the armed forces during peacetime. The ratification of the Saeima is indispensable to all international agreements dealing with issues resolved by legislation.

THE PRESIDENT OF THE REPUBLIC

According to a constitutional amendment adopted by the Saeima in December 1997, the President of the Republic is elected by a secret ballot of the Saeima for a period of four years. A majority of no fewer than 51 votes is required for his/her election. No person of less than 40 years of age may be elected President of the Republic. The office of President is not compatible with any other office, and the President may serve for no longer than two consecutive terms.

The President represents the State in an international capacity; he/she appoints Latvian representatives abroad, and receives representatives of foreign states accredited to Latvia; implements decisions of the Saeima concerning the ratification of international treaties; is Head of the Armed Forces; appoints a Commander-in-Chief in time of war; and has the power to declare war on the basis of a decision of the Saeima.

The President has the right to pardon criminals serving penal sentences; to convene extraordinary meetings of the Cabinet of Ministers for the discussion of an agenda prepared by him/her, and to preside over such meetings; and to propose the dissolution of the Saeima. The President may be held criminally accountable if the Saeima sanctions thus with a majority vote of no fewer than two-thirds of its members.

THE CABINET OF MINISTERS

The Cabinet comprises the Prime Minister and the ministers nominated by him/her. This task is entrusted to the Prime Minister by the President of the Republic. All state administrative institutions are subordinate to the Cabinet, which, in turn, is accountable to the Saeima. If the Saeima adopts a vote expressing 'no confidence' in the Prime Minister, the entire Cabinet must resign. The Cabinet dis-cusses all draft laws presented by the ministries as well as issues concerning the activities of the ministries. If the State is threatened by foreign invasion or if events endangering the existing order of the State arise, the Cabinet has the right to proclaim a state of emergency.

THE JUDICIARY

All citizens are equal before the law and the courts. Judges are independent and bound only by law. The appointment of judges is confirmed by the Saeima. Judges may be dismissed from office against their will only by a decision of the Supreme Court. The retiring age for judges is stipulated by law. Judgment may be passed solely by institutions that have been so empowered by law and in such a manner as specified by law. A Constitutional Court was established in 1996 to examine the legality of legislation.

The Government

HEAD OF STATE

President: VAIRA VIĶE-FREIBERGA (inaugurated 8 July 1999; re-elected 20 June 2003; inaugurated 8 July 2003).

CABINET OF MINISTERS
(April 2004)

A coalition of the Greens' and Farmers' Union (GFU—ZZS), the First Party of Latvia (LPP) and the People's Party.

Prime Minister: INDULIS EMSIS (GFU—ZZS).

Deputy Prime Minister: AINĀRS ŠLESERS (LPP).

Minister of Defence: ATIS SLAKTERIS (People's Party).

Minister of Foreign Affairs: RIHARDS PĪKS (People's Party).

Minister of Finance: OSKARS SPURDZIŅŠ (People's Party).

Minister of the Economy: JURIS LUJĀNS (LPP).

Minister of the Interior: ĒRIKS JĒKABSONS (LPP).

Minister of Education and Science: JURIS RADZEVIČS (LPP).

Minister of Agriculture: MĀRTIŅŠ ROZE (GFU–ZZS).

Minister of Culture: HELĒNA DEMAKOVA (People's Party).

Minister of Welfare: DAGNIJA STAĶE (GFU–ZZS).

Minister of Transport: AINĀRS ŠLESERS (acting) (LPP).

Minister of Justice: VINETA MUIŽNIECE (New Era).

Minister of the Environment: RAIMONDS VĒJONIS (GFU–ZZS).

Minister of Health: RINALDS MUCIŅŠ (Independent).

Minister of Regional Development and Local Governments: ANDREJS RADZEVIČS (New Era).

Minister of Special Assignment on Children and Family Affairs: AINĀRS BAŠTIKS (LPP).

Minister of Special Assignment on Social Integration: NILS MUIŽNIEKS (LPP).

MINISTRIES

Chancery of the President: Pils lauk. 3, Rīga 1900; tel. 737-7548; fax 709-2106; e-mail chancery@president.lv; internet www.president.lv.

Office of the Cabinet of Ministers: Brīvības bulv. 36, Rīga 1520; tel. 708-2800; fax 728-0469; e-mail pasts@mk.gov.lv; internet www.mk.gov.lv/lv.

Ministry of Agriculture: Republikas lauk. 2, Rīga 1981; tel. 702-7107; fax 702-7250; internet www.zm.gov.lv.

Ministry of Culture: K. Valdemāra iela 11A, Rīga 1364; tel. 722-4772; fax 722-4916; e-mail culture@com.latnet.lv; internet www.culture.lv.

Ministry of Defence: K. Valdemāra iela 10–12, Rīga 1473; tel. 721-0124; fax 721-2307; e-mail kanceleja@mod.lv; internet www.mod.lv.

Ministry of the Economy: Brīvības iela 55, Rīga 1010; tel. 701-3101; fax 728-0882; e-mail em@em.gov.lv; internet www.em.gov.lv.

Ministry of Education and Science: Vaļņu iela 2, Rīga 1098; tel. 722-2415; fax 721-3992; e-mail izm@izm.gov.lv; internet www.izm.gov.lv.

Ministry of the Environment: Peldu iela 25, Rīga 1494; tel. 702-6400; fax 782-0442; e-mail pasts@vidm.gov.lv; internet www.varam.gov.lv.

Ministry of Finance: Smilšu iela 1, Rīga 1050; tel. 722-6672; fax 709-5503; internet www.fm.gov.lv.

Ministry of Foreign Affairs: Brīvības bulv. 36, Rīga 1395; tel. 701-6210; fax 782-8121; e-mail info@mfa.gov.lv; internet www.am.gov.lv.

Ministry of Health: Brīvības bulv. 36, Rīga 1520.

Ministry of the Interior: Raiņa bulv. 6, Rīga 1050; tel. 721-9210; fax 722-8283; e-mail pc@iem.gov.lv; internet www.iem.gov.lv.

Ministry of Justice: Brīvības bulv. 36, Rīga 1536; tel. 708-8220; fax 728-5575; e-mail info@tm.gov.lv; internet www.jm.gov.lv.

Ministry of Regional Development and Local Governments: Lāčplēša iela 27, Rīga 1011; internet www.raplm.gov.lv.

Ministry of Social Integration: Brīvības bulv. 36, Rīga 1520.

Ministry of Transport: Gogoļa iela 3, Rīga 1743; tel. 722-6922; fax 721-7180; e-mail satmin@sam.gov.lv; internet www.sam.gov.lv.

Ministry of Welfare: Skolas iela 28, Rīga 1331; tel. 702-1600; fax 727-6445; internet www.lm.gov.lv.

Legislature

SAEIMA

Parliament

Jekaba iela 11, Rīga 1811; tel. 708-7111; fax 708-7100; e-mail web@saeima.lv; internet www.saeima.lv.

Chairman: INGRĪDA ŪDRE.

Deputy Chairmen: ERIKS JEKABSONS, JĀNIS STRAUME.

General Election, 5 October 2002

Parties and coalitions	% of votes	Seats
New Era	23.93	26
For Human Rights in a United Latvia*	18.94	25
People's Party	16.71	20
First Party of Latvia†	9.58	10
Greens' and Farmers' Union‡	9.46	12
Conservative Union 'For Fatherland and Freedom'/LNNK	5.39	7
Others	15.99	—
Total	100.00	100

* An electoral bloc composed of the Latvian Socialist Party and the National Harmony Party.

† Including the Christian Democratic Union of Latvia.

‡ Comprising the Latvian Green Party and the Latvian Farmers' Union.

Political Organizations

There were some 40 political organizations registered in Latvia in 2001; among the most influential were:

Centre Party: Latvian Farmers' Union (LFU) (Latvijas Zemnieku savienība): Republikas lauk. 2, Rīga 1010; tel. 702-7163; fax 702-7467; e-mail lzs@latnet.lv; internet www.lzs.lv; f. 1917; re-est. 1990; merged with Political Asscn of Economists 1996; rural, centrist; forms part of the governing Greens' and Farmers' Union; Chair. AUGUSTS BRIGMANIS; 2,850 mems.

Christian Democratic Union of Latvia (CDUL) (Latvijas Kristīgi Demokrātiskā savienība): Jēkaba iela 26, Rīga 1811; tel. 732-3534; fax 783-0333; internet www.kds.lv; f. 1991; Chair. JURIS KOKINS; 600 mems.

Conservative Union 'For Fatherland and Freedom'/LNNK (Aprienība 'Tēvzemei un Brīvībai'/LNNK): Kalēju iela 10, Rīga 1050; tel. 708-7273; fax 708-7268; e-mail agulbe@saeima.lv; internet www.tb.lv; f. 1997; as a result of a merger between the Union 'For Fatherland and Freedom' and the Latvian National Independence Conservative Movement; conservative; Chair. JĀNIS STRAUME; Vice-Chair. VLADIMIRS MAKAROVS.

First Party of Latvia (LPP) (Latvijas Pirmā Partija): Rīga; f. 2002; absorbed New Christian Party in 2003; Christian, centrist; Chair. ERIKS JEKABSONS.

For Latvia's Freedom: Rīga; pro-European Union; forms part of the Centre alliance; Chair. ODISEJS KOSTANDA.

Helsinki-86: A. Čaka iela 28–19, Rīga 1011; tel. 728-0272; as human rights protection group; political status awarded in 1998.

Labour Party: f. 1996; advocates programme for the renewal and restructuring of industry; part of the Centre alliance; Chair. AIVARS KREITUSS.

Latvian Democratic Party: M. Monētu iela 3, Rīga 1050; tel. 728-7739; fax 728-8211; e-mail ldp@ldp.lv; internet www.ldp.lv; f. 1995; fmrly Democratic Party Saimnieks (the Master), name changed 1999; part of the Centre alliance; Chair. ANDRIS AMERIKS; 900 mems.

Latvian Freedom Party: Rīga; f. 2002; social-liberal; Founder ZIEDONIS CEVERS.

Latvian Green Party (Latvijas Zaļā partija): Kalnciema iela 30, Rīga 1046; tel. 761-4272; fax 761-4927; e-mail lzp@zp.lv; internet www.zp.lv; f. 1990; environmental political party; forms part of the governing Greens' and Farmers' Union; co-Chair. INDULIS EMSIS, VIESTURS SILENIEKS, RAIMONDS VEJONIS.

Latvian National Democratic Party (LNDP): Rīga; f. 2000; joined by the unregistered Russian National Unity Party in 2002; Leader YEVGENIY OSIPOV; 1,650 mems.

Latvian Social Democratic Welfare Party: Rīga; f. 1999; against Latvian membership of NATO; Chair. JURIS ZURAVLOVS.

Latvian Social Democratic Workers' Party (Latvijas Sociāldemokrātiskā strādnieku partija—LSDSP): Ranka dambis 1, Rīga 1048; tel. 761-4099; fax 761-4600; e-mail lsdsp@lis.lv; internet www.lsdsp.lv; f. 1999; as a result of a merger with the Latvian Social Democratic Union; Chair. DAINIS IVANS.

Latvian Socialist Party (Latvijas Sociālistiskā Partija): Burtnieku iela 23; tel. and fax 755-5535; internet www.vide.lv/lsp; f. 1994; withdrew from the For Human Rights in a United Latvia bloc in June 2003; Chair. ALFRĒDS RUBIKS.

Latvian United Republican Party: Rīga; f. 2001; Chair. AINARS STRAKIS.

Latvian Way (Latvijas ceļš): Jaunu iela 25/29, Rīga 1050; tel. 728-5539; fax 782-1121; e-mail lc@lc.lv; internet www.lc.lv; f. 1993; unites prominent political figures from Latvia and abroad; Chair. JĀNIS NAGLIS; Dep. Chair. IVĀRS GODMANIS; 900 mems.

National Harmony Party (Tautas Saskanas Partija): Elizabetes iela 23A/15, Rīga 101; tel. 750-8552; fax 728-1619; e-mail tsp@latnet.lv; internet www.tsp.lv; f. 1993; advocates the rapid integration of non-citizens into Latvian society; withdrew from the For Human Rights in a United Latvia bloc in Feb. 2003; Chair. JĀNIS JURKĀNS; Dep. Chair. JĀNIS URBANOVICS.

New Era (Jaunais laiks): Jēkaba Kazarmās, Torna iela 4–3B, Rīga 1050; tel. 720-5472; fax 720-5473; e-mail birojs@jaunaislaiks.lv; internet www.jaunaislaiks.lv; f. 2002; right-wing; Chair. EINĀRS REPŠE.

People's Party (Tautas partija): Dzirnavu iela 68, Rīga; tel. 728-6441; fax 728-6405; e-mail koord1@tautas.lv; internet www.tautaspartija.lv; f. 1998; Chair. ATIS SLAKTERIS; Vice-Chair. JĀNIS LAGZDINS.

Progressive Centre Party: f. 2002; supports President Viķe-Freiberga; Chair. INTA STAMGUTE.

Social Justice and Equal Rights Movement: f. 1996; against membership of the European Union and NATO, and supports the granting of citizenship to all permanent residents of Latvia; also know as the Equality Movement; member of the For Human Rights in a United Latvia alliance; Chair. TATJANA ZDANOKA; 224 mems.

Union of Social Democrats (SDS): Rīga; f. 2002; centre-left; splinter group from Latvian Social Democratic Workers' Party; Chair. EGILS BALDZĒNS; 958 mems.

Diplomatic Representation

EMBASSIES IN LATVIA

Austria: Elizabetes iela 21A, 4th Floor, Apt 11, Rīga 1010; tel. 721-6125; fax 721-4401; Ambassador Dr WOLFGANG JILLY.

Belarus: Jēzusbaznīcas iela 12, Rīga 1050; tel. 722-2560; fax 732-2891; e-mail latvia@belembassy.org; Ambassador VADIM LAMKAU.

Canada: Doma lauk. 4, Rīga 1977; tel. 722-6315; fax 783-0140; e-mail riga@dfait-maeci.gc.ca; internet www.dfait-maeci.gc.ca/dfait/missions/baltiks; Ambassador ROBERT ANDRIGO.

China, People's Republic: Ganību dambis 5, Rīga 1045; tel. 735-7023; fax 735-7025; e-mail chinaemb_lv@mfa.gov.cn; Ambassador JI YANCHI.

Czech Republic: Elizabetes iela 29A, Rīga 1010; tel. 721-7814; fax 721-7821; e-mail zuczriga@parks.lv; internet www.mfa.cz/riga; Ambassador JAN FINFERLE.

Denmark: L. Pils iela 11, Rīga 1863; tel. 722-6210; fax 722-9218; e-mail rixamb@um.dk; internet www.denmark.lv; Ambassador ARNOLD CHRISTIAN DE FINE SKIBSTED.

Estonia: Skolas iela 13, Rīga 1010; tel. 781-2020; fax 781-2029; e-mail embassy.riga@mfa.ee; Ambassador TOOMAS LUKK.

Finland: Kalpaka bulv. 1, Rīga 1605; tel. 707-8800; fax 707-8814; e-mail sanomat.rii@formin.fi; internet www.finland.lv; Ambassador KIRSTI ESKELINEN-LIUKKONEN.

France: Raiņa bulv. 9, Rīga 1050; tel. 703-6600; fax 703-6615; e-mail webmastre.ambafrance-lv@diplomatie.gouv.fr; internet www.ambafrance-lv.org; Ambassador MICHEL FOUCHER.

Germany: Raiņa blvd 13, Rīga 1050; POB 183, 1047 Rīga; tel. 722-9096; fax 782-0223; e-mail mailbox@deutschebotschaft-riga.lv; internet www.deutschebotschaft-riga.lv; Ambassador ECKHART HEROLD.

Israel: Elizabetes iela 2, 3rd Floor, Rīga 1340; tel. 732-0739; fax 783-0170; e-mail press@rig.mfa.gov.il; internet riga.mfa.gov.il; Ambassador GARY KOREN.

Italy: Teātra iela 9, 3rd/4th Floors, Rīga 1050; tel. 721-6069; fax 721-6084; e-mail ambitalia.riga@apollo.lv; internet www.ambitalia.apollo.lv; Ambassador MAURIZIO LO RE.

Japan: Kr. Valdemāra iela 21, Rīga 1010; tel. 781-2001; fax 781-2004; e-mail eoj.001@latnet.lv; Ambassador SEICHIRO OTSUKA.

Lithuania: Rupniecibas iela 24, Rīga 1010; tel. 732-1519; fax 732-1589; e-mail lt@apollo.lv; internet lv.urm.lt; Ambassador OSVALADAS ČIUKŠYS.

Netherlands: Torņu iela 4, Jēkaba Kazarmas 1A, Rīga 1050; tel. 732-6147; fax 732-6151; e-mail nlgovrig@mailbox.riga.lv; internet www.netherlandsembassy.lv; Ambassador NICOLAAS BEETS.

Norway: Zirgu iela 14, POB 1173, Rīga 1050; tel. 781-4100; fax 781-4108; e-mail emb.riga@mfa.no; Ambassador JAN WESSEL HEG.

Poland: Mednieku iela 6B, Rīga 1010; tel. 703-1500; fax 703-1549; e-mail ambpol@apollo.lv; Ambassador TADEUSZ FISZBACH.

Russia: Antonijas iela 2, Rīga 1010; tel. 733-2151; fax 783-0209; e-mail rusembas@junik.lv; internet www.latvia.mid.ru; Ambassador IGOR STUDENNIKOV.

Slovakia: Smilšu iela 8, Rīga 1050; tel. 781-4280; fax 781-4290; e-mail embassy@slovakia.lv; Ambassador JOSEF DRAVECKÝ.

Sweden: A. Pumpura iela 8, Rīga 1010; tel. 768-6600; fax 768-6601; e-mail ambassaden.riga@foreign.ministry.se; internet www.swedenemb.lv; Ambassador GÖRAN HÅKANSSON.

Switzerland: Elizabetes iela 2, 3rd Floor, Rīga 1340; tel. 733-8351; fax 733-8354; e-mail vertretung@rig.rep.admin.ch; internet www.eda.admin.ch/riga; Ambassador ANNE BAUTY.

Ukraine: Kalpaka bulv. 3, Rīga 1010; tel. 724-3082; fax 732-5583; e-mail uaemb@neonet.lv; Ambassador MYRON YANKIV.

United Kingdom: J. Alunāna iela 5, Rīga 1010; tel. 777-4700; fax 777-4707; e-mail british.embassy@apollo.lv; internet www.britain.lv; Ambassador ANDREW TESORIERE.

USA: Raiņa bulv. 7, Rīga 1510; tel. 703-6206; fax 722-2132; e-mail pas@usembassy.lv; internet www.usembassy.lv; Ambassador BRIAN E. CARLSON.

Uzbekistan: Elizabetes iela 11, 2nd Floor, Rīga 1010; tel. 732-2424; fax 732-2306; e-mail posoluz@apollo.lv; Ambassador KOBILJON S. NAZAROV.

Judicial System

Constitutional Court: J. Alunāna iela 1, Rīga 1010; tel. 722-1412; fax 722-0572; e-mail aivars.e@satv.tiesa.gov.lv; internet www.satv.tiesa.gov.lv; f. 1996 to rule on constitutionality of legislation; comprises seven judges, appointed by the Saeima for a term of 10 years; Chair. AIVARS ENDZINŠ; Deputy Chair. ROMĀNS APSĪTIS.

Supreme Court: Brīvības bulv. 36, Rīga 1050; tel. 702-0350; fax 702-0351; Chair. ANDRIS GUĻĀNS.

Office of the Prosecutor-General: Kalpaka bulv. 6, Rīga 1801; tel. 704-4400; fax 704-4449; e-mail gen@lrp.gov.lv; Prosecutor-General JĀNIS MAIZĪTIS.

Religion

From the 16th century the traditional religion of the Latvians was Lutheran Christian. Russian Orthodoxy was the religion of most of the Slav immigrants. After 1940, when Latvia was annexed by the USSR, many places of religious worship were closed and clergymen were imprisoned or exiled. Following the restoration of independence in 1991, religious organizations regained their legal rights, as well as property that had been confiscated during the Soviet occupation. At 1 July 2000 the statutes of 1,095 religious organizations were registered. The total number of congregations was 1,072, of which 308 were Lutheran, 250 Roman Catholic, 118 Pentecostal, 117 Orthodox, 85 Baptists, 66 Old Believers (Orthodox), 45 Adventist, 11 Methodist, seven Hebrew and six Muslim.

Association for Freedom of Religion (AFFOR): Ganībudambis 3–2, Rīga 1045; e-mail ringolds.balodis@apollo.lv; f. 1999 to protect religious freedom in Latvia; Vice-Pres. SINTIJA BALODE.

Board of Religious Affairs: Pils lauk. 4, Rīga 1050; tel. 722-0585; e-mail ringolds.balodis@apollo.lv; f. 2000; govt agency, attached to the Ministry of Justice; Principal Dr RINGOLDS BALODIS.

CHRISTIANITY

Protestant Churches

Consistory of the Evangelical Lutheran Church of Latvia: M. Pils iela 4, Rīga 1050; tel. 722-6057; fax 782-0041; e-mail konsistorija@parks.lv; internet www.lutheran.lv; f. 1922; Archbishop JĀNIS VANAGS.

Latvian Conference of Seventh-day Adventists in Latvia: Baznīcas iela 12A, Rīga 1010; tel. and fax 724-0013; e-mail viesturs@baznica.lv; internet www.adventistu.baznica.lv; f. 1920; Pres. of Council VIESTURS REĶIS.

Union of Baptist Churches in Latvia: Lāčplēša iela 37, Rīga 1011; tel. 722-3379; fax 722-2651; e-mail ildzjur@latnet.lv; f. 1860; Bishop ANDREJS ŠTERNS; Gen. Sec. ILMĀRS HIRŠS.

Union of Latvian Pentecostal Congregations: Laimas iela 14, Jelgava 3000; tel. 302-5011; f. 1989; Bishop JĀNIS OZOLINKEVIČS.

United Methodist Church in Latvia: Klaipēdas iela 56, Liepāja 3401; tel. 343-2161; fax 346-9848; re-est. 1991; Supt ĀRIJS VĪKSNA.

The Roman Catholic Church

Latvia comprises one archdiocese and three dioceses. At 31 December 2002 there were an estimated 434,421 adherents in the country (equivalent to an estimated 19% of the population).

Bishops' Conference
(Conferentia Episcopalis Lettoniae)

M. Pils iela 2A, Rīga 1050; tel. 722-7266; fax 722-0775.

Pres. Cardinal JĀNIS PUJATS.

Archbishop of Rīga: Cardinal JĀNIS PUJATS, Metropolijas Kurija, M. Pils iela 2A, Rīga 1050; tel. 722-7266; fax 722-0775; e-mail curia@e-apollo.lv; internet www.catholic.lv.

The Orthodox Church

Although the Orthodox Church of Latvia has close ties with the Moscow Patriarchate, it has administrative independence. The spiritual head of the Orthodox Church is elected by its Saeima (or assembly).

Synod of the Orthodox Church of Latvia: M. Pils iela 14, Rīga 1050; tel. 722-4345; f. 1850; mems are mostly ethnic Slavs; Bishop ALEKSANDRS KUDRJAŠOV.

Latvian Old Believer Pomor Church: Krasta iela 73, Rīga 1003; tel. 711-3083; fax 714-4513; e-mail oldbel@junik.lv; f. 1760; Head of Central Council IVANS MIZOĻUBOVS (Fr Ioann).

JUDAISM

Hebrew Religious Community of Rīga: Peitavas iela 6/8, Rīga 1050; tel. 722-4549; f. 1764; Rabbi NATAN BARKAN.

OTHER RELIGIOUS GROUPS

International Society for Krishna Consciousness: K. Barona iela 56, Rīga 1011; tel. 227-2490; e-mail padasevanam@mail.delfi.lv; internet www.gauranga.lv; Co-ordinator HARIJIS SAUSS.

Latvijas Dievturu sadraudze (LDS): Rīga; community of Dievturi, celebrating the ancient Latvian animist religion; Leader JĀNIS SILIŅŠ.

The Press

The joint-stock company Preses nams (Press House—q.v.) is the leading publisher of newspapers and magazines in Latvia. In 2002 there were eight daily newspapers, with an average circulation of 183,000. In addition, 211 non-daily newspapers and 365 other periodicals were published in Latvia. The publications listed below are in Latvian, unless otherwise indicated.

DAILIES

Diena (Day): Mūkusalas iela 41, Rīga 1004; tel. 706-3100; fax 706-3190; e-mail diena@diena.lv; internet www.diena.lv; f. 1990; Latvian; social and political issues; Editor-in-Chief SARMĪTE ĒLERTE; circ. 62,000.

Neatkarīgā Rita Avize (Independent Morning Paper): Balasta dambis 3, Rīga 1081; tel. 706-2462; fax 706-2465; e-mail redakcija@nra.lv; internet www.nra.lv; f. 1990; Editor-in-Chief ALDIS BĒRZIŅŠ; circ. 40,000.

Rīgas Balss (Voice of Rīga): Balasta dambis 3, Rīga 1081; tel. 706-4420; fax 706-2400; e-mail lita@rb.lv; f. 1957; city evening newspaper; Latvian and Russian; Editor-in-Chief ANITA DAUKSTE; circ. 56,800 (Mon.–Thurs.), 69,570 (Fri.).

Sports: Balasta dambis 3, Rīga 1081; tel. 246-4117; fax 786-0000; f. 1955; Editor DACE MILLERE; circ. 7,800.

Vakara Ziņas (Evening News): Rīga; tel. 261-7595; fax 261-2383; f. 1993; Editor-in-Chief AINIS SAULĪTIS; circ. 53,000.

WEEKLIES

The Baltic Times: Skunu iela 16, Rīga 1050; tel. 722-4073; fax 722-6041; e-mail editorsdesk@baltictimes.com; internet www.baltictimes.com; f. 1996; news from Estonia, Latvia and Lithuania; English; Man. Dir ANTRA LINARTE; Editor-in-Chief GARY PEACH; circ. 12,000.

Dienas Bizness (Daily Business): a/k 2, Balasta dambis 3, POB 2, Rīga 1081; tel. 706-2622; fax 706-2309; e-mail nberch@db.lv; internet www.db.lv; f. 1992; Editor-in-Chief JURIS PAIDERS; circ. 17,000.

Ieva: Balasta dambis 3, Rīga 1081; tel. 246-3667; fax 246-1438; e-mail ieva@santa.lv; f. 1997; weekly; illustrated journal for women; Latvian; Editor-in-Chief INGA GORBUNOVA; circ. 76,000.

Izglītība un Kultūra (Education and Culture): Torna iela 11, Rīga 1050; tel. 722-8013; fax 722-5632; f. 1948; Editor ANDRA MANGALE; circ. 6,000.

Latvijas Vēstnesis (Latvian Herald): Bruņinieku iela 36-2, Rīga 1001; tel. 229-8833; fax 229-9410; e-mail editor@mail.lv-laiks.lv; internet www.lv-laiks.lv; f. 1993; official newspaper of the Republic of Latvia; Editor-in-Chief OSKARS GERTS; circ. 5,200.

Lauku Avīze (Country Newspaper): Dzirnavu iela 21, Rīga 1010; tel. 709-6600; fax 709-6645; e-mail redakcija@laukuavize.lv; f. 1988; three a week; popular agriculture, politics and sport; Editor-in-Chief VIESTURS SERDĀNS; circ. 75,000.

PRINCIPAL PERIODICALS

Daugava: Balasta dambis 3, Rīga 1081; tel. 728-0290; e-mail ravdin@mailbox.riga.lv; f. 1977; 6 a year; literary journal; Latvian; Editor-in-Chief ZHANNA EZIT; circ. 500.

Karogs (Banner): Kuršu iela 24, Rīga 1006; tel. 755-4145; fax 755-4146; e-mail karogs@apollo.l; f. 1940; literary monthly; Editor-in-Chief IEVA KOLMANE; circ. 2,000.

Klubs: Balasta dambis 3, Rīga 1081; tel. 246-5534; fax 246-5450; e-mail santa@parks.lv; internet www.klubs.lv; f. 1994; monthly; illustrated journal for men; Latvian; Editor-in-Chief AINĀRS ĒRGLIS; circ. 20,000.

Liesma (Flame): Balasta dambis 3, Rīga 1081; tel. 246-6480; f. 1958; monthly; for young people; Editor-in-Chief DAINIS CAUNE; circ. 20,000.

Mans Mazais: Balasta dambis 3, Rīga 1081; tel. 762-8274; fax 246-5450; e-mail mansmazais@santa.lv; f. 1994; monthly; illustrated journal for young parents; Latvian; Editor-in-Chief VITA BEĻAUNIECE; circ. 20,000.

Mūsmājas (Our Home): Meža iela 4, Rīga 1048; tel. 761-5812; fax 786-0002; e-mail dadzis@latnet.lv; f. 1993; monthly; illustrated magazine for housewives; Latvian; Editor-in-Chief ILZE STRAUTIŅA; circ. 50,000.

Rīgas Laiks (Rīga Times): Lāčplēša iela 25, Rīga 1011; tel. 728-7922; fax 783-0542; e-mail pasts@rigaslaiks.lv; internet www.rigaslaiks.lv; f. 1993; monthly; Editor-in-Chief INESE ZANDERE; circ 10,000.

Santa: Balasta dambis 3, POB 32, Rīga 1081; tel. 762-8274; fax 246-5450; e-mail santa@santa.lv; f. 1991; monthly; illustrated journal for women; Latvian; Editor-in-Chief SANTA ANCHA; circ. 42,000.

NEWS AGENCIES

Baltic News Service: Baznīcas iela 8, Rīga 1010; tel. 708-8600; fax 708-8601; e-mail bns@rb.bns.lv; internet bnsnews.bns.lv; f. 1990; news from Latvia, Lithuania, Estonia and the CIS; in English, Russian and the Baltic languages; Dir LIGA MENGELSONA.

LETA (Latvian News Agency): Palasta iela 10, Rīga 1502; tel. 722-2509; fax 722-3850; e-mail leta.marketing@leta.lv; internet www.leta.lv; f. 1919; independent news agency; Chair. MĀRTIŅŠ BARKĀNS.

Foreign Bureau

Reuters (United Kingdom): Kaļķu iela 15, Rīga 1050; tel. 722-2079; fax 724-3139; e-mail reuters@reuters.lv; Bureau Chief ALAN CROSBY.

PRESS ASSOCIATIONS

Latvian Journalists' Union (Latvijas Žurnālistu savienība): Marstaļu iela 2, Rīga 1050; tel. 721-1433; fax 782-0233; e-mail reiterns@zn.apollo.lv; f. 1992; 700 mems; Pres. LIGITA AZOVSKA.

Publishers

Avots (Spring): Aspazijas bulv. 24, Rīga 1050; tel. 721-1394; fax 722-5824; f. 1980; fiction, dictionaries, crafts, hobbies, art, agriculture, law, reference books, etc.; Pres. JĀNIS LEJA.

Elpa (Breath): Doma lauk. 1, Rīga 1914; tel. 721-1776; fax 750-3326; f. 1990; books and newspapers; Pres. MAIRITA SOLIMA.

Jumava: Dzirnavu iela 73, Rīga 1011; tel. and fax 728-0314; e-mail jumava@parks.lv; internet www.jumava.lv; f. 1994; translations, dictionaries, fiction, etc.; Pres. JURIS VISOCKIS.

Kontinents: Elijas iela 17, Rīga 1050; tel. 720-4130; fax 720-4133; e-mail kontinent@parks.lv; internet www.kontinent.lv; f. 1991.

Latvijas Enciklopēdija (Latvian Encyclopedia Publishers): Rīga; tel. 722-0150; fax 782-0113; f. 1963; encyclopedias, dictionaries, reference books; Dir VIKTORS TĒRAUDS.

Nordik: Daugavgrīvas 36–9, Rīga 1007; tel. 760-2672; fax 760-2818; e-mail nordik@nordik.lv; internet www.nordik.lv; sister co, Tapals, at same address; Dir JĀNIS JUŠKA.

Preses nams (Press House): Balasta dambis 3, Rīga 1081; tel. 246-5732; internet www.presesnams.lv; f. 1990; newspapers, magazines, encyclopedias and scientific literature; controlling interest owned by Ventspils Nafta; Dir EGONS LAPIŅŠ.

Jāņa sēta: Elizabetes iela 83–85, Rīga 1050; tel. 709-2290; fax 709-2292; e-mail janaseta@janaseta.lv; internet www.janaseta.lv; f. 1991; travel and culinary books; Dir AIVARS ZVIRBULIS.

Smaile (Peak): Brīvības iela 104, Rīga 1001; tel. 731-5137; f. 1999; fiction, poetry, fine arts; Dir ANDREJS BRIMERBERGS.

Sprīdītis: Kalēju iela 51, Rīga 1050; tel. 728-6516; fax 728-6818; f. 1989; books for children and young people; Dir ANDREJS RIJNIEKS.

Zinātne (Science): Akadēmijas lauk. 1, Rīga 1050; tel. 721-2797; fax 722-7825; e-mail zinatne@navigator.lv; f. 1951; non-fiction, text books, dictionaries, reference books; Dir IEVA JANSONE.

ZVAIGZNE ABC Ltd (Star): K. Valdemāra iela 6, Rīga 1010; tel. 732-4518; fax 750-8798; e-mail info@zvaigzne.lv; internet www.zvaigzne.lv; f. 1966; privately owned since 1993; educational literature, manuals, dictionaries, non-fiction for children and adults, fiction; Pres. VIJA KILBLOKA; 173 employees.

PUBLISHERS' ASSOCIATIONS

Latvian Publishers' Association (Latvijas Grāmatizdevēju asociācija): K. Barona iela 36–4, Rīga 1011; tel. 728-2392; fax 728-0549; e-mail lga@gramatizdeveji.lv; internet www.gramatizdeveji.delfi.lv; f. 1993; 47 mems; Pres. ANITA ROŽKALNE.

Latvian Press Publishers' Association: Balasta dambis 3, Rīga 1081; tel. 911-7060; fax 728-1077; e-mail lpia@age.lv; internet www.lpia.lv; f. 1993; 33 mems; Pres. AIVARS RUDZINSKIS.

WRITERS' UNION

Latvian Writers' Union (Latvijas Rakstnieku savienība): Kuršu iela 24, Rīga 1426; tel. 755-5180; fax 755-4034; 291 mems; Chair. VALDIS RŪMNIEKS.

Broadcasting and Communications

TELECOMMUNICATIONS

In 2002 there were 701,000 main telephone lines in use; 69% of lines were digital in 2001.

Regulatory Organizations

Department of Communications (Ministry of Transport): Gogoļa iela 3, Rīga 1190; tel. 724-2321; fax 782-0636; e-mail diana .ainep@sam.gov.lv; f. 1991; Dir INĀRA RUDAKA.

Public Utilities Commission of Latvia: Brīvības iela 55, Rīga 1010; tel. 709-7200; fax 709-7277; e-mail sprk@sprk.gov.lv; internet www.sprk.lv; in 2001 the Public Utilities Commission of Latvia assumed the regulatory functions of the Telecommunications Tariff Council and other bodies; Chair. INNA STEINBUKA.

Major Service Providers

Latvian Mobile Telephone (SIA Latvijas Mobilais Telefons—LMT): Unijas iela 39, POB 116, Rīga 1039; tel. 777-3200; fax 753-5353; e-mail info@lmt.lv; internet www.lmt.lv; f. 1992; 24.5% owned by Sonera Holding BV (Finland), 24.5% owned by TeliaSonera AB (Sweden), 23.0% owned by SIA Lattelekom, 23.0% owned by Digitālais Latvijas radio un televīzijas centrs, a/s; Gen. Man. JURIS BINDE; 150 employees.

Radiokom: Elizabetes iela 45–47, Rīga 1010; Dir JANA BALODE.

SIA Lattelekom: Vaļņu iela 30, Rīga 1050; tel. 705-5222; fax 705-5001; e-mail gstrautma@exchange.telekom.lv; internet www .lattelekom.lv; f. 1992; partially privatized; 49% owned by TeliaSonera AB (Sweden); Pres. GUNDARS STRAUTMANIS; 6,500 employees.

Tele2: Kurzemes pr. 3, Rīga 1067; tel. 706-0069; fax 706-0176; internet www.tele2.lv; f. 1991; owned by Tele2 AB (Sweden); fmrly Baltkom GSM; Pres. BILL BUTLER; 110 employees.

Telecommunication Association of Latvia: Rm 702, Academic lauk. 1, Rīga 1050; tel. 722-6962; e-mail kaiva@mail.lv; Pres. PĒTERIS ŠMIDRE.

BROADCASTING

Amendments to the broadcasting law approved in October 1998 required greater use of the Latvian language in all programmes. Foreign programmes were restricted to 25% of daily broadcast time.

Regulatory Organization

National Broadcasting Council of Latvia: Smilšu iela 1–3, Rīga 1939; tel. 722-1848; fax 722-0448; e-mail tvcounc@mailbox.riga.lv; internet www.nrtp.lv; f. 1992; defends social interests and maintains free accessibility to information; Chair. OJĀRS RUBENIS.

Radio

Latvijas Radio (Latvian Radio): Doma lauk. 8, Rīga 1505; tel. 720-6722; fax 720-6709; internet www.radio.org.lv; f. 1925; state-operated service; broadcasts in Latvian, Russian and English; Dir-Gen. DZINTRIS KOLĀTS.

Alise Plus: Raiņa iela 28, Daugavpils 5403; e-mail alise_plus@ daugavpils.apollo.lv; 24-hour transmissions in Russian and Latvian.

European Hit Radio: Elijas iela 17, Rīga 1050; tel. 957-5757; fax 720-4407; e-mail radio@superfm.lv; internet www.europeanhitradio .com; f. 1994; 24-hour transmissions in Latvian, Russian, Estonian, Lithuanian and English; Pres. UGIS POLIS; Dir RICHARD ZAKSS.

Latvijas Kristīgais Radio: Lāčplēša iela 37, Rīga 1011; tel. 721-3704; fax 782-0633; e-mail lkz@am.lv; 24-hour transmissions in Latvian and Russian.

Radio Ef-Ei: Atbrvōsanas aleja 98, Rēzekne 4600; e-mail efei@ mailbox.riga.lv; 24-hour transmissions in Russian and Latvian.

Radio Imanta: Tērbatas iela 1, Valmiera 4201; tel. 420-7349; fax 420-7350; e-mail radio.imanta@tl.lv; internet www.radioimanta.lv; 24-hour transmissions in Russian and Latvian; Chief Editor NILS INTERBERGS.

Radio Mazsalaca: Avotu iela 13, Mazsalaca 4215; 15 hours daily in Latvian.

Radio Merkūrijs: Bērzpils iela 2A, Balvi 4501; e-mail merkurijs@ ridzene.lv; 24-hour transmissions in Latvian and Russian.

Radio Mix FM: L. Nometņu iela 62, Rīga 1002; 24-hour transmissions in Russian.

Radio Rīgai: Televīzijas centrs, Zaķusalas krastmala 3, Rīga 1509; 24-hour transmissions in Latvian.

Radio Saules Iela: Saules iela 8A, Cēsis 4100; 24-hour transmissions in Latvian.

Radio Sigulda: L. Paegles iela 3, Sigulda 2150; 24-hour transmissions in Latvian.

Radio SWH: Skanstes iela 13, Rīga 1013; internet www.radio.swh .lv.

Radio Trīs: Vaļņu iela 5, Cēsis 4101; tel. 412-4566; fax 412-7041; e-mail radio@radio3.lv; internet www.radio3.lv; f. 1994; 24-hour transmissions in Latvian; Dir EGILS VISKRINTS.

Radio Zemgale: Grāfa laukums 6, Lecava 3913; e-mail rz@apollo .lv; internet www.radiozemgalei.lv; f. 2000; 24 hours daily in Latvian; Dir DACE DUBKEVIČA.

Television

Latvijas Televīzija (Latvian Television): Zaķusalas krastmala 3, Rīga 1509; tel. 720-0315; fax 720-0025; e-mail ltv@ltv.lv; internet www.ltv.lv; f. 1954; state-operated service; two channels in Latvian (Channel II also includes programmes in Russian, Polish, Ukrainian, German, English and French); Dir EDGARS KOTS.

LNT (Latvian Independent Television): Elijas iela 17, Rīga 1050; tel. 707-0200; fax 782-1128; e-mail lnt@lnt.lv; internet www.lnt.lv; f. 1996; entertainment, news reports; Dir-Gen. ANDREJS ĒĶIS.

Finance

(cap. = capital; res = reserves; dep. = deposits; m. = million; brs = branches; amounts in LVL)

BANKING

A crisis in the banking sector in 1995 was contained by early 1996. Reorganization of the sector subsequently took place. At the end of 2002 there were 22 banks in operation.

Central Bank

Bank of Latvia (Latvijas Banka): K. Valdemāra iela 2A, Rīga 1050; tel. 702-2300; fax 702-2420; e-mail info@bank.lv; internet www.bank .lv; f. 1922; cap. 25.0m., res 66.8m., dep. 205.7m. (Dec. 2002); Gov. and Chair. of Bd ILMĀRS RIMŠĒVIČS.

Commercial Banks

Aizkraukles Banka: Elizabetes iela 23, Rīga 1010; tel. 777-5555; e-mail bank@ab.lv; internet www.ab.lv; f. 1993; cap. 51,541.0 (1997); Chair. of Bd ALEKSANDRS BERGMANIS.

A/S Vereinsbank Rīga: Elizabetes iela 63, Rīga 1050; tel. 708-5500; fax 708-5507; e-mail info@vereinsbank.lv; internet www .vereinsbank.lv; f. 1997; 100% owned by Vereins- und Westbank AG (Germany); cap. 13.9m., res. 0.0m., dep. 84.6m. (Dec. 2002); Pres. THOMAS SCHÜTZE.

Baltic Transit Bank (Baltijas Tranzītu Banka): 13. Janvāra iela 3, Rīga 1050; tel. 702-4747; fax 721-1985; e-mail btb@btb.lv; internet www.btb.lv; f. 1992; joint-stock commercial bank; merged with Rīgas Naftas un Kimijas Banka in 1999; cap. 8.6m., res −0.5m., dep. 135.9m. (Dec. 2002); Pres. and Chair. of Bd EDGARS DUBRA; 30 brs.

Business Bank of Latvia (Latvijas Biznesa Banka): 3 Antonijas iela, Rīga 1010; tel. 777-5800; fax 777-5849; e-mail pstbox@lbb.lv; internet www.lbb.lv; f. 1992; 99.72% owned by Moscow Municipal Bank—Bank of Moscow (Russian Federation); cap. 4.9m., res −0.8m., dep 15.4m. (Dec. 2002); Chair. and Pres. GEORGIJS DRAGILEVS.

Economic Commercial Bank of Latvia—Lateko (Latvijas Ekonomiskā Komercbanka): E. Birznieka-Upiša iela 21, Rīga 1011; tel. 704-1100; fax 704-1111; e-mail latbk@lateko.lv; internet www .lateko.lv; f. 1992; cap 7.2m., res 0.0m., dep. 173.1m. (Dec. 2002); Pres. OSKARS GULĀNS.

AS Hansabanka: Kaļķu iela 26, Rīga 1050; tel. 702-4444; fax 702-4400; e-mail info@hansabanka.lv; internet www.hansabanka.lv; f. 1992; present name since 1996; merged with Latvijas Zemes banka (Land Bank) 1999, merged with Ventspils ABB 2000; 99.9% owned by Hansapank (Estonia); cap. 46.0m., res 8.2m., dep. 542.1m. (Dec. 2002); Chair. of Bd INGRIDA BLUMA.

JSC Latvian Trade Bank (Latvijas Tirdzniecības Banka): Trijadibas iela 4, Rīga 1048; tel. 761-1818; fax 786-0077; e-mail ltb@ltblv .com; internet www.ltblv.com; f. 1991; 99.4% owned by Moscow Business World Bank (Russia); cap. 3.0m., res 0.7m., dep. 40.8m. (Dec. 2002); Pres. and Chair. ARMANDS STEINBERGS; Vice-Chair. DZINTARS PELCBERGS.

Māras banka: Lāčplēša iela, Rīga 1011; tel. 728-6661; fax 728-2788; e-mail info@marasbanka.lv; internet www.marasbanka.lv; f. 1997;

privately owned; mortgage banking; cap. 3.5m., res 0.9m., dep. 16.8m. (Dec. 2002); Chair. of Council NIKOLAJS SIGURDS BULMANIS; Gen. Man. INGA GULBE.

Mortgage and Land Bank of Latvia (Latvijas Hipoteku un Zemes Banka): Doma lauk. 4, Rīga 1977; tel. 722-2945; fax 782-0143; e-mail banka@hipo.lv; internet www.hipo.lv; f. 1993; state-owned; cap. 17.9m., res 4.6m., dep. 141.2m. (Dec. 2002); Pres. and Chair. of Bd INESIS FEIFERIS; 32 brs.

Multibanka: Elizabetes iela 57, Rīga 1772; tel. 728-9546; fax 782-8232; e-mail info@multibanka.com; internet www.multibanka.lv; f. 1994; cap. 4.3m., res 0.3m., dep. 86.2m. (Dec. 2002); Chair. GVIDO SENKANS; Pres. SVETLANA DZENE.

NORD/LB Latvija JSC: Smilšu iela 6, Rīga 1803; tel. 701-5204; fax 732-3449; e-mail office@nordlb.lv; internet www.nordlb.lv; f. 1989; fmrly Rīgas Komercbanka PLC; operations suspended in March 1999; re-opened as Pirmā Latvijas Komercbanka in Oct. 1999; name changed to Pirmā Banka JSC in June 2001, and as above in April 2003; 98.9% owned by Norddeutsche Landesbank Girozentrale (Germany); cap. 20.2m., res 1.5m., dep. 118.7m. (Dec. 2002); Pres. and Chair. of Bd JÜRGEN MACHALETT; 10 brs.

Ogre Commercial Bank (Ogres Komercbanka): 36 Brīvības iela, Ogre 5001; tel. 701-6520; fax 701-6522; e-mail info@okb.lv; internet portal.okb.lv; f. 1993; 81.4% owned by Salamandra Baltik; cap. 3.3m., res 0.1m., dep. 119.1m. (Dec. 2002); Pres. and Chair. VOLDEMARS EIHE.

Parex Bank (Parekss Banka): Smilšu iela 3, Rīga 1522; tel. 701-0000; fax 701-0001; e-mail inquiry@parex.lv; internet www.parex.lv; f. 1992; 50.93% owned by Europe Holding Ltd; cap. 50.0m., res 3.8m., dep. 843.2m. (Dec. 2002); Pres. VALERY KARGIN; Chair. VICTOR KRASOVITSKY; 5 brs.

Rietumu Bank (Western Bank): Brīvības iela 54, Rīga 1011; tel. 702-5555; fax 702-5588; e-mail info@rietumu.lv; internet www.rietumu.lv; f. 1992; cap. and res 31.2m., dep. 412m. (Dec. 2003); merged with Saules Banka in July 2001; Pres. and Chief Exec. MICHAEL J. BOURKE.

Trust Commercial Bank (Trasta komercbanka): Miesnieku iela 9, Rīga 1050; tel. 702-7777; fax 702-7700; e-mail info@tkb.lv; internet www.tkb.lv; f. 1989; present name adopted 1996; cap. 3.6m., res – 0.4m., dep. 24.8m. (Dec. 2002); Pres. GUNDARS GRIEZE.

Unibank (A/S Latvijas Unibanka): L. Pils iela 23, Rīga 1050; tel. 721-2808; fax 721-5335; e-mail sekretars@unibanka.lv; internet www.unibanka.lv; f. 1993; 98.5% owned by Skandinaviska Enskilda Banken AB (Sweden); cap. 37.1m., res 3.8m., dep. 620.0m. (Dec. 2002); Pres. and Chair. ANDRIS BĒRZIŅŠ; 68 brs.

Savings Bank

JSC Latvijas Krājbanka (Latvian Savings Bank): Palasta iela 1, Rīga 1954; tel. 709-2001; fax 721-2083; e-mail info@lkb.lv; internet www.krajbanka.lv; f. 1924 as Post Office Savings Bank, name changed as above 1998; 7.1% state-owned; cap. 9.1m., res –0.1m., dep. 152.1m. (Dec. 2002); Pres. ANDRIS NATRINS; 10 brs.

Regulatory Authority

Financial and Capital Markets Commission (FCMC): Kungu iela 1, Rīga 1050; tel. 777-4800; fax 722-5755; e-mail fktk@fktk.lv; internet www.fktk.lv; f. 2001; Chair. ULDIS CERPS.

Banking Association

Association of Latvian Commercial Banks: Pērses iela 9–11, Rīga 1011; tel. 728-4528; fax 782-8170; e-mail bankas@latnet.lv; f. 1992; 21 mems; Pres. TEODORS TVERIJONS.

INSURANCE

At the end of 1999 there were 27 insurance companies in Latvia.

Balta Insurance Company Ltd: Vaļņu iela 1, Rīga 1050; tel. 722-9660; fax 782-1014; e-mail balta@balta.lv; automobile, property, freight, travel, agricultural insurance; Pres. ANDRIS LAIZĀNS.

Balva: K. Valdemāra iela 36, Rīga 1010; tel. 750-6955; fax 750-6956; e-mail balva@balva.lv; internet www.balva.lv; f. 1992; non-life insurance; Pres. VASILY RAGOZIN.

JSIC ERGO Latvija: Unijas iela 45, Rīga 1035; tel. 784-0101; fax 784-0102; e-mail info@ergo.lv; bought by Alte Leipziger (Germany) in 2000; all types of risk insurance; Pres. of Bd ILMARS VEIDE.

Estora Reinsurance Co: Elizabetes iela 14, Rīga 1010; tel. 733-3335; fax 733-3898; e-mail estora@estora.com; internet www.estora.com; f. 1992; reinsurance; Dir-Gen. JERGENIJS TOLOČKOVS.

Ezerzeme: Raiņa iela 28, Daugavpils 5403; tel. 542-2555; fax 542-2177; f. 1992; state, private firm, personal property, long- and short-term life, life, domestic animals, accident, freight, travel, funeral insurance; Chair. of Bd PĒTERIS SAVOSTJANOVS.

Helga Joint Stock Insurance Company: Elizabetes iela 20, Rīga 1050; tel. 7243-074; fax 7243-067; e-mail helga@parks.lv.

Latva: Vaļņu iela 1, Rīga 1912; tel. 721-2341; fax 721-0134; e-mail latva@latva.lv; f. 1940; state insurance co; accident, passenger, child and adult life insurance; Chair. MARGARITA PABĒRZA.

Rīga Insurance Company: Grēcinieku iela 22–24, Rīga 1050; tel. 721-1764; fax 722-3437; general liability, professional liability, health, motor, natural disasters, fire, freight insurance; Pres. AIVARS BERGERS.

Union Unlimited: tel. 221-3150; fax 222-5397; travel, property, athletes', freight, state, co-operative, joint-stock, credit, medical, accident insurance; Chair. of Bd AIVARS SALIŅŠ.

COMMODITY AND STOCK EXCHANGES

Latgale Exchange (Latgales birža): Sakņu iela 29, Daugavpils 5403; tel. 542-6044; fax 542-6351; f. 1992; Gen. Dir ANATOLII BOTUSHANSKII.

Latvian Universal Exchange (Latvijas Universālā birža): Rīga; tel. 721-2559; fax 722-4515; f. 1991; Pres. JĀNIS VALTERS.

Rīga Stock Exchange (Rīgas Fondu birža): Doma lauk. 6, Rīga 1885; tel. 721-2431; fax 722-9411; e-mail rfb@rfb.lv; internet www.rfb.lv; f. 1993; Pres. GUNTARS KOKOREVICS.

Trade and Industry

GOVERNMENT AGENCY

Latvian Privatization Agency: K. Valdemāra iela 31, Rīga 1010; tel. 702-1358; fax 783-0363; e-mail lpa@mail.bkc.lv; internet www.lpa.bkc.lv; f. 1994; Dir-Gen. ARNIS OZOLNIEKS.

DEVELOPMENT ORGANIZATIONS

Interlatvija: Kalpaka bulv. 1, Rīga 1010; tel. 733-3602; f. 1987; seeks to promote exports, imports and the establishment of joint ventures; Dir-Gen. MĀRIS FORSTS.

Latvian Investment and Development Agency: Pērses iela 2, Rīga 1442; tel. 703-9400; fax 703-9401; e-mail invest@liaa.gov.lv; internet www.liaa.gov.lv; f. 1993; promotion of business development in Latvia and foreign markets; Dir JURIS KANELS.

CHAMBER OF COMMERCE

Latvian Chamber of Commerce and Industry (Latvijas Tirdzniecības un rūpniecības kamera): K. Valdemāra iela 35, Rīga; tel. 722-5595; fax 782-0092; e-mail info@chamber.lv; internet www.chamber.lv; f. 1934; re-est. 1990; Pres. ANDRIS LARMANIS; Dir-Gen. JĀNIS LEJA.

INDUSTRIAL AND TRADE ASSOCIATIONS

Latvian Association of Business Consultants: Brīvības bulv. 91, Rīga 1001; tel. 727-9807; fax 727-9808; e-mail lbka@lbka.lv; internet www.lbka.lv; f. 1995; Man. Dir DAINIS LOCANS.

Latvian Export Association (Latvijas Eksporta Asociācija): Valmieras iela 41, Rm 11, Rīga; tel. and fax 770-1213; Pres. IVAR STRAUTINSH.

UTILITIES
Regulatory Authority

Public Utilities Commission of Latvia (PUC) (Sabiedrisko Pakalpojumu Regulēšanas Komisija): Brīvības bulv. 55, Rīga 1010; tel. 709-7200; fax 709-7277; e-mail sprk@sprk.gov.lv; internet www.sprk.lv; f. 2001 to replace the Energy Regulation Council; multi-sector regulator overseeing electricity, gas, telecommunications, post and railway sectors; Chair. INNA STEINBUKA.

Electricity
Major suppliers include:

Augstspriegauma tikls: Jatnieku iela 95, Daugavpils 5410.

Austrumu Electricity: A. Pumpura iela 5, Daugavpils 5404.

Centralie elektriskie tikli: Stopinu pagasts, Lici 2118.

Dienvidu Electricity Network: Elektribas iela 10, Jelgava 3001.

Latvenergo: Pulkveža brieža 12, Rīga 1230; tel. 732-8309; e-mail webadm@energo.lv; internet www.energo.lv; state-owned producer and distributor; Pres. KĀRLIS MIĶELSONS; 7,127 employees.

Northern-eastern Electricity Network (LATVENERGO): Mednieku 3, Aizkraukle 5101; tel. 518-1530; fax 518-1539.

Rigas elektrotikls: Pernavas iela 19, Rīga 1012.

Vangazu elektrikis: Gaujas iela 24, Vangazi 2136; tel. and fax 299-5535.

Vats: Talsu iela 84, Ventspils 3602.

Western Electricity Network: Rīga iela 56, Liepāja 3401; tel. 342-3532; fax 342-3105.

Ziemelu Electricity Network: Raiņa iela 14, Valmiera 4201.

Gas

Major suppliers include:

Aga: Katrinas iela 5, Rīga 1045.

Elme L: Aplokciema iela 3, Rīga 1034.

Energija-G: Maskavas iela 85, Rīga 1003.

Gazes transports: Bikernieku iela 111, Rīga 1079.

Katlinieks: Lugazu iela 14, Rīga 1045.

Lanteks: Pernavas iela 42-3, Rīga 1009.

Latvian Gas (Latvijas gaze): A. Briana iela 6, Rīga 1001; tel. 736-9132; fax 782-1406; e-mail latvijas_gaze@lg.lv; internet www.lg.lv; partially privatized in 2000–01; 8% state-owned; Chair. Māris Gailis; 2,817 employees.

Latvijas Propāna Gāze: Kurzemes prospekts 19, Rīga 1067; tel. 741-3709; fax 741-3712; e-mail lpg@lsg.lv; internet www.lsg.lv; f. 2000; purchase, sale and shipment of liquefied petroleum gas.

Remifa: Abolu iela 3, Rīga 1058.

Rīgas gaze: Vagornu iela 20, Rīga 1009.

SIIL: Pushkina iela 3, Rīga 1050.

Saullekts: Virsu iela 11, Rīga 1035.

VITEG: Bruņinieku iela 108, Rīga 1009.

Vitne: Maskavas iela 457, Rīga 1063.

Water

Major suppliers include:

Aizkraukles udens: Tornu iela 1, Aizkraukle 5101.

A/S Madonas udens: Raiņa iela 54, Madona 4801; tel. 480-7071; fax 486-0106; e-mail udens@kvarcs.lv.

Bauskas udenssaimnieciba: Birzu iela 8a, Bauska 3901; tel. 396-0565; fax 396-0566; e-mail baude@apollo.lv.

Buvenergo: Stabu iela 58, Rīga 1011.

Daugavpils Water (Municipal Ltd): Udensvada iela 3, Daugavpils 5403.

JS & J Udenmeistars: Ramulu iela 1, Rīga 1005.

Liepajas udens: K. Valdemāra iela 12, Liepāja 3401; tel. 541-1416; fax 541-0769; e-mail dmeu@dpu.lv.

Rīgas udens (Rīga Water): Basteja bulv. l, k. 5, Rīga 1495; tel. 708-8555; fax 722-2660; e-mail office@ru.lv; internet www.rw.lv; water supply and sewage treatment.

Udens inzinieri: Gānibu dambis 26–601, Rīga 1005.

Udensvada un Kanalizacijas saimnieciba: Udensvada iela 4, Jelgava 3001.

TRADE UNIONS

Free Trade Union Confederation of Latvia (LBAS): Bruņinieku iela 29–31, Rīga 1001; tel. 727-0351; fax 727-6649; e-mail intern@latnet.lv; internet www.lbas.lv; f. 1990; Pres. Juris Radzevics.

Transport

RAILWAYS

In 2002 there were 2,270 km of railways on the territory of Latvia. In 2003 Latvian railways carried 23.0m. passengers and 48.4m. metric tons of freight.

Latvian Railway (Latvijas Dzelzceļš): Gogoļa iela 3, Rīga 1547; tel. 583-4940; fax 782-0231; e-mail info@ldz.lv; internet www.ldz.lv; f. 1993; state joint-stock co; Dir-Gen. Andris Zorgevics.

ROADS

In 2000 Latvia's total road network was 73,202 km, of which 7,011 km were main roads.

Latvian Road Administration: Gogoļa iela 3, Rīga 1050; tel. 702-8169; fax 702-8171; e-mail lad@lad.lv; internet www.lad.lv; Chair. Olafs Kronlaks.

SHIPPING

At 31 December 2002 the Latvian-registered merchant fleet numbered 158 vessels, with a combined total displacement of 88,741 grt. In 2003 some 50.9m. metric tons of freight were transported through the country's three main (Ventspils, Rīga and Liepāja) and seven smaller ports. Ventspils is particularly important for the shipping of petroleum and fuel exports and is included in a special economic zone; Rīga and Ventspils operate in a free port regime.

Maritime Department: Gogoļa iela 3, Rīga 1743; tel. 702-8198; fax 733-1406; e-mail krastins@sam.gov.lv; internet www.sam.gov.lv; Dir Aigars Krastiņš.

Port Authorities

Liepāja Port Authority: Liepāja Special Economic Zone, Feniksa iela 4, Liepāja 3401; tel. 342-7605; fax 348-0252; e-mail authority@lsez.lv; internet www.lsez.lv; Man. Dir Aivars Boja.

Rīga Commercial Port: Eksporta iela 15, Rīga 1227; tel. 732-9224; fax 783-0215; e-mail rto@mail.bkc.lv; internet www.rto.lv; Pres. Aivars Taurins.

Rīga Fishing Seaport: Atlantijas iela 27, Rīga 1020; tel. 235-1514; fax 235-3168; Dir G. Shevchuk.

Rīga Port Authority: Eksporta iela 6, Rīga 1010; tel. 703-0800; fax 783-0051; e-mail rop@mail.rop.lv; internet www.rop.lv; f. 1992; Chief Exec. Leonids Loginovs.

Ventspils Free Port Authority: Jāņa iela 19, Ventspils 3601; tel. 362-2586; fax 362-1297; e-mail vbparvalde@apollo.lv; internet www.ventspils.lv; f. 1991; Chief Exec. Imants Sarmulis.

Ventspils Commercial Port Authority: Dzintaru iela 22, Ventspils 3602; tel. 362-2821; fax 366-8870; e-mail vcp@vcp.lv; Pres. Valeriy Pashuta.

Shipping Companies

Latvian Shipping Co (LASCO) (Latvijas Kugniecība): Basteja bulv. 2, Rīga 1807; tel. 702-0111; fax 782-8106; e-mail lsc@lsc.riga.lv; internet www.latshipcom.lv; f. 1991; tanker, reefer, LPG and dry cargo transportation; partially privatized in 2002; Pres. Andris Klaviņš.

Rīga Shipping Co: Balasta dambis 9, Rīga 1048; tel. 760-1133; fax 786-0243; e-mail riga@shipping.lv; internet www.rigashipping.lv; f. 1994; complete technical management of ships including crewing; Dir Miks Ekbaums.

CIVIL AVIATION

There are two international airports, at Rīga and at Jelgava (southwest of Rīga). The Department of Aviation of the Ministry of Transport co-ordinates the financing of air transport in Latvia, and the Civil Aviation Administration supervises the operation and safety of flights.

Civil Aviation Administration of Latvia: Rīga Airport, Rīga 1053; tel. 720-7307; fax 720-7417; internet www.caa.lv; Dir-Gen. Māris Gorodcovs.

Department of Aviation: Gogoļa iela 3, Rīga 1743; tel. 702-8209; fax 721-7180; Dir Arnis Muižnieks.

AirBaltic Corpn AS: Rīga Airport, Rīga 1053; tel. 720-7069; fax 720-7369; e-mail info@airbaltic.lv; internet www.airbaltic.com; f. 1995; 52.6% govt-controlled, 47.2% owned by Scandinavian Airlines System (Sweden); operates services to 16 destinations in Scandinavia, the Baltic states and Western Europe; Pres. and Chief Exec. Bertolt Flick.

Baltic Express Line: Dzirnavu iela 100, Rīga 1010; tel. 728-1037; fax 728-4806; e-mail bel@binet.lv; internet www.binet.lv/home/bel/english; f. 1993; flights to Bulgaria, Egypt, Greece, Spain and Turkey; Pres. Boris Beloussov; Dir Valeriy Litavar.

A/C Inversija: Rīga Airport, Rīga 1053; tel. 720-7095; fax 720-7476; e-mail inversija@latnet.lv; f. 1988; cargo service; operates routes to destinations in Europe and the Far East; Dir-Gen. Sefim Brook.

Latpass Airline (SIA Latpass Aviolīnijas): Pils laukums 2/5, Rīga 1050; tel. 720-7626; fax 722-6738; e-mail latpass@latpass.lv; internet www.latpass.lv.

RAF-AVIA: Jura Alunana iela 2a, Rīga 1010; tel. 732-4661; fax 732-4671; e-mail rafavia@mail.interfers.lv; internet www.rafavia.com; f. 1991; scheduled and charter flights; Pres. Jurijs Hmelevskii.

Tourism

Among Latvia's principal tourist attractions are the historic centre of Rīga, with its medieval and art nouveau buildings, the extensive beaches of the Baltic coastline, and Gauja National Park, which stretches east of the historic town of Sigulda for nearly 100 km along the Gauja river. Sigulda also offers winter sports facilities. Revenue from tourism in 2002 was some US \$161m. Foreign tourist arrivals numbered 360,927, of whom 15.4% were from Finland, 13.4% from Germany and 10.1% from Russia.

Latvia Tours: Kaļķu iela 8, Rīga 1050; tel. 708-5001; fax 782-0020; e-mail hq@latviatours.lv; internet www.latviatours.lv; Dir GUNDEGA ZELTIŅA.

Latvian Tourism Development Agency: Pils lauk. 4, Rīga 1050; tel. and fax 722-9945; e-mail tda@latviatourism.lv; internet www .latviatourism.lv; f. 1993; Dir AIVARS KALNINSCARON.

LEBANON

Introductory Survey

Location, Climate, Language, Religion, Flag, Capital

The Republic of Lebanon lies in western Asia, bordered by Syria to the north and east, and by Israel and the Palestinian Autonomous Areas to the south. The country has a coastline of about 220 km (135 miles) on the eastern shore of the Mediterranean Sea. The climate varies widely with altitude. The coastal lowlands are hot and humid in summer, becoming mild (cool and damp) in winter. In the mountains, which occupy much of Lebanon, the weather is cool in summer, with heavy snowfalls in winter. Rainfall is generally abundant. The official language is Arabic, which is spoken by almost all of the inhabitants. French is widely used as a second language, while Kurdish and Armenian are spoken by small ethnic minorities. At December 2003 there were 394,532 Palestinian refugees registered in Lebanon. The major religions are Islam and Christianity, and there is a very small Jewish community. In the early 1980s it was estimated that 57% of Lebanon's inhabitants were Muslims, with about 43% Christians. The principal Muslim sects are Shi'a and Sunni, while there is also a significant Druze community. By the 1980s it was generally considered that Shi'a Muslims, totalling an estimated 1.2m., constituted Lebanon's largest single community. Most Christians adhere to the Roman Catholic Church, principally the Maronite rite. There are also Armenian, Greek and Syrian sects (both Catholic and Eastern Orthodox) and small groups of Protestants. The national flag (proportions 2 by 3) has three horizontal stripes, of red, white (half the depth) and red, with a representation of a cedar tree (in green and brown) in the centre of the white stripe. The capital is Beirut.

Recent History

Lebanon, the homeland of the ancient Phoenicians, became part of the Turkish Ottoman Empire in the 16th century, and following the dissolution of the Ottoman Empire after the First World War (1914–18), a Greater Lebanese state was created by the Allied powers. The new state was formed in order to meet the nationalist aspirations of the area's predominantly Christian population, but it also included largely Muslim-populated territories traditionally considered to be part of Syria. Lebanon was administered by France, under a League of Nations mandate, from 1920 until independence was declared on 26 November 1941. A republic was established in 1943, and full autonomy was granted in January 1944.

Religious and cultural diversity is Lebanon's defining feature. At the time of independence Christians formed a slight majority of the population, the largest single community (nearly 30% of the total) being the Maronite Christians, who mostly inhabited the north of the country and the capital, Beirut. Other Christian groups included Greek Orthodox communities, Greek Catholics and Armenians. The Muslim groups were the Sunnis, living mainly in the coastal towns of Sur (Tyre), Saida (Sidon) and Beirut, the Shi'ites, a predominantly rural community in southern Lebanon and the northern Beka'a valley, and, in much smaller numbers, the Druzes, an ancient community in central Lebanon. The relative size of the various communities provided the basis for the unwritten 'national pact' of 1943, whereby executive and legislative posts were to be shared in the ratio of six Christians to five Muslims, and seats in the Chamber of Deputies (renamed the National Assembly in March 1979) were distributed on a religious, rather than a politico-ideological, basis. The convention according to this 'confessional' arrangement was that the President was a Maronite Christian, the Prime Minister a Sunni Muslim, and the President of the National Assembly a Shi'a Muslim.

Lebanon's first President, from 1943 until 1952, was Sheikh Bishara el-Khoury. His successor was Camille Chamoun, whose reforms included the enfranchisement of women. Following elections to the Chamber of Deputies in 1957 there was considerable unrest, mainly among Muslims who mistrusted Chamoun's pro-Western foreign policy and advocated Lebanon's closer alignment with Syria and Egypt. In July 1958 Chamoun appealed to the USA for military assistance; US forces remained in Beirut until October, by which time peace had been restored. Meanwhile, Chamoun was persuaded not to seek a further presidential term, and the Chamber elected Gen. Fouad Chehab as his successor. Chehab, who took office in September 1958, adopted a foreign policy of non-alignment, and introduced state provision of health, education and other services. In 1964 he was succeeded by Charles Hélou, who continued many of Chehab's policies but was faced by increasing controversy over the status of Palestinians in Lebanon.

After the establishment of Israel in 1948, and during the subsequent Arab–Israeli wars, thousands of Palestinians fled to Lebanon, where most were housed in refugee camps in the south of the country. Following the creation of the Palestine Liberation Organization (PLO) in 1964, military training centres for Palestinian guerrilla fighters were established in the camps. From 1968 these self-styled *fedayeen* ('martyrs') began making raids into Israel, provoking retaliatory attacks by Israeli forces. In 1969 there were clashes between Lebanese security forces and the *fedayeen*. Many Christians, particularly the Maronites, advocated strict government control over the Palestinians' activities, but the majority of Muslims strongly supported Palestinian operations against Israel.

Hélou's successor, Sulayman Franjiya, took office in 1970. During his presidency the Palestinian issue was exacerbated by an influx of Palestinian fighters expelled from Jordan in July 1971. Conflict between Israeli forces and Palestinians based in Lebanon intensified, while Christian groups began their own armed campaign against the *fedayeen*. In July 1974 Palestinian forces clashed with militia of the Phalangist Party (the Phalanges Libanaises, or al-Kata'eb, a militant right-wing Maronite Christian group). From April 1975 the conflict between the Palestinians and Phalangists quickly descended into full-scale civil war between the Lebanese National Movement (LNM) of left-wing Muslims (including Palestinians), led by Kamal Joumblatt of the Parti Socialiste Progressiste (PSP, a mainly Druze-supported group), and conservative Christian groups, mainly the Phalangist militia. Constitutional issues overtook the status of Palestinians as the main divisive issue, with the LNM advocating an end to the 'confessional' system, claiming this unduly favoured Christians (who by now were generally accepted as no longer forming a majority of the population). Despite diplomatic efforts by Arab and Western countries, no durable cease-fire was achieved until October 1976, largely as a result of intervention in the conflict (in order to prevent an outright LNM victory) by Syrian forces in mid-1976. Under the terms of the cease-fire a 30,000-strong Arab Deterrent Force (ADF), composed mainly of Syrian troops, entered Lebanon.

President Franjiya was succeeded by Elias Sarkis in September 1976, and Prime Minister Rashid Karami by Selim al-Hoss in December. Legislative elections, due in April 1976, were postponed for an initial period of 26 months—the term of the Chamber of Deputies was subsequently extended further. Although the constitutional *status quo* remained intact, more than 30,000 people had died in the civil war and the militias of the various warring factions controlled most of the country. East Beirut and much of northern Lebanon was controlled by the Lebanese Forces (LF), a coalition of Maronite militias formed in September 1976; West Beirut was controlled by Muslim groups; and Palestinians dominated much of south-west Lebanon.

In March 1978 Israeli forces advanced into southern Lebanon in a counter-attack against forces of Fatah (the Palestine National Liberation Movement), the main guerrilla group within the PLO. UN Security Council Resolution 425, adopted on 17 March, demanded an Israeli withdrawal from Lebanon (thereby respecting its territorial integrity, sovereignty and independence) and also established a UN Interim Force in Lebanon (UNIFIL, see p. 68), initially of 4,000 troops. Israeli forces withdrew in June, but transferred control of a border strip to the pro-Israeli Christian militias of Maj. Saad Haddad. In October, following several months of renewed fighting in Beirut between Syrian troops of the ADF and right-wing Christian militias, the ADF states agreed on a peace plan (the Beiteddin Declaration), which aimed to restore the authority of the Lebanese Government and army. Attempts to implement the plan were unsuccessful, however, and Lebanon's fragmentation deepened.

Al-Hoss resigned the premiership in June 1980 and was replaced in October by Chafic al-Wazzan. In August 1982, in an election boycotted by most Muslim deputies, the renamed National Assembly designated Bachir Gemayel (the younger son of the founder of the Phalangist Party and commander of the LF) to succeed President Sarkis. The President-elect was assassinated in September, and his brother, Amin, was elected in his place. Following the assassination, Phalangist forces (with the apparent complicity of occupying Israeli forces) entered the Palestinian refugee camps of Sabra and Chatila, in west Beirut, killing some 2,000 refugees. Israeli forces had re-entered Lebanon in June 1982, with the declared aim of finally eliminating the PLO's military threat to Israel's northern border. Israeli troops quickly defeated Palestinian forces in south-west Lebanon and surrounded the western sector of Beirut, trapping more than 6,000 Palestinian fighters there. A US-led diplomatic initiative resulted in an agreement enabling the PLO fighters to disperse among several Arab states, and a multinational peace-keeping force was deployed in Beirut. (In September 1983 intense fighting between rival factions of Fatah resulted in a truce agreement, brokered by Saudi Arabia and Syria, which led to a second evacuation of some 4,000 Palestinian fighters, most notably of the PLO Chairman, Yasser Arafat, who was exiled to Tunisia.) Negotiations between Lebanon and Israel began in December 1982, culminating in May 1983 in an agreement to end all hostilities (including the theoretical state of war that had existed between the two countries since 1948) and to withdraw all foreign troops from Lebanon. However, Syria did not recognize the accord, leaving 40,000 of its own troops and 7,000 PLO fighters in the Beka'a valley and northern Lebanon. Israel, meanwhile, redeployed a reduced force of 10,000 troops along the Awali river, south of Beirut. Maj. Saad Haddad's South Lebanon Army (SLA) was to police southern areas as Israel's role lessened. Meanwhile, the multinational force in Beirut (comprising some 5,800 mainly French, Italian and US personnel) was drawn increasingly into the fighting, coming under frequent attack from Muslim militias who opposed its tantamount support for the Christian-led Government. In October 241 US and 58 French marines were killed in suicide bombings by Muslim groups.

The failure to conclude a peaceful settlement, and in particular the resumption of heavy fighting in February 1984 (which the reconstituted, US-trained Lebanese army was unable to suppress), led to the resignation of Prime Minister al-Wazzan, followed shortly afterwards by the withdrawal of the USA, Italy and the United Kingdom from the peace-keeping force. French troops were withdrawn in March. By this time successive defeats had left Gemayel's forces with effective control only in the mainly Christian-populated east Beirut. In March President Gemayel abrogated the May 1983 agreement with Israel, and in April 1984, with Syrian support, he formed a Government of National Unity under former premier Rashid Karami. The Lebanese army failed to gain control of Beirut, and Gemayel's efforts to obtain approval for constitutional reform, already constrained by his fear of alienating his Christian supporters, were further undermined by divisions within the Cabinet.

The Israeli Government formed by Shimon Peres in September 1984 pledged to withdraw Israeli forces from Lebanon. However, while the Lebanese authorities demanded that UNIFIL police the Israeli–Lebanese border, by the time the Israeli withdrawal was completed, in June 1985, Israel had ensured that a narrow buffer zone, policed by the SLA (now commanded by Gen. Antoine Lahad), was in place along the border. With the Israeli presence in Lebanon reduced to a token force, Syria withdrew about one-third of its troops from the Beka'a valley in July, leaving some 25,000 in position.

Sporadic conflict persisted throughout 1985, but in December the leaders of the three main Lebanese militias (the Druze forces, Amal and the LF) signed an accord in the Syrian capital, Damascus, providing for an immediate cease-fire and for the cessation of the civil war within one year. The militias were to be disarmed and disbanded, and a new constitutional regime was to be introduced within three years. However, the militias of the Sunni Murabitoun and the Iranian-backed Shi'ite Hezbollah were not parties to the agreement, which was also opposed by influential Christian elements. Furthermore, there were clashes later in December between supporters of the agreement within the LF and those who resented the concessions made by their leader, Elie Hobeika. In January 1986 Hobeika was forced into exile and replaced as LF leader by Samir Geagea, who, in urging renegotiation of the Damascus accord, effectively ended any prospect of its implementation.

During 1986 Palestinian guerrillas resumed rocket attacks on settlements in northern Israel, provoking retaliatory air attacks by Israel on targets in the Beka'a valley and southern Lebanon. Meanwhile, Hezbollah escalated its attacks on SLA positions within the Israeli buffer zone, and also clashed with UNIFIL. Fighting between Palestinian guerrillas and Shi'ite Amal militiamen for control of the refugee camps in south Beirut escalated in May, before a cease-fire was imposed around the camps in June, as part of a Syrian-sponsored peace plan for Muslim west Beirut. The activities of the Amal, Druze and Sunni militias in west Beirut were temporarily curtailed by the deployment of Lebanese and Syrian troops, but fighting across the so-called 'Green Line', which had effectively divided the area from Christian east Beirut since early 1984, continued. By the time Amal and the PLO agreed in September 1987 to end hostilities, more than 2,500 people had died in the 'war of the camps'. Despite renewed fighting near Sidon in October, in January 1988, avowedly as a gesture of support for the *intifada* (uprising) by Palestinians in the Israeli-occupied territories, the Amal leader, Nabih Berri, announced an end to the siege of the Palestinian refugee camps in Beirut and southern Lebanon.

Prime Minister Karami was killed in a bomb explosion in June 1987. Selim al-Hoss (Prime Minister in 1976–80) was appointed acting premier. In 1988 a political crisis developed as it proved impossible to find a successor to President Gemayal (whose term of office was due to end) that was acceptable to all the warring factions. The three leading contenders for the presidency were Gen. Michel Awn (Commander-in-Chief of the Lebanese army), Raymond Eddé (leader of the Maronite Bloc National) and Sulayman Franjiya (President in 1970–76). Franjiya was Syria's preferred candidate but was notably opposed by Geagea, who apparently ensured that the National Assembly was inquorate when it convened for the election in August 1988. In September the USA and Syria agreed to support another candidate, Mikhail ad-Daher, but Christian army and LF leaders remained opposed to the imposition of any candidate by foreign powers. Gemayel's term of office expired later in the month, when a further attempt by the National Assembly to hold an election was inquorate. The outgoing President appointed an interim military administration, comprising three Christians and three Muslims, with Gen. Awn as Prime Minister. However, there was political confusion as the three nominated Muslim officers immediately refused to serve in the new administration, while two Christian members of the al-Hoss Government resigned, signalling their recognition of the interim military administration. The constitutional crisis, with two Governments claiming legitimacy, was further complicated in November, when the Minister of Defence in the al-Hoss Government dismissed Awn as Commander-in-Chief of the Lebanese army; however, Awn retained the loyalty of large sections of the military and thus remained its *de facto* leader.

In September 1989, following six months of fighting in Beirut between Awn's Lebanese army and Syrian forces, a Tripartite Arab Committee—formed in May by an emergency session of Arab leaders, and comprising King Hassan of Morocco, King Fahd of Saudi Arabia and President Chadli of Algeria—announced a peace plan whereby, most notably, the Lebanese National Assembly would meet to discuss a draft charter of national reconciliation. The Committee's charter was approved by the Syrian Government and the leaders of Lebanon's Muslim militias. Gen. Awn initially rejected its terms, on the grounds that it did not provide for the withdrawal of Syrian forces, but he was forced to relent, in view of support for the charter by almost every Arab country, as well as the USA, the USSR, the United Kingdom and France; a cease-fire accordingly took effect. The National Assembly subsequently met in Ta'if, Saudi Arabia, to discuss the charter, which was finally approved (with some amendments) in October by 58 of the 62 attending deputies (of the 99 deputies elected in May 1972, only 73 survived); it became known as the 'Ta'if agreement'. The charter provided for the transfer of executive power from the presidency to a cabinet, with portfolios divided equally between Christian and Muslim ministers. The number of seats in the National Assembly was to be increased to 108, comprising equal numbers of Christian and Muslim deputies. Following the election of a President and the formation of a new government, all militias involved in the Lebanese conflict were to be disbanded within six months, while the internal security forces would be strengthened; the Syrian armed forces would assist the new Government in implementing the security plan for a maximum of two years.

The National Assembly elected René Mouawad, a Maronite Christian deputy and a former Minister of Education and Arts, as President in early November 1989. The Assembly also unanimously endorsed the Ta'if agreement. However, Awn, who denounced the agreement as a betrayal of Lebanese sovereignty, declared the presidential election unconstitutional and its result null and void, proclaiming himself President. Mouawad was assassinated only 17 days after his election. The National Assembly again convened and elected Elias Hrawi (who had stood against Mouawad earlier in the month) as the new President; the legislature also voted to extend its own term until 1994. A new Cabinet was formed by Selim al-Hoss in late November 1989.

The Christian communities were divided over the Ta'if agreement, and Geagea's refusal to reject the agreement precipitated violent clashes between his LF and Awn's forces in January 1990: by March more than 800 people had been killed in inter-Christian fighting. (Gaegea eventually announced the LF's recognition of the al-Hoss Government, and hence the Ta'if agreement, in April.) In August the National Assembly duly approved amendments to the Constitution, in accordance with the agreement, increasing the number of seats in the National Assembly to 108, to be divided equally between Muslims and Christians. On 21 September the Second Lebanese Republic was officially inaugurated when President Hrawi formally endorsed the amendments. In October Awn and his forces (who continued to reject the Ta'if agreement) were expelled from east Beirut by Syrian forces and units of the Lebanese army loyal to Hrawi. The Lebanese army began to deploy in Beirut in December, by which time all militia forces had withdrawn from the city. In the same month al-Hoss submitted his Government's resignation, and Hrawi invited Omar Karami (Minister of Education and Arts in the outgoing administration) to form a government of national unity, as stipulated by the Ta'if agreement. By early 1991 the Lebanese army was established in most major southern Lebanese towns; by September the militias had been largely disbanded (although Hezbollah maintained armaments in southern Lebanon and the Beka'a valley). In May 1991 the National Assembly approved amendments to the electoral law, and in June the Cabinet appointed 40 deputies to fill the seats that had become vacant since the 1972 election as well as the nine new seats created under the Ta'if agreement. In August 1991 the National Assembly approved a general amnesty for crimes perpetrated during the civil war, although its terms excluded several specified crimes committed during 1975–90. Under a presidential pardon, Awn was allowed to leave the French embassy compound (where he had been sheltering since his defeat in 1990) and to depart for exile in France.

In May 1991 Lebanon and Syria signed a bilateral treaty establishing formal relations in political, military and economic affairs, and confirming the role of the Syrian army as guarantor of the security plans enshrined in the Ta'if agreement. Israel immediately condemned the treaty as a further step towards the formal transformation of Lebanon into a Syrian protectorate, while its opponents within Lebanon denounced it as a threat to the country's independence. In September Lebanon and Syria concluded a mutual security agreement. Syrian forces began to withdraw from Beirut in March 1992, in preparation for their scheduled withdrawal to eastern Lebanon by September. Israel, meanwhile, reasserted its intention of maintaining a military presence in the buffer zone, and its support for the SLA, by launching severe attacks on Palestinian bases in southern Lebanon in June 1991. Lebanese forces began to take up positions in Sidon at the beginning of July. Initial resistance from Palestinians loyal to Arafat was swiftly overcome, and an agreement was concluded with the PLO to allow the Lebanese army to assume control of the area. Israeli military activity against Hezbollah targets in southern Lebanon intensified in late 1991, and the conflict escalated further following the assassination by the Israeli air force of the Secretary-General of Hezbollah, Sheikh Abbas Moussawi, in February 1992.

The deteriorating economic situation in early 1992, combined with allegations of government corruption and incompetence, and a series of general strikes, provoked the resignation of Karami and his Cabinet in May. Subsequent talks in Damascus between President Hrawi and the Syrian leadership led to the reappointment of Rashid Solh as Prime Minister (a position that he had previously held in 1974–75). In July 1992 the National Assembly approved a new electoral law whereby the number of seats in the Assembly was raised from 108 to 128, to be divided equally between Christian and Muslim deputies. The Government's intention to conduct legislative elections in mid-1992 had prompted Christian groups to threaten a boycott of the polls, since it was not certain that Syrian forces would have withdrawn to the eastern area of the Beka'a valley by that time, in accordance with the Ta'if agreement. The Government, for its part, stated that the Lebanese army was not yet able to guarantee the country's security in the absence of Syrian troops.

Lebanon's first legislative elections for 20 years were held in three rounds, on 23 August (in the governorates of the North and the Beka'a valley), 30 August (Beirut and Mount Lebanon) and 6 September 1992 (South and An-Nabatiyah). Electoral turn-out was low (averaging 32%), especially in Maronite districts where leaders had urged a boycott. Hezbollah, contesting the elections for the first time as a political party, enjoyed considerable success in southern constituencies. The Amal leader, Nabih Berri, was appointed President of the new National Assembly in October, and Hrawi invited Rafik Hariri, a Lebanese-born Saudi Arabian business executive, to form a new government, amid hopes that he would restore some confidence in the Lebanese economy and oversee the country's reconstruction. Hariri's Cabinet was dominated by technocrats, and the system of distributing portfolios on an entirely 'confessional' basis was somewhat diluted. It emerged after the elections that Syria would only withdraw its armed forces from Lebanon once a comprehensive peace treaty had been concluded between Syria and Israel.

In December 1992 the Lebanese army took up positions in southern suburbs of Beirut for the first time in eight years, apparently meeting no resistance from Hezbollah, which had hitherto effectively controlled the areas. In mid-1993 the Lebanese Government was said to be attempting to curtail the activities of the Damascus-based Popular Front for the Liberation of Palestine—General Command (PFLP—GC), which had begun to mount guerrilla attacks on Israeli military positions from southern Lebanon. In July Israeli armed forces launched their heaviest artillery and air attacks on targets in southern Lebanon since 1982. The declared aim of 'Operation Accountability' was to eradicate the threat posed by Hezbollah and Palestinian guerrillas, and to create a flow of refugees so as to compel the Lebanese and Syrian authorities to take action against these groups. According to Lebanese sources, the week-long offensive displaced some 300,000 civilians towards the north and resulted in 128 (mainly civilian) deaths. Although a US-brokered cease-fire 'understanding' entered effect at the end of July 1993, hostilities continued in subsequent months.

In June 1994 Hezbollah reported that 26 of its fighters had been killed in an Israeli air attack on one of its training camps in the Beka'a valley; Hezbollah responded with rocket attacks into the security zone and northern Israel. In October an Israeli attack on the town of An-Nabatiyah at-Tahta (Nabatiyah), in which seven civilians died, was apparently provoked by the deaths of 22 people in a bomb attack, attributed to militants of the Palestinian group Hamas, in the Israeli city of Tel-Aviv: hitherto, Israeli operations in Lebanon had tended to be in reprisal for terrorist activity in the security zone. Clashes in southern Lebanon in December reportedly resulted in the killing by Hezbollah of several members of the Israeli military and SLA, and seemingly prompted a retaliatory bomb attack on a suburb of southern Beirut, in which a senior Hezbollah official was killed. Israeli attacks south of Beirut in January 1995 targeted alleged PFLP—GC bases.

In March 1994, meanwhile, the National Assembly approved legislation instituting the death penalty for what were termed 'politically motivated' murders. Shortly afterwards the Maronite LF was proscribed (on the grounds that it had sought the country's partition) and its leader, Samir Geagea, was arrested and charged, along with several of his associates, in connection with the murder, in October 1990, of Dany Chamoun, son of former President Camille Chamoun and the leader of the right-wing Maronite Parti National Libéral (PNL), and with the bombing of a Maronite church outside Beirut in January 1994. In September Gaegea was reportedly relieved of the organization's leadership and his recognition of the Ta'if agreement revoked; the LF command had also reportedly countermanded Geagea's formal dissolution, under the Ta'if agreement, of the organization's militia status. (A successor political organization, the Lebanese Forces Party, had been created in September 1990.) In June 1995 Geagea and a co-defendant were convicted of instigating the murder of Chamoun, and were (together with seven others convicted *in absentia*) sentenced to death; the sentences were immediately commuted to life imprisonment with hard labour. In July 1996 Geagea was acquitted of involvement in the Maronite church bombing. However, by mid-1997, as a result of further convictions, Gaegea had received another two death sentences (one for ordering the assassination of another Maronite rival in 1990, and the other for attempting to assassinate the Minister of Defence, Michel Murr, in 1991—both of which were later commuted to life imprisonment); another sentence of life imprisonment for orchestrating the death of Prime Minister Rashid Karami in 1987; and a 10-year gaol term for attempting to recruit and arm militiamen after 1991 (when all militias had been banned).

In October 1995 the National Assembly voted to amend the Constitution to extend President Hrawi's mandate for a further three years. Prime Minister Hariri had sought an extension of the presidential term in the stated interest of promoting stability in the economic reconstruction process, and the amendment had been facilitated following intervention by Syria to resolve a procedural dispute between Hariri and the President of the National Assembly, Nabih Berri.

Elections to the National Assembly took place, in five rounds, in August–September 1996. Pro-Hariri candidates enjoyed considerable success in the first three rounds of voting (in Mount Lebanon, North Lebanon and Beirut governorates), with the Prime Minister himself winning the largest number of votes at the third round; there were, however, allegations of vote-buying involving Hariri's supporters in Beirut. In the fourth and fifth rounds (in the South and An-Nabatiyah, and in the Beka'a valley) an electoral alliance led by Amal and Hezbollah was reported to have won all but one of the total 46 seats. Prior to the fifth round Syria had redeployed some 12,000 of its estimated 30,000 troops in Lebanon to the eastern part of the Beka'a valley. (Under the terms of the Ta'if agreement, the redeployment should have been completed in 1992.) The overall rate of participation averaged about 45%, suggesting that many voters had disregarded demands particularly by Awn, Gemayel and other exiled figures for a boycott of the polls. Berri was re-elected President of the National Assembly when the new legislature convened in October 1996. Hrawi invited Hariri to form a new government: the distribution of portfolios in the new Cabinet (named in early November, following consultations with Syrian leaders) among the country's various interests remained largely unchanged.

In April 1996 Israel commenced a sustained military offensive (code-named 'Operation Grapes of Wrath') in southern Lebanon and suburbs to the south of Beirut, aimed at preventing rocket attacks by Hezbollah on settlements in northern Israel—which Hezbollah claimed were in response to deliberate attacks on Lebanese civilians by Israeli armed forces or their proxies. Some 400,000 Lebanese were displaced northwards, and the shelling by Israeli forces of a UNIFIL base at Qana, which resulted in the deaths of more than 100 Lebanese civilians who had been sheltering there, and of four UNIFIL soldiers, provoked international condemnation. After more than two weeks of hostilities a cease-fire 'understanding' took effect in late April 1996. As in 1993, this was effectively a compromise confining the conflict to the area of the security zone, recognizing both Hezbollah's right to resist Israeli occupation and Israel's right to self-defence; the 'understanding' also envisaged the establishment of an Israel-Lebanon Monitoring Group (ILMG), comprising representatives of Israel, Lebanon, Syria, France and the USA, to supervise the cease-fire. According to the Israeli authorities, Operation Grapes of Wrath resulted in no Israeli deaths, while 170–200 Lebanese civilians, in addition to some 50 fighters, were killed. Hezbollah claimed to have sustained minimal casualties, and its military capacity appeared largely undiminished. A subsequent UN report on the killing of Lebanese civilians at Qana concluded that it was 'unlikely' that the shelling of the UNIFIL base had, as claimed by the Israelis, been the result of 'gross technical and/or procedural errors'. Prior to the first meeting of the ILMG, in July 1996, Israel and Hezbollah reportedly exchanged prisoners and bodies of members of their armed forces for the first time since 1991. However, despite the April 1996 cease-fire 'understanding', sporadic clashes continued during 1997–98. The extent of Israeli casualties as a result of the occupation of southern Lebanon prompted a vocal campaign within Israel for a unilateral withdrawal from the security zone. In April 1998 Israel's 'inner' Security Cabinet voted to adopt UN Security Council Resolution 425, but with the stipulation that Lebanon provide guarantees of the security of Israel's northern border. Lebanon, however, emphasized that Resolution 425 demanded

an unconditional withdrawal, and stated that neither would it be able to guarantee Israel's immunity from attack, nor would it be prepared to deploy the Lebanese army in southern Lebanon for this purpose; furthermore, Lebanon could not support the continued presence there of the SLA. Concern was also expressed that a unilateral withdrawal from Lebanon in the absence of a comprehensive Middle East peace settlement might foment regional instability.

Meanwhile, in late 1996 the Government had ordered the closure of about 150 radio and 50 television stations; licences to broadcast political items had been granted to only a limited number of stations, most of which were owned by prominent political figures. In September 1997 the authorities began to close down unlicensed broadcasters, and in December the Minister of the Interior, deputy premier Michel Murr, prohibited a televised satellite broadcast, from France, by Gen. Awn, on the grounds that such transmissions were undermining national security. The ban provoked a violent demonstration in Beirut, which resulted in a number of protestors being arrested and tried on charges of defying restrictions on public demonstrations imposed in 1993. (Awn's interview was eventually broadcast in January 1998 by a private terrestrial channel.)

Voting in Lebanon's first municipal elections since 1963 took place, in four rounds, in May–June 1998. At the first round (in Mount Lebanon governorate) Hezbollah won convincing victories in Beirut's southern suburbs, while right-wing organizations opposed to the Government also took control of several councils. At the second round, in North Lebanon, efforts failed to achieve an inter-community balance in Tripoli, where a council comprising 23 Muslims and only one Christian was elected; elsewhere in the governorate there was notable success for candidates loyal to Samir Geagea. However, a joint list of candidates supported by Hariri and Berri won control of the Beirut council at the third round, while Berri's Amal gained overall control in Tyre. At the final round of voting (in the Beka'a valley) Hezbollah candidates were largely defeated by their pro-Syrian secular rivals and by members of the governorate's leading families. Other than in Beirut, the rate of voter participation was high (about 70%). (Municipal elections did not take place in southern Lebanon until September 2001, following the withdrawal of Israeli troops in 2000.)

As President Hrawi's mandate neared completion in 1998, the Commander-in-Chief of the armed forces, Gen. Emile Lahoud, emerged as a suitable successor: his strong leadership, firm stance on corruption and success in having reconstructed the army following the civil war, were thought likely to assist the process of political reform and economic regeneration. Moreover, Syria, which remained a major influence on Lebanese politics, endorsed Lahoud's candidacy, despite his strong nationalist tendency. To enable Lahoud's appointment, the National Assembly overwhelmingly adopted an exceptional amendment to Article 49 of the Constitution—which requires that senior civil servants resign their post two years prior to seeking political office—and Lahoud was duly elected President on 15 October, with the approval of all 118 National Assembly deputies present (the vote was boycotted by the Druze leader, Walid Joumblatt, and his supporters). Lahoud took office on 24 November; law enforcement and the elimination of official corruption were identified as priorities for his administration. Hariri unexpectedly declined an invitation from Lahoud to form a new government, and at the beginning of December Selim al-Hoss (who had headed four administrations during the civil war) was designated Prime Minister. His new Cabinet, which was almost halved in size (to 16 members), included only two ministers from the previous administration—Michel Murr notably retained the post of deputy premier as well as the interior portfolio. Several 'reformists' were appointed to the Cabinet, which excluded representatives of the various 'confessional' blocs and former militia leaders whose rivalries had frequently undermined previous governments. Hezbollah declined to participate in the new Government. At the Cabinet's first session, held later in December, Gen. Michel Sulayman was appointed to succeed Lahoud as head of the armed forces. The al-Hoss Government's programme emphasized anti-corruption measures (corruption, coupled with wasted expenditure, was estimated to have cost the State US $4,500m. since 1990), economic liberalization and reduction of the public debt, as well as accelerated electoral reform. To that effect the judiciary was granted powers to investigate a number of political scandals and bring former high-ranking officials to trial. The incoming Government also revoked the five-year ban on the holding of public demonstrations.

Clashes persisted in southern Lebanon following Israel's 'adoption' of Resolution 425, amid continuing protests of violations of the April 1996 cease-fire 'understanding'. In May 1998 at least 10 people were killed in an Israeli air raid on a Fatah training camp in the central Beka'a valley; in August at least nine Israelis were injured when rockets were fired into northern Israel, in retaliation for the death of an Amal commander near Tyre. In two separate incidents in November, seven Israeli soldiers were killed as a result of attacks by Hezbollah on Israeli patrols in the occupied zone. There were further serious exchanges in December, when 13 civilians were injured by Hezbollah rocket attacks in northern Israel, launched in reprisal for an Israeli air-strike in southern Lebanon in which eight civilians were killed. In January 1999 Israel's Security Cabinet voted to respond to future Hezbollah offensives by targeting infrastructure in central and northern Lebanon (thereby extending the conflict beyond suspected guerrilla bases in the south). Hostilities escalated in February, when Israeli forces annexed the village of Arnoun, just outside the occupied zone; Israel also launched intensive air attacks on Hezbollah targets, following an ambush in the security zone in late February that had killed Brig.-Gen. Erez Gerstein, the commander of the Israeli army's liaison unit with the SLA.

In 1999 the Palestinian militant organizations in Lebanon were riven by factional infighting, and both the Lebanese and Syrian Governments undertook measures to seek to bring the groups to order. In May a senior official of the Fatah faction of the PLO and his wife were killed in Sidon by unidentified gunmen, believed to be PLO activists opposed to Fatah's willingness to negotiate with Israel, while a car bomb in southern Lebanon shortly afterwards seriously wounded another Fatah official, leading to fears of a renewed cycle of violence between the rival Palestinian factions. In October a senior Fatah commander, Sultan Abu al-Aynayn (a close ally of Yasser Arafat), was sentenced to death *in absentia* by a military court in Beirut, having been found guilty of leading a militia and of encouraging anti-Government rebellion. (In December 2000, again *in absentia*, al-Aynayn was convicted of weapons-trafficking and of plotting terrorist actions in southern Lebanon; he was sentenced to 15 years' imprisonment.) Two other Fatah leaders in southern Lebanon were detained by the Lebanese military in November 1999, on charges of murder and of plotting bomb attacks during the 1980s; five further officials of the organization were reportedly arrested in late 1999 and early 2000. In January 2000 the Government ordered a judicial enquiry into the recent upsurge in sectarian violence.

Meanwhile, in January 1999 the Lebanese authorities agreed to upgrade the status of travel documents issued to Palestinians residing in Lebanon to allow them to be treated as holders of Lebanese passports. However, in the months prior to the resumption of 'final status' talks between Israeli and Palestinian negotiators in late 1999, the issue of Palestinian refugees in Lebanon assumed particular importance. In July the Lebanese Government had been angered by an announcement made by the new Israeli Prime Minister, Ehud Barak, elected in May, that the refugees would under no circumstances be permitted to return to Israel, and that 'a solution should be found in the countries where they are now living'. President Lahoud responded by demanding that any permanent peace agreement should guarantee the right of Palestinians to return home; he subsequently initiated legislation to prevent Palestinian refugees in Lebanon from being granted Lebanese citizenship.

During his election campaign Prime Minister Barak had pledged to withdraw Israeli forces from southern Lebanon by July 2000. In June 1999 the SLA completed a unilateral withdrawal from the enclave of Jezzine, in the north-east of the occupied zone. Following further Hezbollah attacks on northern Israel, in late June the outgoing administration of Binyamin Netanyahu ordered a series of air-strikes against infrastructure targets in central and southern Lebanon—the heaviest aerial bombardment since 'Operation Grapes of Wrath' in 1996. In December 1999 the Israeli Government issued an apology to the Lebanese authorities, after at least 15 Lebanese schoolchildren were injured as a result of an assault by its forces. The incident came amid an escalation in Hezbollah operations following the resumption of Israeli-Syrian peace negotiations. In that month an 'understanding in principle' was reportedly reached between Israel and Syria in order to curb the fighting in southern Lebanon, although the informal cease-fire ended in late January

2000 when a senior SLA commander was killed; the deaths of three Israeli soldiers at the end of the month led Israel to declare that peace talks with Syria (now again postponed indefinitely) could resume only if Syria took action to restrain Hezbollah. In mid-February, after suffering further military casualties in the security zone, Israel announced that its Prime Minister would henceforth be empowered to order immediate retaliatory raids against Hezbollah without discussion with the Security Cabinet. In March the Israeli Cabinet voted unanimously to withdraw its forces from southern Lebanon by July, even if no agreement had been reached on the Israeli-Syrian track of the Middle East peace process. In April, having released 13 Lebanese prisoners held without trial for more than a decade as 'bargaining counters' for Israeli soldiers missing in Lebanon, Israel gave the UN official notification that it intended to withdraw its forces from southern Lebanon 'in one phase' by 7 July. The Lebanese Government made the unprecedented admission that it would accept a UN peace-keeping force in southern Lebanon after the Israeli withdrawal. On 23 May Israel's Security Cabinet voted to accelerate the withdrawal of its remaining troops from Lebanon, after Hezbollah had taken control of about one-third of southern Lebanon following the evacuation by the SLA of outposts transferred to its control by the Israeli army. Both the Israeli Government and the UN had expected the withdrawal to take place on 1 June; however, the rapid and chaotic withdrawal of Israeli forces from southern Lebanon was completed on 24 May, almost six weeks ahead of Barak's original deadline. In June the UN Security Council officially declared that the Israeli withdrawal had been completed. However, both the Lebanese Government and Hezbollah maintained that Israel was still required to depart from territory known as Shebaa Farms and to release all Lebanese prisoners. (The UN maintains that Shebaa Farms is part of territory captured by Israel from Syria, and as such must be considered under the Israeli-Syrian track of the peace process.) In July a limited contingent of UNIFIL troops began to redeploy close to the Lebanese border with Israel, to fill the vacuum created by the departure of Israeli forces. At the same time the UN Security Council voted to extend UNIFIL's mandate for a further six months. In August a Joint Security Force of some 1,000 Lebanese troops and Internal Security Forces reportedly deployed in southern Lebanon (other than in the border area), charged with the provision of general security in the territory. Responsibility for the border with Israel remained with UNIFIL (whose troops in Lebanon now numbered some 5,600). Meanwhile, in June 2000 the Lebanese authorities initiated a military trial against more than 2,500 former SLA militiamen, who were charged with having collaborated with Israel during its occupation of southern Lebanon; some of the defendants were tried *in absentia* (many SLA members, fearing reprisals, had fled with the departing Israeli army). By January 2001 an estimated 2,041 alleged collaborators were reported to have been convicted.

Elections to the National Assembly took place on 27 August (Mount Lebanon and North Lebanon) and 3 September 2000 (Beirut, the Beka'a valley, An-Nabatiyah and the South). For the first time since 1972 Lebanese citizens in the former Israeli-occupied zone of southern Lebanon participated in the elections. Voting patterns in the first round swiftly indicated a rejection of al-Hoss's premiership, as the Druze leader, Walid Joumblatt (one of former premier Rafik Hariri's staunchest allies), secured an overwhelming victory in Mount Lebanon governorate. Moreover, the election of Pierre Gemayel, son of Amin Gemayel, in the Maronite Northern Metn district was regarded as a considerable reverse for President Lahoud. Voter participation was an estimated 51%, apparently indicating that the electorate had largely ignored appeals by some Christian parties for a boycott of the poll. At the second round of voting, Hariri's Al-Karamah (Dignity) list proceeded to secure 18 of the 19 assembly seats in Beirut; al-Hoss lost his own seat in the legislature. In the south an alliance of Hezbollah and Amal candidates took all the governorate's 23 seats, while Hezbollah enjoyed similar successes in the Beka'a. Independent monitors reported numerous instances of electoral malpractice. Overall, Hariri was reported to have the support of between 92–106 of the 128 seats in the new legislature. In late October President Lahoud formally appointed Rafik Hariri to the premiership. The composition of his radically altered Cabinet (newly expanded to 30 members) was announced a few days later, with Issam Fares named as Deputy Prime Minister and Elias Murr, the son-in-law of President Lahoud and a non-parliamentarian, replacing his father, Michel Murr, as Minister of the Interior and of Municipal and

Rural Affairs. (Resistance and Development, the party list including Hezbollah, had declined to join the Government.) Hariri and President Lahoud were reported to have reached an informal 'power-sharing' agreement, according to which Hariri would be responsible for economic policy and the President would take charge of defence and foreign affairs.

Divisions between pro- and anti-Syrian elements within Lebanon had become increasingly vocal in the aftermath of the Israeli withdrawal from southern Lebanon in May 2000 and the death of Syria's President Hafiz al-Assad in the following month. An unofficial visit to Beirut by his successor, Bashar al-Assad, for meetings with key Lebanese politicians shortly before the legislative elections appeared to indicate that he intended to continue his late father's role as power-broker in Lebanon. However, the decisive rejection of the Syrian-backed Government of Selim al-Hoss, combined with Joumblatt's electoral successes, appeared to suggest a redefinition of Syria's role in Lebanon. In late September Maronite bishops issued a statement urging the departure of the Syrian military from Lebanon. Nabih Berri (who had been re-elected as President of the National Assembly) reported that the Lebanese and Syrian Governments were preparing to hold discussions concerning the imminent redeployment of Syrian troops, although this was denied by Syria. While the Maronite community and other Christian groups maintained that the departure of Syrian forces was necessary in order for full Lebanese sovereignty to be attained, both President Lahoud and Prime Minister Hariri continued to defend Syria's military presence. In December Syria—which had never previously confirmed that it was holding Lebanese prisoners—freed 46 Lebanese political prisoners (including many Christians who had been detained by Syrian troops during 1975–1990), apparently as a gesture of 'goodwill'. In January 2001 the Lebanese Government established a commission to examine the issue of Lebanese prisoners held in Syria. In the same month a Jordanian newspaper reported that the former Christian militia leader, Gen. Michel Awn, had declared himself ready to return to Lebanon from exile in France in order to appear before the Lebanese judiciary. In mid-March the Lebanese authorities ordered a large deployment of army and security forces to Beirut, to contain protest actions led by students demanding the complete withdrawal of Syrian troops from the country. The mass protests followed renewed calls by Awn for his supporters to hold peaceful demonstrations against Syria. It was reported in early April that President Lahoud had urged pro- and anti-Syrian elements in Lebanon to begin a national dialogue in an attempt to defuse rising tensions, while the Government banned all unlicensed protests against Syria.

The outbreak of the so-called 'al-Aqsa *intifada*' in the Palestinian territories of the West Bank and Gaza in September 2000 resulted in a renewed crisis in the Middle East, prompting uncertainty in Lebanon about the permanence of the Israeli withdrawal, particularly as Hezbollah had renewed its campaign against the Israeli military. In early October Hezbollah fighters captured three Israeli soldiers in Shebaa Farms, with the demand that Israel release 19 Lebanese and dozens of Palestinians from Israeli detention. The UN Secretary-General, Kofi Annan, visited Beirut for talks regarding the soldiers' release; however, in the following week a senior Israeli army reservist and businessman was kidnapped in Switzerland, apparently by Hezbollah (which claimed that the officer was working for Israeli intelligence). The killing of an Israeli soldier in Shebaa Farms at the end of November prompted Israel to launch air-strikes against suspected Hezbollah targets in southern Lebanon. In mid-November the UN Security Council had urged the Lebanese Government to comply with international law by deploying its armed forces on the Israeli border with southern Lebanon (where Hezbollah still controlled the line of withdrawal, or 'Blue Line'), but Lebanon rejected such a deployment until Israel had signed a comprehensive peace treaty with both Lebanon and Syria. At the end of January 2001 the UN Security Council voted to extend UNIFIL's mandate in Lebanon until the end of July, when its operational strength was to be reduced to about 4,500—the number of troops deployed prior to the Israeli withdrawal.

The Lebanese leadership was generally pessimistic as to the prospects for peace in the Middle East following the election, in February 2001, of Likud leader Ariel Sharon as Israeli Prime Minister. (Most Lebanese hold Sharon responsible for the deaths of 2,000 Palestinian refugees in the Sabra and Chatila camps in September 1982—at which time he was Israel's Minister of Defence.) In mid-February 2001 Israel launched mortar attacks close to Shebaa Farms, in reprisal for the death of an Israeli soldier in a bomb attack there. Tensions escalated once again in mid-April: Israel responded to the killing by Hezbollah of another of its soldiers in Shebaa Farms with the first military action against Syrian troops since 1996, launching air raids on a Syrian radar base to the east of Beirut. According to Syrian sources, at least one Syrian soldier died in the attack, which Israel claimed had been provoked by Syria's sponsorship of Hezbollah.

In late April 2001 Rafik Hariri visited Washington, DC, for discussions with US President George W. Bush, during which he urged the US Administration to increase its involvement in international diplomatic efforts to revive the Middle East peace process; at the same time, President Lahoud urged the European Union (EU, see p. 208), and in particular France, to do likewise. During a visit by Lahoud to France in late May President Jacques Chirac urged the Lebanese Government to send its army to the southern border zone in order to prevent the Israeli–Palestinian violence from spreading to Lebanon. However, Lahoud insisted that Lebanon would not deploy its forces along the Blue Line prior to the conclusion of a comprehensive Middle East peace settlement.

In mid-June 2001 Syria withdrew an estimated 6,000–10,000 troops from the largely Christian eastern and southern suburbs of Beirut and from Mount Lebanon, and redeployed the majority to the Beka'a valley. However, Syria's withdrawal from the Lebanese capital was widely regarded as merely symbolic, since Syria retained 15 military bases in strategic parts of Beirut. In early August the Maronite patriarch, Cardinal Sfeir, and the Druze leader, Walid Joumblatt, held discussions, apparently to indicate a new era of 'reconciliation' between the two communities. Within days, however, the mainly pro-Syrian army intelligence service began mass arrests of Maronite Christians (mostly members of the banned LF or supporters of Gen. Awn) who were again demanding a complete Syrian withdrawal from Lebanon. Many Christian and Muslim deputies condemned the detentions as 'unconstitutional', while protesters demonstrating against the growing influence of the military clashed with police. Hariri's political standing appeared to have been weakened by the security forces' actions, which had been undertaken when he was out of the country, as in mid-August the National Assembly approved legislation granting increased powers to President Lahoud. In early September Maronite bishops again issued a strong criticism of Syria's dominance of Lebanese affairs. It was reported at this time that up to seven Syrians had been killed in Lebanon during the past month.

Israel launched a further air attack on a Syrian radar station in eastern Lebanon at the beginning of July 2001 (wounding up to three Syrian soldiers and a Lebanese conscript), again apparently in response to an assault by Hezbollah against the Israeli military in Shebaa Farms. At the end of July the UN Security Council voted for an extension of UNIFIL's mandate for a further six months; the peace-keeping force was to be reduced in size from 4,500 to 3,600 troops, with the possibility that its status would be downgraded to that of an observer mission (this was implemented before the expiry of the six-month mandate). In early October Hezbollah guerrillas broke what had effectively been a three-month cease-fire by launching an attack against two Israeli military positions in Shebaa Farms, to which Israeli forces responded by shelling a Hezbollah patrol in the area. Israel alleged, furthermore, that Hezbollah was directly involved in the Palestinian *intifada*, and was supplying weapons to Palestinians in the West Bank and Gaza. (Hezbollah's leadership initially denied this; however, in early March 2002 Sheikh Nasrallah admitted that two Lebanese militants detained in Jordan had been attempting to smuggle weapons into the West Bank.) In January 2002 Hezbollah again carried out cross-border mortar attacks against military targets in Israel, provoking Israeli air raids across southern Lebanon. In that month the UN Security Council expressed concern regarding recent Israeli violations of Lebanese airspace, and criticized Hezbollah for its frequent interference with the freedom of movement of UNIFIL. The UN again urged the Lebanese Government to deploy its army along the Blue Line. The observer mission's mandate was extended for a further six months from 31 January, and for the same period from the end of July. By the end of 2002 the strength of the force had been reduced to some 2,000 troops. A new UN resolution approved in January 2003 extended UNIFIL's mandate until 31 July. The mandate was subsequently extended until 31 January 2004, and again to 31 July.

Lebanon's political and religious leadership were unequivocal in their condemnation of the September 2001 suicide attacks on New York and Washington, DC. Lebanese Shi'ites feared, however, that Hezbollah might be targeted in any retaliatory campaign against militant Islamist groups deemed to be involved in terrorism. In mid-October Muslim clerics in Lebanon issued a ruling in support of the Afghan people following the commencement of US-led military action in Afghanistan against the Taliban regime and alleged bases of the al-Qa'ida (Base) organization, the militant Islamist network held by the USA to be principally responsible for September's atrocities. Three Lebanese men, believed to be members of Hezbollah involved in the 1985 hijacking of a US commercial flight, had been included on a list of 22 'most wanted' terrorist suspects, published in early October 2001 by the US Federal Bureau of Investigation. Lebanese security forces detained two men in Tripoli in mid-October, on charges of plotting terrorist actions against US targets in the Middle East. (In mid-March 2002 a military court sentenced one of the defendants to a three-year prison term, and the other to 18 months' imprisonment, both with hard labour.) Nevertheless, Lebanese officials refuted claims by Jordanian officials to have uncovered a plot by the Lebanese-based Palestinian militant group Asbat al-Ansar to attack foreign embassies in Beirut. In early November 2001 the Lebanese Government resisted US pressure to freeze the assets of Hezbollah, included on a new US list of proscribed 'terrorist' groups, insisting that it regarded Hezbollah as a legitimate organization of resistance against Israeli occupation.

In late January 2002 Elie Hobeika, the former leader of the Christian LF militia, was killed (along with three aides and two bystanders) in a car bombing in Beirut. A previously unknown anti-Syrian group, styled the 'Lebanese for a Free and Independent Lebanon', claimed responsibility for the attack, alleging that Hobeika was a 'Syrian agent'. Israel denied in the strongest terms assertions made by some Lebanese sources that Israeli interests had instigated the killing, since Hobeika had declared his willingness to give evidence to an investigation being carried out by a Belgian court into alleged 'crimes against humanity' by Ariel Sharon, owing to his implication in the massacre of Palestinians in Sabra and Chatila refugee camps in 1982 (see above). Hobeika was the first prominent Lebanese politician to be assassinated since the civil war ended in 1990. (A Belgian appeals court judged the case against Sharon to be inadmissible at the end of June 2002.)

In early 2002 it was feared that rising tensions between Israel and Lebanon might escalate into a 'second front' of Arab–Israeli conflict; in February Iran denied allegations made by Israeli officials that it was supplying Hezbollah with vast consignments of *Katyusha* rockets and had sent a number of its Revolutionary Guards to Lebanon. At the end of March Hezbollah initiated cross-border mortar, missile and machine-gun attacks against Israeli military targets in Shebaa Farms, asserting that these were in retaliation for Israeli violations of Lebanese airspace. Israel responded to the escalation of Hezbollah attacks by shelling suspected militant bases in southern Lebanon. In early April Lebanese security forces arrested nine Palestinians on charges of plotting to launch rocket assaults against northern Israel. Meanwhile, the UN condemned Hezbollah for increasing the instability along the Blue Line, and also for an incident in which five members of UNIFIL allegedly came under attack by Hezbollah guerrillas near Shebaa Farms. In response to Hezbollah attacks on the Shebaa Farms in August, the Israeli Government responded by targeting suspected Hezbollah bases in southern Lebanon, and issued a firm warning to Lebanon and Syria that they must take immediate action to end such attacks.

Meanwhile, in early March 2002, President Bashar al-Assad of Syria undertook an historic visit to Beirut for discussions with President Lahoud. This first official visit by a Syrian leader to Beirut since 1947 was welcomed by many Lebanese as a formal recognition by Syria of Lebanese sovereignty. The talks resulted in several agreements regarding closer economic co-operation, including a pledge by Syria to reduce the cost of imported natural gas. It was reported in early April 2002 that Syrian troops were soon to redeploy from central Lebanon to the Beka'a valley, thus fulfilling one of the requirements of the 1989 Ta'if agreement. The redeployment was expected to lead to an improvement in Syrian-Lebanese relations, although hundreds of Syrian intelligence officers were likely to remain in central Lebanon.

In late March 2002 Beirut hosted the annual summit meeting of the Council of the Arab League, at which the principal issue under discussion was a peace initiative for the Middle East proposed by Crown Prince Abdullah of Saudi Arabia. However, only 10 out of 22 Arab heads of state attended the summit, while President Mubarak of Egypt and King Abdullah of Jordan reportedly declined to participate in the discussions as a demonstration of solidarity with the President of the Palestinian (National) Authority (PA), Yasser Arafat, who was effectively blockaded by Israeli forces in the West Bank. At the conclusion of the summit, Arab leaders unanimously endorsed the Saudi peace initiative. Incorporated in the Beirut Declaration, this required from Israel a complete withdrawal from all Arab territories occupied in June 1967, and what were termed 'territories still occupied in southern Lebanon', a 'just solution' to the issue of Palestinian refugees, and acceptance of the establishment of a sovereign Palestinian state in the West Bank and Gaza Strip with East Jerusalem as its capital; in return, the Arab states undertook to consider the Arab–Israeli conflict at an end, to sign a peace agreement with Israel, and to establish normal relations with Israel within this comprehensive peace framework. The initiative was, however, rejected by Israel, which maintained that it would lead to the destruction of the State of Israel. The US Secretary of State, Colin Powell, visited both Lebanon and Syria in mid-April 2002, as part of a wider mission to the region; the Lebanese leadership maintained its stance that its obligation to respect the Blue Line did not exclude resistance (by Hezbollah) to 'liberate' Shebaa Farms, while President al-Assad gave no indication that he would exert his influence to halt Hezbollah offensives from southern Lebanon against Israel.

In late May 2002 Jihad Jibril, the head of the PFLP—GC's military operations and son of the group's leader, was killed by a car bomb in west Beirut. The Lebanese security forces blamed inter-Palestinian rivalries for the assassination, although many PFLP—GC officials held the Israeli intelligence services responsible. In August two people were killed and six others injured in the worst factional fighting at the Ain al-Hilweh Palestinian refugee camp for several years. Tensions escalated following the arrest of an Islamist militant the previous month (accused of killing three Lebanese army intelligence officers) by the Lebanese army, aided by Fatah. (In early September the Israeli daily, *Ha'aretz*, alleged that the violence at Ain al-Hilweh was linked to the presence there of up to 200 al-Qa'ida militants who had returned from the war in Afghanistan.) Clashes between the Lebanese army and Palestinian militants occurred at the normally relatively calm al-Jalil refugee camp, near Ba'albak (Ba'albek), in September, which left one soldier and three Palestinians dead, and at least 11 others wounded. Lebanese soldiers had entered the camp in search of a wanted man and removed a cache of armaments from offices of the Fatah Revolutionary Council, an organization founded by the militant leader Abu Nidal, who was found dead in Baghdad, Iraq, in August.

Tensions between Israel and Lebanon were heightened again in September 2002, owing to a dispute regarding access to drinking water supplies in Israel's former security zone in southern Lebanon. Israel claimed that a Lebanese project to supply water from a tributary of the Hasbani river to recently repopulated villages close to the border would affect the flow of water to Israel, and issued a direct threat of military action against Lebanon should the authorities there proceed with the project. While the USA sent a team of experts to the region to attempt to negotiate a peaceful solution to the water dispute, in early October the UN issued a report stating that the construction of a new water pumping station in southern Lebanon did not contravene any international agreements. President Lahoud inaugurated the controversial project in mid-October.

In early September 2002, meanwhile, the Lebanese Government closed down a Christian opposition-controlled television station, Murr Television, and its sister radio station, Radio Mount Lebanon, claiming that they had (among other charges) undermined relations with Syria and violated electoral legislation banning party political broadcasts during a recent by-election in the Metn district, where one of the stations' owners, the nephew of interior minister Elias Murr, had won the seat. The ruling against Murr Television was upheld by a higher court at the end of December and a final appeal was rejected in late April 2003, resulting in the station's permanent closure.

Lebanon's economic crisis dominated the domestic political agenda in late 2002 and early 2003. In late November 2002 international donors attending a conference in Paris, France, agreed to provide Lebanon with an aid package worth some

US \$4,300m. to assist the country with its heavy burden of debt and to finance development projects. In mid-April 2003, following weeks of reported disagreements between members of the Cabinet over economic and other domestic policies, the Prime Minister, Rafik Hariri, tendered his resignation and that of his Government. (The National Assembly was reported to have few objections to the proposed Budget Law 2003 and approved the legislation broadly unchanged.) However, after his premiership was endorsed by the Lebanese parliament, Hariri was asked by President Lahoud to form a new 30-member Cabinet. The new Lebanese Government, announced two days after Hariri's resignation, brought in 11 new ministers, including Jean Obeid, who replaced Mahmoud Hammoud as Minister of Foreign Affairs and Emigrants. Hammoud was named as the new Minister of Defence. The new Cabinet was widely considered to be the most pro-Syrian for more than a decade; it contained no members of the Christian opposition, nor of Hezbollah (who were said to have been willing to join the new administration).

In mid-February 2003 Syria commenced the redeployment of more than 4,000 troops stationed in northern Lebanon, under the terms of the Ta'if agreement; the withdrawal was reportedly carried out over several months. However, despite the decreasing Syrian military presence in the country, Syria was still believed to be exerting considerable influence over Lebanese domestic affairs, and was accused of organizing rocket attacks against a television station owned by Hariri, after the Lebanese Prime Minister had called for an Arab-Israeli dialogue during an official visit to Brazil. In August a prominent member of Hezbollah, Ali Hussein Saleh, was killed when a car bomb exploded in Beirut; the Lebanese and Syrian Governments both accused Israel of having carried out the attack, a charge which Israel rebutted. (Saleh was known to have been involved in operations against Israeli forces prior to their withdrawal from southern Lebanon in 2000.) In the same month Israel accused Syria of initiating another Hezbollah attack against the Israeli military in Shebaa Farms.

In May 2003 it was reported that Lebanese security forces had arrested at least nine suspected al-Qa'ida operatives in Sidon. The suspects were accused of plotting to attack the US embassy in Beirut and to kidnap members of the Lebanese Cabinet. Moreover, they were believed to be linked to the al-Qa'ida militants thought to be in hiding in the Ain al-Hilweh refugee camp. In December 27 Lebanese were found guilty, and given varying prison sentences, on charges of carrying out bomb attacks against mostly US and British businesses in Lebanon between the end of 2002 and April 2003. However, a military court in Beirut acquitted three defendants of plotting to assassinate the US ambassador to Lebanon.

In early November 2003 the Israeli Cabinet agreed to release more than 400 Palestinian, Lebanese (mostly Hezbollah) and other Arab prisoners in exchange for the remains of the three soldiers kidnapped by Hezbollah in 2000 (see above), as well as the return of the Israeli businessman, Elhanan Tannenbaum. Israel also hoped to receive information on the fate of a missing Israeli airman, Ron Arad, who had been shot down over Lebanon in 1986, and was still believed to be held in Lebanese detention. Germany, which had mediated the negotiations between Israel and Hezbollah, oversaw the exchange, and on 29 January 2004 the first 30 Lebanese and other Arab prisoners to be released by Israel were flown to the airport at Cologne, Germany, where they were exchanged for Tannenbaum and the remains of the Israeli soldiers. The remaining Palestinian prisoners, and the remains of 59 Lebanese militants held by Israel, were later released at Israeli border posts. Only a few days prior to the prisoner exchange, Israel launched an air attack against Hezbollah positions in southern Lebanon, in response to a Hezbollah rocket attack on Israeli soldiers who were using bulldozers to clear minefields in the border zone. Hezbollah carried out further attacks in Shebaa Farms in late March.

Government

Under the 1926 Constitution (as subsequently amended), legislative power is held by the National Assembly (called the Chamber of Deputies until 1979), with 128 members elected by universal adult suffrage for four years (subject to dissolution), on the basis of proportional representation. Seats are allocated on a religious or 'confessional' basis (divided equally between Christians and Muslims). The President of the Republic (who must be a Maronite Christian) is elected for six years by the National Assembly. The President, in consultation with depu-

ties and the President of the National Assembly, appoints the Prime Minister (a Sunni Muslim) and other ministers to form the Cabinet, in which executive power is vested. The Ta'if agreement of October 1989, which was incorporated into the Constitution in August 1990, stated that cabinet portfolios must be distributed equally between Christian and Muslim ministers.

Defence

In August 2003 the Lebanese armed forces numbered 72,100 (army 70,000, air force 1,000, navy 1,100). Paramilitary forces included an estimated 13,000 members of the Internal Security Force. Hezbollah's active members numbered some 2,000 in August 2003. At that time there were also an estimated 16,000 Syrian troops in Lebanon. Israeli armed forces and the Israeli-backed South Lebanon Army (SLA) withdrew from Lebanon in May 2000. Government expenditure on defence was budgeted at £L870,000m. in 2003.

The UN Interim Force in Lebanon (UNIFIL, see p. 68) observer mission numbered 1,991 troops at the end of January 2004, assisted by about 50 military observers of the UN Truce Supervision Organization (UNTSO).

Economic Affairs

In 2002, according to estimates by the World Bank, Lebanon's gross national income (GNI), measured at average 2000–02 prices, was US \$17,726m., equivalent to \$3,990 per head (or \$4,470 per head on an international purchasing-power parity basis). During 1990–2002, it was estimated, the population increased at an average annual rate of 1.7%, while gross domestic product (GDP) per head increased, in real terms, by an average of 4.3% per year. Overall GDP increased, in real terms, at an average annual rate of 6.1% in 1990–2002; although zero growth was registered in 2000, GDP growth of some 1.3% was recorded in 2001. According to the Ministry of Finance, GDP increased by 2% in 2002.

According to the UN Economic and Social Commission for Western Asia (ESCWA), agriculture (including hunting, forestry and fishing) contributed an estimated 9.9% of GDP in 2002. According to FAO data, some 3.2% of the labour force were employed in the sector in that year. The principal crops are potatoes, citrus fruits, tomatoes, cucumbers and onions. Viticulture is also significant. Hashish is a notable, albeit illegal, export crop, although the Government is attempting to persuade growers to switch to other crops. The GDP of the agricultural sector was estimated to have increased by an average of 2.0% annually in 1994–2002, although agricultural GDP declined by an estimated 0.7% in 1999. According to FAO data, agricultural production increased by 6.1% in 2000, but declined by 5.8% in 2001; however, an increase of 6.4% was recorded in 2002.

The industrial sector (including manufacturing, construction and power) contributed 18.7% of GDP in 2002, according to estimates by ESCWA. Some 25.9% of the labour force were employed in industry in 1997. Lebanon's only mineral resources consist of small reserves of lignite and iron ore, and their contribution to GDP is insignificant. The GDP of the industrial sector decreased by an estimated average of 0.7% per year in 1994–2002; however, industrial GDP grew by an estimated 3.7% in 1998 and by 1.4% in 1999.

ESCWA figures indicate that manufacturing contributed an estimated 9.7% of GDP in 2002. The sector employed about 10% of the labour force in 1985. The most important branches have traditionally been food-processing, petroleum refining, textiles and furniture and woodworking. Manufacturing GDP was estimated to have decreased at an average annual rate of 4.7% in 1994–2002.

Energy is derived principally from thermal power stations, using imported petroleum (which accounted for 94.3% of total electricity production in 2000). However, in order to meet Lebanon's growing energy requirements, plans for the construction of an offshore pipeline—capable of importing 6m.–9m. cu m of natural gas per day from Syria—were scheduled for completion in 2003. A second pipeline was planned that would enable Lebanon to import an estimated 9m. cu m of natural gas per day from Egypt and 3m. cu m per day from Syria by 2005.

The services sector contributed an estimated 71.4% of GDP in 2002, according to ESCWA data. In 1997 some 65.1% of the working population were employed in the sector, which has traditionally been dominated by trade and finance (accounting for an estimated 32.2% and 13.7% of GDP, respectively, in 2002). Financial services, in particular, withstood many of the disruptions inflicted on the economy by the civil conflict, although the Beirut Stock Exchange did not recommence trading until

1996. Lebanon is also becoming increasingly important as a centre for telecommunications. Recent efforts to revive the tourist industry have met with considerable success, and have been a major source of growth in the construction industry. Tourist arrivals increased by 13.1% in 1998, by 6.7% in 1999 and by 10.1% in 2000 (despite the regional impact of the Israeli–Palestinian crisis, which has partly undermined the revival of Lebanon's tourist industry). Numbers of tourist arrivals from Gulf and other Arab states were reported to be increasing in 2001 and 2002. The GDP of the services sector increased at an average annual rate of some 2.8% in 1994–2002; the sector's GDP was estimated to have increased by 5.9% in 1998 and by 2.0% in 1999.

In 2003 Lebanon recorded a trade deficit of US $5,644m. The principal markets for exports in 2002 were Switzerland (which took 12.6% of Lebanese exports in that year) and Saudi Arabia (9.2%); other significant purchasers included the United Arab Emirates and Syria. The principal supplier of imports in 2002 was Italy (10.8%); Germany, France and the USA were also important suppliers. The principal exports in 2003 were jewellery, machinery and electrical equipment, and food products. The principal imports in that year were mineral products, machinery and electrical equipment, chemical products, and vehicles.

In 2003 Lebanon recorded an overall budget deficit of £L2,591,000m., equivalent to 29.4% of recorded expenditure (compared with a forecast deficit of £L2,125,000m. in the Budget Law 2003). Budget forecasts for 2004 projected a deficit of £L2,850,000m., equivalent to 30.8% of budgeted expenditure. At the end of 2001 Lebanon's total external debt was US $12,450m., of which $8,957m. was long-term public debt. The cost of debt-servicing in that year was equivalent to 50.9% of the value of exports of goods and services. According to the Ministry of Finance, Lebanon's total domestic and external debt totalled L£50,193,000m. at the end of 2003. The annual rate of inflation averaged 23.9% in 1990–97. However, this reflected high rates of inflation in the aftermath of the civil war; consumer prices decreased by an average of 0.9% in 2000, but increased by 1.3% in 2001 and by 4.3% in 2002. In 1997, according to official figures, 8.5% of the labour force were unemployed (representing a significant decline from a level of 35% in 1990), although youth unemployment was reported to be much higher.

Lebanon is a member of the Arab Fund for Economic and Social Development (see p. 144), the Arab Monetary Fund (see p. 145) and the Islamic Development Bank (see p. 275). A customs union with Syria entered into effect in January 1999, and in 2002 the creation of a free-trade zone was under discussion. Lebanon is also involved in efforts to finalize establishment of a Greater Arab Free Trade Area. A Euro-Mediterranean Association Agreement was signed with the European Union (EU, see p. 208) in June 2002. Lebanon has observer status with the World Trade Organization (see p. 343), and was undergoing negotiations with a view to becoming a full member of the organization in 2004.

By the end of the 1990s the Lebanese Government had achieved considerable success in rehabilitating and expanding basic infrastructure, as envisaged under the first phase of its Horizon 2000 investment programme, which covers the period 1995–2007. The second phase was to focus on development of social infrastructure, with investment of US $5,000m. envisaged on education, health and sanitation projects in 1998–2002. The reconstruction process was undertaken with the support of the international donor community, which in late 1996 pledged grants and concessionary loans totalling some $3,200m. However, GDP growth since 1996 has been considerably lower than the targeted annual average of 8% under Horizon 2000. The principal factors inhibiting growth have been identified as the failure to control both the budget deficit and the accumulated public debt (equivalent to 185% of GDP by the end of 2003). In early 1999 the World Bank agreed to disburse some $600m. in concessionary loans over a three-year period, and in April 2000 the EU granted its first aid programme to Lebanon (worth around $47.9m.). However, in 1999 the Lebanese economy was in recession, owing to the decline in domestic demand and inadequate levels of job creation; no overall growth was recorded in 2000. The withdrawal of Israeli troops from southern Lebanon in May 2000 brought about an acceleration of the country's economic reconstruction, despite the high costs involved in rehabilitation projects for the south. The return of Rafik Hariri to the Lebanese premiership in October afforded further optimism, particularly in the construction sector. The new Government pledged to stimulate growth by reducing taxation and import duties, by encouraging the privatization of state-owned enterprises, and by controlling public expenditure in order to reduce the state debt. Liberalization of trade, both regionally and through association with the EU, was also identified as a priority. In October 2001 the IMF recommended a devaluation of the Lebanese pound as a means of easing the Government's fiscal crisis. A value-added tax of 10% was introduced in February 2002. Although the National Assembly approved the Budget Law 2003 in January of that year, the Cabinet continued to debate the proposed economic reforms, which included tax increases, further privatization of state concerns and reductions in public spending, and a failure to reach a consensus led to the resignation of Hariri and his Cabinet in April (although a new Government was subsequently formed under Hariri). Furthermore, throughout 2003 and early 2004 the planned privatization of several vital state-owned interests, notably Electricité du Liban, Middle East Airlines and the mobile telephone network, was delayed as a result of ongoing political disagreements. The Lebanese economy was expected to suffer from the effects of the temporary loss of trade with Iraq, as a result of the conflict there during early 2003 (see the chapter on Iraq), which also had an effect on the tourist industry in Lebanon. Meanwhile, in early 2001 international donors apparently agreed to provide the Lebanese authorities with $458m., in order to assist the economic reform programme. An aid package totalling an estimated $4,300m. was agreed by international donors in late November 2002, in order to provide further assistance with Lebanon's debt restructuring and to finance development projects. Such funding, in addition to the willingness of the Lebanese to tolerate economic austerity, as well as eventual progress towards a Middle East peace settlement, will be essential to the restoration of international competitiveness and enhanced investment.

Education

There are state-controlled primary and secondary schools, but private institutions provide the main facilities for secondary and higher education. Education is not compulsory, but state education is provided free of charge. Primary education begins at six years of age and lasts for five years. Secondary education, beginning at the age of 11, lasts for a further seven years, comprising a first cycle of four years and a second of three years. In 1996 the total enrolment at primary and secondary schools was equivalent to 94% of all school-age children (93% of boys; 95% of girls); enrolment at secondary schools in that year was equivalent to 81% of the appropriate age-group (males 78%; females 84%). Some 87,957 Lebanese students were enrolled at the country's seven universities in the 1996/97 academic year. In 1998 Lebanon secured a loan of US $60m. from the World Bank, in order to restructure the country's system of technical and vocational education. Lebanon has the highest literacy rate in the Arab world. Expenditure on education by the central Government in 2003 was some £L810,000m. (9.4% of total budgetary expenditure).

Public Holidays

2004: 1 January (New Year's Day), 1 February* (Id al-Adha, Feast of the Sacrifice), 9 February (Feast of St Maron), 22 February* (Muharram, Islamic New Year), 2 March* (Ashoura), 22 March (Arab League Anniversary), 9–12 April (Greek Orthodox Easter), 12 April (Easter, Western Church), 2 May* (Mouloud/Yum an-Nabi, birth of Muhammad), 20 May (Ascension Day, Western Church), 15 August (Assumption), 12 September* (Leilat al-Meiraj, ascension of Muhammad), 1 November (All Saints' Day), 14 November* (Id al-Fitr, end of Ramadan), 22 November (Independence Day), 25 December (Christmas Day).

2005: 1 January (New Year's Day), 21 January* (Id al-Adha, Feast of the Sacrifice), 9 February (Feast of St Maron), 10 February* (Muharram, Islamic New Year), 19 February* (Ashoura), 22 March (Arab League Anniversary), 28 March (Easter, Western Church), 21 April* (Mouloud/Yum an-Nabi, birth of Muhammad), 29 April–2 May (Greek Orthodox Easter),

5 May (Ascension Day, Western Church), 15 August (Assumption), 2 September* (Leilat al-Meiraj, ascension of Muhammad), 1 November (All Saints' Day), 4 November* (Id al-Fitr, end of Ramadan), 22 November (Independence Day), 25 December (Christmas Day).

* These holidays are determined by the Islamic lunar calendar and may vary by one or two days from the dates given.

Weights and Measures

The metric system is in force.

Statistical Survey

Source (unless otherwise stated): Central Administration for Statistics, Beirut; internet www.cas.gov.lb; Direction Générale des Douanes, Beirut.

Area and Population

AREA, POPULATION AND DENSITY

Area (sq km)	10,452*
Population (official estimate)	
15 November 1970†	
Males	1,080,015
Females	1,046,310
Total	2,126,325
Population (UN estimates at mid-year)‡	
2000	3,478,000
2001	3,537,000
2002	3,596,000
Density (per sq km) at mid-2002	344.0

* 4,036 sq miles.
† Figures are based on the results of a sample survey, excluding Palestinian refugees in camps. The total number of registered Palestinian refugees in Lebanon was 394,532 at 31 December 2003.
‡ Source: UN, *World Population Prospects: The 2002 Revision.*

PRINCIPAL TOWNS
(population in 2003)*

Beirut (capital)	1,171,000	Jounieh	79,800
Tarabulus (Tripoli)	212,900	Zahleh	76,600
Saida (Sidon)	149,000	Baabda	58,500
Sur (Tyre)	117,100	Ba'albak (Ba'albek)	29,800
An-Nabatiyah at-			
Tahta (Nabatiyah)	89,400	Alayh	26,700

* Figures are rounded.

Source: Stefan Helders, *World Gazetteer* (internet www.world-gazetteer.com).

BIRTHS AND DEATHS
(UN estimates, annual averages)

	1985–90	1990–95	1995–2000
Birth rate (per 1,000)	27.8	24.5	20.4
Death rate (per 1,000)	7.8	6.8	5.5

Source: UN, *World Population Prospects: The 2002 Revision.*

2001 (official estimates, numbers registered): Live births 83,693; Marriages 32,225; Deaths 17,568.

2002 (official estimates, numbers registered): Live births 76,405; Marriages 31,653; Deaths 17,294.

Expectation of life (WHO estimates, years at birth): 69.8 (males 67.6; females 72.0) in 2002 (Source: WHO, *World Health Report*).

EMPLOYMENT
(ISIC major divisions)

	1975	1985*
Agriculture, hunting, forestry and fishing	147,724	103,400
Manufacturing	139,471	45,000
Electricity, gas and water	6,381	10,000
Construction	47,356	25,000
Trade, restaurants and hotels	129,716	78,000
Transport, storage and communications	45,529	20,500
Other services	227,921	171,000
Total	**744,098**	**452,900**

* Estimates.

1997 (provisional estimates at mid-year): Total employed 1,246,000; Unemployed 116,000; Total labour force 1,362,000.

Source: National Employment Office.

Health and Welfare

KEY INDICATORS

Total fertility rate (children per woman, 2002)	2.2
Under-5 mortality rate (per 1,000 live births, 2002)	32
HIV/AIDS (% of persons aged 15–49, 1994)	0.09
Physicians (per 1,000 head, 1997)	2.10
Hospital beds (per 1,000 head, 1997)	2.7
Health expenditure (2001): US $ per head (PPP)	673
Health expenditure (2001): % of GDP	12.2
Health expenditure (2001): public (% of total)	28.1
Access to water (% of persons, 2000)	100
Access to sanitation (% of persons, 2000)	99
Human Development Index (2001): ranking	83
Human Development Index (2001): value	0.752

For sources and definitions, see explanatory note on p. vi.

Agriculture

PRINCIPAL CROPS
('000 metric tons)

	2000	2001	2002
Wheat	108.1	139.5	119.0
Barley	9.4	8.1	17.1
Potatoes	275.0	257.0	397.1
Sugar beet.	341.7	15.2	14.0*
Almonds	24.7	23.9	23.0
Olives	189.5	85.8	92.0*
Cabbages	18.4	20.9	20.9*
Lettuce.	41.8	40.6	40.6*
Tomatoes	235.0	247.0	247.0*
Cauliflower	11.5	13.2	13.2*
Pumpkins, squash and gourds	24.2	16.6	16.6*
Cucumbers and gherkins . . .	149.4	161.0	161.0*
Aubergines (Eggplants) . . .	27.9	21.6	21.6*
Dry onions	157.6	144.2	144.2*
Garlic	11.0	11.0	11.0*
Green beans	45.9	41.6	41.6*
Green broad beans	9.0	10.6	10.6*
Carrots	8.2	10.8	10.8*
Other vegetables	72.4	70.0	70.0*
Bananas	65.6	66.7	66.7*
Oranges	152.4	155.8	155.8*
Tangerines, mandarins, clementines and satsumas . .	49.8	46.1	46.1*
Lemons and limes	103.7	103.1	103.1*
Grapefruit and pomelo . . .	11.8	11.5	11.5*
Apples	126.7	112.0	112.0*
Pears	36.6	30.8	30.8*
Apricots	20.0	19.6	19.6*
Cherries	45.4	42.3	42.3*
Peaches and nectarines	29.7	27.6	27.6*
Plums	25.7	34.2	34.2*
Strawberries	27.3	29.7	29.7*
Grapes	112.6	116.2	116.2*
Watermelons	57.0	61.0	61.0*
Cantaloupes and other melons	21.6	14.9	14.9*
Figs	17.8	16.5	16.5*
Other fruits and berries. . .	41.0	37.2	37.2*

* FAO estimate.

Source: FAO.

LIVESTOCK
('000 head, year ending September)

	2000	2001	2002*
Horses*	6	6	6
Mules*	6	6	6
Asses*	25	25	25
Cattle	77	78	60
Pigs	26	23	20
Sheep	354	329	350
Goats	417	399	421
Poultry*	31,000	32,000	33,000

* FAO estimates.

Source: FAO.

LIVESTOCK PRODUCTS
('000 metric tons)

	2000	2001	2002
Beef and veal*	41.7	37.8	75.6
Mutton and lamb*	5.8	17.0	13.2
Goat meat*	2.5	3.0	3.2
Pig meat*	2.3	2.2	1.9
Poultry meat	113.1	117.4	129.0
Cows' milk	158.4	167.2	193.5
Sheep's milk	22.8	22.2	22.9
Goats' milk	26.9	27.3	29.9
Cheese*	16.1	16.7	18.9
Hen eggs	43.2	44.4	46.2
Cattle hides*	2.7	2.4	4.9
Sheepskins*	0.8	2.3	1.8
Wool: greasy*	1.7	1.7	1.8

* FAO estimates.

Source: FAO.

Forestry

ROUNDWOOD REMOVALS
('000 cubic metres, excluding bark)

	2000	2001	2002
Industrial wood*	7	7	7
Fuel wood	19	82†	82†
Total	26	89†	89†

* Assumed unchanged since 1992 (FAO estimates).
† FAO estimate.

Source: FAO.

SAWNWOOD PRODUCTION
(FAO estimates, '000 cubic metres, including railway sleepers)

	2000	2001	2002
Total (all broadleaved)* . . .	9	9	9

* Assumed to be unchanged since 1991.

Source: FAO.

Fishing

(metric tons, live weight)

	1999	2000	2001
Capture	3,560	3,666	3,670
Groupers and seabasses . . .	250	230	240
Porgies and seabreams . . .	450	450	400
Surmullets (Red mullets). . .	200	250	200
Barracudas	200	200	250
Mullets	300	—	400
Scorpionfishes	150	150	100
Carangids	350	450	400
Clupeoids	500	700	500
Tuna-like fishes	400	500	450
Mackerel-like fishes	300	350	350
Marine crustaceans	125	55	55
Aquaculture	300	400	300
Rainbow trout	300	400	300
Total catch	3,860	4,066	3,970

Source: FAO, *Yearbook of Fishery Statistics*.

Mining

(estimates, '000 metric tons)

	1999	2000	2001
Salt (unrefined)	3.5	3.5	3.5

Source: US Geological Survey.

Industry

SELECTED PRODUCTS
('000 metric tons, unless otherwise indicated)

	2000	2001	2002
Olive oil*	5.3†	5.8†	5.8‡
Sunflower seed oil*‡	1.5	2.0	2.0
Raw sugar*	34.2†	1.9‡	1.9‡
Wine*‡	17.0	16.0	16.0
Beer*‡	12.1	17.0	17.0
Plywood ('000 cubic metres)*‡	34	34	34
Paper*‡	42	42	42
Cement	2,808§	2,700§	2,852‖

* Source: FAO.
† Unofficial figure.
‡ FAO estimate(s).
§ Source: US Geological Survey.
‖ Source: Central Administration for Statistics, Beirut.

Electric energy (provisional, million kWh): 9,072 in 2002.

Finance

CURRENCY AND EXCHANGE RATES

Monetary Units
100 piastres = 1 Lebanese pound (£L).

Sterling, Dollar and Euro Equivalents (31 December 2003)
£1 sterling = £L2,690.4;
US $1 = £L1,507.5;
€1 = £L1,904.0;
£L10,000 = £3.717 sterling = $6.634 = €5.252.

Exchange Rate: The official exchange rate has been maintained at US $1 = £L1,507.5 since September 1999.

BUDGET
(£L '000 million)*

Revenue	2002	2003	2004†
Tax revenue	4,036	4,726	4,645
Taxes on income, profits and capital gains	650	1,000	1,045
Taxes on property	332	400	350
Domestic taxes on goods and services	1,940	2,296	2,499
Taxes on international trade and transactions	879	780	550
Other taxes	235	250	201
Other current revenue	1,465	1,749	1,755
Income from public enterprises	898	1,180	1,296
Administrative fees and charges	444	415	376
Fines and confiscations	11	27	6
Other	112	127	77
Total	5,500	6,475	6,400

Expenditure	2001	2002	2003
General public services	1,379	1,308	1,396
Defence	986	903	870
Public order and safety	395	370	356
Education	813	792	810
Health	315	290	285
Social security and welfare	218	159	163
Housing and community amenities	85	76	80
Recreational and cultural affaitrs and services	77	64	50
Religious affairs and services	7	3	3
Economic services	1,130	792	423
Agriculture	65	39	36
Manufacturing, fuel and energy	24	14	10
Transport and communications	279	188	140
Other purposes	761	552	237
Multi-functional expenditures	4,500	4,619	4,163
Total	9,900	9,375	8,600
Current	8,712	8,551	8,203
Capital	1,188	824	397

* Figures, which are rounded, represent the consolidated operations of the central Government's General Budget and the Council for Development and Reconstruction. The accounts of other central government units with individual budgets (including the general social security scheme) are excluded.
† Provisional.

2004 ('000 £L million, provisional): Expenditure 9,250.

Source: Ministry of Finance.

INTERNATIONAL RESERVES
(US $ million at 31 December)

	2001	2002	2003
Gold*	2,561.1	3,216.3	3,833.5
IMF special drawing rights	24.3	27.3	30.7
Reserve position in IMF	23.7	25.6	28.0
Foreign exchange	4,965.8	7,190.9	12,460.8
Total	7,574.9	10,460.1	16,353.0

* Valued at US $277.78 per troy ounce in 2001; $348.84 per ounce in 2002 and at $415.78 per ounce in 2003.

Source: IMF, *International Financial Statistics*.

MONEY SUPPLY
(£L '000 million at 31 December)

	2001	2002	2003
Currency outside banks	1,381.7	1,375.3	1,530.6
Demand deposits at commercial banks	889.6	1,072.3	1,258.1
Total money (incl. others)	2,365.2	2,544.4	2,827.8

Sources: IMF, *International Financial Statistics*; Banque du Liban.

COST OF LIVING
(Consumer Price Index for Beirut; base: December 1998 = 100)

	2000	2001	2002
Food and beverages	93.7	94.5	93.9
Water, electricity and gas	105.5	104.9	n.a.
Clothing and footwear	104.7	108.4	117.1
Transport and communications	109.9	111.6	133.0
All items (incl. others)	99.8	101.1	105.4

NATIONAL ACCOUNTS
(UN estimates, £L '000 million at current prices*)

Expenditure on the Gross Domestic Product

	2000	2001	2002
Government final consumption expenditure	2,914.2	3,062.8	3,230.3
Private final consumption expenditure	26,555.1	27,372.5	28,279.8
Increase in stocks }			
Gross fixed capital formation. }	5,434.9	5,311.4	5,211.6
Total domestic expenditure	34,904.2	35,746.7	36,721.7
Exports of goods and services	2,547.5	2,685.3	2,839.5
Less Imports of goods and services	12,203.8	12,426.7	12,723.7
GDP in purchasers' values	25,247.9	26,005.3	26,837.5
GDP at constant 1995 prices	20,005.2	20,405.3	20,915.5

Gross Domestic Product by Economic Activity

	2000	2001	2002
Agriculture, hunting, forestry and fishing	2,624.1	2,640.9	2,665.2
Manufacturing	2,524.7	2,570.4	2,607.1
Electricity, gas and water	1,681.3	1,722.2	1,759.8
Construction	753.1	693.4	649.6
Trade, restaurants and hotels	8,122.9	8,378.4	8,648.7
Transport, storage and communications	743.3	784.6	826.9
Finance and insurance	3,313.7	3,490.4	3,674.7
Real estate and business services	1,124.5	1,135.5	1,151.4
Government services	1,954.3	2,014.9	2,090.3
Other community, social and personal services	2,406.0	2,574.7	2,763.9
GDP in purchasers' values	25,247.9	26,005.4	26,837.6

* Figures are rounded.

Source: UN Economic and Social Commission for Western Asia, *National Accounts Studies of the ESCWA Region* (2000).

BALANCE OF PAYMENTS
(US $ million)

	1998	1999	2000
Exports of goods f.o.b.	716	678	718
Imports of goods c.i.f.	−7,060	−6,206	−6,228
Trade balance	−6,344	−5,528	−5,510
Services, income and current transfers (net)	481	−98	−120
Current balance	−5,863	−5,626	−5,630
Capital account (net)	5,375	5,887	5,341
Overall balance	−487	261	−289

Source: Ministry of Economy and Trade.

2001 (US $ million): Exports 889; Imports −7,291; *Trade balance* −6,402 (source: Ministry of Finance).

2002 (US $ million): Exports 1,045; Imports −6,445; *Trade balance* −5,399 (source: Ministry of Finance).

2003 (US $ million): Exports 1,524; Imports −7,168; *Trade balance* −5,644 (source: Ministry of Finance).

External Trade

PRINCIPAL COMMODITIES
(US $ million)*

Imports c.i.f.	1999	2000	2001
Live animals and animal products	349.8	336.1	359.4
Vegetable products	355.5	328.7	361.9
Prepared foodstuffs; beverages, spirits and vinegar; tobacco and manufactured substitutes	463.6	415.3	502.7
Mineral products	613.4	1,095.6	1,340.6
Products of chemical or allied industries	574.8	525.5	595.4
Plastics, rubber and articles thereof	230.6	222.0	257.8
Textiles and textile articles	386.2	352.0	464.7
Natural or cultured pearls, precious or semi-precious stones, precious metals and articles thereof; imitation jewellery; coin	461.7	423.3	363.9
Base metals and articles thereof	407.3	382.1	426.7
Machinery and mechanical appliances; electrical equipment; sound and television apparatus	910.2	800.4	999.0
Vehicles, aircraft, vessels and associated transport equipment	615.2	555.3	712.6
Total (incl. others)	6,206.5	6,227.9	7,291.1

Exports f.o.b.	1999	2000	2001
Vegetable products	52.3	48.5	49.8
Prepared foodstuffs; beverages, spirits and vinegar; tobacco and manufactured substitutes	74.0	72.5	99.7
Products of chemical or allied industries	84.9	88.4	88.1
Paper-making material; paper and paperboard and articles thereof	54.4	53.5	60.2
Textiles and textile articles	54.6	41.5	77.0
Natural or cultured pearls, precious or semi-precious stones, precious metals and articles thereof; imitation jewellery; coin	95.6	126.8	140.9
Base metals and articles thereof	78.6	63.1	65.2
Machinery and mechanical appliances; electrical equipment; sound and television apparatus	72.8	74.8	114.4
Total (incl. others)	676.8	714.3	889.3

* Figures are calculated on the basis of the official dollar rate, which is the previous month's average exchange rate of Lebanese pounds per US dollar.

Sources: Ministry of Economy and Trade; Banque du Liban.

2002 (US $ million): *Imports:* Prepared foodstuffs, beverages, spirits and vinegar, tobacco and manufactured substitutes 475; Mineral products 974; Products of chemical or allied industries 633; Machinery and mechanical appliances, electrical equipment, sound and television apparatus 863; Vehicles, aircraft, vessels and associated transport equipment 572; Others 2,929; Total 6,445. *Exports:* Prepared foodstuffs, beverages, spirits and vinegar, tobacco and manufactured substitutes 102; Products of chemical or allied industries 108; Natural or cultured pearls, precious or semi-precious stones, precious metals and articles thereof, imitation jewellery, coin 215; Base metals and articles thereof 79; Machinery and mechanical appliances, electrical equipment, sound and television apparatus 120; Others 421; Total 1,045 (Source: Ministry of Finance).

2003 (US $ million): *Imports:* Prepared foodstuffs, beverages, spirits and vinegar, tobacco and manufactured substitutes 477; Mineral products 1,190; Products of chemical or allied industries 716; Machinery and mechanical appliances, electrical equipment, sound and television apparatus 873; Vehicles, aircraft, vessels and associated transport equipment 696; Others 3,217; Total 7,168. *Exports:* Prepared foodstuffs, beverages, spirits and vinegar, tobacco and manufactured substitutes 150; Products of chemical or allied industries 115; Natural or cultured pearls, precious or semi-precious stones, precious metals and articles thereof, imitation jewellery, coin 464; Base metals and articles thereof 115; Machinery and mechanical appliances, electrical equipment, sound and television apparatus 179; Others 501; Total 1,524 (Source: Ministry of Finance).

PRINCIPAL TRADING PARTNERS
(US $ million)*

Imports c.i.f.	2000	2001	2002
Belgium	108.0	135.3	207.0
China, People's Republic	287.1	410.9	655.9
Egypt	85.5	106.2	202.6
France	526.5	614.9	779.5
Germany	519.6	623.1	878.4
Greece	157.2	142.0	109.3
India	61.2	64.5	107.0
Indonesia	55.5	72.7	n.a.
Ireland	80.0	52.8	n.a.
Italy	679.9	708.4	1,045.2
Japan	210.9	235.4	327.8
Korea, Republic	74.7	100.7	116.0
Malaysia	44.5	73.6	n.a.
Netherlands	124.6	129.2	222.1
Russia	215.2	409.4	370.8
Saudi Arabia	165.0	259.5	209.4
Spain	136.3	184.3	263.3
Switzerland	431.5	333.7	402.8
Syria	283.3	327.9	312.5
Taiwan	69.9	77.4	n.a.
Thailand	67.1	75.2	n.a.
Turkey	138.5	237.2	390.0
Ukraine	88.4	125.8	154.1
United Kingdom	243.4	284.7	380.9
USA	457.4	515.0	700.5
Total (incl. others)	6,083.9	7,103.5	9,717.8

Exports f.o.b.	2000	2001	2002
Belgium	12.8	12.1	33.7
Canada	7.6	20.9	n.a.
Cyprus	10.2	11.0	n.a.
Egypt	23.4	23.9	41.7
France	36.8	38.2	29.7
Germany	17.7	17.2	n.a.
Greece	7.1	14.4	n.a.
India	13.9	14.2	n.a.
Iraq	33.4	68.0	107.2
Italy	18.0	26.2	34.2
Jordan	31.2	30.7	53.3
Kuwait	26.3	27.8	48.9
Malta	11.0	n.a.	27.0
Netherlands	14.2	15.7	23.6
Saudi Arabia	77.7	85.4	144.8
Spain	18.9	18.2	25.3
Switzerland	51.0	63.2	199.3
Syria	25.8	35.2	114.0
Turkey	23.2	24.8	48.5
United Arab Emirates	74.9	72.9	142.8
United Kingdom	11.0	14.3	31.2
USA	46.4	60.8	80.7
Total (incl. others)	604.6	755.8	1,576.4

* Imports by country of production; exports by country of last consignment.

Source: Ministry of Economy and Trade.

Transport

ROAD TRAFFIC
(motor vehicles in use)

	1995	1996*	1997*
Passenger cars (incl. taxis)	1,197,521	1,217,000	1,299,398
Buses and coaches	5,514	5,640	6,833
Lorries and vans	79,222	81,000	85,242
Motorcycles and mopeds	53,317	54,450	61,471

* Estimates.

Source: International Road Federation, *World Road Statistics*.

SHIPPING
Merchant Fleet
(registered at 31 December)

	2000	2001	2002
Number of vessels	105	99	89
Total displacement ('000 grt)	362.7	301.7	229.3

Source: Lloyd's Register-Fairplay, *World Fleet Statistics*.

International Sea-borne Freight Traffic
('000 metric tons)

	1988	1989	1990
Goods loaded	148	150	152
Goods unloaded	1,120	1,140	1,150

Source: UN, *Monthly Bulletin of Statistics*.

2001 ('000 metric tons, Beirut port only): Goods loaded 330; Goods unloaded 5,134.

2002 ('000 metric tons, Beirut port only): Goods loaded 393; Goods unloaded 4,827.

CIVIL AVIATION
(revenue traffic on scheduled services)

	1997	1998	1999
Kilometres flown (million)	21	20	20
Passengers carried ('000)	857	716	719
Passenger-km (million)	2,116	1,504	1,288
Total ton-km (million)	319	247	222

Source: UN, *Statistical Yearbook*.

Tourism

FOREIGN TOURIST ARRIVALS
('000)*

Country of nationality	1998	1999	2000
Australia	24.3	27.6	30.6
Canada	22.3	28.1	30.2
Egypt	39.2	34.4	35.7
France	58.5	67.0	64.8
Germany	27.1	30.0	35.4
Iran	6.0	14.0	23.2
Italy	14.7	15.8	14.7
Jordan	53.6	61.0	69.6
Kuwait	40.2	41.1	47.6
Saudi Arabia	71.1	82.6	98.3
Sri Lanka	16.6	10.3	16.5
United Kingdom	22.0	22.3	24.3
USA	31.4	40.4	43.3
Total (incl. others)	630.8	673.3	741.6

* Figures exclude arrivals of Syrian nationals, Palestinians and students.

Source: World Tourism Organization, *Yearbook of Tourism Statistics*.

Tourism receipts (US $ million): 1,221 in 1998; 673 in 1999; 742 in 2000 (Source: World Tourism Organization).

Communications Media

	1998	1999	2000
Television receivers ('000 in use)	1,120	1,150	1,170
Telephones ('000 main lines in use)	620.0	650.0	681.5
Mobile cellular telephones ('000 subscribers).	505.3	627.0	743.0
Personal computers ('000 in use)	125	150	175
Internet users ('000) .	100	200	300

2002: Telephones ('000 main lines in use) 678.8; Mobile cellular telephones ('000 subscribers) 775.1; Internet users ('000) 400.

Personal computers ('000 in use): 200 in 2001.

Radio receivers ('000 in use): 2,850 in 1997.

Facsimile machines (number in use): 3,000 in 1992.

Daily newspapers (1996): 15 titles; average circulation (estimate, '000 copies) 435.

Non-daily newspapers (estimates, 1988): 15 titles; average circulation 240,000 copies.

Sources: UNESCO, *Statistical Yearbook*; UN, *Statistical Yearbook* and International Telecommunication Union.

Education

(1996/97, unless otherwise indicated)

	Institutions	Teachers	Students
Pre-primary	1,938 }		164,397*
Primary.	2,160 }	67,935†	382,309*
Secondary:			
general	n.a. }		292,002*
vocational . . .	275†	7,745	55,848*
Higher	n.a.	10,444‡	81,588‡

* Estimate.
† 1994 figure.
‡ 1995/96 figure.

Sources: UNESCO, *Statistical Yearbook*; Banque du Liban, *Annual Report*.

Adult literacy rate (UNESCO estimates): 86.5% (males 92.4%; females 81.0%) in 2001 (Source: UNDP, *Human Development Report*).

Directory

The Constitution

The Constitution was promulgated on 23 May 1926 and amended by the Constitutional Laws of 1927, 1929, 1943, 1947 and 1990.

According to the Constitution, the Republic of Lebanon is an independent and sovereign state, and no part of the territory may be alienated or ceded. Lebanon has no state religion. Arabic is the official language. Beirut is the capital.

All Lebanese are equal in the eyes of the law. Personal freedom and freedom of the press are guaranteed and protected. The religious communities are entitled to maintain their own schools, on condition that they conform to the general requirements relating to public instruction, as defined by the state. Dwellings are inviolable; rights of ownership are protected by law. Every Lebanese citizen over 21 is an elector and qualifies for the franchise.

LEGISLATIVE POWER

Legislative power is exercised by one house, the National Assembly, with 108 seats (raised, without amendment of the Constitution, to 128 in 1992), which are divided equally between Christians and Muslims. Members of the National Assembly must be over 25 years of age, in possession of their full political and civil rights, and literate. They are considered representative of the whole nation, and are not bound to follow directives from their constituencies. They can be suspended only by a two-thirds majority of their fellow-members. Secret ballot was introduced in a new election law of April 1960.

The National Assembly holds two sessions yearly, from the first Tuesday after 15 March to the end of May, and from the first Tuesday after 15 October to the end of the year. The normal term of the National Assembly is four years; general elections take place within 60 days before the end of this period. If the Assembly is dissolved before the end of its term, elections are held within three months of dissolution.

Voting in the Assembly is public—by acclamation, or by standing and sitting. A quorum of two-thirds and a majority vote is required for constitutional issues. The only exceptions to this occur when the Assembly becomes an electoral college, and chooses the President of the Republic, or Secretaries to the National Assembly, or when the President is accused of treason or of violating the Constitution. In such cases voting is secret, and a two-thirds majority is needed for a proposal to be adopted.

EXECUTIVE POWER

With the incorporation of the Ta'if agreement into the Lebanese Constitution in August 1990, executive power was effectively transferred from the presidency to the Cabinet. The President is elected for a term of six years and is not immediately re-eligible. He is responsible for the promulgation and execution of laws enacted by the National Assembly, but all presidential decisions (with the exception of those to appoint a Prime Minister or to accept the resignation of a government) require the co-signature of the Prime Minister, who is head of the Government, implementing its policies

and speaking in its name. The President must receive the approval of the Cabinet before dismissing a minister or ratifying an international treaty. The ministers and the Prime Minister are chosen by the President of the Republic in consultation with the members and President of the National Assembly. They are not necessarily members of the National Assembly, although they are responsible to it and have access to its debates. The President of the Republic must be a Maronite Christian, and the Prime Minister a Sunni Muslim; the choice of the other ministers must reflect the level of representation of the communities in the Assembly.

Note: In October 1998 the National Assembly endorsed an exceptional amendment to Article 49 of the Constitution to enable the election of Gen. Emile Lahoud, then Commander-in-Chief of the armed forces, as President of the Republic: the Constitution requires that senior state officials relinquish their responsibilities two years prior to seeking public office.

The Government

HEAD OF STATE

President: Gen. EMILE LAHOUD (inaugurated 24 November 1998).

CABINET
(April 2004)

Prime Minister: RAFIK HARIRI.

Deputy Prime Minister: ISSAM FARES.

Minister of Foreign Affairs and Emigrants: JEAN OBEID.

Minister of the Interior and Municipalities: ELIAS MURR.

Minister of National Defence: MAHMOUD HAMMOUD.

Minister of the Displaced: ABDULLAH FARHAT.

Minister of Industry and Oil: ELIAS SKAFF.

Minister of Energy and Water: AYOUB HUMAYED.

Minister of Public Health: SULAYMAN FRANJIYA.

Minister of Social Affairs: ASSAD DIEB.

Minister of Finance: FOUAD SINIORA.

Minister of Education and Higher Education: SAMIR JISR.

Minister of the Environment: FARES BOUEIZ.

Minister of Tourism: ALI HUSSEIN ABDULLAH.

Minister of Public Works and Transport: NAJIB MIQATI.

Minister of Youth and Sports: SEBOUH HOFNANIAN.

Minister of Information: MICHEL SAMAHA.

Minister of Economy and Trade: MARWAN HAMADEH.

Minister of Justice: BAHIJ TABBARA.

Minister of Labour: ASSAD HARDAN.

Minister of Culture: GHAZI ARIDI.

Minister of Agriculture: ALI HASSAN KHALIL.

Minister of Posts and Telecommunications: JEAN-LOUIS KORDAHI.

Minister of State for Administrative Development: KARIM PAKRADOUNI.

Ministers of State without portfolio: ASSEM QANSO, KARAM KARAM, TALAL ARSLAN, KHALIL HRAWI, MICHEL MOUSSA, ABD AR-RAHIM MRAD.

MINISTRIES

Office of the President: Presidential Palace, Baabda, Beirut; tel. (5) 920900; fax (5) 922400; e-mail president_office@presidency.gov.lb; internet www.presidency.gov.lb.

Office of the President of the Council of Ministers: Grand Sérail, place Riad es-Solh, Beirut; tel. (1) 746800; fax (1) 865630.

Ministry of Agriculture: blvd Camille Chamoun, Beirut; tel. (1) 455631; fax (1) 455475; e-mail ministry@agriculture.gov.lb; internet www.agriculture.gov.lb.

Ministry of Culture: Beirut; internet www.culture.gov.lb.

Ministry of the Displaced: Minet el-Hosn, Starco Centre, Beirut; tel. (1) 366373; fax (1) 503040; e-mail mod@dm.net.lb; internet www.ministryofdisplaced.gov.lb.

Ministry of Economy and Trade: rue Artois, Hamra, Beirut; tel. (1) 340503; fax (1) 354640; e-mail postmaster@economy.gov.lb; internet www.economy.gov.lb.

Ministry of Education and Higher Education: Campus de l'Unesco, Beirut; tel. (1) 866430; fax (1) 645844.

Ministry of Energy and Water: Shiah, Beirut; tel. (1) 270256.

Ministry of the Environment: POB 70-1091, Antélias, Beirut; tel. (4) 522222; fax (4) 525080; e-mail webmaster@moe.gov.lb; internet www.moe.gov.lb.

Ministry of Finance: 4e étage, Immeuble MOF, place Riad es-Solh, Beirut; tel. (1) 981057; fax (1) 981059; e-mail infocenter@finance.gov.lb; internet www.finance.gov.lb.

Ministry of Foreign Affairs and Emigrants: rue Sursock, Achrafieh, Beirut; tel. (1) 333100.

> **General Directorate of Emigrants:** Immeuble As-Sultan, Jnah, Beirut; tel. (1) 840921; fax (1) 840924; e-mail director@emigrants.gov.lb; internet www.emigrants.gov.lb.

Ministry of Industry: Ministry of Industry and Oil Bldg, ave Sami Solh, Beirut; tel. (1) 427042; fax (1) 427112; e-mail ministry@industry.gov.lb; internet www.industry.gov.lb.

Ministry of Information: rue Hamra, Beirut; tel. (1) 345800.

Ministry of the Interior and Municipalities: Grand Sérail, place Riad es-Solh, Beirut; tel. (1) 863910; e-mail ministry@interior.gov.lb; internet www.interior.gov.lb.

Ministry of Justice: rue Sami Solh, Beirut; tel. (1) 422953; e-mail justice@ministry.gov.lb; internet www.justice.gov.lb.

Ministry of Labour: Shiah, Beirut; tel. (1) 274140.

Ministry of National Defence: Yarze, Beirut; tel. (5) 920400; fax (5) 951014; e-mail ministry@lebarmy.gov.lb; internet www.lebarmy.gov.lb.

Ministry of Public Health: place du Musée, Beirut; tel. (1) 615716; fax (1) 645099; e-mail minister@public-health.gov.lb; internet www.public-health.gov.lb.

Ministry of Public Works and Transport: Shiah, Beirut; tel. (1) 428980; internet www.public-works.gov.lb.

Ministry of State for Administrative Reform: Immeuble Starco, 5e étage, rue George Picot, Beirut; tel. (1) 371510; fax (1) 371599; e-mail newsletter@omsar.gov.lb; internet www.omsar.gov.lb.

Ministry of Telecommunications: rue Sami Solh, 3e étage, Beirut; tel. (1) 424400; fax (1) 888310; e-mail webmaster@mpt.gov.lb; internet www.mpt.gov.lb.

Ministry of Tourism: POB 11-5344, rue Banque du Liban 550, Beirut; tel. (1) 340940; fax (1) 340945; e-mail mot@lebanon-tourism.gov.lb; internet www.lebanon-tourism.gov.lb.

Ministry of Youth and Sports: Beirut.

Legislature

MAJLIS ALNWAB
(National Assembly)

The equal distribution of seats among Christians and Muslims is determined by law, and the Cabinet must reflect the level of representation achieved by the various religious denominations within that principal division. Deputies of the same religious denomination do not necessarily share the same political, or party allegiances. The distribution of seats is as follows: Maronite Catholics 34; Sunni Muslims 27; Shi'a Muslims 27; Greek Orthodox 14; Druzes 8; Greek-Melkite Catholics 8; Armenian Orthodox 5; Alawites 2; Armenian Catholics 1; Protestants 1; Others 1.

President: NABIH BERRI.

Vice-President: ELIE FERZLI.

General election, 27 August and 3 September 2000

Party list	Seats
Resistance and Development	23
Al-Karamah (Dignity)	18
Ba'albek-Hermel al-Ii'tilafiah (Ba'albek-Hermel Coalition)	9
Al-Jabhar an-Nidal al-Watani (National Defence Front)	8
Wahdal al-Jabal (Mountain Union)	7
Ii'tilafiah (Coalition)	6
Al-Karal (Decision)	6
Al-Kitla al-Chaabi—Elias Shaft (People's Front—Elias Shaft)	5
Al-Wifah al-Matni (Metn Accord)	5
Al-Karamah wah Tajdid (Dignity and Renewal)	5
Al-Karal al-Chaabi (Popular Decision)	3
Al-Wifac at-Tajdid (Reconciliation and Renewal)	3
Al-Irada al-Chaabia (Popular Will)	3
Al-Karamah al-Wataniyah (National Dignity)	2
At-Tawafoc al-Watani (National Understanding)	1
Al-Kitla al-Chaabi—Fouad et-Turk (People's Front—Fouad et-Turk)	1
Lubnan (Lebanon)	1
Al-Hurriya (Freedom)	1
Independents	20
Others	1
Total	**128**

Political Organizations

Amal (Hope): e-mail post@amal-movement.com; internet www.amal-movement.com; f. 1975 as a politico-military organization; Shi'ite political party; Leader NABIH BERRI.

Armenian Revolutionary Federation (ARF) (Tashnag): rue Spears, Beirut; f. 1890; principal Armenian party; historically the dominant nationalist party in the independent Armenian Republic of Yerevan of 1917–21, prior to its becoming part of the USSR; socialist ideology; collective leadership.

Al-Baath (Baath Arab Socialist Party): Beirut; f. 1948; local branch of secular pro-Syrian party with policy of Arab union; Leader ASSEM QANSO.

Al-Baath (Baath Arab Socialist Party): f. 1966 following split in Syrian branch of Al-Baath; part of pro-Iraqi faction of Al-Baath; Sec.-Gen. ABD AL-MAJID RAFEI.

Bloc national libanais (National Bloc): rue Pasteur, Gemmayze, Beirut; tel. (1) 584585; fax (1) 584591; f. 1943; right-wing Lebanese party with policy of power-sharing between Christians and Muslims and the exclusion of the military from politics; Pres. CARLOS EDEH.

Hezbollah (Party of God): Beirut; e-mail hizbollahmedia@hizbollah.org; internet www.hizbollah.org; f. 1982 by Iranian Revolutionary Guards who were sent to Lebanon; militant Shi'ite faction which has become the leading organization of Lebanon's Shi'a community and a recognized political party; demands the withdrawal of Israeli forces from the occupied Shebaa Farms area of southern Lebanon and the release of all Lebanese prisoners from Israeli detention; Chair. MUHAMMAD RA'D; Leader and Sec.-Gen. Sheikh HASAN NASRALLAH.

Al-Katae'b (Phalanges Libanaises, Phalangist Party): POB 992, place Charles Hélou, Beirut; tel. (1) 584107; e-mail admin@kataeb.com; internet www.kataeb.com; f. 1936 by the late Pierre Gemayel; nationalist, reformist, democratic social party; largest Maronite party; 100,000 mems; announced merger with Parti national libéral, May 1979; Pres. MOUNIR EL-HAJJ; Sec.-Gen. JOSEPH ABOU KHALIL.

Lebanese Democratic Movement: Beirut; internet www.ldm.org .lb; Pres. JACQUES TAMER; Sec.-Gen. NAJI HATAB.

An-Najjadé (The Helpers): c/o Sawt al-Uruba, POB 3537, Beirut; f. 1936; Arab socialist unionist party; 3,000 mems; Founder and Pres. ADNANE MOUSTAFA AL-HAKIM.

National Lebanese Front: Beirut; f. 1999; Pres. ERNEST KARAM.

Parti communiste libanais (Lebanese Communist Party): Beirut; e-mail lcparty@inco.com.lb; internet www.lcparty.org; f. 1924; officially dissolved 1948–71; Marxist, much support among intellectuals; Pres. MAURICE NOHRA; Sec.-Gen. KHALID HADDADEH.

Parti national libéral (PNL) (Al-Wataniyin al-Ahrar): POB 165576, rue du Liban, Beirut; tel. (1) 338000; fax (1) 200335; e-mail ahrar@ahrar.org.lb; internet www.al-ahrar.com; f. 1958; liberal reformist secular party, although has traditionally had a predominantly Maronite Christian membership; Pres. DORY CHAMOUN.

Parti national nationaliste syrien: internet www.ssnp.com; f. 1932; banned 1962–69; advocates a 'Greater Syria', composed of Lebanon, Syria, Iraq, Jordan, Palestine and Cyprus; Leader JIBRAN ARAIJI.

Parti socialiste progressiste (At-Takadumi al-Ishteraki—PSP): POB 11-2893, Beirut 1107 2120; tel. (1) 303455; fax (1) 301231; e-mail secretary@psp.org.lb; internet www.psp.org.lb; f. 1949; progressive party, advocates constitutional road to socialism and democracy; over 25,000 mems; mainly Druze support; Pres. WALID JOUMBLATT; Sec.-Gen. SHARIF FAYAD.

Al-Wa'ad (National Secular Democratic Party—Pledge): Beirut; f. 1986 by the late Elie Hobeika; pro-Syrian splinter group of Lebanese Forces (see below); Leader (vacant).

Other parties include the **Independent Nasserite Movement** (Murabitoun; Sunni Muslim Militia; Leader IBRAHIM QULAYAT) and the **Lebanese Popular Congress** (Pres. KAMAL SHATILA). The **Nasserite Popular Organization** and the **Arab Socialist Union** merged in January 1987, retaining the name of the former. The **Islamic Amal** is a breakaway group from Amal, based in Ba'albak (Ba'albek) (Leader HUSSEIN MOUSSAVI). **Islamic Jihad** (Islamic Holy War) is a pro-Iranian fundamentalist guerrilla group (Leader IMAAD MOUGNIEH). The **Popular Liberation Army** (f. 1985 by the late MUSTAFA SAAD) is a Sunni Muslim faction, active in the south of Lebanon. **Tawheed Islami** (the Islamic Unification Movement; f. 1982; Sunni Muslim) and the **Arab Democratic Party** (or the Red Knights; Alawites; pro-Syrian; Leader ALI EID) are based in Tripoli.

The **Lebanese Forces Party** (f. 1990), the political successor to the **Lebanese Forces (LF)** (f. 1976; coalition of Maronite militias), claims still to be active in Lebanon, despite proscription by the Government in 1994 and the arrest, conviction and imprisonment of its leader, SAMIR GEAGEA, on murder charges.

Diplomatic Representation

EMBASSIES IN LEBANON

Algeria: POB 4794, face Hôtel Summerland, rue Jnah, Beirut; tel. (1) 826712; fax (1) 826711; Ambassador AHMAD BOUTEHRI.

Argentina: 2nd Floor, Residence des Jardins, Immeuble Moutran, 161 rue Sursock, Achrafieh, Beirut; tel. (1) 210800; fax (1) 210802; e-mail embarg@cyberia.net.lb; Ambassador JOSÉ PEDRO PICO.

Armenia: POB 70607, rue Jasmin, Mtaileb, Beirut; tel. (4) 418860; fax (4) 402952; e-mail armenia@dm.net.lb; Ambassador AREG HOVHANNISSIAN.

Australia: POB 11-1860, Farra Bldg, Bliss St, Ras Beirut; tel. (1) 374701; fax (1) 374709; e-mail austemle@cyberia.net.lb; internet www.lebanon.embassy.gov.au; Ambassador STEPHANIE SHWABSKY.

Austria: POB 11/3942, 8th Floor, Immeuble Tabaris, 812 ave Charles Malek, Achrafieh, Beirut; tel. (1) 217360; fax (1) 217772; e-mail beirut-ob@bmaa.gv.at; Ambassador Dr HELMUT FREUDENSCHUSS.

Bahrain: Sheikh Ahmed ath-Thani Bldg, Raoucheh, Beirut; tel. (1) 805495; Ambassador MUHAMMAD BAHLOUL.

Belgium: POB 11-1600, Riad es-Solh, Beirut; tel. (1) 976001; fax (1) 976007; e-mail beirut@diplobel.org; internet www.diplomatie.be/beirut; Ambassador FRANÇOISE GUSTIN.

Brazil: POB 40242, Baabda, Beirut; tel. (5) 921256; fax (5) 923001; e-mail braemlib@dm.net.lb; internet www.brazilianembassylb.org; Ambassador MARCUS CAMACHO DE VINCENZI.

Bulgaria: POB 11-6544, Immeuble Hibri, rue de l'Australie 55, Raouche, Beirut; tel. (1) 861352; fax (1) 800265; e-mail bgemb_lb@hotmail.com; Ambassador NIKOLAI ANDREEV.

Canada: POB 60163, 1e étage, Immeuble Coolrite, Autostrade Jal ed-Dib, Beirut; tel. (4) 713900; fax (4) 710595; e-mail berut@dfait-maeci.gc.ca; internet www.dfait-maeci.gc.ca/beirut; Ambassador MICHEL DUVAL.

Chile: Nouvelle Naccache, 2e Bifurcation après La Belle Antique avant Carpacio, Beirut; tel. (4) 418670; fax (4) 418672; e-mail echilelb@dm.net.lb; Ambassador FELIPE DU MONCEAU DE BERGENDAL.

China, People's Republic: POB 11-8227, Beirut 1107 2260; tel. (1) 856133; fax (1) 822492; e-mail emb.prc@dm.net.lb; Ambassador LIU XIANGHUA.

Colombia: 5th Floor, Mazda Centre, Jal ed-Dib, Beirut; tel. (4) 712646; fax (4) 712656; e-mail ebeirut@minrelext.gov.co; Ambassador GEORGINE MALLAT.

Cuba: POB 116874, Immeuble Ghazzal, rue Abd as-Sabbah, rue Sakiet el-Janzir/rue de Vienne, Beirut; tel. (1) 805025; fax (1) 810339; e-mail libancub@embacubalebanon.com; internet www.embacubalebanon.com; Chargé d'affaires EDUARDO IGLESIAS.

Czech Republic: POB 40195, Baabda, Beirut; tel. (5) 468763; fax (5) 922120; e-mail beirut@embassy.mzv.cz; internet www.mzv.cz/beirut; Ambassador MAREK SKOLIL.

Denmark: POB 11-5190, Immeuble 812 Tabaris, 4e étage, ave Charles Malek, Achrafieh, Beirut; tel. (1) 335828; fax (1) 335851; e-mail dk-emb@dm.net.lb; internet www.ambassaden-beirut.dk; Ambassador OLE WØHLERS OLSEN.

Egypt: POB 690, rue Thomas Eddison, Ar-Ramla el-Baida, Beirut; tel. (1) 862932; fax (1) 863751; Ambassador HUSSEIN DERAR.

France: rue de Damas, Beirut; tel. (1) 420000; fax (1) 420007; e-mail ambafr@ciberia.net.lb; internet www.ambafrance-lb.org; Ambassador PHILIPPE LECOURTIER.

Gabon: POB 11-1252, Riad es-Solh, Hadath, Beirut 1107 2080; tel. (5) 924649; fax (5) 924643; Ambassador SIMON NTOUTOUME EMANE.

Germany: POB 11-2820, Riad es-Solh, Beirut 1102-2110; tel. (4) 914444; fax (4) 914450; e-mail germanemb@germanembassy.org.lb; internet www.germanembassy.org.lb; Ambassador GÜNTER RUDOLF KNIESS.

Greece: POB 11-0309, Immeuble Boukhater, rue des Ambassades, Naccache, Beirut; tel. (4) 521700; fax (4) 418774; e-mail hellas.emb@inco.com.lb; Ambassador GEORGES GABRIELIDES.

Holy See: POB 1061, Jounieh (Apostolic Nunciature); tel. (9) 263102; fax (9) 264488; e-mail naliban@terra.net.lb; Apostolic Nuncio Most Rev. LUIGI GATTI (Titular Archbishop of Santa Giusta).

Hungary: POB 90618, Centre Massoud, Fanar, Beirut; tel. (1) 898840; fax (1) 873391; e-mail huembbej@inco.com.lb; Ambassador PÁL JENŐ FÁBIÁN.

India: POB 113-5240, Immeuble Sahmarani, rue Kantari 31, Hamra, Beirut; tel. (1) 353892; fax (1) 869806; e-mail indembei@dm.net.lb; Ambassador NANTU SARKAR.

Indonesia: Ave Palais Presidential, rue 68, Secteur 3, Baabda, Beirut; tel. (5) 924682; fax (5) 924678; e-mail indobay@cyberia.net.lb; internet www.welcome.to/indobey; Ambassador SYAM SOEMANAGARA.

Iran: POB 5030, Beirut; tel. (1) 821224; fax (1) 821230; Ambassador MASSOUD IDRIS KARMANSHAHI.

Italy: Immeuble Assicurazioni Generali, Beirut; tel. (1) 985200; fax (1) 985303; e-mail ambital@ambitaliabeirut.org; internet www.ambitaliabeirut.org; Ambassador FRANCO MISTRETTA.

Japan: POB 11-3360, Army St, Zkak al-Blat, Serail Hill, Beirut; tel. (1) 985751; fax (1) 989754; e-mail japanemb@japanemb.org.lb; internet www.lb.emb-japan.go.jp; Ambassador TOKUMITSU MURAKAMI.

Jordan: POB 109, Beirut 5113; tel. (5) 922500; fax (5) 922502; e-mail joremb@dm.net.lb; Ambassador ANMAR AL-HMOUD.

Korea, Republic: POB 40-290, Baabda, Beirut; tel. (5) 953167; fax (5) 953170; e-mail koremadm@dm.net.lb; Ambassador YOUNG-SUN KIM.

Kuwait: Rond-point du Stade, Bir Hassan, Beirut; tel. (1) 822515; fax (1) 840613; internet www.kuwaitinfo.net; Ambassador ALI SULEIMAN AS-SAEID.

Mexico: POB 70-1150, Antélias, Beirut; tel. (4) 418871; fax (4) 418873; e-mail embamex@dm.net.lb; internet www.embamex.org.lb; Ambassador ARTURO PUENTE ORTEGA.

Morocco: Bir Hassan, Beirut; tel. (1) 859829; fax (1) 859839; e-mail sifmar@cyberia.net.lb.

Netherlands: POB 167190, Netherlands Tower, ave Charles Malek, Achrafieh, Beirut; tel. (1) 204663; fax (1) 204664; e-mail nlgovbei@sodetel.net.lb; internet www.netherlandsembassy.org.lb; Ambassador G. J VAN EPEN.

Norway: Immeuble Dimashki, rue Bliss, Ras Beirut, Beirut; tel. (1) 372977; fax (1) 372979; Ambassador SVEIN SEVJE.

Pakistan: POB 135506, Immeuble Shell, 11e étage, Raoucheh, Beirut; tel. (1) 863041; fax (1) 864583; e-mail pakemblb@cyberia.net.lb; Ambassador KHALID M. MIR.

Philippines: POB 136631, 1er et 2e étages, Immeuble Design, rue Abdullah Machnouk, Beirut; tel. (1) 791092; fax (1) 791095; e-mail beirutpe@cyberia.net.lb; Ambassador RAMONITO S. MARINO.

Poland: POB 40-215, Immeuble Khalifa, ave Président Sulayman Franjiya 52, Baabda, Beirut; tel. (5) 924881; fax (5) 924882; e-mail polamb@cyberia.net.lb; Ambassador WALDEMAR MARKIEWICZ.

Qatar: POB 11-6717, 1er étage, Immeuble Deebs, Shouran, Beirut; tel. (1) 865271; fax (1) 810460; e-mail beirut@mofa.gov.qa; Ambassador JABOR BIN ABDULLAH AS-SWAIDI.

Romania: Route du Palais Presidentiel, Baabda, Beirut; tel. (5) 924848; fax (5) 924747; e-mail romembey@inco.com.lb; Ambassador AUREL CALIN.

Russia: rue Mar Elias et-Tineh, Wata Mseitbeh, Beirut; tel. (1) 300041; fax (1) 303837; Ambassador BORIS BOLOTINE.

Saudi Arabia: POB 136144, Kuraitem, Beirut; tel. (1) 860351; fax (1) 861524; e-mail lbemb@mofa.gov.sa; Ambassador FUAD BIN SADEK MUFTI.

Spain: POB 11-3039, Palais Chehab, Hadath Antounie, Beirut; tel. (5) 464120; fax (5) 464030; e-mail embesplb@mail.mae.es; Ambassador MIGUEL ANGEL CARRIEDO.

Sri Lanka: Baabda, Beirut; tel. (5) 924765; fax (5) 924768; e-mail slemblbn@cyberia.net.lb; Ambassador MUHAMMAD ISMAIL MUHSEN.

Sudan: POB 2504, Hamra, Beirut; tel. (1) 350057; fax (1) 353271; Ambassador SAYED AHMAD AL-BAKHIT.

Switzerland: POB 11-172, Riad al-Solh, Beirut 1107 2020; tel. (1) 324129; fax (1) 324167; e-mail vertretung@bey.rep.admin.ch; Ambassador THOMAS LITSCHER.

Tunisia: Hazmieh, Mar-Takla, Beirut; tel. (5) 457431; fax (5) 950434; Ambassador FETHI HOUIDI.

Turkey: POB 70-666, zone II, rue 3, Rabieh, Beirut; tel. (4) 520929; fax (4) 407557; e-mail trbebeyr@intracom.net.lb; Ambassador CELALETTIN KART.

Ukraine: POB 431, Jardin al-Bacha, Jisr al-Bacha, Sin el-Fil, Beirut; tel. (1) 510527; fax (1) 510531; e-mail ukrembassy@inco.com.lb; internet www.ukremblebanon.com; Ambassador VALERII RYLACH.

United Arab Emirates: Immeuble Wafic Tanbara, Jnah, Beirut; tel. (1) 857000; fax (1) 857009; Ambassador MUHAMMAD HAMAD OMRAN.

United Kingdom: POB 11-471, Embassies Complex, Army St, Zkak al-Blat, Serail Hill, Beirut; tel. (1) 990400; fax (1) 990420; e-mail britemb@cyberia.net.lb; internet www.britishembassy.org.lb; Ambassador JAMES WATT.

USA: POB 70-840, Antélias, Aoucar, Beirut; tel. (4) 542600; fax (4) 544136; e-mail pas@inco.com.lb; internet www.usembassy.gov.lb; Ambassador VINCENT M. BATTLE.

Uruguay: POB 6045, Centre Stella Marris, 7e étage, rue Banque du Liban, Jounieh; tel. (9) 636529; fax (9) 636531; e-mail uruliban@dm.net.lb; Ambassador ALBERTO VOSS RUBIO.

Venezuela: POB 603, Immeuble Baezevale House, 5e étage, Zalka, Beirut; tel. (1) 888701; fax (1) 900757; e-mail embavene@dm.net.lb; Ambassador EFRAIN SILVA MENDEZ.

Yemen: Bir Hassan, Beirut; tel. (1) 852688; fax (1) 821610; e-mail yemenembassy@yemenembassy-lebanon.org; internet www.yemenembassy-lebanon.org; Ambassador AHMAD ABDULLAH AL-BASHA.

Note: Lebanon and Syria have very close relations but do not exchange formal ambassadors. Libya closed its embassy in Beirut in September 2003 but still maintains diplomatic relations with Lebanon.

Judicial System

Law and justice in Lebanon are administered in accordance with the following codes, which are based upon modern theories of civil and criminal legislation:

Code de la Propriété (1930).

Code des Obligations et des Contrats (1932).

Code de Procédure Civile (1933).

Code Maritime (1947).

Code de Procédure Pénale (Code Ottoman Modifié).

Code Pénal (1943).

Code Pénal Militaire (1946).

Code d'Instruction Criminelle.

The following courts are now established:

(a) Fifty-six **'Single-Judge Courts'**, each consisting of a single judge, and dealing in the first instance with both civil and criminal cases; there are seventeen such courts at Beirut and seven at Tripoli.

(b) Eleven **Courts of Appeal**, each consisting of three judges, including a President and a Public Prosecutor, and dealing with civil and criminal cases; there are five such courts at Beirut.

First President of the Courts of Appeal of Beirut: TANIOS EL-KHOURY.

(c) Four **Courts of Cassation**, three dealing with civil and commercial cases and the fourth with criminal cases. A Court of Cassation, to be properly constituted, must have at least three judges, one being the President and the other two Councillors. If the Court of Cassation reverses the judgment of a lower court, it does not refer the case back but retries it itself.

General Prosecutor of Cassation: ADNAN ADOUM.

(d) **State Consultative Council**, which deals with administrative cases.

President of the State Consultative Council: GHALEB GHANEM.

(e) **The Court of Justice**, which is a special court consisting of a President and four judges, deals with matters affecting the security of the State; there is no appeal against its verdicts.

In addition to the above, the Constitutional Council considers matters pertaining to the constitutionality of legislation. Military courts are competent to try crimes and misdemeanours involving the armed and security forces. Islamic (*Shari'a*), Christian and Jewish religious courts deal with affairs of personal status (marriage, death, inheritance, etc.).

President of the Constitutional Council: AMIN FARIS NASSER.

Chief of the Military Court: Brig.-Gen. MAHER SAFI ED-DIN.

Religion

Of all the regions of the Middle East, Lebanon probably presents the closest juxtaposition of sects and peoples within a small territory. Estimates for 1983 assessed the sizes of communities as: Shi'a Muslims 1.2m., Maronites 900,000, Sunni Muslims 750,000, Greek Orthodox 250,000, Druzes 250,000, Armenians 175,000. The Maronites, a uniate sect of the Roman Catholic Church, inhabited the old territory of Mount Lebanon, i.e. immediately east of Beirut. In the south, towards the Israeli frontier, Shi'a villages are most common, while between the Shi'a and the Maronites live the Druzes (divided between the Yazbakis and the Joumblatis). The Beka'a valley has many Greek Christians (both Roman Catholic and Orthodox), while the Tripoli area is mainly Sunni Muslim.

CHRISTIANITY

The Roman Catholic Church

Armenian Rite

Patriarchate of Cilicia: Patriarcat Arménien Catholique, rue de l'Hôpital orthodoxe, Jeitawi, Beirut 2078 5605; tel. (1) 570555; fax (1) 570560; e-mail teyrouzjean@terra.net.lb; f. 1742; established in Beirut since 1932; includes patriarchal diocese of Beirut, with an estimated 10,400 adherents (31 December 2002); Patriarch Most Rev. NERSES BEDROS XIX TARMOUNI; Protosyncellus Rt Rev. VARTAN ACHKARIAN (Titular Bishop of Tokat (Armenian Rite)).

Chaldean Rite

Diocese of Beirut: Evêché Chaldéen de Beyrouth, POB 373, Hazmieh, Beirut; tel. (5) 459088; fax (5) 457731; e-mail chaldepiscopus@hotmail.com; an estimated 10,000 adherents (31 December 2002); Bishop of Beirut MICHEL KASSARJI.

Latin Rite

Apostolic Vicariate of Beirut: Vicariat Apostolique, POB 11-4224, Riad el-Solh, Beirut 1107-2160; tel. (9) 236101; fax (9) 236102; e-mail vicariatlat@hotmail.com; an estimated 15,000 adherents (31 December 2002); Vicar Apostolic PAUL DAHDAH (Titular Archbishop of Arae in Numidia).

Maronite Rite

Patriarchate of Antioch and all the East: Patriarcat Maronite, Bkerké; tel. (9) 915441; fax (9) 938844; e-mail jtawk@bkerke.org.lb; includes patriarchal dioceses of Jounieh, Sarba and Jobbé; the Maronite Church in Lebanon comprises four archdioceses and six dioceses, with an estimated 1,431,983 adherents (31 December 2002); Patriarch Cardinal NASRALLAH PIERRE SFEIR.

Archbishop of Antélias: Most Rev. JOSEPH MOHSEN BÉCHARA, Archevêché Maronite, POB 70400, Antélias; tel. (4) 410020; fax (4) 921313.

Archbishop of Beirut: Most Rev. PAUL YOUSSEF MATAR, Archevêché Maronite, 10 rue Collège de la Sagesse, Achrafieh, Beirut; tel. (1) 561980; fax (1) 561931; also representative of the Holy See for Roman Catholics of the Coptic Rite in Lebanon.

Archbishop of Tripoli: Most Rev. YOUHANNA FOUAD EL-HAGE, Archevêché Maronite, POB 104, rue al-Moutran, Karm Sada, Tripoli; tel. (6) 624324; fax (6) 629393; e-mail rahmat@inco.com.lb.

Archbishop of Tyre: Most Rev. MAROUN KHOURY SADER, Archevêché Maronite, Tyre; tel. (7) 740059; fax (7) 344891.

Melkite Rite

Patriarch of Antioch: Patriarcat Grec-Melkite Catholique, POB 22249, 12 ave az-Zeitoon, Bab Charki, Damascus, Syria; tel. (1) 5441030; fax (1) 5418966; e-mail pat.melk@scs-net.org; the Melkite Church in Lebanon comprises seven archdioceses, with an estimated 385,400 adherents (31 December 2002); The Patriarch of Antioch and all the East, of Alexandria and of Jerusalem Most Rev. GRÉGOIRE III LAHAM.

Archbishop of Ba'albek: Most Rev. CYRILLE SALIM BUSTROS, Archevêché Grec-Catholique, Ba'albek; tel. (8) 370200; fax (8) 373986.

Archbishop of Baniyas: Most Rev. ANTOINE HAYEK, Archevêché de Panéas, Jdeidet Marjeyoun; tel. (3) 814487; fax (7) 830007.

Archbishop of Beirut and Gibail: JOSEPH KALLAS, Archevêché Grec-Melkite-Catholique, POB 11–901, 655 rue de Damas, Beirut; tel. (1) 616104; fax (1) 616109; e-mail agmcb@terra.net.lb.

Archbishop of Saida (Sidon): Most Rev. GEORGES KWAÏTER, Archevêché Grec-Melkite-Catholique, POB 247, rue el-Moutran, Sidon; tel. (7) 720100; fax (7) 722055; e-mail mkwaiter@inco.com.lb.

Archbishop of Tripoli: Most Rev. GEORGE RIASHI, Archevêché Grec-Catholique, rue al-Kanaess, Tripoli; tel. (6) 435989; fax (6) 441716.

Archbishop of Tyre: Most Rev. JEAN ASSAAD HADDAD, Archevêché Grec-Melkite-Catholique, POB 257, Tyre; tel. (7) 740015; fax (7) 349180; e-mail eegc@inco.com.lb.

Archbishop of Zahleh and Furzol: Most Rev. ANDRÉ HADDAD, Archevêché Grec-Melkite-Catholique, Saidat en-Najat, Zahleh; tel. (8) 800333; fax (8) 822406.

Syrian Rite

Patriarchate of Antioch: Patriarcat Syrien Catholique d'Antioche, rue de Damas, POB 116/5087, Beirut 1106-2010; tel. (1) 615892; fax (1) 616573; e-mail psc_lb@yahoo.com; jurisdiction over about 150,000 Syrian Catholics in the Middle East, including (at 31 December 2002) 14,500 in the diocese of Beirut; Patriarch: Most Rev. IGNACE PIERRE ABDEL AHAD VIII; Protosyncellus Mgr GEORGES MASRI.

The Anglican Communion

Within the Episcopal Church in Jerusalem and the Middle East, Lebanon forms part of the diocese of Jerusalem (see the chapter on Israel).

Other Christian Groups

Armenian Apostolic Orthodox: Armenian Catholicosate of Cilicia, POB 70317, Antélias, Beirut, Lebanon; tel. (4) 410001; fax (4) 419724; e-mail cathcil@cathcil.org; internet www.cathcil.org; f. 1441 in Cilicia (now in Turkey), transferred to Antélias, Lebanon, 1930; Leader His Holiness ARAM (KESHISHIAN) I (Catholicos of Cilicia); jurisdiction over an estimated 1m. adherents in Lebanon, Syria, Cyprus, Kuwait, Greece, Iran, the United Arab Emirates, the USA and Canada.

National Evangelical Synod of Syria and Lebanon: POB 70890, Antélias, Beirut; tel. (4) 525030; fax (4) 411184; e-mail nessl@minero.net; 80,000 adherents (2003); Gen. Sec. Rev. JOSEPH QASSAB.

Patriarchate of Antioch and all the East (Greek Orthodox): Patriarcat Grec-Orthodoxe, POB 9, Damascus, Syria; tel. (11) 5424400; fax (11) 5424404; e-mail info@antiochpat.org; internet www.antiochpat.org; Patriarch His Beatitude IGNATIUS (HAZIM) IV.

Patriarchate of Antioch and all the East (Syrian Orthodox): Patriarcat Syrien Orthodoxe, Bab Toma, POB 22260, Damascus, Syria; tel. 5432401; fax 5432400; Patriarch IGNATIUS ZAKKA I IWAS.

Supreme Council of the Evangelical Community in Syria and Lebanon: POB 70/1065, rue Rabieh 34, Antélias; tel. (4) 525036; fax (4) 405490; e-mail suprcoun@minero.net; Pres. Rev. Dr SALIM SAHIOUNY.

Union of the Armenian Evangelical Churches in the Near East: POB 11-377, Beirut; tel. (1) 565628; fax (1) 565629; e-mail uaecne@cyberia.net.lb; f. 1846 in Turkey; comprises about 30 Arme-nian Evangelical Churches in Syria, Lebanon, Egypt, Cyprus, Greece, Iran, Turkey and Australia; 7,500 mems (1990); Pres. Rev. MEGRDICH KARAGOEZIAN; Gen. Sec. SEBOUH TERZIAN.

ISLAM

Shi'a Muslims: Leader Imam Sheikh SAYED MOUSSA AS-SADR (went missing during visit to Libya in August 1978); President of the Supreme Islamic Council of the Shi'a Community of Lebanon, ABD AL-AMIR QABALAN; Beirut.

Sunni Muslims: Grand Mufti of Lebanon, Dar el-Fatwa, rue Ilewi Rushed, Beirut; tel. (1) 422340; Leader SG Sheikh Dr MUHAMMAD RASHID QABBANI.

Druzes: Supreme Spiritual Leader of the Druze Community, Beirut; tel. (1) 341116; Political Leader WALID JOUMBLATT.

Alawites: a schism of Shi'ite Islam; there are an estimated 50,000 Alawites in northern Lebanon, in and around Tripoli.

JUDAISM

Jews: Leader CHAHOUD CHREIM (Beirut).

The Press

DAILIES

Al-Amal (Hope): rue Libérateur, Beirut; tel. (1) 382992; f. 1939; Arabic; organ of the Phalangist Party; Chief Editor ELIAS RABABI; circ. 35,000.

Al-Anwar (Lights): c/o Dar Assayad, POB 11-1038, Hazmieh, Beirut; tel. (5) 456374; fax (5) 452700; e-mail info@alanwar.com; internet www.alanwar.com; f. 1959; Arabic; independent; supplement, Sunday, cultural and social; published by Dar Assayad SAL; Editors-in-Chief MICHEL RAAD, RAFIC KHOURY; circ. 14,419.

Ararat: POB 756, Beirut 175158; tel. and fax (1) 565599; f. 1937; Armenian; Communist; Editor-in-Chief SARKIS NAJARIAN; circ. 5,000.

Aztag: POB 80-860, Shaghzoyan Cultural Centre, Bourj Hammoud; tel. (1) 258526; fax (1) 258529; e-mail aztag@inco.com.lb; internet www.aztagdaily.com; f. 1927; Armenian; Editor-in-Chief SHAHANE KANDARIAN; circ. 6,500.

Al-Bairaq (The Standard): Immeuble Dimitri Trad, rue Issa Maalouf, Ashrafieh, Beirut; tel. (1) 216393; fax (1) 338928; e-mail dalwl@dm.net.lb; f. 1913; Arabic; published by Dar Alf Leila wa Leila Publishing House; politics, society; circ. 10,000.

Bairut: Beirut; f. 1952; Arabic.

Ach-Chaab (The People): POB 5140, Beirut; f. 1961; Arabic; Nationalist; Propr and Editor MUHAMMAD AMIN DUGHAN; circ. 7,000.

Ach-Chams (The Sun): Beirut; f. 1925; Arabic.

Ach-Charq (The East): POB 11-0838, rue Verdun, Riad es-Solh, Beirut; tel. (1) 810820; fax (1) 866105; e-mail info@elshark.com; f. 1926; Arabic; Gen. Dir and Editor-in-Chief AOUNI AL-KAAKI.

Daily Star: 6th Floor, Marine Tower, rue de la Sainte Famille, Achrafieh, Beirut; tel. (1) 587277; fax (1) 561333; e-mail webmaster@dailystar.com.lb; internet www.dailystar.com.lb; f. 1952; English; Publr and Editor-in-Chief JAMIL K. MROUE; circ. 10,550.

Ad-Diyar (The Homeland): an-Nahda Building, Yarze, Beirut; tel. (5) 923830; fax (5) 923773; e-mail aldiyar2002@yahoo.com; f. 1987; Arabic; Propr CHARLES AYYUB.

Ad-Dunya (The World): Beirut; f. 1943; Arabic; political; Chief Editor SULIMAN ABOU ZAID; circ. 25,000.

Al-Hakika (The Truth): Beirut; Arabic; published by Amal.

Al-Hayat (Life): POB 11-987, Immeuble Gargarian, rue Emil Eddé, Hamra, Beirut; tel. (1) 352674; fax (1) 866177; internet www.alhayat.com; f. 1946; Arabic; independent; circ. 196,800.

Al-Jarida (The (News) Paper): POB 220, place Tabaris, Beirut; f. 1953; Arabic; independent; Editor ABDULLAH SKAFF; circ. 22,600.

Al-Jumhuriya (The Republic): Beirut; f. 1924; Arabic.

Journal al-Haddis: POB 300, Jounieh; f. 1927; Arabic; political; Owner GEORGES ARÈGE-SAADÉ.

Al-Khatib (The Speaker): rue Georges Picot, Beirut; Arabic.

Al-Kifah al-Arabi (The Arab Struggle): POB 5158-14, Immeuble Rouche-Shams, Beirut; tel. (1) 860132; fax (1) 808281; internet www.kifaharabi.com; f. 1974; Arabic; political, socialist, Pan-Arab; Publr and Chief Editor WALID HUSSEINI.

Lisan ul-Hal (The Organ): rue Châteaubriand, Beirut; e-mail lebanon@lissan-ul-hal.com; internet www.lissan-ul-hal.com; f. 1877; Arabic; Editor GEBRAN HAYEK; circ. 33,000.

Al-Liwa' (The Standard): POB 11-2402, Beirut; tel. (1) 735749; fax (1) 735742; internet www.aliwaa.com.lb; f. 1963; Arabic; Propr ABD AL-GHANI SALAM; Editor SALAH SALAM; circ. 26,000.

Al-Mustuqbal: Beirut; tel. (1) 797770; fax (1) 797779; e-mail contactus@almustaqbal.com.lb; internet www.almustaqbal.com.lb; f. 1999; Owner RAFIK HARIRI; Editor HANI HAMMOUD; circ. 20,000.

An-Nahar (The Day): Immeuble Cooperative de Presse, rue Banque du Liban, Hamra, Beirut; tel. (1) 340960; fax (1) 344567; e-mail annahar@annahar.com.lb; internet www.annahar.com.lb; f. 1933; Arabic; independent; Pres. and Gen. Man. GEBRAN TUENI; Editor-in-Chief OUNSI EL-HAJJ; circ. 50,000.

An-Nass (The People): POB 4886, ave Fouad Chehab, Beirut; tel. (1) 308695; fax (1) 376610; f. 1959; Arabic; Editor-in-Chief HASSAN YAGHI; circ. 22,000.

An-Nida (The Appeal): Beirut; f. 1959; Arabic; published by the Lebanese Communist Party; Editor KARIM MROUÉ; circ. 10,000.

An-Nidal (The Struggle): Beirut; f. 1939; Arabic.

L'Orient-Le Jour: POB 166495, rue Banque du Liban, Beirut; tel. (1) 340560; e-mail redaction@lorient-lejour.com.lb; internet www .lorient-lejour.com.lb; f. 1942; French; independent; Chair. MICHEL EDDÉ; Dir CAMILLE MENASSA; Editorial Dir AMINE ABOU-KHALED; Editor ISSA GORAÏEB; circ. 23,000.

Rayah (Banner): POB 4101, Beirut; Arabic.

Le Réveil: Beirut; tel. (1) 890700; f. 1977; French; Editor-in-Chief JEAN SHAMI; Dir RAYMOND DAOU; circ. 10,000.

Sada Lubnan (Echo of Lebanon): Beirut; f. 1951; Arabic; Lebanese Pan-Arab; Editor MUHAMMAD BAALBAKI; circ. 25,000.

As-Safir: POB 113/5015, Immeuble as-Safir, rue Monimina, Hamra, Beirut 1103-2010; tel. (1) 350080; fax (1) 349431; e-mail co-ordinator@assafir.com; internet www.assafir.com; f. 1974; Arabic; political; Publr TALAL SALMAN; Editor-in-Chief JOSEPH SAMAHA; circ. 50,000.

Sawt al-Uruba (The Voice of Europe): POB 3537, Beirut; f. 1959; Arabic; organ of the An-Najjadé Party; Editor ADNANE AL-HAKIM.

Le Soir: POB 1470, rue de Syrie, Beirut; f. 1947; French; independent; Dir DIKRAN TOSBATH; Editor ANDRÉ KECATI; circ. 16,500.

Telegraf—Bairut: rue Béchara el-Khoury, Beirut; f. 1930; Arabic; political, economic and social; Editor TOUFIC ASSAD MATNI; circ. 15,500 (5,000 outside Lebanon).

Al-Yaum (Today): Beirut; f. 1937; Arabic; Editor WAFIC MUHAMMAD CHAKER AT-TIBY.

Az-Zamane: Beirut; f. 1947; Arabic.

Zartonk: POB 11-617, rue Nahr Ibrahim, Beirut; tel. and fax (1) 566709; e-mail zartonk@dm.net.lb; f. 1937; Armenian; official organ of Armenian Liberal Democratic Party; Man. Editor BAROUYR H. AGHBASHIAN.

WEEKLIES

Al-Alam al-Lubnani (The Lebanese World): POB 462, Beirut; f. 1964; Arabic, English, Spanish, French; politics, literature and social economy; Editor-in-Chief FAYEK KHOURY; Gen. Editor CHEIKH FADI GEMAYEL; circ. 45,000.

Achabaka (The Net): c/o Dar Assayad SAL, POB 11-1038, Hazmieh, Beirut; tel. (5) 450406; fax (5) 452700; f. 1956; Arabic; society and features; Founder SAID FREIHA; Editor GEORGE IBRAHIM EL-KHOURY; circ. 139,775.

Al-Ahad (Sunday): Beirut; Arabic; political; organ of Hezbollah; Editor RIAD TAHA; circ. 32,000.

Al-Akhbar (The News): Beirut; f. 1954; Arabic; published by the Lebanese Communist Party; circ. 21,000.

Al-Anwar Supplement: c/o Dar Assayad, POB 1038, Hazmieh, Beirut; tel. (5) 450406; fax (5) 452700; cultural-social; every Sunday; supplement to daily *Al-Anwar*; Editor ISSAM FREIHA; circ. 90,000.

Assayad (The Hunter): C/o Dar Assayad, POB 11-1038, Hazmieh, Beirut; tel. (5) 450406; fax (5) 452700; f. 1943; Arabic; political and social; circ. 76,192.

Dabbour: Place du Musée, Beirut; tel. (1) 616770; fax (1) 616771; e-mail addabbour@yahoo.com; internet www.addabbour.com; f. 1922; Arabic; Editor JOSEPH RICHARD MUKARZEL; circ. 12,000.

Ad-Dyar: Immeuble Bellevue, rue Verdun, Beirut; f. 1941; Arabic; political; circ. 46,000.

Al-Hadaf (The Target): Beirut; tel. (1) 420554; f. 1969; organ of Popular Front for the Liberation of Palestine (PFLP); Arabic; Editor-in-Chief SABER MOHI ED-DIN; circ. 40,000.

Al-Hawadess (Events): POB 1281, rue Clémenceau, Beirut; published from London (183–185 Askew Rd, W12 9AX); tel. (20) 8740-4500; fax (20) 8749-9781; f. 1911; Arabic; news; Editor-in-Chief MELHIM KAVAM; circ. 120,000.

Al-Hiwar (Dialogue): Beirut; f. 2000; Arabic; Chair. FOUAD MAKHZOUMI; Editor-in-Chief SAM MOUNASSA.

Al-Hurriya (Freedom): Beirut; f. 1960; Arabic; organ of the Democratic Front for the Liberation of Palestine; Editor DAOUD TALHAME; circ. 30,000.

Al-Iza'a (Broadcasting): POB 462, rue Selim Jazaerly, Beirut; f. 1938; Arabic; politics, art, literature and broadcasting; Editor FAYEK KHOURY; circ. 11,000.

Al-Jumhur (The Public): POB 1834, Moussaitbé, Beirut; f. 1936; Arabic; illustrated weekly news magazine; Editor FARID ABU SHAHLA; circ. 45,000, of which over 20,000 outside Lebanon.

Kul Shay' (Everything): POB 3250, rue Béchara el-Khoury, Beirut; Arabic.

Magazine: POB 1404, Immeuble Sayegh, rue Sursock, Beirut; tel. (1) 202070; fax (1) 202663; e-mail info@magazine.com.lb; internet www.magazine.com.lb; f. 1956; French; political, economic and social; published by Editions Orientales SAL; Pres. CHARLES ABOU ADAL; circ. 18,000.

Massis: c/o Patriarcat Arménien Catholique, rue de l'Hôpital Libanais Jeitawi, 2400 Beirut; Armenian; Catholic; Editor Fr ANTRANIK GRANIAN; circ. 2,500.

Al-Moharrir (The Liberator): Beirut; f. 1962; Arabic; circ. 87,000; Gen. Man. WALID ABOU ZAHR.

Monday Morning: POB 165612, Immeuble Dimitri Trad, rue Issa Maalouf, Ashrafieh, Beirut; tel. (1) 200961; fax (1) 335079; e-mail mondaymorning@mmorning.com; internet www.mmorning.com; f. 1971; political and social affairs; published by Dar Alf Leila wa Leila Publishing House; circ. 15,000.

Al-Ousbou' al-Arabi (Arab Week): POB 1404, Immeuble Sayegh, rue Sursock, Beirut; tel. (1) 202070; fax (1) 202663; e-mail info@ arabweek.com.lb; internet www.arabweek.com.lb; f. 1959; Arabic; political and social; published by Editions Orientales SAL; Pres. CHARLES ABOU ADAL; circ. 88,407 (circulates throughout the Arab World).

Phoenix: POB 113222, Beirut; tel. (1) 346800; fax (1) 346359; for women; published by Al-Hasna.

Ar-Rassed: Beirut; Arabic; Editor GEORGE RAJJI.

Revue du Liban (Lebanon Review): Immeuble Dimitri Trad, rue Issa Maalouf, Achrafieh, Beirut; tel. (1) 338930; fax (1) 335079; e-mail rdl@rdl.com.lb; internet www.rdl.com.lb; f. 1928; French; political, social, cultural; published by Dar Alf Leila wa Leila Publishing House; Publr MELHEM KARAM; Gen. Man. MICHEL MISK; circ. 22,000.

Sabah al-Khair (Good Morning): Beirut; Arabic; published by the Syrian Nationalist Party.

Samar: c/o Dar Assayad, POB 11-1038, Hazmieh, Beirut; tel. (5) 452700; fax (5) 452957; Arabic; for teenagers; published by Dar Assayad SAL.

Ash-Shira' (The Sail): POB 13-5250, Beirut; tel. (1) 70300; fax (1) 866050; Arabic; Editor HASSAN SABRA; circ. 40,000.

OTHER SELECTED PERIODICALS

Alam at-Tijarat (Business World): Immeuble Strand, rue Hamra, Beirut; f. 1965; monthly; commercial; Editor NADIM MAKDISI; international circ. 17,500.

Al Computer, Communications and Electronics: c/o Dar Assayad, POB 1038, Hazmieh, Beirut; tel. (5) 456374; fax (5) 452700; f. 1984; monthly; computer technology; published by Dar Assayad International; Chief Editor ANTOINE BOUTROS.

Arab Construction World: POB 13–5121, Chouran, Beirut 1102-2802; tel. (1) 352413; fax (1) 352419; e-mail info@acwmag.com; internet www.acwmag.com; f. 1985; every two months; English and Arabic; published by Chatila Publishing House; Publr FATHI CHATILA; Editor-in-Chief RIYADH CHEHAB; circ. 10,614.

Arab Defense Journal: c/o Dar Assayad, POB 11-1038, Hazmieh, Beirut; tel. (5) 456373; fax (5) 452700; e-mail assayad@inco.com.lb; f. 1976; monthly; military; published by Dar Assayad International; Chief Editor Gen. WADIH JUBRAN; circ. 24,325 (Jan.–June 1999).

Arab Economist: POB 11–6068, Beirut; monthly; published by Centre for Economic, Financial and Social Research and Documentation SAL; Chair. HEKMAT KASSIR.

Arab Water World: POB 13–5121, Chouran, Beirut 1102-2802; tel. (1) 352413; fax (1) 352419; e-mail info@awwmag.com; internet www .awwmag.com; f. 1977; every two months; English and Arabic;

published by Chatila Publishing House; Editor-in-Chief FATHI CHATILA; circ. 8,443.

The Arab World: POB 567, Jounieh; tel. and fax (9) 935096; e-mail maamanculture@lynx.net.lb; internet www.biblib.com; f. 1985; 24 a year; published by Dar Naaman lith-Thaqafa; Editor NAJI NAAMAN.

L'Argus de l'Economie Libanaise: POB 16–5403, rue Arguse Sodeco, Beirut; tel. (1) 219113; e-mail argus@cyperia.net.lb; monthly; Arabic, French and English; economic bulletin; circ. 1,000.

Le Commerce du Levant: Kantari, Immeuble Kantari Corner, 11e étage, Beirut 2021-2502; tel. (1) 362361; fax (1) 360379; e-mail lecommerce@inco.com.lb; internet www.lecommercedulevant.com; f. 1929; monthly; French; commercial and financial; publ. by Société de la Presse Economique; Chief Editor NICOLAS SBIEH; circ. 15,000.

Déco: POB 11–1404, Immeuble Sayegh, rue Sursock, Beirut; tel. (1) 202070; fax (1) 202663; e-mail info@decomag.com.lb; internet www.decomag.com.lb; f. 2000; quarterly; French; architecture and interior design; published by Editions Orientales SAL; Pres. CHARLES ABOU ADAL; circ. 14,000.

Fairuz Lebanon: c/o Dar Assayad, POB 11-1038, Hazmieh, Beirut; tel. (5) 456374; fax (5) 452700; f. 1982; monthly; Arabic; for women; also *Fairuz International*; published by Dar Assayad International; Chief Editor ELHAM FREIHA.

Fann at-Tasswir: POB 16-5947, Beirut; tel. (1) 498950; monthly; Arabic; photography.

Al Fares: c/o Dar Assayad, POB 11-1038, Hazmieh, Beirut; tel. (5) 456374; fax (5) 452700; f. 1991; monthly; Arabic; men's interest; published by Dar Assayad International; Chief Editor ELHAM FREIHA.

Al-Idari (The Manager): c/o Dar Assayad, POB 11-1038, Hamzieh, Beirut; tel. (5) 456374; fax (5) 452700; f. 1975; monthly; Arabic; business management, economics, finance and investment; published by Dar Assayad International; Pres. and Gen. Man. BASSAM FREIHA; Chief Editor HASSAN EL-KHOURY; circ. 31,867.

Al-Intilak (Outbreak): Al-Intilak Printing and Publishing House, POB 4958, Beirut; tel. (1) 302018; e-mail tonehnme@cyberia.net.lb; f. 1960; monthly; Arabic; literary; Chief Editor MICHEL NEHME.

Al-Jeel (The Generation): Beirut; monthly; Arabic; literary.

Al-Khalij Business Magazine: POB 11-8440, Beirut; tel. (1) 345568; fax (1) 602089; e-mail massaref@dm.net.lb; f. 1981; fmrly based in Kuwait; 6 a year; Arabic; Editor-in-Chief ZULFICAR KOBEISSI; circ. 16,325.

Lebanese and Arab Economy: POB 11-1801, Sanayeh, Beirut; tel. (1) 744160; fax (1) 353395; e-mail info@.ccib.org.lb; internet www.ccib.org.lb; f. 1951; monthly; Arabic, English and French; Publr Beirut Chamber of Commerce and Industry.

Majallat al-Iza'at al-Lubnaniat (Lebanese Broadcasting Magazine): c/o Radio Lebanon, rue des Arts et Métiers, Beirut; tel. (1) 863016; f. 1959; monthly; Arabic; broadcasting affairs.

Al-Mar'a: POB 1404, Immeuble Sayegh, rue Sursock, Beirut; tel. (1) 202070; fax (1) 202663; e-mail info@almara.com.lb; internet www.ediori.com.lb; f. 2000; monthly; Arabic; for women; published by Editions Orientales SAL; Pres. CHARLES ABOU ADAL; circ. 20,000.

Middle East Food: POB 13-5121, Chouran, Beirut 1102-2802; tel. (1) 352413; fax (1) 352419; e-mail info@mefmag.com; internet www.mefmag.com; every two months; published by Chatila Publishing House; Editor-in-Chief SAAD ED-DIN CHEHAB; circ. 9,341.

Al-Mouktataf (The Selection): Beirut; monthly; Arabic; general.

Al-Mukhtar (Reader's Digest): Beirut; monthly; general interest.

Qitaboul A'lamil A'rabi (The Arab World Book): POB 567, Jounieh; tel. and fax (9) 935096; e-mail naaman@lynx.net.lb; internet www.biblib.com; f. 1991; 6 a year; Arabic; published by Dar Naaman lith-Thaqafa; Editor NAJI NAAMAN.

Rijal al-Amal (Businessmen): Beirut; f. 1966; monthly; Arabic; business; Publr and Editor-in-Chief MAHIBA AL-MALKI; circ. 16,250.

Scoop: POB 165612, rue Issa Maalouf, Sioufi, Beirut; tel. (1) 482185; fax (1) 490307; weekly; general interest; published by La Régie Libanaise de Publicité; circ. 100,000.

As-Sihafa wal I'lam (Press and Information): POB 567, Jounieh; tel. and fax (9) 935096; e-mail naamanculture@lynx.net.lb; internet www.biblib.com; f. 1987; 12 a year; Arabic; published by Dar Naaman lith-Thaqafa; Editor NAJI NAAMAN.

Siyassa was Strategia (Politics and Strategy): POB 567, Jounieh; tel. and fax (9) 935096; e-mail naamanculture@lynx.net.lb; internet www.biblib.com; f. 1981; 36 a year; Arabic; published by Dar Naaman lith-Thaqafa; Editor NAJI NAAMAN.

Tabibok (Your Doctor): POB 90434, Beirut; tel. in Syria (963-11) 2212980; fax (963-11) 3738901; e-mail sskabbani@mail.sy; f. 1956; monthly; Arabic; medical, social, scientific; Editor Dr SAMI KABBANI; circ. 90,000.

Takarir Wa Khalfiyat (Background Reports): c/o Dar Assayad, POB 11-1038, Hamzieh, Beirut; tel. (5) 456374; fax (5) 452700; f. 1976; tri-monthly; Arabic; political and economic bulletin; published by Dar Assayad SAL.

At-Tarik (The Road): Beirut; monthly; Arabic; cultural and theoretical; published by the Parti communiste libanais; circ. 5,000.

Travaux et Jours (Works and Days): Rectorat de l'Université Saint-Joseph, rue de Damas, Beirut; tel. (1) 611172; fax (1) 423369; e-mail travauxetjours@usj.edu.lb; internet www.usj.edu.lb; f. 1961; publ. twice a year; French; political, social and cultural; Editor MOUNIR CHAMOUN.

Welcome to Lebanon and the Middle East: Beirut; f. 1959; monthly; English; on entertainment, touring and travel; Editor SOUHAIL TOUFIK ABOU JAMRA; circ. 6,000.

NEWS AGENCIES

National News Agency (NNA): Hamra, Beirut; tel. (1) 342290; fax (1) 746031; e-mail nna-leb@nna-leb.gov.lb; internet www.nna-leb.gov.lb; state-owned; Dir KHALIL KHOURY.

Foreign Bureaux

Agence France-Presse (AFP): POB 11-1461, Immeuble Najjar, rue de Rome, Beirut; tel. (1) 347461; fax (1) 350318; e-mail afp_bey@inco.com.lb; internet www.afp.com; Dir PASCAL MALLET.

Agenzia Nazionale Stampa Associata (ANSA) (Italy): POB 113/6545, 2e étage, Immeuble Safieddine, rue Rashid Karame, Beirut; tel. (1) 787237; fax (1) 787236; e-mail ansa@sodetel.net.lb; Correspondent FURIO MORRONI.

Associated Press (AP) (USA): POB 3780, Immeuble Shaker et Oueini, place Riad es-Solh, Beirut; tel. (1) 985190; fax (1) 985196; e-mail info@ap.org; internet www.ap.org; Correspondent SAM F. GHATTAS.

Kuwait News Agency (KUNA): 8th Floor, Arsku Centre, Beirut; tel. (1) 354377; fax (1) 602088; e-mail kunabt@inco.com.lb; Bureau Chief SULTAN AL-MADIRI.

Kyodo Tsushin (Japan): POB 13-5060, Immeuble Makarem, rue Makdessi, Ras Beirut, Beirut; tel. (1) 863861; Correspondent IBRAHIM KHOURY.

Middle East News Agency (MENA) (Egypt): POB 2268, rue Mneimneh, Sarolla Descent, Hamra, Beirut; tel. (1) 754142; fax (1) 754141; e-mail mena_lb@sodetel.net.lb; internet mena.org.eg.

Reuters (United Kingdom): POB 11-1006, Immeuble Hibat al-Maarad, place Riad es-Solh, Beirut; tel. (1) 983885; fax (1) 983889; e-mail samia.nakhoul@reuters.com; internet www.reuters.com; Bureau Chief SAMIA NAKHOUL.

Rossiiskoye Informatsionnoye Agentstvo—Novosti (RIA—Novosti) (Russia): POB 11-1086, Beirut; tel. (1) 300219; fax (1) 314168; e-mail novosti@cyberia.net.lb; Dir KONSTANTIN MAXIMOV.

United Press International (UPI) (USA): Suite 302, 3rd Floor, Block D, Gefinor Centre, Clemenceau, Beirut; tel. (1) 745971; fax (1) 745973; internet www.upi.com; Bureau Man. RIAD KAJ.

Xinhua (New China) News Agency (People's Republic of China): POB 114-5075, Beirut; tel. (1) 830359.

BTA (Bulgaria), INA (Iraq), JANA (Libya), Prensa Latina (Cuba) and Saudi Press Agency (SPA) are also represented in Lebanon.

PRESS ASSOCIATION

Lebanese Press Order: POB 3084, ave Saeb Salam, Beirut; tel. (1) 865519; fax (1) 865516; e-mail mail@pressorder.org; internet www.pressorder.org; f. 1911; 18 mems; Pres. MUHAMMAD AL-BAALBAKI; Vice-Pres. GEORGES SKAFF; Sec. ABD AL-KARIM EL-KHALIL.

Publishers

Dar al-Adab: POB 11-4123, Beirut; tel. and fax (1) 861633; e-mail d_aladab@cyberia.net.lb; f. 1953; dictionaries, literary and general; Man. RANA IDRISS; Editor-in-Chief SAMAH IDRISS.

Arab Institute for Research and Publishing (Al-Mouasasah al-Arabiyah Lildirasat Walnashr): POB 11-5760, Beirut; tel. and fax (1) 751438; e-mail mkayyali@nets.com.jo; f. 1969; Dir. MAHER KAYYALI; works in Arabic and English.

Arab Scientific Publishers BP: POB 13-5574, Immeuble Ein at-Tenah Reem, rue Sakiet al-Janzir, Beirut; tel. (1) 811385; fax (1) 860138; e-mail bchebaro@asp.com.lb; internet www.asp.com.lb; computer science, biological sciences, cookery, travel; Pres. BASSAM CHEBARO.

Dar Assayad Group (SAL and International): POB 11-1038, Hazmieh, Beirut; tel. (5) 457260; fax (5) 452700; e-mail assayad@

inco.com.lb; internet www.darassayad.net; f. 1943; Dar Assayad International founded in 1983; publishes in Arabic *Al-Anwar* (daily, plus weekly supplement), *Assayad* (weekly), *Achabaka* (weekly), *Background Reports* (three a month), *Arab Defense Journal* (monthly), *Fairuz Lebanon* (monthly, plus international monthly edition), *Al-Idari* (monthly), *Al Computer, Communications and Electronics* (monthly), *Al-Fares* (monthly); has offices and correspondents in Arab countries and most parts of the world; CEO BASSAM FREIHA; Gen. Man. ELHAM FREIHA.

Chatila Publishing House: POB 13-5121, Chouran, Beirut 1102-2802; tel. (1) 352413; fax (1) 352419; e-mail info@chatilapublishing .com; internet www.chatilapublishing.com; publishes *Arab Construction World* (every two months), *Arab Water World* (every two months), *Middle East Food* (every two months), *Middle East and World Food Directory* (bi-annual), *Middle East and World Water Directory* (bi-annual).

Edition Française pour le Monde Arabe (EDIFRAMO): POB 113-6140, Immeuble Elissar, rue Bliss, Beirut; tel. (1) 862437; Man. TAHSEEN S. KHAYAT.

Editions Orientales SAL: POB 1404, Immeuble Sayegh, rue Sursock, Beirut; tel. (1) 202070; fax (1) 202663; e-mail info@ediori.com .lb; internet www.ediori.com.lb; political and social newspapers and magazines; Pres. and Editor-in-Chief CHARLES ABOU ADAL.

Geoprojects SARL: POB 113–5294, Immeuble Barakat, 13 rue Jeanne d'Arc, Beirut; tel. (1) 344236; fax (1) 353000; e-mail allprint@ cyberia.net.lb; f. 1978; regional issues, travel; Man. Dir TAHSEEN KHAYAT.

Dar el-Ilm Lilmalayin: POB 1085, Centre Metco, rue Mar Elias, Beirut 2045–8402; tel. (1) 306666; fax (1) 701657; e-mail malayin@ malayin.com; internet www.malayin.com; f. 1945; dictionaries, encyclopaedias, reference books, textbooks, Islamic cultural books; CEO TAREF OSMAN.

Institute for Palestine Studies, Publishing and Research Organization (IPS): POB 11-7164, rue Anis Nsouli, off Verdun, Beirut; tel. and fax (1) 868387; e-mail ipsbrt@palestine-studies.org; internet palestine-studies.org; f. 1963; independent non-profit Arab research organization; to promote better understanding of the Palestine problem and the Arab–Israeli conflict; publishes books, reprints, research papers, etc.; Chair. Dr HISHAM NASHABE; Exec. Sec. Prof. WALID KHALIDI.

The International Documentary Center of Arab Manuscripts: POB 2668, Immeuble Hanna, Ras Beirut, Beirut; e-mail alafaq@ cyberia.net.lb; f. 1965; publishes and reproduces ancient and rare Arabic texts; Propr ZOUHAIR BAALBAKI.

Dar al-Kashaf: POB 112091, rue Assad Malhamee, Beirut; tel. (1) 296805; f. 1930; publishers of *Al-Kashaf* (Arab Youth Magazine), maps, atlases and business books; printers and distributors; Propr M. A. FATHALLAH.

Khayat Book and Publishing Co SARL: 90–94 rue Bliss, Beirut; Middle East, Islam, history, medicine, social sciences, education, fiction; Man. Dir PAUL KHAYAT.

Dar al-Kitab al-Lubnani: Beirut; tel. (1) 861563; fax (1) 351433; f. 1929; Man. Dir HASSAN EZ-ZEIN.

Librairie du Liban Publishers: POB 11-9232, Beirut; tel. (9) 217944; fax (9) 217734; e-mail psayegh@librairie-du-liban.com.lb; internet www.librairie-du-liban.com.lb; f. 1944; publisher of children's books, dictionaries and reference books; distributor of books in English and French; Man. Dirs HABIB SAYEGH, PIERRE SAYEGH.

Dar al-Maaref Liban SARL: Beirut; tel. (1) 931243; f. 1959; children's books and textbooks in Arabic; Man. Dir Dr FOUAD IBRAHIM; Gen. Man. JOSEPH NACHOU.

Dar al-Machreq SARL: POB 946, Beirut; tel. (1) 202423; e-mail machreq@cyberia.net.lb; internet www.darelmachreq.com.lb; f. 1848; religion, art, Arabic and Islamic literature, history, languages, science, philosophy, school books, dictionaries and periodicals; Man. Dir CAMILLE HÉCHAIMÉ.

Dar Naamān lith-Thaqāfa: POB 567, Jounieh; tel. and fax (9) 935096; e-mail naamanculture@lynx.net.lb; internet www.biblib .com; f. 1979; publishes *Mawsou'atul 'Alamil 'Arabiyyil Mu'asser* (Encyclopaedia of Contemporary Arab World), *Mawsou'atul Waqa'e'il 'Arabiyya* (Encyclopaedia of Arab Events), *Qitāboul A'lamil A'rabi, Siyassa was Strategia, As-Sahafa wal I'lam* in Arabic and *The Arab World* in English; Propr NAJI NAAMAN; Exec. Man. MARCELLE AL-ASHKAR.

Dar an-Nahar SAL: POB 11-226, rue de Rome, Hamra, Beirut; tel. (1) 347176; fax (1) 738159; e-mail fadit@annahar.com.lb; f. 1967; a Pan-Arab publishing house; Pres. GHASSAN TUÉNI; Dir FADI TUÉNI.

Naufal Group SARL: POB 11-2161, Immeuble Naufal, rue Sourati, Beirut; tel. (1) 354898; fax (1) 354394; e-mail naufalgroup@terra.net .lb; f. 1970; subsidiary cos Macdonald Middle East Sarl, Les Editions Arabes; encyclopaedias, fiction, children's books, history, law and literature; Man. Dir TONY NAUFAL.

Publitec Publications: POB 166142, Beirut; tel. (1) 495401; fax (1) 493330; e-mail publitecpublications@hotmail.com; internet www .whoswhointhearabworld.info; f. 1965; publishes *Who's Who in Lebanon* and *Who's Who in the Arab World*; Pres. CHARLES GEDEON; Man. KRIKOR AYVAZIAN.

Dar ar-Raed al-Lubnani: POB 93, Immeuble Kamal al-Assad, Hazmieh, Sammouri, Beirut; tel. (5) 450757; f. 1971; CEO RAYED SAMMOURI.

Rihani Printing and Publishing House: Beirut; f. 1963; Propr ALBERT RIHANI; Man. DAOUD STEPHAN.

World Book Publishing: POB 11-3176, rue Emile Eddé, Beirut; tel. (1) 349370; fax (1) 351226; e-mail rafic@wbpbooks.com; internet www.arabook.com; f. 1929; literature, education, philosophy, current affairs, self-help, children's books; Chair. SAID EZ-ZEIN; Man. Dir RAFIC EZ-ZEIN.

Broadcasting and Communications

TELECOMMUNICATIONS

Regulatory Authority

Direction Générale des Télécommunications pour l'Exploitation et la Maintenance: Ministry of Telecommunications (see above); Dir-Gen. ABDUL M. YOUSSEF.

Service Providers

France-Télécom Mobile Liban (FTML): POB 50257, Beirut; tel. (3) 391850; fax (3) 391859; internet www.ftml.com.lb; f. 1994; operates Cellis (see below); Chair. and Gen. Man. SALAH BOURAAD.

Cellis: Beirut; internet www.cellis.com.lb; f. 1995; provides mobile cellular telephone services.

LibanCell SAL: POB 136406, Immeuble LibanCell, ave Charles Hélou, Beirut; tel. (1) 566111; fax (1) 564184; e-mail info@libancell .com.lb; internet www.libancell.com.lb; provides mobile cellular telephone services; Chair. HUSSEIN RIFAI.

BROADCASTING

Radio

Radio Liban: rue Arts et Métiers, Beirut; tel. (1) 346880; part of the Ministry of Information; f. 1937; Dir-Gen. QASSEM HAGE ALI.

The Home Service broadcasts in Arabic on short wave, and the Foreign Service broadcasts in Portuguese, Armenian, Arabic, Spanish, French and English.

Television

Lebanese Broadcasting Corporation (LBC) Sat Ltd: POB 111, Zouk; tel. (9) 850850; fax (9) 850916; e-mail lbcsat@lbcsat.com.lb; internet www.lbcsat.com; f. 1985 as Lebanese Broadcasting Corporation International; name changed 1996; operates satellite channel on Arabsat 2A; programmes in Arabic, French and English; Chair. Sheikh PIERRE ED-DAHER.

Télé-Liban (TL) SAL: POB 11-5055, Hazmieh, 4848 Beirut; tel. and fax (1) 793000; fax (1) 950286; e-mail tl@tele-liban.com.lb; f. 1959; commercial service; programmes in Arabic, French and English on three channels; privatization pending in 2001; Chair. and Dir-Gen. IBRAHIM EL-KHOURY; Dep. Dir-Gen. MUHAMMAD S. KARIMEH.

Future Television: White House, rue Spears, Sanayeh, Beirut; tel. (1) 355355; fax (1) 753434; e-mail future@future.com.lb; internet www.future.com.lb; commercial; privately-owned; Owner RAFIK HARIRI; Gen. Man. NADIM AL-MONLA.

Al-Manar (Lighthouse): rue Abd an-Nour, Haret Hreik, Beirut; tel. (1) 276000; fax (1) 555953; e-mail info@manartv.com; internet www .manartv.com; f. 1991; television station owned by Lebanese Communication Group (LCG) and partly controlled by Hezbollah; operates satellite channel since May 2000; Chair. of Bd NAYEF KRAYEM.

During 1996–98 the Government took measures to close down unlicensed private broadcasters, and to restrict the activities of those licensed to operate. In particular, the broadcasting of news and political programmes by private satellite television channels was banned.

Finance

(cap. = capital; dep. = deposits; res = reserves; m. = million;
brs = branches)

BANKING

Beirut was, for many years, the leading financial and commercial centre in the Middle East, but this role was destroyed by the civil conflict. To restore the city as a regional focus for investment banking is a key element of the Government's reconstruction plans.

Central Bank

Banque du Liban: POB 11-5544, rue Masraf Loubnane, Beirut; tel. (1) 750000; fax (1) 747600; e-mail bdlit@bdl.gov.lb; internet www.bdl .gov.lb; f. 1964 as successor in Lebanon to the Banque de Syrie et du Liban; cap. 1,914,036m. (Dec. 2003), dep. £L12,322,000m. (Dec. 2001); Gov. Riad Salameh; 9 brs.

Principal Commercial Banks

Allied Bank SAL: POB 113-7165, Allied House Bldg, ave Charles Malek, St Nicolas, Achrafieh, Beirut; tel. (1) 326757; fax (1) 200660; internet www.alliedbank.com.lb; f. 1962; renamed as above following takeover by Groupe Méditerranée in 2001; cap. £L15,000m., res £L12,911m., dep. £L348,859m. (Dec. 2001); Chair. and Gen. Man. Mustafa H. Razian; 14 brs.

Al Mawarid Bank SAL: POB 113-6260, Immeuble Yared, 3e étage, rue Abd al-Aziz, Beirut; tel. (1) 350612; fax (1) 744277; e-mail mail@ almawarid.com.lb; internet www.almawarid.com.lb; f. 1980; cap. £L12,500m., res £L3,146m., dep. £L620,742m. (June 2003); Chair. and Gen. Man. Salim Kheireddine; 12 brs.

Arab Finance House (AFH): POB 11-273, Riad es-Solh, Beirut 1107 2020; tel. (1) 329595; fax (1) 329797; e-mail info@ arabfinancehouse.com; internet www.arabfinancehouse.com; f. 2004; first Islamic bank in Lebanon; commercial and investment banking; cap. US $60m.

Bank of Beirut SAL: POB 11-7354, Bank of Beirut SAL Bldg, Foch St, Beirut Central District, Beirut; tel. and fax (1) 983999; e-mail executive@bankofbeirut.com.lb; internet www.bankofbeirut.com.lb; f. 1973; absorbed Transorient Bank 1999, Beirut Riyad Bank 2003; cap. £L45,600m. (Dec. 2003), res £L107,208m., dep. £L2,458,020m. (Dec. 2000); Chair. and Gen. Man. Salim G. Sfeir; 41 brs.

Bank of Beirut and the Arab Countries SAL: POB 11-1536, Immeuble de la Banque, 250 rue Clémenceau, Riad es-Solh, Beirut 1107 2080; tel. (1) 366630; fax (1) 374299; e-mail marketing@bbac .com.lb; internet www.bbac.net; f. 1956; cap. £L72,000m., res £L54,142m., dep. £L2,092,817m. (Dec. 2000); Chair. and Gen. Man. Ghassan T. Assaf; 30 brs.

Bank of Kuwait and the Arab World SAL: POB 113-6248, Immeuble Belle Vue, Ain at-Tineh, Verdun, Beirut; tel. and fax (1) 866306; e-mail bkaw@sodetel.net.lb; f. 1959; cap. £L28,000m., res £L6,882m., dep. £L472,647m. (Dec. 2003); Chair. and Gen. Man. Abdul Razzak Achour; 13 brs.

Bank Al-Madina SAL: POB 113-7221, Immeuble Bank Al-Madina, rue Commodore, Hamra, Beirut; tel. (1) 351296; fax (1) 343762; e-mail intdep@bankal-madina.com; internet www.bankal-madina .com; f. 1982; cap. £L45,540m., res £3,017m., dep. £L868,243m. (Dec. 2001); Hon. Chair. and Gen. Man. Dr Adnan Abou Ayyash; Chair. and Gen. Man. Sheikh Ibrahim Abou Ayyash; 18 brs.

Banque Audi SAL: POB 11-2560, Riad es-Solh, Beirut 1107 2808; tel. (1) 994000; fax (1) 990555; e-mail bkaudi@audi.com.lb; internet www.audi.com.lb; f. 1962; acquired Orient Credit Bank 1997 and Banque Nasr 1998; became part of Audi-Saradar Group in 2004; cap. £L45,799m., dep. £L6,388,818m. (Dec. 2002); Chair. and Gen. Man. Raymond W. Audi; 66 brs.

Banque de Crédit National SAL: POB 110-204, Centre Gefinor, Bloc B, 15e étage, rue Clémenceau, Beirut; tel. (1) 752777; fax (1) 752555; e-mail bcnsafra@dm.net.lb; f. 1920; cap. £L11,000m., res £L2,443m., dep. £L17,809m. (Dec. 1998); Pres., Chair. and Gen. Man. Charles A. Junod.

Banque de l'Industrie et du Travail SAL: POB 11-3948, Riad es-Solh, Beirut 1107 2150; tel. (4) 712539; fax (4) 712538; e-mail international@bitbank.com.lb; internet www.bitbank.com.lb; f. 1960; cap. £L4,000m., res £L2,207m., dep. £L369,080m. (Dec. 2002); Chair. and Gen. Man. Sheikh Fouad Jamil el-Khazen; Dir and Gen. Man. Nabil N. Khairallah; 12 brs.

Banque Libano-Française SAL: POB 11-0808, Tour Liberty, rue de Rome, Beirut 1107-2804; tel. (1) 791332; fax (1) 340350; e-mail info@eblf.com; internet www.eblf.com; f. 1967; cap. £L100,000m., res £L214,794m., dep. £L4,584,240m. (Dec. 2002); Chair. and Gen. Man. Farid Raphael; 29 brs.

Banque de la Méditerranée SAL: POB 11-348, 482 rue Clémenceau, Beirut 2022 9302; tel. (1) 373937; fax (1) 362706; f. 1944; cap. £L530,000m., res £L50,120m., dep. £L6,330,253m. (Dec. 2002); Pres., Chair. and Gen. Man. Dr Mustafa H. Razian; 49 brs.

Banque Misr-Liban SAL: rue Riad es-Solh, Beirut 1107 2010; tel. (1) 980399; fax (1) 980604; e-mail mail@bml.com.lb; internet www .bml.com.lb; f. 1929; cap. £L27,000m. (Dec. 2002), res £L22,424m., dep. £L653,678m. (Dec. 2003); Chair. Muhammad Barakat; Gen. Man. Muhammad Zahran; 15 brs.

Banque Saradar SAL: POB 11-1121, Beirut 1107-2805; tel. (4) 416804; fax (4) 404494; e-mail saradar@saradar.com; internet www .saradar.com; f. 1948; became part of Audi-Saradar Group in 2004; cap. £L40,000m.(Dec. 2000), res £L110,000m., dep. £L2,092,000m. (Dec. 2002); Chair. and Gen. Man. Mario Joe Saradar; 8 brs.

BEMO (Banque Européenne pour le Moyen-Orient) SAL: POB 16-6353, Immeuble BEMO, place Sassine, ave Elias Sarkis, Achrafieh, Beirut; tel. (1) 200505; fax (1) 330780; e-mail bemosal@dm.net .lb; internet www.bemo.com.lb; f. 1964; cap. £L44,055m., res £L12,175m., dep. £L575,751m. (Dec. 2002); Pres. and Gen. Man. Henry Y. Obegi; 6 brs.

BLOM Bank SAL: POB 11-1912, Immeuble BLOM Bank, rue Rachid Karameh, Verdun, Beirut 1107 2807; tel. (1) 743300; fax (1) 738946; e-mail blommail@blom.com.lb; internet www.blom.com.lb; f. 1951 as Banque du Liban et d'Outre-Mer; renamed as above 2000; cap. £L192,500m., res £L412,329m., dep. £L9,685,473m. (Dec. 2002); Pres., Chair. and Gen. Man. Dr Naaman Azhari; Vice-Chair. and Gen. Man. Samer Azhari; 42 brs.

Byblos Bank SAL: POB 11-5605, ave Elias Sarkis, Achrafieh, Beirut; tel. (1) 335200; fax (1) 335540; e-mail byblosbk@byblosbank .com.lb; internet www.byblosbank.com; f. 1959; merged with Banque Beyrouth pour le Commerce SAL 1997; acquired Byblos Bank Europe SA 1998, Wedge Bank Middle East SAL 2001 and ABN AMRO Bank Lebanon 2002; cap. £L246,028m., res £L175,728m., dep. £L7,069,903m. (Dec. 2002); Pres., Chair. and Gen. Man. Dr François Semaan Bassil; 69 brs in Lebanon, 4 abroad.

Creditbank SAL: POB 16-5795, Immeuble Crédit Bancaire SAL, 680 blvd Bachir Gemayel, Achrafieh, Beirut 1100 2802; tel. (1) 218183; fax (1) 200483; e-mail info@creditbank.com.lb; internet www.creditbank.com.lb; f. 1981 as Crédit Bancaire SAL; renamed as above following merger with Crédit Lyonnais Liban SAL 2002; cap. £L23,445m., res £L14,883m., dep. £L441,574m. (Dec. 2002); Chair. and Gen. Man. Tarik Khalifeh; 11 brs.

Crédit Libanais SAL: POB 16-6729, Centre Sofil, ave Charles Malek, Beirut 1100 2811; tel. (1) 200028; fax (1) 325713; e-mail info@ creditlibanais.com.lb; internet www.creditlibanais.com.lb; f. 1961; cap. £L80,000m., res £L166,368m., dep. £L2,917,931m. (Dec. 2002); Pres., Chair. and Gen. Man. Dr Joseph M. Torbey; 52 brs in Lebanon, 2 abroad.

Federal Bank of Lebanon SAL: POB 11-2209, Immeuble Renno, ave Charles Malek, St Nicolas, Beirut; tel. (1) 212300; fax (1) 215847; e-mail federal@cyberia.net.lb; f. 1952; cap. £L9,845m. (Dec. 2001), res £L2,069m., dep. £L302,893m. (Dec. 2003); Chair. and Gen. Man. Ayoub Farid Michel Saab; Vice-Chair. and Dep. Gen. Man. Fadi Michel Saab; 8 brs.

First National Bank SAL: POB 113-5453, Immeuble Immobilia, rue Hamra, Beirut 1103 2040; tel. (1) 738502; fax (1) 343396; e-mail info@fnb.com.lb; internet www.fnb.com.lb; f. 1996; acquired Société Bancaire du Liban SAL 2002; cap. £L47,964m., res £L2,607m., dep. £L856,008m. (Dec. 2002); Pres. and Chair. Rami R. en-Nimer.

Fransabank SAL: POB 11-0393, Riad es-Solh, Beirut 1107 2803; tel. (1) 340180; fax (1) 354572; e-mail fsb@fransabank.com; internet www.fransabank.com; f. 1978 as merger of Banque Sabbag and Banque Française pour le Moyen Orient SAL; acquired Banque Tohmé SAL 1993, Universal Bank SAL 1999, United Bank of Saudi and Lebanon SAL 2002 and Banque de la Beka'a SAL 2003; cap. £L233,114m., res £L92,720m., dep. £L3,941,853m. (Dec. 2001); Chair. Adnan Kassar; Vice-Chair. Adel Kassar; 52 brs.

Intercontinental Bank of Lebanon SAL: POB 11-5292, Immeuble Ittihadiah, ave Charles Malek, Beirut 1107 2190; tel. (1) 200350; fax (1) 204505; e-mail ibl@ibl.com.lb; f. 1961; cap. £L20,000m., res £L19,770m., dep. £L1,364,028m. (Dec. 2003); Chair. and Gen. Man. Selim Habib; 11 brs.

Jammal Trust Bank SAL: POB 11-5640, Immeuble Jammal, rue Verdun, Beirut; tel. (1) 805702; fax (1) 864170; e-mail services@ jammalbank.com.lb; internet www.jammalbank.com.lb; f. 1963 as Investment Bank, SAL; cap. £L26,692m., res £L25,887m., dep. £L229,769m. (Dec. 2001); Pres. and Chair. Ali Abdullah Jammal; 20 brs in Lebanon, 4 in Egypt.

Lebanese Canadian Bank: POB 11-2520, Immeuble Ghantous, blvd Dora, Riad es-Solh, Beirut 1107-2110; tel. (1) 250222; fax (1) 250777; e-mail lebcan@lebcanbank.com; internet www.lebcanbank .com; f. 1960; cap. £L52,606m., res £L10,368m., dep. £L1,438,410m.

(Dec. 2002); Pres., Chair. and Gen. Man. Georges Zard Abou Jaoudé; 16 brs.

Lebanese Swiss Bank SAL: POB 11-9552, Immeuble Hoss, 6e étage, rue Emile Eddé, Hamra, Beirut; tel. (1) 354501; fax (1) 346242; e-mail lbs@t-net.com.lb; f. 1973; cap. £L24,000m., res £L15,649m., dep. £L380,906m. (Dec. 2002); Pres., Chair. and Gen. Man. Dr Tanal Sabbah; 7 brs.

Lebanon and Gulf Bank SAL: POB 113-6404, Immeuble Rinno, 585 rue de Lyon, Hamra, Beirut; tel. (1) 755500; fax (1) 756500; e-mail lgbmail@lgb.com.lb; internet www.lgb.com.lb; f. 1963 as Banque de Crédit Agricole, name changed 1980; cap. £L30,000m., res £L5,593m., dep. £L938,548m. (Dec. 2002); Pres., Chair. and Gen. Man. Abd al-Hafiz Mahmoud Itani; 10 brs.

Middle East and Africa Bank SAL: POB 14-5958, Beirut 1105 2080; tel. (1) 826740; fax (1) 841190; e-mail meabhof@cyberia.net.lb; internet www.meabank.com; f. 1991; cap. US $16m., dep. US $214m., total assets US $245m. (Dec. 2002); Pres., Chair. and Gen. Man. Hassan Hejeij; 5 brs.

National Bank of Kuwait (Lebanon) SAL: POB 11-5727, BAC Bldg, Sanayeh Sq., Justinien St, Riad es-Solh, Beirut 1107 2200; tel. (1) 741111; fax (1) 747866; e-mail info@nbk.com.lb; internet www.nbk.com.lb; f. 1963 as Rifbank, name changed 1996; cap. £L40,020m., res £L5,362m., dep. £L243,425m. (Dec. 2002); Chair. Ibrahim Dabdoub; Gen. Man. Hany Sherif; 9 brs.

Near East Commercial Bank SAL: POB 16-5766, 6e étage, Centre Sofil, ave Charles Malek, St Nicolas, Achrafieh, Beirut; tel. (1) 200331; fax ; e-mail necb@dm.net.lb; f. 1978; cap. £L11,500m., res £L734m., dep. £L191,911m. (Dec. 2002); Chair. and Gen. Man. Paul Caland; 5 brs.

North Africa Commercial Bank SAL: POB 11-9575, Centre Aresco, rue Justinian, Beirut; tel. (1) 346320; fax (1) 346322; e-mail nacb@sodetel.net.lb; f. 1973; cap. £L45,687m., res £L15m., dep. £L638,762m. (Dec. 2002); Pres. and Chair. Aboubaker Ali Sherif; Gen. Man. Hadi I. Engim; 2 brs.

Saudi Lebanese Bank SAL: POB 11-6765, Immeuble Ash-Shua'a, Riad es-Solh, Beirut 1107 2220; tel. (1) 868987; fax (1) 790250; e-mail slbl@inco.com.lb; f. 1979 as Lebanese Saudi Credit SAL, name changed as above 1981; cap. £L40,000m., res £L15,244m., dep. £L675,651m. (Dec. 1997); Pres., Chair. and Gen. Man. Dr Moustafa Razian; 6 brs.

Société Générale de Banque au Liban (SGBL): POB 11-2955, rond-point Salomé, Sin el-Fil, Beirut; tel. (1) 499813; fax (1) 502820; e-mail sgbl@sgbl.com.lb; internet www.sgleb.com; f. 1953 as Société Générale Libano Européenne de Banque SAL (SGLEB); absorbed Inaash Bank SAL 2000; name changed as above 2001; cap. £L117,366m., res £L67,064m., dep. £L3,160,944m. (Dec. 2002); Pres. and Chair Maurice Sehnaoui; 43 brs in Lebanon, 18 abroad.

Société Nouvelle de la Banque de Syrie et du Liban SAL (SNBSL): POB 11-957, Highway, Dbayé, Beirut; tel. (1) 402420; fax (1) 404561; e-mail snbsl@snbsl.com.lb; f. 1963; cap. £L36,225m., res £L7,748m., dep. £L654,899m. (Dec. 2003); Chair. Ramsay A. El-Khoury; Gen. Man. Habib Kahawati; 17 brs.

Standard Chartered Bank SAL: POB 70216, Antélias, Beirut; tel. and fax (4) 542474; internet www.standardchartered.com/lb; f. 1979; acquired Metropolitan Bank SAL 2000; cap. £L12,000m., res £L329m., dep. £L107,000m. (Dec. 2003); Chair. Zahid Rahim; CEO Aamir Hussein; 5 brs.

Syrian Lebanese Commercial Bank SAL: POB 113-5127, Immeuble Cinéma Hamra, rue Hamra, Hamra, Beirut; tel. (1) 341262; fax (1) 341208; e-mail hamra@slcbk.com; internet www.slcb.com.lb; f. 1974; cap. £L45,000m., res £L6,986m., dep. £L399,228m. (Dec. 2002); Pres., Chair. and Gen. Man. Tarek as-Sarraj; 3 brs.

United Credit Bank SAL: POB 13-5086, 5e étage, Immeuble Al-Madina, rue Rashid Karameh, Beirut; tel. (1) 792795; fax (1) 795096; f. 1982 as Commercial Facilities Bank SAL; name changed as above 1998; cap. £L14.3m., dep. £L29.6m. (Dec. 1999); Pres., Chair. and Gen. Man. Dr Adnan M. Abou Ayyash; 4 brs.

Development Bank

Audi Investment Bank SAL: POB 16-5110, Banque Audi Plaza, Bab Idriss, Beirut; tel. (1) 994000; fax (1) 999406; e-mail info@aib.com.lb; internet www.aib.com.lb; f. 1974 as Investment and Finance Bank, present name since 1996; medium- and long-term loans, 100% from Lebanese sources; owned by Banque Audi SAL (99.3%); cap. £L25,075m., res £L13,586m., dep. £L620,014m. (Dec. 2001); Pres., Chair. and Gen. Man. Raymond Wadih Audi.

Principal Foreign Banks

Arab Bank plc (Jordan): POB 11-1015, rue Riad es-Solh, Beirut; tel. (1) 980246; fax (1) 980803; e-mail beirut@arabbank.com.lb; f.

1930; cap. £L31,700m., res £L31,100m.; dep. £L2,001,400m. (Dec. 2001); Exec. Vice-Pres. and Regional Man. Dr Hisham Bsat.

Banque Nationale de Paris Intercontinentale SA (BNPI) (France): POB 11-1608, Tour el Ghazal/BNPI, ave Fouad Chehab, Beirut; tel. (1) 333717; fax (1) 200604; e-mail bnpi.liban@bnpi.com.lb; internet www.bnpi-liban.bnpparibas.com; f. 1944; part of the BNP Paribas group (France); total assets £L2,061,529m. (Dec. 2000); Pres. Henri Tyan; Gen. Man. Guy Lepinard.

Citibank NA (USA): POB 113-579, Centre Gefinor, Bloc E, rue Clémenceau, Beirut; tel. (1) 738400; fax (1) 738406; cap. £L7,943m., res £L738m., dep. £L171,860m. (Dec. 2000); CEO Elia Samaha.

Habib Bank (Overseas) Ltd (Pakistan): POB 5616, Fadlallah Centre, 1st Floor, blvd esh-Shiah, Musharaffieh, Beirut; tel. (1) 558992; e-mail habibbkbey@t-net.com.lb; Gen. Man. Muhammad Shahab Khattack.

HSBC Bank Middle East (United Kingdom): POB 11-1380, HSBC Bldg, Minet el-Hosn, Riad es-Solh, Beirut 1107-2080; tel. (1) 377477; fax (1) 372362; internet www.lebanon.hsbc.com; f. 1946; cap. £L10,750m. (Dec. 1999); CEO Kevin Smorthwaite; 5 brs.

Jordan National Bank SA: POB 5186, Immeuble Diamond Tower, rue Verdun, Beirut; tel. (1) 797078; fax (1) 794955; e-mail jnbobs@netgate.com.lb; cap. £L7,961m., dep. £L121,964m. (Dec. 1997); Regional Gen. Man. Rafic Aramouni; 3 brs.

Saudi National Commercial Bank: POB 11-2355, Riad es-Solh, Beirut 1107 2100; tel. (1) 860863; fax (1) 867728; e-mail sncb@sncb.com.lb; cap. £L10,000m., res £L7,933m., dep. £L87,470m. (Dec. 2002); Gen. Man. Hani Houssami.

Numerous other foreign banks have representative offices in Beirut.

Banking Association

Association of Banks in Lebanon: POB 976, Association of Banks in Lebanon Bldg, Gouraud St, Saifi, Beirut; tel. (1) 970500; fax (1) 970501; e-mail abl@abl.org.lb; internet www.abl.org.lb; f. 1959; serves and promotes the interests of the banking community in Lebanon; mems: 60 banks and 7 banking rep. offices; Pres. Dr Joseph Torbey; Gen. Sec. Dr Makram Sader.

STOCK EXCHANGE

Beirut Stock Exchange (BSE): POB 11-3552, 4e étage, Bloc A3, Immeuble Azareih, Beirut; tel. (1) 993555; fax (1) 993444; e-mail bse@bse.com.lb; internet www.bse.com.lb; f. 1920; recommenced trading in January 1996; 10 cttee mems; Cttee Pres. Dr Fadi Khalaf.

INSURANCE

About 80 insurance companies were registered in Lebanon in the late 1990s, although less than one-half of these were operational. An insurance law enacted in mid-1999 has increased the required capital base for insurance firms and provided tax incentives for mergers within the sector.

Arabia Insurance Co SAL: POB 11-2172, Arabia House, rue de Phénicie, Beirut; tel. (1) 363610; fax (1) 365139; e-mail arabia@arabia-ins.com.lb; internet www.arabiainsurance.com; f. 1944; cap. £L51,000m.; Chair. Dr Hisham Bsat; Gen. Man. Fady Shammas; 20 brs.

Bankers Assurance SAL: POB 11-4293, Immeuble Capitole, rue Riad es-Solh, Beirut; tel. (1) 988777; fax (1) 984004; e-mail mail@bankers-assurance.com; internet www.bankers.com.lb; f. 1972; Chair. Saba Nader; Gen. Man. Eugène Nader.

Commercial Insurance Co (Lebanon) SAL: POB 4351, Centre Starco, Beirut; POB 84, Jounieh; tel. (1) 373070; fax (1) 373071; e-mail comins@commercialinsurance.com.lb; internet www.commercialinsurance.com.lb; f. 1962; Chair. Max R. Zaccar.

Compagnie Libanaise d'Assurances SAL: POB 3685, rue Riad es-Solh, Beirut; tel. (1) 868988; f. 1951; cap. £L3,000m. (1991); Chair. Jean F. S. Aboujaoudé; Gen. Man. Jihad Shaker.

Al-Ittihad al-Watani: POB 11-1270, Jisr al-Wati, Immeuble Al-Ittihad al-Watani, Beirut; tel. (1) 330840; e-mail webmaster@alittihadalwatani.com.lb; internet www.alittihadalwatani.com.lb; f. 1947; cap. £L30m.; Chair. Joe I. Kairouz; Exec. Dir Tannous Feghali.

Libano-Suisse Insurance Co SAL: POB 11-3821, Beirut 1107-2150; tel. (1) 374900; fax (1) 368724; e-mail insure@libano-suisse.com; internet www.libano-suisse.com.lb; f. 1959; cap. £L4,050m. (2000); Chair. Michel Pierre Pharaon; Gen. Man. Samir Nahas.

Al-Mashrek Insurance and Reinsurance SAL: POB 16-6154, Immeuble Al-Mashrek, 65 rue Aabrine, Achrafieh, Beirut 1100 2100; tel. (1) 204666; fax (1) 337625; e-mail amirco@inco.com.lb; f. 1962; cap. £L5,000m., (1999); Chair. and Gen. Man. Abraham Matossian.

'La Phénicienne' SAL: POB 11-5652, Immeuble Hanna Haddad, rue Amine Gemayel, Sioufi, Beirut; tel. (1) 425484; fax (1) 424532; f. 1964; Chair. and Gen. Man. TANNOUS C. FEGHALI.

Société Nationale d'Assurances SAL: POB 11-4805, Immeuble SNA, Hazmieh, Beirut; tel. (1) 956600; fax (1) 956624; e-mail sna@sna.com.lb; internet www.sna.com.lb; f. 1963; Chair. ANTOINE WAKIM.

Trade and Industry

DEVELOPMENT ORGANIZATIONS

Council for Development and Reconstruction (CDR): POB 116-5351, Tallet es-Serail, Beirut; tel. (1) 643982; fax (1) 647947; e-mail general@cdr.gov.lb; internet www.cdr.gov.lb; f. 1977; an autonomous public institution reporting to the Cabinet, the CDR is charged with the co-ordination, planning and execution of Lebanon's public reconstruction programme; it plays a major role in attracting foreign funds; Pres. JAMAL ITANI; Sec.-Gen. JOSEPH HADDAD.

Investment Development Authority of Lebanon (IDAL): POB 113-7251, Cristal Bldg 1145, Hussein el-Adhab St, Nijmeh Sq., Beirut; tel. (1) 983306; fax (1) 983302; e-mail mail@idal.com.lb; internet www.idal.com.lb; f. 1994; state-owned; Chair. and Gen. Man. SAMIH BARBIR.

Société Libanaise pour le Développement et la Reconstruction de Beyrouth (SOLIDERE): POB 11-9493, 149 rue Saad Zagholoul, Beirut; tel. (1) 980650; fax (1) 980662; e-mail solidere@solidere.com.lb; internet www.solidere.com.lb; f. 1994; real estate co responsible for reconstruction of Beirut Central District; Chair. NASSER SHAMMA'A; Gen. Man. MOUNIR DOUAIDY.

CHAMBERS OF COMMERCE AND INDUSTRY

Federation of the Chambers of Commerce, Industry and Agriculture in Lebanon: POB 11-1801, Immeuble Elias Abd-an Nour, Achrafieh, Beirut; internet www.cci-fed.org.lb; Pres. ADNAN KASSAR; Gen. Sec. MICHEL BITAR.

Chamber of Commerce, Industry and Agriculture of Beirut and Mount Lebanon: POB 11-1801, rue Justinian, Sanayeh, Beirut; tel. (1) 744160; fax (1) 353395; e-mail info@ccib.org.lb; internet www.ccib.org.lb; f. 1898; 32,000 mems; Pres. ADNAN KASSAR; Dir-Gen. Dr WALID NAJA.

Chamber of Commerce, Industry and Agriculture of Tripoli and North Lebanon: rue Bechara Khoury, Tripoli; tel. (6) 425600; fax (6) 442042; e-mail abdallahg@cciat.org.lb; internet www.cciat.org.lb; Chair. ABDALLAH GHANDOUR.

Chamber of Commerce, Industry and Agriculture in Sidon and South Lebanon: POB 41, rue Maarouf Saad, Sidon; tel. (7) 720123; fax (7) 722986; e-mail chamber@ccias.org.lb; internet www.ccias.org.lb; f. 1933; Pres. MOHAMAD ZAATARI.

Chamber of Commerce, Industry and Agriculture of Zahleh and Beka'a: POB 100, Zahleh; tel. (8) 802602; fax (8) 800050; internet www.cciaz.org.lb; f. 1939; 2,500 mems; Pres. EDMOND JREISSATI.

EMPLOYERS' ASSOCIATION

Association of Lebanese Industrialists: Chamber of Commerce and Industry Bldg, 5e étage, Sanayeh, Beirut; tel. (1) 350280; fax (1) 350282; e-mail ali@ali.org.lb; internet www.ali.org.lb; Pres. FADY ABBOUD; Gen. Man. SAAD S. OUEINI.

UTILITIES

Electricity

Electricité du Liban (EdL): POB 131, Immeuble de l'Electricité du Liban, 22 rue du Fleuve, Beirut; tel. (1) 442556; fax (1) 583084; internet www.edl.gov.lb; f. 1954; state-owned; scheduled for privatization from 2003; Dir-Gen. KAMAL F. HAYEK.

Water

From the late 1990s the Government began a process of establishing five new regional water authorities (in the governorates of the North, South, Beka'a, Beirut and Mount Lebanon), to replace the existing water authorities and committees. Under the re-organization the new authorities were to operate under the super-vision of the Ministry of Energy and Water.

Beirut Water Supply Office: Beirut; Pres. LUCIEN MOBAYAD.

North Lebanon Water Authority: Chair. and Gen. Man. JAMAL ABD AL-LATIF KARIM.

South Lebanon Water Authority: Chair. and Gen. Man. AHMAD HASSAN NIZAM.

TRADE UNION FEDERATION

Confédération Générale des Travailleurs du Liban (CGTL): POB 4381, Beirut; f. 1958; 300,000 mems; only national labour centre in Lebanon and sole rep. of working classes; comprises 18 affiliated federations including all 150 unions in Lebanon; Chair. GHNEIM AZ-ZOGHBI; Pres. ELIAS ABU RIZQ.

Transport

RAILWAYS

Office des Chemins de Fer de l'Etat Libanais et du Transport en Commun: POB 11–0109, Gare St Michel, Nahr, Beirut; tel. (1) 587211; fax (1) 447007; since 1961 all railways in Lebanon have been state-owned. The original network of some 412 km is no longer functioning. However, the Lebanese authorities have agreed a rail reconstruction project involving a section of the network between Tripoli and the Syrian border; Dir-Gen. RADWAN BOU NASSER ED-DIN.

ROADS

At 31 December 1996 Lebanon had an estimated 6,350 km of roads, of which 2,170 km were highways, main or national roads and 1,370 km were secondary or regional roads. The total road network was estimated at 7,300 km in 1999. The two international motor-ways are the north–south coastal road and the road connecting Beirut with Damascus in Syria. Among the major roads are that crossing the Beka'a and continuing south to Bent-Jbail and the Shtaura–Ba'albek road. Hard-surfaced roads connect Jezzine with Moukhtara, Bzebdine with Metn, Meyroub with Afka and Tannourine. A road construction project, costing some US $100m., was planned for Beirut in the late 1990s. A new 8-km highway, linking around 26 villages in southern Lebanon, was inaugurated in August 2000.

SHIPPING

A two-phase programme to rehabilitate and expand the port of Beirut is currently under way. In the second phase, which com-menced in early 1997, the construction of an industrial free zone, a fifth basin and a major container terminal are envisaged, at an estimated cost of US $1,000m. Tripoli, the northern Mediterranean terminus of the oil pipeline from Iraq (the other is Haifa, Israel—not in use since 1948), is also a busy port, with good equipment and facilities. Jounieh, north of Beirut, is Lebanon's third most impor-tant port. A new deep-water sea port is to be constructed south of Sidon. The reconstructed port of an-Naqoura, in what was then the 'security zone' along the border with Israel, was inaugurated in June 1987.

Port Authorities

Gestion et Exploitation du Port de Beyrouth: POB 1490, Beirut; tel. (1) 580210; fax (1) 585835; e-mail pob-mis@dm.net.lb; internet www.portdebeyrouth.com; Pres., Dir-Gen. and Man. Dir HASSAN KAMEL KRAYTEM; Harbour Master MAROUN KHOURY.

Service d'Exploitation du Port de Tripoli: El Mina, Tripoli; tel. (6) 601225; fax (6) 220180; e-mail tport@terra.net.lb; f. 1959; Har-bour Master MARWAN BAROUDI.

Principal Shipping Companies

Youssef A Abourahal and Hanna N Tabet: POB 11-5890, Imme-uble Ghantous, autostrade Dora, Beirut; tel. (1) 263872.

Ets Paul Adem: Centre Moucarri, 6e étage, autostrade Dora, Beirut; tel. and fax (1) 582421.

Ademar Shipping Lines: POB 175-231, Beirut; tel. (1) 444100; fax (1) 444101.

Agence Générale Maritime (AGEMAR) SARL: POB 9255, Centre Burotec, 7e étage, rue Pasteur, Beirut; tel. (1) 583885; fax (1) 583884; Dirs S. MEDLEJ, N. MEDLEJ.

Amin Kawar & Sons (Jordan): Beirut; tel. (1) 352525; fax (1) 353842; internet www.kawar.com; f. 1963; Chair. and Man. Dir TAWFIQ AMIN KAWAR.

Arab Shipping and Chartering Co: POB 1084, Immeuble Ghan-dour, ave des Français, Beirut; tel. (1) 371044; fax (1) 373370; e-mail arabship@dm.net.lb; agents for China Ocean Shipping Co.

Associated Levant Lines SAL: POB 110371, Immeuble Mercedes, autostrade Dora, Beirut; tel. (1) 255366; fax (1) 255362; e-mail tgf-all@dm.net.lb; Dirs T. GARGOUR, N. GARGOUR, H. GARGOUR.

Wafic Begdache: Immeuble Wazi, 4e étage, rue Moussaitbé, Beirut; tel. (1) 319920; fax (1) 815002; e-mail mody@lebaneseshipping.com.

Bulk Traders International: POB 70-152, Centre St Elie, Bloc A, 6e étage, Antélias, Beirut; tel. (4) 410724; fax (4) 402842; e-mail bulk@cyberia.net.lb.

Continental Ship Management SARL: POB 901413, Centre Dora Moucarri, 8e étage, appt 804, Beirut; tel. (1) 583654; fax (1) 584440.

O. D. Debbas & Sons: Head Office: POB 166678, Immeuble Debbas, 530 blvd Corniche du Fleuve, Beirut; tel. (1) 585253; fax (1) 587135; e-mail oddebbas@oddebbas.com; internet www.oddebbas .com; f. 1892; Man. Dir OIDIH ELIE DEBBAS.

Dery Shipping Lines Ltd: POB 5720-113, Beirut; tel. (1) 862442; fax (1) 344146.

Diana K Shipping Co: POB 113-5125, Immeuble Ajouz, rue Kenedi, Ein Mreisseh, Beirut; tel. (1) 363314; fax (1) 369712; e-mail dianak@cyberia.net.lb; Marine Dept Man. Capt. AMIN HABBAL.

Fauzi Jemil Ghandour: POB 1084, Beirut; tel. (1) 373376; fax (1) 360048; e-mail alifgand@dm.net.lb; agents for Denizçlik Bankasi TAO (Denizvollari); Ecuadorian Line, Festival Shipping and Tourist Enterprises Ltd.

Gezairi Chartering and Shipping Co (GEZACHART): POB 11-1402, Immeuble Gezairi, place Gezairi, Ras Beirut; tel. (1) 783783; fax (1) 784784; e-mail gezachart@gezairi.com; internet www.gezairi .com; ship management, chartering, brokerage.

Gulf Agency Co (Lebanon) Ltd: POB 4392, Beirut; tel. (1) 446086; fax (1) 446097; e-mail gacleltd@dm.net.lb; f. 1969; Gen. Man. SIMON G. BEJJANI.

Lebanese Navigators Co SARL: Beirut; tel. (1) 603335; fax (1) 603334.

Medawar Shipping Co SARL: POB 8962/11, Immeuble Kanafani, rue al-Arz, Saifi, Beirut; tel. (1) 447277; fax (1) 447662.

Mediterranean Feedering Co SARL: POB 70-1187, Immeuble Akak, autostrade Dbayeh, Beirut; tel. (1) 403056; fax (1) 406444; e-mail mfcbeirut@attmail.com; Man. Dir EMILE AKEF EL-KHOURY.

Orient Shipping and Trading Co SARL: POB 11-2561, Immeuble Moumneh, no 72, rue Ain al-Mraisseh 54, Beirut; tel. (1) 644252; fax (1) 602221; Dirs ELIE ZAROUBY, EMILE ZAROUBY.

Rassem Shipping Agency: POB 11-8460, Immeuble Agha, Raoucheh, Beirut; tel. (1) 866372; fax (1) 805593.

Riga Brothers: POB 17-5134, Immeuble Mitri Haddad, rue du Port, Beirut; tel. (1) 406882.

G. Sahyouni & Co SARL: POB 17-5452, Mar Mikhael, Beirut 1104 2040; tel. (1) 257046; fax (1) 241317; e-mail lloydsbey@inco.com.lb; f. 1989; agents for Baltic Control Lebanon Ltd., SARL, and Lloyds; Man. Dir GEORGE SHYOUNI; Financial Man. HENRY CHIDIAC.

Sinno Trading and Navigation Agency: Immeuble Moumneh, rue Ain Mretseh, Beirut; Chair. MUHIEDDINE F. SINNO; Man. Dir AHMED JABBOURY.

A Sleiman Co & Sons: Immeuble Saroulla, 3e étage, rue Hamra, Beirut; tel. (1) 354240; fax (1) 340262.

Union Shipping and Chartering Agency SAL: POB 2856, Immeuble Ghandour, ave des Français, Beirut; tel. (1) 373376; fax (1) 360048; e-mail unichart@dm.net.lb; agents for Croatia Line, Jadroslobodna, Jugo Oceania, Atlanska Plovidba, Jadroplov and Maruba S.C.A.

CIVIL AVIATION

Services from the country's principal airport, in Beirut, were subject to frequent disruptions after 1975; its location in predominantly Muslim west Beirut made it virtually inaccessible to non-Muslims. In 1986 a new airport, based on an existing military airfield, was opened at Halat, north of Beirut, by Christian concerns, but commercial operations from the airport were not authorized by the Government. Services to and from Beirut by Middle East Airlines (MEA) were suspended, and the airport closed, at the end of January 1987, after the Maronite LF militia shelled the airport and threatened to attack MEA aircraft if services from their own airport, at Halat, did not receive official authorization. Beirut airport was reopened in May, after the LF accepted government assurances that Halat would receive the necessary authorization for civil use. However, the commission concluded that Halat did not possess the facilities to cater for international air traffic. Some 2.4m. passengers used Beirut International Airport in 2001. In late 2001 a major expansion project at the airport was completed, at an estimated cost of US $600m.; facilities included a new terminal building and two new runways, increasing handling capacity to 6m. passengers a year.

MEA (Middle East Airlines, Air Liban SAL): POB 206, Headquarters MEA, blvd de l'Aéroport, Beirut; tel. (1) 628888; fax (1) 629260; e-mail mea@mea.net.lb; internet www.mea.com.lb; f. 1945; acquired Lebanese International Airways in 1969; privatization scheduled from 2003; regular services throughout Europe, the Middle East, North and West Africa, and the Far East; Chair. MUHAMMAD EL-HOUT; Commercial Man. NIZAR KHOURY.

Trans-Mediterranean Airways SAL (TMA): Beirut International Airport, POB 11–3018, Beirut; tel. (1) 629210; fax (1) 629219; e-mail cargo@tma.com.lb; internet www.tma.com.lb; f. 1953; scheduled services, charter activities and aircraft lease operations covering Europe, the Middle East, Africa and the Far East; also provides handling, storage and maintenance services; Chair. and Pres. FADI N. SAAB.

Tourism

Before the civil war, Lebanon was a major tourist centre, and its scenic beauty, sunny climate and historic sites attracted some 2m. visitors annually. In 1974 tourism contributed about 20% of the country's income. Since the end of the civil conflict, tourist facilities (in particular hotels) have begun to be reconstructed, and the Government has chosen to concentrate its efforts on the promotion of cultural as well as conference and exhibition-based tourism. In 1999 UNESCO declared Beirut as the Cultural Capital of the Arab World. Lebanon is also being promoted as an 'eco-tourism' destination. Excluding Syrian visitors, the annual total of tourist arrivals increased from 177,503 in 1992 to 741,648 in 2000. Tourism receipts reached an estimated US $1,221m. in 1998; however, receipts fell to $742m. in 2000. Of total arrivals in 2000, 38.8% were from Arab countries (excluding Syria) and 30.9% from Europe.

National Council of Tourism in Lebanon (NCTL): POB 11-5344, rue Banque du Liban 550, Beirut; tel. (1) 343196; fax (1) 343279; e-mail tourism@cyberia.net.lb; internet www .lebanon-tourism.gov.lb; government-sponsored autonomous organization responsible for the promotion of tourism; overseas offices in Paris (France) and Cairo (Egypt); Pres. FOUAD FAWAZ; Dir-Gen. NASSER SAFIEDDINE.

LESOTHO

Introductory Survey

Location, Climate, Language, Religion, Flag, Capital

The Kingdom of Lesotho is a land-locked country, entirely surrounded by South Africa. The climate is generally mild, although cooler in the highlands: lowland temperatures range from a maximum of 32°C (90°F) in summer (October to April) to a minimum of −7°C (20°F) in winter. Rainfall averages about 725 mm (29 ins) per year, mostly falling in summer. The official languages are English and Sesotho. About 90% of the population are Christians. The largest denominations are the Roman Catholic, Lesotho Evangelical and Anglican Churches. The national flag (official proportions 2 by 3) is divided diagonally from lower hoist to upper fly, with the hoist triangle of white bearing, in brown silhouette, a traditional Basotho shield with crossed knobkerrie (club), barbed assegai (spear) and a thyrsus of ostrich feathers, and the fly triangle comprising a blue diagonal stripe and a green triangle. The capital is Maseru.

Recent History

Lesotho was formerly Basutoland, a dependency of the United Kingdom. In 1868, at the request of the Basotho people's chief, the territory became a British protectorate. Basutoland was annexed to Cape Colony (now part of South Africa) in 1871, but detached in 1884. It became a separate British colony and was administered as one of the High Commission Territories in southern Africa (the others being the protectorates of Bechuanaland, now Botswana, and Swaziland). The British Act of Parliament that established the Union of South Africa in 1910 also provided for the possible inclusion in South Africa of the three High Commission Territories, subject to local consent: the native chiefs opposed requests by successive South African Governments for the transfer of the three territories.

Within Basutoland a revised Constitution, which established the colony's first Legislative Council, was introduced in 1956. A new document, granting limited powers of self-government, was adopted in September 1959. Basutoland's first general election, on the basis of universal adult suffrage, took place on 29 April 1965, and full internal self-government was achieved the following day. Moshoeshoe II, Paramount Chief since 1960, was recognized as King. The Basutoland National Party (BNP), a conservative group supporting limited co-operation with South Africa, narrowly won a majority of the seats in the new Legislative Assembly. The BNP's leader, Chief Leabua Jonathan, failed to win a seat, but won a by-election in July 1965, whereupon he became Prime Minister. Basutoland became independent, as Lesotho, on 4 October 1966. The new Constitution provided for a bicameral legislature, comprising the 60-seat National Assembly and the 33-member Senate; executive power was vested in the Cabinet, which was presided over by the Prime Minister. The King was designated Head of State.

The BNP, restyled the Basotho National Party, remained in power at independence. A constitutional crisis arose in December 1966, when King Moshoeshoe II attempted to obtain wider personal powers, but in January 1967 the King signed an undertaking to abide by the Constitution. A general election was held in January 1970, at which the opposition Basotho Congress Party (BCP), a pan-Africanist group led by Dr Ntsu Mokhehle, appeared to have won a majority of seats in the National Assembly. Chief Jonathan declared a state of emergency, suspended the Constitution and arrested several BCP organizers. The election was annulled, and the legislature prorogued. King Moshoeshoe was placed under house arrest and subsequently exiled, although he returned in December after accepting a government order banning him from participating in politics. The country was thus effectively under the Prime Minister's personal control. An interim National Assembly, comprising the former Senate (mainly chiefs) and 60 members nominated by the Cabinet, was inaugurated in April 1973. The state of emergency was revoked in July. However, following a failed coup attempt in January 1974 by alleged supporters of the BCP, Chief Jonathan introduced stringent security laws. Mokhehle and other prominent members of the BCP went into exile abroad, and the party split into two factions, internal and external. The latter, led by Mokhehle, was supported by the Lesotho Liberation Army (LLA), which was responsible for terrorist attacks in Lesotho during the late 1970s and the 1980s. (The South African Government consistently denied allegations that it supported the LLA.)

Although Lesotho was economically dependent on South Africa, and the Government's official policy during the 1970s was one of 'dialogue' with its neighbour, Chief Jonathan repeatedly criticized the apartheid regime, and supported the then banned African National Congress of South Africa (ANC). In December 1982 South African forces launched a major assault on the homes of ANC members in Maseru, killing more than 40 people. In August 1983 South Africa threatened to impose sanctions unless Lesotho expelled or repatriated 3,000 South African refugees. Two groups of refugees were subsequently reported to have left Lesotho. None the less, Lesotho's persistent refusal to sign a joint non-aggression pact led South Africa to impound consignments of armaments destined for Lesotho, and again, in August 1984, to threaten economic sanctions.

The Parliament Act of May 1983 repealed the emergency order of 1970 that had suspended the Constitution. In January 1985 the National Assembly was dissolved. Legislative elections scheduled for September were cancelled in August, when no opposition candidates were nominated: the opposition parties claimed that their prospective candidates had been denied access to the voters' rolls and had therefore been prevented from securing sufficient signatures to qualify for nomination. BNP candidates in all 60 constituencies were thus returned to office unopposed.

In December 1985 South African commando troops were held responsible by the Lesotho Government for a raid in Maseru in which nine people (including several ANC members) were killed. South Africa imposed a blockade on the border with Lesotho from the beginning of 1986. Five of Lesotho's opposition leaders were arrested on their return from talks in South Africa, and there were reports of fighting between factions of the armed forces. On 20 January Chief Jonathan's Government was overthrown in a coup led by Maj.-Gen. Justin Lekhanya, the head of the armed forces. A Military Council, chaired by Lekhanya, was established. The 1983 Parliament Act was revoked, and it was announced that executive and legislative powers were to be vested in King Moshoeshoe, assisted by the Military Council and a (mainly civilian) Council of Ministers. About 60 ANC members were subsequently deported from Lesotho, and the South African blockade was ended. In March 1986 the Military Council suspended all formal political activity. In September the Council of Ministers was restructured, giving increased responsibility to Lekhanya, and the Military Council held discussions with the leaders of the five main opposition parties.

Although the South African Government denied having any part in the coup, the Lekhanya regime proved to be more amenable to South Africa's regional security policy. In March 1986 it was announced that the two countries had reached an informal agreement whereby neither would allow its territory to be used for attacks against the other. Moreover, the Lesotho Government did not join other African states in pressing for international economic sanctions against South Africa. By August more than 200 South African refugees, believed to be ANC members, were reported to have been expelled from Lesotho (although the Lesotho Government did not permit their extradition directly to South Africa). In March 1988 Lesotho and South Africa reached final agreement on the Lesotho Highlands Water Project (LHWP), a major scheme to supply water to South Africa.

In May 1988 Mokhehle was allowed to return to Lesotho after 14 years of exile. In 1989 the LLA was said to have disbanded, and by 1990 the two factions of the BCP had apparently reunited under Mokhehle's leadership. Meanwhile, in mid-1989 elements within the Government reportedly sought the resignation of Lekhanya from the chairmanship of the Military Council, in response to widespread reports implicating him in the fatal shooting, in 1988, of a civilian: it was claimed that Lekhanya had falsely attributed responsibility for the incident to a subordinate. At a subsequent inquest Lekhanya admitted the truth of the allegations; nevertheless, a verdict of justifiable homicide was recorded.

In February 1990 Lekhanya dismissed three members of the Military Council and one member of the Council of Ministers, accusing them of 'insubordination'. When Moshoeshoe refused to approve new appointments to the Military Council, Lekhanya suspended the monarch's executive and legislative powers, which were assumed by the Military Council in March. Moshoeshoe (who remained Head of State) was exiled in the United Kingdom. Lekhanya announced that a general election would take place during 1992; however, party political activity remained outlawed. In June 1990 a National Constituent Assembly (including Lekhanya, members of the Council of Ministers, representatives of banned political parties, traditional chiefs and business leaders) was inaugurated to draft a new constitution. In October Lekhanya invited the King to return from exile. Moshoeshoe responded that his return would be conditional upon the ending of military rule and the establishment of an interim government, pending the readoption of the 1966 Constitution. On 6 November 1990 Lekhanya promulgated an order dethroning the King with immediate effect. Lesotho's 22 principal chiefs elected Moshoeshoe's elder son, Prince David Mohato Bereng Seeiso, as the new King; on 12 November he acceded to the throne, as King Letsie III, having undertaken to remain detached from politics.

On 30 April 1991 Lekhanya was deposed in a coup organized by disaffected army officers. Col (later Maj.-Gen.) Elias Phitsoane Ramaema succeeded Lekhanya as Chairman of the Military Council. Ramaema repealed the ban on party political activity, and by July the National Constituent Assembly had completed the draft Constitution. In May 1992 Lesotho and South Africa agreed to establish diplomatic relations at ambassadorial level. Following talks in the United Kingdom with Ramaema, former King Moshoeshoe returned from exile in July.

The general election was eventually held on 27 March 1993. The BCP secured all 65 seats in the new National Assembly, winning 54% of the votes cast. Although international observers pronounced the election to have been generally free and fair, the BNP—which took 16% of the votes—rejected the result, alleging that there had been widespread irregularities, and later declined the new administration's offer of two seats in the restored Senate. On 2 April Mokhehle was inaugurated as Prime Minister, and King Letsie swore allegiance to the new Constitution, under the terms of which he remained Head of State with no executive or legislative powers; executive authority was vested in the Cabinet.

A mutiny in November 1993 by about 50 junior officers in the national army, the Royal Lesotho Defence Force (RLDF), was apparently precipitated by a proposal to place the military under the command of a senior member of the LLA—as part of government efforts to integrate its former armed wing with the RLDF. Four senior army officers were subsequently reported to have resigned their posts. Skirmishes near Maseru in January 1994 escalated into more serious fighting between some 600 rebel troops and a 150-strong contingent of forces loyal to the Government, reportedly resulting in the deaths of at least five soldiers and three civilians. Following mediation efforts involving representatives of Botswana, South Africa, Zimbabwe, the Commonwealth (see p. 172), the Organization of African Unity (OAU, now the African Union, see p. 137) and the UN, a truce entered force, and at the beginning of February the rival factions surrendered their weapons and returned to barracks. In April, however, the Deputy Prime Minister, Selometsi Baholo (who also held the finance portfolio), was killed during an abduction attempt by disaffected troops. In the following month police-officers demanding increased pay and allowances briefly held hostage the acting finance minister, Mpho Malie (the Minister of Information and Broadcasting). Agreement was subsequently reached on increased allowances, and the Government announced the formation of an independent commission to review salary structures in the public sector.

A commission to investigate the armed forces unrest of January and April 1994 began work in July. In that month Mokhehle appointed a commission of inquiry into the dethronement of King Moshoeshoe II. In August King Letsie petitioned the High Court to abolish the commission on the grounds of bias on the part of its members. On 17 August Letsie announced that he had dissolved the National Assembly, dismissed the Government and suspended sections of the Constitution, citing 'popular dissatisfaction' with the BCP administration. Although several thousand people gathered outside the royal palace in Maseru in support of the deposed Government, army and police support for Letsie's 'royal coup' was evident, and subsequent clashes between demonstrators and the security forces reportedly resulted in five deaths. A well-known human rights lawyer, Hae Phoofolo, was appointed Chairman of a transitional Council of Ministers, and the Secretary-General of the BNP, Evaristus Retselisitsoe Sekhonyana, was appointed Minister of Foreign Affairs. Phoofolo identified as a priority for his administration the amendment of the Constitution to facilitate the restoration of Moshoeshoe; in the mean time, King Letsie was to act as executive and legislative Head of State.

The suspension of constitutional government was widely condemned outside Lesotho. The Presidents of Botswana, South Africa and Zimbabwe led diplomatic efforts to restore the elected Government, supported by the OAU and the Commonwealth. The USA withdrew financial assistance, and several other countries threatened sanctions. Following negotiations in South Africa, in September 1994 King Letsie and Mokhehle signed an agreement, guaranteed by Botswana, South Africa and Zimbabwe, providing for the restoration of Moshoeshoe II as reigning monarch and for the restitution of the elected organs of government; the commission of inquiry into Moshoeshoe's dethronement was to be abandoned; all those involved in the 'royal coup' were to be immune from prosecution; the political neutrality of the armed forces and public service was to be guaranteed, and consultations were to be undertaken with the aim of broadening the democratic process. Moshoeshoe was restored to the throne on 25 January 1995, undertaking not to interfere in politics. Letsie took the title of Crown Prince.

Meanwhile, in October 1994 Sekhonyana was ordered to pay a substantial fine (or be sentenced to two years' imprisonment), after being convicted of sedition and the incitement to violence of army and police troops against former LLA members earlier in the year. The director and another senior officer of the National Security Service (NSS) were held hostage by junior officers (who were demanding improved terms and conditions of service, as well as the officers' enforced retirement and prosecution on charges of attempted murder, corruption and breach of security laws) for two weeks in March 1995, and were released only after intervention by the Commonwealth Secretary-General. In September the human rights organization Amnesty International urged the Mokhehle Government to act to eliminate abuses of human rights by the security forces, condemning what it alleged were arbitrary arrests and incommunicado detentions, as well as the ill-treatment of detainees.

In April 1995 government representatives and military officials from Lesotho met with their counterparts from Botswana, South Africa and Zimbabwe to discuss progress in the restoration of constitutional order in Lesotho. The conference examined the recommendations of the commission of inquiry into the army mutiny of 1994: these included a streamlining of existing forces, a clearer definition of their functions, and improved training. In May 1995 two people were shot dead in Maseru during rioting that had erupted while police were maintaining an indefinite 'go slow', as part of their continuing salary campaign. Apparently in an attempt to deter further indiscipline, the Government announced 15% salary increases for the armed and security forces, thus bringing their pay into line with remuneration for other public-sector employees. In August a 5,000-strong demonstration was organized in Maseru to protest against proposed legislation to debar public servants from trade union membership and Mokhehle's plans to reduce earlier salary increases that were now said to have been granted in error.

King Moshoeshoe was killed in a motor accident on 15 January 1996. The College of Chiefs subsequently elected Crown Prince David to succeed his father, and the prince was restored to the throne, resuming the title King Letsie III, on 7 February. Like his father in January 1995, King Letsie undertook not to involve the monarchy in any aspect of political life.

In February 1996 premises of the national radio service were seized by a small group that broadcast an apparently groundless statement that the Government had been overthrown. The alleged perpetrators of the 'false coup'—Makara Sekautu, the President of the opposition United Party, together with two former members of the Lesotho Defence Force (LDF, as the RLDF had been redesignated) and a former member of the NSS—were subsequently charged with high treason; in March 1997 three of the accused, including Sekautu, were given custodial sentences.

In February 1997 the LDF was mobilized to quell a rebellion at the police headquarters in Maseru. More than 100 police-officers were arrested, and 10 alleged leaders of the rebellion were remanded in custody on charges of sedition and contravention of internal security legislation. Further individuals were subsequently indicted, and charges of high treason added. Two of the instigators of the mutiny fled to South Africa, where they were subsequently granted political asylum. In July 2000 23 police-officers were convicted of sedition, two of contravention of internal security legislation and three acquitted on both counts. All of the accused were acquitted of high treason.

Meanwhile, in April 1997 the National Assembly approved legislation for a reduction in the age of eligibility to vote (from 21 to 18 years), and for the establishment of a three-member Independent Electoral Commission (IEC). In June, following a protracted struggle between rival factions for control of the party, Mokhehle resigned from the BCP and formed the Lesotho Congress for Democracy (LCD), to which he transferred executive power. Mokhehle's opponents denounced the move as a 'political coup', declaring that he should have resigned from the premiership and sought a dissolution of the National Assembly and new elections. However, some 38 members of the National Assembly joined the LCD. In July Molapo Qhobela was elected leader of the BCP. There was further controversy in August, when the Speaker of the National Assembly designated the BCP as the official opposition party. In October members of the Senate (most of whom apparently refused to recognize the legitimacy of Mokhehle's Government) voted to suspend discussion of proposed legislation, pending the King's response to appeals for the dissolution of the National Assembly. At the first annual conference of the LCD, held in January 1998, Mokhehle resigned as leader, and was made Honorary Life President of the party. In February Deputy Prime Minister Bethuel Pakalitha Mosisili was elected to succeed him as party leader. (Mokhehle died in January 1999.)

Elections to an expanded National Assembly took place on 23 May 1998. An application by the three main opposition parties—the BCP, the BNP and the Marematlou Freedom Party (MFP)—for a postponement of the poll, on the grounds that the IEC had not allowed sufficient time for parties to examine the electoral register, had been rejected by the High Court. The LCD secured an overwhelming victory, winning 78 of the Assembly's 80 seats (with some 60.7% of the votes cast); the BNP, which took one seat (with 24.5% of the votes), was the only other party to win representation. Voting for one seat was postponed, owing to the death of a candidate. The IEC and observers representing the Southern African Development Community (SADC, see p. 331) and the Commonwealth concluded that the polls had been generally free and fair. However, the opposition protested that the outcome of the poll reflected fraud on the part of the LCD, and demonstrations in Maseru to denounce the result were reportedly attended by thousands of activists. Mosisili was elected Prime Minister by the National Assembly in late May, and a new Government was appointed in June. At the end of June the BCP, the BNP and the MFP appealed to the High Court to annul the election results; in the following month the Court ordered the IEC to permit the opposition parties to inspect election documents.

In August 1998 opposition activists began a mass vigil outside the royal palace; within one week some 2,000 people were reported to have joined the protest against the outcome of the poll. Tensions escalated as LCD militants blocked access roads to the capital, in a stated attempt to prevent supplies of weapons to the protesters, while it was reported that a government official attempting to flee the country had been stoned to death after opening fire on an opposition blockade. Following consultations involving the Lesotho Government and the main opposition parties, with mediation by the Government of South Africa, Mosisili announced the establishment of an independent commission, comprising representatives of the SADC 'troika' of Botswana, South Africa and Zimbabwe, to investigate the conduct and results of the May election. The commission was to be chaired by Pius Langa, the Deputy President of South Africa's Constitutional Court. The LDF failed to disperse the protesters outside the palace, and further clashes were reported between opposition and LCD activists.

Meanwhile, revelations that state funds had been used to purchase farmland for the Commander of the LDF, Lt-Gen. Makhula Mosakeng, fuelled opposition allegations of the Commander's complicity in corruption and vote-rigging. (Mosakeng stated that the land had been acquired for army, rather than personal, use.) Rumours of political divisions within the army were apparently confirmed in September 1998, when Mosakeng

and several of his senior colleagues were detained by junior officers (who were reported to have been angered by the recent dismissal of an officer who had countermanded orders to disperse protesters by force). Mosakeng announced his resignation and stated that 26 members of the military command had been dismissed.

By mid-September 1998 frustration was evident at delays in releasing the report of the Langa Commission. Protesters marched to the government complex in Maseru (where the South African Minister of Defence was meeting with government representatives and army officers) and subsequently to the South African High Commissioner's residence. The blockade forced the closure of government offices, and essential public services were paralysed as civil servants reportedly joined the protest. The Langa Commission's report, which was finally released on 17 September, expressed serious concerns at apparent irregularities and discrepancies in the conduct of the May general election, but the Commission was 'unable to state that the invalidity of the elections had been conclusively established'. There was considerable confusion in the days following the publication of the report. Rumours that the Mosisili Government had been overthrown were denied; however, it was confirmed that Lesotho had appealed to SADC for assistance, in view of a breakdown in security. On 22 September an SADC peace-keeping force, initially comprising 600 South African troops and 200 from Botswana, entered Lesotho. In response to criticism that he had not consulted King Letsie prior to requesting external military assistance, Mosisili stated that the monarch had, by harbouring opposition protesters in the palace grounds, contributed to the instability that had necessitated SADC intervention. (It was subsequently reported that the King had been prevented from making a broadcast to the nation.) Within Lesotho, there was widespread outrage at what was perceived as an effective 'invasion' by South Africa, and the SADC force encountered unexpectedly strong resistance. There was sustained fighting between the intervention force and rebel units of the LDF before strategic points, including military bases and the Katse Dam (part of the LHWP essential to the supply of water to South Africa), were secured, while rioting in Maseru and other towns targeted in particular South African interests and caused widespread destruction. Mosakeng and his officers, who had fled to South Africa earlier in the month, returned to resume the army command on 24 September: Mosakeng stated that his resignation had been exacted under duress and, since it had not been approved by the King, was invalid. According to figures subsequently released by the Lesotho authorities, three days of fighting resulted in the deaths of 18 members of the LDF and of 47 civilians; nine members of the South African army were killed during the operation. In addition, as many as 4,000 refugees were reported to have crossed into South Africa.

Following meetings with representatives of the SADC 'troika', in early October 1998 it was reported that the LCD and the main opposition parties had agreed in principle that fresh elections should be held within 15–18 months. In the mean time, the IEC was to be restructured, and the electoral system was to be reviewed, with the aim of ensuring wider inclusion in political affairs (many parties felt that the simple majority voting system was incompatible with the nature of Lesotho's political evolution). Tensions again escalated after shots were fired at an LCD rally east of Maseru. The opposition denied claims by the ruling party of an attempt to assassinate the Prime Minister and his deputy, who were attending the rally; further violence at the meeting reportedly resulted in the deaths of two opposition activists. None the less, inter-party talks proceeded, and in mid-October agreement was reached on a transitional structure, designated the Interim Political Authority (IPA), to comprise representatives of 12 political parties, as well as government and parliamentary delegates, to oversee preparations for fresh elections to the National Assembly.

Shortly after the conclusion of this interim settlement it was announced that some 30 members of the LDF had been arrested on suspicion of involvement in the army rebellion of September 1998. The opposition subsequently expressed considerable concern at the alleged ill-treatment of the detainees and denounced continuing operations by SADC units to locate suspected mutineers who had failed to return to barracks following the suppression of the rebellion. Multi-party talks took place in Pretoria, South Africa, during November, but progress towards the establishment of the IPA was impeded after warrants were issued for the arrest, on murder charges, of several opposition activists, including two leading members of the BCP and BNP youth wings. The opposition parties stated that they would not co-operate in arrangements for the IPA until outstanding security matters, including the release of all rebel soldiers, had been expedited. A court martial in October 1999 ruled against the discharge of a total of 38 members of the LDF accused of mutiny.

The BNP leader, Evaristus Sekhonyana, died in November 1998. The party elected Justin Lekhanya to succeed him in March 1999. The withdrawal of the SADC intervention force was completed in May. This force was immediately succeeded by a new SADC mission, comprising some 300 military personnel from South Africa, Botswana and (subsequently) Zimbabwe, which remained until May 2000, assisting in the retraining and restructuring of the LDF.

Meanwhile, the 24-member IPA was inaugurated on 9 December 1998. After protracted consultations, the IPA announced in September 1999 that the number of seats in the National Assembly was to be increased by 50, to 130, effective from the elections scheduled for April 2000, with seats to be allocated according to a combination of proportional representation and simple majority voting. However, arbitration was required to resolve divisions within the IPA as to the number of seats to be decided by each method, and it was not until December 1999 that a Commonwealth-brokered agreement was signed, providing for 80 seats to be allocated on the basis of simple majority in single-member constituencies, and 50 by proportional representation. The mandate of the IPA was to be extended until elections took place. In the mean time, the Presidents of South Africa, Botswana, Mozambique and Zimbabwe, together with the UN, OAU and Commonwealth Secretaries-General, were to act as guarantors to ensure the implementation of the accord.

In February 2000 the IPA accused the Government of reneging on the December 1999 accord, after the LCD-dominated National Assembly voted to submit the proposed electoral changes to a referendum. Further arbitration concluded in May 2000 that the elections should proceed within 10–12 months. In July the IEC identified 26 May 2001 as the provisional date for the elections; however, delays in enacting legislation concerning voter registration and the electoral model caused the abandonment of this date.

In April 2000 the establishment of a commission of inquiry to investigate political events during July–November 1998 was announced. The commission, comprising three senior judges and chaired by Nigel Leon, met for the first time in June 2000 and heard evidence from several public figures. However, a number of opposition politicians criticized the commission, expressing doubts as to its impartiality. In August three LDF members were convicted by a court martial of participation in the mutiny of September 1998 and sentenced to a combined 29 years' imprisonment; a further 33 LDF members were convicted in November. The Leon commission of inquiry, which submitted its report to Prime Minister Mosisili in October 2001, rejected demands for a general amnesty to be granted to perpetrators of violence during the period under review, recommending the indictment of a number of opposition politicians and members of the armed forces. The commission also proposed measures aimed at ensuring the political neutrality of the armed forces and the police, and the establishment of an informal body, comprising the King, traditional chiefs and representatives of the armed forces, the police, the NSS, churches, political organizations, and the industrial and agricultural sectors, to discuss issues affecting Basotho.

In January 2001 a congress of the LCD re-elected Mosisili as leader of the party, for a five-year term. Shakhane Mokhehle, the incumbent and brother of the party's founder, was defeated in the election to the post of Secretary-General of the LCD by the Minister in the Prime Minister's Office, Sephiri Motanyane. In a minor cabinet reshuffle in July Mokhehle, who had disputed the results of the LCD elections, was dismissed as Minister of Justice, Human Rights and Rehabilitation, Law and Constitutional Affairs. Deputy Prime Minister Kelebone Maope resigned from the Government in September and broke away from the LCD, together with Mokhehle, to form a new opposition party, the Lesotho People's Congress (LPC), to prepare for forthcoming elections. By mid-October a total of 27 deputies had defected from the LCD to join the LPC, which was declared the main opposition party. Mosisili made new cabinet appointments in October, in an effort to consolidate his position ahead of the elections.

In mid-January 2002 a protracted dispute over the leadership of the BCP, which had been ongoing since the late 1990s, also appeared to be resolved, when the High Court ruled in favour of Tseliso Makhakhe's leadership of the party. Qhobela subsequently formed a new party, known as the Basutoland African Congress (BAC), which had been the name of the BCP in 1952–59.

Meanwhile, divisions over the electoral model, notably regarding the number of seats to be allocated by proportional representation, had continued to impede progress towards the elections in 2001. In January 2002 Parliament finally approved amendments to the electoral legislation, providing for the expansion of the National Assembly to 120 members, with 80 to be elected on a constituency basis and 40 selected by proportional representation.

The LCD won a resounding victory at the general election, which took place on 25 May 2002, retaining 77 of the 78 contested constituency seats, with 54.9% of the valid votes cast. The BNP became the second largest legislative party, securing 21 of the 40 seats allocated by proportional representation (known as compensatory seats), with 22.4% of the votes cast; the LPC won one constituency seat and four compensatory seats. Voting in two constituencies was postponed, owing to the deaths of candidates. Of the remaining 15 compensatory seats, the National Independent Party secured five, the BAC and the BCP both won three, while four smaller parties each took one seat. Mosisili was re-elected Prime Minister by the National Assembly in early June, and a new Cabinet was subsequently appointed.

In May 2002 Masupha Sole, the former Chief Executive of the Lesotho Highlands Development Authority, who was alleged to have accepted some US $2m. in bribes over a 10-year period from companies awarded contracts to work on the LHWP, was convicted on 13 charges of bribery and fraud; in the following month he was sentenced to 57 years' imprisonment, of which he was to serve 18 years. A Canadian construction company was found guilty in September of paying bribes to Sole in return for a contract to work on the LHWP, and was subsequently fined M22m. (although this was reduced to M15m. by the Lesotho Court of Appeal in August 2003). A German company was also convicted of bribery in August 2003, receiving a M10m. fine.

Meanwhile, the Government declared a state of famine in April 2002, following a period of severe weather conditions, which had damaged crop production; in December the UN World Food Programme estimated that about one-quarter of the population would require emergency food aid during 2003. The rate of infection with HIV/AIDS among people aged 15–49 stood at 31% at the end of 2001, one of the highest in the world. In January 2003 antiretroviral drugs became available to pregnant women infected with HIV in order to reduce mother-to-child transmission.

In mid-November 2003 police in Maseru used rubber bullets and tear gas to disperse protesters demonstrating against low wages; it was reported that up to three people were killed and more than 100 injured in the clashes. The police action was widely condemned, although the Government stated that the demonstrators had failed to follow the agreed route and had damaged property. The Factory Workers' Union, which had organized the protest, claimed that it had been peaceful. In February 2004 the Government declared a state of emergency in response to severe food shortages following a long period of drought; it was estimated that some 57,000 metric tons of food aid would be required to feed 600,000–700,000 people in 2004.

As exemplified by South Africa's prominent role in the resolution of the 1994 constitutional crisis and by its intervention in the political crisis of September 1998, Lesotho's internal affairs continue to be strongly influenced by South Africa. Long-standing problems of border security and, in particular, the issue of disputed land in South Africa's Free State (formerly Orange Free State) have periodically caused friction between the two countries. During a two-day state visit to Lesotho in July 1995, President Nelson Mandela of South Africa advocated the pursuit of mutually-beneficial policies of regional integration, and he and Prime Minister Mokhehle agreed that the issue of sovereignty in Free State should be discussed by 'appropriate' authorities. Relations between the two countries were strained in August 2000 when Lesotho withdrew its support shortly before the scheduled signing of an agreement with Botswana, Namibia and South Africa on the management of water resources from the Orange river. In September an official at the South African High Commission was killed in Maseru. Representatives of both countries met in Pretoria in November and recommended increased co-operation in areas including education and criminal justice. During a visit to Lesotho by President Thabo Mbeki of South Africa in April 2001, it was agreed to replace an intergovernmental liaison committee that had been established following SADC intervention in 1998 (see above) with a joint binational commission at ministerial level, with the aim of enhancing bilateral relations. Relations between Lesotho and South Africa were further enhanced in May 2002, when their ministers of foreign affairs signed the Joint Bilateral Commission of Co-operation programme, which aimed to raise Lesotho from its current status as a 'least developed country' by 2007.

Government

Lesotho is an hereditary monarchy. Under the terms of the Constitution, which came into effect following the March 1993 election, the King, who is Head of State, has no executive or legislative powers. The College of Chiefs is theoretically empowered, under traditional law, to elect and depose the King by a majority vote. Executive power is vested in the Cabinet, which is headed by the Prime Minister. Legislative power is exercised by the National Assembly, which is elected, at intervals of no more than five years, by universal adult suffrage in the context of a multi-party political system. A system of mixed member proportional representation was introduced at the general election of May 2002, when the National Assembly was expanded to 120 members (80 elected by simple majority in single-member constituencies and 40 selected from party lists). The upper house, the Senate, comprises traditional chiefs and 11 nominated members. Lesotho comprises 10 administrative districts, each with an appointed district co-ordinator.

Defence

Military service is voluntary. The Lesotho Defence Force (LDF) comprised 2,000 men in August 2003. The creation of a new commando force unit, the first professional unit in the LDF, was announced in October 2001, as part of ongoing efforts to restructure the armed forces. Projected budgetary expenditure on defence for 2003 was M250m.

Economic Affairs

In 2002, according to estimates by the World Bank, Lesotho's gross national income (GNI), measured at average 2000–02 prices, was US $981m., equivalent to $470 per head (or $2,710 per head on an international purchasing-power parity basis). During 1990–2002, it was estimated, the population increased at an average annual rate of 1.8%, while gross domestic product (GDP) per head increased, in real terms, by an average of 2.0% per year. Overall GDP increased, in real terms, at an average annual rate of 3.9% in 1990–2002; growth in 2002 was 3.8%.

Agriculture, forestry and fishing contributed 16.7% of GDP in 2002, and employed some 37.6% of the labour force in mid-2001. The principal agricultural exports are wool and mohair, cereals and live animals. The main subsistence crops are maize, sorghum and wheat. Lesotho remains a net importer of staple foodstuffs, largely owing to its vulnerability to adverse climatic conditions, especially drought; it was estimated that the country might be able to produce only 10% of its cereal requirements in 2004. During 1990–2002 agricultural GDP decreased at an average annual rate of 0.2%. Agricultural GDP decreased by 1.6% in 2002.

Industry (including mining, manufacturing, construction and power) provided 41.6% of GDP in 2002, and engaged 27.9% of the labour force in 1990. During 1990–2002 industrial GDP increased by an average of 9.0% per year. Industrial GDP increased by 9.0% in 2002.

Mining contributed 0.1% of GDP in 2002. Lesotho has reserves of diamonds, which during the late 1970s provided more than 50% of visible export earnings, but large-scale exploitation of these ceased in 1982; however, it is planned to reopen the Letseng-la Terai mine, and industrial mining at other sites is envisaged. Lesotho also possesses deposits of uranium, lead and iron ore, and is believed to have petroleum deposits. The GDP of the mining sector increased by an average of 3.0% per year in 1996/97–2002/03; growth in 2002/03 was 8.8%.

Manufacturing contributed 19.2% of GDP in 2002. During 1990–2002 manufacturing GDP increased by an average of 6.5% per year; growth in 2002 was 8.0%.

The Lesotho Highlands Water Project (LHWP) provides hydroelectricity sufficient for all Lesotho's needs and for export to South Africa; phases 1A and 1B were inaugurated in 1998 and 2004, respectively. The scheme was expected to be completed by about 2030. Prior to the LHWP more than 90% of Lesotho's energy requirements were imported from South Africa. Imports of fuel and energy comprised an estimated 18.5% of the total value of imports in 1995.

The services sector contributed 41.7% of GDP in 2002. During 1990–2002 the GDP of the services sector increased at an average annual rate of 2.7%. Services GDP decreased by 0.7% in 2001, but increased by 3.6% in 2002.

In 2002 Lesotho recorded a visible trade deficit of US $381.2m. and a deficit of $118.8m. on the current account of the balance of payments. In 2000 the principal source of imports (85.3%) was the Southern African Customs Union (SACU—i.e. chiefly South Africa—see below), which was also the second largest market for exports (40.7%), behind the USA (57.5%). The principal exports in 2002 were clothing, foodstuffs and footwear. The principal imports in 2001 were manufactured goods, food and live animals, and machinery and transport equipment.

In the financial year ending 31 March 2003 there was an overall budgetary deficit of M328m. (equivalent to 4.2% of GDP in that year). Lesotho's external debt totalled US $592.5m. at the end of 2001, of which $573.3m. was long-term public debt. In that year the cost of debt-servicing was equivalent to 12.4% of revenue from exports of goods and services. The annual rate of inflation averaged 10.4% in 1990–2002; consumer prices declined by an average of 9.7% in 2001, but increased by 33.2% in 2002. It was estimated that 31.4% of the labour force were unemployed in July 2002. In 2002 an estimated 62,200 Basotho were employed as miners in South Africa (compared with some 95,900 in 1997).

Lesotho is a member of the Common Monetary Area (with Namibia, South Africa and Swaziland), and a member of SACU (with Botswana, Namibia, South Africa and Swaziland). Lesotho also belongs to the Southern African Development Community (SADC, see p. 331).

Impediments to economic development in Lesotho include vulnerability to drought and serious land shortages, combined with the country's dependence on South Africa (the Lesotho currency, the loti, is fixed at par with the South African rand, exposing Lesotho to fluctuations within the South African economy). From 1988 Lesotho undertook major economic reforms, supported by the IMF and other donors. However, by the late 1990s the strong growth that had prevailed for most of the decade was being eroded, while retrenchment in the South African gold-mining sector resulted in a marked decline in remittances from Basotho working abroad. The Government accelerated its programme of privatization in 2000, with, most notably, the sale of a 70% holding in the Lesotho Telecommunications Corporation. Under a utilities reform project, initiated in May 2001, the Lesotho Electricity Corporation began a restructuring process in preparation for transfer to private ownership. An agreement was reached with South Africa in January 2001 to restructure bilateral economic relations and to increase mutual co-operation for economic development. In March the IMF approved a three-year loan of some US $31m., under the Poverty Reduction and Growth Facility, on condition that Lesotho encouraged private economic activity, limited the role of the public sector and strengthened fiscal stability. The Lesotho Revenue Authority, intended to improve the administration of taxation and other revenue, commenced operations in January 2003, and a value-added tax was introduced in July of that year. The textile industry has benefited considerably from the USA's African Growth and Opportunities Act (AGOA), for which Lesotho was first declared eligible in April 2001; under its terms, textiles and clothing made in Lesotho have unlimited access to the US market, and by early 2002 exports of these products to the USA had increased by nearly 40%. Lesotho's qualification for the benefits of the AGOA attracted interest from foreign investors in Lesotho, notably Taiwanese textile manufacturers. By mid-2003 an estimated 50,000 Basotho were employed in the textile industry, with further expansion planned. Strong textile exports, together with marked expansion in the GDP of the mining sector, were key factors contributing to favourable economic growth in 2001–03. However, adverse weather conditions led to severe food shortages during the same period, and substantial external assistance was required as agricultural productivity declined.

Education

All primary education is available free of charge, and is provided mainly by the three main Christian missions (Lesotho Evangelical, Roman Catholic and Anglican), under the direction of the Ministry of Education. Education at primary schools is officially compulsory for seven years between six and 13 years of age. Secondary education, beginning at the age of 13, lasts for up to five years, comprising a first cycle of three years and a second of two years. Of children in the relevant age-groups in 2000/01, 78% (males 75%; females 82%) were enrolled at primary schools, while only 21% (males 16%; females 26%) were enrolled at secondary schools. Some 3,266 students were enrolled at the National University of Lesotho, at Roma, in 2002. The budget for 2000/01 allocated M600.6m. to education and community services (representing 20.7% of total government expenditure).

Public Holidays

2004: 1 January (New Year's Day), 11 March (Moshoeshoe Day), 9–12 April (Easter), 1 May (Workers' Day), 20 May (Ascension Day), 25 May (Africa Day and Heroes' Day), 17 July (King's Birthday), 4 October (National Independence Day), 25 December (Christmas Day), 26 December (Boxing Day).

2005: 1 January (New Year's Day), 11 March (Moshoeshoe Day), 25–28 March (Easter), 1 May (Workers' Day), 5 May (Ascension Day), 25 May (Africa Day and Heroes' Day), 17 July (King's Birthday), 4 October (National Independence Day), 25 December (Christmas Day), 26 December (Boxing Day).

Weights and Measures

The metric system of weights and measures is in force.

Statistical Survey

Source (unless otherwise stated): Bureau of Statistics, POB 455, Maseru 100; tel. 323852; fax 310177; internet www.bos.gov.ls/.

Area and Population

AREA, POPULATION AND DENSITY

Area (sq km)	30,355*
Population (census results)†	
12 April 1986 (provisional)	1,447,000
14 April 1996 (provisional)	1,862,275
Population (official estimate at May)	
2002	2,200,000
Density (per sq km) at May 2002	72.5

* 11,720 sq miles.

† Excluding absentee workers in South Africa, numbering 152,627 (males 129,088; females 23,539) in 1976.

‡ Source: UN, *World Population Prospects: The 2002 Revision.*

DISTRICTS

(*de jure* population at 2001 demographic survey, provisional)

District	Population
Berea	300,557
Butha-Buthe	126,907
Leribe	362,339
Mafeteng	238,946
Maseru	477,599
Mohale's Hoek	206,842
Mokhotlong	89,705
Qacha's Nek	80,323
Quthing	140,641
Thaba-Tseka	133,680
Total	**2,157,539**

PRINCIPAL TOWNS

(population at 1986 census)

Maseru (capital)	109,400	Hlotse	9,600
Maputsoa	20,000	Mohale's Hoek	8,500
Teyateyaneng	14,300	Quthing	6,000
Mafeteng	12,700		

Source: Stefan Helders, *World Gazetteer* (www.world-gazetteer.com).

Mid-2001 (UN estimate, including suburbs): Maseru, population 271,000 (Source: UN, *World Urbanization Prospects: The 2001 Revision*).

BIRTHS AND DEATHS

(UN estimates, annual averages)

	1985–90	1990–95	1995–2000
Birth rate (per 1,000)	38.8	34.6	32.6
Death rate (per 1,000)	14.2	13.4	16.7

Source: UN, *World Population Prospects: The 2002 Revision.*

Expectation of life (WHO estimates, years at birth): 35.7 (males 32.9; females 38.2) in 2002 (Source: WHO, *World Health Report*).

ECONOMICALLY ACTIVE POPULATION

(ILO estimates, '000 persons at mid-1990)

	Males	Females	Total
Agriculture, etc.	130	150	280
Industry	183	13	196
Manufacturing	8	7	15
Services	134	91	225
Total	**447**	**254**	**701**

Source: ILO.

Mid-2002 (estimates in '000): Agriculture, etc. 279; Total 719 (Source: FAO).

In 2000 about 17% of the total adult male labour force were in employment in South Africa.

Health and Welfare

KEY INDICATORS

Total fertility rate (children per woman, 2002)	3.9
Under-5 mortality rate (per 1,000 live births, 2001)	132
HIV/AIDS (% of persons aged 15–49, 2001)	31.00
Physicians (per 1,000 head, 1995)	0.05
Health expenditure (2001): US $ per head (PPP)	101
Health expenditure (2001): % of GDP	5.5
Health expenditure (2001): public (% of total)	78.9
Access to water (% of persons, 2000)	91
Access to sanitation (% of persons, 2000)	92
Human Development Index (2001): ranking	137
Human Development Index (2001): value	0.510

For sources and definitions, see explanatory note on p. vi.

Agriculture

PRINCIPAL CROPS

('000 metric tons)

	2000	2001	2002*
Wheat	51	18	51
Maize	158	103	300
Sorghum	45	38	46
Roots and tubers*	90	90	90
Dry beans	8	11	8
Dry peas	6	3	3
Vegetables*	18	18	18
Fruit*	13	13	13

* FAO estimate(s).

Source: FAO.

LIVESTOCK
('000 head, year ending September)

	1999	2000*	2001*
Cattle	571	560	540
Sheep	936	850	850
Goats	730	650	650
Pigs*	63	65	65
Horses*	98	100	100
Asses*	152	154	154
Mules*	1	1	1
Poultry*	1,700	1,800	1,800

* FAO estimates.
2002: Figures assumed to be unchanged from 2001 (FAO estimates).
Source: FAO.

LIVESTOCK PRODUCTS
(FAO estimates, '000 metric tons)

	1999	2000	2001
Cows' milk	23	24	24
Beef and veal	11	11	8
Mutton and lamb	3	3	3
Goat meat	2	2	2
Pig meat	3	3	3
Poultry meat	2	2	2
Game meat	4	4	4
Hen eggs	1	2	2
Wool (greasy)	2	3	3

2002: Production assumed to be unchanged from 2001 (FAO estimates).
Source: FAO.

Forestry

ROUNDWOOD REMOVALS
(FAO estimates, '000 cubic metres, excluding bark)

	2000	2001	2002
Total (all fuel wood)	2,022	2,028	2,034

Source: FAO.

Fishing

(metric tons, live weight)

	1999*	2000*	2001
Capture	30	32	24
Common carp	18	20	8
North African catfish	2	2	2
Other freshwater fishes	10	10	14
Aquaculture	4	8	8
Common carp	4	8	8
Total catch	34	40	32

* FAO estimates.
Source: FAO, *Yearbook of Fishery Statistics*.

Finance

CURRENCY AND EXCHANGE RATES
Monetary Units
100 lisente (singular: sente) = 1 loti (plural: maloti).

Sterling, Dollar and Euro Equivalents (31 December 2003)
£1 sterling = 11.8504 maloti;
US $1 = 6.6400 maloti;
€1 = 8.3863 maloti;
1,000 maloti = £84.39 = $150.60 = €119.24.

Average Exchange Rate (maloti per US $)
2001	8.6092
2002	10.5407
2003	7.5648

Note: The loti is fixed at par with the South African rand.

BUDGET
(million maloti, year ending 31 March)

Revenue*	1998/99	1999/2000	2000/01
Tax revenue	1,694.7	1,888.8	1,941.9
Taxes on net income and profits	387.0	419.5	468.8
Company tax	65.0	58.5	126.3
Individual income tax	278.0	306.5	314.7
Taxes on goods and services	270.9	283.2	343.6
Sales tax	233.3	238.0	279.8
Petrol levy	35.9	43.6	62.0
Taxes on international trade and transactions	1,034.4	1,183.1	1,126.1
Customs duties	1,033.4	1,183.1	1,126.1
Non-tax revenue	478.9	424.0	684.7
Administative fees, charges and non-industrial sales	67.8	142.7	162.4
Total	2,173.6	2,312.8	2,626.6

Expenditure†	1998/99	1999/2000	2000/01
General public services	836.1	1,623.9	884.8
Public order, safety and defence	394.6	489.8	397.4
Health, social security and welfare	227.5	243.9	286.4
Education and community services	652.6	694.3	600.6
Economic services	542.5	517.6	303.0
Agriculture and rural development	125.4	151.7	108.2
Commerce, tourism and industry	49.4	51.3	39.5
Water, energy and mining	121.7	139.6	30.1
Roads	228.3	116.9	87.8
Other transport and communications	17.7	58.1	37.4
Unallocable and other purposes	179.8	293.7	823.2
Total	2,438.5	3,373.4	2,895.8
Current	1,942.7	2,318.5	2,382.6
Capital†	495.8	1,054.9	515.3

* Excluding grants received (million maloti): 120.0 in 1998/99; 130.0 in 1999/2000; 125.6 in 2000/01.
† Including lending minus repayments.
Source: IMF, *Lesotho: Statistical Annex* (May 2002).

INTERNATIONAL RESERVES
(US $ million at 31 December)

	2000	2001	2002
IMF special drawing rights	0.66	0.58	0.60
Reserve position in IMF	4.61	4.45	4.82
Foreign exchange	412.62	381.46	n.a.
Total	417.89	386.49	n.a.

Source: IMF, *International Financial Statistics*.

MONEY SUPPLY
(million maloti at 31 December)

	2000	2001	2002
Currency outside banks	139.34	147.14	179.68
Demand deposits at commercial banks	873.73	939.04	1,099.15
Total money (incl. others)	1,035.96	1,292.27	1,278.83

Source: IMF, *International Financial Statistics*.

COST OF LIVING
(Consumer Price Index; base: 1995 = 100)

	2000	2001	2002
All items	147.1	132.9	177.0

Source: IMF, *International Financial Statistics*.

NATIONAL ACCOUNTS
(million maloti at current prices)

Expenditure on the Gross Domestic Product
(year ending 31 March)

	1998/99	1999/2000	2000/01
Government final consumption expenditure.	1,814.2	2,135.1	2,123.2
Private final consumption expenditure.	4,373.7	5,338.6	5,679.4
Increase in stocks	−84.1	−86.7	−133.7
Gross fixed capital formation	2,471.0	2,105.0	2,270.5
Total domestic expenditure.	8,574.8	9,492.0	9,939.4
Exports of goods and services . } *Less* Imports of goods and services }	3,493.0	3,758.6	3,562.2
GDP in purchasers' values .	5,081.8	5,733.4	6,377.2
GDP at constant 1995 prices	3,857.8	3,952.1	4,079.0

Source: IMF, *Lesotho: Statistical Annex* (May 2002).

Gross Domestic Product by Economic Activity

	2000	2001	2002
Agriculture, forestry and fishing .	1,002.9	1,087.8	1,178.1
Mining and quarrying .	7.6	9.1	10.0
Manufacturing .	909.4	1,054.4	1,353.0
Electricity, gas and water .	317.8	365.7	348.9
Construction .	984.3	1,055.6	1,220.4
Trade, restaurants, and hotels .	570.7	629.0	738.8
Transport and communications .	192.0	225.8	256.8
Finance, insurance, real estate and business services .	548.4	613.3	662.6
Government services.	1,087.1	1,167.6	1,284.4
Sub-total .	5,620.2	6,208.3	7,053.0
Less Imputed bank service charge	215.1	221.3	242.4
GDP at factor cost.	5,405.2	5,987.2	6,810.5
Indirect taxes.	558.5	621.8	720.1
GDP in purchasers' values .	5,963.7	6,608.9	7,530.6

BALANCE OF PAYMENTS
(US $ million)

	2000	2001	2002
Exports of goods f.o.b.	211.1	278.6	354.8
Imports of goods f.o.b.	−727.6	−678.6	−736.0
Trade balance .	−516.5	−400.0	−381.2
Exports of services	42.7	40.5	35.4
Imports of services	−42.5	−49.0	−55.5
Balance on goods and services	−516.4	−408.5	−401.4
Other income received .	288.8	235.3	177.8
Other income paid .	−62.6	−56.7	−16.4
Balance on goods, services and income .	−290.2	−229.9	−240.0
Current transfers (net) .	138.8	134.7	121.3
Current balance .	−151.4	−95.1	−118.8
Capital account (net) .	22.0	16.8	23.4
Direct investment from abroad.	117.8	117.0	80.8
Other investment assets .	−19.1	−20.2	0.7
Other investment liabilities .	−13.5	−8.2	4.0
Net errors and omissions .	62.1	155.4	−115.7
Overall balance .	17.8	165.7	−125.3

Source: IMF, *International Financial Statistics*.

External Trade

PRINCIPAL COMMODITIES

Imports c.i.f. (million maloti)	1999	2000	2001
Food and live animals .	787.8	928.7	768.7
Beverages and tobacco .	33.7	115.6	386.6
Crude materials, inedible except fuels .	177.7	228.6	167.7
Mineral fuels and lubricants .	323.7	840.8	317.0
Animal and vegetable oils, fats and waxes .	54.2	104.2	67.0
Chemicals and related products .	309.4	254.6	525.1
Manufactured goods .	715.6	558.7	1,026.5
Machinery and transport equipment .	674.6	426.4	620.0
Miscellaneous manufactured articles .	458.5	486.7	797.3
Total (incl. others) .	3,888.5	4,236.2	5,119.1

Total imports (million maloti): 8,120.0 in 2002 (Source: IMF, *International Financial Statistics*).

Exports (million maloti)	1999	2000	2001
Food and live animals .	63.9	50.2	133.1
Beverages and tobacco .	73.2	65.3	215.7
Crude materials, inedible, except fuels .	66.0	3.4	71.9
Chemicals and related products .	29.5	6.4	14.0
Manufactured goods .	59.3	9.8	89.7
Machinery and transport equipment .	62.3	180.1	193.4
Miscellaneous manufactured articles .	692.7	2,012.2	1,705.7
Total (incl. others) .	1,046.9	2,327.5	2,425.9

Total exports (million maloti): 3,852.0 in 2002 (Source: IMF, *International Financial Statistics*).

PRINCIPAL TRADING PARTNERS
(million maloti)

Imports*	1998	1999	2000
Africa .	4,615.7	4,737.7	4,316.2
SACU† .	4,614.9	4,736.4	4,309.3
Asia .	370.9	372.4	526.0
Hong Kong .	22.2	31.0	70.3
Taiwan .	203.1	192.2	294.6
European Union .	105.7	83.7	42.7
North America .	70.1	50.0	104.8
Canada .	45.1	41.9	97.2
Total (incl. others) .	5,199.9	5,288.8	5,050.5

Exports	1998	1999	2000
Africa .	691.9	556.0	592.5
SACU† .	690.6	554.4	591.8
European Union .	6.0	1.9	1.8
North America .	371.6	494.9	858.3
Canada .	3.8	5.7	22.5
USA .	367.8	489.2	835.8
Total (incl. others) .	1,071.1	1,054.1	1,453.3

* Valuation exclusive of import duties. Figures also exclude donated food.
† Southern African Customs Union, of which Lesotho is a member; also including Botswana, Namibia, South Africa and Swaziland.

Source: IMF, *Lesotho: Statistical Annex* (May 2002).

Transport

ROAD TRAFFIC
(estimates, motor vehicles in use at 31 December)

	1994	1995	1996
Passenger cars	9,900	11,160	12,610
Lorries and vans	20,790	22,310	25,000

Source: IRF, *World Road Statistics*.

CIVIL AVIATION
(traffic on scheduled services)

	1997	1998	1999
Kilometres flown (million) . . .	0	1	0
Passengers carried ('000) . . .	10	28	1
Passenger-km (million)	3	9	0
Total ton-km (million)	0	1	0

Source: UN, *Statistical Yearbook*.

Tourism

	1996	1997	1998
Tourist arrivals*	311,802	323,868	289,819
From South Africa. . . .	295,926	301,869	281,906
Tourism receipts (US $ million) .	19	20	n.a.

* Figures refer to arrivals at frontiers from visitors abroad and include same-day visitors.

Source: World Tourism Organization, *Yearbook of Tourism Statistics*.

1999: Tourist arrivals 186,000; Tourism receipts (US $ million) 19 (Source: World Bank).

Communications Media

	2000	2001	2002
Television receivers ('000 in use) .	35	n.a.	n.a
Telephones ('000 main lines in use)	22.2	n.a.	34.0
Mobile cellular telephones ('000 subscribers).	21.6	33.0	92.0
Internet users ('000)	4.0	5.0	n.a

Facsimile machines (number in use, year ending 31 March 1996): 569.

Radio receivers ('000 in use): 104 in 1997.

Daily newspapers (1996): 2 (average circulation 15,000 copies).

Non-daily newspapers (1996): 7 (average circulation 74,000 copies).

Sources: UNESCO, *Statistical Yearbook*; International Telecommunication Union.

Education

(2002)

	Institu-tions	Teachers	Students		
			Males	Females	Total
Primary	1,333	8,908	209,024	209,644	418,668
Secondary:					
general . . .	224	3,384	35,467	45,663	81,130
technical and vocational . .	8	172	1,040	818	1,859
teacher training .	1	108	1,206	533	1,739
University . . .	1	n.a.	1,567	1,699	3,266

Adult literacy rate (UNESCO estimates): 83.9% (males 73.3%; females 93.9%) in 2001 (Source: UN Development Programme, *Human Development Report*).

Directory

The Constitution

The Constitution of the Kingdom of Lesotho, which took effect at independence in October 1966, was suspended in January 1970. A new Constitution was promulgated following the March 1993 general election. Its main provisions, with subsequent amendments, are summarized below

Lesotho is an hereditary monarchy. The King, who is Head of State, has no executive or legislative powers. Executive authority is vested in the Cabinet, which is headed by the Prime Minister, while legislative power is exercised by the 120-member National Assembly, which comprises 80 members elected on a single-member constituency basis and 40 selected by a system of proportional representation. The National Assembly is elected, at intervals of no more than five years, by universal adult suffrage in the context of a multi-party political system. There is also a Senate, comprising 22 traditional chiefs and 11 nominated members. The Prime Minister is the official head of the armed forces.

The Government

HEAD OF STATE

King: HM King LETSIE III (acceded to the throne 7 February 1996).

CABINET
(April 2004)

Prime Minister and Minister of Defence and National Security: BETHUEL PAKALITHA MOSISILI.

Deputy Prime Minister and Minister of Education: ARCHIBALD LESAO LEHOHLA.

Minister of Local Government: Dr PONTS'O SUZAN MATUMELO SEKATLE.

Minister of Home Affairs and Public Safety: MOTSOAHAE THOMAS THABANE.

Minister of Tourism, Environment and Culture: LEBOHANG NTSINYI.

Minister of Natural Resources (Water, Lesotho Water Highlands Project, Energy, Mining and Technology): MONYANE MOLELEKI.

Minister of Foreign Affairs: MOHLABI KENNETH TSEKOA.

Minister of Trade, Industry, Co-operatives and Marketing: MPHO MELI MALIE.

Minister of Agriculture and Food Security: Dr RAKORO PHORORO.

Minister of Forestry and Land Reclamation: LINCOLN RALECHATE MOKOSE.

Minister of Communications, Science and Technology: MAMPHONO KHAKETLA.

Minister of Public Works and Transport: MOFELEHETSI SALOMONE MOERANE.

Minister of Gender, Youth, Sports and Recreation: MATHABISO LEPONO.

Minister of Finance and Development Planning: TIMOTHY THAHANE.

Minister of Health and Social Welfare: Dr MOTLOHELOA PHOOKO.

Minister of Employment and Labour: SELLO CLEMENT MACHAKELA.

Minister of Justice, Human Rights and Rehabilitation, Law and Constitutional Affairs: REFILOE MASEMENE.

Minister in the Prime Minister's Office: (vacant).

MINISTRIES

Office of the Prime Minister: POB 527, Maseru 100; tel. 311000; fax 310578; internet www.lesotho.gov.ls.

Ministry of Agriculture and Food Security: POB 24, Maseru 100; tel. 316407; fax 310906.

Ministry of Communications, Science and Technology: POB 36, Maseru 100; tel. 323561; fax 310264.

Ministry of Defence and National Security: POB 527, Maseru 100; tel. 316570; fax 310518.

Ministry of Education: POB 47, Maseru 100; tel. 312814; fax 310562.

Ministry of Employment and Labour: Private Bag A116, Maseru 100; tel. 322602; fax 310374.

Ministry of Finance and Development Planning: POB 395, Maseru 100; tel. 311101; fax 310964.

Ministry of Foreign Affairs: POB 1387, Maseru 100; tel. 311150; fax 310642.

Ministry of Forestry and Land Reclamation: POB 24, Maseru 100; tel. 316407; fax 310146; e-mail agric@ilesotho.com.

Ministry of Gender, Youth, Sports and Recreation: POB 10993, Maseru 100; tel. 311006; fax 310506.

Ministry of Health and Social Welfare: POB 514, Maseru 100; tel. 314404; fax 310467.

Ministry of Home Affairs and Public Safety: POB 174, Maseru 100; tel. 323771; fax 310319.

Ministry of Justice, Human Rights and Rehabilitation, Law and Constitutional Affairs: POB 402, Maseru 100; tel. 322683; fax 311092; e-mail ps@justice.gov.ls.

Ministry of Local Government: POB 174, Maseru 100; tel. 323771; fax 310587.

Ministry of Natural Resources: POB 772, Maseru 100; tel. 323163; fax 310520.

Ministry of Public Works and Transport: POB 20, Maseru 100; tel. 311362; fax 310125.

Ministry of Tourism, Environment and Culture: POB 52, Maseru 100; tel. 313034; fax 310194; e-mail ps@tourism.gov.ls.

Ministry of Trade, Industry, Co-operatives and Marketing: POB 747, Maseru 100; tel. 312938; fax 310644.

Legislature

PARLIAMENT

National Assembly

Speaker: NTLHOI MOTSAMAI.

General Election, 25 May 2002

Party	Consti-tuency seats	Compen-satory seats*	Total seats
Lesotho Congress for Democracy .	77	—	77
Basotho National Party	—	21	21
Lesotho People's Congress . . .	1	4	5
National Independent Party. . .	—	5	5
Basotho Congress Party	—	3	3
Basutoland African Congress . .	—	3	3
Lesotho Workers' Party	—	1	1
Marem_atlou Freedom Party. . .	—	1	1
National Progressive Party . . .	—	1	1
Popular Front for Democracy . .	—	1	1
Total	**78†**	**40**	**118†**

* Allocated by proportional representation.

† Voting in two constituencies was postponed, owing to the deaths of candidates.

Senate

Speaker: Chief SEMPE LEJAHA.

The Senate is an advisory chamber, comprising 22 traditional chiefs and 11 members appointed by the monarch.

Political Organizations

Basotho Congress Party (BCP): POB 111, Maseru 100; tel. 8737076; f. 1952; Leader TSELISO MAKHAKHE.

Basotho Democratic Alliance (BDA): Maseru; f. 1984; Pres. S. C. NKOJANE.

Basotho National Party (BNP): POB 124, Maseru 100; f. 1958; Leader JUSTIN METSING LEKHANYA; Sec.-Gen. LESETELI MALEFANE; 280,000 mems.

Basutoland African Congress (BAC): Maseru; f. 2002 following split in the BCP; Leader MOLAPO QHOBELA; Sec.-Gen. MAHOLELA MANDORO.

Khokanyana-Phiri Democratic Alliance: Maseru; f. 1999; alliance of opposition parties.

Christian Democratic Party: Maseru.

Communist Party of Lesotho (CPL): Maseru; f. 1962; banned 1970–91; supported mainly by migrant workers employed in South Africa; Sec.-Gen. MOKHAFISI KENA.

Kopanang Basotho Party (KBP): Maseru; f. 1992; campaigns for women's rights; Leader LIMAKATSO NTAKATSANE.

National Independent Party (NIP): Maseru; f. 1984; Pres. ANTHONY C. MANYELI.

National Progressive Party (NPP): Maseru; f. 1995 following split in the BNP; Leader Chief PEETE NKOEBE PEETE.

Popular Front for Democracy (PFD): Maseru; f. 1991; Leader LEKHETHO RAKUANE.

Social Democratic Party: Maseru; Leader MASITISE SELESO.

Lesotho Congress for Democracy (LCD): Maseru; f. 1997 as a result of divisions within the BCP; Chair. SELLO CLEMENT MACHAKELA; Leader BETHUEL PAKALITHA MOSISILI; Sec.-Gen. SEPHIRI ENOCH MOTANYANE; 200,000 mems.

Lesotho Labour Party (LLP): Maseru; f. 1991; Leader PATRICK SALIE.

Lesotho People's Congress (LPC): f. 2001 following split in the LCD; Interim Leader KELEBONE ALBERT MAOPE; Interim Sec.-Gen. SHAKHANE MOKHEHLE.

Lesotho Workers' Party (LWP): f. 2001; Leader BILLY MACAEFA.

Marematlou Freedom Party (MFP): POB 0443, Maseru 105; tel. 315804; f. 1962; Leader VINCENT MOEKETSE MALEBO; Dep. Leader THABO LEANYA; 300,000 mems.

Sefate Democratic Union (SDU): Maseru; Leader BOFIHLA NKUEBE.

United Democratic Party (UDP): POB 776, Maseru 100; f. 1967; Chair. BEN L. SHEA; Leader CHARLES D. MOFELI; Sec.-Gen. MOLOMO NKUEBE; 26,000 mems.

United Party (UP): Maseru; Pres. MAKARA SEKAUTU.

Diplomatic Representation

EMBASSIES AND HIGH COMMISSIONS IN LESOTHO

China, People's Republic: POB 380, Maseru 100; tel. 316521; fax 310489; Ambassador QIU BOHUA.

Denmark: Site 16, Industrial Area, POB 1259, Maseru 100; tel. 313630; fax 310138; Ambassador ALF JÖNSSON.

Korea, Democratic People's Republic: Maseru; Ambassador AN KYONG HYON.

South Africa: Lesotho Bank Tower, 10th Floor, Kingsway, Private Bag A266, Maseru 100; tel. 315758; fax 310128; e-mail sahcis@lesoff .co.za; High Commissioner M. JAPHET NDLOVU.

United Kingdom: Linare Rd, POB MS521, Maseru 100; tel. 313961; fax 310120; e-mail hcmaseru@bhc.org.ls; internet www.bhc .org.ls; High Commissioner FRANCIS MARTIN.

USA: 254 Kingsway, POB 333, Maseru 100; tel. 312666; fax 310116; e-mail info@embassy.org.ls; internet www.usembassy.org.ls; Ambassador ROBERT GEERS LOFTIS.

Judicial System

HIGH COURT

The High Court is a superior court of record, and in addition to any other jurisdiction conferred by statute it is vested with unlimited original jurisdiction to determine any civil or criminal matter. It also has appellate jurisdiction to hear appeals and reviews from the subordinate courts. Appeals may be made to the Court of Appeal.

Chief Justice: JOSEPH LEBONA KHEOLA.

Judges: M. L. LEHOHLA, W. C. M. MAQUTU, B. K. MOLAI, T. E. MONAPATHI, K. GUNI, G. MOFOLO, M. RAMODIBEDI, S. PEETE, M. HLAJOANE.

COURT OF APPEAL

Judges: T. Browde, R. N. Leon, J. N. Steyn, G. Friedman, M. Ramodibedi.

SUBORDINATE COURTS

Each of the 10 districts possesses subordinate courts, presided over by magistrates.

JUDICIAL COMMISSIONERS' COURTS

These courts hear civil and criminal appeals from central and local courts. Further appeal may be made to the High Court and finally to the Court of Appeal.

CENTRAL AND LOCAL COURTS

There are 71 such courts, of which 58 are local courts and 13 are central courts which also serve as courts of appeal from the local courts. They have limited civil and criminal jurisdiction.

Religion

About 90% of the population profess Christianity.

CHRISTIANITY

African Federal Church Council: POB 70, Peka 340; f. 1927; co-ordinating org. for 48 African independent churches; Co-ordinator Rev. S. Mohono.

Christian Council of Lesotho: Maseru 100; tel. 313639; fax 310310; e-mail ccl@email.co.ls; f. 1973; six mem. and four assoc. mem. churches; Chair. Rev. S. E. Nthabane; Sec. Catherine Ramokhele.

The Anglican Communion

Anglicans in Lesotho are adherents of the Church of the Province of Southern Africa. The Metropolitan of the Province is the Archbishop of Cape Town, South Africa. Lesotho forms a single diocese, with an estimated 100,000 members.

Bishop of Lesotho: Rt Rev. Joseph Mahapu Tsubella, Bishop's House, POB 87, Maseru 100; tel. 311974; fax 310161; e-mail diocese@ilesotho.com.

The Roman Catholic Church

Lesotho comprises one archdiocese and three dioceses. At 31 December 2002 there were some 965,608 adherents of the Roman Catholic Church, equivalent to 51.1% of the population.

Lesotho Catholic Bishops' Conference

Catholic Secretariat, POB 200, Maseru 100; tel. 312525; fax 310294. f. 1972; Pres. Rt Rev. Evaristus Thatho Bitsoane (Bishop of Qacha's Nek).

Archbishop of Maseru: Most Rev. Bernard Mohlalisi, Archbishop's House, 19 Orpen Rd, POB 267, Maseru 100; tel. 312565; fax 310425; e-mail archmase@lesoff.co.za.

Other Christian Churches

African Methodist Episcopal Church: POB 223, Maseru 100; tel. 322616; f. 1903; 11,295 mems.

Dutch Reformed Church in Africa: POB 454, Maseru 100; tel. 314669; f. 1957; 7,396 mems (1991).

Lesotho Evangelical Church: POB 260, Maseru 100; tel. 323942; f. 1833; independent since 1964; Moderator Rev. G. L. Sibolla; Exec. Sec. Rev. A. M. Thebe; 211,000 mems (1990).

Methodist Church of Southern Africa: POB 81, Maseru 100; tel. 322412; f. 1927; Supt Rev. D. Senkhane; c. 10,000 mems and adherents (1989).

Other denominations active in Lesotho include the Apostolic Faith Mission, the Assemblies of God, the Full Gospel Church of God and the Seventh-day Adventists. There are also numerous African independent churches.

BAHÁ'Í FAITH

National Spiritual Assembly: POB 508, Maseru 100; tel. 312346; fax 310092; e-mail bahailesotho@lesotho.com; mems resident in 443 localities.

The Press

Lentsoe la Basotho: POB 353, Maseru 100; tel. 323561; fax 310003; e-mail lbmin@lesoff.co.za; f. 1974; weekly; Sesotho; publ. by

Ministry of Communications, Science and Technology; Editor Kahliso Lebenya; circ. 14,000.

Leselinyana la Lesotho (Light of Lesotho): POB 7, Morija 190; tel. 360244; fax 360005; f. 1863; fortnightly; Sesotho, with occasional articles in English; publ. by Lesotho Evangelical Church; Editor A. B. Thoalane; circ. 10,000.

Lesotho Today: POB 36, Maseru 100; tel. 323586; fax 310003; weekly; English; publ. by Ministry of Communications, Science and Technology; Editor T. Tsepane; circ. 7,000.

Lesotho Weekly: POB 353, Maseru 100; weekly.

Makatolle: POB 111, Maseru 100; tel. 850990; f. 1963; weekly; Sesotho; Editor M. Ramangoei; circ. 2,000.

The Mirror: POB 903, Maseru 100; tel. 315602; fax 310216; f. 1986; weekly; English; Editor Nat Molomo; circ. 4,000.

MoAfrika: POB 7234, Maseru 100; tel. 325034; f. 1990; weekly; Sesotho; Editor-in-Chief Candi Ramainoane; circ. 5,000.

Moeletsi oa Basotho: Mazenod Institute, POB 18, Mazenod 160; tel. 350465; fax 350010; f. 1933; weekly; Roman Catholic; Sesotho; Editor Fr F. S. Shopane; circ. 20,000.

Mopheme (the Survivor): POB 14184, Maseru; tel. and fax 311670; e-mail mopheme@lesoff.co.za; internet www.lesoffice.co.za/news; weekly; English; Editor Lawrence Keketso; circ. 2,500.

Public Eye: POB 14129, Maseru; tel. 3201414; fax 310614; e-mail voicemed@lesoff.co.za; internet www.publiceye.co.ls; f. 1997; weekly; English; Editor Bethuel Thai; circ. 18,000.

Shoeshoe: POB 36, Maseru 100; tel. 323561; fax 310003; quarterly; women's interest; publ. by Ministry of Communications, Science and Technology.

Southern Star: POB 7590, Maseru; tel. 312269; fax 310167; e-mail b&a-holdings@ilesotho.com; weekly; English; Editor Frank Boffoe; circ. 1,500.

The Sun: POB 1013, Maseru; weekly; English; Editor M. Ranouku; circ. 6,500.

Thebe ea Khotso: POB 15303, Maseru; Sesotho; Editor Mohapi Motba; circ. 7,000.

NEWS AGENCIES

Lesotho News Agency (LENA): POB 36, Maseru 100; tel. 315317; fax 326408; e-mail l_lenanews@hotmail.com; internet www.lena.gov.ls; f. 1986; Dir Nkoe Thakali; Editor Violet Maraisane.

Foreign Bureau

Inter Press Service (IPS) (Italy): c/o Lesotho News Agency, POB 36, Maseru 100; Correspondent Lebohang Lejakane.

Publishers

Longman Lesotho (Pty) Ltd: POB 1174, 104 Christie House, Orpen Rd, Maseru 100; tel. 314254; fax 310118; e-mail connie.burford@pearsoned.com ; Man. Dir Seymour R. Kikine.

Macmillan Boleswa Publishers Lesotho (Pty) Ltd: POB 7545, Maseru 100; tel. 317340; fax 310047; e-mail macmillan@lesoff.co.ls.

Mazenod Institute: POB 39, Mazenod 160; tel. 350224; f. 1933; Roman Catholic; Man. Fr B. Mohlalisi.

Morija Sesuto Book Depot: POB 4, Morija 190; tel. and fax 360204; f. 1862; owned by the Lesotho Evangelical Church; religious, educational and Sesotho language and literature.

St Michael's Mission: The Social Centre, POB 25, Roma; tel. 316234; f. 1968; religious and educational; Man. Dir Fr M. Ferrange.

Government Publishing House

Government Printer: POB 268, Maseru; tel. 313023.

Broadcasting and Communications

TELECOMMUNICATIONS

Telecom Lesotho: POB 1037, Maseru 100; tel. 211100; fax 310183; internet www.telecom.co.ls; 70% holding acquired by the Mountain Kingdom Communications consortium in 2000; 30% state-owned; CEO A. Van Der Veer; Chair. Dr Daniel Phororo.

VCL Communications: Development House, Kingsway Rd, POB 7387, Maseru 100; tel. 212000; fax 311079; f. 1996; jt venture between Telecom Lesotho and Vodacom (Pty) Ltd; operates mobile cellular telephone network.

BROADCASTING

Lesotho National Broadcasting Service: POB 552, Maseru 100; tel. 323561; fax 310003; programmes in Sesotho and English; radio transmissions began in 1964 and television transmissions in 1988; Dir MOLAHLEHI LETLOTLO; Dir of Programming MAMONYANE MATSABA.

Finance

(cap. = capital; res = reserves; dep. = deposits; m. = million; brs = branches; amounts in maloti)

BANKING

Central Bank

Central Bank of Lesotho: cnr Airport and Moshoeshoe Rds, POB 1184, Maseru 100; tel. 314281; fax 310051; e-mail cbl@centralbank.org.ls; internet www.centralbank.org.ls; f. 1980; bank of issue; cap. 25.0m., res 2,591.6m., dep. 1,497.7m. (Dec. 2001); Gov. and Chair. E. M. MATEKANE.

Commercial Banks

Lesotho Bank: Central Services, Lesotho Bank Towers, Kingsway, POB 1053, Maseru 100; tel. 314333; fax 310348; f. 1972; transferred to majority private ownership in Aug. 1999; 70% owned by Standard Bank Lesotho Ltd; commercial bank, also carries out development banking functions; total assets 1,031.4m. (2001); Chair. M. FAKO; Exec. Dir C. ADDIS; 15 brs.

Nedbank Lesotho: Standard Bank Bldg, 1st Floor, Kingsway, POB 1001, Maseru 100; tel. 312696; fax 310025; e-mail georgego@nedcor.co.za; fmrly Standard Chartered Bank Lesotho Ltd; owned by Nedcor Bank Ltd (South Africa); cap. 20m., res 21.5m., dep. 704.2m. (Dec. 2002); Chair. W. P. FROST; 3 brs and 7 agencies.

Standard Bank Lesotho Ltd: Bank Bldg, 1st Floor, Kingsway, POB 115, Maseru 100; tel. 312423; fax 310068; e-mail horst@ilesotho.com; internet www.standardbank.co.ls; f. 1957 as Barclays Bank DCO; fmrly Stanbic Bank Lesotho Ltd, present name since 1997; owned by Standard Bank Investment Corpn Ltd; cap. 16.5m., total assets 532.5m. (Dec. 2001); Chair. ROBERT E. NORVAL; Exec. Dir V. KENNEDY; 5 brs and 2 agencies.

Development Bank

Lesotho Building Finance Corpn (LBFC): Private Bag A59, Maseru 100; tel. 313514; fax 310348; state-owned; Man. Dir N. MONYANE; 3 brs.

INSURANCE

Alliance Insurance Co Ltd: POB 1118, Maseru West 105; tel. 312357; fax 310313; e-mail alliance@alliance.co.ls; Man. Dir JOHANN PIENAAR.

Lesotho National Insurance Corpn (Pty) Ltd: Private Bag A96, Lesotho Insurance House, Kingsway, Maseru 100; tel. 313031; fax 310007; e-mail inig@lesoff.co.za; f. 1977; Chair. Dr M. SENAOANA; CEO M. MOLELEKOA.

Mamoth Insurance: Christie House, 4th Floor, POB 1659, Maseru 100; e-mail mamoth@adelfng.co.za; internet www.mamoth.co.ls; f. 1998; Chair. THABO RAMOKGOPA.

Metropolitan Life Ltd: POB 645, Maseru; tel. 323970; fax 317126; Regional Man. E. L. TSHABALALA.

Aon Lesotho (Pty) Ltd: 5th Floor, Postal Services Building, Kingsway, Maseru; POB 993, Maseru 100; tel. 22313540; fax 310033; f. 1969; 55% holding acquired by Aon Holdings BV Rotterdam in 2000, 5% state-owned; Chair. MIKE W. CHURCH; Man. Dir Z. Z. MOHAPELOA.

Thebe Insurance Brokers (Lesotho) (Pty) Ltd: Options Bldg, 1st Floor, Pioneer Rd, Private Bag A244, Maseru 100; tel. 313018; fax 310513; Chair. C. J. SOUNES; Man. Dir D. T. MALING.

Trade and Industry

GOVERNMENT AGENCIES

Privatization Unit: c/o Ministry of Finance and Development Planning, Private Bag A249, Maseru 100; tel. 317902; fax 317551; e-mail mmashologu@privatization.gov.ls; Dir MOTHUSI MASHOLOGU.

Trade Promotion Unit: c/o Ministry of Trade, Industry, Co-operatives and Marketing, POB 747, Maseru 100; tel. 322138; fax 310121.

DEVELOPMENT ORGANIZATIONS

Basotho Enterprises Development Corpn (BEDCO): POB 1216, Maseru 100; tel. 312094; fax 310455; e-mail bedco@lesoff.co.za; f. 1980; promotes and assists in the establishment and development of small-scale Basotho-owned enterprises; CEO SIMON PHAWANE.

Lesotho Highlands Development Authority: Lesotho Bank Towers, 3rd Floor, POB 7332, Maseru 100; tel. 311280; fax 310060; internet www.lhda.org.ls; f. 1986 to supervise the Highlands Water Project (internet www.lhwp.org.ls), being undertaken jtly with South Africa; Chair. H. M. MHLANGA; CEO LIPHAPANG ELIAS POTLOANE.

Lesotho National Development Corpn (LNDC): Development House, 1st Floor, Kingsway Rd, Private Bag A96, Maseru 100; tel. 312012; fax 310038; e-mail info@lndc.org.ls; internet www.lndc.org.ls; f. 1967; 90% state-owned; cap. M40m.; interests include candle, carpet, tyre-retreading, explosives, fertilizer, clothing, jewellery and furniture factories, potteries, two diamond prospecting operations, an abattoir, a diamond-cutting and polishing works, a housing co, a brewery and an international hotel with a gambling casino; Chair. MPHO MELI MALIE (Minister of Trade, Industry, Co-operatives and Marketing); CEO SOPHIA MOHAPI.

Lesotho Co-operatives Handicrafts: Maseru; f. 1978; marketing and distribution of handicrafts; Gen. Man. KHOTSO MATLA.

CHAMBER OF COMMERCE

Lesotho Chamber of Commerce and Industry: POB 79, Maseru 100; tel. 323482; fax 310414; e-mail lcci@lesoff.co.za.

INDUSTRIAL AND TRADE ASSOCIATIONS

Livestock Marketing Corpn: POB 800, Maseru 100; tel. 322444; f. 1973; sole org. for marketing livestock and livestock products; liaises closely with marketing boards in South Africa; projects include an abattoir, tannery, poultry and wool and mohair scouring plants; Gen. Man. S. R. MATLANYANE.

Produce Marketing Corpn: Maseru; f. 1974; Gen. Man. M. PHOOFOLO.

EMPLOYERS' ORGANIZATION

Association of Lesotho Employers: POB 1509, Maseru 100; tel. 315736; e-mail alemp@ilesotho.com; f. 1961; represents mems in industrial relations and on govt bodies, and advises the Govt on employers' concerns; Pres. BRIAN McCARTHY; Exec. Dir T. MAKEKA.

UTILITIES

Lesotho Electricity Corpn: POB 423, Maseru 100; tel. 312236; fax 310093; internet www.lec.co.ls; f. 1969; transfer to the private sector scheduled for 2004; Man. Dir S. L. MHAVILLE.

Lesotho Water and Sewerage Authority: POB 426, Maseru 100; tel. 312449; fax 312006; e-mail makhoalibe@wasa.co.ls; Chair. S. MAKHOALIBE.

TRADE UNIONS

Construction and Allied Workers Union of Lesotho (CAWULE): Private Bag A445, Maseru 100; tel. 333035.

Factory Workers' Union (FAWU): Maseru; f. 2003; Pres. KHABILE TSILO; Sec.-Gen. BILLY MACAEFA.

Lesotho Clothing and Allied Workers' Union (Lecawu): Maseru; Sec.-Gen. DANILE MARAISANE.

Lesotho General Workers' Union: POB 322, Maseru 100; f. 1954; Chair. J. M. RAMAROTHOLE; Sec. T. MOTLOHI.

Lesotho Transport and Telecommunication Workers' Union: Maseru 100; f. 1959; Pres. M. BERENG; Sec. P. MOTRAMAI.

Lesotho University Teachers' and Researchers' Union (LUTARU): Maseru.

National Union of Construction and Allied Workers: Maseru; f. 1967; Pres. L. PUTSOANE; Sec. T. TLALE.

National Union of Printing, Bookbinding and Allied Workers: PO Mazenod 160; f. 1963; Pres. G. MOTEBANG; Gen. Sec. CLEMENT RATSIU.

Union of Shop Distributive and Allied Workers: Maseru 100; f. 1966; Pres. P. BERENG; Sec. J. MOLAPO.

Transport

RAILWAYS

Lesotho is linked with the South African railway system by a short line (2.6 km in length) from Maseru to Marseilles, on the Bloemfontein–Natal main line.

ROADS

In 1999 Lesotho's road network totalled 5,940 km, of which 1,084 km were main roads and 1,950 km were secondary roads. About 18.3% of roads were paved. In 1996 the International Development Association granted US $40m. towards the Government's rolling five-year road programme. From 1996/67 an extra-budgetary Road Fund was to finance road maintenance. In March 2000 a major road network was opened, linking Maseru with the Mohale Dam.

CIVIL AVIATION

King Moshoeshoe I International Airport is at Thota-Moli, some 20 km from Maseru; in January 2002 the Government announced plans for its expansion. There are 27 smaller airfields in Lesotho. International services between Maseru and Johannesburg are operated by South African Airlink.

Lesotho Airways Corpn: POB 861, Maseru 100; tel. 324507; fax 310617; domestic and international passenger services; privatized 1999; Man. Dir MICHAEL SCHRIENER.

Tourism

Spectacular mountain scenery is the principal tourist attraction, and a new ski resort was opened in 2003. In 1999 there were 186,000 tourist arrivals, and receipts from tourism totalled about US $19m.

Lesotho Tourist Board (Boto Ea Tsa Boeti Lesotho): POB 1378, Maseru 100; tel. 313760; fax 310108; e-mail infomsu@ltb.org .ls; f. 1983; Man. Dir MANDISA MASHOLOGU.

LIBERIA

Introductory Survey

Location, Climate, Language, Religion, Flag, Capital

The Republic of Liberia lies on the west coast of Africa, with Sierra Leone and Guinea to the north, and Côte d'Ivoire to the east. The climate is tropical, with temperatures ranging from 18°C (65°F) to 49°C (120°F). English is the official language but the 16 major ethnic groups speak their own languages and dialects. Liberia is officially a Christian state, though some Liberians hold traditional beliefs. There are about 670,000 Muslims. The national flag (proportions 10 by 19) has 11 horizontal stripes, alternately of red and white, with a dark blue square canton, containing a five-pointed white star, in the upper hoist. The capital is Monrovia.

Recent History

Founded by liberated black slaves from the southern USA, Liberia became an independent republic in 1847. The leader of the True Whig Party (TWP), William Tubman, who had been President of Liberia since 1944, died in July 1971 and was succeeded by his Vice-President, William R. Tolbert, who was re-elected in October 1975. The TWP's monopoly of power was increasingly criticized, and in 1978 a major opposition group, the Progressive Alliance of Liberia, was formed.

In April 1980 Tolbert was assassinated in a military coup, led by Master Sgt (later Commander-in-Chief) Samuel Doe, who assumed power as Chairman of the newly established People's Redemption Council (PRC), suspending the Constitution and proscribing all political parties. The new regime attracted international criticism for its summary execution of 13 former senior government officials who had been accused of corruption and mismanagement. In July 1981 all civilian ministers received commissions, thus installing total military rule.

A draft Constitution was approved by 78.3% of registered voters in a national referendum in July 1984. In the same month Doe dissolved the PRC and appointed a 58-member Interim National Assembly, comprising 36 civilians and all the members of the former PRC. The ban on political organizations was repealed in the same month, to enable parties to secure registration prior to presidential and legislative elections, which were due to take place in October 1985. In August 1984 Doe founded the National Democratic Party of Liberia (NDPL) and formally announced his candidature for the presidency. By early 1985 a total of 11 political parties had been formed; however, two influential parties, the Liberian People's Party (LPP) and the United People's Party (UPP), were proscribed, and only three parties besides the NDPL—the Liberian Action Party (LAP), the Liberia Unification Party (LUP) and the Unity Party (UP)—were eventually permitted to participate in the elections. Doe won the presidential election, receiving 50.9% of the votes. At the concurrent elections to the bicameral National Assembly, the NDPL won 22 of the 26 seats in the Senate and 51 of the 64 seats in the House of Representatives.

On 6 January 1986 Doe was inaugurated as President. He appointed a new Cabinet (which largely comprised members of the previous administration). Six members of the opposition parties continued to boycott the National Assembly, and their seats were taken by NDPL representatives at a by-election in December. In March 1988 Gabriel Kpolleh, the leader of the LUP, was among several people arrested on charges of planning to overthrow the Government. In October he and nine others were sentenced to 10 years' imprisonment for treason.

In December 1989 an armed insurrection by rebel forces began in the north-eastern border region of Nimba County. In early 1990 several hundred deaths ensued in fighting between the Liberian army (the Armed Forces of Liberia—AFL) and the rebels, who claimed to be members of a hitherto unknown opposition group, the National Patriotic Front of Liberia (NPFL), led by a former government official, Charles Taylor. The fighting swiftly degenerated into a war between Doe's ethnic group, the Krahn, and the local Gio and Mano tribes, and many thousands of people took refuge in neighbouring Guinea and Côte d'Ivoire. By April the NPFL had gained control of a large part of Nimba County. Following the advance of rebels on the capital, Monrovia, in May, most foreign residents were evacuated. NPFL forces entered Monrovia in July; Taylor's authority as self-proclaimed President of his own interim administration, known as the National Patriotic Reconstruction Assembly, was, however, challenged by a faction of the NPFL, led by Prince Yormie Johnson, whose troops rapidly secured control of parts of Monrovia. In the subsequent conflict both government and rebel forces were responsible for numerous atrocities against civilians. The Economic Community of West African States (ECOWAS, see p. 196) repeatedly failed to negotiate a cease-fire, and in late August it dispatched a military force to restore peace in the region. Doe and Johnson agreed to accept this monitoring group (ECOMOG, see p. 198), but its initial occupation of the port area of Monrovia encountered armed opposition by Taylor's forces.

On 30 August 1990 exiled representatives of Liberia's principal political parties and other influential groups met at a conference convened by ECOWAS in the Gambian capital, Banjul, where they elected Dr Amos Sawyer, the leader of the LPP, as President of an Interim Government of National Unity (IGNU). Doe was taken prisoner by Johnson's rebel Independent National Patriotic Front of Liberia (INPFL) on 9 September, and was killed on the following day. In early October, following Taylor's rejection of a proposed peace settlement, ECOMOG began an offensive aimed at establishing a neutral zone in Monrovia separating the three warring factions. By mid-October ECOMOG had gained control of central Monrovia. On 22 November Sawyer was inaugurated as Interim President, under the auspices of ECOWAS, in Monrovia. Later that month, following ECOWAS-sponsored negotiations in the Malian capital, Bamako, the AFL, the NPFL and the INPFL signed a cease-fire agreement. By January 1991 all rebel forces had withdrawn from Monrovia, and in that month Sawyer nominated ministers to the IGNU. Legislative power was vested in a 28-member Interim National Assembly, which represented the principal political factions, including the INPFL; however, the NPFL refused to participate. On 19 April a national conference re-elected Sawyer as Interim President and appointed a member of the INPFL, Peter Naigow (a former minister in Doe's administration), as Vice-President. In June Sawyer nominated a new Council of Ministers, which was subsequently approved by the Interim National Assembly. In August, however, the INPFL representatives, including Naigow, resigned from the IGNU, after Sawyer denounced the execution, apparently at Johnson's instigation, of four members of the INPFL who had reportedly complied with arrangements to relinquish weapons to ECOMOG.

In April, after members of the NPFL perpetrated several incursions into Sierra Leone, Sierra Leonean forces entered Liberian territory and launched retaliatory attacks, while the NPFL reportedly advanced within Sierra Leone. It was reported that NPFL forces were supporting a Sierra Leonean resistance movement, the Revolutionary United Front (RUF), in attacks against government forces of that country (see the chapter on Sierra Leone). In September members of a newly emerged rebel movement, comprising former supporters of Doe, the United Liberation Movement of Liberia for Democracy (ULIMO), initiated attacks from Sierra Leone against NPFL forces in north-western Liberia.

At the end of October 1991 a summit meeting between Sawyer and Taylor, which took place in Yamoussoukro, Côte d'Ivoire, under the aegis of an ECOWAS five-nation committee, resulted in a peace agreement whereby the troops of all warring factions were to be disarmed and restricted to camps, while the NPFL was to relinquish the territory under its control to ECOMOG. It was also agreed that all Liberian forces would be withdrawn from Sierra Leone, and that a demilitarized zone, under the control of ECOMOG, would be created along Liberia's border with Sierra Leone. However, the NPFL failed to disarm and restrict its forces to camps within the time limit that had been stipulated in the peace agreement. In January 1992 the Interim Election Commission and Supreme Court were established, in accordance with the peace accord. At the end of April, in response to pressure from within the NPFL, Taylor announced that NPFL troops were to withdraw from the border with Sierra Leone; ULIMO also agreed to co-operate in the implementation of the Yamoussoukro accord. In May ECOMOG began to disarm the rebel factions and to deploy troops in territory controlled by the NPFL, and, despite continued fighting between ULIMO and NPFL forces, established a demilitarized zone along the border with Sierra Leone.

In August 1992 ULIMO launched a renewed offensive in western Liberia, gaining control of Bomi and Grand Cape Mount Counties. In October the NPFL claimed that Nigerian aircraft under ECOMOG command had bombed its bases at Kakata and Harbel (the site of the Robertsfield International Airport and the country's principal rubber plantation), near Monrovia, and at Buchanan, following an NPFL attack on ECOMOG forces stationed in the Monrovia region. The NPFL subsequently captured a number of strategic areas on the outskirts of Monrovia; more than 100,000 civilians took refuge from the conflict in central Monrovia. An ECOWAS summit meeting in Cotonou, Benin, demanded that ULIMO and the NPFL observe an immediate cease-fire, and threatened to impose economic sanctions. Hostilities continued, however, and ECOMOG forces (who were supported by members of the AFL and militia loyal to the IGNU) began retaliatory attacks against NPFL positions around Monrovia. In late October it was reported that ECOMOG units had captured the INPFL base at Caldwell, near Monrovia, and that Johnson had surrendered. (The INPFL was subsequently disbanded.) In November the UN Security Council adopted a resolution imposing a mandatory embargo on the supply of armaments to Liberia, and authorized the UN Secretary-General to send a special representative to the country.

In December 1992 ECOMOG claimed that it had regained control of the strategic positions on the outskirts of Monrovia that had been seized by the NPFL in October. In early 1993 ECOMOG began to advance in south-eastern Liberia, recapturing Harbel, while ULIMO was reported to have gained control of Lofa County in the west. In March ULIMO accepted an invitation from Sawyer to join the IGNU; ULIMO forces in Monrovia were subsequently disarmed. Following a major offensive, ECOMOG announced in April that it had gained control of Buchanan (which was reopened to shipping later that year). In June some 600 refugees were found to be have been killed at the Harbel rubber plantation. Taylor denied accusations by the IGNU of NPFL involvement.

In July 1993 a conference, attended by the factions involved in the hostilities, was convened (under the auspices of the UN and ECOWAS) in Geneva, Switzerland. Following several days of negotiations, the IGNU, the NPFL and ULIMO agreed to a cease-fire (to be monitored by a joint committee of the three factions, pending the deployment of UN observers and a reconstituted peace-keeping force), and to the establishment of a transitional government. The peace accord was formally signed in Cotonou on 25 July. Under its terms, the IGNU was to be replaced by the Liberian National Transitional Government (LNTG), with a five-member transitional Council of State and a 35-member Transitional Legislative Assembly (comprising 13 representatives of the IGNU, 13 of the NPFL and nine of ULIMO), pending presidential and general elections. In response to demands by Taylor, the dominance in ECOMOG of the Nigerian contingent was to be considerably reduced, and the peace-keeping force was to be supplemented with additional troops from other African states.

The cease-fire came into effect at the end of July 1993; however, ECOMOG subsequently accused the NPFL of violating the Cotonou accord by repeatedly entering territory under its control. In August the IGNU, the NPFL and ULIMO each appointed a representative to the Council of State, while a list of nine candidates, nominated by the three factions, elected the two remaining members (who were representatives of the IGNU and ULIMO respectively) from among their number. Dr Bismark Kuyon, a member of the IGNU, was subsequently elected Chairman of the Council of State. Shortly afterwards, however, Kuyon announced that the inauguration of the Council of State (originally scheduled to take place on 24 August) was to be postponed, pending the clear implementation of the process of disarmament.

In September 1993 a report by a UN mission concluded that AFL troops had perpetrated the massacre at Harbel (which had been widely attributed to the NPFL), and implied that ECOMOG had deliberately failed to identify those responsible. In the same month the UN Security Council approved the establishment of a 300-member UN Observer Mission in Liberia

(UNOMIL), which was to co-operate with ECOMOG and the Organization of African Unity (now the African Union, see p. 137) in overseeing the transitional process. In October the Transitional Legislative Assembly was established, in accordance with the peace agreement. Sawyer dismissed Kuyon (who had reportedly dissociated himself from the IGNU's refusal to relinquish power prior to disarmament) and appointed Philip Banks, hitherto Minister of Justice, in his place.

Meanwhile, it was feared that renewed hostilities in several areas of the country would jeopardize the peace accord. An armed faction styling itself the Liberia Peace Council (LPC), which reportedly comprised members of the Krahn ethnic group from Grand Gedeh County, joined by a number of disaffected AFL troops, emerged in September 1993 and subsequently entered into conflict with the NPFL in south-eastern Liberia. In December fighting between ULIMO and a newly formed movement, the Lofa Defence Force (LDF), was also reported in Lofa County. The NPFL denied involvement with the LDF, which occupied territory previously controlled by ULIMO in the northwest.

In February 1994 the Council of State elected David Kpomakpor, a representative of the IGNU, as its Chairman. In early March units belonging to UNOMIL and the new ECOMOG force (which had been supplemented by contingents from Tanzania and Uganda) were deployed, and the disarmament of all factions commenced. On 7 March the Council of State was inaugurated; it was envisaged that the presidential and legislative elections (originally scheduled for February) would take place in September. However, the disarmament process was subsequently impeded by an increase in rebel activity: in addition to continuing hostilities involving the LDF and the LPC, more than 200 people were killed in clashes within ULIMO between members of the Krahn and Mandingo ethnic groups, particularly in the region of Tubmanburg (in Bomi County, where the organization was officially based). The hostilities, which followed the dispute earlier that month between the leader of ULIMO, Alhaji G. V. Kromah (a Mandingo), and the Chairman of the organization's military wing, Maj.-Gen. Roosevelt Johnson (a Krahn), were prompted by resentment among the Krahn at the predominance of the Mandingo in ULIMO's representation in the transitional institutions.

In April 1994 UNOMIL's mandate was extended, pending the completion of the transitional process. In May, following prolonged controversy over the allocation of principal portfolios, a 19-member Cabinet was installed, comprising seven representatives of the NPFL, seven of ULIMO and five of the former IGNU. In July, however, Kromah's faction (henceforth referred to as ULIMO—K) initiated an offensive to recapture Tubmanburg, which was under the control of Roosevelt Johnson's forces (ULIMO—J). Also in July the UN Security Council urged the LNTG to convene a meeting of the armed factions to discuss a programme for disarmament. Later that month the Minister of Labour in the LNTG, Thomas Woewiyu, accused Taylor of responsibility for atrocities perpetrated against civilians.

In early September 1994 (when the original mandate of the LNTG was due to expire) a meeting, chaired by Rawlings, of the NPFL, the AFL and ULIMO—K took place in Akosombo, Ghana. On 12 September Taylor, Kromah and the Chief of Staff of the AFL, Lt-Gen. Hezekiah Bowen, signed a peace accord providing for the immediate cessation of hostilities and for the establishment later that month of a reconstituted Council of State, in which four of the five members were to be nominated, respectively, by the three factions and a civilian Liberian National Conference (LNC—which had been convened in Monrovia at the end of August). Meanwhile, following clashes between dissident members of the NPFL and troops loyal to Taylor, the dissidents' Central Revolutionary Council (CRC) announced that Taylor had been deposed and replaced by Woewiyu, who indicated that he was not prepared to accept the Akosombo agreement. In mid-September disaffected members of the AFL, led by a former officer who had served in the Doe administration, Gen. Charles Julu, seized the presidential mansion, but were subsequently overpowered by ECOMOG forces. (Almost 80 members of the AFL, including Julu, were later arrested, and a further 2,000 troops were disarmed by ECOMOG.) Later that month the CRC, apparently in alliance with elements of the AFL, ULIMO, the LPC and the LDF, took control of Taylor's base at Gbarnga (in the central Bong County); forces loyal to Taylor had retreated to the town of Palala, to the east of Gbarnga, while Taylor was said to have taken refuge in Côte d'Ivoire.

In October 1994 both the ECOMOG and UNOMIL contingents were reduced in size, in view of the lack of progress achieved in the peace process. In November a conference, attended by Bowen, Taylor, Woewiyu, the leader of the LPC, Dr George Boley, and the leader of the LDF, François Massaquoi, together with representatives of the LNC and the LNTG, was convened in the Ghanaian capital, Accra, to discuss preparations for the installation of a reconstituted Council of State. Meanwhile, it was reported that the NPFL had regained control of much of the territory, including Gbarnga, that the CRC had captured in September. On 22 December the participants of the peace conference reached agreement for a cease-fire to enter into force later that month and reaffirmed the terms of the Akosombo agreement, including provisions for the establishment of demilitarized zones throughout Liberia and for the installation of a reconstituted Council of State—to comprise a single representative of each of the NPFL, ULIMO, the 'Coalition Forces' (a loose alliance comprising the CRC, the LPC, the LDF and elements of the AFL), and the LNC, with a fifth member elected jointly by the NPFL and ULIMO from traditional rulers. New institutions were to be installed on 1 January 1996, following multi-party elections. Later in December 1994 the UN Security Council extended the mandate of UNOMIL (now comprising 90 observers) until April 1995, while the Nigerian Government reduced its ECOMOG contingent to 6,000 (from about 10,000), in accordance with its stated aim gradually to withdraw from Liberia. The cease-fire, which entered into force on 28 December, was widely observed.

In April 1995 hostilities between the NPFL and the LPC resumed near Buchanan; renewed fighting in other parts of Liberia was also reported. At the end of April Tanzania withdrew its 800-strong ECOMOG contingent, in response to the failure of the UN to disburse funds that had been pledged to the Tanzanian Government. In May an ECOWAS summit meeting, convened in the Nigerian capital to discuss the Liberian conflict, failed to resolve the outstanding issues; it was subsequently announced that the installation of the Council of State was to be postponed until the factions demonstrated commitment to the implementation of the cease-fire and the disarmament process. Peace negotiations, which resumed in Monrovia in July, were again boycotted by Taylor.

Negotiations regarding the composition of the Council of State were impeded by Taylor's persistent demand to be granted its chairmanship. On 19 August 1995, following a further ECOWAS summit meeting in Abuja, the armed factions (the NPFL, ULIMO—K, the LPC, the CRC, the LDF, ULIMO—J and the AFL) finally signed a compromise agreement providing for the installation of a reconstituted Council of State, which was to remain in power, pending elections, for one year. An academic with no factional affiliations, Prof. Wilton Sankawulo, was to assume the office of Chairman, while the other seats were to be allocated to Taylor, Kromah, Boley, the LNC representative, Oscar Quiah, and a traditional ruler who had been nominated by ULIMO and the NPFL, Chief Tamba Taylor. Later that month a cease-fire entered into force, in compliance with the terms of the peace accord. The Council of State was formally installed on 1 September, whereupon the UN special representative announced that the elections were to take place on 20 August 1996. The Council of State subsequently appointed a transitional Council of Ministers, comprising members of the seven factions that had signed the Abuja agreement. Later in September the UN Security Council extended UNOMIL's mandate until the end of January 1996.

In November 1995 a demilitarized zone was established between NPFL and ULIMO—K forces in the region of St Paul River (between Bong and Lofa Counties). Deployment of ECOMOG forces commenced, in accordance with the Abuja peace terms, in December. Following continued clashes between the ULIMO factions, however, ULIMO—J attacked ECOMOG troops in the region of Tubmanburg. ECOMOG suspended deployment of its forces, and launched a counter-offensive in an attempt to restore order. Hostilities continued in early 1996, with large numbers of civilians killed or displaced.

In February 1996 military and executive officials within ULIMO—J issued a resolution to the effect that Johnson had been replaced as leader of the movement in the interests of the peace process. In March the Council of State announced the removal of Johnson from the Council of Ministers. Clashes erupted between the two factions of ULIMO—J, in which forces loyal to Johnson allegedly killed a supporter of the new leadership. The Council of State subsequently ordered that Johnson be

arrested on charges of murder. Johnson, however, refused to surrender to the authorities, and became effectively besieged in his private residence in Monrovia. In April government forces, led by Charles Taylor, engaged in hostilities with Johnson's supporters, in an effort to force him to surrender. The principal factions represented in the transitional authorities thus became involved in the conflict: elements of the LPC and AFL (which were predominantly Krahn) supported Johnson's forces, while the NPFL and ULIMO—K opposed them. Fighting rapidly intensified in central Monrovia, resulting in the displacement of large numbers of civilians, who fled the capital or took refuge in embassy compounds. ECOMOG (which had refrained from military intervention) deployed its forces in the region of Monrovia, with the aim of negotiating between the warring factions. Following a lull in the fighting, however, some of Johnson's supporters launched attacks in the residential area of Mamba Point (where embassies and offices of humanitarian organizations were situated) and seized a number of civilians as hostages. The US Government began to evacuate US citizens, and other foreign nationals, from the US embassy (where some 20,000 civilians had taken shelter). Johnson's supporters, together with their hostages, took to former army barracks (the Barclay Training Centre) in Monrovia; NPFL and ULIMO—K forces subsequently surrounded the barracks, where several thousand civilians were also sheltered. As the evacuation of foreign nationals continued, the US Government dispatched five warships to the region, with the stated aim of ensuring the protection of US diplomatic staff in Monrovia. Later in April 1996 a further cease-fire agreement was negotiated under the aegis of the US Government, the UN and ECOWAS. Under the terms of the accord, ECOMOG troops were subsequently deployed throughout Monrovia, while most of the remaining hostages were released by Johnson's supporters.

In May 1996, during the absence of Johnson (who had left the country under US protection, to attend a planned ECOWAS summit meeting), the NPFL launched a further attack against the Barclay Training Centre, prompting large numbers of civilians to flee to Monrovia Free Port. At the end of May the UN Security Council renewed the mandate of UNOMIL for a further three months, but warned the armed factions that international support would be withdrawn if fighting continued; UNOMIL was henceforth to comprise only the five military and 20 civilian personnel remaining in the country following the evacuation of a further 93 observers in April. In June Johnson's supporters agreed to disarm and to leave the Barclay Training Centre, while an ECOWAS arbitration mission commenced discussions with the faction leaders in an effort to restore the peace process.

In August 1996, at an ECOWAS conference in Abuja, the principal faction leaders (apart from Johnson, who remained abroad) signed a further peace agreement, whereby a reconstituted Council of State was to be installed by the end of that month, with a former senator, Ruth Perry, replacing Sankawulo as Chairman; Taylor and Boley were to remain members of the new administration. Under a revised schedule, elections were to take place at the end of May 1997, and power was to be transferred to an elected government by mid-June, while the armed factions were to have been dissolved by the end of January of that year. In order to implement the new timetable, ECOMOG (which then numbered 8,500) was to be reinforced by personnel from several west African states. At the end of August 1996 the mandate of UNOMIL was again extended.

Perry was inaugurated as Chairman of the Council of State in early September 1996; Johnson was again allocated a ministerial portfolio in a subsequent reorganization of the Cabinet. The faction leaders subsequently ordered their forces to disarm and to remove road-blocks in territory under their control. ECOMOG troops were deployed in strategic regions, including Kakata and Buchanan, and committees comprising ECOMOG and UNOMIL officials, together with representatives of the armed factions, began to visit remote areas of the country to verify the implementation of the disarmament process. Subsequent progress in disarming the members of the various factions was slow, owing, in part, to delays in the delivery of logistical equipment pledged by the international community to ECOMOG. Following the expiry of the deadline for the completion of the disarmament process, which had been extended to early February 1997, ECOMOG announced that about 91% of the rebel forces (who numbered 30,000–35,000, according to revised estimates) had relinquished their armaments.

In January 1997 Taylor announced that the NPFL had been officially dissolved, in accordance with the peace agreement; the movement was subsequently reconstituted as a political organization, the National Patriotic Party (NPP). In the same month Kromah declared that ULIMO—K had also ceased to exist as a military organization, and was to be reconstituted as the All Liberian Coalition Party (ALCOP). Meanwhile, political parties that had become inactive during the civil conflict were revived, and new groupings applied for official registration. In March Taylor, Kromah and Boley resigned from the Council of State, in compliance with the peace agreement, to allow their candidacy in the forthcoming elections. From March a number of west African countries began to dispatch additional contingents to reinforce ECOMOG (which was expected to be enlarged to about 16,000 personnel prior to the elections), with the USA providing logistical and financial assistance. In May, however, following a request by several political parties, the elections were postponed until 19 July to allow all the newly registered organizations sufficient time for preparation.

A 10-day registration process commenced at the end of June 1997. A total of 13 presidential candidates had emerged by this time, among them Ellen Johnson-Sirleaf (a political exile who had served in the Doe administration and subsequently a UN official, who was to contest the election on behalf of the UP). Taylor conducted a large-scale electoral campaign, financed by profits accrued from unofficial exports and his private radio station, Kiss FM. Despite demands for a further postponement, the elections proceeded on 19 July. The Independent Elections Commission announced on 23 July that Taylor had been elected President, with 75.3% of votes cast; Johnson-Sirleaf (who had been widely expected to be Taylor's strongest challenger) received only 9.6% of the votes. In the concurrent elections to the bicameral legislature (at which seats were allocated on a proportionate basis), the NPP secured 49 seats in the 64-member House of Representatives and 21 seats in the 26-member Senate, the UP won seven seats in the House of Representatives and three in the Senate, while ALCOP obtained three seats in the House of Representatives and two in the Senate. Kromah (who had won only 4.0% of the votes) subsequently declared that serious irregularities had occurred, but international observers declared the conduct of the elections to have been 'free and fair'. Taylor's overwhelming victory was generally ascribed to the widely held perception that he was the candidate most likely to achieve long-term stability in the country.

Taylor was inaugurated as President on 2 August 1997, and subsequently nominated a 19-member Cabinet, which was approved by the Senate. The new Government retained several members of the previous transitional administration, including Johnson and Woewiyu. A nine-member National Security Council, comprising several government ministers, the Chief of Staff of the Armed Forces and the Commander of ECOMOG, was established with the aim of ensuring the maintenance of civil order.

At an ECOWAS summit meeting, in Abuja, at the end of August 1997 it was agreed that the ECOMOG force was to be reconstituted and would henceforth assist in the process of national reconstruction, including the restructuring of the armed and security forces, and the maintenance of security; it was further envisaged that ECOMOG's mandate (officially due to expire on 2 February 1998) would be extended in agreement with the Liberian Government. Following the military coup in Sierra Leone in May 1997, ECOMOG was authorized to enforce international sanctions against the new junta led by Maj. Johnny Paul Koroma (see the chapter on Sierra Leone). In October, however, Taylor announced that he opposed the use of military force to oust the Koroma regime, and that ECOMOG would no longer be permitted to launch offensives against Sierra Leone from Liberian territory. Taylor ordered the closure of Liberia's border with Sierra Leone in response to civil disorder within that country, and announced the formation of a 1,000-member security force to be deployed at the joint border. At the end of October Taylor established a National Human Rights Commission, which was empowered to investigate complaints of human rights violations.

In November 1997, following several months of rumours of the influence in Guinea of Liberian rebels (principally members of the former ULIMO), constituting a threat to security in both countries, it was reported that some 30 members of ULIMO had been arrested in southern Guinea. The alleged presence of former Liberian factions in Guinea was discussed at a meeting between Taylor and the Guinean President, Gen. Lansana Conté, in December. Taylor subsequently appointed Kromah (who had taken up residence in Guinea following his electoral

defeat in July) to the post of Chairman of a National Commission on Reconciliation, which was to undertake a major programme to reconstruct public facilities in Liberia. Also in December several members of the Gbarnga security services were arrested in connection with the killing of a former member of the NPFL, Samuel Saye Dokie, and three of his relatives; it was reported that Dokie had been involved in the attempt to overthrow the NPFL leadership in August 1994. Civilian organizations subsequently demanded that the Government initiate an independent investigation into the deaths.

By early 1998 the number of ECOMOG troops had been reduced to about 5,000. Following Taylor's insistence that the Liberian authorities be accorded control of the restructuring of the armed forces, the Government had notified ECOWAS of its desire for ECOMOG to withdraw formally by 2 February, and had requested that Nigeria, Ghana, Burkina Faso and Niger continue to provide military assistance. (In January the Government removed from service some 2,400 members of the AFL, including senior officials, with the apparent aim of reducing the dominance of the Krahn ethnic group.) Following the seizure of the Sierra Leonean capital, Freetown, by ECOMOG troops, Taylor protested that the arrest by ECOMOG of about 25 senior members of Sierra Leone's ousted junta at James Spriggs Payne Airport was an infringement of Liberian territory. The Liberian Government recalled its ambassador in Nigeria for consultations, and subsequently submitted a formal complaint to ECOWAS.

In March 1998 violent clashes erupted in Monrovia between the security forces and Johnson's supporters; Johnson subsequently claimed that members of Taylor's special security forces had attacked his private residence. ECOMOG troops were deployed to prevent further violence, and, in an attempt to ease tension in the capital, Johnson was removed from the Cabinet and appointed ambassador to India. In the same month Kromah, who had expressed concern regarding his own safety, was removed from his position as Chairman of the National Commission on Reconciliation. Later that month, following increasing tension between ECOMOG troops and Liberian security forces, the Government and ECOWAS signed an agreement revising ECOMOG's mandate in the country; the contingent was henceforth banned from intervening in civil disputes. Also in June the House of Representatives approved legislation providing for the creation of a further county, River Gee, in south-eastern Liberia.

In September 1998 security forces attempted to arrest Johnson (who had not yet assumed his ambassadorial post), pursuing him to the US embassy compound, where he and a number of his supporters had taken refuge; some 50 people were killed in ensuing clashes between members of the security forces and Johnson's followers. (It was reported that, following the attacks on Johnson's Krahn supporters by the security forces, a further 4,000 Krahn had fled to Sierra Leone.) The Government subsequently announced that Johnson, Kromah and 21 of their associates had been charged with treason, following an abortive coup attempt, and demanded that US embassy officials relinquish Johnson to Liberian authority. After discussions with the Liberian authorities, however, US officials transported Johnson to Sierra Leone. In response to an incursion by Liberian security forces into the US embassy compound during the fighting, the US Government temporarily closed the embassy and deployed a naval vessel near the Liberian coast to facilitate the evacuation of US nationals in the event of an escalation of violence in Monrovia. The Liberian Government subsequently issued a formal apology to the USA and announced that an investigation would be conducted into the incident, in co-operation with the US authorities. In October 32 people (several, including Johnson, *in absentia*) were formally charged with treason; their trial commenced in November. In the same month Taylor reorganized the Cabinet.

By November 1998 most of the ECOMOG forces in Liberia had been redeployed in Sierra Leone, owing to increased rebel activity in that country, and to continued tension between the Liberian Government and ECOMOG officials; about 2,000 Nigerian and Ghanaian ECOMOG troops remained in Monrovia. In late December the Government closed Liberia's border with Sierra Leone, in response to the escalation in civil conflict in the neighbouring country, and pledged support for the administration of President Ahmed Kabbah. In January 1999 it was announced that further ECOMOG troops in Liberia were to be relocated to Sierra Leone, following a major offensive by RUF forces against Freetown. A small number of ECOMOG forces remained in Liberia to supervise a programme for the destruction of armaments surrendered by the former armed factions. Later that month Taylor dismissed US and British allegations that the Liberian Government was providing clandestine military support to the RUF. In April 13 of the defendants on trial for treason were convicted and sentenced to 10 years' imprisonment.

In April 1999 unidentified forces, who were believed to have entered the country from Guinea, attacked the northern town of Voinjama, in Lofa County, temporarily taking hostage several western European diplomats. AFL troops subsequently regained control of the town, and Taylor submitted a formal protest to the Guinean Government (which denied that the offensive had been staged from Guinean territory). In August members of a rebel movement, styled the Joint Forces for the Liberation of Liberia (JFLL—reported to comprise former members of ULIMO—K), attacked principal towns in Lofa County from Guinea. Some 80 aid workers, including six foreign nationals, were taken hostage by the JFLL, but were released a few days later, following negotiations by humanitarian relief officials. Taylor ordered the closure of the border with Guinea and declared a temporary state of emergency in Lofa County. In September the Guinean authorities claimed that unidentified Liberian rebels had launched attacks on border villages in southern Guinea, killing some 28 civilians. At an ECOWAS meeting on relations between Liberia and Guinea, which took place in Abuja later that month, it was agreed that a commission would be established to address the issue of security at the border between Liberia, Guinea and Sierra Leone. The border was reopened in February 2000.

Taylor effected a number of cabinet changes in September and October 1999, and again in January 2000. At the beginning of May the Government announced that it had initiated a programme to restructure the armed forces, with the aim of reducing them substantially in size and establishing an ethnic balance. In that month Taylor assisted in negotiating the release of UN personnel taken hostage by the RUF in Sierra Leone (q.v.). In June the Vice-President, Enoch Dogolea, died, apparently as a result of a deterioration in his health following a longstanding illness. He was replaced in July by a former ambassador, Moses Zeh Blah, who had been nominated by Taylor. The Government subsequently established a commission to investigate the circumstances of Dogolea's death, following rumours, strongly denied by Taylor, that he had been murdered.

Meanwhile, reports of increased activity by Liberian dissidents, both in Sierra Leone, where rebels had allied with Kamajor militia, and in Guinea, resulted in a further deterioration in relations between the Liberian authorities and the Governments of those countries. In July 2000 rebel forces again launched an offensive from Guinean territory against Voinjama. A hitherto unknown movement, known as Liberians United for Reconciliation and Democracy (LURD), believed to be a grouping of former members of the armed factions (particularly ULIMO–K), claimed responsibility for the attacks. Taylor and Conté subsequently conducted further discussions, with mediation from the Malian President, Alpha Oumar Konaré. In August Johnson-Sirleaf and a further 14 prominent opposition leaders (many of whom were abroad) were charged with alleged involvement with the LURD dissidents.

In September 2000 Conté claimed that Liberian and Sierra Leonean refugees in Guinea were supporting the activity of rebels attempting to overthrow his Government (see the chapter on Guinea), and ordered them to leave the country. Following a further rebel attack on the Guinean border town of Macenta, staged from Liberian territory, government forces bombarded the Liberian town of Zorzor, 220 km north-east of Monrovia, where dissident Liberian forces were based. In early October tripartite discussions between Liberia, Guinea and Sierra Leone were initiated. In January 2001, however, the Liberian Government withdrew its ambassador in Guinea, following further Guinean bombardment of towns in the Foya district of northern Liberia. In the same month a committee of the UN Security Council reported that the Liberian Government actively supported the RUF and proposed the imposition of UN sanctions against Liberia. In early February the authorities announced that the Commander of the RUF, Sam Bockarie, had left the country, and that the rebels' liaison office had been closed. In early March the UN Security Council renewed the embargo on the supply of armaments to Liberia and voted in favour of a 12-month ban on diamond exports from Liberia and restrictions on the foreign travel of senior government and military officials; these latter measures were, however, deferred for a period of two months to allow the Government time to comply with demands that it expel RUF members from Liberia and end financial and military aid to the rebels. (In October 2000 the US Government had announced the imposition of diplomatic sanctions against Taylor, his relatives and close associates, prohibiting them from entering the USA until Liberia withdrew support for the RUF.) In late March 2001 Taylor expelled the ambassadors of Guinea and Sierra Leone from Liberia, claiming that they had been engaged in activity incompatible with their office, and announced the closure of the border with Sierra Leone. The Sierra Leonean authorities subsequently retaliated by ordering the Liberian chargé d'affaires to leave the country.

In April 2001 François Massaquoi, the former leader of the LDF, and Minister of Youth and Sport since 1997, was killed, after LURD forces fired on the helicopter transporting him to Voinjama. The Government subsequently intensified operations to suppress the continuing insurgency in northern Lofa County, near the border with Guinea. By May, however, the LURD claimed to have gained control of that region, and to have advanced to the neighbouring newly created Gbarpolu County, prompting the displacement of several thousand civilians. Early that month, in response to Taylor's perceived failure to comply with UN demands, the embargo on exports of diamonds from Liberia, together with the travel restrictions on senior government and military officials, entered into effect. Taylor condemned the imposition of UN sanctions, claiming that he had ended all connections with the RUF, while a large demonstration was staged in Monrovia in protest at the measures.

In July 2001 Taylor offered a general amnesty to active rebel supporters and to opposition members in exile who had been charged with treason or associated crimes. In August the Government announced that its order of expulsion against the ambassadors of Guinea and Sierra Leone accredited to Liberia had been formally withdrawn, following a request by ECOWAS. In September Johnson-Sirleaf (who had been charged with supporting anti-Government activities) returned to Monrovia under the terms of the general amnesty. In October a five-member UN commission issued a report recommending the extension of the existing sanctions against Liberia. The UN report also stated that the Liberian Government continued to use revenue generated by the timber industry and maritime activities to finance illicit trade in armaments with the RUF, and proposed the imposition of additional sanctions on timber exports.

By early 2002 LURD forces had gained considerable territory from government troops, and continued to advance southwards towards Monrovia. At the end of January it was reported that the insurgents had briefly occupied the village of Sawmill, 80 km north of Monrovia, and had gained control of much of the surrounding region. Thousands of civilians took refuge in Monrovia in early February, after LURD members attacked the town of Klay, in Bomi County, 30 km north-west of the capital. In response to the continued failure of government troops to halt the rapid approach of LURD forces towards Monrovia, Taylor declared a national state of emergency on 8 February (which was subsequently ratified by the legislature, and was to be revised after three months). Later that month the Government announced that it was to establish a permanent security presence at the country's northern border with Sierra Leone and Guinea. (At that time 50,000–60,000 civilians were internally displaced, according to estimates by the office of the UN High Commissioner for Refugees.) At the beginning of March the leader of LURD, Sekou Damate Conneh, announced that his forces aimed to depose Taylor and install a transitional administration in Monrovia. The rebels declared a few days later that they were prepared to enter into dialogue with government officials, but demanded that Taylor be excluded from discussions. The Government insisted that it would not contemplate the negotiation of a power-sharing agreement with the movement. Later that month a meeting of representatives of the Liberian authorities and opposition was convened at Abuja, under the aegis of ECOWAS; the discussions were regarded as preparatory to a National Reconciliation Conference, which was scheduled to take place in July. (However, representatives of LURD failed to attend the negotiations, purportedly owing to the logistical difficulties in travelling to Abuja.) At the conclusion of the discussions delegates representing 29 political and civil society associations, including major opposition leaders, urged the Government and LURD forces to declare a cease-fire.

Nevertheless, fighting continued, particularly at Liberia's northern border with Guinea. At the end of March ECOWAS imposed travel restrictions on the LURD leadership, on the grounds that the movement had initiated renewed hostilities against the Government.

On 6 May 2002 the UN Security Council adopted a resolution extending the armaments and diamond embargoes, and the travel ban, for a further 12 months. The resolution indicated that, if an effective certification scheme were established, Liberian diamonds proven to be legally mined would be exempted from the embargo, and also urged Liberia to introduce internationally verifiable systems to ensure that revenue derived from the maritime registry and the timber industry be used only for legitimate purposes. Also in May the Liberian legislature extended for a further six months the national state of emergency, after LURD forces gained further territory, seizing control of Gbarnga, in Bong County. In July Taylor reorganized the Government, appointing a former prominent member of the NPFL and an associate, Charles Bright, as Minister of Finance. In September 12 registered political parties attended a National Peace and Reconciliation Conference to discuss preparations for forthcoming elections. In the same month Taylor ended the national state of emergency and the ban on political demonstrations, announcing that government forces had regained control of much of the territory captured by the LURD, including the significant town of Bopolu, 100 km north-west of Monrovia.

In December 2002 a US newspaper published evidence resulting from an investigation into the financing of the al-Qa'ida (Base) terrorist network, which implicated the Governments of Liberia and Burkina Faso. Taylor subsequently denied that the Liberian authorities had assisted members of the al-Qa'ida movement to operate an illicit diamond trade in the country, prior to the terrorist attacks against the USA on 11 September 2001. In January 2003 the electoral commission announced that presidential and legislative elections were to take place on 14 October. In February LURD forces recaptured Bopolu, and resumed their advance towards Monrovia, causing large numbers of civilians to take refuge in the capital. By April Gbarnga had also been reoccupied by the rebels, and government and LURD forces were engaged in intensive fighting for control of the town of Ganta, 180 km north-east of Monrovia. On 6 May the UN Security Council renewed the existing embargoes in force against Liberia for a further year, and imposed an additional ban on timber exports (which was to enter into effect in early July for an initial period of 10 months). On the following day the Liberian authorities announced that Bockarie (who had been indicted by the Special Court established in Sierra Leone to try suspects of war crimes committed during the 10-year conflict in the country) had been killed in Liberia during an attempt to arrest him. Subsequently, however, officials at the Special Court claimed that Bockarie and his immediate family had been captured and murdered by Liberian security forces to prevent him from testifying against prominent regional leaders.

Peace discussions, attended by Taylor and LURD, commenced in Accra on 4 June 2003, but were disrupted by the announcement of Taylor's indictment for war crimes by the Special Court, in connection with his alleged longstanding involvement with the RUF. On the following day Taylor returned to Monrovia, where he immediately announced that the authorities had suppressed an attempted coup, involving some of his senior officials and supported by unspecified foreign powers. It was reported that some 30 government members, including Vice-President Blah, had been detained in connection with the alleged coup attempt. (Blah was reinstated one week later.) On the same day LURD forces launched a major attack on Monrovia from the movement's base in Tubmanburg, and rapidly reached the capital's western outskirts, causing an exodus from refugee camps towards the city centre. On 7 June a government counter-offensive forced the rebels to withdraw back over a strategic bridge, which separated the western suburbs from the city centre. LURD's political leadership issued an ultimatum demanding Taylor's resignation, and French military forces commenced the evacuation of foreign nationals in response to the increasingly critical situation. (By that time the Liberian authorities estimated that about 400 civilians and military personnel had been killed in the fighting around Monrovia, while 50,000 civilians had become internally displaced, and humanitarian conditions had greatly deteriorated.) Following the arrival of a MODEL delegation, the peace discussions in Ghana resumed on 9 June. Repeated demands by LURD for

Taylor's resignation as a precondition to the suspension of hostilities, and Taylor's insistence that his indictment by the Sierra Leone Special Court be withdrawn, impeded progress. On 17 June, however, a cease-fire agreement was signed by the LURD and MODEL leaders, and by the Minister of Defence, Daniel Chea, on behalf of the Liberian Government. Immediately beforehand, government troops recaptured Greenville, forcing LURD to withdraw to positions some 35 km from Monrovia. The cease-fire agreement required the deployment of a multinational stabilization force and a 30-day period of discussions to resolve outstanding issues, prior to the adoption of a comprehensive peace accord, which would result in the formation of a new transitional government, and would also make provisions for future elections.

Shortly after the cease-fire agreement was signed in Accra, however, Taylor declared that he would remain in office at least until the end of his presidential term in January 2004, and rejected the Special Court indictment against him. Serious breaches of the cease-fire were reported, and on 26 June 2003, after the resumption of heavy fighting between government and rebel forces in and around Monrovia, in which about 300 civilians were killed, US President George W. Bush urged Taylor to resign. On the following day the rebel leadership declared a unilateral cease-fire (which was, however, rapidly abandoned). At the end of June the UN Secretary-General recommended to the Security Council that a multinational peace-keeping force be deployed in Liberia in response to the critical humanitarian situation, and urged US military intervention. On 6 July Taylor announced that he had accepted, in principle, an offer of asylum from the Nigerian Head of State, Olusegun Obasanjo, but stipulated that he would not leave the country until a peace-keeping operation was installed. Following continued appeals from Liberian civilians for foreign intervention to prevent the humanitarian disaster, a US mission of military observers was dispatched to Liberia. Despite increasing international support for US intervention, however, Bush indicated that he would only deploy peace-keeping troops in Liberia after Taylor had left the country and a West African mission had restored order. Later in July, after the rebel offensive to oust Taylor had reached the centre of the capital, the US embassy compound (in which some 10,000 Liberian civilians had taken refuge) was repeatedly bombarded. On 21 of that month about 100 US marines were flown in to defend the building, while US naval vessels were stationed off the Liberian coast. Demonstrations were staged outside the US embassy in support of demands for full-scale intervention to halt the carnage. Meanwhile, following the resumption of discussions between the government, LURD and MODEL delegations in Accra, it was announced that a peace accord, based on the terms of the failed cease-fire agreement, had been drafted.

On 22 July 2003 a summit meeting of ECOWAS Heads of State was convened in the Senegalese capital, Dakar. Following pressure from the UN Secretary-General, the West African delegates agreed on the following day to dispatch an initial 1,300 Nigerian peace-keeping troops (including a battalion redeployed from neighbouring Sierra Leone) to Liberia. On 1 August the UN Security Council officially authorized the establishment of a multinational force with a maximum strength of 3,250 troops, to be known as the ECOWAS Mission in Liberia (ECOMIL), which was to restore security to allow the distribution of emergency humanitarian assistance, and prepare for the deployment of a longer-term UN stabilization force (envisaged for October). The first Nigerian troops, which began to arrive in Monrovia on 4 August, were welcomed by the civilian population. On 11 August, following continued pressure from West African Governments and the international community, Taylor relinquished power to Vice-President Blah, before leaving Liberia for exile in the town of Calabar, in south-eastern Nigeria. Blah was inaugurated as interim Head of State, pending the installation of a government of national unity, which was the subject of continuing negotiations between the government and rebel delegations in Accra. Taylor's departure fulfilled the main demand of the rebel leadership, and was received with celebrations in Monrovia. Rebels ceded control of Monrovia Free Port to ECOMIL, and a further 200 US military personnel arrived in Liberia to support the peace operation. Meanwhile, an impasse at the Accra peace discussions was resolved, after the LURD delegation abandoned a demand that it be allocated the vice-presidency in the new administration. On 18 August delegates of the incumbent Government, rebel factions, political opposition and civil organizations, under the aegis of the UN, reached a comprehensive peace agreement, which provided for the establishment of a transitional power-sharing government and legislature, to comprise representatives of the participating groupings. Under the accord, Blah was to transfer power to the new administration on 14 October, all armed militia were to be disbanded, and democratic elections were to be conducted by October 2005. On 21 August 2003 the delegations elected Gyude Bryant, a prominent church figure and leader of the LAP, as Chairman of the transitional administration. Perceived as being most neutral, Bryant defeated a further two candidates for the office, Johnson-Sirleaf and Rudolph Sherman of the TWP. By the end of August a UN Joint Monitoring Committee had been dispatched to Monrovia, and ECOMIL troops (then numbering 1,500) were slowly taking control of rebel-held territory, although renewed fighting was reported in Bong County, northeast of Monrovia.

On 19 September 2003 the UN Security Council formally established the UN Mission in Liberia (UNMIL, see p. 70), which was mandated to support the transitional authorities and the implementation of the August peace agreement; the first contingent, of about 4,000, commenced deployment in the country (replacing ECOMIL) on 1 October. On 14 October, under the terms of the peace agreement, Bryant was officially inaugurated as Chairman of the two-year power-sharing administration, the National Transitional Government, while the leader of the UPP, Wesley Johnson, became Vice-Chairman. At the same time a 76-member unicameral legislature, the National Transitional Legislative Assembly, comprising representatives of the groupings signatory to the August agreement and 15 deputies nominated by the counties, was installed. A prominent member of LURD, George Dweh, was subsequently elected Speaker of the new Assembly. Shortly before his inauguration, Bryant had signed an agreement for the resumption of diplomatic relations with the Government of the People's Republic of China, which was expected to finance substantially reconstruction projects in the country (thereby ending links with Taiwan). Later in October the former administration, LURD and MODEL (which were each allocated five ministries in the National Transitional Government) submitted ministerial nominees for approval by the legislature (although MODEL remained undecided on the selection of two representatives). Of the former Taylor loyalists, Chea retained the post of Minister of Defence, while LURD representatives were awarded the portfolios of justice and finance, and the leader of MODEL, Thomas Nimely Yaya, became Minister of Foreign Affairs. (However, the political opposition and civil society groups failed to agree on representatives for the remaining six portfolios divided between them, and it seemed increasingly unlikely that the new administration would operate effectively.) In early December the International Criminal Police Organization (INTERPOL) issued an arrest notice against Taylor (who remained in Nigeria) for suspected war crimes.

On 7 December 2003, in accordance with the peace agreement, UNMIL began a programme of disarmament and demobilization, involving an estimated 40,000 former combatants; it was announced a few days later that some 11,000 had surrendered armaments. However, the process was suspended later that month, following further armed clashes in parts of the country, to allow more time for the deployment of UNMIL. On 22 December the UN Security Council adopted a resolution maintaining the embargoes on imports of armaments and on exports of timber and diamonds for a minimum of one year, but declared that these would be ended in response to progress in the peace process and in efforts by the National Transitional Government to prevent the illicit exploitation of resources; a UN commission was to submit a report on conditions to the Security Council by mid-2004. Also in December 2003 the leadership of the former Government, LURD and MODEL issued a joint demand to be awarded the remaining portfolios in the National Transitional Government allocated to the unarmed political opposition and civil society, as a precondition to compliance with the disarmament process. Opposition parties and civil society organizations responded by threatening to withdraw from the power-sharing administration, and UN officials rejected the demand of the former combatant groups. In January 2004 it was reported that Conneh's wife, Aisha, had ousted him from the leadership of LURD, with the support of other military commanders, resulting in the division of the movement. LURD and MODEL continued to demand Bryant's resignation from the chairmanship of the interim administration as a precondition to disarmament. UNMIL (which at the end of that month totalled about

11,500 uniformed personnel, including 500 troops contributed by the People's Republic of China) announced the establishment of three permanent garrisons in former rebel-controlled territory (where violent unrest was most prevalent). Later that month it was reported that the voluntary repatriation of refugees from Sierra Leone had commenced. In March the UN Security Council adopted a resolution in favour of 'freezing' Taylor's financial assets, which were reported to have been largely misappropriated from government revenue. On 23 March, after the remaining ministerial portfolios were designated, Bryant finally inaugurated the National Transitional Government. In mid-April UNMIL resumed the disarmament programme; by the end of that month more than 18,000 former combatants had relinquished their weapons.

Government

Under the Constitution of January 1986, legislative power is vested in the bicameral National Assembly, comprising the 26-member Senate and the 64-member House of Representatives. Executive power is vested in the President, who holds office for a six-year term (renewable only once). The President, who appoints the Cabinet (subject to the approval of the Senate), is directly elected by universal adult suffrage, as are members of the Assembly. Members of the House of Representatives are elected for a term of six years, and senators for a term of nine years. Following a peace agreement in August 2003, a power-sharing National Transitional Government and a 76-member unicameral legislature, the National Transitional Legislative Assembly, replaced the previous organs of government on 14 October for a two-year period, after which a democratically elected administration was to be established. (The National Transitional Government was officially inaugurated on 23 March 2004.) There were 13 counties at the time of the 1997 senatorial elections; two further counties were created in 1998 and 2001, respectively.

Defence

The total strength of the Armed Forces of Liberia (AFL) at August 2003 was estimated at 11,000–15,000. In 2000 a government programme to restructure the AFL officially commenced; it was envisaged that the AFL was to be reorganized to comprise an army of about 4,000, a navy of 1,000 and an air force of 300. In 2002 military expenditure was estimated at US $25m.

Following a major rebel offensive against the capital in June 2003, the Economic Community of West African States (ECOWAS) agreed in July to dispatch a Nigerian-led peace-keeping contingent to Liberia. On 1 August the UN Security Council authorized the establishment of the multinational force, the ECOWAS Mission in Liberia (ECOMIL), which was to restore security and prepare for the deployment of a longer-term UN stabilization force. The UN Mission in Liberia (UNMIL, see p. 70), which was officially established on 19 September and replaced ECOMIL on 1 October, was mandated to support the implementation of a comprehensive peace agreement, and a two-year transitional administration. With a total authorized strength of up to 15,000, at the end of January 2004 UNMIL numbered 10,903 troops, 108 military observers, and 442 civilian police, supported by 198 international civilian police and 10 local staff.

Economic Affairs

In 2002, according to IMF estimates, Liberia's gross domestic product (GDP) was US $489m., equivalent to $150 per head. During 1990–2002, it was estimated, the population increased at an average annual rate of 2.6%, while there was no discernible increase in GDP per head. Overall GDP increased, in real terms, at an average annual rate of 2.6% in 1990–2002; growth was 4.2% in 2002.

Agriculture (including forestry and fishing) contributed an estimated 76.9% of GDP in 2002. An estimated 66.6% of the labour force were employed in the sector in that year. The principal cash crops are rubber (which accounted for an estimated 39.0% of export earnings in 2002), cocoa and coffee. The principal food crops are rice, cassava, sweet potatoes, yams, plantains and bananas. Timber production has traditionally represented an important source of export revenue, providing an estimated 57.7% of export earnings in 2002. Agricultural GDP, according to the IMF, declined at an average annual rate of 5.5% in 1990–2002; the GDP of the agricultural sector increased by 21.5% in 2000, by 5.9% in 2001 and by an estimated 4.6% in 2002.

Industry (including mining, manufacturing, construction and power) contributed an estimated 7.4% of GDP in 2002, and employed 8% of the labour force in 1999. Industrial GDP, according to the IMF, declined at an average annual rate of 14.8% in 1988–2002; the GDP of the industrial sector increased by 61.6% in 2000, but declined by 2.8% in 2001 and by an estimated 24.4% in 2002.

Mining contributed less than 0.1% of GDP in 2002, and engaged 5.1% of the employed labour force in 1980. Gold and diamonds are mined, and Liberia possesses significant amounts of barytes and kyanite. The production and export of mineral products were severely disrupted from 1990, as a result of the civil conflict. In 1997 total mineral reserves were estimated to include more than 10m. carats of diamonds and 3m. troy oz of gold. In the late 1990s illicit mining and export of diamonds remained widespread, while official revenue from the mining sector (amounting to only about US $1m.) was mainly derived from local production of alluvial gold and diamonds. The GDP of the mining sector, according to the IMF, declined at an average annual rate of 40.1% in 1988–2002; mining GDP increased by 49.8% in 2000, but declined by 74.9% in 2001 and by an estimated 69.9% in 2002.

Manufacturing provided an estimated 5.4% of GDP in 2002, and engaged about 1.2% of the employed labour force in 1980. Manufacturing GDP, according to the IMF, declined at an average annual rate of 5.6% in 1990–2002; the GDP of the manufacturing sector increased by 62.8% in 2000, but by only 0.9% in 2001, and declined by an estimated 23.7% in 2002.

Energy is derived from the consumption of fossil fuels (62.2%) and from hydroelectric power (37.8%). Imports of mineral fuels and lubricants comprised an estimated 20.0% of the value of total imports in 2002.

The services sector contributed an estimated 15.7% of GDP in 2002, and employed about 22% of the labour force in 1999. The GDP of the services sector, according to the IMF, declined at an average annual rate of 3.6% in 1990–2002; however, the GDP of the sector increased by 15.0% in 2000, by 3.2% in 2001 and by an estimated 7.0% in 2002.

Liberia's large open-registry ('flag of convenience') merchant shipping fleet has become an increasingly significant source of foreign exchange. In 2002 revenue from Liberia's maritime programme accounted for an estimated 18.4% of total revenue.

In 2002 Liberia recorded an estimated visible trade deficit of US $25.6m., and there was a deficit of $28.7m. on the current account of the balance of payments. In 2002 the principal source of imports (25.5%) was the Republic of Korea; other major suppliers in that year were Japan, Germany and France. The principal market for exports in 2002 was Germany (55.8%); other important purchasers were Poland and France. The principal exports in 2002 were timber and rubber. The principal imports in that year were food (particularly rice) and live animals, mineral fuels (principally petroleum), machinery and transport equipment, and basic manufactures.

Liberia's overall budgetary deficit was US $7.4m. (equivalent to 1.3% of GDP) in 2002, according to IMF estimates. The country's external debt totalled $1,987m. at the end of 2001, of which $1,012m. was long-term public debt. In that year the cost of debt-servicing was equivalent to 0.6% of the value of exports of goods and services. Consumer prices increased by 12.2% in 2001 and by an estimated 14.2% in 2002. In early 2002 unemployment was estimated at about 87% of the labour force.

Liberia is a member of the Economic Community of West African States (ECOWAS, see p. 196) and the Mano River Union (see p. 360), both of which aim to promote closer economic co-operation in the region.

Prior to the 1989–96 civil conflict, exports of iron ore, rubber and forestry products accounted for a significant proportion of Liberia's gross national income. Following the occupation of significant regions by rebel forces, production of these commodities was severely disrupted, although some informal exports continued. After elections in July 1997, the new Government announced that national revenue had dwindled to a negligible amount, while debt arrears had increased dramatically, and introduced measures to regain control of public expenditure. Substantial levels of growth were recorded in subsequent years (although GDP remained at about one-third of the pre-conflict level), while domestic production, particularly of timber, rubber and rice, increased steadily. In 2000 a new tax system was introduced, and currency reforms were implemented, and the financial position of the central bank was strengthened. Most significantly, however, a progressive deterioration in Liberia's

relations with donors and external creditors resulted in a suspension in the disbursement of post-conflict financial assistance. In May 2001 a UN ban on exports of diamonds from Liberia was imposed (see Recent History), and economic recovery began to slow considerably in that year, with rubber, logging and farming activity disrupted by continued rebel operations in parts of the country and failure to repair infrastructure damaged during the 1989–96 conflict. In March 2003 the IMF suspended Liberia's voting and related rights in the Fund, owing to the country's continued arrears. In June a major rebel offensive against the capital, Monrovia, to oust President Charles Taylor resulted in a critical humanitarian situation, which attracted international attention. After Taylor relinquished power in early August, rebel forces ceded partial control of Monrovia to peace-keeping troops and commercial activity began to normalize. (However, a dramatic decline in foreign-exchange reserves, already at low levels, was partially attributed to looting by Taylor and his associates.) A comprehensive power-sharing agreement between the Government and rebels, signed on 18 August, provided for the the installation of a power-sharing administration, the National Transitional Government, on 14 October (see Recent History). The Chairman of the National Transitional Government immediately introduced measures to remove monopolies on the import of rice and fuel, resulting in a rapid reduction in prices. Major infrastructural projects, including the restoration of water and electricity to Monrovia, were initiated, while, for the first time since the 1989–96 conflict, the extensive rehabilitation of roads, with financial assistance from the People's Republic of China, was planned. Following the deployment of the UN Mission in Liberia from 1 October 2003, significant progress was reported in the disarmament of former rebel combatants, and humanitarian conditions continued to improve, although sporadic hostilities continued in some parts of the country. The illegal production of diamonds continued in some regions, and at the end of the year the UN Security Council extended the embargoes in force against Liberia. In early February 2004, however, a UN-sponsored conference of international donors pledged some US $520m. (exceeding expectations) to support reconstruction and humanitarian efforts, and projects for infrastructural rehabilitation and employment creation. The resumption of relations with the IMF was expected to be a priority for the authorities, and emergency assistance from the Fund would be dependent on the security situation, and on the ability to operate of the National Transitional Government.

Education

Primary and secondary education are available free of charge. Education is officially compulsory for nine years, between seven and 16 years of age. Primary education begins at seven years of age and lasts for six years. Secondary education, beginning at 13 years of age, lasts for a further six years, divided into two cycles of three years each. Following elections in July 1997, the new Government aimed to rehabilitate large numbers of children who had been recruited to fight for the armed factions during the period of civil conflict. In 1999, following a programme of rehabilitation and reconstruction, the number of primary schools in the country increased to more than 4,500 (compared with 1,500 in 1998), while the number of secondary schools rose to 461 (compared with 241 in the previous year). In 1999/2000, according to UNESCO estimates, 83.4% of children in the relevant age-group (95.6% of boys; 71.2% of girls) were enrolled at primary schools, while the equivalent ratio for secondary enrolment was 20.3% of children in the appropriate age-group (23.7% of boys; 16.9% of girls). In early 2002 it was reported that only 40% of children of school age had access to educational facilities. In 1998 20,804 students were enrolled at institutes providing higher education, including the University of Monrovia, the Cuttington University College (controlled by the Protestant Episcopal Church), a college of technology and a computer science institute. The Government announced that about 10.9% of projected 1999 budget expenditure was allocated to education. A comprehensive peace agreement, signed on 18 August 2003, provided for the disbanding of all rebel groups, and the reintegration of recruited child combatants.

Public Holidays

2004: 1 January (New Year's Day), 11 February (Armed Forces Day), 12 March (Decoration Day), 15 March (J. J. Robert's Birthday), 9 April (Good Friday), 11 April (Fast and Prayer Day), 14 May (National Unification Day), 26 July (Independence Day), 24 August (Flag Day), 6 November (Thanksgiving Day), 12

November (National Memorial Day), 29 November (President Tubman's Birthday), 25 December (Christmas Day).

2005: 1 January (New Year's Day), 11 February (Armed Forces Day), 12 March (Decoration Day), 15 March (J. J. Robert's Birthday), 25 March (Good Friday), 11 April (Fast and Prayer Day), 14 May (National Unification Day), 26 July (Independence

Day), 24 August (Flag Day), 6 November (Thanksgiving Day), 12 November (National Memorial Day), 29 November (President Tubman's Birthday), 25 December (Christmas Day).

Weights and Measures

Imperial weights and measures, modified by US usage, are in force.

Statistical Survey

Sources (unless otherwise stated): the former Ministry of Planning and Economic Affairs, POB 9016, Broad Street, Monrovia.

Area and Population

AREA, POPULATION AND DENSITY

Area (sq km)	97,754*
Population (census results)	
1 February 1974	1,503,368
1 February 1984 (provisional)	
Males	1,063,127
Females.	1,038,501
Total	2,101,628
Population (UN estimates at mid-year)†	
2000	2,943,000
2001	3,099,000
2002	3,239,000
Density (per sq km) at mid-2002 . . .	33.1

* 37,743 sq miles.

† Source: UN, *World Population Prospects: The 2002 Revision.*

ADMINISTRATIVE DIVISIONS
(population at 1984 census)

Counties:				
Bomi . .	66,420	Nimba . . .	313,050
Bong . .	255,813	Rivercess .	37,849
Grand Bassa . .	159,648	Sinoe . .	64,147
Grand Cape Mount	79,322	*Territories:*	
Grand Gedeh .	102,810	Gibi . . .	66,802
Lofa . .	247,641	Kru Coast . .	35,267
Maryland . .	85,267	Marshall. .	31,190
Montserrado .	544,878	Sasstown . .	11,524
		Total	2,101,628

Note: The counties of Grand Kru and Margibi were subsequently established. Two further counties, River Gee and Gbarpolu, were created in 1998 and 2001, respectively.

PRINCIPAL TOWNS
(2003)

Monrovia (capital) .	550,200	Harbel. . . .	17,700
Zwedru . . .	35,300	Tubmanburg . .	16,700
Buchanan. . .	27,300	Gbarnga . .	14,200
Yekepa . . .	22,900	Greenville. . .	13,500
Harper . . .	20,000	Ganta . . .	11,200
Bensonville . .	19,600		

Source: Stefan Helders, *World Gazetteer* (internet www.world-gazetteer.com).

BIRTHS AND DEATHS
(UN estimates, annual averages)

	1985–90	1990–95	1995–2000
Birth rate (per 1,000) . . .	49.8	50.1	49.9
Death rate (per 1,000) . . .	19.0	24.2	21.5

Source: UN, *World Population Prospects: The 2002 Revision.*

Expectation of life (WHO estimates, years at birth): 41.8 (males 40.1; females 43.7) in 2002 (Source: WHO, *World Health Report*).

ECONOMICALLY ACTIVE POPULATION

	1978	1979	1980
Agriculture, forestry, hunting and fishing	355,467	366,834	392,926
Mining.	25,374	26,184	28,047
Manufacturing . . .	6,427	6,631	7,102
Construction . . .	4,701	4,852	5,198
Electricity, gas and water .	245	246	263
Commerce	18,668	19,266	20,636
Transport and communications .	7,314	7,549	8,086
Services	49,567	51,154	54,783
Others	28,555	29,477	31,571
Total	**496,318**	**512,193**	**548,615**

Mid-2002 (estimates in '000): Agriculture, etc. 823; Total labour force 1,235 (Source: FAO).

Health and Welfare

KEY INDICATORS

Total fertility rate (children per woman, 2002).	6.8
Under-5 mortality rate (per 1,000 live births, 2001) . . .	235
HIV/AIDS (% of persons aged 15–49, 1999).	2.80
Physicians (per 1,000 head, 1997)	0.02
Health expenditure (2001): US $ per head (PPP)	127
Health expenditure (2001): % of GDP	4.3
Health expenditure (2001): public (% of total)	75.9

For sources and definitions, see explanatory note on p. vi.

Agriculture

PRINCIPAL CROPS
('000 metric tons)

	2000	2001	2002
Rice (paddy)	183.4	145.0*	110.0*
Sweet potatoes†	18	18	18
Cassava (Manioc) . . .	440.5	480.0†	480.0†
Taro (Coco yam)†. . . .	22	26	26
Yams†	20	20	20
Sugar cane†	250	255	255
Coconuts	7†	7*	7*
Oil palm fruit†	174	174	174
Vegetables and melons†. . .	76	76	76
Bananas†	110	110	110
Plantains†.	40	40	40
Oranges†	7	7	7
Pineapples†	7	7	7
Natural rubber (dry weight)* . .	105	107	108

* Unofficial figure(s).

† FAO estimate(s).

Source: FAO.

LIVESTOCK
(FAO estimates, '000 head, year ending September)

	2000	2001	2002
Cattle	36	36	36
Pigs	130	130	130
Sheep	210	210	210
Goats	220	220	220
Chickens	4,000	5,000	5,000
Ducks	200	200	200

Source: FAO.

LIVESTOCK PRODUCTS
(FAO estimates, metric tons)

	2000	2001	2002
Pig meat	4,400	4,400	4,400
Poultry meat	6,600	8,200	8,200
Other meat	8,316	8,816	8,816
Cows' milk	715	715	715
Hen eggs	4,320	4,320	4,320

Source: FAO.

Forestry

ROUNDWOOD REMOVALS
(FAO estimates, '000 cubic metres, excluding bark)

	2000	2001	2002
Sawlogs, veneer logs and logs for sleepers	157	157	157
Other industrial wood	180	180	180
Fuel wood	4,725	4,925	5,133
Total	5,062	5,262	5,470

Source: FAO.

SAWNWOOD PRODUCTION
('000 cubic metres, including railway sleepers)

	2000	2001	2002
Total (all broadleaved)	10	20	30

Source: FAO.

Fishing

(metric tons, live weight, capture)

	1999	2000	2001
Freshwater fishes	4,000	4,000	4,000
West African croakers	1,025	327	210
Dentex	936	588	671
Sardinellas	1,112	887	1,358
Other clupeoids	509	355	331
Bigeye tuna	112	201	175
Marlins, sailfishes, etc.	550	870	294
Swordfish	39	42	34
Sharks, rays, skates, etc.	1,599	1,675	647
Total catch (incl. others)	15,472	11,726	11,286

Source: FAO, *Yearbook of Fishery Statistics*.

Mining

	1999	2000	2001
Diamonds ('000 carats)	200	170	170
Gold (kilograms)*	1,000	1,000	1,000

* Figures refer to the metal content of ores.

Source: US Geological Survey.

Iron ore (metal content, '000 metric tons): 2,490 in 1990; 804 in 1991; 1,142 in 1992 (Source: UN, *Industrial Commodity Statistics Yearbook*).

Industry

SELECTED PRODUCTS

	1999	2000	2001*
Gold (ounces)	550	701	1,431
Diamonds (carats)	8,728	22,220	3,885
Beer (litres)	3,113,463	2,942,873	2,143,706

* Year to September.

Source: IMF, *Liberia: Statistical Appendix* (July 2002).

Electric energy (million kWh, estimates): 504 in 1998; 519 in 1999; 524 in 2000 (Source: UN, *Industrial Commodity Statistics Yearbook*).

Palm oil (FAO estimates, '000 metric tons): 42 in 2000; 42 in 2001; 42 in 2002 (unofficial figure) (Source: FAO).

Cement ('000 metric tons): 15 in 1999; 15 in 2000; 15 in 2001 (Source: US Geological Survey).

Finance

CURRENCY AND EXCHANGE RATES

Monetary Units
100 cents = 1 Liberian dollar (L $).

Sterling, Dollar and Euro Equivalents (31 October 2003)
£1 sterling = L $71.89;
US $1 = L $42.50;
€1 = L $49.39;
L $1,000 = £13.91 = US $23.53 = €20.25.

Average Exchange Rate (L $ per US $)
2000   40.9525
2001   48.5833
2002   61.7542

Note: The aforementioned data are based on market-determined rates of exchange. Prior to January 1998 the exchange rate was a fixed parity with the US dollar (L $1 = US $1).

BUDGET
(US $ million)

Revenue*	2000	2001	2002
Tax revenue	74.3	60.7	70.3
Taxes on income and profits	15.9	11.5	14.4
Companies	4.8	4.2	7.2
Individuals	9.3	6.1	6.7
Taxes on goods and services	17.3	19.7	25.5
Petroleum sales tax	7.2	6.1	6.7
Maritime revenue	17.9	11.0	13.4
Taxes on international trade	23.2	18.6	17.0
Taxes on imports	22.9	18.4	16.8
Taxes on exports	3.3	0.1	0.2
Other revenue	4.6	4.1	2.4
Total	78.9	64.9	72.7

Expenditure	2000	2001	2002
Current expenditure	47.8	40.7	26.0
Wages and salaries	18.4	17.6	13.4
Other goods and services	21.3	18.2	5.9
Subsidies and transfers	3.0	0.9	0.4
Debt service	5.1	4.0	6.3
Capital expenditure†	35.7	32.6	54.1
Total	83.6	73.3	80.1

* Excluding grants received (US $ million): 6.3 in 2000; 4.6 in 2001; 0.0 in 2002.
† Includes expenditure related to national security.

Source: IMF, *Liberia: Selected Issues and Statistical Appendix* (September 2003).

INTERNATIONAL RESERVES
(US $ million at 31 December)

	2000	2001	2002
Reserve position in IMF.	0.03	0.03	0.04
Foreign exchange.	0.23	0.44	3.26
Total	0.27	0.48	3.30

Source: IMF, *International Financial Statistics*.

MONEY SUPPLY
(L $ million at 31 December)

	2000	2001	2002
Currency outside banks*	698.3	845.1	1,045.0
Demand deposits at commercial banks	898.8	851.6	1,318.2
Total money	1,597.0	1,703.4†	2,363.2

* Figures refer only to amounts of Liberian coin in circulation. US notes and coin also circulate, but the amount of these in private holdings is unknown. The amount of Liberian coin in circulation is small in comparison to US currency.
† Including others.

Source: IMF, *International Financial Statistics*.

COST OF LIVING
(Consumer Price Index; base: May 1998 = 100)

	1999	2000	2001
Food	103.1	101.7	97.7
Fuel and light	109.9	122.7	135.3
Clothing	104.8	104.8	112.2
Rent	109.0	126.2	130.2
All items (incl. others)	105.6	111.1	124.6

Source: IMF, *Liberia: Selected Issues and Statistical Appendix* (September 2003).

NATIONAL ACCOUNTS
(at current prices)

Expenditure on the Gross Domestic Product
(L $ million)

	1987	1988	1989
Government final consumption expenditure.	143.9	136.3	141.6
Private final consumption expenditure.	713.9	733.3	656.8
Increase in stocks*	7.0	3.5	4.0
Gross fixed capital formation	120.4	115.3	96.8
Statistical discrepancy	22.9	39.1	48.2
Total domestic expenditure.	1,008.1	1,027.5	947.4
Exports of goods and services	438.2	452.3	521.4
Less Imports of goods and services	356.8	321.5	275.2
GDP in purchasers' values	1,089.5	1,158.3	1,193.6
GDP at constant 1981 prices	1,015.0	1,043.7	1,072.8

* Figures refer only to stocks of iron ore and rubber.
Source: UN, *National Accounts Statistics*.

Gross Domestic Product by Economic Activity
(US $ million)

	2000	2001*	2002*
Agriculture, hunting, forestry and fishing	400.0	391.0	432.2
Mining and quarrying	1.0	0.2	0.1
Manufacturing	38.1	43.1	30.3
Electricity, gas and water	3.0	3.0	2.8
Construction	8.0	8.7	8.3
Trade, restaurants and hotels	21.1	21.2	20.3
Transport, storage and communications	24.4	24.3	28.2
Finance, insurance, real estate and business services	15.1	14.6	13.9
Government services.	16.9	14.1	12.3
Other services	13.9	14.2	13.6
GDP in purchasers' values*.	541.5	534.4	561.8

* Estimates.
Source: IMF, *Liberia: Selected Issues and Statistical Appendix* (September 2003).

BALANCE OF PAYMENTS
(US $ million)

	2000	2001	2002*
Exports of goods f.o.b.	120.3	127.9	147.2
Imports of goods c.i.f.	−185.2	−196.9	−172.8
Trade balance	−64.9	−69.0	−25.6
Services (net)	13.9	14.7	16.1
Balance on goods and services.	−51.0	−54.3	−9.5
Income (net)	−116.8	−109.4	−84.8
Balance on goods, services and income	−167.8	−163.7	−94.3
Current transfers (net)	85.2	53.4	65.6
Current balance	−82.7	−110.3	−28.7
Capital balance (net)	0.5	−10.2	−22.5
Net errors and omissions	−33.0	30.8	−15.5
Overall balance	−115.2	−89.7	−66.6

* Estimates.

Source: IMF, *Liberia: 2002 Article IV Consultation, Overdue Financial Obligations to the Fund—Review Following Declaration of Ineligibility, and Decision on Suspension of Voting and Related Rights—Staff Report; Staff Statement; Public Information Notice and Press Release on the Executive Board Discussion; and Statement by the Executive Director for Liberia* (September 2003).

External Trade

PRINCIPAL COMMODITIES
(US $ million)

Imports c.i.f.	2000	2001	2002*
Food and live animals	53.9	61.3	56.6
Rice	27.5	27.6	38.1
Beverages and tobacco	6.3	6.1	6.5
Crude materials, inedible (excl. fuel)	6.6	3.8	3.1
Mineral fuels and lubricants	40.7	42.9	34.5
Petroleum	38.7	40.8	32.8
Chemicals and related products	14.3	8.7	8.6
Basic manufactures	20.8	18.4	11.4
Machinery and transport equipment	30.0	35.4	17.5
Miscellaneous manufactured articles	9.3	17.6	27.7
Total (incl. others)	185.2	196.9	172.8

Exports f.o.b.	2000	2001	2002*
Rubber	57.1	54.0	57.4
Timber	61.0	69.2	84.9
Cocoa	0.6	0.5	—
Total (incl. others)	120.3	127.9	147.2

* Estimates.

Source: IMF, *Liberia: Selected Issues and Statistical Appendix* (September 2003).

PRINCIPAL TRADING PARTNERS
(US $ million)*

Imports c.i.f.	1986	1987	1988
Belgium-Luxembourg	8.5	11.2	15.0
China, People's Repub.	7.1	14.7	4.8
Denmark	10.6	7.6	5.9
France (incl. Monaco)	6.5	6.4	4.7
Germany, Fed. Repub.	32.7	52.3	39.5
Italy	2.5	2.2	7.3
Japan	20.1	15.0	12.0
Netherlands	20.6	26.8	14.4
Spain	2.5	6.6	3.1
Sweden	2.4	0.6	4.6
United Kingdom	24.2	18.4	12.7
USA	42.5	58.0	57.7
Total (incl. others)	259.0	307.6	272.3

Exports f.o.b.	1986	1987	1988
Belgium-Luxembourg	29.2	23.2	28.2
France (incl. Monaco)	33.1	33.2	33.2
Germany, Fed. Repub.	114.5	109.2	108.1
Italy	70.3	63.4	63.2
Japan	4.9	1.0	4.8
Netherlands	14.4	11.5	10.5
Spain	16.4	17.8	13.4
United Kingdom	7.2	8.8	6.3
USA	93.2	73.9	74.6
Total (incl. others)	408.4	382.2	396.3

* Imports by country of origin; exports by country of last consignment.

Source: UN, *International Trade Statistics Yearbook*.

Transport

RAILWAYS
(estimated traffic)

	1991	1992	1993
Passenger-km (million)	406	417	421
Freight ton-km (million)	200	200	200

Source: UN Economic Commission for Africa, *African Statistical Yearbook*.

ROAD TRAFFIC
(estimates, vehicles in use at 31 December)

	1994	1995	1996
Passenger cars	13,720	10,340	9,400
Goods vehicles	26,000	28,420	32,000

Source: International Road Federation, *World Road Statistics*.

1998 ('000s of vehicles): Passenger cars: 17.4; Commercial vehicles: 10.7 (Source: UN, *Statistical Yearbook*).

SHIPPING
Merchant Fleet
(registered at 31 December)

	2000	2001	2002
Number of vessels	1,557	1,556	1,535
Displacement ('000 gross registered tons)	51,450.9	51,784.0	50,400.2

Source: Lloyd's Register-Fairplay, *World Fleet Statistics*.

International Sea-borne Freight Traffic
(estimates, '000 metric tons)

	1991	1992	1993
Goods loaded	16,706	17,338	21,653
Goods unloaded	1,570	1,597	1,608

Source: UN Economic Commission for Africa, *African Statistical Yearbook*.

CIVIL AVIATION
(traffic on scheduled services)

	1990	1991	1992
Passengers carried ('000)	32	32	32
Passenger-km (million)	7	7	7
Total ton-km (million)	1	1	1

Source: UN, *Statistical Yearbook*.

Communications Media

	1995	1996	1997
Radio receivers ('000 in use)	675	715	790
Television receivers ('000 in use)	56	60	70
Telephones ('000 main lines in use)	5	5	6
Daily newspapers:			
number	8	6	n.a.
average circulation ('000 copies, estimates)	35	35	n.a.

Sources: UNESCO, *Statistical Yearbook*; UN, *Statistical Yearbook*.

Telephones ('000 main lines in use): 6.5 in 1998; 6.6 in 1999; 6.7 in 2000 (Source: International Telecommunication Union).

Internet users ('000): 0.1 in 1998; 0.3 in 1999; 0.5 in 2000 (Source: International Telecommunication Union).

Education
(1998)

		Students		
	Teachers	Males	Females	Total
Pre-primary	6,158	n.a.	n.a.	111,590
Primary	10,047	227,953	167,658	395,611
Secondary	6,621	69,523	44,355	113,878
General	n.a.	55,759	38,367	94,126
Technical and vocational	n.a.	13,764	5,988	19,752
Higher	633	16,817	3,987	20,804

Source: UNESCO Institute for Statistics.

Adult literacy rate (UNESCO estimates): 54.8% in 2001 (Source: UN, *Human Development Report*).

Directory

The Constitution

The Constitution of the Republic of Liberia entered into effect on 6 January 1986, following its approval by national referendum in July 1984. Its main provisions are summarized below.

PREAMBLE

The Republic of Liberia is a unitary sovereign state, which is divided into counties for administrative purposes. There are three separate branches of government: the legislative, the executive and the judiciary. No person is permitted to hold office or executive power in more than one branch of government. The fundamental human rights of the individual are guaranteed.

LEGISLATURE

Legislative power is vested in the bicameral National Assembly, comprising a Senate and a House of Representatives. Deputies of both chambers are elected by universal adult suffrage. Each county elects two members of the Senate for a term of nine years, while members of the House of Representatives are elected by legislative constituency for a term of six years. Legislation requires the approval of two-thirds of the members of both chambers, and is subsequently submitted to the President for endorsement. The Constitution may be amended by two-thirds of the members of both chambers.

EXECUTIVE

Executive power is vested in the President, who is Head of State and Commander-in-Chief of the armed forces. The President is elected by universal adult suffrage for a term of six years, and is restricted to a maximum of two terms in office. A Vice-President, who is also President of the Senate, is elected at the same time as the President. The President appoints a Cabinet, and members of the judiciary and armed forces, with the approval of the Senate. The President is empowered to declare a state of emergency.

JUDICIARY

Judicial power is vested in the Supreme Court and any subordinate courts, which apply both statutory and customary laws in accordance with standards enacted by the legislature. The judgements of the Supreme Court are final and not subject to appeal or review by any other branch of government. The Supreme Court comprises one Chief Justice and five Associate Justices. Justices are appointed by the President, with the approval of the Senate.

POLITICAL PARTIES AND ELECTIONS

Political associations are obliged to comply with the minimum registration requirements imposed by the Elections Commission. Organizations that endanger free democratic society, or that organize, train or equip groups of supporters, are to be denied registration. Prior to elections, each political party and independent candidate is required to submit statements of assets and liabilities to the Elections Commission. All elections of public officials are determined by an absolute majority of the votes cast. If no candidate obtains an absolute majority in the first ballot, a second ballot is conducted between the two candidates with the highest number of votes. Complaints by parties or candidates must be submitted to the Elections Commission within seven days of the announcement of election results. The Supreme Court has final jurisdiction over challenges to election results.

The Government

HEAD OF STATE

Chairman of the National Transitional Government: GYUDE BRYANT (took office 14 October 2003).

NATIONAL TRANSITIONAL GOVERNMENT
(April 2004)

Vice-Chairman: WESLEY JOHNSON.

Minister of Agriculture: GEORGE KAMMIE.

Minister of Commerce and Industry: SAMUEL WULU.

Minister of Defence: DANIEL CHEA.

Minister of Education: Dr EVELYN WHITE-KANDAKAI.

Minister of Finance: LUSINE KAMARA.

Minister of Foreign Affairs: THOMAS YAYA NIMLEY.

Minister of Gender Development: VABA GAYFLOR.

Minister of Health and Social Welfare: Dr PETER COLEMAN.

Minister of Information: Dr C. WILLIAM.

Minister of Internal Affairs: DAN H. MORIAS.

Minister of Justice: KABINEH JANNEH.

Minister of Labour: LAVELI SUPUWOOD.

Minister of Lands, Mines and Energy: JONATHAN MASON.

Minister of National Security: LOSAY KENDOR.

Minister of Planning and Economic Affairs: CHRISTIAN HERBERT.

Minister of Posts and Telecommunications: EUGENE LENN NAGBE.

Minister of Public Works: IRWIN COLEMAN.

Minister of Rural Development: E. C. B. JONES.

Minister of Transport: VAMBA KANNEH.

Minister of Youth and Sport: WHEATONIA DIXON-BARNES.

Minister of State for Presidential Affairs: JACKSON DOE.

MINISTRIES

Office of the President: Executive Mansion, POB 10-9001, Capitol Hill, 1000 Monrovia 10; e-mail emansion@liberia.net.

Ministry of Agriculture: Tubman Blvd, POB 10-9010, 1000 Monrovia 10; tel. 226399.

Ministry of Commerce and Industry: Ashmun St, POB 10-9014, 1000 Monrovia 10; tel. 226283.

Ministry of Defence: Benson St, POB 10-9007, 1000 Monrovia 10; tel. 226077.

Ministry of Education: E. G. N. King Plaza, Broad St, POB 10-1545, 1000 Monrovia 10; tel. and fax 226216.

Ministry of Finance: Broad St, POB 10-9013, 1000 Monrovia 10; tel. 226863.

Ministry of Foreign Affairs: Mamba Point, POB 10-9002, 1000 Monrovia 10; tel. 226763.

Ministry of Gender Development: Monrovia.

Ministry of Health and Social Welfare: Sinkor, POB 10-9004, 1000 Monrovia 10; tel. 226317.

Ministry of Information: Capitol Hill, POB 10-9021, 1000 Monrovia 10; tel. and fax 226269.

Ministry of Internal Affairs: cnr Warren and Benson Sts, POB 10-9008, 1000 Monrovia 10; tel. 226346.

Ministry of Justice: Ashmun St, POB 10-9006, 1000 Monrovia 10; tel. 227872.

Ministry of Labour: Mechlin St, POB 10-9040, 1000 Monrovia 10; tel. 226291.

Ministry of Lands, Mines and Energy: Capitol Hill, POB 10-9024, 1000 Monrovia 10; tel. 226281.

Ministry of National Security: 1000 Monrovia 10.

Ministry of Planning and Economic Affairs: Broad St, POB 10-9016, 1000 Monrovia 10; tel. 226962.

Ministry of Posts and Telecommunications: Carey St, 1000 Monrovia 10; tel. 226079.

Ministry of Presidential Affairs: Executive Mansion, Capitol Hill, 1000 Monrovia 10; tel. 228026.

Ministry of Public Works: Lynch St, POB 10-9011, 1000 Monrovia 10; tel. 227972.

Ministry of Rural Development: POB 10-9030, 1000 Monrovia 10; tel. 227938.

Ministry of Transport: 1000 Monrovia 10.

President and Legislature

PRESIDENT

On 11 August 2003 President Charles Taylor relinquished office before leaving Liberia for exile in Nigeria. Representatives of the incumbent Government, rebel factions, political opposition and civil organizations reached a comprehensive peace agreement on 18 August, providing for the establishment of a transitional power-sharing government and legislature. On 21 August Gyude Bryant was elected as Chairman of a National Transitional Government, defeating Ellen Johnson-Sirleaf and Rudolph Sherman.

LEGISLATURE

Under a comprehensive peace agreement, signed on 18 August 2003, a 76-member unicameral transitional legislature, known as the National Transitional Legislative Assembly (NTLA), was installed in October. The NTLA comprised 12 representatives of the previous Government, 12 each of two former rebel groups, 18 of political parties, seven of civil society and special interest groups, and 15 nominated by the 15 counties.

Speaker: GEORGE DWEH.

Political Organizations

At the end of January 1997 the armed factions in Liberia officially ceased to exist as military organizations; a number of them were reconstituted as political parties, while long-standing political organizations re-emerged. Elections in July of that year were contested by 13 political associations. A number of political associations opposing the Government continued to be based in the USA.

All Liberian Coalition Party (ALCOP): f. 1997 from elements of the fmr armed faction of Alhaji G. V. Kromah, the United Liberation Movement of Liberia for Democracy; Chair. DAVID KORTIE.

Citizens' Development Party (CDP): Monrovia; f. 2002 by mems of fmr rebel group the Independent National Front of Liberia; Leader Prince YORMIE JOHNSON.

Collaborating Liberian Political Parties (CLPP): Monrovia; alliance of 12 parties opposing the Govt, led by the True Whig Party.

Free Democratic Party (FDP): Monrovia; Leader Dr GEORGE T. WASHINGTON.

Liberian Action Party (LAP): Monrovia; f. 1984; Leader GYUDE BRYANT.

Liberian National Union (LINU): Monrovia; Leader HENRY MONIBA.

Liberian People's Party (LPP): Monrovia; f. 1984 by fmr mems of the Movement for Justice in Africa; Leader TOGBA-NAH TIPOTEH.

Liberian Unification Party (LUP): Monrovia; f. 1984; Leader LAVELI SUPUWOOD.

Movement for the Defence of Human Rights (MODHAR): 152 Carey St, Monrovia; tel. 227334; Chair. NIGBA WIAPLAH (acting).

Movement for Democratic Change in Liberia: Monrovia; Chair. NOHN REBECCA KIDAU.

National Democratic Party of Liberia (NDPL): Monrovia; f. 1997 from the fmr armed faction the Liberia Peace Council; Leader Dr GEORGE E. SAIGBE BOLEY.

National Patriotic Party (NPP): Monrovia; f. 1997 from the fmr armed faction the National Patriotic Front of Liberia; won the majority of seats in legislative elections in July; Chair. CYRIL ALLEN; Sec.-Gen. JOHN WHITFIELD.

National Reformation Party (NRP): Monrovia; Leader MARTIN SHERIF.

People's Democratic Party of Liberia (PDPL): Monrovia; Leader FIYAH GBOLIE.

People's Progressive Party (PPP): Monrovia; Leader CHEA CHEAPOO.

Reformation Alliance Party (RAP): Monrovia; Leader HENRY BOIMAH FAHNBULLEH.

True Whig Party (TWP): Monrovia; Leader RUDOLPH SHERMAN.

United People's Party (UPP): Monrovia; f. 1984 by fmr mems of the Progressive People's Party, which led opposition prior to April 1980 coup; Leader WESLEY JOHNSON.

Unity Party (UP): Monrovia; f. 1984; Leader ELLEN JOHNSON-SIRLEAF.

In August 2003 the following two main rebel movements in conflict with government forces signed a peace agreement, which provided for their inclusion in a power-sharing administration:

Liberians United for Reconciliation and Democracy (LURD): emerged 1999, largely comprising fmr mems of United Liberation Movement of Liberia for Democracy; supported by Guinean Govt; Chair. since 1999, SEKOU DAMATE CONNEH, reportedly replaced with wife, AISHA CONNEH, Jan. 2004, resulting in split.

Movement for Democracy in Liberia (MODEL): based in Zwedru, Grand Gedeh County; emerged 2001; largely Krahn; assoc. with supporters of fmr Pres. Samuel Doe; Chair. THOMAS NIMELY YAYA.

Diplomatic Representation

EMBASSIES IN LIBERIA

Algeria: Capitol By-Pass, POB 2032, Monrovia; tel. 224311; Chargé d'affaires a.i. MUHAMMAD AZZEDINE AZZOUZ.

Cameroon: 18th St and Payne Ave, Sinkor, POB 414, Monrovia; tel. 261374; Ambassador VICTOR E. NDIBA.

China, People's Republic: Tubman Blvd, Congotown, POB 5970, Monrovia; tel. 228024; fax 226740; Ambassador YEONG-CHO CHEN.

Congo, Democratic Republic: Spriggs Payne Airport, Sinkor, POB 1038, Monrovia; tel. 261326; Ambassador (vacant).

Côte d'Ivoire: Tubman Blvd, Sinkor, POB 126, Monrovia; tel. 261123; Ambassador CLÉMENT KAUL MELEDJE.

Cuba: 17 Kennedy Ave, Congotown, POB 3579, Monrovia; tel. 262600; Ambassador M. GAUNEANO CARDOSO TOLEDO.

Egypt: POB 462, Monrovia; tel. 226226; fax 226122; Ambassador FATHY GUERGIS BESHARA.

Ghana: cnr 11th St and Gardiner Ave, Sinkor, POB 471, Monrovia; tel. 261477; Ambassador ERNEST AMOA-AWUA.

Guinea: Monrovia; Ambassador ABDOULAYE DORÉ.

Lebanon: 12th St, Monrovia; tel. 262537; Chargé d'affaires a.i. GABRIEL GEARA.

Libya: Monrovia; Ambassador MUHAMMAD UMARAT-TABI.

Morocco: Tubman Blvd, Congotown, Monrovia; tel. 262767; Chargé d'affaires a.i. Dr MOULAY ABBES AL-KADIRI.

Nigeria: Congotown, POB 366, Monrovia; tel. 227345; fax 226135; Ambassador JOSHUA IROHA.

Russia: Payne Ave, Sinkor, POB 2010, Monrovia; tel. 261304; Ambassador VASILII S. BEBKO.

Senegal: Monrovia; Ambassador MOCTAR TRAORÉ.

Sierra Leone: Tubman Blvd, POB 575, Monrovia; tel. 261301; Ambassador KEMOH SALIA-BAO.

USA: 111 United Nations Drive, Mamba Point, POB 10-0098, Monrovia; tel. 226370; fax 226148; e-mail montgomery@state.gov; internet www.usembassy.state.gov/monrovia; Ambassador JOHN W. BLANEY.

Judicial System

In February 1982 the People's Supreme Tribunal (which had been established following the April 1980 coup) was renamed the People's Supreme Court, and its Chairman and members became the Chief Justice and Associate Justices of the People's Supreme Court. The judicial system also comprised People's Circuit and Magistrate Courts. The five-member Supreme Court (composed of representatives of the interim Government and of the NPFL) was established in January 1992 to adjudicate in electoral disputes.

Chief Justice of the Supreme Court of Liberia: HENRY REED COOPER.

Religion

Liberia is officially a Christian state, although complete religious freedom is guaranteed. Christianity and Islam are the two main religions. There are numerous religious sects, and many Liberians hold traditional beliefs.

CHRISTIANITY

Liberian Council of Churches: 16 St, Sinkor, POB 10-2191, 1000 Monrovia; tel. 226630; fax 226132; f. 1982; 11 mems, two assoc. mems, one fraternal mem.; Pres. Rt Rev. Dr W. NAH DIXON; Gen. Sec. Rev. STEVEN W. MUIN.

The Anglican Communion

The diocese of Liberia forms part of the Church of the Province of West Africa, incorporating the local Protestant Episcopal Church. Anglicanism was established in Liberia in 1836, and the diocese of Liberia was admitted into full membership of the Province in 1982. In 1985 the Church had 125 congregations, 39 clergy, 26 schools and about 20,000 adherents in the country. The Metropolitan of the Province is the Bishop of Koforidua, Ghana.

Bishop of Liberia: Rt Rev. EDWARD NEUFVILLE, POB 10-0277, 1000 Monrovia 10; tel. 224760; fax 227519.

The Roman Catholic Church

Liberia comprises the archdiocese of Monrovia and the dioceses of Cape Palmas and Gbarnga. At 31 December 2002 there were an estimated 161,885 adherents in the country, equivalent to 5.7% of the total population.

Catholic Bishops' Conference of Liberia

POB 10-2078, 1000 Monrovia 10; tel. 227245; fax 226175.

f. 1998; Pres. Most Rev. MICHAEL KPAKALA FRANCIS (Archbishop of Monrovia).

Archbishop of Monrovia: Most Rev. MICHAEL KPAKALA FRANCIS, Archbishop's Office, POB 10-2078, 1000 Monrovia 10; tel. 227245; fax 226411; e-mail kpakala1936@hotmail.com.

Other Christian Churches

Assemblies of God in Liberia: POB 1297, Monrovia; f. 1908; 14,578 adherents, 287 churches; Gen. Supt JIMMIE K. DUGBE, Sr.

Lutheran Church in Liberia: POB 1046, Monrovia; tel. 226633; fax 226262; e-mail lwfliberia@compuserve.com; 35,600 adherents; Pres. Bishop SUMOWARD E. HARRIS.

Providence Baptist Church: cnr Broad and Center Sts, Monrovia; f. 1821; 2,500 adherents, 300 congregations, 6 ministers, 8 schools; Pastor Rev. A. MOMOLUE DIGGS.

The Liberia Baptist Missionary and Educational Convention, Inc: POB 390, Monrovia; tel. 222661; f. 1880; Pres. Rev. J. K. LEVEE MOULTON; Nat. Vice-Pres. Rev. J. GBANA HALL; Gen. Sec. CHARLES W. BLAKE.

United Methodist Church in Liberia: cnr 12th St and Tubman Blvd, POB 1010, 1000 Monrovia 10; tel. 223343; f. 1833; c. 68,300 adherents, 600 congregations, 700 ministers, 394 lay pastors, 121 schools, one university; Resident Bishop Rev. Dr JOHN G. INNIS; Sec. Rev. Dr SAMUEL J. QUIRE, Jr.

Other active denominations include the National Baptist Mission, the Pentecostal Church, the Presbyterian Church in Liberia, the Prayer Band and the Church of the Lord Aladura.

ISLAM

The total community numbers about 670,000.

National Muslim Council of Liberia: Monrovia; Leader Shaykh KAFUMBA KONNAH.

The Press

NEWSPAPERS

The Inquirer: Benson St, POB 20-4209, Monrovia; tel. and fax 227105; independent; Man. Editor PHILIP WESSEH.

Monrovia Guardian: Monrovia; independent; Editor SAM O. DEAN.

The New Liberian: Monrovia; govt-owned.

News: ACDB Bldg, POB 10-3137, Carey Warren St, Monrovia; tel. 227820; e-mail imms@afrlink.com; independent; weekly; Chair. WILSON TARPEH; Editor-in-Chief JEROME DALIEH.

PERIODICALS

The Kpelle Messenger: Kpelle Literacy Center, Lutheran Church, POB 1046, Monrovia; Kpelle-English; monthly; Editor Rev. JOHN J. MANAWU.

Liberia Orbit: Voinjama; e-mail orbit@tekmail.com; internet www .liberiaorbit.org; national current affairs; Editor LLOYD SCOTT.

Liberian Post: e-mail info@Liberian.org; internet www.Liberian .tripod.com/Post0.html; independent internet magazine; tourist information; Publr WILLEM TIJSSEN.

New Democrat: Monrovia; e-mail newdemnews@yahoo.com; internet www.newdemocrat.org; national news and current affairs.

Patriot: Congotown 1000, Monrovia; internet www.allaboutliberia .com/patriot.htm.

The People Magazine: Bank of Liberia Bldg, Suite 214, Carey and Warren Sts, POB 3501, Monrovia; tel. 222743; f. 1985; monthly; Editor and Publr CHARLES A. SNETTER.

PRESS ORGANIZATIONS

Liberia Institute of Journalism: Kashour Bldg, 2nd Floor, cnr Broad and Johnson Sts, POB 2314, Monrovia; tel. 227327; e-mail lij@kabissa.org; internet www.kabissa.org/lij; Dir VINICIUS HODGES.

Press Union of Liberia: Benson St, POB 20-4209, Monrovia; tel. and fax 227105; e-mail pul@kabissa.org; internet www.kabissa.org/ pul; f. 1985; Pres. JAMES G. KIAZOLU.

NEWS AGENCIES

Liberian News Agency (LINA): POB 9021, Capitol Hill, Monrovia; tel. and fax 226269; e-mail lina@afrlink.com; Dir-Gen. ERNEST KIAZOLY (acting).

Foreign Bureaux

Agence France-Presse (AFP): Monrovia; Rep. JAMES DORBOR.

United Press International (UPI) (USA): Monrovia; Correspondent T. K. SANNAH.

Xinhua (New China) News Agency (People's Republic of China): Adams St, Old Rd, Congotown, POB 3001, Monrovia; tel. 262821; Correspondent SUN BAOYU.

Reuters (United Kingdom) is also represented in Liberia.

Broadcasting and Communications

TELECOMMUNICATIONS

Liberia Telecommunications Corpn: Monrovia; tel. 227523; Man. Dir JOE GBALAH.

BROADCASTING

Radio

Liberia Communications Network: Congotown 1000, Monrovia; govt-operated; broadcasts information, education and entertainment 24 hours daily in English, French and several African languages; short-wave service.

Liberia Rural Communications Network: POB 10-02176, 1000 Monrovia 10; tel. 271368; f. 1981; govt-operated; rural development and entertainment programmes; Dir J. RUFUS KAINE (acting).

Radio Veritas: Monrovia; Catholic; independent; nation-wide shortwave broadcasts; operations suspended by the Govt early 2002.

Star Radio: Sekou Toure Ave, Mamba Point, Monrovia; tel. 226820; fax 227360; e-mail star@liberia.net; independent news and information station; f. July 1997 by Fondation Hirondelle, Switzerland, with funds from the US Agency for International Development; broadcasts in English, French and 14 African languages; operations suspended by the Govt March 2000; ban on transmissions ended Nov. 2003; Dir GEORGE BENNETT.

Television

Liberia Broadcasting System: POB 594, Monrovia; tel. 224984; govt-owned; Pres. BOCKARIE MUSA.

Finance

(cap. = capital; res = reserves; dep. = deposits; m. = million; br. = branch; amounts in Liberian dollars, unless otherwise indicated)

BANKING

Following intensive fighting between government and rebel forces in the capital in mid–2003, it was reported that commercial banks had resumed operations at the end of August. At this time, however, only four (of a total of 18 deposit banks established since 1954) were active, the remainder having been closed as a result of poor bank management or the 1989–96 civil conflict. The Liberian Bank for Development and Investment is the only locally owned bank.

Central Bank

Central Bank of Liberia: Warren and Carey Sts, POB 2048, Monrovia; tel. 226144; fax 227928; f. 1974 as National Bank of Liberia; name changed March 1999; bank of issue; cap. and res 17.1m., dep. 70.7m. (1986); Gov. ELI SALEEBY.

Other Banks

Ecobank Liberia Ltd: Ashmun and Randall Sts, POB 4825, Monrovia; tel. 226428; fax 227029; e-mail ecobanklr@ecobank.com; internet www.ecobank.com; commenced operations Aug. 1999; cap. and res US $2.1m., total assets US $10.2m. (Dec. 2001); Chair. EUGENE H. COOPER; Man. Dir OFONG AMBAH.

International Bank (Liberia) Ltd: 64 Broad St, POB 10-292, Monrovia; tel. 226279; fax 226159; e-mail ncreative69@yahoo.com; internet www.liberian-connection.com; f. 1948 as International Trust Co of Liberia; name changed April 2000; cap. 2m. (1989), dep. 96.4m. (Dec. 1996); Pres. F. A. GUIDA; 1 br.

Liberian Bank for Development and Investment (LBDI): Ashmun and Randall Sts, POB 547, Monrovia; tel. 227140; fax 226359; e-mail lbdi@liberia.net; f. 1961; cap. and res US $12.5m., total assets US $26.8m. (Dec. 2001); Chair. NATHANIEL BARNES; Pres. FRANCIS A. DENNIS.

Liberian Trading and Development Bank Ltd (TRADEVCO): 57 Ashmun St, POB 10-293, Monrovia; tel. 226072; fax 226471; e-mail tradebank@hotmail.com; f. 1955; wholly-owned subsidiary of Mediobanca SpA (Italy); cap. and res 3.2m., dep. 64.7m. (June 1995); Pres. GIORGIO PICOTTI; CEO SILVIO VIGOTTI.

Banking Association

Liberia Bankers' Association: POB 292, Monrovia; mems include commercial and development banks; Pres. LEN MAESTRE.

INSURANCE

American International Underwriters, Inc: Carter Bldg, 39 Broad St, POB 180, Monrovia; tel. 224921; general; Gen. Man. S. B. MENSAH.

American Life Insurance Co: Carter Bldg, 39 Broad St, POB 60, Monrovia; f. 1969; life and general; Vice-Pres. ALLEN BROWN.

Insurance Co of Africa: 64 Broad St, POB 292, Monrovia; f. 1969; life and general; Pres. SAMUEL OWAREE MINTAH.

National Insurance Corpn of Liberia (NICOL): LBDI Bldg Complex, POB 1528, Sinkor, Monrovia; tel. 262429; f. 1983; state-owned; sole insurer for Govt and parastatal bodies; also provides insurance for the Liberian-registered merchant shipping fleet; Man. Dir MIATTA EDITH SHERMAN.

Royal Exchange Assurance: Ashmun and Randall Sts, POB 666, Monrovia; all types of insurance; Man. RONALD WOODS.

United Security Insurance Agencies Inc: Randall St, POB 2071, Monrovia; life, personal accident and medical; Dir EPHRAIM O. OKORO.

Trade and Industry

GOVERNMENT AGENCIES

Budget Bureau: Capitol Hill, POB 1518, Monrovia; tel. 226340; Dir EMMANUEL GARDNER.

General Services Agency (GSA): Sinkor, Monrovia; tel. 226745; Dir-Gen. EDWARD T. FARLEY.

DEVELOPMENT ORGANIZATIONS

Forestry Development Authority: POB 3010, 1000 Monrovia; tel. 224940; fax 226000; f. 1976; responsible for forest management and conservation; Man. Dir DEMETRIOUS B. TAYLOR.

Liberia Industrial Free Zone Authority: Bushrod Island, POB 9047, Monrovia; f. 1975; 98 mems; Man. Dir GBAI M. GBALA.

National Investment Commission (NIC): Fmr Executive Mansion Bldg, POB 9043, Monrovia; tel. 226685; internet www.nic.gov.lr; f. 1979; autonomous body negotiating investment incentives agreements on behalf of Govt; promotes agro-based and industrial development; Chair. SOMAH PAYGAI.

CHAMBER OF COMMERCE

Liberia Chamber of Commerce: POB 92, Monrovia; tel. 223738; f. 1951; Pres. DAVID A. B. JALLAH; Sec.-Gen. LUESETTE S. HOWELL.

INDUSTRIAL AND TRADE ASSOCIATIONS

Liberian Produce Marketing Corpn: POB 662, Monrovia; tel. 222447; f. 1961; govt-owned; exports Liberian produce, provides industrial facilities for processing of agricultural products and participates in agricultural development programmes; Man. Dir ISAIAH TEASELY.

Liberian Resources Corpn (LIBRESCO): controls Liberia's mineral resources; 60% govt-owned; 40% owned by South African co, Amalia Gold.

EMPLOYERS' ASSOCIATION

National Enterprises Corpn: POB 518, Monrovia; tel. 261370; importer, wholesaler and distributor of foodstuffs, and wire and metal products for local industries; Pres. EMMANUEL SHAW, Sr.

UTILITIES

Electricity

Liberia Electricity Corpn: Waterside, POB 165, Monrovia; tel. 226133; Man. Dir JOSEPH MAYAR.

TRADE UNIONS

Congress of Industrial Organizations: 29 Ashmun St, POB 415, Monrovia; Pres. Gen. J. T. PRATT; Sec.-Gen. AMOS N. GRAY; 5 affiliated unions.

Labor Congress of Liberia: 71 Gurley St, Monrovia; Sec.-Gen. P. C. T. SONPON; 8 affiliated unions.

Liberian Federation of Labor Unions: J. B. McGill Labor Center, Gardnersville Freeway, POB 415, Monrovia; f. 1980 by merger; Sec.-Gen. AMOS GRAY; 10,000 mems (1983).

Transport

RAILWAYS

Railway operations were suspended in 1990, owing to the civil conflict. Large sections of the 480-km rail network were subsequently dismantled.

Bong Mining Co Ltd: POB 538, Monrovia; tel. 225222; fax 225770; f. 1965; Gen. Man. HANS-GEORG SCHNEIDER.

Liberian Mining Co: Monrovia; tel. 221190; govt-owned; assumed control of LAMCO JV Operating Co in 1989.

National Iron Ore Co Ltd: POB 548, Monrovia; f. 1951; Gen. Man. S. K. DATTA RAY.

ROADS

In 1999 the road network in Liberia totalled an estimated 10,600 km, of which about 657 km were paved. The main trunk road is the Monrovia–Sanniquellie motor road, extending north-east from the capital to the border with Guinea, near Ganta, and eastward through the hinterland to the border with Côte d'Ivoire. Trunk roads run through Tapita, in Nimba County, to Grand Gedeh County and from Monrovia to Buchanan. A bridge over the Mano river connects with the Sierra Leone road network, while a main road links Monrovia and Freetown (Sierra Leone). Although principal roads were officially reopened to commercial traffic in early 1997, following the 1989–96 armed conflict, much of the infrastructure remained severely damaged. The National Transitional Government, installed in October 2003, planned extensive rehabilitation of the road network, including a highway linking Monrovia with Harper, which was to be funded by the People's Republic of China.

SHIPPING

In December 2002 Liberia's open-registry fleet (1,535 vessels), the second largest in the world (after Panama) in terms of gross tonnage, had a total displacement of 50.4m. grt. Commercial port activity in Liberia was frequently suspended from 1990, as a result of the armed conflict, but resumed in late 1996. In early 2004 the Liberian authorities announced that the rehabilitation of Monrovia Free Port would require funding of some US $40m.

Bureau of Maritime Affairs: Tubman Blvd, POB 10-9042, 1000 Monrovia 10; tel. and fax 226069; e-mail maritime@liberia.net; internet www.maritime.gov.lr; Commissioner BENONI UREY.

Liberia National Shipping Line (LNSL): Monrovia; f. 1987; jt venture by the Liberian Govt and private German interests; routes to Europe, incl. the United Kingdom and Scandinavia.

National Port Authority: POB 1849, Monrovia; tel. 226646; fax 226180; e-mail natport@liberia.net; f. 1967; administers Monrovia Free Port and the ports of Buchanan, Greenville and Harper; Man. Dir CHEAYEE Z. DOE.

CIVIL AVIATION

Liberia's principal airports are Robertsfield International Airport, at Harbel, 56 km east of Monrovia, and James Spriggs Payne

Airport, at Monrovia. Following the suspension of air services in mid-2003, owing to the intensive conflict in Monrovia (see Recent History), the Belgian airline, SN Brussels Airlines, resumed flights into Robertsfield International Airport in October. However, it was reported that continued lack of regulation of civil aviation in Liberia was contributing to illicit trade. The new National Transitional Government and the UN Mission in Liberia deployed from October

planned the urgent rehabilitation of both airports in order to improve security and facilitate peace-keeping operations.

ADC Liberia Inc: Monrovia; f. 1993; services to the United Kingdom, the USA and destinations in West Africa.

Air Liberia: POB 2076, Monrovia; f. 1974 by merger; state-owned; scheduled passenger and cargo services; Man. Dir JAMES K. KOFA.

LIBYA

Introductory Survey

Location, Climate, Language, Religion, Flag, Capital

The Great Socialist People's Libyan Arab Jamahiriya extends along the Mediterranean coast of North Africa. Its neighbours are Tunisia and Algeria to the west, Niger and Chad to the south, Egypt to the east, and Sudan to the south-east. The climate is very hot and dry. Most of the country is part of the Sahara, an arid desert, but the coastal regions are cooler. Average temperatures range from 13°C (55°F) to 38°C (100°F), but a maximum of 57.3°C (135°F) has been recorded in the interior. Arabic is the official language, although English and Italian are also used in trade. Almost all of the population are Sunni Muslims. The national flag (proportions 2 by 3) is plain green. The administrative capital was formerly Tripoli (Tarabulus), but under a decentralization programme announced in September 1988 most government departments and the legislature were relocated to Sirte (Surt), while some departments were transferred to other principal towns.

Recent History

Libya, formerly an Italian colony and occupied by British and French troops in 1942, attained independence as the United Kingdom of Libya on 24 December 1951. Muhammad Idris as-Sanusi, Amir of Cyrenaica, became King Idris of Libya. British and US forces maintained bases in Libya in return for economic assistance; however, the discovery of petroleum reserves in 1959 greatly increased the country's potential for financial autonomy.

King Idris was deposed in September 1969, in a bloodless revolution led by a group of young nationalist army officers. A Revolution Command Council (RCC) was established, with Col Muammar al-Qaddafi as Chairman, and a Libyan Arab Republic was proclaimed. British and US military personnel withdrew from Libya in 1970, and in 1972 British oil interests in Libya were nationalized.

The Arab Socialist Union (ASU) was established in June 1971 as the country's sole political party. People's Congresses and Popular Committees were formed, and an undertaking was made to administer the country in accordance with Islamic principles. The General National Congress of the ASU (which comprised members of the RCC, leaders of the People's Congresses and Popular Committees and of trade unions and professional organizations) held its first session in January 1976; it was subsequently restyled the General People's Congress (GPC).

In March 1977 the GPC endorsed constitutional changes, recommended by Qaddafi, whereby the official name of the country was changed to the Socialist People's Libyan Arab Jamahiriya. Power was vested in the people through the GPC and its constituent parts. The RCC was dissolved, and a General Secretariat of the GPC (with Qaddafi as Secretary-General) was established. The GPC elected Qaddafi as Revolutionary Leader of the new state. The Council of Ministers was replaced by a General People's Committee, initially with 26 members—each a secretary of a department.

In March 1979 Qaddafi resigned from the post of Secretary-General of the General Secretariat of the GPC to devote more time to 'preserving the revolution'. The creation in early 1984 of the post of Secretary for External Security and of an office, attached to the Secretariat for Foreign Liaison, to 'combat international terrorism', combined with repressive measures to curb the activity of dissidents, apparently reflected Qaddafi's increasing sensitivity to the growth of opposition groups—principally the National Front for the Salvation of Libya (NFSL), which he accused foreign governments of fostering. In 1986 the country's official name was changed to the Great Socialist People's Libyan Arab Jamahiriya.

From 1988, in an apparent attempt to allay domestic dissatisfaction and international criticism, Qaddafi initiated a series of liberalizing economic and political reforms. In foreign policy he adopted a more pragmatic approach to his ambition of achieving Maghreb union (see below), and to his relations with other Arab and African countries. Within Libya he accused the Revolutionary Committees (young, pro-Qaddafi activists) of murdering political opponents of his regime. Qaddafi encour-

aged the reopening of private businesses, in recognition of the inadequacy of state-sponsored supermarkets, and declared an amnesty for all prisoners, other than those convicted of violent crimes or of conspiring with foreign powers. Libyan citizens were guaranteed freedom to travel abroad, and the powers of the Revolutionary Committees were curbed. The GPC created a People's Court and People's Prosecution Bureau to replace the revolutionary courts, and approved a charter of human rights. In August Qaddafi announced that the army was to be replaced by a force of 'Jamahiri Guards', which would be supervised by 'people's defence committees'. In September it was decided to relocate all but two of the secretariats of the GPC, mostly to the town of Sirte (Surt), 400 km east of Tripoli, and in January 1989 Qaddafi announced that all state institutions, including the state intelligence service and the official Libyan news agency, were to be abolished.

In October 1990 the GPC implemented extensive changes to the General People's Committee, creating three new secretariats and electing a new Secretary-General, Abu Sa'id Omar Durdah, as well as 11 new secretaries. Three of the five-member General Secretariat of the GPC were replaced, and Abd ar-Raziq as-Sawsa was appointed Secretary-General of the GPC. There was a further reorganization of the General People's Committee in October–November 1992. The former Secretary for Economic Planning, Omar al-Muntasir, was named Secretary for Foreign Liaison and International Co-operation. Regarded as a moderate, al-Muntasir's appointment was viewed by some observers as a sign of Libya's willingness to resume dialogue with the West over the Lockerbie issue (see below).

Western media reported in October 1993 that elements loyal to Qaddafi had suppressed an attempted military *coup d'état*, and that Libya's second-in-command, Maj. Abd as-Salam Jalloud, was among many placed under house arrest. Qaddafi denied that a coup had been attempted, but the appointment of known loyalists to senior positions in the General People's Committee was announced in January 1994. Most notably, Abd al-Majid al-Aoud, a member of Qaddafi's closest personal entourage, replaced Durdah, a close associate of Jalloud, as Secretary-General.

At its annual convention in March 1997 the GPC made changes to the composition and structure of the General People's Committee. Muhammad Ahmad al-Manqush was appointed Secretary-General of the Committee in December, as part of a further reorganization. The Secretariat for Arab Unity was abolished in a restructuring of the General People's Committee in December 1998, in accordance with Qaddafi's recently stated intention to forge closer relations with African rather than Arab countries.

In January 2000 Qaddafi unexpectedly attended the opening session of the GPC, at the end of which he demanded that the budget for 2000 be redrafted, with a view to channelling petroleum revenues into education, health and public services. Furthermore, he urged that the current administrative system, based on General People's Committees, be abandoned in favour of an alternative form of government. Accordingly, a radical decentralization of the Government was announced in March, whereby almost all of the People's Committees were dissolved and their responsibilities devolved mainly to local level: only those areas described as 'sovereign' were to remain under the control of the General People's Committee, now led by Mubarak Abdallah ash-Shamikh (hitherto responsible for housing and utilities). Most notably, Ali Abd as-Salam at-Turayki was allocated the new post of Secretary for African Unity, being replaced as Secretary for Foreign Liaison and International Co-operation by Abd ar-Rahman Muhammad Shalgam, while Muhammad Abdallah Bait al-Mal retained the post of Secretary for Finance. In July it was reported that Bait al-Mal, along with the President of the Central Bank of Libya and a further 22 senior Libyan bankers, had been implicated in allegations of financial impropriety. They were suspected of having granted unsecured loans to several prominent figures, including a number of senior army officers. Al-Ujayli Abd as-Salam Burayni replaced Bait al-Mal as Secretary for Finance in October, when a further restructuring of the General People's Committees was announced.

In late September 2000 clashes occurred throughout the country between Libyans and nationals of several other African countries. The confrontations were believed to reflect resentment within Libya at the increasing numbers of black African migrants entering the country. A large number of Chadians and Sudanese were reportedly killed in incidents in the town of Az-Zawiyah, some 30 km west of Tripoli, and thousands more were interned in military camps. The Nigerian embassy in Tripoli was ransacked, and Libyan youths were also held responsible for an attack on a camp which was razed to the ground. The General People's Congress announced its intention formally to investigate the incidents, and in mid-October the evacuation and deportation of migrant workers from Nigeria, Chad, Niger, Sudan and Ghana commenced. It was estimated that as a result of the clashes more than 100 Africans had been killed and as many as 30,000 migrants had left Libya. Qaddafi subsequently apportioned blame for the incidents on 'foreign hostile hands' opposed to his plans to create an African Union. In May 2001 two Libyans, four Nigerians and one Ghanaian were sentenced to death for their roles in the violence. A further 12 defendants were sentenced to life imprisonment.

In early September 2001 a minor reorganization of the General People's Committee was announced, including the creation of a new Secretariat for Infrastructure, Urban Planning and Environment, to be headed by Hutaywish Faraj al-Hutaywish. In November it was announced that more than 40 government and bank officials had been sentenced to varying terms of imprisonment for corruption and embezzlement; reportedly among those convicted was Secretary for Finance Burayni, who received a one-year prison sentence for negligence, although he continued to appear on official government lists. In late December Shukri Muhammad Ghanem was appointed to replace Abd es-Salem Ahmad Jouir as Secretary for the Economy and Trade.

In mid-January 2003 Libya was elected to chair the session of the UN Human Rights Commission scheduled to be held in March. For the first time since the formation of the Commission in 1947, the decision was voted upon, with Libya securing 33 of the 53 votes, with 17 countries, including the United Kingdom, abstaining; the USA, Canada and Guatemala opposed the proposal. Libya's election was widely criticized by a number of international human rights organizations.

In mid-June 2003 Qaddafi dismissed ash-Shamikh from the post of Secretary of the GPC, replacing him with Ghanem, who was succeeded as Secretary for the Economy and Trade by Abd al-Qadir Balkheir. It was also announced that the Secretariat for African Unity had been merged with the Secretariat for Foreign Liaison and International Co-operation; Shalgam assumed responsibility for both portfolios. There were reports that Qaddafi had demanded the complete privatization of leading economic sectors, including the petroleum industry, and had proposed that the Libyan economy be opened up to investment from both domestic and foreign companies.

In early March 2004 Qaddafi announced a reorganization of the General People's Committee, which included the creation of four new secretariats (for national security, youth and sport, training and labour, and culture) and the restoration of the Secretariat for Energy, which had been abolished in early 2000. Muhammad Ali al-Houeiz replaced Burayni as Secretary for Finance, while Ali Omar Abu Bakr was appointed Secretary of Justice.

Various plans for Pan-Arab unity led to the formation, in January 1972, of the Federation of Arab Republics, comprising Libya, Egypt and Syria. In 1972 Libya concluded an agreement with Egypt to merge the two countries in 1973. Neither union was effective, and proposals for union with Tunisia in 1974, Syria in 1980, Chad in 1981, Morocco in 1984, Algeria in 1987 and Sudan in 1990 also proved abortive.

Relations with Egypt, already tense following the failure of the Libya-Egypt union, further deteriorated when President Anwar Sadat launched the October 1973 war against Israel without consulting Qaddafi. In common with the other members of the League of Arab States (the Arab League, see p. 278), Libya strongly objected to Sadat's peace initiative with Israel which culminated in the signing of the Camp David accords in 1978, and Libya also condemned the proposals for Middle East peace that were agreed by other Arab states in Fez, Morocco, in 1982. From the late 1980s, none the less, Egypt and Libya forged a close relationship, with Egypt acting as an intermediary between Libya and Western nations.

In 1973 Libyan forces occupied the 'Aozou strip', a reputedly mineral-rich region of 114,000 sq km in the extreme north of Chad, to which it laid claim on the basis of an unratified border treaty concluded by Italy and France in 1935. Thereafter, Libya became embroiled in the lengthy struggle for political control between rival forces in Chad (q.v.). During 1987 intense fighting took place for control of north-western Chad, and in August President Hissène Habré's forces advanced into the 'Aozou strip', occupying the town of Aozou. Libya responded by bombing towns in northern Chad, and recaptured Aozou. In September Chadian forces destroyed an airbase 100 km inside Libya (allegedly a base for Libyan raids on Chad). Later in September the two countries agreed to observe a cease-fire sponsored by the Organization of African Unity (OAU, now African Union—AU, see p. 137), and in October 1988 Libya and Chad restored diplomatic relations. In August 1989, with Algerian mediation, Chad and Libya concluded an agreement to attempt to resolve the dispute over sovereignty of the 'Aozou strip' through a political settlement. Accordingly, the issue was submitted to the International Court of Justice in The Hague, Netherlands, which in February 1994 ruled against Libya's claim. All Libyan troops remaining in the 'Aozou strip' were withdrawn in May. In June Libya and Chad concluded a treaty of friendship, neighbourly terms and co-operation. In May 1998 Qaddafi made his first visit to Chad for 17 years, and in November the two countries officially opened two of their common border posts. Chad's President Idriss Deby (who had overthrown Habré in 1990) and members of his administration made several visits to Libya after 1997 and in January 2002 Libyan mediation resulted in the brokering of a peace agreement between the Chadian Government and the rebel Mouvement pour la démocratie et la justice au Tchad, which had been in conflict since late 1998.

Libya's outspoken criticism of other Arab regimes, and perceived interference in the internal affairs of other countries, led to years of relative political isolation. However, in 1987 Qaddafi sought to realign Libyan policy with that of the majority of Arab states. Qaddafi was reconciled in March with Yasser Arafat's Fatah wing of the Palestine Liberation Organization (PLO—against which he had previously advocated revolt, owing to its more moderate policies) and attempted to reunite the opposing factions of the Palestinian movement. In September Libya re-established 'fraternal' links with Iraq, modifying its support for Iran in the Iran–Iraq War.

A summit meeting of North African Heads of State, held in Morocco in February 1989, concluded a treaty proclaiming the Union du Maghreb arabe (UMA—Union of the Arab Maghreb, see p. 362), comprising Algeria, Libya, Mauritania, Morocco and Tunisia. The treaty envisaged the establishment of a council of heads of state; regular meetings of ministers of foreign affairs; and the eventual free movement of goods, people, services and capital throughout the countries of the region. During 1989–92 the member states formulated 15 regional co-operation conventions. In February 1993, however, it was announced that, in view of the differing economic orientations of each signatory, no convention had actually been implemented, and the UMA's activities were to be limited. UMA leaders met in April 1994 (and subsequently on an annual basis). In 1994 Libya threatened to leave the UMA unless member states ceased to comply with UN sanctions imposed on Libya (see below), and in 1995 it refused to assume the chairmanship of the organization, owing to their continuing compliance.

In February 1997, at a meeting hosted by Libya and attended by the Presidents of Sudan, Chad, Mali and Niger, and government ministers from Egypt, Burkina Faso and Tunisia, a treaty establishing the Community of Sahel-Saharan States (COMESSA, now CEN-SAD, see p. 359) was signed. CEN-SAD's general secretariat was temporarily located in Tripoli, and provisions were made for the establishment of a development bank, a council of heads of state and an executive council.

Libya's relations with the USA, which had been strained for many years, deteriorated significantly under the presidency of Ronald Reagan (1981–89) who accused the Libyan Government of sponsoring international terrorism. In January 1986 Reagan severed all economic and commercial relations with Libya, and in March Libyan forces fired missiles at US fighter aircraft which were challenging Libya's attempts to enforce recognition of the whole of the Gulf of Sirte as its territorial waters. In two retaliatory attacks US fighters destroyed missile and radar facilities in the town of Sirte, and four Libyan patrol boats in the Gulf. In April US military aircraft bombed military installations, airports and official buildings, as well as alleged terrorist training camps and communication centres in Tripoli and Benghazi. The US Administration claimed in justification to have irrefutable proof of Libyan involvement in terrorist attacks and plots against US targets in Europe and the Middle East. A total of 101 people, including many civilians, were reported to have died in the raids. Tensions increased in late 1988 after Reagan stated that the USA was considering military action against a factory at Rabta, outside Tripoli, where Libya was allegedly preparing to manufacture chemical weapons.

In November 1991 the US and British Governments announced that they would seek to extradite two Libyan citizens, Abd al-Baset Ali Muhammad al-Megrahi (a former head of security of Libyan Arab Airlines) and Al-Amin Khalifa Fhimah (an employee of the airline), alleged to have been responsible for an explosion that destroyed a Pan American World Airways (Pan Am) passenger aircraft over Lockerbie, Scotland, in December 1988, resulting in the deaths of 270 people. The Libyan Government denied any involvement in the bombing, and recommended that the allegations be investigated by a neutral body. In January 1992 the UN Security Council adopted a resolution (No. 731) demanding Libya's compliance with requests for the extradition of its two nationals and its co-operation with a French inquiry into the bombing over Niger, in September 1989, of a UTA passenger airline, in which all 171 passengers and crew had been killed. Libya's offer to try on its own territory the two men accused of the Lockerbie bombing was rejected by the USA, the United Kingdom and France, which urged the UN to impose sanctions on Libya. On 31 March 1992 the UN Security Council adopted a resolution (No. 748) imposing economic sanctions against Libya if it refused to comply with Resolution 731, and commit itself to a renunciation of international terrorism, by 15 April. Sanctions, including the severance of international air links, the prohibition of trade in arms and the reduction of Libya's diplomatic representation abroad, were duly imposed on the specified date. In May, at Qaddafi's instigation, 1,500 People's Congresses were convened in Libya and abroad, to enable the country's citizens to decide the fate of the two Lockerbie suspects and their response to the UN sanctions. The GPC announced in the following month its decision to allow the two Lockerbie suspects to be tried abroad, provided that the proceedings were 'fair and just'.

In August 1993 the USA, the United Kingdom and France announced that they would request the UN Security Council to strengthen the sanctions in force against Libya if, by 1 October, Libya had still not complied with Resolutions 731 and 748. The Libyan Government rejected this ultimatum, but stated its willingness to commence discussions with those three countries on an appropriate venue for the trial of the two Lockerbie suspects. In October the UN Secretary-General, Dr Boutros Boutros-Ghali, met the Libyan Secretary for Foreign Liaison and International Co-operation, but failed to secure agreement on a timetable for the surrender of the two suspects to either the USA or the United Kingdom. In November the Security Council adopted a resolution (No. 883) providing for the strengthening of the economic sanctions in force against Libya in the event of the country's failure fully to comply with Resolutions 731 and 748 by 1 December. The sanctions, which were duly applied, included the closure of all Libyan Arab Airlines' offices abroad; a ban on the sale of equipment and services for the civil aviation sector; the sequestration of all Libyan financial resources overseas; and a ban on the sale to Libya of specified items for use in the petroleum and gas industries.

In January 1994 the Scottish lawyer representing the two Lockerbie suspects stated that they might be willing to stand trial in The Hague; this was subsequently endorsed as an appropriate venue by Qaddafi. In February, however, US President Bill Clinton recommended that an embargo should be imposed on Libya's sales of petroleum (which accounted for some 98% of its export earnings) if the country continued to defy the international community. In January 1995 British media published a US intelligence report, compiled in March 1991, that alleged that the Lockerbie bombing had been perpetrated by Palestinian agents at the bidding of a former Iranian Minister of the Interior, in retaliation for the attack on an Iran Air passenger flight, mistakenly shot down by a US aircraft carrier in July 1988. It had been variously claimed that Iranian, Syrian and Palestinian agents—sometimes separately, sometimes in collaboration—had been responsible for the explosion. Never-

theless, both the US and the British authorities remained convinced that there was sufficient evidence to continue to seek the extradition of the two Libyan suspects who had been formally indicted for the offence in the USA and Scotland.

In mid-1996, following its repeated failure to persuade the UN to agree yet more stringent sanctions against Libya, the US Congress approved unilateral 'secondary' sanctions against Libya (and Iran). The Iran-Libya Sanctions Act (ILSA) sought to penalize companies operating in US markets that were investing more than US $40m. (later amended to $20m.) in Libya's oil and gas industries.

In July 1997 the Arab League, which had been criticized by Qaddafi for its lack of support, formally proposed that the two Libyan suspects in the Lockerbie case be tried by Scottish judges under Scottish law in a neutral country. In September the members of the League urged a relaxation of the air embargo on Libya and voted to defy UN sanctions by permitting aircraft carrying Qaddafi, and other flights for religious or humanitarian purposes, to land on their territory.

In April 1998 the official spokesman for the families of the British victims of the Lockerbie bombing, together with an expert in Scottish law, held talks with Qaddafi in Libya, following which it was reported that Qaddafi had agreed to allow the two Libyan suspects to stand trial in the Netherlands under Scottish law. In August the United Kingdom and the USA proposed that the trial be held in the Netherlands under Scottish law and presided over by Scottish judges. The UN Security Council adopted a resolution (No. 1192) welcoming the initiative and providing for the suspension of sanctions upon the arrival in the Netherlands of the two suspects; additional sanctions were threatened if the Libyan authorities did not comply with the resolution.

In December 1998 the UN Secretary-General, Kofi Annan, held a meeting with Qaddafi in Libya in an attempt to expedite a trial. Shortly afterwards the GPC, which had been asked to consider the matter, endorsed the principle of a trial of the Lockerbie suspects, but requested that the USA and the United Kingdom remove 'all remaining obstacles'. In a bid to break the impasse arising from Qaddafi's demand that the trial include a panel of international judges, envoys from Saudi Arabia and South Africa were dispatched to Libya in January 1999 to negotiate with Qaddafi. In February it was reported that the envoys had reached an understanding with the Libyan leader whereby UN observers would be allowed to monitor the two Libyan suspects during the trial, to ensure that they were not questioned by US and British agents, and afterwards, if they were convicted and imprisoned in Scotland. The diplomatic initiative culminated in March with a visit by President Nelson Mandela of South Africa to Libya, during which Qaddafi undertook to surrender the suspects by 6 April. The two Libyans duly arrived for trial in the Netherlands on 5 April and were transferred to Camp Zeist, a former US airbase near Utrecht designated Scottish territory for the purposes of the trial, where they were formally arrested and charged with murder, conspiracy to murder and contravention of the 1982 Aviation Security Act. The UN Security Council immediately voted to suspend sanctions against Libya indefinitely, although they were not to be permanently revoked until Libya had met with other conditions stipulated in UN Security Council Resolution 1192 (including the payment of compensation to the families of victims of the Lockerbie bombing). The USA refused to remove 'secondary' sanctions against Libya (see above), but subsequently announced that it would permit the sale of food and medical items to Libya on a 'case-by-case' basis. In June 1999 the US and Libyan ambassadors to the UN took part in what represented the first official contact between the two countries in 18 years. During the talks the USA informed Libya that it could not support a permanent end to UN sanctions until Libya had fully complied with Resolution 1192; thus in July Kofi Annan reported to the Security Council that he was unable to secure support for the permanent revocation of sanctions against Libya.

The two Libyan suspects appeared before the Scottish court in the Netherlands for the first time in December 1999, at a pre-trial hearing to decide on the jurisdiction of the Scottish court. The presiding Scottish judge ruled that the two suspects could be tried on all three charges, and that they could be described as members of the Libyan intelligence services. (Defence lawyers had argued that to describe the Libyans as members of the intelligence services was irrelevant and prejudicial.) The trial of al-Megrahi and Fhimah eventually commenced on 3 May 2000;

both pleaded not guilty to the charges brought against them, and defence lawyers accused a number of organizations, including militant Palestinian resistance groups, of perpetrating the bombing.

In early January 2001 prosecution lawyers unexpectedly announced that they would no longer pursue charges of conspiracy to murder and contravention of the 1982 Aviation Security Act. Accordingly, the trial proceeded on the sole charge of murder. On 31 January 2001 the judges announced that they had unanimously found al-Megrahi guilty of the murder of 270 people and sentenced him to life imprisonment, with the recommendation that he serve a minimum of 20 years. The judges accepted that al-Megrahi was a member of the Libyan intelligence services, and although they acknowledged their awareness of what they termed 'uncertainties and qualifications' in the case, they concluded that the evidence against him combined to form 'a real and convincing pattern' which left them with no reasonable doubt as to his guilt. Fhimah, however, was unanimously acquitted, owing to lack of proof, and freed to return to Libya. Despite mounting pressure from Arab League states, the British Government asserted that sanctions against Libya would not be permanently revoked until Libya accepted responsibility for the bombing and paid 'substantial' compensation. The newly inaugurated US President, George W. Bush, also indicated his support for this stance, and in July 2001 ILSA was extended for a further five-year term.

Meanwhile, demands for further investigation into the bombing, and Qaddafi's role in it, were rejected by senior Scottish legal officials, who stated that there was insufficient evidence to justify any further proceedings against those alleged to have abetted al-Megrahi, despite the fact that he had apparently not acted alone. Lawyers for al-Megrahi subsequently lodged an appeal against the conviction. The appeal hearing, before five Scottish judges, began at Camp Zeist in late January 2002. Al-Megrahi's lawyers based their case on what they termed new 'strong circumstantial evidence', which raised the possibility that the bomb had been placed on the aircraft at London, United Kingdom, and not in Malta, as the trial judges had concluded. In mid-March the appeal was unanimously rejected, and al-Megrahi was transferred to a prison in Scotland to begin his sentence. In late February Qaddafi's eldest son, Seif al-Islam (whose increasingly prominent role fuelled speculation that he was being prepared as an eventual successor to the Libyan leader), had indicated that Libya would pay compensation to the families of those killed in the Lockerbie bombing, regardless of the outcome of the appeal. Former South African President Nelson Mandela visited al-Megrahi in prison in June to assess the conditions of his imprisonment and concluded that al-Megrahi's detention in solitary confinement amounted to psychological persecution. Mandela requested that al-Megrahi be allowed to serve the remainder of his sentence in a Muslim country, suggesting Egypt, Morocco or Tunisia as possibilities. Nevertheless, in August the British Secretary of State for Foreign and Commonwealth Affairs pledged that al-Megrahi would serve the full term of his sentence in Scotland.

In July 1999 Libya and the United Kingdom reached agreement on the full restoration of diplomatic relations after Qaddafi issued a statement in which he accepted Libya's 'general responsibility' for the death of Yvonne Fletcher, a British policewoman who was shot outside the Libyan People's Bureau in London in 1984, and agreed to co-operate with the investigation into the killing. The payment by Libya, in November 1999, of compensation to the victim's family facilitated the reopening of the British embassy in Tripoli the following month. In January 2000, however, the British Government confirmed that its customs officials had, in late 1999, seized a consignment of *Scud* missile parts which had arrived in the United Kingdom from Taiwan and was bound for Libya via Malta. (It subsequently transpired that the parts had been impounded in mid-1999, prior to the full restoration of diplomatic relations between the United Kingdom and Libya.) Despite this incident and the delivery of the Lockerbie trial verdict, the normalization of relations between the United Kingdom and Libya progressed and in March 2001 Libya appointed an ambassador to the United Kingdom for the first time in 17 years. In early August 2002 a minister of the British Foreign and Commonwealth Office visited Libya for talks with Qaddafi: this was the first visit by a British government minister to Libya for some 20 years. After the meeting it was reported that Libya had given strong indications that it was ready to accept responsibility for the Lockerbie bombing, while the Libyan Secretary for Foreign Affairs declared that Libya

was ready 'in principle' to take steps to compensate the relatives of victims. Qaddafi had also expressed his willingness to co-operate with the international community on issues such as weapons of mass destruction and the 'war against terror'.

In March 2003 it was reported that, following negotiations in London between senior British, US and Libyan representatives, Libya had agreed to accept civil responsibility for the actions of its officials in the Lockerbie case and would pay US $10m. in compensation to the families of the victims. Payment of the compensation was to be a three-stage process: $4m. would be paid to each family on the permanent lifting of UN sanctions; a further $4m. would follow upon the removal of unilateral US sanctions; and a final payment of $2m. would be made when Libya was removed from the list of countries that the USA deemed to support international terrorism. However, Libya would pay only an additional $1m. to each family if the USA did not complete the second and third stages. The following month the Libyan Secretary for Foreign Liaison and International Co-operation, Abd ar-Rahman Muhammad Shalgam, confirmed that Libya would accept responsibility for the actions of its civilians, although both the United Kingdom and the USA stated that they had not received official notification of Libya's position.

Negotiations continued during mid-2003 and on 16 August Libya delivered a letter to the President of the UN Security Council stating that it accepted 'responsibility for the actions of its officials' in the Lockerbie bombing; agreed to pay compensation to the families of the victims; pledged co-operation in any further Lockerbie inquiry; agreed to continue its co-operation in the 'war against terror'; and to take practical measures to ensure that such co-operation was effective. Following the transfer of US $2,700m. in compensation to the International Bank of Settlements, the United Kingdom submitted a draft resolution to the Security Council requesting the formal lifting of UN sanctions against Libya. It was feared, however, that France, which had demanded a similar amount of compensation for families of victims of the UTA bombing in 1989 (see above), would veto the resolution unless Libyan officials agreed to an additional payment. The United Kingdom, France and the USA eventually agreed to postpone the vote on the draft resolution to allow more time for an agreement to be reached between the groups representing families of the UTA victims and the Libyan authorities. US President Bush insisted that his Administration would maintain unilateral sanctions against Libya until the Libyan Government addressed ongoing US concerns such as the infringement of human rights in the country and the pursuit of weapons of mass destruction.

In early September 2003, following an intervention by the French President, Jacques Chirac, the Libyan Government and the families of the UTA bombing reached partial agreement on the payment of additional compensation to the victims' relatives. On 12 September 13 of the 15 members of the UN Security Council approved the lifting of the sanctions imposed against Libya; France and the USA abstained from the vote. Later that month Libya announced its intention to commence dialogue with the USA aimed at normalizing bilateral relations. Nevertheless, the US Administration continued to insist that unilateral sanctions would remain in place. In October talks between Libya and France aimed at reaching a final settlement regarding the issue of compensation for the UTA bombing were suspended following a number of disagreements between the two sides. However, in early January 2004 Libya agreed to pay an additional US $170m. to the relatives of the victims; the payment was to be made in four equal instalments, resulting in the families of each victim receiving an additional $1m.

Meanwhile, in October 2003 an official of the US Department of State accused Libya of having increased its efforts to purchase components for biological and chemical weapons since the lifting of UN sanctions the previous month, and warned that Libya would be added to the group of countries described by President Bush as forming an 'axis of evil' (comprising Iran, Iraq and the Democratic People's Republic of Korea). In mid-December, however, in an unexpected development, the British Prime Minister, Tony Blair, announced that Libya had agreed to disclose and dismantle its programme to develop weapons of mass destruction and long-range ballistic missiles. The statement was the culmination of nine months of clandestine negotiations between Qaddafi and British and US diplomats during which the Libyan authorities had reportedly shown evidence of a 'well advanced' nuclear weapons programme, as well as the existence of large quantities of chemical weapons and bombs designed to carry poisonous gas. Libya also agreed to adhere to the Chemical Weapons Convention and to sign an additional protocol allowing the International Atomic Energy Agency (IAEA) to carry out random inspections of its facilities. Later that month the Director-General of the IAEA, Muhammad el-Baradei, stated that inspectors from the UN agency would visit Libya by the end of December in order to commence the process of dismantling Libya's weapons development projects. Upon visiting a number of sites in Tripoli in late December el-Baradei insisted that these projects had been in the initial stages of development, contradicting the assessment given by the United Kingdom and the USA. In early January 2004 the US Department of State confirmed that British and US intelligence agents had, in October 2003, intercepted a shipment of centrifuges capable of developing weapons-grade uranium destined for Tripoli, which the USA believed had prompted Qaddafi to take the final steps towards abandoning Libya's nuclear weapons programme. It was announced in mid-January 2004 that Libya had ratified the IAEA's Comprehensive Nuclear Test Ban Treaty earlier in that month.

Further disagreements in January 2004 between the USA, the United Kingdom and the IAEA concerning their respective roles in the process of dismantling Libya's weapons facilities were finally resolved late that month: it was agreed that US and British officials would be responsible for destroying and removing the nuclear material and that the IAEA would verify that the dismantling process was complete. Later in January a delegation from the US Congress visited Libya; however, President Bush again reiterated that there were no imminent plans to remove US sanctions. In early February Libyan officials held talks with the US Assistant Secretary of State in London and it was also confirmed that an American diplomat had been stationed in the US interests section of the Belgian embassy in Tripoli, providing the USA with its first permanent diplomatic presence in Libya for 25 years. Also in February Shalgam visited London for talks with his British counterpart and Prime Minister Blair; this represented the first meeting between cabinet-level ministers of the two countries in more than 20 years.

In late February 2004 the Secretary of the GPC, Shukri Muhammad Ghanem, caused controversy when he claimed that compensation was being paid to the families of the Lockerbie victims in order to 'buy peace' and avoid sanctions, and that the country did not accept responsibility for the Lockerbie bombing; he also denied any Libyan involvement in the murder of Fletcher. The following day, however, Shalgam issued a statement in which he announced his regret at Ghanem's comments and reiterated that Libya stood by its acceptance of responsibility for the Lockerbie bombing. The USA subsequently lifted the restrictions on its citizens travelling to Libya, and although trade sanctions remained in place, it was anticipated that a number of US companies would soon be permitted to conduct business in Libya. In early March Libya signed an additional IAEA protocol allowing the agency to carry out random inspections of its nuclear facilities; moreover, Libya commenced the destruction of its supplies of chemical weapons and transported all of its remaining nuclear weapons-related equipment to the USA. Later that month the Organization for the Prohibition of Chemical Weapons verified that Libya's declaration of its chemical weapons inventory (submitted to the UN in early March) had been accurate, after a series of inspections had been carried out by the agency's officials.

In late March 2004 William Burns, the US Assistant Secretary of the Bureau of Near Eastern Affairs, became the highest-ranking US official to visit Libya in more than 30 years; the principal issues under discussion were further moves towards the lifting of US sanctions on Libya and the restoration of normal bilateral relations. Two days later Blair visited Tripoli and held talks with Qaddafi, after which the British Prime Minister stated that there was genuine hope for a 'new relationship', while Qaddafi insisted that he was willing to join the international 'war against terror'. It was also announced that British police-officers would travel to Libya in early April to continue investigations into the murder of Fletcher. In late April the USA announced that it would remove the restrictions that prevented US petroleum companies and banks from conducting commercial activities in Libya and that Libyan students would be allowed to study in the USA.

In January 2000 (shortly after the revelation of the seizure of missile parts by the United Kingdom) the European Union (EU, see p. 208) withdrew an invitation to Qaddafi, issued by the Commission President, Romano Prodi, to visit the European Commission headquarters in Brussels, Belgium, on the grounds that Libya had not accepted EU conditions regarding commitment to human rights, democracy, free trade and support for the Middle East peace process. Apparently in reprisal, Libya immediately announced major commercial contracts with Russia and the People's Republic of China. Qaddafi none the less attended the EU-Africa summit meeting in Cairo, Egypt, in April, at which talks with Prodi and other European officials were described as 'positive'. Relations with the EU, and particularly with France, generally improved following talks in early 1996 between Libyan and EU representatives in Belgium. In July Qaddafi granted the French authorities investigating the 1989 bombing of the UTA passenger aircraft unprecedented access to Libyan evidence. This resulted in February 1998 in a judge's decision to try *in absentia* six Libyans suspected of involvement in the attack, and in March 1999 a French court sentenced the six suspects *in absentia* to life imprisonment. The French authorities issued international arrest warrants for the Libyans, and threatened to intensify sanctions against Libya if it did not impose the verdicts on the accused. In July Libya began payment of some US $31m. in compensation to the families of those killed in the bomb attack. France stated that this represented an acknowledgement by Libya of the responsibility of its citizens for the bombing, although attempts by French lawyers on behalf of the victims' families to prosecute Qaddafi for complicity in the bombing of the aircraft were unsuccessful. Nevertheless, it was announced in January 2004 that Libya had agreed to pay an additional US $170m. to the relatives of the victims (for further details, see above). In late April Qaddafi, who was visiting Europe for the first time in 15 years, met with several senior EU politicians in Brussels and addressed the European Commission.

In October 1996, meanwhile, the German authorities announced that evidence existed to prove the Libyan Government's direct involvement in a bomb attack on a discothèque in Berlin in 1986. Arrest warrants were subsequently issued for the four Libyans suspected of carrying out the bombing, but in March 1997 a German parliamentary delegation recommended that regular contact between the German Parliament and the GPC should continue. In April 1998 Libya resolved to allow the German authorities to question the Libyan suspects. In May the two countries signed an agreement on economic co-operation. Following a lengthy trial, in mid-November 2001 a court in Berlin sentenced four people, including a Libyan national, to between 12 and 14 years' imprisonment for their involvement in the bomb attack. Although Qaddafi's personal complicity in the incident could not be proven, the presiding judge stated that there was sufficient evidence to ascertain that the bombing had been carried out by members of the Libyan secret service and employees of the Libyan People's Bureau in the former East Germany. In August 2003 the Qaddafi Foundation, a charity run by Seif al-Islam Qaddafi, offered to compensate the relatives of the three victims of the Berlin bomb attack.

In February 1998 a Spanish minister visited Tripoli, following an announcement of Spain's intention to renew political and economic ties with Libya. However, the decision by France, Spain, Italy and Portugal to create a rapid reaction force in the Mediterranean was strongly condemned by Qaddafi. In July Italy formally apologized for its colonial rule of Libya, and commitments were made to improve bilateral relations. The Italian Minister of Foreign Affairs, Lamberto Dini, visited Libya in April 1999, immediately after the suspension of international sanctions. Italy's Prime Minister, Massimo D'Alema, travelled to Libya in December, thus becoming the first EU premier to visit the country since 1992. In December 2000 the Libyan Secretary for Foreign Liaison and International Co-operation attended talks with Dini in Rome, at which accords regarding political consultation, visas and the removal of landmines were signed. In September 2003, just days after the lifting of UN sanctions against Libya, the Spanish Prime Minister, José María Aznar López, visited Tripoli for talks with Qaddafi.

In mid-1998 Qaddafi announced his intention to ally Libya more closely with African rather than Arab countries; later in the year numerous African heads of state visited Tripoli, all of whom defied UN sanctions by travelling to Libya by air (see above). In October, as further evidence of his dissatisfaction with Arab states, Qaddafi changed the name of Libya's mission to the Arab League from 'permanent' to 'resident'. In September 1999, on the occasion of the 30th anniversary of his seizure of power, Qaddafi hosted an extraordinary OAU summit in Sirte. Qaddafi presented his vision of a United States of Africa, and demanded that Africa be given veto power on the UN Security Council. The 'Sirte Declaration', a final document adopted by the 43 attending heads of state and government, called for the strengthening of the OAU, the establishment of a pan-African parliament, African monetary union and an African court of justice. At a further extraordinary summit of the OAU in Sirte in early March 2001 it was announced that the organization's member states had overwhelmingly endorsed the proposals to declare the formation of the AU. In early July 2002 Qaddafi travelled to Durban, South Africa, for the 38th and final summit of the OAU, which saw the formal creation of the new AU, chaired by South African President Thabo Mbeki. During the summit Mbeki and numerous other African heads of state attempted to persuade Qaddafi to abandon his hostility towards the New Partnership for Africa's Development, a contract between Africa and the international community under which, in exchange for aid and investment, the African states agreed to strive towards democracy and good governance. After the summit Qaddafi visited Mozambique, Zimbabwe and Malawi. In October Libya notified the Arab League of its intention to withdraw from the organization. Although no official reason for the withdrawal was given, reports indicated that senior Libyan officials had cited the Arab League's 'inefficiency' in dealing with the crises in Iraq and the Palestinian territories as its motives. Arab League ministers of foreign affairs subsequently convened to request that Libya reconsider its decision to withdraw, although it appeared unlikely that Libya would relent. In March 2003 Libyan officials confirmed that the threat of withdrawal was 'serious and official'. Qaddafi's growing influence in Africa was also somewhat checked in January 2003 following the removal of some 300 Libyan troops from the Central African Republic, to whose Government they had been providing protection. In the previous month an agreement between Libya and Zimbabwe which would have resulted in the exchange of Libyan fuel for Zimbabwean beef, sugar and tobacco was abandoned. Attempts to revive the trade pact in mid-2003, which would have resulted in Zimbabwe mortgaging its petroleum assets to Libya, proved unsuccessful, and the abolition of the Secretariat for African Unity in mid-2003 was widely interpreted as evidence of the failure of Qaddafi's African policy.

In early January 2004 it was reported that a senior Israeli diplomat had held talks in Paris in December 2003 with Libyan representatives, with the aim of establishing diplomatic relations between the two countries. While an Israeli official confirmed that a meeting had taken place, the Libyan Government denied that any contact had been made.

Government

Power is vested in the people through People's Congresses, Popular Committees, Trade Unions, Vocational Syndicates, and with the General People's Congress (GPC) and its General Secretariat. The Head of State is the Revolutionary Leader, elected by the GPC. Executive power is exercised by the General People's Committee. The country is divided into three provinces, 10 governorates and 1,500 administrative communes.

Defence

Libya's active armed forces totalled 76,000 (including an estimated 38,000 conscripts) in August 2003: army 45,000; air force 23,000; navy 8,000. Military service is by selective conscription, lasting up to two years. There was additionally a People's Militia of 40,000 reserves. Libya's defence budget in 2002 was an estimated LD 680m.

Economic Affairs

In 1989, according to estimates by the World Bank, Libya's gross national income (GNI), measured at average 1987–89 prices, was US $23,333m., equivalent to $5,310 per head. (In 1994, according to unofficial estimates, GNI at current prices was $26,000m., equivalent to $5,650 per head.) During 1990–2002, it was estimated, the population increased at an average annual rate of 2.1%, while, according to the IMF, gross domestic product (GDP) per head declined, in real terms, by an average of 0.7% per year. Overall GDP increased, in real terms, at an average annual rate of 1.7% in 1990–2002. Real GDP increased by 0.5% in 2001, but declined by 0.2% in 2002.

Agriculture (including forestry and fishing) contributed an estimated 8.6% of GDP in 2001, and engaged 17.9% of the employed labour force in 1996. The principal subsistence crops are wheat and barley; other crops include watermelons, potatoes, onions, olives, tomatoes, dates and citrus fruits. Output is limited by climatic conditions and irrigation problems, although

cultivable land was being significantly increased by the Great Man-made River Project, whereby water was to be carried from the south of the country to the north and thence to the east and west. However, the highly ambitious nature of the scheme has provided engineers with serious difficulties and by early 2004, after 20 years of construction work, the project remained little more than half completed. Agriculture is based mainly on animal husbandry; sheep are the principal livestock, but goats, cattle, camels, horses and poultry are also kept. During 1994–2001 agricultural GDP increased at an average annual rate of 1.6%; the sector's GDP increased by 1.7% in 2000 and by 2.7% in 2001.

Industry (including mining, manufacturing, construction and power) contributed an estimated 50.5% of GDP in 2001, and engaged 29.9% of the employed labour force in 1996. Virtually all of the industrial sector is state-controlled. During 1994–2001 the GDP of the industrial sector increased at an average annual rate of 1.5%; industrial GDP increased by 3.5% in 2000 and by 3.9% in 2001.

Mining contributed 36.1% of GDP in 2001, but engaged only 2.5% of the employed labour force in 1996. The petroleum and natural gas sector contributed 34.1% of GDP in 2001, and engaged 1.7% of the employed labour force in 1996. Libya's economy depends almost entirely on its petroleum and natural gas resources. The National Oil Corporation of Libya (NOC) controls about three-quarters of the petroleum produced in Libya, largely through production-sharing agreements. At the end of 2002 proven recoverable reserves of petroleum were estimated at 29,500m. barrels, sufficient to enable production to be maintained—at that year's levels, averaging 1.38m. barrels per day (b/d)—until 2061. With effect from 1 April 2004 Libya's production quota within the Organization of the Petroleum Exporting Countries (OPEC, see p. 317) was 1,258,000 b/d. Libya's natural gas reserves are extensive (estimated at 1,310,000m. cu m at the end of 2002). Libya also has reserves of iron ore, salt, limestone, clay, sulphur and gypsum. The GDP of the mining sector decreased, in real terms, by an annual average of 0.4% in 1994–2001; mining GDP declined by 1.3% in 2000, but increased by 3.0% in 2001.

Manufacturing contributed 5.9% of GDP in 2001, and engaged 10.5% of the employed labour force in 1996. The principal manufacturing activity is petroleum refining. There are three refineries, at Brega, Ras Lanouf and Az-Zawiyah. A petrochemicals site is located at Brega, and in the late 1990s there were plans to construct a new petrochemicals complex at Ras Lanouf. Other important manufacturing activities were the production of iron, steel and cement, and the processing of agricultural products. The GDP of the manufacturing sector increased at an average annual rate of 3.6% during 1994–2001; the sector's GDP increased by 2.2% in 2000 and by 2.5% in 2001.

Energy is derived almost exclusively from oil-fired power. Libya is a net exporter of fuels (less than 10% of petroleum production is used for domestic energy requirements), with imports of energy products comprising only an estimated 0.2% of the value of merchandise imports in 1998.

Services contributed 40.9% of GDP in 2001, and engaged 52.2% of the employed labour force in 1996. Visitor arrivals declined from 1.8m. in 1995 to 962,559 in 2000. Receipts from tourism in 1999 amounted to US $28m. In an attempt to stimulate growth in the tourism sector, the Government invested heavily in 1996–2001 to expand and rehabilitate tourism infrastructure. During 1994–2001 the GDP of the services sector increased at an annual average rate of 2.3%; services GDP increased by 3.3% in 2000 and by 2.8% in 2001.

In 1999 Libya recorded a visible trade surplus of US $2,762m., and there was a surplus of $1,984m. on the current account of the balance of payments. In 1999 the principal sources of imports were Italy (which provided 18.3% of total imports), Germany (14.5%), the Republic of Korea, the United Kingdom and France. The principal market for exports in that year was Italy (37.8%); Germany, Spain, France and Viet Nam were also important purchasers. The petroleum sector is overwhelmingly Libya's principal generator of exports revenue: exports of mineral fuels, lubricants, etc. accounted for 94.8% of Libya's export earnings in 1997. The principal imports were machinery and transport equipment, basic manufactures, and food and live animals.

There was a projected budgetary surplus of LD 3,128m. in 2003. In the previous year a surplus of LD 939m. had been recorded. Libya's total external debt was about US $3,800m. at the end of 1999, according to estimates quoted by the *Middle*

East Economic Digest. According to the same source, the rate of inflation averaged an estimated 24.0% in 1999, compared with 5.6% in 1997. The rate of unemployment was unofficially estimated to be about 30% in 2003.

Libya is a member of the Arab Monetary Fund (see p. 145), the Council of Arab Economic Unity (see p. 187), the Islamic Development Bank (see p. 275), the Organization of Arab Petroleum Exporting Countries (see p. 311), OPEC (see p. 317) and the Union du Maghreb arabe (Union of the Arab Maghreb, see p. 362).

During 2003–04 prospects for the major improvement and modernization of the Libyan economy were bolstered by a number of extremely important political decisions. The appointment in mid-2003 of Shukri Muhammad Ghanem, a former Libyan representative to OPEC, as Secretary of the GPC precipitated a new phase of economic reform; Ghanem swiftly announced plans to divest more than 360 state-owned entities during 2004 and to establish a stock exchange, although he emphasized that the privatization scheme would not involve companies in the hydrocarbons or chemical sectors. In September 2003 the decision to accept civil responsibility for the Lockerbie bombing facilitated the formal removal of UN sanctions, which had been imposed in 1992 and suspended in 1999 (see Recent History). Although the USA initially remained unwilling to remove unilateral 'secondary' sanctions imposed on Libya in 1996, thus excluding US companies from signing potentially lucrative contracts, it was anticipated that large numbers of European and Asian petroleum companies would seek to take advantage of the opportunities to assume increased roles in the further development of the country's hydrocarbons industry. However, in April 2004 the USA lifted the sanctions which had outlawed commercial activities and financial transactions between Libyan and US companies. Meanwhile, in late 2003 the Libyan Government pledged to increase petroleum production capacity to more than 2m. b/d by 2010. Libya also possesses considerable reserves of natural gas, with major potential for further discoveries. An underwater pipeline linking Libya with Italy, scheduled to be completed in late 2004, is expected to enable some 8,000m. cu m per year of natural gas to be exported to Europe. Libya also elicited praise from the IMF following the country's first ever Article IV consultation in August 2003, although the Fund identified Libya's main challenge as the generation of sufficient growth and employment opportunities to absorb the rapidly growing labour force; indeed, unemploy-ment remained at around 30%. The devaluation of the dinar by more than 50% in early 2002 and the exchange rate reform carried out in mid-2003 were expected to increase the flow of foreign direct investment into the country. Despite forecast GDP growth of 5.6% in 2003, Libya's reliance on petroleum revenues remained a major concern. Attempts are under way, however, to develop the country's largely untapped tourism potential after the enactment of a five-year investment plan, at a cost some US $7,000m., and the improvement in relations with many Western countries in the wake of Libya's decision to abandon its nuclear weapons programme, provided further optimism for economic development.

Education

Education is compulsory for children between six and 15 years of age. Primary education begins at the age of six and lasts for nine years. In 1992 primary enrolment included 96% of the relevant age-group (males 97%; females 96%). Secondary education, from the age of 15, lasts for three years. In 1992 secondary enrolment was equivalent to 98% of pupils in the relevant age-group. Libya also has institutes for agricultural, technical and vocational training. There are 13 universities. In 1992 enrolment in tertiary education was equivalent to 18.4% of the relevant age-group (males 19.2%; females 17.6%).

Public Holidays

2004: 1 February* (Id al-Adha, Feast of the Sacrifice), 22 February* (Islamic New Year), 2 March* (Ashoura), 28 March (Evacuation Day), 2 May* (Mouloud, Birth of Muhammad), 11 June (Evacuation Day), 1 September (Revolution Day), 12 September* (Leilat al-Meiraj, ascension of Muhammad), 7 October (Evacuation Day), 14 November* (Id al-Fitr, end of Ramadan).

2005: 21 January* (Id al-Adha, Feast of the Sacrifice), 10 February* (Islamic New Year), 19 February* (Ashoura), 28 March (Evacuation Day), 21 April* (Mouloud, Birth of Muhammad), 11 June (Evacuation Day), 1 September (Revolution Day), 2 September* (Leilat al-Meiraj, ascension of Muhammad), 7 October (Evacuation Day), 4 November* (Id al-Fitr, end of Ramadan).

*These holidays are dependent on the Islamic lunar calendar and may vary by one or two days from the dates given.

Weights and Measures

The metric system is in force.

Statistical Survey

Sources (unless otherwise stated): National Corporation for Information and Documentation; Census and Statistical Dept, Secretariat of Planning, Sharia Damascus 40, 2nd Floor, Tripoli; tel. (21) 3331731.

Area and Population

AREA, POPULATION AND DENSITY

Area (sq km)	1,775,500*
Population (census results)	
August 1995 (provisional)	
Males	2,236,943
Females	2,168,043
Total	4,404,986†
2003 (provisional)	5,678,484
Population (UN estimates at mid-year)	
2000	5,237,000
2001	5,340,000
2002	5,445,000
Density (per sq km) at census of 2003	3.2

* 685,524 sq miles.
† Excluding 406,916 non-Libyans.
Sources: UN, *World Population Prospects: The 2002 Revision*; National Authority for Information and Authentication.

POPULATION BY REGION
(1995 census, provisional figures)

Al-Batnan	151,240		Misratah (Misurata) .	488,573
Jebel Akhdar . . .	381,165		Najghaza . . .	244,553
Banghazi (Benghazi)	665,615		Tarabulus (Tripoli) .	1,313,996
Al-Wosta	240,574		Az-Zawiyah (Zawia) .	517,395
Al-Wahat	62,056		Jebel Gharbi . . .	316,970
Al-Jufra	39,335		Fazzan (Fezzan) . .	314,029
Sofuljin	76,401		**Total**	4,811,902

PRINCIPAL TOWNS
(population at census of 2003)

Tarabulus (Tripoli,				
the capital) . . .	1,149,957		Az-Zawiyah (Zawia) .	197,177
Banghazi (Benghazi)	636,992		Al-Jabal al-Akhader .	194,185
Misratah (Misurata) .	360,521		Ajdabiya (Ejdabia) .	165,839
Almirqeb	328,292		Garyan (Ghryan) . .	161,408
Turhona and				
Misllatah . . .	296,092		Sirte (Surt) . . .	156,839
Al-Jfara	289,340		Surman and	
			Subratha . . .	152,521
An-Niikat al-Ghames	208,954			

Source: National Authority for Information and Authentication.

BIRTHS, MARRIAGES AND DEATHS

	Registered live births		Registered marriages*		Registered deaths*	
	Number	Rate (per 1,000)	Number	Rate (per 1,000)	Number	Rate (per 1,000)
1994 . .	98,423	20.1	19,190	3.9	14,036	2.9
1995 . .	88,779	17.9	21,358	4.3	13,538	4.6
1996 . .	90,428	17.8	18,743	3.7	12,281	2.4

* Registration is incomplete.

Source: UN, *Demographic Yearbook*.

Expectation of life (WHO estimates, years at birth): 72.6 (males 70.4; females 75.5) in 2002 (Source: WHO, *World Health Report*).

EMPLOYMENT

(official estimates, '000 persons)

	1994	1996*
Agriculture, forestry and fishing	213.4	219.5
Mining and quarrying	29.9	31.0
Manufacturing	124.1	128.5
Electricity, gas and water	33.7	35.5
Construction	168.3	171.0
Trade, restaurants and hotels	70.7	73.0
Transport, storage and communications . .	97.7	104.0
Financing, insurance, real estate and business services	18.7	22.0
Other services	434.8	439.5
Total	**1,191.3**	**1,224.0**
Libyans	1,035.2	1,092.1
Non-Libyans	156.1	131.9

* Figures for 1995 are not available.

Health and Welfare

KEY INDICATORS

Total fertility rate (children per woman, 2002)	3.1
Under-5 mortality rate (per 1,000 live births, 2001) . . .	19
HIV/AIDS (% of persons aged 15–49, 2001)	0.24
Physicians (per 1,000 head, 1997)	1.28
Hospital beds (per 1,000 head, 1997)	4.3
Health expenditure (2001): US $ per head (PPP)	239
Health expenditure (2001): % of GDP	2.9
Health expenditure (2001): public (% of total)	56.0
Access to water (% of persons, 2000)	72
Access to sanitation (% of persons, 2000)	97
Human Development Index (2001): ranking	61
Human Development Index (2001): value	0.783

For sources and definitions, see explanatory note on p. vi.

Agriculture

PRINCIPAL CROPS

('000 metric tons)

	2000	2001	2002
Wheat	125†	130*	130*
Barley	80†	80*	80*
Potatoes	190	195	195*
Dry broad beans*	13	13	13
Almonds*	31	31	31
Groundnuts (in shell) *	25	26	26
Olives*	180	170	170
Tomatoes*	225	160	160
Pumpkins, squash and gourds* .	29	29	29
Cucumbers and gherkins* . .	11	11	12
Chillies and green peppers* . .	15	15	15
Green onions and shallots* . .	53	53	53
Dry onions*	180	180	182
Green peas*	12	12	12
Green broad beans*	15	15	15
Carrots*	24	24	24
Other vegetables*	76	76	76
Oranges*	43	43	43
Tangerines, mandarins, etc. * . .	10	10	10
Lemons and limes*	14	14	14
Apples*	47	47	47
Apricots*	17	17	17
Peaches and nectarines* . . .	10	10	10
Plums*	33	33	33
Grapes*	40	40	40
Watermelons*	214	216	218
Cantaloupes and other melons* .	27	27	27
Figs*	30	30	30
Dates*	133	133	134

* FAO estimate(s).
† Unofficial figure.

Source: FAO.

LIVESTOCK

('000 head, year ending September)

	2000	2001	2002
Horses*	46	46	46
Asses*	30	30	30
Cattle*	210	220	220
Camels*	71	72	72
Sheep	4,124	4,125*	4,130*
Goats	1,263†	1,265*	1,265*
Poultry*	25	25	25

* FAO estimate(s).
† Unofficial figure.

Source: FAO.

LIVESTOCK PRODUCTS

(FAO estimates, '000 metric tons)

	2000	2001	2002
Beef and veal	8	7	7
Mutton and lamb	27	27	27
Goat meat	6	6	6
Poultry meat	99	99	99
Cows' milk	135	137	138
Sheep's milk	55	56	56
Goats' milk	15	15	15
Hen eggs	59	59	59
Wool: greasy	9	9	9
Wool: scoured	2	2	2
Cattle hides	1	1	1
Sheepskins	6	6	6

Source: FAO.

Forestry

ROUNDWOOD REMOVALS
(FAO estimates, '000 cubic metres, excl. bark)

	2000	2001	2002
Sawlogs, veneer logs and logs for sleepers*	63	63	63
Other industrial wood	53	53	53
Fuel wood*	536	536	536
Total	652	652	652

* Annual output assumed to be unchanged since 1978.

Source: FAO.

SAWNWOOD PRODUCTION
(FAO estimates, '000 cubic metres, incl. railway sleepers)

	2000	2001	2002
Total (all broadleaved)*	31	31	31

* Annual output assumed to be unchanged since 1978.

Source: FAO.

Fishing

(FAO estimates, metric tons, live weight)

	1999	2000	2001
Capture	32,850	33,387	33,239
Groupers	4,000	4,000	4,000
Bogue	2,500	2,500	2,500
Porgies and seabreams	4,000	4,000	4,000
Red mullet	4,000	4,000	4,000
Jack and horse mackerels	3,000	3,000	3,000
Sardinellas	7,000	7,000	7,000
Northern bluefin tuna	1,195	1,550	1,940
'Scomber' mackerels	3,000	3,000	3,000
Aquaculture	100	100	100
Total catch (incl. others)	32,950	34,487	33,339

Source: FAO, *Yearbook of Fishery Statistics.*

Mining

(estimates, '000 metric tons, unless otherwise indicated)

	2000	2001	2002
Crude petroleum ('000 barrels)	538,000	520,000	502,000
Natural gas (million cu m)*	11,000	11,400	11,000
Salt	40	40	40
Gypsum (crude)	175	150	150

* Figures refer to gross volume. The dry equivalent (estimates, million cubic metres) was: ; 5,400 in 2000; 5,600 in 2001; 5,700 in 2002.

Source: US Geological Survey.

Industry

SELECTED PRODUCTS
('000 metric tons, unless otherwise indicated)

	1998	1999	2000
Olive oil (crude)	8	9	7
Paper and paperboard	6	6	6
Jet fuels	1,339	1,352	1,453
Motor spirit (petrol)	1,970	1,991	2,030
Naphthas	1,998	2,007	2,007
Kerosene	274	277	297
Gas-diesel (distillate fuel) oil	4,272	4,319	4,662
Residual fuel oils	4,834	4,908	4,330
Liquefied petroleum gas:			
from natural gas plants	685*	353	353
from petroleum refineries	263	238	271
Petroleum bitumen (asphalt)	106	100	111
Cement	3	3	3
Electric energy (million kWh)	19,496	20,044	20,044*

* Provisional or estimated figure(s).

2001 ('000 metric tons): Olive oil (crude) 6; Paper and paperboard 6.

Source: UN, *Industrial Commodity Statistics Yearbook.*

Finance

CURRENCY AND EXCHANGE RATES

Monetary Units
1,000 dirhams = 1 Libyan dinar (LD).

Sterling, Dollar and Euro Equivalents (31 December 2003)
£1 sterling = 2.320 dinars;
US $1 = 1.300 dinars;
€1 = 1.642 dinars
100 Libyan dinars = £43.09 = $76.90 = €60.89

Average Exchange Rate (US $ per Libyan dinar)
2001   1.5382
2002   0.8266
2003   0.7690

Note: In March 1986 the value of the Libyan dinar was linked to the IMF's special drawing right (SDR). Between November 1994 and November 1998 the official mid-point exchange rate was SDR 1 = 525 dirhams (LD 1 = SDR 1.90476). In February 1999 a rate of LD 1 = SDR 1.577 (SDR 1 = 634.1 dirhams) was introduced, but from September 1999 to September 2000 the value of the dinar fluctuated. In September 2000 a new rate of LD 1 = SDR 1.4204 (SDR 1 = 704.03 dirhams) was established, but in June 2001 the Libyan dinar was devalued to SDR 1.224 (SDR 1 = 816.99 dirhams). The latter rate remained in effect until the end of December 2001. In January 2002 the value of the Libyan dinar was adjusted to SDR 0.608 (SDR 1 = LD 1.64474): a devaluation of 50.3%.

BUDGET
(projections, LD million)

Revenue	2001	2002	2003*
Budgetary revenue	5,842	8,645	9,168
Hydrocarbon budget allocation	3,607	6,551	7,214
Non-hydrocarbon tax revenue	2,056	1,150	1,159
Taxes on income and profits	381	506	n.a.
Taxes on international trade	1,531	379	320
Other tax revenue	143	266	—
Non-hydrocarbon non-tax revenue	179	944	795
Extrabudgetary revenue	1,747	2,717	4,122
Total	7,589	11,362	13,290

Expenditure	2001	2002	2003*
Current	5,830	7,085	6,601
Administrative budget	3,537	4,050	4,375
Expenditure on goods and services	3,161	3,552	3,676
Wages and salaries	2,297	2,413	2,437
Interest payments	75	—	123
Subsidies and other current transfers	301	499	576
Extrabudgetary current expenditure	2,293	3,034	2,226
Oil reserve fund	1,797	2,459	1,600
Defence	496	575	626
Capital	1,813	3,339	3,561
Development budget	1,539	2,936	2,820
Extrabudgetary capital expenditure	274	403	741
Total	7,642	10,423	10,162

* Projected figures.

Source: IMF, *Staff Report* (October 2003).

INTERNATIONAL RESERVES
(US $ million at 31 December)

	2000	2001	2002
Gold*	194	194	194
IMF special drawing rights	538	554	610
Reserve position in IMF	515	497	538
Foreign exchange	11,408	13,749	13,621
Total	12,655	14,994	14,963

* Valued at US $42 per troy ounce.

Source: IMF, *International Financial Statistics*.

MONEY SUPPLY
(LD million at 31 December)

	2000	2001	2002
Currency outside banks	2,711.0	2,577.4	2,630.5
Private-sector deposits at Central Bank	200.8	297.8	349.3
Demand deposits at commercial banks	4,363.1	4,370.1	4,753.6
Total money (incl. others)	7,313.5	7,402.7	7,734.7

Source: IMF, *International Financial Statistics*.

COST OF LIVING
(Consumer Price Index, excluding rent, for Tripoli; base: 1979 = 100)

	1982	1983	1984
Food	134.9	152.9	169.5
Clothing	141.1	150.6	169.4
All items (incl. others)	137.6	152.2	165.8

Source: ILO, *Yearbook of Labour Statistics*.

NATIONAL ACCOUNTS
(LD million at current prices)
National Income and Product

	1983	1984	1985
Compensation of employees	2,763.1	2,865.8	2,996.2
Operating surplus	5,282.7	4,357.8	4,572.4
Domestic factor incomes	8,045.8	7,223.6	7,568.6
Consumption of fixed capital	436.1	457.5	481.6
Gross domestic product (GDP) at factor cost	8,481.9	7,681.1	8,050.2
Indirect taxes	470.0	462.2	389.0
Less Subsidies	146.7	130.0	162.2
GDP in purchasers' values	8,805.2	8,013.3	8,277.0
Factor income from abroad	200.2	142.8	122.5
Less Factor income paid abroad	989.0	727.7	397.9
Gross national product	8,016.4	7,428.4	8,001.6
Less Consumption of fixed capital	436.1	457.5	481.6
National income in market prices	7,580.3	6,970.9	7,520.0
Other current transfers from abroad	8.6	2.3	2.6
Less Other current transfers paid abroad	25.2	27.9	16.0
National disposable income	7,563.7	6,945.3	7,506.6

Source: UN, *National Accounts Statistics*.

Expenditure on the Gross Domestic Product

	1998	1999	2000*
Government final consumption expenditure	3,339.0	3,101.6	3,615.9
Private final consumption expenditure	8,071.6	8,513.5	7,962.3
Increase in stocks	127.2	45.7	40.0
Gross fixed capital formation	1,396.6	1,536.0	2,281.2
Total domestic expenditure	12,934.4	13,196.8	13,899.4
Exports of goods and services	2,467.6	3,374.3	6,185.6
Less Imports of goods and services	2,660.7	2,432.9	2,690.3
GDP in purchasers' values	12,741.3	14,138.2	17,394.7

* Preliminary figures.

Source: Central Bank of Libya.

Gross Domestic Product by Economic Activity

	1999	2000*	2001*
Agriculture, forestry and fishing	1,449.9	1,439.7	1,512.5
Mining and quarrying	4,219.2	6,974.5	6,349.0
Petroleum and natural gas	3,995.9	6,661.0	6,009.0
Manufacturing	863.1	972.9	1,040.0
Electricity, gas and water	270.4	291.8	309.5
Construction	803.6	1,087.1	1,185.0
Trade, restaurants and hotels	1,693.3	1,700.3	1,803.5
Transport, storage and communications	1,211.7	1,252.0	1,315.5
Finance, insurance and real estate	776.2	831.6	881.0
Public services	2,429.2	2,665.8	2,779.0
Other services	358.6	404.5	429.5
Total	14,075.2	17,620.2	17,604.5

* Preliminary figures.

Source: Central Bank of Libya.

BALANCE OF PAYMENTS
(US $ million)

	1997	1998	1999
Exports of goods f.o.b.	9,876	6,328	6,758
Imports of goods f.o.b.	−7,160	−5,857	−3,996
Trade balance	2,716	471	2,762
Exports of services	33	47	55
Imports of services	−920	−1,016	−918
Balance on goods and services	1,829	−498	1,899
Other income received	640	633	507
Other income paid	−354	−259	−218
Balance on goods, services and income	2,115	−124	2,187
Current transfers received	4	5	6
Current transfers paid	−244	−272	−210
Current balance	1,875	−391	1,984
Direct investment abroad	−282	−304	−210
Direct investment from abroad	−82	−152	−119
Portfolio investment assets	−774	−212	−3
Other investment assets	−1,040	−164	−293
Other investment liabilities	1,294	277	−346
Net errors and omissions	878	432	−372
Overall balance	1,869	−513	641

Source: IMF, *International Financial Statistics*.

External Trade

PRINCIPAL COMMODITIES
(distribution by SITC, US $ million, excl. military goods)

Imports c.i.f.	1997
Food and live animals	1,119.4
Cereals and cereal preparations	519.9
Meal and flour of wheat and meslin	185.0
Chemicals and related products	417.9
Basic manufactures	1,126.2
Textile yarn, fabrics, etc.	170.9
Iron and steel	398.2
Tubes, pipes and fittings	314.1
Machinery and transport equipment	2,012.4
Machinery specialized for particular industries	251.6
General industrial machinery, equipment and parts	554.8
Electrical machinery, apparatus, etc.	462.2
Road vehicles and parts*	562.4
Passenger motor cars (excl. buses)	314.8
Miscellaneous manufactured articles	658.5
Clothing and accessories (excl. footwear)	223.6
Total (incl. others)	5,592.9

* Data on parts exclude tyres, engines and electrical parts.

Exports f.o.b.	1997
Mineral fuels, lubricants, etc.	8,557.4
Petroleum, petroleum products, etc.	8,386.7
Crude petroleum oils, etc.	6,897.5
Refined petroleum products	1,489.2
Gasoline and other light oils	282.3
Residual fuel oils	1,206.9
Chemicals and related products	294.2
Total (incl. others)	9,028.7

Source: UN, *International Trade Statistics Yearbook*.

PRINCIPAL TRADING PARTNERS
(US $ million)*

Imports c.i.f.	1997	1999†
Australia	89.0	27.6
Austria	51.2	44.9
Belgium‡	101.1	68.1
Canada	150.5	54.5
China, People's Republic	86.9	86.5
Egypt	129.0	69.2
France (incl. Monaco)	345.5	227.6
Germany	717.8	599.3
Greece	69.8	38.3
Ireland	75.7	14.7
Italy	882.2	755.9
Japan	455.3	203.3
Korea, Republic	168.6	321.9
Malta	63.9	66.4
Morocco	117.0	115.8
Netherlands	141.7	81.8
Spain	148.6	115.9
Sweden	94.0	62.7
Switzerland-Liechtenstein	219.3	170.8
Tunisia	220.5	141.6
Turkey	164.4	27.1
United Kingdom	436.3	265.9
USA	78.7	84.0
Total (incl. others)	5,592.9	4,140.4

Exports f.o.b.	1997	1999†
Austria	466.0	87.0
Egypt	84.7	94.1
France (incl. Monaco)	411.2	509.8
Germany	1,353.3	1,507.1
Greece	256.9	186.1
Italy	3,267.6	2,987.0
Netherlands	77.4	81.8
Portugal	127.2	20.6
Spain	825.6	1,084.5
Switzerland-Liechtenstein	393.6	105.2
Tunisia	384.7	320.6
Turkey	508.9	5.7
United Kingdom	202.0	104.4
Viet Nam	—	449.1
Yugoslavia	171.6	14.4
Total (incl. others)	9,028.7	7,905.1

* Imports by country of origin; exports by country of destination. Figures exclude trade in gold.
† Figures for 1998 are not available.
‡ Figures for 1997 include trade with Luxembourg.

Source: UN, *International Trade Statistics Yearbook*.

Transport

ROAD TRAFFIC
(motor vehicles in use at 31 December)

	1995	1996
Passenger cars	794,525	809,514
Buses and coaches	1,424	1,490
Goods vehicles	342,918	356,038
Motorcycles and mopeds	1,078	1,112

Source: IRF, *World Road Statistics*.

SHIPPING

Merchant Fleet
(registered at 31 December)

	2000	2001	2002
Number of vessels	142	140	140
Total displacement ('000 grt)	433.7	250.8	164.9

Source: Lloyd's Register-Fairplay, *World Fleet Statistics*.

International Sea-borne Freight Traffic
(estimates, '000 metric tons)

	1991	1992	1993
Goods loaded	57,243	59,894	62,491
Goods unloaded	7,630	7,710	7,808

Source: UN Economic Commission for Africa, *African Statistical Yearbook.*

CIVIL AVIATION
(traffic on scheduled services)

	1996	1997	1998
Kilometres flown (million) . . .	4	4	4
Passengers carried ('000) . .	639	571	571
Passenger-km (million)	412	377	377
Total ton-km (million)	33	30	27

Source: UN, *Statistical Yearbook.*

Tourism

VISITOR ARRIVALS BY COUNTRY OF ORIGIN*

	1998	1999	2000
Algeria.	30,776	39,193	85,181
Egypt	336,325	374,388	372,914
Morocco	20,108	24,350	23,088
Tunisia	404,716	428,871	400,843
Total (incl. others)	850,292	965,307	962,559

* Including same-day visitors (excursionists).

Source: World Tourism Organization, *Yearbook of Tourism Statistics.*

Tourism Receipts (US $ million): 18 in 1998; 28 in 1999 (Source: World Tourism Organization).

Communications Media

	2000	2001	2002
Telephones ('000 main lines in use)	605	610	610
Mobile cellular telephones ('000 subscribers)	40	50	50
Internet users ('000)	10	20	20

1994: Book production (titles) 26.

1996: Daily newspapers 4 (estimated average circulation 71,000).

1997: Radio receivers ('000 in use) 1,350; Television receivers ('000 in use) 730.

Sources: UNESCO, *Statistical Yearbook*; International Telecommunication Union.

Education

(1995/96, unless otherwise indicated)

	Institutions	Teachers	Students
Primary and preparatory: general	2,733*	122,020	1,333,679
Primary and preparatory: vocational	168	n.a.	22,490
Secondary: general . . .	n.a.	17,668	170,573
Secondary: teacher training.	n.a.	2,760†	23,919
Secondary: vocational . .	312	n.a.	109,074
Universities	13	n.a.	126,348

* 1993/94.
† 1992/93.

Source: partly UNESCO, *Statistical Yearbook.*

Adult literacy rate (UNESCO estimates): 80.8.% (Males 91.3%; Females 69.3%) in 2001 (Source: UNDP, *Human Development Report*).

Directory

The Constitution

The Libyan Arab People, meeting in the General People's Congress in Sebha from 2–28 March 1977, proclaimed its adherence to freedom and its readiness to defend it on its own land and anywhere else in the world. It also announced its adherence to socialism and its commitment to achieving total Arab Unity; its adherence to the moral human values; and confirmed the march of the revolution led by Col Muammar al-Qaddafi, the Revolutionary Leader, towards complete People's Authority.

The Libyan Arab People announced the following:

(i) The official name of Libya is henceforth The Socialist People's Libyan Arab Jamahiriya.

(ii) The Holy Koran is the social code in The Socialist People's Libyan Arab Jamahiriya.

(iii) The Direct People's Authority is the basis for the political order in The Socialist People's Libyan Arab Jamahiriya. The People shall practise its authority through People's Congresses, Popular Committees, Trade Unions, Vocational Syndicates, and The General People's Congress, in the presence of the law.

(iv) The defence of our homeland is the responsibility of every citizen. The whole people shall be trained militarily and armed by general military training, the preparation of which shall be specified by the law.

The General People's Congress in its extraordinary session held in Sebha issued four decrees:

The first decree announced the establishment of The People's Authority in compliance with the resolutions and recommendations of the People's Congresses and Trade Unions.

The second decree stipulated the choice of Col Muammar al-Qaddafi, the Revolutionary Leader, as Secretary-General of the General People's Congress.

The third decree stipulated the formation of the General Secretariat of the General People's Congress (see The Government, below).

The fourth decree stipulated the formation of the General People's Committee to carry out the tasks of the various former ministries (see The Government, below).

In 1986 it was announced that the country's official name was to be The Great Socialist People's Libyan Arab Jamahiriya.

The Government

HEAD OF STATE*

Revolutionary Leader: Col MUAMMAR AL-QADDAFI (took office as Chairman of the Revolution Command Council 8 September 1969).

Second-in-Command: Maj. ABD AS-SALAM JALLOUD.
* Qaddafi himself rejects this nomenclature and all other titles.

GENERAL SECRETARIAT OF THE GENERAL PEOPLE'S CONGRESS
(April 2004)

Secretary: MUHAMMAD AZ-ZANATI.

Assistant Secretary for Popular Congresses: AHMAD MUHAMMAD IBRAHIM.

Assistant Secretary for Popular Committees: Dr ABD AL-KADER MUHAMMAD AL-BAGHDADI.

Secretary for Culture and Mass Mobilization: ABD AL-HAMID AS-SID ZINTANI.

Secretary for Trade Unions, Leagues and Professional Unions: ABDALLAH IDRIS IBRAHIM.

Secretary for Social Affairs: SALIMA SHAIBAN ABD AL-JABAR.

Secretary for Infrastructure, Urban Planning and Environment: Dr SALIM AHMAD FUNAYT.

Secretary for Human Resources: Dr AL-BAGHDADI ALI AL-MAHMOUDI.

Secretary for Foreign Affairs: SULEIMAN SASI ASH-SHAHUMI.

Secretary for Economy: ABD AS-SALAM AHMAD NUWEIR.

Secretary for Legal Affairs and Human Rights: MUHAMMAD ABDALLAH AL-HARARI.

Secretary for Security Affairs: MUFTAH ABD AS-SALAM BUKAR.

GENERAL PEOPLE'S COMMITTEE
(April 2004)

Secretary: SHUKRI MUHAMMAD GHANEM.

Deputy Secretary for Production: Dr AL-BAGHDADI ALI AL-MAHMOUDI.

Secretary for Justice: ALI OMAR ABU BAKR.

Secretary for Finance: MUHAMMAD ALI AL-HOUEIZ.

Secretary for Foreign Liaison and International Co-operation: ABD AR-RAHMAN MUHAMMAD SHALGAM.

Secretary for Tourism: AMMAR AT-TAEF.

Secretary for the Economy and Trade: ABD AL-QADIR BALKHEIR.

Secretary for Infrastructure, Urban Planning and Environment: AT-TAHER AL-JUHAIMI.

Secretary for Energy: FATHI BEN SHATWAN.

Secretary for National Security: NASSER AL-MUBRAK.

Secretary for Youth and Sport: ALI SHAYERI.

Secretary for Culture: MAHDI MBIRESH.

Secretary for Training and Labour: MAATUK MUHAMMAD MAATUK.

Legislature

GENERAL PEOPLE'S CONGRESS

The Senate and House of Representatives were dissolved after the *coup d'état* of September 1969, and the provisional Constitution issued in December 1969 made no mention of elections or a return to parliamentary procedure. However, in January 1971 Col Qaddafi announced that a new legislature would be appointed, not elected; no date was mentioned. All political parties other than the Arab Socialist Union were banned. In November 1975 provision was made for the creation of the 1,112-member General National Congress of the Arab Socialist Union, which met officially in January 1976. This later became the General People's Congress (GPC), which met for the first time in November 1976 and in March 1977 began introducing the wide-ranging changes outlined in the Constitution (above).

Secretary-General: ABD AR-RAZIQ SAWSA.

Political Organizations

In June 1971 the Arab Socialist Union (ASU) was established as the country's sole authorized political party. The General National Congress of the ASU held its first session in January 1976 and later became the General People's Congress (see Legislature, above).

The following groups are in opposition to the Government:

Ansarollah Group: f. 1996.

Fighting Islamic Group: claimed responsibility for subversive activities in early 1996; seeks to establish an Islamic regime.

Islamic Martyrs' Movement (IMM): Spokesman ABDALLAH AHMAD.

Libyan Baathist Party.

Libyan Change and Reform Movement: breakaway group from NFSL.

Libyan Conservatives' Party: f. 1996.

Libyan Constitutional Grouping.

Libyan Democratic Authority: f. 1993.

Libyan Democratic Conference: f. 1992.

Libyan Democratic Movement: f. 1977; external group.

Libyan Movement for Change and Reform: f. 1994; based in London, United Kingdom.

Libyan National Alliance: f. 1980 in Cairo, Egypt.

Libyan National Democratic Rally.

Movement of Patriotic Libyans: f. 1997.

National Front for the Salvation of Libya (NFSL): e-mail visitor@nfsl-libya.com; internet www.nfsl-libya.com; f. 1981 in Khartoum, Sudan; aims to replace the existing regime by a democratically-elected govt; Leader MUHAMMAD MEGARIEF.

Diplomatic Representation

EMBASSIES IN LIBYA

Afghanistan: POB 4245, Sharia Mozhar al-Aftes, Tripoli; tel. (21) 75192; fax (21) 609876; Ambassador (vacant).

Algeria: Sharia Kairauan 12, Tripoli; tel. (21) 4440025; fax (21) 3334631; Ambassador MUHAMMAD KAMAL REZAG BARA.

Argentina: POB 932, Gargaresh, Madina Syahia, Tripoli; tel. (21) 4834956; fax (21) 4840928; e-mail embartrip@hotmail.com; Ambassador MANUEL A. FERNÁNDEZ SALORIO.

Armenia: Tripoli.

Austria: POB 3207, Sharia Khalid ibn al-Walid, Garden City, Tripoli; tel. (21) 4443379; fax (21) 4440838; e-mail austroamb_tripolis@hotmail.com; Ambassador Dr ROBERT KARAS.

Bangladesh: POB 5086, Hadaba al-Khadra, Villa Omran al-Wershafani, Tripoli; tel. (21) 900856; fax (21) 4906616; Ambassador M. SHAFIULLAH.

Belgium: Tower 4, Floor 5, That el-Imad, Tripoli; tel. (21) 3350117; fax (21) 3350118; Ambassador JACQUES SCAVEE.

Benin: POB 6676 254 rue Oumaween, Cité EC Analous, Tripoli; tel. (21) 830990; fax (21) 834569; Ambassador LAFIA CHABI.

Bosnia and Herzegovina: POB 84373, Sharia ben Ashour, Tripoli; tel. and fax (21) 602162; Ambassador MUHAMMAD KUPOSOVIĆ.

Brazil: POB 2270, Sharia ben Ashour, Tripoli; tel. (21) 3614894; fax (21) 3614895; e-mail brcastripoli@lttnet.net; Ambassador JOAQUIM PALMEIRO.

Bulgaria: POB 2945, Sharia Talha ben Abdullah 5–7, Tripoli; tel. (21) 3609988; fax (21) 3609990; e-mail bulem_lib@hotmail.com; Ambassador LYUDMIL SPASOV.

Burkina Faso: POB 81902, Tripoli; tel. (21) 71221; fax (21) 72626; Ambassador YOUSSOUF SANGARE.

Burundi: POB 2817, Sharia Ras Hassan, Tripoli; tel. (21) 608848; Ambassador ZACHARIE BANYIYEZAKO.

Canada: Tripoli; Chargé d'affaires a.i. GEORGE JACOBY.

Chad: POB 1078, Sharia Muhammad Mussadeq 25, Tripoli; tel. (21) 4443955; Ambassador IBRAHIM MAHAMAT TIDEI.

China, People's Republic: POB 5329, Andalous, Gargaresh, Tripoli; tel. (21) 830860; Ambassador HUANG JIEMEN.

Cuba: POB 83738, Andalous, Gargaresh, Tripoli; tel. (21) 71346; Ambassador RAÚL RODRÍGUEZ RAMOS.

Cyprus: POB 3284, Sharia Ad-Dhul 60, Ben Ashour, Tripoli; tel. (21) 3601274; fax (21) 3613516; e-mail cyprusembassy@mail.lttnet.net; Ambassador ARGYROS ANTONIOU.

Czech Republic: POB 1097, Sharia Ahmad Lutfi Sayed, Sharia ben Ashour, Tripoli; tel. (21) 3615436; fax (21) 3615437; e-mail tripoli@embassy.mzv.cz; Ambassador PAVEL ŘEZÁČ.

Egypt: The Grand Hotel, Tripoli; tel. (21) 605500; fax (21) 4445959; Ambassador HANY KHALLAF.

Equatorial Guinea: Tripoli.

Eritrea: Tripoli; Ambassador UTHMAN MUHAMMAD UMAR.

Finland: POB 2508, Tripoli; tel. and fax (21) 4831132; Chargé d'affaires ULLA-MAIJA SUOMINEN.

France: POB 312, Sharia Beni al-Amar, Hay Andalous, Tripoli; tel. (21) 4774 891; fax (21) 4778266; internet ambafrance-ly.org; Ambassador JEAN-JACQUES BEAUSSOU.

Germany: POB 302, Sharia Hassan al-Mashai, Tripoli; tel. (21) 3330554; fax (21) 4448968; e-mail germanembassytrip@web.de; Ambassador DIETMAR GREINEDER.

Ghana: POB 4169, Andalus 21/A, nr Funduk Shati Gargeresh, Tripoli; tel. (21) 4772534; fax (21) 4773557; e-mail ghaemb@all-computers.com; Ambassador GEORGE KUMI.

Greece: POB 5147, Sharia Jalal Bayar 18, Tripoli; tel. (21) 3338563; fax (21) 3336689; e-mail grembtri@hotmail.com; Ambassador Dr PANAYOTIS THEODORACOPOULOS.

Guinea: POB 10657, Andalous, Tripoli; tel. (21) 4772793; fax (21) 4773441; e-mail magatte@lttnet.net; Ambassador ABDUL AZIZ SOUMAH.

Holy See: Tripoli; Apostolic Nuncio Most Rev. Luigi Conti (Titular Archbishop of Gratiana, resident in Malta).

Hungary: POB 4010, Sharia Talha ben Abdullah, Tripoli; tel. (21) 3618218; fax (21) 3618220; e-mail hungemtpi@lttnet.com; Ambassador Andras Szabo.

India: POB 3150, 16 Sharia Mahmud Shaltut, Tripoli; tel. (21) 4441835; fax (21) 3337560; e-mail indemtrip@mail.link.net.mt; Ambassador Appunni Ramesh.

Iran: Tripoli; e-mail iran_em_tripoli@hotmail.com; Ambassador Muhammad Menhaj.

Italy: POB 912, Sharia Vahran 1, Tripoli; tel. (21) 3334133; fax (21) 3331673; e-mail ambasciate.tripoli@esteri.it; Ambassador Claudio Pacifico.

Japan: Tower 4, That al-Imad Complex, Sharia Organization of African Unity, Tripoli; tel. (21) 607463; fax (21) 607462; Ambassador Akira Watanabe.

Korea, Democratic People's Republic: Tripoli; Ambassador Ri Pyong Ho.

Korea, Republic: POB 4781, Gargaresh, Tripoli; tel. (21) 4831322; fax (21) 4831324; Ambassador Huh Bang-Bin.

Kuwait: POB 2225, Beit al-Mal Beach, Tripoli; tel. (21) 4440281; fax (21) 607053; Chargé d'affaires Khaled Motlaq ad-Duwaila.

Lebanon: POB 927, Sharia Omar bin Yasser Hadaek 20, Tripoli; tel. (21) 3333733; Ambassador Mounir Khoreish.

Malaysia: POB 6309, Hai Andalus, Tripoli; tel. (21) 4830854; fax (21) 4831496; e-mail mwtripoli@lttnet.net; Ambassador: Datuk Shapii bin Abu Samah.

Mali: Sharia Jaraba Saniet Zarrouk, Tripoli; tel. (21) 4444924; Ambassador El Bekaye Sidi Moctar Kounta.

Malta: POB 2534, Sharia Ubei ben Ka'ab, Tripoli; tel. (21) 3611181; fax (21) 3611180; e-mail rvellalaurenti@yahoo.com; Ambassador Dr Richard Vella Laurenti.

Mauritania: Sharia Eysa Wokwak, Tripoli; tel. (21) 4443223; Ambassador Yahia Muhammad el-Hadi.

Morocco: POB 908, Sharia ben Ashour, Tripoli; tel. (21) 600110; fax (21) 4445757; Ambassador Driss Alaoui.

Netherlands: POB 3801, Sharia Jalal Bayar 20, Tripoli; tel. (21) 4441549; fax (21) 4440386; Ambassador Jan-Jaap van de Velde.

Nicaragua: Tripoli; Ambassador Guillermo Espinosa.

Niger: POB 2251, Fachloun Area, Tripoli; tel. (21) 4443104; Ambassador Amadou Tidjani Ali.

Nigeria: POB 4417, Sharia Bashir al-Ibrahim, Tripoli; tel. (21) 4443038; Ambassador Prof. Dandatti Abd al-Kadir.

Pakistan: POB 2169, Sharia Abdul Karim al-Khattabi 16, Maidan al-Qadasia, Tripoli; tel. (21) 4440072; fax (21) 4444698; Ambassador Khawar Rashid Pirzada.

Philippines: POB 12508, Andalous, Gargaresh, Tripoli; tel. and fax (21) 4833966; Ambassador Mukhtar M. Muallam.

Poland: POB 519, Sharia ben Ashour 61, Tripoli; tel. (21) 3608569; fax (21) 3615199; Ambassador Jakub Wolski.

Qatar: POB 3506, Sharia ben Ashour, Tripoli; tel. (21) 4446660; Chargé d'affaires Hassan Ahmad Abu Hindi.

Romania: POB 5085, Sharia Ahmad Lotfi Sayed, Sharia ben Ashour, Tripoli; tel. (21) 3615295; fax (21) 3607597; e-mail ambaromatrip@hotmail.com; Chargé d'affaires a.i. Mircea Has.

Russia: POB 4792, Sharia Mustapha Kamel, Tripoli; tel. (21) 3330545; fax (21) 4446673; Ambassador Aleksei B. Podtserob.

Rwanda: POB 6677, Villa Ibrahim Musbah Missalati, Andalous, Tripoli; tel. (21) 72864; fax (21) 70317; Chargé d'affaires Christophe Habimana.

Saudi Arabia: Sharia Kairauan 2, Tripoli; tel. (21) 30485; Chargé d'affaires Muhammad Hassan Bandah.

Serbia and Montenegro: POB 1087, Sharia Turkia 14–16, Tripoli; tel. (21) 3330819; fax (21) 3334114; e-mail yuambtripoli@yahoo.com; Ambassador Dr Vasilije Ilić.

Sierra Leone: Tripoli; Ambassador el Hadj Mohammed Samura.

Slovakia: POB 5721, 3km, Hay al-Andalus, Gergarsh, Tripoli; tel. (21) 4781388; fax (21) 4781387; e-mail slovembtrp@mwc.ly; Ambassador Ján Bóry.

Spain: POB 2302, Sharia el-Amir Abd al-Kader al-Jazairi 36, Tripoli; tel. (21) 3336797; fax (21) 4443743; Ambassador José Luis Tapia Vicente.

Sudan: POB 1076, Sharia Gargarish, Tripoli; tel. (21) 4775387; fax (21) 4774781; e-mail sudtripoli@hotmail.com; Ambassador Osman M. O. Dirar.

Switzerland: POB 439, Sharia ben Ashour, Tripoli; tel. (21) 3614118; fax (21) 3614238; Ambassador Paul Koller.

Syria: POB 4219, Sharia Muhammad Rashid Reda 4, Tripoli (Relations Office); tel. (21) 3331783; Head Munir Borkhan.

Togo: POB 3420, Sharia Khaled ibn al-Walid, Tripoli; tel. (21) 4447551; fax (21) 3332423; Ambassador Tchao Sotou Bere.

Tunisia: POB 613, Sharia Bashir al-Ibrahim, Tripoli; tel. (21) 3331051; fax (21) 4447600; High Representative Mansour Ezzeddine.

Turkey: POB 947, Sharia Zaviya Dahmani, Tripoli; tel. (21) 3337717; fax (21) 3337686; e-mail trablus.be@mfa.gov.tr; Ambassador Riza Erkmenoğlu.

Uganda: POB 80215, Sharia ben Ashour, Tripoli; tel. (21) 604471; fax (21) 4831602; Ambassador William N. Hakiza.

Ukraine: POB 4555, Sharia ben Ashour, Ares, Tripoli; tel. (21) 3608665.

United Kingdom: POB 4206, Tripoli; tel. (21) 3343630; fax (21) 3343634; e-mail belibya@hotmail.com; internet www.britain-in-libya.org; Ambassador Anthony Layden.

Venezuela: POB 2584, Sharia ben Ashour, Jamaa as-sagaa Bridge, Tripoli; tel. (21) 3600408; fax (21) 3600407; Ambassador Julio César Pineda.

Viet Nam: POB 587, Sharia Talha ben Abdullah, Tripoli; tel. (21) 833704; fax (21) 830494; Ambassador Dang San.

Yemen: POB 4839, Sharia Ubei ben Ka'ab 36, Tripoli; tel. (21) 607472; Ambassador Ali Aidarous Yahya.

Judicial System

The judicial system is composed, in order of seniority, of the Supreme Court, Courts of Appeal, and Courts of First Instance and Summary Courts.

All courts convene in open session, unless public morals or public order require a closed session; all judgments, however, are delivered in open session. Cases are heard in Arabic, with interpreters provided for aliens.

The courts apply the Libyan codes which include all the traditional branches of law, such as civil, commercial and penal codes, etc. Committees were formed in 1971 to examine Libyan law and ensure that it coincides with the rules of Islamic *Shari'a*. The proclamation of People's Authority in the Jamahiriya provides that the Holy Koran is the law of society.

Attorney-General: Salim Muhammad Salim.

SUPREME COURT

The judgments of the Supreme Court are final. It is composed of the President and several Justices. Its judgments are issued by circuits of at least three Justices (the quorum is three). The Court hears appeals from the Courts of Appeal in civil, penal, administrative and civil status matters.

President: Hussein Muktar al-Bueishi.

COURTS OF APPEAL

These courts settle appeals from Courts of First Instance; the quorum is three Justices. Each court of appeal has a court of assize.

COURTS OF FIRST INSTANCE AND SUMMARY COURTS

These courts are first-stage courts in the Jamahiriya, and the cases heard in them are heard by one judge. Appeals against summary judgments are heard by the appellate court attached to the court of first instance, whose quorum is three judges.

PEOPLE'S COURT

Established by order of the General People's Congress in March 1988.

President: Abd ar-Raziq Abu Bakr as-Sawsa.

PEOPLE'S PROSECUTION BUREAU

Established by order of the General People's Congress in March 1988.

Secretary: Muhammad Ali al-Misurati.

Religion

ISLAM

The vast majority of Libyan Arabs follow Sunni Muslim rites, although Col Qaddafi has rejected the Sunnah (i.e. the practice, course, way, manner or conduct of the Prophet Muhammad, as followed by Sunnis) as a basis for legislation.

Chief Mufti of Libya: Sheikh TAHIR AHMAD AZ-ZAWI.

CHRISTIANITY

The Roman Catholic Church

Libya comprises three Apostolic Vicariates and one Apostolic Prefecture. At 31 December 2002 there were an estimated 74,000 adherents in the country.

Apostolic Vicariate of Benghazi: POB 248, Benghazi; tel. (91) 9096563; fax (61) 9081599; e-mail vicarapost@hotmail.com; Vicar Apostolic Mgr SYLVESTER CARMEL MAGRO (Titular Bishop of Saldae).

Apostolic Vicariate of Derna: c/o POB 248, Benghazi; Vicar Apostolic (vacant).

Apostolic Vicariate of Tripoli: POB 365, Dahra, Tripoli; tel. (21) 3331863; fax (21) 3334696; e-mail bishoptripolibya@hotmail.com; Vicar Apostolic Mgr GIOVANNI INNOCENZO MARTINELLI (Titular Bishop of Tabuda).

The Anglican Communion

Within the Episcopal Church in Jerusalem and the Middle East, Libya forms part of the diocese of Egypt (q.v.).

Other Christian Churches

The Coptic Orthodox Church is represented in Libya.

The Press

Newspapers and periodicals are published either by the Jamahiriya News Agency (JANA), by government secretariats, by the Press Service or by trade unions.

DAILIES

Ash-Shams: Tripoli; internet www.alshames.com.

Az-Zahf al-Akhdar (The Green March): POB 14373–6998, Tripoli; fax (21) 4772502; e-mail info@azzahfalakhder.com; internet www .azzahfalakhder.com; ideological journal of the Revolutionary Committees.

PERIODICALS

Al-Amal (Hope): POB 4845, Tripoli; internet alalmalmag.com; monthly; social, for children; published by the Press Service.

Ad-Daawa al-Islamia (Islamic Call): POB 2682, Sharia Sawani, km 5, Tripoli; tel. (21) 4800294; fax (21) 4800293; f. 1980; weekly (Wednesdays); Arabic, English, French; cultural; published by the World Islamic Call Society; Eds MUHAMMAD IMHEMED AL-BALOUSHI, ABDULAHI MUHAMMAD ABDUL-JALEEL.

Al-Fajr al-Jadid (The New Dawn): Press Building, Sharia al-Jamhariya, Tripoli; tel. (21) 3606393; fax (21) 3605728; internet www.alfajraljadeed.com; f. 1969; publ. by JANA; bi-monthly.

Economic Bulletin: POB 2303, Tripoli; tel. (21) 3337106; monthly; published by JANA.

Al-Jamahiriya: POB 4814, Tripoli; tel. (21) 4449294; internet www .aljamahiria.com; f. 1980; weekly; Arabic; political; published by the revolutionary committees.

Al-Jarida ar-Rasmiya (The Official Newspaper): Tripoli; irregular; official state gazette.

Libyan Arab Republic Gazette: Secretariat of Justice, NA, Tripoli; weekly; English; published by the Secretariat of Justice.

Risalat al-Jihad (Holy War Letter): POB 2682, Tripoli; tel. (21) 3331021; f. 1983; monthly; Arabic, English, French; published by the World Islamic Call Society.

Scientific Bulletin: POB 2303, Tripoli; tel. (21) 3337106; monthly; published by JANA.

Ath-Thaqafa al-Arabiya (Arab Culture): POB 4587, Tripoli; f. 1973; weekly; cultural; circ. 25,000.

Al-Usbu ath-Thaqafi (The Cultural Week): POB 4845, Tripoli; weekly.

Al-Watan al-Arabi al-Kabir (The Greater Arab Homeland): Tripoli; f. 1987.

NEWS AGENCIES

Jamahiriya News Agency (JANA): POB 2303, Sharia al-Fateh, Tripoli; tel. (21) 3402606; fax (21) 3402624; e-mail mail@ jamahiriyanews.com; internet www.jamahiriyanews.com; branches

and correspondents throughout Libya and abroad; serves Libyan and foreign subscribers.

Foreign Bureaux

Informatsionnoye Telegrafnoye Agentstvo Rossii—Telegrafnoye Agentstvo Suverennykh Stran (ITAR—TASS) (Russia): Sharia Mustapha Kamel 10, Tripoli; Correspondent GEORG SHELENKOV.

ANSA (Italy) is also represented in Tripoli.

Publishers

Ad-Dar al-Arabia Lilkitab (Maison Arabe du Livre): POB 3185, Tripoli; tel. (21) 4447287; f. 1973 by Libya and Tunisia.

Al-Fatah University, General Administration of Libraries, Printing and Publications: POB 13543, Tripoli; tel. (21) 621988; f. 1955; academic books.

General Co for Publishing, Advertising and Distribution: POB 921, Sirte (Surt); tel. (54) 63170; fax (54) 62100; general, educational and academic books in Arabic and other languages; makes and distributes advertisements throughout Libya.

Broadcasting and Communications

TELECOMMUNICATIONS

General Directorate of Posts and Telecommunications: POB 81686, Tripoli; tel. (21) 3604101; fax (21) 3604102; Dir-Gen. ABU ZAID JUMA AL-MANSURI.

General Post and Telecommunications Co: POB 886, Sharia Zawia, Tripoli; tel. (21) 3600777; fax (21) 3609515; f. 1985; Chair. FARAJ AMARI.

BROADCASTING

Radio

Great Socialist People's Libyan Arab Jamahiriya Broadcasting Corporation: POB 9333, Tripoli; POB 119, al-Baida; tel. (21) 3332451; internet www.ljbc.net; f. 1957; broadcasts in Arabic and English from Tripoli and Benghazi; from September 1971 special daily broadcasts to Gaza and other Israeli-occupied territories were begun.

Voice of Africa: POB 4677, Sharia al-Fateh, Tripoli; tel. (21) 4449209; fax (21) 4449875; f. 1973 as Voice of the Greater Arab Homeland; adopted current name in 1998; broadcasts in Arabic, French and English; transmissions in Swahili, Hausa, Fulani and Amharic scheduled to begin in 2000; Dir-Gen. ABDALLAH AL-MEGRI.

Television

People's Revolution Broadcasting TV: POB 333, Tripoli; f. 1968; broadcasts in Arabic; additional channels broadcast for limited hours in English, Italian and French; Dir YOUSUF DEBRI.

Finance

(cap. = capital; res = reserves; dep. = deposits; LD = Libyan dinars; m. = million; brs = branches)

BANKING

Central Bank

Central Bank of Libya: POB 1103, Sharia al-Malik Seoud, Tripoli; tel. (21) 3333591; fax (21) 4441488; e-mail infoh@cbl-ly.com; internet www.cbl-ly.com; f. 1955 as National Bank of Libya, name changed to Bank of Libya 1963, to Central Bank of Libya 1977; bank of issue and central bank carrying govt accounts and operating exchange control; commercial operations transferred to National Commercial Bank 1970; cap. LD 100m., res LD 4,648.1m., dep. LD 5,527.0m. (Dec. 2001); Gov. and Chair. Dr AHMAD M. MENESI.

Other Banks

Ahli Bank: Jadu; f. 1998; private bank.

Gumhouria Bank: POB 396, Sharia Emhemed Megrief, Tripoli; tel. (21) 3333553; fax (21) 3339489; f. 1969 as successor to Barclays Bank International in Libya; known as Masraf al-Jumhuriya until March 1977, and as Jamahiriya Bank until December 2000; wholly-owned subsidiary of the Central Bank; throughout Libya; cap.

LD 40.0m., res LD 79.5m., dep. LD 1,714.2m. (Dec. 2001); Chair. MUHAMMAD A. SHOKRI; 70 brs.

Libyan Arab Foreign Bank: POB 2542, Tower 2, Dat al-Imad Complex, 2542 Tripoli; tel. (21) 3350155; fax (21) 3350164; f. 1972; offshore bank wholly owned by Central Bank of Libya; cap. LD 222.0m., res LD 57.0m., dep. LD 7,432.3m. (Dec. 2002); Chair. and Gen. Man. MUHAMMAD H. LAYAS.

National Commercial Bank SAL: POB 543, HO G.S.P.L.A.J., al-Baida; tel. (21) 3612267; fax (21) 3610306; f. 1970 to take over commercial banking division of Central Bank (then Bank of Libya) and brs of Aruba Bank and Istiklal Bank; wholly owned by Central Bank of Libya; cap. LD 35m., res LD 63.4m., dep. LD 1,545.6m. (Dec. 1998); Chair. and Gen. Man. BADER A. ABU AZIZA; 49 brs.

Sahara Bank SPI: POB 270, Sharia 1 September 10, Tripoli; tel. (21) 3339804; fax (21) 3337922; f. 1964 to take over br. of Banco di Sicilia; 82% owned by Central Bank of Libya; cap. LD 525,000, res LD 52.5m., dep. LD 488.4m. (March 1988); Chair. and Gen. Man. OMAR A. SHABOU; 20 brs.

Umma Bank SAL: POB 685, 1 Giaddat Omar el-Mokhtar, Tripoli; tel. (21) 3334031; fax (21) 3332505; e-mail ummabank@umma-bank .com; internet www.umma-bank.com; f. 1969 to take over brs of Banco di Roma; wholly owned by Central Bank of Libya; cap. LD 23m., res LD 25.3m., dep. LD 1,393.8m. (Dec. 2001); Chair. and Gen. Man. AYAD DAHAIM; 38 brs.

Wahda Bank: POB 452, Fadiel Abu Omar Sq., El-Berkha, Benghazi; tel. (61) 24709; fax (61) 3337592; f. 1970 to take over Bank of North Africa, Commercial Bank SAL, Nahda Banking Bank, Société Africaine de Banque SAL, Kafila al-Ahly Bank; 87%-owned by Central Bank of Libya; cap. LD 36m., res LD 106.1m., dep. LD 1,553.3m. (Dec. 1999); Chair. and Gen. Man. Dr MUHAMMAD M. GHADBAN; 59 brs.

INSURANCE

Libya Insurance Co: POB 64, Sharia Jamal Abdul Nasser, Zawia; tel. (23) 629768; fax (23) 629490; f. 1964; merged with Al-Mukhtar Insurance Co in 1981; all classes of insurance; Man. BELAID ABU GHALIA.

Trade and Industry

There are state trade and industrial organizations responsible for the running of industries at all levels, which supervise production, distribution and sales. There are also central bodies responsible for the power generation industry, agriculture, land reclamation and transport.

GOVERNMENT AGENCY

Great Man-made River Authority (GMRA): Sharia Ben-Ghasir, Tripoli; tel. (21) 3600042; fax (21) 3619437; e-mail info@gmrwua .com; internet www.gmrwua.com; supervises construction of pipeline carrying water to the Libyan coast from beneath the Sahara desert, to provide irrigation for agricultural projects; Sec. for the Great Man-made River project ABD AL-MAJID AL-AOUD.

DEVELOPMENT ORGANIZATIONS

Arab Organization for Agricultural Development: POB 12898, Zohra, Tripoli; tel. and fax (21) 3619275; e-mail arabagri@lycos.com; responsible for agricultural development projects.

General National Organization for Industrialization: Sharia San'a, Tripoli; tel. (21) 3334995; f. 1970; a public org. responsible for the devt of industry.

Kufra and Sarir Authority: Council of Agricultural Development, Benghazi; f. 1972 to develop the Kufra oasis and Sarir area in southeast Libya.

CHAMBERS OF COMMERCE

Benghazi Chamber of Commerce, Trade, Industry and Agriculture: POB 208 and 1286, Benghazi; tel. (61) 95142; fax (61) 80761; f. 1956; Pres. Dr SADIQ M. BUSNAINA; Gen. Man. YOUSUF AL-JIAMI; 45,000 mems.

Tripoli Chamber of Commerce, Industry and Agriculture: POB 2321, Sharia Najed 6–8, Tripoli; tel. (21) 3336855; fax (21) 3332655; f. 1952; Pres. ABDALLAH AL-BARONE; Dir-Gen. RAMADAN A. ZEREG; 60,000 mems.

UTILITIES

Electricity

General Electricity Company of Libya (Gecol): POB 668, Tripoli; Sec. of People's Cttee OMRAN IBRAHIM ABUKRAA.

STATE HYDROCARBONS COMPANIES

Until 1986 petroleum affairs in Libya were dealt with primarily by the Secretariat of the General People's Committee for Petroleum. This body was abolished in March 1986, and sole responsibility for the administration of the petroleum industry passed to the national companies which were already in existence. The Secretariat of the General People's Committee for Petroleum was re-established in March 1989 and incorporated into the new Secretariat for the General People's Committee for Energy in October 1992. This was dissolved in March 2000, and responsibility for local oil policy transferred to the National Oil Corporation, under the supervision of the General People's Committee. Since 1973 the Libyan Government has entered into participation agreements with some of the foreign oil companies (concession holders), and nationalized others. It has concluded 85%–15% production-sharing agreements with various oil companies.

National Oil Corporation (NOC): POB 2655, Tripoli; tel. (21) 4446180; fax (21) 3331390; e-mail info@noclibya.com; internet www .noclibya.com; f. 1970 to undertake joint ventures with foreign cos; to build and operate refineries, storage tanks, petrochemical facilities, pipelines and tankers; to take part in arranging specifications for local and imported petroleum products; to participate in general planning of oil installations in Libya; to market crude oil and petroleum and petrochemical products and to establish and operate oil terminals; from 2000 responsible for deciding local oil policy, under supervision of General People's Committee; Chair. Dr ABD AL-HAFID ZLITNI.

Oilinvest International: Tripoli; wholly-owned subsidiary of the NOC; Chair. and Gen. Man. AHMAD ABD AL-KARIM AHMAD.

Agip North Africa and Middle East Ltd—Libyan Branch: POB 346, Tripoli; tel. and fax (21) 3335135; Sec. of People's Cttee A. M. CREUI.

Arabian Gulf Oil Co (AGOCO): POB 263, Benghazi; tel. (61) 28931; fax (21) 49031; Chair. F. SAID.

Az-Zawiyah Oil Refining Co: POB 15715, Zawia; tel. (23) 20125; fax (23) 605948; f. 1973; Gen. Man. H. LASOUD.

Brega Oil Marketing Co: POB 402, Sharia Bashir as-Saidawi, Tripoli; tel. (21) 4440830; f. 1971; Chair. Dr DOKALI B. AL-MEGHARIEF.

International Oil Investments Co: Tripoli; f. 1988, with initial capital of $500m. to acquire 'downstream' facilities abroad; Chair. MUHAMMAD AL-JAWAD.

National Drilling and Workover Co: POB 1454, 208 Sharia Omar Mukhtar, Tripoli; tel. (21) 3332411; f. 1986; Chair. IBRAHIM BAHI.

Ras Lanouf Oil and Gas Processing Co (RASCO): POB 1971, Ras Lanouf, Benghazi; tel. (21) 3605177; fax (21) 607924; f. 1978; Chair. MAHMUD ABDALLAH NAAS.

Sirte Oil Co: POB 385, Marsa el-Brega, Tripoli; tel. (21) 607261; fax (21) 601487; f. 1955 as Esso Standard Libya, taken over by Sirte Oil Co 1982; absorbed the National Petrochemicals Co in October 1990; exploration, production of crude oil, gas, and petrochemicals, liquefaction of natural gas; Chair. M. M. BENNIRAN.

Umm al-Jawaby Petroleum Co: POB 693, Tripoli; Chair. and Gen. Man. MUHAMMAD TENTTOUSH.

Waha Oil Co: POB 395, Tripoli; tel. (21) 3331116; fax (21) 3337169; Chair. SALEH M. KAABAR.

Zueitina Oil Co: POB 2134, Tripoli; tel. (21) 3338011; fax (21) 3339109; f. 1986; Chair. of Management Cttee M. OUN.

TRADE UNIONS

General Federation of Producers' Trade Unions: POB 734, Sharia Istanbul 2, Tripoli; tel. (21) 4446011; f. 1952; affiliated to ICFTU; Sec.-Gen. BASHIR IHWIJ; 17 trade unions with 700,000 mems.

General Union for Oil and Petrochemicals: Tripoli; Chair. MUHAMMAD MITHNANI.

Pan-African Federation of Petroleum Energy and Allied Workers: Tripoli; affiliated to the Organisation of African Trade Union Unity.

Transport

Department of Road Transport and Railways: POB 14527, Sharia Az-Zawiyah, Secretariat of Communications and Transport Bldg, Tripoli; tel. (21) 609011; fax (21) 605605; Dir-Gen. Projects and Research MUHAMMAD ABU ZIAN.

RAILWAYS

There are, at present, no railways in Libya. In mid-1998, however, the Government invited bids for the construction of a 3,170 km-railway, comprising one branch, 2,178 km in length, running from north to south, and another, 992 km in length, running from east to west. The railway may eventually be linked to other North African rail networks.

ROADS

The most important road is the 1,822-km national coast road from the Tunisian to the Egyptian border, passing through Tripoli and Benghazi. It has a second link between Barce and Lamluda, 141 km long. Another national road runs from a point on the coastal road 120 km south of Misurata through Sebha to Ghat near the Algerian border (total length 1,250 km). There is a branch 247 km long running from Vaddan to Sirte (Surt). A 690-km road, connecting Tripoli and Sebha, and another 626 km long, from Ajdabiya in the north to Kufra in the south-east, were opened in 1983. The Tripoli–Ghat section (941 km) of the third, 1,352-km-long national road was opened in September 1984. There is a road crossing the desert from Sebha to the frontiers of Chad and Niger.

In addition to the national highways, the west of Libya has about 1,200 km of paved and macadamized roads and the east about 500 km. All the towns and villages of Libya, including the desert oases, are accessible by motor vehicle. In 1999 Libya had 47,590 km of paved roads.

SHIPPING

The principal ports are Tripoli, Benghazi, Mersa Brega, Misurata and as-Sider. Zueitina, Ras Lanouf, Mersa Hariga, Mersa Brega and as-Sider are mainly oil ports. A pipeline connects the Zelten oilfields with Mersa Brega. Another pipeline joins the Sarir oilfield with Mersa Hariga, the port of Tobruk, and a pipeline from the Sarir field

to Zueitina was opened in 1968. A port is being developed at Darnah. Libya also has the use of Tunisian port facilities at Sand Gabès, to alleviate congestion at Tripoli. At 31 December 2002 Libya's merchant fleet consisted of 140 vessels, with a combined displacement of 164,901 grt.

General National Maritime Transport Co: POB 80173, Sharia Ahmad Sharif 2, Tripoli; tel. (21) 3333155; fax (21) 6361664; f. 1971 to handle all projects dealing with maritime trade; Chair. SAID MILUD AL-AHRASH.

CIVIL AVIATION

There are four international airports: Tripoli International Airport, situated at ben Gashir, 34 km (21 miles) from Tripoli; Benina Airport 19 km (12 miles) from Benghazi; Sebha Airport; and Misurata Airport. There are a further 10 regional airports. A US $800m. programme to improve the airport infrastructure and air traffic control network was approved in mid-2001.

Libyan Arab Airlines: POB 2555, ben Fernas Bldg, Sharia Haiti, Tripoli; tel. (21) 3617638; fax (21) 3614815; f. 1989 by merger of Jamahiriya Air Transport (which in 1983 took over operations of United African Airlines) and Libyan Arab Airlines (f. 1964 as Kingdom of Libya Airlines and renamed 1969); passenger and cargo services from Tripoli, Benghazi and Sebha to destinations in Europe, North Africa, the Middle East and Asia; domestic services throughout Libya; Chief Exec. SABRI ABDALLAH.

Tourism

The principal attractions for visitors to Libya are Tripoli, with its beaches and annual International Fair, the ancient Roman towns of Sabratha, Leptis Magna and Cyrene, and historic oases. There were 962,559 visitor arrivals in 2000; in 1999 receipts totalled some US $28m.

Department of Tourism and Fairs: POB 891, Sharia Omar Mukhtar, Tripoli; tel. (21) 3332255; fax (21) 4448385; Head of Fairs MUHAMMAD ELGADI.

General Board of Tourism: POB 91871, Tripoli; tel. and fax (21) 503041; Chair. MUHAMMAD SEALNA.

LIECHTENSTEIN

Introductory Survey

Location, Climate, Language, Religion, Flag, Capital

The Principality of Liechtenstein is in central Europe. The country lies on the east bank of the Upper Rhine river, bordered by Switzerland to the west and south, and by Austria to the north and east. Liechtenstein has an Alpine climate, with mild winters. The average annual temperature is about 10°C, while average annual rainfall is about 1,000 mm. The official language is German, of which a dialect—Alemannish—is spoken. Almost all of the inhabitants profess Christianity, and about 78% are adherents of the Roman Catholic Church. The national flag (proportions 3 by 5) consists of two equal horizontal stripes, of royal blue and red, with a golden princely crown, outlined in black, in the upper hoist. The capital is Vaduz.

Recent History

Liechtenstein has been an independent state since 1719, except while under French domination briefly in the early 19th century. In 1919 Switzerland assumed responsibility for Liechtenstein's diplomatic representation, replacing Austria. In 1920 a postal union with Switzerland was agreed, and in 1924 a treaty was concluded with Switzerland whereby Liechtenstein was incorporated in a joint customs union. Franz Josef II succeeded as ruling Prince in 1938. In 1950 Liechtenstein became a party to the Statute of the International Court of Justice, and in 1978 it was admitted to the Council of Europe (see p. 190). Liechtenstein became a member of the UN in September 1990 (hitherto the country had been a member of some UN specialized agencies). In the following year Liechtenstein became a full member of the European Free Trade Association (EFTA, see p. 205).

After 42 years as the dominant party in government, the Fortschrittliche Bürgerpartei Liechtensteins (FBP—Progressive Citizens' Party of Liechtenstein) was defeated by the Vaterländische Union (VU—Patriotic Union) at a general election to the Landtag (parliament) in February 1970. Four years later the FBP regained its majority. At the general election to the Landtag in February 1978, the VU, led by Hans Brunhart, won eight of the 15 seats, although with a minority of the votes cast, while the remaining seats were taken by the FBP, led by Dr Walter Kieber, the Head of Government since March 1974. After protracted negotiations, Brunhart replaced Kieber in April 1978. At the general election in February 1982, the distribution of seats remained unchanged, although the VU gained a majority of votes. Following a referendum in July 1984, women were granted the right to vote on a national basis. However, women were still not permitted to vote on communal affairs in three of Liechtenstein's 11 communes until April 1986, when they were finally accorded full voting rights. (In 1992 an amendment to the Constitution took effect which declared equality between men and women.) In August 1984 Prince Franz Josef transferred executive power to his son, Prince Hans-Adam, although he remained titular Head of State until his death in November 1989, when he was succeeded by Hans-Adam (Hans-Adam II).

The composition of the Landtag remained unchanged following a general election in February 1986, when women voted for the first time in a national poll. In January 1989 the Landtag was dissolved by Prince Hans-Adam, following a dispute between the VU and the FBP regarding the construction of a new museum to accommodate the royal art collection. At the subsequent general election, which took place in March 1989, the number of seats in the Landtag was increased from 15 to 25; the VU retained its majority, securing 13 seats, while the FBP took the remaining 12 seats.

At the next general election, which took place in February 1993, the VU lost its majority, taking only 11 of the Landtag's 25 seats. The FBP again returned 12 representatives, and two seats were won by an environmentalist party, the Freie Liste (FL—Free List). Lengthy negotiations resulted in the formation of a new coalition between the FBP and the VU, in which the FBP was the dominant party, and Markus Büchel of the FBP became Head of Government. In September, however, following a unanimous vote in the Landtag expressing 'no confidence' in his leadership, Büchel was dismissed from his post, and Prince Hans-Adam dissolved the legislature. At a further general election, which was held in October, the VU regained its parliamentary majority, winning 13 seats, while the FBP took 11 seats and the FL secured one seat. The VU became the dominant party in a new coalition with the FBP, with Mario Frick of the VU as Head of Government.

In October 1992 almost 2,000 people demonstrated in Vaduz to protest against a threat by Prince Hans-Adam that he would dissolve the Landtag if deputies did not submit to his wish to hold a proposed referendum to endorse Liechtenstein's entry to the nascent European Economic Area (EEA) shortly in advance of a similar vote in Switzerland. The Prince believed that the outcome of the Swiss plebiscite might be prejudicial to that of the Liechtenstein vote, and that, in the event of voters' rejecting EEA membership at an early referendum, Liechtenstein might still be able to join other EFTA members in applying for admission to the European Community (EC—now European Union—EU, see p. 208). A compromise was reached, whereby the referendum was scheduled to take place shortly after the Swiss vote, while the Government agreed actively to promote a vote in favour of the EEA and to explore the possibility of applying to the EC should EEA membership be rejected. (The authorities subsequently decided that admission to the EU would not be beneficial to the Principality.) At the referendum in December, although Switzerland's voters had rejected accession to the EEA, Liechtenstein's membership was approved by 55.8% of those who voted (about 87% of the Principality's electorate); consequently, the two countries' joint customs union was renegotiated. In April 1995 a further national referendum was held, at which 55.9% of those who voted (around 82% of the electorate) approved the revised customs arrangements. Liechtenstein joined the EEA at the beginning of May.

In March 1996 the Landtag adopted a unanimous motion of loyalty in the hereditary monarchy, after Prince Hans-Adam offered to resign (following tension between the Prince and the legislature—see above). At the next general election, which took place in February 1997, the VU retained its majority with 13 seats, while the FBP secured 10 and the FL two seats. Frick remained Head of Government. In April the FBP withdrew from the ruling coalition, leaving a single party (the VU) to govern alone for the first time since 1938. The constitutional role of the ruling Prince came under renewed scrutiny in 1997, when, against the wishes of the Landtag, Prince Hans-Adam refused to reappoint Dr Herbert Wille, a senior judge who had advocated that constitutional issues should be decided by the Supreme Court rather than the Monarch. Dr Wille subsequently presented a formal complaint to the European Court of Human Rights, which ruled, in November 1999, that Prince Hans-Adam had restricted Wille's right to free speech; the Prince was required to pay 100,000 Swiss francs in costs.

In December 1999 Prince Hans-Adam II requested an Austrian prosecutor, Kurt Spitzer, to investigate allegations in the German press based on an unpublished report of April 1999 by the German secret service that international criminals were using financial institutions in Liechtenstein to 'launder' the proceeds of organized crime. As a result, five people were placed under investigative arrest in May 2000, including the brothers of both the Deputy Head of Government and of one of the principality's most senior judges; all five were later released without charge. In his final report, which was released at the end of August, Spitzer concluded that Liechtenstein was no more culpable of money-laundering than other countries in Europe. He blamed the current problems on the principality's over-bureaucratic and inefficient banking system and the poor application of existing legislation designed to combat economic crimes; criminal proceedings were initiated against two judges for abusing their authority. Spitzer also revealed that a money-laundering investigation was under way against Herbert Batliner, a prominent lawyer who had been implicated in the party-funding scandal involving Germany's former Chancellor, Helmut Kohl, and his party, the Christian Democratic Union, and in another case involving proceeds from drugs-trafficking in Colombia. In June the Financial Action Task Force on Money

Laundering (FATF), a commission of the Organisation for Economic Co-operation and Development (OECD, see p. 295) included Liechtenstein on a list of countries considered unco-operative in international attempts to combat money-laundering. In an effort to reverse some of the damage done to the country's international reputation, the Liechtenstein Bankers' Association announced in July that anonymous accounts would be abolished. In the same month the Government approved the establishment of a new financial investigative unit within the police force and measures to accelerate legal assistance to foreign countries in money-laundering investigations. Legislation was promulgated in December requiring financial institutions to maintain tighter controls over accounts and transactions, including the abolition of anonymous accounts. Liechtenstein was removed from the FATF's list of unco-operative countries in 2001, and, in October of that year, the Government appointed the former head of the Swiss anti-money-laundering authority, Daniel Thelesklaf, to administer a new financial surveillance unit, which was to enforce new regulations requiring banks and lawyers to be able to verify the identity of their clients. However, Liechtenstein was among seven jurisdictions identified on an OECD list as 'unco-operative tax havens' lacking financial transparency in April 2002, under its initiative to abolish 'harmful tax practices'. OECD urged these to amend their national financial legislation or face possible sanctions beginning in April 2003.

In the general election that took place on 9 and 11 February 2001 the VU lost its parliamentary majority, securing only 41.1% of the votes cast (11 of the 25 seats in the Landtag), while the FBP won 49.9% (13 seats) and the FL obtained 8.8% (one seat); voter participation was 86.7% of the electorate. The VU administration's popularity had been adversely affected by an unresolved dispute with Prince Hans-Adam over his demands for constitutional changes, notably with regard to appointments in the judiciary (the Prince advocated that judges be nominated by the reigning Monarch rather than by parliamentary deputies); the Prince claimed that these amendments would benefit the people, whilst the VU regarded them as an attempt to extend the royal prerogative. A new Government comprising solely the FBP, under the leadership of Otmar Hasler, took office on 5 April. The Prince had previously announced that if he failed to secure the support of the new Government for his proposed constitutional reforms, he would seek a national referendum; in December he also threatened to leave the Principality and take up residence in Vienna, Austria (where he owned considerable property).

The issue of constitutional reform was finally resolved by a national referendum, held on 14 and 16 March 2003, in which the participation rate was 87.7% of the electorate. Following an acrimonious campaign Prince Hans-Adam won an overwhelming majority of the votes cast, with 64.3% to 35.7% in favour of granting the Prince new powers. As a result of the referendum, the Prince gained the right to dismiss a government even if it retained parliamentary confidence, to appoint an interim administration pending elections, to preside over a panel to select judges, to veto laws by not signing them within a six-month period and to adopt emergency legislation. Conversely citizens could now force a referendum on any subject (including the future of the monarchy) by collecting a minimum of 1,500 signatures. A compromise proposal put forward by a cross-party group that included the former Premier Mario Frick (the Volksinitiative für Verfassungsfrieden—People's Initiative for Constitutional Peace), which suggested that a princely veto could be overruled by a referendum and sought to limit the Prince's use of emergency legislation to times of war, received the support of only 16.5% of the voters. The overwhelming support for the Prince's proposed changes was partially attributed to widespread fear that, if fulfilled, his threat of self-imposed exile as a symbolic monarch would cause economic decline and social upheaval. Prince Hans-Adam dismissed the findings of a commission established by the Council of Europe, which stated that the constitutional amendments would constitute a retrograde step for democracy and could lead to the isolation of Liechtenstein in Europe. On 15 August 2003 Prince Hans-Adam announced his intention to transfer power to his son, Prince Alois, on 15 August 2004. Prince Hans-Adam was, however, to remain as Head of State.

In the latter half of the 20th century Liechtenstein's relations with the Czech Republic and Slovakia were strained. This stemmed from the expulsion of ethnic Germans from Czechoslovakia and the confiscation of their land (without compensation)

following the Second World War, under the controversial Beneš Decrees. The Liechtenstein royal family lost a large part of its estates during this time—including the castles of Feldsberg and Eisgrub, now estimated to be worth some €100m. Liechtenstein, which was a sovereign, neutral state throughout both the First and Second World Wars, claimed that it was unfairly grouped together with Germany under the terms of the Decrees. Czechoslovakia, however, considered the Liechtenstein royal family to have been collaborators with the Nazi regime in Germany during the Second World War, and that its action was thus legitimate. At the beginning of the 21st century the Czech Republic and Slovakia still refused to recognize Liechtenstein as a sovereign state. In October 2003 Prince Hans-Adam blocked the entry of the Czech Republic and Slovakia (along with that of the eight other EU accession states) into the European Economic Area (EEA); the 10 countries were due to become members of the EU on 1 May 2004 and would, under normal circumstances, have automatically joined the EEA. Their accession to the EEA was delayed until November 2003, when Liechtenstein agreed to sign the enlargement treaty on the EEA; Slovakia subsequently agreed immediately to establish diplomatic relations with Liechtenstein. Liechtenstein reiterated its demand that the Czech Republic and Slovakia acknowledge that the Principality was a sovereign, neutral state through both World Wars. To do so, however, would expose these two countries to the possibility of legal action being brought against them by Liechtenstein for the illegal seizure of land.

Government

The Constitution of the hereditary Principality provides for a unicameral Landtag (parliament), comprising 25 members, who are elected by universal adult suffrage for a term of four years (subject to dissolution), on the basis of proportional representation. A five-member Government is nominated by the reigning Prince, on the recommendation of the Landtag, for four years. In March 2003 constitutional changes were approved by a referendum which extended the powers of the monarch; he was empowered to dismiss governments (even if they retained parliamentary confidence), appoint an interim administration pending an election, approve judicial nominees, veto laws and invoke emergency legislation. Citizens could force an referendum on any subject, including the future of the monarchy, by collecting 1,500 signatures.

Defence

Although Liechtensteiners under the age of 60 years are liable to military service in an emergency, there has been no standing army since 1868 and there is only a small police force, with 63 members.

Economic Affairs

In 1997 Liechtenstein's gross national product (GNP) per head was estimated by the World Bank to be US $50,000, at average 1995–97 prices, ranking as the highest in the world at that time. During 1986–95 the population increased at an average annual rate of 1.4%. During 1990–99, it was estimated, GDP grew at an average annual rate of 1.6%; GDP increased by 4.5% in 1998 but declined by 0.9% in 1999.

Following the Second World War, the importance of agriculture declined in favour of industry. Within the agricultural sector the emphasis is on cattle-breeding, dairy-farming and market gardening. The principal crops are maize and potatoes. In addition, wine is produced, and forestry is a significant activity. In 2002 1.3% of those employed in Liechtenstein worked in agriculture (including forestry).

In 2002 44.9% of those employed in Liechtenstein worked in industrial activity (including mining and quarrying, processing industries, energy and water supply and construction). The metal, machinery and precision instruments industry is by far the most prominent sector. Other important areas are the pharmaceutical, textiles and ceramics industries.

In 1999 some 92.9% of energy requirements were imported from other countries. In that year natural gas supplied 24.2% of energy requirements, electricity 23.6%, fuel oil 23.5%, motor fuel (petrol) 19.2%, diesel 8.2% and firewood 1.2%.

In 2002 53.9% of those employed in Liechtenstein worked in the services sector. Financial services are of great importance. Numerous foreign corporations, holding companies and foundations (estimated to number about 75,000) have nominal offices in Liechtenstein, benefiting from the Principality's stable political situation, tradition of bank secrecy (although stricter banking legislation was introduced in 1997 and in 2000–02, partly to increase the transparency of the sector) and low fiscal charges. Such enterprises pay no tax on profit or income, contributing instead an annual levy on capital or net worth. These levies account for about 20% of the Principality's annual direct revenue. In 1980 Liechtenstein adopted legislation to increase controls on foreign firms, many of which were thereafter subject to audit and entered in the public register. Following the Principality's accession to the European Economic Area (EEA) in 1995, the registration of foreign banks was permitted. New legislation governing insurance companies was approved in 1996, and during the late 1990s the insurance sector expanded rapidly. The building and hotel trades and other service industries are also highly developed.

With a very limited domestic market, Liechtenstein's industry is export-orientated. In 2002 total exports amounted to 2,813.5m. Swiss francs (with imports totalling 1,360.5m. Swiss francs). Switzerland is the principal trading partner, receiving 12.7% of exports in 1998. In that year members of the European Union (EU, see p. 208) accounted for 37.8% of total exports. Specialized machinery, artificial teeth and other materials for dentistry, and frozen food are important exports. The sale of postage stamps, mainly to tourists, provided about 3.0% of the national income in 1997.

The 2002 budget envisaged a deficit of 46.5m. Swiss francs. The annual average rate of inflation increased from 1.9% in 1988 to 5.9% in 1991, decreasing again, to 0.5%, in 1997. Traditionally the unemployment rate has been negligible; in 1999 the rate of unemployment (as a percentage of those employed) was 1.2%. More than one-third of Liechtenstein's population are resident foreigners, many of whom provide the labour for industry, while in December 1999 9,741 workers crossed the borders from Austria and Switzerland each day to work in the Principality.

Liechtenstein has important economic links with neighbouring Switzerland. It is incorporated in a customs union with that country, and uses the Swiss franc as its currency. Liechtenstein became a member of the European Free Trade Association (EFTA, see p. 205) in May 1991, and the EEA in May 1995. The Principality is also a member of the European Bank for Reconstruction and Development (EBRD, see p. 203).

Education

Compulsory education begins at seven years of age. Basic instruction is given for five years at a primary school (Primarschule), after which a pupil may transfer to a lower secondary school (Oberschule) or secondary school (Realschule) for four years, or to the Liechtensteinisches Gymnasium (grammar school) for eight years. There is no university. Many Liechtensteiners continue their studies at universities in Austria and Switzerland. Liechtenstein has a further education college for the study of philosophy, a technical college (Fachhochschule), a music school, an art school, an adult education centre and a school for mentally disabled children. Government expenditure on education totalled 95m. Swiss francs in 1999 (15.1% of total expenditure).

Public Holidays

2004: 1 January (New Year's Day), 2 January (St Berchtold's Day), 6 January (Epiphany), 2 February (Candelmas), 24 February (Shrove Tuesday), 19 March (St Joseph's Day), 9 April (Good Friday), 12 April (Easter Monday), 1 May (Labour Day), 20 May (Ascension Day), 31 May (Whit Monday), 10 June (Corpus Christi), 15 August (Assumption and National Holiday), 8 September (Nativity of the Virgin Mary), 1 November (All Saints' Day), 8 December (Immaculate Conception), 25 December (Christmas), 26 December (St Stephen's Day).

2005: 1 January (New Year's Day), 2 January (St Berchtold's Day), 6 January (Epiphany), 2 February (Candelmas), 8 February (Shrove Tuesday), 19 March (St Joseph's Day), 25 March (Good Friday), 28 March (Easter Monday), 1 May (Labour Day), 5 May (Ascension Day), 16 May (Whit Monday), 26 May (Corpus Christi), 15 August (Assumption and National Holiday), 8 September (Nativity of the Virgin Mary), 1 November (All Saints' Day), 8 December (Immaculate Conception), 25 December (Christmas), 26 December (St Stephen's Day).

Weights and Measures

The metric system is in force.

Statistical Survey

Source: Amt für Volkswirtschaft, Gerberweg 5, 9490 Vaduz; tel. 2366876; fax 2366895; e-mail info.statistik@avw.llv.li; internet www.avw .llv.li.

AREA AND POPULATION

Area: 160.0 sq km (61.8 sq miles).

Population: 29,868 (incl. 11,432 resident aliens) at census of December 1992; 33,863 (incl. 11,566 resident aliens) at 31 December 2002.

Density (31 December 2002): 211.6 per sq km.

Principal Towns (population at 31 December 2002): Schaan 5,573; Vaduz (capital) 5,038; Triesen 4,558; Balzers 4,312; Eschen 3,886; Mauren 3,516; Triesenberg 2,607.

Births, Marriages and Deaths (2001): Live births 401 (12.1 per 1,000); Marriages 199 (6.0 per 1,000); Deaths 220 (6.6 per 1,000).

Employment (2002): Agriculture and forestry 366; Industry and skilled trades 12,927 (Mining and quarrying 47, Processing industries 10,256, Energy and water supply 190, Construction 2,434); Services 15,521 (Retail, repairs, etc. 2,255, Hotels and restaurants 818, Transport and communications 1,103, Banking and insurance 2,130, Real estate, business services, etc. 2,608, Legal consultancy and trust management 1,795, Public administration 1,432, Education 849, Health and social services 1,417, Other services 1,114); *Total* 28,814.

HEALTH AND WELFARE

Key Indicators

Under-5 Mortality Rate (per 1,000 live births 2001): 11.

Physicians (per 1,000 head, 1997): 1.31 (Source: Statistik des Fürstentums Liechtenstein, *Statistisches Jahrbuch (1998)*).

For sources (unless specified) and definitions, see explanatory note on p. vi.

AGRICULTURE, ETC.

Principal Crops (metric tons, 1987): Wheat 460; Oats 4; Barley 416; Silo-maize 27,880; Potatoes 1,040. *2002:* Grapes 150 metric tons (FAO estimate) (Source: partly FAO).

Livestock (2003): Cattle 5,314; Pigs 1,979; Horses 408; Sheep 3,070; Goats 241; Hens 9,975.

Dairy Produce (2002): Total production 13,292 metric tons.

Forestry ('000 cubic metres, 2002): Roundwood removals (excl. bark) 22 (Sawlogs, veneer logs and logs for sleepers 18, Fuel wood 4). Source: FAO.

FINANCE

Currency and Exchange Rates: Swiss currency: 100 Rappen (centimes) = 1 Franken (Swiss franc). *Sterling, Dollar and Euro Equivalents* (31 December 2003): £1 sterling = 2.2075 Franken; US $1 = 1.2369 Franken; €1 = 1.5622 Franken; 100 Franken = £45.30 = $80.85 = €64.01. For average exchange rate, see chapter on Switzerland.

Budget (estimates, '000 Swiss francs, 2002): Revenue 776,904; Expenditure 823,404.

EXTERNAL TRADE

Total Imports ('000 Swiss francs, 2002): 1,360,517.

Total Exports ('000 Swiss francs, 2002): 2,813,509.

TRANSPORT

Road Traffic (registered motor vehicles, December 2003): Passenger cars 23,524; Commercial vehicles 2,560; Motorcycles 2,980.

TOURISM

Arrivals by Country of Residence (2002): Austria 2,286; France 1,345; Germany 17,140; Italy 1,887; Netherlands 1,159; Switzerland 13,014; United Kingdom 1,806; USA 2,253; Total (incl. others) 48,727.

COMMUNICATIONS MEDIA

Newspapers (1995): 3 (total circulation 10,450 copies).

Radio Receivers (1997): 12,382 in use.

Television Receivers (1997): 11,979 in use.

Telephones (2000): 20,072 main lines in use (Source: International Telecommunication Union).

Mobile Cellular Telephones (2000): 14,743 subscribers (Source: International Telecommunication Union).

EDUCATION

(2003/04)

Kindergarten: 58 schools; 60 teachers*; 815 pupils.
Primary: 14 schools; 144 teachers; 2,290 pupils.
Lower secondary: 3 schools; 33 teachers; 438 pupils.
Secondary: 5 schools; 62 teachers*; 735 pupils.
Grammar: 1 school; 41 teachers; 738 pupils.
Music: 1 school; 91 teachers; 2,458 pupils.
Technical: 1 school; 214 teachers; 597 pupils.
* School year 1998/99.

Directory

The Constitution

Under the Constitution of 5 October 1921, the monarchy is hereditary in the male line. The reigning Prince, who is constitutionally responsible for foreign affairs, exercises legislative power jointly with the Landtag (parliament). The Landtag comprises 25 members, who are elected for a term of four years (subject to dissolution) by universal adult suffrage, on a basis of proportional representation. Under the Constitution (as amended in 1969, 1984 and 2003), all citizens of over 20 years of age are eligible to vote. The voters participate directly in legislation through referendums.

In a referendum on 14 and 16 March 2003 the electorate approved constitutional amendments extending the powers of the monarch. He was awarded the right to dismiss governments (even if they retained parliamentary confidence), to appoint an interim administration pending fresh elections, to veto laws by not signing them within a six-month period, to dismiss individual ministers, subject to approval by members of the Landtag, to preside over a panel to select judges (with a casting vote) and to invoke emergency legislation. Citizens were accorded the right to force a referendum on any subject, including the future of the monarchy, by collecting 1,500 signatures.

In accordance with a treaty concluded with Switzerland in 1924, Liechtenstein is incorporated in Swiss customs territory, and uses Swiss currency, customs and postal administration.

The Government

HEAD OF STATE

Ruling Prince: Prince HANS-ADAM II (Prince of Liechtenstein, Duke of Troppau and Jägerndorf, Count of Rietberg—succeeded 13 November 1989).

In August 2003 Prince Hans-Adam announced his intention to hand executive power to his son, Alois, on 15 August 2004. Prince Hans-Adam was to remain as the Head of State.

GOVERNMENT
(April 2004)

All members of the Government belong to the Fortschrittliche Bürgerpartei Liechtensteins (FBP).

Prime Minister (also responsible for Government Affairs; Family and Equal Opportunities; Finance; Construction and Public Works): OTMAR HASLER.

Deputy Prime Minister (also responsible for Education; Transport and Communications; Justice): RITA KIEBER-BECK.

Government Councillors: HANSJÖRG FRICK (Public Health; Social Affairs; Economy), Dr ALOIS OSPELT (Home Affairs; Cultural Affairs; Sports; Environment; Land Use; Agriculture and Forestry), Dr ERNST WALCH (Foreign Affairs).

GOVERNMENT OFFICES

Regierungsgebäude: 9490 Vaduz; tel. 2366111; fax 2366022.

Legislature

LANDTAG

President: KLAUS WANGER (FBP).

Vice-President: Dr PETER WOLFF (VU).

General Election, 9 and 11 February 2001

Party	% of votes	Seats
FBP (Progressive Citizens' Party of Liechtenstein)	49.9	13
VU (Patriotic Union)	41.1	11
FL (Free List)	8.8	1
Total	100.0*	25

* Including spoilt ballots.

Political Organizations

Fortschrittliche Bürgerpartei Liechtensteins (FBP) (Progressive Citizens' Party of Liechtenstein): Aeulestr. 56, Postfach 1213, 9490 Vaduz; tel. 2377940; fax 2377949; e-mail marcus.vogt@ fbp.li; internet www.fbp.li; f. 1918; Chair. JOHANNES MATT; Sec. MARCUS VOGT.

Freie Liste (FL) (Free List): Im Bretscha 4, Postfach 177, 9494 Schaan; e-mail fliste@lie-net.li; internet www.freieliste.li; f. 1985; progressive ecological party; Chair. KARIN JENNI.

Vaterländische Union (VU) (Patriotic Union): Fürst-Franz-Josef-Str. 13, 9490 Vaduz; tel. 2320832; fax 2322632; internet www .vu-online.li; f. 1936 by merger of the People's Party (f. 1918) and the Heimatdienst movement; Chair. OSWALD KRANZ; Sec.-Gen. JÜRGEN NIGG.

Diplomatic Representation

According to an arrangement concluded in 1919, Switzerland has agreed to represent Liechtenstein's interests in countries where it has diplomatic missions and where Liechtenstein is not represented in its own right. In so doing, Switzerland always acts only on the basis of mandates of a general or specific nature, which it may either refuse or accept, while Liechtenstein is free to enter into direct relations with foreign states or to establish its own additional missions. Liechtenstein has an embassy in Bern (Switzerland), a non-resident ambassador to Austria and a non-resident ambassador to the Holy See, as well as a permanent representative to the Council of Europe in Strasbourg (France) and a permanent mission to the UN in New York (USA). There are 37 consular representatives accredited to Liechtenstein.

Judicial System

CIVIL COURTS

Landgericht (County Court): 9490 Vaduz; tel. 2366111; fax 2366539; Court of First Instance; one presiding judge; Presiding Judge Dr BENEDIKT MARXER.

Obergericht (Superior Court): 9490 Vaduz; Court of Second Instance; bench of five judges; Presiding Judge Lic. Iur. MAX BIZOZZERO.

Oberster Gerichtshof (Supreme Court): 9490 Vaduz; Court of Third Instance; bench of five judges; Presiding Judge Dr HANSJÖRG RÜCK.

CRIMINAL COURTS

Landgericht (Petty Sessions): 9490 Vaduz; tel. 2366111; fax 2366539; for summary offences; Presiding Judge LOTHAR HAGEN.

Schöffengericht (Court of Assizes): 9490 Vaduz; for minor misdemeanours; bench of three judges; Presiding Judge Dr BENEDIKT MARXER.

Kriminalgericht (Criminal Court): bench of five judges; Presiding Judge Dr LOTHAR HAGEN.

Obergericht (Superior Court): Court of Second Instance; bench of five judges; Presiding Judge Lic. Iur. MAX BIZOZZERO.

Oberster Gerichtshof (Supreme Court): Court of Third Instance; bench of five judges; Presiding Judge Dr HANSJÖRG RÜCK.

ADMINISTRATIVE COURTS

Verwaltungsgerichtshof (Administrative Court of Appeal): 9490 Vaduz; appeal against decrees and decisions of the Government may be made to this court; five members; Presiding Judge Lic. Iur. ANDREAS BATLINER.

State Court: 9490 Vaduz; five members; exists for the protection of Public Law; Presiding Judge Lic. Iur. HARRY GSTÖHL.

Religion

CHRISTIANITY

The Principality comprises a single archdiocese, Vaduz, created in 1997, which is directly responsible to the Holy See. At 31 December 2002 there were an estimated 25,642 adherents (some 76.5% of the population). The few Protestants (7.3%) belong to the parish of Vaduz.

Archdiocese of Vaduz: Erzbischöfliche Kanzlei, Fürst-Franz-Josef-Str. 112, Postfach 103, 9490 Vaduz; tel. 2332311; fax 2332324; e-mail ebv@supra.net; Archbishop Most Rev. WOLFGANG HAAS.

The Press

Apotheke und Marketing: Fürst-Johannes-Str. 70, 9494 Schaan; tel. 2332585; fax 2332586; e-mail info@am-verlag.com; internet www.am-verlag.com; Editor RALF DOEKEN; circ. 22,000.

Liechtensteiner Vaterland: Fürst-Franz-Josef-Str. 13, 9490 Vaduz; tel. 2361616; fax 2361617; e-mail redaktion@vaterland.li; internet www.vaterland.li; f. 1913; daily (Monday to Saturday); organ of the VU; Editor GÜNTHER FRITZ; circ. 10,295.

Liechtensteiner Volksblatt: Zollstr. 13, 9494 Schaan; tel. 2375151; fax 2375155; e-mail redaktion@volksblatt.li; internet www.volksblatt.li; f. 1878; daily (Monday to Saturday); organ of the FBP; Chief Editor MARTIN FROMMELT; circ. 7,515.

Liechtensteiner Wochenzeitung: 9494 Schaan; tel. 2361692; fax 2361699; e-mail liewo@lie-net.li; f. 1993; weekly (Sunday); Dir HANS-PETER RHEINBERGER; Editors SANDRA CASALINI, JOACHIM BATLINER.

PRESS AGENCY

Presse- und Informationsamt (Press and Information Office): Regierungsgebäude, 9490 Vaduz; tel. 2366721; fax 2366460; e-mail info@pia.llv.li; internet www.presseamt.li; f. 1962; Dir DANIELA CLAVADETSCHER.

Publishers

Buch und Verlagsdruckerei: Landstr. 153, 9494 Schaan; tel. 2361836; fax 2361840; e-mail bvd@bvd.li.

van Eck Publishers: Haldenweg 8, 9495 Triesen; tel. 3923000; fax 3922277; e-mail vaneck@datacomm.ch; f. 1982; art, local interest, juvenile, golf, crime fiction; Man. Dirs FRANK P. VAN ECK, PETER GÖPPEL.

A. R. Gantner Verlag KG: Industriestr. 105A, Postfach 131, 9491 Ruggell; tel. 3771808; fax 3771802; e-mail bgc@adon.li; botany; Dir BRUNI GANTNER-CAPLAN.

Liechtenstein-Verlag AG: Herrengasse 21, Postfach 339, 9490 Vaduz; tel. 2396010; fax 2396019; e-mail flbooks@verlag_ag.lol.li; f. 1947; belles-lettres and legal and scientific books; agents for international literature; Man. ALBART SCHIKS.

Litag Anstalt—Literarische, Medien und Künstler Agentur: Industriestr. 105A, Postfach 131, 9491 Ruggell; tel. 3771808; fax 3771802; e-mail bgc@adon.li; f. 1956; Dir BRUNI GANTNER-CAPLAN.

Sändig Reprint Verlag Wohlwend: Am Schrägen Weg 12, 9490 Vaduz; tel. 2323627; fax 2323649; e-mail saendig@adon.li; internet www.saendig.com; f. 1965; natural sciences, linguistics, free-masonry, fiction, folklore, music, history; Dir CHRISTIAN WOHLWEND.

Topos Verlag AG: Industriestr. 105A, Postfach 551, 9491 Ruggell; tel. 3771111; fax 3771119; e-mail topos@supra.net; internet www.topos.li; f. 1977; law, politics, literature, social science, periodicals; Dir GRAHAM A. P. SMITH.

Broadcasting and Communications

TELECOMMUNICATIONS

Amt für Kommunikation: Kirchstr. 10, 9490 Vaduz; tel. 2366488; fax 2366489; e-mail office@ak.liv.li; internet www.ak.li; regulatory body; Dir STEFAN BECKER.

Telecom FL AG: Austr. 77, 9490 Vaduz; tel. 2377400; fax 2377401; e-mail telecom-fl@telecom-fl.com; internet www.telecom-fl.com; f. 1999.

BROADCASTING

Radio Liechtenstein: Dorfstr. 24, 9495 Triesen; tel. 3991313; fax 3991399; e-mail redaktion@radiol.li; internet www.radiol.li; f. 1995.

Finance

(cap. = capital; res = reserves; dep. = deposits; m. = millions; brs = branches; amounts in Swiss francs)

BANKING

Anlage- und Geschäfts-Bank AG: Egertastr. 10, 9490 Vaduz; tel. 2655353; fax 2655363.

Bank von Ernst (Liechtenstein) AG: POB 112, Egertastr. 10, 9492 Vaduz; tel. 2655353; fax 2655363; e-mail info@bve.li; internet www.bve.li; wholly owned by Bank von Ernst & Cie AG (Switzerland); cap. 25m., res 7m., dep. 157m. (Dec. 2001); Gen. Mans MAX CADERAS, ERNST WEDER.

Bank Frick & Co. AG: Landstr. 8, Postfach 43, 9496 Balzers; tel. 3882121; fax 3882122; e-mail bank@bfc.li; internet www.bfc.li.

Centrum Bank AG: Kirchstr. 3, Postfach 1168, 9490 Vaduz; tel. 2383838; fax 2383839; e-mail cbk@centrumbank.li; internet www.centrumbank.li; f. 1993; cap. 20m., res 68m., dep. 826m. (Dec. 2001); Dirs Dr PETER MARXER, Dr PETER GOOP, Dr PETER MARXER, Jr, Dr HERBERT OBERHUBER.

Hypo Investment Bank (Liechtenstein) AG: Austr. 59, 9490 Vaduz; tel. 2655656; fax 2655699; e-mail info@hib.li; internet www.hib.li; Chair. Dr ANDREAS INSAM.

LGT Bank in Liechtenstein Ltd: Herrengasse 12, Postfach 85, 9490 Vaduz; tel. 2351122; fax 2351522; e-mail info@lgt.com; internet www.lgt.com; f. 1920; present name adopted 1996; cap. 291m., res 804m., dep. 9,479m. (Dec. 2001); Chair. Prince PHILIPP OF LIECHTENSTEIN; CEO THOMAS PISKE; 2 brs.

Liechtensteinische Landesbank AG (State Bank): Städtle 44, Postfach 384, 9490 Vaduz; tel. 2368811; fax 2368822; e-mail llb@llb.li; internet www.llb.li; f. 1861; present name adopted 1955; cap. 172m., res 652m., dep. 9,524m. (Dec. 2002); Chair. ERWIN VOGT; Exec. Dir Dr JOSEPH FEHR; brs in Schaan, Triesenberg, Eschen and Balzers.

Neue Bank AG: Marktgass 20, Postfach 1533, 9490 Vaduz; tel. 2360808; fax 2329260; e-mail info@neuebankag.li; internet www.neuebankag.li.

Raiffeisen Bank (Liechtenstein) AG: Landstr. 140, 9494 Schaan; tel. 2370707; fax 2370777; e-mail info@raiffeisen.li; internet www.raiffeisen.li; f. 1998; total assets 517m. (June 2002).

Swissfirst Bank (Liechtenstein) AG: Austr. 61, Postfach, 9490 Vaduz; tel. 2393333; fax 2393300; e-mail swissfirst@swissfirst.li; internet www.swissfirst.li.

Verwaltungs- und Privat-Bank AG (Private Trust Bank Corporation): Im Zentrum, Postfach 885, 9490 Vaduz; tel. 2356655; fax 2356500; e-mail info@vpbank.li; internet www.vpbank.li; f. 1956; cap. 86m., res 557m., dep. 7,130m. (Dec. 2001); Chair. HANS BRUNHART; Gen. Man. ADOLF E. REAL; 4 brs.

Vorarlberger Volksbank AG: Heiligkreuz 42, Postfach, 9490 Vaduz; tel. 2376930; fax 2376948; e-mail info@volksbank.li; internet www.volksbank.li; Man. Dirs DANIEL BECK, GERHARD HAMEL.

INSURANCE

AIG Life Insurance Co (Liechtenstein) Ltd: Landstr. 38, 9494 Schaan; tel. 2376880; fax 2376889; e-mail info@aiglife.ch; internet www.aiglife.ch; f. 1996.

Alters- und Hinterlassenen-Versicherung (AHV) (Old Age and Survivors' Insurance): 9490 Vaduz; tel. 2381616; fax 2381600; e-mail postmaster@ahv.li; internet www.ahv.li; state-owned; Dir GERHARD BIEDERMANN.

Amisia Fluss-Kasko Versicherungs-AG: Pflugstr. 20, 9490 Vaduz; tel. 2376760; fax 2333050.

AXA Nordstern Versicherungs-AG: Neugasse 15, 9490 Vaduz; tel. 2375010; fax 2375019; e-mail kundendienst@axa-nordstern.li; internet www.axa-nordstern.li; f. 1995.

CapitalLeben Versicherung AG: Landstr. 126A, 9494 Schaan; tel. 2374837; fax 2374848; e-mail office@capitalleben.li; internet www .capitalleben.li; f. 1997; life insurance; Chair. KLAUS OSTERTAG; Man. Dirs Dr MARKUS HETZER, ALEXANDER T. SKREINER.

Fortuna Lebens-Versicherungs-AG: Stadtle 35, 9490 Vaduz; tel. 2361545; fax 2361546; e-mail fl.service@fortuna.li; internet www .fortuna.li; f. 1996; Man. HEINER KEIL.

Swisscom Re AG: Schmedgass 6, 9490 Vaduz; tel. 2301665; fax 2301666; Man. Dirs BERNHARD LAMPERT, URS LUGINBÜHL, MARCEL VON VIVIS, THOMAS WITTBJER.

Transmarine Insurance Co Ltd: Aeulestr. 38, 9490 Vaduz; tel. 2334488; fax 2334489; f. 1996.

Valorlife Lebensversicherungs-AG: Landstr. 114, 9495 Triesen; tel. 3992950; fax 3992959; e-mail info@valorlife.com; internet www .valorlife.com.

Trade and Industry

CHAMBER OF COMMERCE

Liechtenstein Chamber of Commerce and Industry (LCCI): Josef-Rheinberger-Str. 11, 9490 Vaduz; tel. 2375511; fax 2375512; e-mail info@lcci.li; internet www.lcci.li; f. 1947; Pres. MICHAEL HILTI; Gen. Man. JOSEF BECK; 42 mems.

INDUSTRIAL ASSOCIATION

Vereinigung Bäuerlicher Organisationen im Fürstentum Liechtenstein (VBO) (Agricultural Union): Postfach 351, 9493 Mauren; tel. 3759050; fax 3759051; e-mail vbo@kba.li; Pres. THOMAS BÜCHEL; Sec. KLAUS BÜCHEL.

UTILITY

Gas

Liechtensteinische Gasversorgung: Im Rietacker 4, 9494 Schaan; tel. 2361555; fax 2361566; Dir ANTON GERNER.

TRADE UNIONS

Gewerbe- und Wirtschaftskammer für das Fürstentum Liechtenstein (Trades' Union): Zollstr. 23, 9494 Schaan; tel. 2377788; fax 2377789; e-mail gwk@gwk.li; internet www.gwk.li; f. 1936; aims to protect the interests of Liechtenstein artisans and tradespeople; Pres. ARNOLD MATT; Sec. OLIVER GERSTGRASSER; 3,000 mems.

Liechtensteiner Arbeitnehmer-Verband (Employees' Association): 9495 Triesen; tel. 3993838; fax 3993839; e-mail lanv@supra .net; internet www.lanv.li; Pres. ALICE FEHR; Sec. ALBERT JEHLE.

Transport

RAILWAYS

Liechtenstein is traversed by some 18.5 km of railway track, which is administered by Austrian Federal Railways. There is a station at Nendeln, as well as two halts at Schaan and Schaanwald. A local service connects Feldkirch in Austria and Buchs in Switzerland via Liechtenstein, and the Arlberg express (Paris to Vienna) passes through the Principality.

ROADS

Modern roads connect the capital, Vaduz, with all the towns and villages in the Principality. The Rhine and Samina valleys are connected by a tunnel 740 m long. Public transport is provided by a well-developed network of postal buses.

INLAND WATERWAYS

A canal of 26 km, irrigating the Rhine valley, was opened in 1943.

Tourism

Liechtenstein has an Alpine setting in the Upper Rhine area. The principal tourist attractions include a renowned postal museum, a National Museum and the Liechtenstein State Art Collection at Vaduz, as well as the Prince's castle (although this is closed to the public) and two ruined medieval fortresses at Schellenberg. Annually about two-fifths of foreign tourists visit the winter sports resort at Malbun, in the south-east of the Principality. For summer visitors there are some 400 km of hiking trails and an extensive network of cycling paths. In 2002 Liechtenstein received 48,727 foreign visitors.

Liechtenstein Tourismus: Postfach 139, 9490 Vaduz; tel. 2396300; fax 2396301; e-mail info@tourismus.li; internet www .tourismus.li; Dir ROLAND BÜCHEL.

LITHUANIA

Introductory Survey

Location, Climate, Language, Religion, Flag, Capital

The Republic of Lithuania (formerly the Lithuanian Soviet Socialist Republic) is situated on the eastern coast of the Baltic Sea, in north-eastern Europe. It is bounded by Latvia to the north, by Belarus to the south-east, by Poland to the south-west and by the Russian territory of Kaliningrad to the west. Lithuania's maritime position moderates an otherwise continental-type climate. Temperatures range from an average of –4.9°C (23.2°F) in January to a July mean of 17.0°C (62.6°F). Rainfall levels vary considerably from region to region: in the far west the annual average is 700 mm–850 mm (28 ins–33 ins), but in the central plain it is about 600 mm (24 ins). The official language is Lithuanian. The predominant religion is Christianity. Most ethnic Lithuanians are Roman Catholics by belief or tradition, but there are small communities of Lutherans and Calvinists, as well as a growing number of modern Protestant denominations. Adherents of Russian Orthodoxy are almost exclusively ethnic Slavs, while most Tatars have retained an adherence to Islam. The national flag (proportions 1 by 2) consists of three equal horizontal stripes of yellow (top), green and red (bottom). The capital is Vilnius.

Recent History

Prior to annexation by the Russian Empire in 1795, Lithuania was united in a Commonwealth with Poland. In 1915, after the outbreak of the First World War, it was occupied by German troops. A 'Lithuanian Conference' was convened in September 1917, which demanded the re-establishment of an independent Lithuanian state and elected a 'Lithuanian Council', headed by Antanas Smetona; it proceeded to declare independence on 16 February 1918. The new state survived both a Soviet attempt to create a Lithuanian-Belarusian Soviet republic and a Polish campaign aimed at reincorporating Lithuania. In October 1920 Poland annexed the region of Vilnius, but was forced to recognize the rest of Lithuania as an independent state (with its temporary capital at Kaunas). Soviet Russia had recognized Lithuanian independence in the Treaty of Moscow, signed in July. Lithuania's first Constitution, which declared Lithuania a parliamentary democracy, was adopted in August 1922. In December 1926 Antanas Smetona seized power in a military coup d'état and established an authoritarian regime, which endured until 1940.

According to the 'Secret Protocols' to the Treaty of Non-Aggression (the Molotov-Ribbentrop Pact), signed on 23 August 1939 by the USSR and Germany, Lithuania was to be part of the German sphere of influence. However, the Nazi-Soviet Treaty on Friendship and Existing Borders, agreed in September (following the outbreak of the Second World War), permitted the USSR to take control of Lithuania. In October Lithuania was compelled to agree to the stationing of 20,000 Soviet troops on its territory. In return, the USSR granted the city and region of Vilnius (which had been seized by Soviet troops in September) to Lithuania. In June 1940 the USSR dispatched a further 100,000 troops to Lithuania and forced the Lithuanian Government to resign. A Soviet-approved People's Government was formed. Elections to a People's Seim (parliament), which only pro-Soviet candidates were permitted to contest, took place in July. The Seim proclaimed the Lithuanian Soviet Socialist Republic on 21 July, and on 3 August Lithuania formally became a Union Republic of the USSR. The establishment of Soviet rule was followed by the arrest and imprisonment of many Lithuanian politicians and government officials.

Some 210,000 people, mainly Jews, were killed during the Nazi occupation of Lithuania (1941–44). The return of the Soviet Army, in 1944, was not welcomed by most Lithuanians, and anti-Soviet partisan warfare continued until 1952. Lithuanian agriculture was forcibly collectivized and rapid industrialization was implemented. Meanwhile, some 150,000 people were deported, and leaders and members of the Roman Catholic Church were persecuted and imprisoned. Lithuanian political parties were disbanded, and political power became the exclusive preserve of the Communist Party of Lithuania (CPL), the local branch of the Communist Party of the Soviet Union (CPSU). The leader (First Secretary) of the CPL in 1940–74 was Antanas Sniečkus.

A significant dissident movement was established during the 1960s and 1970s. There were demonstrations in Kaunas in May 1972, in support of demands for religious and political freedom. With the introduction of the policy of glasnost (openness) by the Soviet leader, Mikhail Gorbachev, in the mid-1980s, a limited discussion of previously censored aspects of Lithuanian history appeared in the press. Dissident groups took advantage of a more tolerant attitude to political protests, organizing a demonstration in August 1987 to denounce the Nazi-Soviet Pact. However, in February 1988 security forces were deployed to prevent the public celebration of the 70th anniversary of Lithuanian independence. This, together with frustration among the intelligentsia at the slow pace of reform in the republic, led to the establishment in June of the Lithuanian Movement for Reconstruction (Sąjūdis). Sąjūdis organized mass demonstrations to protest against environmental pollution, the suppression of national culture and 'russification', and to condemn the signing of the Molotov-Ribbentrop Pact. The movement appealed to the CPL to support a declaration of independence and the recognition of Lithuanian as the state language. The latter demand was adopted by the Lithuanian Supreme Soviet (legislature) in November, and traditional Lithuanian state symbols were restored. Other concessions made by the CPL during 1988 included the restoration of Independence Day as a public holiday and the return of buildings to the Roman Catholic Church.

Sąjūdis won 36 of the 42 popularly elected seats at elections to the all-Union Congress of People's Deputies in March 1989. Thereafter, the CPL began to adopt a more radical position, in an attempt to retain some measure of popular support. On 18 May the CPL-dominated Supreme Soviet approved a declaration of Lithuanian sovereignty, which asserted the supremacy of Lithuania's laws over all-Union legislation. Public debate concerning the legitimacy of Soviet rule in Lithuania intensified: a commission of the Lithuanian Supreme Soviet declared the establishment of Soviet power in 1940 to have been unconstitutional and, in August, on the 50th anniversary of the signing of the Pact with Nazi Germany, more than 1m. people participated in a 'human chain' extending from Tallinn in Estonia, through Latvia, to Vilnius.

Despite denunciations of Baltic nationalism by the all-Union authorities, the Lithuanian Supreme Soviet continued to adopt reformist legislation, including the establishment of freedom of religion and the legalization of a multi-party system. In December 1989 the CPL declared itself an independent party, no longer subordinate to the CPSU, adopting a new programme that condemned communist policies of the past and declared support for multi-party democracy and independent statehood. Shortly afterwards a group of former CPL members who were opposed to independence formed a separate movement, the Lithuanian Communist Party on the CPSU Platform (LCP). Meanwhile, Algirdas Brazauskas, First Secretary of the CPL since October 1988, was elected Chairman of the Presidium of the Lithuanian Supreme Soviet, defeating three other candidates, including Romualdas Ozolas, a leading member of Sąjūdis. None the less, Sąjūdis remained the dominant political force in the republic, and its supporters won an overall majority in the elections to the Lithuanian Supreme Soviet in February–March 1990. This new, pro-independence parliament elected Vytautas Landsbergis, the Chairman of Sąjūdis, to replace Brazauskas as its Chairman (de facto President of Lithuania), and on 11 March declared the restoration of Lithuanian independence: Lithuania thus became the first of the Soviet republics to make such a declaration. The legislature (restyled the Supreme Council) also restored the pre-1940 name of the country (the Republic of Lithuania) and suspended the USSR Constitution on Lithuanian territory. Kazimieras Prunskienė, a member of the CPL and hitherto a Deputy Chairman of the Council of Ministers, was appointed to be the first Prime Minister of the restored republic.

The Lithuanian declarations were condemned by a special session of the all-Union Congress of People's Deputies as unconstitutional, and Soviet forces occupied CPL buildings in Vilnius and took control of newspaper presses. An economic embargo was imposed on Lithuania in April, and vital fuel supplies were suspended; it remained in force for more than two months, until Lithuania agreed to a six-month moratorium on the independence declaration, pending formal negotiations. However, talks, which began in August, were soon terminated by the Soviet Government, and in January 1991 Landsbergis revoked the suspension of the declaration of independence, since negotiations on Lithuania's status had not resumed. Tension increased in the republic when the Soviet authorities dispatched to Vilnius troops (led by the special OMON units) of the Soviet Ministry of Internal Affairs, who occupied former CPSU properties that had been nationalized by the Lithuanian Government. Landsbergis mobilized popular support to help to defend the parliament building, which he believed to be under threat. In mid-January 13 people were killed and about 500 injured, when Soviet troops seized the broadcasting centre in Vilnius. (In August 1999 six former officers of the LCP were convicted of complicity in attempts to overthrow the Lithuanian Government in January 1991, and sentenced to between three and 12 years' imprisonment.)

Meanwhile, policy differences had arisen within the Lithuanian leadership, and earlier in January 1991 Prunskienė and her Council of Ministers had resigned after the Supreme Council refused to sanction proposed price increases. Gediminas Vagnorius, a member of the Supreme Council, was appointed Prime Minister. The military intervention strengthened popular support for independence. A referendum on this issue took place on 9 February, at which 90.5% of voters expressed support for the re-establishment of an independent Lithuania and for the withdrawal of the USSR army from the republic. In common with five other Soviet republics, Lithuania refused to conduct the all-Union referendum on the future of the USSR, which was held in March. (Voting did take place unofficially in predominantly Russian- and Polish-populated areas of Lithuania, where the majority endorsed the preservation of the USSR.)

A series of attacks by OMON forces on members of the nascent Lithuanian defence force and on the customs posts on the border with Belarus, combined with the seizure of power in Moscow by the State Committee for the State of Emergency (SCSE) in August 1991, led to fears in Lithuania that there would be a renewed attempt to overthrow the Landsbergis administration and reimpose Soviet rule. Soviet military vehicles entered Vilnius, but did not prevent the convening of an emergency session of the Supreme Council, which condemned the SCSE and issued a statement supporting Boris Yeltsin, President of the Russian Federation. As the coup collapsed, the Lithuanian Government ordered the withdrawal of Soviet forces from the republic and banned the LCP. (The successor party to the CPL, the Lithuanian Democratic Labour Party—LDLP, was not banned.) The Government also began to assume effective control of the country's borders. The failed coup prompted the recognition of Lithuanian independence by other states, and on 6 September the USSR State Council recognized the independence of Lithuania and the other Baltic republics (Estonia and Latvia), all three of which were admitted to the UN and the Conference on (now Organization for) Security and Co-operation in Europe (OSCE, see p. 302) later in the month.

During the first half of 1992 there was an increasing polarity within the Supreme Council between Sąjūdis deputies and those of the mainly left-wing opposition parties, most prominently the LDLP, led by Brazauskas. In April 10 members of the Council of Ministers criticized Vagnorius's 'dictatorial' methods, and two ministers subsequently resigned. Vagnorius tendered his resignation as Prime Minister in May, but remained in the post until July, when the legislature approved a motion of 'no confidence' in his leadership. The Seimas (as the Supreme Council had been renamed) appointed Aleksandras Abišala, a close associate of Landsbergis, as Prime Minister; a new Council of Ministers was named shortly afterwards. Meanwhile, the growing division within the legislature had led to a boycott by pro-Sąjūdis deputies, rendering it frequently inquorate. In July, however, the Seimas approved a new electoral law, whereby Lithuania's first post-Soviet legislative elections, scheduled for late 1992, would be held under a mixed system of majority voting (for 71 seats) and proportional representation on the basis of party lists (70 seats).

The LDLP emerged as the leading party in the elections to the Seimas, which took place on 25 October and 15 November 1992, winning a total of 73 of the 141 seats. The defeat of Sąjūdis (which, in alliance with the Citizens' Charter of Lithuania, secured only 30 seats) was largely attributed to popular disenchantment with its management of economic reform. The Christian Democratic Party of Lithuania (CDPL), which was closely aligned with Sąjūdis, won 16 seats. Also on 25 October a referendum approved a new Constitution, which was adopted by the Seimas on 6 November. Pending an election to the new post of President of the Republic, Brazauskas was elected by the Seimas to be its Chairman and acting Head of State. In December 1992 Brazauskas appointed Bronislovas Lubys (hitherto a Deputy Prime Minister) as Prime Minister. Lubys formed a new coalition Council of Ministers, retaining six members of the previous Government and including only three representatives of the LDLP.

The presidential election, on 14 February 1993, was won by Brazauskas, with some 60% of the votes cast. His only rival was Stasys Lozoraitis, Lithuania's ambassador to the USA. Brazauskas subsequently announced his resignation from the LDLP. In March Adolfas Šleževičius replaced Lubys as Prime Minister. In the following month Šleževičius was appointed Chairman of the LDLP. In May a new political organization, the Conservative Party of Lithuania (CP), also known as the Homeland Union (Lithuanian Conservatives), was formed. Mainly comprising former members of Sąjūdis, and chaired by Landsbergis, the CP rapidly established itself as the principal opposition party. (In December Sąjūdis announced its transformation into a 'public movement', a development that further reflected its diminishing influence.)

Persistent allegations of high-level corruption, combined with reports of ideological divisions within the LDLP, as well as several ministerial resignations or dismissals during 1993–94, suggested that the Government was increasingly unstable. The right-wing opposition repeatedly questioned the Government's competence and demanded fresh legislative elections. Increasing popular support for the CP was confirmed at local elections in March 1995, when the party won some 29% of the votes, while its close ally, the CDPL, received 17%; the LDLP took only 20%.

The Minister of the Economy, Aleksandras Vasiliauskas, resigned in October 1995, following the collapse of several small commercial banks and in view of the slow progress achieved in the privatization programme. In November the Government survived its second vote of 'no confidence', initiated by the conservative opposition, which accused the LDLP of economic mismanagement. The banking crisis culminated in December with the suspension of the operations of the country's two largest commercial banks, the Lithuanian Joint-Stock Innovation Bank (LJIB) and Litimpex Bank, owing to insolvency; senior officials of both institutions were arrested on charges of fraud. In January 1996 it was revealed that Šleževičius had withdrawn funds from the LJIB only two days before the bank's suspension; however the Prime Minister refused to submit to opposition demands that he resign. Later in January Romasis Vaitekūnas resigned as Minister of the Interior, following intense public criticism of his handling of the crisis; it was revealed that Vaitekūnas had also withdrawn funds from the LJIB before its closure. Kazys Ratkevičius, the Chairman of the Bank of Lithuania (the central bank) also resigned. Šleževičius initially disregarded a presidential decree that he should leave office, which was upheld by the Seimas in February. He was replaced as Prime Minister by Laurynas Mindaugas Stankevičius, hitherto Minister of Government Reforms and Local Governments. Šleževičius also resigned as Chairman of the LDLP, and was succeeded by Česlovas Juršėnas, the Chairman of the Seimas. In October Šleževičius was charged with abuse of office, in connection with the collapse of the LJIB.

A general election took place in two rounds on 20 October and 10 November 1996. The results confirmed the substantial loss of popular support for the LDLP, which retained only 12 seats in the Seimas. The CP achieved a total of 70 seats, and the right-wing CDPL secured 16. The right-wing Lithuanian Centre Union won 13 seats and the Lithuanian Social Democratic Party (LSDP) 12. Some 53% of eligible voters participated in the first round, and about 40% took part in the second. Following the election, a coalition agreement was signed by the leaders of the CP and the CDPL. Landsbergis was elected Chairman of the Seimas at the assembly's first sitting in late November, and shortly afterwards the Seimas approved the appointment of

Vagnorius as Prime Minister. His Government was dominated by members of the CP, with three representatives of the CDPL and two of the Centre Union. In January 1997 the Minister of Finance, Rolandas Matiliauskas, resigned, amid allegations of financial impropriety. The Prosecutor-General, Valdas Nikitinas, also resigned, following criticism of his handling of investigations into the financial crises of 1995. In November 1997 the Seimas approved new legislation whereby the Government's voucher scheme for privatization was to be superseded by a simplified cash system. A new Fund for State Property and the Restoration of People's Savings was to be responsible for the distribution and investment of revenue derived from the scheme, much of which was to be used to compensate individuals whose savings had depreciated as a result of the recent crises.

Meanwhile, in July 1997 the Seimas had announced that a presidential election would be conducted on 21 December. Brazauskas did not seek re-election, and in the first round of voting none of the seven candidates won the overall majority of votes needed to secure the presidency. In a second round of voting on 4 January 1998 the second-placed candidate after the first round, Valdas Adamkus (a former environmental protection executive, who had been naturalized in the USA), narrowly defeated Artūras Paulauskas (a prominent lawyer and deputy Prosecutor-General, supported by the Lithuanian Liberal Union), with 50.4% of the votes. The new President immediately endorsed the mandate of the incumbent Government, and in March Vagnorius was confirmed as Prime Minister by the Seimas. In April Paulauskas announced the formation of a new, centre-left political party, the New Union (also known as the Social Liberals), which hoped to attract the support of young voters.

A serious conflict of interests between Adamkus and Vagnorius intensified in April 1999, following the President's public criticism of what he regarded as the Government's inadequate attempts to eradicate corruption in the public sector. In mid-April the President urged the coalition parties to consider appointing a new government. Although Vagnorius secured the confidence of the Seimas in a non-binding vote, at the end of the month he announced his intention to resign. In mid-May Adamkus invited the Mayor of Vilnius, Rolandas Paksas (a member of the CP), to form a new government. His Council of Ministers, announced at the beginning of June, was again formed from a coalition led by the CP and the CDPL. In October Paksas indicated that he would not endorse an agreement to sell a one-third stake in the state-owned Mažeikiai NAFTA petroleum refinery to a US oil company, Williams International, under the terms of which Lithuania would be required to provide long-term financing of some 1,400m. litai (more than twice the price paid by the US company), in order to offset the refinery's debts and shortfall in working capital. None the less, the Council of Ministers endorsed the sale, which was strongly supported by Adamkus and the majority of the CP, prompting the resignations of the Ministers of National Economy and of Finance, and, in late October, of Paksas. The Minister of Social Security and Labour, Irena Degutienė (who had assumed the interim premiership following Vagnorius's resignation earlier in the year), was again appointed acting Prime Minister, but she declined an invitation to form a new government. At the end of October Adamkus nominated Andrius Kubilius, the First Deputy Chairman of the Seimas, as Prime Minister. Kubilius' Council of Ministers, named in early November and approved by the legislature one week later, retained largely the same membership as the previous administration. Following the appointment of the new Government, the Lithuanian Centre Union announced that it was to become an opposition party; the party's leader, Romualdas Ozolas, had resigned as a Deputy Chairman of the Seimas after criticizing Landsbergis (who chaired both the CP and the legislature). In mid-November Paksas announced his resignation from the CP; in early December he was elected Chairman of the Lithuanian Liberal Union.

Local elections in mid-March 2000 resulted in considerable successes for parties of the left, most notably the centre-left New Union, which had campaigned against the sale of principal state properties to foreign interests. A lack of support for the CP apparently precipitated a split in the party, as several deputies established a 'moderate' faction in the Seimas, thus depriving the CP-CDPL coalition of an automatic majority in the legislature. In late April the President announced that legislative elections would be held on 8 October. In the following month the country's two largest left-wing parties, the LSDP and the LDLP, agreed to contest the election in alliance. The New Democracy

Party and the Lithuanian Russians' Union subsequently joined the alliance, which was known as the A. Brazauskas Social Democratic Coalition, after the former President, who had been elected Honorary Chairman.

The legislative elections took place as scheduled, with the participation of 28 political parties and alliances; some 56.2% of eligible voters took part. The CP won only nine seats (compared with 70 in 1996). The Social Democratic Coalition obtained the largest representation, with 51 seats. However, the Lithuanian Liberal Union (with 34 seats) and the New Union (with 29), which had formed an informal alliance prior to the elections, subsequently signed a coalition agreement and, with the support of the Lithuanian Centre Union, the Modern Christian-Democratic Union and deputies from single-seat constituencies, secured the 71 seats necessary to obtain a parliamentary majority. On 26 October Rolandas Paksas was approved as Prime Minister, obtaining the support of 79 votes in the Seimas; the leader of the New Union, Artūras Paulauskas, was elected Chairman of the Seimas. The new Council of Ministers was appointed at the end of the month. Jonas Lionginas of the Lithuanian Liberal Union, who had briefly occupied the post of Minister of Finance in 1999, was re-appointed to the Government, and Antanas Valionis of the New Union became Minister of Foreign Affairs. However, in the months following its appointment a number of ministers resigned from the cabinet, including the Minister of the Economy, Eugenijus Maldeikis, who was replaced by Eugenijus Gentvilas. Formalizing their electoral alliance, the LDLP merged with the LSDP at a joint congress held in late January 2001; the LSDP thereby became the single party with the greatest number of seats in the Seimas, and Brazauskas was elected its Chairman. Further political consolidation took place in May, when the CDPL merged with the Christian Democratic Union to form the Lithuanian Christian Democrats.

In mid-June 2001 the six New Union cabinet members resigned their portfolios, following disagreements with the Lithuanian Liberal Union over privatization of the energy sector and economic reform, and criticism of the Prime Minister's style of leadership. Paksas was subsequently unable to form an alternative coalition Government and, despite surviving a vote of 'no confidence', resigned on 20 June; Eugenijus Gentvilas was appointed interim Prime Minister. Hopes that the previous coalition could be resurrected were short-lived; the Government had struggled for much of its brief existence, owing to the two parties' ideological differences, and the New Union sought a new alliance with the LSDP. At the end of the month President Adamkus offered the post of Prime Minister to Brazauskas, who was confirmed in the post on 3 July. The LSDP did not, however, offer the New Union a formal coalition agreement, but instead agreed to an informal accord, which granted the New Union the same six cabinet positions from which it had withdrawn in June (including the foreign affairs portfolio). The Minister of Defence, Linas Linkevičius, formerly of the Lithuanian Liberal Union, was also re-appointed to the cabinet, having declared himself an independent. In September Paksas resigned as Chairman of the Lithuanian Liberal Union, in compliance with demands from within the party; Gentvilas was appointed acting Chairman, and was confirmed in the post in October. In late December Paksas and 10 other deputies left the parliamentary faction of the Lithuanian Liberal Union, owing, in part, to its failure to nominate Paksas as First Deputy Chairman of the Seimas, and amid indications that he would be unable to rely on the party's support were he to stand as a candidate in the presidential election due to take place in 2002. Paksas and the former Lithuanian Liberal Union deputies were formally expelled from the party in January 2002, and in March they founded the rightist Lithuanian Liberal Democratic Party (LLDP), with Paksas as its Chairman.

The results of the first round of voting in the presidential election, held on 22 December 2002, were inconclusive. Adamkus failed to secure an overall majority, obtaining 35.5% of the votes cast, while Paksas was the second-placed candidate, with 19.7% of the votes; parliamentary Chairman Artūras Paulauskas received 8.3%. A second round took place on 5 January 2003, in which Paksas obtained 54.7% of the votes cast, defeating Adamkus, with 45.3%, despite the fact that most major political parties had expressed support for the latter candidate. However, Paksas had pursued a populist campaign, and observers noted that Adamkus appeared to have lost popularity through his implementation of pro-market economic reforms. Paksas was inaugurated as President on 26 February.

On 4 March Brazauskas was re-appointed as Prime Minister; he re-nominated the existing Council of Ministers, with the exception of the Minister of Health Care, Konstantinas Dobrovolskis of the New Union. Dobrovolskis was replaced by Juozas Olekas of the LSDP. Following the presidential election, Paksas resigned as Chairman of the LLDP, and Valentinas Mazuronis was elected as his successor in early March. The Minister of the Interior, Juozas Bernatonis, resigned in late April; he was replaced by Virgilijus Bulovas. In late May Andrius Kubilius was elected as Chairman of the CP, in succession to Vytautas Landsbergis. At the end of the month the Lithuanian Centre Union, the Lithuanian Liberal Union and the Modern Christian-Democratic Union merged to form the Lithuanian Liberal and Centre Union, with Artūras Zuokas as Chairman. In June a faction of the Lithuanian Centre Union that did not support the merger founded the National Centre Party, and elected Romualdas Ozolas as its Chairman. In November the CP absorbed the Lithuanian Rightist Union, and in February 2004 it merged with the Lithuanian Union of Political Prisoners and Deportees. The resulting party was renamed the Homeland Union—Lithuanian Conservatives, Political Prisoners and Deportees and Christian Democrats (HU).

Meanwhile, following the nomination by President Paksas of a new Director-General of the State Security Department, in late October 2003 a classified departmental report was disclosed, which claimed to provide evidence of links between the presidential adviser on national security, Remigijus Acas, and Yurii Borisov, an ethnic Russian with purported connections with organized crime groups, who had contributed significant funds to Paksas' presidential election campaign. It was revealed that in April Paksas had signed a presidential decree permitting Borisov to hold dual citizenship, despite warnings from the State Security Department that he was suspected of involvement in the illegal trading of weapons. In early November an emergency session of the Seimas established a special parliamentary commission to investigate Paksas' alleged links with Russian organized crime and the associated threat to national security, and the Prosecutor-General launched a criminal investigation into Borisov. Paksas subsequently dismissed a number of his senior advisers, but refused to appear before the commission. In early December the Seimas approved the commission's conclusion that the President's conduct had jeopardized national security, and the following day both Brazauskas and Paulauskas appealed for the President's resignation. On 18 December the Seimas approved a draft resolution to initiate impeachment proceedings against Paksas, and a 12-member investigative commission was subsequently established to consider the charges.

On 18 February 2004 the investigative commission endorsed six charges, which were to form the basis for the impeachment of the President: that Paksas represented a threat to national security; that he had failed to protect classified information; that he had attempted illegally to influence the operations of private companies; that he was unable to reconcile his public and private interests; that he had hindered the operations of state institutions; and that he had failed to prevent his advisers from abusing their positions. The following day the Seimas voted to initiate formal impeachment proceedings and, in the mean time, agreed to seek a ruling from the Constitutional Court as to whether the charges technically constituted a breach of the Constitution. Paksas continued to deny the charges against him, and in late February he demanded that the Seimas initiate impeachment proceedings against the parliamentary Chairman, Artūras Paulauskas, whom he accused of the unauthorized disclosure of the confidential State Security Department report that had been made public in October 2003 (the request was rejected, on the grounds that the Constitution provided only for the impeachment of deputies, and not of the parliamentary Chairman). On 24 March Paksas unexpectedly announced the nomination of Borisov as a presidential adviser, but he subsequently retracted the nomination, alleging that it had been prompted by a blackmail attempt. In response to this development, on the following day the Seimas adopted a resolution urging Paksas to resign; Borisov was placed under house arrest for having violated a pledge to avoid contact with the President. At the end of March the Constitutional Court ruled that the President had severely violated the Constitution by granting Borisov dual citizenship in exchange for financial support; failing to protect state secrets; and using his presidential office illegally to influence the actions of a company's share-holders. The ruling was followed by a parliamentary vote

on Paksas' impeachment, which took place on 6 April. In the event, Paksas was removed from office, after the necessary three-fifths' majority in the Seimas narrowly supported impeachment on the three charges confirmed by the Constitutional Court. Paulauskas immediately assumed the presidency, in an acting capacity, pending a presidential election, and subsequently suspended his membership of the New Union, in compliance with the Constitution. The presidential election was scheduled for 13 June.

Whereas Lithuania's Baltic neighbours, Estonia and Latvia, have large national minorities, ethnic Lithuanians constitute the overwhelming majority of the republic's population: in January 1997 ethnic Lithuanians represented some 81% of the total, while the two largest minority groups, Russians and Poles, represented 8% and 7%, respectively, of the total population. As a result, the requirements for naturalization of non-ethnic Lithuanians have been less stringent than in the neighbouring Baltic republics, where national identity has been perceived in some quarters as being under threat. Under new citizenship laws adopted in late 1989, all residents, regardless of ethnic origin, were eligible to apply for naturalization; by early 1993 more than 90% of the country's non-ethnic-Lithuanian residents had been granted citizenship. None the less, the Lithuanian population declined by some 184,000 between 1989 and 2001. In an attempt to counter emigration (in particular to the USA), in September 2002 the Seimas approved legislation permitting Lithuanian citizens to hold dual citizenship, thereby facilitating the subsequent return of Lithuanian nationals to the country.

Mainly because of its citizenship laws, Lithuania's relations with Russia have been less strained than those of Estonia and Latvia. Negotiations for the withdrawal of the estimated 38,000 former Soviet troops remaining in Lithuania, which were held between the Lithuanian and Russian Governments during 1992, resulted, in September, in an agreement by Russia to repatriate all the troops by the end of August 1993. The final troops left, as scheduled, on 31 August, whereupon full state sovereignty was perceived as having been restored in Lithuania.

In November 1993 Lithuania and Russia signed several agreements, including an accord on most-favoured nation status in bilateral trade, and another concerning the transportation, via Lithuania, of Russian military equipment and troops from the Russian exclave of Kaliningrad Oblast. However, there was disagreement between the two countries during 1994, following Lithuania's decision to introduce new regulations governing military transits. A compromise appeared to have been reached in January 1995, when the Lithuanian Government extended until December the existing procedure for military transits; Russia duly indicated that the agreement on bilateral trade would enter into force immediately. In October 1997 President Brazauskas undertook the first official visit to Russia by a Baltic head of state since the disintegration of the former USSR. During the visit a state border delimitation treaty was signed by both sides, and bilateral co-operation agreements on joint economic zones, and on the Baltic continental shelf, were also concluded. The border treaty was ratified by the Seimas in October 1999, but was not ratified by the Russian side until May 2003. Lithuania expressed support for an agreement between the European Union (EU, see p. 208) and Russia in late 2002, which proposed simplified visa arrangements for Russian citizens traversing Lithuania to reach the exclave of Kaliningrad. New transit arrangements were implemented in Lithuania at the beginning of February 2003. However, tensions between the two countries emerged in late February 2004, when Lithuania expelled three Russian diplomats suspected of espionage; Russia reciprocated by expelling three diplomatic personnel from the Lithuanian embassy in Moscow.

Lithuania's relations with neighbouring Poland were largely concerned with the status of the Polish minority in Lithuania (and likewise with the ethnic Lithuanian population in Poland). Following the failed coup attempt of August 1991 in Moscow, leaders of councils in Polish-populated regions of Lithuania were dismissed, in response to their alleged support for the coup, and direct rule was introduced. However, in January 1992 Lithuania and Poland signed a 'Declaration on Friendly Relations and Neighbourly Co-operation', which guaranteed the rights of the respective ethnic minorities and also recognized the existing border between the two countries. A full treaty of friendship and co-operation was signed by the respective Heads of State in April 1994. The treaty, notably, did not include a condemnatory reference to Poland's occupation of the region of Vilnius in 1920–39 (a provision that had originally been demanded by Lithuania). An agreement on free trade was signed by the two countries in June 1996, and during 1997 the Lithuanian and Polish Governments established regular forums for inter-presidential and inter-parliamentary discussion.

Among the former Soviet republics, Lithuania enjoys closest relations with Estonia and Latvia, with which it shares strong cultural and historical ties. Relations between the three states are co-ordinated through the consultative inter-parliamentary Baltic Assembly, the Council of Baltic Sea States (see p. 188) and the Baltic Council (see p. 369). A series of tripartite meetings of the Baltic states during 1997 resulted in agreements to further liberalize trade, to combat illegal activity and to renew efforts to gain entry to the North Atlantic Treaty Organization (NATO, see p. 289). In January 1998 the Presidents of the three states met President Bill Clinton of the USA in Washington, DC, and all parties signed a Charter of Partnership, described as a framework for the development of closer political and economic ties. At a meeting in Sigulda, Latvia, in July, the three countries' premiers agreed further to harmonize their respective customs procedures and labour movement regulations. Lithuania's relations with Latvia were, none the less, strained as a result of disagreements over the demarcation of the countries' maritime border. In October 1995 the Lithuanian Government protested at Latvia's signature of a preliminary agreement with two foreign petroleum companies to explore oilfields in the disputed waters. Tension increased following the ratification of the agreement by the Latvian parliament in October 1996, although in July 1999 the two countries signed an agreement on the Delimitation of the Territorial Sea, Exclusive Economic Zone and Continental Shelf in the Baltic Sea. However, protests from the Latvian fishing industry prevented the agreement from being ratified by the Latvian parliament and, therefore, Lithuania's ratification was invalidated. In December 2000 a protocol was signed for the re-demarcation of the land border between the two countries.

Lithuania has pursued close co-operation with, and eventual integration into, the political, economic and defence systems of western Europe, notably seeking full membership of the EU. A number of political and economic agreements concluded between the EU and the Baltic states in 1995, with the aim of facilitating their membership, came into effect on 1 February 1998. In December 1999 a summit meeting of EU Heads of State and Government in Helsinki, Finland, endorsed proposals to begin accession talks with a number of countries, including Lithuania; formal negotiations commenced in February 2000. As a concession to achieve EU membership, the Government approved a draft national energy strategy in September 1999, which provided for the decommissioning of the first unit of the Ignalina nuclear power plant by 2005. In June 2002 Lithuania agreed to decommision the plant's remaining unit in 2009, in return for a significant contribution from the EU towards the cost of the endeavour. In December 2002 Lithuania, and nine other countries, were formally invited to join the EU on 1 May 2004; at a national referendum, held on 10–11 May 2003, over 91.1% of participants voted in favour of membership. Meanwhile, in November 2002 Lithuania was one of seven countries invited to join NATO in 2004. In common with Estonia and Latvia, Lithuania regarded membership of the Alliance as the principal guarantee of the country's security, and it became a full member on 29 March 2004.

Government

Under the terms of the Constitution that was approved in a national referendum on 25 October 1992, supreme legislative authority resides with the Seimas (Parliament), which has 141 members, elected by universal adult suffrage for a four-year term. (In total, 71 deputies are directly elected by majority vote, with the rest being selected from party lists, on the basis of proportional representation.) The President of the Republic (who is Head of State) is elected by direct popular vote for a period of five years (and a maximum of two consecutive terms). Executive power is vested in the Council of Ministers. This is headed by the Prime Minister, who is appointed by the President with the approval of the Seimas. For administrative purposes, Lithuania is divided into 10 counties.

Defence

Until independence Lithuania had no armed forces separate from those of the USSR. The Department of State Defence (established in April 1990) was reorganized as the Ministry of Defence in October 1991. In 1998 the Baltic states agreed to establish a joint airspace observation system (BALTNET), a defence college and a peace-keeping battalion (BALTBAT). A Baltic naval unit (BALTRON) was established in mid-1998. In August 2003 Lithuania's active armed forces totalled an estimated 12,700 (including 1,000 centrally controlled personnel and a 1,950-strong Voluntary National Defence Force): army 7,950 (including 3,027 conscripts), navy 650 (including 300 conscripts) and air force 1,150. There was also a paramilitary of 14,600, including a border guard of 5,000. Military service is compulsory and lasts for 12 months. Defence expenditure in 2002 amounted to some 906m. litai. The budget for 2003 allocated 1,100m. litai to defence. Lithuania became a full member of the North Atlantic Treaty Organization (NATO, see p. 289) on 29 March 2004. In early April BALTNET was formally absorbed into NATO's Integrated Air Defence System.

Economic Affairs

In 2002, according to estimates by the World Bank, Lithuania's gross national income (GNI), measured at average 2000–02 prices, was US $12,715m., equivalent to $3,660 per head (or $9,880 per head on an international purchasing-power parity basis). During 1990–2002 the population decreased by an annual average of 0.5%, while gross domestic product (GDP) per head declined, in real terms, by an average of 1.0% per year. Overall GDP decreased, in real terms, by an average of 1.5% annually. However, real GDP increased by 6.3% in 2001 and by 6.8% in 2002.

Agriculture (including hunting, forestry and fishing) contributed 7.2% of GDP in 2002, when it engaged 17.8% of the employed population. The principal crops are cereals, sugar beet, potatoes and vegetables. In 1991 legislation was adopted permitting the restitution of land to its former owners, and the privatization of state-owned farms and reorganization of collective farms was initiated. By the mid-1990s almost 40% of arable land was privately cultivated. Legislation approved in January 2003 authorized the sale of agricultural land to foreign owners, although its implementation was to be subject to a seven-year transition period. Real agricultural GDP decreased, in real terms, by an annual average of 1.5% during 1990–2001. The GDP of the sector decreased by 6.9% in 2001, but increased by 3.0% in 2002.

Industry (including mining, manufacturing, construction and power) contributed 34.7% of GDP in 2002, when the sector engaged 27.5% of the employed population. According to World Bank estimates, industrial GDP declined by an annual average of 7.0%, in real terms, during 1990–2001; however, the GDP of the sector increased by 16.4% in 2001 and by 4.0% in 2002.

In 2001 mining and quarrying contributed 0.7% of GDP, and it provided just 0.3% of employment in 2002. Lithuania has significant reserves of peat and materials used in construction (limestone, clay, dolomite, chalk, and sand and gravel), as well as small deposits of petroleum and natural gas. Real mining GDP increased by 18.9% in 2000 and by 30.6% in 2001. In terms of production, the GDP of the sector increased by 13.0% in 2003, according to preliminary official data.

The manufacturing sector provided 23.1% of GDP in 2002, when it engaged 18.5% of the employed labour force. Based on the value of output, the principal branches of manufacturing in 1996 were food products (particularly dairy products—accounting for 9.5% of the total), refined petroleum products, textiles and clothing, and chemicals. The World Bank estimated that manufacturing GDP declined, in real terms, by an annual average of 7.6% during 1990–2001. However, sectoral GDP increased by 4.0% in 2002 and, according to preliminary official figures, manufacturing GDP increased by 14.1% in 2003, in terms of production.

In 2000 nuclear power accounted for 75.7% of gross electricity production, followed by natural gas, which accounted for 15.3%. Lithuania has substantial petroleum-refining and electricity-generating capacities, which enable it to export refined petroleum products and electricity. In 1999 Lithuania exported an estimated 55.9% of its gross electricity production. In 2003 imports of mineral products accounted for 18.2% of the total value of merchandise imports, according to provisional figures.

The services sector contributed 58.0% of GDP in 2002, when it provided 54.7% of total employment. The Baltic port of Klaipėda is a significant entrepôt for regional trade. The GDP of the services sector decreased, in real terms, by an annual average of 0.2% in 1990–2001. However, real services GDP increased by 2.6% in 2001 and by 5.9% in 2002.

In 2002 Lithuania recorded a visible trade deficit of US $1,314.9m., and there was a deficit of $720.7m. on the current account of the balance of payments. In 2003 the principal source of imports was Russia (accounting for 22.2% of the total, according to preliminary figures); other major sources were Germany and Poland. Switzerland was the main market for exports in that year (accounting for an estimated 11.7% of the total, according to preliminary figures). Other principal markets were Russia, Germany, Latvia, the United Kingdom and France. According to preliminary data, in 2003 the principal exports were mineral products (representing an estimated 19.7% of total exports), followed by vehicles and transportation equipment (15.2%), textiles (13.6%), machinery and electrical equipment (11.1%), chemical products (6.6%) and miscellaneous manufactured articles (6.1%). The principal imports were machinery and electrical equipment (representing an estimated 18.8% of total imports), mineral products (18.2%), vehicles and transportation equipment (15.7%), chemical products (8.6%), textiles (7.5%), base metals (6.0%), and plastics and rubber (5.3%).

In 2001, according to IMF estimates, there was a budgetary deficit of 171.8m. litai (equivalent to 0.4% of GDP). Lithuania's total external debt was US $5,248m. at the end of 2001, of which $2,359m. was long-term public debt. In that year the cost of debt-servicing was equivalent to 31.0% of the value of exports of goods and services. Annual inflation averaged 62.1% in 1991–2002. The average annual rate of inflation declined from 1,021% in 1991 to 24.6% by 1996. In 2002 the rate of inflation was 0.3%, and deflation of 1.4% was recorded in 2003. The average rate of unemployment was 12.4% in 2003, when 203,900 people were officially registered as unemployed.

Lithuania is a member, as a 'Country of Operations', of the European Bank for Reconstruction and Development (EBRD, see p. 203), as well as of the IMF and the World Bank. An agreement on a free-trade area between Lithuania, Latvia and Estonia entered into force in April 1994. In December 2000 Lithuania became a member of the World Trade Organization (WTO, see p. 343). Lithuania became an associate member of the European Union (EU, see p. 208) in June 1995. In February 2000 Lithuania officially commenced the negotiation process towards full membership, and it acceded on 1 May 2004.

By the mid-1990s the Government's stabilization programme had achieved modest success: the development of the private sector was well advanced, most prices had been liberalized and progress had been achieved in restructuring the financial sector. However, the economy contracted in 1999, largely owing to the economic crisis in Russia in 1998. Following the controversial sale of part of the Government's stake in the Mažeikiai NAFTA petroleum refinery in late 1999 (see Recent History), other major privatizations were initiated from 2000, and much was achieved in the way of recovery in that year. The last remaining state-owned bank was privatized in 2002, and energy-sector privatization was under way. The initial phase of the privatization of the gas utility, Lietuvos Dujos, was completed in 2002, and further shares were divested in early 2004; the privatization of a major electricity-distribution company, Vakaru skirstomieji tinklai, had also been finalized by early 2004. Meanwhile, in an effort to facilitate increased integration with EU economies and further reorientate foreign trade, from February 2002 the national currency's fixed rate of exchange was linked to the common European currency, the euro, instead of the US dollar, resulting in increased business confidence and investment and lower import costs. In June of that year formal agreement had been reached with the EU on the closure of the Ignalina nuclear power plant; the first of the plant's reactors was to be decom-

missioned in 2005 and the second in 2009, in return for substantial financing from the EU to compensate for the costs incurred. Reforms were implemented in 2002, and there were changes to taxation legislation and the pensions system, as well as new regulations to combat money 'laundering' (the processing of illicitly obtained funds into legitimate holdings), and the introduction of a new labour code at the beginning of 2003. Macroeconomic performance was better than anticipated in 2002–03, stimulated by improved domestic demand, and came despite the deceleration in economic growth recorded throughout much of Europe. In 2003 GDP increased by 8.9%, according to preliminary official figures (Lithuania's highest rate of growth since independence), and gentle deflation was recorded (assisted by increased local competition and the depreciation of the dollar against the euro). The country's anticipated fiscal deficit for 2004, equivalent to some 3.3% of GDP (just over the 3% limit set by the EU), was based on the need for increased expenditure in order to meet EU accession requirements. Lithuania planned to adopt the euro in 2007.

Education

Education, beginning at seven years of age, is free and compulsory until the age of 16. There are three principal levels of education: comprehensive (from seven to 16 years of age), vocational schools and schools of further education (16–18) and higher. There are three principal types of comprehensive school: primary (Grades 1–4), basic (Grades 5–9) and secondary (Grades 10–12). From January 2003 a uniform tuition fee was to be introduced for students of higher education, although there were to be exemptions for the highest achievers. There are three main types of comprehensive school: primary, basic and secondary. In 2001/02 95.4% of the relevant age-group was enrolled in primary education, while enrolment in secondary education was equivalent to 94.1%. In the 2002/03 academic year 594,300 students were enrolled in 2,172 comprehensive schools. The majority of pupils continue their education after the age of 16 years. In 2002/03 there were 82 vocational schools, 51 schools of higher education and 19 universities. Total enrolment at universities was 119,600 in that year. In 1991 the first private schools were opened; by 1999 there were 38 private schools or colleges and one private university. Lithuanian is the main language of instruction, although in 1999/2000 7.7% of students at comprehensive schools were taught in Russian and 3.8% were taught in Polish. The state budget for 2001 allocated 925.5m. litai (7.3% of total expenditure) to education.

Public Holidays

2004: 1 January (New Year's Day), 16 February (Day of the Restoration of the Lithuanian State), 11 March (Day of the Re-establishment of Independence), 12 April (Easter Monday), 1 May (Mothers' Day), 6 July (Anniversary of the Coronation of Grand Duke Mindaugas of Lithuania), 15 August (Assumption), 1 November (All Saints' Day), 25–26 December (Christmas).

2005: 1 January (New Year's Day), 16 February (Day of the Restoration of the Lithuanian State), 11 March (Day of the Re-establishment of Independence), 28 March (Easter Monday), 1 May (Mothers' Day), 6 July (Anniversary of the Coronation of Grand Duke Mindaugas of Lithuania), 15 August (Assumption), 1 November (All Saints' Day), 25–26 December (Christmas).

Weights and Measures

The metric system is in force.

Statistical Survey

Source (unless otherwise indicated): Department of Statistics to the Government of Lithuania (Statistics Lithuania), Gedimino pr. 29, Vilnius 2600; tel. (523) 64822; fax (523) 64845; e-mail statistika@mail.std.lt; internet www.std.lt.

Area and Population

AREA, POPULATION AND DENSITY

Area (sq km).	65,300*
Population (census results)	
12 January 1989†	3,674,802
6 April 2001	
Males	1,629,148
Females.	1,854,824
Total	3,483,972
Population (official estimates at 1 January)	
2001	3,486,998
2002	3,475,586
2003	3,462,553
Density (per sq km) at 1 January 2003	53.0

* 25,212 sq miles.
† Figure refers to the *de jure* population. The *de facto* total was 3,689,779.
‡ Provisional figure, rounded.

POPULATION BY ETHNIC GROUP
(permanent inhabitants at 2001 census)*

	'000	%
Lithuanian	2,907.3	83.5
Polish .	235.0	6.7
Russian .	219.8	6.3
Belarusian	42.9	1.2
Total (incl. others) .	3,484.0	100.0

* Figures are provisional.

ADMINISTRATIVE DIVISIONS
(at 1 January 2003)

County	Area (sq km)	Population	Density (per sq km)
Alytus .	5,425	186,340	34.3
Kaunas	8,089	696,143	86.1
Klaipėda	5,209	383,945	73.7
Marijampolė	4,463	187,607	42.0
Panevėžys.	7,881	297,521	37.8
Šiauliai	8,540	367,166	43.0
Tauragė	4,411	133,473	30.3
Telšiai .	4,350	179,137	41.2
Utena .	7,201	183,131	25.4
Vilnius .	9,731	848,090	87.2
Total .	65,300	3,462,553	53.0

PRINCIPAL TOWNS
(population at 2001 census)

Vilnius (capital) . .	542,287	Šiauliai . . .	133,883
Kaunas . . .	378,943	Panevėžys. . . .	119,749
Klaipėda	192,954	Alytus	71,491

2002 (official estimate at 1 January): Vilnius 553,373.

BIRTHS, MARRIAGES AND DEATHS

	Registered live births		Registered marriages		Registered deaths	
	Number	Rate (per 1,000)	Number	Rate (per 1,000)	Number	Rate (per 1,000)
1996 . .	39,066	10.8	20,433	5.7	42,896	11.9
1997 . .	37,812	10.6	18,796	5.3	41,143	11.5
1998 . .	37,019	10.4	18,486	5.2	40,757	11.5
1999 . .	36,415	10.3	17,868	5.1	40,003	11.3
2000 . .	34,149	9.8	16,906	4.8	38,919	11.1
2001 . .	31,546	9.1	15,764	4.5	40,399	11.6
2002 . .	30,014	8.6	16,151	4.7	41,072	11.8
2003* . .	30,516	8.8	16,988	4.9	41,028	11.9

* Provisional figures.

Expectation of life (WHO estimates, years at birth): 71.9 (males 66.2; females 77.6) in 2002 (Source: WHO, *World Health Report*).

IMMIGRATION AND EMIGRATION
('000 persons)

	2000	2001	2002
Immigrants	1.5	4.7	5.1
Emigrants	2.6	7.3	7.1

EMPLOYMENT
(annual averages, '000 persons)*

	2000	2001	2002
Agriculture, hunting and forestry .	258.1	231.3	249.8
Fishing	3.5	2.6	0.8
Mining and quarrying . . .	3.1	2.8	4.3
Manufacturing . . .	254.0	243.2	260.6
Electricity, gas and water . . .	33.7	35.1	28.4
Construction . . .	83.7	84.8	93.2
Wholesale and retail trade; repair of motor vehicles, motorcycles and personal and household goods . . .	200.4	205.7	211.2
Hotels and restaurants . . .	27.1	25.8	28.0
Transport, storage and communications	90.5	86.0	87.4
Financial intermediation . . .	14.5	10.9	14.0
Real estate, renting and business activities . . .	43.2	41.1	54.9
Public administration and defence; compulsory social security . .	73.7	71.9	81.3
Education	161.0	155.0	138.9
Health and social work . . .	96.5	99.6	94.6
Other community, social and personal service activities . .	53.6	51.9	53.8
Other activities not adequately defined	1.4	4.2	4.9
Total	1,397.8	1,351.8	1,405.9
Unemployed	273.7	284.0	224.4
Total labour force	1,671.5	1,635.8	1,630.3
Males	845.0	830.1	828.9
Females	826.5	805.7	801.4

* Official estimates based on results of 2001 census.

Health and Welfare

KEY INDICATORS

Total fertility rate (children per woman, 2002).	1.3
Under-5 mortality rate (per 1,000 live births, 2001)	9
HIV/AIDS (% of persons aged 15–49, 2001).	0.07
Physicians (per 1,000 head, 1998)	3.95
Hospital beds (per 1,000 head, 2000)	10.1
Health expenditure (2001): US $ per head (PPP)	478
Health expenditure (2001): % of GDP	6.0
Health expenditure (2001): public (% of total)	70.5
Human Development Index (2001): ranking	45
Human Development Index (2001): value	0.824

For sources and definitions, see explanatory note on p. vi.

Agriculture

PRINCIPAL CROPS
('000 metric tons)

	2000	2001	2002
Wheat	1,237.6	1,076.3	1,217.6
Barley	859.6	776.2	871.1
Rye	311.4	231.1	170.2
Oats	82.9	84.3	97.5
Buckwheat	14.8	12.7	10.6
Triticale (wheat-rye hybrid)	130.9	143.8	145.3
Other cereals	20.6	19.8	18.5
Potatoes	1,791.6	1,054.4	1,531.3
Sugar beet	881.6	880.4	1,052.4
Dry peas	49.7	30.0	35.9*
Other pulses*	23.5	22.2	27.0
Rapeseed	81.0	64.8	105.6
Cabbages	125.7	121.3	112.0*
Tomatoes	5.1	4.4	4.0*
Cucumbers and gherkins	12.0	8.0	10.0*
Dry onions	20.3	22.7	20.0*
Carrots	65.3	61.6	54.5*
Green peas	6.0	5.0	5.0*
Other vegetables*	98.3	99.0	84.5
Apples	98.6	151.1	145.0†
Pears	3.0	4.0	4.0†

* Unofficial figure(s).
† FAO estimate.
Source: FAO.

LIVESTOCK
('000 head at 1 January)

	2000	2001	2002
Horses	75	68	64
Cattle	898	748	752
Pigs	936	868	1,011
Sheep	14	12	12
Goats	25	23	24
Chickens	6,372	5,576	6,576
Turkeys	400*	400*	434
Rabbits	85	82	74

* FAO estimate.
Source: FAO.

LIVESTOCK PRODUCTS
('000 metric tons, unless otherwise indicated)

	2000	2001	2002
Beef and veal	75.4	63.9	44.7
Pig meat	84.5	91.6	94.9
Poultry meat	25.1	29.7	32.8
Cows' milk	1,724.7	1,729.8	1,770.9
Cheese	48.3	57.6	57.5*
Butter	19.3	18.2	17.4
Eggs	38.7	41.6	44.7
Honey	0.8	0.8	1.3
Cattle hides (fresh)*	10.7	8.1	6.3

* FAO estimate(s).
Source: FAO.

Forestry

ROUNDWOOD REMOVALS
('000 cubic metres, excl. bark)

	2000	2001	2002
Sawlogs, veneer logs and logs for sleepers	2,900	2,700	3,220
Pulpwood	1,100	1,490	1,620
Other industrial wood	50	30	20
Fuel wood	1,450	1,480	1,440
Total	5,500	5,700	6,300

Source: FAO.

SAWNWOOD PRODUCTION
('000 cubic metres, incl. railway sleepers)

	2000	2001	2002
Coniferous (softwood)	1,000	900	900*
Broadleaved (hardwood)*	300	300	300
Total	1,300	1,200	1,200*

* FAO estimate(s).
Source: FAO.

Fishing

(metric tons, live weight)

	1999	2000	2001
Capture	72,962	78,987	151,931
Atlantic cod	4,371	4,721	3,852
Atlantic redfishes	3,884	6,687	20,182
Jack and horse mackerels	20,657	25,464	15,226
Atlantic herring	1,313	1,198	1,639
Sardinellas	8,680	6,324	4,167
European sprat	3,117	1,682	3,135
European anchovy	13,774	16,137	8,441
Chub mackerel	2,105	3,871	2,798
Atlantic mackerel	4,936	2,085	1,949
Northern prawn	4,167	6,376	5,413
Aquaculture	1,650	1,996	2,001
Common carp	1,650	1,921	1,957
Total catch	74,612	80,983	153,932

Source: FAO, *Yearbook of Fishery Statistics*.

Mining

('000 metric tons, unless otherwise indicated)

	2000	2001	2002
Crude petroleum	232	316	471
Dolomite ('000 cubic metres)	735	524	384
Limestone	1,060	850	894
Clay ('000 cubic metres)	247	177	171
Peat	380	259	259

Industry

SELECTED PRODUCTS
('000 metric tons, unless otherwise indicated)

	2000	2001	2002
Sausages and smoked meat products	55.8	55.2	52.7
Flour	204.9	211.5	213.9
Mayonnaise	8.6	10.1	10.7
Refined sugar	126.6	108.7	138.3
Beer ('000 hectolitres)	210.5	219.3	268.3
Wine ('000 hectolitres)	403	429	493
Cigarettes (million)	7,200	n.a.	n.a.
Cotton fabrics (million sq m)	55.1	43.5	42.6
Linen fabrics (million sq m)	17.8	15.3	15.0
Fabrics of man-made fibres	17.7	10.1	16.1
Footwear—excl. rubber and plastic ('000 pairs)*	700	900	900
Rubber and plastic footwear ('000 pairs)*	400	400	200
Plywood ('000 cubic metres)	21.2	27.6	27.6
Particle board ('000 cubic metres)	194.1	236.5	230.9
Paper	12.3	13.9	10.4
Paperboard	41.0	54.3	67.3
Motor spirit (petrol)	4,659	6,544	6,448
Sulphuric acid	809	465	874
Mineral and chemical fertilizers	924	832	1,161
Nitrogenous fertilizers	595	611	737
Cement	570	500*	600*
Cast iron	23.2	24.6	17.5
Television receivers ('000)	207.2	143.2	348.3
Refrigerators and freezers ('000)	216.3	320.4	399.0
Bicycles ('000)	254	323	344
Electric energy (million kWh)*	11,400	14,300	17,700

* Figures are rounded.

Finance

CURRENCY AND EXCHANGE RATES

Monetary Units
100 centas = 1 litas (plural: litai).

Sterling, Dollar and Euro Equivalents (31 December 2003)
£1 sterling = 4.930 litai;
US $1 = 2.762 litai;
€1 = 3.489 litai;
100 litai = £20.29 = $36.20 = €28.67.

Note: In June 1993 Lithuania reintroduced its national currency, the litas, replacing a temporary coupon currency, the talonas, at a conversion rate of 1 litas = 100 talonai. The talonas had been introduced in May 1992, initially circulating alongside (and at par with) the Russian (formerly Soviet) rouble. An official mid-point exchange rate of US $1 = 4.00 litai was in operation from 1 April 1994 until 1 February 2002. From 2 February 2002 the litas was linked to the euro, with the exchange rate set at €1 = 3.4528 litai.

BUDGET
(million litai)*

Revenue†	1999	2000	2001
Tax revenue	10,452.0	10,316.8	10,697.4
Taxes on income, profits and capital gains	1,398.8	1,334.7	1,273.0
Corporate	360.8	311.7	259.2
Individual	1,038.0	1,023.0	1,013.8
Social security contributions	3,405.5	3,597.7	3,678.0
Domestic taxes on goods and services	5,433.5	5,239.5	5,596.9
Excises	1,643.4	1,459.8	1,643.0
General sales, turnover or value-added taxes	3,741.9	3,698.2	3,831.4
Taxes on international trade	192.6	142.9	133.8
Other current revenue	585.6	775.8	1,032.6
Administrative fees and charges, non-industrial and incidental sales	207.9	188.2	537.7
Capital revenue	13.4	42.7	29.2
Total	11,051.0	11,135.3	11,759.2

Expenditure‡	1999	2000	2001
General public services	530.9	519.2	599.6
Defence	440.4	589.3	755.4
Public order and safety	871.6	829.7	833.0
Education	749.3	724.0	925.5
Health	1,945.0	1,956.6	2,028.9
Social security and welfare	4,519.8	4,574.6	4,480.1
Recreational, cultural and religious affairs and services	272.4	232.7	233.4
Economic affairs and services	1,540.3	1,577.6	1,527.2
Agriculture, forestry, fishing and hunting	561.1	731.6	587.7
Transport and communications	833.5	720.6	680.6
Other purposes	2,386.1	1,443.5	1,233.7
Interest payments	626.7	771.0	741.7
Total	13,260.8	12,447.3	12,616.8
Current	11,120.9	11,533.6	11,499.5
Capital	2,139.9	913.7	1,117.3

* Figures refer to the consolidated accounts of the central Government, comprising the operations of the central budget, the Guarantee Fund and Fund for Financial Support to Bankrupted Enterprises, Privatization Funds, the Road Fund, Social Security Funds and others.
† Excluding grants received (million litai): 239.9 in 2001.
‡ Excluding lending minus repayments (million litai): 796.8 in 1999; −727.3 in 2000; −445.9 in 2001.

Source: IMF, *Government Finance Statistics Yearbook.*

INTERNATIONAL RESERVES
(US $ million at 31 December)

	2000	2001	2002
Gold*	47.10	51.47	63.82
IMF special drawing rights	1.32	18.43	53.44
Reserve position in IMF	0.02	0.02	0.02
Foreign exchange	1,310.21	1,599.27	2,295.86
Total	1,358.65	1,669.19	2,413.14

* National valuation.
Source: IMF, *International Financial Statistics.*

MONEY SUPPLY
(million litai at 31 December)

	2000	2001	2002
Currency outside banks	2,658.3	2,919.9	3,756.4
Demand deposits at banking institutions	3,002.6	3,808.0	4,553.0
Total money (incl. others)	5,672.6	6,744.5	8,329.2

Source: IMF, *International Financial Statistics.*

COST OF LIVING
(Consumer Price Index; base: 1993 = 100)

	1999	2000	2001
Food (incl. beverages)	17,997.5	17,562.6	18,193.3
Fuel and light	783.6	914.8	933.0
Clothing	343.7	341.0	326.7
Rent	682.1	698.0	714.8
All items (incl. others)	19,750.8	19,937.4	20,195.9

Source: ILO.

All items (base: 2001 = 100): 100.3 in 2002; 98.8 in 2003.

NATIONAL ACCOUNTS
(million litai at current prices)

Expenditure on the Gross Domestic Product

	1999	2000	2001
Final consumption expenditure	37,146.7	38,566.7	40,124.1
Households	27,441.8	28,580.7	30,407.3
Non-profit institutions serving households	71.2	132.3	119.2
General government	9,633.8	9,853.7	9,597.6
Gross capital formation	9,858.2	9,025.9	9,979.8
Gross fixed capital formation	9,614.2	8,565.3	9,784.6
Changes in inventories	229.1	448.9	186.0
Acquisitions, *less* disposals, of valuables	14.9	11.7	9.2
Total domestic expenditure	47,004.9	47,592.6	50,103.9
Exports of goods and services	16,952.9	20,436.5	24,182.3
Less Imports of goods and services	21,349.5	23,331.2	26,788.6
GDP in market prices	42,608.3	44,697.9	47,497.6
GDP at constant 2000 prices	42,608.3	44,697.9	47,497.6

Gross Domestic Product by Economic Activity

	1999	2000	2001
Agriculture, hunting and forestry	3,191.8	3,174.3	3,039.8
Fishing	22.9	26.7	28.8
Mining and quarrying	178.8	279.0	317.6
Manufacturing	6,985.1	7,981.6	8,767.7
Electricity, gas and water supply	1,660.1	1,540.9	1,786.1
Construction	2,949.4	2,429.9	2,597.0
Wholesale and retail trade	6,065.9	6,685.0	7,478.3
Hotels and restaurants	652.1	619.0	676.7
Transport, storage and communications	4,003.7	5,013.1	5,384.6
Financial intermediation	868.2	881.0	987.5
Real estate, renting and business activities	3,186.4	3,403.7	3,554.6
Public administration and defence	2,678.2	2,786.9	2,474.6
Education	2,655.2	2,595.9	2,722.6
Health and social work	1,542.6	1,466.3	1,464.7
Other community, social and personal service activities	1,237.7	1,302.8	1,404.1
Private households with employed persons	31.0	37.6	43.6
Sub-total	37,909.3	40,223.8	42,728.3
Less Financial intermediation services indirectly measured	612.7	590.5	593.4
Gross value added in basic prices	37,296.6	39,633.3	42,134.9
Taxes *less* subsidies on products	5,311.7	5,064.5	5,362.8
GDP in purchasers' values	42,608.3	44,697.8	47,497.7

BALANCE OF PAYMENTS
(US $ million)

	2000	2001	2002
Exports of goods f.o.b.	4,050.4	4,889.0	6,028.4
Imports of goods f.o.b.	−5,154.1	−5,997.0	−7,343.3
Trade balance	−1,103.8	−1,108.0	−1,314.9
Exports of services	1,058.8	1,157.0	1,463.7
Imports of services	−678.7	−700.3	−915.0
Balance on goods and services	−723.7	−651.4	−766.1
Other income received	185.5	205.7	191.6
Other income paid	−379.3	−385.5	−375.0
Balance on goods, services and income	−917.5	−831.1	−949.5
Current transfers received	246.8	262.0	231.7
Current transfers paid	−4.3	−4.5	−2.9
Current balance	−674.9	−573.6	−720.7
Capital account (net)	2.1	1.4	56.5
Direct investment abroad	−3.7	−7.1	−17.7
Direct investment from abroad	378.9	445.8	712.5
Portfolio investment assets	−141.4	26.2	−124.5
Portfolio investment liabilities	405.9	238.0	148.8
Financial derivatives assets	—	18.3	19.6
Financial derivatives liabilities	—	−19.6	−22.7
Other investment assets	39.9	−225.0	154.7
Other investment liabilities	22.8	300.9	177.7
Net errors and omissions	128.3	153.6	78.5
Overall balance	158.0	359.0	462.7

External Trade

PRINCIPAL COMMODITIES
(million litai)

Imports c.i.f.	2001	2002	2003*
Vegetable products	692.7	712.1	767.6
Prepared foodstuffs; beverages, spirits and vinegar; tobacco and manufactured substitutes	990.7	1,003.1	1,081.4
Mineral products	5,385.8	5,030.9	5,447.6
Products of the chemical or allied industries	2,338.7	2,447.4	2,586.3
Plastics, rubber and articles thereof	1,340.9	1,479.2	1,593.7
Textiles and textile articles	2,226.7	2,244.8	2,240.6
Base metals and articles thereof	1,328.5	1,922.0	1,809.3
Machinery and mechanical appliances; electrical equipment; sound and television apparatus	4,250.6	4,939.6	5,633.1
Vehicles, aircraft, vessels and associated transport equipment	2,923.2	4,624.3	4,692.8
Total (incl. others)	25,413.2	28,562.2	29,967.5

Exports f.o.b.	2001	2002	2003*
Live animals and animal products	853.6	788.3	864.1
Vegetable products	497.1	412.9	658.0
Prepared foodstuffs; beverages, spirits and vinegar; tobacco and manufactured substitutes	886.3	914.2	1,019.3
Mineral products	4,287.9	3,830.8	4,344.9
Products of the chemical or allied industries	1,179.9	1,306.7	1,465.9
Plastics, rubber and articles thereof	536.5	571.3	613.5
Wood cork and articles thereof; wood charcoal; manufactures of straw, esparto, etc.	964.6	1,094.3	1,191.2
Textiles and textile articles	2,994.1	3,058.1	2,997.3
Base metals and articles thereof	680.9	958.1	734.3
Machinery and mechanical appliances; electrical equipment; sound and television apparatus	1,960.2	2,030.8	2,449.8
Vehicles, aircraft, vessels and associated transport equipment	1,694.0	3,247.5	3,360.0
Miscellaneous manufactured articles	769.8	1,001.4	1,352.2
Total (incl. others)	18,332.0	20,290.7	22,062.4

* Preliminary figures.

PRINCIPAL TRADING PARTNERS
(million litai)

Imports c.i.f.	2001	2002	2003*
Belarus	483.4	424.2	448.3
Belgium	497.9	529.8	487.7
China, People's Republic	500.2	673.6	927.1
Czech Republic	344.1	367.1	450.4
Denmark	742.0	832.8	853.6
Estonia	274.9	301.0	420.9
Finland	582.3	648.1	736.1
France	956.7	1,099.8	1,251.6
Germany	4,377.7	4,851.2	4,855.0
Italy	1,073.0	1,386.1	1,304.6
Japan	482.4	609.9	671.5
Kazakhstan	37.0	400.5	n.a.
Latvia	392.4	454.7	478.5
Netherlands	598.2	642.1	764.8
Norway	245.0	416.2	n.a.
Poland	1,233.0	1,366.3	1,551.2
Russia	6,428.0	6,070.7	6,662.9
Spain	323.5	362.5	398.1
Sweden	771.4	932.3	1,051.7
Ukraine	414.3	466.2	436.3
United Kingdom	851.8	939.0	998.8
USA	771.9	811.8	892.8
Total (incl. others)	25,413.2	28,562.2	29,967.5

Exports f.o.b.	2001	2002	2003*
Belarus	714.5	650.8	699.6
Belgium	299.5	388.7	474.1
Denmark	822.2	1,037.9	1,026.6
Estonia	595.2	773.9	952.3
Finland	255.1	239.1	332.1
France	601.3	834.3	1,123.1
Germany	2,303.1	2,103.9	2,185.2
Italy	369.3	565.8	479.6
Latvia	2,316.3	1,955.0	2,131.0
Netherlands	538.6	639.2	746.8
Norway	239.1	485.0	513.4
Poland	1,148.3	721.7	743.8
Russia	2,019.7	2,469.9	2,231.8
Spain	247.4	220.5	195.0
Sweden	671.3	853.3	882.3
Switzerland	107.7	337.2	2,575.7
Turkey	260.2	352.8	371.4
Ukraine	618.9	527.5	525.0
United Kingdom	2,532.6	2,727.2	1,401.4
USA	696.8	714.7	642.1
Total (incl. others)	18,332.0	20,290.7	22,062.4

* Preliminary figures.

Transport

RAILWAYS
(traffic)

	2000	2001	2002
Passenger journeys ('000)	8,852	7,718	7,217
Passenger-km (million)	611	533	498
Freight transported ('000 metric tons)	30,712	29,174	36,650
Freight ton-km (million)	8,919	7,741	9,767

ROAD TRAFFIC
(public transport and freight)

	2000	2001	2002
Passenger journeys ('000)	372,684	346,401	347,783
Passenger-km (million)	2,154	2,119	2,046
Freight transported ('000 metric tons)	45,013	45,075	45,047
Freight ton-km (million)	7,769	8,274	10,709

ROAD TRAFFIC
(motor vehicles in use at 31 December)

	2000	2001	2002
Passenger cars	1,172,394	1,133,477	1,180,945
Buses and coaches	15,069	15,171	15,376
Lorries and vans	88,346	89,373	93,508
Motorcycles and mopeds	19,842	20,244	21,017

INLAND WATERWAYS

	2000	2001	2002
Passenger journeys ('000)	1,299.9	1,323.6	2,890.2
Passenger-km (million)	2	1	3
Freight transported ('000 metric tons)	852.4	543.3	515.0
Freight ton-km (million)	1	1	1

SHIPPING

Merchant Fleet
(registered at 31 December)

	2000	2001	2002
Number of vessels	185	175	184
Total displacement ('000 grt)	434.2	393.3	435.3

Source: Lloyd's Register-Fairplay, *World Fleet Statistics.*

International Sea-borne Freight Traffic
('000 metric tons)

	1999	2000	2001
Goods loaded	12,864	18,552	18,144
Goods unloaded	2,796	4,296	4,224

Source: UN, *Monthly Bulletin of Statistics.*

CIVIL AVIATION
(traffic on scheduled services)

	2000	2001	2002
Passengers carried ('000)	343	363	376
Passenger-km (million)	461	484	524
Freight transported (million metric tons)	3.3	3.3	3.4

Source: UN, *Statistical Yearbook.*

Kilometres flown: 10 million in 1998.

Tourism

FOREIGN VISITORS BY COUNTRY OF ORIGIN
(arrivals at accommodation establishments)

	1999	2000	2001
Belarus	12,971	14,034	19,195
Estonia	12,499	11,425	14,011
Finland	20,960	22,775	21,282
Germany	48,390	52,089	54,479
Latvia	27,354	24,750	27,252
Poland	33,288	37,477	45,820
Russia	24,890	28,282	44,859
Sweden	14,099	15,174	14,013
United Kingdom	13,332	13,383	11,138
USA	12,479	13,120	13,310
Total (incl. others)	293,247	299,938	349,662

Source: Lithuanian State Department of Tourism, Vilnius.

Receipts from tourism (US $ million): 550.4 in 1999; 391.3 in 2000; 383.0 in 2001 (Source: Bank of Lithuania).

Communications Media

	2000	2001	2002
Television receivers ('000) . . .	1,560	n.a.	n.a.
Telephones ('000 main lines in use)	1,187.7	1,151.7	935.9
Mobile cellular telephones ('000 subscribers).	524.0	932.0	1,631.6
Personal computers ('000 in use) .	240	260	n.a.
Internet users ('000).	225	250	n.a.
Book titles (incl. brochures). . .	3,709	4,402	4,858
Newspapers: number	361	368	354
Newspapers: average circulation ('000 copies)	2,271	2,562	2,328
Other periodicals.	465	484	529

1997: Radio receivers ('000 in use) 1,900; Facsimile machines (number in use) 6,200.

Sources: International Telecommunication Union; UNESCO, *Statistical Yearbook*; UN, *Statistical Yearbook* and Ministry of Education and Science, Vilnius.

Education

(2002/03)

	Institutions	Teachers*	Students*
Comprehensive schools	2,172	50,200	594,300
Vocational schools	82	4,700	44,400
Schools of further education . .	51	5,300	48,600
Universities	19	8,900	119,600

* Figures are rounded.

Source: Ministry of Education and Science, Vilnius.

Teachers (1999): Pre-primary schools 12,526; Primary and general secondary schools 52,000; Vocational schools 5,032.

Adult literacy rate (UNESCO estimates): 99.6% (males 99.7%; females 99.5%) in 2001 (Source: UN Development Programme, *Human Development Report*).

Directory

The Constitution

The Constitution was approved in a national referendum on 25 October 1992 and adopted by the Seimas on 6 November. The following is a summary of its main provisions:

THE STATE

The Republic of Lithuania is an independent and democratic republic; its sovereignty is vested in the people, who exercise their supreme power either directly or through their democratically elected representatives. The powers of the State are exercised by the Seimas (Parliament), the President of the Republic, the Government and the Judiciary. The most significant issues concerning the State and the people are decided by referendum.

The territory of the republic is integral. Citizenship is acquired by birth or on other grounds determined by law. With certain exceptions established by law, no person may be a citizen of Lithuania and of another state at the same time. Lithuanian is the state language.

THE INDIVIDUAL AND THE STATE

The rights and freedoms of individuals are inviolable. Property is inviolable, and the rights of ownership are protected by law. Freedom of thought, conscience and religion are guaranteed. All persons are equal before the law. No one may be discriminated against on the basis of sex, race, nationality, language, origin, social status, religion or opinion. Citizens may choose their place of residence in Lithuania freely, and may leave the country at their own will. Citizens are guaranteed the right to form societies, political parties and associations. Citizens who belong to ethnic communities have the right to foster their language, culture and customs.

SOCIETY AND THE STATE

The family is the basis of society and the State. Education is compulsory until the age of 16. Education at state and local government institutions is free of charge at all levels. State and local government establishments of education are secular, although, at the request of parents, they may offer classes in religious instruction. The State recognizes traditional Lithuanian and other churches and religious organizations, but there is no state religion. Censorship of mass media is prohibited. Ethnic communities may independently administer the affairs of their ethnic culture, education, organizations, etc. The State supports ethnic communities.

NATIONAL ECONOMY AND LABOUR

Lithuania's economy is based on the right to private ownership and freedom of individual economic activity. Every person may freely choose an occupation, and has the right to adequate, safe and healthy working conditions, adequate compensation for work, and social security in the event of unemployment. Trade unions may be freely established and may function independently. Employees have the right to strike in order to protect their economic and social interests. The state guarantees the right of citizens to old-age and disability pensions, as well as to social assistance in the event of unemployment, sickness, widowhood, etc.

THE SEIMAS

Legislative power rests with the Seimas. It comprises 141 members, elected for a four-year term on the basis of universal, equal and direct suffrage by secret ballot. Any citizen who has attained 25 years of age may be a candidate for the Seimas. Members of the Seimas may not be found criminally responsible, may not be arrested, and may not be subjected to any other restrictions of personal freedom, without the consent of the Seimas. The Seimas convenes for two regular four-month sessions every year.

The Seimas considers and enacts amendments to the Constitution; enacts laws; adopts resolutions for the organization of referendums; announces presidential elections; approves or rejects the candidature of the Prime Minister, as proposed by the President of the Republic; establishes or abolishes government ministries, upon the recommendation of the Government; supervises the activities of the Government, with the power to express a vote of 'no confidence' in the Prime Minister or individual ministers; appoints judges to the Constitutional Court and the Supreme Court; approves the state budget and supervises the implementation thereof; establishes state taxes and other obligatory payments; ratifies or denounces international treaties whereto the republic is a party, and considers other issues of foreign policy; establishes administrative divisions of the republic; issues acts of amnesty; imposes direct administration and martial law, declares states of emergency, announces mobilization, and adopts decisions to use the armed forces.

THE PRESIDENT OF THE REPUBLIC

The President of the Republic is the Head of State. Any Lithuanian citizen by birth, who has lived in Lithuania for at least the three preceding years, who has reached 40 years of age and who is eligible for election to the Seimas, may be elected President of the Republic. The President is elected by the citizens of the republic, on the basis of universal, equal and direct suffrage by secret ballot, for a term of five years. No person may be elected to the office for more than two consecutive terms.

The President resolves basic issues of foreign policy and, in conjunction with the Government, implements foreign policy; signs international treaties and submits them to the Seimas for ratification; appoints or recalls, upon the recommendation of the Government, diplomatic representatives of Lithuania in foreign states and international organizations; appoints, upon the approval of the Seimas, the Prime Minister, and charges him/her with forming the Government, and approves its composition; removes, upon the approval of the Seimas, the Prime Minister from office; appoints or dismisses individual ministers, upon the recommendation of the Prime Minister; appoints or dismisses, upon the approval of the Seimas, the Commander-in-Chief of the armed forces and the head of the Security Service.

THE GOVERNMENT

Executive power is held by the Government of the republic (Council of Ministers), which consists of the Prime Minister and other ministers. The Prime Minister is appointed and dismissed by the President of the Republic, with the approval of the Seimas. Ministers are appointed by the President, on the nomination of the Prime Minister.

The Government administers the affairs of the country, protects the inviolability of the territory of Lithuania, and ensures state security and public order; implements laws and resolutions of the Seimas as well as presidential decrees; co-ordinates the activities of the ministries and other governmental institutions; prepares the draft state budget and submits it to the Seimas; executes the state budget and reports to the Seimas on its fulfilment; drafts legislative proposals and submits them to the Seimas for consideration; establishes and maintains diplomatic representation with foreign countries and international organizations.

JUDICIAL SYSTEM

The judicial system is independent of the authority of the legislative and executive branches of government. It consists of a Constitutional Court, a Supreme Court, a Court of Appeal, and district and local courts (for details, see section on Judicial System below).

The Government

HEAD OF STATE

President: Artūras Paulauskas (acting).

COUNCIL OF MINISTERS
(May 2004)

Prime Minister: Algirdas Mykolas Brazauskas.

Minister of the Economy: Petras Čėsna.

Minister of Finance: Algirdas Butkevičius.

Minister of National Defence: Linas Antanas Linkevičius.

Minister of Culture: Roma Žakaitienė.

Minister of Social Security and Labour: Vilija Blinkevičiūtė.

Minister of Justice: Vytautas Markevičius.

Minister of Transport and Communications: Zigmantas Balčytis.

Minister of Health Care: Juozas Olekas.

Minister of Foreign Affairs: Antanas Valionis.

Minister of the Interior: Virgilijus Bulovas.

Minister of Agriculture and Forestry: Jeronimas Kraujelis.

Minister of Education and Science: Algirdas Monkevičius.

Minister of the Environment: Arūnas Kundrotas.

MINISTRIES

Office of the President: S. Daukanto 3/8, Vilnius 2008; tel. (526) 28986; fax (521) 26210; e-mail info@president.lt; internet www .president.lt.

Office of the Prime Minister: Gedimino pr. 11, Vilnius 2039; tel. (526) 63874; fax (521) 63877; e-mail kasp@lrvk.lt; internet www.lrvk .lt.

Ministry of Agriculture and Forestry: Gedimino pr. 19, Vilnius 2025; tel. (523) 91001; fax (521) 24440; e-mail zum@zum.lt; internet www.zum.lt.

Ministry of Culture: J. Basanavičiaus 5, Vilnius 2600; tel. (526) 19486; fax (526) 23120; e-mail culture@muza.lt; internet www.muza .lt.

Ministry of the Economy: Gedimino pr. 38/2, Vilnius 2600; tel. (526) 22416; fax (526) 23974; e-mail pr@po.ekm.lt; internet www .ekm.lt.

Ministry of Education and Science: A. Volano 2/7, Vilnius 2691; tel. (527) 43126; fax (526) 12077; e-mail smmin@smm.lt; internet www.smm.lt.

Ministry of the Environment: Jakšto 4/9, Vilnius 2694; tel. (526) 16148; fax (521) 20847; e-mail kanceliarja@aplinkuma.lt; internet www.gamta.lt.

Ministry of Finance: J. Tumo-Vaižganto 8A/2, Vilnius 2600; tel. (523) 90005; fax (521) 26387; e-mail finmin@finmin.lt; internet www .finmin.lt.

Ministry of Foreign Affairs: J. Tumo-Vaižganto 2, Vilnius 2600; tel. (523) 62444; fax (523) 13090; e-mail urm@urm.lt; internet www .urm.lt.

Ministry of Health Care: Vilniaus 33, Vilnius 2001; tel. (526) 21625; fax (521) 24601; e-mail webmaster@sam.lt; internet www .sam.lt.

Ministry of the Interior: Šventaragio 2, Vilnius 2600; tel. (527) 18451; fax (527) 18551; e-mail atstovasspaudai@vrm.lt; internet www.vrm.lt.

Ministry of Justice: Gedimino pr. 30/1, Vilnius 2600; tel. (526) 24670; fax (526) 25940; e-mail tm1@utic.tm.lt.

Ministry of National Defence: Totorių 25/3, Vilnius 2001; tel. (526) 24821; fax (521) 26082; e-mail vis@kam.lt; internet www.kam .lt.

Ministry of Social Security and Labour: A. Vivulskio 11, Vilnius 2693; tel. (526) 03790; fax (526) 03813; e-mail post@socmin.lt; internet www.socmin.lt.

Ministry of Transport and Communications: Gedimino pr. 17, Vilnius 2679; tel. (523) 93911; fax (521) 24335; e-mail transp@transp .lt; internet www.transp.lt.

President and Legislature

PRESIDENT

Presidential Election, First Ballot, 22 December 2002

Candidates	Valid votes cast	% of valid votes cast
Valdas Adamkus	514,154	35.53
Rolandas Paksas	284,559	19.66
Artūras Paulauskas	120,238	8.31
Vytautas Šerenas	112,215	7.75
Vytenis Povilas Andriukaitis	105,584	7.30
Kazimieras Prunskienė	72,925	5.04
Juozas Edvardas Petraitis	54,139	3.74
Eugenijus Gentvilas	44,562	3.08
Julius Veselka	32,293	2.23
Algimantas Matulevičius	32,137	2.22
Others	74,311	5.14
Total	**1,447,117**	**100.00**

Second Ballot, 5 January 2003

Candidates	Valid votes cast	% of valid votes cast
Rolandas Paksas	777,769	54.71
Valdas Adamkus	643,870	45.29
Total	**1,421,639**	**100.00**

LEGISLATURE

SEIMAS
(Parliament)

Gedimino pr. 53, Vilnius 01109; tel. (523) 96212; fax (523) 96330; e-mail bendrasis@lrs.lt; internet www.lrs.lt.

Chairman: Česlovas Juršėnas (acting).

Deputy Chairmen: Vytenis Povilas Andriukaitis, Artūras Skardžius, Gintaras Steponavičius.

General Election, 8 October 2000

Parties	% of votes	Seats
A. Brazauskas Social Democratic Coalition*	31.1	51
Lithuanian Liberal Union	17.3	34
New Union (Social Liberals)	19.6	29
Conservative Party of Lithuania	8.6	9
Lithuanian Farmers' Party	4.1	4
Christian Democratic Party of Lithuania	3.1	2
Lithuanian Centre Union	2.9	2
Lithuanian Poles' Electoral Action	1.9	2
Christian-Democratic Union	4.2	1
Moderate Conservative Union	2.0	1
Lithuanian Freedom Union	1.3	1
Young Lithuania National Party	1.2	1
Modern Christian-Democratic Union	—	1

Parties— *continued*	% of votes	Seats
Independents	—	3
Others	2.6	0
Total	**100.0**	**141**

*Comprising the Lithuanian Democratic Labour Party and the Lithuanian Social Democratic Party (the two parties formally merged under the latter name in 2001), the New Democracy Party (which merged with the Lithuanian Peasants' Party to form the Peasants' and New Democracy Union in 2002) and the Lithuanian Russians' Union.

Political Organizations

In mid-2003 37 political parties were registered with the Ministry of Justice.

Homeland Union (HU) (Homeland Union—Lithuanian Conservatives, Political Prisoners and Deportees and Christian Democrats) (Tėvynės Sąjunga—TS): Gedimino pr. 15, Vilnius 2001; tel. and fax (523) 96450; e-mail info@tslk.lt; internet www.tslk.lt; f. 1993 from elements of Sąjūdis, as the Conservative Party of Lithuania (Homeland Union); absorbed the Lithuanian Rightist Union in Nov. 2003; merged with the Lithuanian Union of Political Prisoners and Deportees in Feb. 2004, and name changed as above; Chair. ANDRIUS KUBILIUS; 60,000 mems.

Lithuanian Christian Democrats: Pylimo 36/2, Vilnius 2001; tel. (526) 26126; fax (521) 27387; e-mail lkdp@takas.lt; internet www .lkdp.lt; f. 1904; re-est. 1989; formed in 2001 by merger of the Christian Democratic Party of Lithuania and the Christian Democratic Union; Chair. VALENTINAS STUNDYS; 12,000 mems.

Lithuanian Citizens' Alliance: Vilnius; tel. (527) 33394; f. 1996; Chair. MEČISLAV VAŠKOVIČ.

Lithuanian Economic Party: Vilnius; tel. (526) 31564; fax (526) 51380; f. 1995; Chair. KLEMENSAS ŠEPUTIS; 1,500 mems.

Lithuanian Freedom Union: Kaunas; tel. (372) 02594; f. 1994; Chair. VYTAUTAS ŠUSTAUSKAS.

Lithuanian Green Party: Antakalnio 46–40, Vilnius 2055; tel. (374) 25566; fax (374) 25207; e-mail zigmasvaisvila@lrs.lt; internet www.zalieji.lt; f. 1989; Chair. RŪTA GAJAUSKAITE; 400 mems.

Lithuanian Justice Party: Nemuno 19, Kaunas; tel. (372) 09382; f. 1995; Chair. BRONIUS SIMANAVIČIUS.

Lithuanian Labour Party: Vilnius; f. 2003; Chair. VIKTOR USPASKIKH.

Lithuanian Liberal Democratic Party (LLDP): Pylimo 27/14, Vilnius 2000; tel. (526) 23493; e-mail sekretoriatas@ldp.lt; internet www.ldp.lt; f. 2002; right-wing; Chair. VALENTINAS MAZURONIS; 1,500 mems.

Lithuanian Liberal and Centre Union: A. Jakšto 9, Vilnius 2001; tel. (523) 13264; fax (527) 91910; e-mail lls@lls.lt; internet www.lls.lt; f. 2003; by a merger of the Lithuanian Centre Union, the Lithuanian Liberal Union and the Modern Christian-Democratic Union; Chair. ARTŪRAS ZUOKAS; over 5,000 mems.

Lithuanian Life Logics Party: Vilnius; f. 1996; Chair. VYTAUTAS BERNATONIS.

Lithuanian National Union: Gedimino pr. 22, Vilnius 2600; tel. (526) 24935; fax (526) 17310; e-mail lietauta@takas.lt; internet www .lts.lt; f. 1924; refounded 1989; Chair. GEDIMINAS SAKALNIKAS; 3,000 mems.

Lithuanian People's Party: Pelesos 1/2, Vilnius; tel. (526) 30429; f. 1996; Chair. VYTAUTAS LAZINKA.

Lithuanian Poles' Electoral Action (AWPL): Didžioji 40, Vilnius 2601; tel. (521) 23388; f. 1994; Chair. WALDEMAR TOMASZEWSKI; 1,000 mems.

Lithuanian Polish People's Party (Polska Partia Ludowa): Vilnius; Chair. ANTONINA POLTAWIEC.

Lithuanian Political Prisoners' Party: Kipro Petrausko pr. 38, Kaunas 3005; tel. and fax (377) 95494; f. 1995; Chair. ZIGMAS MEDINECKAS.

Lithuanian Reform Party: Gedimino pr. 2, Vilnius; tel. (521) 25800; f. 1996; Chair. ALGIRDAS PILVELIS.

Lithuanian Republican Party: Pramonės pr. 3–62, Kaunas 3031; tel. (373) 51214; e-mail respublikos_varpai@takas.lt; internet respublikosvarpai.5u.com; active 1922–29; re-est. 1991; Chair. KAZIMIERAS PETRAITIS; 2,450 mems.

Lithuanian Russians' Union: Savanorių pr. 11–70, Vilnius 2015; tel. (523) 96636; fax (526) 24248; e-mail sergejus.dmitrijevas@lrs.lt; internet www.sojuzrus.visiems.lt; f. 1995; contested the 2000 legislative election as part of the A. Brazauskas Social Democratic Coalition; Chair. SERGEJ DMITRIJEV; 1,200 mems.

Lithuanian Social Democratic Party (LSDP): Barboros Radvilaites 1, Vilnius 2600; tel. (526) 13907; fax (526) 15420; e-mail info@ lsdp.lt; internet www.lsdp.lt; absorbed the Lithuanian Democratic Labour Party in 2001; Chair. ALGIRDAS BRAZAUSKAS; 11,000 mems.

Lithuanian Social Justice Union: Žirmūnų 30A–42, Vilnius; tel. (527) 32055; f. 1996; Chair. KAZIMIERAS JONAS JOCIUS.

Lithuanian Socialist Party: Šeškinės 65/58, Vilnius 2010; tel. (524) 19765; f. 1994; Chair. ALBINAS VISOCKAS; 800 mems.

Moderate Conservative Union: Odminių g. 5, Vilnius 2002; tel. (521) 26876; fax (521) 26880; e-mail info@nks.lt; internet www.nks .lt; f. 2000; centre-right; Chair. GEDIMINAS VAGNORIUS.

National Centre Party (NCP): Vilnius; f. 2003 by former members of the Lithuanian Centre Union unwilling to merge into the Lithuanian Liberal and Centre Union (q.v.); Chair. ROMUALDAS OZOLAS; 1,000 mems.

National Progress Party: Vilnius ; tel. (523) 96656; fax (523) 96779; e-mail egidijus.klumbys@lrs.lt; internet www.tpp.lt; active 1916–24, re-est. 1994; Chair. EGIDIJUS KLUMBYS; 1,100 mems.

New Union (Social Liberals): Gedimino pr. 10/1, Vilnius 2001; tel. (521) 07600; fax (521) 07602; e-mail centras@nsajunga.lt; internet www.nsajunga.lt; f. 1998; centre-left; Chair. VILIJA BLINKEVIČIŪTĖ (acting).

Peasants' and New Democracy Union: A. Jakšto 9–22, Vilnius 2001; tel. and fax (526) 15613; e-mail ndpartija@takas.lt; internet www.5ci.lt/ndmp; f. 2001 by the merger of the New Democracy Party and the Lithuanian Peasants' Party (Lithuanian Farmers' Party); Chair. KAZIMIERAS PRUNSKIENĖ; 1,500 mems.

Young Lithuania National Party ('Jaunoji Lietuva'): Čiurlionio 9/2, Vilnius 2009; tel. (372) 26254; fax (527) 03217; e-mail jaunalietuviai@is.lt; internet www.is.lt/jaunalietuviai; f. 1994; Chair. STANISLOVAS BUŠKEVIČIUS; 1,000 mems.

Diplomatic Representation

EMBASSIES IN LITHUANIA

Austria: Gaono g. 6, Vilnius; tel. (526) 60580; fax (527) 91363; e-mail a80645@post.omnitel.net; Ambassador MICHAEL SCHWARZINGER.

Belarus: Mindango 13, Vilnius 2600; tel. (526) 62200; fax (526) 62212; internet www.belarus.lt; Ambassador ULADZIMIR GARKUN.

China, People's Republic: Algirdo 36, Vilnius 2006; tel. (521) 62861; fax (521) 62682; e-mail chinaemb_lithuania@mfa.gov.cn; internet www.chinaembassy.lt; Ambassador CHEN YUMING.

Czech Republic: Tilto g. 1–2, Vilnius 2000; tel. (526) 61040; fax (526) 61066; e-mail vilnius@embassy.mzv.cz; Ambassador PETR VOZNICA.

Denmark: T. Kosciuškos 36, Vilnius 01100; tel. (521) 53434; fax (523) 12300; e-mail vnoamb@um.dk; internet www.denmark.lt; Ambassador EVA JANSON.

Estonia: Mickevičiaus 4A, Vilnius 2004; tel. (527) 80200; fax (527) 80201; e-mail sekretar@estemb.lt; Ambassador REIN OIDEKIVI.

Finland: Klaipėdos 6, Vilnius 2600; tel. (521) 21621; fax (521) 22463; e-mail sanomat.vil@formin.fi; internet www.finland.lt; Ambassador TAINA KIEKKO.

France: Švarco g. 1, Vilnius 2600; tel. (521) 22979; fax (521) 24211; e-mail ambafrance.vilnius@diplomatie.gouv.fr; internet www .ambafrance-lt.org; Ambassador GUY YELDA.

Germany: Z. Sierakausko 24/8, Vilnius 2600; tel. (521) 31815; fax (521) 31812; e-mail germ.emb@takas.lt; internet www .deutschebotschaft-wilna.lt; Ambassador Dr ALEXANDER VON ROM.

Holy See: Kosciuškos g. 28, Vilnius 2001; tel. (521) 23696; fax (521) 24228; e-mail nuntiusbalt@aiva.lt; Apostolic Nuncio Most Rev. PETER STEPHAN ZURBRIGGEN (Titular Archbishop of Glastonia— Glastonbury).

Italy: Tauro 12, Vilnius 2001; tel. (521) 20620; fax (521) 20405; e-mail ambasciata@ambitvilnius.lt; Ambassador BERNARDO UGUCCIONI.

Kazakhstan: Birutes 20A/35 , Vilnius 2004; tel. (521) 22123; fax (521) 33701; e-mail kazakhstan@embassy.lt; internet kazakhstan .embassy.lt; Ambassador RASHID IBRAYEV.

Latvia: M. K. Čiurlionio 76, Vilnius 2600; tel. (521) 31260; fax (521) 31130; e-mail lietuva@latvia.balt.net; internet latvia.balt.net; Ambassador MAIRA MORA.

Norway: D. Poškos 59, Vilnius 2004; tel. (527) 26926; fax (527) 26964; e-mail emb.vilnius@mfa.no; internet www.norvegija.lt; Ambassador KÅRE HAUGE.

Poland: Smėlio 20A, Vilnius 2055; tel. (527) 09001; fax (527) 09007; internet www.polandembassy.lt; Ambassador JERZY BAHR.

Romania: Vivulskio 19, Vilnius; tel. (523) 10527; fax (523) 10652; e-mail ambromania@post.omnitel.net; internet www.romania.lt; Chargé d'affaires a.i. CONSTANTIN BUDIANU.

Russia: Latvių 53/54, Vilnius 2600; tel. (527) 21763; fax (527) 23877; e-mail rusemb@rusemb.lt; Ambassador BORIS TSEPOV.

Sweden: Didžioji 16, Vilnius 2600; tel. (526) 85010; fax (526) 85030; e-mail ambassaden.vilnius@foreign.ministry.se; internet www .swedishembassy.lt; Ambassador JAN PALMSTIERNA.

Turkey: Didžioji 37, Vilnius 2001; tel. (526) 49570; fax (521) 23277; e-mail turemvil@eunet.lt; Ambassador ALI NAZIM BELGER.

Ukraine: Teatro 4, Vilnius 2600; tel. (521) 21536; fax (521) 20475; e-mail ukrembassy@post.5ci.lt; internet www.5ci.lt/ukrembassy; Ambassador BORYS KLYMCHUK.

United Kingdom: Antakalnio 2, Vilnius 2055; tel. (524) 62900; fax (524) 62901; e-mail be-vilnius@britain.lt; internet www.britain.lt; Ambassador COLIN ROBERTS.

USA: Akmenų 6, Vilnius 2600; tel. (521) 23031; fax (523) 12819; e-mail mail@usembassy.lt; internet www.usembassy.lt; Ambassador STEPHEN D. MULL.

Judicial System

The organs of justice are the Supreme Court, the Court of Appeal, district courts, local courts of administrative areas and a special court—the Commercial Court. The Seimas (Parliament) appoints and dismisses from office the judges of the Supreme Court in response to representations made by the President of the Republic (based upon the recommendation of the chairman of the Supreme Court). Judges of the Court of Appeal are appointed by the President with the approval of the Seimas (on the recommendation of the Minister of Justice), while judges of district and local courts are appointed and dismissed by the President. The Council of Judges submits recommendations to the President of the Republic concerning the appointment of judges, as well as their promotion, transfer or dismissal from office.

The Constitutional Court decides on the constitutionality of acts of the Seimas, as well as of the President and the Government. It consists of nine judges, who are appointed by the Seimas for a single term of nine years; one-third of the Court's members are replaced every three years.

The Office of the Prosecutor-General is an autonomous institution of the judiciary, comprising the Prosecutor-General and local and district prosecutors' offices which are subordinate to him. The Prosecutor-General and his deputies are appointed for terms of seven years by the President, subject to approval by the Seimas, while the prosecutors are appointed by the Prosecutor-General. The Office of the Prosecutor-General incorporates the Department for Crime Investigation. The State Arbitration decides cases of business litigation. A six-volume Civil Code, in accordance with European Union and international law, came into effect in 2001, replacing the Soviet civil legal system, which had, hitherto, remained in operation.

Constitutional Court: Gedimino pr. 36, Vilnius 2600; tel. (521) 26398; fax (521) 27975; e-mail mailbox@lrkt.lt; internet www.lrkt.lt; f. 1993; Chair. EDIGIJUS KURIS.

Court of Appeal: Gedimino pr. 40/1, Vilnius 2600; tel. (526) 26876; fax (526) 18039; Chair. VYTAUTAS MILIUS.

Supreme Court: Gynėjų 6, Vilnius 2725; tel. (526) 10560; fax (526) 27950; e-mail lat@tic.lt; internet www.lat.litlex.lt; Chair. VYTAUTAS GREIČIUS.

Office of the Prosecutor-General: A. Smetonos 4, Vilnius 01515; tel. (526) 62305; fax (526) 62317; e-mail cekelil@lrgp.lt; Prosecutor-General ANTANAS KLIMAVIČIUS.

Religion

Lithuania adopted Christianity at the end of the 14th century. However, the country's geographical position and history have long predetermined a diversity of religious communities. The restoration of independence, in 1991, stimulated the revival of religious practice, which was widely suppressed or banned during the Soviet period. Traditional religious communities were re-established and new ones came into existence. In 2001 there were 923 traditional and 176 non-traditional religious organizations registered in the country.

CHRISTIANITY

The Roman Catholic Church

Roman Catholicism has been the principal religious affiliation in Lithuania for more than 600 years (it was adopted by the Lithuanian State in 1387). The Roman Catholic Church in Lithuania comprises two archdioceses and five dioceses. There are seminaries at Vilnius, Kaunas and Telšiai. At 31 December 2002 the Roman Catholic Church estimated there to be 2.8m. adherents in Lithuania (equivalent to some 80% of the population).

Lithuanian Bishops' Conference
(Conferentia Episcopalis Lituaniae)
Skapo 4, Vilnius 2001; tel. (521) 25455; fax (521) 20972; e-mail lvk@ post.omnitel.net.
f. 1996; Pres. Cardinal AUDRYS JUOZAS BAČKIS (Archbishop of Vilnius).

Archbishop of Kaunas: Most Rev. SIGITAS TAMKEVIČIUS, Rotušės 14A, Kaunas 3000; tel. (374) 09026; fax (373) 20090; e-mail kurija@ kn.lcn.lt; internet www.kaunas.lcn.lt.

Archbishop of Vilnius: Cardinal AUDRYS JUOZAS BAČKIS, Šventaragio 4, Vilnius 2001; tel. (526) 27098; fax (521) 22807; e-mail vilncnsis@takas.lt.

The Byzantine Rite Catholic (Uniate) Church

Established in 1596 by the Lithuanian Brasta (Brest) Church Union, the Uniate Church is headed by the Metropolitan Archbishop of Lviv (Ukraine) and is under the judicial protection of the Roman Catholic Church of Lithuania. At 1 January 1996 there were five communities, with three priests, one monastic order and one church returned to the adherents in Vilnius.

Representation of the Order of St Basil the Great in Lithuania: Aušros Vartų 7B, Vilnius 2001; tel. (521) 22578; Centre of the Byzantine Rite Catholics (Uniates) in Lithuania; Superior PAVLO JACHIMEC.

Orthodox Churches

Russian Orthodox Church

The first communities appeared during the 12th century and the first monastery was established in Vilnius in 1597. While Lithuania formed part of the Russian Empire (1795–1915), Orthodoxy was considered the state religion. The Vilnius and Lithuanian Eparchy of the Russian Orthodox Church is under the jurisdiction of the Moscow Patriarchate. At 1 January 1996 there were 41 communities (with 30 clergymen and 41 churches). There were an estimated 180,000 adherents in 2001.

Vilnius and Lithuanian Eparchy of the Russian Orthodox Church: Aušros Vartų 10, Vilnius 2001; tel. (521) 27765; Metropolit CHRYZOSTOM (Georgii Martishkin).

Lithuanian Old Believers Pomor Church

The first communities settled in Lithuania in 1679 and the Church was established in 1709. At 1 January 1996 there were approximately 34,000 adherents (mainly ethnic Russians) in 58 communities, with 23 clergymen and 50 churches.

Supreme Council of the Old Believers (Pomor) Church in Lithuania: Naujininkų 20, Vilnius 2030; tel. (526) 95271; f. 1925; Chair. MARK SEMIONOV (acting).

Protestant Churches

Lithuanian Evangelical Lutheran Church

The first parishes were established in 1539–69. In 1563 the Evangelical Church divided into Lutheran and Reformed Churches. Church attendance revived after 1990. The Lithuanian Evangelical Lutheran Church comprises one diocese. At 1 January 1998 there were approximately 30,000 adherents in 54 parishes (with 18 priests and 41 churches).

Consistory of the Lithuanian Evangelical Lutheran Church: Tumo-Vaizganto 50, Tauragė 5900; tel. and fax (446) 61145; e-mail konsistorija@takas.lt; Bishop JONAS KALVANAS.

Lithuanian Evangelical Reformed Church

The first parishes were established after 1563. At 1 January 1996 there were approximately 12,000 adherents in 11 parishes (with two pastors and nine churches).

Lithuanian Evangelical Reformed Church: POB 661, Vilnius 2049; tel. and fax (524) 50656; Pres. of Synodie Collegium POVILAS A. JAŠINSKAS.

Lithuanian Baptist Union and Other Churches

Parliament awarded the Baptist Union 'recognized' status in July 2001, the first religious community to be awarded this status. There has been a Baptist presence in Lithuania since the 18th century. The United Methodist Church, the New Apostolic Church, the Pentecostal Union and the Adventist Church ETH are all similarly seeking such status, beyond their current one of simply being registered.

ISLAM

Sunni Islam is the religion of the ethnic Tatars of Lithuania. The first Tatar communities settled there in the 14th century. The first mosque in Vilnius was erected in 1558. At 1 January 1996 there were five Tatar religious communities (with 10 clergymen, four mosques and one prayer house). In 2001 there were an estimated 5,000 adherents in Lithuania.

Sunni Muslim Religious Centre—Muftiate in Lithuania: A. Vivulskio 3, Vilnius 2006; tel. (524) 25124; fax (526) 03451; e-mail ramazanas@is.lt; internet www.islam.is.lt; f. 1998; Mufti ROMUALDAS KRINICKIS.

JUDAISM

The first Jewish communities appeared in Lithuania in the 15th century. In the 15th–17th centuries Lithuania was an important centre of Jewish culture and religion. Before the Second World War approximately 250,000 Jews lived in Lithuania; an estimated 90% were murdered during the German occupation (1941–44). At 1 January 1996 there were five Judaic religious communities, with two synagogues (in Vilnius and Kaunas). There were an estimated 5,000 adherents in Lithuania in 2001.

Jewish Community of Lithuania: Pylimo 4, Vilnius 2001; tel. (526) 13003; fax (521) 27915; e-mail jewishcom@post.5ci.lt; internet www.litjews.org; f. 1992 to replace and expand the role of the Jewish Cultural Society; Chair. SIMONAS ALPERAVIČIUS; Chief Rabbi SAMUEL KAHN (London, United Kingdom).

The Press

In 2002 there were 354 newspapers and 529 periodicals published in Lithuania.

The publications listed below are in Lithuanian, except where otherwise indicated.

PRINCIPAL NEWSPAPERS

Kauno diena (Kaunas Daily): Vytauto pr. 27, Kaunas 3687; tel. (373) 41971; fax (374) 23404; e-mail redakcija@kaunodiena.lt; internet www.kaunodiena.lt; f. 1945; 6 a week; Editor-in-Chief AUŠRA LEKA; circ. 50,000.

Klaipėda: Šauliu 21, Klaipėda 5800; tel. (463) 97701; e-mail office@klaipeda.daily.lt; internet www.klaipeda.daily.lt; Editor ANTANAS STANEVIČIUS.

Kurier Wileński (Vilnius Express): Laisvės pr. 60, Vilnius 2056; tel. (524) 27901; fax (524) 27265; f. 1953; 5 a week; in Polish; Editor-in-Chief CZESŁAW MALEWSKI; circ. 8,000.

Lietuvos aidas (Echo of Lithuania): Maironio 1, Vilnius 2710; tel. (526) 15208; fax (521) 24876; e-mail centr@aidas.lt; internet www.aidas.lt; f. 1917; re-est. 1990; 5 a week; Editor-in-Chief ROMA GRINIŪTĖ-GRINBERGIENĖ; circ. 20,000.

Lietuvos rytas (Lithuania's Morning): Gedimino pr. 12A, Vilnius 2001; tel. (527) 43600; fax (527) 43700; e-mail daily@lrytas.lt; internet www.lrytas.lt; f. 1990; 6 a week in Lithuanian, with 3 supplements per week; Editor-in-Chief GEDVYDAS VAINAUSKAS; circ. 65,000 (Mon.–Fri.), 200,000 (Sat.).

Lietuvos žinios (Lithuanian News): Kęstučiog. 4, Vilnius; tel. (527) 54904; fax (527) 53131; e-mail lzinios@lzinios.lt; internet www.lzinios.lt; 6 a week; Editor-in-Chief RYTAS STASELIS.

Respublika (Republic): A. Smetonos 2, Vilnius 2600; tel. (521) 23112; fax (521) 23538; f. 1989; 6 a week in Lithuanian, with 5 Russian editions per week; Editor-in-Chief VITAS TOMKUS; circ. 55,000.

Šiaulių kraštas: P. Višinskio g. 26, Šiauliai 77155; tel. (415) 91555; fax (415) 24581; e-mail redakcija@skrastas.lt; internet www.skrastas.lt.

Vakarinės naujienos (Evening News): Laisvės pr. 60, Vilnius 2056; tel. (524) 28052; fax (524) 28563; e-mail info@vnaujienos.lt; internet www.vnaujienos.lt; f. 1958; 5 a week; in Lithuanian and Russian; Editor RIČARDAS JARMALAVIČIUS; circ. 15,000.

Vakaro žinios (Evening News): Jogailos g. 11/2-11, Vilnius 2600; tel. and fax (526) 16875; e-mail vakarozinios@takas.lt; daily; circ. 70,000.

Vakarų ekspresas (Western Express): H. Manto 2, Klaipėda 5800; tel. (462) 18074; fax (463) 10102; e-mail sek.ve@balt.net; internet www.vakaru-ekspresas.lt; f. 1990; 6 a week; Editor-in-Chief GINTARAS TOMKUS; circ. 15,000.

Verslo žinios (Business News): J. Jasinskio 16A, Vilnius 2001; tel. (525) 26300; fax (525) 26313; e-mail info@vzinios.lt; internet www.vz.lt; f. 1994; 5 a week; circ. 9,000.

PRINCIPAL PERIODICALS

Apžvalga (Review): Pylimo 362, Vilnius 2001; tel. (526) 11151; fax (526) 10503; f. 1990; fortnightly; publ. by Christian Democratic Party of Lithuania; Editor-in-Chief DARIUS VILIMIAS; circ. 2,000.

Artuma: M. Daukšos 21, Kaunas 44282; tel. and fax (370) 209683; f. 1989; monthly; Editor-in-Chief VANDA IBIANSKA; circ. 3,000.

Dienovidis (Midday): Pilies 23A, Vilnius 2001; tel. (521) 21911; fax (521) 23101; e-mail dienovidis@takas.lt; f. 1990; weekly; Editor-in-Chief ALDONA ŽEMAITYTĖ; circ. 4,500.

Ekho Litvy (Echo of Lithuania): Laisvės pr. 60, Vilnius 2056; tel. (524) 28463; fax (524) 28463; e-mail echo.litvy@aunet.lt; f. 1940; daily; in Russian; Editor-in-Chief ALGIMANTAS ZHUKAS; circ. 5,000.

Genys (Woodpecker): Geležinio Vilko 12, Vilnius 2001; tel. (523) 13621; fax (523) 13622; f. 1940; monthly; illustrated; for 8–12-year-olds; Editor-in-Chief VYTAUTAS RAČICKAS; circ. 5,000.

Kultūros barai (Domains of Culture): Latako 3, Vilnius 2001; tel. (526) 16696; fax (526) 10538; e-mail kulturosbarai@takas.lt; internet www.eurozine.com; f. 1965; monthly; Editor-in-Chief BRONYS SAVUKYNAS; circ. 3,000.

Laima: Saltoniškių 29/3, Vilnius 2004; tel. (527) 28083; fax (527) 21614; e-mail laima@redakcija.lt; internet www.redakcija.lt/laima; f. 1993; monthly; lifestyle and feature magazine for women; Editor-in-Chief GITANA BUKAUSKIENĖ; circ. 30,000.

Liaudies kultūra (Ethnic Culture): Barboros Radvilaitės 8, Vilnius 2600; tel. (526) 13412; fax (521) 24033; e-mail lfcc@lfcc.lt; internet www.lfcc.lt/lk; f. 1988; 6 a year; Editor-in-Chief DALIA ANTANINA RASTENIENĖ; circ. 1,100.

Lietuvos sportas (Lithuanian Sports): Odminių 3, Vilnius 2600; tel. and fax (526) 16757; f. 1922; re-est. 1992; 3 a week; Editor-in-Chief BRONIUS ČEKANAUSKAS; circ. 18,000.

Lietuvos ūkis (Lithuanian Economy): Algirdo 31, Vilnius 2600; tel. (521) 36718; fax (522) 36445; f. 1921; monthly; Editor-in-Chief ALGIRDAS JASIONIS; circ. 3,000.

Literatūra ir menas (Literature and Art): Z. Sierakausko 15, Vilnius 2009; tel. (523) 33189; fax (523) 33181; e-mail lmenas@takas.lt; internet www.culture.lt/lmenas; f. 1946; weekly; publ. by the Lithuanian Writers' Union; Editor-in-Chief KORNELIJUS PLATELIS; circ. 3,000.

Lithuania in the World: T. Vrublevskio 6, Vilnius 2600; tel. (526) 14432; fax (526) 13521; e-mail lw.magazine@post.omnitel.net; internet www.kryptis.lt/lithuania; f. 1993; 6 a year; in English; Editor-in-Chief STASYS KAŠAUSKIS; circ. 15,000.

Magazyn Wileński (Vilnius Journal): Laisvės pr. 60, Vilnius 2056; tel. (524) 27718; fax (524) 29065; e-mail magazyn@magwil.lt; internet www.magwil.lt; f. 1990; monthly; political, cultural; in Polish; Editor-in-Chief MICHAŁ MACKIEWICZ; circ. 5,000.

Metai (Year): K. Sirvydo 6, Vilnius 2600; tel. (526) 17344; f. 1991; monthly; journal of the Lithuanian Writers' Union; Editor-in-Chief DANIELIUS MUŠINSKAS; circ. 2,000.

Mokslas ir gyvenimas (Science and Life): Antakalnio g. 36, Vilnius 10305; tel. and fax (523) 41572; e-mail mgredacija@takas.lt; internet ausis.gf.vu.lt/mg/; f. 1957; monthly; popular and historical science; Editor-in-Chief JUOZAS BALDAUSKAS; circ. 3,500.

Moksleivis (Schoolmate): A. Jakšto 8–10, Vilnius 2600; tel. (526) 27604; f. 1959; monthly; Editor-in-Chief ALGIMANTAS ZURBA; circ. 14,000.

Moteris (Woman): Vykinto 7, Vilnius 2004; tel. and fax (521) 24741; e-mail redakcija@moteris.lt; internet www.moteris.lt; f. 1952; monthly; popular, for women; Editor-in-Chief EGLE STRIAUKIENE; circ. 40,000.

Mūsų gamta (Our Nature): Rudens 33B, Vilnius 2600; tel. (526) 96964; f. 1964; 6 a year; Editor-in-Chief VYTAUTAS KLOVAS; circ. 2,500.

Naujasis Židinys (New Hearth): Tilto g. 8/3, Vilnius 2001; tel. (522) 20311; fax (521) 22363; f. 1991; monthly; religion and culture; Editor-in-Chief SAULIUS DRAZDAUSKAS; circ. 1,200.

Nemunas: Gedimino 45, Kaunas 3000; tel. (373) 22244; f. 1967; monthly; journal of the Lithuanian Writers' Union; Editor-in-Chief ALGIMANTAS MIKUTA; circ. 1,500.

Panele (Young Miss): Vykinto 7, Vilnius 2004; tel. (527) 15900; fax (527) 15901; e-mail magazine@panele.lt; internet www.panele.lt; f. 1994; monthly; popular, for ages 12–25; Editor-in-Chief JURGA SIMKIENE; circ. 66,000.

7 meno dienos (7 Days of Art): Bernardinų 10, Vilnius 2001; tel. (526) 13039; fax (526) 11926; e-mail 7md@culture.lt; internet www.culture.lt/7menodienos; f. 1992; weekly; Editor-in-Chief LINAS VILD-ŽIŪNAS; circ. 2,000.

Sandora (Covenant): Dominikonų 6, Vilnius 2001; tel. (521) 22141; fax (521) 20598; e-mail sandora@hotmail.com; f. 1989; monthly; Editor-in-Chief ELVYRA KUČINSKAITĖ; circ. 9,000.

Švyturys (Beacon): Maironio 1, Vilnius 2600; tel. (526) 10791; fax (526) 14690; f. 1949; monthly; politics, economics, history, culture, fiction; Editor-in-Chief JUOZAS BAUŠYS; circ. 10,000.

Tremtinys (Deportee): Laisvės 39, Kaunas 3000; tel. (372) 09530; f. 1988; weekly; publ. by the Lithuanian Union of Political Prisoners and Deportees; Editor-in-Chief ROMUALDAS JURGELIONIS; circ. 4,000.

Valstiečių laikraštis (Farmer's Newspaper): Laisvės pr. 60, Vilnius 2056; tel. and fax (524) 21281; e-mail redakcija@valstietis.lt; internet www.valstietis.lt; f. 1940; 2 a week; Editor-in-Chief JONAS ŠVOBA; circ. 78,000.

Vasario 16 (16 February): J. Gruodžio 9–404, Kaunas 3000; tel. (372) 25219; f. 1988; fortnightly; journal of the Lithuanian Democratic Party; Sec. PRIMAS NOREIKA; circ. 1,600.

NEWS AGENCIES

Baltic News Service (BNS): Jogailos g. 9/1, Vilnius 2001; tel. (523) 12410; fax (526) 81515; e-mail bns@bns.lt; f. 1991; Dir JURGITA LITVINIENĖ (acting).

ELTA (Lithuanian News Agency): Gedimino pr. 21/2, Vilnius 2600; tel. (526) 28864; fax (526) 19507; e-mail zinias@elta.lt; internet www.elta.lt; f. 1920; Dir KĘSTUTIS JANKAUSKAS.

Publishers

Alma littera: A. Juozapavičiaus 6/2, Vilnius 2600; tel. (527) 28246; fax (5) 28026; e-mail post@almali.lt; internet www.almali.lt; f. 1990; fiction, children's books, textbooks; Dir-Gen. ARVYDAS ANDRIJAUSKAS.

Baltos lankos (White Meadows): Mėsinių 4, Vilnius 2001; tel. (521) 20126; fax (521) 20152; e-mail baltos.lankos@post.omnitel.net; internet www.baltoslankos.lt; f. 1992; literature, humanities, social sciences, fiction and textbooks; Editor SAULIUS ŽUKAS.

Eugrimas: Šilutės 42A, Vilnius 08212; tel. and fax (527) 33955; e-mail info@eugrimas.lt; internet www.eugrimas.lt; f. 1995; academic and professional literature, incl. economics, education, law and politics; Dir EUGENIJA PETRULIENĖ.

Katalikų pasaulis (Catholic World): Dominikonų 6, Vilnius 2001; tel. (521) 22422; fax (526) 26462; f. 1990; Dir KĘSTUTIS LATOŽA.

Lietuvos rašytojų sąjungos leidykla (Lithuanian Writers' Union Publishers): K. Sirvydo 6, Vilnius 01101; tel. and fax (526) 28945; e-mail info@rsleidykla.lt; internet www.rsleidykla.lt; f. 1990; fiction, essays, literary heritage, children's books; Dir GIEDRE SORIENE.

Mintis (Idea): Z. Sierakausko 15, Vilnius 2600; tel. (523) 32943; fax (521) 63157; f. 1949; philosophy, history, law, economics, tourist information; Dir ALEKSANDRAS KRASNOVAS.

Mokslo ir enciklopedijų leidybos institutas (Science and Encyclopedia Publishing Institute): L. Asanavičiūtės 23, Vilnius 04315; tel. (524) 58526; fax (524) 58537; e-mail meli@meli.lt; internet www.meli.lt; f. 1992; encyclopedias, science and reference books, dictionaries, higher education textbooks, books for the general reader; Dir RIMANTAS KARECKAS.

Presvika: Pamėnkalnio 25–11, Vilnius 01113; tel. (526) 23182; fax (526) 23110; e-mail presvika@vilnius.balt.net; internet www.presvika.lt; f. 1996; psychological and educational literature, textbooks and fiction; Dir VIOLETA BILAIŠYTĖ.

Šviesa (Light): Vytauto 25, Kaunas 3000; tel. (373) 41834; fax (373) 42032; e-mail sviesa@balt.net; internet www.sviesa.lt; f. 1945; textbooks and pedagogical literature; Dir JONAS BARCYS.

Tyto alba: J. Jasinskio 10, Vilnius 2001; tel. and fax (524) 98602; e-mail tytoalba@taide.lt; internet www.tytoalba.lt; f. 1993; literature in translation; Dir LOLITA VARANAVIČIENĖ.

Vaga (Furrow): Gedimino pr. 50, Vilnius 2600; tel. (526) 26443; fax (526) 16902; e-mail vaga@post.omnitel.net; internet www.lietus.lt/vaga; f. 1945; fiction, non-fiction, art, children's books; Dir ARTURAS MICKEVIČUS.

Vyturys (Lark): J. Tumo-Vaižganto 2, Vilnius 2600; tel. and fax (526) 29407; f. 1985; fiction and non-fiction for children and youth; Dir ALEKSAS BOČIAROVAS.

Lithuanian Publishers' Association: K. Sirvydo 6, Vilnius 2000; tel. and fax (526) 17740; e-mail lla@centras.lt; f. 1989; Pres. SAULIUS ZUKAS.

Broadcasting and Communications

TELECOMMUNICATIONS

Regulatory Authority

Communications Regulatory Authority (Ryšių Reguliavimo Tarnyba): Algirdo 27, Vilnius 03219; tel. (521) 05633; fax (521) 61564; e-mail rrt@rrt.lt; internet www.rrt.lt; f. 2001; Dir TOMAS BARAKAUSKAS.

Major Service Provider

Lietuvos Telekomas AB: Savanorių pr. 28, Vilnius 2001; tel. (521) 27755; fax (521) 26655; e-mail info@telecom.lt; internet www.telecom.lt; f. 1992; privatized 1998; operates public telecommunications network, repairs telecommunications equipment; monopoly withdrawn in 2003; Gen. Man. ARŪNAS ŠIKŠTA; 3,200 employees.

UAB Eurocom: Naugarduko g. 99, Vilnius 03202; tel. (527) 44699; fax (527) 44612; e-mail eurocom@eurocom.lt; internet www.eurocom.lt; f. 2001; fixed line and mobile telecommunications service provider; a subsidiary of VP Market; Dir KĘSTUTIS SKREBYS.

Omnitel UAB: T. Ševčenkos 25, Vilnius 03503; tel. (698) 63333; fax (527) 45574; e-mail info@omnitel.net; internet www.omnitel.lt; f. 1991 as Litcom; 90% owned by Telia Sonera (Sweden); largest mobile GSM communications provider in Lithuania; Pres. ANTANAS JUOZAS ZABULIS.

UAB Tele2: POB 147, Vilnius 2000; tel. (684) 00212; fax (523) 66301; e-mail tele2@tele2.lt; internet www.tele2.lt; f. 1999; owned by Tele2 AB (Sweden); provider of GSM, internet and fixed-line telecommunications services; Chief Exec. PETRAS MASIULIS.

BROADCASTING

Lietuvos Radijo ir televizijos komisija (Radio and Television Commission of Lithuania): Vytenio 6, Vilnius 03113; tel. (523) 30660; fax (526) 47125; e-mail lrtk@rtk.lt; internet www.rtk.lt; f. 1996; licensing and licence compliance.

Radio

Lietuvos radijas ir televizija (Lithuanian Radio and Television): S. Konarskio 49, Vilnius 2600; tel. (523) 63000; fax (523) 63208; e-mail forel@lrtv.lt; internet www.lrtv.lt; f. 1926; govt-owned; Chair. MARCELIJUS MARTINAITIS; Gen. Dir KĘSTUTIS PETRAUSKIS.

Lietuvos radijas (Lithuanian Radio): S. Konarskio 49, Vilnius 2600; tel. (523) 63010; fax (521) 35333; internet www.lrtv.lt/lt_lr.htm; f. 1926; broadcasts in Lithuanian, Russian, Polish, Yiddish, Belarusian and Ukrainian; Dir JŪRATĖ LAUČIŪTĖ.

A2: Vilnius; tel. (526) 41229; e-mail a2@post.inet.lt; internet www.a2.lt; private, commercial.

Aukštaitijos radijas: Laisvės 1, Panevėžys 5300; tel. and fax (455) 96969; e-mail armac@laineta.lt; private, commercial; Dir ALGIRDAS ŠATAS.

Bumsas: Smiltelės 13–64, Klaipėda 5802; tel. (463) 20909; fax (463) 22020; e-mail bumsas@bumsas.lt; internet www.bumsas.lt; private, commercial; Dir DALIUS NOREIKA.

FM 99: Rotuses 2, POB 119, Alytus 4580; tel. (315) 77711; fax (315) 74646; e-mail fm99@fm99.lt; internet www.fm99.lt; private, commercial; Dir LIUDAS RAMANAUSKAS.

Kapsai: P. Armino 71, Marijampolė 4520; tel. and fax (343) 54512; e-mail kapsai@mari.omnitel.net; internet www1.omnitel.net/kapsai; private, commercial; Dir RAIMUNDAS MARUSKEVIČIUS.

Kauno fonas 105.4: Radastu 2, Kaunas 3000; tel. (373) 30390; fax (373) 30368; e-mail reklama@kaunoradijas.lt; internet www.kaunoradijas.lt; private, commercial; Dir ORESTAS MINDERIS.

Labas FM: Naugarduko 91, Vilnius 2006; tel. (521) 63591; internet www.labasfm.lt; Dir DARIUS UZKURAITIS.

Laisvoji banga: Naugarduko 91, Vilnius 2006; tel. (521) 63836; fax (521) 63591; e-mail radio@lbanga.lt; internet www.lbanga.lt; private, commercial; Dir VYTAUTAS BARTKUS.

Laluna: M. Mazvydo 11, Klaipėda 5800; tel. and fax (463) 43232; e-mail laluna@laluna.lt; internet www.laluna.lt; private, commercial; Dir RUSLANAS ALEKSANDRAVIČIUS.

M-1: Laisvės pr. 60, Vilnius 2056; tel. (523) 60360; fax (523) 60366; e-mail m-1@m-1.lt; internet www.m-1.lt; private, commercial; Dir-Gen. HUBERTAS GRUSNYS.

Mazeikiu aidas: Sodu 13–93, Mazeikiai 5500; tel. (443) 65095; fax (443) 65600; private, commercial; Dir ALINA JONIKAITĖ.

Nevėzio radijas: Kniaudiskiu 87/84 P.d. 107, Panevėžys 5304; tel. (454) 23922; fax (455) 96888; e-mail rolka@nradijas.lt; private, commercial; Dir ALVYDAS ADUKONIS.

Pukas: Šaldytuvu 25, Kaunas 3002; tel. (373) 42424; fax (373) 42434; e-mail boss@pukas.lt; f. 1991; private, commercial; Dir KĘSTUTIS PŪKAS.

Radiocentras: Laisvės pr. 60, Vilnius 2056; tel. (521) 28706; fax (524) 29073; e-mail biuras@radiocentras.lt; internet www .radiocentras.lt; private, commercial; Dir-Gen. M. GARBERIS.

Ratekona: P.d. 3300, Vilnius 2013; tel. (685) 76840; fax (521) 52171; e-mail consult@zilionis.cjb.net; f. 1994; private, commercial; Dir SIGITAS ZILIONIS.

Saules radijas: Dvaro 88, Šiauliai 5400; tel. (414) 22431; fax (414) 32816; e-mail src@siauliai.aiva.lt; private, commercial; Editor-in-Chief VALENTINAS DIDZGALVIS.

Tau: Draugystės 19, Kaunas 3031; tel. (373) 52790; fax (373) 52128; e-mail info@tau.balt.net; internet www.tau.lt; private, commercial; Dir ALGIRDAS KEPEŽINSKAS.

Titanika: Sporto 6, Kaunas 3000; tel. (372) 03404; fax (372) 08222; e-mail titanika@kaunas.sav.lt; internet www.kaunas.sav.lt/titanika/; private, commercial.

Ventus: Montuotoju 2, Mazeikiai 5500; tel. (443) 96225; fax (443) 96226; e-mail admin@ventus.lt; internet www.ventus.lt; private, commercial; Dir-Gen. GIEDRIUS STELMOKAS.

V. Mečkausko firma 'Versmės' radijas ir televizija: Pergalės 57–9, Elektrėnai 26001; tel. (528) 39543; fax (528) 39616; e-mail mesta@one.lt.

Všį Kauno radijas ir televizija: S. Daukanto 28A, Kaunas 3000; tel. (373) 21010; fax (373) 22570; e-mail kaunas@lrtv.lt; Dir P. GARNYS.

Žemaitijos radijas: Mažeikių 18, Telšiai 5610; tel. (444) 74433; fax (444) 75445; e-mail zemaitijos@radijas.lt; internet www.radijas.lt; private, commercial; Dir ALGIMANTAS GINČIAUSKIS.

UAB Znad Wilii radijo stotis: Laisvės pr. 60, Vilnius 2056; tel. (524) 90870; fax (527) 84446; e-mail radio@znadwilii.lt; internet www.znadwilii.lt; f. 1992; private, commercial; Dir-Gen. MIROSLAVAS JUCHNEVIČIUS.

Television

Lietuvos radijas ir televizija: see Radio.

Lietuvos televizija: S. Konarskio 49, Vilnius 2600; tel. (523) 63100; fax (521) 63282; e-mail romas@litv.lt; programmes in Lithuanian, Russian, Polish, Ukrainian and Belarusian; Dir ROMAS JANKAUSKAS.

Aidas: Birutes 42, Trakai 4050; tel. (528) 52480; mainly relays German programmes; private, commercial; Dir ČESLOVAS RULEVIČIUS.

Baltijos televizija: Laisvės pr. 60, Vilnius 2056; tel. (524) 28917; fax (524) 26623; e-mail webmaster@btv.lt; internet www.btv.lt; broadcasts own programmes and relays German, Polish and US broadcasts; private, commercial; Dir-Gen. GINTARAS SONGAILA.

Kaunas plius: P.d. 2040, Kaunas 3000; tel. (372) 20650; fax (372) 20640; private, commercial; Pres. HENRIKAS ZUKAUSKAS.

LNK TV (Laisvas ir nepriklausomas kanalas): Šeškinės 20, Vilnius 07156; tel. (521) 24061; fax (524) 31054; e-mail info@lnk.lt; internet www.lnk.lt; private, commercial; Dir PAULIUS KOVAS.

PAN-TV: Laisvės 26–211, Panevėžys 5300; tel. (454) 64267; fax (454) 35889; private, commercial; Dir SAULIUS BUKELIS.

Raseiniu TV: Vytauto Didziojo 10, Raseiniai 4400; tel. (428) 53955; fax (428) 53735; e-mail mirkliai@raseiniai.omnitel.net; Dir KĘSTUTIS SKAMARAKAS.

Šiaulių TV: Aušros al. 48, Šiauliai 5400; tel. and fax (415) 23809; private; Dir STASYS SUŠINSKAS.

TV3: Nemencines 4, Vilnius 2016; tel. (523) 16131; fax (527) 64253; e-mail postmaster@tv3.lt; internet www.tv3.lt; broadcasts own programmes (20% of schedule) in Lithuanian and English, and relays international satellite channels; private, commercial; Dir VILMA MARČIULEVIČIUTE.

Vilniaus TV: Vivulskio 23, Vilnius 2600; tel. (521) 35560; fax (523) 37904; e-mail vk@mail.iti.lt; internet www.vtv.lt; f. 1994; private, commercial; Dir LEONAS REMEIKA.

Finance

(cap. = capital; res = reserves; dep. = deposits; m. = million; brs = branches; amounts in litai, unless otherwise stated)

BANKING

In the early 1990s, following independence, comprehensive reforms were made to the banking system, beginning with the establishment of a central bank, the Bank of Lithuania. During 1995 several commercial banks became bankrupt, and the crisis resulted in the eventual closure of 16 of the 28 banks in operation. As a result, the Government devised a programme, in consultation with the IMF and the World Bank, to secure and restructure the banking system. At the end of 2001 nine banks were operating under a licence from the Bank of Lithuania; there were also four branches of foreign banks, and five representative offices of foreign banks in Lithuania.

Central Bank

Bank of Lithuania (Lietuvos bankas): Gedimino pr. 6, Vilnius 2001; tel. (526) 80029; fax (526) 28124; e-mail info@lb.lt; internet www.lb.lt; f. 1922; re-est. 1990; central bank, responsible for bank supervision; cap. 100m., res 413.3m., dep. 3,270.2m. (Dec. 2002); Chair. of Bd REINOLDIJUS ŠARKINAS.

Commercial Banks

Bank of Vilnius (Vilniaus bankas AB): Gedimino pr. 12, Vilnius 2600; tel. (526) 82514; fax (526) 82333; e-mail info@vb.lt; internet www.vb.lt; f. 1990 as Spaudos Bankas; absorbed AB Bankas Hermis in 2000; 98.9% owned by Skandinaviska Enskilda Banken AB (Sweden); cap. 154.4m., res 530.3m., dep. 5,406.1m. (Dec. 2002); Pres. and Chief Exec. JULIUS NIEDVARAS; 18 brs.

AB Bankas Hansabankas: Savanorių pr. 19, Vilnius 2009; tel. (526) 84444; fax (522) 32433; e-mail info@hansa.lt; internet www .hansa.lt; f. 2001 by merger of Lieutuvos Taupomasis Bankas and Hansabankas; name changed as above in April 2003; 99.25% owned by Hansapank (Estonia); cap. 370.3m., res −81.6m., dep. 3,729.0m. (Dec. 2002); Chair. of Bd GIEDRIUS DUSEVIČIUS.

AB Bankas NORD/LB Lietuva: J. Basanavičiaus 26, Vilnius 2600; tel. (523) 93444; fax (521) 39057; e-mail info@nordlb.lt; internet www.nordlb.lt; f. 1992 as AB Lietuvos Žemės Ūkio Bankas; name changed as above in May 2003; 93.09% owned by Norddeutsche Landesbank Girozentrale (Germany); cap. 176.6m., res 33.8m., dep. 1,631.0m. (Dec. 2002); Chair. THOMAS S. BUERKLE; 46 brs.

Medical Bank (Medicinos Bankas): Pamėnkalnio 40, Vilnius 2600; tel. (521) 23321; fax (526) 24481; e-mail info@medbank.lt; internet www.medbank.lt; f. 1992; cap. 34.3m., res −3.1m., dep. 109.4m. (Dec. 2002); Chair. of Bd KĘSTUTIS OLSAUSKAS; 7 brs.

AB Parex Bankas: K. Kalinausko 13, Vilnius 2009; tel. (526) 64600; fax (526) 64601; e-mail info@parex.lt; internet www.parex.lt; f. 1996; cap. 31.0m. , res 0.9m., dep. 128.1m. (Dec. 2002); Chair. and Chief Exec. JANIS TUKANS; 6 brs.

UAB Sampo Bankas: Gelezinio Vilko 18A, Vilnius 2004; tel. (521) 09400; fax (521) 09409; e-mail bankas@sampo.lt; internet www .sampo.lt; f. 1994; fmrly Lithuanian Development Bank; present name adopted 2001; 99.99% owned by Sampo plc (Finland); cap. 53.1m., res 3.3m., dep. 318.3m. (Dec. 2002); Chair. of Bd GINTAUTAS GALVANAUSKAS.

Šiaulių Bankas AB: Tilžės 149, Šiauliai 5400; tel. (415) 22117; fax (414) 30774; e-mail info@sb.lt; internet www.sb.lt; f. 1992; cap. 38.0m., res 5.4m., dep. 398.5m. (Dec. 2002); Chair. ALGIRDAS BUTKUS; 8 brs.

Snoras Bank: A. Vivulskio 7, Vilnius 2600; tel. (526) 62700; fax (523) 10155; e-mail info@snoras.com; internet www.snoras.com; f. 1992; cap. 163.5m., dep. 655.1m., total assets 884.0m. (Dec. 2001); Chair. of Management Bd RAIMONDAS BARANAUSKAS; 10 brs.

AB Ūkio Bankas: J. Gruodžio 9, Kaunas 3000; tel. (373) 01301; fax (373) 23188; e-mail ub@ub.lt; internet www.ub.lt; f. 1989; cap. 90.7m., res −8.9m., dep. 608.1m. (Dec. 2002); Chair. of Bd and Chief Exec. EDITA KARPAVIČIENE; 12 brs.

Property Banks

Turto Bank: Kestucio 46, Vilnius 2600; tel. (527) 80900; fax (527) 51155; e-mail info@turtas.lt; internet www.turtas.lt; f. 1996; cap. 8.9m., total assets 1,001.9m. (Dec. 2000); recovery of non-performing loans, administration of Ministry of Finance loans; Chair. of Bd STEPONAS VYTAUTAS JURNA; 6 brs.

Banking Association

Association of Lithuanian Banks: Ankštoji g. 5, Vilnius 2600; tel. (524) 96669; fax (524) 96139; e-mail info@lba.lt; f. 1991; Pres. EDUARDAS VILKELIS; 10 mems.

COMMODITY EXCHANGES

National Commodity Exchange: Laisvės 35, Kaunas 3000; tel. (372) 24498; fax (376) 20726; f. 1992; Pres. Vytautas Vinkleris; 16 mems.

Baltic Exchange: Pylimo 2/6, Vilnius 2001; tel. (521) 61195; fax (521) 26842; f. 1991; Pres. Vytautas Jakelis; 16 mems.

STOCK EXCHANGE

National Stock Exchange: Konstitucijos pr. 23, Vilnius 2600; tel. (527) 23871; fax (527) 24894; e-mail office@nse.lt; internet www.nse.lt; f. 1993; Pres. Rimantas Busila.

Trade and Industry

GOVERNMENT AGENCIES

Fund for State Property and Restoration of People's Savings: Vilnius; f. 1997; supervises distribution and uses of revenues derived from privatization.

Lithuanian Development Agency for Small and Medium-sized Enterprises (SMEDA): Gedimino pr. 38/2, Vilnius 01104; tel. (526) 19219; fax (526) 19207; e-mail info@svv.lt; internet www.svv.lt; f. 1996; under the Ministry of the Economy; Dir Arvydas Darulis.

State Property Fund: Vilnius 16, Vilnius 01507; tel. (526) 84999; fax (526) 84997; e-mail info@vtf.lt; internet www.vtf.lt; f. 1995; privatization and management of state-owned and municipal property; Dir Povilas Milašauskas.

DEVELOPMENT AGENCY

National Regional Development Agency: Lukiskiu 5–502, Vilnius 2005; tel. and fax (523) 34151; e-mail nrda@nrda.lt; internet www.nrda.lt; f. 1999 by the Asscn of Lithuanian Chambers of Commerce, Industry and Crafts; Dir Auridas Skibiniauskas.

CHAMBERS OF COMMERCE

Association of Lithuanian Chambers of Commerce, Industry and Crafts: J-Tumo-Vaižganto 9/1–63A, Vilnius 01108; tel. (526) 12102; fax (526) 12112; e-mail info@chambers.lt; internet www.chambers.lt; f. 1992; mem. of International Chamber of Commerce and of Asscn of European Chambers of Commerce and Industry; Dir-Gen. Rimas Varkulevičius.

Kaunas Chamber of Commerce, Industry and Crafts: K. Donelaičio 8, Kaunas 3000; POB 2111, Kaunas; tel. (372) 01491; fax (372) 08330; e-mail chamber@chamber.lt; internet www.chamber.lt; f. 1925; re-est. 1991; Pres. M. Rondomanskas.

Klaipėda Chamber of Commerce, Industry and Crafts: POB 148, Klaipėda 5800; tel. (464) 10628; fax (464) 10626; e-mail krppr@klaipeda.omnitel.net; Pres. Sigitas Paulauskas; Dir Viktoras Krolis.

Marijampolė Chamber of Commerce and Industry: Kęstučio 9/20, Marijampolė 4520; tel. (343) 55568; fax (343) 56346; Pres. Vygandas Matulis.

Panevėžys Chamber of Commerce, Industry and Crafts: Respublikos 34, Panevėžys 5319; tel. (454) 63687; fax (454) 62227; e-mail panevezys@chambers.lt; internet www.ccic.lt; f. 1991; Pres. Vytautas Šidlauskas; Gen. Dir Vytautas Kazakevičius.

Šiauliai Chamber of Commerce, Industry and Crafts: Vilniaus 88, Šiauliai 76285; tel. (41) 523224; fax (41) 523903; e-mail siauliai@chambers.lt; internet www.rumai.lt; f. 1993; Dir-Gen. Rimundas Domarkas.

Vilnius Chamber of Commerce, Industry and Crafts: Algirdo 31, Vilnius 2600; tel. (521) 35550; fax (521) 35542; e-mail vilnius@cci.lt; internet www.cci.lt; f. 1991; Pres. Vytas Navickas; 427 mems.

INDUSTRIAL ASSOCIATION

Lithuanian Industrialists' Confederation: A. Vienuolio 8, Vilnius 2001; tel. (521) 25217; fax (527) 23320; f. 1989; Pres. Bronislovas Lubys.

EMPLOYERS' ORGANIZATION

Lithuanian Business Employers' Confederation: A. Rotundo 5, Vilnius 2600; tel. (526) 29729; fax (526) 20448; e-mail lvdk@post.omnitel.net; internet 195.182.80.20/lvdk; f. 1999; Pres. Viktor Uspaskich.

UTILITIES

Energy System of Lithuania: Zveju 14, Vilnius 2600; tel. (527) 34638; fax (521) 26736; Gen. Dir Anzelmas Bacialiskas.

Electricity

Lietuvos energija AB (Lithuanian Power): Zveju 14, Vilnius 2600; tel. (527) 82406; fax (521) 26736; e-mail lietuvos.energija@lpc.lt; internet www.lpc.lt; f. 1995; restructured in 2000; Man. Dir Rymantas Juozaitis; 11,500 employees.

Alytus Electric Utility: Pramonės 7, Alytus 4580; tel. (315) 25745; fax (315) 34827; e-mail aet@lpc.lt; f. 1962; transmission and distribution; 127,000 customers (Dec. 1996); Dir Vitas Blazauskas.

Klaipėda Electric Utility: Liepu 64A, Klaipėda 5799; tel. (463) 15064; fax (463) 15056; f. 1957; transmission and distribution; 218,000 customers (Dec. 1996); Dir Vytautas Girdvainis.

Rytų Skirstomieji Tinklai AB (RST): Senamiesčio 102B, Panevėžys 5319; tel. (455) 04459; fax (454) 81394; e-mail pet@pet.lt; internet rytis.rst.lt; f. 1957; distribution of electricity in eastern Lithuania; scheduled for privatization; 156,000 customers (Dec. 2002); Dir Leonas Mikalajūnas.

Šiauliai Electric Utility: Tilžės 68, Šiauliai 5409; tel. (415) 94459; fax (415) 53041; e-mail info@set.lpc.lt; f. 1957; transmission and distribution; 190,000 customers (Jan. 2002); Dir Vincas Ponelis.

Utena Electric Utility: Uzpaliu 87, Utena 4910; tel. (389) 62150; fax (389) 62196; e-mail utenoset@uet.lpc.lt; f. 1964; transmission and distribution; 113,900 customers (Jan. 2001); Dir Jurgis Dumbrava.

JSC Vakaru skirstomieji tinklai (VST): Kestučio 36, Kaunas 3000; tel. (373) 09259; fax (373) 09269; e-mail vest@vest.lt; internet www.vest.lt; f. 2001; distribution in central and western Lithuania; 96.5% of shares divested to NDX Energija in 2003–04; Chief Exec. Darius Nedzinskas; 3,000 employees.

Vilnius Electric Utility: Motoru 2, Vilnius 2038; tel. (521) 67465; fax (521) 67467; f. 1957; transmission and distribution; 268,000 customers (Dec. 1996); Dir Rimantas Milisauskas.

Gas

Lietuvos Dujos (Lithuanian Gas): Aguonų 24, Vilnius 2600; tel. (523) 60210; fax (523) 60200; e-mail lt@lietuvosdujos.lt; internet www.dujos.lt; f. 1995; natural gas transmission and distribution; 24% state-owned; 36% owned by Ruhrgas AG (Germany); 34% of shares divested to Gazprom (Russia) in 2004; Chair. Eike Benke; Gen. Man. Vikoras Valentukevičius; 4,300 employees.

TRADE UNIONS

Christian Farmers' Union of Lithuania: V. Mykolaičio-Putino 5, Vilnius 2009; tel. and fax (523) 12029; f. 1919; re-est. 1995; 10 regional brs; 6,000 mems; Chair. Juozas Aleknavičius.

Lithuanian Labour Federation: V. Mykolaičio-Putino 5/140, Vilnius 2600; tel. and fax (523) 12029; e-mail ldforg@ldf.lt; internet www.ldf.lt; f. 1919; re-est. 1991; 20,000 mems; Chair. Kazimieras Kuzminskas; Sec.-Gen. Regina Rekesiene.

Lithuanian Trade Unions Centre: Basanavičiaus 29A, Vilnius 2600; tel. (526) 14888; fax (526) 60217; f. 1993; 13 affiliated unions with 140,000 mems; Chair. Algirdas Kvedaravičius.

Lithuanian Union of Free Trade Unions: J. Jasinskio 9, Vilnius 2600; tel. (526) 10921; fax (526) 19078; f. 1992; 8 affiliated unions with 50,000 mems; Chair. Algirdas Sysas.

Lithuanian Workers' Union: V. Mykolaičio-Putino 5, Vilnius 2009; tel. (526) 21743; fax (521) 33295; e-mail ltds@takas.lt; internet www.darbininkas.lt; f. 1989; 28 regional brs; 7 federations; 52,000 mems; Pres. Aldona Balsiené.

Transport

RAILWAYS

In 2002 there were 1,775 km of railway track in use in Lithuania; in the same year some 122 km of track were electrified. Main lines link Vilnius with Rīga (Latvia), Minsk (Belarus), Kaliningrad (Russia) and Warsaw (Poland), via the Belarusian town of Grodno.

Lithuanian Railways (Lietuvos geležinkeliai AB): Mindaugo 12–14, Vilnius 2600; tel. (526) 93300; fax (526) 18323; e-mail 24@litrail.lt; internet www.litrail.lt; f. 1991; Gen. Dir K. Dirgela; 15,500 employees.

ROADS

In 2002 the total length of the road network was 77,148 km. The motorway network totalled 417 km and some 90% of roads were paved.

Lithuanian Road Administration (Lietuvos automobilių kelių direkcija): J. Basanaviciaus 36/2, Vilnius 03109; tel. (521) 31361; fax (521) 31362; e-mail info@lra.lt; internet www.lra.lt; Gen. Dir VIRGAUDAS PUODZIUKAS.

SHIPPING

The main port is at Klaipėda. During the Soviet period the port was used as an important transit facility, with some 90% of its total traffic being transit trade to and from the republics of the USSR. This role diminished with the establishment of Lithuanian independence in 1991. In 2002 there were 477 km of inland navigable waterways.

Port Authority

Klaipėda State Seaport Authority: J. Janonio 24, Klaipėda 5800; tel. (464) 99799; fax (464) 99777; e-mail info@port.lt; internet www .port.lt.

Shipowning Company

Public Company 'Lithuanian Shipping Company' (AB Lietuvos Jūrų Laivininkystė): Malunininku 3, Klaipėda 5813; tel. (463) 93105; fax (463) 93119; e-mail gp@ljl.lt; internet www.ljl.lt; f. 1969; partially privatized in June 2001; 73.24% state-owned; transportation of cargo; Gen. Dir VYTAUTAS VISMANTAS.

CIVIL AVIATION

Lithuania has air links with Western European destinations and with cities in the former USSR. The state airline, Lietuvos aviali-nijos, is based at the international airports at Vilnius and Kaunas. An airport at Šiauliai opened for international flights at the end of 1993.

Directorate of Civil Aviation (Oro Navigacija): Rodūnės kelias 2, Vilnius 2023; tel. (527) 39102; fax (527) 39161; e-mail info@ans.lt; internet www.ans.lt; Gen. Dir ALGIMANTAS RAŠČIUS.

Lithuanian Airlines (Lietuvos avialinijos): A. Gustaičio 4, Vilnius 2038; tel. (523) 06017; fax (521) 66828; e-mail info@lal.lt; internet www.lal.lt; f. 1991; state-owned; operates passenger and cargo flights to regional and European destinations; Dir-Gen. STASYS JARMALAVIČIUS.

Aviakompanija Lietuva (Air Lithuania): Veiverių 132, Karmelava Airport, Kaunas 3018; tel. (373) 91420; fax (372) 26030; e-mail hdoffice@airlithuania.lt; internet www.airlithuania.lt; f. 1991; state-owned; became subsidiary of Lithuanian Airlines in August 1997; scheduled for privatization in 2004; operates passenger and cargo services to Europe; Chair. and Dir-Gen. TOMAS LAURINAITIS.

Tourism

Tourist attractions in Lithuania include the historic cities of Vilnius, Kaunas, Kėdainiai, Trakai and Klaipėda, coastal resorts, such as Palanga and Kuršiu Nerija, and picturesque countryside. There were some 350 private travel agencies in operation in 1999 and some 349,662 tourists visited the country in 2001; tourist receipts in that year totalled US $383.0m.

Lithuanian State Department of Tourism: A. Juozapavičiaus 13, Vilnius 09311; tel. (521) 08796; fax (521) 08753; e-mail vtd@ tourism.lt; internet www.tourism.lt; Dir ALVITIS LUKOSEVICIUS.

LUXEMBOURG

Introductory Survey

Location, Climate, Language, Religion, Flag, Capital

The Grand Duchy of Luxembourg is a land-locked country in Western Europe. It is bordered by Belgium to the west and north, by France to the south, and by Germany to the east. The climate is temperate, with cool summers and mild winters. In Luxembourg-Ville the average temperature ranges from 1°C (33°F) in January to 18°C (64°F) in July, while annual rainfall averages 782 mm. Letzeburgish (Luxembourgish), a German-Moselle-Frankish dialect, is the spoken language and became the official language in 1985. French is generally used for administrative purposes, while German is the principal written language of commerce and the press. Almost all of the inhabitants profess Christianity: about 88% are Roman Catholics and a small minority are Protestants. The national flag (proportions 3 by 5) consists of three equal horizontal stripes, of red, white and blue. The capital is Luxembourg-Ville (Lützelburg).

Recent History

As a founder member of the European Community (EC—now European Union—EU, see p. 208), of which Luxembourg-Ville is one of the main bases, Luxembourg has played a significant role in progress towards European integration since the Second World War. Luxembourg's commitment to such integration was exemplified by its status as one of the original signatories to the June 1990 Schengen Agreement (named after the town in Luxembourg where the accord was signed), which binds signatories to the abolition of internal border controls.

The Belgo-Luxembourg Economic Union (BLEU) has existed since 1921, except for the period from 1940–44, when the Grand Duchy was subject to wartime occupation by Germany. In 1948 the Benelux Economic Union (see p. 359) was inaugurated between Belgium, Luxembourg and the Netherlands, becoming effective in 1960, and establishing the three countries as a single customs area in 1970.

In November 1964 Grand Duchess Charlotte abdicated, after a reign of 45 years, and was succeeded by her son, Prince Jean.

Pierre Werner, leader of the Parti Chrétien Social (PCS), became Prime Minister in February 1959. After the fall of the Government in October 1968, Werner headed a coalition of the PCS and the Parti Démocratique ('Liberals') from January 1969 until May 1974. At a general election in May 1974, the PCS lost its political dominance for the first time since 1919, and in June a centre-left coalition between the Parti Ouvrier Socialiste Luxembourgeois (POSL) and the Parti Démocratique Luxembourgeois (PDL) was formed under the premiership of Gaston Thorn, the Minister of Foreign Affairs since 1969. At the next general election, which took place in June 1979, the PCS increased its strength in the 59-member Chambre des Députés from 18 to 24 seats. In July Werner again formed a coalition Government, comprising his party and the PDL, which held 15 seats.

At a general election in June 1984 the PCS again secured the largest number of seats (25) in the enlarged 64-member legislature. However, the success of the POSL, which took 21 seats (compared with 14 in the previous election), was widely attributed to general dissatisfaction with an economic austerity programme, which had been introduced during the early 1980s, and with the rising level of unemployment. A centre-left coalition was formed in July 1984 between the PCS and the POSL, with Jacques Santer of the PCS (hitherto Minister of Finance, Labour and Social Security) as Prime Minister. New elections to the Chambre des Députés (whose membership had been reduced to 60 in January 1989) took place in June 1989. The PCS, the POSL and the PDL each lost three seats (returning, respectively, 22, 18 and 11 deputies). In the following month Santer was again sworn in as the head of a coalition Government, which comprised equal numbers of representatives from the PCS and the POSL. At the next general election, in June 1994, the PCS and the POSL each lost one representative in the Chambre des Députés, winning 21 and 17 seats respectively; the PDL secured 12 seats. The PCS-POSL coalition was renewed, and Santer was reappointed Prime Minister. In January 1995 Santer took office as President of the Commission of the EU. He was succeeded as Prime Minister by Jean-Claude Juncker, hitherto Minister of the Budget, of Finance and of Labour.

In January 1998 the Minister of the Environment and of Health, Johny Lahure, resigned from his posts following the disclosure of a financial scandal within the Ministry of Health, and in May 1999 the President of the National Audit Office, Gérard Reuter, was suspended from office, pending investigation into allegations of mismanagement and fraud.

The two governing parties both recorded losses at the general election held concurrently with elections to the European Parliament on 13 June 1999, the PCS emerging with 19 seats and the POSL with 13. The main opposition party, the PDL, increased its representation from 12 to 15 seats, while the Comité d'Action pour la Démocratie et la Justice took seven seats (an increase of two). The environmentalist party, Déi Gréng, retained its five seats in the Chambre des Députés. Juncker, who remained as Prime Minister, subsequently formed a new centre-right coalition of his PCS and the PDL, which took office in early August; the POSL thus returned to opposition for the first time in 15 years.

In March 1998 Grand Duke Jean conferred broad constitutional powers upon his son and heir, Prince Henri, permitting him to deputize for the Grand Duke in all official capacities, including the signing of legislation, and in late December 1999 Grand Duke Jean announced his intention to abdicate the following year. On 7 October 2000 the Grand Duke's eldest son, Prince Henri, succeeded him as Head of State.

Luxembourg's banking secrecy laws have for many years been a cause of concern regarding the activities of banks and individual depositors benefiting from such legislation. Attempts by the EC, in the early 1990s, to impose more uniform regulations on the conduct of financial services in its member countries, in conjunction with the world-wide liquidation, in July 1991, of the Bank of Credit and Commerce International, the holding company and a subsidiary of which were incorporated in Luxembourg, focused renewed attention on Luxembourg's regulatory procedures. In April 1993 legislation was introduced which permitted the confiscation of deposits in Luxembourg banks accruing from suspected illegal drugs-related activities. Further legislation was introduced in 1997 which extended the State's powers of confiscation to include funds believed to be derived from other illegal sources, including arms-smuggling. During 1997 Luxembourg's financial sector came under renewed scrutiny when the Belgian authorities conducted an investigation into alleged widespread tax evasion by Belgian citizens and companies based in the Grand Duchy. The German authorities also launched a similar investigation. Luxembourg was further criticized for refusing, as did Switzerland, to endorse the code of conduct with respect to tax 'havens' drafted by the Organisation for Economic Co-operation and Development (OECD, see p. 295) in April 1998. During 1998 Luxembourg also opposed European Commission moves towards European taxation harmonization, which would oblige Luxembourg to impose tax on non-residents' interest and dividend income for the first time, thereby reducing the attraction of Luxembourg as a financial centre. In May 2000, however, Luxembourg for the first time endorsed reforms, proposed by a report by the OECD, aimed at limiting the use of bank secrecy laws in order to evade paying taxes; the report did, however, acknowledge the legitimacy of bank secrecy. In October the Chambre des Députés approved a relaxation of bank secrecy laws to facilitate co-operation with the US Internal Revenue Service in its attempts to halt tax evasion.

In December 2000 the Government was very active during negotiations regarding the Treaty of Nice, which aimed to reform the institutions of the EU in light of its forthcoming enlargements. The terms of the Treaty substantially safeguarded Luxembourg's privileged position in the EU: Luxembourg was to continue to have a European Commissioner, to maintain its six seats in the European Parliament and to continue to enjoy a voting weight in the Council of the European Union out of proportion to its size. Consequently it was no surprise that, in July 2001, the Chambre des Députés ratified the Treaty by a large majority, making the Grand Duchy the third EU member state to do so. At the same time, Luxembourg continued, much to the frustration of most of its EU partners, to oppose the removal from Luxembourg-Ville of the Secretariat of the European Parliament, together with its 1,500 staff, whose continued presence in the Grand Duchy was considered by the Luxembourg Government to be vital to the local economy.

The leaders and ministers responsible for foreign affairs from seven of the EU's smaller states (Luxembourg, Austria, Belgium, Finland, the Netherlands, Ireland and Portugal) met in Luxembourg in early April 2003 to prepare a unified position against the potential diminution of their powers by the Convention on the Future of Europe, which aimed to draft the EU's first constitution. Notably, they were opposed to a French and German initiative to install an elected President for the Council of the European Union, to replace the current system whereby the presidency is rotated among the members every six months, on the grounds that the latter effectively guaranteed smaller countries a role in EU policy formation.

In June 2002 new legislation was enacted which enabled women who had never worked and therefore not contributed to a pension fund to be entitled to receive a pension in their own right from the age of 60 years. The following month laws to assist first-time house buyers were introduced. Also in July controversial new legislation allowing for the expansion of Findel Airport was approved.

Elections to both the national legislature and the European Parliament were scheduled for 13 June 2004. Juncker, who was considered one of the most likely candidates to replace Romano Prodi as President of the European Commission, nevertheless affirmed his commitment to domestic politics.

Popular opposition in Luxembourg to a potential US-led military campaign in Iraq to remove the regime of Saddam Hussain culminated in nation-wide demonstrations on 15 February 2003. The Government's opposition to the military intervention (which was undertaken without the support of a UN resolution), although muted, adversely affected relations with the USA. Following the removal of the Iraqi regime, however, the Government announced the allocation of €3.5m. for the financing of a humanitarian aid programme for Iraq. In March Parliament approved the secondment of 10 officers and men to the International Security and Assistance Force in Afghanistan (ISAF), and, as part of the EU's first ever military operation, that of one officer to the Union's peace-keeping mission to the former Yugoslav republic of Macedonia. Four EU countries, Luxembourg, Belgium, France and Germany, all of which had opposed the US-led military campaign in Iraq, held a special summit in April to discuss defence matters, at which it was agreed to establish an autonomous European military command headquarters near Brussels. The plan, which provoked protests from the USA and the United Kingdom, was superseded in December by a compromise agreement between France, Germany and the United Kingdom to create an EU 'planning cell' within existing defence structures.

Government

Luxembourg is an hereditary and constitutional monarchy. Legislative power is exercised by the unicameral Chambre des Députés, with 60 members elected by universal adult suffrage for five years (subject to dissolution) on the basis of proportional representation. Some legislative functions are also entrusted to the advisory Conseil de l'Etat, with 21 members appointed for life by the Grand Duke, but decisions made by this body can be overruled by the legislature.

Executive power is vested in the Grand Duke, but is normally exercised by the Council of Ministers, led by the President of the Government (Prime Minister). The Grand Duke appoints ministers, but they are responsible to the legislature. Luxembourg is divided into three districts (Luxembourg, Diekirch, Grevenmacher), 12 cantons and 118 municipalities.

Defence

Luxembourg was a founder member of NATO in 1949. Compulsory military service was abolished in 1967, but Luxembourg maintains an army of volunteers, totalling 900, and a gendarmerie numbering 612 (in August 2003). Defence expenditure in the budget for 2003 was about €204m. In March 1987 the country became a signatory of the Benelux military convention, together with Belgium and the Netherlands. This aimed at the standardization of training methods and of military equipment in the three countries. Luxembourg committed 100 troops to the proposed joint EU rapid reaction force, which was to be ready to be deployed by 2003.

Economic Affairs

In 2002, according to estimates by the World Bank, Luxembourg's gross national income (GNI), measured at average 2000–02 prices, was US $17,221m., equivalent to $38,830 per head (or $51,060 per head on an international purchasing-power parity basis). During 1990–2002, it was estimated, the population increased at an average rate of 1.3% per year, while gross domestic product (GDP) per head grew, in real terms, by an average of 3.7% per year. Overall GDP increased, in real terms, at an average annual rate of 5.1% in 1990–2002; growth in 2002 was 0.8%.

Agriculture (including forestry and fishing) contributed 0.5% of GDP in 2002. In the same year an estimated 1.3% of the employed labour force were engaged in the agricultural sector. The principal crops are cereals, potatoes and wine grapes. Livestock-rearing is also of some importance. According to the IMF, agricultural GDP declined at an average annual rate of 0.4% in 1990–95 and, according to the World Bank, it grew by 1.3% per year during 1995–2000. However, in 2000, real agricultural GDP fell by 0.5%.

Industry (including mining, manufacturing, construction and power) provided 16.6% of GDP and engaged an estimated 22.4% of the employed labour force in 2002. Industrial GDP increased, in real terms, at an average annual rate of 0.3% in 1990–95 and by 5.0% per year in 1995–2000; it rose by 9.3% in 1999 and by 5.2% in 2000.

Manufacturing activities, excluding power and water, constitute the most important industrial sector, contributing 9.5% of GDP and engaging 11.9% of the employed work-force in 2002. Although the country's deposits of iron ore are no longer exploited, the iron and steel industry remains one of the most important sectors of the Luxembourg economy; metal manufactures accounted for an estimated 28.1% of total exports in 2001. The Luxembourg steel industry is dominated by Arcelor, which was formed in June 2001 by the merger of the Luxembourg-based Aciéries Réunies de Burbach-Eich-Dudelange SA—ARBED and the steel companies Usinor, of France, and Aceralia, of Spain, to form the world's largest steel group. In January 2003 Arcelor announced that no further investment would be made in the two smelting furnaces in the Val du Fensch and that hot-phase production would gradually cease. The steelworks, which employed around 1,500 workers and contributed 85% of the Val du Fensch's annual revenue, would eventually close in 2010. Machinery and equipment provided 24.0% of total exports in 2001. Other important branches of manufacturing are basic manufactures and chemicals and related products. According to the IMF, real manufacturing GDP increased by an average of 1.5% per year in 1990–95 and, according to the World Bank, by 4.7% per year in 1995–2000; it grew by 7.5% in 1999 and by 6.1% in 2000.

In 2000 53.1% of electricity was derived from natural gas and 27.7% from hydroelectric installations. Fuel imports comprised 7.1% of the value of total imports in 2000.

The services sector contributed 82.8% of GDP and engaged 76.4% of the employed labour force in 2002. Favourable laws governing banking secrecy and taxation have encouraged the development of Luxembourg as a major international financial centre. Financial services contributed 21.9% of GDP in 2001. In 2003 there were 178 banks in Luxembourg, and about 23,000 people were employed in banking activities. In 2002 there were 14,335 holding companies registered in Luxembourg. Stock exchange activities (notably the 'Eurobond' market and investment portfolio management) are also prominent; at April 2000 Luxembourg's investment fund sector was the biggest in Europe, with assets of €848,000m. At the end of 2000 there were 94 approved insurance companies in Luxembourg, as well as 264 reinsurance companies. According to the IMF, the GDP of the services sector increased, in real terms, at an average annual rate of 6.8% in 1990–95 and, according to World Bank figures, by 6.2% per year in 1995–2000; it rose by 3.6% in 1999 and by 8.2% in 2000.

In 2002, according to IMF figures, Luxembourg recorded a visible trade deficit of US $2,163m.; however, there was a surplus on the current account of the balance of payments of $1,636m. Other members of the European Union (EU, see p. 208) account for much of Luxembourg's foreign trade (supplying 89.9% of imports and purchasing 84.5% of exports, according to provisional figures for 2002). In 2002 the principal source of imports (34.8%) was Belgium; other major providers were Germany (26.3%), France (15.3%) and the Netherlands (5.1%). The principal market for exports in that year was Germany (25.1%); other major purchasers were France (19.8%), Belgium (11.9%), the United Kingdom (7.4%) and Italy (5.8%). The principal exports in 2002 were manufactured goods, particularly metal manufactures, and machinery and transport equipment. The principal imports were machinery, transport equipment, manufactured articles, notably metal manufactures, and chemical products.

In 2002 a small budgetary surplus, of €500,000, was recorded. Government debt was equivalent to 6.2% of GDP in 1999. The annual rate of inflation averaged 2.2% in 1990–2002; consumer prices rose by 2.7% in 2001 and by 2.1% in 2002. Unemployment averaged 3.8% in 2003. Cross-border commuters from neighbouring states totalled 94,500 in 2002, constituting more than one-third of the total employed in Luxembourg.

Luxembourg was a founder member of the EU and of the Benelux Economic Union (see p. 359). Luxembourg is also a member of the European Bank for Reconstruction and Development (see p. 203), and the European System of Central Banks (ESCB), inaugurated in 1998 (see European Central Bank).

Luxembourg's economy expanded at an average annual rate of more than 5% during 1985–2000, recording increases in GDP even in the early 1990s when neighbouring countries were in recession. In January 1999 Luxembourg participated in the adoption of the euro as the single unit of currency for transactions throughout the eurozone and as an internationally traded currency in the 11 EU countries participating in economic and monetary union. The country's economic success was based on its development as an international financial centre, following the decline in the importance of the country's previously dominant iron and steel industry. In order to promote the country's long-term prospects, the IMF recommended tax reform, the restructuring of the pension system, the introduction of measures to improve the flexibility of the labour market and continuing support to the financial sector through effective supervision. Government proposals to reduce corporate and personal taxes, and to promote private pension savings took effect from the budget of 2002. The IMF also warned that the rapid growth of the late 1990s was unlikely to be replicated in the future and that the sharp rise in expenditure at central government level might become unsustainable. This economic growth, which has ensured buoyant public finances, was achieved with virtually no inflationary effect, although an increase in petroleum prices provoked a steep rise in inflation, of 3%, in early 2003 (the annual average was estimated to be 2.1%). A strengthening euro was expected to help reduce inflation in early 2004, leading to a predicted annual average of 2%. Rapid economic expansion in Luxembourg has attracted an increasing number of cross-border workers from neighbouring countries, who accounted for more than one-third of the work-force in 2002. These workers pay social security contributions in Luxembourg but retire to their native countries to spend their pensions, which are financed by Luxembourg. The solution advanced by the Government was to eschew further job creation in favour of the development of high-technology industries (with a substantial value added), which do not require a larger work-force. This plan was also expected to help to diversify the economy away from too great a dependence on the financial sector, the future profitability of which was likely to be eroded by the effects of EU integration, including the harmonization of taxation and regulatory structures. The financial sector had anticipated with consternation the potential consequences of the removal of banking secrecy at the behest of the EU. Its apprehensions were allayed, at least temporarily, when the new EU taxation rules concerning overseas investments, which were highly favourable to Luxembourg, were agreed in early 2003. They allowed Luxembourg (as well as Austria and Belgium) to retain banking

secrecy for at least the next six years, while other EU countries were to begin exchanging account details from 2005 in an attempt to eliminate tax fraud. Instead, in Luxembourg, Austria and Belgium a withholding tax would be levied on non-residents' savings. The tax would rise incrementally from 15% in 2005 to 35% in 2010. Crucially, Switzerland would have to apply the same rate of tax, thus avoiding 'capital flight' from Luxembourg. Luxembourg also secured an agreement that it would not be forced to exchange banking information in the future without parallel action from Switzerland (which was extremely unlikely). Luxembourg also hoped to diversify into the potentially lucrative cross-border pensions fund market, and had already installed a flexible regulatory regime in order to take full advantage of pending EU legislation (expected to be adopted in 2005) allowing pension-fund providers to offer services and products to customers across the EU. A comparatively modest increase in GDP, of 2.5%, was forecast for 2004. It was predicted that in the same year the fiscal deficit would exceed 3% of GDP.

Education

Education in Luxembourg is compulsory from the age of four to 15 years. Primary education begins at six years of age and lasts for six years. German is the initial language of instruction at primary level. French is added to the programme in the second year, and replaces German as the language of instruction at higher secondary level.

At the age of 12, children can choose between secondary school (lycée) and technical education (lycée technique). The first year of secondary school is a general orientation course on comprehensive lines, which is then followed by a choice between two sections: the Classical Section, with an emphasis on Latin, and the Modern Section, which stresses English and other modern languages. The completed secondary course lasts seven years, and leads to the Certificat de Fin d'Etudes Secondaires, which qualifies for university entrance. The technical education course (six to eight years) leads either to a vocational diploma, a technician's diploma (diplôme de technicien) or a technical baccalaureate diploma (bac technique) and is devised in three parts: an orientation and observation course, an intermediate course and an upper course.

The Centre Universitaire was established in 1969, offering one-year or two-year courses in the humanities, sciences and law and economics, as well as training courses for lawyers and teachers, following which the students generally attend other European universities. The Institut Supérieur de Technologies (IST) is an institute for higher education at university level in civil engineering, electrical engineering, applied computer sciences and mechanical engineering.

Central government expenditure on national education, vocational training and sport in 2003 was projected at €662.3m. (equivalent to around 12% of total current expenditure).

Public Holidays

2004: 1 January (New Year's Day), 23 February (Carnival), 12 April (Easter Monday), 1 May (Labour Day), 20 May (Ascension Day), 31 May (Whit Monday), 23 June (National Day), 15 August (Assumption), 6 September (Luxembourg City Fête, Luxembourg City only), 1 November (All Saints' Day), 25 December (Christmas), 26 December (St Stephen's Day).

2005: 1 January (New Year's Day), 7 February (Carnival), 28 March (Easter Monday), 1 May (Labour Day), 5 May (Ascension Day), 16 May (Whit Monday), 23 June (National Day), 15 August (Assumption), 5 September (Luxembourg City Fête, Luxembourg City only), 1 November (All Saints' Day), 25 December (Christmas), 26 December (St Stephen's Day).

Weights and Measures

The metric system is in force.

Statistical Survey

Source (unless otherwise stated): Service Central de la Statistique et des Etudes Economiques (STATEC), Ministère de l'Economie, 6 blvd Royal, BP 304, 2013 Luxembourg; tel. 478-42-52; fax 46-42-89; e-mail statec.post@statec.etat.lu; internet www.statec.lu.

AREA AND POPULATION

Area: 2,586 sq km (999 sq miles).

Population: 384,634 at census of 1 March 1991; 439,539 (males 216,540, females 222,999) at census of 15 February 2001; 448,300 (males 221,000, females 227,300) official estimate at January 2003.

Density (January 2003): 173.4 per sq km.

Principal Towns ('000, 2003 estimates): Luxembourg-Ville (cap-

LUXEMBOURG

ital) 78.3; Esch-sur-Alzette 27.6; Differdange 18.6; Dudelange 17.5; Pétange 14.1; Sanem 13.5; Hesperange 10.8.

Births, Marriages and Deaths (2002): Live births 5,345 (birth rate 12.0 per 1,000); Marriages 2,022 (marriage rate 4.5 per 1,000); Deaths 3,744 (death rate 8.4 per 1,000).

Expectation of Life (WHO estimates, years at birth): 78.8 (males 75.7; females 81.7) in 2002. Source: WHO, *World Health Report*.

Immigration and Emigration (2002): Arrivals 12,101; Departures 9,452.

Employment (estimates, '000 persons, incl. armed forces, 2002): Agriculture, hunting, forestry and fishing 3.6; Mining and quarrying 0.3; Manufacturing 34.0; Electricity, gas and water supply 1.6; Construction 28.1; Wholesale and retail trade, repair of motor vehicles, motorcycles and personal and household goods 39.8; Hotels and restaurants 13.1; Transport, storage and communications 23.6; Financial intermediation 33.1; Real estate, renting and business activities 46.3; Public administration and defence; compulsory social security 14.9; Education 12.8; Health and social work 17.5; Other community, social and personal service activities 10.5; Private households with employed persons 6.6; *Total employed* 285.7.

HEALTH AND WELFARE

Key Indicators

Total Fertility Rate (children per woman, 2002): 1.7.

Under-5 Mortality Rate (per 1,000 live births, 2001): 5.

HIV/AIDS (% of persons aged 15–49, 2000): 0.16.

Physicians (per 1,000 head, 2001): 2.5.

Hospital Beds (per 1,000 head, 2001): 6.9.

Health Expenditure (2001): US $ per head (PPP): 2,905.

Health Expenditure (2001): % of GDP: 6.0.

Health Expenditure (2001): public (% of total): 89.9.

Human Development Index (2001): ranking: 15.

Human Development Index (2001): value: 0.930.
For sources and definitions, see explanatory note on p. vi.

AGRICULTURE, ETC.

Principal Crops ('000 metric tons, 2002): Wheat 71.7; Rye 7.4; Barley 51.8; Oats 10.2; Triticale (wheat-rye hybrid) 23.0; Potatoes 20.1; Rapeseed 12.5; Cabbages 130.0 (FAO estimate); Tomatoes 130.0 (FAO estimate); Onions 75.0 (FAO estimate); Mushrooms 15.0 (FAO estimate); Apples 11.2; Grapes 21.2.

Livestock (2002): Cattle 197,257; Horses 3,126 (2001); Pigs 79,665; Sheep 9,104; Poultry 77,968.

Livestock Products ('000 metric tons, 2002): Beef and veal 10,738; Pigmeat 11,700; Chicken meat 15,608 (FAO estimate); Milk 270,665; Cheese 3.0 (1996).

Forestry ('000 cubic metres, 2002): *Roundwood Removals* (excl. fuel wood) 135 (Sawlogs, veneer logs and logs for sleepers 68, Pulpwood 67 (unofficial figure); *Sawnwood Production* (FAO estimates, incl. railway sleepers) 133 (Coniferous 113, Broadleaved 20). Source: FAO.

INDUSTRY

Selected Products ('000 metric tons, unless otherwise indicated, 2002): Crude steel 2,736; Rolled steel products 3,947; Wine ('000 hl) 153.9.

FINANCE

Currency and Exchange Rates: 100 cent = 1 euro (€). *Sterling and Dollar Equivalents* (31 December 2003): £1 sterling = 1.41306 euros; US $1 = 0.79176 euros; 100 euros = £70.77 = $0.79177. *Average Exchange Rate* (euros per US dollar): 1.0854 in 2000; 1.1175 in 2001; 1.0625 in 2002. Note: The national currency was formerly the Luxembourg franc. From the introduction of the euro, with Luxembourg's participation, on 1 January 1999, a fixed exchange rate of €1 = 40.3399 Luxembourg francs was in operation. Euro notes and coins were introduced on 1 January 2002. The euro and local currency circulated alongside each other until 28 February, after which the euro became the sole legal tender.

Budget (provisional, '000 million euros, 2003): *Revenue:* Direct taxes 3,122.4; Indirect taxes 2,877.5; Other current revenue 305.4; Capital revenue 44.4; Total 6,349.7. *Expenditure:* Ministry of Agriculture, Viticulture and Rural Development 72.1; Ministry of the Civil Service and Administrative Reform 377.7; Ministry of Culture, Further Education and Research 148.5; Ministry of the Economy 19.1; Ministry of the Environment 25.7; Ministry of Family Affairs, Social Solidarity and Youth 931.6; Ministry of Finance 185.7; Ministry of Foreign Affairs, External Trade, Co-operation, Humanitarian Action and Defence 213.1; Ministry of Health 63.1; Ministry of the Interior 451.6; Ministry of Justice 71.1; Ministry of Labour and Employment 138.4; Ministry of National Education, Vocational Training and Sport 662.3; Ministry of Public Works 113.3; Ministry of Small Business, Tourism and Housing 64.5; Ministry of Social Security 1,421.4; Ministry of State 103.6; Ministry of Transport 450.9; Ministry of Women's Affairs 7.6; Total current expenditure 5,521.4; Capital expenditure 827.8; Total 6,349.2.

International Reserves (US $ million at 31 December 2002): Gold 26.05; IMF special drawing rights 9.14, Reserve position in IMF 142.41; Total 151.72. Source: IMF, *International Financial Statistics*.

Money Supply (million euros at 31 December 2002): Currency issued 653.0*; Demand deposits at banking institutions 48,161.1. Source: IMF, *International Financial Statistics*.
*Currency put into circulation by the Banque Centrale du Luxembourg was €9,932m.

Cost of Living (Consumer Price Index; base: 1995 = 100): All items 111.0 in 2001; 113.3 in 2002; 114.7 in 2003. Source: IMF, *International Financial Statistics*.

Expenditure on the Gross Domestic Product (million euros at current prices, 2002): Final consumption expenditure 13,702.0 (Households 9,249.3, Non-profit institutions serving households 368.8, General government 4,083.9); Gross capital formation 4,574.6 (Gross fixed capital formation 4,744.1, Changes in inventories 61.0, Acquisitions, less disposals, of valuables −230.5); *Total domestic expenditure* 18,276.6; Exports of goods and services 32,464.7; *Less* Imports of goods and services 28,400.9; *GDP in purchasers' values* 22,340.5.

Gross Domestic Product by Economic Activity (million euros at current prices, 2002): Agriculture, hunting, forestry and fishing 130.6; Mining and quarrying 37.7; Manufacturing 2,262.9; Electricity, gas and water supply 279.4; Construction 1,389.6; Wholesale and retail trade, repair of motor vehicles, motorcycles and personal and household goods 2,152.7; Hotels and restaurants 469.1; Transport and communications 2,135.6; Financial services 6,810.9; Real estate, renting and business activities 4,407.7; Public administration and defence; compulsory social security 1,313.8; Education 893.7; Health and social work 913.0; Other community, social and personal service activities 578.5; Private households with employed persons 122.4; *Sub-total* 23,897.6; *Less* Financial intermediation services indirectly measured 3,989.7; *Gross value added in basic prices* 19,908.0; Taxes on products 2,667.9; *Less* subsidies on products 235.4; *GDP in market prices* 22,340.5.

Balance of Payments (US $ million, 2002): Exports of goods f.o.b. 9,609; Imports of goods f.o.b. −11,772; *Trade balance* −2,163; Exports of services 20,353; Imports of services −13,604; *Balance on goods and services* 4,587; Other income received 49,701; Other income paid −51,969; *Balance on goods, services and income* 2,319; Current transfers received 2,678; Current transfers paid −3,361; *Current balance* 1,636. Source: IMF, *International Financial Statistics*.

EXTERNAL TRADE

Principal Commodities (million euros, provisional 2002): *Imports:* Food and live animals 896.8; Beverages and tobacco 384.7; Crude materials (inedible) except fuels 647.1; Mineral fuels, lubricants, etc. 985.0; Chemicals and related products 1,244.5; Metal manufactures 1,338.0; Other basic manufactures 996.3; Machinery and other equipment 2,385.4; Transport equipment 1,970.2; Miscellaneous manufactured articles 1,440.1; Total (incl. others) 12,166.7. *Exports:* Food and live animals 442.6; Chemicals and related products 609.9; Metal manufactures 2,415.7; Other basic manufactures 1,390.8; Machinery and other equipment 2,055.1; Transport equipment 462.7; Miscellaneous manufactured articles 1,290.5; Total (incl. others) 9,065.5.

Principal Trading Partners (million euros, provisional, 2002): *Imports:* Belgium 4,122.9; France 1,872.0; Germany 3,213.7; Japan 133.0; Italy 239.8; Netherlands 620.8; United Kingdom 513.4; USA 532.0; Total (incl. others) 12,204.3. *Exports:* Austria 111.0; Belgium 1,076.5; France 1,796.68; Germany 2,275.7; Italy 523.92; Netherlands 398.2; Spain 439.5; Sweden 102.6; United Kingdom 673.4; USA 292.0; Total (incl. others) 9,055.0.

TRANSPORT

Railways (traffic, million, 2002): Passenger-kilometres 268; Freight ton-kilometres 613.

Road Traffic (motor vehicles in use at 1 January 2002): Cars 287,245; Motorcycles 12,671; Buses and coaches 1,176; Goods vehicles 22,691; Tractors 26,126; Total (incl. others) 341,351.

River Traffic (Port of Mertert, '000 metric tons, 2001): Goods loaded 475, Goods unloaded 1,161.

Civil Aviation (traffic on scheduled services, 2002): Passengers carried 1,517,000; Freight (metric tons) 578,944.

TOURISM

Foreign Tourist Arrivals (at accommodation establishments): 851,589 in 2000; 829,246 in 2001; 875,845 in 2002.

Arrivals by Country (2002): Belgium 187,088; France 75,111; Germany 112,270; Italy 23,181; Netherlands 249,807; United Kingdom 55,947; USA 24,354; Total (incl. others) 875,845.

COMMUNICATIONS MEDIA

Facsimile Machines: 20,000 in use (1998).

Mobile Cellular Telephones: 455,000 subscribers (2002).

Telephones: 346,800 main lines in use (2002).

Personal Computers ('000 in use): 230 (2002).

Internet Users ('000): 165 (2002).

Daily Newspapers: 5 (1998).

Book Production: 513 titles (1997).

Radio Receivers: 285,000 in use (1997).

Television Receivers: 260,000 in use (2000).
Sources: partly UNESCO, *Statistical Yearbook;* International Telecommunication Union.

EDUCATION
(2001/02)

Nursery: 799 teachers; 10,850 pupils.

Primary: 2,895 teachers; 31,963 pupils.

Secondary, Middle, Vocational and Technical: 3,206 teachers (state sector only); 9,942 pupils (secondary), 21,598 pupils (middle, vocational and technical).

Higher Institute of Technology: 360 students.

Teacher Training: 394 students.

Other University-level: 7,891 students, incl. 5,688 studying abroad.

Directory

The Constitution

The Constitution now in force dates back to 17 October 1868, but in 1919 a constituent assembly introduced some important changes, declaring that the sovereign power resided in the nation, that all secret treaties were denounced and that deputies were to be elected by a list system by means of proportional representation, on the basis of universal adult suffrage. Electors must be citizens of Luxembourg and must have attained 18 years of age. Candidates for election must have attained 21 years of age. The Grand Duke, who is Sovereign, chooses government ministers, may intervene in legislative questions and has certain judicial powers. There is a single-chamber legislature, the Chamber of Deputies (Chambre des Députés), with 60 members elected for five years. There are four electoral districts, the North, the Centre, the South and East. By the law of 9 October 1956 the Constitution was further revised to the effect that: 'The exercise of prerogatives granted by the Constitution to the legislative, executive and judiciary powers, can, by treaty, be temporarily vested in institutions of international law.' The Constitution was further amended on 12 December 1994, 12 July 1996 (introducing a Constitutional Court) and 12 January 1998. In addition to the Council of Ministers, which consists of the President of the Government (Prime Minister) and at least three other ministers, the State Council (which is the supreme administrative tribunal and which also fulfils certain legislative functions) comprises 21 members nominated for life by the Sovereign.

The Government

HEAD OF STATE

Grand Duke: HRH Henri Albert Félix Marie Guillaume (succeeded to the throne 7 October 2000).

Marshal of the Court: Henri Ahlborn.

COUNCIL OF MINISTERS
(April 2004)

A coalition of the Parti Chrétien Social (PCS) and the Parti Démocratique Luxembourgeois (PDL).

Prime Minister and Minister of State and of Finance: Jean-Claude Juncker (PCS).

Deputy Prime Minister and Minister of Foreign Affairs and External Trade, and of the Civil Service and Administrative Reform: Lydie Polfer (PDL).

Minister of Agriculture, Viticulture and Rural Development, and of Small Business, Tourism and Housing: Fernand Boden (PCS).

Minister of Family Affairs, Social Solidarity and Youth, and of Women's Affairs: Marie-Josée Jacobs (PCS).

Minister of Culture, Further Education and Research, and of Public Works: Erna Hennicot-Schoepges (PCS).

Minister of the Interior: Michel Wolter (PCS).

Minister of Justice, and of the Treasury and Budget: Luc Frieden (PCS).

Minister of National Education, Vocational Training and Sport: Anne Brasseur (PDL).

Minister of the Economy and of Transport: Henri Grethen (PDL).

Minister of Co-operation, Humanitarian Action and Defence, and of the Environment: Charles Goerens (PDL).

Minister of Health and of Social Security: Carlo Wagner (PDL).

Minister of Labour and Employment, of Parliamentary Relations, of Religious Affairs, and Minister delegate of Communications: François Biltgen (PDL).

Secretary of State for the Civil Service and Administrative Reform: Joseph Schaak (PDL).

Secretary of State for the Environment: Eugène Berger (PDL).

MINISTRIES

Office of the Prime Minister: Hôtel de Bourgogne, 4 rue de la Congrégation, 2910 Luxembourg; tel. 478-21-06; fax 46-17-20.

Ministry of Agriculture, Viticulture and Rural Development: 1 rue de la Congrégation, 1352 Luxembourg; tel. 478-25-00; fax 46-40-27; internet www.etat.lu/MA.

Ministry of the Civil Service and Administrative Reform: 63 ave de la Liberté, BP 1807; 1018 Luxembourg; tel. 478-31-06; fax 648-36–16; e-mail Ministere-FonctionPublique@mfp.etat.lu; internet www.etat.lu.

Ministry of Communications: 18 montée de la Pétrusse, 2945 Luxembourg; tel. 478-67-10; fax 40-89-40; e-mail officielle.boite@mz.etat.lu; internet www.etat.lu/mss.

Ministry of Culture, Further Education and Research: 20 montée de la Pétrusse, 2273 Luxembourg; tel. 478-66-19; fax 40-24-27; internet www.ltam.lu/culture.

Ministry of the Economy: 19–21 blvd Royal, 2449 Luxembourg; tel. 478-41-37; fax 46-04-48; e-mail info@eco.public.lu; internet www.eco.public.lu.

Ministry of the Environment: 18 montée de la Pétrusse, 2327 Luxembourg; tel. 478-68-24; fax 40-04-10; e-mail ministere_environment@mev.etat.lu; internet www.emwelt.lu.

Ministry of Family Affairs, Social Solidarity and Youth: 12–14 ave Emile Reuter, 2919 Luxembourg; tel. 478-65–00; fax 478-65-70.

Ministry of Finance: 3 rue de la Congrégation, 2931 Luxembourg; tel. 478-26-35; fax 47-52-41; internet www.etat.lu/FI.

Ministry of Foreign Affairs, Trade, Co-operation, Humanitarian Action and Defence: 6, rue de la Congrégation, 1352, Luxembourg; tel. 478-1; fax 22-20-48; e-mail officielle.boite@mae.etat.lu; internet www.mae.lu.

Ministry of Health: Villa Louvigny, allée Marconi, 2120, Luxembourg; tel. 478-55-00; fax 46-79-63; e-mail ministere-sante@ms.etat.lu; internet www.etat.lu/MS.

Ministry of the Interior: 19 rue Beaumont, 1219 Luxembourg; tel. 478-46-26; fax 22-11-25; internet www.etat.lu/MI.

Ministry of Justice: 16 blvd Royal, 2934 Luxembourg; tel. 478-45-06; fax 22-76-61; internet www.mj.public.lu.

Ministry of Labour and Employment: 26 rue Zithe, 2763 Luxembourg; tel. 478-61-22; fax 48-63-25; e-mail Jean.Zahlen@mt.etat.lu; internet www.etat.lu/MT.

Ministry of National Education, Vocational Training and Sport: 29 rue Aldrigen, BP 180, 2011 Luxembourg; tel. 478-51-51; fax 478-51-10; e-mail pisa@men.lu; internet www.men.lu.

Ministry of Public Works: 4 blvd F. D. Roosevelt, 2450 Luxembourg; tel. 478-33-00; fax 22-31-60; e-mail webmaster@tp.etat.lu; internet www.etat.lu/MTP.

Ministry of Religious Affairs: 4 rue de la Congrégation, 2910 Luxembourg; tel. 478-1; fax 46-17-20.

Ministry of Small Business, Tourism and Housing: 6 ave E. Reuter, 2937 Luxembourg; tel. 478-47-15; fax 478-11-87; internet www.etat.lu/MCMT.

Ministry of Social Security: 26 rue Zithe, 2763 Luxembourg; tel. 478-63-11; fax 478-63-28; e-mail Romain.Fehr@mss.etat.lu; internet www.etat.lu/MSS.

Ministry of State: 4 rue de la Congrégation, 1352 Luxembourg; tel. 478-21-00; fax 46-17-20; e-mail ministere.etat@me.etat.lu; internet www.etat.lu.

Ministry of Transport: 19–21 blvd Royal, 2449 Luxembourg; tel. 478-44-11; fax 46-43-15.

Ministry of Women's Affairs: 12–14 ave E. Reuter, 2921 Luxembourg; tel. 478-58-14; fax 24-18-86; e-mail promotionfeminine@mpf.etat.lu; internet www.mpf.lu.

Legislature

CHAMBRE DES DÉPUTÉS
(Chamber of Deputies)

President: JEAN SPAUTZ (Parti Chrétien Social).

General Election, 13 June 1999

Party	Seats
Parti Chrétien Social	19
Parti Démocratique Luxembourgeois	15
Parti Ouvrier Socialiste Luxembourgeois	13
Comité d'Action pour la Démocratie et la Justice	7
Déi Gréng	5
Déi Lénk	1
Total	**60**

Advisory Councils

Conseil Economique et Social: 31 blvd Konrad Adenauer, BP 1306, 1013 Luxembourg; tel. 43-58-51; fax 42-27-29; e-mail ces@ces.etat.lu; internet www.etat.lu/CES; f. 1966; consultative body on economics and social affairs; 35 mems; Pres. GASTON REINESCH; Sec.-Gen. MARIANNE NATI-STOFFEL.

Conseil d'Etat: 5 rue Sigefroi, 2536 Luxembourg; tel. 47-30-71; fax 46-43-22; e-mail conseil@ce.smtp.etat.lu; internet www.etat.lu/CE; 21 mems nominated for life by the Sovereign; Pres. PIERRE MORES; Vice-Pres CLAUDE BICHELER, CHARLES RUPPERT.

Political Organizations

Comité d'Action pour la Démocratie et la Justice: 9 rue de la Loge, 1945 Luxembourg; tel. 46-37-42; fax 46-37-45; e-mail adr@chd.lu; internet www.adr.lu; f. 1989; present name adopted 1994; conservative; campaigns to secure improved pension rights for private-sector employees; Pres. ROBERT MEHLEN; Sec.-Gen. FERNAND GREISEN.

Déi Gréng (Greens): BP 454, 2014 Luxembourg; tel. 46-37-40-1; fax 46-37-43; e-mail greng@greng.lu; internet www.greng.lu; f. 1983; fmrly Déi Gréng Alternativ (Green Alternative Party); merged with the Gréng Lëscht Ekologesch Initiativ (Green List Ecological Initiative) in 1995; advocates 'grass-roots' democracy, environmental protection, social concern and increased aid to developing countries; Secs ABBES JACOBY, CHRISTIAN BOMB.

Déi Lénk (The Left): BP 817, 2018 Luxembourg; tel. 26-20-20-72; fax 46-69-66-960; e-mail sekretariat@dei-lenk.lu; internet www.dei-lenk.lu; f. 1999; individual membership; no formal leadership.

Parti Chrétien Social (PCS) (Christian Social Party): 4 rue de l'Eau, BP 826, 2018 Luxembourg; tel. 22-57-31-1; fax 47-27-16; e-mail csv@csv.lu; internet www.csv.lu; f. 1914; advocates political stability, sustained economic expansion, ecological and social progress; 9,500 mems; Pres. FRANÇOIS BILTGEN; Sec.-Gen. JEAN-LOUIS SCHILTZ.

Parti Communiste Luxembourgeois (PCL/KPL) (Communist Party): 2 rue Astrid, 1143 Luxembourg; tel. 44-60-66; e-mail zeiluvol@pt.lu; f. 1921; Pres. ALI RUCKERT.

Parti Démocratique Luxembourgeois (PDL) (Democratic Party): BP 510, 2015 Luxembourg Luxembourg; tel. 22-41-84-1; fax 47-10-07; e-mail groupdp@dp.lu; internet www.dp.lu; liberal; Leader LYDIE POLFER; Sec.-Gen. HENRI GRETHEN.

Parti Ouvrier Socialiste Luxembourgeois (POSL) (Socialist Workers' Party): 37 rue de St Esprit, 1475 Luxembourg; tel. 45-59-91; fax 45-65-75; e-mail info@lsap.lu; internet www.lsap.lu; f. 1902; social democrat; 6,000 mems; Pres. JEAN ASSELBORN; Sec.-Gen. LUCIEN LUX.

Diplomatic Representation

EMBASSIES IN LUXEMBOURG

Austria: 3 rue des Bains, 1212 Luxembourg; tel. 47-11-88; fax 46-39-74; e-mail luxemburg-ob@bmaa.gv.at; Ambassador WALTER HAGG.

Belgium: 4 rue des Girondins, 1626 Luxembourg; tel. 44-27-46-1; fax 45-42-82; e-mail luxembourg@diplobel.org; Ambassador INGEBORG KRISTOFFERSEN.

Cape Verde: 46 rue Goethe, 1637 Luxembourg; tel. 26-48-09-48; fax 26-48-09-49; Chargé d'affaires a.i. OCTAVIO BENTO GOMES.

China, People's Republic: 2 rue Van der Meulen, 2152 Luxembourg; tel. 43-69-91-1; fax 42-24-23; Ambassador SUN RONGMIN.

Denmark: 4 bvld Royal, 2449 Luxembourg; tel. 22-21-22-1; fax 22-21-24; e-mail luxamb@um.dk; Ambassador IB RITTO ANDREASEN.

Finland: 2 rue Heine, 1720 Luxembourg; tel. 49-55-51-1; fax 49-46-40; e-mail sanomat.lux@formin.fi; Ambassador SAULI FEODOROW.

France: 8b blvd Joseph II, BP 359, 2013 Luxembourg; tel. 45-72-71-1; fax 45-72-71-227; Ambassador PIERRE CARRIGUE-GUYONNAUD.

Germany: 20–22 ave Emile Reuter, BP 95, 2010 Luxembourg; tel. 45-34-45-1; fax 45-56-04; internet webplaza.pt.lu/public/dtbotlux; Ambassador ROLAND LOHKAMP.

Greece: 117 val Ste Croix, 1371 Luxembourg; tel. 44-51-93; fax 45-01-64; Ambassador PANAYOTIS MACRIS.

Ireland: 28 route d'Arlon, 1140 Luxembourg; tel. 45-06-10; fax 45-88-20; e-mail luxembourg@iveagh.irlgov.ie; Ambassador MICHAEL HOEY.

Italy: 5–7 rue Marie-Adélaïde, 2128 Luxembourg; tel. 44-36-44-1; fax 45-55-23; e-mail italamb@ambitalialux.lu; Ambassador RAFFAELE CAMPANELLA.

Japan: 62 ave de la Faïencerie, BP 92, 2010 Luxembourg; tel. 464-15-11; fax 46-41-76; Ambassador MASAHIRO ANDO.

Netherlands: 5 rue C. M. Spoo, 2546 Luxembourg; tel. 22-75-70; fax 40-30-16; e-mail nlgovlux@pt.lu; Ambassador JOHAN S. L. GUALTHÉRIE VAN WEEZEL.

Portugal: 24 rue Guillaume Schneider, 2522 Luxembourg; tel. 46-61-90-1; fax 46-51-69; e-mail embport@pt.lu; Ambassador PAULO COUTO BARBOSA.

Romania: 41 blvd de la Pétrusse, 2320 Luxembourg; tel. 45-51-59; fax 45-51-63; e-mail ambroum@pt.lu; Ambassador TUDOREL POSTOLACHE.

Russia: Château de Beggen, 1719 Luxembourg; tel. 42-23-33; fax 42-23-34; Ambassador OLEG KRIVONOGOV.

Spain: 4–6 blvd E. Servais, 2535 Luxembourg; tel. 46-02-55; fax 47-48-50; Ambassador RICARDO ZALACAIN JORGE.

Sweden: 2 rue Heine, 1720 Luxembourg; tel. 29-68-34; fax 29-69-09; e-mail ambassaden.luxemburg@foreign.ministry.se; internet www.swedenabroad.com/luxembourg; Ambassador AGNETA SÖDERMAN.

Switzerland: 25A blvd Royal, BP 469, 2014 Luxembourg; tel. 22-74-74-1; fax 22-74-74-20; e-mail vertretung@lux.rep.admin.ch; Ambassador INGRID APELBAUM-PIDOUX.

Turkey: 49, rue Siggy vu Letzebuerg, 1933 Luxembourg; tel. 44-32-81; fax 44-32-81-34; e-mail ambturq@pt.lu; Ambassador ERDORL TÜMER.

United Kingdom: 14 blvd Roosevelt, 2450 Luxembourg; tel. 22-98-64; fax 22-98-67; e-mail britemb@pt.lu; internet webplaza.pt.lu/public/britemb; Ambassador JAMES CLARK.

USA: 22 blvd E. Servais, 2535 Luxembourg; tel. 46-01-23; fax 46-14-01; internet www.amembassy.lu; Ambassador PETER TERPELUK, Jr.

Judicial System

The lowest courts in Luxembourg are those of the Justices of the Peace, of which there are three, at Luxembourg-Ville, Esch-sur-Alzette and Diekirch. These are competent to deal with civil, commercial and criminal cases of minor importance. Above these are the two District Courts, Luxembourg being divided into the judicial districts of Luxembourg and Diekirch. These are competent to deal with civil, commercial and criminal cases. The Superior Court of Justice includes both a court of appeal, hearing decisions made by District Courts, and the Cour de Cassation. As the judicial system of the Grand Duchy does not employ the jury system, a defendant is acquitted if a minority of the presiding judges find him or her guilty. The highest administrative court is the Comité du Contentieux du Conseil d'Etat. Special tribunals exist to adjudicate upon various matters of social administration such as social insurance. The department of the Procureur Général (Attorney-General) is responsible for the administration of the judiciary and the supervision of judicial police investigations. In July 1996 an amendment to the Constitution introduced a Constitutional Court.

Judges are appointed for life by the Grand Duke, and are not removable except by judicial sentence.

President of the Superior Court of Justice: PAUL KAYSER.

Attorney-General: CAMILLE WAMPACH.

Religion

CHRISTIANITY

The Roman Catholic Church

For ecclesiastical purposes, Luxembourg comprises a single archdiocese, directly responsible to the Holy See. At 31 December 2002 there were an estimated 380,000 adherents in the country, representing about 86% of the total population.

Archbishop of Luxembourg: Most Rev. FERNAND FRANCK, Archevêché, 4 rue Génistre, BP 419, 2014 Luxembourg; tel. 46-20-23; fax 47-53-81; e-mail archeveche@cathol.lu.

The Anglican Communion

Within the Church of England, Luxembourg forms part of the diocese of Gibraltar in Europe.

Chaplain: Rev. CHRISTOPHER LYON, 89 rue de Muhlenbach, 2168 Luxembourg; tel. and fax 43-95-93; e-mail chris.lyon@anglican.lu; internet www.anglican.lu; English-speaking church (Anglican Chaplaincy).

Protestant Church

The Evangelical Church in the Grand Duchy of Luxembourg: rue de la Congrégation, 1352 Luxembourg; tel. 22-96-70; fax 46-71-88; e-mail mail@protestant.lu; internet www.protestant.lu; f. 1818 as Protestant Garnison Church, 1868 as community for the Grand Duchy; there are about 1,500 Evangelicals; Pres. Pasteur MICHEL FAULLIMMEL.

JUDAISM

Chief Rabbi: JOSEPH SAYAGH, 34 rue Alphouse Munchen, 2172 Luxembourg; tel. 45-23-66; fax 25-04-30.

The Press

DAILIES

Lëtzebuerger Journal: Résidence de Beauvoir, 51 rue de Strasbourg, BP 2101, 1021 Luxembourg; tel. 49-30-33; fax 49-20-65;

internet www.journal.lu; f. 1948; organ of the Democratic Party; Editor ROB ROEMEN; circ. 13,500 (1993).

Luxemburger Wort: 2 rue Christophe Plantin, 2988 Luxembourg; tel. 49-93-1; fax 49-93-38-4; e-mail wort@wort.lu; internet www.wort.lu; f. 1848; German; Catholic; Christian Democrat; Chief Editor LÉON ZECHES; circ. 87,126 (2000).

Le Républicain Lorrain: 7 rue d'Esch, BP 2211, 1022 Luxembourg; tel. and fax 44-77-44-37-01; f. 1963; French; Head of Publicity MARC TURMES; circ. 16,200 (1999).

Tageblatt/Zeitung fir Letzebuerg: 44 rue du Canal, 4050 Esch-sur-Alzette; tel. 54-71-31-1; fax 54-71-30; e-mail tageblatt@tageblatt.lu; internet www.tageblatt.lu; f. 1913; French and German; Dir ALVIN SOLD; circ. 29,601 (1998).

Zeitung vum Lëtzeburger Vollek: BP 3008, 1030 Luxembourg; tel. 44-60-66-1; fax 44-60-66-66; internet www.zlv.lu; f. 1946; organ of the Communist Party; Dir FRANÇOIS HOFFMANN; circ. 8,000 (1992).

PERIODICALS

AutoRevue: BP 231, 2012 Luxembourg; tel. 22-99-3; f. 1948; monthly; illustrated; Publr PAUL NEYENS; circ. 12,000.

Carrière: BP 2535, 1025 Luxembourg; tel. 85-89-19; fax 85-89-19; e-mail carrieremag@logic.lu; internet www.logic.lu/carriere; f. 1988; women's interest; French and German; Editor MONIQUE MATHIEU; circ. 5,000.

Echo de l'Industrie: 7 rue Alcide de Gasperi, BP 1304, 1013 Luxembourg; tel. 43-53-66-1; fax 43-23-28; e-mail echo@fedil.lu; f. 1920; monthly; industry, commerce; publ. by Fédération des Industriels Luxembourgeois; Dir NICOLAS SOISSON; circ. 2,100.

Handelsblad/Le Journal du Commerce: 31 blvd Konrad Adenauer, BP 482, 2014 Luxembourg; tel. 43-94-44; fax 43-94-50; f. 1945; 6 a year; journal of the Confédération du Commerce Luxembourgeois; circ. 2,100.

D'Handwierk: 2 circuit de la Foire Internationale, BP 1604, 1016 Luxembourg; tel. 42-45-11-1; fax 42-45-25; e-mail info@fda.lu; internet www.federation-des-artisans.lu; monthly; organ of the Fédération des Artisans and the Chambre des Métiers; circ. 7,000.

Horesca—Informations: 7 rue Alcide de Gasperi, BP 2524, 1025 Luxembourg; tel. 42-13-55-1; fax 42-13-55-299; e-mail info@horesca.lu; internet www.horesca.lu; monthly; hotel trade, tourism, gastronomy; Editor DAVE GIANNANDREA; circ. 6,000.

Le Jeudi: 15 rte d'Esch, 1368 Luxembourg; tel. 22-05-50; fax 22-05-44; e-mail redaction@le-jeudi.lu; internet www.lejeudi.lu; f. 1997; weekly; French; Dir DANIÈLE FONCK; circ. 10,854 (1998).

De Konsument: 55 rue des Bruyères, 1274 Howald; tel. 49-60-22-1; fax 49-49-57; e-mail ulc@pt.lu; internet www.ulc.lu; 12 a year; consumer affairs.

De Lëtzeburger Bauer: 16 blvd d'Avranches, 2980 Luxembourg; tel. 48-81-61-1; fax 40-03-75; e-mail letzeburger.bauer@netline.lu; f. 1944; weekly; journal of Luxembourg farming; circ. 7,500.

D'Lëtzeburger Land: 59 rue Glesener, BP 2083, 1020 Luxembourg; tel. 48-57-57; fax 49-63-09; e-mail land@land.lu; internet www.land.lu; f. 1954; weekly; political, economic, cultural affairs; Man. Editor MARIO HIRSCH; circ. 6,500.

Lux-Post: Editions Saphir, 23 rue des Gênets, 1621 Luxembourg; tel. 49-53-63; fax 48-53-70; local news; four regional edns; French and German.

Muselzeidung: 30 rue de Trèves, POB 36, 6701 Grevenmacher; tel. 75-87-47; fax 75-84-32; e-mail burton@pt.lu; f. 1981; regional magazine; monthly; German; Editor TANIA USELDINGER.

OGB-L Aktuell/Actualités: 4002 Esch-sur-Alzette; tel. 54-05-45-1; fax 54-16-20; e-mail ogbl@first-luxembourg.lu; internet www.ogb-l.lu; f. 1919; monthly; journal of the Confederation of Independent Trade Unions of Luxembourg; circ. 43,000.

Revue/D'Letzebuerger Illustréiert: 2 rue Dicks, BP 2755, 1027 Luxembourg; tel. 49-81-81-1; fax 48-77-22; e-mail revue@revue.lu; internet www.revue.lu; f. 1945; weekly; illustrated; Man. Dir GUY LUDIG; Editor-in-Chief CLAUDE WOLF; circ. 31,000.

Revue Technique Luxembourgeoise: 4 blvd Grande-Duchesse Charlotte, 1330 Luxembourg; tel. 45-13-54; fax 45-09-32; internet www.aliai.lu; f. 1908; quarterly; technology.

Sauerzeidung: 30 rue de Trèves, BP 36, 6701 Grevenmacher; tel. 75-87-47; fax 75-84-32; e-mail burton@pt.lu; internet www.muselzeidung.lu; f. 1988; regional newspaper; monthly; German; Publr EUGENE BURTON; circ. 10,000.

Soziale Fortschrett (LCGB): 11 rue du Commerce, BP 1208, Luxembourg; tel. 49-94-24-1; fax 49-94-24-49; internet www.lcgb.lu; f. 1921; monthly; journal of the Confederation of Christian Trade Unions of Luxembourg; Pres. ROBERT WEBER; circ. 36,000.

Télécran: 2 rue Christophe Plantin, BP 1008, 1010 Luxembourg; tel. 49-93-50-0; fax 49-93-59-0; e-mail telecran@telecran.lu; internet www.telecran.lu; f. 1978; TV and family weekly; illustrated; Man. Editor FERN MORBACH; circ. 46,500.

Transport: 13 rue du Commerce, BP 2615, 1026 Luxembourg; tel. 22-67-86-1; fax 22-67-09; e-mail syprolux@pt.lu; fortnightly; circ. 3,800.

Woxx: 51 ave de la Liberté, BP 684, 2016 Luxembourg; tel. 29-79-99-0; fax 29-79-79; e-mail woxx@woxx.lu; internet www.woxx.lu; f. 1988 as GréngeSpoun; weekly; social, ecological, environmental and general issues; Secs ROBERT GARCIA, RICHARD GRAF, RENÉE WAGENER; circ. 3,000.

NEWS AGENCIES

Among the foreign bureaux in Luxembourg are:

Agence Europe SA: BP 428, 2014 Luxembourg; tel. 22-00-32; fax 46-22-77; e-mail info@agenceurope.com; internet www.agenceurope.com.

Reuters Ltd (United Kingdom): 25C blvd Royal, BP 915, 2449 Luxembourg; Bureau Chief JEAN-MARC PAUFIQUE.

Agence France-Presse, Associated Press (USA), and United Press International (USA) are also represented in Luxembourg.

PRESS ASSOCIATIONS

Association Luxembourgeoise des Editeurs de Journaux: 2 rue Christophe Plantin, 2988 Luxembourg; tel. 49-93-200; fax 49-93-38-6; e-mail direction@saint-paul.lu; internet www.saint-paul.lu; Pres. ALVIN SOLD; Sec. CHARLES RUPPERT.

Association Luxembourgeoise des Journalistes: BP 14732, 1027 Luxembourg; tel. 46-09-52; fax 51-82-36; e-mail secr@alj.lu; Pres. JEAN-CLAUDE WOLFF.

Publishers

Editions François Mersch: BP 231, 2012 Luxembourg; tel. 22-99-3; history, photography.

Editions Guy Binsfeld: 14 Place du Parc, 2313 Luxembourg; tel. 49-68-68; fax 40-76-09; e-mail binsfeld@binsfeld.lu; internet www.editionsguybinsfeld.lu; f. 1979; Man. Dir GUY BINSFELD.

Editions Phi: BP 321, 4004 Esch-sur-Alzette; tel. 54-13-82-820; fax 54-13-87; e-mail editions.phi@editpress.lu; internet www.phi.lu; f. 1980; fmrly Editions Francis van Maele; literature, art; Dir A. THOME.

Editions Schortgen: 121 rue de l'Alzette, BP 367, 4004 Esch-sur-Alzette; tel. 54-64-87; fax 53-05-34; art, literature, factual, cuisine, comics; Dir JEAN-PAUL SCHORTGEN.

Editpress Luxembourg SA: 44 rue du Canal, BP 147, 4050 Esch-sur-Alzette; tel. 54-71-31-1; fax 54-71-30; e-mail tageblatt@tageblatt.lu; internet www.tageblatt.lu; Dir ALVIN SOLD.

Edouard Kutter: BP 319, 2013 Luxembourg; tel. 22-35-71; fax 47-18-84; e-mail kuttered@pt.lu ; internet www.kutter.lu; art, photography, facsimile edns on Luxembourg.

Imprimerie Joseph Beffort: 7 rue Pletzer, 8080 Luxembourg; tel. 25-44-55-1; fax 25-44-19; internet www.beffort.lu; f. 1869; scientific, economic reviews.

Saint-Paul Luxembourg SA: 2 rue Christophe Plantin, 2988 Luxembourg; tel. 49-93-1; fax 49-93-38-6; e-mail editions@isp.lu; internet www.isp.lu; f. 1887; Dir CHARLES RUPPERT.

PUBLISHERS' ASSOCIATIONS

Fédération Luxembourgeoise des Editeurs de Livres: 31 blvd Konrad Adenauer, BP 482, 2014 Luxembourg; tel. 43-94-44-1; fax 43-94-50; e-mail info@clc.lu; internet www.clc.lu; Pres. ALBERT DAMING.

Fédération Luxembourgeoise des Travailleurs du Livre: 26A rue de Pulvermühl, 2356 Luxembourg; tel. 42-24-18; fax 42-24-19; e-mail fltl@pt.lu; f. 1864; Pres. GUST STEFANETTI; Sec. LOUIS PINTO.

Broadcasting and Communications

TELECOMMUNICATIONS

Regulatory Authority

Institut Luxembourgeois de Régulation (ILR): 45 allée Scheffer, 2922 Luxembourg; tel. 45-88-45-1; fax 45-88-45-88; e-mail ilr@ilr.lu; internet www.ilr.lu; Dir ODETTE WAGENER.

Major Service Providers

Cegecom SA: 3 rue Jean Piret, BP 2708, 1027 Luxembourg; tel. 26-49-91; fax 26-49-96-99; e-mail info@cegecom.net; internet www.cegecom.lu; Man. Dir FRANÇOIS THYS.

Coditel SA: BP 78, 6905 Niederanven; tel. 34-93-93-1; fax 34-93-98; e-mail info@coditel.lu; internet www.coditel.lu; Dir CHRISTIAN DURLET.

Entreprise des Postes et Télécommunications (EPT): 8A ave Monterey, 2020 Luxembourg; tel. 47-65-1; fax 47-51-10; e-mail registry@pt.lu; internet www.telecom.lu; f. 1992; post, telecommunications and internet service provider; Pres. MARCEL GROSS.

Equant (Global One Communications SA): 201 rte de Thionville, 5885 Howald; tel. 27-30-11; fax 27-30-13-01; e-mail info.luxembourg@equant.com; internet www.equant.com; telecommunications operator; Dir (Sales) VIRGINIE LÉGER.

LUXGSM: 8A ave Monterey, 2020 Luxembourg; tel. 47-65-1; fax 47-51-10; internet www.luxgsm.lu; f. 1993; mobile cellular telephone operator; subsidiary of Entreprise des Postes et Télécommunications; Dir MARCEL GROSS.

GTS Bénélux: 8 rue Henri Schnadt, 2530 Luxembourg; tel. 33-35-11; fax 33-36-11-1; e-mail info@gtsgroup.lu; internet www.gtsgroup.lu.

Tango: 177 rue de Luxembourg, 8077 Bertrange; tel. 27-77-71-01; fax 27-77-78-88; e-mail info@tango.lu; internet www.tele2.lu; fmrly Millicom Luxembourg; fixed and mobile telephony, as well as data network and Internet services; owned by Tele2 AB.

3C Communications SA: 75 rte de Longwy, 8080 Bertrange; tel. 27-75-01-01; fax 27-75-02-50; internet www.ccc.lu; fmrly Télé 2 Luxembourg; operates Internet payments, credit card transactions and public telephones; owned by Tele2 AB.

BROADCASTING

Regulatory Authority

Commission Indépendante de la Radiodiffusion Luxembourgeoise: Luxembourg.

Radio

Eldoradio: 47 Mühlenweg, BP 1344, 1013 Luxembourg; tel. 40-95-09-1; fax 40-95-09-509; e-mail eldoradio@eldoradio.lu; internet www.eldoradio.lu; music station.

Radio 100,7: 45a ave Monterey, BP 1833, 2163 Luxembourg; tel. 44-00-44-1; fax 44-00-44-940; e-mail dweyler@100komma7.lu; internet www.100komma7.lu; f. 1993; non-commercial cultural broadcaster.

Radio Ara: 2 rue de la Boucherie, BP 266, 2012 Luxembourg; tel. 22-22-89; fax 22-22-66; e-mail radioara@pt.lu; internet www.ara.lu; music broadcaster.

Radio DNR: 12 rue Christophe Plantin, 2988 Luxembourg; tel. 40-70-60; fax 40-81-63; internet www.dnr.lu; e-mail dnr@dnr.lu.

Radio Latina: 2 rue Astrid, BP 1915, 1019 Luxembourg; tel. 29-95-96-1; fax 40-24-76; programmes for foreign communities in Luxembourg.

Radio LRB: BP 8, 3201 Bettembourg; tel. 52-44-88; fax 52-44-88; e-mail info@lrb.lu; internet www.lrb.lu.

Radio WAKY Power FM 107: POB 70, 5801 Hesperange; tel. 48-20-85; fax 48-21-13; internet www.radio.lu; English and Letzeburgish.

RTL Group: 45 blvd Pierre Frieden, 2850 Luxembourg; tel. 42-14-21; fax 42-142-27-60; internet www.rtlgroup.com; f. 2000 by merger of CLT-UFA and Pearson TV; 90.2% owned by Bertelsmann AG (Germany); 9.8% public ownership; 37 radio stations and television channels in 8 countries; CEO DIDIER BELLENS; Chair. JUAN ABELLÓ.

RTL Radio Lëtzeburg: tel. 42-14-23; fax 42-14-22-737; e-mail info@rtl.lu; broadcasts in Luxembourgish; Station Man. FERNAND MATHES; Chief Editor MARIE LINSTER.

SES Astra: Château de Betzdorf, 6815 Betzdorf; tel. 710-725-1; fax 710-725-227; internet www.ses-astra.com; f. 2001; owned by SES Global; operates 13 satellites (broadcasting 1,300 digital and analogue television and radio channels) including the ASTRA 1A television satellite (launched in 1988), ASTRA 1B (1991), ASTRA 1C (1993), ASTRA 1D (1994), ASTRA 1E (1995), ASTRA 1F (1996), ASTRA 1G (1997), ASTRA 1H (1999), ASTRA 2A (1998), ASTRA 2B (2000), ASTRA 2C(2001), ASTRA 2D(2000), ASTRA 3A (2002); Chair. ROMAIN BAUSCH; CEO FERDINAND KAYSER.

Sunshine Radio: 40 rue de Bragance, 1255 Luxembourg; tel. 22-57-92; fax 22-57-92; English and Letzeburgish.

Television

RTL Télé Lëtzeburg: 177 rue de Luxembourg, 8077 Bertrange; tel. 42-14-23; fax 42-14-23-753; e-mail online@rtl.lu; internet www.rtl .lu; subsidiary of RTL Group.

Finance

(cap. = capital; res = reserves; dep. = deposits; m. = million; brs = branches; amounts in euros unless otherwise indicated)

BANKING

In 2003 there were 178 banks in Luxembourg, most of which were subsidiaries or branches of foreign banks; a selection of the principal banks operating internationally is given below.

Central Bank

Banque centrale du Luxembourg: 2 blvd Royal, 2983 Luxembourg; tel. 47-74-1; fax 47-74-49-10; e-mail sg@bcl.lu; internet www .bcl.lu; f. 1998; represents Luxembourg within the European System of Central Banks (ESCB); cap. 25.0m., res 114.7m., dep. 7,429.3m. (Dec. 2003); Pres. YVES MERSCH; Exec. Dirs ANDRÉE BILLON, SERGE KOLB.

Principal Banks

ABN Amro Bank (Luxembourg) SA: 46 ave J. F. Kennedy, 185 Luxembourg; tel. 26-07-1; fax 26-07-29-99; internet www.abnamro .lu; f. 1991 by merger; cap. 372.0m., res 38.5m., dep. 4,642.8m. (Dec. 2001); Chair. M. H. REUCHLIN; Man. Dir PETER AELBERS.

Banca di Roma International SA: 26 blvd Royal, BP 692, 2449 Luxembourg; tel. 47-79-06-1; fax 47-79-06-228; e-mail info@ bancaroma.lu; internet www.bancaroma.lu; f. 1992 by merger; cap. 120.0m., res 72.2m., dep. 1,915.9m. (Dec. 2002); Chair. GIANFRANCO IMPERATORI; Gen. Man. ALESSANDRO AGNOLUCCI.

Banca Nazionale del Lavoro International SA: 51 rue des Glacis, BP 286, 2012 Luxembourg; tel. 22-50-31; fax 22-36-08; e-mail info@bnli.lu; f. 1977; cap. 25.0m., res 6.1m., dep. 2,145.6m. (Dec. 2002); Pres. RODOLFO RINALDI; Gen. Man. FABIO DI VINCENZO.

Bank Sarasin Benelux SA: 287–289 route d'Arlon, 1150 Luxembourg; tel. 45-78-80-1; fax 45-23-96; e-mail infolux@sarasin.com; internet www.sarasin.lu; f. 1988; cap. 16.3m., res 18.3m., dep. 926m. (Dec. 2003); Chair. GUIDO VAN BERKEL; Man. Dir THOMAS WITTLIN.

Bankgesellschaft Berlin International SA: 30 blvd Royal, 2449 Luxembourg; tel. 47-78-1; fax 47-78-20-29; e-mail contact@ bankgesellschaft.lu; internet www.bankgesellschaft.lu; f. 1995 by merger; cap. 57.0m., res 132.4m., dep. 5,764.1m. (Dec. 2001); Chair. SERGE DEMOLIÈRE; Man. Dirs HORST-DIETER HOCHSTETTER, UWE JUNGER-WIRTH.

Banque et Caisse d'Epargne de l'Etat, Luxembourg: 1 place de Metz, 1930 Luxembourg; tel. 40-15-1; fax 40-15-20-99; internet www .bcee.lu; f. 1856 as Caisse de l'Epargne de l'Etat du Grand-Duché de Luxembourg, name changed as above 1989; govt-owned; cap. 173.5m., res 702.6m., dep. 32,975.0m. (Dec. 2002); Chair. VICTOR ROD; Pres. and CEO RAYMOND KIRSCH; 96 brs.

Banque Degroof Luxembourg SA: 7 blvd Joseph II, BP 902, 2019 Luxembourg; tel. 45-35-45-1; fax 25-07-21; e-mail degroof@tcp.ip.lu; cap. 37.0m., res 51.7m., dep. 1,279.7m. (Sep. 2002); Chair. ALAIN PHILIPPSON; Man. Dir GEERT DE BRUYNE.

Banque LBLux SA: 3 rue Jean Monnet, BP 602, 2180 Luxembourg; tel. 42-43-41; fax 42-43-45-099; e-mail bank@lblux.lu; internet www .lblux.lu; f. 1973; cap. 18,288.0m., res 787.3m., dep. 187,924.7m. (Dec. 2001); Chair. Dr PETER KAHN; Man. Dirs HENRI STOFFEL, ALEX MEYER.

Banque Générale du Luxembourg SA: 50 ave John F. Kennedy, 2951 Luxembourg; tel. 42-42-1; fax 42-42-25-79; e-mail info@bgl.lu; internet www.bgl.lu; f. 1919; Fortis Bank Luxembourg SA merged into the above in Nov. 2001; cap. 350.0m., res 692.7m., dep. 33,765.9m. (Dec. 2001); Chair. MARCEL MART; 40 brs.

Banque Ippa et Associés SA: 34 ave de la Liberté, BP 1134, 1011 Luxembourg; tel. 26-29-26-29; fax 26-29-26-26; e-mail customer@bia .lu; internet www.bia.lu; f. 1989 as Banque Ippa et Associés; current name adopted in 2000 following merger with Bank Anhyp Luxembourg SA; cap. 15.0m., res 2.8m., dep. 654.8m. (2001); Chair. AFFIED BOUCKAERT; Man. Dir YVES LAHAYE.

Banque de Luxembourg SA: 14 blvd Royal, BP 466, 2014 Luxembourg; tel. 49-92-41; fax 47-26-65; e-mail bllux@pt.lu; internet www.banquedeluxembourg.com; f. 1937; 71% owned by Crédit Industriel d'Alsace et de Lorraine; cap. 100.0m., res 197.7m., dep. 10,782.5m. (Dec. 2002); Chair. ROBERT RECKINGER; 4 brs.

Banque Raiffeisen SC: 28 blvd Royal, BP 111, 2011 Luxembourg; tel. 46-21-51; fax 47-14-69; internet www.raiffessen.lu; f. 1926 as Caisse Centrale Raiffeisen SC, name changed as above July 2001; res 55.4m., dep. 1,951.5m. (Dec. 2001); Pres. PAUL LAUTERBOUR; Chair. and Gen. Man. ALPHONSE SINNES.

Banque Safra Luxembourg SA: 10A blvd Joseph II, BP 887, 2018 Luxembourg; tel. 45-47-73; fax 45-47-86; internet www.safra.lu; cap. Swiss francs 24.2m., res Swiss francs 131.7m., dep. Swiss francs 3,952.9m. (Dec. 2001); Chair. JOSEPH SAFRA; Man. Dir JORGE ALBERTO KININSBERG.

BNP Paribas Luxembourg: 10A blvd Royal, 2093 Luxembourg; tel. 46-46-1; fax 46-46-41-41; cap. 100.0m., res 160.0m., dep. 17,000.0m. (Dec. 2001); Chair. VIVIEN LEVY-GARBOUA; Gen. Mans ALAIN BAILLY, PATRICE CROCHET.

Clearstream Banking SA: 42 ave JF Kennedy, 1855 Luxembourg; tel. 243-0; fax 24-33-80-00; e-mail marketing@clearstream.com; internet www.clearstream.com; f. 1970 as Cedelbank, name changed as above Jan. 2000; private bank; acts as the central bank's securities depository; cap. 56.8m., res 16.8m., dep. 4,325.1m. (Dec. 2000); Chair. ROBERT R. DOUGLASS; CEO ANDRÉ ROELANTS.

Commerzbank International SA: 11 rue Notre Dame, BP 303, 2013 Luxembourg; tel. 47-79-11-1; fax 47-79-11-270; e-mail cisal@ commerzbank.com; internet www.commerzbank.lu; f. 1969; cap. 579.8m., res 1,370.2m., dep. 8,172.0m. (Dec. 2002); Pres. and Chair. KLAUS-PETER MULLER; Man. Dir BERND HOLZENTHAL; Gen. Man. ADRIEN NEY.

Crédit Agricole Indosuez Luxembourg SA: 39 allée Scheffer, BP 1104, 1011 Luxembourg; tel. 47-67-1; fax 46-24-42; internet www .e-private.com; f. 1969; present name adopted 1997; cap. 3,000.0m. Luxembourg francs; res 869.8m. Luxembourg francs, dep. 282,919.5m. Luxembourg francs (Dec. 2001); Chair. JACQUES HAFFNER; Man. Dir and Gen. Man. CHARLES HAMER.

Crédit Lyonnais Luxembourg SA: 26A blvd Royal, BP 32, 2094 Luxembourg; tel. 47-68-31-1; fax 42-68-31-501; e-mail info@ creditlyonnais.lu; internet www.creditlyonnais.lu; cap. 55m., res 23,170m. (Dec. 2001); Pres. PATRICE DURAND; Gen. Man. PIERRE-PAUL COCHET.

Crédit Suisse (Luxembourg) SA: 56 Grand-Rue, BP 40, 2010 Luxembourg; tel. 46-00-11-1; fax 46-32-70; cap. Swiss francs 25.0m., res Swiss francs 40.0m., dep. Swiss francs 2,584.4m. (Dec. 2001); Pres. ALEXANDRE ZELLER; Man. Dir HANS-ULRICH HÜGLI.

Danske Bank International SA: 2 rue du Fossé, 2011 Luxembourg; tel. 46-12-75-1; fax 47-30-78; e-mail information@lu .danskebank.com; internet www.danskebank.com/lu; f. 1976; cap. 146.9m., res 12.9m., dep. 563.2m. (Dec. 2002); Chair. SVEN ERIK LYSTBØK; Man. Dir MOGENS HOLM.

DekaBank Deutsche Girozentrale Luxembourg SA: 38 ave J. F. Kennedy, 1855 Luxembourg; tel. 22-09-11; fax 34-09-38-09; e-mail info@dekabank.lu; internet www.dekabank.lu; f. 1971 as Deutsche Girozentrale International SA, name changed as above after merger with DekaBank Luxembourg SA in Jan. 2002; cap. 25.6m., res 83.6m., dep. 7,199.3m. (Dec. 2001); Chair. AXEL WEBER; Man. Dir BRUNO STUCKENBROEKER.

Deutsche Bank Luxembourg SA: 2 blvd Konrad Adenauer, 1115 Luxembourg; tel. 42-12-21; fax 42-12-24-49; internet www .deutsche-bank.lu; f. 1970 as Deutsche Bank Compagnie Financière Luxembourg; cap. 215.0m., res 839.1m., dep. 48,421.5m. (Dec. 2002); CEO ERNST WILHELM CONTZEN.

Deutsche Postbank International SA: Airport Center, 2 route des Trèves, 2633 Senningerberg; tel. 34-95-31-1; fax 34-95-32-550; e-mail deutsche.postbank@postbank.lu; internet www.postbank.de; f. 1993; cap. 145.0m., res 47.0m., dep. 8,929m. (Dec. 2003); Chair. LOUKAS RIZOS; Gen. Mans CHRISTOPH SCHMITZ, JOCHEN BEGAS.

Dexia Banque Internationale à Luxembourg (Dexia BIL): 69 route d'Esch, 2953 Luxembourg; tel. 45-90-1; fax 45-90-20-10; e-mail contact@dexia-bil.lu; internet www.dexia-bil.lu; f. 1856 as Banque Internationale à Luxembourg, name changed as above in 2000; 99.9% owned by Dexia SA; cap. 141.2m., res 1,350.2m., dep. 40.4m. (Dec. 2003); Chair. FRANÇOIS NARMON; CEO MARC HOFFMANN; 42 brs.

Dresdner Bank Luxembourg SA: 26 rue de Marché-aux-Herbes, 2097 Luxembourg; tel. 47-60-1; fax 47-60-33-1; e-mail info@ Dresdner-Bank.lu; internet www.dresdner-bank.lu; f. 1967; cap. 125.0m., res 891.5m., dep. 16,074.6m. (Dec. 2002); Chair. Dr BERND FAHRHOLZ; Pres. WOLFGANG A. BAERTZ; Man. Dirs Dr WALTER H. DRAISBACH, REINHARD H. KRAFFT.

DZ Bank International SA: 4 rue Thomas Edison, BP 661, 2016 Luxembourg; tel. 44-90-31; fax 44-90-32-00-1; e-mail info@dzi.lu; internet www.dzi.lu; f. 1978; previously called DG Bank Luxembourg SA, name changed as above in November 2001 after merger with GZ Bank International SA; 70.15% owned by DG International Beteiligungsgesellschaft, 27.27% owned by Finanzverbund Beteiligungsgesellschaft; cap. 80.7m., res 198.4m., dep. 13,725.3m. (Dec. 2001); Chair. HEINZ HILGERT; Man. Dirs WOLFGANG KÖHLER, BERNHARD SINGER, FRANZ SCHULZ, NORBERT FRIEDRICH, FRANK MÜLLER.

EFG Private Bank (Luxembourg) SA: 5 rue Jean Monnet, BP 897, 2018 Luxembourg; tel. 42-07-24-1; fax 42-07-24-650; f. 1986; cap. 70.0m., res 10.0m., dep. 1,245.0m. (Dec. 2001); Chair. PAUL MUNCHEN; Man. Dir FRANÇOIS RIES.

HSBC Private Bank (Luxembourg) SA: 32 blvd Royal, BP 733, 2017 Luxembourg; tel. 47-93-31-1; fax 47-93-31-337; e-mail hrlu@hsbcrepublic.com; internet www.hsbcpb.com; f. 1985; cap. 53.0m., res 33.9m., dep. 2,534.5m. (Dec. 2002); Chair. MICHAEL S. ELIA; Man. Dir and CEO DAVID LEVY.

HSBC Trinkhaus & Burkhardt (International) SA: 1–7 rue Nina et Julien Lefèvre, BP 579, 2015 Luxembourg; tel. 47-18-47-1; fax 47-18-47-64-1; f. 1977; cap. 15.5m., res 51.8m., dep. 1,366.2m. (Dec. 2000); Pres. Dr S. ROMETSCH; Man. Dirs HANS-JOACHIM ROSTECK, JÖRG MEIER.

HSH Nordbank International SA: 2 rue Jean Monnet, BP 612, 2016 Luxembourg; tel. 42-41-41-1; fax 42-41-97; e-mail info@hsh-nordbank-int.com; internet www.hsh-nordbank-int.com; f. 1977; cap. 43.0m., res 182.1m., dep. 7,350.0m. (Dec. 2003); Chair. FRANZ SALES WAAS.

HVB Banque Luxembourg SA: 4 rue Alphonse Weicker, 2721 Luxembourg; tel. 42-72-1; fax 42-72-45-00; e-mail contact@hypovereinsbank.lu; internet www.hypovereinsbank.lu; f. 1998 by merger of Hypobank International SA and Vereinsbank International SA Luxembourg, name changed as above in Oct. 2001; cap. 238.0m., res 635.0m., dep. 34,296.0m. (Dec. 2002); Pres. and Chair. Dr WOLFGANG SPRISSLER; Man. Dirs ERNST-DIETER WIESNER, GUNNAR HOMANN, BERND JANIETZ.

IKB International SA: 12 rue Erasme, BP 771, 2017 Luxembourg; tel. 42-37-77; e-mail ikb.luxembourg@ikb.de; internet www.ikb.de; f. 1979; cap. 52.5m., res 77.8m., dep. 6,767.5m. (November 2003); Chair. STEFAN ORTSEIFEN.

IMI Bank (Lux) SA: 8 ave de la Liberté, BP 1022, 1010 Luxembourg; tel. 40-45-75-1; fax 49-36-22; e-mail postmaster@imi.lu; internet www.imi.lu; f. 1990; cap. 68.3m., res 8.5m., dep. 5,082.5m. (Dec. 2002); Chair. CARLO CORRADINI; CEO CARLO SGARBI; Gen. Man. GABRIELE DALLA TORRE.

ING BHF-BANK International SA: 283 route d'Arlon, BP 258, 2012 Luxembourg; tel. 45-76-76-1; fax 45-83-20; f. 1972 as BHF Bank, name changed as above on 17 Dec. 2002; cap. 26.0m., res 46.5m., dep. 4,098.4m. (Dec. 2003); Chair. ROLAND SCHARFF; Man. Dirs Dr HARTMUT ROTHACKER, FRANK RYBKA.

ING Luxembourg SA: 52 route d'Esch, 1470 Luxembourg; tel. 44-99-11; fax 44-99-12-31; internet www.ing.lu; f. 1960 as Crédit Européen SA, changed name as above April 2003; owned by ING Belgium SA/NV; cap. 73.0m., res 219.0m., dep. 7,799.0m. (Dec. 2002); Chair PHILLIPE DAMAS; Man. Dir BRUNO COLMANT; 18 brs.

Kredietbank SA Luxembourgeoise: 43 blvd Royal, 2955 Luxembourg; tel. 47-97-1; fax 47-26-67; internet www.kbl.lu; f. 1949; cap. 189.0m., res 828.7m., dep. 19,032.8m. (Dec. 2001); Pres. ETIENNE VERWILGHEN; 5 brs.

LRI (Landesbank Rheinland-Pfalz International SA): 10–12 blvd Roosevelt, BP 84, 2010 Luxembourg; tel. 47-59-21-1; fax 47-59-21-314; e-mail info@lri.lu; internet www.lri.lu; f. 1978; cap. 216.0m., res 148.2m., dep. 8,886.6m. (Dec. 2002); Chair. PAUL K. SCHMINKE; Man. Dirs ALAIN BAUSTERT, ROBY HAAS.

Norddeutsche Landesbank Luxembourg SA: 26 route d'Arlon, BP 121, 2011 Luxembourg; tel. 45-22-11-1; fax 45-22-11-31-9; f. 1972; cap. 205.0m., res 248.5m., dep. 22,760.0m. (Dec. 2002); Man. Dir JOCHEN PETERMANN.

Nordea Bank SA: 672 rue de Neudorf-Findel, BP 562, 2015 Luxembourg; tel. 43-88-71; fax 43-93-52; e-mail nordea@nordea.lu; internet www.nordea.lu; f. 1976 as Privatbanken International (Denmark) SA, Luxembourg, changed name to Unibank SA in 1990, present name adopted Feb. 2001; cap. 25.0m., res 135.5m., dep. 2,087.5m. (Dec. 2002); Chair. CHRISTIAN CLAUSEN; Man. Dir JHON MORTENSEN.

Sanpaolo Bank SA: 12 ave de la Liberté, BP 2062, 1020 Luxembourg; tel. 40-37-60-1; fax 49-53-91; f. 1981 as Sanpaolo-Lariano Bank SA, name changed as above 1995; cap. 70.0m., res 4.4m., dep. 3,628.3m. (Dec. 2001); Chair. MARCO MAZZUCCHELLI; Man. Dir DORIANO DEMI.

SEB Private Bank SA: 6A Circuit de la Foire Internationale, BP 487, 2014 Luxembourg; tel. 26-23-1; fax 26-23-20-01; internet www.sebprivatebank.com; f. 1977 as Skandinaviska Enskilda Banken (Luxembourg) SA, merged with sister bank and name changed to S-E-Banken Luxembourg SA in 1994, present name adopted in 1999; merged with BfG Bank Luxembourg SA March 2001; cap. 118.0m.,

res 102.4m., dep. 1,624.8m. (Dec. 2002); Chair. ULF PETERSON; Man. Dir LARS BJERREK.

Société Européenne de Banque SA: 19–21 blvd du Prince Henri, BP 21, 2010 Luxembourg; tel. 46-14-11; fax 22-37-55; e-mail seb@pt.lu; f. 1976; cap. 45.0m., res 32.0m., dep. 3,391.5m. (Dec. 2001); Chair. ANGELO CALOIA; Man. Dir CLAUDE DESCHENAUX.

Société Générale Bank & Trust: 11 ave Emile Reuter, BP 1271, 1012 Luxembourg; tel. 22-88-51; fax 22-88-59; e-mail sgbt.lu@socgen.com; internet www.sgbt.lu; f. 1956 as International and General Finance Trust; cap. 179.0m., res 90.8m., dep. 10,332.4m. (Dec. 2001); Chair. PIERRE MATHÉ; Man. Dir ALBERT LE DIRAC'H.

UBS (Luxembourg) SA: 36–38 Grand-Rue, BP 2, 2010 Luxembourg; tel. 45-12-11; fax 45-12-12-700; f. 1998 by merger of Swiss Bank Corporation (Luxembourg) SA and Union de Banques Suisses (Luxembourg) SA; cap. Swiss francs 150m., res Swiss francs 418.6m., dep. Swiss francs 15,911m. (Dec. 2001); Chair. RAOUL WEIL; Man. Dir ROGER HARTMANN.

WestLB International SA: 32–34 blvd Grande-Duchesse Charlotte, BP 420, 2014 Luxembourg; tel. 44-74-11; fax 44-74-12-10; e-mail info@westlb.lu; internet www.westlb.lu; f. 1972; subsidiary of WestLB AG (Germany); cap. 65.0m., res 172.9m., dep. 14,448.0m. (Dec. 2000); Pres. GERHARD ROGGEMANN; Man. Dirs Dr GEORG BISSEN, FRANZ RUF.

Banking Association

Association des Banques et Banquiers Luxembourg (ABBL): 20 rue de la Poste, BP 13, 2010 Luxembourg; tel. 46-36-60-1; fax 46-09-21; e-mail mail@abbl.lu; internet www.abbl.lu; f. 1939; Dir LUCIEN THIEL.

STOCK EXCHANGE

Société de la Bourse de Luxembourg SA: 11 ave de la Porte-Neuve, BP 165, 2011 Luxembourg; tel. 47-79-36-1; fax 47-32-98; e-mail info@bourse.lu; internet www.bourse.lu; f. 1928; Chair. RAYMOND KIRSCH; CEO MICHEL MAQUIL.

INSURANCE

At the end of 2000 there were 94 approved insurance companies and, in addition, 264 reinsurance companies. A selection of insurance companies is given below:

Aon Insurance Managers (Luxembourg) SA: 19 rue de Bitbourg, BP 593, 2015 Luxembourg; tel. 22-34-221; fax 47-02-51; e-mail lambert_schroeder@aon.com; f. 1994; Man. Dir. LAMBERT SCHROEDER.

Assurances Mutuelles d'Europe: 47 blvd Joseph II, BP 787, 2017 Luxembourg; tel. 47-46-93; fax 47-46-90; e-mail ame@ame.lu; internet www.ame.lu.

AXA Assurances Luxembourg: 7 rue de la Chapelle, 1325 Luxembourg; tel. 45-30-20-1; fax 45-83-39; e-mail info@axa.lu; internet www.axa.lu; f. 1977; all branches and life; Chair. PIERRE BULTEZ.

Fortis Luxembourg Assurances: 16 blvd Royal, 2449 Luxembourg; tel. 24-18-58-1; fax 24-18-58-905; e-mail info@fortis.lu; internet www.fortis.lu; life and non-life insurance.

Le Foyer, Groupe d'Assurances: 6 rue Albert Borschette, 1246 Luxembourg; tel. 43-74-37; fax 43-83-22; e-mail contact@lefoyer.lu; internet www.lefoyer.lu; f. 1922; all branches and life.

La Luxembourgeoise SA d'Assurances: 10 rue Aldringen, 1118 Luxembourg; tel. 47-61-1; fax 47-61-30-0; e-mail groupell@lalux.lu; internet www.lalux.lu; f. 1989; all branches of non-life; Chair. GABRIEL DEIBENER; Dir-Gen. PIT HENTGEN.

West of England Shipowners' Mutual Insurance Asscn (Luxembourg): 33 blvd du Prince Henri, BP 841, 1724 Luxembourg; tel. 47-00-67-1; fax 22-52-53; internet www.westpandi.com; f. 1970; marine mutual insurance; Gen. Man. PHILIP ASPDEN.

Trade and Industry

GOVERNMENT AGENCY

Société Nationale de Crédit et d'Investissement (SNCI): 7 rue du St-Esprit, BP 1207, 1012 Luxembourg; tel. 46-19-71-1; fax 46-19-79; e-mail snci@snci.lu; internet www.snci.lu; f. 1978; cap. and res €401m. (Dec. 2000), dep. €275.5m., assets €722.8m. (1998); SNCI finances participations in certain cos, provides loans for investment and research and development projects, provides export credit; Chair. EVA KREMER; Gen. Man. GEORGES BOLLIG.

CHAMBER OF COMMERCE

Chambre de Commerce du Grand-Duché de Luxembourg: 7 rue Alcide de Gasperi, 2981 Luxembourg-Kirchberg; tel. 42-39-39-1; fax 43-83-26; e-mail chamcom@cc.lu; internet www.cc.lu; f. 1841; Pres. JOSEPH KINSCH; 35,000 mems.

INDUSTRIAL AND TRADE ASSOCIATIONS

Centrale Paysanne Luxembourgeoise: 16 blvd d'Avranches, 2980 Luxembourg; tel. 48-81-61-1; fax 40-03-75; f. 1945; Pres. CARLO RAUS; Sec. LUCIEN HALLER; groups all agricultural organizations.

Chambre d'Agriculture: 261 route d'Arlon, BP 81, 8001 Strassen; tel. 31-38-76; fax 31-38-75; e-mail chaagri@pt.lu; Pres. MARCO GAASCH; Sec.-Gen. ROBERT LEY.

Confédération Luxembourgeoise du Commerce (CLC): 7 rue Alcide de Gasperi, BP 482, 2014 Luxembourg; tel. 43-94-44; fax 43-94-50; e-mail info@clc.lu; internet www.clc.lu; f. 1909; Pres. NORBERT FRIOB; Sec.-Gen. THIERRY NOTHUM; 3,500 mems.

Fédération des Artisans du Grand-Duché de Luxembourg: 2 circuit de la Foire Internationale, BP 1604, 1016 Luxembourg; tel. 42-45-11-1; fax 42-45-25; e-mail info@fda.lu; internet www.federation-des-artisans.lu; f. 1905; Chair. NORBERT GEISEN; Dir ROMAIN SCHMIT; 4,000 mems.

Fédération des Industriels Luxembourgeois (FEDIL): 1st Floor, 31 blvd Konrad Adenauer, BP 1304, 1013 Luxembourg; tel. 43-53-66-1; fax 43-23-28; e-mail fedil@fedil.lu; internet www.fedil.lu; f. 1918; Pres. CHARLES KROMBACH; Administrative Dir NICOLAS SOISSON; c. 450 mems.

Groupement des Industries Sidérurgiques Luxembourgeoises (Federation of Iron and Steel Industries in Luxembourg): BP 1704, 1017 Luxembourg; tel. 48-00-01; fax 48-35-32; f. 1927; Pres. FERNAND WAGNER (Arcelor); Dir PIERRE REITER.

UTILITIES

Regulatory Authority

Service de l'Energie de l'Etat (SEE): 34 ave de la Porte-Neuve, 2227 Luxembourg, BP 10, 2010 Luxembourg; tel. 46-97-46-1; fax 22-25-24; e-mail see.administration@eg.etat.lu; internet www.etat.lu/SEE; f. 1967; civil service department with responsiblity for testing, standardization and certification; Dir JEAN-PAUL HOFFMANN.

Electricity

CEGEDEL (Compagnie Grand-Ducale d'Electricité de Luxembourg): 2089 Luxembourg; tel. 26-24-1; fax 26-24-6100; e-mail mail@cegedel.lu; internet www.cegedel.lu; f. 1928; produces and distributes electricity; 33% state-owned; Chair. ROLAND MICHEL; Dir-Gen. ROMAIN BECKER.

Gas

SUDGAZ SA: BP 383, 4004 Esch-sur-Alzette; tel. 55-66-55-1; fax 57-20-44; e-mail contact@sudgaz.lu; internet www.sudgaz.lu; f. 1899; gas distribution co; Man. Dir WILL HOFFMANN; Dir JO SIMON.

TRADE UNIONS

Confédération Générale du Travail du Luxembourg (CGT)/Onofhaengege Gewerkschaftbond-Letzeburg (OGB-L) (Luxembourg General Confederation of Labour): 60 blvd J. F. Kennedy, BP 149, 4002 Esch-sur-Alzette; tel. 54-05-45-1; fax 54-16-20; e-mail see-l@ogb-l.lu; internet www.ogb-l.lu; f. 1921; Pres. JOHN CASTEGNARO; 52,000 mems (1998).

Landesverband Luxemburger Eisenbahner, Transportarbeiter, Beamten und Angestellten (National Union of Luxembourg Railway and Transport Workers and Employees): 63 rue de Bonnevoie, 1260 Luxembourg; tel. 48-70-44-1; fax 48-85-25; e-mail info@landesverband.lu; internet www.fncttfel.lu; f. 1909; affiliated to CGT and International Transport Workers' Federation; Pres. NICO WENNMACHER; Gen. Sec. GUY GREIVELDING; 8,000 mems.

Lëtzebuerger Chrëschtleche Gewerkschaftsbond (LCGB) (Confederation of Christian Trade Unions): 11 rue du Commerce, BP 1208, 1012 Luxembourg; tel. 49-94-24-1; fax 49-94-24-49; e-mail info@lcgb.lu; internet www.lcgb.lu; f. 1921; affiliated to European Trade Union Confederation and World Confederation of Labour; Pres. ROBERT WEBER; Gen. Sec. MARC SPAUTZ; 40,000 mems.

Transport

RAILWAYS

At 1 January 2002 there were 274 km of electrified railway track.

Société Nationale des Chemins de Fer Luxembourgeois: 9 place de la Gare, BP 1803, 1018 Luxembourg; tel. 49-90-1; fax 49-90-44-70; e-mail ainfo@cfl.lu; internet www.cfl.lu; Pres. JEANNOT WARINGO; Dir and CEO ALEX KREMER.

ROADS

At 1 January 2003 there were 2,873 km of roads, of which motorways comprised 125 km.

Ministry of Public Works: (see Ministries).

INLAND WATERWAYS AND SHIPPING

Rhine shipping has direct access to the Luxembourg inland port of Mertert as a result of the canalization of the Moselle River. An 'offshore' shipping register was established in 1991.

CIVIL AVIATION

There is an international airport near Luxembourg-Ville.

Luxair (Société Luxembourgeoise de Navigation Aérienne): Aéroport de Luxembourg, 2987 Luxembourg; tel. 47-98-42-81; fax 47-98-42-89; e-mail info@luxair.lu; internet www.luxair.lu; f. 1962; regular services to destinations in Europe and North Africa; Pres. and CEO CHRISTIAN HEINZMANN.

Cargolux Airlines International SA: Aéroport de Luxembourg, 2990 Luxembourg; tel. 42-11-1; fax 43-54-46; e-mail info@cargolux.com; internet www.cargolux.com; f. 1970; regular international all-freighter services; technological development; owned by Luxair, a consortium of Luxembourg banks and Swissair; Dir and CEO ULRICH OGIERMANN.

Tourism

Many tourist resorts have developed around the ruins of medieval castles such as Clerf, Esch/Sauer, Vianden and Wiltz. The Benedictine Abbey at Echternach is also much visited. There is a thermal centre at Mondorf-les-Bains, supplied by three mineralized springs. In addition, there are numerous footpaths and hiking trails. Luxembourg-Ville, with its many cultural events and historical monuments, is an important centre for congresses. In 2002 there were 875,845 tourist arrivals at hotels and similar establishments.

Office National du Tourisme (ONT): 68–70 blvd de la Pétrusse, BP 1001, 1010 Luxembourg; tel. 42-82-82-1; fax 42-82-82-38; e-mail info@ont.lu; internet www.ont.lu; f. 1931; 191 mems; Chair. M. SCHANK; Dir ROBERT L. PHILIPPART.

THE FORMER YUGOSLAV REPUBLIC OF MACEDONIA

Introductory Survey

Location, Climate, Language, Religion, Flag, Capital

The former Yugoslav republic of Macedonia (FYRM) is situated in south-eastern Europe. The FYRM is a land-locked state and is bounded by Serbia and Montenegro to the north, Albania to the west, Greece to the south and Bulgaria to the east. The republic is predominantly mountainous with a continental climate, although the Vardar (Axiós) river valley, which bisects the country from north-west to south-east, across the centre of the republic and into Greece, has a mild Mediterranean climate with an average summer-time temperature of 27°C (80°F). The official language of the republic, under the Constitution of November 1991, was originally stipulated as Macedonian. Constitutional amendments adopted in November 2001 accorded minority languages, such as Albanian, the status of official languages in communities where speakers constitute 20% of the population. Most of the population is nominally Christian and of the Eastern Orthodox faith. The ethnic Macedonians (who accounted for 66.6% of the total population according to the 1994 census) are adherents of the Macedonian Orthodox Church, which is autocephalous, but not recognized by other Orthodox churches. Most of the ethnic Albanians (officially recorded as 22.7% of the population) are Muslims, as are the majority of the remaining minority groups. The national flag (proportions 1 by 2) comprises, in the centre of a red field, a yellow disc, tangential to which eight yellow rays extend to the edges of the flag. The capital is Skopje.

Recent History

After the First World War, during which Macedonia was occupied by the Bulgarians and the Central Powers of Austria-Hungary and Germany, Vardar Macedonia, the area now known as the former Yugoslav republic of Macedonia (FYRM), became part of the new Kingdom of Serbs, Croats and Slovenes (formally named Yugoslavia in 1929). In the Second World War, however, the Bulgarian occupation of 1941–44 disillusioned many Yugoslav Macedonians. From 1943 Tito's Partisans (Josip Broz—alias Tito—was the General Secretary of the banned Communist Party of Yugoslavia) began to increase their support in the region, and after the war the new Federal People's Republic of Yugoslavia and its communist rulers resolved to include a Macedonian nation as a federal partner (having rejected the idea of a united Macedonia under Bulgaria). A distinct Macedonian identity was promoted, and a linguistic policy that encouraged the establishment of a Macedonian literary language distinct from Bulgarian and Serbian, together with the consolidation of an historical and cultural tradition, increased Macedonian self-awareness. In 1967 the Orthodox Church in Macedonia declared itself autocephalous, a move strongly contested by the Serbian Orthodox Church.

The presence of a large ethnic Albanian minority in western Macedonia added to Macedonian insecurities. The proximity of neighbouring Kosovo (a province of Serbia with a majority ethnic Albanian population) and demands, from the late 1960s, for the creation of a Yugoslav Albanian republic alarmed the Macedonian authorities, which became particularly active against Albanian nationalism from 1981. In 1989 the communists amended the republican Constitution to allow for the introduction of a multi-party system; however, Macedonia was declared to be a 'nation-state' of the ethnic Macedonians, and mention of the 'Albanian and Turkish minorities' was excluded. Tension continued into the early 1990s, with the new Constitution of 1991 also refusing to specify the republic (with its new sovereign status) as a 'homeland' of the Albanians as well as the Macedonians, although it was enacted only by avoiding reference to official languages—a move designed to satisfy one of the requirements stipulated by the European Community (EC, now European Union, EU, see p. 208) for recognition of the new independent state. In January 1992 an unofficial referendum (declared illegal by the Macedonian authorities) resulted in a 99.9% vote in favour of territorial and political autonomy for the ethnic Albanian population.

In February 1990 the newly established Movement for All-Macedonian Action (MAMA) organized several large demonstrations to protest against the oppression of fellow nationals in Albania, Bulgaria and Greece. In June a more fundamentalist nationalist party, the Internal Macedonian Revolutionary Organization—Democratic Party for Macedonian National Unity (IMRO—DPMNU), led by Ljubčo Georgievski, declared its support for the return of territories then within Serbia. The republican communist leader, Petar Gosev, President of the renamed League of Communists of Macedonia—Party for Democratic Reform (LCM—PDR), also condemned the threat of Serbian nationalism.

In November and December 1990 the first multi-party elections to a unicameral republican Sobranie (Assembly) were held in Macedonia. The MAMA and the IMRO—DPMNU, which had formed an electoral alliance, the Front for Macedonian National Unity, to counter the strong support for the ruling LCM—PDR, alleged irregularities after failing to win any seats at the first round. Following two further rounds of voting, however, the IMRO—DPMNU unexpectedly emerged as the single party with the most seats (a total of 37) in the 120-member Sobranie. The LCM—PDR won 31 seats and the two predominantly Albanian parties (the Party for Democratic Prosperity—PDP and the People's Democratic Party) a total of 25. The republican branch of the federal Alliance of Reform Forces (ARF, subsequently the Liberal Party of Macedonia—LPM) won 19 seats. Since no party or alliance controlled an overall majority of the seats, negotiations to establish a coalition administration began; finally, in January 1991 Kiro Gligorov of the LCM—PDR was elected President of the Republic, with Georgievski as Vice-President, and Stojan Andov of the ARF was elected President of the Sobranie. The three parties agreed to support a government largely comprising members without political affiliation. In March the Sobranie approved a new administration, headed by Nikola Kljušev. The LCM—PDR was renamed the Social Democratic Alliance of Macedonia (SDAM) in April.

On 25 January 1991 the Sobranie unanimously adopted a motion declaring the republic a sovereign territory. The Macedonian administration was, none the less, active in subsequent attempts to mediate in the growing crisis in Yugoslavia. After the June declarations of Croatian and Slovenian 'dissociation' and the later descent into civil war, Macedonia became wary of Serbian domination of the remaining federal institutions, declaring its neutrality and emphasizing its sovereign status. On 8 September a republican referendum (boycotted by the ethnic Albanian population) overwhelmingly supported the sovereignty of Macedonia.

Georgievski resigned the vice-presidency in October 1991, and the IMRO—DPMNU announced that it had joined the opposition, on the grounds that, despite having the largest representation in the Sobranie, it had been excluded from the decision-making process. The preparation of the new Constitution was delayed by the IMRO—DPMNU's proposal for an introductory nationalist statement, which was strongly opposed by the predominantly ethnic Albanian parties. Although the final version did not declare Macedonia to be the 'motherland' of the Macedonian people, it failed to grant the Albanian language official equality with Macedonian. On 17 November the Constitution was endorsed by 96 of the 120 Assembly members: the majority of ethnic Albanian deputies and three IMRO—DPMNU deputies did not support its enactment.

The complete withdrawal of federal troops from Macedonia in March 1992, in conjunction with the adoption in April of a new Constitution in the Federal Republic of Yugoslavia (FRY), referring only to Serbia and Montenegro, effectively signalled Yugoslav acceptance of Macedonian secession from the federation.

Macedonia established diplomatic relations with Slovenia in March, and with Croatia in April.

Macedonian affairs were subsequently dominated by the question of wider international recognition. The republic, while no longer part of Yugoslavia, was unable to act as an independent nation in the international community. Bulgaria recognized the state of Macedonia (although not the existence of a distinct Macedonian nationality or language) in January 1992, closely followed by Turkey in February, provoking mass protests in Thessaloníki, the capital of the Greek region of Macedonia. The Greek authorities insisted that 'Macedonia' was a purely geographical term (delineating an area that included a large part of northern Greece), and expressed fears that the republic's independence under the name 'Macedonia' might foster a false claim to future territorial expansion. Greece was instrumental in the formulation of an EC policy, adopted in early 1992, that the republic should be awarded no formal recognition of independence until stringent constitutional requirements had been fulfilled. In May Gligorov rejected a statement by the EC that it was 'willing to recognize Macedonia as a sovereign and independent state within its existing borders under a name that can be accepted by all concerned'. Negotiations with Greece ended in failure in June. In July a motion expressing 'no confidence' in the Government received overwhelming support in the Sobranie, and large demonstrations were staged in Skopje in protest at the EC declaration and the Government's failure to gain international recognition for an independent Macedonia. The Government resigned later in the month. The IMRO—DPMNU failed to form a new coalition and, eventually, in September Branko Crvenkovski, the Chairman of the SDAM, was installed as Prime Minister of a coalition Government.

The adoption of a new flag in August 1992 attracted particular opposition from Greece, which objected to the depiction outside Greece of the 'Vergina Star' (regarded as an ancient Greek symbol of Philip of Macedon and Alexander the Great). As a result of a blockade of petroleum deliveries imposed on Macedonia by Greece, by September reserves at the Skopje petroleum refinery were exhausted. In February 1993 Greece agreed to international arbitration over the issue of Macedonia's name, undertaking to abide by its final outcome. On 8 April the republic was admitted to the UN under the temporary name of 'the former Yugoslav republic of Macedonia', pending settlement of the issue of a permanent name by international mediators. However, Greece continued to assert, and the FYRM to deny, that the use of the 'Vergina Star' emblem and the name 'Macedonia' implied territorial claims on the northern Greek province of Macedonia; international mediation efforts achieved little, and in October the Greek Government announced that Greece was to withdraw from UN-sponsored negotiations on the issue of a permanent name. In January 1994 Greece requested that the other nations of the EU prevail upon the FYRM (which was by this time recognized by all the other EU member states) to make concessions concerning its name, flag and Constitution, and threatened to ban trade with the FYRM if these preconditions were not fulfilled. From February (shortly after Russia and the USA had formally recognized the FYRM) Greece blocked all non-humanitarian shipments to the FYRM from the port of Thessaloníki, and also road and rail transport links with the FYRM; the Greek consulate in Skopje was subsequently closed. In April the European Commission, which contested that the Greek embargo was in violation of EU trade legislation, initiated legal proceedings against Greece at the Court of Justice of the European Communities. In April 1995, however, the Court issued a preliminary opinion that the embargo was not in breach of Greece's obligations under the Treaty of Rome. Meanwhile, Greece agreed to resume negotiations in April with the FYRM, under the auspices of the UN; in May the Organization for Security and Co-operation in Europe (OSCE, see p. 302) announced that it was to join the mediation efforts. In September an interim accord was signed at the UN headquarters in New York, USA, by the FYRM Minister of Foreign Affairs and his Greek counterpart. The agreement provided for the mutual recognition of existing frontiers and respect for the sovereignty and political independence of each state, and for the free movement of goods and people between the two countries. Greece was to end its trade embargo and veto on the FYRM's entry into international organizations, while the FYRM undertook to abandon its use of the Vergina emblem in any form, and to amend parts of its Constitution that had been regarded by Greece as 'irredentist'. (The issue of a permanent name for the FYRM was to be the subject of further negotiations.) In early October the Sobranie approved a new state flag, depicting an eight-rayed sun in place of the Vergina emblem. The interim accord was ratified by the Sobranie on 9 October, and was formally signed in Skopje by representatives of the FYRM and Greece on 13 October. The border between the two countries was subsequently reopened.

The Albanian Government formally recognized the FYRM in April 1993. However, relations between the Macedonian authorities and the country's ethnic Albanian minority continued to deteriorate. In November several ethnic Albanians were arrested in the western towns of Gostivar and Tetovo (both of which had predominantly Albanian populations) and in Skopje. The Government stated that the arrests had been made following the discovery of a conspiracy to form paramilitary groups, with the eventual aim of establishing an Albanian republic in the west of the country. Further arrests followed, and in June 1994 Mithat Emini, the former General Secretary of the PDP, was sentenced to eight years' imprisonment, after being convicted of conspiring to engage in hostile activity; nine others received custodial sentences of between five and eight years. (In February 1995 all the sentences were reduced by two years.)

In February 1994, after several months of disunity, the PDP split when a faction led by Xheladin Murati (the Deputy President of the Sobranie) and including the PDP's representatives in the Government and in the legislature, withdrew from the party's congress. The remaining grouping, led by Arben Xhaferi, made more radical demands regarding the status of ethnic Albanians in the FYRM. Organizations representing ethnic Albanians protested that inadequate preparations for a national census, conducted in mid-1994, effectively prevented the full enumeration of the ethnic Albanian community. It was reported that many ethnic Albanians boycotted the census, despite appeals by their political leaders for full participation. Following the publication of the census results, ethnic Albanian groups continued to assert that their community was considerably larger than officially indicated. The sentencing of Emini and his co-defendants prompted ethnic Albanian deputies to boycott the Sobranie in July (although they resumed their seats to defeat a motion, proposed by the IMRO—DPMNU, expressing 'no confidence' in the Government). Murati resigned from the leadership of his PDP faction (and from his role at the Sobranie) later in July, reportedly in protest at the sentences; he was succeeded as party leader by Abdurahman Aliti.

Gligorov, representing the Alliance for Macedonia (an electoral coalition of the SDAM, the LPM and the Socialist Party of Macedonia—SPM) was re-elected to the presidency on 16 October 1994, winning 78.4% of the valid votes cast; his only challenger was Ljubiša Georgievski of the IMRO—DPMNU. A first round of voting to the new Sobranie took place on the same day. The IMRO—DPMNU, which failed to secure any seats, alleged widespread electoral fraud in both elections, and boycotted the second round of legislative voting, which took place on 30 October (a third round was necessary in 10 constituencies on 13 November, owing to irregularities in earlier rounds). The final results confirmed that the Alliance for Macedonia had won the majority of seats in the Sobranie (with the SDAM taking 58, the LPM 29 and the SPM eight seats). Aliti's 'moderate' PDP, which had been legally recognized as the successor to the original party, secured 10 seats; members of the 'radical' PDP had been obliged to stand as independent candidates (Xhaferi was among the independent candidates to be elected). Gligorov subsequently requested that Branko Crvenkovski form a new government, and the SDAM-led administration, which also included members of the LPM, Aliti's PDP and the SPM, was approved by the Sobranie in December.

Tensions were exacerbated by efforts by the ethnic Albanian community to establish an Albanian-language university in Tetovo, following continued claims by ethnic Albanian groups that the education system of the FYRM disadvantaged ethnic minorities. Despite government objections that to establish such an institution would be unconstitutional, the university was formally established in December 1994. In February 1995 the opening of the university provoked considerable unrest; an ethnic Albanian was killed in clashes with security forces, and several people were arrested, including the university's rector, who was charged with incitement to resistance. Following negotiations with the PDP, the authorities agreed to withdraw police reinforcements from Tetovo (while continuing to assert that the university was illegal). In July 1996 five of the university's founders, including its rector, received custodial sentences for inciting the riots, prompting protests by ethnic Albanians in Tetovo and other parts of the country. (In May 2000 the

Sobranie approved legislation granting the university at Tetovo legal status as a private foundation, and in January 2004 further legislation was passed, transforming it into a state university.)

In October 1995 Gligorov was injured in a car-bomb attack in Skopje, which was condemned by all political parties; he resumed full presidential duties in January 1996. Meanwhile, divisions had emerged within the Alliance for Macedonia. Despite appeals for unity by Gligorov, the alliance that had supported his election to the presidency collapsed, and the LPM was excluded from the Government following a reallocation of portfolios in February. Andov resigned as President of the Sobranie in early March, stating that Crvenkovski had acted unconstitutionally in expelling the LPM from the Government. A new penal code, under which the death penalty was abolished, entered into force in November.

In September 1996, prior to local elections scheduled for 17 November, the Sobranie approved legislation reorganizing the territorial division of the FYRM into 123 municipalities. In October three opposition parties, the IMRO—DPMNU, the DP and the newly established Movement for All-Macedonian Action (MAAK)—Conservative Party, formed a coalition to contest the elections. Xhaferi's faction, which had been reconstituted as the Party of Democratic Prosperity of Albanians in Macedonia (PDPAM), and the (also ethnic Albanian) National Democratic Party (NDP) agreed to present joint candidates in some parts of the country. Following the first round of the local elections, opposition parties claimed that the electoral lists had been falsified by the Government to ensure favourable results for the SDAM. The SDAM received the greatest number of votes, followed by the coalition led by the IMRO—DPMNU, and the PDP. Observers from the Council of Europe (see p. 190) declared that, overall, the elections had been conducted fairly.

In January 1997, following a campaign by ethnic Albanian students, legislation was adopted to permit Albanian to become the language of instruction at the teacher-training faculty of the university at Skopje. This provoked outrage among Macedonian students at the faculty, and a series of protests by university and secondary school students ensued. Ethnic tensions were further compounded by the civil conflict in Albania in early 1997.

A financial scandal emerged in March 1997, involving the embezzlement of funds invested in 'pyramid' savings schemes. Crvenkovski pledged an investigation to identify those responsible for the losses sustained by large numbers of investors, and several officials, including the Deputy Governor of the central bank, were subsequently arrested on suspicion of involvement. Although the Government won a vote of confidence in its management of the affair, the LPM deputies withdrew from the parliamentary chamber to register their disapproval of the measures undertaken. In April the Government announced plans to reimburse losses incurred by investors, following the failure of a major savings institution in the south-western town of Bitola; in the following month the Sobranie approved the replacement of the Governor of the central bank, who was believed to have been involved in the failure of the investment scheme. Earlier in the month the IMRO—DPMNU had organized a demonstration in Skopje to demand the resignation of the Government, and Crvenkovski subsequently reorganized the Cabinet. (In early June 1998 the owner of the institution in Bitola was sentenced to eight years' imprisonment, and four government financial officials also received custodial terms.)

In May 1997 ethnic Albanians in Gostivar took part in protests against a ruling by the Constitutional Court that prohibited the use of the Albanian flag in the FYRM. A number of municipalities with a predominantly ethnic Albanian population refused to comply with the order of the Court, and in June the President of the Constitutional Court issued a statement demanding that the Government enforce the ruling. In early July the Sobranie adopted legislation stipulating that the use of the Albanian flag, and flags of other ethnic minorities, would only be permitted on national holidays, with the Macedonian flag being displayed at the same time. None the less, the mayors of Gostivar and Tetovo continued to refuse to comply with the order of the Constitutional Court, and government officials forcibly removed Albanian flags that had been displayed at municipal buildings. Ensuing protests in Gostivar resulted in violent clashes between security forces and demonstrators, as a result of which three ethnic Albanians were killed; some 500 protesters were arrested. Security forces were finally withdrawn from Gostivar and Tetovo later in July. A report on the violence submitted to the Sobranie by the Ministry of the Interior was

rejected by ethnic Albanian deputies, who condemned the actions of the security forces. In September the mayor of Gostivar, Rufi Osmani, received a custodial sentence of some 13 years (reduced to seven years in February 1998), after being convicted on charges of inciting ethnic tension and rebellion, while the Chairman of the municipal council was sentenced to three years' imprisonment for failing to adopt the ruling of the Constitutional Court. In April the Democratic Party of Albanians (DPA—which had been formed in July 1997 by the amalgamation of the PDPAM and the NDP) announced that it was to withdraw its representatives from all government bodies, in protest at Osmani's imprisonment.

At the end of August 1998 the PDP and the DPA established an electoral alliance, in advance of the forthcoming elections to the Sobranie. In early September the IMRO—DPMNU and the newly formed Democratic Alternative (DA) formed an electoral coalition, styled For Changes. Later that month, following clashes between ethnic Albanian activists and security forces, a number of ethnic Albanians were arrested on suspicion of involvement in a series of bomb attacks in principal towns earlier that year, for which the Kosovo Liberation Army (KLA—Ushtria Clirimtare e Kosoves, see below) had claimed responsibility.

After the first round of the legislative elections, held, as scheduled, on 18 October 1998, a second round of voting proceeded on 1 November; the For Changes alliance secured an absolute majority in the Sobranie, with 58 seats, while the SDAM obtained 29, and the alliance of the PDP and the DPA 24 seats. Owing to irregularities, a further round of voting took place in two electoral districts, at which one seat was won by the For Changes alliance, and the other by the PDP–DPA alliance. Later in November the leader of the IMRO—DPMNU, Ljubčo Georgievski, was nominated to the office of Prime Minister. The DPA was subsequently invited to join the governing coalition of the IMRO—DPMNU and the DA. In early December the Cabinet, comprising 14 representatives of the IMRO—DPMNU, eight of the DA and five of the DPA, was formed. In early December the DPA leadership formally reversed its decision to withdraw its representatives from government bodies, in view of its participation in the new Cabinet. At the end of December the Sobranie approved legislation (supported by the new Government) providing for the release of some 8,000 prisoners, among them Osmani. In January 1999, however, Gligorov refused to approve the amnesty, which he claimed to be unconstitutional. In February the amnesty legislation was resubmitted to the Sobranie (in accordance with the Constitution) and subsequently adopted by the government parties.

The first round of the presidential election, on 31 October 1999, was contested by six candidates: Tito Petkovski, representing the SDAM, secured 33.2% of the votes cast, and Boris Trajkovski, the IMRO—DPMNU candidate (who had hitherto served as deputy foreign minister), won 20.6%; Vasil Tupurkovski, the DA leader, took 16.0%, and Muharem Nexipi, the DPA candidate, 14.8%. Since no candidate had secured an outright majority of the votes, a second round was contested by the two leading candidates, Petkovski and Trajkovski, on 14 November; Trajkovski was elected to the presidency with about 52.8% of the votes cast (after DPA and DA voters transferred support to his candidacy). The SDAM disputed the results of the election, alleging widespread malpractice, particularly in the west of the country. In late November the Supreme Court upheld a legal appeal by the SDAM against the results, and ruled that a further ballot take place in some western regions. A partial round, affecting about 10% of the total electorate, consequently took place on 5 December. However, the overall results were virtually unchanged after the ballot, with Trajkovski receiving some 52.9% of the votes cast. Although the SDAM again claimed that irregularities had taken place, Petkovski finally accepted Trajkovski's election to the presidency. Trajkovski, who was formally inaugurated as President on 15 December, pledged to aim for greater democracy and stability in the country. Following negotiations between the two leaders of the For Changes coalition, Georgievski and Tupurkovski, the IMRO—DPMNU, DA and DPA reached agreement on the formation of a new Government later that month. The coalition Cabinet, which contained seven new ministers (including Tupurkovski, who became a Deputy Prime Minister), was formally approved by the Sobranie on 27 December.

In January 2000 the Government announced that amendments to the Constitution, which would allow higher education to be conducted in the language of ethnic minorities, would be submitted for approval by the Sobranie. In April legislation was adopted, obliging the authorities to return property expropriated under the communist regime. In the same month disaffected members of IMRO—DPMNU, headed by a former Minister of Finance, Boris Zmejkovski, established a breakaway faction, which became known as 'Real' IMRO. In May the SDAM, the Liberal-Democratic Party (LDP) and the Democratic League—Liberal Party established an electoral alliance. In July Georgievski reorganized the Cabinet, reducing the number of ministries from 21 to 14. Local government elections took place in two rounds on 10 and 24 September, amid reports of numerous violent incidents. After a further round of voting took place, owing to electoral irregularities, it was announced at the end of the month that the parties of the government coalition had secured 75 of the 123 municipalities. Following prolonged dissent between Georgievski and Tupurkovski, the DA withdrew from the coalition Government and from the Sobranie at the end of November. Georgievski subsequently formed a new Cabinet, which, for the first time, included members of the LDP.

In early 2001 ethnic Albanian militants, members of the self-styled National Liberation Army (NLA—which had emerged as the successor movement to the KLA), began to infiltrate northern parts of the FYRM from Kosovo, clashing with Macedonian security forces. In early March NLA forces seized the border village of Tanusevci, north of Skopje, prompting counter-attacks from government troops. The border with Kosovo was officially closed, after senior government officials visiting the border region were attacked and temporarily besieged by the NLA. Although the authorities succeeded in regaining control of Tanusevci, in mid-March NLA forces (reported to number about 200) attempted to occupy Tetovo. The Government imposed curfew regulations in Tetovo, but rejected the demands of Macedonian nationalists, who demonstrated in Skopje in favour of the introduction of martial law. Following an appeal by the Government to the international community for military assistance, the North Atlantic Treaty Organization (NATO, see p. 289) announced that a further 1,000 troops were to be deployed at the border with Kosovo to prevent the NLA from receiving supplies from the province. (The NATO troops stationed in the FYRM had only a mandate to provide logistical support to KFOR.) On 21 March the UN Security Council adopted Resolution 1345, condemning the nationalist violence in the FYRM as constituting a threat to the stability of the region. Despite reports that the ethnic Albanian rebels aimed to establish a 'greater Albania' (to comprise Kosovo, northern and western FYRM and the Presevo Valley), the NLA insisted that the conflict had been initiated to pressurize the Macedonian Government to institute constitutional changes guaranteeing equal rights for ethnic Albanians. Government forces staged a major counter-offensive against the rebels, who had refused to comply with an ultimatum to cease hostilities. The prolonged bombardment of rebel positions resulted in a withdrawal by the NLA from the Tetovo region, and hostilities temporarily subsided in early April. However, at the end of the month eight members of the Macedonian security forces were killed in an NLA attack near the border with Kosovo. Their funeral precipitated rioting and attacks by Macedonians on Albanian-owned property in the southern town of Bitola. Government troops subsequently launched an offensive against rebel ethnic Albanian positions at the border villages of Vakcince and Slupcane, near Kumanovo, after two further members of the armed forces were killed.

Meanwhile, in early April 2001, following the temporary suppression of the insurgency, inter-party discussions regarding the ethnic Albanian demands commenced. After signing a Stabilization and Association Agreement with the EU, the Government pledged to initiate political, social and economic reforms by mid-2001. Ethnic Albanian proposals included the postponement of the national census, due to take place in May, until October, to allow the return of refugees who had fled the conflict; state funding for the university at Tetovo; and the conversion of the state television's third service into an Albanian-language channel. However, the Government continued to oppose principal demands that the Constitution be amended to grant the ethnic Albanian population (hitherto officially categorized as a minority) equal rights with the Macedonian population, and Albanian the status of a second official language.

In early May 2001, following the resumption of intensive hostilities in the north of the country, the Government announced that the declaration of a state of war (which would allow the authorities to adopt emergency powers and Trajkovski to rule by decree) was under debate; the declaration, which required the approval of a two-thirds' majority in the Sobranie, was strongly opposed by ethnic Albanian deputies. Intensive discussions ensued between the principal political parties, attended by the EU High Representative responsible for foreign and security policy, Javier Solana Madariaga, and the NATO Secretary-General, Lord Robertson of Port Ellen, who visited Skopje to urge the Government to continue dialogue with the ethnic Albanian minority; it was agreed that the SDAM, the DPA and the PDP would join a government of national unity, and the parliamentary debate on the declaration of a state of war was suspended. The PDP subsequently demanded that the Government declare a cease-fire in the conflict in the north, as a precondition to the ethnic Albanian party's participation in the new Cabinet. After the government offensive against the rebels was temporarily suspended, the Government of national unity (which was again headed by Georgievski) was approved by the Sobranie on 13 May. NLA leaders stated that the rebel movement (which still held several villages) would continue hostilities until the Government agreed to enter into negotiations.

On 8 June 2001 Trajkovski announced proposals for a comprehensive peace plan, which provided for the proportional representation of ethnic Albanians at all levels of government, the increased official use of the Albanian language, and a partial amnesty for NLA combatants. Solana subsequently announced his support for the plan; however, the NLA demanded that the Government end hostilities and enter into negotiations on constitutional reforms, and rebel forces seized the town of Aracinovo, only some 6 km east of Skopje. Later in June the Government announced the suspension of its offensive against the NLA, following pressure from international envoys. However, violent protests were staged by Macedonian nationalists at the parliament building in Skopje, in response to the NATO-mediated cease-fire arrangement at Aracinovo, which was perceived to be lenient towards the ethnic Albanian rebels. On 29 June NATO formally approved an operation to deploy a 3,500-member multinational force in the FYRM to assist in the disarmament of the NLA, which was, however, conditional on the imposition of a lasting cease-fire. On 5 July the Government announced that an official cease-fire agreement had been signed by both sides, and negotiations resumed between leaders of the principal Macedonian and ethnic Albanian parties regarding a permanent peace settlement. However, Georgievski and his nationalist cabinet supporters strongly opposed proposals, detailed by EU and US special envoys, for the extension of the use of the Albanian language, and accused international mediators of sympathizing with the rebels. After minor violations, the cease-fire collapsed after 17 days, when the NLA launched further attacks on government forces deployed at villages near Tetovo. (By that time some 60,000 ethnic Albanians had fled to Kosovo, while a further 30,000 had become internally displaced.) International diplomatic efforts subsequently intensified, following renewed fears of widespread civil conflict. On 26 July, after discussions between Trajkovski, Solana and Robertson, it was announced that an accord had been reached to restore the cease-fire between government forces and the ethnic Albanian rebels, who had agreed to withdraw from newly captured territory near Tetovo. At the end of July further negotiations on the peace proposals, between Macedonian and ethnic Albanian representatives, commenced at the western town of Ohrid. Progress in the discussions was reported in early August, following the resolution of the two main issues of contention (the extension of the official use of the Albanian language and the right to proportional representation of the ethnic Albanian community in the security forces). In response to increasing pressure from the EU and the USA, the Government announced a unilateral cease-fire, and on 13 August the Macedonian and ethnic Albanian leaders at Ohrid signed a framework peace agreement, providing for the amendment of the Constitution to grant greater rights to the ethnic Albanian community. On the following day the NLA leader, Ali Ahmeti, agreed that the NLA, numbering an estimated 2,500–3,000, would relinquish its armaments to NATO troops. Following an assessment of the security situation, NATO announced that the cease-fire was generally being observed, and on 22 August the activation order for a NATO mission, Operation Essential Harvest, was released. The force, which finally comprised 4,500 troops (of whom the United Kingdom contributed about 1,900), had a mandate to disarm the ethnic Albanian combatants and destroy their weapons within 30 days of its deployment. Contention ensued, after the Ministry of Internal Affairs claimed the NLA to be in possession of some 85,000 armaments; however, NATO estimated the number of weapons to be collected at 3,000–4,000.

In early September 2001 parliamentary debate on constitutional reform was delayed by mass nationalist protests against the peace plan. Macedonian nationalist parties in the legislature continued to dispute the extent of a number of the proposed amendments, while ethnic Albanian representatives insisted that attempts to limit the proposals, or to submit them to a referendum, would provoke renewed conflict. Meanwhile, investigators from the International Criminal Tribunal for the former Yugoslavia (ICTY, see p. 16) at the Hague, Netherlands, had been dispatched to the FYRM to conduct preliminary inquiries into the killing of six ethnic Albanian civilians in the village of Ljuboten in early August; the nationalist Minister of Internal Affairs, Ljube Boskovski, was suspected of responsibility for the massacre. On 26 September NATO's 30-day disarmament programme was declared to have been successful, with the collection of some 3,875 armaments. On the same day the establishment of a further, reduced NATO mission, Operation Amber Fox, was authorized. (In response to international pressure, the Government had invited NATO to retain a military presence in the country, despite domestic opposition.) The new mission, comprising 700 troops, together with 300 forces already stationed in the FYRM, was deployed under German leadership, with a three-month renewable mandate to protect EU and OSCE monitors supervising the implementation of the peace agreement. On 27 September Ahmeti announced that the NLA had been formally dissolved, following the completion of the disarmament process. In early October the EU criticized delays in implementing constitutional reforms, after Macedonian parties announced that the legislative process would be suspended pending the release of 14 Macedonian civilians allegedly seized by the NLA earlier that year. Following pressure from Trajkovski, and further diplomatic visits by Solana and Robertson, who urged acceptance of the plan, discussion on the measures resumed in the Sobranie. Later that month Trajkovski approved plans for the deployment of ethnically-mixed security units in regions formerly held by the NLA. Cease-fire violations by dissident former NLA combatants were reported in the northwest of the country in early November.

On 16 November 2001 the Sobranie finally adopted 15 main amendments to the existing Constitution (although the extent of some provisions had been reduced at the insistence of the Macedonian parties). The principal reforms were: the revision of the Constitution's preamble to include a reference to members of non-ethnic Macedonian communities as citizens of the country; the introduction in the Sobranie of a 'double majority' system, whereby certain legislation would require the approval of a minority group; the establishment of Albanian as the second official language in communities where ethnic Albanians comprised more than 20% of the population; and the right to proportional representation for ethnic Albanians in the Constitutional Court, all areas of government administration, and the security forces. The adoption of the reforms was received with approval by the international community. Later in November the SDAM and the allied LDP withdrew from the coalition Government (which was subsequently reorganized), on the grounds that their participation was no longer necessary.

In early December 2001 NATO extended the mandate of Operation Amber Fox until 26 March 2002, and it was subsequently extended until 26 June. An EU-sponsored international donor conference on economic assistance for the FYRM, originally scheduled to take place in October 2001, was further postponed in December, pending the implementation of additional reforms. In January 2002 new legislation providing for the devolution of greater authority to local government (thereby granting a measure of self-rule to predominantly ethnic Albanian regions) was approved by the Sobranie, and the donor conference duly took place in March (see Economic Affairs). Also in January a Deputy Prime Minister, Dosta Dimovska (who was considered to be a moderate), resigned from the Government, following disagreement with Georgievski over issues relating to the deployment of security units in previously NLA-controlled villages. In February the three principal ethnic Albanian political parties (the DPA, the PDP and the NDP) and the former NLA leadership officially established a co-ordinating council, confirming speculation that Ahmeti would enter domestic politics. In March the Sobranie adopted legislation granting immunity from prosecution to several thousand former NLA insurgents (excluding those indictable by the ICTY), in accordance with the peace settlement. In May the mandate of Operation Amber Fox was further extended, to 26 October. In accordance with the peace agreement, the Sobranie was dissolved on 18 July, prior to legislative elections, which were scheduled for 15 September and were to be monitored by the OSCE.

In May 2002 Ahmeti established a new political party, the Democratic Union for Integration (DUI), which was believed to comprise mainly former NLA combatants. Later that month two ministers belonging to 'Real' IMRO resigned from the Government, on the grounds that former NLA members had become dominant within the principal ethnic Albanian parties. In the same month the Sobranie approved legislation whereby Albanian became an official language, in accordance with the Ohrid peace accord. At the end of August fears of a resurgence in violence emerged, after ethnic Albanians took hostage five Macedonian civilians at Gostivar; large numbers of security forces surrounded an ethnic Albanian base and killed two of the kidnappers. However, the elections to the legislature took place peacefully on 15 September, attracting commendation from the international community, after OSCE observers declared them to have been conducted democratically. Georgievski's Government was removed from power by a 10-party alliance (led by the SDAM and the LDP), known as Together for Macedonia, which secured 60 of the 120 seats in the Sobranie. (IMRO—DPMNU won 33 seats and the newly established DUI 16 seats.) Allegations of malpractice by the outgoing Government were rejected by the electoral commission. The Together for Macedonia alliance and the DUI subsequently signed an agreement for the establishment of a coalition Government (which was, however, to exclude former NLA combatants). The new, 18-member administration, comprising members of the SDAM, the LDP and the DUI, headed by Crvenkovski, was officially approved by the Sobranie on 1 November.

In October 2002 NATO agreed to extend the mandate of Operation Amber Fox until December (following controversy within the Government over plans for the contingent to be replaced by EU forces). On 14 December Operation Amber Fox was succeeded by a 450-member mission, Allied Harmony, with a mandate to protect international monitors and advise Macedonian security forces. On 31 March 2003 this contingent was replaced by an EU-led mission, known as Operation Concordia, comprising 350 military personnel; 13 EU member states and 14 non-EU nations were to participate in the force. The purpose of the operation, which was deployed at the official request of Trajkovski, was to maintain security in order to facilitate the implementation of the Ohrid peace agreement. Meanwhile, in early 2003 a newly emerged ethnic Albanian extremist group, the Albanian National Army (ANA), threatened to launch a military offensive against the Government. The ANA, which favoured the creation of a 'greater Albania', had claimed responsibility for a number of bomb attacks, including one against the regional court at Struga. In September ethnic Albanian militants clashed with a security patrol at the border with Kosovo; several of the rebels were killed in the incident (which was regarded as the most serious since August 2001). The authorities subsequently dispatched security forces to the region in an operation to suppress dissident activity (a measure that was criticized by the DUI).

Meanwhile, in April 2003 Georgievski announced his resignation from the leadership of the IMRO—DPMNU; he was replaced in late May by Nikola Gruevski. In early November Ljuben Paunovski, a member of the IMRO—DPMNU and a former Minister of Defence, was sentenced to over five years' imprisonment, on charges of the embezzlement of public funds during his time in office. In the same month Crvenkovski replaced four ministers, including those responsible for the economy and finance portfolios, in a major government reorganization (which was believed to reflect his concern at a lack of economic progress). Nikola Popovski (a member of the SDAM and hitherto President—speaker of the Sobranie), replaced the leader of the LDP, Petar Gosev, as Deputy Prime Minister and Minister of Finance. Later that month Ljupco Jordanovski, also of the SDAM, was elected as the new parliamentary speaker. In early December Tupurkovski's DA, the SPM and the Democratic Alliance of Pavle Trajanov, a former Minister of Internal Affairs, established a new opposition alliance, known as Third Path.

On 15 December 2003 Operation Concordia was replaced by a 200-member EU mission, Operation Proxima, which, in addition to maintaining security and combating organized crime in the country, was to advise the Macedonian police forces. At the end of September a meeting of EU Ministers of Foreign Affairs had approved the deployment of the contingent in the FYRM for a minimum of one year. In February 2004 the Government prepared to redemarcate municipal boundaries, as part of a process of administrative decentralization included in the provisions of the Ohrid agreement. However, approval of the draft legislation in the Sobranie was expected to be problematic, owing to widespread popular opposition to the proposals.

On 26 February 2004 President Trajkovski, together with eight government officials, was killed, when an aircraft transporting him to a international investment conference in Bosnia and Herzegovina crashed in a southern, mountainous region of the country, east of the Croatian port of Dubrovnik. Trajkovski had been popular domestically, and his funeral on 5 March was attended by the NATO Secretary-General and the Heads of State and of Government of some 30 nations. Jordanovski, as speaker of the Sobranie, assumed the presidency in an acting capacity, pending an election, which, under the terms of the Constitution, was to take place within 40 days. Officials of the NATO-commanded Stabilization Force (SFOR) stationed in Bosnia and Herzegovina denied Macedonian media reports that SFOR air controllers had been responsible for the crash. In early March Jordanovski announced that the presidential election would take place on 14 April, in accordance with the Constitution. Crvenkovski was expected to be a leading presidential candidate, and later in March he was officially nominated by the SDAM to represent the party. The IMRO—DPMNU elected a parliamentary deputy, Sasko Kedev, as its presidential candidate, while two former NLA commanders, the DUI Secretary-General, Gzim Ostreni, and Zudi Xhelili of the DPA were also to contest the election. (Boskovski's independent candidacy was rejected by the electoral commission, on the grounds that he failed to meet the requirement of having been resident in the FYRM for 10 years.) The OSCE announced that it was to dispatch an observer mission to monitor the election, and campaigning officially commenced at the end of March. Crvenkovski won 42.5% of the votes cast on 14 April; since he failed to secure the 50% of the votes necessary to be elected outright, a second round between him and Kedev (who had won 34.1% of the votes) was scheduled. On 28 April Crvenkovski was elected to the presidency with 62.7% of the votes. Kedev immediately claimed that widespread malpractice had been perpetrated and appealed against the election results, which were, however, upheld by OSCE monitors. Crvenkovski was inaugurated on 12 May.

Both the September 1995 interim agreement with Greece and the November Dayton peace accord (for further details, see the chapter on Bosnia and Herzegovina) were of great significance in promoting diplomatic and external economic links for the FYRM, despite the still unresolved issue of a permanent name for the country. The FYRM was admitted to the Council of Europe in late September, and to the OSCE in mid-October; in the following month the FYRM joined NATO's 'Partnership for Peace' (see p. 291) programme. The agreement with Greece facilitated the establishment of full diplomatic relations with the EU from January 1996, and negotiations subsequently began for a co-operation accord; a declaration on co-operation was, furthermore, signed with the European Free Trade Association (see p. 205) in early April. By the end of 1996 more than 75 countries had recognized the FYRM, with about two-thirds using the country's constitutional name, the Republic of Macedonia. The FYRM Government signed a Stabilization and Association Agreement with the EU in April 2001, which came into effect on 1 April 2004. A formal application for membership of the EU was submitted the Irish Taoiseach (Prime Minister) and President of the European Council, Bertie Ahern, on 22 March 2004 (having been postponed from February, owing to the death of President Trajkovski—see above).

In July 1995 the FYRM and Turkey signed a 20-year co-operation agreement and a mutual security accord. Turkey, together with Albania, Bulgaria and Italy, was involved (between February 1994 and October 1995) in providing trading routes whereby the FYRM could bypass the Greek blockade. None the less, the issue of ethnic Albanians' rights in the FYRM was a frequent source of tension with Albania, and relations with Bulgaria continued to be impeded, specifically, by the question of its recognition of a distinct Macedonian language and nationality.

Although the FYRM formally supported the UN embargo on the FRY, there was frequent evidence that the FYRM Government permitted violations of the blockade. Regular trade with both Greece and the FRY resumed in late 1995, while discussions continued between Macedonian, Greek and UN officials regarding the issue of a permanent name for the FYRM. By 1999 the FYRM's relations with Greece had improved significantly, and in December the two countries signed an agreement on military co-operation. At the end of 2000 the principal border crossing between the FYRM and Greece was reopened.

An agreement signed by the FYRM and the FRY in early April 1996, regulating bilateral relations and promoting mutual co-operation, was regarded as particularly significant in formalizing the FRY's recognition of the FYRM as a sovereign state. Although criticized by most opposition groups within the FYRM, the agreement, since it took into account the position of ethnic Serbs in the FYRM, was welcomed by representatives of the ethnic-Serb community—which constituted about 2% of the total population in 1994, according to census results—who were campaigning for constitutional recognition as a distinct ethnic group of the FYRM. Meanwhile, the FYRM, Bosnia and Herzegovina, Croatia and Slovenia were co-operating in efforts to secure international recognition for all the former republics as successor states to the SFRY, and thereby win access to a share of the assets of the former Yugoslavia. In September the FRY Prime Minister, Radoje Kontić, on his first official visit to the FYRM, signed seven bilateral agreements. The Governments of the FYRM and Serbia and Montenegro (which reconstituted from the FRY in February 2003) increased bilateral co-operation in a number of areas, particularly measures to combat organized crime and promote regional stability.

In late 1992 the UN Security Council approved the deployment of members of the UN Protection Force along the FYRM's border with the FRY and Albania, in an effort to protect the FYRM from any external threat to its security; in March 1995 the operation in the FYRM was renamed the UN Preventive Deployment Force (UNPREDEP). In June 1996 the USA and the FYRM exchanged diplomatic notes regulating the status of US troops participating in UNPREDEP. Following a reduction in UNPREDEP's authorized strength by the Security Council, the US contingent of military personnel was placed under direct US administration. In April 1997 the mandate of UNPREDEP was extended to the end of May, in view of the civil disorder in Albania (q.v.); it was further extended in June and December. Following the civil unrest in Albania, a number of border incursions by armed groups of Albanian rebels were reported, and in September two members of the FYRM's security forces were killed in a clash with Albanians who had entered the country illegally. In October the Ministers of Defence of the FYRM and Albania signed an agreement providing for increased security along the joint border between the two countries.

In the first months of 1998 increasing clashes were reported in Kosovo between members of the Serbian security forces and the KLA, a paramilitary movement established by ethnic Albanians. In late July the UN Security Council extended the mandate of UNPREDEP until 28 February 1999 and agreed to increase the size of the contingent from 750 to about 1,100, with the aim of reinforcing border control. In early December 1998, following discussions between President Gligorov and NATO officials, it was announced that a NATO 'extraction force' was to be deployed in the FYRM to effect the evacuation of OSCE monitors in Kosovo in the event of large-scale conflict. In late February 1999 the People's Republic of China vetoed a UN Security Council resolution to extend the mandate of UNPREDEP for a further six months, following a decision by the FYRM Government to extend diplomatic recognition to Taiwan, which also prompted the People's Republic of China to suspend diplomatic relations with the FYRM. In the same month additional NATO troops began to assemble near the FYRM border with Kosovo (where the 2,300-member 'extraction force', principally comprising French and British troops, was already stationed). Diplomatic efforts failed, however, and NATO forces commenced an intensive aerial bombardment of strategic targets in the FRY in late March. Ethnic Serbs in the FYRM subsequently increased demonstrations against the presence of NATO forces in the country. The NATO air offensive precipitated increased reprisals by Serbian security forces against the ethnic Albanian population in Kosovo and by early April some 140,000 refugees had fled to the FYRM. The FYRM Government denied foreign allegations of the maltreatment by its security forces of the Kosovar refugees, and complained of delays in assistance from the EU. By mid-April about 14,000 NATO troops were deployed near the FYRM border with Kosovo, and were involved in assisting the refugees. Owing to concern over internal destabilization, the FYRM authorities repeatedly closed the border with Kosovo to prevent the continued arrival of large numbers of ethnic Albanians, and demanded that the international community fulfil pledges to accept a proportion of the refugees. By late May some 60,000 refugees had been transported from the FYRM for provisional resettlement abroad, while an estimated 250,000 remained in the country. In early June the strength of NATO forces stationed in the FYRM was increased to 16,000. Shortly afterwards the Yugoslav Government accepted a peace plan which provided for the withdrawal of Serbian forces from Kosovo, the return of ethnic Albanian refugees and the deployment of a NATO-led Kosovo Peace Implementation Force (KFOR). NATO troops, which were to be deployed under the KFOR mandate, entered Kosovo from the FYRM. On 20 June NATO announced that the air campaign had officially ended, following the withdrawal of Serbian forces from Kosovo. Large numbers of ethnic Albanian refugees subsequently began to return to Kosovo from the FYRM. Some 4,000 NATO troops remained in the FYRM, with a mandate to provide logistical support to KFOR.

In early 2001 an ethnic Albanian insurgency spread into the FYRM from Kosovo (see above). In June the FYRM and the People's Republic of China agreed to restore diplomatic relations (thereby ensuring Chinese support in the UN Security Council for the deployment of a NATO peace-keeping operation from August); Taiwan subsequently announced the severance of relations with the FYRM. In March 2002 Trajkovski and the head of the UN Interim Administration Mission in Kosovo (UNMIK) agreed to establish a joint committee to discuss border issues. In March 2004 the FYRM Minister of Foreign Affairs met the Head of UNMIK and NATO and US envoys for emergency discussions on Kosovo, following an outbreak of ethnic Albanian violence in the province's ethnically divided town of Kosovska Mitrovica, amid concern that the clashes would result in further destabilization in the FYRM.

Government

According to the 1991 Constitution, which was amended in November 2001, legislative power is vested in the Sobranie (Assembly), with 120 members, elected for a four-year term by universal adult suffrage (85 in single-seat constituencies and 35 members by proportional representation). The President is directly elected for a five-year term, and appoints a Prime Minister to head the Government. The Ministers are elected by the Sobranie. For the purposes of local government, the FYRM is divided into 123 municipalities. However, in early 2004 there were plans to reduce the number of administrative districts to 62, as part of a process of decentralization included in the provisions of the Ohrid agreement.

Defence

In August 2003 the armed forces of the FYRM totalled 12,850 in active service (including 5,200 conscripts): army 11,650, air force 800, marine force 400. Paramilitary forces comprised a police force of 7,600, of which some 5,000 were armed. Conscription was introduced in April 1992, and military service lasts for six months. On 31 March 2003 the existing North Atlantic Treaty Organization (NATO, see p. 289) contingent in the FYRM was replaced by a European Union (EU, see p. 208) mission, known as Operation Concordia, which was, in turn, replaced on 15 December by a 200-member EU police mission, Operation Proxima. Expenditure on defence was budgeted at about 7,400m. new denars in 2003.

Economic Affairs

In 2002, according to World Bank estimates, the FYRM's gross national income (GNI), measured at average 2000–02 prices, was US $3,456m., equivalent to $1,700 per head (or $6,210 per head on an international purchasing-power parity basis). During 1990–2002, it was estimated, the population increased by an average of 0.6% per year, while gross domestic product (GDP) per head declined, in real terms, at an average annual rate of 1.0%. Overall GDP declined, in real terms, at an average annual rate of 0.5% in 1990–2002; real GDP declined by 4.5% in 2001, but increased by 0.3% in 2002.

Agriculture (including hunting, forestry and fishing) contributed an estimated 11.8% of GDP in 2002, when 23.9% of the employed labour force were engaged in the sector. Dairy farming is significant, and the principal agricultural exports are tobacco, vegetables and fruit. The wine industry is of considerable importance, and the FYRM is also a producer of wheat, maize and barley. During 1990–2002, according to the World Bank, the GDP of the agricultural sector increased, in real terms, at an average annual rate of 0.2%; real agricultural GDP declined by 10.8% in 2001, but increased by 2.1% in 2002.

In 2002 industry contributed an estimated 28.9% of GDP and engaged 33.3% of the employed labour force. During 1990–2002, according to the World Bank, the GDP of the industrial sector declined, in real terms, at an average annual rate of 3.8%; real industrial GDP declined by 6.5% in 2001 and by 5.6% in 2002.

Mining contributed an estimated 0.6% of GDP and engaged 1.2% of the employed labour force in 2002. The only major mining activity is the production of lignite (brown coal), although there are also deposits of iron, zinc, lead, copper, chromium, manganese, antimony, silver, gold and nickel. Production in the mining and quarrying sector increased at an average annual rate of 5.9% in 1996–2000.

The manufacturing sector contributed an estimated 18.6% of GDP in 2002, and engaged 23.6% of the employed labour force. In 1996 the principal branches of the sector, measured by gross value of output, were food products (accounting for 19.1% of the total), textiles and clothing (11.9%), machinery (11.0%), chemicals, and iron and steel. The GDP of the manufacturing sector decreased, in real terms, at an average annual rate of 5.3% in 1990–2002; real manufacturing GDP declined by 3.9% in 2001 and by 5.4% in 2002.

Energy is derived principally from coal and lignite, which provided 79.8% of the electricity generated in 2000. The first stage of a pipeline from the Bulgarian border to carry natural gas to the FYRM from Russia became operational in late 1995. A 214-km pipeline, which was to transport petroleum from the Greek port of Thessaloníki to Skopje, was inaugurated in July 2002. Imports of mineral fuels accounted for 13.2% of the value of total imports in 2002.

Services accounted for an estimated 59.3% of GDP and engaged 42.8% of the employed labour force in 2002. Regional instability, notably ethnic hostilities in the north of the FYRM in 2001, has had an adverse impact on tourist activity. During 1990–2002, according to the World Bank, the GDP of the services sector increased, in real terms, at an average annual rate of 0.9%; services GDP declined by 1.6% in 2001, but rose by 3.6% in 2002.

In 2002 the FYRM recorded a visible trade deficit of US $767.6m., while there was a deficit of $325.3m. on the current account of the balance of payments. In 2002 the principal source of imports was Germany (accounting for 14.3%); other major sources were Greece, the FRY, Slovenia, Bulgaria, Russia and Italy. The principal market for exports in that year was the FRY (22.1%); other important purchasers were Germany, Greece, the USA, Italy and Croatia. The principal exports in 2002 were miscellaneous manufactured articles (notably clothing and accessories), basic manufactures (particularly iron and steel), beverages and tobacco, food and live animals, machinery and transport equipment, and chemicals. The main imports in that year were machinery and transport equipment (particularly road vehicles and parts), basic manufactures, mineral fuels and lubricants (notably petroleum and petroleum products), food and live animals, chemical products and miscellaneous manufactured articles.

The FYRM recorded an overall budgetary deficit of 13,019m. new denars (equivalent to 5.4% of GDP) in 2002. The fiscal deficit was estimated to have declined to 3,412m. new denars (equivalent to 1.4% of GDP) in 2003. At the end of 2001 the FYRM's total external debt was estimated at US $1,423m., of which $1,136m. was long-term public debt. In that year the cost of debt-servicing was equivalent to 12.9% of the value of exports of goods and services. The annual rate of inflation averaged 67.6% in 1990–2002. Consumer prices increased by 1.8% in 2002. The rate of unemployment was estimated at some 31.9% in 2002.

The FYRM is a member of the IMF and the European Bank for Reconstruction and Development (EBRD, see p. 203). It become a member of the World Trade Organization (WTO, see p. 343) in April 2003.

The FYRM's economic prospects were significantly improved by the removal, in late 1995, of the Greek embargo on trade with the FYRM and the UN sanctions against the FRY, which had severely disrupted the FYRM's trading links. Progress was achieved through mass privatization, and a stock exchange was opened in Skopje in March 1996. The NATO aerial bombardment of the FRY in March–June 1999, resulting in a mass influx of refugees from Kosovo, strained the FYRM's resources. Following the end of the conflict, however, Macedonian enterprises profited from involvement in the reconstruction of infrastructural damage in Kosovo, and from Serbia's economic regeneration. A significant improvement in relations between Greece and the FYRM also provided for substantial Greek investment. The introduction of value-added tax in 2000 proved successful, and in November the IMF approved a new three-year loan to support the Government's economic reforms. However, ethnic hostilities in the north of the country in early 2001 (see Recent History) prompted renewed fears of widespread civil conflict, and a substantial deterioration of the fiscal position ensued. Following the negotiation of a peace agreement in August, the authorities requested considerable donor assistance to finance the reconstruction of damaged infrastructure and housing, and the relocation of displaced civilians. A Stabilization and Association Agreement was signed with the European Union (EU) in April. A major donor aid conference, sponsored by the EU and the World Bank, finally took place in March 2002; international donors pledged a total of US $515m. to support reconstruction. In September the Government, which had been widely regarded as responsible for mismanagement and widespread corruption, was replaced. Measures to investigate suspected embezzlement in public institutions and to combat further malpractice were immediately introduced. In October the WTO formally approved the FYRM's accession, and it became a full member in April 2003. A further stand-by credit agreement with the IMF was signed in early 2003, and in October the Fund approved the disbursement of further funds. (An agreement providing for the continuance of IMF-recommended policies was expected to be negotiated on the expiry of the existing arrangement in June 2004.) The Government's success in adhering to IMF conditions of fiscal restraint and fulfilling targets for growth and low inflation was commended; however, reduced state expenditure (resulting in a lower than anticipated budgetary deficit) caused delays in implementing investment projects. The Government also proved slow to introduce measures to reform the pension system and privatize or close loss-making enterprises, which would adversely affect unemployment. None the less, economic growth was projected to accelerate in 2004–05, as a result of increased external funding and private investment. The death of President Boris Trajkovski on 26 February 2004 (see above) produced conditions of political uncertainty in the country, prior to an election in April; the country's formal application for membership of the EU, due to take place on the same day, was finally submitted on 22 March. Furthermore, an outbreak of ethnic Albanian violence in Kosovo in March prompted fears of renewed destabilization in the FYRM.

Education

Elementary education is provided free of charge, and is officially compulsory for all children between the ages of seven and 15 years. Various types of secondary education, beginning at 15 years of age and lasting for four years, are available to those who qualify. In 1999/2000 primary enrolment included 93.6% of children in the relevant age-group (males 94.0%, females 93.1%), while the comparable ratio for secondary education was equivalent to 83.6% (males 85.0%; females 82.2%). The Constitution guarantees nationals the right to elementary and secondary education in their mother tongue. In 2001/02 Albanian was the language of education in 275 primary schools and 24 secondary schools, Turkish in 55 primary schools and five secondary schools, and Serbian in 13 primary schools. There are universities at Skopje and at Bitola. In July 2000 new legislation permitted the use of Albanian and other languages in private tertiary institutions, and an Albanian-language university (the South-East Europe University) at Tetovo opened as a private institution, with funding from the international community, in November 2001. In early 2004, under further amendments to legislation on higher education, the Albanian-language Tetovo University (previously declared illegal) became the third state-funded university, and was expected to open for the 2004/05 academic year. In 2002/03 some 45,624 students were enrolled in tertiary education. Expenditure on education by the central Government in 2002 was budgeted at 7,591m. denars (11.4% of total expenditure).

Public Holidays

2004: 1 January (New Year), 6–7 January (Christmas), 8 March (International Women's Day), 11–12 April (Orthodox Easter), 1 May (Labour Day), 24 May (Day of the Apostles St Cyril and St Methodius), 2 August (National Day), 8 September (Independence Day).

2005: 1 January (New Year), 6–7 January (Christmas), 8 March (International Women's Day), 1 May (Labour Day), 1–2 May (Orthodox Easter), 24 May (Day of the Apostles St Cyril and St Methodius), 2 August (National Day), 8 September (Independence Day).

Weights and Measures

The metric system is in force.

Statistical Survey

Source (unless otherwise indicated): State Statistical Office of the Republic of Macedonia, 91000 Skopje, Dame Gruev 4, POB 506; tel. (2) 114904; fax (2) 111336; e-mail info@stat.gov.mk; internet www.stat.gov.mk.

Area and Population

AREA, POPULATION AND DENSITY

Area (sq km)	25,713*
Population (census results)	
31 March 1991†	2,033,964
20 June 1994‡	
Males	974,255
Females	971,677
Total	1,945,932
Population (official estimates at 31 December)	
2001	2,031,112
2002	2,049,000
Density (per sq km) at 31 December 2002	79.7

* 9,928 sq miles.

† The total refers to the *de jure* population, i.e. persons with a permanent residence in the country, including residents temporarily abroad (regardless of the duration of their absence). Other persons present in Macedonia were excluded.

‡ Figures from the 1994 census refer to persons with an official place of residence in the country (including those temporarily abroad for less than a year) and persons from other countries who have been granted a residence permit in Macedonia and have been present there for at least a year.

PRINCIPAL ETHNIC GROUPS
(census results)

	1991	1994
Macedonian	1,328,187	1,295,964
Albanian	441,987	441,104
Turkish	77,080	78,019
Roma (Gypsy)	52,103	43,707
Serbian	42,775	40,228
Muslim	31,356	15,418
Vlach	7,764	8,601
Total (incl. others)	2,033,964	1,945,932

PRINCIPAL TOWNS
(population at 1994 census)

Skopje (capital) . .	444,299		Veles	46,798
Bitola	77,464		Štip	41,730
Kumanovo . . .	71,853		Ohrid	41,146
Prilep	68,148		Strumica . . .	34,067
Tetovo	50,344			

BIRTHS, MARRIAGES AND DEATHS*

	Registered live births Number	Rate (per 1,000)	Registered marriages Number	Rate (per 1,000)	Registered deaths Number	Rate (per 1,000)
1994	33,487	17.2	15,736	8.1	15,771	8.1
1995	32,154	16.3	15,823	8.0	16,338	8.3
1996	31,403	15.8	14,089	7.1	16,063	8.1
1997	29,478	14.8	14,072	7.0	16,596	8.3
1998	29,244	14.6	13,993	7.0	16,870	8.4
1999	27,309	13.5	14,172	7.0	16,789	8.3
2000	29,308	14.5	14,255	7.0	17,253	8.5
2001	27,010	13.3	13,267	6.5	16,919	8.3

* Prior to 1994, rates per 1,000 are not comparable with figures for later years.

Expectation of life (WHO estimates, years at birth): 72.0 (males 69.0; females 75.1) in 2002 (Source: WHO, *World Health Report*).

ECONOMICALLY ACTIVE POPULATION
(sample surveys, '000 persons aged 15 years and over, at April)

	2001*	2002
Agriculture, hunting and forestry	149.2	133.6
Fishing	0.3	0.7
Mining and quarrying	9.3	6.9
Manufacturing	149.2	132.4
Electricity, gas and water	16.5	14.8
Construction	35.6	32.8
Wholesale and retail trade, repair of motor vehicles, motorcycles and articles for personal use and for households	66.7	64.3
Hotels and restaurants	12.4	11.2
Transport, storage and communications	33.2	32.6
Financial intermediation	8.8	8.4
Real estate, renting and business activities	10.4	11.1
Public administration and defence, compulsory social security	33.9	33.0
Education	27.0	33.7
Health and social work	26.9	26.2
Total employed†	599.3	561.3

* October.
† Including others.

Source: IMF, *Former Yugoslav Republic of Macedonia: Selected Issues and Statistical Appendix* (May 2003).

Health and Welfare

KEY INDICATORS

Total fertility rate (children per woman, 2002)	1.9
Under-5 mortality rate (per 1,000 live births, 2001)	26
HIV/AIDS (% of persons aged 15–49, 2001)	<0.10
Physicians (per 1,000 head, 2002)	4.6
Hospital beds (per 1,000 head, 2002)	9.8
Health expenditure (2001): US $ per head (PPP)	331
Health expenditure (2001): % of GDP	6.8
Health expenditure (2001): public (% of total)	84.9
Human Development Index (2001): ranking	60
Human Development Index (2001): value	0.784

For sources and definitions, see explanatory note on p. vi.

Agriculture

PRINCIPAL CROPS
('000 metric tons)

	2000	2001	2002
Wheat	299.0	246.0	267.2
Rice (paddy)	18.5	7.9	8.9
Barley	110.0	91.5	128.4
Maize	125.0	117.3	140.2
Rye	8.2	9.5	7.1
Potatoes	164.0	173.0	183.1
Sugar beet	56.0	38.0	43.8
Dry beans	13.6	11.7	13.8
Sunflower seed	10.0*	5.5	8.8
Cabbages	70.4	75.3	71.0
Tomatoes	134.7	126.3	109.5
Cucumbers and gherkins†	22	22	22
Chillies and green peppers	112.0	117.0	108.1
Dry onions	36.3	30.6	34.6
Green beans	17.7	17.5	13.8
Other vegetables	22.5	23.1	22.6
Apples	84.3	38.4	63.3
Pears	8.9	6.5	7.7
Peaches and nectarines	9.5	4.6	6.3
Plums	23.4	13.3	23.8
Cherries (incl. sour)	6.6	5.4	6.4
Grapes	264.3	229.8	119.0
Watermelons and other melons	125.0	133.1	152.4
Other fruits	10.6	7.4	6.6
Tobacco (leaves)	22.2	23.2	22.0

* Unofficial figure.
† FAO estimates.

Source: FAO.

LIVESTOCK
('000 head, year ending September)

	2000	2001	2002
Horses	57	57*	57*
Cattle	270	265†	259
Pigs	226	204	196
Sheep	1,289	1,251	1,234
Poultry	3,350*	3,350*	2,900

* FAO estimate.
† Unofficial figure.

Source: FAO.

LIVESTOCK PRODUCTS
('000 metric tons)

	2000	2001	2002
Beef and veal	6.3	6.9*	6.7
Mutton and lamb	4.5†	5.9†	4.6
Pig meat	9.3	8.4	10.6
Poultry meat	4.8	4.7	4.0
Cows' milk	220.2	200.9	198.4
Sheep's milk	40.2	47.5	51.6
Butter†	9.5	9.5	9.5
Cheese†	1.4	1.4	1.4
Poultry eggs	25.5	22.2	19.4
Honey	1.1	1.0	0.9
Wool: greasy	1.9	1.9	1.9
Cattle hides†	1.3	1.3	1.3
Sheepskins†	0.9	1.1	1.1

* Unofficial figure.
† FAO estimate(s).

Source: FAO.

Forestry

ROUNDWOOD REMOVALS
('000 cubic metres, excl. bark)

	2000	2001	2002
Sawlogs, veneer logs and logs for sleepers	164	125	104
Pulpwood	5	—	—
Other industrial wood	8	10	8
Fuel wood	875	605	603
Total	1,052	740	715

Source: FAO.

SAWNWOOD PRODUCTION
('000 cubic metres, incl. railway sleepers)

	2000	2001	2002
Coniferous (softwood)	8	6	6
Broadleaved (hardwood). . . .	28	17	15
Total	36	23	21

Source: FAO.

Fishing

(metric tons, live weight)

	1999	2000	2001
Capture	135	208	128
Freshwater fishes	113	77	13
Trouts	22	131	115
Aquaculture	1,669	1,626	1,053
Common carp	215	238	153
Bleak	130	110	70
Other freshwater fishes . . .	210	330	221
European eel	60	50	32
Trouts	788	705	454
Huchen	244	173	110
White fishes	22	20	13
Total catch	1,804	1,834	1,181

Source: FAO, *Yearbook of Fishery Statistics.*

Mining

('000 metric tons)

	1999	2000	2001
Lignite.	7,277.6	7,514.8	8,142.1
Copper concentrates*	37.8	42.4	25.0
Lead concentrates*	12.3	16.2	9.1
Zinc concentrates*	10.2	12.2	5.7
Gypsum (crude)	76.2	60.0	74.0

* Figures refer to the metal content of concentrates.

Industry

SELECTED PRODUCTS
('000 metric tons, unless otherwise indicated)

	1999	2000	2001
Vegetable oils: refined	11.3	15.6	15.4
Flour	140.4	n.a.	n.a.
Refined sugar.	43.0	31.9	18.0
Beer ('000 hectolitres)	651.9	659.8	622.2
Spirits ('000 hectolitres). . . .	25.2	16.1	16.9
Soft drinks ('000 hectolitres) . .	685.2	907.5	858.1
Cigarettes (million)	17,758	8,690	7,802
Wool yarn: pure and mixed . .	0.5	0.5	0.4
Cotton yarn: pure and mixed . .	2.3	2.5	1.1
Woven cotton fabric (million sq metres)	6.1	3.8	5.2
Woven woollen fabrics (million sq metres)	0.8	0.6	1.0
Leather footwear ('000) . . .	2,488	2,129	1,073
Paper and paperboard	20.6	20.5	21.0
Sulphuric acid	87.8	108.6	101.1
Motor spirit (petrol)	266.8	99.0	65.3
Gas-diesel (distillate fuel) oil . .	203.6	258.6	142.4
Residual fuel oils (Mazout) . . .	248.2	376.9	281.5
Cement	563.3	801.1	585.5
Ferro-alloys	77.5	58.5	3.0
Lead: unwrought.	46.8	n.a.	n.a.
Zinc: unwrought	4.0	n.a.	n.a.
Electric energy (million kWh) . .	6,821.7	6,786.6	6,356.1

Finance

CURRENCY AND EXCHANGE RATES

Monetary Units
100 deni = 1 new Macedonian denar.

Sterling, Dollar and Euro Equivalents (30 October 2003)
£1 sterling = 88.27 new denars;
US $1 = 52.18 new denars;
€1 = 60.64 new denars;
1,000 new denars = £11.33 = $19.16 = €16.49.

Average Exchange Rate (new denars per US $)
2001   68.037
2002   64.350
2003   54.322

Note: The Macedonian denar was introduced in April 1992, replacing (initially at par) the Yugoslav dinar. In May 1993 a new Macedonian denar, equivalent to 100 of the former units, was established as the sole legal tender.

BUDGET
(million new denars)*

Revenue†	2001	2002	2003
Tax revenue	47,564	54,387	50,932
Personal income tax	7,247	7,514	7,713
Profit tax	3,006	2,625	3,184
Sales tax	17,133	20,521	22,792
Excises	10,681	10,715	10,297
Import duties	6,111	6,335	6,596
Non-tax revenue	3,833	2,971	4,853
Total	51,397	57,358	55,785

Expenditure	2001	2002	2003
Current expenditure	56,683	59,310	50,900
Wage, salaries and allowances .	16,407	18,339	20,785
Other purchases of goods and services	19,825	13,803	7,576
Refugees and poverty-related expenditure	582	389	416
Transfers	15,669	23,452	19,359
Interest payments	4,200	3,328	2,764
Capital expenditure	7,380	8,221	6,081
Enterprise sector reform and public administration reform	1,183	1,832	2,026
Other expenditure	117	1,014	190
Total	65,363	70,378	59,197

* Figures refer to transactions of the central Government, excluding the operations of extrabudgetary funds.
† Excluding foreign grants received (million new denars): 415 in 2001; 0 in 2002; 0 in 2003.

Source: IMF, *Former Yugoslav Republic of Macedonia: First Review Under the Stand-by Arrangement and Request for Waiver of Applicability of Performance Criteria—Staff Report; Staff Statement; Press Release on the Executive Board Discussion* (November 2003).

INTERNATIONAL RESERVES
(US $ million at 31 December)

	2001	2002	2003
Gold*	53.7	67.8	37.1
IMF special drawing rights . .	2.2	6.1	0.3
Foreign exchange	742.9	715.9	897.8
Total	798.8	789.8	935.2

* National valuation.

Source: IMF, *International Financial Statistics*.

MONEY SUPPLY
(million new denars at 31 December)

	2001	2002	2003
Currency outside banks	14,134	14,136	14,177
Demand deposits at deposit money banks	11,168	12,255	12,800
Total (incl. others)	22,392	27,722	27,152

Source: IMF, *International Financial Statistics*.

COST OF LIVING
(Consumer price index; base: 2001=100)

	1999	2000	2002
Food	93.9	93.5	101.8
Tobacco and beverages	85.8	97.8	101.0
Fuel and light	75.6	96.2	101.0
Clothing (incl. footwear)	101.1	98.7	106.8
Rent and water	82.6	89.8	104.1
Transport and communications .	74.6	91.3	102.1
All items (incl. others)	89.6	94.8	101.8

NATIONAL ACCOUNTS
(million new denars at current prices)

National Income and Product

	1994	1995	1996
Compensation of employees . . .	95,546	104,503	109,183
Operating surplus	9,218	17,337	18,587
Domestic factor incomes . . .	104,764	121,840	127,770
Consumption of fixed capital . .	20,558	23,290	23,628
Gross domestic product (GDP) at factor cost	125,322	145,130	151,398
Indirect taxes	25,315	27,781	28,235
Less Subsidies	4,228	3,390	3,190
GDP in purchasers' values . .	146,409	169,521	176,444
Factor income from abroad . . .	432	1,206	1,778
Less Factor income paid abroad .	2,462	2,283	2,966
Gross national product (GNP) .	144,379	168,445	175,256
Less Consumption of fixed capital .	20,558	23,290	23,628
National income in market prices	123,821	145,155	151,628
Other current transfers from abroad	17,711	16,320	18,997
Less Other current transfers paid abroad	7,819	7,494	10,518
National disposable income . .	133,713	153,981	160,106

Expenditure on the Gross Domestic Product

	1999	2000	2001
Government final consumption expenditure	43,009	43,021	57,983
Private final consumption expenditure	145,693	175,965	163,788
Increase in stocks	6,461	12,351	8,043
Gross fixed capital formation . .	34,710	38,332	34,716
Total domestic expenditure . .	229,873	269,669	264,530
Exports of goods and services . .	88,143	114,209	99,091
Less Imports of goods and services	109,007	147,489	129,780
GDP in purchasers' values . .	209,010	236,389	233,841
GDP at constant 1995 prices .	187,684	196,223	187,342

Gross Domestic Product by Economic Activity

	2000	2001	2002*
Agriculture, hunting and forestry	23,756	22,933	24,398
Fishing	14	24	25
Industry†	53,163	50,940	48,423
Construction	13,361	11,801	11,462
Wholesale and retail trade . .	25,402	26,076	29,077
Hotels and restaurants . . .	3,463	3,410	3,788
Transport and communications .	21,261	21,694	24,213
Financial services	7,342	7,420	8,445
Real estate and business services‡	17,931	18,935	18,804
Public administration and defence	14,333	14,445	15,249
Education	8,266	8,048	8,353
Health care and social work . .	8,987	8,690	9,119
Other community, social and personal services	5,217	5,552	5,699
Sub-total	202,496	199,968	207,055
Less Imputed bank service charge	5,153	4,738	5,393
GDP at basic prices . . .	197,344	195,230	201,660
Taxes on products . . . . } *Less* Subsidies on products . . }	39,045	38,611	37,230
GDP in purchasers' values .	236,389	233,841	238,890

* Estimates.
† Including mining, manufacturing and electricity. Figures exclude crafts and trades, listed separately.
‡ Including imputed rents of owner-occupied dwellings.

BALANCE OF PAYMENTS
(US $ million)

	2000	2001	2002
Exports of goods f.o.b.	1,320.7	1,155.4	1,110.5
Imports of goods f.o.b.	−2,011.1	−1,681.8	−1,878.1
Trade balance	**−690.4**	**−526.4**	**−767.6**
Exports of services	316.7	244.6	253.0
Imports of services	−268.0	−263.8	−277.8
Balance on goods and services	**−641.7**	**−545.6**	**−792.3**
Other income received	41.6	52.6	51.0
Other income paid	−87.3	−93.3	−82.4
Balance on goods, services and income	**−687.3**	**−586.3**	**−823.6**
Current transfers received	788.2	725.7	655.3
Current transfers paid	−173.3	−383.0	−157.0
Current balance	**−72.4**	**−243.6**	**−325.3**
Capital account (net)	0.3	1.3	8.3
Direct investment abroad	0.6	−0.9	−0.1
Direct investment from abroad	174.5	441.5	77.2
Portfolio investment assets	−0.8	3.2	1.1
Portfolio investment liabilities	−0.1	0.4	0.1
Other investment assets	−77.7	−98.1	245.4
Other investment liabilities	193.7	−20.4	−116.4
Net errors and omissions	61.0	2.3	−12.2
Overall balance	**279.2**	**85.6**	**−122.1**

Source: IMF, *International Financial Statistics*.

External Trade

PRINCIPAL COMMODITIES
(distribution by SITC, US $ million)

Imports c.i.f.	2000	2001	2002
Food and live animals	211.6	194.0	246.5
Meat and meat preparations	63.3	61.7	70.9
Cereals and cereal preparations	40.1	31.3	45.7
Crude materials (inedible) except fuels	54.5	47.1	50.1
Mineral fuels, lubricants, etc.	289.8	234.2	263.2
Petroleum, petroleum products etc.	255.7	192.8	205.7
Chemicals and related products	188.5	172.4	211.7
Basic manufactures	270.2	207.0	264.8
Iron and steel	57.2	34.8	44.6
Machinery and transport equipment	409.8	283.3	408.0
Machinery specialized for particular industries	63.6	51.5	53.5
General industrial machinery equipment and parts	51.7	44.2	49.2
Electrical machinery, apparatus etc. (excl. telecommunications and sound equipment)	61.7	47.7	70.9
Road vehicles and parts*	137.8	62.2	131.0
Miscellaneous manufactured articles	103.3	109.5	113.3
Total (incl. others)	2,093.9	1,693.6	1,995.2

* Data on parts exclude tyres, engines and electrical parts.

Exports f.o.b.	2000	2001	2002
Food and live animals	65.8	64.9	74.7
Vegetables and fruit	30.5	30.1	36.0
Beverages and tobacco	129.4	121.5	124.9
Beverages	44.3	46.5	48.7
Tobacco and tobacco manufactures	85.1	75.0	76.2
Crude materials (inedible) except fuels	49.0	37.5	35.4
Chemicals and related products	59.8	60.5	69.3
Basic manufactures	487.3	372.6	316.2
Textile yarn, fabrics, etc.	36.9	37.3	35.8
Iron and steel	289.4	195.7	156.1
Non-ferrous metals	90.4	73.4	62.0
Machinery and transport equipment	83.2	76.6	74.5
Electrical machinery, apparatus etc. (excl. telecommunications and sound equipment)	46.5	46.9	42.0
Miscellaneous manufactured articles	378.2	376.3	388.9
Clothing and accessories (excl. footwear)	317.9	320.5	334.1
Footwear	38.4	37.4	35.8
Total (incl. others)	1,322.6	1,157.5	1,115.5

PRINCIPAL TRADING PARTNERS
(US $ million)

Imports c.i.f.	2000	2001	2002
Austria	41.7	43.9	53.3
Bulgaria	97.6	103.3	128.5
Croatia	57.9	46.4	55.2
France	38.6	30.3	53.1
Germany	253.3	215.0	284.7
Greece	201.6	184.6	237.9
Hungary	31.4	17.4	28.7
Italy	111.1	107.8	118.6
Japan	22.0	16.8	22.6
Netherlands	45.3	45.8	51.9
Poland	20.9	15.4	21.8
Russia	191.9	139.7	125.4
Slovenia	144.2	118.9	129.7
Sweden	31.7	18.8	17.7
Switzerland-Liechtenstein	28.2	23.3	28.3
Turkey	52.4	46.6	59.3
Ukraine	205.8	86.2	72.7
United Kingdom	32.0	26.3	32.8
USA	83.1	51.6	58.7
Yugoslavia	190.4	158.0	185.2
Total (incl. others)	2,093.9	1,693.6	1,995.2

Exports f.o.b.	2000	2001	2002
Albania	12.8	10.0	13.9
Belgium	23.9	7.5	10.4
Bosnia and Herzegovina	23.2	16.3	18.3
Bulgaria	26.9	20.8	21.8
Croatia	47.7	58.5	59.1
Cyprus	20.9	1.6	0.6
France	14.9	16.0	24.8
Germany	257.5	238.7	234.0
Greece	84.1	101.1	117.0
Italy	90.8	91.2	81.9
Netherlands	36.0	45.4	44.7
Russia	10.4	13.9	14.4
Slovenia	26.4	21.0	21.7
Spain	13.2	21.5	14.6
Switzerland-Liechtenstein	35.7	38.9	27.6
United Kingdom	27.2	26.7	28.9
USA	165.7	99.4	77.4
Yugoslavia	335.1	267.0	246.4
Total (incl. others)	1,322.6	1,157.5	1,115.5

Transport

RAILWAYS
(traffic)

	2000	2001	2002
Passenger journeys ('000) . . .	1,862	1,344	930
Passenger-km (million)	176	133	98
Freight carried ('000 metric tons).	3,231	2,799	2,208
Freight net ton-km (million) . .	527	462	334

ROAD TRAFFIC
(motor vehicles in use at 31 December)

	2000	2001	2002
Motorcycles	3,729	4,483	2,918
Passenger cars	299,588	309,562	307,581
Buses	2,498	2,620	2,497
Commercial vehicles. . . .	20,763	21,727	20,213
Special vehicles	8,552	9,554	10,292
Tractors and working vehicles . .	1,417	1,560	918

INLAND WATERS
(lake transport)

	2000	2001	2002
Passengers carried ('000) . . .	10	3	6
Passenger-km ('000)	321	117	389

CIVIL AVIATION
(traffic on scheduled services)

	1997	1998	1999
Kilometres flown (million) . .	5	5	7
Passengers carried ('000) . .	250	295	488
Passenger-kilometres (million). .	285	328	599
Total ton-kilometres (million) . .	27	31	57

Source: UN, *Statistical Yearbook*.

Tourism

TOURISTS BY COUNTRY OF ORIGIN*

	2000	2001	2002
Albania	24,747	6,419	9,086
Bulgaria	27,623	8,484	11,703
Croatia.	4,651	2,609	4,097
France	4,768	2,313	2,542
Germany	10,349	4,860	6,084
Greece	21,304	10,637	14,677

— continued	2000	2001	2002
Italy	4,410	2,511	3,076
Netherlands	6,809	1,564	2,016
Russia	3,078	1,647	1,246
Slovenia	5,288	2,658	3,837
Turkey.	6,700	3,101	5,180
Ukraine	6,347	3,405	908
United Kingdom	6,693	4,357	3,916
USA	15,312	7,099	6,997
Yugoslavia	35,522	16,429	23,239
Total (incl. others)	224,016	98,946	122,861

* Figures refer to arrivals from abroad at accommodation establishments.

Tourism receipts (US $ million): 37 in 1999; 37 in 2000; 23 in 2001 (Source: World Tourism Organization).

Communications Media

	2000	2001	2002
Television receivers ('000 in use) .	570	n.a.	n.a.
Telephones ('000 subscribers) . .	507.3	538.5	578.3
Mobile cellular telephones ('000 subscribers).	99.9	221.3	366.3
Internet users ('000).	n.a.	70.0	n.a.
Book production: titles*. . . .	727	737	1,102
Book production: copies ('000)*. .	968	1,061	1,899
Daily newspapers: titles. . .	6	8	9
Daily newspapers: average circulation ('000 copies) . .	32,640	43,689	45,536
Non-daily newspapers: titles . .	33	29	30
Non-daily newspapers: average circulation ('000 copies) . .	2,619	2,961	2,618

* Including pamphlets.

Radio receivers ('000 in use): 410 in 1997.

Facsimile machines (number in use): 3,000 in 1997.

Sources: mainly International Telecommunication Union; UNESCO, *Statistical Yearbook*; and UN, *Statistical Yearbook*.

Education

(2001/02, unless otherwise indicated)

	Institutions	Teachers	Students
Primary	1,010	13,508	242,707
Secondary	95	5,550	92,068
University level*	29	1,487	44,731
Other higher*	1	32	893

* 2002/03 figures.

Adult literacy rate (latest available): Males 97%; Females 91% (Source: UNICEF, *The State of the World's Children*).

Directory

The Constitution

The Constitution of the former Yugoslav republic of Macedonia was promulgated on 17 November 1991. The September 1995 interim agreement with Greece required guarantees that the Macedonian Constitution enshrined or implied no claim to territory beyond the country's existing borders. Some amendment of the 1991 document was thus necessitated. Following the framework agreement between the principal Macedonian and ethnic Albanian parties, reached in August 2001 (see Recent History), the Constitution was revised on 16 November to include 15 principal amendments. The following is a summary of the main provisions of the Constitution, which describes the country as the Republic of Macedonia:

GENERAL PROVISIONS

The Republic of Macedonia is a sovereign, independent, democratic state, where sovereignty derives from democratically elected citizens, referendums and other forms of expression. The citizens of the Republic of Macedonia are defined as the Macedonian people, as well as citizens living within its borders who are, *inter alia*, ethnic Albanians, ethnic Turks, ethnic Serbs and Vlach. The fundamental values defined by the Constitution are: basic human rights, free expression of nationality, the rule of law, a policy of pluralism and the free market, local self-government, entrepreneurship, social justice and solidarity, and respect for international law. State power is divided into legislative, executive and judicial power.

BASIC RIGHTS

The following rights and freedoms are guaranteed and protected in the Republic: the right to life, the inviolability of each person's physical and moral integrity, the right to freedom of speech, public appearance, public information, belief, conscience and religion, and the freedom to organize and belong to a trade union or a political party. All forms of communication and personal data are secret, and the home is inviolable.

The Macedonian language is the official language in use throughout the Republic of Macedonia. Any other language spoken by at least 20% of the population (such as Albanian) is also an official language. The official personal documentation of citizens speaking an official language other than Macedonian will also be issued in that language.

Military and semi-military associations, which do not belong to the Armed Forces of the Republic, are prohibited.

Any citizen who has reached the age of 18 years has the right to vote and to be elected to organs of government. The right to vote is equal, general and direct, and is realized in free elections by secret ballot. The proportional representation of each community must be assured in the public services and in all areas of public life. Citizens enjoy equal freedoms and rights without distinction as to sex, race, colour, national and social origin, political and religious conviction, material and social position. All religious creeds are separate from the State and are equal under the law. They are identified, *inter alia*, as the Macedonian Orthodox Church, the Islamic Community of Macedonia, the Roman Catholic Church, the Evangelic Methodist Church and the Jewish Community. The members of all such communities are free to establish schools and other charitable institutions in the fields of culture, art and education.

GOVERNMENT

Legislature
Legislative power resides with the Sobranie (assembly), which consists of between 120 and 140 deputies elected for four years. The Sobranie adopts and amends the Constitution, enacts laws and gives interpretations thereof, adopts the budget of the Republic, decides on war and peace, chooses the Government, elects judges and releases them from duty. The Sobranie may decide, by a majority vote, to call a referendum on issues within its competence. A decision is adopted at a referendum if the majority of voters taking part in the ballot votes in favour of it and if more than one-half of the electorate participates in the vote. The Sobranie forms a Council for Inter-Ethnic Relations, comprising seven representatives from each of the ethnic Macedonian and Albanian communities, and five representatives of other nationalities living in the state. Parliamentary legislation on issues of culture and identity, particularly in the areas of language and education, can only be adopted if a majority of the deputies representing these communities votes in favour, in addition to the overall majority. Three of the nine judges of the Constitutional Court and three of the seven members of the Republican Judicial Council must also be elected by a double majority vote.

President
The President of the Republic represents the country and is responsible for ensuring respect for the Constitution and laws. He is Commander of the Armed Forces and appoints the Prime Minister. He appoints three members of the Security Council of the Republic (of which he is President) and ensures that the Council reflects the composition of the country's population.

Ministers
Executive power in the Republic resides with the Prime Minister and Ministers, who are not permitted concurrently to be deputies in the Sobranie. The Ministers are elected by the majority vote of all the deputies in the Sobranie. The Ministers implement laws and the state budget, and are responsible for foreign and diplomatic relations.

Judiciary
Judicial power is vested in the courts, and is autonomous and independent. The Supreme Court is the highest court. The election and dismissal of judges is proposed by the Republican Judicial Council.

Local Government
Legislation at local and municipal level is adopted by a two-thirds' majority vote of the total number of representatives. Legislation regulating such areas as local finance, elections and municipal boundaries must be adopted by a majority of the representatives representing the minority communities, as well as by an overall majority. In units of local self-government, citizens participate in decision-making on issues of local relevance directly, and through representatives.

OTHER PROVISIONS
The Sobranie elects an Ombudsman to ensure that constitutional rights are upheld, particularly the principles of non-discrimination and fair representation of the respective communities in public life. Revision of the Constitution must be approved by a two-thirds'

majority in the Sobranie. Certain articles, such as the Preamble and those relating to local councils and minority rights, also require a majority of the vote by deputies from the minority communities.

The Government

HEAD OF STATE

President of the Republic: BRANKO CRVENKOVSKI (elected 28 April 2004; inaugurated 12 May 2004).

GOVERNMENT
(May 2004)

A coalition of the Social Democratic Alliance of Macedonia (SDAM), the Liberal-Democratic Party (LDP) and the Democratic Union for Integration (DUI).

Prime Minister: HARI KOSTOV (SDAM) (designate).

Deputy Prime Minister and Minister of Finance: NIKOLA POPOVSKI (SDAM).

Deputy Prime Minister, with responsibility for Political Systems: MUSA XHAFERI (DUI).

Deputy Prime Minister, with responsibility for European Integration: RADMILA SHEKERINSKA (SDAM).

Minister of Defence: VLADO BUCHKOVSKI (SDAM).

Minister of Internal Affairs: HARI KOSTOV (SDAM).

Minister of Justice: IXHET MEHMETI (DUI).

Minister of Foreign Affairs: ILINKA MITREVA (SDAM).

Minister of the Economy: STEVCO JAKIMOVSKI (LDP).

Minister of Transport and Communications: AGRON BUXHAKU (DUI).

Minister of Agriculture, Forestry and Water Resources: SLAVKO PETROV (LDP).

Minister of Labour and Social Welfare: JOVAN MANASIEVSKI (LDP).

Minister of Education and Science: AZIZ POLOZHANI (DUI).

Minister of Culture: BLAGOJA STEFANOVSKI (SDAM).

Minister of Health: REXHEP SELMANI (DUI).

Minister of Local Self-Government: ALEKSANDAR GESHTAKOVSKI (SDAM).

Minister of the Environment and Urban Planning: LJUBOMIR JANEVI (SDAM).

Minister without Portfolio: VLADO POPOVSKI (LDP).

MINISTRIES

Office of the President: 1000 Skopje, 11 Oktomvri bb; tel. (2) 3113318; fax (2) 3112147; internet www.president.gov.mk.

Office of the Prime Minister: 1000 Skopje, Ilindenska bb; tel. (2) 3115455; fax (2) 3112561; e-mail office@primeminister.gov.mk; internet www.primeminister.gov.mk.

Ministry of Agriculture, Forestry and Water Resources: 1000 Skopje, Leninova 2; tel. (2) 3134477; fax (2) 3239429; internet www.mzsv.gov.mk.

Ministry of Culture: 1000 Skopje, Ilindenska bb; tel. (2) 3118022; fax (2) 3127112; internet www.gov.mk/kultura.

Ministry of Defence: 1000 Skopje, Orce Nikolov bb; tel. and fax (2) 3119577; fax (2) 3227835; e-mail info@morm.gov.mk; internet www.morm.gov.mk.

Ministry of the Economy: 1000 Skopje, Bote Bocevski 9; tel. (2) 384470; fax (2) 384472; e-mail ms@mt.net.mk; internet www.ms.gov.mk.

Ministry of Education and Science: 1000 Skopje, Dimitrija Čupovski 9; tel. (2) 3117896; fax (2) 3118414; e-mail mofk@mofk.gov.mk; internet www.mofk.gov.mk.

Ministry of the Environment and Urban Planning: 1000 Skopje, ul. Drezdenska 52; tel. (2) 3366930; fax (2) 3366931; e-mail info@moe.gov.mk; internet www.moe.gov.mk.

Ministry of Finance: 1000 Skopje, Dame Gruev 14; tel. (2) 3117288; fax (2) 3117280; internet www.finance.gov.mk.

Ministry of Foreign Affairs: 1000 Skopje, Dame Gruev 6; tel. (2) 3115266; fax (2) 3115790; e-mail mailmnr@mnr.gov.mk; internet www.mnr.gov.mk.

Ministry of Health: 1000 Skopje, Vodnjanska bb; tel. (2) 3147147; fax (2) 3113014; internet www.zdravstvo.com.mk.

Ministry of Internal Affairs: 1000 Skopje, Dimitar Mirchev bb; tel. (2) 3117222; fax (2) 3112468.

Ministry of Justice: 1000 Skopje, Dimitrija Čupovski 9; tel. (2) 3117277; fax (2) 3226975; internet www.covekovi-prava.gov.mk.

Ministry of Labour and Social Welfare: 1000 Skopje, Dame Gruev 14; tel. (2) 3117787; fax (2) 3118242; e-mail mtsp@mt.net.mk; internet www.mtsp.gov.mk.

Ministry of Local Self-Government: 1000 Skopje, Dimitrija Čupovski 9; tel. (2) 3106302; fax (2) 3106303; internet www.mls.gov .mk.

Ministry of Sports and Youth: 1000 Skopje, Jurij Gagarin 15; tel. (2) 3393408; fax (2) 3384472.

Ministry of Transport and Communications: 1000 Skopje, plostad Crvena skopska opstina 4; tel. (2) 3126228; fax (2) 3123292.

President and Legislature

PRESIDENT

Presidential Election, First Ballot, 14 April 2004

Candidate	Votes	% of votes
Branko Crvenkovski (SDAM)	385,347	42.47
Sasko Kedev (IMRO—DPMNU)	309,132	34.07
Gzim Ostreni (DUI)	134,208	14.79
Zidi Xhelili (DPA).	78,714	8.67
Total	907,401	100.00

Second Ballot, 28 April 2004

Candidate	Votes	% of votes
Branko Crvenkovski (SDAM)	553,522	62.70
Sasko Kedev (IMRO—DPMNU)	329,271	37.30
Total	882,793	100.00

SOBRANIE
(Assembly)

President: Dr LJUBCO JORDANOVSKI, 1000 Skopje, 11 Oktomvri bb; tel. (2) 3112255; fax (2) 3237947; e-mail sobranie@sobranie.mk; internet www.sobranie.mk.

General Election, 15 September 2002*

Party	Votes	% of votes	Seats
Together for Macedonia† . .	494,744	40.46	60
IMRO—DPMNU‡	298,404	24.41	33
DUI	114,913	11.85	16
DPA	63,695	5.21	7
PDP	28,397	2.32	2
NDP	26,237	2.15	1
SPM	25,976	2.12	1
Others	140,345	11.48	—
Total	1,222,711	100.00	120

* Of the 120 members of the Assembly, 85 were elected in single-member constituencies. The remaining 35 were elected by a national system of proportional representation, in which voters chose from lists of candidates submitted by individual parties or by groups of parties.

† Electoral coalition of 10 parties, led by the SDAM.

‡ The IMRO—DPMNU contested the elections in alliance with the LPM.

Political Organizations

Democratic Alliance: Skopje; f. 2000; Chair. PAVLE TRAJANOV.

Democratic Alliance of Serbs in Macedonia (Demokratski Savez Srba u Makedoniji—DSSM): Skopje; f. 1994; Chair. BORIVOJE RISTIĆ.

Democratic Alternative (DA) (Demokratska Alternativa): c/o Sobranje, 1000 Skopje, 11 Oktomvri bb; tel. (2) 3062713; fax (2) 3063089; internet www.da.org.mk; f. 1998; formed an electoral alliance with the IMRO—DPMNU; Chair. VASIL TUPURKOVSKI.

Democratic League—Liberal Party: Skopje, Gale Hristov k. 3-6; tel. (2) 3263523; Leader XHEMIL IDRIZI.

Democratic Muslim Party: Skopje; f. 2001; Leader TEFIK KADRI.

Democratic Party of Albanians (DPA): Tetovo, Maršal Tito 2; tel. and fax (44) 7332572; e-mail polsh-polsh@yahoo.com; f. July 1997 by a merger of the Party of Democratic Prosperity of Albanians in Macedonia (f. 1994) and the National Democratic Party (f. 1990); officially registered in July 2002; absorbed the National Democratic Party (f. 2001) and the Republican Party of Albanians (f. 2002) in June 2003; Chair. ARBEN XHAFERI.

Democratic Party of Serbs in Macedonia (DPSM): Skopje, 27 Mart 11; tel. (2) 3254274; f. 1996; Pres. DRAGISA MILETIĆ.

Democratic Party of Turks in Macedonia (DPTM) (Demokratska Partija na Turcite va Makedonija): Skopje, bul. Krste Misirkova 67; tel. (2) 3114696; Leader ERDOĞAN SARACH.

Democratic Party of Yugoslavs of Macedonia (DPYM) (Demokratska Partija Jugoslovena Makedonije—DPJM): Skopje; f. 1993; Chair. ZIVKO LEKOSKI; Gen. Sec. BOGDAN MICKOSKI.

Democratic Union for Integration (DUI) (Demokratska Unija za Integracija): Tetovo; f. 2002; ethnic Albanian, dominated by former mems of rebel National Liberation Army; Chair. ALI AHMETI; Sec.-Gen. GZIM OSTRENI.

Front for Albanian National Unification (FANU): emerged in 2003 as political wing of rebel Albanian National Army; supports creation of 'greater Albania'; Sec.-Gen. ALBAN VJOSA.

Internal Macedonian Revolutionary Organization ('Real') **('Real' IMRO)** (Vnatrešno-Makedonska Revolucionerna Organizacija—VMRO): Skopje; f. 2000 by fmr mems of the IMRO—DPMNU; centre-right; Chair. BORIS ZMEJKOVSKI.

Internal Macedonian Revolutionary Organization—Democratic Party for Macedonian National Unity (IMRO—DPMNU) (Vnatrešno-Makedonska Revolucionerna Organizacija—Demokratska Partija za Makedonsko Nacionalno Edinstvo—VMRO—DPMNE): 1000 Skopje, Petar Drapshin br. 36; tel. (2) 3111441; fax (2) 3211586; e-mail info@vmro-dpmne.org.mk; internet www.vmro-dpmne.org.mk; nationalist; formed an electoral alliance with the Democratic Alternative; Pres. NIKOLA GRUEVSKI; Sec. DEN DONCEV.

Liberal-Democratic Party (LDP) (Liberalno-Demokratska Partija): Skopje, Ilindenska bb; tel. and fax (2) 3116106; e-mail contact@ldo.org.mk; internet www.ldp.org.mk; f. 1996 by a merger of the Liberal Party and the Democratic Party; Leader PETAR GOSEV.

Liberal Party of Macedonia (LPM) (Liberalna Partija na Makedonije): 1000 Skopje; tel. (2) 464955; e-mail lpm@mt.net.mk; internet www.liberalna.org.mk; Leader STOJAN ANDOV.

Macedonian Democratic Party: Tetovo, Bazaar 3; tel. (44) 20826; fax (44) 24860; Leader TOMISLAV STOJANOVSKI.

Movement for all-Macedonian Action (MAAK)—Conservative Party: Skopje, Maksim Gorki 18/111; tel. (2) 116540; f. 1996; right-wing nationalist; Leader STRASO ANGELOVSKI.

Party of Democratic Action—Islamic Way (Stranka Demokratske Akcije—Islamski Put): Tetovo, Ilindenska 191; tel. (44) 32113; Leader MAZLAM KENAN.

Party for Democratic Prosperity (PDP) (Partija za Demokratski Prosperitet): Tetovo, Karaorman 62; tel. (44) 25709; f. 1990; split 1994; predominantly ethnic Albanian and Muslim party; Chair. ABDYLMENAF BEXHETI; Sec.-Gen. NASER ZYBERI.

Party for the Full Emancipation of Romanies in Macedonia (Demokratska Progresivna Partija na Romite od Makedonija): Skopje, Shuto Orizari bb; tel. (2) 3612726; Leader FAIK ABDIĆ.

Social Democratic Alliance of Macedonia (SDAM) (Socijaldemokratski Sojuz na Makedonije—SDSM): 1000 Skopje, Bihačka 8; tel. (2) 3135380; fax (2) 3120462; e-mail contact@sdsm.org.mk; internet www.sdsm.org.mk; f. 1943; name changed from League of Communists of Macedonia—Party of Democratic Reform in 1991; led alliance, Together for Macedonia, which was elected to govt in Sept. 2002; Chair. BRANKO CRVENKOVSKI; Gen. Sec. GEORGI SPASOV.

Social Democratic Party of Macedonia (Socijaldemokratska Partija na Makedonije): Skopje, bul. Kliment Ohridski 54; tel. and fax (2) 3134077; Leader BRANKO JANEVSKI.

Socialist Party of Macedonia (SPM) (Socijalistiska Partija na Makedonije): 1000 Skopje, 11 Oktomvri 17; tel. (2) 3228015; fax (2) 3220075; f. 1990; left-wing; Chair. LJUBISAV IVANOV; Vice-Chair. BLAGOJE FILIPOVSKI.

Union of Ethnic Croats: Skopje; f. 1996; Pres. MARIJA DAMJANOVSKA.

Union of Roma in Macedonia (Sojuz na Romite od Makedonija): Skopje.

Diplomatic Representation

EMBASSIES IN THE FORMER YUGOSLAV REPUBLIC OF MACEDONIA

Albania: 1000 Skopje, Hristijan Todorovski-Karposh 94; tel. (2) 2614636; fax (2) 2614200; e-mail ambshquip@lotus.mpt.com.mk; Ambassador VLADIMIR PRELJA.

Austria: 1000 Skopje, Vasil Stefanovski 7; tel. (2) 3109550; fax (2) 3130237; e-mail austramb@unet.com.mk; Ambassador PHILIP HOYOS.

Bosnia and Herzegovina: 1000 Skopje, Mile Pop-Jordanov 56; tel. (2) 3086216; fax (2) 3086221; Ambassador Dr SAVA ČEKLIČ.

Bulgaria: 1000 Skopje, Zlatko Shnaider 3; tel. (2) 3229444; fax (2) 3116139; e-mail bgemb@unet.com.mk; Ambassador ALEKSANDAR YORDANOV.

China, People's Republic: 1000 Skopje, 474 No 20; tel. (2) 3213163; fax (2) 3212500; Ambassador ZHANG WANXUE.

Croatia: 1000 Skopje, Mitropolit Teodosij Gologanov 59; tel. (2) 3127350; fax (2) 3127417; e-mail velhrskp@mpt.com.mk; Ambassador ALEKSANDAR MILOŠEVIĆ.

France: 1000 Skopje, Salvador Aljende 73; tel. (2) 3118749; fax (2) 3117760; e-mail franamba@nic.mpt.com.mk; internet www.ambafrnce-mk.org; Ambassador VÉRONIQUE BUJON-BARRÉ.

Germany: 1000 Skopje, Leninska 59; tel. (2) 3093900; fax (2) 3093899; e-mail dtboskop@unet.com.mk; internet www.deutschebotschaft-skopje.com.mk; Ambassador Dr IRENE HINRICHSEN.

Hungary: 1000 Skopje, Mirka Ginova 27; tel. (2) 3063423; fax (2) 3063070; e-mail hungemb@mt.net.mk; Ambassador Dr FERENC PÓKA.

Iran: 1000 Skopje, Gjorgji Peskov 6; tel. (2) 3118020; fax (2) 3118502; e-mail iri-emb@unet.cpm.mk; Chargé d'affaires a.i. MOSLEM SABERI.

Italy: 1000 Skopje, 8 Udarna brig. 22; tel. (2) 3117430; fax (2) 3117087; e-mail segreteria@ambasciata.org.mk; internet www.ambasciata.org.mk; Ambassador Dr GIORGIO MARINI.

Netherlands: 1000 Skopje, Leninova 69–71; tel. (2) 3129319; fax (2) 3129309; e-mail nethemb@mt.com.mk; internet www.nlembassy.org.mk; Ambassador FRÉDÉRIQUE MARIA DE MAN.

Norway: 1000 Skopje, Mitropolit Teodosie Gologanov 59/2A; tel. (2) 3129165; fax (2) 3111138; e-mail embskp@mfa.no; Ambassador DAG MALMER HALVORSEN.

Poland: 1000 Skopje, Djuro Djakovic 50; tel. and fax (2) 3119744; e-mail ambpol@unet.com.mk; Ambassador ANDRZEJ DOBRZYŃSKI.

Romania: 1000 Skopje, Rajko Zinzifov 42; tel. (2) 3228055; fax (2) 3228036; e-mail romanamb@on.net.mk; Ambasssador MIRCEA CRISTE.

Russia: 1000 Skopje, Pirinska 44; tel. (2) 3117160; fax (2) 3117808; e-mail rusembas@mol.com.mk; f. 1994; Ambassador AGARON ASATUR.

Serbia and Montenegro: 1000 Skopje, Pitu Guli 8; tel. (2) 3129298; fax (2) 3129427; e-mail yuamb@unet.com.mk; Ambassador BISERKA MATIĆ SPASOJEVIĆ.

Slovenia: 1000 Skopje, Vodnjanska 42; tel. (2) 3178730; fax (2) 3176631; e-mail vsk@mzz-dkp.gov.si; Ambassador MARJAN ŠIFTAR.

Switzerland: 1000 Skopje, Maksim Gorki 19; tel. (2) 3128300; fax (2) 3116205; e-mail vertretung@sko.rep.admin.ch; internet www.eda.admin.ch/skopje; Ambassador STEFAN MELLEN.

Turkey: 1000 Skopje, Slavej Planina bb; tel. (2) 3113270; fax (2) 3117024; e-mail turkish@mol.com.mk; Ambassador MEHMET TAŞER.

United Kingdom: 1000 Skopje, Dimitrija Čupovski 26, 4th Floor; tel. (2) 3299299; fax (2) 3299236; e-mail beskopje@mt.net.com; internet www.britishembassy.org.mk; Ambassador GEORGE EDGAR.

USA: 1000 Skopje, Ilindenska bb; tel. (2) 3116180; fax (2) 3118105; e-mail usis@usemb-skopje.mpt.com.mk; internet usembassy.mpt.com.mk; Ambassador LAWRENCE BUTLER.

Judicial System

The FYRM has 27 Courts of First Instance and three Courts of Appeal. The Republican Judicial Council, which comprises seven members elected by the Sobranie for a term of six years, proposes the election or dismissal of judges to the Sobranie. The Constitutional Court, comprising nine judges elected by the Sobranie with a mandate of nine years, is responsible for the protection of constitutional and legal rights, and ensures that there is no conflict in the exercise of legislative, executive and judicial powers. The Supreme Court is the highest court in the country, and guarantees the equal administration of legislation by all courts

Constitutional Court of the Republic of Macedonia: 1000 Skopje, 12 Udarna brig. 2; tel. (2) 3165153; fax (2) 3119355; e-mail usud@usud.gov.mk; Pres. Dr TODOR DŽUNOV.

Supreme Court: 1000 Skopje, Krste Misirkova bb; tel. (2) 3234064; fax (2) 3237538; Pres. SIMEON GELEVSKI.

Republican Judicial Council: 1000 Skopje, Lazar Lichenoski 13; tel. (2) 3213084; fax (2) 3116458; Pres. TIHOMIR VELKOVSKI.

Office of the Public Prosecutor: 1000 Skopje, Krste Misirkova bb; tel. (2) 3229314; Public Prosecutor ALEKSANDR PRCEVSKI.

Religion

Most ethnic Macedonians are adherents of the Eastern Orthodox Church, and since 1967 there has been an autocephalous Macedonian Orthodox Church. However, the Serbian Orthodox Church refuses to recognize it, and has persuaded the Ecumenical Patriarch and other Orthodox Churches not to do so either. There are some adherents of other Orthodox rites in the country. Those Macedonian (and Bulgarian) Slavs who converted to Islam during the Ottoman era are known as Pomaks and are included as an ethnic group of Muslims. The substantial Albanian population is mostly Muslim (mainly Sunni, but some adherents of a Dervish sect); there are a few Roman Catholic Christians and a small Jewish community.

CHRISTIANITY

Macedonian Orthodox Church: Skopje, Betovenova bb, POB 69; tel. (2) 3230697; fax (2) 3230685; Metropolitan See of Ohrid revived in 1958; autocephaly declared 1967; 1.5m. mems; comprises seven bishoprics in Macedonia and three abroad; Head of Church and Archbishop of Ohrid and Macedonia Metropolitan Archbishop MIHAIL RIĆ (of Skopje).

The Roman Catholic Church

The diocese of Skopje, suffragan to the archdiocese of Vrhbosna (Bosnia and Herzegovina), covers most of the FYRM. The Bishop is also Apostolic Exarch for Catholics of the Byzantine Rite in the FYRM. At 31 December 2002 there were an estimated 3,500 adherents of the Latin Rite in the diocese, and the country had 11,367 adherents of the Byzantine Rite.

Bishop of Skopje: Rt Rev. JOAKIM HERBUT, Biskupski Ordinarijat, 1000 Skopje, Risto Šiškov 31; tel. and fax (2) 3164123; e-mail katbiskupija@mt.net.mk.

ISLAM

Islamic Community of Macedonia: Skopje, Chairska 52; tel. (2) 3117530; fax (2) 3117883; e-mail bim@bim.org.mk; internet www.bim.org.mk; formerly headquarters of the Skopje Region, one of the four administrative divisions of the Yugoslav Muslims; Leader Hadži ARIF EMINI.

JUDAISM

Jewish Community: 1000 Skopje, Borka Taleski 24.

The Press

In 2002 a total of 39 newspapers and 178 magazines were published in the FYRM.

PRINCIPAL DAILY NEWSPAPERS

Bechuk: 1000 Skopje, MOST Ltd, Dame Gruev 5; tel. (2) 3117377; fax (2) 3118638; e-mail vesnik@utrinski.com.mk; internet www.int.utrinskivesnik.com.mk; Dir EROL RIZAOV; Editor-in-Chief BRANKO TRICKOVSKI.

Denes: 1000 Skopje, M. H. Jasmin 50; tel. (2) 3110239; fax (2) 3110150; e-mail denes@unet.com.mk; internet www.denes.com.mk; Dir GEORGI AJANOVSKI; Editor NIK DENES.

Dnevnik: 1000 Skopje, Teodosij Gologanov 28; tel. (2) 3297555; fax (2) 3297554; e-mail dnevnik@dnevnik.com.mk; internet www.dnevnik.com.mk; independent; country's most popular daily newspaper; Editor-in-Chief BRANKO GEROSKI.

Flaka e vëllazërimit (Flame of Brotherhood): 1000 Skopje, Mito Hadživasilev bb; tel. (2) 3112025; fax (2) 3224829; f. 1945; re-launched 1994; Albanian-language newspaper; Editor-in-Chief ABDULHADI ZULFIQARI; circ. 4,000.

Nova Makedonija: 1000 Skopje, Mito Hadživasilev bb; tel. (2) 3237455; fax (2) 3118238; internet www.novamakedonija.com.mk; f. 1944; morning; in Macedonian; Editor-in-Chief GEORGI AJANOVSKI; circ. 25,000.

Utrinski Vesnik: Skopje; internet int.utrinskivesnik.com.mk; country's second largest newspaper.

Večer: 1000 Skopje, Mito Hadživasilev bb; tel. (2) 3111537; fax (2) 3238327; internet www.vecer.com.mk; f. 1963; evening; in Macedonian; Editor-in-Chief Stojan Nasev; circ. 29,200.

Vest: Skopje; internet www.vest.com.mk; pro-Government; tabloid.

PERIODICALS

Delo: Skopje, Petar Drapshin 26; tel. (2) 3231949; fax (2) 3115748; f. 1993; weekly; nationalist; Editor-in-Chief Bratislav Taskovski.

Fokus: Skopje, Zheležniča 53; tel. (2) 3111327; fax (2) 3111685; weekly; independent; Editor-in-Chief Nikola Mladenov.

Macedonian Times: 1000 Skopje, Vasil Gorgov 39; tel. and fax (2) 3121182; e-mail mian@mian.com.mk; internet www.unet.com.mk/mian; f. 1994; monthly; politics and current affairs; English; Editor-in-Chief Jovan Pavloski.

Puls: 1000 Skopje, Mito Hadživasilev bb; tel. (2) 3117124; fax (2) 3118024; weekly; Editor-in-Chief Mirce Tomovski.

Roma Times: Skopje; e-mail mail@dostae.net.mk; internet www.dostae.net.mk/mk/press_mk_roma.htm; f. 2001; 3 a week; circ. 3,000.

Sport Magazine: 1000 Skopje, Mito Hadživasilev Jasmin bb; tel. and fax (2) 3116254; e-mail lav@unet.com.mk; f. 1991; weekly; circ. 6,000.

Trudbenik: Skopje, Udarna brigada 12; weekly; organ of Macedonian Trade Unions; Editor Simo Ivanovski.

NEWS AGENCIES

Macedonian Information Agency: 1000 Skopje, Bojmija K/2; tel. (2) 2461600; fax (2) 2464048; e-mail mia@mia.com.mk; internet www.mia.com.mk; f. 1992; 24-hr news service in Macedonian, Albanian and English; Exec. Dir Zivko Georgievski.

Makfax: 1000 Skopje, Goce Delčev bb, POB 738; tel. (2) 3110125; fax (2) 3110184; e-mail makfax@unet.com.mk; internet www.makfax.com.mk; f. 1993; independent; provides daily regional news service; Macedonian, Albanian and English.

PRESS ASSOCIATION

Journalists' Association of Macedonia: 1000 Skopje, Gradskizid 13, POB 498; tel. and fax (2) 3116447; Pres. Stojan Nasev.

Publishers

Detska radost/Nova Makedonija: 1000 Skopje, Mito Hadživasilev Jasmin bb; tel. (2) 3213059; fax (2) 3225830; f. 1944; children's books; Dir Kiril Donev.

Kultura: 1000 Skopje, Sv. Kliment Ohridski 68a; tel. (2) 3111332; fax (2) 3228608; e-mail ipkultura@simt.com.mk; f. 1945; history, philosophy, art, poetry, children's literature and fiction; in Macedonian; Dir Dimitar Baševski.

Kulturen Život: 1000 Skopje, Ruzveltova 6; tel. (2) 3239134; f. 1971; Editor Ljubica Arsovska.

Makedonska kniga: 1000 Skopje, 11 Oktomvri; tel. (2) 3224055; fax (2) 3236951; f. 1947; arts, non-fiction, novels, children's books; Dir Sande Stojčevski.

Matica Makedonska: 1000 Skopje, ul. Maršal Tito br. 43/1-6; tel. (2) 3230358; fax (2) 3229244; f. 1991; Dir Rade Siljan.

Metaforum: 1000 Skopje, Goce Delčev 6; tel. (2) 3114890; fax (2) 3115634; f. 1993; Dir Ružica Bilko.

Misla: 1000 Skopje, Partizanski odredi 1; tel. (2) 3221844; fax (2) 3118439; f. 1966; modern and classic Macedonian and translated literature; Pres. Zlata Bunteslea.

Naša kniga: 1000 Skopje, Maksim Gorki 21, POB 132; tel. (2) 3228066; fax (2) 3116872; f. 1948; Dir Stojan Lekovski.

Prosvetno delo: 1000 Skopje, Dimitrija Čupovski 15; tel. (2) 3117255; fax (2) 3225434; f. 1945; works of domestic writers and textbooks in Macedonian for elementary, professional and high schools; fiction and scientific works; Dir Dr Krste Angelovski.

Tabernakul: 1000 Skopje, POB 251, Mihail Cokov; tel. (2) 3127073; fax (2) 3115329; e-mail contact@tabernakul.com.mk; internet www.tabernakul.com.mk; f. 1989; Dir Cvetan Vraživirski.

Broadcasting and Communications

TELECOMMUNICATIONS

Makedonski Telekomunikacii (MT): 1000 Skopje, Direkcija, Orce Nikolov bb; tel. (2) 3141141; fax (2) 3126244; e-mail info@mpt.com.mk; internet www.mt.com.mk; 51% of shares divested to the Matáv Hungarian Telecommunications Co in Jan. 2001; Chief Exec. Dan Doncev.

BROADCASTING

Radio

Makedonska Radio-Televizija (MRT): 1000 Skopje, Goce Delčev bb; tel. (2) 3236839; fax (2) 3111821; e-mail mkrtvcor@mt.com.mk; internet www.mkrtv.com.mk; f. 1944; fmrly Radiotelevizija Skopje, name changed 1991; 3 radio channels; broadcasts in Macedonian, Albanian, Turkish, Serb, Roma and Vlach; Dir-Gen. Gordana Stosić; Dir of Radio Grigori Popovski.

Antenna 5 Radio: 1000 Skopje, Tetovska 35; tel. (2) 3111911; fax (2) 3113281; e-mail mail@antenna5.com.mk; internet www.antenna5.com.mk; 12 transmitters broadcast to 80% of the country.

Television

Makedonska Radio-Televizija (MRT): 1000 Skopje, Goce Delčev bb; tel. (2) 3112200; fax (2) 3111821; e-mail gstosic@unet.com.mk; internet www.mkrtv.com.mk; f. 1964; fmrly Radiotelevizija Skopje, name changed 1991; state broadcasting co; 3 television services; broadcasts in Macedonian, Albanian, Turkish, Serb, Roma and Vlach; Dir-Gen. Gordana Siosie; Dir of Television Ljubčo Tozija.

Al Television: 1000 Skopje, Pero Nakov bb; tel. (2) 2550350; fax (2) 2551970; e-mail altv@al.com.mk; internet www.al.com.mk; Gen. Man. Darko Perusevski.

SITEL Television: Skopje; tel. (2) 3116566; fax (2) 3114898; e-mail sitel@unet.com.mk; internet www.sitel.com.mk; Gen. Man. Govan Ivanovski.

Finance

(cap. = capital; res = reserves; dep. = deposits; m. = million; amounts in new Macedonian denars, unless otherwise indicated; brs = branches)

BANKS

At the end of 2002 there were 21 commercial banks and 17 savings houses in the FYRM; of these, the three largest banks managed about 64% of banking system assets and some 73% of total deposits. A programme to privatize the banking sector was completed in early 2000. State ownership of banks was about 14% and foreign ownership amounted to some 45% of total bank capital at the end of 2002.

National Bank

Narodna Banka na Makedonija (National Bank of the Republic of Macedonia): 1000 Skopje, POB 401, Kompleks banki bb; tel. (2) 3108108; fax (2) 3113481; e-mail governorsoffice@nbrm.gov.mk; internet www.nbrm.gov.mk; central bank and bank of issue; cap. and res 8,267.0m., dep. 18,886.1m. (Dec. 2002); Gov. Ljube Trpeski.

Selected Banks

Alpha Banka a.d.—Skopje: 1000 Skopje, Dame Gruev 1, POB 564; tel. (2) 3116433; fax (2) 3116830; e-mail kreditnabank@mt.net.mk; f. 1993 as Kreditna Banka a.d.; name changed as above in 2002; cap. 185.8m., res 601.5m., dep. 1,151.6m. (Dec. 2002); Chair. Spyros Filaretos; 3 brs.

Balkanska Banka: 1000 Skopje, Maksim Gorki 6; tel. (2) 3286100; fax (2) 3132186; e-mail balkbank@mt.net.mk; internet www.bbs.com.mk; f. 1993; cap. 308.2m., res 311.4m., dep. 896.3m. (Dec. 2002); Gen. Man. Kiril Pendev.

Eksport-Import Banka a.d.—Skopje: 91000 Skopje, DTC Paloma Bjanka, Dame Gruev 16; tel. (2) 3133411; fax (2) 3112744; e-mail info@eximb.com.mk; internet www.eximb.com.mk; f. 1994; cap. 601.4m., res 162.6m., dep. 1,645.3m. (Dec. 2001); Pres. Metodija Smilenski.

Eurostandard Banka a.d. Skopje: 1000 Skopje, Vasil Glavinov St, 2nd Floor, TCC Plaza; tel. (2) 3228444; fax (2) 3224095; e-mail info@eurostandard.com.mk; internet www.eurostandard.com.mk; f. 2001; cap. 548.6m., res 0.2m., dep. 678.7m. (Dec. 2002); Pres. Rodolfo Pizzocheri.

InvestBanka a.d. Skopje: 1000 Skopje, Makedonija 9/11; tel. (2) 3114166; fax (2) 3135367; internet www.investbanka.com.mk; f.

1992; cap. 575.0m., res 3.6m., dep. 1,218.8m. (Dec. 2002); Pres. SVETLANA PENDAROVSKA.

Izvozna I. Kreditna Banka a.d.: 1000 Skopje, Partizanski odredi 3, POB 421; tel. (2) 3129147; fax (2) 3122393; e-mail ikbanka@ikbanka.com.mk; internet www.ikbanka.com.mk; f. 1993; cap. 408.3m., res 276.2m., dep. 883.0m. (Dec. 2002); Pres. PANCE MANCEVSKI.

Komercijalna Banka a.d.—Skopje: 1000 Skopje, Kej Dimitar Vlahov 4; tel. (2) 3107107; fax (2) 3124064; e-mail contact@kbnet .com.mk; internet www.kbnet.com.mk; f. 1955 as Komunalna Banka; name changed as above in 1991; cap. 2,139.8m., res 950.1m., dep. 21,865.9m. (Dec. 2002); Pres. TRAJKO DAVITKOVSKI; 33 brs.

Makedonska Banka a.d.—Skopje: 91000 Skopje, Blok 12/2, bul. VMRO br. 3, POB 505; tel. (2) 3117111; fax (2) 3117191; e-mail info@makbanka.com.mk; internet www.makbanka.com; f. 1972; name changed in 1994; cap. 239.6m., res 515.2m., dep. 1,813.2m. (Dec. 2000); Pres. ALEKSANDAR NIKOLOVSKI.

Ohridska Banka a.d.—Ohrid: 6000 Ohrid, Makedonski Prosvetiteli 19; tel. (46) 206600; fax (46) 254130; e-mail obinfo@ob.com.mk; internet www.ob.com.mk; cap. 636.8m., res 136.7m., dep. 2,929.4m. (Dec. 2002); Pres. NAUM HADZILEGA; Chair. VANGEL NIKOLOSKI.

Radobank a.d. Skopje: 1000 Skopje, Jurij Gagarin 17; tel. (2) 3093300; fax (2) 3080453; e-mail radobank@radobank.com.mk; internet www.radobank.com.mk; f. 1993; Chair. RUBIN GRADOVSKI.

Stopanska Banka a.d.—Bitola: 97000 Bitola, Dobrivoe Radosavljević 21; tel. (47) 37048; fax (47) 223876; e-mail stbbt@mt.net .mk; f. 1948 as Komunalna Banka Bitola; name changed as above in 1995; cap. 896.9m., res 180.2m., dep. 2,433.1m. (Dec. 2002); Pres. VANGEL TORKOV.

Stopanska Banka a.d.—Skopje: 1000 Skopje, 11 Oktomvri 7; tel. (2) 3295295; fax (2) 3114503; e-mail sbank@stb.com.mk; internet www.stb.com.mk; f. 1944; cap. 3,602.2m., res 1.1m., dep. 18,116.7m. (Dec. 2002); privatized in April 2000; Chair. TAKIS ARAPOGLOU; 23 brs.

Teteks—Kreditna Bank a.d.: 1000 Skopje, POB 198; tel. (2) 3119206; fax (2) 3222370; e-mail tebank@mol.com.mk; f. 1993 as Teteks Banka; name changed as above, following merger with Kreditna Banka a.d. Bitola; cap. 272.9m., res 2.2m., dep. 784.4m. (Dec. 1995); Pres. GLIGORIE GOGOVSKI.

Tetovska Banka a.d. Tetovo: Tetovo, Marshal Tito 14; tel. (44) 335280; fax (44) 335274; e-mail tbtb@mt.net.mk; f. 1995; cap. 518.0m., res 14.5m., dep. 638.8m. (Dec. 2002); Dir ATANAS SPIROSKI.

Tutunska Banka a.d. Skopje: 1000 Skopje, 12-ta Udarna brigada bb, POB 702; tel. (2) 3105601; fax (2) 3105681; e-mail tbanka1@tb .com.mk; internet www.tb.com.mk; f. 1985; cap. 533.5m., res 1,115.6m., dep. 4,359.6m. (Dec. 2002); Pres. BORIS ZAKRAJSEK.

STOCK EXCHANGE

Skopje Stock Exchange: 1000 Skopje, Mito Hadživasilev Jasmin 20; tel. (2) 3122055; fax (2) 3122069; e-mail mse@unet.com.mk; internet www.mse.org.mk; f. 1996; Chair. EVGENI ZOGRAFSKI.

INSURANCE

Stock Co for Insurance and Reinsurance 'Makedonija'—Skopje: 1000 Skopje, 11 Oktomvri 25; tel. (2) 3115188; fax (2) 3115374; internet www.qbe.com; f. 1945; stock company for insurance and reinsurance.

Trade and Industry

GOVERNMENT AGENCY

Agency of Information: 1000 Skopje, Guro Gakovik 64; tel. (2) 3214723; fax (2) 3115659; e-mail sinf@sinf.gov.mk; internet www .sinf.gov.mk; Dir VEBI BEXHETI.

Privatization Agency of the Republic of Macedonia: 1000 Skopje, Nikola Vapcarov 7, POB 410; tel. (2) 3117564; fax (2) 3126022; e-mail agency@mpa.org.mk; internet www.mpa.org.mk; Dir MARINA NAKEVA-KAVRAKOVA.

Securities and Exchange Commission: 1000 Skopje, Kuzman Josifovski Pitu 1, POB 859; tel. and fax (2) 3114199; e-mail khv@sec .gov.mk; internet www.sec.gov.mk; Pres. NIKOLA GRUEVSKI.

CHAMBERS OF COMMERCE

Economic Chamber of Macedonia: 1000 Skopje, Dimitrija Čupovski 13; tel. (2) 3118088; fax (2) 3116210; e-mail ic@ic .mchamber.org.mk; internet www.mchamber.org.mk; f. 1962; Pres. DUŠAN PETRESKI.

Regional Chamber of Commerce of Skopje: 1000 Skopje, Partizanski odredi 2, POB 509; tel. (2) 3112511; fax (2) 3116419; e-mail regkomsk@regkom.org.mk; Pres. BORIS DIMOVSKI.

UTILITIES

Electricity

Electric Power Industry of Macedonia (Elektrostopanstvo na Makedonija): 1000 Skopje, Bate Bacevski br. 9; tel. (2) 3111077; fax (2) 3227827; production, transfer and distribution of electric power.

TRADE UNIONS

Federation of Trade Unions of Macedonia: 1000 Skopje; tel. (2) 3231374; fax (2) 3115787; Pres. VANCO MURATOVSKI; 320,000 mems.

Transport

RAILWAYS

In 2002 the rail network totalled 699 km, of which 233 km were electrified. From 2000 the European Investment Bank made a series of loans to finance the modernization of the railways.

Makedonski Železnici (MZ) (Macedonian Railways): 1000 Skopje, železnička 50; tel. (2) 3227903; fax (2) 3462330; e-mail mzdir@mt.net .mk; f. 1992; Dir-Gen. RATKO STEFANOVSKI.

ROADS

The FYRM's road network totalled 12,974 km in 2002, of which about 6,806 km were paved. The principal road links Tabanovtse, at the border with Serbia and Montenegro, and Bogoroditsa, at the border with Greece. In July 2003 the European Bank for Reconstruction and Development (EBRD) granted the FYRM a US $45m. loan in support of two major road-construction projects.

Fund for National and Regional Roads: 1000 Skopje, Dame Gruev 14; tel. (2) 3118044; fax (2) 3220535; e-mail tanjam@mpt.net .mk.

CIVIL AVIATION

The FYRM has two international airports, at Petrovets, 25 km from Skopje, and at Ohrid.

Adria Airways: 1000 Skopje, Gradski zid, blok 11; tel. (2) 3117009; fax (2) 3235531.

Avioimpex: 1000 Skopje, Oktomvri K14 11; tel. (2) 3239933; fax (2) 3119348; e-mail axx@lotus.mpt.com.mk; internet www.avioimpex .com; f. 1992; flights within Europe; Pres. ILIJA SMILEV.

Macedonian Airlines (MAT): 1000 Skopje, Vasil Glavinov 3; tel. (2) 3292333; fax (2) 3229576; e-mail mathq@mat.com.mk; internet www.mat.com.mk; f. 1994; domestic services and flights within Europe; Man. Dir DUSKO GRUEVSKI.

Palair Macedonian Airlines: 1000 Skopje, Kuzman Jusifovski Pitu bb; tel. (2) 3115868; fax (2) 3238238; f. 1991; domestic services and flights within Europe and to the USA, Canada and Australia; Chair. BITOLJANA VANJA.

Tourism

Following independence in 1991, the FYRM's tourist industry (formerly a major source of foreign exchange) experienced a decline, largely owing to the country's proximity to the conflict in other republics of the former Yugoslavia, domestic instability and the sanctions imposed by Greece. Receipts from tourism totalled US $37m. in 2000, but continuing regional instability, including fighting in the north of the FYRM, adversely affected tourism in 2001, when receipts amounted to just $23m; tourist arrivals declined dramatically, from 224,016 in 2000 to 98,946 in 2001, although they recovered somewhat, to 122,861, in 2002.

Tourist Association of Macedonia: 1000 Skopje, Dame Gruev 28/5; tel. (2) 3290862; e-mail tarm@mt.net.mk; internet www.tarm .org.mk.

Tourist Association of Skopje: 1000 Skopje, POB 399, Dame Gruev, blok 3; tel. (2) 3118498; fax (2) 3230803.

MADAGASCAR

Introductory Survey

Location, Climate, Language, Religion, Flag, Capital

The Republic of Madagascar comprises the island of Madagascar, the fourth largest in the world, and several much smaller offshore islands, in the western Indian Ocean, about 500 km (300 miles) east of Mozambique, in southern Africa. The inland climate is temperate; in Antananarivo temperatures are generally between 8°C (48°F) and 27°C (81°F), with cooler, dryer weather between May and October. The coastal region is tropical, with an average daily maximum temperature of 32°C (90°F). The rainy season extends from November to April in the highlands (average annual rainfall is 1,000 mm–1,500 mm) but is more prolonged on the coast, where average annual rainfall can reach 3,500 mm. The official language is Malagasy, and government acts are published in both Malagasy and French. Hova and other dialects are also widely spoken. More than 50% of the population follow animist beliefs, while about 43% are Christians and the remainder are Muslims. The national flag (proportions 2 by 3) has a vertical white stripe (one-third of the length) at the hoist and two equal horizontal stripes, of red and green, in the fly. The capital is Antananarivo (formerly Tananarive).

Recent History

A French possession since 1896, Madagascar became an autonomous state within the French Community in October 1958, as the Malagasy Republic. In May 1959 Philibert Tsiranana, leader of the Parti social démocrate (PSD), was elected President. The country achieved full independence on 26 June 1960. Prior to independence France supported the PSD, which was identified with the majority coastal tribes (côtiers), as an alternative to the more nationalistic highland people, the Merina, who were the traditional ruling group in the island.

After 1967 the economy deteriorated, and there was growing opposition to the Government's alleged authoritarianism and subservience to French interests. In May 1972, following civil unrest, President Tsiranana transferred full powers to the Army Chief of Staff, Gen. Gabriel Ramanantsoa. In October 1973 pro-Government parties secured a decisive victory in legislative elections. A prolonged crisis followed an attempted military coup in December 1974, and in early February 1975 Ramanantsoa transferred power to Col Richard Ratsimandrava, hitherto Minister of the Interior; however, Ratsimandrava was assassinated shortly afterwards. On 12 February Brig.-Gen. Gilles Andriamahazo assumed power and imposed martial law. All political parties were suspended. In June Andriamahazo was succeeded as Head of State by Lt-Commdr (later Adm.) Didier Ratsiraka, a côtier and a former Minister of Foreign Affairs, who became Chairman of the Supreme Revolutionary Council (SRC).

In a referendum in December 1975 more than 94% of voters approved a new Constitution, which provided for radical administrative and agrarian reforms, and the appointment of Ratsiraka as President of the Republic for a term of seven years. The country's name was changed to the Democratic Republic of Madagascar, and a 'Second Republic' was proclaimed. In January 1976 the civilian element in the Government was increased, and representatives of different regions and parties were included. In March the Avant-garde de la révolution malgache (AREMA—Antoky Ny Revolosiona Malagasy) was founded as the nucleus of the Front national pour la défense de la révolution socialiste malgache (FNDR), the only political organization permitted by the Constitution.

At local government elections in March–June 1977 AREMA secured the majority of votes, resulting in division within the FNDR. The left-wing Mouvement national pour l'indépendance de Madagascar (Monima Ka Miviombio, known as Monima), led by Monja Jaona, withdrew from the FNDR and was subsequently proscribed. At legislative elections in June AREMA secured 112 of the 137 seats in the National People's Assembly. A new Council of Ministers was formed in August, and the membership of the SRC was extended to include leaders of the former political parties and additional côtiers, in an effort to restore political equilibrium.

In October 1980 the arrest of Jaona (who was accused of inciting resentment against the Government) prompted demonstrations. Civil unrest continued in 1981, despite Monima's decision, in March, to rejoin the FNDR and Jaona's subsequent appointment to the SRC. In November 1982 Ratsiraka was re-elected President, receiving 80.2% of the votes cast. Jaona was removed from the SRC in December, following his appeal for a general strike in protest against the election results. At elections to the National People's Assembly in August 1983 AREMA won 117 of the 137 seats. Open dissatisfaction with the Government's policies persisted, however.

In February 1988 the Prime Minister, Col Désiré Rakotoarijaona, resigned, owing to poor health, and was replaced by Lt-Col Victor Ramahatra, formerly Minister of Public Works. Ratsiraka was re-elected to the presidency in March 1989 for a further seven-year term, with 62.7% of the total votes cast. In April rioting followed opposition allegations of electoral irregularities. At legislative elections in May AREMA won 120 seats. The Mouvement pour le pouvoir prolétarien (Mpitolona ho amin'ny Fonjakan'ny Madinika—MFM), which obtained only seven seats, rejected the official results, alleging electoral misconduct. The Elan populaire pour l'unité nationale (Vonjy Iray Tsy Mivaky, known as Vonjy) secured four seats, AKFM/Fanavaozana (a newly formed group, comprising former members of the Parti du congrès de l'indépendance de Madagascar—AKFM), won three seats, the original AKFM two seats, and Monima only one seat.

In August 1989 Ratsiraka assented to opposition demands for discussions about the future role and structure of the FNDR. In September AREMA secured the majority of votes in local government elections. In December the National People's Assembly adopted a constitutional amendment abolishing the requirement for political parties to be members of the FNDR (thereby effectively dissolving the FNDR), despite opposition from MFM deputies.

In March 1990 the Government formally permitted the resumption of multi-party politics. Numerous new organizations emerged, while other parties that had hitherto operated within the FNDR became official opposition movements. Several pro-Government political associations joined AREMA to form a new coalition, the Mouvement militant pour le socialisme malgasy (MMSM). The principal opposition movements included the Union nationale pour le développement et la démocratie (UNDD) and the MFM (restyled the Mouvement pour le progrès de Madagascar, or Mpitolona ho amin'ny Fandrosoan'ny Madagasikara). An informal alliance, the Comité des forces vives—subsequently known as Forces vives (FV, Hery Velona)—was formed by 16 opposition factions, and trade unions and other groups.

In December 1990 the National People's Assembly approved the abolition of press censorship and the establishment (in partnership with the Government) of private broadcasting stations. In May 1991 legislation providing for extensive constitutional amendments was submitted to the National People's Assembly. Opposition parties criticized the proposals, on the grounds that the revised Constitution would retain references to socialism. In June opposition leaders applied to the Constitutional High Court to effect Ratsiraka's removal from office, while the FV organized demonstrations in support of its demands for the resignation of the President and the convening of a national conference to draft a new constitution. Ratsiraka refused to resign. Later in June the FV formed a 'parallel' administration, which it termed the 'Provisional Government'.

In July 1991 the FV organized a general strike, warning that it would continue until the Government acceded to its demands for constitutional reform. Subsequent negotiations between the MMSM and the FV achieved little. The FV appointed Jean Rakotoharison, a retired army general, as President of the 'Provisional Government', and Albert Zafy, the leader of the UNDD, as its Prime Minister. However, Manandafy Rakotonirina, the leader of the MFM, rejected the formation of the 'Provisional Government', favouring further negotiations, and withdrew his party from the FV. Members of the 'Provisional

Government' subsequently occupied the premises of six official government ministries. Later in July Ratsiraka ordered the detention of several members of the 'Provisional Government' and imposed a state of emergency in Antananarivo. The FV withdrew from negotiations with the MMSM, in protest against the arrests, while the French Government appealed to Ratsiraka to release the opposition leaders. In response to increasing public pressure, Ratsiraka dissolved the Council of Ministers and pledged to organize a constitutional referendum before the end of 1991. Members of the 'Provisional Government' were released from custody, and Ratsiraka repealed legislation that authorized the detention of opponents of the Government.

In August 1991 Ratsiraka appointed Guy Razanamasy, the mayor of Antananarivo, as Prime Minister. In the same month a number of demonstrators were killed when an anti-Government rally was violently suppressed by the presidential guard. Negotiations between the MMSM and the FV were again suspended, and the armed forces withdrew their support for Ratsiraka. Later that month Ratsiraka declared Madagascar to be a federation of six states, with himself as President, and claimed to command the support of five provinces where AREMA continued to hold the majority of seats in regional councils. However, the FV disregarded the proclamation and continued to demand that Ratsiraka relinquish the presidency. At the end of August Razanamasy formed an interim Government, not including members of the FV or the MFM, which was condemned by opposition leaders.

On 31 October 1991 representatives of the Government, the FV, the MFM, church leaders and the armed forces signed an agreement providing for the suspension of the Constitution and the creation of a transitional Government, which was to remain in office for a maximum period of 18 months, pending presidential and legislative elections. The SRC and the National People's Assembly were to be replaced by interim bodies, respectively the High State Authority for Transition to the Third Republic and the National Committee for Economic and Social Regeneration. On an interim basis, Ratsiraka was to remain as President of the Republic and Razanamasy as Prime Minister. Zafy was designated President of the High State Authority, which was to comprise 18 representatives of the FV, seven of the MFM and six of the MMSM. Rakotonirina and Pastor Richard Andriamanjato, the leader of AKFM/Fanavaozana, were appointed as joint Presidents of the 131-member National Committee for Economic and Social Regeneration. The power to appoint or to dismiss government ministers, hitherto vested in the President, was granted to Razanamasy. A new constitution was to be submitted to a national referendum by the end of 1991. Zafy subsequently rejected the agreement, on the grounds that Ratsiraka was to retain the nominal post of Commander-in-Chief of the Armed Forces. In November Razanamasy formed a new interim Government, which included three representatives of the MFM and one MMSM member. Francisque Ravony, of the MFM, was appointed to the new post of Deputy Prime Minister. Owing to Zafy's refusal to participate in the Government, 10 portfolios that had been allocated to the FV remained vacant. Later in November, however, Zafy agreed to accept the presidency of the High State Authority.

In December 1991 Razanamasy announced that the formation of the coalition Government had proved unsuccessful, and 11 ministers, including Ravony, resigned. Razanamasy appointed a larger Government of national consensus, in which 14 (of 36) portfolios were allocated to the FV. In January 1992 it was announced that all political factions had now accepted the terms of the October 1991 agreement. The institutions that had been established by the accord were to prepare for the constitutional referendum, now scheduled for June 1992, and for local, presidential and legislative elections, which were to take place by the end of the year. In February regional debates took place to compile proposals for the new constitution, which was to be drafted (together with an electoral code) by a National Forum. Also in February the High State Authority for Transition to the Third Republic announced the dissolution of the SRC and the National People's Assembly, in accordance with the October 1991 agreement, and indicated that a new body was to be created to supervise local elections, replacing the existing system of government, based on village assemblies (*fokontany*). However, the MMSM claimed that the High State Authority was not empowered to dissolve the local government structure. The Government subsequently announced that control of local government was to be transferred from elected councils to special

delegations, and that security commissions were to be established to organize the *fokontany*.

At the National Forum, which was convened in March 1992, the MMSM agreed to abandon its proposals for the creation of a federal republic, but continued to profess adherence to a decentralized system of government. At the end of March, following a decision by the Forum to restrict the President to two terms of office (thereby debarring Ratsiraka from contesting the presidential election), supporters of the MMSM attacked the conference hall during a session of the Forum.

The draft Constitution of the Third Republic, as submitted to the Government in April 1992, envisaged a unitary state and provided for a bicameral legislature, comprising a Senate and a National Assembly. Two-thirds of the members of the Senate were to be selected by an electoral college, with the remaining one-third to be appointed by the President, while the 184-member National Assembly was to be elected by universal suffrage, under a system of proportional representation, for a four-year term. The authority of the President was reduced, and executive power was vested in the Prime Minister, who was to be appointed by the National Assembly. (The stipulation in the draft Constitution that the President be restricted to two terms of office had, however, been withdrawn.) Ratsiraka reiterated his intention to contest the presidential election and demanded that a draft providing for a federal system of government also be submitted to the forthcoming referendum, as an alternative to the National Forum's proposals.

In August 1992 supporters of a federal system of government took control of the airport and the radio and television stations at Antsiranana, and announced the establishment of a federal directorate in the town; similar incidents followed at Toamasina, in the east, and Toliary, in the south-west of the country. The new Constitution was approved by 72.2% of votes cast in a national referendum on 19 August. Federalists forcibly prevented the electorate from voting in a number of regions, and several people were killed in clashes between supporters of the MMSM and members of the FV at Toamasina. Later that month the armed forces regained control of the towns that had been occupied by the federalists.

In September 1992 several prominent political figures, including Zafy and Rakotonirina, announced that they were to contest the forthcoming presidential election. Divisions emerged within the FV after a number of constituent parties presented alternative candidates to Zafy, the alliance's official candidate. Later in September the National Forum's electoral code was submitted to a committee of government officials and church leaders, which proposed that the stipulation restricting the President to two terms of office be incorporated in the code. Shortly afterwards MMSM supporters unilaterally declared Antsiranana, Toliary, Toamasina and Fianarantsoa (in central Madagascar) to be federal states, and suspended infrastructural links between these provinces and Antananarivo. In October federalists in Antsiranana, apparently supported by members of the presidential guard, took hostage members of the FV and seized control of the radio and television stations. Razanamasy declared the unilateral proclamation of independence of the four provinces to be illegal, but initiated negotiations with the federalists, in an effort to prevent disruption of the presidential election. Later that month there were further clashes in Toliary between supporters of the FV and federalists, led by Monja Jaona, who had declared himself to be Governor of the province. At the end of October, however, the federalists agreed to participate in the presidential election, although the MMSM continued officially to reject the new Constitution.

The presidential election took place on 25 November 1992, contested by eight candidates. Zafy secured 45.1% of votes cast, and Ratsiraka 29.2%. Prior to a second round of voting, on 10 February 1993, the remaining six candidates withdrew in favour of Zafy, who thus secured 66.7% of the votes cast. Zafy's inauguration, on 27 March, was accompanied by violent clashes between security forces and federalists in the north. In accordance with the Constitution, Zafy resigned as President of the UNDD at a party congress in May; Emmanuel Rakotovahiny, the Minister of State for Agriculture and Rural Development, was elected as his successor.

Several constituent parties of the FV that had not supported Zafy in the first round of the presidential election subsequently presented independent lists of candidates for the forthcoming legislative elections; the remaining parties in the alliance became known as Forces vives Rasalama (Hery Velona Rasalama—HVR). Violence intensified prior to polling: two people were killed, and 40 (including Jaona) arrested, after security forces attacked federalists who had occupied the prefecture at Toliary. The elections, to a reduced 138-member National Assembly, took place on 16 June 1993, and were contested by 121 political associations. The HVR secured 46 seats, the MFM 15, and a new alliance of pro-Ratsiraka parties 11 seats. The official results indicated that parties supporting Zafy had won 75 seats in the National Assembly. In August Francisque Ravony was elected Prime Minister and formed a new Council of Ministers. Richard Andriamanjato was elected President of the National Assembly.

By early 1994, owing to frequent party realignments, Ravony no longer commanded a majority in the legislature. In June government proposals for economic reforms were rejected by the National Assembly. Nevertheless, in July a motion of censure against Ravony's Government was rejected. In the same month scheduled elections to establish new regional authorities (already postponed from October 1993) were further delayed, owing to lack of agreement regarding proposals for decentralization. In August 1994, following negotiations with the HVR, Ravony formed a new Council of Ministers.

In October 1994 controversy over a local subsidiary enterprise, Flamco Madagascar, which had failed to reimburse funds advanced by the Government, prompted increased division between Ravony and Andriamanjato regarding economic policy. Meanwhile, opposition leaders demanded the removal of Zafy, Ravony and Andriamanjato, amid general resentment towards the Government, which had been precipitated by an increase in the rate of inflation resulting from the flotation of the Malagasy franc. At a regional congress of AREMA, which took place at the end of October, Ratsiraka urged the resignation of Ravony and dissolution of the Government. In the same month pro-Andriamanjato sections of the HVR demanded the dismissal of three government ministers, including the Minister of Finance and the Budget, José Yvon Raserijaona, on the grounds of incompetence, subsequently joining the opposition in urging Ravony's resignation, after he failed to replace the three ministers concerned. In January 1995 Ravony dismissed the Governor of the central bank, who had approved the financial transaction with Flamco Madagascar, at the insistence of the IMF and World Bank, and (apparently as a concession to Andriamanjato) also dismissed Raserijaona, assuming the finance and budget portfolio himself.

In July 1995, apparently at Zafy's instigation, deputies belonging to the HVR, the UNDD and AKFM/Fanavaozana proposed a motion of censure against Ravony in the National Assembly (which was, however, rejected by a large majority). Zafy subsequently announced that he was unable to co-operate with Ravony and decreed that a constitutional amendment empowering the President, rather than the National Assembly, to select the Prime Minister, be submitted for approval in a national referendum. Ravony indicated that he would resign after the referendum, regardless of the outcome. In August Ravony formed a new Council of Ministers, comprising representatives of the parliamentary majority that had supported him in the previous month. The referendum proceeded in September, at which the constitutional amendment was approved by 63.6% of votes cast. Ravony duly resigned in October, and Zafy appointed Rakotovahiny as Prime Minister. Rakotovahiny's Council of Ministers included several members of the outgoing administration, although the leader of the HVR, Alain Ramaroson (the only member of the HVR to be allocated a portfolio), refused to join the Government. In accordance with government plans to restructure local government, elections to 1,400 new communes took place on 5 November. An abstention rate of 60% was recorded, and a decline in support for the HVR was apparent.

Following the installation of the new Government, disagreement between Rakotovahiny and the Minister of the Budget, Finance and Planning, Jean Claude Raherimanjato, delayed the adoption of the budget for 1996. In addition, dissension emerged between the parties that supported Zafy over the composition of the Council of Ministers; in December 1995 associates of Andriamanjato demanded that an alternative cabinet be appointed. In April 1996 an attempt by Raherimanjato to dismiss senior ministry officials (which Rakotovahiny refused to endorse) prompted industrial action by civil servants at the Ministry of the Budget, Finance and Planning. In the same month opposition members took part in further demonstrations to demand Zafy's resignation. In May a motion of censure against Rakotovahiny's Government, apparently instigated by Raherimanjato,

was approved by a large majority in the National Assembly. Rakotovahiny submitted his administration's resignation, and Zafy appointed Norbert Ratsirahonana, hitherto President of the Constitutional High Court, as Prime Minister.

Zafy refused to approve the new Government initially proposed by Ratsirahonana, insisting on the inclusion of five UNDD members who had served in the previous Council of Ministers. In protest, most of the opposition deputies consequently left the legislative chamber when the Prime Minister presented the new Government to the National Assembly in June 1996. Ratsirahonana, however, won a vote of confidence in the legislature in July, by associating the vote with legislation providing for the implementation of economic reforms stipulated by the IMF and the World Bank. On 26 July a motion in the National Assembly to remove Zafy from office for numerous contraventions of the Constitution was supported by 99 of 131 votes cast. (Meanwhile, local elections, which had been scheduled for August, and were to replace the existing six provinces with 28 regions, were postponed as a result of the presidential crisis.) The Constitutional High Court endorsed the President's impeachment in September, upholding the majority of the charges against him; Zafy maintained that his impeachment was illegal, but resigned the same day. Ratsirahonana was appointed interim President by the Constitutional High Court, pending an election; he formed a new interim Government that represented the majority in the National Assembly and excluded members of the UNDD. Zafy announced his intention to contest the forthcoming election, as did Ratsiraka, Ratsirahonana and Ravony. In October Ravony withdrew from the presidential election and, unexpectedly, declared his support for Zafy.

In all, 15 candidates stood in the first round of the presidential election, which proceeded peacefully on 3 November 1996; Ratsiraka (with 36.6% of the votes cast) and Zafy (with 23.4%) qualified to contest the second round. The head of LEADER/Fanilo, Herizo Razafimahaleo, obtained 15.1%, and Ratsirahonana 10.1%, of the votes. Razafimahaleo urged his supporters to vote for Ratsiraka. None of the unsuccessful candidates chose to support Zafy, who declared his intention, if elected, to retain Ratsirahonana (who had successfully concluded an agreement with the IMF in August) as Prime Minister; Ratsirahonana, however, refused to endorse either candidate. At the second round, which took place on 29 December, Ratsiraka narrowly won, with 50.71% of the valid votes cast, although more than 50% of the registered electorate abstained from voting. Ratsiraka was inaugurated as President on 9 February. He appointed Pascal Rakotomavo (a former Minister of Finance) as Prime Minister. Rakotomavo's Government included Razafimahaleo as Deputy Prime Minister in charge of Foreign Affairs. During a visit to France in March, Ratsiraka discussed plans to effect constitutional change by referendum.

In May 1997 legislative elections, which had been scheduled for August, were postponed, officially to allow time for identity cards to be issued to voters. The opposition, led by Zafy, denounced the delay as a violation of the Constitution and, in early August, demanded the resignation of the Government and of the Constitutional High Court (which had endorsed the extension of the existing legislature's mandate), as well as the dissolution of the National Assembly. In August a commission that had been appointed by the Prime Minister to draft constitutional amendments presented its proposals. However, apparently following intervention from Andriamanjato, who was said to have insisted that the National Assembly alone was responsible for constitutional revision, regional forums, attended by local officials and representatives of non-governmental organizations, were held in September to put forward proposals for one constitutional project. (Ratsiraka had originally favoured submitting two alternatives to a referendum, one for a federal state, the other for a decentralized, unitary state.) A new constitution was then to be drafted by a 15-member National Consultative Commission, nominated by Ratsiraka, Rakotomavo and Andriamanjato. Meanwhile, in October the Government condemned declarations apparently made by Zafy and his supporters that Antsiranana had become a 'liberated territory'.

In January 1998 Ratsiraka invited political leaders to attend discussions on constitutional reform, although Hery Miara-dia, an opposition grouping led by Zafy, and members of the Panorama Group, a more moderate alliance led by Ravony and Ratsirahonana, refused to participate. None the less, Ratsiraka subsequently announced that a constitutional referendum would take place on 15 March 1998, to be followed by legislative elections. The draft amendments to the Constitution envisaged a 'federal-style' state, composed of six autonomous provinces, and also provided for increased presidential powers.

In February 1998 a motion of impeachment against Ratsiraka failed to gain the requisite two-thirds' majority in the National Assembly. Later that month the principal opposition parties urged voters to boycott the forthcoming referendum, claiming that the Government had ignored the views presented at the regional forums and the proposals of the National Consultative Commission, and had deliberately delayed discussion on legislation proposed by Rakotonirina (who had chaired the Commission) whereby any draft constitution would require the approval of more than 50% of all registered voters in order to become law. The referendum proceeded on 15 March 1998, when extensive revisions to the Constitution were narrowly endorsed by 50.96% of votes cast. Rakotonirina's proposed legislation was approved by the National Assembly later that month. However, Ratsiraka referred the legislation back to the National Assembly, and in April it was rejected after further deliberation.

Elections to an expanded National Assembly followed on 17 May 1998, under a new electoral law. Of the 150 seats, 82 were to be filled from single-member constituencies, with the remaining deputies to be elected by a system of proportional representation in 34 two-member constituencies. Ratsiraka's party, AREMA, performed well in the elections, winning 63 seats, while the pro-presidential LEADER/Fanilo and the Rassemblement pour le socialisme et la démocratie (RPSD) secured 16 and 11 seats, respectively. Ratsirahonana's party, Ny asa vita no ifampitsara (AVI), emerged as the strongest opposition party, with 14 seats, while Zafy's new party—Asa, Faharaminana, Fampandrasoana, Arinda (AFFA)—won six seats; independent candidates took 32 seats. Several leading political figures failed to secure re-election, notably Andriamanjato, and Rakotonirina and Germain Rakotonirainy, the leaders of the MFM (which won only three seats). The AVI and 24 independent deputies were subsequently reported to have joined the AREMA majority, leaving the AFFA and the remaining independents as the only significant parliamentary opposition. In July Tantely Andrianarivo, hitherto Deputy Prime Minister, was appointed as Prime Minister, retaining responsibility for finance and the economy. The 31-member Council of Ministers was dominated by AREMA, with the key portfolios largely unchanged; 12 new ministers were appointed.

The first local government elections—communal voting for 20,000 councillors and 1,392 mayors—since the reintroduction of the three-tier system of local government (provinces, regions and communes), under the amended Constitution of 1998, took place on 14 November 1999. The greatest successes were recorded by independent (or nominally independent) candidates. Most notably, Marc Ravalomanana, the head of the country's largest agro-industrial processor, Tiko, was elected mayor of Antananarivo; Ravalomanana had been a principal donor of electoral funds to the AVI, but had stood as an independent. Roland Ratsiraka, a nephew of the President, was elected independent mayor of Toamasina, while Zafy failed to secure election to the post of mayor of Diego Garcia. Following the party's poor performance in the elections, Pierrot Rajaonarivelo, the Deputy Prime Minister, resigned as Secretary-General of AREMA. Regional elections were postponed.

Provincial elections took place on 3 December 2000 to elect 336 councillors, as a preliminary step to the decentralization of certain powers to six autonomous provinces (legislation on the organization of which had been approved by the National Assembly in August). Voter participation in the capital was reported to have been very low, at about 30%, following calls by various organizations, including opposition parties and the Christian Council of Churches in Madagascar, for a boycott of the elections. It was reported that AREMA had secured control of most of the major towns, although the AVI won a majority of seats in Antananarivo.

On 18 March 2001 a 1,727-member electoral college, which included mayors and local councillors, elected 60 members of the new Senate. AREMA won 49 of the 60 seats, while LEADER/Fanilo secured five seats and opposition parties a total of six, including two for the AVI. President Ratsiraka subsequently named the remaining 30 senators who would constitute the 90-seat upper house.

A presidential election took place on 16 December 2001, contested by six candidates, including Ratsiraka, Zafy, Razafimahaleo and Marc Ravalomanana. According to the official results, Ravalomanana, whose candidacy was supported by a number of opposition parties, most notably the AVI, the RPSD

and the MFM, secured 46.21% of the votes cast and Didier Ratsiraka 40.89%, thereby necessitating a second round of voting. However, Ravalomanana's own electoral observers disputed this result, claiming that he had won an outright victory, with 52.15% of the votes, and demanded a public comparison of voting records. The opposition was supported in these demands by international electoral observers. A re-count was subsequently conducted, and on 25 January 2002 the Constitutional High Court endorsed the official results and ruled that a second round of voting should take place within 30 days. Ravalomanana rejected this verdict and called for a national strike in protest. Some 500,000 people responded by gathering in Antananarivo; government offices, public utilities and banks ceased operations, and air traffic was suspended. Ravalomanana's supporters also closed the central bank in order to prevent Ratsiraka from withdrawing special funds from the treasury. Strike action continued, in varying forms, for eight weeks. Following a meeting between Ravalomanana and Ratsiraka in mid-February, negotiations were conducted between their representatives, with mediation by the Organization of African Unity (OAU); Ratsiraka's delegates rejected Ravalomanana's proposals for the formation of an interim government and new appointments to the Constitutional High Court and electoral committee. Meanwhile, the Minister of the Armed Forces, Gen. Marcel Ranjeva, declared that the army would remain neutral in the electoral dispute.

On 22 February 2002 Ravalomanana accelerated events by unilaterally declaring himself President in an inaugural ceremony in Antananarivo attended by 100,000 supporters. The President of the Senate immediately declared Ravalomanana's proclamation to be illegal, and it was widely condemned by the international community. In response, President Ratsiraka declared a three-month 'state of national necessity', according himself broad powers, including the right to pass laws by decree. On 26 February Ravalomanana named Jacques Sylla, a former Minister of Foreign Affairs under Zafy's presidency, as his Prime Minister. On the following day Ratsiraka's Minister of Foreign Affairs and Minister of Post and Telecommunications both resigned. Meanwhile, after weeks of largely peaceful protests, violent clashes erupted between supporters of Ratsiraka and Ravalomanana in Antananarivo, prompting Ratsiraka to decree martial law and appoint a military governor, Gen. Léon-Claude Raveloarison, in the capital. None the less, Ravalomanana proceeded with the formation of his rival Government in early March, while opposition supporters erected barricades against the army and set fire to the military headquarters; 17 of those appointed to Ravalomanana's administration were successfully installed in government offices, accompanied by large crowds of supporters and unopposed by the military. On the same day the governors of the five remaining provinces of the country declared their allegiance to Ratsiraka, recognizing his hometown, Toamasina (where Ratsiraka and his ministers had relocated) as a temporary 'alternative capital'. A few days later Gen. Ranjeva resigned as Minister of the Armed Forces, shortly after Ravalomanana's rival Government had taken control of his offices in Antananarivo. Gen. Raveloarison resigned as military governor of Antananarivo some three weeks after his appointment, having failed to apply martial law and order troops to end protests, on the grounds that this would have incurred deaths. Later in March 58 of Madagascar's 150 deputies attended a parliamentary session called by Ravalomanana and elected an interim President of the National Assembly.

An OAU mission held talks with Ravalomanana and Ratsiraka in March 2002, in an attempt to resolve the ongoing political crisis, but its proposal for a 'government of national reconciliation' was rejected by both sides. In late March four supporters of Ravalomanana were killed, and a further 28 injured, during clashes with the security forces in Fianarantsoa, bringing the estimated number of deaths in the protests since January to 25. At the beginning of April, supporters of Ratsiraka, who had erected roadblocks to isolate Antananarivo in February, destroyed two of the bridges located on its supply routes to the rest of the island, in an effort to intensify the effective siege of the capital, which was already suffering from severe fuel shortages. The situation fostered fears of ethnic conflict, with Ravalomanana supported by the predominantly Merina population of Antananarivo and the central highlands, and Ratsiraka by the *côtiers*. This concern was exacerbated by Ravalomanana's appeal for his supporters to overthrow the roadblocks around the capital, declaring the country to be in a state of war and listing the names of those considered to be enemies. The OAU condemned Ravalomanana's statements as incitement to violence.

On 10 April 2002 the Supreme Court ruled that there had been irregularities in the appointment, shortly before the presidential election, of six of the nine judges of the Constitutional High Court, which had endorsed the official results; one week later the Supreme Court annulled the disputed results and ordered a re-count of the votes. On the following day Ratsiraka and Ravalomanana signed a peace accord in Dakar, Senegal, where they had been holding talks under the auspices of the OAU and the UN, and with mediation by the Presidents of Senegal, Benin, Côte d'Ivoire and Mozambique. Following the completion of the re-count, in late April, the Constitutional High Court ruled that Ravalomanana had secured the presidency, with 51.46% of the votes cast, while Ratsiraka had won 35.90%. Ratsiraka, who had failed to remove the blockade of Antananarivo (in contravention of the Dakar accord), refused to accept the Court's decision. Nevertheless, Ravalomanana was inaugurated as President on 6 May, largely without international recognition, and appointed a new Council of Ministers later that month. Four of the country's six provincial governors, who were loyal to Ratsiraka, subsequently threatened to secede. Ravalomanana and Ratsiraka failed to reach agreement at further talks in Dakar in early June. Heavy fighting ensued, as troops loyal to Ravalomanana conducted a military offensive against areas controlled by Ratsiraka, securing two provincial capitals, Mahajanga and Toliary, in mid-June.

In mid-June 2002 Ravalomanana dissolved the Government that he had formed in May, immediately reappointing Sylla as Prime Minister; however, despite nominating six new members of the Council of Ministers, he failed to appoint a government of national unity. At the end of June the USA recognized Ravalomanana as the legitimate leader of Madagascar; endorsement soon followed from France and, in contravention of the policy of the OAU, Senegal. Meanwhile, the OAU suspended Madagascar from its meetings, pending the staging of free and fair elections leading to the establishment of a legitimate government; this decision was upheld by the African Union (AU, see p. 137), which replaced the OAU in July. In early July Ravalomanana's government troops took control of Antsiranana and Toamasina, and Ratsiraka sought exile in France; this apparent admission of defeat allowed for an international conference to take place in Paris, France, on the donation of aid for the reconstruction of Madagascar. The new Government was in full control of the island by the middle of the month. Ravalomanana replaced the 30 presidentially appointed members of the Senate, with the approval of the Constitutional High Court, despite the fact that those appointed by Ratsiraka had been appointed for a tenure of six years. In August six of the nine members of the Constitutional High Court were also replaced. In early October Ravalomanana dismissed Narisoa Rajaonarivony as Deputy Prime Minister and Minister of Finance and Development and altered the portfolio of Benjamin Andriamparany Radavidson from Minister of Economy and Planning to that of Minister of the Economy, Finance and the Budget.

In mid-October 2002 the National Assembly was dissolved in preparation for legislative elections, brought forward from May 2003, in response to pressure from aid donors, in order to finalize the legitimacy of Ravalomanana's mandate. At the elections, which took place on 15 December 2002, Ravalomanana's party, Tiako i Madagasikara (TIM—I Love Madagascar), won 104 of the 160 seats and the pro-Ravalomanana Firaisankinam-Pirenena, an alliance of the AVI and elements of the RPSD, secured a further 22 seats; notably, 23 independent deputies were elected, and the formerly incumbent AREMA party won only three seats. (Foreign observers were permitted to be present at the elections for the first time in Malagasy electoral history.) In mid-January 2003 a new Government was appointed, which included 10 new ministers and was reduced in overall size from 30 to 20 ministers; the former Minister of Public Works, Jean Lahiniriako, was elected President of the National Assembly. Madagascar's suspension from meetings of the AU—hitherto the only remaining significant authority not to have recognized the new Government—was formally revoked at the organization's General Assembly in July of that year; the legitimacy of the Ravalomanana administration was thus considered finally to have been established. Meanwhile, various members of the former Ratsiraka administration were arrested and tried in court, including the former Governors of Fianarantsoa and Toamasina. In August former President Ratsiraka was sentenced, *in absentia*, to 10 years' hard labour for the embezzlement of public funds and declared unfit for public office.

Local elections took place in two rounds on 9 and 23 November 2003 in rural and urban areas, respectively. The TIM performed well in both sets of elections, securing mayorships in 27 of the country's 45 largest cities and towns, followed by independents, who won nine. Notably, Roland Ratsiraka, the nephew of the former President, was re-elected independent mayor of Toamasina, having been suspended from this post several months earlier over allegations of financial mismanagement. AREMA boycotted the polls. In December former Prime Minister Andrianarivo was sentenced to 12 years' hard labour and fined 42,000m. francs MG for embezzling public funds and endangering state security; however, in the following month he was authorized to seek medical treatment abroad. In January 2004 Ravalomanana restructured and reshuffled the Council of Ministers, reducing its membership to 17 ministers and two secretaries of state. Several former supporters of Ratsiraka were appointed in order to diversify the ethnic composition of the Government, which had hitherto been dominated by the Merina. In March the President granted pardons to those sentenced to less than three years' imprisonment for involvement with the pro-Ratsiraka resistance; those with more serious sentences would have the right to apply individually for an amnesty. The worst cyclone to strike the island in several decades occurred in March, resulting in some 200 deaths, including those of passengers on a ferry *en route* from the Comoros, and the displacement of thousands of people, as well as the widespread destruction of infrastructure; international aid was forthcoming in response.

Madagascar's foreign policy is officially non-aligned: while it formerly maintained close links with communist countries (particularly the People's Republic of China, the Democratic People's Republic of Korea and the former USSR), the Zafy Government established relations with Israel, South Africa and the Republic of Korea. Relations with France have been affected by disputes over compensation for nationalized French assets and over the continuing French claim to the Iles Glorieuses, north of Madagascar, and three other islets in the Mozambique Channel. In 1980 the UN voted in favour of restoring all the disputed islets to Madagascar. In early 1986 the Government announced the extension of Madagascar's exclusive economic zone to include the Iles Glorieuses and the three islets. In 1997 government announcements regarding future privatization plans in Madagascar prompted renewed appeals from France for compensation for nationalized French assets. In response, the Government allocated some 50,000m. francs MG as initial compensation in the budget for 1998. In February 2000 it was agreed that the Iles Glorieuses would be co-administered by France, Madagascar and Mauritius, without prejudice to the question of sovereignty. In April 2004, during a state visit to Madagascar by Prime Minister Paul Bérenger of Mauritius, political and economic co-operation agreements between the two countries were signed.

Relations with the People's Republic of China were strengthened in January 1999, during a visit by Vice-President Hu Jintao; agreements were signed on the expansion of bilateral economic relations and China's provision of preferential loans to Madagascar. In September 2000 the representative office for Taiwan in Madagascar was closed down, following an official visit by the Malagasy Minister of Foreign Affairs to China. (It was claimed that this was carried out by the Government in support of the 'one China' policy; however, the Taiwanese claimed that the office had never functioned effectively.)

Government

The Constitution of the Third Republic was endorsed by national referendum on 19 August 1992, but was extensively revised by amendments that were endorsed by national referendum on 15 March 1998. The amended Constitution enshrines a 'federal-style' state, composed of six autonomous provinces, each with a provincial council (holding legislative power) elected by universal suffrage for a term of five years. Each provincial council elects a governor, who appoints up to 12 general commissioners to exercise executive power in the province. The first local elections (for communal councillors and mayors) under the restored three-tier system of provinces, regions and communes, as envisaged in the Constitution, took place in November 1999. Provincial elections were held in December 2000. The Constitution provides for a bicameral legislature, comprising a Senate (established in March 2001) and a National Assembly. Two-thirds of the members of the Senate are elected by the autonomous provinces, and the remaining one-third of the members are appointed by the President, while the National Assembly is elected by universal suffrage for a five-year term of office. The constitutional Head of State is the President, who is elected for a term of five years, and can be re-elected for two further terms. The President appoints the Prime Minister and, on the latter's recommendation, the other members of the Council of Ministers.

Defence

At 1 August 2003 total armed forces numbered about 13,500 men: army 12,500, navy 500 and air force 500. There is a paramilitary gendarmerie of 8,100. The defence budget for 2003 was estimated at 330,000m. francs MG.

Economic Affairs

In 2002, according to estimates by the World Bank, Madagascar's gross national income (GNI), measured at average 2000–02 prices, was US $3,913m., equivalent to about $240 per head (or $720 per head on an international purchasing-power parity basis). During 1990–2002, it was estimated, the population increased at an average annual rate of 2.9%, while gross domestic product (GDP) per head decreased, in real terms, by an average of 2.0% per year. Overall GDP increased, in real terms, at an average annual rate of 0.9% in 1990–2002; GDP increased by 6.0% in 2001, but decreased by 11.9% in 2002.

In 2002 the agricultural sector (including forestry and fishing) accounted for 31.5% of GDP and employed an estimated 73.4% of the labour force. Rice, the staple food crop, is produced on some 50% of cultivated land. Since 1972, however, imports of rice have been necessary to supplement domestic production. The most important cash crops are vanilla (which accounted for 24.1% of total export revenue in 2002), cloves and coffee. Following a long drought in 2003, vanilla production was estimated to have halved in that year, leading to a dramatic escalation in world prices. Sugar, coconuts, tropical fruits, cotton and sisal are also cultivated. Cattle-farming is important. Sea fishing by coastal fishermen (particularly for crustaceans) is being expanded, while vessels from the European Union fish for tuna and prawns in Madagascar's exclusive maritime zone, within 200 nautical miles (370 km) of the coast, in return for compensation. According to the World Bank, agricultural GDP increased by an average of 1.7% per year in 1990–2002; the sector's GDP increased by 4.0% in 2001, but declined by 1.4% in 2002.

Industry (including mining, manufacturing, construction and power) contributed 14.3% of Madagascar's GDP in 2002, and employed about 5.5% of the labour force in 1999. According to the World Bank, industrial GDP increased at an average annual rate of 0.2% in 1990–2002; the sector's GDP increased by 7.6% in 2001, but declined by 25.1% in 2002.

The mining sector contributed only 0.3% of GDP in 1991 and, together with manufacturing, engaged about 1.5% of the labour force in 1993. However, Madagascar has sizeable deposits of a wide range of minerals, principally chromite (chromium ore), which, with graphite and mica, is exported, together with small quantities of semi-precious stones. A proposed major project to resume the mining of ilmenite (titanium ore) in south-eastern Madagascar, which would generate US $550m. over a 30-year period but which had prompted considerable controversy on environmental grounds, received approval from the Government in 2001, pending the completion of further studies. Other potential mineral projects included the exploitation of an estimated 100m. metric tons of bauxite in the south-east of the country, and of nickel and cobalt deposits in central Madagascar. Following exploratory drilling for petroleum at three offshore areas in the early 1990s, it was announced that only non-commercial deposits of oil and gas had been discovered, although contracts for further exploration were granted in 1997 and 1999. The mining of sapphires commenced in southern Madagascar in 1998, but in March 1999 the Government ordered the suspension of sapphire mining pending the results of studies into the effects of exploitation on the environment; however, unauthorized mining continued on a wide scale.

Manufacturing contributed 10.9% of GDP in 2002. The petroleum refinery at Toamasina, using imported petroleum, provides a significant share of export revenue. Other important branches of manufacturing are textiles and clothing, food products, beverages and chemical products. The introduction of a new investment code in 1990 and the creation of a number of export processing zones achieved some success in attracting foreign private investment, particularly in the manufacturing branches of textiles, cement, fertilizers and pharmaceuticals.

According to the World Bank, manufacturing GDP remained constant in 1990–2002; the GDP of the sector increased by 10.7% in 2001, but decreased by 25.1% in 2002.

Energy generation depends on imports of crude petroleum (which accounted for 29.7% of the value of total imports in 2002) to fuel thermal installations, although hydroelectric resources have also been developed, and accounted for an estimated 67.6% of electricity production in 2001. In 2004 the Government was in the process of privatizing the national electricity and water utility, Jiro sy rano Malagasy (JIRAMA).

The services sector accounted for 54.2% of GDP in 2002, and engaged some 10.9% of the labour force in 1993. According to the World Bank, the GDP of the services sector increased by an average of 1.3% per year in 1990–2002; services GDP increased by 6.1% in 2001, but declined by 11.1% in 2002.

In 2002 Madagascar recorded a visible trade deficit of US $117m., and there was a deficit of $298m. on the current account of the balance of payments. The principal source of imports in 2001 was France (21.5%); other major suppliers were the People's Republic of China and South Africa. France was also the principal market for exports (accounting for 29.7% of exports in that year); the USA was also an important purchaser. The principal exports in 2002 were vanilla, crustaceans and cloves. The principal imports in that year included petroleum, raw materials and spare parts, consumer goods, equipment goods and food.

Madagascar's overall budget deficit for 2002 was estimated at 1,863,100m. francs MG (equivalent to 6.2% of GDP). Madagascar's external debt totalled US $4,160m. at the end of 2001, of which $3,793m. was long-term public debt. In the same year the cost of debt-servicing was estimated to be equivalent to 43.3% of the value of exports of goods and services. The annual rate of inflation averaged 15.7% in 1990–2001; consumer prices increased by 6.9% in 2001 and by 15.9% in 2002. About 6% of the labour force was estimated to be unemployed in 1995.

Madagascar is a member of the Indian Ocean Commission (see p. 360) and of the Common Market for Eastern and Southern Africa (COMESA, see p. 171). An application was made to join the Southern African Development Community (SADC, p. 331) in 2003.

Madagascar's dominant agricultural sector is vulnerable to adverse climatic conditions, including cyclones, and to fluctuations in the market prices of the country's principal exports. In December 2000 the IMF and the World Bank agreed to support a comprehensive debt reduction package under the enhanced initiative for heavily indebted poor countries (HIPCs). The IMF approved a loan, of US $103m., in March 2001 under the Poverty Reduction and Growth Facility (PRGF). Also in March Madagascar was declared eligible to benefit from the USA's African Growth and Opportunity Act, allowing duty free access to the US market, and both exports to the USA and foreign investment in Madagascar increased dramatically as a result. In December the IMF reported that economic performance had been favourable in 2001, but expressed concern at the persistently high level of poverty in the country. Economic activity was paralysed from the beginning of 2002—amid political uncertainty caused by the disputed presidential election (see Recent History)—by the strikes called by Marc Ravalomanana and the blockades ordered by Didier Ratsiraka. In February the World Bank estimated that the strike was costing Madagascar up to $14m. per day (the entire annual savings from debt-relief) and that 50,000 jobs were threatened. The closure of the central bank from the end of January also resulted in the freezing of the nation's assets, rendering Madagascar unable to service its debts and at risk of default; real GDP for the year declined by 11.9%. Companies in the export processing zone (specializing in textiles for export) and in the agricultural sector were severely affected by the political crisis, being highly dependent on foreign purchasers and the transportation network; tourism also was drastically curtailed. In July international donors pledged some $2,300m. (one-half of which was to be supplied by the Bretton Woods institutions) over a period of four years towards the reconstruction and development of the country; this subsequently enabled the authorities to repay the arrears on all external payments. From August the foreign-exchange markets reopened and the currency remained broadly stable after an initial decline. In October the IMF fully disbursed a structural adjustment credit of $100m., and in November it approved an Emergency Economic Recovery Credit and other loans aimed at public-sector management and private-sector development; in December the Fund granted $15m. under the PRGF and extended the arrangement until November 2004, in addition to allotting $4m. in interim assistance under the HIPC initiative. The economy recovered well in 2003, with growth estimated at some 9.6% and slower inflation, and a Poverty Reduction Strategy Paper was adopted in July. However, the country suffered from a particularly severe cyclone in March 2004, which adversely affected infrastructure of the aquaculture, rice and vanilla sectors, undermining the GDP growth rate of 6% and inflation rate of 5% forecast for that year. In response, the IMF immediately released $35m. in funds and extended the PRGF further, to March 2005. Meanwhile, Madagascar's new currency, the ariary (which had been introduced in July 2003 to replace the franc MG), depreciated considerably in early 2004, prompting significant increases in food and fuel prices, but optimism with regard to potential foreign investment.

Education

Six years' education, to be undertaken usually between six and 13 years of age, is officially compulsory. Madagascar has both public and private schools, although legislation that was enacted in 1978 envisaged the progressive elimination of private education. Primary education generally begins at the age of six and lasts for five years. Secondary education, beginning at 11 years of age, lasts for a further seven years, comprising a first cycle of four years and a second of three years. In 2000/01 primary enrolment included 68% of children in the relevant age-group (males 67%; females 68%), while, according to UNESCO estimates, in 1998/99 secondary enrolment included 11% of children in the relevant age-group (males 11%; females 12%). In 1998/99 31,013 students attended institutions providing tertiary education. In 1999 the OPEC Fund granted a loan worth US $10m. to support a government programme to improve literacy standards and to increase access to education. In 2001 the Arab Bank for Economic Development in Africa granted a loan of $8m. to finance a project in support of general education. The budget for 2001 allocated 736,600m. francs MG (14.0% of total expenditure) to education.

Public Holidays

2004: 1 January (New Year), 29 March (Martyr's Day, Commemoration of 1947 Rebellion), 12 April (Easter Monday), 1 May (Labour Day), 20 May (Ascension Day), 25 May (Organization of African Unity Day), 30 May (Whitsun), 26 June (Independence Day), 15 August (Assumption), 1 November (All Saints' Day), 25 December (Christmas), 30 December (Anniversary of the Democratic Republic of Madagascar).

2005: 1 January (New Year), 28 March (Easter Monday), 29 March (Martyr's Day, Commemoration of 1947 Rebellion), 1 May (Labour Day), 5 May (Ascension Day), 15 May (Whitsun), 25 May (Organization of African Unity Day), 26 June (Independence Day), 15 August (Assumption), 1 November (All Saints' Day), 25 December (Christmas), 30 December (Anniversary of the Democratic Republic of Madagascar).

Weights and Measures

The metric system is in force.

Statistical Survey

Source (unless otherwise stated): Institut National de la Statistique de Madagascar, BP 485, Anosy Tana, 101 Antananarivo; e-mail dginstat@dts.mg; internet rova.cite.mg/instat; tel. (20) 2227418.

Area and Population

AREA, POPULATION AND DENSITY

Area (sq km)	587,041*
Population (census results)	
1974–75†	7,603,790
1–19 August 1993	
Males	5,991,171
Females.	6,100,986
Total	12,092,157
Population (official estimates at mid-year)‡	
1999	14,650,000
2000	15,085,000
2001	15,529,000
Density (per sq km) at mid-2001	26.5

* 226,658 sq miles.

† The census took place in three stages: in provincial capitals on 1 December 1974; in Antananarivo and remaining urban areas on 17 February 1975; and in rural areas on 1 June 1975.

‡ Source: IMF, *Madagascar: Selected Issues and Statistical Appendix* (January 2003).

PRINCIPAL ETHNIC GROUPS
(estimated population, 1974)

Merina (Hova)	. .	1,993,000	Sakalava	470,156*
Betsimisaraka	. .	1,134,000	Antandroy . . .	412,500
Betsileo		920,600	Antaisaka. . . .	406,468*
Tsimihety. . . .		558,100		

* 1972 figure.

PRINCIPAL TOWNS
(population at 1993 census)

Antananarivo (capital). . .	1,103,304	Mahajanga (Majunga) . . .	106,780
Toamasina (Tamatave). . .	137,782	Toliary (Tuléar) . . .	80,826
Antsirabé	126,062	Antsiranana (Diégo-	
Fianarantsoa. . .	109,248	Suarez)	59,040

2001 (estimated population, incl. Renivohitra and Avaradrano): Antananarivo 1,111,392.

BIRTHS AND DEATHS

	1999	2000	2001
Birth rate (per 1,000)	43.0	42.5	42.0
Death rate (per 1,000)	14.1	13.8	13.5

Source: African Development Bank.

Expectation of life (WHO estimates, years at birth): 56.3 (males 54.4; females 58.4) in 2002 (Source: WHO, *World Health Report*).

ECONOMICALLY ACTIVE POPULATION
('000 persons)

	1991	1992	1993
Agriculture	4,926	5,057	5,100
Manufacturing and mining . . .	82	84	86
Construction	44	45	46
Trade, banking and insurance . .	141	145	149
Transport and telecommunications	40	41	42
Administration	180	193	208
Other activities*	240	246	243
Total labour force	5,653	5,811	5,874

* Including artisans and domestic servants.

Labour force ('000 persons): 6,165 in 1994; 6,350 in 1995; 6,540 in 1996; 6,737 in 1997.

Source: IMF, *Madagascar: Recent Economic Developments and Selected Issues* (August 2000).

1993 census (persons aged 10 years and over): Total labour force 5,299,563 (males 3,181,509; females 2,118,054) (Source: ILO, *Yearbook of Labour Statistics*).

Mid-2002 (estimates in '000): Agriculture, etc. 5,941; Total labour force 8,097 (Source: FAO).

Health and Welfare

KEY INDICATORS

Total fertility rate (children per woman, 2002).	5.7
Under-5 mortality rate (per 1,000 live births, 2001) . . .	136
HIV/AIDS (% of persons aged 15–49, 2001).	0.29
Physicians (per 1,000 head, 1996)	10.7
Hospital beds (per 1,000 head, 1999)	0.5
Health expenditure (2001): US $ per head (PPP)	20
Health expenditure (2001): % of GDP	2.0
Health expenditure (2001): public (% of total)	65.9
Access to water (% of persons, 2000).	47
Access to sanitation (% of persons, 2000)	42
Human Development Index (2001): ranking	149
Human Development Index (2001): value	0.468

For sources and definitions, see explanatory note on p. vi.

Agriculture

PRINCIPAL CROPS
('000 metric tons)

	1999	2000	2001
Rice (paddy)	2,570	2,480	2,662
Maize	175	170	180
Potatoes	291	287	295
Sweet potatoes	520	513	525
Cassava (Manioc)	2,461	2,463	2,510
Taro (Coco yam)†	160	190	200
Sugar cane	2,180	2,189	2,208
Dry beans	82*	74	75
Other pulses†	18	20	19
Groundnuts (in shell) . . .	34	35	35
Coconuts†	85	84	85
Oil palm fruit†	22	21	21
Cottonseed	20*	16†	17†
Tomatoes†	23	22	22
Other vegetables†	333	322	322
Bananas†	265	290	290
Oranges†	85	83	83
Mangoes†	206	210	210
Avocados†	24	23	23
Pineapples†	52	51	51
Cashewapple†	69	68	68
Other fruits†	167	166	166
Coffee (green).	65	58	64
Vanilla	2	1	2
Cinnamon (Canella)†	2	2	2
Cloves	15	16*	16†
Cotton (lint)*	14	11	11
Sisal	17	17	17
Tobacco (leaves)	2	2	1

* Unofficial figure(s).
† FAO estimate(s).

Source: FAO.

LIVESTOCK
('000 head, year ending September)

	2000	2001	2002*
Cattle	10,364	10,500*	10,500
Pigs*	1,450	1,600	1,600
Sheep	584	633	650
Goats	1,033	1,180	1,200
Chickens	21,540	24,050	24,000
Ducks*	3,900	3,800	3,800
Geese*	3,100	3,000	3,000
Turkeys*	2,000	1,900	2,000

* FAO estimate(s).

Source: FAO.

LIVESTOCK PRODUCTS
(FAO estimates, '000 metric tons)

	2000	2001	2002
Cows' milk	535	535	535
Beef and veal	148	147	147
Pig meat	63	70	70
Poultry meat	64	67	67
Hen eggs	15	15	15
Honey	4	4	4
Cattle hides	21	21	21

Source: FAO.

Forestry

ROUNDWOOD REMOVALS
('000 cubic metres, excl. bark)

	2000	2001	2002
Sawlogs, veneer logs and logs for sleepers	70	70*	74
Pulpwood	23	23	23
Fuel wood*	9,637	9,919	10,202
Total	9,730	10,012	10,299

* FAO estimate(s).

Source: FAO.

SAWNWOOD PRODUCTION
('000 cubic metres, incl. railway sleepers)

	2000	2001	2002
Coniferous (softwood)	4	4*	4*
Broadleaved (hardwood)	481	396	91
Total	485	400	95

* FAO estimate.

Source: FAO.

Fishing

('000 metric tons, live weight)

	1999	2000	2001
Capture	129.6	132.1	135.6
Cyprinids	4.0	4.0	4.0
Cichlids	21.5	21.5	21.5
Other freshwater fishes	4.5	4.5	4.5
Narrow-barred Spanish mackerel	12.0	12.0	12.0
Other marine fishes	74.4	75.1	78.6
Shrimps and prawns	10.5	12.1	11.8
Aquaculture	5.8*	7.3*	7.7
Brine shrimp	3.5	4.8	5.4
Total catch	135.4*	139.4	143.3

Note: Figures exclude aquatic plants ('000 metric tons, capture only): 1.9 in 1999; 5.8 in 2000; 5.0 in 2001. Also excluded are crocodiles, recorded by number rather than weight, and shells. The number of Nile crocodiles caught was: 4,302 in 1999; 6,606 in 2000; 9,408 in 2001. The catch of marine shells (in metric tons) was: 8 in 1999; 74 in 2000; 32 in 2001.
* FAO estimate.

Source: FAO, *Yearbook of Fishery Statistics*.

Mining

(metric tons)

	1999	2000	2001
Chromite*	144	131,293	23,637
Salt	26,131	25,530	25,928
Graphite (natural)	16,137	40,328	2,013
Mica	54	66	90

* Figures refer to gross weight. The estimated chromium content is 27%.

Industry

SELECTED PRODUCTS
(metric tons, unless otherwise indicated)

	1999	2000	2001
Raw sugar	61,370	62,487	67,917
Beer ('000 hectolitres)	610.1	645.5	691.7
Cigarettes	3,839	4,139	4,441
Woven cotton fabrics (million metres)	20.4	23.3	29.6
Leather footwear ('000 pairs)	460	570	n.a.
Plastic footwear ('000 pairs)	375	303	291
Paints	1,918	1,487	1,554
Soap	15,884	15,385	15,915
Motor spirit—petrol ('000 cu metres)	98.0	122.6	128.3
Kerosene ('000 cu metres)	65.0	65.2	75.1
Gas-diesel (distillate fuel) oil ('000 cu metres)	119.0	150.4	150.2
Residual fuel oils ('000 cu metres)	198.8	225.7	247.2
Cement	45,701	50,938	51,882
Electric energy (million kWh)*	721.3	779.8	833.9

* Production by the state-owned utility only, excluding electricity generated by industries for their own use.

Finance

CURRENCY AND EXCHANGE RATES

Monetary Units

5 iraimbilanja = 1 ariary.

Sterling, Dollar and Euro Equivalents (31 December 2003)

£1 sterling = 10,746.2 francs MG;
US $1 = 6,021.3 francs MG;
€1 = 7,604.9 francs MG;
100,000 francs MG = £9.305 = $16.607 = €13.149.

Average Exchange Rate (Malagasy francs per US $)

2001	6,588.5
2002	6,832.0
2003	6,210.0

Note: A new currency, the ariary, was introduced on 31 July 2003 to replace the franc malgache (franc MG). The old currency was to remain legal tender until 30 November. Some figures in this survey are still given in terms of francs MG.

GENERAL BUDGET
('000 million francs MG)*

Revenue†	1999	2000	2001
Budgetary revenue	2,667	3,068	3,029
Tax revenue	2,580	2,972	2,906
Taxes on income, profits and capital gains	398	467	595
Corporate	207	236	301
Individual	190	231	293
Domestic taxes on goods and services	661	865	804
General sales, turnover or value-added tax	389	513	536
Excises	128	160	110
Fiscal monopoly profits	111	179	146
Taxes on international trade and transactions	1,481	1,591	1,452
Import duties	1,481	1,591	1,452
Other revenue	87	96	123
Non-budgetary revenue	—	—	—
Total	2,667	3,068	3,029

Expenditure‡	1999	2000	2001
Current expenditure	2,175.0	2,402.6	3,081.7
General services	695.0	880.0	1,067.5
Defence	382.8	319.7	428.4
Education	392.0	555.5	736.6
Health	150.3	182.6	265.4
Social and community services	34.1	46.3	48.0
Economic services	143.2	160.9	163.2
Agriculture	55.9	83.2	72.4
Public works	41.7	18.8	25.3
Other purposes	760.4	577.3	801.0
Interest on government debt	492.8	612.3	591.9
Operations financed by counterpart funds	n.a.	2.0	1.4
Capital expenditure	1,615.9	1,766.1	2,180.9
Total	3,790.9	4,168.7	5,262.6

* Figures exclude the net cost of structural reforms ('000 million francs MG): 369.7 in 1999; 582.7 in 2000; 223.1 in 2001.
† Excluding grants received ('000 million francs MG): 842.5 in 1999; 946.7 in 2000; 1,161.6 in 2001. Also excluded is divestment revenue ('000 million francs MG): 51.8 in 1999; 46.3 in 2000; 104.1 in 2001.
‡ Excluding adjustment for changes in payment arrears.

Source: IMF, *Madagascar: Selected Issues and Statistical Appendix* (January 2003).

INTERNATIONAL RESERVES
(US $ million at 31 December)

	2000	2001	2002
IMF special drawing rights	0.0	0.1	0.0
Foreign exchange	285.1	398.2	363.2
Total	285.2	398.4	363.2

Source: IMF, *International Financial Statistics.*

MONEY SUPPLY
('000 million francs MG at 31 December)

	2000	2001	2002
Currency outside banks	1,789.1	2,159.6	2,330.1
Demand deposits at deposit money banks	2,228.9	3,074.1	3,297.8
Total money	4,018.0	5,233.7	5,627.9

Source: IMF, *International Financial Statistics.*

COST OF LIVING
(Consumer Price Index for Madagascans in Antananarivo; base: 1992 = 100)

	1999	2000	2001
Food	428.4	489.4	120.5
All items*	414.0	463.1	200.7

* Excluding rent.
Source: UN, *Monthly Bulletin of Statistics.*

NATIONAL ACCOUNTS
('000 million francs MG at current prices)

Expenditure on the Gross Domestic Product

	2000	2001	2002
Government final consumption expenditure	2,063.8	2,639.0	2,585.0
Private final consumption expenditure	22,483.0	24,001.0	25,387.0
Increase in stocks / Gross fixed capital formation	4,250.0	5,340.0	4,839.0
Total domestic expenditure	28,796.8	31,980.0	32,811.0
Exports of goods and services	7,984.0	8,627.0	4,871.0
Less Imports of goods and services	10,539.0	10,764.0	7,624.0
GDP in purchasers' values	26,242.0	29,843.0	30,058.0
GDP at constant 1984 prices	2,331.0	2,471.0	2,157.0

Source: IMF, *International Financial Statistics.*

Gross Domestic Product by Economic Activity

	1998	1999	2000
Agriculture, hunting, forestry and fishing	5,719.4	6,366.1	6,858
Mining and quarrying			
Manufacturing	2,549.3	2,916.7	3,412
Electricity, gas and water			
Construction	296.4	355.0	396
Trade, restaurants and hotels	2,386.3	2,624.2	2,927
Transport, storage and communications	3,654.5	4,034.7	4,501
Government services	1,051.4	1,266.0	1,412
Other services	3,285.7	3,948.5	4,404
Sub-total	18,943.1	21,511.2	23,912
Less imputed bank charges	237.6	308.6	329
GDP at factor cost	18,705.5	21,202.6	23,583
Indirect taxes, *less* subsidies	1,637.9	2,176.5	2,659
GDP in purchasers' values	20,343.4	23,379.1	26,242

Source: IMF, *Madagascar: Selected Issues and Statistical Appendix* (December 2001).

2001: Primary sector 7,679; Secondary sector 4,015; Tertiary sector 16,070; Sub-total 27,764; *Less* imputed bank charges 233; GDP at factor cost 27,531; Indirect taxes, *less* subsidies 2,312; GDP in purchasers' values 29,843.

2002: Primary sector 8,963; Secondary sector 4,078; Tertiary sector 15,421; Sub-total 28,462; *Less* imputed bank charges 196; GDP at factor cost 28,265; Indirect taxes, *less* subsidies 1,777; GDP in purchasers' values 30,042.

BALANCE OF PAYMENTS
(US $ million)

	2000	2001	2002
Exports of goods f.o.b.	823.7	928	486
Imports of goods f.o.b.	−997.5	−955	−603
Trade balance	−173.7	−27	−117
Exports of services	364.1	351	224
Imports of services	−522.1	−511	−398
Balance on goods and services	−331.7	−187	−291
Other income received	22.4	24	26
Other income paid	−64.1	−106	−101
Balance on goods, services and income	−373.4	−270	−366
Current transfers received	121.9	114	88
Current transfers paid	−31.3	−15	−21
Current balance	−282.8	−170	−298
Capital account (net)	115.0	113	58
Direct investment from abroad	83.0	93	8
Other investment assets	−87.3	−128	42
Other investment liabilities	−26.3	−103	−104
Net errors and omissions	38.6	−57	11
Overall balance	−160.0	−253	−283

Source: IMF, *International Financial Statistics.*

External Trade

PRINCIPAL COMMODITIES
(US $ million)

Imports c.i.f.	1997	1998	1999
Food and live animals	56.4	62.3	58.3
Cereals and cereal preparations	35.7	39.0	40.7
Rice	16.8	16.3	23.7
Mineral fuels, lubricants and related materials	120.9	104.1	122.2
Petroleum, petroleum products and related materials	119.6	103.2	122.0
Crude petroleum and oils obtained from bituminous materials	78.2	51.1	69.6
Petroleum products, refined	38.9	50.4	50.7
Gas oils	26.3	31.1	32.4
Chemicals and related products	72.7	66.0	56.8
Medicinal and pharmaceutical products	23.8	18.7	17.7
Basic manufactures	90.9	100.8	76.4
Machinery and transport equipment	146.9	144.3	135.6
General industrial machinery and equipment	16.9	18.1	17.2
Electric machinery, apparatus and appliances	20.9	19.4	21.1
Road vehicles	55.3	55.0	45.6
Miscellaneous manufactures	41.3	43.8	37.0
Total (incl. others)	573.1	556.8	505.3

2001 (US $ million): Food 65.7; Energy (petroleum) 131.8; Equipment goods 128.7; Raw materials and spare parts 103.1; Consumer goods 103.9; Other imports (including EPZ) 344.8; *Total* 878.0.

2002 (US $ million): Food 46.2; Energy (petroleum) 162.8; Equipment goods 68.8; Raw materials and spare parts 75.6; Consumer goods 70.0; Other imports (including EPZ) 124.2; *Total* 547.6.

Exports f.o.b.	1997	1998	1999
Food and live animals	150.4	98.3	83.3
Fish, crustaceans and molluscs and preparations thereof	69.0	20.6	10.2
Vegetables and fruit	17.3	16.3	16.9
Fruit, preserved	7.9	7.9	10.2
Coffee, tea, cocoa, spices	59.3	59.9	51.2
Coffee, unroasted, husks and skins	32.8	40.3	16.6
Spices	25.2	17.9	33.0
Vanilla	9.6	7.1	12.1
Cloves	12.2	9.2	17.9
Crude materials, inedible, except fuels	36.0	32.3	23.1
Basic manufactures	63.1	51.9	87.5
Textile yarn, fabrics, made-up articles and related products	50.8	43.4	68.3
Textile yarn	6.0	5.5	18.3
Yarn of wool or animal hair	1.5	0.9	12.1
Cotton fabrics, woven	17.5	33.1	31.2
Fabrics, woven, of silk, noil or other waste silk	20.3	0.0	9.4
Precious and semi-precious stones, not mounted, set or strung	8.0	4.9	15.2
Miscellaneous manufactures	6.4	9.1	19.6
Total (incl. others)	277.8	234.6	232.8

Source: UN, *International Trade Statistics Yearbook*.

2002 (US $ million): Crustaceans 67.8; Coffee 2.2; Cloves 22.8; Vanilla 90.2; Cotton fabrics 5.3; Total (incl. others) 375.0.

PRINCIPAL TRADING PARTNERS
(US $ million)

Imports	1997	1998	1999
Belgium-Luxembourg	12.0	7.3	—
China, People's Repub.	25.3	24.1	33.8
France	131.7	121.6	104.7
Germany	24.9	36.3	23.5
India	10.1	10.9	10.4
Iran	50.6	44.6	62.9
Italy	14.1	11.2	8.2
Japan	34.8	29.9	25.8
Malaysia	5.8	5.9	7.1
Netherlands	6.9	5.6	4.9
Pakistan	11.6	9.1	10.5
Romania	0.9	7.4	—
Singapore	7.2	3.5	7.0
SACU*	55.3	33.8	25.8
United Kingdom	13.3	12.7	8.8
USA	25.6	19.8	15.0
Total (incl. others)	573.1	556.8	505.3

* Southern African Customs Union, comprising Botswana, Lesotho, Namibia, South Africa and Swaziland.

2001: France 21.5%; People's Republic of China 9.1%; South Africa 5.5%; Japan 4.4%; USA 4.2%; Mauritius 2.9% (Source: IMF, *Madagascar: Selected Issues and Statistical Appendix*, January 2003).

Exports	1997	1998	1999
Belgium-Luxembourg	8.5	6.1	—
France	125.6	101.6	88.1
Germany	13.5	10.6	14.9
Italy	8.2	8.6	11.5
Japan	25.0	4.6	3.3
Mauritius	10.9	16.1	9.4
Netherlands	2.9	1.5	1.6
Portugal	0.9	3.0	1.5
Singapore	8.4	6.4	17.4
Spain	6.4	3.4	2.9
United Kingdom	8.9	6.6	5.2
USA	10.5	14.1	12.6
Total (incl. others)	277.8	234.6	232.8

Source: UN, *International Trade Statistics Yearbook*.

2001: France 29.7%; USA 13.9%; Mauritius 2.6% (Source: IMF, *Madagascar: Selected Issues and Statistical Appendix*, January 2003).

Transport

RAILWAYS
(traffic)

	1997	1998	1999
Passengers carried ('000)	359	293	273
Passenger-km (millions)	37	35	31
Freight carried ('000 metric tons)	227	213	141
Ton-km (millions)	81	71	46

Source: Réseau National des Chemins de Fer Malagasy.

ROAD TRAFFIC
(vehicles in use)

	1994	1995	1996*
Passenger cars	54,821	58,097	60,480
Buses and coaches	3,797	4,332	4,850
Lorries and vans	35,931	37,232	37,972
Road tractors	488	560	619

* Estimates.

Source: IRF, *World Road Statistics*.

SHIPPING

Merchant Fleet
(registered at 31 December)

	2000	2001	2002
Number of vessels	105	104	103
Displacement ('000 gross registered tons)	43.7	43.4	34.8

Source: Lloyd's Register-Fairplay, *World Fleet Statistics.*

International Sea-borne Freight Traffic
('000 metric tons)

	1987	1988	1989
Goods loaded:			
Mahajanga	17	18	29.4
Toamasina	252	350	360.6
other ports	79	100	137.4
Total	348	468	527.4
Goods unloaded:			
Mahajanga	37	32	30.8
Toamasina	748	778	708.9
other ports	48	53	52.0
Total	833	863	791.7

1990 ('000 metric tons): Goods loaded 540; Goods unloaded 984 (Source: UN, *Monthly Bulletin of Statistics*).

CIVIL AVIATION
(traffic on scheduled services)

	1996	1997	1998
Kilometres flown (million) . . .	8	9	9
Passengers carried ('000) . .	542	575	318
Passenger-km (million)	659	758	718
Total ton-km (million)	85	98	94

Source: UN, *Statistical Yearbook.*

Tourism

TOURIST ARRIVALS BY NATIONALITY

	1999	2000	2001
Canada and USA.	6,913	6,402	6,808
France	74,657	88,039	95,316
Germany	5,530	6,403	6,808
Italy	8,295	8,004	8,510
Japan	2,489	2,055	3,404
Mauritius	3,871	4,526	8,510
Réunion	11,060	14,406	17,021
Switzerland	2,765	3,201	3,404
United Kingdom	4,148	4,802	5,106
Total (incl. others)	138,253	160,071	170,208

Tourism receipts (US $ million): 91 in 1998; 100 in 1999; 116 in 2000.

Source: World Tourism Organization, mainly *Yearbook of Tourism Statistics.*

Communications Media

	1999	2000	2001
Television receivers ('000 in use) .	360	375	n.a.
Telephones ('000 main lines in use)	50.2	56.7	58.4
Mobile cellular telephones ('000 subscribers).	35.8	63.1	147.5
Personal computers ('000 in use) .	30	n.a.	40
Internet users ('000)	25	30	35

Source: International Telecommunication Union.

1995: Radio receivers ('000 in use) 2,850; Book production (incl. pamphlets): titles 131, copies ('000) 292; Daily newspapers: number 6, circulation ('000 copies) 59 (Source: UNESCO, *Statistical Yearbook*).

1996: Radio receivers ('000 in use) 2,950; Book production (incl. pamphlets): titles 119, copies ('000) 296; Daily newspapers: number 5, circulation ('000 copies) 66 (Source: UNESCO, *Statistical Yearbook*).

1997: Radio receivers ('000 in use) 3,050 (Source: UNESCO, *Statistical Yearbook*).

Education

(1998, unless otherwise indicated)

	Institu-tions	Tea-chers	Pupils		
			Males	Females	Total
Pre-primary* . . .	n.a.	n.a.	28,657	29,186	57,843
Primary	14,438	42,678	1,024,286	988,130	2,012,416
Secondary: general .	n.a.	18,987†	168,634	165,616	334,250
Secondary: teacher training‡ . . .	n.a.	58	199	142	341
Secondary: vocational§ . . .	n.a.	1,092	5,708	2,430	8,138
Tertiary	6	1,471	16,826	14,187	31,013

* 1994/95 figures.
† UNESCO estimate.
‡ 1993/94 figures.
§ 1995/96 figures, public education only.

Source: UNESCO, Institute for Statistics.

Adult literacy rate (UNESCO estimates): 67.3% (males 74.2%; females 60.6%) in 2001 (Source: UN Development Programme, *Human Development Report*).

Directory

The Constitution

The Constitution of the Third Republic of Madagascar was endorsed by national referendum on 19 August 1992, but was substantially altered by amendments that were endorsed in a national referendum on 15 March 1998. The amended Constitution enshrines a 'federal-style' state, composed of six autonomous provinces—each with a governor and up to 12 general commissioners (holding executive power) and a provincial council (holding legislative power). It provides for a government delegate to each province, who is charged with supervising the division of functions between the state and the province. The bicameral legislature consists of the National Assembly (the lower house), which is elected by universal adult suffrage, under a mixed system of single-seat constituencies and a form of proportional representation, for a five-year term of office. The Constitution also provides for a Senate (the upper house), of which one-third of the members are presidential nominees and two-thirds are elected in equal numbers by the provincial councillors and mayors of each of the six autonomous provinces, for a term of six years. The constitutional Head of State is the President. If no candidate obtains an overall majority in the presidential election, a second round of voting is to take place a maximum of 30 days after the publication of the results of the first ballot. Any one candidate can be elected for a maximum of three five-year terms. The powers of the President were greatly increased by constitutional amendments of March 1998: he has the power to determine general state policy in the Council of Ministers, to call referendums on all matters of national importance, and to dissolve the National Assembly not less than one year after a general election. Executive power is vested in a Prime Minister, who is appointed by the President. The President appoints the Council of Ministers, on the recommendation of the Prime Minister.

The Government

HEAD OF STATE

President: MARC RAVALOMANANA (inaugurated 6 May 2002, following a disputed presidential election—see Recent History).

COUNCIL OF MINISTERS
(April 2004)

Prime Minister: JACQUES SYLLA.

Deputy Prime Minister in charge of Economic Programmes and Minister of Transport, Public Works and Regional Planning: ZAZA MANITRANJA RAMANDIMBIARISON.

Minister of the Economy, Finance and the Budget: BENJAMIN ANDRIAMPARANY RADAVIDSON.

Minister of Justice and Keeper of the Seals: LALA HENRIETTE RATSIHAROVALA.

Minister of Foreign Affairs: Gen. MARCEL RANJEVA.

Minister of the Interior and Administrative Reform: Gen. SOJA.

Minister of Defence: Maj.-Gen. PETERA BEHAJAINA.

Minister of National Education and Scientific Research: HAJA NIRINA RAZAFINJATOVO.

Minister of Health and Family Planning: ANDRY RASAMINDRAKOTROKA.

Minister of the Population, Social Protection and Leisure: ZAFILAZA.

Minister of Industry, Trade and the Development of the Private Sector: MEJAMIRADO RAZAFIMIHARY.

Minister of the Civil Service, Labour and Social Legislation: JEAN THÉODORE RANJIVASON.

Minister of the Environment, Water and Forests: Gen. CHARLES SYLVAIN RABOTOARISON.

Minister of Energy and Mining: JACQUES H. RABARISON.

Minister of Agriculture, Livestock and Fisheries: HARISON EDMOND RANDRIAIMANANA.

Minister of Telecommunications, Post and Communications: CLERMONT GERVAIS MAHAZAKA.

Minister of Youth and Sports: HENRI FRANÇOIS VICTOR RANDRIANJATOVO.

Minister of Culture and Tourism: JEAN-JACQUES RABENIRINA.

Secretary of State for Decentralization and Regional and Communal Development at the Ministry of the Interior and Administrative Reform: ENIAVASOA.

Secretary of State for Public Security at the Ministry of the Interior and Administrative Reform: LUCIEN VICTOR RAZAKANIRINA.

MINISTRIES

Office of the Prime Minister: BP 248, Mahazoarivo, 101 Antananarivo; tel. (20) 2225258; fax (20) 2235258.

Ministry of Agriculture, Livestock and Fisheries: BP 301, Ampandrianomby, 101 Antananarivo; tel. (20) 2227227; fax (20) 2226561.

Ministry of the Civil Service, Labour and Social Legislation: BP 270, Cité des 67 Hectares, Tsaralalana, 101 Antananarivo; tel. (20) 2223082; fax (20) 2233856.

Ministry of Culture and Tourism: BP 305, Antaninarenina, 101 Antananarivo; tel. (20) 2227477; fax (20) 2229848.

Ministry of Defence: BP 08, Ampahibe, 101 Antananarivo; tel. (20) 2222211; fax (20) 2235420; e-mail mdn@wanadoo.mg.

Ministry of the Economy, Finance and the Budget: BP 61, Antaninarenina, 101 Antananarivo; tel. (20) 2264681; fax (22) 2234530; e-mail cabmefb@dts.mg; internet www.mefb.gov.mg.

Ministry of Energy and Mining: BP 527, Immeuble de l'Industrie, Antaninarenina, 101 Antananarivo; tel. (20) 2228928; fax (20) 2232554; internet www.cite.mg/mine.

Ministry of the Environment, Water and Forests: rue Farafaty, BP 571 Ampandrianomby, 101 Antananarivo; tel. (20) 2240908; fax (20) 2241919.

Ministry of Foreign Affairs: BP 836, Anosy, 101 Antananarivo; tel. (20) 2221198; fax (20) 2234484.

Ministry of Health and Family Planning: BP 88, Ambohidahy, 101 Antananarivo; tel. (20) 2263121; fax (20) 2264228; e-mail cabminsan@dts.mg.

Ministry of Industry, Trade and the Development of the Private Sector: BP 527, Immeuble de l'Industrie, Antaninarenina, 101 Antananarivo; tel. (20) 2232251; fax (20) 2228024; e-mail celenv-mind@dts.mg; internet www.industrie.gov.mg.

Ministry of the Interior and Administrative Reform: BP 833, Anosy, 101 Antananarivo; tel. (20) 2223084; fax (20) 2235579.

Ministry of Justice: rue Joel Rakotomalala, BP 231, Faravohitra, 101 Antananarivo; tel. (20) 2237684; fax (20) 2264458; e-mail minjust.roger@simicro.mg; internet www.justice.gov.mg.

Ministry of National Education and Scientific Research: BP 4163, Tsimbazaza, 101 Antananarivo; tel. (20) 2229423; fax (20) 2234508; internet www.refer.mg/edu/minesup.

Ministry of the Population, Social Protection and Leisure: BP 723, Ambohijatovo, 101 Antananarivo; tel. (20) 2227691; fax (20) 2264823; internet www.madapopulation.net.

Ministry of Telecommunications, Post and Communications: Antaninarenina, 101 Antananarivo; tel. (20) 2223267; fax (20) 2235894.

Ministry of Transport, Public Works and Regional Planning: BP 4139, 101 Antananarivo; tel. (20) 2223215; fax (20) 2220890; e-mail viceprimature@mttpat.gov.mg.

Ministry of Youth and Sports: Ambohijatovo, Place Goulette, BP 681, 101 Antananarivo; tel. (20) 2227780; fax (20) 2234275.

Secretariat for Decentralization and Regional and Communal Development: BP 24 bis, 101 Antananarivo; tel. (20) 2235881; fax (20) 2237516.

Secretariat for Public Security: BP 23 bis, 101 Antananarivo; tel. (20) 2221029; fax (20) 2231861.

President and Legislature

PRESIDENT

Presidential Election, 16 December 2001

Candidate	% of votes
Marc Ravalomanana	51.46
Adm. (retd) Didier Ratsiraka	35.90
Others	12.64
Total	100.00

LEGISLATURE

Senate

President: GUY RAJEMISON RAKOTOMAHARO.

Senatorial Election, 18 March 2001

Party	Seats
AREMA	49
LEADER/Fanilo	5
Independents	3
AVI	2
AFFA	1
Total	60*

*Elected by a 1,727-member electoral college of provincial councillors and mayors. An additional 30 seats were appointed by the President.

National Assembly

President: JEAN LAHARINIKO.

General Election, 15 December 2002

Party	Seats
TIM	104
FP	22
AVI	20
RPSD	2
RPSD	5
AREMA	3
MFM	2
LEADER/Fanilo	1
Independents	23
Total	**160**

Political Organizations

Following the restoration of multi-party politics in March 1990, more than 120 political associations emerged, of which six secured representation in the National Assembly in 2002. The following were among the more influential political organizations in early 2004:

Association pour la renaissance de Madagascar (Andry sy riana enti-manavotra an'i Madigasikara) (AREMA): f. 1975 as Avant-garde de la révolution malgache; adopted present name 1997; party of former Pres. RATSIRAKA (now in exile); control disputed between two factions, headed by Gen. Sec. PIERROT RAJAONARIVELO (in exile), and Asst. Gen. Sec. PIERRE RAHARIJAONA.

Comité pour la Réconciliation Nationale (CRN): Antananarivo; f. 2002; opposition; Chair. ALBERT ZAFY.

Firaisankinam-Pirenena (FP—Front Patriotique): f. 2002 as an alliance, consisting of AVI and mems of RPSD, to co-operate with TIM in the legislative elections of 2002.

Herim-Bahoaka Mitambatra (HBM) (Union of Popular Forces): formed part of the coalition supporting Pres. Ravalomanana prior to the presidential election; Leader TOVONANAHARY RABERSITONTA.

LEADER/Fanilo (Torch): f. 1993 as a party of 'non-politicians'; Leader Prof. MANASSE ESOAVELOMANDROSO.

Mouvement pour le progrès de Madagascar (Mpitolona ho amin'ny fandrosoan'ny Madagasikara) (MFM): 101 Antananarivo; f. 1972 as Mouvement pour le pouvoir prolétarien (MFM), adopted present name in 1990; advocates liberal and market-orientated policies; Leader MANANDAFY RAKOTONIRINA; Sec.-Gen. GERMAIN RAKOTONIRAINY.

Ny asa vita no ifampitsara (AVI—People are judged by the work they do): f. 1997 to promote human rights, hard work and development; Leader NORBERT RATSIRAHONANA.

Rassemblement pour le socialisme et la démocratie (RPSD): f. 1993 by fmr mems of PSD; also known as Renaissance du parti social-démocratique; Jean-Eugène Voninahitsy formed a breakaway party known as the RPSD Nouveau in 2003; Leader EVARISTE MARSON.

Tiako i Madagasikara (TIM—I Love Madagascar): internet www.tim-madagascar.org; f. 2002; supports Pres. Ravalomanana; Pres. RAZOHARIMIHAJA SOLOFONANTENAINA; Sec.-Gen. JACQUES SYLLA.

Toamasina Tonga Saina (TTS): pro-AREMA party.

Diplomatic Representation

EMBASSIES IN MADAGASCAR

China, People's Republic: Ancien Hôtel Panorama, BP 1658, 101 Antananarivo; tel. (20) 2240129; fax (20) 2240215; Ambassador XU JINGHU.

Egypt: LOT MD 378 Ambalatokana Mandrosoa Ivato, BP 4082, 101 Antananarivo; tel. (20) 2245497; fax (20) 2245379; Ambassador AZZAH ABD AL-FATAH NASSIR.

France: 3 rue Jean Jaurès, BP 204, 101 Antananarivo; tel. (20) 2239898; fax (20) 2239927; e-mail ambatana@dts.mg; Ambassador CATHERINE BOIVINEAU.

Germany: 101 rue du Pasteur Rabeony Hans, BP 516, Ambodirotra, 101 Antananarivo; tel. (20) 2223802; fax (20) 2226627; e-mail amballem@dts.mg; Ambassador Dr DIETER HUBERTUS ZEISLER.

Holy See: Amboniloha Ivandry, BP 650, 101 Antananarivo; tel. (20) 2242376; fax (20) 2242384; e-mail noncapmg@dts.mg; Apostolic Nuncio Most Rev. BRUNO MUSARÒ (Titular Archbishop of Abari).

India: 4 làlana Emile Rajaonson, Tsaralalana, BP 1787, 101 Antananarivo; tel. (20) 2223334; fax (20) 2233790; e-mail indembmd@bow.dts.mg; Ambassador SIBABRATA TRIPATHI.

Indonesia: 26–28 rue Patrice Lumumba, BP 3969, 101 Antananarivo; tel. (20) 2224915; fax (20) 2232857; Chargé d'affaires a.i. SLAMET SUYATA SASTRAMIHARDZA.

Iran: route Circulaire, Lot II L43 ter, 101 Antananarivo; tel. (20) 2228639; fax (20) 2222298; Ambassador (vacant).

Italy: 22 rue Pasteur Rabary, BP 16, Ankadivato, 101 Antananarivo; tel. (20) 2221217; fax (20) 2223814; e-mail ambanta@simicro.mg; Ambassador RENATO VOLPINI.

Japan: 8 rue du Dr Villette, BP 3863, Isoraka, 101 Antananarivo; tel. (20) 2226102; fax (20) 2221769; Ambassador OSAMU YOSHIHARA.

Korea, Democratic People's Republic: 101 Antananarivo; tel. (20) 2244442; Ambassador RI YONG HAK.

Libya: Lot IIB, 37A route Circulaire Ampandrana-Ouest, 101 Antananarivo; tel. (20) 2221892; Chargé d'affaires a.i. Dr MOHAMED ALI SHARFEDIN AL-FITURI.

Mauritius: Anjaharay, route Circulaire, BP 6040, Ambanidia 101, Antananarivo; tel. (20) 2221864; fax (20) 2221939; Ambassador GHISLAINE HENRY.

Russia: BP 4006, Ivandry-Ambohijatovo, 101 Antananarivo; tel. (20) 2242827; fax (20) 2242642; Ambassador YURII N. MERZLIAKOV.

South Africa: Antananarivo; Ambassador WALTER THEMBA THABETHE.

Switzerland: BP 118, 101 Antananarivo; tel. (20) 2262997; fax (20) 2228940; e-mail swiemant@wanadoo.mg; Chargé d'affaires a.i. ROSMARIE SCHELLING.

United Kingdom: Lot II I164 ter, Alarobia, Amboniloha, BP 167, 101 Antananarivo; tel. (20) 2249378; fax (20) 2249381; e-mail ukembant@simicro.mg; Ambassador BRIAN DONALDSON.

USA: 14–16 rue Rainitovo, Antsahavola, BP 620, 101 Antananarivo; tel. (20) 2221257; fax (20) 2234539; Ambassador WANDA L. NESBITT.

Judicial System

HIGH CONSTITUTIONAL COURT

Haute Cour Constitutionnelle: POB 835, Ambohidahy, 101 Antananarivo; tel. (20) 2266061; e-mail hcc@simicro.mg; internet www.simicro.mg/hcc; interprets the Constitution and rules on constitutional issues; nine mems; Pres. JEAN-MICHEL RAJAONARIVONY.

HIGH COURT OF JUSTICE

Haute Cour de Justice: 101 Antananarivo; nine mems.

SUPREME COURT

Cour Suprême: Palais de Justice, Anosy, 101 Antananarivo; Pres. ALICE RAJAONAH (acting); Attorney-General COLOMBE RAMANANTSOA (acting); Chamber Pres YOLANDE RAMANGASOAVINA, FRANÇOIS RAMANANDRAIBE.

COURT OF APPEAL

Cour d'Appel: Palais de Justice, Anosy, 101 Antananarivo; Pres. AIMÉE RAKOTONIRINA; Pres of Chamber CHARLES RABETOKOTANY, PÉTRONILLE ANDRIAMIHAJA, BAKOLALAO RANAIVOHARIVONY, BERTHOLIER RAVELONTSALAMA, LUCIEN RABARIJHON, NELLY RAKOTOBE, ARLETTE RAMAROSON, CLÉMENTINE RAVANDISON, GISÈLE RABOTOVAO, JEAN-JACQUES RAJAONA.

OTHER COURTS

Tribunaux de Première Instance: at Antananarivo, Toamasina, Antsiranana, Mahajanga, Fianarantsoa, Toliary, Antsirabé, Ambatondrazaka, Antalaha, Farafangana and Maintirano; for civil, commercial and social matters, and for registration.

Cours Criminelles Ordinaires: tries crimes of common law; attached to the Cour d'Appel in Antananarivo but may sit in any other large town. There are also 31 Cours Criminelles Spéciales dealing with cases concerning cattle.

Tribunaux Spéciaux Economiques: at Antananarivo, Toamasina, Mahajanga, Fianarantsoa, Antsiranana and Toliary; tries crimes specifically relating to economic matters.

Tribunaux Criminels Spéciaux: judges cases of banditry and looting; 31 courts.

Religion

It is estimated that more than 50% of the population follow traditional animist beliefs, some 41% are Christians (about one-half of whom are Roman Catholics) and some 7% are Muslims.

CHRISTIANITY

Fiombonan'ny Fiangonana Kristiana eto Madagasikara (FFKM)/Conseil Chrétien des Eglises de Madagascar/Christian Council of Churches in Madagascar: Vohipiraisama, Ambohijatovo-Atsimo, BP 798, 101 Antananarivo; tel. (20) 2229052; f. 1980; four mems and one assoc. mem.; Pres. Pastor EDMOND RAZAFIMAHALEO; Gen. Sec. Rev. LALA ANDRIAMIHARISOA.

Fiombonan'ny Fiangonana Protestanta eto Madagasikara (FFPM)/Fédération des Eglises Protestantes à Madagascar/Federation of the Protestant Churches in Madagascar: VK 3 Vohipiraisana, Ambohijatovo-Atsimo, BP 4226, 101 Antananarivo; tel. (20) 2220144; f. 1958; two mem churches; Pres. Pastor EDMOND RAZAFIMAHEFA; Gen. Sec. Rev. Dr ROGER ANDRIATSIRATAHINA.

The Anglican Communion

Anglicans are adherents of the Church of the Province of the Indian Ocean, comprising six dioceses (four in Madagascar, one in Mauritius and one in Seychelles). The Archbishop of the Province is the Bishop of Antananarivo. The Church has about 160,000 adherents in Madagascar, including the membership of the Eklesia Episkopaly Malagasy (Malagasy Episcopal Church), founded in 1874.

Bishop of Antananarivo (also Archbishop of the Province of the Indian Ocean): Most Rev. RÉMI JOSEPH RABENIRINA, Evêché Anglican, Lot VK57 ter, Ambohimanoro, 101 Antananarivo; tel. (20) 2220827; fax (20) 2261331; e-mail eemdanta@dts.mg.

Bishop of Antsiranana: Rt Rev. ROGER CHUNG PO CHEN, Evêché Anglican, BP 278, 201 Antsiranana; tel. (20) 8222650; e-mail eemdants@dts.mg.

Bishop of Mahajanga: Rt Rev. JEAN-CLAUDE ANDRIANJAFIMANANA, BP 169, 401 Mahajanga; e-mail eemdmaha@dts.mg.

Bishop of Toamasina: Rt Rev. JEAN PAUL SOLO, Evêché Anglican, rue James Seth, BP 531, 501 Toamasina; tel. (20) 5332163.

The Roman Catholic Church

Madagascar comprises four archdioceses and 16 dioceses. At 31 December 2002 the number of adherents in the country represented about 24% of the total population.

Bishops' Conference

Conférence Episcopale de Madagascar, 102 bis, rue Cardinal Jerôme Rakotomalala, BP 667, 101 Antananarivo; tel. (20) 2220478; fax (20) 2224854; e-mail ecar@vitelcom.mg.

f. 1969; Pres. Most Rev. FULGENCE RABEONY (Archbishop of Toliary).

Archbishop of Antananarivo: Cardinal ARMAND RAZAFINDRATANDRA, Archevêché, Andohalo, BP 3030, 101 Antananarivo; tel. (20) 2220726; fax (20) 2264181; e-mail didih@simicro.org.

Archbishop of Antsiranana: Most Rev. MICHEL MALO, Archevêché, BP 415, 201 Antsiranana; tel. (82) 21605; e-mail coord.diocesaine@blueline.mg.

Archbishop of Fianarantsoa: Most Rev. FULGENCE RABEMAHAFALY, Archevêché, place Mgr Givelet, BP 1440, Ambozontany, 301 Fianarantsoa; tel. (20) 7550027; fax (20) 7551436; e-mail ecarfianar@vitelcom.mg.

Archbishop of Toliary: Most Rev. FULGENCE RABEONY, Archevêché, Maison Saint Jean, BP 30, 601 Toliary; tel. (20) 9442416; e-mail diocesetulear@dts.mg.

Other Christian Churches

Fiangonan' i Jesoa Kristy eto Madagasikara/Eglise de Jésus-Christ à Madagascar: Lot 11 B18, Tohatohabato Ranavalona 1, Trano 'Ifanomezantsoa', BP 623, 101 Antananarivo; tel. (20) 2226845; fax (20) 2226372; e-mail fjkm@dts.mg; f. 1968; Pres. Rev. EDMOND RAZAFIMAHEFA; Gen. Sec. Rev. CHARLES RAKOTONIRINA; 2m. mems.

Fiangonana Loterana Malagasy (Malagasy Lutheran Church): BP 1741, 101 Antananarivo; tel. (20) 2222347; Pres. Rev. BENJAMIN RABENOROLAHY; 600,000 mems.

The Press

In December 1990 the National People's Assembly adopted legislation guaranteeing the freedom of the press and the right of newspapers to be established without prior authorization.

PRINCIPAL DAILIES

Bulletin de l'Agence Nationale d'Information 'Taratra' (ANTA): 3 rue du R. P. Callet, Behoririka, BP 386, 101 Antananarivo; tel. (20) 2221171; f. 1977; French; Man. Dir JEANNOT FENO.

L'Express de Madagascar: BP 3893, 101 Antananarivo; tel. (20) 2221934; fax (20) 2262894; e-mail lexpress@malagasy.com; internet www.lexpressmada.com; f. 1995; French and Malagasy; Editor (vacant); circ. 10,000.

Gazetiko: BP 1414 Ankorondrano, 101 Antananarivo; tel. (20) 2269779; fax (20) 2227351; e-mail gazetikom@yahoo.fr; Malagasy.

La Gazette de la Grande Ile: Lot II, W 23 L Ankorahotra, Antananarivo; tel. (20) 2261377; fax (20) 2265188; e-mail admin@lagazette-dgi.com; internet www.lagazette-dgi.com; French; Pres. LOLA RASOAMAHARO; circ. 20,000.

Imongo Vaovao: 11K 4 bis Andravoahangy, BP 7014, 101 Antananarivo; tel. (20) 2221053; f. 1955; Malagasy; Dir CLÉMENT RAMAMONJISOA; circ. 10,000.

Madagascar Tribune: Immeuble SME, rue Ravoninahitriniarivo, BP 659, Ankorondrano, 101 Antananarivo; tel. (20) 2222635; fax (20) 2222254; e-mail tribune@bow.dts.mg; internet www.madagascar-tribune.com; f. 1988; independent; French and Malagasy; Editor RAHAGA RAMAHOLIMIHASO; circ. 12,000.

Maresaka: 12 làlana Ratsimba John, Isotry, 101 Antananarivo; tel. (20) 2223568; f. 1953; independent; Malagasy; Editor M. RALAIARIJAONA; circ. 5,000.

Midi Madagasikara: làlana Ravoninahitriniarivo, BP 1414, Ankorondrano, 101 Antananarivo; tel. (20) 2269779; fax (20) 2227351; e-mail midi@dts.mg; internet www.dts.mg/midi; f. 1983; French and Malagasy; Dir MAMY RAKOTOARIVELO; circ. 25,500.

Les Nouvelles: Antananarivo; in French and Taratra; f. 2003; Editor-in-Chief CHRISTIAN CHADEFAUX.

PRINCIPAL PERIODICALS

Basy Vava: Lot III E 96, Mahamasina Atsimo, 101 Antananarivo; tel. (20) 2220448; f. 1959; Malagasy; Dir GABRIEL RAMANANJATO; circ. 3,000.

Bulletin de la Société du Corps Médical Malgache: Imprimerie Volamahitsy, 101 Antananarivo; Malagasy; monthly; Dir Dr RAKOTOMALALA.

Dans les Médias Demain (DMD): Immeuble Jeune Afrique, 58 rue Tsiombikibo, BP 1734, Ambatovinaky, 101 Antananarivo; tel. (20) 2263615; fax (20) 2230629; e-mail dmd@dts.mg; internet www.dmd.mg; f. 1986; independent; economic information and analysis; weekly; Dir HONORÉ RAZAFINTSALAMA; circ. 4,000.

Feon'ny Mpiasa: Lot M8, Isotry, 101 Antananarivo; trade union affairs; Malagasy; monthly; Dir M. RAZAKANAIVO; circ. 2,000.

Fiaraha-Miasa: BP 1216, 101 Antananarivo; Malagasy; weekly; Dir SOLO NORBERT ANDRIAMORASATA; circ. 5,000.

Gazetinao: Lot IPA 37, BP 1758, Anosimasina, 101 Antananarivo; tel. (20) 2261979; e-mail jamesdigne@caramail.com; f. 1976; French and Malagasy; monthly; Editors-in-Chief ANDRIANIAINA RAKOTOMAHANINA, JAMES FRRANKLIN; circ. 3,000.

Isika Mianakavy: Ambatomena, 301 Fianarantsoa; f. 1958; Roman Catholic; Malagasy; monthly; Dir J. RANAIVOMANANA; circ. 21,000.

Journal Officiel de la République de Madagascar: BP 248, 101 Antananarivo; tel. (20) 2265010; fax (20) 2225319; e-mail segma.gvt@dts.mg; f. 1883; official announcements; Malagasy and French; weekly; Dir HONORÉE ELIANNE RALALAHARISON; circ. 1,545.

Journal Scientifique de Madagascar: BP 3855, Antananarivo; f. 1985; Dir Prof. MANAMBELONA; circ. 3,000.

Jureco: BP 6318, Lot IVD 48 bis, rue Razanamaniraka, Behoririka, 101 Antananarivo; tel. (20) 2255271; e-mail jureco@malagasy.com; internet www.jureco.com; law and economics; monthly; French; Dir MBOARA ANDRIANARIMANANA.

Lakroan'i Madagasikara: BP 1169, Maison Jean XXIII, Mahamasina Sud, 101 Antananarivo; tel. (20) 2221158; fax (20) 2224020; e-mail lakroa@dts.mg; internet lakroa.free.fr; f. 1927; Roman Catholic; French and Malagasy; weekly; Dir LOUIS RASOLO; circ. 25,000.

La Lettre de Madagascar (LLM): Antananarivo; f. 2003; 2 a month; in French and English; economic; Editor-in-Chief DANIEL LAMY.

Mada—Economie: 15 rue Ratsimilaho, BP 3464, 101 Antananarivo; tel. (20) 2225634; f. 1977; reports events in south-east Africa; monthly; Editor RICHARD-CLAUDE RATOVONARIVO; circ. 5,000.

Mpanolotsaina: BP 623, 101 Antananarivo; tel. (20) 2226845; fax (20) 2226372; e-mail fjkm@dts.mg; religious, educational; Malagasy; quarterly; Dir RAYMOND RAJOELISOL.

New Magazine: BP 7581, Newprint, Route des Hydrocarbures, 101 Antananarivo; tel. (20) 2233335; fax (20) 2236471; e-mail newmag@dts.mg; internet www.dts.mg/newmag; 2 a month; in French; Dir CLARA RAVOAVAHY.

Ny Mpamangy-FLM: 9 rue Grandidier Isoraka, BP 538, Antsahamanitra, 101 Antananarivo; tel. (20) 2232446; f. 1882; monthly; Dir Pastor JEAN RABENANDRASANA; circ. 3,000.

Ny Sakaizan'ny Tanora: BP 538, Antsahaminitra, 101 Antananarivo; tel. (20) 2232446; f. 1878; monthly; Editor-in-Chief DANIEL PROSPER ANDRIAMANJAKA; circ. 5,000.

PME Madagascar: rue Hugues Rabesahala, BP 953, Antsakaviro, 101 Antananarivo; tel. (20) 2222536; fax (20) 2234534; f. 1989; French; monthly; economic review; Dir ROMAIN ANDRIANARISOA; circ. 3,500.

Recherche et Culture: BP 907, 101 Antananarivo; tel. (20) 2226600; f. 1985; publ. by French dept of the University of Antananarivo; 2 a year; Dir GINETTE RAMAROSON; circ. 1,000.

Revue Ita: BP 681, 101 Antananarivo; tel. (20) 2230507; f. 1985; controlled by the Ministry of Population, Women's Affairs and Children; monthly; Dir FILS RAMALANJAONA; circ. 1,000.

Revue de l'Océan Indien: Communication et Médias Océan Indien, rue H. Rabesahala, BP 46, Antsakaviro, 101 Antananarivo; tel. (20) 2222536; fax (20) 2234534; e-mail roi@dts.mg; internet www.madatours.com/roi; f. 1980; monthly; French; Man. Dir GEORGES RANAIVOSOA; Sec.-Gen. HERY M. A. RANAIVOSOA; circ. 5,000.

Sahy: Lot VD 42, Ambanidia, 101 Antananarivo; tel. (20) 2222715; f. 1957; political; Malagasy; weekly; Editor ALINE RAKOTO; circ. 9,000.

Sosialisma Mpiasa: BP 1128, 101 Antananarivo; tel. (20) 2221989; f. 1979; trade union affairs; Malagasy; monthly; Dir PAUL RABEMANANJARA; circ. 5,000.

Vaovao: BP 271, 101 Antananarivo; tel. (20) 2221193; f. 1985; French and Malagasy; weekly; Dir MARC RAKOTONOELY; circ. 5,000.

NEWS AGENCIES

Agence Nationale d'Information 'TARATRA' (ANTA): 7 rue Jean Ralaimongo, Ambohiday, BP 386, 101 Antananarivo; tel. and fax (20) 2236047; e-mail anta@blanbir.mg; f. 1977; Man. Dir JOÉ ANACLET RAKOTOARISON.

Foreign Bureaux

Associated Press (AP) (USA): BP 73, 101 Antananarivo; tel. (20) 2241944; e-mail zadefo@malagasy.com; Correspondent (vacant).

Korean Central News Agency (KCNA) (Democratic People's Republic of Korea): 101 Antananarivo; tel. (20) 2244795; Dir KIM YEUNG KYEUN.

Xinhua (New China) News Agency (People's Republic of China): BP 1656, 101 Antananarivo; tel. (20) 2229927; Chief of Bureau WU HAIYUN.

Reuters (United Kingdom) is also represented in Madagascar.

Publishers

Edisiona Salohy: BP 4226, 101 Antananarivo; Dir MIRANA VOLOLOARISOA RANDRIANARISON.

Editions Ambozontany Analamalintsy: BP 7553, 101 Antananarivo; tel. (20) 2243111; e-mail editionsj@wanadoo.mg; f. 1962; religious, educational, historical, cultural and technical textbooks; Dir Fr GUILLAUME DE SAINT PIERRE RAKOTONANDRATONIARIVO.

Foibe Filankevitry Ny Mpampianatra (FOFIPA): BP 202, 101 Antananarivo; tel. (20) 2227500; f. 1971; textbooks; Dir Frère RAZAFINDRAKOTO.

Imprimerie Nouvelle: PK 2, Andranomahery, route de Majunga, BP 4330, 101 Antananarivo; tel. (20) 2221036; fax (20) 2269225; e-mail nouvelle@wanadoo.mg; Dir EUGÈNE RAHARIFIDY.

Imprimerie Takariva: 4 rue Radley, BP 1029, Antanimena, 101 Antananarivo; tel. (20) 2222128; f. 1933; fiction, languages, school textbooks; Man. Dir PAUL RAPATSALAHY.

Madagascar Print and Press Co (MADPRINT): rue Rabesahala, Antsakaviro, BP 953, 101 Antananarivo; tel. (20) 2222536; fax (20) 2234534; f. 1969; literary, technical and historical; Dir GEORGES RANAIVOSOA.

Maison d'Edition Protestante Antso: 19 rue Venance Manifatra, Imarivolanitra, BP 660, 101 Antananarivo; tel. (20) 2220886; fax (20) 2226372; e-mail fjkm@dts.mg; f. 1972; religious, school, social, political and general; Dir HANS ANDRIAMAMPIANINA.

Nouvelle Société de Presse et d'Edition (NSPE): Immeuble Jeune Afrique, 58 rue Tsiombikibo, BP 1734, Ambatorinaky, 101 Antananarivo; tel. (20) 2227788; fax (20) 2230629.

Office du Livre Malgache: Lot 111 H29, Andrefan' Ambohijanahary, BP 617, 101 Antananarivo; tel. (20) 2224449; f. 1970; children's and general; Sec.-Gen. JULIETTE RATSIMANDRAVA.

Société Malgache d'Edition (SME): BP 659, Ankorondrano, 101 Antananarivo; tel. (20) 2222635; fax (20) 2222254; e-mail tribune@bow.dts.mg; f. 1943; general fiction, university and secondary textbooks; Man. Dir RAHAGA RAMAHOLIMIHASO.

Société Nouvelle de l'Imprimerie Centrale (SNIC): làlana Ravoninahitriniarivo, BP 1414, 101 Antananarivo; tel. (20) 2221118; e-mail mrakotoa@dts.mg; f. 1959; science, school textbooks; Man. Dir MAMY RAKOTOARIVELO.

Société de Presse et d'Edition de Madagascar: Antananarivo; non-fiction, reference, science, university textbooks; Man. Dir RAJAOFERA ANDRIAMBELO.

Trano Printy Fiangonana Loterana Malagasy (TPFLM): BP 538, 9 ave Général Gabriel Ramanantsoa, 101 Antananarivo; tel. (20) 2223340; fax (20) 2262643; e-mail impluth@dts.mg; f. 1877; religious, educational and fiction; Man. RAYMOND RANDRIANATOANDRO.

Government Publishing House

Imprimerie Nationale: BP 38, 101 Antananarivo; tel. (20) 2223675; all official publs; Dir JEAN DENIS RANDRIANIRINA.

Broadcasting and Communications

TELECOMMUNICATIONS

Mobile cellular telephone networks are operated by Antaris, Sacel and Telecel.

Office Malagasy d'Etudes et de Régulation des Télécommunications (OMERT): BP 99991, Route des Hydrocarbures-Alarobia, 101 Antananarivo; tel. (20) 2242119; fax (20) 2221516; e-mail omert@dts.mg; internet www.omert.mg; f. 1997; Gen. Man. GILBERT ANDRIANIRINA RAJAONASY.

Société Anonyme Télécom Malagasy (TELMA): BP 763, 101 Antananarivo; tel. (20) 2242705; fax (20) 2242654; e-mail rakotoar@bow.dts.mg; internet www.telma.net; 68% owned by Distacom (Hong Kong); Chair. DAVID WHITE; Dir-Gen. BRUNO ANTRIATAVISON.

BROADCASTING

Radio

In 2001 there were an estimated 127 radio stations.

Radio MBS (Malagasy Broadcasting System): BP 11137, Anosipatrana, Antananarivo; tel. (20) 2266702; fax (20) 2268941; e-mail marketing@mbs.mg; internet www.mbs.mg; broadcasts by satellite; Man. SARAH RAVALOMANANA.

Radio Nationale Malagasy: BP 442, Anosy, 101 Antananarivo; tel. (20) 2221745; fax (20) 2232715; e-mail radmad@dts.mg; internet www.takelaka.dts/radmad; state-controlled; broadcasts in French and Malagasy; Dir ALAIN RAJAONA.

Le Messager Radio Evangélique: BP 1374, 101 Antananarivo; tel. (20) 2234495; broadcasts in French, English and Malagasy; Dir JOCELYN RANJARISON.

Radio Antsiva: Lot VA, BP 6323, 21 Ambohitantely, 101 Antananarivo; tel. (20) 2265789; internet www.antsiva.mg; broadcasts in French, English and Malagasy; Dir ISMAËL RAZAFINARIVO.

Radio Feon'ny Vahoaka (RFV): 103 Immeuble Ramaroson, 8e étage, 101 Antananarivo; tel. (20) 2233820; broadcasts in French and Malagasy; Dir ALAIN RAMAROSON.

Radio Korail: 101 Antananarivo; tel. and fax (20) 2224494; f. 1993; broadcasts in French and Malagasy; Dir ALAIN RAJAONA.

Radio Lazan'iarivo (RLI): Lot V A49, Andafiavaratra, 101 Antananarivo; tel. (20) 2229016; fax (20) 2267559; e-mail rli@simicro.mg; broadcasts in French, English and Malagasy; Dir IHOBY RABARIJOHN.

Radio Tsioka Vao (RTV): Tana; tel. (20) 2221749; f. 1992; broadcasts in French, English and Malagasy; Dir DETKOU DEDONNAIS.

Television

In 2001 there were an estimated 13 television stations.

MA TV: BP 1414 Ankorondrano, 101 Antananarivo; tel. (20)

2220897; fax (20) 2234421; e-mail matv@dts.mg; internet www
.matvonline.tv.

MBS Television (Malagasy Broadcasting System): BP 11137, Anosipatrana, Antananarivo; tel. (20) 2266702; fax (20) 2268941; e-mail
journaltv@mbs.mg; internet www.mbs.mg; broadcasts in French
and Malagasy.

Radio Télévision Analamanga: Immeuble Fiaro, 101 Antananarivo; e-mail rta@rta.mg; internet www.rta.mg; including four
provincial radio stations; Dir-Gen. J. C. AUCHAN.

Télévision Nasionaly Malagasy: BP 1202, 101 Antananarivo; tel.
(20) 2222381; state-controlled; broadcasts in French and Malagasy;
Dir-Gen. RAZAFIMAHEFA HERINIRINA LALA.

Finance

(cap. = capital; res = reserves; dep. = deposits; m. = million;
brs = branches; amounts in Malagasy francs)

BANKING

Central Bank

Banque Centrale de Madagascar: ave de la Révolution Socialiste
Malgache, BP 550, 101 Antananarivo; tel. (20) 2221751; fax (20)
2234532; e-mail banque-centrale@banque-centrale.mg; internet
www.banque-centrale.mg; f. 1973; bank of issue; cap. 1,000m., res
62,865.8m., dep. 3,036,929.7m. (Dec. 2001); Gov. GASTON RAVELO-
JAONA.

Other Banks

Bank of Africa (BOA)—Madagascar: 2 place de l'Indépendance,
BP 183, 101 Antananarivo; tel. (20) 2239100; fax (20) 2229408;
e-mail boamg.dg@bkofafrica.com; internet www.bkofafrica.net; f.
1976 as Bankin'ny Tantsaha Mpamokatra, name changed as above
1999; 15% state-owned; commercial bank, specializes in micro-
finance; cap. 40,000m., res 11,476.9m., dep. 1,384,551.7m. (Dec.
2002); Pres. PAUL DERREUMAUX; Gen. Man. ALAIN LEPATRE LAMONTAGNE;
46 brs.

Banque Malgache de l'Océan Indien (BMOI) (Indian Ocean
Malagasy Bank): place de l'Indépendance, BP 25 Bis, Antaninarenina, 101 Antananarivo; tel. (20) 2234609; fax (20) 2234610; e-mail
bmoi.sm@simicro.mg; internet www.bmoi.mg; f. 1990; 75% owned by
BNP Paribas SA (France); cap. 30,000m., res 98,900m., dep.
1,389,200m. (Dec. 2002); Pres. GASTON RAMENASON; Dir-Gen. JEAN-
CLAUDE HERIDE; 8 brs.

Banque de Solidarité Malgache (SBM): rue Andrianary Rat-
ianarivo Antsahavola 1, 101 Antananarivo; tel. (20) 2266607; fax
(20) 2266608; e-mail sbmm@dts.mg; f. 1996; cap. and res 20,873.4m.,
dep. 186,682.8m. (Dec. 2002); Chair. CHAITLALL GUNNESS; Gen. Man.
KRISHNADUTT RAMBOJUN.

BFV—Société Générale: Làlana Jeneraly Rabetevitra 14, BP 196,
Antananarivo 101; tel. (20) 2220691; fax (20) 2234554; f. 1977 as
Banky Fampandrosoana ny Varotra; changed name in 1998; 70%
owned by Société Générale (France) and 30% state-owned; cap.
70,000m., res 6,572m., dep. 754,126m. (Dec. 2000); Chief Exec. JEAN-
PIERRE DUCROQUET; 24 brs.

BNI—Crédit Lyonnais Madagascar: 74 rue du 26 Juin 1960, BP
174, 101 Antananarivo; tel. (20) 2223951; fax (20) 2233749; e-mail
stdg@bni.mg; internet www.bni.mg; f. 1976 as Bankin 'ny Indostria;
32.58% state-owned; cap. 13,500m., res 128,102m., dep. 1,700,780m.
(Dec. 2002); Pres. and Chair. EVARISTO MARSON; Dir-Gen. DOMINIQUE
TISSIER; 22 brs.

Union Commercial Bank SA (UCB): 77 rue Solombavambahoaka
Frantsay, Antsahavola, BP 197, 101 Antananarivo; tel. (20)
2227262; fax (20) 2228740; e-mail ucb.int@dts.mg; f. 1992; 70%
owned by Mauritius Commercial Bank Ltd; cap. 6,000m., res
60,087.6m., dep. 327,141.9m. (Dec. 2002); Pres. RAYMOND HEIN; Gen.
Man. HENRI FLEUROT; 3 brs.

INSURANCE

ARO (Assurances Réassurances Omnibranches): Antsahavola,
BP 42, 101 Antananarivo; tel. (20) 2220154; fax (20) 2234464; e-mail
arol@dts.mg; Pres. FRANCIS RAKOTO; Dir-Gen. JEAN-BAPTISTE GUERRA.

Assurance France-Madagascar: 7 rue Rainitovo, BP 710, 101
Antananarivo; tel. (20) 2223024; fax (20) 2269201; e-mail l.afm@
wanadoo.mg; f. 1951; Dir RAKOUTH ZAFIARISOA.

Compagnie Malgache d'Assurances et de Réassurances:
Immeuble 'Ny Havana', Zone des 67 Ha, BP 3881, 101 Antananarivo;
tel. (20) 2226760; fax (20) 2224303; f. 1968; cap. 16,050m. (1996);
Dir-Gen. BERA RAZANAKOLONA.

Mutuelle d'Assurances Malagasy (MAMA): Lot 1F, 12 bis, rue
Rainibetsimisaraka, Ambalavao-Isotry, BP 185, 101 Antananarivo;
tel. (20) 2222508; Pres. FRÉDÉRIC RABARISON.

Ny Havana: BP 3881, Antananarivo 101; tel. (20) 2226760; fax (20)
2224303; Dir-Gen. BERA RAZANAKOLONA.

Société Malgache d'Assurances (SMA—ASCOMA): 13 rue Patrice Lumumba, BP 673, 101 Antananarivo; tel. (20) 2223162; fax (20)
2222785; e-mail ascoma@simicro.mg; f. 1952; Dir VIVIANE RAMANITRA.

Trade and Industry

DEVELOPMENT ORGANIZATIONS

**Office des mines nationales et des industries stratégiques
(OMNIS):** 21 làlana Razanakombana, BP 1 bis, 101 Antananarivo;
tel. (20) 2224439; fax (20) 2222985; e-mail omnis@simicro.mg; f.
1976; promotes the exploration and exploitation of mining resources,
in particular oil resources; Dir-Gen. Gen. RANDRIANAFIDISOA.

**Société d'Etude et de Réalisation pour le Développement
Industriel (SERDI):** Antananarivo; tel. (20) 2221335; f. 1966; Dir-
Gen. RAOILISON RAJAONARY.

CHAMBER OF COMMERCE

**Fédération des Chambres de Commerce, d'Industrie et
d'Agriculture de Madagascar:** 20 rue Paul Dussac, BP 166, 101
Antananarivo; tel. (20) 2221567; 12 mem. chambers; Pres. JEAN
RAMAROMISA; Chair. HENRI RAZANATSEHENO; Sec.-Gen. HUBERT RATSIAN-
DAVANA.

TRADE ASSOCIATION

Société d'Intérêt National des Produits Agricoles (SINPA):
BP 754, rue Fernand-Kasanga, Tsimbazaza, Antananarivo; tel. (20)
2220558; fax (20) 2220665; f. 1973; monopoly purchaser and distributor of agricultural produce; Chair. GUALBERT RAZANAJATOVO; Gen.
Man. JEAN CLOVIS RALIJESY.

EMPLOYERS' ORGANIZATIONS

Groupement des Entreprises de Madagascar (GEM): Kianja
MDRM sy Tia Tanindrazana, BP 1338, 101 Antananarivo; tel. (20)
23841; e-mail gem@simicro.mg; f. 1973; eight nat. syndicates and
five regional syndicates comprising 725 cos and 49 directly affiliated
cos; Pres. GASTON RAMENASON; Sec.-Gen. ZINAH RASAMUEL RAVALOSON.

**Groupement National des Exportateurs de Vanille de Mada-
gascar (GNEV):** BP 21, Antalaha; tel. (13) 20714532; fax (13)
20816017; e-mail rama.anta@sat.blueline.mg; 18 mems; Pres. JEAN
GEORGES RANDRIAMIHARISOA.

Syndicat des Importateurs et Exportateurs de Madagascar: 2
rue Georges Mandel, BP 188, 101 Antananarivo; Pres. M. FONTANA.

Syndicat des Industries de Madagascar: Immeuble Kobana
Soanierana; BP 1695, 101 Antananarivo; tel. (20) 2223608; fax (20)
2233043; f. 1958; Chair. NAINA ANDRIANTSITOHAINA.

Syndicat des Planteurs de Café: 37 làlana Razafimahandry, BP
173, 101 Antananarivo.

Syndicat Professionnel des Agents Généraux d'Assurances:
Antananarivo; f. 1949; Pres. SOLO RATSIMBAZAFY; Sec. IHANTA RAN-
DRIAMANDRANTO.

UTILITIES

Electricity and Water

Jiro sy Rano Malagasy (JIRAMA): BP 200, 149 rue Rainandria-
mampandry, Faravohitra, 101 Antananarivo; tel. (20) 2220031; fax
(20) 2233806; e-mail dgjirama@wanadoo.mg; f. 1975; state-owned;
controls production and distribution of electricity and water; Chair.
PATRICK RAMIARAMANANA; Dir-Gen. DESIRÉ RASIDY.

TRADE UNIONS

**Cartel National des Organisations Syndicales de Madagascar
(CARNOSYAMA):** BP 1035, 101 Antananarivo.

**Confédération des Travailleurs Malagasy Révolutionnaires
(FISEMARE):** Lot IV N 76-A, Ankadifotsy, BP 1128, Befelatanana-
Antananarivo 101; tel. (20) 2221989; fax (20) 2267712; f. 1985; Pres.
PAUL RABEMANANJARA.

Confédération des Travailleurs Malgaches (Fivomdronam-
ben'ny Mpiasa Malagasy—FMM): Lot IVM 133 A Antetezanafo-
voany I, BP 846, 101 Antananarivo; tel. (20) 2224565; f. 1957; Sec.-
Gen. JEANNOT RAMANANA; 30,000 mems.

Fédération des Syndicats des Travailleurs de Madagascar (Firaisan'ny Sendika eran'i Madagaskara—FISEMA): Lot III, rue Pasteur Isotry, 101 Antananarivo; f. 1956; Pres. DESIRÉ RALAMBOTA-HINA; Sec.-Gen. M. RAZAKANAIVO; 8 affiliated unions representing 60,000 mems.

Sendika Kristianina Malagasy (SEKRIMA) (Christian Confederation of Malagasy Trade Unions): Soarano, route de Mahajanga, BP 1035, 101 Antananarivo; tel. (20) 2223174; f. 1937; Pres. MARIE RAKOTOANOSY; Gen. Sec. RAYMOND RAKOTOARISAONA; 158 affiliated unions representing 40,000 mems.

Union des Syndicats Autonomes de Madagascar (USAM): Ampasadratsarahoby, Lot 11 H67, Faravohitra, BP 1038, 101 Antananarivo; Pres. NORBERT RAKOTOMANANA; Sec.-Gen. VICTOR RAHAGA; 46 affiliated unions representing 30,000 mems.

Transport

RAILWAYS

In 2001 there were 893 km of railway, including four railway lines, all 1-m gauge track. The northern system, which comprised 720 km of track, links the east coast with Antsirabé, in the interior, via Moramanga and Antananarivo, with a branch line from Moramanga to Lake Alaotra and was privatized in 2001. The southern system, which comprised 163 km of track, links the east coast with Fianarantsoa.

Réseau National des Chemins de Fer Malagasy: 1 ave de l'Indépendance, BP 259, Soarano, 101 Antananarivo; tel. (20) 2220521; fax (20) 2222288; f. 1909; in the process of transfer to private sector; Administrator DANIEL RAZAFINDRABE.

Madarail: tel. and fax (20) 2234599; e-mail madarail@wanadoo.mg; f. 2001; Bolloré, France; operated by Comazar, South Africa; operates the northern network of the Madagascan railway; Gen. Dir PATRICK STEVENAERT.

ROADS

In 2001 there were an estimated 49,837 km of classified roads; about 11.6% of the road network was paved. In 1987 there were 39,500 km of unclassified roads, used only in favourable weather. A road and motorway redevelopment programme, funded by the World Bank (€300m.) and the European Union (EU—€61m.), began in June 2000. In August 2002 the EU pledged undertook to disburse US $10m. for the reconstruction of 11 bridges destroyed during the political crisis in that year. In 2003 Japan pledged $28m. to build several bridges and a 15km bypass.

INLAND WATERWAYS

The Pangalanes Canal runs for 600 km near the east coast from Toamasina to Farafangana. In 1984 the Government initiated a project to rehabilitate more than 200 km of the canal by 1988, at a cost of 18.5m. Malagasy francs. In 1990 432 km of the canal between Toamasina and Mananjary were navigable.

SHIPPING

There are 18 ports, the largest being at Toamasina, which handles about 70% of total traffic, and Mahajanga. In 1987 Madagascar received foreign loans totalling US $34.8m., including a credit of $16m. from the World Bank, to finance a project to rehabilitate 10 ports.

Compagnie Générale Maritime (CGM): BP 69, 501 Toamasina; tel. (20) 5332312; fax (20) 5331037; f. 1976 by merger; Dir-Gen. GILLES-LOUIS TROIANO.

Compagnie Malgache de Navigation (CMN): rue Toto Radona, BP 1621, 101 Antananarivo; tel. (20) 2225516; f. 1960; coasters; 13,784 grt; 97.5% state-owned; privatization pending; Pres. ELINAH BAKOLY RAJAONSON; Dir-Gen. ARISTIDE EMMANUEL.

Navale et Commerciale Havraise Peninsulaire (NCHP): rue Rabearivelo Antsahavola, BP 1021, 101 Antananarivo; tel. (20) 2222502; Rep. JEAN-PIERRE NOCKIN.

Société Nationale Malgache des Transports Maritimes (SMTM): 6 rue Indira Gandhi, BP 4077, 101 Antananarivo; tel. (20) 2227342; fax (20) 2233327; f. 1963; 59% state-owned; privatization pending; services to Europe; Chair. ALEXIS RAZAFINDRATSIRA; Dir-Gen. ANDRIONORO RAMANANTSOA.

CIVIL AVIATION

The Ivato international airport is at Antananarivo, while the airports at Mahajanga, Toamasina and Nossi-Bé can also accommodate large jet aircraft. There are 211 airfields, two-thirds of which are privately owned. In 1996 the Government invited tenders for a rehabilitation project, which was to include nine of the major airports. Later that year the Government authorized private French airlines to operate scheduled and charter flights between Madagascar and Western Europe.

Aviation Civile de Madagascar (ACM): BP 4414, 101 Tsimbazaza-Antananarivo; tel. (20) 2222162; fax (20) 2224726; e-mail acm@acm.mg; Pres. NARIFERA RAOBANITRA; Dir-Gen. FRANÇOIS XAVIER RANDRIAMAHANDRY.

Société Nationale Malgache des Transports Aériens (Air Madagascar): 31 ave de l'Indépendance, BP 437, 101 Antananarivo; tel. (20) 2222222; fax (20) 2225728; e-mail airmad@dts.mg; internet www.air-mad.com; f. 1962; 89.58% state-owned; transfer to the private sector pending; managed by Lufthansa Consulting since 2001; extensive internal routes connecting all the principal towns; external services to France, Germany, Italy, Singapore, the Comoros, Kenya, Mauritius, Réunion, Seychelles and South Africa; Pres. NIRINA ANDRIAMANERASOA; Gen. Dirs ROLLAND BESOA RAZAFIMAHARO, JAMES ANDRIANALISOA.

Transports et Travaux Aériens de Madagascar: 17 ave de l'Indépendance, Analakely, Antananarivo; tel. (20) 2222222; fax (20) 2224340; e-mail tamdg@dts.mg; f. 1951; provides airline services; Administrators LALA RAZAFINDRAKOTO, FRANÇOIS DANE.

Tourism

Madagascar's attractions include unspoiled scenery, many unusual varieties of flora and fauna, and the rich cultural diversity of Malagasy life. In 2001 a total of 170,208 tourists visited Madagascar. Revenue from tourism in 2000 was estimated at US $116m. The number of hotel rooms increased from some 3,040 in 1991 to an estimated 7,207 in 1999.

Direction du Tourisme de Madagascar: Ministry of Culture and Tourism, Tsimbazaza, BP 610, 101 Antananarivo; tel. (20) 2226298; fax (20) 2278953; e-mail mintour@dts.mg; internet www.madagascar-contacts.com/mintourcomfr.

La Maison du Tourisme de Madagascar: place de l'Indépendance, BP 3224, 101 Antananarivo; tel. (20) 2235178; fax (20) 2269522; e-mail mtm@simicro.mg; internet www.tourisme.madagascar.com; Exec. Dir ANDRÉ ANDRIAMBOAVONJY.

MALAWI

Introductory Survey

Location, Climate, Language, Religion, Flag, Capital

The Republic of Malawi is a land-locked country in southern central Africa, with Zambia to the west, Mozambique to the south and east, and Tanzania to the north. Lake Malawi forms most of the eastern boundary. The climate is tropical, but much of the country is sufficiently high above sea-level to modify the heat. Temperatures range from 14°C (57°F) to 18°C (64°F) in mountain areas, but can reach 38°C (100°F) in low-lying regions. There is a rainy season between November and April. The official language is English, although Chichewa is being promoted as the basis for a 'Malawi Language'. Some 80% of the population profess Christianity, while a further 13%, largely Asians, are Muslims. Most of the remaining Malawians follow traditional beliefs, although there is also a Hindu minority. The national flag (proportions 2 by 3) has three equal horizontal stripes, of black, red and green, with a rising sun, in red, in the centre of the black stripe. The capital is Lilongwe.

Recent History

Malawi was formerly the British protectorate of Nyasaland. In 1953 it was linked with two other British dependencies, Northern and Southern Rhodesia (now Zambia and Zimbabwe), to form the Federation of Rhodesia and Nyasaland. Elections in August 1961 gave the Malawi Congress Party (MCP), led by Dr Hastings Kamuzu Banda, a majority of seats in the Legislative Council. Dr Banda became Prime Minister in February 1963, and the Federation was dissolved in December. Nyasaland gained independence, as Malawi, on 6 July 1964. The country became a republic and a one-party state, with Banda as its first President, on 6 July 1966. Malawi created a major controversy among African states in 1967 by officially recognizing the Republic of South Africa. In 1971 Banda, named Life President in that year, became the first African head of state to visit South Africa. In 1976, however, Malawi recognized the communist-backed Government in Angola in preference to the South African-supported forces. Malawi did not recognize the 'independence' granted by South Africa to four of its African 'homelands'.

Until 1993 all Malawian citizens were obliged to be members of the MCP; no political opposition was tolerated, and only candidates who had been approved by Banda were allowed to contest elections to the National Assembly. In 1979 Banda openly admitted that a letter bomb that injured the exiled leader of the Socialist League of Malawi (LESOMA), Dr Attati Mpakati, had been sent on his instructions. In March 1983 Mpakati was assassinated in Zimbabwe, although the Malawi Government denied any responsibility for his death. In May of that year Orton Chirwa and his wife, Vera, the leaders of the Malawi Freedom Movement (MAFREMO), were sentenced to death for treason, although Banda subsequently commuted the sentences to life imprisonment. (Orton Chirwa died in prison in October 1992; Vera Chirwa was pardoned and released in January 1993.)

Frequent reorganizations of the Cabinet effectively prevented the emergence of any political rival to Banda. However, it was reported in 1983 that a conflict had developed between Dick Matenje, the Minister without Portfolio in the Cabinet and Secretary-General of the MCP, and John Tembo, the Governor of the Reserve Bank of Malawi, concerning the eventual succession to Banda. In May the authorities reported that Matenje and three other senior politicians had died in a road accident; Malawian exiles claimed that the four men had been shot while attempting to flee the country. (In January 1994 a former police-officer claimed to have taken part in the shootings, under official orders; the Banda Government, however, rejected calls for an official inquiry.) In August 1984 Banda reorganized the MCP Executive Committee; the important post of party Secretary-General remained vacant, however, until the appointment of Gwandaguluwe Chakuamba in October 1993 (see below).

At elections to the National Assembly in May 1987 213 members of the MCP contested 69 of the 112 elective seats in the Assembly. Some 33 candidates were elected unopposed, and several elective seats were not filled. Banda subsequently nom-inated further members to the Assembly, bringing its total membership to 116 in 1989. In January 1992 Tembo (now widely regarded as Banda's probable successor) was appointed Minister of State in the President's Office. Legislative elections took place in June: 96 of the elective seats (by then numbering 141) were contested by 630 members of the MCP, while 45 candidates were returned unopposed. Five seats remained vacant, after some candidates were disqualified. An additional 10 members of the Assembly were subsequently nominated by Banda.

Opposition to the Government intensified during 1992: in March Malawi's Roman Catholic bishops published an open letter criticizing the Government's alleged abuses of human rights. In April Chakufwa Chihana, a prominent trade union leader who had demanded multi-party elections, was arrested. In May industrial unrest in the southern city of Blantyre escalated into violent anti-Government riots, which spread to the capital, Lilongwe, and reportedly resulted in 38 deaths. Later in the month Western creditors suspended all but urgent humanitarian aid to Malawi, pending improvements in the Government's human rights record. In July Chihana was charged with sedition, and in August the police detained 11 church leaders and prohibited a planned rally by pro-democracy supporters. In September opposition activists formed the Alliance for Democracy (AFORD), a pressure group operating within Malawi, under the chairmanship of Chihana, which aimed to campaign for democratic political reform. Another opposition grouping, the United Democratic Front (UDF), was formed in October. In that month Banda conceded that a referendum on the introduction of a multi-party system would take place. However, in November the Government banned AFORD. In the following month Chihana was found guilty of sedition and sentenced to two years' hard labour (reduced to nine months' in March 1993). In January 1993 LESOMA merged with the Malawi Democratic Union to form the United Front for Multi-party Democracy. In March MAFREMO dissolved itself, and its membership joined AFORD.

The referendum on the introduction of a multi-party system was held on 14 June 1993, monitored by UN representatives. Despite evidence of MCP attempts to disrupt the opposition's activities prior to the poll, 63.2% of those who participated (some 63.5% of the electorate) voted for an end to single-party rule. Banda rejected opposition demands for the immediate installation of an interim government of national unity. He agreed, however, to the establishment of a National Executive Council to oversee the transition to a multi-party system and the holding of free elections, and of a National Consultative Council to implement the necessary amendments to the Constitution. Both councils were to include members of the Government and the opposition. Banda announced an amnesty for thousands of political exiles, and stated that a general election would be held, on a multi-party basis, within a year. In late June the Constitution was amended to allow the registration of political parties other than the MCP: by mid-August five organizations, including AFORD and the UDF, had been accorded official status.

In September 1993 Banda carried out an extensive cabinet reshuffle, relinquishing the post of Minister of External Affairs, which he had held since 1964. In October 1993 Banda underwent neurological surgery in South Africa. Interim executive power was assumed by a three-member Presidential Council, chaired by the new Secretary-General of the MCP, Chakuamba. (Chakuamba, a former government minister, had been released in July from a 22-year prison sentence, imposed for sedition in 1981.) The two other members, Tembo and the Minister of Transport and Communications, Robson Chirwa, were also senior MCP officials. In November 1993 a further cabinet reshuffle relieved Banda of all ministerial responsibilities. Later in November the National Assembly approved a Constitutional Amendment Bill, which, *inter alia*, abolished the institution of life presidency, ended the requirement that election candidates be members of the MCP, repealed the right of the President to nominate members of the legislature exclusively from the MCP, and lowered the minimum voting age from 21 to 18 years. The

Assembly also amended the Public Security Act to outlaw detention without trial.

Having made a rapid and unexpected recovery, Banda resumed full presidential powers in December 1993. Shortly afterwards, in response to increasing pressure from the opposition, the Government amended the Constitution to provide for the appointment of an acting President in the event of the incumbent's being incapacitated. In February 1994 the MCP announced that Banda was to be the party's presidential candidate in the forthcoming general election (scheduled for May); Chakuamba was named as the MCP's candidate for the vice-presidency. Also in February the National Assembly approved an increase in the number of elective seats in the legislature from 141 to 177.

Meanwhile, the MCP announced in September 1993 that members of the Malawi Young Pioneers (MYP), a notorious paramilitary section of the ruling party, were to be gradually disarmed. In December, following the murder of three soldiers by MYP members, the regular army acted to close MYP offices and camps. In the ensuing violence, exacerbated by long-standing tensions between the army and the MYP, 32 people were reported to have been killed. Banda appointed a Minister of Defence (having hitherto held personal responsibility for defence) to oversee the MYP disarmament process and investigate army grievances. By early 1994 the authorities stated that the disarmament had been satisfactorily completed; it was known, however, that several thousand MYP members had crossed the border into Mozambique to take refuge in rebel bases. In January the Governments of Malawi and Mozambique agreed to a programme for the repatriation of MYP members. In the following month the MYP was officially disbanded, although it was subsequently reported that many armed MYP members remained in hiding in Mozambique (see below).

On 16 May 1994 the National Assembly adopted a provisional Constitution, which provided for the appointment of a Constitutional Committee and of a human rights commission, and abolished the system of 'traditional' courts. Malawi's first multi-party parliamentary and presidential elections took place on 17 May. In the presidential election the Secretary-General of the UDF, (Elson) Bakili Muluzi (a former government minister and MCP Secretary-General), took 47.3% of the votes cast, defeating Banda (who won 33.6% of the votes). Eight parties contested the legislative elections: of these, the UDF won 84 seats in the National Assembly, the MCP 55 and AFORD 36. (Voting was repeated in two constituencies where irregularities had been found, as a result of which the UDF and MCP each won a further seat.) The distribution of seats was strongly influenced by regional affiliations, with AFORD winning all of the Northern Region's seats, and the MCP and UDF particularly successful in the Central and Southern Regions, respectively. The Constitution was introduced for a one-year period on 18 May; it was to be subject to further review prior to official ratification one year later.

President Muluzi and his Vice-President, Justin Malewezi, were inaugurated on 21 May 1994. The stated aims of the new administration were to alleviate poverty and ensure food security, and to combat corruption and the mismanagement of resources. Three prisons where abuses of human rights were known to have taken place were closed. The new UDF-dominated Government also proclaimed an amnesty for the country's remaining political prisoners, and commuted all death sentences to terms of life imprisonment. Attempts to recruit members of AFORD into a coalition administration failed, owing to disagreements regarding the allocation of senior portfolios, and in June AFORD and the MCP agreed to function as an opposition front. The Muluzi Government was thus deprived of a majority in the National Assembly, which was inaugurated at the end of June. In August it was announced that Banda, while remaining honorary Life President of the MCP, was to retire from active involvement in politics. Chakuamba, as Vice-President of the party, effectively became the leader of the MCP.

In September 1994 a number of AFORD members were appointed to the Government, including Chihana as Second Vice-President and Minister of Irrigation and Water Development. In January 1995 AFORD announced an end to its co-operation with the MCP. Meanwhile, the creation of the post of Second Vice-President had necessitated a constitutional amendment, and provoked severe criticism from the MCP. Moreover, the National Constitutional Conference recommended that the post be abolished. In March, however, the National Assembly (in the absence of MCP deputies, who boycotted the vote) approved the retention of the second vice-presidency; the Assembly also endorsed recommendations for the establishment—although not before May 1999—of a second chamber of parliament, as well as a constitutional clause requiring that senior state officials declare all personal assets within two months of assuming their post. The Constitution took effect on 18 May 1995.

In June 1994 Muluzi established an independent commission of inquiry to investigate the deaths of Matenje and his associates in May 1983. In January 1995, in accordance with the findings of the commission, Banda was placed under house arrest and Tembo and two former police-officers were detained; the four were charged with murder and conspiracy to murder. A former inspector-general of police was charged later in the month. Cecilia Kadzamira, Tembo's niece and the former President's 'Official Hostess', was charged, in April, with conspiracy to murder and was subsequently released on bail. The trial opened later that month, but was immediately adjourned, owing to Banda's failure to appear in court (his defence counsel asserted that he was too ill to stand trial) and to the failure of the state prosecution to submit certain evidence to the defence. Hearings resumed, in Banda's absence, in July. In September Tembo and the two former police-officers were granted bail, and most restrictions on Banda's movements were ended. The case against Kadzamira was abandoned in December, owing to lack of evidence, and later in the month Banda, Tembo and the other defendants were found not guilty of conspiracy to murder and conspiracy to defeat justice. The Director of Public Prosecutions subsequently appealed against the verdict, complaining that the presiding judge had effectively instructed the jury to acquit the defendants. In January 1996 an MCP-owned newspaper printed a statement by Banda in which he admitted that he might unknowingly have been responsible for brutalities perpetrated under his regime and apologized to Malawians for 'pain and suffering' inflicted during his presidency. Meanwhile, in July 1995 Tembo and four other members of the Banda regime were charged with conspiring to murder the bishops who had published criticisms of the former administration in 1992. (The charges were withdrawn 'in the interests of national reconciliation' in October 2000.)

In July 1995 lawyers acting for Banda demanded that Muluzi explain the apparent payment of a substantial sum to a witness in the trial of Banda and his associates. Meanwhile, there were further allegations that the Muluzi administration had been involved in dubious financial transactions. It emerged, in mid-1995, that the President had authorized the payment of some 6.2m. kwacha from the state poverty alleviation account to UDF deputies (to enable the payment of loans to their constituents); there was also evidence of the involvement of government ministers in the smuggling of maize to neighbouring countries. Moreover, it was claimed that few ministers had complied with the constitutional requirement regarding the declaration of assets. An investigation of Banda's financial interests was initiated in September. In February 1996 Muluzi announced that an independent Anti-Corruption Bureau was to be established to investigate allegations of corruption.

In July 1995 the UDF and AFORD signed a formal co-operation agreement. In December, however, Chihana warned that AFORD might withdraw from the coalition Government, alleging that the UDF was using public funds to secure political influence, and complaining of a lack of openness in the Muluzi administration. Chihana resigned from the Government in May 1996, expressing his intention to devote himself more fully to the work of his party. The post of Second Vice-President remained vacant following a subsequent reorganization of the Cabinet. In late May another AFORD minister resigned. In June AFORD withdrew from its coalition with the UDF, declared that remaining AFORD ministers should resign, and appointed a 'shadow cabinet'. Five members were dismissed from AFORD's National Executive, and another was suspended, having refused to relinquish their ministerial posts. AFORD and the MCP insisted that AFORD ministers should be regarded as members of the UDF. The rejection of this demand resulted in a parliamentary boycott by both opposition parties. At the beginning of December the AFORD ministers remaining in the Cabinet asserted that they were independent and had not joined the UDF. In March 1997 AFORD stated that the party would continue its boycott until the ministers resigned both their government posts and parliamentary seats. In April the MCP and AFORD ended their parliamentary boycott, following a meeting with Muluzi at which he had allegedly promised to amend the Constitution to prevent parliamentary delegates from changing their political affiliation without standing for re-election.

In January 1997 it was announced that Banda was to be charged with embezzling state funds for the establishment of a private school; however, in May he was discharged as unfit to attend court. In July the Supreme Court dismissed an appeal against the acquittal, in December 1995, of Banda and Tembo on murder charges, shortly after Muluzi reportedly requested that all criminal cases against Banda be discontinued. Also in July 1997 Banda announced his intention to resign as President of the MCP. In November Banda died in South Africa, where he had been undergoing emergency medical treatment. He was accorded a state funeral, with full military honours, which was attended by some 100,000 Malawians.

In June 1998 the National Assembly approved legislation providing for the introduction of a single-ballot electoral system to replace the existing multiple-ballot system and for a strengthening of the authority and independence of the Electoral Commission. In November legislation was adopted to allow presidential and parliamentary elections to run concurrently (as Muluzi's term was due to end several weeks earlier than that of the National Assembly), and the elections were subsequently scheduled for 18 May 1999. An electoral alliance between the MCP and AFORD, which was officially announced in February 1999, created serious divisions within the MCP, when the party's leader and presidential candidate, Chakuamba, chose Chihana, the leader of AFORD, as the candidate for the vice-presidency, in preference to Tembo. Thousands of Tembo's supporters were reported to have mounted protests to demand Chakuamba's resignation. The Chakuamba-Chihana partnership also provoked a wider dispute with the UDF and the Electoral Commission, which claimed that the arrangement was unconstitutional. In February the National Assembly adopted a controversial report by the Electoral Commission that recommended the creation of a further 72 parliamentary seats, including an additional 42 in the Southern Region, a UDF stronghold. In response to widespread opposition to the proposals, however, only 16 of the 72 seats were approved.

Having been postponed twice, the presidential and legislative elections were held on 15 June 1999. Muluzi was re-elected to the presidency, securing 51.37% of the votes cast, while Chakuamba obtained 43.30%. Turn-out was high, with some 93.8% of registered voters reported to have participated. At the elections to the expanded National Assembly the ruling UDF won 93 seats, while the MCP secured 66 seats, AFORD 29 and independent candidates four. (Owing to the death of a candidate, voting in the remaining constituency was postponed until October, when the seat was won by the UDF.) The opposition disputed the results, and violent clashes ensued in the northern districts. Despite declarations from international observers that the elections were largely free and fair, the MCP-AFORD alliance filed two petitions with the High Court, challenging Muluzi's victory and the results in 16 districts. The opposition alleged irregularities in the voter registration process and claimed that Muluzi's victory was unconstitutional, as he had failed to gain the support of 50% of all registered voters. None the less, Muluzi was inaugurated later in June, and a new Cabinet was appointed. In mid-August the UDF regained a parliamentary majority when the four independent deputies decided to ally themselves with the UDF, of which they had previously been members.

Chakuamba, who had maintained a boycott of the new parliament pending the result of his party's challenge to the outcome of the elections, was suspended from the chamber in June 2000. Tembo assumed the leadership of the opposition and appointed his supporters to prominent posts within the MCP. Chakuamba was reinstated in September, and a dispute between the two factions ensued. In October the opposition's petitions against the election results were dismissed by the High Court.

Muluzi reorganized the Cabinet in March 2000 and again in August, following the resignation of a deputy minister who had been charged with manslaughter. In October a report was published criticizing the Malawian Government for the purchase of a new fleet of cars for the use of government officials, allegedly with money donated in aid by the United Kingdom. In November, following these and other allegations of corruption made against several ministers, Muluzi dismissed the entire Cabinet and announced direct presidential rule, before appointing a new administration some days later. Brown Mpinganjira, the Minister of Transport and Public Works, Cassim Chilumpha, the Minister of Education, Science and Technology, and Peter Chupa, the Minister of Labour and Vocational Training, were not reappointed. They were subsequently investigated for their alleged involvement in the corrupt awarding of a number of construction contracts. Mpinganjira, who claimed the accusations were politically motivated, was charged with receiving illegal payments in December.

The country's first multi-party local elections were held in November 2000. The MCP was disqualified from contesting a number of wards where both factions of the party had submitted nominations. Amid allegations of electoral malpractice, the UDF secured victory in 610 of the 860 contested wards, AFORD winning 120 seats and the MCP 84.

Mpinganjira was acquitted of the corruption charges in January 2001 and subsequently formed a new political movement, the National Democratic Alliance (NDA). It was reported that five members of the National Assembly had joined the NDA by February. Meanwhile, in January 2001 deputies from the Tembo faction of the MCP ensured the approval by the National Assembly of a UDF proposal to abandon plans (ostensibly for financial reasons) for the creation of a second legislative chamber, the Senate, which would have had powers to impeach the President; AFORD boycotted the vote. In February Chilumpha was arrested on charges of corruption connected with campaigning for the June 1999 elections. In March 2001 six people were arrested and charged with treason for allegedly planning a coup against Muluzi; the leader of the plot was said to be Sudi Sulaimana, a political activist who had previously been arrested in 1993 for attempting to overthrow Banda. However, Chakuamba claimed that the Government had fabricated the plot in order to curb the activities of its political opponents. In October Mpinganjira was arrested and charged with treason for alleged involvement in the March coup attempt, but was released after a court ruled that his detention was unconstitutional. Meanwhile, in June, at a rally in Lilongwe, 37 of the 41 MCP district chairmen publicly endorsed Tembo as their new leader, declaring that they had lost confidence in Chakuamba; however, the latter dismissed the significance of the endorsement. In November seven deputies who had joined the NDA, including Mpinganjira and Makhumula, were excluded from the National Assembly for abandoning the political parties for which they had been elected, an action proscribed by law since May, when the UDF acted to prevent defections to the NDA; Sam Mpasu, the Speaker, defied an order of the High Court restraining him from expelling the deputies. Also in November the UDF-dominated National Assembly approved a motion to commence impeachment proceedings against three High Court judges for allegedly favouring the opposition, despite objections from the International Commission of Jurists, religious leaders and civil rights groups.

In January 2002 Muluzi effected a minor cabinet reshuffle, notably dismissing Mathews Chikaonda as Minister of Finance and Economic Planning. In the mean time, negotiations between Chihana and Muluzi on the possible formation of a government of national unity had created divisions within AFORD. The minister responsible for poverty alleviation, Leonard Mangulama, was dismissed in August after a report was published implicating him in the sale of emergency maize reserves to Kenya when Minister of Agriculture and Irrigation Development. A minor reorganization of ministerial portfolios took place in September. In the same month it was reported that Mpinganjira had fled the country following the murder of a supporter of the UDF in late August. In October Tembo was convicted of contempt of court for organizing a convention of the MCP in June, in defiance of a court injunction.

Proposed legislation to change the Constitution to allow Muluzi to seek a third presidential term failed to gain the requisite support of two-thirds of the members of the National Assembly in July 2002. A further attempt to introduce a constitutional amendment also failed in January 2003, when the bill was withdrawn; the Minister of Commerce and Industry, Peter Kaleso, was dismissed in that month in a minor cabinet reshuffle, as he had been expected to vote against the amendment. The UDF declared that it would hold a referendum on the issue later in the year. However, in late March Muluzi declared that he would not seek a third presidential term, and proposed Dr Bingu wa Mutharika, recently appointed Minister of Economic Planning and Development, as his successor, to contest the presidential election scheduled for May 2004. (Mutharika had represented the United Party at the 1999 presidential election, but subsequently defected to the UDF.) Two days later, in early April 2003, Muluzi dismissed his entire Cabinet, apparently without explanation. However, several ministers reported that Muluzi had imposed the appointment of Mutharika on the party without sufficient consultation, and suggested that they had been dismissed for expressing opposition to the President's decision; Muluzi appointed a new administration later that month.

In May 2003, at a party convention in Blantyre that was disrupted by violent incidents, Tembo and Chakuamba, were elected, respectively, as President and Vice-President of the MCP. Tembo was subsequently named as the MCP's candidate to contest the 2004 presidential election, despite some opposition within the party and doubts over his eligibility to stand, owing to his conviction for contempt of court in October 2002 (see above). In December 2003, however, the Supreme Court of Appeal overturned Tembo's conviction. Chakuamba subsequently resigned from the MCP and formed the Republican Party (RP). On 1 January 2004 Justin Malewezi, Malawi's First Vice-President and Minister responsible for Privatization, announced his resignation from the UDF for what were termed 'personal reasons'. He did not, however, relinquish his position in the Government, stating that he would remain in office, but on leave, until after the presidential election had taken place. One week after leaving the UDF Malewezi joined the People's Progressive Movement (PPM), an opposition party founded in April 2003. Later in January 2004 Aleke Banda, who had resigned from the UDF in May 2003, was elected as President of the PPM, while Malewezi was chosen as its Vice-President. In February 2004 the Government initiated legal proceedings aimed at having Malewezi's position within the Cabinet declared vacant on the grounds that he had resigned as Vice-President 'by implication or by his own conduct'. Meanwhile, in late January six opposition parties, including the PPM and the RP, announced their formation of the Mgwirizano Coalition to contest the forthcoming presidential election; Chakuamba was elected as the coalition's presidential candidate in February. Malewezi subsequently announced that he would contest the election as an independent. A minor cabinet reshuffle was effected in late February, and Muluzi appointed Hetherwick Ntaba, the leader of the New Congress for Democracy (NCD), as Minister of Energy and Mining at the end of March, following the NCD's decision to join the UDF-AFORD electoral alliance. Presidential and legislative elections were to take place on 18 May, but were subsequently postponed, in compliance with a judicial ruling, until 20 May after the opposition lodged complaints of irregularities in the voters' register.

Despite being the only African country to have maintained full diplomatic relations with South Africa during the apartheid era, Malawi joined the Southern African Development Co-ordination Conference (subsequently the Southern African Development Community, see p. 331), which originally aimed to reduce the dependence of southern African countries on South Africa.

Relations with Mozambique were frequently strained during the early and mid-1980s by the widely held belief that the Banda regime was supporting the Resistência Nacional Moçambicana (Renamo—see the chapter on Mozambique). Following the death of President Machel of Mozambique in an air crash in South Africa in October 1986, the South African Government claimed that documents discovered in the wreckage revealed a plot by Mozambique and Zimbabwe to overthrow the Banda Government. Angry protests from Malawi were answered by denials of the accusations from the Mozambican and Zimbabwean Governments. In December, however, Malawi and Mozambique signed an agreement on defence and security matters, which was believed to include co-operation in eliminating Renamo operations. In July 1988, during an official visit to Malawi, President Chissano of Mozambique stated that he did not believe Malawi to be supporting Renamo. In December of that year Malawi, Mozambique and the office of the UN High Commissioner for Refugees (UNHCR) signed an agreement to promote the voluntary repatriation of an estimated 650,000 Mozambican refugees who had fled into Malawi during the previous two years. However, by mid-1992 the number of Mozambican refugees in Malawi had reportedly reached 1m. Large numbers of refugees returned to Mozambique in 1993–94, but in May 1995 Malawi demanded the repatriation of the remainder—estimated to total some 39,000—stating that food aid and other assistance to those who failed to leave would be reduced. The programme of the Malawi-Mozambique-UNHCR commission officially ended in November: it was estimated that a total of 1m. refugees had been repatriated. None the less, the continued presence of more than 2,000 MYP members in Mozambique (many of whom were said to have been harboured in Renamo bases) remained a cause of concern. In October it was announced that the two countries were to establish a commission to locate renegade MYP members and persuade them to return to Malawi.

In October 2001 the Danish Government was forced to recall its ambassador to Lilongwe after the Malawian Ministry of Foreign Affairs and International Co-operation alleged that the ambassador had made derogatory comments about Muluzi; the ambassador had recently commissioned an audit report on aid from the Danish Government, owing to suspicions that funds might have been misused. In January 2002 Denmark announced that it was to withdraw all financial assistance to Malawi, owing to negative political developments in the country, and subsequently closed its embassy in Lilongwe. In June 2003 the Malawian authorities surrendered into the custody of US officials five men who were suspected by the US Central Intelligence Agency of having links with the militant Islamist al-Qa'ida (Base) organization. The five suspects, described as 'prohibited immigrants' by the Malawian authorities, were subsequently removed from Malawi via Zimbabwe.

Government

The Head of State is the President, who is elected by universal adult suffrage, in the context of a multi-party political system, for a term of five years. Executive power is vested in the President, and legislative power in the National Assembly, which has 193 elective seats. Members of the Assembly are elected for five years, by universal adult suffrage, in the context of a multi-party system. Cabinet ministers are appointed by the President. The country is divided into three administrative regions (Northern, Central and Southern), sub-divided into 24 districts.

Defence

Malawi's active defence forces at 1 August 2003 comprised a land army of 5,300, a marine force of 220 and an air force of 80; all form part of the army. There was also a paramilitary police force of 1,500. Expenditure on defence in the 2001/02 budget was 1,032m. kwacha (equivalent to 2.4% of total expenditure).

Economic Affairs

In 2002, according to estimates by the World Bank, Malawi's gross national income (GNI), measured at average 2000–02 prices, was US $1,728m., equivalent to $160 per head (or $570 per head on an international purchasing-power parity basis). During 1990–2002, it was estimated, the population increased at an average annual rate of 2.0%, while gross domestic product (GDP) per head increased, in real terms, by an average of 0.9% per year. Overall GDP increased, in real terms, at an average annual rate of 2.9% in 1990–2002; real GDP increased by 1.8% in 2002 and by 4.4% in 2003.

Measured at constant 1994 prices, agriculture (including forestry and fishing) contributed 38.1% of GDP in 2003, and engaged an estimated 82.1% of the labour force in 2002. The principal cash crops are tobacco (which accounted for 56.9% of total export earnings in 2002), tea and sugar cane. The principal food crops are maize, potatoes, cassava, plantains, groundnuts and pulses. Periods of severe drought and flooding have necessitated imports of basic foods in recent years. In March 2004 the Government forecast a 24% decline in maize production in that year, owing to late and erratic rainfall. During 1990–2002, according to the World Bank, agricultural GDP increased at an average annual rate of 5.4%. According to official figures, growth in agricultural GDP was 2.4% in 2002 and 6.8% in 2003.

Industry (including manufacturing, mining, construction and power) contributed 15.6% of GDP in 2003, and engaged 4.5% of the employed labour force in 1998. During 1990–2002, according to the World Bank, industrial GDP increased by an average of 1.4% per year. Industrial GDP decreased by 1.5% in 2002, but increased by 4.1% in 2003.

Mining and quarrying contributed 1.1% of GDP in 2003, and engaged less than 0.1% of the employed labour force in 1998. Limestone, coal and gemstones are mined, and there are plans to develop deposits of bauxite, high-calcium marble and graphite. There are also reserves of phosphates, uranium, glass sands, asbestos and vermiculite. In August 2000 an Australian company announced its intention to establish a uranium mine in northern Malawi, near the border with Tanzania; it was anticipated that production would commence in 2005. Environmental and financial concerns have delayed plans to exploit an estimated 30m. metric tons of bauxite deposits at Mount Mulanje.

The GDP of the mining sector increased at an average annual rate of 15.1% in 1994–2003, according to official figures; mining GDP decreased by 38.6% in 2002, but increased by 23.4% in 2003.

Manufacturing contributed 10.6% of GDP in 2003, and engaged 2.7% of the employed labour force in 1998. During 1990–2002, according to the World Bank, manufacturing GDP increased by an average of 0.1% per year. Manufacturing GDP decreased by 0.1% in 2002, but increased by 1.2% in 2003.

Production of electrical energy is by hydroelectric (principally) and thermal installations. Some 90% of energy for domestic use is derived from fuel wood. In October 1997 an agreement was signed to link Malawi's electricity system to the Cahora Bassa hydroelectric dam in Mozambique, but completion of the project was not expected until 2006. In October 2000 a hydroelectric power plant, with a generation capacity of 64 MW, was opened at Kapichira. In January 2001 the Government introduced a campaign to widen access to electricity, especially in rural areas; in 2001 only 4% of Malawians had access to electricity. In 2003 the Government was examing the possibility of establishing coal-fired power stations. Imports of fuel comprised an estimated 9.6% of the value of total imports in 1998.

The services sector contributed 46.3% of GDP in 2003, and engaged 11.0% of the employed labour force in 1998. The GDP of the services sector increased by an average of 2.0% per year in 1990–2002, according to the World Bank. Services GDP increased by 3.2% in 2002 and by 2.8% in 2003.

In 2002 Malawi recorded a visible trade deficit of US $150.8m., while there was a deficit of $200.7m. on the current account of the balance of payments. In 2001 the principal source of imports was South Africa (39.7%); Zimbabwe and Zambia were also notable suppliers. South Africa was also the principal market for exports (19.1%) in that year; other important markets were the USA, Germany, Japan and the Netherlands. The principal exports in 2002 were tobacco, tea and sugar. The principal imports in 1998 were machinery and transport equipment (particularly road vehicles and parts), basic manufactures, food and live animals (notably cereals and cereal preparations), chemicals and related products, and mineral fuels.

In the financial year ending 30 June 2002 Malawi's overall budget deficit was an estimated 10,959m. kwacha (equivalent to 8.1% of GDP). The country's external debt totalled US $2,602m. at the end of 2001, of which $2,483m. was long-term public debt. In that year the cost of debt-servicing was equivalent to 7.8% of exports of goods and services. The annual rate of inflation averaged 28.8% in 1990–2002; consumer prices increased by an average of 22.7% in 2001 and by 14.8% in 2002. Some 1.1% of the labour force were unemployed in 1998.

Malawi is a member of the Southern African Development Community (see p. 331) and also of the Common Market for Eastern and Southern Africa (COMESA, see p. 171). Nine members of COMESA, including Malawi, became inaugural members of the COMESA Free Trade Area in October 2000. The country belongs to the International Tea Promotion Association (see p. 357) and to the International Tobacco Growers' Association (see p. 357).

Upon assuming office in May 1994, the Muluzi administration inherited an economy weakened not only by natural impediments to growth (including Malawi's land-locked position, the vulnerability of the dominant agricultural sector to drought, and a high rate of population growth), but also by the severe mismanagement of economic affairs by the Banda regime. The Muluzi Government continued policies of economic liberalization and diversification initiated in the last years under Banda. However, by 1997, as adherence to the programme slackened, the budget deficit widened and GDP growth slowed, leading to the suspension of IMF disbursements. In October 1999 the IMF approved a loan worth US $10.6m. in support of the Government's economic programme for 1999–2000. However, a significant decline in revenue from tobacco exports adversely affected the economy in 2000, and GDP growth failed to meet expected targets. The devaluation of the kwacha continued throughout 2000–03. (From May 2000 the central bank discontinued its policy of quoting an exchange rate for the kwacha

and allowed the markets to determine the currency's relative value.) In November 2000 Malawi was granted debt relief equating to $1,000m. under the World Bank's initiative for heavily indebted poor countries (HIPCs), and in December the IMF approved a loan of some $65m. under its Poverty Reduction and Growth Facility (PRGF), disbursing $9m. immediately. Structural reforms planned for 2001 included the continuing restructuring of the civil service and of the tax system, in addition to progress with the privatization of state-owned enterprises. However, unsatisfactory progress in the implementation of the IMF-supported economic programme repeatedly delayed the first review of performance under the PRGF arrangement, and thus further disbursements. Moreover, in late 2001 and early 2002 the European Union (EU), the USA and other donors suspended aid to Malawi, in response to concerns regarding corruption and economic mismanagement. In April 2002 Malawi was suspended from the HIPC initiative over allegations of corruption concerning the sale of its grain reserves. Meanwhile, in February President Muluzi declared a state of national disaster and appealed for $21.6m. in international aid, as an estimated 70% of the population were seriously affected by food shortages, following severe flooding in 2001. In response, the USA provided some $29m. of aid in August; in the following months the IMF and the International Development Association provided emergency financial aid packages, and the World Bank approved grants and loans worth around $100m. to improve agricultural production and disaster management. In July 2003, in conjunction with the World Bank, the Government launched a financial management, transparency and accountability project, aimed at improving economic governance. In October the IMF finally completed the first review of Malawi's economic performance under the PRGF arrangement approved in December 2000, authorizing the disbursement of some $9m. The Fund extended the arrangement until December 2004, and agreed to resume interim assistance under the HIPC initiative. The EU and other donors also conditionally agreed to resume lending to Malawi, and in early 2004 the EU was preparing a three-year programme, worth €45m., to counter food insecurity in Malawi.

Education

Primary education is officially compulsory, beginning at six years of age and lasting for eight years. Secondary education, which begins at 14 years of age, lasts for four years, comprising two cycles of two years. According to UNESCO estimates, in 1999/2000 primary enrolment included 69% of children in the relevant age-group (males 66%; females 71%), while in 2000/01 secondary enrolment included 25% of children in the relevant age-group (males 27%; females 23%). A programme to expand education at all levels has been undertaken; however, the introduction of free primary education in September 1994 led to the influx of more than 1m. additional pupils, resulting in severe overcrowding in schools. In January 1996 the International Development Association granted US $22.5m. for the training of 20,000 newly recruited teachers, appointed in response to the influx. In mid-1997 additional funding was provided by the African Development Bank for the construction of primary and secondary schools. The University of Malawi had 3,565 students in 1999. Some students attended institutions in the United Kingdom and the USA. Estimated expenditure on education in the 2001/02 budget was 6,790m. kwacha (equivalent to 15.8% of total expenditure).

Public Holidays

2004: 1 January (New Year's Day), 15 January (John Chilembwe Day), 3 March (Martyrs' Day), 9–12 April (Easter), 1 May (Labour Day), 14 June (Freedom Day), 6 July (Republic Day), 11 October (Mothers' Day), 25–26 December (Christmas).

2005: 1 January (New Year's Day), 15 January (John Chilembwe Day), 3 March (Martyrs' Day), 25–28 March (Easter), 1 May (Labour Day), 14 June (Freedom Day), 6 July (Republic Day), 10 October (Mothers' Day), 25–26 December (Christmas).

Weights and Measures

The metric system is in use.

Statistical Survey

Sources (unless otherwise indicated): National Statistical Office of Malawi, POB 333, Zomba; tel. 524377; fax 525130; e-mail enquiries@statistics.gov.mw; internet www.nso.malawi.net; Reserve Bank of Malawi, POB 30063, Capital City, Lilongwe 3; tel. 780600; fax 782752; internet www.rbm.malawi.net.

Area and Population

AREA, POPULATION AND DENSITY

Area (sq km)	118,484*
Population (census results)	
1–21 September 1987	7,988,507
1–21 September 1998	
Males	4,867,563
Females.	5,066,305
Total	9,933,868
Population (UN estimates at mid-year)†	
2000	11,370,000
2001	11,627,000
2002	11,871,000
Density (per sq km) at mid-2002	100.2

* 45,747 sq miles. The area includes 24,208 sq km (9,347 sq miles) of inland water.

† Source: UN, *World Population Prospects: The 2002 Revision.*

Ethnic groups (1977 census): Africans 5,532,298; Europeans 6,377; Asians 5,682; others 3,103.

REGIONS
(census of September 1998)

Region	Area (sq km)*	Population	Density (per sq km)	Regional capital
Southern	31,753	4,633,968	145.9	Blantyre
Central	35,592	4,066,340	114.2	Lilongwe
Northern . . .	26,931	1,233,560	45.8	Mzuzu
Total	94,276	9,933,868	105.4	

* Excluding inland waters, totalling 24,208 sq km.

PRINCIPAL TOWNS
(population at census of September 1998)

Blantyre	502,053	Karonga	27,811
Lilongwe (capital)	440,471*	Kasungu	27,754
Mzuzu	86890	Mangochi	26,570
Zomba	65915		

* Including Limbe.
Source: Thomas Brinkoff, *City Population* (internet www.citypopulation.de).

BIRTHS AND DEATHS
(UN estimates, annual averages)

	1985–90	1990–95	1995–2000
Birth rate (per 1,000)	51.7	49.4	48.2
Death rate (per 1,000)	19.9	20.1	22.5

Source: UN, *World Population Prospects: The 2002 Revision.*

Expectation of life (WHO estimates, years at birth): 40.2 (males 39.8; females 40.6) in 2002 (Source: WHO, *World Health Report*).

ECONOMICALLY ACTIVE POPULATION*
(persons aged 10 years and over, 1998 census)

	Males	Females	Total
Agriculture, hunting, forestry and fishing	1,683,006	2,082,821	3,765,827
Mining and quarrying	2,206	293	2,499
Manufacturing	94,545	23,938	118,483
Electricity, gas and water . . .	6,656	663	7,319
Construction	70,196	3,206	73,402
Trade, restaurants and hotels . .	176,466	80,923	257,389
Transport, storage and communications	29,438	3,185	32,623
Financing, insurance, real estate and business services . . .	10,473	3,484	13,957
Public administration	82,973	18,460	101,433
Community, social and personal services	52,980	33,016	85,996
Total employed.	2,208,940	2,249,989	4,458,929
Unemployed	34,697	15,664	50,361
Total labour force	2,243,637	2,265,653	4,509,290

* Excluding armed forces.

Mid-2002 (estimates in '000): Agriculture, etc. 4,686; Total 5,705 (Source: FAO).

Health and Welfare

KEY INDICATORS

Total fertility rate (children per woman, 2002).	6.1
Under-5 mortality rate (per 1,000 live births, 2001) . . .	183
HIV/AIDS (% of persons aged 15–49, 2001).	15.00
Hospital beds (per 1,000 head, 1998)	1.34
Health expenditure (2001): US $ per head (PPP)	39
Health expenditure (2001): % of GDP	7.8
Health expenditure (2001): public (% of total)	35.0
Access to water (% of persons, 2000)	57
Access to sanitation (% of persons, 2000)	77
Human Development Index (2001): ranking	162
Human Development Index (2001): value	0.387

For sources and definitions, see explanatory note on p. vi.

Agriculture

PRINCIPAL CROPS
('000 metric tons)

	2000	2001	2002
Rice (paddy)	72	93	92
Maize	2,501	1,589	1,557
Millet	20	20	21
Sorghum	37	37	39
Potatoes	2,037	2,852	1,061
Cassava (Manioc)	2,757*	3,313	1,540
Dry beans	58	60*	94
Chick-peas*	35	35	35
Cow peas (dry)*	54	54	54
Pigeon peas*	79	79	79
Groundnuts (in shell)	117	148	158
Sunflower seed	3	4	4
Cabbages*	28	28	28
Tomatoes*	35	35	35
Onions (dry)*	18	18	18
Other vegetables*	175	175	175
Mangoes*	33	33	33
Bananas*	93	93	93
Plantains*	200	200	200
Other fruits*	185	150	186
Sugar cane*	2,000	1,900	1,900
Coffee (green)†	4	4	4
Tea	45	37	38*
Tobacco (leaves)	99	83	69
Cotton (lint)*	10	10	10

* FAO estimate(s).
† Unofficial figure.

Source: FAO.

LIVESTOCK
('000 head, year ending September)

	2000	2001	2002
Cattle	763	749	750*
Pigs	468	436	456
Sheep	112	115	115*
Goats	1,689	1,670	1,700*
Poultry*	15,000	15,200	15,200

* FAO estimate(s).

Source: FAO.

LIVESTOCK PRODUCTS
(FAO estimates, '000 metric tons)

	2000	2001	2002
Beef and veal	16	16	16
Goat meat	6	6	6
Pig meat	22	20	20
Poultry meat	15	15	15
Cows' milk	35	35	35
Hen eggs	20	20	20

Source: FAO.

Forestry

ROUNDWOOD REMOVALS
(FAO estimates, '000 cubic metres, excluding bark)

	2000	2001	2002
Sawlogs, veneer logs and logs for sleepers*	130	130	130
Other industrial wood	390	390	390
Fuel wood	4,964	4,996	5,029
Total	5,484	5,516	5,549

* Output assumed to be unchanged since 1993.

Source: FAO.

SAWNWOOD PRODUCTION
('000 cubic metres, including railway sleepers)

	1991*	1992†	1993
Coniferous (softwood)	28	28	30
Broadleaved (hardwood)	15	15	15†
Total	43	43	45

* Unofficial figures.
† FAO estimate(s).
1994–2002: Annual production as in 1993 (FAO estimates).

Source: FAO.

Fishing

('000 metric tons, live weight)

	1999	2000*	2001
Capture	45.4	43.0	40.7
Cyprinids	8.3	7.5	6.3
Tilapias	6.8	6.2	5.2
Cichlids	18.8	19.0	20.5
Torpedo-shaped catfishes	8.5	7.6	6.4
Other freshwater fishes	3.0	2.7	2.3
Aquaculture	0.6	0.5	0.6
Total catch	46.0	43.5	41.3

* FAO estimates.

Source: FAO, *Yearbook of Fishery Statistics*.

Mining

('000 metric tons, unless otherwise indicated)

	2000	2001	2002
Coal	34.3	34.4	41.9
Limestone	144.0	167.0	175.0
Lime	21.9	3.6	1.2
Gemstones (kilograms)	16,390	16,500*	16,500*
Aggregate ('000 cubic metres)	80.8	595.0	155.7

* Estimate.

Source: US Geological Survey.

Industry

SELECTED PRODUCTS
('000 metric tons, unless otherwise indicated)

	1999	2000	2001
Raw sugar	108	96	107
Beer ('000 hectolitres)	684	739	1,033
Blankets ('000)	478	574	281
Cement	104	198	111
Electric energy (million kWh)	883	886	n.a.

Source: UN, *Industrial Commodity Statistics Yearbook*.

2000 ('000 metric tons): Raw sugar 96; Cement 198.

Finance

CURRENCY AND EXCHANGE RATES

Monetary Units
100 tambala = 1 Malawi kwacha (K).

Sterling, Dollar and Euro Equivalents (31 October 2003)
£1 sterling = 183.32 kwacha;
US $1 = 108.37 kwacha;
€1 = 125.95 kwacha;
1,000 Malawi kwacha = £5.455 = $9.228 = €7.940.

Average Exchange Rate (kwacha per US $)
2000   59.5438
2001   72.1973
2002   76.6866

BUDGET
(K million, year ending 30 June)

Revenue*	1999/2000	2000/01	2001/02†
Tax revenue‡	14,353.3	19,285	20,168
Taxes on income and profits	6,590.5	8,740	9,338
Companies	2,569.8	3,140	2,987
Individuals	4,020.7	5,601	6,350
Taxes on goods and services	5,833.7	8,169	8,772
Surtax	5,189.3	6,091	6,472
Excise duties	644.4	2,078	2,250
Taxes on international trade	2,242.0	2,905	2,540
Import duties	2,200.6	2,385	2,396
Non-tax revenue	1,454.9	1,595	2,495
Departmental receipts	1,050.0	1,036	1,202
Total	**15,808.1**	**20,880**	**22,663**

Expenditure	1999/2000	2000/01	2001/02†
General public services	5,805	14,609	14,729
Defence	698	989	1,032
Public order and safety	881	1,164	1,633
Education	3,395	4,337	6,790
Health	1,975	2,275	4,334
Social security and welfare	1,680	1,392	307
Housing and community amenities	1,946	2,015	113
Recreational, cultural and other social services	61	74	61
Economic affairs and services	4,935	6,914	6,489
Agriculture and natural resources	2,058	1,541	2,356
Transport and communications	2,523	3,540	2,940
Unallocable expenditure	3,251	4,114	10,119
Total	**23,189**	**35,822**	**43,051**

* Excluding grants received (K million): 6,296 in 1999/2000; 10,353 in 2000/01; 9,429 in 2001/02.
† Estimates.
‡ After deduction of tax refunds (K million): 432 in 1999/2000; 460 in 2000/01; 373 in 2001/02.

Source: IMF, *Malawi: Selected Issues and Statistical Appendix* (August 2002).

INTERNATIONAL RESERVES
(US $ million at 31 December)

	2000	2001	2002
Gold*	0.54	0.54	0.51
IMF special drawing rights	0.47	0.84	0.09
Reserve position in IMF	2.91	2.85	3.11
Foreign exchange	243.52	203.05	161.98
Total	**247.45**	**207.28**	**165.69**

* National valuation.

Source: IMF, *International Financial Statistics*.

MONEY SUPPLY
(K million at 31 December)

	2000	2001	2002
Currency outside banks	4,144.9	4,208.5	6,198.1
Demand deposits at commercial banks	4,934.4	5,473.0	6,455.0
Total money (incl. others)	**9,198.0**	**10,014.4**	**12,738.8**

Source: IMF, *International Financial Statistics*.

COST OF LIVING
(National Consumer Price Index; base: 1990 = 100)

	2000	2001	2002
Food (incl. beverages)	1,611.7	1,895.4	2,198.4
Clothing (incl. footwear)	764.2	997.3	1,166.9
All items (incl. others)	**1,478.0**	**1,813.5**	**2,081.0**

Source: ILO.

NATIONAL ACCOUNTS
Expenditure on the Gross Domestic Product
(K million at current prices)

	2001	2002	2003
Government final consumption expenditure	19,591.3	45,110.3	52,527.3
Private final consumption expenditure	97,634.2	119,876.6	143,226.7
Increase in stocks	1,360.0	1,414.1	1,558.8
Gross fixed capital formation	15,740.8	14,110.2	14,674.7
Total domestic expenditure	**134,326.3**	**180,514.2**	**211,987.5**
Exports of goods and services	34,044.9	35,596.6	44,859.1
Less Imports of goods and services	45,291.2	62,103.3	72,835.7
GDP in purchasers' values	**123,080.0**	**154,007.5**	**184,011.0**
GDP at constant 1994 prices	**12,582.2**	**12,803.7**	**13,373.3**

Gross Domestic Product by Economic Activity
(K million at constant 1994 prices)

	2001	2002	2003
Agriculture, forestry and fishing	4,810	4,926	5,261
Mining and quarrying	202	124	153
Manufacturing	1,456	1,454	1,471
Electricity and water	176	186	195
Construction	273	311	341
Distribution	2,782	2,826	2,892
Transport and communications	546	625	639
Finance, insurance and business services	1,019	1,082	1,147
Ownership of dwellings	190	195	200
Private social services	279	287	295
Government services	1,216	1,208	1,226
Sub-total	**12,947**	**13,224**	**13,819**
Less Imputed bank service charges	365	420	446
GDP at factor cost	**12,582**	**12,804**	**13,373**

BALANCE OF PAYMENTS
(US $ million)

	2000	2001	2002
Exports of goods f.o.b.	403.1	427.9	422.4
Imports of goods f.o.b.	−462.0	−472.2	−573.2
Trade balance	**−58.8**	**−44.3**	**−150.8**
Exports of services	34.3	43.6	49.4
Imports of services	−167.1	−171.4	−221.9
Balance on goods and services	**−191.7**	**−172.1**	**−323.3**
Other income received	33.3	12.2	6.0
Other income paid	−50.5	−42.6	−44.5
Balance on goods, services and income	**−209.0**	**−202.5**	**−361.8**
Current transfers received	143.1	148.8	170.0
Current transfers paid	−7.6	−6.2	−8.9
Current balance	**−73.5**	**−60.0**	**−200.7**
Direct investment from abroad	26.0	19.3	5.9
Other investment liabilities	162.8	194.1	128.1
Net errors and omissions	−23.9	−221.5	156.7
Overall balance	**91.4**	**−68.0**	**90.0**

Source: IMF, *International Financial Statistics*.

External Trade

PRINCIPAL COMMODITIES
(distribution by SITC, US $ million)

Imports c.i.f.	1996	1997	1998
Food and live animals	56.5	67.5	97.9
Cereals and cereal preparations	41.5	45.7	78.4
Maize (unmilled)	11.2	14.5	55.1
Flour of wheat or of meslin	19.8	22.7	13.6
Mineral fuels, lubricants, etc.	72.0	94.0	57.4
Petroleum, petroleum products, etc.	70.8	93.4	56.9
Refined petroleum products	67.1	89.8	55.1
Chemicals and related products	118.6	125.8	79.0
Medicinal and pharmaceutical products	16.6	23.7	11.2
Manufactured fertilizers	56.7	37.6	29.9
Nitrogenous fertilizers (mineral or chemical)	35.0	21.4	13.7
Artificial resins, plastic materials, etc.	13.5	23.9	10.9
Basic manufactures	128.5	148.2	131.4
Paper, paperboard, etc.	21.4	25.3	18.6
Textile yarn, fabrics, etc.	42.9	45.5	39.4
Iron and steel	23.5	19.8	24.3
Machinery and transport equipment	206.4	272.8	161.2
Machinery specialized for particular industries	25.2	90.6	24.1
General industrial machinery, equipment and parts	19.5	18.7	24.1
Telecommunications and sound equipment	33.6	13.1	7.7
Road vehicles and parts*	93.0	111.3	69.5
Passenger motor cars (excl. buses)	19.9	20.0	13.2
Goods vehicles (lorries and trucks)	33.4	47.6	32.1
Motor vehicles for goods transport, etc.	32.1	45.9	26.9
Miscellaneous manufactured articles	32.9	48.4	38.1
Total (incl. others)	644.8	800.3	598.7

* Excluding tyres, engines and electrical parts.

Exports f.o.b.	1994	1995
Food and live animals	79.9	79.5
Sugar, sugar preparation and honey	24.8	19.6
Sugar and honey	24.8	19.6
Raw beet and cane sugars	17.6	16.1
Coffee, tea, cocoa and spices	45.3	44.1
Unroasted coffee, husks and skins	14.8	15.4
Tea	30.0	26.6
Beverages and tobacco	198.7	300.0
Tobacco and tobacco manufactures	198.2	295.6
Unmanufactured tobacco; tobacco refuse	196.7	293.8
Unstripped tobacco	67.9	70.7
Stripped or partly stripped tobacco	128.9	223.1
Crude materials (inedible) except fuels	10.5	11.3
Basic manufactures	20.0	17.0
Textile yarn, fabrics, etc.	15.1	11.0
Woven cotton fabrics (excl. narrow or special fabrics)	12.0	7.0
Unbleached fabrics (not mercerized)	10.8	6.4
Machinery and transport equipment	13.3	8.6
Miscellaneous manufactured articles	12.6	14.9
Clothing and accessories (excl. footwear)	11.2	13.3
Total (incl. others)	337.1	433.3

Source: UN, *International Trade Statistics Yearbook*.

1996 (K million): Total imports c.i.f. 9,544.9; Total exports f.o.b. 7,214.1 (Tobacco 4,408.0; Sugar 522.8; Tea 400.3; Cotton 227.6).

1997 (K million): Total imports c.i.f. 12,847.7; Total exports f.o.b. 8,827.4 (Tobacco 5,426.6; Tea 673.3; Cotton 477.9; Sugar 467.3).

1998 (K million): Total imports c.i.f. 17,998; Total exports f.o.b. 16,533 (Tobacco 9,678.7; Tea 1,249.0; Sugar 1,178.7; Cotton 155.9).

1999 (K million): Total imports c.i.f. 28,488.0; Total exports f.o.b. 20,318.0 (Tobacco 12,110.0; Tea 1,730.0; Sugar 860.0).

2000 (K million): Total imports c.i.f. 32,252.2; Total exports f.o.b. 23,630.4 (Tobacco 14,200.0; Tea 2,250.0; Sugar 2,340.0).

2001 (K million): Total imports c.i.f. 39,479.9; Total exports f.o.b. 31,816.5 (Tobacco 18,360.0; Tea 2,460.0; Sugar 3,980.0).

2002 (K million): Total imports c.i.f. 53,657.1; Total exports f.o.b. 31,416.0 (Tobacco 17,890.0; Tea 2,830.0; Sugar 2,680.0).

Sources (for 1996–2002): Malawi Government, *Economic Report*; IMF, *International Financial Statistics*; Reserve Bank of Malawi.

PRINCIPAL TRADING PARTNERS
(US $ million)

Imports	1999	2000	2001
France	10.0	5.1	6.1
Germany	30.1	13.0	17.3
Japan	16.6	12.7	12.4
Mozambique	5.3	12.1	13.3
Netherlands	4.0	7.4	3.6
South Africa	258.2	260.2	252.3
United Kingdom	31.2	18.1	13.0
USA	9.5	14.4	16.3
Zambia	66.1	62.8	69.3
Zimbabwe	80.3	92.3	101.5
Total (incl. others)	631.6	621.6	636.0

Exports	1999	2000	2001
France	8.6	8.8	11.3
Germany	72.1	29.3	55.9
Japan	21.1	46.5	37.6
Mozambique	2.5	0.6	0.7
Netherlands	43.0	28.6	26.8
South Africa	74.7	85.9	94.8
United Kingdom	16.0	15.3	19.6
USA	69.1	53.8	76.5
Zambia	2.6	2.2	2.4
Zimbabwe	7.0	8.1	8.9
Total (incl. others)	482.4	441.6	497.2

Transport

RAILWAYS
(traffic)

	1996	1997	1998
Passengers carried ('000)	339,000	452,000	349,000
Freight ('000 metric tons)	132,000	167,000	197,000

Source: Ministry of Finance and Economic Planning, *Economic Report 1999*.

ROAD TRAFFIC
(estimates, motor vehicles in use at 31 December)

	1994	1995	1996
Passenger cars	23,520	25,480	27,000
Lorries and vans	26,000	29,000	29,700

Source: International Road Federation, *World Road Statistics*.

SHIPPING

Inland waterways
(lake transport)

	1996	1997	1998
Freight ('000 metric tons)	13,000	10,000	14,000
Passengers carried ('000)	191,000	133,000	115,000

Source: Ministry of Finance and Economic Planning, *Economic Report 1999*.

CIVIL AVIATION
(traffic on scheduled services)

	1997	1998	1999
Kilometres flown (million)	3	3	2
Passengers carried ('000)	158	158	112
Passenger-kilometres (million)	336	337	224
Total ton-kilometres (million)	33	33	21

Source: UN, *Statistical Yearbook*.

Tourism

FOREIGN TOURIST ARRIVALS BY COUNTRY OF RESIDENCE

	1999	2000	2001
Mozambique	20,924	18,300	36,500
North America	6,995	3,000	14,500
South Africa*	16,680	15,000	28,500
United Kingdom and Ireland	22,383	17,200	27,500
Zambia	38,195	34,200	39,600
Zimbabwe	20,350	18,700	28,500
Total (incl. others)	254,352	228,106	266,300

* Includes South Africa, Botswana, Lesotho and Swaziland.

Source: World Tourism Organization, *Yearbook of Tourism Statistics*.

Tourism receipts (US $ million): 20 in 1999; 27 in 2000; 27 in 2001 (Source: World Bank).

Communications Media

	2000	2001	2002
Telephones ('000 main lines in use)	45.0	54.1	73.1
Mobile cellular telephones ('000 subscribers)	49.5	55.7	86.0
Internet users ('000)	15.0	20.0	27.0

Radio receivers ('000 in use): 4,929 in 1998.

Television receivers ('000 in use): 27 in 1999.

Facsimile machines (number in use): 1,250 in 1997.

Book production: 117 titles in 1996.

Daily newspapers: 5 in 1996; estimated average circulation 25,000 copies in 1995.

Non-daily newspapers: 4 in 1996 (estimated average circulation 120,000 copies).

Sources: UNESCO, *Statistical Yearbook*; UN, *Statistical Yearbook*; International Telecommunication Union.

Education

(1998)

	Institu-tions	Teachers	Students Males	Students Females	Students Total
Primary*†	3,160	340,375	1,057,273	1,045,151	2,102,424
Secondary†	n.a.	18,197	531,771	414,358	946,309
Tertiary	n.a.	509	8,303	3,176	11,479

* 1997 figures.
† UNESCO estimates.

Source: UNESCO Institute for Statistics.

Adult literacy rate (UNESCO estimates): 61.0% (males 75.0%; females 47.6%) in 2001 (Source: UN Development Programme, *Human Development Report*).

Directory

The Constitution

A new Constitution, replacing the (amended) 1966 Constitution, was approved by the National Assembly on 16 May 1994, and took provisional effect for one year from 18 May. During this time the Constitution was to be subject to review, and the final document was promulgated on 18 May 1995. The main provisions (with subsequent amendments) are summarized below:

THE PRESIDENT

The President is both Head of State and Head of Government. The President is elected for five years, by universal adult suffrage, in the context of a multi-party political system. The Constitution provides for up to two Vice-Presidents.

PARLIAMENT

Parliament comprises the President, the Vice-President(s) and the National Assembly. The National Assembly has 193 elective seats, elections being by universal adult suffrage, in the context of a multi-party system. Cabinet ministers who are not elected members of parliament also sit in the National Assembly. The Speaker is appointed from among the ordinary members of the Assembly. The parliamentary term is normally five years. The President has power to prorogue or dissolve Parliament.

In 1995 the National Assembly approved proposals for the establishment of a second chamber, the Senate, to be implemented in 1999. The chamber was not established by that date, however, and in January 2001 the National Assembly approved a proposal to abandon plans for its creation.

EXECUTIVE POWER

Executive power is exercised by the President, who appoints members of the Cabinet.

The Government

HEAD OF STATE

President: Dr (ELSON) BAKILI MULUZI (took office 21 May 1994; re-elected 15 June 1999).

First Vice-President: JUSTIN MALEWEZI.

CABINET
(April 2004)

President and Head of Government: Dr BAKILI MULUZI.

First Vice-President: JUSTIN MALEWEZI.

Second Vice-President and Minister of Agriculture, Irrigation and Food Security: CHAKUFWA CHIHANA.

Minister of Natural Resources and Environmental Affairs: ULADI MUSSA.

Minister of Foreign Affairs and International Co-operation: LILIAN PATEL.

Minister of Justice: PAUL MAULIDI.

Attorney-General: PETER FACHI.

Minister of Finance: FRIDAY JUMBE.

Minister of Economic Planning and Development: Dr BINGU WA MUTHARIKA.

Minister of Home Affairs and Internal Security: MONJEZA MALUZA.

Minister of Tourism, Parks and Wildlife: WALLACE CHIUME.

Minister of Youth, Sports and Culture: PHILLIP BWANALI.

Minister of Commerce and Industry: SAMUEL LEMMOTH MPASU.

Minister of Energy and Mining: HETHERWICK NTABA.

Minister of Health and Population: YUSUF MWAWA.

Minister of Transport and Public Works: CLEMENT STAMBULI.

Minister of Lands, Physical Planning and Surveys: THENGO MALOYA.

Minister of Housing: SAMUEL KALIYOMA PHUMISA.

Minister of Education, Science and Technology: GEORGE MTAFU.

Minister of Water Development: DUMBO LEMANI.

Minister of Defence: RODWELL MUNYENYEMBE.

Minister of Information: HENDERSON MABETI.

Minister of Privatization: HENRY PHOYA.

Minister of Gender and Community Services: ALICE SUMANI.

Minister of Labour and Vocational Training: BOB KHAMISA.

Minister without Portfolio: CHIPIMPHA MUGHOGHO.

Minister of State for Presidential Affairs: KEN LIPENGA.

Minister of State in the President's Office, responsible for the HIV/AIDS Programmes: MARY KAPHWEREZA BANDA.

Minister of State in the President's Office, responsible for People with Disabilities: SUSAN CHITIMBE.

Minister of State in the President's Office, responsible for Districts and Local Government Administration: SALIM BAGUS.

Minister of State in the President's Office, responsible for Statutory Corporations: RAPHAEL MHONE.

Minister of State, responsible for Poverty Alleviation Programmes and Disaster Management: BERNARD CHISALE.

There were also 14 Deputy Ministers.

MINISTRIES

Office of the President and Cabinet: Private Bag 301, Capital City, Lilongwe 3; tel. 1782655; fax 1783654.

Ministry of Agriculture, Irrigation and Food Security: POB 30144, Capital City, Lilongwe 3; tel. 1783450; fax 1784299.

Ministry of Commerce and Industry: POB 30366, Capital City, Lilongwe 3; tel. 1780244; fax 1780680.

Ministry of Defence: Private Bag 339, Lilongwe 3; tel. 1782200; fax 1781282.

Ministry of District and Local Government Administration: POB 30312, Lilongwe 3; tel. 1784500; fax 1782130.

Ministry of Economic Planning and Development: Lilongwe.

Ministry of Education, Science and Technology: Private Bag 328, Capital City, Lilongwe 3; tel. 1784800; fax 1782873.

Ministry of Energy and Mining: Lilongwe.

Ministry of Finance: POB 30049, Capital City, Lilongwe 3; tel. 1782199; fax 1781679.

Ministry of Foreign Affairs and International Co-operation: POB 30315, Capital City, Lilongwe 3; tel. 1731788; fax 1781516.

Ministry of Gender and Community Services: Private Bag 330, Capital City, Lilongwe 3; tel. 1780411; fax 1780826.

Ministry of Health and Population: POB 30377, Capital City, Lilongwe 3; tel. 1783044; fax 1783109.

Ministry of HIV/AIDS Programmes: Lilongwe.

Ministry of Housing: Lilongwe.

Ministry of Information: Private Bag 310, Lilongwe 3; tel. 1783233; fax 1784568.

Ministry of Justice: Private Bag 333, Capital City, Lilongwe 3; tel. 1788411; fax 1788332; e-mail justice@sdnp.org.mw; internet www.sdnp.org.mw/ruleoflaw.

Ministry of Labour and Vocational Training: Private Bag 344, Capital City, Lilongwe 3; tel. 1783277; fax 1783805; e-mail labour@eo.wn.apc.org.

Ministry of Lands, Physical Planning and Surveys: Private Bag 311, Lilongwe 3; tel. 1784766; fax 1781389.

Ministry of Natural Resources and Environmental Affairs: Private Bag 350, Lilongwe 3; tel. 1782600; fax 1780260.

Ministry of Privatization: Lilongwe.

Ministry of Statutory Corporations: POB 30061, Lilongwe 3; tel. 1784266; fax 1784110.

Ministry of Tourism, Parks and Wildlife: Private Bag 326, Lilongwe 3; tel. 1775499; fax 1770650; e-mail tourism@malawi.net.

Ministry of Transport and Public Works: Private Bag 322, Capital City, Lilongwe 3; tel. 1780344; fax 1784678.

Ministry of Water Development: Tikwere House, Private Bag 390, Capital City, Lilongwe 3; tel. 1782600; fax 1780260.

Ministry of Youth, Sports and Culture: POB 30387, Lilongwe 3.

President and Legislature

PRESIDENT

Presidential Election, 15 June 1999

Candidate	Votes	% of votes
Bakili Muluzi (UDF)	2,442,685	51.37
Gwandaguluwe Chakuamba (MCP-AFORD)	2,106,790	44.30
Kamulepo Kalua (MDP) . . .	67,856	1.43
Rev. Daniel Nkhumbwe (CNU) . .	24,347	0.51
Bingu wa Mutharika (UP) . .	22,073	0.46
Invalid votes	91,671	1.93
Total	4,755,422	100.00

NATIONAL ASSEMBLY

Speaker: DAVIS KATSONGA.

General Election, 15 June 1999

Party	Seats
UDF	93
MCP	66
AFORD	29
Independents	4
Total*	192

* Voting in the remaining constituency was postponed, owing to the death of a candidate. The seat was won by a candidate of the UDF at a by-election in October.

Political Organizations

Alliance for Democracy (AFORD): Private Bag 28, Lilongwe; f. 1992; in March 1993 absorbed membership of fmr Malawi Freedom Movement; Pres. CHAKUFWA CHIHANA; First Vice-Pres. KALUNDI CHIRWA; Sec.-Gen. WALLACE CHIUME.

Congress for the Second Republic (CSR): Leader KANYAMA CHIUME.

Forum Party (FP): f. 1997; Leader KALONGA STAMBULI.

Malawi Congress Party (MCP): Private Bag 388, Lilongwe 3; tel. 1730388; f. 1959; sole legal party 1966–93; Pres. JOHN TEMBO; Sec.-Gen. KATE KAINJA.

Malawi Democratic Party (MDP): Pres. KAMLEPO KALUA.

Malawi Democratic Union (MDU): Pres. JAMES TABUNA DISENTIKUBA.

Malawi Forum for Unity and Development (MAFUNDE): f. 2002; aims to combat corruption and food shortages; Pres. GEORGE MNESA.

Mass Movement for the Young Generation (MM): Lilongwe; f. 1998; Interim Pres. CHAIMA BANDA.

Movement for Genuine Democratic Change (MGODE): Lilongwe; f. 2003 by fmr mems of AFORD; Pres. SAM KANDODO BANDA; Nat. Chair. GREENE LULILO MWAMONDWE; Sec.-Gen. RODGER NKWAZI.

National Democratic Alliance (NDA): POB 994, Blantyre; tel. 1842593; e-mail nda-mw@yahoo.com; internet www.geocities.com/nda_mw; f. 2001 by fmr mems of UDF; Pres. BROWN MPINGANJIRA; Chair. JAMES MAKHUMULA.

New Congress for Democracy (NCD): Lilongwe; f. 2004 by fmr mems of MCP; Pres. HETHERWICK NTABA.

New Dawn for Africa (NDA): Lilongwe; f. 2003; Pres. THOM CHIUMIA.

Pamodzi Freedom Party (PFP): Lilongwe; f. 2002; Interim Pres. RAINSFORD CHIGADULA NDIWO.

People's Progressive Movement: f. 2003 by fmr mems of the UDF; Pres. ALEKE KADONAPHANI BANDA.

Republican Party (RP): f. 2004; Leader GWANDAGULUWE CHAKUAMBA.

Social Democratic Party (SDP): Pres. ISON KAKOME.

United Democratic Front (UDF): POB 5446, Limbe; internet www.udf.malawi.net; f. 1992; Chair. Dr BAKILI MULUZI; Sec.-Gen. KENNEDY MAKWANGWALA.

United Front for Multi-party Democracy (UFMD): f. 1992 by three exiled political groups: the Socialist League of Malawi, the Malawi Freedom Party and the Malawi Democratic Union; Pres. EDMOND JIKA.

United Party (UP): f. 1997.

The Movement for the Restoration of Democracy in Malawi (f. 1996) is based in Mozambique and consists of fmr Malawi Young Pioneers; it conducts occasional acts of insurgency.

Diplomatic Representation

EMBASSIES AND HIGH COMMISSIONS IN MALAWI

China (Taiwan): Area 40, Plot No. 9, POB 30221, Capital City, Lilongwe 3; tel. 1773611; fax 1774812; e-mail rocemml@malawi.net; Ambassador CHEN HSI-TSAN.

Egypt: POB 30451, Lilongwe 3; tel. 1780668; fax 1780691; e-mail egy_emb_Malawi@yahoo.com; Ambassador ADEL EL-MELIGUI.

Germany: POB 30046, Lilongwe 3; tel. 1772555; fax 1770250; e-mail germanemb@malawi.net; Ambassador Dr FRANZ RING.

Mozambique: POB 30579, Lilongwe 3; tel. 1784100; fax 1781342; e-mail mozambique@malawi.net; High Commissioner JORGE DE SOUSA MATEUS.

Norway: Private Bag B323, Lilongwe 3; tel. 1774211; fax 1772845; e-mail emb.lilongwe@mfa.no; Ambassador ASBJØRN EIDHAMMER.

South Africa: Kang'ombe House, 3rd Floor, City Centre, POB 30043, Lilongwe 3; tel. 1773722; fax 1772571; e-mail sahc@malawi.net; High Commissioner N. M. C. SELEKA.

United Kingdom: British High Commission Bldg, Capital Hill, POB 30042, Lilongwe 3; tel. 1772400; fax 1772657; e-mail bhclilongwe@fco.gov.uk; High Commissioner NORMAN LING.

USA: Area 40, Plot 18, POB 30016, Lilongwe 3; tel. 1773166; fax 1770471; internet usembassy.state.gov/malawi; Ambassador STEVEN A. BROWNING.

Zambia: POB 30138, Lilongwe 3; tel. 1782635; fax 1784349; High Commissioner Col (retd) LAWRENCE M. H. HAAMAUNDU.

Zimbabwe: POB 30187, Lilongwe 3; tel. 1784988; fax 1782382; e-mail zimhighcomllw@malawi.net; Ambassador E. T. MANYIKA.

Judicial System

The courts administering justice are the Supreme Court of Appeal, High Court and Magistrates' Courts.

The High Court, which has unlimited jurisdiction in civil and criminal matters, consists of the Chief Justice and five puisne judges. Traditional Courts were abolished under the 1994 Constitution. Appeals from the High Court are heard by the Supreme Court of Appeal in Blantyre.

High Court of Malawi

POB 30244, Chichiri, Blantyre 3; tel. 1670255; fax 1670213; e-mail highcourt@sdnp.org.mw; internet www.judiciary.mw.

Registrar H. S. POTANI.

Chief Justice: RICHARD A. BANDA.

Justices of Appeal: L. A. UNYOLO, H. M. MTEGHA, J. B. KALAILE, D. G. TAMBALA, A. S. E. MSOSA.

High Court Judges: M. P. MKANDAWIRE, I. J. MTAMBO, D. F. MWAUNGULU, A. K. C. NYIRENDA, D. S. L. KUMANGE, G. M. CHIMASULA PHIRI, E. B. Z. KUMITSONYO, CHIUDZA BANDA, L. B. T. NDOVIE, W. M. HANJA, E. B. TWEA, R. R. MZIKAMANDO, J. M. ANSAH, R. R. CHINANGWA, A. CHIPETA.

Religion

About 75% of the population profess Christianity. The Asian community includes Muslims and Hindus, and there is a small number of African Muslims. Traditional beliefs are followed by about 10% of the population.

CHRISTIANITY

Malawi Council of Churches: POB 30068, Capital City, Lilongwe 3; tel. 1783499; fax 1783106; f. 1939; 19 mems and 12 associates; Chair. Rt Rev. JAMES TENGATENGA; Gen. Sec. Rev. Dr A. C. MUSOPOLE.

The Anglican Communion

Anglicans are adherents of the Church of the Province of Central Africa, covering Botswana, Malawi, Zambia and Zimbabwe. The Church comprises 12 dioceses, including three in Malawi. The Archbishop of the Province is the Bishop of Botswana. There are about 80,000 adherents in Malawi.

Bishop of Lake Malawi: Rt Rev. PETER NATHANIEL NYANJA, POB 30349, Capital City, Lilongwe 3; tel. 1797858; fax 1797548; e-mail nyanja@comw.net.

Bishop of North Malawi: Rt Rev. CHRISTOPHER JOHN BOYLE, POB 120, Mzuzu; tel. 1331486; fax 1333805; e-mail bishopboyle@sdnp.org.mw.

Bishop of Southern Malawi: Rt Rev. JAMES TENGATENGA, POB 30220, Chichiri, Blantyre 3; tel. 1641218; fax 1641235; e-mail angsoma@clcom.net; internet www.clcom.net/angsoma.

Protestant Churches

Church of Central Africa (Presbyterian): Blantyre Synod: POB 413, Blantyre; tel. and fax 1633942; comprises three synods in Malawi (Blantyre, Livingstonia and Nkhoma); Co-ordinator Rev. J. J. MPHATSE; Gen. Sec. MATIYA NKHOMA; more than 1m. adherents in Malawi.

Evangelical Association of Malawi: Lilongwe; tel. and fax 1730373; e-mail evangelicalassmw@malawi.net; Chair. Rev. MVULA J. MVULA; Gen. Sec. FRANCIS MKANDAWIRE.

The Indigenous Baptist Convention of Malawi: POB 51083, Limbe; tel. 1643224; Chair. Rev. S. L. MALABWANYA; Gen. Sec. Rev. M. T. KACHASO GAMA.

The Lutheran Church of Central Africa: POB 748, Blantyre; tel. 1630821; fax 1630821; f. 1963; evangelical and medical work; Co-ordinator J. M. JANOSEK; 35,000 mems. in Malawi.

Seventh-day Adventists: POB 951, Blantyre; tel. 1620264; fax 1620528; e-mail 1016631763@malawi.net; Pres. B. E. MALOPA; Exec. Sec. R. R. MZUMARA.

The African Methodist Episcopal Church, the Churches of Christ, the Free Methodist Church, the Pentecostal Assemblies of God and the United Evangelical Church in Malawi are also active.

The Roman Catholic Church

Malawi comprises one archdiocese and six dioceses. At 31 December 2002 some 19.4% of the total population were adherents of the Roman Catholic Church.

Episcopal Conference of Malawi

Catholic Secretariat of Malawi, Chimutu Rd, POB 30384, Capital City, Lilongwe 3; tel. 1782066; fax 1782019; e-mail ecm@malawi.net. f. 1969; Pres. Most Rev. TARCISIUS GERVAZIO ZIYAYE (Archbishop of Blantyre).

Archbishop of Blantyre: Most Rev. TARCISIUS GERVAZIO ZIYAYE, Archbishop's House, POB 385, Blantyre; tel. and fax 1637905.

BAHÁ'Í FAITH

National Spiritual Assembly: POB 30922, Lilongwe 3; tel. 1771713; e-mail bahaimalawi@africa-online.net; f. 1970; mems resident in over 1,500 localities.

The Press

ABA Today: POB 5861, Limbe; f. 1982; monthly; publ. by African Businessmen's Association of Malawi.

Blantyre Handbook: Centraf Associates, POB 30462, Chichiri, Blantyre; f. 1978; quarterly.

Boma Lathu: POB 494, Blantyre; tel. 1620266; fax 1620039; e-mail manabt@Malawi.net; internet www.mafor.malawi.net; f. 1973; monthly; Chichewa; publ. by the Ministry of Information; circ. 100,000.

Business and Development News: POB 829, Development House, Victoria Avenue, Blantyre; f. 1973; monthly.

Business Monthly: POB 906646, Blantyre 9; tel. 16301114; fax 1620039; e-mail aluviza@miw.healthnet.org; f. 1995; 6 a year; English; economic, financial and business news; Editor ANTHONY LIVUZA; circ. 10,000.

The Daily Times: Private Bag 39, Blantyre; tel. 1671445; fax 1671114; e-mail dailytimes@malawi.net; f. 1895; Mon.–Fri.; English; Editor-in-Chief VELS MACHOA; circ. 11,500.

Kuunika: POB 17, Nkhoma, Lilongwe; f. 1909; monthly; Chichewa; Presbyterian; Editor Rev. M. C. NKHALAMBAYAUSI; circ. 6,000.

Malawi Life: Private Bag 39, Ginnery Corner, Blantyre; tel. 1671566; f. 1991; monthly magazine; English.

Malawi Government Gazette: Government Printer, POB 37, Zomba; tel. 1523155; f. 1894; weekly.

Malawi News: Private Bag 39, Blantyre; tel. 1671566; fax 1671114; e-mail dailytimes@malawi.net; internet www.blantyre-newspapers .com; f. 1895; weekly; English, Chichewa; Editor HORACE SOMANJE; circ. 20,000.

Medical Quarterly: Centraf Associates, POB 30462, Chichiri, Blantyre; f. 1980; quarterly; English; journal of the Medical Association of Malawi.

The Mirror: POB 30721, Blantyre; tel. 1675043; f. 1994; weekly; English; Editor-in-Chief GEORGE TUKHUWA; circ. 10,000.

Moni: POB 5592, Limbe; tel. 1651139; fax 1641126; e-mail mpp@ clcom.net; f. 1964; monthly; Chichewa and English; circ. 40,000.

Moyo: Health Education Unit, POB 30377, Lilongwe 3; bi-monthly; English; publ. by Ministry of Health and Population; Editor-in-Chief W. G. BOMBA.

Nation: POB 30408, Chichiri, Blantyre; tel. 1673703; fax 1674343; internet www.nation.malawi.net; f. 1993; weekly; English; independent; Editor ALFRED NTONGA; circ. 10,000.

National Magazine: Blantyre Newspapers Ltd, Blantyre; tel. 1671566; fax 16711114; f. 1991; monthly.

Odini: POB 133, Lilongwe; tel. 1721135; fax 1721141; f. 1949; fortnightly; Chichewa and English; Roman Catholic; Dir P. I. AKOMENJI; circ. 12,000.

This is Malawi: POB 494, Blantyre; tel. 1620266; fax 1620807; e-mail alivuza@malawi.net; internet www.maform.malawi.net; f. 1964; monthly; English and Chichewa edns; publ. by the Dept of Information; Editor ANTHONY LIVUZA; circ. 12,000.

The Weekly Chronicle: POB 40521, Lilongwe; f. 1993; weekly; English, independent; Editor WILLIE ZINGANI; circ. 5,000.

NEWS AGENCIES

Malawi News Agency (MANA): Mzuza; tel. 1636122; f. 1966.

Foreign Bureau

Newslink Africa (UK): POB 2688, Blantyre; Correspondent HOBBS GAMA.

Publishers

Christian Literature Association in Malawi: POB 503, Blantyre; tel. 1620839; f. 1968; general and religious publs in Chichewa and English; Gen. Man. J. T. MATENJE.

Likuni Press and Publishing House: POB 133, Lilongwe; tel. 1721388; fax 1721141; f. 1949; publs in English and Chichewa; Gen. Man. (vacant).

Mzuzu Publishing Co: POB 225, Nkhata Bay; tel. 1352353; f. 1977; Exec. Chair. M. W. KANYAMA CHIUME.

Popular Publications: POB 5592, Limbe; tel. 1651833; fax 1641126; e-mail mpp@clcom.net; f. 1961; general and religious; Gen. Man. VALES MACHILA.

Government Publishing House

Government Printer: POB 37, Zomba; tel. 1523155.

Broadcasting and Communications

TELECOMMUNICATIONS

Malawi Telecommunications Ltd (MTL): Lamya House, Masauko Chipembere Highway, POB 537, Blantyre; tel. 1620977; fax 1624445; e-mail mtlceo@malawi.net; f. 2000 following division of

Malawi Posts and Telecommunications Corpn into two separate entities; partial privatization to be completed in 2004; CEO EMMANUEL MAHUKA.

Mobile Systems International (MSI): f. 1998; operates the Celtel mobile cellular telephone network; Man. Dir DAVID BAMFORD.

Telekom Networks Malawi (TNM): tel. 1641088; fax 1642805; e-mail nasirbah@malawi.net; operates mobile cellular telephone network; CEO NASIR BAHARONI.

BROADCASTING

Radio

Malawi Broadcasting Corpn: POB 30133, Chichiri, Blantyre 3; tel. 1671222; fax 1671257; e-mail dgmbc@malawi.net; f. 1964; statutory body; semi-commercial, partly state-financed; two channels; programmes in English, Chichewa, Chitumbuka, Lomwe and Yao; Chair. Maj. Gen. B. NAMWAL; Dir-Gen. OWEN MAUNDE (acting); Dir of News and Current Affairs M. M. KASINJA.

Television

Television Malawi (TVM): f. 1999; broadcasts 55 hours per week, of which 10 hours are produced locally; relays programmes from France, Germany, South Africa and the United Kingdom; Chair. MOHAMMED KULESI.

Finance

(cap. = capital; res = reserves; dep. = deposits; m. = million; brs = branches; amounts in kwacha)

BANKING

Central Bank

Reserve Bank of Malawi: POB 30063, Capital City, Lilongwe 3; tel. 1770600; fax 1772752; e-mail reserve-bank@rbm.malawi.net; internet www.rbm.malawi.net; f. 1965; bank of issue; cap. 306.0m., res 3,627.3m., dep. 14,267.9m. (Dec. 2001); Gov. Dr ELIAS E. NGALANDE BANDA; Gen. Mans E. J. KAMBALAME, C. S. R. CHUKA; br. in Blantyre.

Commercial Banks

Finance Bank Malawi Ltd: Finance House, Victoria Ave, POB 421, Blantyre; tel. 1624232; fax 1622957; e-mail finbank@malawi .net; cap. and res 213.6m., total assets 1,817.3m. (Dec. 2001); Chair. Dr R. L. MAHTANI; Man. Dir A. S. PILLAI.

Loita Investment Bank Ltd: Loita House, Victoria Ave, Private Bag 389, Chichiri, Blantyre 3; tel. 1620099; fax 1622683; e-mail lib@ mw.loita.com; internet www.loita.com; cap. 65.0m., res 25.6m., dep. 2,218.3m. (Dec. 2002); Chair. N. JUSTIN CHINYATA; Gen. Man. JEROME BISSAY; 2 brs.

National Bank of Malawi: Victoria Ave, POB 945, Blantyre; tel. 1620622; fax 1620606; e-mail executive@natbankmw.com; internet www.natbank.co.mw; f. 1971; cap. 453m., res 609m., dep. 10,292m. (Dec. 2002); Chair. Dr M. A. P. CHIKAONDA; CEO T. J. O. BARNES; 13 brs; agencies throughout Malawi.

Stanbic Bank Ltd: POB 1111, Blantyre; tel. 1620144; fax 1620360; e-mail malawi@stanbic.com; internet www.stanbic.com; f. 1970 as Commercial Bank of Malawi; name changed as above June 2003; 8% state-owned; cap. 200m., res 290m., dep. 7,554m. (Dec. 2001); Chair. ELVAS B. KADZAKO; Man. Dir VICTOR MBEWE; 13 brs.

Development Bank

IndeBank Ltd: Indebank House, Kaushong Rd, Top Mandala, POB 358, Blantyre; tel. 1620055; fax 1623353; e-mail indebank@malawi .net; f. 1972 as Investment and Development Bank of Malawi Ltd; cap. 80.0m., total assets 1,342.2m. (Dec. 2001); provides loans to statutory corpns and to private enterprises in the agricultural, industrial, tourism, transport and commercial sectors; Chair. S. MALATA; Gen. Man. AGNES VARELA.

Merchant Banks

First Merchant Bank Ltd: First House, Glyn Jones Road, POB 122, Blantyre; tel. 1621955; fax 1621978; e-mail fmb.headoffice@ fmbmalawi.com; internet www.fmbmalawi.com; cap. and res 242.8m., total assets 3,514.9m. (Dec. 2001); Chair. RASIKBHAI C. KANTARIA; Gen. Man. SEETHARAMAN SRINIVASAN.

Leasing and Finance Co of Malawi Ltd: Indebank House, 1st Floor, Top Mandala, POB 1963, Blantyre; tel. 1620233; fax 1620275; e-mail lfc@malawi.net; f. 1986; subsidiary of First Merchant Bank

Ltd since June 2002; cap. 8.0m., total assets 596.1m. (Sept. 2001); Gen. Man. J. N. WHITEHEAD.

National Finance Co Ltd: Plantation House, POB 261, Blantyre; tel. 1623670; fax 1620549; e-mail natfin@malawi.net; internet www .natbank.co.mw; f. 1958; subsidiary of National Bank of Malawi; cap. and res 87.0m., total assets 243.1m. (Dec. 2001); Chair. T. J. O. BARNES; Gen. Man. M. T. BAMFORD.

Savings Bank

Malawi Savings Bank: Umoyo House, Victoria Ave, POB 521, Blantyre; tel. 1625111; fax 1621089; e-mail msb@msb.malawi.net; state-owned; total assets 777.5m. (2001); Chair. P. CHILAMBE; Gen. Man. IAN C. BONONGWE.

STOCK EXCHANGE

Malawi Stock Exchange: Able House, Ground Floor, cnr Hannover Ave and Chilembwe Rd, POB 2598, Blantyre; tel. 1821783; fax 1624353; f. 1995; Chair. C. MPANDE; CEO THOM MPINGANJIRA.

INSURANCE

National Insurance Co Ltd: NICO House, POB 501, Blantyre; tel. 1622699; fax 1622364; e-mail nico@nico.malawi.net; f. 1971; transferred to private sector in 1998; cap. and res 104.7m. (Sept. 1997); offices at Blantyre, Lilongwe, Mzuzu and Zomba; agencies countrywide; CEO and Man. Dir FELIX L. MLUSU.

Old Mutual Malawi: POB 393, Blantyre; tel. 1620677; fax 1622649; e-mail oldmutual@malawi.net; f. 1845; Gen. Man. MARIUS WALTERS.

Royal Insurance Co of Malawi Ltd: POB 442, Blantyre; tel. 1624044; fax 1623862; Gen. Man. ROBERT G. NDUNGU.

United General Insurance Co Ltd: POB 383, Blantyre; tel. 1621577; fax 1621980; e-mail ugi@malawi.net; Gen. Man. I. KUMWENDA.

Trade and Industry

GOVERNMENT AGENCIES

Malawi Export Promotion Council: Delamere House, POB 1299, Blantyre; tel. 1620499; fax 1635429; e-mail mepco@malawi.net; f. 1974; Gen. Man. G. I. L. MANGOCHI.

Malawi Investment Promotion Agency (MIPA): Aquarius House, Private Bag 302, Lilongwe 3; tel. 1770800; fax 1771781; e-mail mipall@malawi.net; internet www.mipa.malawi.net; f. 1993; promotes and facilitates local and foreign investment; CEO TED A. KALEBE.

Privatization Commission: POB 937, Blantyre; tel. 1623655; fax 1621248; f. 1996; to oversee privatization programme.

DEVELOPMENT ORGANIZATIONS

Agricultural Development and Marketing Corpn (ADMARC): POB 5052, Limbe; tel. 1640500; fax 1640486; f. 1971; govt agency; markets agricultural crops produced by smallholder farmers; exports confectionery-grade groundnut kernels, maize, cassava and sunflower seed; primary marketing of tobacco, wheat and beans, peas and other seeds; co-operates with commercial cos in the cultivation and processing of agricultural produce; in process of privatization in 2004; Chair. J. STEVENS.

Malawi Development Corpn (MDC): MDC House, Glyn Jones Rd, POB 566, Blantyre; tel. 1620100; fax 1620584; e-mail mdcgm@ malawi.net; internet www.mdc.co.mw; f. 1964; state-owned; provides finance and management advice to commerce and industry; 23 subsidiary and assoc. cos; Chair. Dr JERRY A. A. JANA; Gen. Man. PATRICK A. MAKINA.

Small Enterprise Development Organization of Malawi (SEDOM): POB 525, Blantyre; tel. 1622555; fax 1622781; e-mail sedom@sdnp.org.mw; f. 1982; financial services and accommodation for indigenous small- and medium-scale businesses.

CHAMBER OF COMMERCE

Malawi Chamber of Commerce and Industry: Chichiri Trade Fair Grounds, POB 258, Blantyre; tel. 1671988; fax 1671147; e-mail mcci@eo.wn.apc.org; f. 1892; 400 mems; Chair. MARK KATSONGO PHIRI.

INDUSTRIAL AND TRADE ASSOCIATIONS

Smallholder Coffee Farmers Trust: POB 20133, Luwinga, Mzuzu 2; tel. 1332899; fax 1332902; e-mail mzuzucoffee@malawi .net; producers and exporters of arabica coffee.

Smallholder Sugar Authority: Blantyre.

Smallholder Tea Authority: POB 80, Thyolo.

Tea Association of Malawi Ltd: POB 930, Blantyre; tel. 1671355; fax 1671427; f. 1936; 20 mems; Man. Dir G. D. BANDA.

Tobacco Association of Malawi: POB 31360, Lilongwe 3; tel. 1773099; fax 1773493; e-mail tama@eomw.net; f. 1929; 60,000 mems; Pres. ALBERT W. KAMULAGA; Exec. Sec. S. Y. L. CHIRAMBO.

Tobacco Exporters' Association of Malawi Ltd: Private Bag 403, Kanengo, Lilongwe 4; tel. 1710663; fax 1710668; e-mail tobacco-exporters@sndp.org.mw; f. 1930; 9 mems; Chair. CHARLES A. M. GRAHAM; Exec. Sec. H. M. MBALE.

EMPLOYERS' ORGANIZATIONS

Employers' Consultative Association of Malawi (ECAM): POB 2134, Blantyre; tel. and fax 1670715; e-mail ecam@malawi.net; f. 1963; 250 mems; Chair. H. C. MVULA; Exec. Dir V. F. SINJANI.

Master Builders', Civil Engineering Contractors' and Allied Trades' Association: POB 311, Blantyre; tel. and fax 1624754; e-mail bes@malawi.net; f. 1955; 41 mems (2003); Chair. E. BIZZARO.

Master Printers' Association of Malawi: POB 2460, Blantyre; tel. 1670608; f. 1962; 21 mems; Chair. PAUL FREDERICK.

Motor Traders' Association: POB 311, Blantyre; tel. and fax 1624754; e-mail bes@malawi.net; f. 1954; 24 mems (2003); Chair. A. R. OSMAN.

UTILITY

Electricity

Electricity Supply Commission of Malawi (ESCOM): ESCOM House, Haile Selassie Rd, POB 2047, Blantyre; tel. and fax 1622008; f. 1966; controls electricity distribution; Chair. FRANK JIYA; CEO REYNOLD DUNCAN.

TRADE UNIONS

Trades Union Congress of Malawi (TUCM): POB 5094, Limbe; f. 1964; 6,500 mems; Chair. KEN WILLIAM MHANGO; Gen. Sec. EATON V. LAITA; the following are among the principal affiliated unions:

> **Building Construction, Civil Engineering and Allied Workers' Union:** Limbe; tel. 1650598; f. 1961; 6,000 mems; Chair. W. I. SOKO; Gen. Sec. G. SITIMA.

> **Railway Workers' Union of Malawi:** POB 5393, Limbe; tel. 1640844; f. 1954; 3,000 mems; Pres. THOMAS CHISAKANIZA; Gen. Sec. MACDONALD LUWANJA.

Other unions affiliated to the TUCM are the Commercial and Allied Workers' Union, the Civil Servants' Trade Union, the Hotels, Food and Catering Workers' Union, the Local Government Employees' Union, the Plantation and Agricultural Workers' Union, the Teachers' Union of Malawi, the Textile, Garment, Guards and Leather Workers' Union, the Transport and General Workers' Union and the Sugar Plantation and Allied Workers' Union. The TUCM and its affiliated unions had a total membership of 450,000 in 1995.

Transport

RAILWAYS

The Central East African Railways Co (fmrly Malawi Railways) operates between Nsanje (near the southern border with Mozambique) and Mchinji (near the border with Zambia) via Blantyre, Salima and Lilongwe, and between Nkaya and Nayuchi on the eastern border with Mozambique, covering a total of 797 km. The Central East African Railways Co and Mozambique State Railways connect Malawi with the Mozambican ports of Beira and Nacala. These links, which traditionally form Malawi's principal trade routes, were effectively closed during 1983–85, owing to insurgent activity in Mozambique. The rail link to Nacala was reopened in October 1989; however, continued unrest and flooding in Mozambique prevented full use of the route until the completion of a programme of improvements in September 2000; the service was temporarily suspended in 2002 while safety was improved. There is a rail/lake interchange station at Chipoka on Lake Malawi, from where vessels operate services to other lake ports in Malawi.

Central East African Railways Co Ltd: POB 5144, Limbe; tel. 1640844; fax 1643262; f. 1994 as Malawi Railways Ltd; sold to a consortium owned by Mozambique's Empresa Nacional dos Portos e Caminhos de Ferro de Moçambique and the USA's Railroad Corpn in mid-1999 and subsequently renamed as above; CEO ROBERT MORTENSEN; Gen. Man. BRANDLEY KNAPP.

ROADS

In 1997 Malawi had a total road network of some 16,451 km, of which 4,520 km were main roads and 2,768 km were secondary roads; about 19.0% of the road network was paved. In 1999 the total road network was estimated at 28,400 km. In addition, unclassified community roads total an estimated 10,000 km. All main roads, and most secondary roads, are all-weather roads. Major routes link Lilongwe and Blantyre with Harare (Zimbabwe), Lusaka (Zambia) and Mbeya and Dar es Salaam (Tanzania). A 480-km highway along the western shore of Lake Malawi links the remote Northern Region with the Central and Southern Regions. A project to create a new trade route, or 'Northern Corridor', through Tanzania, involving road construction and improvements in Malawi, was completed in 1992.

Road Transport Operators' Association: Chitawira Light Industrial Site, POB 30740, Chichiri, Blantyre 3; tel. 1670422; fax 1671423; e-mail rtoa@sdnp.org.mw; f. 1956; 200 mems (2004); Chair. E. MUHOMED.

CIVIL AVIATION

Lilongwe (formerly Kamuzu) International Airport was opened in 1982. There is another main airport, at Blantyre, which serves a number of regional airlines, and three domestic airports.

Air Malawi Ltd: 4 Robins Rd, POB 84, Blantyre; tel. 1620811; fax 1620042; e-mail enquiries@airmalawi.net; internet www.airmalawi.net; f. 1967; restructuring in preparation for privatization began in 1999; scheduled domestic and regional services, scheduled services to the United Kingdom suspended in June 1999; Chair. B. G. BOWLER; CEO FRANCIS PELEKAMOYO.

Tourism

Fine scenery, beaches on Lake Malawi, big game and an excellent climate form the basis of the country's tourist potential. The number of foreign visitor arrivals declined from 254,352 in 1999 to 228,106 in 2000, but rose to 266,300 in 2001; receipts from tourism totalled US $27m. in 2001.

Department of Tourism: POB 402, Blantyre; tel. 1620300; fax 1620947; f. 1969; responsible for tourist policy; inspects and licenses tourist facilities, sponsors training of hotel staff and publishes tourist literature; Dir of Tourism Services F. MASIMBE.

Tourism Development and Investment Co (TDIC): Blantyre; f. 1988 by Malawi Development Corpn to operate hotels and tours; Chief Exec. FRANCIS MBILIZI.

MALAYSIA

Introductory Survey

Location, Climate, Language, Religion, Flag, Capital

The Federation of Malaysia, situated in South-East Asia, consists of 13 states. Eleven of these are in Peninsular Malaysia, in the southern part of the Kra peninsula (with Thailand to the north and the island of Singapore to the south), and two, Sabah and Sarawak, are on the north coast of the island of Borneo, two-thirds of which comprises the Indonesian territory of Kalimantan. Sarawak also borders Brunei, a coastal enclave in the north-east of the state. The climate is tropical; there is rain in all seasons and temperatures are generally between 22°C (72°F) and 33°C (92°F), with little variation throughout the year. The official language is Bahasa Malaysia, based on Malay, but English is also widely used. Chinese, Tamil and Iban are spoken by minorities. Islam is the established religion, practised by about 53% of the population (including virtually all Malays), while about 19%, including most of the Chinese community, follow Buddhism. The Indians are predominantly Hindus. There is a minority of Christians among all races, and traditional beliefs are practised, particularly in Sabah and Sarawak. Malaysia's national flag (proportions 1 by 2) has 14 horizontal stripes, alternating red and white, with a blue rectangular canton, containing a yellow crescent and a 14-pointed yellow star, in the upper hoist. The capital is Kuala Lumpur. A new administrative capital, Putrajaya, has been developed south of Kuala Lumpur.

Recent History

The 11 states of Malaya, under British protection, were united as the Malayan Union in April 1946 and became the Federation of Malaya in February 1948. An armed communist offensive began in 1948, and was not effectively suppressed until the mid-1950s. After 1960 the remainder of the banned Communist Party of Malaya (CPM) took refuge in southern Thailand. Meanwhile, Malaya was granted independence, within the Commonwealth, on 31 August 1957.

Malaysia was established on 16 September 1963, through the union of the independent Federation of Malaya (renamed the States of Malaya), the internally self-governing state of Singapore, and the former British colonies of Sarawak and Sabah (North Borneo). Singapore left the federation in August 1965, reducing the number of Malaysia's component states from 14 to 13. The States of Malaya were designated West Malaysia in 1966 and later styled Peninsular Malaysia.

In 1970 serious inter-communal rioting, engendered by Malay resentment of the Chinese community's economic dominance and of certain pro-Chinese electoral results, precipitated the resignation of Tunku Abdul Rahman, who had been Prime Minister of Malaya (and subsequently of Malaysia) since independence. The new Prime Minister, Tun Abdul Razak, widened the Government coalition, dominated by the United Malays National Organization (UMNO), to create a national front, Barisan Nasional (BN). The BN originally comprised 10 parties, absorbing most of the former opposition parties. In January 1976 the Prime Minister died and was succeeded by the Deputy Prime Minister, Dato' Hussein bin Onn.

Political stability was subsequently threatened by the resurgence of the communist guerrilla movement, which conducted a series of terrorist attacks in Peninsular Malaysia during 1976–78. However, CPM activity subsequently declined, owing to co-operation between Malaysia and Thailand in military operations along their common border. In 1987, in a Thai-sponsored amnesty, about 700 Malaysian communists surrendered to the Thai authorities. In December 1989, following a year of negotiations with the Thai Government, the remaining 1,188 rebels (including recruits from Thailand and Singapore) agreed to terminate all armed activities. The peace agreements, signed by the leader of the CPM and representatives of the Malaysian and Thai Governments, made provision for the resettlement of the insurgents in either Malaysia or Thailand and their eventual participation in legitimate political activity in Malaysia.

In October 1977 the expulsion of the Chief Minister (Menteri Besar) of Kelantan from the dominant Parti Islam se Malaysia (PAS—Islamic Party of Malaysia) resulted in violent political disturbances in Kelantan and the declaration of a state of emergency by the federal Government. Direct rule was imposed in Kelantan, and the PAS was expelled from the BN coalition in December. In the federal and state elections of July 1978 Hussein consolidated the position of the BN, while the PAS, in opposition, suffered a serious reversal. In 1978, following the federal Government's rejection of proposals for a Chinese university, racial and religious tensions re-emerged.

In July 1981 Hussein was succeeded as Prime Minister by Dato' Seri Dr Mahathir Mohamad, Deputy Prime Minister since 1976. Mahathir called a general election in April 1982; the BN coalition won convincingly in all states and increased its overall strength in the House of Representatives.

At an election for the Sabah State Legislative Assembly in April 1985, a new political party, the Parti Bersatu Sabah (PBS—Sabah United Party) obtained more than one-half of the seats; Sabah thus became the only state that was not controlled by the BN. The legality of the new PBS Government was challenged by Muslim opponents, and in February 1986 the Chief Minister (Ketua Menteri) called a further election. In the May election the PBS won an increased majority of seats in the Assembly, and in June the BN agreed to admit the PBS into its ruling coalition, together with the United Sabah National Organization (USNO), which had been expelled in 1984.

In February 1986 Mahathir's leadership of the federal Government and of UMNO was challenged when Datuk Musa Hitam, the Deputy Prime Minister, resigned from the Government, owing to 'irreconcilable differences' with Mahathir. However, Musa retained his position as Deputy President of UMNO. During the following months Musa's supporters became increasingly critical of Mahathir, and divisions within the party widened. At an early general election in August, the BN coalition took 148 of the 177 seats in an enlarged House of Representatives: UMNO secured 83 seats, while the Malaysian Chinese Association (MCA) won 17. Of the opposition parties, the Democratic Action Party (DAP) won 24 seats, having gained support from ethnic Chinese voters who were disillusioned with the MCA. In state elections held simultaneously, the BN retained control of all the State Legislative Assemblies in Peninsular Malaysia. Several ministers who had supported Musa were subsequently demoted or removed from the Government.

In early 1987 there was a serious challenge for the presidency of UMNO from Tengku Razaleigh Hamzah, the Minister of Trade and Industry. At the UMNO General Assembly in April, none the less, Mahathir was elected UMNO President for the third time (and thus retained the position of Prime Minister at the head of the BN coalition), albeit with a greatly reduced majority. The General Assembly also narrowly elected Abdul Ghafar Baba (who had replaced Musa as Deputy Prime Minister in February 1986) as UMNO Deputy President, a position that Musa had previously occupied. Mahathir subsequently announced the resignation of Razaleigh and of Datuk Rais Yatim, the Minister of Foreign Affairs, from the Cabinet, and the dismissal of several other pro-Razaleigh ministers.

Criticism of Mahathir's leadership persisted during 1987, both from within UMNO and from other political parties. At the same time, racial tensions intensified in various parts of the country over Chinese-language education, religion and other issues. In October–November, allegedly to prevent violent racially-motivated riots between Chinese and Malays over politically sensitive issues, 106 people were detained under the provisions of the Internal Security Act (ISA), which allows detention without trial on grounds of national security. Those detained included politicians from all parties (most notably the leader of the DAP, Lim Kit Siang), lawyers, journalists and leaders of pressure groups. Three newspapers were closed by the Government, and political rallies were prohibited. In November the Government introduced legislation to impose stringent penalties on editors and publishers disseminating what the Government regarded as 'false' news. From December the Minister of Information was empowered to monitor all radio and television broadcasts, and to revoke the licence of any private broadcasting company not conforming with 'Malaysian values'. By April 1989 all the detainees under the ISA had been released (although often under restrictive conditions).

In February 1988 the High Court gave a ruling on a suit filed in the previous June by dissatisfied members of UMNO, who claimed that, since some of the delegations taking part in the UMNO elections of April 1987 had not been legally registered, the elections should be declared null and void. On account of the irregularities, the Court ruled that UMNO was an 'unlawful society' and that there had been 'no election at all'. Mahathir maintained that the ruling did not affect the legal status of the Government, and the Head of State, Tunku Mahmood Iskandar, expressed support for Mahathir. Later in February 1988 Mahathir announced that UMNO Baru (New UMNO) had been formed and that members of the original party would have to re-register in order to join. In March it was stated that Razaleigh and his supporters were to be excluded from the new party. The assets of UMNO Baru (hereafter referred to as UMNO) were 'frozen' and placed under judicial control until the party's legal status had been resolved; they were finally returned in September 1994.

Tension between the executive and the judiciary was intensified by Parliament's approval in March 1988 of constitutional amendments limiting the power of the judiciary to interpret laws. The Lord President of the Supreme Court, Tun Mohammed Salleh bin Abas, wrote to the Head of State to complain about government attempts to reduce the independence of the judiciary, and was subsequently dismissed from office. In June 1989 the Government further limited the powers of the judiciary when it introduced a security law, removing the right of persons being detained under provisions of the ISA to have recourse to the courts.

In September 1988 Razaleigh and 12 others followed two earlier dissidents and left the BN coalition to join the opposition in the House of Representatives as independents. They were joined in October by Musa. In December Musa and his supporters drafted a six-point resolution (the Johore Declaration), specifying the terms under which they would consent to join UMNO. These terms were accepted by UMNO in January 1989 but were binding only in the state of Johore. Following the defeat at a by-election in that month of an opposition representative by an MCA candidate with UMNO support, Musa announced his membership of UMNO, prompting a further eight dissident representatives in Johore to join the party.

In March 1989 Razaleigh's movement established an alliance with the fundamentalist PAS. In May Razaleigh's party registered as Semangat '46 (Spirit of 1946, a reference to the year of foundation of the original UMNO). The DAP, whose followers were largely urban Chinese, agreed to co-operate with Semangat '46 and the PAS, but refused to join a formal alliance, owing to their opposition to the PAS's proclaimed policy of forming an Islamic state in Malaysia. In June a former breakaway faction from the PAS, Barisan Jama'ah Islamiah Sa-Malaysia, left the BN coalition to join Semangat '46, the PAS and the Parti Hisbul Muslimin Malaysia in an opposition coalition, Angkatan Perpaduan Ummah (APU—Muslim Unity Movement). APU subsequently won a by-election by a small margin in Trengganu. In May and August, however, the BN won three by-elections. In December Mahathir held a cordial but unproductive meeting with Razaleigh, in an attempt to heal the rift in the ethnic Malay community.

A general election took place in October 1990. The opposition parties formed an informal electoral alliance, Gagasan Rakyat (People's Might). (Gagasan Rakyat was formally registered in April 1992, and Razaleigh was elected as Chairman in July.) Prior to the election the PBS withdrew from the BN and aligned itself with the opposition. Despite the defection of the PBS (which won the 14 seats that it contested), the BN controlled 127 of the 180 seats in the enlarged House of Representatives, thus retaining the two-thirds' majority necessary to amend the Constitution. The opposition's share of the seats increased from 37 to 53. However, Semangat '46 won only eight seats (compared with the 12 that it had held previously) of a total of 61 that it contested. Elections to 11 of the 13 State Legislative Assemblies (excluding Sabah and Sarawak) took place simultaneously. The BN obtained a majority of seats in every state except Kelantan, where APU won every seat in both the federal and state elections. Mahathir subsequently declared that it would be difficult for the federal Government to co-operate with the opposition state administrations in Sabah and Kelantan.

In November 1990, at a meeting of the UMNO General Assembly, Mahathir and Abdul Ghafar Baba were unanimously re-elected, respectively, as President and Deputy President of the party. Two incumbent Vice-Presidents of UMNO, Dato' Anwar Ibrahim, the Minister of Education, and Datuk Abdullah Ahmad Badawi, a former Minister of Defence (who had been dismissed in 1987 for supporting Razaleigh's leadership challenge), were re-elected; Datuk Seri Sanusi Junid, the Minister of Agriculture, was also elected a Vice-President. In February 1991 Mahathir announced cabinet changes, appointing Anwar, widely regarded as the probable future leader of UMNO, as Minister of Finance and Abdullah, his long-standing rival, as Minister of Foreign Affairs.

In January 1991 the Chief Minister of Sabah and President of the PBS, Datuk Seri Joseph Pairin Kitingan, was arrested and charged with corruption. It was widely conjectured that his arrest and his press adviser's detention, under the ISA, were politically motivated. In May UMNO secured its first seat in Sabah, in a by-election necessitated by the defection to UMNO of USNO's founder and President, Tun Mustapha Harun. Shortly afterwards Jeffrey Kitingan (the brother of the Chief Minister) was detained under the ISA, accused of plotting Sabah's secession from Malaysia.

At the UMNO General Assembly in November 1991, Mahathir made reference to the nine hereditary rulers' supposed abuse of privilege for personal gain. In February 1992 a delegation of senior UMNO representatives (excluding Mahathir) presented the Sultans with a memorandum that alleged interference by the rulers in both political and commercial spheres. UMNO criticism of the Sultans was widely suspected to be due, in part, to the Sultan of Kelantan's open support for Razaleigh (a prince of Kelantan) in the 1990 general election. In July 1992 four of the nine Sultans approved a Proclamation of Constitutional Principles, drafted in consultation with UMNO, establishing a code of conduct for the Sultans. There was further controversy in November when the Sultan of Johore assaulted a sports official. (In 1977, before he became Sultan, Mahmood Iskandar was convicted of 'culpable homicide' but was pardoned by his father, the Sultan.) Mahathir, who in 1983 had successfully forced the Sultans to surrender their right to refuse assent to laws passed by Parliament, proposed to remove the rulers' constitutional immunity from prosecution. In January 1993 Parliament approved amendments ending the Sultans' legal immunity, curtailing their power to pardon the offences of family members, and allowing parliamentary criticism of their misdeeds. Under the terms of the Constitution, however, the Sultans' privileges could not be restricted without the consent of the Conference of Rulers, comprising the nine Sultans. The Sultans indicated initially that they would approve the amendments, but, two hours before Parliament met, the rulers rejected the changes entirely. Mahathir responded by withdrawing from the Sultans various customary royal privileges (many of them financial) not stipulated in the Constitution. A constitutional crisis was averted when, in February, the Conference of Rulers agreed to the amendments with the inclusion of slight modifications; they were thus finally adopted with royal consent in March.

In August 1993, despite earlier assertions that he would not challenge the incumbent Ghafar, Anwar announced his decision to contest the post of UMNO Deputy President in the party's divisional elections, which Mahathir had postponed until November. The post was particularly significant as the Deputy President of UMNO was traditionally also accorded the position of Deputy Prime Minister and would be regarded as Mahathir's probable successor. In October Mahathir was returned unopposed as President of UMNO. Ghafar submitted his resignation as Deputy Prime Minister, seemingly in protest against Mahathir's failure actively to support his candidacy for the party post. By November Anwar, representing the *Malayu baru* (new Malays—younger, urban, mainly professional Malays who had prospered as a result of economic expansion), had secured overwhelming support for his candidacy, prompting the more traditional Ghafar to withdraw from the contest (the latter also resigned from UMNO). Anwar was duly elected Deputy President of UMNO, and all three vice-presidential posts were won by his self-styled 'Vision Team', which comprised Tan Sri Haji Muhyiddin Yassim (the Chief Minister—Menteri Besar—of Johore), Datuk Seri Najib Razak (the Minister of Defence) and Tan Sri Dato' Mohammed Haji Mohammed Taib (the Chief Minister—Menteri Besar—of Selangor). Anwar was appointed Deputy Prime Minister in December.

In April 1993 USNO, now led by Tun Mustapha Amirkahar (the son of Tun Mustapha Harun), left the opposition in the

Sabah State Legislative Assembly to form a coalition with the ruling PBS. Prior to the announcement six of the 11 elected representatives of USNO joined UMNO. USNO's defection prompted the federal Government successfully to seek the party's deregistration in August, on the grounds that it had breached its own statutes. In the same month Tun Mustapha Harun was appointed to the federal post of Minister of Sabah Affairs.

In January 1994 Pairin Kitingan dissolved the Sabah State Legislative Assembly in preparation for elections, although the Assembly's mandate did not expire until 1995. Shortly afterwards Pairin Kitingan was convicted on charges of corruption by the High Court. (Hearings had begun in January 1992.) He was, however, fined less than the minimum RM 2,000 that was required to disqualify him from office. Although Pairin Kitingan gained popular sympathy owing both to his perceived victimization in the corruption case and to his resistance to federal encroachment on Sabahan authority, a faction emerged in the PBS that favoured more harmonious relations with the federal Government. Former members of the deregistered USNO joined the PBS for the election, and the party also gained the support of Tun Mustapha Harun, who had resigned from his federal position of Minister of Sabah Affairs and as a member of UMNO in January. (Tun Mustapha Harun died in January 1995.) At the election, which took place on 18–19 February 1994, the PBS won a narrow majority, securing 25 of the 48 elective seats. Shortly before his inauguration as Chief Minister, however, Pairin Kitingan was informed that the state ruler, Tan Sri Mohamad Said Keruak, was too ill to carry out the ceremony. PBS leaders accused Said of allowing the BN time to persuade the PBS legislators to defect. Pairin Kitingan was finally sworn in as Chief Minister two days later. In March, however, several PBS members did defect to the opposition; among these was Jeffrey Kitingan, who announced the formation of a breakaway party, the Parti Demokratik Sabah Bersatu (PDSB—United Sabah Democratic Party). Jeffrey Kitingan had been released from detention under the ISA in December 1993: although he was initially confined to Seremban town in Negeri Sembilan for two years, all restrictions on him were swiftly revoked, encouraging suspicions of an agreement with the federal authorities. Pairin Kitingan tried to call new elections, but Said refused to sign the order of dissolution of the Assembly. On 17 March 1994 Pairin Kitingan resigned as Chief Minister, and on the following day Tan Sri Sakaran Dandai, a leader of the Sabah wing of UMNO, was sworn in at the head of a new administration.

In June 1994 the BN coalition agreed to admit two breakaway parties from the PBS, the Parti Demokratik Sabah (Sabah Democratic Party), led by Datuk Bernard Dompok, and the Parti Bersatu Rakyat Sabah (PBRS—United Sabah People's Party), led by Joseph Kurup, but refused to accept the application for membership of a third, Setia (Sabah People's United Democratic Party). In the same month it was announced that Dompok and Jeffrey Kitingan were to be appointed to the federal Government: in August Dompok became Minister in the Prime Minister's Department and Jeffrey Kitingan Deputy Minister for Housing and Local Government. Also in June Jeffrey Kitingan was cleared of corruption in the High Court.

In May 1994 the House of Representatives approved the 1994 Constitution (Amendment) Act, which further restricted the powers of the monarchy and provided for the restructuring of the judiciary. Hitherto the Yang di-Pertuan Agong (Head of State) had been competent to withhold assent from and return legislation, within 30 days, to Parliament for further consideration. The amendment required the Yang di-Pertuan Agong to give his assent to a bill within 30 days; if he failed to do so, the bill would, none the less, become law. The changes to the judiciary in the amendment included the creation of a Court of Appeal, the restyling of the Supreme Court as the Federal Court and of the Lord President as the Chief Justice.

From June 1994 the Government took action to suppress the activities of Al-Arqam, an Islamic sect which had been founded by Ashaari Muhammad in 1968. Al-Arqam was believed to have about 10,000 members in Malaysia, many of whom were public servants, and was alleged to control considerable assets. Although Al-Arqam had traditionally eschewed politics, the Government asserted that the group was a threat to national security and denounced its Islamic teachings as 'deviationist'; moreover, the Malaysian authorities accused it of training a military force in Thailand, although this was denied by both Al-Arqam and the Thai Government. In July UMNO threatened to expel party members who refused to leave Al-Arqam, and in

early August the National Fatwa (Islamic Advisory) Council banned the sect on the grounds that its doctrine contravened Islamic principles.

A general election took place on 24–25 April 1995. Following an often acrimonious election campaign, in which opposition parties complained of biased coverage by the media and undemocratic practices by the Mahathir Government (including the manipulation of electoral boundaries to its own advantage), the BN won an overwhelming majority, taking 162 of the 192 seats in the House of Representatives (with some 64% of the total votes cast). The PBS won eight of Sabah's federal seats, including those held by Jeffrey Kitingan and Dompok. Although this constituted a loss of six seats, it was an indication that, despite the BN's assumption of power at state level through the defection of former PBS members of the legislature, the PBS remained a significant political force in Sabah. The BN also retained control of 10 of the 11 State Legislative Assemblies for which voting took place, in most cases securing a two-thirds' majority. In Kelantan, which remained the only state under opposition control, a coalition of the PAS and Semangat '46 took 35 of the 43 state seats.

Despite his overwhelming election victory, Mahathir's position appeared vulnerable during the divisional elections of UMNO in 1995. The defeat of several Mahathir supporters was widely attributed to the influence of Anwar's associates, and prompted speculation that Anwar might challenge Mahathir for the leadership. In November, however, UMNO's General Assembly adopted an unprecedented resolution to avoid any contest for the two senior party positions in 1996; Anwar finally declared that he would not challenge Mahathir, and Mahathir for the first time said that he would retire in the near future and again named Anwar as his successor.

Semangat '46 was formally dissolved in October 1996, and its members were admitted to UMNO. At that month's UMNO General Assembly Mahathir and Anwar were, as anticipated, returned unopposed to their posts. In contrast to the 1993 party elections, in which Anwar's supporters had been particularly successful, a large proportion of Mahathir loyalists were now elected. Notably, in the elections for the vice-presidencies, Muhyiddin Yassim, the only member of Anwar's 'Vision Team' who had remained loyal to the Deputy President, was defeated by Dato' Abdullah Ahmad Badawi (the Minister of Foreign Affairs, who had been a vice-president prior to 1993); Najib Razak and Mohammad Taib were re-elected. However, the Minister of International Trade and Industry, Dato' Seri Paduka Rafidah Aziz, a Mahathir loyalist, who had been investigated in 1994 by the Anti-Corruption Agency for corrupt share-dealing, was defeated as head of the women's wing by an Anwar-backed candidate, while Rahim was ousted from the youth-wing leadership by another supporter of Anwar. No former member of Semangat '46, including Razaleigh, secured a position on the UMNO Supreme Council.

In October 1996 the PAS announced that it was to abandon its attempt (of some six years' standing) to replace secular criminal laws with *hudud*, the Islamic criminal code, in Kelantan, unless this was approved by the federal Government: Mahathir was known to be strongly opposed to such a policy. The PAS won a by-election for the State Legislative Assembly in Kelantan in January 1997. Although the PAS took the seat by only a narrow margin (the seat had been won convincingly at the previous election by a Semangat '46 candidate), the results were nevertheless indicative of Razaleigh's weakened position in the state.

In May 1997 Mahathir appointed Anwar as Acting Prime Minister while he took two months' leave of absence from the post. On his return, Mahathir's response to the currency crisis affecting the region, following Thailand's effective devaluation of the baht in early July, was widely perceived to have exacerbated Malaysia's economic position. His criticism of international investors resulted in further losses to the value of both the currency and shares on the stock exchange. Meanwhile, Anwar benefited politically from the situation, appearing to act responsibly in reassuring investors and rescinding the newly imposed financial restrictions. Political opponents, however, attempted to undermine Anwar through the circulation of a series of letters accusing him of sexual indiscretions. International criticism of Mahathir's outspokenness prompted popular demonstrations of support for the premier within Malaysia and near unanimous support for a vote of confidence in his leadership, which was held in the House of Representatives during November. In the same month Mahathir announced the formation of an executive authority to address the economic crisis, the National Economic

Action Council. The composition of the Council, including the appointment of the former Minister of Finance, Dato' Paduka Daim Zainuddin, as Executive Director of the Council, was approved by the Cabinet in January 1998. At the UMNO annual convention in September 1997 Mahathir criticized the increasing tendency of Malaysian Muslims to attach excessive importance to external symbols of Islam (such as beards and headscarves) and warned of the dangers of extremism. Mahathir's speech, which was resented by many Muslims, followed the widely publicized arrest, in June, of three Muslim women for taking part in a beauty contest in Selangor. The arrests prompted debate concerning the position of women in Malaysian society and resulted in demands for the reform of the Islamic Syariah (Shariah) courts; a *fatwa* (religious edict) had the force of law in the state in which it was issued, which arguably violated the liberties of Malaysians as guaranteed under the federal Constitution. In November 10 men were detained under the ISA for disseminating Shia Muslim teachings (Malaysian Muslims belong predominantly to the Sunni sect) which were perceived as militant and a threat to national security. Many non-governmental organizations (NGOs) and political parties called for the detainees to be released or allowed to stand trial under the Sedition Act.

At internal elections for divisional committee members in UMNO, which took place in March 1998, most of Mahathir's supporters retained their positions. However, evidence of a growing divide between Mahathir and Anwar became apparent at the UMNO annual party congress held in June, where Ahmad Zahid Hamidi, the head of the youth wing of UMNO and one of Anwar's supporters, made a speech attacking what he termed the debilitating impact of corruption in the party. Zahid's speech, which was reminiscent of Anwar's recent condemnation of corruption and political restrictions, was perceived as an attack on the party's leadership; Mahathir responded by publishing a list of hundreds of people and companies who had received privatization contracts in recent years, which included close associates of Anwar and members of his family. During the following weeks Mahathir acted to counter the influence of Anwar. He promoted Daim Zainuddin (a close personal ally) to the position of Minister of Special Functions in charge of economic development, thus undermining Anwar's position as Minister of Finance. It was suggested that the rift between Mahathir and Anwar was a result of economic policy divisions. (Mahathir's solution to the economic crisis lay in protectionism and continued expansion, in contrast to Anwar's support for austerity measures.) These allegations were, however, formally denied by Mahathir. Mahathir also dismissed newspaper editors close to Anwar and ordered the arrest of an associate of Anwar on firearms charges, which carried the death penalty under Malaysian law. The resignation in August of the Governor (a close ally of Anwar) and Deputy Governor of the central bank, reportedly owing to a disagreement over policy with Mahathir, served as an indication of the intensification of the rift within the Government. Supporters loyal to the Prime Minister responded to the perceived threat to Mahathir's leadership by circulating a brochure entitled 'Fifty Reasons Why Anwar Cannot Become Prime Minister', in which Anwar was accused of sexual offences and corruption.

Allegations of Anwar's supposed sexual misconduct increased throughout the months following the UMNO congress, and, following Anwar's refusal to resign, culminated in Mahathir's dismissal of Anwar as Deputy Prime Minister and Minister of Finance on 2 September 1998, on the grounds that he was morally unfit to hold office. On the following day Anwar was expelled from UMNO, and affidavits accusing him of sexual impropriety were filed with the High Court. The allegations were denied by Anwar, who asserted that they constituted part of a high-level political conspiracy to discredit him. Anwar began a tour of the country, drawing extensive support for his calls for the wide-ranging reform of the political system from the many thousands who attended his public appearances. His supporters adopted the slogan *'reformasi'* (reform), which had united the popular forces that ousted President Suharto in Indonesia. In mid-September Anwar's adoptive brother, Sukma Darmawan Samitaat Madja, and a former speech-writer for Anwar, Munawar Ahmad Anees, were each sentenced to six months' imprisonment after they confessed to illegal homosexual activity with Anwar. The following day, at a meeting attended by at least 40,000 people in Kuala Lumpur, Anwar called directly for Mahathir's resignation; he was arrested shortly afterwards and detained under the ISA. A further 17 people, including a number

of close associates of Anwar, were also detained under the same act. Anwar's arrest provoked demonstrations of protest, which erupted into violence when demonstrations involving up to 60,000 people were violently dispersed by the security forces; 132 people were arrested.

Following Anwar's arrest, his wife, Wan Azizah Wan Ismail, emerged as the *de facto* leader of the opposition movement, making appearances at rallies attended by Anwar's supporters and condemning her husband's detention. Despite a restriction order issued against Wan Azizah, barring her from holding rallies at her residence, demonstrations in protest at Anwar's detention continued to be held throughout September 1998 and became the forum for demands for widespread political reform and the removal of the restrictions on freedom of speech and assembly imposed under the ISA. Anwar finally appeared in court in Petaling Jaya at the end of September, where he pleaded not guilty to five charges of corruption and five charges of sexual impropriety. Allegations made by Anwar, who appeared in court with visible bruising to his face, that he had been severely beaten while in police custody and had subsequently been denied medical attention for a number of days, provoked expressions of extreme concern from foreign Governments—in particular from the Presidents of the Philippines and Indonesia—and prompted the UN Secretary-General, Kofi Annan, to urge the Malaysian Government to ensure humane treatment for Anwar. The Malaysian Government initially dismissed Anwar's claims of assault; however, it was subsequently announced that a special investigation would be established. In December the Inspector-General of the Malaysian police force, Tan Sri Abdul Rahim Noor, resigned after an initial inquiry blamed the police for the injuries Anwar had received. Malaysia's Attorney-General publicly admitted in January 1999 that Anwar had been assaulted by the police while in custody, and a Royal Commission of Inquiry into Anwar's injuries, which was completed in March, found Rahim Noor to be personally responsible for the beating. In accordance with the recommendations of the inquiry, in April Rahim Noor was charged with assaulting Anwar. In March 2000 Rahim Noor was sentenced to two months' imprisonment and fined RM 2,000 after pleading guilty to a lesser charge of assault against Anwar.

Anwar's trial on four charges of corruption (which referred to efforts allegedly made by him in 1997 to obtain through the police written denials that he was guilty of sexual misconduct and sodomy) began in November 1998. The presiding judge ruled that official foreign observers were not to be allowed at the trial. The credibility of the prosecution was undermined by the professed willingness of a principal witness to lie under oath, the withdrawal by a witness for the prosecution of his claims to have engaged in illegal homosexual activity with Anwar and the retraction by Anwar's adoptive brother and his speech-writer of their confessions, which they claimed had been obtained through police coercion. The defence suffered a number of reverses during the trial: in November the judge sentenced one of Anwar's lawyers to three months' imprisonment for contempt of court, because of a motion he had filed on behalf of Anwar to have two of the prosecutors dismissed from the case; the charges against Anwar were unexpectedly amended in January 1999, with the emphasis being shifted from sexual misconduct to abuse of power (the amendment meant that the prosecution would no longer have to prove that Anwar had committed sexual offences, but only that he had attempted to use his position to influence the police to quash the investigation into the allegations, effectively making it far easier for the prosecution to obtain a conviction). In addition, the judge ruled that all evidence given by several witnesses was inadmissible, despite requests from Anwar's lawyers that some parts of the testimony be retained as evidence for the defence. Following a disagreement between the defence and the presiding judge over the judge's refusal to hear a motion tabled by the defence that he be dismissed, the defence team refused to sum up its case, and the trial was ended abruptly in late March. In mid-April Anwar was found guilty on each of the four charges of corruption and a sentence of six years' imprisonment was imposed (under Malaysian law, this would be followed by a five-year period of disqualification from political office). Following the delivery of the verdict, supporters of the former Deputy Prime Minister clashed with security forces outside the court. Violent protests continued for the next three days, resulting in the arrest of 18 demonstrators. Following the trial, the three prosecution witnesses who had withdrawn their testimony against Anwar were charged with perjury. In late April Anwar was further charged with one count of illegal homosexual activity, to which he pleaded not guilty; it was announced that four other similar charges and one additional corruption charge against him had been suspended.

On the first day of Anwar's second trial in early June 1999 the prosecution amended the wording of its charge, changing the month and year (for the second time) in which the alleged crimes were supposedly committed. The trial was adjourned in September and Anwar was sent for medical examination following claims by the defence that Anwar had proven high levels of arsenic in his blood and was quite possibly the victim of deliberate poisoning. In the same month some 10,000 Anwar supporters gathered to demonstrate against the Government's treatment of the former Deputy Prime Minister and Minister of Finance; following the protests, several prominent allies of Anwar were reported to have been arrested. Anwar's trial resumed in late September, however, after medical tests found that Anwar showed no clinical signs of arsenic poisoning, although concerns over Anwar's health continued to be expressed in October. In his testimony in court in October and November, Anwar made potentially damaging allegations of corruption against members of the Government (including the Minister of Finance, Daim, and the Minister of Domestic Trade and Consumer Affairs, Dato' Seri Megat Junid bin Megat Ayob) who he alleged had conspired to remove him from office. In mid-November the trial of Anwar was adjourned indefinitely without explanation; supporters of Anwar claimed that the adjournment was a government attempt to silence him in the approach to the general election, which was to be held in late November. The trial resumed on 25 January 2000, but was adjourned again in late February at the request of the defence. Meanwhile, in April 2000 the Court of Appeal upheld Anwar's conviction on four charges of corruption.

Anwar suffered a further set-back in early June 2000, after the Court of Appeal rejected his plea for a stay of proceedings, ordering the trial on charges of sodomy to continue. In July the presiding judge ordered Anwar's defence lawyers to conclude their case, although they protested that they had intended to call further witnesses. Despite an indefinite postponement of the verdict, initially scheduled for early August, by the judge, and several police warnings, some 200 protesters gathered outside the High Court in a pro-Anwar rally. The High Court found Anwar guilty of sodomy, sentencing him to a further nine years' imprisonment, thus bringing his term to a total of 15 years. His adopted brother, Sukma Darmawan, was sentenced to six years' imprisonment and four strokes of the cane for the same offence. Although the verdict of guilty had been widely expected, observers were surprised by the severity of the sentence and by the judge's ruling that the punishments should be served consecutively rather than concurrently.

Although Anwar had been effectively removed from public office for 15 years, the affair continued to receive prominence in the media. Anwar was hospitalized in November, suffering from an acute back problem that required critical surgery. The Government refused a request for Anwar to travel abroad for surgery and, after becoming exasperated at Anwar's indecision, in April 2001 issued an ultimatum to Anwar either to accept treatment in a state hospital or return to his cell. He returned to his cell in May. In the same month public prosecutors announced that the remaining charges of corruption and sodomy against him were to be abandoned and, in July, Anwar lodged an appeal against his sodomy conviction. Meanwhile, in June 2001 the contempt verdict passed against one of Anwar's lawyers was overturned after the High Court ruled that the lawyer had been acting only in the interests of his client. In July 2002 Anwar lost his final appeal against his corruption conviction. In October of the same year Mahathir launched bankruptcy proceedings against Anwar, following his refusal to pay the costs of a defamation lawsuit he had brought against the Prime Minister in 1999. In April 2003 Anwar's appeal against his final conviction for sodomy was rejected by the Court of Appeal. Despite speculation that the accession of Abdullah Badawi to the premiership in October 2003 (see below) would bring about a change in the Government's stance towards Anwar, in January 2004 a court denied his application for bail pending the result of a further appeal against his sodomy conviction.

In January 1999, meanwhile, prior to the closure of the first trial of Anwar, Mahathir effected a major cabinet reorganization, in which Abdullah Badawi was appointed as Deputy Prime Minister and Minister for Home Affairs (a post relinquished by Mahathir) and Daim Zainuddin was allocated the finance port-

folio, which had been assumed by Mahathir following the dismissal of Anwar in September 1998. Also in January 1999 the UMNO Supreme Council announced its decision to postpone for 18 months elections for senior posts within the party, previously scheduled to be held in June, effectively preventing any potential challenge to Mahathir's leadership from within the party. The BN won a significant victory in the elections to the State Legislative Assembly in Sabah on 12–13 March, securing 31 of the 48 seats; Mahathir indicated, however, that the result would not induce him to call an early general election. In early April a new opposition party, the Parti Keadilan Nasional (PKN—National Justice Party), was launched by Wan Azizah in anticipation of the general election; the new party reportedly aimed to establish itself as a multi-ethnic and multi-religious party and declared that its first act, should it come to power, would be to seek a royal pardon for Anwar. Anwar himself, however, did not join the new party. Despite its stated aspirations to multi-ethnicity, the initial membership of the party appeared to be predominantly Muslim.

In November 1999 the Government unexpectedly announced that a general election was to be held later the same month. The opposition expressed dissatisfaction at the limited period of time allowed by the Government for campaigning in advance of the election. At the election, which was held on 29 November, a decisive victory was won by the governing BN coalition, which gained 148 of a total of 193 seats in the House of Representatives, thereby retaining the two-thirds' majority required to allow the Government to amend the Constitution. The opposition coalition, the Barisan Alternatif (Alternative Front—which had been formed by the PAS, the PKN, the DAP and the Parti Rakyat Malaysia (PRM—Malaysian People's Party) in June 1999 and which subsequently selected Anwar as its prime ministerial candidate) won a total of 42 seats, while the opposition PBS (which remained outside the Barisan Alternatif) secured three seats. Despite the BN's victory in the general election, UMNO experienced a significant loss of support amongst Malay voters (mainly to the PAS which secured 27 seats) and lost 23 seats, including those of four cabinet ministers. The party also performed poorly in the assembly elections held simultaneously in 11 Malaysian states: the PAS secured control of the state legislature in Trengganu, retained power in Kelantan and made significant gains in Mahathir's home state of Kedah. This erosion of confidence in UMNO was widely believed to be a result of the Government's treatment of Anwar and the concomitant decline of public confidence in the country's institutions, including the police and the judicial system. While there were a number of new appointments to the Cabinet, which was announced in early December, many of the key portfolios remained unchanged. In an unexpected move, however, Mahathir promoted the unelected academic, Musa Mohamad, neither an existing government minister nor a member of UMNO, to the influential post of Minister of Education; Musa replaced Dato' Seri Najib Abdul Razak, a former potential successor to Mahathir, who was transferred to the less powerful Ministry of Defence in what was perceived by many as an effective demotion. Also in December Mahathir announced that he intended this (his fifth) term of office to be his last, and for the first time formally identified the Deputy Prime Minister, Abdullah Ahmad Badawi, as his preferred successor. In the same month the Barisan Alternatif nominated Fadzil Nor, President of the PAS, as the new parliamentary leader of the opposition. He replaced Lim Kit Siang, who had lost his seat in the general election in November 1999 and who in early December resigned as the Secretary-General of the DAP in acknowledgement of the party's poor performance in the elections, which was largely attributed to ethnic Chinese alarm at the prospect of an Islamic state as envisaged by the DAP's electoral partner, the PAS.

In May 2000, at the UMNO party elections, Mahathir and Abdullah were formally elected President and Deputy President of the party, respectively. However, despite consolidating his own position within UMNO, Mahathir came under increasing pressure from both the opposition and the BN.

Recognizing the need for change in order to improve the increasingly unfavourable public image of the Government, in November 2000 the Prime Minister appointed Mohamed Dzaiddin Abdullah as the new Chief Justice, in a bid to enhance the credibility of the judiciary, tarnished by the Anwar trials. Later that month UMNO held a special general assembly, at which measures were approved to revitalize the image of the party and to attract more young professionals, including women. These developments failed to prevent the opposition PKN from taking a seat from the BN coalition at a by-election in the Lunas constituency of Kedah. The loss, thought to be due to the thousands of ethnic Chinese and young voters who had joined the electorate since the 1999 election, was unexpected, as the BN had held the Lunas seat since independence in 1957.

In April 2001 the Minister of Finance, Daim Zainuddin, decided to take a two-month leave of absence. The leave was seen as having been enforced by Mahathir, who wanted to distance himself from criticism arising from two controversial nationalization agreements involving the heavily-indebted Malaysia Airlines and Time dotCom (the telecommunications unit of the Renong Group) in late 2000, both companies being connected to protégés of Daim. In June 2001 Daim formally resigned from his post, following widespread allegations that he had taken advantage of public funds to help business associates. Mahathir assumed the finance portfolio on an interim basis.

Possibly fearing a split in the Malay vote over the Anwar affair, Mahathir attempted to strengthen support by using the race issue in August 2000, when he criticized Suqiu, the Malaysian Chinese Organizations' Election Appeals Committee, branding some of its members extremists and likening them to communists for urging the abolition of the New Vision Policy. The policy had for 30 years ensured favouritism for the Malay majority in education and commerce, in an attempt to reduce the inequality of wealth between Malays and Chinese. The effect of the criticism may have been merely to alienate Chinese supporters, integral to the BN's 1999 victory, although Suqiu did withdraw its demands after a series of meetings with UMNO in January 2001. In early March Mahathir confirmed that the New Vision Policy, due to end in 2001, was to be extended for a further 10 years.

In January 2000, meanwhile, government suppression of dissent increased significantly. Three prominent members of the opposition were arrested; the deputy leader of the DAP and Anwar's legal representative, Karpal Singh, and the Vice-President of the PKN, Marina Yusoff, were charged under the Sedition Act, while Mohamad Ezam Mohamad Noor was charged under the Official Secrets Act. In the same month the editor and the printer of the popular PAS newspaper, *Harakah*, were also charged with sedition in connection with an article concerning the trial of Anwar that reportedly included a quote accusing the authorities of conspiring against him. The arrests were perceived by observers to constitute an attempt by the Government to curb the influence of the PAS following the party's strong performance in the general election. In early March 2000 the Government acted to restrict sales of *Harakah*, ordering that the newspaper be published just twice a month instead of twice weekly and restricting sales of the publication to members of the PAS only. In an apparent further attempt by the Government to stifle the expression of dissent in the national press, the group editor of the *New Straits Times*, Kadir Jasin, was forced to resign in January following the publication of an editorial which questioned the decision by the UMNO Supreme Council to reject demands that the party's two most senior positions be contested from within the party in the forthcoming UMNO internal elections (the Supreme Council proposed instead that Mahathir and Abdullah Ahmad Badawi be renominated for the party presidency and vice-presidency unopposed). In January 2002 public prosecutors abandoned the sedition charges against Karpal Singh. No explanation was given for the decision.

The Anwar issue continued to incite public unrest, and in April 2000 a protest to mark the anniversary of Anwar's conviction for corruption was broken up by riot police, 48 PKN activists being arrested. Public criticism of the Government, and subsequent detentions, became more frequent after Anwar's second conviction, as confidence in Mahathir's leadership continued to decline. Mohamad Ezam Mohamad Noor was arrested in March 2001 as a result of allegedly seditious comments, despite already being on trial for releasing a secret report on corruption. A month later he was detained again, along with six other opposition leaders, including Tian Chua and the PKN youth Vice-Chairman, N. Gobala Krishnan, under the ISA (which allows for detention without trial for up to two years). The aim of these arrests seemed to be to dissuade protesters from gathering for the second anniversary of Anwar's conviction. The effect was significant as only 2,000 demonstrators defied the authorities' ban to attend the peaceful 'Black 14' rally, named after and coinciding with the date of Anwar's first conviction, 14 April. The seven detainees were not immediately released after the rally, however, and three more arrests were made under the

ISA. During late April the PKN youth leaders, Dr Badrul Amin Baharom and Loman Noor Adam, were arrested, as was the human rights activist, Badarudiin Ismail, thus bringing the total of recent detainees under the provisions of the ISA to 10. In August 2002 Mohamad Ezam Mohamad Noor was sentenced to a two-year prison term, having been convicted of 'leaking' state secrets. In June 2003 he was freed on bail, pending an appeal against his conviction.

In early August 2001 an extraordinary session of the Court of Final Appeal heard arguments against the detention of five people under the ISA. Significantly, the judges ruled that the onus was on the State to produce evidence that those arrested posed a real threat to national security. Meanwhile, Nik Adli Nik Abdul Aziz, son of PAS spiritual leader Datuk Haji Nik Abdul Aziz Nik Mat, became one of 10 men detained under the Act on suspicion of membership of the Kumpulan Mujahidin Malaysia (KMM), an Islamist fundamentalist group believed to be engaged in a long-term plot to overthrow the Government. Seven of those taken into custody were also members of the PAS. Soon afterwards 25 supporters of Anwar Ibrahim were freed from prison and promptly rearrested on new charges, before being granted bail. In September the Government announced that Nik Adli Nik Abdul Aziz was to be detained for two years without trial under the provisions of the ISA. Eight of the nine men arrested with him were also imprisoned. Human rights activists accused the Government of exploiting the aftermath of the terrorist attacks on the USA in the same month (see the chapter on the USA) to suppress national opposition groups. Further arrests continued to be made under the ISA, as the Government tightened its control of national security.

In September 2001 the opposition was destabilized by the withdrawal of the DAP from the Barisan Alternatif. The party accused the PAS of alienating Chinese voters through its support for an Islamic state. In the same month an election in Malaysia's largest state, Sarawak, confirmed the strength of the ruling coalition. The BN won 60 out of 62 available seats in the state legislature. The DAP secured one seat; an independent candidate the other. Neither the PAS—contesting an election in the region for the first time—nor the PKN achieved any success. In November the PBS decided to rejoin the Government following more than a decade of absence from power; the party was formally readmitted to the BN in January 2002. Also in January, at a by-election in the Perlis district of Indera Kayangan, the PKN, supporting the cause of Anwar Ibrahim, was heavily defeated by Mahathir's BN. The PAS accused the Government of using devious methods to exploit popular fear of Islamist militancy in the aftermath of the September terrorist attacks and thus secure a resounding victory in the election.

On 21 November 2001 Sultan Salahuddin Abdul Aziz Shah Al-Haj ibni Al-Marhum Sultan Hisamuddin Alam Shah Al-Haj died at the age of 75. On 13 December the Raja of Perlis, Tuanku Syed Sirajuddin Syed Putra Jamalullail, was sworn in as the new monarch, following his election by secret ballot from amongst the remaining eight Malay rulers. The Sultan of Trengganu continued as his deputy.

In December 2001 a court convicted 19 members of the Islamist cult al-Ma'unah of treason for plotting to overthrow the Government. The men had been arrested following the murder of two hostages during a confrontation with security forces after a weapons robbery in July 2000. Ten other cult members had pleaded guilty to lesser charges and received 10-year prison terms. Three of the sect's ringleaders were sentenced to death for their part in the armed rebellion. The remaining men were given life terms. (In November 2003 15 members of the cult, who had played only minor roles in the robbery and who later expressed remorse for their actions, were released, having been held under the ISA.) In the same month *The Sun* published a story claiming the existence of a plot to assassinate Prime Minister Mahathir. The story was later proved to be false and more than one-half of the editorial staff were dismissed, leading to allegations that the authorities had plotted to discredit the newspaper and thus more easily subject it to Malaysia's rigorous censorship laws. In January 2002 the Government announced further measures intended to stifle potential sources of dissent, stating that, with effect from May 2002, students and staff at public universities would be required to sign a pledge declaring allegiance to their king, country and government. Students had played a leading role in the protests that had followed the dismissal of Anwar Ibrahim in 1998.

In June 2002, during a speech to the annual congress of UMNO, Prime Minister Mahathir made the dramatic announcement that he intended to resign from the Government, with immediate effect. However, he was persuaded to withdraw his resignation shortly afterwards and, following some discussion, it was decided that he would remain in power until October 2003, when he would be succeeded by the Deputy Prime Minister, Abdullah Ahmad Badawi. During the transition period Abdullah would assume increased responsibility for the running of the Government. Meanwhile, Fadzil Nor, President of the PAS, died following complications arising from heart surgery; Abdul Hadi Awang assumed the party leadership on an interim basis.

In July 2002 Abdul Hadi Awang announced the imposition of Islamic law in Terengganu state, of which he was the Chief Minister. The Government continued to oppose efforts to enforce the new law code, however. In the same month, at a by-election to the Kedah seat of Pendang, which had become vacant upon the death of Fadzil Nor, the BN secured a narrow victory.

In October 2002 police arrested five men, believed to be members of the regional terrorist organization Jemaah Islamiah, under the ISA. The arrests brought the total number of ISA detainees to approximately 70. Members of Jemaah Islamiah were believed to be responsible for the recent terrorist attack on the Indonesian island of Bali (see the chapter on Indonesia), which had resulted in the deaths of 202 people, including many tourists. In November the ISA attracted renewed criticism when a court ordered the release of Nashar-uddin Nasir, who had been detained under its provisions since April of that year, on the grounds that no evidence had been provided to substantiate claims that he had engaged in terrorist activities. The Government, in contravention of the judicial order, rearrested him almost immediately after his release. It was announced subsequently that the ISA was to be strengthened in order to prevent further challenges by the courts. Meanwhile, Prime Minister Mahathir announced the appointment of Datuk Dr Jamaluddin Jarjis as Minister of Finance II; Mahathir himself continued to hold the other finance portfolio.

In May 2003 Minister of Transport Ling Liong Sik announced his resignation. In the following month it was announced that three members of the PKN who had been imprisoned under the ISA for more than two years were to be released. In August the PKN merged with the smaller PRM, forming the Parti Keadilan Rakyat Malaysia (PKR), in advance of the general election scheduled to be held in 2004. It was hoped that the merger would strengthen opposition to the BN and promote Anwar's cause. The President of the PKN, Wan Azizah, continued as President of the new party. In September it was announced that nine suspected members of the KMM who had been detained under the ISA in August 2001, including Nik Adli Nik Abdul Aziz, would be imprisoned for a further two years.

On 31 October 2003 Prime Minister Mahathir Mohamed retired, having spent 22 years in power; his designated successor, Deputy Prime Minister Abdullah Ahmad Badawi, was then sworn in as Prime Minister. Upon his accession to the premiership, Abdullah announced that he did not intend to appoint a deputy immediately and that there would be no initial reorganization of the Cabinet. Abdullah retained the home affairs portfolio and, in addition, assumed Mahathir's role as Minister of Finance. In November Abdullah was also endorsed as the new Chairman of the BN. Meanwhile, the PAS announced plans to transform Malaysia fully into an Islamic state should it come to power, attracting criticism not only from non-Muslim members of the BN but also from political allies of the PAS, including the PKR. In January 2004 the new Prime Minister effected his first cabinet reorganization, nominating Minister of Defence Najib Razak as Deputy Prime Minister in what was widely perceived to be his most significant appointment. Amongst other changes, the economist Nor Mohamed Yakcop became Minister of Finance II, replacing Jamaluddin Jarjis, who was allocated the domestic trade and consumer affairs portfolio.

In February 2004, as a result of an ongoing anti-corruption campaign initiated by the new Prime Minister, both the Minister of Land and Co-operative Development, Tan Sri Datuk Kasitah bin Gaddam, and the former head of the national steel company Perwaja Steel Bhd, Eric Chia Eng Hock, were arrested and charged with corruption. Kasitah announced his resignation shortly afterwards. Meanwhile, in the same month a national service programme was introduced with the intention of promoting national unity; conscripts were to perform military service for three months. In early March Abdullah announced that Parliament was to be dissolved and a general election held

later in that month, several months before the constitutional deadline of November. Later in March it was reported that six suspected Indonesian members of Jemaah Islamiah had been captured in Malaysia and were being held under the ISA, bringing the total number of suspected militants detained under the ISA to 96.

On 21 March 2004, following a brief campaign period, elections took place to an enlarged 219-member House of Representatives and to 12 of the 13 State Legislative Assemblies (Sarawak was exempted, having held elections to its legislature in September 2001). The BN secured a commanding victory, winning 198 of the 219 seats in the House of Representatives and taking control of 11 of the 12 State Legislative Assemblies, including that of Terengganu, which had previously been governed by the PAS. The PAS retained control of Kelantan by a narrow margin. The DAP secured 12 seats in the House of Representatives, followed by the PAS, which won seven (compared with 27 at the election of 1999) and the PKR, which retained only one seat, that held by Wan Azizah. Having been sworn in again as head of government, Abdullah Badawi subsequently announced a major reorganization of his Cabinet, which was enlarged through the creation of two new ministries—the Ministry of Federal Territories and the Ministry of Natural Resources and the Environment—and the division of three existing ministries, those of Home Affairs, Education and Culture, Arts and Tourism. Abdullah retained the finance portfolio and that of internal security, created following the division of the Ministry of Home Affairs. Najib Razak continued as Deputy Prime Minister and Minister of Defence.

Malaysia's foreign policy was dominated by its membership of the regional grouping, the Association of South East Asian Nations (ASEAN, see p. 154), founded in 1967. Mahathir was instrumental in bringing Myanmar into ASEAN in 1997 under the Policy of Constructive Engagement. Malaysia also played an integral role in bringing together the military junta and Aung San Suu Kyi for negotiations in late 2000, although it was thought that financial considerations might have been significant, with a promise of direct investment in Myanmar by PETRONAS in return for a semblance of progress on the part of the junta. Mahathir's visit to Myanmar in January 2001 confirmed Malaysia's interest in Myanmar, a possible alternative source of natural gas. In September 2001 the Myanma leader, Gen. Than Shwe, paid an official visit to Malaysia during which a number of bilateral agreements were signed. In August 2002 Mahathir visited Myanmar again; during his visit he met with Aung San Suu Kyi and, it was thought, attempted to encourage the junta to engage in further dialogue with the opposition.

Relations with Singapore had always been characterized by mistrust, after the city-state left the Federation of Malaya in 1965. Resentment increased as Singapore advanced more swiftly than Malaysia economically, creating a certain acrimonious competition between the two countries. As Malaysia also developed, however, bilateral relations became more cordial, and co-operation increased. The visit in August 2000 by Singapore's Senior Minister and figurehead, Lee Kuan Yew, to Mahathir in Kuala Lumpur demonstrated the growing convergence of the two countries' viewpoints. In September 2001 Lee Kuan Yew travelled to Kuala Lumpur again, on a visit intended to further enhance ties between the two countries. Relations were threatened from early 2002, however, as tensions arose over the renegotiation of a 1961 agreement by which Malaysia supplied Singapore with water. Negotiations took place in July and October 2002 in an attempt to resolve the problems arising from the water dispute, but without success. It was feared that the issue would have to be referred to an international court of arbitration to secure its resolution. In February 2003 Prime Minister Mahathir stated that, while Malaysia would cease to supply Singapore with untreated water in 2011, it would continue to supply filtered water, at a reasonable price, for as long as necessary. Following the retirement of Mahathir in October 2003, bilateral relations showed signs of improvement under new Prime Minister Abdullah Badawi. In January 2004 Abdullah reciprocated visits with his Singaporean counterpart, Goh Chok Tong, and discussed the tensions in the relationship.

In January 1993 Gen. Fidel Ramos visited Malaysia, the first Philippine President to do so since 1968, owing to strained relations over the Philippines' claim to Sabah. Mahathir and Ramos agreed to establish a joint commission to address bilateral problems. In February 1994 Mahathir made the first official visit by a Malaysian head of government to the Philippines. Relations with the Philippines, however, were strained in April

2000, when Muslim separatists from the southern Philippines abducted a group of tourists from the Malaysian resort of Sipadan, off the coast of Sabah. Following a similar kidnapping incident in September, the Malaysian Government dispatched an additional 600 troops to the region.

Relations with Indonesia generally improved from the mid-1990s. In June 1996 the two countries agreed on joint measures to limit the flow of illegal workers into Malaysia. Wide-ranging amendments to the Immigration Act in Malaysia in October 1996 failed to halt the flow of illegal immigrants, which was blamed for rising social tensions. The regional economic crisis, which began in mid-1997, led to an increase in illegal immigrants arriving in Malaysia and prompted Malaysia to begin a repatriation programme to Indonesia and elsewhere. Violent protests against deportation took place in detention centres in March 1998. In addition, groups of illegal Indonesian immigrants entered the compounds of several foreign embassies and the office of the UN High Commissioner for Refugees in March and April and requested political asylum to prevent their repatriation to the Indonesian province of Aceh, where they claimed that, as members of secessionist groupings, they would be subject to persecution. Some of the immigrants were subsequently granted asylum by Denmark and Norway. In November 2000 Malaysia and Indonesia agreed to intensify border patrols, after four Malaysians were detained by Indonesian police in June of that year for allegedly stealing logs.

Relations with both Indonesia and the Philippines, meanwhile, were strained in 1998 following the arrest in September of the former Malaysian Deputy Prime Minister and Minister of Finance, Anwar Ibrahim: both the President of Indonesia and the President of the Philippines made explicit criticisms of the Malaysian Government regarding its treatment of Anwar. Although the controversy surrounding Anwar's treatment receded as an international issue in 1999, bilateral relations with the Philippines were adversely affected by President Estrada's granting of an audience to Anwar's wife, Wan Azizah Wan Ismail, when she visited the Philippines in April. The new President of Indonesia, Abdurrahman Wahid, demonstrated the close relations between Indonesia and Malaysia by visiting Kuala Lumpur immediately after his election in October 1999.

In August 2001 President Wahid's successor, Megawati Sukarnoputri, visited Malaysia on the final stage of her tour of ASEAN nations. In the same month the new President of the Philippines, Gloria Macapagal Arroyo, also paid her first official visit to the country. However, relations with Indonesia soon threatened to deteriorate again. In 2001 the Government announced that it would deport 10,000 Indonesian illegal immigrants each month in an attempt to tighten controls on foreign labour in the country at a time of economic slowdown. In December 2001 and January 2002 a series of riots by Indonesian labourers led Prime Minister Mahathir to comment that Malaysia might give workers of different nationalities preference in the labour market owing to the problems caused by the illegal immigrants. In late January a temporary ban was imposed on new workers arriving from Indonesia. Soon afterwards the Indonesian Government issued a formal apology for the behaviour of its workers and stated that it hoped the trouble caused would not affect an otherwise harmonious relationship. Relations with the Philippines were also threatened in November 2001 when the authorities arrested the fugitive Philippine rebel leader, Nur Misuari, on charges of attempting to enter Malaysia illegally. After much indecision, he was finally deported in January 2002 to face trial in Manila (see the chapter on the Philippines). In May 2002 Malaysia, Indonesia and the Philippines signed an anti-terrorism pact enabling them to exchange intelligence and to launch joint police operations, in an effort to combat regional terrorist organizations; Thailand and Cambodia also acceded to the pact later in the year. In August the implementation of new legislation requiring that all illegal immigrants leave the country, or face penalties including fines, imprisonment and caning, strained relations with both the Philippines and Indonesia, as the majority of the workers affected were citizens of those countries. In September the Malaysian Government announced that, owing to diplomatic pressure, exacerbated by public protests being held in Indonesia and the Philippines over the apparently inhumane nature of the expulsions, deportations were being temporarily halted. In early 2004 relations with Indonesia were threatened again when the Indonesian Government called for a global boycott of Malaysian timber, following the release of a report alleging that protected trees from Indonesia were being smuggled across the joint border, 'laundered' and re-exported. The Government denied the claims.

In 1994 Malaysian and Indonesian officials commenced discussions to resolve their conflicting claims to the sovereignty of two small islands off the coast of Borneo, Sipadan and Ligitan. In October 1996 an agreement was reached by both countries to refer the issue to the International Court of Justice (ICJ, see p. 18). In December 2002 the ICJ ruled that Malaysia would be awarded sovereignty of the islands, thus bringing an end to the dispute. Another territorial claim being pursued through negotiations was the dispute with Singapore over the island of Batu Putih (Pedra Branca). In February 2003 the two countries finally signed a formal agreement referring the dispute to the ICJ. Malaysia is also involved with Brunei, Viet Nam, the People's Republic of China, the Philippines and Taiwan in disputed sovereignty claims over the Spratly Islands in the South China Sea. In November 2002 the ASEAN member states approved a Code of Conduct for the islands; the agreement was also sanctioned by China.

Relations with Thailand were strained at the end of 1995 following the killing by the Malaysian navy of two Thai citizens fishing illegally in Malaysian waters. In December the two countries agreed to establish a committee to resolve a long-standing dispute over fishing rights. In February 1996 relations deteriorated, owing to Thailand's opposition to Malaysia's construction of a 27-km wall (completed in 1997) along its border with Thailand, intended to deter illegal immigration from that country. However, in January 1997 the two countries agreed to co-operate in preventing Bangladeshi migrant workers from entering Malaysia and in expediting the return of illegal Thai workers from Malaysia. The arrest in January 1998 of three Thai Muslim separatists by the Malaysian authorities and their deportation to Thailand demonstrated continued co-operation between the two countries since Malaysia was often regarded as a place of sanctuary for Muslim separatists in southern Thailand. Relations between Malaysia and Thailand were further enhanced in April, when the two countries signed an agreement to share equally the natural gas produced in an offshore area to which both countries had territorial claims. However, the Thai Minister of Foreign Affairs, Surin Pitsuwan, was amongst a number of international political figures who expressed concern at the arrest and detention of the former Deputy Prime Minister and Minister of Finance, Anwar Ibrahim, in September. In April 2001 the Thai Prime Minister, Thaksin Shinawatra, made his first official visit to the country on a trip intended to enhance co-operative ties. Bilateral talks were also held in January 2002 in an attempt to resolve problems arising from a planned project to build a gas pipeline between the two countries. In January 2004 new Prime Minister Abdullah Badawi visited Thailand for security discussions, following several attacks believed to have been perpetrated by separatists along the Thai side of the joint border. The two countries agreed to co-operate in efforts to bring an end to the violence and began joint border patrols. The Thai Government subsequently announced that it intended to fence off parts of the border, owing to speculation that those responsible for the attacks might be taking refuge in Malaysia.

Malaysia's relations with the People's Republic of China remained extremely cordial, with Malaysia frequently offering public support to China, particularly in response to US criticism. Mahathir paid another of a long series of official visits to China in November 2000, and the Chinese Premier, Zhu Rongji, made an official visit to Malaysia in November 1999. In May 2001 the Yang di-Pertuan Agong paid an official state visit to China at the invitation of the Chinese President, Jiang Zemin.

Mahathir's proposal to establish an East Asian Economic Caucus (EAEC), a trade group intended to exclude the USA, met with considerable resistance from the US Government (which continued to promote the US-dominated Asia-Pacific Economic Co-operation forum—APEC, see p. 147) and Australia. In July 1993 ASEAN agreed, despite the continuing reluctance of Japan to participate, that the EAEC should operate as an East Asian interest group within APEC. In November 1999 (although Mahathir was absent owing to the Malaysian general election) the third informal summit meeting of the 10 ASEAN countries and the Republic of China, Japan and the Republic of Korea took place. At the meeting it was agreed to hold annual East Asian summits of all 13 nations and to strengthen present economic co-operation with the distant aim of forming an East Asian bloc with a common market and monetary union. This ambition was brought closer in April 2001 when, at a meeting of ASEAN countries which China, Japan and the Republic of Korea also attended, plans were agreed for a network of currency 'swap' arrangements to prevent a repetition of the regional financial crisis of 1997.

In 1999 Mahathir objected to Australia's leadership of the UN-mandated peace-keeping mission in East Timor (now Timor-Leste, following the territory's accession to independence in May 2002), the UN Transitional Administration in East Timor (UNTAET), claiming that an ASEAN-led mission would be more appropriate. Other ASEAN members were, however, reluctant to assume responsibility for the peace-keeping body and Australia and East Timor both objected to the notion of Malaysia leading transitional arrangements, owing to its close relations with Indonesia. Only after the intervention of the UN Secretary-General did Malaysia finally contribute limited personnel to UNTAET. In February 2001 Malaysia announced that it would open a liaison office in Dili, East Timor, which became an embassy upon the declaration of East Timor as a fully independent state in May 2002.

In July 1997 Mahathir (who was often regarded as the international spokesperson for developing countries) indicated that he might submit a proposal to the UN to review its 1948 Universal Declaration of Human Rights, with regard to the specific priorities of less developed countries. While this sentiment was supported by many Asian countries, the USA reacted angrily to any suggestion of compromise on the issue of human rights. Relations with the USA were also strained by the involvement of Malaysia's national petroleum corporation, PETRONAS, in a consortium that signed an agreement during September to invest in Iran, in contravention of US sanctions against Iran. In October Mahathir paid a formal visit to Cuba, the first such visit by a Malaysian leader, and urged Malaysian firms to invest in the country, in defiance of US legislation which threatened reprisals against firms conducting business with Cuba. Bilateral relations deteriorated further in the same month following Mahathir's suggestion that the economic crisis in the South-East Asian region was due to hostile Jewish currency speculation aimed at preventing progress among Muslim nations. A resolution tabled by 34 members of the US Congress calling for the withdrawal of the remarks or Mahathir's resignation was condemned by Mahathir and the Malaysian press. Relations with the USA were further strained in 1998 following US condemnation of the detention and treatment of the former Deputy Prime Minister and Minister of Finance, Anwar Ibrahim; the Malaysian Government was particularly angered by a speech delivered at the APEC summit meeting in Kuala Lumpur in November by the US Vice-President, Albert Gore, in which Gore expressed support for the movement for political reform in Malaysia. During a speech to UMNO members in June 1999, Mahathir criticized the influence on the country of non-Malaysians (and, in particular, ethnic Europeans), who Mahathir claimed were attempting to 're-colonize' Malaysia. Relations with the USA were improved with a visit by Adm. Dennis Blair, the Commander-in-Chief of the US Pacific Command, to Kuala Lumpur in January 2001. At his meeting with Mahathir, the first between the Prime Minister and a US Pacific commander, the two countries agreed to extend military co-operation. However, the new US President, George W. Bush, insisted that any further improvement in relations would depend on better treatment for Anwar Ibrahim and other detained members of the Malaysian opposition.

In September 2001 bilateral ties with the USA were greatly strengthened when Mahathir moved quickly to condemn attacks on the US mainland thought to have been carried out by the al-Qa'ida terrorist network. However, during a meeting with the US President at an APEC summit meeting in Shanghai that month, Mahathir refused to lend his Government's support to the US-led retaliatory attacks on Afghanistan that began in October, voicing his concerns at the large numbers of civilian casualties resulting from the raids. At a meeting of ASEAN leaders in November, Malaysia agreed to co-operate with other member nations in the fight against terrorism. In January 2002 the USA congratulated the Malaysian Government on its demonstration of support for the international coalition against terrorism, following the detention of at least 15 suspected terrorists. However, it demanded assurances that the suspects would receive a fair trial under the ISA. In October it was reported that the US Government had requested that Malaysia be the host for a regional anti-terrorism training centre.

While Mahathir made clear his opposition to the US-led campaign to remove the regime of Saddam Hussein in Iraq in

2003, relations with the USA remained generally stable, owing largely to the Government's ongoing operation against suspected domestic terrorists, which was in line with the global anti-terrorism campaign being pursued by the Bush Administration. However, in October 2003, at a summit meeting of the Organization of the Islamic Conference (OIC, see p. 314) held in Putrajaya, Prime Minister Mahathir attracted criticism from the USA, Israel and several European countries when he attacked what he described as Jewish subjugation of Islamic countries during his opening address to the meeting. The Government later issued an apology for the comments. In early 2004 relations with the USA were threatened when new Prime Minister Abdullah Badawi accused the USA of using unreliable intelligence to implicate Malaysia in a global nuclear smuggling network. The US Government had alleged that a company owned by Abdullah's son had supplied components to the network.

In June 1997 the inauguration took place of a group that aimed to foster economic co-operation among Muslim developing countries, the Developing-Eight (D-8), comprising Malaysia, Bangladesh, Egypt, Indonesia, Iran, Nigeria, Pakistan and Turkey. Malaysia continued to express its close relationship with Arab countries after it denounced US and British air strikes against Iraq in February 2001, while demanding the removal of UN sanctions.

Government

Malaysia is a federation of 13 states. The capital, Kuala Lumpur, is a separate Federal Territory, as is the island of Labuan and the newly developed administrative capital of Putrajaya. The Head of State, or Supreme Head of Malaysia, is a monarch (Yang di-Pertuan Agong), elected for a five-year term (with a Deputy Head of State) by and from the hereditary rulers of nine of the states. The monarch acts on the advice of Parliament and the Cabinet. Parliament consists of the Dewan Negara (Senate) and the Dewan Rakyat (House of Representatives). The Senate has 70 members, including 44 appointed by the Head of State, four of which are from the Federal Territories, and 26 elected members, two chosen by each of the 13 State Legislative Assemblies. The House of Representatives consists of 219 members (increased from 193 at the March 2004 general election), elected for five years by universal adult suffrage: 165 from Peninsular Malaysia (including 11 from Kuala Lumpur and one from Putrajaya), 28 from Sarawak and 26 from Sabah (including one from Labuan). The Head of State appoints the Prime Minister and, on the latter's recommendation, other ministers. The Cabinet is responsible to Parliament. The country is divided into 137 administrative districts.

Defence

Malaysia participates in the Five-Power Defence Arrangements with Australia, New Zealand, Singapore and the United Kingdom. In August 2003 the active armed forces totalled 104,000 men: army 80,000, navy 14,000 and air force 10,000. In February 2004 a programme of national service was introduced, initially on an experimental basis, requiring conscripts to perform three months of military service. Reserve forces numbered 51,600 (army 50,000, navy 1,000, air force 600). Paramilitary forces in 2003 included a General Operations Force (formerly the Police Field Force) of 18,000 men and a People's Volunteer Corps with about 240,000 members. Federal budget plans for 2003 allocated RM 7,700m. to defence.

Economic Affairs

In 2002, according to estimates by the World Bank, Malaysia's gross national income (GNI), measured at average 2000–02 prices, was US $85,956m., equivalent to $3,540 per head (or $8,280 per head on an international purchasing-power parity basis). During 1990–2002, it was estimated, the population increased at an annual average of 2.4%, while gross domestic product (GDP) per head increased, in real terms, by an average of 3.7% per year. Overall GDP increased, in real terms, at an average annual rate of 6.2% in 1990–2002. According to the Bank Negara Malaysia (BNM), GDP increased by 4.1% in 2002 and by 5.2% in 2003.

Agriculture (including forestry and fishing) contributed 9.1% of GDP in 2003, according to the BNM. The sector engaged 15.2% of the employed labour force in 2000. The principal subsistence crop is rice. Malaysia is the world's leading producer of palm oil, exports of which contributed an estimated 6.5% of the value of total merchandise exports in 2003. Other important cash crops include rubber (which accounted for 1.2% of total exports in 2003), cocoa, coconuts, bananas, tea and pineapples. Sawlogs accounted for only an estimated 0.6% of total exports in 2003, owing to a government policy of sustainable management which led to the imposition of restrictions on exports of logs in 1993. During 1990–2002, according to the Asian Development Bank (ADB), agricultural GDP increased, in real terms, at an average annual rate of 0.5%. According to the BNM, agricultural GDP increased by 3.0% in 2002 and by 5.5% in 2003.

Industry (including mining, manufacturing, construction and utilities) contributed 47.0% of GDP in 2003. The sector engaged 37.0% of the employed labour force in 2000. During 1990–2002, according to the ADB, industrial GDP increased, in real terms, at an average annual rate of 7.3%. According to the BNM, industrial GDP grew by 3.9% in 2002 and by 7.0% in 2003.

Mining contributed 10.0% of GDP in 2003. However, it engaged only 0.4% of the employed labour force in 2000. At the end of 2002 estimated proven gas reserves stood at 2,120,000m. cu m, and petroleum reserves at 3,000m. barrels. Petroleum production in 2002 averaged 833,000 barrels per day from Malaysia's 33 oilfields, enough to sustain production for less than 11 years. At that year's level, natural gas production could be sustained for less than 43 years. Exports of crude petroleum provided an estimated 5.0% of total export earnings in 2003. Malaysia is one of the world's leading producers of tin, although in 2003 sales of this commodity accounted for only 0.1% of total export revenue. Bauxite, copper, iron, gold and coal are also mined. The GDP of the mining sector increased at an average annual rate of 4.3% in 1990–2002, according to the ADB. Mining GDP increased by 3.7% in 2002 and by 4.8% in 2003, according to the BNM.

Manufacturing (the largest export sector) contributed 30.2% of GDP in 2003. The manufacturing sector engaged 27.6% of the employed labour force in 2000. The most important branches of manufacturing include electrical machinery and appliances, food products, metals and metal products, non-electrical machinery, transport equipment, rubber and plastic products, chemical products, wood products and furniture. During 1990–2002 manufacturing GDP increased, in real terms, at an average annual rate of 8.1%. Manufacturing GDP increased by 4.0% in 2002 and by 8.2% in 2003.

Energy is derived principally from Malaysia's own reserves of hydrocarbons. The country's dependence on petroleum as a source of electric energy declined from 55.9% in 1990 to 8.8% in 2000. The share contributed by natural gas increased from 22.0% to 78.5% over the same period. In 2000 hydropower and coal accounted for 10.1% and 2.6%, respectively, of the country's electricity production, which reached 75,300m. kWh in 2002. Construction of a controversial 2,400-MW hydroelectric dam at Bakun, in Sarawak, was postponed in 1997, owing to the financial crisis. In early 2004 construction of the dam had yet to commence, as the Government was considering making further reductions to the scale of the project. Imports of mineral fuels comprised 4.7% of the value of merchandise imports in 2002.

The services sector contributed 43.9% of GDP in 2003. It engaged 47.8% of the employed labour force in 2000. Tourism makes a significant contribution to the economy. Tourist arrivals rose from almost 12.8m. in 2001 to 13.3m. in 2002; receipts from the sector reached RM 25,781.1m. in the latter year. However, it was feared that, in the aftermath of the terrorist attack in Bali in October 2002 (see the chapter on Indonesia), Malaysia's tourism sector might be adversely affected; following the attack, warnings were issued by several foreign governments against travel to Malaysia. In 2003 these fears were borne out when tourist arrivals declined to 10.6m. In 2003 the financial and real estate sector, along with business services, contributed 10.9% of GDP. The banking system in Malaysia was severely damaged by the regional financial crisis in 1997; a series of mergers subsequently took place as part of plans to consolidate the sector. The GDP of the services sector increased by an average of 7.8% per year in 1990–2002. Services GDP grew by 4.2% in 2002 and by 3.9% in 2003.

In 2002 Malaysia recorded a visible trade surplus of US $18,135m., with a surplus of $7,190m. on the current account of the balance of payments. In 2003 the principal source of imports (providing 17.4% of the total) was Japan; other major suppliers were the USA (15.2%), Singapore (12.0%), the People's Republic of China and the Republic of Korea. The principal market for exports (18.0%) was the USA; other significant purchasers were Singapore (16.4%) and Japan (10.9%). The principal imports in 2002 were machinery and transport equipment, basic manufactures and chemicals. The principal exports

in 2003 were electrical machinery and parts (particularly semiconductors and electronic equipment), chemicals, textiles, palm oil and products, crude petroleum and liquefied natural gas.

In 2002 there was a federal budgetary deficit of approximately RM 20,253m. The 2004 budget envisaged expenditure of RM 112,500m., resulting in a deficit equivalent to 3.3% of GDP. At the end of 2001 Malaysia's external debt totalled US $43,351m., of which $24,068m. was long-term public debt. The cost of debt-servicing in that year was equivalent to 6.0% of the value of exports of goods and services. The annual rate of inflation averaged 3.2% in 1990–2002. Consumer prices increased by an average of 1.4% in 2001 and by 1.8% in 2002. In 2002 3.5% of the labour force were unemployed.

Malaysia is a member of the UN Economic and Social Commission for Asia and the Pacific (ESCAP, see p. 31), the Asian Development Bank (ADB, see p. 151), the Association of South East Asian Nations (ASEAN, see p. 154), the Colombo Plan (see p. 359) and Asia-Pacific Economic Co-operation (APEC, see p. 147), all of which aim to accelerate economic progress in the region. In January 1992 the member states of ASEAN agreed to establish a free-trade zone, the ASEAN Free Trade Area (AFTA). The original target for the reduction of tariffs to between 0% and 5% was 2008, but this was subsequently advanced to 2003 and then 2002, when AFTA was formally established. Malaysia itself, however, was granted a three-year delay in January 2001 for the opening of its politically-sensitive automotive industry to the free-trade agreements, fearing competition from Thailand.

In September 1998 the Malaysian Government introduced controversial capital controls to limit the repercussions of regional developments and ensure stability in domestic prices and exchange rates. The ringgit was fixed at 3.80 to the US dollar and from 1 October became non-convertible overseas. These and other measures enabled Malaysia to reduce interest rates and raise domestic demand without destabilizing the currency. The economy therefore made a rapid recovery from the regional economic crisis of 1997/98, and the last of the capital controls for non-residents were removed in May 2001, although the ringgit 'peg' remained in place. In July 1999, meanwhile, the Government intensified its efforts towards the reform of the financial sector, announcing plans for the forcible restructuring of the country's numerous banks and finance companies. By August 2001 51 banks had merged under the plans, highlighting the substantial progress made in financial sector reforms. In April 2001 the Government announced the Eighth Malaysia Plan (EMP), which gave economic projections for 2001–05. According to the EMP, the economy was to grow at an average annual rate of 7.5% over the next five years. The Government also expected to achieve a substantial reduction in levels of poverty. Despite the economic recovery of 1999–2000, however, foreign investment in Malaysia decreased in 2001, partly owing to the increasing attractiveness of the People's Republic of China as a destination for foreign investment, before rising in 2002. In 2002, while global demand for Malaysia's principal export commodities, such as electrical and electronic goods, remained slow, an increase in the prices of palm oil, crude petroleum and chemicals, amongst others, contributed to a recovery in exports. Following the retirement of Prime Minister Mahathir Mohamad in October 2003, his successor, Abdullah Ahmad Badawi, deferred several large-scale infrastructure projects and launched an anti-corruption campaign in an attempt to reduce public spending. He also announced his intention to focus on developing the country's agricultural sector and to prioritize educational reforms. A significant downturn in exports in the second half of 2003 was largely attributable to a contraction in the electronics sector; it was feared that the relocation of many electronics companies to China had affected sectoral expansion. GDP expanded by 5.2% in 2003 and, in the same year, the budget deficit was equivalent to 5.5% of GDP. Despite increasing pressure for a review of the viability of the currency 'peg', owing to a decline in the value of the US dollar from late 2003, the arrangement was expected to remain in place in 2004. The Government predicted GDP growth of between 5.5% and 6.0% for the year. However, reforms to the country's education and health sectors would continue to be necessary in the long term, in order to minimize Malaysia's reliance on foreign direct investment and on exports to drive economic growth.

Education

Under the Malaysian education system, free schooling is provided at government-assisted schools for children between the ages of six and 18 years. There are also private schools, which receive no government financial aid. Education is compulsory for 11 years between the ages of six and 16 years. Bahasa Malaysia is the main medium of instruction, while English is taught as a second language; Chinese and Tamil are used for instruction only in primary institutions. In January 2003 new legislation came into effect, requiring that all mathematics and science classes in schools be taught in English. Primary education begins at six years of age and lasts for six years. In 1997 the number of pupils attending primary schools was equivalent to 101% of children in the relevant age-group (males 101%; females 101%). Secondary education, beginning at the age of 12, lasts for seven years, comprising a first cycle of three years and a second of four. Pupils may attend vocational and technical secondary schools instead of the final four years of academic education. In 1997 the total enrolment at secondary schools was equivalent to 64% of the school-age population (males 59%; females 69%). In 1997 Malaysia had 11 state universities and three private universities; in 1995 total enrolment at tertiary level was equivalent to 12% of the relevant age-group. In October 1994 the Government introduced a bill that would allow foreign universities to establish branch campuses in Malaysia. From the end of that year the Government permitted the use of English as a medium of instruction in science and engineering subjects at tertiary level. At the seventh ASEAN summit meeting in November 2001 it was decided that the town of Bandar Nusajaya in Johor would be the location for the first ASEAN university. It would be Malaysia's second international university.

Federal budget expenditure for 2002 allocated RM 16,982m. (24.7% of total expenditure) to education.

Public Holidays

Each state has its own public holidays, and the following federal holidays are also observed:

2004: 22–23 January* (Chinese New Year), 1 February† (Hari Raya Haji, Feast of the Sacrifice), 22 February† (Muharram, Islamic New Year), 1 May (Labour Day), 2 May† (Mouloud, Prophet Muhammad's Birthday), 2 June (Vesak Day), 5 June (Official Birthday of HM the Yang di-Pertuan Agong), 31 August (National Day), 12 November‡ (Deepavali), 14 November† (Hari Raya Puasa, end of Ramadan), 25 December (Christmas Day).

2005: 21 January† (Hari Raya Haji, Feast of the Sacrifice), 9–10 February* (Chinese New Year), 10 February† (Muharram, Islamic New Year), 21 April† (Mouloud, Prophet Muhammad's Birthday), 1 May (Labour Day), 22 May (Vesak Day), 5 June (Official Birthday of HM the Yang di-Pertuan Agong), 31 August (National Day), 1 November‡ (Deepavali), 4 November† (Hari Raya Puasa, end of Ramadan), 25 December (Christmas Day).

* The first two days of the first moon of the lunar calendar.

† These holidays are dependent on the Islamic lunar calendar and may vary by one or two days from the dates given.

‡ Except Sabah and Sarawak.

Weights and Measures

The metric system is in force. There is also a local system of weights and measures:

1 cupak = 1 quart (1.1365 litres);

1 gantang = 1 gallon (4.5461 litres);

1 tahil = 11/3 ounces (37.8 grams);

16 tahils = 1 kati = 11/3 lb (604.8 grams);

100 katis = 1 picul = 1331/3 lb (60.48 kg);

40 piculs = 1 koyan = 5,3331/3 lb (2,419.2 kg).

Statistical Survey

Sources (unless otherwise stated): Department of Statistics, Blok C6, Parcel C, Pusat Pentadbiran Kerajaan Persekutuan, 62514 Putrajaya; tel. (3) 88857000; fax (3) 88889248; e-mail jpbpo@stats.gov.my; internet www.statistics.gov.my; Departments of Statistics, Kuching and Kota Kinabalu. Note: Unless otherwise indicated, statistics refer to all states of Malaysia.

Area and Population

AREA, POPULATION AND DENSITY

Area (sq km)	
Peninsular Malaysia.	131,686
Sabah (incl. Labuan)	73,711
Sarawak	124,450
Total	329,847*
Population (census results)	
14 August 1991	18,379,655
5–20 July 2000	
Males	11,853,432
Females.	11,421,258
Total	23,274,690
Population (official estimate at mid-year)	
2002	24,530,000
Density (per sq km) at mid-2002	74.4

* 127,355 sq miles.

PRINCIPAL ETHNIC GROUPS
(at census of August 1991)*

	Peninsular Malaysia	Sabah†	Sarawak	Total
Malays and other indigenous groups	8,433,826	1,003,540	1,209,118	10,646,484
Chinese.	4,250,969	218,233	475,752	4,944,954
Indians.	1,380,048	9,310	4,608	1,393,966
Others	410,544	167,790	10,541	588,875
Non-Malaysians	322,229	464,786	18,361	805,376
Total	14,797,616	1,863,659	1,718,380	18,379,655

* Including adjustment for underenumeration.
† Including the Federal Territory of Labuan.

Mid-1997 (estimates, '000 persons): Malays 10,233.2; Other indigenous groups 2,290.9; Chinese 5,445.1; Indian 1,541.7; Others 685.7; Non-Malaysians 1,468.9; Total 21,665.5.

STATES
(census of 5–20 July 2000)

	Area (sq km)	Population*	Density (per sq km)	Capital
Johor (Johore)	18,987	2,740,625	144.3	Johore Bahru
Kedah	9,425	1,649,756	175.0	Alor Star
Kelantan	15,024	1,313,014	87.4	Kota Bahru
Melaka (Malacca)	1,652	635,791	384.9	Malacca
Negeri Sembilan (Negri Sembilan)	6,644	859,924	129.4	Seremban
Pahang	35,965	1,288,376	35.8	Kuantan
Perak	21,005	2,051,236	97.7	Ipoh
Perlis	795	204,450	257.2	Kangar
Pulau Pinang (Penang)	1,031	1,313,449	1,274.0	George Town
Sabah	73,619	2,603,485	35.4	Kota Kinabalu
Sarawak	124,450	2,071,506	16.6	Kuching
Selangor	7,960	4,188,876	526.2	Shah Alam
Terengganu (Trengganu)	12,955	898,825	69.4	Kuala Trengganu
Federal Territory of Kuala Lumpur.	243	1,379,310	5,676.2	—
Federal Territory of Labuan	92	76,067	826.8	Victoria
Total	329,847	23,274,690	70.6	

* Including adjustment for underenumeration.

PRINCIPAL TOWNS
(population at 2000 census)

Kuala Lumpur		Kuala Terengganu	
(capital)*	1,297,526	(Kuala Trengganu)	250,528
		Seremban	246,441
Ipoh	566,211	Kota Baharu (Kota	
Kelang (Klang)	563,173	Bahru)	233,673
		Sandakan	220,000†
Petaling Jaya	438,084	Taiping‡	183,320
Shah Alam	319,612	George Town	
Kuantan	283,041	(Penang)	180,573

* The new town of Putrajaya is now the administrative capital.
† Provisional.
‡ Excluding a part of Pondok Tanjong, which is in the District of Kerian.
Source: Thomas Brinkhoff, *City Population* (internet www.citypopulation.de).

Mid-2001 (UN estimate, incl. suburbs): Kuala Lumpur 1,410,000 (Source: UN, *World Urbanization Prospects: The 2001 Revision*).

BIRTHS AND DEATHS

	Registered live births		Registered deaths	
	Number	Rate (per 1,000)	Number	Rate (per 1,000)
1993	541,760	27.7	87,594	4.5
1994	537,611	26.7	90,051	4.5
1995	539,234	24.9	95,025	4.4
1996	540,866	25.5	95,520	4.5
1997	537,104	24.8	97,042	4.5
1998	554,573	25.0	97,906	4.4

Source: UN, mainly *Demographic Yearbook*.

1999 (rates per 1,000): Births 25.4; Deaths 4.6 (Source: Ministry of Health, Kuala Lumpur).

2000 (provisional, rates per 1,000): Births 24.5; Deaths 4.4 (Source: Ministry of Health, Kuala Lumpur).

2001 (provisional, rates per 1,000): Births 22.3; Deaths 4.4 (Source: Ministry of Health, Kuala Lumpur).

2002 (provisional, rates per 1,000): Births 21.8; Deaths 4.4 (Source: Ministry of Health, Kuala Lumpur).

Expectation of life (WHO estimates, years at birth): 72.0 (males 69.6; females 74.7) in 2002 (Source: WHO, *World Health Report*).

ECONOMICALLY ACTIVE POPULATION*
(sample surveys, ISIC major divisions, '000 persons aged 15 to 64 years)

	1998	1999	2000
Agriculture, forestry and fishing	1,401	1,389	1,408
Mining and quarrying	42	42	41
Manufacturing	2,277	2,379	2,559
Electricity, gas and water	70	72	75
Construction	810	804	755
Trade, restaurants and hotels	1,437	1,449	1,584
Transport, storage and communications	435	442	462
Finance, insurance, real estate and business services	418	420	509
Government services	875	877	981
Other services	832	867	899
Total employed	8,597	8,741	9,271
Unemployed	284	269	302
Total labour force	8,881	9,010	9,573

* Excluding members of the armed forces.
Source: IMF, *Malaysia: Statistical Appendix* (October 2001).

2002 ('000 persons): Total employed 9,452.6; Unemployed 343.5; Total labour force 9,886.2.

Health and Welfare

KEY INDICATORS

Total fertility rate (children per woman, 2002)	2.9
Under-5 mortality rate (per 1,000 live births, 2001)	8
HIV/AIDS (% of persons aged 15–49, 2001)	0.35
Physicians (per 1,000 head, 1996)	2.01
Health expenditure (2001): US $ per head (PPP)	345
Health expenditure (2001): % of GDP	3.8
Health expenditure (2001): public (% of total)	53.7
Human Development Index (2001): ranking	58
Human Development Index (2001): value	0.790

For sources and definitions, see explanatory note on p. vi.

Agriculture

PRINCIPAL CROPS
('000 metric tons)

	2000	2001	2002
Rice (paddy)	2,141	2,094	2,091
Maize*	65	67	70
Sweet potatoes†	41	41	41
Cassava (Manioc)†	380	380	370
Other roots and tubers†	45	44	44
Sugar cane†	1,600	1,600	1,600
Groundnuts (in shell)†	6	6	6
Coconuts	734*	700†	738†
Oil palm fruit†	56,600	58,950	58,390
Cabbages†	47	37	37
Tomatoes†	10	10	10
Pumpkins, squash and gourds†	14	14	14
Cucumbers and gherkins†	40	50	45
Other vegetables and melons†	250	245	240
Watermelons	86	96	91
Mangoes	20	20	20
Pineapples†	92	86	87
Papayas†	60	65	65
Bananas†	540	530	500
Oranges†	12	12	12
Other fruit (excl. melons)†	299	301	300
Coffee (green)†	18	20	22
Cocoa beans	70	58	48
Tea (made)	6*	5*	5†
Tobacco (leaves)	7	9	12
Natural rubber	615	546	589

* Unofficial figure(s).
† FAO estimate(s).

Source: FAO.

LIVESTOCK
('000 head, year ending September)

	2000	2001	2002
Cattle	724	742	748
Buffaloes	142	148	154
Goats	233	247	248
Sheep	157	129	118
Pigs	1,808	1,973	1,824
Chickens	123,650	149,586	160,843
Ducks*	13,000	13,000	13,000

* FAO estimates.
Source: FAO.

LIVESTOCK PRODUCTS
('000 metric tons)

	2000	2001	2002
Beef and veal*	18	19	21
Buffalo meat*.	3	3	4
Pig meat	160	168	207
Poultry meat*.	771	781	836
Cows' milk	30	32	37
Buffaloes' milk*	7	7	7
Hen eggs	391	411	432
Other poultry eggs	10	10	11
Cattle and buffalo hides*	3	3	4

* FAO estimates.

Source: FAO.

Forestry

ROUNDWOOD REMOVALS
('000 cubic metres, excl. bark)

	2000	2001	2002
Sawlogs, veneer logs and logs for sleepers	15,095	16,161	17,913
Fuel wood*	3,346	3,286	3,228
Total	18,441	19,447	21,141

* FAO estimates.

Source: FAO.

SAWNWOOD PRODUCTION
('000 cubic metres, incl. railway sleepers)

	2000	2001	2002
Total (all broadleaved)	5,590	4,696	4,594

Source: FAO.

Fishing

('000 metric tons, live weight)

	1999	2000	2001
Capture	1,251.8	1,289.2	1,234.7
Threadfin breams	39.7	32.5	28.9
Indian scad	70.2	84.2	77.4
Marine clupeoids	45.5	33.6	40.8
Kawakawa	57.3	58.1	56.1
Yellowstripe scad	41.3	44.3	39.9
Indian mackerels	111.4	98.1	99.5
Prawns and shrimps	90.5	96.0	77.5
Squids	40.3	54.4	45.3
Aquaculture	155.1	151.8	158.2
Blood cockle	79.9	64.4	70.8
Total catch	1,406.9	1,441.0	1,392.9

Note: Figures exclude crocodiles, recorded by number rather than by weight. The number of estuarine crocodiles caught was: 120 in 1999; 559 in 2000; 375 in 2001. Also excluded are shells and corals. Catches of turban shells (FAO estimates, metric tons) were: 80 in 1999; 80 in 2000; 80 in 2001. Catches of hard corals (FAO estimates, metric tons) were: 4,000 in 1999; 4,000 in 2000; 4,000 in 2001.

Source: FAO, *Yearbook of Fishery Statistics*.

Mining

PRODUCTION
(metric tons, unless otherwise indicated)

	2000	2001	2002*
Tin-in-concentrates	6,307	4,972	4,215
Bauxite	123,000	64,000	40,000
Iron ore†	259,000	376,000	404,000
Kaolin	233,885	364,458	258,273
Gold (kg)	4,026	3,965	4,289
Silver (kg)§	5	3	n.a.
Barytes	7,274	649	1,602
Hard coal	382,942	497,733	352,513
Crude petroleum ('000 barrels)	249,159	243,696	255,922
Natural gas (million cu m)‡	56,929	58,751	61,091
Ilmenite†	124,801	129,750	106,046
Zirconium†	3,642	3,768	5,293

* Data are preliminary.

† Figures refer to the gross weight of ores and concentrates.

‡ Including amount reinjected, flared and lost.

§ Includes by-product from a copper mine in Sabah, tin mines in Peninsular Malaysia and gold mines in Peninsular Malaysia and Sarawak.

Sources: Minerals and Geoscience Dept; US Geological Survey; UN, *Statistical Yearbook for Asia and the Pacific*.

Industry

SELECTED PRODUCTS
('000 metric tons, unless otherwise indicated)

	2001	2002	2003
Canned fish, frozen shrimps/prawns	40.1	42.2	47.6
Palm oil (crude)	11,804	11,908	n.a.
Refined sugar	1,210.4	1,404.8	1,424.1
Soft drinks ('000 litres)	501.6	440.2	521.4
Cigarettes (metric tons)	25,618	23,079	23,971
Woven cotton fabrics (million metres)	177.4	166.4	160.5
Veneer sheets ('000 cu metres)	1,173.2	1,089.6	956.3
Plywood ('000 cu metres)	3,937.5	3,972.3	4,171.4
Kerosene and jet fuel	3,293.1	3,170.7	3,056.6
Liquefied petroleum gas	2,308.0	2,945.4	3,188.2
Inner tubes and pneumatic tyres ('000)	26,391	27,107	27,873
Rubber gloves (million pairs)	12,256.3	12,207.7	15,072.2
Earthen brick and cement roofing tiles (million)	1,196.1	1,315.6	1,579.0
Cement	13,820	14,336	17,227
Iron and steel bars and rods	2,691.3	3,221.5	3,385.8
Refrigerators for household use ('000)	186.0	172.1	184.5
Television receivers ('000)	9,501.2	10,409.7	9,915.2
Radio receivers ('000)	28,839	21,735	27,640
Semiconductors (million)	13,524	15,036	15,932
Electronic transistors (million)	19,989	20,401	24,206
Integrated circuits (million)	17,457	19,916	23,269
Passenger motor cars ('000)*	383.6	418.8	342.7
Commercial vehicles('000)*	62.7	72.3	80.8
Motorcycles and scooters ('000)	235.9	242.4	256.3

* Vehicles assembled from imported parts.

Tin (smelter production of primary metal, metric tons): 28,913 in 1999; 26,228 in 2000; 32,566 (preliminary figure) in 2001 (Source: US Geological Survey).

Source (unless otherwise indicated): Bank Negara Malaysia, Kuala Lumpur.

Finance

CURRENCY AND EXCHANGE RATES

Monetary Units
100 sen = 1 ringgit Malaysia (RM—also formerly Malaysian dollar).

Sterling, US Dollar and Euro Equivalents (31 December 2003)
£1 sterling = RM 6.7819;
US $1 = RM 3.8000;
€1 = RM 4.7994;
RM 100 = £14.75 = US $26.32 = €20.84.

Exchange Rate
A fixed exchange rate of US $1 = RM 3.8000 has been in effect since September 1998

FEDERAL BUDGET
(RM million)

Revenue	2000	2001	2002
Tax revenue	47,173	61,492	66,860
Taxes on income and profits	29,156	42,097	44,351
Companies (excl. petroleum)	13,905	20,770	24,642
Individuals	7,015	9,436	9,889
Petroleum	6,010	9,858	7,636
Export duties	1,032	867	803
Import duties	3,599	3,193	3,668
Excises on goods	3,803	4,130	4,745
Sales tax	5,968	7,356	9,243
Service tax	1,701	1,927	2,214
Other revenue	14,692	18,076	16,655
Total	**61,864**	**79,567**	**83,515**

Expenditure	2000	2001	2002
Defence and security	6,958	8,310	9,030
Economic Services	6,637	5,150	6,015
Agriculture and rural development	1,323	1,366	1,446
Trade and industry	3,761	1,870	1,838
Transport	1,286	1,672	2,069
Social services	18,784	21,757	24,798
Education	12,923	14,422	16,982
Health	4,131	4,680	5,152
Transfer payments	2,524	5,561	5,778
Debt service charges	9,055	9,634	9,670
Pensions and gratuities	4,187	4,711	5,134
General administration	8,401	8,636	8,274
Total	**56,547**	**63,757**	**68,699**

Source: Bank Negara Malaysia, Kuala Lumpur.

FEDERAL DEVELOPMENT EXPENDITURE
(RM million)

	2000	2001	2002
Defence and security	2,332	3,287	4,333
Social services	11,076	15,384	18,043
Education	7,099	10,363	12,436
Health	1,272	1,570	1,503
Housing	1,194	1,269	1,808
Economic services	11,639	12,725	12,433
Agriculture and rural development	1,183	1,394	1,364
Public utilities	1,517	1,092	1,808
Trade and industry	3,667	4,830	3,474
Transport	4,863	5,042	5,401
General administration	2,894	3,839	1,168
Total	**27,941**	**35,235**	**35,977**

Source: Bank Negara Malaysia, Kuala Lumpur.

INTERNATIONAL RESERVES
(US $ million at 31 December)

	2000	2001	2002
Gold*	53	51	56
IMF special drawing rights	105	125	151
Reserve position in IMF	792	764	790
Foreign exchange	28,625	29,585	33,280
Total	**29,576**	**30,526**	**34,277**

* Valued at SDR 35 per troy ounce.

Source: IMF, *International Financial Statistics*.

MONEY SUPPLY
(RM million at 31 December)

	2000	2001	2002
Currency outside banks	22,263	22,148	23,897
Demand deposits at commercial banks	54,520	57,791	63,892
Total money (incl. others)	**80,656**	**83,882**	**91,932**

Source: IMF, *International Financial Statistics*.

COST OF LIVING
(Consumer Price Index; base 2000 = 100)

	1999	2001	2002
Food	98.1	100.7	101.4
Beverages and tobacco	99.1	100.7	101.8
Clothing and footwear	101.8	97.4	95.2
Rent and other housing costs, heating and lighting	98.6	101.4	102.1
Furniture, domestic appliances, tools and maintenance	100.0	100.1	99.7
Medical care	98.0	102.9	105.4
Transport and communications	98.0	103.6	110.4
Education and leisure	99.4	99.9	100.1
Other goods and services	99.1	100.7	101.8
All items	**98.5**	**101.4**	**103.2**

Source: Bank Negara Malaysia, Kuala Lumpur.

NATIONAL ACCOUNTS
(RM million at current prices)

Expenditure on the Gross Domestic Product

	2001	2002	2003 *
Government final consumption expenditure	42,097	50,015	53,893
Private final consumption expenditure	150,644	159,506	169,813
Change in stocks	−3,268	1,251	−1,456
Gross fixed capital formation	83,345	83,764	87,089
Total domestic expenditure	**272,818**	**294,536**	**309,339**
Exports of goods and services	389,256	415,040	450,592
Less Imports of goods and services	327,765	348,918	367,918
GDP in purchasers' values	**334,309**	**360,658**	**392,012**
GDP at constant 1987 prices	**210,640**	**219,309**	**230,710**

* Preliminary figures.

Source: Bank Negara Malaysia, Kuala Lumpur.

Gross Domestic Product by Economic Activity

	2001	2002	2003
Agriculture, forestry and fishing	27,006	32,550	37,115
Mining and quarrying	33,976	34,029	40,666
Manufacturing	101,924	110,461	122,458
Electricity, gas and water	11,262	11,759	12,543
Construction	14,163	14,606	14,910
Trade, restaurants and hotels	48,708	50,946	52,679
Transport, storage and communications	23,688	24,680	26,201
Finance, insurance, real estate and business services	42,346	43,221	44,371
Government services	23,895	27,625	29,037
Other services	23,371	24,764	25,902
Sub-total	350,339	374,641	405,882
Import duties	5,841	6,793	6,824
Less Imputed bank service charges	21,870	20,776	20,694
GDP in purchasers' values	334,309	360,658	392,012

Source: Bank Negara Malaysia, Kuala Lumpur.

BALANCE OF PAYMENTS
(US $ million)

	2000	2001	2002
Exports of goods f.o.b.	98,429	87,981	93,383
Imports of goods f.o.b.	−77,602	−69,597	−75,248
Trade balance	20,827	18,383	18,135
Exports of services	13,941	14,455	14,878
Imports of services	−16,747	−16,657	−16,448
Balance on goods and services	18,020	16,182	16,565
Other income received	1,986	1,847	2,139
Other income paid	−9,594	−8,590	−8,734
Balance on goods, services and income	10,412	9,439	9,970
Current transfers received	756	537	661
Current transfers paid	−2,680	−2,689	−3,442
Current balance	8,488	7,287	7,190
Direct investment abroad	−2,026	−267	−1,905
Direct investment from abroad	3,788	554	3,203
Portfolio investment liabilities	−2,145	−666	−836
Other investment assets	−5,565	−2,702	−4,597
Other investment liabilities	—	−830	1,868
Net errors and omissions	−3,221	−2,394	−391
Overall balance	−1,009	999	3,657

Source: IMF, *International Financial Statistics*.

External Trade

PRINCIPAL COMMODITIES
(RM million)

Imports c.i.f.	2000	2001	2002
Food and live animals	11,393	12,277	12,471
Beverages and tobacco	709	924	1,396
Crude materials (inedible) except fuels	7,096	6,891	6,839
Mineral fuels, lubricants, etc.	14,973	14,706	14,386
Animal and vegetable oils and fats	604	793	1,270
Chemicals	22,372	20,704	21,523
Basic manufactures	32,596	29,297	30,918
Machinery and transport equipment	195,728	169,609	187,624
Miscellaneous manufactured articles	17,659	15,730	17,085
Other commodities and transactions	8,330	9,298	9,997
Total	311,459	280,229	303,508

Exports f.o.b.	2000	2001	2002
Food and live animals	6,470	6,581	7,494
Beverages and tobacco	1,215	1,308	1,283
Crude materials (inedible) except fuels	10,288	7,565	8,441
Mineral fuels, lubricants, etc.	35,903	32,288	30,715
Animal and vegetable oils and fats	12,937	12,343	17,927
Chemicals	14,278	14,318	16,726
Basic manufactures	25,788	24,115	24,887
Machinery and transport equipment	233,379	202,828	212,068
Miscellaneous manufactured articles	29,925	29,171	30,454
Other commodities and transactions	3,088	3,767	4,480
Total	373,270	334,284	354,475

Source: Asian Development Bank, *Key Indicators of Developing Asian and Pacific Countries*.

PRINCIPAL TRADING PARTNERS
(RM million)

Imports c.i.f.	2001	2002	2003
Australia	5,944	5,415	4,802
China, People's Republic	14,473	23,328	25,897
France	4,349	4,263	4,565
Germany	10,451	11,188	14,758
Hong Kong	7,064	8,809	8,233
India	2,934	2,442	2,561
Indonesia	8,536	9,683	11,196
Ireland	3,811	2,678	1,553
Italy	2,865	2,517	2,410
Japan	53,750	53,813	53,412
Korea, Republic	11,249	16,006	16,250
Philippines	6,987	9,862	9,928
Singapore	35,352	36,243	36,928
Taiwan	15,930	16,848	15,026
Thailand	11,120	11,982	14,215
United Kingdom	6,846	5,966	5,987
USA	44,881	51,679	46,823
Total (incl. others)	280,229	302,589	307,266

Exports f.o.b.	2001	2002	2003
Australia	7,795	8,011	9,607
China, People's Republic	14,683	19,961	24,467
France	3,569	5,170	6,662
Germany	7,766	7,962	9,140
Hong Kong	15,437	20,165	23,285
India	5,992	6,690	9,541
Indonesia	5,930	6,801	8,085
Japan	44,393	39,690	41,757
Korea, Republic	11,108	11,832	11,173
Netherlands	15,438	13,136	12,914
Philippines	4,892	5,071	5,264
Singapore	56,643	60,525	62,689
Taiwan	12,167	13,202	13,463
Thailand	12,756	15,087	17,394
United Kingdom	8,759	8,327	8,779
USA	67,618	69,293	68,786
Total (incl. others)	334,284	354,078	382,303

Source: Bank Negara Malaysia, Kuala Lumpur.

Transport

RAILWAYS
(traffic, Peninsular Malaysia and Singapore)

	1998	1999	2000
Passenger-km (million)	1,397	1,313	1,220
Freight ton-km (million)	992	908	917

Source: UN, *Statistical Yearbook*.

ROAD TRAFFIC
(registered motor vehicles at 31 December)

	1998*	1999*	2000
Passenger cars	3,517,484	3,852,693	4,212,567
Buses and coaches	45,643	47,674	48,662
Lorries and vans	599,149	642,976	665,284
Road tractors	286,898	304,135	315,687
Motorcycles and mopeds	4,692,183	5,082,473	5,356,604

* Source: International Road Federation, *World Road Statistics*; data for 1999 are estimates.

SHIPPING

Merchant Fleet
(registered at 31 December)

	2000	2001	2002
Number of vessels	865	882	915
Total displacement ('000 grt)	5,328.1	5,207.1	5,394.4

Source: Lloyd's Register-Fairplay, *World Fleet Statistics*.

Sea-borne Freight Traffic*
(Peninsular Malaysia, international and coastwise, '000 metric tons)

	1998	1999	2000
Goods loaded	35,206	39,755	42,547
Goods unloaded	48,314	54,854	56,537

* Including transhipments.
Source: UN, *Monthly Bulletin of Statistics*.

CIVIL AVIATION
(traffic on scheduled services)

	1997	1998	1999
Kilometres flown (million)	183	189	207
Passengers carried ('000)	15,592	13,654	14,985
Passenger-km (million)	28,698	29,372	33,708
Total ton-km (million)	3,777	3,777	4,431

Source: UN, *Statistical Yearbook*.

Tourism

TOURIST ARRIVALS BY COUNTRY OF RESIDENCE*

	2001	2002	2003
Brunei	309,529	256,952	215,634
China, People's Republic	453,246	557,647	350,597
Indonesia	777,449	769,128	621,651
Japan	397,639	354,563	213,527
Singapore	6,951,594	7,547,761	5,922,306
Taiwan	249,811	209,706	137,419
Thailand	1,018,797	1,166,937	1,152,296
United Kingdom	262,423	239,294	125,569
Total (incl. others)	12,775,073	13,292,010	10,576,915

* Including Singapore residents crossing the frontier by road through the Johore Causeway.

Tourism receipts (RM million): 17,335.4 in 2000; 24,221.5 in 2001; 25,781.1 in 2002.

Source: Malaysia Tourism Promotion Board.

Communications Media

	1999	2000	2001
Television receivers ('000 in use)*	3,800	3,900	n.a.
Telephones ('000 main lines in use)	4,430.8	4,634.3	4,710.0
Mobile cellular telephones ('000 subscribers)	2,990.0	4,960.8	7,128.0
Personal computers ('000 in use)*	1,500	2,400	3,000
Internet users ('000)*	2,500	3,700	6,500

Radio receivers ('000 in use, 1997): 9,100.

Facsimile machines ('000 in use): 175.0* in 1998.

Mobile cellular telephones ('000 subscribers): 8,500 in 2002.

Book production (1999): 5,084 titles (29,040,000 copies in 1996)†.

Newspapers (1996): 42 dailies (average circulation 3,345,000 copies); 44 non-dailies (average circulation 1,424,000 copies).

Periodicals (1992): 25 titles (average circulation 996,000 copies).
* Estimate(s).
† Including pamphlets (106 titles and 646,000 copies in 1994).

Sources: International Telecommunication Union; UNESCO, *Statistical Yearbook*; UN, *Statistical Yearbook*.

Education

(January 2003, unless otherwise indicated)

	Institutions	Teachers	Students
Primary	7,498	174,189	2,996,780
Secondary	1,881	126,544	2,061,168
Regular	1,682	113,032	1,951,225
Fully residential	45	2,623	25,897
Vocational	1	29	96
Technical	85	7,093	38,291
Religious	55	2,971	36,998
Special	3	150	602
Special Model	8	504	7,147
Sports	2	142	912
Tertiary*	48	14,960	210,724
Universities	9	7,823	97,103
Teacher training	31	3,220	46,019
MARA Institute of Technology	1	2,574	42,174

* 1995 figures.

Source: Ministry of Education.

Pre-primary: 9,743 schools (1994); 20,352 teachers (1994); 459,015 pupils (1995) (Source: UNESCO, *Statistical Yearbook*).

Adult literacy rate (UNESCO estimates): 87.9% (males 91.7%; females 84.0%) in 2001 (Source: UN Development Programme, *Human Development Report*).

Directory

Note: in 2003–04 telephone and fax numbers in Malaysia remained in the process of change. See www.telekom.com.my for further details.

The Constitution

The Constitution of the Federation of Malaya became effective at independence on 31 August 1957. As subsequently amended, it is now the Constitution of Malaysia. The main provisions are summarized below.

SUPREME HEAD OF STATE

The Yang di-Pertuan Agong (King or Supreme Sovereign) is the Supreme Head of Malaysia.

Every act of government is derived from his authority, although he acts on the advice of Parliament and the Cabinet. The appointment of a Prime Minister lies within his discretion, and he has the right to refuse to dissolve Parliament even against the advice of the Prime Minister. He appoints the Judges of the Federal Court and the High Courts on the advice of the Prime Minister. He is the Supreme Commander of the Armed Forces. The Yang di-Pertuan Agong is elected by the Conference of Rulers, and to qualify for election he must be one of the nine hereditary Rulers. He holds office for five years or until his earlier resignation or death. Election is by secret ballot on each Ruler in turn, starting with the Ruler next in precedence after the late or former Yang di-Pertuan Agong. The first Ruler to obtain not fewer than five votes is declared elected. The Deputy Supreme Head of State (the Timbalan Yang di-Pertuan Agong) is elected by a similar process. On election the Yang di-Pertuan Agong relinquishes, for his tenure of office, all his functions as Ruler of his own state and may appoint a Regent. The Timbalan Yang di-Pertuan Agong exercises no powers in the ordinary course, but is immediately available to fill the post of Yang di-Pertuan Agong and carry out his functions in the latter's absence or disability. In the event of the Yang di-Pertuan Agong's death or resignation he takes over the exercise of sovereignty until the Conference of Rulers has elected a successor.

CONFERENCE OF RULERS

The Conference of Rulers consists of the Rulers and the heads of the other states. Its prime duty is the election by the Rulers only of the Yang di-Pertuan Agong and his deputy. The Conference must be consulted in the appointment of judges, the Auditor-General, the Election Commission and the Services Commissions. It must also be consulted and concur in the alteration of state boundaries, the extension to the federation as a whole, of Islamic religious acts and observances, and in any bill to amend the Constitution. Consultation is mandatory in matters affecting public policy or the special position of the Malays and natives of Sabah and Sarawak. The Conference also considers matters affecting the rights, prerogatives and privileges of the Rulers themselves.

FEDERAL PARLIAMENT

Parliament has two Houses—the Dewan Negara (Senate) and the Dewan Rakyat (House of Representatives). The Senate has a membership of 70, comprising 26 elected and 44 appointed members. Each state legislature, acting as an electoral college, elects two Senators; these may be members of the State Legislative Assembly or otherwise. The Yang di-Pertuan Agong appoints the other 44 members of the Senate; these include four Senators representing the three Federal Territories—Kuala Lumpur, Labuan and Putrajaya. Members of the Senate must be at least 30 years old. The Senate elects its President and Deputy President from among its members. It may initiate legislation, but all proposed legislation for the granting of funds must be introduced in the first instance in the House of Representatives. All legislative measures require approval by both Houses of Parliament before being presented to the Yang di-Pertuan Agong for the Royal Assent in order to become law. A bill originating in the Senate cannot receive Royal Assent until it has been approved by the House of Representatives, but the Senate has delaying powers only over a bill originating from and approved by the House of Representatives. Senators serve for a period of three years, but the Senate is not subject to dissolution. Parliament can, by statute, increase the number of Senators elected from each state to three. The House of Representatives consists of 219 elected members (see Amendments). Of these, 165 are from Peninsular Malaysia (including 11 from Kuala Lumpur and one from Putrajaya), 28 from Sarawak and 26 from Sabah (including one from Labuan). Members are returned from single-member constituencies on the basis of universal adult franchise. The term of the House of Representatives is limited to five years, after which time a fresh

general election must be held. The Yang di-Pertuan Agong may dissolve Parliament before then if the Prime Minister so advises.

THE CABINET

To advise him in the exercise of his functions, the Yang di-Pertuan Agong appoints the Cabinet, consisting of the Prime Minister and an unspecified number of Ministers (who must all be Members of Parliament). The Prime Minister must be a citizen born in Malaysia and a member of the House of Representatives who, in the opinion of the Yang di-Pertuan Agong, commands the confidence of that House. Ministers are appointed on the advice of the Prime Minister. A number of Deputy Ministers (who are not members of the Cabinet) are also appointed from among Members of Parliament. The Cabinet meets regularly under the chairmanship of the Prime Minister to formulate policy.

PUBLIC SERVICES

The Public Services, civilian and military, are non-political and owe their loyalty not to the party in power but to the Yang di-Pertuan Agong and the Rulers. They serve whichever government may be in power, irrespective of the latter's political affiliation. To ensure the impartiality of the service, and its protection from political interference, the Constitution provides for a number of Services Commissions to select and appoint officers, to place them on the pensionable establishment, to determine promotion and to maintain discipline.

THE STATES

The heads of nine of the 13 states are hereditary Rulers. The Ruler of Perlis has the title of Raja, and the Ruler of Negeri Sembilan that of Yang di-Pertuan Besar. The rest of the Rulers are Sultans. The heads of the States of Melaka (Malacca), Pinang (Penang), Sabah and Sarawak are each designated Yang di-Pertua Negeri and do not participate in the election of the Yang di-Pertuan Agong. Each of the 13 states has its own written Constitution and a single Legislative Assembly. Every state legislature has powers to legislate on matters not reserved for the Federal Parliament. Each State Legislative Assembly has the right to order its own procedure, and the members enjoy parliamentary privilege. All members of the Legislative Assemblies are directly elected from single-member constituencies. The head of the state acts on the advice of the State Government. This advice is tendered by the State Executive Council or Cabinet in precisely the same manner in which the Federal Cabinet tenders advice to the Yang di-Pertuan Agong.

The legislative authority of the state is vested in the head of the state in the State Legislative Assembly. The executive authority of the state is vested in the head of the state, but executive functions may be conferred on other persons by law. Every state has its own Executive Council or Cabinet to advise the head of the state, headed by its Chief Minister (Ketua Menteri in Melaka, Pinang, Sabah and Sarawak and Menteri Besar in other states), and collectively responsible to the state legislature. Each state in Peninsular Malaysia is divided into administrative districts, each with its District Officer. Sabah is divided into four residencies: West Coast, Interior, Sandakan and Tawau, with headquarters at Kota Kinabalu, Keningau, Sandakan and Tawau, respectively. Sarawak is divided into five Divisions, each in charge of a Resident—the First Division, with headquarters at Kuching; the Second Division, with headquarters at Simanggang; the Third Division, with headquarters at Sibu; the Fourth Division, with headquarters at Miri; the Fifth Division, with headquarters at Limbang.

AMENDMENTS

From 1 February 1974, the city of Kuala Lumpur, formerly the seat of the Federal Government and capital of Selangor State, is designated the Federal Territory of Kuala Lumpur. It is administered directly by the Federal Government and returns five members to the House of Representatives.

In April 1981 the legislature approved an amendment empowering the Yang di-Pertuan Agong to declare a state of emergency on the grounds of imminent danger of a breakdown in law and order or a threat to national security.

In August 1983 the legislature approved an amendment empowering the Prime Minister, instead of the Yang di-Pertuan Agong, to declare a state of emergency.

The island of Labuan, formerly part of Sabah State, was designated a Federal Territory as from 16 April 1984.

The legislature approved an amendment increasing the number of parliamentary constituencies in Sarawak from 24 to 27. The amendment took effect at the general election of 20–21 October 1990. The total number of seats in the House of Representatives, which had increased to 177 following an amendment in August 1983, was thus expanded to 180.

In March 1988 the legislature approved two amendments relating to the judiciary (see Judicial System).

In October 1992 the legislature adopted an amendment increasing the number of parliamentary constituencies from 180 to 192. The Kuala Lumpur Federal Territory and Selangor each gained three seats, Johor two, and Perlis, Kedah, Kelantan and Pahang one. The amendment took effect at the next general election (in April 1995).

In March 1993 an amendment was approved which removed the immunity from prosecution of the hereditary Rulers.

In May 1994 the House of Representatives approved an amendment which ended the right of the Yang di-Pertuan Agong to delay legislation by withholding his assent from legislation and returning it to Parliament for further consideration. Under the amendment, the Yang di-Pertuan Agong was obliged to give his assent to a bill within 30 days; if he failed to do so, the bill would, none the less, become law. An amendment was simultaneously approved restructuring the judiciary and introducing a mandatory code of ethics for judges, to be drawn up by the Government.

In 1996 an amendment was approved, increasing the number of parliamentary constituencies from 192 to 193.

In July 2001 an amendment was approved banning all discrimination on grounds of gender.

From 1 February 2001 the city of Putrajaya, formerly part of Selangor State, was designated a Federal Territory.

In 2003 the legislature approved an amendment increasing the number of parliamentary constituencies from 193 to 219. The amendments took effect at the next general election (in March 2004).

The Government

SUPREME HEAD OF STATE

HM Yang di-Pertuan Agong: HM Tuanku SYED SIRAJUDDIN IBNI AL-MARHUM SYED PUTRA JAMALULLAIL (Raja of Perlis) (took office 13 December 2001).

Deputy Supreme Head of State

Timbalan Yang di-Pertuan Agong: HRH Sultan MIZAN ZAINAL ABIDIN (Sultan of Terengganu).

THE CABINET
(April 2004)

Prime Minister and Minister of Finance and of Internal Security: Dato' Seri ABDULLAH BIN Haji AHMAD BADAWI.

Deputy Prime Minister and Minister of Defence: Dato' Seri NAJIB BIN Tun Haji ABDUL RAZAK.

Minister of Housing and Local Government: Dato' ONG KAH TING.

Minister of Foreign Affairs: Datuk Seri SYED HAMID BIN SYED JAAFAR ALBAR.

Minister of Home Affairs: Datuk AZMI KHALID.

Minister of International Trade and Industry: Dato' Seri Paduka RAFIDAH BINTI AZIZ.

Minister of Domestic Trade and Consumer Affairs: Datuk SHAFIE APDAL.

Minister of Transport: Dato' CHAN KONG CHOY.

Minister of Energy, Water and Communications: Datuk Seri Dr LIM KENG YAIK.

Minister of Works: Dato' Seri S. SAMY VELLU.

Minister of Youth and Sports: Datuk AZALINA OTHMAN SAID.

Minister of Education: Datuk HISHAMMUDDIN Tun HUSSEIN.

Minister of Higher Education: Datuk Dr SHAFIE MOHD SALLEH.

Minister of Information: Datuk Paduka ABDUL KADIR Sheikh FADZIR.

Minister of Human Resources: Datuk Dr FONG CHAN ONN.

Minister of Natural Resources and the Environment: Datuk Seri ADENAN SATEM.

Minister of Plantation Industries and Commodities: Datuk PETER CHIN FAH KUI.

Minister of Arts, Culture and Heritage: Datuk Seri Dr RAIS YATIM.

Minister of Tourism: Datuk LEO MICHAEL TOYAD.

Minister of Science, Technology and Innovations: Datuk Dr JAMALUDDIN JARJIS.

Minister of Health: Datuk Dr CHUA SOI LEK.

Minister of Agriculture and Agro-Based Industry: Tan Sri Dato' Haji MUHYIDDIN BIN Haji MOHD YASSIN.

Minister of Rural and Regional Development: Datuk ABDUL AZIZ SHAMSUDDIN.

Minister of Federal Territories: Tan Sri MOHAMED ISA ABDUL SAMAD.

Minister of Entrepreneur and Co-operative Development: Datuk MOHAMED KHALED NORDIN.

Minister of Women, Family and Community Development: Datuk SHAHRIZAT BTE ABDUL JALIL.

Minister of Finance II: NOR MOHAMED YAKCOP.

Ministers in the Prime Minister's Department: Tan Sri BERNARD GILUK DOMPOK, Dato' Seri MOHAMED NAZRI BIN ABDUL AZIZ, Datuk MUSTAPA BIN MOHAMED, Datuk Seri MOHD RADZI BIN Sheikh AHMAD, Prof. Datuk Dr ABDULLAH BIN MOHD ZIN, Datuk Dr MAXIMUS JOHNITY ONGKILI.

MINISTRIES

Prime Minister's Office (Jabatan Perdana Menteri): Blok Utama, Tingkat 1–5, Pusat Pentadbiran Kerajaan Persekutuan, 62502 Putrajaya; tel. (3) 88888000; fax (3) 88883424; e-mail ppm@pmo.gov.my; internet www.pmo.gov.my.

Ministry of Agriculture and Agro-Based Industry: Tingkat 4, Wisma Tani, Jalan Sultan Salahuddin, 50624 Kuala Lumpur; tel. (3) 26982011; fax (3) 26913758; e-mail admin@moa.my; internet www.agrolink.moa.my.

Ministry of Arts, Culture and Heritage: Menara Dato' Onn, 34th–36th Floors, POB 5–7, Putra World Trade Centre, 45 Jalan Tun Ismail, 50694 Kuala Lumpur; tel. (3) 26937111; fax (3) 26941146; e-mail mocat@tourism.gov.my; internet www.mocat.gov.my.

Ministry of Defence (Kementerian Pertahanan): Wisma Pertahanan, Jalan Padang Tembak, 50634 Kuala Lumpur; tel. (3) 26921333; fax (3) 26914163; e-mail cpa@mod.gov.my; internet www.mod.gov.my.

Ministry of Domestic Trade and Consumer Affairs (Kementerian Perdagangan Dalam Negeri Dan Hal Ehwal Pengguna): Tingkat 33, Menara Dayabumi, Jalan Sultan Hishamuddin, 50632 Kuala Lumpur; tel. (3) 22742100; fax (3) 22745260; e-mail menteri@kpdnhq.gov.my; internet www.kpdnhq.gov.my.

Ministry of Education (Kementerian Pendidikan): Blok J, Tingkat 7, Pusat Bandar Damansara, 50604 Kuala Lumpur; tel. (3) 2586900; fax (3) 2543107; e-mail webmaster@moe.gov.my; internet www.moe.gov.my.

Ministry of Energy, Water and Communications: Wisma Damansara, 1st Floor, Jalan Semantan, 50668 Kuala Lumpur; tel. (3) 20875000; fax (3) 20957901; e-mail webmaster@ktkm.gov.my; internet www.ktkm.gov.my.

Ministry of Entrepreneur and Co-operative Development: Tingkat 22–26, Medan MARA, Jalan Raja Laut, 50652 Kuala Lumpur; tel. (3) 26985022; fax (3) 26917623; e-mail nazri@kpun.gov.my; internet www.kpun.gov.my.

Ministry of Federal Territories: Putrajaya.

Ministry of Finance (Kementerian Kewangan): Kompleks Kementerian Kewangan, Precinct 2, Pusat Pentadbiran Kerajaan Persekutuan, 62592 Putrajaya; tel. (3) 88823000; fax (3) 88823892; e-mail mk1@treasury.gov.my; internet www.treasury.gov.my.

Ministry of Foreign Affairs (Kementerian Luar Negeri): Wisma Putra, 1 Jalan Wisma Putra, 62602 Putrajaya; tel. (3) 88874000; fax (3) 88891717; e-mail webmaster@kln.gov.my; internet www.kln.gov.my.

Ministry of Health (Kementerian Kesihatan): Jalan Cenderasari, 50590 Kuala Lumpur; tel. (3) 26985077; fax (3) 26985964; e-mail CJM@moh.gov.my; internet www.moh.gov.my.

Ministry of Higher Education: Kuala Lumpur.

Ministry of Home Affairs (Kementerian Dalam Negeri): Blok D1, Parcel D, Pusat Pentadbiran Kerajaan Persekutuan, 62546 Putrajaya; tel. (3) 88868000; e-mail irg@kdn.gov.my; internet www.kdn.gov.my.

Ministry of Housing and Local Government (Kementerian Perumahan dan Kerajaan Tempatan): Paras 4 and 5, Blok K, Pusat Bandar Damansara, 50782 Kuala Lumpur; tel. (3) 2547033; fax (3) 2547380; e-mail menteri@kpkt.gov.my; internet www.kpkt.gov.my.

Ministry of Human Resources (Kementerian Sumber Manusia): Level 6–9, Blok D3, Parcel D, Pusat Pentadbiran Kerajaan Perseku-tuan, 62502 Putrajaya; tel. (3) 88865000; fax (3) 88893381; e-mail mhr@po.jaring.my; internet www.jaring.my/ksm.

Ministry of Information (Kementerian Penerangan): 5th Floor, Wisma TV, Angkasapuri, 50610 Kuala Lumpur; tel. (3) 2825333; fax (3) 2821255; e-mail webmaster@kempen.gov.my; internet www .kempen.gov.my.

Ministry of Internal Security: Putrajaya.

Ministry of International Trade and Industry (Kementerian Perdagangan Antarabangsa dan Industri): Blok 10, Kompleks Pejabat Kerajaan, Jalan Duta, 50622 Kuala Lumpur; tel. (3) 62033022; fax (3) 62031303; e-mail mitiweb@miti.gov.my; internet www.miti.gov.my/.

Ministry of Natural Resources and the Environment: Kuala Lumpur.

Ministry of Plantation Industries and Commodities: Menara Dayabumi, 6th–8th Floors, Jalan Sultan Hishamuddin, 50654 Kuala Lumpur; tel. (3) 22747511; fax (3) 22745014; e-mail webeditor@kpu.gov.my; internet www.kpu.gov.my.

Ministry of Rural and Regional Development: Aras 5–9, Blok D9, Parcel D, Pusat Pentadbiran Kerajaan Persekutuan, 62606 Putrajaya; tel. (3) 88863500; fax (3) 88892096; e-mail info@kplb.gov .my; internet www.kplb.gov.my.

Ministry of Science, Technology and Innovations: Level 4, Blok C5, Parcel C, Federal Government Administrative Centre, 62662 Putrajaya; tel. (3) 88858000; fax (3) 88892980; e-mail mastic@ mastic.gov.my; internet www.moste.gov.my.

Ministry of Tourism (Kementerian Pelancongan): Kuala Lumpur.

Ministry of Transport (Kementerian Pengangkutan): Wisma Per-dana, Level 5–7, Blok D5, Parcel D, Federal Government Admin-istrative Centre, 62502 Putrajaya; tel. (3) 88866000; fax (3) 88892537; e-mail LeeLC@mot.gov.my; internet www.mot.gov.my.

Ministry of Women, Family and Community Development: Wisma Bumi Raya, Floors 19–21, Jalan Raja Laut, 50562 Kuala Lumpur; tel. (3) 26925022; fax (3) 26937353; e-mail adminkpn@ kempadu.gov.my; internet www.kempadu.gov.my.

Ministry of Works (Kementerian Kerja Raya): Ground Floor, Blok A, Kompleks Kerja Raya, Jalan Sultan Salahuddin, 50580 Kuala Lumpur; tel. (3) 27111100; fax (3) 27116612; e-mail menteri@kkr .gov.my; internet www.kkr.gov.my.

Ministry of Youth and Sports (Kementerian Belia dan Sukan): Blok G, Jalan Dato' Onn, 50570 Kuala Lumpur; tel. (3) 26932255; fax (3) 26932231; e-mail webmaster@kbs.gov.my; internet www.kbs .gov.my.

Legislature

PARLIAMENT

Dewan Negara
(Senate)

The Senate has 70 members, of whom 26 are elected. Each State Legislative Assembly elects two members. The Supreme Head of State appoints the remaining 44 members, including four from the three Federal Territories.

President: Tan Sri MICHAEL CHEN WING SUM.

Dewan Rakyat
(House of Representatives)

The House of Representatives has a total of 219 members: 165 from Peninsular Malaysia (including 11 from Kuala Lumpur and one from the Federal Territory of Putrajaya), 28 from Sarawak and 26 from Sabah (including one from the Federal Territory of Labuan).

Speaker: Tan Sri MUHAMMAD ZAHIR ISMAIL.

Deputy Speaker: Datuk LIM SI CHENG.

General Election, 21 March 2004

Party	Seats
Barisan Nasional (National Front)	198
United Malays National Organization	109
Malaysian Chinese Association	31
Parti Pesaka Bumiputera Bersatu	11
Parti Gerakan Rakyat Malaysia	10
Malaysian Indian Congress	9
Parti Bansa Dayak Sarawak	6
Sarawak United People's Party	6
Parti Bersatu Sabah	4
Sabah Progressive Democratic Party	4
United Kadazan People's Organization	4
Sabah Progressive Party	2
Parti Bersatu Rakyat Sabah	1
Parti Progresif Pendukuk Malaysia	1
Democratic Action Party	12
Parti Islam se Malaysia	7
Parti Keadilan Rakyat	1
Independents	1
Total	**219**

The States

JOHOR
(Capital: Johor Bahru)

Sultan: HRH Tuanku MAHMOOD ISKANDAR IBNI AL-MARHUM Sultan ISMAIL.

Menteri Besar: Datuk Haji ABDUL GHANI OTHMAN.

State Legislative Assembly: 56 seats: Barisan Nasional 55; Parti Islam se Malaysia 1; elected March 2004.

KEDAH
(Capital: Alor Star)

Sultan: HRH Tuanku Haji ABDUL HALIM MU'ADZAM SHAH IBNI AL-MARHUM Sultan BADLISHAH.

Menteri Besar: Datuk SYED RAZAK SYED ZAIN BARAKBAH.

State Legislative Assembly: 36 seats: Barisan Nasional 31; Parti Islam se Malaysia 5; elected March 2004.

KELANTAN
(Capital: Kota Baharu)

Sultan: HRH Tuanku ISMAIL PETRA IBNI AL-MARHUM Sultan YAHAYA PETRA.

Menteri Besar: Tuan Guru Haji Nik ABDUL AZIZ BIN Nik MAT.

State Legislative Assembly: 45 seats: Parti Islam se Malaysia 24; Barisan Nasional 21; elected March 2004.

MELAKA (MALACCA)
(Capital: Melaka)

Yang di-Pertua Negeri: HE Tun Datuk Sri UTAMA SYED AHMAD Al-Haj BIN SYED MAHMUD SHAHABUDIN.

Ketua Menteri: Datuk WIRA MOHAMED ALI RUSTAM.

State Legislative Assembly: 28 seats: Barisan Nasional 26; Democratic Action Party 2; elected March 2004.

NEGERI SEMBILAN
(Capital: Seremban)

Yang di-Pertuan Besar: Tuanku JA'AFAR IBNI AL-MARHUM Tuanku ABDUL RAHMAN.

Menteri Besar: Datuk MOHAMAD HASAN.

State Legislative Assembly: 36 seats: Barisan Nasional 34; Democratic Action Party 2; elected March 2004.

PAHANG
(Capital: Kuantan)

Sultan: HRH Haji AHMAD SHAH AL-MUSTA'IN BILLAH IBNI AL-MARHUM Sultan ABU BAKAR RI'AYATUDDIN AL-MU'ADZAM SHAH.

Menteri Besar: Dato' ADNAN BIN YAAKOB.

State Legislative Assembly: 41 seats: Barisan Nasional 40; Democratic Action Party 1; elected March 2004.

PERAK
(Capital: Ipoh)

Sultan: HRH Sultan Tuanku AZLAN MUHIBUDDIN SHAH IBNI AL-MARHUM Sultan YUSUF IZUDDIN GHAFARULLAH SHAH.

Menteri Besar: Dato' Seri DiRaja MOHAMAD TAJOL ROSLI.

State Legislative Assembly: Pejabat Setiausaha Kerajaan Negeri, Perak Darul Ridzuan, Bahagian Majlis, Jalan Panglima Bukit Gantang Wahab, 30000 Ipoh; tel. (05) 2410451; fax (05) 2552890; e-mail master@perak.gov.my; internet www.perak.gov.my; 59 seats: Barisan Nasional 52; Democratic Action Party 7; elected March 2004.

PERLIS
(Capital: Kangar)

Regent: Tuanku SYED FAIZUDDIN PUTRA IBNI Tuanku SYED SIRAJUDDIN PUTRA JAMALULAIL.

Menteri Besar: Dato' Seri SHAHIDAN KASSIM.

State Legislative Assembly: internet www.perlis.gov.my; 15 seats: Barisan Nasional 14; Parti Islam se Malaysia 1; elected March 2004.

PINANG (PENANG)
(Capital: George Town)

Yang di-Pertua Negeri: HE Datuk ABDUL RAHMAN Haji ABBAS.

Ketua Menteri: Tan Sri Dr KOH TSU KOON.

State Legislative Assembly: 40 seats: Barisan Nasional 38; Democratic Action Party 1; Parti Islam se Malaysia 1; elected March 2004.

SABAH
(Capital: Kota Kinabalu)

Yang di-Pertua Negeri: HE Datuk AHMADSHAH ABDULLAH.

Ketua Menteri: Datuk Seri MUSA AMAN.

State Legislative Assembly: Dewan Undangan Negeri Sabah, Aras 4, Bangunan Dewan Undangan Negeri Sabah, Peti Surat 11247, 88813 Kota Kinabalu; tel. (88) 427533; fax (88) 427333; e-mail pejduns@sabah.gov.my; internet www.sabah.gov.my; 60 seats: Barisan Nasional 59; Independents 1; elected March 2004.

SARAWAK
(Capital: Kuching)

Yang di-Pertua Negeri: HE Tun Datuk Patinggi Abang Haji MUHAMMED SALAHUDDIN.

Ketua Menteri: Datuk Patinggi Tan Sri Haji ABDUL TAIB BIN MAHMUD.

State Legislative Assembly: Bangunan Dewan Undangan Negeri, 93502 Petra Jaya, Kuching, Sarawak; tel. (82) 441955; fax (82) 440790; e-mail mastapaj@sarawaknet.gov.my; internet www.dun.sarawak.gov.my; 62 seats: Barisan Nasional 60; Democratic Action Party 1; Independents 1; elected September 2001.

SELANGOR
(Capital: Shah Alam)

Sultan: Tuanku IDRIS SALAHUDDIN ABDUL AZIZ SHAH.

Menteri Besar: MOHAMAD KHIR TOYO.

State Legislative Assembly: 56 seats: Barisan Nasional 54; Democratic Action Party 2; elected March 2004.

TERENGGANU
(Capital: Kuala Terengganu)

Sultan: HRH Sultan Tuanku MIZAN ZAINAL ABIDIN IBNI AL-MARHUM Sultan MAHMUD.

Menteri Besar: Datuk IDRIS JUSOH.

State Legislative Assembly: 32 seats: Barisan Nasional 28; Parti Islam se Malaysia 4; elected March 2004.

Political Organizations

Barisan Nasional (BN) (National Front): Suites 1–2, 8th Floor, Menara Dato' Onn, Pusat Dagangan Dunia Putra, Jalan Tun Ismail, 50480 Kuala Lumpur; tel. (3) 2920384; fax (3) 2934743; e-mail info@bn.org.my; internet www.bn.org.my; f. 1973; the governing multiracial coalition of 14 parties; Chair. Dato' Seri ABDULLAH BIN Haji AHMAD BADAWI; Sec.-Gen. Dato' Datuk Sri MOHAMMED RAHMAT; Comprises:

Liberal Democratic Party: Tingkat 2, Lot 1, Wisma Jasaga, POB 1125, Sandakan, 90712 Sabah; tel. (89) 271888; fax (89) 288278; e-mail ldpkk@tm.net.my; Chinese-dominated; Pres. Datuk CHONG KAH KIAT; Sec.-Gen. Datuk ANTHONY LAI VAI MING.

Malaysian Chinese Association (MCA): Wisma MCA, 8th Floor, 163 Jalan Ampang, POB 10626, 50720 Kuala Lumpur; tel. (3) 21618044; fax (3) 21619772; e-mail info@mca.org.my; internet www.mca.org.my; f. 1949; c. 1,033,686 mems; Pres. Dato' ONG KAH TING; Sec.-Gen. Dato' Seri Dr TING CHEW PEH.

Malaysian Indian Congress (MIC): Menara Manickavasagam, 6th Floor, 1 Jalan Rahmat, 50350 Kuala Lumpur; tel. (3) 4424377; fax (3) 4427236; internet www.mic.malaysia.org; f. 1946; 401,000 mems (1992); Pres. Dato' Seri S. SAMY VELLU; Sec.-Gen. Dato' G. VADIVELOO.

Parti Bansa Dayak Sarawak (PBDS) (Sarawak Native People's Party): 622 Jalan Kedandi, Tabuan Jaya, POB 2148, Kuching, Sarawak; tel. (82) 365240; fax (82) 363734; f. 1983 by fmr mems of Sarawak National Party; Pres. Datuk DANIEL TAJEM.

Parti Bersatu Rakyat Sabah (PBRS) (United Sabah People's Party): POB 20148, Luyang, Kota Kinabalu, 88761 Sabah; tel. and fax (88) 269282; f. 1994; breakaway faction of PBS; mostly Christian Kadazans; Leader Datuk JOSEPH KURUP.

Parti Bersatu Sabah (PBS) (Sabah United Party): Block M, Lot 4, 2nd and 3rd Floors, Donggongon New Township, 89500 Penampang, Sabah; ; tel. (88) 714891; fax (88) 718067; e-mail hq@pbs-sabah.org; internet www.pbs-sabah.org; f. 1985; multiracial party, left the BN in 1990 and rejoined in Jan. 2002; Pres. Datuk Seri JOSEPH PAIRIN KITINGAN; Sec.-Gen. Datuk RADIN MALLEH.

Parti Gerakan Rakyat Malaysia (GERAKAN) (Malaysian People's Movement): Tingkat 5, Menara PGRM, 8 Jalan Pudu Ulu Cheras, 56100 Kuala Lumpur; tel. (3) 92876868; fax (3) 92878866; e-mail gerakan@gerakan.org.my; internet www.gerakan.org.my; f. 1968; 300,000 mems; Pres. Dato' Seri Dr LIM KENG YAIK; Sec.-Gen. CHIA KWANG CHYE.

Parti Pesaka Bumiputera Bersatu (PBB) (United Traditional Bumiputra Party): Lot 401, Jalan Bako, POB 1953, 93400 Kuching, Sarawak; tel. (82) 448299; fax (82) 448294; f. 1983; Pres. Tan Sri Datuk Patinggi Amar Haji ABDUL TAIB MAHMUD; Dep. Pres. Datuk ALFRED JABU AK NUMPANG.

Parti Progresif Penduduk Malaysia (PPP) (People's Progressive Party): 27–29A Jalan Maharajalela, 50150 Kuala Lumpur; tel. (3) 2441922; fax (3) 2442041; e-mail info@ppp.com.my; internet www.jaring.my/ppp/; f. 1953 as Perak Progressive Party; joined the BN in 1972; Pres. Datuk M. KAYVEAS.

Sabah Progressive Party (SAPP) (Parti Maju Sabah): Lot 23, 2nd Floor, Bornion Centre, 88300 Kota Kinabalu, Sabah; tel. (88) 242107; fax (88) 254799; e-mail sapp@po.jaring.my; internet www.sapp.org.my; f. 1994; non-racial; Pres. Datuk YONG TECK LEE; Sec.-Gen. RICHARD YONG WE KONG.

Sarawak Progressive Democratic Party (SPDP): Lot 4319–4320, Jalan Stapok, Sungai Maong, 93250 Kuching, Sarawak; tel. (82) 311180; fax (82) 311190; f. 2003 by breakaway faction of Sarawak National Party; Pres. Datuk WILLIAM MAWAN ANAK IKOM; Sec.-Gen. Agung Dr JUDSON SAKAI TAGAL.

Sarawak United People's Party (SUPP): 7 Jalan Tan Sri Ong Kee Hui, POB 454, 93710 Kuching, Sarawak; tel. (82) 246999; fax (82) 256510; e-mail supp@po.jaring.my; internet www.sarawak.com.my/supp/; f. 1959; Sarawak Chinese minority party; Pres. Datuk Dr GEORGE CHAN HONG NAM; Sec.-Gen. SIM KHENG HUI.

United Kadazan People's Organization (UPKO): Penampang Service Centre, Km 11, Jalan Tambunan, Peti Surat 420, 89507 Penampang, Sabah; tel. (88) 718182; fax (88) 718180; e-mail n4upko@yahoo.com; internet www.upko.org.my; f. 1994 as the Parti Demokratik Sabah (PDS—Sabah Democratic Party); formed after collapse of PBS Govt by fmr leaders of the party, represents mostly Kadazandusun, Rungus and Murut communities; Pres. Tan Sri BERNARD GILUK DOMPOK.

United Malays National Organization (Pertubuhan Kebangsaan Melayu Bersatu—UMNO Baru) (New UMNO): Menara Dato' Onn, 38th Floor, Jalan Tun Dr Ismail, 50480 Kuala Lumpur; tel. (3) 40429511; fax (3) 40412358; e-mail email@umno.net.my; internet www.umno.org.my; f. 1988 to replace the original UMNO (f. 1946) which had been declared an illegal organization, owing to the participation of unregistered branches in party elections in April 1987; Supreme Council of 45 mems; 2.5m. mems; Pres. Dato' Seri ABDULLAH BIN Haji AHMAD BADAWI; Sec.-Gen. Tan Sri MOHD KHALIL BIN YAACOB.

Angkatan Keadilan Insan Malaysia (AKIM) (Malaysian Justice Movement): f. 1994 by fmr members of PAS and Semangat '46; Pres. HAMBALI YAZID.

Barisan Alternatif (Alternative Front): Kuala Lumpur; f. June 1999 to contest the general election; opposition electoral alliance originally comprising the PAS, the DAP, the PKN and the PRM; the DAP left in Sept. 2001.

Barisan Jama'ah Islamiah Sa-Malaysia (Berjasa) (Front Malaysian Islamic Council—FMIC): Kelantan; f. 1977; pro-Islamic; 50,000 mems; Pres. Dato' Haji WAN HASHIM BIN Haji WAN ACHMED; Sec.-Gen. MAHMUD ZUHDI BIN Haji ABDUL MAJID.

Bersatu Rakyat Jelata Sabah (Berjaya) (Sabah People's Union): Natikar Bldg, 1st Floor, POB 2130, Kota Kinabalu, Sabah; f. 1975; 400,000 mems; Pres. Haji MOHAMMED NOOR MANSOOR.

Democratic Action Party (DAP): 24 Jalan 20/9, 46300 Petaling Jaya, Selangor; tel. (3) 7578022; fax (3) 7575718; e-mail dap .Malaysia@pobox.com; internet www.malaysia.net/dap; f. 1966; main opposition party; advocates multiracial society based on democratic socialism; 12,000 mems; Chair. LIM KIT SIANG; Sec.-Gen. M. KULA SEGARAN (acting).

Democratic Malaysia Indian Party (DMIP): f. 1985; Leader V. GOVINDARAJ.

Kongres Indian Muslim Malaysia (KIMMA): Kuala Lumpur; tel. (3) 2324759; f. 1977; aims to unite Malaysian Indian Muslims politically; 25,000 mems; Pres. AHAMED ELIAS; Sec.-Gen. MOHAMMED ALI BIN Haji NAINA MOHAMMED.

Malaysian Solidarity Party: Kuala Lumpur.

Parti Hisbul Muslimin Malaysia (Hamim) (Islamic Front of Malaysia): Kota Bahru, Kelantan; f. 1983 as an alternative party to PAS; Pres. Datuk ASRI MUDA.

Parti Ikatan Masyarakat Islam (Islamic Alliance Party): Terengganu.

Parti Islam se Malaysia (PAS) (Islamic Party of Malaysia): Pejabat Agung PAS Pusat, Lorong Haji Hassan, off Jalan Batu Geliga, Taman Melewar, 68100 Batu Caves, Selangor Darul Ehsan; tel. (3) 61895612; fax (3) 61889520; e-mail editor@parti-pas.org; internet www.parti-pas.org; f. 1951; seeks to establish an Islamic state; 700,000 mems; Pres. ABDUL HADI AWANG; Sec.-Gen. NASHARUDIN MAT ISA.

Parti Keadilan Masyarakat (PEKEMAS) (Social Justice Party): Kuala Lumpur; f. 1971 by fmr mems of GERAKAN; Chair. SHAHAR-YDDIN DAHALAN.

Parti Keadilan Rakyat (PKR) (People's Justice Party): 75A Jalan Lawan Pedang 13/27, Tadisma Business Park, 40000 Shah Alam, Selangor; tel. (3) 55133416; fax (3) 55129646; e-mail contact@ partikeadilanrakyat.org; internet www.partikeadilanrakyat.org; f. Aug. 2003 following merger between Parti Keadilan Nasional (PKN) and Parti Rakyat Malaysia (PRM); Pres. WAN AZIZAH WAN ISMAIL; Sec.-Gen. ABDUL RAHMAN OTHMAN.

Parti Nasionalis Malaysia (NasMa): f. 1985; multiracial; Leader ZAINAB YANG.

Parti Rakyat Jati Sarawak (PAJAR) (Sarawak Native People's Party): 22A Jalan Bampeylde, 93200 Kuching, Sarawak; f. 1978; Leader ALI KAWI.

Persatuan Rakyat Malaysian Sarawak (PERMAS) (Malaysian Sarawak Party): Kuching, Sarawak; f. March 1987 by fmr mems of PBB; Leader Haji BUJANG ULIS.

Pertubuhan Bumiputera Bersatu Sarawak (PBBS) (United Sarawak National Association): Kuala Lumpur; f. 1986; Chair. Haji WAN HABIB SYED MAHMUD.

Pertubuhan Rakyat Sabah Bersatu (United Sabah People's Organization—USPO): Kota Kinabalu, Sabah.

Sabah Chinese Party (PCS): Kota Kinabalu, Sabah; f. 1986; Pres. Encik FRANCIS LEONG.

Sabah Chinese Consolidated Party (SCCP): POB 704, Kota Kinabalu, Sabah; f. 1964; 14,000 mems; Pres. JOHNNY SOON; Sec.-Gen. CHAN TET ON.

Sarawak National Party (SNAP): 304–305 Bangunan Mei Jun, 1 Jalan Rubber, POB 2960, 93758 Kuching, Sarawak; tel. (82) 254244; fax (82) 253562; f. 1961; deregistered Nov. 2002 but deregistration deferred indefinitely in April 2003 following appeal; Pres. EDWIN DUNDANG BUGAK; Sec.-Gen. STANLEY JUGOL.

Setia (Sabah People's United Democratic Party): Sabah; f. 1994.

United Malaysian Indian Party: aims to promote unity and economic and social advancement of the Indian community; Sec. KUMAR MANOHARAN.

Diplomatic Representation

EMBASSIES AND HIGH COMMISSIONS IN MALAYSIA

Afghanistan: 2nd Floor, Wisma Chinese Chamber, 258 Jalan Ampang, 50450 Kuala Lumpur; tel. (3) 42569400; fax (3) 42566400; e-mail murad1@tm.net.my; internet www.afghanembassykl.org; Chargé d'affaires a.i. AMANULLAH JAYHOON.

Albania: 2952 Jalan Bukit Ledang, off Jalan Duta, 50480 Kuala Lumpur; tel. (3) 20937808; fax (3) 20937359; Chargé d'affaires a.i. HAJDAR MUNEKA.

Algeria: 5 Jalan Mesra, off Jalan Damai, 55000 Kuala Lumpur; tel. (3) 21488159; fax (3) 21488154; Ambassador RACHID BLADEHANE.

Argentina: 3 Jalan Semantan Dua, Damansara Heights, 50490 Kuala Lumpur; tel. (3) 20950176; fax (3) 20952706; e-mail emsia@pd .jaring.my; Ambassador ALFREDO MORELLI.

Australia: 6 Jalan Yap Kwan Seng, 50450 Kuala Lumpur; tel. (3) 21465555; fax (3) 21415773; e-mail info@australia.org.my; internet www.australia.org.my; High Commissioner JAMES WISE.

Austria: MUI Plaza, 7th Floor, Jalan P. Ramlee, POB 10154, 50704 Kuala Lumpur; tel. (3) 21484277; fax (3) 21489813; e-mail kuala-lumpur-ob@bmaa.gv.at; Ambassador Dr OSWALD SOUKOP.

Bangladesh: Block 1, Lorong Damai 7, Jalan Damai, 55000 Kuala Lumpur; tel. (3) 21487490; fax (3) 21413381; e-mail bddoot@pc .jaring.my; High Commissioner MOHAMMED MASOOD AZIZ.

Belgium: 8A Jalan Ampang Hilir, 55000 Kuala Lumpur; tel. (3) 42525733; fax (3) 42527922; e-mail kualalumpur@diplobel.org; Ambassador ROLAND VAN REMOORTELE.

Bosnia and Herzegovina: JKR 854, Jalan Bellamy, 50460 Kuala Lumpur; tel. (3) 21440353; fax (3) 21426025; e-mail hsomun@ hotmail.com; Ambassador HAJRUDIN SOMUN.

Brazil: 22 Pesiaran Damansara Endah, Damansara Heights, 50490 Kuala Lumpur; tel. (3) 20948607; fax (3) 20955086; e-mail brazil@po .jaring.my; Ambassador EDGARD TELLES RIBEIRO.

Brunei: Tingkat 19, Menara Tan & Tan, Jalan Tun Razak, 50400 Kuala Lumpur; tel. (3) 21612800; fax (3) 2631302; e-mail bhckl@ brucomkul.com.my; High Commissioner Dato' Paduka Haji ABDULLAH BIN Haji MOHAMMAD JAAFAR.

Cambodia: 46 Jalan U Thant, 55000 Kuala Lumpur; tel. (3) 42573711; fax (3) 42571157; e-mail reckl@tm.net.my; Ambassador KEO PUTH REASMEY.

Canada: POB 10990, 50732 Kuala Lumpur; tel. (3) 27183333; fax (3) 27183399; e-mail klmpr-td@dfait-maeci.gc.ca; internet www .dfait-maeci.gc.ca/kualalumpur; High Commissioner MELVYN L. MACDONALD.

Chile: 8th Floor, West Block 142-C, Jalan Ampang, Peti Surat 27, 50450 Kuala Lumpur; tel. (3) 21616203; fax (3) 21622219; e-mail eochile@ppp.nasionet.net; internet www.chileembassy-malaysia .com.my; Ambassador ROBERTO IBARRA GARCÍA.

China, People's Republic: 229 Jalan Ampang, 50450 Kuala Lumpur; tel. (3) 21428495; fax (3) 21414552; e-mail cn@tm.net.my; Ambassador HU ZHENGYUE.

Colombia: Level 26, UOA Centre, 19 Jalan Pinang, 50450 Kuala Lumpur; tel. (3) 21645488; fax (3) 21645487; e-mail ekualalumpur@ minrelext.gov.co; Chargé d'affaires a.i. YOBANI VELASQUEZ QUINTERO.

Croatia: 3 Jalan Menkuang, off Jalan Ru Ampang, 55000 Kuala Lumpur; tel. (3) 42535340; fax (3) 42535217; e-mail croemb@tm.net .my; Chargé d'affaires a.i. ZELJKO BELAJ.

Cuba: 20 Lingkungan U Thant, off Jalan U Thant, 55000 Kuala Lumpur; tel. (3) 42516808; fax (3) 42520428; e-mail malacub@po .jaring.my; internet www.cubaemb.com.my; Ambassador PEDRO MONZÓN BARATA.

Czech Republic: 32 Jalan Mesra, off Jalan Damai, 55000 Kuala Lumpur; tel. (3) 21427185; fax (3) 21412727; e-mail kualalumpur@ embassy.mzv.cz; internet www.mzv.cz/kualalumpur; Ambassador Dr VÍTĚZSLAV GREPL.

Denmark: POB 10908, 50728 Kuala Lumpur; tel. (3) 20322001; fax (3) 20322012; e-mail kulamb@un.dk; internet www.denmark.com .my; Ambassador LASSE REIMANN.

Ecuador: 10th Floor, West Block, Wisma Selangor Dredging, 142-C Jalan Ampang, 50450 Kuala Lumpur; tel. (3) 21635078; fax (3) 21635096; e-mail embecua@po.jaring.my; Ambassador Dr MARCO TULIO CORDERO ZAMORA.

Egypt: 28 Lingkungan U Thant, POB 12004, 55000 Kuala Lumpur; tel. (3) 42568184; fax (3) 42573515; e-mail egyembkl@tm.net.my; Ambassador MOHAMED AFIFI.

Fiji: Level 2, Menara Chan, 138 Jalan Ampang, 50450 Kuala Lumpur; tel. (3) 27323335; fax (3) 27327555; e-mail fhckl@pd.jaring .my; High Commissioner Adi SAMANUNU Q. TALAKULI CAKOBAU.

Finland: Level 5, Wisma Chinese Chamber, 258 Jalan Ampang, 50450 Kuala Lumpur; tel. (3) 42577746; fax (3) 42577793; e-mail sanomat.kul@formin.fi; Ambassador UNTO JUHANI TURUNEN.

France: 196 Jalan Ampang, 50450 Kuala Lumpur; tel. (3) 20535500; fax (3) 20535501; e-mail ambassade .kuala-lumpur-amba@diplomatie.gouv.fr; internet www .ambafrance-my.org; Ambassador JACQUES LAPOUGE.

Germany: 26th Floor, Menara Tan & Tan, 207 Jalan Tun Razak, 50400 Kuala Lumpur; tel. (3) 21709666; fax (3) 21619800; e-mail contact@german-embassy.org.my; internet www.german-embassy .org.my; Ambassador JUERGEN A. R. STAKS.

Ghana: 14 Ampang Hilir, off Jalan Ampang, 55000 Kuala Lumpur; tel. (3) 42526995; fax (3) 42578698; e-mail ghcomkl@tm.net.my; High Commissioner JOHN BENTUM-WILLIAMS.

Guinea: 5 Jalan Kedondong, off Jalan Ampang Hilir, Kuala Lumpur; tel. (3) 42576500; fax (3) 42511500; e-mail mwcnakry@ sotelgui.net.gn; Ambassador MAMADOU TOURÉ.

Hungary: City Square Centre, 30th Floor, Empire Tower, Jalan Tun Razak, 50400 Kuala Lumpur; tel. (3) 21637914; fax (3) 21637918; e-mail huembkl@tm.net.my; Ambassador LÁSZLÓ VÁR-KONYI.

India: 2 Jalan Taman Duta, off Jalan Duta, 50480 Kuala Lumpur; tel. (3) 20933510; fax (3) 20933507; e-mail highcomm@po.jaring.my; High Commissioner VEENA SIKRI.

Indonesia: 233 Jalan Tun Razak, POB 10889, 50400 Kuala Lumpur; tel. (3) 21452011; fax (3) 21417908; e-mail kbrikl@po.jaring .my; internet www.kbrikl.org.my; Ambassador K. P. H. RUSDIHARDJO.

Iran: 1 Lorong U Thant Satu, off Jalan U Thant, 55000 Kuala Lumpur; tel. (3) 42514824; fax (3) 42562904; e-mail ir_emb@tm.net .my; internet www.iranembassy.com.my; Ambassador MOHAMMAD GHASEM MOHEB ALI.

Iraq: 2 Jalan Langgak Golf, off Jalan Tun Razak, 55000 Kuala Lumpur; tel. (3) 21480555; fax (3) 21414331; Chargé d'affaires a.i. Dr MAHMOUD AL-MSAFIR.

Ireland: Ireland House, The Amp Walk, 218 Jalan Ampang, POB 10372, 50450 Kuala Lumpur; tel. (3) 21612963; fax (3) 21613427; e-mail ireland@po.jaring.my; Ambassador DANIEL MULHALL.

Italy: 99 Jalan U Thant, 55000 Kuala Lumpur; tel. (3) 42565122; fax (3) 42573199; e-mail embassyit@italy-embassy.org.my; internet www.italy-embassy.org.my; Ambassador ANACLETO FELICANI.

Japan: 11 Pesiaran Stonor, off Jalan Tun Razak, 50450 Kuala Lumpur; tel. (3) 21427044; fax (3) 21672314; internet www.my .emb-japan.go.jp; Ambassador MASAKI KONISHI.

Jordan: 2 Jalan Kedondong, off Jalan Ampang Hilir, 55000 Kuala Lumpur; tel. (3) 42521268; fax (3) 42528610; e-mail jordanembassy@ po.jaring.my; Ambassador MAZEN JUMA.

Kazakhstan: POB 21, Wisma Selangor Dredging, 3rd Floor, South Block, 142A Jalan Ampang, 50540 Kuala Lumpur; tel. (3) 21664144; fax (3) 21668553; e-mail klkazemb@po.jaring.my; Ambassador IKRAM ADYRBEKOV.

Kenya: Kuala Lumpur Empire Tower Unit, 38C, 38th Floor, 182 Jalan Tun Razak, 50400 Kuala Lumpur; tel. (3) 21645015; fax (3) 21645017; e-mail kenya@po.jaring.my; High Commissioner JAMES K. KARUGA.

Korea, Democratic People's Republic: 4 Jalan Persiaran Madge, off Jalan U Thant, 55000 Kuala Lumpur; tel. (3) 42569913; fax (3) 42569933; Ambassador KIM WON HO.

Korea, Republic: Lot 9 and 11, Jalan Nipah, off Jalan Ampang, 55000 Kuala Lumpur; tel. (3) 42512336; fax (3) 42521425; e-mail korem-my@mofat.go.kr; Ambassador LEE YOUNG-JOON.

Kuwait: 229 Jalan Tun Razak, 50400 Kuala Lumpur; tel. (3) 21410033; fax (3) 21426126; e-mail q8kl@pd.jaring.my; Ambassador FAHAD HEJER SHAOWF AL-METAIRI.

Kyrgyzstan: 10 Lorong Damai 9, 55000 Kuala Lumpur; tel. (3) 21649862; fax (3) 21632024; e-mail kyrgyz@tm.net.my; Ambassador GULNARA KYSKARAYEVA.

Laos: 12A Pesiaran Madge, off Jalan Ampang Hilir, 55000 Kuala Lumpur; tel. (3) 42511118; fax (3) 42510080; Ambassador CHALEUNE WARINTHRASAK.

Libya: 6 Jalan Madge, off Jalan U Thant, 55000 Kuala Lumpur; tel. (3) 21411035; fax (3) 21413549; Ambassador Dr AHMAD MOHAMED ALI AL-HANESH.

Luxembourg: Menara Keck Seng Bldg, 16th Floor, 203 Jalan Bukit Bintang, 55100 Kuala Lumpur; tel. (3) 21433134; fax (3) 21433157;

e-mail emluxem@po.jaring.my; Chargé d'affaires a.i. CHARLES SCHMIT.

Mauritius: Lot W17-B1 and C1, 17th Floor, West Block, Wisma Selangor Dredging, Jalan Ampang, 50450 Kuala Lumpur; tel. (3) 21636306; fax (3) 21636294; e-mail maur@tm.net.my; High Commissioner S. K. S. DUSOWOTH.

Mexico: Menara Tan & Tan, 22nd Floor, 207 Jalan Tun Razak, 50400 Kuala Lumpur; tel. (3) 21646362; fax (3) 21640964; e-mail embamex@po.jaring.my; internet www.embamex.org.my; Ambassador ALFREDO PÉREZ BRAVO.

Morocco: Wisma Selangor Dredging, 3rd Floor, East Block, 142B Jalan Ampang, 50450 Kuala Lumpur; tel. (3) 21610701; fax (3) 21623081; e-mail sifmakl@tm.net.my; Ambassador BADRE EDDINE ALLALI.

Myanmar: 12 Jalan Ru, off Jalan Ampang Hilir, 55000 Kuala Lumpur; tel. (3) 42560280; fax (3) 42568320; e-mail mekl@tm.net .my; Ambassador U HLA MAUNG.

Namibia: 11 Jalan Mesra, off Jalan Damai, 55000 Kuala Lumpur; tel. (3) 21433595; fax (3) 21417803; e-mail namhckl@po.jaring.my; High Commissioner NEVILLE MELVIN GERTZA.

Nepal: Suite 13A-01, 13th Floor, Wisma MCA, 163 Jalan Ampang, 40450 Kuala Lumpur; tel. (3) 21645934; fax (3) 21648659; Chargé d'affaires a.i. DEEPAK DHITAL.

Netherlands: The Amp Walk, 7th Floor, 218 Jalan Ampang, POB 10543, 50450 Kuala Lumpur; tel. (3) 21686200; fax (3) 21686240; e-mail nlgovkl@netherlands.org.my; internet www.netherlands.org .my; Ambassador J. C. F. VON MÜHLEN.

New Zealand: Menara IMC, 21st Floor, 8 Jalan Sultan Ismail, 50250 Kuala Lumpur; tel. (3) 20782533; fax (3) 20780387; e-mail nzhckl@po.jaring.my; High Commissioner GEOFF RANDAL.

Nigeria: 85 Jalan Ampang Hilir, 55000 Kuala Lumpur; tel. (3) 42517843; fax (3) 42524302; e-mail nighcomm@tm.net.my; High Commissioner Dr R. O. AKEJU (acting).

Norway: Suite CD, 53rd Floor, Empire Tower, Jalan Tun Razak, 50400 Kuala Lumpur; tel. (3) 21637100; fax (3) 21637108; e-mail emb.kualalumpur@mfa.no; Ambassador ARILD EIK.

Oman: 109 Jalan U Thant, 55000 Kuala Lumpur; tel. (3) 42577378; fax (3) 42571400; e-mail omanemb@po.jaring.my; Ambassador Sheikh GHAZI BIN SAID BIN ABDULLAH AL BAHR AL RAWAS.

Pakistan: 132 Jalan Ampang, 50450 Kuala Lumpur; tel. (3) 21618877; fax (3) 21645958; e-mail parepklumpur@po.jaring.my; internet www3.jaring.my/pakistanhc/; High Commissioner Maj.-Gen. (retd) TALAT MUNIR.

Papua New Guinea: 11 Lingkungan U Thant, off Jalan U Thant, 55000 Kuala Lumpur; tel. (3) 42575405; fax (3) 42576203; e-mail you@yourdomain.com; High Commissioner PETER P. MAGINDE.

Peru: Wisma Selangor Dredging, 6th Floor, South Block 142-A, Jalan Ampang, 50450 Kuala Lumpur; tel. (3) 21633034; fax (3) 21633039; e-mail info@embperu.com.my; internet www.embperu .com.my; Ambassador JAVIER GONZALES.

Philippines: 1 Changkat Kia Peng, 50450 Kuala Lumpur; tel. (3) 21484233; fax (3) 21483576; e-mail philgov@tm.net.my; internet www.philembassykl.org.my; Ambassador ROMUALDO ANOVER ONG.

Poland: 495 Bt 4½ Jalan Ampang, 68000 Ampang, Selangor; tel. (3) 42576733; fax (3) 42570123; e-mail polamba@tm.net.my; Ambassador EUGENIOSZ SAWICKI.

Romania: 114 Jalan Damai, off Jalan Ampang, 55000 Kuala Lumpur; tel. (3) 21423172; fax (3) 21448713; e-mail romemb@tm.net .my; Chargé d'affaires a.i. DRAGOS SERBANESCU.

Russia: 263 Jalan Ampang, 50450 Kuala Lumpur; tel. (3) 42567252; fax (3) 42576091; e-mail ruemvvl@tm.net.my; Ambassador VLADIMIR NIKOLAEVICH MOROZOV.

Saudi Arabia: Level 4, Wisma Chinese Chamber, 258 Jalan Ampang, 50450 Kuala Lumpur; tel. (3) 42579433; fax (3) 42578751; e-mail saembssy@tm.net.my; Ambassador HAMED MOHAMMED YAHYA.

Senegal: 5 Persiaran Ampang, 55000 Kuala Lumpur; tel. (3) 42567343; fax (3) 42563205; e-mail senamb_mal@yahoo.fr; Ambassador AMADOU FAYE.

Seychelles: 12th Floor, West Block, Wisma Selangor Dredging, POB 24, 142C Jalan Ampang, 50450 Kuala Lumpur; tel. (3) 21635726; fax (3) 21635729; e-mail seyhicom@po.jaring.my; High Commissioner LOUIS SYLVESTRE RADEGONDE.

Singapore: 209 Jalan Tun Razak, 50400 Kuala Lumpur; tel. (3) 21616277; fax (3) 21616343; e-mail shckl@po.jaring.my; internet www.mfa.gov.sg/kl; High Commissioner ASHOK KUMAR MIRPURI.

Slovakia: 11 Jalan U Thant, 55000 Kuala Lumpur; tel. (3) 21150016; fax (3) 21150014; e-mail slovemb@tm.net.my; Ambassador MILAN TANCAR.

South Africa: 12 Lorong Titiwangsa, Taman Tasik Titiwangsa, Setapak, 53200 Kuala Lumpur; tel. (3) 40244456; fax (3) 40249896; e-mail sahcpol@tm.net.my; internet www.afrikaselatan.com; High Commissioner Dr ABRAHAM SOKHAYA NKOMO.

Spain: 200 Jalan Ampang, 50450 Kuala Lumpur; tel. (3) 21484868; fax (3) 21424582; e-mail embespmy@mail.mae.es; Ambassador ALVARO IRANZO GUTIÉRREZ.

Sri Lanka: 116 Jalan Damai, off Jalan Ampang, 55000 Kuala Lumpur; tel. (3) 21612199; fax (3) 21612219; e-mail slhicom@putra.net.my; internet www.kuala-lumpur.mission.gov.lk; High Commissioner BERNADINE ROSE SANANAYAKE.

Sudan: 2A Persiaran Ampang, off Jalan Ru, 55000 Kuala Lumpur; tel. (3) 42569104; fax (3) 42568107; e-mail sudanikuala@hotmail.com; Ambassador MOHAMED ADAM ISMAIL.

Swaziland: Suite 22.03 and 03 (A), Menara Citibank, 165 Jalan Ampang, 50450 Kuala Lumpur; tel. (3) 21632511; fax (3) 21633326; e-mail swazi@tm.net.my; High Commissioner MABILI D. DLAMIMI.

Sweden: Wisma Angkasa Raya, 6th Floor, 123 Jalan Ampang, POB 10239, 50708 Kuala Lumpur; tel. (3) 21485433; fax (3) 21486325; e-mail ambassaden.kuala-lumpur@foreign.ministry.se; internet www.embassyofswedenmy.org; Ambassador BRUNO BEIJER.

Switzerland: 16 Persiaran Madge, 55000 Kuala Lumpur; tel. (3) 21480622; fax (3) 21480935; e-mail vertretung@kua.rep.admin.ch; Ambassador Dr PETER A. SCHWEIZER.

Syria: Suite 23.03, 23rd Floor, Menara Tan & Tan, Jalan Tun Razak, 50400 Kuala Lumpur; tel. (3) 21634110; fax (3) 21634199; Chargé d'affaires a.i. ABDUL AZIZ ALI.

Thailand: 206 Jalan Ampang, 50450 Kuala Lumpur; tel. (3) 21488222; fax (3) 21486527; e-mail thaikul@mfa.go.th; Ambassador CHAISIRI ANAMARN.

Timor-Leste: 62 Jalan Ampang Hilir, 55000 Kuala Lumpur; tel. (3) 42562046; fax (3) 42562016; e-mail embaixada_tl_kl@yahoo.com; Ambassador DJAFAR AMUDE ALKATIRI.

Turkey: 118 Jalan U Thant, 55000 Kuala Lumpur; tel. (3) 42572225; fax (3) 42572227; e-mail turkbe@tm.net.my; Ambassador KORAY TARGAY.

Ukraine: 22nd Floor, Suite 22.02, Menara Tan & Tan, 207 Jalan Tun Razak, 50400 Kuala Lumpur; tel. (3) 21669552; fax (3) 21664371; e-mail emb_my@mfa.gov.ua; Chargé d'affaires VALENTYN VELYCHKO.

United Arab Emirates: 1 Gerbang Ampang Hilir, off Persiaran Ampang Hilir, 55000 Kuala Lumpur; tel. (3) 42535221; fax (3) 42535220; e-mail uaemal@tm.net.my; Ambassador NASSER SALMAN ALABOODI.

United Kingdom: 185 Jalan Ampang, 50450 Kuala Lumpur; tel. (3) 21702200; fax (3) 21442370; e-mail political.kualalumpur@fco.gov.uk; internet www.britain.org.my; High Commissioner BRUCE CLEGHORN.

USA: 376 Jalan Tun Razak, POB 10035, 50700 Kuala Lumpur; tel. (3) 21685000; fax (3) 21422207; internet www.usembassymalaysia.org.my; Ambassador MARIE T. HUHTALA.

Uruguay: 6 Jalan 3, Taman Tun Abdul Razak, 68000 Ampang, Selangor Darul Bhsan; tel. (3) 42518831; fax (3) 42517878; e-mail urukual@po.jaring.my; Ambassador ROBERTO PABLO TOURINO TURNES.

Uzbekistan: 2 Jalan 12, Taman Tun Abdul Razak, 68000 Ampang, Selangor; tel. (3) 42532406; fax (3) 42535406; e-mail uzbekemb@streamyx.com; Ambassador AYBEK KHASANOV.

Venezuela: Suite 20-05, 20th Floor, Menara Tan & Tan, 207 Jalan Tun Razak, 50400 Kuala Lumpur; tel. (3) 21633444; fax (3) 21636819; e-mail venezuela@po.jaring.my; internet www.venezuela.org.my; Ambassador Maj.-Gen. (retd) NOEL ENRIQUE MARTÍNEZ OCHOA.

Viet Nam: 4 Jalan Persiaran Stonor, 50450 Kuala Lumpur; tel. (3) 21484036; fax (3) 21483270; e-mail daisevn@putra.net.my; Ambassador NGUYEN QUOC DUNG.

Yemen: 7 Jalan Kedondong, off Jalan Ampang Hilir, 55000 Kuala Lumpur; tel. (3) 42511793; fax (3) 42511794; e-mail yemenkl@tm.net.my; Ambassador Dr ABDUL NASSER ALI ABDO MUNIBARI.

Zimbabwe: 124 Jalan Sembilan, Taman Ampang Utama, 68000 Ampang, Selangor Darul Ehsan; tel. (3) 42516779; fax (3) 42517252; e-mail zhck@tm.net.my; Ambassador LUCAS PANDE TAVAYA.

Judicial System

The two High Courts, one in Peninsular Malaysia and the other in Sabah and Sarawak, have original, appellate and revisional jurisdiction as the federal law provides. Above these two High Courts is the Court of Appeal, which was established in 1994; it is an inter-mediary court between the Federal Court and the High Court. When appeals to the Privy Council in the United Kingdom were abolished in 1985 the former Supreme Court became the final court of appeal. Therefore, at that stage only one appeal was available to a party aggrieved by the decision of the High Court. Hence, the establishment of the Court of Appeal. The Federal Court (formerly the Supreme Court) has, to the exclusion of any other court, jurisdiction in any dispute between states or between the Federation and any state; and has special jurisdiction as to the interpretation of the Constitution. The Federal Court is headed by the Chief Justice (formerly the Lord President); the other members of the Federal Court are the President of the Court of Appeal, the two Chief Judges of the High Courts and the Federal Court Judges. Members of the Court of Appeal are the President and the Court of Appeal judges, and members of the High Courts are the two Chief Judges and their respective High Court judges. All judges are appointed by the Yang di-Pertuan Agong on the advice of the Prime Minister, after consulting the Conference of Rulers. In 1993 a Special Court was established to hear cases brought by or against the Yang di-Pertuan Agong or a Ruler of State (Sultans).

The Sessions Courts, which are situated in the principal urban and rural centres, are presided over by a Sessions Judge, who is a member of the Judicial and Legal Service of the Federation and is a qualified barrister or a Bachelor of Law from any of the recognized universities. Their criminal jurisdiction covers the less serious indictable offences, excluding those that carry the death penalty. Civil jurisdiction of a Sessions Court is up to RM 250,000. The Sessions Judges are appointed by the Yang di-Pertuan Agong.

The Magistrates' Courts are also found in the main urban and rural centres and have both civil and criminal jurisdiction, although of a more restricted nature than that of the Sessions Courts. The Magistrates consist of officers from the Judicial and Legal Service of the Federation. They are appointed by the State Authority in which they officiate on the recommendation of the Chief Judge.

There are also Syariah (Shariah) courts for rulings under Islamic law. In July 1996 the Cabinet announced that the Syariah courts were to be restructured with the appointment of a Syariah Chief Judge and four Court of Appeal justices, whose rulings would set precedents for the whole country.

Prior to February 1995 trials for murder and kidnapping in the High Courts were heard with jury and assessors, respectively. The amendment to the Criminal Procedure Code abolished both the jury and the assessors systems, and all criminal trials in the High Courts are heard by a judge sitting alone. In 1988 an amendment to the Constitution empowered any federal lawyer to confer with the Attorney-General to determine the courts in which any proceedings, excluding those before a Syariah court, a native court or a court martial, be instituted, or to which such proceedings be transferred.

Federal Court of Malaysia
Bangunan Sultan Abdul Samad, Jalan Raja, 50506 Kuala Lumpur; tel. (3) 26939011; fax (3) 26932582; internet www.kehakiman.gov.my.

Chief Justice of the Federal Court: Tan Sri Dato' Sri AHMAD FAIRUZ bin Dato' Sheikh ABDUL HALIM.

President of the Court of Appeal: (vacant).

Chief Judge of the High Court in Peninsular Malaysia: Dato' HAIDAR BIN MOHAMED NOOR.

Chief Judge of the High Court in Sabah and Sarawak: Datuk STEVE SHIP LIM KIONG.

Attorney-General: ABDUL GANI PATAIL.

Religion

Islam is the established religion but freedom of religious practice is guaranteed. Almost all ethnic Malays are Muslims, representing 53% of the total population in 1985. In Peninsular Malaysia 19% followed Buddhism (19% in Sarawak and 8% in Sabah), 7% were Christians (29% in Sarawak and 24% in Sabah), and Chinese faiths, including Confucianism and Daoism, were followed by 11.6%. Sikhs and other religions accounted for 0.5%, while 2%, mostly in Sabah and Sarawak, were animists.

Malaysian Consultative Council of Buddhism, Christianity, Hinduism and Sikhism (MCCBCHS): 8 Jalan Duku, off Jalan Kasipillai, 51200 Kuala Lumpur; tel. (3) 40414669; fax (3) 40444304; e-mail hsangam@po.jaring.my; f. 1981; a non-Muslim group.

ISLAM

President of the Majlis Islam: Datuk Haji MOHD FAUZI BIN Haji ABDUL HAMID (Kuching, Sarawak).

Jabatan Kemajuan Islam Malaysia (JAKIM) (Department of Islamic Development Malaysia): Aras 4–9, Block D7, Pusat Pentadbiran Persekutuan, 62502 Putrajaya; tel. (3) 88864000; e-mail faizal@islam.gov.my; internet www.islam.gov.my.

Istitut Kefahaman Islam Malaysia (IKIM) (Institute of Islamic Understanding Malaysia): 2 Langgak Tunku, off Jalan Duta, 50480 Kuala Lumpur; tel. (3) 62010889; fax (3) 62014189; internet www.ikim.gov.my.

BUDDHISM

Malaysian Buddhist Association (MBA): MBA Building, 113, 3¼ Miles, Jalan Klang, 58000 Kuala Lumpur; tel. (3) 7815595; e-mail mbapg@po.jaring.my; internet www.jaring.my/mba; f. 1959; the national body for Chinese-speaking monks and nuns and temples from the Mahayana tradition; Pres. Venerable CHEK HUANG.

Young Buddhist Association of Malaysia (YBAM): 10 Jalan SS2/75, 47300 Petaling Jaya, Selangor; tel. (3) 78764591; fax (3) 78762770; e-mail ybamhq@po.jaring.my; internet www.ybam.org.my; f. 1970.

Buddhist Missionary Society Malaysia (BMSM): 123 Jalan Berhala, off Jalan Tun Sambanthan, 50470 Brickfields, Kuala Lumpur; tel. (3) 22730150; fax (3) 22740245; e-mail president@bmsm.org.my; internet www.bmsm.org.my; f. 1962 as Buddhist Missionary Society; Pres. ANG CHOO HONG.

Malaysian Fo Kuang Buddhist Association: 2 Jalan SS3/33, Taman University, 47300 Petaling Jaya, Selangor.

Buddhist Tzu-Chi Merit Society (Malaysia): 24 Jesselton Ave, 10450 Pinang; e-mail mtzuchi@po.jaring.my; internet www.tzuchi.org.my.

Sasana Abhiwurdhi Wardhana Society: 123 Jalan Berhala, off Jalan Tun Sambanthan, 50490 Kuala Lumpur; f. 1894; the national body for Sri Lankan Buddhists belonging to the Theravada tradition.

CHRISTIANITY

Majlis Gereja-Gereja Malaysia (Council of Churches of Malaysia): 26 Jalan Universiti, 46200 Petaling Jaya, Selangor; tel. (3) 7567092; fax (3) 7560353; e-mail cchurchm@tm.net.my; internet www.ccmalaysia.org; f. 1947; 16 mem. churches; 8 associate mems; Pres. Most Rev. Datuk YONG PING CHUNG (Anglican Bishop of Sabah); Gen. Sec. Rev. Dr HERMEN SHASTRI.

The Anglican Communion

Malaysia comprises three Anglican dioceses, within the Church of the Province of South East Asia.

Primate: Most Rev. Datuk YONG PING CHUNG (Bishop of Sabah).

Bishop of Kuching: Rt Rev. MADE KATIB, Bishop's House, POB 347, 93704 Kuching, Sarawak; tel. (82) 240187; fax (82) 426488; e-mail bkg@pc.jaring.my; has jurisdiction over Sarawak, Brunei and part of Indonesian Kalimantan (Borneo).

Bishop of Sabah: Most Rev. Datuk YONG PING CHUNG, Rumah Bishop, Jalan Tangki, POB 10811, 88809 Kota Kinabalu, Sabah; tel. (88) 247008; fax (88) 245942; e-mail pcyong@pc.jaring.my.

Bishop of West Malaysia: Rt. Rev. Tan Sri Dr LIM CHENG EAN, Bishop's House, 14 Pesiaran Stonor, 50450 Kuala Lumpur; tel. (3) 20312728; fax (3) 20313225; e-mail diocese@tm.net.my.

The Baptist Church

Malaysia Baptist Convention: 2 Jalan 2/38, 46000 Petaling Jaya, Selangor; tel. (3) 77823564; fax (3) 77833603; e-mail mbcpj@tm.net.my; Chair. Dr TAN ENG LEE.

The Methodist Church

Methodist Church in Malaysia: 69 Jalan 5/31, 46000 Petaling Jaya, Selangor; tel. (3) 79541811; fax (3) 79541788; e-mail methmas@tm.net; 140,000 mems; Bishop Dr PETER CHIO SING CHING.

The Presbyterian Church

Presbyterian Church in Malaysia: Joyful Grace Church, Jalan Alsagoff, 82000 Pontian, Johor; tel. (7) 711390; fax (7) 324384; Pastor TITUS KIM KAH TECK.

The Roman Catholic Church

Malaysia comprises two archdioceses and six dioceses. At 31 December 2002 approximately 3.2% of the population were adherents.

Catholic Bishops' Conference of Malaysia, Singapore and Brunei

Xavier Hall, 133 Jalan Gasing, 46000 Petaling Jaya, Selangor; tel. and fax (3) 79581371; e-mail cbcmsb@pc.jaring.my.

Pres. Most Rev. NICHOLAS CHIA (Archbishop of Singapore).

Archbishop of Kuala Lumpur: Most Rev. MURPHY NICHOLAS XAVIER PAKIAM, Archbishop's House, 528 Jalan Bukit Nanas, 50250 Kuala Lumpur; tel. (3) 20788828; fax (3) 20313815; e-mail mpakiam@pd.jaring.my.

Archbishop of Kuching: Most Rev. JOHN HA TIONG HOCK, Archbishop's Office, 118 Jalan Tun Abang Haji Openg, POB 940, 93718 Kuching, Sarawak; tel. (82) 242634; fax (82) 425724; e-mail johnha@pd.jaring.my.

BAHÁ'Í FAITH

Spiritual Assembly of the Bahá'ís of Malaysia: 4 Lorong Titiwangsa 5, off Jalan Pahang, 53200 Kuala Lumpur; tel. (3) 40235183; fax (3) 40226277; e-mail nsa-sec@bahai.org.my; internet www.bahai.org.my; mems resident in 800 localities.

The Press

PENINSULAR MALAYSIA DAILIES

English Language

Business Times: Balai Berita 31, Jalan Riong, 59100 Kuala Lumpur; tel. (3) 22822628; fax (3) 22825424; e-mail bt@nstp.com.my; internet www.btimes.com.my; f. 1976; morning; Editor ZAINUL ARIFIN; circ. 15,000.

Malay Mail: Balai Berita 31, Jalan Riong, 59100 Kuala Lumpur; tel. (3) 22822829; fax (3) 22821434; e-mail malaymail@nstp.com.my; internet www.mmail.com.my; f. 1896; afternoon; Editor FAUZI OMAR; circ. 75,000.

Malaysiakini: 2–4 Jalan Bangsa-Utang 9, 59000 Kuala Lumpur; tel. (3) 22835567; fax (3) 22892579; e-mail editor@malaysiakini.com; internet www.malaysiakini.com; Malaysia's first on-line newspaper; English and Malay; Editor STEVEN GAN.

New Straits Times: Balai Berita 31, Jalan Riong, 59100 Kuala Lumpur; tel. (3) 2823322; fax (3) 2821434; e-mail news@nstp.com.my; internet www.nst.com.my; f. 1845; morning; Group Editor-in-Chief KALIMULLAH MASHEERUL HASSAN; circ. 190,000.

The Edge: G501–G801, Levels 5–8, Block G, Phileo Damansara I, Jalan 16/11, off Jalan Damansara, 46350 Petaling Jaya, Selangor; tel. (3) 76603838; fax (3) 76608638; e-mail eeditor@bizedge.com; internet www.theedgedaily.com; f. 1996; weekly, with daily internet edition; business and investment news.

The Star: 13 Jalan 13/6, 46200 Petaling Jaya, POB 12474, Selangor; tel. (3) 7581188; fax (3) 7551280; e-mail msd@thestar.com.my; internet www.thestar.com.my; f. 1971; morning; Group Chief Editor NG POH TIP; circ. 192,059.

The Sun: Sun Media Corpn Sdn Bhd, Lot 6, Jalan 51/217, Section 51, 46050 Petaling Jaya, Selangor Darul Ehsan; tel. (3) 7946688; fax (3) 7952624; e-mail editor@sunmg.po.my; f. 1993; Editor-in-Chief HO KAY TAT; Man. Dir TAN BOON KEAN; circ. 82,474.

Chinese Language

China Press: 80 Jalan Riong, 59100 Kuala Lumpur; tel. (3) 2828208; fax (3) 2825327; circ. 206,000.

Chung Kuo Pao (China Press): 80 Jalan Riong, 59100 Kuala Lumpur; tel. (3) 2828208; fax (3) 2825327; f. 1946; Editor POON CHAU HUAY; Gen. Man. NG BENG LYE; circ. 210,000.

Guang Ming Daily: 19 Jalan Semangat, 46200 Petaling Jaya, Selangor; tel. (3) 7582888; fax (3) 7575135; circ. 87,144.

Kwong Wah Yit Poh: 19 Jalan Presgrave, 10300 Pinang; tel. (4) 2612312; fax (4) 2615407; e-mail editor@kwongwah.com.my; internet www.kwongwah.com.my; f. 1910; morning; Chief Editor TAN AYE CHOO; circ. 72,158.

Nanyang Siang Pau (Malaysia): 1 Jalan SS7/2, 47301 Petaling Jaya, Selangor; tel. (3) 78776000; fax (3) 78776855; e-mail editor@nanyang.com.my; internet www.nanyang.com.my; f. 1923; morning and evening; Editor-in-Chief WONG KAM HOR; circ. 185,000 (daily), 223,000 (Sunday).

Shin Min Daily News: 31 Jalan Riong, Bangsar, 59100 Kuala Lumpur; tel. (3) 2826363; fax (3) 2821812; f. 1966; morning; Editor-in-Chief CHENG SONG HUAT; circ. 82,000.

Sin Chew Jit Poh (Malaysia): 19 Jalan Semangat, POB 367, Jalan Sultan, 46200 Petaling Jaya, Selangor; tel. (3) 7582888; fax (3) 7570527; internet www.sinchew-i.com; f. 1929; morning; Chief Editor LIEW CHEN CHUAN; circ. 227,067 (daily), 230,000 (Sunday).

Malay Language

Berita Harian: Balai Berita 31, Jalan Riong, 59100 Kuala Lumpur; tel. (3) 2822323; fax (3) 2822425; e-mail bharian@bharian.com.my; internet www.bharian.com.my; f. 1957; morning; Group Editor AHMAD REJAL ARBEE; circ. 350,000.

Metro Ahad: Balai Berita 31, Jalan Riong, 59100 Kuala Lumpur; tel. (3) 2822328; fax (3) 2824482; e-mail metahad@nstp.com.my; internet www.metroahad.com.my; circ. 132,195.

Mingguan Perdana: 48 Jalan Siput Akek, Taman Billion, Kuala Lumpur; tel. (3) 619133; Group Chief Editor KHALID JAFRI.

Utusan Malaysia: 46M Jalan Lima, off Jalan Chan Sow Lin, 55200 Kuala Lumpur; tel. (3) 2217055; fax (3) 2220911; e-mail corpcomm@utusan.com.my; internet www.utusan.com.my; Editor ABDUL AZIZ ISHAK; circ. 239,385.

Watan: 23–1 Jalan 9A/55A, Taman Setiawangsa, 54200 Kuala Lumpur; tel. (3) 4523040; fax (3) 4523043; circ. 80,000.

Tamil Language

Malaysia Nanban: 11 Jalan Murai Dua, Batu Kompleks, off Jalan Ipoh, 51200 Kuala Lumpur; tel. (3) 6212251; fax (3) 6235981; circ. 45,000.

Tamil Nesan: 28 Jalan Yew, Pudu, 55100 Kuala Lumpur; tel. (3) 2216411; fax (3) 2210448; f. 1924; morning; Editor V. VIVEKANANTHAN; circ. 35,000 (daily), 60,000 (Sunday).

Tamil Osai: 19 Jalan Murai Dua, Batu Kompleks, Jalan Ipoh, Kuala Lumpur; tel. (3) 671644; circ. 21,000 (daily), 40,000 (Sunday).

Tamil Thinamani: 9 Jalan Murai Dua, Batu Kompleks, Jalan Ipoh, Kuala Lumpur; tel. (3) 66719; Editor S. NACHIAPPAN; circ. 18,000 (daily), 39,000 (Sunday).

SUNDAY PAPERS

English Language

New Sunday Times: Balai Berita 31, Jalan Riong, 59100 Kuala Lumpur; tel. (3) 2822328; fax (3) 2824482; e-mail news@nstp.com.my; f. 1932; morning; Group Editor (vacant); circ. 191,562.

Sunday Mail: Balai Berita 31, Jalan Riong, 59100 Kuala Lumpur; tel. (3) 2822328; fax (3) 2824482; e-mail smail@nstp.com.my; f. 1896; morning; Editor JOACHIM S. P. NG; circ. 75,641.

Sunday Star: 13 Jalan 13/6, 46200 Petaling Jaya, POB 12474, Selangor Darul Ehsan; tel. (3) 7581188; fax (3) 7551280; f. 1971; Editor DAVID YEOH; circ. 232,790.

Malay Language

Berita Minggu: Balai Berita 31, Jalan Riong, 59100 Kuala Lumpur; tel. (3) 2822328; fax (3) 2824482; e-mail bharian@bharian.com.my; f. 1957; morning; Editor Dato' AHMAD NAZRI ABDULLAH; circ. 421,127.

Mingguan Malaysia: 11A The Right Angle, Jalan 14/22, 46100 Petaling Jaya; tel. (3) 7563355; fax (3) 7577755; f. 1964; Editor MOHD HASSAN MOHD NOOR; circ. 543,232.

Utusan Zaman: 11A The Right Angle, Jalan 14/22, 46100 Petaling Jaya; tel. (3) 7563355; fax (3) 7577755; f. 1939; Editor MUSTAFA FADULA SUHAIMI; circ. 11,782.

Tamil Language

Makkal Osai: 11 Jalan Murai Dua, Batu Kompleks, off Jalan Ipoh, 51200 Kuala Lumpur; tel. (3) 6212251; fax (3) 6235981; circ. 28,000.

PERIODICALS

English Language

Her World: Berita Publishing Sdn Bhd, Balai Berita, 31 Jalan Riong, 59100 Kuala Lumpur; tel. (3) 2824322; fax (3) 2828489; monthly; Editor ALICE CHEE LAN NEO; circ. 35,000.

Malaysia Warta Kerajaan Seri Paduka Baginda (HM Government Gazette): Percetakan Nasional Malaysia Berhad, Jalan Chan Sow Lin, 50554 Kuala Lumpur; tel. (3) 92212022; fax (3) 92220690; e-mail pnmb@po.jaring.my; fortnightly.

Malaysian Agricultural Journal: Ministry of Agriculture, Publications Unit, Wisma Tani, Jalan Sultan Salahuddin, 50624 Kuala Lumpur; tel. (3) 2982011; fax (3) 2913758; f. 1901; 2 a year.

Malaysian Forester: Forestry Department Headquarters, Jalan Sultan Salahuddin, 50660 Kuala Lumpur; tel. (3) 26988244; fax (3) 26925657; e-mail skthai@forestry.gov.my; f. 1931; quarterly; Editor THAI SEE KIAM.

The Planter: Wisma ISP, 29–33 Jalan Taman U Thant, POB 10262, 50708 Kuala Lumpur; tel. (3) 21425561; fax (3) 21426898;

e-mail isphq@tm.net.my; internet www.isp.org.my; f. 1919; publ. by Isp Management (M); monthly; Editor W. T. PERERA; circ. 4,000.

Young Generation: 11A The Right Angle, Jalan 14/22, 46100 Petaling Jaya, Selangor; tel. (3) 7563355; fax (3) 7577755; monthly; circ. 50,000.

Chinese Language

Mister Weekly: 2A Jalan 19/1, 46300 Petaling Jaya, Selangor; tel. (3) 7562400; fax (3) 7553826; f. 1976; weekly; Editor WONG AH TAI; circ. 25,000.

Mun Sang Poh: 472 Jalan Pasir Puteh, 31650 Ipoh; tel. (5) 3212919; fax (5) 3214006; bi-weekly; circ. 77,958.

New Life Post: 80M Jalan SS21/39, Damansara Utama, 47400 Petaling Jaya, Selangor; tel. (3) 7571833; fax (3) 7181809; f. 1972; bi-weekly; Editor LOW BENG CHEE; circ. 231,000.

New Tide Magazine: Nanyang Siang Pau Bldg, 2nd Floor, Jalan 7/2, 47301 Petaling Jaya, Selangor; tel. (3) 76202118; fax (3) 76202131; e-mail newtidemag@hotmail.com; f. 1974; monthly; Editor NELLIE OOI; circ. 39,000.

Malay Language

Dewan Masyarakat: Dewan Bahasa dan Pustaka, POB 10803, 50926 Kuala Lumpur; tel. (3) 2481011; fax (3) 2484211; f. 1963; monthly; current affairs; Editor ZULKIFLI SALLEH; circ. 48,500.

Dewan Pelajar: Dewan Bahasa dan Pustaka, Jalan Wisma Putra, POB 10803, 50926 Kuala Lumpur; tel. (3) 2481011; fax (3) 2484211; f. 1967; monthly; children's; Editor ZALEHA HASHIM; circ. 100,000.

Dewan Siswa: POB 10803, 50926 Kuala Lumpur; tel. (3) 2481011; fax (3) 2484208; monthly; circ. 140,000.

Gila-Gila: 38-1, Jalan Bangsar Utama Satu, Bangsar Utama, 59000 Kuala Lumpur; tel. (3) 22824970; fax (3) 22824967; fortnightly; circ. 70,000.

Harakah: Jabatan Penerangan dan Penyelidikan PAS, 28A Jalan Pahang Barat, Off Jalan Pahang, 53000 Kuala Lumpur; tel. (3) 40213343; fax (3) 40212422; e-mail hrkh@pc.jaring.my; internet www.harakahdaily.com; two a month; Malay; organ of the Parti Islam se Malaysia (PAS—Islamic Party of Malaysia); Editor ZULKIFLI SULONG.

Jelita: Berita Publishing Sdn Bhd, 16–20 Jalan 4/109E, Desa Business Park, Taman Desa, off Jalan Klang Lama, 58100 Kuala Lumpur; tel. (3) 7620811; fax (3) 76208114; e-mail jelita@beritapub.com.my; internet www.jelita.com.my; monthly; fashion and beauty magazine; Editor ROHANI PA' WAN CHIK; circ. 80,000.

Mangga: 11A The Right Angle, Jalan 14/22, 46100 Petaling Jaya, Selangor; tel. (3) 7563355; fax (3) 7577755; monthly; circ. 205,000.

Mastika: 11A The Right Angle, Jalan 14/22, 46100 Petaling Jaya, Selangor; tel. (3) 7363355; fax (3) 7577755; monthly; Malayan illustrated magazine; Editor AZIZAH ALI; circ. 15,000.

Utusan Radio dan TV: 11A The Right Angle, Jalan 14/22, 46100 Petaling Jaya, Selangor; tel. (3) 7363355; fax (3) 7577755; fortnightly; Editor NORSHAH TAMBY; circ. 115,000.

Wanita: 11A The Right Angle, Jalan 14/22, 46100 Petaling Jaya, Selangor; tel. (3) 7563355; fax (3) 7577755; monthly; women; Editor NIK RAHIMAH HASSAN; circ. 85,000.

Punjabi Language

Navjiwan Punjabi News: 52 Jalan 8/18, Jalan Toman, Petaling Jaya, 46050 Selangor; tel. (3) 7565725; f. 1950; weekly; Assoc. Editor TARA SINGH; circ. 9,000.

SABAH DAILIES

Api Siang Pau (Kota Kinabalu Commercial Press): 24 Lorong Dewan, POB 170, Kota Kinabalu; f. 1954; morning; Chinese; Editor Datuk LO KWOCK CHUEN; circ. 3,000.

Borneo Mail (Nountan Press Sdn Bhd): 1 Jalan Bakau, 1st Floor, off Jalan Gaya, 88999 Kota Kinabulu; tel. (88) 238001; fax (88) 238002; English; circ. 14,610.

Daily Express: News House, 16 Jalan Pasar Baru, POB 10139, 88801 Kota Kinabalu; tel. (88) 256422; fax (88) 238611; e-mail sph@tm.net.my; internet www.dailyexpress.com.my; f. 1963; morning; English, Bahasa Malaysia and Kadazan; Editor-in-Chief SARDATHISA JAMES; circ. 30,000.

Hwa Chiaw Jit Pao (Overseas Chinese Daily News): News House, 16 Jalan Pasar Baru, POB 10139, 88801 Kota Kinabalu; tel. (88) 256422; e-mail sph@tm.net.my; internet www.dailyexpress.com.my; f. 1936; morning; Chinese; Editor HII YUK SENG; circ. 30,000.

Merdeka Daily News: Lot 56, BDC Estate, Mile 1½ North Road, POB 332, 90703 Sandakan; tel. (89) 214517; fax (89) 275537; e-mail merkk@tm.net.my; f. 1968; morning; Chinese; Editor-in-Chief FUNG KON SHING; circ. 8,000.

New Sabah Times: Jalan Pusat Pembangunan Masyarakat, off Jalan Mat Salleh, 88100 Kota Kinabalu; POB 20119, 88758 Kota Kinabalu; tel. (88) 230055; fax (88) 241155; internet www .newsabahtimes.com.my; English, Malay and Kadazan; Editor-in-Chief EDDY LOK; circ. 30,000.

Syarikat Sabah Times: Kota Kinabalu; tel. (88) 52217; f. 1952; English, Malay and Kadazan; circ. 25,000.

Tawau Jih Pao: POB 464, 1072 Jalan Kuhara, Tawau; tel. (89) 72576; Chinese; Editor-in-Chief STEPHEN LAI KIM YEAN.

SARAWAK DAILIES

Berita Petang Sarawak: Lot 8322, Lorong 7, Jalan Tun Abdul Razak, 93450 Kuching; POB 1315, 93726 Kuching; tel. (82) 480771; fax (82) 489006; f. 1972; evening; Chinese; Chief Editor HWANG YU CHAI; circ. 12,000.

Borneo Post: 40 Jalan Tuanku Osman, POB 20, 96000 Sibu; tel. (84) 332055; fax (84) 321255; internet www.borneopost.com.my; morning; English; Man. Dir LAU HUI SIONG; Editor NGUOI HOW YIENG; circ. 60,000.

International Times: Lot 2215, Jalan Bengkel, Pending Industrial Estate, POB 1158, 93724 Kuching; tel. (82) 482215; fax (82) 480996; e-mail news@intimes.com; internet www.intimes.com.my; f. 1968; morning; Chinese; Editor LEE FOOK ONN; circ. 37,000.

Malaysia Daily News: 7 Island Rd, POB 237, 96009 Sibu; tel. (84) 330211; tel. (84) 320540; f. 1968; morning; Chinese; Editor WONG SENG KWONG; circ. 22,735.

Sarawak Tribune and Sunday Tribune: Lot 231, Jalan Nipah, off Jalan Abell, 93100 Kuching; tel. (82) 424411; fax (82) 420358; internet www.jaring.my/tribune; f. 1945; English; Editor FRANCIS SIAH; circ. 29,598.

See Hua Daily News: 40 Jalan Tuanku Osman, POB 20, 96000 Sibu; tel. (84) 332055; fax (84) 321255; f. 1952; morning; Chinese; Man. Editor LAU HUI SIONG; circ. 80,000.

United Daily News: internet www.uniteddaily.com.my; f. 2004 following merger between Chinese Daily News and Miri Daily News; morning; Chinese; Dep. Publr WONG KEH HUONG; circ. 35,000.

PERIODICALS

Pedoman Rakyat: Malaysian Information Dept, Mosque Rd, 93612 Kuching; tel. (82) 240141; f. 1956; monthly; Malay; Editor SAIT BIN HAJI YAMAN; circ. 30,000.

Pembrita: Malaysian Information Services, Mosque Rd, 93612 Kuching; tel. (82) 247231; f. 1950; monthly; Iban; Editor ALBAN JAWA; circ. 20,000.

Sarawak Gazette: Sarawak Museum, Jalan Tun Abang Haji Openg, 93566 Kuching; tel. (82) 244232; fax (82) 246680; e-mail museum@po.jaring.my; f. 1870; 2 a year; English; Chief Editor Datu Haji SALLEH SULAIMAN.

Utusan Sarawak: Lot 231, Jalan Nipah, off Jalan Abell, POB 138, 93100 Kuching; tel. (82) 424411; fax (82) 420358; internet www .tribune.com.my/tribune; f. 1949; Malay; Editor Haji ABDUL AZIZ Haji MALIM; circ. 32,292.

NEWS AGENCIES

Bernama (Malaysian National News Agency): Wisma Bernama, 28 Jalan 1/65A, off Jalan Tun Razak, POB 10024, 50700 Kuala Lumpur; tel. (3) 2945233; fax (3) 2941020; e-mail sjamil@bernama.com; internet www.bernama.com; f. 1968; general and foreign news, economic features and photo services, public relations wire, screen information and data services, stock market on-line equities service, real-time commodity and monetary information services; daily output in Malay and English; in June 1990 Bernama was given the exclusive right to receive and distribute news in Malaysia; Gen. Man. SYED JAMIL JAAFAR.

Foreign Bureaux

Agence France-Presse (AFP): 26 Hotel Equatorial, 1st Floor, Jalan Treacher, 2610520 Kuala Lumpur; tel. (3) 2691906; fax (3) 2615606; Correspondent MERVIN NAMBIAR.

Associated Press (AP) (USA): Wisma Bernama, 28 Jalan 1/65A, off Jalan Tun Razak, POB 12219, Kuala Lumpur; tel. (3) 2926155; Correspondent HARI SUBRAMANIAM.

Inter Press Service (IPS) (Italy): 32 Jalan Mudah Barat, Taman Midah, 56000 Kuala Lumpur; tel. (3) 9716830; fax (3) 2612872; Correspondent (vacant).

Press Trust of India: 114 Jalan Limau Manis, Bangsar Park, Kuala Lumpur; tel. (3) 940673; Correspondent T. V. VENKITACHALAM.

United Press International (UPI) (USA): Room 1, Ground Floor, Wisma Bernama, Jalan 1/65A, 50400 Kuala Lumpur; tel. (3) 2933393; fax (3) 2913876; Rep. MARY LEIGH.

Reuters (United Kingdom) and Xinhua (People's Republic of China) are also represented in Malaysia.

PRESS ASSOCIATION

Persatuan Penerbit-Penerbit Akhbar Malaysia (Malaysian Newspaper Publishers' Asscn): Unit 706, Block B, Phileo Damansara 1, 9 Jalan 16/11, off Jalan Damansara, 46350 Petaling Jaya; tel. (3) 76608535; fax (3) 76608532; e-mail mnpa@macomm.com.my; Chair. ROSELINA JOHARI.

Publishers

KUALA LUMPUR

Arus Intelek Sdn Bhd: Plaza Mont Kiara, Suite E-06-06, Mont Kiara, 50480 Kuala Lumpur; tel. (3) 62011558; fax (3) 62018698; e-mail arusintelek@po.jaring.my; Man. Datin AZIZAH MOKHZANI.

Berita Publishing Sdn Bhd: Balai Berita, 31 Jalan Riong, 59100 Kuala Lumpur; tel. (3) 2824322; fax (3) 2821605; internet www.jelita .com.my; education, business, fiction, cookery; Man. ABDUL MANAF SAAD.

Dewan Bahasa dan Pustaka (DBP) (Institute of Language and Literature): POB 10803, 50926 Kuala Lumpur; tel. (3) 21481011; fax (3) 21444460; e-mail aziz@dbp.gov.my; internet www.dbp.gov.my; f. 1956; textbooks, magazines and general; Chair. Tan Sri KAMARUL ARIFFIN MOHAMED YASSIN; Dir-Gen. Dato' Haji A. AZIZ DERAMAN.

International Law Book Services: Lot 4.1, Wisma Shen, 4th Floor, 149 Jalan Masjid India, 50100 Kuala Lumpur; tel. (3) 2939864; fax (3) 2928035; e-mail gbc@pc.jaring.my; Man. Dr SYED IBRAHIM.

Jabatan Penerbitan Universiti Malaya (University of Malaya Press): University of Malaya, Lembah Pantai, 50603 Kuala Lumpur; tel. (3) 79574361; fax (3) 79574473; e-mail hamedi@um.edu.my; internet www.um.edu.my/umpress; f. 1954; general fiction, literature, economics, history, medicine, politics, science, social science, law, Islam, engineering, dictionaries; Chief Editor Dr HAMEDI MOHD ADNAN.

Malaya Press Sdn Bhd: Kuala Lumpur; tel. (3) 5754650; fax (3) 5751464; f. 1958; education; Man. Dir LAI WING CHUN.

Pustaka Antara Sdn Bhd: Lot UG 10–13, Upper Ground Floor, Kompleks Wilayah, 2 Jalan Munshi Abdullah, 50100 Kuala Lumpur; tel. (3) 26980044; fax (3) 26917997; e-mail pantara@tm.net .my; textbooks, children's, languages, fiction; Man. Dir Datuk ABDUL AZIZ BIN AHMAD.

Utusan Publications and Distributors Sdn Bhd: 1 and 3 Jalan 3/91A, Taman Shamelin Perkasa, Cheras, 56100 Kuala Lumpur; tel. (3) 9856577; fax (3) 9846554; e-mail rose@utusan.com.my; internet www.upnd.com.my; school textbooks, children's, languages, fiction, general; Exec. Dir ROSELINA JOHARI.

JOHOR

Penerbitan Pelangi Sdn Bhd: 66 Jalan Pingai, Taman Pelangi, 80400 Johor Bahru; tel. (7) 3316288; fax (7) 3329201; e-mail ppsb@ po.jaring.my; internet www.pelangibooks.com; children's books, guidebooks and reference; Man. Dir SAMUEL SUM KOWN CHEEK.

Textbooks Malaysia Sdn Bhd: 49 Jalan Tengku Ahmad, POB 30, 85000 Segamat, Johor; tel. (7) 9318323; fax (7) 9313323; school textbooks, children's fiction, guidebooks and reference; Man. Dir FREDDIE KHOO.

NEGERI SEMBILAN

Bharathi Press: 166 Taman AST, POB 74, 70700 Seremban, Negeri Sembilan Darul Khusus; tel. (6) 7622911; f. 1939; Mans M. SUBRAMANIA BHARATHI, BHARATHI THASAN.

PINANG

Syarikat United Book Sdn Bhd: 187–189 Lebuh Carnarvon, 10100 Pulau Pinang; tel. (4) 61635; fax (4) 615063; textbooks, children's, reference, fiction, guidebooks; Man. Dir CHEW SING GUAN.

SELANGOR

Federal Publications Sdn Bhd: Lot 46, Subang Hi-Tech Industrial Park, Batu Tiga, 40000 Shah Alam, Selangor; tel. (3) 56286888; fax (3) 56364620; e-mail fpsb@tpg.com.my; f. 1957; computer, children's magazines; Gen. Man. STEPHEN K. S. LIM.

FEP International Sdn Bhd: 6 Jalan SS 4c/5, POB 1091, 47301 Petaling Jaya, Selangor; tel. (3) 7036150; fax (3) 7036989; f. 1969; children's, languages, fiction, dictionaries, textbooks and reference; Man. Dir Lim Mok Hai.

Mahir Publications Sdn Bhd: 39 Jalan Nilam 1/2, Subang Sq., Subang Hi-Tech Industrial Park, Batu Tiga, 40000 Shah Alam, Selangor; tel. (3) 7379044; fax (3) 7379043; e-mail mahirpub@tm.net.my; Gen. Man. Zainora binti Muhamad.

Minerva Publications (NS) Sdn Bhd: 51 Jalan SG 3/1, Tan Sri Gombak, Batu Caves, 68100 Selangor; tel. (3) 61882876; fax (3) 61883876; e-mail minerva@streamyx.com; internet www.minervaa.com; f. 1974; general, children's, reference, medical, law; Dir and Chief Editor Sujaudeen; Man. Dir Thanjudeen.

Pearson Education Malaysia Sdn Bhd: Lot 2, Jalan 215, off Jalan Templer, 46050 Petaling Jaya, Selangor; tel. (3) 77820466; fax (3) 77818005; e-mail inquiry@pearsoned.com.my; internet www.pearsoned.com.my; textbooks, mathematics, physics, science, general, educational materials; Dir Wong Wee Woon; Man. Wong Mei Mei.

Pelanduk Publications (M) Sdn Bhd: 12 Jalan SS 13/3E, Subang Jaya Industrial Estate, 47500 Subang Jaya, Selangor; tel. (3) 7386885; fax (3) 7386575; e-mail pelpub@tm.net.my; internet www.pelanduk.com; Man. Jackson Tan.

Penerbit Fajar Bakti Sdn Bhd: 4 Jalan U1/15, Sekseyen U1, Hicom-Glenmarie Industrial Park, 40150 Shah Alam, Selangor; tel. (3) 7047011; fax (3) 7047024; e-mail edes@pfb.po.my; school, college and university textbooks, children's, fiction, general; Man. Dir Edda de Silva.

Penerbit Pan Earth Sdn Bhd: 11 Jalan SS 26/6, Taman Mayang Jaya, 47301 Petaling Jaya, Selangor; tel. (3) 7031258; fax (3) 7031262; Man. Stephen Cheng.

Penerbit Universiti Kebangsaan Malaysia: Universiti Kebangsaan Malaysia, 43600 UKM, Selangor; tel. (3) 8292840; fax (3) 8254375; Man. Hasrom bin Haron.

Pustaka Delta Pelajaran Sdn Bhd: Wisma Delta, Lot 18, Jalan 51A/22A, 46100 Petaling Jaya, Selangor; tel. (3) 7570000; fax (3) 7576688; e-mail dpsb@po.jaring.my; economics, language, environment, geography, geology, history, religion, science; Man. Dir Lim Kim Wah.

Pustaka Sistem Pelajaran Sdn Bhd: Lot 17–22 and 17–23, Jalan Satu, Bersatu Industrial Park, Cheras Jaya, 43200 Cheras, Selangor; tel. (3) 9047558; fax (3) 9047573; Man. T. Thiru.

Sasbadi Sdn Bhd: 103A Jalan SS 21/1A, Damansara Utama, 47400 Petaling Jaya, Selangor; tel. (3) 7182550; fax (3) 7186709; Man. Law King Hui.

SNP Panpac (Malaysia) Sdn Bhd: Lot 3, Jalan Saham 23/3, Kawasan MIEL Phase 8, Section 23, 40300 Shah Alam, Selangor Darul Ehsam; tel. (3) 55481088; fax (3) 55481080; e-mail eastview@snpo.com.my; f. 1980; fmrly SNP Eastview Publications Sdn Bhd; school textbooks, children's, fiction, reference, general; Dir Chia Yan Heng.

Times Educational Sdn Bhd: 22 Jalan 19/3, 46300 Petaling Jaya, Selangor; tel. (3) 7571766; fax (3) 7573607; textbooks, general and reference; Man. Foong Chui Lin.

GOVERNMENT PUBLISHING HOUSE

Percetakan Nasional Malaysia Bhd (Malaysia National Printing Ltd): Jalan Chan Sow Lin, 50554 Kuala Lumpur; tel. (3) 2212022; fax (3) 2220690; fmrly the National Printing Department, incorporated as a company under govt control in January 1993.

PUBLISHERS' ASSOCIATION

Malaysian Book Publishers' Association: 306 Block C, Glomac Business Centre, 10 Jalan SS 6/1 Kelana Jaya, 47301 Petaling Jaya, Selangor; tel. (3) 7046628; fax (3) 7046629; e-mail mabopa@po.jaring.my; internet www.mabopa.com.my; f. 1968; Pres. Ng Tieh Chuan; Hon. Sec. Kow Ching Chuan; 95 mems.

Broadcasting and Communications

TELECOMMUNICATIONS

Celcom (Malaysia) Sdn Bhd: Wisma Telekom Semarak, 82 Jalan Raja Muda Abdul Aziz, 503000 Kuala Lumpur; tel. (3) 26873838; e-mail cpr@celcom.com.my; internet www.celcom.com.my; f. 1988; private co licensed to operate mobile cellular telephone service; merged with TM Cellular Sdn Bhd in 2003; Chair. Dr Mohamed Munir bin Abdul Majid; CEO Dato' Mohamed Yunus Ramli bin Abbas.

DiGi Telecommunications Sdn Bhd: Lot 30, Jalan Delima 1/3, Subang Hi-Tech Industrial Park, 40000 Shah Alam, Selangor; tel. (3) 57211800; fax (3) 57211857; internet www.digi.com.my; private co licensed to operate mobile telephone service; Chair. Tan Sri Dato' Seri Vincent Tan Chee Yioun; CEO Tore Johnsen.

Jabatan Telekomunikasi Malaysia (JTM) (Department of Telecommunications): c/o Ministry of Energy, Communications and Multimedia, Wisma Damansara, 3rd Floor, Jalan Semantan, 50668 Kuala Lumpur; tel. (3) 20875000; fax (3) 20957901; internet www.ktkm.gov.my; regulatory body for telecommunications industry.

Maxis Communications Bhd: Menara Maxis, Aras 18, Kuala Lumpur City Centre, 50088 Kuala Lumpur; tel. (3) 23307000; fax (3) 23300008; internet www.maxis.com.my; f. 1995; provides mobile, fixed line and multimedia services; approx. 3.25m. subscribers in 2003; CEO Jamaludin Ibrahim; Chair. Datuk Megat Zaharuddin bin Megat Mohamed Noor.

Telekom Malaysia Bhd: Level 51, North Wing, Menara Telekom, off Jalan Pantai Baru, 50672 Kuala Lumpur; tel. (3) 22401221; fax (3) 22832415; internet www.telekom.com.my; f. 1984; public listed co responsible for operation of basic telecommunications services; 74% govt-owned; 4.22m. fixed lines (95% of total); Chair Haji Muhammad Radzi bin Haji Mansor; Chief Exec. Dr Md Khir Abdul Rahman.

Technology Resources Industries Bhd (TRI): Menara TR, 23rd Floor, 161B Jalan Ampang, 50450 Kuala Lumpur; tel. (3) 2619555; fax (3) 2632018; operates mobile cellular telephone service; Chair. and Chief Exec. Tan Sri Dato' Tajudin Ramli.

Time dotCom Bhd: Wisma Time, 1st Floor, 249 Jalan Tun Razak, 50400 Kuala Lumpur; tel. (3) 27208000; fax (3) 27200199; internet www.time.com.my; f. 1996 as Time Telecommunications Holdings Bhd; name changed as above in Jan. 2000; state-controlled co licensed to operate trunk network and mobile cellular telephone service; Chair. Dato' Wan Muhamad Wan Ibrahim; Man. Dir Tan See Yin.

BROADCASTING

Regulatory Authority

Under the Broadcasting Act (approved in December 1987), the Minister of Information is empowered to control and monitor all radio and television broadcasting, and to revoke the licence of any private company violating the Act by broadcasting material 'conflicting with Malaysian values'.

Radio Televisyen Malaysia (RTM): Dept of Broadcasting, Angkasapuri, Bukit Putra, 50614 Kuala Lumpur; tel. (3) 22825333; fax (3) 2824735; e-mail helpdesk@rtm.net.my; internet www.rtm.net.my; f. 1946; television introduced 1963; supervises radio and television broadcasting; Dir-Gen. Jaafar Kamin; Dep. Dir-Gen. Tamimuddin Abdul Karim.

Radio

Radio Malaysia: Radio Televisyen Malaysia (see Regulatory Authority), POB 11272, 50740 Kuala Lumpur; tel. (3) 2823991; fax (3) 2825859; f. 1946; domestic service; operates six networks; broadcasts in Bahasa Malaysia, English, Chinese (Mandarin and other dialects), Tamil and Aborigine (Temiar and Semai dialects); Dir of Radio Madzhi Johari.

Suara Islam (Voice of Islam): Islamic Affairs Division, Prime Minister's Department, Blok Utama, Tingkat 1–5, Pusat Pentadbiran Kerajaan Persekutuan, 62502 Putrajaya; internet www.smpke.jpm.my; f. 1995; Asia-Pacific region; broadcasts in Bahasa Malaysia on Islam.

Suara Malaysia (Voice of Malaysia): Wisma Radio, Angkasapuri, POB 11272, 50740 Kuala Lumpur; tel. (3) 22887824; fax (3) 22847594; f. 1963; overseas service in Bahasa Malaysia, Arabic, Myanmar (Burmese), English, Bahasa Indonesia, Chinese (Mandarin/Cantonese), Tagalog and Thai; Controller of Overseas Service Stephen Sipaun.

Radio Televisyen Malaysia—Sabah: Jalan Tuaran, 88614 Kota Kinabalu; tel. (88) 213444; fax (88) 223493; f. 1955; television introduced 1971; a dept of RTM; broadcasts programmes over two networks for 280 hours a week in Bahasa Malaysia, English, Chinese (two dialects), Kadazan, Murut, Dusun and Bajau; Dir of Broadcasting Jumat Engson.

Radio Televisyen Malaysia—Sarawak: Broadcasting House, Jalan P. Ramlee, 93614 Kuching; tel. (82) 248422; fax (82) 241914; e-mail pvgrtmsw@tm.net.my; f. 1954; a dept of RTM; broadcasts 445 hours per week in Bahasa Malaysia, English, Chinese, Iban, Bidayuh, Melanau, Kayan/Kenyah, Bisayah and Murut; Dir of Broadcasting Norhyati Ismail.

Rediffusion Sdn Bhd: Rediffusion House, 17 Jalan Pahang, 53000 Kuala Lumpur; tel. (3) 4424544; fax (3) 4424614; f. 1949; two programmes; 44,720 subscribers in Kuala Lumpur; 11,405 subscribers in Pinang; 6,006 subscribers in Province Wellesley; 20,471 subscribers in Ipoh; Gen. Man. Rosni B. Rahmat.

Time Highway Radio: Wisma Time, 10th Floor, Jalan Tun Razak, 50400 Kuala Lumpur; tel. (3) 27202993; fax (3) 27200993; e-mail chief@thr.fm; internet www.thr.fm; f. 1994; serves Kuala Lumpur region; broadcasts in English; CEO Abdul Aziz Hamdan.

Television

Measat Broadcast Network Systems Sdn Bhd: Kuala Lumpur; internet www.astro.com.my; nation-wide subscription service; Malaysia's first satellite, Measat 1, was launched in January 1996; a second satellite was launched in October of that year; Chair. T. Ananda Krishnan.

Mega TV: Kuala Lumpur; internet www.megatv.com.my; subscription service; began broadcasting in November 1995; 5 foreign channels; initially available only in Klang Valley; 40%-owned by the Govt.

MetroVision: 33 Jalan Delima, 1/3 Subang Hi-Tech Industrial Park, 40000 Shah Alam, Selangor; tel. (3) 7328000; fax (3) 7328932; e-mail norlin@metrovision.com.my; internet www.metrovision.com .my; began broadcasting in July 1995; commercial station; operates only in Klang Valley; 44%-owned by Senandung Sesuria Sdn Bhd, 56%-owned by Metropolitan Media Sdn Bhd; Man. Dr Sabri Abdul Rahman.

Radio Televisyen Malaysia—Sabah: see Radio.

Radio Televisyen Malaysia—Sarawak: see Radio.

Sistem Televisyen Malaysia Bhd (TV 3): 3 Persiaran Bandar Utama, Bandar Utama, 47800 Petaling, Selangor Darul Ehsan; tel. (3) 77266333; fax (3) 77261333; internet www.tv3.com.my; f. 1983; Malaysia's first private television network, began broadcasting in 1984; Chair. Dato' Mohd Noor Yusof; Man. Dir Hisham Dato' Abd. Rahman.

Televisyen Malaysia: Radio Televisyen Malaysia (see Regulatory Authority); f. 1963; operates two national networks, TV1 and TV2; Controller of Programmes Ismail Mohamed Jah.

Under a regulatory framework devised by the Government, the ban on privately owned satellite dishes was ended in 1996.

Finance

(cap. = capital; auth. = authorized; res = reserves; dep. = deposits; m. = million; brs = branches; amounts in ringgit Malaysia)

BANKING

In January 2004 there were 46 domestic commercial banks, merchant banks and finance companies. In February 2000 the Government announced that it had approved plans for the creation of up to 10 banking groups to be formed through the merger of existing institutions. By August 2001 51 banks had merged under the terms of these plans. In February 2004 53 banks held offshore licences in Labuan.

Central Bank

Bank Negara Malaysia: Jalan Dato' Onn, 50480 Kuala Lumpur; tel. (3) 26988044; fax (3) 2912990; e-mail info@bnm.gov.my; internet www.bnm.gov.my; f. 1959; bank of issue; financial regulatory authority; cap. 100.0m., res 30,143.0m., dep. 101,586.1m. (Dec. 2002); Gov. Tan Sri Dato' Sri Zeti Akhtar Aziz; 6 brs.

Regulatory Authority

Labuan Offshore Financial Services Authority (LOFSA): Level 17, Main Office Tower, Financial Park Labuan, Jalan Merdeka, 87000 Labuan; tel. (87) 408188; fax (87) 413328; e-mail communication@lofsa.gov.my; internet www.lofsa.gov.my; regulatory body for the International Offshore Financial Centre of Labuan established in October 1990; Chair. Datuk Zeti Akhtar Aziz (Gov. of Bank Negara Malaysia); Dir-Gen. Rosnah Omar.

Commercial Banks

Peninsular Malaysia

ABN Amro Bank Bhd: Levels 25–27, MNI Twins, Tower II, 11 Jalan Pinang, POB 10094, 50704 Kuala Lumpur; tel. (3) 21626666; fax (3) 21625692; e-mail info@abnamro.com.my; internet www .abnamromalaysia.com; f. 1963.

Affin Bank Bhd: Menara AFFIN, 17th Floor, Jalan Raja Chulan, 50200 Kuala Lumpur; tel. (3) 20559000; fax (3) 20261415; e-mail head.ccd@affinbank.com.my; internet www.affinbank.com.my; f. 1975 as Perwira Habib Bank Malaysia Bhd; name changed to Perwira Affin Bank Bhd 1994; merged with BSN Commercial Bank

(Malaysia) Bhd Jan. 2001, and name changed as above; cap. 1,017.3m., res 150.1m., dep. 16,882.3m. (Dec. 2002); Chair. Gen. Tan Sri Dato' Seri Ismail Haji Omar; Pres. and CEO Dato' Abdul Hamidy Abdul Hafiz; 110 brs.

Alliance Bank Malaysia Bhd: Menara Multi-Purpose, Ground Floor, Capital Sq., 8 Jalan Munshi Abdullah, 50100 Kuala Lumpur; POB 10069, 50704 Kuala Lumpur; tel. (3) 26948800; fax (3) 26946727; e-mail multilink@alliancebg.com.my; internet www .alliancebank.com.my; f. 1982 as Malaysian French Bank Berhad; name changed to Multi-Purpose Bank Bhd 1996; name changed as above Jan. 2001, following acquisition of six merger partners; cap. 596.5m., res 540.4m., dep. 13,535.1m. (March 2003); Chair. Tan Sri Abu Talib Othman; Chief Exec. Dir Ng Siek Chuan; 79 brs.

AmBank Bhd: 22nd Floor, Bangunan AmBank Group, 55 Jalan Raja Chulan, 50200 Kuala Lumpur; POB 10980, 50732 Kuala Lumpur; tel. (3) 20782633; fax (3) 20316453; e-mail customercare@ ambg.com.my; internet www.ambg.com.my; f. 1994; fmrly Arab-Malaysian Bank Bhd; name changed as above 2002; cap. 435.5m., res –94.2m., dep. 7,966.6m. (March 2002); Chair. Tan Sri Dato' Azman Hashim; Man. Dir Kung Beng Hong.

Bangkok Bank Bhd (Thailand): 105 Jalan Tun H. S. Lee, 50000 Kuala Lumpur; tel. (3) 2324555; fax (3) 2388569; e-mail bbb@tm.net .my; f. 1958; cap. 100.0m., res 68.0m., dep. 541.9m. (Dec. 2002); Chair. Albert Cheok Saychuan; CEO Chalit Tayjasanant; 1 br.

Bank of America Malaysia Bhd: Wisma Goldhill, Jalan Raja Chulan, 50200 Kuala Lumpur; tel. (3) 20321133; fax (3) 20319087; internet www.bankofamerica.com.my; cap. 135.8m., res 177.2m., dep. 546.7m. (Dec. 2002); Chair. Kathleen M. Sifer.

Bank of Nova Scotia Bhd: POB 11056, Menara Boustead, 69 Jalan Raja Chulan, 50734 Kuala Lumpur; tel. (3) 21410766; fax (3) 21412160; e-mail bns.kualalumpur@scotiabank.com; internet www .scotiabank.com.my; f. 1973; cap. 122.4m., res 222.6m., dep. 1,806.1m. (Oct. 2002); Man. Dir Rasool Khan.

Bank of Tokyo-Mitsubishi (Malaysia) Bhd (Japan): 1 Leboh Ampang, 50100 Kuala Lumpur; tel. (3) 20789100; fax (3) 20708340; e-mail edpbtm@tm.net.my; f. 1996 following merger of the Bank of Tokyo and Mitsubishi Bank; cap. 200m., res 516.1m., dep. 1,832.5m. (Dec. 2002); Chair. Yoshihiro Watanabe; Pres. and CEO Hiroyuki Kudo.

Bank Pembangunan & Infrastruktur Malaysia Bhd: Menara Bank Pembangunan, POB 12352, Jalan Sultan Ismail, 50774 Kuala Lumpur; tel. (3) 26152020; fax (3) 26928520; e-mail bpimb-pr@ bpimb.com.my; internet www.bpimb.com.my; f. 1973; cap. 1,000m. (Dec. 1999); dep. 2,190m. (Dec. 2000); Man. Dir and CEO Tan Sri Datuk Dr Aris Othman; Chair. Datuk Mohamed Adnan bin Ali; 13 brs.

Bumiputra Commerce Bank Bhd: 6 Jalan Tun Perak, 50050 Kuala Lumpur; tel. (3) 26983022; fax (3) 26986628; internet www .bcb.com.my; f. 1999 following merger of Bank Bumiputra Malaysia Bhd with Bank of Commerce Bhd; cap. 1,708.3m., res 1,834.9m., dep. 49,473.5m. (Dec. 2001); Chair. Tan Sri Radin Soenarno al-Haj; Man. Dir and CEO Dr Rozali Mohamed Ali; 249 brs.

Citibank Bhd (USA): 165 Jalan Ampang, POB 10112, 50450 Kuala Lumpur; tel. (3) 2325334; fax (3) 2328763; internet www.citibank .com.my; f. 1959; cap. 121.7m., res 1,454.5m., dep. 17,804.1m. (Dec. 2001); Country Officer Piyush Gupta; 3 brs.

Deutsche Bank (Malaysia) Bhd (Germany): 18–20 Menara IMC, 8 Jalan Sultan Ismail, 50250 Kuala Lumpur; tel. (3) 20536788; fax (3) 20319822; f. 1994; cap. 125.0m., res 226.9m., dep. 1,980.7m. (Dec. 2002); Man. Dir Kuah Hun Liang.

EON Bank Bhd: Wisma Cyclecarri, 11th Floor, 288 Jalan Raja Laut, 50350 Kuala Lumpur; tel. (3) 26941188; fax (3) 26949588; e-mail eontsy@tm.net.my; internet www.eonbank.com.my; f. 1963; fmrly Kong Ming Bank Bhd; merged with Oriental Bank Bhd, Jan. 2001; cap. 1,329.8m., res 278.5m., dep. 17,757.8m. (Dec. 2002); Chair. Tan Sri Dato' Seri Mohamed Saleh bin Sulong; 46 brs.

Hong Leong Bank Bhd: Wisma Hong Leong, Level 3, 18 Jalan Perak, 50450 Kuala Lumpur; tel. (3) 21642828; fax (3) 27156365; internet www.hlb.com.my; f. 1905; fmrly MUI Bank Bhd; merged with Wah Tat Bank Bhd, Jan. 2001; cap. 1,433.2m., res 1,278.6m., dep. 22,097.4m. (June 2002); Chair. Tan Sri Quek Leng Chan; Man. Dir James Lim Cheng Poh; 72 brs.

HSBC Bank Malaysia Bhd (Hong Kong): 2 Leboh Ampang, POB 10244, 50912 Kuala Lumpur; tel. (3) 20700744; fax (3) 20702678; e-mail manager.public.affairs@hsbc.com.my; internet www.hsbc .com.my; f. 1860; fmrly Hongkong Bank Malaysia Bhd; adopted present name in 1999; cap. 114.5m., res 1,526.3m., dep. 20,342.3m. (Dec. 2001); Chair. Arman Mehta.

Malayan Banking Bhd (Maybank): Menara Maybank, 14th Floor, 100 Jalan Tun Perak, 50050 Kuala Lumpur; tel. (3) 20708833; fax (3) 20702611; e-mail publicaffairs@maybank.com.my; internet www.maybank2u.com; f. 1960; acquired Pacific Bank Bhd, Jan.

2001; merged with PhileoAllied Bank (Malaysia) Bhd, March 2001; cap. 3,550.2m., res 2,968.0m., dep. 96,978.2m. (June 2002); Chair. Tan Sri MOHAMED BASIR BIN AHMAD; Pres. and CEO Datuk AMIRSHAM A. AZIZ; 327 domestic brs, 30 overseas brs.

OCBC Bank (Malaysia) Bhd: Tingkat 1–8, Wisma Lee Rubber, Jalan Melaka, 50100 Kuala Lumpur; tel. (3) 26920344; fax (3) 26926518; internet www.ocbc.com.my; f. 1932; cap. 287.5m., res 1,624.0m., dep. 17,527.1m. (Dec. 2002); Chair. Tan Sri Dato' NASRUDDIN BAHARI; CEO ALBERT YEOH BEOW TIT; 25 brs.

Public Bank Bhd: Menara Public Bank, 146 Jalan Ampang, 50450 Kuala Lumpur; tel. (3) 21638888; fax (3) 21639917; internet www.publicbank.com.my; f. 1965; merged with Hock Hua Bank Bhd, March 2001; cap. 2,314.5m., res 3,381.7m., dep. 38,737.4m. (Dec. 2002); Chair. Tan Sri Dato' Dr TEH HONG PIOW; 216 domestic brs, 3 overseas brs.

RHB Bank Bhd: Towers Two and Three, RHB Centre, 426 Jalan Tun Razak, 50400 Kuala Lumpur; tel. (3) 92878888; fax (3) 92879000; e-mail md_ceo@rhbbank.com.my; internet www.rhbbank.com.my; formed in 1997 by a merger between DCB Bank Bhd and Kwong Yik Bank Bhd; acquired Sime Bank Bhd in mid-1999; merged with Bank Utama (Malaysia) Bhd, May 2003; cap. 3,318.1m., res 1,420.8m., dep. 38,994.4m. (June 2002); Chair. Dato' ALI BIN HASSAN; Man. Dir and CEO (vacant); 148 brs.

Southern Bank Bhd: Level 3, Menara Southern Bank, 83 Medan Setia Satu, Plaza Damamsara, Bukit Damansara, 50490 Kuala Lumpur; tel. (3) 2573000; fax (3) 3817200; e-mail info@sbbgroup.com.my; internet www.sbbgroup.com.my; f. 1963; merged with Ban Hin Lee Bank Bhd, July 2000; cap. 1,122.8m., res 883.1m., dep. 19,829.7m. (Dec. 2001); Chair. Tan Sri OSMAN S. CASSIM; CEO Dato' TAN TEONG HEAN; 105 domestic brs, 1 overseas br.

Standard Chartered Bank Malaysia Bhd: 1st Floor, 2 Jalan Ampang, 50450 Kuala Lumpur; tel. (3) 20726555; fax (3) 2010621; internet www.standardchartered.com.my.

United Overseas Bank (Malaysia) Bhd: Menara UOB, Jalan Raja Laut, POB 11212, 50450 Kuala Lumpur; tel. (3) 26927722; fax (3) 26981228; e-mail uobmtre@uob.com.my; internet www.uob.com.my; f. 1920; merged with Chung Khiaw Bank (Malaysia) Bhd in 1997 and with Overseas Union Bank (Malaysia) Bhd in 2002; cap. 470m., res 1,130.8m., dep. 15,174.1m. (Dec. 2002); Pres. WEE EE CHEONG; Dir and CEO FRANCIS LEE CHIN YONG; 25 brs.

Merchant Banks

Affin Merchant Bank Bhd: Menara Boustead, 27th Floor, 69 Jalan Raja Chulan, POB 1124, 50200 Kuala Lumpur; tel. (3) 2423700; fax (3) 2424982; e-mail general@affinmerchantbank.com.my; internet www.affinmerchantbank.com.my; f. 1970 as Permata Chartered Merchant Bank Bhd; name changed as above March 2001; cap. 187.5m., res 122.2m., dep. 1,519.3m. (Dec. 2001); Chair. Tan Sri YAACOB MOHAMED ZAIN; CEO Datin ZURAIDAH ATAN-SHARARIMAN.

Alliance Merchant Bank Bhd: Menara Multi-Purpose, 20th Floor, Capital Sq., 8 Jalan Munshi Abdullah, 50100 Kuala Lumpur; tel. (3) 26927788; fax (3) 26928787; e-mail ambb@alliancemerchant.com.my; internet www.alliancemerchant.com.my; f. 1974 as Amanah-Chase Merchant Bank Bhd; name changed as above Jan. 2001, following merger with Bumiputra Merchant Bankers Bhd; cap. 365.0m., res 54.3m., dep. 1,809.5m. (March 2003); Chair. Tan Sri ABU TALIB OTHMAN; Chief Exec. Dir T. JEYARATNAM.

AmMerchant Bank Bhd: 22nd Floor, Bangunan AmBank Group, 55 Jalan Raja Chulan, 50200 Kuala Lumpur; tel. (3) 20782644; fax (3) 20314891; e-mail customercare@ambg.com.my; internet www.ambg.com.my; f. 1975; fmrly Arab-Malaysian Merchant Bank Bhd; name changed as above 2002; cap. 300.0m., res 367.3m., dep. 11,372.0m. (March 2002); Chair. Tan Sri Dato' AZMAN HASHIM; Man. Dir CHEAH TEK KUANG; 4 brs.

Aseambankers Malaysia Bhd: Menara Maybank, 33rd Floor, 100 Jalan Tun Perak, 50050 Kuala Lumpur; tel. (3) 20591888; fax (3) 20784194; e-mail faudziah@aseam.com.my; internet www.aseam.com.my; f. 1973; cap. 50.1m., res 152.3m., dep. 2,962.2m. (June 2002); CEO and Dir AGIL NATT; Chair. Dato' MOHAMED BASIR AHMAD; 2 brs.

Commerce International Merchant Bankers Bhd: Bangunan CIMB, 10th Floor, Jalan Semantan, Damansara Heights, 50490 Kuala Lumpur; tel. (3) 2536688; fax (3) 2535522; e-mail info@cimb.com.my; f. 1974; cap. 319.2m., res 876.7m., dep. 6,774.6m. (Dec. 2002); Chair. Dato' MOHAMED NOR BIN MOHAMED YOUSOF.

Malaysian International Merchant Bankers Bhd: Wisma Cyclecarri, 21st Floor, 288 Jalan Raja Laut, 50350 Kuala Lumpur; tel. (3) 26910200; fax (3) 26948388; internet www.mimb.com.my; f. 1970; shareholders' funds 265m. (Dec. 2003); Chair. Dato' ZULKIFLI BIN ALI; 1 br.

Public Merchant Bank Bhd: 25th Floor, Menara Public Bank, 146 Jalan Ampang, 50450 Kuala Lumpur; tel. (3) 21669382; fax (3) 21669362; f. 1973 as Asian International Merchant Bankers Bhd; became Sime Merchant Bankers Bhd 1996; name changed as above 2000; cap. 165.0m., res –28.9m., dep. 1,086.6m. (Dec. 2002); Chair. Datuk ISMAIL BIN ZAKARIA.

RHB Sakura Merchant Bankers Bhd: Tower Three, 9th Floor, RHB Centre, 426 Jalan Tun Razak, 50400 Kuala Lumpur; tel. (3) 92873888; fax (3) 92878000; e-mail publicaffairs@rhb.com.my; internet www.rhb.com.my; f. 1974; cap. 338.6m., res 409.4m., dep. 2,735.4m. (June 2002); Chair. Datuk AZLAN ZAINOL; Man. Dir (vacant).

Southern Investment Bank Bhd: 11th Floor, Wisma Genting, Jalan Sultan Ismail, 50250 Kuala Lumpur; tel. (3) 20594188; fax (3) 20722964; e-mail sibb@sibb.com.my; internet www.sibb.com.my; f. 1988; fmrly Perdana Merchant Bankers Bhd; cap. 77.9m., res –32.2m., dep. 216.7m. (Dec. 2000); Chair. Dato' Nik IBRAHIM KAMIL; CEO YAP FAT (acting).

Utama Merchant Bank Bhd: Central Plaza, 27th Floor, Jalan Sultan Ismail, 50250 Kuala Lumpur; POB 12406, 50776 Kuala Lumpur; tel. (3) 21438888; fax (3) 21430357; e-mail umbb@umbb.po.my; internet www.cmsb.com.my/ubg; f. 1975 as Utama Wardley Bhd, name changed 1996; cap. 223.0m., res 63.6m., dep. 992.6m. (Dec. 1999); Chair. Nik HASHIM BIN Nik YUSOFF; CEO DONNY KWA SOO CHUAN; 1 br.

Co-operative Bank

Bank Kerjasama Rakyat Malaysia Berhad: Bangunan Bank Rakyat, Jalan Tangsi, Peti Surat 11024, 50732 Kuala Lumpur; tel. (3) 2985011; fax (3) 2985981; f. 1954; 83,095 mems. of which 823 were co-operatives (Dec. 1996); Chair. Dr YUSUF YACOB; Man. Dir Dato' ANUAR JAAFAR; 67 brs.

Development Banks

Bank Industri & Teknologi Malaysia Bhd (Industrial Development Bank of Malaysia): Level 28, Bangunan Bank Industri, Bandar Wawasan, 1016 Jalan Sultan Ismail, POB 10788, 50724 Kuala Lumpur; tel. (3) 26929088; fax (3) 26985701; e-mail pru@bankindustri.com.my; internet www.bankindustri.com.my; f. 1979; govt-owned; finances long-term, high-technology projects, shipping and shipyards and engineering (plastic, electrical and electronic); cap. 670.5m., res 10.1m., dep. 3,485.1m. (Dec. 2000); Chair. Tan Sri Dato' OTHMAN MOHD RIJAL; Man. Dir Encik MD NOOR YUSOFF.

Sabah Development Bank Bhd: SDB Tower, Wisma Tun Fuad Stephens, POB 12172, 88824 Kota Kinabalu, Sabah; tel. (88) 232177; fax (88) 261852; e-mail sdbank@po.jaring.my; internet www.borneo-online.com.my/sdb; f. 1977; wholly owned by State Government of Sabah; cap. 350m., res –135.2m., dep. 754.4m. (Dec. 2001); Chair. PETER SIAU; Man. Dir and CEO PETER LIM.

Islamic Banks

Bank Islam Malaysia Bhd: Darul Takaful, 14th Floor, Jalan Sultan Ismail, 50250 Kuala Lumpur; tel. (3) 26935842; fax (3) 26922153; e-mail bislam@po.jaring.my; internet www.bankislam.com.my; f. 1983; cap. 500m., res 527.2m., dep. 10,929.9m. (June 2002); Chair. Dato' MOHAMED YUSOFF BIN MOHAMED NASIR; Man. Dir Dato' Haji AHMAD TAJUDIN ABDUL RAHMAN; 83 brs.

Bank Muamalat Malaysia Bhd: Menara Bumiputra, 21 Jalan Melaka, 50913 Kuala Lumpur; tel. (3) 26988787; fax (3) 26910388; e-mail webmaster@muamalat.com.my; internet www.muamalat.com.my; f. 1999; CEO Tuan Haji MOHD SHUKRI HUSSIN; 40 brs.

'Offshore' Banks

ABN Amro Bank, Labuan Branch: Level 9 (A), Main Office Tower, Financial Park Labuan, Jalan Merdeka, 87000 Labuan; tel. (87) 423008; fax (87) 421078; Man. ANTHONY RAJAN.

Al-Hidayah Investment Bank (Labuan) Ltd: Level 7 (C), Main Office Tower, Financial Park Labuan, Jalan Merdeka, 87000 Labuan; tel. (87) 451660; fax (87) 583088.

AMInternational (L) Ltd: Level 12 (B), Block 4, Office Tower, Financial Park Labuan, Jalan Merdeka, 87000 Labuan; tel. (87) 413133; fax (87) 425211; e-mail felix-leong@ambg.com.my; internet www.ambg.com.my; CEO PAUL ONG WHEE SEN.

AmMerchant Bank Bhd, Labuan Branch: Level 12 (B), Block 4, Office Tower, Financial Park Labuan, Jalan Merdeka, 87000 Labuan; tel. (87) 413133; fax (87) 425211; Gen. Man. PAUL ONG WHEE SEN.

Bank Islam (L) Ltd: Level 15, Block 4, Office Tower Penthouse B, Financial Park Labuan, Jalan Merdeka, 87000 Labuan; tel. (87) 451802; fax (87) 451800; e-mail bislamln@tm.net.my; CEO MOHAMAD NAJIB SHAHARUDDIN.

Bank of America, National Trust and Savings Association, Labuan Branch: Level 13 (D), Main Office Tower, Financial Park Labuan, Jalan Merdeka, 87000 Labuan; tel. (87) 411778; fax (87) 424778; Gen. Man. Pengiran Nur Farhah Ooi Abdullah.

Bank of East Asia Ltd, Labuan Offshore Branch: Level 10 (C), Main Office Tower, Financial Park Labuan, Jalan Merdeka, 87000 Labuan; tel. (87) 451145; fax (87) 451148; e-mail bealbu@hkbea.com.my; Gen. Man. Thomas Wong Wai Yip.

Bank Muamalat Malaysia Bhd, Labuan Branch: Level 15 (A1), Main Office Tower, Financial Park Labuan, Jalan Merdeka, 87000 Labuan; tel. (87) 412898; fax (87) 451164; e-mail fuad@muamalat.com.my; Gen. Man. Zainol Rashid Khairuddin.

Bank of Nova Scotia, Labuan Branch: Level 10 (C2), Main Office Tower, Financial Park Labuan, Jalan Merdeka, 87000 Labuan; tel. (87) 451101; fax (87) 451099; Man. Kwan Sing Hung.

Bank of Tokyo-Mitsubishi Ltd, Labuan Branch: Level 12 (A & F), Main Office Tower, Financial Park Labuan, Jalan Merdeka, 87000 Labuan; tel. (87) 410487; fax (87) 410476; e-mail pulaubtm@tm.net.my; Gen. Man. Waturu Tanaka.

Barclays Bank PLC: Level 5(A), Main Office Tower, Financial Park Labuan, Jalan Merdeka, 87000 Labuan; tel. (87) 425571; fax (87) 425575; e-mail barclay@tm.net.my; Man. Miaw Siaw Loong.

Bayerische Landesbank Girozentrale, Labuan Branch: Level 14 (C), Block 4, Office Tower, Financial Park Labuan, Jalan Merdeka, 87000 Labuan; tel. (87) 422170; fax (87) 422175; e-mail blblab@tm.net.my; Exec. Vice-Pres., CEO and Gen. Man. Louise Paul.

BNP Paribas, Labuan Branch: Level 9 (E), Main Office Tower, Financial Park Labuan, Jalan Merdeka, 87000 Labuan; tel. (87) 422328; fax (87) 419328; e-mail bnpkul@tm.net.my; Gen. Man. Yap Siew Ying.

Bumiputra Commerce Bank (L) Ltd: Level 14 (B), Main Office Tower, Financial Park Labuan, Jalan Merdeka, 87000 Labuan; tel. (87) 410302; fax (87) 410313; e-mail bumitrst@tm.net.my; Gen. Man. Asaraf Abu Bakar.

Cathay United Bank, Labuan Branch: Level 3 (C), Main Office Tower, Financial Park Labuan, Jalan Merdeka, 87000 Labuan; tel. (87) 452168; fax (87) 453678; Gen. Man. Yeh Pin Hung.

CIMB (L) Ltd: Unit 11 (B1), Level 11, Main Office Tower, Financial Park Labuan, Jalan Merdeka, 87000 Labuan; tel. (87) 451608; fax (87) 451610; CEO Adha Amir Abdullah.

Citibank Malaysia (L) Ltd: Level 11 (F), Main Office Tower, Financial Park Labuan, Jalan Merdeka, 87000 Labuan; tel. (87) 421181; fax (87) 419671; Gen. Man. Clara Lim Ai Cheng.

City Credit Investment Bank Ltd: Level 11 (D1), Main Office Tower, Financial Park Labuan, Jalan Merdeka, 87000 Labuan; tel. (87) 582268; fax (87) 581268; Dir Abdul Rahman Abdullah.

Commercial IBT Bank, Labuan Branch: 02-01 2nd Floor, Wisma Lucas Kong, 40185 Jalan Merdeka, 87000 Labuan; tel. (87) 411868; fax (87) 416818; e-mail aong@cibtbank.com; Pres. Dir Dr Adrian Ong Chee Beng.

Commerzbank AG, Labuan Branch: Level 6 (E), Main Office Tower, Financial Park Labuan, Jalan Merdeka, 87000 Labuan; tel. (87) 416953; fax (87) 413542; Prin. Officer Ho Kah Heng.

Crédit Agricole Indosuez, Labuan Branch: Level 11 (C), Main Office Tower, Financial Park Labuan, Jalan Merdeka, 87000 Labuan; tel. (87) 425118; fax (87) 424998; Gen. Man. Boon Eong Tan.

Crédit Industriel et Commercial: Level 11 (C2), Main Office Tower, Financial Park Labuan, Jalan Merdeka, 87000 Labuan; tel. (87) 452008; fax (87) 452009; Gen. Man. Yeow Tiang Hui.

Crédit Lyonnais, Labuan Branch: Level 6 (B), Main Office Tower, Financial Park Labuan, Jalan Merdeka, 87000 Labuan; tel. (87) 408331; fax (87) 439133; Man. Clement Wong.

Crédit Suisse First Boston, Labuan Branch: Level 10 (B), Main Office Tower, Financial Park Labuan, Jalan Merdeka, 87000 Labuan; tel. (87) 425381; fax (87) 425384; Gen. Man. Rudolf Zaugg.

Danaharta Managers (L) Ltd: Tingkat 10, Bangunan Setia 1, 15 Lorong Dungun, Bukit Damansara, 50490 Kuala Lumpur; tel. (3) 2531122; fax (3) 2534375; Gen. Man. (vacant).

Deutsche Bank AG, Labuan Branch: Level 9 (G2), Main Office Tower, Financial Park Labuan, Jalan Merdeka, 87000 Labuan; tel. (87) 439811; fax (87) 439866; Man. Dir Kuah Hun Liang.

Development Bank of Singapore (DBS Bank) Ltd, Labuan Branch: Level 12 (E), Main Office Tower, Financial Park Labuan, Jalan Merdeka, 87000 Labuan; tel. (87) 423375; fax (87) 423376; Gen. Man. Kevin Wong.

Dresdner Bank AG, Labuan Branch: Level 13 (C), Main Office Tower, Financial Park Labuan, Jalan Merdeka, 87000 Labuan; tel. (87) 419271; fax (87) 419272; Gen. Man. Jamaludin Nasir.

ECM Libra Investment Bank Ltd: Level 3I (1), Main Office Tower, Financial Park Complex, Jalan Merdeka, 87000 Labuan; tel. (87) 408525; fax (87) 408527.

Hongkong & Shanghai Banking Corporation, Offshore Banking Unit: Level 11 (D), Main Office Tower, Financial Park Labuan, Jalan Merdeka, 87000 Labuan; tel. (87) 417168; fax (87) 417169; Man. Prem Kumar.

ING Bank NV: Level 8 (B2), Main Office Tower, Financial Park Labuan, Jalan Merdeka, 87000 Labuan; tel. (87) 425733; fax (87) 425734; Gen. Man. Milly Tan.

International Commercial Bank of China: Level 7 (E2), Main Office Tower, Financial Park Labuan, Jalan Merdeka, 87000 Labuan; tel. (87) 581688; fax (87) 581668; Gen. Man. Tai Chi-Hsien.

J. P. Morgan Chase Bank, Labuan Branch: Level 5 (F), Main Office Tower, Financial Park Labuan, Jalan Merdeka, 87000 Labuan; tel. (87) 424384; fax (87) 424390; e-mail fauziah.hisham@chase.com; Gen. Man. Leong Ket Ti.

J. P. Morgan Malaysia Ltd: Unit 5 (F), Level 5, Main Office Tower, Financial Park Labuan, Jalan Merdeka, 87000 Labuan; tel. (87) 459000; fax (87) 451328; Gen. Man. Leong Ket Ti.

KBC Bank NV, Labuan Branch: Level 3 (B), Main Office Tower, Financial Park Labuan, Jalan Merdeka, 87000 Labuan; tel. (87) 581778; fax (87) 583787; Gen. Man. Kong Kok Chee.

Lloyds TSB Bank PLC: Lot B, 11th Floor, Wisma Oceanic, Jalan OKK Awang Besar, 87007 Labuan; tel. (87) 418918; fax (87) 411928; e-mail labuan@lloydstsb.com.my; Dir and Gen. Man. Barry Francis Lea.

Macquarie Bank Ltd, Labuan Branch: Unit Level 3 (A), Main Office Tower, Financial Park Labuan, Jalan Merdeka, 87000 Labuan; tel. (87) 583080; fax (87) 583088; Division Dir Darren Woodward.

Maybank International (L) Ltd: Level 16 (B), Main Office Tower, Financial Park Labuan, Jalan Merdeka, 87000 Labuan; tel. (87) 414406; fax (87) 414806; e-mail millmit@tm.net.my; Gen. Man. Lam Hee.

Mizuho Corporate Bank Ltd, Labuan Branch: Level 9 (B and C), Main Office Tower, Financial Park Labuan, Jalan Merdeka, 87000 Labuan; tel. (87) 417766; fax (87) 419766; Gen. Man. Isaku Tanimura.

Natexis Banque Populaires: Level 9 (G), Main Office Tower, Financial Park Labuan, Jalan Merdeka, 87000 Labuan; tel. (87) 581009; fax (87) 583009; Gen. Man. Rizal Abdullah.

National Australia Bank, Labuan Branch: Level 12 (C2), Main Office Tower, Financial Park Complex, Jalan Merdeka, 87008 Labuan; tel. (87) 426386; fax (87) 428387; e-mail natausm@po.jaring.my; Gen. Man. Lionel Lim.

OSK Investment Bank (Labuan) Ltd: Lot 3B, Level 5, Wisma Lazenda, Jalan Kemajuan, Labuan; tel. (87) 581885; fax (87) 582885; Prin. Officer Ong Leong Huat.

Oversea-Chinese Banking Corporation Ltd, Labuan Branch: Level 8 (C), Main Office Tower, Financial Park Labuan, Jalan Merdeka, 87000 Labuan; tel. (87) 423381; fax (87) 423390; Gen. Man. Bernard Fernando.

Public Bank (L) Ltd: Level 8 (A and B), Main Office Tower, Financial Park Labuan, Jalan Merdeka, 87000 Labuan; tel. (87) 411898; fax (87) 413220; Man. Alexander Wong.

RHB Bank (L) Ltd: Level 15 (B), Main Office Tower, Financial Park Labuan, Jalan Merdeka, 87000 Labuan; tel. (87) 417480; fax (87) 417484; Gen. Man. Toh Ay Leng.

RUSD Investment Bank, Inc.: Level 4–A1, Main Office Tower, Financial Park Labuan, Jalan Merdeka, 87000 Labuan; tel. (87) 452100; fax (87) 543100; Man. Dir Naseeruddin A. Khan.

Société Générale, Labuan Branch: Level 11 (B), Main Office Tower, Financial Park Labuan, Jalan Merdeka, 87000 Labuan; tel. (87) 421676; fax (87) 421669; Gen. Man. Ramzan Abu Tahir.

Standard Chartered Bank Offshore Labuan: Level 10 (F), Main Office Tower, Financial Park Labuan, Jalan Merdeka, 87000 Labuan; tel. (87) 417200; fax (87) 417202; Gen. Man. Edward Ng.

Sumitomo Mitsui Banking Corpn, Labuan Branch: Level 12 (B and C), Main Office Tower, Financial Park Labuan, Jalan Merdeka, 87000 Labuan; tel. (87) 410955; fax (87) 410959; Gen. Man. Junichi Ikeno.

UBS AG, Labuan Branch: Level 5 (E), Main Office Tower, Financial Park Labuan Complex, Jalan Merdeka, 87000 Labuan; tel. (87) 421743; fax (87) 421746; Man. Zelie Ho Swee Lum.

UFJ Bank Ltd, Labuan Branch: Level 10 (D), Main Office Tower, Financial Park Labuan, Jalan Merdeka, 87000 Labuan; tel. (87) 419200; fax (87) 419202; Gen. Man. MASAYUKI KUNISHIGE.

United Overseas Bank Ltd, Labuan Branch: Level 6 (A), Main Office Tower, Financial Park Labuan, Jalan Merdeka, 87000 Labuan; tel. (87) 424388; fax (87) 424389; Gen. Man. HO FONG KUN.

United World Chinese Commercial Bank: Level 3 (C), Main Office Tower, Financial Park Labuan, Jalan Merdeka, 87000 Labuan; tel. (87) 452168; fax (87) 453678; Gen. Man. PIN HUNG YEH.

Banking Associations

Association of Banks in Malaysia (ABM): UBN Tower, 34th Floor, 10 Jalan P. Ramlee, 50250 Kuala Lumpur; tel. (3) 20788041; fax (3) 20788004; e-mail banks@abm.org.my; internet www.abm.org.my; f. 1973; Chair. Dr ROZALI BIN MOHAMED ALI; Exec. Dir WONG SUAN LYE.

Institute of Bankers Malaysia: Wisma IBI, 5 Jalan Semantan, Damansara Heights, 50490 Kuala Lumpur; tel. (3) 20956833; fax (3) 20952322; e-mail ibbm@ibbm.org.my; internet www.ibbm.org.my; Chair. Tan Sri Dato' Dr ZETI AKHTAR AZIZ.

Malayan Commercial Banks' Association: POB 12001, 50764 Kuala Lumpur; tel. (3) 2983991.

Persatuan Institusi Perbankan Tanpa Faedah Malaysia (Association of Islamic Banking Institutions Malaysia—AIBIM): Tingkat 9, Menara Tun Razak, Jalan Raja Laut, 50350 Kuala Lumpur; tel. (3) 26932936; fax (3) 26910453; e-mail secretariat@aibim.com.my; internet www.aibim.com.my.

STOCK EXCHANGES

Kuala Lumpur Stock Exchange (KLSE): Exchange Sq., Bukit Kewangan, 50200 Kuala Lumpur; tel. (3) 20267099; fax (3) 27102308; e-mail commsdept@klse.com.my; internet www.klse.com.my; f. 1973; in 1988 KLSE authorized the ownership of up to 49% of Malaysian stockbroking companies by foreign interests; 283 mems (April 2003); 921 listed cos (March 2004); merged with Malaysian Exchange for Securities Dealing and Automated Quotation Bhd (MESDAQ) in March 2002; Chair. MOHAMAD AZLAN HASHIM; Pres. Dato' MOHD SALLEH BIN ABDUL MAJID.

Malaysia Derivatives Exchange Bhd (MDEX): 10th Floor, Exchange Sq., Bukit Kewangan, 50200 Kuala Lumpur; tel. (3) 20708199; fax (3) 20702376; e-mail info@mdex.com.my; internet www.mdex.com.my; f. 2001 as a result of the merger of the Kuala Lumpur Options and Financial Futures Exchange Bhd (KLOFFE) and the Commodity and Monetary Exchange of Malaysia; multi-product futures exchange; Exec. Chair. Dato' ABDUL JABBAR BIN ABDUL MAJID; Gen. Man. RAGHBIR SINGH BHART.

Regulatory Authority

Securities Commission (SC): 3 Persiaran Bukit Kiara, Bukit Kiara, 50490 Kuala Lumpur; tel. (3) 62048000; fax (3) 62015078; e-mail cau@seccom.com.my; internet www.sc.com.my; f. 1993; Chair. Datuk ALI ABDUL KADIR.

INSURANCE

From 1988 onwards, all insurance companies were placed under the authority of the Central Bank, Bank Negara Malaysia. In 1997 there were 69 insurance companies operating in Malaysia; nine reinsurance companies, 11 composite, 40 general and life and two takaful insurance companies.

Principal Insurance Companies

Allianz General Insurance Malaysia Bhd: Wisma UOA II, Floors 23 and 23A, 21 Jalan Pinang, 50450 Kuala Lumpur; tel. (3) 21623388; fax (3) 21626387; e-mail partner@allianz.com.my; internet www.allianz.com.my; f. 2001; CEO WILLIAM MEI YORK LIANG; Chair. Tan Sri RAZALI ISMAIL.

Allianz Life Insurance Malaysia Bhd: Wisma UOA II, Floors 23 and 23A, 21 Jalan Pinang, 50450 Kuala Lumpur; tel. (3) 21623388; fax (3) 21626387; e-mail partner@allianz.com.my; internet life.allianz.com.my; fmrly MBA Life Assurance Sdn Bhd; Chief Financial Officer CHARLES ONG ENG CHOW.

Asia Insurance Co Ltd: Bangunan Asia Insurance, 2 Jalan Raja Chulan, 50200 Kuala Lumpur; tel. (3) 2302511; fax (3) 2323606; f. 1923; general.

Capital Insurance Bhd: 38 Jalan Ampang, POB 12338, 50774 Kuala Lumpur; tel. (3) 2308033; fax (3) 2303657; Gen. Man. MOHD YUSOF IDRIS.

Commerce Life Assurance Bhd: 338 Jalan Tunku Abdul Rahman, 50100 Kuala Lumpur; tel. (3) 26123600; fax (3) 26987035; internet www.xlife.com.my; f. 1992 as AMAL Assurance Bhd; name changed as above in 1999.

Great Eastern Life Assurance (Malaysia) Bhd: Menara Great Eastern, 303 Jalan Ampang, 50450 Kuala Lumpur; tel. (3) 42598888; fax (3) 42590500; e-mail wecare@lifeisgreat.com.my; internet www.lifeisgreat.com.my; Dir and CEO ALEX FOONG SOO HAH.

John Hancock Life Insurance (Malaysia) Bhd: Menara John Hancock, 12th Floor, 6 Jalan Gelenggang, Damansara Heights, 50490 Kuala Lumpur; tel. (3) 20948055; fax (3) 20935487; internet www.jhancock.com.my; f. 1963; life and non-life insurance; fmrly British American Life and General Insurance Bhd; Chair. Tan Sri Dato' Haji YAHYA BIN ABDUL WAHAB; Man. Dir KHOR HOCK SENG.

Hong Leong Assurance Sdn Bhd: Menara HLA, 26th Floor, Jalan Kia Peng, 50450 Kuala Lumpur; tel. (3) 76501818; fax (3) 27101735; internet www.hla.com.my; Chair. Tan Sri QUEK LENG CHAN.

ING Insurance Bhd: Menara ING, 84 Jalan Raja Chulan, POB 10846, 50927 Kuala Lumpur; tel. (3) 21617255; fax (3) 21610549; internet www.ing.com.my; f. 1987; fmrly Aetna Universal Insurance Bhd; Chair. Tengku ABDULLAH IBNI AL-MARHUM Sultan ABU BAKAR.

Jerneh Insurance Corpn Sdn Bhd: Wisma Jerneh, 12th Floor, 38 Jalan Sultan Ismail, POB 12420, 50788 Kuala Lumpur; tel. (3) 2427066; fax (3) 2426672; f. 1970; general; Gen. Man. GOH CHIN ENG.

Malaysia National Insurance Sdn Bhd: Tower 1, 26th Floor, MNI Twins, 11 Jalan Pinang, 50450 Kuala Lumpur; tel. (3) 21769000; fax (3) 21769090; internet www.mni.com.my; f. 1970; life and general; CEO MOHAMED NAJIB ABDULLAH.

Malaysian Co-operative Insurance Society Ltd: Wisma MCIS, Jalan Barat, 46200 Petaling Jaya, Selangor; tel. (3) 7552577; fax (3) 7571563; e-mail info@mcis.po.my; internet www.mcis.com.my/mcis; f. 1954; CEO L. MEYYAPPAN.

Mayban Assurance Bhd: Mayban Assurance Tower, Dataran Maybank, 1 Jalan Maarof, 50000 Kuala Lumpur; tel. (3) 22972888; fax (3) 22972828; e-mail mayassur@tm.net.my; internet www.maybank2u.com.my; Chair. Tan Sri MOHAMED BASIR AHMAD.

MBf Insurans Sdn Bhd: Plaza MBf, 5th Floor, Jalan Ampang, POB 10345, 50710 Kuala Lumpur; tel. (3) 2613466; fax (3) 2613466; Man. MARC HOOI TUCK KOK.

MCIS Zürich Insurance Bhd: Wisma MCIS Zürich, Jalan Barat, 46200 Petaling Jaya, Selangor; tel. (3) 79552577; fax (3) 79574780; e-mail info@mciszurich.com.my; internet www.mciszurich.com.my; CEO Datuk L. MEYYAPPAN; Chair. Dato' MOHAMAD WAHIDUDDIN BIN ABDUL WAHAB.

Multi-Purpose Insurans Bhd: Menara Multi-Purpose, 9th Floor, Capital Square, 8 Jalan Munshi Abdullah, 50100 Kuala Lumpur; tel. (3) 26919888; fax (3) 26945758; e-mail info@mpib.com.my; fmrly Kompas Insurans Bhd; Senior Gen. Mans WONG FOOK WAH, VISWANATH A. L. KANDASAMY.

Overseas Assurance Corpn Ltd: Wisma Lee Rubber, 21st Floor, Jalan Melata, 50100 Kuala Lumpur; tel. (3) 2022939; fax (3) 2912288; Gen. Man. A. K. WONG.

Progressive Insurance Sdn Bhd: Plaza Berjaya, 9th, 10th and 15th Floors, 12 Jalan Imbi, POB 10028, 50700 Kuala Lumpur; tel. (3) 2410044; fax (3) 2418257; Man. JERRY PAUT.

RHB Insurance Bhd: Tower 1, 4th Floor, RHB Centre, Jalan Tun Razak, 50450 Kuala Lumpur; tel. (3) 9812731; fax (3) 9812729; Man. MOHAMMAD ABDULLAH.

Sime AXA Assurance Bhd: Wisma Sime Darby, 15th Floor, Jalan Raja Laut, 50350 Kuala Lumpur; tel. (3) 2937888; fax (3) 2914672; e-mail hkkang@simenet.com; Gen. Man. HAK KOON KANG.

South-East Asia Insurance Bhd: Tingkat 9, Menara SEA Insurance, 1008 Jalan Sultan Ismail, 50250 Kuala Lumpur; POB 6120 Pudu, 55916 Kuala Lumpur; tel. (3) 2938111; fax (3) 2930111; internet www.sea.com.my; CEO HASHIM HARUN.

UMBC Insurans Sdn Bhd: Bangunan Sime Bank, 16th Floor, Jalan Sultan Sulaiman, 50000 Kuala Lumpur; tel. (3) 2328733; fax (3) 2322181; f. 1961; CEO ABDULLAH ABDUL SAMAD.

United Oriental Assurance Sdn Bhd: Wisma UOA, 36 Jalan Ampang, 50450 Kuala Lumpur; tel. (3) 2302828; fax (3) 2324250; e-mail uoa@uoa.po.my; f. 1976; CEO R. NESARETNAM.

Trade and Industry

GOVERNMENT AGENCIES

Danamodal Nasional Bhd (Danamodal): 10th Floor, Bangunan Sime Bank, Jalan Sultan Sulaiman, 50000 Kuala Lumpur; tel. (3) 20312255; fax (3) 20310786; e-mail info@danamodal.com.my; internet www.bnm.gov.my/danamodal/main2bck.htm; f. 1998 to recapitalize banks and restructure financial institutions, incl.

arranging mergers and consolidations; Man. Dir MARIANUS VONG SHIN TZOI; Chair. Raja Datuk ARSHAD Raja Tun UDA.

Federal Agricultural Marketing Authority (FAMA): Bangunan Fama Point, Lot 17304, Jalan Persiaran 1, Bandar Baru Selayang, 68100 Batu Caves, Selangor Darul Ehsan; tel. (3) 61389622; fax (3) 61365597; internet agrolink.moa.my/fama; f. 1965 to supervise, co-ordinate and improve marketing of agricultural produce, and to seek and promote new markets and outlets for agricultural produce; Chair. AZIZI MEOR NGAH; Dir-Gen. HARON A. RAHIM.

Federal Land Development Authority (FELDA): Jalan Maktab, 54000 Kuala Lumpur; tel. (3) 2935066; fax (3) 2920087; f. 1956; govt statutory body formed to develop land into agricultural smallholdings to eradicate rural poverty; 893,150 ha of land developed (1994); involved in rubber, oil palm and sugar-cane cultivation; Chair. Raja Tan Sri MUHAMMAD ALIAS; Dir-Gen. MOHAMED FADZIL YUNUS.

Khazanah Nasional: 21 Putra Place 100, Ilu Putra, 50350 Kuala Lumpur; e-mail knb@po.jaring.my; f. 1994; state-controlled investment co; assumed responsibility for certain assets fmrly under control of the Minister of Finance Inc.; holds 40% of Telekom Malaysia Bhd, 40% of Tenaga Nasional Bhd, 6.6% of HICOM Bhd and 17.8% of PROTON; Chair. Datuk Seri Dr MAHATHIR MOHAMAD.

Malaysia Export Credit Insurance Bhd: Bangunan Bank Industri, 17th Floor, Bandar Wawsan, 1016 Jalan Sultan Ismail, POB 11048, 50734 Kuala Lumpur; tel. (3) 26910677; fax (3) 26910353; e-mail mecib@mecib.com.my; internet www.mecib.com.my; f. 1977; wholly owned subsidiary of Bank Industri Malaysia Technologi Bhd; provides insurance, financial guarantee and other trade-related services for exporters of locally manufactured products and for banking community; cap. RM 150m., exports declared RM 1,020m. (2003); Gen. Man. EN. AMINURRASHID ZULKIFLY; 67 employees.

Malaysia External Trade Development Corpn (MATRADE): Wisma Sime Darby, Jalan Raja Laut, 50350 Kuala Lumpur; tel. (3) 26947259; fax (3) 26947362; e-mail info@hq.matrade.gov.my; internet www.matrade.gov.my; f. 1993; responsibility for external trade development and promotion; CEO MERLYN KASIMIR.

Malaysian Institute of Economic Research: Menara Dayabumi, 9th Floor, Jalan Sultan Hishamuddin, POB 12160, 50768 Kuala Lumpur; tel. (3) 22725897; fax (3) 22730197; e-mail Admin@mier.po.my; internet www.mier.org.my; Exec. Dir MOHAMED ARIFF.

Malaysian Palm Oil Board (MPOB): Lot 6, SS6, Jalan Perbandaran, 47301 Kelana Jaya, Selangor; tel. (3) 7035544; fax (3) 7033533; internet porla.gov.my; f. 2000 by merger of Palm Oil Registration and Licensing Authority and Palm Oil Research Institute of Malaysia; Dir-Gen. Dato' MOHD YUSOF BASIR.

Malaysian Timber Industry Board (Lembaga Perindustrian Kayu Malaysia): 13–17 Menara PGRM, Jalan Pudu Ulu, POB 10887, 50728 Kuala Lumpur; tel. (3) 9822235; fax (3) 9851477; e-mail mtib@po.jaring.my; internet www.gov.my; f. 1968 to promote and regulate the export of timber and timber products from Peninsular Malaysia; Chair. Dato' Dr Haji ABDULLAH BIN MOHD TAHIR; Dir-Gen. Dato' Haji ABDUL RASHID MAT AMIN.

Muda Agricultural Development Authority (MADA): MADA HQ, Ampang Jajar, 05990 Alor Setar, Kedah; tel. (4) 7728255; fax (4) 7722667; internet www.mada.gov.my; Chair. Dato' Seri SYED RAZAK BIN SYED ZAIN.

National Economic Action Council: NEAC-MTEN, Office of the Minister of Special Functions, Level 2, Block B5, Federal Government Administrative Centre, 62502 Putrajaya, Selangor Darul Ehsan; tel. (88) 883333; internet www.neac.gov.my/; Exec. Dir Dato' MUSTAPA MOHAMED.

National Information Technology Council (NITC): Kuala Lumpur; Sec. Datuk Tengku Dr MOHD AZZMAN SHARIFFADEEN.

National Timber Certification Council: Kuala Lumpur; Chair. CHEW LYE TENG.

Pengurusan Danaharta Nasional Bhd (Danaharta): Tingkat 10, Bangunan Setia 1, 15 Lorong Dungun, Bukit Damansara, 50490 Kuala Lumpur; tel. (3) 20931122; fax (3) 20934360; internet www.danaharta.com.my; f. 1998 to acquire non-performing loans from the banking sector and to maximize the recovery value of those assets; Man. Dir ZUKRI SAMAT.

Perbadanan Nasional Bhd (PERNAS): Kuala Lumpur; tel. (3) 2935177; f. 1969; govt-sponsored; promotes trade, banking, property and plantation development, construction, mineral exploration, steel manufacturing, inland container transportation, mining, insurance, industrial development, engineering services, telecommunication equipment, hotels and shipping; cap. p.u. RM 116.25m.; 10 wholly owned subsidiaries, over 60 jointly owned subsidiaries and 18 assoc. cos; Chair. Tunku Dato' SHAHRIMAN BIN Tunku SULAIMAN; Man. Dir Dato' A. RAHMAN BIN HAMIDON.

DEVELOPMENT ORGANIZATIONS

Fisheries Development Authority of Malaysia: 7th—11th Floors, Wisma PKNS, Jalan Raja Laut, 50784 Kuala Lumpur; tel. (3) 26177000; fax (3) 26911931; e-mail info@kim.moa.my; internet agrolink.moa.my/lkim; Dir-Gen. Dato' Sheikh AHMAD BIN Sheikh LONG.

Johor Corporation: 13th Floor, Menara Johor Corporation, Kotaraya, 80000 Johor Bahru; tel. (7) 2232692; fax (7) 2233175; e-mail pdnjohor@jcorp.com.my; internet www.jcorp.com.my; development agency of the Johor state govt; Chief Exec. Dato' H. MUHAMMAD ALI.

Kumpulan FIMA Bhd (Food Industries of Malaysia): Kompleks FIMA, International Airport, Subang, Selangor; tel. (3) 7462199; f. 1972; fmrly govt corpn, transferred to private sector in 1991; promotes food and related industry through investment on its own or by co-ventures with local or foreign entrepreneurs; oil palm, cocoa and fruit plantation developments; manufacturing and packaging, trading, supermarkets and restaurants; Man. Dir Dato' MOHD NOOR BIN ISMAIL; 1,189 employees.

Majlis Amanah Rakyat (MARA) (Trust Council for the People): Bangunan Medan MARA, 13th Floor, 21 Jalan Raja Laut, 50609 Kuala Lumpur; tel. (3) 26915111; fax (3) 26913620; internet www.mara.gov.my; f. 1966 to promote, stimulate, facilitate and undertake economic and social development; to participate in industrial and commercial undertakings and jt ventures; Chair. Tan Sri NAZRI AZIZ.

Malaysian Agricultural Research and Development Institute (MARDI): POB 12301, General Post Office, 50774 Kuala Lumpur; tel. (3) 89437111; fax (3) 89483664; e-mail saharan@mardi.my; internet www.mardi.my; f. 1969; research and development in food and tropical agriculture; Dir-Gen. Dr SAHARAN BIN Haji ANANG.

Malaysian Industrial Development Authority (MIDA): Wisma Damansara, 6th Floor, Jalan Semantan, POB 10618, 50720 Kuala Lumpur; tel. (3) 2553633; fax (3) 2557970; e-mail promotion@mida.gov.my; internet www.mida.gov.my; f. 1967; Chair. Tan Sri Datuk ZAINAL ABIDIN BIN SULONG; Dir-Gen. Dato' ZAINUN AISHAH AHMAD.

Malaysian Industrial Development Finance Bhd: Bangunan MIDF, 195A Jalan Tun Razak, 50400 Kuala Lumpur; tel. (3) 21610066; fax (3) 21615973; e-mail inquiry@midf.com.my; internet www.midf.com.my; f. 1960 by the Govt, banks, insurance cos; industrial financing, advisory services, project development, merchant and commercial banking services; Man. Dir Dato' MOHAMED SALLEHUDDIN BIN OTHMAN.

Malaysian Pepper Marketing Board: Tanah Putih, POB 1653, 93916 Kuching; tel. (82) 331811; fax (82) 336877; e-mail pmb@pepper.po.my; internet www.sarawakpepper.gov.my/sarawakpepper; f. 1972; responsible for the statutory grading of all Sarawak pepper for export, licensing of pepper dealers and exporters, trading and the development and promotion of pepper grading, storage and processing facilities; Gen. Man. GRUNSIN AYOM.

Pinang Development Corporation: 1 Pesiaran Mahsuri, Bandar Bayan Baru, 11909 Bayan Lepas, Pinang; tel. (4) 6340111; fax (4) 6432405; e-mail enquiry@pdc.gov.my; internet www.pdc.gov.my; f. 1969; development agency of the Pinang state government; Chair. Tan Sri Dr KOH TSU KOON.

Sarawak Economic Development Corpn: Menara SEDC, 6th–11th Floors, Sarawak Plaza, Jalan Tunku Abdul Rahman, POB 400, 93902 Kuching; tel. (82) 416777; fax (82) 424330; e-mail ssedc@pop1.jaring.my; internet www.sedc.com.my; f. 1972; statutory org. responsible for commercial and industrial development in Sarawak either solely or jtly with foreign and local entrepreneurs; responsible for the development of tourism infrastructure; Chair. Datuk Haji TALIB ZULPILIP.

Selangor State Development Corporation (PKNS): Persiaran Barat, off Jalan Barat, 46505 Petaling Jaya, Selangor; tel. (3) 79572955; fax (3) 79575250; e-mail general@pkns.gov.my; internet www.pkns.gov.my; f. 1964; partially govt-owned; Corporate Man. YUSOF OTHMAN.

CHAMBERS OF COMMERCE

The Associated Chinese Chamber of Commerce: Wisma Chamber, 4th Floor, Lot 214, Jalan Bukit Mata, 93100 Kuching; tel. (82) 428815; fax (82) 429950; e-mail kcjong@pc.jaring.my; f. 1965; Pres. TIONG SU KOUK; Sec. Gen. LEE KHIM SIN.

Associated Chinese Chambers of Commerce and Industry of Malaysia: 8th Floor, Office Tower, Plaza Berjaya, 12 Jalan Imbi, 55100 Kuala Lumpur; tel. (3) 2452503; fax (3) 2452562; e-mail acccim@mol.net.my; internet www.acccim.org.my; Pres. Dato' LIM GUAN TEIK; Exec. Sec. ONG KIM SENG.

Malay Chamber of Commerce Malaysia: Plaza Pekeliling, 17th Floor, Jalan Tun Razak, 50400 Kuala Lumpur; tel. (3) 4418522; fax

(3) 4414502; f. 1957 as Associated Malay Chambers of Commerce of Malaya; name changed as above 1992; Pres. Tan Sri Dato' TAJUDIN RAMLI; Sec.-Gen. ZAKI SAID.

Malaysian Associated Indian Chambers of Commerce and Industry: 116 Jalan Tuanku Abdul Rahman, 2nd Floor, 50100 Kuala Lumpur; tel. (3) 26931033; fax (3) 26911670; e-mail klsicci@po .jaring.my; internet www.maicci.com; f. 1950; Pres. Dato' K. KENNETH ESWARAN; Hon. Sec.-Gen. MUTHUSAMY V. V. M. SAMY; 8 brs.

Malaysian International Chamber of Commerce and Industry (MICCI) (Dewan Perniagaan dan Perindustrian Antarabangsa Malaysia): C-8-8, 8th Floor, Block C, Plaza Mont' Kiara, 50480 Kuala Lumpur; tel. (3) 62017708; fax (3) 62017705; e-mail micci@micci.com; internet www.micci.com; f. 1837; brs in Pinang, Perak, Johor, Melaka and Sabah; 1,100 corporate mems; Pres. P. J. DINGLE; Exec. Dir STEWART J. FORBES.

National Chamber of Commerce and Industry of Malaysia: 37 Jalan Kia Peng, 50450 Kuala Lumpur; tel. (3) 2419600; fax (3) 2413775; e-mail nccim@po.jaring.my; internet www.nccim.org.my/ nccim; f. 1962; Pres. Tan Sri TAJUDIN RAMLI; Sec.-Gen. Dato' ABDUL HALIM ABDULLAH.

Sabah Chamber of Commerce and Industry: Jalan Tiga, Sandakan; tel. (89) 2141; Pres. T. H. WONG.

Sarawak Chamber of Commerce and Industry (SCCI): POB A-841, Kenyalang Park Post Office, 93806 Kuching; tel. (82) 237148; fax (82) 237186; e-mail phtay@pc.jaring.my; internet www.cmsb .com.my/scci; f. 1950; Chair. Datuk Haji MOHAMED AMIN Haji SATEM; Dep. Chair. Datuk Abang Haji ABDUL KARIM Tun Abang Haji OPENG.

South Indian Chamber of Commerce of Sarawak: 37C India St, Kuching; f. 1952; Pres. HAJA NAZIMUDDIN BIN ABDUL MAJID; Vice-Pres. SYED AHMAD.

INDUSTRIAL AND TRADE ASSOCIATIONS

Federation of Malaysian Manufacturers: Wisma FMM, 3 Persiaran Dagang, PJU 9 Bandar Sri Damansara, 52200 Kuala Lumpur; tel. (3) 62761211; fax (3) 62741266; e-mail webmaster@ fmm.org.my; internet www.fmm.org.my; f. 1968; 2,145 mems (Jan. 2004); Pres. JEN (B.) Dato' MUSTAFA MANSUR; CEO LEE CHENG SUAN.

Federation of Rubber Trade Associations of Malaysia: 138 Jalan Bandar, 50000 Kuala Lumpur; tel. (3) 2384006.

Malayan Agricultural Producers' Association: Kuala Lumpur; tel. (3) 42573988; fax (3) 42573113; f. 1997; 464 mem. estates and 115 factories; Pres. Tan Sri Dato' Haji BASIR BIN ISMAIL; Dir MOHAMAD BIN AUDONG.

Malaysian Iron and Steel Industry Federation: 28E, 30E, 5th Floor, Block 2, Worldwide Business Park, Jalan Tinju 13/50, Section 13, 40675 Shah Alam, Selangor; tel. (3) 55133970; fax (3) 55133891; e-mail misif@po.jaring.my; Chair. Tan Sri Dato' SOONG SIEW HOONG; 150 mems.

Malaysian Oil Palm Growers' Council: Bangunan Getah Asli I, 3rd Floor, 148 Jalan Ampang, POB 10747, 50724 Kuala Lumpur; tel. (3) 2615088; fax (3) 2612504; f. 1953.

Malaysian Pineapple Industry Board: Wisma Nanas, 5 Jalan Padi Mahsuri, Bandar Baru UDA, 81200 Johor Bahru; tel. (7) 2361211; fax (7) 2365694; e-mail mpib@tm.net.my; Dir-Gen. Tuan Haji ISMAIL BIN ABD JAMAL.

Malaysian Rubber Products Manufacturers' Association: 1 Jalan USJ 11/1J, Subang Jaya, 47620 Petaling Jaya, Selangor; tel. (3) 56316150; fax (3) 56316152; e-mail mrpma@po.jaring.my; internet www.mrpma.com; f. 1952; Pres. Tan Sri Datuk ARSHAD AYUB; 144 mems.

Malaysian Rubber Board: 148 Jalan Ampang, 50450 Kuala Lumpur; tel. (3) 92062000; fax (3) 21634492; e-mail dg@lgm.gov.my; internet www.lgm.gov.my; f. 1998; implements policies and development programmes to ensure the viability of the Malaysian rubber industry; regulates the industry (in particular, the packing, grading, shipping and export of rubber); Dir-Gen. Dato' ABDUL HAMID BIN SAWAL.

Malaysian Wood Industries Association: 19B, 19th Floor, Menara PGRM, 8 Jalan Pudu Ulu, Cheras, 56100 Kuala Lumpur; tel. (3) 92821778; fax (3) 92821779; e-mail mwia@tm.net.my; f. 1957.

National Tobacco Board Malaysia (Ibu Pejabat Lembaga Tembakau Negara): Kubang Kerian, POB 198, 15720 Kota Bharu, Kelantan; tel. (9) 7652933; fax (9) 7655640; e-mail ltnm@ltn.gov.my; Dir-Gen. TEO HUI BEK.

Northern Malaya Rubber Millers and Packers Association: 22 Pitt St, 3rd Floor, Suites 301–303, 10200 Pinang; tel. (4) 620037; f. 1919; 153 mems; Pres. HWANG SING LUE; Hon. Sec. LEE SENG KEOK.

Palm Oil Refiners' Association of Malaysia (PORAM): Kuala Lumpur; tel. (3) 2488893; f. 1975 to promote the palm oil refining industry; Chair. Datuk ROBERT W. K. CHAN; 27 mems.

Rubber Industry Smallholders' Development Authority (RISDA): 4½ Miles, Jalan Ampang, 50450 Kuala Lumpur; tel. (3) 4564022; Dir-Gen. MOHD ZAIN bin Haji YAHYA.

Tin Industry Research and Development Board: West Block, 8th Floor, Wisma Selangor Dredging, Jalan Ampang, POB 12560, 50782 Kuala Lumpur; tel. (3) 21616171; fax (3) 21616179; e-mail mcom@po.jaring.my; Chair. MOHAMED AJIB ANUAR; Sec. MUHAMAD NOR MUHAMAD.

EMPLOYERS' ORGANIZATIONS

Malaysian Employers' Federation: 3A06–3A07, Block A, Pusat Dagangan Phileo Damansara II, 15 Jalan 16/11, off Jalan Damansara, 46350 Petaling Jaya, Selangor; tel. (3) 79557778; fax (3) 79559008; e-mail mef-hq@mef.po.my; internet www.mef.org.my; f. 1959; Pres. JAFAR ABDUL CARRIM; private-sector org. incorporating 10 employer organizations and 3,447 individual enterprises, including:

Association of Insurance Employers: c/o Royal Insurance (M) Sdn Bhd, Menara Boustead, 5th Floor, 69 Jalan Raja Chulan, 50200 Kuala Lumpur; tel. (3) 2410233; fax (3) 2442762; Pres. NG KIM HOONG.

Commercial Employers' Association of Peninsular Malaysia: c/o The East Asiatic Co (M) Bhd, 1 Jalan 205, 46050 Petaling Jaya, Selangor; tel. (3) 7913322; fax (3) 7913561; Pres. HAMZAH Haji GHULAM.

Malayan Commercial Banks' Association: see Banking Associations, above.

Malaysian Chamber of Mines: West Block, Wisma Selangor Dredging, 8th Floor, Jalan Ampang, 50350 Kuala Lumpur; tel. and fax (3) 21616171; e-mail mcom@po.jaring.my; internet www .mcom.com.my; f. 1914; promotes and protects interests of Malaysian mining industry; Pres. Ir ABDUL RAHMAN DAHAN; Exec. Dir MUHAMAD NOR MUHAMAD.

Malaysian Textile Manufacturers' Association: Wisma Selangor Dredging, 9th Floor, West Block, 142C Jalan Ampang, 50450 Kuala Lumpur; tel. (3) 21621587; fax (3) 21623953; e-mail textile@po.jaring.my; internet www.fashion-asia.com; Pres. BAHAR AHMAD; Exec. Dir CHOY MING BIL; 230 mems.

Pan Malaysian Bus Operators' Association: 88 Jalan Sultan Idris Shah, 30300 Ipoh, Perak; tel. (5) 2549421; fax (5) 2550858; Sec. Datin TEOH PHAIK LEAN.

Sabah Employers' Consultative Association: Dewan SECA, No. 4, Block A, 1st Floor, Bandar Ramai-Ramai, 90000 Sandakan, Sabah; tel. and fax (89) 272846; Pres. E. M. KHOO.

Stevedore Employers' Association: 5 Pengkalan Weld, POB 288, 10300 Pinang; tel. (4) 2615091; Pres. ABDUL RAHMAN MAIDIN.

UTILITIES

Electricity

Energy Commission of Malaysia: Levels 15, 19 and 20, Menara Dato' Onn, Putra World Centre, Jalan Tun Ismail, Kuala Lumpur; internet www.st.gov.my; f. 2002; regulatory body supervising electricity and gas supply.

Tenaga Nasional Bhd: 129 Jalan Bangsar, POB 11003, 50732 Kuala Lumpur; tel. (3) 2825566; fax (3) 2823274; e-mail webadmin@ tnb.com.my; internet www.tnb.com.my; f. 1990 through the corporatization and privatization of the National Electricity Board; 53% govt-controlled; generation, transmission and distribution of electricity in Peninsular Malaysia; generating capacity of 7,573 MW (65% of total power generation); also purchases power from 12 licensed independent power producers; Chair. JAMALUDDIN JARIS; CEO Dato' FUAD B. JAAFAR (acting).

Sabah Electricity Board (SEB): Wisma Lembaga Letrik Sabah, 88673 Kota Kinabalu; tel. (88) 211699; generation, transmission and distribution of electricity in Sabah.

Sarawak Electricity Supply Corpn (SESCO): POB 149, Kuching, Sarawak; tel. (82) 441188; fax (82) 444434; internet www .sesco.com.my; generation, transmission and distribution of electricity in Sarawak.

Gas

Energy Commission of Malaysia: see above.

Gas Malaysia Sdn Bhd: 5 Jalan Serendah 26/17, Seksyen 26, Peti Surat 7901, 40732 Shah Alam, Selangor Darul Ehsan; tel. (3) 51923000; e-mail ccu@gasmalaysia.com; internet www.gasmalaysia .com; f. 1992; Chair. Tan Sri Datuk Dr AHMAD TAJUDDIN ALI; CEO MUHAMAD NOOR HAMID.

Water

Under the federal Constitution, water supply is the responsibility of the state Governments. In 1998, owing to water shortages, the National Water Resources Council was established to co-ordinate management of water resources at national level. Malaysia's sewerage system is operated by Indah Water Konsortium, owned by Prime Utilities.

National Water Resources Council: c/o Ministry of Works, Jalan Sultan Salahuddin, 50580 Kuala Lumpur; tel. (3) 2919011; fax (3) 2986612; f. 1998 to co-ordinate management of water resources at national level through co-operation with state water boards; Chair. Dato' Seri Dr MAHATHIR BIN MOHAMAD.

Regulatory Authorities

Johor State Regulatory Body: c/o Pejabat Setiausaha Kerajaan Negeri Johor, Aras 1, Bangunan Sultan Ibrahim, Jalan Bukit Timbalan, 80000 Johor Bahru; tel. (7) 223850; Dir Tuan Haji OMAR BIN AWAB.

Kelantan Water Department: Tingkat Bawah Blok 6, Kota Darul Naim, 15503 Kota Bahru, Kelantan; tel. (9) 7475240; Dir Tuan Haji WAN ABDUL AZIZ BIN WAN JAAFAR.

Water Supply Authorities

Kedah Public Works Department: Bangunan Sultan Abdul Halim, Jalan Sultan Badlishah, 05582 Alor Setar, Kedah; tel. (4) 7334041; fax (4) 7341616; Dir Dr NORDIN BIN YUNUS.

Kelantan Water Sdn Bhd: 14 Beg Berkunci, Jalan Kuala Krai, 15990 Kota Bahru, Kelantan; tel. (10) 9022222; fax (10) 9022236; Dir PETER NEW BERKLEY.

Kuching Water Board: Jalan Batu Lintang, 93200 Kuching, Sarawak; tel. (82) 240371; fax (82) 244546; Dir DAVID YEU BIN TONG.

Labuan Public Works Department: Jalan Kg. Jawa, POB 2, 87008 Labuan; tel. (87) 414040; fax (87) 412370; Dir Ir ZULKIFLY BIN MADON.

LAKU Management Sdn Bhd: Soon Hup Tower, 6th Floor, Lot 907, Jalan Merbau, 98000 Miri; tel. (85) 442000; fax (85) 442005; e-mail chuilin@pd.jaring.my; serves Miri, Limbang and Bintulu; CEO YONG CHIONG VAN.

Melaka Water Corpn: Tingkat Bawah, 1 10–13, Graha Maju, Jalan Graha Maju, 75300 Melaka; tel. (6) 2825233; fax (6) 2837266; Ir ABDUL RAHIM SHAMSUDI.

Negeri Sembilan Water Department: Wisma Negeri, 70990 Seremban; tel. (6) 7622314; fax (6) 7620753; Ir Dr MOHD AKBAR.

Pahang Water Supply Department (Jabatan Bekalan Air Pahang): 9–10 Kompleks Tun Razak, Bandar Indera Mahkota, 25582 Kuantan, Pahang; tel. (9) 5721222; fax (9) 5721221; e-mail p-jba@pahang.gov.my; Dir Ir Haji ISMAIL BIN Haji MAT NOOR.

Pinang Water Supply Department: Level 29, KOMTAR, 10000 Pinang; tel. (4) 6505462; fax (4) 2645282; e-mail lyc@sukpp.gov.my; f. 1973; Gen. Man. Datuk Ir LEE YOW CHING.

Perak Water Board: Jalan St John, Peti Surat 589, 30760 Ipoh, Perak; tel. (5) 2551155; fax (5) 2556397; Dir Ir SANI BIN SIDIK.

Sabah Water Department: Wisma MUIS, Blok A, Tingkat 6, Beg Berkunci 210, 88825 Kota Kinabalu; tel. (88) 232364; fax (88) 232396; Man. Ir BENNY WANG.

SAJ Holdings Sdn Bhd: Bangunan Ibu Pejabat SAJ Holdings, Jalan Garuda, Larkin, POB 262, 80350 Johor Bahru; tel. (7) 2244040; fax (7) 2236155; e-mail support@saj.com.my; internet www .saj.com.my; f. 1999; Exec. Chair. Dir Dato' Haji HAMDAN BIN MOHAMED.

Sarawak Public Works Department: Wisma Seberkas, Jalan Tun Haji Openg, 93582 Kuching; tel. (82) 244041; fax (82) 429679; Dir MICHAEL TING KUOK NG.

Selangor Water Department: POB 5001, Jalan Pantai Baru, 59990 Kuala Lumpur; tel. (3) 2826244; fax (3) 2827535; f. 1972; Dir Ir LIEW WAI KIAT.

Sibu Water Board: Km 5, Jalan Salim, POB 405, 96007 Sibu, Sarawak; tel. (84) 211001; fax (84) 211543; e-mail swbs@swb.gov .my; Man. DANIEL WONG PARK ING.

Terengganu Water Department: Tkt 3, Wisma Negeri, Jalan Pejabat, 20200 Kuala Terengganu; tel. (9) 6222444; fax (9) 6221510; Ir Haji WAN NGAH BIN WAN.

TRADE UNIONS

In 1995 there were 502 trade unions, 56% of which were from the private sector. About 8.2% of the Malaysian work-force of 7.9m. belonged to unions.

Congress of Unions of Employees in the Public Administrative and Civil Services (CUEPACS): a nat. fed. with 53 affiliates, representing 120,150 govt workers (1994).

Malaysian Trades Union Congress: Wisma MTUC, 10–5, Jalan USJ 9/5T, 47620 Subang Jaya, Selangor; POB 3073, 46000 Petaling Jaya, Selangor; tel. (3) 80242953; fax (3) 80243224; e-mail mtuc@tm .net.my; internet www.mtuc.org.my; f. 1949; 241 affiliated unions; Pres. ZAINAL RAMPAK; Sec.-Gen. G. RAJASEKARAN.

Principal affiliated unions:

All Malayan Estates Staff Union: POB 12, 46700 Petaling Jaya, Selangor Darul Ehsan; tel. (3) 7249533; e-mail mes@po.jaring.my; 2,654 mems; Pres. TITUS GLADWIN; Gen. Sec. D. P. S. THAMOTHARAM.

Amalgamated Union of Employees in Government Clerical and Allied Services: 32A Jalan Gajah, off Jalan Yew, Pudu, 55100 Kuala Lumpur; tel. (3) 9859613; fax (3) 9838632; 6,703 mems; Pres. IBRAHIM BIN ABDUL WAHAB; Gen. Sec. MOHAMED IBRAHIM BIN ABDUL WAHAB.

Chemical Workers' Union: Petaling Jaya, Selangor; 1,886 mems; Pres. RUSIAN HITAM; Gen. Sec. JOHN MATHEWS.

Electricity Industry Workers' Union: 55-2 Jalan SS 15/8A, Subang Jaya, 47500 Petaling Jaya, Selangor; tel. (3) 7335243; 22,000 mems; Pres. ABDUL RASHID; Gen. Sec. P. ARUNASALAM.

Federation of Unions in the Textile, Garment and Leather Industry: c/o Selangor Textile and Garment Manufacturing Employees Union, 9D Jalan Travers, 50470 Kuala Lumpur; tel. (3) 2742578; f. 1989; four affiliates; Pres. ABDUL RAZAK HAMID; Gen. Sec. ABU BAKAR IBRAHIM.

Harbour Workers' Union, Port Kelang: 106 Persiaran Raja Muda Musa, Port Kelang; 2,426 mems; Pres. MOHAMED SHARIFF BIN YAMIN; Gen. Sec. MOHAMED HAYAT BIN AWANG.

Kesatuan Pekerja Tenaga Nasional Bhd: 30 Jalan Liku Bangsar, POB 10400, 59100 Kuala Lumpur; tel. (3) 2745657; 10,456 mems; Pres. MOHAMED ABU BAKAR; Gen. Sec. IDRIS BIN ISMAIL.

Kesatuan Pekerja-Pekerja FELDA: 2 Jalan Maktab Enam, Melalui Jalan Perumahan Gurney, 54000 Kuala Lumpur; tel. (3) 26929972; fax (3) 26913409; 2,900 mems; Pres. INDERA PUTRA Haji ISMAIL; Gen. Sec. MOHAMAD BIN ABDUL RAHMAN.

Kesatuan Pekerja-Pekerja Perusahaan Membuat Tekstil dan Pakaian Pulau Pinang dan Seberang Prai: 23 Lorong Talang Satu, Prai Gardens, 13600 Prai; tel. (4) 301397; 3,900 mems; Pres. ABDUL RAZAK HAMID; Gen. Sec. KENNETH STEPHEN PERKINS.

Malayan Technical Services Union: 3A Jalan Menteri, off Jalan Cochrane, 55100 Kuala Lumpur; tel. (3) 92851778; fax (3) 92811875; 6,500 mems; Pres. Haji MOHAMED YUSOP Haji HARMAIN SHAH; Gen. Sec. SAMUEL DEVADASAN.

Malaysian Rubber Board Staff Union: POB 10150, 50908 Kuala Lumpur; tel. (3) 4565102; 1,108 mems; Pres. JUDE MICHAEL; Gen. Sec. NG SIEW LAN.

Metal Industry Employees' Union: Metalworkers' House, 5 Lorong Utara Kecil, 46200 Petaling Jaya, Selangor; tel. (3) 79567214; fax (3) 79550854; e-mail mieum@tm.net.my; 15,491 mems; Pres. KAMARUSZAMAN BIN MANSOR; Gen. Sec. JACOB ENGKATESU.

National Union of Commercial Workers: Bangunan NUCW, 98A–D Jalan Masjid India, 50100 Kuala Lumpur; POB 12059, 50780 Kuala Lumpur; tel. (3) 2927385; fax (3) 2925930; f. 1959; 11,937 mems; Pres. TAIB SHARIF; Gen. Sec. C. KRISHNAN.

National Union of Plantation Workers: 428 A, B, Jalan 5/46, Gasing Indah, POB 73, 46700 Petaling Jaya, Selangor; tel. (3) 77827622; fax (3) 77815321; e-mail sangkara@mail.tm.net.my; f. 1990; 41,000 mems; Pres. AWI BIN AWANG; Gen. Sec. G. SANKARAN.

National Union of PWD Employees: 32B Jalan Gajah, off Jalan Yew, 55100 Kuala Lumpur; tel. (3) 9850149; 5,869 mems; Pres. KULOP IBRAHIM; Gen. Sec. S. SANTHANASAMY.

National Union of Telecoms Employees: Wisma NUTE, 17A Jalan Bangsar, 59200 Kuala Lumpur; tel. (3) 2821599; fax (3) 2821015; 15,874 mems; Pres. MOHAMED SHAFIE B. P. MAMMAL; Gen. Sec. MOHD JAFAR BIN ABDUL MAJID.

Non-Metallic Mineral Products Manufacturing Employees' Union: 99A Jalan SS 14/1, Subang Jaya, 47500 Petaling Jaya, Selangor; tel. (3) 56352245; fax (3) 56333863; e-mail nonmet@tm.net .my; 10,000 mems; Pres. ABDULLAH ABU BAKAR; Sec. S. SOMAHSUNDRAM.

Railwaymen's Union of Malaya: Bangunan Tong Nam, 1st Floor, Jalan Tun Sambathan (Travers), 50470 Kuala Lumpur; tel. (3) 2741107; fax (3) 2731805; 5,500 mems; Pres. ABDUL GAFFOR BIN IBRAHIM; Gen. Sec. S. VEERASINGAM.

Technical Services Union—Tenaga Nasional Bhd: Bangunan Keselamatan, POB 11003, Bangsar, Kuala Lumpur; tel. (3) 2823581; 3,690 mems; Pres. RAMLY YATIM; Gen. Sec. CLIFFORD SEN.

Timber Employees' Union: 10 Jalan AU 5c/14, Ampang, Ulu Kelang, Selangor; 7,174 mems; Pres. Abdullah Meton; Gen. Sec. Minhat Sulaiman.

Transport Workers' Union: 21 Jalan Barat, Petaling Jaya, 46200 Selangor; tel. (3) 7566567; 10,447 mems; Pres. Norashikin; Gen. Sec. Zainal Rampak.

Independent Federations and Unions

Kongres Kesatuan Guru-Guru Dalam Perkhidmatan Pelajaran (Congress of Unions of Employees in the Teaching Services): Johor; seven affiliates; Pres. Ramli bin Mohd Johan; Sec.-Gen. Kassim bin Haji Haron.

Malaysian Medical Association: MMA House, 4th Floor, 124 Jalan Pahang, 53000 Kuala Lumpur; tel. (3) 40420617; fax (3) 40418187; e-mail mma@tm.net.my; internet www.mma.org.my; 10 affiliates; Pres. Datuk Dr N. Arumugarn.

National Union of Bank Employees: NUBE Bldg, 61 Jalan Ampang, POB 12488, 50780 Kuala Lumpur; tel. (3) 20789800; fax (3) 20703800; e-mail nubehq@pd.jaring.my; internet www.nube.org .my; 27,000 mems; Gen. Sec. J. Solomon.

National Union of Journalists: 30b Jalan Padang Belia, 50470 Kuala Lumpur; tel. (3) 2742867; fax (3) 2744776; f. 1962; 1,700 mems; Gen. Sec. Onn Ee Seng.

National Union of Newspaper Workers: 11b Jalan 20/14, Paramount Garden, 46300 Petaling Jaya, Selangor; tel. (3) 78768118; fax (3) 78751490; e-mail nunwl@tm.net.my; 3,000 mems; Pres. Gan Hoe Jian; Gen. Sec. R. Chandrasekaran.

Sabah

Sabah Banking Employees' Union: POB 11649, 88818 Kota Kinabalu; internet sbeukk@tm.net.my; 729 mems; Gen. Sec. Lee Chi Hong.

Sabah Civil Service Union: Kota Kinabalu; f. 1952; 1,356 mems; Pres. J. K. K. Voon; Sec. Stephen Wong.

Sabah Commercial Employees' Union: Sinsuran Shopping Complex, Lot 3, Block N, 2nd Floor, POB 10357, 88803 Kota Kinabalu; tel. (88) 225971; fax (88) 213815; e-mail sceu-kk@tm.net.my; f. 1957; 980 mems; Gen. Sec. Rebecca Chin.

Sabah Medical Services Union: POB 11257, 88813 Kota Kinabalu; tel. (88) 242126; fax (88) 242127; e-mail smsu65@hotmail .com; 4,000 mems; Pres. Kathy Lo Nyuk Chin; Gen. Sec. Laurence Vun.

Sabah Petroleum Industry Workers' Union: POB 1087, Kota Kinabalu; 168 mems; Gen. Sec. Thien Fook Shin.

Sabah Teachers' Union: POB 10912, 88810 Kota Kinabalu; tel. (88) 420034; fax (88) 431633; f. 1962; 3,001 mems; Pres. Kwan Ping Sin; Sec.-Gen. Patrick Y. C. Chok.

Sarawak

Kepak Sarawak (Kesatuan Pegawai-Pegawai Bank, Sarawak): POB 62, Bukit Permata, 93100 Kuching, Sarawak; tel. (19) 8549372; e-mail kepaksar@tm.net.my; bank officers' union; 1,430 mems; Gen. Sec. Dominic Ch'ng Yung Ted.

Sarawak Commercial Employees' Union: POB 807, Kuching; 1,636 mems; Gen. Sec. Song Swee Liap.

Sarawak Teachers' Union: 139a Jalan Rock, 1st Floor, 93200 Kuching; tel. (82) 245727; fax (82) 245757; e-mail swktu@po.jaring .my; internet www.geocities.com/swktu; f. 1965; 12,832 mems; Pres. William Ghani Bina; Sec.-Gen. Thomas Huo Kok Sen.

Transport

RAILWAYS

Peninsular Malaysia

The state-owned Malayan Railways had a total length of 1,672 km in Peninsular Malaysia in 1996. The main railway line follows the west coast and extends 782 km from Singapore, south of Peninsular Malaysia, to Butterworth (opposite Pinang Island) in the north. From Bukit Mertajam, close to Butterworth, the Kedah line runs north to the Thai border at Padang Besar where connection is made with the State Railway of Thailand. The East Coast Line, 526 km long, runs from Gemas to Tumpat (in Kelantan). A 21-km branch line from Pasir Mas (27 km south of Tumpat) connects with the State Railway of Thailand at the border station of Sungei Golok. Branch lines serve railway-operated ports at Port Dickson and Telok Anson as well as Port Klang and Jurong (Singapore). An express rail link connecting central Kuala Lumpur and the new Kuala Lumpur International Airport (KLIA) opened in 2001.

Keretapi Tanah Melayu Bhd (KTMB) (Malayan Railways): KTMB Corporate Headquarters, Jalan Sultan Hishamuddin, 50621 Kuala Lumpur; tel. (3) 22757142; fax (3) 27105706; e-mail pro@ktmb .com.my; internet www.ktmb.com.my; f. 1885; incorporated as a co under govt control in Aug. 1992; privatized in Aug. 1997; managed by the consortium Marak Unggal (Renong, DRB and Bolton); Chair. Tan Sri Dato' Thong Yaw Hong.

Sabah

Sabah State Railway: Karung Berkunci 2047, 88999 Kota Kinabalu; tel. (88) 254611; fax (88) 236395; 134 track-km of 1-m gauge (1995); goods and passenger services from Tanjong Aru to Tenom, serving part of the west coast and the interior; diesel trains are used; Gen. Man. Ir Benny Wang.

ROADS

Peninsular Malaysia

Peninsular Malaysia's road system is extensive, in contrast to those of Sabah and Sarawak. In 1999 the road network in Malaysia totalled an estimated 65,877 km, of which 16,206 km were highways and 31,777 km secondary roads; 75.8% of the network was paved.

Sabah

Jabatan Kerja Raya (Public Works Department): 88582 Kota Kinabalu, Sabah; tel. (88) 244333; fax (88) 237234; e-mail pos@jkr .sabah.gov.my; maintains a network totalling 14,297 km, of which 1,230 km were trunk roads in 1997; the total included 5,011 km of sealed roads; Dir David Chiu Siong Seng.

Sarawak

Jabatan Kerja Raya (Public Works Department): 88582 Kota Kinabalu, Sabah; tel. (88) 244333; fax (88) 237234; e-mail pos@jkr .sabah.gov.my; road network totalling 10,979 km, of which 3,986 km were sealed roads; Dir David Chiu Siong Seng.

SHIPPING

The ports in Malaysia are classified as federal ports, under the jurisdiction of the federal Ministry of Transport, or state ports, responsible to the state ministries of Sabah and Sarawak.

Peninsular Malaysia

The federal ports in Peninsular Malaysia are Klang (the principal port), Pinang, Johor and Kuantan.

Johor Port Authority: POB 66, 81707 Pasir Gudang, Johor; tel. (7) 2517721; fax (7) 2517684; e-mail jport@lpj.com.my; internet www.lpj .gov.my; f. 1973; Gen. Man. Mohd Rozali bin Mohd Ali.

Johor Port Bhd: POB 151, 81707 Pasir Gudang, Johor; tel. (7) 2525888; fax (7) 2522507; e-mail joport@silicon.net.my; internet www.joport.com.my; Exec. Chair. Dato' Mohd Taufik Abdullah.

Klang Port Authority: POB 202, Jalan Pelabuhan, 42005 Port Klang, Selangor; tel. (3) 31688211; fax (3) 31670211; e-mail pka_admin@pka.gov.my; f. 1963; Gen. Man. Datin Paduka O. C. Phang.

Kuantan Port Authority: Tanjung Gelang, POB 161, 25720 Kuantan, Pahang; tel. (9) 5833201; fax (9) 5833866; e-mail lpk@po .jaring.my; internet www.1pktn.gov.my; f. 1974; Gen. Man. Khairul Anuar bin Abdul Rahman.

Penang Port Commission: POB 143, 10710 Pinang; tel. (4) 2633211; fax (4) 2626211; e-mail sppp@po.jaring.my; internet www .penangport.gov.my; f. 1956; Gen. Man. Dato' Capt. Haji Abdul Rahim Abdul Aziz.

Sabah

The chief ports are Kota Kinabalu, Sandakan, Tawau, Lahad Datu, Kudat, Semporna and Kunak and are administered by the Sabah Ports Authority. Many international shipping lines serve Sabah. Local services are operated by smaller vessels. The Sapangar Bay oil terminal, 25 km from Kota Kinabalu wharf, can accommodate oil tankers of up to 30,000 dwt.

Sabah Ports Authority: Bangunan Ibu Pejabat LPS, Jalan Tun Fuad, Tanjung Lipat, Locked Bag 2005, 88617 Kota Kinabalu, Sabah; tel. (88) 538400; fax (88) 223036; e-mail sabport@po.jaring .my; internet www.infosabah.com.my/spa; Gen. Man. Alex Lee.

Sarawak

There are four port authorities in Sarawak: Kuching, Rajang, Miri and Bintulu. Kuching, Rajang and Miri are statutory ports, while Bintulu is a federal port. Kuching port serves the southern region of Sarawak, Rajang port the central region, and Miri port the northern region.

Kuching Port Authority: Jalan Pelabuhan, Pending, POB 530, 93710 Kuching, Sarawak; tel. (82) 482144; fax (82) 481696; e-mail kuport@po.jaring.my; f. 1961; Gen. Man. CHOU CHII MING.

Rajang Port Authority: 96000 Sibu, Sarawak; tel. (84) 319004; fax (84) 318754; e-mail rajang@po.jaring.my; f. 1970; Gen. Man. Haji BAHRIN Haji ADENG.

Principal Shipping Companies

Achipelego Shipping (Sarawak) Sdn Bhd: Lot 267/270, Jalan Chan Chin Ann, POB 2998, 93758 Kuching; tel. (82) 412581; fax (82) 416249; Gen. Man. MICHAEL M. AMAN.

Malaysia Shipping Corpn Sdn Bhd: Office Tower, Plaza Berjaya, Suite 14C, 14th Floor, 12 Jalan Imbi, 55100 Kuala Lumpur; tel. (3) 21418788; fax (3) 21429214; Chair. Y. C. CHANG.

Malaysian International Shipping Corpn Bhd (National Shipping Line of Malaysia): Suite 3–8, Tingkat 3, Wisma MISC, 2 Jalan Conlay, 50450 Kuala Lumpur; tel. (3) 2428088; fax (3) 2486602; e-mail zzainala@miscnote1.miscbhd.com; internet www.misc-bhd .com; f. 1968; regular sailings between the Far East, South-East Asia, Australia, Japan and Europe; also operates chartering, tanker, haulage and warehousing and agency services; major shareholder, Petroliam Nasional Bhd (PETRONAS); Chair. Tan Sri Dato' MOHD HASSAN BIN MARICAN; Man. Dir Dato' Haji MOHD ALI BIN Haji YASIN.

Perbadanan Nasional Shipping Line Bhd (PNSL): Kuala Lumpur; tel. (3) 2932211; fax (3) 2930493; f. 1982; specializes in bulk cargoes; Chair. Tunku Dato' SHAHRIMAN BIN Tunku SULAIMAN; Exec. Dep. Chair. Dato' SULAIMAN ABDULLAH.

Persha Shipping Agencies Sdn Bhd: Bangunan Mayban Trust, Penthouse Suite, Jalan Pinang, 10200 Pinang; tel. (4) 2612400; fax (4) 2623122; Man. Dir MOHD NOOR MOHD KAMALUDIN.

Syarikat Perkapalan Kris Sdn Bhd (The Kris Shipping Co Ltd): 3AO7 Block A, Kelana Centre Point, 3 Jalan SS7/19, Kelana Jaya; POB 8428, 46789 Petaling Jaya, Selangor; tel. (3) 7046477; fax (3) 7048007; domestic services; Chair. Dato' Seri SYED NAHAR SHAHABUDIN; Gen. Man. ROHANY TALIB; Dep. Gen. Man. THO TEIT CHANG.

Trans-Asia Shipping Corpn Sdn Bhd: Unit 715–718, Block A, Kelana Business Centre, 97 Jalan SS7/2, Kelana Jaya, 47301 Petaling Jaya, Selangor; tel. (3) 78802020; fax (4) 78802200; e-mail ahmad@tasco.com.my; internet www.tasco.com.my; Man. Dir LEE CHECK POH.

CIVIL AVIATION

The new Kuala Lumpur International Airport (KLIA), situated in Sepang, Selangor (50 km south of Kuala Lumpur) began operations in June 1998, with an initial capacity of 25m.–30m. passengers a year, rising to 45m. by 2020. It replaced Subang Airport in Kuala Lumpur (which was renamed the Sultan Abdul Aziz Shah Airport in 1996). An express rail link between central Kuala Lumpur and KLIA opened in early 2001. There are regional airports at Kota Kinabalu, Pinang, Johor Bahru, Kuching and Pulau Langkawi. In addition, there are airports catering for domestic services at Alor Star, Ipoh, Kota Bahru, Kuala Terengganu, Kuantan and Melaka in Peninsular Malaysia, Sibu, Bintulu and Miri in Sarawak and Sandakan, Tawau, Lahad Datu and Labuan in Sabah. There are also numerous smaller airstrips.

Department of Civil Aviation (Jabatan Penerbangan Awam Malaysia): Aras B1, 1, 2 and 3, Blok D5, Parcel D, Pusat Pentadbiran Kerajaan Persekutuan, 62502 Putrajaya; tel. (3) 88866000; fax (3) 88891541; internet www.dca.gov.my; Dir-Gen. Dato' KOK SOO CHON.

Air Asia Sdn Bhd: Wisma HICOM, 6th Floor, 2 Jalan Usahawan, U1/8, Seksyen Ul, 40150 Shah Alam, Selangor; tel. (3) 2028007; fax (3) 2028137; internet www.airasia.com; f. 1993; a second national airline, with a licence to operate domestic, regional and international flights; 85%-owned by HICOM.

Berjaya Air: Apprentice Training Bldg, 1st Floor, Mas Complex B (Hangar 1), Lapangan Terbang Sultan Abdul Aziz Shah, Shah Alam, Selangor, 47200 Kuala Lumpur; tel. (3) 7476828; fax (3) 7476228; e-mail berjayaa@tm.net.my; f. 1989; scheduled and charter domestic services; Pres. Dato TENGKU ADNAN MANSOR.

Malaysia Airlines: 32nd Floor, Bangunan MAS, Jalan Sultan Ismail, 50250 Kuala Lumpur; tel. (3) 21655140; fax (3) 21633178; e-mail grpcomm@malaysiaairlines.com.my; internet www .malaysiaairlines.com.my; f. 1971 as the Malaysian successor to the Malaysia Singapore Airlines (MSA); known as Malaysian Airline System (MAS) until Oct. 1987; services to 33 domestic points and to 79 international destinations; Chair. Tan Sri Datuk Seri AZIZAN ZAINUL ABIDIN.

Pelangi Airways Sdn Bhd: Kuala Lumpur; tel. (3) 2624453; fax (3) 2624515; internet www.asia123.com/pelangi/home.htm; f. 1988; domestic scheduled passenger services; Chair. Tan Sri SAW HWAT LYE.

Transmile Air Sdn Bhd: Wisma Semantan, Mezzanine 2, Block B, 12 Jalan Gelenggang, Bukit Damansara, 50490 Kuala Lumpur; tel. (3) 2537718; fax (3) 2537719; f. 1992; scheduled and charter regional and domestic services for pasengers and cargo; Chair. Tan Sri ZAINOL MAHMOOD.

Tourism

Malaysia has a rapidly-growing tourist industry, and tourism remains an important source of foreign-exchange earnings. In 2003 some 10.6m. tourists visited Malaysia. In 2002 tourist receipts totalled RM 25,781.1m.

Malaysia Tourism Promotion Board: Menara Dato' Onn, 17th, 24th–27th, 30th Floors, Putra World Trade Centre, Jalan Tun Ismail, 50480 Kuala Lumpur; tel. (3) 26935188; fax (3) 26935884; e-mail tourism@tourism.gov.my; internet www.tourism.gov.my; f. 1972 to co-ordinate and promote activities relating to tourism; Chair. Datuk Paduka ABDUL KADIR Haji Sheikh FADZIR; Dir-Gen. Datuk ABDULLAH JONID.

Sabah Tourist Association: Kota Kinabalu; tel. (88) 211484; internet www.sabahtourist.com.my; f. 1963; 55 mems; parastatal promotional org.; Chair. CLEMENT LEE.

Sarawak Tourism Board: Levels 6 and 7, Bangunan Yayasan Sarawak, Jalan Masjid, 93400 Kuching; ; tel. (82) 423600; fax (82) 416700; e-mail stb@sarawaktourism.com; internet www .sarawaktourism.com; f. 1995; CEO ABANG Haji KASHIM ABANG MORSHIDI.

THE MALDIVES
Introductory Survey

Location, Climate, Language, Religion, Flag, Capital

The Republic of Maldives (commonly referred to as 'the Maldives') is in southern Asia. The country, lying about 675 km (420 miles) south-west of Sri Lanka, consists of 1,190 small coral islands (of which 200 are inhabited), grouped in 26 natural atolls (but divided, for administrative purposes, into 20 atolls), in the Indian Ocean. The climate is hot and humid. The average annual temperature is 27°C (80°F), with little daily or seasonal variation, while annual rainfall is generally between 2,540 mm and 3,800 mm (100 ins to 150 ins). The national language is Dhivehi (Maldivian), which is related to Sinhala. Islam is the state religion, and most Maldivians are Sunni Muslims. The national flag (proportions 2 by 3) is red, with a green rectangle, containing a white crescent, in the centre. The capital is Malé.

Recent History

The Maldives, called the Maldive Islands until April 1969, formerly had an elected Sultan as head of state. The islands were placed under British protection, with internal self-government, in 1887. They became a republic in January 1953, but the sultanate was restored in February 1954. The Maldives became fully independent, outside the Commonwealth, on 26 July 1965. Following a referendum, the country became a republic again in November 1968, with Amir Ibrahim Nasir, Prime Minister since 1957, as President.

In 1956 the Maldivian and British Governments agreed to the establishment of a Royal Air Force staging post on Gan, an island in the southernmost atoll, Addu. In 1975 the British Government's decision to close the base and to evacuate British forces created a large commercial and military vacuum. In October 1977 President Nasir rejected an offer of an annual payment of US $1m. from the USSR to lease the former base on Gan, announcing that he would not lease the island for military purposes, nor lease it to a superpower. In 1981 the President announced plans to establish an industrial zone on Gan. By 1990 there were two factories (producing ready-made garments) operating on Gan. The airport on Gan, which links the capital, Malé, with the south, is now fully operational and is due to become an international airport in the near future.

A new Constitution, promulgated in 1968, vested considerable powers in the President, including the right to appoint and dismiss the Prime Minister and the Cabinet of Ministers.

In March 1975, following rumours of a coup conspiracy, President Nasir dismissed the Prime Minister, Ahmed Zaki, and the premiership was abolished. Unexpectedly, President Nasir announced that he would not seek re-election at the end of his second term in 1978. To succeed him, the Majlis (legislature) chose Maumoon Abdul Gayoom, Minister of Transport under Nasir, who was approved by referendum in July 1978 and took office in November. President Gayoom announced that his main priority would be the development of the poor rural regions, while in foreign affairs the existing policy of non-alignment would be continued.

Ex-President Nasir left the country after his resignation, but the authorities subsequently sought his return to the Maldives, where he was required to answer charges of misappropriating government funds. In 1980 President Gayoom confirmed an attempted coup against the Government and implicated Nasir in the alleged plot. Nasir was to stand trial, in his absence, on these and other charges. In April 1981 Ahmed Naseem, former Deputy Minister of Fisheries and brother-in-law of Nasir, was sentenced to life imprisonment for plotting to overthrow President Gayoom. Nasir himself denied any involvement in the coup, and attempts to extradite him from Singapore were unsuccessful. (In July 1990, however, President Gayoom officially pardoned Nasir *in absentia*, in recognition of the role that he had played in winning national independence.) In 1983 another unsuccessful plot against President Gayoom was reported. In September he was re-elected as President, for a further five years, by a national referendum (with 95.6% of the popular vote). In September 1988 Gayoom was again re-elected unopposed, for a third five-year term, obtaining a record 96.4% of the popular vote.

A third, and more serious, attempt to depose President Gayoom took place in November 1988, when a sea-borne mercenary force, which was composed of around 80 alleged Sri Lankan Tamil separatists (led by a disaffected Maldivian businessman, Abdullah Luthufi), landed in Malé and endeavoured to seize control of important government installations. At the request of President Gayoom, however, the Indian Government dispatched an emergency contingent of 1,600 troops, which rapidly and successfully suppressed the attempted coup. Nineteen people were reported to have been killed in the fighting. In September 1989 the President commuted to life imprisonment the death sentences imposed on 12 Sri Lankans and four Maldivians, who took part in the aborted coup. The Indian Government withdrew its remaining 160 troops from the Maldives in November.

In February 1990, despite alleged opposition from powerful members of the privileged élite, President Gayoom announced that, as part of proposals for a broad new policy of liberalization and democratic reform, he was planning to introduce legislation, in the near future, enabling him to distribute powers, currently enjoyed by the President alone, amongst other official bodies. A further sign of growing democratization in the Maldives was the holding of discussions by the President's Consultative Council, in early 1990, concerning freedom of speech (particularly in the local press). In April, however, it became apparent that some Maldivians opposed political change, when three pro-reform members of the Majlis received anonymous death threats. A few months later, following the emergence of several politically outspoken magazines, including *Sangu* (The Conchshell), there was an abrupt reversal of the Government's policy regarding the liberalization of the press. All publications not sanctioned by the Government were banned, and a number of leading writers and publishers were arrested.

As part of a major cabinet reshuffle in May 1990, President Gayoom dismissed the Minister of State for Defence and National Security, Ilyas Ibrahim (who also held the Trade and Industries portfolio and headed the State Trading Corporation), from his post, following the latter's abrupt and unannounced departure from the country. The Government later disclosed that Ibrahim (Gayoom's brother-in-law) was to have appeared before a presidential special commission investigating alleged embezzlement and misappropriation of government funds. On his return to the Maldives in August, Ibrahim was placed under house arrest. In March 1991, however, the special commission concluded that there was no evidence of involvement, either direct or indirect, by Ibrahim in the alleged financial misdeeds; in the same month the President appointed Ilyas Ibrahim as Minister of Atolls Administration. In April the President established an anti-corruption board, which was to investigate allegations of corruption, bribery, fraud, misappropriation of government funds and property, and misuse of government office.

In early August 1993, a few weeks before the Majlis vote on the presidential candidate, Gayoom was informed that Ilyas Ibrahim, whose position as Minister of Atolls Administration had afforded him the opportunity to build a political base outside Malé (where he already enjoyed considerable popularity), was seeking the presidency and attempting to influence members of the Majlis (at that time, the Majlis nominated and elected by secret ballot a single candidate, who was presented to the country in a referendum). In the Majlis vote, held in late August, the incumbent President, who had previously been unanimously nominated for the presidency by the legislature, obtained 28 votes, against 18 for his brother-in-law. For his allegedly unconstitutional behaviour, however, Ibrahim was charged with attempting to 'influence the members of the Majlis' and he promptly left the country. Ibrahim was subsequently tried *in absentia* and sentenced to 15 years' imprisonment. In addition, his brother, Abbas Ibrahim, was removed from his post as Minister of Fisheries and Agriculture. (Ilyas Ibrahim returned to the Maldives in 1996 when he was placed under house arrest; this restriction was lifted in 1997.)

In October 1993 Gayoom was re-elected as President, for a further five years, by a national referendum in which he obtained 92.8% of the popular vote. Following his re-election, the President carried out an extensive cabinet reshuffle and a far-reaching reorganization of government bodies, including the establishment of two new ministries (that of Youth, Women's Affairs and Sports and that of Information and Culture), in order to increase efficiency and to further democratic reform.

In November 1994, at an official ceremony marking Republic Day, President Gayoom outlined various measures intended to strengthen the political system and to advance the process of democratization. These included the granting of greater autonomy and responsibilities to members of the Cabinet of Ministers, the introduction of regulations governing the conduct of civil servants (in order to increase their accountability), the introduction of democratic elections to island development committees and atoll committees, and the establishment of a Law Commission to carry out reforms to the judicial system.

In November 1996 President Gayoom effected an extensive cabinet reshuffle and a reorganization of government bodies, including the establishment of a Supreme Council for Islamic Affairs, which was to be under direct presidential control and was to advise the Government on matters relating to Islam. In early 1997 President Gayoom announced that the Citizens' Special Majlis (which was established in 1980 with the specific task of amending the Constitution) had resolved to complete the revision of the Constitution during that year and to implement the amended version by 1 January 1998. The Citizens' Special Majlis finished its 17-year-long task in early November 1997 (passing the amendments by 88 votes to two votes). The revised Constitution was ratified by the President on 27 November and came into effect, as planned, on 1 January 1998. Under the new 156-article Constitution, a formal, multi-candidate contest was permitted for the legislature's nomination for the presidency; no restriction was placed on the number of terms a president may serve; for administrative purposes, the number of atolls was increased from 19 to 20; the Majlis, which was henceforth known as the People's Majlis, was enlarged from 48 to 50 seats; the Citizens' Special Majlis was renamed the People's Special Majlis; the rights of the people were expanded; parliamentary immunity was introduced; the office of auditor-general was created; the post of commissioner of elections was constitutionalized; ministers were afforded greater power; public officers were made more accountable; parliamentary questions were allowed; and judges and magistrates were obliged to take special oaths of loyalty.

In September 1998 five individuals declared their candidacy for the presidency; the People's Majlis unanimously voted by secret ballot for the incumbent President Gayoom to go forward to the national referendum. In the referendum, which was held in mid-October, Gayoom was re-elected as President for a fifth term in office, obtaining 90.9% of the popular vote. Following his re-election, the President carried out a cabinet reorganization, including the establishment of two new ministries (that of Communications, Science and Technology and that of Human Resources, Employment and Labour). In an unexpected move, Ilyas Ibrahim was appointed to hold the new portfolio of transport and civil aviation.

In November 1999 elections for 42 members of the 50-seat People's Majlis were conducted (on a non-partisan basis). In an attempt to strengthen and develop the Maldivian system of public administration, the President established an Advisory Committee on Public-Sector Reform and Modernization and a Network of Senior Government Officials in November 1999 and February 2000, respectively. At the end of May 2000 the Minister of State for Finance and Treasury, Arif Hilmy, resigned owing to ill health, and was replaced by Mohamed Jaleel. In September the Comprehensive Nuclear Test Ban Treaty was ratified by the Maldives. As part of a government initiative to promote the advancement of women in public life, President Gayoom appointed a woman as the new Island Chief of Himmafushi in June 2001. In December a woman was appointed as Atoll Chief of Vaavu Atoll (the first woman to be assigned a senior executive position of an atoll). In October the President announced his support for the USA in its global 'war on terror', launched in reponse to the suicide attacks in New York and Washington, DC, USA in September.

Meanwhile, in early 2001 an attempt by 42 prominent Maldivians, including members of the People's Majlis, former cabinet ministers and businessmen, to register the newly formed Maldivian Democratic Party (MDP) was blocked by the People's Majlis on the grounds that the existence of political parties would encourage divisions among the public and, therefore, be counter-productive. It was believed by some, however, that President Gayoom had enforced the decision and, in doing so, had acted unconstitutionally.

In early September 2002 an armed passenger attempted to hijack an Air Seychelles aircraft en route from Mumbai (India) to the Seychelles, via Malé. Airline staff managed to overpower the hijacker, who was arrested in Malé; no other passengers were injured. It was reported that the suspect, an Indian national, and his assistant, an Indian citizen also on the flight, wanted to divert the aeroplane to another destination.

In October 2002 the President carried out a partial government reorganization. Meanwhile, in July three journalists were charged with defamation and inciting violence and sentenced to life imprisonment (their assistant was sentenced to a term of 10 years) for writing articles criticizing the President and the Government. In early 2003 international activists demanded the release of the detainees, claiming that the journalists had not advocated violent opposition to President Gayoom or the Government, and that they had only been exercising their right to freedom of speech. In July a businessman was sentenced to life imprisonment for publishing an article via the internet urging that the Government be overthrown. Later that month the human rights organization Amnesty International issued a report citing frequent cases of arbitrary detentions, unfair trials and long-term imprisonment and torture of political opponents in the Maldives. The human rights group urged the Government to release political prisoners, investigate allegations of torture and reform the criminal justice system. The Maldives authorities strongly rejected the allegations.

In September 2003 detainees at a prison in Malé held protests in response to the death of a fellow prisoner. Reports of the violent suppression of the rioting by the country's National Security Service (NSS), and the death of another two detainees, prompted major anti-Government protests in the capital (the first ever during President Gayoom's tenure). Large numbers of alleged demonstrators were subsequently arrested, and a curfew was imposed on the city. Gayoom appealed for calm and announced an investigation into the death of the prisoners (the number of fatalities later increased to four, after one died in prison). Eleven members of the NSS were arrested for their involvement, and the Deputy Chief of the NSS and Police Commissioner, Brig. Adam Zahir, was removed (he was appointed executive director of the Ministry of Information, Arts and Culture until his reinstatement as Police Commissioner in mid-February 2004 after the inquiry cleared him of any misconduct). Amnesty International reiterated demands for an end to widespread political repression and to the violation of human rights and for reform of the judicial system.

On 25 September 2003, nevertheless, Gayoom was re-elected unanimously by secret ballot in the People's Majlis for a sixth presidential term, defeating three other candidates. His re-election was ratified at a public referendum on 17 October, where he secured 90.3% of the votes cast. On 12 November, one day after his new term began, President Gayoom effected a cabinet reorganization. Dr Mohamed Munavvar, the Attorney-General, and Ibrahim Hussain Zaki, the Minister of Planning and National Development, were dismissed in the reshuffle. President Gayoom gave no reason for the changes, although it was alleged that the two had been removed for supporting reformers attempting to register a political party. Gayoom also announced that the judicial system, executive and legislature would be reformed over the next five years (without specifying what the changes would be) and that a human rights commission would be established in Malé. In the same month, political activists decided to establish the MDP (which had been prevented from registering as a political party in the Maldives in 2001—see above) in exile in Sri Lanka, in response to the rise in discontent with the Maldives Government. In December the Maldives authorities blocked access to the MDP's website. In mid-February 2004 members of the MDP claimed that more than 15 of its supporters had been arrested in Malé in an alleged attempt to disrupt a planned protest march; however, the Government asserted that the raids were aimed at criminal offenders and that only eight people had been detained.

In December 2003 a Human Rights Commission was established. At the end of that month a report by the Presidential Commission investigating the death of four prisoners in September 2003 (see above) was submitted to President Gayoom. In his speech on the findings of the Commission to the People's Majlis in January 2004, Gayoom stated that the security personnel involved in the prisoners' deaths had acted illegally and would be prosecuted. The President also announced that a programme of penal reform was under way. However, an exiled spokesman for the banned opposition MDP, Mohamed Latheef, criticized the report, claiming that the names of those responsible for the deaths had been omitted from the report, and demanded the President's resignation.

In November 1989, meanwhile, the Maldives hosted an international conference, with delegates from other small island nations, to discuss the threat posed to low-lying island countries by the predicted rise in sea-level caused by heating of the earth's atmosphere as a result of pollution (the 'greenhouse effect'). In June 1990 an Environmental Research Unit, which was to operate under the Ministry of Planning and the Environment, was established in the Maldives. The Maldives again expressed its serious concern with regard to problems of world-wide environmental pollution when it hosted the 13th conference of the UN's Intergovernmental Panel on Climate Change (IPCC, see p. 132) in September 1997. In September 1999 a special session of the UN General Assembly was convened in New York to address the specific problems faced by the 43-member Alliance of Small Island States (see p. 368) (including the Maldives), notably climate change, rising sea levels and globalization. At the UN Millennium Summit meeting in September 2000 the President of the Maldives again took the opportunity to urge leaders to address environmental issues. The Government expressed its grave disappointment and concern at the USA's decision in April 2001 to reject the Kyoto Protocol to the UN's Framework Convention on Climate Change. The rest of the international community adopted the protocol in July after many of the targets had been reduced. The USA proposed an alternative initiative in February 2002; however, most states dismissed it as ineffective. In early March the Maldives, Kiribati and Tuvalu announced their decision to take legal action against the USA for refusing to sign the Kyoto Protocol (thus contributing to global warming which has produced the rising sea levels that threaten to submerge the islands). President Gayoom attended the South Asian Regional Conference on Ecotourism in India in January 2002. At the World Summit on Sustainable Development held in September 2002 in Johannesburg, South Africa, President Gayoom warned the international community that low-lying islands were at greater risk than ever before. He called for urgent action, including the universal ratification and implementation of the Kyoto Protocol, to prevent a global environmental catastrophe. On his return to the Maldives, the President stated that some progress had been made in certain areas, although the decisions were not as far-reaching as desired by small island nations.

The Maldives is a founder member of the South Asian Association for Regional Co-operation (SAARC, see p. 329), which was formally constituted in December 1985, and the country became a full member of the Commonwealth in June 1985. The Maldives' international standing was enhanced in November 1990, when it successfully hosted the fifth SAARC summit meeting, which was held in Malé. In October 1995 the Maldives opened its third resident diplomatic mission (in addition to those in Sri Lanka and at the UN headquarters in New York) in London, United Kingdom. The 11th SAARC Summit Conference of heads of state and government took place in early January 2002 in Kathmandu, Nepal, despite rising tensions between India and Pakistan. The member countries signed two conventions on the promotion of child welfare in South Asia (proposed by President Gayoom) and the prevention and combat of the trafficking of women and children for prostitution. At the 12th SAARC Summit Conference in early January 2004, held in the Pakistani capital of Islamabad, the members agreed to form a South Asia Free Trade Area by 1 January 2006. The leaders also signed the Social Charter and agreed on the Additional Protocol on Terrorism. In April 2003 the number of countries with which the Maldives had established diplomatic relations stood at 136.

Government

Legislative power is held by the unicameral People's Majlis, with 50 members, including 42 elected for five years by universal adult suffrage (two by the National Capital Island and two from each of the 20 atolls) and eight appointed by the President. Executive power is vested in the President, who is elected by secret ballot by the People's Majlis (under the 1998 constitutional revisions, more than one candidate may be nominated for election) and endorsed in office for five years by a national referendum. He governs with the assistance of an appointed Cabinet of Ministers, which is responsible to the

People's Majlis. The country has 21 administrative districts: the capital is under direct central administration while the 20 atolls are each under an atoll chief (verin) who is appointed by the President, under the general guidance of the Minister of Atolls Administration.

Economic Affairs

In 2002, according to estimates by the World Bank, the Maldives' gross national income (GNI), measured at average 2000–02 prices, was US $598m., equivalent to $2,090 per head. During 1990–2002, it was estimated, the population increased at an average annual rate of 2.5%, while gross domestic product (GDP) per head increased, in real terms, by an average of 4.6% per year during 1990–2001. Overall GDP increased, in real terms, at an average annual rate of 7.3% in 1990–2001. According to the Asian Development Bank (ADB, see p. 151), GDP growth increased to 6.0% in 2002, but slowed to 4.2% in 2003. An initial projection of GDP growth for 2004 was 2.8%.

Agriculture and fishing contributed an estimated 9.4% of GDP (at constant 1995 prices) in 2002. About 14% of the total working population were employed in the sector (more than 10% in fishing) in 2000. In 2002 revenue from exports of marine products totalled 716.7m. rufiyaa, thus accounting for 61.7% of total export earnings. In February 1999 the Kooddoo Fisheries Complex in the South Huvadhu Atoll, the largest fisheries project ever implemented in the Maldives, was officially opened. In January 2001 the fresh fish export market was opened to the private sector. Small quantities of various fruits, vegetables and cereals are produced, but virtually all of the principal staple foods have to be imported. The dominant agricultural activity (not including fishing) in the Maldives is coconut production. Agricultural GDP increased, in real terms, by an annual average of 1.9% in 1990–2002. Real agricultural GDP grew by 1.7% in 2001 and by 1.4% in 2002.

Industry (including mining, manufacturing and construction) employed about 19% of the working population in 2000, and provided an estimated 15.5% of GDP in 2002.

Mining and quarrying contributed an estimated 0.6% of GDP in 2002, and employed 0.5% of the working population in 2000. No reserves of petroleum or natural gas have, as yet, been discovered in Maldivian waters.

The manufacturing sector employed 13% of the working population in 2000. Including electricity, gas and water, the manufacturing sector contributed 11.7% of GDP in 2002. There are only a small number of 'modern' manufacturing enterprises in the Maldives, including fish-canning, garment-making and soft-drink bottling. Although cottage industries (such as the weaving of coir yarn and boat-building) employ nearly one-quarter of the total labour force, there is little scope for expansion, owing to the limited size of the domestic market. Because of its lack of manufacturing industries, the Maldives has to import most essential consumer and capital goods. In the late 1980s and 1990s traditional handicrafts, such as lacquer work and shell craft, revived as a result of the expansion of the tourism sector. Manufacturing GDP increased, in real terms, by an annual average of 5.8% in 1990–2002. Real manufacturing GDP grew by 2.7% in 2001 and by 1.5% in 2002.

Energy is derived principally from petroleum, imports of which comprised 11.8% of the cost of imports in 2001. Owing to a surge in commercial activities and a significant increase in construction projects in Malé, demand for electricity in the capital grew rapidly in the late 1980s and early 1990s. Accordingly, plans were formulated in late 1991 to augment the generating capacity of the power station in Malé and to improve the distribution network. By early 1998 20 islands had been provided with electricity (equivalent to about 60% of the total population). In early 2001 the third phase of the Malé power project, further to increase the capital's power supply, was under way. In December the ADB agreed to provide a loan to improve the supply of electricity to some 40 outer islands.

Following the decline of the shipping industry in the 1980s, tourism gained in importance as an economic sector, and by 1989 it had overtaken the fishing industry as the Maldives' largest source of foreign exchange. In 1999 the tourism sector provided 18.5% of GDP. In 2001 tourist arrivals decreased by 1.3%, compared with the previous year, to reach 460,984, owing to the global economic slowdown and concerns over travel safety and stability in the South Asian region after the terrorist attacks on the USA in September. By the end of 2002, however, tourist arrivals had increased by 5.1%; receipts from tourism in that year reached an estimated 892.1m. rufiyaa. In 2003 tourist arrivals increased by 16.3% to reach 563,593. In late 2001 a four-year plan was under way to convert 12 islands into holiday resorts and to increase the number of hotel beds by 4,000. The services sector contributed 75.1% of GDP in 2002. Compared with the previous year, the GDP of the services sector expanded by 4.3% in 2002.

In 2002 the Maldives recorded a visible trade deficit of US $211.1m., and there was a deficit of $44.0m. on the current account of the balance of payments. In 2002 the principal source of imports was Singapore (accounting for 25.8% of the total); other major sources were Sri Lanka, India and France. The principal market for exports was the USA (accounting for 38.4% of the total); other major purchasers were Sri Lanka, Thailand and Japan. The principal exports were marine products (tuna being the largest export commodity) and clothing. The principal imports were machinery and mechanical appliances and electrical equipment, mineral products and textile and textile articles.

Foreign grant aid in 2000 totalled an estimated US $17.7m.; Japan is the Maldives' largest aid donor (disbursing $11.9m. in 1997). The 2003 budget envisaged expenditure of 3,826.5m. rufiyaa and revenue of 2,987.8m., including grants of 113.4m. rufiyaa. The budgetary deficit increased significantly to the equivalent of 7.8% of GDP in 2002 and was expected to reach about 8.5% of GDP in 2003. The Maldives' total external debt was US $234.9m. at the end of 2001, of which $180.7m. was long-term public debt. In that year the cost of debt-servicing was equivalent to 4.6% of revenue from exports of goods and services. During 1990–2002 the average annual rate of inflation was 6.1%. Consumer prices increased by only 0.7% in 2001, and by 0.9% in 2002 (despite a July 2001 8% devaluation of the rufiyaa). According to the ADB, 2.0% of the labour force were unemployed in 2001.

The Maldives is a member of the UN Economic and Social Commission for Asia and the Pacific (ESCAP, see p. 31), the ADB, the Colombo Plan (see p. 359) and the South Asian Association for Regional Co-operation (SAARC, see p. 329).

One result of the rapid growth and increasing importance of the tourism sector in the Maldives in the late 1990s was the Government's efforts to improve the infrastructure (including development of communication systems, sanitation and water supply). By 1999 the Maldivian telecommunications company, DHIRAAGU, had provided telephone facilities to all of the inhabited islands. In mid-1999 DHIRAAGU signed a 47m.-rufiyaa contract with a French telecommunications company for the supply and implementation of a mobile cellular telephone system for the Maldives. By February 2004 more than 72,000 inhabitants had subscribed to mobile cellular telephones, with coverage reaching more than 70% of the population. In mid-2000 DHIRAAGU launched its 'Instant Internet Access'. However, despite a recovery in fish exports and buoyant tourism receipts in the latter half of the 1990s, the current-account deficit persisted and the trade deficit continued to grow. In April 2000 Air Maldives, a joint venture between the Government and a Malaysian company, Naluri Bhd, permanently ceased operating international flights, owing to estimated losses of US $50m.–$70m. This outcome adversely affected the tourist industry and business confidence. The tourist industry suffered further in 2001, owing to the suicide attacks on the USA and the subsequent military action in Afghanistan. The fisheries sector, however, fared better. In early 2001 the Government opened up the export of fresh and canned fish to the private sector, and in that year the Maldives Industrial Fisheries Company recorded a 13% increase in sales of fish, compared with the previous year. In 2002 the fisheries sector continued to expand (earnings from fish exports increased by 35%, compared with the previous year) and tourism gradually began to recover. The current-account deficit, however, remained high and the fiscal deficit continued to grow, largely owing to an increase in government expenditure. Furthermore, the islands continued to experience a shortage of domestic labour: in 2003 about 33,765 expatriate workers (mainly from India, Sri Lanka and Bangladesh) were employed in the Maldives, and it was estimated that in 1999 almost 20% of the country's GDP went to non-Maldivians. Although the growth in overall GDP declined in 2003, the tourist industry improved substantially and the fishing industry continued to expand. The Government pledged to continue to open up the public sector to private investment in 2004. In January President Gayoom announced that the 2004 budget would focus on accelerating social and economic progress. The Government had

commenced the introduction of necessary reforms for the development of the financial market. In June 2000 the Maldives was one of more than 30 countries and territories named by the Organisation for Economic Co-operation and Development (OECD, see p. 295) as unfair tax havens, but was subsequently removed from the list. Meanwhile, public expenditure needs to be further curtailed for the Government to make any significant progress in strengthening the economy. The high average annual rate of population growth (estimated at 2.7% in 1990–95), which has placed a heavy burden on the economy in general and on the congested capital island of Malé in particular, is an issue that is effectively being addressed (according to the results of the March 2000 census, the rate of population increase had fallen to 1.9% in 1995–2000). From 1997, in an attempt to solve the problem of overcrowding in Malé, the artificially constructed island of Hulhumalé was developed as a suburb to relieve congestion in the capital. The first group of people was appointed to move to the island in early 2004. The demand for local construction and transport generated by this project and other regional development programmes was expected to benefit the economy. In March 2002 the Maldives and the ADB signed a partnership agreement to reduce poverty. Some of the aims were to reduce absolute poverty from 43% in 1998 to 25% by 2015 and to promote involvement of local communities in public sector decision-making. Two other key issues that require prompt attention are: the protection of the fragile environment to ensure sustainable economic growth; and an improvement in Maldivian teaching standards in order to upgrade the national skills base.

Education

Education is not compulsory. There are three types of formal education: traditional Koranic schools (Makthab), Dhivehi-language primary schools (Madhrasa) and English-language primary and secondary schools. Schools of the third category are the only ones equipped to teach a standard curriculum. In 1984 a national curriculum was introduced in all schools. In 1989 the Government established a National Council on Education to oversee the development of education in the Maldives. Primary education begins at six years of age and lasts for five years. Secondary education, beginning at the age of 11, lasts for up to seven years, comprising a first cycle of five years and a second of two years. In 2000/01 the total enrolment at primary and secondary schools was equivalent to 101% of the school-age population. In 2000/01 primary enrolment was equivalent to 131% of children in the relevant age-group (boys 131%; girls 131%); the comparable ratio for secondary enrolment was 55% (boys 53%; girls 57%). The construction of the first secondary school outside Malé was completed, on Hithadoo Island in Addu Atoll, in 1992. There is a full-time vocational training centre, a teacher-training institute, an institute of hotel and catering services (opened in 1987), an Institute of Management and Administration, a Science Education Centre, an Islamic education centre, and a Non-formal Education Centre (renamed as Centre for Continuing Education in October 2002). The Maldives Institute of Technical Education, which was completed in late 1996, was expected to alleviate the problem of the lack of local skilled labour. The Maldives College of Higher Education, which was established to provide a uniform framework and policies for post-secondary education institutes, was opened in late 1998. Projected budgetary expenditure on education by the central Government in 2003 was 698.5m. rufiyaa, representing 18.3% of total spending.

Public Holidays

2004: 1 February* (Id al-Adha, feast of the Sacrifice), 22 February* (Islamic New Year), 21 April* (National Day), 2 May* (Birth of the Prophet Muhammad), 26–27 July (Independence Days), 15 October* (Ramadan begins), 3 November (Victory Day), 11–12 November (Republic Days), 14 November* (Id al-Fitr, end of Ramadan), 10 December (Fishermen's Day).

2005: 21 January* (Id al-Adha, feast of the Sacrifice), 10 February* (Islamic New Year), 10 April* (National Day), 21 April* (Birth of the Prophet Muhammad), 26–27 July (Independence Days), 5 October* (Ramadan begins), 3 November (Victory Day), 4 November* (Id al-Fitr, end of Ramadan), 11–12 November (Republic Days), 10 December (Fishermen's Day).

*These holidays are dependent on the Islamic lunar calendar and may vary by one or two days from the dates given.

Statistical Survey

Sources (unless otherwise stated): Ministry of Planning and National Development, Ghaazee Bldg, 4th Floor, Ameer Ahmed Magu, Malé 20-05; tel. 322919; fax 327351; internet www.planning.gov.mv.

AREA AND POPULATION

Area: 298 sq km (115 sq miles).

Population: 244,814 at census of 25 March 1995; 270,101 (males 137,200, females 132,901) at census of 31 March–7 April 2000; 276,000 (official estimate) at mid-2001.

Density (mid-2001): 926 per sq km.

Principal Town (population, 2000 census): Malé (capital) 74,069.

Births and Deaths (provisional, 2001): Registered live births 4,882 (birth rate 17.7 per 1,000); Registered deaths 1,079 (death rate 3.9 per 1,000).

Expectation of Life (WHO estimates, years at birth): 66.1 (males 66.5; females 65.6) in 2002. Source: WHO, *World Health Report*.

Economically Active Population (persons aged 12 years and over, census of April 2000): Agriculture, hunting and forestry 2,495; Fishing 9,294; Mining and quarrying 473; Manufacturing 11,081; Electricity, gas and water 1,132; Construction 3,691; Trade, restaurants and hotels 15,606; Transport, storage and communications 7,873; Financing, insurance, real estate and business services 1,690; Community, social and personal services 18,089; Activities not adequately defined 14,821; *Total employed* 86,245 (males 57,351, females 28,894); Unemployed 1,742 (males 928, females 814); *Total labour force* 87,987 (males 58,279, females 29,708).

HEALTH AND WELFARE

Key Indicators

Total Fertility Rate (children per woman, 2002): 5.4.

Under-5 Mortality Rate (per 1,000 live births, 2001): 77.

HIV/AIDS (% of persons aged 15–49, 2001): 0.06.

Physicians (per 1,000 head, 1996): 0.40.

Hospital Beds (per 1,000 head, 1996): 0.76.

Health Expenditure (2001): US $ per head (PPP): 263.

Health Expenditure (2001): % of GDP: 6.7.

Health Expenditure (2001): public (% of total): 83.5.

Access to Water (% of persons, 2000): 100.

Access to Sanitation (% of persons, 2000): 56.

Human Development Index (2001): ranking: 86.

Human Development Index (2001): value: 0.751.

For sources and definitions, see explanatory note on p. vi.

AGRICULTURE, ETC.

Principal Crops (metric tons, 1992): Coconuts (number of nuts) 13,442,737, Finger millet 5.7, Maize 1.6, Cassava 31.6, Sweet potatoes 13.8, Taro (Colocasia) 141.7, Alocasia 522.3, Onions 0.1, Chillies 40.3, Sorghum 2.0.

Coconuts (number): 18.9m. in 2000; 27.2m. in 2001; 43.5m. in 2002.

Sea Fishing ('000 metric tons, 2001): Total catch 125.8 (Skipjack tuna—Oceanic skipjack 88.0; Yellowfin tuna 15.2; Sharks, rays, skates, etc. 11.9) (Source: FAO, *Yearbook of Fishery Statistics*). *2002* ('000 metric tons): Total catch 164.3 (Skipjack tuna—Ocean skipjack 115.3; Yellowfin tuna 25.3).

INDUSTRY

Selected Products ('000 metric tons, 2001): Frozen fish 14.2; Salted, dried or smoked fish 6.9; Canned fish 7.2. Source: UN, *Industrial Commodity Statistics Yearbook*.

Electric Energy (million kWh): 116.5 in 2000; 130.3 in 2001; 140.8 in 2002.

FINANCE

Currency and Exchange Rates: 100 laari (larees) = 1 rufiyaa (Maldivian rupee). *Sterling, Dollar and Euro Equivalents* (31 December 2003): £1 sterling = 22.844 rufiyaa; US $1 = 12.800 rufiyaa; €1 = 16.166 rufiyaa; 1,000 rufiyaa = £43.77 = $78.13 = €61.86. *Average Exchange Rate* (rufiyaa per US dollar): 12.242 in 2001; 12.800 in 2002; 12.800 in 2003. Note: Between October 1994 and July 2001 the mid-point rate of exchange was maintained at US $1 = 11.77 rufiyaa. In July 2001 a new rate of $1 = 12.80 rufiyaa was introduced.

Budget (forecasts, million rufiyaa, 2003): *Revenue*: Tax revenue 1,130.9; Other current revenue 1,695.7; Capital revenue 47.8; Total 2,874.4, excl. grant received (113.4). *Expenditure*: General public services 800.7; Defence 466.6; Education 698.5; Health 395.9; Social security and welfare 123.8; Community programmes 560.6; Economic services 645.6 (Agriculture 34.8, Trade and industry 8.6, Electricity, gas and water 44.6, Transport and communications 517.6, Tourism 40.0); Interest on public debt 134.8; Total 3,826.5 (Current 2,367.5, Capital 1,459.0), excl. net lending (–124.2).

International Reserves (US $ million at 31 December 2003): IMF special drawing rights 0.45; Reserve position in IMF 2.31; Foreign exchange 156.73; Total 159.49. Source: IMF, *International Financial Statistics*.

Money Supply (million rufiyaa at 31 December 2003): Currency outside banks 624.90; Demand deposits at commercial banks 1,398.76; Total money (incl. others) 2,105.35. Source: IMF, *International Financial Statistics*.

Cost of Living (Consumer price index; base: 1995 = 100): All items 114.6 in 2000 (Food, excl. fish, 107.5; Fish 192.6; Clothing and footwear 102.6; Housing 106.6); 115.4 in 2001 (Food, excl. fish, 118.5; Fish 151.9; Clothing and footwear 101.6; Housing 108.4); 116.4 in 2002 (Food, excl. fish, 125.4; Fish 143.6; Clothing and footwear 97.7; Housing 106.8).

Gross Domestic Product by Economic Activity (revised estimates, million rufiyaa at constant 1995 prices, 2002): Agriculture 188.6; Fishing 494.7; Coral and sand mining 41.5; Manufacturing, electricity and water supply 849.6; Construction 229.0; Wholesale and retail trade, tourism 2,458.0; Transport and communications 998.0; Finance, real estate and business services 966.8; Public administration 862.9; Education, health and social services 141.9; *Sub-total* 7,230.9; *Less* Financial intermediation services indirectly measured 272.5; *GDP at factor cost* 6,958.4; Other taxes, *less* subsidies 684.3; *GDP in purchasers' values* 7,642.7.

Balance of Payments (US $ million, 2002): Exports of goods f.o.b. 133.6; Imports of goods f.o.b. –344.7; *Trade balance* –211.1; Exports of services 355.5; Imports of services –111.2; *Balance on goods and services* 33.2; Other income received 4.1; Other income paid –40.7; *Balance on goods, services and income* –3.4; Current transfers received 9.6; Current transfers paid –50.2; *Current balance* –44.0; Direct investment from abroad 11.7; Other investment assets 36.0; Other investment liabilities 31.2; Net errors and omissions –27.1; *Overall balance* 7.8. Source: IMF, *International Financial Statistics*.

Official Development Assistance (US $ million, 2000): Bilateral 12.1; Multilateral 7.2; *Total* 19.3 (Grants 17.7, Loans 1.6); *Per Caput Assistance* (US $): 71.4. Source: UN, *Statistical Yearbook for Asia and the Pacific*.

EXTERNAL TRADE

Principal Commodities (million rufiyaa, 2002): *Imports*: Live animals; animal products 292.7 (Dairy produce, eggs, honey and edible products 159.1); Vegetable products 370.8 (Edible vegetables 131.7; Edible fruits and nuts, peel of citrus or melons 104.3); Prepared food, beverages, spirits and tobacco 439.5 (Beverages, spirits and vinegar 110.0); Mineral products 819.2 (Salt, sulphur, earth and stone, lime and cement 163.0; Mineral fuels, oils, waxes, bituminous substances 656.1); Chemicals and allied industries 271.5; Plastics, rubber and articles thereof 128.2 (Plastics and articles thereof 112.37); Wood, wood charcoal, cork, straw, plaiting materials and articles thereof 141.5 (Wood and articles of wood; wood charcoal 136.3); Paper-making material, paper and paperboard and articles thereof 127.3; Textile and textile articles 593.9 (Cotton incl. yarns and woven fabrics thereof 167.3); Articles of stone, plaster, cement, asbestos, mica or similar materials, glass and glassware 89.5; Base metal and articles of base metal 250.1; Machinery and mechanical appliances; electrical equipment, parts and accessories 930.6 (Nuclear reactors, boilers, machinery and mechanical appliances, computers 490.2; Electrical machinery and equipment and parts thereof, telecommunications equipment, sound recorders, television recorders 440.3); Vehicles, aircraft, vessels and associated transport equipment 203.1 (Vehicles other than railway or tramway rolling stock 65.0; Aircraft, spacecraft and parts thereof 66.2); Miscellaneous manufactured articles 204.2 (Furniture, bedding, cushions, lamps and light fittings, illuminated signs, nameplates, prefabricated buildings 158.6); Total (incl. others) 5,014.0. *Exports*: Marine products 716.7 (Fresh or chilled tuna 131.2; Fresh or chilled reef fish 21.3; Frozen tuna 222.0; Dried tuna 115.8; Sea cucumber 38.0; Canned fish 128.9; Live reef fish 22.5; Other marine products 9.8); Apparel and clothing accessories 443.7; Total (incl. others) 1,161.7.

Principal Trading Partners (million rufiyaa, 2002): *Imports*: Australia 143.1, Canada 78.0, Denmark 80.8, France 297.4, Germany 60.9, Hong Kong 115.6, India 536.5, Indonesia 156.6, Italy 55.7, Japan 91.3, Malaysia 260.1, Netherlands 53.2, New Zealand 31.1, Singapore 1,293.6, Sri Lanka 761.97, Thailand 167.0, United Arab Emirates 358.5, United Kingdom 82.5, USA 63.9; Total (incl. others) 5,014.0. *Exports*: Germany 38.9, Hong Kong 22.2, Japan 133.4, Singapore 32.3, Sri Lanka 178.4, Thailand 170.0, United Kingdom 110.5, USA 445.9; Total (incl. others) 1,161.7.

TRANSPORT

Road Traffic (registered motor vehicles, 2002): Passenger cars 1,986; Taxis 608; Buses, coaches and vans 644; Lorries and tractors 730; Motorcycles and mopeds 15,957; Total (incl. others) 21,843. Source: Ministry of Transport and Civil Aviation, Malé.

Merchant Shipping Fleet (displacement, '000 gross registered tons at 31 December): 78.4 in 2000; 66.6 in 2001; 58.1 in 2002. Source: Lloyd's Register-Fairplay, *World Fleet Statistics*.

International Shipping (freight traffic, '000 metric tons, 1990): Goods loaded 27; Goods unloaded 78. Source: UN, *Monthly Bulletin of Statistics*.

Civil Aviation (traffic on scheduled services, 1999): Passengers carried 344,000; Passenger-km (million) 501. Source: UN, *Statistical Yearbook*.

TOURISM

Foreign Visitors by Country of Nationality (2002): Austria 10,480; France 31,228; Germany 63,212; Italy 114,9557; Japan 43,705; Switzerland 31,707; United Kingdom 80,377; Total (incl. others) 484,680. *2003:* Total foreign visitors 563,593 (Italy 140,304). Source: Ministry of Tourism, Malé.

Tourism Receipts (million rufiyaa): 693.3 in 2000; 715.9 in 2001 (estimate); 892.1 in 2002 (estimate). Source: Ministry of Tourism, Malé.

COMMUNICATIONS MEDIA

Radio Receivers (July 2000): 29,724 registered.

Television Receivers (July 2000): 10,701 registered.

Telephones (main lines in use): 24,432 in 2000; 27,242 in 2001; 28,651 in 2002.

Mobile Cellular Telephones (2002): 41,899.

Personal Computers (2001): 6,000 in use.

Internet Users (2002): 1,067 registered subscribers. Sources: Ministry of Planning and National Development, Malé; International Telecommunication Union.

EDUCATION

Pre-primary: 148 schools (2000); 12,886 pupils (2002); 411 teachers (2000).

Primary: 230 schools (2000); 68,242 pupils (2002); 2,221 teachers (2000).

Middle (2000): 222 schools; 27,293 pupils; 1,025 teachers.

Lower Secondary: 74 schools (2000); 23,903 pupils (2002); 1,134 teachers (2000).

Higher Secondary: 2 schools (2000); 1,131 pupils (2002); 53 teachers (2000).

Teacher Training (1999): 171 students.

Vocational: 11 schools (1986); 151 students (2000); 54 teachers (1986). Source: mainly Ministry of Education, Malé.

Adult Literacy Rate (UNESCO estimates): 97.0% (males 97.1%; females 96.9%) in 2001. Source: UN Development Programme, *Human Development Report*.

Directory

The Constitution

Following a referendum in March 1968, the Maldive Islands (renamed the Maldives in April 1969) became a republic on 11 November 1968. On 27 November 1997 the President ratified a new 156-article Constitution, which was to replace the 1968 Constitution; the new Constitution came into effect on 1 January 1998. The main constitutional provisions are summarized below:

STATE, SOVEREIGNTY AND CITIZENS

The Maldives shall be a sovereign, independent, democratic republic based on the principles of Islam, and shall be a unitary State, to be known as the Republic of Maldives. In this Constitution, the Republic of Maldives shall hereinafter be referred to as 'the Maldives'.

The powers of the State of the Maldives shall be vested in the citizens. Executive power shall be vested in the President and the Cabinet of Ministers, legislative power shall be vested in the People's Majlis (People's Council) and the People's Special Majlis, and the power of administering justice shall be vested in the President and the courts of the Maldives.

The religion of the State of the Maldives shall be Islam. The national language of the Maldives shall be Dhivehi.

FUNDAMENTAL RIGHTS AND DUTIES OF CITIZENS

Maldivian citizens are equal before and under the law and are entitled to the equal protection of the law. No Maldivian shall be deprived of citizenship, except as may be provided by law. No person shall be arrested or detained, except as provided by law. Any Maldivian citizen subjected to oppressive treatment shall have the right to appeal against such treatment to the concerned authorities and to the President.

The following are guaranteed: inviolability of residential dwellings and premises; freedom of education; inviolability of letters, messages and other means of communication; freedom of movement; the right to acquire and hold property; protection of property rights; the right to work; and freedom of expression, assembly and association.

Loyalty to the State and obedience to the Constitution and to the law of the Maldives shall be the duty of every Maldivian citizen, irrespective of where he may be.

THE PRESIDENT

The President shall be the Head of State, Head of Government and the Commander-in-Chief of the Armed Forces and of the Police.

The President shall be elected by secret ballot by the People's Majlis (more than one candidate may be nominated for election) and endorsed in office for five years by a national referendum.

In addition to the powers and functions expressly conferred on or assigned to the President by the Constitution and law, the President shall have the power to execute the following: appointment to and removal from office of the Vice-President, Chief Justice, Speaker and Deputy Speaker of the People's Majlis, Ministers, Attorney-General, Atoll Chiefs, judges, Auditor-General and Commissioner of Elections; appointment and dissolution of the Cabinet of Ministers; presiding over meetings of the Cabinet of Ministers; making a statement declaring the policies of the Government at the opening session of the People's Majlis every year; promulgating decrees, directives and regulations, as may be required from time to time for the purposes of ensuring propriety of the affairs of the Government and compliance with the provisions of the Constitution and law; holding public referendums on major issues; the declaration of war and peace.

While any person holds office as President, no proceedings shall be instituted or continued against him in any court or tribunal in respect of anything done or omitted to be done by him either in his official or private capacity.

A motion to remove the President from office may be considered in the People's Majlis only when one-third of the members of the Majlis have proposed it and two-thirds of the Majlis have resolved to consider it.

In the event that the presidency becomes vacant by reason of death, resignation or removal from office, the Speaker of the People's Majlis shall discharge the functions as Acting President from the time of occurrence of such vacancy. He shall continue to discharge these functions until a three-member Council is elected by a secret ballot of the People's Majlis to administer the State.

The President shall have the right to appoint at his discretion a Vice-President to discharge the duties and responsibilities assigned by the President.

THE CABINET OF MINISTERS

There shall be a Cabinet of Ministers appointed by the President, and the Cabinet shall be presided over by the President. The Cabinet of Ministers shall consist of the Vice-President (if any), Ministers charged with responsibility for Ministries and the Attorney-General.

The Cabinet of Ministers shall discharge the functions assigned to it by the President. The following shall be included in the said functions: to assist the President in formulating government policy on important national and international matters and issues; to advise the President on developing the Maldives economically and socially; to assist the President in the formulation of the annual state budget and government bills to be submitted to the People's Majlis; and to advise the President on the ratification of international treaties and agreements signed by the Maldivian Government with foreign administrations that require ratification by the State.

The President may, at his discretion, remove any Minister or the Attorney-General from office.

In the event of a vote of no confidence by the People's Majlis in a member of the Cabinet of Ministers, such member shall resign from office.

The President may dissolve the Cabinet of Ministers if, in his opinion, the Cabinet of Ministers is unable effectively to discharge its functions. Upon dissolution of the Cabinet of Ministers, the President shall inform the People's Majlis of the fact, specifying the reasons thereof, and shall appoint a new Cabinet of Ministers as soon as expedient.

THE PEOPLE'S MAJLIS

Legislative power, except the enactment of the Constitution, shall be vested in the People's Majlis. The People's Majlis shall consist of 50 members, of whom eight members shall be appointed by the President, two members elected from Malé and two members elected from each of the atolls. The duration of the People's Majlis shall be five years from the date on which the first meeting of the People's Majlis is held after its election. The Speaker and Deputy Speaker of the People's Majlis shall be appointed to and removed from office by the President. The Speaker shall not be a member of the People's Majlis, whereas the Deputy Speaker shall be appointed from among the members of the People's Majlis.

There shall be three regular sessions of the People's Majlis every year. The dates for the commencement and conclusion of these sessions shall be determined by the Speaker. An extraordinary sitting of the People's Majlis shall only be held when directed by the President. With the exception of the matters that, in accordance with the Constitution, require a two-thirds' majority for passage in the People's Majlis, all matters proposed for passage in the People's Majlis shall be passed by a simple majority.

Prior to the commencement of each financial year, the Minister of Finance shall submit the proposed state budget for approval by the People's Majlis.

A bill passed by the People's Majlis shall become law and enter into force upon being assented to by the President.

A motion expressing want of confidence in a member of the Cabinet of Ministers may be moved in the People's Majlis.

THE PEOPLE'S SPECIAL MAJLIS

The power to draw up and amend the Constitution of the Maldives shall be vested in the People's Special Majlis. The People's Special Majlis shall consist of: members of the Cabinet of Ministers, members of the People's Majlis, 42 members elected from Malé and the atolls, and eight members appointed by the President.

Any article or provision of the Constitution may be amended only by a law passed by a majority of votes in the People's Special Majlis and assented to by the President.

THE JUDICIARY

The High Court shall consist of the Chief Justice and such number of Judges as may be determined by the President. The Chief Justice and the Judges of the High Court shall be appointed by the President.

All appeals from the courts of the Maldives shall, in accordance with regulations promulgated by the President, be heard by the High Court. The High Court shall hear cases determined by the President to be filed with the High Court from among the proceedings instituted by the State.

There shall be in the Maldives such number of courts at such places as may be determined by the President. The judges of the courts shall be appointed by the President.

PROCLAMATION OF EMERGENCY

Where the President has determined that the security of the Maldives or part thereof is threatened by war, foreign aggression or civil unrest, the President shall have the right to issue a Proclamation of Emergency. While the Proclamation is in force, the President shall have the power to take and order all measures expedient to protect national security and public order. Such measures may include the suspension of fundamental rights and laws. A Proclamation of Emergency shall initially be valid for a period of three months. The Proclamation may be extended, if approved by the People's Majlis, for a period determined by the People's Majlis.

GENERAL PROVISIONS

No bilateral agreement between the Government of the Maldives and the government of a foreign country and no multilateral agreement shall be signed or accepted by the Government of the Maldives unless the President has authorized in writing such signature or acceptance. In the event that such agreement requires ratification by the Maldives, such agreement shall not come into effect unless the President has ratified the same on the advice of the Cabinet of Ministers.

The Government

HEAD OF STATE

President: MAUMOON ABDUL GAYOOM (took office 11 November 1978; re-elected 30 September 1983, 26 September 1988, 1 October 1993, 16 October 1998 and 17 October 2003).

THE CABINET OF MINISTERS
(April 2004)

Minister of Defence and National Security and of Finance and Treasury: MAUMOON ABDUL GAYOOM.

Minister of Fisheries, Agriculture and Marine Resources: ABDULLA KAMALUDDEEN.

Minister of Foreign Affairs: FATHULLA JAMEEL.

Minister of Women's Affairs, Family Development and Social Security: ANEESA AHMED.

Minister of Education: Dr MAHMOOD SHAUGEE.

Minister of Trade and Industries: ABDULLA YAMEEN.

Minister of Health: AHMED ABDULLA.

Minister of Justice: AHMED ZAHIR.

Minister of Tourism: HASSAN SOBIR.

Minister of Transport and Civil Aviation: ILYAS IBRAHIM.

Minister of Planning and National Development: HAMDOON HAMEED.

Minister of Home Affairs and Environment: ISMAIL SHAFEEU.

Minister of Communication, Science and Technology: MIDHATH HILMY.

Minister of Construction and Public Works: UMAR ZAHIR.

Minister of Atolls Administration: ABDULLA HAMEED.

Minister of Youth Development and Sports: Dr MOHAMED ZAHIR HUSSAIN.

Minister of Information, Arts and Culture: IBRAHIM HUSSAIN MANIKU.

Minister of Employment and Labour: ABDUL RASHEED HUSSAIN.

Minister of State for Presidential Affairs: MOHAMED HUSSAIN.

Minister of State for Defence and National Security: ABDUL SATTAR ADAM.

Minister of State for Finance and Treasury: MOHAMED JALEEL.

Minister of State and Auditor-General: ISMAIL FATHY.

Attorney-General: Dr HASSAN SAEED.

MINISTRIES

President's Office: Boduthakurufaanu Magu, Malé 20-05; tel. 323701; fax 325500; internet www.presidencymaldives.gov.mv.

Attorney-General's Office: Huravee Bldg, Malé 20-05; tel. 323809; fax 314109.

Ministry of Atolls Administration: Faashana Bldg, Boduthakurufaanu Magu (North), Malé 20-05; tel. 323070; fax 327750.

Ministry of Communication, Science and Technology: Bank of Maldives Bldg, 5th Floor, Boduthakurufaanu Magu, Malé 20-05; tel. 331695; fax 331694; e-mail secretariat@mcst.gov.mv; internet www.mcst.gov.mv.

Ministry of Construction and Public Works: Izzuddeen Magu, Malé 20-01; tel. 323234; fax 328300; e-mail mcpw@dhivehinet.net.mv.

Ministry of Defence and National Security: Bandaara Koshi, Ameer Ahmed Magu, Malé 20-05; tel. 322607; fax 332689; e-mail admin@defence.gov.mv.

Ministry of Education: Ghaazee Bldg, 2nd Floor, Ameer Ahmed Magu, Malé 20-05; tel. 323262; fax 321201; e-mail educator@dhivehinet.net.mv; internet www.moe.gov.mv.

Ministry of Finance and Treasury: Block 379, Ameenee Magu, Malé 20-03; tel. 317590; fax 324432; e-mail minfin@dhivehinet.net.mv.

Ministry of Fisheries, Agriculture and Marine Resources: Ghaazee Bldg, Ground Floor, Ameer Ahmed Magu, Malé 20-05; tel. 322625; fax 326558; internet www.fishagri.gov.mv.

Ministry of Foreign Affairs: PA Complex, 5th Floor, Hilaalee Magu, Maafannu, Malé 10-307; tel. 323400; fax 323841; e-mail admin@foreign.gov.mv.

Ministry of Health: Ameenee Magu, Malé 20-03; tel. 328887; fax 328889; e-mail moh@dhivehinet.net.mv; internet www.health.gov.mv.

Ministry of Home Affairs and Environment: Huravee Bldg, 3rd Floor, Ameer Ahmed Magu, Malé 20-05; tel. 324861; fax 322286; e-mail env@environment.gov.mv; internet www.environment.gov.mv.

Ministry of Human Resources, Employment and Labour: Ghaazee Bldg, 4th Floor, Ameer Ahmed Magu, Malé 20-05; e-mail info@manpowermaldives.org; internet www.manpowermaldives.org.

Ministry of Information, Arts and Culture: Buruzu Magu, Malé 20-04; tel. 323836; fax 326211; e-mail informat@dhivehinet.net.mv; internet www.maldivesinfo.gov.mv.

Ministry of Justice: Justice Bldg, Orchid Magu, Malé 20-05; tel. 322303; fax 325447; internet www.justice.gov.mv.

Ministry of Planning and National Development: Ghaazee Bldg, 4th Floor, Ameer Ahmed Magu, Malé 20-05; tel. 322919; fax 327351; internet www.planning.gov.mv.

Ministry of Tourism: Bank of Maldives Bldg, 4th Floor, Boduthakurufaanu Magu, Malé 20-05; tel. 323228; fax 323229.

Ministry of Trade and Industries: Ghaazee Bldg, 1st Floor, Ameer Ahmed Magu, Malé 20-05; tel. 323668; fax 323840; e-mail trademin@dhivehinet.net.mv; internet www.investmaldives.com.

Ministry of Transport and Civil Aviation: Huravee Bldg, Ameer Ahmed Magu, Malé 20-05; tel. 323992; fax 323994; e-mail admin@transport.gov.mv; internet www.transport.gov.mv.

Ministry of Women's Affairs and Social Security: Umar Shopping Arcade, 2nd and 4th Floors, Chaandhanee Magu, Malé 20-02; tel. 323687; fax 316237; internet www.urcmaldives.gov.mv.

Ministry of Youth Development and Sports: Ghaazee Bldg, Ameeruahmed Magu, Malé 20-02; tel. 326986; fax 327162; e-mail youthspo@dhivehinet.net.mv; internet www.youthsports.gov.mv.

Legislature

PEOPLE'S MAJLIS

The People's Majlis (People's Council) comprises 50 members, of whom eight are appointed by the President, two elected by the people of Malé and two elected from each of the 20 atolls (for a five-year term). The most recent election was held on 19 November 1999.

Speaker: ABDULLA HAMEED.

Deputy Speaker: ABDUL RASHEED HUSSAIN.

Political Organizations

There are no political parties in the Maldives. There is, however, an opposition party, composed of mainly exiled Maldivians, based in Colombo, Sri Lanka:

Maldivian Democratic Party (MDP): Colombo, Sri Lanka; e-mail secretariat@maldiviandemocraticparty.org; internet www.maldiviandemocraticparty.org; f. 2001 ; denied official registration in the Maldives; reconstituted in Colombo in 2003; Spokesperson MOHAMED LATHEEF.

Diplomatic Representation

HIGH COMMISSIONS IN THE MALDIVES

Bangladesh: H. High Grove, 6 Hithaffinivaa Magu, Malé; tel. 315541; fax 315543; e-mail bdootmal@dhivehinet.net.mv; High Commissioner ABDUL LATIF (acting).

India: H. Athireege-Aage, Ameeru Ahmed Magu, Malé; tel. 323015; fax 324778; High Commissioner S. M. GAVAI.

Pakistan: G. Penta Green, Majeedhee Magu, Malé; tel. 322024; fax 321832; High Commissioner AMIR MUHAMMAD KHAN.

Sri Lanka: H. Sakeena Manzil, Medhuziyaaraiyh Magu, Malé 20-05; tel. 322845; fax 321652; e-mail highcom@dhivehinet.net.mv; High Commissioner T. ZAROOK A. SAMSUDEEN.

Judicial System

The administration of justice is undertaken in accordance with Islamic (*Shari'a*) law. In 1980 the Maldives High Court was established. There are four courts in Malé, and 200 island courts, one in every inhabited island. All courts, with the exception of the High Court, are under the control of the Ministry of Justice.

In January 1999 the Government declared that the island court of each atoll capital would thenceforth oversee the administration of justice in that atoll. At the same time it was announced that arrangements were being made to appoint a senior magistrate in each atoll capital.

HIGH COURT

Chief Justice: MOHAMED RASHEED IBRAHIM.

Judges:, ABDUL GHANEE MOHAMED, AHMED HAMEED FAHMY, ALI HAMEED MOHAMED.

In February 1995 the President established a five-member Advisory Council on Judicial Affairs. The Council was to function under the President's Office (equivalent, in this respect, to a Supreme Court) and was to study and offer counsel to the President on appeals made to the President by either the appellant or the respondent in cases adjudicated by the High Court. The Council was also to offer such counsel as and when requested by the President on other judicial matters.

ADVISORY COUNCIL ON JUDICIAL AFFAIRS

Members: MOOSA FATHY, ABDULLA HAMEED, DR MOHAMED MUNAVVAR, Prof. MOHAMED RASHEED IBRAHIM, AL-SHEIKH HASSAN YOOSUF.

Religion

Islam is the state religion, and the Maldivians are Sunni Muslims. In mid-1991 there were 724 mosques and 266 women's mosques throughout the country.

In late 1996 a Supreme Council for Islamic Affairs was established, under the authority of the President's Office. The new body was to authorize state policies with regard to Islam and to advise the Government on Islamic affairs.

Musthashaaru of the Supreme Council for Islamic Affairs: MOOSA FATHY.

President of the Supreme Council for Islamic Affairs: MOHAMED RASHEED IBRAHIM.

Deputy President of the Supreme Council for Islamic Affairs: AHMED FAROOG MOHAMED.

The Press

In 1993 the Government established a National Press Council to review, monitor and further develop journalism in the Maldives.

DAILIES

Aafathis Daily News: Feeroaz Magu, Maafannu, Malé 20-02; tel. 318609; fax 312425; e-mail aafathis@dhivehinet.net.mv; internet www.aafathisnews.com.mv; f. 1979; daily; Dhivehi and English; Editor AHMED ZAHIR; circ. 3,000.

Haveeru Daily: Ameenee Magu, POB 20103, Malé; tel. 325671; fax 323103; e-mail haveeru@haveeru.com.mv; internet www.haveeru .com.mv; f. 1979; Dhivehi and English; Chair. MOHAMED ZAHIR HUSSAIN; Editor ALI RAFEEQ; circ. 4,500.

Miadhu News: G. Mascot, Koimalaa Hingun, Malé 20-02; tel. 320700; fax 320500; e-mail miadhu@dhivehinet.net.mv; internet www.miadhu.com; daily newspaper; Propr IBRAHIM RASHEED MOOSA; Chair. AHMED ABDULLA.

PERIODICALS

Adduvas: Malé; f. 2000; weekly; news, entertainment, health issues and social affairs.

Dheenuge Magu (The Path of Religion): The President's Office, Boduthakurufaanu Magu, Malé 20-05; tel. 323701; fax 325500; e-mail info@presidencymaldives.gov.mv; f. 1986; weekly; Dhivehi; religious; publ. by the President's Office; Editor President MAUMOON ABDUL GAYOOM; Dep. Editor MOHAMED RASHEED IBRAHIM; circ. 7,500.

Dhivehingetharika (Maldivian Heritage): National Centre for Linguistic and Historical Research, Soasun Magu, Malé 20-05; tel. 323206; fax 326796; e-mail nclhr@dhivehinet.net.mv; internet www .qaumiyyath.gov.mv; f. 1998; Dhivehi; Maldivian archaeology, history and language.

Faiythoora: National Centre for Linguistic and Historical Research, Soasun Magu, Malé 20-05; tel. 323206; fax 326796; e-mail nclhr@dhivehinet.net.mv; internet www.qaumiyyath.gov.mv; f. 1979; monthly magazine; Dhivehi; Maldivian history, culture and language; Editor Uz ABDULLA HAMEED; circ. 800.

Furadhaana: Ministry of Information, Arts and Culture, Buruzu Magu, Malé 20-04; tel. 321749; fax 326211; e-mail informat@ dhivehinet.net.mv; internet www.maldives-info.com; f. 1990; monthly; Dhivehi; Editor IBRAHIM MANIK; circ. 1,000.

Jamaathuge Khabaru (Community News): Centre for Continuing Education, Salahudeen Bldg, Malé 20-04; tel. 328772; fax 322223; monthly; Dhivehi; Editor AHMED ZAHIR; circ. 1,500.

Maldives Marine Research Bulletin: Marine Research Centre, Ministry of Fisheries, Agriculture and Marine Resources, H. White Waves, Malé 20-06; tel. 322328; fax 322509; e-mail marine@fishagri .gov.mv; f. 1995; biannual; fisheries and marine research; Asst Dir-Gen. AHMED HAFIZ.

Maldives News Bulletin: Maldives News Bureau, Ministry of Information, Arts and Culture, Buruzu Magu, Malé 20-04; tel. 323838; fax 326211; e-mail informat@dhivehinet.net.mv; internet www.maldives-info.com; weekly; English; Editor ALI SHAREEF; circ. 350.

Monday Times: H. Neel Villa, Boduthakunufaanu Magu, Malé; tel. and fax 315084; e-mail info@mondaytimes.com.mv; internet www .mondaytimes.com.mv; f. 2000; weekly; Editor MOHAMED BUSHRY.

Our Environment: Forum of Writers on the Environment, c/o Ministry of Planning and National Development, Ghaazee Bldg, Ameer Ahmed Magu, Malé 20-05; tel. 324861; fax 327351; f. 1990; monthly; Dhivehi; Editor FAROUQ AHMED.

Rasain: Ministry of Fisheries, Agriculture and Marine Resources, Ghaazee Bldg, Ameer Ahmed Magu, Malé 20-05; tel. 322625; fax 326558; e-mail fishagri@dhivehinet.net.mv; f. 1980; annual; fisheries development.

Samugaa: Malé; f. 1995; publ. by the Government Employees' Club.

NEWS AGENCIES

Haveeru News Service (HNS): POB 20103, Malé; tel. 313825; fax 323103; e-mail haveeru@dhivehinet.net.mv; internet www.haveeru .com; f. 1979; Chair. MOHAMED ZAHIR HUSSAIN; Man. Editor AHMED ZAHIR.

Hiyama News Agency: H. Navaagan, Malé 20-05; tel. 322588.

Maldives News Bureau (MNB): Ministry of Information, Arts and Culture, Buruzu Magu, Malé 20-04; tel. 323836; fax 326211; e-mail informat@dhivehinet.net.mv; internet www.maldives-info.com.

Broadcasting and Communications

TELECOMMUNICATIONS

Ministry of Communication, Science and Technology (Post and Telecommunication Section): Telecom Bldg, Husnuheena Magu, Malé 20-04; tel. 323344; fax 320000; e-mail telecom@ dhivehinet.net.mv; regulatory authority; Dir-Gen. (Post and Telecommunication Section) HUSSAIN SHAREEF; Dir MOHAMED AMIR.

Dhivehi Raajjeyge Gulhun Ltd (DHIRAAGU): Medhuziyaaraiy Magu, Malé 20-03; tel. 322802; fax 322800; e-mail info@dhiraagu .com.mv; internet www.dhiraagu.com.mv; f. 1988; jointly owned by the Maldivian Government (55%) and by Cable and Wireless PLC of the United Kingdom (45%); functions under Ministry of Communication, Science and Technology; operates all national and international telecommunications services in the Maldives (incl. internet service–Dhivehinet); Chair. ISMAIL SHAFEEU; CEO and Gen. Man. ISMAIL WAHEED.

RADIO

Radio Eke: Malé.

Voice of Islam: Malé.

Voice of Maldives (VOM) (Dhivehi Raajjeyge Adu): Moonlight Higun, Malé 20-06; tel. 325577; fax 328357; radio broadcasting began in 1962 under name of Malé Radio; name changed as above in 1980; three channels; home service in Dhivehi (0530 hrs–2245 hrs daily) and English (1700 hrs–1900 hrs daily); Dir-Gen. IBRAHIM MANIK.

TELEVISION

Television Maldives: Buruzu Magu, Malé 20-04; tel. 323105; fax 325083; television broadcasting began in 1978; two channels: TVM broadcasts for an average of 6–7 hrs daily and TVM Plus (f. 1998) broadcasts for 10 hrs daily; covers a 40-km radius around Malé; Dir-Gen. HUSSAIN MOHAMED; Dep. Dirs MOHAMED NASHID, ABDUL MUHUSIN.

Finance

(cap. = capital; brs = branches; amounts in US dollars unless otherwise stated)

BANKING

Central Bank

Maldives Monetary Authority (MMA): Umar Shopping Arcade, 3rd Floor, Chandhanee Magu, Maafannu, Malé 20-01; tel. 323783; fax 323862; e-mail mail@mma.gov.mv; internet www.mma.gov.mv; f. 1981; bank of issue; supervises and regulates commercial bank and foreign-exchange dealings and advises the Govt on banking and monetary matters; authorized cap. 4m. rufiyaa (2001); Gov. President MAUMOON ABDUL GAYOOM; Vice-Gov. MOHAMED JALEEL; Gen. Man. ABDUL GHAFOOR.

Commercial Bank

Bank of Maldives (PLC) Ltd (BML): 11 Boduthakurufaanu Magu, Malé 20-094; tel. 322948; fax 328233; e-mail info@bml.com .mv; internet www.bankofmaldives.com.mv; f. 1982; 75% state-owned, 25% privately-owned; cap. 36.5m., res 156m., dep. 1,677m. (2002); Chair. IBRAHIM ZUHAIR; Gen. Man. and CEO SERENE HO OI KHUEN; 17 brs.

Foreign Banks

Bank of Ceylon (Sri Lanka): Aage Bldg, Boduthakurufaanu Magu, Malé; tel. 323045; fax 320575; e-mail bcmale@dhivehinet.net.mv; internet www.bankofceylon.net; Country Man. ROY JAYASUNDARA; 1 br.

Habib Bank Ltd (Pakistan): Ship Plaza, Ground Floor, 1/6 Orchid Magu, POB 20121, Malé; tel. 322051; fax 326791; e-mail hblmale@ dhivehinet.net.mv; Vice-Pres. and Chief Man. MUHAMMAD JAMIL ANJUM.

The Hongkong and Shanghai Banking Corpn Ltd (Hong Kong): MTCC Bldg, 1st Floor, Boduthakurufaanu Magu, Malé 20–05; tel. 330770; fax 312072; e-mail sarathweerakoon@hsbc.com.lk; Country Man. SARATH WEERAKOON.

State Bank of India: Boduthakurufaanu Magu, Malé 20-05; tel. 320860; fax 323053; e-mail sbimale@dhivehinet.net.mv; CEO G. N. DASH.

DEVELOPMENT FINANCE ORGANIZATION

Housing Development Finance Corpn: Gaadhoo Bldg, 3rd Floor, Henveiru, Malé; f. 2004 to provide public housing loans; 100% state-owned; Chair. IBRAHIM NAEEM.

INSURANCE

Allied Insurance Co of the Maldives (Pte) Ltd: 04–06 STO Trade Centre, Orchid Magu, Malé; tel. 324612; fax 325035; e-mail allied@dhivehinet.net.mv; internet www.alliedmaldives.com; f. 1985; all classes of non-life insurance; operated by State Trading Organisation (see below); Chief Exec. MOHAMED MANIKU; Gen. Man. ISMAIL RIZA.

Trade and Industry

GOVERNMENT AGENCIES

Foreign Investment Services Bureau (FISB): Malé; tel. 323890; fax 323756; e-mail trademin@dhivehinet.net.mv; internet www.investmaldives.com; under administration of Ministry of Trade and Industries; Dir-Gen. AHMED NASEEM.

Maldives Housing and Urban Development Board: Malé; Dir ABDUL AZEEZ; Dep. Dir ABDULLAH SODIQ.

CHAMBER OF COMMERCE AND INDUSTRY

Maldives National Chamber of Commerce and Industry (MNCCI): G. Viyafaari Hiya, Ameenee Magu, Malé 20-04; tel. 326634; fax 310233; e-mail mncci@dhivehinet.net.mv; internet www.mncci.com; f. 1978; merged with the Maldivian Traders' Association in 2000; Pres. MOHAMED SOLIH; Sec.-Gen. ABDULLAH FAIZ.

INDUSTRIAL AND TRADE ASSOCIATIONS

The Maldives Association of Construction Industry (MACI): Malé; f. 2003; Chair. ABDULLA MOHAMED; Sec.-Gen. AMIN IBRAHIM.

Sri Lanka Trade Centre: Girithereyege Bldg, 3rd Floor, Hithaffinivaa Magu, Malé; tel. 315183; fax 315184; e-mail dirsltc@avasmail.com.mv; f. 1993 to facilitate and promote trade, tourism, investment and services between Sri Lanka and the Maldives; Dir M. I. SUFIYAN.

State Trading Organization PLC (STO): STO Bldg, 7 Haveeree Higun, Malé 20-02; tel. 323279; fax 325218; e-mail sto@dhivehinet.net.mv; internet www.stomaldives.com; f. 1964 as Athirimaafannuge Trading Account, renamed as above in 1976; became public limited company in 2001; state-controlled commercial organization; under administration of independent Board of Directors; imports and distributes staple foods, fuels, pharmaceuticals and general consumer items; acts as purchaser for govt requirements; undertakes long-term development projects; Man. Dir MOHAMED MANIKU; Dir ISMAIL IBRAHIM.

UTILITIES

Electricity

Maldives Electricity Bureau: Malé; tel. 328753; fax 323840; e-mail trademin@dhivehinet.net.mv; f. 1998; under administration of Ministry of Trade and Industries; regulatory authority.

State Electric Co (STELCO) Ltd: Ameenee Magu, Malé; tel. 320982; fax 327036; e-mail admin@stelco.com.mv; internet www.stelco.com.mv; f. 1997 to replace Maldives Electricity Board; under administration of Ministry of Trade and Industries; provides electricity, consultancy services, electrical spare parts service, etc.; operates 22 power stations; installed capacity 32,921 kW (Dec. 2000); Chair. ABDULLAH YAMEEN; Man. Dir ABDUL SHAKOOR.

Gas

Maldive Gas Pvt Ltd: Thilafushi, Malé Atoll; f. 1999; as a jt venture between State Trading Organisation and Champa Gas and Oil Co; Chair. MOHAMED MANIK.

Water

Maldives Water and Sanitation Authority (MWSA): Malé; f. 1973; Dir FAROOQ MOHAMED HASSAN.

Malé Water and Sewerage Co: Ameenee Magu, Machangolhi, POB 20148, Malé 20-375; tel. 323209; fax 324306; e-mail mwsc@dhivehinet.net.mv; f. 1995; 70% govt-owned; produces approximately 5,000 cu m tons of fresh, desalinated water daily, using seven plants; provides water and sewerage services to the islands of Malé, Hulhumalé and Villingili; provides water services to the island of Maafushi; Chair. HASSAN SOBIR; Gen. Man. MOHAMED AHMED DIDI.

Transport

Maldives Transport and Contracting Co Ltd (MTCC): MTCC Bldg, 5th Floor, Boduthakurufaanu Magu, POB 263, Malé 20-181; tel. 326822; fax 323221; e-mail info@mtcc.com.mv; internet www.mtcc.com.mv; f. 1980; 60% state-owned, 40% privately owned; marine transport, civil and technical contracting, harbour development, shipping agents for general cargo, passenger liners and oil tankers; Man. Dir MOHAMED IBRAHIM; Chair. UMAR ZAHIR.

SHIPPING

Vessels operate from the Maldives to Sri Lanka and Singapore at frequent intervals, also calling at points in India, Pakistan, Myanmar (formerly Burma), Malaysia, Bangladesh, Thailand, Indonesia and the Middle East. In December 2002 the merchant shipping fleet of the Maldives numbered 58 vessels, with a combined displacement of 58,130 grt. Smaller vessels provide services between the islands on an irregular basis. Malé is the only port handling international traffic. In 1986 a new commercial harbour was opened in Malé. The Malé Harbour Development Project was implemented during 1991–97, and improved and increased the capacity and efficiency of Malé Port.

Maldives Ports Authority (MPA): Commercial Harbour, Malé 20-02; tel. 329339; fax 325293; e-mail maldport@dhivehinet.net.mv; f. 1986; under administration of Ministry of Transport and Civil Aviation; Man. Dir ISMAIL SHAFEEQ.

Island Enterprises Pvt Ltd: Maaram, 1st Floor, Ameeru Ahmed Magu, Henveiru, POB 20169, Malé 20-05; tel. 323531; fax 325645; e-mail info@ielmaldives.com; internet www.iemaldives.com; f. 1978; fleet of eight vessels; exporters of frozen fish, owners of processing plant, shipping agents, chandlers, cruising agents, surveyors and repairs; Man. Dir OMAR MANIK.

Precision Marine Pvt Ltd: Maaram, 1st Floor, Ameeru Ahmed Magu, Henveiru, POB 20169, Malé 20-05; tel. 323531; fax 325645; e-mail fiberbot@dhivehinet.net.mv; internet www.pmlboatyard.com.mv; subsidiary of Island Enterprises Pvt Ltd; mfrs and repairers of fibreglass boats, launches, yachts, marine sports equipment, etc.; Dir OMAR MANIK.

Madihaa Co (Pvt) Ltd: 1/40 Shaheed Ali Higun, Malé; tel. 327812; fax 322251; e-mail madicom@dhivehinet.net.mv; f. 1985; imports and exports fresh fruit and vegetables, construction raw materials, confectionary items and soft drinks; Man. Dir MOOSA AHMED.

Maldives National Shipping Ltd: Ship Plaza, 2nd Floor, 1/6 Orchid Magu, POB 2022, Malé 20-02; tel. 323871; fax 324323; e-mail mns@dhivehinet.net.mv; f. 1965; 100% state-owned; fleet of three container vessels; br. in Singapore; Gen. Man. AIMON JAMEEL.

Matrana Enterprises (Pvt) Ltd: 97 Majeedhee Magu, Malé; tel. 321733; fax 322832; Sr Exec. MOHAMED ABDULLA.

Villa Shipping and Trading Co (Pvt) Ltd: Villa Bldg, POB 2073, Malé; tel. 325195; fax 325177; e-mail villa@dhivehinet.net.mv; Man. Dir QASIM IBRAHIM.

CIVIL AVIATION

The existing airport on Hululé Island near Malé, which was first opened in 1966, was expanded and improved to international standard with financial assistance from abroad and, as Malé International Airport, was officially opened in 1981. Charter flights from Europe subsequently began. In addition, there are four domestic airports covering different regions of the country: one on Gan Island, Addu Atoll, another on Kadhdhoo Island, Hadhdhummathi Atoll, another on Hanimaadhoo Island, South Thiladhummathi Atoll, and another on Kaadedhdhoo Island, South Huvadhu Atoll. The airport on Gan Island was expected to be capable of servicing international flights in the near future. Construction of a fifth domestic airport, in Raa Atoll Dhuvaafaru, was scheduled to begin in 1994. In early 1995 there were 10 helipads in use in the Maldives.

Maldives Airport Co Ltd: Malé International Airport, Hululé; tel. 323506; fax 325034; e-mail enquiry@airports.com.mv; internet www.airports.com.mv; f. 2000; 100% govt-owned; under administration of Ministry of Transport and Civil Aviation; Man. Dir AHMED ALI MANIKU.

Air Maldives Ltd: 26 Ameer Ahmed Magu, Henveiru, POB 2049, Malé 20-05; tel. 328454; fax 318757; e-mail airmldvs@dhivehinet.net.mv; f. 1974; 51% govt-owned, 49% owned by Naluri Bhd (Malaysia); under administration of Ministry of Transport and Civil Aviation; domestic flights; operated international flights until March 2000; national carrier.

Island Aviation Services Ltd: Malé; e-mail info@island.com.mv; internet www.island.com.mv; f. 2000; 100% govt-owned; operates domestic flights (suspended by Air Maldives Ltd in April 2000); Chair. ABDULLA YAMEEN; Man. Dir BANDHU IBRAHIM SALEEM.

Maldivian Air Taxi: Malé International Airport, Hululé, POB 2023, Malé; tel. 315201; fax 315203; e-mail mat@mat.com.mv; internet www.mataxi.com; f. 1993; seaplane services between Malé and outer islands; operates 15 aircraft; Chair. LARS ERIK NIELSEN; Gen. Man. AUM FAWZY.

Ocean Air (Pvt) Ltd: Malé; scheduled domestic flights between Malé and Gan.

Trans Maldivian Airways (Pvt) Ltd: POB 2079, Malé; tel. 325708; fax 323161; e-mail mail@tma.com.mv; internet www.tma .com.mv; f. 1989 as Hummingbird Island Airways Pvt Ltd, name changed as above in 2000; operates 12 floatplanes; Man. Dir BRAM STELLER.

Tourism

The tourism industry brings considerable foreign exchange to the Maldives. The islands' attractions include white sandy beaches, excellent diving conditions and multi-coloured coral formations. By April 2001 there were 87 island resorts in operation, and 16,428 hotel beds were available. The annual total of foreign visitors increased from only 29,325 in 1978 to 467,154 in 2000. Tourist arrivals decreased to 460,984 in 2001, before rising to 484,680 in 2002 and to 563,593 in 2003. Revenue from tourism was estimated at 892.1m. rufiyaa in 2002. A plan was implemented in late 2001 to convert 12 islands into resorts and to increase the number of hotel beds by some 4,000 by 2005.

Maldives Association of Tourism Industry (MATI): Gadhamoo Bldg, 3rd Floor, Henveiru, Malé; tel. 326640; fax 326641; e-mail mati@dhivehinet.net.mv; f. 1984; promotes and develops tourism; Chair. MOHAMED UMAR MANIKU; Sec.-Gen. S. I. MOHAMED.

Maldives Tourism Promotion Board: Bank of Maldives Bldg, 4th Floor, Boduthakurufaanu Magu, Malé 20-05; tel. 323228; fax 323229; e-mail mtpb@visitmaldives.com.mv; internet www .visitmaldives.com; f. 1998.

Air Maldives Travel Bureau/Tourist Information: Arrival Hall, Malé International Airport, Hululé; tel. 325511 (Ext. 8240); fax 325056; f. 1997.

MALI

Introductory Survey

Location, Climate, Language, Religion, Flag, Capital

The Republic of Mali is a land-locked country in West Africa, with Algeria to the north, Mauritania and Senegal to the west, Guinea and Côte d'Ivoire to the south, and Burkina Faso and Niger to the east. The climate is hot throughout the country. The northern region of Mali is part of the Sahara, an arid desert. It is wetter in the south, where the rainy season is from June to October. Temperatures in Bamako are generally between 16°C (61°F) and 39°C (103°F). The official language is French but a number of other languages, including Bambara, Fulfulde, Sonrai, Tamashek, Soninke and Dogon, are widely spoken. It is estimated that about 80% of the population are Muslims and 18% follow traditional animist beliefs; under 2% are Christians. The national flag (proportions 2 by 3) has three equal vertical stripes, of green, gold and red. The capital is Bamako.

Recent History

Mali, as the former French West African colony of Soudan, merged in April 1959 with Senegal to form the Federation of Mali, which became independent on 20 June 1960. Senegal seceded two months later, and the remnant of the Federation was proclaimed the Republic of Mali on 22 September 1960. Its first President was Modibo Keita, the leader of the Union soudanaise—Rassemblement démocratique africain (US—RDA), who pursued authoritarian socialist policies. Mali withdrew from the Franc Zone (see p. 255) in 1962, and developed close relations with the communist bloc. Economic difficulties caused Mali to return to the Franc Zone in 1968, although the country was not fully reintegrated into the Zone's monetary union until 1984.

Keita dissolved the elected legislature in January 1968. Following a series of purges of US—RDA and public officials, Keita was overthrown in November of that year by a group of junior army officers, who assumed power as the Comité militaire pour la libération nationale (CMLN). The Constitution was abrogated, and all political activity was banned. Lt (later Gen.) Moussa Traoré became Head of State and President of the CMLN, while Capt. Yoro Diakité became President of the Government (Prime Minister). In September 1969 Traoré assumed the presidency of the Government, demoting Diakité to a lesser ministerial post.

A draft Constitution, providing for the establishment of a one-party state at the end of a five-year transitional period of military rule, was approved by a national referendum in June 1974. Keita died in custody in 1977, prompting anti-Government demonstrations. The single political party, the Union démocratique du peuple malien (UDPM), was officially constituted in March 1979, and presidential and legislative elections took place in June. Traoré, the sole candidate for the presidency, was elected for a five-year term; a single list of UDPM candidates for the 82-member Assemblée nationale was elected for a four-year term.

A constitutional amendment in September 1981 increased the presidential term of office to six years and reduced that of the legislature to three years. Elections to the Assemblée nationale were thus held in June 1982 and June 1985, with UDPM candidates being elected unopposed on both occasions. In June 1985 Traoré was re-elected President, reportedly obtaining 99.9% of the votes cast. He relinquished the defence portfolio to a close associate, Gen. Sékou Ly, in June 1986, and appointed Dr Mamadou Dembélé to the restored office of Prime Minister. The office of Prime Minister was again abolished in June 1988, and Traoré resumed responsibility for defence. At legislative elections later in June only about one-half of the incumbent deputies were returned to office, after provision was made for as many as three UDPM-nominated candidates to contest each seat.

Meanwhile, a long-standing territorial dispute between Mali and Burkina Faso, concerning the Agacher strip (a reputedly mineral-rich area of their common border), escalated into armed conflict in December 1985, resulting in some 50 deaths. The International Court of Justice (ICJ), to which the issue had been referred in 1983, urged both countries to withdraw their troops from the disputed zone, and in January 1986, following regional mediation, troops were withdrawn from the area. The two states resumed full diplomatic relations in June, and in December accepted the ICJ's ruling that each be awarded sovereignty over one-half of the territory.

In March 1990 Traoré initiated a nation-wide series of conferences to consider the exercise of democracy within and by the UDPM. Mali's first cohesive opposition movements began to emerge in that year, among them the Comité national d'initiative démocratique (CNID) and the Alliance pour la démocratie au Mali (ADEMA), which together organized mass pro-democracy demonstrations in December.

In January 1991 Traoré assigned the defence portfolio to Brig.-Gen. Mamadou Coulibaly. The security forces harshly repressed violent pro-democracy demonstrations in Bamako in March 1991: official figures later revealed that 106 people were killed, and 708 injured, in three days of unrest. On 26 March it was announced that Traoré had been arrested. A military Conseil national de réconciliation (CNR), led by Lt-Col (later Gen.) Amadou Toumani Touré, the commander of the army's parachute regiment, assumed power, and the Constitution and its institutions were abrogated. The CNR was succeeded by a 25-member Comité de transition pour le salut du peuple (CTSP), chaired by Touré. It was announced that a national conference would be convened, and that the armed forces would relinquish power to democratic institutions in January 1992. Soumana Sacko (who had briefly been Minister of Finance and Trade in 1987) returned to Mali from the Central African Republic to head a transitional, civilian-dominated government.

The transitional regime affirmed its commitment to the economic adjustment efforts of recent years, and undertook the reform of Malian political life. Among those arrested in subsequent months were Gen. Ly (Minister of the Interior and Basic Development at the time of the violently repressed demonstrations in early 1991), Mamadou Coulibaly and the former army Chief of Staff, Ousmane Coulibaly. In July 1991 an amnesty for most political prisoners detained under Traoré was proclaimed, and provision made for the legalization of political parties. The CNID was registered as the Congrès national d'initiative démocratique, and ADEMA adopted the additional title of Parti pan-africain pour la liberté, la solidarité et la justice. Pre-independence parties, banned for many years, re-emerged, most notably the US—RDA.

The National Conference began in July 1991. Over a period of two weeks its 1,800 delegates adopted a draft Constitution (of what was designated the Third Republic of Mali), an electoral code and a charter governing the activities of political parties. In August seven government ministers and about one-half of the members of the CTSP were replaced, following reports implicating them in acts of repression earlier in the year. In November the period of transition to democratic rule was extended until March 1992. The delay was attributed principally to the CTSP's desire to conclude a peace agreement with Tuareg rebels in the north of the country (see below). The draft Constitution was finally submitted to a national referendum on 12 January 1992, when it was endorsed by 99.8% of those who voted (about 43% of the registered electorate).

Municipal elections proceeded on 19 January 1992, at which 23 of the 48 authorized parties presented candidates, and in which ADEMA enjoyed the greatest success, winning 214 of 751 municipal seats. At the elections to the Assemblée nationale, on 23 February and 8 March, ADEMA won 76 of the 129 seats, the CNID took nine seats, and the US—RDA eight. The date for the transition to civilian rule was again postponed, and the first round of the presidential election eventually proceeded on 12 April, contested by nine candidates. The leader of ADEMA, Alpha Oumar Konaré, won the largest share of the votes cast (some 45%). He and his nearest rival, Tiéoulé Mamadou Konaté (of the US—RDA), proceeded to a second round, on 26 April, at which Konaré secured 69% of the votes. Overall, only about 20% of the electorate were reported to have voted in the presidential election; a similar turn-out was reported in the legislative polls. Konaré was inaugurated as President on 8 June. He appointed Younoussi Touré (hitherto the national director of the Banque centrale des états de l'Afrique de l'ouest) as Prime Minister. Touré's first Council of Ministers was dominated by members of ADEMA, although a small number of portfolios were allocated to representatives of the US—RDA and of the Parti pour la démocratie et le progrès (PDP).

The trial of Traoré and his associates began in November 1992. In February 1993 Traoré, Ly, Mamadou Coulibaly and Ousmane Coulibaly were sentenced to death, having been convicted, *inter alia*, of premeditated murder at the time of the March 1991 unrest. The Supreme Court rejected appeal proceedings in May 1993; however, Konaré subsequently indicated that no death penalty would be exacted under his presidency. Charges remained against Traoré, his wife and several others in connection with the 'economic crimes' of the former administration.

Touré resigned in April 1993, following violent disturbances in Bamako, involving students and school pupils disaffected by the adverse effects of economic austerity measures. The new Prime Minister, Abdoulaye Sekou Sow (hitherto Minister of State, responsible for Defence), implemented an extensive reorganization of the Government. The Council of Ministers remained dominated by ADEMA, but also included representatives of other parties, including the CNID; Sow was not himself a member of any political party. Following the resignation of ADEMA's Vice-President, Mohamed Lamine Traoré, from a senior government post, a major reorganization of the Council of Ministers was effected in November. ADEMA remained the most prominent party in the new Government, which also incorporated members of the CNID, the PDP, the Rassemblement pour la démocratie et le progrès (RDP) and, for a brief period, prior to their withdrawal, representatives of the US—RDA.

Meanwhile, a programme of austerity measures, announced in September 1993, provoked considerable political controversy and failed to prevent the suspension of assistance by the IMF and the World Bank. The 50% devaluation of the CFA franc, in January 1994, exacerbated differences regarding economic policy within the Government. Sow resigned in February, and was replaced by Ibrahim Boubacar Keita, since November 1993 the Minister of Foreign Affairs, Malians Abroad and African Integration, and a member of ADEMA's 'radical' wing, which was opposed to Sow's economic policies. The subsequent withdrawal from the coalition of the CNID and the RDP prompted the appointment of a new Government, again dominated by ADEMA; the PDP in turn withdrew (although its representative in the Council of Ministers resigned from the party in order to retain his portfolio).

Mali's first national forum took place in December 1994; the Prime Minister and other government members answered questions submitted by members of the public on any matter of national concern. The forum was broadcast nationally, and was held on an annual basis thereafter.

Following the election of Keita as President of ADEMA in September 1994, Mohamed Lamine Traoré and other prominent figures resigned from the party and subsequently formed the Mouvement pour l'indépendance, la renaissance et l'intégration africaine (MIRIA). In January 1995 a party established by supporters of the UDPM, the Mouvement patriotique pour le renouveau (MPR), was granted official status. In October the Parti pour la renaissance nationale (PARENA), comprising several leading members of the CNID, who alleged excessive dominance by the party Chairman, Mountaga Tall, was registered. PARENA and ADEMA established a political alliance in February 1996, and PARENA's leaders, Yoro Diakité and Tiébilé Dramé, were appointed to the Government in July. In October it was announced that a prominent member of the MPR and former minister under Traoré, Mady Diallo, had been arrested, together with several armed forces officers, following the discovery of a plot to assassinate Konaré, Keita and other government ministers. Diallo was later released, but was rearrested in April 1997. The trial of Diallo and six army officers accused of plotting to overthrow President Konaré began in March 1998, and in March 1999 the seven were sentenced to prison terms of 15–18 months.

In early 1997 the first round of legislative elections was postponed from 9 March until 13 April, when, despite opposition demands for further delay, voting proceeded accordingly. More than 1,500 candidates, mainly representing 36 of the country's 61 registered political parties, sought election to the enlarged (147-seat) Assemblée nationale. As early results indicated that ADEMA was the only party to have won seats outright at this round, the main opposition parties denounced the results as fraudulent and announced their intention to withdraw from the second round. Although independent monitors described the poll as flawed, but not fraudulent, the opposition parties also withdrew their candidates from the forthcoming presidential and municipal elections. On 24 April the Constitutional Court invalidated the results of the first round of voting, citing irregularities in the conduct of the poll.

The presidential election was postponed, by one week, until 11 May 1997. Konaré stated that he did not wish to be the sole candidate and appealed to the opposition to participate. In early May the leader of the Parti pour l'unité, la démocratie et le progrès, Mamadou Maribatou Diaby, announced that he was prepared to contest the presidency. The Constitutional Court rejected an opposition petition for the cancellation of the poll. According to the final results, Konaré was re-elected to the presidency, securing 95.9% of the valid votes cast. Although members of the radical opposition, which had campaigned for a boycott by voters, stated that the low rate of participation (28.4% of the registered electorate) effectively invalidated Konaré's victory, the turn-out was higher than that recorded at the 1992 presidential election. At the end of the month the municipal elections were postponed indefinitely.

Violent protests occurred in Bamako in June 1997, as Konaré was sworn in for a second term of office. Five opposition leaders, among them Tall (the CNID Chairman), Almamy Sylla (the RDP President and leader of the radical opposition collective) and Sogal Maïga (the MPR Secretary-General), were subsequently arrested and charged with various offences, including incitement to violence. They were released on bail in mid-June, shortly after the first round of the legislative elections (due on 6 July) had been postponed by two weeks. Meanwhile, several opposition activists had been sentenced to three months' imprisonment for their part in recent disturbances.

A small number of opposition parties announced their intention to present candidates for the Assemblée nationale, but the radical collective, known as the Collectif des partis politiques de l'opposition (COPPO), at this time numbering 18 parties of varying political tendencies, reiterated its refusal to re-enter the electoral process. Violent disturbances, in which two deaths were reported, preceded the first round of legislative voting on 20 July 1997, which was contested by 17 parties (including five 'moderate' opposition parties) and a number of independent candidates. COPPO again asserted that its appeal for a boycott had been heeded, and that the low rate of participation by voters (at about 12% of the registered electorate in Bamako, and 22% outside the capital) would render the new parliament illegitimate. A second round of voting was necessary for eight seats on 3 August. The final results allocated 130 of the 147 seats to ADEMA, eight to PARENA, four to the Convention démocratique et sociale (CDS), three to the Union pour la démocratie et le développement (UDD) and two to the PDP.

By September 1997 there were indications that ADEMA was willing to consider a degree of compromise in order to defuse tensions. Konaré held a meeting with some 20 opposition leaders, including representatives of COPPO, at which he presented proposals for a broadly based coalition government. A new Council of Ministers, under Keita, was appointed in mid-September. Although it was emphasized that this was not a transitional government, the new administration included, in addition to members of ADEMA and its allies, a small number of representatives of the moderate opposition parties (among them the UDD and PDP). Further measures intended to promote national reconciliation were implemented, and in December Konaré formally commuted a total of 21 death sentences, including, most notably, those imposed on ex-President Traoré and his associates. However, although several parties had withdrawn from COPPO, little progress was made towards a full political reconciliation. In February 1998 13 radical opposition parties confirmed their intention to boycott the municipal elections (scheduled for 19 April), stating that the voters' register remained unreliable, and denouncing the Government for planning the elections in the absence of a wider political settlement. The municipal elections were subsequently postponed.

In April 1998 former US President Jimmy Carter visited Bamako to mediate between the Government and opposition. He recommended that the opposition recognize Konaré's legitimacy as elected President, that a new electoral commission be formed, and that new electoral lists be prepared prior to municipal elections. The radical opposition accepted the principle of mediation, but reiterated their demands for Konaré's resignation.

The cohesion of the opposition was undermined in May, when Daba Diawara, the leader of a 'moderate' faction of the US—RDA, announced his willingness to recognize Konaré as President. In July 1998 Diawara was elected as Chairman of the US—RDA, and members who opposed political reconciliation were expelled.

The municipal elections finally commenced on 21 June 1998, with voting in 19 communes, amid sporadic violence, in which one death was reported, while several members of the CNID were arrested on attempted sabotage charges. The remaining COPPO parties boycotted the elections, in which turn-out was estimated at 25.5% overall. Elections in the majority of communes (some 682) were scheduled to take place in November 1998; however, in September it was announced that voting was to be postponed until April 1999, to allow for the resolution of outstanding administrative problems and, furthermore, for negotiations on participation by all political tendencies.

In October 1998 the trial for 'economic crimes' began in Bamako of ex-President Traoré, his wife Mariam, her brother, Abraham Douah Cissoko (the former head of customs), a former Minister of Finance and Trade, Tiénan Coulibaly, and the former representative in France of the Banque de développement du Mali, Moussa Koné. In January 1999 Traoré, his wife and brother-in-law were sentenced to death, having been convicted of 'economic crimes' to the value of some US $350,000 (the original charges had cited embezzled funds amounting to $4m.). Coulibaly and Koné were acquitted. In September Konaré commuted the death sentences to terms of life imprisonment. Meanwhile, in municipal voting, held in May and June 1999, ADEMA won more than one-half of the contested seats; more than 30 parties contested the elections, although significant elements of the radical opposition maintained their boycott.

Clashes were reported in July 1999 in Gao and Kidal between members of the Arab and Kounta communities. Ten people were reportedly killed in the violence, and security forces were deployed in the area to prevent further disturbances. Meanwhile, ethnic violence was also reported in the Kayes region, where eight people were killed in a dispute between Soninké farmers and Fulani (Peul) herders. Numerous disputes between the two groups had been reported in the area since early 1999, but at the end of July a government-brokered peace agreement was signed by representatives of both communities and by the President of the Assemblée nationale. In August further clashes between the Arab and Kounta communities resulted in nine deaths. The Minister of the Interior subsequently visited the area in an attempt to restore order; in October, however, renewed clashes between the two groups were reported to have killed up to 40 people.

In February 2000 Keita submitted his Government's resignation. Observers suggested that the resignation had been prompted by widespread discontent with Keita's leadership within ADEMA, and also by Keita's desire to promote his candidature in the presidential election, scheduled for 2002. An extensively reorganized Council of Ministers was subsequently appointed. The new Prime Minister, Mandé Sidibé, was widely regarded as a supporter of economic reform. In June Choguel Kokala Maïga, the leader of the MPR, was among opposition leaders who announced their intention to participate fully in the elections to be held in 2002, stating that conditions for electoral fairness and transparency seemed likely to be achieved.

In July 2000 the Assemblée nationale approved legislation providing for state funding of political parties. The Assemblée also adopted a revision of the Constitution proposed by Konaré, according to which some 50 articles of the 1992 document would be amended, subject to approval by referendum. Significant proposed changes to the Constitution included authorization for people of dual nationality to stand in presidential elections, the abolition of the Supreme Court and the creation of a new press regulatory body. Also in July COPPO, which now comprised 15 parties and was led by Almamy Sylla of the RDP, announced that it would henceforth participate in the electoral process.

Keita resigned from the leadership of ADEMA in October 2000, following the announcement that his opponents within the party had succeeded in calling an extraordinary congress of the party, to be held in late November. Prominent members of this reformist grouping within ADEMA included the Minister of the Armed Forces and Former Combatants, Soumeylou Boubèye Maïga, and the Minister of Facilities, National Development, the Environment and Town Planning, Soumaïla Cissé. At the congress, several new members were appointed to the ADEMA's executive committee, and Dioncounda Traoré was elected as the new Chairman of the party. None the less, Keita insisted that he would continue to seek election as President of Mali in 2002. A minor ministerial reshuffle was effected in June 2001, in which two ministers who had been implicated in cases of alleged corruption were dismissed. In July a new party led by Keita, the Rassemblement pour le Mali (RPM), was officially registered.

In November 2001 Konaré indefinitely postponed a referendum, which had been due to take place in December, on the constitutional amendments adopted by the legislature in July 2000, following pressure from opposition parties and the judiciary. In January 2002 Soumaïla Cissé was elected as ADEMA's candidate for the forthcoming presidential election. In March Modibo Keita, hitherto Secretary-General at the presidency, was appointed as Prime Minister, following Sidibé's resignation to contest the presidency as an independent candidate. Ahmed El Madani Diallo, the Minister of Rural Development, also resigned from the Government later that month and announced his presidential candidacy. In early April it was reported that 16 opposition parties, including the CNID, the RPM and the MPR, had formed an electoral alliance, Espoir 2002, agreeing to support a single opposition candidate (generally expected to be Ibrahim Boubacar Keita, who was to contest the election on behalf of the RPM) in the event of a second round of voting. Twenty-four candidates registered to contest the election, notably including Gen. (retd) Amadou Toumani Touré, the leader of the 1991 coup and subsequent transitional regime, who was supported by an alliance of 23 political parties, including MIRIA, PARENA and the US—RDA.

At the first round of the presidential election, which was held on 28 April 2002, Touré secured the largest share of the votes cast, with 28.7%, followed by Cissé, with 21.3%, and Keita, with 21.0%. Of the remaining 21 candidates, none received more than 4% of the votes cast. As no candidate had secured an overall majority, Touré and Cissé contested a second round of voting on 12 May. Touré, supported by more than 40 parties, including those of Espoir 2002, was elected to the presidency, with 65.0% of the votes cast. The electoral process was marred by allegations of fraud and incompetence, which led the Constitutional Court to annul 25% of the votes cast in the first ballot. None the less, international observers described the elections as generally free, fair and open. Touré was inaugurated as President on 8 June, and subsequently formed an interim Government, comprising 21 ministers. The new Prime Minister and Minister of African Integration, Ahmed Mohamed Ag Hamani, was regarded as a technocrat; in addition to having previously held various ministerial posts under Traoré, he had, more recently, served as ambassador to Belgium and to Morocco and as High Commissioner of the Organisation pour la mise en valeur du fleuve Sénégal (see p. 360). Despite the support that Touré had received from the parties of the Espoir 2002 grouping in the presidential election, it was emphasized that the newly elected President was not affiliated to any particular political party, and would be prepared to govern with any future parliamentary majority. Meanwhile, in late May, in the stated interests of national reconciliation, Konaré announced that Traoré and his wife were to be pardoned. However, Traoré denounced the gesture as politically motivated, and only left prison in mid-July, after Konaré's term of office had ended.

The elections to the Assemblée nationale further demonstrated the clear lack of any one dominant political grouping in Mali, while the rate of participation, at 25.7% nation-wide, in the second round, was low. The first round of polls, which was held on 14 July 2002, was largely inconclusive. According to provisional results, issued by the Ministry of Territorial Administration and Local Government after the second round, held on 28 July, ADEMA had won the largest number of seats (57) in the new Assemblée, although remaining short of the overall majority that the party had held in the outgoing legislature. However, as a result of various irregularities in the conduct of the polls, several thousand votes were invalidated; following the publication, in early August, of revised results by the Constitutional Court, the RPM emerged as the single largest party, with 46 of the 147 seats (although 20 of its seats had been won in local electoral alliances with other parties of the Espoir 2002 grouping), while ADEMA secured 45 seats. Other parties of Espoir 2002 obtained a further 21 seats, giving a total of 66 to supporters of the RPM, while the pro-ADEMA Alliance pour la République et la démocratie won an additional six seats, giving a total of 51. The CNID received 13 seats, while parties belonging to an informal alliance supportive of President Touré, the Alliance pour l'alternance et le changement (ACC), including

PARENA and the US—RDA, won a total of 10 seats. A recently formed party led by a former student activist, Cheick Oumar Sissoko, the Parti de la solidarité africaine pour la démocratie et l'indépendance, won six seats, and six independent candidates were elected. The Constitutional Court declared void the results of voting in eight constituencies in Sikasso, in the south, and Tin-Essako, in the north, owing to administrative flaws; by-elections were scheduled to be held in October. In early September 19 deputies, comprising those of the ACC parties, several independent deputies and other declared supporters of Touré, formed a grouping within the legislature, with the declared intention of forming a stable presidential majority. Later in the month Ibrahim Boubakar Keita was elected President of the Assemblée nationale. Meanwhile, in mid-August Mamadou Bamou Touré resigned as Secretary-General of the US—RDA.

In mid-October 2002 Touré announced the formation of a Government of National Unity, comprising 21 ministers and seven minister-delegates. Although many of the principal posts remained unchanged from the interim administration appointed in June, one notable appointment was that of Bassari Touré, a former official of the World Bank, as Minister of the Economy and Finance, who was expected to institute an expedited process of reform. The new Government stated that improvements to the health and education systems were among its priorities, as was the introduction of measures to alleviate the consequences of recent price rises in foodstuffs, electricity and water. Meanwhile, ADEMA increased its representation in the Assemblée nationale to 53 deputies, becoming the largest party grouping, following its victory in by-elections in all eight constituencies where elections were rerun on 20 October. A minor government reorganization was announced in mid-November.

In mid-2003 a split in ADEMA resulted in the formation, by Cissé, of a new party, the Union pour la République et la démocratie, which held its inaugural conference in early June. However, as Cissé's responsibilities as a commissioner of the Union économique et monétaire ouest-africaine meant that he was prohibited from political activity, former Prime Minister Younoussi Touré was elected as the interim Chairman of the party. In late August clashes between adherents of rival Islamic groups, apparently provoked by a dispute over land, resulted in 13 deaths in the west of the country. In early October the principal trade union federation, the Union nationale des travailleurs du Mali, called a two-day strike in protest at what it described as the Government's failure to improve workers' conditions, or to reduce utility charges, since the 2002 elections.

In November 2003 the Council of Ministers proposed legislation that, subject to its approval by the Assemblée nationale, would provide for political parties to receive state funding; in order to be eligible for such funding, the sum of which was to be determined by the number of deputies and local councillors elected, parties were to be required to have a national head office and to present their accounts for auditing to the Supreme Court on an annual basis. Some 54 parties were stated to qualify for funding at this time. In February 2004 the Government announced that municipal elections, initially scheduled to be held on 25 April, had been postponed until 23 May.

In late April 2004 Ag Hamani tendered his resignation as Prime Minister, apparently in response to a request by President Touré. A new administration was appointed in early May, in which new appointments were made to several key posts, among these Moktar Ouane as Minister of Foreign Affairs and International Co-operation, and Aboubacar Traoré as Minister of the Economy and Finance.

A predominant concern in the first half of the 1990s was the rebellion in the north of Mali, which began as large numbers of Tuareg nomads, who had migrated to Algeria and Libya at times of drought, began to return to West Africa (see also the chapter on Niger). A Tuareg attack in June 1990 on Menaka (in northeastern Mali, near the border with Niger) precipitated a state of emergency in the Gao and Tombouctou regions, and the armed forces began a campaign against the nomads. A peace accord signed in January 1991 in Tamanrasset, Algeria, by representatives of the Traoré Government and delegates from two Tuareg groups, the Mouvement populaire de l'Azaouad (MPA) and the Front islamique-arabe de l'Azaouad (FIAA), failed to provide a lasting solution to the conflict. Following the overthrow of the Traoré regime, the transitional administration affirmed its commitment to the Tamanrasset accord, and Tuareg groups were represented in the CTSP. However, unrest continued. At the time of the National Conference it was reported that at least 150 members of the armed forces had been killed since 1990; meanwhile, thousands of Tuaregs, Moors and Bella (the descendants of the Tuaregs' black slaves, some of whom remained with the nomads) had fled to neighbouring countries.

In February 1992, following negotiations between representatives of the Malian Government and of the Mouvements et fronts unifiés de l'Azaouad (MFUA), comprising the MPA, the FIAA and the Armée révolutionnaire de l'Azaouad (ARLA), with Algerian mediation, a truce entered into force, and a commission of inquiry was inaugurated to examine acts of violence perpetrated and losses suffered during the conflict; the more militant Front populaire de libération de l'Azaouad (FPLA) was not reported to have attended the talks. Following further discussions, the Malian authorities and the MFUA signed a draft 'National Pact' in April. Although sporadic attacks continued, particularly against members of the northern majority Songhaï, provisions of the National Pact were implemented: joint patrols were established, and in November President Konaré visited the north to inaugurate new administrative structures. In February 1993 the Malian Government and the MFUA signed an accord facilitating the integration of an initial 600 Tuaregs into the national army. In May Rhissa Ag Sidi Mohamed, the leader of the FPLA, expressed satisfaction at the success of early efforts to repatriate refugees, and he and his supporters returned from their base in Burkina to Mali. In that month it was announced that the office of the UN High Commissioner for Refugees (UNHCR) was to oversee a two-year voluntary repatriation programme, whereby 12,000 refugees would be resettled from southern Algeria to Mali by the end of 1993. However, the assassination, in February 1994, of the MPA's military leader—now, in accordance with the Pact, a senior officer in the Malian army—resulted in several weeks of clashes between the MPA and the ARLA, which was blamed for his death.

In May 1994 the Malian authorities and Tuareg leaders reached agreement regarding the integration of 1,500 former rebels into the Malian army and of a further 4,860 Tuaregs into civilian sectors. The success of the agreement was, however, undermined by an intensification of disorder in northern Mali. Meanwhile, a Songhaï-dominated black resistance movement, the Mouvement patriotique malien Ghanda Koy ('Masters of the Land'), emerged, amid rumours of official complicity in its offensives against the Tuaregs. In June one of the leaders of the FIAA died as a result of a clash with members of the armed forces. Meeting in Tamanrasset shortly afterwards, the Malian authorities and the MFUA endorsed a reinforcement of the army presence in areas affected by the violence, and agreed procedures for the more effective integration of Tuareg fighters. Despite a serious escalation of violence in July, the ministers responsible for foreign affairs of Mali, Algeria, Burkina Faso, Libya, Mauritania and Niger met in Bamako in August to discuss the Tuareg issue, and a new agreement for the voluntary repatriation from Algeria of Malian refugees was reached: Although MFUA leaders welcomed the agreement, pledged the reconciliation of the Tuareg movements, and reiterated their commitment to the National Pact, sporadic hostilities continued.

In October 1994 both the Government and the MFUA appealed for an end to the violence, following an attack on Gao (for which the FIAA claimed responsibility) and retaliatory action, as a result of which 66 deaths were officially reported. A new Minister of the Armed Forces and Veterans was appointed shortly afterwards, and the authorities subsequently appeared to adopt a less conciliatory approach to the dissident rebel groups, with the FIAA becoming increasingly marginalized in the peace process. In January 1995 representatives of the FPLA and Ghanda Koy issued a joint statement appealing for an end to hostilities in the north, and for the implementation of the Pact. Further discussions involving Tuareg groups, Ghanda Koy and representatives of local communities resulted in the signing, in April, of an agreement providing for co-operation in resolving hitherto contentious issues. In May representatives of the organs of state, the MFUA and Ghanda Koy toured the north, as well as refugee areas in Algeria, Burkina and Mauritania, in order to promote awareness of the peace process; Konaré also visited those countries, appealing to refugees to return and participate in the process of reconstruction. In June the FIAA announced an end to its armed struggle, and expressed its willingness to join national reconciliation efforts. In July a meeting, in Tombouctou, of representatives of the Government and of Mali's creditors agreed development strategies for the northern regions, incorporating the restoration of civilian local government, education and health-care facilities and basic utilities. A programme for the encampment of former rebels, in preparation for their eventual integration into the national army or civilian structures, began in November and ended in February 1996, by which time some 3,000 MFUA fighters and Ghanda Koy militiamen had registered and surrendered their weapons. The MFUA and Ghanda Koy subsequently issued a joint statement affirming their adherence to Mali's Constitution, national unity and territorial integrity, urging the full implementation of the National Pact and associated accords and proclaiming the 'irreversible dissolution' of their respective movements.

In September 1997 the graduation of MFUA and Ghanda Koy contingents in the gendarmerie was reported as marking the accomplishment of the integration of all fighters within the national armed and security forces. In October the former FPLA leader, Rhissa Ag Sidi Mohamed, who had not previously been regarded as a party to the peace process, returned to Mali and expressed willingness to join efforts to consolidate peace and promote the development of the north. None the less the Ministers of Justice and of the Armed Forces and Veterans expressed concern that the continued proliferation of weapons, as well as the inadequacy of military and administrative structures in the north, could result in renewed clashes. In November 2000 it was reported that Malian government forces had been dispatched to end widespread banditry by an armed group, led by Ibrahim Bahanga, a former Tuareg rebel, in the Kidal area, near to the border with Algeria. In September 2001 Bahanga reportedly announced that his forces were to cease hostilities, following talks with a state official.

The presence of large numbers of refugees from the conflict in northern Mali dominated Mali's relations with its neighbours during the 1990s, and even after the completion of the process of repatriation in mid-1998 (and the conclusion of a UNHCR programme in June 1999) the north of the country remained vulnerable to cross-border banditry. In May 1998 the ministers responsible for the interior of Mali, Mauritania and Senegal met with a view to strengthening co-operation and border controls, and in December Mali and Senegal agreed to improve border security. In February 1999 Mali and Algeria agreed to revive their joint border committee to promote development and stability in the region. In March Konaré visited Mauritania to discuss border stability; however, in June a dispute over watering rights escalated into an armed conflict between neighbouring Malian and Mauritanian communities, in which 13 people were killed. The two Governments responded to the disturbances by increasing border controls and by sending a joint delegation to the villages involved. In August 1999 at a meeting in Dakar, Senegal, the Malian, Mauritanian and Senegalese ministers responsible for the interior agreed to establish an operational unit drawn from the police forces of the three countries in order to ensure security in the area of their joint border.

Concerns about insecurity in the region re-emerged in mid-2003, following reports, in late July, that some 15 German, Swiss and Dutch tourists, said to have been kidnapped in February by Islamist militants allegedly associated with the Groupe salafiste pour la prédication et le combat in southern Algeria, had been smuggled into Mali. Following negotiations with the kidnappers, conducted by a former rebel Tuareg leader, Iyad Ag Agaly, 14 hostages were released in mid-August (the remaining hostage had reportedly died earlier from heatstroke). In late October the Malian Minister of the Armed Forces and War Veterans, Mahamane Kalil Maïga, visited Algeria and met the Chief of Staff of the Algerian Army, Lt-Gen. Muhammad Lamari, to discuss security in the region. In March 2004 Mali announced that it was to increase anti-terrorism co-operation with the authorities in Algeria, Chad and Niger.

France remains an important trading partner and the principal donor of bilateral aid. From mid-1996 a series of expulsions from France of illegal immigrants, including many Malians, was generally criticized in Mali. The issue of immigration was a principal focus of discussions during a visit by the French Prime Minister, Lionel Jospin, in December 1997. Progress was achieved in September 1998, with the establishment of a Franco-Malian joint committee on immigration, intended to promote co-operation on the repatriation of migrants and their reintegration into Malian society. The new Government formed in October 2002 included a Minister-delegate for Malians Abroad and African Integration, and the issue of immigration

was, again, a principal topic of discussion when the French Minister of the Interior, Internal Security and Local Freedoms, Nicolas Sarkozy, visited Mali later that month. During a visit to Mali in October 2003, the French President, Jacques Chirac, held talks with officials on the country's economic development, as well as illegal immigration.

President Konaré regarded the development of a wider international role for Mali as a priority in foreign policy, and Mali has contributed actively to UN peace-keeping forces. Following an official visit by Konaré to Washington, DC, in November 1997, when he met US President Bill Clinton, US military instructors were dispatched to Mali to train Malian troops for peace-keeping missions. Mali contributed troops to a regional surveillance mission, and the UN peace-keeping force that succeeded it, in the Central African Republic between February 1997 and February 2000, and to an enlarged peace-keeping force of the Economic Community of West African States (ECOWAS)— ECOMOG (see p. 198)—prior to elections in Liberia in 1997.

In February 1999 some 488 Malian troops joined ECOMOG forces in Sierra Leone, although the Malian authorities emphasized that these troops would take on a purely peace-keeping role. However, following widespread demands in Mali for a withdrawal, during August the majority of the force departed Sierra Leone; it was later announced that seven Malian soldiers had been killed and 10 seriously injured while serving in Sierra Leone. As Chairman of ECOWAS, in March 2001 Konaré hosted a mini-summit, attended by the leaders of the three countries of the Mano River Union (see p. 360), Sierra Leone, Liberia and Guinea, in Bamako on the subject of the peace process in Sierra Leone. Konaré sought to emphasize the role of Mali in ECOWAS, and in November 2000 a 120-member ECOWAS parliament, which was to promote regional co-operation, was inaugurated in Bamako.

Mali has in recent years forged closer relations with Libya, and was a founder member of the Community of Sahel-Saharan States (see p. 359), established in Tripoli in 1997. In early 2004 some 30 US military instructors were dispatched to Mali to train troops in techniques to combat banditry and international terrorism.

Government

The Constitution of the Third Republic, which was approved in a national referendum on 12 January 1992, provides for the separation of the powers of the executive, legislative and judicial organs of state. Executive power is vested in the President of the Republic, who is elected for five years by universal suffrage. The President appoints a Prime Minister, who, in turn, appoints a Council of Ministers. Legislative power is vested in the 147-seat unicameral Assemblée nationale, elected for five years by universal suffrage. Elections take place in the context of a multi-party political system.

Mali has eight administrative regions, each presided over by a governor, and a district government in Bamako. Following a significant revision of local government structures in 1999, and a further minor revision in 2001, the number of elected mayors across Mali increased from 19 to 703. The Constitution makes provision for the establishment of a High Council of Local Communities.

Defence

In August 2003 the active Malian army numbered about 7,350 men, including a naval force of about 50 men (with patrol boats on the River Niger) and an air force of 400. Paramilitary forces comprised the gendarmerie (1,800), republican guard (2,000), militia (3,000) and national police (1,000). Military service is by selective conscription and lasts for two years. The defence budget for 2003 was estimated at 52,000m. francs CFA.

Economic Affairs

In 2002, according to estimates by the World Bank, Mali's gross national income (GNI), measured at average 2000–02 prices, was US $2,770m., equivalent to $240 per head (or $840 on an international purchasing-power parity basis). During 1990–2002, it was estimated, the population increased at an average annual rate of 2.5%, while gross domestic product (GDP) per head increased, in real terms, by an average of 1.8% per year. Overall GDP increased, in real terms, at an average annual rate of 4.3% in 1990–2002. Real GDP increased by 1.5% in 2001 and by 9.6% in 2002, according to the World Bank, largely as a result of a significant increase in the cotton crop. However, the IMF estimated real GDP growth in 2001 and 2002 at 13.3% and 4.4%, respectively, based on a revised methodology of compiling national accounts.

Agriculture (including livestock-rearing, forestry and fishing) contributed 37.1% of GDP in 2002. An estimated 79.9% of the labour force were employed in the sector in that year. Mali is among Africa's foremost producers and exporters of cotton (exports of which contributed an estimated 22.4% of the value of merchandise exports in 2002). Cotton production increased significantly in 2001/02, to a record 570,900 metric tons, reflecting a marked expansion in the area of land cultivated for the crop in that year; output declined to 439,700 tons in 2002/03. Shea-nuts (karité nuts), groundnuts, vegetables and mangoes are also cultivated for export. The principal subsistence crops are millet, sorghum, fonio, rice and maize. Cereal imports remain necessary in most years, although a crop of 2,300m. tons was forecast for 2002/03, some 22% more than in the previous year. The livestock-rearing and fishing sectors make an important contribution to the domestic food supply and (in the case of the former) to export revenue, although both are highly vulnerable to drought. According to the World Bank, agricultural GDP increased by an average of 3.2% per year in 1990–2002, declining by 13.0% in 2001, but increasing by 19.5% in 2002. According to the IMF, however, agricultural GDP increased by 31.7% in 2001, but declined by an estimated 4.4% in 2002. (Figures for the agricultural sector were particularly affected by the revised methodology for calculating national accounts, principally owing to a change in the timing of recording agricultural output: for example, crops produced and marketed in the 2001/02 season would now be recorded in the data for 2001.)

Industry (including mining, manufacturing, construction and power) contributed 26.4% of GDP in 2002. According to the World Bank, industrial GDP increased at an average annual rate of 8.8% in 1990–2001. Industrial GDP increased by 26.1% in 2001 and by 20.0% in 2002, according to the IMF.

Mining contributed 11.7% of GDP in 2002. The importance of the sector has increased with the successful exploitation of the country's gold reserves: exports of gold contributed 65.2% of the value of total exports in 2002. Output of gold has increased significantly since the mid-1990s, as new mining facilities have commenced operations, and by 2002 exports of gold had increased to 66.1 metric tons, yielding 411,600m. francs CFA, compared with 6.6 tons (39,800m. francs CFA) in 1996. In 2001 Mali became the third largest gold producer in Africa, and further increases in production were anticipated. Salt, diamonds, marble and phosphate rock are also mined. The future exploitation of deposits of iron ore and uranium is envisaged. According to the IMF, the GDP of the mining sector increased at an average annual rate of 46.8% in 1996–2002; growth in mining GDP reached 181.3% in 1997, before slowing to an estimated 23.1% by 2002.

The manufacturing sector, including electricity and water, contributed 7.5% of GDP in 2002. The main areas of activity are agro-industrial (chiefly the processing of cotton, sugar and rice). Brewing and tobacco industries are represented, and some construction materials are produced for the domestic market. According to the World Bank, manufacturing GDP increased at an average annual rate of 2.7% in 1990–2001. Manufacturing GDP declined by 14.1% in 2001, according to the IMF, but increased by an estimated 25.6% in 2002.

Of total electric energy generated in 1995, about 80% was derived from hydroelectric installations. Mali began to receive power supplies from the Manantali hydroelectric project (constructed and operated under the auspices of the Organisation pour la mise en valeur du fleuve Sénégal—OMVS) from December 2001, and there were also plans to link the Malian network with those of Côte d'Ivoire, Burkina Faso and Ghana. An agreement on energy supply was also reached with Algeria in February 1998. In July 2000 Belgium provided a loan of 2,600m. francs CFA for the construction of two high-voltage power stations in Bamako. Imports of petroleum products comprised 17.5% of the value of merchandise imports in 2002.

The services sector contributed 36.5% of GDP in 2002. In preparation for the African Nations Cup football tournament, which Mali hosted in early 2002, the Government began to implement a social development programme, 'Mali 2002', which was also intended to develop the tourism industry. Under the programme, the construction of two new international airports was envisaged, as well as other infrastructural improvements. According to the World Bank, the GDP of the services sector increased at an average annual rate of 2.9% in 1990–2001.

Services GDP increased by 5.7% in 2001 and by an estimated 1.1% in 2002, according to the IMF.

In 2002 Mali recorded a visible trade surplus of an estimated 133,100m. francs CFA, while there was a deficit of 99,700m. francs CFA on the current account of the balance of payments. In 2002 the principal sources of imports were Côte d'Ivoire and France (which supplied, respectively, 17.0% and 13.5% of total imports). The largest market for exports were Thailand (which accounted for 14.7% of total exports), India (8.1%) and Germany (5.3%). The principal exports in 2002 were gold and cotton, together comprising 87.6% of total exports. The principal imports in that year were machines and vehicles, chemical products, petroleum products, foodstuffs and construction materials.

In 2002, according to IMF estimates, Mali recorded an overall budget deficit of 85,200m. francs CFA, equivalent to 3.6% of GDP. Mali's total external debt was US $2,890m. at the end of 2001, of which $2,616m. was long-term public debt. In that year the cost of debt-servicing was equivalent to 8.8% of the value of exports of goods and services. The annual rate of inflation averaged 4.0% in 1990–2002. Consumer prices increased by 5.1% in 2002.

Mali is a member of numerous international and regional organizations, including the Economic Community of West African States (ECOWAS, see p. 196), the West African organs of the Franc Zone (see p. 256), the African Groundnut Council (see p. 355), the Liptako-Gourma Integrated Development Authority (see p. 360), the Niger Basin Authority (see p. 361) and the OMVS (see p. 360).

Mali's economic development is hindered by its vulnerability to drought, its dependence on imports and its narrow range of exports. The country also lacks facilities for the processing of its important cotton crop; it was reported in 2002 that only 1% of Mali's cotton crop was processed in the country. In August 1999 the IMF approved a loan for Mali under the Enhanced Structural Adjustment Facility (ESAF), equivalent to about US $633m., in support of the Government's programme of economic reform for 1999–2002. (The facility was subsequently extended for a further year.) Mali's external debt remains at a high level, despite a rescheduling of commitments along concessionary lines by official creditors in 1996, the granting of some $870m. in debt-service relief under the initiative of the IMF and the World Bank for heavily indebted poor countries (HIPCs) in 2000, and the cancellation by France, in September 2002, of €80m. of bilateral debt; in March 2003 the Bretton Woods institutions announced that Mali had reached completion point under the terms of the HIPC initiative, thus becoming eligible for additional debt-relief. Mali's strong economic performance in 2001–02 was largely attributable to favourable climatic conditions, resulting in large cotton and cereal crops, and an increase in gold production. GDP growth was forecast to slow to 3.2% in 2003, largely owing to the effects of the political crisis in Côte d'Ivoire (through which more than 70% of Mali's external trade, excluding gold, was previously shipped, and where some 800,000 Malians reside), although agricultural output in Mali was projected to increase by around 11% as a result of good rainfall. The Government of Prime Minister Ahmed Mohamed Ag Hamani, appointed in October 2002, announced its commitment to the IMF-supported programme of reforms, and to a Poverty Reduction Strategy Paper agreed by the previous administration and the Fund in May 2002. The Government announced various infrastructural projects, including proposals to improve access to water and electricity supplies in rural areas, and the construction of a highway to link Kita, west of Bamako, with Saraya in eastern Senegal. The Government also pursued a programme of privatization, notably transferring the railway from Bamako to Dakar, Senegal, to private management in 2003. In addition, the cotton sector was undergoing restructuring and a partial transfer to private ownership, having been adversely affected by a decline in international prices during the late 1990s, and the transfer of the state oilseed-processing plant to private ownership was scheduled to take place in 2004. None the less, in the absence of a more diversified economic base, Mali's economy remained vulnerable both to external shocks and to fluctuations in the terms of trade of its principal import and export commodities.

Education

Education is provided free of charge and is officially compulsory for nine years between seven and 16 years of age. Primary education begins at the age of seven and lasts for six years. Secondary education, from 13 years of age, lasts for a further six years, generally comprising two cycles of three years. The rate of school enrolment in Mali is among the lowest in the world: in 1997 total enrolment at primary and secondary schools excluding Medersas (Islamic schools) was equivalent to only 32% of the school-age population (males 39%; females 25%). In 2000/01 primary enrolment was equivalent to 61% of the appropriate age-group (males 71%; females 51%), while in 1998/99 secondary enrolment was equivalent to only 15% (males 20%; females 10%). Tertiary education facilities include the national university, developed in the mid-1990s. Hitherto many students have received higher education abroad, mainly in France and Senegal. Estimated budgetary expenditure on education in 2000 was 64,930m. francs CFA, equivalent to 15.6% of total government expenditure in that year.

Public Holidays

2004: 1–2 January (New Year's Day), 20 January (Armed Forces Day), 1 February* (Tabaski, Feast of the Sacrifice), 25 March (Commemoration of the overthrow of Moussa Traoré), 12 April (Easter Monday), 1 May (Labour Day), 2 May* (Mouloud, Birth of the Prophet), 25 May (Africa Day, anniversary of the OAU's foundation), 1 June* (Baptism of the Prophet), 22 September (Independence Day), 14 November* (Korité, end of Ramadan), 25 December (Christmas).

2005: 1 January (New Year's Day), 20 January (Armed Forces Day), 21 January* (Tabaski, Feast of the Sacrifice), 25 March (Commemoration of the overthrow of Moussa Traoré), 28 March (Easter Monday), 21 April* (Mouloud, Birth of the Prophet), 1 May (Labour Day), 20 May* (Baptism of the Prophet), 25 May (Africa Day, anniversary of the OAU's foundation), 22 September (Independence Day), 4 November* (Korité, end of Ramadan), 25 December (Christmas).

*These holidays are determined by the Islamic lunar calendar and may vary by one or two days from the dates given.

Weights and Measures

The metric system is in force.

Statistical Survey

Source (unless otherwise stated): Direction Nationale de la Statistique et de l'Informatique, BP 12, Bamako; tel. 22-24-55; fax 22-71-45.

Area and Population

AREA, POPULATION AND DENSITY

Area (sq km)	1,240,192*
Population (census results)†	
1–30 April 1987	7,696,348
17 April 1998	
Males	4,847,436
Females.	4,943,056
Total	9,790,492
Population (UN estimates at mid-year)‡	
2000	11,904,000
2001	12,256,000
2002	12,623,000
Density (per sq km) at mid-2002	10.2

* 478,841 sq miles.
† Figures are provisional and refer to the *de jure* population.
‡ Source: UN, *World Population Prospects: The 2002 Revision*; Figures have not been revised to take account of the 1998 census result.

ETHNIC GROUPS (percentage of total, 1995): Bambara 36.5; Peul 13.9; Sénoufo 9.0; Soninké 8.8; Dogon 8.0; Songhaï 7.2; Malinké 6.6; Diola 2.9; Bobo and Oulé 2.4; Tuareg 1.7; Moor 1.2; Others 1.8 (Source: La Francophonie).

ADMINISTRATIVE DIVISIONS

(*de jure* population at 1998 census, provisional figures)

District				
Bamako	1,016,167	Mopti		1,475,274
Regions		Kayes		1,372,019
Sikasso	1,780,042	Tombouctou . .		461,956
Ségou	1,679,201	Gao		397,516
Koulikoro . . .	1,565,838	Kidal		42,479

PRINCIPAL TOWNS*

(*de jure* population at 1998 census, provisional figures)

Bamako (capital) .	1,016,167	Koutiala . . .	74,153
Sikasso	113,813	Kayes	67,262
Ségou	90,898	Gao	54,903
Mopti	79,840	Kati	49,756

* With the exception of Bamako, figures refer to the population of communes (municipalities).

BIRTHS AND DEATHS

(UN estimates, annual averages)

	1985–90	1990–95	1995–2000
Birth rate (per 1,000)	49.6	49.7	49.8
Death rate (per 1,000)	18.3	17.3	16.9

Source: UN, *World Population Prospects: The 2002 Revision*.

Expectation of life (WHO estimates, years at birth): 44.8 (males 43.9; females 45.7) in 2002 (Source: WHO, *World Health Report*).

ECONOMICALLY ACTIVE POPULATION

('000 persons, ILO estimates, 1990)

	Males	Females	Total
Agriculture, hunting, forestry and fishing	1,990	1,846	3,837
Industry	55	33	88
Manufacturing	40	32	72
Services	352	195	547
Total	**2,437**	**2,106**	**4,544**

Source: ILO.

2002 ('000 persons, estimates): Agriculture, etc. 4,735; Total labour force 5,929 (Source: FAO).

Health and Welfare

KEY INDICATORS

Total fertility rate (children per woman, 2002)	7.0
Under-5 mortality rate (per 1,000 live births, 2001) . .	231
HIV/AIDS (% of persons aged 15–49, 2001)	1.65
Physicians (per 1,000 head, 1994)	0.05
Hospital beds (per 1,000 head, 1998)	0.24
Health expenditure (2001): US $ per head (PPP) . . .	30
Health expenditure (2001): % of GDP	4.3
Health expenditure (2001): public (% of total)	38.6
Access to water (% of persons, 2000)	65
Access to sanitation (% of persons, 2000)	69
Human Development Index (2001): ranking	172
Human Development Index (2001): value	0.337

For sources and definitions, see explanatory note on p. vi.

Agriculture

PRINCIPAL CROPS

('000 metric tons)

	2000	2001	2002
Wheat	6.1	9.1	10.1
Rice (paddy)	742.6	932.6	926.5
Maize	214.5	299.4	320.5
Millet	759.1	792.5	1,034.2
Sorghum	564.7	516.7	951.4
Fonio	22.7	21.4	13.7
Sweet potatoes	47.1	68.9	74.5
Cassava (Manioc)	14.8	17.7	24.2
Yams	15.4	36.8	47.8
Sugar cane	313.0	285.2	300.0
Pulses	153.0	157.0*	157.0*
Groundnuts (in shell) . . .	193.1	196.0	257.1
Karité nuts (Sheanuts)* . . .	85	85	85
Cottonseed*	100	229	245
Tomatoes	36.5	35.1	49.7
Dry onions	20.3	30.2	28.5
Other vegetables*	242.1	252.5	252.8
Mangoes	25.9	33.1	29.1
Cotton (lint)	100.8†	230.0*	246.0*

* FAO estimate(s).
† Unofficial figure.
Source: FAO.

LIVESTOCK

('000 head, year ending September)

	2000	2001	2002
Cattle	6,620	6,735	6,819
Sheep	6,200*	6,039†	6,150*
Goats	9,849	8,691†	8,850*
Pigs	66	83	85*
Horses*	165	165	170
Asses*	680	680	700
Camels*	467	467	470
Chickens	25,000*	23,364	25,500*

* FAO estimate(s).
† Unofficial figure.
Source: FAO.

LIVESTOCK PRODUCTS

(FAO estimates, '000 metric tons)

	2000	2001	2002
Beef and veal	91.0	97.5	97.5
Mutton and lamb	26.3	25.6	26.3
Goat meat	36.4	33.6	34.3
Chicken meat	29.2	27.2	29.6
Camel meat	7.4	7.4	7.5
Game meat	17.0	17.0	18.0
Other meat	4.6	5.2	5.3
Cows' milk	161.7	167.8	166.6
Sheeps' milk	96.0	90.0	93.0
Goats' milk	195.9	180.0	183.0
Camels' milk	54.6	54.6	54.9
Cattle hides (fresh)	14.0	15.0	15.0
Sheepskins (fresh)	6.1	5.9	6.1
Goatskins (fresh)	5.2	4.8	4.9

Source: FAO.

Forestry

ROUNDWOOD REMOVALS

(FAO estimates, '000 cubic metres, excl. bark)

	2000	2001	2002
Sawlogs, veneer logs and logs for sleepers	4	4	4
Other industrial wood	409	409	409
Fuel wood	4,731	4,788	4,846
Total	**5,143**	**5,200**	**5,258**

Source: FAO.

SAWNWOOD PRODUCTION

('000 cubic metres, incl. railway sleepers)

	1987	1988	1989
Total (all broadleaved)	11	13	13*

* FAO estimate.

1990–2002: Annual production as in 1989 (FAO estimates).
Source: FAO.

Fishing

('000 metric tons, live weight)

	1999	2000	2001*
Capture	98.5	109.9	100.0
Nile tilapia	26.8	33.0	30.0
Bottlenose fishes	n.a.	7.7	7.0
Characins	8.4	5.5	5.0
Black catfishes	3.7	4.4	4.0
North African catfish . . .	15.1	27.5	25.0
Upsidedown catfishes . . .	4.1	3.3	3.0
Nile perch	5.1	6.6	6.0
Other freshwater fishes . .	35.4	22.0	20.0
Aquaculture	0.1	0.0	0.0
Total catch	**98.6**	**109.9**	**100.0**

* FAO estimates.
Source: FAO, *Yearbook of Fishery Statistics*.

Mining

(estimates, metric tons, unless otherwise indicated)

	1999	2000	2001
Gold (kg)*	23,690	28,717	42,288
Silver (kg)	1,000	1,000	n.a.
Gypsum	500	500	500
Salt	6,000	6,000	6,000

* Reported figures, excluding artisanal output, estimated at 2,000 kg per year.

Sources: mainly US Geological Survey and Banque centrale des états de l'Afrique de l'ouest.

Industry

SELECTED PRODUCTS
('000 metric tons, unless otherwise indicated)

	1998	1999	2000
Raw sugar*	28.5	31.2†	29.1
Salted, dried or smoked fish*	6.8	6.4	8.0
Cigarettes ('000 packets)	50.9	51.4	n.a.
Cement‡	10	10	10
Electric energy (million kWh)§	498	404	412

* Data from FAO.
† Unofficial figure.
‡ Data from the US Geological Survey.
§ Provisional or estimated figures.

2001: Raw sugar ('000 metric tons) 28.0 (Data from FAO); Salted, dried or smoked fish ('000 metric tons) 7.9 (Data from FAO).

2002: Raw sugar ('000 metric tons) 32.0 (Data from FAO).

Source: mainly UN, *Industrial Commodity Statistics Yearbook*.

Finance

CURRENCY AND EXCHANGE RATES

Monetary Units
100 centimes = 1 franc de la Communauté financière africaine (CFA).

Sterling, Dollar and Euro Equivalents (31 December 2003)
£1 sterling = 926.91 francs CFA;
US $1 = 519.36 francs CFA;
€1 = 655.96 francs CFA;
10,000 francs CFA = £10.79 = $19.25 = €15.24.

Average Exchange Rate (francs CFA per US $)
2001   733.04
2002   696.99
2003   581.20

Note: An exchange rate of 1 French franc = 50 francs CFA, established in 1948, remained in force until January 1994, when the CFA franc was devalued by 50%, with the exchange rate adjusted to 1 French franc = 100 francs CFA. This relationship to French currency remained in effect with the introduction of the euro on 1 January 1999. From that date, accordingly, a fixed exchange rate of €1 = 655.957 francs CFA has been in operation.

BUDGET
('000 million francs CFA)*

Revenue†	2000	2001	2002
Budgetary revenue	245.5	292.6	354.7
Tax revenue	233.3	281.6	323.5
Taxes on net income and profits	28.5	40.4	45.1
Enterprises	11.5	19.4	13.8
Individuals	15.2	19.1	28.4
Payroll tax	4.8	5.6	6.5
Property taxes	6.9	0.3	0.4
Taxes on goods and services	54.9	65.5	72.0
Value-added tax	35.1	43.2	42.9
Taxes on international trade	124.4	154.1	180.3
Customs duties	29.3	34.2	42.8
Value-added tax on imports	46.5	68.0	83.8
Petroleum import duties	33.5	28.3	30.2
Other tax revenue	13.8	15.7	19.3
Stamp duties	7.5	9.5	9.9
Other current revenue	12.2	11.0	31.2
Special funds and annexed budgets	24.4	27.5	33.7
Total	269.9	320.1	388.4

Expenditure‡	2000	2001	2002
Budgetary expenditure	393.5	458.0	529.2
Current expenditure	200.2	279.8	308.7
Wages and salaries	73.1	85.8	93.5
Goods and services	75.2	91.8	109.0
Transfers and subsidies	35.9	87.6	87.8
Interest payments (scheduled)	16.0	14.6	18.4
Capital expenditure	193.3	178.2	220.5
Externally financed	133.3	116.3	140.3
Equipment and investment	60.0	61.9	80.2
Special funds and annexed budgets	24.4	27.5	33.7
Total	417.9	485.5	562.9

* Figures represent a consolidation of the central government budget, special funds and annexed budgets.
† Excluding grants received ('000 million francs CFA): 90.0 in 2000; 83.6 in 2001; 85.8 in 2002.
‡ Excluding net lending ('000 million francs CFA): −2.5 in 2000; −10.6 in 2001; −4.9 in 2002, and HIPC initiative spending ('000 million francs CFA): 0.9 in 2000; 16.8 in 2001; 30.9 in 2002.

Sources: IMF, *Mali: Selected Issues and Statistical Annex* (January 2004).

INTERNATIONAL RESERVES
(excluding gold, US $ million at 31 December)

	2000	2001	2002
IMF special drawing rights	0.1	0.4	0.0
Reserve position in IMF	11.4	11.1	12.0
Foreign exchange	369.7	337.4	582.4
Total	381.2	348.9	594.4

Source: IMF, *International Financial Statistics*.

MONEY SUPPLY
(million francs CFA at 31 December)

	2000	2001	2002
Currency outside banks	146,911	179,046	247,483
Demand deposits	143,630	197,808	238,218
Total money (incl. others)	291,151	377,204	486,060

Source: IMF, *International Financial Statistics*.

COST OF LIVING
(Consumer Price Index for Bamako: base: 1996 = 100)

	2000	2001	2002
Food, beverages and tobacco	95.7	103.3	110.9
Clothing	104.4	109.5	109.3
Housing, water, electricity and gas	104.8	110.0	117.5
All items (incl. others)	101.4	106.6	112.0

Source: Banque centrale des états de l'Afrique de l'ouest.

NATIONAL ACCOUNTS
('000 million francs CFA at current prices)

Expenditure on the Gross Domestic Product

	2000	2001	2002
Final consumption expenditure	1,704.3	1,856.5	1,919.1
Households	1,393.5	1,509.7	1,550.1
Non-profit institutions serving households			
General government	310.8	346.8	369.0
Gross capital formation	380.1	552.4	486.9
Gross fixed capital formation	362.8	433.2	438.3
Changes in inventories	17.3	119.2	48.4
Acquisitions, less disposals, of valuables			
Total domestic expenditure	2,084.4	2,408.9	2,406.0
Exports of goods and services	458.6	642.4	746.3
Less Imports of goods and services	659.9	847.5	792.8
GDP in market prices	1,883.1	2,203.8	2,359.3

Source: IMF, *International Financial Statistics*.

Gross Domestic Product by Economic Activity

	2000	2001	2002
Agriculture, livestock-rearing, forestry and fishing	637.8	778.0	799.2
Mining	113.3	206.4	251.3
Manufacturing	121.5	123.1	162.2
Electricity, gas and water	26.2	30.2	36.7
Construction and public works	99.2	110.8	119.2
Transport, storage and communications	299.6	301.6	281.4
Trade	146.5	153.9	158.4
Other market services	81.4	92.4	97.2
Non-market services	211.6	232.9	250.2
GDP at factor cost	1,737.1	2,029.3	2,155.8
Import duties	146.0	174.5	203.5
GDP in purchasers' values	1,883.1	2,203.8	2,359.3

Source: Banque centrale des états de l'Afrique de l'ouest.

BALANCE OF PAYMENTS
('000 million francs CFA)

	2000	2001	2002*
Exports of goods f.o.b.	388.1	531.2	631.4
Imports of goods f.o.b.	−421.5	−538.4	−498.3
Trade balance	−33.5	−7.2	133.1
Exports of services	70.5	110.8	123.6
Imports of services	−238.4	−308.9	−290.8
Balance on goods and services	−201.4	−205.3	−34.1
Other income (net)	−69.9	−121.7	−160.9
Balance on goods, services and income	−271.3	−327.0	−195.0
Private transfers (net)	44.3	51.1	58.5
Official transfers (net)	45.7	48.4	36.8
Current balance	−181.2	−227.5	−99.7
Capital account (net)	61.1	62.1	75.2
Private finance (net)	72.3	27.1	47.0
Official finance (net)	49.2	42.0	61.0
Net errors and omissions	26.4	63.6	12.9
Overall balance	27.8	−32.9	96.4

* Estimated figures.

Source: IMF, *Selected Issues and Statistical Annex* (January 2004).

External Trade

PRINCIPAL COMMODITIES
(distribution by SITC, US $ million)

Imports c.i.f.	1998	1999	2000
Food and live animals	145.4	136.9	93.4
Dairy products and birds' eggs	24.7	25.1	15.9
Milk and cream	24.3	24.8	15.9
Milk and cream, preserved, concentrated or sweetened	24.0	24.2	15.7
Cereals and cereal preparations	43.1	38.1	25.6
Rice, semi-milled or wholly milled	22.4	20.3	9.3
Sugar, sugar preparations and honey	30.1	27.5	17.2
Sugar and honey	29.8	27.1	16.9
Refined sugar, etc.	29.3	26.4	16.5
Mineral fuels, lubricants, etc.	113.7	115.5	169.9
Petroleum, petroleum products, etc.	112.3	113.9	168.6
Petroleum products, refined	110.7	112.0	167.2
Chemicals and related products	127.5	127.6	101.0
Medicinal and pharmaceutical products	23.5	27.5	24.3
Fertilizers, manufactured	50.1	37.8	29.4
Nitrogen-phosphorus-potassium fertilizer	36.7	21.5	17.8
Basic manufactures	110.5	142.2	108.5
Non-metallic mineral manufactures	31.8	32.5	38.6
Lime, cement and fabricated construction materials	26.8	24.0	33.6
Cement	25.3	22.5	30.5
Iron and steel	32.4	45.5	18.5
Machinery and transport equipment	193.9	248.0	237.9
Power generating machinery and equipment	15.2	26.3	27.9
Machinery specialized for particular industries	47.1	44.8	58.1
Civil engineering, contractors' plant, equipment and parts	22.2	23.0	39.3
Construction and mining machinery	14.1	12.9	28.7
General industrial machinery, equipment and parts	23.5	26.1	18.7
Electrical machinery, apparatus, appliances and parts	23.0	25.3	24.1
Road vehicles	72.6	96.1	82.7
Passenger motor vehicles (excl. buses)	23.2	27.3	22.4
Lorries and motor vehicles for special purposes	26.3	31.3	38.3
Motor vehicles for the transport of goods or materials	26.3	31.3	38.3
Miscellaneous manufactured articles	23.7	30.0	29.6
Total (incl. others)	736.6	823.8	759.1

Exports f.o.b.	1997	1998	1999
Food and live animals . .	14.7	61.7	59.3
Live animals chiefly for food . .	9.3	50.0	53.3
Crude materials (inedible) except fuels . . .	264.6	286.6	227.2
Textile fibres (not wool tops) and their wastes (not in yarn)	263.1	284.4	226.5
Raw cotton, excl. linters, not carded or combed . . .	254.5	284.1	217.6
Basic manufactures . . .	1.9	5.9	17.3
Gold, non-monetary (excl. gold ores and concentrates) . .	16.1	236.8	240.2
Total (incl. others)	302.4	619.7	571.0

Source: UN, *Industrial Trade Statistics Yearbook*.

2000 ('000 million francs CFA): Total imports c.i.f. 589.40; Total exports f.o.b. 388.13 (Source: IMF, *International Financial Statistics*).

2001 ('000 million francs CFA): Total imports c.i.f. 741.90; Total exports f.o.b. 530.50 (Source: IMF, *International Financial Statistics*).

SELECTED TRADING PARTNERS
(US $ million)

Imports	2000	2001	2002
China, People's Repub. . . .	38.3	25.2	23.8
Côte d'Ivoire	227.6	223.8	242.9
France (incl. Monaco) . . .	167.0	198.4	192.1
Germany	50.6	64.8	56.3
Total (incl. others)	1,268.4	1,364.4	1,426.7

Exports	2000	2001	2002
Belgium	7.7	2.6	5.1
Brazil	23.1	8.7	1.0
France (incl. Monaco) . . .	4.2	4.7	6.5
Germany	13.2	6.3	8.6
India	11.0	12.2	13.2
Indonesia	1.1	4.7	3.8
Spain	3.9	5.4	8.4
Thailand	37.6	28.8	23.9
United Kingdom	9.2	1.9	4.8
Total (incl. others)	235.5	153.5	163.1

Source: IMF, *Mali: Selected Issues and Statistical Annex* (January 2004).

Transport

RAILWAYS
(traffic)

	1997	1998	1999
Passengers ('000).	862	790	778
Freight carried ('000 metric tons) .	565	566	536
Passenger-km (million)	223	218	210
Freight ton-km (million) . . .	258	256	241

ROAD TRAFFIC
(estimates, motor vehicles in use)

	1994	1995	1996
Passenger cars	24,250	24,750	26,190
Lorries and vans	16,000	17,100	18,240

Source: IRF, *World Road Statistics*.

CIVIL AVIATION
(traffic on scheduled services)*

	1997	1998	1999
Kilometres flown (million) . . .	3	3	3
Passengers carried ('000) . . .	86	91	84
Passenger-km (million)	242	258	235
Total ton-km (million)	38	38	36

* Including an apportionment of the traffic of Air Afrique.

Source: UN, *Statistical Yearbook*.

Communications Media

	1999	2000	2001
Television receivers ('000 in use) .	140	160	n.a.
Telephones ('000 main lines in use)	33.8	39.2	49.9
Mobile cellular telephones ('000 subscribers).	6.4	10.4	45.3
Personal computers ('000 in use) .	11	13	14
Internet users ('000)	7.0	18.8	30.0

Source: International Telecommunication Union.

Book production (first editions, excluding pamphlets): 14 titles (28,000 copies) in 1995 (Source: UNESCO, *Statistical Yearbook*).

Daily newspapers (1996): Number 3; Estimated average circulation ('000 copies) 12 (Source: UNESCO, *Statistical Yearbook*).

Radio receivers ('000 in use): 570 in 1997 (Source: UNESCO, *Statistical Yearbook*).

Tourism

	1998	1999	2000*
Tourist arrivals ('000)	83	87	91
Tourism receipts (US $ million) .	50	50	50

* Estimates.

Sources: World Tourism Organization.

Education
(1998/99, unless otherwise indicated)

	Institutions	Teachers	Males	Females	Total
Pre-primary	212	1,050	10,056	15,085	25,141
Primary*	2,871	15,447†	565,743	393,192	958,935
Secondary: general	n.a.	7,663	127,214	63,702	190,916
technical and vocational . .	n.a.		16,070	10,714	26,784
teacher training‡ .	n.a.	77§	1,052	494	1,596
Tertiary	n.a.	960	n.a.	n.a.	18,662

* Data exclude Medersas (Islamic schools).
† National estimate.
‡ 1997/98 figures, unless otherwise indicated.
§ 1996/97 figure.

Source: mainly UNESCO Institute for Statistics and Ministry of Education, Bamako.

2003/04: *Pre-primary*: 318 institutions; 971 teachers; 35,000 students (rounded figure); *Primary and Secondary (general)*: 8,714 institutions; 36,064 teachers; 1,650,803 students; *Secondary (general)*: 2,127 teachers; 68,925 students; *Secondary (technical and vocational)*: 763 teachers; 40,000 students (rounded figure); *Tertiary*: 37,635 students (Source: Office of the Secretary-General of the Government, Bamako).

Adult literacy rate (UNESCO estimates): 26.4% (males 36.7%; females 16.6%) in 2001 (Source: UN Development Programme, *Human Development Report*).

Directory

The Constitution

The Constitution of the Third Republic of Mali was approved in a national referendum on 12 January 1992. The document upholds the principles of national sovereignty and the rule of law in a secular, multi-party state, and provides for the separation of the powers of the executive, legislative and judicial organs of state.

Executive power is vested in the President of the Republic, who is Head of State and is elected for five years by universal adult suffrage. The President appoints the Prime Minister, who, in turn, appoints other members of the Council of Ministers.

Legislative authority is exercised by the unicameral 147-member Assemblée nationale, which is elected for five years by universal adult suffrage.

The Constitution guarantees the independence of the judiciary. Final jurisdiction in constitutional matters is vested in a Constitutional Court.

The rights, freedoms and obligations of Malian citizens are enshrined in the Constitution. Freedom of the press and of association are guaranteed.

The Government

HEAD OF STATE

President: Gen. (retd) AMADOU TOUMANI TOURÉ (took office 8 June 2002).

COUNCIL OF MINISTERS
(May 2004)

Prime Minister: OUSMANE ISSOUFI MAÏGA.

Minister of the Environment and Decontamination: NANCOUMA KÉITA.

Minister of Planning and Territorial Development: MARIMATIA DIARRA.

Minister of Stock-breeding and Fisheries: OUMAR IBRAHIMA TOURÉ.

Minister of Crafts and Tourism: BAH N'DIAYE.

Minister of National Education: MAMADOU LAMINE TRAORÉ.

Minister of Industry and Trade: CHOGUEL KOKALA MAÏGA.

Minister of Territorial Administration and Local Communities: Gen. KAFOUGOUNA KONÉ.

Minister of Foreign Affairs and International Co-operation: MOKTAR OUANE.

Minister of Malians Abroad and African Integration: OUMAR HAMADOUN DICKO.

Minister of Agriculture: SEYDOU TRAORÉ.

Minister of Communication and New Information Technologies: GAOUSSOU DRABO.

Minister of Mining, Energy and Water Resources: AHMED DIANE SEMEGA.

Minister of Culture: CHEICK OUMAR SISSOKO.

Minister of Social Development, Solidarity and the Elderly: DJIBRIL TANGARA.

Minister of the Economy and Finance: ABOUBACAR TRAORÉ.

Minister of the Civil Service, the Reform of the State and Relations with the Institutions: BADI OULD GANFOUD.

Minister of Employment and Professional Training: DIALLO M'BODJI SÈNE.

Minister of the Promotion of Investment and of Small- and Medium-sized Enterprises, Government Spokesperson: OUSMANE THIAM.

Minister for the Promotion of Women, Children and the Family: BERTHÉ AÏSSATA BENGALY.

Minister of Defence and Veterans: MAMADOU CLAZIÉ SISSOUMA.

Minister of Justice, Keeper of the Seals: FANTA SYLLA.

Minister of State-Administered Estates and Housing Affairs: SOUMARÉ AMINATA SIDIBÉ.

Minister of Health: MAÏGA ZEINAB MINT YOUBA.

Minister of Capital Works and Transport: ABDOULAYE KOÏTA.

Minister of Internal Security and Civil Protection: Col SADJO GASSAMA.

Minister of Youth and Sports: MOUSSA BALLA DIAKITÉ.

Minister of Housing and Town Planning: MODIBO SYLLA.

Minister, Secretary-General of the Government: FOUSSEYNI SAMAKE.

MINISTRIES

Office of the President: BP 1463, Koulouba, Bamako; tel. 222-25-72; fax 223-00-26; e-mail presidence@koulouba.pr.ml; internet www.koulouba.pr.ml.

Office of the Prime Minister: quartier du Fleuve, BP 790, Bamako; tel. 223-06-80; fax 222-85-83.

Office of the Secretary-General of the Government: BP 14, Koulouba, Bamako; tel. 222-25-52; fax 222-70-50; e-mail sgg@sgg.gov.ml; internet www.sgg.gov.ml.

Ministry of Agriculture: BP 1676, Bamako; tel. 222-27-85.

Ministry of Capital Works and Transport: Bamako; tel. 222-39-37.

Ministry of the Civil Service, the Reform of the State and Relations with the Institutions: Bamako.

Ministry of Communication and New Information Technologies: quartier du Fleuve, BP 116, Bamako; tel. 222-26-47; fax 223-20-54.

Ministry of Crafts and Tourism: Badalabougou, Semagesco, BP 2211, Bamako; tel. 223-64-50; fax 223-82-01; e-mail malitourisme@afribone.net.ml; internet www.malitourisme.com.

Ministry of Culture: Korofina, BP 4075, Bamako; tel. 224-66-63; fax 224-57-27; e-mail info@culture.gov.ml; internet w3.culture.gov.ml.

Ministry of Defence and Veterans: route de Koulouba, BP 2083, Bamako; tel. 222-50-21; fax 223-23-18.

Ministry of the Economy and Finance: BP 234, Koulouba, Bamako; tel. 222-51-56; fax 222-01-92.

Ministry of Employment and Professional Training: Bamako.

Ministry of the Environment and Decontamination: Bamako; tel. 223-05-39.

Ministry of Foreign Affairs and International Co-operation: Koulouba, Bamako; tel. 222-83-14; fax 222-52-26; e-mail info@maliensdelexterieur.gov.ml; internet www.maliensdelexterieur.gov.ml.

Ministry of Health: BP 232, Koulouba, Bamako; tel. 222-53-02; fax 223-02-03.

Ministry of Housing and Town Planning: Bamako.

Ministry of Industry and Trade: quartier du Fleuve, BP 234, Koulouba, Bamako; tel. 222-43-87; fax 222-88-53.

Ministry of Internal Security and Civil Protection: Bamako; tel. 222-34-31.

Ministry of Justice: quartier du Fleuve, BP 97, Bamako; tel. 222-26-42; fax 223-00-63.

Ministry of Malians Abroad and African Integration: Bamako.

Ministry of Mining, Energy and Water Resources: BP 238, Bamako; tel. 222-41-84; fax 222-21-60.

Ministry of National Education: BP 71, Bamako; tel. 222-57-80; fax 222-21-26; e-mail info@education.gov.ml; internet www.education.gov.ml.

Ministry of Planning and Territorial Development: Bamako.

Ministry of the Promotion of Investment and of Small- and Medium-sized Enterprises: Bamako.

Ministry for the Promotion of Women, Children and the Family: Torokorobougou, BP 2688, Bamako; tel. 228-74-42; fax 228-75-04; e-mail mpfef@fib.com.

Ministry of Social Development, Solidarity and the Elderly: Bamako; tel. 223-23-01.

Ministry of State-Administered Estates and Housing Affairs: Bamako; tel. 223-63-44.

Ministry of Stock-breeding and Fisheries: Bamako.

Ministry of Territorial Administration and Local Communities: face Direction de la RCFM, BP 78, Bamako; tel. 222-42-12; fax 223-02-47; internet w3.matcl.gov.ml.

Ministry of Youth and Sports: route de Koulouba, BP 91, Bamako; tel. 222-31-53; fax 223-10-87.

President and Legislature

PRESIDENT

Presidential Election, First Ballot, 28 April 2002

Candidates	Votes	% of votes
Gen. (retd) Amadou Toumani Touré		
(Independent)	449,176	28.71
Soumaïla Cissé (ADEMA)	333,525	21.31
Ibrahim Boubacar Keïta (RPM)	329,143	21.03
Tiébilé Dramé (PARENA)	62,493	3.99
Mountaga Tall (CNID)	58,695	3.75
Moussa Balla Coulibaly (UDD)	50,211	3.21
Choguel Kokala Maïga (MPR)	42,469	2.71
Mamadou Bakary Sangaré (CDS)	34,603	2.21
Mandé Sidibé (Independent)	31,389	2.01
Ahmed El Madani Diallo (Independent)	25,584	1.63
Daba Diawara (PIDS)	17,156	1.10
Others	130,332	8.33
Total	**1,564,776**	**100.00**

Second Ballot, 12 May 2002

Candidates	Votes	% of votes
Gen. (retd) Amadou Toumani Touré		
(Independent)	926,243	65.01
Soumaïla Cissé (ADEMA)	498,503	34.99
Total	**1,424,746**	**100.00**

ASSEMBLÉE NATIONALE

Assemblée nationale: BP 284, Bamako; tel. 221-57-24; fax 221-03-74; e-mail mamou@blonba.malinet.ml; internet www.animali.org.

President: IBRAHIM BOUBACAR KEÏTA.

General Election, 14 and 28 July 2002*

Parties and alliances	Seats
Alliance pour la démocratie au Mali—Parti pan-africain pour la liberté, la solidarité et la justice (ADEMA)	53
Rassemblement pour le Mali (RPM)	46†
Congrès national d'initiative démocratique—Faso Yiriwa Ton (CNID)	13
Rassemblement pour la démocratie et le travail (RDT)	7
Parti de la solidarité africaine pour la démocratie et l'indépendance (SADI)	6
Convention démocratique et sociale (CDS)	4
Bloc pour la démocratie et l'intégration africaine—Faso Jigi (BDIA)	3
Union soudanaise—Rassemblement démocratique africaine (US—RDA)/Rassemblement national pour la démocratie (RND)	3
Mouvement patriotique pour le renouveau (MPR)	2
Rassemblement malien pour le travail (RAMAT)	2
Parti pour la démocratie et le renouveau—Dounkafa Ton (PDR)	1
Parti pour la renaissance nationale (PARENA)	1
Independents	6
Total	**147**

*These figures include the results of voting in eight constituencies where the elections were rerun on 20 October 2002.

† Including 20 seats won in coalitions with other parties.

Advisory Councils

Constitutional Court: BP 213, Bamako; tel. 222-56-32; fax 223-42-41; f. 1994; Pres. ABDARAHMAN BABA TOURÉ; Sec.-Gen. BOUBACAR TAHOUATI.

Economic, Social and Cultural Council: Koulouba, Bamako; tel. 222-43-68; fax 222-84-52; e-mail cesc@cefib.com; f. 1987; Pres. MOUSSA BALLA COULIBALY.

High Council of Communities: Bamako; compulsorily advises the Govt on issues relating to local and regional development; comprises national councillors, elected indirectly for a term of five years; Sec-Gen. MAMANI NASSIRE.

Political Organizations

In mid-2002 there were some 87 functioning political groups in Mali. In early 2004 the most active parties and political groupings included:

Alliance pour l'alternance et le changement (ACC): Bamako; f. 2002 prior to legislative elections by supporters of Pres. Touré; 28 constituent parties in May 2002; Pres. IBRAHIM BOUBACAR BÂH.

Bloc pour la démocratie et l'intégration africaine—Faso Jigi (BDIA): rue du RDA, Missira, porte 41, BP E 1413, Bamako; tel. 221-45-22; fax 220-82-93; f. 1993; liberal and democratic; Leader YOUSSOUF TRAORÉ.

Mouvement pour l'indépendance, la renaissance et l'intégration africaine (MIRIA): Dravéla Bolibana, rue 417, porte 66, Bamako; tel. 229-29-81; f. 1994 following split in ADEMA; Pres. MOHAMED LAMINE TRAORÉ.

Parti pour la démocratie et le renouveau—Dounkafa Ton (PDR): Niaréla, rue 428, porte 94, près Carré des Martyrs, Bamako; f. 1998; Pres. ADAMA KONÉ; Leader KALILOU SAMAKE.

Parti pour la renaissance nationale (PARENA): rue Soundiata, porte 1397, Ouolofobougou, Bamako; tel. 223-49-54; fax 222-29-08; e-mail info@parena.org.ml; internet www.parena.org.ml; f. 1995 following split in CNID; Pres. TIÉBILÉ DRAMÉ; Sec.-Gen. AMIDOU DIABATÉ.

Rassemblement malien pour le travail (RAMAT): Marché, Hippodrome, rue 224, porte 1393, BP E 2281, Bamako; f. 1991; Leader ABDOULAYE MACKO.

Rassemblement national pour la démocratie (RND): Niaréla, route Sotuba, porte 1892, Hamdallaye, Bamako; tel. 229-73-88; fax 221-73-88; f. 1997 by 'moderate' breakaway group from RDP; Pres. ABDOULAYE GARBA TAPO.

Union des forces démocratiques pour le progrès—Samaton (UFDP): Djicoroni Para, carré Son Président, Bamako; tel. 223-17-66; f. 1991; Sec.-Gen. Col YOUSSOUF TRAORÉ.

Union soudanaise—Rassemblement démocratique africain (US—RDA): Missira, porte 41, BP E 1413, Bamako; tel. and fax 221-45-22; f. 1946; sole party 1960–68, banned 1968–1991; 'moderate' faction split from party in 1998; Hon. Pres. Dr MAMADOU EL-BÉCHIR GOLOGO; Sec.-Gen. (vacant).

Alliance pour la République et la démocratie: Bamako; f. 2001; Pres. MOUSSA BABA COULIBALY.

Alliance pour la démocratie au Mali—Parti pan-africain pour la liberté, la solidarité et la justice (ADEMA): rue Fankélé, porte 145, BP 1791, Bamako-Coura; tel. 222-03-68; internet www.adema-pasj.org; f. 1990 as Alliance pour la démocratie au Mali; Pres. DIONCOUNDA TRAORÉ; Sec.-Gen. MARIMATIA DIARRA.

Union pour la démocratie et le développement (UDD): ave OUA, porte 3626, Sogoniko, BP 3275, Bamako; tel. 222-46-94; f. 1991 by supporters of ex-Pres. Traoré; Leader MOUSSA BABA COULIBALY.

Convention démocratique et sociale (CDS): N'Tomikorobougou, rue 673, porte 108, Bamako; tel. 222-62-76; f. 1996; Chair. MAMADOU BAKARY SANGARÉ.

Convention parti du peuple (COPP): Hippodrome, BP 9012, Bamako; f. 1996; Pres. Me MAMADOU GACKOU.

Espoir 2002: Bamako; f. 2001; Spokesman Me MOUNTAGA TALL; 16 constituent parties in March 2002.

Congrès national d'initiative démocratique—Faso Yiriwa Ton (CNID): 58 rue 429, Niarela, BP 2572, Bamako; tel. 221-42-75; fax 222-83-21; e-mail cnid@cefib.com; f. 1991; Chair. Me MOUNTAGA TALL; Sec.-Gen. N'DIAYE BA.

Mouvement patriotique pour le renouveau (MPR): chez Choguel Maïga, Baco-Djicoroni ACI, Bamako; tel. 222-40-23; f. 1995; Pres. Dr CHOGUEL KOKALA MAÏGA.

Parti pour l'indépendance, la démocratie et la solidarité (PIDS): Hippodrome, rue 300, porte 426, Bamako; f. 2001 by dissidents from US—RDA; Pres. DABA DIAWARA.

Rassemblement pour la démocratie et le progrès (RDP): Niarela, rue 485, porte 11, BP 2110, Bamako; tel. 221-30-92; fax 222-67-95; f. 1991; Pres. ALMAMY SYLLA.

Rassemblement pour la démocratie et le travail (RDT): Bamako; tel. 222-25-58; f. 1991; Leader AMADOU ALI NIANGADOU.

Rassemblement pour le Mali (RPM): Hippodrome, rue 228, porte 1164, Bamako; tel. 221-69-40; fax 221-69-56; e-mail rpm@viky.net; internet www.rpm.org.ml; f. 2001; Pres. IBRAHIM BOUBACAR KEITA; Sec.-Gen. Dr BOCARY TRETA.

Parti de la solidarité africaine pour la démocratie et l'indépendance (SADI): Djélibougou, rue 246, porte 559, BP 3140, Bamako; tel. 224-87-82; f. 2002; Leader CHEICK OUMAR SISSOKO.

Parti pour la démocratie et le progrès (PDP): Niarela, rue 428, porte 94, BP 2351, Bamako; tel. 224-16-75; f. 1991; Leader MADY KONATÉ.

Parti malien pour le développement et le renouveau (PMDR): Sema I, rue 76, porte 62, BP 553, Badalabougou, Bamako; tel. 222-25-58; f. 1991; social democratic; Pres. Me ABDOUL WAHAB BERTHE.

Union pour la République et la démocratie (URD): Bamako; f. 2003 by fmr mems of ADEMA (q.v.) allied to 2002 presidential candidate Soumaïla Cissé; Pres. YOUNOUSSI TOURÉ (acting).

Diplomatic Representation

EMBASSIES IN MALI

Algeria: Sogoninko BP 02, Bamako; tel. 220-51-76; fax 222-93-74; Ambassador MOHAMED ANTAR DAOUD.

Burkina Faso: route INRSP, Hippodrome, BP 9022, Bamako; tel. 223-31-71; fax 221-92-66; e-mail ambafaso@datatech.toolnet.org; Ambassador Prof. SANNÉ MOHAMED TOPAN.

Canada: route de Koulikoro, immeuble Séméga, BP 198, Hippodrome, Bamako; tel. 221-22-36; fax 221-43-62; e-mail bmako@dfait-macci.gc.ca; Ambassador LOUISE OUIMET.

China, People's Republic: route de Koulikoro, Hippodrome, BP 112, Bamako; tel. 221-35-97; fax 222-34-43; e-mail amchimali@spider.toolnet.org; Ambassador WEI WENHUA.

Côte d'Ivoire: square Patrice Lumumba, immeuble CNAR, BP E 3644, Bamako; tel. 222-03-89; fax 222-13-76; Ambassador ABOUBACAR SIRIKI DIABATÉ.

Cuba: Niarela, Bamako; tel. 221-02-89; fax 221-02-93; Ambassador ARMANDO GARCÍA.

Egypt: BP 44, Badalabougou-est, Bamako; tel. 222-35-65; fax 222-08-91; e-mail mostafa@datatech.net.ml; Ambassador MOHAMED EL-GHOBARI.

France: square Patrice Lumumba, BP 17, Bamako; tel. 222-29-51; fax 222-31-36; e-mail ambassade@france-mali.org.ml; Ambassador NICOLAS NORMAND.

Germany: Badalabougou-est, rue 14, porte 334, BP 100, Bamako; tel. 222-32-99; fax 222-96-50; e-mail allemagne.presse@afribone.net.ml; Ambassador INGMAR BRENTLE.

Ghana: Bamako; Ambassador KWADKO AFOAKWA SARPONG.

Guinea: Immeuble Saybou Maïga, quartier du Fleuve, BP 118, Bamako; tel. 222-30-07; fax 221-08-06; Ambassador MOHAMED LAMINE JO SOUMAH.

Iran: Hippodrome, ave al-Quds, BP 2136, Bamako; tel. 221-76-38; fax 221-07-31; Ambassador HEDAYATOLAH GHAREDAGHI.

Libya: Badala Ouest, face Palais de la Culture, BP 1670, Bamako; tel. 222-34-96; fax 222-66-97; Ambassador Dr SALAHEDDIN AHMED ZAREM.

Mauritania: route de Koulikoro, Hippodrome, BP 135, Bamako; tel. 221-48-15; fax 222-49-08; Ambassador MOHAMED SIE'AHMED OULD LECKHALE.

Morocco: rue 25, porte 80, BP 2013, Badalabougou-est, Bamako; tel. 222-21-23; fax 222-77-87; e-mail sifamali@afribone.net.ml; Ambassador MOHAMED RCHOUK.

Netherlands: rue 437, BP 2220, Hippodrome, Bamako; tel. 221-56-11; fax 221-36-17; e-mail bam@minbuza.nl; Ambassador Dr R. H. BUIKEMA.

Nigeria: BP 57, Badala-est; tel. 221-53-28; fax 222-39-74; e-mail ngrbko@malinet.ml; Ambassador MOHAMMED SANI KANGIWA.

Russia: BP 300, Niarela, Bamako; tel. 221-55-92; fax 221-99-26; e-mail ambrusse_mali@datatech.toolnet.org; Ambassador ANATOLII I. KLIMENKO.

Saudi Arabia: Villa Bal Harbour, 28 Cité du Niger, BP 81, Bamako; tel. 221-25-28; fax 221-50-64; e-mail mlemb@mofa.gov.sa; Chargé d'affaires a.i. KHALED OMAR ABDRABUH.

Senegal: quartier du Fleuve, BP 42, Bamako; tel. 222-82-74; fax 221-17-80; Ambassador AMADOU DEME.

South Africa: Bâtiment Diarra, Hamdallaye, ACI-2000, BP 2015, Bamako; tel. 229-29-25; fax 229-29-26; e-mail bamako@foreign.gov.za; internet www.saemali.info; Ambassador Dr P. T. MATHOMA.

Tunisia: quartier du Fleuve, Bamako; tel. 223-28-91; fax 222-17-55; Ambassador BÉCHIR MSAKNI.

USA: angle rue Rochester NY, ave Mohamed V, BP 34, Bamako; tel. 222-54-70; fax 222-37-12; e-mail webmaster@usa.org.ml; internet w3.usa.org.ml; Ambassador VICKI HUDDLESTON.

Judicial System

The 1992 Constitution guarantees the independence of the judiciary.

High Court of Justice: Bamako; competent to try the President of the Republic and ministers of the Government for high treason and for crimes committed in the course of their duties, and their accomplices in any case where state security is threatened; mems designated by the mems of the Assemblée nationale, and renewed annually.

Supreme Court: BP 7, Bamako; tel. 222-24-06; e-mail csupreme@afribone.net.ml; f. 1969; comprises judicial, administrative and auditing sections; judicial section comprises five chambers, administrative section comprises two chambers, auditing section comprises three chambers; Pres. ASKIA M'BARAKOU TOURÉ; Sec.-Gen. ALKAÏDY SANIBIÉ TOURÉ.

President of the Bar: Me MAGATTÉ SÈYE.

There are three Courts of Appeal, seven Tribunaux de première instance (Magistrates' Courts) and also courts for labour disputes.

Religion

According to the UN Development Programme's *Human Development Report*, around 80% of the population are Muslims, while 18% follow traditional animist beliefs and under 2% are Christians.

ISLAM

Association Malienne pour l'Unité et le Progrès de l'Islam (AMUPI): Bamako; state-endorsed Islamic governing body.

Chief Mosque: place de la République, Bagadadji, Bamako; tel. 221-21-90.

Haut Conseil Islamique: Bamako; f. 2002; responsible for management of relations between the Muslim communities and the State; Pres. MODY SYLLA (acting).

CHRISTIANITY

The Roman Catholic Church

Mali comprises one archdiocese and five dioceses. At 31 December 2002 there were an estimated 227,891 Roman Catholics, comprising about 2.0% of the total population.

Bishops' Conference

Conférence Episcopale du Mali, Archevêché, BP 298, Bamako; tel. 222-67-84; fax 222-67-00; e-mail cemali@afribone.net.ml.

f. 1973; Pres. Most Rev. JEAN-GABRIEL DIARRA (Bishop of San).

Archbishop of Bamako: JEAN ZERBO, Archevêché, BP 298, Bamako; tel. 222-54-99; fax 222-52-14; e-mail mgrjeanzerbo@afribone.net.ml.

Other Christian Churches

There are several Protestant mission centres, mainly administered by US societies.

BAHÁ'Í FAITH

National Spiritual Assembly: BP 1657, Bamako; e-mail ntirandaz@aol.com.

The Press

The 1992 Constitution guarantees the freedom of the press. In 2000 there were six daily newspapers, 18 weekly or twice-weekly publications and six monthly or twice-monthly publications.

DAILY NEWSPAPERS

Les Echos: Hamdallaye, ave Cheick Zayed, porte 2694, BP 2043, Bamako; tel. 229-62-89; fax 226-76-39; e-mail jamana@malinet.ml; f. 1989; publ. by Jamana cultural co-operative; circ. 30,000; Dir ALEXIS KALAMBRY; Editor-in-Chief ABOUBACAR SALIPH DIARRA.

L'Essor: square Patrice Lumumba, BP 141, Bamako; tel. 222-36-83; fax 222-47-74; e-mail info@essor.gov.ml; internet www.essor.gov.ml; f. 1949; pro-Govt newspaper; Editor SOULEYMANE DRABO; circ. 3,500.

Info Matin: rue 56/350, Bamako Coura, BP E 4020, Bamako; tel. 223-82-09; fax 223-82-27; e-mail redaction@info-matin.com; internet www.info-matin.com; independent; Dir SAMBI TOURÉ; Editor-in-Chief MOHAMED SACKO.

Société des Télécommunications du Mali (SOTELMA): route de Koulikoro, BP 740, Bamako; tel. 222-77-38; fax 221-30-22; e-mail segal@sotelma.ml; f. 1990; state-owned; 49% privatization proposed; Pres. and Dir-Gen. KAFFA FOMMA DICKO.

Le Républicain: 116 rue 400, Dravéla-Bolibana, BP 1484, Bamako; tel. 229-09-00; fax 229-09-33; e-mail republicain@cefib.com; f. 1992; independent; Dir SALIF KONÉ.

PERIODICALS

26 Mars: Badalabougou-Sema Gesco, Lot S13, BP MA 174, Bamako; tel. 229-04-59; f. 1998; weekly; independent; Dir BOUBACAR SANGARÉ.

L'Aurore: Niaréla 298, rue 438, BP 3150, Bamako; tel. and fax 221-69-22; e-mail aurore@timbagga.com.ml; f. 1990; 2 a week; independent; Dir KARAMOKO N'DIAYE.

Le Canard Enchanté: Immeuble Koumara, bloc 104, Centre Commercial, Bamako; tel. 673-47-59; f. 2002; weekly; satirical; Dir OUMAR BABI.

Le Carrefour: ave Cheick Zayed, Hamdallaye, Bamako; tel. 223-98-08; e-mail journalcarrefour@yahoo.fr; f. 1997; Dir MAHAMANE IMRANE COULIBALY.

Citoyen: Bamako; f. 1992; fortnightly; independent.

Le Continent: AA 16, Banankabougou, BP E 4338, Bamako; tel. and fax 229-57-39; e-mail le_continent@yahoo.fr; f. 2000; weekly; Dir IBRAHIMA TRAORÉ.

Le Courrier: 230 ave Cheick Zayed, Lafiabougou Marché, BP 1258, Bamako; tel. and fax 229-18-62; e-mail journalcourrier@webmails.com; f. 1996; weekly; Dir SADOU A. YATTARA; also *Le Courrier Magazine*, monthly.

L'Indépendant: Immeuble ABK, Hamdallaye ACI, BP E 1040, Bamako; tel. and fax 223-27-27; e-mail independant@cefib.com; 2 a week; Dir SAOUTI HAÏDARA.

L'Inspecteur: Immeuble Nimagala, bloc 262, BP E 4534, Bamako; tel. 672-47-11; e-mail inspecteurmali@yahoo.fr; f. 1992; weekly; Dir ALY DIARRA.

Jamana—Revue Culturelle Malienne: BP 2043, Bamako; BP E 1040; e-mail jamana@malinet.ml; f. 1983; quarterly; organ of Jamana cultural co-operative.

Journal Officiel de la République du Mali: Koulouba, BP 14, Bamako; tel. 222-59-86; fax 222-70-50; official gazette.

Kabaaru: Village Kibaru, Bozola, Bamako; f. 1983; state-owned; monthly; Fulbé (Peul) language; rural interest; Editor BADAMA DOUCOURÉ; circ. 5,000.

Kabako: rue 228, porte 474, Hippodrome, BP E 731, Bamako; tel. 221-29-12; f. 1991; weekly; general; Dir DIABY MACORO CAMARA.

Kibaru: Village Kibaru, Bozola, BP 1463, Bamako; f. 1972; monthly; state-owned; Bambara and three other languages; rural interest; Editor NIANZÉ SAMAKÉ; circ. 5,000.

Liberté: Immeuble Sanago, Hamdallaye Marché, BP E 24, Bamako; tel. 228-18-98; e-mail ladji.guindo@cefib.com; f. 1999; weekly; Dir ABDOULAYE LADJI GUINDO.

Le Malien: rue 497, porte 277, Badialan III, BP E 1558, Bamako; tel. 223-57-29; fax 229-13-39; e-mail lemalien2000@yahoo.fr; f. 1993; weekly; Dir SIDI KEITA.

Match: 97 rue 498, Lafiabougou, BP E 3776, Bamako; tel. 229-18-82; e-mail bcissouma@yahoo.fr; f. 1997; 2 a month; sports; Dir BABA CISSOUMA.

Musow: Bamako; e-mail musow@musow.com; internet www.musow.com; women's interest.

Nyéléni Magazine: Niaréla 298, rue 348, BP 13150, Bamako; tel. 229-24-01; f. 1991; monthly; women's interest; Dir MAÏMOUNA TRAORÉ.

L'Observateur: Galérie Djigué, rue du 18 juin, BP E 1002, Bamako; tel. and fax 223-06-89; e-mail belcotamboura@hotmail.com; f. 1992; 2 a week; Dir BELCO TAMBOURA.

Le Reflet: Immeuble Kanadjigui, Route de Koulikoro, Boulkassoumbougou, BP E 1688, Bamako; tel. 224-39-52; fax 223-23-08; e-mail lereflet@afribone.malinet.ml; weekly; fmrly *Le Carcan*; present name adopted Jan. 2001; Dir ABDOUL KARIM DRAMÉ.

Le Scorpion: r230 ave Cheick Zayed, Lafiabougou Marché, BP 1258, Bamako; tel. and fax 229-18-62; f. 1991; weekly; Dir MAHAMANE HAMÈYE CISSÉ.

Le Tambour: rue 497, porte 295, Badialan III, BP E 289, Bamako; tel. and fax 222-75-68; e-mail tambourj@yahoo.fr; f. 1994; 2 a week; Dir YÉRO DIALLO.

Tatou Sports: BP 98, Sikasso; tel. 262-02-46; Dir SAÏD DIARRASSOUBA.

NEWS AGENCIES

Agence Malienne de Presse et Publicité (AMAP): square Patrice Lumumba, BP 141, Bamako; tel. 222-36-83; fax 222-47-74; e-mail amap@afribone.net.ml; f. 1977; Dir SOULEYMANE DRABO.

Foreign Bureau

Agence France-Presse (AFP): BP 778, Bamako; tel. 222-07-77.

IPS (Italy) and Xinhua (New China) News Agency (People's Republic of China) are also represented in Mali.

PRESS ASSOCIATIONS

Association des Editeurs de la Presse Privée (ASSEP): BP E 1002, Bamako; tel. 671-31-33; e-mail belcotamboura@hotmail.com; Pres. BELCO TAMBOURA.

Association des Femmes de la Presse Privée: Porte 474, rue 428, BP E 731, Bamako; tel. 221-29-12; Pres. FANTA DIALLO.

Association des Journalistes Professionels des Médias Privés du Mali (AJPM): BP E 2456, Bamako; tel. 222-19-15; fax 223-54-78; Pres. MOMADOU FOFANA.

Association des Professionnelles Africaines de la Communication (APAC MALI): Porte 474, rue 428, BP E 731, Bamako; tel. 221-29-12; Pres. MASSIRÉ YATTASSAYE.

Maison de la Presse de Mali: 17 rue 619, Darsalam, BP E 2456, Bamako; tel. 222-19-15; fax 223-54-78; e-mail maison.presse@afribone.net.ml; internet www.mediamali.org; independent media association; Pres. SADOU A. YATTARA.

Union Interprofessionnelle des Journalistes et de la Presse de Langue Française (UIJPLF): rue 42, Hamdallaye Marché, BP 1258, Bamako; tel. 229-98-35; Pres. MAHAMANE HAMÉYE CISSÉ.

Union Nationale des Journalistes Maliens (UNAJOM): BP 141, Bamako; tel. 222-36-83; fax 223-43-13; e-mail amap@afribone.net.ml; Pres. OUSMANE MAÏGA.

Publishers

EDIM SA: ave Kassé Keïta, BP 21, Bamako; tel. 222-40-41; f. 1972 as Editions Imprimeries du Mali, reorg. 1987; general fiction and non-fiction, textbooks; Chair. and Man. Dir ALOU TOMOTA.

Editions Donniya: Cité du Niger, BP 1273, Bamako; tel. 221-46-46; fax 221-90-31; e-mail donniya@malinet.ml; internet www.cefib.com/impcolor/donniya.htm; f. 1996; general fiction, history, reference and children's books in French and Bambara.

Le Figuier: 151 rue 56, Semal, BP 2605, Bamako; tel. and fax 223-32-11; e-mail lefiguier@afribone.net.ml; f. 1997; fiction and non-fiction.

Editions Jamana: BP 2043, Bamako; tel. 229-62-89; fax 229-76-39; e-mail jamana@malinet.ml; f. 1988; literary fiction, poetry, reference; Dir BA MAÏRA SOW.

Editions Teriya: BP 1677, Bamako; tel. 224-11-42; theatre, literary fiction; Dir GAOUSSOU DIAWARA.

Broadcasting and Communications

TELECOMMUNICATIONS

Ikatel: Bamako; f. 2003; fixed-line and mobile cellular telecommunications; jtly owned by France Telecom and Société Nationale des Télécommunications du Sénégal; Dir-Gen. ALIOUNE N'DIAYE; 100,000 subscribers (2003).

Malitel: Bamako; tel. 222-47-31; fax 222-47-30; e-mail malitel@cefib.com; internet www.malitel.com; f. 1999; operates fixed-line telephone services, also mobile and cellular telecommunications in Bamako, Kayes, Mopti, Ségou and Sikasso; 47,000 subscribers to mobile cellular telecommunications services (2003).

Société des Télécommunications du Mali (SOTELMA): route de Koulikoro, BP 740, Bamako; tel. 222-77-38; fax 221-30-22; e-mail segal@sotelma.ml; f. 1990; state-owned; 49% privatization proposed; Pres. and Dir-Gen. KAFFA FOMMA DICKO.

BROADCASTING

Radio

Office de Radiodiffusion-Télévision Malienne (ORTM): BP 171, Bamako; tel. 221-20-19; fax 221-42-05; e-mail ortm@afribone .net.ml; internet www.ortm.net; Dir-Gen. SIDIKI KONATÉ; Dir of Radio OUMAR TOURÉ.

Radio Mali–Chaîne Nationale: BP 171, Bamako; tel. 221-20-19; fax 221-42-05; e-mail ortm@spider.toolnet.org; f. 1957; state-owned; radio programmes in French, Bambara, Peulh, Sarakolé, Tamachek, Sonrai, Moorish, Wolof, English.

Chaîne 2: Bamako; f. 1993; radio broadcasts to Bamako.

In late 2003 there were an estimated 130 community, commercial and religious radio stations broadcasting in Mali.

Fréquence 3: Bamako; f. 1992; commercial.

Radio Balanzan: BP 419, Ségou; tel. 232-02-88; commercial.

Radio Bamakan: Marché de Médine, BP E 100, Bamako; tel. and fax 221-27-60; e-mail radio.bamakan@ifrance.com; f. 1991; community station; 104 hours of FM broadcasts weekly; Man. MODIBO DIALLO.

Radio Espoir: BP 1399, Bamako; tel. 220-67-08; f. 2000; Dir MAURICE SOGOBA.

Radio Foko de Ségou Jamana: BP 2043, Bamako; tel. 232-00-48; fax 222-76-39; e-mail radiofoko@cefib.com.

Radio Guintan: Magnambougou, BP 2546, Bamako; tel. 220-09-38; f. 1994; community radio station; Dir RAMATA DIA.

Radio Jamana: BP 2043, Bamako; tel. 229-62-89; fax 229-76-39; e-mail jamana@malinet.net.

Radio Kayira: Djélibougou Doumanzana, BP 3140, Bamako; tel. 224-87-82; fax 222-75-68; f. 1992; community station; Dir OUMAR MARIKO.

Radio Klédu: Cité du Niger, BP 2322, Bamako; tel. 221-00-18; f. 1992; commercial; Dir FADIALA DEMBÉLÉ.

Radio Liberté: BP 5015, Bamako; tel. 223-05-81; f. 1991; commercial station broadcasting 24 hours daily; Dir ALMANY TOURÉ.

Radio Patriote: Korofina-Sud, BP E 1406, Bamako; tel. 224-22-92; f. 1995; commercial station; Dir MOUSSA KEÏTA.

Radio Rurale: Plateau, BP 94, Kayes; tel. 253-14-76; e-mail rrk@ afribone.net.ml; f. 1988; community stations established by the Agence de coopération culturelle et technique (ACTT); transmitters in Niono, Kadiolo, Bandiagara and Kidal; Dir FILY KEÏTA.

Radio Sahel: BP 394, Kayes; tel. 252-21-87; f. 1991; commercial; Dir ALMAMY S. TOURÉ.

Radio Tabalé: Bamako-Coura, BP 697, Bamako; tel. and fax 222-78-70; f. 1992; independent public-service station; broadcasting 57 hours weekly; Dir TIÉMOKO KONÉ.

La Voix du Coran et du Hadit: Grande Mosquée, BP 2531, Bamako; tel. 221-63-44; f. 1993; Islamic station broadcasting on FM in Bamako; Dir El Hadj MAHMOUD DICKO.

Radio Wassoulou: BP 24, Yanfolila; tel. 265-10-97; commercial.

Radio France International, the Voix de l'Islam and the Gabonese-based Africa No. 1 began FM broadcasts in Mali in 1993; broadcasts by Voice of America and the World Service of the British Broadcasting Corpn are also transmitted via private radio stations.

Television

Office de Radiodiffusion-Télévision Malienne (ORTM): see Radio; Dir of Television BALY IDRISSA SISSOKO.

Multicanal SA: Quinzambougou, BP E 1506, Bamako; tel. 221-49-64; e-mail sandrine@multi-canal.com; internet www.multi-canal .com; private subscription broadcaster; relays international broadcasts; Pres. ISMAÏLA SIDIBÉ.

TV Klédu: 600 ave Modibo Keïta, BP E 1172, Bamako; tel. 223-90-00; fax 223-70-50; e-mail info@tvkledu.com; internet www.cefib.com/ tvkledu; private cable TV operator; relays international broadcasts; Pres. MAMADOU COULIBALY.

Finance

(cap. = capital; res = reserves; dep. = deposits; m. = million; brs = branches; amounts in francs CFA)

BANKING

Central Bank

Banque Centrale des Etats de l'Afrique de l'Ouest (BCEAO): BP 206, Bamako; tel. 222-37-56; fax 222-47-86; internet www.bceao .int; f. 1962; HQ in Dakar, Senegal; bank of issue for the mem. states of Union économique et monétaire ouest-africaine (UEMOA, comprising Benin, Burkina Faso, Côte d'Ivoire, Guinea-Bissau, Mali, Niger, Senegal and Togo); cap. and res 859,313m., total assets 5,671,675m. (Dec. 2002); Gov. CHARLES KONAN BANNY; Dir in Mali IDRISSA TRAORÉ; brs at Mopti and Sikasso.

Commercial Banks

Bank of Africa—Mali (BOA): 418 ave de la Marné, Bozola, BP 2249, Bamako; tel. 221-47-61; fax 221-46-53; e-mail boama.dg@ bkofafrica.com; internet www.bkofafrica.net/mali.htm; f. 1983; cap. and res 4,586m., total assets 81,237m. (Dec. 2002); Dir-Gen. JEAN-PIERRE IMBERT; 5 brs.

Banque Commerciale du Sahel (BCS–SA): ave Kassé Keïta, BP 2372, Bamako; tel. 221-01-95; fax 221-97-82; e-mail bcs@cefib.com; f. 1980; fmrly Banque Arabe Libyo-Malienne pour le Commerce Extérieur et le Développement; 91.3% owned by Libyan-Arab Foreign Bank; cap. 1,100m., total assets. 22,555m. (Dec. 2000); Pres. FANGA-TIGUI DOUMBIA; Dir-Gen. MOHAMED SAED EL ATRACH; 1 br.

Banque de l'Habitat du Mali (BHM): rue de Métal Soudan, quartier du Fleuve, BP 2614, Bamako; tel. 222-91-90; fax 222-93-50; e-mail bhm@bhm.malinet.ml; f. 1990; present name adopted 1996; 37.1% owned by Institut National de Prévoyance Social, 25.9% by Agence Cession Immobilière; cap. 4,000m, total assets 52,811m. (Dec. 2001); Pres. and Dir-Gen. MAMADOU SAMBA DIARRA; 1 br.

Banque International pour le Commerce et l'Industrie au Mali (BICI–Mali): Immeuble Nimagala, blvd du Peuple, BP 72, Bamako; tel. 223-33-70; fax 223-33-73; e-mail bicim-sa@cefib.com; f. 1998; 50% owned by SFOM Interafrica (Switzerland), 20% by BNP Paribas (France), 15% by Banque Mauritanienne pour le Commerce International (Mauritania); cap. 2m., total assets 33.7m. (Dec. 2001); Pres. and Dir-Gen. LUC-MARIE VIDAL; 1 br.

Banque Internationale pour le Mali (BIM): ave de l'Indépendance, BP 15, Bamako; tel. 222-51-11; fax 222-45-66; e-mail bim@bim .com.ml; f. 1980; present name adopted 1995; 61.5% state-owned; privatization pending; cap. 4,255m., res 1,099m., dep. 78,806m. (Dec. 2002); Pres. and Dir-Gen. DIAKARYA KEITA; 7 brs.

Banque Malienne de Crédit et de Dépôts: ave Mobido Keita, BP 45, Bamako; tel. 222-53-36; fax 222-79-50; e-mail bmcd@malinet.ml; 100% state-owned; transfer to private-sector ownership proposed.

Ecobank Mali: place de la Nation, quartier du Fleuve, BP E 1272, Bamako; tel. 223-33-00; fax 223-33-05; e-mail ecobank@malinet.ml; f. 1998; 50% owned by Ecobank Transnational Inc., 18% by Ecobank Bénin, 15% by Ecobank Togo; cap. 2,525m., dep. 25,175m., total assets 37,318m. (Dec. 2001); Pres. SEYDOU DJIM SYLLA; Dir-Gen. KASSIM ABOU KABASSI; 2 brs.

Development Banks

Banque de Développement du Mali (BDM-SA): ave Modibo Keita, quartier du Fleuve, BP 94, Bamako; tel. 222-20-50; fax 222-50-85; e-mail info@bdm-sa.com; internet www.bdm-sa.com; f. 1968; absorbed Banque Malienne de Crédit et de Dépôts in 2001; 20% state-owned, 20% owned by BCEAO, 20% by Banque ouest-africaine de développement; cap. 3,760m., total assets 258,180m. (Dec. 2001); Pres. and Dir-Gen. ABDOULAYE DAFFÉ; 14 brs.

Banque Malienne de Solidarité (BMS): ave du Fleuve, Immeuble Dette Publique, 2e étage, BP 1280, Bamako; tel. and fax 223-50-43; e-mail bms-sa@bms-sa.com; f. 2002; cap. 2.4m.; 1 br.

Banque Nationale de Développement Agricole—Mali (BNDA—Mali): Immeuble BNDA, blvd du Mali, ACI 2000, BP 2424, Bamako; tel. 229-64-64; fax 229-25-75; e-mail bnda@bndamali .com; f. 1981; 40.6% state-owned, 21.2% owned by Agence française de développement (France), 20.0% owned by Deutsche Entwicklangs Gesellschaft (Germany), 18.2% owned by BCEAO; cap. 9,968m. (Dec. 2002), total assets 75,820m. (Dec. 2001); Pres. and Dir-Gen. MOUSSA KALIFA TRAORÉ; 22 brs.

Financial Institutions

Direction Générale de la Dette Publique: Immeuble ex-Caisse Autonome d'Amortissement, quartier du Fleuve, BP 1617, Bamako;

tel. 222-29-35; fax 222-07-93; management of the public debt; Dir NAMALA KONÉ.

Equibail Mali: rue 376, porte 1319, Niarela, BP E 566, Bamako; tel. 21-37-77; fax 21-37-78; e-mail equip.ma@bkofafrica.com; internet www.bkofafrica.net/jeux_de_cadres/equibail/equibail_mali/equibail_mali.htm; f. 1999; 50.2% owned by African Financial Holding, 17.5% by Bank of Africa—Benin; cap. 300m. (Dec. 2002); Mems of Administrative Council RAMATOULAYE TRAORÉ, PAUL DERREUMAUX, LÉON NAKA.

Société Malienne de Financement (SOMAFI): blvd du 22 octobre 1946, BP E 3643, Bamako; tel. 222-18-66; fax 222-18-69; e-mail somafi@malinet.ml; f. 1997; cap. and res 137m., total assets 1,217m. (Dec. 1999); Pres. M. SYLLA; Man. Dir ERIC LECLÈRE.

STOCK EXCHANGE

Bourse Régionale des Valeurs Mobilières (BRVM): Chambre de Commerce et de l'Industrie du Mali, place de la Liberté, BP E 1398, Bamako; tel. 223-23-54; fax 223-23-59; e-mail abocoum@brvm.org; f. 1998; national branch of BRVM (regional stock exchange based in Abidjan, Côte d'Ivoire, serving the mem. states of UEMOA); Man. AMADOU DJÉRI BOCOUM.

INSURANCE

Les Assurances Générales de France (AGF): ave du Fleuve, BP 190, Bamako; tel. 222-58-18.

Assurance Colina Mali SA: BP E 154, Bamako; tel. 222-57-75; fax 223-24-23; e-mail c-mali@colina-sa.com; f. 1990; cap. 1,000m.; Dir-Gen. MARYUONNE SIDIRE.

Caisse Nationale d'Assurance et de Réassurance du Mali (CNAR): BP 568, Bamako; tel. 222-64-54; fax 222-23-29; f. 1969; state-owned; cap. 50m.; Dir-Gen. F. KEITA; 10 brs.

Compagnie d'Assurance Privée—La Soutra: BP 52, Bamako; tel. 222-36-81; fax 222-55-23; f. 1979; cap. 150m.; Chair. AMADOU NIONO.

Compagnie d'Assurance et de Réassurance de Mali: BP 1822, Bamako; tel. 222-60-29.

Compagnie d'Assurance Sabu Nyuman: Bamako Coura 135–136, BP 1822, Bamako; tel. 222-60-29; fax 222-57-50; f. 1984; cap. 250m.; Dir-Gen. MOMADOU SANOGO.

Gras Savoye Mali: ave Amílcar Cabral, angle rue 224, porte 1052, Hippodrome, BP 9032, Bamako; tel. 221-41-93; fax 221-42-71; e-mail grassavoye.mali@afribone.net.ml; internet www.grassavoye.com; affiliated to Gras Savoye (France); Man. ALASSANE TOURÉ.

Lafía Assurances: ave de la Nation, BP 1542, Bamako; tel. 222-35-51; fax 222-52-24; f. 1983; cap. 50m.; Dir-Gen. ABDOULAYE TOURÉ.

Trade and Industry

GOVERNMENT AGENCIES

Centre d'Etudes et de Promotion Industrielle (CEPI): BP 1980, Bamako; tel. 222-22-79; fax 222-80-85.

Direction Nationale des Affaires Economiques (DNAE): Bamako; tel. 222-23-14; fax 222-22-56; involved in economic and social affairs.

Direction Nationale des Travaux Publics (DNTP): ave de la Liberté, BP 1758, Bamako; tel. and fax 222-29-02; administers public works.

Guichet Unique–Direction Nationale des Industries: rue Titi Niare, Quinzambougou, BP 96, Bamako; tel. and fax 222-31-66.

Office National des Produits Pétroliers (ONAP): quartier du Fleuve, rue 315, porte 141, BP 2070, Bamako; tel. 222-28-27; fax 222-44-83; e-mail onap@datatech.toolnet.org; Dir-Gen. ABDOULAYE YAYA SECK.

Office du Niger: BP 106, Ségou; tel. 232-02-92; fax 232-01-43; f. 1932; taken over from the French authorities in 1958; restructured in mid-1990s; cap. 7,139m. francs CFA; principally involved in cultivation of food crops, particularly rice; Pres. and Man. Dir NANCOMA KEÏTA.

Office des Produits Agricoles du Mali (OPAM): BP 132, Bamako; tel. 222-37-55; fax 221-04-06; e-mail opam@datatech.toolnet.org; f. 1965; state-owned; manages National (Cereals) Security Stock, administers food aid, responsible for sales of cereals and distribution to deficit areas; cap. 5,800m. francs CFA; Pres. and Dir-Gen. ABDOULAYE KOITA.

DEVELOPMENT ORGANIZATIONS

Agence Française de Développement (AFD): Quinzambougou, Route de Sotuba, BP 32, Bamako; tel. 221-28-42; fax 221-86-46; internet www.afd.fr; fmrly Caisse Française de Développement; Dir in Mali DOMINIQUE DORDAIN.

Office de Développement Intégré du Mali-Ouest (ODIMO): square Patrice Lumumba, Bamako; tel. 222-57-59; f. 1991 to succeed Office de Développement Intégré des Productions Arachidières et Céréalières; development of diversified forms of agricultural production; Man. Dir ZANA SANOGO.

Service de Coopération et d'Action Culturelle: square Patrice Lumumba, BP 84, Bamako; tel. 221-83-38; fax 221-83-39; administers bilateral aid from France; Dir BERTRAND COMMELIN.

CHAMBER OF COMMERCE

Chambre de Commerce et d'Industrie du Mali: place de la Liberté, BP 46, Bamako; tel. 222-50-36; fax 222-21-20; e-mail ccim@cefip.com; f. 1906; Pres. MAMADOU LAMINE TOUNKARA; Sec.-Gen. DABA TRAORÉ.

EMPLOYERS' ASSOCIATIONS

Association Malienne des Exportateurs de Légumes (AMELEF): Bamako; f. 1984; Pres. BADARA FAGANDA TRAORÉ; Sec.-Gen. BIRAMA TRAORÉ.

Association Malienne des Exportateurs de Ressources Animales (AMERA): Bamako; tel. 222-56-83; f. 1985; Pres. AMBARKÉ YERMANGORE; Admin. Sec. ALI HACKO.

Fédération Nationale des Employeurs du Mali (FNEM): BP 2445, Bamako; tel. 221-63-11; fax 221-90-77; f. 1980; Pres. MOUSSA MARY BALLA COULIBALY; Permanent Sec. LASSINA TRAORÉ.

UTILITIES

Electricity

Energie du Mali (EDM): square Patrice Lumumba, BP 69, Bamako; tel. 222-30-20; fax 222-84-30; e-mail sekou.edm@cefib.com; f. 1960; 60% owned by Saur International (France); planning, construction and operation of power-sector facilities; cap. 7,880m. francs CFA; Pres. YORO DIAKITÉ; Dir-Gen. HAROUNA DIAKITÉ; 1,401 employees (2001).

Enertech GSA: marché de Lafiabougou, BP 1949, Bamako; tel. 222-37-63; fax 222-51-36; f. 1994; cap. 20m. francs CFA; solar energy producer; Dir MOCTAR DIAKITÉ.

Société de Gestion de l'Energie de Manantali (SOGEM): Immeuble 790, Hippodrome, rue 335 x 336, BP 4015, Bamako; tel. 221-03-92; fax 221-11-22; to generate and distribute electricity from the Manantali HEP project, under the auspices of the Organisation pour la mise en valeur du fleuve Sénégal.

Gas

Maligaz: route de Sotuba, BP 5, Bamako; tel. 222-23-94; gas distribution.

TRADE UNION FEDERATION

Union nationale des travailleurs du Mali (UNTM): Bourse du Travail, blvd de l'Indépendance, BP 169, Bamako; tel. 222-36-99; fax 223-59-45; f. 1963; 13 national and 8 regional unions, and 52 local organizations; Sec.-Gen. SIAKA DIAKITÉ.

There are, in addition, several non-affiliated trade unions.

Transport

RAILWAYS

Mali's only railway runs from Koulikoro, via Bamako, to the Senegal border. The line continues to Dakar, a total distance of 1,286 km, of which 729 km is in Mali. The track is in very poor condition, and is frequently closed during the rainy season. In 1995 the Governments of Mali and Senegal agreed to establish, with a view to privatization, a joint company to operate the Bamako–Dakar line. Some 536,000 metric tons of freight were handled on the Malian railway in 1999. Plans exist for the construction of a new rail line linking Bamako with Kouroussa and Kankan, in Guinea.

Régie du Chemin de Fer du Mali (RCFM): BP 260, Bamako; tel. 222-59-68; fax 222-83-88; e-mail rcfm@cefib.com; internet www.promali.org/rcfm; f. 1960; transferred to private management in 2003; Pres. DIAKARIDIA SIDIBÉ; Man. Dir SAMBA SIMPARA.

ROADS

The Malian road network in 1999 comprised 17,107 km, of which about 1,500 km were main roads. About 2,760 km of the network were paved. A bituminized road between Bamako and Abidjan (Côte d'Ivoire) provides Mali's main economic link to the coast; construction of a road linking Bamako and Dakar (Senegal) is to be financed by the European Development Fund. The African Development Bank also awarded a US $31.66m. loan to fund the Kankan–Kouremale–Bamako road between Mali and Guinea. A road across the Sahara to link Mali with Algeria is also planned.

Compagnie Malienne de Transports Routiers (CMTR): BP 208, Bamako; tel. 222-33-64; f. 1970; state-owned; Man. Dir MAMADOU TOURÉ.

INLAND WATERWAYS

The River Niger is navigable in parts of its course through Mali (1,693 km) during the rainy season from July to late December. The River Senegal was, until the early 1990s, navigable from Kayes to Saint-Louis (Senegal) only between August and November, but its navigability was expected to improve following the inauguration, in 1992, of the Manantali dam, and the completion of works to deepen the river-bed.

Compagnie Malienne de Navigation (COMANAV): BP 10, Koulikoro; tel. 226-20-94; fax 226-20-09; f. 1968; 100% state-owned; river transport; Pres. and Man. Dir YACOUBA DIALLO.

Société Navale Malienne (SONAM): Bamako; tel. 222-60-52; fax 222-60-66; f. 1981; transferred to private ownership in 1986; Chair. ALIOUNE KEÏTA.

Société Ouest-Africaine d'Entreprise Maritime (SOAEM): rue Mohamed V, BP 2428, Bamako; tel. 222-58-32; fax 222-40-24; maritime transport co.

CIVIL AVIATION

The principal airport is at Bamako-Senou. The other major airports are at Bourem, Gao, Goundam, Kayes, Kita, Mopti, Nioro, Ségou, Tessalit and Tombouctou. There are about 40 small airfields. Mali's airports are being modernized with external financial assistance.

Direction Nationale de l'Aéronautique Civile: Bamako; tel. 222-55-24.

Air Affaires Mali: BP E 3759, Badalabougou, Bamako; tel. 222-61-36.

STA Trans African Airlines: quartier du Fleuve, BP 775, Bamako; tel. 222-44-44; fax 221-09-81; e-mail sta-airlines@sta-airlines.com; internet www.sta.aero; f. 1984 as Société des Transports Aériens; privately-owned; local, regional and international services; Man. Dir MELHEM ELIE SABBAGUE.

Tourism

Mali's rich cultural heritage is promoted as a tourist attraction. In 1999 the Government launched a three-year cultural and tourism development programme centred on Tombouctou, Gao and Kidal. An estimated 91,000 tourists visited Mali in 2000, when receipts from tourism totalled some US $50m.

Office Malien du Tourisme et de l'Hôtellerie (OMATHO): BP 191, Bamako; tel. 222-56-73; fax 222-55-41; e-mail tombouctou2000@tourisme.gov.ml; internet w3.tourisme.gov.ml; f. 1995; Dir-Gen. HAWA KEÏTA.

MALTA

Introductory Survey

Location, Climate, Language, Religion, Flag, Capital

The Republic of Malta is in southern Europe. The country comprises an archipelago in the central Mediterranean Sea, consisting of the inhabited islands of Malta, Gozo and Comino, and the uninhabited islets of Cominotto, Filfla and St Paul's. The main island, Malta, lies 93 km (58 miles) south of the Italian island of Sicily and 288 km (179 miles) east of the Tunisian coast, the nearest point on the North African mainland. The climate is warm, with average temperatures of 22.6°C (72.7°F) in summer and 13.7°C (56.6°F) in winter. Average annual rainfall is 578 mm (22.8 ins). Maltese and English are the official languages, although Italian is widely spoken. About 91% of the inhabitants are Christians belonging to the Roman Catholic Church. The national flag (proportions 2 by 3) consists of two equal vertical stripes, white at the hoist and red at the fly, with a representation of the George Cross, edged with red, in the upper hoist. The capital is Valletta, on the island of Malta.

Recent History

Malta, which had been a Crown Colony of the United Kingdom since 1814, became an independent sovereign state, within the Commonwealth, on 21 September 1964. The Government, led by Dr Giorgio Borg-Olivier of the Nationalist Party (Partit Nazzjonalista—PN), negotiated defence and financial aid agreements, effective over a 10-year period, with the United Kingdom.

In June 1971 the Malta Labour Party (Partit Laburista—MLP), led by Dom Mintoff, assumed power after winning a general election. Pursuing a policy of non-alignment, the Government concluded agreements for cultural, economic and commercial co-operation with Italy, Libya, Tunisia, the USSR, several East European countries, the USA, the People's Republic of China and others, and received technical assistance, notably from Libya. The MLP Government abrogated the 1964 Mutual Defence and Assistance Agreement with the United Kingdom. This agreement was replaced in 1972 by a new seven-year agreement, under which Malta was to receive substantially increased rental payments for the use of military facilities by the United Kingdom and other members of the North Atlantic Treaty Organization (NATO, see p. 289). British troops were finally withdrawn in March 1979.

Malta became a republic in December 1974. The MLP retained power at general elections held in September 1976 and in December 1981, when it secured a majority of three seats in the House of Representatives, although obtaining only 49.1% of the votes cast. The PN, which had received 50.9% of the votes cast, contested the result, refused to take its seats in the House of Representatives, and organized a campaign of civil disobedience. In March 1983 the PN terminated its legislative boycott, but immediately withdrew again, in protest against a government resolution to loosen ties with the European Community (EC, now the European Union—EU, see p. 208). Although Mintoff promised constitutional amendments and weekly consultations with the opposition, these arrangements collapsed in June, when the Government blamed the PN for a bomb attack on government offices. In November a police raid on the PN headquarters was alleged to have discovered a cache of arms and ammunition.

In June 1983 the House of Representatives approved controversial legislation, under which about 75% of church property was to be expropriated to provide finance for a programme of universal free education and the abolition of fee-paying church schools. Opponents of the measure denounced it as both unconstitutional and a violation of religious liberty, and in September 1984 the courts disallowed the legislation. In April 1984 the House approved legislation forbidding any school to accept fees (including voluntary gifts and donations). The Roman Catholic Archbishop of Malta rejected the government conditions and closed all church schools, in response to growing tensions and public unrest. A strike by state school teachers in October and November further polarized opinion, but an agreement was reached in November, when the schools were re-opened.

Mintoff retired in December 1984 and was replaced as Prime Minister by the new leader of the MLP, Dr Carmelo Mifsud Bonnici. In April 1985 the Government reached agreement with the Roman Catholic Church, providing for the phased introduction of free education in church secondary schools, and guaranteeing the autonomy of church schools. However, in July 1988 the enforced introduction of new licensing procedures for church schools led to demands by the Roman Catholic Church that the State should reduce its supervisory powers over church education.

At a general election held in May 1987 the PN obtained 50.9% of the votes cast but won only 31 of the 65 seats in the House of Representatives, while the MLP, with 48.9% of the votes cast, won the remaining 34 seats. However, in accordance with a constitutional amendment that had been adopted in January (see Government, below), the PN was allocated four additional seats, giving it a majority of one in the legislature, thus ending the MLP's 16-year tenure in office. The leader of the PN, Dr Eddie Fenech Adami, became Prime Minister. The PN secured an increased majority of three seats over the MLP at a general election held in February 1992. This result was widely interpreted as an endorsement of the PN's pro-EC policies.

Malta has maintained a policy of non-alignment in its international relations, and has negotiated economic co-operation agreements with many countries. In 1984 the Governments of Malta and Libya signed a five-year treaty of co-operation, which included an undertaking by Libya to provide military training. The treaty signified a return to the previously close relations between the two countries, which had deteriorated in 1980, owing to a dispute over a maritime boundary (eventually resolved by the International Court of Justice in 1985). Malta has an association agreement with the EU, originally signed in 1970 and periodically renewed. On becoming Prime Minister in May 1987, Fenech Adami declared that the Government, while retaining Malta's non-aligned status and its links with Libya, would seek closer relations with the USA and other Western countries, and would apply for full membership of the EC.

A formal application for full membership of the EC was submitted by the Maltese Government in July 1990. In June 1993 the EC Commission recommended that, subject to the Government of Malta's satisfying EC requirements for regulatory reforms in financial services, competition and consumer protection, favourable consideration should be given to the future accession of Malta to the EU. In June 1994 the Council of the EU affirmed that the next phase of enlargement, following the (then) expected accession to the EU in January 1995 of Austria, Finland, Norway and Sweden, would involve Malta and Cyprus. In June 1995 the EU affirmed that full negotiations on Malta's accession were to begin six months after the conclusion of the 1996 Intergovernmental Conference.

Domestic opposition to Maltese accession to the EU had been led by the MLP, on the grounds that EU agricultural policies would increase the cost of living, and that integration into the EU would conflict with the Republic's traditional neutrality in its foreign relations. In September 1996 the PN Government, seeking to confirm its mandate to pursue the goal of full membership of the EU, called a general election for the following month. Although the PN contested the election on its record of economic success, the Government's introduction of value-added tax (VAT), as a precondition of Malta's admission to the EU, had proved unpopular with the electorate, and its proposed abolition by the MLP (which would concurrently disqualify Malta from EU membership), was widely regarded as the decisive factor in the election. With a participation rate of 97.1% of eligible voters, the MLP secured 50.7% of the votes cast, as against 47.8% for the PN. The MLP obtained 35 seats in the House of Representatives, with the PN receiving 34 seats. (As the MLP actually won three seats less than the PN in the election, four seats were added to its final total, giving it a one-seat majority in the House.) Dr Alfred Sant, the leader of the MLP, formed a new Government with the declared intention of replacing the 1970 association agreement (see above) with new arrangements providing for an eventual 'free-trade zone' between Malta and the EU. The MLP also emphasized its commitment to the advancement of Malta's financial services sector.

In February 1997 the Government announced the initiation of a 'national discussion' of proposals to legalize divorce. However, the imposition of tax increases and levies on public utilities substantially diminished the Government's popularity. Sant called a general election for September, three years earlier than constitutionally required, and in the poll, for which there was a participation rate of 95.4%, the PN, led by Fenech Adami, obtained a five-seat majority, having obtained 51.8% of votes cast, with the MLP receiving 48.0%. Immediately following the election, Fenech Adami reactivated Malta's application for full membership of the EU. In December 1999 the European Commission agreed that accession negotiations could begin in February 2000, and in the following month the President of the Commission paid an official visit to the island. In November 2000 the Commission published a report which stated that Malta was among the best-equipped economically of those countries seeking to join the EU. Further action was required in Malta to reduce state aid (notably the politically sensitive LM 15m. annual subsidy to the island's dry docks), to implement privatization plans and to strengthen tax and customs administrations. There were also some environmental issues that required attention, notably the inadequate sewerage system.

Accession talks for the EU were formally concluded on 13 December 2002 in Copenhagen. Malta had obtained 77 exemptions in the discussions aimed largely at protecting its industrial and agricultural sectors but also including cultural issues, such as the right to maintain the predominantly Roman Catholic country's ban on divorce. A non-binding referendum was called for 8 March 2003 to determine whether the country would join the EU. Support for membership of the EU was led by the ruling PN of Fenech Adami and opposition to it by Sant's MLP, which told voters to abstain, vote against the motion to join or spoil their ballots. Following an acrimonious campaign, 53.65% of the votes cast were in favour of joining, with 46.35% against. Sant refused to concede defeat, however, arguing that since the turnout had been only 91% of the electorate the vote in support of membership of the EU did not represent an absolute majority. Fenech Adami, whose mandate expired in 2004, called a general election for 12 April 2003, four days before the proposed signing of the EU accession treaty by 10 applicant countries, including Malta.

At the general election that took place on 12 April 2003 96% of the electorate participated; the PN won 51.8% of the votes, while the MLP received 47.5% and the environmentalist Alternattiva Demokratika (Green Party) 0.7%. Fenech Adami was sworn in as Prime Minister on 14 April, announced the new Cabinet the following day (which included two new ministries with responsibility for rural affairs and the environment and for youth and the arts) and signed the EU accession treaty in Athens, Greece, on 16 April. The House of Representatives eventually ratified the treaty on 14 July by 34 votes to 25 (with six members boycotting the vote), and the President signed it on 16 July. Malta thus became a full member of the EU on 1 May 2004.

Malta's accession to the EU marked the beginning of a change in the country's politics. Since independence Malta's politics had been deeply partisan and bitterly polarized over who could best govern the archipelago, or more recently over whether to join the EU. Following the 2003 general election, however, the parties moved towards unity and consensus in order to obtain the maximum benefits for Malta from its EU membership. The MLP, which had previously been opposed outright to accession, accepted the result of the general election as a final arbiter of Maltese opinion on the question. Accordingly, following the MLP's defeat at the polls, the party leadership decided to embrace majority public opinion and work within the reality of EU membership. This decision proved to be divisive, and was resisted by a 'fundamentalist wing' of the MLP led by Carmelo Mifsud Bonnici, the former MLP leader and Prime Minister. However, delegates at a subsequent party conference agreed that the MLP would not withdraw Malta from the EU if and when the party came to power. Moreover, it was agreed that the incumbent Government would henceforth be able to rely on the MLP's support in its efforts to ensure that Malta received six seats in the European Parliament, rather than the four or five seats proposed by other, larger member states, and that the EU Constitution guaranteed the principle of equality of member states. In January 2004 the Minister of Foreign Affairs, Dr Joe Borg, was named as Malta's first European Commissioner.

On 7 February 2004 Fenech Adami used the occasion of his 70th birthday to announce his intention to resign as leader of the PN. He had always maintained that he would relinquish this post, and that of Prime Minister, when he reached 70 years of age, and he indicated that he would step down as Prime Minister once the party had appointed his successor. At a party conference on 29 February the Deputy Prime Minister and Minister for Social Policy, Dr Lawrence Gonzi, was elected as the PN's new leader. Gonzi took 59.3% of the delegates' votes and won the leadership contest after his nearest rival, John Dalli, the Minister for Finance and Economic Affairs, withdrew, thereby obviating the need for a second round of voting. (None the less, a second round was held as a formality; Gonzi took 94% of the votes cast.) Fenech Adami duly resigned from his seat in the House of Representatives and from his post as Prime Minister, and Gonzi was sworn in on 23 March 2004. On his assumption of the premiership he stated that his main priorities in the post would be full participation in the EU, the creation of jobs and the establishment of a sounder economy.

On 29 March 2004 Fenech Adami was elected President by the House of Representatives, by 33 votes to 29. His appointment was controversial, as party leaders had not traditionally stood for the post, and it was bitterly opposed by the MLP. Fenech Adami was sworn in as Malta's seventh President on 4 April 2004.

Malta is a member of the Council of Europe (see p. 190) and the Organization for Security and Co-operation in Europe (see p. 302). Participation by Malta in the NATO 'Partnership for Peace' programme formally commenced in 1995, but was suspended by the MLP Government during 1996–98.

Government

Under the 1974 Constitution, legislative power is held by the unicameral House of Representatives, whose 65 members are elected by universal adult suffrage for five years (subject to dissolution) on the basis of proportional representation. The Constitution was amended in January 1987 to ensure that a party that received more than 50% of the total votes cast in a general election would obtain a majority of seats in the legislature (by the allocation—if necessary—of extra seats to that party). The President is the constitutional Head of State, elected for a five-year term by the House, and executive power is exercised by the Cabinet. The President appoints the Prime Minister and, on the latter's recommendation, other Ministers. The Cabinet is responsible to the House.

Defence

In August 2003 the armed forces of Malta comprised a regular army of 2,140. Military service is voluntary. Budgetary expenditure on defence in 2003 was estimated at LM 11.5m.

Economic Affairs

In 2001, according to estimates by the World Bank, Malta's gross national income (GNI), measured at average 1999–2001 prices, was US $3,632m., equivalent to $9,200 per head (or $16,790 per head on an international purchasing-power parity basis). During 1990–2002, it was estimated, the population increased at an average annual rate of 0.8%, while during 1990–2001 gross domestic product (GDP) per head increased, in real terms, at an average annual rate of 3.5%. Overall GDP increased, in real terms, at an average annual rate of 4.4% in 1990–2001; GDP declined by 0.7% in 2001.

Agriculture (including hunting, forestry and fishing) contributed an estimated 2.8% of GDP in 2002. Some 1.9% of the working population were employed in the sector in 2003. The principal export crop is potatoes. Tomatoes and other vegetables, cereals (principally wheat and barley) and fruit are also cultivated. Livestock and livestock products are also important, and efforts are being made to develop the fishing industry. Exports of food and live animals accounted for 6.9% of total exports in 2000. According to FAO figures, Malta's agricultural production increased at an average rate of 1.7% per year in 1990–2002. Output rose by 2.7% in 2001, but declined by 4.4% in 2002.

Industry (including mining, manufacturing and construction) provided an estimated 26.3% of GDP in 2002, and engaged 29.8% of the employed labour force in 2003. Industrial production (including electricity and water, but excluding construction) increased at an average rate of 12.2% per year in 1990–96. It rose by 11.0% in 1995, but declined by 4.7% in 1996.

Mining and quarrying, together with construction, contributed 3.4% of GDP in 2002, and engaged 7.8% of the employed labour force in 2003 (mining and quarrying alone engaged just 0.7% of the employed labour force). The mining sector's output expanded at an average annual rate of 18.3% in 1990–96.

Production rose by 26.6% in 1995 and by 11.0% in 1996. The principal activities are stone and sand quarrying. There are reserves of petroleum in Maltese offshore waters, and petroleum and gas exploration is proceeding.

Manufacturing (excluding government enterprises) contributed an estimated 22.9% of GDP in 2002. Some 19.2% of the working population were employed in the manufacturing sector in 2003. Based on the gross value of output, the principal branches of manufacturing, excluding ship-repairing, in 1999 were transport equipment and machinery (accounting for 54.7% of the total), food products and beverages (12.4%) and textiles, footwear and clothing (8.4%). Manufacturing production increased at an average rate of 7.6% per year in 1990–96. It advanced by 8.1% in 1995, but declined by 6.2% in 1996.

Energy is derived principally from imports of crude petroleum (the majority of which is purchased, at preferential rates, from Libya) and coal. Imports of mineral fuels comprised 8.2% of the value of total imports in 2001.

Services (including public utilities and other government enterprises) provided 70.9% of GDP in 2002, and engaged 68.3% of the employed labour force in 2003. Tourism is a major source of foreign exchange earnings. In 2003 Malta received 1,126,601 foreign visitors, and revenue from the sector reached LM 260.7m. in 2001. In 2003 some 8.7% of the employed labour force were engaged in hotels and catering establishments.

In 2002 Malta recorded a visible trade deficit of US $424.5m., and there was a deficit of $83.9m. on the current account of the balance of payments. More than two-thirds of Malta's trade is with the countries of the European Union (EU, see p. 208). In 2001 the principal source of imports (accounting for 19.9% of the total) was Italy (including San Marino); other major suppliers were France (15.0%), the USA (11.6%) and the United Kingdom (10.0%). The USA was the principal market for exports (taking 19.8% of the total); other significant purchasers of exports were Germany (13.1%), Singapore (11.8%) and France (9.3%). The principal domestic exports in 2003 were machinery and transport equipment, accounting for 67.2% of the total, and miscellaneous manufactured articles (20.8%). The principal imports were machinery and transport equipment, accounting for 48.4%, basic manufactures (11.4%), and miscellaneous manufactured articles (11.2%).

In 2002 Malta recorded a budgetary deficit of LM 48.3m. (equivalent to 2.9% of GDP in that year). At the end of 1997 Malta's external debt totalled US $1,034m., of which $125m. was long-term public debt. In that year the cost of debt-servicing was equivalent to 2.1% of the value of exports of goods and services. The annual rate of inflation averaged 2.9% in 1990–2001; consumer prices increased by 2.4% in 2000 and by 2.9% in 2001. In 2003 8.2% of the labour force were unemployed.

Malta is a member of the World Trade Organization (WTO, see p. 343) and of the European Bank for Reconstruction and Development (EBRD, see p. 203).

Malta signed an association agreement with the European Community (EC, now EU) in 1970, allowing favourable trading conditions for Malta, together with economic assistance from that organization. In July 1990 Malta formally applied for full membership of the EC, and in June 1993 the European Commission confirmed Malta's eligibility for eventual accession to the EU. However, following the transfer of power to the Malta Labour Party in October 1996, the new Government announced that EU membership would not be sought, although it was proposed eventually to replace the 1970 association agreement with the formation of a 'free-trade zone' affording Malta certain commercial and social links with the EU. On resuming office in September 1998, the Nationalist Party resumed negotiations for full membership of the EU. Accession talks formally ended on 13 December 2002 and in a non-binding referendum on 8 March 2003 53.6% voted in favour of membership of the EU compared with 46.3% against. The decision to proceed with accession to the EU was confirmed by the victory of the Nationalist Party (Partit Nazzjonalista) in a general election on the 12 April. On 16 April Malta signed the EU accession treaty in Athens, Greece, with nine other applicant countries, all of whom joined the EU on 1 May 2004.

Following the closure, in 1979, of the British military base and naval docks, on which Malta's economy had been largely dependent, successive governments have pursued a policy of restructuring and diversification. The domestic market is limited, owing to the small population. There are few natural resources, and almost all raw materials have to be imported. Malta's development has therefore been based on the promotion of the island as an international financial centre and on manufacturing for export (notably in non-traditional fields, such as electronics, information technology and pharmaceuticals), together with the continuing development of tourism. Following its accession to power in 1998 the Nationalist Government attempted to address the budget deficit. A budget reduction programme, which included limits on public-sector expenditure (particularly wage increases), a privatization programme and more stringent efforts to combat the country's high level of tax evasion and the large 'parallel' economy, aimed to reduce the deficit to 3% of GDP by 2004. It was also hoped that privatization would increase investment in Malta's inadequate infrastructure. Malta's small-scale, open economy was particularly affected by the terrorist attacks on the USA in September 2001, the SARS (severe acute respiratory syndrome) health scare and the US-led military action in Iraq in early 2003, all of which adversely affected Malta's important tourism industry. In late 2003, with accession to the EU imminent, structural reforms were also making their mark on the Maltese economy. During 2003 employment in manufacturing fell by some 1,150 jobs, although this was offset by a rise in employment in the service sector. In other respects, Malta faced the same challenges as the other EU member states whose ranks it joined on 1 May 2004: restraining government expenditure, modernizing the welfare state, removing labour market inflexibilities, boosting international competitiveness, and generating stronger economic growth. Likewise, pensions reform was a priority: expenditure on old-age pensions was expected to more than double during 2004–24, to about 11% of GDP, according to the IMF. Moreover, in line with present trends, the number of workers supporting one pensioner was forecast to decrease from four to two over the same period.

Education

Education is compulsory between the ages of five and 16 years, and is available free of charge in government schools and institutions, from kindergarten to university. Kindergarten education is provided for three- and four-year-old children. Primary education begins at five years of age and lasts for six years. Secondary education, beginning at 11 years of age, lasts for a maximum of seven years, but this period is extended in the case of technology and vocational courses. After completing five years of secondary-level education, students having the necessary qualifications may opt to follow a higher academic or technical or vocational course. In October 1999 there were 80 state primary schools, 22 state secondary schools and 11 junior lyceums, which offer a more challenging curriculum. The junior college, administrated by the University, prepares students specifically for a university course. About 30% of the student population attend schools administered by the Roman Catholic Church, from kindergarten to higher secondary level. The Government subsidizes the provision of free education for students in church schools. In 1999/2000 enrolment at primary and secondary schools was equivalent to 98% of the school-age population. Enrolment at primary schools in that year included 99.1% of both boys and girls in the relevant age-group, while the comparable ratio for secondary enrolment was 88.9% (males 88.7%; females 89.0%). Higher education is available at the University of Malta, at which approximately 7,500 students were enrolled in 1999. There are also a number of technical institutes, specialist schools and an extended skill-training scheme for trade-school leavers. The Government also provides adult education courses. Of total recurrent budgetary expenditure in 2002 LM 47.5m. (7.4%) was allocated to education.

Public Holidays

2004: 1 January (New Year's Day), 10 February (St Paul's Shipwreck), 19 March (St Joseph), 31 March (Freedom Day), 9 April (Good Friday), 1 May (St Joseph the Worker), 7 June (Memorial of 1919 Riot), 29 June (St Peter and St Paul), 15 August (Assumption), 8 September (Our Lady of Victories), 21 September (Independence Day), 8 December (Immaculate Conception), 14 December (Republic Day), 25 December (Christmas).

2005: 1 January (New Year's Day), 10 February (St Paul's Shipwreck), 19 March (St Joseph), 25 March (Good Friday), 31 March (Freedom Day), 1 May (St Joseph the Worker), 7 June (Memorial of 1919 Riot), 29 June (St Peter and St Paul), 15

August (Assumption), 8 September (Our Lady of Victories), 21 September (Independence Day), 8 December (Immaculate Conception), 14 December (Republic Day), 25 December (Christmas).

Carnival is also celebrated each year on the Saturday to Tuesday before Ash Wednesday. This will be 21–24 February in 2004; 5–8 February in 2005.

Weights and Measures

The metric system is in force.

Statistical Survey

Source (unless otherwise stated): National Statistics Office, Lascaris, Valletta; tel. 21223221; fax 21249841; e-mail nso@magnet.mt; internet www.nso.gov.mt.

AREA AND POPULATION

Area: 316 sq km (122 sq miles).

Population: 378,132 (males 186,836, females 191,296) at census of 26 November 1995 (figures refer to *de jure* population); 397,296 (males 196,836, females 200,460) at 31 December 2002 (incl. 10,358 non-Maltese residents).

Density (Maltese only, 31 December 2002): 1,224 per sq km.

Principal Towns (estimated total population at 31 December 2002): Birkirkara 22,334; Qormi 18,553; Mosta 17,936; Zabbar 15,057; San Gwann 12,723; Sliema 12,575; Valletta (capital) 7,173.

Births, Marriages and Deaths (2002): Registered live births 3,805 (birth rate 9.9 per 1,000); Marriages 2,240 (marriage rate 5.8 per 1,000); Registered deaths 3,031 (death rate 7.9 per 1,000).

Expectation of Life (WHO estimates, years at birth): 78.1 (males 75.9; females 80.3) in 2002. Source: WHO, *World Health Report*.

Migration (2002): Emigrants 96 (all to United Kingdom); Returning emigrants 382; Non-Maltese nationals settling in the islands 533.

Economically Active Population (September 2003): Agriculture, hunting and forestry 2,181; Fishing 548; Mining and quarrying 1,058; Manufacturing 28,080; Electricity, gas and water supply 4,174; Construction 10,438; Wholesale and retail trade; repair of motor vehicles, motorcycles and personal and household goods 21,189; Hotels and restaurants 12,736; Transport, storage and communications 12,061; Financial intermediation 5,515; Real estate, renting and business activities 8,033; Public administration and defence; compulsory social security 13,290; Education 11,508; Health and social work 9,340; Other community, social and personal service activities 5,817; Private households with employed persons 438; Extra-territorial organizations and bodies 196; *Total employed* 146,602; Unemployed 13,166; *Total labour force* 159,768 (males 110,038, females 49,730).

HEALTH AND WELFARE

Key Indicators

Total Fertility Rate (children per woman, 2001): 1.8.

Under-5 Mortality Rate (per 1,000 live births, 2001): 5.

HIV/AIDS (% of persons aged 15–49, 2001): 0.13.

Physicians (per 1,000 head, 1998): 2.6.

Hospital Beds (per 1,000 head, 1995): 5.43.

Health Expenditure (2001): US $ per head (PPP): 813.

Health Expenditure (2001): % of GDP: 8.8.

Health Expenditure (2001): public (% of total): 68.5.

Access to Water (% of persons, 2000): 100.

Access to Sanitation (% of persons, 2000): 100.

Human Development Index (2001): ranking: 33.

Human Development Index (2001): value: 0.856.

For sources and definitions, see explanatory note on p. vi.

AGRICULTURE, ETC

Principal Crops ('000 metric tons, 2002): Wheat 9.6*; Barley 2.2*; Potatoes 27.5; Cabbages 3.9; Tomatoes 11.0; Cauliflowers 6.4; Pumpkins, squash and gourds 1.3*; Dry onions 4.4; Garlic 0.6; Green broad beans 1.4; Other vegetables 7.4*; Melons 13.9*; Citrus fruit 1.0*; Grapes 1.2; Other fruits and berries 3.8*.
*FAO estimate. Source: FAO.

Livestock ('000 head, year ending September 2002): Cattle 18.0*; Pigs 79.3; Sheep 6.6; Goats 2.2; Rabbits 0.2*; Chickens 1.0; Horses 1.0*; Asses 0.5*; Mules 0.3*.
*FAO estimate. Source: FAO.

Livestock Products ('000 metric tons, 2002): Beef and veal 1.6; Pig meat 10.4; Rabbit meat 1.4*; Poultry meat 5.7; Cows' milk 44.3; Sheep's milk 2.0; Poultry eggs 5.4.
*FAO estimate. Source: FAO.

Fishing (metric tons, live weight 2001): Capture 882 (Common dolphinfish 303, Northern bluefin tuna 219, Swordfish 89); Aquaculture 1,235 (European seabass 196, Gilthead seabream 1,039); *Total catch* 2,117. Source: FAO, *Yearbook of Fishery Statistics*.

INDUSTRY

Production (gross output, excl. ship-repairing, LM '000, 1999): Stone quarrying and sand pits 3,825; Food and beverages 125,442; Tobacco products 24,226; Textiles, footwear and clothing (incl. leather products) 85,174; Wood and wood products (excl. furniture) 1,346; Printing, publishing and allied trades 51,249; Rubber, chemicals, and non-metallic products 89,375; Metals 23,562; Transport equipment and machinery 554,863; Construction 56,341; Furniture 57,784; Miscellaneous industries 715; Total (incl. others) 1,074,402.

FINANCE

Currency and Exchange rates: 1,000 mils = 100 cents = 1 Maltese lira (LM; plural: liri). *Sterling, Dollar and Euro Equivalents* (31 December 2003): £1 sterling = 611.3 mils; US $1 = 342.5 mils; €1 = 432.6 mils; LM 100 = £163.60 = $291.97 = €231.17. *Average Exchange Rate* (US $ per Maltese lira): 2.2121 in 2001; 2.5074 in 2002; 2.9197 in 2003.

Budget (LM million, 2002): *Revenue:* Income tax 190.2; Customs and excise 59.8; Value-added tax 117.5; Social security 181.1; Grants and loans 13.3; Total (incl. others) 771.0. *Expenditure:* Recurrent expenditure 646.0 (of which Social security 190.7; Education 47.5); Public debt servicing 75.7; Capital expenditure 97.7; Total 819.3.

International Reserves (US $ million at 31 December 2002): Gold 1.2; IMF special drawing rights 39.3; Reserve position in IMF 54.7; Foreign exchange 2,115.2; Total 2,210.4. Source: IMF, *International Financial Statistics*.

Money Supply (LM million at 31 December 2002): Currency outside banks 436.8; Demand deposits at commercial banks 241.8; Total money (incl. others) 680.1. Source: IMF, *International Financial Statistics*.

Cost of Living (Retail Price Index; base: 1995 = 100): All items 112.6 in 2000; 115.9 in 2001; 118.5 in 2002. Source: IMF, *International Financial Statistics*.

Gross Domestic Product (LM '000 at current market prices, provisional): 1,562,752 in 2000; 1,634,362 in 2001; 1,680,444 in 2002.

Expenditure on Gross Domestic Product (provisional, LM '000 at current prices, 2002): Government final consumption expenditure 340,898; Private final consumption expenditure 1,081,840; Changes in stocks –67,952; Gross fixed capital formation 350,695; *Total domestic expenditure* 1,705,481; Exports of goods and services 1,472,928; *Less* Imports of goods and services 1,497,965 *GDP in purchasers' values* 1,680,444.

Gross Domestic Product by Economic Activity (provisional, LM '000 at current prices, 2002): Agriculture, hunting, forestry and fishing 39,297; Mining and quarrying (incl. construction) 48,315; Manufacturing 326,468; Transport, storage and communications 88,704; Wholesale and retail trade 155,319; Insurance, banking and real estate 132,182; Government enterprises 92,893; Public administration 233,368; Property income 138,088; Other private services 170,235; *GDP at factor cost* 1,424,869; Indirect taxes 268,614; *Less* Subsidies 13,039; *GDP in purchasers' values* 1,680,444.

Balance of Payments (US $ million, 2002): Exports of goods f.o.b. 2,243.4; Imports of goods f.o.b. -2,667.8; *Trade balance* -424.5; Exports of services 1,096.6; Imports of services -737.5; *Balance on goods and services* -65.3; Other income received 836.4; Other income paid -841.3; *Balance on goods, services and income* -70.2; Current transfers received 238.1; Current transfers paid -251.8; *Current balance* -83.9; Capital account (net) 6.3; Direct investment abroad -0.1; Direct investment from abroad -425.2; Portfolio investment assets -414.3; Portfolio investment liabilities -1.7; Other investment assets -520.9; Other investment liabilities 1,579.2; Net errors and omissions 148.5; *Overall balance* 287.9. Source: IMF, *International Financial Statistics*.

EXTERNAL TRADE

Principal Commodities (LM million, provisional, 2003): *Imports c.i.f.*: Food and live animals 116.8; Mineral fuels, lubricants, etc. 102.1; Chemicals 103.2; Basic manufactures 145.3; Machinery and transport equipment 619.2; Miscellaneous manufactured articles 143.0; Total (incl. others) 1,279.8. *Exports (excl. re-exports) f.o.b.*: Food and live animals 33.3; Basic manufactures 44.9; Machinery and transport equipment 549.4; Miscellaneous manufactured articles 170.3; Total (incl. others) 817.5.

Selected Trading Partners (US $ million, 2001): *Imports:* France (incl. Monaco) 409.3; Germany 238.9; Italy (incl. San Marino) 543.8; Singapore 182.3; United Kingdom 273.5; USA 315.3; Total (incl. others) 2,726.8. *Exports*: France (incl. Monaco) 182.8; Germany 255.8; Singapore 230.9; Switzerland (incl. Liechtenstein) 132.4; United Kingdom 169.5; USA 388.0; Total (incl. others) 1,958.8. Source: UN, *International trade Statistics Yearbook*.

TRANSPORT

Road Traffic (motor vehicles in use, December 2002): Private cars 195,055, Commercial vehicles 43,852, Minibuses 399, Coaches and buses 734, Motorcycles 13,097; Total (incl. others) 261,329.

Shipping: *Merchant Fleet* (31 December 2002): Vessels 1,350; Total displacement 26,331,381 grt (Source: Lloyds Register-Fairplay, *World Fleet Statistics*). *International Freight Traffic* (metric tons, 2001): Goods loaded 319,972; Goods unloaded 1,453,574.

Civil Aviation (traffic on scheduled services, 1999): Kilometres flown (million) 24; Passengers carried ('000) 1,421; Passenger-km (million) 2,320; Total ton-km (million) 214. Source: UN, *Statistical Yearbook*.

TOURISM

Tourist Arrivals: 1,180,145 in 2001; 1,133,814 in 2002; 1,126,601 in 2003.

Arrivals by Country of Origin (provisional, 2003): Austria 28,416; Belgium 23,724; France 76,384; Germany 125,811; Italy 94,175; Netherlands 44,395; United Kingdom 459,565; Total (incl. cruise passengers and others) 1,126,601.

Tourism Receipts (LM million): 254.6 in 1998; 271.4 in 1999; 268.2 in 2000; 260.7 in 2001.

COMMUNICATIONS MEDIA

Radio Receivers (1997): 255,000 in use*.

Television Receivers (1999): 212,000 in use*.

Telephones (main lines, 2003): 208,271 in use.

Facsimile Machines (1996): 6,000 in use (estimate)†.

Mobile Cellular Telephones (2003): 289,992 subscribers.

Personal Computers (2001): 90,000 in use‡.

Internet Users (2002): 82,880.

Book Production (1996): 458 titles.

Daily Newspapers (1999): 4 titles (combined average circulation 54,000 copies per issue).

Non-daily Newspapers (1999): 10 titles.

Other Periodicals (1992): 359 titles*.
* Source: UN, *Statistical Yearbook*.
† Source: UNESCO, *Statistical Yearbook*.
‡ Source: International Telecommunication Union.

EDUCATION

Pre-primary (1999/2000): 131 schools; 910 teachers; 10,039 students.

Primary (1999/2000): 126 schools; 1,501 teachers; 34,261 students.

Secondary (1999/2000): *General:* 75 schools; 2,561 teachers; 27,254 students; *Vocational:* 23 schools; 526 teachers; 1,647 students; *Junior College* (1995/96): 1 school; 1,800 students.

Universities, etc. (1999/2000): 754 teachers; 6,362 students.

Adult Literacy Rate (UNESCO estimates): 92.3% (males 91.5%; females 93.0%) in 2001. Source: UN Development Programme, *Human Development Report*.
Source: UNESCO, *Statistical Yearbook*.

Directory

The Constitution

On 13 December 1974 the Independence Constitution of 1964 was substantially amended to bring into effect a Republican Constitution, under the terms of which Malta became a democratic republic within the Commonwealth, founded on work and on respect for the fundamental rights and freedoms of the individual. The new Constitution provided for the creation of the office of President of Malta to replace that of Governor-General.

The religion of the Maltese people is recognized to be the Roman Catholic Apostolic Religion, and the Church Authorities have the constitutional right and duty to teach according to its principles. The religious teaching of the Roman Catholic Church is provided in all state schools as part of compulsory education.

The Constitution provides that the national language and the language of the Courts is Maltese but that both Maltese and English are official languages.

An independent Public Services Commission, consisting of three to five members, is appointed by the President, on the advice of the Prime Minister, to make recommendations to the Prime Minister concerning appointments to public office and the dismissal and disciplinary control of persons holding public office.

The Constitution also provides for an Employment Commission, consisting of a chairman and four other members, the function of which is to ensure that, in respect of employment, no distinction, exclusion or preference that is not justifiable is made or given in favour of or against any person by reason of his or her political opinion.

The Judicature is independent.

Radio and television broadcasting is controlled by an independent authority.

DECLARATION OF PRINCIPLES

The Constitution upholds the right to work and to reasonable hours of work, the safeguarding of rights of women workers, the encouragement of private economic enterprise, the encouragement of co-operatives, the provision of free and compulsory primary education, and the provision of social assistance and insurance.

FUNDAMENTAL RIGHTS AND FREEDOMS OF THE INDIVIDUAL

The Constitution provides for the protection of the right to life, freedom from arbitrary arrest or detention, protection of freedom of conscience, protection from discrimination on the grounds of race, etc.

THE PRESIDENT

Under the Constitution, the office of President becomes vacant after five years from the date of appointment made by resolution of the House of Representatives. The President appoints the Prime Minister, choosing the member of the House of Representatives who is judged to be ablest to command the confidence of a majority of the members. On the advice of the Prime Minister, the President appoints the other ministers, the Chief Justice, the Judges and the Attorney-General.

THE CABINET

The Cabinet consists of the Prime Minister and such number of other ministers as recommended by the Prime Minister.

PARLIAMENT

The House of Representatives consists of such number of members, being an odd number and divisible by the number of divisions, as

Parliament by law determines from time to time. In future the electoral divisions are not to be fewer than nine and not more than 15, as Parliament may from time to time determine. The normal life of the House of Representatives is five years, after which a general election is held. Election is by universal adult suffrage on the basis of proportional representation. The age of majority is 18 years. Under a constitutional amendment adopted in January 1987, it was ensured that a party receiving more than 50% of the total votes cast in a general election would obtain a majority of seats in the House of Representatives, by the allocation (if necessary) of extra seats to that party.

NEUTRALITY AND NON-ALIGNMENT

In January 1987 a constitutional amendment was adopted, aiming to entrench in the Constitution Malta's status of neutrality and adherence to a policy of non-alignment, and stipulating that no foreign military base was to be permitted on Maltese territory.

The Government

HEAD OF STATE

President: Dr EDWARD (EDDIE) FENECH ADAMI (took office 4 April 2004).

THE CABINET
(April 2004)

Prime Minister and Minister for Finance: Dr LAWRENCE GONZI.

Deputy Prime Minister and Minister for Justice and Home Affairs: Dr TONIO BORG.

Minister of Education, Youth and Employment: Dr LOUIS GALEA.

Minister of Foreign Affairs and Investment Promotion: JOHN DALLI.

Minister for Tourism and Culture: Dr FRANCIS ZAMMIT DIMECH.

Minister for Competitiveness and Communications: CENSU GALEA.

Minister for Resources and Infrastructure: NINU ZAMMIT.

Minister for Gozo: GIOVANNA DEBONO.

Minister of Health, the Elderly and Community Care : Dr LOUIS DEGUARA.

Minister for Information Technology and Investment: Dr AUSTIN GATT.

Minister for Rural Affairs and the Environment: GEORGE PULLICINO.

Minister for Urban Development and Road: JESMOND MUGLIETT.

Minister for the Family and Social Solidarity: DOLORES CRISTINA.

PARLIAMENTARY SECRETARIES (ATTACHED TO MINISTRIES)

Parliamentary Secretary in the Office of the Prime Minister: ANTHONY ABELA.

Parliamentary Secretary in the Ministry of Finance: TONIO FENECH.

Parliamentary Secretary in the Ministry of Justice and Home Affairs: CARMELO MIFSUD BONNICI.

Parliamentary Secretary in the Ministry of Foreign Affairs and Investment Promotion: MICHAEL FRENDO.

Parliamentary Secretary for Small Business and the Self-Employed in the Ministry of Competitiveness and Communications: EDWIN VASSALLO.

Parliamentary Secretary for the Elderly and Community Care in the Ministry of Health, the Elderly and Community Care: HELEN D'AMATO.

Parliamentary Secretary for Agriculture and Fisheries in the Ministry of Rural Affairs and the Environment: FRANCIS AGIUS.

MINISTRIES

Office of the President: The Palace, Valletta CMR 02; tel. 21221221; fax 21241241; e-mail president@gov.mt; internet president.gov.mt.

Office of the Prime Minister: Auberge de Castille, Valletta CMR 02; tel. 21242560; fax 21249888; internet www.opm.gov.mt.

Ministry for Competitiveness and Communications: Casa Leoni, St Joseph High Rd, St Venera CMR 02; tel. 21485100; fax 21493744; e-mail info.mtc@gov.mt; internet www.mtc.gov.mt.

Ministry for Education, Youth and Employment: Great Siege Rd, Floriana CMR 02; tel. 21250909; fax 21221634; e-mail communications.moed@magnet.mt; internet www.education.gov.mt.

Ministry for Family and Social Solidarity: Palazzo Ferreria, 310 Republic St, Valletta CMR 02; tel. 25903100; fax 25903121; internet www.msp.gov.mt.

Ministry of Finance: Maison Demandols, South St, Valletta CMR 02; tel. 21226263; fax 21250965; e-mail info.mof@gov.mt; internet mfea.gov.mt.

Ministry of Foreign Affairs and Investment Promotion: Palazzo Parisio, Merchants St, Valletta CMR 02; tel. 21242853; fax 21237822; internet www.foreign.gov.mt.

Ministry for Gozo: St Francis Sq., Victoria VCT 112, Gozo; tel. 21561482; fax 21559360; internet www.gozo.gov.mt.

Ministry of Health, the Elderly and Community Care: Palazzo Castellania, 15 Merchants St, Valletta CMR 02; tel. 21224071; fax 22992655; internet www.health.gov.mt.

Ministry for Information Technology and Investment: 168 Triq id-Dejqa, Valletta CMR 02; tel. 21226808; fax 21250700; internet www.miti.gov.mt.

Ministry for Justice and Home Affairs: Auberge d'Aragon, Independence Sq., Valletta CMR 02; tel. 25960000; fax 21242609; internet www.mjha.gov.mt.

Ministry for Resources and Infrastructure: Block B, Floriana CMR 02; tel. 21222378; fax 21243306; internet www.mri.gov.mt.

Ministry for Rural Affairs and the Environment: Barriera Wharf, Valletta CMR 02; tel. 22952000; fax 22952212; internet www.mrae.gov.mt.

Ministry of Tourism and Culture: Auberge d'Italie, Merchants St., Valetta CMR 02; tel. 22981306; fax 22981301; e-mail marisa.delorenzo@gov.mt; internet www.tourism.gov.mt.

Ministry for Urban Development and Roads: House of Four Winds, Hastings Gdns, Valletta CMR 02; tel. 21225200; fax 21248937.

Legislature

HOUSE OF REPRESENTATIVES

Speaker: ANTON TABONE.

General Election, 12 April 2003

Party	Votes	%	Seats
Partit Nazzjonalista (Nationalist Party)	146,172	51.8	35
Malta Labour Party (Partit Laburista)	134,092	47.5	30
Alternattiva Demokratika (Green Party)	1,929	0.7	—
Others	20	0.0	—
Total	282,213	100.0	65

Political Organizations

Alternattiva Demokratika (Green Party): 149 Archbishop St, Valletta; tel. 21240334; fax 21224745; e-mail alternattiva@usa.net; internet www.alternattiva.org.mt; f. 1989; emphasizes social and environmental issues; Chair. Dr HARRY VASSALLO; Sec.-Gen. MARIO MALLIA.

Malta Labour Party (MLP) (Partit Laburista): National Labour Centre, Mile End Rd, Hamrun HMR 02; tel. 21249900; fax 21244204; e-mail mlp@mlp.org.mt; internet www.mlp.org.mt; f. 1921; democratic socialist; Leader Dr ALFRED SANT; Pres. EMMLE CUSCHIERI; Gen. Sec. JIMMY MAGRO; 39,000 mems.

Partit Nazzjonalista (Nationalist Party—PN): Herbert Ganado St, Pietà HMR 08; tel. 21243641; fax 21243640; e-mail pn@pn.org.mt; internet www.pn.org.mt; f. 1880; Christian democratic; advocates full membership of the EU; Leader Dr LAWRENCE GONZI; Sec.-Gen. JOE SALIBA; 31,000 mems.

Diplomatic Representation

EMBASSIES AND HIGH COMMISSIONS IN MALTA

Australia: Villa Fiorentina, Ta'Xbiex Terrace, Ta'Xbiex MSD 11; tel. 21338201; fax 21344059; e-mail aushicom@vol.net.mt; High Commissioner RICHARD POLK.

China, People's Republic: Karmnu Court, Lapsi St, St Julian's; tel. 21384695; fax 21344730; Ambassador ZU QINSHUN.

Egypt: Villa Mon Rêve, 10 Sir Temi Zammit St, Ta'Xbiex MSD 11; tel. 21333259; fax 21319230; Ambassador YEHYA IBRAHIM EL-RAMLAWY.

France: POB 408, Valletta CMR 01; 130 Melita St, Valletta CMR 01; tel. 21233430; fax 21233528; e-mail france@global.net.mt; Ambassador PATRICK CHRISMANT.

Germany: 'Il-Piazzetta', Entrance B, 1st Floor, Tower Rd, Sliema, SLM 16; POB 48, Marsa, GPO 01; tel. 21336531; fax 21333976; e-mail germanembassy@waldonet.net.mt; Ambassador GEORG MERTEN.

Holy See: Villa Cor Jesù, Tal-Virtù Rd, Tal-Virtù, Rabat (Apostolic Nunciature); tel. 21453422; fax 21453423; e-mail apost@mail.keyworld.net; Apostolic Nuncio Most Rev. FÉLIX DEL BLANCO PRIETO (Titular Archbishop of Vannida).

India: Regional Rd, St Julian's SGN 02; tel. 21344302; fax 21344259; internet www.incore.com/india/traveli.embassy.html; High Commissioner SURENDRA KUMAR.

Italy: 5 Vilhena St, Floriana; tel. 21233157; fax 21235339; e-mail ambitalia@waldonet.net.mt; Ambassador Dr GIANCARLO RICCIO.

Libya: Dar Jamahariya, Notabile Rd, Balzan; tel. 21486347; fax 21483939; Secretary of People's Bureau ALI SALEH MOHAMED NAGEM.

Russia: Ariel House, Anthony Schembri St, Kappara, San Gwann; tel. 21371905; fax 21372131; e-mail rusemb@keyworld.net; Ambassador SERGEI S. ZOTOV.

Tunisia: Valletta Rd, Attard BZN 03; tel. 21417171; fax 21413414; e-mail at.lavalette@maltanet.net; Ambassador ABDESSALEM HETIRA.

United Kingdom: 7 St Anne St, Floriana VLT 15; tel. 21233134; fax 21242001; e-mail bhc@vol.net.mt; internet www.britain.com.mt; High Commissioner HOWARD J. S. PEARCE.

USA: Development House, 3rd Floor, St Anne St, Floriana; tel. 21235960; fax 21243229; Ambassador ANTHONY GIOIA.

Judicial System

The legal system consists of enactments of the Parliament of Malta, and those of the British Parliament not repealed or replaced by enactments of the Maltese legislature. Maltese Civil Law derives largely from Roman Law, while British Law has significantly influenced Maltese public law.

The Courts are: Constitutional Court, Court of Appeal, Court of Criminal Appeal, Civil Court, Criminal Court, Commercial Court, Court of Magistrates, Juvenile Court and Small Claims Tribunal.

Chief Justice and President of the Court of Appeal and the Constitutional Court: Dr VINCENT A. DE GAETANO.

Judges: CARMEL A. AGIUS, JOSEPH D. CAMILLERI, JOSEPH A. FILLETTI, FRANCO DEPASQUALE, ANTON DEPASQUALE, FRANK G. CAMILLERI, ALBERTO J. MAGRI, NOEL ARRIGO, GEOFFREY VALENZIA, GIANNINO CARUANA DEMAJO, GINO CAMILLERI, CARMELO FARRUGIA SACCO, RAYMOND PACE, DAVID P. SCICLUNA.

Attorney-General: ANTHONY BORG BARTHET.

Religion

CHRISTIANITY

The Roman Catholic Church

Malta comprises one archdiocese and one diocese. At 31 December 2002 there were 368,446 adherents in the country, representing about 92.7% of the total population.

Bishops' Conference

Conferenza Episcopale Maltese, Archbishop's Curia, Floriana; tel. 21234317; fax 21223307; e-mail info@maltachurch.org.mt.

f. 1971; Pres. Most Rev. JOSEPH MERCIECA (Archbishop of Malta).

Archbishop of Malta: Most Rev. JOSEPH MERCIECA, Archbishop's Curia, Floriana; POB 29, Valletta; tel. 21234317; fax 21223307; e-mail info@maltachurch.org.mt.

Bishop of Gozo: Rt Rev. NIKOL JOSEPH CAUCHI, Chancery Office, POB 1, Republic St, Victoria VCT 103, Gozo; tel. 21556661; fax 21551278; e-mail diocese@gozodiocese.org.

The Anglican Communion

Malta forms part of the diocese of Gibraltar in Europe.

Church of England: Pro-Cathedral of St Paul, Independence Sq., Valletta VLT 12; tel. 21225714; fax 21225867; e-mail anglican@onvol.net; internet www.vol.net.mt/anglicansmalta; Bishop of Gibraltar in Europe Rt Rev. GEOFFREY ROWELL (resident in England); Suffragan Bishop Rt Rev. DAVID HAMID (resident in England); Archdeacon of Italy and Malta Ven. GORDON REID (resident in Italy); Senior Chaplain and Chancellor of the Pro-Cathedral Rev. Canon ALAN WOODS.

The Press

DAILIES

The Malta Independent: Standard House, Birkirkara Hill, St Julian's STJ 09; tel. 21345888; fax 21344860; e-mail tmi@maltanet.net; English; Editor Fr NOEL GRIMA.

In-Nazzjon: Herbert Ganado St, POB 37, Pietà HMR 08; tel. 21243641; fax 21242886; e-mail news@media.link.com.mt; internet www.media.link.com.mt; f. 1970; Maltese; publ. by Media.link Communications; Editor JOHN ZAMMIT; circ. 20,000.

L-Orizzont: Union Print Co, A-41 Industrial Estate, Valletta Rd, Marsa HMR 15; tel. 21244557; fax 21238484; e-mail unionprint@kemmunet.net.mt; f. 1962; Maltese; Editor FRANS GHIRXI; circ. 25,000.

The Times: Allied Newspapers Ltd, 341 St Paul St, Valletta VLT 07; tel. 21241464; fax 21247901; e-mail daily@timesofmalta.com; internet www.timesofmalta.com; f. 1935; English; Editor VICTOR AQUILINA; circ. 23,000.

WEEKLIES

Il-Gens: Media Centre, National Rd, Blata il-Bajda HMR 02; tel. 25699119; fax 25699123; e-mail gens@mediacentre.org.mt; internet www.mediacentre.org.mt; f. 1988; Maltese; Editor NICHOLAS BALDACCHINO; circ. 13,000.

Il-Gwida: Mercury Publicity Services, POB 83, Valletta CMR 01; tel. and fax 21220932; Maltese and English; radio, television and entertainment guide; Editor JOE CALLEJA; circ. 12,000.

Il-Mument: Herbert Ganado St, POB 37, Pietà HMR 08; tel. 21243641; fax 21240839; e-mail nazzjon@mbox.vol.net.mt; f. 1972; Maltese; Editor VICTOR CAMILLERI; circ. 25,000.

Kulhadd: Centru Nazzjonali Laburista, Mile End Rd, Hamrun, HMR 02; tel. 21235313; fax 21240717; e-mail kulhadd@keyworld.net; f. 1993; Maltese; Editor FELIX AGIUS.

Lehen is-Sewwa: Catholic Institute, Floriana VLT 16; tel. and fax 21225847; e-mail lehenissewwa@vol.net.mt; internet www.lehenissewwa.com.mt; f. 1928; Roman Catholic; Editor PAUL SALIBA; circ. 10,000.

The Malta Business Weekly: Standard House, Birkirkara Hill, St Julian's STJ 09; tel. 21345888; fax 21346062; e-mail tmbw@mail.independent.com.mt; internet www.maltabusinessweekly.com; f. 1994; English; Editor DAVID JOHN KELLEHER.

The Malta Financial and Business Times: Newsworks Ltd, 2nd Floor, Cali Bldgs, Vjal ir-Rihan, San Gwann SGN 07; tel. 21382741; fax 21385075; e-mail businesstimes@newsworksltd.com; internet www.businesstimes.com.mt; f. 1999; Editor SAVIOUR BALZAN.

The Malta Independent on Sunday: Standard House, Birkirkara Hill, St Julian's STJ 09; tel. 21345888; fax 21344884; e-mail amanduca@independent.com.mt; internet www.independent.com.mt; English; Editor ANTHONY MANDUCA.

The Sunday Times: Allied Newspapers Ltd, POB 328, Valletta CMR 01; tel. 21241464; fax 21240806; e-mail Sunday@timesofmalta.com; internet www.timesofmalta.com; f. 1922; English; Editor LAURENCE GRECH; circ. 40,000.

It-Tórca (The Torch): Union Press, A 41, Marsa Industrial Estate, Marsa HMR 15; tel. 21244557; fax 21238484; e-mail unionprint@kemmunet.net.mt; f. 1944; Maltese; Editor ALFRED BRIFFA; circ. 30,000.

SELECTED PERIODICALS

BASE: Valletta; tel. 21245779; fax 21245778; quarterly; Editor JACQUELINE FENECH.

Commercial Courier: Malta Chamber of Commerce, Exchange Bldgs, Republic St, Valletta VLT 05; tel. 21247233; fax 21245223; e-mail admin@chamber.org.mt; monthly; Editor KEVIN J. BORG; circ. 1,500.

The Employer: Malta Employers' Asscn, 35/1 South St, Valletta VLT 11; tel. 21222992; fax 21230227; e-mail mea@maltanet.net; internet www.maltanet.net/mea; Editor JOSEPH FARRUGIA.

Industry Today: Development House, St Anne St, Floriana VLT 01; tel. 21234428; fax 21240702; e-mail info@foi.org.mt; internet www.foi.org.mt; journal of the Malta Fed. of Industry; quarterly; Editor EDWIN CALLEJA; circ. 1,000.

Malta Business Online: 33/4 St. Nicholas Bldgs, Abate Rigord St, Ta'Xbiex MSD 12; tel. 21342704; fax 21316694; e-mail mbo@tcin.com; internet www.mbo.com.mt; f. 1986 as Business Review; monthly; publ. by E-business Ltd; Editor STEPHEN P. D'ALESSANDRO.

Malta Government Gazette: Department of Information, 3 Castille Pl., Valletta CMR 02; tel. 21250550; fax 21239170; e-mail info@gov.mt; internet www.doi.gov.mt; f. 1813; official notices; Maltese and English; 2 a week; circ. 3,000.

Malta In Figures: National Statistics Office, Lascaris, Valetta CMR 02; tel. 21223221; fax 21249841; e-mail nso@gov.mt; internet www.nso.gov.mt; official statistics; annual.

Malta This Month: Advantage Advertising Ltd, 3rd Floor, Regency House, Republic St, Valletta VLT 04; tel. 21249924; fax 21249927; e-mail advantage@onvol.net; publ. by Air Malta; monthly; Editor PETER DARMANIN.

The Retailer: Association of General Retailers and Traders, Exchange Bldgs, Republic St, Valletta VLT 05; tel. 21230459; fax 21246925; monthly; Editor VINCENT FARRUGIA.

The Teacher: Teachers' Institute, 213 Republic St, Valletta VLT 03; tel. 21237815; fax 21244074; e-mail info@mut.org.mt; internet www.mut.org.mt; journal of the Malta Union of Teachers; quarterly; Editor JOSEPH P. DEGIOVANNI.

Xpress: 149 Archbishop St, Valletta; tel. 21240334; fax 21224745; publ. of the Alternattiva Demokratika; Maltese; monthly; Editor NEIL SPITERI.

NEWS AGENCIES

Agence France-Presse (AFP): 370 Zabbar Rd, Fgura PLA 16; tel. 21693210; Correspondent MARIA INGUANEZ.

Agenzia Nazionale Stampa Associata (ANSA) (Italy): c/o The Sunday Times, Allied Newspapers Ltd, 341 St Paul St, POB 328, Valletta CMR 01; tel. 21224406; fax 21240806; e-mail lgrech@timesofmalta.com; Correspondent LAURENCE GRECH.

Associated Press (AP) (USA): c/o The Times, Allied Newspapers Ltd, 341 St Paul St, Valletta VLT 07; tel. 21241464; fax 21247901; e-mail gcini@timesofmalta.com; Correspondents VICTOR AQUILINA, GEORGE CINI.

Jamahiriya News Agency (JANA) (Libya): 239 St Paul's St, POB 270, Valletta; tel. 21239392; fax 21239405; Correspondent F. M. HEWAT.

Reuters (United Kingdom): 119 Censu Busuttid St, Halin 11; tel. 21415171; fax 21247901; e-mail cscicluna@timesofmalta.com; Correspondent CRISTOPHER SCICLUNA.

United Press International (USA): 1 The Elms, Dahlet Ic-Cipress, Attard; tel. 21423068; fax 21247901; Correspondent VICTOR AQUILINA.

Publishers

Gozo Press: Mgarr Rd, Ghajnsielem, Gozo; tel. 21551534; e-mail gozopress@onvol.net; popular and academic; Dir JOHN SULTANA.

Progress Press Co Ltd: Strickland House, 341 St Paul St, POB 328, Valletta VLT 07; tel. 21241464; fax 21241336; e-mail vbuhagiar@timesofmalta.com; f. 1957; educational and textbooks, fiction, guidebooks; Chair. RONALD AGIUS; Man. Dir WILFRID B. ASCIAK.

Publishers Enterprises Group (PEG) Ltd: PEG Bldg, UB7 Industrial Estate, San Gwann SGN 09; tel. 21440083; fax 21488908; e-mail contact@peg.com.mt; internet www.peg.com.mt; f. 1983; educational, children's, cookery, technical, tourism, leisure; Man. Dir EMANUEL DEBATTISTA.

University of Malta Press: University Campus, Msida MSD 06; tel. 21313416; fax 21344879; e-mail mupl@mus.com.mt; f. 1953; Maltese folklore, history, law, bibliography and language.

Broadcasting and Communications

All broadcasting services are under the overall supervision of the Broadcasting Authority.

TELECOMMUNICATIONS

Maltacom PLC: POB 40, Marsa CMR 01; tel. 21212121; fax 25945895; e-mail info@maltacom.com; internet www.maltacom.com; f. 1975; operates all telecommunications services; 60% govt-owned, 40% held by private-sector investors; Chair. SONNY PORTELLI.

Go Mobile: Fra Diego St, Marsa HMR 12; tel. 21246200; fax 21234314; mobile cellular subsidiary; CEO Prof. JUANITO CAMILLERI.

BROADCASTING

Regulatory Authority

Malta Broadcasting Authority: Mile End Rd, Hamrun HMR 02; tel. 21247908; fax 21240855; e-mail info@ba-malta.org; internet www.ba-malta.org; f. 1961; statutory body responsible for the supervision and regulation of sound and television broadcasting; Chair. Chief Justice Emeritus Dr JOSEPH SAID PULLICINO; CEO Dr KEVIN AQUILINA.

Radio and Television

Bay Radio: St George's Bay, St Julian's STJ 02; tel. 21373813; fax 21376113; e-mail 897@bay.com.mt; Station Man. TERRY FARRUGIA.

Campus FM: Old Humanities Bldg, University of Malta, Msida MSD 06; tel. 21333313; fax 21314485; e-mail campusfm@um.edu.mt; internet www.campusfm.um.edu.mt.

Capital Radio: MEDIA Co-op Ltd, 87 Ursada St, Valletta; tel. 21233078; fax 21239701; e-mail capital@maltanet.net; internet www.capitalradio.com.mt; Station Man. JOHN MALLIA.

Island Sound Radio: 46 Robert Samut Sq., Floriana VLT 14; tel. 21249141; fax 21249785; News Co-ordinator BERNIE LYNCH.

Media.link Communications Co Ltd: Dar Centrali, Herbert Ganado St, Pietà HMR 08; tel. 21243641; fax 21243640; e-mail antona@vol.net.mt; internet www.media.link.com.mt.

  Net TV: Dar Centrali, Herbert Ganado St, Pietà HMR 08; tel. 21243641; fax 21226645; CEO ANTON ATTARD.

  Radio 101: Independence Point, Herbert Ganado St, Pietà HMR 08; tel. 21241164; fax 21564111; Head of News PIERRE PORTELLI.

Mediapact Ltd: Centrepoint, B'Kara By-pass, B'Kara; tel. 21443131; fax 21443232; internet www.maxplus.com.mt; operates television channel Max Plus.

Melita Cable PLC: 333 rue d'Argens, Gzira GZR 04; tel. 21345470; fax 21345435; e-mail info@melitacable.com; internet www.melitacable.com; CEO FRANK LEITER.

Multi Media Education and Broadcasting Centre: Maria Regina School, Mile End Rd, Hamrun HMR 02; tel. 21239274; fax 21240701; operates television channel Education 22.

One Productions Ltd: A28B, Industrial Estate, Marsa LQA 06; tel. 21226634; fax 21248249; e-mail livetv@super1.com; internet www.super1.com; f. 1999; owned by Malta Labour Party; Chair RENALD DALLI; CEO ALBERT MARSHALL.

  Super One Radio: tel. 21244905; fax 21231472; e-mail radio@super1.com; broadcasts 24 hours daily.

  Super One Television: A28B Industrial Estate, Marsa LQA 06; tel. 25682568; fax 21231472; e-mail kullhadd@keyworld.net; broadcasts 126 hours weekly; CEO RENALD DALLI.

Public Broadcasting Services Ltd: St Luke's Rd, G'Mangia MSD 09; tel. 21225051; fax 21246697; e-mail info@pbs.com.mt; internet www.pbs.com.mt; f. 1991; govt-owned; operates national radio and television services: Radio 'Radju Malta', 'FM Bronja' and 'Radju Parlament'; Television Malta and Channel 12; Chair. MICHAEL MALLIA; CEO ANDREW PSAILA.

Radio Calypso: Oasis, Mons. P. Pace St, Victoria VCT 111, Gozo; tel. 21563000; fax 21563565; e-mail info@calypso102.com; internet www.calypso102.com; News Editor PIERRE MEYLAK.

Radju MAS: 15 Old Mint St, Valletta VLT 12; tel. 21237755; fax 21247246; Editor Mgr FORTUNATO MIZZI.

RTK Radio: Media Centre, National Rd, Blata il-Bajda HMR 02; tel. 25699100; fax 25699151; e-mail vformosa@mediacentre.org.mt; internet www.rtk.org.mt; f. 1992; radio station of the Catholic Church of Malta; Chair. VICTOR FORMOSA.

Smash TV and Radio: Smash Communications, Thistle Lane, Paola PLA 19; tel. 21697829; fax 21697830; f. 1992; Man. Dir JOSEPH BALDACCHINO.

Finance

(cap. = capital; res = reserves; dep. = deposits; m. = million;
br. = branch; amounts in Maltese liri, unless otherwise stated)

BANKING

Central Bank

Central Bank of Malta: Castille Place, POB 378, Valletta CMR 01;
tel. 25500000; fax 25502500; e-mail info@centralbankmalta.com;
internet www.centralbankmalta.com; f. 1968; bank of issue; cap.
5m., res 91m., dep. 356m. (June 2003); Gov. MICHAEL C. BONELLO.

Commercial Banks

APS Bank Ltd: APS House, 24 St Anne Sq., Floriana VLT 16; tel.
21226644; fax 21226202; e-mail headoffice@apsbank.com.mt;
internet www.apsbank.com.mt; f. 1910; cap. 5m., res 6m., dep. 195m.
(Dec. 2003); Chair. Prof. EMMANUEL P. DELIA; CEO EDWARD CACHIA; 5
brs.

Bank of Valletta PLC: BOV Centre, High St, Sliema SLM 16; tel.
21333084; fax 23213700; e-mail customercare@bov.com; internet
www.bov.com; f. 1974; cap. 13.8m., res 113.1m., dep. 1,428.3m.
(Sept. 2003); merged with Valletta Investment Bank Ltd in Oct.
2000; Chair. JOSEPH F. X. ZAHRA; 41 brs.

HSBC Bank Malta PLC: 233 Republic St, Valletta VLT 05; tel.
21245281; fax 21485857; e-mail info@hsbcmalta.com; internet www
.hsbcmalta.com; f. 1975 as Mid-Med Bank; Maltese Govt's 67%
interest acquired by Midland Bank International Financial Services
Ltd 1999; cap. and res 110m., dep. 1,289m. (June 2002); Chair.
ALBERT MIZZI; CEO CHRISTOPHER HOTHERSALL; 45 brs and agencies.

Lombard Bank Malta PLC: 67 Republic St, Valletta VLT 05; tel.
21240442; fax 21247442; e-mail mail@lombardmalta.com; internet
www.lombardmalta.com; f. 1969; cap. 4m., res 7m., dep. 160m. (June
2003); Chair. CHRISTIAN LEMMERICH; CEO JOSEPH SAID; 6 brs.

Principal 'Offshore' Banks

First International Merchant Bank PLC: Plaza Commercial
Centre, 7th Floor, Bisazza St, Sliema SLM 15; tel. 21322100; fax
21322122; e-mail info@fimbank.com; internet www.fimbank.com; f.
1994; cap. US $23m., res US $8m., dep. US $89m. (Dec. 2002); Chair.
NAJEEB H. M. AL-SALEH; Pres. CLAUDE L. ROY.

Izola Bank Ltd: 53/58 East St, Valletta VLT 06; tel. 21241258; fax
21241250; Gen. Man. ANDREW MIFSUD.

Volksbank Malta Ltd: 53 Dingli St, Sliema SLM 09; tel. 21336100;
fax 21336090; e-mail info@volksbank.com.mt; f. 1995; Chair.
MAURICE MIZZI; Man. Dir THOMAS HAVLIK.

STOCK EXCHANGE

Malta Stock Exchange: Garrison Chapel, Castille Pl., Valletta
CMR 01; tel. 21244051; fax 25696316; e-mail borza@maltanet.net;
internet www.borzamalta.com.mt; f. 1992; Chair. ALFRED MALLIA.

INSURANCE

Aon Malta Ltd: 53 Mediterranean Bldg, Abate Rigord St, Ta'Xbiex
MSD 12; tel. 23433234; fax 21341597; e-mail info@aon.com.mt;
internet www.aon.com.mt; f. 1976; Chair. ALFREDO SCOTTI; Man. Dir
JOSEPH CUTAJAR.

Middle Sea Insurance PLC: Middle Sea House, Floriana VLT 16;
tel. 21246262; fax 21248195; e-mail middlesea@middlesea.com;
internet www.middlesea.com; f. 1981; Chair. MARIO C. GRECH; Gen.
Man. JOSEPH M. RIZZO.

Numerous foreign insurance companies, principally British, Canadian and Italian, are represented in Malta by local agents.

Trade and Industry

GOVERNMENT AGENCIES

Malta External Trade Corporation Ltd (METCO): Trade
Centre, Industrial Estate, San Gwann SGN 09; POB 8, San Gwann
SGN 01; tel. 21446186; fax 21496687; e-mail info@metco.net;
internet www.metco.net; f. 1989; promotes exports and external
trade; Chair. ANTHONY S. DIACONO; Gen. Man. STEPHEN SULTANA.

Malta Financial Services Authority: Notabile Rd, Attard BKR
14; tel. 21441155; fax 21441189; e-mail communications@mfsa.com
.mt; internet www.mfsa.com.mt; promotes and supervises the financial services sector, incl. banking and investments; regulates activities of Malta Stock Exchange; houses Malta's Companies Registry;
Chair. Prof. JOSEPH V. BANNISTER; CEO JOSEPH DEMANUELE.

Malta Freeport Terminals Ltd: Freeport Centre, Port of Marsaxlokk, Kalafrana BBG 05; tel. 21650200; fax 21654814; e-mail
marketing@maltafreeport.com.mt; internet www.maltafreeport
.com.mt; f. 1988; container terminals and distribution centre; also
operates petroleum products terminal and general warehousing
facilities; Chair. MARK PORTELLI.

Malta Investment Management Co Ltd (MIMCOL): Trade
Centre, San Gwann Industrial Estate, B'Kara SGN 09; tel.
21497970; fax 21499568; e-mail info@mimcol.com; internet www
.mimcol.com; f. 1988; manages govt investments in domestic commercial enterprises and encourages their transfer to private-sector
ownership; Chair. IVAN FALZON.

DEVELOPMENT ORGANIZATION

Malta Development Corporation (MDC): POB 141, Marsa GPO
01; tel. 21441888; fax 21441887; e-mail info@mdc.com.mt; internet
www.investinmalta.com; f. 1967; administers govt programme of
investment incentives; liaises between industry and the Govt and
assists foreign cos; maintains offices in Italy, Germany and the USA;
Chair. FRANCIS VASSALLO.

CHAMBER OF COMMERCE

Malta Chamber of Commerce and Enterprise: Exchange Bldgs,
Republic St, Valletta VLT 05; tel. 21233873; fax 21245223; e-mail
admin@chamber.org.mt; internet www.chamber.org.mt; f. 1848;
Pres. LOUIS APAP-BOLOGNA; 1,000 mems.

EMPLOYERS' ORGANIZATIONS

Malta Employers' Association: 35/1 South St, Valletta VLT 11;
tel. 21222992; fax 21230227; e-mail mea@maltanet.net; internet
www.maltanet.net/mea; f. 1965; Pres. ARTHUR MUSCAT; Dir-Gen.
JOSEPH FARRUGIA.

Malta Federation of Industry: Development House, St Anne St,
Floriana VLT 01; tel. 21234428; fax 21240702; e-mail info@foi.org
.mt; internet www.foi.org.mt; f. 1946; nat. org. for industry; 300
corporate mems; Pres. ANTON BORG; Dir-Gen. EDWIN CALLEJA.

UTILITIES

Electricity

Enemalta Corporation: Church Wharf, Marsa HMR 01; POB 6,
Hamrun HMR 01; tel. 21223601; fax 21243055; e-mail info@
enemalta.com.mt; internet www.enemalta.com.mt; f. 1977; state
energy corpn; purchases and distributes petroleum products and
operates two oil-fired power stations for electricity generation; distributes electricity, petroleum products and LPG; Chair. TANCRED
TABONE.

Water

Water Services Corporation: Qormi Rd, Luqa LQA 05; tel.
21249851; fax 21223016; e-mail water@wsc.com.mt; internet www
.wsc.com.mt; f. 1991; govt agency responsible for the production and
distribution of drinking water and the local sewerage system; Chair.
MICHAEL FALZON; CEO ANTHONY RIZZO.

TRADE UNIONS

In June 1998 there were 34 registered trade unions (with a combined
membership of 81,700).

Confederation of Malta Trade Unions (CMTU): 9C M. A. Vas-
salli St, Valletta VLT 13; tel. 21237313; fax 21250146; e-mail cmtu@
maltanet.net; f. 1958; affiliated to the World Confed. of Labour, to
the Commonwealth Trade Union Council and to the European Trade
Union Confed.; Pres. ALFRED BUHAGIAR; Gen. Sec. CHARLES MAGRO;
32,400 mems.

The principal affiliated unions include:

Association of General Retailers & Traders Union (GRTU):
Exchange Bldgs, Republic St, Valletta VLT 05; tel. 21230459; fax
21246925; f. 1948; Pres. CHARLES J. BUSUTTIL; Sec. PHILIP FRENCH;
6,400 mems.

Malta Union of Teachers: Teachers' Institute, 213 Republic St,
Valletta VLT 03; tel. 21237815; fax 21244074; e-mail info@mut
.org.mt; internet www.mut.org.mt; f. 1919; Pres. J. BENCINI; Gen.
Sec. JOSEPH P. DEGIOVANNI; 5,770 mems.

Union Haddiema Maghqudin (UHM): 'Dar Reggie Miller', St
Thomas St, Floriana VLT 15; tel. 21220847; fax 21246091; e-mail
uhm@maltanet.net; internet www.uhm.org.mt; f. 1966; Pres. G.
TANTI; Sec.-Gen. G. VELLA; 25,793 mems.

The General Workers' Union (GWU): Workers' Memorial Bldg,
South St, Valletta VLT 11; tel. 21244300; fax 21242975; e-mail info@
gwu.org.mt; internet www.gwu.org.mt; f. 1943; affiliated to the Int.

Confed. of Free Trade Unions, to the European Trade Union Confed. and to the Commonwealth Trade Union Confed.; Pres. SALV SAMMUT; CEO and Gen. Sec. TONY ZARB; 48,758 mems.

Transport

RAILWAYS

There are no railways in Malta.

ROADS

In 1999 there were 1,742 km of roads. About 96.2% of roads are paved. Bus services serve all parts of the main island and most parts of Gozo.

Public Transport Directorate: Sa Maison Rd, Pietà MSD 08; tel. 21255165; fax 21255175; e-mail pta@maltanet.net; internet www .maltatransport.com; f. 1989; regulatory body for public transport in Malta, part of Malta Transport Authority; Chair. C. DEMICOLI.

Roads Department: Cannon Rd, St Venera CMR 02; tel. 21483609; fax 21243753; e-mail carmel.zammit@magnet.mt; Chair. C. DEMI-COLI; CEO M. FALZON.

SHIPPING

Malta's national shipping register is open to ships of all countries. At 31 December 2002 Malta's merchant fleet comprised 1,350 vessels, with a total displacement of 26,331,381 gross registered tons. The island's dry dock facilities are also an important source of revenue.

Malta Maritime Authority: Ports Directorate, Marina Pinto, Valletta VLT 01; tel. 21222203; fax 21250365; e-mail info@mma.gov.at; internet www.mma.gov.mt; f. 1991; govt agency supervising the administration and operation of ports and yachting centres, and of vessel registrations under the Maltese flag; Chair. Dr MARC BONELLO.

Bianchi & Co (1916) Ltd: Palazzo Marina, 143 St Christopher St, Valletta VLT 02; tel. 21232241; fax 21232991; e-mail info@bianchi .com.mt; Man. Dir R. BIANCHI.

Cassar & Cooper Ltd: Valletta Bldgs, 54 South St, POB 311, Valletta, VLT 11; tel. 21232221; fax 21237864; e-mail info@ cassar-cooper.com; internet www.cassar-cooper.com; Dir MICHAEL COOPER.

O. F. Gollcher & Sons Ltd: 19 Zachary St, POB 268, Valletta VLT 10; tel. 25691100; fax 21234195; e-mail contact@gollcher.com; internet www.gollcher.com; Dir MARK GOLLCHER.

Medserv Ltd: Malta Freeport, Port of Marsaxlokk, Birzebbugia BBG 07; tel. 22202302; fax 22202328; e-mail info@medservmalta .com; Dir ANTHONY J. DUNCAN.

Mifsud Brothers Ltd: 27 South St, Valletta VLT 11; tel. 21232157; fax 21221331; e-mail info@mbl.com.mt; internet www.mbl.com.mt; f. 1860; shipping and travel agents; Man. Dir IVAN MIFSUD.

S. Mifsud & Sons Ltd (SMS): 131 East St, Valletta VLT 06; tel. 21233127; fax 21234180; cargo and ferry services between Malta/Catania, Reggio di Calabria; Dir ADRIAN S. MIFSUD.

Ripard, Larvan & Ripard Ltd: 156 Ta'Xbiex Seafront, Gzira GZR 03; tel. 21335591; fax 21343419; e-mail chandlery@rlryachting.com; Man. Dir CHRISTIAN RIPARD.

Sea Malta Co Ltd: Flagstone Wharf, Marsa HMR 12; tel. 21232230; fax 21225776; e-mail info@seamalta.com.mt; internet www .seamalta.com.mt; f. 1973; govt-owned national shipping line; operates roll-on/roll-off services between Malta, France, Italy, Northern Europe, Sicily, Spain and Tunisia; represents shipping line that operates passenger service between Malta and Libya; agency and insurance services, ship management, freight forwarding, shipbroking, bunkering, warehouse and passenger services; Chair. MAR-LENE MIZZI; Gen. Man. JOSEPH BUJEGA.

Sullivan Shipping Agencies Ltd: Exchange Bldgs, Republic St, Valletta VLT 05; tel. 21245127; fax 21233417; e-mail info@ sullivanshipping.com.mt; Dir JOHN E. SULLIVAN.

Thomas Smith & Co Ltd: 12 St Christopher St, Valletta VLT 06; tel. 21245071; fax 21242056; e-mail info@tcsmith.com; internet www .tcsmith.com; Man. Dir JOE GERADA.

Virtu Steamship Co Ltd: 3 Princess Elizabeth Terrace, Ta'Xbiex MSD 11; tel. 21345220; fax 21314533; f. 1945; ship-owners; ship agents; shipbrokers; Malta–Sicily express passenger ferry service; Man. Dir F. A. PORTELLI.

CIVIL AVIATION

Malta International Airport is situated at Gudja (8 km from Valletta). In 1998 a total of 2.74m. passengers (excluding passengers in transit) passed through the airport.

Air Malta PLC: Luqa LQA 01; tel. 21690890; fax 21673241; e-mail info@airmalta.com.mt; internet www.airmalta.com; f. 1973; national airline with a 96.4% state shareholding; scheduled passenger and cargo services to mainland Europe, the United Kingdom, Sicily, North Africa and the Middle East; charter services to the United Kingdom and mainland Europe; CEO ERNST FUNK.

Tourism

Malta offers climatic, scenic and historical attractions, including fine beaches. Tourism forms a major sector of Malta's economy, generating foreign exchange earnings of LM 260.7m. in 2001; in 2003 tourist arrivals totalled 1,126,601.

Malta Tourism Authority: Auberge d'Italie, 229 Merchant St., Valletta CMR 02; tel. 22915000; fax 22915893; e-mail info@ visitmalta.com; internet www.mta.com.mt; Chair. CHRIS GRECH; CEO LESLIE VELLA.

THE MARSHALL ISLANDS

Introductory Survey

Location, Climate, Language, Religion, Flag, Capital

The Republic of the Marshall Islands consists of two groups of islands, the Ratak ('sunrise') and Ralik ('sunset') chains, comprising 29 atolls (some 1,225 islets) and five islands, and covering about 180 sq km (70 sq miles) of land. The territory lies within the area of the Pacific Ocean known as Micronesia (which includes Kiribati, Tuvalu and other territories). The islands lie about 3,200 km (2,000 miles) south-west of Hawaii and about 2,100 km (1,300 miles) south-east of Guam. Rainfall decreases from south to north, with January, February and March being the driest months, although seasonal variations in rainfall and temperature are generally small. The native population comprises various ethno-linguistic groups, but English is widely understood. The principal religion is Christianity. The national flag (proportions 100 by 190) is dark blue, with a representation of a white star (with 20 short and four long rays) in the upper hoist; superimposed across the field are two progressively-wider stripes (orange above white), running from near the lower hoist corner to near the upper fly corner. The capital is the Dalap-Uliga-Darrit Municipality, on Majuro Atoll.

Recent History

The first European contact with the Marshall and Caroline Islands was by Spanish expeditions in the 16th century, including those led by Alvaro de Saavedra and Fernão de Magalhães (Ferdinand Magellan), the Portuguese navigator. The islands received their name from the British explorer, John Marshall, who visited them at the end of the 18th century. Spanish sovereignty over the Marshall Islands was recognized in 1886 by the Papal Bull of Pope Leo XIII, which also gave Germany trading rights there (German trading companies had been active in the islands from the 1850s). In 1899 Germany bought from Spain the Caroline Islands and the Northern Mariana Islands (except Guam, which had been ceded to the USA after the Spanish–American War of 1898). In 1914, at the beginning of the First World War, Japan occupied the islands, and received a mandate for its administration from the League of Nations in 1920. After the capture of the islands by US military forces in 1944 and 1945, most of the Japanese settlers were repatriated, and in 1947 the UN established the Trust Territory of the Pacific Islands (comprising the Caroline Islands, the Marshall Islands and the Northern Mariana Islands), to allow the USA to administer the region. The territory was governed by the US Navy from 1947 until 1951, when control passed to a civil administration—although the Northern Mariana Islands remained under military control until 1962.

From 1965 onwards there were increasing demands for local autonomy. In that year the Congress of Micronesia was formed; in 1967 a commission was established to examine the future political status of the islands. In 1970 it declared Micronesians' rights to sovereignty over their own lands, of self-determination, to their own constitution and to revoke any form of free association with the USA. In 1977, after eight years of negotiations, President Jimmy Carter announced that his administration intended to adopt measures to terminate the trusteeship agreement by 1981.

On 9 January 1978 the Marianas District achieved separate status as the Commonwealth of the Northern Mariana Islands (q.v.), but remained legally a part of the Trusteeship until 1986. The Marshall Islands District drafted its own Constitution, which came into effect on 1 May 1979, and the four districts of Yap, Truk (now Chuuk), Ponape (now Pohnpei) and Kosrae ratified a new Constitution, to become the Federated States of Micronesia (q.v.), on 10 May 1979. In the Palau District a referendum in July 1979 approved a proposed local constitution, which came into effect on 1 January 1981, when the district became the Republic of Palau (q.v.).

The USA signed a Compact of Free Association with the Republic of Palau in August 1982, and with the Marshall Islands and the Federated States of Micronesia in October of that year. The trusteeship of the islands was due to end after the principle and terms of the Compacts had been approved by the respective peoples and legislatures of the new countries, by the US Congress and by the UN Security Council. Under the Compacts, the four countries (including the Northern Mariana Islands) would be independent of each other and would manage their internal and foreign affairs separately, while the USA would be responsible for defence and security. Moreover, Marshallese citizens were granted the right to live and work in the USA. The Compacts with the Federated States of Micronesia and the Marshall Islands were approved in plebiscites in June and September 1983 respectively. The Congress of the Federated States of Micronesia ratified the country's decision in September. Under the Compact with the Marshall Islands, the USA was to retain its military bases in the Marshall Islands for at least 15 years and, over the same period, was to provide annual aid of US $30m.

The Compact between the Marshall Islands and the USA came into effect on 21 October 1986, following its approval by the islands' Government. In November President Ronald Reagan issued a proclamation formally ending US administration of Micronesia. The first President of the Republic of the Marshall Islands was Iroijlaplap (paramount chief) Amata Kabua, who was re-elected in 1984, 1988, 1992 and 1995. In December 1990 the UN Security Council finally ratified the termination of the trusteeship agreement; the Marshall Islands became a member of the UN in 1991. Prior to their scheduled expiry in 2001, the terms of Compact were extended for a further two year period, pending negotiation of new arrangements (see below).

The Marshall Islands' atolls of Bikini and Enewetak were used by the USA for experiments with nuclear weapons: Bikini in 1946–58 and Enewetak in 1948–58. A total of 67 such tests were carried out during this period. The native inhabitants of Enewetak were evacuated before tests began, and were allowed to return to the atoll in 1980, after much of the contaminated area had supposedly been rendered safe. The inhabitants of Bikini Atoll campaigned for similar treatment, and in 1985 the US Administration agreed to decontaminate Bikini Atoll over a period of 10–15 years. In 1985 the entire population of Rongelap Atoll, which had been engulfed by radioactive fallout from the tests at Bikini in 1954, was forced to resettle on Mejato Atoll, after surveys suggested that levels of radiation there remained dangerous. In April 2001, following the adoption by the USA of a new standard of radioactivity considered to be acceptable, some six times lower than the previous level, the Tribunal announced that Ailuk Atoll was to be evacuated and environmental studies conducted.

Under the terms of the Compact, the US Government consented to establish a US $150m. Nuclear Claims Fund to settle claims against the USA resulting from nuclear testing in the Marshall Islands during the 1940s and 1950s. Accordingly, the Marshall Islands Nuclear Claims Tribunal was established in 1988, with jurisdiction to 'render final determination upon all claims past, present and future, of the Government, citizens and nationals of the Marshall Islands' in respect of the nuclear testing programme. A compensation programme was implemented in 1991 for personal injuries deemed to have resulted from the testing programme. Following an approach defined in legislation adopted by the US Congress in 1990, which established a 'presumptive' programme of compensation for specified diseases contracted by US civilian and military personnel who had been physically present in what was termed the 'affected area' during periods of atmospheric testing in Nevada, the Marshall Islands Nuclear Claims Tribunal initially identified 25 diseases for which credible evidence demonstrated a significant statistical relationship between exposure to radiation and subsequent development of a disease; in response to the findings of later studies, the Tribunal's list had by 2003 been extended to include 11 further conditions. Compensation awards totalling $83m. had by the end of 2003 been made to, or on behalf of, 1,865, individuals who had contracted one or more of these conditions. Additionally, an award of some $578m. had been ordered in May 2000 in respect of a class action brought by the people of Enewetak for loss of and damage to property; and an award of $563m. had been made in March 2002 in settlement of a class action brought by the peoples of Bikini Atoll; settlements of similar class actions by the peoples of Rongelap and Utrik Atolls were being finalized, while a new class action had been submitted by the people of Ailuk Atoll. However, only $45.8m. had been made available for actual payment of awards decided by the Tribunal; furthermore, less than $6m. remained of the original value of the Fund. In view of the inadequacy of the Fund to meet the compensation awards made by the Tribunal, in September 2000 the Marshall Islands Government formally petitioned the US Congress for a renegotiation of the settlement agreed under the Compact; the basis of the petition, which sought additional compensation amounting to $2,000m., was an article of the agreement providing for what were termed 'Changed Circumstances'.

In January 1994, meanwhile, several senior members of the Marshall Islands' legislature, the Nitijela, demanded that the US authorities release detailed information on the effects of its nuclear-testing programme in the islands. In July documentation released by the US Department of Energy gave conclusive evidence that Marshall Islanders had been deliberately exposed to high levels of radiation in order that its effects on their health could be studied by US medical researchers. Further evidence emerged during 1995 that the USA had withheld the medical records of islanders involved in radiation experiments (which included tritium and chromium-51 injections and genetic and bone-marrow transplant experiments).

Despite the publication of a study conducted by US scientists (in 1992) into contamination levels on Bikini atoll, which suggested that radiation levels there remained dangerous, in February 1997 a group of Bikini Islanders returned for the first time since 1946 to assist in the rehabilitation of the atoll for resettlement. The operation was to involve the removal of radioactive topsoil (although the matter of its disposal presented a serious problem) and the saturation of the remaining soil with potassium, which was believed to inhibit the absorption of radioactive material by root crops. In early 1999 the Nuclear Claims Tribunal demanded the adoption of US Environmental Protection Agency standards in the rehabilitation of contaminated islands, claiming that Marshall Islanders deserved to receive the same treatment as US citizens would in similar circumstances. The US Department of Energy, however, expressed strong resistance to the suggestion. In February 2001 a report published by an eminent Japanese scientist stated that radiation levels on Rongelap Island, according to research conducted in 1999, had now declined to such a level that human habitation of the island was again possible. In early 2004 the Marshall Islands protested that a reduction, decided upon by the US Department of Energy without consultation with Island representatives, of some US $740,000 in congressional funding allocated to nuclear test-related studies would result in the closure of a centre on Bikini Atoll used to support scientific studies at the former test site.

Another atoll in the Marshall Islands, Kwajalein, has been used since 1947 as a target for the testing of missiles fired from California, USA. The Compact as ratified in 1986 committed the US Government to provide an estimated US $170m. in rent over a period of 30 years for land used as the site of a missile-tracking station, and a further $80m. for development projects. The inhabitants of Kwajalein Atoll were concentrated on the small island of Ebeye, adjacent to the US base on Kwajalein Island, before a new programme of weapons-testing began in 1961. Consequent overcrowding reportedly led to numerous social problems on Ebeye. In 1989 the Marshall Islands Government agreed that the USA could lease a further four islands in the atoll, for five years, for the purpose of military tests. A further lease agreement was signed in 1995 for the use of Biken Island (in Aur Atoll) and Wake Island in the missile-testing programme. The issue of the Kwajalein lease proved to be one of the most controversial aspects of the renegotiated terms of the Compact, as signed in 2003 (see below). In January 2003 it was announced that the Marshall Islands Government and the USA had reached agreement on new terms extending the lease of the Kwajalein site, previously scheduled to end in 2016, until 2066 (with the USA retaining the right to extend the lease by 20 years). The renegotiated terms envisaged that payments for use of the site would be increased from $13.5m. annually to $16.9m. (including continued provision of $1.9m. annually in social funding for the residents of Ebeye), with a further increase, to more than $19.9m. per year, to enter into effect from 2014. However, Kwajalein landowners, who deemed the new terms unacceptable, asserted that the new arrangement was invalid, since they had not consented, as constitutionally required, to its terms.

Following legislative elections in November 1995, at which eight incumbent members of the 33-seat Nitijela were defeated, Kabua was re-elected for a fifth term. The President died in December 1996. Iroijlaplap Imata Kabua, a cousin of the late President, was elected as his successor on 13 January 1997.

In 1996 the Nitijela approved legislation allowing for the introduction of gambling in the islands, in order to provide an additional source of revenue. However, income earned from the venture did not fulfil expectations. Moreover, a vociferous campaign by local church leaders to revoke the legislation led to fierce debate in the Nitijela in early 1998. Divisions within the Cabinet ensued, with three members supporting the President's pro-gambling stance and four others opposing. In April the Nitijela voted to repeal the law legalizing gambling: several influential politicians (including Imata Kabua) known to have major gambling interests were disqualified from voting. A second bill containing further measures to ensure the prohibition of all gambling activity in the islands was narrowly approved. Three ministers who had supported the anti-gambling legislation were dismissed in a cabinet reorganization in August. In the following month one of the dismissed ministers proposed a motion of 'no confidence' in Kabua. The President and his supporters boycotted subsequent sessions of the Nitijela, thereby rendering the legislature inquorate and effectively precluding the vote, as well as delaying the approval of the budget for the impending financial year. Despite opposition claims that Kabua's continued absence from the Nitijela violated the terms of the Constitution, the motion of 'no confidence' in Kabua was eventually defeated by a margin of one vote in October.

At legislative elections held in November 1999 the opposition United Democratic Party (UDP) secured a convincing victory over the incumbent administration, winning 18 of the 33 seats in the Nitijela. Five senior members of the outgoing Government were defeated, including the Ministers of Finance and of Foreign Affairs and Trade—both of whom had played a prominent role in the establishment of diplomatic relations with Taiwan in 1998 (see below). The former Nitijela Speaker, Kessai Note, was elected President on 3 January 2000 (the islands' first non-traditional leader to assume the post). The UDP Chairman, Litokwa Tomeing, became Speaker of the legislature. Note subsequently appointed a 10-member Cabinet, and reiterated his administration's intention to pursue anti-corruption policies. In May a task-force was established by the Government for the purposes of investigating misconduct and corruption; it was hoped that the task-force would help to render government more accountable.

In November 2000 it was reported that finance officials had discovered that Imata Kabua had used funds granted to the Marshall Islands under the terms of the Compact of Free Association to pay off a personal loan, although the former President denied any wrongdoing. In mid-January 2001 Imata Kabua and former ministers in his Government, including the former Minister of Education, Justin DeBrum, presented a 'no confidence' motion against President Note to the Nitijela. Although it was suggested that the vote had been intended to delay the publication of a report into mismanagement and corruption on the part of the former Government, DeBrum stated that the motion resulted from a number of failings by the Note Government, including its unwillingness to renegotiate land rental payments with the USA for the use of the military base on Kwajalein Atoll and also the development of an economic relationship between the Note Government and Rev. Sun Myung Moon, the founder of the Unification Church (known as the 'Moonies'). However, the Government was successful in defeating the vote by a margin of 19 to 14.

In September 2000 the Nitijela approved legislation to ensure the closer regulation of the banking and financial sector. In May of that year the Group of Seven industrialized nations (G-7) had expressed its view that the Marshall Islands had become a significant centre for the 'laundering' of money generated by international criminal activity, and, in June the Marshall Islands was one of more than 30 countries and territories criticized by the Organisation for Economic Co-operation and Development (OECD, see p. 295) for the provision of inappropriate 'offshore' financial establishments. OECD threatened to implement sanctions against 'unco-operative tax havens' unless reforms were introduced before July 2001. Following a commendation from the IMF on a series of new measures to combat fraud, including specific legislation and the establishment of a Domestic Financial Intelligence Unit, in October 2002 the Financial Action Task Force on Money Laundering (see p. 363) removed the Marshall Islands from its list of countries judged to be unhelpful in the combating of international financial crime.

Negotiations began between the US and Marshall Islands Governments in July 2001 to renew the provisions of the Compact of Free Association ratified in 1986, which was due to expire at the end of September 2001. A two-year extension was permitted while negotiations were under way, during which time annual assistance to the Marshall Islands was to increase by some US $5.5m. An agreement was originally scheduled for early 2002 in order to allow adequate time for the US Congress to review it and to approve the requisite legislation (by 1 October 2003), but the procedure was postponed until early May 2002 after the Marshall Islands Government submitted a proposal seeking financing of more than $1,000m. over 15 years. The Government had also objected to being allocated 25%–30% less in US grant assistance per caput than that apportioned to the Federated States of Micronesia since the year 2000. In a further attempt to increase the national income, the Government sought to raise significantly the level of taxes levied on the Kawajalein base (see above). In early November 2002 the USA and the Marshall Islands Government announced a programme of direct funding of $822m., to be disbursed over 20 years, in addition to the expansion of many US government services in the islands. It was envisaged that the Marshall Islands would receive some $30.5m. a year; furthermore, a trust fund would be established, to which the USA would contribute $7m. annually in order to provide a means of income after the termination of direct US assistance in 2023. The amended Compact of Free Association was signed by the Governments of the Marshall Islands and the USA in May 2003, at which time a number of issues—including a requirement for an initial US payment into a Kwajalein landowners' trust fund, and consideration of the 'Changed Circumstances' petition—remained to be resolved. Under the new Compact, Marshall Islanders would for the first time require passports in order to enter the USA. They would, however, retain the right to enter the USA to live, work and study, and would no longer be required to obtain work authorization documentation before taking up employment in the USA. Other than the issue of the Kwajalein lease, a principal obstacle to the negotiation of Compact amendments had been that of immigration: the USA, increasingly preoccupied by issues of homeland security, had been notably concerned to prevent future sales of Marshallese passports (a controversial programme of which had been implemented in the 1990s, although this had officially been suspended in 1997). The US authorities had also sought to close a loophole in the original Compact provisions that had effectively allowed the unmonitored adoption of Marshallese children by US citizens. Final terms, including the restoration of some rights of access to US health care and education programmes, were approved by the US Congress in November 2003, and ratified by President George W. Bush in December.

At a general election held on 17 November 2003 the UDP returned 20 Senators to the 33-member Nitijela. The opposition grouping Ailin Kein Ad (Our Islands), which had campaigned against the terms of the renewed Compact and which received particularly strong support from Marshall Islanders resident in the USA, secured 10 seats (the re-election of the incumbent Ailin Kein Ad Senator for Ailinglaplap Atoll was decided following a recount of votes conducted in late January 2004). Note was re-elected for a second presidential term in a vote held in the Nitijela on 4 January 2004, defeating Justin DeBrum, the candidate of Ailin Kein Ad, by 20 votes to nine. He and his new Cabinet were sworn in on 12 January.

In 1989 a UN report on the 'greenhouse effect' (heating of the earth's atmosphere) predicted a possible resultant rise in sea-level of some 3.7 m by 2030, which would completely submerge the Marshall Islands. The islands' Government strongly criticized the Australian Government's refusal, at the conference on climate change in Kyoto, Japan, in December 1997, to reduce its emission of pollutant gases known to contribute to the 'greenhouse effect'. Furthermore, in early 2002 the Intergovernmental Panel on Climate Change (IPCC) projected that during the 21st century global sea-level rises would submerge over 80% of Majuro atoll. However, the Marshall Islands Government has itself caused regional concerns regarding pollution, notably with regard to the possible establishment of large-scale facilities for the storage of nuclear waste. Criticism by the US Government of the plans, announced in 1994, was strongly denounced by the Marshall Islands authorities, which claimed that the project constituted the only opportunity for the country to generate sufficient income for the rehabilitation of contaminated islands and the provision of treatment for illnesses caused by the US nuclear-test programme. In mid-1997 President Imata Kabua announced the indefinite suspension of the project (despite the initiation of a feasibility study into the development of a nuclear waste storage facility). None the less, the Government approved plans for a new feasibility study on the subject in April 1998. The new Minister of Foreign Affairs appointed by President Note in January 2000 was known to be strongly opposed to the scheme.

In November 1998 the Marshall Islands established full diplomatic relations with Taiwan. The action was immediately condemned by the People's Republic of China, which in December severed diplomatic ties with the islands, closing its embassy in Majuro and suspending all intergovernmental agreements. The Marshall Islands Government insisted that it wished to maintain cordial relations with both governments. The Note administration, which took office in January 2000, emphasized its commitment to the maintenance of diplomatic relations with Taiwan. In February 2001 a proposed visit by a flotilla of Taiwanese naval vessels to the Marshall Islands was vetoed by the USA, on the grounds that the defence protocol of the Compact of Free Association prohibited such a visit.

Government

The Constitution of the Republic of the Marshall Islands, which became effective on 1 May 1979, provides for a parliamentary form of government, with legislative authority vested in the 33-member Nitijela. The Nitijela (members of which are elected, by popular vote, for a four-year term) elects the President of the Marshall Islands (also a four-year mandate) from among its own members. Under the terms of the Compact of Free Association, the Republic of the Marshall Islands is a sovereign, self-governing state. The first Compact was was signed by the Governments of the Marshall Islands and the USA on 25 June 1983, and was effectively ratified by the US Congress on 14 January 1986. A revised Compact was signed by the Governments of the two countries on 1 May 2003; it was ratified by the US Congress in November 2003, and signed by US President George W. Bush in December of that year.

Local governmental units are the municipalities and villages. Elected Magistrates and Councils govern the municipalities. Village government is largely traditional.

Defence

Under the terms of the Compact of Free Association as ratified in 1986 and amended in 2003, the defence of the Marshall Islands is the responsibility of the USA, which maintains a military presence on Kwajalein Atoll.

Economic Affairs

In 2001, according to estimates by the World Bank, the Marshall Islands' gross national income (GNI), measured at average 1999–2001 prices, was US $115m., equivalent to $2,190 per head. During 1990–2001, it was estimated, the population increased at an average annual rate of 2.0%, while gross domestic product (GDP) declined, in real terms, at an average rate of 1.5% per year. According to the Asian Development Bank (ADB), GDP decreased by 3.1% in 2000, but increased by 1.6% in 2001 and by 3.8% in 2002.

Agriculture is mainly on a subsistence level. The sector (including fishing and livestock-rearing) contributed an estimated 13.7% of GDP in 1999/2000. According to FAO, the sector engaged 6,000 people in 2001. The principal crops are coconuts, cassava and sweet potatoes. In 2000 some 2,706 short tons of copra were produced (a decrease of 19.2% compared with the previous year), and in that year exports of coconut oil and copra accounted for 31.0% of the total value of exports. Copra production suffered a severe decline in the late 1990s, following sustained low prices, an ageing tree stock and a reduction in the number of government-owned vessels used for transport purposes. The fishing sector incorporates a commercial tuna-fishing industry, including a tuna-canning factory and transhipment base on Majuro. The cultivation of seaweed was developed extensively in 1992, and in 1994 a project to cultivate blacklip pearl oysters on Arno Atoll was undertaken with US funding. The sale of fishing licences is an important source of revenue and earned the islands an estimated US $3m. in 2000/01. The Marshall Islands expected to receive annual revenues of some $21m. following the renewal of a treaty between the USA and the Forum Fisheries Agency (FFA) group of Pacific island nations in 2003. In 2001 the Japanese Government funded the construction of a commercial fishing base at Jaluit Atoll. According to initial estimates by the ADB, compared with the previous year the GDP of the agricultural sector declined by 13.9% in 1998, but increased by 1.7% in 1999 and by 3.7% in 2000.

Industrial activities (including mining, manufacturing, construction and power) contributed an estimated 15.1% of GDP in 1999/2000, and engaged 9.4% of the employed labour force in 1988. Between 1990 and 1999 industrial GDP declined at an average annual rate of 1.5%. According to provisional estimates by the ADB, compared with the previous year the GDP of the industrial sector rose by 1.3% in 1999 and by 3.7% in 2000. The islands have few mineral resources, although there are high-grade phosphate deposits on Ailinglaplap Atoll.

Manufacturing activity, which provided 1.8% of GDP in 1999/2000, consists mainly of the processing of coconuts (to produce copra and coconut oil) and other agricultural products and of fish (see above). According to the ADB, the manufacturing sector engaged a total of 800 workers in 2000.

The services sector provided an estimated 71.3% of GDP in 1999/2000. The international shipping registry experienced considerable expansion following the political troubles in Panama in 1989, and continued to expand in the mid-1990s (largely as a result of US ships' re-flagging in the islands). The shipping industry also benefited from the construction of a floating dry-dock on Majuro in 1995. Tourist receipts reached US $4m. in 1999. The number of tourist arrivals rose from 5,246 in 2000 to 5,399 in 2001. According to initial estimates by the ADB, compared with the previous year the GDP of the services sector expanded by only 0.2% in 1998, before contracting by 0.5% in 1999 and by 0.8% in 2000.

In the financial year ending 30 September 2001 the Marshall Islands recorded an estimated trade deficit of US $52.2m., but a surplus of $14.4m. on the current account of the balance of payments. The only significant domestic exports in 2000 were coconut products and fish. The principal imports included mineral fuels and lubricants (which accounted for 43.6% of total expenditure on merchandise imports), food and live animals, and machinery and transport equipment. In that year the principal sources of imports were the USA (which provided 61.4% of total imports) and Japan (5.1%). The USA was also the principal export destination, receiving 71.2% of total exports.

A budgetary surplus equivalent to 9.1% of GDP was forecast for 2001/02. Financial assistance from the USA, in accordance with the terms stipulated in the Compact of Free Association, contributes a large part of the islands' revenue. Aided by an increase in this support, estimates for 2001/02 envisaged a rise in budgetary expenditure to US $74m. (compared with $66m. in the previous year). Recurrent expenditure was projected to increase from $55m. in 2000/01 to $59m. in 2001/02. The islands' external debt was estimated at $67.0m. in 2000/01. In that year the cost of debt-servicing (including repayments) was equivalent to 168.7% of the value of exports of goods and services. The Marshall Islands received $551 of aid per caput in 2003. In 2000/01 budgeted aid from the USA amounted to $20.7m. (35% of which was to be provided under the Compact agreement). The US aid budget for 2002 included a grant of $2.5m. to the Marshall Islands for an extension of the Military Use and Operating Rights Agreement (in addition to its mandatory annual payments of support for Enewetak Atoll and the Compact of Free Association). Aid is also provided by Japan and Taiwan. According to the ADB, annual inflation in Majuro averaged 5.7% in 1990–1999. Consumer prices were estimated to have increased by an annual average of 1.6% in 2000 and by an estimated 0.8% in both 2001 and 2002. The unemployment rate stood at 30.0% of the economically active population in 2000.

The Marshall Islands is a member of the Pacific Community (see p. 323), the Pacific Islands Forum (see p. 325), the South Pacific Regional Trade and Economic Co-operation Agreement (SPARTECA, see p. 328), the UN Economic and Social Commission for Asia and the Pacific (ESCAP, see p. 31) and the Asian Development Bank (ADB, see p. 151). In early 1996 the Marshall Islands and other countries and territories of Micronesia established the Council of Micronesian Government Executives. The new body aimed to facilitate discussion of economic developments in the region, and to examine possibilities for reducing the considerable cost of shipping essential goods between the islands.

The introduction, from the mid-1990s, of retrenchment measures in the public sector was welcomed by several international financial organizations and supported by the ADB. However, it was subsequently observed that reform of the public sector, which until the recession of the mid-1990s had employed up to one-half of the economically-active population, had been accompanied by a decline in employment in the private sector, leading to a very high rate of unemployment (according to US assessments, the highest of any US-affiliated state in the Pacific) and emigration. In 1999 the Kabua Government reduced import duties by more than 50% on many items, in an attempt to revitalize the local economy. Reforms to promote the private sector were also announced. During the 1990s the Marshall Islands sought to diversify its international economic relations. The Marshall Islands has since 1998 notably benefited from numerous economic agreements with Taiwan, worth an estimated US $20m., which have financed many projects including the construction of roads, the acquisition of boats, and the development of the agricultural sector. However, concern was expressed by the ADB in 1999 that reliance on external aid was hampering economic reform in the Marshall Islands (in 2000 bilateral and multilateral aid to the Marshall Islands totalled $57.2m.) In June 2001 the ADB approved a programme of low-interest loans totalling $12m., urging the Government to use it to improve budgeting and accounting practices. In December 2002 the ADB approved a further total of $7.25m. in loans and grants in order to improve the country's infrastructure. Nevertheless, it was considered that reforms of the public sector in the mid-1990s, combined with low world prices for Marshallese products, had contributed directly to the islands' economic decline. The lack of internationally marketable natural resources and the remote location of the islands also present major difficulties for the Marshall Islands Government in its efforts to revitalize and expand the economy. Attempts to overcome these obstacles, including the introduction of passport sales and efforts to promote gambling and 'offshore' financial services (see Recent History) have generated political controversy, both domestically and internationally. None the less, in October 2002 the Marshall Islands was removed from the Financial Action Task Force (FATF) list of Non Co-operative Countries and Territories following the successful implementation of a series of regulatory measures (see above). The Government has also been able to obtain a further source of income by expanding ship registrations, to the effect that in 2002 the Marshallese merchant fleet was reportedly the sixth largest in the world. A notable feature of the amended Compact of Free Association, which was signed by the Governments of the Marshall Islands and the USA in May 2003 (see Recent History), was the planned gradual decrement in grant assistance over the 20-year period of the renewed Compact. It was intended that this would represent less of a strain on the Marshall Islands' economy than had the five-yearly reductions in funding implemented under the original Compact, in compensation for which the Marshall Islands had implemented a number of projects such as the controversial sale of passports. The new terms also provided for the establishment of a trust fund, revenue from which would supersede US direct assistance from 2003.

Education

Education is compulsory between the ages of six and 14. In 1999 a total of 12,421 children attended the 103 primary schools of the Marshall Islands. A total of 2,667 pupils were enrolled at 16 secondary schools in 1999. The College of the Marshall Islands (which became independent from the College of Micronesia in 1993) is based on Majuro. In 1995 the University of the South Pacific opened an extension centre on Majuro. The Fisheries and Nautical Center offers vocational courses for Marshall islanders seeking employment in the fishing industry or on passenger liners, cargo ships and tankers. Government expenditure on education in the 1997/98 budget was estimated at $10.0m., equivalent to 23.5% of total recurrent budgetary spending.

Public Holidays

2004: 1–2 January (New Year), 1 March (Nuclear Victims' Remembrance Day), 9 April (Good Friday), 30 April (Constitution Day), 4 July (Fishermen's Day), 6 September (Dri-Jerbal), 24 September (Manit—Culture Day), 17 November (President's Day), 3 December (Kamolol—Gospel Day), 25 December (Christmas).

2005 (provisional): 1–2 January (New Year), 1 March (Nuclear Victims' Remembrance Day), 25 March (Good Friday), 1 May (Constitution Day), 4 July (Fishermen's Day), 5 September (Dri-Jerbal), 30 September (Manit—Culture Day), 18 November (President's Day), 2 December (Kamolol—Gospel Day), 25 December (Christmas).

Weights and Measures

With certain exceptions, the imperial system is in force. One US cwt equals 100 lb; one long ton equals 2,240 lb; one short ton equals 2,000 lb. A policy of gradual voluntary conversion to the metric system is being undertaken.

Statistical Survey

AREA AND POPULATION

Area: 181.4 sq km (70.0 sq miles) (land only); two island groups, the Ratak Chain (88.1 sq km) and the Ralik Chain (93.3 sq km).

Population: 43,380 at census of 13 November 1988; 50,848 (males 26,034, females 24,814) at census of June 1999. *By Island Group* (1999): Ratak Chain 30,932 (Majuro Atoll 23,682); Ralik Chain 19,916 (Kwajalein Atoll 10,903).

Density (1999 census): 280.3 per sq km.

Births and Deaths (estimates, 1999): Birth rate 41.8 per 1,000; Death rate 4.9 per 1,000.

Expectation of Life (WHO estimates, years at birth): 62.7 (males 61.1; females 64.6) in 2002. Source: WHO, *World Health Report*.

Economically Active Population (2000): Agriculture, forestry and fishing 2,100; Manufacturing 800; Activities not adequately defined 7,400; *Total employed* 10,300; Unemployed 4,500; *Total labour force* 15,000. Source: Asian Development Bank, *Key Indicators of Developing Asian and Pacific Countries*.

HEALTH AND WELFARE

Key Indicators

Total Fertility Rate (children per woman, 2002): 5.5.

Under-5 Mortality Rate (per 1,000 live births, 2001): 66.

Physicians (per 1,000 head, 1996): 0.42.

Health Expenditure (2001): US $ per head (PPP): 343.

Health Expenditure (2001): % of GDP: 9.8.

Health Expenditure (2001): public (% of total): 64.7.
For sources and definitions, see explanatory note on p. vi.

AGRICULTURE, ETC.

Principal Crops, Livestock and Livestock Products: see the chapter on the Federated States of Micronesia.

Fishing (metric tons, live weight): Total catch 37,098 in 2001. Source: FAO, *Yearbook of Fishery Statistics*.

INDUSTRY

Electric Energy (million kWh)* 64.1 in 1998; 62.9 in 1999; 63.0 in 2000. Source: Asian Development Bank, *Key Indicators of Developing Asian and Pacific Countries*.
* Figures refer to Majuro only.

FINANCE

Currency and Exchange Rates: United States currency is used: 100 cents = 1 United States dollar (US $). *Sterling and Euro Equivalents* (31 December 2003): £1 sterling = US $1.7847; €1 = US $1.26; US $100 = £56.03 = €79.12.

Budget (estimates, US $ million, year ending 30 September 2002): *Revenue:* Recurrent 24.8 (Tax 18.6, Non-tax 6.2); Grants 58.8; Total 83.6. *Expenditure:* Recurrent 58.7; Capital (incl. net lending) 15.3; Total 74.0. Source: Asian Development Bank, *Key Indicators of Developing Asian and Pacific Countries*.

Cost of Living (Consumer Price Index for Majuro; base: Oct.–Dec. 1982 = 100): All items 197.1 in 2000; 198.7 in 2001; 200.3 in 2002. Source: Asian Development Bank, *Key Indicators of Developing Asian and Pacific Countries*.

Gross Domestic Product by Economic Activity (estimates, US $ million at current prices, year ending 30 September 2001): Agriculture 14.0; Mining 0.3; Manufacturing 1.6; Electricity, gas and water 3.2; Construction 11.2; Trade 17.5; Transport and communications 6.0; Finance 15.8; Public administration 30.9; *Sub-total* 100.5; Import duties 6.7; *Less* Imputed bank service charges 5.5; *GDP in purchasers' values* 101.7. Source: Asian Development Bank, *Key Indicators of Developing Asian and Pacific Countries*.

Balance of Payments (estimates, US $ million, year ending 30 September 2001): Merchandise exports f.o.b. 8.3; Merchandise imports c.i.f. –60.5; *Trade balance* –52.2; Exports of services 35.0; Imports of services –13.2; *Balance on goods and services* –30.4; Private unrequited transfers (net) 0.7; Official unrequited transfers (net) 44.1; *Current balance* 14.4; Capital account (net) –22.0; Net errors and omissions 9.3; *Overall balance* 1.7. Source: Asian Development Bank, *Key Indicators of Developing Asian and Pacific Countries*.

EXTERNAL TRADE

Principal Commodities (estimates, US $ million, 2000): *Imports:* Food, live animals, beverages and tobacco 7.4; Crude materials, inedible, except fuels 2.9; Mineral fuels, lubricants and related materials 29.7; Animal and vegetable oils and fats 2.9; Chemicals 0.2; Basic manufactures 4.0; Machinery and transport equipment 11.5; Miscellaneous manufactured articles 1.9; Goods not classified by kind 7.7; Total 68.2. *Exports:* Coconut oil (crude) 1.1; Copra cake 1.2; Pet fish 0.5; Total (incl. others) 7.3. Source: mainly Asian Development Bank, *Key Indicators of Developing Asian and Pacific Countries*.

Principal Trading Partners (estimates, US $ million, 2000): *Imports:* Australia 1.4; Hong Kong 1.3; Japan 3.5; New Zealand 0.9; USA 41.9; Total (incl. others) 68.2. *Exports:* USA 5.2; Total (incl. others) 7.3. Source: mainly Asian Development Bank, *Key Indicators of Developing Asian and Pacific Countries*.

TRANSPORT

Road Traffic (vehicles registered, 1999): Trucks 64; Pick-ups 587; Sedans 1,404; Jeeps 79; Buses 75; Vans 66; Scooters 47; Other motor vehicles 253.

Shipping: *Merchant Fleet* (at 31 December 2002): Vessels 428; Displacement ('000 grt) 14,673 (Source: Lloyd's Register-Fairplay, *World Fleet Statistics*). *International Sea-borne Freight Traffic* (estimates, '000 metric tons, 1990):* Goods loaded 29; Goods unloaded 123 (Source: UN, *Monthly Bulletin of Statistics*).
* Including the Northern Mariana Islands, the Federated States of Micronesia and Palau.

Civil Aviation (traffic on scheduled services, 1998): Passengers carried 32,000; Passenger-km 20 million. Total ton-km 2 million. Source: UN, *Statistical Yearbook*.

TOURISM

Tourist Arrivals: 4,622 in 1999; 5,246 in 2000; 5,444 in 2001.

Arrivals by Country (2001): Australia 190; Fiji 94; Japan 996; Kiribati 283; Federated States of Micronesia 203; Philippines 222; USA 2,039; Total (incl. others) 5444.

Tourism Receipts (US $ million): 3 in 1998; 4 in 1999; 4 in 2000. Sources: World Tourism Organization, *Yearbook of Tourism Statistics*, and Marshall Islands Visitor Authority.

COMMUNICATIONS MEDIA

Telephones (main lines in use): 4,200 in 2001*.

Mobile Cellular Telephones (subscriptions): 500 in 2001*.

Facsimile Machines (number): 160 in 1996†.

Personal Computers: 4,000 in 2001*.

Internet Users: 900 in 2001*.

Non-daily Newspaper: 1 (average circulation 10,000 copies) in 1996‡.

* Source: International Telecommunication Union.

† Source: UN, *Statistical Yearbook*.

‡ Source: UNESCO, *Statistical Yearbook*.

EDUCATION

Primary (1998): 103 schools; 548 teachers; 12,421 pupils enrolled.

Secondary (1998): 16 schools; 162 teachers; 2,667 pupils enrolled.

Higher (1994): 1 college; 25 teachers; 1,149 students enrolled.

Directory

The Constitution

On 1 May 1979 the locally-drafted Constitution of the Republic of the Marshall Islands became effective. The Constitution provides for a parliamentary form of government, with legislative authority vested in the 33-member Nitijela. Members of the Nitijela are elected by a popular vote, from 25 districts, for a four-year term. There is an advisory council of 12 high chiefs, or Iroij. The Nitijela elects the President of the Marshall Islands (who also has a four-year mandate) from among its own members. The President then selects members of the Cabinet from among the members of the Nitijela. On 25 June 1983 the final draft of a Compact of Free Association was signed by the Governments of the Marshall Islands and the USA, and the Compact was effectively ratified by the US Congress on 14 January 1986. An amended Compact was signed by the Governments of the two countries on 1 May 2003; final terms were ratified by the US Congress in November, and signed by the US President in December of that year. By the terms of the Compact, free association recognizes the Republic of the Marshall Islands as an internally sovereign, self-governing state, whose policy concerning foreign affairs must be consistent with guide-lines laid down in the Compact. Full responsibility for defence lies with the USA, which undertakes to provide regular economic assistance. The economic and defence provisions of the Compact are renewable after 15 years, but the status of free association continues indefinitely.

The Government

HEAD OF STATE

President: KESSAI H. NOTE (took office 10 January 2000; re-elected by the Nitijela 4 January 2004).

THE CABINET
(April 2004)

Minister in Assistance to the President: WITTEN T. PHILIPPO.

Minister of Education: WILFRED I. KENDALL.

Minister of Finance: BRENSON S. WASE.

Minister of Transportation and Communication: MICHAEL M. KONELIOS.

Minister of Health and Environment: ALVIN T. JACKLICK.

Minister of Public Works: MATTLAN ZACKHRAS.

Minister of Internal Affairs: REIN MORRIS.

Minister of Justice: DONALD CAPELLE.

Minister of Resources and Development: JOHN M. SILK.

Minister of Foreign Affairs and Trade: GERALD ZACKIOS.

MINISTRIES

Office of the President: Govt of the Republic of the Marshall Islands, POB 2, Majuro, MH 96960; tel. (625) 3213; fax (625) 4021; e-mail presoff@ntamar.net.

Ministry of Education: POB 3, Majuro, MH 96960; tel. (625) 5262; fax (625) 7735/3861; e-mail secmoe@ntamar.net.

Ministry of Finance: POB D, Majuro, MH 96960; tel. (625) 7420; fax (625) 3607; e-mail secfin@ntamar.net.

Ministry of Foreign Affairs and Trade: POB 1349, Majuro, MH 96960; tel. (625) 3181; fax (623) 4979; e-mail mofatadm@ntamar.net.

Ministry of Health and Environment: POB 16, Majuro, MH 96960; tel. (625) 3355; fax (625) 3432; e-mail mipamohe@ntamar.net.

Ministry of Internal Affairs: POB 18, Majuro, MH 96960; tel. (625) 8240/8718; fax (625) 5353; e-mail rmihpo@ntamar.net.

Ministry of Justice: c/o Office of the Attorney General, Majuro, MH 96960; tel. (625) 3201/8245; fax (625) 3323; e-mail agoffice@ntamar.net.

Ministry of Public Works: POB 1727, Majuro, MH 96960; tel. (625) 8911; fax (625) 3005; e-mail rndadm@ntamar.net.

Ministry of Resources and Development: POB 1727, Majuro, MH 96960; tel. (625) 3206/3277; fax (625) 5447; e-mail rndsec@ntamar.net.

Ministry of Transportation and Communication: POB 1079, Majuro, MH 96960; tel. (625) 3129/8869; fax (625) 3486; e-mail rmimotc@ntamar.net.

STATE TRIBUNAL

Nuclear Claims Tribunal: POB 702, Majuro, MH 96960; tel. (625) 3396; fax (625) 3389; e-mail nctmaj@ntamar.net; internet www.nuclearclaimstribunal.com; f. 1988; authorized under Section 177 of the first Compact of Free Association between the Government of the Marshall Islands and the Government of the USA to decide all claims arising from the nuclear testing programme conducted by the USA in the Marshall Islands in 1946–1958; Chair. JAMES H. PLASMAN; Defender of the Fund PHILIP A. OKNEY; Public Advocate BILL GRAHAM.

Legislature

THE NITIJELA

The Nitijela (lower house) consists of 33 elected Senators. The most recent national election was held on 17 November 2003, as a result of which the United Democratic Party held 20 seats and Ailin Kein Ad 10.

Speaker: Sen. LITOKWA TOMEING.

THE COUNCIL OF IROIJ

The Council of Iroij is the upper house of the bicameral legislature, comprising 12 tribal chiefs who advise the Presidential Cabinet and review legislation affecting customary law, land tenure or any traditional practice.

Chairman: Iroij KOTAK LOEAK.

Political Organizations

Ailin Kein Ad (Our Islands): Majuro; f. 2002; opposed to President Note; Leader TONY DEBRUM.

United Democratic Party: Majuro; Chair. LITOKWA TOMEING.

Diplomatic Representation

EMBASSIES IN THE MARSHALL ISLANDS

China (Taiwan): A5-6, Lojkar Village, Long Island, POB 1229, Majuro, MH 96960; tel. (247) 4141; fax (247) 4143; e-mail eoroc@ntamar.net; Ambassador LIEN-GENE CHEN.

Japan: A-1 Lojkar Village, POB 300, Majuro, MH 96960; tel. (247) 7463; fax (247) 7493; Ambassador KENRO IINO.

USA: POB 1379, Majuro, MH 96960; tel. (247) 4011; fax (247) 4012; e-mail publicmajuro@state.gov; internet usembassy.state.gov/majuro; Ambassador GRETA N. MORRIS.

Judicial System

The judicial system consists of the Supreme Court and the High Court, which preside over District and Community Courts, and the Traditional Rights Court.

Supreme Court of the Republic of the Marshall Islands: POB 378, Majuro, MH 96960; tel. (625) 3201; fax (625) 3323; e-mail jutrep@ntamar.com; Chief Justice DANIEL CADRA.

High Court of the Republic of the Marshall Islands: Majuro; Chief Justice CARL INGRAM.

District Court of the Republic of the Marshall Islands: Majuro, MH 96960; tel. (625) 3201; fax (625) 3323; Presiding Judge BOKEPOK HELAI.

Traditional Rights Court of the Marshall Islands: Majuro, MH 96960; customary law only; Chief Judge RAILEY ALBERILTAR.

Religion

The population is predominantly Christian, mainly belonging to the Protestant United Church of Christ. The Roman Catholic Church, Assembly of God, Bukot Nan Jesus, Seventh-day Adventists, the Church of Jesus Christ of Latter-day Saints (Mormons), the Full Gospel and the Bahá'í Faith are also represented.

CHRISTIANITY

The Roman Catholic Church

The Apostolic Prefecture of the Marshall Islands included 4,601 adherents at 31 December 2002.

Prefect Apostolic of the Marshall Islands: Rev. Fr JAMES C. GOULD, POB 8, Majuro, MH 96960; tel. (625) 6675; fax (625) 5520; e-mail catholic@ntamar.com.

Protestant Churches

The Marshall Islands come under the auspices of the United Church Board for World Ministries (475 Riverside Drive, New York, NY 10115, USA); Sec. for Latin America, Caribbean and Oceania Dr PATRICIA RUMER.

BAHÁ'Í FAITH

National Spiritual Assembly: POB 1017, Majuro, MH 96960; tel. (247) 3512; fax (247) 7180; e-mail nsamarshallislands@yahoo.com; internet www.mh.bahai.org; mems resident in 50 localities; Sec. Dr IRENE J. TAAFAKI.

The Press

Kwajalein Hourglass: POB 23, Kwajalein, MH 96555; tel. (355) 3539; e-mail jbennett@kls.usaka.smdc.army.mil; internet www.smdc.army.mil/KWAJ/Hourglass/Hourglass.html; f. 1954; 2 a week; Editor JIM BENNETT; circ. 2,300.

Marshall Islands Journal: POB 14, Majuro, MH 96960; tel. (625) 8143; fax (625) 3136; e-mail journal@ntamar.com; f. 1970; weekly; Editor GIFF JOHNSON; circ. 3,700.

Broadcasting and Communications

TELECOMMUNICATIONS

National Telecommunications Authority (NTA): POB 1169, Majuro, MH 96960; tel. (625) 3852; fax (625) 3952; e-mail aefowler@ntamar.net; internet www.ntamar.com; privatized in 1991; sole provider of local and long-distance telephone services and internet communications in the Marshall Islands; Chair. ALEX C. BING; Pres. and Gen. Man. ALAN FOWLER.

BROADCASTING

Radio

Radio Marshalls V7AB: POB 3250, Majuro, MH 96960; tel. (625) 8411; fax (625) 5353; govt-owned; commercial; programmes in English and Marshallese; Station Man. ANTARI ELBON.

Marshall Islands Broadcasting Co: POB 19, Majuro, MH 96960; tel. (625) 3250; fax (625) 3505; privately-owned; Chief Information Officer PETER FUCHS.

Television

Alele Museum Foundation: POB 629, Majuro, MH 96960; tel. and fax (625) 3226; broadcasts educational programmes.

Marshalls Broadcasting Co Television: POB 19, Majuro, MH 96960; tel. (625) 3413; privately-owned; Chief Information Officer PETER FUCHS.

The US Dept of Defense operates a radio station and a television station (24 hours a day) for the military base on Kwajalein Atoll.

Finance

(cap. = capital; res = reserves; dep. = deposits; amounts in US dollars)

BANKING

Bank of Guam (USA): POB C, Majuro, MH 96960; tel. (625) 3322; fax (625) 3444; internet www.bankofguam.com; Man. ROMY A. ANGEL; brs in Ebeye, Kwajalein and Majuro.

Bank of the Marshall Islands: POB J, Majuro, MH 96960; tel. (625) 3636; fax (625) 3661; e-mail bankmar@ntamar.com; internet www.angelfire.com/ms/bankofMI; f. 1982; 40% govt-owned; dep. 46,767.8m., total assets 58,806.5m. (Dec. 2002); Chair. GRANT LABAUN; Gen. Man. PATRICK CHEN; brs in Majuro, Ebeye and Santo.

Marshall Islands Development Bank: POB 1048, Majuro, MH 96960; tel. (625) 3230; fax (625) 3309; f. 1989; total assets 19.5m. (Dec. 1992); lending suspended in 2003; Man. Dir AMON TIBON.

INSURANCE

Majuro Insurance Company: POB 60, Majuro, MH 96960; tel. (625) 8885; fax (625) 8188; Man. LUCY RUBEN.

Marshalls Insurance Agency: POB 113, Majuro, MH 96960; tel. (625) 3366; fax (625) 3189; Man. TOM LIKOVICH.

Moylan's Insurance Underwriters (Marshall) Inc: POB 727, Majuro, MH 96960; tel. (625) 3220; fax (625) 3361; e-mail marshalls@moylansinsurance.com; internet www.moylansinsurance.com; Pres. JOEL PHILLIP.

Trade and Industry

DEVELOPMENT ORGANIZATIONS AND STATE AUTHORITIES

Marshall Islands Environmental Protection Authority: PO Box 1322, Majuro, MH 96960; tel. (625) 3035; fax (625) 5202; e-mail eparmi@ntamar.net; Dir ABRAHAM HICKIN (acting).

Marshall Islands Development Authority: Majuro, MH 96960; Gen. Man. DAVID KABUA.

Marshall Islands Marine Resources Authority: Majuro, MH 96960; Dir DANNY WASE.

Kwajalein Atoll Development Authority (KADA): POB 5159, Ebeye Island, Kwajalein, MH 96970; Dir JEBAN RIKLON.

Tobolar Copra Processing Authority: POB G, Majuro, MH 96960; tel. (625) 3494; fax (625) 7206; e-mail tobolar@ntamar.com; Gen. Man. MIKE SLINGER.

CHAMBER OF COMMERCE

Majuro Chamber of Commerce: Majuro, MH 96960; Pres. KIRTLEY PINHO.

UTILITIES

Electricity

Marshalls Energy Company: POB 1439, Majuro, MH 96960; tel. (625) 3829; fax (625) 3397; e-mail meccorp@ntamar.net; Gen. Man. WILLIAM F. ROBERTS.

Kwajalein Atoll Joint Utility Resource (KAJUR): POB 5819, Ebeye Island, Kwajalein, MH 96970; tel. (329) 3799; fax (329) 3722.

Water

Majuro Water and Sewage Services: POB 1751, Majuro, MH 96960; tel. (625) 8934; fax (625) 3837; e-mail mwsc@ntamar.net; internet www.omip.org/majuro.html; Man. HACKNEY TAKJU.

CO-OPERATIVES

These include the Ebeye Co-op, Farmers' Market Co-operative, Kwajalein Employees' Credit Union, Marshall Is Credit Union, Marshall Is Fishermen's Co-operative, and the Marshall Is Handicraft Co-operative.

Transport

ROADS

Macadam and concrete roads are found in the more important islands. In 1996 there were 152 km of paved roads in the Marshall Islands, mostly on Majuro and Ebeye. Other islands have stone and coral-surfaced roads and tracks. In 1997 the Marshall Islands received a grant of some US $0.5m. from Japan for a road-improvement project on Majuro. The project was to form part of an extensive programme costing US $15m., and was completed in 1999.

SHIPPING

The Marshall Islands operates an 'offshore' shipping register. In mid-2003 the merchant fleet comprised 569 vessels, with a combined displacement of some 17.5m. grt.

Vessel Registry:

Marshall Islands Maritime and Corporate Administrators Inc: 11495 Commerce Park Drive, Reston, VA 20191-1507, USA; tel. (703) 620-4880; fax (703) 476-8522; e-mail info@register-iri.com; internet www.register-iri.com.

The Trust Company of the Marshall Islands Inc: Trust Company Complex, Ajeltake Island, POB 1405, Majuro, MH 96960; tel. (247) 3018; fax (247) 3017; e-mail tcmi@ntamar.net; Pres. GUY EDISON CLAY MAITLAND.

CIVIL AVIATION

In 1995 the Marshall Islands, Kiribati, Nauru and Tuvalu agreed to begin discussions on the establishment of a joint regional airline. In 1997 the Marshall Islands signed a bilateral agreement on international air transport with the Federated States of Micronesia. Continental Micronesia operates three flights a week from Honolulu and Guam; Air Marshall Islands provides a daily domestic service; and Aloha Airlines provides a weekly service from Honolulu to Kwajalein and to Majuro.

Air Marshall Islands (AMI): POB 1319, Majuro, MH 96960; tel. (625) 3731; fax (625) 3730; e-mail amihdq@ntamar.net; internet www.airmarshallislands.com; f. 1980; internal services for the Marshall Islands; international operations ceased in early 1999; also charter, air ambulance and maritime surveillance operations; agency for Aloha airlines; Chair. KUNIO LAMARI; CFO NEIL ESCHERRA.

Continental Micronesia: POB 156, Majuro; tel. (625) 3209; fax (625) 3730; international flights between Majuro, the Federated States of Micronesia, Guam and Honolulu; also internal services between Majuro and Kwajalein; based in Hagåtña, Guam; Man. LEO SION.

Tourism

Tourism, which has been hindered by the difficulty of gaining access to the islands and a lack of transport facilities, was expected to develop significantly from the late 1990s, owing to the establishment of major resort complexes on Majuro and on Mili Atoll, funded at an estimated cost of US $1,000m. by South Korean investors. There were 5,444 tourist arrivals in 2001. In that year some 37.5% of visitors came from the USA and 18.3% from Japan. The islands' attractions include excellent opportunities for diving, game-fishing and the exploration of sites and relics of Second World War battles. The Marshall Islands Visitor Authority has implemented a short-term tourism development programme focusing on special-interest tourism markets. In the longer term the Visitor Authority planned to promote the development of small-island resorts throughout the country.

Marshall Islands Visitor Authority: POB 5, Majuro, MH 96960; tel. (625) 6482/5581; fax (625) 6771; e-mail tourism@ntamar.net; internet www.visitmarshallislands.com; f. 1997; Chair. KIRT PINHO.

MAURITANIA
Introductory Survey

Location, Climate, Language, Religion, Flag, Capital

The Islamic Republic of Mauritania lies in north-west Africa, with the Atlantic Ocean to the west, Algeria and the disputed territory of Western Sahara (occupied by Morocco) to the north, Mali to the east and south, and Senegal to the south. The climate is hot and dry, particularly in the north, which is mainly desert. Average annual rainfall in the capital in the 1990s was 131 mm (5.1 ins). The 1991 Constitution designates Arabic (which is spoken by the Moorish majority) as the official language, and Arabic, Poular, Wolof and Solinke as the national languages. The black population in the south is largely French-speaking, and French is widely used in commercial and business circles. Islam is the state religion, and the inhabitants are almost all Muslims. The national flag (proportions 2 by 3) comprises a green field, bearing, on the vertical median, a yellow five-pointed star between the upward-pointing horns of a yellow crescent. The capital is Nouakchott.

Recent History

Mauritania, formerly part of French West Africa, achieved full independence on 28 November 1960 (having become a self-governing member of the French Community two years earlier). Moktar Ould Daddah, leader of the Mauritanian Assembly Party (MAP) and Prime Minister since June 1959, became Head of State at independence, and was elected President in August 1961. All parties subsequently merged with the MAP to form the Mauritanian People's Party (MPP), with Ould Daddah as Secretary-General, and Mauritania became a one-party state in 1964. In 1973 Mauritania joined the League of Arab States (see p. 278), and withdrew from the Franc Zone in the following year, as part of a general trend towards the establishment of closer relations with Arab nations.

Under a tripartite agreement of November 1975, Spain ceded Spanish (now Western) Sahara to Mauritania and Morocco, to be apportioned between them. The agreement took effect in February 1976, when Mauritania occupied the southern portion of the territory. Fighting ensued between Moroccan and Mauritanian troops and the guerrilla forces of the Frente Popular para la Liberación de Saguia el-Hamra y Río de Oro (the Polisario Front), which sought independence for Western Sahara. Attacks within Mauritania by Polisario forces proved highly damaging to the economy. Diplomatic links with Algeria, which supported Polisario bases within its borders, were severed in March 1976. Meanwhile, relations with Morocco improved, following that country's renunciation of territorial claims that included Mauritania, and in mid-1977 a joint defence pact was formed.

By 1977 Mauritania was spending two-thirds of its budget on defending territory that promised no economic benefits. The disruption of iron-ore exports, combined with the effects of drought, had brought the country almost to bankruptcy. In July 1978 Ould Daddah was deposed in a bloodless coup, led by the armed forces Chief of Staff, Lt-Col (later Col) Moustapha Ould Mohamed Salek, who took power as Chairman of a Military Committee for National Recovery (MCNR). Polisario immediately declared a cease-fire with Mauritania, but the continuing presence of several thousand Moroccan troops in Mauritania impeded a full settlement. Amid continuing political instability, in April 1979 the MCNR was replaced by a Military Committee for National Salvation (MCNS). Salek continued to head the MCNS, but relinquished the post of Prime Minister to Lt-Col Ahmed Ould Bouceif. The MCNS adopted a new charter, assuming legislative power for itself and separating the roles of Head of State and Head of Government. Ould Bouceif died in an air crash in May, and the MCNS appointed Lt-Col Mohamed Khouna Ould Haidalla in his place. Salek resigned in June, and was replaced as titular Head of State by Lt-Col Mohamed Mahmoud Ould Ahmed Louly. In July Polisario announced a resumption of hostilities against Mauritania. Later that month the Organization of African Unity (OAU, now the African Union, see p. 137) recommended that a referendum be held to determine the future of the disputed region. These events provided the impetus for Mauritania's withdrawal from the war: Ould Haidalla renounced Mauritania's territorial claims in Western Sahara, and a peace treaty was signed with Polisario in August. Morocco announced its annexation of the entire territory, and diplomatic relations between Mauritania and Algeria were re-established.

Ould Haidalla succeeded Louly as Head of State in January 1980; he retained the posts of Prime Minister and Minister of Defence until December, when Sid'Ahmed Ould Bneijara was appointed premier in a largely civilian Council of Ministers. Although a draft Constitution, envisaging a multi-party system, was prepared, an attempted coup in March 1981 prompted Ould Haidalla to end civilian participation in the Government. The new Prime Minister, Lt-Col (later Col) Maawiya Ould Sid'Ahmed Taya (a prominent member of the MCNS and the army Chief of Staff) assumed the defence portfolio in April, and the draft Constitution was abandoned. Another coup plot was discovered in February 1982, resulting in the arrest and imprisonment of its leaders, Salek and Ould Bneijara.

In March 1984 widespread student unrest was denounced by the Government as a Libyan-backed 'destabilization plot'. Ould Haidalla again assumed the positions of Prime Minister and Minister of Defence, reappointing Col Taya as army Chief of Staff. On 12 December, while Ould Haidalla was temporarily absent from the country, Taya assumed the presidency in a bloodless coup and also took the defence portfolio in the new Government. An amnesty was proclaimed for all political prisoners and exiles, including Ould Daddah (then in exile in Tunisia), Salek and Ould Bneijara. Ould Haidalla was detained upon his return to Mauritania, but was released, with five of his associates, in December 1988.

Meanwhile, an escalation of ethnic tensions threatened internal stability. In late 1986 the conviction of 20 prominent black activists, on charges of 'undermining national unity', led to civil disturbances and to increased activity by organizations opposed to what they claimed to be the oppression of black Mauritanians by the light-skinned Moorish community. Following the discovery of a coup plot in October 1987, three military officers of the black Toucouleur ethnic group were sentenced to death, and 41 others were imprisoned. In January 1988 it was reported that more than 500 black personnel had been expelled from the armed forces, as a result of disturbances following the executions of the convicted officers.

In late 1990 many arrests followed the disclosure of an alleged coup plot, in which the Senegalese Government denied any involvement (see below). As part of clemency measures, announced from March 1991, the Government stated that almost all Mauritania's political prisoners had been freed, although other sources disputed this statement.

At a national referendum on 12 July 1991, a draft Constitution, which accorded extensive powers to the presidency and provided for the introduction of a multi-party political system, was supported by 97.9% of those who voted (85.3% of the registered electorate), according to official reports. Pending the installation of the organs of State provided for in the new document, Taya and the MCNS were to remain in power. Meanwhile, legislation permitting the registration of political parties was promulgated: among the first organizations to be accorded official status was the Democratic and Social Republican Party (DSRP), which was closely linked with Taya.

Taya was elected President on 17 January 1992, with 62.7% of the votes cast, defeating by three other candidates; his nearest rival was Ahmed Ould Daddah, with 32.8%. The rate of voter participation was 51.7%. The defeated candidates alleged electoral fraud and appealed unsuccessfully to the Supreme Court to declare the election invalid. Independent observers reported that they did not regard the poll as fraudulent. Unrest in the aftermath of the election resulted in at least two deaths and about 160 arrests.

Six opposition parties withdrew their candidates prior to legislative elections, which were held on 6 and 13 March 1992, protesting that certain electoral procedures were unduly favourable to the DSRP. Taya's party took 67 of the 79 seats in the National Assembly, and independent candidates won 10 of the remaining twelve seats; a low rate of participation by voters was reported. Following elections to the Senate, on 3 and 10 April, the new, 56-member upper house (which was elected by municipal leaders) included 36 DSRP members and 17 independents (one other party had, unsuccessfully, presented candidates for election); three seats were reserved for representatives of Mauritanians resident abroad. Taya was inaugurated as President on 18 April. He named the hitherto Minister of Finance, Sidi Mohamed Ould Boubacar, as Prime Minister, to lead a Government that included three black ministers, one opposition representative, and only one member of the military.

In May 1993 the National Assembly approved legislation pardoning all those convicted of offences perpetrated in connection with 'armed operations and acts of violence and terrorism' in the three years preceding Taya's inauguration as elected President. Opponents of the measure protested that it exonerated members of the armed forces for crimes committed during a period of severe repression of the black community.

The DSRP secured control of 172 of Mauritania's 208 administrative districts at Mauritania's first multi-party municipal elections, held in January and February 1994. Ahmed Ould Daddah's Union of Democratic Forces—New Era (UDF—NE) won control of 17 districts, the remainder being taken by independent candidates. Shortly before the first round of voting, a prominent human rights activist, Cheikh Sadibou Camara (who was also a member of an opposition party, the Union for Democracy and Progress—UDP), had been detained for several days, apparently in response to allegations that he had reported to a visiting delegation of international human rights organizations that children of Harratin (mainly dark-skinned Moors who had formerly been slaves) had been abducted and sold into slavery: Mauritanian law regards any reference to a return to slavery (which had been prohibited by law on several occasions, most recently in 1980) as injurious to national unity.

In September 1994 more than 90 alleged members of illicit Islamist organizations were arrested, although in October an amnesty was granted to the detainees following the broadcast of 'confessions', in which several detainees, including prominent members of the UDF—NE, had admitted their membership of reputedly extremist groups. The Taya Government subsequently prohibited the delivery of political speeches in places of worship and outlawed several Islamist organizations.

Government changes in February 1995 included the appointment of new Ministers of Finance and of Defence. Internal tensions within the UDF—NE threatened to undermine the influence of the party, as dissident groups complained of excessive centralization around Ould Daddah's leadership; in March a movement that had previously belonged to the UDF—NE announced that it was to join the DSRP. In July several UDF—NE members were reported to have defected to the UDP. In mid-1995, none the less, six opposition parties (including the UDF—NE and the UDP) announced that they had agreed a series of joint demands regarding future elections, including the compilation of an accurate voters' register, the formulation of a new electoral code, and guarantees of judicial independence.

In October 1995 the Taya administration declared the Iraqi ambassador *persona non grata* and demanded his departure from Mauritania. The expulsion coincided with reports of a foiled coup in Mauritania, allegedly sponsored by the Iraqi Government, which, it was claimed, had funded 'secret organizations' to conduct espionage in Mauritania, and a series of arrests ensued; among those detained were two parliamentarians (one from the DSRP, the other from the UDP), the Secretary-General of the National Assembly and army officers. In December 52 defendants stood trial on charges of forming an illegal organization; all 52 were discharged on appeal in January 1996.

In January 1996 Taya appointed Cheikh el Avia Ould Mohamed Khouna (hitherto Minister of Fisheries and Marine Economy) as Prime Minister, and a new Council of Ministers was formed. At legislative elections held on 11 and 18 October, the DSRP won 71 of the 79 seats in the National Assembly. The Rally for Democracy and Unity (RDU), closely allied with the administration, also secured a seat. Action for Change (AC), which sought to represent the interests of Harratin, was the only opposition party to obtain representation in the Assembly; six independent candidates also secured election. The UDP, which had participated in the first round of the elections, withdrew from the second round in protest at what it alleged were unfair electoral procedures. Later in October the Prime Minister named a new Council of Ministers.

In January 1997 several opposition leaders, including Messaoud Ould Boulkheir, the AC Chairman, were arrested on charges of maintaining 'suspicious relations' with Libya. Although Ould Boulkheir and several others had been freed by February, five other opposition activists received prison sentences for conspiring to break the law; in April four of the five convicted were acquitted on appeal. In February five prominent opposition parties, including the AC and the UDF—NE, formed a coalition, the Forum of Opposition Parties (FOP), which subsequently announced that it would boycott the forthcoming presidential election.

At the presidential election, held on 12 December 1997, and contested by four candidates, Taya was returned to office with 90.9% of the valid votes cast; his nearest rival, Mohamed Lemine Ch'Bih Ould Cheikh Melainine (who had resigned from the DSRP in 1996), won 7.0% of the vote. Opposition parties alleged that there had been widespread electoral fraud and disputed the official rate of voter participation, of 73.8%. Taya subsequently appointed Mohamed Lemine Ould Guig, a university academic, as Prime Minister, and a new Council of Ministers, which included three women, was installed. In November 1998 Cheikh el Avia Ould Mohamed Khouna (who had previously held the post in 1996–97) was again appointed Prime Minister.

Meanwhile, in March 1998 internal divisions in the UDF—NE resulted in a split in the party into two rival factions, led by Ahmed Ould Daddah and Moustapha Ould Bedreddine. In December Ould Daddah and two other members of his faction were placed under house arrest after they demanded that a public inquiry be held into allegations that Mauritania had agreed to allow Israeli nuclear waste to be stored underground in its territory. They were acquitted in March 1999 of charges of threatening public order. In November the Government banned the pro-Iraqi Baathist National Vanguard Party (Taliaa), a constituent member of the FOP, following its criticism of the Mauritanian Government's decision to establish full diplomatic relations with Israel in the previous month. In April 2000 Ould Daddah was detained two days prior to a meeting of the UDF—NE, at which he was expected to address the acquisition of wealth by associates of President Taya. Ould Daddah was released after five days, although a ban on public gatherings implemented following his arrest remained in force. In June security forces used tear gas to disperse a meeting of at least 4,000 UDF—NE members in Nouadhibou. In August concerns regarding increasing press censorship were heightened by the Government's seizure of copies of four weekly news publications; according to an international press freedom group, Reporters sans frontières, seven publications had been subject to such seizures since the beginning of 2000, in accordance with press legislation that permitted the Government to suppress the distribution of any publication it regarded as likely to 'undermine the principles of Islam or the credibility of the State'. A government reshuffle took place in September.

From October 2000, following the onset of the second Palestinian *intifada* (uprising) in Israel and the Palestinian Autonomous Areas (q.v.), the Mauritanian Government experienced increasing pressure from opposition groups, including the UDF—NE, to break off diplomatic relations with Israel. In October several pro-Palestinian demonstrations in Nouakchott and Nouadhibou led to violent anti-Israeli protests. Arrests of members of clandestine Islamist groups and of UDF—NE activists were reported. In late October the Council of Ministers officially dissolved the UDF—NE, on the grounds that the party had incited violence and sought to damage Mauritanian national interests. Several members of the party's executive committee were detained in November. A demonstration in Nouadhibou by supporters of the UDF—NE reportedly attracted 15,000 protesters (the party was believed to have around 100,000 members). Ould Daddah refused to recognize the dissolution of the party, and the UDF—NE's partners in the FOP condemned the Government's action as unconstitutional. Six detained officials of the party began a hunger strike, although four of these were released by the end of November. Meanwhile, the faction of the UDF—NE led by Moustapha Ould Bedreddine, which remained authorized, restyled itself as the Union of Progressive Forces (UPF).

In December 2000 President Taya announced that an element of proportional representation would be introduced in subsequent elections to the National Assembly, and that the State would seek to facilitate funding and equal access to the media for all parties, although independent candidacies were to be prohibited. The National Assembly approved these measures in January 2001, although the radical opposition, including the FOP, continued to demand the establishment of an independent electoral commission and the reregistration of the banned Taliaa and the UDF—NE. Also in January, a government reshuffle included the appointment of a new Minister of Foreign Affairs and Co-operation, Dah Ould Abdi. In April it was announced that six new political groupings had been officially recognized, including a breakaway group from the AC, the Alliance for Justice and Democracy. A further minor government reshuffle was effected in mid-May. Meanwhile, in early April Mohamed Lemine Ch'Bih Ould Cheikh Melainine, now the leader of the Popular Front (PF—a constituent party of the FOP), was arrested on charges of conspiring with Libya to commit acts of sabotage and terrorism. Human rights groups criticized the conduct of his trial, including its relocation from Nouakchott to the remote town of Aïoun and the refusal to grant visas to prominent legal observers from overseas. In mid-June Melainine was sentenced to five years' imprisonment; in protest at this decision, the Mauritanian Renewal Party, one of the new parties officially registered in April, announced its withdrawal from the governing coalition.

Some 15 political parties contested legislative and municipal elections held on 19 and 26 October 2001, at which an electoral turn-out of some 55% was reported. The DSRP won 64 of the 81 seats in the enlarged National Assembly, and the RDU and the UDP, which were now both allied with the ruling party, each secured three seats. The AC was the most successful of the opposition parties, winning four seats, while the UPF and the newly formed Rally of Democratic Forces (RDF), which replaced the banned UDF—NE, also each took three seats, and the PF secured the remaining seat. The DSRP secured control of more than four-fifths of Mauritania's districts at the concurrent municipal elections, although opposition parties secured control of six of the capital's nine districts. In November President Taya reappointed Cheikh el Avia Ould Mohamed Khouna as Prime Minister, and the Council of Ministers was reshuffled; 14 ministers from the previous administration were retained.

In January 2002 Ould Daddah was elected President of the RDF; four former vice-presidents of the UDF—NE were also appointed to the 12-member executive committee of the RDF. In that month the Government officially dissolved the AC. The Minister of Communication and Relations with Parliament, Cheyakh Ould Ely, accused the party of promoting racism and extremism, and of attempting to undermine national unity and good relations with Senegal. In February the Supreme Court rejected an appeal by the AC against its dissolution. At partial senatorial elections, held in April, the RDF won one seat, the first time that part of the radical opposition had secured representation in the Senate, in which the DSRP enjoyed a large majority. In August the Convention for Change (CC), an organization including many former members of the AC, and led by Ould Boulkheir, was denied the right to register as a political party; it was reported that a government spokesman had declared that the CC was simply a renamed form of the AC and, as such, a continued threat to national unity.

In October 2002 the UFP announced that it was to organize a series of meetings intended to promote a 'national dialogue' between the authorities and the opposition parties; the first such meeting was scheduled to occur at the end of October. However, later that month seven other opposition parties, including the CC (which remained banned), the PF and the RDF, formed a new grouping, the United Opposition Framework (UOF), which also stated as its purpose the co-ordination of dialogue between the opposition and the Government pertaining to democratic reform; the UFP was, notably, excluded from the UOF, reportedly at the initiative of the RFD. Consequently, the initial meeting proposed by the UFP was postponed indefinitely, and, expressing discontent at the situation, in mid-November the UFP announced its withdrawal from the National Assembly. As a result of the withdrawal of the three UFP deputies from the Assembly, the group of opposition deputies was dissolved, as it was now reduced to eight members, less than the 10 required for the formation of a parliamentary group. None the less, the UFP emphasized that it remained prepared to participate in any dialogue on democratic reform together with other opposition groups. On 27 October a government reorganization was effected. Notably, Dah Ould Abdi was replaced as Minister of Foreign Affairs and Co-operation by Mohamed Ould Tobar; new Ministers of Rural Development and the Environment and of Health were also appointed.

In March 2003 US-led military action in Iraq, aimed at ousting the regime of Saddam Hussain, prompted protests in Mauritania, with widespread demonstrations held to demand that the Government break off diplomatic relations with Israel and with the two principal nations involved in the conflict, the United Kingdom and the USA. As opposition to the Government's broadly pro-US stance intensified in early May, police raided the headquarters of a tolerated—although not officially authorized—Baathist party, the National Renaissance Party (NRP—Nouhoudh). Three leaders of the NRP, including its Secretary-General, Mohamed Ould Abdellahi Ould Eyye, were arrested on unspecified charges; 13 other Baathists were also arrested over a period of four days, including the Secretary-General of the former Taliaa party. (Ten of those arrested were later charged with attempting to re-establish Taliaa.) The Government's increasing intolerance of radical opposition movements targeted not only secularist Arab nationalist groupings, but also Islamist activists: a senior member of the RDF, Mohamed Jemil Ould Mansour, who was also the leader of a committee opposed to the normalization of relations between Mauritania and Israel, was one of several prominent Islamists and religious leaders arrested. The Government also stated that it would close any mosques that were being used for political purposes or that incited hatred against Jews.

Meanwhile, in late March 2003 the registration of a new party, the Alliance for Democracy in Mauritania (ADEMA), was refused by the authorities, which stated that the party represented an attempt to re-establish the banned AC. However, while the leader of ADEMA, Zein El Abidine Sy, had been a member of the executive committee of the AC, the new party denied any association with the former group.

In early May 2003 Taya effected a minor government reorganization, dismissing Cheyakh Ould Ely, the Minister of Communication and Relations with Parliament, who, although a member of the DSRP, was considered a pan-Arab nationalist. The appointment of Abdellahi Ould Souleimane Ould Cheikh Sidya, reportedly a close relation of Ahmed Ould Daddah, as Minister of Economic and Development Affairs was apparently aimed at attracting supporters of the RDF to the Government, while the appointment of Lembrabott Ould Mohamed Lemine as Minister of Culture and Islamic Affairs was regarded as an attempt to reduce tensions between the Government and Islamic communities. However, at the end of May the publication of a pro-Islamist weekly journal, *Ar-Rayah*, was suspended, and nine Baathists were convicted by a Nouakchott court of engaging in illegal political activity. In early June four Islamic cultural associations were closed down, and, according to opposition reports, more than 100 alleged Islamists were detained, 36 of whom (including Ould Mansour) were charged with plotting against the constitutional order.

The tensions that had been escalating throughout the first half of 2003 culminated in an attempted *coup d'état*, which commenced on 8 June. Exchanges of fire were reported near the presidential palace and at other strategic locations in Nouakchott. According to official reports, 15 people (including six civilians) died in ensuing clashes between the insurgents and the security forces, with a further 68 people injured; the most senior figure to be killed was the Chief of Staff of the Armed Forces, Col Mohamed Lamine Ould Ndiayane. Government forces regained control of the city on 9 June. Although the exact identity and motives of the rebels were unclear, reports named the leaders of the coup as Saleh Ould Hnana, a former colonel and Baathist sympathizer, who had been expelled from the Mauritanian armed forces in 2002, and Mohammed Ould Sheikhna, a squadron leader in the national air force; Taya subsequently stated, however, that Islamists had been responsible for the rebellion. (Other sources claimed that the attempted coup had been prompted by tribal rivalries.)

In the days following the restoration of order at least 12 alleged rebel leaders were arrested, including Ould Sheikhna, although the whereabouts of Ould Hnana remained unknown. Meanwhile, more than 30 detained Islamists, who had been freed during the disorder, were reported to have surrendered themselves to the authorities, although Ould Mansour fled to Senegal before later being granted political asylum in Belgium. In mid-June 2003 several senior officials, including the Chief of Staff of the National Gendarmerie, the President of the High Court of Justice and the Mayor of Nouakchott, were replaced by new appointees regarded as loyal to the President. In July another suspected coup leader, Lt Didi Ould M'Hamed, who had fled to Senegal, was extradited to Mauritania; it was subsequently announced that he would face a civil trial.

In early July 2003 Taya appointed a new Prime Minister: Sghaïr Ould M'Barek, a Harratin, was regarded as a close ally of the President. A new Government was subsequently formed. Although several of the high-ranking officials who had been arrested in mid-June had been released from custody by mid-July, it was reported that the former Prime Minister, Cheikh el Avia Ould Mohamed Khouna, had been detained after having sought political asylum in Spain. Further arrests of Islamists were reported throughout the month. In early August more than 80 members of the military who had been arrested following the attempted coup were released, although many more remained in detention. In mid-August Ould Mansour (who remained in exile in Belgium) announced the formation of a new opposition movement, the Mauritanian Forum for Reform and Democracy. At the end of the month Ould Cheikh Melainine was freed, having been granted a presidential pardon. Some 41 Islamists had also been released from detention by the end of the month, although others continued to face charges. In early September it was announced that some 30 members of the military, including 20 senior officers, were to be tried in connection with the coup attempt.

In mid-October 2003 the Constitutional Council announced that six candidates, including Taya, Ahmed Ould Daddah, Ould Boulkheir and former President Ould Haidalla, were to be permitted to contest the forthcoming presidential election, which was scheduled for 7 November. Ould Haidalla was widely regarded as the most credible challenger to Taya; the former President's campaign attracted the support of several prominent Islamists and secular Arab nationalists, as well as a number of proponents of liberal reform. On 3 November Ould Haidalla's home was raided by police, apparently in response to reports that illicit weapons were being stored at the property. On 5 November police used tear gas to disperse a demonstration in Nouakchott organized by supporters of Ould Haidalla, Ahmed Ould Daddah and Ould Boulkheir in protest at the raid. On 6 November Ould Haidalla and four of his close associates were detained; the State Prosecutor announced that all five were to be charged with planning a *coup d'état* and endangering national security, although they were released without charge later that day. Voting in the presidential election proceeded on 7 November, in largely calm conditions. According to official results, Taya won 66.7% of the votes cast, followed by Ould Haidalla, with 18.7%, Ahmed Ould Daddah, with 6.9%, and Ould Boulkheir, with 5.0%. Some 60.8% of the electorate participated in the election. Opposition candidates accused the Government of perpetrating fraud at the election, which international observers had not been permitted to monitor. On 13 November Taya announced the formation of a new Government, which included eight new appointees, among them Mohamed Vall Ould Bellal as Minister of Foreign Affairs and Co-operation, although most of the other principal posts remained unchanged.

In mid-November 2003 the trial of Ould Haidalla (who had again been arrested on 9 November) and 14 of his supporters, on charges of seeking to obtain power by force and by threatening the strategic interests of Mauritania, commenced in Nouakchott; one of Ould Haidalla's sons was additionally accused of having accepted US $1m. from Libya as an inducement to destabilize Mauritania. (In late December the Government claimed that the Libyan authorities had provided significant financial support for Ould Haidalla's election campaign.) The trial concluded at the end of December, when Ould Haidalla and four of his co-defendants, including his son, were convicted of plotting to overthrow the Head of State; they received five-year suspended sentences, during which time they were forbidden to engage in political activity, and were fined the equivalent of $1,600 each. Four others received lesser sentences and fines.

In mid-January 2004 the Constitutional Council rejected an appeal by Ould Haidalla that the results of the presidential election be annulled. Also in January Ould Mansour was arrested following his return to Mauritania, although he was released, subject to certain conditions, later in the month. In mid-February Ould Haidalla announced that he intended to form a new political party. The DSRP won 15 of the 18 seats contested at partial elections to the Senate, held on 9 and 16 April, while its ally, the RDU, secured its first senatorial representation. The opposition Popular Progressive Alliance also obtained legislative representation for the first time, winning two seats.

A long-standing border dispute with Senegal was exacerbated by the deaths, in April 1989, of two Senegalese farmers, who had been involved in a dispute regarding grazing rights with Mauritanian livestock-breeders. The ensuing crisis served to illustrate the persistence of mutual ethnic and economic rivalries. Mauritanian nationals resident in Senegal were attacked, and their businesses (primarily those of the retail trade) looted, while Senegalese nationals in Mauritania and black Mauritanians suffered similar aggression. By early May it was believed that several hundred people, mostly Senegalese, had been killed. Operations to repatriate nationals of both countries commenced, with international assistance. Amid allegations that the Mauritanian authorities had begun to instigate expulsions of the indigenous black population to Senegal or to Mali, a prominent human rights organization, Amnesty International, expressed concern at the reported violation of black Mauritanians' rights. Mauritania and Senegal suspended diplomatic relations in August 1989, and sporadic outbreaks of violence were reported later that year. OAU mediation efforts in early 1990 were thwarted by military skirmishes in the border region, resulting in several deaths. In late 1990 the Senegalese Government denied accusations made by the Mauritanian authorities that it was implicated in an alleged attempt to overthrow Taya. In December the arrests of large numbers of black Mauritanians were reported. In early 1991 Mauritanian naval vessels were reported to have opened fire on Senegalese fishing boats, apparently in Senegal's territorial waters; in March several deaths were reported to have resulted from a military engagement on Senegalese territory, following an incursion by Senegalese troops into Mauritania.

Following renewed diplomatic activity, diplomatic relations with Senegal were resumed in April 1992, and the process of reopening the border began in May. However, Mauritanian refugees in Senegal insisted that, as long as the Taya Government refused to recognize their national identity (*mauritanité*) and land and property rights, they would not return to Mauritania. In September 1993 the Mauritanian authorities announced that Senegalese nationals would henceforth be required to fulfil certain criteria, including currency-exchange requirements, before being allowed to remain in (or to enter) Mauritania. In January 1996 several hundred Mauritanian refugees staged demonstrations in northern Senegal, protesting at the Mauritanian Government's proposed repatriation programme, and insisting that their earlier demands be met and that the repatriation process be organized by the office of the UN High Commissioner for Refugees in co-operation with the two Governments. By late 2000 the number of Mauritanian refugees in Senegal had declined to 19,800 (compared with 65,500 in mid-1995). (At the end of 2002, however, 19,777 Mauritanian refugees still remained in Senegal.) Meanwhile, in early June 2000 relations between Mauritania and Senegal deteriorated after Mauritania accused the new Senegalese administration of relaunching an irrigation project, which involved the use of joint waters from the Senegal river, in contravention of the Organisation pour la mise en valeur du fleuve Sénégal project (see p. 361). The dispute escalated when the Mauritanian authorities requested that all of its citizens living in Senegal return home and issued the estimated 100,000 Senegalese nationals living in Mauritania with a 15-day deadline by which to leave the country. In mid-June, following mediation by King Muhammad VI of Morocco and the Presidents of The Gambia and Mali, the Mauritanian Minister of the Interior announced that the decision to expel Senegalese citizens had been withdrawn and that Mauritanians living in Senegal could remain there. President Wade of Senegal visited Mauritania later that month and announced that the irrigation project had been abandoned. In April 2001 President Taya's presence as guest of honour at a ceremony in Dakar to commemorate the 41st anniversary of the independence of Senegal demonstrated an improvement in relations between the countries. Presidents Taya and Wade met again in July 2003, when negotiations were conducted on a range of bilateral and international issues; Wade reiterated his support for Taya's administration, following the attempted coup in Nouakchott in the previous month. The extradition of one of the suspected coup plotters from Senegal to Mauritania was also regarded as evidence of a strengthening of relations.

Meanwhile, in April 1994 Mauritania, Mali and Senegal agreed to strengthen military co-operation in order to improve joint border security. In mid-1996, at the conclusion of a meeting in Nouakchott of their ministers responsible for the interior, the three countries established joint security measures on their common borders. In August 1999 representatives of the Malian, Senegalese and Mauritanian Governments signed an agreement, which provided for the establishment of a special operational unit drawn from the police forces of the three countries to combat border crime.

Diplomatic relations between Mauritania and Morocco were severed in 1981, following accusations, denied by both countries, of involvement in mutual destabilization attempts. In 1983 Mauritania sought to improve relations between the Maghreb countries (Algeria, Morocco, Mauritania, Tunisia and Libya) and was a signatory of the Maghreb Fraternity and Co-operation Treaty, drafted by Algeria and Tunisia. Relations with Morocco again deteriorated from February 1984, when Mauritania announced its recognition of the Sahrawi Arab Democratic Republic (the Western Saharan state proclaimed by Polisario in 1976), although Taya restored diplomatic relations with Morocco in April 1985. In February 1989 Mauritania was a founder member, with Algeria, Libya, Morocco and Tunisia, of the Union of the Arab Maghreb (UMA, see p. 362), although relations with Libya were reported to have deteriorated from the mid-1990s; Libya was a particularly vehement critic of Mauritania's decision to establish and maintain full diplomatic relations with Israel. Diplomatic relations with Libya, severed in 1995, were none the less restored in March 1997. In September 2001 King Muhammad VI of Morocco paid a three-day official visit to Mauritania, aimed at improving bilateral relations between the two countries. In March 2004 President Taya led an official delegation to Morocco, and again met with King Muhammad.

Mauritania's relations with France deteriorated abruptly in 1999, following the arrest by the French authorities in July of Ali Ould Dah, a captain in the Mauritanian army, who was attending a training course in France. Ould Dah was charged with the torture, in 1991, of fellow Mauritanian soldiers suspected of participating in the unsuccessful attempt to overthrow the Taya administration in 1990. The Mauritanian Government responded by suspending military co-operation with France and introducing visas for French nationals visiting Mauritania. In late September a court in Montpellier, France, ordered Ould Dah's release from custody, although he was required to remain in France until the end of legal proceedings. By April 2000, however, Ould Dah had illicitly returned to Mauritania. Relations with France appeared to improve following the election of a new, centre-right, Government there in 2002, and in September of that year the French Minister of Defence, Michèle Alliot-Marie, met Taya in Nouakchott, and affirmed that co-operation between the two countries was to be strengthened. The French Minister of Foreign Affairs, Dominique de Villepin, visited Mauritania in mid-June 2003, shortly after the attempted *coup d'état* had been suppressed, when he expressed renewed support for the Taya administration; it was announced that French military cooperation with Mauritania was to recommence later in the year.

In November 1995 Mauritania signed an agreement to recognize and establish relations with Israel. In October 1998 Mauritania's Minister of Foreign Affairs and Co-operation visited Israel, where he held talks with the Prime Minister, Binyamin Netanyahu. The Arab League strongly criticized the visit, claiming that it contravened the League's resolutions on the suspension of the normalization of relations with Israel, and threatened to impose sanctions on Mauritania. Widespread controversy was provoked both domestically, and in Arab countries, by the establishment of full diplomatic relations between Mauritania and Israel in October 1999. (Of Arab countries, only Egypt and Jordan had taken such a step, under the terms of their respective peace treaties with Israel.) Following the resumption of the Palestinian uprising in September 2000, the Mauritanian Government came under renewed pressure to suspend diplomatic relations with Israel. Notably, in protest against Mauritanian policy towards Israel, Iraq refused admittance to a Mauritanian aircraft that was to bring humanitarian aid to Iraq in November 2000, and in March 2001 Syria reduced its diplomatic representation in Nouakchott to the level of a chargé d'affaires, and closed its cultural centre in Mauritania. A visit by the Mauritanian Minister of Foreign Affairs and Co-operation, Dah Ould Abdi, to Israel in May 2001, when he met Israeli Prime Minister Ariel Sharon and President Moshe Katsav, and entered into negotiations with the Minister of Foreign Affairs, Shimon Peres, provoked further controversy, particularly as a result of an appeal by the Arab League, issued earlier that month, for all member countries to cease political contacts with Israel. A further meeting between Peres, Taya and Ould Abdi, in Nouakchott, in October 2002, provoked further controversy. Despite widespread public opposition to the US-led military campaign against Iraq, which intensified in March 2003, the authorities in Nouakchott refused to support the regime of Saddam Hussain. In July of that year the Mauritanian Government announced its support for the establishment of an Iraqi Governing Council, which had been appointed by the US-led Coalition Provisional Authority in that month.

Mauritania withdrew from the Economic Community of West African States (see p. 196), with effect from 31 December 2000, owing to decisions adopted by the organization at its summit in December 1999, including the integration of the armed forces of member states and the removal of internal border controls and tariffs.

Government

The Constitution that was approved in a national referendum on 12 July 1991 vests executive power in the President of the Republic (who is elected by universal adult suffrage for a period of six years). The bicameral legislature comprises an 81-member National Assembly (elected by universal suffrage for five years, with 20% of its membership being elected by a form of proportional representation, with effect from the elections held in October 2001) and a 56-member Senate (elected by municipal leaders with a six-year mandate—part of its membership being elected every two years). All elections are conducted in the context of a multi-party political system. The President of the Republic is empowered to appoint a Prime Minister, who is designated Head of Government.

For the purpose of local administration, Mauritania is divided into 13 wilaya (regions), comprising a total of 53 moughataa (counties), which are subdivided into 216 communes (districts).

Defence

In August 2003 the total armed forces were estimated to number 15,750 men: army 15,000, navy about 500, air force 250. Full-time membership of paramilitary forces totalled about 5,000. Military service is by authorized conscription, and lasts for two years. The defence budget for 2003 was estimated at UM 5,000m.

Economic Affairs

In 2002, according to estimates by the World Bank, Mauritania's gross national income (GNI), measured at average 2000–02 prices, was US $1,163m., equivalent to $410 per head (or $1,740 on an international purchasing-power parity basis). During 1990–2002, it was estimated, the population increased at an average annual rate of 3.0%, while gross domestic product (GDP) per head increased, in real terms, by an average of 1.2% per year. According to the World Bank, overall GDP increased, in real terms, at an average annual rate of 4.2% in 1990–2002; GDP increased by 4.6% in 2001 and by 5.1% in 2002. (According to IMF figures, GDP growth in 2001 and 2002 was 4.0% and 3.3%, respectively.)

Agriculture (including forestry and fishing) contributed 20.8% of GDP in 2002. In that year about 52.4% of the labour force were employed in the sector. Owing to the unsuitability of much of the land for crop cultivation, output of staple foods (millet, sorghum, rice and pulses) is insufficient for the country's needs. Livestock-rearing is the principal occupation of the rural population. Fishing, which in 2002 provided 43.4% of export earnings, supplies 5%–10% of annual GDP and up to 30% of budgetary revenue, and also makes a significant contribution to domestic food requirements. During 1990–2002, according to the World Bank, agricultural GDP increased by an average of 4.4% per year. Agricultural GDP declined by 0.2% in 2001, but increased by 2.0% in 2002.

Industry (including mining, manufacturing, construction and power) provided 29.4% of GDP in 2002. An estimated 11.6% of the labour force were employed in the industrial sector in 1994. During 1990–2002, according to the World Bank, industrial GDP increased at an average annual rate of 2.6%. Industrial GDP increased by 1.4% in 2001 and by 4.8% in 2002.

Mining contributed 12.2% of GDP in 2002. The principal activity in this sector is the extraction of iron ore, exports of which contributed 55.6% of total merchandise export earnings in 2002. Gypsum, salt, gold and copper are also mined. Other exploitable mineral resources include diamonds, phosphates, sulphur, peat, manganese and uranium. In October 1999 highly valuable blue granite deposits were discovered in the north of the country. Many international companies were involved in offshore petroleum exploration in Mauritania in the early 2000s, with reserves at the offshore Shafr el Khanjar and Chinguetti fields estimated at 450m.–1,000m. barrels; production was expected to commence in 2006. In September 2000 a five-year programme intended to accelerate the growth of the mining sector commenced, with a US $16.5m. loan from the World Bank. The GDP of the mining sector declined by an average of 4.3% per year in 1998–2002, according to the IMF. Mining GDP declined by 9.2% in 2001 and by 7.3% in 2002.

The manufacturing sector contributed 8.9% of GDP in 2002. Fish-processing (which contributed 3.9% of GDP in 2002) is the most important activity. The processing of minerals (including imported petroleum) is also of some significance. According to the World Bank, manufacturing GDP increased at an average annual rate of 1.6% in 1990–2002; it increased by 5.9% in 2001 and by 1.3% in 2002.

Mauritania began to utilize electricity generated at hydro-electric installations constructed under the austpices of theOr-ganisation pour la mise en valeur du fleuve Sénégal (OMVS) in late 2002, thus reducing the country's dependence on power generated at thermal stations. Imports of petroleum products comprised 8.8% of the value of merchandise imports in 2001.

The services sector contributed 49.9% of GDP in 2002, and engaged an estimated 25.8% of the labour force in 1994. According to the World Bank, the combined GDP of the services sector increased by an average rate of 5.1% per year during 1990–2002. Services GDP increased by 8.5% in 2001 and by 7.0% in 2002.

In 2002 Mauritania recorded a visible trade deficit of an estimated US $87.7m. and a deficit of an estimated $51.2m. on the current account of the balance of payments. In 2002 the principal source of imports (20.8%) was France; other major suppliers were the Belgo-Luxembourg Economic Union, Spain and Germany. The principal markets for exports in that year were Italy (14.8%), France (14.4%), Spain and the Belgo-Lux-embourg Economic Union. The principal exports in 2002 were iron ore and fish, crustaceans and molluscs. The principal imports in 2001 were capital goods, foodstuffs, vehicles and components, construction materials and petroleum products.

Mauritania's overall budget surplus for 2002 was UM 20,900m., equivalent to 7.8% of GDP. Mauritania's total external debt was US $2,164m. at the end of 2001, of which $1,865m. was long-term public debt. In that year the cost of debt-servicing was equivalent to 22.8% of the value of exports of goods and services. The annual rate of inflation averaged 5.7% in 1990–2002; consumer prices increased by an average of 4.7% in 2001 and by 3.9% in 2002. The overall rate of unemployment in 2000 was 28.9%.

Mauritania is a member of the Islamic Development Bank (see p. 275), of the OMVS (see p. 361) and of the Union of the Arab Maghreb (see p. 362).

Mauritania's economy is largely dependent on fishing and on the exploitation of iron ore, although the exploitation of petro-leum reserves, principally at offshore locations, was expected to contribute significantly to GDP growth from the mid-2000s. Economic adjustment programmes have been undertaken since the late 1980s, including agreements with the IMF and the World Bank, resulting in the liberalization and restructuring of the economy. In July 1999 the IMF approved a three-year loan worth US $56.5m. under its Enhanced Structural Adjustment Facility (ESAF) to support the Government's 1999–2002 eco-nomic programme. In February 2000 Mauritania became one of the first countries to receive assistance under the joint IMF/World Bank initiative for heavily indebted poor countries, which would amount to a reduction of Mauritania's debt by $622m.; in June 2002 Mauritania became the sixth country to reach 'completion point' under the initiative. In July 2003 a further arrangement, worth some $8.8m., was agreed with the

IMF for 2003–05, under the Poverty Reduction and Growth Facility (PRGF—the successor of the ESAF). From the late 1980s government revenue has been bolstered by the sale of fishing licences to foreign fleets. In 2001 the European Union (EU) renewed its fishing agreement with Mauritania. In return for increased financial aid (of some €430m. during 2001–06), EU vessels were granted improved fishing rights in Mauritania's waters. In the early 2000s the services sector was a major source of economic growth, in particular in the areas of trade, transport and telecommunications, while considerable potential exists for the expansion of activities related to tourism. Significant improvements to the communications infrastructure, under way and planned in the mid-2000s, were expected to facilitate con-tinued growth in the services sector; in particular, the con-struction of a new highway linking the two principal cities, Nouakchott and Nouadhibou, was expected to improve pros-pects for both tourism and external trade. Although a drought in late 2002, which resulted in a depleted cereals harvest and a lower than average fish catch, ensured that growth in that year, was lower than anticipated, economic indicators in the early 2000s were generally favourable. A substantial reorganization and simplification of the taxation system was implemented in 2003, and, following initial difficulties, the transfer to majority private ownership of the state electricity company was expected to be completed by mid-2004. Meanwhile, further economic progress remained largely dependent on the diversification of Mauritania's production base. GDP growth of 5.4% was pro-jected for 2003.

Education

Primary education, which is officially compulsory, begins at six years of age and lasts for six years. In 2000/01 total enrolment at primary schools included 64% of children in the relevant age-group (66% of boys; 62% of girls), according to UNESCO esti-mates. Secondary education begins at 12 years of age and lasts for six years, comprising two cycles of three years each. Total enrolment at public secondary schools in 2000/01 included only 14% of children in the appropriate age-group (16% of boys; 13% of girls), according to UNESCO estimates. In 1998/99 a total of 12,912 students were enrolled at Mauritania's four higher edu-cation institutions (including the Université de Nouakchott, which was opened in 1983). In 2001 a UN project was initiated to address sexual inequality in the Mauritanian education system, which was particularly evident at higher education institutions, where only 16.6% of students were female in 1998. Total expenditure on education in 1998 was UM 6,197.8m. (equivalent to 27.5% of total government expenditure). In 1999 total expenditure on education amounted to UM 6,557.6m.

Public Holidays

2004: 1 January (New Year's Day), 1 February* (Tabaski—Id al-Adha, Feast of the Sacrifice), 22 February* (Islamic New Year), 1 May (Labour Day), 2 May* (Mouloud, Birth of Muhammad), 25 May (African Liberation Day, anniversary of the OAU's founda-tion), 10 July (Armed Forces Day), 12 September* (Leilat al-Meiraj, Ascension of Muhammad), 14 November* (Korité—Id al-Fitr, end of Ramadan), 28 November (Independence Day).

2005: 1 January (New Year's Day), 21 January* (Tabaski—Id al-Adha, Feast of the Sacrifice), 10 February* (Islamic New Year), 21 April* (Mouloud, Birth of Muhammad), 1 May (Labour Day), 25 May (African Liberation Day, anniversary of the OAU's foundation), 10 July (Armed Forces Day), 2 September* (Leilat al-Meiraj, Ascension of Muhammad), 4 November* (Korité—Id al-Fitr, end of Ramadan), 28 November (Independence Day).

*These holidays are determined by the Islamic lunar calendar and may vary by one or two days from the dates given.

Weights and Measures

The metric system is in force.

Statistical Survey

Source (unless otherwise stated): Office National de la Statistique, BP 240, Nouakchott; tel. 525-28-80; fax 525-51-70; e-mail webmaster@ons.mr; internet www.ons.mr.

Area and Population

AREA, POPULATION AND DENSITY

Area (sq km)	1,030,700*
Population (census results)	
5–20 April 1988	1,864,236†
1–15 November 2000‡	
Males	1,241,712
Females.	1,266,447
Total	2,508,159
Population (UN estimates at mid-year)§	
2001	2,724,000
2002	2,807,000
Density (per sq km) at mid-2002	2.7

* 397,950 sq miles.

† Including an estimate of 224,095 for the nomad population.

‡ Figures include nomads, totalling 128,163 (males 66,007, females 62,156), enumerated during 10 March–20 April 2001.

§ Source: UN, *World Population Prospects: The 2002 Revision*.

ETHNIC GROUPS (percentage of total, 1995): Moor 81.5; Wolof 6.8; Toucouleur 5.3; Sarakholé 2.8; Peul 1.1; Others 2.5 (Source: La Francophonie).

REGIONS

(census of November 2000)

Region	Area ('000 sq km)	Population*	Chief town
Hodh Ech Chargui . .	183	281,600	Néma
Hodh el Gharbi . . .	53	212,156	Aïoun el Atrous
Assaba	37	242,265	Kiffa
Gorgol	14	242,711	Kaédi
Brakna	33	247,006	Aleg
Trarza	68	268,220	Rosso
Adrar	215	69,542	Atâr
Dakhlet-Nouadhibou .	22	79,516	Nouadhibou
Tagant	95	76,620	Tidjikja
Guidimagha	10	177,707	Sélibaby
Tiris Zemmour . . .	253	41,121	Zouïrât
Inchiri	47	11,500	Akjoujt
Nouakchott (district) .	1	558,195	Nouakchott
Total	**1,030**	**2,580,159**	

* Including nomad population, enumerated during 10 March–20 April 2001.

PRINCIPAL TOWNS

(population at census of 2000*)

Nouakchott (capital).	588,195	Kiffa	32,716
Nouadhibou . . .	72,337	Bougadoum . . .	29,045
Rosso	48,922	Atâr	24,021
Boghé	37,531	Boutilimit. . . .	22,257
Adel Bagrou . . .	36,007	Theiekane. . . .	22,041
Kaédi	34,227	Ghabou	21,700
Zouïrât	33,929	Mal	20,488

* With the exception of Nouakchott, figures refer to the population of communes (municipalities), and include nomads.

BIRTHS AND DEATHS

(UN estimates, annual averages)

	1985–90	1990–95	1995–2000
Birth rate (per 1,000)	42.6	42.4	42.6
Death rate (per 1,000)	16.8	16.2	15.5

Source: UN, *World Population Prospects: The 2002 Revision*.

Expectation of life (WHO estimates, years at birth): 52.1 (males 49.8; females 54.5) in 2002 (Source: WHO, *World Health Report*).

ECONOMICALLY ACTIVE POPULATION

(census of 2000, persons aged 10 years and over, including nomads)

	Males	Females	Total
Agriculture, hunting, forestry and fishing	219,771	94,535	314,306
Mining and quarrying	5,520	249	5,769
Manufacturing	18,301	11,855	30,156
Electricity, gas and water . . .	2,655	182	2,837
Construction	15,251	311	15,562
Trade, restaurants and hotels . .	83,733	24,799	108,532
Transport, storage and communications	17,225	691	17,916
Financing, insurance, real estate and business services	1,557	454	2,011
Community, social and personal services	72,137	26,583	98,720
Other and unspecified	33,350	22,608	55,958
Total	**469,500**	**182,267**	**651,767**

Health and Welfare

KEY INDICATORS

Total fertility rate (children per woman, 2002).	5.8
Under-5 mortality rate (per 1,000 live births, 2001) . . .	183
HIV/AIDS (% of persons aged 15–49, 1999).	0.52
Physicians (per 1,000 head, 1995)	0.14
Hospital beds (per 1,000 head, 1990)	0.67
Health expenditure (2001): US $ per head (PPP) . . .	45
Health expenditure (2001): % of GDP	3.6
Health expenditure (2001): public (% of total)	72.4
Access to water (% of persons, 2000).	37
Access to sanitation (% of persons, 2000)	33
Human Development Index (2001): ranking	154
Human Development Index (2001): value	0.454

For sources and definitions, see explanatory note on p. vi.

Agriculture

PRINCIPAL CROPS

('000 metric tons)

	2000	2001	2002
Rice (paddy)	76.2	67.2*	67.9*
Maize*	5.5	7.8	6.0
Millet*	7.3	3.1	0.4
Sorghum*	95.3	83.7	25.4
Roots and tubers†	6.1	6.3	6.5
Cow peas†	22	24	24
Other pulses†	16	16	16
Oilseeds†	5	5	5
Vegetables†	3.7	3.9	3.9
Dates†	15	15	22
Watermelons†	10	11	11

* Unofficial figures.

† FAO estimates.

Source: FAO.

LIVESTOCK
('000 head, year ending September)

	1999	2000	2001*
Cattle	1,433	1,476	1,500
Goats	4,784†	5,023†	5,100
Sheep	7,176†	7,535†	7,600
Asses*	157	157	158
Horses*	20	20	20
Camels	1,206	1,230†	1,230
Chickens*	4,100	4,100	4,100

* FAO estimates.
† Unofficial figure.

2002: Figures assumed to be unchanged from 2001 (FAO estimates).

Source: FAO.

LIVESTOCK PRODUCTS
('000 metric tons)

	1999	2000	2001
Beef and veal*	10.3	10.4	10.5
Mutton and lamb†	17.1	18.0	18.0
Goat meat†	11.4	12.0	12.0
Camel meat†	18.5	19.0	19.0
Chicken meat†	4.0	4.0	4.0
Camel milk†	21.3	21.5	21.5
Cows' milk†	112.0	113.8	115.5
Sheep's milk†	84.2	84.2	84.2
Goats' milk†	101.3	101.3	101.3
Cheese†	2.0	2.0	2.1
Hen eggs†	4.9	4.9	4.9
Cattle hides†	1.5	1.6	1.6
Sheepskins†	2.3	2.4	2.4
Goatskins†	1.4	1.4	1.4

* Unofficial figures.
† FAO estimates.

2002: Figures assumed to be unchanged from 2001 (FAO estimates).

Source: FAO.

Forestry

ROUNDWOOD REMOVALS
(FAO estimates, '000 cubic metres, excluding bark)

	2000	2001	2002
Sawlogs, veneer logs and logs for sleepers	1	1	1
Other industrial wood	5	5	5
Fuel wood	1,428	1,464	1,502
Total	1,434	1,470	1,508

Source: FAO.

Fishing

(FAO estimates, '000 metric tons, live weight)

	1999	2000	2001
Freshwater fishes	5.0	5.0	5.0
Sardinellas	4.0	4.0	4.0
Cuttlefishes and bobtail squids	4.1	4.3	4.7
Other squids	2.4	2.4	2.1
Octopuses	12.8	13.8	13.3
Total catch (incl. others)	76.0	80.8	83.6

Source: FAO, *Yearbook of Fishery Statistics*.

Mining

('000 metric tons)

	1999	2000	2001
Gypsum*	100	100	100
Iron ore: gross weight	10,401†	11,450†	10,300
Iron ore: metal content	7,475†	7,500	7,300
Salt*	5.5	5.5	5.5

* Estimated production.
† Reported production.

Source: US Geological Survey.

Industry

SELECTED PRODUCTS
('000 metric tons, unless otherwise indicated)

	1999	2000	2001
Frozen fish*	23.2	24.7	27.0
Salted, dried and smoked fish*	0.9	1.0	0.9
Electric energy (million kWh)	226.7	227.2.	251.5

* Data from FAO.

Source: partly UN, *Industrial Commodity Statistics Yearbook*.

Finance

CURRENCY AND EXCHANGE RATES

Monetary Units
  5 khoums = 1 ouguiya (UM).

Sterling, Dollar and Euro Equivalents (30 September 2003)
  £1 sterling = 440.16 ouguiyas;
  US $1 = 263.00 ouguiyas;
  €1 = 306.45 ouguiyas;
  1,000 ouguiyas = £2.272 = $3.802 = €3.263.

Average Exchange Rate (ouguiyas per US $)
  2001   255.629
  2002   271.739
  2003   263.030

BUDGET
('000 million ouguiyas)

Revenue*	2000	2001	2002
Budgetary revenue	57.9	51.8	101.1
Tax revenue	33.3	36.4	38.7
Taxes on income and profits	10.6	11.3	12.1
Taxes on goods and services	16.5	18.2	19.5
Value-added tax	7.8	9.3	10.4
Turnover taxes	4.8	4.3	4.3
Tax on petroleum products	2.1	2.6	2.6
Taxes on international trade	5.5	6.1	6.3
Other current revenue	23.0	13.0	62.5
Fishing royalties and penalties	16.4	5.3	51.8
Revenue from public enterprises	4.1	3.6	4.9
Capital revenue	1.6	2.4	2.3
Special accounts	0.1	0.0	0.0
Statistical discrepancy	—	—	-2.4
Total	58.0	51.8	101.1

Expenditure	2000	2001	2002
Current expenditure	39.4	42.6	52.4
Wages and salaries	11.0	12.2	13.0
Goods and services	13.0	14.3	21.6
Transfers and subsidies . .	3.9	4.4	4.6
Military expenditure . . .	4.2	4.4	4.9
Interest on public debt . . .	7.4	7.2	8.3
Capital expenditure and net lending	28.7	23.1	32.0
Fixed capital formation . .	16.9	20.5	29.0
Restructuring and net lending .	11.8	2.6	2.9
Total	68.1	65.6	84.4

* Excluding grants received ('000 million ouguiyas): 2.7 in 2000; 4.0 in 2001; 4.2 in 2002.

Source: IMF, *Islamic Republic of Mauritania: Statistical Appendix* (October 2003).

INTERNATIONAL RESERVES
(US $ million at 31 December)

	2000	2001	2002
Gold*	3.1	3.1	3.1
IMF special drawing rights . . .	0.4	0.2	0.2
Foreign exchange	279.5	284.3	396.0
Total	283.0	287.6	399.3

* Valued at market-related prices.

Source: IMF, *International Financial Statistics*.

MONEY SUPPLY
(million ouguiyas at 31 December)

	2000	2001	2002
Currency outside banks	6,402	6,688	6,282
Demand deposits at deposit money banks	17,749	21,033	22,628
Total money (incl. others) . .	24,151	27,721	28,910

Source: IMF, *International Financial Statistics*.

COST OF LIVING
(Consumer Price Index in Nouakchott; base: July 1985 = 100)

	2000	2001	2002
Food (incl. beverages) . . .	271.1	288.8	301.6
Clothing (incl. footwear) . . .	220.1	225.0	226.4
Rent	262.5	271.0	285.1
All items (incl. others) . . .	254.0	265.9	276.4

Source: IMF, *Islamic Republic of Mauritania: Statistical Appendix* (October 2003).

NATIONAL ACCOUNTS

Expenditure on the Gross Domestic Product
(million ouguiyas at current prices)

	2000	2001	2002
Government final consumption expenditure	38,696	38,408	49,674
Private final consumption expenditure*	151,605	178,611	206,890
Increase in stocks . . . . } Gross fixed capital formation . }	73,616	86,766	88,899
Total domestic expenditure .	263,917	303,785	345,463
Exports of goods and services .	90,945	96,967	103,684
Less Imports of goods and services	125,423	149,434	180,091
GDP in purchasers' values .	229,439	251,318	269,056
GDP at constant 1985 prices .	89,350	92,930	96,031

* Including public enterprises.

Source: IMF, *Islamic Republic of Mauritania: Statistical Appendix* (October 2003).

Gross Domestic Product by Economic Activity
(million ouguiyas at current prices)

	2000	2001	2002
Agriculture, hunting, forestry and fishing	45,536	47,188	50,436
Mining and quarrying	31,224	31,741	29,521
Manufacturing	19,018	21,121	21,491
Electricity, gas and water . . } Construction . . . . . . }	14,343	17,242	20,253
Trade, restaurants and hotels .	41,030	44,512	47,965
Transport and communications .	20,786	25,508	29,233
Public administration	23,371	26,378	29,465
Other services	12,150	13,175	14,340
GDP at factor cost	207,458	226,865	242,703
Indirect taxes, *less* subsidies . .	21,981	24,453	26,353
GDP in purchasers' values .	229,439	251,318	269,056

Source: IMF, *Islamic Republic of Mauritania: Statistical Appendix* (October 2003).

BALANCE OF PAYMENTS
(US $ million)

	2000	2001	2002*
Exports of goods f.o.b.	344.7	338.6	330.3
Imports of goods f.o.b.	−336.2	−372.3	−418.0
Trade balance	8.5	−33.7	−87.7
Services (net)	−133.3	−194.4	−59.0
Balance on goods and services .	−124.8	−228.1	−146.7
Private unrequited transfers (net) .	35.4	47.9	30.4
Official transfers	63.4	75.6	65.1
Current balance	−26.0	−104.5	−51.2
Direct investment	40.1	92.2	117.6
Official medium- and long-term loans	−28.0	−30.0	−31.9
Other capital and errors and omissions	6.7	−22.5	21.1
Overall balance	−7.2	−64.8	55.6

* Estimates.

Source: IMF, *Islamic Republic of Mauritania: Statistical Appendix* (October 2003).

External Trade

PRINCIPAL COMMODITIES
(million ouguiyas)

Imports c.i.f.	1999	2000	2001
Capital goods	13,100	n.a.	24,800
Petroleum products	8,700	6,500	8,400
Food products	23,100	15,100	12,200
Vehicles and components . .	7,300	n.a.	8,900
Construction materials . . .	2,800	n.a.	8,700
Total (incl. others)	64,000	74,500	95,500

Exports f.o.b.	1999	2000	2001
Iron ore	45,600	46,800	47,700
Fish, crustaceans and molluscs .	32,400	35,900	36,300
Total (incl. others)	78,200	85,600	88,900

2002 ($ US million): *Imports c.i.f.*: Petroleum products 107.6; Total imports (incl. others) 418.0. *Exports f.o.b.*: Iron ore 183.8, Fish, crustaceans and molluscs 143.5; Total exports (incl. others) 330.3 (Source: IMF, *Islamic Republic of Mauritania: Statistical Appendix* (October 2003)).

PRINCIPAL TRADING PARTNERS
(US $ million)*

Imports c.i.f.	2000	2001	2002
Belgium-Luxembourg	32.9	31.4	36.8
France	94.5	89.2	86.9
Germany	17.2	21.3	23.2
Italy	21.9	22.1	17.6
Japan	9.2	9.8	16.2
Netherlands	10.0	10.7	14.0
Spain	21.8	21.5	27.9
United Kingdom	8.5	7.2	14.0
USA	9.6	16.0	14.4
Total (incl. others)	336.2	372.3	418.0

Exports c.i.f.	2000	2001	2002
Belgium-Luxembourg	30.8	28.9	33.9
France	63.5	50.7	47.6
Germany	13.2	20.8	35.7
Italy	47.4	51.0	48.8
Japan	53.0	27.1	21.0
Portugal	7.6	7.0	7.8
Spain	38.1	42.2	39.9
United Kingdom	5.4	5.4	1.5
Total (incl. others)	344.7	338.6	330.3

* Data are compiled on the basis of reporting by Mauritania's trading partners. Data detailing imports and exports of trade with developing and emerging countries were not available.
Source: IMF, *Islamic Republic of Mauritania: Statistical Appendix* (October 2003).

Transport

RAILWAYS

1984: Passengers carried 19,353; Passenger-km 7m.; Freight carried 9.1m. metric tons; Freight ton-km 6,142m.

Freight ton-km (million): 6,365 in 1985; 6,411 in 1986; 6,473 in 1987; 6,535 in 1988; 6,610 in 1989; 6,690 in 1990; 6,720 in 1991; 6,810 in 1992; 6,890 in 1993 (figures for 1988–93 are estimates) (Source: UN Economic Commission for Africa, *African Statistical Yearbook*).

ROAD TRAFFIC
('000 motor vehicles in use)

	1996	1997	1998
Passenger cars	5.2	5.3	5.4
Commercial vehicles	6.0	6.3	6.6

Source: UN, *Statistical Yearbook*.

SHIPPING
Merchant Fleet
(registered at 31 December)

	2000	2001	2002
Number of vessels	144	141	142
Total displacement ('000 grt)	49.2	47.4	47.6

Source: Lloyd's Register-Fairplay, *World Fleet Statistics*.

International Sea-borne Freight Traffic
(Port of Nouadhibou, '000 metric tons)

	1996	1997	1998
Goods loaded	11,623	11,906	11,450
Goods unloaded	139	119	119

Source: Port Autonome de Nouadhibou.

CIVIL AVIATION
(traffic on scheduled services)*

	1997	1998	1999
Kilometres flown (million)	4	4	4
Passengers carried ('000)	245	250	187
Passenger-km (million)	324	340	290
Total ton-km (million)	46	46	41

* Including an apportionment of the traffic of Air Afrique.
Source: UN, *Statistical Yearbook*.

Tourism

Tourist arrivals (estimates, '000): 24 in 1999.

Receipts from tourism (US $ million): 20 in 1998; 28 in 1999 (Source: World Tourism Organization).

Communications Media

	1998	1999	2000
Television receivers ('000 in use)	231	247	n.a.
Telephones ('000 main lines in use)	15.0	16.5	19.0
Facsimile machines (number in use)	2,600	3,300	n.a.
Mobile cellular telephones ('000 subscribers)	n.a.	n.a.	7.1
Personal computers ('000 in use)*	15	20	25
Internet users ('000)*	1	3	5

2001: Personal computers ('000 in use) 27*; Internet users ('000) 7*.

* Estimate(s).

Daily newspapers (1996): Number 2; Estimated average circulation ('000 copies) 12.

Radio receivers ('000 in use, 1997): 570.

Sources: UNESCO, *Statistical Yearbook*; UN, *Statistical Yearbook*; International Telecommunication Union.

Education
(1998/99, unless otherwise indicated)

	Institutions	Teachers	Students Males	Students Females	Students Total
Pre-primary*	36	108	n.a.	n.a.	800
Primary	2,676	7,366	178,672	167,550	346,222
Secondary:†					
general	n.a.	2,185	35,192	24,837	60,029
technical and vocational	3‡		1,148	534	1,682
teacher training	2‡	43§	803§	327§	1,130§
Tertiary	4§	270§	n.a.	n.a.	12,912

* 1992/93 figures.
† Data refer to public education only.
‡ 1991/92 figure.
§ 1995/96 figure.

1999/2000: Primary: 355,822 students; Secondary: 63,735 students.

Adult literacy rate (UNESCO estimates): 40.7% (males 51.1%; females 30.7%) in 2001 (Source: UN Development Programme, *Human Development Report*).

Sources: mainly UNESCO Institute for Statistics and Ministry of National Education, Nouakchott.

Directory

While no longer an official language under the terms of the 1991 Constitution (see below), French is still widely used in Mauritania, especially in the commercial sector. Many organizations are therefore listed under their French names, by which they are generally known.

The Constitution

The Constitution of the Arab and African Islamic Republic of Mauritania was approved in a national referendum on 12 July 1991.

The Constitution provides for the establishment of a multi-party political system. The President of the Republic is elected, by universal adult suffrage (the minimum age for voters being 18 years), for a period of six years: no limitations regarding the renewal of the presidential mandate are stipulated. Legislative power is vested in a National Assembly (al Jamiya al-Wataniyah—elected by universal suffrage for a period of five years) and in a Senate (Majlis al-Shuyukh—elected by municipal leaders with a six-year mandate, part of its membership being elected every two years). The President of the Republic is empowered to appoint a Head of Government or Prime Minister. Provision is also made for the establishment of a Constitutional Council and a High Council of Islam (both of which were inaugurated in 1992), as well as an Economic and Social Council.

The Constitution states that the official language is Arabic, and that the national languages are Arabic, Pular, Wolof and Solinké.

The Government

HEAD OF STATE

President: Col Maawiya Ould Sid'Ahmed Taya (took office 12 December 1984; elected President 17 January 1992; re-elected 12 December 1997 and 7 November 2003).

COUNCIL OF MINISTERS
(April 2004)

Prime Minister: Sghaïr Ould M'Barek.

Minister of Foreign Affairs and Co-operation: Mohamed Vall Ould Bellal.

Minister of National Defence: Baba Ould Sidi.

Minister of Justice: Diabira Bakary.

Minister of the Interior, Posts and Telecommunications: Kaba Ould Aléwa.

Minister of Finance: Mahfoudh Ould Mohamed Ali.

Minister of Economic Affairs and Development: Abdellahi Ould Souleimane Ould Cheikh Sidya.

Minister of Culture, Youth and Sports: Hamoud Ould M'Hamed.

Minister of Fisheries and the Maritime Economy: Ba Mamadou M'Baré.

Minister of Trade, Crafts and Tourism: Mohamed Lemine Ould Khattry.

Minister of Mines and Industry: Zeidane Ould H'Meyda.

Minister of Rural Development and the Environment: Ahmedou Ould Ahmedou.

Minister of Equipment and Transport: Ba Bocar Soulé.

Minister of Water Resources and Energy: Cheikh Saadbouh Camara.

Minister of National Education: Elhacen Ould Mohamed.

Minister of the Civil Service and Labour: Salka Mint Bilal.

Minister of Health and Social Affairs: Isselmou Ould Abdel Kader.

Minister of the Struggle against Illiteracy and of Islamic Orientation and Basic Education: Mohamed Mahmoud Ould Boyé.

Minister of Communication and Relations with Parliament: Hammoud Ould Abdi.

Minister, Secretary-General of the Presidency: Diallo Abou Moussa.

Secretary of State to the Prime Minister, responsible for New Technologies: Fatimetou Mint Mohamed Saleck.

Secretary of State at the Ministry of Foreign Affairs and Co-operation, responsible for Maghreb Affairs: Abdel Kader Ould Mohamed.

Secretary of State at the Ministry of Health and Social Affairs, responsible for the Status of Women: Zeinebou Mint Mohamed.

Secretary-General of the Government: Diallo Abou Moussa.

MINISTRIES

Office of the President: Présidence de la République, BP 184, Nouakchott; tel. and fax 525-26-36; internet www.mauritania.mr.

Office of the Prime Minister: Nouakchott.

Ministry of the Civil Service and Labour: BP 193, Nouakchott; tel. and fax 525-84-10.

Ministry of Communication and Relations with Parliament: Nouakchott.

Ministry of Culture, Youth and Sports: BP 223, Nouakchott; tel. 525-11-30.

Ministry of Economic Affairs and Development: 303 Ilot C, BP 5150, Nouakchott; tel. 529-06-93; fax 529-06-01; e-mail cdhlcpi@opt .mr.

Ministry of Equipment and Transport: BP 237, Nouakchott; tel. 525-33-37.

Ministry of Finance: BP 181, Nouakchott; tel. 525-20-20.

Ministry of Fisheries and the Maritime Economy: BP 137, Nouakchott; tel. 525-24-76; fax 525-31-46.

Ministry of Foreign Affairs and Co-operation: BP 230, Nouakchott; tel. 525-26-82; fax 525-28-60.

Ministry of Health and Social Affairs: BP 177, Nouakchott; tel. 525-20-52; fax 525-22-68.

Ministry of the Interior, Posts and Telecommunications: BP 195, Nouakchott; tel. 525-36-61; fax 525-36-40; e-mail paddec@ mauritania.mr.

Ministry of Justice: BP 350, Nouakchott; tel. 525-10-83; fax 525-70-02.

Ministry of Mines and Industry: BP 199, Nouakchott; tel. 525-30-83; fax 525-69-37; e-mail mmi@mauritania.mr.

Ministry of National Defence: BP 184, Nouakchott; tel. 525-20-20.

Ministry of National Education: BP 387, Nouakchott; tel. 525-12-37; fax 525-12-22.

Ministry of Rural Development and the Environment: BP 366, Nouakchott; tel. 525-15-00; fax 525-74-75.

Ministry of the Struggle against Illiteracy and of Islamic Orientation and Basic Education: Nouakchott.

Ministry of Trade, Crafts and Tourism: BP 182, Nouakchott; tel. 525-35-72; fax 525-76-71.

Ministry of Water Resources and Energy: BP 4913, Nouakchott; tel. 525-71-44; fax 529-42-87; e-mail saadouebih@yahoo.fr.

Office of the Secretary-General of the Government: BP 184, Nouakchott.

President and Legislature

PRESIDENT

Presidential Election, 7 November 2003

	Votes	% of votes
Maawiya Ould Sid'Ahmed Taya	438,915	66.69
Mohamed Khouna Ould Haidalla	123,244	18.73
Ahmed Ould Daddah	45,314	6.89
Messaoud Ould Boulkheir	33,089	5.03
Moulay el-Hassen Ould Jiyed	9,768	1.48
Aicha Mint Jiddane	3,100	0.47
Total*	658,148	100.00

* Including 4,718 votes of abstention, equivalent to 0.72% of votes.

NATIONAL ASSEMBLY
(al Jamiya al-Wataniyah)

National Assembly (al Jamiya al-Wataniyah): ave de l'Indépendance, BP 185, Nouakchott; tel. 525-11-30; fax 525-70-78; internet www.mauritania.mr/assemble.

President: RACHID OULD SALEH.

General Election, 19 and 26 October 2001

	Seats
Democratic and Social Republican Party (DSRP) . .	64
Action for Change (AC)	4
Rally for Democracy and Unity (RDU)	3
Rally of Democratic Forces (RDF)	3
Union for Democracy and Progress (UDP)	3
Union of Progressive Forces (UPF)	3
Popular Front (PF)	1
Total	**81**

SENATE
(Majlis al-Shuyukh)

Senate (Majlis al-Shuyukh): ave de l'Indépendance, BP 5838, Nouakchott; tel. 525-68-77; fax 525-73-73.

President: BOUBOU FARBA DIENG.

The 54 members of the Senate are indirectly elected for a term of six years, with one-third of the seats renewable every two years. After the most recent election, held on 9 and 16 April 2004, the strength of the parties was as follows:

	Seats
Democratic and Social Republican Party (DSRP) . . .	45
Popular Progressive Alliance (PPA)	2
National Union for Democracy and Development (NUDD)	1
Rally of Democratic Forces (RDF)	1
Rally for Democracy and Unity (RDU)	1
Union for Democracy and Progress (UDP)	1
Unattached	3
Total	**54**

Advisory Councils

Constitutional Council: f. 1992; includes six mems, three nominated by the Head of State and three designated by the Presidents of the Senate and National Assembly; Pres. ABDOULLAH OULD ELY SALEM; Sec.-Gen. MOHAMED OULD M'REIZIG.

Economic and Social Council: Nouakchott.

Political Organizations

The organizations listed below were among the most significant officially registered parties in early 2004, unless otherwise stated.

Alliance for Democracy in Mauritania (ADEMA): Nouakchott; f. 2003; registration refused; Leader ZEIN EL ABIDINE SY.

Alliance for Youth and Democracy (AYD): Nouakchott; Leader CISSE AMADOU CHIEKHOU.

Democratic Alliance: Nouakchott; f. 2001; Leader MOHAMED OULD TALEB OTHMAN.

Democratic and Social Republican Party (DSRP): Nouakchott; tel. 525-58-55; e-mail prds@prds.mr; internet www.prds.mr; f. 1991; absorbed Movement of Independent Democrats in 1995; Pres. Col MAAWIYA OULD SID'AHMED TAYA; Sec.-Gen. Dr BOULLAHA OULD MEGUEYA; 451,333 mems (2000).

Mauritanian Labour Party: Nouakchott; f. 2001; Leader MOHAMED HAFID OULD DENNA.

Mauritanian Liberal Democrats: Nouakchott; f. 2001; Leader MUSTAPHA OULD LEMRABET.

Mauritanian Party for Renewal and Construction: Nouakchott; f. 2001; Leader MOULAY EL-HASSEN OULD JIYED.

National Renaissance Party (NRP—Nouhoudh) (El Nouhoudh El Watani): Nouakchott; f. 2001; Baathist; although not officially recognized, the party's existence was tolerated by authorities prior to May 2003, when several senior leaders of the party were arrested,

and its headquarters closed by police; Sec.-Gen MOHAMED OULD ABDELLAHI OULD EYYE.

National Union for Democracy and Development (NUDD): f. 1997; Leader TIDJANE KOITA.

Rally for Democracy and Unity (RDU): f. 1991; supports Govt of Pres. Taya; Chair. AHMED OULD SIDI BABA.

Third Generation: Nouakchott; f. 2001; Leader LEBAT OULD JEH.

Union for Democracy and Progress (UDP): Ilot V, no. 70, Tevragh Zeina, BP 816, Nouakchott; tel. 525-52-89; fax 525-29-95; e-mail www.udp.mr; f. 1993; Pres. NAHA HAMDI MOUKNASS; Sec.-Gen. AHMED AHMED BEDDA.

Union of Progressive Forces (UPF) (Ittihad Quwa al-Taqaddum): Nouakchott; e-mail ufpweb2@yahoo.fr; internet www.ufpweb.org; f. 2000, following the enforced dissolution of the fmr Union of Democratic Forces—New Era, which it had existed as a faction thereof since 1998; Pres. MOHAMED OULD MAOULOUD; Sec.-Gen. MOHAMED EL MOUSTAPHA OULD BEDREDDINE.

United Opposition Framework (UOF) (al-Itar al-Muwahhad li-al-Mu'aradah): f. 2002 to replace Forum of Opposition Parties; coalition of radical opposition parties; mems include:

> **Alliance for Justice and Democracy:** Nouakchott; f. 2000 as breakaway group from fmr Action for Change (which was subsequently prohibited); seeks to represent the interests of Harratins; Leader KABEH ABDOULAYE.

> **Convention for Change (CC):** Nouakchott; f. 2002 to replace the banned Action for Change, to represent the interests of Harratin (black Moors who had fmrly been slaves); refused registration by Govt in Aug. 2002; Chair. MESSAOUD OULD BOULKHEIR; Sec.-Gen. IBRAHIM ASSAR.

> **Popular Front (PF):** Nouakchott; f. 1998; social-liberal; Leader MOHAMED LEMINE CH'BIH OULD CHEIKH MELAININE.

> **Popular Progressive Alliance (PPA):** Nouakchott; f. 1991; Sec.-Gen. MOHAMED HASSAOUD OULD ISMAËL.

> **Rally of Democratic Forces (RDF):** f. 2001 by fmr mems of the officially dissolved Union of Democratic Forces—New Era (f. 1991); Sec.-Gen. AHMED OULD DADDAH.

Unauthorized, but influential, is the Islamic **Ummah Party** (the Constitution prohibits the operation of religious political organizations), founded in 1991 and led by Imam SIDI YAHYA, and the Baathist **National Vanguard Party (Taliaa)**, which was officially dissolved by the Government in 1999 and is led by AHMEDOU OULD BABANA. The clandestine **Mauritanian African Liberation Forces (MALF)** was founded in 1983 in Senegal to represent Afro-Mauritanians (internet flamnet.fr.fm; Pres. SAMBA THIAM). A further group based in exile is the **Arab-African Salvation Front Against Slavery, Racism and Tribalism—AASF** (e-mail faas@caramail.com; internet membres.lycos.fr/faas). In mid-2003 the **Mauritanian Forum for Reform and Democracy**, based in Brussels, Belgium, was formed by opponents of the Taya regime in exile; it stated as its principal aims the promotion of peaceful change in Mauritania and the reinforcement of Islamic principles (Pres. MOHAMED JEMIL MANSOUR, Sec.-Gen. ABOU BAKR BENELMARWANI).

Diplomatic Representation

EMBASSIES IN MAURITANIA

Algeria: Tevragh Zeina, BP 625, Nouakchott; tel. 525-35-69; fax 525-47-77; Ambassador ABDELKRIM BEN HOCINE.

China, People's Republic: Tevragh Zeina, BP 257, Nouakchott; tel. 525-20-70; fax 525-24-62; e-mail www.ambchine@opt.mr; Ambassador LI GUOXUE.

Congo, Democratic Republic: Tevragh Zeina, BP 5714, Nouakchott; tel. 525-46-12; fax 525-50-53; e-mail ambardc.rim@caramail .com; Chargé d'affaires a.i. TSHIBASU MFUAD.

Egypt: Villa no. 167, Tevragh Zeina, BP 176, Nouakchott; tel. 525-21-92; fax 525-33-84; Ambassador AHMED NABAWI.

France: rue Ahmed Ould M'Hamed, BP 231, Nouakchott; tel. 525-17-40; fax 525-69-38; e-mail ambafrance.nouakchott-amba@ diplomatie.gouv.fr; internet www.france-mauritanie.mr; Ambassador PATRICK NICOLOSO.

Germany: Tevragh Zeina, BP 372, Nouakchott; tel. 525-17-29; fax 525-17-22; e-mail amb-allemagne@toptechnology.mr; Ambassador Dr BERND MORAST.

Israel: Ilot A516, Tevragh Zeina, BP 5714, Nouakchott; tel. 525-82-35; fax 525-46-12; e-mail info@nouakchott.mfa.gov.il; Ambassador BOAZ BISMUTH (designate).

Kuwait: Tevragh Zeina, BP 345, Nouakchott; tel. 525-33-05; fax 525-41-45.

Libya: BP 673, Nouakchott; tel. 525-52-02; fax 525-50-53.

Mali: Tevragh Zeina, BP 5371, Nouakchott; tel. 525-40-81; fax 525-40-83; e-mail ambmali@hotmail.com; Ambassador MOUSSA KALILOU COULIBALY.

Morocco: 569 ave de Gaulle, Tevragh Zeina, BP 621, Nouakchott; tel. 525-14-11; fax 529-72-80; e-mail sifmanktt@mauritel.mr; Ambassador ABDERRAHMANE BENOMAR.

Nigeria: Ilot P9, BP 367, Nouakchott; tel. 525-23-04; fax 525-23-14; Ambassador Alhaji BALA MOHAMED SANI.

Qatar: BP 609, Nouakchott; tel. 525-23-99; fax 525-68-87; e-mail nouakchoti@mofa.gov.qa; Ambassador MOHAMMED MOUBARAK AL-MO-HANNADI.

Russia: BP 221, Nouakchott; tel. 525-19-73; fax 525-52-96; e-mail ambruss@opt.mr; Ambassador LEONID V. ROGOV.

Saudi Arabia: Las Balmas, Zinat, BP 498, Nouakchott; tel. 525-26-33; fax 525-29-49; e-mail mremb@mofa.gov.sa; Ambassador MOHAMED AL FADH EL ISSA.

Senegal: BP 2511, Nouakchott; tel. 525-72-90; fax 525-72-91.

Spain: BP 232, Nouakchott; tel. 525-20-80; fax 525-40-88; e-mail ambespmr@correo.mae.es; Ambassador ENRIQUE RUIZ MOLERO.

Syria: Tevragh Zeina, BP 288, Nouakchott; tel. 525-27-54; fax 525-45-00.

Tunisia: BP 681, Nouakchott; tel. 525-28-71; fax 525-18-27; Ambassador ABDEL WEHAB JEMAL.

United Arab Emirates: BP 6824, Nouakchott; tel. 525-10-98; fax 525-09-92.

USA: rue Abdallaye, BP 222, Nouakchott; tel. 525-26-60; fax 525-15-92; e-mail aemnouak@opt.mr; Ambassador JOHN W. LIMBERT.

Yemen: Tevragh Zeina, BP 4689, Nouakchott; tel. 525-55-91; fax 525-56-39.

Judicial System

The Code of Law was promulgated in 1961 and subsequently modified to incorporate Islamic institutions and practices. The main courts comprise three courts of appeal, 10 regional tribunals, two labour tribunals and 53 departmental civil courts. A revenue court has jurisdiction in financial matters. The members of the High Court of Justice are elected by the National Assembly and the Senate.

Shari'a (Islamic) law was introduced in February 1980. A special Islamic court was established in March of that year, presided over by a magistrate of Islamic law, assisted by two counsellors and two *ulemas* (Muslim jurists and interpreters of the Koran). A five-member High Council of Islam, appointed by the President, advises upon the conformity of national legislation to religious precepts, at the request of the President.

Audit Court (Cour des Comptes): Nouakchott; audits all govt institutions; Pres. SOW ADAMA SAMBA.

High Council of Islam (al-Majlis al-Islamiya al-A'la'): Nouakchott; f. 1992; Pres. AHMED OULD NEINI.

High Court of Justice: Nouakchott; f. 1961; comprises an equal number of appointees elected from their membership by the National Assembly and the Senate, following each partial or general renewal of those legislative bodies; competent to try the President of the Republic in case of high treason, and the Prime Minister and members of the Government in case of conspiracy against the state.

Supreme Court: BP 201, Palais de Justice, Nouakchott; tel. 525-21-63; f. 1961; comprises an administrative chamber, a civil and commercial chamber, a social and employment chamber and a criminal chamber; also functions as the highest court of appeal; Pres. MOHAMED KABR OULD KHATTRI.

Religion

ISLAM

Islam is the official religion, and the population are almost entirely Muslims of the Malekite rite. The major religious groups are the Tijaniya and the Qadiriya. Chinguetti, in the region of Adrar, is the seventh Holy Place in Islam. A High Council of Islam (see above, Judicial System) supervises the conformity of legislation to Muslim orthodoxy.

CHRISTIANITY

Roman Catholic Church

Mauritania comprises the single diocese of Nouakchott, directly responsible to the Holy See. The Bishop participates in the Bishops' Conference of Senegal, Mauritania, Cape Verde and Guinea-Bissau, based in Dakar, Senegal. At 31 December 2002 there were an estimated 4,500 adherents, mainly non-nationals, in the country.

Bishop of Nouakchott: Most Rev. MARTIN ALBERT HAPPE, Evêché, BP 5377, Nouakchott; tel. 525-04-27; fax 525-37-51; e-mail diocesenouakchott@yahoo.com.

The Press

Of some 400 journals officially registered in Mauritania in mid-2000, less than 20 were regular, widely available publications. In mid-2003 the regularly circulating press included the following:

Al-Akhbar: BP 5346, Nouakchott; tel. 525-08-94; fax 525-37-57; f. 1995; weekly; Arabic.

Al-Qalam/Le Calame: BP 1059, Nouakchott; tel. 529-02-34; fax 525-75-55; e-mail calame@compunet.mr; internet www.calame.8k .com; f. 1994; weekly; Arabic and French; independent; Editors-in-Chief RIYAD OULD AHMED EL-HADI (Arabic edn), HINDOU MINT AININA (French edn).

Le Carrefour: Nouakchott; Dir MOUSSA OULD SAMBA SY.

Châab: BP 371, Nouakchott; tel. 525-29-40; fax 525-85-47; daily; Arabic; also publ. in French *Horizons*; publ. by Agence Mauritanienne de l'Information; Dir-Gen. MOHAMED EL-HAFED OULD MAHAM.

Challenge: BP 1346, Nouakchott; tel. and fax 529-06-26.

Ech-tary: BP 1059, Nouakchott; tel. 525-50-65; fortnightly; Arabic; satirical.

L'Essor: BP 5310, Nouakchott; tel. 529-19-83; fax 525-04-07; e-mail sidiel2000@yahoo.fr; monthly; economics; Dir SIDI EL-MOCTAR CHEÏGUER; circ. 2,500.

El-Anba: BP 3901, Nouakchott; tel. and fax 525-99-27.

L'Eveil-Hebdo: BP 587, Nouakchott; tel. 525-67-14; fax 525-87-54; e-mail eveil@caramail.com; f. 1991; weekly; independent; Publr MAMADOU SY.

Inimich al-Watan: Nouakchott; independent; Arabic; Dir of Publication MOHAMED OULD ELKORY.

Journal Officel: BP 188, Nouakchott; tel. 525-33-37; fax 525-34-74; fortnightly.

Maghreb Hebdo: BP 5266, Nouakchott; tel. 525-98-10; fax 525-98-11; f. 1994; weekly; Dir KHATTRI OULD DIÈ.

Nouakchott-Info: BP 1905, Nouakchott; tel. 525-02-71; fax 525-54-84; e-mail nouakinfo@toptechnology.mr; f. 1995; daily; independent; Arabic and French; Dir CHEIKHNA OULD NENNI; Editor ISSELMAI OULD MOUSTAPHA.

L'Opinion Libre: Nouakchott; weekly; Editor ELY OULD NAFA.

Rajoul Echarée: Nouakchott; e-mail rajoul_echaree@ toptechnology.mr; weekly; independent; Arabic; Dir SIDI MOHAMED OULD YOUNÈS.

Ar-Rayah (The Banner): Nouakchott; e-mail team@rayah.info; internet www.rayah.info; f. 1997; independent; weekly; pro-Islamist; publication prohibited in May 2003; Editor AHMED OULD WEDIAA.

Le Rénovateur: Nouakchott; every 2 months; f. 2001; Editor Chiekh TIDIANE DIA.

La Tribune: BP 6227, Nouakchott; tel. 525-44-92; fax 525-02-09; Editor-in-Chief MOHAMMED FALL OULD OUMÈRE.

NEWS AGENCIES

Agence Mauritanienne de l'Information (AMI): BP 371, Nouakchott; tel. 525-29-40; fax 525-45-87; e-mail ami@mauritania.mr; internet www.mauritania.mr/ami; fmrly Agence Mauritanienne de Presse; state-controlled; news and information services in Arabic and French; Dir MOHAMED CHEIKH OULD SIDI MOHAMED.

Foreign Bureaux

Foreign bureaux represented in Mauritania include Agence France-Presse, Reuters (UK) and Xinhua (New China) News Agency (People's Republic of China).

Publishers

Imprimerie Commerciale et Administrative de Mauritanie: BP 164, Nouakchott; textbooks, educational.

Imprimerie Nationale: BP 618, Nouakchott; tel. 525-44-38; fax 525-44-37; f. 1978; state-owned; Pres. RACHID OULD SALEH; Man. Dir ISSIMOU MAHJOUB.

Government Publishing House

Société Nationale d'Impression: BP 618, Nouakchott; Pres. MOUSTAPHA SALECK OULD AHMED BRIHIM.

Broadcasting and Communications

TELECOMMUNICATIONS

Mauritel: BP 7000, Nouakchott; tel. 525-23-40; fax 525-17-00; e-mail webmaster@mauritel.mr; internet www.mauritel.mr; fmrly Société Mauritanienne des Télécommunications; 46% state-owned, 34% owned by Maroc Télécom (Morocco), 20% owned by Abdallahi Ould Noueigued group; Dir Col AHMEDOUL OULD MOHAMED EL KORY.

El-Jawel Mauritel Mobiles: ave du Roi Fayçal, Nouakchott; tel. 29-63-36; fax 29-53-16; e-mail infos@mauritelmobiles.mr; internet www.mauritel.mr; f. 2000; operates a mobile cellular telephone network (El Jawal) in Nouakchott and more than 20 other locations nation-wide.

Société Mauritano-Tunisienne de Télécommunications (Mattel): Nouakchott; f. 2000; privately owned Mauritanian-Tunisian co; operates mobile cellular communications network in Nouakchott and more than 10 other locations nation-wide.

BROADCASTING

Radio

Radio de Mauritanie (RM): ave Nasser, BP 200, Nouakchott; tel. and fax 525-21-64; e-mail rm@mauritania.mr; f. 1958; state-controlled; five transmitters; radio broadcasts in Arabic, French, Sarakolé, Toucouleur and Wolof; Dir SID BRAHIM OULD HAMDINOU.

Television

Télévision de Mauritanie (TVM): BP 5522, Nouakchott; tel. 525-40-67; fax 525-40-69; Dir YESLEM OULD EBNOU ABDEM.

Finance

(cap. = capital; res = reserves; dep. = deposits; m. = million; brs= branches; amounts in ouguiyas)

BANKING

Central Bank

Banque Centrale de Mauritanie (BCM): ave de l'Indépendance, BP 623, Nouakchott; tel. 525-22-06; fax 525-27-59; e-mail anima@bnm.mr; f. 1973; bank of issue; total assets 200m. (2001); Chief. Exec. ABDELLAHI NOUEIGUED; 4 brs.

Commercial Banks

Banque al-Amana pour le développement et l'Habitat (BADH): BP 5559, Nouakchott; tel. 525-34-90; fax 525-34-95; e-mail badh@opt.mr; f. 1996; 50% privately owned; cap. 1,500m., total assets 3,278m. (Dec. 2001); Pres. AHAMED SALEM OULD BOUNA MOKHTAR; Dir-Gen. MOHAMMED OULD OUMAROU; 4 brs.

Banque pour le Commerce et l'Industrie (BCI): ave Nasser, BP 5050, Nouakchott; tel. 529-28-76; fax 529-28-79; e-mail bci@opt.mr; f. 1999; cap. 1,000m. (Dec. 1999); Pres. and Dir-Gen. ISSELMOU OULD DIDI OULD TAJEDINE; 5 brs.

Banque pour le Commerce et l'Investissement en Mauritanie (Bacim-Bank): Nouakchott; f. 2002; privately-owned; cap. US $4m. (Feb. 2002); Pres. and Dir-Gen. AHMED OULD EL WAFI.

Banque Mauritanienne pour le Commerce International (BMCI): Immeuble Afarco, ave Nasser, BP 622, Nouakchott; tel. 525-28-26; fax 525-20-45; e-mail info@bmci.mr; internet www.bmci.mr; f. 1974; privately-owned; cap. 3,000m., total assets 19,842m. (Dec. 2001); Pres. and Dir-Gen. MOULAY OULD HACEN OULD ABASS; 10 brs.

Banque Nationale de Mauritanie (BNM): ave du Roi Fayçal, BP 614, Nouakchott; tel. 525-26-02; fax 525-33-97; e-mail bnm10@bnm.mr; f. 1989; privately-owned; cap. 2,500m., res 2,485m., dep. 20,030m. (Dec. 2003); Pres. and Dir-Gen. MOHAMED OULD NOUEIGUED; 11 brs.

Chinguitty Bank: ave Nasser, BP 626, Nouakchott; tel. 525-21-42; fax 525-23-82; f. 1972; 50% owned by Libyan Arab Foreign Bank,

50% state-owned; cap. 3,500m. (Dec. 2001), total assets 11,852m. (Dec. 1999); Pres. M. EL HASSEN OULD SALEH; Gen. Man. DAW AMAR ABDALLA; 2 brs.

Générale de Banque de Mauritanie pour l'Investissement et le Commerce SA (GBM): ave de l'Indépendance, BP 5558, Nouakchott; tel. 525-36-36; fax 525-46-47; e-mail gbm@infotel.opt.mr; f. 1995; 65% privately-owned, 30% owned by Banque Belgolaise (Belgium); cap. 1,500m, res. 5,607.8., dep. 12,304.0m. (Dec. 2002); Pres. and Dir-Gen. MOHAMED HMAYEN OULD BOUAMATOU; 1 br.

Islamic Bank

Banque al-Wava Mauritanienne Islamique (BAMIS): 758, rue 22–018 ave du Roi Fayçal, BP 650, Nouakchott; tel. 525-14-24; fax 525-16-21; e-mail bamis@bamis.mr; internet www.bamis.mr; f. 1985; fmrly Banque al-Baraka Mauritannienne Islamique; majority share privately owned, 15.2% owned by Groupe Dallah Al Baraka; cap. 2,000m., res 2,585m., dep. 8,826m. (Dec. 2002); Pres. MOHAMED ABDELLAHI OULD ABDELLAHI; Dir-Gen. MOHAMED ABDELLAHI OULD SIDI; Exec. Dir MOHAMED OULD TAYA; 2 brs.

INSURANCE

Assurances Générales de Mauritanie: BP 2141, avenue Charles de Gaulle TZA Ilot A 667, Nouakchott; tel. 529-29-00; fax 529-29-11; Man. MOULAYE ELY BOUAMATOU.

Cie Nationale d'Assurance et de Réassurance (NASR): 12 ave Gamal-Abdel-Nasser, BP 163, Nouakchott; tel. 525-26-50; fax 525-18-18; f. 1994; state-owned; Pres. ABDELLAHI OULD MOCTAR; Dir-Gen. ABDERRAHMANE OULD BOUBOU.

Société Anonyme d'Assurance et de Réassurance (SAAR): ave J. F. Kennedy, Immeuble El-Mamy, BP 2841, Nouakchott; tel. 525-30-56; fax 525-25-36; e-mail saar@infotel.mr; f. 1999; Pres. and Dir-Gen. AHMED BEZEID OULD MED LEMINE.

TAAMIN: BP 5164, Nouakchott; tel. 529-40-01; fax 529-40-02; e-mail taamin@toptechnology.mr; Pres. and Dir-Gen. MOULAYE EL HASSEN OULD MOCTAR EL HASSEN.

Trade and Industry

DEVELOPMENT ORGANIZATIONS

Agence Française de Développement (AFD): rue Mamadou Kouaté prolongée, BP 5211, Nouakchott; tel. 525-25-25; fax fax 525-49-10; e-mail afd@mauritel.mr; internet www.afd.fr; Dir in Mauritania GILLES CHAUSSE.

Mission Française de Coopération et d'Action Culturelle: BP 203, Nouakchott; tel. 525-21-21; fax 525-20-50; e-mail mcap.coop.france@opt.mr; administers bilateral aid from France; Dir MAURICE DADOUCHE.

Société Nationale pour le Développement Rural (SONADER): BP 321, Nouakchott; tel. 521-18-00; fax 525-32-86; e-mail sonader@toptechnology.mr; f. 1975; Dir AHMED OULD BAH OULD CHEIKH SIDIA.

CHAMBER OF COMMERCE

Chambre de Commerce, d'Industrie et d'Agriculture de Mauritanie: BP 215, Nouakchott; tel. 525-22-14; fax 525-38-95; f. 1954; Pres. MAHMOUD OULD AHMEDOU; Dir HABIB OULD ELY.

INDUSTRIAL AND TRADE ASSOCIATIONS

NAFTEC, SA: BP 679, Nouakchott; tel. 525-26-51; fax 525-25-42; e-mail naftec@toptechnology.mr; f. 1980; cap. UM 120m.; majority-owned by Naftec (Algeria), Mauritanian Govt is a minority shareholder; import and distribution of petroleum products; fmrly Société Mauritanienne de Commercialisation des Produits Pétroliers; Dir-Gen. A. GHIMOOZ.

Société Mauritanienne de Commercialisation de Poissons, SA (SMCP): Avenida Media, BP 259, Nouadhibou; tel. 524-53-90; fax 524-55-66; f. 1984; cap. UM 500m.; Govt is a minority shareholder; until 1992 monopoly exporter of demersal fish and crustaceans; Pres. MOHAMED SALEM OULD LEKHAL; Dir-Gen. BOIJEL OULD HEMEID.

Société Nationale d'Importation et d'Exportation (SONIMEX): BP 290, Nouakchott; tel. 525-14-72; fax 525-30-14; f. 1966; cap. UM 914m.; 74% state-owned; import of foodstuffs and textiles, distribution of essential consumer goods, export of gum arabic; Pres. HAMOUD OULD AHMEDOU; Dir-Gen. (vacant).

EMPLOYERS' ORGANIZATION

General Confederation of Mauritanian Employers (CGEM) (Confédération Générale des Employeurs de Mauritanie): BP 383,

Nouakchott; tel. 525-21-60; fax 525-33-01; e-mail germe@opt.mr; f. 1960; professional asscn for all employers active in Mauritania; Pres. MOHAMED BOUAMATOU.

UTILITIES

Electricity

Société Mauritanienne d'Electricité (SOMELEC): BP 355, Nouakchott; tel. 525-23-08; fax 525-39-95; f. 2001; state-owned; privatization planned for 2004; production and distribution of electricity; Dir-Gen. Col AHMEDOU OULD MOHAMED EL-KORI.

Gas

Société Mauritanienne des Gaz (SOMAGAZ): POB 5089, Nouakchott; tel. 525-18-71; fax 529-47-86; e-mail somagaz@compunet.mr; production and distribution of butane gas; Dir-Gen. MOHAMED YAHYA OULD MOHAMED EL-MOCTAR.

Water

Société Nationale d'Eau (SNDE): ave 42-096, no. 106, Tevragh-Zeina, BP 796, Nouakchott; tel. 525-52-73; fax 525-19-52; e-mail mfoudail@infotel.mr; f. 2001; Dir-Gen. THIAM SAMBA.

TRADE UNIONS

Confédération Générale des Travailleurs de Mauritanie: Nouakchott; f. 1992; obtained official recognition in 1994.

Confédération Libre des Travailleurs de Mauritanie: Nouakchott; f. 1995; Sec.-Gen. SAMORI OULD BEYI.

Union des Travailleurs de Mauritanie (UTM): Bourse du Travail, BP 630, Nouakchott; f. 1961; Sec.-Gen. ABDERAHMANE OULD BOUBOU; 45,000 mems.

Transport

RAILWAYS

A 670-km railway connects the iron-ore deposits at Zouérate with Nouadhibou; a 40-km extension services the reserves at El Rhein, and a 30-km extension those at M'Haoudat. Motive power is diesel-electric. The Société Nationale Industrielle et Minière (SNIM) operates one of the longest (2.4 km) and heaviest (22,000 metric tons) trains in the world.

SNIM—Direction du Chemin de Fer et du Port: BP 42, Nouadhibou; tel. 574-51-74; fax 574-53-96; e-mail m.khalifa.beyah@snim.com; internet www.snim.fr; f. 1963; Gen. Man. MOHAMED SALECK OULD HEYINE; Dir KHALIFA OULD BEYAH.

ROADS

In 1999 there were about 7,891 km of roads and tracks, of which only 2,090 km were paved. The 1,100-km Trans-Mauritania highway, completed in 1985, links Nouakchott with Néma in the east of the country. Plans exist for the construction of a 7,400-km highway, linking Nouakchott with the Libyan port of Tubruq (Tobruk). In August 1999 the Islamic Development Bank granted Mauritania a loan worth US $9.4m. to help finance the rebuilding of the Chouk–Kiffa road. The construction of a 470-km highway between Nouakchott and Nouadhibou commenced in the early 2000s.

Société Mauritanienne des Transports (SOMATRA): Nouakchott; tel. 525-29-53; f. 1975; Pres. CHEIKH MALAININE ROBERT; Dir-Gen. MAMADOU SOULEYMANE KANE.

INLAND WATERWAYS

The River Senegal is navigable in the wet season by small coastal vessels as far as Kayes (Mali) and by river vessels as far as Kaédi; in the dry season as far as Rosso and Boghé, respectively. The major river ports are at Rosso, Kaédi and Gouraye.

SHIPPING

The principal port, at Point-Central, 10 km south of Nouadhibou, is almost wholly occupied with mineral exports. In 1998 the port handled 11.6m. metric tons of cargo, and cleared 3,804 vessels. There is also a commercial and fishing port at Nouadhibou. The deep-water Port de l'Amitié at Nouakchott, built and maintained with assistance from the People's Republic of China, was inaugurated in 1986. The port, which has a total capacity of about 1.5m. tons annually, handled 843,000 tons in 1998 (compared with 479,791 tons in 1990); the port cleared 453 vessels in 1998 (compared with 244 in 1990). In 2001 Mauritania's merchant fleet consisted of 141 vessels and had a total displacement of 47,394 grt.

Port Autonome de Nouakchott (Port de l'Amitié): BP 267/5103, El Mina, Nouakchott; tel. 525-14-53; fax 525-16-15; f. 1986; deep-water port; Dir-Gen. MOUSTAPHA OULD ABDALLAH.

Port Autonome de Nouadhibou: BP 236, Nouadhibou; tel. 574-51-34; f. 1973; state-owned; Pres. HABIB ELY; Dir-Gen. BÉBAHA OULD AHMED YOURA.

Shipping Companies

Cie Mauritanienne de Navigation Maritime (COMAUNAM): 119 ave Gamal-Abdel-Nasser, BP 799, Nouakchott; tel. 525-36-34; fax 525-25-04; f. 1973; 51% state-owned, 49% owned by Govt of Algeria; nat. shipping co; forwarding agent, stevedoring; Chair. MOHAND TIGHILT; Dir-Gen. KAMIL ABDELKADER.

Société d'Acconage et de Manutention en Mauritanie (SAMMA): BP 258, Nouadhibou; tel. 574-52-63; fax 574-52-37; f. 1960; freight and handling, shipping agent, forwarding agent, stevedoring; Dir-Gen. DIDI OULD BIHA.

Société Générale de Consignation et d'Entreprises Maritimes (SOGECO): BP 351, Nouakchott; tel. 525-22-02; fax 525-39-03; f. 1973; shipping agent, forwarding, stevedoring; Man. Dir SID' AHMED ABEIDNA.

Société Mauritanienne pour la Pêche et la Navigation (SMPN): BP 40254, Nouakchott; tel. 525-36-38; fax 525-37-87; e-mail smpn@toptechnology.mr; Dir-Gen. ABDALLAHI OULD ISMAIL.

VOTRA: BP 454, Nouakchott; tel. 525-24-10; fax 525-31-41; Dir-Gen. ABDERRAHMANE OULD CHOUAÏB.

CIVIL AVIATION

There are international airports at Nouakchott, Nouadhibou and at Néma, and 23 smaller airstrips. Facilities at Nouakchott were expanded considerably in the late 1980s and early 1990s.

Air Mauritanie (Société Mixte Air Mauritanie): BP 41, Nouakchott; tel. 525-22-11; fax 525-38-15; e-mail reservation@airmauritanie.mr; internet www.airmauritanie.mr; f. 1974; 11% state-owned; domestic, regional and international passenger and cargo services; Dir-Gen. SIDI ZEIN.

Tourism

Mauritania's principal tourist attractions are its historical sites, several of which have been listed by UNESCO under its World Heritage Programme, and its game reserves and national parks. Some 24,000 tourists visited Mauritania in 1999. Receipts from tourism in 1999 totalled an estimated US $28m.

Office National du Tourisme: BP 246, Nouakchott; tel. 525-35-72; f. 2002; Dir KHADIJÉTOU MINT BOUBOU.

SOMASERT: BP 42, Nouadhibou; tel. 574-90-42; fax 574-90-43; subsidiary of SNIM; responsible for promoting tourism, managing hotels and organizing tours; Dir-Gen. ABDERRAHMANE OULD DOUA.

MAURITIUS
Introductory Survey

Location, Climate, Language, Religion, Flag, Capital

The Republic of Mauritius lies in the Indian Ocean. The principal island, from which the country takes its name, lies about 800 km (500 miles) east of Madagascar. The other main islands are Rodrigues, the Agalega Islands and the Cargados Carajos Shoals (St Brandon Islands). The climate is maritime subtropical and generally humid. The average annual temperature is 23°C (73°F) at sea-level, falling to 19°C (66°F) at an altitude of 600 m (about 2,000 ft). Average annual rainfall varies from 890 mm (35 ins) at sea-level to 5,080 mm (200 ins) on the highest parts. Tropical cyclones, which may be severe, occur between September and May. Most of the population are of Indian descent. The most widely spoken languages in 1990 were Creole (35.9%) and Bhojpuri (32.5%). English is the country's official language, and Creole (derived from French) the lingua franca. The principal religious group are Hindus, who comprise more than 50% of the population. About 30% are Christians and 17% are Muslims. The national flag (proportions 2 by 3) has four equal horizontal stripes, of red, blue, yellow and green. The capital is Port Louis.

Recent History

The islands of Mauritius and Rodrigues, formerly French possessions, passed into British control in 1810. Subsequent settlement came mainly from East Africa and India, and the European population has remained largely French-speaking.

A ministerial form of government was introduced in 1957. The first elections under universal adult suffrage, held in 1959, were won by the Mauritius Labour Party (MLP), led by Dr (later Sir) Seewoosagur Ramgoolam. Mauritius became independent, within the Commonwealth, on 12 March 1968, with Ramgoolam as Prime Minister.

In November 1965 the United Kingdom transferred the Chagos Archipelago (including the atoll of Diego Garcia), a Mauritian dependency about 2,000 km (1,250 miles) north-east of the main island, to the newly created British Indian Ocean Territory (BIOT, q.v.). Mauritius has subsequently campaigned for the return of the islands, which have been developed as a major US military base. Mauritius also claims sovereignty of the French-held island of Tromelin, about 550 km (340 miles) to the north-west.

During the 1970s political opposition to successive coalition governments formed by Ramgoolam was led by a radical left-wing group, the Mouvement Militant Mauricien (MMM), founded by Paul Bérenger. Although the MMM became the largest single party in the Legislative Assembly following a general election in December 1976, Ramgoolam was able to form a new coalition Government with the support of the Parti Mauricien Social Démocrate (PMSD), which represented traditional Franco-Mauritian and Creole interests. However, social unrest and rising unemployment undermined popular support for the Government, and at a general election in June 1982 the MMM, in alliance with the Parti Socialiste Mauricien (PSM), won all 60 contested seats on the main island. Anerood (later Sir Anerood) Jugnauth, the leader of the MMM, became Prime Minister, and Bérenger Minister of Finance.

The MMM/PSM coalition collapsed in March 1983, when Bérenger and his supporters resigned, following differences concerning economic policy and the status of Creole (which the MMM had sought to make the official language). Jugnauth formed a new Government and a new party, the Mouvement Socialiste Militant (MSM), which subsequently merged with the PSM. A general election took place in August, at which an electoral alliance of the MSM, the MLP and the PMSD, led by Sir Gaëtan Duval, gained a legislative majority. Jugnauth formed a new coalition Government, in which Duval became Deputy Prime Minister. The MLP, however, withdrew from the coalition in February 1984.

In December 1985 four members of the Legislative Assembly were arrested in the Netherlands on charges of drugs-smuggling. Four ministers resigned after Jugnauth refused to comment on allegations that other deputies were involved in the affair. In July 1986 three ministers resigned, citing lack of confidence in Jugnauth's leadership, although in the following month the MLP agreed to rejoin the government coalition.

In late 1986 a government commission of inquiry into the drugs scandal implicated three members of the Legislative Assembly, all of whom supported the government alliance, and in early 1987 a further six coalition deputies were accused by the commission of involvement in the affair. A general election followed in August. The MSM again formed an electoral alliance with the PMSD and the MLP, the three parties obtaining 39 of the 62 elective seats (although they received only 49.8% of total votes cast). Bérenger, who failed to secure a seat, transferred his functions as leader of the opposition in the Legislative Assembly to Dr Paramhansa Nababsingh (while Bérenger himself replaced Nababsingh as Secretary-General of the MMM). A new coalition, led by Jugnauth, took office in September, and the Government subsequently announced plans to make Mauritius a republic within the Commonwealth. In August 1988, following a disagreement over employment policies, the PMSD withdrew from the coalition. Two attempts on Jugnauth's life (in November 1988 and March 1989) were ascribed by him to criminals involved in drugs-trafficking.

In July 1990 the MSM and the MMM agreed to form an alliance to contest the next general election, and to promote constitutional measures allowing Mauritius to become a republic within the Commonwealth. This proposal, however, was jointly opposed by the MLP and the PMSD, prompting Jugnauth to dismiss the MLP leader, Sir Satcam Boolell, from the Government, together with two dissident ministers from the MSM. A further three ministers representing the MLP also resigned, leaving only one MLP member in the Government. Boolell subsequently relinquished the leadership of the MLP to Dr Navinchandra Ramgoolam (the son of the late Sir Seewoosagur Ramgoolam). In September Jugnauth formed a new coalition Government, in which Nababsingh was appointed a Deputy Prime Minister.

Jugnauth dissolved the Legislative Assembly in August 1991. At the subsequent general election, which took place on 15 September, an alliance of the MSM, the MMM and the small Mouvement des Travaillistes Démocrates (MTD), won 57 of the 62 directly elected seats, while the MLP/PMSD alliance obtained three seats. The two remaining seats were secured by the Organisation du Peuple Rodriguais (OPR). Four 'additional' seats were subsequently allocated to members of the MLP/PMSD alliance. Jugnauth formed a new government coalition, to which nine representatives of the MMM (including Bérenger, who became Minister of External Affairs) and one representative of the MTD were appointed. Shortly afterwards Duval resigned from the Legislative Assembly.

In December 1991 the Legislative Assembly approved the constitutional framework for the country's transition to a republic within the Commonwealth. Following the proclamation of the Republic of Mauritius on 12 March 1992, the Legislative Assembly was redesignated as the National Assembly, and the incumbent Governor-General, Sir Veerasamy Ringadoo, became interim President. Later in March the Government announced its choice of Cassam Uteem, the Minister of Industry and Industrial Technology and a member of the MMM, to assume the presidency in June. Uteem was duly elected President by the National Assembly; Sir Rabindrah Ghurburrun, a member of the MMM, took office as Vice-President.

Controversial political manoeuvres in the National Assembly by the government coalition followed the announcement in October 1992 by Ramgoolam that he was to return to the United Kingdom to complete legal studies (while retaining the leadership of the MLP), despite a constitutional stipulation that the mandate of a parliamentary deputy who failed to attend sessions of the National Assembly for a period of more than three months would be suspended. Plans by Ramgoolam to return to Mauritius to attend subsequent parliamentary meetings were thwarted by Jugnauth, who, in December, unexpectedly curtailed a session of the National Assembly, and, in January 1993, convened a further session without prior notice. Legal proceedings, initiated by the MSM, to exclude Ramgoolam from the

National Assembly were subsequently dismissed by the Supreme Court.

The government coalition came under increasing pressure during 1993, amid intensifying disputes between the MSM and the MMM. In August, following an unexpected success by the PMSD in municipal by-elections in a constituency that traditionally supported the MMM, a meeting between Bérenger and Ramgoolam prompted speculation that an MMM/MLP alliance was contemplated. Shortly afterwards Jugnauth dismissed Bérenger from the Council of Ministers, on the grounds that he had repeatedly criticized government policy.

The removal of Bérenger precipitated a serious crisis within the MMM, whose political bureau decided that the other nine members of the party who held ministerial portfolios should remain in the coalition Government. Led by Nababsingh, the Deputy Prime Minister, and Jean-Claude de l'Estrac, the Minister of Industry and Industrial Technology, supporters of the pro-coalition faction announced in October 1993 that Bérenger had been suspended as Secretary-General of the MMM. Bérenger and his supporters responded by expelling 11 MMM officials from the party, and seeking a legal ban on Nababsingh and de l'Estrac from using the party name. The split in the MMM led in November to a government reshuffle, in which the remaining two MMM ministers supporting Bérenger were replaced by members of the party's pro-coalition faction.

In April 1994 the MLP and the MMM announced that they had agreed terms for an alliance to contest the next general elections. Under its provisions, Ramgoolam was to be Prime Minister and Bérenger the Deputy Prime Minister, with ministerial portfolios allocated on the basis of 12 ministries to the MLP and nine to the MMM. In the same month, three deputies from the MSM, who had been close associates of a former Minister of Agriculture dismissed two months earlier, withdrew their support from the Government.

Nababsingh and the dissident faction of the MMM, having lost Bérenger's legal challenge for the use of the party name, formed a new party, the Renouveau Militant Mauricien (RMM), which formally commenced political activity in June 1994. In the same month Jugnauth declared that the Government, which retained a cohesive parliamentary majority, would remain in office to the conclusion of its mandate in September 1996.

During the course of a parliamentary debate in November 1994, Bérenger and de l'Estrac accepted a mutual challenge to resign their seats in the National Assembly and to contest by-elections. In the following month the MSM indicated that it would not oppose RMM candidates in the two polls. In January 1995, however, Jugnauth unsuccessfully sought to undermine the MLP/MMM alliance by offering electoral support to the MLP. The by-elections, held in February, were both won by MLP/MMM candidates, and Bérenger was returned to the National Assembly. Following these results, Jugnauth opened political negotiations with the PMSD, whose leader, Xavier-Luc Duval (the son of Sir Gaëtan Duval), entered the coalition as Minister of Industry and Industrial Technology and Minister of Tourism. The post of Attorney-General and Minister of Justice was also allocated to the PMSD, and Sir Gaëtan Duval agreed to act as an economic adviser to the Prime Minister. As a result, however, of widespread opposition within the PMSD to participation in the coalition, Xavier-Luc Duval left the Government in October, and Sir Gaëtan Duval subsequently resumed the leadership of the party. The Minister for Rodrigues, representing the OPR, also left the Government.

In November 1995 the Government was defeated in a parliamentary vote, requiring a two-thirds' majority, to introduce a constitutional requirement for instruction in oriental languages to be provided in primary schools. Jugnauth dissolved the National Assembly, and at the subsequent general election in December the MLP/MMM alliance won a decisive victory: of the 62 elected seats, the MLP secured 35 seats, the MMM obtained 25 seats and the OPR two seats. Under constitutional arrangements providing representation for unsuccessful candidates attracting the largest number of votes, Sir Gaëtan Duval re-entered the National Assembly, together with two members of the Mouvement Rodriguais and a representative of Hizbullah, an Islamic fundamentalist group. Ramgoolam became Prime Minister of the new MLP/MMM coalition, with Bérenger as Deputy Prime Minister with responsibility for foreign and regional relations. Sir Gaëtan Duval died in May 1996 and was succeeded in the National Assembly and as leader of the PMSD by his brother, Hervé Duval, although Xavier-Luc Duval continued to command a significant following within the party.

The MLP/MMM coalition began to experience strain in June 1996, when austerity proposals aroused considerable opposition from Bérenger and the MMM. The Minister of Finance, Rundheersing Bheenick, subsequently resigned, and the finance portfolio remained under the supervision of Ramgoolam until November, when an extensive reallocation of ministerial responsibilities was carried out. More serious divisions began to emerge within the coalition Government in late 1996, when differences were reported between Ramgoolam and Bérenger over the allocation of ministerial responsibilities and the perception by the MMM of delays in the implementation of social and economic reforms. In January 1997 rumours had begun to circulate of a possible political alliance between the MMM and the MSM, and in March it was reported that Ramgoolam intended to seek support from certain members of the PMSD should the MMM decide to withdraw from the Government. Bérenger's criticism of the coalition's performance intensified in the following months, and culminated in June in his dismissal from the Government and the consequent withdrawal of the MMM from the coalition. Following unsuccessful efforts by Ramgoolam to draw the PMSD into a new administration, an MLP Council of Ministers was formed by Ramgoolam, who additionally assumed Bérenger's former responsibilities for foreign affairs. Bheenick returned to the Government as Minister of Economic Development and Regional Co-operation. Ahmed Rashid Beebeejaun, Minister of Land Transport, Shipping and Public Safety in the former coalition, left the MMM and retained his former portfolio as an independent. Ramgoolam emphasized his determination to remain in office for the full legislative term to December 2000. On 28 June 1997 the National Assembly re-elected Cassam Uteem to a second five-year term as President. A prominent supporter of the MLP, Angidi Verriah Chettiar, was elected Vice-President.

Following the dissolution of the MLP/MMM alliance, Bérenger sought to assume the leadership of a consolidated political opposition to the Government. In August 1997 two small parties, the Mouvement Militant Socialiste Mauricien (MMSM) and the Rassemblement pour la Réforme (RPR), agreed to support Bérenger in this aim. The alliance was extended to include a breakaway faction of the PMSD, known as the 'Vrais Bleus', under the leadership of Hervé Duval, who had been replaced as party leader by his nephew, Xavier-Luc Duval, an opponent of co-operation with the MMM.

In April 1998 the MMM, the MMSM, the RPR and the 'Vrais Bleus' formed an electoral coalition, the Alliance Nationale, to contest a by-election for a vacant seat in the National Assembly. The seat, which was retained by the MLP, had also been sought by Jugnauth on behalf of the MSM, which remained unrepresented in the National Assembly. Jugnauth, seeking to revitalize his party's prospects in preparation for the next general election (which was constitutionally required to take place by December 2000), subsequently entered negotiations with Bérenger for an electoral alliance, and in December 1998 both parties agreed terms for a joint list of candidates. Ramgoolam, following a reshuffle of the Council of Ministers in October, announced proposals in the following month for an all-party review of the electoral system, with a view to considering the adoption of proportional representation.

In February 1999 Mauritius experienced three days of serious rioting, following the death in police custody of a popular Creole musician. The public disorders, during which three deaths and damage estimated at £20m. were caused, were widely interpreted as an indication of the resentment felt by the Creole community, which has remained at the margin of the Republic's economic prosperity. Lesser disturbances took place on Rodrigues, whose population is predominantly Creole, in early May. During the following months escalating social tensions in Mauritius were evidenced by a number of violent confrontations involving members of several of the island's various ethnic and religious communities, and in December the Government enacted legislation granting it wide powers to suppress public disorder.

The MLP announced in mid-1999 its endorsement of the candidature of Xavier-Luc Duval for a legislative by-election to be held in September. Duval, after obtaining the vacant seat, joined the Government as Minister of Industry, Commerce, Corporate Affairs and Financial Services, following an extensive government reshuffle completed at the end of the month. The selection in October of Pravind Jugnauth, the son of Sir Aneerood Jugnauth, as Deputy Leader of the MSM gave rise to speculation that Sir Aneerood was contemplating retirement from politics and intended his son to be his successor. It also provoked divisions within the informal alliance that had been formed between the MMM and the MSM in February 1999.

None the less, in August 2000 the MSM/MMM alliance was made official, in advance of the imminent general election, on the basis that Jugnauth would lead as Prime Minister for three years in the event of victory, before assuming the more honorary role of President, thus allowing Bérenger to become Prime Minister for the remaining two years. In the same month both the Minister of Social Security and National Unity, Prakash Bundhun, and the Minister of Health, Nundhkeshwarsingh Deerpalsingh, resigned, following separate allegations of fraud and investigations by the Economic Crime Office; Deerpalsingh was subsequently arrested.

A general election was held on 11 September 2000. There was a high rate of participation, with 81% of the 790,000 registered electors casting their ballots. The MSM/MMM alliance achieved a significant victory, winning 54 of the 62 directly elected seats in the National Assembly, while the MLP/PMSD alliance gained only six seats and the OPR two seats. As agreed, Sir Anerood Jugnauth became Prime Minister again, while Paul Bérenger was appointed Deputy Prime Minister and Minister of Finance. A new Council of Ministers was appointed one week later.

In November 2000 the British High Court of Justice ruled that the eviction of several thousand inhabitants of the Chagos Archipelago between 1967 and 1973, to allow the construction of a US military base on the atoll of Diego Garcia, had been unlawful, and overturned a 1971 ordinance preventing the islanders from returning to the Archipelago. (The majority of the displaced islanders had been resettled in Mauritius, which had administered the Chagos Archipelago until its transfer to BIOT in 1965.) Following the ruling, the Mauritian Government declared its right to sovereignty over the islands to be indisputable and sought international recognition as such. Jugnauth stated that he would be prepared to negotiate with the USA over the continued presence of the military base. The United Kingdom responded that it would return the islands if, as had been maintained for many years, the USA was prepared to move out of the base on Diego Garcia. India declared its support for the Mauritian Government's claim to sovereignty, as part of the close relationship being encouraged between the two countries.

Municipal elections were held on 7 October 2001; the ruling MSM/MMM alliance won 115 of the country's 226 council seats and secured control of all five municipalities. In November exiled Chagos islanders demonstrated outside the British High Commission in Port Louis, in support of their demands for compensation from the British Government. In February 2002 legislation allowing the displaced islanders to apply for British citizenship received royal assent in the United Kingdom. At that time the British Government was also examining the feasibility of a return to the Chagos Archipelago for the islanders, who continued to seek compensation.

In January 2002 a commission on constitutional and electoral reform presented its proposals at a series of public forums, before submitting them to the Government for consideration. Recommendations included the introduction of a system of proportional representation in legislative elections and a reinforcement of presidential powers. In mid-February controversial legislation on the prevention of terrorism was finally promulgated by the Chief Justice of the Supreme Court, Arianga Pillay, acting as interim President, following the resignations of both President Uteem and his successor, Vice-President Chettiar, over the issue. The legislation had been rejected by opposition parties and proved unpopular with many sections of society for arrogating excessive powers to the authorities and infringing on citizens' rights. On 25 February Karl Offman was elected as President by an extraordinary session of the National Assembly, which was boycotted by opposition deputies. Although formally elected for five years, Offman was to relinquish the presidency to Jugnauth in October 2003; in preparation for this, in April 2003 Jugnauth announced his resignation from the leadership of the MSM, to be succeeded by his son, Pravind. In January of that year the Minister of Housing and Land, Mookhesswur Choonee, resigned from his post, following his arrest on suspicion of illegally having sold state-owned land to a private investor. His duties were subsequently appended to those of the Minister of Local Government and Rodrigues, Georges Lesjongard. However, after the charges against him were dropped, Choonee rejoined the Government in May 2004.

In August 2003, in preparation for the transfer of governing roles, a constitutional amendment was approved by the National Assembly to increase the powers of the President, giving the incumbent the right to refuse a request from the Prime Minister to dissolve the legislature following a vote of 'no confidence'. As agreed, on 1 October Offman resigned as President and was replaced, in an acting capacity, by the Vice-President, Raouf Bundhun, pending the election by the National Assembly of Sir Anerood Jugnauth as his successor one week later. Jugnauth had resigned as Prime Minister on 30 September and was immediately replaced by Paul Bérenger, who appointed a new Council of Ministers. On 23 December Bérenger effected a government reshuffle, notably appointing Jaya Krishna Cuttaree as Minister of Foreign Affairs, International Trade and Regional Co-operation. During his first months in office Bérenger conducted a premiership active in international diplomacy, visiting two of the country's principal trading partners, India and France, and signing co-operation agreements with Madagascar. In early 2004 he also renewed the campaign to reclaim sovereignty of the Chagos Archipelago from the United Kingdom, on the basis that international law does not allow the dismemberment of a country before independence, and of Tromelin Island from France.

Government

Constitutional amendments, which were approved by the Legislative Assembly (henceforth known as the National Assembly) in December 1991 and came into effect on 12 March 1992, provided for the establishment of a republic. The constitutional Head of State is the President of the Republic, who is elected by a simple majority of the National Assembly for a five-year term of office. Legislative power is vested in the unicameral National Assembly, which comprises the Speaker, 62 members elected by universal adult suffrage for a term of five years, up to eight 'additional' members (unsuccessful candidates who receive the largest number of votes at a legislative election, to whom seats are allocated by the Electoral Supervisory Commission to ensure a balance in representation of the different ethnic groups), and the Attorney-General (if not an elected member). Executive power is vested in the Prime Minister, who is appointed by the President and is the member of the National Assembly best able to command a majority in the Assembly. The President appoints other ministers, on the recommendation of the Prime Minister.

Defence

The country has no standing defence forces, although at 1 August 2003 paramilitary forces were estimated to number 2,000, comprising a special mobile force of 1,500, to ensure internal security, and a coastguard of 500. Projected budgetary expenditure on defence for 2003 was Rs 240m.

Economic Affairs

In 2002, according to estimates by the World Bank, Mauritius' gross national income (GNI), measured at average 2000–02 prices, was US $4,669m., equivalent to $3,850 per head (or $10,530 per head on an international purchasing-power parity basis). During 1990–2002, it was estimated, the population increased at an average annual rate of 1.1%, while gross domestic product (GDP) per head increased, in real terms, by an average of 4.1% per year. Overall GDP increased, in real terms, at an average annual rate of 5.3% in 1990–2002; growth in 2002 was 4.4%.

Agriculture (including hunting, forestry and fishing) contributed 5.9% of GDP in 2003, according to provisional estimates, and engaged 9.3% of the employed labour force in that year. The principal cash crops are sugar cane (sugar accounted for 19.8% of export earnings in 2003, according to provisional figures), tea and tobacco. Food crops include potatoes and vegetables. Poultry farming is also practised. During 1990–2002, according to the World Bank, the GDP of the agricultural sector increased, in real terms, at an average rate of 1.1% per year; growth in 2002 was 7.8%.

Industry (including mining, manufacturing, construction and utilities) contributed 28.5% of GDP in 2003, according to provisional estimates, and engaged 37.1% of the employed labour force in that year. During 1990–2002, according to the World Bank, industrial GDP increased, in real terms, at an average annual rate of 5.6%; growth in 2002 was 5.3%. Mining is negligible, accounting for only 0.3% of employment and 0.1% of GDP in 2003.

Manufacturing contributed 20.3% of GDP in 2003, according to provisional estimates, and engaged 27.2% of the employed labour force in that year. The principal branches of manufacturing are textiles and clothing and food products, mainly sugar. Clothing (excluding footwear) provided 58.9% of export earnings in 2003. Factories in the Export Processing Zone (EPZ) process import raw materials to produce goods for the export market. Textile firms accounted for 88.4% of total EPZ employment in 1998 and 84.4% of EPZ exports (mainly in the form of clothing) in 1997. Other important products include fish preparations, watches and clocks, and precious stones. Export receipts from EPZ products represented almost 76.4% of total export earnings in 1999. During 1990–2002, according to the World Bank, the GDP of the manufacturing sector, increased, in real terms, at an average annual rate of 5.4%; growth in 2002 was 5.5%.

Electric energy is derived principally from thermal (oil-fired) and hydroelectric power stations. Bagasse (a by-product of sugar cane) is also used as fuel for generating electricity; in 1992 a programme was initiated to enable Mauritius eventually to derive 15% of its energy requirements from bagasse. Imports of refined petroleum products comprised 9.4% of the value of merchandise imports in 2003, according to provisional figures. Thermal energy accounted for 95.6% of electricity generated in 2002.

The services sector contributed 65.6% of GDP in 2003, according to provisional estimates, and engaged 53.5% of the employed labour force in that year. Tourism is the third most important source of revenue, after agriculture and manufacturing. The number of foreign tourist arrivals increased to 702,018 in 2003 from 422,000 in 1995. Receipts from tourism were estimated to total Rs 19,397m. in 2003. An 'offshore' banking sector and a stock exchange have operated since 1989. According to the World Bank, the real GDP of the services sector increased at an average annual rate of 6.3% in 1990–2001; growth in 2001 was 6.7%.

In 2002 Mauritius recorded a visible trade deficit of US $188.1m., and there was a surplus of $259.2m. on the current account of the balance of payments. In 2003 the principal source of imports (12.1%) was South Africa; other major suppliers were France (11.8%), India and the People's Republic of China. The principal market for exports (30.8%) was the United Kingdom; other significant purchasers were France and the USA. The principal exports in 2003 were clothing and sugar. The principal imports in that year were refined petroleum products and textile yarn and fabrics.

In 2001/02 there was an estimated budgetary deficit of Rs 8,144m. (equivalent to 5.9% of GDP). Mauritius' external debt totalled US $1,724m. at the end of 2001, of which $765m. was long-term public debt. In that year the cost of debt-servicing was equivalent to 6.9% of the value of exports of goods and services. The annual rate of inflation averaged 6.6% in 1990–2001. Consumer prices increased by an average of 4.2% in 2000 and 5.4% in 2001. About 9.9% of the labour force were unemployed in 2003.

Mauritius is a member of the Common Market for Eastern and Southern Africa (COMESA, see p. 171), the Southern African Development Community (SADC, see p. 331) and the Indian Ocean Commission (IOC, see p. 360), which aims to promote regional economic co-operation. Mauritius was among the founder members of the Indian Ocean Rim Association for Regional Co-operation (IOR—ARC, see p. 360) in 1997.

Mauritius' economy was traditionally dependent on sugar production, and economic growth was therefore vulnerable to adverse climatic conditions and changes in international prices for sugar. However, since the 1980s the Government has pursued a successful policy of diversification, encouraging labour-intensive manufacturing (particularly of clothing) in the EPZ, and extensive reforms have been implemented with IMF support. Port Louis has been established as a free port. Since the mid-1990s the Government has continued to promote further measures to achieve economic diversification and liberalization, aimed at encouraging foreign investment and increasing export revenue. The expansion of tourism has also been actively promoted. The geographical location of Mauritius, as well as a number of incentive measures implemented by the Government, has contributed to its successful establishment as an international financial centre. By the late 1990s the island had become a significant provider of 'offshore' banking and investment services for a number of south Asian countries (particularly India), as well as for members of SADC and IOR—ARC groupings. Since 1999 the Prime Minister has also promoted the country as

a future hub of communications and information technology, as a means of encouraging the next stage of economic development and transferring the emphasis towards services. The construction of a free zone 'cybercity' was initiated, with an investment of US $110m. from India, and in 2000 a South Africa–Far East underwater fibre optic cable was laid, linking Port Louis to both regions. However, a number of issues remained of concern, including growing unemployment, high inflation, excessive public debt, inadequate labour-force skills and an ageing population. A record drought in 1998–2000 caused an estimated Rs 2,000m. of damage and reduced the sugar harvest by an estimated 40%. In August 2001 the Prime Minister announced a restructuring and centralization plan for the sugar industry, whereby 7,000 workers were to be invited to retire over three years and several factories were closed, in order to reduce costs and improve international competitiveness. The textile industry, the country's second largest foreign-exchange earner, was eroded by the transfer, in 2000, of the operations of more than 20 major Mauritian manufacturers to Madagascar, owing to lower costs in that country. Furthermore, in January 2002 more than 1,000 textile workers in the EPZ were made redundant, owing to a decline in trade following the suicide attacks on the USA in September 2001; exports to the USA had previously been expected to increase, as a result of the USA's African Growth and Opportunity Act (AGOA), which granted duty-free access to the US market for textile products from Mauritius. The expiry of the preferential Multi-Fibre Agreement with the EU in December 2004 will pose a further threat to the textiles industry, exposing it to direct competition from countries with lower labour costs, particularly those in Asia. The budgetary deficit was somewhat reduced in 2003, but remained a concern, as did the high level of unemployment. The Government's focus on funding and developing education was an effort to match the skills of the work-force to the requirements of the the economy. Growth of some 5.1% and inflation of 4% were forecast by the Government for 2004.

Education

Education is officially compulsory for seven years between the ages of five and 12. Primary education begins at five years of age and lasts for six years. Secondary education, beginning at the age of 11, lasts for up to seven years, comprising a first cycle of three years and a second of four years. Primary and secondary education are available free of charge. In 2001/02 the number of children attending primary schools incuded 95% of the appropriate age-group (males 95%; females 95%), while the comparable ratio for secondary schools was 64% (males 63%; females 65%). The education system provides for instruction in seven Asian languages (65% of primary school children were studying at least one of these in 2001). The Government exercises indirect control of the large private sector in secondary education (in 2002 only 40 of 143 schools were state administered). The University of Mauritius had 3,667 students in 1997/98; in addition, many students receive further education abroad. Of total expenditure by the central Government in 2001/02, Rs 4,742m. (14.4%) was for education, according to provisional figures.

Public Holidays

2004: 1–2 January (New Year), 22 January (Chinese New Year), 1 February (Abolition of Slavery), 5 February (Thaipoosam Cavadee), 18 February (Maha Shivaratree), 12 March (National Day), 21 March (Ougadi), 1 May (Labour Day), 15 August (Assumption), 19 September (Ganesh Chathurti), 2 November (Arrival of the Workers), 12 November (Divali), 14 November* (Id al-Fitr, end of Ramadan), 25 December (Christmas Day).

2005: 1–2 January (New Year), 25 January (Thaipoosam Cavadee), 1 February (Abolition of Slavery), 8 February (Maha Shivaratree), 9 February (Chinese New Year), 12 March (National Day), 9 April (Ougadi), 1 May (Labour Day), 15 August (Assumption), 7 September (Ganesh Chathurti), 1 November (Divali), 2 November (Arrival of the Workers), 4 November* (Id al-Fitr, end of Ramadan), 25 December (Christmas Day).

*This holiday is dependent on the Islamic lunar calendar and may vary by one or two days from the dates given.

Weights and Measures

The metric system is in standard use.

Statistical Survey

Source (unless otherwise stated): Central Statistical Office, LIC Centre, President John F. Kennedy St, Port Louis; tel. 212-2316; fax 211-4150; e-mail cso@intnet.mu; internet ncb.intnet.mu/cso.

Area and Population

AREA, POPULATION AND DENSITY

Area (sq km)	2,040*
Population (census results)	
1 July 1990	1,058,942†
2 July 2000‡	
Males	583,949
Females.	595,188
Total	1,179,137
Population (official estimates at mid-year)§	
2001	1,199,881
2002	1,210,196
2003	1,222,811
Density (per sq km) at mid-2003§	599.4

* 788 sq miles.
† Including an adjustment of 2,115 for underenumeration.
‡ Excluding an adjustment for underenumeration.
§ Islands of Mauritius and Rodrigues only (area 1,969 sq km).

ISLANDS

	Area (sq km)	Population 1990 census	Population 2000 census
Mauritius . . .	1,865	1,024,571*	1,143,069
Rodrigues . . .	104	34,204	35,779
Other islands . .	71	167	289

* Including adjustment for underenumeration.

ETHNIC GROUPS: Island of Mauritius, mid-1982: 664,480 Indo-Mauritians (507,985 Hindus, 156,495 Muslims), 264,537 general population (incl. Creole and Franco-Mauritian communities), 20,669 Chinese.

LANGUAGE GROUPS
(census of 2 July 2000)*

Arabic	806	Marathi	16,587
Bhojpuri . . .	361,250	Tamil	44,731
Chinese . . .	16,972	Telegu. . . .	18,802
Creole	454,763	Urdu	34,120
English . . .	1,075	Other languages .	169,619
French. . . .	21,171	Not stated . .	3,170
Hindi	35,782	**Total** . . .	1,178,848

* Figures refer to the languages of cultural origin of the population of the islands of Mauritius and Rodrigues only. The data exclude an adjustment for underenumeration.

POPULATION BY DISTRICT
(2002, provisional figures)

Plaine Wilhems . .	366,700	Riv du Rempart . .	101,800
Flacq	130,900	Moka	77,200
Port Louis. . .	129,700	Savanne . . .	67,800
Pamplemousses . .	126,400	Black River . .	64,000
Grand Port . .	109,500	Rodrigues . . .	36,200

PRINCIPAL TOWNS
(census of 2 July 2000)

Port Louis (capital)	144,303	Curepipe . . .	78,920
Beau Bassin/Rose Hill . . .	103,872	Quatre Bornes . .	75,884
Vacoas/Phoenix . .	100,066		

Source: Thomas Brinkhoff, *City Population* (internet www.citypopulation.de).

BIRTHS, MARRIAGES AND DEATHS*

	Registered live births		Registered marriages		Registered deaths	
	Number	Rate (per 1,000)	Number	Rate (per 1,000)	Number	Rate (per 1,000)
1996	20,763	18.3	10,700	9.4	7,670	6.8
1997	20,012	17.4	10,887	9.5	7,986	7.0
1998	19,434	16.7	10,898	9.4	7,839	6.8
1999	20,311	17.3	11,295	9.6	7,944	6.8
2000	20,205	17.0	10,963	9.2	7,982	6.7
2001	19,696	16.4	10,635	8.9	7,983	6.7
2002	19,983	16.5	10,484	8.6	8,310	6.9
2003	19,986	16.3	10,451	8.5	8,236	6.7

* Figures refer to the islands of Mauritius and Rodrigues only. The data are tabulated by year of registration, rather than by year of occurrence.

Expectation of life (WHO estimates, years at birth): 71.9 (males 68.4; females 75.5) in 2002 (Source: WHO, *World Health Report*).

ECONOMICALLY ACTIVE POPULATION
(persons aged 12 years and over)

	2001	2002	2003
Agriculture, forestry and fishing .	54,300	46,900	46,200
Sugar cane	28,100	21,600	19,900
Mining and quarrying	1,300	1,300	300
Manufacturing	143,500	139,500	134,800
EPZ	91,000	85,700	80,000
Electricity and water	3,000	3,100	3,000
Construction	43,500	44,100	45,700
Wholesale and retail trade, repair of motor vehicles and household goods	65,100	67,400	70,200
Hotels and restaurants . . .	24,200	25,400	26,500
Transport, storage and communications	31,600	33,400	34,600
Financial intermediation . . .	7,500	7,500	7,900
Real estate, renting and business activities	14,300	14,300	14,600
Public administration and defence.	36,200	38,200	39,200
Education	23,300	24,300	25,800
Health and social work . . .	12,300	12,700	13,400
Other services	30,700	32,000	32,700
Total employed*	490,800	490,100	494,900
Males	321,600	324,000	327,300
Females.	169,200	166,100	167,600
Unemployed	47,700	50,800	54,400
Total labour force	538,500	540,900	549,300

* Includes foreign workers.

Health and Welfare

KEY INDICATORS

Total fertility rate (children per woman, 2002). . . .	2.0
Under-5 mortality rate (per 1,000 live births, 2001) . . .	19
HIV/AIDS (% of persons aged 15–49, 2001). . . .	0.10
Physicians (per 1,000 head, 1995)	0.85
Hospital beds (per 1,000 head, 1994)	3.07
Health expenditure (2001): US $ per head (PPP) . . .	323
Health expenditure (2001): % of GDP	3.4
Health expenditure (2001): public (% of total)	59.5
Access to water (% of persons, 2000).	100
Access to sanitation (% of persons, 2000)	99
Human Development Index (2001): ranking	62
Human Development Index (2001): value	0.779

For sources and definitions, see explanatory note on p. vi.

Agriculture

PRINCIPAL CROPS
('000 metric tons)

	2000	2001	2002
Potatoes	13.8	16.3	13.3
Sugar cane	5,109.5	5,792.3	4,873.9
Coconuts	1.5	1.5	1.9*
Cabbages	10.8	11.7	8.2
Lettuce	1.7	2.4	2.2
Tomatoes	9.7	12.4	11.7
Cauliflower	2.0	1.8	1.8
Pumpkins, squash and gourds	7.8	7.9	8.0*
Cucumbers and gherkins	9.0	9.0*	9.0*
Aubergines (Eggplants)	1.6	1.6*	1.6*
Dry onions	11.1	11.0	7.1
Carrots	11.5	12.0	8.6
Other vegetables*	22.0	23.5	21.8
Bananas	8.5	11.0	7.2
Pineapples	3.4	6.0	1.9
Other fruit*	1.2	1.2	1.2
Tea (made)	1.3	1.5	1.4
Tobacco (leaves)	0.6	0.6	0.5

* FAO estimate(s).

Source: FAO.

LIVESTOCK
(FAO estimates, '000 head, year ending September)

	2000	2001	2002
Cattle	27	28	28
Pigs	12	12	11
Sheep	10	12	12
Goats	94	95	93
Chickens	7,700	8,900	9,800

Source: FAO.

LIVESTOCK PRODUCTS
('000 metric tons)

	2000	2001	2002
Beef and veal	3	2	2
Poultry meat	21	27	29
Cows' milk	5	4	4
Hen eggs*	5	5	5

* FAO estimates.

Source: FAO.

Forestry

ROUNDWOOD REMOVALS
('000 cubic metres, excl. bark)

	1999	2000	2001
Sawlogs, veneer logs and logs for sleepers	7	5	5
Other industrial wood	6	3	3
Fuel wood	12	10	9
Total	25	18	17

SAWNWOOD PRODUCTION
('000 cubic metres, incl. railway sleepers)

	1999	2000	2001
Coniferous (softwood)	4	2	2
Broadleaved (hardwood)	1	1	1
Total	5	3	3

2002: Production as in 2001 (FAO estimates).

Source: FAO.

Fishing
(metric tons, live weight)

	1999	2000	2001
Capture	12,205	9,615	10,694
Unicorn cod	285	347	340
Groupers and seabasses	826	863	938
Emperors (Scavengers)	4,598	4,698	4,008
Goatfishes	509	541	556
Spinefeet (Rabbitfishes)	461	448	450
Skipjack tuna	2,361	305	8
Yellowfin tuna	742	226	125
Octopuses	299	303	347
Aquaculture	85	87	59
Total catch	12,290	9,702	10,753

Source: FAO, *Yearbook of Fishery Statistics*.

Industry

SELECTED PRODUCTS
(metric tons, unless otherwise indicated)

	1999	2000	2001
Frozen fish	3,922	4,700	n.a.
Canned fish	18,992	20,173	n.a.
Raw sugar	373,294	569,289	645,598
Molasses*	132,000	144,000	174,100
Beer and stout (hectolitres)	358,450	374,970	328,100*
Cigarettes (million)	979	976	n.a.
Iron bars and steel tubes	45,000	46,125	48,000*
Fertilizers	85,300	87,400	83,000*
Electric energy (million kWh)	1,559	1,600	1,659

* Rounded figure(s).

2002 (metric tons, unless otherwise indicated): Raw sugar 520,900; Molasses 140,200; Beer and stout 348,400 hectolitres; Electric energy 1,715 million kWh.

Finance

CURRENCY AND EXCHANGE RATES

Monetary Units
100 cents = 1 Mauritian rupee.

Sterling, Dollar and Euro Equivalents (31 December 2003)
£1 sterling = 46.56 rupees;
US $1 = 26.09 rupees;
€1 = 32.95 rupees;
1,000 Mauritian rupees = £21.48 = $38.33 = €30.35.

Average Exchange Rate (Mauritian rupees per US $)
2001 29.129
2002 29.962
2003 27.901

BUDGET
(million rupees, year ending 30 June)

Revenue	1999/2000	2000/01*	2001/02†
Tax revenue	20,373	20,189	21,519
Taxes on property	1,206	1,324	1,299
Domestic taxes on goods and services	9,339	9,466	10,821
Taxes on international trade	6,935	6,349	5,893
Other tax revenue	12	11	13
Non-tax revenue	2,966	2,338	3,451
Property income	1,862	1,660	1,783
Other non-tax revenue	604	658	1,059
Foreign grants	161	199	317
Total	23,500	22,707	25,286

Expenditure	1999/2000	2000/01	2001/02†
Public administration and security	4,767	5,363	5,722
General public services . . .	2,524	2,917	2,906
Public order and safety . . .	2,004	2,193	2,546
Community & social services . .	13,951	15,494	18,029
Education	3,987	4,357	4,742
Health	2,256	2,547	2,872
Social security	5,563	6,160	6,670
Economic services	4,192	4,175	3,734
Agriculture, forestry, fishing and hunting	1,260	1,329	1,269
Transportation and communications	1,102	1,855	881
Other functions	4,733	6,388	5,456
Public debt interest	3,856	5,527	4,541
Total expenditure	27,643	31,420	32,941
Lending minus repayments. . .	167	−1,574	490
Total expenditure and lending minus repayments	27,810	29,846	33,430

* Revised estimates.
† Provisional figures.

Source: IMF, *Mauritius: Selected Issues and Statistical Appendix* (October 2003).

INTERNATIONAL RESERVES
(US $ million at 31 December)

	2001	2002	2003
Gold*	12.3	12.3	21.1
IMF special drawing rights. . .	21.1	23.2	25.6
Reserve position in IMF. . .	18.2	19.7	32.5
Foreign exchange.	796.3	1,184.5	1,519.2
Total	847.9	1,239.7	1,598.4

* Valued at market-related prices.

Source: IMF, *International Financial Statistics*.

MONEY SUPPLY
(million rupees at 31 December)

	2001	2002	2003
Currency outside banks	7,329.0	8,286.0	9,347.0
Demand deposits at deposit money banks	7,974.9	9,759.0	10,940.5
Total money (incl. others). . .	15,451.7	18,156.6	20,401.1

Source: IMF, *International Financial Statistics*.

COST OF LIVING
(Consumer Price Index; base: July 1996–June 1997 = 100)

	1999	2000	2001
Food and non-alcoholic beverages .	117.1	118.6	123.4
Alcoholic beverages and tobacco .	144.0	156.4	168.1
Clothing and footwear	112.0	114.9	116.3
Fuel and electricity	100.5	106.3	122.4
Housing and household operations	110.2	118.9	122.2
All items (incl. others)	117.1	122.0	128.6

NATIONAL ACCOUNTS
(provisional, million rupees in current prices)
Components of the Gross National Product

	2001	2002	2003
Compensation of employees . .	49,347	52,621	58,011
Operating surplus . . . . . } Consumption of fixed capital . . }	67,084	71,059	77,676
Gross domestic product (GDP) at factor cost . . .	116,431	123,680	135,687
Indirect taxes	15,661	18,223	21,219
Less Subsidies	848	1,124	934
GDP in purchasers' values . .	131,244	140,779	155,972
Factor income received from abroad. . . . . } *Less* Factor income paid abroad . }	393	396	−793
Gross national product (GNP) at market prices	131,637	141,175	155,179

Expenditure on the Gross Domestic Product
(estimates)

	2001	2002*	2003†
Government final consumption expenditure.	16,751	18,292	20,365
Private final consumption expenditure.	80,112	88,038	96,541
Increase in stocks‡	−2,396	−133	1,591
Gross fixed capital formation . .	29,798	31,369	35,550
Total domestic expenditure. .	124,265	137,566	154,047
Exports of goods and services . .	90,463	88,301	89,812
Less Imports of goods and services	82,636	83,964	86,953
GDP in purchasers' values . .	132,092	141,903	156,906

* Revised estimates.
† Preliminary estimates.
‡ Including statistical discrepancies.

Gross Domestic Product by Economic Activity

	2001*	2002*	2003†
Agriculture, hunting, forestry, and fishing	8,469	7,928	8,546
Mining and quarrying	150	75	80
Manufacturing	27,423	28,277	29,402
Electricity, gas and water . . .	2,634	3,012	3,453
Construction	6,540	7,319	8,384
Wholesale and retail trade, repair of motor vehicles and personal goods	13,745	14,715	15,825
Hotels and restaurants	7,430	7,550	7,990
Transport, storage and communications	15,124	16,894	18,845
Financial intermediation . . .	11,473	11,890	13,627
Real estate, renting and business activities	10,499	11,727	13,118
Public administration and defence; compulsory social security . .	7,455	8,118	9,315
Education	5,224	5,746	6,493
Health and social work	3,311	3,730	4,314
Other services	4,407	4,871	5,464
Sub-total	123,884	131,852	144,856
Less Imputed bank service charges	6,290	6,900	7,650
GDP at basic prices . . .	117,594	124,952	137,206
Taxes on products, *less* subsidies	14,498	16,951	19,700
GDP in purchasers' values . .	132,092	141,903	156,906

* Revised estimates.
† Provisional estimates.

BALANCE OF PAYMENTS
(US $ million)

	2000	2001	2002
Exports of goods f.o.b.	1,552.2	1,628.2	1,830.2
Imports of goods f.o.b.	−1,944.4	−1,846.0	−2,018.3
Trade balance	−392.1	−217.7	−188.1
Exports of services	1,070.2	1,222.0	1,134.8
Imports of services	−762.5	−810.1	−786.5
Balance on goods and services.	−84.5	194.1	160.2
Other income received . . .	48.7	75.2	74.8
Other income paid	−64.9	−60.9	−65.1
Balance on goods, services and income	−100.7	208.4	169.9
Current transfers received . . .	167.6	193.1	188.3
Current transfers paid	−103.8	−125.4	−98.9
Current balance	−36.9	276.1	259.2
Capital account (net)	−0.6	−1.4	−1.9
Direct investment abroad . .	−13.0	−2.9	−1.2
Direct investment from abroad. .	265.6	−27.7	27.6
Portfolio investment assets . . .	−18.8	−17.7	−18.3
Portfolio investment liabilities .	−120.4	−1.6	0.9
Other investment assets . . .	−307.6	−336.9	−440.5
Other investment liabilities .	452.1	138.9	554.9
Net errors and omissions . . .	10.1	−78.6	−39.6
Overall balance	230.6	−51.8	341.1

Source: IMF, *International Financial Statistics*.

External Trade

PRINCIPAL COMMODITIES
(million rupees)

Imports c.i.f.	2001*	2002	2003*
Food and live animals . . .	8,235	11,289	10,311
Fish and fish preparations .	1,754	3,985	2,555
Crude materials (inedible) except fuels	1,787	1,813	1,542
Mineral fuels, lubricants, etc. .	6,504	6,634	7,169
Refined petroleum products .	5,532	5,673	6,268
Chemicals.	4,777	5,012	5,779
Basic manufactures	17,694	18,744	18,817
Textile yarn, fabrics, etc . .	10,738	4,332	4,285
Cotton fabrics. . . .	n.a.	2,785	2,362
Machinery and transport equipment	13,132	13,543	14,865
Machinery specialized for particular industries . .	3,631	2,583	2,234
General industrial machinery, equipment and parts		2,026	1,971
Telecommunications and sound equipment . . .	n.a.	1,373	2,229
Other electrical machinery, apparatus, etc.	n.a.	1,980	2,233
Road motor vehicles . . .	2,755	2,718	2,800
Aircraft, marine vessels and parts	1,967	770	1,390
Miscellaneous manufactured articles	5,015	6,317	6,507
Total (incl. others)	58,115	64,608	66,389

Exports f.o.b.†	2001*	2002	2003*
Food and live animals	10,909	11,862	11,637
Sugar	8,138	8,869	8,430
Basic manufactures	3,535	2,641	2,657
Textile yarn, fabrics, etc. . .	2,225	1,161	2,088
Miscellaneous manufactured articles	27,219	27,811	27,277
Clothing and accessories (excl. footwear)	25,094	25,516	25,005
Total (incl. others)	42,474	43,022	42,448

* Provisional.

† Excluding re-exports (million rupees): 1,944 in 2001 (provisional); 8,657 in 2002; 9,672 in 2003 (provisional). Also excluded are stores and bunkers for ships and aircraft (million rupees): 1,937 in 2001 (provisional); 2,214 in 2002; 2,044 in 2003 (provisional).

From 2002 data include transactions of Mauritius Freeport.

PRINCIPAL TRADING PARTNERS
(million rupees)*

Imports c.i.f.	2001	2002	2003†
Argentina	n.a.	899	732
Australia	2,383	2,587	2,153
Bahrain	n.a.	1,106	2,571
Belgium	796	930	946
China, People's Repub. . . .	4,154	5,434	5,516
France	5,431	7,131	7,845
Germany	3,137	2,217	2,159
Hong Kong	1,381	1,201	1,051
India	4,656	4,725	5,435
Indonesia	n.a.	1,249	1,131
Italy	1,911	2,092	2,102
Japan	2,139	2,287	2,322
Korea, Repub..	n.a.	1,068	693
Madagascar	n.a.	667	1,342
Malaysia	1,711	1,838	2,020
Pakistan	n.a.	812	1,022
Saudi Arabia	n.a.	1,484	1,638
Seychelles	n.a.	991	218
Singapore	1,223	1,418	1,663
South Africa	8,031	8,116	8,020
Spain	n.a.	1,189	1,114
Switzerland	1,267	996	922
Taiwan	1,040	1,549	1,166
Thailand	n.a.	975	963
United Arab Emirates . . .	n.a.	1,731	486
United Kingdom	2,108	2,371	2,166
USA	1,827	1,791	1,727
Total (incl. others)	58,115	64,608	66,389

Exports f.o.b.	2001	2002	2003†
Belgium	732	873	954
France	7,938	9,983	9,616
Germany	1,584	1,558	1,554
Italy	1,605	1,915	1,913
Japan	n.a.	794	452
Madagascar	2,012	2,029	3,254
Netherlands	777	831	857
Portugal	742	559	664
Réunion	532	1,166	1,534
South Africa	n.a.	576	787
Spain	701	653	660
Switzerland	n.a.	492	526
United Kingdom	13,822	15,680	16,035
USA	8,774	9,920	9,083
Total (incl. others)	44,418	51,679	52,120

* Imports by country of origin; exports by country of destination.

† Provisional.

Transport

ROAD TRAFFIC
(motor vehicles registered at 31 December)

	2001	2002	2003
Private vehicles: cars	89,748	95,635	101,928
Private vehicles: motorcycles and mopeds	119,953	122,801	125,602
Commercial vehicles: buses . .	2,408	2,450	2,460
Commercial vehicles: taxis . . .	5,318	5,801	5,979
Commercial vehicles: goods vehicles	31,582	32,986	33,997

SHIPPING

Merchant Fleet
(registered at 31 December)

	2000	2001	2002
Number of vessels	40	42	45
Total displacement ('000 grt) . .	91.2	96.9	62.7

Source: Lloyd's Register-Fairplay, *World Fleet Statistics*.

Sea-borne Freight Traffic
('000 metric tons)

	2000	2001	2002
Goods unloaded	3,677	4,362	3,961
Goods loaded*	1,514	1,365	947

* Excluding ships' bunkers.

CIVIL AVIATION
(traffic)

	1999	2000	2001
Aircraft landings*	7,612	8,349	8,765
Freight unloaded (metric tons). .	20,290	20,113	18,100†
Freight loaded (metric tons) . .	20,695	21,156	20,800†

* Commercial aircraft only.
† Figures are rounded.

Tourism

FOREIGN TOURIST ARRIVALS

Country of Residence	2001	2002	2003
France	197,595	202,869	200,229
Germany	50,866	53,762	53,970
India	18,890	20,898	25,367
Italy	37,343	38,263	39,774
Réunion	91,140	96,375	95,679
South Africa	47,882	42,685	45,756
Switzerland	18,427	17,371	17,929
United Kingdom	77,888	80,667	91,210
Total (incl. others)	660,318	681,648	702,018

Tourism earnings (million rupees): 18,166 in 2001; 18,328 in 2002; 19,397 in 2003.

Communications Media

	2000	2001	2002
Telephones ('000 main lines in use)	280.9	306.8	327.2
Mobile cellular telephones ('000 subscribers).	180	300	350
Personal computers ('000 in use)	120	130	n.a.
Internet users ('000)	87	158	180
Television sets licensed ('000) . .	223.9	235.4	241.4
Daily newspapers	6	6	6
Non-daily newspapers	35	35	34

1995: Facsimile machines (number in use) 20,000; Book production: titles 64, copies ('000) 116.

1996: Facsimile machines (number in use) 25,000; Book production: titles 80, copies ('000) 163.

1997: Facsimile machines (number in use) 28,000.

Sources: partly UNESCO, *Statistical Yearbook*; UN, *Statistical Yearbook*; International Telecommunication Union.

Education

(March 2003)

	Institutions	Teachers	Students*
Pre-primary	1,092	2,508	38,620
Primary	291	5,465	129,616
Secondary	175	5,938	103,847
Technical and vocational . .	114	433	7,326

* By enrolment.

Adult literacy rate (UNESCO estimates): 84.8% (males 88.0%; females 81.7%) in 2001 (Source: UN Development Programme, *Human Development Report*).

Directory

The Constitution

The Mauritius Independence Order, which established a self-governing state, came into force on 12 March 1968, and was subsequently amended. Constitutional amendments providing for the adoption of republican status were approved by the Legislative Assembly (henceforth known as the National Assembly) on 10 December 1991, and came into effect on 12 March 1992. The main provisions of the revised Constitution are listed below:

HEAD OF STATE

The Head of State is the President of the Republic, who is elected by a simple majority of the National Assembly for a five-year term of office. The President appoints the Prime Minister (in whom executive power is vested) and, on the latter's recommendation, other ministers.

COUNCIL OF MINISTERS

The Council of Ministers, which is headed by the Prime Minister, is appointed by the President and is responsible to the National Assembly.

THE NATIONAL ASSEMBLY

The National Assembly, which has a term of five years, comprises the Speaker, 62 members elected by universal adult suffrage, a maximum of eight additional members and the Attorney-General (if not an elected member). The island of Mauritius is divided into 20 three-member constituencies for legislative elections. Rodrigues returns two members to the National Assembly. The official language of the National Assembly is English, but any member may address the Speaker in French.

The Government

HEAD OF STATE

President: Sir ANEROOD JUGNAUTH (took office 7 October 2003).
Vice-President: RAOUF BUNDHUN.

COUNCIL OF MINISTERS
(May 2004)

Prime Minister and Minister of Defence and Home Affairs: PAUL RAYMOND BÉRENGER.

Deputy Prime Minister and Minister of Finance and Economic Development: PRAVIND KUMAR JUGNAUTH.

Minister of Foreign Affairs, International Trade and Regional Co-operation: JAYA KRISHNA CUTTAREE.

Minister of Housing and Lands, and Minister of Small and Medium Enterprises: GEORGES PIERRE LESJONGARD.

Minister of Social Security, National Solidarity and Senior Citizens' Welfare and Reform Institutions: SAMIOULLAH LAUTHAN.

Minister of Public Infrastructure and Land Transport: ANIL KUMAR BACHOO.

Minister of Public Utilities: ALAN GANOO.

Minister of Agriculture, Food Technology and Natural Resources: NANDCOOMAR BODHA.

Minister of the Environment and the National Development Unit: RAJESH ANAND BHAGWAN.

Minister of Labour, Industrial Relations and Employment: SHOWKUTALLY SOODHUN.

Minister of Civil Service Affairs and Administrative Reform: AHMAD SULLIMAN JEEWAH.

Minister of Tourism and Leisure: ANIL KUMARSINGH GAYAN.

Minister of Women's Rights, Child Development and Family Welfare: MARIE ARIANNE NAVARRE-MARIE.

Minister of Health and Quality of Life: ASHOCK KUMAR JUGNAUTH.

Minister of Education and Scientific Research: LOUIS STEVEN OBEEGADOO.

Minister of Fisheries: SYLVIO LOUIS MICHEL.

Minister of Arts and Culture: MOTEE RAMDASS.

Minister of Commerce and Co-operatives: PREMDUT KOONJOO.

Minister of Industry, Financial Services and Corporate Affairs: KHUSHHAL CHAND KHUSHIRAM.

Minister of Local Government and Solid Waste Management: MOOKHESSWUR CHOONEE.

Minister of Information Technology and Telecommunications: DEELCHAND JEEHA.

Attorney-General and Minister of Justice and Human Rights: EMMANUEL JEAN LEUNG SHING.

Minister of Training, Skills Development, Productivity and External Communications: SANGEET FOWDAR.

Minister of Youth and Sports: RAVI RAJ YERRIGADOO.

Minister of Shipping, Rodrigues and Outer Islands: PRITHVIRAJ AUROOMOOGA PUTTEN.

MINISTRIES

President's Office: Clarisse House, Vacoas, Port Louis; tel. 697-0077; fax 697-2347; e-mail statepas@intnet.mu; internet ncb.intnet.mu/president.htm.

Prime Minister's Office: Government Centre, Port Louis; tel. 202-9010; fax 208-8619; internet primeminister.gov.mu.

Ministry of Agriculture, Food Technology and Natural Resources: Renganaden Seeneevassan Bldg, 9th Floor, Port Louis; tel. 212-7946; fax 212-4427; e-mail moa-headoffice@mail.gov.mu; internet agriculture.gov.mu.

Ministry of Arts and Culture: Renganaden Seeneevassen Bldg, 7th Floor, cnr Pope Hennessy and Maillard Sts, Port Louis; tel. 212-9993; fax 212-9366; e-mail minoac@intnet.mu; internet culture.gov.mu.

Ministry of Civil Service Affairs and Administrative Reform: New Government Centre, 7th Floor, Port Louis; tel. 201-1886; fax 212-9528; e-mail civser@intnet.mu; internet civilservice.gov.mu.

Ministry of Commerce and Co-operatives: Life Insurance Corpn of India Bldg, 3rd Floor, John F. Kennedy St, Port Louis; tel. 208-4812; fax 208-9263; e-mail pscoop@intnet.mu; internet cooperatives.gov.mu.

Ministry of Defence and Home Affairs: Government Centre, 4th Floor, Port Louis; internet ncb.intnet.mu/dha/ministry.

Ministry of Education and Scientific Research: IVTB House, Pont Fer, Phoenix; tel. 601-5200; fax 698-2550; e-mail moeps@mail.gov.mu; internet ministry-education.gov.mu.

Ministry of the Environment and the National Development Unit: Ken Lee Tower, Barracks St, Port Louis; tel. 212-3363; fax 212-8324; e-mail admenv@internet.mu; internet environment.gov.mu.

Ministry of Finance and Economic Development: Government House, Ground Floor, Port Louis; tel. 201-2557; fax 208-9823; e-mail mof@bow.intnet.mu; internet mof.gov.mu.

Ministry of Fisheries: Life Insurance Corpn of India Bldg, 4th Floor, John F. Kennedy St, Port Louis; tel. 211-2470; fax 208-1929; internet fisheries.gov.mu.

Ministry of Foreign Affairs, International Trade and Regional Co-operation: New Government Centre, 5th Floor, Port Louis; tel. 201-1648; fax 208-8087; e-mail mfa@mail.gov.mu; internet foreign.gov.mu.

Ministry of Health and Quality of Life: Emmanuel Anquetil Bldg, Sir Seewoosagur Ramgoolam St, Port Louis; tel. 201-1912; fax 208-0376; e-mail mohql@intnet.mu; internet health.gov.mu.

Ministry of Housing and Lands: Moorgate House, Port Louis; tel. 212-6022; fax 212-7482; internet housing.gov.mu.

Ministry of Industry, Financial Services and Corporate Affairs: Air Mauritius Centre, 7th Floor, John F. Kennedy St, Port Louis; tel. 210-7100; fax 212-8201; e-mail mind@mail.gov.mu; internet industry.gov.mu.

Ministry of Information Technology and Telecommunications: Air Mauritius Centre, Level 9, John F. Kennedy St, Port Louis; tel. 210-0201; fax 212-1673; e-mail mtel@mail.gov.mu; internet telecomit.gov.mu.

Ministry of Justice and Human Rights: Renganaden Seeneevassen Bldg, 2nd Floor, Port Louis; tel. 212-2139; fax 212-6742; e-mail sgo@intnet.mu; internet attorneygeneral.gov.mu.

Ministry of Labour, Industrial Relations and Employment: Victoria House, cnr St Louis and Barracks Sts, Port Louis; tel. 207-2600; fax 212-3070; e-mail mol@mail.gov.mu; internet labour.gov.mu.

Ministry of Local Government and Solid Waste Management: Emmanuel Anquetil Bldg, 3rd Floor, cnr Sir Seewoosagur Ramgoolam and Jules Koenig Sts, Port Louis; tel. 201-1216; fax 208-9729; e-mail mlg@mail.gov.mu; internet localgovernment.gov.mu.

Ministry of Public Infrastructure and Land Transport: Moorgate House, 4th Floor, Sir W. Newton St, Port Louis; tel. 208-3063; fax 208-7149; internet publicinfrastructure.gov.mu.

Ministry of Public Utilities: Medcor Bldg, 10th Floor, John F. Kennedy St, Port Louis; tel. 210-3994; fax 208-6497; e-mail minpuuti@intnet.mu; internet publicutilities.gov.mu.

Ministry of Social Security, National Solidarity and Senior Citizens' Welfare and Reform Institutions: Renganaden Seeneevassen Bldg, Jules Koenig St, Port Louis; tel. 212-9813; fax 212-8190; e-mail mssns@intnet.mu; internet socialsecurity.gov.mu.

Ministry of Tourism and Leisure: Air Mauritius Centre, Level 12, John F. Kennedy St, Port Louis; tel. 211-7930; fax 208-6776; e-mail mot@intnet.mu; internet tourism.gov.mu.

Ministry of Training, Skills Development, Productivity and External Communications: NPF Bldg, 6th Floor, cnr Jules Koenig and Maillard Sts, Port Louis; tel. 212-5051; fax 212-5820; e-mail mhrd@intnet.mu; internet training.gov.mu.

Ministry of Women's Rights, Child Development and Family Welfare: CSK Bldg, cnr Remy Ollier and Emmanuel Anquetil Sts, Port Louis; tel. 240-1377; fax 240-7717; e-mail mwfwcd@bow.intnet.mu; internet women.gov.mu.

Ministry of Youth and Sports: Emmanuel Anquetil Bldg, 3rd Floor, Sir Seewoosagur Ramgoolam St, Port Louis; tel. 201-2543; fax 211-2986; e-mail mys@mail.gov.mu; internet youthsport.gov.mu.

Legislature

NATIONAL ASSEMBLY

Speaker: PREMNATH RAMNAH.

General Election, 11 September 2000

Party	Seats*
Mouvement Socialiste Militant (MSM)/Mouvement Militant Mauricien (MMM)	54
Mauritius Labour Party (MLP)/Parti Mauricien Social Démocrate (PMSD)	6
Organisation du Peuple Rodriguais (OPR)	2

* Additional members were to be appointed from the unsuccessful candidates who attracted the largest number of votes.

Political Organizations

Comité d'Action Musulman (CAM): Port Louis; f. 1958; Muslim support; Pres. YOUSSUF MOHAMMED.

Hizbullah: Port Louis; Islamist; Leader CEHL MEEAH.

Mauritius Labour Party (MLP) (Parti Travailliste): 7 Guy Rozemont Sq., Port Louis; tel. 212-6691; e-mail labour@intnet.mu; internet www.labour.intnet.mu; f. 1936; formed an alliance with the Parti Mauricien Social Démocrate for the 2000 election; Leader Dr NAVINCHANDRA RAMGOOLAM; Chair. JEAN-FRANÇOIS CHAUMIÈRE; Sec.-Gen. SARAT DUTT LALLAH.

Mouvement Militant Mauricien (MMM): 21 Poudrière St, Port Louis; tel. 212-6553; fax 208-9939; internet mmm.intnet.mu; f. 1969; socialist; formed an alliance with the Mouvement Socialiste Militant for the 2000 election and subsequently a coalition govt; Chair. AHMAD JEEWAH; Leader PAUL BÉRENGER; Sec.-Gen. IVAN COLLENDAVELLOO.

Mouvement Rodriguais: Port Mathurin, Rodrigues; tel. 831-1876 (Port Mathurin); tel. and fax 686-8859 (Port Louis); f. 1992; represents the interests of Rodrigues; Leader JOSEPH (NICHOLAS) VON-MALLY.

Mouvement Socialiste Militant (MSM): Sun Trust Bldg, 31 Edith Cavell St, Port Louis; tel. 212-8787; fax 208-9517; e-mail request@msmsun.com; internet www.msmsun.com; f. 1983 by fmr mems of the MMM; dominant party in subsequent coalition govts until Dec. 1995 and again in 2000; Leader PRAVIND JUGNAUTH; Chair. JOE LESJONGARD; Sec.-Gen. VISHWANATH SAJADAH.

Organisation du Peuple Rodriguais (OPR): Port Mathurin, Rodrigues; represents the interests of Rodrigues; Leader LOUIS SERGE CLAIR.

Parti Mauricien Social Démocrate (PMSD): Melville, Grand Gaube; also known as the Parti Mauricien Xavier-Luc Duval (PMXD); centre-right; formed an alliance with the Mauritius Labour Party for the 2000 election; Leader CHARLES GAËTAN XAVIER-LUC DUVAL; Sec.-Gen. JACQUES PANGLOSE.

Minor parties include the **Mouvement Militant Socialiste Mauricien** (Leader MADUN DULLOO), the **Rassemblement pour la Réforme** (Leader SHEILA BAPPOO), the **Renouveau Militant Mauricien** (Leader Dr PARAMHANSA (PREM) NABABSINGH), the **'Vrais Bleus'** (Leader HERVÉ DUVAL), the **Parti Socialiste Ouvrier** (Sec.-Gen. DIDIER EDMOND), the **Rassemblement pour l'Organisation des Créoles, Lalit** and the **Mouvement Républicain**.

Diplomatic Representation

EMBASSIES AND HIGH COMMISSIONS IN MAURITIUS

Australia: Rogers House, 2nd Floor, John F. Kennedy St, POB 541, Port Louis; tel. 208-1700; fax 208-8878; e-mail austhc@intnet.mu; internet www.ahcmauritius.org; High Commissioner IAN McCONVILLE.

China, People's Republic: Royal Rd, Belle Rose, Rose Hill; tel. 454-9111; fax 464-6012; Ambassador WANG FUYUAN.

Egypt: Forest Lane, Floreal, POB 8, Port Louis; tel. 696-5012; fax 686-5575; Ambassador MAGDA HOSNI NASR AHMED.

France: 14 St George St, Port Louis; tel. 202-0100; fax 202-0110; e-mail ambafr@intnet.mu; internet www.ambafrance-mu.org; Ambassador HENRI VIGNAL.

India: Life Insurance Corpn of India Bldg, 6th Floor, John F. Kennedy St, POB 162, Port Louis; tel. 208-3775; fax 208-6859; High Commissioner PRIPURAN SINGH HAER.

Madagascar: Guiot Pasceau St, Floreal, POB 3, Port Louis; tel. 686-5015; fax 686-7040; Ambassador BRUNO RANARIVELO.

Pakistan: 9A Queen Mary Ave, Floreal, Port Louis; tel. 698-8501; fax 698-8405; e-mail pareportlouis@hotmail.com; High Commissioner SYED HASAN JAYED.

Russia: Queen Mary Ave, POB 10, Floreal, Port Louis; tel. 696-1545; fax 696-5027; e-mail rusemb.mu@intnet.mu; Ambassador V. M. NESTERUSHKIN.

South Africa: BAI Bldg, 4th Floor, 25 Pope Hennessy St, POB 908, Port Louis; tel. 212-6925; fax 212-6936; High Commissioner AJAY KUMAR BRAMDEO.

United Kingdom: Les Cascades Bldg, 7th Floor, Edith Cavell St, POB 1063, Port Louis; tel. 202-9400; fax 202-9408; e-mail bhc@intnet.mu; High Commissioner DAVID SNOXELL.

USA: Rogers House, 4th Floor, John F. Kennedy St, Port Louis; tel. 208-4400; fax 208-9534; e-mail usembass@intnet.mu; internet mauritius.usembassy.gov; Ambassador JOHN PRICE.

Judicial System

The laws of Mauritius are derived both from the French Code Napoléon and from English Law. The Judicial Department consists of the Supreme Court, presided over by the Chief Justice and eight other Judges who are also Judges of the Court of Criminal Appeal and the Court of Civil Appeal. These courts hear appeals from the Intermediate Court, the Industrial Court and 10 District Courts. The Industrial Court has special jurisdiction to protect the constitutional rights of the citizen. There is a right of appeal in certain cases from the Supreme Court to the Judicial Committee of the Privy Council in the United Kingdom.

Chief Justice: ARIANGA PILLAY.

Senior Puisne Judge: B. SIK YUEN.

Puisne Judges: V. BOOLELL, K. P. MATADEEN, R. N. NARAYEN, E. BALANCY, P. LAM SHANG LEEN.

Religion

Hindus are estimated to comprise more than 50% of the population, with Christians accounting for some 30% and Muslims 17%. There is also a small Buddhist community.

CHRISTIANITY

The Anglican Communion

Anglicans in Mauritius are within the Church of the Province of the Indian Ocean, comprising six dioceses (four in Madagascar, one in Mauritius and one in Seychelles). The Archbishop of the Province is the Bishop of Antananarivo, Madagascar. In 1983 the Church had 5,438 members in Mauritius.

Bishop of Mauritius: Rt Rev. IAN ERNEST, Bishop's House, Phoenix; tel. 686-5158; fax 697-1096; e-mail dioang@intnet.mu.

Presbyterian Church of Mauritius

Minister: Pasteur ANDRÉ DE RÉLAND, 11 Poudrière St, Port Louis; tel. 208-2386; f. 1814.

The Roman Catholic Church

Mauritius comprises a single diocese, directly responsible to the Holy See, and an apostolic vicariate on Rodrigues. At 31 December 2002 there were an estimated 278,251 adherents in the country, representing about 24.3% of the total population.

Bishop of Port Louis: Rt Rev. MAURICE PIAT, Evêché, 13 Mgr Gonin St, Port Louis; tel. 208-3068; fax 208-6607; e-mail eveche@intnet.mu.

BAHÁ'Í FAITH

National Spiritual Assembly: POB 538, Port Louis; tel. 212-2179; mems resident in 190 localities.

ISLAM

Mauritius Islamic Mission: Noor-e-Islam Mosque, Port Louis; Imam S. M. BEEHARRY.

The Press

DAILIES

China Times: 24 Emmanuel Anquetil St, POB 325, Port Louis; tel. 240-3067; f. 1953; Chinese; Editor-in-Chief LONG SIONG AH KENG; circ. 3,000.

Chinese Daily News: 32 Rémy Ollier St, POB 316, Port Louis; tel. 240-0472; f. 1932; Chinese; Editor-in-Chief WONG YUEN MOY; circ. 5,000.

L'Express: 3 Brown Sequard St, POB 247, Port Louis; tel. 202-8200; fax 208-8174; e-mail sentinelle@bow.intnet.mu; internet www.lexpress-net.com; f. 1963; English and French; Editor-in-Chief JEAN-CLAUDE DE L'ESTRAC; circ. 35,000.

Maurice Soir: Port Louis; f. 1996; Editor SYDNEY SELVON; circ. 2,000.

Le Mauricien: 8 St George St, POB 7, Port Louis; tel. 208-3251; fax 208-7059; e-mail redaction@lemauricien.com; internet www.lemauricien.com; f. 1907; English and French; Editor-in-Chief GILBERT AHNEE; circ. 35,000.

L'Observateur: Port Louis; f. 1997; French.

Le Quotidien: Port Louis; tel. 211-4800; fax 211-7479; e-mail quotidie@bow.intnet.mu; f. 1996; English and French; Dirs JACQUES DAVID, PATRICK MICHEL; circ. 30,000.

Le Socialiste: Manilall Bldg, 3rd Floor, Brabant St, Port Louis; tel. 208-8003; fax 211-3890; English and French; Editor-in-Chief VEDI BALLAH; circ. 7,000.

The Sun: 31 Edith Cavell St, Port Louis; tel. 212-4820; fax 208-9517; English and French; Editor-in-Chief SUBASH GOBIN; circ. 4,000.

The Tribune: Port Louis; f. 1999; Publr HARISH CHUNDUNSING.

WEEKLIES AND FORTNIGHTLIES

5-Plus Dimanche: Résidence des Palmiers, 198 Royal Rd, Beau Bassin; tel. 454-3353; fax 454-3420; f. 1994; English and French; Editor-in-Chief FINLAY SALESSE; circ. 30,000.

5-Plus Magazine: Résidence des Palmiers, 198 Royal Rd, Beau Bassin; tel. 454-3353; fax 454-3420; f. 1990; English and French; Editor-in-Chief PIERRE BENOÎT; circ. 10,000.

Business Magazine: TN Tower, 1st Floor, 13 St George St, Port Louis; tel. 211-1925; fax 211-1926; f. 1993; English and French; Editor-in-Chief LYNDSAY RIVIÈRE; circ. 6,000.

Le Croissant: cnr Velore and Noor Essan Mosque Sts, Port Louis; tel. 240-7105; English and French; Editor-in-Chief RAYMOND RICHARD NAUVEL; circ. 25,000.

Le Dimanche: 5 Jemmapes St, Port Louis; tel. 212-5887; fax 212-1177; e-mail ledmer@intnet.mu; f. 1961; English and French; Editor RAYMOND RICHARD NAUVEL; circ. 25,000.

La Gazette des Iles: Port Louis; historical journal.

L'Hebdo-Militant: Port Louis.

Impact News: 6 Grandcourt, Port Louis; tel. 240-8567; English and French; Editor-in-Chief CADER SAIB.

Lalit de Klas: 153B Royal Rd, G.R.N.W., Port Louis; tel. 208-2132; English, French and Creole; Editor ASHOK SUBRON.

Le Lotus: 73 Prince of Wales St, Rose Hill; tel. 208-4068; English and French; Editor-in-Chief MOGANADEN PILLAY.

Le Mag: Industrial Zone, Tombeay Bay; tel. 247-1005; fax 247-1061; f. 1993; English and French; Editor (vacant); circ. 8,000.

Mauritius Times: 23 Bourbon St, Port Louis; tel. and fax 212-1313; e-mail mtimes@intnet.mu; internet www.mauritiustimes.com; f. 1954; English and French; Editor-in-Chief MADHUKAR RAMLALLAH; circ. 15,000.

Le Militant Magazine: 7 Lord Kitchener St, Port Louis; tel. 212-6050; fax 208-2291; f. 1989; English and French; Editor-in-Chief MITRADEV PEERTHUM; circ. 2,000.

Mirror: 39 Emmanuel Anquetil St, Port Louis; tel. 240-3298; Chinese; Editor-in-Chief NG KEE SIONG; circ. 4,000.

News on Sunday: Port Louis; tel. 211-5902; fax 211-7302; e-mail newsonsunday@hotmail.com; internet www.newsonsunday.com; f. 1996; weekly; Editor MICHAEL LYNCH; circ. 15,000.

Le Nouveau Militant: 21 Poudrière St, Port Louis; tel. 212-6553; fax 208-2291; f. 1979; publ. by the Mouvement Militant Mauricien; English and French; Editor-in-Chief J. RAUMIAH.

Le Rodriguais: Saint Gabriel, Rodrigues; tel. 831-1613; fax 831-1484; f. 1989; Creole, English and French; Editor JACQUES EDOUARD; circ. 2,000.

Star: Port Louis; tel. 212-2736; fax 211-7781; e-mail starpress@intnet.mu; internet www.mauriweb.com/star; English and French; Editor-in-Chief REZA ISSACK.

Style: Port Louis; women's interest; weekly.

Sunday: Port Louis; tel. 208-9516; fax 208-7059; f. 1966; English and French; Editor-in-Chief SUBASH GOBIN.

La Vie Catholique: 28 Nicolay Rd, Port Louis; tel. 242-0975; fax 242-3114; e-mail viecatho@intnet.mu; internet pages.intnet.mu/lavie; f. 1930; weekly; English, French and Creole; Editor-in-Chief Fr GEORGES CHEUNG; circ. 8,000.

Week-End: 8 St George St, Port Louis; tel. 208-3252; fax 208-3248; internet www.lemauricien.com/weekend; f. 1966; French and English; Editor-in-Chief GÉRARD CATEAUX; circ. 80,000.

Week-End Scope: 8 St George St, Port Louis; tel. 208-3251; fax 208-7059; internet www.lemauricien.com/wes; English and French; Editor-in-Chief AHMAD SALARBUX.

OTHER SELECTED PERIODICALS

CCI-INFO: 3 Royal St, Port Louis; tel. 208-3301; fax 208-0076; e-mail mcci@intnet.mu; internet www.mcci.org; English and French; f. 1995; publ. of the Mauritius Chamber of Commerce and Industry.

Ciné Star Magazine: 64 Sir Seewoosagur Ramgoolam St, Port Louis; tel. 240-1447; English and French; Editor-in-Chief ABDOOL RAWOOF SOOBRATTY.

Education News: Edith Cavell St, Port Louis; tel. 212-1303; English and French; monthly; Editor-in-Chief GIAN AUBEELUCK.

Le Message de L'Ahmadiyyat: c/o Ahmadiyya Muslim Asscn, POB 6, Rose Hill; tel. 464-1747; fax 454-2223; e-mail darussalaam@intnet.mu; French; monthly; Editor-in-Chief MOHAMMAD AMEEN JOWAHIR; circ. 3,000.

Le Progrès Islamique: 51B Solferino St, Rose Hill; tel. 467-1697; fax 467-1696; f. 1948; English and French; monthly; Editor DEVINA SOOKIA.

La Voix d'Islam: Parisot Rd, Mesnil, Phoenix; f. 1951; English and French; monthly.

Publishers

Boukié Banané (The Flame Tree): 5 Edwin Ythier St, Rose Hill; tel. 454-2327; fax 465-4312; e-mail limem@intnet.mu; internet pages.intnet.mu/develop; f. 1979; Morisien literature, poetry and drama; Man. Dir DEV VIRAHSAWMY.

Business Publications Ltd: TN Tower, 1st Floor, St George St, Port Louis; tel. 211-1925; fax 211-1926; f. 1993; English and French; Dir LYNDSAY RIVIÈRE.

Editions du Dattier: 82 Goyavier Ave, Quatre Bornes; tel. 466-4854; fax 446-3105; e-mail dattier@intnet.mu; English and French; Dir JEAN-PHILIPPE LAGESSE.

Editions de l'Océan Indien: Stanley, Rose Hill; tel. 464-6761; fax 464-3445; e-mail eoibooks@intnet.mu; f. 1977; textbooks, literature; English, French and Asian languages; Gen. Man. (vacant).

Editions Le Printemps: 4 Club Rd, Vacoas; tel. 696-1017; fax 686-7302; e-mail elp@bow.intnet.mu; Man. Dir A. I. SULLIMAN.

Editions Vizavi: 9 St George St, Port Louis; tel. 211-3047; e-mail vizavi@intnet.mu; Dir PASCALE SIEW.

Broadcasting and Communications

TELECOMMUNICATIONS

Information and Communication Technologies Authority (ICTA): Jade House, 1st floor, cnr Rémy Ollier and Jumman Mosque Sts, Port Louis; tel. 217-222; fax 217-777; e-mail icta@intnet.mu; internet www.icta.mu; f. 1999; regulatory authority; Chair. ASHOK RADHAKISSOON.

Mauritius Telecom Ltd: Telecom Tower, Edith Cavell St, Port Louis; tel. 203-7000; fax 208-1070; e-mail ceo@mauritiustelecom.com.mu; internet www.mauritiustelecom.com; f. 1992; 40% owned by France Telecom; privatized in 2000; provides all telecommunications services, including internet and digital mobile cellular services; Chair. Dr PREM NABABSING; Chief Exec. JOHN LEUNG YINKO.

BROADCASTING

In 1997 the Supreme Court invalidated the broadcasting monopoly held by the Mauritius Broadcasting Corporation.

Radio

Mauritius Broadcasting Corpn: Broadcasting House, Louis Pasteur St, Forest Side; tel. 675-5001; fax 676-7332; e-mail mbc@intnet.mu; internet mbc.intnet.mu; f. 1964; independent corpn operating five national radio services and three television channels; Chair. TORRIDEN CHELLAPERMAL; Dir-Gen. HOOTESH RAMBURN.

Radio One: Port Louis; f. 2002; owned by Sentinelle media group; news and entertainment; Dir-Gen. JEAN-MICHEL FONTAINE.

Top FM: Harbour Front, 6th Floor, cnr Queen Elizabeth and John Kennedy Sts, Port Louis; tel. 213-2121; fax 213-2222; e-mail topfm@intnet.mu; internet www.servihoo.com/channels/media/radios/topfm; f. 2003; part of the International Broadcasting Group, in partnership with the Sunrise Group; Chair. BALKRISHNA KAUNHYE.

A further two private stations, Radio Plus and Sunrise Radio, were issued licences in early 2002.

Television

Independent television stations were to commence broadcasting from 2002, as part of the liberalization of the sector.

Mauritius Broadcasting Corpn: see Radio.

Finance

(cap. = capital; res = reserves; dep. = deposits; m. = million; brs = branches; amounts in Mauritian rupees, unless otherwise stated)

BANKING

Central Bank

Bank of Mauritius: Sir William Newton St, POB 29, Port Louis; tel. 208-4164; fax 208-9204; e-mail bomrd@bow.intnet.mu; internet bom.intnet.mu; f. 1966; bank of issue; cap. 10.0m., res 14,205.9m., dep. 9,662.5m. (June 2002); Gov. RAMESWURLALL BASANT ROI; Man. Dir BABOO RAJENDRANATHSING GUJADHUR.

Principal Commercial Banks

Bank of Baroda: Sir William Newton St, POB 553, Port Louis; tel. 208-1504; fax 208-3892; e-mail bobgen@intnet.mu; cap. and res 19.9m., dep. 396m. (March 1998); Pres. R. A. ALMEIDA; 6 brs.

Barclays Bank PLC, Mauritius: Sir William Newton St, POB 165, Port Louis; tel. 208-2685; fax 208-2720; f. 1919; absorbed Banque Nationale de Paris Intercontinentale in 2002; cap. 100.0m., res 616.1m., dep. 6,886.7m. (Dec. 2001); Dir JACQUES DE NAVACELLE; 16 brs.

First City Bank Ltd: 16 Sir William Newton St, POB 485, Port Louis; tel. 208-5061; fax 208-5388; e-mail info@firstcitybank-mauritius.com; internet www.firstcitybank-mauritius.com; f. 1991 as the Delphis Bank Ltd; merged with Union International Bank in 1997; private bank; taken over by consortium in 2002; 51.6% owned by the Development Bank of Mauritius; cap. 420.1m., res 34.2, dep. 4,530.5m. (June 2002); Chair. B. CHOORAMUN; Chief Exec. ROHIT AUKLE.

Hongkong and Shanghai Banking Corpn Ltd (HSBC): place d'Armes, POB 50, Port Louis; tel. 208-1801; fax 210-0400; e-mail hsbcmauritius@hsbc.co.mu; internet www.hsbc.co.mu; f. 1916; CEO SANJIV BHASIN.

Indian Ocean International Bank Ltd: 34 Sir William Newton St, POB 863, Port Louis; tel. 208-0121; fax 208-0127; f. 1978; cap. 100.5m., res 177.0m., dep. 2,713.0m. (June 2002); Pres. VALAYDON VISWANATHEN; 8 brs.

Mauritius Commercial Bank Ltd: MCB Centre, 9–15 Sir William Newton St, Port Louis; tel. 202-5000; fax 208-7054; e-mail publicrelations@mcb.co.mu; internet www.mcbgroup.com; f. 1838; cap. 582.6m., res 7,303.0m., dep. 74,646.3m. (June 2002); Pres. JACQUES F. HAREL; Gen. Man. PIERRE GUY NOËL; 41 brs.

South East Asian Bank Ltd: Max City Bldg, 2nd Floor, cnr Rémy Ollier and Louis Pasteur Sts, POB 13, Port Louis; tel. 216-8826; fax 241-7379; e-mail seab@intnet.mu; f. 1989; cap. and res 114.7m., dep. 1,001.3m. (Dec. 2000); Chief Exec. VINCENT LEE; Chair. Tan Sri Dato' ABDUL KHALID BIN SAHAN; 5 brs.

State Bank of Mauritius Ltd: State Bank Tower, 1 Queen Elizabeth II Ave, POB 152, Port Louis; tel. 202-1111; fax 202-1234; e-mail sbm@sbm.intnet.mu; internet www.sbm-online.com; f. 1973; cap. 336.2m., res 4,273.9m., dep. 27,044.9m. (June 2003); Chair. Sir DEWOONARAIN DOOKUN; Chief Exec. MUNI KRISHNA T. REDDY; 42 brs.

Development Bank

Development Bank of Mauritius Ltd: La Chaussée, POB 157, Port Louis; tel. 208-0241; fax 208-8498; e-mail dbm@intnet.mu; internet www.dbm-ltd.com; f. 1964; 65% govt-owned; cap. 125m., res 1,130.0m., total assets 3,981.3m. (June 2001); Chair. A. HOSSEN; Man. Dir B. CHOORAMUN.

Principal 'Offshore' Banks

Banque Internationale des Mascareignes Ltd: Le Caudan Waterfront, 4th Floor, Barkly Wharf, POB 489, Port Louis; tel. 212-4978; fax 212-4983; e-mail bim@intnet.mu; internet www.bim.intnet

.mu; f. 1991; jt venture of Banque de la Réunion (50.5%), Mauritius Commercial Bank Ltd (35%) and Crédit Lyonnais Global Banking, France (14.5%); cap. US $6.0m., res $1.5m., dep. $106.5m. (Dec. 2001); Chair. JEAN-CLAUDE CLARAC; Gen. Man. YVES NAMY.

SBI International (Mauritius) Ltd: Harbour Front Bldg, 7th Floor, John F. Kennedy St, POB 376, Port Louis; tel. 212-2054; fax 212-2050; e-mail sbilmaur@intnet.mu; f. 1989; 98% owned by the State Bank of India; cap. US $10.0m., res $9.0m., dep. $93.9m. (Mar. 2003); Chair. A. K. PURWAR; Man. Dir M. C. MULAY.

Bank of Baroda, Banque Nationale de Paris Intercontinentale, Barclays Bank PLC, African Asian Bank, PT Bank International Indonesia, Investec Bank (Mauritius) and HSBC Bank PLC also operate 'offshore' banking units.

STOCK EXCHANGE

Financial Services Commission: Harbour Front Bldg, 4th Floor, John F. Kennedy St, Port Louis; tel. 210-7000; fax 208-7172; e-mail fscmauritius@intnet.mu; internet www.fscmauritius.org; f. 2001; regulatory authority for securities, insurance and global business activities; Chief Exec. IQBAL RAJAHBALEE.

Stock Exchange of Mauritius: Cascades Bldg, 2nd Floor, Edith Cavell St, Port Louis; tel. 212-9541; fax 208-8409; e-mail stockex@bow.intnet.mu; internet www.semdex.com; f. 1989; 11 mems; Chair. JEAN DE FONDAUMIÈRE; CEO SUNIL BENIMADHU.

INSURANCE

Albatross Insurance Co Ltd: 22 St George St, POB 116, Port Louis; tel. 207-9007; fax 208-4800; e-mail headoffice@albatross.mu; internet www.albatross-insurance.com; f. 1975; Chair. TIMOTHY TAYLOR; Man. Dir JEAN DE LA HOGUE.

Anglo-Mauritius Assurance Society Ltd: Swan Group Centre, 10 Intendance St, POB 837, Port Louis; tel. 202-8600; fax 208-8956; e-mail anglomtius@intnet.mu; internet www.groupswan.com; f. 1951; Chair. J. CYRIL LAGESSE; CEO JEAN DE FONDAUMIÈRE.

British American Insurance Co (Mauritius) Ltd: BAI Bldg, 25 Pope Hennessy St, POB 331, Port Louis; tel. 202-3600; fax 208-3713; e-mail bai@intnet.mu; f. 1920; Chair. DAWOOD RAWAT; Man. Dir HEINRICH K. DE KOCK.

Ceylinco Stella Insurance Co Ltd: 36 Sir Seewoosagur Ramgoolam St, POB 852, Port Louis; tel. 208-0056; fax 208-1639; e-mail stellain@intnet.mu; internet www.stellain.com; f. 1977; Chair. and Man. Dir R. KRESHAN JHOBOO.

Indian Ocean General Assurance Ltd: 35 Corderie St, POB 865, Port Louis; tel. 212-4125; fax 212-5850; e-mail iogaltd@intnet.mu; f. 1971; Chair. SAM M. CUNDEN; Man. Dir D. A. CUNDEN.

Island Insurance Co Ltd: Labourdonnais Court, 5th Floor, cnr Labourdonnais and St George Sts, Port Louis; tel. 212-4860; fax 208-8762; e-mail island.ins@intnet.mu; f. 1998; Chair. CARRIM A. CURRIMJEE; Man. Dir OLIVIER LAGESSE.

Jubilee Insurance (Mauritius) Ltd: PCL Bldg, 4th Floor, 43 Sir William Newton St, POB 301, Port Louis; tel. 210-3678; fax 212-7970; e-mail jubilee@intnet.mu; f. 1998; Chair. and CEO AUGUSTINE J. HATCH.

Lamco International Insurance Ltd: 12 Barracks St, Port Louis; tel. 212-0233; fax 208-0630; e-mail lamco@intnet.mu; internet www.lamcoinsurance.com; f. 1978; Chair. A. B. ATCHIA.

Life Insurance Corpn of India: LIC Centre, John F. Kennedy St, Port Louis; tel. 212-5316; fax 208-6392; e-mail liccmm@intnet.mu; f. 1956; Chief Man. HEMANT BHARGAVA.

Mauritian Eagle Insurance Co Ltd: 1st Floor, IBL House, Caudan Waterfront, POB 854, Port Louis; tel. 203-2200; fax 208-8608; e-mail meagle@meagle.intnet.mu; internet www.iblgroup.com/mauritianeagle; f. 1973; Chair. P. D'HOTMAN DE VILLIERS; Exec. Dir G. LAN HUN KUEN.

Mauritius Union Assurance Co Ltd: 4 L'Homme St, POB 233, Port Louis; tel. 208-4185; fax 212-2962; e-mail mua@bow.intnet.mu; internet www.muaco.com; f. 1948; Chair. Sir MAURICE LATOUR-ADRIEN; Gen. Man. JEAN-NOËL LAM CHUN.

The New India Assurance Co Ltd: Bank of Baroda Bldg, 3rd Floor, 15 Sir William Newton St, Port Louis; tel. 208-1442; fax 208-2160; e-mail niasurance@intnet.mu; f. 1935; Chief Man. A. K. JAIN.

La Préservatrice Foncière: 6 Dumas St, Port Louis; tel. 212-1352; fax 208-3604; Dirs MAURICE MARTIN, FRANÇOIS MARTIN.

La Prudence Mauricienne Assurances Ltée: Le Caudan Waterfront, 2nd Floor, Barkly Wharf, POB 882, Port Louis; tel. 207-2500; fax 208-8936; e-mail prudence@intnet.mu; Chair. ROBERT DE FROBERVILLE; Man. Dir FÉLIX MAUREL.

Rainbow Insurance Co Ltd: 23 Edith Cavell St, POB 389, Port Louis; tel. 212-5767; fax 208-8750; f. 1976; Chair. B. Gokulsing; Man. Dir Previn Renburg.

State Insurance Co of Mauritius Ltd (SICOM): SICOM Bldg, Sir Célicourt Antelme St, Port Louis; tel. 208-5406; fax 208-7662; e-mail email@sicom.intnet.mu; internet sicom.intnet.mu; f. 1975; Chair. A. F. Ho Chan Fong; Man. Dir K. Bhoojedhur-Obeegadoo.

Sun Insurance Co Ltd: 2 St George St, Port Louis; tel. 208-0769; fax 208-2052; f. 1981; Chair. Sir Kailash Ramdanee; Man. Dir A. Musbally.

Swan Insurance Co Ltd: Swan Group Centre, 10 Intendance St, POB 364, Port Louis; tel. 211-2001; fax 208-6898; e-mail swan@intnet.mu; f. 1955; Chair. J. M. Antoine Harel; CEO Jean de Fondaumière.

L. and H. Vigier de Latour Ltd: Les Jamalacs Bldg, Old Council St, Port Louis; tel. 212-2034; fax 212-6056; Chair. and Man. Dir L. J. D. Henri Vigier de Latour.

Trade and Industry

GOVERNMENT AGENCIES

Agricultural Marketing Board (AMB): Dr G. Leclézio Ave, Moka; tel. 433-4025; fax 433-4837; e-mail agbd@intnet.mu; markets certain locally produced and imported food crops; also collects and distributes milk and provides cold store facilities.

Mauritius Meat Authority: Abattoir Rd, Roche Bois, POB 612, Port Louis; tel. 242-5884; fax 242-4695; e-mail msa@bow.intnet.mu; licensing authority; controls and regulates sale of meat and meat products; also purchases and imports livestock and markets meat products.

Mauritius Sugar Authority: Ken Lee Bldg, 2nd Floor, Edith Cavell St, Port Louis; tel. 208-7466; fax 208-7470; e-mail msa@bow .intnet.mu; internet www.mns.intnet.mu/msa.htm; Chair. S. Seebaluck; Exec. Dir G. Rajpati.

Mauritius Tea Board: Wooton St, Curepipe Rd, Curepipe; tel. 675-3497; fax 676-1445; regulates and controls the activities of the tea industry; Gen. Man. A. Seepergauth.

DEVELOPMENT ORGANIZATIONS

Mauritius Freeport Authority (MFA): Trade and Marketing Centre, 1st Floor, Freeport Zone 6, Mer Rouge; tel. 206-2500; fax 206-2600; e-mail mfa@freeport.gov.mu; internet www.efreeport .com; f. 1990; Chair. Kavydass Ramano; Dir-Gen. Rajakrishna Chellapermal.

Mauritius Industrial Development Authority (MIDA): BAI Bldg, 2nd Floor, 25 Pope Hennessy St, POB 1184, Port Louis; tel. 208-7750; fax 208-5965; e-mail media@intnet.mu; internet ncb .intnet.mu/mida; f. 1985 to promote the export of goods and services and to encourage export-orientated investment; Chair. (vacant); CEO Elizabeth Ah Chong.

Mauritius Infocom Development Authority: Port Louis; f. 2001; responsible for both the Mauritius Telecommunications Authority and the National Computer Board.

Mauritius Investment Board: Port Louis; f. 2000 to promote international investment, business and services.

State Investment Corpn Ltd (SIC): Air Mauritius Centre, 15th Floor, John F. Kennedy St, Port Louis; tel. 212-2978; fax 208-8948; e-mail sicadmin@intnet.mu; provides support for new investment and transfer of technology, in agriculture, industry and tourism; Man. Dir Seilendra Gokhool; CEO Rajiv Beeharry.

CHAMBERS OF COMMERCE

Chinese Chamber of Commerce: Port Louis; tel. 208-0946; fax 242-1193; Pres. Jean Kok Shun.

Mauritius Chamber of Commerce and Industry: 3 Royal St, Port Louis; tel. 208-3301; fax 208-0076; e-mail mcci@intnet.mu; internet www.mcci.org; f. 1850; 416 mems; Pres. Marday Venkatasamy; Sec.-Gen. Mahmood Cheeroo.

INDUSTRIAL ASSOCIATION

Mauritius Sugar Producers' Association: Plantation House, Duke of Edinburgh Ave, Port Louis; tel. 212-0295; fax 212-5727; e-mail mspa@intnet.mu; Chair. Georges Leungshing; Dir P. de Labauve d'Arifat.

EMPLOYERS' ORGANIZATION

Mauritius Employers' Federation: Cernée House, 1st Floor, Chaussée St, Port Louis; tel. 212-1599; fax 212-6725; e-mail info@mef-online.org; internet www.mef-online.org; f. 1962; Pres. (vacant); Dir Dr Azad Jeetun.

UTILITIES

Electricity

Central Electricity Board: Royal Rd, POB 40, Curepipe; tel. 675-5010; fax 675-7958; e-mail ceb@intnet.mu; internet ceb.intnet.mu; f. 1952; state-operated; scheduled for privatization; Chair. Prof. A. Brij Kishore Baguant; Gen. Man. Paul van Niekerk.

Water

Central Water Authority: Royal Rd, St Paul-Phoenix; tel. 601-5000; fax 686-6264; e-mail cwa@bow.intnet.mu; internet www.ncb .intnet.mu/putil/cwa; state-operated; scheduled for privatization; f. 1971; Gen. Man. Rohit Mungra; Exec. Chair. H. K. Booluck.

TRADE UNIONS

Federations

Federation of Civil Service Unions (FCSU): Jade Court, Rm 308, 3rd Floor, Jummah Mosque St, Port Louis; tel. 216-1977; fax 216-1475; e-mail f.c.s.u.@intnet.mu; f. 1957; 67 affiliated unions with 25,000 mems (2000); Pres. Rashid Imrith; Sec. Soondress Sawmynaden.

General Workers' Federation: 13 Brabant St, Port Louis; tel. 212-3338; Pres. Farook Auchoybur; Sec.-Gen. Devanand Ramjuttun.

Mauritius Federation of Trade Unions: Arc Bldg, 3rd Floor, cnr Sir William Newton and Sir Seewoosagur Ramgoolam Sts, Port Louis; tel. 208-9426; f. 1958; four affiliated unions; Pres. Farook Hossenbux; Sec.-Gen. R. Mareemootoo.

Mauritius Labour Congress: 8 Louis Victor de la Faye St, Port Louis; tel. 212-4343; fax 208-8945; f. 1963; 55 affiliated unions with 70,000 mems (1992); Pres. Nurdeo Luchmun Roy; Gen. Sec. Jugdish Lollbeeharry.

Principal Unions

Government Servants' Association: 107A Royal Rd, Beau Bassin; tel. 464-4242; f. 1945; Pres. A. H. Malleck-Amode; Sec.-Gen. S. P. Torul; 14,000 mems (1984).

Government Teachers' Union: 3 Mgr Gonin St, POB 1111, Port Louis; tel. 208-0047; fax 208-4943; f. 1945; Pres. Jugdish Lollbeeharry; Sec. Sheikh Nashir Ramjan; 4,358 mems (1998).

Nursing Association: Royal Rd, Beau Bassin; tel. 464-5850; f. 1955; Pres. Cassam Kureeman; Sec.-Gen. Francis Supparayen; 2,040 mems (1980).

Organization of Artisans' Unity: 42 Sir William Newton St, Port Louis; tel. 212-4557; fax 212-4557; f. 1973; Pres. Auguste Follet; Sec. Roy Ramchurn; 2,874 mems (1994).

Plantation Workers' Union: 8 Louis Victor de la Faye St, Port Louis; tel. 212-1735; f. 1955; Pres. C. Bhagirutty; Sec. N. L. Roy; 13,726 mems (1990).

Port Louis Harbour and Docks Workers' Union: 19B Poudrière St, Port Louis; tel. 208-2276; Pres. M. Veerabadren; Sec.-Gen. Gerard Bertrand; 2,198 mems (1980).

Sugar Industry Staff Employees' Association: 1 Rémy Ollier St, Port Louis; tel. 212-1947; f. 1947; Chair. T. Bellerose; Sec.-Gen. G. Chung Kwan Fang; 1,450 mems (1997).

Textile, Clothes and Other Manufactures Workers' Union: Thomy d'Arifat St, Curepipe; tel. 676-5280; Pres. Padmatee Teeluck; Sec.-Gen. Désiré Guildaree.

Union of Bus Industry Workers: 19B Poudrière St, Port Louis; tel. 212-3338; Pres. Babooa; Sec.-Gen. F. Auchoybur; 1,783 mems (1980).

Union of Employees of the Ministry of Agriculture and other Ministries: 28 Hennessy Ave, Quatre-Bornes; tel. 465-1935; e-mail bruno5@intnet.mu; f. 1989; Sec. Bruneau Dorasami; 2,500 mems (Dec. 2003).

Union of Labourers of the Sugar and Tea Industry: Royal Rd, Curepipe; f. 1969; Sec. P. Ramchurn; 2,150 mems (1980).

Transport

RAILWAYS

There are no operational railways in Mauritius.

ROADS

In 2001 there were 2,000 km of classified roads, of which 60km were motorways, 950 km were other main roads, and 592 km were secondary roads. About 98% of the road network is paved. An urban highway links the motorways approaching Port Louis. A motorway connects Port Louis with Plaisance airport.

SHIPPING

Mauritius is served by numerous foreign shipping lines. In 1990 Port Louis was established as a free port to expedite the development of Mauritius as an entrepôt centre. In 1995 the World Bank approved a loan of US $30.5m. for a programme to develop the port. At 31 December 2002 Mauritius had a merchant fleet of 45 vessels, with a combined displacement of 62,690 grt.

Mauritius Ports Authority: Port Administration Bldg, POB 379, Mer Rouge, Port Louis; tel. 206-5400; fax 240-0856; e-mail mauport@intnet.mu; internet www.mauport.com; f. 1976; Chair. (vacant); Dir-Gen. Capt. JEAN WONG CHUNG TOI.

Ireland Blyth Ltd: IBL House, Caudan, Port Louis; tel. 203-2000; fax 208-1014; e-mail iblinfo@ibl.intnet.mu; internet www.iblgroup.com; Chair. ARNAUD DALAIS; CEO P. D'HOTMAN DE VILLIERS; 2 vessels.

Islands Services Ltd: Rogers House, 5 John F. Kennedy St, POB 60, Port Louis; tel. 208-6801; fax 208-5045; services to Indian Ocean islands; Chair. Sir RENÉ MAINGARD; Exec. Dir Capt. RENÉ SANSON.

Mauritius Shipping Corpn Ltd: St James Court, Suite 417/418, St Denis St, Port Louis; tel. 210-6120; fax 210-5176; e-mail mauriship@intnet.mu; internet www.mrushipping.com; f. 1985; state-owned; Pres. B. P. DAUMOO.

Société Mauricienne de Navigation Ltée: 1 rue de la Reine, POB 53, Port Louis; tel. 208-3241; fax 208-8931; e-mail iblsh@bow.intnet .mu; Man. Dir Capt. FRANÇOIS DE GERSIGNY.

CIVIL AVIATION

Sir Seewoosagur Ramgoolam International Airport is at Plaisance, 4 km from Mahébourg. Proposals are being considered for the construction of a second airport, at Plaine-les-Roches, in the north of the island.

Air Mauritius: Air Mauritius Centre, John F. Kennedy St, POB 441, Port Louis; tel. 207-7070; fax 208-8331; e-mail mkcare@ airmauritius.intnet.mu; internet www.airmauritius.com; f. 1967; 51% state-owned; services to 28 destinations in Europe, Asia, Australia and Africa; CEO ARJOON SUDDHOO; Chair. and Man. Dir VINOD CHIDAMBARAM.

Tourism

Tourists are attracted to Mauritius by its scenery and beaches, the pleasant climate and the blend of cultures. Accommodation capacity totalled 17,776 beds in 2000. The number of visitors increased from 300,670 in 1990 to 702,018 in 2003, when the greatest numbers of visitors were from France (28.5%), Réunion (13.6%) and the United Kingdom (13.0%). Gross revenue from tourism in 2003 was estimated at Rs 19,397m.

Mauritius Tourism Promotion Authority: Air Mauritius Centre, 11th Floor, John F. Kennedy St, Port Louis; tel. 210-1545; fax 212-5142; e-mail mtpa@intnet.mu; internet www.mauritius.net; Chair. GUY HUGNIN; Dir Dr KARL A. MOOTOOSAMY.

MEXICO

Introductory Survey

Location, Climate, Language, Religion, Flag, Capital

The United Mexican States is bordered to the north by the USA, and to the south by Guatemala and Belize. The Gulf of Mexico and the Caribbean Sea lie to the east, and the Pacific Ocean and Gulf of California to the west. The climate varies with altitude. The tropical southern region and the coastal lowlands are hot and wet, with an average annual temperature of 18°C (64°F), while the highlands of the central plateau are temperate. Much of the north and west is arid desert. In Mexico City, which lies at about 2,250 m (nearly 7,400 ft) above sea-level, temperatures are generally between 5°C (42°F) and 25°C (78°F). The country's highest recorded temperature is 58°C (136°F). The principal language is Spanish, spoken by more than 90% of the population, while about 8% speak indigenous languages, of which Náhuatl is the most widely spoken. Almost all of Mexico's inhabitants profess Christianity, and about 90% are adherents of the Roman Catholic Church. The national flag (proportions 4 by 7) has three equal vertical stripes from hoist to fly, of green, white and red, with the state emblem (a brown eagle, holding a snake in its beak, on a green cactus, with a wreath of oak and laurel beneath) in the centre of the white stripe. The capital is Mexico City.

Recent History

Conquered by Hernán Cortés in the 16th century, Mexico was ruled by Spain until the wars of independence of 1810–21. After the war of 1846, Mexico ceded about one-half of its territory to the USA. Attempts at political and social reform by the anti-clerical Benito Juárez precipitated civil war in 1857–60, and the repudiation of Mexico's external debts by Juárez in 1860 led to war with the United Kingdom, the USA and France. The Austrian Archduke Maximilian, whom France tried to install as Emperor of Mexico, was executed, on the orders of Juárez, in 1867. Order was restored during the dictatorship of Porfirio Díaz, which lasted from 1876 until the Revolution of 1910. The Constitution of 1917 embodied the aims of the Revolution by revising land ownership, by drafting a labour code and by curtailing the power of the Roman Catholic Church. From 1929–2000 the country was dominated by the Partido Revolucionario Institucional (PRI), for much of that time in an effective one-party system, although a democratic form of election was maintained. However, allegations of widespread electoral malpractice persistently arose in connection with PRI victories.

In presidential elections held in July 1976 the PRI candidate, José López Portillo, was elected with almost 95% of the votes cast. In 1977 López Portillo initiated reforms to increase minority party representation in the legislature and to widen democratic participation. The high level of political participation in the presidential election of July 1982 (held amid a financial crisis) was without precedent, with left-wing groups taking part for the first time; however, the PRI's candidate, Miguel de la Madrid Hurtado, was successful. The concurrent elections to the Cámara Federal de Diputados (Federal Chamber of Deputies) resulted in another overwhelming victory for the PRI, which performed strongly in the single-member constituencies. On taking office in December, the new President embarked on a programme of major economic reform, giving precedence to the repayment of Mexico's debts, a policy which imposed severe financial constraints upon the middle and lower classes and which led to growing disaffection among traditional PRI supporters. Notably, the Partido Acción Nacional (PAN), an opposition party, made important gains at municipal elections in two state capitals in mid-1983. The PRI's effective response ensured success at the remaining elections, but provoked opposition allegations of widespread electoral fraud. Contrary to expectations, at gubernatorial and congressional elections conducted in July 1985, the PRI secured all seven of the available state governorships and won 288 of the 300 directly elective seats in the Cámara.

The formation of a major left-wing alliance, the Partido Mexicano Socialista—PMS (comprising six parties), in 1987 and, in particular, the emergence of a dissident faction, the Corriente Democrática (CD), within the PRI in 1986 were disturbing political developments for the ruling party. In early 1988 the CD and four left-wing parties (including the PMS coalition) formed an electoral alliance, the Frente Democrático Nacional (FDN), headed by CD leader Cuauhtémoc Cárdenas Solórzano. The legitimacy of the PRI victory at the presidential and congressional elections, conducted in July, was fiercely challenged by the opposition groups, following a delay in the publication of official results, reports of widespread electoral fraud and the failure of the Federal Electoral Commission to release details of results from almost 50% of polling stations. Moreover, Cárdenas claimed victory on behalf of the broad-left coalition; for the first time ever, the opposition secured seats in the Senado (Senate), while the PRI suffered defeats in the Distrito Federal and at least three other states.

In August 1988 the new Congreso de la Unión (Congress) was installed and immediately assumed the function of an electoral college, in order to investigate the claims of both sides. In September the allocation of 200 seats in the Cámara by proportional representation afforded the PRI a congressional majority and effective control of the electoral college. Opposition members withdrew from the Cámara in protest at the PRI's obstruction of the investigation, enabling the ruling party to ratify Carlos Salinas de Gortari as the new President with 50.7% of the votes cast. Cárdenas was credited with 31.1% of the ballot. The results, although widely regarded as having been manipulated by the PRI, revealed a considerable erosion in support for the party, particularly among the traditional bastions of the trade unions, peasant groups and bureaucracy.

President Salinas took office in December 1988, declaring that his administration's priorities would include renegotiating the foreign debt and combating poverty, fraud and corruption. During 1989, despite the Government's active reinforcement of its commitment to the elimination of corruption, the initiative was undermined by the implication of police and security forces in a succession of abuses of human rights.

Agreements on rescheduling Mexico's vast foreign debts were reached with the 'Paris Club' of official creditors in 1989, and with some 450 commercial banks in early 1990. Success for the Government in financial negotiations with creditors was largely dependent upon its ability to provide evidence of a stable and developing domestic economy. In January 1989 a Pact for Economic Stability and Growth was implemented, with the agreement of employers' organizations and trade unions, and was subsequently extended until the end of 1994. None the less, the country experienced severe labour unrest in 1989 in support of greater pay increases and in protest at the Government's divestment programme.

In May 1989, following the dissolution of the FDN earlier in the year, supporters of the CD, together with the PMS, formed the Partido de la Revolución Democrática (PRD), under the leadership of Cárdenas. During the year political opposition to the PRI was strengthened by success in gubernatorial and municipal elections, and by further accusations against the PRI of electoral fraud. In October proposed constitutional amendments were approved with the unexpected support of the PAN. A 'governability clause', whereby an absolute majority of seats in the Cámara would be awarded to the leading party, should it receive at least 35% of the votes at a general election, was criticized by the PRD.

In July 1991 the Federal Electoral Code was approved by the Cámara with support from all represented parties, except the PRD. The legislation contained provisions for the compilation of a new electoral roll, the issue of more detailed identification cards for voters, the modification of the Federal Electoral Institute (IFE), and the creation of a Federal Electoral Tribunal. The PRD was highly critical of many of the provisions, including alleged procedural obstacles to the formation of political alliances, and the power given to the President to appoint the head of the IFE (the Secretary of the Interior) and to nominate six 'independent' lawyers to its executive.

In June 1990, in response to continuing allegations of federal police complicity in abuses of human rights, President Salinas announced the creation of the National Commission for Human

Rights (CNDH). Opposition groups and independent human rights organizations were critical of the Government's stipulation that the Commission should be excluded from addressing cases relating to political campaigns or electoral processes. In October the Government proposed legislation transferring responsibility for the interrogation of suspected criminals from the federal judicial police to the public magistrate's office. The proposed legislation also sought to undermine the validity of confession alone (often allegedly extracted under torture) as sufficient grounds for conviction.

The PRI continued to secure disputed electoral success at municipal and state level in 1991. At mid-term congressional elections in August, the party won 290 of the 300 directly elective seats in the Cámara (plus 30 of the 200 seats awarded by proportional representation) and 31 of the 32 contested seats in the Senado. The return to the level of support that the PRI had enjoyed prior to the 1988 elections was largely attributed to the success of the Government's programme of economic reform. The election results were less encouraging for the opposition; the PAN secured 10 directly elective seats in the Cámara and its first seat in the Senado, but the PRD failed to win a directly elective seat in either congressional house.

In November 1991 President Salinas announced proposals for constitutional reform with regard to agriculture, education and religion. Concern was expressed by PRI traditionalists that the agricultural reform programme and the proposals for the devolution of federal responsibility for education might jeopardize the PRI's broad base of support from the rural community and from the 1.2m.-strong teachers' union. Legislation to enact the agrarian reform was adopted in March 1992. Reform proposals to grant legal recognition to the Roman Catholic Church received congressional approval in December 1991, and constitutional restrictions on the Church were ended by a new law, promulgated by the President in January 1992. A National Agreement for the Modernization of Basic Education was agreed between the federal Government, state governments and the national teachers' union in May 1992.

PRI victories at gubernatorial and legislative elections in several states during 1993 were denounced by the opposition as fraudulent. In July President Salinas presented an electoral reform proposal (approved by the Congreso in September), which included provisions for greater access to the media for all parties, restrictions on party funding, and improved impartiality of supervision. Other measures sought to increase the representation of minority parties in the Senado, and to end over-representation of larger parties in the Cámara. The 'governability clause' introduced in 1989 was to be removed. Divisions within the PRI emerged in November, following the selection of Luis Donaldo Colosio, the Secretary of Social Development, as the party's candidate in the presidential elections. Additional electoral reforms, which claimed to end PRI control of the IFE, received congressional approval in March 1994, but failed to appease PRD leaders, who demanded that the incumbent head of the IFE should be replaced by an impartial president elected by the IFE's newly created six-member commission.

On 1 January 1994 armed Indian groups numbering 1,000–3,000 took control of four municipalities of the southern state of Chiapas. The rebels issued the Declaration of the Lacandona Jungle, identifying themselves as the Ejército Zapatista de Liberación Nacional—EZLN (after Emiliano Zapata, who championed the land rights of Mexican peasants during the 1910–17 Revolution), and detailed a series of demands for economic and social change in the region, culminating in a declaration of war against the Government and a statement of intent to depose the 'dictator', President Salinas. A charismatic rebel spokesman, identified as 'subcomandante Marcos', stated that the insurgency had been timed to coincide with the implementation of the North American Free Trade Agreement (NAFTA—see below), which the rebels considered to be the latest in a series of segregative government initiatives adopted at the expense of indigenous groups. During the first day of the uprising the insurgents killed several police officials and abducted some prominent local figures, including a former Chiapas state governor. On 10 January the Government announced a unilateral cease-fire and an amnesty (effective from 22 January) for those EZLN members prepared to surrender arms. Manuel Camacho Solís was appointed head of a peace and reconciliation commission in Chiapas on the same day. He enlisted the help of Samuel Ruiz, Bishop of San Cristóbal de las Casas, one of Chiapas' largest towns, in an attempt to foster a peaceful dialogue with the EZLN, although sporadic

fighting continued throughout January. Negotiations in February and March concluded with the publication of a document detailing 34 demands of the EZLN, and the Government's response to them. A preliminary accord was reached following the Government's broad acceptance of many of the rebels' stipulations, including an acceleration of the wide-ranging anti-poverty programme in the region, the incorporation of traditional Indian structures of justice and political organization, and a commitment from the Government to investigate the impact of NAFTA and recent land-reform legislation on Indian communities. Official figures suggested that 100–150 guerrillas, soldiers and civilians had been killed during the conflict, while the Roman Catholic Church estimated that there had been as many as 400 casualties. In June the EZLN announced that the Government's peace proposal had been rejected by an overwhelming majority of the movement's supporters. However, a similar majority had rejected the resumption of hostilities with the security forces, and had endorsed the extension of the cease-fire pending renewed bilateral discussions. In response, Salinas was critical of the work of the peace and reconciliation commission, prompting the resignation of Camacho Solís, who was replaced by Jorge Madrazo Cuéllar, the head of the CNDH.

Meanwhile, in March 1994 the PRI's presidential candidate, Colosio, was assassinated at a campaign rally. Mario Aburto Martínez, arrested at the scene of the murder, was later identified as the apparently motiveless assassin. However, speculation that Colosio had been the victim of a conspiracy within the PRI establishment increased following the arrest, in connection with the incident, of a number of party members associated with police and intelligence agencies. The PRI subsequently named Ernesto Zedillo Ponce de León, a former cabinet minister who had most recently been acting as Colosio's campaign manager, as the party's presidential candidate. Zedillo was elected President on 21 August, with 48.8% of the votes, ahead of the PAN candidate, Diego Fernández de Cevallos (25.9%), and the PRD candidate, Cuauhtémoc Cárdenas (16.6%). The PRI also achieved considerable success at the concurrent congressional elections, securing all of the directly elected seats in the Senado and all but 23 of the directly elected seats in the Cámara. Zedillo was considered to have conducted an unremarkable electoral campaign (during which he had promised to suspend the privilege of the *dedazo*—the presidential right to nominate PRI officials), and he was the first PRI presidential candidate to receive less than 50% of the votes. Despite the participation of some 70,000 impartial monitors and the attendance of a UN advisory technical team, numerous incidents of electoral malpractice were reported.

Zedillo identified the immediate aims of his administration as the promotion of the independence of the judiciary, the separation of party political activity from the functions of federal government and the further reform of the electoral system. Public confidence in the impartiality and ability of the judiciary had been seriously undermined by the inconsistency and confusion surrounding recent investigations into the deaths of Colosio and José Francisco Ruiz Massieu (see below). Zedillo's appointment of a senior member of the PAN to the post of Attorney-General in a new Cabinet announced in November 1994, together with the disclosure, in December, of more detailed plans for judicial reform, sought to restore the prestige of the judiciary.

The report of a special investigation into Colosio's murder, published in July 1994, concluded that Aburto Martínez had acted alone in the assassination, reversing the findings of a preliminary investigation which had suggested the existence of a number of conspirators. The report provoked public incredulity, and President Salinas commissioned a further independent investigation. Speculation that Colosio had been the first victim of a politically motivated campaign of violence, conducted by a cabal of senior PRI traditionalists in order to check the advance of the party's reformist wing, intensified following the murder, in September, of the PRI Secretary-General, José Francisco Ruiz Massieu, although responsibility for Ruiz Massieu's death was initially attributed to the powerful Golfo drugs cartel. In October Aburto Martínez was sentenced to 42 years' imprisonment for Colosio's murder. In February 1995, however, a report issued by the Attorney-General was highly critical of all previous investigations of the incident, concluding that the assassination had involved at least two gunmen. (An alleged second gunman was acquitted in August 1996.) Meanwhile, in November 1994 Ruiz Massieu's brother, Mario, resigned his post as Deputy Attorney-General, claiming that senior PRI officials, including the party's

President and Secretary-General, had impeded his investigation into his brother's death, in an attempt to protect the identities of those responsible for the assassination. In February 1995 Raúl Salinas de Gortari, brother of former President Salinas, was arrested on charges of complicity in Ruiz Massieu's murder, and in April Fernando Rodríguez González (a former employee at the Cámara, who was charged with hiring the assassins) implicated several new conspirators, including five state Governors. Mario Ruiz Massieu was subsequently detained in the USA. Attempts by the Mexican Government to secure his extradition were frustrated. In October two men were each sentenced to 18 years' imprisonment for perpetrating the murder of the PRI Secretary-General. In October 1996 the case against Raúl Salinas was prejudiced further by the discovery of a body buried in the grounds of his property in Mexico City. The deceased was initially assumed to be Manuel Muñoz Rocha, a former federal congressman who was alleged to have been Salinas's accomplice in the assassination of Ruiz Massieu and who had disappeared shortly after the incident. In December Jorge Madrazo Cuéllar was appointed Attorney-General to replace Lozano Gracia, who had failed to reveal that scientific evidence proved that the body exhumed was not that of Muñoz Rocha.

In March 1995, following the arrest of his brother, former President Salinas began a solitary public campaign to discredit the new administration and to defend himself from accusations of responsibility for the country's economic crisis and from allegations that he had obstructed attempts to bring to justice those responsible for Colosio's death. Salinas's efforts culminated in a highly-publicized but brief hunger strike which prompted the Attorney-General to issue a statement confirming that there was no evidence that Salinas had impeded the Colosio murder inquiry. Some days later Salinas left the country. Raúl Salinas was convicted of murder and sentenced to 50 years' imprisonment in January 1999; the sentence was later reduced to almost 28 years. (However, in August 2002 he was additionally charged with the embezzlement of up to 209m. new pesos from a secret presidential fund under his brother's control.) In September 1999 Mario Ruiz Massieu committed suicide in the USA while awaiting trial on charges of 'laundering' money gained from drugs-trafficking; he left a note repeating his earlier accusations against the PRI and blaming Zedillo and other senior officials for his own death and the assassination of Colosio.

By October 1994 tensions in Chiapas had increased and the EZLN announced its withdrawal from negotiations with the Government. Violent confrontations between left- and right-wing groups, peasants and landowners and EZLN supporters and security forces increased in the weeks preceding the inauguration of the controversially elected PRI Governor, Eduardo Robledo Rincón. A second national democratic convention in November endorsed a campaign of civil disorder to disrupt the Governor's inauguration, but voted to resume negotiations with the Government. Fears that the Government might again seek a military solution to the crisis were aroused following the installation by opposition groups of a parallel state administration for Chiapas in December. Such concerns were initially dispelled by both sides' adoption of a more conciliatory approach to negotiations during December 1994 and January 1995, and by the establishment of a national mediation commission, the Comisión Nacional de Intermediación (CONAI), led by Bishop Ruiz. However, in February President Zedillo announced the resumption of a military offensive against EZLN positions in Chiapas, following the discovery of a number of illegal arsenals in Mexico City and Veracruz. Zedillo also issued warrants for the arrest of several EZLN leaders, including subcomandante Marcos, who was identified as Rafael Sebastián Guillén Vicente. Some days later the Government appeared to adjust this stance: military operations in the region were suspended while Robledo Rincón announced a temporary leave of absence from the post of Governor of Chiapas. The warrants for the arrest of EZLN leaders were subsequently suspended, and in March the Law for Dialogue, Conciliation and Honourable Peace in Chiapas was enacted by the Government, with the support of all major political parties. The Law was welcomed by EZLN spokesmen and formal discussions between the two sides began in San Andrés Larraínzar in April.

Existing tensions between peasant groups and the authorities were exacerbated in July 1995 by the arrest of a number of police officials implicated in the shooting of 17 members of a local peasant workers' organization in the state of Guerrero in June. A CNDH report contradicted Governor Rubén Figueroa's assertion that the security forces had been acting in self-defence. In January 1996 it was announced that four former state officials and a number of police officers had been arrested in connection with the incident; Figueroa resigned in March. In April the Supreme Court ruled that Figueroa and several others had deliberately suppressed information regarding the massacre.

In August 1995 an unofficial plebiscite organized by the EZLN in Mexico City and the state of Chiapas recorded an almost equal division of support from around 1.2m. voters for the guerrilla movement's evolution into an independent political force and for its alignment with an existing political body. In February 1996 the EZLN and the Government signed an agreement in San Andrés Larraínzar on the guarantee of cultural, linguistic and local government rights for indigenous groups, although the issue of land reform was not addressed. However, the EZLN announced its withdrawal from the peace negotiations in September as the agreement had not been implemented. In December the Comisión de Concordia y Pacificación (COCOPA), a multi-party congressional committee charged with finding a peace settlement, presented draft legislation on indigenous rights based on the San Andrés Larraínzar agreement. Although the bill was supported by the EZLN, it was rejected by the Government on the grounds that it threatened national sovereignty. In January 1997, in an apparent attempt to renew dialogue with the Zapatistas, the authorities released seven alleged EZLN members from prison.

In June 1996 some 100 members of a previously unknown guerrilla group, the Ejército Popular Revolucionario (EPR), commemorated the first anniversary of the Guerrero shootings (see above) by staging a rally in the village of Aguas Blancas, Guerrero. The Government responded by launching a major military offensive in the state, resulting in the capture of eight alleged EPR members. In August the EPR announced its allegiance to a new political grouping, the Partido Popular Revolucionario Democrático, and launched armed attacks, claiming self-defence, on government installations in the states of Guerrero, México and Oaxaca; 17 people were killed and at least 21 were injured during the assaults. Concurrently, subcomandante Marcos sent an open letter to the EPR, distancing the EZLN from the new guerrilla group. Although the military intensified its counter-insurgency campaign in September, at the end of the month the EPR announced a temporary unilateral cease-fire in Guerrero in order not to impede mayoral and legislative elections. The EPR also declared a unilateral cease-fire in México state in the weeks preceding the municipal elections. In January 1997 the authorities arrested Benigno Guzmán Martínez, said to be the EPR leader, bringing to 85 the total number of supposed EPR members arrested since mid-1996. (During 1997 the EPR continued to launch sporadic attacks. In June 1998 the armed forces killed 11 EPR members and arrested 21 others during a military offensive in Guerrero state.)

The Government's ongoing attempts to effect political reform were reactivated in January 1996 at a meeting of some 50 civil and political groups. However, subsequent discussions were regularly interrupted during early 1996 by the demands of opposition parties for the annulment of a number of disputed election results. In July the PRI, the PAN, the PRD and the Partido del Trabajo (PT, a labour party) reached consensus on reforms that would include introducing a directly elected Governor of the Distrito Federal, increasing and regulating public financing for political parties, employing proportional representation in elections to the Senado, granting a right of vote to Mexican citizens resident abroad, and allowing the IFE greater independence. The reforms received congressional approval in August. However, in November, in apparent response to their diminishing share of the vote in recent municipal elections, PRI traditionalists secured the adoption by the Cámara of a series of amendments to the electoral reform bill, increasing public funding in 1997 for political parties by some 476%, pronouncing that to exceed campaign finance limits would no longer be a criminal or electoral offence, expanding the Government's access to the media, and restricting the right of opposition parties to form coalitions.

Internal tensions in the PRI became increasingly apparent during 1996. At the party's National Assembly, PRI traditionalists retaliated against the progressive faction by voting to alter the prerequisites for senior government positions. The new conditions would have prevented the selection of President Zedillo and of most of his Cabinet. Nevertheless, in December one of Zedillo's close allies, Humberto Roque Villanueva, replaced Oñate as party president.

In May 1996 Zedillo dismissed Mexico City's chief of police following public outcry at the violent tactics employed by his officers to disperse a group of striking teachers in the capital. In the following months hundreds of police employees throughout the country were dismissed for incompetence or corruption, while army officers were increasingly appointed to positions within the police force. In March 1997 some 2,500 members of Mexico City's police force were replaced by army personnel, and in October an élite police unit was disbanded after accusations that as many as 35 of its members were implicated in the torture and murder of three youths in September. Several officers at the anti-abduction unit in the state of Morelos were also accused of torture and murder in early 1998, precipitating the resignation of the state's PRI Governor in May.

At elections held on 6 July 1997 for all 500 members of the Cámara the PRI lost its overall majority for the first time, while the PRD and the PAN made substantial gains. At concurrent elections held for one-quarter of the seats in the Senado the PRI retained its overall majority, albeit significantly reduced, while the PAN and the PRD increased their representation. In addition, the PRI was defeated by the PAN in two of six gubernatorial elections conducted at the same time. Most significant, however, was the election of Cárdenas, the PRD candidate, as Governor of the Distrito Federal, who secured 47.8% of the votes cast, compared with 25.6% by Alfredo del Mazo, a PRI traditionalist. The electoral defeats suffered by the PRI exacerbated tensions within the party and prompted the resignation of its president, Roque Villanueva, in September. Several PRI members had defected to the PRD, some of whom were selected as candidates in gubernatorial elections. The PRI remained divided on the issue of the selection of candidates for senior government positions as the prerequisites agreed at the National Assembly in the previous year (see above) reduced significantly the number of eligible party members.

The first opposition-dominated Cámara convened in September 1997. The PAN, the PRD, the Partido Verde Ecologista de México (PVEM) and the PT agreed an informal alliance, as a result of which opposition parties succeeded in taking control of important legislative committees, including those concerning the budget, the interior and anti-corruption. It was anticipated that this would lead to the closer scrutiny of government expenditure and to the possible removal of the largely discretionary funds controlled by Zedillo.

Despite attempts by the COCOPA to resume peace negotiations, clashes between EZLN supporters and the security forces in the state of Chiapas continued during 1997. The Government came under criticism for increasing its military presence in the state and for expelling foreign human rights activists from the region. In September, in an attempt to rally support for their cause, several thousand Zapatistas and their sympathizers staged a peaceful demonstration in Mexico City, during which the EZLN inaugurated the Frente Zapatista de Liberación Nacional, a political force created in 1996 to embody the Zapatistas' ideology. The prospect of reaching a peaceful solution in Chiapas was undermined in November 1997 by an apparent assassination attempt on Bishop Ruiz, allegedly by members of Paz y Justicia, a paramilitary group financed by anti-EZLN landowners. In December, moreover, there was widespread disquiet at the killing of 45 Indians in a church in the village of Acteal, in the municipality of Chenalhó, Chiapas. Some 58 residents of Chenalhó were arrested subsequently, including the mayor, Jacinto Arias. Meanwhile, Chuayffet, the Secretary of the Interior, and Julio César Ruiz Ferro, the Governor of Chiapas, were forced to resign, following criticism of their roles in the events leading to the Acteal massacre. Both Francisco Labastida Ochoa and Roberto Albores Guillén, who succeeded Chuayffet and Ruiz Ferro, respectively, made conciliatory gestures towards the EZLN. In February Zedillo announced the appointment of a new government peace negotiator; nevertheless, the military presence in Chiapas increased, purportedly to disarm paramilitary groups in the region. In April 1998 Gen. Julio César Santiago Díaz, who had been acting chief of staff of Chiapas state police at the time of the massacre, was arrested and charged with failing to intervene to prevent the bloodshed. In September 1999 Jacinto Arias was convicted on charges of supplying the weapons used in the massacre and sentenced to 35 years' imprisonment. In November 2002 18 people were each sentenced to 36 years' imprisonment for their involvement in the deaths as part of a paramilitary group with links to the PRI; they joined 70 others previously convicted.

In March 1998, following President Zedillo's unsuccessful attempt to persuade the COCOPA to revise the draft law that it had presented in December 1996, Labastida announced draft legislation on indigenous rights and culture. The COCOPA, the PAN and the EZLN rejected the proposals on the grounds that they failed to comply with the San Andrés Larraínzar agreement. The EZLN, angered by the Government's failure to consult with the Zapatistas, demanded that certain preconditions be met before it resumed dialogue with the authorities. In June Bishop Ruiz resigned from the CONAI, accusing the Government of behaving in an increasingly aggressive manner towards the Commission, and of weakening reconciliation efforts. Concurrently, the CONAI announced its dissolution. During May and June eight Zapatista sympathizers were killed and more than 100 were arrested when the security forces attempted to dismantle two 'autonomous municipalities' (villages which, with EZLN support, had declared themselves outside federal and state control) in Chiapas.

In November 1998 bilateral talks were held in San Cristóbal de las Casas, during which the EZLN expressed regret at the dissolution of the CONAI, and reiterated its preconditions for entering into dialogue with the Government. In March 1999 some 5,000 Zapatistas conducted a nation-wide unofficial plebiscite to determine, *inter alia*, the level of support for the recognition of Indian rights, the San Andrés Larraínzar agreement and the demilitarization of Chiapas. According to the EZLN, 2.5m. people participated in the poll, of whom 97% concurred with Zapatista demands.

The Government made efforts to initiate negotiations with the EZLN in September 1999, when, in an open letter to the Zapatistas, the Secretary of the Interior, Diódoro Carrasco, proposed independent (although not international) mediation and the establishment of a special judicial authority to investigate paramilitary activities in Chiapas. Furthermore, a number of Zapatista sympathizers were released from prison. Meanwhile, Samuel Ruiz retired as Bishop of San Cristóbal de las Casas in January 2000. Despite appeals from Ruiz and Indian groups, the Vatican declined to appoint Ruiz's coadjutor, Raúl Vera López (who had in December been named Bishop of Saltillo), as his successor.

The popularity of the PRI appeared to recover during 1998, with the ruling party winning seven of the 10 governorships contested that year, and performing well in municipal and local elections. In March 1999 José Antonio González Fernández, hitherto Secretary of Labour, became the first elected President of the PRI.

In May 1998, at the culmination of a three-year counter-narcotics operation, the US authorities made more than 160 arrests in Mexico and indicted three Mexican financial groups on charges of laundering the profits from cocaine cartels; a further nine banks were implicated in the scandal. (It was estimated that drugs cartels in Mexico and Colombia laundered some US $8,000m. annually through Mexican financial institutions.) The Zedillo administration, which in March had admitted that a small financial group had been purchased by drugs-traffickers in 1995, protested that it had not been informed about the operation, despite bilateral agreements on drugs-trafficking intelligence.

Meanwhile, in mid-1998 the PRI encountered strong opposition in the Congreso to its proposals to convert into public debt liabilities to the value of some $65,000m. assumed by the bank rescue agency, the Fondo Bancario de Protección al Ahorro (FOBAPROA), after the financial crisis of late 1994. Frustrated by the Government's refusal to release full details about the rescue programme, in August the PRD issued a list of more than 300 business executives who were alleged to have benefited from the scheme, and conducted a nation-wide survey to determine the level of support for the PRI's proposal. The PRD claimed that 3m. people participated in the poll, of whom 94% opposed the Government's plans. In December revised legislation establishing a successor to the FOBAPROA was approved by the Cámara. The PAN abandoned demands for the resignation of the Governor of the central bank, Guillermo Ortiz, who had held the finance portfolio at the time of the rescue programme, while the Government was forced to concede that FOBAPROA's liabilities would not automatically become public debt. Congressional approval would thenceforth be required annually for part of the budget for bonds issued to refinance FOBAPROA's liabilities. FOBAPROA's successor, the Instituto de Protección al Ahorro Bancario was created in May 1999.

In April 1999 a warrant was issued for the arrest of the outgoing Governor of the state of Quintana Roo, Mario Villanueva, only hours after the end of his term. Villanueva, who had already fled the state to escape what he claimed was political persecution, was alleged to have been involved in drugs-trafficking and to have links with the Juárez cartel. Villanueva was arrested in Cancún in late May 2001, and in January 2002 a federal court in New York, USA, presented a formal request for his extradition; he was alleged to have assisted two cartel leaders, also threatened with extradition, in the smuggling of 200 tons of cocaine from Colombia to the USA.

In November 1999 the PRI held its first ever nation-wide open primaries to select its candidate for the presidential election. Following a bitterly fought contest, the former Secretary of the Interior, Francisco Labastida Ochoa defeated the Governor of Tabasco, Roberto Madrazo Pintado to secure the PRI nomination. Meanwhile, in September, the PAN's only presidential aspirant, Vicente Fox Quesada, who had recently resigned as Governor of Guanajuato state, was approved as the party's candidate for the election. In October Cárdenas, who had resigned as Governor of the Distrito Federal in the previous month, was formally nominated as the PRD's candidate. By the close of registration in January 2000 six presidential candidates had emerged: Labastida, Cárdenas (standing for the PRD-dominated Alianza por México—AM), Fox (representing a PAN-PVEM alliance known as the Alianza por el Cambio—AC), Manuel Camacho Solís, the leader of the Partido de Centro Democrático, Gilberto Rincón Gallardo, the President of Democracia Social, and Porfirio Muñoz Ledo, representing the Partido Auténtico de la Revolución Mexicana.

In the presidential election held on 2 July 2000, Fox secured 43.5% of the votes cast, while Labastida won 36.9% and Cárdenas 17.0%. Fox was thus elected President, ending the PRI's 71-year hegemony in Mexican government. In the concurrent elections to the Congreso the AC secured 223 of the 500 seats (208 of them won by the PAN, 15 by the PVEM, compared with 209 won by the PRI and 68 by the parties of the AM. The PRI remained the largest grouping in the Senado, however, with 60 seats, compared with 51 held by the AC and 17 by the AM. Fox announced that, upon taking office, he would establish a commission to investigate 'past events', while stating that his primary motive in doing so was 'national reconciliation', rather than retribution. To the same end, he declared he would invite members of the PRI and the PRD to join his first Cabinet. The governorship of the Distrito Federal, contested on the same day as the federal elections, was won by Andrés Manuel López Obrador of the PRD, who secured some 34.5% of the votes cast, compared with his nearest rival, Santiago Creel Miranda of the PAN, who obtained some 33.4% of the ballot.

Meanwhile, in August 2000, the Secretary of Tourism in the outgoing Zedillo administration, Oscar Espinosa Villareal, suddenly resigned his position and disappeared. Espinosa had been under investigation on allegations of embezzlement relating to his term, in 1994–97, as the last appointed Regent of the Distrito Federal. He was subsequently extradited from Nicaragua, where he had claimed asylum, and in August 2001 was committed to stand trial on charges of embezzlement. The trial had yet to begin in mid-2004; however, in October 2003 the Secretariat of State for Public Function barred Espinosa from holding public office for five years and fined him 300,000 pesos.

Fox took office as President on 1 December 2000, stating that his priorities were a reduction in poverty, improved relations with the USA and peace and reconciliation within Mexico. His first Cabinet contained members of the PAN, PRI and other parties, in addition to a number of prominent figures from commerce and academia. The PRD declined an offer of three cabinet portfolios, however, stating that it did not support Fox's economic or social policies.

Upon taking office President Fox announced that 53 military checkpoints in Chiapas were to be abandoned and that proposed legislation based on the San Andrés Larraínzar peace accords would be reintroduced to the Congreso. In response, subcomandante Marcos issued a statement stating that negotiations could be reopened on three conditions: that seven military bases in the state be abandoned, that EZLN prisoners be released and that the proposed legislation be enacted. Four of the seven bases were immediately closed and a number of EZLN activists released. In January 2001 the Government announced a series of new proposals aimed at the restoration of peace in Chiapas, including the establishment of offices in the state's major towns to facilitate liaison among the parties involved. In

February subcomandante Marcos, other Zapatista leaders and numerous other campaigners for indigenous rights began a tour of Mexico, which culminated in Mexico City in early March, where a rally in the capital's main square, attended by an estimated 150,000 people, was held in support of congressional approval of the proposed indigenous-rights legislation. Following a congressional vote four EZLN leaders were permitted to address both legislative chambers and, on 28 March, the EZLN announced that formal dialogue with the Government would recommence, although its other demands had not been met. Subcomandante Marcos successfully negotiated the dismantling of the remaining three garrisons in Chiapas, and in April the Congreso approved amendments to six articles of the Constitution, which recognized and guaranteed indigenous political, legal, social and economic rights, and prohibited discrimination against Indians based on race and tribal affiliation. However, the legislation fell short of granting indigenous peoples the right to autonomy over land and natural resources; in response, the EZLN suspended all contact with the Government.

Controversy arose in the state of Yucatán in February 2001, when the PRI-led state government defied an order by the Federal Electoral Commission to dissolve the state electoral commission, following allegations of a pro-PRI bias within its ranks in the months preceding the gubernatorial election. PRI activists barricaded themselves in the commission's headquarters and refused to allow federal officers to enter the building; the election was eventually won in May by Patricio Patrón Laviada, representing a PAN-led alliance. Furthermore, in July Eugenio Elorduy of the PAN defeated the PRI candidate in the gubernatorial election in Baja California, while in November the PRD candidate Lazaro Cárdenas (grandson of President Cárdenas—1934–40), defeated the PRI incumbent to become governor of the southern state of Michoacán, further evidence that the PRI was continuing to lose support in its traditional strongholds.

In October 2001 the Government announced that eight parties, including the PRI and the PRD, had signed the Acuerdo Político para el Desarrollo Nacional (Political Agreement for National Development), designed to facilitate law-making. Under the terms of the Agreement, the parties promised to support government measures to improve public finances and to deregulate the energy and telecommunications sectors. Nevertheless, the Government continued to encounter congressional opposition to its proposed fiscal reforms.

Although the elimination of corruption and an improvement in human rights were priorities in Fox's electoral campaign, little was done to address these issues in the President's first year in office. The country's poor human rights record was highlighted in late 2001 by the assassination in October of the leading civil liberties lawyer, Digna Ochoa, and by the publication, in December, of an Amnesty International report alleging that Mexican security forces were involved in widespread human rights violations. In response, President Fox announced an official inquiry into the 'disappearance' of 532 people detained by security forces in the 1970s and 1980s. In February 2002 Fox ordered the immediate release of Gen. José Francisco Gallardo, who had been sentenced to 28 years' imprisonment in 1993 after being convicted of misappropriating military property. Human rights groups and supporters of Gallardo had maintained that the charges were fabricated and that he had been incarcerated after demanding a reform of the military justice system.

In January 2002 the Government announced that an investigation was to be held into allegations that the state petroleum company, PEMEX, had covertly funded the election campaign of the PRI presidential candidate, Francisco Labastida, in 2000. The affair centred on the alleged diversion of 1,580m. new pesos in PEMEX funds into PRI accounts by two leaders of the petroleum workers' union, the Sindicato de Trabajadores Petroleros de la República Mexicana (STPRM), Carlos Romero Deschamps and Ricardo Aldana. In May a former director of PEMEX, Manuel Gómez-Peralta, was detained in connection with the allegations; furthermore, a former PEMEX President, Rogelio Montemayor, was arrested in Houston, Texas (USA) in October. In September the Attorney-General requested that Deschamps and Aldana be stripped of their right (as deputy and senator, respectively) to immunity from prosecution. In mid-September 2003 the Cámara was scheduled to vote on the removal of Aldana's immunity; however, one week before the vote was due the lower chamber, in which the PRI enjoyed a majority, approved a PRI-proposed motion to have the issue dealt with by a congressional committee, rather than in the Cámara itself. In early 2003 the PRI was fined 1,000m. new pesos by the IFE. Meanwhile, in October 2002 opposition parties demanded that President Fox allow the re-opening of investigations into allegations that the PAN organization Amigos de Fox, responsible for Fox's presidential campaign, had received substantial illegal foreign funding. (The investigation had been suspended on grounds of banking secrecy, but had been ordered to recommence by the electoral tribunal in May.) The PRI threatened to initiate a congressional investigation unless the Amigos de Fox's accounts were made public. In October 2003 the IFE fined both the PAN and the PVEM for receiving illegal campaign funding from Amigos de Fox.

In March 2002 Roberto Madrazo Pintado, the former Governor of Tabasco won the PRI leadership, although there were subsequent allegations of electoral fraud from his opponent Beatrix Paredes's supporters. In March Luis Felipe Bravo Mena was elected President of the PAN and, in the same month, Rosario Robles Berlanga was elected President of the PRD.

In May 2002 27 Zapotec Indians were killed in suspicious circumstances at Agua Fría, in Santiago Textitlán, Oaxaca; state authorities arrested 17 villagers, but local Indian organizations claimed that paramilitary groups had been involved in the attacks. Following the incident, an Amnesty International official denounced the state Attorney-General's office for abuses. In July protests by farmers and Zapatistas over the proposed construction of a new international airport for Mexico City descended into violence; in subsequent clashes with the police one person was killed and 31 injured. In response, the protestors, who were opposed to proposed legislation expropriating their land, threatened to kill 12 hostages (a further three hostages were later taken). The Government subsequently reversed its policy on the project.

In his annual 'Informe' address in September 2002, President Fox urged the Congreso to support legislation for structural reform, particularly of the electricity sector, and stressed the need for partnership between President and legislature. This, however, proved difficult to achieve, particularly in the midst of allegations and counter-allegations of electoral financial malpractice between the PRI and the PAN. In November there was conflict over both a proposed delay in the extension of value-added tax (VAT), and the introduction of a so-called 'luxuries tax', proposed by the PRD. Furthermore, in December the PRD obstructed legislation proposing the reduction in the number of lower-house seats elected by proportional representation (from 200 to 100).

The Fox administration had pledged to address the problem of drugs-trafficking. A subsequent increased fight against narcotics had led to an average of 23 arrests per day during 2002 (including the leaders of the Tijuana and Gulf cocaine cartels in March and May, respectively). However, the anti-drugs programme was itself the subject of an anti-corruption drive in the same year that led to a number of specialized army units being dismantled. Meanwhile, in November the investigation into the 'guerra sucia' (dirty war) of the late 1970s resulted in the conviction of Brigadier-Gen. Mario Acosta and Gen. Francisco Quirós on charges of protecting the operations of the Juárez cartel; they also faced charges over the disappearance of 143 activists. In the same month a special investigation by the Office of the Public Prosecutor accused Elba Esther Gordillo Morales, the PRI Secretary-General, of involvement in the deaths of several teachers while she was head of the Sindicato Nacional de Trabajadores de la Educación (SNTE) teachers' union; the accusations were supported by the dissident Coordinadora Nacional de Trabajadores de la Educación (CNTE), which additionally claimed that Gordillo had illegally transferred SNTE funds to the presidential campaign of Labastida in 2000. In December the CNTE, supported by farmers and Zapatistas, forced their way into the Congreso building to demand that more funding be given to rural areas, education and poverty reduction. Also in December the Government succeeded in gaining congressional approval for a conservative budget for 2003, despite obstruction by the PRI and PRD (see Economic Affairs).

In January 2003 the Secretary of Foreign Affairs, Jorge Castañeda, resigned, prompting President Fox to carry out a cabinet reshuffle. Castañeda was replaced by the Secretary of the Economy, Luis Ernesto Derbez Bautista, who in turn was succeeded by Fernando Canales Barragán, the Governor of Nuevo León. In April the Comptroller-General, Francisco Barrio Terrazas, resigned in order to stand in the mid-term elections that were scheduled to be held in July. Meanwhile, in February conflicts within the PRD had led to the cancellation of internal elections for candidates for the July elections. Instead, candidates were picked by the national committee, and included a number of recent PRI converts who had left the party following the electoral funding scandal of 2002.

Municipal elections, held in the state of México in March 2003, saw the PAN lose its majority in the state legislature to the PRI, which contested the ballot in conjunction with the PVEM. President Fox's negative reaction to the US-led military campaign against the regime of Saddam Hussain in Iraq in March–April (see below), as well as the consequent deterioration in relations with the USA, resulted in an increase in public support for his Government; nevertheless, in the mid-term congressional elections on 6 July, the PAN's representation in the Cámara was reduced from 205 to 153 seats. In contrast, the PRI increased its lower-house representation to 224 seats (from 209), as did the PRD, securing 95 seats (compared with 52 seats in the previous legislature). The opposition's gains, however, were marred by an electoral turn-out of only 42%. In the concurrently-held gubernatorial elections, the PRI and its allies won three of the six states contested, while PAN candidates were successful in two states. In the state of Colima, the victory of the PRI candidate, Gustavo Vázquez, was initially disallowed owing to accusations that the incumbent PRI Governor had unduly influenced the election; however, Vázquez was eventually inaugurated as Governor on 31 December.

In late July 2003 the Minister of Tourism, Leticia Navarro, resigned. She was replaced by Rodolfo Elizondo Torres, hitherto the President's spokesperson. In early September President Fox effected a further minor cabinet reshuffle. Ernesto Martens Rebolledo was replaced as Secretary of Energy by Felipe Calderón Hinjosa, while Alberto Cárdenas Jiménez succeeded Victor Lichtinger Waisman as Secretary of the Environment and Natural Resources. Both new ministers were PAN members.

In August 2003 the Government came under criticism, both at home and abroad, over its human rights record. Amnesty International published a report, Muertes Intolerables, that accused the Government of inefficiency and negligence in investigating the murders of an estimated 370 women in Juárez over the previous 10 years; in October a commissioner was appointed to investigate the crimes. Also in August the Government announced the dismissal of the deputy foreign minister responsible for human rights, Mariclaire Acosta, and subsequent incorporation of her office into the Department of Global Affairs. The Government claimed that progress made in the field of human rights meant the office was superfluous. In early November the Supreme Court ruled that prosecution for murders could proceed, even in cases where no body had been found. The ruling enabled prosecutions for human rights abuses committed during the 'dirty war' of the late 1970s to proceed; in February 2004 Miguel Nazar Haro, former director of the covert Dirección General de Seguridad, was arrested in connection with the disappearance of left-wing activist Jesús Piedra Ibarra in 1975.

On 10 August 2003 the EZLN declared that 30 municipalities in Chiapas, hitherto under Zapatista control, were to be granted autonomy. Thirty Juntas de Buen Gobierno would oversee the transition from military to civilian control in these areas. The announcement was interpreted as an attempt by the EZLN to move from being an armed force to a political party.

On 1 September 2003, in his third annual 'Informe' address, President Fox called for support for his Government's proposed energy, tax and labour reforms. In early November the Government presented its budget to the Congreso. Among the proposals was a plan to lower the rate of VAT from 15% to 10%, and to extend it to apply to food and medicine. This proposal was rejected by the Cámara, and the PRI, the largest congressional party, subsequently presented its own budget proposals to the legislature. However, divisions appeared within that party, ostensibly over the alternative proposals. In December 118 PRI deputies voted to replace Elba Esther Gordillo Morales as PRI leader in the Cámara with Emilio Chauyfett. Gordillo, who had originally supported the Government's proposed budget, refused to accept her dismissal and continued to rely on the support of 104 PRI deputies. It was widely believed that the underlying reason for the split was who would secure the PRI nomination for the presidential election that was due in 2006: Gordillo or the party president, Roberto Madrazo Pintado. (In mid-March 2004 Gordillo resigned her seat in the Cámara; however, she maintained her position as PRI Secretary-General and was re-elected to the SNTE presidency in the same month.) On 31 December the Cámara finally approved amended fiscal proposals. The 2004 budget made no changes to VAT or income tax, while spending was increased in areas such as health and infrastructure. Furthermore, the Government abandonded controversial measures to privatize or close state-run companies.

In March 2004 a scandal emerged surrounding the PRD Governor of the Distrito Federal, Andrés Manuel López Obrador, who was a likely candidate in the 2006 presidential election. A videotape appeared to show López Obrador's finance chief, Gustavo Ponce Meléndez, gambling large amounts at a casino in Las Vegas (USA). A further video recording came to light that apparently showed the Governor's former private secretary, René Bejarano, accepting money from a prominent Argentine businessman, Carlos Ahumada, who was accused of corruption. López Obrador denied any knowledge of either incident and claimed that a 'dirty tricks' campaign was being waged against him. At the end of the month Jorge Castañeda, the former Secretary of Foreign Affairs, announced his intention to stand as an independent candidate in the presidential election.

Mexico's foreign policy has been determined largely by relations with the USA. The rapid expansion of petroleum production from the mid-1970s onwards gave Mexico a new independence, empowering it to favour the left-wing regimes in Cuba and Nicaragua, opposed by the USA, during the 1980s. In February 1985 relations between Mexico and the USA deteriorated following the murder of an agent of the US Drug Enforcement Administration (DEA) by Mexican drugs-traffickers. The situation worsened in April 1990, when a Mexican physician was abducted, in Mexico, by agents employed by the DEA, and transported to the USA to be arrested on charges relating to the murder. The Mexican authorities considered this action to be in violation of the existing US-Mexican extradition treaty, and refused to recognize the legality of the trial (which was dismissed in December 1992 owing to lack of evidence). Meanwhile, relations between Mexico and the USA remained tense, largely because of disagreement over the problem of illegal immigration from Mexico into the USA and Mexico's failure to take effective action against the illegal drugs trade. This situation improved following the deportation to the USA in 1996 of Juan García Abrego, the alleged head of the Golfo drugs cartel. In February 1997 Mexico's credibility in combating drugs-trafficking was seriously undermined when Gen. Jesús Gutiérrez Rebollo, the head of the counter-narcotics agency, was dismissed and charged with receiving payment from Amado Carrillo Fuentes, the head of the Juárez drugs cartel. (He was later sentenced to more than 30 years' detention.) However, later in February 1997 the new head of the Golfo drugs cartel was arrested, and in March the USA 'certified' Mexico as a country co-operating in its campaign against drugs-trafficking. In May, shortly before the first official visit to the country by the US President, Bill Clinton, Mexico's discredited counter-narcotics agency was disbanded and replaced with a specially trained anti-drugs unit. During his visit, Clinton concluded agreements on border co-operation (further to accords signed during 1996) and on measures to combat the illegal trade in drugs and weapons. In March 1998 Mexico was 'certified' again; however, bilateral relations were strained in May, when a major US counter-narcotics operation was conducted in Mexico, without Mexican authorization. None the less, additional co-operation agreements were signed by the two countries in early 1999, and Mexico was duly 'certified' again. In March 2000 Mexico was again 'certified' by the USA for its co-operation in the campaign against drugs-trafficking. Upon taking office in late 2000, Fox criticized the practice of 'certification', declaring it unilateral, and advocated its abolition. Despite the new President's hostility, and ongoing concerns regarding corruption in the army and law enforcement agencies, the 'certification' was reaffirmed in March 2001. Following a modification of the USA's certification process in 2002, in September 2003 Mexico appeared in a list of countries deemed to be major illicit drugs-producing or -trafficking countries by the USA. It was estimated that 70% of cocaine destined for the USA passed through Mexico. In August 2002 Fox cancelled a scheduled visit to the USA in protest at the execution of a Mexican national in Texas. In early 2003 a ruling by the International Court of Justice prevented the execution of Mexican prisoners in the USA, pending the legal resolution of the issue.

In December 1992 Mexico, the USA and Canada formally approved NAFTA, which duly took effect from 1 January 1994. Among NAFTA's provisions are the gradual reduction of tariffs on 50% of products over a period of 10–15 years (some 57% of tariffs on agricultural trade between the USA and Mexico was removed immediately), and the establishment, by Mexico and the USA, of a North American Development Bank (NADBank) charged with the funding of initiatives for the rehabilitation of the two countries' common border. From January 2003 tariffs on a number of agricultural products were reduced or removed entirely, provoking widespread discontent among Mexico's 25m.-strong rural community. In particular, they pointed to the greater subsidies received by US farmers (US $200,000m. in 2003, over US $10,000m. in Mexico), and to a poor transport infrastructure, which resulted in higher costs. A pledge by President Fox in May 2002 to repay Mexico's 'water debt' to the USA had also angered Mexican farmers. Following the collapse, in September 2003, of the fifth Ministerial Conference of the World Trade Organization (WTO) in Cancún, Mexico joined the group of developing countries led by Brazil (originally known as the G-20, then the G-22, but subsequently renamed the G-19) that opposed the US-EU policy of subsidizing agricultural products. In late December 2003 the Government banned imports of beef from the USA following the discovery of a case of bovine spongiform encephalopathy (BSE) in a cow in Washington; restrictions were partially lifted in early March 2004.

The Fox Government sought to persuade the US Administration of George W. Bush (2001–) to adopt a more liberal position on Mexican immigrants to the USA. In July 2001 President Bush proposed a possible amnesty for all illegal Mexican immigrants in the USA (estimated to number 3m. in 2001). US trade unions, once opposed to such an idea on the grounds that it would undermine the interests of US workers, indicated their support for the proposal. In August the US Senate voted to ban Mexican trucks operating outside a 32 km zone north of the US–Mexican border. In response, the Mexican Government threatened to impose trade sanctions, claiming that the ban contravened NAFTA regulations. However, in December President Bush, who had opposed the ban, approved legislation allowing Mexican trucks unrestricted access to US highways, although more rigorous safety inspections were to be introduced. In early September President Fox visited Washington, DC, where he addressed the US Congress, in an attempt to regularize the flow of Mexican immigrants to the USA by the end of 2001. However, progress on immigration policy was suspended following the terrorist attacks in the USA on 11 September, and proposals to tighten security on the US-Mexican border were included in the budget presented to the US Congress in February 2002. In the following month, nevertheless, following a summit meeting in Monterrey, the two Presidents announced a 'smart border' partnership agreement, intended to facilitate the legal entry of Mexican people and goods into the USA while, at the same time, securing the frontier against possible acts of terrorism. Attempts to regularize the status of illegal Mexican immigrants in the USA led to the preliminary introduction of identity cards in Texas in May.

In September 2002, however, Fox requested that the emphasis in US-Mexican relations be shifted back to bilateral issues, which had been neglected in favour of border security. Also in September, Mexico unilaterally withdrew from the Inter-American Treaty of Reciprocal Assistance (the Rio Treaty), the defence pact linking Mexico to the USA, resulting in a downturn in relations with the USA. In March 2003, with Mexican public opinion strongly against armed intervention to remove the regime of Saddam Hussein in Iraq, President Fox risked a further deterioration of relations with both the USA and Spain by stating his opposition to war. His opposition was all the more significant owing to Mexico's place as one of the five non-permanent members of the UN Security Council. Although US sources maintained this would not affect bilateral relations, it was likely that recent progress made on immigration issues would be, at least temporarily, halted, while US-Mexico border trade decreased significantly following the commencement of the US-led military campaign in Iraq. In January 2004 the announcement of a revised US immigration initiative, which offered significantly less to Mexican immigrants in the USA than had been hoped, was met with disappointment by the Mexican Government, which had hoped to increase freedom of movement between the two countries. In the same month US officials began managing the security arrangements for US bound flights leaving Mexico City's airport. In March, following a summit with the President Bush in Texas, President Fox announced that the USA had agreed to relax certain immigration restrictions for Mexicans.

In April 2004 Mexico's relations with Cuba were strained after Mexico voted in favour of a UN motion to censure Cuba for human rights abuses. In early May the Cuban leader, Fidel Castro Ruz, criticized Mexico's stance and accused the Fox Government of interference in the island's affairs. In response, President Fox expelled the Cuban ambassador from the country and recalled the Mexican ambassador in Havana.

In January 1991 a preliminary free-trade agreement was signed with Honduras, Guatemala, El Salvador, Nicaragua and Costa Rica, in order to facilitate the negotiation of bilateral agreements between Mexico and each of the five countries, leading to free trade in an increasing range of products over a six-year period. During the 1990s Mexico concluded agreements for greater economic co-operation and increased bilateral trade with Colombia and Venezuela (as the Group of Three—G-3 (see p. 360), established in 1994), with Bolivia, Costa Rica and with the European Union (EU, see p. 208). A free trade accord with Nicaragua came into force in 1998; a similar accord with Chile was signed in 1998 and came into force in the following year. A further trade agreement with Guatemala, Honduras and El Salvador (the Northern Triangle) was concluded in 2000. In March 2000 Mexico and the EU signed a free-trade agreement, the first to be signed between the EU and a Latin American country. The accord provided for the gradual elimination of tariffs on industrial and agricultural products, the progressive liberalization of trade in services, and preferential access to public procurement; it also obliged the signatories to respect democratic principles and human rights. In October 2003 Mexico signed an Organization of American States agreement on regional security, which was also aimed at increasing co-operation on social and environmental issues. In a series of meetings held in late 2003, Mexico supported the Brazilian Government in demanding revisions to the proposed Free Trade Area of the Americas, due to come into force in 2005, negotiations towards which were ongoing in 2004. In March 2004 Mexico concluded an economic association agreement with Japan.

Government

Mexico is a federal republic comprising 31 states and a Distrito Federal—Federal District (around the capital). Under the 1917 Constitution, legislative power is vested in the bicameral Congreso de la Unión, elected by universal adult suffrage. The Senado has 128 members (four from each state and the Distrito Federal), serving a six-year term. The Cámara Federal de Diputados, directly elected for three years, has 500 seats, of which 300 are filled from single-member constituencies. The remaining 200 seats, allocated so as to achieve proportional representation, are filled from parties' lists of candidates. Executive power is held by the President, directly elected for six years at the same time as the Senado. He governs with the assistance of an appointed Cabinet. Each state has its own constitution and is administered by a Governor (elected for six years) and an elected chamber of deputies. The Distrito Federal is also administered by a Governor.

Defence

Military service, on a part-time basis (four hours per week), is compulsory for conscripts selected by lottery, for one year. In August 2003 the active armed forces totalled 192,770: 144,000 in the army (including some 60,000 conscripts), 37,000 in the navy (including naval air force and marines) and 11,770 in the air force. There is a rural defence militia numbering 14,000. The reserve numbered 300,000. Defence expenditure for 2003 was budgeted at 31,700m. new pesos.

Economic Affairs

In 2002, according to estimates by the World Bank, Mexico's gross national income (GNI), measured at average 2000–02 prices, was US $596,703m., equivalent to $5,910 per head (or $8540 per head on an international purchasing-power parity basis). During 1990–2002, it was estimated, the population increased at an average annual rate of 1.6%, while gross domestic product (GDP) per head increased, in real terms, by an average of 1.3% per year. Overall GDP increased, in real terms, at an average annual rate of 2.9% in 1990–2002; GDP increased by 0.7% in 2002.

Agriculture (including forestry and fishing) contributed an estimated 4.0% of GDP in 2002 and engaged about 18.1% of the employed labour force in 2001. The staple food crops are maize, wheat, sorghum, barley, rice, beans and potatoes. The principal cash crops are coffee, cotton, sugar cane, and fruit and vegeta-

bles (particularly tomatoes). Livestock-raising and fisheries are also important. During 1990–2001, according to World Bank estimates, agricultural GDP increased at an average annual rate of 1.6%; agricultural GDP rose by 0.6% in 2000 and by 1.9% in 2001. The reduction and eventual removal of import tariffs proposed under NAFTA was a significant blow to Mexico's agriculture sector, which had lower subsidies and higher overhead costs than in the USA; the elimination of tariffs on 21 products in January 2003 was offset by a US $10,000m. aid programme, announced in November 2002.

Industry (including mining, manufacturing, construction and power) engaged an estimated 25.9% of the employed labour force in 2001, and provided an estimated 26.1% of GDP in 2002. During 1990–2001 industrial GDP increased by an average of 3.3% per year; industrial GDP increased by 6.1% in 2000, but decreased by 3.5% in 2001.

Mining contributed an estimated 1.3% of GDP in 2002, and engaged an estimated 0.3% of the employed labour force in 2001. During 1990–2001 the GDP of the mining sector increased by an average of 1.9% per year; mining GDP increased by 3.8% in 2000 and by 0.8% in 2001. Mexico has large reserves of petroleum (which accounted for 7.9% of total export earnings in 2001) and natural gas. Zinc, salt, silver, copper, celestite and fluorite are also major mineral exports. In addition, mercury, bismuth, antimony, cadmium, manganese and phosphates are mined, and there are significant reserves of uranium.

Manufacturing provided an estimated 20.4% of GDP in 2002, and engaged an estimated 18.9% of the employed labour force in 2001. Manufacturing GDP increased by an annual average of 3.6% in 1990–2001; the sector increased by 6.9% in 2000, but decreased by 3.0% in 2001. In 2001 the most important branches of manufacturing (based on value of output) were metals and machinery, food, beverages and tobacco, and chemicals. By December 2000 Mexico had 3,703 *maquiladora* export plants (where intermediate materials produced on US territory are processed or assembled on the Mexican side of the border), providing an estimated 1.3m. jobs and making an increasingly significant contribution to the sector (accounting for an estimated 48.6% of total revenue from manufacturing exports in 2002).

Energy is derived principally from mineral fuels and lubricants and hydroelectric power. In 2000 some 47.5% of total output of electricity production was derived from petroleum, 19.8% came from natural gas, 16.2% was derived from hydroelectric plants and 9.3% came from coal-powered plants. During the late 1990s the Government initiated a programme to deregulate the energy sector; in 1997 private consortia were awarded concessions to build and lease power-stations in Mexico. In 2001 fuel imports accounted for 3.0% of total merchandise imports. In late 2001 the Governments of Mexico and Guatemala reached agreement, under the regional 'Plan Puebla-Panamá' (a series of joint transport, industry and tourism projects intended to integrate the Central American region), to link their electricity grids. In 2002 the Government's planned reform of the energy sector faced congressional opposition. In 2003, according to the state concern Petróleos Mexicanos (PEMEX), oil production was 3,371,000 barrels per day, while production of natural gas was 4,498m. cu ft per day.

The services sector contributed an estimated 69.9% of GDP in 2002, and engaged an estimated 55.6% of the employed labour force in 2001. According to government figures, the GDP of the sector increased by an average of 3.7% per year in 1990–2001; the sector experienced growth of 7.4% in 2000 and of 1.0% in 2001. Tourism is one of Mexico's principal sources of foreign exchange. In 2002 there were an estimated 19.7m. foreign visitors to Mexico (mostly from the USA and Canada), providing revenue of US $8,858m.

In 2002 Mexico recorded a visible trade deficit of an estimated US $7,995m., and there was a deficit of $14,069m. on the current account of the balance of payments. In 2002 the principal source of imports (63.4%) was the USA, which was also the principal market for exports (89.1%). The principal exports in that year were electric and electronic products, parts for road vehicles, and industrial machinery and the principal imports were electric and electronic products, industrial machinery and transport equipment. In 2002 imports from Mercosur (Mercado Común del Sur, or Southern Common Market, see p. 335) countries almost doubled, while exports decreased slightly.

In 2002 there was an estimated budgetary deficit of 135,098.0m. new pesos, equivalent to 2.2% of GDP. Mexico's external debt totalled an estimated US $158,290m. at the end of

2001, of which $86,199m. was long-term public debt. In that year the cost of debt-servicing was equivalent to 26.1% of the value of exports of goods and services. The average annual rate of inflation was 16.1% in 1990–2002. Consumer prices increased by an average of 5.0% in 2002. Some 1.9% of the total labour force were officially recorded as unemployed in 2002, according to ILO figures.

Mexico is a member of the Inter-American Development Bank (IDB, see p. 257), and of the Latin American Integration Association (see p. 277). Mexico was admitted to the Asia-Pacific Economic Co-operation group (APEC, see p. 147) in 1993, and joined the Organisation for Economic Co-operation and Development (OECD, see p. 295) in 1994. Mexico is also a signatory nation to the North American Free Trade Agreement (NAFTA, see p. 288). In mid-March 2004 Mexico concluded a free trade agreement with Japan.

Mexico's economic development, centred on the expansion of the petroleum industry, was impeded from the mid-1980s by the decrease in international petroleum prices, in addition to the persistent problems of the flight of capital, the depreciation of the peso, a shortage of foreign exchange and vast foreign debt. A programme of tax reform and economic liberalization was undertaken from the late 1980s, but in late 1994 and early 1995 a sharp devaluation of the peso provoked a financial crisis, necessitating a stringent policy of economic adjustment and the procurement of substantial international credit facilities. During 1995–97 a state agency, FOBAPROA, assumed some US $65,000m. in bank liabilities as a result of the crisis. In 1998, despite a dramatic decline in the price of petroleum and the adverse effects of a fall in the value of the peso against the US dollar, GDP growth of 5.0% was recorded, not least because of the strength of the manufacturing sector. A reform of the banking sector was undertaken in May 1999, creating the Instituto para la Protección al Ahorro Bancario to manage the assets previously assumed by FOBAPROA and removing all restrictions on foreign ownership of banks. In 1999 economic performance was again favourable and in 2000 GDP growth accelerated to 6.6%, reflecting continuing strong export growth, particularly in the *maquiladora* industries. However, there was an economic slowdown in 2001; GDP declined by 0.2%, with the *maquiladora* sector being particularly badly affected, contracting by 8.9% in that year. In 2003 the *maquiladora* sector continued to suffer from decreasing export revenues and decreasing employment. In 2002 remittances from Mexicans living in the USA were estimated to be $13,270m., or 2.2% of GDP. The 2003 budget, passed in December 2002, set a strict fiscal deficit of 0.5% of GDP; finances were boosted in early 2003 by a massive increase in crude petroleum export prices, as a result of uncertain supplies from Venezuela and the US-led military campaign in Iraq, as well as by a weak new peso (oil revenues were paid in US dollars). Free trade became a prominent issue in the latter half of 2003; at the fifth Ministerial Conference of the World Trade Organization, held in Cancún in September, Mexico joined the so-called G-20 (subsequently renamed the G-19) group of developing nations opposed to the developed world's agricultural subsidies. Ongoing negotiations over the proposed Free Trade Area of the Americas also ran into difficulties in late 2003 over each country's level of participation. NAFTA, which reached its 10th anniversary on 1 January 2004, also faced criticism from various sectors. It was claimed that although Mexican agricultural exports had doubled during the 10 years that NAFTA had been in place, 1.3m. jobs had been lost in the agricultural sector. In 2003 the Mexican economy was adversely affected by the sluggish economy of its largest trading partner, the USA. At the same time, the People's Republic of China, with its lower labour costs, threatened Mexico's position as the second largest exporter to the USA. In August 2003 unemployment reached a six-year high of 4.0%. Throughout the second half of 2003 the Government experienced problems in convincing a hostile Congreso to approve its reform agenda. In December President Fox was forced to abandon the Government's commitment to the privatization, closure or merger of several state-run companies in order that his proposed budget receive congressional approval. A revised and more moderate budget, which included increased expenditure on agriculture, education and anti-poverty programmes was eventually passed by the Congreso in late December. Economic growth in 2004 was predicted to be 3.1%, and the Banco Central forecast that the rate of inflation would be 3% in that year.

Education

Education in state schools is provided free of charge and is officially compulsory. It covers six years of primary education, beginning at six years of age, and three years of secondary education, either general or technical, from the age of 12 . This can then be followed by another three-year cycle of higher or specialized secondary education. In 1996 the total enrolment at primary and secondary schools was equivalent to 90% of the school-age population (males 90%; females 89%). In 2000/2001 year 99% of children in the relevant age-group were enrolled in primary education (males 99%; females 101%), while UNESCO estimated that 60% of children in the relevant age-group were enrolled in secondary schools (males 57%; females 62%). In 2001/02 there were an estimated 4,183 institutes of higher education, attended by 2,147,100 students. In 2002 there were 56 universities in Mexico. In 2001/02 nursery schools for the indigenous population numbered 8,487, while there were 9,065 primary schools for the indigenous population. However, in spite of the existence of more than 80 indigenous languages in Mexico, there were few bilingual secondary schools. Total enrolment at primary school was 14,843,400 students in 2001/02; in that year 6,112,900 students were enrolled at all levels of secondary education. The National Agreement for the Modernization of Basic Education (agreed between the Federal Government, state governments and the national teachers' union in 1992) envisaged the future devolution of federal responsibility for education, to state and municipal bodies. Federal expenditure on education in 2000 was an estimated 216,548m. new pesos (equivalent to 24.7% of total central government expenditure). In November 2002 the Congreso Nacional approved legislation establishing a lower limit on education expenditure equivalent to 8% of GDP.

Public Holidays

2004: 1 January (New Year's Day), 5 February (Constitution Day), 22 March (for Birthday of Benito Juárez), 8 April (Maundy Thursday)*, 9 April (Good Friday)*, 3 May (for Labour Day), 5 May (Anniversary of the Battle of Puebla)*, 16 September (Independence Day), 12 October (Discovery of America), 1 November (All Saints' Day)*, 2 November (All Souls' Day)*, 22 November (for Anniversary of the Revolution), 12 December (Day of Our Lady of Guadalupe)*, 25 December (Christmas).

2005: 1 January (New Year's Day), 5 February (Constitution Day), 21 March (Birthday of Benito Juárez), 24 March (Maundy Thursday)*, 25 March (Good Friday)*, 2 May (for Labour Day), 5 May (Anniversary of the Battle of Puebla)*, 16 September (Independence Day), 12 October (Discovery of America), 1 November (All Saints' Day)*, 2 November (All Souls' Day)*, 21 November (for Anniversary of the Revolution), 12 December (Day of Our Lady of Guadalupe)*, 25 December (Christmas).

*Widely-celebrated unofficial holidays.

Weights and Measures

The metric system is in force.

Statistical Survey

Sources (unless otherwise stated): Dirección General de Estadística, Instituto Nacional de Estadística, Geografía e Informática (INEGI), Edif. Sede, Avda Prolongación Héroe de Nacozari 2301 Sur, 20270 Aguascalientes, Ags; tel. (14) 918-1948; fax (14) 918-0739; internet www.inegi.gob.mx; Banco de México, Avda 5 de Mayo 2, Apdo 98 bis, 06059 México, DF; tel. (55) 5237-2000; fax (55) 5237-2370; internet www.banxico.org.mx; Banco Nacional de Comercio Exterior, SNC, Periférico Sur 4333, 3°, Col. Jardines en la Montaña, 14210 México, DF; tel. (55) 5449-9424; fax (55) 5449-9223; internet www.bancomext.com.

Area and Population

AREA, POPULATION AND DENSITY

Area (sq km)	
Continental	1,959,248
Islands.	5,127
Total	1,964,375*
Population (census results)	
5 November 1995	91,158,290
14 February 2000	
Males	47,592,253
Females.	49,891,159
Total	97,483,412
Population (UN estimates at mid-year)†	
2001	100,456,000
2002	101,965,000
Density (per sq km) at mid-2002	51.9

* 758,449 sq miles.

† Source: UN, *World Population Prospects: The 2002 Revision*.

ADMINISTRATIVE DIVISIONS
(at census of 14 February 2000)

States	Area (sq km)*	Population	Density (per sq km)	Capital
Aguascalientes (Ags) . .	5,623	944,285	167.9	Aguascalientes
Baja California (BC) . . .	71,540	2,487,367	34.8	Mexicali
Baja California Sur (BCS) .	73,937	424,041	5.7	La Paz
Campeche (Camp.) . .	57,718	690,689	12.0	Campeche
Chiapas (Chis) .	73,680	3,920,892	53.2	Tuxtla Gutiérrez
Chihuahua (Chih.) . .	247,490	3,052,907	12.3	Chihuahua
Coahuila (de Zaragoza) (Coah.) . .	151,447	2,298,070	15.2	Saltillo
Colima (Col.) . .	5,629	542,627	96.4	Colima
Distrito Federal (DF) . . .	1,485	8,605,239	5,794.8	Mexico City
Durango (Dgo) .	123,364	1,448,661	11.7	Victoria de Durango
Guanajuato (Gto) .	30,617	4,663,032	152.3	Guanajuato
Guerrero (Gro) .	63,618	3,079,649	48.4	Chilpancingo de los Bravos
Hidalgo (Hgo) .	20,855	2,235,591	107.2	Pachuca de Soto
Jalisco (Jal.) . . .	78,624	6,322,002	80.4	Guadalajara
México (Méx.) .	22,332	13,096,686	586.5	Toluca de Lerdo
Michoacán (de Ocampo) (Mich.) .	58,672	3,985,667	67.9	Morelia
Morelos (Mor.) .	4,894	1,555,296	317.8	Cuernavaca
Nayarit (Nay.) .	27,861	920,185	33.0	Tepic
Nuevo León (NL) .	64,206	3,834,141	59.7	Monterrey
Oaxaca (Oax.) .	93,348	3,438,765	36.8	Oaxaca de Juárez
Puebla (Pue.) .	34,246	5,076,686	148.2	Heroica Puebla de Zaragoza
Querétaro (de Arteaga) (Qro) .	11,659	1,404,306	120.4	Querétaro
Quintana Roo (Q.Roo) . .	42,544	874,963	20.6	Ciudad Chetumal
San Luis Potosí (SLP) . . .	61,165	2,299,360	37.6	San Luis Potosí

States— continued	Area (sq km)*	Population	Density (per sq km)	Capital
Sinaloa (Sin.) .	57,334	2,536,844	44.2	Culiacán Rosales
Sonora (Son.) .	179,527	2,216,969	12.3	Hermosillo
Tabasco (Tab.) .	24,747	1,891,829	76.4	Villahermosa
Tamaulipas (Tam.) .	80,155	2,753,222	34.3	Ciudad Victoria
Tlaxcala (Tlax.) .	3,988	962,646	241.4	Tlaxcala de Xicohténcatl
Veracruz-Llave(Ver.) . .	71,856	6,908,975	96.2	Jalapa Enríquez
Yucatán (Yuc.) .	39,675	1,658,210	41.8	Mérida
Zacatecas (Zac.) .	75,412	1,353,610	17.9	Zacatecas
Total . . .	.1,959,248	97,483,412	49.8	—

* Excluding islands.

PRINCIPAL TOWNS
(population at census of 14 February 2000)

Ciudad de México (Mexico City, capital)	8,605,239	Querétaro. . . .	536,463
Guadalajara . . .	1,646,183	Torreón . . .	502,964
Ecatepec de Morelos (Ecatepec) . .	1,621,827	San Nicolás de los Garzas . . .	496,879
Heroica Puebla de Zaragoza (Puebla).	1,271,673	Santa María Chimalhuacán (Chimalhuacán) .	482,530
Nezahualcóyotl . .	1,225,083	Atizapán de Zaragoza . . .	467,544
Ciudad Juárez . .	1,187,275	Tlaquepaque . . .	458,674
Tijuana . . .	1,148,681	Toluca de Lerdo (Toluca). . . .	435,125
Monterrey. . . .	1,110,909	Cuautitlán Izcalli .	433,830
León	1,020,818	Victoria de Durango (Durango) . .	427,135
Zapopan . . .	910,690	Tuxtla Gutiérrez . .	424,579
Naucalpan de Juárez (Naucalpan) . .	835,053	Veracruz Llave (Veracruz) . . .	411,582
Tlalnepantla de Baz (Tlalnepantla) . .	714,735	Reynosa . . .	403,718
Guadalupe . . .	669,842	Benito Juárez (Cancún) . . .	397,191
Mérida . . .	662,530	Matamoros . . .	376,279
Chihuahua . . .	657,876	Jalapa Enríquez (Xalapa) . . .	373,076
San Luis Potosí . .	629,208	Villahermosa. . . .	330,846
Acapulco de Juárez (Acapulco) . .	620,656	Mazatlán . . .	327,989
Aguascalientes . .	594,092	Cuernavaca . . .	327,162
Saltillo . . .	562,587	Valle de Chalco (Xico) . . .	322,784
Morelia . . .	549,996	Irapuato . . .	319,148
Mexicali . . .	549,873	Tonalá. . . .	315,278
Hermosillo . . .	545,928	Nuevo Laredo . . .	308,828
Culiacán Rosales (Culiacán) . .	540,823		

BIRTHS, MARRIAGES AND DEATHS*

	Registered live births		Registered marriages		Registered deaths	
	Number	Rate (per 1,000)	Number	Rate (per 1,000)	Number	Rate (per 1,000)
1994	2,904,389	25.6	671,640	7.2	419,074	4.5
1995	2,750,444	25.0	658,114	7.3	430,278	4.6
1996	2,707,718	24.4	670,523	6.9	436,321	4.5
1997	2,698,425	23.7	707,840	7.5	440,437	4.7
1998	2,668,428	23.0	n.a.	n.a.	444,665	n.a.
1999	2,769,089	22.3	743,856	n.a.	443,950	n.a.
2000	2,798,339	21.1	707,422	7.1	437,667	4.2
2001	2,767,610	20.5	665,434	6.6	443,127	4.2

* Data are tabulated by year of registration rather than by year of occurrence. However, birth registration is incomplete. According to UN estimates, the average annual rates in 1990–1995, were: births 27.0 per 1,000; deaths 5.2 per 1,000 and in 1995–2000: births 24.6 per 1,000; deaths 5.0 per 1,000 (Source: UN, *World Population Prospects: The 2002 Revision*).

Expectation of life (UN estimates, years at birth): 74.4 (males 71.7; females 77.0) in 2002 (Source: WHO *World Health Report*).

ECONOMICALLY ACTIVE POPULATION

(sample surveys, '000 persons aged 12 years and over, April–June)

	1999	2000	2001
Agriculture, hunting and forestry	8,048.6	6,901.8	6,920.7
Fishing	160.1	158.9	153.7
Mining and quarrying	133.4	155.6	127.2
Manufacturing	7,344.8	7,546.7	7,373.0
Electricity, gas and water supply	193.1	188.5	194.9
Construction	2,158.0	2,527.6	2,396.9
Wholesale and retail trade; repair of motor vehicles, motorcycles and personal and household goods	6,582.4	8,524.5	8,839.2
Hotels and restaurants	1,807.5	1,844.4	1,982.2
Transport, storage and communications	1,738.5	1,730.6	1,776.7
Financial intermediation	302.7	293.0	280.2
Real estate, renting and business activities	1,156.7	1,177.9	1,224.4
Public administration and defence, compulsory social security	1,728.3	1,739.4	1,682.1
Education	1,722.9	1,877.5	1,971.6
Health and social work	1,024.8	1,062.6	1,039.1
Other community, social and personal services activities	3,094.5	1,322.6	1,226.4
Private households with employed persons	1,707.4	1,770.9	1,673.1
Extra-territorial organizations and bodies	151.0	159.8	0.9
Activities not adequately defined	14.5	1.7	142.0
Total employed	39,069.1	38,983.8	39,004.3
Unemployed	682.3	650.0	678.5
Total labour force	39,751.4	39,633.8	39,682.8
Males	26,436.9	26,073.5	26,165.3
Females	13,314.5	13,560.3	13,517.5

Source: ILO.

2002: Total employed 40,302.0; Unemployed 783.7; Total labour force 41,085.7 (males 26,888, females 14,197.8).

Source: ILO.

Health and Welfare

KEY INDICATORS

Total fertility rate (children per woman, 2002)	2.5
Under-5 mortality rate (per 1,000 live births, 2001)	29
HIV/AIDS (% of persons aged 15–49, 2000)	0.28
Physicians (per 1,000 head, 2000)	1.8
Hospital beds (per 1,000 head, 2000)	1.1
Health expenditure (2001): US $ per head (PPP)	544
Health expenditure (2001): % of GDP	6.1
Health expenditure (2001): public (% of total)	44.3
Access to water (% of persons, 2000)	86
Access to sanitation (% of persons, 2000)	73
Human Development Index (2001): ranking	55
Human Development Index (2001): value	0.800

For sources and definitions, see explanatory note on p. vi.

Agriculture

PRINCIPAL CROPS

('000 metric tons)

	2000	2001	2002
Wheat	3,493	3,275	3,236
Rice (paddy)	351	227	227
Barley	713	762	737
Maize	17,557	20,134	19,299
Oats	32	89	64
Sorghum	5,842	6,567	5,206
Potatoes	1,627	1,628	1,483
Sugar cane	44,100*	47,250*	45,635
Dry beans	888	1,063	1,549
Chick-peas	234	326	235
Soybeans (Soya beans)	102	122	87
Groundnuts (in shell)	142	120	75
Coconuts*	1,117	1,100	959
Safflower seed	96	111	53
Cottonseed	123	152	68
Cabbages	171	216	197
Lettuce	192	213	228
Tomatoes	2,086	2,183	1,990
Cauliflower*	205	200	200
Pumpkins, squash and gourds*	530	560	470
Cucumbers and gherkins*	410	420	433
Chillies and green peppers	1,735	1,871	1,784
Green onions and shallots	905	1,029	1,131
Dry onions*	100	102	100
Carrots	377	356	378
Green corn*	298	191	186
Bananas	1,863	1,983	2,077
Oranges	3,813	4,035	3,844
Tangerines, mandarins, clementines and satsumas	314	365	360*
Lemons and limes	1,661	1,594	1,680
Grapefruit and pomelos	263	320	269
Apples	338	443	428
Peaches and nectarines	147	176	198
Strawberries	141	131	142
Grapes	372	436	363
Watermelons	1,049	970	858
Cantaloupes and other melons*	500	510	510
Mangoes	1,559	1,577	1,528
Avocados	907	940	901
Pineapples	522	626	660
Papayas	672	873	876
Coffee (green)	338	303	313
Cocoa beans	28	47	45
Pimento and allspice*	55	55	55
Cotton (lint)	78	97	43
Tobacco (leaves)	45	41	22

* FAO estimate(s).

Source: FAO.

LIVESTOCK
('000 head, year ending September)

	2000	2001	2002
Horses*	6,250	6,255	6,255
Mules*	3,280	3,280	3,280
Asses*	3,250	3,260	3,260
Cattle	30,524	30,621	30,700*
Pigs	16,087	17,584	18,000*
Sheep	6,046	6,165	6,260*
Goats	8,704	8,702	9,600*
Chickens*	476,000	497,600	520,800
Ducks*	8,000	8,100	8,100
Turkeys*	3,000	5,850	5,850

* Estimate(s).

Source: FAO.

LIVESTOCK PRODUCTS
('000 metric tons)

	2000	2001	2002
Beef and veal	1,409	1,445	1,451
Mutton and lamb	33	36	38
Goat meat	39	39	42
Pig meat	1,030	1,058	1,070
Horse meat*	79	79	79
Poultry meat	1,863	1,976	2,123
Cows' milk	9,311	9,472	9,658
Goats' milk	131	140	146
Butter	15	15	15
Cheese	147	153	156
Evaporated and condensed milk*	153	156	158
Hen eggs	1,788	1,892	1,901
Cattle hides	175†	176*	176*
Honey	59	59	59

* FAO estimate(s).
† Unofficial figure.

Source: FAO.

Forestry

ROUNDWOOD REMOVALS
('000 cubic metres, excl. bark)

	2000	2001	2002
Sawlogs, veneer logs and logs for sleepers	6,651*	6,176	6,176*
Pulpwood	1,234*	1,028	1,028*
Other industrial wood	220*	216	216*
Fuel wood*	37,561	37,736	37,913
Total	**45,666**	**45,156**	**45,333**

* FAO estimate(s).

Source: FAO.

SAWNWOOD PRODUCTION
('000 cubic metres, incl. railway sleepers)

	1999*	2000*	2001
Coniferous (softwood)	2,904	2,904	2,904*
Broadleaved (hardwood)	206	206	483
Total	**3,110**	**3,110**	**3,387**

* FAO estimate(s).

2002: Production assumed to be unchanged from 2001 (FAO estimates).

Source: FAO.

Fishing
('000 metric tons, live weight)

	1999	2000	2001
Capture	1,205.6	1,315.6	1,398.6
Tilapias	59.3	68.8	60.3
California pilchard (sardine)	345.5	478.2	609.8
Yellowfin tuna	121.9	102.3	135.5
Chub mackerel	69.4	45.2	3.8
Marine shrimps and prawns	66.5	61.6	57.5
American cupped oyster	39.3	48.1	48.6
Jumbo flying squid	58.0	56.2	73.7
Aquaculture	48.4	53.9	76.1
Total catch (incl. others)	**1,254.0**	**1,369.5**	**1,474.7**

Note: Figures exclude aquatic plants ('000 metric tons, capture only): 32.1 in 1999; 33.6 in 2000; 46.9 in 2001. Also excluded are aquatic mammals and crocodiles (recorded by number rather than by weight), shells and corals. The number of Morelet's crocodiles caught was: 2 in 1999; 1,288 in 2000; 3,643 in 2001. The catch of marine shells (metric tons) was: 965 in 1999; 464 in 2000; 463 in 2001 (FAO estimate).

Source: FAO, *Yearbook of Fishery Statistics*.

Mining
(metric tons, unless otherwise indicated)

	2000	2001	2002*
Antimony†	52	81	208
Arsenic†	2,522	2,381	1,945
Barytes	127,668	142,017	132,836
Bismuth†	1,112	1,390	1,126
Cadmium†	1,297	1,434	1,399
Coal	8,230,115	6,986,027	6,116,270
Coke	2,235,032	2,065,483	1,656,437
Copper†	338,999	5,518	308,388
Crude petroleum ('000 barrels per day)	3,012	3,127	3,177
Celestite	157,420	145,789	109,314
Dolomite	403,664	670,797	518,412
Feldspar	334,439	329,591	348,670
Flourite	635,230	619,468	666,379
Gas (million cu ft per day)	4,679	4,511	4,423
Gold (kg)†	25,822	28,749	23,254
Graphite	30,330	21,442	15,956
Iron†	6,795,406	5,269,820	5,750,563
Lead†	160,607	148,625	112,244
Manganese†	156,117	99,751	65,483
Molybdenum†	6,886	5,518	3,428
Phosphate rock	1,052,464	787,283	458,710
Silica	1,802,545	1,720,211	1,826,665
Silver†	2,746,852	3,030,437	2,852,138
Sulphur	851,427	878,180	885,492
Wollastonite	30,836	39,830	28,259
Zinc†	358,576	427,273	391,711

* Provisional figures.
† Figures for metallic minerals refer to metal content of ores.

Industry

SELECTED PRODUCTS
('000 metric tons, unless otherwise indicated)

	1999	2000	2001
Wheat flour	2,457	2,538	2,611
Other cereal flour	1,878	1,179	1,667
Raw sugar	2,804	2,531	3,018
Beer ('000 hectolitres)	57,905	59,851	61,632
Soft drinks ('000 hectolitres)	119,083	126,460	130,050
Cigarettes (million units)	59,492	56,383	56,057
Cotton yarn (pure and mixed)	21	21	19
Tyres ('000 units)*	17,386	16,780	13,533
Cement	31,958	33,429	32,239
Gas stoves—household ('000 units)	3,165	3,973	4,021
Refrigerators—household ('000 units)	2,083	2,049	2,071
Lorries, buses, tractors, etc. ('000 units)	462	554	529
Passenger cars ('000 units)	988	1,294	1,273
Washing machines—household ('000 units)	1,593	1,720	1,636
Electric energy (million kWh)	228,910	228,873	n.a.

* Tyres for road motor vehicles.

Source: UN, *Industrial Commodity Statistics Yearbook*.

Finance

CURRENCY AND EXCHANGE RATES

Monetary Units
100 centavos = 1 Mexican nuevo peso.

Sterling, Dollar and Euro Equivalents (31 December 2003)
£1 sterling = 20.053 nuevos pesos;
US $1 = 11.236 nuevos pesos;
€1 = 14.191 nuevos pesos;
1,000 Mexican nuevos pesos = £49.87 = $89.00 = €70.47.

Average Exchange Rate (nuevos pesos per US $)
2001   9.34234
2002   9.6560
2003   10.7890

Note: Figures are given in terms of the nuevo (new) peso, introduced on 1 January 1993 and equivalent to 1,000 former pesos.

BUDGET*
(million new pesos)

Revenue	2000	2001	2002
Taxation	581,703.4	654,870.3	729,429.6
Income taxes	258,754.2	285,523.1	319,316.9
Value-added tax	189,606.0	208,408.1	218,260.5
Excise tax	81,544.1	110,688.8	136,493.0
Import duties	32,861.4	28,902.1	27,431.7
Other taxes	18,937.7	21,348.2	26,074.6
Other revenue	286,564.3	284,244.2	259,852.3
Royalties	210,955.2	203,751.6	158,507.1
Petroleum royalties	196,143.2	187,606.6	139,841.9
Total revenue	868,267.7	939,114.5	989,281.9

Expenditure	2000	2001	2002
Programmable expenditure	589,402.2	631,773.7	744,831.2
Current expenditure	507,609.8	539,425.7	607,587.9
Consumption	120,437.1	123,092.3	170,816.2
Personal services	86,479.9	93,132.1	101,734.6
Transfers	387,799.3	416,333.4	471,312.5
Capital expenditure	81,792.4	92,348.0	137,243.3
Transfers	62,346.2	76,044.3	122,044.0
Non-programmable expenditure	362,680.9	365,176.9	379,548.7
Interest and fees	176,461.0	166,826.4	158,550.2
Revenue sharing	178,136.2	196,931.2	214,890.9
Total expenditure	952,083.1	996,950.6	1,124,379.9

* Figures refer to the consolidated accounts of the central Government, including government agencies and the national social security system. The budgets of state and local governments are excluded.

Source: Dirección General de Planeación Hacendaria.

INTERNATIONAL RESERVES*
(US $ million at 31 December)

	2000	2001	2002
IMF special drawing rights	366	356	392
Reserve position in the Fund	—	—	308
Foreign exchange	35,142	44,384	49,895
Total	35,509	44,741	50,594

* Excluding gold reserves ($357 million at 30 September 1989).

Source: IMF, *International Financial Statistics*.

MONEY SUPPLY
(million new pesos at 31 December)

	2000	2001	2002
Currency outside banks	182,237	199,177	232,467
Demand deposits at deposit money banks	266,975	317,377	358,808
Total money (incl. others)	450,738	527,672	618,680

Source: IMF, *International Financial Statistics*.

COST OF LIVING
(Consumer Price Index; base: 1990 = 100)

	1999	2000	2001
Food, beverages and tobacco	473.6	503.4	530.5
Electricity, gas and water	654.4	819.1	891.7
Clothing and footwear	425.7	470.1	497.2
Rent	493.8	549.9	586.1
All items (incl. others)	491.9	538.6	572.9

2002: Food, beverages and tobacco 551.7; All items 601.7.

Source: ILO.

NATIONAL ACCOUNTS

National Income and Product
(million new pesos at current prices)

	1998	1999	2000
Compensation of employees	1,176,936	1,434,759	1,714,421
Operating surplus	1,943,622	2,309,085	2,736,485
Domestic factor incomes	3,120,558	3,743,844	4,450,906
Consumption of fixed capital	397,224	461,860	523,557
Gross domestic product at factor cost	3,517,782	4,205,704	4,974,463
Indirect taxes	346,901	404,370	527,891
Less Subsidies	18,333	16,388	16,982
GDP in purchasers' values	3,846,350	4,593,686	5,485,372

Source: ECLAC, *Statistical Yearbook for Latin America and the Caribbean*.

Expenditure on the Gross Domestic Product
('000 million new pesos at current prices)*

	2000	2001	2002
Government final consumption expenditure	609.72	686.03	723.51
Private final consumption expenditure	3,683.74	4,056.83	4,304.56
Increase in stocks	130.30	72.76	84.98
Gross fixed capital formation	1,174.12	1,144.85	1,161.68
Total domestic expenditure	5,597.88	5,960.47	6,274.73
Exports of goods and services	1,704.08	1,598.52	1,673.47
Less Imports of goods and services	1,810.58	1,730.39	1,795.38
GDP in purchasers' values	5,491.37	5,828.59	6,152.83
GDP at constant 1993 prices	1,602.54	1,599.79	1,611.67

* Figures are rounded to the nearest 10 million new pesos.

Source: IMF, *International Financial Statistics*.

Gross Domestic Product by Economic Activity
(million new pesos at current prices)

	2000	2001	2002
Agriculture, forestry and fishing .	202,010	218,770	225,879
Mining and quarrying . . .	70,178	72,144	75,501
Manufacturing	1,013,598	1,037,134	1,060,438
Electricity, gas and water . .	54,941	62,526	76,342
Construction	257,906	262,631	275,293
Trade, restaurants and hotels . .	1,065,694	1,105,047	1,163,226
Transport, storage and communications	556,840	595,607	628,129
Finance, insurance, real estate and business services	605,499	642,115	710,099
Community, social and personal services	1,215,204	1,380,406	1,483,433
Sub-total	5,041,870	5,376,380	5,698,339
Less Imputed bank service charge	61,084	90,770	102,070
GDP at factor cost	4,980,786	5,285,606	5,596,269
Indirect taxes, *less* subsidies . .	510,909	542,984	556,560
GDP in purchasers' values . .	5,491,373	5,828,591	6,152,829

Note: Totals may not be equal to the sum of component parts, owing to rounding.

BALANCE OF PAYMENTS
(US $ million)

	2000	2001	2002
Exports of goods f.o.b.	166,456	158,443	160,682
Imports of goods f.o.b.	−174,457	−168,398	−168,677
Trade balance	−8,001	−9,955	−7,995
Exports of services . . .	13,752	12,699	12,740
Imports of services	−17,363	−17,194	−17,659
Balance on goods and services	−11,612	−14,450	−12,914
Other income received	6,049	5,098	4,053
Other income paid	−19,594	−17,997	−15,462
Balance on goods, services and income	−25,157	−27,349	−24,323
Current transfers received . . .	7,001	9,338	10,289
Current transfers paid	−29	−22	−35
Current balance	−18,185	−18,033	−14,069
Direct investment abroad . . .	—	−4,405	−969
Direct investment from abroad . .	15,483	25,335	13,627
Portfolio investment assets . . .	1,290	3,857	1,134
Portfolio investment liabilities . .	−11,560	−9,304	−10,397
Other investment assets . . .	5,808	−3,287	11,601
Other investment liabilities . .	−7,784	−11,055	−9,228
Net errors and omissions . . .	3,667	942	1,049
Overall balance	−11,281	−15,950	−7,252

Source: IMF, *International Financial Statistics*.

External Trade

PRINCIPAL COMMODITIES
(distribution by SITC, US $ million)

Imports f.o.b.	1999	2000	2001
Food and live animals . . .	5,909.8	7,050.7	8,314.3
Crude materials (inedible) except fuels	4,156.7	4,902.1	4,688.6
Mineral fuels, lubricants and related materials	3,181.4	5,618.3	5,635.8
Chemicals and related products	12,309.6	14,892.5	15,269.7
Basic manufactures	25,444.1	33,422.8	31,941.1
Textile yarn, fabrics, etc. . .	4,928.6	6,252.6	6,045.0
Machinery and transport equipment.	71,585.5	95,897.0	98,634.5
Power-generating machinery and equipment	5,410.6	6,890.4	6,598.1

Imports f.o.b.— *continued*	1999	2000	2001
Machinery specialized for particular industries . .	4,844.5	5,386.7	4,710.1
General industrial machinery and equipment and parts	8,309.7	10,281.1	10,366.1
Office machines and automatic data-processing equipment . .	4,357.5	5,774.9	8,374.2
Telecommunciations and sound equipment	6,898.4	9,771.8	10,017.6
Other electrical machinery, apparatus, etc. . . .	27,002.1	36,388.3	38,020.7
Switchgear, resistors, printed circuits, switchboards, etc.. .	6,472.5	8,486.5	9,644.6
Thermionic valves, tubes, etc. .	10,106.0	14,279.5	14,467.6
Electronic microcircuits . .	5,604.8	8,937.7	8,669.5
Road vehicles and parts* . .	12,157.1	18,964.4	18,309.5
Parts and accessories for cars, buses, lorries, etc.*	8,230.1	12,054.8	11,192.7
Miscellaneous manufactured articles.	18,022.6	23,294.9	23,763.6
Articles of plastic materials, etc. .	5,613.0	7,265.2	7,265.3
Total (incl. others)	146,064.6	190,790.5	190,365.2

* Data on parts exclude tyres, engines and electrical parts.

Exports f.o.b.	1999	2000	2001
Food and live animals . . .	5,999.6	6,472.1	6,419.4
Mineral fuels, lubricants, etc. .	9,731.0	16,052.8	12,639.3
Petroleum, petroleum products, etc.	9,604.8	15,964.1	12,493.3
Crude petroleum oils, etc. . .	8,858.8	14,878.5	11,597.9
Chemicals and related products	4,402.5	5,253.1	5,326.2
Basic manufactures	12,120.2	13,848.2	12,810.9
Machinery and transport equipment.	81,258.9	98,281.3	95,497.4
Power-generating machinery and equipment	5,731.6	6,222.4	6,047.3
General industrial machinery equipment and parts . . .	4,475.4	5,171.9	5,074.3
Office machines and automatic data-processing equipment . .	9,760.3	11,756.7	13,188.4
Automatic data-processing machines and units . . .	6,398.9	8,137.8	9,692.5
Telecommunications and sound equipment	14,379.5	19,221.1	19,142.2
Colour television receivers . .	5,156.1	5,727.4	6,239.0
Other electrical machinery apparatus, etc.	21,756.8	26,063.9	22,285.9
Equipment for distributing electricity.	6,008.2	6,719.8	5,949.7
Insulated electric wire, cable etc.	5,977.2	6,673.9	5,898.4
Road vehicles and parts* . . .	23,383.4	27,898.1	27,825.2
Passenger motor cars (excl. buses).	12,407.5	16,296.7	15,297.4
Goods vehicles (lorries and trucks)	4,101.5	4,815.7	6,447.6
Parts and accessories for cars, buses, lorries, etc.*	5,107.9	5,812.5	5,579.3
Miscellaneous manufactured articles.	19,379.9	22,607.6	22,454.4
Clothing and accessories (excl. footwear)	7,772.9	8,631.3	8,012.0
Total (incl. others)	136,262.8	166,191.7	158,684.6

* Data on parts exclude tyres, engines and electrical parts.

Source: UN, *International Trade Statistics Yearbook*.

2002 (US $ million, preliminary figures): *Imports f.o.b.*: Agricultural products 4,871.9; Manufactured goods 160,622.8; Total (incl. others) 168,678.9; *Exports f.o.b.*: Agricultural products 3,263.5; Mineral products 13,510.81; Manufactured goods 143,160.4; Total (incl. others) 160,682.0.

PRINCIPAL TRADING PARTNERS*
(US $ million)

Imports c.i.f.	2000	2001	2002†
Brazil	1,802.9	2,101.3	2,565.0
Canada	4,016.6	4,234.9	4,480.3
China, People's Republic	2,879.6	4,027.3	6,274.4
China (Taiwan)	1,994.3	3,015.3	4,250.1
France	1,466.6	1,577.0	1,806.8
Germany	5,758.4	6,079.6	6,065.8
Italy	1,849.4	2,100.3	2,171.1
Japan	6,465.7	8,085.7	9,348.6
Korea, Republic	3,690.4	3,531.7	3,910.0
Malaysia	1,353.7	2,006.2	1,993.2
Spain	1,430.0	1,827.4	2,223.9
USA	127,817.7	114,061.6	106,921.9
Total (incl. others)	174,457.8	168,396.5	168,678.9

Exports f.o.b.	2000	2001	2002†
Canada	3,353.1	3,069.5	2,806.0
USA	147,898.3	140,483.9	143,256.9
Total (incl. others)	166,454.8	158,442.9	160,762.7

* Imports by country of origin; exports by country of destination.
† Preliminary data.

Transport

RAILWAYS
(traffic, million)

	2000	2001	2002*
Passenger-kilometres	82	67	66
Freight ton-kilometres	48,333	47,336	47,809

* Preliminary data.

ROAD TRAFFIC
(estimates, vehicles in use at 31 December)

	1998	1999	2000
Passenger cars	9,378,587	9,842,006	10,443,489
Buses and coaches	108,690	109,929	111,756
Lorries and vans	4,403,953	4,639,860	7,931,590

Source: International Road Federation, *World Road Statistics*.

SHIPPING

Merchant Fleet
(registered at 31 December)

	2000	2001	2002
Number of vessels	631	633	658
Total displacement ('000 grt)	883.2	908.1	937.2

Source: Lloyd's Register-Fairplay, *World Fleet Statistics*.

Sea-borne Shipping
(domestic and international freight traffic, '000 metric tons)

	2000	2001*
Goods loaded	176,694	179,400
Goods unloaded	67,558	65,031

* Provisional.

CIVIL AVIATION
(traffic on scheduled services)

	1997	1998	1999
Kilometres flown (million)	308	308	368
Passengers carried ('000)	17,752	18,685	19,263
Passenger-km (million)	24,065	25,976	27,847
Total ton-km (million)	2,333	2,556	2,742

Source: UN, *Statistical Yearbook*.

Passengers carried ('000): 33,974 in 2000; 33,673 in 2001; 34,131 in 2002 (preliminary).

Freight carried ('000 tons): 379 in 2000, 351 in 2001, 352 in 2002 (preliminary).

Source: *Informe de Gobierno, 2002*.

Tourism

	2000	2001	2002*
Tourist arrivals ('000)	20,641	19,810	19,667
Border tourists ('000)	10,050	9,659	9,784
Total expenditure (US $ million)	8,295	8,401	8,858

* Preliminary.

Source: Secretaría de Turismo de México.

Communications Media

	2000	2001	2002
Television receivers ('000 in use)	28,000	n.a.	n.a.
Telephone ('000 main lines in use)	12,332.6	13,533.0	14,941.6
Mobile cellular telephones ('000 subscribers)	14,073.7	20,136.0	25,928.3
Personal computers ('000 in use)	5,000	6,900	n.a.
Internet users ('000)	2,712.4	3,500.0	4,663.4

Radio receivers ('000 in use): 31,000 in 1997.

Facsimile machines ('000 in use): 285 in 1997.

Daily newspapers (1996): Number 295; Average circulation 9,030,000.

Non-daily newspapers (1996): Number 23; Average circulation 620,000.

Sources: International Telecommunication Union; UNESCO, *Statistical Yearbook*; UN, *Statistical Yearbook*.

Education

(estimates, 2001/02)

	Institutions	Teachers	Students*
Pre-primary	73,384	179,985	3,432.3
Primary	99,230	609,654	14,843.4
Secondary (incl. technical)	29,104	317,111	5,480.2
Intermediate: professional/technical	1,592	30,914	356.3
Intermediate: Baccalaureate	8,995	188,554	2,764.2
Higher (incl. post-graduate)	4,183	216,804	2,147.1

* Figures are in thousands.

Source: Secretaría de Educación Pública.

Adult literacy rate (UNESCO estimates): 91.4% (males 93.5%; females 89.5%) in 2001 (Source: UN Development Programme, *Human Development Report*).

Directory

The Constitution

The present Mexican Constitution was proclaimed on 5 February 1917, at the end of the revolution, which began in 1910, against the regime of Porfirio Díaz. Its provisions regarding religion, education and the ownership and exploitation of mineral wealth reflect the long revolutionary struggle against the concentration of power in the hands of the Roman Catholic Church and the large landowners, and the struggle which culminated, in the 1930s, in the expropriation of the properties of the foreign petroleum companies. It has been amended from time to time.

GOVERNMENT

The President and Congress

The President of the Republic, in agreement with the Cabinet and with the approval of the Congreso de la Unión (Congress) or of the Permanent Committee when the Congreso is not in session, may suspend constitutional guarantees in case of foreign invasion, serious disturbance, or any other emergency endangering the people.

The exercise of supreme executive authority is vested in the President, who is elected for six years and enters office on 1 December of the year of election. The presidential powers include the right to appoint and remove members of the Cabinet and the Attorney-General; to appoint, with the approval of the Senado (Senate), diplomatic officials, the higher officers of the army, and ministers of the supreme and higher courts of justice. The President is also empowered to dispose of the armed forces for the internal and external security of the federation.

The Congreso is composed of the Cámara Federal de Diputados (Federal Chamber of Deputies) elected every three years, and the Senado whose members hold office for six years. There is one deputy for every 250,000 people and for every fraction of over 125,000 people. The Senado is composed of two members for each state and two for the Distrito Federal. Regular sessions of the Congreso begin on 1 September and may not continue beyond 31 December of the same year. Extraordinary sessions may be convened by the Permanent Committee.

The powers of the Congreso include the right to: pass laws and regulations; impose taxes; specify the criteria on which the Executive may negotiate loans; declare war; raise, maintain and regulate the organization of the armed forces; establish and maintain schools of various types throughout the country; approve or reject the budget; sanction appointments submitted by the President of the Supreme Court and magistrates of the superior court of the Distrito Federal; approve or reject treaties and conventions made with foreign powers; and ratify diplomatic appointments.

The Permanent Committee, consisting of 29 members of the Congreso (15 of whom are deputies and 14 senators), officiates when the Congreso is in recess, and is responsible for the convening of extraordinary sessions of the Congreso.

The States

Governors are elected by popular vote in a general election every six years. The local legislature is formed by deputies, who are changed every three years. The judicature is specially appointed under the Constitution by the competent authority (it is never subject to the popular vote).

Each state is a separate unit, with the right to levy taxes and to legislate in certain matters. The states are not allowed to levy interstate customs duties.

The Federal District

The Distrito Federal consists of Mexico City and several neighbouring small towns and villages. The first direct elections for the Governor of the Distrito Federal were held in July 1997; hitherto a Regent had been appointed by the President.

EDUCATION

According to the Constitution, the provision of educational facilities is the joint responsibility of the federation, the states and the municipalities. Education shall be democratic, and shall be directed to developing all the faculties of the individual students, while imbuing them with love of their country and a consciousness of international solidarity and justice. Religious bodies may not provide education, except training for the priesthood. Private educational institutions must conform to the requirements of the Constitution with regard to the nature of the teaching given. The education provided by the states shall be free of charge.

RELIGION

Religious bodies of whatever denomination shall not have the capacity to possess or administer real estate or capital invested therein. Churches are the property of the nation; the headquarters of bishops, seminaries, convents and other property used for the propagation of a religious creed shall pass into the hands of the state, to be dedicated to the public service of the federation or of the respective state. Institutions of charity, provided they are not connected with a religious body, may hold real property. The establishment of monastic orders is prohibited. Ministers of religion must be Mexican; they may not criticize the fundamental laws of the country in a public or private meeting; they may not vote or form associations for political purposes. Political meetings may not be held in places of worship.

A reform proposal, whereby constitutional restrictions on the Catholic Church were formally ended, received congressional approval in December 1991 and was promulgated as law in January 1992.

LAND AND MINERAL OWNERSHIP

Article 27 of the Constitution vests direct ownership of minerals and other products of the subsoil, including petroleum and water, in the nation, and reserves to the Federal Government alone the right to grant concessions in accordance with the laws to individuals and companies, on the condition that they establish regular work for the exploitation of the materials. At the same time, the right to acquire ownership of lands and waters belonging to the nation, or concessions for their exploitation, is limited to Mexican individuals and companies, although the State may concede similar rights to foreigners who agree not to invoke the protection of their governments to enforce such rights.

The same article declares null all alienations of lands, waters and forests belonging to towns or communities made by political chiefs or other local authorities in violation of the provisions of the law of 25 June 1856,* and all concessions or sales of communally-held lands, waters and forests made by the federal authorities after 1 December 1876. The population settlements which lack ejidos (state-owned smallholdings), or cannot obtain restitution of lands previously held, shall be granted lands in proportion to the needs of the population. The area of land granted to the individual may not be less than 10 hectares of irrigated or watered land, or the equivalent in other kinds of land.

The owners affected by decisions to divide and redistribute land (with the exception of the owners of farming or cattle-rearing properties) shall not have any right of redress, nor may they invoke the right of amparo† in protection of their interests. They may, however, apply to the Government for indemnification. Small properties, the areas of which are defined in the Constitution, will not be subject to expropriation. The Constitution leaves to the Congreso the duty of determining the maximum size of rural properties.

In March 1992 an agrarian reform amendment, whereby the programme of land-distribution established by the 1917 Constitution was abolished and the terms of the ejido system of tenant farmers were relaxed, was formally adopted.

Monopolies and measures to restrict competition in industry, commerce or public services are prohibited.

A section of the Constitution deals with work and social security.

On 30 December 1977 a Federal Law on Political Organizations and Electoral Procedure was promulgated. It includes the following provisions:

Legislative power is vested in the Congreso de la Unión which comprises the Cámara Federal de Diputados and the Senado. The Cámara shall comprise 300 deputies elected by majority vote within single-member electoral districts and up to 100 deputies (increased to 200 from July 1988) elected by a system of proportional representation from regional lists within multi-member constituencies. The Senado comprises two members for each state and two for the Distrito Federal, elected by majority vote.

Executive power is exercised by the President of the Republic of the United Mexican States, elected by majority vote.

Ordinary elections will be held every three years for the federal deputies and every six years for the senators and the President of the Republic on the first Sunday of July of the year in question. When a vacancy occurs among members of the Congreso elected by majority vote, the house in question shall call extraordinary elections, and when a vacancy occurs among members of the Cámara elected by proportional representation it shall be filled by the candidate of the same party who received the next highest number of votes at the last ordinary election.

Voting is the right and duty of every citizen, male or female, over the age of 18 years.

A political party shall be registered if it has at least 3,000 members in each one of at least half the states in Mexico or at least 300 members in each one of at least half of the single-member constituencies. In either case the total number of members must be no less than 65,000. A party can also obtain conditional registration if it has been active for at least four years. Registration is confirmed if the party obtains at least 1.5% of the popular vote. All political parties shall have free access to the media.

In September 1993 an amendment to the Law on Electoral Procedure provided for the expansion of the Senado to 128 seats, representing four members for each state and the Distrito Federal, three to be elected by majority vote and one by proportional representation.

* The Lerdo Law against ecclesiastical privilege, which became the basis of the Liberal Constitution of 1857.
† The Constitution provides for the procedure known as juicio de amparo, a wider form of habeas corpus, which the individual may invoke in protection of his constitutional rights.

The Government

HEAD OF STATE

President: Vicente Fox Quesada (took office 1 December 2000).

CABINET
(April 2004)

Secretary of the Interior: Santiago Creel Miranda Semblanza.

Secretary of Foreign Affairs: Dr Luis Ernesto Derbez Bautista.

Secretary of National Defence: Gen. Girardo Clemente Ricardo Vega García.

Secretary of the Navy: Adm. Marco Antonio Peyrot González.

Secretary of Public Security and Judicial Services: Dr Alejandro Gertz Manero.

Secretary of Finance and Public Credit: Francisco Gil Díaz.

Secretary of Social Development: Josefina Vázquez Mota.

Secretary of the Environment and Natural Resources: Ing. Alberto Cárdenas Jiménez.

Secretary of Energy: Lic. Felipe de Jesús Calderón Hinojosa.

Secretary of Economy: Fernando Canales Clariond.

Secretary of Agriculture, Livestock, Rural Development, Fisheries and Food: Javier Usabiaga Arroyo.

Secretary of Communications and Transport: Pedro Cerisola y Weber.

Secretary of Public Function: Eduardo Ramero Ramos.

Secretary of Public Education: Dr S. Reyes Tamez Guerra.

Secretary of Health: Dr Julio José Frenk Mora.

Secretary of Labour and Social Welfare: Carlos María Abascal Carranza.

Secretary of Agrarian Reform: Florencio Salazar Adame.

Secretary of Tourism: Rodolfo Elizondo Torres.

Attorney-General: Gen. Rafael Marcial Macedo de la Concha.

SECRETARIATS OF STATE

Office of the President: Los Pinos, Puerta 1, Col. San Miguel Chapultepec, 11850 México, DF; tel. (55) 5515-3717; fax (55) 5510-8713; internet www.presidencia.gob.mx.

Secretariat of State for Agrarian Reform: Avda Dr Vertiz 800, 1°, Col. Narvarte, 03020 México, DF; tel. (55) 273-9180; fax (55) 273-2481; internet www.sra.gob.mx.

Secretariat of State for Agriculture, Livestock, Rural Development, Fisheries and Food: Insurgentes Sur 476, 13°, Col. Roma Sur, 06760 México, DF; tel. (55) 5584-0096; fax (55) 5584-0268; e-mail c.informacion@sagar.gob.mx; internet www.sagarpa.gob.mx.

Secretariat of State for Communications and Transport: Avda Universidad y Xola, Cuerpo C, 1°, Col. Narvarte, 03028 México, DF; tel. (55) 5723-9300; fax (55) 5519-9748; e-mail www .sct@sct.gob.mx; internet www.sct.gob.mx.

Secretariat of State for the Economy: México, DF; fax (55) 5229-6134; internet www.economia.gob.mx.

Secretariat of State for Energy: Insurgentes Sur 552, 3°, Col. Roma Sur, 06769 México, DF; tel. (55) 5448-6033; fax (55) 5448-

6055; e-mail energia1@energia.gob.mx; internet www.energia.gob .mx.

Secretariat of State for the Environment and Natural Resources: Blvd Adolfo Ruíz Cortines, 4209, 3°, Col. Jardines en la Montaña, Tlalpan, 14210 México, DF; tel. (55) 5628-0600; fax (55) 5628-0644; internet www.semarnat.gob.mx.

Secretariat of State for Finance and Public Credit: Palacio Nacional, primer patio Mariano, 3°, Col. Centro, 06066 México, DF; tel. (55) 5518-5420; fax (55) 5542-2821; internet www.shcp.gob.mx.

Secretariat of State for Foreign Affairs: Avda Ricardo Flores Magón 2, 3°, Col. Guerrero, 06995 México, DF; tel. (55) 9157-4330; fax (55) 5782-4109; e-mail comment@sre.gob.mx; internet www.sre .gob.mx.

Secretariat of State for Health: Lieja 7, 1° Col. Juárez, 06600 México, DF; tel. (55) 5553-0758; fax (55) 5553-7917; e-mail ssa@mail .ssa.gob.mx; internet www.ssa.gob.mx.

Secretariat of State for the Interior: Bucareli 99, 1°, Col. Juárez, 06069 México, DF; tel. (55) 5592-1141; fax (55) 5546-5350; internet www.gobernacion.gob.mx.

Secretariat of State for Labour and Social Welfare: Edif. A, 4°, Anillo Periférico Sur 4271, 4°, Col. Fuentes del Pedregal, 14149 México, DF; tel. (55) 5645-3965; fax (55) 5645-5594; e-mail correo@ stps.gob.mx; internet www.stps.gob.mx.

Secretariat of State for National Defence: Manuel Avila Camacho, esq. Avda Industria Militar, 3°, Col. Lomas de Sotelo, 11600 México, DF; tel. (55) 5395-5936; fax (55) 5557-1370; e-mail comsoc@ mail.sedena.gob.mx; internet www.sedena.gob.mx.

Secretariat of State for the Navy: Eje 2 Ote, Tramo Heroica, Escuela Naval Militar 861, Col. Los Cipreses, 04830 México, DF; tel. (55) 5684-8188; fax (55) 5679-6411; internet www.semar.gob.mx.

Secretariat of State for Public Education: República de Argentina 28, 2°, Col. Centro, 06029 México, DF; tel. (55) 5510-2557; fax (55) 5329-6873; e-mail educa@sep.gob.mx; internet www.sep.gob .mx.

Secretariat of State for Public Function: Insurgentes Sur 1735, 10°, Col. Guadalupe Inn, 01020 México, DF; tel. (55) 3003-4090; fax (55) 5662-4763; e-mail ltacher@secodam.gob.mx; internet www .secodam.gob.mx.

Secretariat of State for Public Security and Judicial Services: Londres 102, 7°, Col. Juaréz, 06600 México, DF; e-mail ssp@ snsp.gob.mx; internet www.ssp.gob.mx.

Secretariat of State for Social Development: Avda Reforma 116, 17°, Col. Juárez, Cuauhtémoc, 06600 México, DF; tel. (55) 5328-5000; fax (55) 5271-8862; e-mail secretaridadelramo@sedesol.gob .mx; internet www.sedesol.gob.mx.

Secretariat of State for Tourism: Presidente Masarik 172, Col. Polanco, 11587 México, DF; tel. (55) 5250-8555; fax (55) 5255-3112; internet www.mexico-travel.com.

Office of the Attorney-General: Paseo de la Reforma 211, 2°, Col. Cuauhtémoc, 06500 México, DF; tel. (55) 5626-9600; fax (55) 5626-4447; internet www.pgr.gob.mx.

State Governors
(April 2004)

Aguascalientes: Felipe González Gonzales (PAN).

Baja California: Eugenio Elorduy Walther (PAN).

Baja California Sur: Leonel Cota Montaño (PRD-PT-PVEM).

Campeche: Jorge Carlos Hurtado Valdez (PRI).

Chiapas: Pablo Salazar Mendiguchía (Ind.).

Chihuahua: Lic. Patricio Martínez García (PRI).

Coahuila (de Zaragoza): Enrique Martínez y Martínez (PRI).

Colima: Gustavo Alberto Vázquez Montes (PRI).

Distrito Federal: Andrés Manuel López Obrador (PRD).

Durango: Lic. Angel Sergio Guerrero Mier (PRI).

Guanajuato: Juan Carlos Romero Hicks (PAN).

Guerrero: René Juárez Cisneros (PRI).

Hidalgo: Manuel Angel Núñez Soto (PRI).

Jalisco: Lic. Francisco Ramirez Acuña (PAN).

México: Lic. Arturo Montiel Rojas (PRI).

Michoacán (de Ocampo): Lazaro Cárdenas Batel (PRD).

Morelos: Lic. Sergio Estrada Cajigal Ramírez (PAN).

Nayarit: Antonio Echevarría (PAN-PRD-PT-PVEM).

Nuevo León: Lic. JOSÉ NATIVIDAD GONZÁLEZ PARÁS (PRI-PVEM-PLM-Fuerza Ciudadana).

Oaxaca: JOSÉ MURAT CASAB (PRI).

Puebla: MELQUIADES MORALES FLORES (PRI).

Querétaro (de Arteaga): FRANCISCO GARRIDO PATRÓN (PAN).

Quintana Roo: JOAQUÍN HENDRICKS DÍAZ (PRI).

San Luis Potosí: MARCELO DE LOS SANTOS FRAGA (PAN).

Sinaloa: JUAN S. MILLÁN LIZARRAGA (PRI).

Sonora: JOSÉ EDUARDO ROBINSON BOURS CASTELO (PRI-PVEM).

Tabasco: MANUEL ANDRADE DÍAZ (PRI).

Tamaulipas: TOMÁS YARRINGTON RUVALCABA (PRI).

Tlaxcala: ALFONSO SÁNCHEZ ANAYA (PRD-PT-PVEM).

Veracruz-Llave: MIGUEL ALEMÁN VELAZCO (PRI).

Yucatán: PATRICIO PATRÓN LAVIADA (PAN-PRD-PT-PVEM).

Zacatecas: Lic. RICARDO MONREAL AVILA (PRD).

President and Legislature

PRESIDENT

Election, 2 July 2000

Candidate	Number of votes	% of votes
Vicente Fox Quesada (Alianza por el Cambio*)	15,988,740	43.47
Francisco Labastida Ochoa (PRI)	13,576,385	36.91
Cuauhtémoc Cárdenas Solórzano (Alianza por México)	6,259,048	17.02
Others	957,455	2.60
Total	**36,781,628**	**100.00**

*An alliance of the PAN and the PVEM.

CONGRESO DE LA UNIÓN

Senado
(Senate)

President: ENRIQUE JACKSON RAMÍREZ.

Elections, 2 July 2000

Party	Seats
Partido Revolucionario Institucional (PRI)	60
Partido Acción Nacional (PAN)*	46
Partido de la Revolución Democrática (PRD)†	15
Partido Verde Ecologista de México (PVEM)*	5
Convergencia por la Democracia (CD)†	1
Partido del Trabajo (PT)†	1
Total	**128**

*Contested the elections jointly as the Alianza por el Cambio.
†Contested the elections as part of the Alianza por México.

Cámara Federal de Diputados
(Federal Chamber of Deputies)

President: ARMANDO SALINAS TORRE.

Elections, 6 July 2003

Party	Seats
Partido Revolucionario Institucional (PRI)	224
Partido Acción Nacional (PAN)	153
Partido de la Revolución Democrática (PRD)	95
Partido Verde Ecologista de México (PVEM)	17
Partido del Trabajo (PT)	6
Convergencia por la Democracia (CD)	5
Total	**500**

Political Organizations

To retain legal political registration, parties must secure at least 1.5% of total votes at two consecutive federal elections. Several of the parties listed below are no longer officially registered but continue to be politically active.

Convergencia: Louisiana 113, Col. Nápoles 03810, México, DF; tel. (55) 5543-8513; internet www.convergencia.org.mx; f. 1995 as Convergencia por la Democracia; Pres. DANTE DELGADO RANNAURO; Sec.-Gen. ALEJANDRO CHANONA BURGUETE.

Democracia Social: San Borja 416, Col. del Valle, 03100 México, DF; tel. (55) 5559-2875; f. 1999; Pres. GILBERTO RINCÓN GALLARDO.

Fuerza Ciudadana: Rochester 94, Col. Napoles 03810, México, DF; tel. (55) 5523-9512; e-mail info@fuerzaciudadana.org.mx; internet www.fuerzaciudadana.org.mx; f. 2002; Pres. JORGE ALCOCER VILLANUEVA; Sec.-Gen. EMILIO CABALLERO URDIALES.

México Posible: Dr Vértiz 1200, Col. Letrán Valle, 03650 México, DF; tel. 5243-6061; e-mail correo@mexicoposible.org.mx; internet www.mexicoposible.org.mx; f. 2002; minority rights.

Partido Acción Nacional (PAN): Avda Coyoacán 1546, Col. del Valle, México, DF; tel. (55) 5200-4000; e-mail correo@cen.pan.org.mx; internet www.pan.org.mx; f. 1939; democratic party; 150,000 mems; Pres. LUIS FELIPE BRAVO MENA; Sec.-Gen. MANUEL ESPINO BARRIENTOS.

Partido Alianza Social (PAS): Édison 89, Col. Tabacalera, 06030 México, DF; tel. (55) 5592-5688; fax (55) 5566-1665; internet www.pas.org.mx; Pres. GUILLERMO CALDERÓN DOMÍNGUEZ; Sec.-Gen. ADALBERTO ROSAS LÓPEZ.

Partido Auténtico de la Revolución Mexicana (PARM): Pueblo 286, 1°, Col. Roma, 06700 México, DF; tel. (55) 5514-9676; f. 1954 to sustain the ideology of the Mexican Political Constitution of 1917; 191,500 mems; Pres. CARLOS GUZMÁN PÉREZ.

Partido de Centro Democrático (PCD): Amores 923, Col. del Valle, Deleg. Benito Juárez, 03100 México, DF; tel. (55) 5575-3101; fax (55) 5575-8888; e-mail pcdcen@pcd2000.org.mx; centrist party; f. 1997; Leader MANUEL CAMACHO SOLÍS.

Partido del Frente Cardenista de Reconstrucción Nacional (PFCRN): Avda México 199, Col. Hipódromo Condesa, 06170 México, DF; f. 1972; Marxist-Leninist; fmrly Partido Socialista de los Trabajadores; 132,000 mems; Pres. RAFAEL AGUILAR TALAMANTES; Sec.-Gen. GRACO RAMÍREZ ABREU.

Partido Liberal México (PLM): Nuevo Leon 80, Col. Condesa 06180, México, DF; tel. (55) 5211-32958; e-mail plm@plm.org.mx; internet www.plm.org.mx; f. 2002; Pres. C. SALVADOR ORDAZ MONTES DE OCA.

Partido México Posible—La Nueva Política: Abasolo 8, Col. El Carmen 04100, México, DF; tel. (55) 5659-0807; fax (55) 5659-0778; e-mail correo@mexicoposible.org.mx; internet www.mexicoposible.org.mx; f. 2002; focus on the rights of women and indigenous peoples, and ecological issues; Pres. PATRICIA MERCADO CASTRO; Sec.-Gen. WILFRIDO ISAMÍ SALZAR RULE.

Partido Popular Socialista (PPS): Avda Alvaro Obregón 185, Col. Roma, 06797 México, DF; tel. (55) 5533-0816; fax (55) 5525-7131; internet www.pps.org.mx; f. 1948; left-wing party; Sec.-Gen. MANUEL FERNÁNDEZ FLORES.

Partido de la Revolución Democrática (PRD): Monterrey 50, Col. Roma, 06700 México, DF; tel. (55) 5525-6059; fax (55) 5208-7833; internet www.prd.org.mx; f. 1989 by the Corriente Democrática (CD) and elements of the Partido Mexicano Socialista (PMS); centre-left; Pres. LEONEL GODOY; Sec.-Gen. CARLOS NAVARRETE RUIZ.

Partido Revolucionario Institucional (PRI): Insurgentes Norte 59, Edif. 2, subsótano, Col. Buenavista, 06359 México, DF; tel. (55) 5591-1595; fax (55) 5546-3552; internet www.pri.org.mx; f. 1929 as the Partido Nacional Revolucionario, but is regarded as the natural successor to the victorious parties of the revolutionary period; broadly based and centre govt party; Pres. ROBERTO MADRAZO PINTADO; Sec.-Gen. ELBA ESTHER GORDILLO MORALES; opinion groups within the PRI include: the Corriente Crítica Progresista, the Corriente Crítica del Partido, the Corriente Constitucionalista Democratizadora, Corriente Nuevo PRI XIV Asamblea, Democracia 2000, México Nuevo and Galileo.

Partido Social Demócrata Mexicano (PSDM): Edisón 89, Col. Revolución, 06030 México, DF; tel. (55) 5592-5688; fax (55) 5535-0031; f. 1975 as Partido Demócrata Mexicano; adopted current name in 1998; Christian Democrat party; 450,000 mems; Pres. BALTASAR IGNACIO VALADEZ MONTOYA.

Partido de la Sociedad Nacionalista (PSN): Magdalena 117, Col. del Valle 03100, México, DF; tel. (55) 5682-5960; e-mail psn@psn.org.mx; internet www.psn.org.mx; Pres. GUSTAVO RIOJAS SANTANA.

Partido del Trabajo (PT): Avda Cuauhtémoc 47, Col. Roma, 06700 México, DF; tel. and fax (55) 5525-8419; internet www.pt.org.mx; f. 1991; labour party; Leader ALBERTO ANAYA GUTIÉRREZ.

Partido Verde Ecologista de México (PVEM): Medicina 74, esq. Avda Copilco, Universidad, Del. Coyoacán, 04360 México, DF; tel. and fax (55) 5658-7172; e-mail pve@infosel.net.mx; internet www

.pvem.org.mx; f. 1987; ecologist party; Leader BERNARDO DE LA GARZA HERRERA.

The following parties are not legally recognized:

Frente Zapatista de Liberación Nacional: Zapotecos 7, Col. Obrera, 06800 México, DF; tel. and fax (55) 5761-4236; e-mail fzln@org.mx; internet www.fzln.org.mx; f. 1996; political force embodying the ideology of the EZLN; Leader JAVIER ELORRIAGA.

Illegal organizations active in Mexico include the following:

Ejército Popular Revolucionario (EPR): internet www.pengo.it/PDPR-EPR/; f. 1994; left-wing guerrilla group active in southern states.

Ejército Revolucionario Popular Insurgente (ERPI): f. 1996; left-wing guerrilla group active in Guerrero, Morelos and Oaxaca; Leader JACOBO SILVA NOGALES.

Ejército Zapatista de Liberación Nacional (EZLN): internet www.ezln.org; f. 1993; left-wing guerrilla group active in the Chiapas region; Leader 'Subcomandante INSURGENTE MARCOS'.

Frente Democrático Oriental de México Emiliano Zapata (FDOMEZ): peasant org.

Partido Popular Revolucionario Democrático: internet www.pengo.it/PDPR-EPR; f. 1996; political grouping representing the causes of 14 armed peasant orgs, including the EPR and the PROCUP.

Partido Revolucionario Obrerista y Clandestino de Unión Popular (PROCUP): internet www.pengo.it/PDPR-EPR/; peasant org.

Diplomatic Representation

EMBASSIES IN MEXICO

Algeria: Sierra Madre 540, Col. Lomas de Chapultepec, 11000 México, DF; tel. (55) 5520-6950; fax (55) 5540-7579; e-mail embjargl@iwm.com.mx; Ambassador ABDELKADER TAFFAR.

Angola: Schiller 503, Col. Polanco, 11580 México, DF; tel. (55) 5545-5883; fax (55) 5545-2733; e-mail luanda@data.net.mx; Ambassador JOSÉ JAIME FURTADO GONCALVEZ.

Argentina: Manuel Avila Camacho 1, 7°, Col. Lomas de Chapultepec, 11000 México, DF; tel. (55) 5520-9430; fax (55) 5540-5011; e-mail embajadaargentina@prodigy.net.mx; Ambassador OSCAR GUILLERMO GALIE.

Australia: Rubén Darío 55, Col. Polanco, 11580 México, DF; tel. (55) 1101–2200; fax (55) 5203-8431; e-mail dima-mexico.city@dsat.gov.au; internet www.mexico.embassy.gov.au; Ambassador GRAEME JOHN WILSON.

Austria: Sierra Tarahumara 420, Col. Lomas de Chapultepec, Del. Miguel Hidalgo, 11000 México, DF; tel. (55) 5251-1606; fax (55) 5245-0198; e-mail mexiko-ob@bmaa.gv.at; internet www.embajadadeaustria.com.mx; Ambassador Dr RUDOLF LENNKH.

Belgium: Musset 41, Col. Polanco, 11550 México, DF; tel. (55) 5280-0758; fax (55) 5280-0208; e-mail Mexico@diplobel.org; internet www.diplobel.org/mexico; Ambassador MICHEL DELFOSSE.

Belize: Bernardo de Gálvez 215, Col. Lomas de Chapultepec, 11000 México, DF; tel. (55) 5520-1274; fax (55) 5520-6089; e-mail embelize@prodigy.net.mx; Ambassador SALVADOR AMÍN FIGUEROA.

Bolivia: Insurgentes Sur 263, 6°, esq. Alvaro Obregón, Col. Roma Sur, 06760 México, DF; tel. (55) 5564-5415; fax (55) 5564-5298 ext. 19; e-mail embajada@embol.org.mx; Ambassador RAFAEL CAPRA JEMIO.

Brazil: Lope de Armendáriz 130, Col. Lomas Virreyes, 11000 México, DF; tel. (55) 5201-4531; fax (55) 5520-4929; e-mail embrasil@brasil.org.mx; internet www.brasil.org.mx; Ambassador LUIZ AUGUSTO DE ARAUJO CASTRO.

Bulgaria: Paseo de la Reforma 1990, Col. Lomas de Chapultepec, 11000 México, DF; tel. (55) 5596-3283; fax (55) 5596-1012; e-mail ebulgaria@yahoo.com; Ambassador IVAN CHRISTOV.

Canada: Schiller 529, Col. Polanco, 11560 México, DF; tel. (55) 5724-7900; fax (55) 5724-7980; e-mail embajada@canada.org.mx; internet www.canada.org.mx; Ambassador GAËTAN LAVERTU.

Chile: Andrés Bello 10, 18°, Col. Polanco, 11560 México, DF; tel. (55) 5280-9681; fax (55) 5280-9703; e-mail echilmex@prodigy.net.mx; internet www.embajadadechile.com/mx; Ambassador CARLOS FERNANDO MOLINA VALLEJO.

China, People's Republic: Avda San Jerónimo 217B, Del. Álvaro Obregón 01090, México, DF; tel. (55) 5616-0609; fax (55) 5616-0460; e-mail embchina@data.net.mx; internet www.embajadachina.org.mx; Ambassador REN JINGYU.

Colombia: Paseo de la Reforma 379, Col. Lomas de Chapultepec, 11000 México, DF; tel. (55) 5525–0277; fax (55) 5209–2876; e-mail emcolmex@prodigy.net.mx; internet www.colombiaenmexico.org; Ambassador LUIS IGNACIO GUZMÁN RAMÍREZ.

Costa Rica: Río Po 113, Col. Cuauhtémoc, 06500 México, DF; tel. (55) 5525-7764; fax (55) 5511-9240; e-mail embcrica@ri.redint.com; Ambassador RONALD GURDIÁN MARCHENA.

Cuba: Presidente Masaryk 554, Col. Polanco, 11560 México, DF; tel. and fax (55) 5280-8039; fax 5280–0839; e-mail cancilleria@embacuba.com.mx; internet www.embacuba.com/mx; Ambassador JORGE BOLAÑOS SUÁREZ (expelled May 2004).

Cyprus: Sierra Gorda 370, Col. Lomas de Chapultepec, 11000 México, DF; tel. (55) 5202-7600; fax (55) 5520-2693; e-mail chipre@data.net.mx; Ambassador ANTONIS TOUMAZIS.

Czech Republic: Cuvier 22, esq. Kepler, Col. Nueva Anzures, 11590 México, DF; tel. (55) 5531-2777; fax (55) 5531-1837; e-mail mexico@embassy.mzv.cz; internet www.czechembassy.org; Ambassador VERA ZEMANOVÁ.

Denmark: Tres Picos 43, Apdo 105-105, Col. Chapultepec Morales, 11580 México, DF; tel. (55) 5255-3405; fax (55) 5545-5797; e-mail mexamb@um.dk; internet www.danmex.org; Ambassador SØREN HASLUND.

Dominican Republic: República de Guatemala 84, Centro Histórico, Del. Cuauhtémoc, 06020, México, DF; tel. (55) 5542–3593; fax (55) 5542–3553; e-mail embadomi@data.net.mx; internet www.embajadadominicana.com.mx; Ambassador CÁNDIDO GÉRON ARAUJO.

Ecuador: Tennyson 217, Col. Polanco, 11560 México, DF; tel. (55) 5545-3141; fax (55) 5254-2442; e-mail mecuamex@prodigy.net.mx; Ambassador FRANCISCO HERRERA ARAÚZ.

Egypt: Alejandro Dumas 131, Col. Polanco, 11560 México, DF; tel. (55) 5281-0823; fax (55) 5282-1294; e-mail embofegypt@prodigy.net.mx; Ambassador MAMDOUH SHAWKY MOUSTAFA.

El Salvador: Temístocles 88, Col. Polanco, 11560 México, DF; tel. and fax (55) 5281-5725; e-mail embesmex@webtelmex.net.mx; Ambassador FRANCISCO FLOR IMENDIA MAZA.

Finland: Monte Pelvoux 111, 4°, Col. Lomas de Chapultepec, Del. Miguel Hidalgo, 11000 México, DF; tel. (55) 5540-6036; fax (55) 5540-0114; e-mail finmex@prodigy.net.mx; internet www.finlandia.org.mx; Ambassador ILKKA HEISKANEN.

France: Campos Elíseos 339, Col. Polanco, 11560 México, DF; tel. (55) 9171-9700; fax (55) 9171-9703; e-mail webmaster@francia.org.mx; internet www.francia.org.mx; Ambassador PHILIPPE FAURE.

Germany: Lord Byron 737, Col. Polanco, 11560 México, DF; tel. (55) 5283-2200; fax (55) 5281-2588; e-mail info@embajada-alemana.org.mx; internet www.embajada-alemana.org.mx; Ambassador EBERHARD KOLSCH.

Greece: Sierra Gorda 505, Col. Lomas de Chapultepec, 11010 México, DF; tel. (55) 5520-2070; fax (55) 5202-4080; e-mail grecemb@prodigy.net.mx; Ambassador DIONYSSIUS KODELLAS.

Guatemala: Esplanada 1025, Col. Lomas de Chapultepec, 11000 México, DF; tel. (55) 5540-7520; fax (55) 5202-1142; e-mail embaguate@mexis.com; Chargé d'affaires a.i. SILVIA ELENA ARÉVALO DE LEÓN.

Haiti: Pres. Don Martín 53, Del. Miguel Hidalgo 11500, México, DF; tel. (55) 5557-2065; fax (55)5395-1654; e-mail ambadh@mail.internet.com.mx; Ambassador PIERRE-JEAN IDALBERT.

Holy See: Calle Juan Pablo II 118, Col. Guadalupe Inn, Del. Alvaro Obregón, 01020 México, DF; tel. (55) 5663-3999; fax (55) 5663-5308; e-mail nuntiusmex@infosel.net.mx; Apostolic Nuncio Most Rev. GIUSEPPE BERTELLO (Titular Archbishop of Urbisaglia).

Honduras: Alfonso Reyes 220, Col. Hipódromo Condesa, 06170 México, DF; tel. (55) 5211-5747; fax (55) 5211-5425; e-mail emhonmex@mail.internet.com.mx; Ambassador RENÉ BECERRA ZELAYA.

Hungary: Paseo de las Palmas 2005, Col. Lomas de Chapultepec, 11000 México, DF; tel. (55) 5596-0523; fax (55) 5596-2378; e-mail secretaria@embajadahungria.com.mx; internet embajadahungria@vantel.net.mx; Ambassador GYULA NÉMETH.

India: Musset 325, Col. Polanco, 11550 México, DF; tel. (55) 5531-1050; fax (55) 5254-2349; e-mail inembmex@prodigy.net.mx; internet www.indembassy.org; Ambassador SURINDER SINGH GILL.

Indonesia: Julio Verne 27, Col. Polanco, 11560 México, DF; tel. (55) 5280-6363; fax (55) 280-7062; e-mail kbrimex@prodigy.net.mx; Ambassador AHWIL LUTHAN.

Iran: Paseo de la Reforma 2350, Col. Lomas Altas, 11950 México, DF; tel. (55) 9172–2691; fax (55) 9172–2694; e-mail iranembmex@hotmail.com; Ambassador MOHAMMAD RUHI SEFAT.

Iraq: Paseo de la Reforma 1875, Col. Lomas de Chapultepec, 11000 México, DF; tel. (55) 5596-09833; fax (55) 5596-0254; A chargé d'affaires has been appointed by the Iraqi Governing Council.

Ireland: Cerrada Blvd M. Avila Camacho 76, Third Floor, Col. Lomas de Chapultepec, 11000 México, DF; tel. (55) 5520-5803; fax (55) 5520-5892; e-mail embajada@irlanda.org.mx; Ambassador ART AGNEW.

Israel: Sierra Madre 215, Col. Lomas de Chapultepec, 11000 México, DF; tel. (55) 5201-1500; fax (55) 5201-1555; e-mail embisrael@prodigy.net.mx; Ambassador DAVID DADONN.

Italy: Paseo de las Palmas 1994, Col. Lomas de Chapultepec, 11000 México, DF; tel. (55) 5596-3655; fax (55) 5596-2472; e-mail info@embitalia.org.mx; internet www.embitalia.org.mx; Ambassador FRANCO TEMPESTA.

Jamaica: Schiller 326, 8°, Col. Chapultepec Morales, Del. Miguel Hidalgo, 11570 México, DF; tel. (55) 5250-6804; fax (55) 5250-6160; e-mail embjamaicamex@infosel.net.mx; Ambassador VILMA KATHLEEN MCNISH.

Japan: Paseo de la Reforma 395, Col. Cuauhtémoc, Apdo 5-101, 06500 México, DF; tel. (55) 5211-0028; fax (55) 5207-7743; e-mail embjapmx@mail.internet.com.mx; internet www.internet.com.mx-embjapon; Ambassador MUTSUYOSHI NISHIMURA.

Korea, Democratic People's Republic: Eugenio Sue 332, Col. Polanco, 11550 México, DF; tel. (55) 5545-1871; fax (55) 5203-0019; e-mail dpkoreaemb@prodigy.net.mx; Ambassador RI KANG SE.

Korea, Republic: Lope de Armendáriz 110, Col. Lomas Virreyes, 11000 México, DF; tel. (55) 5202-9866; fax (55) 5540-7446; e-mail coremex@prodigy.net.mx; Ambassador KYU-HYUNG CHO.

Lebanon: Julio Verne 8, Col. Polanco, 11560 México, DF; tel. (55) 5280-5614; fax (55) 5280-8870; e-mail embalib@prodigy.net.mx; Ambassador NOUHAD MAHMOUD.

Malaysia: Calderón de la Barca 215, Col. Polanco, 11550 México, DF; tel. (55) 5254-1118; fax (55) 5254-1295; e-mail mwmexico@infosel.net.mx; Ambassador MOHAMMED ABDUL HALIM BIN ABDUL RAHMAN.

Morocco: Paseo de las Palmas 2020, Col. Lomas de Chapultepec, 11020 México, DF; tel. (55) 5245-1786; fax (55) 5245-1791; e-mail sifamex@infosel.net.mx; internet www.marruecos.org.mx; Chargé d'affaires a.i. NOUREDDINE KHALIFA.

Netherlands: Edif. Calakmul, Avda Vasco de Quiroga 3000, 7°, Col. Santa Fe, 01210 México, DF; tel. (55) 5258-9921; fax (55) 5258-8138; e-mail nlgovmex@nlgovmex.com; internet www.paisesbajos.com.mx; Ambassador JAN-JAAP VAN DE VELDE.

New Zealand: Jaime Balmes 8, 4°, Col. Polanco, 11510 México, DF; tel. (55) 5283-9460; fax (55) 5283-9480; e-mail kiwimexico@compuserve.com.mx; Ambassador PAUL TIPPING.

Nicaragua: Prado Norte 470, Col. Lomas de Chapultepec 11000, México, DF; tel. (55) 5540-5625; fax (55) 5520-6961; e-mail embanic@prodigy.net.mx; Ambassador LEOPOLDO RAMÍREZ EVA.

Nigeria: Paseo de las Palmas 1875, Col. Lomas de Chapultepec 11000, México, DF; tel. (55) 5596-1274; fax (55) 5245-0105; e-mail nigembmx@att.net.mx; Chargé d'affaires a.i. CLEMENT ONOJA ADUKU.

Norway: Avda de los Virreyes 1460, Col. Lomas Virreyes, 11000 México, DF; tel. (55) 5540-3486; fax (55) 5202-3019; e-mail emb.mexico@mfa.no; internet www.noruega.org.mx; Ambassador HELGE SKAARA.

Pakistan: Hegel 512, Col. Chapultepec Morales, 11570 México, DF; tel. (55) 5203-3636; fax (55) 5203-9907; Ambassador Agha JEHANGIR ALI KHAN.

Panama: Horacio 1501, Col. Polanco 11560, México, DF; tel. (55) 5557-6159; fax (55) 5395-4269; e-mail embpanmx@prodigy.net.mx; internet www.embpanamamexico.com; Ambassador DIONISO DE GRACIA GUILLÉN.

Paraguay: Homero 415, 1°, esq. Hegel, Col. Polanco, 11570 México, DF; tel. (55) 5545-0405; fax (55) 5531-9905; e-mail embapar@prodigy.net.mx; Ambassador JOSÉ FÉLIX FERNÁNDEZ ESTIGARRIBIA.

Peru: Paseo de la Reforma 2601, Col. Lomas Reforma, 11000 México, DF; tel. (55) 5570-2443; fax (55) 5259-0530; e-mail embaperu@prodigy.net.mx; Ambassador ALFREDO AROSEMENA FERREYROS.

Philippines: Sierra Gorda 175, Col. Lomas de Chapultepec 11000 México, DF; tel. (55) 5202-8456; fax (55) 5202-8403; e-mail ambamexi@mail.internet.com.mx; Ambassador JUSTO O. ORROS, Jr.

Poland: Cracovia 40, Col. San Ángel, 01000 México, DF; tel. (55) 5550-4700; fax (55) 5616-0822; e-mail ambrpmx1@mail.cpesa.com.mx; Ambassador GABRIEL BESZLEJ.

Portugal: Avda Alpes 1370, Lomas de Chapultepec, 11000 México, DF; tel. (55) 5520-7897; fax (55) 5520-4688; e-mail embpomex@prodigy.net.mx; Ambassador MANUEL MARCELO MONTEIRO CURTO.

Romania: Sófocles 311, Col. Polanco, 11560 México, DF; tel. (55) 5280-0197; fax (55) 5280-0343; e-mail ambromaniei@prodigy.net.mx; internet www.gilbert.ro; Ambassador VASILE DAN.

Russia: José Vasconcelos 204, Col. Hipódromo Condesa, 06140 México, DF; tel. (55) 5273-1305; fax (55) 5273-1545; e-mail embrumex@mail.internet.com.mx; Ambassador KONSTANTIN MOZEL.

Saudi Arabia: Paseo de las Palmas 2075, Col. Lomas de Chapultepec, 11000 México, DF; tel. (55) 5596-8845; fax (55) 5251-8587; e-mail saudiemb@prodigy.net.mx; Ambassador HASSAN TALAT NAZER.

Serbia and Montenegro: Montañas Rocallosas Ote 515, Col. Lomas de Chapultepec, 11000 México, DF; tel. (55) 5520-0524; fax (55) 5520-9927; e-mail ambayumex@att.met.mx; Ambassador VESNA PESIĆ.

Slovakia: Julio Verne 35, Col. Polanco, 11560 México, DF; tel. (55) 5280-6669; fax (55) 5280-6294; e-mail embslovakia@mexis.com; Ambassador BRANISLAV HITKA.

South Africa: Andrés Bello 10, 9°, Edif. Forum, Col. Polanco, 11560 México, DF; tel. (55) 5282-9260; fax (55) 5282-9260; e-mail safrica@prodigy.net.mx; Ambassador MALCOLM GRANT FERGUSON.

Spain: Galileo 114, esq. Horacio, Col. Polanco, 11550 México, DF; tel. (55) 5282-2271; fax (55) 5282-1520; e-mail embaes@prodigy.net.mx; Ambassador MARÍA CRISTINA BARRIOS Y ALMAZOR.

Sweden: Paseo de las Palmas 1375, 11000 México, DF; tel. (55) 9178-5010; fax (55) 5540-3253; e-mail info@suecia.com.mx; internet www.suecia.com.mx; Ambassador EWA POLANO.

Switzerland: Paseo de las Palmas 405, 11°, Torre Optima, Col. Lomas de Chapultepec, 11000 México, DF; tel. (55) 5520-3003; fax (55) 5520-8685; e-mail vertretung@mex.rep.admin.ch; internet www.eda.admin.ch/mexico_emb; Ambassador GIAN FEDERICO PEDOTTI.

Thailand: Paseo de la Reforma 930, Col. Lomas de Chapultepec 11000, México, DF; tel. (55) 5540-4551; fax (55) 5540-4817; e-mail thaimex@infosel.net.mx; Ambassador PLERNPIT POTIGANOND.

Turkey: Monte Libano 885, Col. Lomas de Chapultepec 11000, México, DF; tel. (55) 5282-5446; fax (55) 5282-4894; e-mail turkem@mail.internet.com.mx; Ambassador MEHMET NURI EZEN.

Ukraine: Sierra Paracaima 396, Col. Lomas de Chapultepec 11000, México, DF; tel. (55) 5282-4789; fax (55) 5540-3606; e-mail ukrainembasy@mexis.com; Ambassador OLEXANDER TARANENKO.

United Kingdom: Río Lerma 71, Col. Cuauhtémoc, 06500 México, DF; tel. (55) 5242-8500; fax (55) 5242-8517; e-mail ukinmex@att.net.mx; internet www.embajadabritanica.com.mx; Ambassador DENISE HOLT.

USA: Paseo de la Reforma 305, Col. Cuauhtémoc, 06500 México, DF; tel. (55) 5080-2000; fax (55) 5080-2150; internet www.usembassy-mexico.gov; Ambassador ANTONIO O. GARZA, Jr.

Uruguay: Hegel 149, 1°, Col. Chapultepec Morales, 11560 México, DF; tel. (55) 5545-3342; fax (55) 5531-4029; e-mail uruazte@ort.org.mx; Ambassador SAMUEL LICHTENSZTEJN TEZLER.

Venezuela: Schiller 326, Col. Chapultepec Morales, 11570 México, DF; tel. (55) 5203-4233; fax (55) 5203-5072; e-mail venez-mex@embajadadevenezuela.com.mxn; Ambassador LINO MARTÍNEZ SALAZAR.

Viet Nam: Sierra Ventana 255, Col. Lomas de Chapultepec, 11000 México, DF; tel. (55) 5540-1632; fax (55) 5540-1612; e-mail dsqvn@terra.com.mx; Chargé d'affaires a.i. LE VAN THINH.

Judicial System

The principle of the separation of the judiciary from the legislative and executive powers is embodied in the 1917 Constitution. The judicial system is divided into two areas: the federal, dealing with federal law, and the local, dealing only with state law within each state.

The federal judicial system has both ordinary and constitutional jurisdiction and judicial power is exercised by the Supreme Court of Justice, the Electoral Court, Collegiate and Unitary Circuit Courts and District Courts. The Supreme Court comprises two separate chambers: Civil and Criminal Affairs, and Administrative and Labour Affairs. The Federal Judicature Council is responsible for the administration, surveillance and discipline of the federal judiciary, except for the Supreme Court of Justice.

In March 2002 there were 146 Collegiate Circuit Courts (Tribunales Colegiados), 58 Unitary Circuit Courts (Tribunales Unitarios) and 219 District Courts (Juzgados de Distrito). Mexico is divided into 26 judicial circuits. The Circuit Courts may be collegiate, when dealing with the derecho de amparo (protection of constitutional rights of an individual), or unitary, when dealing with appeal cases. The Collegiate Circuit Courts comprise three magistrates with residence in the cities of México, Toluca, Guadalajara, Monterrey, Hermosillo, Puebla, Boca del Río, Xalapa, Torreón, San Luis Potosí, Villahermosa, Morelia, Mazatlán, Oaxaca, Mérida, Mexicali, Guanajuato, Chihuahua, Cuernavaca, Ciudad Victoria, Tuxtla Gutiérrez, Chilpancingo, Querétaro, Pachuca, Zacatecas, Aguascalientes, Tepic and Durango. The Unitary Circuit Courts comprise one magistrate with residence mostly in the same cities as given above.

SUPREME COURT OF JUSTICE

Supreme Court of Justice, Pino Suárez 2, Col. Centro, Del. Cuauhtémoc, 06065 México, DF; tel. (55) 5522-0096; fax (55) 5522-0152; internet www.scjn.gob.mx.

Chief Justice: MARIANO AZUELA GÜITRÓN.

First Chamber—Civil and Criminal Affairs

President: JOSÉ DE JESÚS GUDIÑO PELAYO.

Second Chamber—Administrative and Labour Affairs

President: GUILLERMO I. ORTIZ MAYAGOITIA.

Religion

CHRISTIANITY

The Roman Catholic Church

The prevailing religion is Roman Catholicism, but the Church, disestablished in 1857, was for many years, under the Constitution of 1917, subject to state control. A constitutional amendment, promulgated in January 1992, officially removed all restrictions on the Church. For ecclesiastical purposes, Mexico comprises 14 archdioceses, 65 dioceses, five territorial prelatures and two eparchates (both directly subject to the Holy See). An estimated 90% of the population are adherents.

Bishops' Conference

Conferencia del Episcopado Mexicano (CEM), 54760 Cuautitlán Izcalli, Prolongación Rio Acatlán, Lago de Guadalupe; tel. (55) 5877-2663; fax (55) 5877-2603.

Pres. LUIS MORALES REYES (Archbishop of San Luis Potosí).

Archbishop of Acapulco: FELIPE AGUIRRE FRANCO, Arzobispado, Quebrada 16, Apdo 201, 39300 Acapulco, Gro; tel. and fax (744) 482-0763; e-mail buenpastor@acabtu.com.mx.

Archbishop of Antequera/Oaxaca: HÉCTOR GONZÁLEZ MARTÍNEZ, Independencia 700, Apdo 31, 68000 Oaxaca, Oax.; tel. (951) 64822; fax (951) 65580; e-mail antequera@oax1.telmex.net.mx.

Archbishop of Chihuahua: JOSÉ FERNÁNDEZ ARTEAGA, Arzobispado, Avda Cuauhtémoc 1828, Apdo 7, 31020 Chihuahua, Chih.; tel. (614) 10-3202; fax (614) 10-5621; e-mail curiao1@chih1.telmex.net.mx.

Archbishop of Durango: HÉCTOR GONZÁLEZ MARTÍNEZ, Arzobispado, 20 de Noviembre 306 Poniente, Apdo 116, 34000 Durango, Dgo; tel. (618) 114242; fax (618) 128881; e-mail arqdgo@logicnet.com.mx.

Archbishop of Guadalajara: Cardinal JUAN SANDOVAL IÑÍGUEZ, Arzobispado, Liceo 17, Apdo 1-331, 44100 Guadalajara, Jal.; tel. (33) 614-5504; fax (33) 658-2300; e-mail arzgdl@arquinet.com.mx.

Archbishop of Hermosillo/Sonora: JOSÉ ULISES MACÍAS SALCEDO, Arzobispado, Dr Paliza 81, Apdo 1, 83260 Hermosillo, Son.; tel. (658) 13-2138; fax (658) 13-1327; e-mail obispo@rtn.uson.mx.

Archbishop of Jalapa: SERGIO OBESO RIVERA, Arzobispado, Avda Manuel Avila Camacho 73, Apdo 359, 91000 Jalapa, Ver.; tel. (932) 12-0579; e-mail arzobispadoal_xal@infosel.net.mx.

Archbishop of Mexico City: Cardinal NORBERTO RIVERA CARRERA, Curia del Arzobispado de México, Durango 90, 5°, Col. Roma, Apdo 24433, 06700 México, DF; tel. (55) 5208-3200; fax (55) 5208-5350; e-mail armexico@proyect.com.

Archbishop of Monterrey: FRANCISCO ROBLES, Zuazua 1100 con Ocampo, Apdo 7, 64000 Monterrey, NL; tel. (81) 345-2466; fax (81) 345-3557; e-mail curia@sdm.net.mx.

Archbishop of Morelia: ALBERTO SUÁREZ INDA, Arzobispado, Apdo 17, 58000 Morelia, Mich; tel. (443) 120523; fax (443) 123744; e-mail suarezi@prodigy.net.mx.

Archbishop of Puebla de los Angeles: ROSENDO HUESCA PACHECO, Avda 2 Sur 305, Apdo 235, 72000 Puebla, Pue.; tel. (222) 32-4591; fax (222) 46-2277; e-mail rhuesca@mail.cem.org.mx.

Archbishop of San Luis Potosí: LUIS MORALES REYES, Arzobispado, Francisco Madero 300, Apdo 1, 78000 San Luis Potosí, SLP; tel. (444) 12-4555; fax (444) 12-7979; e-mail adiosclp@mail.cem.org.mx.

Archbishop of Tlalnepantla: RICARDO GUÍZAR DÍAZ, Arzobispado, Avda Juárez 42, Apdo 268, 54000 Tlalnepantla, Méx.; tel. (55) 5565-3944; fax (55) 5565-2751; e-mail rguizar@mail.cem.org.mx.

Archbishop of Yucatán: EMILIO CARLOS BERLIE BELAUNZARÁN, Arzobispado, Calle 58 501, 97000 Mérida, Yuc.; tel. (999) 28-5720; fax (999) 23-7983; e-mail acm@sureste.com.

The Anglican Communion

Mexico is divided into five dioceses, which form the Province of the Anglican Church in Mexico, established in 1995.

Bishop of Cuernavaca: MARTINIANO GARCÍA MONTIEL, Minerva 1, Las Delicias, 62330 Cuernavaca, Mor.; tel. and fax (777) 15-2870; e-mail diovca@giga.com.mx.

Bishop of Mexico City: SERGIO CARRANZA GÓMEZ, Avda San Jerónimo 117, Col. San Ángel, 01000 México, DF; tel. and fax (55) 5616-2205; e-mail diomex@avantel.net.

Bishop of Northern Mexico: GERMÁN MARTÍNEZ MÁRQUEZ (currently suspended), Simón Bolívar 2005 Nte, Col. Mitras Centro, 64460 Monterrey, NL; tel. and fax (81) 48-7362; e-mail dionte@infosel.com.mx.

Bishop of South-Eastern Mexico: BENITO JUÁREZ MARTÍNEZ, Avda Las Américas 73, Col. Aguacatl, 91130 Jalapa, Ver.; tel. and fax (932) 144387; e-mail dioste@prodigy.net.mx.

Bishop of Western Mexico: SAMUEL ESPINOZA VENEGAS (currently suspended), Javier Gamboa 255, Col. Sector Juarez 44100, Guadalajara, Jal.; tel. (33) 3615-5070; fax (33) 615-4413; e-mail diocte@vianet.com.mx.

Protestant Churches

Federación Evangélica de México: Motolinia 8, Of. 107, Del. Cuauhtémoc, 1830, 06002, México, DF; tel. (55) 5585-0594; f. 1926; Pres. Prof. MOISES MÉNDEZ; Exec. Sec. Rev. ISRAEL ORTIZ MURRIETA.

Iglesia Evangélica Luterana de México: Mina Pte 5808, Nuevo Larado, Tamps; Pres. ENCARNACIÓN ESTRADA; 3,000 mems.

Iglesia Metodista de México, Asociación Religiosa: Miravelle 209, Col. Albert 03570, México, DF; tel. (55) 5539-3674; internet www.iglesia-metodista.org.mx; f. 1930; 55,000 mems; 370 congregations; comprises seven episcopal areas; Bishop (Mexico) GRACIELA ALVAREZ DELGADO; Bishop (North-East) ANTONI AGUIÑA MARQUÉZ; Bishop (North-Central) GABRIEL LOZADA VALDEZ, Bishop (East) RAÚL ROSAS GONZÁLEZ; Bishop (North) ISAÍAS RÁMOS CORONA, Bishop (South-East) ENRIQUE FLORES BARRERA.

National Baptist Convention of Mexico: Vizcaínas Ote 16, Altos, 06080 México, DF; tel. (55) 5518-2691; fax (55) 5521-0118; internet www.bautistas.org.mx/cnbm; f. 1903; Pres. ROLANDO GUTIÉRREZ CORTÉS.

BAHÁ'Í FAITH

National Spiritual Assembly of the Bahá'ís of Mexico: Emerson 421, Col. Chapultepec Morales, 11570 México, DF; tel. (55) 5545-2155; fax (55) 5255-5972; e-mail bahaimex@mx.inter.net; internet www.bahaimex.org; mems resident in 978 localities.

The Press

DAILY NEWSPAPERS

México, DF

La Afición: Ignacio Mariscal 23, Apdo 64 bis, Col. Tabacalera, 06030 México, DF; tel. (55) 5546-4780; fax (55) 5546-5852; e-mail opino@aguila.el-universal.com.mx; f. 1930; sport, entertainment, news; Pres. Lic. JUAN FRANCISCO EALY ORTIZ; Gen. Man. ANTONIO GARCÍA SERRANO; circ. 85,000.

La Crónica de Hoy: Grupo Editorial Convergencia, SA de CV, Balderas 333, 6°, Col. Centro, 06040 México, DF; tel. (52) 5512-4412; internet www.cronica.com.mx; Pres. JORGE KAHWAGI GASTINE.

Cuestión: Laguna de Mayrán 410, Col. Anáhuac, 11320 México, DF; tel. (55) 5260-0499; fax (55) 5260-3645; e-mail cuestion@compuserve.com; internet www.cuestion.com.mx; f. 1980; midday; Dir-Gen. Lic. ALBERTO GONZÁLEZ PARRA; circ. 48,000.

El Día: Insurgentes Norte 1210, Col. Capultitlán, 07370 México, DF; tel. (55) 5729-2155; fax (55) 5537-6629; e-mail cduran@servidor.unam.mx; f. 1962; morning; Dir-Gen. José Luis Camacho López; circ. 50,000.

Diario de México: Chimalpopoca 38, Col. Obrera, 06800 México, DF; tel. (55) 5588-3831; fax (55) 5578-7650; e-mail diamex@rtn.net.mx; f. 1948; morning; Dir-Gen. Federico Bracamontes Gálvez; Dir Rafael Lizardi Durán; circ. 76,000.

Esto: Guillermo Prieto 7, 1°, 06470 México, DF; tel. and fax (55) 5591-0866; e-mail esto@oem.com.mx; internet www.oem.com.mx; f. 1941; morning; sport; Pres. Lic. Mario Vázquez Raña; Dir Carlos Trapaga Barrientos; circ. 400,000, Mondays 450,000.

Excélsior: Reforma 18, Apdo 120 bis, Col. Centro, 06600 México, DF; tel. (55) 5566-2200; fax (55) 5566-0223; e-mail foro@excelsior.com.mx; internet www.excelsior.com.mx; f. 1917; morning; independent; Dir Regino Díaz Redondo; Gen. Man. Juventino Olivera López; circ. 200,000.

El Financiero: Lago Bolsena 176, Col. Anáhuac entre Lago Peypus y Lago Onega, 11320 México, DF; tel. (55) 5227-7600; fax (55) 5254-6427; e-mail pilar@elfinanciero.com.mx; internet www.elfinanciero.com.mx; f. 1981; financial; Dir-Gen. Pilar Estandía de Cárdenas; circ. 147,000.

El Heraldo de México: Dr Lucio, esq. Dr Velasco, Col. Doctores, 06720 México, DF; tel. (55) 5578-7022; fax (55) 5578-9824; e-mail heraldo@iwm.com.mx; internet www.heraldo.com.mx; f. 1965; morning; Dir-Gen. Gabriel Alarcón Velázquez; circ. 209,600.

La Jornada: Francisco Petrarca 118, Col. Chapultepec Morales, 11570 México, DF; tel. (55) 5262-4300; fax (55) 5262-4354; e-mail jornada@condor.dqsca.unam.mx; internet http://unam.netgate.net/jornada; f. 1984; morning; Dir-Gen. Lic. Carmen Lira Saade; Gen. Man. Lic. Jorge Martínez Jiménez; circ. 106,471, Sundays 100,924.

Novedades: Balderas 87, esq. Morelos, Col. Centro, 06040 México, DF; tel. (55) 5518-5481; fax (55) 5521-4505; internet www.unam.netgate.net/novedades; f. 1936; morning; independent; Pres. and Editor-in-Chief Romulo O'Farrill, Jr; Vice-Pres. José Antonio O'Farrill Avila; circ. 42,990, Sundays 43,536.

Ovaciones: Lago Zirahuén 279, 20°, Col. Anáhuac, 11320 México, DF; tel. (55) 5328-0700; fax (55) 5260-2219; e-mail ovaciones@televisa.com.mx; f. 1947; morning and evening editions; Pres. and Dir-Gen. Lic. Alberto Ventosa Aguilera; circ. 130,000; evening circ. 100,000.

La Prensa: Basilio Badillo 40, Col. Tabacalera, 06030 México, DF; tel. (55) 5228-9947; fax (55) 5521-8209; e-mail prensa@oem.com.mx; internet www.oem.com.mx; f. 1928; morning; Pres. and Dir-Gen. Lic. Mario Vázquez Raña; circ. 270,000.

Reforma: Avda México Coyoacán 40, Col. Sta Cruz Atoyac, 03310 México, DF; tel. (55) 5628-7100; fax (55) 5628-7188; internet www.reforma.infosel.com; f. 1993; morning; Pres. and Dir-Gen. Alejandro Junco de la Vega; circ. 94,000.

El Sol de México: Guillermo Prieto 7, 20°, Col. San Rafael, 06470 México, DF; tel. (55) 5566-1511; fax (55) 5535-5560; e-mail info@oem.com.mx; internet www.elsoldemexico.com.mx; f. 1965; morning and midday; Pres. and Dir-Gen. Lic. Mario Vázquez Raña; Dir Pilar Ferreira García; circ. 76,000.

El Universal: Bucareli 8, Apdo 909, Col. Centro, 06040 México, DF; tel. (55) 5709-1313; fax (55) 5510-1269; e-mail redaccio@servidor.unam.mx; internet www.el-universal.com.mx; f. 1916; morning; independent; centre-left; Pres. and Dir-Gen. Lic. Juan Francisco Ealy Ortiz; circ. 165,629, Sundays 181,615.

Unomásuno: Retorno de Correggio 12, Col. Nochebuena, 03720 México, DF; tel. (55) 5563-9911; fax (55) 5598-8821; e-mail cduran@servidor.unam.mx; f. 1977; morning; left-wing; Pres. Manuel Alonso Muñoz; Dir Rafael Cardona S.; circ. 40,000.

PROVINCIAL DAILY NEWSPAPERS

Baja California

El Mexicano: Carretera al Aeropuerto s/n, Fracc. Alamar, Apdo 2333, 22540 Tijuana, BC; tel. (664) 21-3400; fax (664) 21-2944; f. 1959; morning; Dir and Gen. Man. Eligio Valencia Roque; circ. 80,000.

El Sol de Tijuana: Rufino Tamayo 4, Zona Río, 22320 Tijuana, BC; tel. (664) 34-3232; fax (664) 34-2234; e-mail soltij@oem.com.mx; internet www.oem.com.mx; f. 1989; morning; Pres. and Dir-Gen. Lic. Mario Vázquez Raña; circ. 50,000.

La Voz de la Frontera: Avda Madero 1545, Col. Nueva, Apdo 946, 21100 Mexicali, BC; tel. (686) 53-4545; fax (686) 53-6912; e-mail lavoz@oem.com.mx; internet www.oem.com.mx; f. 1964; morning; independent; Pres. and Dir-Gen. Mario Vázquez Raña; Gen. Man. Lic. Mario Valdés Hernández; circ. 65,000.

Chihuahua

El Diario: Publicaciones del Chuviscar, SA de CV, Avda Universidad 1900, Col. San Felipe, Chihuahua, Chih.; tel. (614) 429-0700; internet www.diario.com.mx; www.eldiariodechihuahua.com.mx; f. 1976; Pres. Osvaldo Rodríguez Borunda.

El Heraldo de Chihuahua: Avda Universidad 2507, Apdo 1515, 31240 Chihuahua, Chih.; tel. (614) 13-9339; fax (614) 13-5625; e-mail elheraldo@buzon.online.com.mx; f. 1927; morning; Pres. and Dir-Gen. Lic. Mario Vázquez Raña; Dir. Lic. Javier H. Contreras; circ. 27,520, Sundays 31,223.

Coahuila

La Opinión: Blvd Independencia 1492 Ote, Apdo 86, 27010 Torreón, Coah.; tel. (871) 13-8777; fax (871) 13-8164; internet www.editoriallaopinion.com.mx; f. 1917; morning; Pres. Francisco A. González; circ. 40,000.

El Siglo de Torreón: Avda Matamoros 1056 Pte, Apdo 19, 27000 Torreón, Coah.; tel. (871) 12-8600; fax (871) 16-5909; internet www.elsiglodetorreon.com.mx; f. 1922; morning; Pres. Olga De Juambelz y Horcasitas; circ. 38,611, Sundays 38,526.

Vanguardia: Blvd Venustiano Carranza 1918, República Oriente, 25280 Saltillo, Coah.; tel. (844) 411-0835; e-mail hola@vanguardia.com.mx; internet www.vanguardia.com.mx.

Guanajuato

El Nacional: Carretera Guanajuato–Juventino Rosas, km 9.5, Apdo 32, 36000 Guanajuato, Gto; tel. (477) 33-1286; fax (477) 33-1288; f. 1987; morning; Dir-Gen. Arnoldo Cuéllar Ornelas; circ. 60,000.

Jalisco

El Diario de Guadalajara: Calle 14 2550, Zona Industrial, 44940 Guadalajara, Jal.; tel. (33) 612-0043; fax (33) 612-0818; f. 1969; morning; Pres. and Dir-Gen. Luis A. González Becerra; circ. 78,000.

El Informador: Independencia 300, Apdo 3 bis, 44100 Guadalajara, Jal.; tel. (33) 614-6340; fax (33) 614-4653; internet www.informador.com.mx; f. 1917; morning; Editor Jorge Álvarez del Castillo; circ. 50,000.

El Occidental: Calzada Independencia Sur 324, Apdo 1-699, 44100 Guadalajara, Jal.; tel. (33) 613-0690; fax (33) 613-6796; f. 1942; morning; Dir Lic. Ricardo del Valle del Peral; circ. 49,400.

México

ABC: Avda Hidalgo Ote 1339, Centro Comercial, 50000 Toluca, Méx.; tel. (722) 179880; fax (722) 179646; e-mail miled1@mail.miled.com; internet www.miled.com; f. 1984; morning; Pres. and Editor Miled Libien Kaui; circ. 65,000.

Diario de Toluca: Allende Sur 209, 50000 Toluca, Méx.; tel. (722) 142403; fax (722) 141523; f. 1980; morning; Editor Anuar Maccise Dib; circ. 22,200.

El Heraldo de Toluca: Salvador Díaz Mirón 700, Col. Sánchez Colín, 50150 Toluca, Méx.; tel. (722) 173453; fax (722) 122535; f. 1955; morning; Editor Alberto Barraza Sánchez A; circ. 90,000.

El Mañana: Avda Hidalgo Ote 1339, Toluca, Méx.; tel. (722) 179880; fax (722) 178402; e-mail miled1@mail.miled.com; internet www.miled.com; f. 1986; morning; Pres. and Editor Miled Libien Kaui; circ. 65,000.

Rumbo: Allende Sur 205, Toluca, Méx.; tel. (722) 142403; fax (722) 141523; f. 1968; morning; Editor Anuar Maccise Dib; circ. 10,800.

El Sol de Toluca: Santos Degollado 105, Apdo 54, 50050 Toluca, Méx.; tel. (722) 150340; fax (722) 147441; f. 1947; morning; Pres. and Dir-Gen. Lic. Mario Vázquez Raña; circ. 42,000.

Michoacán

La Voz de Michoacán: Blvd del Periodismo 1270, Col. Arriaga Rivera, Apdo 121, 58190 Morelia, Mich.; tel. (443) 327-3712; fax (443) 327-3728; e-mail lavoz@mail.giga.com; internet www.voznet.com.mx; f. 1948; morning; Dir-Gen. Lic. Miguel Medina Robles; circ. 50,000.

Morelos

El Diario de Morelos: Morelos Sur 817, Col. Las Palmas, 62000 Cuernavaca, Mor.; tel. (777) 14-2660; fax (777) 14-1253; internet www.diariodemorelos.com.mx; morning; Dir-Gen. Federico Bracamontes; circ. 47,000.

Nayarit

Meridiano de Nayarit: E. Zapata 73 Pte, Apdo 65, 63000 Tepic, Nay.; tel. (321) 20145; fax (321) 26630; internet www.meridiano.com.mx; f. 1942; morning; Dir Dr David Alfaro; circ. 60,000.

El Observador: Allende 110 Ote, Despachos 203-204, 63000 Tepic, Nay.; tel. (321) 24309; fax (321) 24309; morning; Pres. and Dir-Gen. Lic. LUIS A. GONZÁLEZ BECERRA; circ. 55,000.

Nuevo León

ABC: Platón Sánchez Sur 411, 64000 Monterrey, NL; tel. (81) 344-4480; fax (81) 344-5990; e-mail abc2000@mexis.com; f. 1985; morning; Pres. GONZALO ESTRADA CRUZ; Dir-Gen. GONZALO ESTRADO TORRES; circ. 40,000, Sundays 45,000.

El Diario de Monterrey: Eugenio Garza Sada 2245 Sur, Col. Roma, Apdo 3128, 647000 Monterrey, NL; tel. (81) 359-2525; fax (81) 359-1414; internet www.diariodemonterrey.com; f. 1974; morning; Dir-Gen. Lic. FEDERICO ARREOLA; circ. 80,000.

El Norte: Washington 629 Ote, Apdo 186, 64000 Monterrey, NL; tel. (81) 345-3388; fax (81) 343-2476; internet www.elnorte.com.mx; f. 1938; morning; Man. Dir Lic. ALEJANDRO JUNCO DE LA VEGA; circ. 133,872, Sundays 154,951.

El Porvenir: Galeana Sur 344, Apdo 218, 64000 Monterrey, NL; tel. (81) 345-4080; fax (81) 345-7795; internet www.elporvenir.com.mx; f. 1919; morning; Dir-Gen. JOSÉ GERARDO CANTÚ ESCALANTE; circ. 75,000.

El Sol: Washington 629 Ote, Apdo 186, 64000 Monterrey, NL; tel. (81) 345-3388; fax (81) 343-2476; internet www.infosel.com.mx; f. 1922; evening (except Sundays); Man. Dir Lic. ALEJANDRO JUNCO DE LA VEGA; circ. 45,300.

Oaxaca

El Imparcial: Armenta y López 312, Apdo 322, 68000 Oaxaca, Oax.; tel. (951) 516-2812; fax (951) 516-0050; internet www.imparoax.com.mx; f. 1951; morning; Dir-Gen. Lic. BENJAMÍN FERNÁNDEZ PICHARDO; circ. 17,000, Sundays 20,000.

Puebla

El Sol de Puebla: Avda 3 Ote 201, Apdo 190, 72000 Puebla, Pue.; tel. (222) 42-4560; fax (222) 46-0869; internet www.oem.com.mx; f. 1944; morning; Pres. and Dir-Gen. Lic. MARIO VÁZQUEZ RAÑA; circ. 67,000.

San Luis Potosí

El Heraldo: Villerías 305, 78000 San Luis Potosí, SLP; tel. (444) 812-3312; fax (444) 812-2081; e-mail heraldsl@prodigy.net.mx; internet www.elheraldodesanluis.com.mx; f. 1954; morning; Dir-Gen. ALEJANDRO VILLASANA MENA; circ. 60,620.

Momento: Zenón Fernández y Leandro Valle, Col. Jardines del Estadio, 78280 San Luis Potosí, SLP; tel. (444) 814-4444; fax (444) 812-2020; f. 1975; morning; Dir-Gen. Lic. EMILIO MANUEL TRINIDAD ZALDÍVAR; circ. 60,000.

Pulso: Galeana 485, 78000 San Luis Potosí, SLP; tel. (444) 812-7575; fax (444) 812-3525; internet www.pulsoslp.com.mx; morning; Dir-Gen. MIGUEL VALLADARES GARCÍA; circ. 60,000.

El Sol de San Luis: Avda Universidad 565, Apdo 342, 78000 San Luis Potosí, SLP; tel. and fax (444) 812-4412; f. 1952; morning; Pres. and Dir-Gen. Lic. MARIO VÁZQUEZ RAÑA; Dir JOSÉ ANGEL MARTÍNEZ LIMÓN; circ. 60,000.

Sinaloa

El Debate de Culiacán: Madero 556 Pte, 80000 Culiacán, Sin.; tel. (667) 16-6353; fax (667) 15-7131; e-mail redaccion@debate.com.mx; internet www.debate.com.mx; f. 1972; morning; Dir ROSARIO I. OROPEZA; circ. 23,603, Sundays 23,838.

Noroeste Culiacán: Grupo Periodicos Noroeste, Angel Flores 282 Ote, Apdo 90, 80000 Culiacán, Sin.; tel. (667) 713-2100; fax (667) 712-8006; e-mail cschmidt@noroeste.com.mx; internet www.noroeste.com.mx; f. 1973; morning; Pres. MANUEL J. CLOUTHIER; Editor RODOLFO DIAZ; circ. 35,000.

El Sol de Sinaloa: Blvd G. Leyva Lozano y Corona 320, Apdo 412, 80000 Culiacán, Sin.; tel. (667) 13-1621; f. 1956; morning; Pres. Lic. MARIO VÁZQUEZ RAÑA; Dir JORGE LUIS TÉLLEZ SALAZAR; circ. 30,000.

Sonora

El Imparcial: Sufragio Efectivo y Mina 71, Col. Centro, Apdo 66, 83000 Hermosillo, Son.; tel. (658) 59-4700; fax (658) 17-4483; e-mail impar@imparcial.com.mx; internet www.imparcial.com.mx; f. 1937; morning; Pres. and Dir-Gen. JOSÉ SANTIAGO HEALY LOERA; circ. 32,083, Sundays 32,444.

Tabasco

Tabasco Hoy: Avda de los Ríos 206, 86035 Villahermosa, Tab.; tel. (993) 16-3333; fax (993) 16-2135; internet www.tabascohoy.com.mx; f. 1987; morning; Dir-Gen. MIGUEL CANTÓN ZETINA; circ. 52,302.

Tamaulipas

El Bravo: Morelos y Primera 129, Apdo 483, 87300 Matamoros, Tamps; tel. (871) 160100; fax (871) 162007; e-mail elbravo@riogrande.net.mx; f. 1951; morning; Pres. and Dir-Gen. JOSÉ CARRETERO BALBOA; circ. 60,000.

El Diario de Nuevo Laredo: González 2409, Apdo 101, 88000 Nuevo Laredo, Tamps; tel. (867) 128444; fax (867) 128221; internet www.diario.net; f. 1948; morning; Editor RUPERTO VILLARREAL MONTEMAYOR; circ. 68,130, Sundays 73,495.

Expresión: Calle 3a y Novedades 1, Col. Periodistas, 87300 Matamoros, Tamps; tel. (871) 174330; fax (871) 173307; morning; circ. 50,000.

El Mañana de Reynosa: Prof. Lauro Aguirre con Matías Canales, Apdo 14, 88620 Ciudad Reynosa, Tamps; tel. (899) 921-9950; fax (899) 924-9348; internet www.elmananarey.com.mx; f. 1949; morning; Dir-Gen. HERIBERTO DEANDAR MARTÍNEZ; circ. 65,000.

El Mundo: Ejército Nacional 201, Col. Guadalupe, 89120 Tampico, Tamps; tel. (833) 134084; fax (833) 134136; f. 1918; morning; Dir-Gen. ANTONIO MANZUR MARÓN; circ. 54,000.

La Opinión de Matamoros: Blvd Lauro Villar 200, Apdo 486, 87400 Matamoros, Tamps; tel. (871) 123141; fax (871) 122132; e-mail opinion1@tamps1.telmex.net.mx; f. 1971; Pres. and Dir-Gen. JUAN B. GARCÍA GÓMEZ; circ. 50,000.

Prensa de Reynosa: Matamoros y González Ortega, 88500 Reynosa, Tamps; tel. (899) 23515; fax (899) 223823; f. 1963; morning; Dir-Gen. FÉLIX GARZA ELIZONDO; circ. 60,000.

El Sol de Tampico: Altamira 311 Pte, Apdo 434, 89000 Tampico, Tamps; tel. (833) 12-3566; fax (833) 12-6986; internet www.oem.com.mx; f. 1950; morning; Dir-Gen. Lic. RUBÉN DÍAZ DE LA GARZA; circ. 77,000.

Veracruz

Diario del Istmo: Avda Hidalgo 1115, 96400 Coatzacoalcos, Ver.; tel. (921) 48802; fax (921) 48514; e-mail info@istmo.com.mx; internet www.diariodelistmo.com; f. 1979; morning; Dir-Gen. JAÍR BENJAMÍN ROBLES BARAJAS; circ. 64,600.

El Dictamen: 16 de Septiembre y Arista, 91700 Veracruz, Ver.; tel. (229) 311745; fax (229) 315804; f. 1898; morning; Pres. CARLOS ANTONIO MALPICA MARTÍNEZ; circ. 38,000, Sundays 39,000.

Yucatán

Diario de Yucatán: Calle 60, No 521, 97000 Mérida, Yuc.; tel. (999) 23-8444; fax (999) 42-2204; internet www.yucatan.com.mx; f. 1925; morning; Dir-Gen. CARLOS R. MENÉNDEZ NAVARRETE; circ. 54,639, Sundays 65,399.

El Mundo al Día: Calle 62, No 514A, 97000 Mérida Yuc.; tel. (999) 23-9933; fax (999) 24-9629; e-mail nmerida@cancun.novenet.com.mx; f. 1964; morning; Pres. ROMULO O'FARRILL, Jr; Gen. Man. Lic. GERARDO GARCÍA GAMBOA; circ. 25,000.

Por Esto!: Calle 60, No 576 entre 73 y 71, 97000 Mérida, Yuc.; tel. (999) 24-7613; fax (999) 28-6514; internet www.poresto.net; f. 1991; morning; Dir-Gen. MARIO R. MENÉNDEZ RODRÍGUEZ; circ. 26,985, Sundays 28,727.

Zacatecas

Imagen: Avda Revolución 24, Col. Tierra y Libertad, Guadalupe, Zac.; tel. and fax (492) 923-4412; internet www.imagenzac.com.mx; Dir-Gen. EUGENIO MERCADO.

SELECTED WEEKLY NEWSPAPERS

Bolsa de Trabajo: San Francisco 657, 9A, Col. del Valle, 03100 México, DF; tel. (55) 5536-8387; f. 1988; employment; Pres. and Dir-Gen. MÓNICA ELÍAS CALLES; circ. 30,000.

El Heraldo de León: Hermanos Aldama 222, Apdo 299, 37000 León, Gto; tel. (477) 713-1194; fax (477) 714-3464; e-mail heraldo@el-heraldo-bajio.com; internet www.el-heraldo-bajio.com; f. 1957; Pres. and Dir-Gen. MAURICIO BERCÚN LÓPEZ; circ. 85,000.

Segundamano: Insurgentes Sur 813-501, Col. Nápoles, 03810 México, DF; tel. (55) 5729-3737; fax (55) 5687-9635; f. 1986; Dir-Gen. LUIS MAGAÑA MAGAÑA; circ. 105,000.

GENERAL INTEREST PERIODICALS

Car and Driver: Alabama 113, Col. Nápoles, 03810 México, DF; tel. (55) 5523-5201; fax (55) 5536-6399; f. 1999; monthly; Pres. PEDRO VARGAS G.; circ. 80,000.

Casas & Gente: Ediarte, SA de CV, Amsterdam 112, 06100 México, DF; tel. (55) 5286-7794; fax (55) 5211-7112; e-mail informac@casasgente.com; internet www.casasgente.com; 10 a year; interior design; Dir-Gen. NICOLÁS H. SÁNCHEZ-OSORIO.

Conozca Más: Vasco de Quiroga 2000, Col. Santa Fe, 01210 México, DF; tel. (55) 5261-2600; fax (55) 5261-2704; f. 1990; monthly; scientific; Dir Eugenio Mendoza; circ. 90,000.

Contenido: Buffon 46, 9°, Col. Anzures, 11590 México, DF; tel. (55) 5531-3162; fax (55) 5545-7478; f. 1963; monthly; popular appeal; Dir Armando Ayala A.; circ. 124,190.

Cosmopolitan (México): Vasco de Quiroga 2000, Col. Santa Fe, 01210 México, DF; tel. (55) 5261-2600; fax (55) 5261-2704; f. 1973; monthly; women's magazine; Dir Sara María Castany; circ. 260,000.

Fama: Avda Eugenio Garza Sada 2245 Sur, Col. Roma, Apdo 3128, 64700 Monterrey, NL; tel. (81) 359-2525; fortnightly; show business; Pres. Jesús D. González; Dir Raúl Martínez; circ. 350,000.

Impacto: Avda Ceylán 517, Col. Industrial Vallejo, Apdo 2986, 02300 México, DF; tel. (55) 5587-3855; fax (55) 5567-7781; f. 1949; weekly; politics; Man. and Dir-Gen. Juan Bustillos Orozco; circ. 115,000.

Kena Especiales: Romero de Terreros 832, Col. del Valle, 03100 México, DF; tel. (55) 5543-1032; fax (55) 5669-3465; e-mail armonia@ netsevice.com.mx; f. 1977; fortnightly; women's interest; Dir-Gen. Lic. Liliana Moreno G; circ. 100,000.

Letras Libres: Presidente Carranza 210, Col. Coyoacán, 04000 México, DF; tel. (55) 5554-8810; fax (55) 5658-0074; e-mail correo@ letraslibres.com; internet www.letraslibres.com; monthly; culture; Chief Editor Julio Trujillo.

Marie Claire: Editorial Televisa, SA de CV, Vasco de Quiroga 2000, Col. Santa Fe, 01210 México, DF; tel. (55) 5261-2600; fax (55) 5261-2704; f. 1990; monthly; women's interest; Editor Louise Mereles; circ. 80,000.

Mecánica Popular: Vasco de Quiroga 2000, Edif. E, Col. Santa Fe, Deleg. Alvaro Obregón, 01210 Mexico, DF; tel. (55) 5261-2600; fax (55) 5261-2705; e-mail mecanica.popular@siedi.spin.com.mx; f. 1947; monthly; crafts and home improvements; Dir Andrés Jorge; circ. 247,850.

Men's Health: Vasco de Quiroga 2000, Col. Santa Fe, 01210 México, DF; tel. (55) 5261-2645; fax (55) 5261-2733; e-mail mens.health@ editorial.televisa.com.mx; f. 1994; monthly; health; Editor Juan Antonio Sempere; circ. 130,000.

Muy Interesante: Vasco de Quiroga 2000, Col. Santa Fe, 01210 México, DF; tel. (55) 5261-2600; fax (55) 5261-2704; f. 1984; monthly; scientific devt; Dir Pilar S. Hoyos; circ. 250,000.

Proceso: Fresas 7, Col. del Valle, 03100 México, DF; tel. (55) 5629-2090; fax (55) 5629-2092; f. 1976; weekly; news analysis; Pres. Julio Scherer García; circ. 98,784.

La Revista Peninsular: Calle 35, 489 x 52 y 54, Centro, Mérida, Yuc.; e-mail revista@sureste.com; internet www.larevista.com.mx; weekly; news and politics; Dir-Gen. Rodrigo Menéndez Cámara.

Selecciones del Reader's Digest: Avda Lomas de Sotelo 1102, Col. Loma Hermosa, Apdo 552, Naucalpan, 11200 México, DF; tel. (55) 5395-7444; fax (55) 5395-3835; f. 1940; monthly; Dir Avdon Coria; circ. 611,660.

Siempre!: Vallarta 20, Apdo 32-010, Col. Revolución, 06030 México, DF; tel. (55) 5566-9355; fax (55) 566-9355; e-mail siempre@data.net .mx; f. 1953; weekly; left of centre; Dir Lic. Beatriz Pagés Rebollar de Nieto; circ. 100,000.

Tele-Guía: Vasco de Quiroga 2000, Col. Santa Fe, 01210 México, DF; tel. (55) 5261-2600; fax (55) 5261-2704; f. 1952; weekly; television guide; Editor María Eugenia Hernández; circ. 375,000.

Tiempo Libre: Holbein 75 bis, Col. Nochebuena, 03720 México, DF; tel. (55) 5611-7332; fax (55) 5611-3874; e-mail info@tiempolibre.com .mx; internet www.tiempolibre.com.mx; f. 1980; weekly; entertainment guide; Dir-Gen. Angeles Aguilar Zinser; circ. 95,000.

Tú: Vasco de Quiroga 2000, Col. Santa Fe, 01210 México, DF; tel. (55) 5261-2600; fax (55) 5261-2730; f. 1980; monthly; Editor María Antonieta Salamanca; circ. 275,000.

TV y Novelas: Vasco de Quiroga 2000, Col. Santa Fe, 01210 México, DF; tel. (55) 5261-2600; fax (55) 5261-2704; f. 1982; weekly; television guide and short stories; Dir Jesús Gallegos; circ. 460,000.

Ultima Moda: Morelos 16, 6°, Col. Centro, 06040 México, DF; tel. (55) 5518-5481; fax (55) 5512-8902; f. 1966; monthly; fashion; Pres. Romulo O'Farrill, Jr; Gen. Man. Lic. Samuel Podolsky Rapoport; circ. 110,548.

Vanidades: Vasco de Quiroga 2000, Col. Santa Fe, 01210 México, DF; tel. (55) 5261-2600; fax (55) 5261-2704; f. 1961; fortnightly; women's magazine; Dir Sara María Barceló de Castany; circ. 290,000.

Visión: Homero 411, 5°, Col. Polanco, 11570 México, DF; tel. (55) 5531-4914; fax (55) 5531-4915; e-mail 74174.3111@compuserve.com; offices in Santafé de Bogotá, Buenos Aires and Santiago de Chile; f.

1950; fortnightly; politics and economics; Gen. Man. Roberto Bello; circ. 27,215.

Vogue (México): Grupo Idéas de México, SA de CV, México, DF; tel. (55) 5095-8066; fax (55) 5530-2828; internet www.vogue.com.mx; f. 1999; monthly; women's fashion; circ. 208,180.

SPECIALIST PERIODICALS

Boletín Industrial: Goldsmith 37-403, Col. Polanco, 11550 México, DF; tel. (55) 5280-6463; fax (55) 5280-3194; e-mail bolind@Viernes .iwm.com.mx; internet www.bolind.com.mx; f. 1983; monthly; Dir-Gen. Humberto Valadés Díaz; circ. 36,000.

Comercio: Río Tíber 87, 06500 México, DF; tel. (55) 5514-0873; fax (55) 5514-1008; f. 1960; monthly; business review; Dir Raúl Horta; circ. 40,000.

Gaceta Médica de México: Academia Nacional de Medicina, Unidad de Congresos del Centro Médico Nacional Siglo XXI, Bloque B, Avda Cuauhtémoc 330, Col. Doctores, 06725 México, DF; tel. (55) 5578-2044; fax (55) 5578-4271; e-mail gacetamx@starnet.net.mx; f. 1864; every 2 months; medicine; Editor Dr Luis Benítez; circ. 20,000.

Manufactura: Sinaloa 149, 1°, Col. Roma, 06700 México, DF; tel. (55) 5511-1537; fax (55) 5208-1265; e-mail publicidad@expansion .com.mx; internet www.expansion.com.mx; f. 1994; monthly; industrial; Dir-Gen. Alejandro Serna Barrera; circ. 29,751.

Negobancos (Negocios y Bancos): Bolívar 8-103, Apdo 1907, Col. Centro, 06000 México, DF; tel. (55) 5510-1884; fax (55) 5512-9411; e-mail nego_bancos@mexico.com; f. 1951; fortnightly; business, economics; Dir Alfredo Farrugia Reed; circ. 10,000.

ASSOCIATIONS

Asociación Nacional de Periodistas A.C.: Luis G. Obregón 17, Desp. 209, Col. Centro, 06020 México, DF; tel. (55) 5702-1546.

Federación Latinoamericana de Periodistas (FELAP): Nuevo Leon 144, 1°, Col. Hipódromo Condesa, 06170 México, DF; tel. (55) 5286-6055; fax (5) 286-6085.

NEWS AGENCIES

Agencia de Información Integral Periodística, SA (AIIP): Tabasco 263, Col. Roma, Delegación Cuauhtémoc, 06700 México, DF; tel. (55) 8596-9643; fax (55) 5235-3468; e-mail aiipsa@axtel.net; internet www.aiip.com.mx; f. 1987; Dir-Gen. Miguel Herrera López.

Agencia Mexicana de Información (AMI): Avda Cuauhtémoc 16, Col. Doctores, 06720 México, DF; tel. (55) 5761-9933; e-mail info@ red-ami.com; internet www.ami.com.mx; Dir-Gen. José Luis Becerra López; Gen.-Man. Eva Vázquez López.

Notimex, SA de CV: Morena 110, 3°, Col. del Valle, 03100 México, DF; tel. (55) 5420-1100; fax (55) 5682-0005; e-mail comercial@ notimex.com.mx; internet www.notimex.com.mx; f. 1968; services to press, radio and TV in Mexico and throughout the world; Dir-Gen. Dr Jorge Medina Viedas.

Foreign Bureaux

Agence France-Presse (AFP): Torre Latinoamericana, 9°, Eje Central y Madero 1, 06007 México, DF; tel. (55) 5518-5494; fax (55) 5510-4564; e-mail redaccion.mexico@afp.com; Bureau Chief Paul Rutler.

Agenzia Nazionale Stampa Associata (ANSA) (Italy): Emerson 150, 2°, Col. Chapultepec Morales, 11570 México, DF; tel. (55) 5255-3696; fax (55) 5255-3018; e-mail ansamexico@prodigy.net.mx; Bureau Chief Marco Brancaccia.

Associated Press (AP) (USA): Paseo de la Reforma 350, Col. Juárez 06600, México, DF; tel. (55) 5080-3400; fax (55) 5208-2684; e-mail apmexico@ap.org; Bureau Chief Eloy O. Aguilar.

Deutsche Presse-Agentur (dpa) (Germany): Avda Cuauhtémoc 16-301, Col. Doctores, 06720 México, DF; tel. (55) 5578-4829; fax (55) 7561-0762; e-mail info@dpa.com.mx; Bureau Chief Klaus Blume.

EFE (Spain): Lafayette 69, Col. Anzures, 11590 México, DF; tel. (55) 5545-8256; fax (55) 5254-1412; e-mail direccion@efe.com.mx; Bureau Chief Manuel Fuentes García.

Informatsionnoye Telegrafnoye Agentstvo Rossii—Telegrafnoye Agentsvo Suverennykh Stran (ITAR—TASS) (Russia): Monte Líbano 965, Col. Lomas de Chapultepec 11000, México, DF; tel. (55) 5202-4831; fax (55) 5202-4879; e-mail itartass@ prodigy.net; Bureau Chief Igor Varlamov.

Inter Press Service (IPS) (Italy): Avda Cuauhtémoc 16-403, Col. Doctores, Del. Cuauhtémoc, 06720 México, DF; tel. (55) 5578-0417; fax (55) 5578-2094; e-mail mex@ipservespanol.org; Chief Correspondent Diego Cevallos Rojas.

Jiji Tsushin-Sha (Japan): Sevilla 9, 2°, Col. Juárez, Del. Cuauhtémoc, 06600 México, DF; tel. (55) 5528-9651; fax (55) 5511-0062; Bureau Chief FUJIO IKEDA.

Kyodo Tsushin (Japan): Cerro Dios de Hacha 66, Col. Romero de Terreros 04310, México, DF; tel. (55) 5554-7199; fax (55) 5658-2957; e-mail kyodonews@mexis.com; Bureau Chief MASAHARU NANAMI.

Maghreb Arabe Presse (Morocco): Miguel de Cervantes Saavedra 448, 4°, Col. Irrigación 11500, México, DF; tel. (55) 1997-2558; fax (55) 1997-6198; e-mail mohammedtanji@hotmail.com; Correspondent MOHAMMED TANJI.

Prensa Latina (Cuba): Edif. B, Dpto 504, Insurgentes Centro 125, Col. San Rafael, Del. Cuauhtémoc, 06470 México, DF; tel. (55) 5546-6015; fax (55) 5592-0570; e-mail plenmex@mail.internet.com.mx; Chief Correspondent Lic. AISSA GARCÍA GOREIA.

Reuters Ltd (United Kingdom): Manuel Ávila Camacho 36, Edif. Torre Esmeralda 11, 19°, Col. Lomas de Chapultepec 11000, México, DF; tel. (55) 5282-7000; fax (55) 5282-7171; internet about.reuters.com/latam; e-mail mexicocity.newsroom@reuters.com; Bureau Chief KIERAN MICHAEL MURRAY.

Viet Nam News Agency (VNA) (Viet Nam): Río Pánuco 180, Col. Cuauhtemoc 06500, México, DF; tel. (55) 5514-9013; fax (55) 5514-1015; e-mail vnamex@prodigy.net.mx; Correspondent PHAM PHOI.

Xinhua (New China) News Agency (People's Republic of China): Francisco I. Madero 17, Col. Tlacopac, 01040 México, DF; tel. (55) 5662-8548; fax (55) 5662-9028; e-mail xinhuamx@xinhuanet.com; Bureau Chief SONG XINDE.

ASSOCIATION

Asociación de Corresponsales Extranjeros en México (ACEM): Avda Cuauhtémoc 16, 1°, Col. Doctores, Del. Cuauhtémoc, 06720 México, DF; tel. (55) 5588-3241; fax (55) 5588-6382.

Publishers

México, DF

Aguilar, Altea, Taurus, Alfaguara, SA de CV: Avda Universidad 767, Col. del Valle, 03100 México, DF; tel. (55) 5688-8966; fax (55) 5604-2304; e-mail sealtiel@santillana.com.mx; f. 1965; general literature; Dir SEALTIEL ALATRISTE.

Arbol Editorial, SA de CV: Avda Cuauhtémoc 1430, Col. Sta Cruz Atoyac, 03310 México, DF; tel. (55) 5688-4828; fax (55) 5605-7600; e-mail editorialpax@maxis.com; f. 1979; health, philosophy, theatre; Man. Dir GERARDO GALLY TEOMONFORD.

Artes de México y del Mundo, SA de CV: Plaza Río de Janeiro, Col. Roma, 06700 México, DF; tel. (55) 5525-5905; fax (55) 5525-5925; e-mail artesdemexico@artesdemexico.com; internet www.artesdemexico.com; f. 1988; art, design, poetry.

Editorial Avante, SA de CV: Luis G. Obregón 9, 1°, Apdo 45-796, Col. Centro, 06020 México, DF; tel. (55) 5510-8804; fax (55) 5521-5245; e-mail editorialavante@editorialavante.com.mx; internet www.editorialavante.com.mx; f. 1948; educational, drama, linguistics; Man. Dir Lic. MARIO A. HINOJOSA SAENZ.

Editorial Azteca, SA: Calle de la Luna 225–227, Col. Guerrero, 06300 México, DF; tel. (55) 5526-1157; fax (55) 5526-2557; f. 1956; religion, literature and technical; Man. Dir ALFONSO ALEMÓN JALOMO.

Librería y Ediciones Botas, SA de CV: Justo Sierra 52, Apdo 941, 06020 México, DF; tel. (55) 5702-4083; fax (55) 5702-5403; e-mail botas@mail.nextgeninter.net.mx; internet members.nbci.com/botas; f. 1910; history, law, philosophy, literature, fine arts, science, language, economics, medicine; Dir ANDRÉS BOTAS HERNÁNDEZ.

Cía Editorial Continental, SA de CV (CECSA): Renacimiento 180, Col. San Juan Tlihuaca, Azcapotzalco, 02400 México, DF; tel. (55) 5561-8333; fax (55) 5561-5231; e-mail info@patriacultural.com.mx; f. 1954; business, technology, general textbooks; Pres. CARLOS FRIGOLET LERMA.

Ediciones de Cultura Popular, SA: Odontología 76, Copilco Universidad, México, DF; f. 1969; history, politics, social sciences; Man. Dir URIEL JARQUÍN GALVEZ.

Ediciones CUPSA: Centro de Comunicación Cultural CUPSA, Apdo 97 bis, 06000 México, DF; tel. (55) 5546-2100; f. 1958; biblical studies, theology, church history, devotional materials, hymn books; Dir ELISA TOSTADO.

Editorial Diana, SA de CV: Arenal No 24, Edif. Norte, Ex-Hacienda Guadalupe, Chimalistac, Del. Álvaro Obregón, 01050 México, DF; tel. (55) 5089-1220; fax (55) 5089-1230; e-mail jlr@diana.com.mx; internet www.editorialdiana.com.mx; f. 1946; general trade and technical books; Pres. and CEO JOSÉ LUIS RAMÍREZ.

Edamex, SA de CV: Heriberto Frias 1104, Col. del Valle, 03100 México, DF; tel. (55) 5559-8588; fax (55) 5575-0555; e-mail info@edamex.com; internet www.edamex.com; arts and literature, sport, journalism, education, philosophy, food, history, children's, health, sociology; Dir-Gen. MONICA COLMENARES.

Ediciones Era, SA de CV: Calle del Trabajo 31, Col. La Fama, Tlalpan, 14269 México, DF; tel. (55) 5528-1221; fax (55) 5606-2904; e-mail edicionesera@laneta.apc.org; internet www.edicionesera.com.mx; f. 1960; general and social science, art and literature; Gen. Man. NIEVES ESPRESATE XIRAU.

Editorial Everest Mexicana, SA: Calzada Ermita Iztapalapa 1631, Col. Barrio San Miguel del Iztapalapa, 09360 México, DF; tel. (55) 5685-1966; fax (55) 5685-3433; f. 1980; general textbooks; Gen. Man. JOSÉ LUIS HUIDOBRO LEÓN.

Espasa Calpe Mexicana, SA: Pitágoras 1139, Col. del Valle, 03100 México, DF; tel. (55) 5575-5022; f. 1948; literature, music, economics, philosophy, encyclopaedia; Man. FRANCISCO CRUZ RUBIO.

Fernández Editores, SA de CV: Eje 1 Pte México-Coyoacán 321, Col. Xoco, 03330 México, DF; tel. (55) 5605-6557; fax (55) 5688-9173; f. 1943; children's literature, textbooks, educational toys, didactic material; Man. Dir LUIS GERARDO FERNÁNDEZ PÉREZ.

Editorial Fondo de Cultura Económica, SA de CV: Carretera Picacho-Ajusco 227, Col. Bosques del Pedregal, 14200 México, DF; tel. (55) 5227-4672; fax (55) 5227-4640; e-mail editorial@fce.com.mx; f. 1934; economics, history, philosophy, children's books, science, politics, psychology, sociology, literature; Dir Lic. MIGUEL DE LA MADRID.

Editorial Grijalbo, SA de CV: Calzada San Bartolo-Naucalpan 282, Col. Argentina, Apdo 17-568, 11230 México, DF; tel. (55) 5358-4355; fax (55) 5576-3586; e-mail diredit@grijalbo.com.mx; internet www.randomhousemondadori.com.mx; f. 1954; owned by Mondadori (Italy); general fiction, history, sciences, philosophy, children's books; Man. Dir AGUSTÍN CENTENO RÍOS.

Nueva Editorial Interamericana, SA de CV: Cedro 512, Col. Atlampa, Apdo 4-140, 06450 México, DF; tel. (55) 5541-6789; fax (55) 5541-1603; f. 1944; medical publishing; Man. Dir RAFAEL SÁINZ.

Distribuidora Intermex, SA de CV: Lucio Blanco 435, Azcapotzalco, 02400 México, DF; tel. (55) 5230-9500; fax (55) 5230-9516; e-mail pmuhechi@televisa.com.mx; f. 1969; romantic fiction; Gen. Dir Lic. ALEJANDRO PAILLÉS.

McGraw-Hill Interamericana de México, SA de CV: Cedro 512, Col. Atlampa Cuauhtémoc, 06450 México, DF; tel. (55) 5576-7304; fax (55) 5628-5367; e-mail mcgraw-hill@infosel.net.mx; internet www.mcgraw-hill.com.mx; education, business, science; Man. Dir CARLOS RIOS.

Editorial Joaquín Mortiz, SA de CV: Insurgentes Sur 1162, 3°, Col. del Valle, 03100 México, DF; tel. (55) 5575-8585; fax (55) 5559-3483; f. 1962; general literature; Man. Dir Ing. HOMERO GAYOSO ANIMAS.

Editorial Jus, SA de CV: Plaza de Abasolo 14, Col. Guerrero, 06300 México, DF; tel. (55) 526-0616; fax (55) 5529-0951; f. 1938; history of Mexico, law, philosophy, economy, religion; Man. TOMÁS G. REYNOSO.

Ediciones Larousse, SA de CV: Dinamarca 81, Col. Juárez, 06600 México, DF; tel. (55) 5208-2005; fax (55) 5208-6225; f. 1965; Man. Dir DOMINIQUE BERTÍN GARCÍA.

Editora Latino Americana, SA: Guatemala 10-220, México, DF; popular literature; Dir JORGE H. YÉPEZ.

Editorial Limusa, SA de CV: Balderas 95, 1°, Col. Centro, 06040 México, DF; tel. (55) 5521-2105; fax (55) 5512-2903; e-mail limusa@noriega.com.mx; internet www.noriega.com.mx; f. 1962; science, general, textbooks; Pres. CARLOS NORIEGA MILERA.

Editorial Nuestro Tiempo, SA: Avda Universidad 771, Desp. 103-104, Col. del Valle, 03100 México, DF; tel. (55) 5688-8768; fax (55) 5688-6868; f. 1966; social sciences; Man. Dir ESPERANZA NACIF BARQUET.

Editorial Oasis, SA: Avda Oaxaca 28, 06700 México, DF; tel. (55) 5528-8293; f. 1954; literature, pedagogy, poetry; Man. MARÍA TERESA ESTRADA DE FERNÁNDEZ DEL BUSTO.

Editorial Orión: Sierra Mojada 325, 11000 México, DF; tel. (55) 5520-0224; f. 1942; archaeology, philosophy, psychology, literature, fiction; Man. Dir SILVA HERNÁNDEZ BALTAZAR.

Editorial Patria, SA de CV: Renacimiento 180, Col. San Juan Tlihuaca, Azcapotzalco, 02400 México, DF; tel. (55) 5561-6042; fax (55) 5561-5231; e-mail info@patriacultural.com.mx; f. 1933; fiction, general trade, children's books; Pres. CARLOS FRIGOLET LERMA.

Editorial Planeta Mexicana, SA de CV: Clavijero 70, Col. Esperanza, México, DF; tel. (55) 5533-1250; internet www

.editorialplaneta.com.mx; general literature, non-fiction; part of Grupo Planeta (Spain); Man. Dir JOAQUIN DÍEZ-CANEDO.

Editorial Porrúa Hnos, SA: Argentina 15, 5°, 06020 México, DF; tel. (55) 5702-4574; fax (55) 5702-6529; e-mail servicios@porrua.com; internet www.porrua.com; f. 1944; general literature; Dir JOSÉ ANTONIO PÉREZ PORRÚA.

Editorial Posada, SA de CV: Eugenia 13, Desp. 501, Col. Nápoles, 03510 México, DF; tel. (55) 5682-0660; f. 1968; general; Dir-Gen. CARLOS VIGIL ZUBIETA.

Editorial Quetzacoatl, SA: Medicina 37, Local 1 y 2, México, DF; tel. (55) 5548-6180; Man. Dir ALBERTO RODRÍGUEZ VALDÉS.

Medios Publicitarios Mexicanos, SA de CV: Avda México 99-103, Col. Hipódromo Condesa, 06170 México, DF; tel. (55) 5574-2858; fax (55) 5574-2668; e-mail editorial@mpm.com.mx; internet www.mpm.com.mx; f. 1958; advertising media rates and data; Man. FERNANDO VILLAMIL ÁVILA.

Reverté Ediciones, SA de CV: Río Pánuco 141A, 06500 México, DF; tel. (55) 5533-5658; fax (55) 5514-6799; e-mail 101545.2361@ compuserve.com; f. 1955; science, technical, architecture; Man. RAMÓN REVERTÉ MASCÓ.

Salvat Mexicana de Ediciones, SA de CV: Presidente Masarik 101, 5°, 11570 México, DF; tel. (55) 5250-6041; fax (55) 5250-6861; medicine, encyclopaedic works; Dir GUILLERMO HERNÁNDEZ PÉREZ.

Siglo XXI Editores, SA de CV: Avda Cerro del Agua 248, Col. Romero de Terreros, Del. Coyoacán, 04310 México, DF; tel. (55) 5658-7999; fax (55) 5658-7599; e-mail informes@sigloxxieditores .com.mx; internet www.sigloxxieditores.com.mx; f. 1966; art, economics, education, history, social sciences, literature, philology and linguistics, philosophy and political science; Dir-Gen. Lic. JAIME LABASTIDA OCHOA; Gen. Man. Ing. JOSÉ MARIA CASTRO MUSSOT.

Editorial Trillas, SA: Avda Río Churubusco 385 Pte, Col. Xoco, Apdo 10534, 03330 México, DF; tel. (55) 5688-4233; fax (55) 5601-1858; e-mail trillas@ovinet.com.mx; internet www.trillas.mx; f. 1954; science, technical, textbooks, children's books; Man. Dir FRANCISCO TRILLAS MERCADER.

Universidad Nacional Autónoma de México: Dirección General de Fomento Editorial, Avda del Iman 5, Ciudad Universitaria, 04510 México, DF; tel. (55) 5622-6581; fax (55) 5665-2778; f. 1935; publications in all fields; Dir-Gen. ARTURO VELÁZQUEZ JIMÉNEZ.

Estado de México

Pearson Educación de México, SA de CV: Calle 4, 25, Fraccionamiento Industrial Alce Blanco, Naucalpan de Juárez 53370, Méx.; tel. (55) 5387-0700; fax (55) 5358-6445; internet www.pearson.com .mx; f. 1984; educational books under the imprints Addison-Wesley, Prentice Hall, Allyn and Bacon, Longman and Scott Foresman; Pres. STEVE MARBAN.

ASSOCIATIONS

Cámara Nacional de la Industria Editorial Mexicana: Holanda 13, Col. San Diego Churubusco, 04120 México, DF; tel. (55) 5688-2011; fax (55) 5604-3147; e-mail cepromex@caniem.com; internet www.caniem.com; f. 1964; Pres. ANTONIO RUANO FERNÁNDEZ; Gen. Man. CLAUDIA DOMÍNGUEZ MEJÍA.

Instituto Mexicano del Libro, AC: México, DF; tel. (55) 5535-2061; Pres. KLAUS THIELE; Sec.-Gen. ISABEL RUIZ GONZÁLEZ.

Organización Editorial Mexicana, SA: Guillermo Prieto 7, 06470 México, DF; tel. (55) 5566-1511; fax (55) 5566-0694; e-mail info@oem .com.mx; internet www.oem.com.mx; Pres. Lic. MARIO VÁZQUEZ RAÑA.

Prensa Nacional Asociada, SA (PRENASA): Insurgentes Centro 114-411, 06030 México, DF; tel. (55) 5546-7389.

Broadcasting and Communications

TELECOMMUNICATIONS

Regulatory Authorities

Comisión Federal de Telecomunicaciones (Cofetel): Bosque de Radiatas 44, 4°, Col. Bosques de las Lomas, 05120 México, DF; tel. (55) 261-4000; fax (55) 5261-4000; e-mail información@cft.gob.mx; internet www.cofetel.gob.mx; Pres. JORGE ARREDONDO MARTÍNEZ.

Dirección General de Concesiones y Permisos de Telecomunicaciones: Unidad Contel Sga, Avda de las Telecomunicaciones s/n, Ixtapalapa, 09310 México, DF; tel. (55) 5692-0077; Dir Ing. SERGIO CERVANTES.

Dirección General de Telecomunicaciones: Lázaro Cárdenas 567, 11°, Ala Norte, Col. Narvarte, 03020 México, DF; tel. (55) 5519-9161; Dir-Gen. Ing. ENRIQUE LUENGAS H.

Principal Operators

Alestra: Paseo de las Palmas 405, Col. Lomas de Chapultepec, 11000 México, DF; internet www.alestra.com.mx; 49% owned by AT&T; Dir-Gen. ROLANDO ZUBIRÁN SHETLER.

America Movil, SA de CV (Telcel): Lago Alberto, 366 Col. Anáhuac, 11320 México, DF; internet www.telcel.com; CEO DANIEL HAJJ.

Avantel: Liverpool 88, Col. Juárez, 06600 México, DF; e-mail webmaster@avantel.com.mx; internet www.avantel.net.mx; f. 1994; Dir-Gen. OSCAR RODRÍGUEZ MARTÍNEZ.

Carso Global Telecom, SA de CV: Insurgentientes Sur 3500, Col. Peña Pobre, 14060 México DF; tel. (55) 5726-3686; fax (55) 5238-0601; internet www.cgtelecom.com.mx; Chair. CARLOS SLIM DOMIT.

Iusacell, SA de CV: Avda Prolongación Paseo de la Reforma 1236, Col. Santa Fe, 05438 México, DF; internet www.iusacell.com.mx; f. 1989; operates mobile cellular telephone network; Dir-Gen. GUSTAVO GUZMÁN SEPÚLVEDA.

Telecomunicaciones de México (TELECOMM): Torre Central de Telecomunicaciones Eje Central Lázaro Cárdenas 567, 11°, Ala Norte, Col. Narvarte, 03020 México, DF; tel. (55) 5629-1166; fax (55) 5559-9812; internet www.sct.gob.mx; govt-owned; Dir-Gen. ANDRÉS FIGUEROA COBIÁN.

Telefónica México: Avda Gómez Morín 350, Col. Valle del Campestre, 66265 San Pedro Garsa García, NL; tel. (81) 368-1900; internet www.pegascopcs.com.mx; operates mobile telephone service Telefónica Móviles (MoviStar), telecommunications co Telefónica Data; controls Pegaso, Cedetel, Norcel, Movitel and Baja Celular; owned by Telefónica, SA (Spain).

Teléfonos de México, SA de CV (Telmex): Parque Via 198, Of. 701, Col. Cuauhtémoc, 06599 México, DF; tel. (55) 5222-5462; fax (55) 5545-5500; internet www.telmex.com.mx; Dir-Gen. CARLOS SLIM DOMIT.

BROADCASTING

Regulatory Authorities

Cámara Nacional de la Industria de Radio y Televisión (CIRT): Horacio 1013, Col. Polanco Reforma, Del. Miguel Hidalgo, 11550 México, DF; tel. (55) 5726-9909; fax (55) 5545-6767; e-mail cirt@cirt.com.mx; internet www.cirt.com.mx; f. 1942; Pres. JORGE MENDOZA GARZA.

Dirección General de Radio, Televisión y Cine (RTC): Secretaria de Gobernación, Bucareli 99, Col. Juaréz, Del. Cuahtémoc, 06600 México, DF; internet www.rtc.gob.mx; tel. (55) 5566-0262.

Dirección de Normas de Radiodifusión: Eugenia 197, 1°, Col. Narvarte, 03020 México, DF; tel. (55) 5590-4372; e-mail amilpg@sct .gob.mx; internet www.sct.gob.mx; licence-issuing authority; Dir Dr ALFONSO AMILPAS.

Instituto Mexicano de Televisión: Anillo Periférico Sur 4121, Col. Fuentes del Pedregal, 14141 México, DF; tel. (55) 5568-5684; Dir-Gen. Lic. JOSÉ ANTONIO ALVAREZ LIMA.

Radio

In 2002 there were 1,142 commercial radio stations in Mexico. Among the most important commercial networks are:

ARTSA: Avda de Los Virreyes 1030, Col. Lomas de Chapultepec, 11000 México, DF; tel. (55) 5202-3344; fax (55) 5202-6940; Dir-Gen. Lic. GUSTAVO ECHEVARRÍA ARCE.

Corporación Mexicana de Radiodifusión: Tetitla 23, esq. Calle Coapa, Col. Toriello Guerra, 14050 México, DF; tel. (55) 5424-6380; fax (55) 5666-5422; e-mail comentarios@cmr.com.mx; internet www .cmr.com.mx; Pres. ENRIQUE BERNAL SERVÍN; Dir-Gen. OSCAR BELTRÁN.

Firme, SA: Gauss 10, Col. Nueva Anzures, 11590 México, DF; tel. (55) 55250-7788; fax (55) 5250-7788; Dir-Gen. LUIS IGNACIO SANTIBÁÑEZ.

Grupo Acir, SA: Monte Pirineos 770, Col. Lomas de Chapultepec, 11000 México, DF; tel. (55) 5540-4291; fax (55) 5540-4106; f. 1965; comprises 140 stations; Pres. FRANCISCO IBARRA LÓPEZ.

Grupo Radio Centro, SA de CV: Constituyentes 1154, Col. Lomas Atlas, Del. Miguel Hidalgo, 11950 México, DF; tel. (55) 5728-4947; fax (55) 5259-2915; f. 1965; comprises 100 radio stations; Pres. ADRIÁN AGUIRRE GÓMEZ; Dir-Gen. Ing. GILBERTO SOLIS SILVA.

Grupo Siete Comunicácion: Montecito 38, 31°, Of. 33, México, DF; tel. (55) 5488-0887; e-mail jch@gruposiete.com.mx; internet www.gruposiete.com.mx; f. 1997; Pres. Lic. FRANCISCO JAVIER SÁNCHEZ CAMPUZANO.

Instituto Mexicano de la Radio (IMER): Mayorazgo 83, 2°, Col. Xoco, 03330 México, DF; tel. (55) 5628-1730; f. 1983; Dir-Gen. CARLOS LARA SUMANO.

MVS Radio Stereorey y FM Globo: Mariano Escobedo 532, Col. Anzures, 11590 México, DF; tel. (55) 5203-4574; fax (55) 5255-1425; e-mail vargas@data.net.mx; f. 1968; Pres. Lic. JOAQUÍN VARGAS G; Vice-Pres. Lic. ADRIÁN VARGAS G.

Núcleo Radio Mil: Insurgentes Sur 1870, 01030 México, DF; tel. (55) 5662-6060; f. 1960; comprises seven radio stations in Mexico City and three provincial radio stations; Pres. and Dir-Gen. Lic. E. GUILLERMO SALAS PEYRÓ.

Organización Radio Centro: Artículo 123, No 90, Col. Centro, 06050 México, DF; tel. (55) 5709-2220; fax (55) 512-8588; nine stations in Mexico City; Pres. MARÍA ESTHER GÓMEZ DE AGUIRRE.

Organización Radiofónica de México, SA: Tuxpan 39, 8°, Col. Roma Sur, 06760 México, DF; tel. (55) 5264-2025; fax (55) 5264-5720; Pres. JAIME FERNÁNDEZ ARMENDÁRIZ.

Radio Cadena Nacional, SA (RCN): Lago Victoria 78, Col. Granada, 11520 México, DF; tel. (55) 2624-0401; e-mail loregonzalez@rcn.com.mx; internet www.rcn.com.mx; f. 1948; Pres. RAFAEL C. NAVARRO ARRONTE; Dir-Gen. SERGIO FAJARDO ORTIZ.

Radio Comerciales, SA de CV: Avda México y López Mateos, 44680 Guadalajara, Jal.; tel. (33) 615-0852; fax (33) 630-3487; 7 major commercial stations.

Radio Educación: Angel Urraza 622, Col. del Valle, 03100 México, DF; tel. (55) 5559-6169; fax (55) 5575-6566; f. 1924; Gen. Dir LUIS ERNESTO PI OROZCO.

Radio Fórmula, SA: Privada de Horacio 10, Col. Polanco, 11560 México, DF; tel. (55) 282-1016; Dir Lic. ROGERIO AZCARRAGA.

Radiodifusoras Asociadas, SA de CV (RASA): Durango 331, 2°, Col. Roma, 06700 México, DF; tel. (55) 5553-6620; fax (55) 5286-2774; f. 1956; Pres. JOSÉ LARIS ITURBIDE; Dir-Gen. JOSÉ LARIS RODRÍGUEZ.

Radiodifusores Asociados de Innovación y Organización, SA: Emerson 408, Col. Chapultepec Morales, 11570 México, DF; tel. (55) 5203-5577; fax (55) 5545-2078; Dir-Gen. Lic. CARLOS QUIÑONES ARMENDÁRIZ.

Radiorama, SA de CV: Reforma 56, 5°, 06600 México, DF; tel. (55) 5566-1515; fax (55) 5566-1454; Dir JOSÉ LUIS C. RESÉNDIZ.

Representaciones Comerciales Integrales: Avda Chapultepec 431, Col. Juárez, 06600 México, DF; tel. (55) 5533-6185; Dir-Gen. ALFONSO PALMA V.

Sistema Radio Juventud: Pablo Casals 567, Prados Providencia, 44670 Guadalajara, Jal.; tel. (33) 641-6677; fax (33) 641-3413; f. 1975; network of several stations including Estereo Soul 89.9 FM; Dirs ALBERTO LEAL A., J. JESÚS OROZCO G., GABRIEL ARREGUI V.

Sistema Radiofónico Nacional, SA: Baja California 163, Of. 602, 06760 México, DF; tel. (55) 5574-0298; f. 1971; represents commercial radio networks; Dir-Gen. RENÉ C. DE LA ROSA.

Sociedad Mexicana de Radio, SA de CV (SOMER): Gutenberg 89, Col. Anzures, 11590 México, DF; tel. (55) 5255-5297; fax (55) 5545-0310; Dir-Gen. EDILBERTO HUESCA PERROTIN.

Television

In 2002 there were 468 television stations. Among the most important are:

Asesoramiento y Servicios Técnicos Industriales, SA (ASTISA): México, DF; tel. (55) 5585-3333; commercial; Dir ROBERTO CHÁVEZ TINAJERO.

MVS (Multivisión): Blvd Puerto Aéreo 486, Col. Moctezuma, 15500 México, DF; tel. (55) 5764-8100; internet www.mvs.com; subscriber-funded.

Once TV: Carpio 475, Col. Casco de Santo Tomás, 11340 México, DF; tel. (55) 5356-1111; fax (55) 5396-8001; e-mail canal11@vmredipn.ipn.mx; f. 1959; Dir-Gen. ALEJANDRA LAJOUS VARGAS.

Tele Cadena Mexicana, SA: Avda Chapultepec 18, 06724 México, DF; tel. (55) 5535-1679; commercial, comprises about 80 stations; Dir Lic. JORGE ARMANDO PIÑA MEDINA.

Televisa, SA de CV: Edif. Televicentro, Avda Chapultepec 28, Col. Doctores, 06724 México, DF; tel. (55) 5709-3333; fax (55) 5709-3021; e-mail webmaster@televisa.com.mx; internet www.televisa.com; f. 1973; commercial; began broadcasts to Europe via satellite in Dec. 1988 through its subsidiary, Galavisión; 406 affiliated stations; Chair. and CEO EMILIO AZCÁRRAGA JEAN; Vice-Pres. ALEJANDRO BURILLO AZCÁRRAGA.

Televisión Azteca, SA de CV: Anillo Periférico Sur 4121, Col. Fuentes del Pedregal, 14141 México, DF; tel. (55) 5420-1313; fax (55) 5645-4258; e-mail webtva@tvazteca.com; internet tvazteca.todito

.com; f. 1992; assumed responsibility for former state-owned channels 7 and 13; Pres. RICARDO B. SALINAS PLIEGO.

Televisión de la República Mexicana: Mina 24, Col. Guerrero, México, DF; tel. (55) 5510-8590; cultural; Dir EDUARDO LIZALDE.

As a member of the Intelsat international consortium, Mexico has received communications via satellite since the 1960s. The launch of the Morelos I and Morelos II satellites, in 1985, provided Mexico with its own satellite communications system. The Morelos satellites were superseded by a new satellite network, Solidaridad, which was inaugurated in early 1994. In late 1997 Mexico's three satellites (grouped in a newly-formed company, SatMex) were transferred to private ownership.

Finance

(cap. = capital; dep. = deposits; m. = million; res = reserves; amounts in new pesos unless otherwise stated)

BANKING

The Mexican banking system is comprised of the Banco de México (the central bank of issue), multiple or commercial banking institutions and development banking institutions. Banking activity is regulated by the Federal Government.

Commercial banking institutions are constituted as *Sociedades Anónimas*, with wholly private social capital. Development banking institutions exist as *Sociedades Nacionales de Crédito*, participation in their capital is exclusive to the Federal Government, notwithstanding the possibility of accepting limited amounts of private capital. In 2000 there were 34 commercial banks operating in Mexico.

All private banks were nationalized in September 1982. By July 1992, however, the banking system had been completely returned to the private sector. Legislation removing all restrictions on foreign ownership of banks received congressional approval in 1999.

Supervisory Authority

Comisión Nacional Bancaria y de Valores (National Banking and Securities Commission): Insurgentes Sur 1971, Torre Norte, Sur y III, Col. Guadalupe Inn, Del. Álvaro Obregón, 01020 México, DF; tel. and fax (55) 5724-6000; e-mail info@cnbv.gob.mx; internet www.cnbv.gob.mx; f. 1924; govt commission controlling all credit institutions in Mexico; Pres. JONATHAN DAVIS ARZAC.

Central Bank

Banco de México (BANXICO): Avda 5 de Mayo 2, Col Centro, Del Cuauhtémoc, 06059 México, DF; tel. (55) 5237-2000; fax (55) 5237-2370; e-mail comsoc@banxico.org.mx; internet www.banxico.org.mx; f. 1925; currency issuing authority; became autonomous on 1 April 1994; cap. 4,433m., res 15,921m., dep. 465,858.0m. (Dec. 2002); Gov. Dr. GUILLERMO ORTIZ MARTÍNEZ; 6 brs.

Commercial Banks

Banamex: Avda Isabel la Católica 44, 1°, Col. Centro Histórico, Del. Cuauhtémoc, 06000 México, DF; tel. (55) 5720-7091; fax (55) 5920-7323; internet www.banamex.com; f. 1884; transferred to private ownership in 1991; merged with Citibank México, SA in 2001; cap. 41,790.8m., res –17,382.8m., dep. 243,630.6m. (Dec. 1998); Dir-Gen. ROBERTO HERNÁNDEZ RAMÍREZ; 1,260 brs.

Banca Serfín, SA: Paseo de la Reforma 500, Mod. 409, 4°, Col. Lomas de Santa Fe, 01219 México, DF; tel. (55) 5259-8860; fax (55) 5257-8387; internet www.serfin.com.mx; f. 1864; merged with Banco Continental Ganadero in 1985; transferred to private ownership in Jan. 1992; acquired by Banco Santander Central Hispano (Spain) in Dec. 2000; cap. 6,616.0m., res 788.9m., dep. 92,363.6m. (Dec. 2002); CEO ADOLFO LAGO ESPINOSA; 554 brs.

Banco del Bajío, SA: Avda Manuel J. Clouthier 508, Col. Jardines del Campestre, 37128 León, Gto; tel. (477) 710-4600; fax (477) 710-4693; e-mail internacional@bajionet.com.mx; internet www.bajionet.com.mx; f. 1994; cap. 933.2m., res –41.3m., dep. 8,093.1m. (Dec. 2002); Gen. Man. CARLOS DE LA CERDA SERRANO.

Banco Mercantil del Norte, SA (BANORTE): Avda Morones Prieto 2312 Pte, 2°, Col Lomas de San Francisco, 64710 Monterrey, NL; tel. (81) 3319-7200; fax (81) 3319-5216; internet www.banorte.com; f. 1899; merged with Banco Regional del Norte in 1985; cap. 5,351.8m., res 1,332.8m., dep. 179,725.6m. (Dec. 2002); Chair. ROBERTO GONZÁLEZ BARRERA; 457 brs.

Banpaís, SNC: Paseo de la Reforma 359, Col. Cuauhtémoc, 06500 México, DF; tel. (55) 5208-2044; fax (55) 5533-1223; f. 1892 as Banco de Nuevo León, present name 1978; merged with Banco Latino in 1985; transferred to private ownership in 1991; cap. 636,000m. old pesos, res 28,000m. old pesos, dep. 8,390,000m. old pesos (Dec. 1992); Chair. Lic. CARLOS SALES GUTIÉRREZ; 160 brs.

HSBC México: Paseo de la Reforma 156, Col. Juarez, Cuauhtémoc, 06600 México, DF; tel. and fax (55) 5721-2222; fax (55) 5721-2626; f. 1941; bought by HSBC (UK) in 2002; name changed from Banco Internacional, SA (BITAL) in 2004; cap. 14,962.0m., res 662.1m., dep. 141,533.3m. (Dec. 2002); Gen. Man. and CEO SANDY FLOCKHART.

Scotiabank Inverlat, SA: Miguel Avila Camacho 1, 19°, Col. Lomas de Chapultepec, 11009 México, DF; tel. (55) 5229-2929; fax (55) 5229-2114; internet www.inverlat.com.mx; f. 1977 as Multibanco Comermex, SA; changed name to Banco Inverlat, SA 1995; 55% holding acquired by Scotiabank Group (Canada) and name changed as above 2001; cap. 2,8957.8m., res 1,240.1m., dep. 73,860.3m. (Dec. 2002); CEO ANATOL VON HANN; 371 brs.

Development Banks

Banco Nacional de Comercio Exterior, SNC (BANCOMEXT): Periférico Sur 433, Col. Jardines en la Montaña, 14210 México, DF; tel. (55) 5449-9020; fax (55) 5449-9028; internet www.bancomext.com; f. 1937; cap. 17,613.8m., res −10,524.2.3m., dep. 45,201.0m. (Dec. 2001); Man. Dir ENRIQUE VILATELA RIBA.

Banco Nacional de Crédito Rural, SNC (BANRURAL): Agrarismo 227, Col. Escandón, 11800 México, DF; tel. (55) 5273-1300; fax (55) 5584-2664; e-mail contacto@banrural.gob.mx; internet www.banrural.gob.mx; f. 1975; provides financing for agriculture and normal banking services; in liquidation March 2004; cap. 1,791,569m., res −155,439m. old pesos, dep. 623,402m. old pesos (Sept. 1992); Dir-Gen. ALFREDO GÓMEZ AGUIRRE; 187 brs.

Banco Nacional del Ejército, Fuerza Aérea y Armada, SNC (BANJERCITO): Avda Industria Militar 1055, 2°, Col. Lomas de Sotelo, 11200 México, DF; tel. (55) 5557-5728; fax (55) 5395-0909; internet www.banjercito.com.mx; f. 1947; cap. 11,035m. old pesos, res 1,780.7m. old pesos, dep. 139,184.5m. old pesos (Sept. 1990); Dir-Gen. Gral-Bgda FERNANDO MILLÁN VILLEGAS; 17 brs.

Banco Nacional de Obras y Servicios Públicos, SNC (BANOBRAS): Tecoyotitla 100, 3°, esq. Francia, Col. Florida, 01030 México, DF; tel. (55) 5723-6202; fax (55) 5723-6108; e-mail bneumann@banobras.gob.mx; internet www.banobras.gob.mx; f. 1933; govt-owned; cap. 8,176.4m., res 1,743.1m., dep. 118,041.0m. (Dec. 2001); Chair. Dr GUILLERMO ORITZ MARTINEZ.

BBVA Bancomer, SA: Centro Bancomer, Avda Universidad 1200, Col. Xoco, 03339 México, DF; tel. (55) 5621-3434; fax (55) 5621-3230; internet www.bancomer.com.mx; f. 2000 by merger of Bancomer (f. 1864) and Mexican operations of Banco Bilbao Vizcaya Argentaria (Spain); privatized 2002; cap. 67,283.2m., res −22,306.5m., dep. 358,537.3m. (Dec. 2002); Chair. EUGENIO GARZA LAGÜERA.

Nacional Financiera, SNC: Insurgentes Sur 1971, Torre IV, 13°, Col. Guadalupe Inn, 01020 México, DF; tel. (55) 5325-6700; fax (55) 5661-8418; e-mail info@nafin.gob.mx; internet www.nafin.com; f. 1934; Chair. JOSÉ ANGEL GURRIA TREVINO; Pres. CARLOS SALES GUTTIERREZ; 32 brs.

Foreign Bank

Dresdner Bank Mexico, SA: Bosque de Alisos 47B, 4°, Col. Bosques de las Lomas, 05120 México, DF; tel. (55) 5258-3000; fax (55) 5258-3100; e-mail Mexico@dbla.com; f. 1995; Man. Dir LUIS NIÑO DE RIVERA.

BANKERS' ASSOCIATION

Asociación de Banqueros de México: 16 de Setiembre 27, Col. Centro Histórico, 06000 México, DF; tel. (55) 5752-4305; internet www.abm.org.mx; f. 1928; fmrly Asociación Mexicano de Bancos; Pres. MANUEL MEDINA MORA; Dir-Gen. Lic. ADOLFO RIVAS MARTIN DEL CAMPO; 52 mems.

STOCK EXCHANGE

Bolsa Mexicana de Valores, SA de CV: Paseo de la Reforma 255, Col. Cuauhtémoc, 06500 México, DF; tel. (55) 5726-6600; fax (55) 5591-0642; e-mail cinforma@bmv.com.mx; internet www.bmv.com.mx; f. 1894; Pres. Lic. MANUEL ROBELDA GONZALES DE CASTILLA; Dir-Gen. Ing. GERARDO FLORES DEUCHLER.

INSURANCE

México, DF

ACE Seguros: Bosques de Alisos, 47-A, 1°, Col. Bosques de las Lomas, 5120 México, DF; tel. (5) 258-5800; fax (5) 258-5899; e-mail info@acelatinamerica.com; f. 1990; fmrly Seguros Cigna.

Aseguradora Cuauhtémoc, SA: Manuel Avila Camacho 164, 11570 México, DF; tel. (55) 5250-9800; fax (55) 5540-3204; f. 1944;

general; Exec. Pres. JUAN B. RIVEROLL; Dir-Gen. JAVIER COMPEÁN AMEZCUA.

Aseguradora Hidalgo, SA: Presidente Masarik 111, Col. Polanco, Del. Miguel Hidalgo, 11570 México, DF; f. 1931; life; Dir-Gen. JOSÉ GÓMEZ GORDOA; Man. Dir HUMBERTO ROQUE VILLANUEVA.

La Continental Seguros, SA: Francisco I. Madero, 1, 10°, 06007 México, DF; tel. (55) 5518-1670; fax (55) 5510-3259; f. 1936; general; Pres. Ing. TEODORO AMERLINCK Y ZIRIÓN; Vice-Pres. Ing. RODRIGO AMERLINCK Y ASSERETO.

ING Comercial América—Seguros: Insurgentes Sur 3900, Col. Tlalpan, 14000 México, DF; tel. (55) 5169-2500; internet www.comercialamerica.com.mx; f. 1936 as La Comercial; acquired by ING Group in 2000; life, etc.; Pres. GLENN HILLIARS; Dir-Gen. Ing. ADRIÁN PÁEZ.

La Nacional, Cía de Seguros, SA: México, DF; f. 1901; life, etc.; Pres. CLEMENTE CABELLO; Chair. Lic. ALBERTO BAILLERES.

Pan American de México, Cía de Seguros, SA: México, DF; f. 1940; Pres. Lic. JESS N. DALTON; Dir-Gen. GILBERTO ESCOBEDA PAZ.

Royal & SunAlliance Mexico: Blvd Adolfo López Mateos 2448, Col. Altavista, 01060 México, DF; tel. (55) 5723-7999; fax (55) 5723-7941; e-mail omar.antonio@mx.royalsun.com; internet www.royalsun.com.mx; f. 1941; acquired Seguros BBV-Proburta in 2001; general, except life.

Seguros América Banamex, SA: Avda Revolución 1508, Col. Guadalupe Inn, 01020 México, DF; f. 1933; Pres. AGUSTÍN F. LEGORRETA; Dir-Gen. JUAN OROZCO GÓMEZ PORTUGAL.

Seguros Azteca, SA: Insurgentes 102, México, DF; f. 1933; general including life; Pres. JUAN CAMPO RODRÍGUEZ.

Seguros Constitución, SA: Avda Revolución 2042, Col. La Otra Banda, 01090 México, DF; tel. (55) 5550-7910; f. 1937; life, accident; Pres. ISIDORO RODRÍGUEZ RUIZ; Dir-Gen. ALFONSO DE ORDUÑA Y PÉREZ.

Seguros el Fénix, SA: México, DF; f. 1937; Pres. VICTORIANO OLAZÁBAL E; Dir-Gen. JAIME MATUTE LABRADOR.

Seguros Internacional, SA: Abraham González 67, México, DF; f. 1945; general; Pres. Lic. GUSTAVO ROMERO KOLBECK.

Seguros de México, SA: Insurgentes Sur 3496, Col. Peña Pobre, 14060 México, DF; tel. (55) 5679-3855; f. 1957; life, etc.; Dir-Gen. Lic. ANTONIO MIJARES RICCI.

Seguros La Provincial, SA: México, DF; f. 1936; general; Pres. CLEMENTE CABELLO; Chair. ALBERTO BAILLERES.

Seguros La República, SA: Paseo de la Reforma 383, México, DF; f. 1966; general; 43% owned by Commercial Union (United Kingdom); Pres. LUCIANO ARECHEDERRA QUINTANA; Gen. Man. JUAN ANTONIO DE ARRIETA MENDIZÁBAL.

Guadalajara, Jal.

Nueva Galicia, Compañía de Seguros Generales, SA: Guadalajara, Jal.; f. 1946; fire; Pres. SALVADOR VEYTIA Y VEYTIA.

Monterrey, NL

Seguros Monterrey Aetna, SA: Avda Diagonal Sta Engracia 221 Ote, Col. Lomas de San Francisco, 64710 Monterrey, NL; tel. (81) 319-1111; fax (81) 363-0428; f. 1940; casualty, life, etc.; Dir-Gen. FEDERICO REYES GARCÍA.

Seguros Monterrey del Círculo Mercantil, SA, Sociedad General de Seguros: Padre Mier Pte 276, Monterrey, NL; f. 1941; life; Gen. Man. CARMEN G. MASSO DE NAVARRO.

Insurance Association

Asociación Mexicana de Instituciones de Seguros, AC: Fco I Madero 21, Col. Tlacopac San Angel, 01140 México, DF; tel. (55) 5662-6161; e-mail aglez@amis.com.mx; internet www.amis.com.mx; f. 1946; all insurance cos operating in Mexico are mems; Pres. JOSÉ LUIS LLAMOSAS PORTILLA; Dir-Gen. RECAREDO ARIAS JIMÉNEZ.

Trade and Industry

GOVERNMENT AGENCIES

Comisión Nacional Forestal (CONAFOR): Carretera a Nogales s/n, Esq. Periférico Pte. 5°, San Juan de Ocotán, 45019 Zapopan, Jal.; tel. (33) 3777-7077; fax (33) 3110-0820; e-mail transparencia@conafor.gob.mx; internet www.conafor.gob.mx; f. 2001; Supt Ing. RAFAEL ORDOÑEZ VILLAGRÁN.

Comisión Nacional de Precios: Avda Juárez 101, 17°, México 1, DF; tel. (55) 510-0436; f. 1977; national prices commission; Dir-Gen. JESÚS SÁNCHEZ JIMÉNEZ.

Comisión Nacional de los Salarios Mínimos (CNSM): Avda Cuauhtémoc 14, 2°, Col. Doctores, 06720 México 7, DF; tel. (55) 5761-5778; fax (55) 5578-5775; internet www.consami.gob.mx; f. 1962, in accordance with Section VI of Article 123 of the Constitution; national commission on minimum salaries; Pres. Lic. BASILIO GONZÁLEZ-NUÑEZ; Tech. Dir ALIDA BERNAL COSIO.

Consejo Mexicano de Comercio Exterior (CONCE): Eugenio Sue 94, Polanco, 11560 México, DF; tel. (52) 5281-0595; e-mail comce@comce.org.mx; internet www.comce.org.mx; f. 1999 to promote international trade; Chair. FEDERICO SADA GONZÁLEZ.

Consejo Nacional de Comercio Exterior, AC (CONACEX): Avda Parque Fundidora 501, Of. 95E, Edif. CINTERMEX, Col. Obrera, 64010 Monterrey, NL; tel. (81) 369-0284; fax (81) 369-0293; e-mail conacex@technet.net.mx; internet www.technet.net.mx/conacex; f. 1962 to promote national exports; Chair. Ing. JAVIER PRIETO DE LA FUENTE; Pres. Lic. JUAN MANUEL QUIROGA LAM.

Consejo de Recursos Minerales: Felipe Angeles s/n Carr. México-Pachuca, km 93.5, Col. Venta Prieta, 42080 Pachuca, HI; tel. (771) 771-4016; fax (771) 771-3252; e-mail geoinfo@coremisgm.gob.mx; internet www.coremisgm.gob.mx; f. 1957; govt agency for the devt of mineral resources; Dir-Gen. Ing. FRANCISCO JOSÉ ESCANDÓN VALLE.

Instituto Nacional del Consumidor: Insurgentes Sur 1228, 10°, Col. del Valle Tlacoquemecatl, 03210 México, DF; tel. (55) 5559-2478; fax (55) 5559-0123; f. 1976; national institute for consumer protection; Dir-Gen. MARGARITA ORTEGA VILLA.

Instituto Nacional de Investigaciones Nucleares (ININ): Centro Nuclear de México, Km 36.5, Carreterra México–Toluca, 52045 Ocoyoacac, Méx.; tel. (55) 5329-7219; fax (55) 5329-7298; e-mail osg@nuclear.inin.mx; internet www.inin.mx; f. 1979 to plan research and devt of nuclear science and technology, as well as the peaceful uses of nuclear energy, for the social, scientific and technological devt of the country; administers the Secondary Standard Dosimetry Laboratory, the Nuclear Information and Documentation Centre, which serves Mexico's entire scientific community; the 1 MW research reactor which came into operation, in 1967, supplies part of Mexico's requirements for radioactive isotopes; also operates a 12 MV Tandem van de Graaff. Mexico has two nuclear reactors, each with a generating capacity of 654 MW; the first, at Laguna Verde, became operational in 1989 and is administered by the Comisión Federal de Electricidad (CFE); Dir-Gen. M. EN C. JOSÉ RAÚL ORTÍZ MAGAÑA.

Instituto Nacional de Pesca (National Fishery Institute): Pitágoras 1320, Col. Sta Cruz Atoyac, 03310 México, DF; tel. (55) 5688-1469; fax (55) 5604-9169; e-mail compean@inp.semarnat.gob.mx; internet http://inp.semarnat.gob.mx/; f. 1962; Dir GUILLERMO COMPEAN JIMÉNEZ.

Procuraduría Federal del Consumidor: Dr Carmona y Valle 11, Col. Doctores, 06720 México, DF; tel. (55) 5761-3021; f. 1975; consumer protection; Dir IGNACIO PICHARDO PAGAZA.

DEVELOPMENT ORGANIZATIONS

Comisión Coordinadora de la Industria Siderúrgica: México, DF; f. 1972; co-ordinating commission for the devt of the iron and steel industries; Dir-Gen. Lic. ALFREDO ADE TOMASINI.

Comisión Nacional de las Zonas Aridas: Blvd Venustiano Carranza 1623, Col. República, 25280 Saltillo, Coah.; tel. 01844-416000 ext. 36; e-mail uenlace@conaza.gob.mx; internet www.conaza.gob.mx; f. 1970; commission to co-ordinate the devt and use of arid areas; Dir-Gen. Ing. MANUEL AGUSTÍN REED SEGOVIA.

Fideicomiso de Fomento Mineiro (FIFOMI): Puente de Tecamachalco 26, 2°, Col. Lomas de Chapultepec, 11000 México, DF; tel. (55) 5202-0968; e-mail nroque@fifomi.gob.mx; internet www.fomentomineiro.gob.mx; trust for the development of the mineral industries; Dir-Gen. NORBERTO DE JESÚS ROQUE DÍAZ DE LEÓN.

Fideicomisos Instituídos en Relación con la Agricultura (FIRA): México, DF; tel. (55) 5550-7011; internet www.fira.gob.mx; Dir Ing. ANTONIO BACA DÍAZ; a group of devt funds to aid agricultural financing, under the Banco de México, comprising:

   Fondo de Garantía y Fomento para la Agricultura, Ganadería y Avicultura (FOGAGA): f. 1954.

   Fondo Especial para Financiamientos Agropecuarios (FEFA): f. 1965.

   Fondo Especial de Asistencia Técnica y Garantía para Créditos Agropecuarios (FEGA): f. 1972.

Instituto Mexicano del Petróleo (IMP): Avda Eje Central Lázaro Cárdenas 152, Apdo 14-805, 07730 México, DF; tel. (55) 5567-6600; fax (55) 5567-6047; internet www.imp.mx; f. 1965 to foster devt of the petroleum, chemical and petrochemical industries; Dir GUSTAVO CHAPELA CASTAÑARES.

CHAMBERS OF COMMERCE

Confederación de Cámaras Nacionales de Comercio, Servicios y Turismo (CONCANACO) (Confederation of National Chambers of Commerce): Balderas 144, 3°, Col. Centro, 06079 México, DF; tel. (55) 5772-9300; fax (55) 5709-1152; internet www.concanacored.com; f. 1917; Pres. RAÚL ALEJANDRO PADILLA OROZCO; Dir-Gen. Lic. CARLOS MORA ÁLVAREZ; comprises 283 regional Chambers.

Cámara de Comercio, Servicios y Turismo Ciudad de México (CANACO) (Chamber of Commerce, Services and Tourism of Mexico City): Paseo de la Reforma 42, 3°, Col. Centro, Apdo 32005, 06048 México, DF; tel. (55) 5592-2677; fax (55) 5592-2279; internet www.ccmexico.com.mx; f. 1874; 50,000 mems; Dir-Gen. Lic. EDUARDO GARCÍA VILLASEÑOR.

Cámara Nacional de la Industria de Transformación (CANACINTRA): Avda San Antonio 256, Col. Ampliación Nápoles, México, DF; tel. (55) 5482-3000; internet webmaster@canacintra.org.mx; internet www.canacintra.org.mx; represents majority of smaller manufacturing businesses; Pres. YEIDCKOL POLEVNSKY GURWITZ.

Chambers of Commerce exist in the chief town of each state as well as in the larger centres of commercial activity.

CHAMBERS OF INDUSTRY

The 64 Industrial Chambers and 32 Associations, many of which are located in the Federal District, are representative of the major industries of the country.

Central Confederation

Confederación de Cámaras Industriales de los Estados Unidos Mexicanos (CONCAMIN) (Confed. of Industrial Chambers): Manuel María Contreras 133, 8°, Col. Cuauhtémoc, 06500 México, DF; tel. (55) 5566-7822; fax (55) 5535-6871; e-mail cetin@solar.sar.net; internet www.concamin.org.mx; f. 1918; represents and promotes the activities of the entire industrial sector; Pres. ALEJANDRO MARTÍNEZ GALLARDO; Dir-Gen. RENÉ ESPINOSA Y TORRES ESTRADA.

INDUSTRIAL AND TRADE ASSOCIATIONS

Asociación Nacional de Importadores y Exportadores de la República Mexicana (ANIERM) (National Association of Importers and Exporters): Monterrey 130, Col. Roma-Cuauhtémoc, 06700 México, DF; tel. (55) 5564-8618; fax (55) 5584-5317; f. 1944; Pres. RODRIGO GUERRA B.; Vice-Pres. Lic. HUMBERTO SIMONEEN ARDILA.

Azúcar, SA de CV: Insurgentes Sur 1079, Col. Nochebuena, 03910 México, DF; tel. (5) 563-7100; f. 1983 to develop the sugar industry; Dir Ing. EDUARDO A. MACGREGOR BELTRÁN.

Comisión de Fomento Minero: Puente de Tecamachalco 26, Lomas de Chapultepec, 11000 México, DF; tel. (55) 5540-2906; f. 1934 to promote the devt of the mining sector; Dir Lic. LUIS DE PABLO SERNA.

Comisión Nacional del Cacao (Conadeca): México, DF; tel. (55) 5286-9495; f. 1973 to promote the cultivation, industrialization and the marketing of cocoa; Dir-Gen. Lic. JULIO DERBEZ DEL PINO.

Comisión Nacional de Fruticultura (Conafrut): Querétaro, Qro; tel. (463) 570-2499; f. 1961 to develop the production, industrialization and marketing of fruits; Dir Lic. FRANCISCO MERINO RÁBAGO.

Comisión Nacional de Inversiones Extranjeras: Blvd Avila Camacho 1, 11°, 11000 México, DF; tel. (55) 5540-1426; fax (55) 5286-1551; f. 1973; commission to co-ordinate foreign investment; Exec. Sec. Dr CARLOS CAMACHO GAOS.

Comisión Nacional de Seguridad Nuclear y Salvaguardias (CNSNS): Dr Barragán 779, Col. Narvarte, 03020 México, DF; tel. (55) 5095-3240; fax (55) 095-3295; e-mail swaller@cnsns.gob.mx; f. 1979; nuclear regulatory agency; Dir-Gen. JUAN EIBENSCHUTZ HARTMAN.

Comisión Petroquímica Mexicana: México, DF; to promote the devt of the petrochemical industry; Tech. Sec. Ing. JUAN ANTONIO BARGÉS MESTRES.

Compañía Nacional de Subsistencias Populares (CONASUPO): Avda Insurgentes Sur 489, 4°, Col. Hipódromo Condesa, 06100 México, DF; tel. (55) 5272-0472; fax (55) 5272-0607; f. 1965 to protect the income of small farmers, improve the marketing of basic farm commodities and supervise the operation of rural co-operative stores; Dir Lic. JAVIER BONILLA GARCÍA.

Consejo Empresarial Mexicano para Asuntos Internacionales (CEMAI): Homero 517, 7°, Col. Polanco, 11570 México, DF; tel. (55) 5250-7033; fax (55) 5531-1590.

Consejo Mexicano del Café: Lope de Vega 125, 1°, Col. Chapultepec Morales, 115700 México, DF; tel. and fax (55) 5254-2334; e-mail cmc@sagar.gob.mx; internet www.sagarpa.gob.mx/cmc.

Fondo de Operación y Financiamiento Bancario a la Vivienda: Ejército Nacional 180, 7°, 8° y 11°, Col. Anzures, 11590 México, DF; tel. (55) 5255-4199; fax (55) 5203-7304; f. 1963 to promote the construction of low-cost housing through savings and credit schemes; devt fund under the Banco de México; Dir-Gen. Lic. MANUEL ZEPEDA PAYERAS.

Instituto del Fondo Nacional de la Vivienda para los Trabajadores (INFONAVIT): Barranca del Muerto 280, 4°, Col. Guadalupe Inn., Del. Alvaro Obregón, 01029 México, DF; tel. (55) 5660-2423; f. 1972 to finance the construction of low-cost housing for the working classes; Dir JOSÉ JUAN DE OLLOQUI Y LABASTIDA.

Instituto Mexicano del Café (Inmecafé): Carretera Jalapa-Veracruz km 4, Campo Experimental Garnica, Jalapa, Ver.; tel. (55) 5250-5543; f. 1958; sponsors cultivation to increase domestic and foreign sales of coffee; Dir-Gen. JESÚS SALAZAR TOLEDANO.

Instituto Nacional de Investigaciones Forestales y Agropecuarios (INIFAP) (National Forestry and Agricultural Research Institute): Apdo 6-882, 06600 México, DF; tel. (55) 5687-7451; f. 1985; conducts research into plant genetics, management of species and conservation; Exec. Dir Dr MANUEL R. VILLA ISSA.

Tabacos Mexicanos, SA de CV (TABAMEX): México, DF; tel. (55) 5395-5477; fax (55) 5395-6836; f. 1972 to foster the cultivation, industrialization and marketing of tobacco; Dir-Gen. GUSTAVO CARVAJAL MORENO.

EMPLOYERS' ORGANIZATIONS

Consejo Coordinador Empresarial (CCE): Paseo de la Reforma 255, 11°, Col. Cuauhtémoc, 06500 México, DF; tel. (55) 592-3910; fax (55) 592-3857; internet www.cce.org.mx; f. 1974; co-ordinating body of private sector; Pres. LUIS GERMÁN CÁRCOBA; Dir FRANCISCO CALDERÓN.

Consejo Mexicano de Hombres de Negocios (CMHN): México, DF; represents leading businesspeople; affiliated to CCE (q.v.); Pres. EUGENIO CLARIOND REYES.

STATE HYDROCARBONS COMPANY

Petróleos Mexicanos (PEMEX): Avda Marina Nacional 329, 44°, Col. Huasteca, 11300 México, DF; tel. (55) 5254-2044; fax (55) 5531-6354; internet www.pemex.com; f. 1938; govt agency for the exploitation of Mexico's petroleum and natural gas resources; Dir-Gen. RAÚL MUÑOZ LEOS; 106,900 employees.

UTILITIES

Regulatory Authorities

Comisión Nacional del Agua: Avda Insurgentes Sur 2140, 2°, Col. Chimalistac, Del. Alvaro Obregón, 01070 México, DF; tel. (55) 5661-3806; e-mail webmaster@cna.gob.mx; internet www.cna.gob.mx; commission to administer national water resources; Dir CRISTOBAL JAIME JAQUEZ.

Comisión Reguladora de Energía: Horacio 1750, Col. Los Morales, 11510 México, DF; tel. (55) 5283-1500; internet www.cre.gob.mx; f. 1994; commission to control energy policy and planning; Pres. DIONISIO PÉREZ-JÁCOME.

Secretariat of State for Energy: see section on The Government (Secretariats of State).

Electricity

Comisión Federal de Electricidad (CFE): Río Ródano 14, 7°, Col. Cuauhtémoc, 06598 México, DF; tel. (55) 5207-3704; fax (55) 5553-6424; internet www.cfe.gob.mx; state-owned power utility; Dir-Gen. ALFREDO ELÍAS AYUB.

Luz y Fuerza del Centro: Melchor Ocampo 171, 7°, Col. Tlaxpana, 11379 México, DF; tel. (55) 629-7100; fax (55) 5518-0083; internet www.lfc.gob.mx; operates electricity network in the centre of the country; Dir-Gen. ALFONSO CASO AGUILAR.

Gas

Gas Natural México (GNM): Monterrey, NL; internet www.gasnaturalmexico.com.mx; f. 1994; distributes natural gas in the states of Tamaulipas, Aguascalientes, Coahuila, San Luis Potosí, Guanajuato, Nuevo León and México and the in Distrito Federal; subsidiary of Spanish co Gas Natural.

Petróleos Mexicanos (PEMEX): see State Hydrocarbons Company, above: distributes natural gas.

TRADE UNIONS

Congreso del Trabajo (CT): Avda Ricardo Flores Magón 44, Col. Guerrero, 06300 México 37, DF; tel. (55) 5583-3817; f. 1966; trade union congress comprising trade union federations, confederations, etc.; Pres. Lic. HÉCTOR VALDÉS ROMO.

Confederación Regional Obrera Mexicana (CROM) (Regional Confederation of Mexican Workers): República de Cuba 60, México, DF; f. 1918; Sec.-Gen. IGNACIO CUAUHTÉMOC PALETA; 120,000 mems, 900 affiliated syndicates.

Confederación Revolucionaria de Obreros y Campesinos (CROC) (Revolutionary Confederation of Workers and Farmers): Hamburgo 250, Col. Juárez, 06600 México, DF; f. 1952; Sec.-Gen. ALBERTO JUÁREZ BLANCAS; 120,000 mems in 22 state federations and 8 national unions.

Confederación Revolucionaria de Trabajadores (CRT) (Revolutionary Confederation of Workers): Dr Jiménez 218, Col. Doctores, México, DF; f. 1954; Sec.-Gen. MARIO SUÁREZ GARCÍA; 10,000 mems; 10 federations and 192 syndicates.

Confederación de Trabajadores de México (CTM) (Confederation of Mexican Workers): Vallarta 8, México, DF; f. 1936; admitted to ICFTU; Sec.-Gen. LEONARDO RODRÍGUEZ ALCAINE; 5.5m. mems.

Federación Obrera de Organizaciones Femeniles (FOOF) (Workers' Federation of Women's Organizations): Vallarta 8, México, DF; f. 1950; women workers' union within CTM; Sec.-Gen. HILDA ANDERSON NEVÁREZ; 400,000 mems.

Federación Nacional de Sindicatos Independientes (National Federation of Independent Trade Unions): Isaac Garza 311 Ote, 64000 Monterrey, NL; tel. (8) 375-6677; internet www.fnsi.org.mx; f. 1936; Sec.-Gen. JACINTO PADILLA VALDEZ; 230,000 mems.

Federación de Sindicatos de Trabajadores al Servicio del Estado (FSTSE) (Federation of Unions of Government Workers): Gómez Farías 40, Col. San Rafael, 06470 México, DF; f. 1938; Sec.-Gen. Lic. JOEL AYALA; 2.5m. mems; 80 unions.

Frente Unida Sindical por la Defensa de los Trabajadores y la Constitución (United Union Front in Defence of the Workers and the Constitution): f. 1990 by more than 120 trade orgs to support the implementation of workers' constitutional rights.

Unión General de Obreros y Campesinos de México, Jacinto López (UGOCM-JL) (General Union of Workers and Farmers of Mexico, Jacinto López): José María Marroquí 8, 2°, 06050 México, DF; tel. (55) 5518-3015; f. 1949; admitted to WFTU/CSTAL; Sec.-Gen. JOSÉ LUIS GONZÁLEZ AGUILERA; 7,500 mems, over 2,500 syndicates.

Unión Nacional de Trabajadores (UNT) (National Union of Workers): México, DF; internet www.unt.org.mx; f. 1998; Leader FRANCISCO HERNÁNDEZ JUÁREZ.

A number of major unions are non-affiliated; they include:

Frente Auténtico de los Trabajadores (FAT).

Pacto de Unidad Sindical Solidaridad (PAUSS): comprises 10 independent trade unions.

Sindicato Nacional de Trabajadores Mineros, Metalúrgicos y Similares de la República Mexicana (Industrial Union of Mine, Metallurgical and Related Workers of the Republic of Mexico): Avda Dr Vertiz 668, Col. Narvarte, 03020 México, DF; tel. (55) 5519-5690; f. 1933; Sec.-Gen. NAPOLEON GÓMEZ URRUTIA; 86,000 mems.

Sindicato Nacional de Trabajadores de la Educación (SNTE): Venezuela 44, Col. Centro, México, DF; tel. (55) 5702-0005; fax (55) 5702-6303; teachers' union; Pres. ELBA ESTHER GORDILLO MORALES; Sec.-Gen. TOMÁS VÁZQUEZ VIGIL; 1.2m. mems.

Coordinadora Nacional de Trabajadores de la Educación (CNTE): dissident faction; Leader TEODORO PALOMINO.

Sindicato de Trabajadores Petroleros de la República Mexicana (STPRM) (Union of Petroleum Workers of the Republic of Mexico): Zaragoza 15, Col. Guerrero, 06300 México, DF; tel. (55) 5546-0912; close links with PEMEX; Sec.-Gen. CARLOS ROMERO DESCHAMPS; 110,000 mems; includes:

Movimiento Nacional Petrolero: reformist faction; Leader HEBRAÍCAZ VÁSQUEZ.

Sindicato de Trabajadores Ferrocarrileros de la República Mexicana (STFRM) (Union of Railroad Workers of the Republic of Mexico): Avda Ricardo Flores Magón 206, Col. Guerrero, México 3, DF; tel. (55) 5597-1011; f. 1933; Sec.-Gen. VÍCTOR F. FLORES MORALES; 100,000 mems.

Sindicato Unico de Trabajadores Electricistas de la República Mexicana (SUTERM) (Sole Union of Electricity Workers of the Republic of Mexico): Río Guadalquivir 106, Col. Cuauhtémoc, 06500 México, DF; tel. (55) 5207-0578; Sec.-Gen. LEONARDO RODRÍGUEZ ALCAINE.

Sindicato Unico de Trabajadores de la Industria Nuclear (SUTIN): Viaducto Río Becerra 139, Col. Nápoles, 03810 México, DF; tel. (55) 5523-8048; fax (55) 5687-6353; e-mail sutin@nuclear

.inin.mx; internet www.prodigyweb.net.mx/sutin; Sec.-Gen. RICARDO FLORES BELLO.

Unión Obrera Independiente (UOI): non-aligned.

The major agricultural unions are:

Central Campesina Independiente: Dr E. González Martínez 101, México, DF; Leader ALFONSO GARZÓN SANTIBÁÑEZ.

Confederación Nacional Campesina (CNC): Mariano Azuela 121, Col. Santa María de la Ribera, México, DF; Sec.-Gen. Lic. BEATRIZ PAREDES RANGEL.

Confederación Nacional Ganadera: Calzada Mariano Escobedo 714, Col. Anzures, México, DF; tel. (55) 5203-3506; Pres. Ing. CÉSAR GONZÁLEZ QUIROGA; 300,000 mems.

Consejo Agrarista Mexicano: México, DF; Sec.-Gen. HUMBERTO SERRANO.

Unión Nacional de Trabajadores Agriculturas (UNTA).

Transport

Road transport accounts for about 98% of all public passenger traffic and for about 80% of freight traffic. Mexico's terrain is difficult for overland travel. As a result, there has been an expansion of air transport and there were 83 international and national airports, plus 2,418 landing fields and feeder airports, in 1992. In 2002 plans to build a new airport in the capital were postponed after conflict over the proposed site. International flights are provided by a large number of national and foreign airlines. Mexico has 140 seaports, 29 river docks and a further 29 lake shelters. More than 85% of Mexico's foreign trade is conducted through maritime transport. In the 1980s the Government developed the main industrial ports of Tampico, Coatzacoalcos, Lázaro Cárdenas, Altamira, Laguna de Ostión and Salina Cruz in an attempt to redirect growth and to facilitate exports. The port at Dos Bocas, on the Gulf of Mexico, was one of the largest in Latin America when it opened in 1999. A 300-km railway link across the isthmus of Tehuantepec connects the Caribbean port of Coatzacoalcos with the Pacific port of Salina Cruz.

In 1992, as part of an ambitious divestment programme, the Government announced that concessions would be offered for sale to the private sector, in 1993, to operate nine ports and 61 of the country's airports. The national ports authority was to be disbanded, responsibility for each port being transferred to Administraciones Portuarias Integrales (APIs). In 1998 plans were announced for public share offerings in 35 airports. From 1997 the national railway system underwent privatization granted under 50-year concessions.

Secretariat of State for Communications and Transport: see section on The Government (Secretariats of State).

Aeropuertos y Servicios Auxiliares (ASA): Avda 602 N°.161, Col. San Juan de Aragón, Del. V. Carranza, 15620 México, DF; tel. (55) 5786-9526; fax (55) 5786-9709; internet www.asa.gob.mx; Dir-Gen. ERNESTO VALESCO LEÓN.

Caminos y Puentes Federales (CAPUFE): e-mail contacto@ capufe.gob.mx; internet www.capufe.gob.mx; Dir-Gen. MANUEL ZUBIRIA MAQUEO.

STATE RAILWAYS

In 2002 there were 26,690 km of main line track. In 2001 the railway system carried an estimated 242,000 passengers and 47,336m. freight ton-km. Ferrocarriles Nacionales de México (FNM), government-owned since 1937, was liquidated in 2001 following a process of restructuring and privatization. In July 2003 plans were announced for the construction of suburban train system for the Valle de México.

Ferrocarril del Noreste: Avda Manuel L. Barragán 4850, Col. Hidalgo, 64281 Monterrey, NL; tel. (81) 8305-7931; fax (81) 8305-7766; e-mail tfm@tfm.com.mx; internet www.tfm.com.mx; concession awarded to Transportación Ferroviaria Mexicana (TFM) in 1997; 4,251 km of line, linking Mexico City with the ports of Lázaro Cárdenas, Veracruz, Tampico, Altamira and Matamoros and the US border at Nuevo Laredo; Dir-Gen. M. MOHAR.

Ferrocarril Pacifico-Norte: Avda Baja California 200, Col. Roma Sur, 06760 México, DF; internet www.ferromex.com.mx; 50-year concession awarded to Grupo Ferroviario Mexicano, SA, (GFM) commencing in 1998; owned by Grupo México, SA de CV; operates through wholly-owned subsidiary Ferrocarril Mexicano, SA de CV (FERROMEX); 7,500 km of track and Mexico's largest rail fleet; Dir of Operations Ing. LORENZO REYES RETANA.

Ferrocarril del Sureste (Ferrosur): Jaime Balmes 11, 4°, Col. Los Morales Polanco, 11510 México, DF; tel. (55) 5387-6500; fax (55) 5387-6533; 50-year concession awarded to Grupo Tribasa in 1998; 66.7% sold to Empresas Frisco, SA de CV, in 1999, owned by Grupos Carso, SA de CV; Dir GUILLERMO MUÑOZ LARA.

Servicio de Transportes Eléctricos del Distrito Federal (STE): Avda Municipio Libre 402, Col. San Andrés Tetepilco, México, DF; tel. (55) 5539-6500; fax (55) 5672-4758; e-mail infoste@ df.gob.mx; internet www.ste.df.gob.mx; suburban tram route with 17 stops upgraded to light rail standard to act as a feeder to the metro; also operates bus and trolleybus networks; Dir-Gen. Dra FLORENCIA SERRANIA SOTO.

Sistema de Transporte Colectivo (Metro): Delicias 67, 06070 México, DF; tel. (55) 5709-1133; fax (55) 5512-3601; internet www .metro.df.gob.mx; f. 1967; the first stage of a combined underground and surface railway system in Mexico City was opened in 1969; 10 lines, covering 158 km, were operating, in 1998, and five new lines, bringing the total distance to 315 km, are to be completed by 2010; the system is wholly state-owned and the fares are partially subsidized; Dir-Gen. Dr JAVIER GONZÁLEZ GARZA.

ROADS

In 2002 there were an estimated 340,937 km of roads, of which 33% were paved. The construction of some 4,000 km of new four-lane toll highways, through the granting of govt concessions to the private sector, was undertaken during 1989–93. In mid-1997 the Govt announced that it would repurchase almost one-half of the road concessions granted in an attempt to stimulate road construction.

Long-distance buses form one of the principal methods of transport in Mexico, and there are some 600 lines operating services throughout the country.

Dirección General de Autotransporte Federal: Calzada de las Bombas 411, 11°, Col. San Bartolo Coapa, 04800 México, DF; tel. (55) 5684-0757; co-ordinates long distance bus services.

SHIPPING

At the end of 2002 Mexico's registered merchant fleet numbered 658 vessels, with a total displacement of 937,231 grt. The Government operates the facilities of seaports. In 1989–94 US $700m. was spent on port development, much of it from the private sector. In 1994–95 management of several ports were transferred to the private sector.

Coordinación General de Puertos y Marina Mercante (CGPMM): Avda Nuevo León 210, Col. Hipódromo, 06100 México, DF03310 México, DF; tel. (55) 5723-9300; e-mail cgpmmweb@sct.gob .mx; Dir CÉSAR PATRICIO REYES ROEL.

Port of Acapulco: Puertos Mexicanos, Malecón Fiscal s/n, Acapulco, Gro.; tel. (744) 22067; fax (744) 31648; Harbour Master Capt. RENÉ F. NOVALES BETANZOS.

Port of Coatzacoalcos: Administración Portuaria Integral de Coatzacoalcos, SA de CV, Interior recinto portuario s/n Coatzacoalcos, 96400 Ver.; tel. (921) 214-6744; fax (921) 214-6758; e-mail apicoa@apicoatza.com; internet www.apicoatza.com; Dir-Gen. Ing. GILBERTO ANTÓNIO RIOS RUÍZ.

Port of Dos Bocas: Administración Portuaria Integral de Dos Bocas, SA de CV, Carretera Federal Puerto Ceiba-Paraíso 414, Col. Quintín Arzuz Paraíso, 86600 Tabasco, Tab.; tel. (933) 353-2744; e-mail dosbocas@apidosbocas.com; internet www.apidosbocas.com.

Port of Manzanillo: Administración Portuaria Integral de Manzanillo, SA de CV, Avda Tte Azueta 9, Col. Burócrata, 28250 Manzanillo, Col.; tel. (314) 331–1400; fax (314) 332–1005; e-mail comercializacion@apimanzanillo.com.mx; internet www .apimanzanillo.com.mx; Dir-Gen. Capt. HÉCTOR MORA GÓMEZ.

Port of Tampico: Administración Portuaria Integral de Tampico, SA de CV, Edif. API de Tampico, 1°, Recinto Portuario, 89000 Tampico, Tamps.; tel. (833) 212-4660; fax (833) 212-5744; e-mail apitam@puertodetampico.com.mx; internet www.puertodetampico .com.mx; Gen. Dir Ing. RAFAEL MESEGUER LIMA.

Port of Veracruz: Administración Porturia Integral de Veracruz, SA de CV, Marina Mercante 210, 7°, 91700 Veracruz, Ver.; tel. (229) 32-1319; fax (229) 32-3040; e-mail portverc@infosel.net.mx; internet apiver.com; privatized in 1994; Port Dir JUAN JOSÉ SÁNCHEZ ESQUEDA.

Petróleos Mexicanos (PEMEX): Edif. 1917, 2°, Avda Marina Nacional 329, 44°, Col. Anáhuac, 11300 México, DF; tel. (55) 5531-6053; Dir-Gen. J. R. MOCTEZUMA.

Transportación Marítima Mexicana, SA de CV: Avda de la Cúspide 4755, Col. Parques del Pedregal, Del. Tlalpan, 14010 México, DF; tel. (55) 5652-4111; fax (55) 5665-3566; internet www .tmm.com.mx; f. 1955; cargo services to Europe, the Mediterranean, Scandinavia, the USA, South and Central America, the Caribbean and the Far East; Pres. JUAN CARLOS MERODIO; Dir-Gen. JAVIER SEGOVIA.

CIVIL AVIATION

There were 57 international airports in Mexico in 2002.

Aerocalifornia: Aquiles Serdán 1955, 23000 La Paz, BCS; tel. (612) 26655; fax (612) 53993; e-mail aeroll@aerocalifornia.uabcs.mx; f.

1960; regional carrier with scheduled passenger and cargo services in Mexico and the USA; Chair. PAUL A. ARECHIGA.

Aerocancún: Edif. Oasis 29, Avda Kukulcan, esq. Cenzontle, Zona Hotelera, 77500 Cancún, Q. Roo; tel. (988) 32475; fax (988) 32558; charter services to the USA, South America, the Caribbean and Europe; Dir-Gen. JAVIER MARANON.

Aerocaribe: Aeropuerto Internacional, Zona Hangares, 97291 Mérida, Yuc.; tel. (999) 46-1307; fax (999) 46-1330; e-mail qamsc@mail.interaccess.mx.com; internet www.aerocaribe.com; f. 1975; operates a network of domestic passenger flights from Cancún and Mérida; subsidiary of Mexicana; Pres. JAIME VALENZUELA TAMARIZ.

Aerocozumel: Aeropuerto Internacional, Apdo 322, Cozumel, 77600 Q. Roo; tel. (987) 23456; fax (987) 20877; f. 1978; charter airline; subsidiary of Mexicana; Dir JAIME VALENZUELA TAMARIZ.

Aeromar, Transportes Aeromar: Aeropuerto Internacional, Zona E, Hangar 7, 15620 México, DF; tel. (55) 5756-0282; fax (55) 5756-0174; e-mail web.aeromar@aeromar.com.mx; internet www.aeromar.com.mx; f. 1987; scheduled domestic passenger and cargo services; Dir-Gen. JUAN I. STETA.

Aerovías de México (Aeroméxico): Paseo de la Reforma 445, 3°, Torre B, Col. Cuauhtémoc, 06500 México, DF; tel. (55) 5133-4000; fax (55) 5133-4619; internet www.aeromexico.com; f. 1934 as Aeronaves de México, nationalized 1959; fmrly Aeroméxico until 1988, when, following bankruptcy, the Govt sold a 75% stake to private investors and a 25% stake to the Asociación Sindical de Pilotos de México; services between most principal cities of Mexico and the USA, Brazil, Peru, France and Spain; CEO ARTURO BARAHONA; Pres. and Chair. ALFONSO PASQUEL.

Mexicana (Compañía Mexicana de Aviación, SA de CV): Xola 535, 30°, Col. del Valle, Apdo 12813, 03100 México, DF; tel. (55) 5448-3000; tel. 01771247; fax (55) 5687-8786; e-mail dirgenmx@mexicana.com.mx; internet www.mexicana.com; f. 1921; operated as private co, until July 1982, when the Govt took a 58% stake; in 1989 it was returned to private ownership; international services between Mexico City and the USA, Central America and the Caribbean; domestic services; Pres. and CEO FERNANDO P. FLORES.

Tourism

Tourism remains one of Mexico's principal sources of foreign exchange. Mexico received an estimated 19.7m. foreign visitors in 2002, and receipts from tourists in that year were estimated at US $8,858m. More than 90% of visitors come from the USA and Canada. The country is famous for volcanoes, coastal scenery and the great Sierra Nevada (Sierra Madre) mountain range. The relics of the Mayan and Aztec civilizations and of Spanish Colonial Mexico are of historic and artistic interest. Zihuatanejo, on the Pacific coast, and Cancún, on the Caribbean, were developed as tourist resorts by the Government. In 1998 there were 392,402 hotel rooms in Mexico. The government tourism agency, FONATUR, encourages the renovation and expansion of old hotels and provides attractive incentives for the industry. FONATUR is also the main developer of major resorts in Mexico.

Secretariat of State for Tourism: see section on The Government (Secretariats of State).

Fondo Nacional de Fomento al Turismo (FONATUR): Insurgentes Sur 800, 17°, Col. del Valle, 03100 México, DF; tel. (55) 5448-4200; internet www.fonatur.gob.mx; f. 1956 to finance and promote the devt of tourism; Dir Lic. JOHN MCCARTHY.

THE FEDERATED STATES OF MICRONESIA

Introductory Survey

Location, Climate, Language, Religion, Flag, Capital

The Federated States of Micronesia forms (with Palau, q.v.) the archipelago of the Caroline Islands, about 800 km east of the Philippines. The Federated States of Micronesia comprises 607 islands and includes (from west to east) the states of Yap, Chuuk (formerly Truk), Pohnpei (formerly Ponape) and Kosrae. The islands are subject to heavy rainfall, although precipitation decreases from east to west. January, February and March are the driest months, although seasonal variations in rainfall and temperature are generally small. Average annual temperature is 27°C (81°F). The native population consists of various ethno-linguistic groups, but English is widely understood. The principal religion is Christianity, much of the population being Roman Catholic. The national flag (proportions 10 by 19) consists of four five-pointed white stars, arranged as a circle, situated centrally on a light blue field. The capital is Kolonia, on Pohnpei.

Recent History

The Federated States of Micronesia was formerly part of the US-administered Trust Territory of the Pacific Islands (for history up to 1965, see the chapter on the Marshall Islands).

From 1965 there were increasing demands for local autonomy within the Trust Territory of the Pacific Islands. In that year the Congress of Micronesia was formed, and in 1967 a commission was established to examine the future political status of the islands. In 1970 it declared Micronesians' rights to sovereignty over their own lands, to self-determination, to devise their own constitution and to revoke any form of free association with the USA. In May 1977, after eight years of negotiations, US President Jimmy Carter announced that his administration intended to adopt measures to terminate the trusteeship agreement by 1981. Until 1979 the four districts of Yap, Truk (Chuuk since 1990), Ponape (Pohnpei since 1984) and Kosrae were governed by a local Administrator, appointed by the President of the USA. However, on 10 May 1979 the four districts ratified a new Constitution to become the Federated States of Micronesia. The Constitution was promulgated in 1980.

The USA signed the Compact of Free Association with the Republic of Palau in August 1982, and with the Marshall Islands and the Federated States of Micronesia in October. Under the Compacts, the four countries (including the Northern Mariana Islands) became independent of each other and took charge of both their internal and foreign affairs separately, while the USA remained responsible for defence and security. The Compact was approved by plebiscite in the Federated States of Micronesia in June 1983, and was ratified by the islands' Congress in September.

In May 1986 the UN Trusteeship Council endorsed the US Government's request for the termination of the existing trusteeship agreement with the islands. US administration of the Federated States of Micronesia was formally ended in November of that year. The UN Security Council ratified the termination of the trusteeship agreement in December 1990. Ponape was renamed Pohnpei in November 1984, when its Constitution came into effect. Truk was renamed Chuuk in January 1990, when its new Constitution was proposed (being later adopted). The Federated States of Micronesia was admitted to the UN in September 1991.

The incumbent President (since 1987), John Haglelgam, was replaced by Bailey Olter, a former Vice-President, in May 1991. At congressional elections in March 1995 Olter was re-elected to the Pohnpei Senator-at-Large seat, and in early May he was re-elected to the presidency unopposed. Similarly, Jacob Nena was re-elected as Vice-President. Allegations that financial mismanagement by the Governor of Chuuk, Sasao Gouland, had resulted in state debts of some US $20m. led to his resignation in June 1996, in order to avoid impeachment proceedings. In July Olter suffered a stroke. Jacob Nena served as acting President during Olter's absence from office, and in May 1997 was sworn in as President of the country. (Olter died in February 1999.)

Congressional elections took place in early March 1997 for the 10 Senators elected on a two-yearly basis, at which all of the incumbents were returned to office. A referendum held concurrently on a proposed amendment to the Constitution (which envisaged increasing the allocation of national revenue to the state legislatures from 50% to 80% of the total budget) was approved in Chuuk and Yap, but rejected in Pohnpei and Kosrae.

Allegations of government interference in the media became widespread when the editor of the country's principal newspaper, *FSM News*, was refused permission to re-enter the islands in June 1997. The Government had sought to deport the editor (who was a Canadian national) following publication in the periodical of reports on government spending, which the authorities claimed were false and malicious. It was also thought that by enforcing the exclusion order, the Government hoped to suppress the publication in the newspaper of information relating to alleged corruption among public officials. The newspaper ceased publication in late 1997.

In February 1998 Congress approved proposals to restructure and reorganize the Cabinet. Several ministerial portfolios were consequently merged or abolished, with the aim of reducing government expenditure. Congressional elections took place on 2 March 1999, at which President Nena was re-elected to the Kosrae Senator-at-Large seat and Vice-President Leo Falcam to the Pohnpei Senator-at-Large seat. On 11 May Congress elected Falcam as President and the Chuuk Senator-at-Large, Redley Killion, as Vice-President.

A first round of renegotiations of the Compact of Free Association (certain terms of which were due to expire in 2001) was completed in late 1999. The USA and the Federated States of Micronesia pledged to maintain defence and security relations. It was also agreed that the USA would continue to provide economic aid to the islands and assist in the development of the private sector, as well as in promoting greater economic self-sufficiency. In July 2001 the USA offered annual assistance of US $61m. and a trust fund of $13m., and expressed concern that the $2,600m. it had given to Micronesia and the Marshall Islands since 1986 had been mismanaged. The Compact's funding terms for Micronesia were originally due to expire on 3 November 2001, but negotiations regarding a new Compact were not completed by this time. Funding was, nevertheless, continued at the Compact's 15-year average level while negotiations remained in progress. Following a proposal by the USA in April 2002 to extend economic assistance for a period of 20 years, a new draft funding structure was agreed, and in March the US budget projections for 2004 granted Micronesian citizens access to private health care resources in the USA as part of the Federated States' continued entitlement to US federal programmes. On 1 May 2003 the amended Compact of Free Association was signed by representatives of the two countries in Pohnpei. The new Compact envisaged direct annual grants of $76.2m. in 2004, in addition to a further $16m. annually, which was to be paid into a Trust Fund for Micronesia. From 2007, direct grants were to decrease by some $800,000, with this amount being transferred to the trust fund. (The total amount to be paid prior to the expected termination of US assistance in 2023 amounted, in 2004 terms, to some $1,760m.) Furthermore, the Micronesian Government also undertook to provide frequent, strictly monitored audit information on all US funding in order to ensure greater accountability. In October 2003 final agreement was reached on some outstanding security and immigration issues, and the US Congress approved the amended Compact in November. President George W. Bush signed the pact in December, although in mid-2004 it awaited approval by the Micronesian Congress. Nevertheless, there remained widespread concern in the Federated States of Micronesia that the new Compact represented a substantial overall reduction in annual income over the long term. Moreover, the formula for the distribution of Compact funds to each of Micronesia's states and the removal of certain US subsidies remained the subject of considerable controversy.

In September 2002 unrest occurred on the Faichuk islands, part of Chuuk, where the Faichuk Commission for Statehood continued its campaign to secede from Chuuk and gain equal status within the Federation. Local dissatisfaction worsened in September following allegations of electoral manipulation against the village mayor of Udot island, with a large crowd appearing to support attempts by local security forces to prevent the mayor's arrest.

Also in September 2002 a referendum was held on a number of proposed amendments to the Constitution. The prospective changes included a provision for the direct election of presidential candidates, the extension of the right of islanders to hold dual citizenship and changes to the distribution formula for Compact of Free Association funds. However, the measures did not receive the required three-quarters' majority of votes and were thus rejected.

At congressional elections held on 6 March 2003 President Leo Falcam unexpectedly failed to achieve re-election to a further four-year term as Senator-at-Large for Pohnpei. In mid-May Congress appointed the Senator-at-Large for Yap, Joseph J. Urusemal, to the presidency. The elections were the subject of some controversy, as it appeared that elected officials had disbursed a portion of the 2002 US funding for Micronesia in order to enhance their electoral prospects. The alleged misallocation of funds was reportedly a significant factor in the worsening fiscal positions of Chuuk, Pohnpei and Kosrae. Moreover, perceptions of official accountability continued to deteriorate in 2003; in November three serving congressmen were indicted for their role in an alleged fraud involving some $1.2m. in public funds. In January, the National Congress approved a resolution to dismiss the judge assigned to the case; President Urusemal lodged a petition against the measure. Also in January, national congressmen attempted to introduce legislation effectively absolving public officials from corruption allegations relating to Compact of Free Association funds. The proposals caused widespread public hostility, and several representatives of state legislatures threatened to secede from the federation unless the measure were withdrawn. In March 2004 the so-called 'amnesty bill' was returned to a Congressional sub-committee for further discussion.

In December 1996 a state of emergency was declared after a typhoon wreaked devastation on the islands of Yap. Flooding and mudslides in Pohnpei in April 1997, as a result of heavy rain, caused the deaths of more than 20 people; another typhoon in mid-1997 left several people dead. Furthermore, in early 1998 a state of emergency was declared, owing to severe drought throughout the islands, believed to have been caused by El Niño (a periodic warming of the tropical Pacific Ocean). In July 2002 at least 49 people died and extensive damage was caused to crops and buildings on Chuuk during a severe tropical storm. In December the islands suffered further damage (albeit without loss of life) when a typhoon struck. President George W. Bush of the USA declared Micronesia a federal disaster area and ordered emergency US funding and resources to be allocated to the relief effort. A further typhoon which struck Yap in April 2004 left 1,200 people homeless; the US Government offered to assume 75% of the cost of the recovery effort. In late 2000 marine biologists issued a warning regarding the erosion of the islands' coastlines, caused by the destruction of the coral reefs by pollution, overfishing and increasing sea temperatures. Furthermore, in late 2003 concerns over environmental pollution increased, due to environmental damage caused by former US and Japanese military equipment submerged in Micronesian waters. A former US Navy oil tanker submerged off the remote Ulithi Atoll was reported at this time to be leaking. Meanwhile, in September 2003 President Urusemal urged the UN General Assembly to work towards halting climate change and its consequent effects on sea-levels and weather systems.

In May 2000 a state of emergency was declared on Pohnpei, following an outbreak of cholera. In August the Government announced a vaccination scheme for the entire population over two years of age. Import restrictions were introduced on the surrounding islands. Pohnpei was officially declared free of cholera on 16 February 2001. During the epidemic some 20

people had died and a further 3,525 were estimated to have been infected.

In February 2003 Pohnpei hosted the first Summit of Micronesian Leaders. At the second summit, held in Koror, Palau, in March 2004, President Urusemal and the leaders of Palau, the Northern Mariana Islands and Guam undertook to increase co-operation between the Pacific island states in the areas of tourism and the environment.

Government

On 10 May 1979 the locally drafted Constitution of the Federated States of Micronesia, incorporating the four states of Kosrae, Yap, Ponape (later Pohnpei) and Truk (later Chuuk), became effective. The federal legislature, the Congress, comprises 14 members (Senators). The four states each elect one 'Senator-at-Large', for a four-year term. The remaining 10 Senators are elected for two-year terms: their seats are distributed in proportion to the population of each state. Each of the four states also has its own Constitution, Governor and legislature. The federal President and Vice-President are elected by the Congress from among the four Senators-at-Large; the offices rotate among the four states. (By-elections are then held for the seats to which the President and Vice-President had been elected.) In November 1986 the Compact of Free Association was signed by the Governments of the Federated States of Micronesia and the USA. Certain of its terms, due to expire in 2001, were renegotiated in late 1999, and an amended Compact was signed by the Governments of both countries on 1 May 2003. By the terms of the Compact, the Federated States of Micronesia is a sovereign, self-governing state.

Local government units are the municipalities and villages. Elected Magistrates and Councils govern the municipalities. Village government is largely traditional.

Defence

The USA is responsible for the defence of the Federated States of Micronesia.

Economic Affairs

In 2002, according to estimates by the World Bank, gross national income (GNI) in the Federated States of Micronesia, measured at average 1999–2002 prices, was US $242m., equivalent to $1,980 per head. During 1990–2002, it was estimated, the population increased at an average annual rate of 2.0%, while gross domestic product (GDP) per head decreased, in real terms, by an average of 0.5% per year. Overall GDP increased, in real terms, an average annual rate of 1.6% in 1990–2002; growth in 2002 was 2.0%.

Agriculture is mainly on a subsistence level, although its importance is diminishing. The principal crops are coconuts (from which some 500 short tons of copra were produced in 2001), bananas, betel-nuts, cassava and sweet potatoes. White peppercorns are produced on Pohnpei. The sector (including forestry and fishing) contributed 19.1% to GDP in 1996 and engaged 55.3% of the employed labour force in 2000. Exports of bananas accounted for 1.2% of export earnings in 1999, while exports of marine products accounted for 91.9% of total export revenue in that year. Fees earned from fisheries licensing agreements, mainly with Japan, account for a substantial percentage of domestic budgetary revenue. In 1999/2000 fishing access fees totalled $16.8m.

Industry (including mining, manufacturing, utilities and construction) provided 3.9% of GDP in 1996. There is little manufacturing, other than garment production (in Yap) and the manufacture of buttons using trochus shells. The sector provided 1.4% of GDP in 1996 and engaged 3.5% of the employed labour force in 1994. The islands are dependent on imported fuels (which accounted for 20.3% of the value of total imports in 1999).

The services sector provided an estimated 77.0% of GDP in 1996 (with government services alone contributing 42.1%). A total of 6,015 people were employed by the national and state Governments in 1996/97. Tourism is an increasingly important industry; it was hoped that several projects to improve communications would further stimulate tourism, hitherto hindered by the territory's remote situation. The industry was identified in a report by the Asian Development Bank (ADB) in mid-1995 as having the greatest potential for development and thus contribution to the islands' economic growth. In 2001, however, the number of visitor arrivals declined to 15,265, compared with 20,051 in the previous year.

In the financial year ending September 2001 there was a visible trade deficit of an estimated US $130.8m., but an estimated surplus of $3.3m. on the current account of the balance of payments. The principal sources of imports in 1999 were the USA (which supplied 43.9% of the total) and Australia (19.8%). Japan was the principal market for exports in 1999, purchasing 83.9% of the total. In 1999 the main imports were food and live animals (24.8% of the total), mineral fuels and lubricants (20.3%), machines and transport equipment (19.5%) and basic manufactures (18.9%). The dominant exports were fish and fish products, mainly in the form of re-exports to Japan by foreign vessels (accounting for 91.9% of total export earnings in 1999).

In 1999/2000 there was an estimated budget surplus of US $0.4m. However, the fiscal surpluses reported for 2002 and 2003 were estimated to have been resulted primarily from increased US aid payments. The Federated States of Micronesia relies heavily on financial assistance, particularly from the USA, which according to the IMF provided an estimated $97.7m. (equivalent to 42.1% of GDP) in 2002. At the end of the 2000/01 financial year the islands' total external debt was estimated at US $58m., and in that year the cost of debt-servicing was forecast by the ADB to be equivalent to 22.0% of the value of exports of goods and services. However, by the end of 2002 the Government had successfully repaid its outstanding commercial debt; the public debt-service ratio, meanwhile, declined sharply to 6.0% of the value of exports. According to the ADB, the inflation rate steadily decreased from an estimated annual average of 6.0% in 1993 to 1.5% in 1998, before rising to 2.6% in 1999 and to 3.2% in 2000, then declining to 2.6% in 2001. According to the ADB, some 2.6% of the labour force were unemployed in 2000.

The Federated States of Micronesia is a member of the Pacific Community (see p. 323), the Pacific Islands Forum (see p. 325), the South Pacific Regional Trade and Economic Co-operation Agreement (SPARTECA, see p. 328), the UN Economic and Social Commission for Asia and the Pacific (ESCAP, see p. 31) and the Asian Development Bank (ADB, see p. 151). In November 2002 the Federated States of Micronesia was announced as the location of the headquarters for the Tuna Commission, a new multilateral agency to manage migratory fish stocks in the central and western Pacific region. The organization's remit included the management of waters outside each nation's 200-mile exclusive economic zone, in accordance with the framework established under the 1995 UN Fish Stocks Agreement. The Council of Micronesian Government Executives, of which the Federated States of Micronesia was a founder member in 1996, aims to facilitate discussion of economic developments in the region and to examine possibilities for reducing the considerable cost of shipping essential goods between the islands.

The islands are vulnerable to adverse climatic conditions, as was illustrated in late 1997 and early 1998, when a prolonged drought caused problems throughout the islands, and in 2002 following a series of tropical storms. The country's prospects for economic development are, furthermore, constrained by the islands' remote position and lack of marketable commodities. An extremely high rate of natural increase in the population has exacerbated certain economic problems, but is, however, partially offset by an annual emigration rate of more than 2%. With the renegotiation of several terms of the Compact of Free Association from late 1999 (see Recent History), the USA emphasized its continued commitment to the economic development of the islands, including the promotion of greater self-sufficiency, in return for improved accountability regarding US funding by the Micronesia Government. In December 2000 the ADB approved a US $8m. loan to fund a six-year reform programme of the health and education sectors, and followed this in December 2001 with a further loan of $13m., targeted at job creation, increasing production for both domestic and export markets, and the development of a competitive services sector. However, the private sector continued to be constrained by the disproportionately high cost of domestic labour, rates of pay in the public sector having risen substantially in recent years as a result of the large external inflows (although public sector salaries were 'frozen' under the 2004 budget). Moreover, an IMF report released in February 2003 noted that infrastructure for the private sector remained underdeveloped, notwithstanding the authorities' largely positive oversight of the banking sector. Further criticism was attached to the private sector's role as an effective provider of services to the public sector, and the public sector's tendency to operate in unequal competition with private-sector interests. Concerns also continued as to the relative lack of progress in restructuring the economy in preparation for the potentially dramatic impact of the decline and eventual withdrawal of direct US aid in 2023 (upon the expiry of the Compact as amended in 2003): according to the UN, bilateral and multilateral aid to Micronesia totalled $101.6m. in 2000, the latter accounting for only $5.0m. of the total. The trust fund for Micronesia established to alleviate such pressures upon expiry of the Compact was expected to remain vulnerable to international economic performance, the majority of this capital being invested in US stock markets. Moreover, it was considered in some quarters that the amended Compact of Free Association represented a substantial real reduction in Micronesia's grant income.

Education

Primary education, which begins at six years of age and lasts for eight years, is compulsory. Secondary education, beginning at 14 years of age, comprises two cycles, each of two years. The Micronesia Maritime and Fisheries Academy, which was opened in Yap in 1990, provides education and training in fisheries technology at secondary and tertiary levels. The College of Micronesia offers two- and three-year programmes leading to a degree qualification. A summit meeting was held in September 2000 to discuss the improvement and reform of the education sector. In 1997 Micronesia had a student-teacher ratio of 17. An average of 37% of students remained in education from first grade to graduation.

Public Holidays

2004: 1 January (New Year's Day), 9 April (Good Friday, Pohnpei only), 10 May (Constitution Day), 24 October (United Nations Day), 3 November (Independence Day), 25 December (Christmas Day).

2005: 1 January (New Year's Day), 25 March (Good Friday, Pohnpei only), 10 May (Constitution Day), 24 October (United Nations Day), 3 November (Independence Day), 25 December (Christmas Day).

Weights and Measures

With certain exceptions, the imperial system is in force. One US cwt equals 100 lb; one long ton equals 2,240 lb; one short ton equals 2,000 lb. A policy of gradual voluntary conversion to the metric system is being undertaken.

Statistical Survey

Note: Further statistics relating to the Federated States of Micronesia are to be found in the chapter on the Marshall Islands

AREA AND POPULATION

Area: 700 sq km (270.3 sq miles): Chuuk (294 islands) 127 sq km; Kosrae (5 islands) 110 sq km; Pohnpei (163 islands) 344 sq km; Yap (145 islands) 119 sq km.

Population: 105,506 (53,923 males, 51,583 females) at census of 18 September 1994; 107,008 (males 54,191, females 52,817) at 2000 census (provisional). *By State* (2000): Chuuk 53,595; Kosrae 7,686; Pohnpei 34,486; Yap 11,241.

Density (2000): 153 per sq km. *By State* (per sq km): Chuuk 422.0; Kosrae 70.0; Pohnpei 100.3; Yap 94.5.

Births and Deaths (2000, official estimates): Birth rate 27.1 per 1,000; Death rate 6.0 per 1,000.

Expectation of Life (WHO estimates, years at birth): 66.5 (males 64.9; females 68.1) in 2002. Source: WHO, *World Health Report*.

Economically Active Population ('000 persons, 2000): Agriculture, forestry and fishing 17.25; Total employed (incl. others) 31.21;

Unemployed 0.82; Total labour force 32.02. Source: Asian Development Bank, *Key Indicators of Developing Asian and Pacific Countries.*

HEALTH AND WELFARE

Key Indicators

Total Fertility Rate (children per woman, 2002): 3.8.

Under-5 Mortality Rate (per 1,000 live births, 2001): 24.

Physicians (per 1,000 head, 1999): 0.57.

Hospital Beds (per 1,000 head, 1989): 3.47.

Health Expenditure (2001): US $ per head (PPP): 319.

Health Expenditure (2001): % of GDP: 7.8.

Health Expenditure (2001): public (% of total): 72.0 .
For sources and definitions, see explanatory note on p. vi.

AGRICULTURE, ETC.

Principal Crops* (FAO estimates, '000 metric tons, 2002): Coconuts 140; Cassava 12; Bananas 2; Sweet potatoes 3. Source: FAO.

Livestock* (FAO estimates, '000 head, year ending September 2002): Pigs 32; Cattle 14; Goats 4; Poultry 185. Source: FAO.

Livestock Products* ('000 metric tons, 2002): Beef and veal 245; Pig meat 873; Poultry meat 135; Hen eggs 175; Cattle hides 45. Source: FAO.
* Including the Northern Mariana Islands, the Marshall Islands and Palau.

Fishing ('000 metric tons, live weight, 2001): Skipjack tuna 10.3; Yellowfin tuna 5.3; Bigeye tuna 1.5 (FAO estimate); Total capture (incl. others) 18.1 (FAO estimate). Source: FAO, *Yearbook of Fishery Statistics.*

FINANCE

Currency and Exchange Rates: United States currency is used: 100 cents = 1 United States dollar (US $). *Sterling and Euro Equivalents* (31 December 2003): £1 sterling = US $1.7847; €1 = US $1.26; US $100 = £56.32 = €79.12.

Budget (estimates, US $ million, year ending 30 September 2002): *Revenue:* Domestic 46.2 (Tax 28.4, Non-tax 17.8); Grants 114.2; Total 160.4. *Expenditure:* Recurrent 129.1; Capital 25.7; Total 154.8. Source: Asian Development Bank, *Key Indicators of Developing Asian and Pacific Countries.*

Gross Domestic Product by Economic Activity (US $ million at current prices, 1996): Agriculture, forestry and fishing 34.7; Mining and quarrying 0.7; Manufacturing 2.6; Electricity, gas and water 1.9; Construction 1.9; Wholesale and retail trade 39.5; Hotels and restaurants 4.1; Transport, storage and communications 8.5; Finance, real estate and business services 5.5; Government services 76.5; Other services 5.6; *GDP in purchasers' values* 181.5. Source: IMF, *Federated States of Micronesia: Recent Economic Developments* (August 1998).

Balance of Payments (estimates, US $ million, year ending 30 September 2002): Merchandise exports (incl. re-exports) f.o.b. 16.1; Merchandise imports f.o.b. –93.2; *Trade balance* –77.1; Exports of services 36.2; Imports of services –49.8; *Balance on goods and services* –90.7; Private unrequited transfers 2.3; Official unrequited transfers 97.1; *Current balance* 8.7; Capital transfers (net) 36.8; Net errors and omissions –21.6; *Overall balance* 24.1. Source: Asian Development Bank, *Key Indicators of Developing Asian and Pacific Countries.*

EXTERNAL TRADE

Principal Commodities (estimates, US $'000, 1999): *Imports:* Food and live animals 3,053; Beverages and tobacco 738; Crude materials (inedible) except fuel 52; Mineral fuels, lubricants, etc. 2,503; Chemicals 534; Basic manufactures 2,326; Machinery and transport equipment 2,406; Miscellaneous manufactured articles 701; Total (incl. others) 12,328. *Exports:* Fish 1,956; Bananas 25; Total (incl. others) 2,128. Source: Asian Development Bank, *Key Indicators of Developing Asian and Pacific Countries.*

Principal Trading Partners (US $'000, 1999): *Imports:* Australia 2,440; Japan 1,536; USA 5,409; Total (incl. others) 12,328. *Exports:* Japan 1,785; Marshall Islands 23; Total (incl. others) 2,128. Source: Asian Development Bank, *Key Indicators of Developing Asian and Pacific Countries.*

TRANSPORT

Shipping: *Merchant Fleet* (registered at 31 December 2002): Vessels 19; Total displacement ('000 grt) 13.4. Source: Lloyd's Register-Fairplay, *World Fleet Statistics.*

TOURISM

Foreign Tourist Arrivals: 16,140 in 1999; 20,051 in 2000; 15,265 in 2001. Source: World Tourism Organization, *Yearbook of Tourism Statistics.*

Tourist Arrivals by Country of Residence (2001): Australia 516; Japan 3,118; Other Asia (including Philippines, Republic of Korea, People's Republic of China, Taiwan, etc.) 9,183; USA 6,903; Total (incl. others) 15,265. Source: World Tourism Organization, *Yearbook of Tourism Statistics.*

COMMUNICATIONS MEDIA

Telephones ('000 main lines in use, 2001): 10.0*.

Facsimile Machines (number in use, 1998): 539*.

Radio Receivers (1996): 22,000 in use.

Internet Users ('000, 2000): 4.0*.

Television Receivers (1996): 19,800 in use.

* Source: International Telecommunication Union.

EDUCATION

Primary (1995): 174 schools; 1,051 teachers (1984); 27,281 pupils.

Secondary (1995): 24 schools; 314 teachers (1984); 6,898 pupils.

Tertiary (1994): 1,461 students.
Source: UN, *Statistical Yearbook for Asia and the Pacific.*

Directory

The Constitution

On 10 May 1979 the locally-drafted Constitution of the Federated States of Micronesia, incorporating the four states of Kosrae, Yap, Ponape (formally renamed Pohnpei in November 1984) and Truk (renamed Chuuk in January 1990), became effective. Each of the four states has its own Constitution, elected legislature and Governor. The Constitution guarantees fundamental human rights and establishes a separation of the judicial, executive and legislative powers. The federal legislature, the Congress of the Federated States of Micronesia, is a unicameral parliament with 14 members, popularly elected. The executive consists of the President, elected by the Congress, and a Cabinet. The Constitution provides for a review of the governmental and federal system every 10 years.

In November 1986 the Compact of Free Association was signed by the Governments of the Federated States of Micronesia and the USA. By the terms of the Compact, the Federated States of Micronesia is an internally sovereign, self-governing state, whose policy concerning foreign affairs must be consistent with guide-lines laid down in the Compact. Full responsibility for defence lies with the

USA, and the security arrangements may be terminated only by mutual agreement. Furthermore, the Compact guaranteed exclusivity to US military forces in Micronesia's waters. The Governments of the Federated States of Micronesia and the USA signed an amended Compact on 1 May 2003, whereby its terms where renewed until 2023. The agreement was approved by the US Congress in November 2003 and ratified by President George W. Bush in December. The status of free association continues indefinitely.

The Government

HEAD OF STATE

President: Joseph J. Urusemal (took office 14 July 2003).

Vice-President: Redley Killion.

THE CABINET
(April 2004)

Secretary of the Department of Finance and Administration: NICK L. ANDON.

Secretary of the Department of Foreign Affairs: SEBASTIAN L. ANEFAL.

Secretary of the Department of Economic Affairs: ISHMAEL LEBEHN (acting).

Secretary of the Department of Health, Education and Social Services: Dr JEFFERSON B. BENJAMIN.

Secretary of the Department of Justice: HARRY SEYMOUR (acting).

Secretary of the Department of Transportation, Communications and Infrastructure: AKALLINO H. SUSAIA.

Public Defender: BEAUTEAN C. WORSWICK.

GOVERNMENT OFFICES

Office of the President: POB PS-53, Palikir, Pohnpei, FM 96941; tel. 320-2228; fax 320-2785.

Department of Economic Affairs: POB PS-12, Palikir, Pohnpei, FM 96941; tel. 320-2646; fax 320-5854; e-mail fsmrd@mail.fm; e-mail invest@fsminvest.fm; internet www.fsminvest.fm.

Department of Finance and Administration: POB PS-158, Palikir, Pohnpei, FM 96941; tel. 320-2640; fax 320-2380.

Department of Foreign Affairs: POB PS-123, Palikir, Pohnpei, FM 96941; tel. 320-2641; fax 320-2933; e-mail foreignaffairs@mail.fm.

Department of Health, Education and Social Services: POB PS-70, Palikir, Pohnpei, FM 96941; tel. 320-2872; fax 320-5263.

Department of Justice: POB PS-105, Palikir, Pohnpei, FM 96941; tel. 320-2644; fax 320-2234.

Department of Transportation, Communications and Infrastructure: POB PS-2, Palikir, Pohnpei, FM 96941; tel. 320-2865; fax 320-5853.

Office of the Public Defender: POB PS-174, Palikir, Pohnpei, FM 96941; tel. 320-2648; fax 320-5775.

Public Information Office: POB PS-34, Palikir, Pohnpei, FM 96941; tel. 320-2548; fax 320-4356; e-mail fsmpio@mail.fm; internet www.fsmpio.fm.

The Legislature

CONGRESS OF THE FEDERATED STATES OF MICRONESIA

The Congress comprises 14 members (Senators), of whom four are elected for a four-year term and 10 for a two-year term.

Speaker: PETER M. CHRISTIAN.

STATE LEGISLATURES

Chuuk State Legislature: POB 189, Weno, Chuuk, FM 96942; tel. 330-2234; fax 330-2233; Senate of 10 mems and House of Representatives of 28 mems elected for four years; Gov. ANSITO WALTER.

Kosrae State Legislature: POB 187, Tofol, Kosrae, FM 96944; tel. 370-3002; fax 370-3162; e-mail kosraelc@mail.fm; unicameral body of 14 mems serving for four years; Gov. RENSLEY A. SIGRAH.

Pohnpei State Legislature: POB 39, Kolonia, Pohnpei, FM 96941; tel. 320-2235; fax 320-2505; internet www.fm/pohnpeileg/; 27 representatives elected for four years (terms staggered); Gov. JOHNNY P. DAVID.

Yap State Legislature: POB 39, Colonia, Yap, FM 96943; tel. 350-2108; fax 350-4113; 10 mems, six elected from the Yap Islands proper and four elected from the Outer Islands of Ulithi and Woleai, for a four-year term; Gov. VINCENT A. FIGIR.

Diplomatic Representation

EMBASSIES IN MICRONESIA

Australia: POB S, Kolonia, Pohnpei, FM 96941; tel. 320-5448; fax 320-5449; e-mail australia@mail.fm; internet www.australianembassy.fm; Ambassador BRENDAN F. DORAN.

China, People's Republic: POB 530, Kolonia, Pohnpei, FM 96941; tel. 320-5575; fax 320-5578; e-mail chinaemb@mail.fm; Ambassador ZHANG BINHUA.

Japan: Pami Bldg, 3rd Floor, POB 1847, Kolonia, Pohnpei, FM 96941; tel. 320-5465; fax 320-5470; Chargé d'affaires a.i. HYOSUKE YASUI.

USA: POB 1286, Kolonia, Pohnpei, FM 96941; tel. 320-2187; fax 320-2186; e-mail usembassy@mail.fm; internet www.fm/usembassy; Ambassador LARRY M. DINGER.

Judicial System

Supreme Court of the Federated States of Micronesia: POB PS-J, Palikir Station, Pohnpei, FM 96941; tel. 320-2357; fax 320-2756; Chief Justice ANDON L. AMARAICH.

State Courts and Appellate Courts have been established in Yap, Chuuk, Kosrae and Pohnpei.

Religion

The population is predominantly Christian, mainly Roman Catholic. The Assembly of God, Jehovah's Witnesses, Seventh-day Adventists, the Church of Jesus Christ of Latter-day Saints (Mormons), the United Church of Christ, Baptists and the Bahá'í Faith are also represented.

CHRISTIANITY

The Roman Catholic Church

The Federated States of Micronesia forms a part of the diocese of the Caroline Islands, suffragan to the archdiocese of Agaña (Guam). The Bishop participates in the Catholic Bishops' Conference of the Pacific, based in Fiji. At 31 December 2002 there were 77,733 adherents in the diocese.

Bishop of the Caroline Islands: Most Rev. AMANDO SAMO, Bishop's House, POB 939, Weno, Chuuk, FM 96942; tel. 330-2399; fax 330-4585; e-mail diocese@mail.fm; internet www.diocesecarolines.org.

Other Churches

United Church of Christ in Pohnpei: Kolonia, Pohnpei, FM 96941.

Liebenzell Mission: Rev. Roland Rauchholz, POB 9, Weno, Chuuk, FM 96942; tel. 330-3869.

The Press

Chuuk News Chronicle: POB 244, Wenn, Chuuk, FM 96942; f. 1983; Editor MARCIANA AKASY.

FSM—Job Training Partnership Act News: Pohnpei, FM 96941; f. 1994; monthly; US-funded.

The Island Tribune: Pohnpei, FM 96941; f. 1997; fortnightly.

Micronesia Focus: Pohnpei, FM 96941; f. 1994; Editor KETSON JOHNSON.

The National Union: FSM Public Information Office, POB 490, Kolonia, Pohnpei, FM 96941; tel. 320-2548; f. 1980; 2 a month; Public Information Officer KETSON JOHNSON; circ. 5,000.

Broadcasting and Communications

TELECOMMUNICATIONS

FSM Telecommunication Corporation: POB 1210, Kolonia, Pohnpei, FM 96941; tel. 320-2740; fax 320-2745; e-mail takinaga@mail.fm; internet www.telecom.fm; provides domestic and international services; Gen. Man. TAKURO AKINAGA.

BROADCASTING

Radio

Federated States of Micronesia Public Information Office: POB PS-34, Palikir, Pohnpei, FM 96941; tel. 320-2548; fax 320-4356; e-mail fsmpio@mail.fm; internet www.fsmpio.fm; govt-operated; four regional stations, each broadcasting 18 hours daily; Information Officer KESTER JAMES.

Station V6AH: POB 1086, Kolonia, Pohnpei, FM 96941; programmes in English and Ponapean; Man. DUSTY FREDERICK.

Station V6AI: POB 117, Colonia, Yap, FM 96943; tel. 350-2174; fax 350-4426; programmes in English, Yapese, Ulithian and Satawalese; Man. PETER GARAMFEL.

Station V6AJ: POB 147, Tofol, Kosrae, FM 96944; tel. 370-3040; fax 370-3880; e-mail v6aj@.mail.fm; programmes in English and Kosraean; Man. NENA TOLENNA.

Station V6AK: Wenn, Chuuk, FM 96942; programmes in Chuukese and English; Man. P. J. MAIPI.

Television

Island Cable TV—Pohnpei: POB 1628, Pohnpei, FM 96941; tel. 320-2671; fax 320-2670; e-mail ictv@mail.fm; f. 1991; Pres. BERNARD HELGENBERGER; Gen. Man. DAVID O. CLIFFE.

TV Station Chuuk (TTKK): Wenn, Chuuk, FM 96942; commercial.

TV Station Pohnpei (KPON): Central Micronesia Communications, POB 460, Kolonia, Pohnpei, FM 96941; f. 1977; commercial; Pres. BERNARD HELGENBERGER; Tech. Dir DAVID CLIFFE.

TV Station Yap (WAAB): Colonia, Yap, FM 96943; tel. 350-2160; fax 350-4113; govt-owned; Man. LOU DEFNGIN.

Finance

BANKING

Regulatory Authority

Federated States of Micronesia Banking Board: POB 1887, Kolonia, Pohnpei, FM 96941; e-mail fsmbb@mail.fm; f. 1980; Chair. LARRY RAIGETAL; Commissioner MATTHEW Y. CHIGIYAL.

Banks are also supervised by the US Federal Deposit Insurance Corporation.

Commercial Banks

Bank of the Federated States of Micronesia: POB 98, Kolonia, Pohnpei, FM 96941; tel. 320-2724; fax 370-5359; e-mail bofsmhq@mail.fm; brs in Kosrae, Yap, Pohnpei and Chuuk.

Bank of Guam (USA): POB 367, Kolonia, Pohnpei, FM 96941; tel. 320-2550; fax 320-2562; e-mail bogpohn@mail.fm; internet www.bankofguam.com; Man. VIDA B. RICAFRENTE; brs in Chuuk and Pohnpei.

Development Bank

Federated States of Micronesia Development Bank: POB M, Kolonia, Pohnpei, FM 96941; tel. 320-2840; fax 320-2842; e-mail fsmdb@mail.fm; f. 1979; Chair. IHLEN JOSEPH; Pres. ANNA MENDIOLA; 4 brs.

Banking services for the rest of the islands are available in Guam, Hawaii and on the US mainland.

INSURANCE

Actouka Executive Insurance: POB Q, Kolonia, Pohnpei; tel. 320-5331; fax 320-2331; e-mail mlamar@mail.fm.

Caroline Insurance Underwriters: POB 37, Chuuk; tel. 330-6045; fax 330-2207.

FSM Insurance Group: Kosrae; tel. 370-3788; fax 370-2120.

Moylan's Insurance Underwriters: POB 1448, Kolonia, Pohnpei; tel. 320-2118; fax 320-2519; e-mail pohnpei@moylansinsurance.com.

Oceania Insurance Co: POB 1202, Weno, Chuuk, FM 96942; tel. 330-3036; fax 330-2334; e-mail oceanpac@mail.fm; also owns and manages Pacific Basin Insurance.

Yap Insurance Agency: Yap; tel. 350-2340; fax 350-2341; e-mail tachelioyap@mail.fm.

Trade and Industry

GOVERNMENT AGENCIES

Coconut Development Authority: POB 297, Kolonia, Pohnpei, FM 96941; tel. 320-2892; fax 320-5383; e-mail fsmcda@mail.fm; responsible for all purchasing, processing and exporting of copra and copra by-products in the islands; Gen. Man. NAMIO NANPEI.

Pohnpei Economic Development Authority: POB 738, Kolonia, Pohnpei, FM 96941; tel. 320-2298; fax 320-2775; e-mail eda@mail.fm; Chair. President JOSEPH J. URUSEMAL (*ex officio*); Exec. Dir SHELTEN NETH.

FSM National Fisheries Corporation: POB R, Kolonia, Pohnpei, FM 96941; tel. 320-2529; fax 320-2239; e-mail nfcairfreight@mail.fm; internet www.fsmgov.org/nfc/; f. 1984; established in 1990, with the Economic Devt Authority and an Australian co, the Caroline Fishing Corpn (three vessels); promotes fisheries development; Pres. PETER SITAN.

National Oceanic Resource Management Authority (NORMA): POB PS-122, Palikir, Pohnpei, FM 96941; tel. 320-2700; fax 320-2383; e-mail norma@mail.fm; fmrly Micronesian Fisheries Authority; name changed 2002; responsible for conservation, management and development of tuna resources and for issue of fishing licences; Exec. Dir BERNARD THOULAG; Deputy Dir EUGENE PANGELINAN.

UTILITIES

Chuuk Public Works (CPW): POB 248, Weno, Chuuk, FM 96942; tel. 330-2242; fax 320-4815; e-mail chkpublicworks@mail.fm.

Kosrae Utility Authority: POB 277, Tofol, Kosrae, FM 96944; tel. 370-3799; fax 370-3798; e-mail KUA@mail.fm; corporatized in 1994.

Pohnpei Utility Corporation: POB C, Kolonia, Pohnpei, FM 96941; tel. 320-5606; fax 320-2505; f. 1992; provides electricity, water and sewerage services.

Yap Public Services Corporation: POB 621, Colonia, Yap, FM 96943; tel. 350-2175; fax 350-2331; f. 1996; provides electricity, water and sewerage services.

CO-OPERATIVES

Chuuk: Chuuk Co-operative, Faichuk Cacao and Copra Co-operative Asscn, Pis Fishermen's Co-operative, Fefan Women's Co-operative.

Pohnpei: Pohnpei Federation of Co-operative Asscns (POB 100, Pohnpei, FM 96941), Pohnpei Handicraft Co-operative, Pohnpei Fishermen's Co-operative, Uh Soumwet Co-operative Asscn, Kolonia Consumers' and Producers' Co-operative Asscn, Kitti Minimum Co-operative Asscn, Kapingamarangi Copra Producers' Asscn, Metalanim Copra Co-operative Asscn, PICS Co-operative Asscn, Mokil Island Co-operative Asscn, Ngatik Island Co-operative Asscn, Nukuoro Island Co-operative Asscn, Kosrae Island Co-operative Asscn, Pingelap Consumers' Co-operative Asscn.

Yap: Yap Co-operative Asscn, POB 159, Colonia, Yap, FM 96943; tel. 350-2209; fax 350-4114; e-mail yca@mail.fm; f. 1952; Pres. JAMES GILMAR; Gen. Man. TONY GANNGIYAN; 1,200 mems.

Transport

ROADS

Macadam and concrete roads are found in the more important islands. Other islands have stone and coral-surfaced roads and tracks.

SHIPPING

Pohnpei, Chuuk, Yap and Kosrae have deep-draught harbours for commercial shipping. The ports provide warehousing and transhipment facilities.

Caroline Fisheries Corporation (CFC): POB 7, Kolonia, Pohnpei, FM 96941; tel. 320-5791; fax 320-5791; e-mail cfc@mail.fm; Gen. Man. MILAN KAMBER.

Pacific Shipping Agency: POB 154, Lelu, Kosrae FM 96944; tel. 370-2912; Gen. Man. THEODORE SIGRAH.

Pohnpei Transfer & Storage, Inc.: POB 340, Kolonia, Pohnpei FM 96941; tel. 320-2552; fax 320-2389; e-mail fsmlinejv@mail.fm; Gen. Man. JOE VITT.

Truk Transportation Company (TRANSCO): POB 99, Weno, Chuuk FM 96942; tel. 330-2143; fax 330-2726; e-mail transco@mail.fm; Gen. Man. LINDA MORI HARTMAN.

Waab Transportation Company.: POB 177, Colonia, Yap FM 96943; tel. 350-2301; fax 350-4110; e-mail waabtrans@mail.fm; agents for PM & O Lines (USA); Gen. Man. CYRIL CHUGRAD.

CIVIL AVIATION

The Federated States of Micronesia is served by Continental Micronesia, Air Nauru and Continental Airlines (USA). Pacific Missionary Aviation, based in Pohnpei and Yap, provides domestic air services. There are international airports on Pohnpei, Chuuk, Yap and Kosrae, and airstrips on the outer islands of Onoun and Ta in Chuuk.

Tourism

The tourist industry is a significant source of revenue, although it has been hampered by the lack of infrastructure. Visitor attractions include excellent conditions for scuba-diving (notably in Chuuk Lagoon), Second World War battle sites and relics (many underwater) and the ancient ruined city of Nan Madol on Pohnpei. In 1990 there was a total of 362 hotel rooms. The number of tourist arrivals totalled 15,265 in 2001.

Federated States of Micronesia Visitors Board: Dept of Economic Affairs, National Government, PO Box PS-12, Palikir, Pohnpei, FM 96941; tel. 320-5133; fax 320-3251; e-mail fsminfo@visit-fsm.org; internet www.visit-fsm.org.

Chuuk Visitors Bureau: POB FQ, Weno, Chuuk, FM 96942; tel. 330-4133; fax 330-4194; e-mail cvb@mail.fm.

Kosrae Visitors Bureau: POB 659, Tofol, Kosrae, FM 96944; tel. 370-2228; fax 370-2187; e-mail kosrae@mail.fm; internet www.kosrae.com.

Pohnpei Department of Tourism and Parks: POB 66, Kolonia, Pohnpei, FM 96941; tel. 320-2421; fax 320-6019; e-mail tourismparks@mail.fm; Deputy Chief BUMIO SILBANUZ.

Pohnpei Visitors Bureau: POB 1949, Kolonia, Pohnpei, FM 96941; tel. 320-4851; fax 320-4868; e-mail pohnpeiVB@mail.fm; internet www.visit-pohnpei.fm.

Yap Visitors Bureau: POB 36, Colonia, Yap, FM 96943; tel. 350-2298; fax 350-2571; e-mail yvb@mail.fm; internet www.visityap.com.

MOLDOVA

Introductory Survey

Location, Climate, Language, Religion, Flag, Capital

The Republic of Moldova is a small, land-locked country situated in south-eastern Europe. It includes only a small proportion of the historical territories of Moldova (or Moldavia, in its Russian form), most of which are in Romania, while others (southern Bessarabia and northern Bucovina) are in Ukraine. The republic is bounded to the north, east and south by Ukraine. To the west it borders Romania. The climate is very favourable for agriculture, with long, warm summers and relatively mild winters. Average temperatures in Chișinău range from 21°C (70°F) in July to –4°C (24°F) in January. The Constitution of July 1994 describes the official language as Moldovan (although this is widely considered to be identical to Romanian). Most of the inhabitants of Moldova profess Christianity, the largest denomination being the Eastern Orthodox Church. The national flag (proportions 1 by 2) consists of three equal vertical stripes, of light blue, yellow and red; the yellow stripe has at its centre the arms of Moldova (a shield bearing a stylized bull's head in yellow, set between an eight-pointed yellow star, a five-petalled yellow flower, and a yellow crescent, the shield being set on the breast of an eagle, in gold and red, which holds a green olive branch in its dexter talons, a yellow sceptre in its sinister talons, and a yellow cross in its beak). The capital is Chișinău (Kishinev).

Recent History

The area of the present-day Republic of Moldova corresponds to only part of the medieval principality of Moldova (also known as Moldavia), which emerged as an important regional power in the 15th century. In the following century, however, the principality came under Ottoman domination. Following a period of conflict between the Ottoman and Russian Empires in the late 18th century, Moldova was divided into two parts under the Treaty of Bucharest of 1812: the eastern territory of Bessarabia, situated between the Prut and Dniester (Dnestr or Nistru) rivers (which roughly corresponds to modern Moldova), was ceded to Russia, while the Ottomans retained control of western Moldova. A Romanian nationalist movement evolved in western Moldova and the neighbouring region of Wallachia during the 19th century, culminating in the proclamation of a sovereign Romanian state in 1877, independent of the Ottoman Empire. In 1881 Romania became a kingdom. In June 1918, after the collapse of the Russian Empire, Bessarabia was proclaimed an independent republic, although in November it voted to become part of Romania. This union was recognized in the Treaty of Paris (1920). However, the USSR (established in 1922) refused to recognize Romania's claims to the territory, and in October 1924 formed a Moldovan Autonomous Soviet Socialist Republic (ASSR) on the eastern side of the Dniester, in the Ukrainian Soviet Socialist Republic (SSR). In June 1940 Romania was forced to cede Bessarabia and northern Bucovina to the USSR, under the terms of the Treaty of Non-Aggression (the 'Molotov-Ribbentrop Pact'), concluded with Germany in August 1939. Northern Bucovina, southern Bessarabia and the Kotovsk-Balta region of the Moldovan ASSR were incorporated into the Ukrainian SSR. The remaining parts of the Moldovan ASSR and of Bessarabia were merged to form the Moldovan SSR, which formally joined the USSR on 2 August 1940. Political power in the republic was vested in the Communist Party of Moldova (CPM), a subsidiary of the Communist Party of the Soviet Union (CPSU).

Between July 1941 and August 1944 the Moldovan SSR was reunited with Romania. However, the Soviet Army reannexed the region in 1944, and the Moldovan SSR was re-established. Soviet policy in Moldova concentrated on isolating the region from its historical links with Romania: cross-border traffic virtually ceased, the Cyrillic script was imposed on the Romanian language (which was referred to as Moldovan) and Russian and Ukrainian immigration was encouraged. In the 1950s thousands of ethnic Romanians were deported to Central Asia. Moldova remained among the more conservative republics of the USSR. Two future Soviet leaders, Leonid Brezhnev and Konstantin Chernenko, held prominent positions in the CPM during their early years of CPSU service: Brezhnev as First Secretary (leader) of the CPM in 1950–52, and Chernenko as head of party propaganda in 1948–56.

The policy of *glasnost* (openness), introduced by Soviet leader Mikhail Gorbachev in 1986, allowed the expression within Moldova of opposition to the process of 'russification'. In May 1987 the CPM issued a decree increasing provision for the teaching of Romanian in schools, but this did little to satisfy public opinion. In May 1989 a number of independent cultural and political groups, which had recently emerged, but were denied legal status by the authorities, allied to form the Popular Front (PF). In June some 70,000 people attended a protest demonstration, organized by the PF, on the anniversary of the Soviet annexation of Bessarabia in 1940. This was followed, in August 1989, by mass demonstrations in the capital, Chișinău (Kishinev), in support of proposals by the Moldovan Supreme Soviet (legislature) to declare Romanian the official language of the republic. Following protests by non-ethnic Romanians, the proposals were amended: legislation was enacted providing for Russian to be retained as a language of inter-ethnic communication, but the official language was to be Romanian, written in the Latin script. Following disturbances, and subsequent riots, during the Revolution Day celebrations in Chișinău in November, the First Secretary of the CPM, Semion Grossu, was dismissed. He was replaced by Petru Lucinschi, an ethnic Romanian considered to be more supportive of Gorbachev's reforms.

The increasing influence of the Romanian-speaking population was strongly opposed by other inhabitants of the republic (who, at the 1989 census, comprised some 35% of the total population). In the areas east of the Dniester, where Russians and Ukrainians predominated, the local authorities refused to implement the language law. Opposition to growing Moldovan nationalism was led by the Yedinstvo (Unity) Movement, a group dominated by leading CPM members, and the United Work Collectives, a Slav-dominated organization based among the towns east of the Dniester. Both organizations had strong links with Gagauz Halky (Gagauz People), the most prominent of the political groups representing the 150,000-strong Gagauz minority (a Turkic people). In January 1990 a referendum took place in the eastern town of Tiraspol, in which the predominantly Russian-speaking population voted overwhelmingly to seek greater autonomy for the region beyond the Dniester (Transnistria or Transdnestria).

None of the independent political groups was officially allowed to endorse candidates in elections to the Moldovan Supreme Soviet in February 1990, but individual candidates made clear where their sympathies lay. About 80% of the 380 deputies elected were members of the CPM, but many were also sympathetic to the aims of the PF. The new Supreme Soviet convened in April, whereupon Mircea Snegur, a CPM member supported by the PF, was elected Chairman. In the following month the Government resigned after losing a vote of 'no confidence'. A new Council of Ministers, chaired by a leading economist, Mircea Druc, implemented far-reaching political changes. The CPM's constitutional right to power was revoked, and media organizations belonging to the CPM were transferred to state control. On 23 June the Supreme Soviet adopted a declaration of sovereignty asserting the supremacy of Moldova's Constitution and laws throughout the republic, which was to be known as the Soviet Socialist Republic of Moldova (as opposed to the russified 'Moldavia'). The Supreme Soviet also declared the 1940 annexation of Bessarabia to have been illegal. In September Snegur was elected to the newly instituted post of President of the Republic, and the role of Chairman of the Supreme Soviet became that of a parliamentary speaker.

The actions of the increasingly radical Romanian majority in the legislature provoked further anxiety among the country's ethnic minorities during 1990. In August the Gagauz proclaimed a separate 'Gagauz SSR' in the southern region around Comrat. In the following month east-bank Slavs proclaimed their secession from Moldova and the establishment of the 'Transdnestrian SSR', comprising Moldovan territory east of the Dniester, with its self-styled capital at Tiraspol. Both declarations were immediately annulled by the Moldovan Supreme Soviet. In October Moldovan nationalists sought to thwart elections to a Gagauz Supreme Soviet by sending some 50,000 armed volunteers to the area. Violence was prevented only by the dispatch of Soviet troops to the region. The new Gagauz Supreme Soviet convened in Comrat and elected Stepan Topal as its President. Further inter-ethnic violence occurred east of the Dniester in November, when elections were announced to a Transdnestrian Supreme Soviet. Negotiations in Moscow involving the Moldovan Government, the east-bank Slavs and the Gagauz failed to resolve the crisis, but the elections proceeded without further violence.

In mid-December 1990 an estimated 800,000 people, attending a 'Grand National Assembly', voted by acclamation to reject any new union treaty (which was being negotiated by other Soviet republics). Furthermore, in February 1991 the Moldovan Supreme Soviet resolved not to conduct the all-Union referendum on the future of the USSR, which was scheduled for March, and endorsed proposals for a confederation of states without central control as the preferred replacement for the USSR. Despite the official boycott, some 650,000 people (mostly Russians, Ukrainians and Gagauz) participated in the referendum, voting almost unanimously for the preservation of the USSR. Nevertheless, the ethnic-Romanian-dominated Government and legislature continued the process of de facto secession from the USSR. All-Union enterprises were placed under republican jurisdiction, a Moldovan state bank was established (independent of the USSR Gosbank), the CPM was prohibited from activities in state and government organs, and conscription to the USSR armed forces was not implemented. In May the designation 'Soviet Socialist' was removed from the republic's name and the Supreme Soviet was renamed the Moldovan Parliament. In the same month, following a vote of 'no confidence' by the legislature, Mircea Druc was removed from the post of Prime Minister.

Following the coup attempt in Moscow in August 1991, the commanders of the USSR's South-Western Military District sought to impose a state of emergency in Moldova. However, the republican leadership immediately announced its support for the Russian President, Boris Yeltsin, in his opposition to the coup, and demanded the reinstatement of Gorbachev as President of the USSR. On 27 August, after the coup had collapsed, the Moldovan Parliament and the 'Grand National Assembly' proclaimed Moldova's independence from the USSR. The Government asserted its jurisdiction over the border with Romania and introduced customs posts on the border with Ukraine. In September President Snegur ordered the creation of national armed forces, and assumed control of the republican KGB (state security service), transforming it into a Ministry of National Security. The Government announced that it would no longer participate in any Soviet structures or in negotiations for a new political union. However, in November the leadership did sign a treaty to establish an economic community.

At the election to the republican presidency on 8 December 1991 Snegur, the sole candidate, received 98.2% of the votes cast. On 21 December Moldova was among the 11 signatories to the Alma-Ata (Almaty) Declaration establishing the Commonwealth of Independent States (CIS, see p. 180). The establishment of the CIS led to wider international recognition of Moldova's independence, which had been somewhat delayed by concerns at inter-ethnic tension within the republic. Moldovan affairs during the first half of 1992 were, none the less, dominated by the armed conflict in Transnistria (see below) and by the question of possible unification with Romania, strongly advocated by the ruling PF (which in February was re-formed as the Christian Democratic Popular Front—CDPF). Moreover, a National Council for Reintegration had been established in December 1991, comprising legislators from both Moldova and Romania who were committed to the idea of a unified Romanian state. Within Moldova, however, popular support for unification remained insubstantial. In June 1992 the CDPF-dominated Government announced its resignation, which was attributed to popular opposition to the Government's pro-unification policies, compounded by the severe decline in the standard of living and the Government's inability to curb increasing corruption and lawlessness. Andrei Sangheli, a Deputy Prime Minister in the outgoing administration, was appointed Prime Minister, and a new Government 'of national accord' was formed, led by the Agrarian Democratic Party (ADP), which largely comprised members of the former communist leadership—in particular collective farm managers. Several portfolios that had been

reserved for representatives from Transnistria and Gagauzia were refused. The CDPF became the main opposition party. The ADP declared its commitment to consolidating Moldovan statehood, rejecting any future union with Romania in favour of a closer alignment with Russia and the CIS. The ADP's anti-unification policies were strongly supported by President Snegur, who in January 1993 proposed that the issue be resolved in a referendum. Snegur's proposal was, however, narrowly rejected by Parliament. The ensuing political crisis led to the resignations of both supporters and opponents of union with Romania, including the pro-unification Chairman of Parliament, Alexandru Moşanu. Moşanu was replaced in February by Petru Lucinschi, the former leader of the CPM (which had been banned following the attempted coup in Moscow in 1991).

The ADP made substantial progress with the drafting of a new Moldovan constitution during 1993, although the document could only be ratified by the new Parliament that was due to be elected in early 1994. The draft Constitution provided, *inter alia*, for a reduced, 104-member legislature. Moldova's first multi-party elections were held on 27 February 1994, with the participation of more than 73% of the electorate. On the eve of the elections, the authorities in Gagauzia rescinded their decision to boycott the poll, and the rate of participation in the region was reported to be high. In Transnistria the local leadership did not permit polling stations to open; however, residents were able to vote on the left bank of the Dniester. In all, 13 parties and blocs contested the elections, the results of which demonstrated widespread popular support for parties advocating continued Moldovan independence. The ADP obtained an overall majority in Parliament (56 seats). The successor party to the CPM, the Socialist Party (SP), in alliance with the Slav-based Yedinstvo Movement, won 28 seats. Two pro-unification groups shared the remaining 20 seats: the Peasants' Party of Moldova/Congress of Intelligentsia alliance (11) and the CDPF alliance (nine). The overwhelming lack of support for the pro-unification parties was confirmed in a national referendum on Moldova's statehood on 6 March. Of the 75% of the participating electorate, more than 95% were in favour of continued independence. In late March Andrei Sangheli was re-elected Prime Minister, and Petru Lucinschi was re-elected Chairman of Parliament. A new, smaller Council of Ministers, comprising solely members of the ADP, was appointed in April. In May the CPM was permitted to re-form, as the Moldovan Party of Communists (MPC).

The new Constitution was adopted by Parliament in July 1994 and entered into force in August. As well as establishing the country's permanent neutrality, the Constitution provided for a 'special autonomous status' for Transnistria and Gagauzia within Moldova (the exact terms of which were to be determined at a later date). The official state language was specified as Moldovan (rather than Romanian), although the two languages were acknowledged to be identical. In March–April 1995 thousands of students participated in rallies in Chişinău, demanding that Romanian be redesignated the official state language. In response, Snegur decreed a six-month moratorium on the language issue; meanwhile, a special committee was to examine the matter. In June, following the rejection by the ADP and its allies in Parliament of the proposal that Romanian replace Moldovan in the Constitution as the state language, Snegur resigned his membership of the ADP (which he had joined in 1994). In August 1995 he established the Party of Rebirth and Conciliation (PRC), with the support of several disaffected ADP deputies, as well as one of the Deputy Chairmen of Parliament, Nicolae Andronic (who was removed from his post). There were renewed student rallies in October; in February 1996, none the less, Parliament again rejected the proposed redesignation of the state language.

Some 68% of the registered electorate participated in the presidential election held on 17 November 1996, which was contested by nine candidates. Although Snegur received the largest share of the votes cast (39%), his failure to win an absolute majority necessitated a second round of voting, contested by the incumbent and his closest rival, the ADP-supported Petru Lucinschi (who had secured 28%). The rate of participation was slightly higher (72%) in the second round, held on 1 December, when Lucinschi emerged with 54% of the votes. The authorities in Transnistria again boycotted the poll, and there were reports that residents were prevented from leaving the region to vote on the left bank of the Dniester. Lucinschi was inaugurated as President on 15 January 1997, and a new Government was announced later that month. It retained approximately one-half of the members of the outgoing administration, and was headed by Ion Ciubuc, a non-party economist. In March the leader of the ADP, Dumitru Moțpan, was elected as Lucinschi's successor as Chairman of Parliament (he had hitherto served as a Deputy Chairman).

Relations between Lucinschi and Parliament were strained during 1997, in particular over the progress of economic reforms. Parliamentary elections took place on 22 March 1998. In an apparent rejection of Lucinschi's economic reform programme, the elections were won by the MPC, led by Vladimir Voronin, which took 30.1% of the votes cast (40 of the total seats). The Democratic Convention of Moldova (CDM), an alliance of right-wing parties that included the PRC, under the leadership of Snegur, achieved 19.2% (26 seats), while the Movement for a Democratic and Prosperous Moldova (MDPM) received 18.2% (24 seats) and the Moldovan Party of Democratic Forces 8.8% (11 seats). The remaining 11 parties (including the ADP) failed to secure the minimum 4% of the total votes required for representation. Three independent candidates won seats; the rate of participation was 67%, according to preliminary results. The elections were, once again, boycotted in Transnistria, but voters were permitted to cross the Dniester to vote.

At the first session of the new legislature, convened in late April 1998, Dumitru Diacov was elected Chairman. The Government resigned shortly afterwards. Since none of the political parties had secured an overall parliamentary majority, the new Government, appointed in late May (with Ciubuc retaining his post as Prime Minister), comprised a coalition of members of the MDPM, the CDM and the Moldovan Party of Democratic Forces. Within Parliament, the coalition, called the Alliance for Democracy and Reforms, was led by Snegur. The efficacy of the new Government was swiftly undermined by differences between coalition members, although a motion of 'no confidence' was defeated in November.

In early 1999 there were protests in Chişinău by workers in the education and transport sectors over accumulated wage and pension arrears. Ciubuc resigned as Prime Minister in early February, citing internal divisions. Snegur resigned as parliamentary leader of the government coalition one day later, after his nominee for the premiership, Deputy Prime Minister Nicolae Andronic, was rejected. Shortly afterwards Lucinschi nominated the Mayor of Chişinău, Serafim Urecheanu, as Prime Minister. However, Urecheanu resigned in mid-February, having failed to reach agreement with the parliamentary majority, notably on the issue of strengthening executive powers. Lucinschi had, in the mean time, submitted a presidential bill to Parliament providing for a substantial expansion of the executive's authority over the next two years, which, he maintained, was essential in order to address the economic crisis. Following Urecheanu's resignation, Lucinschi nominated Ion Sturza, the Deputy Prime Minister and Minister of the Economy and Reforms, as Prime Minister. Although Parliament twice failed to endorse his proposed government, Lucinschi nominated Sturza a third time. Confronted with a choice between acceptance or an early general election (the Constitution permits the President to dissolve the legislature if a candidate for the premiership is twice rejected), Parliament approved Sturza's Government in mid-March, with the requisite 52 votes.

Local elections were held in Moldova on 23 May 1999, after which the country was reorganized into nine provinces and two autonomous entities—Gagauzia and Transnistria. A referendum was held on the same day, on the issue of increasing presidential powers. Although initially invalidated because of the low rate of electoral participation, in June the Constitutional Court ruled the referendum, which had approved the President's proposals, to be valid; however, it was to have no judicial effect. In August a controversial draft law on amending the Constitution was published, whereby the President would appoint the prime minister and members of the government and adopt their programme of activity; it was also proposed that the presidential term of office be extended from four to five years and that the number of deputies be reduced from 101 to 70, elected solely on the basis of single-mandate constituencies. In September Lucinschi announced his willingness to cancel a proposed referendum on the issue if parliamentary representatives, together with experts from the Council of Europe (see p. 190), succeeded in proposing revisions to the draft law. In the following month a group of deputies advanced a reform plan for debate in Parliament, which included a proposal that the President be appointed by the legislature. Moreover, in November the Constitutional Court ruled the May referendum to have been illegal, as it had not been announced and prepared by

Parliament; in future the President would not have the right to call plebiscites.

The creation, in October 1999, of a new, independent political bloc, by members of the MDPM and a former deputy of the Moldovan Party of Democratic Forces, weakened the Government's support in Parliament. In the following month Sturza lost a vote of confidence in the legislature, after the defeat of a controversial bill on the privatization of the wine and tobacco industries; the IMF and the World Bank subsequently suspended credits to Moldova (the bill was finally approved in October 2000). In mid-November 1999 Lucinschi nominated the former ambassador to Russia, Valeriu Bobutac, as Prime Minister. Bobutac resigned 10 days later, having failed to secure the necessary support in the legislature. Following the failure of a second candidate, Vladimir Voronin, the President decided to propose a third, rather than dissolve the legislature. After negotiations on the composition of a new government to be led by the former Minister of Communications, Ion Casian, failed, the President nominated Dumitru Braghiş, hitherto Deputy Minister of Economy and Reform. Braghiş was approved as Prime Minister in late December, thus narrowly averting the dissolution of Parliament and new legislative elections.

In early July 2000 Parliament voted, by 92 votes to five, in favour of amending the Constitution to permit the legislature to elect the Head of State. Although President Lucinschi vetoed the proposed constitutional change, Parliament swiftly overturned his decision, and legislation was enacted in late July; the President declared the new law to be in contravention of the non-binding referendum of May 1999. In September 2000 Parliament approved a further amendment to the law on presidential electoral procedure and an alteration to the electoral code, and in mid-October it announced that a presidential election would be held at the beginning of December. Lucinschi, who insisted that the public should retain the right to elect the president, announced that he would not contest the election. In November the MPC selected its First Secretary, Vladimir Voronin, to stand as the party's candidate in the presidential election. Also contesting the election was the Chairman of the Constitutional Court, Pavel Barbalat, who had been proposed by a coalition of the Democratic Party of Moldova (PDM—as the MDPM had been renamed in April), the CDM, the Christian Democratic People's Party (CDPP, formerly the CDPF) and the Moldovan Party of Democratic Forces.

Three rounds of voting in the presidential election proved inconclusive in early December 2000, with neither of the two candidates obtaining the requisite number of votes to secure an overall victory. After Voronin refused to withdraw his candidacy, the PDM, the CDM, the CDPP and the Moldovan Party of Democratic Forces boycotted a fourth round of voting on 21 December, preventing it from taking place (as only 48 out of the necessary quorum of 61 deputies were present), and thereby permitting the President to dissolve the legislature and schedule early parliamentary elections; Lucinschi emphasized the right of the new Parliament to overturn measures introduced by the previous legislature. Parliament was duly dissolved on 12 January 2001, and a general election was scheduled for 25 February. Lucinschi remained in office after the official expiry of his term in mid-January, until a successor could be elected.

At the legislative elections, held as scheduled on 25 February 2001, the MPC won an overall majority in Parliament, securing 49.9% of the votes cast and 71 seats. The Braghiş Alliance, formed by the incumbent Prime Minister, obtained 13.4% of the votes and 19 seats, while the CDPP obtained 8.3% of the votes and 11 seats. The elections, which represented the first communist return to power in the former USSR since its collapse, were described as free and fair by Organization for Security and Co-operation in Europe (OSCE, see p. 302) observers. The rate of voter participation was some 70%. In early March the MPC, which pledged to maintain a multi-party system, again nominated Voronin to stand in the presidential election, which took place on 4 April. Voronin secured 71 votes, Braghiş obtained 15 and another communist candidate, Valerian Cristea, won three; the 11 deputies of the CDPP abstained from voting to express their lack of support for any candidate. Following his inauguration as President on 7 April, Voronin nominated Vasile Tarlev, a former businessman without party affiliation, to head a new government. A new Minister of Energy, Iacob Timciuc, was appointed in early August, and in early September Nicolae Dudău was appointed as Minister of Foreign Affairs.

Proposals put forward in August 2001 by the Minister of Education, Ilie Vancea, according to which the compulsory teaching of Russian language and history was to be introduced to the national curriculum from 2002, were confirmed in December 2001. A demonstration, organized by the CDPP and involving an estimated 3,000 people, took place in Chişinău on 9 January 2002 to protest against the proposed changes to the education system and what was perceived as an attempt by the Government to bring about the russification of Moldova; increasingly large-scale, daily protests continued throughout the month, prompting fears of destabilization and demands for CDPP members to be deprived of their parliamentary immunity. In late January the Ministry of Justice suspended the CDPP from participation in political activities for a period of one month, thus preventing it from organizing further protests. However, in February, following intervention by the Council of Europe, the suspension of the CDPP was annulled in order to allow the party to campaign for local elections, due to be held in April. In mid-February, however, the Constitutional Court ruled the scheduling of early local elections for April, before the expiry of the four-year mandate of the local government officials elected in 1999, to be unconstitutional.

Meanwhile, in early February 2002 both the Deputy Prime Minister and Minister of the Economy, Andrei Cucu, and the reformist Minister of Finance, Mihai Manole, tendered their resignations, prompting international concern that the withdrawal of the only two non-MPC members of the Council of Ministers might hinder the implementation of economic reforms. Protests against the reform of the education system intensified throughout February, eventually prompting Vancea to announce that the controversial legislation would be retracted and to make a public apology. None the less, the domestic crisis prompted Vancea's dismissal on 26 February; he was replaced by Gheorghe Sima, and Zinaida Grecîanîi was appointed as Minister of Finance on the same day. The following day the Minister of the Interior, Vasile Draganel, resigned, amid reports that he had been unwilling to use force to dispel protesters. Draganel was replaced by Gheorghe Papuc, a long-serving member of the security forces.

Despite a ruling by the Supreme Court declaring the ongoing protests to be illegal and demanding that they be halted, in late February 2002 demonstrators began to protest outside the headquarters of the national television company against state censorship and misinformation. In late March the Deputy Chairman of the CDPP, Vlad Cubreacov, who had been involved in organizing the anti-Government protests, was declared missing; thousands of demonstrators subsequently gathered to protest against Cubreacov's disappearance, which members of the CDPP attributed to the Government. At the end of the month the CDPP announced that it had discontinued its anti-Government protests, in compliance with Council of Europe recommendations, but declared that the Government's failure to comply with Council resolutions on, *inter alia*, the granting of independence to the state-owned media and the judiciary would lead to the resumption of demonstrations. In late May Cubreacov was discovered alive near the Transnistrian border, although his kidnappers remained unidentified. In June judicial proceedings against members of the opposition involved in the organization of public protests (including Cubreacov) were suspended indefinitely.

In early June 2002 Parliament approved a new Civil Code. A number of government changes were made in late 2002, including the appointment in December of Vasile Sova to the new post of Minister of Reintegration, with responsibility for the resolution of the issue of Transnistria and the co-ordination of government structures. Also in December the Social Liberal Party absorbed the Moldovan Party of Democratic Forces. Local elections took place on 25 May and 8 June 2003, in which the MPC won the majority of seats, followed by the newly formed Moldova Noastra alliance (Our Moldova—comprising the Alliance of Independents of Moldova, the Moldovan Liberal Party and the Social Democratic Alliance of Moldova). Following the elections, new legislation on administrative reform, approved by the Government in January, came into effect, according to which the nine provinces and two autonomous regions introduced in 1999 were replaced with a structure based on the Soviet system, and comprising 33 districts and one municipality. In July 2003 the parties of the Moldova Noastra bloc formally merged, together with the Popular Democratic Party of Moldova, to form Alianţa Moldova Noastra, led by Dumitru Braghiş, Serafim Urechean and Veaceslav Untilă. In early August Voronin

appointed Marian Lupu as Deputy Prime Minister and Minister of the Economy, replacing Ştefan Odagiu, who had been dismissed in July. Valentin Beniuc succeeded Gheorghe Sima as Minister of Education.

Thousands of protesters took part in opposition demonstrations in November 2003, in protest against the Government's initial support for a Russian proposal for the federalization of Moldova as a solution to the Transnistria issue (see below). The proposals, rejected in late November, had envisaged the installation of a popularly elected president and new, bicameral legislature, with an upper house comprising 13 Moldovan, nine Transnistrian and four Gagauz representatives; Transnistria and Gagauzia were to have been represented at federal level by deputy prime ministers. In early December the Prosecutor-General, Vasile Rusu, resigned, following criticism of his response to the protests; he was replaced by Valeriu Balaban. Further protests took place in December against legislation on nationalities policy, which was submitted to Parliament by Voronin. The new law, which was approved on 19 December, intended to promote the use of Russian as a language of interethnic communication, although Moldovan was to remain the official language, and emphasized Moldovan (as distinct from Romanian) identity. Deputies from the Braghiş Alliance and the CDPP did not participate in the voting.

In February 2004 Andrei Stratan replaced Nicolae Dudău as Minister of Foreign Affairs. In the same month Parliament withdrew the immunity from prosecution of three members of the CDPP, including the party's Chairman, Iurie Rosca, at the request of the Prosecutor-General, to permit their prosecution on charges of organizing and participating in unauthorized protests. From April the Democratic Party of Moldova and the Social Liberal Party agreed to co-operate with the Alianţa Moldova Noastra, in preparation for parliamentary elections in 2005.

Following the proclamation of Transnistria's secession in September 1990, relations between the region and the central Government in Chişinău remained tense. Armed conflict broke out in December 1991, as the leadership of the self-proclaimed republic, opposed to the Government's objective of reunification with Romania, launched a campaign to gain control of Transnistria (with the ultimate aim of unity with Russia). More than six months of military conflict ensued, as Moldovan government troops were dispatched to combat the local Slav militia. The Moldovan Government claimed that the east-bank forces were actively supported by the Russian Government, while the Moldovans were, in turn, accused of receiving military and other assistance from Romania. The situation was complicated by the presence (and alleged involvement in support of the east-bank Slavs) of the former Soviet 14th Army, which was still stationed in the region and jurisdiction over which had been transferred to Russia. Peace negotiations were held at regular intervals, with the participation of Moldova, Russia, Ukraine and Romania; however, none of the agreed cease-fires was observed. By June 1992 some 700 people were believed to have been killed in the conflict, with a further estimated 50,000 people forced to take refuge in neighbouring Ukraine. On 21 July, however, a peace agreement was finally negotiated by Presidents Snegur and Yeltsin, whereby Transnistria was accorded 'special status' within Moldova (the terms of which were to be formulated later). Later in July Russian, Moldovan and Transnistrian peace-keeping troops were deployed in the region to monitor the cease-fire. However, Moldova's relations with Russia remained strained during the remainder of 1992.

Transnistria continued to demand full statehood, and in January 1994 the Moldovan Government accepted proposals by the Conference on Security and Co-operation in Europe (CSCE—later OSCE) for greater autonomy, including economic independence, for Transnistria, within a Moldovan confederation. The Transnistrian leadership expressed its approval of the proposals, and the result of the Moldovan parliamentary elections of the following month (which eliminated the possibility of Moldova's future unification with Romania) further enhanced the prospects for peace in the region. In April President Snegur and the Transnistrian leader, Igor Smirnov, pledged their commitment to holding negotiations for a peaceful resolution of the conflict, based on the CSCE recommendations.

In July 1994, following the adoption of the new Moldovan Constitution, which provided for a 'special autonomous status' for Transnistria, negotiations duly commenced on the details of the region's future status within Moldova. Progress was obstructed, in particular, by disagreement over the future of the

15,000-strong 14th Army, since the Transnistrian leadership demanded the continued presence of the Army in the region as a guarantor of security. In October, however, the Moldovan and Russian Governments reached an agreement, under which Russia was to withdraw the 14th Army within a period of three years, whereupon Transnistria's negotiated 'special autonomous status' would take effect. A referendum (declared illegal by President Snegur) was held in Transnistria in March 1995, in which some 91% of participants voted against the withdrawal of the 14th Army. In late June, however, the withdrawal of weapons and ammunition of the 14th Army was begun. In December a new bicameral legislature was elected in Transnistria. On the same occasion two further referendums were held: 82.7% of the electorate endorsed a new constitution (which proclaimed the region's independence), while 89.7% voted for Transnistria to join the CIS as a sovereign state. In February 1996, however, the CIS ruled out admittance for Transnistria on such terms.

In July 1996 the executive and legislative authorities of Moldova and Transnistria initialled a memorandum, drafted with the aid of Russian, Ukrainian and OSCE mediators, on normalizing relations; this was viewed as an important stage towards defining the 'special status' of Transnistria within a future Moldovan confederation. However, Snegur subsequently declared his opposition to the memorandum, claiming that it effectively formalized Moldova's 'disintegration into two states', and announced that any decision on the issue should be postponed until after the presidential election. Following his election as Moldova's new President in December, Petru Lucinschi announced his intention to sign the memorandum. In that month Igor Smirnov was re-elected 'President' of Transnistria, with more than 70% of the votes cast.

Meanwhile, the withdrawal of contingents of the 14th Army continued, and by early 1997 its strength had reportedly been reduced to some 5,000–6,000 men. None the less, the withdrawal agreement, although signed by the respective Governments, still awaited ratification by the Russian State Duma. In April it was announced that substantial progress had been achieved in the negotiations concerning the status of Transnistria. A new article was added to the memorandum initialled in mid-1996, stating that the two sides would develop relations within the framework of one state, the borders of which would correspond to those of the former Soviet republic of Moldova. The memorandum was signed in Moscow, in early May, by Lucinschi and Smirnov, with Russia and Ukraine acting as guarantors of the document. It was agreed to resume negotiations on the defining of Transnistria's 'special status', and commissions were constituted for that purpose. Representatives of the two sides, meeting in Moscow in October, reached agreement on a number of 'confidence-building measures', and an agreement was signed in Odessa, Ukraine, by Lucinschi, Smirnov, Russian Prime Minister Viktor Chernomyrdin and President Leonid Kuchma of Ukraine on 20 March 1998. A reduction in Moldovan and Transnistrian peace-keeping forces was envisaged, while Russian troops were to remain in Transnistria until a final political settlement was reached.

The success of Snegur's CDM at the March 1998 legislative elections raised concerns among the Transnistrian leadership regarding the future of relations with the Moldovan Government. In June, however, Russian and Moldovan delegations to the joint commission monitoring the Odessa Accords agreed proposals for the composition of peace-keeping forces in the Transnistrian security zone. In late August the joint monitoring commission approved the deployment of Ukrainian peace-keeping forces in the security zone: at this time, there were some 700 troops from each of Moldova, Transnistria and Russia. Meanwhile Moldova's peace-keeping troops were gradually reduced in number (to about 500), and Moldova continued to urge Russia to accelerate the withdrawal of its troops and weaponry from the area. From late May 1999, following local elections in Moldova (in which the region refused to participate), Transnistria was designated an autonomous entity. In July Lucinschi met Smirnov, along with Russian Prime Minister Sergei Stepashin and an OSCE representative in Kiev, Ukraine. Although the negotiations concluded with the signature of a joint declaration on the normalization of relations between Moldova and Transnistria, Smirnov declared that differences remained. At an OSCE summit in İstanbul, Turkey, in November, Russia agreed to withdraw from Transnistria in three stages, with all hardware to be removed by the end of 2001, and all troops by the end of 2002.

In June 2000 the 'Transdnestrian Supreme Soviet' was converted to a reduced, unicameral legislature. Smirnov introduced a form of presidential rule in the following month, and a new cabinet was installed to act as a consultative body; legislative elections were held in December. Meanwhile, in July President Lucinschi established a commission for the settlement of the regional conflict, which was to co-operate with the OSCE and with the Russian and Ukrainian commissions on Transnistria. In August, in Moscow, the Moldovan and 'Transdnestrian' delegations held separate tripartite discussions with the Russian and Ukrainian commissions, but, although new proposals for the resolution of the issue were advanced by the head of the Russian commission, the former Russian Prime Minister, Yevgenii Primakov, no agreement was reached. The new Moldovan President elected in April 2001, Vladimir Vorodin, declared the pursuit of a final political settlement for Transnistria to be a priority but, although a number of bilateral agreements were signed in Tiraspol in May, no substantive progress was made. In June the OSCE welcomed the Moldovan Government's announcement that it was to reduce the strength of its peace-keeping forces in the security zone. A deterioration in Transnistria's relations with the Moldovan Government took place in September, however, following the Government's introduction of new customs procedures, in accordance with World Trade Organization specifications; the withholding of new customs seals from the Transnistrian authorities, thereby preventing the region from conducting its own external economic activities, led to claims that the Moldovan Government was attempting to impose an 'economic blockade' on the region, and the curtailment of negotiations. Igor Smirnov was re-elected as 'President' of the region in an election held on 9 December, receiving almost 82% of the votes cast; the election result was recognized by neither the Moldovan Government nor the international community. A new Transnistrian Government was appointed in February 2002. Meanwhile, the agreed withdrawal of Russian military hardware from the region was subject to delays, partly owing to the obstruction of railway lines by Transnistrians who hoped to gain compensation for the equipment withdrawn. In December 2002 the OSCE amended the deadline agreed in 1999 for the removal of Russian forces from Moldova, extending it for a further year, until 31 December 2003; however, Russia indicated that some troops might remain, with a possible mandate for maintaining peace and stability in the event of agreement on reunification.

In July 2002 mediators from Russia, Ukraine and the OSCE submitted a new draft agreement (the 'Kiev agreement'), according to which Moldova would become a federal state, in which the autonomous territories would maintain their own legislature and constitution; Smirnov permitted participation in talks on the draft, but insisted that recognition of Transnistria's 'independence' was a fundamental prerequisite. On 27 February 2003 the European Union (EU, see p. 208) and the USA, and subsequently other countries, imposed a travel ban on those Transnistrian officials considered to be 'primarily responsible for a lack of co-operation in promoting a political settlement' (in response, in March certain Moldovan officials were deemed *personae non gratae* in Transnistria; the ban was lifted in November). On 28 February the Moldovan Government and the Transnistrian authorities reached preliminary agreement on proposals by President Voronin for the joint drafting of a new constitution, which would be subject to approval by referendum by February 2004 (however, no further progress was made towards organizing a plebiscite on the issue). In mid-November 2003 the Russian President, Vladimir Putin, announced new proposals for a political settlement. Drafted by the deputy head of the presidential administration, Dmitrii Kozak, the plan envisaged the establishment of an 'asymmetrical federation', comprising Moldova and Transnistria, with unified defence, customs and finance systems. The leaders of both Transnistria and Moldova initially responded positively to the proposals, but Voronin withdrew his support in late November, following opposition protests and reservations expressed by the OSCE. The 'Kozak memorandum' had also attracted criticism from some observers, who considered it to serve Russian interests. In February 2004 the Moldovan and Transnistrian sides submitted new proposals for Moldova's federalization to OSCE mediators. However, the Transnistrian authorities considered the new proposals to offer the region insufficient autonomy, and representatives of the Moldovan Government also criticized the draft for its failure to clarify the issue of the continued presence of Russian troops and military equipment in Transnistria. Earlier in the month the Russian Minister of Defence had indicated that, despite the agreements on troop withdrawal reached in 1999 and 2002, Russia intended to maintain troops in the region, in response to the increasing numbers of US troops based in eastern Europe. Also in February 2004 the EU extended the travel restrictions imposed on Transnistrian officials in 2003 for a further one-year period.

During the period of the Transnistrian conflict, in 1991–92, the situation in Gagauzia remained peaceful, although the region continued to demand full statehood. The new Moldovan Constitution, adopted in July 1994, provided for a 'special autonomous status' for Gagauzia, as for Transnistria, and negotiations duly commenced on the details of this status. Agreement was quickly reached between the Government and the Gagauz authorities, and in December the Moldovan Parliament adopted legislation on the 'special status of Gagauz-Eri' (or Gagauzia). The regions of southern Moldova populated by the Gagauz were to enjoy broad self-administrative powers, and Gagauz was to be one of three official languages (with Moldovan and Russian). Legislative power was to be vested in a regional assembly, and a directly elected 'baskan' was to hold a quasi-presidential position. The law on the status of Gagauz-Eri entered into force in February 1995, and in the following month a referendum was held in the region to determine which settlements would form part of the region. Elections to the 35-seat regional assembly (Halk Toplusu) took place in late May–early June. Elections, held simultaneously, to the post of baskan were won by Gheorghe Tabunscic, the First Secretary of the Comrat branch of the MPC. Under the new Constitution, Tabunscic, as Gagauz leader, became a member of the Council of Ministers. At the first session of the assembly, the self-proclaimed 'Gagauz Republic' was declared defunct. Following local elections in Moldova in late May 1999, Gagauzia, like Transnistria, was designated an autonomous entity. Elections to the Halk Toplusu and to the post of baskan were held in late August. Following a second round of voting in early September, Dumitru Croitor was elected as Baskan, with 61.5% of the votes cast. In mid-February 2002 the Halk Toplusu passed a vote of 'no confidence' in Croitor, and scheduled a referendum in the hope of securing his dismissal. However, as the confidence vote had been passed without the required majority, it was declared to be unconstitutional by supporters of Croitor. On 24 February, the date that the referendum was scheduled to take place, the regional security forces reportedly seized the offices of the regional Election Commission, declaring its mandate to have expired and the plebiscite to be illegal. President Voronin subsequently visited the region and demanded the resignations of both Croitor and the Chairman of the Halk Toplusu. Croitor finally resigned at the end of June. At a second round of voting in an election held on 11 October, Gheorghe Tabunscic secured the highest proportion of the votes cast and regained the position of Baskan; a new Government was subsequently approved. On 25 July 2003 the Moldovan Parliament officially recognized the autonomous status of Gagauzia through an amendment to the national Constitution, which awarded the Halk Toplusu the right to self-determination and to propose its own legislation. Legislative elections were held in the region in November and December, in which the MPC and independent candidates each won almost one-half of the seats contested.

Owing to the changing domestic situation, Moldova's membership of the CIS was equivocal from its signature of the Alma-Ata Declaration in December 1991 until early 1994. In August 1993 the Moldovan Parliament failed by four votes to ratify the Alma-Ata Declaration, largely owing to the influence of deputies favouring unification with Romania, thus technically removing Moldova from the CIS. However, it was increasingly recognized that Moldova's economic survival depended on the CIS, and in September President Snegur signed a treaty to join the new CIS economic union. Following Moldova's parliamentary elections of February 1994 and the referendum in March, which strongly endorsed continued independence, Parliament reversed its earlier decision, and in late April it finally ratified membership of the CIS. However, the legislature indicated that Moldova would participate neither in CIS military structures nor in monetary union.

The communist Government elected in 2001 undertook a policy of *rapprochement* with Russia, and on 27 December Parliament ratified a treaty on friendship and co-operation, which had been signed by the two countries' respective Presidents in the previous month. The treaty was ratified by the Russian State Duma in April 2002. Since gaining independence

Moldova has also sought to develop good relations with the neighbouring countries of Ukraine and Romania. Agreement on the delimitation of the Moldovan–Ukrainian border, apart from the Transnistrian section, was reached in November 1997, and the two countries finally defined their border in May 1999.

Relations with Romania were subject to tensions. A basic political treaty, in preparation for six years, was agreed in May 1999 and initialled in April 2000; however, it was not signed, and in late 2003 the Romanian Prime Minister, Adrian Năstase, indicated that the country no longer considered the treaty to be relevant to the political situation. Meanwhile, in February 2000 many Moldovans had applied to obtain Romanian citizenship as formal negotiations on Romania's accession to the EU commenced. The Romanian Government subsequently introduced measures to simplify the application process, angering the Moldovan authorities, since the Constitution did not permit dual citizenship. The situation was resolved when President Lucinschi drafted a new law, allowing Moldovans to hold dual citizenship with Israel, Romania and Russia, which was enacted in August. Moldova and Romania signed several co-operation agreements in July 2001. However, from August Romania expressed concern at the apparent 'russification' of Moldova, in particular following a decision to introduce compulsory Russian-language teaching from 2002 (see above). In March 2002 a Romanian diplomat was expelled from Moldova, after having reportedly met organizers of opposition protests; Romania responded by expelling a Moldovan diplomat. None the less, following a meeting in September between the Presidents of the two countries, held in Beirut, Lebanon, it was agreed to establish working groups to resolve problems in diplomatic relations. From April 2003 ministerial co-operation between Moldova and Romania was resumed, together with discussions on the initiation of negotiations regarding a border agreement; it was confirmed that Romania would not require Moldovan citizens to possess entry visas until its accession to the EU, anticipated in 2007. In May 2003 the Moldovan Parliament passed legislation, which permitted Romanians in Moldova to hold dual citizenship. None the less, in October the Moldovan Government appealed to the Council of Europe for assistance with regard to its deteriorating relations with Romania, after that country failed to sign a bilateral treaty confirming Moldova's borders.

Government

Under the Constitution of 1994, supreme legislative power is held by the unicameral Moldovan Parliament, which is directly elected every four years. Parliament comprises 101 members. The President is Head of State and holds executive power in conjunction with the Council of Ministers, led by the Prime Minister. According to constitutional amendments introduced in July 2000, the President is elected by the legislature for a four-year term. Following local elections in May 1999 the country was reorganized into nine provinces and two autonomous entities—Gagauzia and Transnistria. However, in January 2003 the Government approved new legislation on administrative reform, replacing the nine provinces and two autonomous regions introduced in 1999 with a structure based on the Soviet system, and comprising 33 districts (rayons) and one municipality.

Defence

Following independence from the USSR (declared in August 1991), the Moldovan Government initiated the creation of national armed forces. By August 2003 these were estimated to number 6,910, including an army of 5,560 and an air force of 1,100. There are an estimated 3,400 paramilitary forces, attached to the Ministry of Internal Affairs. Military service is compulsory (with exemptions for students) and lasts for one year. Under an agreement concluded by the Moldovan and Russian Governments in late 1994, the former Soviet 14th Army (under Russian jurisdiction) was to have been withdrawn from Transnistria within three years, but in March 1998 it was agreed that Russian forces would remain in the region until a final political settlement had been reached. In July 2000 it was agreed to withdraw the Russian military presence from Transnistria in three stages, with all hardware to be removed by the end of 2001 and all troops by the end of 2002; the deadline was subsequently extended until December 2003, but both troops and equipment remained in Transnistria at 2004. In early 1994 Moldova joined the North Atlantic Treaty Organization's (NATO) 'Partnership for Peace' (see p. 291) programme. The 2003 budget allocated 102m. Moldovan lei to defence.

Economic Affairs

In 2002, according to estimates by the World Bank, Moldova's gross national income (GNI), measured at average 2000–02 prices, was US $1,671m., equivalent to $460 per head (or $1,560 on an international purchasing-power parity basis). During 1990–2002, it was estimated, the population decreased by an annual average of 0.2%, while gross domestic product (GDP) per head declined, in real terms, at an average rate of 7.1% per year. Overall GDP declined, in real terms, at an average annual rate of 7.3% in 1990–2002; however, GDP increased by 6.1% in 2001 and by 7.2% in 2002.

As a result of its extremely fertile land and temperate climate, Moldova's economy is dominated by agriculture and related industries. Some 85% of the country's terrain is cultivated. In 2002 agriculture contributed some 25.1% of GDP. In 2001 the sector (including hunting, forestry and fishing) provided 51.0% of employment. Principal crops include wine grapes and other fruit, tobacco, vegetables and grain. The wine industry has traditionally occupied a central role in the economy, and was revived after the Soviet Government's anti-alcohol campaign of the mid-1980s. The private ownership of land was legalized in 1991, although the sale of agricultural land was not to be permitted until 2001. Private farmers accounted for an estimated 67% of Moldova's agricultural output in 1999. According to the World Bank, the GDP of the agricultural sector declined, in real terms, at an average rate of 7.9% per year during 1990–2002. Agricultural GDP increased by 4.3% in 2001 and by 2.0% in 2002.

In 2002 industry (including mining, manufacturing, power and construction) contributed 24.2% of GDP; in 2001 the sector provided 13.9% of employment. Between 1990 and 2002, according to the World Bank, industrial GDP declined at an average rate of 11.0% per year. However, real industrial GDP increased by 17.4% in 2001 and by 6.0% in 2002.

Mining and quarrying employed just 0.1% of the working population in 2001. Moldova has extremely limited mineral resources, and there is no domestic production of fuel or non-ferrous metals. Activity is focused primarily on the extraction and processing of industrial minerals such as gypsum, limestone, sand and gravel. Deposits of petroleum and natural gas were discovered in southern Moldova in the early 1990s; total reserves of natural gas have been estimated at 22,000m. cu m.

The manufacturing sector provided 9.1% of employment in 2001 and contributed 18.2% of GDP in 2002. The sector is dominated by food-processing, wine and tobacco production, machine-building and metalworking, and light industry. In 1994 the principal branches, measured by gross value of output, were food-processing and beverages (57.8%), tobacco (4.9%), non-metallic mineral products (4.6%) and textiles (4.0%). According to the World Bank, manufacturing GDP declined, in real terms, by an annual average of 0.4% in 1995–2002. Manufacturing GDP increased by 17.8% in 2001 and by 6.0% in 2002.

Moldova relies heavily on imported energy—primarily natural gas and petroleum products—from Russia, Romania and Ukraine. Moldova was seeking to become self-sufficient in natural gas, following the discovery of gas reserves in the south of the country. A large proportion of natural gas imports supply the Moldoveneasca power station, located in Transnistria, which contributed some 85% of the country's electrical generating capacity in 1996. In 2000 natural gas accounted for 92.3% of electricity production, and coal accounted for 5.0% (compared with 43.8% in 1994). Mineral products comprised an estimated 26.5% of the value of total imports in 2001.

Services accounted for 50.7% of GDP in 2002, and provided 35.1% of total employment in 2001. The GDP of the services sector declined, in real terms, by an annual average of 2.5% in 1991–2002. Services GDP decreased, in real terms, by 0.5% in 2001, but increased by 4.4% in 2002.

In 2002 Moldova recorded a visible trade deficit of US $378.2m., while there was a deficit of $97.3m. on the current account of the balance of payments. In 2002, according to the IMF, the principal source of imports was Ukraine (accounting for 19.6% of the value of total imports). Other major suppliers were Russia, Romania, Italy and Germany. The main market for exports in that year was Russia (37.1% of the value of total exports). Other important purchasers were Ukraine, Italy, Romania and Germany. In 2002 the principal imports were mineral products, machinery and mechanical appliances, chemicals and related products, and textiles. The main exports in that year were food products, beverages and tobacco (accounting for some 41.5% of the value of total exports), textiles and vegetable products.

In 2002 the state budget recorded a deficit of 447m. Moldovan lei (equivalent to 2.0% of GDP). Moldova's total external debt at the end of 2001 was US $1,214m., of which $779m. was long-term public debt. In that year the cost of debt-servicing was equivalent to 19.4% of the value of exports of goods and services. Consumer prices increased by an annual average of 118.8% during 1991–2002. The average rate of inflation was 9.7% in 2001 and 5.5% in 2002. The average rate of unemployment was 7.9% in 2003.

Moldova became a member of the IMF and the World Bank in 1992. It also joined the European Bank for Reconstruction and Development (EBRD, see p. 203). Moldova subsequently became a member of the Organization of the Black Sea Economic Co-operation (see p. 312), and it became a full member of the World Trade Organization (see p. 343) in July 2001.

In common with other former Soviet republics following independence, Moldova's planned transition to a market economic system was hampered by the serious disruptions in inter-republican trade. Another factor that adversely affected economic performance was the armed conflict in Transnistria (the main industrial centre) in the first half of 1992 and the region's subsequent attempts to secede from Moldova (see Recent History). Moldova introduced its own national currency, the Moldovan leu, in November 1993. Although the IMF initially declared itself satisfied with Moldova's accelerated structural reforms, after 1998 the reform process stalled, and lending was repeatedly suspended in 1999–2003. The communist Government elected in 2001 cancelled several privatization agreements and concerns over the possible renationalization of the national airline and the electricity-distribution networks in 2002–03 resulted in reduced investment. The privatization programme, originally scheduled for completion by the end of 2002, had been extended until 2005. Meanwhile, in April 2002 an agreement was signed with the World Bank supporting Moldova's request for the restructuring of its external debt (equivalent to over 150% of GDP), but in August 2003 debt-service payments to bilateral creditors were suspended. The annual rate of consumer-price inflation increased in 2003, to some 18.0%, although inflation was expected to decline to between 4.5% and 8.0% in 2004, and economic growth, of 5%, was expected to be maintained. None the less, there was concern about the sustainability of growth and the country's endemic poverty, and the IMF recommended that the Government implement measures to combat corruption, reduce state interference in economic activity, accelerate privatization and maintain a liberal trade regime.

Education

Education is officially compulsory in Moldova between seven and 16 years of age. Primary education begins at seven years of age and lasts for four years. Secondary education, beginning at 11, lasts for a maximum of seven years, comprising a first cycle of five years and a second of two years. Primary enrolment in 2002 was equivalent to 95% of children in the relevant age-group, and the comparable ratio for secondary enrolment was 88%. In 1997 total enrolment at primary, secondary and tertiary levels was equivalent to 71% of females and 69% of males. In 2002 budgetary expenditure on education was 1,240m. lei (equivalent to 5.6% of GDP).

Public Holidays

2004: 1 January (New Year's Day), 7–8 January (Christmas), 8 March (International Women's Day), 11–12 April (Orthodox Easter), 1 May (Labour Day), 9 May (Victory and Commemoration Day), 27 August (Independence Day), 31 August ('Limbă Noastră', National Language Day).

2005: 1 January (New Year's Day), 7–8 January (Christmas), 8 March (International Women's Day), 1–2 May (Orthodox Easter), 1 May (Labour Day), 9 May (Victory and Commemoration Day), 27 August (Independence Day), 31 August ('Limbă Noastră', National Language Day).

Weights and Measures

The metric system is in force.

Statistical Survey

Principal sources (unless otherwise indicated): State Department for Statistics and Sociology, 2028 Chişinău, şos. Hînceşti 53D; tel. (2) 73-37-74; fax (2) 22-61-46; e-mail dass@statistica.md; internet www.statistica.md.
Note: Most of the figures for 1993–2004 exclude the Transnistria (Transdnestr) region of eastern Moldova, i.e. the area on the left bank of the Dniester (Dnestr or Nistru) river.

Area and Population

AREA, POPULATION AND DENSITY

Area (sq km)	33,800*
Population (census results)†	
17 January 1979	3,949,756
12 January 1989	
Males	2,063,192
Females	2,272,168
Total	4,335,360
Population (official estimates at 1 January)	
2002	3,627,812
2003	3,617,700
2004	3,606,800
Density (per sq km) at January 2004	106.7

* 13,050 sq miles.
† Figures refer to the *de jure* population. The *de facto* total at the 1989 census was 4,337,592 (males 2,058,160, females 2,279,432).

POPULATION BY ETHNIC GROUP
(permanent inhabitants, 1989 census)

	Number	%
Moldovan	2,794,749	64.5
Ukrainian	600,366	13.8
Russian	562,069	13.0
Gagauz	153,458	3.5
Bulgarian	88,419	2.0
Jewish	65,672	1.5
Others and unknown	70,627	1.7
Total	**4,335,360**	**100.0**

ADMINISTRATIVE DIVISIONS
(estimated population at 1 January 2003)

Bălţi	500,900	Taraclia	465,600
Cahul	190,800	Tighina	169,000
Chişinău . . .	1,161,800	Ungheni	260,300
Edinet	279,100	*Autonomous territory*	
Lapusna . . .	2776,300	*of Gagauzia* . .	158,900
Orhei	300,400	*Transnistria and*	
Soroco	274,600	*Tighina (Bender)** .	629,800
		Total	**3,617,700**

* 2001 figure.

PRINCIPAL TOWNS
(estimated population at 1 January 1996)

Chişinău (Kishinev)			
(capital) . . .	655,000	Tighina (Bender) . .	128,000
Tiraspol . . .	187,000	Râbnita (Rybnitsa) .	62,900
Bălţi (Beltsy) . . .	153,500		

2004 (estimate, 1 January): Chişinău 662,200; Bălţi 144,300.

BIRTHS, MARRIAGES AND DEATHS

	Registered live births		Registered marriages		Registered deaths	
	Number	Rate (per 1,000)	Number	Rate (per 1,000)	Number	Rate (per 1,000)
1995 . . .	56,411	13.0	32,775	7.5	52,969	12.2
1996 . . .	51,865	12.0	26,089	6.0	49,748	11.5
1997 . . .	51,286	11.9	26,305	6.1*	51,138	11.9
1998 . . .	46,755	10.9	25,793	6.0*	47,691	11.1
1999† . .	38,501	9.0	23,524	5.5	41,315	9.6
2000† . .	36,939	8.7	21,684	5.1	41,224	9.7
2001 . . .	36,448	10.0	21,200‡	5.8	40,100‡	11.0
2002 . . .	35,705	9.9	21,700‡	6.0	41,900‡	11.6

* Estimate.
† Numbers exclude, but rates include, Transnistria.
‡ Rounded figures.

Sources: partly UN, *Population and Vital Statistics Report; Moldovan Economic Trends.*

Expectation of life (WHO estimates, years at birth): 67.8 (males 64.0; females 71.6) in 2002 (Source: WHO, *World Health Report*).

ECONOMICALLY ACTIVE POPULATION
('000 persons)

	1999	2000	2001
Agriculture, hunting and forestry	730	769.0	763.4
Fishing	1	1.4	1.4
Mining and quarrying	3	1.7	2.0
Manufacturing	135	135.8	136.8
Electricity, gas and water supply .	22	28.5	26.4
Construction	44	44.4	43.2
Wholesale and retail trade; repair of motor vehicles, motorcycles and personal and household goods	135	147.3	144.5
Hotels and restaurants	15	18.0	19.3
Transport, storage and communications	70	63.9	64.3
Financial intermediation . . .	10	8.1	9.2
Real estate, renting and business activities	35	19.5	19.5
Public administration and defence; compulsory social security . .	49	64.5	65.8
Education	137	101.5	100.9
Health and social work	80	74.2	70.7
Other community, social and personal service activities . .	29	28.2	28.2
Private households with employed persons	—	8.6	3.1
Total employed	**1,495**	**1,514.6**	**1,499.0**
Unemployed	187	140.1	117.7
Total labour force	**1,682**	**1,654.6**	**1,616.7**
Males	853	828.0	806.6
Females	829	826.6	810.1

Source: ILO.

2002: Economically active population 1,614,967; Employed 1,505,117; Unemployed 109,850.

2003: Economically active population 1,473,580; Employed 1,356,479; Unemployed 117,102.

Health and Welfare

KEY INDICATORS

Total fertility rate (children per woman, 2002)	1.4
Under-5 mortality rate (per 1,000 live births, 2001) . . .	32
HIV/AIDS (% of persons aged 15–49, 2001)	0.24
Physicians (per 1,000 head, 1998)	3.5
Hospital beds (per 1,000 head, 1996)	12.12
Health expenditure (2001): US $ per head (PPP) . . .	100
Health expenditure (2001): % of GDP	5.1
Health expenditure (2001): public (% of total)	79.2
Access to water (% of persons, 2000)	100
Human Development Index (2001): ranking	108
Human Development Index (2001): value	0.700

For sources and definitions, see explanatory note on p. vi.

Agriculture

PRINCIPAL CROPS
('000 metric tons)

	2000	2001	2002
Wheat	727.7	1,185.2	1,122.3
Barley	133.0	230.9	220.5
Maize	1,031.0	1,117.6	1,192.8
Potatoes	330.0	384.8	324.9
Sugar beet	943.5	1,0845.0	1,116.0
Dry peas	15.0	37.8	22.9
Sunflower seed	268.5	254.5	320.1
Cabbages	43.0	78.6	69.7*
Tomatoes	104.0	105.0	93.0*
Cucumbers and gherkins* . .	19.8	21.3	18.9
Chillies and green peppers* .	71.5	76.9	68.0
Dry onions	53.7	79.0	70.0*
Carrots	26.0	26.0	23.0*
Other vegetables* . . .	49.5	67.1	60.1
Apples	162.4	186.9	271.0
Plums	41.2	59.2	66.8
Grapes	703.8	505.0	660.2
Watermelons	26.3	33.1	36.0
Other fruits*	51.5	71.0	55.9
Tobacco (leaves)	25.3	16.1	11.6

* Unofficial figure(s).
Source: FAO.

LIVESTOCK
('000 head at 1 January)

	2000	2001	2002
Horses	67	71	70*
Cattle	423	394	405
Pigs	683	447	449
Sheep	930	830	835
Goats	100	109	112
Chickens	12,575	13,041	14,119

* FAO estimate.
Source: FAO.

LIVESTOCK PRODUCTS
('000 metric tons)

	2000	2001	2002
Beef and veal	18.1	15.6	15.9
Mutton and lamb . . .	2.3	1.8	1.9
Pig meat	49.7	43.6	44.3
Poultry meat	16.5	19.9	21.1
Cows' milk	554.8	560.6	603.5
Sheep's milk	13.9	13.9	16.2
Goats' milk	4.6	4.9	5.8
Butter	2.5	3.0	3.5
Cheese	4.5	4.6	5.1†
Hen eggs*	32.0	34.5	37.8
Honey	2.0	2.2	2.3
Wool: greasy	2.1	2.1	2.1
Cattle hides (fresh)† . .	2.3	2.3	2.3

* Unofficial figures.
† FAO estimate(s).
Source: partly FAO.

Forestry

ROUNDWOOD REMOVALS
('000 cubic metres, excl. bark)

	1999	2000	2001
Sawlogs, veneer logs and logs for sleepers	3	5	3
Other industrial wood . .	9	24	24*
Fuel wood	36	30	30*
Total	**48**	**59**	**57**

* FAO estimate.
Source: FAO.

SAWNWOOD PRODUCTION
('000 cubic metres, incl. railway sleepers)

	1999	2000	2001
Coniferous (softwood) . . .	—	—	—
Broadleaved (hardwood) . .	6	5	5*
Total	**6**	**5**	**5***

* FAO estimate.
Source: FAO.

Fishing
(metric tons, live weight)

	1999	2000	2001
Capture	309	344	387
Common carp	178	192	212
Crucian carp	104	132	127
Aquaculture	815	990	1,189
Common carp	107	173	105
Crucian carp	105	110	23
Grass carp (White amur) . .	92	99	63
Silver carp	511	608	998
Total catch	**1,124**	**1,334**	**1,576**

Source: FAO, *Yearbook of Fishery Statistics*.

Mining
('000 metric tons)

	1998	1999	2000
Gypsum	19.8	18.5	32.1
Peat*	475	475	475

* Estimated production.
Source: US Geological Survey.

Industry

SELECTED PRODUCTS
('000 metric tons, unless otherwise indicated)

	1999	2000	2001
Vegetable oil	17	22	34
Flour	159	148	122
Raw sugar	99	102	130
Wine ('000 hectolitres)	668	1,073	1,550
Mineral water ('000 hectolitres)	242	306	374
Soft drinks ('000 hectolitres)	142	185	256
Cigarettes (million)	8,731	9,262	9,421
Carpets (million sq m)	0.5	0.4	0.4
Footwear ('000 pairs)	705	998	1,090
Cement	50	222	158
Washing machines ('000 units)	18	25	25
Television receivers ('000 units)	3	2	2
Tractors ('000 units)	0.0	0.2	0.5
Electric energy (million kWh)	4,122	3,294	n.a.

Source: UN, *Industrial Commodity Statistics Yearbook*.

Finance

CURRENCY AND EXCHANGE RATES

Monetary Units
100 bani (singular: ban) = 1 Moldovan leu (plural: lei).

Sterling, Dollar and Euro Equivalents (31 December 2003)
£1 sterling = 23.594 lei;
US $1 = 13.220 lei;
€1 = 16.697 lei;
1,000 Moldovan lei = £42.38 = $75.64 = €59.89.

Average Exchange Rate (Moldovan lei per US$)
2001   12.8651
2002   13.5705
2003   13.9449

Note: The Moldovan leu was introduced (except in the Transnistria region) on 29 November 1993, replacing the Moldovan rouble at a rate of 1 leu = 1,000 roubles. The Moldovan rouble had been introduced in June 1992, as a temporary coupon currency, and was initially at par with the Russian (formerly Soviet) rouble.

STATE BUDGET
(million lei)*

Revenue†	2000	2001	2002
Tax revenue	3,973	4,645	5,827
Taxes on profits	275	350	428
Taxes on personal incomes	265	348	468
Value-added tax	1,333	1,498	2,034
Excises	658	681	330
Taxes on international trade	222	234	333
Social Fund contributions	994	1,304	1,644
Other taxes	227	231	263
Non-tax revenue	806	749	710
Total	**4,779**	**5,394**	**6,537**

Expenditure‡	2000	2001	2002
Current budgetary expenditure	2,922	2,890	3,392
National economy	331	298	417
Social sphere	1,570	1,795	2,489
Education	719	923	1,240
Health care	464	542	792
Interest payments	1,021	797	486
Capital budgetary expenditure	175	206	258
Social Fund expenditure	1,328	1,373	1,900
Project loan spending	252	190	334
Other expenditure	776	926	1,251
Total	**5,453**	**5,585**	**7,135**

* Figures refer to a consolidation of the operations of central (republican) and local governments, including the Social Fund.
† Excluding grants received (million lei): 132 in 2000; 147 in 2001; 73 in 2002.
‡ Excluding net lending (million lei): −32 in 2000; −17 in 2001; −78 in 2002.
Source: IMF, *Republic of Moldova: Statistical Appendix* (February 2004).

INTERNATIONAL RESERVES
(US $ million at 31 December)

	2001	2002	2003
IMF special drawing rights	0.74	0.27	0.04
Reserve position in IMF	0.01	0.01	0.01
Foreign exchange	227.78	268.58	302.22
Total (excl. gold)	**228.53**	**268.86**	**302.27**

Source: IMF, *International Financial Statistics*.

MONEY SUPPLY
(million lei at 31 December)

	2001	2002	2003
Currency outside banks	1,834.20	2,288.56	2,740.52
Demand deposits at commercial banks	665.76	1,271.14	1,674.28
Total money (incl. others)	**2,500.00**	**3,559.80**	**4,415.07**

Source: IMF, *International Financial Statistics*.

COST OF LIVING
(Consumer Price Index; base: Dec. 1994 = 100)

	2000	2001	2002
Food	268.8	297.6	310.4
Non-food goods	238.5	260.6	281.0
Services	629.8	668.0	700.0
All items	**298.7**	**327.8**	**345.8**

Source: *Moldovan Economic Trends*.

NATIONAL ACCOUNTS
(million lei at current prices, excl. Transnistria)

Expenditure on the Gross Domestic Product

	2000	2001	2002*
Government final consumption expenditure†	2,471.8	2,878.0	3,985.7
Private final consumption expenditure	14,030.9	16,384.7	18,640.2
Changes in inventories	1,363.7	1,245.7	1,350.6
Gross fixed capital formation	2,472.5	3,190.0	3,653.3
Total domestic expenditure	**20,338.9**	**23,698.4**	**27,629.8**
Exports of goods and services	7,945.7	9,536.3	12,238.1
Less Imports of goods and services	12,265.1	14,183.0	17,827.5
GDP in purchasers' values	**16,019.6**	**19,051.5**	**22,040.4**

* Preliminary figures.
† Including non-profit institutions.
Source: *Moldovan Economic Trends*.

Gross Domestic Product by Economic Activity

	1998	1999	2000
Agriculture, hunting, forestry and fishing	2,351	3,066	3,919
Mining and quarrying	17	24	23
Manufacturing	1,276	1,613	2,423
Electricity, gas and water supply	229	456	358
Construction	289	409	423
Wholesale and retail trade; repair of motor vehicles, motorcycles and personal and household goods	941	1,885	2,135
Transport, storage and communications	671	1,013	1,434
Other services	2,381	3,226	4,248
Sub-total	**8,155**	**11,692**	**14,963**
Taxes (less subsidies) on products and imports	1,403	1,323	1,976
Less Financial intermediation services indirectly measured	436	693	959
GDP in purchasers' values	**9,122**	**12,322**	**15,980**

BALANCE OF PAYMENTS
(US $ million)

	2000	2001	2002
Exports of goods f.o.b.	476.8	567.2	659.8
Imports of goods f.o.b.	−770.5	−880.3	−1,038.0
Trade balance	−293.6	−313.0	−378.2
Exports of services	164.5	168.1	211.3
Imports of services	−201.7	−207.7	−245.2
Balance on goods and services	−330.8	−352.6	−412.1
Other income received	173.3	235.0	276.5
Other income paid	−123.3	−124.4	−111.2
Balance on goods, services and income	−280.9	−242.0	−246.8
Current transfers received	164.7	162.0	164.2
Current transfers paid	−9.1	−11.7	−14.8
Current balance	−125.3	−91.7	−97.3
Capital account (net)	−14.4	−20.7	−15.3
Direct investment abroad	−0.1	−0.1	−0.4
Direct investment from abroad	136.1	98.2	117.1
Portfolio investment assets	—	−3.2	−1.0
Portfolio investment liabilities	−4.2	−3.5	−26.5
Other investment assets	−28.7	−12.1	−54.3
Other investment liabilities	41.5	−7.4	7.8
Net errors and omissions	−6.7	13.1	15.4
Overall balance	−1.8	−27.3	−54.5

Source: IMF, *International Financial Statistics.*

External Trade

PRINCIPAL COMMODITIES
(US $ million)

Imports	1999	2000	2001
Food and live animals	22.1	40.0	69.3
Beverages and tobacco	11.1	58.1	49.2
Cigarettes	2.8	48.0	33.9
Crude materials, inedible, except fuels	14.7	23.5	34.4
Mineral products	228.0	252.1	237.5
Petroleum petroleum products etc.	69.9	108.5	111.7
Gas, natural and manufactured	102.7	92.8	101.3
Products of chemical or allied industries	51.9	84.4	97.2
Medicinal and pharmaceutical products	21.9	41.9	31.5
Basic manufactures	117.3	146.6	197.3
Textiles and textile articles	51.0	62.7	78.6
Machinery and transport equipment	88.0	109.6	144.6
Total (incl. others)	586.6	777.0	896.6

Exports f.o.b.	1999	2000	2001
Food and live animals	134.5	100.8	117.2
Meat and preparations	22.9	15.7	11.1
Cereals and preparations	30.1	15.9	20.8
Vegetables and fruit	59.1	52.5	61.4
Edible nuts	17.0	17.0	18.3
Fruit or vegetable juices	17.3	15.0	24.0
Beverages and tobacco	143.2	158.2	198.7
Wine of fresh grapes	100.5	114.2	156.4
Crude materials, inedible	38.4	42.3	44.8
Basic manufactures	22.7	34.1	38.6
Machinery and equipment	34.3	29.3	39.2
Miscellaneous manufactures	73.6	92.7	113.8
Apparel and clothing	57.4	75.7	92.7
Total (incl. others)	464.1	471.6	570.2

Source: UN, *International Trade Statistics Yearbook.*

PRINCIPAL TRADING PARTNERS
(US $ million)

Imports c.i.f.	1999	2000	2001
Belarus	22.7	31.9	38.9
Bulgaria	9.4	13.6	20.7
France	12.6	20.0	25.9
Germany	61.4	87.7	85.4
Greece	8.4	15.1	5.3
Hungary	6.9	13.0	18.2
Italy	38.2	48.9	65.4
Netherlands	9.4	8.7	12.8
Poland	8.3	15.5	18.0
Romania	81.6	119.3	93.3
Russia	138.7	119.6	144.1
Turkey	11.8	18.2	19.7
Ukraine	79.2	105.6	152.6
United Kingdom	8.2	9.7	11.7
USA	22.2	48.2	28.1
Total (incl. others)	586.7	777.0	896.6

Exports f.o.b.	1999	2000	2001
Austria	10.0	5.6	8.5
Belarus	21.8	21.8	30.2
Bulgaria	5.3	3.6	3.7
Canada	3.3	2.1	2.3
France	6.4	7.9	8.4
Germany	33.5	36.3	40.8
Greece	5.8	2.4	2.7
Hungary	16.3	4.6	7.2
Italy	25.6	36.4	46.0
Kazakhstan	3.4	4.7	4.5
Poland	5.0	2.0	1.7
Romania	41.3	37.6	38.0
Russia	191.2	209.5	248.7
Ukraine	32.9	35.5	40.8
United Kingdom	3.9	5.4	5.6
USA	14.5	15.6	25.7
Total (incl. others)	464.2	471.4	570.2

Source: UN, *International Trade Statistics Yearbook.*

Transport

RAILWAYS
(traffic)

	1998	1999	2000
Passenger journeys (million)	9.4	5.4	4.8
Passenger-km (million)	656	343	315
Freight transported (million metric tons)	11.1	6.6	8.2
Freight ton-km (million)	2,575	1,191	1,513

ROAD TRAFFIC
(motor vehicles in use)

	1997	1998	1999
Passenger cars	205,973	222,769	232,278
Buses and coaches	11,169	12,917	13,582
Lorries and vans	56,924	57,404	52,430

Source: IRF, *World Road Statistics.*

INLAND WATERWAYS
(traffic)

	1998	1999	2000
Freight transported ('000 metric tons)	13.1	15.9	8.7

CIVIL AVIATION
(traffic)

	1996	1997	1998
Kilometres flown (million) . . .	5	2	4
Passengers carried ('000) . . .	190	46	118
Passenger-km (million)	240	61	146
Total ton-km (million)	23	6	14

Source: UN, *Statistical Yearbook*.

1999: Passengers carried ('000) 200; Passenger-km (million) 240; Freight transported ('000 metric tons) 1.3; Freight ton-km (million) 3.3.

2000: Passengers carried ('000) 220; Passenger-km (million) 253; Freight transported ('000 metric tons) 1.4; Freight ton-km (million) 4.1.

Tourism

FOREIGN VISITOR ARRIVALS
(incl. excursionists)

Country of origin	1999	2000	2001
Belarus	550	546	509
Bulgaria	458	528	295
Germany	277	537	558
Italy	409	594	572
Romania	2,087	2,341	2,076
Russia	2,595	5,146	2,361
Turkey	1,612	2,548	2,405
Ukraine	1,944	1,969	2,261
United Kingdom	615	327	163
USA	889	1,030	1,072
Total (incl. others)	14,088	18,964	15,690

2002: 20,161 tourist arrivals.

2003: 23,598 tourist arrivals.

Receipts from tourism (US $ million): 4 in 1998; 2 in 1999; 4 in 2000.

Sources: World Tourism Organization, *Yearbook of Tourism Statistics*; and World Bank, *World Development Indicators*.

Communications Media

	1999	2000	2001
Television receivers ('000 in use) .	1,300	1,300	n.a.
Telephones ('000 main lines in use)	555.3	583.8	639.2
Facsimile machines (number in use)	716	n.a.	n.a.
Mobile cellular telephones ('000 subscribers)	18.0	132.3	225.0
Personal computers ('000 in use)	35	64	70
Internet users ('000)	25	53	60

Radio receivers ('000 in use): 3,220 in 1997.

Book production (including pamphlets): 921 titles (2,779,000 copies) in 1996.

Daily newspapers: 4 (average circulation 261,000) in 1996.

Non-daily newspapers: 206 (estimated average circulation 1,350,000) in 1996.

Other periodicals: 76 (average circulation 196,000) in 1994.

Sources: UNESCO, *Statistical Yearbook*; International Telecommunication Union.

Education

(2002/03)

	Institutions	Teachers*	Students
Primary	120 }	42,300	19,200
Secondary: general	1,460 }		523,400
Secondary: vocational . . .	83	2,300	22,600
Higher: colleges*	60	1,900	19,900
Higher: universities . . .	45	5,300	95,039

* 2000/01 figures.

Adult literacy rate (UNESCO estimates): 99.0% (males 99.6%; females 98.4%) in 2001 (Source: UN Development Programme, *Human Development Report*).

Directory

The Constitution

The Constitution of the Republic of Moldova, summarized below, was adopted by the Moldovan Parliament on 28 July 1994 and entered into force on 27 August. On 28 July 2000 amendments to the Constitution were enacted, which transformed Moldova into a parliamentary republic. Following alterations to the law on presidential election procedure, approved on 22 September, the President of the Republic was, henceforth, to be elected by the legislature, rather than directly.

GENERAL PRINCIPLES

The Republic of Moldova is a sovereign, independent, unitary and indivisible state. The rule of law, the dignity, rights and freedoms of the people, and the development of human personality, justice and political pluralism are guaranteed. The Constitution is the supreme law. The Constitution upholds principles such as human rights and freedoms, democracy and political pluralism, the separation and co-operation of the legislative, executive and judicial powers of the State, respect for international law and treaties, fundamental principles regarding property, free economic initiative and the right to national identity. The national language of the republic is Moldovan and its writing is based on the Latin alphabet, although the State acknowledges the right to use other languages spoken within the country.

FUNDAMENTAL RIGHTS, FREEDOMS AND DUTIES

The Constitution grants Moldovan citizens their rights and freedoms and lays down their duties. All citizens are equal before the law; they should have free access to justice, are presumed innocent until proven guilty and have a right to an acknowledged legal status.

The State guarantees fundamental human rights, such as the right to life and to physical and mental integrity, the freedoms of movement, conscience, expression, assembly and political associ-ation, and the enfranchisement of Moldovan citizens aged over 18 years. Moldovan citizens have the right of access to information and education, of health security, of establishing and joining a trade union, of working and of striking. The family, orphaned children and the disabled enjoy the protection of the State. Obligations of the citizenry include the payment of taxes and the defence of the motherland.

PARLIAMENT

Parliament is the supreme legislative body and sole legislative authority of Moldova. It consists of 101 members, directly elected for a four-year term. The Chairman of Parliament is elected by members, also for a four-year term. Parliament holds two ordinary sessions per year. The Parliament's basic powers include: the enactment of laws, the holding of referendums, the provision of legislative unity throughout the country, the approval of state policy, the approval or suspension of international treaties, the election of state officials, the mobilization of the armed forces and the declaration of the states of national emergency, martial law and war.

THE PRESIDENT OF THE REPUBLIC

The President of the Republic is the Head of State and is elected by the legislature for a four-year term. A candidate must be aged no less than 40 years, be a Moldovan citizen and a speaker of the official language. The candidate must be in good health and, with his or her application, must submit the written support of a minimum of 15 parliamentarians. A decision on the holding of a presidential election is taken by parliamentary resolution, and the election must be held no fewer than 45 days before the expiry of the outgoing President's term of office. To be elected President, a candidate must obtain the support of three-fifths of the parliamentary quorum. If necessary, further ballots must then be conducted, contested by the two candidates who received the most votes. The candidate who receives more votes becomes President. The post of President may be held by the same person for not more than two consecutive terms.

The President's main responsibilities include the promulgation of laws, the issue of decrees, the scheduling of referendums, the conclusion of international treaties and the dissolution of the Parliament. The President is allowed to participate in parliamentary proceedings. The President, after consultation with the parliamentary majority, is responsible for nominating a Prime Minister-designate and a Government. The President can preside over government meetings and can consult the Government on matters of special importance and urgency. On proposals submitted by the Prime Minister, the President may revoke or renominate members of the Government in cases of vacancies or the reallocation of portfolios. The President is Commander-in-Chief of the armed forces.

If the President has committed a criminal or constitutional offence, the votes of two-thirds of the members of Parliament are required to remove the President from office; the removal must be confirmed by the Supreme Court of Justice, for a criminal offence, and by a national referendum, for a constitutional offence.

THE COUNCIL OF MINISTERS

The principal organ of executive government is the Council of Ministers, which supervises state policy and public administration of the country. The Council of Ministers is headed by a Prime Minister, who co-ordinates the activities of the Government. The Council of Ministers must resign if the Parliament votes in favour of a motion of 'no confidence' in the Council.

LOCAL ADMINISTRATION

For administrative purposes, the Republic of Moldova is divided into districts, towns and villages, in which local self-government is practised. At village and town level, elected local councils and mayors operate as autonomous administrative authorities. At district level, an elected council co-ordinates the activities of village and town councils.

The area on the left bank of the Dniester (Dnestr or Nistru) river, as well as certain other places in the south of the republic (i.e. Gagauzia) may be granted special autonomous status, according to special statutory provisions of organic law*.

JUDICIAL AUTHORITY

Every citizen has the right to free access to justice. Justice shall be administered by the Supreme Court of Justice, the Court of Appeal, tribunals and the courts of law. Judges sitting in the courts of law and the Supreme Court of Justice are appointed by the President following proposals by the Higher Magistrates' Council. They are elected for a five-year term, and subsequently for a 10-year term, after which their term of office expires on reaching the age limit. The Higher Magistrates' Council is composed of 11 magistrates, who are appointed for a five-year term. It is responsible for the appointment, transfer and promotion of judges, as well as disciplinary action against them.

The Prosecutor-General, who is appointed by Parliament, exercises control over the enactment of law, as well as defending the legal order and the rights and freedoms of citizens.

THE CONSTITUTIONAL COURT

The Constitutional Court is the sole authority of constitutional judicature in Moldova. It is composed of six judges, who are appointed for a six-year term. The Constitutional Court's powers include: the enforcement of constitutionality control over laws, decrees and governmental decisions, as well as international treaties endorsed by the republic; the confirmation of the results of elections and referendums; the explanation and clarification of the Constitution; and decisions over matters of the constitutionality of parties. The decisions of the Constitutional Court are final and are not subject to appeal.

CONSTITUTIONAL REVISIONS

A revision of the Constitution may be initiated by one of the following: a petition signed by at least 200,000 citizens from at least one-half of the country's districts and municipalities; no less than one-third of the members of Parliament; the President of the Republic; the Government. Provisions regarding the sovereignty, independence, unity and neutrality of the State may be revised only by referendum.

*In July 2003 a constitutional amendment was approved by Parliament, officially recognizing the autonomous status of Gagauzia.

The Government

HEAD OF STATE

President: VLADIMIR VORONIN (elected 4 April 2001).

COUNCIL OF MINISTERS
(April 2004)

Prime Minister: VASILE TARLEV.

First Deputy Prime Minister: VASILE IOVV.

Deputy Prime Minister: VALERIAN CRISTEA.

Deputy Prime Minister and Minister of Agriculture and the Food Industry: DUMITRU TODOROGLO.

Minister of the Economy: MARIAN LUPU.

Minister of Finance: ZINAIDA GRECÎANII.

Minister of Industry: MIHAI GARŞTEA.

Minister of Energy: IACOB TIMCIUC.

Minister of Transport and Telecommunications: VASILE ZGARDAN.

Minister of Ecology and Natural Resources: CONSTANTIN MIHAILESCU.

Minister of Education: VALENTIN BENIUC.

Minister of Health: ANDREI GHERMAN.

Minister of Labour and Social Protection: VALERIAN REVENCO.

Minister of Culture: VEACESLAV MADAN.

Minister of Justice: VASILE DOLGHIERU.

Minister of Foreign Affairs: ANDREI STRATAN.

Minister of Internal Affairs: GHEORGHE PAPUC.

Minister of Defence: Brig.-Gen. VICTOR GAICIUC.

Minister of Reintegration: VASILE SOVA.

Baskan (Leader) of Gagauzia: GHEORGHE TABUNSCIC.

STATE DEPARTMENTS

Chairman of the State Department for Civil Defence and Emergencies: Col FILIP BEŞLEAGA.

Chairman of the State Department for Construction and Territorial Development: IGOR SEMENOVSCHER.

Chairman of the State Department for Fuel and Energy: VALERIU ICONNICOV.

Chairman of the State Department for Inter-Ethnic Relations: OLGA GONCHAROVA.

Chairman of the State Department for Privatization: NICOLAE GUMENII.

Chairman of the State Department for Standardization and Metrology: (vacant).

Chairman of the State Department for Statistical and Sociological Analysis: VITALIE VALCOV.

MINISTRIES

Office of the President: Chişinău, bd Ştefan cel Mare 154; tel. (22) 23-47-93.

Office of the Council of Ministers: 2033 Chişinău, Piaţa Marii Adunări Naţionale 1; tel. (22) 23-30-92.

Ministry of Agriculture and the Food Industry: 2012 Chişinău, bd Ştefan cel Mare 162; tel. (22) 23-34-27; fax (22) 23-23-68.

Ministry of Culture: 2033 Chişinău, Piaţa Marii Adunări Naţionale 1; tel. (22) 23-39-56; fax (22) 23-23-88.

Ministry of Defence: 2021 Chişinău, şos. Hînceşti 84; tel. (22) 79-98-44; fax (22) 23-45-35; e-mail valeriusu@army.md; internet www.army.md.

Ministry of Ecology and Natural Resources: 2005 Chişinău, str. Cosmonauţilor 9; tel. (22) 22-16-68; fax (22) 22-07-48; e-mail capcelea@moldova.md.

Ministry of the Economy: 2033 Chişinău, Piaţa Marii Adunări Naţionale 1; tel. (22) 23-74-48; fax (22) 23-40-64; e-mail minecon@moldova.md.

Ministry of Education: 2033 Chişinău, Piaţa Marii Adunări Naţionale 1; tel. (22) 23-35-15; fax (22) 23-34-74; e-mail tiron@minedu.moldnet.md.

Ministry of Energy: 2012 Chişinău, str. V. Alecsandri 78; tel. (22) 22-22-64; fax (22) 25-33-42; e-mail mdepen@rambler.ru.

Ministry of Finance: 2005 Chişinău, str. Cosmonauţilor 7; tel. (22) 23-35-75; fax (22) 22-13-07; e-mail protocol@minfin.moldova.md; internet www.moldova.md.

Ministry of Foreign Affairs: 2012 Chişinău, str. 31 August 80; tel. (22) 57-82-07; fax (22) 23-23-02; e-mail secdep@mfa.md; internet www.mfa.md.

Ministry of Health: 2009 Chişinău, str. V. Alecsandri 1; tel. (22) 72-98-60; fax (22) 73-87-81; e-mail sdomente@mednet.md.

Ministry of Industry: 2012 Chişinău, bd Ştefan cel Mare 69; tel. (22) 27-80-59; fax (22) 27-80-00.

Ministry of Internal Affairs: 2012 Chişinău, bd Ştefan cel Mare 75; tel. (22) 22-45-47; fax (22) 22-27-43; e-mail mai@mai.md; internet www.mai.md.

Ministry of Justice: 2012 Chişinău, str. 31 August 1989 82; tel. (22) 23-47-95; fax (22) 23-47-97; e-mail dagri@cni.md.

Ministry of Labour and Social Protection: 2009 Chişinău, str. V. Alecsandri 1; tel. (22) 73-75-72; fax (22) 72-30-00; e-mail mmpsf@cni.md.

Ministry of Transport and Communications: 2012 Chişinău, bd Ştefan cel Mare 134; tel. (22) 22-10-01; fax (22) 24-15-53; e-mail secretary@mci.gov.md; internet mci.gov.md.

STATE DEPARTMENTS

State Department for Civil Defence and Emergencies: Chişinău, str. Gh. Asachi 69; tel. (22) 73-85-01; fax (22) 23-34-30.

State Department for Construction and Territorial Development: Chişinău.

State Department for Fuel and Energy: see Ministry of Energy.

State Department for Inter-Ethnic Relations: Chişinău, A. Matcevici 109/1.

State Department for Privatization: 2012 Chişinău, str. Pushkin 26; tel. (22) 23-43-50; fax (22) 23-43-36; e-mail dep.priv@moldtelecom.md; internet www.privatization.md.

State Department for Standardization and Metrology: 2069 Chişinău, str. E. Coca 28; tel. (22) 74-85-88; fax (22) 75-05-81; e-mail moldovastandard@standart.mldnet.com.

State Department for Statistics and Sociology: 2028 Chişinău, şos. Hînceşti 53; tel. (22) 40-30-00; fax (22) 22-61-46; e-mail moldstat@statistica.md; internet www.statistica.md.

President and Legislature

PRESIDENT

The Moldovan Parliament failed to elect a President in four rounds of voting in December 2000. Therefore, under the terms of the Constitution, Parliament had to be dissolved and legislative elections held before a fresh presidential election could take place. Three candidates contested the presidential election of 4 April 2001. Vladimir Voronin was elected President with 71 votes; Dumitru Braghiş received 15 votes and Valerian Cristea received three votes. The 11 deputies of the Christian Democratic People's Party abstained from voting.

PARLIAMENT

Parlamentul
(Parliament)

2073 Chişinău, bd Ştefan cel Mare 105; tel. (22) 23-33-52; fax (22) 23-30-12; e-mail info@parlament.md; internet www.parlament.md.

Chairman: EUGENIA OSTAPCIUC.

Deputy Chairmen: VADIM MISIN, MIHAIL CAMERZAN.

General Election, 25 February 2001

Parties and alliances	% of votes	Seats
Moldovan Party of Communists	49.93	71
Braghiş Alliance	13.40	19
Christian Democratic People's Party	8.31	11
Other parties, alliances and independents*	28.36	—
Total	100.00	101

* Including the Party of Revival and Conciliation, the Democratic Party of Moldova, the National Liberal Party, the Social Democratic Party of the Republic of Moldova and the National Peasants' Christian Democratic Party.

Political Organizations

Legislation approved in December 2002, which required political organizations to re-register with the Ministry of Justice each year and provide evidence that their membership numbered at least 5,000 people, from among at least one-half of Moldova's districts, was nullified in November 2003. In March of that year 26 political parties were registered with the Ministry of Justice.

Agrarian Democratic Party (ADP) (Partidul Democrat Agrar din Moldova): Chişinău; tel. (22) 22-42-74; fax (22) 22-23-63; f. 1991 by moderates from both the Popular Front of Moldova and the Communist Party of Moldova; supports Moldovan independence, and economic and agricultural reform; Chair. ANATOL POPUŞOI.

Alianţa Moldova Noastra (AMN) (Our Moldova Social Liberal Alliance): Chişinău, str. Puskin 62A; tel. (22) 54-85-38; e-mail vitalia@ch.moldpac.md; f. 2003 by merger of the Alliance of Independents of Moldova, the Moldovan Liberal Party and the Social Democratic Alliance of Moldova, and the Popular Democratic Party of Moldova; supports Moldova's integration into Europe, a market economy and inter-ethnic harmony; Chair. DUMITRU BRAGHIŞ, SERAFIM URECHEAN, VEACESLAV UNTILĂ; c. 100,000 mems.

Christian Democratic People's Party (CDPP) (Partidul Popular Creştin Democrat—PPCD): 2009 Chişinău, str. Nicolae Iorga 5; tel. (22) 23-33-56; fax (22) 23-86-66; e-mail magic@cni.md; internet inima.dnt.md; f. 1989 as the Popular Front of Moldova, renamed 1992, and as above 1999; advocates Moldova's entry into the European Union and NATO; Chair. IURIE ROŞCA.

Civic Dignity Party of Moldova (Partidul Demnităţii Civice din Moldova—PDCM): Chişinău; tel. (22) 49-84-73; f. 1999; Pres. ION LIPCIU.

Democratic Labour Party of Moldova: Chişinău; f. 1993; Pres. ALECSANDRU ARSENI.

Democratic Party of Moldova (PDM) (Partidul Democrat din Moldova): 2001 Chişinău, str. Tighina 32; tel. (22) 27-82-29; fax (22) 27-82-30; e-mail pdm@mtc.md; internet www.pdm.md; f. 1997; centrist; formerly Movement for a Democratic and Prosperous Moldova, name changed in April 2000; formed bloc with the Party of Progressive Forces in Sept. 2001; Chair. DUMITRU DIACOV.

Democratic Unity Party: Chişinău; f. 2001; pro-European, concerned with social issues; Leader SERGIU MOCIANU.

'Green Alliance' Ecological Party of Moldova (Alianţa Verde—PEM–AVE): 2012 Chişinău, str. Sciusev 63; tel. and fax (22) 72-16-43; e-mail iondediu@yahoo.com; f. 1992; represents political ecology and sustainable development; Pres. Prof. ION DEDIU; 10,000 mems.

Moldovan Centrist Union: Chişinău, str. Columna 103B; tel. (22) 22–46–59; f. 2000; splinter group of former Movement for a Democratic and Prosperous Moldova; Chair. MIHAI PETRACHE.

Moldovan Democratic Forum: Chişinău; f. 2001 by the merger of six right-wing parties: the National Liberal Party, the Moldovan Party of Democratic Forces, the National Peasants' Christian Democratic Party, the Party of Social Justice and Order, the New National Moldovan Party and the Party of Civil Dignity.

Moldovan Party of Communists (MPC) (Partidul Comuniştilor din Republica Moldova): 2012 Chişinău, str. N. Iorga 11; tel. (22) 23-46-14; fax (22) 23-36-73; e-mail pcrm@pisem.net; internet www.pcrm.md; fmrly the Communist Party of Moldova (banned Aug. 1991); revived as above 1994; formed a 10-party Left-Centre Union for the 2003 local elections; First Sec. VLADIMIR VORONIN.

National Salvation Movement (NSM): Chişinău; f. 2000; breakaway faction from the National Liberal Party.

Reform Party (PRM): Chişinău, str. Bucureşti 87; tel. (22) 23-26-89; fax (22) 22-80-97; f. 1993; centre-right Christian-Democratic party, which seeks to represent middle-class interests; Leader MIHAI GIMPU; Chair. ŞTEFAN GORDA; 12,000 mems.

Republican Party of Moldova (PRM): Chişinău, str. A. Vlahuţă 11/4; tel. (22) 22-83-18; f. 1999; Pres. VALERI EFREMOV.

Social Liberal Party: Chişinău, str. Bulgară 24B; tel. (22) 27-66-20; fax (22) 22-25-03; e-mail secretariat@psl.md; internet www.psl.md; f. 1999; absorbed the Christian Democratic League of Women and the National Youth League of Moldova; merged with the Party of Democratic Forces in December 2002; Leader OLEG SEREBREAN; Deputy Chair. VALERIU MATEI.

Socialist Party of Moldova (Partidul Socialist din Moldova): Chişinău, str. Calea Ieşilor 61/1, ap. 15; tel. (22) 75-87-62; successor to the former Communist Party of Moldova; favours socialist economic and social policies, defends the rights of Russian and other minorities and advocates CIS membership; Pres. VICTOR MOREV.

Yedinstvo (Unity) Movement: 2009 Chişinău, str. Hînceşti 35; tel. (22) 23-79-52; f. 1989; represents interests of ethnic minorities in Moldova; 35,000 mems; Pres. PETR SHORNIKOV.

Parties and organizations in Transnistria include: the Union of Patriotic Forces (Tiraspol; radical socialist; Leader VASILII YAKOVLEV); the Movement for the Development of Dnestr (Tiraspol; moderate); the United Council of Workers' Collectives (Tiraspol; radical); 'For Accord and Stability' (Tiraspol; moderate); and 'Position' (Tiraspol; moderate; Leader SVETLANA MIGULEA); Russia's Unity—Yedinstvo Party established a branch in Tiraspol in 2000 (founded by the local Union of Industrialists, Agriculturalists and Entrepreneurs).

Parties and organizations in Gagauzia include: the Vatan (Motherland) Party (Comrat; Leader ANDREI CHESHMEJI) and Gagauz Halky (Gagauz People—Comrat; Leader KONSTANTIN TAUSHANDJI).

Diplomatic Representation

EMBASSIES IN MOLDOVA

Belarus: 2009 Chişinău, str. Mateevici 35; tel. (22) 23-83-02; fax (22) 23-83-00; Ambassador VASILY SAKOVICH.

Bulgaria: Chişinău, str. 31 August 1989 125, Hotel Codru; tel. (22) 23-79-83; fax (22) 23-79-08; e-mail amb_bg@mdl.net; Ambassador EVGENII EKHOV.

China, People's Republic: Chişinău, str. Mitropolit Dosoftei 124; tel. (22) 24-85-51; fax (22) 24-75-46; e-mail root@chinam.mldnet .com; Ambassador XU ZHONGKAI.

France: Chişinău, str. 31 August 1989 101A; tel. (22) 22-82-04; fax (22) 22-82-24; e-mail amb-fr@cni.md; internet www.ambafrance.md; Ambassador EDMOND PAMBOUKJIAN.

Germany: 2012 Chişinău, str. Maria Cibotari 35, Hotel Jolly Alon; tel. (22) 20-06-00; fax (22) 23-46-80; e-mail de-botschaft@riscom.md; internet www.de-botschaft.org.md; Ambassador Dr MICHAEL ZICKERICK.

Hungary: 2004 Chişinău, bd Ştefan cel Mare 131; tel. (22) 22-34-04; fax (22) 22-45-13; e-mail huembkiv1@meganet.md; Ambassador Dr SÁNDOR RÓBEL.

Poland: Chişinău, str. Plamadeala 3; tel. (22) 23-85-51; fax (22) 23-85-53; e-mail ambpolsk@ch.moldpac.md; f. 1994; Ambassador PIOTR MARCINIAK.

Romania: Chişinău, str. Bucureşti 66/1; tel. (22) 22-30-37; fax (22) 22-81-29; e-mail ambrom@ch.moldpac.md; Ambassador FILIP TEODORESCU.

Russia: 2004 Chişinău, bd Ştefan cel Mare 153; tel. (22) 23-49-43; fax (22) 23-51-07; e-mail domino@mdl.net; internet www.moldova .mid.ru; Ambassador (vacant).

Turkey: Chişinău, str. Mateevici 57; tel. (22) 24-26-08; fax (22) 22-55-28; e-mail tremb@moldova.md; Ambassador FATMA FIRAT TOPCUOĞLU.

Ukraine: 2004 Chişinău, str. Sfatul Ţării 55; tel. (22) 58-21-51; fax (22) 58-51-08; e-mail emb_md@mfa.gov.ua; Ambassador PETRO CHALYI.

United Kingdom: Chişinău, str. Bănulescu-Bodoni 57/1; tel. (22) 23-89-91; fax (22) 23-89-92; Ambassador BERNARD WHITESIDE.

USA: 2009 Chişinău, str. Mateevici 103; tel. (22) 23-37-72; fax (22) 23-30-44; e-mail rosenquist@chisinaub.us-state.gov; internet www .usembassy.md; Ambassador HEATHER HODGES.

Judicial System

Supreme Court: 2009 Chişinău, str. M. Kogâlniceanu 70; tel. (22) 22-13-67; Chair. VALERIA STERBET.

Constitutional Court

2004 Chişinău, str. A. Lapusneanu 28; tel. (22) 24-05-49; fax (22) 24-52-23; e-mail curtea@constit.mldnet.com; internet www.ccrm.rol .md.

f. 1994; Chair. VICTOR PUSCAS.

Prosecutor-General: VALERIU BALABAN.

Religion

The majority of the inhabitants of Moldova profess Christianity, the largest denomination being the Eastern Orthodox Church. The Gagauz, although of Turkic descent, are also adherents of Orthodox Christianity. The Russian Orthodox Church (Moscow Patriarchy) has jurisdiction in Moldova, but there are Romanian and Turkish liturgies.

Eastern Orthodox Church

In December 1992 the Patriarch of Moscow and All Russia issued a decree altering the status of the Eparchy of Chişinău and Moldova to that of a Metropolitan See. The Government accepted this decree, thus tacitly rejecting the claims of the Metropolitan of Bessarabia (based in Romania). However, at the end of July 2002 the Government agreed to register the Bessarabian Metropolitan Church, following international pressure.

Archbishop of Chişinău and Moldova: VLADIMIR, 2012 Chişinău, str. Mitropolit Dosoftei 85; tel. (22) 22-34-70; fax (22) 22-52-10; e-mail administ@apost.moldpac.md.

Roman Catholic Church

In October 2001 the diocese of Chişinău, covering the whole country, was established. At 31 December 2002 there were an estimated 20,000 Catholics in Moldova.

Bishop of Chişinău: Rt Rev. ANTON COŞA, 2012 Chişinău, str. Mitropolit Dosoftei 85; tel. (22) 22-34-70; fax (22) 22-52-10; e-mail administ@apost.moldpac.md; internet catholic.dnt.md.

The Press

In 1996 there were four daily newspapers published in Moldova (with a combined circulation averaging 261,000 copies). In that year 206 non-daily newspapers were published (with an estimated circulation of 1,350,000). In 1994 there were 76 other periodicals (31 for the general public and 45 for specific readership, with a total circulation of 196,000).

The publications listed below are in Romanian (or Moldovan, as it is officially termed), except where otherwise indicated.

PRINCIPAL NEWSPAPERS

Accente: Chişinău, str. Vlaicu Pîrcălab 45, 405; internet www .accente.com.md; weekly; Editor-in-Chief SERGIU AFANASIU.

Dnestrovskaya Pravda (Dnestr Truth): Tiraspol, str. 25 October 101; tel. and fax (33) 3-46-86; f. 1941; 3 a week; Russian; Editor TATYANA M. RUDENKO; circ. 7,000.

Ekonomicheskoye Obozrenie (Economic Review): Chişinău, bd Ştefan cel Mare 180; tel. (22) 24-69-52; fax (22) 24-69-50; e-mail red@ logos.press.md; internet logos.press.md; f. 1990; weekly; Editor-in-Chief SERGEI MIŞIN.

GP Flux: Chişinău, str. Corobceanu 17; tel. (22) 23-22-14; fax (22) 24-75-29; e-mail secretar@flux.press.md; internet flux.press.md; daily; Editor-in-Chief IGOR BURCIU.

Glasul Naţiunii (Voice of the Nation): Chişinău, str. 31 August 15; tel. and fax (22) 54-31-37; e-mail glasul_natiunii@hotmail.com; 4 a month; Editors VASILE NĂSTASE, EMANUELA JORGA.

Jurnal de Chişinău: 2012 Chişinău, str. Puşkin 22, 4th Floor, Of. 446; tel. (22) 23-40-41; fax (22) 23-42-30; e-mail cotidian@jurnal.md; internet www.jurnal.md; daily; Editor-in-Chief VAL BUTNARU.

Kishinevskiye Obozrevatel (Chişinău Correspondent): Chişinău, bd Ştefan cel Mare 162, 604/7; tel. (22) 21-02-34; fax (22) 21-02-64; e-mail oboz@molodvacc.md; internet www.ko.md; weekly; Russian; Editor-in-Chief IRINA ASTAHOVA.

Kishinevskiye Novosti (Chişinău News): Chişinău, str. Puşkin 22; tel. (22) 23-39-18; fax (22) 23-42-40; e-mail kn@mdl.net; weekly; Russian; Editor-in-Chief SERGEI DROBOT.

Kommersant Moldovy: Chişinău, str. Puşkin 22, 601; tel. (22) 23-36-94; e-mail vartem@commert.press.md; internet www.km.riscom .net; weekly; Russian; Editor-in-Chief ARTEM VARENIŢA.

Komsomolskaye Pravda Moldova: Chişinău, str. Vlaicu Pîrcălab 45; tel. (22) 22-07-13; fax (22) 22-12-74; e-mail ser@kp.md; internet www.kp.md; daily; Russian; Editor-in-Chief SERGEI CIURICOV.

Moldavskie Vedomosti (Moldovan Gazette): Chişinău, str. Bănulescu-Bodoni 21; tel. and fax (22) 23-86-18; e-mail editor@mv.net .md; internet vedomosti.md; weekly; Russian; Editor-in-Chief DMITRII CIUBASENKO.

Moldova Suverană (Sovereign Moldova): 2012 Chişinău, str. Puşkin 22, et. 3; tel. (22) 23-35-38; fax (22) 23-31-96; e-mail cotidian@suverana.press.md; internet www.moldova-suverana.md; f. 1924; daily; organ of the Govt; Editor ION BERLINSCHI; circ. 105,000.

Nezavisimaya Moldova (Independent Moldova): 2012 Chişinău, str. Puşkin 22, 303; tel. (22) 23-36-05; fax (22) 23-31-41; e-mail admin@nm.mldnet.com; internet www.nmmd; f. 1925; daily; organ of the Govt; Russian; Editor IURII TISCENCO; circ. 60,692.

Tinerimya Moldovei/Molodezh Moldovy (Youth of Moldova): Chişinău; f. 1928; 3 a week; editions in Romanian (circ. 12,212) and Russian (circ. 4,274); Editor V. BOTNARU.

Trudovoi Tiraspol (Working Tiraspol): Tiraspol, str. 25 October 101; tel. (33) 3-04-12; f. 1989; main newspaper of the east-bank Slavs; Russian; Editor DIMA KONDRATOVICH.

Viaţă Satului (Life of the Village): 2612 Chişinău, str. Puşkin 22, Casa presei, 4th Floor; tel. (22) 23-03-68; f. 1945; weekly; govt publ.; Editor V. S. SPINEY.

PRINCIPAL PERIODICALS

Basarabia (Bessarabia): 2004 Chişinău, str. 31 August 98, 401; tel. (22) 21-05-13; e-mail libr@mnc.md; f. 1931; fmrly *Nistru*; monthly; journal of the Union of Writers of Moldova; fiction; Editor-in-Chief D. MATKOVSKY.

Chipăruş (Peppercorn): 2612 Chişinău, str. Puşkin 22; tel. (22) 23-38-16; f. 1958; fortnightly; satirical; Editor-in-Chief ION VIKOL.

Femeia Moldovei (Moldovan Woman): 2470 Chişinău, str. 28 June 45; tel. (22) 23-31-64; f. 1951; monthly; popular, for women.

Lanterna Magică (Magic Lantern): Chişinău, str. Puşkin 24, 49; tel. (22) 74-86-43; fax (22) 23-23-88; e-mail lung_ro@yahoo.com; internet www.iatp.md/lanternamagica; f. 1990; publ. by the Ministry of Culture; 6 a year; art, culture.

Literatură şi Artă: 2009 Chişinău, str. Sfatul Ţării 2; tel. (22) 23-82-12; fax (22) 23-82-17; e-mail literatura@moldnet.md; f. 1954; weekly; organ of the Union of Writers of Moldova; literary; Editor NICOLAE DABIJA.

Moldova si Lumea (Moldova and the World): 2012 Chişinău, str. Puşkin 22, 510; tel. (22) 23-75-81; fax (22) 23-40-32; f. 1991; monthly; state-owned; international socio-political review; Editor BORIS STRATULAT.

Noi (Us): Chişinău; tel. (22) 23-31-91; f. 1930; fmrly *Scînteia Leninista*; monthly; fiction; for 12–18-year-olds; Man. VALERIU VOLONTIR; circ. 5,000.

Politica: 2033 Chişinău, bd Ştefan cel Mare 105; tel. (22) 23-74-03; fax (22) 23-32-10; e-mail vppm@cni.md; f. 1991; monthly; political issues.

Săptămína: Chişinău, str. 31 August 107; tel. (22) 22-44-61; fax (22) 21-37-07; e-mail saptamin@mom.mldnet.com; internet www.net .md/saptamina/; weekly magazine; Editor-in-Chief VIOREL MIHAIL.

Sud-Est (South-East): Chişinău, str. Maria Cibotaru 16; tel. (22) 23-26-05; fax (22) 23-22-42; internet www.sud-est.md; f. 1990; publ. by the Ministry of Culture; quarterly; art, culture; Editor-in-Chief VALENTINA TASLAUANA.

NEWS AGENCIES

AP Flux Press Agency: Chişinău, str. Corobceanu 17; tel. (22) 24-92-72; fax (22) 24-91-51; e-mail flux@cni.md; internet flux.press.md; f. 1995; Dir NADINE GOGU.

BASA-press—Moldovan Information and Advertising Agency: 2012 Chişinău, str. Vasile Alecsandri 72; tel. (22) 22-03-90; fax (22) 22-13-96; e-mail basa@basa.md; internet www.basa.md; f. 1992; independent; co-operates with Deutsche Presse-Agentur (Germany); Gen. Dir VALERIU RENITA.

DECA Press Agency: Bălti, str. Independentei 33; tel. (31) 61-385; fax (31) 607-44; e-mail info@deca-press.net; internet www .deca-press.net; f. 1996; local news; non-profit; Dir VITALIE CAZACU.

InfoMarket.MD (Denimax Grup): tel. (22) 27-76-26; e-mail editor@infomarket.md; internet www.infomarket.md; on-line business news; Editor ALECSANDRU BURDEINII.

Infotag News Agency: 2014 Chişinău, str. Kogâlniceanu 76; tel. (22) 23-49-30; fax (22) 23-49-33; e-mail office@infotag.net.md; internet www.infotag.md; f. 1993; leading private news agency; Dir ALEXANDRU TANAS.

Interlic News Agency: 2012 Chişinău, str. M. Cibotari 37, Of. 306; tel. and fax (22) 25-16-49; fax (22) 23-20-67; e-mail red@interlic.md; internet www.interlic.md; f. 1995; independent; Dir IVAN SVEATCENKO.

State Information Agency—Moldpres: 2012 Chişinău, str. Puşkin 22; tel. (22) 23-26-69; fax (22) 23-26-98; e-mail director@ moldpres.md; internet www.moldpres.md; f. 1940 as ATEM, reorganized 1990 and 1994; Dir SIMION ROPOT.

PRESS ASSOCIATIONS

Independent Journalism Centre (IJC): 2012 Chişinău, str. Sciusev 53; tel. (22) 21-36-52; fax (22) 22-66-81; e-mail ijcnews@ijc .iatp.md; internet ijc.iatp.md; f. 1994; non-governmental org.

Independent Press Association (API): Chişinău, str. Corobceanu 15; tel. (22) 21-06-02; fax (22) 20-36-86; e-mail api@ moldtelecom.md; internet api.iatp.md; f. 1997; Pres. ION CIUMEICA.

Mass Media Association of Moldova: Chişinău; internet www .media.ist.md; f. 2000.

Union of Journalists of Moldova: 2012 Chişinău, str. Puşkin 22; tel. and fax (22) 23-34-19; e-mail ujm@moldnet.md; internet www .iatp.md/ujm; f. 1957; Chair. VALERIU SAHARNEANU.

Publishers

In 1996 there were 921 titles (books and pamphlets) published in Moldova (2.8m. copies).

Editura Cartea Moldovei: 2004 Chişinău, bd Ştefan cel Mare 180; tel. (22) 24-65-10; fax (22) 24-64-11; f. 1977; fiction, non-fiction, poetry, art books; Dir DUMITRU FURDUI; Editor-in-Chief RAISA SUVEICA.

Editura Hyperion: 2004 Chişinău, bd Ştefan cel Mare 180; tel. (22) 24-40-22; f. 1976; fiction, literature, arts; Dir VALERIU MATEI.

Editura Lumina (Light): 2004 Chişinău, bd Ştefan cel Mare 180; tel. (22) 24-63-95; f. 1966; educational textbooks; Dir VICTOR STRATAN; Editor-in-Chief ANATOL MALEV.

Editura Ştiinţa (Science): 2028 Chişinău, str. Academiei 3; tel. (22) 73-96-16; fax (22) 73-96-27; e-mail prini@stiinta.asm.md; f. 1959; textbooks, encyclopedias, dictionaries, children's books and fiction in various languages; Dir GHEORGHE PRINI.

Izdatelstvo Kartia Moldoveniaske: Chişinău; tel. (22) 24-40-22; f. 1924; political and literature; Dir N. N. MUMZHI; Editor-in-Chief I. A. TSURKANU.

Broadcasting and Communications

TELECOMMUNICATIONS

Regulatory Authority

Ministry of Transport and Telecommunications: see section on the Government.

Telecommunications Company

Moldcell SA: 2060 Chişinău, str. Belgrad 3; tel. (22) 20-62-06; fax (22) 20-62-07; e-mail moldcell@moldcell.md; internet www.moldcell .md; f. 1999; mobile-telecommunications; owned by Fintur Holdings b.v. (Netherlands).

Moldtelecom SA: 2001 Chişinău, bd Ştefan cel Mare 10; tel. (22) 54-87-97; fax (22) 54-64-19; e-mail office@moldtelecom.md; internet www.moldtelecom.md; f. 1993; telephone communication and internet service provider; scheduled for partial privatization; Gen. Dir STELA SÇOLA.

BROADCASTING

Regulatory Authorities

National Regulatory Agency in Telecommunications and Informatics (ANRTI): 2012 Chişinău, bd Ştefan cel Mare 134; tel. (22) 25-13-17; fax (22) 22-28-85; e-mail office@anrti.md; internet www.anrti.md; f. 2000; Dir IURUE TABIRŢA.

Radio and Television Co-ordinating Council (Consiliul Coordonator al Audiovizualului): 2012 Chişinău, str. Mihai Eminescu 28; tel. (22) 27-75-51; fax (22) 27-74-71; e-mail cca_moldova@mdl.net; internet www.cca.md; regulatory and licensing body; Chair. ION MIHAILO.

State Communication Inspectorate (Inspectoratul de Stat al Comunicatiilor): 2021 Chişinău, str. Drumul Viilor 28-2; tel. (22) 73-53-64; fax (22) 73-39-41; e-mail ciclicci@isc.net.md; f. 1993; responsible for frequency allocations and monitoring, certification of post and communications equipment and services; Dir TEODOR CICLICCI.

Radio

State Radio and Television Company of Moldova (Teleradio) (Televiziunea de Stat a Republicii Moldova): 2028 Chişinău, str. Miorita 1; tel. (22) 72-10-77; fax (22) 72-33-52; e-mail info@trm.md; internet www.trm.md; f. 1994; Dir ILIE TELESCU; Exec. Dir (Radio) SERGIU BATOG.

Radio Moldova: 2028 Chişinău, str. Miorita 1; tel. (22) 72-13-88; fax (22) 72-35-37; f. 1930; broadcasts in Romanian, Russian, Ukrainian, Gagauz and Yiddish.

Television

State Radio and Television Company of Moldova (Teleradio) (Televiziunea de Stat a Republicii Moldova): see Radio; Exec. Dir (Television) VICTOR TABARCA.

TV Moldova (Televiziunea Nationala Moldova): f. 1958; Exec. Dir VICTOR MORARU.

Chişinău Television: 2028 Chişinău, str. Hînceşti 64; tel. (22) 73-91-94; fax (22) 72-35-37; f. 1958; Dir-Gen. ARCADIE GHERASIM.

Finance

(cap. = capital; res = reserves; dep. = deposits; m. = million; brs = branches; amounts in Moldovan lei, unless otherwise stated)

BANKING

The National Bank of Moldova (NBM), established in 1991, is independent of the Government (but responsible to Parliament) and has the power to regulate monetary policy and the financial system. The lack of a stringent regulatory framework and the consequent proliferation of small commercial banks led the Government to introduce, in January 1996, new legislation on financial institutions. All commercial banks were subsequently inspected and a more effective banking supervision was implemented. At September 2003 there were 16 commercial banks in operation.

Central Bank

National Bank of Moldova (Banca Naţională a Moldovei): 2006 Chişinău, bd Renaşterii 7; tel. (22) 22-50-52; fax (22) 22-05-91; e-mail official@bnm.org; internet www.bnm.org; f. 1991; cap. 100.0m., res 257.0m., dep. 638.8m. (Dec. 2001); Gov. LEONID TALMACI; Dep. Gov. DUMITRU URSU.

Commercial Banks

Banca de Finanţe şi Comerţ SA (FinComBank SA—Finance and Trade Bank JSC): 2012 Chişinău, str. Puşkin 26; tel. (22) 22-74-35; fax (22) 22-73-08; e-mail fincom@fcb.mldnet.com; internet www .fincombank.com; f. 1993; cap 87.3m., dep. 279.7m., total assets 457.6m. (Dec. 2003); Chair. VICTOR KHVOROSTOVSKY; 10 brs.

Banca Socială: 2006 Chişinău, str. Bănulescu-Bodoni 61; tel. (22) 22-14-94; fax (22) 22-42-30; e-mail office@socbank.md; internet www .socbank.md; f. 1991; joint-stock commercial bank; cap. 57.6m., res 8.6m., dep. 451.0m. (Feb. 2002); Pres. VLADIMIR SUETNOV; Chair. VALENTIN KUNEV; 18 brs.

BC 'Eximbank' SA (Eximbank Joint-Stock Commercial Bank): 2001 Chişinău, bd Ştefan cel Mare 6; tel. (22) 27-25-83; fax (22) 54-62-34; e-mail info@eximbank.com; internet www.eximbank.com; Chair. MARCEL CHIRCĂ.

BC Unibank SA: 2012 Chişinău, str. G. Bănulescu Bodoni 45; tel. (22) 22-55-86; fax (22) 22-05-30; e-mail welcome@unibank.md; internet www.unibank.md; f. 1993; joint-stock commercial bank; cap. 88.6m., res 5.7m., dep. 200.0m. (Oct. 2003); Pres. CLAUDIA MELNIC; 5 brs.

CB Businessbank SA: 2012 Chişinău, str. Alecsandru cel Bun 97; tel. (22) 20-56-10; fax (22) 22-23-70; e-mail bank@busbank.mldnet .com; internet www.businessbank.md; f. 1997; cap. 72.1m., res 1.1m., dep. 81.1m. (Jan. 2003); Chair. of Bd SERGIU N. BRINZILA.

CB Comerţbank JSC: 2001 Chişinău, str. Hînceşti 38A; tel. (22) 73-99-91; fax (22) 73-99-81; e-mail comertbank@mdl.net; internet www .comertbank.md; f. 1991; cap. 96.0m., total assets 149.9m. (Jan. 2003); Chair. NATALIA ULIYANOVA.

Energbank: 2012 Chişinău, str. Vasile Alecsandri 78; tel. (22) 54-43-77; fax (22) 25-34-09; e-mail office@energbank.com; internet www.energbank.com; f. 1997; cap. 58.3m. (2002), dep. 146.3m., total assets 239.4m. (Jan. 2003); Chair. MIHAIL OGORODNICOV; 31 brs.

EuroCreditBank JSC: 2001 Chişinău, str. Ismail 33; tel. (22) 50-01-01; fax (22) 54-88-27; e-mail info@ecb.md; internet www.ecb.md; f. 2002 to replace Petrolbank; commercial investment bank; cap. 40.1m., res 14.2m., dep. 115.7m. (Dec. 2000); Pres. ALEKSANDR ZHO-LONDKOVSKII; Pres. DUMITRU LUPAN; 2 brs.

Guinea: 2068 Chişinău, str. Alecu Russo 1; tel. (22) 43-05-11; fax (22) 44-41-40; cap. 10.4m., total assets 59.1m. (Jan. 1998); Chair. IURII STASIEV.

IBID-MB (International Bank for Investment and Development): 2067 Chişinău, bd Moscow 21; tel. (22) 34-62-49; fax (22) 34-62-31; cap. 9.6m., total assets 24.7m. (Jan. 1998); Chair. GHEORGHE NECHIT.

Investprivatbank SA: 2001 Chişinău, str. Şciusev 34; tel. (22) 27-43-86; fax (22) 54-05-10; e-mail ipb@ipb.md; internet www.ipb.md; f. 1994; cap. 67.9m., dep. 77.6m., total assets 171.4m. (Dec. 2002); Chair. IVAN CHIRPALOV; 3 brs.

CB Mobiasbanca SA: 2012 Chişinău, bd Ştefan cel Mare 81A; tel. (22) 27-92-69; fax (22) 27-92-70; e-mail info@mobiasbank.com; internet www.mobiasbank.com; f. 1990; acquired Bank-coop in 2001;

commercial bank; cap. US $8.9m., res US $0.8m., dep. US $14.8m. (Jan. 2003); Chair. of Bd VICTOR POPUSOI; 8 brs.

Moldindconbank SA (Moldovan Bank for Industry and Construction): 2012 Chişinău, str. Armeneasca 38; tel. (22) 22-55-21; fax (22) 27-91-95; e-mail info@moldinconbank.com; internet www .moldindconbank.com; f. 1991; joint-stock commercial bank; cap. 29.7m., res 6.2m., dep. 703.5m. (Dec. 2002); Chair. of Bd VALERIAN MIRZAC; 21 brs.

Moldova Agroindbank SA: 2005 Chişinău, str. Cosmonauţilor 9; tel. (22) 21-28-28; fax (22) 22-80-58; e-mail aib@maib.md; internet www.maib.md; f. 1991; joint-stock commercial bank; cap. 51.9m., res 31.1m. (Dec. 2002); Chair. VICTOR MICULEŢ; Pres. NATALIA VRABIE; 45 brs.

Universalbank SA: 2004 Chişinău, bd Ştefan cel Mare 180, et. 4; tel. (22) 29-59-00; fax (22) 249-59-06; e-mail ub@mail.universalbank .md; internet www.universalbank.md; f. 1994; cap. 46.5m., res 8.5m., dep. 92.7m., total assets 205.5m. (Dec. 2001); Chair. of Bd DIANA MOTOLOGA (acting).

Vias: 2002 Chişinău; tel. (22) 54-14-10; fax (22) 54-14-20; cap. 10.3m., total assets 18.1m. (Jan. 1998); Chair. NICOLAE DEDE.

Victoriabank: 2004 Chişinău, str. 31 August 141; tel. (22) 23-30-65; fax (22) 23-39-33; e-mail mail@victoriabank.md; internet www .victoriabank.md; f. 1989; cap. 146.0m., total assets 767.5m. (Dec. 2001); Chair. VICTOR ŢURCANU; 12 brs.

Savings Bank

Banca de Economii a Moldovei SA: 2012 Chişinău, str. Columna 115; tel. (22) 24-47-22; fax (22) 24-47-31; e-mail bem@bem.md; internet www.bem.md; f. 1992; cap. 29.3m., res 4.4m., dep. 862.4m. (Dec. 2002); Pres. RAISA CANTEMIR; 36 brs.

STOCK EXCHANGE

Moldovan Stock Exchange (Bursa de Valori a Moldovei SA): 2001 Chişinău, bd Ştefan cel Mare 73; tel. (22) 27-75-94; fax (22) 27-73-56; e-mail dodu@moldse.md; internet www.moldse.md; f. 1994; Chair. Dr CORNELIU DODU.

INSURANCE

QBE Asito SA: 2005 Chişinău, str. Bănulescu-Bodoni 57/1; tel. and fax (22) 22-62-12; fax (22) 22-11-79; e-mail asito@qbe-asito.com; internet www.qbe-asito.com; f. 1991; 74% owned by QBE Insurance Group (based in Australia); leading insurance co, with 40% market share; Gen. Man. EUGEN SHLOPAK; 1,100 employees.

Trade and Industry

GOVERNMENT AGENCIES

State Department for Privatization: see the section on The Government.

Moldovan Export Promotion Organization (MEPO): 2009 Chişinău, str. Mateevici 65; tel. (22) 27-36-54; fax (22) 22-43-10; e-mail mepo@mepo.net; internet www.mepo.net; f. 1999; assists enterprises in increasing exports and improving business environment; Gen. Dir VALERIU CANNA.

CHAMBER OF COMMERCE

Chamber of Commerce and Industry of the Republic of Moldova: 2012 Chişinău, str. M. Eminescu 28; tel. (22) 22-15-52; fax (22) 24-14-53; e-mail inform@chamber.md; internet www.chamber .md; f. 1969; Chair. GHEORGHE CUCU.

UTILITIES

Regulatory Authority

National Energy Regulatory Agency (ANRE): 2012 Chişinău, str. Columna 90; tel. (22) 54-13-84; fax (22) 22-46-98; e-mail anre@ moldova.md; internet www.anre.moldpac.md; f. 1997; autonomous public institution; Dirs MARIN PROFIR, VASILE CARAFIZI; Gen. Dir NICOLAE TRIBOI.

Electricity

The sector comprises one transmission company, five distribution companies and four power-generation plants.

MoldElectrica IS: f. 2001 to assume the transmission and distribution functions of Moldtranselectro (q.v.).

Reţelele Electrice de Distribuţie Centru SA (RED Centru): 2055 Vatra, str. Luceafarul 13; tel. and fax (22) 50-13-37; e-mail uf@

moldova.com; privatized in 2000; wholly owned by Unión Eléctrica Fenosa (Spain); distribution co.

Reţelele Electrice (mun. Chişinău) SA: Chişinău; privatized in 2000; wholly owned by Unión Eléctrica Fenosa (Spain); distribution co.

Reţelele Electrice de Distribuţie Nord SA (RED Nord): 3121 Bălţi, bd Ştefan cel Mare 180A; tel. (31) 2-20-00; fax (31) 2-33-12; e-mail red-nord@mdl.net; f. 1997; electricity distribution; owns nine regional distribution divisions; Dir GHEORGHE I. PELIN.

Reţelele Electrice de Distribuţie Nord-Vest (RED Nord-Vest): owns six regional distribution divisions.

Reţelele Electrice de Distribuţie Sud SA (RED Sud): 3901 Cahul, str. Tineretului 2; e-mail uf@moldova.com; f. 1997; privatized in 2000; wholly owned by Unión Eléctrica Fenosa (Spain); electricity distribution.

Gas

MoldovaGaz SA: 2005 Chişinău, str. Albisoara 38; tel. (22) 22-32-70; fax (22) 24-00-14; f. May 1999; national gas pipeline and distribution networks; comprises one transmission company and 12 distribution companies; 51% owned by Gazprom (Russia), 35% owned by Moldova and 14% held by Transnistria; Gen. Dir GHENADII ABASCIN (acting).

Moldovatransgas SRL: 5233 Drochia, şos. Tarigrad, POB 24; tel. (52) 24-452; fax (52) 26-238; f. 1986; natural gas transportation, supply and equipment service.

TRADE UNIONS

Confederation of Trade Unions of Moldova: 2012 Chişinău, str. 31 August 129; tel. (22) 23-76-74; fax (22) 23-76-98; e-mail cfsind@cni.md; internet www.csrm.md; f. 1990; Pres. PETRU CHIRIAC.

CONSUMER ORGANIZATION

Central Union of Consumers' Co-operatives of Moldova (Uniunea Centrală a Cooperativelor de Consum din Republica Moldova—MOLDCOOP): 2001 Chişinău, bd Ştefan cel Mare 67; tel. (22) 27-15-95; fax (22) 27-41-50; f. 1925; Chair. PAVEL G. DUBALARI.

Transport

RAILWAYS

Plans for the construction of a new rail link, connecting Chişinău wth Iaşi, Romania, were announced in mid-2002.

Moldovan Railways: 2012 Chişinău, str. Vlaicu Pîrcălab 48; tel. (22) 25-44-08; fax (22) 22-13-80; e-mail secr@railway.md; internet www.railway.md; f. 1992 following the dissolution of the former Soviet Railways (SZhD) organization; total network 1,120.5 km; Dir-Gen. MIRON GAGAUZ.

ROADS

In 2000 Moldova's network of roads totalled 12,691 km (86.1% of which was hard-surfaced), including 3,328 km of main roads and 6,105 km of regional roads.

INLAND WATERWAYS

In 1997 the total length of navigable waterways in Moldova was 424 km. The main river ports are at Tighina (Bender, Bendery), Rîbniţa and Reni. The construction of a maritime port (petroleum terminal) on the River Danube was under way.

SHIPPING

Neptun-M SA: 2064 Chişinău, str. V. Belinski 101; tel. (22) 74-95-51; fax (22) 74-09-01; f. 1992; Gen. Dir VICTOR ANDRUŞCA.

CIVIL AVIATION

Chişinău International Airport and the air-traffic-control operator, Moldatsa, were re-opened in June 2000, after refurbishment funded by the European Bank for Reconstruction and Development (EBRD). Moldova has three civilian airports, in Chişinău, Tiraspol and Bălţi. In 2003 proposals were announced to transform the country's only military airbase, in Marculesti, into a fourth civilian airport.

Civil Aviation Administration: 2026 Chişinău, Aeroportul Chişinău; tel. (22) 52-40-64; fax (22) 52-91-18; e-mail info@caa.md; internet www.caa.md; f. 1993; Dir VLADIMIR SABARIN.

Compania Aeriana Moldova Ltd: 2026 Chişinău, Aeroportul Chişinău; tel. (22) 52-51-62; fax (22) 52-40-40; formerly Air Moldova; Unistar Ventures GmbH (Germany) purchased a stake in June 2000; 51% retained by the state; scheduled and charter passenger and cargo flights to destinations in Europe and the CIS; Dir-Gen. PETER CHEBAN.

Air Moldova International: 2026 Chişinău, Aeroportul Chişinău, 4th Floor; tel. (22) 52-97-91; fax (22) 52-64-14; e-mail info@ami.md; internet www.ami.md; scheduled and charter flights to destinations in Europe and the CIS; Dir-Gen. DORIN TIMCIUC.

Moldavian Airlines SA: 2026 Chişinău, Aeroportul Chişinău; tel. (22) 52-93-56; fax (22) 52-50-64; e-mail sales@mdv.md; internet www.mdv.md; f. 1994; scheduled and charter passenger and cargo flights to destinations in Europe, the Middle East and North Africa; Pres. and Chief Exec. NICOLAE PETROV.

Moldtransavia SRL: 2026 Chişinău, Aeroportul Chişinău; tel. (22) 52-59-71; fax (22) 52-63-99; e-mail mold@travia.mldnet.com; air freight and passenger transportation.

Tourism

There were 23,598 tourist arrivals in 2003, compared with 15,690 in 2001.

Federation of Sport and Tourism of the Republic of Moldova: Chişinău; tel. (22) 44-51-81; e-mail ftsmd@narod.ru; internet www.ftsmd.narod.ru; Pres. IVAN D. ZABUNOV.

Moldova-Tur SA: 2001 Chişinău, bd Ştefan cel Mare 4; tel. (22) 54-03-01; fax (22) 54-04-94; e-mail moldovatur@travers.md; internet www.jpm.md/mtur; f. 1959.

MONACO

Introductory Survey

Location, Climate, Language, Religion, Flag

The Principality of Monaco lies in western Europe. The country is a small enclave in south-eastern France, about 15 km east of Nice. It has a coastline on the Mediterranean Sea but is otherwise surrounded by French territory. The climate is Mediterranean, with warm summers and very mild winters. The official language is French, but Monégasque (a mixture of the French Provençal and Italian Ligurian dialects), Italian and English are also spoken. Most of the population profess Christianity, with about 91% belonging to the Roman Catholic Church. The national flag (proportions 4 by 5) has two equal horizontal stripes, of red and white. The state flag (proportions 4 by 5) displays the princely arms of Monaco (a white shield, held by two monks and superimposed on a pavilion of ermine) on a white background.

History

The Principality of Monaco is an hereditary monarchy, which has been ruled by the Grimaldi dynasty since 1297. It was abolished during the French Revolution but re-established in 1814. In 1861 Monaco became an independent state under the protection of France. The Constitution, promulgated in January 1911, vested legislative power jointly in the Prince and an 18-member Conseil National, selected for a term of five years by a panel comprising nine delegates of the municipality and 21 members elected by universal suffrage. Agreements in 1918 and 1919 between France and Monaco provided for Monaco's incorporation into France should the reigning prince die without leaving a male heir. Prince Louis II, the ruler of Monaco since 1922, died in May 1949, and was succeeded by his grandson, Prince Rainier III. A new Constitution, introduced in December 1962, abolished the formerly-held principle of the divine right of the ruler, and stipulated that the Conseil National be elected by universal adult suffrage.

Supporters of Prince Rainier, grouped in the Union Nationale et Démocratique dominated at five-yearly elections in 1963–88, on all but two occasions taking all 18 seats on the Conseil National. In January 1993, however, two lists of candidates, the Liste Campora (led by Jean-Louis Campora, the President of the football team, AS Monaco) and the Liste Médecin, secured 15 and two seats respectively, while an independent candidate won the remaining seat. At legislative elections in February 1998 UND candidates secured all 18 seats.

Controversy surrounding the use of Monaco's financial sector for the transfer of funds derived from criminal activities intensified in 1998 with the culmination of an investigation into the deposit of US $5.5m. in cash, suspected of originating from the illegal drugs trade, at a bank in Monaco in 1995. The affair led to a crisis in relations between France and the Principality, with the French Government overruling Prince Rainier by refusing to extend the mandate of Monaco's Chief Prosecutor, whom it suspected of not conducting a sufficiently thorough investigation of the scandal. Following further criticisms of Monégasque banking practice by a report by the Organisation for Economic Co-operation and Development (OECD, see p. 295) in April 2000, the French Government published two reports in October, which recommended a rapid revision of the bilateral treaties between Monaco and France, proposing that Monégasque institutions be brought into greater conformity with French excise, fiscal and banking regulations. A further report issued by OECD in April 2002 stated that the fiscal legislation and banking secrecy permitted in Monaco remained in breach of international conventions, although initial suggestions that Monaco, and six other sovereign territories could be subject to financial sanctions in response to this non-compliance were not, in the event, realized.

In March 2002 the electoral law was amended, and in April the Conseil National approved a number of significant constitutional amendments, both moves in part with the intention of progressing Monaco's application for full membership of the Council of Europe (see p. 190), which had been submitted in October 1998. The age of majority was lowered from 21 years to 18 years, and several executive powers of the Prince were transferred to the Conseil National, the size of which was to be increased to 24 members following the elections in 2003. Additionally, the law of succession was modified, to permit succession through the female line.

In late 2002 discontent was reported at a proposal, supported by Campora, to sell AS Monaco to a Ukrainian investment company, Fedcominvest, which was also the football club's principal sponsor. Following a report in *Le Monde*, in December 2002, which alleged that Fedcominvest was involved in 'money laundering', Prince Rainier, who on behalf of the Principality, retained ultimate control over the club, prohibited the proposed sale. The ensuing scandal appeared to be a significant factor in appreciably reducing support for Campora's UND at the legislative elections, held on 9 February 2003, when the UND secured only three seats on the enlarged Conseil National; the remaining 21 seats were awarded to the Union pour Monaco list, led by a former member of the UND, Stéphane Valéri. A further significant factor that was regarded as contributing to the precipitous decline in support for the UND was the continuing delay in progressing Monaco's application for full membership of the Council of Europe, in spite of the constitutional changes approved in 2002.

In late April 2004 the Parliamentary Assembly of the Council of Europe (PACE) ruled that Monaco was entitled to receive special 'guest status' at PACE but that further reforms were required before the Principality could be considered for full membership of the Council; among the principal requirements were the extension of eligibility for several senior government positions, including the Minister of State (who, under the terms of a 1930 treaty, was required to be a French civil servant) to Monégasque citizens, and an enhancement of fiscal regulation.

Monaco participates in the work of a number of international organizations, and in 1993 became a member of the UN.

Government

Legislative power is vested jointly in the Prince, an hereditary ruler, and the 24-member Conseil National, which is elected by universal adult suffrage, partly under a system of proportional representation, for a term of five years. The electorate comprises only Monégasque citizens aged 18 years or over. Executive power is exercised, under the authority of the Prince, by the four-member Council of Government, headed by the Minister of State (a French civil servant selected by the Prince from a list of three candidates presented by the French Government). The Prince represents the Principality in its relations with foreign powers, and signs and ratifies treaties. There is, additionally, a consultative Conseil Communal, elected for a term of four years, headed by a mayor.

Economic Affairs

In 2001, according to World Bank estimates, Monaco's gross national income (GNI), measured at average 1999–2001 prices, was equivalent to approximately US $24,700 per head. In 2000, according to World Bank estimates, GNI, measured at average 1998–2000 prices, was equivalent to approximately $25,200 per head, or approximately $25,700 on an international purchasing-power parity basis. According to UN estimates, Monaco's gross domestic product (GDP) was $847m. in 1995 (equivalent to $26,470 per head). During 1990–95 GDP increased, in real terms, at an average annual rate of 1.1%. GDP grew by 2.2% in 1995. The annual rate of population increase averaged 0.6% in 1990–2000. Monaco has the highest population density of all the independent states in the world.

There is no agricultural land in Monaco. In 1990 a Belgian enterprise established an offshore fish farm for sea bass and sea bream.

Industry (excluding construction and public works) accounted for 11.6% of economic activity in 1993, and engaged some 17.0% of those employed in the private sector in 2002. Industry is mainly light in Monaco. The principal sectors, measured by gross value of output, are chemicals, pharmaceuticals and cosmetics (which together accounted for 46.5% of all industrial revenue in 2002), plastics, micro-electronics and electrical goods, paper and card manufacture, and clothing and textiles.

Service industries represent the most significant sector of the economy in Monaco, contributing 49.1% of total revenue in 1993, and providing employment to 83.0% of those working in the private sector in 2002. Banking and finance accounted for more than 38% of the services sector and employed some 1,400 people in the late 1990s. At the end of 2002 the total value of deposits in Monaco's private banking sector was estimated at €18,600m. By 2002 it was estimated that the share of national revenue provided by the casino had declined to around 5%, while trade accounted for 38.1% of revenue in that year, and banking and financial activities accounted for some 17.5%.

Tourism is also an important source of income, providing an estimated 25% of total government revenue in 1991 and engaging some 20% of the employed labour force in the late 1990s. In 2002 262,520 tourists (excluding excursionists) visited Monaco, representing a decrease of some 2.7%, compared with 2001. Including excursionists, some 4m. people visited the Principality in 1992, and in that year revenue from tourism totalled US $1,300m. The greatest number of visitors (excluding excursionists) in 2002 were from Italy (23.2%), France (15.8%), the United Kingdom (14.5%) and the USA (9.7%). In that year the conference industry accounted for 30.4% of the nights spent at Monaco's foreign hotels.

Monaco's external trade is included in the figures for France. Revenue is derived principally from real estate, light and medium industry, indirect taxation and tourism.

In 2003 there was a budgetary deficit of €23.2m.: expenditure amounted to €616.7m. In 2000 value-added tax (VAT) contributed 52.8% of total government revenue. In the late 1990s it was estimated that less than 3% of the population were unemployed in the Principality.

Monaco is largely dependent on imports from France, owing to its lack of natural resources. There is a severe labour shortage in the Principality, and the economy is reliant on migrant workers (many of whom remain resident in France and Italy). Following the establishment of a casino in the 1860s, tourism became the dominant sector in the economy. In particular, the Principality has sought to establish itself as a major centre of the conference industry; about one-third of the visitors to Monaco in 1994 were connected with this sector, compared with one-10th in the early 1970s. From the 1980s, however, the industry and real estate sectors expanded, as a series of land reclamation projects increased Monaco's area by 20%, and the Principality's railway station was relocated underground. A number of foreign companies and banks are registered in Monaco in order to take advantage of the low rates of taxation on company profits. Since the removal of French restrictions on foreign exchange in 1987, Monaco's banking industry (which includes an 'offshore' sector) has expanded. The opening of a new conference and cultural centre in mid-2000 was expected to result in the further expansion of Monaco's business conference industry. The role of tourism in the economy was expected to grow further, following the construction of a new pier for luxury vessels, completed in August 2002. Further measures, which aimed to create an additional 350 berthing spaces for leisure yachts in Monaco (in addition to the 350 already extant), were announced in 2003, although the number of tourist visits recorded in 2002 was some 12.6% less than in 2000, reflecting weaknesses in the international economy. The shipping and telecommunications industries were also a focus of expansion in the Principality in the early 2000s.

Education

Education follows the French system, and is compulsory for 10 years for children aged six to 16 years. Primary education begins at six years of age and lasts for five years. Secondary education begins at 11 years of age and lasts for seven years. In 1996/97 some 1,919 pupils attended the Principality's seven primary schools, while 2,358 pupils were enrolled in secondary education. Total expenditure on education amounted to 221m. French francs in 1996, equivalent to 6.3% of total budgetary expenditure.

Public Holidays

2004: 1 January (New Year's Day), 27 January (Feast of St Dévote, Patron Saint of the Principality), 12 April (Easter Monday), 1 May (Labour Day), 20 May (Ascension Day), 31 May (Whit Monday), 15 August (Assumption), 1 November (All Saints' Day), 19 November (National Day/Fête du Prince), 8 December (Immaculate Conception), 25–26 December (Christmas).

2005: 1 January (New Year's Day), 27 January (Feast of St Dévote, Patron Saint of the Principality), 28 March (Easter Monday), 1 May (Labour Day), 5 May (Ascension Day), 16 May (Whit Monday), 15 August (Assumption), 1 November (All Saints' Day), 19 November (National Day/Fête du Prince), 8 December (Immaculate Conception), 25–26 December (Christmas).

Weights and Measures

The metric system is in force.

Statistical Survey

Source: (unless otherwise stated): Direction de l'expansion économique, division des statistiques et des études économiques, 9 rue du Gabian, 98000 Monte-Carlo; tel. 93-15-41-59; fax 93-15-87-59.

AREA AND POPULATION

Area: 1.95 sq km.

Population: 29,972 at census of 23 July 1990; 32,020 (males 15,544, females 16,476) at census of July 2000.

Density (July 2000): 16,435 per sq km.

Population by Nationality (2000): French 10,229; Italian 6,410; Monégasque 6,089; Other 9,292.

Districts (population at 2000 census): Monte-Carlo 15,507; Condamine 12,187; Fontvieille 3,292; Monaco-Ville (capital) 1,034.

Births, Marriages and Deaths (2002): Live births 771; Marriages 175; Deaths 564. Source: Monaco—La Mairie.

Expectation of Life (WHO estimates, years at birth): 81.2 (males 77.8; females 84.5) in 2002. Source: WHO, *World Health Report*.

Economically Active Population (incl. non-residents, September 2002): 38,354.

HEALTH AND WELFARE

Key Indicators

Total Fertility Rate (children per woman, 2001): 1.8.

Under-5 Mortality Rate (per 1,000 live births, 2001): 5.

Physicians (per 1,000 head, 1998): 6.64.

Health Expenditure (2001): US $ per head (PPP): 2,016.

Health Expenditure (2001): % of GDP: 7.6.

Health Expenditure (2001): public (% of total): 56.1.

Access to Water (% of persons, 2000): 100.

Access to Sanitation (% of persons, 2000): 100.

For sources and definitions, see explanatory note on p. vi.

FINANCE

Currency and Exchange Rates: French currency: 100 cent = 1 euro (€). *Sterling and Dollar Equivalents* (31 December 2003): £1 sterling = 1.4131 euros; US $1 = 0.7918 euros; 100 euros = £70.77 = $126.30. *Average Exchange Rate* (euros per US dollar): 1.1175 in 2001; 1.0626 in 2002; 0.8860 in 2003. *Note:* The local currency was formerly the French franc, although some Monégasque currency, at par with the French franc, also circulated. From the introduction of the euro, with French participation, on 1 January 1999, a fixed exchange rate of €1 = 6.55957 French francs was in operation. Euro notes and coins were introduced on 1 January 2002. The euro and local currency circulated alongside each other until 17 February, after which the euro became the sole legal tender.

Budget (million euros, 2003): Revenue 593.6; Expenditure 616.7.

EXTERNAL TRADE

Monaco's imports and exports are included in the figures for France.

TRANSPORT

Road Traffic (vehicles in use at 31 December 1996, estimates): Passenger cars 21,120; Buses and coaches 70; Lorries and vans 2,700; Road tractors 80; Motorcycles and mopeds 5,400. Source: IRF, *World Road Statistics*.

TOURISM

Tourist Arrivals (excluding excursionists): 300,185 in 2000; 269,925 in 2001; 262,520 in 2002. Figures refer to arrivals of foreign visitors at hotels and similar establishments.

Tourist Arrivals by Country (2002): France 41,392; Germany 14,983; Italy 60,822; Japan 8,252; Switzerland 8,242; United Kingdom 38,071; USA 25,430; Total (incl. others) 262,520.

COMMUNICATIONS MEDIA

Radio Receivers (1997): 34,000 in use*.

Television Receivers (1997): 25,000 in use*.

Daily Newspapers (1996): 1 title (estimated circulation 8,000 copies—1995)*.

Non-daily Newspapers (1996): 5 titles (estimated circulation 50,000 copies)*.

Telephones (2000): 30,000 main lines in use†.

Facsimile Machines (1992): 1,880 in use‡.

Mobile Cellular Telephones (2000): 18,700 subscribers†.
* Source: UNESCO, *Statistical Yearbook*.
† Source: International Telecommunication Union.
‡ Source: UN, *Statistical Yearbook*.

EDUCATION

(1996/97)

Pre-primary: 9 schools; 46 teachers (1995/96); 996 pupils (males 526; females 470).

Primary: 7 schools; 102 teachers (1995/96); 1,919 pupils (males 1,011; females 908).

General Secondary: 192 teachers; 2,358 pupils (males 1,141; females 1,217).

Vocational: 89 teachers; 528 pupils (males 287; females 241). Source: UNESCO, *Statistical Yearbook*.

Directory

The Constitution

The Constitution of 17 December 1962, as amended on 2 April 2002, vests legislative power jointly in the Prince and the 24-member National Council (Conseil National), which is elected by universal adult suffrage, partly under a system of proportional representation, for a term of five years. Executive power is exercised, under the authority of the Prince, by the four-member Council of Government, headed by the Minister of State. The Constitution maintains the traditional hereditary monarchy, although the principle of the divine right of the ruler is renounced. The law of succession was modified to permit succession through the female line in April 2002. The right of association, trade union freedom and the right to strike are guaranteed. The Supreme Tribunal safeguards fundamental liberties. Constitutional amendments have to be submitted for approval by the Conseil National. Several executive powers of the Prince were transferred to the Conseil National in April 2002.

The Government

HEAD OF STATE

Ruling Prince: HSH Prince RAINIER III (succeeded 9 May 1949).

COUNCIL OF GOVERNMENT
(April 2004)

Minister of State: PATRICK LECLERCQ.

Government Councillor for Finance and Economic Affairs: FRANCK BIANCHERI.

Government Councillor for Public Works and Social Affairs: JOSÉ BADIA.

Government Councillor for the Interior: PHILIPPE DESLANDES.
There is also a Chef de Cabinet (GEORGE GRINDAS).

MINISTRIES

The postal address for all Ministries is: BP 522, MC 98015; tel. 93-15-80-00; fax 93-15-82-17; e-mail centre-info@gouv.mc; internet www.gouv.mc

Ministry of State: place de la Visitation, MC98000; fax 93-15-80-12; e-mail cabminetat@gouv.mc.

Legislature

Conseil National
12 rue Bellando de Castro, MC; tel. 93-30-41-15; fax 93-25-31-90.
The Conseil National (National Council) has 24 members. At the most recent elections, which took place on 9 February 2003, the Union pour Monaco (UPM) list secured 21 seats, with the Union Nationale et Démocratique (UND) controlling the remaining three.

President: STÉPHANE VALÉRI.

Vice-President: CLAUDE BOISSON.

Advisory Councils

Conseil d'état: Monte-Carlo; advises on proposed laws or ordinances submitted for its approval by the Ruling Prince or by the Government, or on any other matter; 12 mems, appt by the Ruling Prince, following the advice of the Director of Judicial Services; Pres. ALAIN GUILLOU; Vice-Pres. NORBERT FRANÇOIS; Sec. PHILIPPE NARMINO.

Conseil de la Couronne: Monte-Carlo; f. 1942; advises the Ruling Prince on matters of state, and must be consulted by the Ruling Prince prior to the implementation of certain constitutional matters, including the signature or ratification of treaties, the dissolution of the Conseil National, questions of naturalization or reintegration, the issuing of pardons or amnesties; seven mems, appointed for renewable terms of three yrs; Pres and three mems are appointed by free choice of the Ruling Prince, the remaining three mems are named by the Ruling Prince and approved by the Conseil National; all mems must hold Monégasque nationality; Pres. CHARLES BALLERIO.

Conseil économique et social: Centre Administratif, 8 rue Louis-Notari, MC; tel. 97-97-77-91; fax 93-50-05-96; f. 1945; advises on economic matters; 33 mems, appointed for a term of three years; 11 mems directly appt by Govt, 11 appt by Govt from list prepared by Union des Syndicats de Monaco, 11 appt by Govt from list prepared by the Fédération Patronale Monégasque; the Ruling Prince appoints Pres. and two Vice-Pres from among the mems; Pres. ANDRÉ GARINO; Vice-Pres ANDRÉ THIBAULT, JACQUES WOLZOK.

Political Organizations

There are no political parties as such in Monaco; however, candidates are generally grouped into lists to contest elections to the Conseil National. Between 1963 and 1992, and 1998 and 2003 the Conseil National was dominated by representatives of the **Union Nationale et Démocratique (UND)**. At the 1993 elections, however, the two main groupings were the **Liste Campora**, led by Jean-Louis Campora, and the **Liste Médecin**, led by Jean-Louis Médecin. The majority of seats at the 2003 elections were secured by the **Union pour Monaco** list.

Diplomatic Representation

There are no embassies in Monaco, but diplomatic relations are maintained at consular level with 55 countries.

Judicial System

The organization of the legal system is similar to that of France. There is one Justice of the Peace, a Tribunal de Première Instance (Court of First Instance), a Cour d'Appel (Court of Appeal), a Cour de Révision (High Court of Appeal), a Tribunal Criminel (Crown Court) and finally the Tribunal Suprême (Supreme Tribunal), which deals with infringements of the rights and liberties provided by the Constitution, and also with legal actions aiming at the annulment of administrative decisions for abusive exercise of power.

Palais de Justice

5 rue Col Bellando de Castro, MC 98000; tel. 93-15-84-11; fax 93-15-85-89.

Director of Judicial Services: ALAIN GUILLOU.
President of the Supreme Tribunal: ROLAND DRAGO.
President of the High Court of Appeal: YVES JOUHAUD.
President of the Court of Appeal: JEAN-FRANÇOIS LANDWERLIN.
President of the Court of First Instance: PHILIPPE NARMINO.

Religion

CHRISTIANITY

The Roman Catholic Church

Monaco comprises a single archdiocese, directly responsible to the Holy See. At 31 December 2002 there were an estimated 29,000 adherents in the Principality, representing about 90.6% of the total population.

Archbishop of Monaco: Most Rev. BERNARD BARSI, Archevêché, 6 rue des Fours, MC 98000; tel. 93-30-77-86; fax 93-30-39-31; e-mail evechedemonaco@aol.com.

The Anglican Communion

Within the Church of England, Monaco forms part of the diocese of Gibraltar in Europe.

Chaplain: (vacant), St Paul's Church House, 22 ave de Grande Bretagne, MC 98000; tel. 93-30-71-06; fax 93-30-50-39; e-mail stpauls@monaco.mc; internet www.stpauls.monaco.mc.

The Principality also has two Protestant churches and a synagogue.

The Press

Gazette Monaco-Côte d'Azur: 1, ave Princesse Alice, MC 98000; tel. 97-97-61-20; fax 93-50-68-27; e-mail lagazette@monte-carlo.mc; f. 1976; monthly; regional information; Dir-Gen. MAX POGGI; Chief Editor NOËLLE BINE-MULLER; circ. 10,000.

Journal de Monaco: Ministère d'Etat, BP 522, MC 98015; tel. 93-15-83-15; fax 93-15-82-17; internet http://www.gouv.mc/DataWeb/jourmon.nsf/(VDate)?OpenView&Start=1&Count=15; f. 1858; edited at the Ministry of State; official weekly; contains texts of laws and decrees; Man. Editor GILLES TONELLI.

Monaco Actualité: 2 rue du Gabian, MC 98000; tel. 92-05-75-36; fax 92-05-75-34; e-mail actualite@monaco.mc; Dir-Gen. MAURICE RICCOBONO; circ. 15,000.

Monaco Hebdo: 27 blvd d'Italie, MC 98000; tel. 93-50-56-52; fax 93-50-19-22; Man. Editor ROBERTO TESTA.

Monte-Carlo Méditerranée: tel. 92-05-67-67; fax 92-05-37-01; Dir-Gen. GÉRARD COMMAN; Chief Editor CAROLE CHABRIER.

French newspapers are widely read, and a special Monaco edition of *Nice-Matin* is published in Nice, France.

NEWS AGENCIES

Monte-Carlo Press: Monte-Carlo; e-mail mcpress@monaco.net; internet mcpress.free.fr; f. 1987.

SPORTEL: 4 blvd du Jardin Exotique, MC 98000; tel. 93-30-20-32; fax 93-30-20-33; e-mail info@sportelmonaco.com; internet www.sportelmonaco.com; sport; Exec. Vice-Pres. DAVID TOMATIS.

Publishers

EDIPROM: Monte-Carlo; tel. 92-05-67-67; fax 92-05-37-01; advertising material, official publications; Pres. GÉRARD COMMAN.

Editions Alphée: 28 rue Comte Félix Gastaldi, MC 98015 Monaco Cédex; tel. 99-99-67-17; fax 99-99-67-18.

Editions EGC: 9 ave du Prince Héréditaire Albert, BP 438, MC 98011 Monaco Cédex; e-mail multiprint@multiprintmc.com; economics, history, literature; Gen. Man. GÉRARD COMMAN.

Editions Victor Gadoury: 57 rue Grimaldi, MC 98000; tel. 93-25-12-96; fax 93-50-13-39; e-mail contact@gadoury.com; internet www.gadoury.com; f. 1967; numismatics.

Editions de l'Oiseau-Lyre SAM: Les Remparts, BP 515, MC 98015 Monaco Cédex; tel. 93-30-09-44; fax 93-30-19-15; e-mail oiseau_lyre@compuserve.com; internet www.oiseaulyre.com; f. 1932; music publishers; Dir KENNETH GILBERT.

Editions de Radio Monte Carlo SAM: Monte-Carlo; tel. 93-15-17-57; general; Pres. JEAN PASTORELLI.

Editions Regain S.N.C. Boy et Cie: Monte-Carlo; tel. 93-50-62-04; f. 1946; fiction, essays, autobiography, travel, religion, philosophy, poetry; Dir-Gen. MICHÈLE G. BOY.

Editions du Rocher: 28 rue Comte Félix Gastaldi, MC 98015; tel. 93-30-33-41; fax 93-50-73-71; f. 1943; scientific, medical, detective and general; Dir JEAN PAUL BERTRAND.

Editions André Sauret SAM: Monte-Carlo; tel. 93-50-67-94; fax 93-30-71-04; art, fiction; Dir RAYMOND LEVY.

Marsu Productions: 9 ave des Castelans, MC 98000; tel. 92-05-61-11; fax 92-05-76-60; e-mail marsuproductions@monaco377.com; internet www.marsupilami.com; comic-strips, children's entertainment.

Monaco Télématique (MCTEL): 25 blvd d'Italie, MC 98004; tel. 92-16-88-88; fax 93-30-45-45; e-mail mctel@mctel.mc; internet www.mctel.mc; scientific and technical.

Broadcasting and Communications

TELECOMMUNICATIONS

Direction du Controle des Concessions et des Télécommunications: 23 ave Prince Héréditaire Albert, MC 98000; tel. 93-15-88-00; fax 97-98-56-57; Dir RAOUL VIORA.

Monaco Telecom: 25 blvd de Suisse, MC 98000; tel. 99-66-63-00; fax 99-66-63-01; e-mail monaco-telecom@monaco-telecom.mc; f. 1997; 51% owned by Vivendi; incorporates the wholly-owned subsidiaries Monaco Telecom International, Monaco Interactive and Société Monégasque de Services de Telecoms; CEO ANTOINE VERAN.

BROADCASTING

Radio

Radio Monte Carlo SAM (RMC): Monte-Carlo; tel. 93-15-16-17; fax 93-15-16-30; the official programme of RMC is broadcast in French on 1,400 m (216 kHz); programmes in French are broadcast on 216 m (1,467 kHz); programmes on RMC may be backed by commercials or by sponsors; 83% owned by the French Government (Société financière de la radiodiffusion); Pres. C. C. SOLAMITO; Dir-Gen. JEAN NOEL TASSEZ.

Riviera Radio: 10–12 quai Antoine 1er, MC 98000; tel. 97-97-94-94; fax 97-97-94-95; e-mail info@rivieraradio.mc; internet www.rivieraradio.mc; broadcasts in English; Man. Dir PAUL KAVANAGH.

Société Monégasque d'Exploitation et d'Études de Radiodiffusion (SOMERA): Monte-Carlo; tel. 93-15-16-17; fax 93-15-16-60; fmr subsidiary of RMC, transferred to Radio-France Internationale in 1996; in French and Arabic; Pres. JEAN-PAUL CLUZEL; Dir-Gen. CHRISTIAN CHARPY.

Trans World Radio SC: BP 349, MC 98007; tel. 92-16-56-00; fax 92-16-56-01; f. 1955; broadcasts evangelical Christian programmes in 190 languages; Pres. DAVID TUCKER; Station Man. THOMAS STREETER.

Television

TVI Monte-Carlo: 8 quai Antoine 1er, MC 98000; tel. 92-16-88-20; fax 93-25-46-39; e-mail tvimc@frateschi.mc; programmes in Italian; CEO LUIGI FRATESCHI.

Société Spéciale d'Entreprises Télé Monte-Carlo: 16 blvd Princesse Charlotte, BP 279, MC 98090; tel. 93-50-59-40; fax 93-25-01-09; internet www.cecchigori.com; f. 1954; Pres. JEAN-LOUIS MÉDECIN.

Finance

(cap. = capital, res = reserves, dep. = deposits, brs = branches,
m. = million, amounts in euros—€)

BANKS

In 2001 a total of 44 banks, including major British, French, Italian and US banks, were represented in the Principality.

Banco Atlantico (Monaco), SAM: Sporting d'Hiver, 2 ave Princesse Alice, BP 147, MC 98003; tel. 92-16-57-57; fax 92-16-57-50; e-mail abcmc@webstore.mc; internet www.batlantico.es; f. 1980; 100% owned by Banco Atlántico (Spain); fmrly 49% owned by Arab Banking Corporation, Bahrain, as ABC Banque Internationale de Monaco; cap. 11.4m., res 7.9m., dep. 316.7m. (Dec. 2000); Chair. OLIMPIO FERNANDEZ; Exec. Dir and Dir-Gen. ANTONIO SALVADOR.

Banque Centrale Monégasque de Crédit: Monte-Carlo; tel. 92-16-52-00; fax 93-30-91-93; f. 1969; Pres. JEAN DEFLASSIEUX; Gen. Man. MARC LANZERINI.

Banque de Gestion Edmond de Rothschild: BP 317, Les Terrasses, 2 ave de Monte-Carlo, MC 98000; tel. 93-10-47-47; fax 93-25-75-57; e-mail banque@lcf-rothschild.mc; internet www.lcf-rothschild.com; f. 1986; present name adopted 1993; cap. 12.0m., res 10.7m., dep. 384.5m. (Dec. 2002); Chair. LEONARDO P. A. POGGI; Gen. Man. GIAMPAOLO BERNINI.

Banque du Gothard (Monaco): La Belle Epoque, 15–17 bis ave d'Ostende, MC 98000; tel. 93-10-66-66; fax 93-50-60-71; e-mail philippe.tronlozai@gottardo.com; internet www.gottardo.com; f. 1994; 100% owned by Banca del Gottardo (Switzerland); cap. 40.0m., res 20.2m., dep. 1,357.5m. (Dec. 2002); Pres. NICOLA MORDASINI.

Banque Sudameris: 47–49 blvd d'Italie, MC 98000; tel. 92-16-51-00; fax 92-16-51-13; e-mail monaco@sudameris.fr; Man. MICHEL DE GIRONDE.

Barclays Bank: 31 ave de la Costa, BP 339, MC 98007; tel. 93-15-35-35; fax 93-25-15-68; Gen. Man. J. B. BUISSON; 3 brs.

Compagnie Monégasque de Banque: 23 ave de la Costa, BP 149, MC 98007; tel. 93-15-77-77; fax 93-25-08-69; e-mail cmb@cmb.mc; internet www.cmb.mc; f. 1976; 34.4% owned by Commerzbank AG (Germany), 33.9% by Intesa Holding International SA (Luxembourg), 17.3% by Mediobanca-Banca di Credito Finanziario SpA (Italy); cap. 111.1m., res 58.9m., dep. 1,408.0m. (Dec. 2002); Chair. ENRICO BRAGGIOTTI.

Crédit Foncier de Monaco (CFM Monaco): 11 blvd Albert 1er, BP 499, MC 98000; tel. 93-10-20-00; fax 93-10-23-50; e-mail info@cfm.mc; internet www.cfm.mc; f. 1922; 77.1% owned by Crédit Agricole Indosuez; cap. 35.0m., res 79.7m., dep. 1,906.4m. (Sep. 2003); Chair. YVES BARSALOU; Gen. Man. HERVÉ CATALA.

Crédit Suisse (Monaco): 27 ave de la Costa, BP 155, MC 98003; tel. 93-15-27-27; fax 93-25-27-59; e-mail alexandre.zeller@cspb.com; f. 1987; cap. 12.0m., res 2.1m., dep. 505.6m. (Dec. 2002); Chair. ALEXANDRE ZELLER.

EFG Eurofinancière d'Investissements: Ville Les Aigles, 15 ave d'Ostende, MC 98000; tel. 93-15-11-11; fax 93-15-11-12; e-mail enquiries_mco@efgbank.com; internet www.efggroup.com; f. 1990; 100% owned by EFG Bank European Financial Group (Switzerland); private banking; cap. 16.0m., res 1.3m., dep. 377.9m. (Dec. 2002); Dir-Gen. GEORGE CATSIAPIS.

HSBC Republic Bank (Monaco): 17 ave d'Ostende, MC 98000; tel. 93-15-25-25; fax 93-15-25-00; internet www.hsbcprivatebank.com; f. 1997 as Republic National Bank of New York (Monaco) SA, present name adopted 2000; owned by HSBC Private Banking Holdings (Suisse—Switzerland); private banking; cap. 86.0m., dep. 2,947.1m., total assets 3,135.9m. (Dec. 2002); Chief Exec. and Dir-Gen. GÉRARD COHEN.

KB Luxembourg (Monaco): 8 ave de Grande Bretagne, BP 262, MC 98005; tel. 92-16-55-55; fax 92-16-53-80; e-mail contact@kblmonaco.com; f. 1996; cap. 7.2m., res 2.1m., dep. 299.4m. (Dec. 2003); Chair. of Bd JEAN-PAUL LOOS.

Société Monégasque de Banque Privée: 9 blvd d'Italie, MC 98000; tel. 93-15-23-23; fax 93-15-23-30; f. 1953; 49.9% owned by Dexia Banque Internationale à Luxembourg SA (Luxembourg), 25.1% by Caixa Holding (Spain), 25.0% by Crèdit Andorrà SA (Andorra); cap. 29.6m., res. 1.1m., dep. 284.3m. (Dec. 2002); Chair. JUAN ANTONIO SAMARANCH; Dir-Gen. JOSEP TRIAS.

UBS (Monaco): 2 ave de Grande Bretagne, BP 189, MC 98007; tel. 93-15-58-15; fax 93-15-58-00; e-mail rolf.meier@ubs.com; internet www.ubs.com/monaco; f. 1956; present name adopted 1998; 100% owned by UBS AG (Switzerland); cap. 9.2m., res 23.9m., dep. 1,913.7m. (Dec. 2002); Chief Exec. PIERRE POYET.

United European Bank—Monaco: 26 blvd d'Italie, BP 319, MC 98007; tel. 93-15-74-74; fax 93-50-15-37; e-mail ueb.monaco@uebmonaco.mc; f. 1956; private banking; Pres.and Chair. GÉRARD LOHIER; Dir-Gen. ERIC GEORGES.

INSURANCE COMPANIES

Eric Blair Insurance: 33 blvd Princesse Charlotte, MC 98000; tel. 93-50-99-66; fax 93-50-14-47; e-mail insure@monaco.mc; internet www.monaco.mc/co/ericblair.

Gramaglia AGF: 14 blvd des Moulins, BP 153, MC 98003; tel. 92-16-59-00; fax 92-16-59-16; e-mail info@gramaglia.mc; internet www.gramaglia.mc; Dir ANTOINE GRAMAGLIA.

Monaco Insurance Services: 3 ave Saint-Charles, BP 113, MC 98008; tel. 93-25-38-58; fax 93-25-74-37; Dir PIERRE AOUN.

Mourenon et Giannotti: 22 blvd Princesse Charlotte, MC 98000; tel. 97-97-08-88; fax 97-97-08-80; f. 1975; Dirs JEAN-PHILIPPE MOURENON, JOSÉ GIANNOTTI.

J.P. Sassi-Drouot Assurances: Monte-Carlo; tel. 93-30-45-88; Dir JEAN-PIERRE SASSI.

Silvain Assurances: 33 blvd Princesse Charlotte, BP 267, MC 98005; tel. 93-25-54-45; fax 93-50-39-05; Dir FRANÇOIS SILVAIN.

Société Française de Recours Cie d'Assurances: 28 blvd Princesse Charlotte, MC 98000; tel. 93-50-52-63; fax 93-50-54-49; Dir FLORIANO CONTE.

Trade and Industry

GOVERNMENT AGENCIES

Conseil Economique et Social: 8 rue Louis Notari, Monte-Carlo; tel. 97-97-77-90; fax 93-50-05-96; consultative org. in six sections dealing with all aspects of Monaco's economy; comprises 30 members who represent, in equal proportions, employers, workers and the Government; named by the Head of State every three years from all nationalities; President must be Monégasque national; Pres. ANDRÉ GARINO; Vice-Pres ANDRÉ THIBAULT, JACQUES WOLZOK.

Direction de l'Action Sanitaire et Sociale: 13 rue Emile de Loth; tel. 93-15-84-20; fax 93-15-81-59; Dir Dr ANNE NEGRE.

Direction des Affaires Culturelles: 4 blvd des Moulins; tel. 93-15-85-15; fax 93-50-66-94; Dir RAINIER ROCCHI.

Direction des Affaires Maritimes: La Capitainerie, quai Jean-Charles Rey, MC 98000; tel. 93-15-86-78; fax 93-15-37-15; Dir PHILIPPE REMY.

Direction du Budget et du Trésor: 10 quai Antoine 1er, 98000 MC; tel. 93-15-87-73; fax 93-15-84-26; Dir SOPHIE THEVENOUX.

Direction des Contentieux: Stade Louis II, Entrée H, 1 ave des Castelans, MC 98018; Dir ISABELLE ROUANET-PASSERON.

Direction du Contrôle des Concessions et des Télécommunications: 23 ave Prince Héréditaire Albert; tel. 93-15-88-00; fax 97-98-56-57; Dir RAOUL VIORA.

Direction de l'Education Nationale, de la Jeunesse et des Sports: Lycée Technique, ave de l'Annonciade; tel. 93-15-80-05; fax 93-15-85-74; e-mail denjs@gouv.mc; internet www.monaco.gouv.mc; Dir YVETTE LAMBIN DE COMBREMONT.

Direction de l'Environnement, de l'Urbanisme et de la Construction: 23 ave Prince Héréditaire Albert; tel. 93-15-22-99; fax 93-15-88-02; Dir MAUD COLLE-GAMERDINGER.

Direction de l'Expansion Economique: 9 rue du Gabian; tel. 93-15-21-74; fax 92-05-75-20; Dir CATHERINE ORECCHIA-MATTHYSSENS.

Direction de la Fonction Publique et des Ressources Humaines: Stade Louis II, entrée H, 1 ave des Castelans; tel. 93-15-81-13; fax 93-15-42-91; Dir CLAUDE COTTALORDA.

Direction de l'Habitat: 24 rue du Gabian; tel. 93-15-80-08; fax 93-15-20-06; Dir MARIE-JOSÉ CALENCO.

Direction de la Prospective et des Etudes d'Urbanisme: 3 ave de Fontveille; tel. 93-15-80-00; fax 93-15-46-60; e-mail prospective@gouv.mc; Dir PATRICE CELLARIO.

Direction des Relations Extérieures: Ministère d'État, Place de la Visitation, MC 98000; tel. 93-15-82-43; fax 93-15-85-54; e-mail relext@gouv.mc; Dir PATRICK LECLERCQ; Sec.-Gen. CLAUDE GIORDAN.

Direction des Services Fiscaux: 57 rue Grimaldi, BP 475, 98012 Monaco Cédex; tel. 93-15-40-54; fax 93-15-81-55; Dir GÉRARD EMMEL.

Direction de la Sûreté Publique: 3–4 rue Louis Notari, BP 465, MC 98012; tel. 93-15-30-15; fax 93-50-65-47; Dir JEAN-FRANÇOIS SAUTIER.

Direction du Travail et des Affaires Sociales: 2 rue Princesse Antoinette; tel. 93-15-88-14; fax 92-16-70-05; Dir THIERRY PICCO.

Trésorerie Générale des Finances: Cour de la Trésorie, Palais de Monaco; tel. 93-15-88-19; fax 93-15-85-75; Treas. YVON BERTRAND.

CHAMBER OF COMMERCE

Jeune Chambre Economique de Monaco: MC 98000; tel. 92-05-20-19; fax 92-05-31-29; e-mail jcemonaco@jcemonaco.mc; internet www.jcemonaco.mc; f. 1963; 102 mems; Pres. JOUMANA YAMMINE.

EMPLOYERS' ASSOCIATION

Fédération Patronale Monégasque (FPM) (Employers' Federation of Monaco): 'Le Coronado', 20 ave de Fontvielle, MC 98000; tel. 92-05-38-92; fax 92-05-20-04; e-mail info@federation-patronale.mc; internet www.federation-patronale.mc; f. 1944; Pres. F. E. GRIFFIN; 23 member orgs, with 1,500 individual mems.

UTILITIES

Electricity and Gas

Société Monégasque de l'Electricité et du Gaz (SMEG): 10 ave de Fontvieille, BP 633, MC 98013 Monaco Cédex; tel. 92-05-05-00; fax 92-05-05-92; e-mail smeg@smeg.mc; internet www.smeg.mc; f. 1890.

Water

Société Monégasque des Eaux (SME): 29 ave Princesse Grace, MC 98000; tel. 93-30-83-67; fax 92-05-05-00.

TRADE UNION

Union des Syndicats de Monaco (USM): 28 blvd Rainier III, 98000 Monaco; tel. 93-30-19-30; fax 93-25-06-73; e-mail usm@usm.mc; internet www.usm.mc; f. 1944; Pres. (vacant); Sec.-Gen. ANGÈLE BRAQUETTI; 35 mem. unions with 2,500 individual mems.

Transport

RAILWAYS

There is 1.7 km of railway track in Monaco running from France to Monte-Carlo. It is operated by the French state railway, the Société Nationale des Chemins de fer Français (SNCF). As part of the Government's policy of land reclamation an underground railway station was opened in 1999, at a cost of 1,930m. francs.

ROADS

In 1999 there were an estimated 50 km of major roads in the Principality.

SHIPPING

Monaco has an estimated docking capacity of 100 cruise ships.

Service de la Marine: 7 ave J.F. Kennedy; tel. 93-15-80-00.

Societe d'Exploitation des Ports de Monaco: Monte-Carlo; f. 2003; 100% state-owned; responsible for management and development of the two principal ports in Monaco, at La Condamine and Fontveille; Pres. ALECO KEUSSEOGLOU.

Shipping Companies

Compagnie pour la Géstion des Affaires Maritimes et Industrielles SAM (COGEMA SAM): 20 blvd de Suisse, MC 98000 Cédex; tel. 93-10-52-70; fax 93-50-03-81; e-mail secretary@ damicoint.com; internet www.cogema-sam.com; CEO MARCO FIORI.

MC Shipping Inc.: Aigue Marine, 24 ave de Fontvielle, BP 658, MC 98013 Cédex; tel. 92-05-94-04; fax 92-05-94-16; Pres. and CEO GUY MOREL.

Olympic Shipping and Management: Monte-Carlo; tel. 93-25-41-41; fax 93-30-07-10.

Société Anonyme Monégasque d'Administration Maritime et Aérienne (SAMAMA): L'Estoril, Bloc B 1er étage, 31 ave Princesse Grace, MC 98000 Cédex; tel. 99-99-51-00; fax 99-99-51-09; e-mail general@samama-monaco.com.

V. Ships Inc: Aigue Marine, 24 ave de Fontvieille, BP 639, MC 98013 Cédex; tel. 92-05-10-10; fax 92-05-94-10; internet www.vships.com; Pres. TULLIO BIGGI; Man. Dir LORENZO MALVAROSA.

CIVIL AVIATION

There is a helicopter shuttle service between the international airport at Nice, France, and Monaco's heliport at Fontvieille.

Heli-Air Monaco SAM: Héliport de Monaco, MC 98000; tel. 92-05-00-50; fax 92-05-00-51; e-mail helico@heliairmonaco.com; internet www.heliairmonaco.com; Pres. JACQUES CROVETTO.

Tourism

Tourists are attracted to Monaco by the Mediterranean climate, dramatic scenery and numerous entertainment facilities, including a casino. In 2002 262,520 tourists (excluding excursionists) visited Monaco. In 1992, when (including excursionists) an estimated 4m. people visited the Principality, revenue from tourism totalled US $1,300m. In that year there were 18 hotels in the Principality.

Direction du Tourisme et des Congrès: 2A blvd des Moulins, MC 98030 Cédex; tel. 92-16-61-16; fax 92-16-60-00; e-mail dtc@ monaco-congres.com; internet www.monaco-congres.com; there are also international conference centres in Monte-Carlo at: Centre de Congrès Auditorium de Monte-Carlo, blvd Louis II, at Centre de Rencontres Internationales, ave d'Ostende, and at Grimaldi Forum, ave Princesse Grace; Dir-Gen. DARIO DELL'ANTONIA; Dir RÉGINE MAY.

Société des Bains de Mer (SBM): place du Casino, BP 139, MC 98007; tel. 92-16-20-00; fax 92-16-38-60; e-mail dva@sbm.mc; internet www.sbm.mc; f. 1863; corpn in which the Government holds a 69.6% interest; controls the entertainment facilities of Monaco, including the casino and numerous hotels, clubs, restaurants and sporting facilities; Chair. JEAN-LUC BIAMONTI; Gen. Man. MICHEL NOVATIN.

MONGOLIA

Introductory Survey

Location, Climate, Language, Religion, Flag, Capital

Mongolia is a land-locked country in central Asia, with the Russian Federation to the north and the People's Republic of China to the south, east and west. The climate is dry, with generally mild summers but very cold winters. Temperatures in Ulan Bator range between −32°C (−26°F) and 22°C (71°F). The principal language is Khalkha Mongolian. Kazakh is spoken in the province of Bayan-Ölgii. There is no state religion, but Buddhist Lamaism is being encouraged once again. The national flag (proportions 1 by 2) has three equal vertical stripes, of red, blue and red, with the 'soyombo' symbol (a combination of abstract devices) in gold on the red stripe at the hoist. The capital is Ulan Bator (Ulaanbaatar).

Recent History

The country was formerly the Manchu province of Outer Mongolia. In 1911, following the republican revolution in China, Mongolian princes declared the province's independence. With support from Tsarist Russia, Outer Mongolia gained autonomy, as a feudal Buddhist monarchy, but Russia accepted Chinese suzerainty over the province in 1915. Following the Russian revolution of 1917, China began to re-establish control in Mongolia in 1919. In 1920 Mongol nationalists appealed to the new Soviet regime for assistance, and in March 1921 they met on Soviet territory to found the Mongolian People's Party (called the Mongolian People's Revolutionary Party (MPRP) from 1924) and established a Provisional People's Government. After nationalist forces, with Soviet help, drove anti-Bolshevik troops from the Mongolian capital, independence was proclaimed on 11 July 1921. Soviet Russia recognized the People's Government in November of that year. In November 1924, after the death of Bogd Khan (King) Javzandamba Khutagt VIII, the Mongolian People's Republic was proclaimed.

The Mongolian People's Republic became increasingly dependent on the USSR's support. The Government conducted campaigns to collectivize the economy and to destroy the power of the nobility and Buddhist priests. In 1932 an armed uprising was suppressed with Soviet assistance. Following a purge of the MPRP and army leadership in 1936–39, power was held by Marshal Khorloogiin Choibalsan as Prime Minister and MPRP leader. The dictatorship of Choibalsan closely followed the pattern of Stalin's regime in the USSR, and its thousands of victims included eminent politicians, military officers, religious leaders and intellectuals. In 1939 a Japanese invasion from Manchuria was repelled by Soviet and Mongolian forces at Khalkhyn Gol (Nomonhan). In keeping with the Yalta agreement, war was declared on Japan in August 1945, four days before the Japanese surrender, and northern China was invaded. In a Mongolian plebiscite in October 1945, it was reported that 100% of the votes were cast in favour of independence, and this was recognized by China in January 1946.

Choibalsan died in January 1952 and was succeeded as Prime Minister by Yumjaagiin Tsedenbal, who had been the Party's First Secretary since 1940. Dashiin Damba became First Secretary of the MPRP in April 1954. In 1955 India became the first non-communist country to recognize Mongolia. Tsedenbal replaced Damba as First Secretary of the MPRP in November 1958, and a new Constitution was adopted in July 1960. Mongolia became a member of the UN in October 1961 and was subsequently accorded diplomatic recognition by the United Kingdom (1963), other Western European and developing countries. By January 1987, when Mongolia was finally granted diplomatic recognition by the USA, it maintained diplomatic relations with more than 100 states.

Jamsrangiin Sambuu, Head of State since July 1954, died in May 1972. He was replaced in June 1974 by Tsedenbal, who remained First Secretary of the MPRP (restyled General Secretary in 1981) but relinquished the post of Chairman of the Council of Ministers to Jambyn Batmönkh. In August 1984 Tsedenbal was removed from the party leadership and state presidency, apparently owing to ill health, and Batmönkh replaced him as General Secretary of the MPRP. In December Batmönkh also became Head of State, while Dumaagiin

Sodnom, hitherto a Deputy Chairman of the Council of Ministers and the Chairman of the State Planning Commission, was appointed Chairman of the Council of Ministers.

By the end of 1988 the MPRP Political Bureau was obliged to admit that economic renewal was not succeeding because of the need for social reforms. Batmönkh advocated greater openness and offered the prospect of multi-candidate elections. He criticized Tsedenbal for the country's 'stagnation', also stating that the former leader had belittled collective leadership.

Between December 1989 and March 1990 there was a great upsurge in public political activity, as several newly formed opposition movements organized a series of peaceful demonstrations in Ulan Bator, demanding political and economic reforms. The most prominent of the new opposition groups was the Mongolian Democratic Union (MDU), founded in December 1989. In January 1990 dialogue was initiated between MPRP officials and representatives of the MDU, including its chief co-ordinator, Sanjaasürengiin Zorig (a lecturer at the Mongolian State University). The emergence of further opposition groups, together with escalating public demonstrations (involving as many as 20,000 people), led to a crisis of confidence within the MPRP. At a party plenum in mid-March 1990 Batmönkh announced the resignation of the entire Political Bureau as well as of the Secretariat of the Central Committee. Gombojavyn Ochirbat, a former head of the Ideological Department of the Central Committee and a former Chairman of the Central Council of Mongolian Trade Unions, was elected the new General Secretary of the party, replacing Batmönkh. A new five-member Political Bureau was formed. The plenum voted to expel the former MPRP General Secretary, Yumjaagiin Tsedenbal, from the party and to rehabilitate several prominent victims of Tsedenbal's purges of the 1960s.

At a session of the People's Great Khural (legislature), held shortly after the MPRP plenum, Punsalmaagiin Ochirbat, hitherto the Minister of Foreign Economic Relations and Supply, was elected Chairman of the Presidium (Head of State), replacing Batmönkh, and other senior positions in the Presidium were reorganized. Dumaagiin Sodnom was dismissed from his post as Chairman of the Council of Ministers and was replaced by Sharavyn Gungaadorj, a Deputy Chairman and Minister of Agriculture and the Food Industry. The Khural also adopted amendments to the Constitution, including the deletion of references to the MPRP as the 'guiding force' in Mongolian society, and approved a new electoral law. It was decided that the next elections to the Khural would be held in mid-1990, and not in 1991 as originally planned. Meanwhile, all limits on personal livestock holdings were removed, and new regulations were introduced to encourage foreign investment in Mongolia. However, in late March 1990 an estimated 13,000 people, dissatisfied with the results of the Khural's session, demonstrated in Ulan Bator to demand the dissolution of the Khural. Opposition leaders declared that the changes introduced by the legislature were insufficient, and demanded the introduction of a multi-party electoral law.

In April 1990 the MPRP held an extraordinary congress, at which more than three-quarters of the membership of the Central Committee was renewed. General Secretary Gombojavyn Ochirbat was elected to the restyled post of Chairman of the party. The Political Bureau was renamed the Presidium, and a new, four-member Secretariat of the Central Committee was appointed. In May the People's Great Khural passed a law on political parties, which legalized the new 'informal' parties through official registration, and also adopted further amendments to the Constitution, introducing a presidential system with a standing legislature called the State Little Khural, elected by proportional representation of parties.

At the July 1990 general election and consequent re-elections, 430 deputies were elected to serve a five-year term: 357 from the MPRP (in some instances unopposed), 16 from the Mongolian Democratic Party (MDP, the political wing of the MDU), 19 shared among the Mongolian Revolutionary Youth League, the Mongolian National Progress Party (MNPP), and the Mongolian Social-Democratic Party (MSDP), and 39 without party affiliation. Under constitutional amendments adopted in May, the People's Great Khural was required to convene at least four times in the five years of its term.

In September 1990 the People's Great Khural elected Punsalmaagiin Ochirbat to be the country's first President, with a five-year term of office; the post of Chairman of the Presidium was abolished. Dashiin Byambasüren was appointed Prime Minister (equivalent to the former post of Chairman of the Council of Ministers) and began consultations on the formation of a multi-party government. The newly restyled Cabinet was elected by the State Little Khural in September and October. Under the amended Constitution, the President, Vice-President and Ministers were not permitted to remain concurrently deputies of the People's Great Khural; therefore, re-elections of deputies to the legislature were held in November.

The 20th Congress of the MPRP, held in February 1991, elected a new 99-member Central Committee, which, in turn, appointed a new Presidium. The Central Committee also elected a new Chairman, Büdragchaagiin Dash-Yondon, the Chairman of the Ulan Bator City Party Committee, who had become a Presidium member in November 1990.

A new Constitution was adopted by an almost unanimous vote of the Great Khural in January 1992, and entered into force in the following month. It provided for a unicameral Mongolian Great Khural, comprising 76 members, to replace the People's Great Khural, following elections to be held in June. (The State Little Khural was abolished.) The country's official name was changed from the Mongolian People's Republic to Mongolia, and the communist gold star was removed from the national flag.

At the elections to the Mongolian Great Khural in June 1992, contested by the MPRP, an alliance of the MDP, the MNPP and the United Party (UP), the MSDP, and six other parties and another alliance, a total of 293 candidates stood for 76 seats in 26 constituencies, comprising the 18 *aimag* (provinces), the towns of Darkhan and Erdenet, and Ulan Bator City (six). A total of 95.6% of the electorate participated in the elections. Candidates were elected by a simple majority, provided that they obtained the support of at least 50% of the electorate in their constituency. The MPRP candidates received some 57% of the total votes, while the candidates of the other parties (excluding independents) achieved a combined total of 40%. The outcome of the election was disproportionate, however, with the MPRP taking 70 seats (71 including a pro-MPRP independent). The remaining seats went to the MDP (two, including an independent), the MSDP, MNPP and UP (one each).

The first session of the Mongolian Great Khural opened in July 1992 with the election of officers, the nomination of Puntsagiin Jasrai (who had served as a Deputy Chairman of the Council of Ministers in the late 1980s) to the post of Prime Minister, and the approval of his Cabinet. Natsagiin Bagabandi, a Vice-Chairman of the MPRP Central Committee, was elected Chairman of the Great Khural. Jambyn Gombojav (Chairman of the People's Great Khural from late 1990 to late 1991) was elected Vice-Chairman of the new Khural. Meanwhile, a National Security Council was established, with the country's President as its Chairman, and the Prime Minister and Chairman of the Great Khural as its members.

In October 1992 the MDP, MNPP, UP and the Mongolian Renewal Party amalgamated to form the Mongolian National Democratic Party (MNDP), with a General Council headed by the MNPP leader, Davaadorjiin Ganbold, and including Sanjaasürengiin Zorig and other prominent opposition politicians. In the same month the MPRP Central Committee was renamed the MPRP Little Khural, and its membership was increased to 169 (and subsequently to 198). The Presidium was replaced by a nine-member Party Leadership Council, headed by Büdragchaagiin Dash-Yondon as its General Secretary.

The Great Khural adopted a Presidential Election Law in March 1993, and direct elections to the presidency were scheduled for 6 June. Lodongiin Tüdev, a member of the Party Leadership Council and Editor-in-Chief of the MPRP organ, *Ünen*, was chosen as the MPRP's candidate, while President Ochirbat was nominated by a coalition of the MNDP and the MSDP. The result of the election was a convincing popular victory for Ochirbat: he received 57.8% of the votes cast, compared with 38.7% for Tüdev.

The MPRP in early 1996 forced through the Great Khural amendments that increased the number of constituencies from 26 to 76, making them all single-seat constituencies, while preserving the majority vote system. To be declared elected, a candidate would have to receive only 25% of the constituency votes. In response, opposition parties formed an election coalition, the Democratic Alliance, which received support from the Mongolian Green Party and the MDU.

At the general election, held on 30 June 1996, a resounding victory was achieved by the Democratic Alliance, which won 50 of the 76 seats in the Great Khural, receiving some 46.7% of the total votes cast. The MPRP took only 25 seats (40.6%), while one seat went to a candidate of the United Heritage Party (UHP). Electoral turn-out was 92.2%. At the legislature's inaugural session, in mid-July, the leader of the MSDP, Radnaasümbereliin Gonchigdorj, was elected to the post of Chairman of the Great Khural. Mendsaikhany Enkhsaikhan, the leader of the Democratic Alliance and the group's choice for Prime Minister, was nominated by President Ochirbat and voted into office. Following the rejection of MPRP demands concerning the allocation of positions in the Great Khural, MPRP members staged a three-day boycott of the legislature, leaving it inquorate and unable to function. After the boycott ended, the MNDP leader, Tsakhiagiin Elbegdorj, was elected Vice-Chairman of the Great Khural; a new Government was formed at the end of July.

Following their election defeat, and amid growing evidence of a rift between supporters of tradition and advocates of the reform process, in July 1996 the MPRP Little Khural elected a new Leadership Council and General Secretary of the party, Nambaryn Enkhbayar. Indications of a split in the party increased in February 1997, when the leaders of the MPRP sought to enforce their uncompromising policies on the party congress. Several prominent dissenting members resigned from the party, and Natsagiin Bagabandi, who had been Chairman of the Great Khural in 1992–96, was elected Chairman of the party.

With 18 May 1997 set by the Great Khural as the date for the presidential election, the MNDP and the MSDP proposed a joint candidate for the post of President—the incumbent, Ochirbat. The MPRP nominated the party Chairman, Bagabandi, while the UHP adopted Jambyn Gombojav, a former Vice-Chairman of the Great Khural. The election was won convincingly by Bagabandi, with some 60.8% of the total votes cast. In a severe setback to the democratic movement, Ochirbat received only 29.8%, a reflection of popular dissatisfaction at the rigorous economic reform policies implemented by the ruling Democratic Alliance. Gombojav obtained 6.6% of the votes.

Following Bagabandi's success in the presidential election, Enkhbayar was elected Chairman of the MPRP in his place. In August 1997 he won a by-election for Bagabandi's former seat in the Great Khural. Almost immediately after assuming his seat in the legislature, Enkhbayar initiated a motion of censure against the Democratic Alliance Government for its performance, but the contentious motion was defeated by the ruling Alliance after two weeks of debate.

In April 1998 the Democratic Alliance decided that, henceforth, the Cabinet was to comprise members of the Great Khural, headed by the leader of the Alliance. Tsakhiagiin Elbegdorj, leader of the MNDP, was thus appointed Prime Minister, and a new Cabinet was formed in May. The Government became embroiled in a dispute over the amalgamation of the state-owned Reconstruction Bank, declared bankrupt after over-extending its credit, with the private Golomt Bank. Amid accusations that Democratic Alliance leaders had obtained loans from the bank shortly before its failure, the MPRP effected a boycott of the Great Khural. The party rejected the Government's reinstatement of Reconstruction Bank and returned to the Great Khural in late July to pursue a vote of 'no confidence' in the Government. The vote was carried by 42 votes to 33, with the support of 15 members of the Democratic Alliance.

In August 1998 the Democratic Alliance nominated as its candidate for Prime Minister Davaadorjiin Ganbold, Chairman of the Economic Standing Committee of the Great Khural (who had been chief Deputy Prime Minister in 1990–92 and President of the MNDP in 1992–96). President Bagabandi rejected Ganbold's nomination, on the grounds of his failure to act to resolve the bank merger crisis in his capacity as Chairman of the Committee. Ganbold was nominated a second time, and again rejected by Bagabandi, who proposed Great Khural member Dogsomyn Ganbold. The Democratic Alliance persisted, and by the end of the month Davaadorjiin Ganbold had been nominated and rejected five times. The Democratic Alliance then proposed Rinchinnyamyn Amarjargal, acting Minister of External Relations and a member of the MNDP General Council. President Bagabandi accepted the nomination, but it was rejected by one vote in the Great Khural in September. Two other candidates were subsequently rejected by Bagabandi.

In October 1998 Sanjaasürengiin Zorig, the Minister of Infrastructure Development, was murdered. Zorig, the founder of the Mongolian Democratic Movement, had not been nominated, but was widely seen as a potential prime ministerial candidate. Following Zorig's state funeral, Bagabandi named six more candidates of his own, including Dogsomyn Ganbold and the Mayor of Ulan Bator, Janlavyn Narantsatsralt. The Democratic Alliance disregarded the presidential list and for the sixth time nominated Davaadorjiin Ganbold. Although the nomination was supported by all 48 Democratic Alliance members of the Great Khural, Bagabandi once again rejected him. The political crisis was then deepened by a new Constitutional Court ruling that members of the Great Khural could not serve concurrently in the Government. Two months later the Democratic Alliance finally nominated Bagabandi's candidate, Janlavyn Narantsatsralt, who was appointed Prime Minister in December. The formation of his Government was completed with the appointment of the last four ministers in January 1999.

Narantsatsralt's Government remained in power for just over six months. In July 1999 the Prime Minister was challenged in the Great Khural over a letter that he had written in January to Yurii Maslyukov, First Deputy Chairman of the Russian Government, in which he seemingly acknowledged Russia's right to privatize its share in the Erdenet joint venture without reference to the Mongolians. Unable to offer a satisfactory explanation, in late July Narantsatsralt lost a vote of confidence, in which MSDP members of the Great Khural voted with the opposition MPRP. The Democratic Alliance nominated Rinchinnyamyn Amarjargal for the post of Prime Minister, but the proposal was immediately challenged by Bagabandi. The President insisted that, following the Constitutional Court ruling of late 1998, he could consider Amarjargal's suitability for nomination in the Great Khural only after the candidate had resigned his seat. After several days of arguments, representatives of the Democratic Alliance and the President adopted a formula that allowed the Great Khural's approval of the prime ministerial nomination and the nominee's resignation of his Great Khural seat to take place simultaneously. Amarjargal was elected Prime Minister at the end of July. The ministers of Narantsatsralt's Government remained in office in an acting capacity until early September, when all but one (the Minister of Law) were reappointed. The formation of the Government was completed in late October with the appointment of Dashpuntsagiin Ganbold as Minister of Law. In November 1999 Amarjargal assumed the presidency of the MNDP, replacing Narantsatsralt.

The 1992 Constitution was amended for the first time in December 1999 by a Great Khural decree supported by all three parliamentary parties, which simplified the procedure for the appointment of the Prime Minister and allowed members of the Great Khural to serve as government ministers while retaining their seats in the legislature. An attempt by the President to veto the decree was defeated by the Great Khural in January 2000, but the Constitutional Court ruled in March that the decree had been illegal. When the Great Khural opened its spring session in April, members rejected the ruling and refused to discuss it. The Constitutional Court's demand for a statement on the issue was disregarded by the Great Khural.

As the general election approached, party political activity increased dramatically. A breakaway grouping of the MNDP reformed the Mongolian Democratic Party, and a faction of the MSDP founded the Mongolian New Social Democratic Party. Sanjaasürengiin Oyuun, the sister of the murdered minister, Zorig, established the Civil Courage Party (CCP, or Irgenii Zorig Nam) drawing away from the MNDP several more members of the Great Khural, and formed an electoral alliance with the Green Party. The MNDP, unable to reconstitute the previously-successful Democratic Alliance with the MSDP, therefore formed a new Democratic Alliance with the Mongolian Believers' Democratic Party.

At the election, held on 2 July 2000, three coalitions and 13 parties were represented by a total of 603 candidates, including 27 independents. The MPRP took 72 of the 76 seats in the Great Khural. Prime Minister Rinchinnyamyn Amarjargal and his entire cabinet lost their seats. The MPRP received 50.2% of the votes cast. The level of participation was 82.4% of the electorate. The party's victory was attributed to widespread popular support for its manifesto of social welfare and poverty reduction, and to the disintegration of the MNDP-MSDP coalition. The MPRP's main support lay in rural constituencies, where it was widely seen as willing and able to halt the economic and social stagnation of the countryside. The Democratic Alliance won 13%

of the votes cast, while the Mongolian Democratic New Socialist Party (MDNSP, which had amalgamated with the Mongolian Workers' Party in 1999) received 10.7% of the votes; each of them won one seat. The MSDP received 8.9% of the votes cast but won no seats.

When the Great Khural opened, Lkhamsürengiin Enebish, the MPRP General Secretary, was elected Chairman (Speaker). The nomination of the MPRP Chairman, Nambaryn Enkhbayar, for the post of Prime Minister was, however, rejected by President Bagabandi, on the grounds that priority be given to the constitutional amendments. After a week of discussions a compromise was reached whereby Enkhbayar's nomination was presented to the Great Khural, while the amendments remained in force pending a Great Khural debate and a full nine-member session of the Constitutional Court. In July 2000 the Great Khural approved Enkhbayar's appointment as Prime Minister by 67 MPRP members' votes to three. Enkhbayar's cabinet was approved in August.

Reflecting the MPRP's emphasis on social issues, Enkhbayar divided the former Ministry of Health and Social Welfare into two separate ministries, the Ministry of Health and the Ministry of Social Protection and Welfare. The Ministry of Law was renamed the Ministry of Justice and Home Affairs and assumed control of the border troops. However, the MSDP alleged that the new Government was acting in violation of the Constitution, by dismissing large numbers of civil servants because of their party affiliation. In late September 2000 the leaders of the MNDP and the MSDP signed a joint declaration announcing that a conference of the parties would be held in early December, to formalize the merging of the two parties. This was done with a view to ensuring the necessary parliamentary basis for the nomination of Radnaasümbereliin Gonchigdorj, the leader of the MSDP, in the presidential election scheduled for 2001.

At the conference on 6 December 2000 five parties—the MNDP, MSDP, the Mongolian Democratic Party, the Believers' Democratic Party and the Democratic Renewal Party—resolved to dissolve themselves and form a new Democratic Party (DP). Dambyn Dorligjav, a former Minister of Defence and director of the Erdenet copper enterprise, was elected Chairman, while Janlavyn Narantsatsralt and the former Minister of the Environment, Sonomtserengiin Mendsaikhan, were elected as vice-chairmen. At its registration in late December the DP claimed a membership of 160,000. The party's National Advisory Committee was formed in February 2001 and comprised two members from each of the Great Khural's 76 constituencies. Members included many of the former leaders of the MNDP and the MSDP who had failed to win seats in the elections of July 2000.

In mid-December 2000 the Great Khural readopted, unchanged and for immediate implementation, the decree of December 1999 amending the 1992 Constitution. The decree was vetoed by the President, and this veto was rejected. The Constitutional Court, however, was unable to meet in full session because the election of replacements for time-expired members was delayed in the Great Khural. President Bagabandi finally set his seal the amendments in May 2001.

In February 2001 the 23rd congress of the ruling MPRP re-elected Prime Minister Nambaryn Enkhbayar as its Chairman, approved the establishment of a new Little Khural of 244 members and enlarged the Party Leadership Council from 11 to 15 members. At the end of September Lkhamsürengiin Enebish, Chairman of the Great Khural and recently re-elected as General Secretary of the MPRP, died; he was succeeded in the latter post by Doloonjingiin Idevkhten and as Chairman of the Great Khural by Sanjbegziin Tömör-Ochir, Secretary of the MPRP.

The presidential election of 20 May 2001 was won by the MPRP's candidate, Natsagiin Bagabandi, who received 57.95% of the votes cast. Radnaasümbereliin Gonchigdorj of the Democratic Party won 36.58% of votes, and Luvsandambyn Dashnyam of the Civil Courage Party received 3.54%.

In January 2001, meanwhile, during one of Mongolia's most severe winters ever, a helicopter carrying 23 people, who were investigating the *zud* (livestock starvation owing to frozen fodder) in the Uvs *aimag* in western Mongolia, crashed, killing eight. The dead included several UN staff and Shagdaryn Otgonbileg, a member of the Great Khural and former director of the Erdenet copper enterprise, who was given a state funeral. Later that month the UN appealed for humanitarian aid to help Mongolian herders, whose animals were dying in huge numbers. In May Otgonbileg's widow Tuyaa was elected Great Khural MPRP member for his Zavkhan 22 constituency unopposed.

In March 2002 Sanjaasürengiin Oyuun's Civil Courage Party merged with Bazarsadyn Jargalsaikhan's Mongolian Republican Party (MRP) to form the Civil Courage Republican Party, under Oyuun's leadership. However, in June 2003 the MRP leader Bazarsadyn Jargalsaikhan withdrew from the merger after disagreement about the formation of a coalition with the DP. Attempts in December to oust Oyuun from the party leadership failed, and in March 2004 she agreed to join the Motherland Democracy coalition comprising Erdenebat's MDNSP and the DP (see below) and prepared to reregister the CCRP as the CCP.

In June 2002, meanwhile, the Great Khural approved the Law on Land and the Law on Land Privatization. Although less than 1% of the country's total territory was to be available for privatization, the laws generated much controversy. From November there were several demonstrations by tractor-driving farmers who were arrested for parking their vehicles on Sükhbaatar Square in Ulan Bator. The demonstrators, led by DP leader Erdeniin Bat-Üül, protested that the poor would be denied land by the 'oligarchy'. The privatization law duly entered into force in May 2003, and privatization was scheduled to be completed by June 2005.

Meanwhile, an effective protest against the Government's silencing of the opposition was made by Lamjavyn Gündalai, a DP member of the Great Khural, who interrupted the Prime Minister's televised address and disrupted the opening ceremony of the autumn 2002 session of the Great Khural by displaying to television cameras a series of placards on which he demanded the right to speak, condemned the imprisonment of journalists and criticized the land privatization programme.

When the 2003 spring session opened at the beginning of April Gündalai again displayed a range of slogans; the President and the Prime Minister were unable to deliver their speeches, and the televised session was suspended. At the end of May Gündalai made a public allegation that there was 'top secret' information that the Minister of Justice and Home Affairs, Tsendiin Nyamdorj, had links with the special services of a foreign country. Nyamdorj denied this, saying that it was an old claim that had previously been refuted, at the time of the 1996 and 2000 elections. A former Director of Intelligence, Jaalkhüügiin Baatar, claimed that Nyamdorj had links with China that he had not explained. Baatar was subsequently arrested, and the DP urged Nyamdorj to resign. In early June Nyamdorj said that he was seeking the prosecution of Baatar, Gündalai and Enkhsaikhan (the last now DP Chairman). In July Gündalai was removed from an aircraft at Ulan Bator airport while on his way via the Republic of Korea to a conference in Singapore. Amidst violent scenes at the headquarters of the DP, he was arrested by plain-clothes policemen for 'violation of the border'. This provoked an uproar regarding the breaching of Gündalai's parliamentary immunity, and the DP sought an investigation by the human rights committee of the Inter-Parliamentary Union (a non-governmental organization based in Geneva, Switzerland). In late July, on the same day as the newspaper *Önöödör* published extracts from the 'top secret' material relating to Nyamdorj, Gündalai was released. It was not clear whether the Chairman of the Great Khural, Sanjbegziin Tömör-Ochir, had been instrumental in this, but a few days previously, in Khövsgöl, Tömör-Ochir had faced public demonstrations over the issue. In August the charges against Gündalai were abandoned on the instructions of the Deputy Chief Prosecutor. Later in the same month, Nyamdorj threatened to sue the DP for libel and 1,000m. tögrög in damages over the party's claims of his alleged links to China. In early August the Motherland Democracy coalition, recently formed by the MDNSP and the DP in preparation for the legislative election of 2004, demanded that Prime Minister Enkhbayar should deal with those responsible for Gündalai's 'illegal arrest' and suspend Nyamdorj. In October Gündalai succeeded, for a third time, in disrupting the opening of the Great Khural's autumn session, with the result that the Prime Minister was once again unable to deliver his report to the cameras. When the Great Khural met in late January 2004 to discuss the affair, Gündalai was not informed and was absent, but members voted not to deprive him of his parliamentary immunity. The investigation of Nyamdorj's complaint had been passed to Ulan Bator's Sükhbaatar district court, but the Procurator ordered the court to resolve the issue within 15 days or to dismiss it.

The National Human Rights Commission's 2003 annual report was highly critical of bureaucracy, corruption and cronyism. The police were accused of numerous cases of brutality; the right of detainees to contact a lawyer was widely abused, the report stated. The National Human Rights Programme was adopted in December. Also in 2003, Damirangiin Enkhbat, who had been suspected of the murder of the Minister of Infrastructure Development Sanjaasürengiin Zorig in 1998 and had since been resident in France, was reported to have been abducted by Mongolian secret agents and subsequently imprisoned in Mongolia. In early 2004 reports from Amnesty International, the human rights organization, suggested that he had been tortured during interrogation.

Two important documents outlining Mongolian foreign policy objectives were published in July 1994. Advocating 'political realism', *The Mongolian National Security Concept* emphasized the importance of maintaining a 'balanced relationship' with Russia and China, while 'strengthening trust and developing all-round good-neighbourly relations and mutually beneficial co-operation with both'. *The Mongolian Foreign Policy Concept* also described as the 'foremost objective' of the country's foreign policy the pursuit of 'friendly relations with Russia and China, and without favouring one or the other to develop co-operation with them in complete equality'. Traditional features and specific aspects of economic co-operation were to be safeguarded. Other priorities listed were: good relations with the USA, Japan, Germany and other highly developed nations of West and East; consolidation of political and economic integration in the Asian region; co-operation with the UN and its various bodies; and sound relations with the newly independent states of eastern Europe and the CIS, as well as with developing countries.

Following the dissolution of the USSR in 1991, co-operation with the Russian Federation, the largest of the successor states, continued. During an official visit to Russia in January 1993, President Ochirbat and the Russian President, Boris Yeltsin, issued a joint statement expressing regret at the execution and imprisonment of Mongolian citizens in the USSR during the Stalinist purges. Ochirbat and Yeltsin also signed a new 20-year Mongolian-Russian Treaty of Friendship and Co-operation to replace the defunct Mongolian-Soviet treaty of 1986. A similar treaty had been signed with Ukraine in November 1992, during the official visit to Mongolia by Ukrainian President Leonid Kravchuk. In November 2000 the Russian President, Vladimir Putin, stayed overnight in Ulan Bator en route to an Asia-Pacific Economic Co-operation (APEC) conference in Brunei. He was the most senior Russian or Soviet visitor to Mongolia since 1974. Presidents Bagabandi and Putin issued a joint declaration on bilateral co-operation and the protection of each other's national interests. Russia affirmed its commitment to guaranteeing Mongolia's security in connection with its nuclear weapons-free status. In March Russia sent food aid to relieve starvation resulting from the severe Mongolian winter during which much livestock had perished (see above). Russian Prime Minister Mikhail Kasyanov officially visited Mongolia in late March 2002, to discuss economic and military co-operation, and also the issue of the latter's outstanding debt of 11,000m. transferable roubles that Moscow claimed it was owed for Soviet aid granted to Mongolia during 1947–91. Mongolia disagreed with Russia's position that the debt should be paid in full at par value with the US dollar. The disagreement disrupted Mongolian-Russian discussions in early 2003 on a new contract for the Erdenet copper-mining joint venture.

However, when the two Prime Ministers did eventually meet in Moscow in July 2003, Mongolia's repayment of the Soviet-era debt was hardly discussed, and the major outcome of the talks was a new five-year agreement on the operation of the Erdenet copper enterprise that preserved Mongolia's 51% ownership of stock. Russia agreed that Mongolia had already repaid the cost of building the Erdenet plant. Otherwise, Mongolia's main concern was to reduce Russian taxes on imports of Mongolian goods. At the end of December Russia announced that it had received Mongolia's payment in settlement of the 'big debt' (as the Mongolians referred to the money Russia claimed it was owed for Soviet aid to Mongolia during 1947–91). Russia had waived 98% of the total debt of 11,400m. transferable roubles and accepted payment of US $250m. Prime Minister Nambaryn Enkhbayar celebrated a political and diplomatic victory for the MPRP Government, but the details of the settlement remained unclear. The two countries had been unable to agree terms for the previous 10 years, especially the equivalence of the now defunct transferable rouble, but also because of Mongolian opposition pressure to offset the cost of damage done to the environment by Soviet military activity. DP leader and ex-Prime Minister Enkhsaikhan pointed out that under the Constitution international agreements were supposed to be approved by the

Great Khural. Former Prime Minister Byambasüren revived charges of Soviet price-fixing, stating that from 1976 Mongolia had been paid only 0.39 roubles for every one rouble of the value of its exports to the USSR but had been charged 1.5 roubles for its imports of Soviet goods.

Relations with the People's Republic of China were good until the onset of the Sino-Soviet dispute in the 1960s. In 1986, however, Sino-Mongolian relations improved significantly when the Chinese Vice-Minister of Foreign Affairs visited Ulan Bator, and the two countries signed agreements on consular relations and trade. In June 1987 a delegation from the Chinese National People's Congress visited Ulan Bator, and in the same month a treaty concerning the resolution of border disputes was initialled by representatives of the two Governments.

Relations between Mongolia and China improved in April 1994, when a new Treaty of Friendship and Co-operation was concluded during a visit to Ulan Bator by the Chinese Premier, Li Peng. An agreement on cultural, economic and technical co-operation was also signed. Mongolia continued to protest in 1995 at the ongoing series of nuclear tests being carried out in China (in the Xinjiang Autonomous Region). Mongolian human rights groups and the Ulan Bator press supported protests in Inner Mongolia against the arrest by the Chinese authorities of Inner Mongolian human rights activists in December. Prime Minister Jasrai's official visit to China in March 1996, focusing on trade and co-operation, appeared not to have been affected by these events. Relations with China were further consolidated in 1997 by the visits to Ulan Bator of Qiao Shi, the Chairman of the National People's Congress Standing Committee, in April, and of Qian Qichen, the Chinese Deputy Premier and Minister of Foreign Affairs, in August.

In June 2003 Chinese President Hu Jintao visited Ulan Bator where he held talks with President Bagabandi and Prime Minister Enhbayar and addressed the Great Khural on the subject of 'neighbourly partnership of mutual trust' which, besides reiterating respect for each other's independence, sovereignty and territorial integrity, embodied in the handling of bilateral relations 'a spirit of consultation, co-operation and friendship'. China granted Mongolia 50m. yuan for the building of a road across their border from Zamyn-Üüd to Erlian.

Mongolia received three important foreign visitors in mid-1999: President Kim Dae-Jung of the Republic of Korea visited in May, and in July official visits were paid by Prime Minister Keizo Obuchi of Japan and President Jiang Zemin of China. In November Prime Minister Amarjargal visited both North and South Korea and also China. In March 2000 he paid an official visit to the United Kingdom. President Bagabandi travelled widely in 2000 and early 2001, visiting Germany, Italy, the Philippines, the USA, India and the Republic of Korea. Nambaryn Enkhbayar's first overseas trip as Prime Minister was to the World Economic Forum in Davos, Switzerland, in January 2001. He subsequently travelled to Japan.

During an official visit to the USA in November 2001, Prime Minister Enkhbayar addressed the UN General Assembly in New York and also had a meeting with President George W. Bush. Enkhbayar reaffirmed the strategic partnership with the USA and urged greater investment in Mongolia. Having condemned the terrorist attacks of 11 September against the USA, he informed President Bush of Mongolia's readiness to allow the use of its air space to help combat terrorism. Following US military action in Iraq in March 2003, some 170 soldiers of the Mongolian army's élite battalion were sent to Iraq for duty with the Polish contingent stationed north of Baghdad.

The seventh British-Mongolian 'Round-Table' Conference in Ulan Bator in September 2002 was attended by a parliamentary secretary of the United Kingdom's Foreign and Commonwealth Office. The Secretary-General of the United Nations, Kofi Annan, paid a brief visit to Mongolia in October 2002. The Dalai Lama visited Ulan Bator in November 2002, travelling via Japan after Russia refused him a visa and Korean Air, the national carrier of South Korea, banned him on the grounds that he posed a security threat. Although his visit was at the invitation of Mongolia's Buddhist leaders rather than of the Government, the Chinese authorities indicated their displeasure by halting rail traffic on their mutual border for 36 hours. The MPRP was accepted as a member of Socialist International at the grouping's 22nd congress in São Paolo, Brazil, in October 2003. Prime Minister Enkhbayar (the MPRP leader) declared that this signified Mongolia's international acceptance as a 'democratic country with a leftist-centrist ideology'.

Government

Supreme legislative power is vested in the 76-member Mongolian Great Khural (Assembly), elected by universal adult suffrage for four years. The Great Khural recognizes the President on his election and appoints the Prime Minister and members of the Cabinet, which is the highest executive body. The President, who is directly elected for a term of four years, is Head of State and Commander-in-Chief of the Armed Forces.

In August 2002 the Great Khural approved the reorganization of government agencies, reducing the number of regulatory agencies to eight and executive agencies to 33. Those subordinated to the Prime Minister included the Chief Directorate of Intelligence, State Property Committee, National Radio and Television, and the Monstame News Agency.

Mongolia is divided into 21 provinces (*aimag*) and one municipality (Ulan Bator), with appointed governors and elected local assemblies.

Defence

Under the 1992 Constitution, the President of Mongolia is, *ex officio*, Commander-in-Chief of the Armed Forces. The defence roles of the President, the Mongolian Great Khural, the Government and local administrations are defined by the Mongolian Law on Defence (November 1993). Mongolia's *Military Doctrine*, a summary of which was issued by the Great Khural in July 1994, defines the armed forces as comprising general purpose troops, air defence troops, construction troops and civil defence troops. The border troops and internal troops, which are not part of the armed forces, are responsible for protection of the borders and of strategic installations, respectively. In August 2003, according to the International Institute for Strategic Studies, Mongolia's defence forces numbered 8,600, comprising an army of 7,500 (of whom 3,300 were thought to be conscripts), 800 air defence personnel and 300 construction troops. There was a paramilitary force of about 7,200, comprising 1,200 internal security troops and 6,000 border guards. Military service is for 12 months (for males aged 18–25 years), but a system of alternative service is being introduced. Defence spending for 2004 was projected at 20,742.3m. tögrög.

Economic Affairs

In 2002, according to estimates by the World Bank, Mongolia's gross national income (GNI), measured at average 2000–02 prices, was US $1,088m., equivalent to $440 per head (or $1,650 per head on an international purchasing-power parity basis). During 1990–2002, it was estimated, the population increased by an average annual rate of 1.3%, while gross domestic product (GDP) per head decreased, in real terms, by an average of 0.9% per year. Overall GDP increased, in real terms, by an average annual rate of 0.4% in 1990–2002. According to Mongolian sources, GDP increased by 4.0% in 2002 and by 5.5% in 2003.

According to figures from the Asian Development Bank (ADB), agriculture (including forestry) contributed 20.7% of GDP in 2002. The sector engaged 44.9% of the employed labour force in 2002. Animal herding is the main economic activity and is practised throughout the country. By mid-1995 more than 90% of all livestock was privately owned. Livestock numbers (sheep, goats, horses, cattle and camels) reached a new record of 33.6m. at the end of 1999 but, following exceptionally severe weather, declined to fewer than 23.7m. in 2002, before recovering to almost 26.2m. in 2003. The principal crops are cereals, potatoes and vegetables. During 1990–2001, according to figures from the World Bank, the GDP of the agricultural sector increased, in real terms, at an average annual rate of 1.8%. According to the ADB, agricultural GDP decreased by 18.5% in 2001 and by 10.5% in 2002.

Industry (comprising manufacturing, mining, construction and utilities) provided 23.5% of GDP in 2002, according to the ADB, and engaged 11.4% of the employed labour force in 2002. According to the World Bank, during 1990–2001 industrial GDP declined, in real terms, at an average rate of 1.8% per year. According to the ADB, the industrial sector's GDP increased by 16.2% in 2001 and by 5.0% in 2002.

Mining contributed 8.6% of GDP in 2002, according to the ADB. Mongolia has significant, largely unexplored, mineral resources and is a leading producer and exporter of copper, gold, molybdenum and fluorspar concentrates. Export of copper concentrate in 2003 was worth an estimated US $159m. The copper-molybdenum works at Erdenet, a Mongolian-Russian joint venture, is the most important mining operation in the country. The value of copper concentrate in Mongolia's total exports, however, decreased from 53.0% in 1995 to 27.6% in

2002. During 2003 a Canadian company continued to upgrade the Oyuu Tolgoi (Turquoise Hill) mineral deposits at Khanbogd, South Gobi, not only raising its estimates of copper and gold content but also finding plentiful supplies of underground water. Copper production was provisionally scheduled to begin in 2006. Other mineral resources include coal, tungsten, tin, uranium and lead. In May 2000 Mongolia's coal reserves were estimated at 150,000m. metric tons. Gold production rose from 4.5 tons in 1995 to 13.7 tons in 2001, before declining to 12.1 tons in 2002. Petroleum reserves were discovered in 1994. Extraction of crude petroleum, from the Tamsag basin, commenced in 1997. According to the ADB, compared with the previous year the GDP of the mining sector expanded by 9.6% in 2001 but decreased by 6.8% in 2002. In 2003, according to official sources, output of coal reportedly rose by 5%, extraction of petroleum and gas by 31.5% and other minerals by 18.1%.

The manufacturing sector accounted for 9.5% of GDP in 2002, according to the ADB. Manufacturing industries are based largely on the products of the agricultural and animal husbandry sector. Mongolia is one of the world's foremost producers of cashmere, and also manufactures garments, leather goods and carpets. The principal branches of manufacturing include food products, textiles and non-metallic mineral products. According to figures from the ADB, manufacturing GDP increased by 31.8% in 2001 and by 12.2% in 2002.

Energy is derived principally from thermal power stations, fuelled by coal. Most provincial centres have thermal power stations or diesel generators, while smaller rural centres generally rely on small diesel generators. In more isolated areas wood, roots, bushes and dried animal dung are used for domestic fuel. The Ulan Bator No. 4 power station, the largest in the country, went into operation in 1985. Its capacity of 380 MW doubled Mongolia's generating capacity. In 2000, according to the World Bank, imports of energy products comprised 19.1% of the total value of merchandise imports. Mongolia imports electricity and petroleum products from Russia. Production of crude petroleum increased sharply from 73,700 barrels in 2001 to 139,200 barrels in 2002.

The services sector contributed an estimated 55.8% of GDP in 2002, according to the ADB, and engaged an estimated 43.7% of the employed labour force in 2000. During 1990–2001, according to figures from the ADB, the GDP of the sector decreased, in real terms, by an average of 0.4% annually. According to the ADB, the GDP of the services sector increased by 8.2% in 2001 and by 12.1% in 2002.

In 2002, according to the IMF, Mongolia recorded a visible trade deficit of US $156.2m., and there was a deficit of $158.0m. on the current account of the balance of payments. In 2003 the trade deficit reached $187.1m. In 2002 the principal source of imports was Russia, supplying 34.1% of the total. Other major suppliers were the People's Republic of China (24.4%), the Republic of Korea (12.2%) and Japan (6.1%). China was the principal market for exports in that year, purchasing 42.4% of the total. Other important purchasers were the USA (31.6%) and Russia (8.6%). The principal imports in 2003 were machinery (20.2%) and mineral products (19.2%). The principal exports in 2003 were minerals (33.3% of the total), textiles and textile products (25.5%) and precious metals and jewellery (23.3%).

The budget for 2004 envisaged a deficit of 85,994.9m. tögrög. Mongolia's total external debt was US $885.0m. at the end of 2001, of which $823.8m. was long-term public debt. In that year the cost of debt-servicing was equivalent to 7.7% of the value of exports of goods and services. The annual rate of inflation averaged 97.5% during 1991–97. According to IMF figures, during 1998–2001 the average annual inflation rate was 9.0%. However, the rate of annual inflation declined to 3.1% in 2002, according to an official source. Annual inflation in 2003 was 4.7%. The number of registered unemployed persons decreased to 38,600 (4.6% of the labour force) at the end of 2000, and to 30,900 by the end of 2002. The number of unregistered unemployed persons was believed to be far greater, with unemployment reaching some 17% of the labour force in 2002. The number of registered unemployed persons in 2003 was 33,300.

In 1989 Mongolia joined the Group of 77 (an organization of developing countries, founded under the auspices of UNCTAD (see p. 47) to promote economic co-operation). In February 1991 Mongolia became a member of the Asian Development Bank (ADB, see p. 151) as well as of the IMF and World Bank. In 1994 the European Union (EU, see p. 208) announced the inclusion of Mongolia in TACIS, the EU's programme of technical assistance

to the Commonwealth of Independent States. In 1997 Mongolia became a member of the World Trade Organization (WTO, see p. 343). In July 1998 Mongolia was admitted to the ASEAN Regional Forum (ARF, see p. 157), and in May 2000 the country became a member of the European Bank for Reconstruction and Development (EBRD, see p. 203). Mongolia is also a member of the UN Economic and Social Commission for Asia and the Pacific (ESCAP, see p. 31).

The Democratic Alliance coalition Government, elected in June 1996, initiated a wide-ranging programme of economic reforms. At the end of that year the Government announced a four-year economic programme and, with the help of external aid, a much-needed restructuring of Mongolia's financial system was instigated. Plans for the transfer of state assets to the private sector were also revealed. By 2000, however, the privatization programme had made little progress. Severe drought in late 1999 was followed in early 2000 by several months of acutely cold weather. In consequence, by mid-2000 an estimated 3m. head of livestock had died. International donors offered financial aid, in response to government appeals, and Red Cross relief teams were mobilized to take food and medicine to isolated herding families suffering extreme hardship. In early 2001 weakened animals faced even more severe conditions, with deep snow and exceptionally low temperatures. The annual livestock census in December 2001 revealed that numbers had decreased by more than 7m. head during the previous three years, and further losses were recorded in 2002. Prime Minister Enkhbayar had expressed concern about the state of the nomadic herding economy, declaring that it was important to improve the quality of stock and raise yields to meet the growing needs of large towns, especially Ulan Bator. He therefore advocated a gradual replacement of traditional nomadic family herding by livestock farming settlements, with adequate provision of winter care for animals and community facilities for herders. The national development plan announced in 2001 aimed to end Mongolia's traditional dependency on nomadic herding and envisaged the building of new towns and urbanizing 90% of the population during the next 30 years. These towns would be linked by a 2,400-km east–west highway, which would serve as a development corridor across the country as well as foster new trade zones on the Russian and Chinese borders. The Great Khural also approved legislation allowing for the privatization of various state industries in the period to 2004. In May 2002 a stake of 76% in the Trade and Development Bank of Mongolia was purchased by Swiss and US interests. APU, the distillery and soft drinks manufacturer, was transferred to the private sector in the same year. The Agricultural Bank was sold to a Japanese-financed company in February 2003, and in December of that year the Mongol Daatgal insurance company was successfully privatized. The State's 80% share in NIC, the oil import company, was purchased by the Mongolian rival distribution company, Petrovis, in February 2004. In June 2002, meanwhile, the Great Khural approved a land privatization law (see History), which proved to be controversial. (The law came into force in May 2003). Mongolia remained dependent on external aid, with public debt having risen to the equivalent of 80% of GDP, the majority of which was owed to foreign institutions. Between 1991 and 2002 Mongolia received a total of US $2,500m. in aid: of this, 52.5% was in the form of grants (of which 46% was allocated for technical assistance) and 47.5% as loans. The Mongolia Consultative Group (formerly the Mongolia Assistance Group) convened in Tokyo, Japan, in November 2003 and promised an aid programme of $335m. in grants and loans for the coming year. Meanwhile, by 2002 there were signs of an improvement in the economy. Foreign investment had increased by US $125,280 in 2001 (38% more than the increase of $90,586 in 2000), mainly owing to renewed interest in Mongolia's copper and gold resources, especially from China (which had accounted for 37% of foreign investment during the preceding three years). The country's foreign-exchange reserves increased from $205.6m. in 2001 to $349.5m. in 2002. In 2002 GDP per head reached US $3,423 in urban areas but was only $1,245 in rural areas, illustrating a marked disparity. The ADB envisaged overall GDP growth of around 5% in 2004.

Education

Ten-year general education is compulsory, beginning at six years of age. Pupils may attend vocational-technical schools from the ages of 16 to 18 years. In 2000/01 703 general schools, with a total enrolment of 494,500 pupils, employed 19,200 teachers. The 36 vocational training schools employed 865 teachers, and had a total enrolment of 12,177 in that year. Many

Mongolian students continue their academic careers at universities and technical schools in Russia and Germany. Government expenditure on education in 2001 amounted to 97,552.7m. tögrög (20.7% of budgetary expenditure). The state budget allocation to the Ministry of Education, Culture and Science for 2004 was 138,382.7m. tögrög (21.6% of planned budgetary expenditure).

Public Holidays

2004: 1 January (New Year), 21–22 February (Tsagaan Sar, lunar new year), 8 March (International Women's Day), 1 June (Children's Day), 11–13 July (National Days), 26 November (Republic Day).

2005: 1 January (New Year), 9–10 February (Tsagaan Sar, lunar new year), 8 March (International Women's Day), 1 June (Children's Day), 11–13 July (National Days), 26 November (Republic Day).

Weights and Measures

The metric system is in force.

Statistical Survey

Unless otherwise indicated, revised by Alan J. K. Sanders

Area and Population

AREA, POPULATION AND DENSITY

Area (sq km)	1,564,116*
Population (census results)	
5 January 1989	2,043,400
5 January 2000	
Males	1,177,981
Females	1,195,512
Total	2,373,493
Population (official estimates at mid-year)	
2000	2,390,000
2001	2,425,000
2002	2,510,000
Density (per sq km) at mid-2002	1.6

* 603,909 sq miles.

ADMINISTRATIVE DIVISIONS
(January 2000 census)

Province (Aimag)	Area ('000 sq km)	Estimated population ('000)	Provincial Centre
Arkhangai	55.3	97.1	Tsetserleg
Bayankhongor	116.0	84.8	Bayankhongor
Bayan-Ölgii.	45.7	91.1	Ölgii
Bulgan	48.7	61.8	Bulgan
Darkhan-Uul	3.3	83.3	Darkhan
Dornod (Eastern) . .	123.6	75.4	Choibalsan
Dornogobi (East Gobi) . .	109.5	50.6	Sainshand
Dundgobi (Central Gobi) .	74.7	51.5	Mandalgobi
Gobi-Altai	141.4	63.7	Altai
Gobi-Sümber	5.5	12.2	Choir
Khentii	80.3	70.9	Öndörkhaan
Khovd	76.1	86.8	Khovd
Khövsgöl	100.6	119.1	Mörön
Orkhon	0.8	71.5	Erdenet
Ömnögobi (South Gobi) .	165.4	46.9	Dalanzadgad
Övörkhangai	62.9	111.4	Arvaikheer
Selenge	41.2	100.0	Sükhbaatar
Sükhbaatar	82.3	56.2	Baruun Urt
Töv (Central)	74.0	99.3	Zuun mod
Ulaanbaatar (Ulan Bator)*	4.7	760.1	(capital city)
Uvs	69.6	90.0	Ulaangom
Zavkhan	82.5	90.0	Uliastai
Total	**1,564.1**	**2,373.5**	

* Ulaanbaatar, including Nalaikh, and Bagakhangai and Baganuur districts beyond the urban boundary, has special status as the capital city.

ETHNIC GROUPS
(January 2000 census)

	Number	%
Khalh (Khalkha)	1,934,700	81.5
Kazakh (Khasag)	103,000	4.3
Dörvöd (Durbet)	66,700	2.8
Bayad (Bayat)	50,800	2.1
Buryat (Buriat)	40,600	1.7
Dariganga	31,900	1.3
Zakhchin	29,800	1.3
Uriankhai	25,200	1.1
Other ethnic groups	82,600	3.5
Foreign citizens	8,100	0.3
Total	**2,373,500**	**100.0**

PRINCIPAL TOWNS
(estimated population, December 1999 unless otherwise indicated)

Ulan Bator (capital) .	869,900*		Erdenet	65,700
Darkhan	72,600		Choibalsan . . .	40,900†

* January 2004.
† January 2000 census.

BIRTHS, MARRIAGES AND DEATHS

	Registered live births		Registered marriages		Registered deaths	
	Number	Rate (per 1,000)	Number	Rate (per 1,000)	Number	Rate (per 1,000)
1996 . .	51,806	22.9	14,188	6.3	17,550	7.7
1997 . .	49,488	21.5	14,421	6.3	16,980	7.4
1998 . .	49,256	21.2	13,908	6.0	15,799	6.8
1999 . .	49,461	21.0	13,722	5.8	16,105	6.8
2000 . .	48,721	20.4	12,601	5.3	15,472	6.5
2001 . .	49,685	20.5	12,393	5.1	15,999	6.6
2002 . .	45,700	18.5	n.a.	n.a.	n.a.	6.0
2003 . .	44,700	17.9	n.a.	n.a.	n.a.	6.0

Source: mainly *Mongolian Statistical Yearbook*.

Expectation of life (WHO estimates, years at birth): 62.9 (males 60.1; females 65.9) in 2002 (Source: WHO, *World Health Report*).

EMPLOYMENT
('000 employees at 31 December)

	1998	1999	2000
Agriculture and forestry	394.1	402.6	393.5
Industry*	97.9	98.8	91.0
Transport and communications	33.4	34.9	34.1
Construction	27.5	27.6	23.4
Trade	n.a.	83.1	83.9
Public administration	n.a.	31.5	34.7
Education			
Science, research and development	42.5	43.2	54.4
Health	35.6	34.8	33.5
Total (incl. others)	809.5	813.6	809.0

Source: *Mongolian Statistical Yearbook.*

Unemployed ('000 registered at 31 December): 49.8 in 1998; 39.8 in 1999; 38.6 in 2000; 40.3 in 2001; 30.9 in 2002; 33.3 in 2003.

2001 ('000 employees at 31 December): Agriculture 402.4; Industry* 93.0; Other sectors 337.0; Total 832.3.

2002 ('000 employees at 31 December): Agriculture 391.4; Industry* 99.2; Other sectors 380.2; Total 870.8.

* Comprising manufacturing (except printing and publishing), mining and quarrying, electricity, water, logging and fishing.

Source: Asian Development Bank, *Key Indicators of Developing Asian and Pacific Countries.*

Health and Welfare

KEY INDICATORS

Total fertility rate (children per woman, 2002)	2.4
Under-5 mortality rate (per 1,000 live births, 2001)	76
HIV/AIDS (% of persons aged 15–49, 2001)	<0.10
Physicians (per 1,000 head, 2001)	2.7
Hospital beds (per 1,000 head, 2001)	7.4
Health expenditure (2001): US $ per head (PPP)	122
Health expenditure (2001): % of GDP	6.4
Health expenditure (2001): public (% of total)	72.3
Access to water (% of persons, 2000)	60
Access to sanitation (% of persons, 2000)	30
Human Development Index (2001): ranking	117
Human Development Index (2001): value	0.661

For sources and definitions, see explanatory note on p. vi.

Agriculture

PRINCIPAL CROPS
(metric tons)

	2001	2002	2003
Cereals*	150,900	125,860	165,000
Potatoes	58,000	51,890	78,700
Other vegetables	44,500	39,720	59,600
Hay	831,490	753,750	830,800

* Mostly wheat, but also small quantities of barley and oats.

LIVESTOCK
(at 31 December)

	2001	2002	2003
Sheep	11,938,100	10,536,600	10,656,400
Goats	9,683,700	9,055,900	10,555,900
Horses	2,190,800	1,970,300	2,950,300
Cattle	2,069,600	1,869,500	1,778,000
Camels	285,500	252,200	255,900

LIVESTOCK PRODUCTS
('000 metric tons, unless otherwise indicated)

	1998	1999	2000
Meat	268.3	289.0	310.6
Beef and veal	99.3	104.6	113.4
Mutton, lamb and goat meat	120.2	128.9	120.0
Sheep's wool: greasy	20.1	20.9	21.7
Raw cashmere	n.a.	3.3	3.3
Milk	430.8	467.0	375.6
Eggs (million)	8.5	9.6	6.7

Source: Mongolian Statistical Directorate.

Forestry

ROUNDWOOD REMOVALS
('000 cubic metres, excl. bark)

	2000	2001	2002
Total	631	631	631

Source: FAO.

SAWNWOOD PRODUCTION
('000 cubic metres, incl. railway sleepers)

	2000	2001	2002
Total	30.5	39.7	28.3

Source: National Statistical Office, *Monthly Bulletin of Statistics.*

Fishing

(metric tons, live weight)

	1999	2000	2001
Total catch (freshwater fishes)	524	425	117

Source: FAO, *Yearbook of Fishery Statistics.*

Mining

(metric tons, unless otherwise indicated)

	2000	2001	2002
Coal	5,019,300	5,134,200	5,307,400
Fluorspar concentrate	210,000	209,000	159,800
Copper concentrate*	357,800	381,400	376,300
Molybdenum concentrate*	2,843	3,028	3,384
Gold (kilograms)	11,808	13,674	12,097
Crude petroleum (barrels)	65,522	73,700	139,200

* Figures refer to the gross weight of concentrates. Copper concentrate has an estimated copper content of 25%, while the metal content of molybdenum concentrate is 47%.

2003 (metric tons): Coal 5,573,800.

Source: National Statistical Office, *Monthly Bulletin of Statistics.*

Industry

SELECTED PRODUCTS

	2000	2001	2002
Flour ('000 metric tons)	40.2	37.7	49.6
Bread ('000 metric tons)	20.2	23.3	21.7
Confectionery ('000 metric tons)	6.0	6.0	6.1
Vodka ('000 litres)	6,595.7	8,626.5	9,436.2
Beer ('000 litres)	3,247.2	4,267.8	3,375.3
Soft drinks ('000 litres)	8,644.7	11,082.7	12,907.3
Cashmere (combed) (metric tons)	450.9	608.4	622.1
Wool; scoured (metric tons)	1,420.0	2,089.7	1,179.6
Felt ('000 metres)	113.9	110.5	112.9
Camelhair blankets ('000)	28.5	43.1	38.2
Spun thread (metric tons)	40.8	45.6	55.9
Knitwear ('000 garments)	1,233.5	2,315.7	5,563.6
Carpets ('000 sq metres)	704.8	614.8	533.9
Leather footwear ('000)	5.6	16.7	9.5
Felt footwear ('000 pairs)	34.0	33.4	16.1
Surgical syringes (million)	16.3	17.7	22.8
Bricks (million)	17.3	21.0	13.2
Lime ('000 metric tons)	37.0	30.1	42.5
Cement ('000 metric tons)	91.7	67.7	147.6
Ferroconcrete ('000 cu metres)	14.8	17.0	11.9
Steel sheet and blanks ('000 metric tons)	20.4	17.2	26.3
Copper (metric tons)	641.1	1,475.9	1,500.0
Electricity (million kWh)	2,239.1	2,367.0	2,463.9

2003 (million kWh): Electricity 2,519.2.

Sources: *Mongolian Statistical Yearbook*, and *Monthly Bulletin of Statistics*.

Finance

CURRENCY AND EXCHANGE RATES

Monetary Units
100 möngö = 1 tögrög (tughrik).

Sterling, Dollar and Euro Equivalents (31 July 2003)
£1 sterling = 1,857.0 tögrög;
US $1 = 1,153.0 tögrög;
€1 = 1,305.0 tögrög;
10,000 tögrög = £5.385 = $8.673 = €7.663.

Average Exchange Rate (tögrög per US $)
2001   1,097.70
2002   1,110.31
2003   1,146.54

BUDGET
(million tögrög)

Revenue	2000	2001	2002
Tax revenue	274,109.2	319,419.2	356,501.1
Income tax	74,088.8	64,965.2	70,921.0
Customs duty	35,741.3	49,648.5	52,344.7
Taxes on goods and services	117,562.3	179,199.1	204,168.5
Value-added tax	74,974.5	106,151.7	117,363.6
Social insurance	38,691.7	46,144.7	53,343.5
Other current revenue	65,555.7	95,657.5	102,932.6
Foreign aid (grants)	3,067.6	9,140.5	6,615.6
Capital revenue (privatization)	7,469.8	327.1	477.7
Total	350,202.2	424,544.3	466,527.0

Expenditure	2001	2002
Goods and services	247,586.4	280,403.9
Wages and salaries	91,622.9	105,262.7
Interest payments	16,190.8	17,703.5
Subsidies and transfers	95,206.1	109,668.1
Capital expenditure	50,335.9	63,738.9
Lending (net)	60,745.5	65,034.8
Total (incl. others)	470,064.7	536,549.3

2000 (million tögrög): Total expenditure 412,926.6.

Source: National Statistical Office.

2003 (million tögrög): Total revenue 535,800.0; Total expenditure 616,500.0 (Source: *Zuuny Medee*).

2004 (forecasts, million tögrög): Total revenue 553,332.7; Total expenditure 639,327.6 (Source: *Töriin Medeelel*).

INTERNATIONAL RESERVES
(US $ million at 31 December)

	2000	2001	2002
Gold*	23.31	50.91	49.79
IMF special drawing rights	0.01	0.02	0.04
Reserve position in IMF	0.05	0.08	0.12
Foreign exchange	178.70	205.60	349.50
Total	202.08	256.61	399.44

* Valued at 4,300 tögrög per gram.

Source: IMF, *International Financial Statistics*.

MONEY SUPPLY
(million tögrög at 31 December)

	2000	2001	2002
Currency outside banks	100,910	109,131	120,755
Demand deposits at deposit money banks	29,842	46,995	66,944
Total money	130,751	156,126	187,699

Source: IMF, *International Financial Statistics*.

COST OF LIVING
(Consumer Price Index for Ulan Bator at December; base: December 1995 = 100)

	1996	1997	1998
Food and beverages	133.7	148.8	150.1
Clothing and footwear	146.0	193.4	213.8
Rent and utilities	172.7	260.1	284.2
All items (incl. others)	144.6	174.2	184.7

Source: National Statistical Office.

All items: 203.1 in 1999; 219.6 in 2000 (Source: Mongolbank, *Monthly Bulletin*).

December 2001 (base: December 2000 = 100): All items 108.0 (Source: Mongolbank, *Monthly Bulletin*).

NATIONAL ACCOUNTS
(million tögrög at current prices, unless otherwise indicated)

Expenditure on the Gross Domestic Product

	2000	2001	2002
Government final consumption expenditure	183,213.3	217,491.3	226,634.7
Private final consumption expenditure	730,006.7	834,662.4	954,321.8
Increase in stocks	46,613.6	50,614.5	63,277.6
Gross fixed capital formation	321,971.1	348,889.5	294,324.1
Total domestic expenditure	1,281,804.7	1,451,657.7	1,538,558.2
Exports of goods and services Less Imports of goods and services	−170,061.1	−205,260.0	−198,990.0
Sub-total	1,111,743.6	1,246,397.7	1,339,568.2
Statistical discrepancy*	−92,857.9	−130,756.6	−108,238.1
GDP in purchasers' values	1,018,885.7	1,115,641.1	1,231,330.1
GDP at constant 1995 prices	632,717.2	638,929.5	664,252.5

* Referring to the difference between the sum of the expenditure components and official estimates of GDP, compiled from the production approach.

Gross Domestic Product by Economic Activity

	2000	2001	2002
Agriculture	296,484.9	277,561.0	254,769.6
Mining	117,161.0	100,832.0	106,063.4
Manufacturing	62,507.3	90,144.3	117,187.6
Electricity, heating and water supply	24,631.7	32,955.3	40,246.6
Construction	19,310.8	21,931.9	26,230.5
Trade	244,583.5	297,831.9	339,880.1
Transport and communications	112,195.8	144,941.2	171,820.8
Finance	571.8	−55.3	10,364.1
Public administration	47,064.0	48,179.5	56,116.9
Other services	94,375.0	101,319.7	108,650.5
GDP in purchasers' values	1,018,885.7	1,115,641.4	1,231,330.1

Source: Asian Development Bank, *Key Indicators of Developing Asian and Pacific Countries.*

BALANCE OF PAYMENTS
(US $ million)

	2000	2001	2002
Exports of goods f.o.b.	535.8	523.2	524.0
Imports of goods f.o.b.	−608.4	−623.8	−680.2
Trade balance	−72.6	−100.6	−156.2
Exports of services	77.7	113.5	183.9
Imports of services	−162.8	−205.4	−265.8
Balance on goods and services	−157.7	−192.5	−238.1
Other income received	13.0	14.8	14.1
Other income paid	−19.5	−16.8	−18.6
Balance on goods, services and income	−164.2	−194.5	−242.6
Current transfers received	25.0	40.3	126.9
Current transfers paid	−16.9	—	−42.3
Current balance	−156.1	−154.2	−158.0
Direct investment from abroad	53.7	43.0	77.8
Other investment assets	−44.3	−5.2	−32.1
Other investment liabilities	80.5	69.2	111.7
Net errors and omissions	−19.3	−32.2	14.1
Overall balance	−85.5	−79.4	−13.4

Source: IMF, *International Financial Statistics.*

External Trade

PRINCIPAL COMMODITIES
(US $ million)

Imports c.i.f.	2001	2002	2003
Vegetable products	51.2	56.3	34.5
Prepared foodstuffs; beverages, spirits and vinegar; tobacco and manufactured substitutes	53.2	54.5	57.9
Mineral products	145.4	122.9	151.5
Products of chemical or allied industries	33.8	33.3	40.9
Textiles and textile articles	63.2	83.7	81.5
Base metals and articles thereof	29.7	29.7	41.3
Machinery and mechanical appliances; electrical equipment; sound and television apparatus	113.4	128.3	158.9
Vehicles, aircraft, vessels and associated transport equipment	69.1	69.8	79.7
Total (incl. others)	637.7	659.0	787.3

Exports f.o.b.	2001	2002	2003
Live animals and animal products	26.4	25.6	18.3
Mineral products	175.2	165.5	199.7
Copper concentrate	147.9	138.0	n.a.
Fluorite concentrate	19.7	13.9	n.a.
Hides, skins and furs	59.0	43.3	48.7
Hides and skins	17.3	9.7	n.a.
Cashmere (dehaired)	54.9	30.1	n.a.
Textiles and textile articles	171.5	136.6	152.9
Knitwear	18.9	17.5	n.a.
Precious metals and jewellery	75.4	119.2	139.8
Gold	74.7	117.6	n.a.
Total (incl. others)	521.5	500.9	600.2

Sources: National Statistical Office, *Monthly Bulletin of Statistics.*

PRINCIPAL TRADING PARTNERS
(US $ million)

Imports c.i.f.	2000	2001	2002
China, People's Republic	125.7	136.1	160.8
Germany	29.7	30.3	29.6
Japan	73.3	55.9	40.5
Korea, Republic	55.5	58.3	80.3
Russia	206.2	225.9	224.6
Singapore	10.6	10.4	10.9
USA	28.4	14.9	22.9
Total (incl. others)	614.5	637.7	659.0

Exports f.o.b.	2000	2001	2002
Australia	12.5	10.0	17.7
China, People's Republic	274.3	238.3	212.2
Japan	8.1	15.7	6.3
Republic of Korea	12.3	20.2	22.3
Russia	45.1	44.9	43.1
United Kingdom	17.5	12.4	17.5
USA	130.3	144.5	158.4
Total (incl. others)	535.8	521.5	500.9

Source: National Statistical Office, *Monthly Bulletin of Statistics.*

Transport

FREIGHT CARRIED
('000 metric tons)

	2001	2002	2003
Rail	10,147.7	11,637.0	12,337.0
Road	1,658.2	1,888.7	5,335.9
Air	2.9	2.4	2.2
Water	1.7	1.8	—
Total	11,810.5	13,529.9	17,675.1

Source: Mongolian Statistical Directorate.

PASSENGERS CARRIED
(million)

	2001	2002	2003
Rail	4.1	4.0	4.0
Road	94.1	101.4	163.7
Air*	0.3	0.3	0.2
Total	98.5	105.7	167.9

* MIAT only.

Source: Mongolian Statistical Directorate.

RAILWAYS
(traffic)

	2001	2002	2003
Passengers carried ('000) . . .	4,556.1	4,000.0	4,001.0
Freight carried ('000 metric tons) .	10,147.7	11,637.0	12,337.0
Freight ton-km (million) . . .	5,287.9	6,461.3	n.a.

Source: Mongolian Statistical Directorate.

ROAD TRAFFIC
(motor vehicles in use)

	1998	1999	2000
Passenger cars	37,795	39,921	44,051
Buses and coaches . . .	4,579	6,012	8,548
Lorries, special vehicles and tankers	29,116	28,907	29,094

2003: Total road vehicles 105,800.

Source: mainly Mongolian Statistical Directorate.

CIVIL AVIATION
(traffic on scheduled services)

	2001	2002	2003
Passengers carried ('000) . . .	254.5	269.5	251.9
Freight carried (tons)	2,970.0	2,400.0	2,200.0

Source: Mongolian Statistical Directorate.

Tourism

FOREIGN ARRIVALS BY NATIONALITY

Country	1998	1999*	2000
China, People's Republic . . .	92,789	58,346	57,546
France	1,819	1,983	1,841
Germany	3,388	3,506	4,206
Japan	11,846	11,775	11,392
Korea, Republic	3,073	5,171	8,039
Russia	63,532	55,782	49,456
United Kingdom	2,251	2,221	2,800
USA	4,622	5,381	6,451
Total (incl. others)	197,424	158,734	158,205

* Figures are provisional. The revised total is 159,745.

Source: *Mongolian Statistical Yearbook*.

2001: Total arrivals 192,051 (Source: National Statistical Office, *Monthly Bulletin of Statistics*).

Tourism receipts (US $ million): 33 in 1998; 28 in 1999 (Source: World Bank).

Communications Media

	1999	2000	2001
Television receivers ('000 in use) .	168.8	169.1	n.a.
Telephones ('000 main lines in use)	104.1	112.2	119.7
Mobile cellular telephones ('000 subscribers).	48.2	75.1	195.0
Personal computers ('000 in use) .	24	n.a.	35
Internet users ('000)	12.0	30.0	40.0
Newspapers printed (million copies)	22.2	18.0	19.2

Radio receivers ('000 in use): 360 in 1997.

Facsimile machines (number in use): 7,963 in 1999.

Book production (1994): 128 titles; 640,000 copies.

Non-daily newspapers (titles): 80 in 1998.

Other periodicals (titles): 24 in 1998.

2002: (telephones, '000 main lines in use): 126.7.

2003: 135,500 main telephone lines in use; 257,600 mobile cellular telephone subscribers.

Sources: UNESCO, *Statistical Yearbook*; UN, *Statistical Yearbook*; International Telecommunication Union; Mongolian Statistical Directorate.

Education

(2000/01)

	Institutions	Teachers	Students
General education schools:			
Primary (grades 1–3) . . .	133		
Incomplete secondary (grades 4–8).	219	19,200	494,500
Complete secondary (grades 9–10)	351		
Vocational schools	36	865	97,100
Higher education:			
Universities and colleges*			
State-owned	38	3,455	56,906
Private	134	1,465	28,064

* Excluding those studying abroad (152 in 1999/2000).

2002/03: General education schools 695; Students at general education schools 527,599; Students at vocational schools 19,500; Students at universities and colleges 98,400.

2003/04: Students at general education schools 548,400.

Pre-school institutions (2000): 27 crèches (1,900 pupils) and 653 kindergartens (79,300 pupils).

Source: Mongolian Statistical Directorate.

Adult literacy rate (UNESCO estimates): 98.5% (males 98.3%; females 98.6%) in 2001 (Source: UN Development Programme, *Human Development Report*).

Directory

The Constitution

The Constitution was adopted on 13 January 1992 and came into force on 12 February of that year. It proclaims Mongolia (*Mongol Uls*), with its capital at Ulan Bator (Ulaanbaatar), to be an independent sovereign republic which ensures for its people democracy, justice, freedom, equality and national unity. It recognizes all forms of ownership of property, including land, and affirms that a 'multi-structured economy' will take account of 'universal trends of world economic development and national conditions'.

The 'citizen's right to life' is qualified by the death penalty for serious crimes, and the law provides for the imposition of forced labour. Freedom of residence and travel within the country and abroad may be limited for security reasons. The citizens' duties are to respect the Constitution and the rights and interests of others, pay taxes, and serve in the armed forces, as well as the 'sacred duty'

to work, safeguard one's health, bring up one's children and protect the environment.

Supreme legislative power is vested in the Mongolian Great Khural (Assembly), a single chamber with 76 members elected by universal adult suffrage for a four-year term, with a Chairman and Vice-Chairman elected from amongst the members. The Great Khural recognizes the President on his election and appoints the Prime Minister and members of the Cabinet. A presidential veto of a decision of the Great Khural can be overruled by a two-thirds majority of the Khural. Decisions are taken by a simple majority.

The President is Head of State and Commander-in-Chief of the Armed Forces. He must be an indigenous citizen at least 45 years old who has resided continuously in Mongolia for the five years before election. Presidential candidates are nominated by parties with seats in the Great Khural; the winning candidate in general presidential elections is President for a four-year term.

The Cabinet is the highest executive body and drafts economic, social and financial policy, takes environmental protection measures, strengthens defence and security, protects human rights and implements foreign policy for a four-year term.

The Supreme Court, headed by the Chief Justice, is the highest judicial organ. Judicial independence is protected by the General Council of Courts. The Procurator General, nominated by the President, serves a six-year term.

Local administration in the 21 *aimag* (provinces) and Ulan Bator is effected on the basis of 'self-government and central guidance', comprising local khurals of representatives elected by citizens and governors (*zasag darga*), nominated by the Prime Minister to serve four-year terms.

The Constitutional Court, which guarantees 'strict observance' of the Constitution, consists of nine members nominated for a six-year term, three each by the Great Khural, the President and the Supreme Court.

The first amendments to the Constitution, adopted by the Mongolian Great Khural in December 2000, despite opposition over procedure from the Constitutional Court, were finally approved by President Bagabandi in May 2001. The main effects of the amendments were to clarify the method of appointment of Prime Ministers, enable decision-making by a simple majority vote, and shorten the minimum length of sessions of the Khural from 75 days to 50.

The Government

PRESIDENCY

President and Commander-in-Chief of the Armed Forces: NATSAGIIN BAGABANDI (elected President of Mongolia 18 May 1997; re-elected 20 May 2001).

Head of Presidential Secretariat: BADAMDORJIIN BATKHISHIG.

Director of the Presidential Information Service: DALANTAIN KHALIUN.

NATIONAL SECURITY COUNCIL

The President heads the National Security Council; the Prime Minister and the Chairman of the Mongolian Great Khural are its members. The Secretary is the President's national security adviser.

Chairman: NATSAGIIN BAGABANDI.

Members: NAMBARYN ENKHBAYAR, SANJBEGZIIN TÖMÖR-OCHIR.

Secretary: DÜGERJAVYN GOTOV.

CABINET
(April 2004)

Prime Minister: NAMBARYN ENKHBAYAR.

General Ministries

Minister of Foreign Affairs: LUVSANGIIN ERDENECHULUUN.

Minister of Finance and Economy: CHÜLTEMIIN ULAAN.

Minister of Justice and Home Affairs: TSENDIIN NYAMDORJ.

Sectoral Ministries

Minister of Nature and the Environment: ULAMBAYARYN BARSBOLD.

Minister of Defence: JÜGDERDEMIDIIN GÜRRAGCHAA.

Minister of Education, Culture and Science: AYUURZANYN TSANJID.

Minister of Infrastructure: BYAMBYN JIGJID.

Minister of Social Welfare and Labour: SHIILEGIIN BATBAYAR.

Minister of Industry and Trade: CHIMIDZORIGIIN GANZORIG.

Minister of Food and Agriculture: DARJAAGIIN NASANJARGAL.

Minister of Health: PAGVAJAVYN NYAMDAVAA.

Head of Government Affairs Directorate: ÖLZIISAIKHANY ENKHTÜVSHIN.

MINISTRIES AND GOVERNMENT DEPARTMENTS

All Ministries and Government Departments are in Ulan Bator.

Prime Minister's Office: State Palace, Sükhbaataryn Talbai 1, Ulan Bator 12; fax 328329; internet www.pmis.gov.mn/primeminister.

Ministry of Defence: Government Bldg 7, Dandaryn Gudamj, Bayanzürkh District, Ulan Bator 61; tel. 458495; fax 451727; e-mail mef@mongolnet.mn; internet www.pmis.gov.mn/mdef/mongolian.

Ministry of Education, Culture and Science: Government Bldg 3, Baga Toiruu 44, Sükhbaatar District, Ulan Bator 210620; tel. 322480; fax 323158; internet www.med.pmis.gov.mn.

Ministry of Finance and Economy: Government Bldg 2, Negdsen Ündestnii Gudamj 5/1, Chingeltei District, Ulan Bator 210646; tel. 320247; fax 322712; internet www.mof.pmis.gov.mn.

Ministry of Food and Agriculture: Government Bldg 9, Enkh Taivny Örgön Chölöö 16A, Bayanzürkh District, Ulan Bator 210349; tel. 450258; fax 452554; e-mail mofa@mofa.pmis.gov.mn; internet www.pmis.gov.mn/food&agriculture.

Ministry of Foreign Affairs: Enkh Taivny Örgön Chölöö 7A, Sükhbaatar District, Ulan Bator 210648; tel. 311311; fax 322127; e-mail mongmer@magicnet.mn; internet www.extmin.mn.

Ministry of Health: Government Bldg 8, Olimpiin Gudamj 2, Sükhbaatar District, Ulan Bator; tel. 323381; fax 320916; e-mail moh@moh.mng.net; internet www.pmis.gov.mn/health/index.

Ministry of Industry and Trade: Block A, Government Bldg 2, Negdsen Ündestnii Gudamj 5/1, Chingeltei District, Ulan Bator 210646; tel. 329222; fax 322595; e-mail mit@mit.pmis.gov.mn; internet www.mit.pmis.gov.mn.

Ministry of Infrastructure: Government Bldg 2, Negdsen Ündestnii Gudamj 5/1, Chingeltei District, Ulan Bator 210646; tel. 326222; fax 310612; e-mail webmaster@mid.pmis.gov.mn; internet www.mid.pmis.gov.mn.

Ministry of Justice and Home Affairs: Government Bldg 5, Khudaldaany Gudamj 6/1, Chingeltei District, Ulan Bator 210646; tel. 322383; fax 325225; e-mail forel@moj.pmis.gov.mn; internet www.pmis.gov.mn/mjus.

Ministry of Nature and the Environment: Government Bldg 3, Baga Toiruu 44, Sükhbaatar District, Ulan Bator 210620; tel. 320943; fax 321401; e-mail mtt@magicnet.mn; internet www.pmis.gov.mn/men.

Ministry of Social Welfare and Labour: Government Bldg 2, Negdsen Ündestnii Gudamj 5/1, Chingeltei District, Ulan Bator 210646; tel. 328559; fax 328634; e-mail mswl@mongolnet.mn.

Government Affairs Directorate (Cabinet Secretariat): State Palace, Sükhbaataryn Talbai 1, Ulan Bator 12; tel. 323501; fax 310011; internet www.pmis.gov.mn/cabinet.

National Statistical Office: Government Bldg 3, Baga Toiruu 44, Sükhbaatar District, Ulan Bator 210620; tel. 322424; fax 324518; e-mail info@nso.mn; internet www.nso.mn.

President and Legislature

PRESIDENT

Office of the President: Ulan Bator; fax 311121; internet www.pmis.gov.mn/president.

Election, 20 May 2001

Candidate	Votes	%
Natsagiin Bagabandi (MPRP)	574,553	57.95
Radnaasümbereliin Gonchigdorj (Democratic Party)	362,684	36.58
Luvsandambyn Dashnyam (Civil Courage Party)	35,139	3.54

MONGOLIAN GREAT KHURAL

Under the fourth Constitution, which came into force in February 1992, the single-chamber Mongolian Great Khural is the State's supreme legislative body. With 76 members elected for a four-year term, the Great Khural must meet for at least 50 working days in every six months. Its Chairman may act as President of Mongolia when the President is indisposed.

Chairman: SANJBEGZIIN TÖMÖR-OCHIR.

Vice-Chairman: JAMSRANGIIN BYAMBADORJ.

General Secretary: NAMSRAIJAVYN LUVSANJAV.

General Election, 2 July 2000

Party	Seats
Mongolian People's Revolutionary Party (MPRP) . .	72
Civil Courage Party*	1
Mongolian Democratic New Socialist Party (MDNSP) .	1
Mongolian National Democratic Party (MNDP)†‡ . .	1
Independent‡	1
Total	**76**

* In coalition with the Mongolian Green Party.
† In coalition with the Mongolian Believers' Democratic Party.
‡ The MNDP was absorbed into the Democratic Party (DP—see Political Organizations, below) in December 2000. The Independent member of the Great Khural subsequently joined the DP.

Political Organizations

Civil Courage Republican Party: Rm 1, Altai College, Sükhbaatar District, Ulan Bator (CPO 13, Box 37); tel. and fax 319006; e-mail oyun@mail.parl.gov.mn; f. 2002 by merger of the Civil Courage Party and Mongolian Republican Party; also known as the Citizen's Will (Republican Party); split announced in 2003; Civil Courage Party and Mongolian Republican Party to be re-registered as independent parties under fmr names; c. 150,000 mems. (Feb. 2003); Chair. SANJAASÜRENGIIN OYUUN.

Democratic Party (DP): Chingisiin Örgön Chölöö 1, Ulan Bator; f. 2000 by amalgamation of the Mongolian National Democratic Party, Mongolian Social-Democratic Party, Mongolian Democratic Party, Mongolian Democratic Renewal Party and the Mongolian Believers' Democratic Party; c. 170,000 mems. (May 2002); Chair. MENDSAIKHANY ENKHSAIKHAN; Sec.-Gen. LÜIMEDIIN GANSÜKH.

Mongolian Communist Party: f. 1999; Chair. L. SHIITER.

Mongolian Democratic New Socialist Party (MDNSP): Erel Co, Bayanzürkh District, Ulan Bator; internet www.mongol.net/mdnsp; f. 1998; amalgamated with Mongolian Workers' Party 1999; 110,000 mems (May 2002); Chair. BADARCHIIN ERDENEBAT.

Mongolian Democratic Party (MDP): Ulan Bator; f. 1990; merged in Oct. 1992 with other parties to form the Mongolian National Democratic Party (MNDP); reconstituted in Jan. 2000, the party won no seats in the 2000 elections, and in Dec. 2000 most members merged with the MDNP and other parties to form the Democratic Party; a splinter group opposed to the merger tried unsuccessfully to challenge the legal status of the DP and then elected a new MDP leadership; Chair. DAMDINDORJIIN NINJ.

Mongolian Democratic Socialist Party: State Property Bldg No. 5, Ulan Bator; 947 mems (1998); Chair. DASHDORJIIN MANDAKH.

Mongolian Green Party: POB 51, Erkh Chölöönii Gudamj 11, Ulan Bator 38; tel. 323871; fax 458859; f. 1990; political wing of the Alliance of Greens; 5,000 mems (March 1997); Chair. DAVAAGIIN BASANDORJ.

Mongolian Liberal Party: f. 1999 as Mongolian Civil Democratic New Liberal Party, renamed 2004; ruling body Little Khural of 90 mems with Leadership Council of nine; Chair. D. BANZRAGCH.

Mongolian Liberal Democratic Party: POB 470, Ulan Bator 44; tel. 151030; fax 310076; e-mail mldp@magicnet.mn; internet www .mldp.mn; f. 1998 as Mongolian Socialist Democratic (Labour) Party; ruling body Political Council; 848 mems (1998); Chair. TÜVSHINBATYN TÖMÖRMÖNKH.

Mongolian National Solidarity Party: Ikh Zasag' Institute Bldg, 4th Horoo, Bayanzürkh District, Ulan Bator; tel. and fax 455736; f. 1994 as Mongolian Solidarity Party; 15,480 mems (March 2002); Chair. NAMSRAIN NYAM-OSOR.

Mongolian New Social Democratic Party: f. 2000 by dissidents of the Mongolian Social-Democratic Party (MSDP); Chair. LANTUUGIIN DAMDINSÜREN.

Mongolian Party of Tradition and Justice: f. 1999; fmrly Mongolian National Democratic Socialist Party; Sec.-Gen. GANTÖMÖRIIN GALINA.

Mongolian People's Party (MPP): Ulan Bator; tel. 311083; f. 1991; forestalled any MPRP plans to revert to its original name, MPP; 2,000 mems (June 1995); in March 2000 some mems (led by Chairman Dembereliin Ölziibaatar) claimed to have merged the MPP with the MPRP; others reaffirmed the MPP's independence at a party congress in April; Chair. Lama DORLIGJAVYN BAASAN.

Mongolian People's Revolutionary Party (MPRP): Baga Toiruu 37/1, Ulan Bator 11; tel. 322745; fax 320368; f. 1921 as Mongolian People's Party; c. 122,000 mems (May 2002); ruling body Party Little Khural (244 mems in Feb. 2001), which elects the Leadership Council; Chair. NAMBARYN ENKHBAYAR; Gen. Sec. DOLOONJINGIIN IDEVKHTEN.

Mongolian Rural Development Party: f. 1995 as the Mongolian Countryside Development Party, reorganized in December 1999; Pres. L. CHULUUNBAATAR.

Mongolian Traditional United Party: Huvisgalchdyn Örgön Chölöö 26, Ulan Bator; tel. 325745; fax 342692; also known as the United Heritage (conservative) Party; f. 1993 as an amalgamation of the United Private Owners' Party and the Independence Party; 14,000 mems (1998); ruling body General Political Council; Chair. ÜRJINGIIN KHÜRELBAATAR.

Society of Russian Citizens: Ulan Bator; represents local Russian long-term residents; Chair. (vacant).

United Socialist Party of Mongols: Ulan Bator; f. 2000; nationalist party; Chair. (vacant).

Diplomatic Representation

EMBASSIES IN MONGOLIA

Bulgaria: Olimpiin Gudamj 8, Ulan Bator (CPO Box 702); tel. and fax 322841; e-mail posolstvobg@magicnet.mn; Ambassador NIKOLAI MARIN.

China, People's Republic: Zaluuchuudyn Örgön Chölöö 5, Ulan Bator (CPO Box 672); tel. 320955; fax 311943; Ambassador GAO SHUMAO.

Cuba: Negdsen Ündestnii Gudamj 18, Ulan Bator (CPOB 710); tel. 323778; fax 327709; e-mail embacuba@mongol.net; Ambassador EDUARDO CASTELLANOS SOTO.

Czech Republic: POB 665, Olimpiin Gudamj 14, Ulan Bator; tel. 321886; fax 323791; e-mail czechemb@mongol.net; internet www .mzv.cz/ulaanbaatar; Ambassador OLDŘICH SOMMER.

France: Diplomatic Corps Bldg, Apartment 48, Ulan Bator 6 (CPO Box 687); tel. 324519; fax 329633; e-mail ambafrance@magicnet.mn; Ambassador NICOLAS CHAPUIS.

Germany: Negdsen Ündestnii Gudamj 7, Ulan Bator (CPO Box 708); tel. 323325; fax 323905; e-mail germanemb_ulanbator@mongol .net; Ambassador MICHAEL VORWERK.

Hungary: Enkh Taivny Gudamj 1, Ulan Bator (CPO Box 668); tel. 323973; fax 311793; e-mail huembuln@mongol.net; Ambassador ISTVÁN BALOGH.

India: Zaluuchuudyn Örgön Chölöö 10, Ulan Bator (CPO Box 691); tel. 329522; fax 329532; e-mail indembmongolia@magicnet.mn; Ambassador GAURI SHANKAR GUPTA.

Japan: Zaluuchuudyn Gudamj 12, Ulan Bator 13 (CPO Box 1011); tel. 320777; fax 313332; e-mail eojmongol@magicnet.mn; internet www.eojmongolia.mn; Ambassador TATSUO TODA.

Kazakhstan: Diplomatic Corps Bldg, Apartment 11, Chingeltei District, Ulan Bator (CPO Box 291); tel. 312240; fax 312204; e-mail kzemby@magicnet.mn; Ambassador J. S. KARYBDZHANOV.

Korea, Republic: Olimpiin Gudamj 10, Ulan Bator (CPO Box 1039); tel. 321548; fax 311157; Ambassador KIM WON-TAE.

Laos: Ikh Toiruu 59, Ulan Bator (CPO Box 1030); tel. 322834; fax 321048; e-mail laoemb@mongol.net; Ambassador VANHEUANG VONGVICHIT.

Poland: Diplomatic Corps Bldg, 95, Apartment 66–67, Ulan Bator 13; tel. 320641; fax 320576; Ambassador KRZYSZTOF DEBNICKI.

Russia: Enkh Taivny Gudamj A-6, Ulan Bator (CPO Box 661); tel. 327851; fax 327018; e-mail embassy_ru@mongol.net; Ambassador OLEG DERKOVSKII.

Turkey: Enkh Taivny Örgön Chölöö 5, Ulan Bator (CPO Box 1009); tel. 313992; fax 313992; e-mail turkemb@mongol.net; Ambassador TANER KARAKAŞ.

United Kingdom: Enkh Taivny Gudamj 30, Ulan Bator 13 (CPO Box 703); tel. 458133; fax 458036; e-mail britemb@magicnet.mn; Ambassador RICHARD AUSTEN.

USA: Ikh Toiruu 59/1, Ulan Bator (CPO Box 1021); tel. 329606; fax 320776; e-mail webmaster@us-mongolia.com; Ambassador PAMELA JO SLUTZ.

Viet Nam: Enkh Taivny Örgön Chölöö 47, Ulan Bator (CPO Box 670); tel. 458917; fax 458923; Ambassador CHAN NGUYEN TICH.

Judicial System

Under the fourth Constitution, judicial independence is protected by the General Council of Courts, consisting of the Chief Justice (Chairman of the Supreme Court), the Chairman of the Constitutional Court, Procurator General, Minister of Law and others. The Council nominates the members of the Supreme Court for approval by the Great Khural. The Chief Justice is chosen from among the members of the Supreme Court and approved by the President for a six-year term. Civil, criminal and administrative cases are handled by Ulan Bator City court, the 21 *aimag* (provincial) courts, *sum* (rural district) and urban district courts, while the system of special courts (military, railway, etc.) is still in place. The Procurator General and his deputies, who play an investigatory role, are nominated by the President and approved by the Great Khural for six-year terms. The Constitutional Court safeguards the constitutional legality of legislation. It consists of nine members, three nominated each by the President, Great Khural and Supreme Court, and elects a Chairman from among its number.

Chief Justice: CHIMEDLKHAMYN GANBAT.

Procurator General: MONGOLYN ALTANKHUYAG.

Chairman of Constitutional Court: NAVAANPERENLEIN JANTSAN.

Religion

The 1992 Constitution maintains the separation of Church and State but forbids any discrimination, declaring that 'the State shall respect religion and religion shall honour the State'. During the early years of communist rule Mongolia's traditional Mahayana Buddhism was virtually destroyed, then exploited as a 'show-piece' for visiting dignitaries (although the Dalai Lama himself was not permitted to visit Mongolia until the early 1980s). The national Buddhist centre is Gandantegchinlen Khiid (monastery) in Ulan Bator, with about 100 lamas and a seminary; it is the headquarters of the Asian Buddhist Conference for Peace. In the early 1990s some 2,000 lamas established small communities at the sites of 120 former monasteries, temples and religious schools, some of which were being restored. These included two other important monasteries, Erdene Zuu and Amarbayasgalant. The Kazakhs of western Mongolia are nominally Sunni Muslims, but their mosques, also destroyed in the 1930s or closed subsequently, are only now being rebuilt or reopened. Traces of shamanism from the pre-Buddhist period still survive. In recent years there has been a new upsurge in Christian missionary activity in Mongolia. However, the Law on State-Church Relations (of November 1993) sought to make Buddhism the predominant religion and restricted the dissemination of beliefs other than Buddhism, Islam and shamanism. The law was challenged by human rights campaigners and Mongolian Christians as unconstitutional.

BUDDHISM

Living Buddha: The Ninth Javzandamba Khutagt (Ninth Bogd), Jambalnamdolchoijinjaltsan (resident in Dharamsala, India).

Gandantegchinlen Monastery: Ulan Bator 58; tel. 360023; Centre of Mongolian Buddhists; Khamba Lama (Abbot) DEMBERELIIN CHOIJAMTS.

Mongolian Buddhist Association: Pres. G. ENKHSAIKHAN.

CHRISTIANITY

Roman Catholic Church

The Church is represented in Mongolia by a single mission. At April 2004 there were 187 Catholics in the country.

Catholic Mission: POB 694, Ulan Bator; tel. 458825; fax 458027; e-mail ccmvatican@magicnet.mn; f. 1992; Superior Bishop WENCESLAO PADILLA.

Cathedral of St. Peter and St. Paul: Bayanzürkh District, Ulan Bator.

Protestant Church

Association of Mongolian Protestants: f. 1990; Pastor M. BOLDBAATAR.

Russian Orthodox Church

Holy Trinity Church: Jukovyn Gudamj 55, Ulan Bator; opened in 1870, closed in 1930; services recommenced 1997 for Russian community; Father ANATOLII FESECHKO.

ISLAM

Muslim Society: f. 1990; Hon. Pres. K. SAIRAAN; Chair. of Central Council M. AZATKHAN.

BAHÁ'Í FAITH

Bahá'í Community: Ulan Bator; tel. 321867; f. 1989; Leader A. ARIUNAA.

The Press

PRINCIPAL NATIONAL NEWSPAPERS

State-owned publications in Mongolia were denationalized with effect from 1 January 1999, although full privatization could not proceed immediately.

MN-Önöödör (Today): Mongol News Co, Ikh Toiruu 20, Ulan Bator; tel. 352504; fax 352501; e-mail mntoday@mobinet.mn; internet www.mongolnews.mn; f. 1996; 304 a year; Editor-in-Chief TS. BALDORJ; circ. 5,500.

Mongolyn Medee (Mongolian News): Erel Group, 13th Khoroo, Bayanzürkh Düüreg, Ulan Bator; tel. 453169; fax 453816; e-mail news-of-mon@magicnet.mn; 256 a year; Editor-in-Chief D. SANDAGSÜREN; circ. 2,900.

Ödriin Sonin (Daily News): Ikh Toiruu, Ulan Bator 20; tel. 99263536; fax 352499; e-mail daily_news@mbox.mn; internet www.dn.mongolmedia.com; f. 1924; restored 1990; fmrly Ardyn Erkh, Ardyn Ündesnii Erkh, Ündesnii Erkh and Ödriin Toli; 312 a year; Editor-in-Chief JAMBALYN MYAGMARSÜREN; circ. 14,200.

Ünen (Truth): Baga Toiruu 11, Ulan Bator; tel. 323847; fax 321287; e-mail unen@magicnet.mn; internet www.unen.mn; f. 1920; publ. by MPRP; 256 a year; Editor-in-Chief TSERENSODNOMYN GANBAT; circ. 8,330.

Zuuny Medee (Century's News): Amaryn Gudamj 1, Ulan Bator 20; tel. 320940; fax 321279; e-mail zuunii_medee@yahoo.com; internet www.zuuniimedee.mn; f. 1991 as *Zasgiin Gazryn Medee*; 312 a year; Editor-in-Chief TSERENDORJIIN TSETSEGCHULUUN; circ 8,000.

PRINCIPAL PERIODICALS

81-r Suvag (Channel 81): POB 367/13, Ulan Bator; tel. 99118359; e-mail channel81@mongolmedia.com; internet www.channel81.mongolmedia.com; publishes views of the Mongolian Newspaper Asscn; 40 a year; Editor-in-Chief JAMSRANGIIN BAYARJARGAL.

Anagaakh Arga Bilig (The Healthy Way of Yin and Yang): POB 1053/13, Ulan Bator; tel. 321367; e-mail arslny7144@magicnet.mn; twice monthly; Editor YA. ARSLAN.

Ardyn Elch (People's Envoy): St. Petersburg Centre, 2nd Floor, Rm 36, Sükhbaataryn Örgön Chölöö; tel. 95252346; fax 314580; monthly; Editor-in-Chief B. TSEDEN.

Bagsh (Teacher): Rm 106, Teachers' College, Ulan Bator; tel. 99183398; f. 1989 by Ministry of Education; 24 a year.

Business Times: Chamber of Commerce and Industry, Government Bldg 1, Rm 806, Erkh Chölöönii Talbai, Ulan Bator; tel. 325374; fax 324620; e-mail bis_times@usa.net; 48 a year; Editor B. SARANTUYAA.

Deedsiin Amidral (Elite's Life): Bldg 6, Rm 207, A. Amaryn Gudamj, POB 536/13, Ulan Bator; tel. 91189399; fax 323847; e-mail elitslife@mongolmedia.com; internet www.elitslife.mongolmedia.com; Editor-in-Chief TSEGMIDIIN CHIMIDDONDOG.

Deedsiin Khüreelen (Elite's Forum): CPO Box 1114, Ulan Bator; tel. 325687; 48 a year; Editor NYAMBUUGIIN BILGÜÜN; circ. 12,000.

Dorno-Örnö (East-West): POB 17/48, Ulan Bator; fax 322613; f. 1978; publ. by Institute of Oriental and International Studies of Acad. of Sciences; scientific and socio-political journal; history, culture, foreign relations; articles in Mongolian; two a year; Editor-in-Chief Dr N. ALTANTSETSEG.

Erüül Mend (Health): Ulan Bator; fax 321278; publ. by Ministry of Health; monthly; Editor-in-Chief SH. JIGJIDSÜREN; circ. 5,600.

Il Tovchoo (Openness): Mongol Nom Co Bldg, Rm 8, Ulan Bator; POB 234, Ulan Bator 46; tel. 325517; e-mail iltovchoo@magicnet.mn; f. 1990; current affairs and cultural news; 36 a year; Editor-in-Chief G. AKIM.

Khani (Spouse): POB 600/49, National Agricultural Co-operative Members' Association Bldg, Rm 103, Enkh Taivny Gudamj 18A-1, Bayanzürkh Düüreg, Ulan Bator; women and family issues; 36 a year; Editor-in-Chief D. OTGONTUYAA; circ. 64,920.

Khöldömör (Labour): Sükhbaataryn Talbai 3, Ulan Bator 210664; tel. 323026; f. 1928; publ. by the Confederation of Mongolian Trade Unions; 36 a year; Editor-in-Chief TSOODOLYN KHULAN; circ. 64,920.

Khökh Tolbo (Blue Spot): POB 306/24, Mon-Azi Co Bldg, Ulan Bator; tel. and fax 313405; 48 a year; Editor-in-Chief BATYN ERDENE-BAATAR; circ. 3,500.

Khuuli Züin Medeelel (Legal Information): Ministry of Justice and Home Affairs, Ulan Bator; f. 1990; 24 a year.

Khuviin Amidral (Private Life): POB 429/44, Ulan Bator 44; tel. 329926; fax 310181; 36 a year; Editor-in-Chief T. AMARDAVAA; circ. 2,900.

Khuviin Soyol (Personal Culture): CPOB 1254, Rm 2, Block 39, behind No. 5 School, Baga Toiruu, Ulan Bator; Editor BEKHBAZARYN BEKHSÜREN.

Khümüün Bichig (People and Script): Montsame, Ulan Bator; tel. 329486; fax 327857; e-mail montsame@pop.mn; current affairs in Mongolian classical script; 36 a year; Editor T. GALDAN; circ. 15,000.

Khümüüs (People): POB 411, Ulan Bator 46; tel. 328732; fax 318363; e-mail khumuus@mongol.net; 48 a year; Editor O. MÖNKH-ERDENE; circ. 21,500.

Khümüüsiin Amidral (People's Life): POB 411, Ulan Bator 46; tel. 328732; fax 318363; e-mail khumuus@mongol.net; 48 a year; Editor B. KHULAN.

Mash Nuuts (Top Secret): POB 113/49, Ulan Bator 49; 24 a year; Editors N. BATDELGER, TS. MÖNKHTUYAA.

Mongol Taims (Mongol Times): Jamyangiin Gudamj 9, Ulan Bator; tel. and fax 458802; 48 a year; Editor CHONOIN KULANDA.

Mongol Törkh (Mongolian Style): POB 418/46, MPRP Bldg, Rm 102, Sükhbaatar Düüreg, Ulan Bator; tel. and fax 311406; 36 a year; Editor D. BADAMGARAV.

Mongoljin Goo (Mongolian Beauty): POB 717/44, Mongolian Women's Federation, Ulan Bator; tel. 320790; fax 367406; e-mail monwofed@magicnet.mn; f. 1990; monthly; Editor J. ERDENECHIMEG; circ. 3,000.

Mongolyn Anagaakh Ukhaan (Mongolian Medicine): CPOB 696/13, Ulan Bator 13; tel. 112306; fax 451807; e-mail nymadawa@hotmail.com; publ. by Scientific Society of Mongolian Physicians, Sub-assembly of Medical Sciences and Mongolian Academy of Sciences; quarterly; Editor-in-Chief Prof. PAGVAJAVYN NYAMDAVAA.

Mongolyn Khödöö (Mongolian Countryside): Mongolian National University, Khan-Uul District, Zaisan, Ulan Bator; tel. 91164884; e-mail tulgaa_h2000@yahoo.com; publ. by Ministry of Agriculture and Industry, and Academy of Agricultural Sciences; monthly; Editor-in-Chief SODNOMDARJAAGIIN BATTULGA.

Montsame—giin Medee (Montsame News): CPOB 1514, Montsame, Ulan Bator; tel. 314507; fax 314511; daily news digest primarily for government departments; 264 a year; Editor B. NAMIN-CHIMED.

Notstoi Medee (Important News): POB 359/20, Maximum Press Co, Ulan Bator; tel. 99133270; Editor B. MÖNKHZUL.

Oroin Medee (Evening News): Bayangol Düüreg, Ulan Bator; tel. 90151080; e-mail e_news@hotmail.com; Editor-in-Chief S. BADAM-RAGCHAA.

Sain Baina Uu? (Hello!): CPOB 1085, Chingisiin Örgön Chölöö 1, Ulan Bator; tel. 310757; fax 372810; internet sain.mongolmedia.com; publ. by the Democratic Party; 48 a year; Editor CH. CHU-LUUNBAATAR.

Serüüleg (Alarm Clock): POB 1094/13, Flat 2, Entrance 1, Block A4, 1-40 Myangat, Ulan Bator; tel. and fax 318006; 40 a year; Editor-in-Chief SENGEEGIIN BAYARMÖNKH; circ. 28,600.

Setgüülch (Journalist): POB 600/46, Ulan Bator; tel. 325388; fax 313912; f. 1982; publ. by Union of Journalists; journalism, politics, literature, art, economy; quarterly; Editor TSENDIIN ENKHBAT.

Shar Sonin (Yellow Newspaper): POB 76/20A, Ulan Bator; tel. 313984; 48 a year; Editor B. ODGEREL.

Shinjlekh Ukhaany Akademiin Medee (Academy of Sciences News): Sükhbaataryn Talbai 3, Ulan Bator; tel. (11) 321993; e-mail MAS@ac.mn; f. 1961; publ. by Academy of Sciences; quarterly; Editor-in-Chief D. REGDEL.

Shuurkhai Zar (Quick Advertisement): POB 151/46A, Ulan Bator Bank Bldg, Rm 104, 1st Floor, Ulan Bator; tel. 313778; e-mail shirevger@mobinet.mn; Editor E. TSEYENKHORLOO.

Tavan Tsagarig (Five Rings): National Olympic Committee, Ikh Toiruu 20, Ulan Bator; tel. 352487; fax 343541; e-mail t_ts_sport@yahoo.com; noc@olympic.mn; Editor-in-Chief SODNOMDARJAAGIIN BATBAATAR.

Töriin Medeelel (State Information): Secretariat of the Mongolian Great Khural, State Palace, Ulan Bator 12; tel. 329612; fax 322866; e-mail elbegsaihan@maild.parl.gov.mn; internet www.parl.gov.mn; f. 1990; presidential and governmental decrees, state laws; 48 a year; circ. 5,000.

Tsenkher Delgets (Light Blue Screen): Ulan Bator; tel. 312010; fax 311850; e-mail bsnews@magicnet.mn; weekly guide to TV and radio programmes; Editor-in-Chief GALIGAAGIIN BAYARSAIKHAN.

Tsonkh (Window): CPOB 1085, Chingisiin Örgön Chölöö 1, Ulan Bator; tel. 310717; publ. by the Democratic Party's Political Department; monthly.

Üg (Word): CPOB 680, Rm 2, Block 8B, 1–40 Myangat, Ulan Bator; tel. 321165; fax 329795; e-mail ugsonin@mol.mn; fmrly the journal of the Mongolian Social Democratic Party (until 2000); Editor B. KHANDOLGOR.

Ulaanbaatar Times (Ulan Bator Times): A. Amaryn Gudamj 1, Ulan Bator 20; tel. and fax 311187; f. 1990 as *Ulaanbaatar*; publ. by Ulan Bator City Govt; weekly; Editor-in-Chief JÜNPERELIIN SARUUL-BUYAN; circ. 2,000.

Utga Zokhiol Urlag (Literature and Art): Union of Writers, Sükhbaataryn Gudamj 11, Ulan Bator 46; tel. 321863; f. 1955; monthly; Editor-in-Chief Ü. KHÜRELBAATAR; circ. 3,000.

Zar Medee (Advertisement News): Government Bldg 5, 1st Floor, Rm 130, Chingeltei Düüreg, Ulan Bator; tel. and fax 324885; e-mail advertisement-news@yahoo.com; personal and company advertisements; 102 a year; Editor D. BAYASGALAN.

Zindaa (Ranking): Kyoküshyuzan Development Fund Bldg, Chingeltei Düüreg, Ulan Bator; tel. 312008; internet www.zindaa.mongolmedia.com; wrestling news; 36 a year; Editor-in-Chief KH. MANDAKHBAYAR.

FOREIGN LANGUAGE PUBLICATIONS

Menggu Xiaoxi Bao (News of Mongolia): Montsame News Agency, CPOB 1514, Ulan Bator; e-mail mgxxbao@yahoo.com; f. 1929 as *Ajilchny Zam*; closed 1991, reopened 1998; 48 a year; in Chinese; Sec. B. MÖNKHTUUL.

Mongolia This Week: Ulan Bator; tel. and fax 318339; e-mail mongoliathisweek@mobinet.mn; internet www.mongoliathisweek.mn; weekly in English, online daily; Editor-in-Chief D. NARANTUYAA; English Editor ERIC MUSTAFA.

Mongoliya Segodnya (Mongolia Today): Box 609, PO 46, Ulan Bator; tel. and fax 324141; e-mail MNSegodnia@mongol.net; weekly; Editor-in-Chief DÜNGER-YAICHILIIN SOLONGO.

The Mongol Messenger: Montsame News Agency, CPOB 1514, Ulan Bator 13; tel. 325512; fax 327857; e-mail monmessenger@magicnet.mn; internet www.mongolmessenger.mn; f. 1991; weekly newspaper in English; Editor-in-Chief B. INDRA; circ. 2,000.

Montsame Daily News: CPOB 1514, Montsame, Ulan Bator; tel. 314574; fax 327857; daily English news digest for embassies, etc.

Novosti Mongolii (News of Mongolia): CPOB 1514, Montsame, Ulan Bator; tel. 310157; fax 327857; e-mail montsame@pop.magicnet.mn; f. 1942; weekly; in Russian; Editor-in-Chief ENKH-BAYARYN RAVDAN.

The UB Post: Mongol News Co, Ikh Toiruu 20, Ulan Bator; tel. 352487; fax 352495; e-mail ubpost@yahoo.com; internet ubpost.mongolnews.mn; f. 1996; weekly; in English; Editor-in-Chief NAMS-RAIN OYUUNBAYAR; circ. 4,000.

NEWS AGENCIES

Montsame (Mongol Tsakhilgaan Medeenii Agentlag) (Mongolian News Agency): Jigjidjavyn Gudamj 8, Ulan Bator 13 (CPO Box 1514); tel. 314502; fax 327857; e-mail montsame@magicnet.mn; internet www.montsame.mn; f. 1921; govt-controlled; Gen. Dir DOR-JIIN ARIUNBOLD (acting); Editor-in-Chief GIVAANDONDOGIIN PÜREV-SAMBUU.

Mongolyn Medee (Mongolian News): operated by Mongolteleviz; Dir D. SANDAGSÜREN.

Foreign Bureaux

Informatsionnoye Telegrafnoye Agentstvo Rossii—Telegrafnoye Agentstvo Suverennykh Stran (ITAR—TASS) (Russia): Khudaldaany Gudamj 4, Rm 323, Ulan Bator; Bureau Chief V. B. IONOV; Correspondent N. A. KERZHENTSEV.

Rossiiskoye Informatsionnoye Agentstvo—Novosti (RIA—Novosti) (Russia): POB 686, Ulan Bator; tel. 327384; Correspondent ALEKSANDR ALTMAN.

Xinhua (New China) News Agency (People's Republic of China): Ulan Bator; tel. 322718; Correspondent LI REN.

Publishers

Mongolian Book Publishers' Association: Ulan Bator; Exec. Dir S. TSERENDORJ.

Mongolian Free Press Publishers' Association: POB 306, Ulan Bator 24; tel. and fax 313405; Pres. BATYN ERDENEBAATAR.

The Government remains the largest publisher, but the ending of the state monopoly has led to the establishment of several small commercial publishers, including Shuvuun Saaral (Ministry of Defence), Mongol Khevlel and Soyombo Co, Mongolpress (Montsame), Erdem (Academy of Sciences), Süülenkhüü children's publishers, Sudaryn Chuulgan, Interpress, Sükhbaatar Co, Öngöt Khevlel, Admon, Odsar, Khee Khas Co, etc. Newspaper publishing fell from 134.1m. copies in 1990 to 21.1m. copies in 1999. Book printing likewise declined, from 96.3m. printer's sheets (each of 16 pages) in 1990 to 19.2m. in 1993. In 1994 128 book titles appeared, with a total of 640,000 copies. The two main press, periodical and book subscription agencies are Mongol Shuudan and Gurvan Badrakh Co.

Broadcasting and Communications

TELECOMMUNICATIONS

Digital exchanges have been installed in Ulan Bator, Darkhan, Erdenet, Sükhbaatar, Bulgan and Arvaikheer, while radio-relay lines have been digitalized between: Ulan Bator–Darkhan–Sükhbaatar; Ulan Bator–Darkhan–Erdenet; and Dashinchilen–Arvaikheer. Mobile telephone companies operate in Ulan Bator and other central towns, in addition to Arvaikheer, Sainshand and Zamyn-Üüd.

Datakom: Negdsen Ündestnii Gudamj 49, Ulan Bator 46; tel. 315544; fax 320210; e-mail sales@datacom.mn; internet www.web.mn; service provider for Magicnet connection to internet; Dir DANGAASÜRENGIIN ENKHBAT.

Micom: Mongol Tsakhilgaan Kholboo Co Bldg, 3rd Floor, Sükhbaataryn Talbai 1, Ulan Bator 210611; tel. 313229; fax 322473; e-mail info@micom.mng.net; internet www.micom.mng.net; Dir R. BATMEND.

MobiCom: Amaryn Gudamj 2, Ulan Bator 210620 (CPO Box 20A); tel. 312222; fax 310411; e-mail mobicom@mobicom-corp.com; mobile telephone service provider; Dir G. BATTÖR.

Moncom: 51 Post Office, Box 207, Ulan Bator; tel. 329409; e-mail ch.enkhmend@hotmail.com; pager services.

Mongolia Telecom: Sükhbaataryn Talbai 1, Ulan Bator 210611 (CPO Box 1166); tel. 320597; fax 325412; e-mail mt@mtcone.net; internet www.mongol.net; 54.6% state-owned, 40.0% owned by Korea Telecom; Pres. and CEO OONOI SHAALUU.

Railcom: Business Services, Ulan Bator Railway Directorate, Ulan Bator; tel. 942600; internet www.railcom.mn; telephone, TV and internet service provider.

Skytel: Montel Co Bldg, 4th Floor, 1st Khoroo, Chingeltei District, Ulan Bator 13; tel. 318488; fax 318487; e-mail skytel@mtcone.net; mobile telephone and voice mail service provider; Mongolia-Republic of Korea joint venture; Marketing Man. G. TÜVSHINTÖGS.

BROADCASTING

A 1,900-km radio relay line from Ulan Bator to Altai and Ölgii provides direct-dialling telephone links as well as television services for western Mongolia. New radio relay lines have been built from Ulan Bator to Choibalsan, and from Ulan Bator to Sükhbaatar and Sainshand. Most of the population is in the zone of television reception, following the inauguration of relays via satellites operated by the International Telecommunications Satellite Organization (INTELSAT).

All provincial centres receive two channels of Mongolian national television; and all district centres can receive television, although only a third can receive Mongolian television.

Head of Mongolian Radio and Television Affairs Directorate: BAASANJAVYN GANBOLD.

Radio

Mongolradio: Khuvisgalyn Zam 3, Ulan Bator 11; tel. 323096; f. 1934; operates for 17 hours daily on three long-wave and one medium-wave frequency, and VHF; programmes in Mongolian (two) and Kazakh; Dir BAARANGIIN PÜREVDASH.

Voice of Mongolia: Ulan Bator; e-mail radiomongolia@magicnet.mn; external service of Mongolradio; broadcasts in Russian, Chinese, English and Japanese on short wave; Dir B. NARANTUYAA.

The World Service of the British Broadcasting Corpn is relayed on 103.1 MHz in Ulan Bator.

AE and JAAG Studio: Amryn Gudamj 2, Ulan Bator 210620, POB 126, Ulan Bator; tel. 310631; fax 326545; e-mail aejaag@magicnet.mn; f. 1996; broadcasts for 4.5–5 hours daily; CEO Z. ALTAI.

FM 100.1: Orkhun Centre (East entrance), No.3 Ger District, Ulan Bator; tel. 305388; Elgen Nutag (Homeland) radio.

FM 102.1: Ulan Bator; 'Homeland' Youth Radio; run by the Open Information Foundation.

FM 103.6: radio station run by TV-9.

FM 106.6: Ulan Bator; f. 2001; Voice of America news and information in Mongolian; English lessons and music.

FM 107 (New Century Radio): Ulan Bator; local entertainment; also relays Voice of America broadcasts in English and Russian; Dir M. BUYANBADRAKH.

Info Radio: Youth Palace, Ulan Bator; tel. 329353; e-mail inforadio@mongol.net; broadcasts on 105.5 MHz.

Khökh Tenger (Blue Sky Radio): Ulan Bator; broadcasts for 12 hours Monday to Saturday and for shorter hours on Sundays on 100.9 MHz and 4850 kHz; Dir L. AMARZAYAA.

Puls-Misheel: Ulan Bator; f. 2001 by Mongolradio and Buryat Puls radio; Russian-language broadcaster on 102.5 MHz, 24 hours; hourly news in Russian and Mongolian.

Radio Ulaanbaatar: Ulan Bator; f. 1995; fmrly *Dörvön Uul* (Four Mountains); broadcasts on 101.6 MHz; Dir U. BULGAN.

There are seven long– and short-wave radio transmitters and 49 FM stations in 23 towns (13 in Ulan Bator).

Television

Mongolteleviz (MTV): Khuvisgalyn Zam 3, Ulan Bator 11 (CPO Box 365); tel. 326663; fax 327234; e-mail mrtv@magicnet.mn; f. 1967; daily morning and evening transmissions of locally-originated material relayed by land-line and via INTELSAT satellites; short news bulletins in English Mon., Wed. and Fri.; state-owned; Dir TSENDIIN ENKHBAT.

MN Channel 25: AE and JAAG Studio, Ulan Bator; broadcasts entertainment in the evening from Tuesday to Sunday; CEO Z. ALTAI.

Sansar: Ikh Toiruu 46, Ulan Bator; tel. 313752; fax 313770; cable television equipment and services; Dir-Gen. TS. ELBEGZAYAA.

TV-5: evening broadcasts from 6 p.m., repeated the following morning.

TV-9: f. 2003; broadcaster for the Ulan Bator area, general entertainment, with 20% religious content; Dir N. DULAMSÜREN.

UBS: Ulaanbaatar Broadcasting System (operated by Ulan Bator City Government); evening broadcasts repeated the following morning except Mondays; Dir-Gen. L. BALKHJAV.

Cable TV companies (29 in total) operate in 19 towns. There are local TV stations in Ulan Bator (three), Darkhan, Sükhbaatar and Baganuur. ORT and RTR may be received via Russian satellites, and Kazakh television is received in Bayan-Ölgii. NHK, Deutsche Welle, RTF and Inner Mongolia (China) Television programmes are relayed in Ulan Bator on Channel 10.

Finance

(cap. = capital; res = reserves; dep. = deposits; m. = million; brs = branches; amounts in tögrög)

BANKING

Before 1990 the State Bank was the only bank in Mongolia, responsible for issuing currency, controlling foreign exchange and allocating credit. With the inauguration of market reforms in Mongolia in the early 1990s, the central and commercial functions of the State Bank were transferred to the newly-created specialized commercial banks: the Bank of Capital Investment and Technological Innovation and the State Bank International. In May 1991 the State Bank became an independent central bank, and the operation of private, commercial banks was permitted. By the end of 1996 there were 15 commercial banks. The performance of these banks was poor, owing to high levels of non-performing loans, inexperienced management and weak supervision. Loss of confidence in the sector resulted in the implementation of extensive restructuring: in November 1996 amendments were made to banking legislation to improve the regulation and supervision of commercial banks, and two major insolvent banks were liquidated. Restructuring continued in the late 1990s and beyond.

Central Bank

Bank of Mongolia (Mongolbank): Baga Toiruu 9, Ulan Bator 46; tel. 322169; fax 311471; e-mail ad@mongolbank.mn; internet www .mongolbank.mn; f. 1924 as the State Bank of the Mongolian People's Republic; cap. 5,000m., res 29,709m., dep. 254,760m. (Dec. 2002); Gov. OCHIRBATYN CHULUUNBAT.

Other Banks

AG Bank—Agricultural Bank (Khan Bank): Enkh Taivny Gudamj 51, Ulan Bator 240149 (POB 185, Ulan Bator 51); tel. and fax 458670; e-mail haanbank_fsd@magicnet.mn; f. 1991; purchased by H and S Securities (Japan) in Feb. 2003; cap. 4,945m. (Dec. 1999), total assets US $75.8m. (Dec. 2003); CEO J. PETER MORROW; 380 brs.

Anod Bank: Khudaldaany Gudamj 18, Ulan Bator 211238 (POB 361, Ulan Bator 13); tel. 327566; fax 313070; e-mail international@ anod.mn; internet www.anod.mn; cap. 3,000m., dep. 33,210m. (Dec. 2002); Dir-Gen. D. ENKHTÖR.

Avtozam Bank (Motor Roads Bank): Bridge-Building Office, Ulan Bator; tel. 381744; fax 368094; f. 1990; cap. 95m.; Dir-Gen. TS. SANGIDORJ.

Aziin Khöröngö Oruulaltyn Bank (Asian Capital Investment Bank): Khölög Group Bldg, Eastern entrance, 2nd Floor, Bayangol District, Ulan Bator; tel. 367386; Dir-Gen. TSEDENGIIN BATBOLD.

Bayanbogd Bank: Sambuugiin Gudamj 11, Ulan Bator; tel. and fax 329942; privately owned; cap. 423.7m., dep. 795.5m. (June 1999); Owner D. ADYAA.

Capital Bank (Capital Bank of Mongolia): Chingeltei Duureg, Sambuugiin Gudamj 48, Ulan Bator 211238; tel. 319247; fax 310833; e-mail center@capitalbank.mn; internet www.capitalbank .mn; cap. 4,000m., res 400m., dep 7,000m. (Jan. 2004); Chair. AGVAANJAMYN ARIUNBOLD; Exec. Dir DAMBADARJAAGIIN JARGALSAIKHAN; 11 brs.

Capitron Bank: Enkh Taivny Örgön Chölöö, Ulan Bator 210648; tel. 327550; fax 315635; e-mail info@capitronbank.mn; internet www.capitronbank.mn; f. 2001; cap. 4,000m., res 5,000m., dep 12,000m. (2002); Exec. Dir A. MÖNKHBAT.

Chingis Khan Bank: Chinggis Khan Bank Bldg, 5th Khoroo, Bayangol District, Ulan Bator; tel. (11) 633105; fax (11) 633185; e-mail chkhbank@magicnet.mn; f. 2001 by Millennium Securities Management Ltd and Coral Sea Holdings Ltd (British Virgin Islands); cap. US $31.4m.

Erel Bank: 'Erel' Co No 2 Bldg, Chingisiin Örgön Chölöö, 3rd Khoroo, Ulan Bator (POB 500, Ulan Bator 36); tel. and fax 343567; e-mail info@erelbank.mn; f. 1997; cap. 3,000m., res 243.6m., dep. 1636.9m. (Oct. 2003); Owner BADARCHIIN ERDENEBAT; CEO GOMBO-JAVYN DORJ.

Export Import Bank: Zamchny Gudamj 1, Bayangol District, Ulan Bator (CPO Box 28/52); tel. 311693; fax 311323; f. 1993 as Ulaanbaatar Bank; cap. 506.8m.; CEO L. SARANGEREL.

Golomt Bank of Mongolia: Bodi Tower, Sükhbaataryn Talbai 3, 4th Floor, Ulan Bator 210620; tel. 311530; fax 312307; e-mail psdc@ golomtbank.com; internet golomtbank.mn; f. 1995 by Mongolian-Portuguese IBH Bodi International Co Ltd; cap. 2,071.7m., res 413.3m., dep. 43,890.6m. (Dec. 2001); Chair. LUVSANVANDANGIIN BOLD; Dir-Gen. D. BAYASGALAN; 10 brs.

Interbank of Mongolia: POB 1130, Interbank Bldg, Sükhbaatar District, Ulan Bator; tel. 327403; fax 328372; e-mail interbank@ mongolnet.mn; internet www.interbank.mn; f. 2001; cap. 2,238.1m., dep. 10,554.8m., total assets 12,908.0m. (Dec. 2002); Gen. Dir KHOR-OLSÜRENGIIN CHINBAT.

Khadgalamjiin Bank (Savings Bank): Khudaldaany Gudamj 6, Ulan Bator 11; tel. 312043; fax 310621; e-mail savbank@magicnet .mn; internet www.savingsbank.mn; f. 1996 as Ardyn Bank; cap. 2,536.8m. (Dec. 2001); Dir-Gen. G. TSERENPÜREV; 37 brs.

Kredit Bank: State Palace Bldg (east side), Sükhbaataryn Talbai, Ulan Bator; tel. (11) 310853; fax (11) 319039; e-mail creditbank@ magicnet.mn; internet www.creditbank.mn; cap. 1,117m. (March 2000).

Mongol Shuudan Bank (Post Bank): Kholboochdyn Gudamj 4, Ulan Bator 13 (POB 874); tel. (11) 310103; fax (11) 311270; e-mail post_bank@mongol.net; internet www.postbank.mn; f. 1993; cap. 3,268.3m., res 624.5m., dep. 35,731.3m. (Dec. 2002); 100% in private ownership; Exec. Dir D. OYUUNJARGAL.

Teever Khögjliin Bank (Transport and Development Bank): Amarsanaagiin Gudamj 2, Bayanzürkh District, Ulan Bator; tel. 458617; Exec. Dir D. ENKHTUYAA; cap. 1,072m.

Trade and Development Bank of Mongolia (Khudaldaa Khögjliin Bank): Khudaldaany Gudamj 6, Ulan Bator 11; tel. 326289; fax 311618; e-mail tdbank@tdbm.mn; internet www.tdbm.mn; f. 1991; carries out Mongolbank's foreign operations; cap. 2,000.0m., res.

3,152.6m., dep. 100,455.8m. (Dec. 2001); 76% equity bought by Banca Commerciale (Lugano) and Gerald Metals (Stanford, CT), May 2002; Exec. Dir SHILEGMAAGIIN MÖNKHBAT.

Tülsh-Erchim Bank (Fuel and Power Bank): Baga Toiruu, Ulan Bator; tel. 310605; fax 310981; f. 1992; Dir M. MYAGMARSÜREN.

Ulaanbaatar Bank: Baga Toiruu 15, Ulan Bator (PO 370, Ulan Bator 46); tel. 312155; fax 311067; e-mail ubbank@magicnet.mn; f. 1998 by Capital City with assistance from the Bank of Taipei (Taiwan); cap. 4,800m.; Dir-Gen. G. BUYANBAT.

XacBank: Yörönkhii said Amaryn Gudamj, Sükhbaatar District, Ulan Bator 210646 (POB 46/721); tel. 318185; fax 328701; e-mail bank@xacbank.org; internet www.xacbank.org; f. 2001; cap. 2.6m., res 0.01m., dep. 8.6m. (2003); Exec. Dir CHULUUNY GANKHUYAG; Chair. STEPHEN MITCHELL.

Zoos Bank: 'Oi Mod' Co Bldg, Choimbolyn Gudamj 6, 2nd Khoroo, Chingeltei District, Ulan Bator (POB 314, Ulan Bator 44); tel. 312107; fax 324450; e-mail zoosbank@mongol.net; internet www .zoosbank.mn; f. 1999; cap. 2,802.2m., res 5.0m., dep. 19,748.1m. (Dec. 2002); Exec. Dir SH. CHUDANJII.

Banking Associations

Bankers' Association: Ulan Bator; Pres. D. NYAMTSEREN; Chair. of Bd S. ORGODOL.

Mongolian Bankers Association: Ulan Bator; e-mail monba@ mongolnet.mn; Pres. LUVSANVANDANGIIN BOLD; Exec. Dir JIGJIDIIN ÜNENBAT.

STOCK EXCHANGE

Stock Exchange: Sükhbaataryn Talbai 2, Ulan Bator; tel. 310501; fax 325170; e-mail mse@mongol.net; internet www.mse.mn; f. 1991; Dir DULAMSÜRENGIIN DORLIGSÜREN.

INSURANCE

Agricultural Insurance Co: Nairamdal District, Ulan Bator; f. 1992; insurance of farm stock, equipment and buildings.

Mongol Daatgal (National Insurance and Reinsurance Co): Ikh Toiruu 11, Ulan Bator 28; tel. 313647; fax 313901; e-mail daatgal@ magicnet.mn; internet www.mongoldaatgal.mn; f. 1934; sold Dec. 2003 to consortium formed by Angara-SKB and Chingis Khan Bank; Chair. and CEO B. JARGALSAIKHAN; Snr Vice-Pres. J. BAT-ORSHIKH; Gen. Man. U. BYAMBASÜREN.

Trade and Industry

GOVERNMENT AGENCIES

Labour Co-ordination Directorate: Khuvisgalchdyn Gudamj 14, Ulan Bator; tel. and fax 327906; Dir D. JANTSAN.

Mineral Resources Authority: Government Bldg 5, Barilgachdyn Talbai 13, Ulan Bator 211238; tel. and fax 310370; e-mail mram@ magicnet.mn; Dir O. CHULUUN.

Mongol Gazryn Tos: Üildverchnii Gudamj, Ulan Bator 37; tel. 61584; e-mail petromon@magicnet.mn; supervises petroleum exploration and development; Dir O. DAVAASAMBUU.

State Industry and Trade Control Service: POB 38/66, Barilgachdyn Talbai, Ulan Bator 38; tel. and fax 328049; e-mail chalkhaajavd@mongolnet.mn; f. 2000; enforces laws and regulations relating to trade and industry, services, consumer rights, and geology and mining; Dir DAMBADARJAAGIIN CHALKHAAJAV.

State Property Committee: Government Bldg 4, Ulan Bator 12; tel. 312460; fax 312798; internet odmaa@spc.gov.mn; supervision and privatization of state property; Chair. LKHANAASÜRENGIIN PÜR-EVDORJ.

DEVELOPMENT ORGANIZATIONS

Economics and Market Research Center: Government Bldg 11, J. Sambuugiin Gudamj 11, Ulan Bator 38; tel. 324258; fax 324620; e-mail emrc@mongolchamber.mm; internet www.mongolchamber .mn; Dir J. BOZKHÜÜKHEN.

Foreign Investment and Foreign Trade Agency (FIFTA): Government Bldg 1, J. Sambuugiin Gudamj 11, Ulan Bator; tel. 326040; fax 324076; e-mail fifta@investnet.mn; internet www.investnet.mn; Chair. BAASANKHÜÜGIIN GANZORIG.

Mongolian Business Development Agency: Yörönkhii said Amaryn Gudamj, Ulan Bator; CPO Box 458, Ulan Bator 13; tel. 311094; fax 311092; e-mail mbda@mongol.net; internet www .mbda-mongolia.org; f. 1994; Gen. Man. D. BAYARBAT.

CHAMBERS OF COMMERCE

Central Asian Chamber of Commerce: PO Box 470, Ulan Bator 44; tel. 38970; fax 311757; Chair. G. TÖMÖRMÖNKH.

Junior Chamber of Commerce: Youth Union Bldg, Ulan Bator; tel. 328694; Chair NATSAGDORJ.

Mongolian National Chamber of Commerce and Industry: Sambuugiin Gudamj 11, Ulan Bator 38; tel. 312501; fax 324620; e-mail chamber@mongolchamber.mn; internet www .mongolchamber.mn; f. 1960; responsible for establishing economic and trading relations, contacts between trade and industrial organizations, both at home and abroad, and for generating foreign trade; organizes commodity inspection, press information, and international exhbns and fairs at home and abroad; registration of trademarks and patents; issues certificates of origin and of quality; Sec. Gen. ENEBISHIIN OYUUNTEGSH; Chair.and CEO SAMBUUGIIN DEMBEREL.

INDUSTRIAL AND TRADE ASSOCIATIONS

Association of Private Herders' Co-operatives: POB 21/787, Ulan Bator 211121; tel. 633601; fax 325935; e-mail mongolherder@ magicnet.mn; f. 1991; Pres. R. ERDENE.

Mongolian Farmers and Flour Producers' Association: AgroPro Business Centre, 19th Khoroo, Bayangol District, Ulan Bator 24; tel. 300114; fax 362875; e-mail agropro@magicnet.mn; f. 1997; research and quality inspection services in domestic farming and flour industry; Pres. SHARAVYN GUNGAADORJ.

Mongolian Franchising Council of the Mongolian National Chamber of Commerce and Industry: Ulan Bator; tel. 327178; fax 324620; e-mail tecd@mongolchamber.mn; Pres. BAATARYN CHADRAA.

Mongolian Marketing Association: Ulan Bator; Pres. D. DAGVADORJ.

Mongolian National Mining Association: Sky Plaza Centre, Olimpiin Gudamj 14, PO Box 46/910, Ulan Bator 210646; tel. 314877; fax 314877; e-mail mongma@mobinet.mn; internet www .owc.org.mn/monnma; f. 1994; provides members of the mining sector with legal protection, and reflects their views in Government mining policy and mineral sector development; Pres. DUGARYN JARGALSAIKHAN; Exec. Dir NAMGARYN ALGAA.

Mongolian Printing Works Association: Ulan Bator; Pres. G. KHAVCHUUR.

Mongolian Wool and Cashmere Federation: Khan-Uul District, Ulan Bator; tel. 341871; fax 342814; Pres. G. YONDONSAMBUU.

EMPLOYERS' ORGANIZATIONS

Employers' and Owners' United Association: Ulan Bator; Exec. Dir. B. SEMBEEJAV.

Federation of Professional Business Women of Mongolia: Ulan Bator 20; tel. and fax 315638; e-mail mbpw@mongolnet.mn; f. 1992; provides education, training, and opportunities for women to achieve economic independence, and the running of businesses; Pres. OCHIRBATYN ZAYAA; 7,000 mems, 14 brs.

Free Labour Managers' Association: Ulan Bator; Pres. N. PÜREVDORJ.

Immovable Property (Real Estate) Business Managers' Association: Ulan Bator; Pres. J. BYAMBADORJ.

Mongolian Management Association: Ulan Bator; Chair. Exec. Council DAGVADORJIIN TSERENDORJ.

Private Business Owners' Association: Ulan Bator; Pres. T. NYAMDORJ.

Private Employers' Association: Ulan Bator; Pres. O. NATSAGDORJ.

Private Industry Owners' Association: Ulan Bator; f. 1990; with 39 mems; Pres. LUVSANBALDANGIIN NYAMSAMBUU.

UTILITIES

Electricity

TsShSG: Ulan Bator; tel. 41294; supervision of electric power network in Ulan Bator; Dir D. BASSAIKHAN.

Water

DShSG: Ulan Bator; tel. 343047; supervision of hot water district heating network in Ulan Bator; Dir SHARAVYN BAASANJAV.

USAG: Khökh Tengeriin Gudamj 5, Ulan Bator 49; tel. 455055; fax 450120; e-mail usag@magicnet.mn; supervision of water supply network in Ulan Bator; Chair. OSORYN ERDENEBAATAR.

IMPORT AND EXPORT ORGANIZATIONS

Agrotekhimpeks: Ulan Bator 32; imports agricultural machinery and implements, seed, fertilizer, veterinary medicines and irrigation equipment.

Arisimpex: Ulan Bator 52; tel. 343007; fax 343008; exports hides and skins, fur and leather goods; imports machinery, chemicals and accessories for leather, fur and shoe industries; Pres. A. TSERENBALJID.

Avtoimpeks: Sonsgolon-2, Ulan Bator (POB 37, Ulan Bator 211137); tel. 331860; fax 331383; f. 1934; privatization pending 1999; imports of vehicles and spare parts, vehicle servicing; Exec. Dir TS. TOGTMOL.

Barter and Border: Khuvisgalchdyn Örgön Chölöö, Ulan Bator 11; tel. 324848; barter and border trade operations.

Böönii Khudaldaa: Songinokhairkhan District, Ulan Bator; wholesale trader; privately-owned; Dir-Gen. OCHBADRAKHYN BALJINNYAM.

Khorshoololimpeks: Tolgoit 37, Ulan Bator (PO Box 262); tel. 332926; fax 331128; f. 1964; exports sub-standard skins, hides, wool and furs, handicrafts and finished products; imports equipment and materials for housing, and for clothing and leather goods; Dir L. ÖLZIIBUYAN.

Kompleksimport: Enkh Taivny Gudamj 7, Ulan Bator; tel. and fax 382718; f. 1963; imports consumer goods, foodstuffs, sets of equipment and turnkey projects; training of Mongolians abroad; stateowned pending privatization in 1999; cap. 3,500m. tögrög.

Makhimpeks: 4th Khoroo, Songinokhairkhan District, Ulan Bator; tel. 63247; fax 632517; e-mail makhimpex@mongol.net; f. 1946; abattoir, meat processing, canning, meat imports and exports; 51% share privatized in 1999; cap. 7,800m. tögrög; Dir H. BATTULGA.

Materialimpex: Teeverchdiin Gudamj 35, Ulan Bator 35; tel. 365125; fax 367904; e-mail miehnco@magicnet.mn; f. 1957; exports cashmere, wool products, animal skins; imports glass, roofing material, dyes, sanitary ware, metals and metalware, wallpaper, bitumen, wall and floor tiles; privatized Feb. 1999 (most shares state-owned); Gen. Dir B. ZORIG; 126 employees.

Mongoleksport Co Ltd: Government Bldg 7, 8th Floor, Erkh Chölöönii Talbai, Ulan Bator 11; tel. 329234; fax 324848; exports wool, hair, cashmere, mining products, antler, skins and hides; Dir-Gen. D. CHIMEDDAMBAA.

Mongolemimpex: Ikh Toiruu 39, Ulan Bator 28; tel. 323961; fax 323877; e-mail moemim@magicnet.mn; procurement and distribution to hospitals and pharmacies of drugs and surgical appliances; Dir-Gen. R. BYAMBAA.

Mongolimpeks: Khuvisgalchdyn Örgön Chölöö, Ulan Bator 11; tel. 326081; exports cashmere, camels' wool, hair, fur, casings, powdered blood and horn, antler, wheat gluten, alcoholic drinks, cashmere and camels' wool knitwear, blankets, copper concentrate, souvenirs, stamps and coins; imports light and mining industry machinery, scientific instruments, chemicals, pharmaceuticals and consumer goods; state-owned; Dir-Gen. DORJPALAMYN DÖKHÖMBAYAR.

Mongol Safari Co: Ulan Bator 38; tel. 360267; fax 360067; e-mail monsafari@magicnet.mn; exports hunting products; imports hunting equipment and technology; organizes hunting and trekking tours; Dir-Gen. U. BUYANDELGER.

Monnoos: POB 450, Ulan Bator 36; tel. 343201; fax 342591; e-mail monnoos@mongolnet.mn; wool trade enterprise; Dir SANJIIN BATOYUUN.

Monos Cosmetics: Sonsgolon Toiruu 5, Songinokhairkhan District 20, POB 62, Ulan Bator 211137; tel. 633257; fax 633117; e-mail info@monoscosmetics.mn; internet www.monoscosmetics.mn; f. 1990; production, export and import of cosmetics; Chair. and CEO BALDANDORJIIN ERDENEKHISHIG; 90 employees.

Monospharma Co Ltd: Chingünjavyn gudamj 9, Bayangol District 2, Ulan Bator 210526; tel. and fax 361419; e-mail monospharma@ mongol.net; f. 1990; production, export and import of medicine, medical equipment and health food; Dir-Gen. LUVSANGIIN KHÜRELBAATAR; 280 employees.

MTT (Mongol Transport Team): POB 582, Ulan Bator 21; tel. 689000; fax 684953; e-mail mtt@mttteam.mn; internet www.mttteam .mn; international freight forwarders by air, sea, rail and road; offices in Beijing, Berlin, Moscow and Prague.

NIC: Yörönkhii said Amaryn Gudamj, Ulan Bator 210646; tel. 321277; fax 327288; e-mail otgon@nicco.mn; 80% state share sold to Petrovis Feb. 2004; imports oil and oil products; Dir-Gen. P. TÜVSHINBAATAR.

Noosimpeks: Ulan Bator 52; tel. 342611; fax 343057; exports scoured sheep's wool, yarn, carpets, fabrics, blankets, mohair and felt boots; imports machinery and chemicals for wool industry.

Nüürs: Ulan Bator 21; tel. 327428; exports and imports in coal-mining field; Man. D. DÜGERJAV.

Packaging: Tolgoit, Ulan Bator; tel. 31053; exports raw materials of agricultural origin, sawn timber, consumer goods, unused spare parts and equipment, and non-ferrous scrap; imports machinery and materials for packaging industry, and consumer goods.

Raznoimpeks: 3rd Khoroo, Bayangol District, Ulan Bator 36; tel. 329465; fax 329901; f. 1933; exports wool, cashmere, hides, canned meat, powdered bone, alcoholic drinks, macaroni and confectionery; imports cotton and woollen fabrics, silk, knitwear, shoes, fresh and canned fruit, vegetables, tea, milk powder, acids, paints, safety equipment, protective clothing, printing and packaging paper; state-owned pending planned privatization of 51% share in 1999; cap. 6,100m. tögrög; Exec. Dir TS. BAT-ENKH.

Tekhnikimport: Ulan Bator; tel. 32336; imports machinery, instruments and spare parts for light, food, wood, building, power and mining industries, road-building and communications; state-owned; Dir-Gen. ERDENIIN GANBOLD.

Tushig Trade Co Ltd: Enkhtaivny Örgön Chölöö, Ulan Bator 44, PO Box 481; tel. 314062; fax 314052; e-mail d.ganbaatar@mongol.net; exports sheep and camel wool, and cashmere goods; imports machinery for small enterprises, foodstuffs and consumer goods; Dir-Gen. D. GANBAATAR.

Tuushin Co Ltd: Yörönkhii said Amaryn Gudamj 2, Ulan Bator 210620; tel. and fax 325909; e-mail tuushin@magicnet.mn; f. 1990; international freight forwarders; transport and forwarding policy and services, warehousing, customs agent; tourism; offices in Beijing, Moscow and Prague; Dir-Gen. N. ZORIGT.

CO-OPERATIVES

Central Association of Consumer Co-operatives: Ulan Bator 20; tel. and fax 329025; f. 1990; wholesale and retail trade; exports animal raw materials; imports foodstuffs and consumer goods; Chair. G. MYANGANBAYAR.

Individual Herdsmen's Co-operatives Association: Ulan Bator; Pres. R. ERDENE.

Mongolian Central Association of Savings and Credit Co-operatives: Ulan Bator; f. ; Pres. E. SANDAGDORJ.

Mongolian Co-operatives Development Centre: Ulan Bator; Dir DANZANGIIN RADNAARAGCHAA.

Mongolian Producer Co-operatives Central Association: Ulan Bator; Pres. CHOGSOMJAVYN BURIAD.

Mongolian United Association of Savings and Credit Co-operatives: Ulan Bator; Pres. TSERENDORJIIN GANKHUYAG.

National Association of Mongolian Agricultural Co-operatives: Enkh Taivny Gudamj 11, Ulan Bator; tel. and fax 358671; Pres. N. NADMID.

Union of Mongolian Production and Services Co-operatives: POB 470, Ulan Bator 210646; tel. 328446; fax 329669; f. 1990; Pres. of Supreme Council (vacant).

TRADE UNIONS

Confederation of Mongolian Trade Unions: Sükhbaataryn Talbai 3, Ulan Bator 11; tel. 327253; fax 322128; brs throughout the country; Chair. GORCHINSÜRENGIIN ADYAA; International Relations Adviser TS. NATSAGDORJ; 450,000 mems (1994).

'Khökh Mongol' (Blue Mongolia) Free Trade Unions: Ulan Bator; f. 1991 by Mongolian Democratic Union; Leader SH. TÖMÖR-BAATAR.

United Association of Free Trade Unions: f. 1990; Pres. SH. DORJPAGMA.

Transport

RAILWAYS

In 1999 the Mongolian Railway had a total track length of 1,815 km. In 1990 it carried 2.6m. passengers and 14.5m. tons of freight (about 70% of total freight traffic). However, traffic by rail later declined, owing to fuel shortages; in 1991 rail freight carriage was 10.3m. tons, falling to 8.6m. tons in 1992. In 2002 the railway carried 4.0m. passengers, and 11.6m. tons of freight (about 86% of total freight traffic was transported by rail).

Ulan Bator Railway: POB 376, Ulan Bator 13; tel. 944401; fax 328360; e-mail slc-mr@magicnet.mn; internet www.mtz.mn; f. 1949; joint-stock co with Russian Federation; Dir RADNAABAZARYN RAASH; First Dep. Dir N. BATMÖNKH.

External Lines: from the Russian frontier at Naushki/Sükhbaatar (connecting with the Trans-Siberian Railway) to Ulan Bator and on to the Chinese frontier at Zamyn-Üüd/Erenhot, connecting with Beijing (total length 1,110 km).

Branches: from Darkhan to Sharyn Gol coalfield (length 63 km); branch from Salkhit near Darkhan, westwards to Erdenet (Erdenet-iin-ovoo open-cast copper mine) in Bulgan Province (164 km); from Bagakhangai to Baganuur coal-mine, south-east of Ulan Bator (96 km); from Khar Airag to Bor-Öndör fluorspar mines (60 km); from Sainshand to Züünbayan oilfield (63 km).

Eastern Railway, linking Mongolia with the Trans-Siberian and Chita via Borzya; from the Russian frontier at Solovyevsk to Choibalsan (238 km), with branch from Chingis Dalan to Mardai uranium mine near Dashbalbar (110 km).

IFFC (International Freight-forwarding Centre)): 2/F Ulan Bator Railway Building, Ulan Bator, CPO Box 376; tel. 312509; fax 313165; e-mail iffc@magicnet.mn; international freight forwarding.

Mongoltrans: Khan-Uul District, Ulan Bator; POB 373, Ulan Bator 211121; tel. 312281; fax 320185; e-mail montrans@magicnet.mn; internet www.magicnet.mn/montrans; rail freight forwarding; offices in Beijing and Moscow; Dir-Gen. B. MYAGMAR.

ROADS

Main roads link Ulan Bator with the Chinese frontier at Zamyn üüd/Erenhot and with the Russian frontier at Altanbulag/Kyakhta. A road from Chita in Russia crosses the frontier in the east at Mangut/Onon (Ölzii) and branches for Choibalsan and Öndörkhaan. In the west and north-west, roads from Biisk and Irkutsk in Russia go to Tsagaannuur, Bayan-Ölgii aimag, and Khankh, on Lake Khövsgöl, respectively. The total length of the road network was 49,250 km in 2003, of which asphalted roads comprised 5,632 km and gravel and improved earth roads comprised 1,801 km. The first section of a hard-surfaced road between Ulan Bator and Bay-ankhongor was completed in 1975. The road from Darkhan to Erdenet was also to be surfaced. Mongolia divides its road system into state-grade and country-grade roads. State-grade roads run from Ulan Bator to provincial centres and from provincial centres to the border. Country-grade roads account for the remaining 41,817 km, but they are mostly rough cross-country tracks.

To mark the millennium, the Government decided to construct a new east–west road, linking the Chinese and Russian border regions via Ölgii, Lake Khar Us, Zavkhan and Arkhangai provinces, Dashin-chilen, Lün, Ulan Bator, Nalaikh, Baganuur, Öndörkhaan and Sümber. Construction was expected to take about 10 years, but because of the cost, the road was not expected to be surfaced for the whole length.

According to a vehicle census reported in December 2000, Mongolia had 81,693 motor vehicles, including 24,671 goods vehicles, 1,683 tankers, 2,740 specialized vehicles (such as ambulances and fire engines), 8,548 buses and trolleybuses, and 44,051 cars. Of these vehicles, 57,814 were privately owned.

There are bus services in Ulan Bator and other large towns, and road haulage services throughout the country on the basis of motor transport depots, mostly situated in provincial centres. However, in some years services have been truncated, owing to fuel shortages.

CIVIL AVIATION

Civil aviation in Mongolia, including the provision of air traffic control and airport management, is the responsibility of the Civil Aviation Directorate of the Ministry of Infrastructure. It supervises the Mongolian national airline (MIAT) and smaller operators such as Khangarid and Tengeriin Ulaach, which operate local flights. There are scheduled services to Ulan Bator (Buyant-Ukhaa) by Aeroflot (Russia) and Air China.

Director-General of Civil Aviation: MANJIIN DAGVA.

Aero Mongolia: Ulan Bator; operates scheduled flights to four *aimag* centres.

Blue Sky Aviation: POB 932, Ulan Bator 13; tel. 312085; fax 322857; e-mail bsa@whizzmail.com; jt venture of Mission Aviation Fellowship and Exodus International; operates charter flights and medical emergency services; Dir PAAVO KILPI; Operations Man. JAV-KHLANTÖGSIIN GANBAATAR.

Khangarid: Room 210, MPRP Bldg, Baga Toiruu 37/1, Ulan Bator; tel. 379935; fax 379973; domestic and international passenger and freight services; Dir L. SERGELEN.

Mongolian Civil Air Transport (MIAT): Buyant-Ukhaa, Ulan Bator; tel. 379935; fax 379919; internet www.miat.com; f. 1956; operated by Air Consulting International (Republic of Ireland) as part of preparations for privatization; scheduled services to Moscow, Irkutsk, Beijing, Seoul, Osaka, Berlin, Höhhot, and to some Mongolian provincial centres; in 2003 MIAT carried some 252,000 passengers and 2,200 tons of freight, and operated 10 aircraft on scheduled services; Dir LUTYN SANDAG.

Tengeriin Ulaach Shine: Buyant-Ukhaa 34-17, Khan-Uul District, Ulan Bator; tel. 983043; fax 379765; internal transport for tourists and businesspeople; Dir L. TÖMÖR.

Tourism

A foreign tourist service bureau was established in 1954, but tourism is not very developed. There are 12 hotels for foreign tourists in Ulan Bator, with some 1,500 beds, and the outlying tourist centres (Terelj, South Gobi, Öndör-Dov and Khujirt) have basic facilities. The country's main attractions are its scenery, wildlife and historical relics. There were 192,051 foreign visitors to Mongolia in 2001, of whom 31,978 had tourist visas. Tourist receipts totalled US $28m.

in 1999. Tourism profits in 2002 amounted to US $102.9m., or 10.2% of GDP.

Juulchin Tourism Corporation of Mongolia: Chingisiin Khaany Örgön Chölöö 5B, Ulan Bator 210543; tel. 328428; fax 320246; e-mail juulchin@Mongol.net; internet www.mongoljuulchin.mn; f. 1954; offices in Berlin, New Jersey, Beijing, Tokyo, Osaka and Seoul; tours, trekking, safaris, jeep tours, expeditions; Exec. Dir S. NERGÜI.

Mongolian Tourism Association: Rm 318, Trade Union Building, Sükhbaataryn Talbai 11, Ulan Bator; tel. (11) 327820; e-mail info@travelmongolia.org; internet www.travelmongolia.org; Pres. TSEVELMAA BAYARSAIKHAN.

Mongolian Tourism Board: Government Bldg 14, Sambuugiin Gudamj 11, Ulan Bator 38; tel. (11) 311102; fax (11) 318492; e-mail mtb@magicnet.mn; internet www.mongoliatourism.gov.mn.

MOROCCO

Introductory Survey

Location, Climate, Language, Religion, Flag, Capital

The Kingdom of Morocco is situated in the extreme north-west of Africa. It has a long coastline on the shores of the Atlantic Ocean and, east of the Strait of Gibraltar, on the Mediterranean Sea, facing southern Spain. Morocco's eastern frontier is with Algeria, while to the south lies the disputed territory of Western Sahara (under Moroccan occupation), which has a lengthy Atlantic coastline and borders Mauritania to the east and south. Morocco's climate is semi-tropical. It is warm and sunny on the coast, while the plains of the interior are intensely hot in summer. Average temperatures are 27°C (81°F) in summer and 7°C (45°F) in winter for Rabat, and 38°C (101°F) and 4°C (40°F) respectively for Marrakesh. The rainy season in the north is from November to April. The official language is Arabic, but a large minority speak Berber. Spanish is widely spoken in the northern regions, and French in the rest of Morocco. The established religion is Islam, and most of the country's inhabitants are Muslims. There are small minorities of Christians and Jews. The national flag (proportions 2 by 3) is red, with a green pentagram (intersecting lines in the form of a five-pointed star), known as 'Solomon's Seal', in the centre. The capital is Rabat.

Recent History

In 1912, under the terms of the Treaty of Fez, most of Morocco became a French protectorate, while a smaller Spanish protectorate was instituted in the north and far south of the country. Spain also retained control of Spanish Sahara (now Western Sahara), and Tangier became an international zone in 1923. A nationalist movement developed in Morocco during the 1930s and 1940s, led by the Istiqlal (Independence) grouping, and on 2 March 1956 the French protectorate achieved independence as the Sultanate of Morocco. Sultan Muhammad V, who had reigned since 1927 (although he had been temporarily removed from office by the French authorities between 1953 and 1955), became the first Head of State. The northern zone of the Spanish protectorate joined the new state in April 1956, and Tangier's international status was abolished in October. The southern zone of the Spanish protectorate was ceded to Morocco in 1958, but no agreement was reached on the enclaves of Ceuta and Melilla, in the north, the Ifni region in the south, or the Saharan territories to the south of Morocco, which all remained under Spanish control. The Sultan was restyled King of Morocco in August 1957, and became Prime Minister in May 1960. He died in February 1961, and was succeeded by his son, Moulay Hassan, who took the title of Hassan II.

Elections to Morocco's first House of Representatives took place in May 1963, and six months later King Hassan relinquished the post of Prime Minister. In June 1965, however, increasing political fragmentation prompted Hassan to declare a 'state of exception', and to resume full legislative and executive powers. The emergency provisions remained in force until July 1970, when a new Constitution was approved. Elections in the following month resulted in a pro-Government majority in the new Chamber of Representatives.

In July 1971 an attempted *coup d'état* was suppressed by forces loyal to the King. Among those subsequently arrested were numerous members of the left-wing Union nationale des forces populaires (UNFP), five of whom were sentenced to death. Although a revised Constitution was approved in March 1972 by popular referendum, a general election did not take place until June 1977. Two-thirds of the deputies in the Chamber of Representatives were directly elected, the remainder being elected by local government councils, professional associations and labour organizations. Supporters of the King's policies won a majority of seats in the new legislature. A Government of national unity was formed, including opposition representatives from Istiqlal and the Mouvement populaire (MP) in addition to the pro-monarchist independents.

In October 1981, when it was announced that the term of office of the Chamber of Representatives was to be extended from four to six years, all 14 deputies belonging to the Union socialiste des forces populaires (USFP) withdrew from the assembly. Elections to the legislature were postponed and an interim Government of national unity was appointed, headed by Muhammad Karim Lamrani (Prime Minister in 1971–72). The new Government included members of the six main political parties: Istiqlal, the MP, the Parti national démocrate (PND), the Rassemblement national des indépendants (RNI), the Union constitutionnelle (UC) and the USFP. The postponed legislative elections took place in September and October 1984. Despite significant gains by the USFP, the Chamber of Representatives was again dominated by the centre-right parties. A new Cabinet, appointed in April 1985, included members of the MP, the PND, the RNI and the UC. Lamrani resigned in September 1986, on grounds of ill health, and was replaced by Az ad-Dine Laraki (hitherto Deputy Prime Minister and Minister of National Education).

In March 1992 King Hassan announced that the Constitution was to be revised and submitted for approval in a national referendum, in preparation for legislative elections (which had been postponed since 1990, pending settlement of the Western Sahara dispute). The King indicated in July that the legislative elections would take place in November, and that voting would be extended to include Western Sahara—irrespective of the UN's progress in organizing a referendum on the territory's status (see below). In August the King dissolved the Government, and named Lamrani as Prime Minister in an interim, non-partisan Government. According to official results, the revised Constitution was overwhelmingly endorsed by 99.96% of those who voted (97.29% of the electorate) in the national referendum, which was held in September; approval was officially reported to be unanimous in major cities and in three of the four provinces of Western Sahara. Under the terms of the new Constitution, the King would retain strong executive powers, including the right to appoint the Prime Minister, although the nomination of government members would henceforth be the prerogative of the premier. The Government would be required to reflect the composition of the Chamber of Representatives, and was obliged to submit its legislative programme for the Chamber's approval; new legislation would automatically be promulgated one month after having been endorsed by parliament, regardless of whether royal assent had been received. Provision was also made for the establishment of a Constitutional Council and of an Economic and Social Council, and guarantees of human rights were enshrined in the document.

Legislative elections eventually took place on 25 June 1993. Parties of the Bloc démocratique—grouping Istiqlal, the USFP, the Parti du progrès et du socialisme (PPS), the Organisation de l'action démocratique et populaire (OADP) and the UNFP—won a combined total of 99 of the 222 directly elective seats in the enlarged chamber. (Within the Bloc, the USFP won 48 seats and Istiqlal 43.) The MP won 33 seats, the RNI 28 and the UC 27. The indirect election (by an electoral college) of the remaining 111 members of the Chamber, which followed on 17 September, was less favourable to the Bloc démocratique, which won only 21 further seats. Of the 333 seats in the Chamber, the USFP now controlled 56, the UC 54, Istiqlal 52, the MP 51, and the RNI 41. The USFP and Istiqlal protested against irregularities in the procedure of the electoral college voting, and demanded the annulment of the indirect election results. In November the King reappointed Lamrani as premier. The new Government comprised technocrats and independents, and did not include any representatives of the parties that had contested the legislative elections. (By-elections took place in April 1994 in 14 constituencies—in all but one of which the Constitutional Council had annulled results of the previous year's legislative elections.)

In December 1993 the Conseil Consultatif des Droits de l'Homme (CCDH), established by the King in April 1990, substantiated allegations made by human rights organizations of the 'disappearance' and detention of political activists; however, it denied the existence of secret detention centres. King Hassan granted an amnesty for 424 (mostly political) prisoners in July 1994: among those released were Morocco's longest serving political detainee and about 100 members of the proscribed Islamist movement Al Adl wa-'l Ihsan (Justice and Charity).

In May 1994 Hassan replaced Lamrani with Abd al-Latif Filali, hitherto Minister of State for Foreign Affairs and Co-operation. Although the new Prime Minister held consultations with the political groupings represented in parliament, the composition of the new Government (in which he retained the foreign affairs portfolio) was effectively unchanged. In July the King appealed to all political parties to participate in a government of national unity, and in October he announced his intention to select a premier from the ranks of the opposition. However, negotiations on the formation of a coalition government failed, apparently owing to the Bloc démocratique's refusal to join an administration in which Driss Basri (a long-serving government member and close associate of the King) remained as Minister of the Interior and Information, and in January 1995 Hassan instructed Filali to form a new cabinet. The interior and information portfolios, were, notably, separated in the new Government: Basri remained Minister of the Interior, while Driss Alaoui M'Daghri, regarded as a 'liberal' technocrat, took responsibility for the restyled Ministry of Communications.

Muhammad Basri, a prominent opposition figure (sentenced to death *in absentia* in 1974) and founder member of both the UNFP and the USFP, returned to Morocco from France in June 1995, after 28 years in exile. It was widely believed that his rehabilitation had been precipitated by the royal amnesty of July 1994 and by the return to Morocco (also from France) in May 1995 of the First Secretary of the USFP, Abd ar-Rahman el-Youssoufi, both of which seemed to indicate a greater level of political tolerance on the part of the Moroccan authorities. In December Abd as-Salam Yassin, the leader of Al Adl wa-'l Ihsan, was briefly released after six years of house arrest, but restrictions on his movement were reinstated after Yassin criticized the Government. Despite the King's assertion that there were no longer any political detainees in Morocco, a report published by the Association marocaine des droits de l'homme (AMDH) in February 1996 claimed that 58 political prisoners (primarily radical Islamists, supporters of independence for Western Sahara and left-wing activists) remained in detention.

In August 1996 the King presented further constitutional amendments, including the creation of an indirectly elected second parliamentary assembly, the Chamber of Advisers, and the introduction of direct elections for all members of the Chamber of Representatives. Most political parties supported the reforms; however, an appeal by the OADP leadership for a boycott of a planned referendum on the amendments led to a split in the party and the subsequent creation of the Parti socialiste démocratique (PSD). According to official results, 83.0% of the electorate participated in the referendum, held in September, with the reforms being approved by 99.6% of voters. Legislation regarding the new bicameral parliament was promulgated in August 1997: the Chamber of Representatives was to comprise 325 members, directly elected for a five-year term; the 270 members of the Chamber of Advisers would be indirectly elected, for a nine-year term, by local councils (which would chose 162 members), chambers of commerce (81) and trade unions (27). Earlier that month a new Cabinet had been named, following the resignation, at the King's behest, of numerous ministers with formal party affiliation in preparation for the forthcoming legislative elections.

At elections to the Chamber of Representatives, held on 14 November 1997, the Bloc démocratique won a combined total of 102 seats (of which the USFP took 57 and Istiqlal 32); the centre-right Entente nationale took 100 (50 secured by the UC, 40 by the MP), and centrist parties 97 (including 46 obtained by the RNI). The Mouvement populaire constitutionnel et démocratique (MPCD), which earlier in the year had formally absorbed members of the Islamist Al Islah wa Attajdid, won nine seats, securing parliamentary representation for the first time. (In October 1998 the MPCD changed its name to the Parti de la justice et du développement—PJD.) According to official results, 58.3% of the eligible electorate participated in the poll. At indirect elections to the Chamber of Advisers, which followed on 5 December, centrist parties won 90 of the seats (42 secured by the RNI, 33 by the Mouvement démocratique et social), the Entente nationale 76 (28 obtained by the UC, 27 by the MP) and the Bloc démocratique 44 (21 won by Istiqlal). In February 1998 the King appointed el-Youssoufi as the new Prime Minister, in an apparent attempt to appease opposition parties dissatisfied with the outcome of the legislative elections. This was the first time since independence that a socialist had been appointed to

the Moroccan premiership. In March a new Cabinet was formed, including members of the USFP, the RNI, Istiqlal, the PPS, the Mouvement nationale populaire (MNP), the Front des forces démocratiques and the PSD.

King Hassan died on 23 July 1999, after several years of ill health. His eldest son, Crown Prince Sidi Muhammad, succeeded as King Muhammad VI. At the end of July the new King decreed an amnesty whereby some 8,000 prisoners were freed and more than 38,000 had their sentences reduced. In August the King ordered the creation within the CCDH of an independent commission to determine levels of compensation for families of missing people and for those subjected to arbitrary detention. In April the CCDH had announced that it had been agreed to compensate the families of 112 people who were now officially acknowledged as having 'disappeared' between 1960 and 1990. Independent Moroccan human rights organizations asserted that the number of missing people amounted to almost 600.

In September 1999 King Muhammad approved the return to Morocco of Abraham Serfaty, a left-wing dissident who had been deported to France in 1991; Serfaty had been granted a passport by the el-Youssoufi administration in 1998, but his return had not been authorized. The family of former opposition leader Mehdi Ben Barka, who had been abducted and subsequently murdered in Paris, France, in 1965, was also permitted to return to Morocco in November. In January 2000 the location was apparently revealed of Ben Barka's burial site, beneath the Courcouronnes mosque in Paris—which was constructed in the mid-1980s with finance from King Hassan II. The French Prime Minister, Lionel Jospin, announced an end to the ban on access to archives where documents relating to the abduction and murder were kept, and later that month a French judge re-opened an inquiry into the disappearance of four men who had been convicted *in absentia* in 1967 of the kidnap of Ben Barka and were believed to have fled to Morocco.

Meanwhile, in November 1999 King Muhammad dismissed the long-serving Minister of State for the Interior, Driss Basri. Basri's removal from office, apparently in response to the violent suppression of protests in Western Sahara in September (see below) was interpreted as a particularly important step towards the modernization of Moroccan society. The new Minister of the Interior, Ahmed Midaoui (a former Director of National Security), immediately pledged to work towards the strengthening of democracy and the reconciliation of the administration and the people of Morocco. Victims of repression and their families, together with left wing political parties and non-governmental organizations, subsequently formed a 'Justice and Trust' organization, which aimed to investigate human rights abuses in Morocco since independence. In April 2000 the Government commenced payments, reportedly totalling 40m. dirhams, in respect of the cases of an initial 40 victims of arbitrary detention, from the fund established in the previous year. Abd as-Salam Yassin was released from house arrest in May.

In early 2000, at the behest of the King, the Government introduced a programme of social reforms, a principal outcome of which would be vastly to improve the social status and legal rights of Moroccan women. Under the 'national action plan', the minimum age of marriage for a woman was to be raised from 15 to 18, polygamy would only be allowed with the permission of the first wife, and women would have equal judicial rights to divorce and to receive a fair division of marital assets. The plan provoked outrage among Islamists, who claimed it would lead to the disintegration of the traditional family and the destruction of Islamic values.

In September 2000 King Muhammad effected a cabinet reorganization, reducing the number of ministerial portfolios from 43 to 33. Notably, the leader of Istiqlal, Abbas el-Fassi, was appointed Minister of Social Development, Solidarity, Employment and Vocational Training. Shortly afterwards indirect elections were held to renew one-third of the seats in the Chamber of Advisers. The RNI won 14 of the 90 seats available, the MNP 12 and the PND 10, with the remaining 54 seats divided among smaller parties.

In March 2001 King Muhammad announced the establishment of a royal commission to revise the country's laws on personal rights and responsibilities; the commission was to be chaired by the First President of the Supreme Court, Driss Dahak, and included leading Islamic scholars and jurists. Meanwhile, the King continued to demonstrate a commitment to greater rights for Moroccan women by appointing women to posts of royal advisers, ambassadors and other senior public offices. In July King Muhammad announced his intention to create a royal institute charged with preserving the language and culture of the country's Berber population, which would also work towards the integration of the Berber language into the education system; the institute was duly established in October. In September Muhammad appointed Driss Jettou, a former Minister of Finance and Industry, as Minister of the Interior; Ahmed Midaoui became an adviser to the King.

In June 2001 the Moroccan authorities granted Jean-Baptiste Parlos, the French judge leading the inquiry into the Ben Barka affair (see above), permission to visit Morocco as part of his investigation. Later that month Ahmed Boukhari, a former member of the Moroccan special services, alleged in an article published in *Le Journal* and in the French daily *Le Monde* that Ben Barka had been kidnapped in Paris by French police-officers in the employ of the Moroccan secret service and taken to a chateau in the south of the city where he died after being tortured by Morocco's then Minister of the Interior, Gen. Muhammad Oufkir; Ben Barka's body was subsequently smuggled out of France in a Moroccan military aircraft and was dissolved in a tank of acid at a torture and detention centre in Rabat. According to Boukhari the bodies of many opponents of King Hassan's regime had been disposed of in this way during the 1960s. The USFP's political bureau demanded that legal proceedings be commenced against Boukhari and the other special services operatives named in his confession, while the Organisation marocaine des droits de l'homme (OMDH) and the AMDH demanded that the Moroccan Government establish an inquiry into the affair. In mid-July 2001 Boukhari received a summons to appear before the French investigation into Ben Barka's disappearance; however, the Moroccan authorities refused to grant Boukhari a passport, and in the following month Boukhari was arrested on charges of cashing cheques for which he had insufficient funds. Boukhari's detention was con-demned by human rights organizations, which claimed that the Moroccan Government was attempting to prevent Boukhari from testifying at the Parlos inquiry. In late August Boukhari was sentenced to one year's imprisonment, although in mid-October the sentence was reduced on appeal to three months and he was released the following month. Three former Moroccan secret service agents cited in Boukhari's revelations announced their intention to sue him for defamation, and in mid-December, after he was found guilty of the charges by a court in Casablanca, he was again imprisoned for three months and ordered to pay compensation of 300,000 dirhams. In December 2002 the Moroccan authorities announced that they would co-operate fully with the French investigation into the Ben Barka affair, and in January 2003 a French judge travelled to Rabat where he interviewed Boukhari about the disappear-ance of Ben Barka.

In late January 2002 el-Youssoufi stated that he would stand down as Prime Minister after the legislative elections scheduled for September, but would remain First Secretary of the USFP. In March the Government agreed a number of changes to the electoral system, including the abandonment of the simple majority system in favour of proportional representation. The Government insisted that the new system would reduce fraudu-lent practices and increase public confidence in the electoral process; at least 10% of the 325 seats in the lower house were to be reserved for women. The general election took place on 27 September 2002. According to official figures, the USFP won the largest number of seats, although its representation in the Chamber of Representatives was reduced from 57 to 50 seats. Istiqlal increased its parliamentary representation to 48 mem-bers, while the PJD took 42 seats, the RNI 41, the MP 27, the MNP 18 and the UC 16. The rate of voter participation was recorded at just 51.6% of the electorate. In early October King Muhammad appointed Jettou as the new Prime Minister, and a new Government was announced the following month. Despite securing the third highest number of seats in the Chamber of Representatives, the PJD was not allocated any ministerial portfolios. The new Cabinet comprised members of the USFD, Istiqlal, the RNI, the MNP, the MP and the PPS, as well as a number of non-affiliated technocrats—one of whom, Al Mus-tapha Sahel, replaced Jettou as Minister of the Interior. Three women were appointed to the Government.

In early May 2003 King Muhammad marked the occasion of the birth of a son and heir to the throne, Prince Moulay Hassan, by ordering the release of an estimated 9,000 prisoners and reducing the gaol terms of a further 38,000. Later that month Ali Lamrabet, the editor of two satirical magazines, was sentenced to four years' imprisonment for 'insulting the King' and 'under-mining the monarchy'. Lamrabet had commenced a hunger strike earlier in May, and his case had been closely followed by a number of international human rights groups. Lamrabet's sentence was subsequently commuted, on appeal, to a term of three years and in late June he ended his hunger strike. In January 2004 Lamrabet was granted a royal pardon and released from prison.

Meanwhile, in mid-May 2003 45 people died and more than 100 others were injured in a series of suicide bomb attacks in central Casablanca, which targeted the Belgian consulate, a Spanish restaurant and a Jewish cultural centre. Among those killed were reported to be 12 suicide bombers, and two other suspected attackers were detained by the security forces along with some 30 others thought to have been involved in the bombings. The Moroccan authorities believed that the bombers were linked to a small Moroccan-based militant Islamist group, al-Assirat al-Moustaquim (Righteous Path), but that the attacks had been orchestrated by an international terrorist network operating in Europe, possibly the al-Qa'ida (Base) organization of the fugitive Saudi Arabian-born Islamist Osama bin Laden. In late May the suspected co-ordinator of the attacks, who had been arrested in Fez, died in police custody as a result of ill health. Days earlier Jettou had led an anti-terrorism march through Casablanca attended by an estimated 1m. people, and later in May stricter anti-terrorism measures were approved by the legislature, which broadened the definition of terrorism to 'any premeditated act, by an individual or a group, that aims to breach public order through terror and violence', and increased the number of offences punishable by the death sentence.

In mid-July 2003 10 of the alleged 31 members of the radical Islamist group Salafia Jihadia, who had been arrested during police operations against Islamist networks in mid-2002, were sentenced to death by a court in Casablanca, having been convicted of murder and attempted murder. Eight of the accused received sentences of life imprisonment, and the remainder given custodial terms of 10–20 years. Salafia Jihadia was widely suspected of being involved in the suicide bomb attacks in Casablanca in May 2003. Later in July it was announced that more than 700 people would be tried in connection with the bomb attacks; 52 defendants subsequently appeared before Casablanca's criminal court, charged with 'forming a criminal band, acting against the security of the state, sabotage and homicide'. In mid-August four men, including the two suspected surviving suicide bombers, received the death sentence for their roles in the violence; 39 others were sentenced to life imprison-ment for plotting further attacks in Essaouira, Agadir and Marrakesh. Some 50 Islamists received various prison sen-tences during September for their alleged roles in attempting to carry out further bomb attacks within Morocco.

Despite the clampdown on Islamist activity in the wake of the Casablanca bombings, King Muhammad continued to pursue his policies of reform and modernization of Moroccan society. In June 2003 it was announced that teaching of the Berber lan-guage in primary schools would commence in the 2003/04 aca-demic year, and that 1,000 Berber teachers had been appointed. It was planned eventually to extend the subject to all levels of the school system. In October King Muhammad announced major revisions to the *mudawana* (family code), which he claimed would promote female equality and protect children's rights. The reforms (as originally outlined in 2000) would raise the legal age of marriage for women from 15 to 18 and simplify the procedure for women seeking a divorce from their husband. Although polygamy was not to be outlawed under the new legislation, women would be able to prevent their husbands from taking a second wife and would also be provided with equal authority and property rights within the marriage. In January 2004 the changes to the *mudawana* were approved by the legislature.

Following the cession of the Spanish enclave of Ifni to Morocco in 1969, political opinion in Morocco was united in opposing the continued occupation by Spain of areas considered to be histor-ically parts of Moroccan territory: namely Spanish Sahara and Spanish North Africa (q.v.)—a number of small enclaves on Morocco's Mediterranean coast. A campaign to annex Spanish Sahara, initiated in 1974, received active support from all Moroccan political parties. In October 1975 King Hassan ordered a 'green march' by more than 300,000 unarmed Moroc-cans to occupy the territory. The marchers were stopped by the Spanish authorities when they had barely crossed the border, but in November Spain agreed to cede the territory to Morocco and Mauritania, to be apportioned equally between them. Spain formally relinquished sovereignty of Spanish Sahara in February 1976. Moroccan troops moved into the territory to confront a guerrilla uprising led by the Frente Popular para la Liberación de Saguia el-Hamra y Río de Oro (the Polisario Front), a national liberation movement supported by Algeria and (later) Libya which aimed to achieve an independent Western Saharan state. On 27 February the Polisario Front declared the 'Sahrawi Arab Democratic Republic' (SADR), and shortly afterwards established a 'Government-in-exile' in Algeria. In protest, Morocco severed diplomatic relations with Algeria.

Moroccan troops inflicted heavy casualties on the insurgents, and ensured the security of Western Sahara's main population centres, but they failed to prevent constant infiltration, harassment and sabotage by Polisario forces. Moreover, Polisario had considerable success against Mauritanian troops, and in August 1979 Mauritania renounced its claim to Saharan territory and signed a peace treaty with the Polisario Front. Morocco immediately asserted its claim to the whole of Western Sahara and annexed the region.

In July 1980 the SADR applied to join the Organization of African Unity (OAU—now African Union, see p. 137) as a sovereign state. Although 26 of the 50 members then recognized the Polisario Front as the rightful government of Western Sahara, Morocco insisted that a two-thirds' majority was needed to confer membership. Morocco rejected an OAU proposal for a cease-fire and a referendum on the territory, and in 1981 heavy fighting resumed in the region. The SADR was accepted as the OAU's 51st member in early 1982, but a threat by 18 members to leave the organization in protest necessitated a compromise whereby the SADR, while remaining a member, agreed not to attend OAU meetings. In late 1984 an SADR delegation did attend a summit meeting of the OAU with little opposition from other states, causing Morocco to resign from the organization. Meanwhile, fighting continued in Western Sahara; decisive victories for Polisario proved impossible, however, as Morocco constructed a 2,500-km defensive wall of sand, equipped with electronic detectors, to surround Western Sahara.

In October 1985 Morocco announced a unilateral cease-fire in Western Sahara, and invited the UN to supervise a referendum to be held there the following January. A series of indirect talks between the two sides, arranged by the UN and the OAU in 1986–87, failed to achieve a solution, and in January 1988 Polisario forces renewed their offensive against Moroccan positions in Western Sahara. In August, however, it was announced that the Polisario Front and Morocco had provisionally accepted a peace plan proposed by the UN Secretary-General, Javier Pérez de Cuéllar, which envisaged the conclusion of a formal cease-fire, a reduction in Moroccan military forces in Western Sahara and the withdrawal of Polisario forces to their bases, to be followed by a referendum on self-determination in Western Sahara. A list of eligible voters was to be based on the Spanish census of 1974. Implementation of the peace process was impeded by a renewed Polisario offensive in September 1988, and Muhammad Abd al-Aziz, President of the SADR, reiterated that the peace plan was accepted in principle only and that direct negotiations with Morocco were still necessary. A meeting in Marrakesh in January 1989 between King Hassan and officials of the Polisario Front and the SADR—the first direct contact for 13 years—was apparently limited to exchanges of goodwill, but was followed, in February, by the announcement of a unilateral cease-fire by Polisario. A further meeting was postponed by Hassan, who in September rejected the possibility of official negotiations with the SADR; later that month Polisario renewed its military attacks on Moroccan positions.

UN Security Council Resolution No. 690 of April 1991 established a peace-keeping force, the UN Mission for the Referendum in Western Sahara (MINURSO, see p. 69), which was to implement the 1988 plan for a referendum on self-determination. In June 1991 Polisario agreed to a formal cease-fire, with effect from 6 September, from which date the 2,000-strong MINURSO delegation would undertake its duties in the region. The cease-fire came into effect as scheduled, and the MINURSO deployment began. Reports at this time suggested that some 30,000 people had entered Western Sahara from Morocco, prompting claims that the Moroccan authorities were attempting to alter the region's demography in advance of the referendum. It was also reported that more than 170,000 Sahrawi who had fled the region since 1976 were being repatriated in order that they might participate in the referendum. By

November 1991 only 200 MINURSO personnel had been deployed in Western Sahara, and the peace process was undermined further by Morocco's failure to withdraw any of its forces from the region (under the terms of the cease-fire agreement, Morocco was to have withdrawn one-half of its 130,000 troops from Western Sahara by mid-September). In May 1992 Pérez de Cuéllar's successor as UN Secretary-General, Dr Boutros Boutros-Ghali, announced that Morocco and Polisario representatives were to begin indirect talks under his auspices. In the same month, however, Morocco appeared to prejudge the result of the proposed referendum by including the population of Western Sahara in the voting lists for its own regional and local elections. In June the SADR Government, which by this time was recognized by 75 countries, appealed to the international community and the UN to condemn alleged Moroccan violations of the cease-fire and to exert pressure for the implementation of the UN peace plan. UN-sponsored negotiations in the USA in September failed to formulate acceptable criteria for the drafting of lists of eligible voters at an eventual referendum.

In March 1993 the UN Security Council approved plans for the holding of the referendum on Western Sahara by the end of the year. In July the first direct negotiations took place between the Moroccan Government and Polisario, although little progress was achieved. In March 1994 Boutros-Ghali submitted a report to the UN Security Council detailing possible procedures for overcoming the impasse on the Western Saharan issue, including the effective withdrawal of the UN from the peace process. (It had been reported in September 1993 that only 360 of the proposed 2,000 UN military personnel were in place.) The Security Council subsequently agreed to a continuation of negotiations for a further three months, and undertook to review the future of MINURSO if a referendum was not organized before the end of the year. In April Polisario accepted the UN programme for the registration of voters. However, the work of a UN voter identification commission, which had been due to commence in June, was delayed by the Moroccan Government's objection to the inclusion of OAU observers in the process.

In May 1995 the Moroccan security forces arrested more than 100 pro-independence Sahrawi who were demonstrating in the Western Sahara capital, el-Aaiún; in the following month a military court sentenced eight student demonstrators to terms of imprisonment ranging from 15 to 20 years, although the sentences were reduced in July to one year's custody. Polisario had, in the meantime, withdrawn from the voter identification process, in protest at the severity of the sentences and at alleged Moroccan violations of the cease-fire. In September the SADR announced the formation of a new 14-member Government, headed by Mahfoud Ali Beïba, and in October the first elected Sahrawi National Assembly was inaugurated in a refugee camp in Tindouf, Algeria.

The UN Security Council voted periodically to extend MINURSO's mandate on a short-term basis, noting in January 1996 that it was improbable that the referendum would take place during that year. In May the Security Council voted to suspend the registration of voters in Western Sahara until 'convincing proof' was offered by the Moroccan Government and the Sahrawi leadership that they would not further obstruct preparations for the referendum. The mandate of MINURSO was extended, but its personnel was to be reduced by 20%.

In April 1996 Amnesty International, a prominent human rights organization, issued a report asserting that Moroccan security forces in Western Sahara were consistently violating human rights. The report suggested that the protection of human rights should become the priority of MINURSO, while it also expressed concern at the abuse of human rights in refugee camps run by Polisario in southern Algeria. (In November 1995 Polisario had released 186 Moroccan prisoners of war; Polisario claimed that they were released originally in 1989, but were refused entry by Morocco on the grounds that no such detainees existed.) In October 1996 the Moroccan authorities released 66 Sahrawi, some of whom had been held in detention since 1977. According to the International Committee of the Red Cross, some 1,920 Moroccans remained incarcerated by the Polisario Front.

In March 1997 the new UN Secretary-General, Kofi Annan, appointed James Baker (a former US Secretary of State) as his Personal Envoy to Western Sahara. Baker visited the region in April, and in June he mediated in talks in Portugal between representatives of Morocco and the SADR. Direct talks, under the auspices of the UN Special Representative, continued in Portugal in August and in the USA in September. The process of voter identification resumed in December for a referendum scheduled to be held one year later. However, disagreement between Morocco and Polisario regarding the eligibility of voters delayed the identification process and led the UN to revise the proposed date for the referendum on several occasions. By September 1998 a total of 147,350 voters had been identified since the commencement of the identification process in August 1994, but the issue of the disputed tribes remained unresolved. In June 1998, meanwhile, as Morocco intensified its efforts to rejoin the OAU, several OAU member states engaged in debate as to whether to expel the SADR from the organization. Support for the SADR within the OAU had declined markedly, with only a minority of member countries continuing to recognize its independent status.

In November 1998, during talks with Moroccan and SADR officials, the UN Secretary-General warned that the UN would withdraw from Western Sahara if the two parties failed to show political will towards resolving the conflict. Annan presented proposals regarding the disputed tribes, the publication of a list of voters not contested by either party, and the repatriation of refugees under the auspices of the UN High Commissioner for Refugees. Although the proposals were accepted by Polisario, the Moroccan authorities expressed reservations. Morocco delayed the signing of a technical agreement with the UN (defining the legal status of MINURSO troops in Western Sahara) until February 1999: Algeria and Mauritania had signed similar accords with the UN in November 1998. In July 1999 MINURSO published a list of 84,251 people provisionally entitled to vote in the referendum, which was scheduled to be held on 31 July 2000.

In February 1999, meanwhile, the SADR announced the formation of a new Government, led by Beïba's predecessor, Bouchraya Hammoudi Bayoune. In September the Polisario Front congress re-elected Muhammad Abd al-Aziz secretary-general of the organization. Abd al-Aziz subsequently effected a reshuffle of the SADR Government; Bayoune retained the premiership and also assumed the interior portfolio. In late September it was reported that Moroccan security forces had violently suppressed demonstrations in el-Aaiún. In October a delegation comprising several ministers of the Moroccan Government was dispatched to el-Aaiún for consultations with the Sahrawi population at the behest of King Muhammad—who had in September established a royal commission to monitor affairs in Western Sahara.

In November 1999 UN officials indicated that the referendum was likely to be subject to a further postponement. In response, Polisario stated that it could not rule out a return to an armed struggle if the referendum did not take place as scheduled. Nevertheless, in late November Polisario released 191 Moroccan prisoners. In December the mandate of MINURSO was once again extended to enable it to complete its work on the identification of possible voters in the referendum. However, the UN Secretary-General subsequently announced it would be impossible to organize the referendum before 2002, owing to the large number of appeals (totalling some 79,000) lodged by those deemed ineligible to vote. In January 2000 it was announced that 86,381 out of a total of 198,481 people identified in Western Sahara would be eligible to vote in the referendum. In February, however, Annan postponed the referendum indefinitely, and warned, furthermore, of the possibility that it might never take place, owing to the persistent differences regarding criteria for eligibility to vote. The mandate of MINURSO was further extended in February. By March the number of appeals lodged had reached over 130,000, and Abd al-Aziz reiterated the threat of the resumption of armed hostilities if Morocco continued to obstruct the UN peace plan.

In April 2000 Baker toured Morocco and Western Sahara, and in London, United Kingdom, in May he chaired the first direct talks between representatives of Morocco and Polisario for three years. Algeria and Mauritania also sent delegations, but the meeting failed to make any substantive progress. MINURSO's mandate was further extended until the end of July, and in late June Baker chaired another meeting of representatives of the four parties in London in an attempt to revive plans for a referendum; however, the talks again ended in failure. In October Annan urged Morocco partially to devolve authority in Western Sahara, stating that if no such concessions were granted, the UN would reactivate plans to hold a referendum in the territory. Concurrently, MINURSO's mandate was extended until the end of February 2001.

In December 2000, to mark the beginning of Ramadan, Polisario released 201 Moroccan prisoners, urging Morocco to release some 150 Sahrawi from detention in Morocco. The Moroccan authorities denied the detention of any Sahrawi in Morocco, and in turn demanded the release of a further 1,500 Moroccans whom they claimed were being held by Polisario. In late February 2001, on the 25th anniversary of the beginning of the Polisario Front's struggle for independence, the Moroccan Minister of the Interior, Ahmed Midaoui, asserted that there remained only one solution to the dispute—that Morocco retain control over its entire territory. Annan had recently issued a report in which he lamented the climate of increased mistrust and bitterness between the two sides, maintaining that this undermined the cease-fire. At the end of February, as MINURSO's mandate was extended for a further two months, Annan announced that if Morocco failed to offer or support some devolution of governmental authority, MINURSO would be directed to begin the process of hearing appeals regarding eligibility to vote in the referendum. A further two-month extension was approved by the UN Security Council in late April, in accordance with recommendations made by the Secretary-General: although Annan had been unable, in his latest report, to report progress towards overcoming the obstacles to implementation of the settlement plan, he expressed his view that 'substantial progress' had been made towards determining whether the Government of Morocco was 'prepared to offer or support some devolution of authority for all the inhabitants and former inhabitants of the Territory'.

In late June 2001 the UN Security Council unanimously approved a compromise resolution (No. 1359), formulated by Baker, which encouraged Polisario and Morocco to discuss an autonomy plan for Western Sahara without abandoning the delayed referendum. The resolution also extended MINURSO's mandate until the end of November. Under the terms of the autonomy proposal the inhabitants of Western Sahara would have the right to elect their own legislative and executive bodies and have control over areas of local government (including budget and taxation, law enforcement, internal security, social welfare, education, commerce, transportation, agriculture, mining, fisheries, environmental policy, urban development, utilities, roads and basic infrastructure) for a period of at least five years, during which Morocco would retain control over defence and foreign affairs. A referendum on the final status of the territory would take place within this five-year period. In late August Baker hosted three days of talks in Wyoming, USA, attended by representatives from Polisario, Mauritania and Algeria; however, Polisario subsequently accused the UN of bowing to Moroccan pressure and in mid-September Polisario announced its formal rejection of Baker's proposal. In late October King Muhammad visited Western Sahara for the first time since his accession to throne, and in early November he granted an amnesty to 56 prisoners in Western Sahara. Later that month the UN Security Council approved Annan's request for an extension of MINURSO's mandate until February 2002, and in early December 2001 William Lacy Swing, a former US ambassador, was appointed the UN Secretary-General's Special Representative for Western Sahara. Tensions between Polisario and Morocco were further exacerbated when, in December, President Jacques Chirac of France (which lends Morocco considerable support on the Western Sahara issue) referred to the territory as part of Morocco. Polisario none the less released a further 115 Moroccan prisoners of war in early January 2002.

In early February 2002 UN legal counsel advised the Secretary-General that the Moroccan Government could not issue exploration licences for petroleum in Western Sahara without the consent of the Sahrawi people; the advice followed a request made by the SADR in late 2001 for clarification on the legality of reconnaissance licences signed by Morocco and two oil companies. Later in February 2002 Annan again expressed disappointment at the continued lack of progress and described the prospects for a settlement as 'rather bleak'. Nevertheless, he outlined four possible measures to be considered by the UN Security Council in order to attempt to resolve the continuing impasse over Western Sahara: to resume attempts to implement the 1988 settlement plan, with or without the agreement of Polisario and the Moroccan Government; to charge Baker with revising his earlier draft framework agreement; to commence discussions regarding the division of the territory; or to terminate MINURSO's mandate. Later that month the UN Security Council approved an extension of the mandate of the peace-keeping force until the end of April. Meanwhile, in early March King Muhammad again visited Western Sahara, vowing not to relinquish any part of the disputed territory. Upon its expiry at the end of April, MINURSO's mandate was renewed for a further three months; during this period consideration would be given to the UN Secretary-General's proposals for resolving the impasse regarding the disputed territory. At the same time UN officials denied reports that James Baker had announced his intention to resign should the Security Council not accord him a mandate to revise the draft framework agreement.

In July 2002 a further 101 Moroccan prisoners of war were released by Polisario. Later that month the UN Security Council admitted that it had been unable to agree on the resolution of the Western Sahara issue (as none of the four proposals had secured the required support), but had voted unanimously to allow Baker to pursue efforts to find a political solution which would provide for self-determination. MINURSO's mandate was extended until the end of January 2003. In that month Baker visited government officials in Mauritania and Algeria, as well as Polisario leader Abd al-Aziz and Morocco's King Muhammad, to present them with the UN's most recent proposal for the settlement of the ongoing dispute. Although no details of the plan were officially disclosed, Baker asked all parties to present their comments on the proposal to him by early March. Just days later, however, it was reported that Polisario had rejected the plan. In an attempt to give the parties more time in which to consider Baker's proposals, the UN Security Council extended MINURSO's mandate until the end of March; it was subsequently extended for a further two months in order to give Baker sufficient time to evaluate the parties' responses to his proposal. In February Polisario had released another 100 Moroccan prisoners of war, although more than 1,100 reportedly remained in detention; the Security Council again urged the release of all prisoners of war.

In late May 2003 Annan formally released details of a new peace plan aimed at ending the Western Sahara dispute and urged Morocco, Polisario and Algeria to accept the proposals. The new plan, known as 'Baker Plan II', proposed immediate self-government for Western Sahara for a period of four to five years, after which time a referendum would be held in order to give all bona fide residents the opportunity to decide the long-term future of the territory. According to the UN Secretary-General, the new peace plan provided a fair and balanced approach to a political solution to the dispute, but he emphasized that it required both sides to make compromises. Annan suggested an extension of MINURSO's mandate for a further two months to enable the Security Council to consider the proposals thoroughly. The Security Council approved Annan's proposals at the beginning of June. At the end of June Polisario, under strong pressure from Algeria, accepted the Baker plan as a basis for negotiation. Morocco, however, refused to accept any 'imposed decision' on Western Sahara.

On 31 July 2003 the UN Security Council unanimously adopted Resolution 1495 concerning Western Sahara. This supported Baker Plan II and called on parties and states of the region to co-operate fully with the Secretary-General and his special envoy in working towards the implementation of the peace plan. MINURSO's mandate was extended until 31 October 2003. Following strong opposition from France, Resolution 1495 did not demand that Morocco and Polisario comply with the plan. Nevertheless, the Spanish permanent representative to the UN, chairing the Security Council, insisted that the resolution provided the two parties with sufficient 'political room' to reach a definite solution to the dispute on the basis of Baker Plan II: this had not imposed a solution on the parties but urged them to resume sustained discussions. Annan invited the parties to act constructively and to work with him and Baker towards acceptance and implementation of the peace plan. Negotiations on specific elements of the plan were expected to take place, in an attempt to make progress towards implementation before the end of the year. However, given what was regarded as Moroccan intransigence, compounded by divisions within the Security Council, it remained unlikely that significant progress would be made. The resolution also called on Polisario to release without further delay all remaining Moroccan prisoners of war, and for Morocco and Polisario to co-operate with the International Committee of the Red Cross (ICRC) to resolve the fate of persons unaccounted for since the beginning of the conflict.

In early August 2003 Annan announced that a former Peruvian diplomat, Alvaro de Soto, would replace Swing as the UN Secretary-General's Special Representative for Western Sahara. In September Polisario released 243 Moroccan prisoners of war, although the ICRC maintained that a further 914 Moroccans were still being held captive by Polisario. In late October Annan again urged Morocco to accept and implement Baker Plan II; concurrently, MINURSO's mandate was extended until January 2004. In November 2003 Polisario released a further 300 Moroccan prisoners of war. In January 2004 MINURSO's mandate was again extended until April, by which time Annan stated that he required a 'final response' from Morocco with regard to Baker Plan II. In late February 100 Moroccans were released from detention by Polisario, although there had been no further progress between the two sides towards implementing the peace agreement. In April MINURSO's mandate was extended until October and the Security Council adopted a resolution urging Morocco and Polisario to accept the UN's plan to grant Western Sahara immediate self-government. Morocco, however, continued to reject this proposal and remained insistent on granting the territory 'autonomy within the framework of Moroccan sovereignty'.

Relations with other North African states improved significantly in the late 1980s. In May 1988 Algeria and Morocco agreed to re-establish diplomatic relations. (Relations with Mauritania had been suspended in 1981 and resumed in April 1985.) In February 1989 North African heads of state, meeting in Marrakesh, signed a treaty establishing the Union du Maghreb arabe (UMA—Union of the Arab Maghreb, see p. 362). The new body, grouping Morocco, Algeria, Libya, Mauritania and Tunisia, aimed to promote trade by allowing the free movement of goods, services and workers. During 1990 bilateral agreements on economic co-operation were concluded by Morocco with Algeria and Libya, and there were further discussions within the UMA on the formation of a North African free-trade area. However, there were political disagreements particularly concerning Algeria's continued support for the Polisario Front, and over Moroccan condemnation of Iraq's invasion of Kuwait in August 1990. In early 1993 it was announced that the five UMA members had decided there should be a 'pause' in the development of a closer union; of 15 conventions signed since the inauguration of the UMA, none had as yet been fully applied. However, the organization continued to hold meetings on an annual basis. In December 1995 King Hassan expressed disapproval at Algeria's continued support for the independence of Western Sahara, and demanded that UMA activities be suspended. An impending UMA summit was subsequently postponed. In March 1999 President Ben Ali of Tunisia made his first official visit to Morocco, during which he pledged to improve bilateral relations and to reactivate the UMA. At bilateral meetings during 2000 with other Maghreb Heads of State King Muhammad pledged to take measures to revive the UMA. A summit meeting of ministers responsible for foreign affairs of the five UMA states proceeded in the Algerian capital in March 2001. However, the meeting, which was to have made preparations for the first summit meeting of UMA heads of state since 1995, quickly broke down following disagreements between Moroccan and Algerian representatives.

Relations with Algeria had been further undermined in mid-1994, by the murder, apparently by radical Islamists, of two Spanish tourists in Marrakesh, which the Moroccan authorities attributed in part to Algerian nationals. The imposition by Morocco of entry restrictions on Algerian citizens prompted the Algerian Government to introduce reciprocal visa restrictions and to close its border with Morocco. Tensions eased somewhat in September, when Algeria announced the appointment of a new ambassador to Morocco, and in October a Moroccan minister attended ceremonies in Algeria to mark the commencement of work on a Maghreb–Europe gas pipeline. In January 1995 three people, including one Algerian, were sentenced to death for their part in acts of terrorism including the murders in Marrakesh; three others were sentenced to life imprisonment. The French security forces made further arrests in connection with the murder of the two Spaniards during 1995–96, and in early 1997 a French court sentenced another 29 alleged conspirators (two Moroccans, the remainder French citizens of Maghreb origin) to terms of imprisonment ranging from one to eight years. The Western Sahara issue remained a source of tension between Morocco and Algeria, but in mid-1998 the Moroccan authorities indicated their desire to normalize relations with Algeria and to reopen the common border. In September 1999, however, Algeria's new President, Abdelaziz Bouteflika, claimed that radical Islamist rebels were launching attacks on Algeria from Morocco, and accused Morocco of ignoring the increasing trade in illicit drugs between the two countries. Bouteflika also criticized Morocco for negotiating a separate trade agreement with the European Union (EU, see p. 208), claiming that this was not in the interests of the UMA. Both Morocco and Algeria none the less subsequently reiterated their commitment to reviving the activities of the UMA. Although relations remained generally co-operative, Bouteflika was vocal in opposing the UN proposals for Western Sahara in mid-2001, which he claimed merely favoured Morocco. In late February 2002, furthermore, Morocco asserted that Algerian support for the partition of Western Sahara risked destabilizing the region; for its part, Algeria accused Morocco of blocking a UN-sponsored solution to the Western Sahara issue. During a visit to Algiers by the Moroccan Minister of Foreign Affairs and Co-operation in mid-June 2003, it was agreed to establish three bilateral commissions to consider political, economic and social matters.

From the late 1990s Morocco was actively involved in wider regional integration efforts, as a member of the Community of Sahel-Saharan States (CEN-SAD, see p. 359), and also through bilateral and multilateral free-trade arrangements; in May 2001, notably, the Governments of Morocco, Iraq, Jordan and Tunisia agreed, at a meeting in Agadir, to establish a free-trade zone. In October Morocco and Mauritania took steps to improve bilateral relations after King Muhammad visited that country.

A visit to Rabat by the Israeli Prime Minister, Itzhak Rabin, in September 1993 was regarded as an indication of improved relations between Morocco and Israel, and of the role played by King Hassan in the Middle East peace process. In September 1994 Morocco became only the second Arab country (after Egypt) to establish direct links with Israel; liaison offices were subsequently opened in Rabat and Tel-Aviv. In March 1997, however, in condemnation of recent Israeli settlement policy, ministers of foreign affairs of the League of Arab States (the Arab League, see p. 278) recommended a number of sanctions against Israel, including the closure of representative missions. In January 2000 Morocco and Israel agreed in principle to upgrade diplomatic relations to ambassadorial level, although no indication was given as to when embassies would be established. In October, however, as the crisis in Israeli–Palestinian relations deepened, Morocco announced that it had closed down Israel's liaison office in Rabat and its own representative office in Tel-Aviv. There was widespread outrage in Morocco in response to the Israeli military offensive in Palestinian-controlled areas of the West Bank from the end of March 2002. A national march in solidarity with the Palestinian people took place in Rabat in early April, attracting more than 1m. people—the biggest demonstration in the Arab world.

Morocco has generally maintained close relations with France. However, the French Government expressed considerable concern following the imposition of death sentences on three defendants in January 1995 (see above), all of whom had been resident in France prior to their arrest. As the development of a Maghreb union slowed, Morocco attempted to improve relations with the EU, which had been critical of Morocco's human rights record. In February 1996, after two years of negotiations, Morocco signed an association agreement with the EU, which provided for greater political and economic co-operation, financial aid and the eventual establishment of a free-trade zone. In March 2000 King Muhammad made his first state visit abroad since acceding to the throne when he attended talks with President Chirac in France. During the visit Muhammad expressed his hope that Morocco would be accorded partnership status with the EU and, ultimately, full membership of the union.

In February 1995, following the approval by the Spanish parliament of statutes of autonomy for the enclaves of Ceuta and Melilla, Morocco intensified its diplomatic campaign to obtain sovereignty over the territories. Relations between Morocco and Spain deteriorated further in April, when responsibility for two bomb explosions in Ceuta was claimed by a guerrilla group suspected by the Spanish authorities of receiving clandestine support from Morocco. Tensions were exacerbated by protracted negotiations between Morocco and the EU to renew fishing licences, although bilateral relations improved after Morocco initialled the fisheries agreement with the EU in November. In February 1996 the Spanish Prime Minister, Felipe González, attended a meeting in Rabat with Prime Minister Filali to discuss ways of increasing contacts in order to avoid similar commercial disputes. Filali made an official visit to Spain in mid-1997, and in January 1998 the two countries established a joint commission to examine security issues including illegal

immigration (to Spain) and drugs-trafficking. Bilateral relations were consolidated further in April, with a visit to Morocco by the Spanish premier, José María Aznar López. In August 1999 Prime Minister el-Youssoufi urged a review of the statutes of Ceuta and Melilla; however, Spain's ruling Partido Popular asserted that no Moroccan sovereignty claims with regard to this issue would be considered. Aznar again visited Morocco in May 2000, and in September, during King Muhammad's first visit to Spain since his accession, two economic co-operation agreements were signed. Nevertheless, relations remained strained owing to lack of progress in negotiations with the EU regarding a new fisheries accord and attacks by Spanish fishermen on lorries carrying Moroccan products through Spanish ports.

In July 2001, in an attempt to limit the increasing number of Moroccans entering Spain illegally, the two countries signed an agreement that would allow as many as 20,000 Moroccans to enter Spain each year in search of employment. In September, however, Spain refuted allegations made by King Muhammad that Spanish criminal associations were responsible for the large increase in numbers of Moroccan economic migrants attempting illegally to cross the Straits of Gibraltar, asserting that collusion between Moroccan police and the smugglers was ongoing. Relations between the two countries deteriorated further later that month after Morocco recalled its ambassador from Spain. The Moroccan Government was critical of border controls introduced by the Spanish authorities for Moroccans entering the Spanish enclaves of Ceuta and Melilla, and the breakdown, in April 2002, of talks on renewing the EU fisheries accord also contributed to strained bilateral relations. A new disagreement erupted at the end of December over maritime boundaries between the Spanish Canary Islands and Morocco's Atlantic coast, following the Spanish Government's decision to grant oil exploration rights around the Canary Islands to a Spanish company, Repsol. Moroccan–Spanish relations were further strained in mid-July 2002 when a small detachment of Moroccan troops occupied the uninhabited rocky islet of Perejil (known as Leila to Morocco), west of the Spanish enclave of Ceuta and close to the Moroccan coastline. Morocco claimed that it was establishing a surveillance post on the island as part of its campaign against illegal emigration and drugs-smuggling. However, Spain insisted that there had been since 1990 an agreement that neither Morocco nor Spain would occupy Perejil, and, with the support of the EU and NATO, demanded the immediate evacuation of Moroccan troops from the island. A few days later Spain's ambassador to Morocco was recalled, and Spanish special forces intervened and forcibly removed Moroccan troops from Perejil. Spanish officials insisted that their troops would be withdrawn if King Muhammad gave assurances that Moroccan forces would not reoccupy the island, and the Spanish Minister of Foreign Affairs, Ana Palacio, stated that Spain had no interest in maintaining a permanent military presence on the island. Both sides emphasized their desire to end the dispute through diplomatic means, and, following mediation by the US Secretary of State, Colin Powell, Spanish forces withdrew from the island. Talks held later in July 2002 in Rabat between Palacio and her Moroccan counterpart Muhammad Benaissa (the first at this level since October 2001) resulted in an accord whereby both states agreed to return to the *status quo ante*. However, a further meeting between Palacio and Benaissa scheduled for September was cancelled by Morocco, which claimed that a Spanish aircraft had landed on the disputed islet. The two sides met again in December when they agreed to establish a number of working groups to address the main issues dividing the countries. By early 2003 relations had improved somewhat: in January Muhammad temporarily allowed Spanish boats to fish in Moroccan waters, and in the following month the two countries agreed to the return of their respective ambassadors. In December Morocco and Spain announced plans to construct a 39-km underwater rail tunnel between the two countries. A number of Moroccans were among a group of suspected militant Islamists detained by the Spanish authorities following a series of bomb attacks on commuter trains in Madrid in March 2004, in which 191 people died.

The Moroccan Government was swift to condemn the September 2001 attacks on New York and Washington, DC, for which the al-Qa'ida network was believed to be responsible. In early June 2002 the Moroccan authorities announced that they had arrested three Saudi nationals who were alleged to be members of an Islamist cell linked to al-Qa'ida that was preparing terrorist attacks on US and British warships in the Strait of Gibraltar. Two of the suspects' wives, both of Moroccan origin, had also been arrested, along with five other Moroccans, for allegedly acting as couriers between the Saudis in Morocco and al-Qa'ida, which had provided them with funds and logistical support. In February 2003 the three Saudis were sentenced to 10 years' imprisonment by a court in Casablanca; six of the Moroccans received sentences ranging from four months to one year for their roles in the plot. Also in February a Moroccan student, Mounir al-Motassadek, who was alleged to have been a member of the cell that had planned and executed the September 2001 attacks was convicted by a court in Hamburg, Germany, of belonging to a terrorist group and of aiding and abetting the murder of 3,066 people. He was sentenced to 15 years' imprisonment. In mid-August 2003 the trial commenced in Hamburg of a second Moroccan student charged with identical offences; however, he was acquitted of all charges in February 2004. In March al-Motassadek's conviction was quashed by the German Federal Criminal Court; he was released from detention in April, pending a retrial in June.

Government

The 1992 Constitution (amended by referendum in 1996) provides for a modified constitutional monarchy, with an hereditary King as Head of State. Legislative power is vested in the Chamber of Representatives, with 325 members directly elected, on the basis of universal adult suffrage, for five years, and in the Chamber of Advisers, with 270 members chosen by electoral colleges (representing mainly local councils, with the remainder selected from professional associations and trade unions) for a nine-year term. Executive power is vested in the King, who appoints (and may dismiss) the Prime Minister and (on the latter's recommendation) other members of the Cabinet. The King may also dissolve the legislature.

Defence

In August 2003 Morocco's active armed forces numbered 196,300, consisting of an army of 175,000 (including an estimated 100,000 conscripts), a navy of 7,800 and an air force of 13,500. In addition, there was a paramilitary 'gendarmerie royale' of 20,000, and a paramilitary 'force auxiliaire' of 30,000 men (including a mobile intervention corps of 5,000). Army reserve forces totalled 150,000. Military service of 18 months is by authorized conscription. Under the 2003 budget, government expenditure on defence was projected at 15,500m. dirhams.

Economic Affairs

In 2002, according to estimates by the World Bank, Morocco's gross national income (GNI), measured at average 2000–02 prices, was US $35,354m., equivalent to $1,190 per head (or $3,690 per head on an international purchasing-power parity basis). During 1990–2002, it was estimated, the population increased at an average annual rate of 1.8%, while gross domestic product (GDP) per head increased, in real terms, by an average of 1.0% per year. According to official figures, overall GDP increased, in real terms, at an average annual rate of 2.5% in 1990–2002; it increased by 7.2% in 2001 and by 3.2% in 2002.

Agriculture (including forestry and fishing) contributed 16.5% of GDP in 2002, and engaged 43.6% of the employed labour force in 2001. The principal crops are cereals (mainly wheat and barley), sugar beet, potatoes, citrus fruit, tomatoes and sugar cane . Almost all of Morocco's meat requirements are produced within the country. The sale of licences to foreign fishing fleets is an important source of revenue. In 2001 seafoods and seafood products accounted for an estimated 9.3% of total exports. During 1990–2002 agricultural GDP increased at an average annual rate of 0.4%. Agricultural GDP declined by 15.7% in 2000, as a result of severe drought; however, it increased by 27.6% in 2001 and by 5.6% in 2002.

Industry (including mining, manufacturing, construction and power) engaged 19.7% of the employed labour force in 2001, and provided 31.1% of GDP in 2002. During 1990–2002 industrial GDP increased by an average of 3.0% per year. Industrial GDP rose by 5.0% in 2001 and by 2.7% in 2002.

Mining and quarrying contributed 1.9% of GDP in 2002; the sector engaged 0.6% of the labour force in 2000. The major mineral exports are phosphate rock and phosphoric acid, which together earned an estimated 12.5% of export revenues in 2001. Morocco is the world's largest exporter of phosphate rock. Petroleum exploration activity was revived at the end of the 1990s, and in August 2000 the discovery of major oil and natural gas reserves in the Talsinnt region of eastern Morocco was announced. Coal, salt, iron ore, barytes, lead, copper, zinc,

silver, gold and manganese are mined. Deposits of nickel, cobalt and bauxite have been discovered. During 1990–2002 mining GDP increased at an average annual rate of 1.3%. Mining GDP increased by 3.0% in 2001 and by 3.2% in 2002.

Manufacturing employed 12.3% of the labour force in 2000, and contributed 20.0% of GDP in 2002. The most important branches, measured by gross value of output, are food-processing, textiles, and chemicals. During 1990–2002 manufacturing GDP was estimated to have increased at an average annual rate of 2.8%. Manufacturing GDP rose by 4.2% in 2001 and by 2.8% in 2002.

Electric energy is derived principally from thermal power stations (which accounted for an estimated 94.5% of production in 2001) using coal and imported petroleum and gas. Facilities for generating hydroelectric and wind power have also been developed. Imports of fuel and energy products comprised an estimated 17.6% of the value of total merchandise imports in 2001.

The services sector contributed 52.4% of GDP in 2002, and engaged 36.7% of the employed labour force in 2001. The tourist industry is generally a major source of revenue, and tourist arrivals reached 2.2m. in 2002. The GDP of the services sector increased by an estimated average of 3.2% per year during 1990–2002. The GDP of the sector rose by 3.8% in 2001 and by 2.8% in 2002.

In 2002 Morocco recorded a visible trade deficit of US $3,036m., but there was a surplus of $1,488m. on the current account of the balance of payments. In 2001 the principal source of imports was France (which provided an estimated 24.1% of merchandise imports); other major suppliers in that year included Spain, the United Kingdom, and Germany. France was also the principal market for exports (32.8%) in 2001; Spain, the United Kingdom and Italy were also important purchasers of Moroccan exports. The principal exports in 2001 were manufactured garments, phosphates and phosphoric acid, hosiery, and seafoods and seafood products. The principal imports in that year were crude petroleum and textiles.

In the financial year ending 30 June 2000 there was a budget deficit of 2,261m. dirhams, equivalent to 0.7% of GDP. Morocco's total external debt in 2000 was US $16,962m., of which $14,325m. was long-term public debt. The cost of debt-servicing in that year was equivalent to 17.8% of exports of goods and services. The annual rate of inflation averaged 3.8% in 1989–2002. Annual inflation slowed to just 0.6% in 2001, but increased to 2.8% in 2002. Some 12.5% of the labour force were unemployed in 2001.

Morocco is a member of the African Development Bank (see p. 135), the Islamic Development Bank (see p. 275) and of the Arab Fund for Economic and Social Development (see p. 144). It is a founder member of the Union du Maghreb arabe (Union of the Arab Maghreb, see p. 362).

Since 1980 the Moroccan authorities have undertaken a series of economic reforms (under the auspices of the IMF), including the reduction of taxes, tariffs and subsidies and the introduction of a more efficient tax system. Efforts to stimulate foreign investment have had considerable success, while a programme of privatization has bolstered government revenue. In March 2000 a trade and co-operation agreement with the European Union (EU) came into effect, which provided for the establishment of a free-trade zone with the EU within 10 years. The Government was able to compensate for the loss of revenue from the fisheries accord with the EU, which expired in 2001, with the sale, for US $1,100m., of Morocco's second mobile cellular telephone operating licence and the partial privatization of Maroc Télécom—35% of which was sold to the French telecommunications company Vivendi for $2,330m. The tourism sector, which contributes an estimated 8% of GDP per year, was adversely affected by the volatile situation in the Middle East from 2002 and the suicide bombings launched against Western targets in Casablanca in May 2003. Nevertheless, the Government continued with ambitious plans to raise the number of tourist visitors to Morocco to 10m. by 2010 and to significantly increase tourism revenues. The 2004 budget forecast GDP growth of 3.0% for that year, although analysts maintained that much higher growth was needed in order to reduce endemic poverty in the country and to stimulate job creation. There were, however, a number of positive macroeconomic developments in 2003–04: the rate of inflation remained low; a balance of payments surplus was recorded; and foreign exchange reserves increased. Furthermore, Morocco and the USA signed a free-trade agreement in early March 2004, and a number of high-profile privatizations were also scheduled for that year.

Education

Morocco has state-controlled primary, secondary and technical schools, and there are also private schools. Education is compulsory for six years, to be undertaken between the ages of seven and 13 years. Primary education begins at seven years of age and lasts for six years. Secondary education, beginning at the age of 13, lasts for up to six years (comprising two cycles of three years). Primary enrolment in 1999 included 79% of children in the relevant age-group (83% of boys; 74% of girls), while secondary enrolment included 38% of the relevant age-group (boys 43%; girls 33%). In 1988 the secondary school graduation examination, the *baccalauréat*, was replaced by a system of continuous assessment. There were 276,018 students enrolled at state universities and equivalent-level institutions in 2002/03. Under the 2002 budget, expenditure on education by the central Government was 25,894m. dirhams (21.8% of total spending).

Public Holidays

2004: 1 January (New Year), 11 January (Independence Manifesto), 1 February* (Eid el-Kebir—Id al-Adha, Feast of the Sacrifice), 22 February* (Islamic New Year), 2 March* (Ashoura), 1 May (Labour Day), 2 May* (Mouloud, Birth of the Prophet), 23 May (National Day), 30 July (Festival of the Throne, anniversary of King Muhammad's accession), 14 August (Oued ed-Dahab Day, anniversary of 1979 annexation), 15 October (Beginning of Ramadan), 6 November (Anniversary of the Green March*), 14 November* (Eid es-Seghir—Id al-Fitr, end of Ramadan), 18 November (Independence Day).

2005: 1 January (New Year), 11 January (Independence Manifesto), 21 January* (Eid el-Kebir—Id al-Adha, Feast of the Sacrifice), 10 February* (Islamic New Year), 19 February* (Ashoura), 21 April* (Mouloud, Birth of the Prophet), 1 May (Labour Day), 23 May (National Day), 30 July (Festival of the Throne, anniversary of King Muhammad's accession), 14 August (Oued ed-Dahab Day, anniversary of 1979 annexation), 5 October* (Beginning of Ramadan), 4 November* (Eid es-Seghir—Id al-Fitr, end of Ramadan), 6 November (Anniversary of the Green March), 18 November (Independence Day).

*These holidays are dependent on the Islamic lunar calendar and may vary by one or two days from the dates given.

Weights and Measures

The metric system is in force.

Statistical Survey

Sources (unless otherwise stated): Direction de la Statistique, BP 178, Rabat 10001; tel. (3) 7773606; fax (3) 7773042; e-mail webmaster@statistic.gov.ma; internet www.statistic.gov.ma; Bank Al-Maghrib, 277 ave Muhammad V, BP 445, Rabat; tel. (3) 7702626; fax (3) 7706677; e-mail dai@bkam.gov.ma; internet www.bkam.ma.
Note: Unless otherwise indicated, the data exclude Western (formerly Spanish) Sahara, a disputed territory under Moroccan occupation.

Area and Population

AREA, POPULATION AND DENSITY

Area (sq km)	710,850*
Population (census results)†	
3 September 1982	
Males	10,205,859
Females.	10,182,358
Total	20,388,217
2 September 1994	26,073,717
Population (official estimates at mid-year)†	
2000	28,705,000
2001	29,170,000
2002	29,631,000
Density (per sq km) at mid-2002	41.7

* 274,461 sq miles. This area includes the disputed territory of Western Sahara, which covers 252,120 sq km (97,344 sq miles).
† Including Western Sahara, with a population of 163,868 (provisional) at the 1982 census and 252,146 at the 1994 census.

REGIONS
(population at 1994 census)

	Area (sq km)	Population	Density (per sq km)
Sud*	394,970	3,234,024	8.2
Tensift	38,445	3,546,768	92.3
Centre.	41,500	6,931,418	167.0
Nord-Ouest	29,955	5,646,716	188.5
Centre-Nord	43,950	3,042,310	69.2
Oriental	82,820	1,768,691	21.4
Centre-Sud	79,210	1,903,790	24.0
Total	**710,850**	**26,073,717**	**36.7**

* Including the prefectures of Boujdour, el-Aaiún, es-Smara and Oued ed-Dahab, which comprise the disputed territory of Western Sahara (area 252,120 sq km; population 252,146).

PRINCIPAL TOWNS
(population at 1994 census)

Casablanca . . .	2,770,560	Kénitra	292,627
Rabat (capital)* .	1,335,996	Tétouan	277,516
Fès (Fez)	769,014	Safi	262,276
Marrakech		Mohammedia . . .	170,063
(Marrakesh) . .	672,506	Khouribga . . .	152,090
Agadir	524,564	El-Jadida . . .	119,083
Tanger (Tangier). .	497,147	Nador	112,450
Meknès	443,214	Ksar-el-Kebir . .	107,065
Oujda	351,878		

* Including Salé and Temara.

Source: Thomas Brinkhoff, *City Population* (internet www.citypopulation.de).

BIRTHS AND DEATHS
(UN estimates, annual averages)

	1985–90	1990–95	1995–2000
Birth rate (per 1,000)	32.3	26.7	24.4
Death rate (per 1,000)	8.9	7.4	6.6

Source: UN, *World Population Prospects: The 2002 Revision.*

Expectation of life (WHO estimates, years at birth): 70.8 (males 68.8; females 72.8) in 2002 (Source: WHO, *World Health Report*).

ECONOMICALLY ACTIVE POPULATION
(sample surveys, '000 persons aged 15 years and over)

	1999	2000	2001
Agriculture, hunting, forestry and fishing	4,048	4,010	3,900
Mining and quarrying	58	55	
Manufacturing	1,153	1,098	1,169
Electricity, gas and water	40	34	
Construction	560	555	598
Wholesale and retail trade	991	1,118	1,155
Transport, storage and communications	279	297	317
Repairing	155	158	
Restaurants and hotels	140	155	835
Financing, insurance, real estate and business services	104	105	
Personal and domestic services	359	372	
General administration	500	482	976
Other community services	440	443	
Activities not adequately defined	17	10	5
Total employed	**8,845**	**8,891**	**8,955**
Unemployed	1,433	1,394	1,275
Total labour force	**10,278**	**10,285**	**10,230**

Health and Welfare

KEY INDICATORS

Total fertility rate (children per woman, 2002)	2.8
Under-5 mortality rate (per 1,000 live births, 2001)	44
HIV/AIDS (% of persons aged 15–49, 2001)	0.08
Physicians (per 1,000 head, 1997)	0.46
Hospital beds (per 1,000 head, 1997)	0.46
Health expenditure (2001): US $ per head (PPP)	199
Health expenditure (2001): % of GDP	5.1
Health expenditure (2001): public (% of total)	39.3
Access to water (% of persons, 2000)	82
Access to sanitation (% of persons, 2000)	75
Human Development Index (2001): ranking	126
Human Development Index (2001): value	0.606

For sources and definitions, see explanatory note on p. vi.

Agriculture

PRINCIPAL CROPS
('000 metric tons)

	2000	2001	2002
Wheat	1,381	3,316	3,357
Rice (paddy)	25	37	17
Barley	467	1,155	1,669
Maize	95	54	199
Oats	15	15	15*
Sorghum	12	10	10*
Other cereals	17	17*	17*
Potatoes	1,090	1,155	1,334
Sweet potatoes	13	6	6
Sugar cane	1,318	1,324	939
Sugar beet	2,883	3,106	2,986
Dry beans	12	12*	12*
Dry broad beans	33	82	80*
Dry peas	6	13	22
Chick-peas	15	32	51
Lentils	3	13	42
Other pulses	45	43	51*
Almonds	65	82	70
Groundnuts (in shell)	39	45	45*
Olives	400	420	420*
Sunflower seed	19	33	16
Cabbages	38	35	33
Artichokes	41	45	47
Asparagus*	36	36	3
Tomatoes	1,165	881	991

— continued	2000	2001	2002
Cauliflowers	24	38	48
Pumpkins, squash and gourds	130	130*	130*
Cucumbers and gherkins	24	25*	25*
Aubergines (Eggplants)	34	35*	35*
Chillies and green peppers	180	180*	143
Dry onions	348	554	610
Green beans	33	33*	11
Green peas	65	79	69
Green broad beans	99	96	104
String beans	37	40	53
Carrots	210	199	233
Carobs*	23	24	24
Other vegetables	380	374	361
Watermelons	219	300	370*
Cantaloupes and other melons	374	380*	380*
Figs	68	69	68
Avacados	13	14	14
Grapes	262	253	275*
Dates	74	32	33
Apples	300	228	373
Pears	30	36	45
Quinces	31	20	30*
Peaches and nectarines	48	46	55
Plums	51	63	43
Strawberries	105	90	90*
Oranges	870	708	723
Tangerines, mandarins, clementines and satsumas	531	263	406
Lemons and limes	14	6	11
Apricots	106	120	85
Bananas	111	119	162
Other fruits and berries	59	58	55*
Tobacco (leaves)	5	6	7

* FAO estimate(s).

Source: FAO.

LIVESTOCK
('000 head, year ending September)

	2000	2001	2002
Cattle	2,675	2,647	2,670
Sheep	17,300	17,172	16,336
Goats	4,931	5,133	5,090
Camels*	36	36	36
Horses	154	155*	155*
Mules	518	520*	520*
Asses	1,099	1,000*	1,000*
Poultry	135	137	137

* FAO estimate(s).

Source: FAO.

LIVESTOCK PRODUCTS
('000 metric tons)

	2000	2001	2002
Beef and veal	140	150	150*
Mutton and lamb	125	125	120*
Goat meat	22	22	21*
Poultry meat	250	255	280
Other meat	38	38	38
Cows' milk	1,185	1,100	1,331
Sheep's milk*	27	27	26
Goats' milk*	35	35	34
Butter*	18	17	20
Cheese*	8	8	8
Poultry eggs	235*	235*	235
Honey	2	3	2
Wool: greasy	40†	40*	40*
Wool: scoured*	17	17	17
Cattle hides (fresh)*	20	20	20
Sheepskins (fresh)*	13	13	13
Goatskins (fresh)*	3	3	3

* FAO estimate(s).
† Unofficial figure.

Source: FAO.

Forestry

ROUNDWOOD REMOVALS
('000 cubic metres, excl. bark)

	2000	2001	2002*
Sawlogs, veneer logs and logs for sleepers	207	201	201
Pulpwood	362	374	374
Fuel wood	487	396	6,932
Total	1,056	971	7,507

* FAO estimates.

Source: FAO.

SAWNWOOD PRODUCTION
('000 cubic metres, incl. railway sleepers)

	1987	1988	1989
Coniferous (softwood)	40	26	43
Broadleaved (hardwood)	40	27	40
Total	80	53	83

1990–2002: Annual production as in 1989.

Source: FAO.

Fishing

('000 metric tons, live weight)

	1999	2000	2001
Capture	745.4	896.6	1,083.3
European pilchard (sardine)	429.7	539.8	763.2
European anchovy	40.2	22.1	47.4
Chub mackerel	17.4	63.4	26.0
Cuttlefish, bobtails and squids	20.2	32.9	17.6
Octopuses	84.6	99.4	112.6
Aquaculture	2.8	1.8	1.4
Total catch (incl. others)	748.2	898.4	1,084.6

Note: Figures exclude aquatic plants ('000 metric tons, capture only): 5.9 in 1999; 6.1 in 2000; 10.0 in 2001.

Mining

('000 metric tons)

	2000	2001	2002*
Hard coal	30.8	1.9	0.3
Crude petroleum	13.0	10.1	12.8
Iron ore†	6.5	8.0	1.6
Copper concentrates†	23.1	19.1	17.8
Lead concentrates†	117.4	110.9	87.4
Manganese ore†	25.8	13.8	17.5
Zinc concentrates†	201.7	174.8	178.4
Phosphate rock‡	19,658	20,724	21,806
Fluorspar (acid grade)	77.0	96.5	94.9
Barytes	343.6	467.1	469.9
Salt (unrefined)	162.4	233.8	266.1
Clay	30.7	40.7	43.2

* Preliminary figures.

† Figures refer to the gross weight of ores and concentrates.

‡ Including production in Western Sahara.

Industry

SELECTED PRODUCTS*
('000 metric tons, unless otherwise indicated)

	1999	2000	2001
Cement	7,194	7,497	8,058
Electric energy (million kWh)	13,264	13,942	14,803
Phosphate fertilizers†	481	631	550
Carpets and rugs ('000 sq m)	638	594	546
Wine‡	49	30	28
Olive oil (crude)	71	46	41
Motor spirit—petrol	391	383	344
Naphthas	507	492	532
Kerosene	96	98	114
Distillate fuel oils	2,539	2,322	2,415
Residual fuel oils	2,508	2,365	2,401
Jet fuel	279	282	271
Petroleum bitumen—asphalt	141	132	127
Liquefied petroleum gas	266	239	n.a.

* Major industrial establishments only.

† Estimated production in terms of phosphoric acid.

‡ Source: FAO.

Source: partly UN, *Industrial Commodity Statistics Yearbook*.

2002 ('000 metric tons): Motor spirit—petrol 377; Naphthas 527; Kerosene 80.1; Distillate fuel oils 2,323; Residual fuel oils 2,000; Petroleum bitumen—asphalt 131.

Finance

CURRENCY AND EXCHANGE RATES

Monetary Units

100 centimes (santimat) = 1 Moroccan dirham.

Sterling, Dollar and Euro Equivalents (31 December 2003)

£1 sterling = 15.62 dirhams;

US $1 = 8.75 dirhams;

€1 = 11.05 dirhams;

1,000 Moroccan dirhams = £64.04 = $114.29 = €90.49.

Average Exchange Rate (dirhams per US $)

2001　11.303
2002　11.021
2003　9.574

GENERAL BUDGET
(million dirhams)

Revenue*	2000	2001	2002†
Tax revenue	85,473	86,971	91,020
Taxes on income and profits	26,841	28,162	30,378
Individual	11,967	15,338	16,353
Corporate	10,124	11,708	12,917
Taxes on international trade	16,636	14,010	14,231
Indirect taxes	36,659	38,994	40,056
VAT	21,476	23,115	23,951
Excises	15,183	15,879	16,105
Registration and stamps	4,162	4,546	4,999
Revenue accruing to the road fund	1,175	1,259	1,356
Non-tax revenue	7,385	8,413	7,241
Dividend and licence income	5,287	4,904	4,244
Total	92,858	95,384	98,261

Expenditure	2000‡	2001	2002†
General public services	4,549	6,658	6,885
Defence	7,872	15,643	16,994
Public order	4,394	9,166	10,096
Education	11,579	23,776	25,894
Health, social security and welfare	2,303	4,954	5,183
Housing	597	993	969
Recreation, culture etc. . . .	443	862	930
Agriculture, mines and energy .	2,179	4,424	5,107
Transport and communications .	2,159	3,452	3,604
General expenditure	6,010	16,890	11,355
Transfers to local governments. .	3,308	6,443	6,935
Other	15,433	25,952	25,047
Total	**60,825**	**119,213**	**118,999**

* Excluding receipts from privatization 18 in 2000; 23,372 in 2001; 621 in 2002.
† Preliminary figures.
‡ Figures refer to the period 1 July–31 December 2000.

Source: IMF, *Morocco, Statistical Appendix* (June 2003).

INTERNATIONAL RESERVES
(US $ million at 31 December)

	2000	2001	2002
Gold*	184	169	193
IMF special drawing rights . .	119	123	122
Reserve position in IMF. . .	92	89	96
Foreign exchange.	4,612	8,262	9,915
Total	**5,007**	**8,643**	**10,326**

* National valuation of gold reserves (706,000 in 2000; 707,000 in 2001; 708,000 in 2002).

Source: IMF, *International Financial Statistics*.

MONEY SUPPLY
(million dirhams at 31 December)

	2000	2001	2002
Currency outside banks . . .	58,169	66,025	69,565
Demand deposits at deposit money banks	156,545	181,099	199,276
Total money (incl. others) . . .	**216,503**	**249,693**	**272,086**

Source: IMF, *International Financial Statistics*.

COST OF LIVING
(Consumer Price Index for urban areas; base: 1989 = 100)

	2000	2001	2002
Food	159.1	157.5	164.2
Clothing	161.3	163.5	166.2
Shelter.	159.2	162.5	165.0
Household equipment	138.2	138.4	139.2
All items (incl. others)	**157.3**	**158.3**	**162.7**

NATIONAL ACCOUNTS
(million dirhams at current prices)

Expenditure on the Gross Domestic Product

	1999	2000*	2001†
Government final consumption expenditure.	66,146	67,689	74,618
Private final consumption expenditure.	214,416	224,883	235,008
Increase in stocks	−1,984	−1,629	2,131
Gross fixed capital formation . .	81,896	85,312	85,264
Total domestic expenditure. .	**360,474**	**376,256**	**397,022**
Exports of goods and services . .	84,663	93,504	105,435
Less Imports of goods and services	99,543	115,693	119,560
GDP in purchasers' values . .	**345,594**	**354,068**	**382,897**
GDP at constant 1980 prices .	**133,622**	**134,927**	**143,648**

* Semi-definitive figures.
† Provisional figures.

Gross Domestic Product by Economic Activity

	2000	2001	2002
Agriculture, hunting, forestry and fishing	48,991.0	59,657.0	64,141.4
Mining and quarrying	7,290.2	7,429.4	7,314.4
Electricity and water	15,354.3	15,390.1	16,236.3
Manufacturing	72,155.1	76,461.9	77,757.0
Construction	18,300.1	19,371.9	19,313.8
Wholesale and retail trade . . .	42,490.1	44,989.4	47,148.9
Hotels and restaurants	8,001.2	8,163.2	7,799.9
Transport and communications .	24,896.9	26,259.4	28,673.1
Public administration and defence; compulsory social security . .	50,489.2	58,253.0	59,972.0
Financial intermediation . . .	17,163.0	18,038.3	19,060.0
Other services	38,130.0	39,308.1	40,897.9
Sub-total	**343,261.1**	**373,321.7**	**388,314.7**
Less Financial intermediation service	17,187.0	18,183.3	19,092.0
Gross value added	**326,074.1**	**355,138.4**	**369,222.7**
Taxes, less subsidies, on products .	28,133.8	28,046.6	28,559.2
GDP at market prices	**354,207.8**	**383,184.5**	**397,781.9**

BALANCE OF PAYMENTS
(US $ million)

	2000	2001	2002
Exports of goods f.o.b.	7,419	7,142	7,861
Imports of goods f.o.b.	−10,654	−10,164	−10,898
Trade balance	**−3,235**	**−3,022**	**−3,036**
Exports of services	3,034	4,029	4,354
Imports of services	−1,884	−2,119	−2,415
Balance on goods and services .	**−2,085**	**−1,111**	**−1,097**
Other income received	276	326	377
Other income paid	−1,149	−1,159	−1,115
Balance on goods, services and income	**−2,958**	**−1,944**	**−1,836**
Current transfers received . . .	2,574	3,670	3,439
Current transfers paid	−118	−120	−115
Current balance	**−501**	**1,606**	**1,488**
Capital account (net)	−6	−9	−6
Direct investment abroad . . .	−59	−97	−28
Direct investment from abroad. .	10	144	81
Portfolio investment liabilities . .	18	−7	−14
Other investment liabilities . .	−954	−1,006	−1,431
Net errors and omissions . . .	114	230	−79
Overall balance	**−1,167**	**861**	**11**

Source: IMF, *International Financial Statistics*.

External Trade

PRINCIPAL COMMODITIES
(million dirhams)

Imports c.i.f.	1999	2000	2001*
Foodstuffs, beverages and tobacco	11,540	14,210	15,348
Wheat	3,817	5,484	6,164
Energy and lubricants	13,000	21,657	21,874
Crude petroleum	8,941	14,710	14,488
Refined petroleum products . .	2,507	4,802	4,744
Crude animal and vegetable products.	5,583	5,803	5,763
Semi-finished products	21,828	24,365	26,387
Chemical products.	3,247	3,441	3,686
Metallurgical products . . .	4,679	5,403	5,533
Finished industrial capital goods	27,026	24,694	22,019
Aircraft, boats and industrial vehicles	3,454	4,000	1,958
Finished consumer products . .	24,323	28,822	29,919
Textile products	10,479	10,740	12,190
Telecommunications receiving equipment	995	4,501	2,398
Total (incl. others)	**105,931**	**122,527**	**124,081**

Exports f.o.b.	1999	2000	2001*
Foodstuffs, beverages and tobacco	14,853	16,751	16,185
Citrus fruit	2,613	2,050	2,026
Crustaceans and molluscs . .	4,422	6,742	4,954
Prepared and preserved fish . .	1,961	2,141	2,543
Energy and lubricants	1,990	2,882	3,098
Crude mineral products	5,979	5,766	6,179
Phosphates	4,462	4,129	4,687
Semi-finished products . . .	13,711	17,063	17,763
Phosphoric acid	5,777	5,365	5,380
Natural and chemical fertilizers	3,107	3,430	4,017
Electronic components (transistors)	1,826	4,253	4,302
Finished industrial capital goods	6,776	4,798	4,449
Electric wire and cable . . .	1,633	2,074	2,512
Finished consumer products . .	28,456	29,753	31,392
Manufactured garments . . .	16,172	16,195	17,164
Hosiery	8,070	8,935	8,861
Total (incl. others)	73,617	78,827	80,440

* Provisional figures.

Source: partly Office des Changes, Rabat.

PRINCIPAL TRADING PARTNERS
(million dirhams)*

Imports c.i.f.	1999	2000	2001†
Algeria	1,364.2	2,023.7	2,179.0
Argentina	704.2	1,066.8	1,651.3
Belgium-Luxembourg . . .	1,866.5	1,952.2	1,762.6
Brazil	2,044.0	1,820.6	3,025.0
Canada	1,355.1	2,404.0	2,534.2
China, People's Republic . .	2,419.9	2,846.4	3,151.5
France	27,275.4	29,438.9	29,854.4
Germany	6,400.9	5,978.4	6,251.0
Iran	2,346.1	3,795.9	3,185.0
Iraq	2,481.3	5,047.6	4,640.3
Italy	5,634.1	5,809.8	6,262.0
Japan	2,359.7	2,069.4	1,889.4
Korea, Republic	918.0	1,261.9	1,452.4
Netherlands	1,892.7	2,067.8	1,948.1
Russia	2,750.2	2,663.2	4,095.2
Saudi Arabia	3,433.3	6,087.8	5,854.2
South Africa	837.9	938.4	1,619.0
Spain	11,771.2	12,092.6	12,806.9
Sweden	1,475.1	2,718.9	1,563.2
Switzerland	1,109.2	1,209.2	1,333.6
Turkey	1,202.6	1,059.7	1,261.8
Ukraine	906.1	1,056.5	1,584.6
United Kingdom	5,722.2	7,559.3	7,699.4
USA	6,929.6	6,836.1	4,557.7
Total (incl. others)	105,931.0	122,526.8	124,080.7

Exports f.o.b.	1999	2000	2001†
Belgium-Luxembourg . . .	1,979.8	2,222.8	2,036.0
Brazil	473.6	730.2	915.5
France	26,309.4	26,392.1	26,391.7
Germany	4,186.8	3,916.8	3,361.0
India	3,550.4	3,297.9	2,894.3
Italy	3,728.0	5,616.3	4,599.5
Japan	2,679.8	3,009.8	2,041.3
Libya	1,130.3	668.7	660.5
Netherlands	1,420.1	1,316.4	2,184.5
Spain	7,867.3	10,220.2	12,274.2
United Kingdom	6,526.6	7,560.0	6,908.8
USA	2,511.8	2,693.5	3,246.0
Total (incl. others)	73,616.7	78,826.7	80,439.6

* Imports by country of production; exports by country of last consignment.
† Provisional figures.

Source: Office des Changes, Rabat.

Transport

RAILWAYS
(traffic)*

	2000	2001	2002
Passenger-km (million) . . .	1,956	2,019	2,145
Freight ton-km (million) . . .	4,650	4,699	4,794

* Figures refer to principal railways only.

ROAD TRAFFIC
(motor vehicles in use at 31 December)

	1996	1997	1998
Passenger cars	1,021,515	1,059,241	1,111,846
Goods vehicles	363,533	379,504	392,602
Motorcycles and scooters . . .	19,417	19,704	19,891

Source: Ministère du Transport et de la Marine Marchande.

SHIPPING

Merchant Fleet
(registered at 31 December)

	2000	2001	2002
Number of vessels	493	485	483
Total displacement ('000 grt) . .	466.9	461.5	501.7

Source: Lloyd's Register-Fairplay, *World Fleet Statistics*.

International Sea-borne Freight Traffic
('000 metric tons)

	2000	2001	2002
Goods loaded	23,384	24,959	24,822
Goods unloaded	29,831	32,591	32,127

CIVIL AVIATION
(traffic on Royal Air Maroc scheduled services)

	1999	2000	2001
Kilometres flown (million) . . .	65.0	67.9	62.8
Passengers carried ('000) . . .	3,460	3,676	3,677
Passenger-km (million)	6,880	7,442	6,642
Total ton-km (million) . . .	678.4	718.5	n.a.

Tourism

FOREIGN TOURIST ARRIVALS BY COUNTRY OF NATIONALITY*

	2000	2001	2002†
France	813,865	840,230	877,465
Germany	211,039	196,700	172,860
Italy	142,426	123,628	112,518
Maghreb countries	63,989	71,454	67,280
Spain	232,245	200,519	201,258
United Kingdom	137,232	135,642	146,511
USA	121,068	97,072	72,845
Total (incl. others)	2,325,505	2,249,662	2,222,267

* Excluding Moroccans resident abroad (1,787,532 in 2000; 1,973,653 in 2001; 1,971,065 in 2002).
† Provisional figures.

Cruise-ship passengers: 180,203 in 2000; 207,260 in 2001; 255,305 in 2002.

Receipts from tourism (provisional, US $ million): 2,040 in 2000; 2,460 in 2001; 2,152 in 2002.

Communications Media

	2000	2001	2002
Television receivers ('000 in use)	4,700	n.a.	n.a.
Telephones ('000 main lines in use)	1,425.0	1,191.3	1,127.4
Mobile cellular telephones ('000 subscribers)	2,342.0	4,771.7	6,198.7
Personal computers ('000 in use)	350	400	400
Internet users ('000)	100	400	500

1996: Book production (titles) 918, ('000 copies) 1,836; Daily newspapers 22 (average circulation 704,000 copies); Other newspapers and periodicals 699 (average circulation 3,671,000 copies).

1997: Radio receivers ('000 in use) 6,640; Telefax stations (number in use) 18,000 (estimate).

Sources: UNESCO, *Statistical Yearbook*; UN, *Statistical Yearbook*; and International Telecommunication Union.

Education

(1999/2000, unless otherwise indicated)

	Institutions	Teachers	Males	Females	Total
				Pupils/Students	
Pre-primary . .	33,577*	43,952	532,076	284,978	817,054
Primary: public . .	5,940	121,763	1,932,806	1,565,120	3,497,926
Primary: private . .	625	5,819	92,595	79,084	171,679
Secondary: general (public)	1,446	84,024‡	785,550	610,346	1,393,896
Secondary: general (private) . . .	218	4,277	26,834	18,258	45,092
Secondary: vocational	69	n.a.	12,810	9,981	22,791
University level* † .	68	9,667	154,314	112,193	266,507

* 1997/98 figure(s).
† Provisional; state institutions only.
‡ Including vocational teachers.

2000/01: Primary 3,842,000 (public 3,644,404; private 177,596); Secondary 1,504,367 (public 1,457,388; private 46,979); University level 265,905.

2001/02: Primary 4,029,112 (public 3,832,356; private 196,756); Secondary 1,610,753 (public 1,561,686; private 49,067); University level 266,621.

2002/03: Primary 4,101,157 (public 3,884,638; private 216,519); Secondary 1,679,077 (public 1,628,490; private 50,587); University level 276,018.

Source: mainly Ministère de l'Education Nationale.

Adult literacy rate (UNESCO estimates): 49.8% (males 62.6%; females 37.2%) in 2001 (Source: UNDP, *Human Development Report*).

Directory

The Constitution

The following is a summary of the main provisions of the Constitution, as approved in a national referendum on 4 September 1992, and as amended by referendum on 13 September 1996.

PREAMBLE

The Kingdom of Morocco, a sovereign Islamic State whose official language is Arabic, constitutes a part of the Great Arab Maghreb. As an African State, one of its aims is the realization of African unity. It adheres to the principles, rights and obligations of those international organizations of which it is a member and works for the preservation of peace and security in the world.

GENERAL PRINCIPLES

Morocco is a constitutional, democratic and social monarchy. Sovereignty pertains to the nation and is exercised directly by means of the referendum and indirectly by the constitutional institutions. All Moroccans are equal before the law, and all adults enjoy equal political rights including the franchise. Freedoms of movement, opinion and speech and the right of assembly are guaranteed. Islam is the state religion. All Moroccans have equal rights in seeking education and employment. The right to strike, and to private property, is guaranteed. All Moroccans contribute to the defence of the Kingdom and to public costs. There shall be no one-party system.

THE MONARCHY

The Crown of Morocco and its attendant constitutional rights shall be hereditary in the line of HM King Hassan II, and shall be transmitted to the oldest son, unless during his lifetime the King has appointed as his successor another of his sons. The King is the symbol of unity, guarantees the continuity of the state, and safeguards respect for Islam and the Constitution. The King appoints, and may dismiss, the Prime Minister and other Cabinet Ministers (appointed upon the Prime Minister's recommendation), and presides over the Cabinet. He shall promulgate adopted legislation within a 30-day period, and has the power to dissolve the Chamber of Representatives and or the Chamber of Advisers. The Sovereign is the Commander-in-Chief of the Armed Forces; makes appointments to civil and military posts; appoints Ambassadors; signs and ratifies treaties; presides over the Supreme Council of the Magistracy, the Supreme Council of Education and the Supreme Council for National Reconstruction and Planning; and exercises the right of pardon. In cases of threat to the national territory or to the action of

constitutional institutions, the King, having consulted the President of the Chamber of Representatives, the President of the Chamber of Advisers and the Chairman of the Constitutional Council, and after addressing the nation, has the right to declare a State of Emergency by royal decree. The State of Emergency shall not entail the dissolution of Parliament and shall be terminated by the same procedure followed in its proclamation.

LEGISLATURE

This consists of a bicameral parliament: the Chamber of Representatives and the Chamber of Advisers. Members of the Chamber of Representatives are elected by direct universal suffrage for a five-year term. Three-fifths of the members of the Chamber of Advisers are elected by electoral colleges of local councils; the remainder are elected by electoral colleges representing chambers of commerce and trade unions. Members of the Chamber of Advisers are elected for a nine-year term, with one-third renewable every three years. Deputies in both chambers enjoy parliamentary immunity. Parliament shall adopt legislation, which may be initiated by members of either chamber or by the Prime Minister. Draft legislation shall be examined consecutively by both parliamentary chambers. If the two chambers fail to agree on the draft legislation the Government may request that a bilateral commission propose a final draft for approval by the chambers. If the chambers do not then adopt the draft, the Government may submit the draft (modified, if need be) to the Chamber of Representatives. Henceforth the draft submitted can be definitively adopted only by absolute majority of the members of the Chamber of Representatives. Parliament holds its meetings during two sessions each year, commencing on the second Friday in October and the second Friday in April.

GOVERNMENT

The Government, composed of the Prime Minister and his Ministers, is responsible to the King and Parliament and ensures the execution of laws. The Prime Minister is empowered to initiate legislation and to exercise statutory powers except where these are reserved to the King. He presents to both parliamentary chambers the Government's intended programme and is responsible for co-ordinating ministerial work.

RELATIONS BETWEEN THE AUTHORITIES

The King may request a second reading, by both Chambers of Parliament, of any draft bill or proposed law. In addition, he may submit proposed legislation to a referendum by decree; and dissolve either Chamber or both if a proposal that has been rejected is approved by referendum. He may also dissolve either Chamber by decree after consulting the Chairman of the Constitutional Council, and addressing the nation, but the succeeding Chamber may not be dissolved within a year of its election. The Chamber of Representatives may force the collective resignation of the Government either by refusing a vote of confidence or by adopting a censure motion. The election of the new Parliament or Chamber shall take place within three months of its dissolution. In the interim period the King shall exercise the legislative powers of Parliament, in addition to those conferred upon him by the Constitution. A censure motion must be signed by at least one-quarter of the Chamber's members, and shall be approved by the Chamber only by an absolute majority vote of its members. The Chamber of Advisers is competent to issue 'warning' motions to the Government and, by a two-thirds' majority, force its resignation.

THE CONSTITUTIONAL COUNCIL

The Constitutional Council consists of six members appointed by the King (including the Chairman) for a period of nine years, and six members appointed for the same period—three selected by the President of the Chamber of Representatives and three by the President of the Chamber of Advisers. One-third of each category of the Council are renewed every three years. The Council is empowered to judge the validity of legislative elections and referendums, as well as that of organic laws and the rules of procedure of both parliamentary chambers, submitted to it.

JUDICIARY

The Judiciary is independent. Judges are appointed on the recommendation of the Supreme Council of the Magistracy presided over by the King.

THE ECONOMIC AND SOCIAL COUNCIL

An Economic and Social Council shall be established to give its opinion on all matters of an economic or social nature. Its constitution, organization, prerogatives and rules of procedure shall be determined by an organic law.

THE HIGH AUDIT COUNCIL

The High Audit Council exercises the general supervision of the implementation of fiscal laws. It ensures the regularity of revenues and expenditure operations of the departments legally under its jurisdiction, as it assesses the management of the affairs thereof. It is competent to penalize any breach of the rules governing such operations. Regional audit councils exercise the supervision of the accounts of local assemblies and bodies, and the management of the affairs thereof.

LOCAL GOVERNMENT

Local government in the Kingdom consists of establishing regions, governorships, provinces and communes.

REVISING THE CONSTITUTION

The King, the Chamber of Representatives and the Chamber of Advisers are competent to initiate a revision of the Constitution. The King has the right to submit the revision project he initiates to a national referendum. A proposal for a revision by either parliamentary chamber shall be adopted only if it receives a two-thirds' majority vote by the chamber's members. Revision projects and proposals shall be submitted to the nation for referendum by royal decree; a revision of the Constitution shall be definitive after approval by referendum. Neither the state, system of monarchy nor the prescriptions related to the religion of Islam may be subject to a constitutional revision.

The Government

HEAD OF STATE

Monarch: HM King Muhammad VI (acceded 23 July 1999).

CABINET
(April 2004)

A coalition of the Union socialiste des forces populaires (USFP); Rassemblement national des indépendants (RNI); Istiqlal; Parti du progrès et du socialisme (PPS); Mouvement national populaire (MNP); Parti socialiste démocratique (PSD); and non-affiliates.

Prime Minister: Driss Jettou.

Minister of State: Abbas el-Fassi (Istiqlal).

Minister of Foreign Affairs and Co-operation: Muhammad Benaissa (RNI).

Minister of the Interior: Al Mustapha Sahel.

Minister of Justice: Muhammad Bouzoubaa (USFP).

Minister of Habous (Religious Endowments) and Islamic Affairs: Ahmed Toufiq.

Minister of Territorial Administration, Water Resources and the Environment: Muhammad el-Yazghi (USFP).

Minister of the Finance and Privatization: Fathallah Oualalou (USFP).

Secretary-General of the Government: Abdessadek Rabiaa.

Minister of Agriculture and Rural Development: Mohand Laenser (MP).

Minister of Employment, Social Development and Solidarity: Mustapha Mansouri.

Minister of National Education and Youth: Habib el-Malki (USFP).

Minister of Higher Education and Scientific Research: Khalid Alioua (USFP).

Minister in charge of the Modernization of the Public Sector: Najib Zerouali (RNI).

Minister of Cultural Affairs: Muhammad Achaari (USFP).

Minister in charge of Human Rights: Muhammad Aujjar (RNI).

Minister of Handicrafts and Social Economy: Muhammad el-Khalifa (Istiqlal).

Minister of Equipment and Transport: Karim Ghellab (Istiqlal).

Minister of Industry, Commerce and Telecommunications: Rachid Talbi el-Alami (RNI).

Minister of Tourism: Adil Douri (Istiqlal).

Minister of Health: Muhammad Cheikh Biadillah.

Minister of Maritime Fisheries: Muhammad Taieb Rhafes (RNI).

Minister in charge of Relations with Parliament: Muhammad Saad el-Alami (Istiqlal).

Minister of Energy and Mining: Muhammad Boutaleb (RNI).

Minister of Communication and Government Spokesperson: Nabil Benabdallah (PPS).

Minister of Foreign Trade: Mustapha Mechahouri (MP).

Minister-delegate to the Prime Minister, in charge of the Administration of National Defence: Abd ar-Rahman Sbai.

Minister-delegate to the Minister of Foreign Affairs and Co-operation: Taieb Fassi Fihri.

Minister-delegate to the Minister of Foreign Affairs and Co-operation, in charge of Moroccans Resident Abroad: Nezha Chekrouni (USFP).

Minister-delegate to the Minister of the Interior: Fouad Ali el-Himma.

Minister-delegate to the Minister of Higher Education and Scientific Research, in charge of Scientific Research: Omar Fassi Fihri (PPS).

Minister-delegate to the Prime Minister, in charge of Economic and General Affairs and the Balancing of the Economy: Abderazzak el-Mossadeq.

Minister-delegate to the Prime Minister, in charge of Housing and Town Planning: Ahmed Toufiq Hjira (Istiqlal).

There are also six Secretaries of State.

MINISTRIES

Office of the Prime Minister: Palais Royal, Le Méchouar, Rabat; tel. (3) 7762709; fax (3) 7769995; e-mail aughar@pm.gov.ma; internet www.pm.gov.ma.

Ministry of Agriculture and Rural Development: Quartier Administratif, Place Abdellah Chefchaouni, BP 607, Rabat; tel. (3) 7760933; fax (3) 7763378; e-mail webmaster@mardrpm.gov.ma; internet www.madrpm.gov.ma.

Ministry of Communication: 10 rue Beni Mellal, Rabat; tel. (3) 7762507; fax (3) 7760828; e-mail webmaster@minicom.gov.ma; internet www.minicom.gov.ma.

Ministry of Cultural Affairs: 10 rue Beni Mellal, Rabat; tel. (3) 7762507; fax (3) 7760828; e-mail webmaster@mincom.gov.ma; internet www.mincom.gov.ma.

Ministry of Economic Planning: ave Al Haj Ahmed Cherkaoui, BP 826, 10004 Rabat; e-mail idoubba@cnd.mpep.gov.ma; internet www.mpep.gov.ma.

Ministry of Employment, Social Development and Solidarity: Rabat; e-mail dfp@dfp.ac.ma; internet www.dfp.ac.ma.

Ministry of Energy and Mining: rue Abou Marouane Essaadi, Agdal, Rabat; tel. (3) 7688830; fax (3) 7688831; e-mail webmaster@mem.gov.ma; internet www.mem.gov.ma.

Ministry of Equipment and Transport: Quartier Administratif, Rabat; tel. (3) 7762811; fax (3) 7765505; internet www.mtpnet.gov.ma.

Ministry of Finance and Privatization: Quartier Administratif, Chella, Rabat; tel. (3) 7760147; fax (3) 7760509; internet www.finances.gov.ma.

Ministry of Foreign Affairs and Co-operation: ave Franklin Roosevelt, Rabat; tel. (3) 7761583; fax (3) 7765508; e-mail mail@maec.gov.ma; internet www.maec.gov.ma.

Ministry of Habous (Religious Endowments) and Islamic Affairs: Al-Mechouar Essaid, Rabat; tel. (3) 7766801; fax (3) 7765282; e-mail webmaster@habous.gov.ma; internet www.habous.gov.ma.

Ministry of Health: 335 rue Larache, blvd Muhammad V, Rabat; tel. (3) 7761121; fax (3) 7768401; e-mail inas@sante.gov.ma; internet www.sante.gov.ma.

Ministry of Higher Education and Scientific Research: 35 ave Ibn Sina, BP 707, Rabat; tel. (3) 7774733; fax (3) 7778028; e-mail dfc@dfc.gov.ma; internet www.dfc.gov.ma.

Ministry in charge of Human Rights: Rabat; tel. (3) 7673131; fax (3) 7671967.

Ministry of Industry, Commerce and Telecommunications: Rabat; tel. (3) 7761868; fax (3) 7766265; e-mail webmaster@mcinet.gov.ma; internet www.mcinet.gov.ma.

Ministry of the Interior: Quartier Administratif, Rabat; tel. (3) 7761868; fax (3) 7762056.

Ministry of Justice: Place Mamounia, Rabat; tel. (3) 7732941; fax (3) 7730772; e-mail kourout@justice.gov.ma; internet www.justice.gov.ma.

Ministry of Maritime Fisheries: BP 476, Agdal, Rabat; e-mail webmaster@mpm.gov.ma; internet www.mpm.gov.ma.

Ministry of National Education and Youth: Bab Rouah, Rabat; tel. (3) 7771822; fax (3) 7779029; internet www.men.gov.ma.

Ministry in charge of Relations with Parliament: Nouveau Quartier Administratif, Rabat; tel. (3) 7775124; e-mail mirepa@mcrp.gov.ma; internet www.mcrp.gov.ma.

Ministry of Territorial Administration, Water Resources and the Environment: 36 ave el-Abtal, Agdal, Rabat; tel. (3) 7772634; fax (3) 7772756; e-mail info@minenv.gov.ma; internet www.minenv.gov.ma.

Ministry of Transport and Merchant Navy: rue Maa al-Ainane, Casier Officiel, BP 759, Rabat; tel. (3) 7774266; fax (3) 7779525.

Ministry of Youth and Sports: blvd Ibn Sina, Rabat; tel. (3) 7680028; fax (3) 7680145; internet www.mjs.gov.ma.

Legislature

MAJLIS AN-NUAB
(Chamber of Representatives)

President: ABD AR-RADHI (USFP).

General Election, 27 September 2002

Party	% of votes	Seats
Union socialiste des forces populaires (USFP)	15.38	50
Istiqlal	14.77	48
Parti de la justice et du développement (PJD)	12.92	42
Rassemblement national des indépendants (RNI)	12.62	41
Mouvement populaire (MP)	8.31	27
Mouvement national populaire (MNP)	5.54	18

Party— *continued*	% of votes	Seats
Union constitutionnelle	4.92	16
Front des forces démocratiques (FFD)	3.69	12
Parti national démocrate (PND)	3.69	12
Parti du progrès et du socialisme (PPS)	3.38	11
Union démocratique (UD)	3.08	10
Mouvement démocratique social (MDS)	2.15	7
Parti socialiste démocratique (PSD)	1.85	6
Parti Al Ahd	1.54	5
Alliance des libertés (ADL)	1.23	4
Parti de la gauche socialist unifiée (PGSU)	0.92	3
Parti de la réforme et du développement (PRD)	0.92	3
Parti marocain libéral (PML)	0.92	3
Parti des forces citoyennes (PFC)	0.62	2
Parti de l'environnement et du développement (PED)	0.62	2
Parti démocratique et de l'indépendance (PDI)	0.62	2
Congrès national ittihadi (CNI)	0.31	1
Total	**100.00**	**325***

* 30 of the 325 seats were reserved for women. Of these 30 seats five were won by the USFP; Istiqlal, the PJD and the RNI each took four seats; the MP, the MNP, the UC, the PND, the FFD and PPS all secured two seats; and the UD received one seat.

MAJLIS AL-MUSTASHARIN
(Chamber of Advisers)

President: MUSTAPHA OKACHA.

Election, 5 December 1997*

	Seats
Rassemblement national des indépendants (RNI)	42
Mouvement démocratique et social (MDS)	33
Union constitutionnelle (UC)	28
Mouvement populaire (MP)	27
Parti national démocrate (PND)	21
Istiqlal	21
Union socialiste des forces populaires (USFP)	16
Mouvement national populaire (MNP)	15
Parti de l'action (PA)	13
Front des forces démocratiques (FFD)	12
Parti du progrès et du socialisme (PPS)	7
Parti social et démocratique (PSD)	4
Parti démocratique pour l'indépendance (PDI)	4
Trade unions	
Confédération Démocratique du Travail (CDT)	11
Union Marocaine du Travail (UMT)	8
Union Générale des Travailleurs Marocains (UGMT)	3
Others	5
Total	**270**

* Of the Chamber of Advisers' 270 members, 162 were elected by local councils, 81 by chambers of commerce and 27 by trade unions.

Note: On 8 September 2000 elections were held to renew one-third of the seats in the Chamber of Advisers. 54 members were elected by local councils and 27 by chambers of commerce. The seats were allocated accordingly: RNI 14 seats; MNP 12; PND 10; MP 9; UC 8; Istiqlal 7; MDS 6; FFD 5; USFP 3; PPS 2; PA 2; PSD two; PDI one. Of the nine seats elected by trade unions the CDT won 4; the UMT 2; the UGTM 2; and the l'Union Nationale des Travailleurs du Maroc (UNMT) won one seat. Further elections were held to renew one-third of the seats in the Chamber of Advisers on 6 October 2003.

Political Organizations

Congrès national ittihadi (CNI): f. 2001; Sec.-Gen. ABDELMAJID BOUZOUBAA.

Front des forces démocratiques (FFD): 13 blvd Tariq ibn Ziad, Rabat; tel. (3) 7661625; fax (3) 7661626; f. 1997 after split from PPS; Sec.-Gen. THAMI EL-KHIARI.

Istiqlal: 4 ave Ibn Toumert, Bab el-Had, Rabat; tel. (3) 7730951; fax (3) 7725354; f. 1944; aims to raise living standards and to confer equal rights on all; stresses the Moroccan claim to Western Sahara; Sec.-Gen. ABBAS EL-FASSI.

Mouvement démocratique et social (MDS): 471 ave Muhammad V, Rabat; tel. (3) 7709110; f. 1996 as Mouvement national démocratique et social after split from MNP; adopted current name in Nov. 1996; Leader MAHMOUD ARCHANE.

Mouvement national populaire (MNP): Souissi, Rabat; tel. (3) 7753623; fax (3) 7759761; f. 1991; centre party; Leader MAHJOUBI AHERDANE.

Mouvement populaire (MP): 66 rue Patrice Lumumba, Rabat; tel. (3) 7767320; fax (3) 7767537; f. 1958; liberal; Sec.-Gen. MOHAND LAENSER.

Mouvement populaire pour la démocratie (MPD): Leader M. EL-KHATIB.

Organisation de l'action démocratique et populaire (OADP): Casablanca; tel. (2) 2262433; fax (2) 2278442; e-mail organisation .oadp@caramail.com; f. 1983; Sec.-Gen. MUHAMMAD BEN SAÏD AÏT IDDER.

Parti de l'action (PA): 113 ave Allal ben Abdallah, Rabat; tel. (3) 7206661; f. 1974; advocates democracy and progress; Sec.-Gen. MUHAMMAD EL IDRISSI.

Parti Al Ahd: f. 2002; Chair. NAJIB EL-OUAZZANI.

Parti de l'avant-garde démocratique socialiste (PADS): BP 2091, 54 ave de la Résistance Océan, Rabat; tel. (3) 7200559; fax (3) 7708491; internet membres.tripod.fr/PADSMAROC/; an offshoot of the USFP; legalized in April 1992; Sec.-Gen. AHMAD BENJELLOUNE.

Parti du congrès national unioniste: Rabat; f. 2001 by dissident members of the USFP; Sec.-Gen. ABDELMAJID BOUZOUBAÀ.

Parti démocratique et de l'indépendance (PDI): Casablanca; tel. (2) 2223359; f. 1946; Sec.-Gen. ABDELWAHED MAACH.

Parti de l'environnement et du développement (PED): f. 2002; Sec.-Gen. AHMAD AL-ALAMI.

Parti des forces citoyennes (PFC): f. 2001; Sec.-Gen. ABDERRAHIM LAHJOUJI.

Parti de la gauche socialiste unifiée (PGSU): Rabat; f. 2001; left-wing coalition comprising the OADP, the MPD, the Activistes de gauche and the Démocrates indépendants; Pres. MUHAMMAD BEN SAÏD AÏT IDDER.

Parti de la justice et du développement (PJD): 5 rue Maati Bakhay, Rabat; tel. (3) 7208862; fax (3) 7208854; e-mail pjd@ maktoub.com; f. 1967 as the Mouvement populaire constitutionnel et démocratique (MPCD); breakaway party from MP; formally absorbed members of the Islamic asscn Al Islah wa Attajdid in June 1996 and adopted current name in Oct. 1998; Sec.-Gen. SAADEDDINE OTHMANI.

Parti marocain libéral (PML): f. 2002; Nat. Co-ordinator MUHAMMAD ZIANE.

Parti national démocrate (PND): 18 rue de Tunis, Rabat; tel. (3) 7732127; fax (3) 7720170; f. 1981 from split within RNI; Sec.-Gen. ABDELLAH KADIRI.

Parti de la reforme et du developpement (PRD): Rabat; f. 2001 by fmr members of the RNI; Leader ABD AR-RAHMANE KOHEN.

Parti du progrès et du socialisme (PPS): 29 ave John Kennedy, Youssoufia, Rabat; tel. (3) 7759464; fax (3) 7759476; f. 1974; successor to the Parti communiste marocain (banned in 1952), and the Parti de la libération et du socialisme (banned in 1969); left-wing; advocates modernization, social progress, nationalization and democracy; 35,000 mems; Sec.-Gen. ISMAIL ALAOUI.

Parti socialiste démocratique (PSD): 1 rue Ibn Moqla, angle les Orangers, Rabat; tel. and fax (3) 7208576; e-mail dsp1@iam.net.ma; f. 1996; breakaway party from OADP; Leader ISSA OUARDIGHI.

Rassemblement national des indépendants (RNI): 6 rue Laos, ave Hassan II, Rabat; tel. (3) 7721420; fax (3) 7733824; f. 1978 from the pro-govt independents' group that formed the majority in the Chamber of Representatives; Leader AHMAD OUSMAN.

Union constitutionnelle (UC): 158 ave des Forces Armées Royales, Casablanca; tel. (2) 2441144; fax (2) 2441141; e-mail uc@ marocnet.net.ma; internet www.mincom.gov.ma/partis/uc; f. 1983; 25-member Political Bureau; Leader (vacant).

Union démocratique (UD): f. 2001; Pres. BOUAZZA IKKEN.

Union nationale des forces populaires (UNFP): 28–30 rue Magellan, BP 747, Casablanca; tel. (2) 2302023; fax (2) 2319301; f. 1959 by Mehdi ben Barka from a group within Istiqlal; left-wing; in 1972 a split occurred between the Casablanca and Rabat sections of the party; Leader MOULAY ABDALLAH IBRAHIM.

Union socialiste des forces populaires (USFP): 17 rue Oued Souss, Agdal, Rabat; tel. (3) 7773905; fax (3) 7773901; e-mail usfp@ mtds.com; internet www.mtds.com/~usfp; f. 1959 as UNFP, became USFP in 1974; left-wing progressive party; 100,000 mems; First Sec. MUHAMMAD EL-YAZGHI.

The following group is active in the disputed territory of Western Sahara:

Frente Popular para la Liberación de Saguia el-Hamra y Río de Oro (Frente Polisario) (Polisario Front): BP 10, el-Mouradia, Algiers; tel. (2) 747907; fax (2) 747206; e-mail dgmae@mail.wissal .dz; f. 1973 to gain independence for Western Sahara, first from Spain and then from Morocco and Mauritania; signed peace treaty with Mauritanian Govt in 1979; supported by Algerian Govt; in February 1976 proclaimed the Sahrawi Arab Democratic Republic (SADR); admitted as the 51st member of the OAU in Feb. 1982 and currently recognized by more than 75 countries worldwide; its main organs are a 33-member National Secretariat, a 101-member Sahrawi National Assembly (Parliament) and a 13-member Govt; Sec.-Gen. of the Polisario Front and Pres. of the SADR MUHAMMAD ABD AL-AZIZ; Prime Minister of the SADR BOUCHRAYA HAMMOUDI BAYOUNE.

Diplomatic Representation

EMBASSIES IN MOROCCO

Algeria: 46–48 blvd Tariq Ibn Ziad, BP 448, 10001 Rabat; tel. (3) 7765591; fax (3) 7762237; e-mail algerabat@iam.net.ma; Ambassador MUHAMMAD LAKHDAR HADJAZI.

Angola: km 4.5, route des Zaêrs, BP 1318, Soussi, Rabat; tel. (3) 7659239; fax (3) 7653703; e-mail amb.angola@iam.net.ma; Ambassador Dr LUIS JOSÉ DE ALMEIDA.

Argentina: 12 rue Mekki Bitaouri, Souissi, 10000 Rabat; tel. (3) 7755120; fax (3) 7755410; e-mail embarat@maghrebnet.net.ma; Ambassador JUAN JOSÉ SANTANDER.

Austria: 2 rue de Tiddes, BP 135, 10000 Rabat; tel. (3) 7764003; fax (3) 7765425; e-mail rabat-ob@bmaa.gv.at; Ambassador Dr GERHARD DEISS.

Bangladesh: 25 ave Tarek Ibn Ziad, Rabat; tel. (3) 7766731; fax (3) 7766729; e-mail bdoot@mtds.com; internet www .bangladeshembassy-morocco.org; Ambassador MOHAMMAD AL-HAROON.

Bahrain: rue beni Hassan, km 6.5, route des Zaêrs, Soussi, Rabat; tel. (3) 7656024; fax (3) 7630732; Ambassador MUSTAPHA KAMAL MUHAMMAD.

Belgium: 6 ave de Marrakech, BP 163, 10001 Rabat; tel. (3) 7764746; fax (3) 7767003; e-mail info@ambabel-rabat.org.ma; Ambassador CHRISTINA FUNES-NOPPEN.

Benin: 30 ave Mehdi Ben Barka, BP 5187, Souissi, 10105 Rabat; tel. (3) 7754158; fax (3) 77754156; Ambassador ALLASSANE YASSO.

Brazil: 3 rue Cadi Benjelloun, La Pinède, BP 414, 10000 Rabat; tel. (3) 7755151; fax (3) 7755291; Ambassador LAURO BARBOSA DA SILVA MOREIRA.

Bulgaria: 4 ave Ahmed El Yazidi, BP 1301, 10000 Rabat; tel. (3) 7765477; fax (3) 7763201; Ambassador Dr GEORGE B. KAREV.

Burkina Faso: 7 rue al-Bouziri, BP 6484, Agdal, 10101 Rabat; tel. (3) 7675512; fax (3) 7675517; e-mail ambfrba@smirt.net.ma; Ambassador ASSIMI KOUANDA.

Cameroon: 20 rue du Rif, BP 1790, Souissi, Rabat; tel. (3) 7754194; fax (3) 7750540; e-mail ambacam@iam.net.ma; Ambassador MAHAMAT PABA SALÉ.

Canada: 13 bis rue Jaafar as-Sadik, BP 709, Agdal, Rabat; tel. (3) 7687400; fax (3) 7687430; Ambassador YVES GAGNON.

Central African Republic: 42 rue Pasteur, BP 770, Agdal, 10000 Rabat; tel. (3) 7734198; Ambassador JOSEPH-VALERY HABYTAT.

Chile: 35 ave Ahmed Balafrej, Souissi, Rabat; tel. (3) 7636065; fax (3) 7636067; e-mail echilema@iam.net.ma; Ambassador ALEJANDRO CARVAJAL.

China, People's Republic: 16 ave Ahmed Balafrej, 10000 Rabat; tel. (3) 7754056; fax (3) 7757519; Ambassador XIONG ZHANQI.

Colombia: Residence place Otman Ibnou Affane, 3eme étage, App. no 12, angle ave 16 Novembre et rue Honaine, Agdal, 10000 Rabat; tel. (3) 7670804; fax (3) 7670802; e-mail emcora@smirt.net.ma; Ambassador GUILLERMO SALAH ZULETTA.

Congo, Democratic Republic: 34 ave de la Victoire, BP 553, 10000 Rabat; tel. (3) 7262280; fax (3) 7262280; Chargé d'affaires a.i. WAWA BAMIALY.

Congo, Republic: ave Imam Malik, 7 rue Senhaja, Soussi, Rabat; tel. (3) 7659966; fax (3) 7659959; Ambassador AIME EMMANUEL YOKA.

Côte d'Ivoire: 21 rue de Tiddas, BP 192, 10001 Rabat; tel. (3) 7763151; fax (3) 7762792; e-mail ambcim@dial.net.ma; Ambassador AMADOU THIAM.

Croatia: 73 rue Marnissa, Souissi, Rabat; tel. (3) 7638824; fax (3) 7638827; e-mail croamb@acdim.net.ma; Ambassador DUBRAVCO ZIPOVČIĆ .

Czech Republic: rue Ait Melloul, BP 410, Souissi, 10001 Rabat; tel. (3) 7755421; fax (3) 7755493; e-mail rabat@embassy.mzv.cz; internet www.mzv.cz/rabat; Ambassador ELEONORA URBANOVA.

Egypt: 31 rue al-Jazair, 10000 Rabat; tel. (3) 7731833; fax (3) 7706821; Ambassador ACHRAF YUSSUF ABDELHALIM ZAÂZAÂ.

Equatorial Guinea: ave President Roosevelt, angle rue d'Agadir 9, Rabat; tel. (3) 7764793; fax (3) 7764704; Ambassador EDOUARDO NDONG ELO NZANG.

Finland: 145 rue Soufiane Ben Wahb, OLM, Rabat; tel. (3) 7762312; fax (3) 7762352; e-mail admin@ambafinrab.org.ma; Ambassador ESKO KIURU.

France: 3 rue Sahnoun, 10000 Rabat; tel. (3) 7689706; fax (3) 7689720; e-mail michel.de-bonnecorse@diplomatie.fr; internet www.ambafrance-ma.org; Ambassador FRÉDÉRIC GRASSET.

Gabon: ave Imam Malik, km 3.5, BP 1239, 10100 Rabat; tel. (3) 7751968; fax (3) 7757550; Ambassador VICTOR AFOUNOUNA.

Gambia: 11 rue Cadi Ben Hammadi Senhaji, Soussi, Rabat; tel. (3) 7638045; fax (3) 7638189; Ambassador MAUDO HARLEY NURU TOURAY.

Germany: 7 Zankat Madnine, BP 235, 10000 Rabat; tel. (3) 7709662; fax (3) 7706851; e-mail amballma@mtds.com; internet www.amballemagne-rabat.com; Ambassador ROLAND MAUCH.

Greece: km 5 route des Zaiers, Villa Chems, Soussi, 10000 Rabat; tel. (3) 7638964; fax (3) 7638990; e-mail ambagrec@iam.net.ma; Ambassador MICHEL CAMBANIS.

Guinea: 15 rue Hamzah, Agdal, 10000 Rabat; tel. (3) 7674148; fax (3) 7672513; Ambassador MAHMADOU SALIOU SYLA.

Holy See: rue Béni M'tir, BP 1303, Souissi, Rabat (Apostolic Nunciature); tel. (3) 7772277; fax (3) 7756213; e-mail nuntius@iam.net.ma; Apostolic Nuncio Most Rev. ANTONIO SOZZO (Titular Archbishop of Concordia).

Hungary: 17 Zankat Aït Melloul, Souissi, BP 5026, Rabat; tel. (3) 7750757; fax (3) 7754123; e-mail huembrba@mtds.com; Ambassador KÁROLY GEDAI.

India: 13 ave de Michlifen, 10000 Rabat; tel. (3) 7671339; fax (3) 7671269; e-mail india@maghrebnet.net.ma; Ambassador INDRAJIT SINGH RATHORE.

Indonesia: 63 rue Béni Boufrah, km 5.9 route des Zaërs, BP 5076, 10105 Rabat; tel. (3) 7757860; fax (3) 7757859; e-mail kbrirabat@iam.net.ma; Ambassador SOEKAMTO WIENARDI.

Iran: ave Imam Malik, BP 490, 10001 Rabat; tel. (3) 7752167; fax (3) 7659118; Ambassador MOHAMMED MASJED JAME'I.

Iraq: 39 blvd Mehdi Ben Barka, 10100 Rabat; tel. (3) 7754466; fax (3) 7759749; a chargé d'affaires a.i. has been appointed by the Iraqi Governing Council.

Italy: 2 rue Idriss al-Azhar, BP 111, 10001 Rabat; tel. (3) 7706592; fax (3) 7706882; e-mail ambasiata@ambitalia.ma; Ambassador ALBERTO CANDILIO.

Japan: 39 ave Ahmed Balafrej, Souissi, 10100 Rabat; tel. (3) 7631782; fax (3) 7750078; e-mail amb-japon@fusion.net.ma; Ambassador HIROMI SATO.

Jordan: Villa al-Wafae, Lot 5, Souissi II, 10000 Rabat; tel. (3) 7751125; fax (3) 7758722; Ambassador MUHAMMAD HASSAN SOLEIMANE AD-DAOUDIA.

Korea, Republic: 41 ave Mehdi Ben Barka, Souissi, 10100 Rabat; tel. (3) 7751767; fax (3) 7750189; e-mail adambco@iam.net.ma; Ambassador JU CHUL-KU.

Kuwait: ave Imam Malik, km 4.3, BP 11, 10001 Rabat; tel. (3) 7751775; fax (3) 7753591; Ambassador SALAH MUHAMMAD AL-BIJAN.

Lebanon: 19 ave Adb al-Karim Ben Jalloun, 10000 Rabat; tel. (3) 7760728; fax (3) 7760949; Ambassador MOUSTAPHA HASSAN MOUSTAPHA.

Liberia: Lotissement no 7, Napabia, rue Ouled Frej, Souissi, Rabat; tel. (3) 7638426; Ambassador JARJAR KAMARA.

Libya: 1 rue Chouaïb Doukkali, BP 225, 10000 Rabat; tel. (3) 7769566; fax (3) 7705200; Ambassador EMBAREK ABDALLAH TURKI.

Malaysia: 17 ave Bir Kacem, Soussi, Rabat; tel. (3) 7658324; fax (3) 7658363; e-mail mwrabat@maghrebnet.net; Ambassador DATUK HAJI MOHD NOR BIN HAJI ATAN.

Mali: 7 rue Thami Lamadour, Souissi, Rabat; tel. (3) 7759125; fax (3) 7754742; Ambassador FOUSSEIN SY.

Mauritania: 6 rue Thami Lamdour, BP 207, Souissi, 10000 Rabat; tel. (3) 7656678; fax (3) 7656680; e-mail ambassadeur@mauritanie.org.ma; Ambassador MOHAMED FADEL OULD DAH.

Mexico: 6 rue Cadi Mohamed Brebi, BP 1789, Souissi, Rabat; tel. (3) 7631969; fax (3) 7768583; e-mail embamexmar@smirt.net.ma; Ambassador JUAN ANTONIO MATEOS.

Netherlands: 40 rue de Tunis, BP 329, 10001 Rabat; tel. (3) 7726780; fax (3) 7733333; e-mail nlgovrab@mtds.com; internet www.mtds.com/nlgovrab; Ambassador JOHANNES A. F. M. REVIS.

Niger: 14 Bis, rue Jabal al-Ayachi, Agdal, Rabat; tel. (3) 7674615; fax (3) 7674629; Ambassador RAMATOU DIORI HAMANI.

Nigeria: 70 ave Omar ibn al-Khattab, BP 347, Agdal, 10001 Rabat; tel. (3) 7671857; fax (3) 7672739; e-mail nigerianrabat@menara.ma; Ambassador ALHAJI ABUBAKAR SHEHO WURNO.

Norway: 9 rue Khenifra, BP 757, Agdal, Rabat; tel. (3) 7764085; fax (3) 7764088; e-mail emb.rabat@mfa.no; Ambassador ARNE AASHEIM.

Oman: 21 rue Hamza, Agdal, 10000 Rabat; tel. (3) 7673788; fax (3) 7674567; Ambassador MAHMOUD BIN ALI MUHAMMAD AR-RAHMAN.

Pakistan: 11 Zankat Azrou, 10000 Rabat; tel. (3) 7762402; fax (3) 7766742; e-mail parerabat@maghrebnet.net.ma; Ambassador Maj. Gen. (Retd) SHUJAAT ALI KHAN.

Peru: 16 rue d'Ifrane, 10000 Rabat; tel. (3) 7723236; fax (3) 7702803; e-mail lepruab@msn.com; Ambassador JORGE ABARCA DEL CARPIO.

Poland: 23 rue Oqbah, Agdal, BP 425, 10000 Rabat; tel. (3) 7771173; fax (3) 7775320; e-mail apologne@iam.net.ma; internet www.ambpologne.ma; Ambassador MIECZYSŁAW JACEK STEPIŃSKI.

Portugal: 5 rue Thami Lamdouar, Souissi, 10000 Rabat; tel. (3) 7756446; fax (3) 7756445; e-mail embport_rabat@hotmail.com; Ambassador JOSÉ MANUEL DE CARVAHLO LAMOIRAS.

Qatar: 4 ave Tarik ibn Ziad, BP 1220, 10001 Rabat; tel. (3) 7765681; fax (3) 7765774; e-mail qe-rabat@mtds.com; Ambassador SAQR MUBARAK AL-MANSOURI.

Romania: 10 rue d'Ouezzane, 10000 Rabat; tel. (3) 7724694; fax (3) 7700196; e-mail amb.roumanie@menara.ma; Ambassador GELU VOICAN VOICULESCU.

Russia: km 4 route des Zaiers, 10100 Rabat; tel. (3) 7753509; fax (3) 7753590; e-mail ambrus@iam.net.ma; Ambassador YURII KOTOV.

Saudi Arabia: 43 place de l'Unité Africaine, 10000 Rabat; tel. (3) 7730171; fax (3) 7768587; e-mail ambassd@goodinfo.net.ma; Ambassador ABD AL-AZIZ KHODJA.

Senegal: 17 rue Cadi ben Hamadi Senhaji, Souissi, 10000 Rabat; tel. (3) 7754171; fax (3) 7754149; Ambassador IBOU IDIAYE.

Serbia and Montenegro: 23 ave Mehdi Ben Barka, Souissi, BP 5014, 10105 Rabat; tel. (3) 7752201; fax (3) 7753258; e-mail youg@iam.net.ma; Chargé d'affaires GOLUB LAZOVIĆ.

South Africa: 34 rue Saadiens, Rabat; tel. (3) 7706760; fax (3) 7706756; e-mail sudaf@mtds.com; Ambassador M. MTUTUZELI. MPEHLE.

Spain: 3 rue Madnine, BP 1354, 10000 Rabat; tel. (3) 7707600; fax (3) 7707387; e-mail infembsp@mtds.com; Ambassador FERNANDO ARIAS-SALGADO Y MONTALVO.

Sudan: 5 ave Ghomara, Souissi, 10000 Rabat; tel. (3) 7752863; fax (3) 7752865; e-mail soudanirab@maghrebnet.net.ma; Ambassador AHMED MEKKI AHMED YAHIA.

Sweden: 159 ave John Kennedy, BP 428, 10000 Rabat; tel. (3) 7759303; fax (3) 7758048; e-mail swedrab@mtds.com; Ambassador NILS ANDERS PETER BRUCE.

Switzerland: Square de Berkane, BP 169, 1001 Rabat; tel. (3) 7706974; fax (3) 7705749; e-mail vertretung@rab.rep.admin.ch; Ambassador DANIEL VON MURALT.

Syria: km 5.2, route des Zaërs, BP 5158, Souissi, Rabat; tel. (3) 7755551; fax (3) 7757522; Ambassador YOUSSEF JOUMAA.

Thailand: 11 rue de Tiddas, BP 4436, Rabat; tel. (3) 7763328; fax (3) 7763920; e-mail thairab@wanadoo.net.ma; Ambassador SIRIWAT SUTHIGASAME.

Tunisia: 6 ave de Fès et 1 rue d'Ifrane, 10000 Rabat; tel. (3) 7730636; fax (3) 7730637; Ambassador SALAH BACCARI.

Turkey: 7 ave Abdelkrim Benjelloun, 10000 Rabat; tel. (3) 7762605; fax (3) 7660476; e-mail amb-tur-rabat@iam.net.ma; Ambassador HUSEYIN NACI AKINCI.

Ukraine: Cite OLM Soussi II, Villa 212, Rabat; tel. (3) 7657840; fax (3) 7754679; e-mail ukremb@iam.net.ma; Ambassador YOURI F. MALKO.

United Arab Emirates: 11 ave des Alaouines, 10000 Rabat; tel. (3) 7702085; fax (3) 7724145; e-mail uaerabat@mtds.com; Ambassador ISSAA HAMAD BUSHAHAB.

United Kingdom: 17 blvd de la Tour Hassan, BP 45, 10001 Rabat; tel. (3) 77238600; fax (3) 7704531; e-mail britemb@mtds.com; internet www.britain.org.ma; Ambassador HAYDON WARREN-GASH.

USA: 2 ave de Muhammad el-Fassi, Rabat; tel. (3) 7762265; fax (3) 7765661; internet www.usembassy-morocco.org.ma; Ambassador THOMAS RILEY.

Venezuela: 58 Lotissement OLM, Villa Yasmine, rue Capitaine Abdeslam el-Moudden el-Alami, Soussi, Rabat; tel. (3) 7650315; fax (3) 7650372; e-mail emvenez@iam.net.ma; Ambassador REBECA SANCHEZ BELLO.

Yemen: 11 rue Abou-Hanifa, Agdal, 10000 Rabat; tel. (3) 7674306; fax (3) 7674769; e-mail yemenembassy@iam.net.ma; Ambassador Dr ALI MTENA HASSAN.

Judicial System

SUPREME COURT

Al-Majlis al-Aala

Hay Ryad, blvd An-Nakhil, Rabat; tel. (3) 7714932; e-mail coursupreme@maghrebnet.net.ma; internet www.maghrebnet.net.ma/cour-supreme/.

Responsible for the interpretation of the law and regulates the jurisprudence of the courts and tribunals of the Kingdom. The Supreme Court sits at Rabat and is divided into six Chambers.

First President: DRISS DAHAK.

Attorney-General: MUHAMMAD ABDELMOUNIM EL-MEJBOUD.

The 21 **Courts of Appeal** hear appeals from lower courts and also comprise a criminal division.

The 65 **Courts of First Instance** pass judgment on offences punishable by up to five years' imprisonment. These courts also pass judgment, without possibility of appeal, in personal and civil cases involving up to 3,000 dirhams.

The **Communal and District Courts** are composed of one judge, who is assisted by a clerk or secretary, and hear only civil and criminal cases.

The seven **Administrative Courts** pass judgment, subject to appeal before the Supreme Court pending the establishment of administrative appeal courts, on litigation with Government departments.

The nine **Commercial Courts** pass judgment, without the possibility of appeal, on all commercial litigations involving up to 9,000 dirhams. They also pass judgment on claims involving more than 9,000 dirhams, which can be appealed against in the commercial appeal courts.

The **Special Court of Justice** presides over crimes and felonies allegedly committed by Government officials or judges involving 25,000 dirhams or more.

The **Permanent Royal Armed Forces' Court** tries offences committed by the armed forces and military officers.

Religion

ISLAM

About 99% of Moroccans are Muslims (of whom about 90% are of the Sunni sect), and Islam is the state religion.

CHRISTIANITY

There are about 69,000 Christians, mostly Roman Catholics.

The Roman Catholic Church

Morocco (excluding the disputed territory of Western Sahara) comprises two archdioceses, directly responsible to the Holy See. At 31 December 2002 there were an estimated 23,150 adherents in the country, representing less than 0.1% of the population. The Moroccan archbishops participate in the Conférence Episcopale Régionale du Nord de l'Afrique (f. 1985), based in Algiers (Algeria).

Archbishop of Rabat: Most Rev. VINCENT LANDEL, Archevêché, 1 rue Hadj Muhammad Riffaï, BP 258, 10001 Rabat; tel. (3) 7709239; fax (3) 7706282; e-mail landel@wanadoo.net.ma.

Archbishop of Tangier: Most Rev. JOSÉ ANTONIO PETEIRO FREIRE, Archevêché, 55 rue Sidi Bouabid, BP 2116, 9000 Tangier; tel. (3) 9932762; fax (3) 9949117; e-mail igletanger@wanadoo.net.ma.

Western Sahara comprises a single Apostolic Prefecture, with an estimated 120 Catholics (2002).

Prefect Apostolic of Western Sahara: Fr ACACIO VALBUENA RODRÍGUEZ, Misión Católica, BP 31, 70001 el-Aaiún; tel. 893270.

The Anglican Communion

Within the Church of England, Morocco forms part of the diocese of Gibraltar in Europe. There are Anglican churches in Casablanca and Tangier.

Protestant Church

Evangelical Church: 33 rue d'Azilal, 20000 Casablanca; tel. (2) 2302151; fax (2) 2444768; e-mail eeam@lesblancs.com; f. 1920; established in eight towns; Pres. Pastor JEAN-LUC BLANC; 1,000 mems.

JUDAISM

There is a Jewish community of some 8,000. In March 1999 the Moroccan authorities reopened the synagogue in Fez, established in the 17th century.

Grand Rabbi of Casablanca: CHALOM MESSAS (President of the Rabbinical Court of Casablanca, Palais de Justice, place des Nations Unies).

The Press

DAILIES

Casablanca

Assahra Al-Maghribia: 88 blvd Muhammad V, Casablanca; tel. (2) 2268860; fax (2) 2203935; f. 1989; Arabic; Dir ABD AL-HAFID ROUISSI.

Al-Bayane (The Manifesto): 62 blvd de la Gironde, BP 13152, Casablanca; tel. (2) 2307882; internet www.casanet.ma/albayane; Arabic and French; organ of the Parti du progrès et du socialisme; Dir ISMAIL ALAOUI; circ. 5,000.

Al-Ittihad al-Ichtiraki (Socialist Unity): 33 rue Emir Abdelkader, BP 2165, Casablanca; tel. (2) 2619400; fax (2) 2619405; Arabic; organ of the Union socialiste des forces populaires; Dir ABDALLAH BOUHLAL; Editor ABD AR-RAHMAN EL-YOUSSOUFI; circ. 110,000.

L'Economiste: 201 blvd Bordeaux, Casablanca; tel. (2) 2271650; fax (2) 2297285; e-mail info@leconomiste.com; internet www.leconomiste.com; f. 1991; French; Dir ABDELMOUNAÏM DILAMI; Editor NADIA SALAH; circ. 24,000.

Libération: 33 rue Emir Abdelkader, Casablanca; tel. (2) 2310062; internet www.liberation.press.ma; f. 1964; French; organ of the Union socialiste des forces populaires; Dir MUHAMMAD AL-YAZGHI.

Maroc Soir: 88 blvd Muhammad V, Casablanca; tel. (2) 2268860; fax (2) 2262969; f. 1971; French; Dir DRISSI EL-ALAMI; circ. 50,000.

Le Matin du Sahara et du Maghreb: 88 blvd Muhammad V, Casablanca; tel. (2) 2268860; fax (2) 2317535; e-mail contact@lematin.press.ma; internet www.lematin.press.ma; f. 1971; French; Dir ABD AL-HAFID ROUISSI; circ. 100,000.

Rissalat al-Oumma (The Message of the Nation): 158 ave des Forces Armées Royales, Casablanca; tel. (2) 2905949; fax (2) 2901926; Arabic; weekly edition in French; organ of the Union constitutionnelle; Dir ABDALLAH FERDAOUS.

Rabat

Al-Alam (The Flag): 11 ave Allal ben Abdallah, BP 141, Rabat; tel. (3) 7732419; fax (3) 7733896; f. 1946; organ of the Istiqlal party; Arabic; literary supplement on Fridays; weekly edition on Mondays; monthly edition on foreign policy; Dir ABD AL-KRIM GHALLAB; circ. 100,000.

Al-Anba'a (Information): ave Allal el-Fassi, Rabat; tel. (3) 7683967; fax (3) 7683970; internet www.alanbaa.press.ma; f. 2000; daily; Arabic; publ. by Ministry of Communication; Dir (Editorial) MUHAMMAD BELGHAZI.

Assyassa al-Jadida: 43 rue Abou Fares al-Marini, BP 1385, Rabat; tel. (3) 7208571; fax (3) 7208573; e-mail assassjdid@maghrebnet.net.ma; f. 1997; Arabic; organ of the Parti socialiste démocratique; Dir ABD AL-LATIF AOUAD; Editor TALAA ASSOUD ALATLASSI.

Al-Maghrib: 6 rue Laos, BP 469, Rabat; tel. (3) 7722708; fax (3) 7722765; f. 1977; French; organ of the Rassemblement national des indépendants (RNI); Dir MUSTAPHA IZNASNI; circ. 15,000.

Al-Mithaq al-Watani (The National Charter): 6 rue Laos, BP 469, Rabat; tel. (3) 7722708; fax (3) 7722765; f. 1977; Arabic; organ of the RNI; Dir MED AUAJJAR; circ. 25,000.

An-Nidal ad-Dimokrati (The Democratic Struggle): 18 rue de Tunis, Rabat; tel. (3) 7730754; fax (3) 7731255; Arabic; organ of the Parti national démocrate; Dir MUHAMMAD ARSALANE AL-JADIDI.

L'Opinion: 11 ave Allal ben Abdallah, Rabat; tel. (3) 7727812; fax (3) 7732181; f. 1965; French; organ of the Istiqlal party; Dir MUHAMMAD IDRISSI KAÏTOUNI; Editor JAMAL HAJJAM; circ. 60,000.

SELECTED PERIODICALS

Casablanca

Achamal: Casablanca; weekly; Arabic; Editor-in-Chief KHALID MECHBAL.

Bulletin Mensuel de la Chambre de Commerce et d'Industrie de la Wilaya du Grand Casablanca: 98 blvd Muhammad V, BP 423, Casablanca; tel. (2) 2264327; monthly; French; Pres. LAHCEN EL-WAFI.

CGEM Infos: angle ave des Forces Armées Royales et rue Muhammad Arrachid, 20100 Casablanca; tel. (2) 2986932; fax (2) 2253845; e-mail cgem@iam.net.ma; weekly; French; Admin. MOUHCINE AYOUCHE.

Construire: 25 rue d'Azilal, Immeuble Ortiba, Casablanca; tel. (2) 2305721; fax (2) 2317577; f. 1940; weekly; French; Dir TALAL BOUCHAIB.

Demain: Casablanca; f. 1997; weekly, French; Dir ALI LAMRABET.

Les Echos Africains: Immeuble SONIR, angle blvd Smiha, rue d'Anjou, BP 13140, Casablanca; tel. (2) 2307271; fax (2) 2319680; f. 1972; monthly; French; news, economics; Dir MUHAMMAD CHOUFFANI EL-FASSI; Editor Mme SOODIA FARIDI; circ. 5,000.

La Gazette du Maroc: ave des Forces Armées Royales, Tour de Habous, 13eme étage, Casablanca; tel. (2) 2313925; fax (2) 2318094; e-mail redaction@lagazettedumaroc.com; internet www .lagazettedumaroc.com; weekly; French; Dir KAMAL LAHLOU.

Al-Ittihad al-Watani Lilkouate ach-Chaabia (National Union of Popular Forces): 28–30 rue Magellan, Casablanca; tel. (2) 2302023; fax (2) 2319301; weekly; Arabic; organ of the Union nationale des forces populaires; Dir MOULAY ABDALLAH IBRAHIM.

Le Journal: Media Trust, 61 ave des F.A.R., Casablanca; tel. (2) 2546670; fax (2) 2446185; e-mail lejournalhebdo@yahoo.fr; internet www.lejournalhebdo.com; weekly; French; news, politics, economics; Dir ABOUBAKR JAMAÏ.

Lamalif: 6 bis rue Defly Dieude, Casablanca; tel. (2) 2220032; f. 1966; monthly; French; economic, social and cultural magazine; Dir MUHAMMAD LOGHLAM.

La Mañana: 88 blvd Muhammad V, Casablanca; tel. (2) 2268860; fax (2) 2203935; f. 1990; Spanish; Dir ABD AL-HAFID ROUISSI.

Maroc Fruits: 22 rue Al-Messaoudi, Casablanca; tel. (2) 2363946; fax (2) 2364041; f. 1958; fortnightly; Arabic and French; organ of the Association des Producteurs d'Agrumes du Maroc; Dir NEJJAI AHMAD MANSOUR; circ. 6,000.

Maroc Soir: 34 rue Muhammad Smiha, Casablanca; tel. (2) 2301271; fax (2) 2317535; f. 1971; French; Dir ABD AL-HAFID ROUISSI; circ. 30,000.

Matin Hebdo: 34 rue Muhammad Smiha, Casablanca; tel. (2) 2301271; weekly; Dir AHMAD AL-ALAMI.

Matin Magazine: 88 blvd Muhammad V, Casablanca; tel. (2) 2268860; fax (2) 2262969; f. 1971; weekly; French; Dir ABD AL-HAFID ROUISSI.

An-Nidal (The Struggle): 10 rue Cols Bleus, Sidi Bousmara, Médina Kédima, Casablanca; f. 1973; weekly; Arabic; organ of the Parti national démocrate; Dir IBRAHIMI AHMAD.

La Nouvelle Tribune: 1 blvd Abd al-Latif Ben Kaddour, angle blvd Zerktouni, Casablanca; tel. (2) 2940911; fax (2) 2940914; e-mail nouvelle-tribune@techno.net.ma; internet www.lanouvelletribune .press.ma; f. 1996; weekly; French; Dir FAHD YATA; circ. 25,000.

Les Nouvelles du Maroc: 28 ave des Forces Armées Royales, Casablanca; tel. (2) 2203031; fax (2) 2277181; weekly; French; Dir KHADIJA S. IDRISSI.

Al-Ousbouaa al-Maghribia: 158 ave des Forces Armées Royales, Casablanca; f. 1984; organ of the Union constitutionnelle; Editor MUSTAFA ALAOUI.

La Quinzaine du Maroc: 53 rue Dumont d'Urville, Casablanca; tel. (2) 2302482; fax (2) 2440426; e-mail mauro@wanadoopro.ma; f. 1951; monthly; English and French; Dir HUBERT MAURO; circ. 20,000.

Revue Marocaine de Droit: 24 rue Nolly, Casablanca; tel. (2) 2273673; quarterly; French and Arabic; Dirs J. P. RAZON, A. KETTANI.

As-Sahifa: Casablanca; weekly; Arabic; Dir ABOUBAKR JAMAI.

Les Temps du Maroc: 88 blvd Muhammad V, Casablanca; tel. (2) 2268860; fax (2) 2262969; e-mail contact@lematin.press.ma; internet www.tempsdumaroc.press.ma; f. 1995; weekly; French; Dir ABD AL-HAFID ROUISSI.

La Vie Economique: 5 blvd ben Yacine, 20300 Casablanca; tel. (2) 2443868; fax (2) 2304542; e-mail vieeco@marocnet.net.ma; internet www.marocnet.net.ma/vieeco; f. 1921; weekly; French; Pres. and Dir JEAN LOUIS SERVAN-SCHREIBER.

La Vie Industrielle et Agricole: 142 blvd Muhammad V, Casablanca; tel. (2) 2274407; 2 a month; French; Dir AHMAD ZAGHARI.

La Vie Touristique Africaine: 142 blvd Muhammad V, Casablanca; tel. (2) 2274407; fortnightly; French; tourist information; Dir AHMAD ZAGHARI.

Rabat

Al-Aklam (The Pens): Rabat; monthly; Arabic; Dir ABD AR-RAHMAN BEN AMAR.

Al-Anba'a (Information): ave Allal el-Fassi, Rabat; tel. (3) 7683967; fax (3) 7683970; internet www.alanbaa.press.ma; f. 2000; weekly; Arabic; publ. by Ministry of Communication; Dir (Editorial) MUHAMMAD BELGHAZI.

Assiassa Al-Jadida: 8 rue Sanaa, BP 1385, Rabat; tel. (3) 7208571; fax (3) 7208573; e-mail aouad@nsimail.com; f. 1996; weekly; Arabic; organ of the Partie socialiste démocratique; Dir ABDELLATIF AOUAD.

Ach-Chorta (The Police): BP 437, Rabat; tel. (3) 7723194; monthly; Arabic; Dir MUHAMMAD AD-DRIF.

Da'ouat Al-Haqq (Call of the Truth): al-Michwar as-Said, Rabat; tel. (3) 7760810; publ. by Ministry of Habous (Religious Endowments) and Islamic Affairs; f. 1957; monthly; Arabic.

Al-Haraka: 66 rue Patrice Lumumba, BP 1317, Rabat; tel. (3) 7768667; fax (3) 7768677; weekly; Arabic; organ of the Mouvement populaire; Dir ALI ALAOUI.

Al-Imane: rue Akenssous, BP 356, Rabat; f. 1963; monthly; Arabic; Dir ABOU BAKER AL-KADIRI.

Al-Irchad (Spiritual Guidance): al-Michwar as-Said, Rabat; tel. (3) 7760810; publ. by Ministry of Habous (Religious Endowments) and Islamic Affairs; f. 1967; monthly; Arabic.

Al-Khansa: 154 ave Souss Mohammadia, Rabat; monthly; Arabic; Dir ABOUZAL AICHA.

Al-Maghribi: Rabat; tel. (3) 7768139; weekly; Arabic; organ of the Parti de l'action; Dir ABDALLAH AL-HANANI.

At-Tadamoun: Rabat; monthly; Arabic; Dir ABD AL-MAJID SEMLALI EL-HASANI.

La Verité: Rabat; weekly; French; Chief Editor ALLAL EL-MALEH.

La Voix du Centre: Rabat; weekly; French; Editor-in-Chief MUSTAPHA SHIMI.

Tangier

Actualités Touristiques: 80 rue de la Liberté, Tangier; monthly; French; Dir TAYEB ALAMI.

Le Journal de Tanger: 11 ave Moulay Abd al-Aziz, BP 420, Tangier; tel. (3) 7946051; fax (3) 7945709; e-mail redact@ journaldetanger.com; internet www.journaldetanger.com; f. 1904; weekly; French, English, Spanish and Arabic; Dir BAKHAT ABD AL-HAQ; circ. 10,000.

NEWS AGENCIES

Maghreb Arabe Presse (MAP): 122 ave Allal ben Abdallah, BP 1049, 10000 Rabat; tel. (3) 7764083; fax (3) 7702734; e-mail direction@map.co.ma; internet www.map.co.ma; f. 1959; Arabic, French, English and Spanish; state-owned; Dir-Gen. MUHAMMAD YASSINE MANSOURI.

Foreign Bureaux

Agence France-Presse (AFP): 2 bis rue du Caire, BP 118, Rabat; tel. (3) 7768943; fax (3) 7700357; f. 1920; Dir IGNACE DALLE.

Agencia EFE (Spain): 14 ave du Kairouane, Rabat; tel. (3) 7723218; fax (3) 7732195; Bureau Chief ALBERTO MASEGOSA GARCÍA-CALAMARTE.

Informatsionnoye Telegrafnoye Agentstvo Rossii—Telegrafnoye Agentstvo Suverennykh Stran (ITAR—TASS) (Russia): 32 rue de la Somme, Rabat; tel. (3) 7750315; Dir OLEG CHIROKOV.

Inter Press Service (IPS) (Italy): Rabat; tel. (3) 7756869; fax (3) 7727183; e-mail ipseumed@hotmail.com; internet www.ips.org; Dir BOULOUIZ BOUCHRA.

Reuters (United Kingdom): 509 Immeuble es-Saada, ave Hassan II, Rabat; tel. (3) 7726518; fax (3) 7722499; Chief Correspondent (North Africa) JOHN BAGGALEY.

Xinhua (New China) News Agency (People's Republic of China): 4 rue Kadi Mekki el-Bitaouri, Souissi, Rabat; tel. (3) 7755320; fax (3) 7754319; Dir ZHUGE CANGLIN.

Publishers

Dar el-Kitab: place de la Mosquée, Quartier des Habous, BP 4018, Casablanca; tel. (2) 2305419; fax (2) 2304581; f. 1948; philosophy, history, Africana, general and social science; Arabic and French; Dir BOUTALEB ABDOU ABD AL-HAY; Gen. Man. KHADIJA EL KASSIMI.

Editions La Porte: 281 blvd Muhammad V, BP 331, Rabat; tel. (3) 7709958; fax (3) 7706476; e-mail la_porte@meganet.net.ma; law, guides, economics, educational books.

Les Editions Maghrébines: Quartier Industrial, blvd E, N 15, Sin Sebaa, Casablanca; tel. (2) 2351797; fax (2) 2355541; f. 1962; general non-fiction.

Government Publishing House

Imprimerie Officielle: ave Yacoub El Mansour, Rabat-Chellah; tel. (3) 7765024; fax (3) 7765179.

Broadcasting and Communications

TELECOMMUNICATIONS

Regulatory Authority

Agence Nationale de Réglementation des Télécommunications (ANRT): Centre d'Affaires, blvd Ar-Ryad; Hay Ryad, BP 2939,10100 Rabat; tel. (3) 7718400; fax (3) 7716489; e-mail webmaster@anrt.net.ma; internet www.anrt.net.ma; f. 1998; Dir-Gen. MUHAMMAD BENCHAABOUN.

Principal Operators

Itissalat al-Maghrib—Maroc Télécom: ave Annakhil Hay Riad, Rabat; tel. (3) 7712626; fax (3) 7714860; internet www.iam.ma; f. 1998 to take over telephone services from the ONPT; partially privatized in 2002; Dir ABDESSALEM AHIZOUNE.

BROADCASTING

Morocco can receive broadcasts from Spanish radio stations, and the main Spanish television channels can also be received in northern Morocco.

Radio

Radiodiffusion-Télévision Marocaine: 1 rue el-Brihi, BP 1042, 1000 Rabat; tel. (3) 7709613; fax (3) 7703208; internet www.maroc .net/rc; govt station; Network A in Arabic, Network B in French, English and Spanish, Network C in Berber and Arabic; Foreign Service in Arabic, French and English; Dir-Gen. MUHAMMAD TRICHA; Dir Radio ABD AR-RAHMAN ACHOUR.

Radio Méditerranée Internationale: 3–5 rue Emsallah, BP 2055, Tangier; tel. and fax (3) 9936363; e-mail medi1@medi1.com; internet www.medi1.com; Arabic and French; Man. Dir PIERRE CASALTA.

Voice of America Radio Station in Tangier: c/o US Consulate-General, chemin des Amoureux, Tangier.

Television

Radiodiffusion-Télévision Marocaine: 1 rue el-Brihi, BP 1042, 1000 Rabat; tel. (3) 7709613; fax (3) 7703208; internet www.maroc .net/rc; govt station; transmission commenced 1962; 45 hours weekly; French and Arabic; carries commercial advertising; Dir-Gen. MUHAMMAD TRICHA; Dir Television FAICAL LAARAICHI.

SOREAD 2M: Société d'études et de réalisations audiovisuelles, km 7.3 route de Rabat, Aïn-Sebaâ, Casablanca; tel. (2) 2667373; fax (2) 2667392; internet www.2m.tv; f. 1988; transmission commenced 1989; public television channel, owned by Moroccan Government (72%) and by private national foreign concerns; broadcasting in French and Arabic; Man. Dir MOSTAFA BENALI.

Finance

(cap. = capital; res = reserves; dep. = deposits; m. = million; brs = branches; amounts in dirhams unless otherwise indicated)

BANKING

Central Bank

Bank Al-Maghrib: 277 ave Muhammad V, BP 445, Rabat; tel. (3) 7702626; fax (3) 7706677; e-mail dai@bkam.gov.ma; internet www

.bkam.ma; f. 1959 as Banque du Maroc; bank of issue; cap. 500m., res 4,869.0m., dep. 37,445.6m. (Dec. 2002); Gov. MUHAMMAD SEQAT.

Other Banks

Banque Centrale Populaire (Crédit Populaire du Maroc): 101 blvd Muhammad Zerktouni, BP 10622, 21100 Casablanca; tel. (2) 2202533; fax (2) 2222699; e-mail bcpinternational@ banquepopulairemorocco.ma; internet www.cpm.co.ma; f. 1961; 51% state-owned, 49% privately-owned; cap. 1,328.5m., res 3,942.1m., total assets 77,641.0m. (Dec. 2001); Pres. and Gen. Man. NOUREDDINE OMARY; 400 brs.

Banque Commerciale du Maroc SA (BCM): 2 blvd Moulay Youssef, BP 11141, 20000 Casablanca; tel. (2) 2298888; fax (2) 2268852; internet www.attijari.com; f. 1911; 20.3% owned by Banco Central Hispano; merger with Wafabank pending; cap. 1,325.0m., res 3,839.8m., dep. 43,269.9m. (Dec. 2001); Chair. and CEO KHALID OUDGHIRI; Gen. Mans ALI IBN MANSOUR, MUHAMMAD KETTANI, BOUKBER JAI; 112 brs.

Banque Marocaine du Commerce Extérieur SA (BMCE): 140 ave Hassan II, BP 13425, 20000 Casablanca; tel. (2) 2200496; fax (2) 2200512; e-mail sgg@bmcebank.co.ma; internet www.bmcebank.co .ma; f. 1959; transferred to majority private ownership in 1995; cap. 1,587.5m., res 3,512.4m., total assets 49,896.1m. (Dec. 2002); Chair. and CEO OTHMAN BEN JELLOUN; 201 brs.

Banque Marocaine pour l'Afrique et l'Orient: 1 place Bandoeng, BP 11183, 20000 Casablanca; tel. (2) 2307070; fax (2) 2301673; f. 1975 to take over British Bank of the Middle East (Morocco); cap. 200.0m., res 1.4m., dep. 2,042.0m. (Dec. 1996); Chair. FARID DELLERO; Gen. Man. SAID IBRAHIMI; 29 brs.

Banque Marocaine pour le Commerce et l'Industrie SA: 26 place des Nations Unies, BP 15573, Casablanca; tel. (2) 2224101; fax (2) 2299402; e-mail bmcisg@casanet.net.ma; internet www.bmcinet .com; f. 1964; transferred to majority private ownership in 1995; cap. 775.2m., res 723.4m., dep. 21,463.9m. (Dec. 2002); Pres. MUSTAPHA FARIS; Gen. Man. JEAN-JACQUES SANTINI; 137 brs.

Banque Nationale pour le Développement Economique (BNDE): 12 place des Alaouites, BP 407, 10000 Rabat; tel. (3) 7706040; fax (3) 7703706; internet www.bnde.co.ma; f. 1959; 34.2% state-owned, 65.8% privately-owned; cap. 600.0m., res 475.8m., dep. 5,200.6m. (Dec. 1999); Chair. and Man. Dir KHALID KADIRI; 14 brs.

Citibank (Maghreb): 52 ave Hassan II, Casablanca; tel. (2) 2224168; fax (2) 2205723; f. 1967; cap. 100m., res 2.5m., dep. 612.6m. (Dec. 1996); Pres. ERIC STOCLET.

Crédit Immobilier et Hôtelier: 187 ave Hassan II, Casablanca; tel. (2) 2479000; fax (2) 2479999; e-mail cih@cih.co.ma; f. 1920; transferred to majority private ownership in 1995; cap. 3,323.4m., res 1,225.4m., dep. 25,195.2m. (Dec. 2001); Pres. MUHAMMAD EL-ALJ; 91 brs.

Crédit du Maroc SA: 48–58 blvd Muhammad V, BP 13579, 20000 Casablanca; tel. (2) 2477000; fax (2) 2477071; e-mail cdmdai@ atlasnet.net.ma; internet www.creditdumaroc.co.ma; f. 1963; cap. 833.8m., res 648.1m., dep. 14,002.8m. (Dec. 2001); Chair. and CEO FRANCIS SAVOYE; 122 brs.

Société Générale Marocaine de Banques SA: 55 blvd Abd al-Moumen, BP 13090, 21100 Casablanca; tel. (2) 2438844; fax (2) 2298809; internet www.sgmaroc.com; f. 1962; cap. 1,170.0m., res 655.7m., dep. 19,348.6m. (Dec. 2001); Pres. ABD AL-AZIZ TAZI; 180 brs.

Société Marocaine de Dépôt et Crédit: 79 ave Hassan II, BP 296, 20000 Casablanca; tel. (2) 2224114; fax (2) 2264498; f. 1974; cap. 625.9m., res 717.8m., total assets 4,811.0m. (Dec. 1998); Chair and Gen. Man. ABD AL-LATIF IDMAHAMMA; 21 brs.

Wafabank: 163 ave Hassan II, 21000 Casablanca; tel. (2) 2200200; fax (2) 2470398; f. 1964 as Cie Marocaine de Crédit et de Banque; merger with Banque Commercial du Maroc pending; cap. 645.8m., res 3,060.2m., total assets 36,610.1m. (Dec. 2002); Pres. and CEO ABDELHAK BENNANI; 91 brs.

Bank Organizations

Association Professionnelle des Intermédiaires de Bourse du Maroc: 71 ave des Forces Armées Royales, Casablanca; tel. (2) 2314824; fax (2) 2314903; f. 1967; groups all banks and brokers in the stock exchange of Casablanca, for studies, inquiries of general interest and contacts with official authorities; 11 mems; Pres. ABD AL-LATIF JOUAHRI.

Groupement Professionnel des Banques du Maroc: 71 ave des Forces Armées Royales, Casablanca; tel. (2) 2314824; fax (2) 2314903; f. 1967; groups all commercial banks for studies, inquiries of general interest, and contacts with official authorities; 18 mems; Pres. ABD AL-LATIF JOUAHRI.

STOCK EXCHANGE

Bourse des Valeurs de Casablanca: ave de l'Armée Royale, Casablanca; tel. (2) 2452626; fax (2) 2452625; e-mail contact@casablanca-bourse.com; internet www.casablanca-bourse.com; f. 1929; Chair. DRISS BENCHEIKH.

INSURANCE

Al-Wataniya: 83 ave des FAR, 20000 Casablanca; tel. (2) 2314850; fax (2) 2313137; internet www.alwataniya.com; Dir-Gen. ABD AL-AZIZ GUESSONS.

Alliance Africaine: 63 blvd Moulay Youssef, 20000 Casablanca; tel. (2) 2200690; fax (2) 2200694; f. 1975; cap. 20m.; Pres. ABD AR-RAHIM CHERKAOUI; Dir-Gen. KHALID CHEDDADI.

Assurances Al-Amane: 122 ave Hassan II, 20000 Casablanca; tel. (2) 2267272; fax (2) 2265664; f. 1975; cap. 120m.; Pres. and Dir-Gen. MUHAMMAD BOUGHALEB.

Atlanta Assurances: BP 13685, 20001 Casablanca; tel. (2) 2436868; fax (2) 2203011; e-mail info@atlanta.ma; f. 1947; cap. 100m.; Dir-Gen. SELLAM SEKKAT.

Cie Africaine d'Assurances: 120 ave Hassan II, 20000 Casablanca; tel. (2) 2224185; fax (2) 2260150; internet www.caa.co.ma; f. 1950; Dir-Gen. JAMAL HAROUCHI.

Cie d'Assurances et de Réassurances SANAD: 3 blvd Muhammad V, BP 13438, 20000 Casablanca; tel. (2) 2260591; fax (2) 2293813; e-mail contact@sanad.ma; internet www.sanad.ma; f. 1975; Chair. MUHAMMAD HASSAN BENSALAH; Dir-Gen. ABDELTIF TAHIRI.

CNIA Assurance: 216 blvd Muhammad Zerktouni, 20000 Casablanca; tel. (2) 2474040; fax (2) 2206081; internet www.cnia.ma; f. 1949; cap. 30m.; Pres. ABDELLATIF AL-RAYES; Dir-Gen. SAID AHMIDOUCH.

La Marocaine Vie: 37 blvd Moulay Youssef, Casablanca; tel. (2) 2206320; fax (2) 2261971; f. 1978; cap. 12m.; Pres. HAMZA KETTANI.

Mutuelle Centrale Marocaine d'Assurances: 16 rue Abou Inane, BP 27, Rabat; tel. (3) 7766960; Pres. ABD AS-SALAM CHERIF D'OUEZZANE; Dir-Gen. YACOUBI SOUSSANE.

Mutuelle d'Assurances des Transporteurs Unis (MATU): 215 blvd Muhammad Zerktouni, Casablanca; tel. (2) 2367097; Dir-Gen. M. BENYAMNA MUHAMMAD.

La Royale Marocaine d'Assurances (RMA): 67–69 ave de l'Armée Royale, BP 13779, 20000 Casablanca; tel. (2) 2312163; fax (2) 2313884; internet www.rma.co.ma; f. 1949; cap. 1,108.0m.; Chair. OTHMAN BEN JELLOUN; Dir-Gen. SÉBASTIEN CASTRO.

Es-Saada, Cie d'Assurances et de Réassurances: 123 ave Hassan II, BP 13860, 20000 Casablanca; tel. (2) 2222525; fax (2) 2262655; e-mail es-saada@techno.net.ma; f. 1961; cap. 50m.; Pres. MEHDI OUAZZANI; Man. Dir SAÏD OUAZZANI.

Société Centrale de Réassurance: Tour Atlas, place Zallaqa, BP 13183, Casablanca; tel. (2) 2308585; fax (2) 2308672; e-mail scr@scrmaroc.com; internet www.scrmaroc.com; f. 1960; cap. 30m.; Chair. MUSTAPHA BAKKOURY; Man. Dir AHMAD ZINOUN.

Société Marocaine d'Assurances à l'Exportation: 24 rue Ali Abderrazak, BP 15953, Casablanca; tel. (2) 2982000; fax (2) 2252070; e-mail smaex@wanadoo.net.ma; internet www.smaex.com; f. 1988; insurance for exporters in the public and private sectors; assistance for export promotion; Pres. and Dir-Gen. MUHAMMAD TAZI; Asst Dir-Gen. ABDELKADER DRIOUACHE.

WAFA Assurance: 1–3 blvd Abd al-Moumen, BP 13420, 20001 Casablanca; tel. (2) 2224575; fax (2) 2209103; e-mail webmaster@wafaassurance.com; internet www.wafaassurance.com; Pres. SAÂD KETTANI; Dir-Gen. JAOUAD KETTANI.

Zurich Cie Marocaine d'Assurances: City Park Centre, 106 rue Abderrahmane Sahraoui, 20000 Casablanca; tel. (2) 2279015; fax (2) 2491729; Pres. and Dir-Gen. BERTO FISLER.

INSURANCE ASSOCIATION

Fédération Marocaine des Sociétés d'Assurances et de Réassurances: 154 blvd d'Anfa, Casablanca; tel. (2) 2391850; fax (2) 2391854; f. 1958; 17 mem. cos; Pres. HAMZA KETTANI.

Trade and Industry

GOVERNMENT AGENCIES

Centre Marocain de Promotion des Exportations (CMPE): 23 blvd Bnou Majid el-Bahar, BP 10937, Casablanca; tel. (2) 2302210; fax (2) 2301793; e-mail cmpe@cmpe.org.ma; internet www.cmpe.org.ma; f. 1980; state org. for promotion of exports; Dir-Gen. MOUNIR M. BENSAID.

Direction de la Privatisation: 1 angle ave Ibn Sina et Oued al-Makhazine, Agdal, Rabat; tel. (3) 7689614; fax (3) 7673299; e-mail minpriv@mtds.com; internet www.minpriv.gov.ma; privatization agency integrated with Ministry of the Economy, Finance, Privatization and Tourism; Dir NAJIB HAJOUI.

Office National des Hydrocarbeures et des Mines (ONHYM): 5 ave Moulay Hassan, BP 99, 10001 Rabat; tel. (3) 7702398; fax (3) 7709411; e-mail sammoud@brpm.org.ma; internet www.brpm.org.ma; f. 1928 as Bureau de Recherches et de Participations Minières; name changed to above in 2003; state agency conducting exploration, valorization and exploitation of hydrocarbons and mineral resources; Dir-Gen. MELLA AMINA BENKHADRA.

Société de Gestion des Terres Agricoles (SOGETA): 35 rue Daïet-Erroumi, BP 731, Agdal, Rabat; tel. (3) 7772834; fax (3) 7772765; e-mail sogeta@acdim.net.ma; f. 1973; oversees use of agricultural land; Man. Dir BACHIR SAOUD.

DEVELOPMENT ORGANIZATIONS

Agence National pour la Promotion de la PME (ANPME): 10 rue Gandhi, BP 211, 10001 Rabat; tel. (3) 7708460; fax (3) 7707695; e-mail anpme@anpme.gov.ma; internet www.anpme.gov.ma; f. 1973 as the Office pour le Développement Industriel; name changed as above in 2002; a state agency to develop industry; Dir-Gen. ECHIHABI LATIFA.

Caisse de Dépôt et de Gestion: place Moulay El-Hassan, BP 408, 10001 Rabat; tel. (3) 7765520; fax (3) 7763849; e-mail cdg@cdg.org.ma; internet www.cdg.org.ma; f. 1959; finances small-scale projects; cap. and res 2,058.1m. dirhams (Dec. 1998); Dir-Gen. MUSTAPHA BAKKOURI; Sec.-Gen. MUSTAPHA MECHAHOURI.

Caisse Marocaine des Marchés (Marketing Fund): Résidence El Manar, blvd Abd al-Moumen, Casablanca; tel. (2) 2259118; fax (2) 2259120; f. 1950; cap. 10m. dirhams; Man. HASSAN KISSI.

Caisse Nationale de Crédit Agricole (Agricultural Credit Fund): 2 ave d'Alger, BP 49, 10001 Rabat; tel. (3) 7725920; fax (3) 7732580; f. 1961; cap. 1,573.5m. dirhams, dep. 3,471.9m. dirhams; Dir-Gen. SAID IBRAHIMI.

Société de Développement Agricole (SODEA): ave Hadj Ahmed Cherkaoui, BP 6280, Rabat; tel. (3) 7770825; fax (3) 7774798; f. 1972; state agricultural devt org; Man. Dir M. SABBARI HASSANI LARBI.

Société Nationale d'Investissement (SNI): 60 rue d'Alger, BP 38, 20000 Casablanca; tel. (2) 2484288; fax (2) 2484303; f. 1966; transferred to majority private ownership in 1994; cap. 10,900m. dirhams; Pres. MOURAD CHERIF; Sec.-Gen. KAMAL EL-AYOUBI.

CHAMBERS OF COMMERCE

La Fédération des Chambres de Commerce et d'Industrie du Maroc: 6 rue d'Erfoud, Rabat-Agdal; tel. (3) 7767078; fax (3) 7767076; f. 1962; groups the 26 Chambers of Commerce and Industry; Pres. AHMAD M'RABET; Dir-Gen. MUHAMMAD LARBI EL HARRAS.

Chambre de Commerce, d'Industrie et de Services de la Wilaya de Rabat-Salé: 1 rue Gandhi, BP 131, Rabat; tel. (3) 7706444; fax (3) 7706768; e-mail ccisrs@ccisrs.org.ma; internet www.ccisrs.org.ma; Pres. OMAR DERRAJI; Dir ZINE EL-ABIDINE AFIA.

Chambre de Commerce et d'Industrie de la Wilaya du Grand Casablanca: 98 blvd Muhammad V, BP 423, Casablanca; tel. (2) 2264327; Pres. LAHCEN EL-WAFI.

INDUSTRIAL AND TRADE ASSOCIATIONS

Office National Interprofessionnel des Céréales et des Légumineuses: 25 ave Moulay Hassan, BP 154, Rabat; tel. (3) 7701735; fax (3) 7709626; f. 1937; Dir-Gen. ABD AL-HAI BOUZOUBAA.

Office National des Pêches: 13 rue Lieutenant Mahroud, BP 16243, 20300 Casablanca; tel. (2) 2240551; fax (2) 2242305; e-mail onp@onp.co.ma; internet www.onp.co.ma; f. 1969; state fishing org.; Man. Dir MAJID KAISSAR EL-GHAIB.

EMPLOYERS' ORGANIZATIONS

Association Marocaine des Industries Textiles et de l'Habillement (AMITH): 92 blvd Moulay Rachid, Casablanca; tel. (2) 2942085; fax (2) 2940587; e-mail mtazi@amith.org.ma; internet www.amith.org.ma; f. 1958; mems 700 textile, knitwear and ready-made garment factories; Pres. SALAH-EDDINE MEZOUAR; Dir-Gen. ABDE LALI BERRADA.

Association des Producteurs d'Agrumes du Maroc (ASPAM): 22 rue al-Messaoudi, Casablanca; tel. (2) 2363946; fax (2) 2364041; f. 1958; links Moroccan citrus growers; has its own processing plants; Pres AHMED MANSOUR NEJJAI.

Association Professionelle des Agents Maritimes, Consignataires de Navires, et Courtiers d'Affrètement du Maroc: Iman Centre No 1, 5ème Etage, rue Arrachid Muhammad (ex rue de la

Plage), Casablanca; tel. (2) 2541112; fax (2) 2541415; e-mail apram@wanadoopro.ma; internet www.apram.ma; Pres. ABDELAZIZ MANTRANCH; 32 mems.

Association Professionnelle des Cimentiers: Casablanca; tel. (2) 2401342; fax (2) 2248208; cement manufacturers.

Confédération Générale des Entreprises du Maroc (CGEM): angle ave des Forces Armées Royales et rue Muhammad Arrachid, 20100 Casablanca; tel. (2) 2252696; fax (2) 2253839; e-mail cgem@cgem.ma; internet www.cgem.ma; Pres. HASSAN CHAMI.

Union Marocaine de l'Agriculture (UMA): 12 place des Alaouites, Rabat; Pres. M. NEJJAI.

UTILITIES

Electricity and Water

Office National de l'Eau Potable (ONEP): 6 bis rue Patrice Lumumba, Rabat; tel. (3) 7650695; fax (3) 7650640; e-mail onepigi@mtds.com; internet www.onep.org; f. 1972; responsible for drinking-water supply; Dir ALI FASSI-FIHRI.

Office National de l'Electricité (ONE): 65 rue Othman Ben Affan, BP 13498, 20001 Casablanca; tel. (2) 2668080; fax (2) 2220038; e-mail offelec@one.org.ma; internet www.one.org.ma; f. 1963; state electricity authority; Chair. AHMAD NAKKOUCHE.

Régie Autonome Intercommunale de Distribution d'Eau et d'Electricité de la Wilaya de Chaouia (RADEEC): industrial and commercial public body providing water and power supplies in the Chaouia region.

Régie Autonome Intercommunale de Distribution d'Eau et d'Electricité de la Wilaya de Tanger (RAID): 5 rue Oqba ibn Naffiy, BP 286, Tanger; tel. (3) 7321414; fax (3) 7322156; water, sewerage and electricity network for Tanger; a concession to manage the services was scheduled to be awarded in 1999.

Régie d'Eau et d'Electricité (RED): Rabat; in 1998 a 30-year concession to manage Rabat's water and power grids was awarded to a consortium of Electricidade de Portugal (Portugal), Urbaser (Spain) and Alborada (Morocco).

Gas

Afriquia Gaz: rue Ibnou el-Ouennanae Ain Sebaa; Casablanca; tel. (2) 2352144; fax (2) 2352239; f. 1992; Morocco's leading gas distributor; transfer to private ownership pending; Dir-Gen. RACHID IDRISSI KAITOUNI.

TRADE UNIONS

Confédération Démocratique du Travail (CDT): 64 rue al-Mourtada, Quartier Palmier, BP 13576, Casablanca; tel. (2) 2994470; fax (2) 2258162; f. 1978; 400,000 mems; Sec.-Gen. MUHAMMAD NOUBIR AMAOUI.

Union Démocratique de l'Agriculture: f. 1997; Sec.-Gen. ABD AR-RAHMAN FILALI.

Union Générale des Travailleurs Marocains (UGTM): 9 rue du Rif, angle Route de Médiouna, Casablanca; tel. (2) 2282144; f. 1960; associated with Istiqlal; supported by unions not affiliated to UMT; 673,000 mems; Sec.-Gen. ABD AR-RAZZAQ AFILAL.

Union Marocaine du Travail (UMT): Bourse du Travail, 232 ave des Forces Armées Royales, Casablanca; tel. (2) 2302292; left-wing and associated with the UNFP; most unions are affiliated; 700,000 mems; Sec. MAHJOUB BEN SEDDIQ.

Union Syndicale Agricole (USA): agricultural section of UMT.

Union Marocaine du Travail Autonome: Rabat; breakaway union from UMT.

Transport

Office National des Transports (ONT): rue al-Fadila, Quartier Industriel, BP 596, Rabat-Chellah; tel. (3) 7797842; fax (3) 7797850; f. 1958; Man. Dir MUHAMMAD LAHBIB EL-GUEDDARI.

RAILWAYS

In 2002 there were 1,907 km of railways, of which 370 km were double track; 1,003 km of lines were electrified and diesel locomotives were used on the rest. In that year the network carried some 14.7m. passengers and 29.9m. metric tons of freight. All services are nationalized. A feasibility study was begun in early 1998 into the construction of a 28-km metro system in Casablanca.

Office National des Chemins de Fer (ONCF): 8 bis rue Abderrahmane El Ghafiki, Rabat-Agdal; tel. (3) 7774747; fax (3) 7774480;

e-mail meziane@oncf.org.ma; internet www.oncf.org.ma; f. 1963; administers all Morocco's railways; Dir-Gen. KARIM GHELLAB.

ROADS

In 2001 there were 57,226 km of classified roads, of which 56.1% were paved.

Cie de Transports au Maroc (CTM—SA): 23 rue Léon l'Africain, Casablanca; tel. (2) 2753677; fax (2) 2765428; e-mail webmaster@ctm.co.m; internet www.ctm.co.ma; agencies in Tangier, Rabat, Meknès, Oujda, Marrakesh, Agadir, El Jadida, Safi, Casablanca, Essaouira, Fez and Ouarzazate; privatized in mid-1993 with 40% of shares reserved for Moroccan citizens; Pres. and Dir-Gen. ABDALLAH LAHLOU.

SHIPPING

According to official figures, Morocco's 21 ports handled 57.0m. tons of goods in 2002. The most important ports, in terms of the volume of goods handled, are Casablanca, Jorf Lasfar, Safi and Mohammadia. Tangier is the principal port for passenger services. Construction work on new ports at Tangier (to handle merchandise traffic) and Agadir commenced in 2000.

Office d'Exploitation des Ports (ODEP): 175 blvd Muhammad Zerktouni, 20100 Casablanca; tel. (2) 2232324; fax (2) 2232325; e-mail administrateur@odep.org.ma; internet www.odep.org.ma; f. 1985; port management and handling of port equipment; Gen. Man. MUSTAPHA BARROUG.

Principal Shipping Companies

Agence Gibmar SA: 3 rue Henri Regnault, Tangier; tel. (3) 7935875; fax (3) 7933239; e-mail agemcemed@mamnet.net.ma; also at Casablanca; regular services from Tangier to Gibraltar; Chair. JAMES PETER GAGGERO; Dir YOUSSEF BENYAHIA.

Cie Chérifienne d'Armement: 5 blvd Abdallah ben Yacine, 21700 Casablanca; tel. (2) 2309455; fax (2) 2301186; f. 1929; regular services to Europe; Man. Dir MAX KADOCH.

Cie Marocaine d'Agences Maritimes (COMARINE): 45 ave de l'Armée Royale, BP 60, 20000 Casablanca; tel. (2) 2311941; fax (2) 2312570; e-mail comarine@marocnet.net.ma.

Cie Marocaine de Navigation (COMANAV): 7 blvd de la Résistance, BP 628, Casablanca 20300; tel. (2) 2303012; fax (2) 2308455; e-mail comanav@comanav.co.ma; internet www.comanav.co.ma; f. 1946; regular services to Mediterranean, North-west European, Middle Eastern and West African ports; tramping; Chair. MUHAMMAD BENHAROUGA.

Intercona SA: 31 ave de la Résistance, Tangier; tel. (3) 9322253; fax (3) 9943863; e-mail intercona@wanadoo.net.ma; f. 1943; daily services from Algeciras (Spain) to Tangier and Ceuta (Spanish North Africa); Dir-Gen. ANDRES VAZQUEZ ESPINOSA.

Limadet-ferry: 3 rue Ibn Rochd, Tangier; tel. (3) 933639; fax (3) 937173; f. 1966; operates between Algeciras (Spain) and Tangier, six daily; Dir-Gen. RACHID BEN MANSOUR.

Société Marocaine de Navigation Atlas: 81 ave Houmane el-Fatouaki, 21000 Casablanca; tel. (2) 2224190; fax (2) 2274401; f. 1976; Chair. HASSAN CHAMI; Man. Dir M. SLAOUI.

Union Maritime Maroc-Scandinave (UNIMAR): 12 rue de Foucauld, BP 746, Casablanca; tel. (2) 2279590; fax (2) 2223883; f. 1974; chemicals; Dir-Gen. ABD AL-WAHAB BEN KIRANE.

Voyages Paquet: Hôtel Royal Mansour, rue Sidi Belyout, 20000 Casablanca; tel. (2) 2311065; fax (2) 2442108; f. 1970; Pres. MUHAMMAD ELOUALI ELALAMI; Dir-Gen. NAÏMA BAKALI ELOUALI ELALAMI.

CIVIL AVIATION

The main international airports are at Casablanca (King Muhammad V), Rabat, Tangier, Marrakesh, Agadir Inezgane, Fez, Oujda, Al-Hocima, el-Aaiún, Ouarzazate and Agadir al-Massira. Construction of a new international airport at al-Aroui, located 25 km south of Nador, began in late 1998. In November 1999 the Arab Fund for Economic and Social Development granted a loan worth US $32.7m. to finance a project to extend and modernize King Muhammad V airport. The project, which includes the construction of a second runway and new terminal buildings, is expected to be completed by 2005.

Office Nationale des Aéroports: BP 8101, Casablanca-Oasis; tel. (2) 2539040; fax (2) 2539901; e-mail onda@onda.ma; internet www.onda.ma; f. 1990; Dir-Gen. ABDELHANINE BENALLOU.

Regional Airlines: Aéroport de Muhammad V, BP 12518, Casablanca; tel. (2) 2538020; fax (2) 2538411; f. 1997; privately-owned; domestic flights and services to southern Spain, Portugal and the Canary Islands; Pres. and CEO MUHAMMAD HASSAN BENSALAH.

Royal Air Maroc (RAM): Aéroport de Casablanca-Anfa; tel. (2) 2912000; fax (2) 2912087; internet www.royalairmaroc.com; f. 1953;

94.4% state-owned; scheduled for partial privatization; domestic flights and services to 35 countries in Western Europe, Scandinavia, the Americas, North and West Africa, the Canary Islands and the Middle East; CEO MUHAMMAD BERRADA.

Tourism

Tourism is Morocco's second main source of convertible currency. The country's attractions for tourists include its sunny climate, ancient sites (notably the cities of Fez, Marrakesh, Meknès and Rabat) and spectacular scenery. There are popular holiday resorts on the Atlantic and Mediterranean coasts. In 2002 foreign tourist arrivals totalled 2.22m., compared with 1.63m. in 1996. Tourist receipts in 2002 totalled an estimated US $2,152m.

Office National Marocain du Tourisme: 31 angle ave al-Abtal et rue Oued Fes, Agdal, Rabat; tel. (3) 7681531; fax (3) 7777437; e-mail visitmorocco@onmt.org.ma; internet www.moroccotourism.org.ma; f. 1918; Dir-Gen. FATHIA BENNIS.

MOZAMBIQUE

Introductory Survey

Location, Climate, Language, Religion, Flag, Capital

The Republic of Mozambique lies on the east coast of Africa, bordered to the north by Tanzania, to the west by Malawi, Zambia and Zimbabwe, and to the south by South Africa and Swaziland. The country has a coastline of about 2,470 km (1,535 miles) on the shores of the Indian Ocean, and is separated from Madagascar, to the east, by the Mozambique Channel. Except in a few upland areas, the climate varies from tropical to sub-tropical. Rainfall is irregular, but the rainy season is usually from November to March, when average temperatures in Maputo are between 26°C (79°F) and 30°C (86°F). In the cooler dry season the average temperatures are 18°C (64°F) to 20°C (68°F) in June and July. Portuguese is the official language, while there are 39 indigenous languages, the most widely spoken being Makhuwa, Tsonga, Sema and Lomwe. Many of the inhabitants follow traditional beliefs. There are about 5m. Christians, the majority of whom are Roman Catholics, and 4m. Muslims. The national flag (proportions 2 by 3) has three equal horizontal stripes, of green, black and yellow, separated by narrow white stripes. At the hoist is a red triangle containing a five-pointed yellow star, on which are superimposed an open book, a hoe and a rifle. The capital is Maputo (formerly Lourenço Marques).

Recent History

Mozambique became a Portuguese colony in the 19th century and an overseas province in 1951. Nationalist groups began to form in the 1960s. The Frente de Libertação de Moçambique (Frelimo—Mozambique Liberation Front) was formed in 1962 and launched a military campaign for independence in 1964. After the coup in Portugal (q.v.) in April 1974, negotiations between Frelimo and the new Portuguese Government resulted in a period of rule in Mozambique by a transitional Government, followed by full independence on 25 June 1975. Samora Machel, leader of Frelimo since the murder of its founder, Eduardo Mondlane, in 1969, became the first President of Mozambique. In February 1977 Frelimo was reconstituted as the Frelimo Party, a 'Marxist-Leninist vanguard party', with restricted membership. Between September and December elections took place to local, district and provincial assemblies and, at national level, to the Assembléia Popular (People's Assembly).

In March 1976 Mozambique closed its border with Rhodesia (now Zimbabwe) and applied economic sanctions against that country. Mozambique was the principal base for Rhodesian nationalist guerrillas, and consequently suffered considerable devastation as a result of offensives launched by Rhodesian government forces against guerrilla camps. The border was reopened in January 1980.

After Zimbabwean independence in April 1980, South Africa adopted Rhodesia's role as supporter of the Mozambican opposition guerrilla group, Resistência Nacional Moçambicana (Renamo), also known as the Movimento Nacional da Resistência de Moçambique. The activities of Renamo subsequently increased, causing persistent disruption to road, rail and petroleum pipeline links from Mozambican ports, which were vital to the economic independence of southern African nations from South Africa. In March 1984 Mozambique and South Africa signed a formal joint non-aggression pact, known as the Nkomati accord, whereby each Government undertook to prevent opposition forces on its territory from launching attacks against the other, and a Joint Security Commission was established. The accord effectively implied that South Africa would withdraw its covert support for Renamo in return for a guarantee by Mozambique that it would prevent any further use of its territory by the then banned African National Congress of South Africa (ANC). However, following an intensification of Renamo activity, in 1985 the Frelimo Government appealed to foreign powers for increased military assistance, and in June it was agreed that Zimbabwe would augment its military presence in Mozambique. A major military offensive against Renamo in July resulted in the capture, in August, of the rebels' national operational command centre and of other major rebel bases in the area. Mozambique subsequently alleged that documents dis- covered at one of the captured Renamo bases revealed that South Africa had repeatedly violated the Nkomati accord by providing material support for the rebels. The Joint Security Commission ceased to meet in 1985.

General elections were scheduled to take place in 1982, but were postponed several times because of the security situation. Legislative elections eventually began in August 1986, but were delayed, owing to the internal conflict. The post of Prime Minister was created in July and allocated to Mário Machungo.

President Machel died in an air crash in South Africa in October 1986. The causes of the incident were unclear, and the Mozambican Ministry of Information declared that it did not exclude the possibility of South African sabotage. In May 1998 it was announced that South Africa's Truth and Reconciliation Commission (TRC) was to examine evidence relating to the crash. The TRC final report stated that the evidence was inconclusive, but a number of questions merited further investigation. In November 1986 the Central Committee of Frelimo appointed Joaquim Alberto Chissano, hitherto Minister for Foreign Affairs, as President. The elections were then resumed. In contrast to the 1977 elections, the voters were given a choice of candidates, with 299 Frelimo nominees for the 250 seats in the Assembléia Popular; nevertheless, all government and party leaders had been re-elected when the poll was completed in December 1986.

In September 1987, amid renewed Renamo activity, talks began with South Africa in an attempt to revive the Nkomati accord. In June 1988, following six months of negotiations, Mozambique, South Africa and Portugal signed an agreement to rehabilitate the Cahora Bassa hydroelectric plant in Mozambique (potentially one of the greatest sources of electricity in southern Africa). In May Mozambican and South African officials had agreed to reactivate the Nkomati accord and to re-establish the Joint Security Commission, and in September Chissano met the South African President, P. W. Botha, in Mozambique. As a result of this meeting, Mozambique and South Africa established a joint commission for co-operation and development.

At Frelimo's fifth congress, held in July 1989, the party's exclusively Marxist-Leninist orientation was renounced, more pragmatic policies were approved, and party membership was opened to Mozambicans from all sectors of society. In January 1990 Chissano announced the drafting of a new constitution, to be presented to the Assembléia Popular for approval later in the year.

In mid-1989 Presidents Daniel arap Moi of Kenya and Robert Mugabe of Zimbabwe agreed to mediate between the Mozambique Government and Renamo. In August Renamo rejected the Government's peace proposals, and demanded recognition as a political entity, the introduction of multi-party elections and the withdrawal of Zimbabwean troops from Mozambique as preconditions for peace. Mediation by Mugabe and Moi came to an end after Renamo refused to attend a meeting between the protagonists that had been arranged to take place in Malawi in June 1990. However, direct talks were held in July in Rome, Italy. In August the Frelimo Central Committee voted unanimously in favour of introducing a multi-party system, with a view to elections planned for 1991. Further talks between the Government and the rebels resulted in an agreement, in December 1990, for a partial cease-fire. Under the terms of the agreement, all Zimbabwean troops present in Mozambique were required to retire to the Beira and Limpopo transport 'corridors' linking Zimbabwe to the Mozambican ports of Beira and Maputo. The cease-fire was confined to these areas.

The agreement in Rome followed the introduction, on 30 November 1990, of a new Mozambican Constitution, formally ending Frelimo's single-party rule and committing the State to political pluralism and a free-market economy, and enshrining private property rights and guarantees of press freedom. The official name of the country was changed from the People's Republic of Mozambique to the Republic of Mozambique. Renamo refused to recognize the new Constitution, declaring that it had been drafted without democratic consultation. The

President was henceforth to be elected by direct universal suffrage, and the legislature was renamed the Assembléia da República (Assembly of the Republic). A new law concerning the formation, structure and function of political parties came into effect in February 1991. In accordance with the Constitution, Renamo would not be recognized as a legitimate political party until it had renounced violence completely.

In December 1990 negotiations between the Government and Renamo resumed in Rome, and a Joint Verification Commission, comprising independent representatives from 10 nations, in addition to those of the Mozambican Government and Renamo, was established to monitor the partial cease-fire. Further talks took place in Rome in January 1991, but collapsed following the presentation of a report by the Joint Verification Commission containing accusations that Renamo had violated the cease-fire agreement, and did not resume until May.

In June 1991 the Government announced that it had uncovered a plot, involving several members of the armed forces, to overthrow Chissano. The leaders of the coup were believed to be opposed to the introduction of a multi-party system and to negotiations with Renamo. In August the Minister of the Interior, Col Manuel José António Mucananda, was detained in connection with the attempted coup. He was, however, exonerated in February 1992, on the grounds that he had been instrumental in bringing the coup attempt to the attention of the authorities, and resumed his ministerial post in April.

In August 1991 a Frelimo party congress undertook further structural changes. The Political Bureau was restyled the Political Commission; Chissano was re-elected as President of the party, while Feliciano Salomão Gundana, Minister of the Presidency, was appointed to the new position of Secretary-General. As part of the democratization of the party, members of the Central Committee were for the first time elected by secret ballot.

In October 1991 Renamo and the Government signed a protocol agreeing fundamental principles and containing a set of mutual guarantees as a basis for a peace accord. Throughout the discussions Renamo continued guerrilla attacks, many of which were launched (despite the Nkomati accord) from South Africa. Under the terms of the protocol, Renamo effectively recognized the legitimacy of the Government and agreed to enter the multi-party political framework. In return, the Government pledged not to legislate on any of the points under negotiation in Rome until a general peace accord had been signed. In November a second protocol, concerning party law, was signed by both parties, enabling Renamo to begin functioning as a political party immediately after the signing of a general peace accord.

In March 1992, following protracted discussions conducted in Rome, a third protocol was signed establishing the principles for the country's future electoral system. Under its terms, the elections, to be held (one year after the signing of the general peace accord) under a system of proportional representation, were to be supervised by international observers. An electoral commission was to be established, with one-third of its members to be appointed by Renamo. Discussions, which resumed in June, reached an impasse over constitutional issues. In July, following meetings with Mugabe and President F. W. de Klerk of South Africa, Chissano announced that he was prepared to meet the Renamo leader, Afonso Macacho Marceta Dhlakama, for direct talks. On 7 August, following three days of discussions in Rome, Chissano and Dhlakama signed a joint declaration committing the two sides to a total cease-fire by 1 October, as part of a General Peace Agreement (Acordo Geral de Paz—AGP). Dhlakama rejected Chissano's offer of an immediate armistice, on the grounds that the mechanisms necessary to guarantee such a truce had first to be implemented.

In September 1992 Chissano and Dhlakama met in Gaborone, Botswana, to attempt to resolve the deadlocked military and security issues. Chissano offered to establish an independent commission to monitor and guarantee the impartiality of the Serviço de Informação e Segurança do Estado (SISE—State Information and Security Service), which Renamo claimed to be merely a continuation of the disbanded political police, the Serviço Nacional de Segurança Popular (National Service of People's Security). In addition, the figure of 30,000 was agreed upon as the number of troops to comprise the joint national defence force.

The AGP was finally signed on 4 October 1992. Under the terms of the agreement, a general cease-fire was to come into force immediately after ratification of the treaty by the legislature. Both the Renamo troops and the government forces were to withdraw to assembly points within seven days of ratification. The new national defence force, the Forças Armadas de Defesa de Moçambique (FADM), would then be created, drawing on equal numbers from each side, with the remaining troops surrendering their weapons to a UN peace-keeping force within six months. A Cease-fire Commission, incorporating representatives from the Government, Renamo and the UN, was to be established to assume responsibility for supervising the implementation of the truce regulations. Overall political control of the peace process was to be vested in a Comissão de Supervisão e Controle (CSC—Supervision and Control Commission), comprising representatives of the Government, Renamo and the UN; its remit was to include supervision of the Cease-fire Commission and other commissions charged with establishing the joint armed forces, reintegrating demobilized soldiers into civilian society, and verifying the withdrawal of foreign troops from Mozambique. In addition, Chissano was to appoint a National Information Commission (COMINFO), with responsibilities including supervision of the SISE. Presidential and legislative elections were to take place, under UN supervision, one year after the signing of the AGP, provided that it had been fully implemented and the demobilization process completed. The AGP was duly ratified by the Assembléia da República and came into force on 15 October. On that day UN observers arrived in Maputo to supervise the first phase of the cease-fire. However, shortly afterwards the Government accused Renamo of systematically violating the accord. Dhlakama subsequently claimed that Renamo's actions had been defensive manoeuvres and, in turn, accused government forces of violating the accord by advancing into Renamo territory.

In November 1992, owing to considerable delays in the formation of the various peace commissions envisaged in the AGP, the timetable for the cease-fire operations was redrafted. In December the UN Security Council finally approved a plan for the establishment of the UN Operation in Mozambique (ONUMOZ), providing for the deployment of some 7,500 troops, police and civilian observers to oversee the process of demobilization and formation of the FADM, and to supervise the forthcoming elections. However, there were continued delays in the deployment of ONUMOZ, since the UN was experiencing difficulty in persuading its member nations to contribute troops. Renamo, moreover, refused to begin confining its forces to assembly points until 65% of the UN force was in place. The location of the 49 assembly points was not agreed until February 1993. In March the peace process was effectively halted when Renamo withdrew from the CSC and the Cease-fire Commission, protesting that proper provisions had not been made to accommodate its officials, and in April Dhlakama announced that his forces would begin to report to assembly points only when Renamo received US $15m. to finance its transition into a political party. Meanwhile, the first UN troops became operational on 1 April, and in mid-April the Zimbabwean troops guarding the Beira and Limpopo 'corridors' were replaced by UN forces, six months behind schedule.

In June 1993 Renamo rejoined the CSC. The commission subsequently agreed to a formal postponement of the election date to October 1994. A meeting in Maputo of international aid donors, also in June 1993, revealed growing impatience among the international community at the repeated delays in the peace process and with Renamo's escalating demands for logistical and financial support. The meeting produced promises of additional support for the peace process, bringing the total pledged by donors to US $520m., including support for the repatriation of 1.5m. refugees from neighbouring countries, the resettlement of 4m.–5m. displaced people and the reintegration of some 80,000 former combatants into civilian life. The UN also agreed to establish a trust fund of $10m. to finance Renamo's transformation into a political party, with the disbursement of funds dependent on UN approval.

Renamo announced new preconditions to the advancement of the peace process in July 1993, insisting initially on the recognition of its own administration, to operate parallel to that of the Government, and later on the appointment of its members to five of the country's 11 provincial governorships. Under the terms of an agreement signed in September, Renamo was to appoint three advisers to each of the incumbent provincial governors to make recommendations relating to the reintegration of areas under Renamo control into a single state administration. It was also agreed that a request be made to the UN to send a police corps to supervise the activities of the national police and ensure neutrality in areas under Renamo control. In

October 1993 the CSC approved a new timetable covering all aspects of the peace process, including the elections in October 1994. In November 1993 the UN Security Council adopted a resolution renewing the mandate of ONUMOZ for a further six months. In addition, it acceded to the joint request by the Government and Renamo for a UN police corps. In the same month consensus was finally reached on the text of the electoral law, which was promulgated at the end of December. At a meeting of the CSC in mid-November an agreement was signed providing for the confinement of troops, to be concluded by the end of the year. However, less than 15% of the total number of troops for confinement entered assembly points.

The National Electoral Commission, which was inaugurated in February 1994, comprised 10 members from the Government, seven from Renamo, three from the other opposition parties and an independent chairman. Later in February the UN Security Council announced that, in response to demands made by Renamo, it would be increasing the membership of the UN police corps monitoring the confinement areas from 128 to 1,144. By the end of February only 50% of troops had entered assembly points, and none had officially been demobilized. In March, in an effort to expedite the confinement process, the Government announced that it was to commence the unilateral demobilization of its troops. Renamo began the demobilization of its troops shortly afterwards. In April Lt-Gen. Lagos Lidimo, the nominee of the Government, and the former Renamo guerrilla commander, Lt-Gen. Mateus Ngonhamo, were inaugurated as the high command of the FADM. In the same month Chissano issued a decree scheduling the presidential and legislative elections for 27–28 October, and in May the UN Security Council renewed the mandate of ONUMOZ for the final period, ending on 15 November.

The confinement and demobilization processes continued to make slow progress, and the deadline for the completion of confinement was consequently extended to 8 July 1994, with demobilization to be completed by 15 August. By that date only 7,375 troops from both sides had enlisted in the FADM; the deadline for registration at confinement points was subsequently extended to 31 August, after which date it was to continue at three centres in the north, centre and south of the country. On 16 August, in accordance with the provisions of the AGP, the government Forças Armadas de Moçambique were formally dissolved and their assets transferred to the FADM, which was inaugurated as the country's official armed forces on the same day.

In August 1994 Renamo formally registered as a political party. In the same month the Partido Liberal e Democrático de Moçambique, the Partido Nacional Democrático and the Partido Nacional de Moçambique formed an electoral coalition, the União Democrática (UD). The presidential and legislative elections took place on 27–29 October. The extension of voting to a third day had become necessary following the withdrawal of Renamo from the elections only hours before the beginning of the poll, claiming that conditions were not in place to ensure free and fair elections. However, following concerted international pressure, Renamo abandoned its boycott after the first day. In the presidential election Chissano secured an outright majority (53.3%) of the votes. His closest rival was Dhlakama, who received 33.7% of the votes. In the legislative elections Frelimo also secured an overall majority, winning 129 of the 250 seats in the Assembléia da República; Renamo obtained 112 seats, and the UD the remaining nine. Dhlakama accepted the results of the elections, although he maintained that there had been irregularities. The UN asserted that the irregularities were insufficient to have affected the overall credibility of the poll, which it declared to have been free and fair—a view endorsed by international observers. Later in November the UN Security Council extended the mandate of ONUMOZ until the end of January 1995. In December 1994 the Cease-fire Commission issued its final report, according to which ONUMOZ had registered a combined total of 91,691 government and Renamo troops during the confinement process, of whom 11,579 had enlisted in the FADM (compared with the 30,000 envisaged in the AGP).

Chissano was inaugurated as President on 9 December 1994, and the new Government, in which all portfolios were assigned to members of Frelimo, was sworn in on 23 December. Demands by Renamo that it be awarded governorships in the five provinces where it won a majority of the votes in the legislative elections were rejected by Chissano. At the first session of the new legislature, which began on 8 December, a dispute concerning the voting procedure employed to elect its Chairman resulted in the withdrawal of the Renamo and UD deputies, who had unsuccessfully demanded a secret ballot; both parties had abandoned their boycott by the end of December, although not before the conclusion of the first session.

By the end of March 1995 all ONUMOZ troops and police had left Mozambique, two months later than originally envisaged, and only a small unit of ONUMOZ officials remained in the country. In February 1996 the Government proposed that municipal elections, which the Constitution stipulated must be conducted no later than October 1996, be held in 1997. Delays in the election process had resulted from a dispute between the parliamentary opposition, which demanded simultaneous local elections throughout Mozambique, and the Government, which sought to hold elections only in those areas that had attained municipal status. In October 1996 parliament approved a constitutional amendment differentiating between municipalities and administrative posts. In August 1997 the Government postponed the elections until 1998, owing to delays in the disbursement by international donors of funding for the voter registration process. In January 1998 Renamo alleged that the voter registration process had been fraudulent, and threatened to boycott the elections unless a further registration of voters was conducted. In April Renamo was among 16 opposition parties that officially withdrew from the elections. Renamo subsequently campaigned vigorously to dissuade the electorate from participating in the ballot. At the elections, which took place on 30 June, Frelimo secured all the mayoral posts and won control of all the municipal authorities contested. However, since very few opposition parties contested the election, Frelimo's main competition came from independent candidates. Moreover, the voter turn-out was only 14.6%, prompting Renamo to demand the annulment of the elections on the grounds that the low level of participation greatly reduced the legitimacy of the newly elected representatives.

In October 1998 the Government published draft constitutional amendments that envisaged substantial changes to the country's political system, including a reduction in presidential powers and concomitant increase in those of the Prime Minister and the legislature. If approved, the amendments would confer the status of 'Head of Government' on the Prime Minister, transferring this from the President—who would remain 'Head of State'. In addition, a Council of State would be formed as a consultative body to advise the President.

Under the Constitution, presidential and legislative elections were to take place by November 1999. However, political disputes and administrative delays threatened to force a postponement of the elections. A principal cause of the delay was Renamo's insistence on the need to reregister the entire electorate. In June Frelimo announced that Chissano would stand as its presidential candidate. In the following month 11 opposition parties, led by Renamo, signed an agreement to contest the forthcoming elections as a coalition, styled Renamo—União Eleitoral (Renamo—UE). The coalition was to present a single list of legislative candidates, with Dhlakama as its presidential candidate.

Presidential and legislative elections took place on 3–5 December 1999. In the presidential contest, Chissano defeated Dhlakama (his sole challenger), taking 52.3% of the valid votes cast. Frelimo secured an outright majority in the legislative elections, winning 133 of the 250 seats in the Assembléia da República; Renamo—UE obtained the remaining seats. Renamo rejected the outcome, claiming that the vote had been fraudulent, and threatened to petition the Constitutional Council to overturn the result. However, international monitors declared that the vote had been free and fair. In January 2000 the Supreme Court—exercising the functions of the Constitutional Council, which had yet to be established—rejected the appeal by Renamo against the results of the elections. Later that month it was reported that, in contravention of legislation requiring political parties to be based in the capital, Renamo had moved its headquarters to Beira, leaving only a small delegation in Maputo. On 15 January Chissano was sworn in for a further five-year presidential term. However, Dhlakama refused to attend the investiture, and Renamo continued to dispute the legitimacy of the newly elected Government.

In February 2000 massive flooding in southern and central areas caused widespread devastation to the country's social and economic infrastructure. The flooding was the worst ever on record, seriously affecting an estimated 2m. people. Some 10% of Mozambique's cultivated land was destroyed, and most of its livestock was lost. Much of the country's transport infrastructure was destroyed, as were many villages. The World Bank estimated the cost of losses at between US $270m. and $430m.

In May 2000 thousands of people took part in a march to mark Workers' Day, demanding the establishment of labour tribunals, which, despite their creation in 1992, had not actually come into existence; workers were also seeking an increase in the minimum wage and the return of price controls. Earlier that month the Prime Minister, Pascoal Mocumbi, condemned comments by Dhlakama, in which he had threatened to regroup demobilized Renamo soldiers and seize control of the country. The Renamo political delegate for Nampula province was later arrested. It was subsequently revealed that negotiations were taking place between Chissano and Renamo. In July a senior member of Renamo, Raul Domingos, was suspended from the party, pending an investigation into negotiations conducted in June between himself and the Minister for Transport and Communications, Tomás Salomão, during which Domingos was alleged to have demanded an estimated US $500,000 to assist in personal loan repayments, up to $1m. per month for Renamo and $10,000 per month for Dhlakama. Domingos was officially expelled from the party in September.

Renamo boycotted the election of the new National Elections Commission (NEC), officially inaugurated in July 2000, on the grounds that it did not recognise the legitimacy of the current Government, and that a review of the current electoral law was needed. Frelimo appointed eight representatives to the 15-member NEC. Demonstrations held by Renamo in November, in protest at the results of the December 1999 elections, resulted in the deaths of some 41 people, following clashes between Renamo and Frelimo supporters. (In June 2001 several Renamo members were found guilty of armed rebellion in relation to the riots, while several police-officers were also prosecuted; a further 14 Renamo members and supporters were imprisoned in January 2002 for their part in the violence.) Moreover, later in November 2000 one of the country's most influential journalists, Carlos Cardoso, was killed in Maputo. It was alleged by Dhlakama that Cardoso had been murdered as a result of an article, published in the newspaper *Metical*, in which he had criticized the Government's involvement in the protests earlier in November. (It was announced in March 2001 that three people, including the former manager of a branch of the Banco Comercial de Moçambique—BCM, had been arrested in connection with Cardoso's murder; shortly before his death Cardoso had apparently uncovered details relating to the theft of some 144,000m. meticais from a branch of the BCM in 1996.) Furthermore, Renamo accused the Government of being responsible for the death of some 83 prisoners (principally Renamo supporters arrested during the protests) in late November; the Government denied the allegations, claiming that the prisoners had died of suffocation due to overcrowding. A subsequent report by the Mozambican Human Rights Association suggested that the prisoners had, in fact, died of suffocation and starvation.

In late December 2000 Dhlakama and Chissano held talks (the first since the disputed election in December 1999) in an attempt to resolve the growing political tension between their two parties. The two leaders agreed to hold further talks in 2001, and to establish inquiries into the violence in November. Moreover, Dhlakama stated that he was prepared to accept the results of the 1999 elections, and Chissano pledged to consult Renamo about future state appointments (notably in the appointment of state governors). However, comments by Dhlakama, accusing Frelimo of violence and intimidation towards Renamo, subsequently jeopardized the future of talks between the two parties. Following a second meeting between the two leaders in January 2001, the two parties appeared to be no closer to achieving a consensus. Nevertheless, it was agreed that a number of working groups (including groups on defence and security, constitutional and parliamentary affairs, and the media) would be established in February. At a further meeting, in March, Chissano referred Dhlakama's demand for the appointment of Renamo governors to the Assembléia da República, whose Frelimo representatives were strongly opposed to accommodating Renamo demands. In protest, Dhlakama ceased negotiations in April.

Floods in central Mozambique in February and March 2001 resulted in some 100 deaths and left an estimated 230,000 people homeless and displaced. In July the Government requested some US $132m. in international aid to assist in the reconstruction of damaged infrastructure, and for the development of measures to prevent a recurrence.

President Chissano announced in May 2001 that he would not stand for re-election on the expiry of his term in 2004, prompting speculation about potential successors, ahead of the eighth Frelimo party congress, to be held in June 2002. At the long-postponed Renamo congress, held in October 2001, Dhlakama was re-elected party President, obtaining over 95% of votes cast; Joaquim Vaz was elected Secretary-General. The holding of a party congress by Renamo for the first time since the end of the civil war, as well as the establishment of a 10-member Political Committee, were regarded as confirmation of the movement's decision to establish itself as a full political party, and to decentralize the party leadership and structure.

In August 2001 Siba-Siba Macuacua, the interim Chairman of Banco Austral, was murdered while investigating corruption allegations at the bank. Macuacua had published a list of more than 1,000 people, including some government officials, who had failed to repay loans to the bank. The investigation into Macuacua's murder proceeded slowly; in March 2004 the Attorney-General, Joaquim Madeira, reported to the Assembléia da República that some 59 people had been questioned in connection with the case.

In November 2001 the Assembléia da República approved legislation prohibiting the process of money 'laundering'. The new measures imposed restrictions on banking and other local financial activities, in an attempt to render them more accountable. Also in that month a former member of the UD, António Palange, founded a new political party, the Congresso dos Democratas Unidos, aimed at promoting national reconciliation and a policy of understanding between the different ethnic and racial groups; Palange stated that economic freedom in Mozambique was the party's principal objective.

In June 2002, at the party's eighth party congress, Frelimo elected Armando Guebuza as its Secretary-General, and thus also its candidate for the 2004 presidential election. During July Renamo's attempt to establish itself as a legitimate opposition party was threatened after Dhlakama dismissed Vaz as Secretary-General, assuming the position himself, and dissolved the party's Political Committee. In September long-standing Renamo opposition to new electoral laws (regarding the composition of a National Elections Commission) was suddenly withdrawn, and a 19-member Commission approved. In October Renamo announced its intention to contest municipal elections (due in 2003) alone, rather than in coalition, while in November 2002 the party regained some stability with the appointment of Viana Magalhaes as Secretary-General. In December, however, further controversy arose when Renamo demanded the exclusion from the Assembléia da República of five deputies who had resigned or been expelled from the party, including Domingos, who had announced his intention to present himself as an independent candidate for the 2004 presidential election. The police were called to the Assembléia to disperse Renamo protesters, who caused an estimated US $11,000 of damage to the building. The former Renamo deputies retained their right to participate in the Assembléia.

Meanwhile, in November 2002, during the trial of six men for Cardoso's murder in 2000, the President's eldest son, Nyimpine Chissano, was accused by three of the defendants of having ordered or paid for the assassination; Nyimpine Chissano denied any involvement in the murder. It was additionally claimed that one of the accused, Aníbal António dos Santos, who had escaped from custody in suspicious circumstances at the beginning of September, was making secret threats against key figures in the trial. In January 2003 all six accused were found guilty of Cardoso's murder; dos Santos, who had been tried *in absentia*, was arrested in South Africa at the end of January, and extradited to Mozambique to serve a prison term of 28 years and six months.

In February 2003, in response to Renamo's decision to run alone in the municipal elections, 10 opposition parties announced the formation of a new coalition, the União Eleitoral, led by Domingos. In October Domingos founded his own party, the Partido para a Paz, Democracia e Desenvolvimento (PPDD). From mid-2003 divisions became apparent within Frelimo between supporters of its presidential candidate, Guebuza, and Chissano loyalists. The Assembléia da República adopted anti-corruption measures in October. The Constitutional Council, which was to supervise elections and determine the constitutionality of new legislation, was inaugurated in early November, with Rui Baltazar dos Santos Alves as its first Chairman. Municipal elections were held on 19 November. Despite allegations by Renamo of irregularities, the elections proceeded smoothly, and their conduct was later commended by an observer mission from the European Union (EU), although voter turn-out, at 24.2%, was low. Frelimo won a majority in 29 municipalities and the mayorship of 28, while Renamo won a majority in only four and the mayorship of five. The results were verified by the Constitutional Council in January 2004. In mid-February Luísa Diogo was appointed as Prime Minister, to replace Mocumbi, who resigned the premiership to take up an executive post in an EU-sponsored initiative specializing in clinical research. Diogo was also to retain the responsibilities of Minister of Planning and Finance, the post she had held under Mocumbi.

During 1995 the activities, principally in the border province of Manica, of a group of mainly Zimbabwean dissidents, known as Chimwenje, came under increasing scrutiny. The group, which was alleged to have links with Renamo, was believed to be preparing for military incursions into Zimbabwe, where it sought the overthrow of President Mugabe. In early 1996 the Chissano Government announced its intention to expel the dissidents from Mozambique. In June, following a series of armed attacks on both sides of the Mozambique–Zimbabwe border, which were believed to have been perpetrated by Chimwenje, the Governments of Mozambique and Zimbabwe agreed to combine and intensify efforts to combat the activities of the dissidents. The group was suppressed in late 1996. During late 2002 and early 2003 Mozambique resettled a number of white Zimbabwean farmers whose land had been appropriated by the Mugabe regime. In January 2004 friction arose when officials in Mozambique's Tete province accused Zimbabwean troops of crossing the border and behaving violently towards the local population.

After independence, Mozambique developed strong international links with the USSR and other countries of the communist bloc, and with neighbouring African states: it is a member of the Southern African Development Community (SADC, see p. 331), founded in 1979, as the Southern African Development Co-ordination Conference, then with the aim of reducing the region's economic dependence on South Africa, principally by developing trade routes through Mozambique. In December 1996 Mozambique, Malawi, Zambia and Zimbabwe (also SADC members) formally agreed to establish the Beira Development Corridor as a trading route avoiding South Africa's ports. In 1993 full diplomatic relations were established with South Africa. In July 1994 Mozambique and South Africa established a new Joint Defence and Security Commission, replacing the Joint Security Commission originally established in 1984. In November 1995 Mozambique was admitted, by special dispensation, as a full member of the Commonwealth (see p. 172).

Government

The Constitution of 30 November 1990 provides for a multiparty political system. Legislative power is vested in the Assembléia da República, with 250 members, who are elected for a five-year term. Members are elected by universal, direct adult suffrage in a secret ballot, according to a system of proportional representation. The President of the Republic, who is Head of State, is directly elected for a five-year term; the President holds executive power and governs with the assistance of an appointed Council of Ministers. Provincial governors, appointed by the President, have overall responsibility for the functions of government within each of the 11 provinces. For the purposes of local government, Mozambique is divided into 33 municipalities.

Defence

In August 2003 total active armed forces were estimated at 8,200 (army 7,000, navy 200, air force 1,000). Military service is compulsory and lasts for two years. Expenditure on defence was budgeted at an estimated 2,000,000m. meticais in 2003.

Economic Affairs

In 2002, according to estimates by the World Bank, Mozambique's gross national income (GNI), measured at average 2000–02 prices, was US $3,869m., equivalent to $210 per head. During 1990–2002, it was estimated, the population increased at an average annual rate of 2.2%, while gross domestic product (GDP) per head increased, in real terms, by an average of 4.2% per year. Overall GDP increased, in real terms, at an average annual rate of 6.6% in 1990–2002; growth in 2002 was 9.9%. According to official figures, growth in 2002 was 8.3%.

Agriculture (including forestry and fishing) contributed 24.3% of GDP in 2002. In mid-2002 an estimated 80.8% of the economically active population were employed in the sector. Fishing is the principal export activity: fish, crustaceans and molluscs accounted for 14.2% of total export earnings in 2001. The principal cash crops are fruit and nuts, cotton, sugar cane and copra. The main subsistence crop is cassava. During 1990–2002, according to the World Bank, agricultural GDP increased by an average of 3.5% per year; growth in 2002 was 7.3%.

Industry (including mining, manufacturing, construction and power) employed 5.6% of the economically active population in 1997, and provided 25.2% of GDP in 2002. During 1990–2002, according to the World Bank, industrial GDP increased at an average annual rate of 14.3%; growth in 2002 was 21.9%.

Mining and quarrying contributed 0.3% of GDP in 2002, and employed 0.5% of the economically active population in 1997. Only coal, bauxite, marble, gold and salt are exploited in significant quantities, although gravel and crushed rocks are also mined. The exploitation of commercially viable levels of graphite began in 1994, but production ceased in 2000. Formal production of bentonite also ceased in 2002, although small amounts were still processed. There are reserves of other minerals, including high-grade iron ore, precious and semi-precious stones, and natural gas. Plans began in 1994 to exploit natural gas reserves at Pande, in the province of Inhambane, which were estimated at 55,000m. cu m. A South African company, SASOL Ltd, was granted a 25-year concession to develop gasfields at Pande and Temane (also in Inhambane province); it was anticipated that the Government would receive revenues of some US $900m. from the project, and the construction of a pipeline to transport the gas to South Africa was completed in 2003. A gas-processing centre was scheduled to open in Temane in early 2004. In 2003 the Government announced that it was to invest $20m. in gas prospecting in Sofala province. In 1999 the largest reserve of titanium in the world (estimated at 100m. metric tons) was discovered in the district of Chibuto, in the province of Gaza; production from the Limpopo Corridor Sands Project in Chibuto was expected to begin in 2007 and last for some 35 years, providing up to 1m. tons of titanium per year. In 2003 plans were announced for the exploitation of further titanium reserves in Nampula province; it was hoped that production would commence in 2005, providing up to 2.5% of GDP. According to government targets, minerals were to account for 10% of exports and 6% of GDP by 2005. According to official figures, mining GDP increased at an average annual rate of 7.1% in 1991–02; growth in 2002 was 2.1%.

Manufacturing contributed 13.2% of GDP in 2002, and employed 3.0% of the economically active population in 1997. A large aluminium smelter, Mozal, was opened in 2000 and expanded in 2003, with the completion of Mozal 2, which was expected to double capacity, to some 506,000 metric tons of aluminium ingots per year. It was estimated that Mozal contributed around 2.1% of GDP in 2002, and unwrought aluminium and alloys accounted for 54.5% of total export earnings in 2001. During 1994–2002, according to the World Bank, manufacturing GDP increased at an average annual rate of 14.0%; growth in 2002 was 6.2%.

Electrical energy is derived principally from hydroelectric power, which provided some 99.6% of total electricity production in 2000. Mozambique's important Cahora Bassa hydroelectric plant on the Zambezi River supplies electricity to South Africa and Zimbabwe. In late 2003 an extended power supply from Cahora Bassa to Zambézia province was opened. From 1999 a consortium involving Mozambican, French and German companies financed a feasibility study for the construction of a hydroelectric power plant at Mepanda Uncua, some 70 km downstream of Cahora Bassa, which would help to support the 900-MW energy requirement of the Mozal smelter. Construction of the plant, which would have a generating capacity of 2,500 MW, was projected to cost some US $1,500m. It was envisaged that power from the plant, which would not be completed before 2007, would also be exported to South Africa. Mozambique currently imports all of its petroleum requirements. Imports of mineral fuels and lubricants comprised 15.9% of the value of total imports in 2001.

The services sector engaged 12.3% of the economically active population in 1997, and contributed 50.5% of GDP in 2002. By the end of the 1990s tourism was the fastest growing sector of the economy, and was estimated to contribute some US $32m. annually to the budget. It was hoped that the formal opening, in April 2002, of the Great Limpopo Transfrontier Park, comprising South Africa's Kruger National Park, Zimbabwe's Gonarezhou National Park and Mozambique's Limpopo National Park, would attract additional tourists. The GDP of the services sector increased by an average of 2.2% per year in 1990–2002, according to the World Bank; services GDP increased by 1.1% in 2001, but declined by 6.2% in 2002.

In 2002 Mozambique recorded a trade deficit of US $581.1m., and there was a deficit of $420.6m. on the current account of the balance of payments. In 2001 the principal source of imports was South Africa (40.3%); Portugal was also a major supplier. In the same year South Africa was the principal market for exports (receiving 15.3%); Zimbabwe was another significant purchaser. The principal exports in 2002 were aluminium, electricity and prawns. The principal imports in 2001 were machinery and transport equipment, refined petroleum products, food and live animals (principally cereals and cereal preparations), basic manufactures and chemicals. Production from the Mozal aluminium smelter almost doubled the value of total exports in 2001, to some $703m.

In 2003 there was an overall budgetary deficit of 5,139,000m. meticais. Mozambique's total external debt was estimated at US $4,466m. at the end of 2001, of which $3,772m. was long-term public debt. In that year the cost of debt-servicing was equivalent to 3.4% of the total value of exports of goods and services. The average annual rate of inflation was 11.9% in 1998–2002; consumer prices increased by an average of 9.0% in 2002. According to official figures, the number of unemployed was 118,000 at the end of 1996.

Mozambique is a member of the Southern African Development Community (SADC, see p. 331). In November 2000 Mozambique was invited by the Common Market for Eastern and Southern Africa (COMESA, see p. 171) to rejoin the organization (Mozambique left COMESA in 1993, when it joined SADC).

In terms of average income, Mozambique is one of the poorest countries in the world. During the 1980s economic development was severely frustrated by the effects of the civil war. Since 1990 there has been considerable progress in liberalizing the economy. Increased production in rural areas, continued structural reform and the partial restoration of the infrastructure contributed to significant GDP growth from 1993, and in 1994–98 Mozambique's economy was one of the fastest growing in the world. In June 1999 the Bretton Woods institutions reduced Mozambique's public debt by almost two-thirds, significantly decreasing the country's annual servicing obligations for the period 1999–2005, and the IMF approved a three-year loan for Mozambique, equivalent to some US $78.5m., under the Enhanced Structural Adjustment Facility (later renamed the Poverty Reduction and Growth Facility—PRGF). In March 2000 the 'Paris Club' of official creditors deferred all payments due on the country's external debt for one year, following severe flooding in southern and central Mozambique, and the IMF increased the PRGF arrangement to some $113m. In April the IMF agreed to grant Mozambique a further $600m. in debt relief under the enhanced terms of the initiative for heavily indebted poor countries. A decline in prices for cashew nuts in 2000–01 (principally as a result of a collapse in demand in India, but also partly owing to the liberalization of Mozambique's cashew-processing industry, as requested by the World Bank) led to economic uncertainty and an increase in the country's trade deficit. None the less, strong economic growth was recorded in 2001, owing to the increased output of the Mozal smelter and a

recovery in the agricultural sector, following the floods in 2000. During 2002 Mozambique's foreign debt was drastically reduced by the cancellation of its obligations to Russia, Italy, Germany and the United Kingdom. In June the IMF commended Mozambique's rapid post-flood recovery, extending the PRGF arrangement by one year. In 2003 foreign investment and aid continued to contribute significantly to infrastructural developments. In October, at a meeting of the World Bank's Consultative Group, donors pledged some $790m. in assistance for 2004, mostly in the form of grants. GDP growth of some 7.0% and inflation of 10.8% were estimated in 2003. Meanwhile, the Government maintained its commitment to the country's Action Plan for the Reduction of Absolute Poverty; it was estimated that 54% of the population were living below the poverty line in 2003, compared with 69% in 1997. GDP growth of 8% was forecast for 2004, largely owing to the expansion of Mozal, and inflation was projected to decline to 9%.

Education

Education is officially compulsory for seven years from the age of seven. Primary schooling begins at seven years of age and lasts for seven years. It is divided into two cycles, of five and two years. Secondary schooling, from 13 years of age, lasts for six years and comprises two cycles, each lasting three years. As a proportion of the school-age population, the total enrolment at primary and secondary schools was equivalent to 49% in 2000/01 (males 56%; females 42%). According to UNESCO estimates, in 2000/01 54% of children in the relevant age-group were enrolled at primary schools (males 59%; females 50%), while secondary enrolment included only 9% of children in the relevant age-group (males 11%; females 8%). There were 7,156 students in public higher education in 1997. Two privately owned higher education institutions, the Catholic University and the Higher Polytechnic Institute, were inaugurated in 1996. In late 2003 it was announced that education would no longer take place solely in Portuguese, but also in some Mozambican dialects. Education was allocated 20.3% of total current government expenditure in 1999.

Public Holidays

2004: 1 January (New Year's Day), 3 February (Heroes' Day, anniversary of the assassination of Eduardo Mondlane), 7 April (Day of the Mozambican Woman), 1 May (Workers' Day), 25 June (Independence Day), 7 September (Victory Day—anniversary of the end of the Armed Struggle), 25 September (Anniversary of the launching of the Armed Struggle for National Liberation, and Day of the Armed Forces of Mozambique), 25 December (National Family Day).

2005: 1 January (New Year's Day), 3 February (Heroes' Day, anniversary of the assassination of Eduardo Mondlane), 7 April (Day of the Mozambican Woman), 1 May (Workers' Day), 25 June (Independence Day), 7 September (Victory Day—anniversary of the end of the Armed Struggle), 25 September (Anniversary of the launching of the Armed Struggle for National Liberation, and Day of the Armed Forces of Mozambique), 25 December (National Family Day).

Weights and Measures

The metric system is in force.

Statistical Survey

Source (unless otherwise stated): Instituto Nacional de Estatística, Comissão Nacional do Plano, Avda Ahmed Sekou Touré 21, CP 493, Maputo; tel. (1) 491054; fax (1) 493547; internet www.ine.gov.mz.

Area and Population

AREA, POPULATION AND DENSITY

Area (sq km)	799,380*
Population (census results)	
1 August 1980	11,673,725†
1 August 1997	
Males	7,714,306
Females	8,384,940
Total	16,099,246

Population (official estimates at mid-year)	
2000	17,242,240
2001	17,656,153
2002	18,082,523
Density (per sq km) at mid-2002	22.6

* 308,641 sq miles. The area includes 13,000 sq km (5,019 sq miles) of inland water.

† Excluding an adjustment for underenumeration. This was estimated to have been 3.8%, and the adjusted total was 12,130,000.

PROVINCES
(at 1 July 2002)

Province	Area (sq km)	Population	Density (per sq km)
Cabo Delgado	82,625	1,525,634	18.5
Gaza	75,709	1,266,431	16.7
Inhambane	68,615	1,326,848	19.3
Manica	61,661	1,207,332	19.6
City of Maputo	300	1,044,618	3,482.1
Maputo province	26,058	1,003,992	38.5
Nampula	81,606	3,410,141	41.8
Niassa	129,056	916,672	7.1
Sofala	68,018	1,516,166	22.3
Tete	100,724	1,388,205	13.7
Zambézia	105,008	3,476,484	33.1
Total	**799,380**	**18,082,523**	**22.6**

PRINCIPAL TOWNS
(population at 1997 census)

Maputo (capital)	966,837	Nacala-Porto	158,248
Matola	424,662	Quelimane	150,116
Beira	397,368	Tete	101,984
Nampula	303,346	Xai-Xai	99,442
Chimoio	171,056	Gurue	99,335

Mid-2001 (UN estimate, incl. suburbs): Maputo 1,134,000 (Source: UN, *World Urbanization Prospects: The 2001 Revision*).

BIRTHS AND DEATHS
(UN estimates, annual averages)

	1985–90	1990–95	1995–2000
Birth rate (per 1,000)	43.7	44.6	43.0
Death rate (per 1,000)	21.1	20.6	21.4

Source: UN, *World Population Prospects: The 2002 Revision*.

Expectation of life (WHO estimates, years at birth): 42.6 (males 41.2; females 43.9) in 2002 (Source: WHO, *World Health Report*).

ECONOMICALLY ACTIVE POPULATION
(persons aged 12 years and over, 1980 census)

	Males	Females	Total
Agriculture, forestry, hunting and fishing	1,887,779	2,867,052	4,754,831
Mining and quarrying	} 323,730	23,064	346,794
Manufacturing			
Construction	41,611	510	42,121
Commerce	90,654	21,590	112,244
Transport, storage and communications	74,817	2,208	77,025
Other services*	203,629	39,820	243,449
Total employed	**2,622,220**	**2,954,244**	**5,576,464**
Unemployed	75,505	19,321	94,826
Total labour force	**2,697,725**	**2,973,565**	**5,671,290**

* Including electricity, gas and water.

Source: ILO, *Yearbook of Labour Statistics*.

1991 (estimates, '000 persons): Agriculture 6,870; Industry 766; Services 798; Total labour force 8,434 (Source: UN Economic Commission for Africa, *African Statistical Yearbook*).

1997 (percentage distribution of economically active population at census of 1 August): Agriculture, forestry and hunting: 91.3% of females, 69.6% of males; Mining: 0.0% of females, 1.0% of males; Manufacturing: 0.8% of females, 5.5% of males; Energy: 0.0% of females, 0.3% of males; Construction: 0.3% of females, 3.9% of males; Transport and Communications: 0.1% of females, 2.3% of males; Commerce and Finance: 4.3% of females, 9.7% of males; Services: 2.2% of females, 3.4% of males; Unknown: 0.9% of females, 1.4% of males.

Mid-2002 (estimates in '000): Agriculture, etc. 7,837; Total labour force 9,696 (Source: FAO).

Health and Welfare

KEY INDICATORS

Total fertility rate (children per woman, 2002)	5.7
Under-5 mortality rate (per 1,000 live births, 2001)	197
HIV/AIDS (% of persons aged 15–49, 2001)	13.00
Hospital beds (per 1,000 head, 1990)	0.87
Health expenditure (2001): US $ per head (PPP)	47
Health expenditure (2001): % of GDP	5.9
Health expenditure (2001): public (% of total)	67.4
Access to water (% of persons, 2000)	60
Access to sanitation (% of persons, 2000)	43
Human Development Index (2001): ranking	170
Human Development Index (2001): value	0.356

For sources and definitions, see explanatory note on p. vi.

Agriculture

PRINCIPAL CROPS
('000 metric tons)

	2000	2001	2002
Rice (paddy)	151	167	167*
Maize	1,019	1,143	1,236†
Millet	49	62†	50†
Sorghum	252	314	314*
Potatoes*	80	80	80
Sweet potatoes*	65	66	66
Cassava (Manioc)	5,362	5,400*	5,400*
Sugar cane	397	400*	400*
Pulses*	205	205	205
Cashew nuts	58	58*	58*
Groundnuts (in shell)	115	109	110*
Coconuts*	264	265	265
Sunflower seed*	11	11	11
Cottonseed	23	24*	24*
Other oil seeds	30	30*	30*
Tomatoes	7	9*	9*
Other vegetables and melons	108	108*	108*
Bananas*	90	90	90
Oranges	13	14*	14*
Grapefruits and pomelos*	13	13	13
Mangoes*	24	24	24
Pineapples*	13	13	13
Papayas*	31	31	31
Other fruits*	90	90	90
Cotton (lint)	11	24†	25†

* FAO estimate(s).
† Unofficial figure.

Source: FAO.

LIVESTOCK
(FAO estimates, '000 head, year ending September)

	1998	1999	2000
Asses	22	23	23
Cattle	1,300	1,310	1,320
Pigs	176	178	180
Sheep	123	124	125
Goats	388	390	392
Chickens	26,000	27,000	28,000

2001–02: Figures assumed to be unchanged from 2000.

Source: FAO.

LIVESTOCK PRODUCTS
(FAO estimates, '000 metric tons)

	1999	2000	2001
Beef and veal	38	38	38
Goat meat	2	2	2
Pig meat	13	13	13
Poultry meat	36	36	36
Cows' milk	60	60	60
Goats' milk	8	8	8
Hen eggs	14	14	14
Cattle hides	5	5	5

Source: FAO.

2002: Figures assumed to be unchanged from 2001 (FAO estimates).

Forestry

ROUNDWOOD REMOVALS
('000 cubic metres, excl. bark)

	1997	1998	1999
Sawlogs, veneer logs and logs for sleepers	129	128	128
Other industrial wood	1,139	1,166	1,191
Fuel wood	16,724	16,724	16,724
Total	17,992	18,018	18,043

2000–02: Production as in 1999 (FAO estimates).

Source: FAO.

SAWNWOOD PRODUCTION
('000 cubic metres, incl. railway sleepers)

	1997	1998	1999
Total	33	28	28

2000–02: Production as in 1999 (FAO estimates).

Source: FAO.

Fishing

(metric tons, live weight)

	1999	2000	2001
Freshwater fishes	1,191	1,275	1,000
Dagaas	9,052	11,813	7,076
Tuna-like fishes	2,635	5,081	3,096
Penaeus shrimps	8,846	9,460	9,479
Knife shrimp	1,611	1,766	1,738
Total catch (incl. others) . . .	33,989	39,065	32,512

Note: Figures exclude crocodiles, recorded by number rather than by weight. The number of Nile crocodiles caught was: 585 in 1999; 718 in 2000; 477 in 2001.

Source: FAO, *Yearbook of Fishery Statistics*.

Mining

('000 metric tons, unless otherwise indicated)

	2000	2001	2002
Bauxite	8.1	8.6	9.1
Bentonite	16.1	17.7	0.0
Coal	16.1	27.6	43.5
Gold (kilograms)*	23.0	22.0	17.0
Gravel and crushed rock ('000 cubic metres)	187.0†	13.0	24.2
Marble (slab) ('000 square metres)	1.8†	15.3	10.0
Salt (marine)†	7.0	10.0	15.0
Natural gas (million cu m) . . .	1.0†	1.0‡	1.0‡

* Figures exclude artisanal gold production; total gold output is estimated at 360 kg–480 kg per year.
† Estimate(s).
‡ Reported figure.

Source: US Geological Survey.

Industry

SELECTED PRODUCTS
('000 metric tons, unless otherwise indicated)

	1999	2000	2001
Flour (cereals other than wheat) .	9	18	23
Wheat flour	125	114	140
Raw sugar	46	39	31
Beer ('000 hl)	95	989	982
Soft drinks ('000 hl)	100	626	670
Cigarettes (million)	1,084	1,417	1,359
Footwear (excl. rubber, '000 pairs) .	7	7	2
Cement	266	348	421
Electric energy (million kWh)* . .	6,864	6,974	n.a.

* Estimates.

Source: UN, *Industrial Commodity Statistics Yearbook*.

2002 ('000 metric tons, reported figure): Groundnut oil 17.0 (estimate); Beer of barley 48.0 (estimate); Cement 274 (Sources: FAO and US Geological Survey).

Finance

CURRENCY AND EXCHANGE RATES

Monetary Units
100 centavos = 1 metical (plural: meticais).

Sterling, Dollar and Euro Equivalents (31 December 2003)
£1 sterling = 42,577.1 meticais;
US $1 = 23,856.7 meticais;
€1 = 30,131.0 meticais;
100,000 meticais = £2.349 = $4.191 = €3.319.

Average Exchange Rate (meticais per US $)
2001   20,703.6
2002   23,678.0
2003   23,782.3

Note: Between April 1992 and October 2000 the market exchange rate was the rate at which commercial banks purchased from and sold to the public. Since October 2000 it has been the weighted average of buying and selling rates of all transactions of commercial banks and stock exchanges with the public.

BUDGET
('000 million meticais)

Revenue*	2001	2002	2003
Taxation	8,589	10,629	13,695
Taxes on income . . .	1,498	2,116	3,235
Domestic taxes on goods and services	5,379	6,404	7,799
Customs duties	1,477	1,851	2,229
Other taxes.	236	258	432
Non-tax revenue	1,027	1,427	1,019
Total	**9,616**	**12,056**	**14,714**

Expenditure	2001	2002	2003
Current expenditure. . . .	10,319	13,469	16,342
Compensation of employees . .	4,898	6,206	7,734
Other goods and services . .	2,400	2,776	2,991
Interest on public debt . . .	478	1,274	1,319
Transfer payments . . .	1,992	2,694	3,075
Others	552	519	1,223
Capital expenditure	12,260	15,487	13,850
Unallocated	115	−206	252
Total	**22,694**	**28,750**	**30,444**

* Excluding grants received ('000 million meticais): 9,637 in 2001; 9,947 in 2002; 10,590 in 2003.

Source: Banco de Moçambique.

INTERNATIONAL RESERVES
(US $ million at 31 December)

	2000	2001	2002
IMF special drawing rights . . .	0.06	0.06	0.07
Reserve position in IMF. . .	0.01	0.01	0.01
Foreign exchange.	725.04	715.50	819.11
Total	**725.11**	**715.57**	**819.19**

Source: IMF, *International Financial Statistics*.

MONEY SUPPLY
('000 million meticais at 31 December)

	2001	2002	2003
Currency outside banks . . .	2,970.4	3,485.5	4,258.8
Demand deposits at commercial banks	6,912.7	8,017.5	9,897.1
Total money (incl. others) . .	**10,066.0**	**11,688.2**	**14,391.8**

Source: IMF, *International Financial Statistics*.

COST OF LIVING
(Consumer Price Index; base: 1998=100)

	2000	2001	2002
Food, beverages and tobacco . .	110	140	151
Clothing and footwear . . .	99	118	126
Firewood and furniture . . .	152	176	190
All items	**118**	**144**	**157**

Source: IMF, *Republic of Mozambique: Statistical Appendix* (November 2003).

NATIONAL ACCOUNTS
('000 million meticais at current prices)

National Income and Product

	1999	2000	2001
Compensation of employees. .	11,173.4	13,672.7	17,522.9
Net operating surplus	7,364.1	10,158.0	7,391.1
Net mixed income	24,859.8	24,187.1	30,803.4
Domestic primary incomes . .	**43,397.3**	**48,017.8**	**55,717.4**
Consumption of fixed capital . .	5,096.1	6,625.3	10,810.0
Gross domestic product (GDP) at factor cost	**48,493.4**	**54,643.1**	**66,527.4**
Taxes on production and imports .	3,472.8	2,330.0	4,674.0
Less Subsidies	53.0	55.7	66.6
GDP in market prices	**51,913.2**	**56,917.4**	**71,134.8**

Expenditure on the Gross Domestic Product

	2000	2001	2002
Government final consumption expenditure	7,730.1	10,325.9	16,178.3
Private final consumption expenditure	44,678.1	51,708.1	61,420.3
Increase in stock . . . . } Gross capital formation . . . }	19,323.0	18,845.1	17,695.5
Total domestic expenditure . .	**71,731.2**	**80,879.1**	**95,294.1**
Exports of goods and services .	7,325.7	15,472.3	20,030.2
Less Imports of goods and services	22,139.3	25,216.7	32,576.9
GDP in purchasers' values .	**56,917.4**	**71,134.8**	**82,747.4**
GDP at constant 1996 prices .	**44,686.4**	**50,483.5**	**54,668.3**

Gross Domestic Product by Economic Activity

	2000	2001	2002
Agriculture and livestock . . .	12,346.2	15,554.8	18,394.6
Fishing	1,378.1	1,600.9	1,612.8
Mining	206.3	254.4	265.2
Manufacturing	6,829.5	9,852.1	10,854.2
Electricity and water	1,280.5	1,465.5	1,853.4
Construction	5,306.7	6,170.4	7,815.6
Wholesale and retail trade . .	12,353.2	14,960.3	17,258.7
Restaurants and hotels . . .	796.7	956.6	1,191.9
Transport and communications .	5,296.8	6,810.8	7,747.4
Financial services	2,240.0	2,785.2	3,087.6
Real estate and business services	1,533.3	1,719.0	1,829.5
Public administration and defence	2,118.1	2,660.6	3,309.5
Education	1,563.7	2,157.2	2,618.4
Health	538.7	692.1	821.9
Other Services	2,797.4	3,372.1	3,749.1
Sub-Total	**56,585.2**	**71,012.0**	**82,409.8**
Less Financial services indirectly measured	965.2	1,315.4	1,513.9
Gross value added in basic prices	**55,619.8**	**69,696.6**	**80,895.9**
Taxes on products . . . . } *Less* Subsidies on products . . }	1,297.5	1,438.3	1,851.2
GDP in market prices . . .	**56,917.4**	**71,134.8**	**82,747.4**

BALANCE OF PAYMENTS
(US $ million)

	2000	2001	2002
Exports of goods f.o.b.	364.0	703.1	681.8
Imports of goods c.i.f.	−1,163.0	−1,063.4	−1,262.9
Trade balance	**−799.0**	**−360.3**	**−581.1**
Exports of services	405.1	310.6	544.8
Imports of services	−648.4	−916.8	−804.2
Balance on goods and services	**−1,042.3**	**−966.5**	**−840.6**
Unrequited official transfers (grants)	563.9	469.3	420.0
Current balance	**−478.4**	**−497.1**	**−420.6**
Foreign borrowing	483.8	156.3	808.5
Amortization	−344.0	−376.5	−162.7
Trade credit	—	—	−127.5
Direct investment (net)	139.1	255.4	156.3
Short-term capital, and errors and omissions (net)	−152.5	41.0	−160.1
Overall balance	**−352.0**	**−420.9**	**94.0**

Source: IMF, *Republic of Mozambique: Statistical Appendix* (November 2003).

External Trade

PRINCIPAL COMMODITIES
(distribution by SITC, US $ million)

Imports c.i.f.	1998	1999	2001*
Food and live animals	169.3	114.1	125.5
Cereals and cereal preparations	100.0	75.9	84.8
Wheat and meslin (unmilled)	30.5	23.9	25.3
Rice (unmilled)	52.0	41.8	45.9
Sugar, sugar preparations and honey	25.1	14.6	7.1
Crude materials (inedible) except fuels	26.2	13.4	16.4
Mineral fuels, lubricants etc.	66.1	73.4	169.5
Petroleum, petroleum products, etc.	55.0	67.9	135.2
Refined petroleum products	53.8	67.2	132.6
Animal and vegetable oils, fats and waxes	12.4	21.0	11.4
Chemicals and related products	54.0	43.4	68.3
Basic manufactures	193.4	79.2	107.1
Non-metallic mineral manufactures	30.6	13.4	23.8
Iron and steel	44.7	14.4	20.7
Manufactures of metals	59.8	19.3	22.4
Machinery and transport equipment	220.2	288.0	232.6
Machinery specialized for particular industries	30.4	23.8	26.4
General industrial machinery, equipment and parts	34.7	24.9	30.4
Electrical machinery, apparatus, etc.	38.6	31.7	46.0
Road vehicles and parts	60.8	168.7	45.4
Passenger motor vehicles (excl. buses)	10.8	41.6	0.0
Road motor vehicles	12.8	32.7	2.2
Motor vehicles for transport of goods	24.5	79.6	27.2
Miscellaneous manufactured articles	62.0	42.6	88.9
Commodities and transactions not classified elsewhere	0.0	1.4	232.5
Total (incl. others)	817.2	685.1	1,063.4

Exports f.o.b.	1998	1999	2001*
Food and live animals	129.3	128.1	141.5
Fish, crustaceans, molluscs and preparations	66.4	74.8	99.7
Crustaceans and molluscs, fresh, frozen or salted	62.1	69.7	94.5
Vegetables and fruit	49.8	42.5	14.5
Fresh or dried fruit and nuts	49.5	40.1	13.9
Crude materials (inedible) except fuels	23.8	38.9	34.8
Cotton	10.9	19.8	16.1
Carded or combed cotton	1.6	13.2	13.0
Mineral fuels, lubricants, etc.	37.6	68.1	66.9
Electric current	37.0	62.9	57.3
Basic manufactures	10.9	5.6	399.6
Aluminium and alloys, unwrought	0.0	0.0	383.1
Machinery and transport equipment	22.4	14.0	17.3
Miscellaneous manufactured articles	9.1	7.2	17.3
Total (incl. others)	244.5	270.6	703.1

* Figures for 2000 not available.

Source: UN, *International Trade Statistics Yearbook*.

2000 (US $ million): Exports: Aluminium 60.2; Prawns 91.5; Electricity 67.0; Cotton 25.5; Timber 14.2; Cashew nuts (unprocessed) 11.9; Total (incl. others) 364.0 (Source: IMF, *Republic of Mozambique: Statistical Appendix*—November 2003).

2002 (US $ million)* *Exports:* Aluminium 361.1 (preliminary); Prawns 63.9; Electricity 107.4; Cotton 20.7; Timber 17.4; Cashew nuts (unprocessed) 16.2; Total (incl. others) 681.8 (Source: IMF, *Republic of Mozambique: Statistical Appendix*—November 2003).

* Figures for 2001 not available.

PRINCIPAL TRADING PARTNERS
(US $ million)

Imports c.i.f.	1998	2000*	2001
China, People's Repub.	12.7	22.2	21.7
France-Monaco	17.2	23.9	12.1
Germany	8.9	8.9	5.9
India	35.2	19.0	25.2
Italy-San Marino-Vatican	8.2	17.3	9.5
Japan	32.3	50.7	6.9
Korea, Republic	n.a.	13.1	4.2
Pakistan	17.6	18.3	30.9
Portugal	64.2	92.4	90.1
Saudi Arabia	32.8	n.a.	n.a.
South Africa	—	425.3	428.5
Southern African Customs Union†	344.7	—	—
Spain	6.5	10.6	20.4
Thailand	10.4	4.5	3.5
United Arab Emirates	12.1	2.7	13.3
United Kingdom	16.3	17.2	12.1
USA	43.6	36.3	19.2
Zimbabwe	19.0	5.1	9.0
Total (incl. others)	817.3	1,157.9	1,063.4

Exports f.o.b.	1999	2000	2001
France-Monaco	2.7	1.8	0.7
Hong Kong	8.0	4.2	5.2
India	32.0	17.9	3.5
Japan	11.6	15.7	29.2
Malawi	4.8	11.0	10.3
Netherlands	4.5	3.8	7.1
Portugal	24.5	42.4	28.2
South Africa	—	53.3	107.6
Southern African Customs Union†	76.2	—	—
Spain	34.5	39.0	26.9
United Kingdom	2.8	3.1	0.2
USA	12.6	17.2	6.8
Zimbabwe	40.2	64.5	37.1
Total (incl. others)	270.9	364.0	703.1

* Figures for 1999 not available.
† Comprises Botswana, Lesotho, Namibia, South Africa and Swaziland.

Source: UN, *International Trade Statistics Yearbook*.

2002 (US $ million): Imports 1,262.9; Exports 681.8 (Source: IMF, *Republic of Mozambique: Statistical Appendix*—November 2003).

Transport

RAILWAYS
(traffic)

	1999	2000	2001
Freight ton-km (million)	721.2	604.8	774.5
Passenger-km (million)	144.7	129.8	142.0

Source: IMF, *Republic of Mozambique: Statistical Appendix* (July 2002).

ROAD TRAFFIC
(motor vehicles in use at 31 December)

	1994	1995*	1996*
Passenger cars	30,977	25,740	4,900
Lorries and vans	10,035	7,520	7,520

* Estimates.
Source: International Road Federation, *World Road Statistics*.

SHIPPING
Merchant Fleet
(registered at 31 December)

	2000	2001	2002
Number of vessels	127	131	131
Total displacement ('000 grt)	37.4	38.0	37.2

Source: Lloyd's Register-Fairplay, *World Fleet Statistics*.

Freight Handled
('000 shipping tons)

	1999	2000	2001
Goods loaded and unloaded	6,118	6,097	7,312

Source: IMF, *Republic of Mozambique: Statistical Appendix* (July 2002).

International Sea-borne Freight Traffic ('000 metric tons, 1990): Goods loaded 2,578; Goods unloaded 3,379 (Source: *UN, Monthly Bulletin of Statistics*).

CIVIL AVIATION
(traffic on scheduled services)

	1997	1998	1999
Kilometres flown (million)	4	4	5
Passengers carried ('000)	188	201	235
Passenger-km (million)	291	295	326
Total ton-km (million)	32	33	36

Source: UN, *Statistical Yearbook*.

Passenger-km (million): 330 in 1999; 378 in 2000; 272 in 2001.

Freight ton-km (million): 6.1 in 1999; 7.2 in 2000; 6.7 in 2001.

Source: IMF, *Republic of Mozambique: Statistical Appendix* (July 2002).

Tourism

TOURIST ARRIVALS BY COUNTRY OF RESIDENCE

Country	2001
Portugal	46,300
South Africa	377,100
Swaziland	15,600
Total (incl. others)	483,700

Source: Ministério de Turismo, Maputo.

Communications Media

	1999	2000	2001
Television receivers ('000 in use)	100	105	n.a.
Telephones ('000 main lines in use)	78.1	85.7	89.5
Mobile cellular telephones ('000 subscribers)	12.2	51.1	152.7
Personal computers ('000 in use)	50	60	70
Internet users ('000)	15	30	30

Source: International Telecommunication Union.

Radio receivers (1997): 730,000 in use.

Facsimile machines (1996): 7,200 in use.

Daily newspapers (1998): 12 (average circulation 43,000).

Non-daily newspapers (1998): 44 (estimated average circulation 187,000).

Periodicals (1998): 32 (average circulation 83,000).

Book production (1984): 66 titles (including 37 pamphlets); 3,490,000 copies (including 360,000 pamphlets).

Sources: UNESCO, *Statistical Yearbook*; UN, *Statistical Yearbook*.

Education
(1998)

	Institutions	Teachers	Students Males	Students Females	Total
Pre-primary*†	5,689	28,705	n.a.	n.a.	1,745,049
Primary	6,263	31,512	1,111,011	807,389	1,918,400
Secondary	75†	8,073	149,902	104,638	254,540
Higher*†	3	954	n.a.	n.a.	7,156

* Public education only.
† 1997 figure(s).
Source: partly UNESCO Institute for Statistics.

2001: 8,165 primary institutions.

Adult literacy rate (UNESCO estimates): 45.2% (males 61.2%; females 30.0%) in 2001 (Source: UN Development Programme, *Human Development Report*).

Directory

The Constitution

The Constitution came into force on 30 November 1990, replacing the previous version, introduced at independence on 25 June 1975 and revised in 1978. Its main provisions, as amended in 1996, are summarized below.

GENERAL PRINCIPLES

The Republic of Mozambique is an independent, sovereign, unitary and democratic state of social justice. Sovereignty resides in the people, who exercise it according to the forms laid down in the Constitution. The fundamental objectives of the Republic include:

The defence of independence and sovereignty;

the defence and promotion of human rights and of the equality of citizens before the law; and

the strengthening of democracy, of freedom and of social and individual stability.

POLITICAL PARTICIPATION

The people exercise power through universal, direct, equal, secret, personal and periodic suffrage to elect their representatives, by referenda and through permanent democratic participation. Political parties are prohibited from advocating or resorting to violence.

FUNDAMENTAL RIGHTS AND DUTIES OF CITIZENS

All citizens enjoy the same rights and are subject to the same duties, irrespective of colour, race, sex, ethnic origin, place of birth, religion, level of education, social position or occupation. In realizing the objectives of the Constitution, all citizens enjoy freedom of opinion, assembly and association. All citizens over 18 years of age are entitled to vote and be elected. Active participation in the defence of the country is the duty of every citizen. Individual freedoms are guaranteed by the State, including freedom of expression, of the press, of assembly, of association and of religion. The State guarantees accused persons the right to a legal defence. No Court or Tribunal has the power to impose a sentence of death upon any person.

STATE ORGANS

Public elective officers are chosen by elections through universal, direct, secret, personal and periodic vote. Legally-recognized political parties may participate in elections.

THE PRESIDENT

The President is the Head of State and of the Government, and Commander-in-Chief of the armed forces. The President is elected by direct, equal, secret and personal universal suffrage on a majority vote, and must be proposed by at least 10,000 voters, of whom at least 200 must reside in each province. The term of office is five years. A candidate may be re-elected on only two consecutive occasions, or again after an interval of five years between terms.

THE ASSEMBLY OF THE REPUBLIC

Legislative power is vested in the Assembléia da República (Assembly of the Republic). The Assembléia is elected by universal direct adult suffrage on a secret ballot, and is composed of 250 Deputies. The Assembléia is elected for a maximum term of five years, but may be dissolved by the President before the expiry of its term. The Assembléia holds two ordinary sessions each year.

THE COUNCIL OF MINISTERS

The Council of Ministers is the Government of the Republic. The Prime Minister assists and advises the President in the leadership of the Government and presents the Government's programme, budget and policies to the Assembléia da República, assisted by other ministers.

LOCAL STATE ORGANS

The Republic is administered in provinces, municipalities and administrative posts. The highest state organ in a province is the provincial government, presided over by a governor, who is answerable to the central Government. There shall be assemblies at each administrative level.

THE JUDICIARY

Judicial functions shall be exercised through the Supreme Court and other courts provided for in the law on the judiciary, which also subordinates them to the Assembléia da República. Courts must safeguard the principles of the Constitution and defend the rights and legitimate interests of citizens. Judges are independent, subject only to the law.

The Government

HEAD OF STATE

President of the Republic and Commander-in-Chief of the Armed Forces: JOAQUIM ALBERTO CHISSANO (took office 6 November 1986; elected President 27–29 October 1994; re-elected 3–5 December 1999).

COUNCIL OF MINISTERS
(April 2004)

Prime Minister and Minister of Planning and Finance: LUÍSA DIOGO.

Minister of Foreign Affairs and Co-operation: Dr LEONARDO DOS SANTOS SIMÃO.

Minister of National Defence: Gen. (retd) TOBIAS DAI.

Minister of Justice: JOSÉ IBRAIMO ABUDO.

Minister of the Interior and Minister in the President's Office, with responsibility for Defence and Security Affairs: ALMERINO DA CRUZ MARCOS MANHENJE.

Minister of State Administration: JOSÉ CHICHAVA.

Minister of Agricultural and Rural Development: HÉLDER MONTEIRO MUTEIA.

Minister of Fisheries: CADMIEL MUTEMBA.

Minister of Industry and Trade: CARLOS ALBERTO MORGADO.

Minister of Mineral Resources and Energy: CASTIGO JOSÉ CORREIA LANGA.

Minister of Transport and Communications: TOMÁS AUGUSTO SALOMÃO.

Minister of Education: ALCIDO EDUARDO NGUENHA.

Minister of Health: FRANCISCO FERREIRA SONGANE.

Minister of Culture: MIGUEL COSTA MKAÍMA.

Minister of Environmental Co-ordination: JOHN WILLIAM KACHAMILA.

Minister of Labour: MÁRIO LAMPIÃO SEVENE.

Minister of Public Works and Housing: ROBERTO COSTLEY-WHITE.

Minister of Youth and Sport: JOEL MATIAS LIBOMBO.

Minister of Women's Affairs and Social Welfare Co-ordination: VIRGÍLIA SANTOS MATABELE.

Minister in the Presidency with responsibility for Parliamentary and Diplomatic Affairs: FRANCISCO CAETANO MADEIRA.

Minister of Tourism: FERNANDO SUMBANE.

Minister of Veterans' Affairs: ANTÓNIO HAMA THAY.

Minister of Higher Education, Science and Technology: LÍDIA MARIA RIBEIRO ARTHUR BRITO.

MINISTRIES

Office of the President: Avda Julius Nyerere 1780, Maputo; tel. (1) 491121; fax (1) 492065.

Office of the Prime Minster: Praça da Marinha Popular, Maputo; tel. (1) 426861; fax (1) 426881; e-mail dgpm.gov@teledata.mz.

Ministry of Agricultural and Rural Development: Praça dos Heróis Moçambicanos, CP 1406, Maputo; tel. (1) 460011; fax (1) 460055; internet www.map.gov.mz.

Ministry of Culture: Avda Patrice Lumumba 1217, CP 1742, Maputo; tel. (1) 420086; fax (1) 429700.

Ministry of Education: Avda 24 de Julho 167, 9° andar, CP 34, Maputo; tel. (1) 492006; fax (1) 492196; internet www.mined.gov.mz.

Ministry of Environmental Co-ordination: Avda Acordos de Lusaka 2115, CP 2020, Maputo; tel. (1) 466245; fax (1) 465849; e-mail jwkacha@virconn.com; internet www.sdnp.mz/ambiente.

Ministry of Fisheries: Rua Consiglieri Pedroso 347, CP 1723, Maputo; tel. (1) 431266; fax (1) 425087; e-mail alfredo@mozpesca .org; internet www.mozpesca.org.

Ministry of Foreign Affairs and Co-operation: Avda Julius Nyerere 4, CP 2787, Maputo; tel. (1) 490222; fax (1) 494070; e-mail minec@zebra.uem.mz; internet www.minec.gov.mz.

Ministry of Health: Avdas Eduardo Mondlane e Salvador Allende 1008, CP 264, Maputo; tel. (1) 427131; fax (1) 427133.

Ministry of Higher Education, Science and Technology: Avda Patrice Lumumba 770, Maputo; tel. (1) 352800; fax (1) 352860; e-mail secretariado@mesct.gov.mz; internet www.mesct.gov.mz.

Ministry of Industry and Trade: Praça 25 de Junho 300, CP 1831, Maputo; tel. (1) 426093.

Ministry of the Interior: Avda Olaf Palme 46/48, CP 290, Maputo; tel. (1) 420131; fax (1) 420084.

Ministry of Justice: Avda Julius Nyerere 33, Maputo; tel. (1) 491613; fax (1) 494264.

Ministry of Labour: Avda 24 de Julho 2351–2365, CP 258, Maputo; tel. (1) 427051; fax (1) 421881.

Ministry of Mineral Resources and Energy: Avda Fernão de Magalhães 34, CP 2904, Maputo; tel. (1) 425680; fax (1) 427103; e-mail minas@minas.co.mz; internet www.minas.co.mz.

Ministry of National Defence: Avda Mártires de Mueda 280, CP 3216, Maputo; tel. (1) 492081; fax (1) 491619.

Ministry of Planning and Finance: Praça da Marinha Popular, CP 272, Maputo; tel. (1) 315013; fax (1) 315060; e-mail dnpo@dnpo .uem.mz; internet www.mozambique.mz/governo/mpf/dnpo.

Ministry of Public Works and Housing: Avda Karl Marx 268, CP 268, Maputo; tel. (1) 420543; fax (1) 421369.

Ministry of State Administration: Rua da Rádio Moçambique 112, CP 4116, Maputo; tel. (1) 426666; fax (1) 428565; internet www .sdnp.org.mz/mae.

Ministry of Tourism: Avda 25 de Setembro 1018, CP 4101, Maputo; tel. (1) 313755; fax (1) 306212; internet www.moztourism .gov.mz.

Ministry of Transport and Communications: Avda Mártires de Inhaminga 336, Maputo; tel. (1) 420223; fax (1) 431028; e-mail celular@zebra.uem.mz; internet www.mtc.gov.mz.

Ministry of Veterans' Affairs: Rua General Pereira d'Eça 35, CP 3697, Maputo; tel. (1) 490601.

Ministry of Women's Affairs and Social Welfare Co-ordination: Rua de Tchamba 86, CP 516, Maputo; tel. (1) 490921; fax (1) 492757; e-mail vmatabele@mimucas.org.mz; internet www .mimucas.org.mz.

Ministry of Youth and Sport: Avda 25 de Setembro 529, CP 2080, Maputo; tel. (1) 312172; e-mail mjd@tvcabo.co.mz; internet www .mjd.gov.mz.

PROVINCIAL GOVERNORS
(April 2004)

Cabo Delgado Province: JOSÉ PACHECO.

Gaza Province: ROSÁRIO MUALEIA.

Inhambane Province: AIRES ALY.

Manica Province: SOARES NHACA.

Maputo Province: ALFREDO NAMITETE.

Nampula Province: ABDUL RAZAK.

Niassa Province: DAVID SIMANGO.

Sofala Province: FELÍCIO ZACARIAS.

Tete Province: TOMÁS MANDLATE.

Zambézia Province: LUCAS CHOMERA.

City of Maputo: ARTUR CANANA.

President and Legislature

PRESIDENT
Presidential Election, 3–5 December 1999

	Votes	% of votes
Joaquim Alberto Chissano (Frelimo)	2,338,333	52.29
Afonso Macacho Marceta Dhlakama (Renamo—União Eleitoral)	2,133,655	47.71
Total*	4,471,988	100.00

*Excluding 320,795 blank votes and 141,569 spoilt votes.

ASSEMBLÉIA DA REPÚBLICA
Chairman: EDUARDO MULEMBUE.
General Election, 3–5 December 1999

	Votes	% of votes	Seats
Frente de Libertação de Moçambique (Frelimo)	2,005,713	48.54	133
Resistência Nacional Moçambicana—União Eleitoral (Renamo—UE)	1,603,811	38.81	117
Partido do Trabalho (PT)	111,139	2.69	—
Partido Liberal e Democrático de Moçambique (Palmo)	101,970	2.47	—
Partido Social, Liberal e Democrático (Sol)	83,440	2.02	—
União Moçambicana de Oposição (UMO)	64,117	1.55	—
União Democrática (UD)	61,122	1.48	—
Total (incl. others)*	4,132,323	100.00	250

*Excluding 462,666 blank votes and 238,772 spoilt votes.

Political Organizations

Aliança Democrática de Moçambique (ADM): Maputo; f. 1994; Co-ordinator JOSÉ PEREIRA BRANQUINHO.

Aliança Independente de Moçambique (Alimo): Maputo; f. 1998; mem. of União Eleitoral; Sec.-Gen. ERNESTO SERGIO.

Confederação Democrática de Moçambique (Codemo): Maputo; f. 1991; Leader DOMINGOS CARDOSO.

Congresso dos Democratas Unidos (CDU): Maputo; f. 2001; Leader ANTÓNIO PALANGE.

Congresso Independente de Moçambique (Coinmo): Pres. VÍTOR MARCOS SAENE; Sec.-Gen. HILDA RABECA TSININE.

Frente de Ação Patriótica (FAP): Maputo; f. 1991; mem. of União Eleitoral; Pres. JOSÉ CARLOS PALAÇO; Sec.-Gen. RAUL DA CONCEIÇÃO.

Frente Democrática Unida—United Democratic Front (UDF): Maputo; mem. of União Eleitoral.

Frente de Libertação de Moçambique (Frelimo): Rua Pereira do Lago 10, Bairro de Sommerschield, Maputo; tel. (1) 490181; fax (1) 490008; e-mail info@frelimo.org.mz; internet www.frelimo.org.mz; f. 1962 by merger of three nationalist parties; reorg. 1977 as a 'Marxist-Leninist vanguard movement'; in July 1989 abandoned its exclusive Marxist-Leninist orientation; Pres. JOAQUIM ALBERTO CHISSANO; Sec.-Gen. ARMANDO GUEBUZA.

Frente Unida de Moçambique—Partido de Convergência Democrática (Fumo—PCD): Avda Mao Tse Tung 230, 1° andar, Maputo; tel. (1) 494044; Sec.-Gen. JOSÉ SAMO GUDO.

Movimento Nacionalista Moçambicana—Partido Moçambicano da Social Democracia (Monamo—PMSD): mem. of União Eleitoral; Sec.-Gen. Dr MÁXIMO DIOGO JOSÉ DIAS.

Partido Agrário de Moçambique (PAM): f. 1991.

Partido Comunista de Moçambique (Pacomo): f. 1995.

Partido do Congresso Democrático (Pacode): Leader VASCO CAMPIRA MAMBOYA ALFAZEMA.

Partido de Convenção Nacional (PCN): Avda 25 Setembro 1123, 3° andar, Maputo; tel. (1) 426891; obtained legal status in 1992; mem. of União Eleitoral; Chair. LUTERO CHIMBIRIMBIRI SIMANGO; Sec.-Gen. Dr GABRIEL MABUNDA.

Partido Democrático de Libertação de Moçambique (Padelimo): based in Kenya; Pres. JOAQUIM JOSÉ NIOTA.

Partido Democrático de Moçambique (Pademo): f. 1991; obtained legal status in 1993; Co-ordinator WEHIA MONAKACHO RIPUA; Gen. Sec. GIMO GUINDILA.

Partido Democrático para a Reconciliação de Moçambique (PAMOMO): mem. of União Eleitoral; Leader ALBERTO MAIOPUE.

Partido Ecologista de Moçambique (PEMO): Maputo; mem. of União Eleitoral.

Partido Independente de Moçambique (Pimo): f. 1993; Leader YAQUB SABINDY; Sec.-Gen. MAGALHÃES BRAMUGY.

Partido Internacionalista Democrático de Moçambique (Pidemo): f. 1993; Leader JOÃO KAMACHO.

Partido Liberal e Democrático de Moçambique (Palmo): obtained legal status 1993; Chair. MARTINS BILAL; Sec.-Gen. ANTÓNIO MUEDO.

Partido Nacional de Obreiros e Camponêses (Panaoc): Leader ARMANDO SIUEIA.

Partido para a Paz, Democracia e Desenvolvimento (PPDD): Quelimane; f. 2003; liberal; Leader RAUL DOMINGOS.

Partido Patriótico Independente de Moçambique: f. 1995; breakaway faction of Pimo.

Partido Popular de Moçambique (PPM).

Partido Progressivo e Liberal de Moçambique (PPLM): f. 1992; Pres. NEVES SERRANO.

Partido do Progresso do Povo de Moçambique (PPPM): Avda 25 Setembro, 1123, 4° andar, Maputo; tel. (1) 426925; f. 1991; obtained legal status 1992; Pres. Dr PADIMBE MAHOSE KAMATI ANDREA; Sec.-Gen. CHE ABDALA.

Partido Renovador Democrático (PRD): obtained legal status 1994; mem. of União Eleitoral; Pres. MANECA DANIEL.

Partido Revolucionário do Povo Socialista Unido de Moçambique (Prepsumo): f. 1992.

Partido Social Democrático (PSD): Leader CARLOS MACHEL.

Partido de Todos os Nativos Moçambicanos (Partonamo): f. 1996; Leader MUSSAGY ABDUL REMANE.

Partido do Trabalho (PT): f. 1993; breakaway faction of PPPM; Pres. MIGUEL MABOTE; Sec.-Gen. LUÍS MUCHANGA.

Partido Social, Liberal e Democrático (Sol): breakaway faction of Palmo; Leader CASIMIRO MIGUEL NHAMITHAMBO.

Partido de Unidade Nacional (PUN): TV Sado 9, Maputo; tel. (1) 419204; mem. of União Eleitoral.

Partido Verde de Moçambique (PVM): Leader BRUNO SAPEMBA.

Regedores e Camponeses de Moçambique (Recamo): f. by ARONE SIJAMO.

Resistência Nacional Moçambicana (Renamo): Avda Julius Nyerere 2541, Maputo; tel. (1) 493107; also known as Movimento Nacional da Resistência de Moçambique (MNR); f. 1976; fmr guerrilla group, in conflict with the Govt between 1976 and Oct. 1992; obtained legal status in 1994; Pres. AFONSO MACACHO MARCETA DHLAKAMA; Sec.-Gen. VIANA MAGALHAES.

União Democrática (UD): f. 1994; Gen. Sec. JOSÉ CHICUARRA MASSINGA.

   Partido Nacional Democrático (Panade): Avda Trabalho 1412, 3° andar, Maputo; tel. (1) 401937; obtained legal status 1993; Leader JOSÉ CHICUARRA MASSINGA.

   Partido Nacional de Moçambique (Panamo): Pres. MARCOS JUMA.

União Democrática de Moçambique (Udemo): f. 1987 as the mil. wing of Unamo, from which it broke away in 1991; adopted present name in 1992; Leader GIMO PHIRI.

União Nacional Moçambicana (Unamo): f. 1987; breakaway faction of Renamo; social democratic; obtained legal status 1992; mem. of União Eleitoral; Pres. CARLOS ALEXANDRE DOS REIS; Sec.-Gen. FLORENCIA JOÃO DA SILVA.

Diplomatic Representation

EMBASSIES AND HIGH COMMISSIONS IN MOZAMBIQUE

Algeria: Rua de Mukumbura 121–125, CP 1709, Maputo; tel. (1) 492070; fax (1) 490582; e-mail ambalger@mail.tropical.co.mz; Ambassador FOUAD BOUTTOURA.

Angola: Avda Kenneth Kaunda 783, Maputo; tel. (1) 493691; fax (1) 493930; Ambassador JOÃO GARCIA BIRES.

Brazil: Avda Kenneth Kaunda 296, CP 1167, Maputo; tel. (1) 492388; fax (1) 490986; e-mail ebrasil@teledata.mz; Ambassador PEDRO LUIZ CARNEIRO DE MENDONÇA.

China, People's Republic: Avda Julius Nyerere 3142, CP 4668, Maputo; tel. (1) 491560; fax (1) 491196; e-mail hxing@emilmoz.mz; Ambassador CHEN DUQING.

Congo, Democratic Republic: Avda Kenneth Kaunda 127, CP 2407, Maputo; tel. (1) 497154; fax (1) 494929; Chargé d'affaires a.i. MULUMBA TSHIDIMBA MARCEL.

Congo, Republic: Avda dos Mártires de Machava 385, Maputo; tel. and fax (1) 493779; Chargé d'affaires a.i. MONSEGNO BASHA OSHEFWA.

Cuba: Avda Kenneth Kaunda 492, CP 387, Maputo; tel. (1) 492444; fax (1) 492700; e-mail embacuba@emilmoz.com; Ambassador EVELIO DORTA GONZÁLEZ.

Denmark: Avda 24 de Julho 1500, CP 4588, Maputo; tel. (1) 303413; fax (1) 303526; e-mail dkembmoz@mail.tropical.co.mz; Ambassador MADS SANDAU-JENSEN.

Egypt: Avda Mao Tse Tung 851, CP 4662, Maputo; tel. (1) 491118; fax (1) 491489; e-mail Egypt@virconn.com; Ambassador MOHAMED EL-ASHMAWI.

Finland: Avda Julius Nyerere 1128, CP 1663, Maputo; tel. (1) 490578; fax (1) 491661; e-mail sanomat.map@formin.fi; Ambassador ILARI RENTAKARI.

France: Avda Julius Nyerere 2361, CP 4781, Maputo; tel. (1) 490444; fax (1) 491727; e-mail ambfrmoz@virconn.com; internet www.ambafrance-mz.org; Ambassador LOUISE AVON.

Germany: Rua Damião de Góis 506, CP 1595, Maputo; tel. (1) 492714; fax (1) 492888; e-mail germaemb@isl.co.mz; Ambassador ROLF-RUDIGER ZIRPEL.

Holy See: Avda Kwame Nkrumah 224, CP 2738, Maputo; tel. (1) 491144; fax (1) 492217; e-mail namoz.secret@teledata.mz; Apostolic Nuncio Most Rev. GEORGE PANIKULAM (Titular Archbishop of Caudium).

Iceland: Avda Zimbabwe 1694, Maputo; tel. (1) 483509; fax (1) 483511; e-mail icemb.maputo@utn.stjr.is; internet www.iceland.org/mo; Ambassador BENEDICT ASGEIRSSON.

India: Avda Kenneth Kaunda 167, CP 4751, Maputo; tel. (1) 492437; fax (1) 492364; e-mail hicomind@tvcabo.co.mz; internet www.hicomind-maputo.org; High Commissioner UPENDRA CHANDRA BARO.

Iran: Avda dos Mártires da Machava 1630, Maputo; tel. (1) 490700; fax (1) 492005; Ambassador ABDUL ALI TAUAKALI.

Ireland: Rua Dom João IV 213, Maputo; tel. (1) 491440; fax (1) 493023; e-mail ireland@vircom.com; Chargé d'affaires a.i. EDWARD JUSTIN CARROLL.

Italy: Avda Kenneth Kaunda 387, CP 976, Maputo; tel. (1) 491605; fax (1) 400503; e-mail ambitel.moz@virconn.net; internet www.italia.gov.mz; Ambassador GUIDO LARCHER.

Japan: Avda Julius Nyerere 2832, CP 11434, Maputo; tel. (1) 499819; fax (1) 498957; Ambassador KAWASI BAAH BOAKGE.

Korea, Democratic People's Republic: Rua da Kaswende 167, Maputo; tel. (1) 491482; Ambassador RO MIN SU.

Libya: Rua Pereira Marinho 294, CP 4434, Maputo; tel. (1) 490662; fax (1) 492450; Ambassador AIAD SALAH ASHAWISH.

Malawi: Avda Kenneth Kaunda 75, CP 4148, Maputo; tel. (1) 492676; fax (1) 490224; High Commissioner ZILILO Q. Y. CHIMAMBO.

Mauritius: Rua Dom Carlos 42, Maputo; tel. (1) 494182; fax (1) 494729; e-mail mhcmoz@virconn.com; High Commissioner DEVARAY VIRAH SAWMY.

Netherlands: Rua de Mukumbura 285, CP 1163, Maputo; tel. (1) 490031; fax (1) 490429; e-mail nlgovmap@virconn.com; Ambassador ARIE C. A. VAN DER WIEL.

Nigeria: Avda Kenneth Kaunda 821, CP 4693, Maputo; tel. (1) 490105; fax (1) 490991; High Commissioner ALBERT G. PIUS OMOTAIO.

Norway: Avda Julius Nyerere 1162, CP 828, Maputo; tel. (1) 480100; fax (1) 480107; e-mail emb.maputo@norad.no; internet www.norway.org.mz; Ambassador HENNING STIRØ.

Portugal: Avda Julius Nyerere 720, CP 4696, Maputo; tel. (1) 490316; fax (1) 491172; e-mail cculmapa@mail.tropical.co.mz; Ambassador ANTÓNIO T. DA CUNHA VALENTE.

Russia: Avda V. Lenine 2445, Maputo; tel. (1) 417372; fax (1) 417515; e-mail embrus@mail.tropical.net; Ambassador VLADIMIR VASLIEVICH ZEMSKIY.

Saudi Arabia: Rua João de Barros 124, Maputo; tel. (1) 490098; fax (1) 494705; Ambassador ALI MAHMOUD EMBAREK.

South Africa: Avda Eduardo Mondlane 41, CP 1120, Maputo; tel. (1) 493030; fax (1) 493029; e-mail sahc@tropical.co.mz; High Commissioner YASMIN JESSIE DUARTE.

Spain: Rua Damião de Góis 347, CP 1331, Maputo; tel. (1) 492025; fax (1) 492055; e-mail embespmz@correo.mae.es; Ambassador JOSÉ ANTÓNIO SALARICH.

Swaziland: Avda Luís Pasteur 1271/68, CP 4711, Maputo; tel. (1) 491601; fax (1) 492117; High Commissioner CARLTON D. DLAMINI.

Sweden: Avda Julius Nyerere 1128, CP 338, Maputo; tel. (1) 490091; fax (1) 490056; e-mail embassy.maputo@sida.se; Ambassador MAJ-INGE KLINGVALL.

Switzerland: Avda Julius Nyerere 1213, CP 135, Maputo; tel. (1) 492432; fax (1) 492474; e-mail swiccmap@mail.tropical.co.mz; Ambassador RUDOLF BAERFUSS.

Tanzania: Avda dos Mártires da Machava 852, Maputo; tel. (1) 490110; fax (1) 491228; e-mail ujamaa@zebra.uem.mz; High Commissioner Issa Mohamed Issa.

United Kingdom: Avda Vladimir I. Lénine 310, CP 55, Maputo; tel. (1) 420111; fax (1) 421666; e-mail bhc@virconn.com; High Commissioner Howard Parkinson.

USA: Avda Kenneth Kaunda 193, CP 783, Maputo; tel. (1) 492797; fax (1) 490114; internet www.usembassy-maputo.gov.mz; Ambassador Helen la Lime.

Zambia: Avda Kenneth Kaunda 1286, CP 4655, Maputo; tel. (1) 492452; fax (1) 491893; High Commissioner Maj.-Gen. Bellon Bestings Chisuta.

Zimbabwe: Avda dos Mártires da Machava 1623, CP 743, Maputo; tel. (1) 490404; fax (1) 492237; e-mail maro@isl.co.mz; Ambassador David Hamhoziripi.

Judicial System

The Constitution of November 1990 provides for a Supreme Court and other judicial courts, an Administrative Court, courts-martial, customs courts, maritime courts and labour courts. The Supreme Court consists of professional judges, appointed by the President of the Republic, and judges elected by the Assembléia da República. It acts in sections, as a trial court of primary and appellate jurisdiction, and in plenary session, as a court of final appeal. The Administrative Court controls the legality of administrative acts and supervises public expenditure.

President of the Supreme Court: Mário Mangaze.

Attorney-General: Joaquim Madeira.

Religion

There are an estimated 5m. Christians and 4m. Muslims, as well as a small Hindu community. Many inhabitants follow traditional beliefs.

CHRISTIANITY

In 1975 educational and medical facilities that had hitherto been administered by churches were acquired by the State. In June 1988 the Government announced that these facilities were to be returned.

Conselho Cristão de Moçambique (Christian Council of Mozambique): Avda Agostino Neto 1584, CP 108, Maputo; tel. (1) 322836; fax (1) 321968; e-mail com-ccmhq@isl.co.mz; internet swan.isl.co.mz/ccm; f. 1948; 22 mems; Pres. Rt Rev. Bernardino Mandlate; Gen. Sec. Rev. Dinis Matsolo.

The Roman Catholic Church

Mozambique comprises three archdioceses and nine dioceses. At 31 December 2002 adherents represented some 21.6% of the total population.

Bishops' Conference

Conferência Episcopal de Moçambique (CEM), Secretariado Geral da CEM, Avda Paulo Samuel Kankhomba 188/RC, CP 286, Maputo; tel. (1) 490766; fax (1) 492174.

f. 1982; Pres. Most Rev. Jaime Pedro Gonçalves (Archbishop of Beira).

Archbishop of Beira: Most Rev. Jaime Pedro Gonçalves, Cúria Arquiepiscopal, Rua Correia de Brito 613, CP 544, Beira; tel. (3) 322313; fax (3) 327639; e-mail arquidbeira@teledata.mz.

Archbishop of Maputo: Most Rev. Francisco Chimoio, Paço Arquiepiscopal, Avda Eduardo Mondlane 1448, CP 258, Maputo; tel. (1) 326240; fax (1) 321873.

Archbishop of Nampula: Most Rev. Tomé Makhweliha, Paço Arquiepiscopal, CP 84, 70100 Nampula; tel. (6) 213025; fax (6) 214194; e-mail arquidioce.npl@teledata.mz.

The Anglican Communion

Anglicans in Mozambique are adherents of the Church of the Province of Southern Africa. There are two dioceses in Mozambique. The Metropolitan of the Province is the Archbishop of Cape Town, South Africa.

Bishop of Lebombo: Rt Rev. Dinis Salomão Sengulane, CP 120, Maputo; tel. (1) 405364; fax (1) 401093; e-mail libombo@zebra.uem.mz.

Bishop of Niassa: Rev. Mark van Koevering, CP 264, Lichinga, Niassa; tel. (7) 12735; fax (7) 12336; e-mail anglican-niassa@maf.org.

Other Churches

Baptist Convention of Mozambique: Avda Maguiguane 386, CP 852, Maputo; tel. (1) 26852; Pres. Rev. Bento Bartolomeu Matusse; 17,443 adherents.

Free Methodist Church: Pres. Rev. Franisse Sando Muvile; 19,895 mems.

Igreja Maná: Rua Francisco Orlando Magumbwe 528, Maputo; tel. (1) 490876; fax (1) 490896; e-mail adm_mocambique@igrejamana.com.

Igreja Reformada em Moçambique (Reformed Church in Mozambique): CP3, Vila Ulongue, Anogonia-Tete; internet www2.gospelcom.net/rec/mozamb.html; f. 1908; Gen. Sec. Dr Wallace E. Chikakuda; 33,000 mems.

Presbyterian Church of Mozambique: Avda Ahmed Sekou Touré 1822, CP 21, Maputo; tel. (1) 421790; fax (1) 428623; e-mail ipmoc@zebra.uem.mz; 100,000 adherents; Pres. of Synodal Council Rev. Mário Nyamuxwe.

Other denominations active in Mozambique include the Church of Christ, the Church of the Nazarene, the United Congregational Church of Mozambique, the United Methodist Church of Mozambique, and the Wesleyan Methodist Church.

ISLAM

Comunidade Mahometana: Avda Albert Luthuli 291, Maputo; tel. (1) 425181; fax (1) 300880; e-mail toranias@zebra.uem.mz; internet www.paginaislamica.8m.com/pg1.htm; Pres. Abdul Assiz Osman Latif.

Islamic Congress of Mozambique: represents Sunni Muslims; Chair. Assane Ismael Maqbul.

Islamic Council of Mozambique: Leader Sheikh Aboobacar Ismael Mangirá.

The Press

DAILIES

Correio da Manha: Avda Filipe Samuel Magaia 528, CP 1756, Maputo; tel. (1) 305322; fax (1) 305321; e-mail refi@virconn.com; internet www.correiodamanha.co.mz; f. 1997; Dir Refinaldo Chilengue.

Diário de Moçambique: Avda 25 de Setembro 1509, 2° andar, CP 2491, Beira; tel. and fax (3) 427312; f. 1981; under state management since 1991; Dir Ezequiel Ambrósio; Editor Faruco Sadique; circ. 16,000.

Expresso da Tarde: Avda Patrice Lumumba 511, 1° andar, Maputo; tel. (1) 314912; e-mail expresso@teledata.mz; subscription only; distribution by fax; Dir Salvador Raimundo Honwana.

Imparcial Fax: Maputo; tel. (1) 308797; fax (1) 308796; e-mail imparcial@emilmoz.com; news-sheet by subscription only, distribution by fax; Dir Migéis Lopes Junior.

Mediafax: Avda Amílcar Cabral 1049, CP 73, Maputo; tel. (1) 430722; fax (1) 302402; e-mail mediafax@mediacoop.co.mz; internet www.mediacoop.odline.com; f. 1992 by co-operative of independent journalists Mediacoop; news-sheet by subscription only, distribution by fax and internet; Editor João Chamusse (acting).

Notícias: Rua Joaquim Lapa 55, CP 327, Maputo; tel. (1) 420119; fax (1) 420575; f. 1926; morning; under state management since 1991; Dir Bernardo Mavanga; Editor Hilário Cossa; circ. 33,000.

WEEKLIES

Campeão: Avda 24 de Julho 3706, CP 2610, Maputo; tel. and fax (1) 401810; sports newspaper; Dir Renato Caldéira; Editor Alexandre Zandamela.

Correio Semanal: Avda Filipe Samuel Magaia 528, CP 1756, Maputo; tel. (1) 305322; fax (1) 305312; Dir Refinaldo Chilengue.

Demos: Avda Mohamed Siad Barre, CP 2457, Maputo; tel. (1) 401420; fax (1) 401420; Dir Virgílio Mabota; Editor Palmira Velasco.

Desafio: Rua Joaquim Lapa 55, Maputo; tel. (1) 305437; fax (1) 305431; Dir Almiro Santos; Editor Boavida Funjua.

Domingo: Rua Joaquim Lapa 55, CP 327, Maputo; tel. (1) 431026; fax (1) 431027; f. 1981; Sun.; Dir Jorge Matine; Editor Moises Mabunda; circ. 25,000.

Fim de Semana: Rua da Resistência 1642, 1° andar, Maputo; tel. (1) 417012; fax (1) 416059; e-mail fsemana@teledata.mz; internet www.fimdesemana.co.mz; f. 1997; independent.

Savana: c/o Mediacoop, Avda Amílcar Cabral 1049, CP 73, Maputo; tel. (1) 301737; fax (1) 302402; e-mail savana@mediacoop.co.mz; internet www.mediacoop.odline.com; f. 1994; Dir KOK NAM; Editor FERNANDO GONÇALVES; circ. 15,000.

Tempo: Avda Ahmed Sekou Touré 1078, CP 2917, Maputo; tel. (1) 26191; f. 1970; magazine; under state management since 1991; Dir ROBERTO UAENE; Editor ARLINDO LANGA; circ. 40,000.

Zambeze: Rua José Sidumo, Maputo; tel. (1) 302019; Dir SALOMÃO MOYANE.

PERIODICALS

Agora: Maputo; tel. (1) 494147; fax (1) 494204; e-mail agora@agora.co.mz; internet www.agora.co.mz; f. 2000; monthly; economics, politics, society; Pres. MARIA DE LOURDES TORCATO; Dir JOVITO NUNES; circ. 5,000.

Agricultura: Instituto Nacional de Investigação Agronómica, CP 3658, Maputo; tel. (1) 30091; f. 1982; quarterly; publ. by Centro de Documentação de Agricultura, Silvicultura, Pecuária e Pescas.

Aro: Avda 24 de Julho 1420, CP 4187, Maputo; f. 1995; monthly; Dir POLICARTO TAMELE; Editor BRUNO MACAME, Jr.

Arquivo Histórico: CP 2033, Maputo; tel. (1) 421177; fax (1) 423428; f. 1987; Editor MARIA INÊS NOGUEIRA DA COSTA.

Boletim da República: Avda Vladimir I. Lénine, CP 275, Maputo; govt and official notices; publ. by Imprensa Nacional da Moçambique.

Maderazinco: Maputo; e-mail maderazinco@yahoo.com; internet www.maderazinco.tropical.co.mz; f. 2002; quarterly; literature.

Moçambique–Novos Tempos: Avda Ahmed Sekou Touré 657, Maputo; tel. (1) 493564; fax (1) 493590; f. 1992; Dir J. MASCARENHAS.

Mozambiquefile: c/o AIM, Rua da Radio Moçambique, CP 896, Maputo; tel. (1) 313225; fax (1) 313196; e-mail aim@tucabo.co.mz; internet www.sortmoz.com/aimnews; monthly; Dir GUSTAVO MAVIZ; Editor PAUL FAUVET.

Mozambique Inview: c/o Mediacoop, Avda Amílcar Cabral 1049, CP 73, Maputo; tel. (1) 430106; fax (1) 302402; e-mail inview@mediacoop.co.mz; internet www.mediacoop.odline.com; f. 1994; 2 a month; economic bulletin in English; Editor WILBERT ZIVISAI.

Portos e Caminhos de Ferro: CP 276, Maputo; English and Portuguese; ports and railways; quarterly.

Revista Médica de Moçambique: Instituto Nacional de Saúde, Ministério da Saúde e Faculdade de Medicina, Universidade Eduardo Mondlane, CP 264, Maputo; tel. (1) 420368; fax (1) 431103; e-mail mdgedge@malarins.uem.mz; f. 1982; 4 a year; medical journal; Editor MARTINHO DGEDGE.

NEWS AGENCIES

Agência de Informação de Moçambique (AIM): Rua da Rádio Moçambique, CP 896, Maputo; tel. (1) 313225; fax (1) 313196; e-mail aim@tucabo.co.mz; internet www.sortmoz.com/aimnews; f. 1975; daily reports in Portuguese and English; Dir GUSTAVO LISSETIANE MAVIE.

Foreign Bureaux

Agence France-Presse (AFP): CP 4650, Maputo; tel. (1) 422940; fax (1) 422940; Correspondent RACHEL WATERHOUSE.

Agência Lusa de Informação (Portugal): Avda Ho Chi Minh 111, Maputo; tel. (1) 427591; fax (1) 421690; e-mail lsa@lusa.pt; Bureau Chief LUÍS ANDRAD DE SÁ.

Agenzia Nazionale Stampa Associata (ANSA) (Italy): Maputo; tel. (1) 430723; fax (1) 421906; Correspondent PAUL FAUVET.

Xinhua (New China) News Agency (China): Rua Coimbra 258, Maputo; tel. (1) 414445.

Reuters (UK) is also represented in Mozambique.

Publishers

Arquivo Histórico de Moçambique: Avda Filipe Samuel Magaia 715, CP 2033, Maputo; tel. (1) 421177; fax (1) 423428; e-mail jneves@zebra.uem.mz; internet www.ahm.uem.mz; Dir JOEL DAS NEVES TEMBE.

Central Impressora: c/o Ministério da Saúde, Avdas Eduardo Mondlane e Salvador Allende 1008, CP 264, Maputo; owned by the Ministry of Health.

Centro de Estudos Africanos: Universidade Eduardo Mondlane, CP 1993, Maputo; tel. (1) 490828; fax (1) 491896; f. 1976; social and political science, regional history, economics; Dir Col SERGIO VIEIRA.

Editora Minerva Central: Rua Consiglieri Pedroso 84, CP 212, Maputo; tel. (1) 22092; f. 1908; stationers and printers, educational, technical and medical textbooks; Man. Dir J. F. CARVALHO.

Editorial Ndjira, Lda: Avda Ho Chi Minh 85, Maputo; tel. (1) 300180; fax (1) 308745.

Empresa Moderna Lda: Avda 25 de Setembro, CP 473, Maputo; tel. (1) 424594; f. 1937; fiction, history, textbooks; Man. Dir LOUIS GALLOTI.

Fundo Bibliográfico de Língua Portuguesa: Avda 25 Setembro 1230, 7° andar, Maputo; tel. (1) 429531; fax (1) 429530.

Instituto Nacional do Livro e do Disco: Avda 24 de Julho 1921, CP 4030, Maputo; tel. (1) 34870; govt publishing and purchasing agency; Dir ARMÉNIO CORREIA.

Moçambique Editora: Rua Armando Tivane 1430, Bairro de Polana, Maputo; tel. (1) 495017; fax (1) 499071; e-mail info@me.co.mz; internet www.me.co.mz; f. 1996; educational textbooks, dictionaries.

Plural Editores: Avda 24 de Julho 414, Maputo; tel. (1) 486828; fax (1) 486829; e-mail plural@pluraleditores.co.mz; internet www.pluraleditores.co.mz; f. 2003; educational textbooks; part of the Porto Editora Group.

Government Publishing House

Imprensa Nacional de Moçambique: Rua da Imprensa, CP 275, Maputo; tel. (1) 423383.

Broadcasting and Communications

TELECOMMUNICATIONS

Telecomunicações de Moçambique (TDM): Rua da Sé 2, CP 25, Maputo; tel. (1) 431921; fax (1) 431944; e-mail rfernandes@tdm.mz; internet www.tdm.mz; f. 1993; Chair. and Man. Dir JOAQUIM RIBEIRA PEREIRA DE CARVALHO.

Telecomunicações Moveis de Moçambique (TMM): Edif. Mcel, Esquina Avda 25 de Setembro e Rua Belmiro Obede Muianga, CP 1463, Maputo; tel. (1) 307870; internet www.mcel.co.mz; f. 1997; subsidiary of TDM; mobile cellular telephone provider, operating Moçambique Celular (mCel).

Vodacom Moçambique: Rua Fereira Maia 74, Maputo; tel. (1) 409272; f. 2002; owned by Vodacom (South Africa); mobile cellular telephone services to commenced operations in Dec. 2003; Chair. HERMENGILDO GAMITO; Man. Dir CLIVE TARR.

Regulatory Authority

Instituto Nacional das Comunicações de Moçambique (INCM): Avda Eduardo Mondlane 123–127, CP 1937, Maputo; tel. (1) 490131; fax (1) 492728; internet www.incm.gov.mz.

BROADCASTING

Radio

Rádio Encontro: Avda Francisco Manyanga, CP 366, Nampula; tel. (6) 215588.

Rádio Feba Moçambique: Avda Julius Nyerere 441, Maputo; tel. (1) 440002.

Rádio Maria: Rua Igreja 156A, Machava, Maputo; tel. (1) 750505; fax (1) 752124; e-mail ramamo@virconn.com; f. 1995; evangelical radio broadcasts; Dir Fr JOO CARLOS H. NUNES.

Rádio Miramar: Avda Zimbabwe 1726, Maputo; tel. (1) 491772; owned by Brazilian religious sect, the Universal Church of the Kingdom of God.

Rádio Moçambique: Rua da Rádio 2, CP 2000, Maputo; tel. (1) 321814; fax (1) 321816; e-mail isepca_mz@yahoo.com.br; internet www.teledata.mz/radiomocambique; f. 1975; programmes in Portuguese, English and vernacular languages; Chair. MANUEL FERNANDO VETERANO.

Rádio Terra Verde: fmrly Voz da Renamo; owned by former rebel movement Renamo; transmitters in Maputo and Gorongosa, Sofala province.

Rádio Trans Mundial Moçambique: Avda Eduardo Mondlane 2998, Maputo; tel. (1) 407358; fax (1) 407357.

Television

Rádio Televisão Klint (RTK): Avda Agostinho Neto 946, Maputo; tel. (1) 422956; fax (1) 493306; Dir CARLOS KLINT.

Televisão Miramar: owned by Brazilian religious sect, the Universal Church of the Kingdom of God.

Televisão de Moçambique (TVM): Avda 25 de Setembro 154, CP 2675, Maputo; tel. (1) 308117; fax (1) 308122; internet www.tvm.co .mz; f. 1981; Pres. ANTÓNIO JÚLIO BOTELHO MONIZ; Dir ANABELA ANDRIANO POULOS.

TV Cabo Moçambique: Avda dos Presidentes 68, CP 1750, Maputo; tel. (1) 480500; fax (1) 499015; e-mail tvcabo@tvcabo.co.mz; internet www.tvcabo.co.mz; cable television and internet services in Maputo.

Finance

(cap. = capital; res = reserves; dep. = deposits; m. = million; brs = branches; amounts in meticais, unless otherwise stated)

BANKING

Central Bank

Banco de Moçambique: Avda 25 de Setembro 1679, CP 423, Maputo; tel. (1) 428150; fax (1) 421912; e-mail cdi@bancomoc.uem .mz; internet www.bancomoc.mz; f. 1975; bank of issue; cap. 248,952m., res 382,168m., dep. 7,443,656m. (Dec. 2001); Gov. ADRIANO AFONSO MALEIANE; 4 brs.

Commercial Banks

Banco Austral: Avda 25 de Setembro 1184, CP 757, Maputo; tel. (1) 428125; fax (1) 330549; e-mail jane.grob@teledata.mz; f. 1977; fmrly Banco Popular de Desenvolvimento (BPD); 60% transferred to private ownership in 1997; renationalized in 2001; 80% of ownership transferred to the Amalgamated Banks of South Africa in Jan. 2002; total assets 3,230,850m. (Dec. 2001); CEO K. MUGANTHAN; 52 brs and agencies.

Banco Comercial e de Investimentos (BCI): Edif. John Orr's, Avda 25 de Setembro 1465, CP 4745, Maputo; tel. (1) 307777; fax (1) 307152; e-mail bcimoz@teledata.mz; internet www.bci.co.mz; f. 1996; 60% owned by Caixa Geral de Depósitos (Portugal); dep.US $290.2m. (Dec. 2003); Chair. ABDUL MAGID OSMAN; 32 brs.

Banco de Desenvolvimento e de Comércio de Moçambique, SARL: Apto 420–425, Avda 25 de Setembro 1230, 4° andar, Maputo; tel. (1) 313040; fax (1) 313047; f. 2000; 42% owned by Montepie Geral (Portugal).

Banco de Fomento, SARL: Avda Julius Nyerere 1016, CP 4233, Maputo; tel. (1) 494010; fax (1) 494401; e-mail bfe.moc@teledata.mz; fmrly Banco de Fomento e Exterior SA, name changed as above 1998; cap. 100,000m., res 49,642m., dep. 1,074,209m. (Dec. 2000); Pres. ARTUR SANTOS SILVA; Man. Dir JOÃO SILVA BENTO.

Banco Internacional de Comércio, SARL: Edif. INSS, Avda 24 de Julho 3549, 2° andar, Maputo; tel. (1) 404080; fax (1) 400745; e-mail icbm@isl.co.mz; f. 1998; total assets US $5.9m. (Dec. 2002); Chair. JOSEPHINE SIVARETNAM; CEO LEE SANG HUAT.

Banco Internacional de Moçambique, SARL (BIM): Avda 25 de Setembro 1800, CP 865, Maputo; tel. (1) 307481; fax (1) 307546; e-mail ecassola@bim.co.mz; internet www.mundobim.co.mz; f. 1995; merged with Banco Comercial de Moçambique in 2001; 50.4% owned by Banco Comercial Português, 23.1% by the state, 16.1% by International Finance Corpn; cap. 500,000m., dep. 12,359,990m. (Dec. 2001); Chair. Dr MÁRIO FERNANDES DA GRAÇA MACHUNGO; 88 brs.

Banco Internacional de Moçambique—Investimento: Avda Kim Il Sung 961, Maputo; tel. (1) 490085; fax (1) 490212; e-mail biminvestimento@bim.co.mz; f. 1998; 50% owned by Banco Internacional de Moçambique, 25% by BCP Investimento and 15% by International Finance Corpn; total assets 102,754m. (Dec. 2000); Chair. Dr MÁRIO FERNANDES DA GRAÇA MACHUNGO; Man. Dir Dr NUNO SALGADO SANTOS.

Banco Standard Totta de Moçambique, SARL: Praça 25 de Junho 1, CP 2086, Maputo; tel. (1) 423041; fax (1) 426967; e-mail admin1@bstm.co.mz; internet www.bstm.co.mz; f. 1966; 60% owned by Banco Totta e Açores, SA; total assets 4,961,388m. (Dec. 2001); Man. Dir JOÃO FILIPE DE LIMA MAYER; 24 brs.

Cooperativa de Poupança e Crédito, SARL: Avda 25 de Setembro 1679, 3° andar, Maputo; tel. (1) 307754; fax (1) 307753; e-mail cpc-sc@teledata.mz.

Novo Banco, SARL: Avda do Trabalho 750, Maputo; tel. and fax (1) 407705; e-mail novobanco@teledata.mz; f. 2000.

Foreign Banks

African Banking Corporation (Moçambique), SARL: Avda 25 de Setembro 1230, 1° andar, CP 1445, Maputo; tel. (1) 306700; fax (1) 306305; e-mail africanbankingcorp@africanbankingcorp.co.mz; internet www.nedbank.com; f. 1999; 100% owned by African Banking Corpn Holdings Ltd (Botswana); fmrly BNP Nedbank (Moçambique), SARL; changed name as above after acquisition in 2002; Chair. BENJAMIN ALFREDO; Man. Dir ZANDILE CHIRESHE.

African Banking Corporation Leasing, SARL: Rua da Imprensa 256, 7° andar, CP 4447, Maputo; tel. (1) 300451; fax (1) 431290; e-mail ulcmoz@mail.tropical.co.mz; 66% owned by African Banking Corpn Holdings Ltd (Botswana); fmrly ULC (Moçambque); changed name as above in 2002; total assets US $1.8m. (Dec. 1998); Chair. ANTÓNIO BRANCO; Gen. Man. VICTOR VISEU.

União Comercial de Bancos (Moçambique), SARL: Avda Friedrich Engels 400, Maputo; tel. (1) 481900; fax (1) 498675; e-mail ucb@tucabo.co.mz; f. 1999; 62.5% owned by Mauritius Commercial Bank Group; total assets US $37.5m. (Dec. 2003); Chair. PHILIPPE ALAIN FORGET; Gen. Man. ROBERT CANTIN.

DEVELOPMENT FUND

Fundo de Desenvolvimento Agrícola e Rural: CP 1406, Maputo; tel. (1) 460349; fax (1) 460157; f. 1987 to provide credit for small farmers and rural co-operatives; promotes agricultural and rural development; Sec. EDUARDO OLIVEIRA.

STOCK EXCHANGE

Bolsa de Valores de Moçambique: Avda 25 de Setembro 1230, Prédio 33, 5° andar, Maputo; tel. (1) 308826; fax (1) 310559; e-mail jussub@bvm.com; Chair. Dr JUSSUB NURMAMAD.

INSURANCE

In December 1991 the Assembléia da República approved legislation terminating the state monopoly of insurance and reinsurance activities.

Companhia de Seguros de Moçambique, IMPAR: Avda 25 de Setembro 1800–17, CP 616, Maputo; tel. (1) 429696; fax (1) 430020; e-mail impar@zebra.uem.mz; f. 1992; Pres. INOCÊNCIO A. MATAVEL; Gen. Man. MANUEL BALANCHO.

Empresa Moçambicana de Seguros, EE (EMOSE): Avda 25 de Setembro 1383, CP 1165, Maputo; tel. (1) 422095; fax (1) 424526; f. 1977 as state insurance monopoly; took over business of 24 fmr cos; privatization pending; cap. 150m.; Gen. Dir VENÂNCIO MONDLANE.

Seguradora Internacional de Moçambique: Maputo; tel. (1) 430959; fax (1) 430241; e-mail simseg@zebra.uem.mz; Pres. MÁRIO FERNANDES DA GRAÇA MACHUNGO.

Trade and Industry

GOVERNMENT AGENCIES

Centro de Promoção de Investimentos (CPI): Rua da Imprensa 332, CP 4635, Maputo; tel. (1) 313295; fax (1) 313325; e-mail cpi@cpi .co.mz; internet www.mozbusiness.gov.mz; encourages foreign investment and jt ventures with foreign firms; evaluates and negotiates investment proposals.

Instituto para a Promoção de Exportações (IPEX): Avda 25 de Setembro 1008, 3° andar, CP 4487, Maputo; tel. (1) 307257; fax (1) 307256; e-mail ipex@teledata.mz; internet www.ipex.gov.mz; f. 1990 for the promotion and co-ordination of national exports abroad; Pres. Dr FELISBERTO FERRÃO.

Unidade Técnica para a Reestruturação de Empresas (UTRE): Rua da Imprensa 256, 7° andar, CP 4350, Maputo; tel. (1) 426514; tel. (1) 421541; e-mail utre@teledata.mz; internet www .tropical.co.mz/~parafric; implements restructuring of state enterprises; Dir MOMADE JUMAS.

CHAMBERS OF COMMERCE

Câmara de Comércio de Moçambique: Rua Mateus Sansão Muthemba 452, CP 1836, Maputo; tel. (1) 491970; fax (1) 492211; f. 1980; Pres. JACINTO VELOSO; Sec.-Gen. MANUEL NOTIÇO.

Mozambique-USA Chamber of Commerce: Rua Mateus Sansão Mutemba 425, Maputo; tel. (1) 492904; fax (1) 492739; e-mail mail@ mail.ccmusa.co.mz; internet www.ccmusa.co.mz.

STATE INDUSTRIAL ENTERPRISES

Empresa Nacional de Carvão de Moçambique (CARBOMOC): Rua Joaquim Lapa 108, CP 1773, Maputo; tel. (1) 427625; fax (1) 424714; f. 1948; mineral extraction and export; transfer to private ownership pending; Dir JAIME RIBEIRO.

Empresa Nacional de Hidrocarbonetos de Moçambique (ENH): Avda Fernão de Magalhães 34, CP 4787, Maputo; tel. (1)

429456; fax (1) 424015; controls concessions for petroleum exploration and production; Dir MÁRIO MARQUES.

Empresa Nacional de Petróleos de Moçambique (PET-ROMOC): Praça dos Trabalhadores 9, CP 417, Maputo; tel. (1) 427191; fax (1) 430181; f. 1977 to take over the Sonarep oil refinery and its associated distribution co; state directorate for liquid fuels within Mozambique, incl. petroleum products passing through Mozambique to inland countries; Dir MANUEL PATRÍCIO DA CRUZ VIOLA.

UTILITIES

Electricity

Electricidade de Moçambique (EDM): Avda Agostinho Neto 70, CP 2447, Maputo; tel. (1) 490636; fax (1) 491048; internet www .mozambique.mz/electricity/index.htm; f. 1977; 100% state-owned; production and distribution of electric energy; Pres. VICENTE VELOSA; Dir FERNANDO RAMOS JULIÃO; 2,700 employees.

Water

Direcção Nacional de Águas: Avda 25 de Setembro 942, 9° andar, CP 1611, Maputo; tel. (1) 420469; fax (1) 421403; e-mail watco@ zebra.uem.mz; internet www.dna.mz; Dir AMÉRICO MUIANGA.

TRADE UNIONS

Freedom to form trade unions, and the right to strike, are guaranteed under the 1990 Constitution.

Confederação de Sindicatos Livres e Independentes de Moçambique (CONSILMO): Sec.-Gen. JEREMIAS TIMANE.

Organização dos Trabalhadores de Moçambique—Central Sindical (OTM—CS) (Mozambique Workers' Organization—Trade Union Headquarters): Rua Manuel António de Sousa 36, Maputo; tel. (1) 426786; fax (1) 421671; e-mail otmcs@teledata.mz; f. 1983 as trade union fed. to replace fmr production councils; officially recognized in 1990; 200,000 mems (1993); Pres. AMOS JUNIOR MATSIUHE; Sec-Gen. JOAQUIM FANHEIRO.

Sindicato Nacional dos Trabalhadores Agro-Pecuários e Florestais (SINTAF): Avda 25 de Setembro 1676, 1° andar, Maputo; tel. (1) 312119; Sec.-Gen. EUSÉBIO LUÍS CHIVULELE.

Sindicato Nacional dos Trabalhadores da Aviação Civil, Correios e Comunicações (SINTAC): Rua de Silves 24, Maputo; tel. (1) 415926; Sec.-Gen. MANUEL SANTOS DOS REIS.

Sindicato Nacional dos Trabalhadores do Comércio, Banca e Seguros (SINTCOBASE): Avda Ho Chi Minh 365, 1° andar, CP 2142, Maputo; tel. (1) 426271; Sec.-Gen. AMÓS JÚNIOR MATSINHE.

Sindicato Nacional dos Trabalhadores da Indústria do Açúcar (SINTIA): Avda das FPLM 1912, Maputo; tel. (1) 460108; f. 1989; Sec.-Gen. ALEXANDRE CÂNDIDO MUNGUAMBE.

Sindicato Nacional dos Trabalhadores da Indústria Alimentar e Bebidas (SINTIAB): Avda Eduardo Mondlane 1267, CP 394, Maputo; tel. and fax (1) 324709; f. 1986; Gen. Sec. SAMUEL FENIAS MATSINHE.

Sindicato Nacional dos Trabalhadores da Indústria de Cajú (SINTIC): Rua do Jardim 574, 1° andar, Maputo; tel. (1) 475300; Sec.-Gen. BOAVENTURA MONDLANE.

Sindicato Nacional dos Trabalhadores da Indústria de Construção Civil, Madeira e Minas (SINTICIM): Rua Joaquim Lapa 22, 4° andar, Maputo; tel. (1) 321159; Sec.-Gen. JEREMIAS TIMANA.

Sindicato Nacional dos Trabalhadores da Indústria Hoteleira, Turismo e Similares (SINTHOTS): Avda Eduardo Mondlane 1267, CP 394, Maputo; tel. (1) 420409; Sec.-Gen. ALBERTO MANUEL NHAPOSSE.

Sindicato Nacional dos Trabalhadores da Indústria Metalúrgica, Metalomecânica e Energia (SINTIME): Avda Olof Palme 245, 1° andar, Maputo; tel. (1) 428588; fax (1) 310508; Sec.-Gen. RUI BENJAMIM COSTA.

Sindicato Nacional dos Trabalhadores da Indústria Química, Borracha, Papel e Gráfica (SINTIQUIGRA): Avda Karl Marx 414, 1° andar, CP 4433, Maputo; tel. (1) 421553; Sec.-Gen. JOAQUIM M. FANHEIRO.

Sindicato Nacional dos Trabalhadores da Indústria Têxtil Vestuário, Couro e Calçado (SINTEVEC): Avda do Trabalho 1276, 1° andar, CP 2613, Maputo; tel. (1) 426753; fax (1) 421671; Sec.-Gen. PEDRO JOAQUIM MANDJAZE.

Sindicato Nacional dos Trabalhadores da Marinha Mercante e Pesca (SINTMAP): Rua Joaquim Lapa 22, 5° andar, No 6, Maputo; tel. (1) 305593; Sec.-Gen. DANIEL MANUEL NGOQUE.

Sindicato Nacional dos Trabalhadores dos Portos e Caminhos de Ferro (SINPOCAF): Avda Guerra Popular, CP

2158, Maputo; tel. (1) 420531; Sec.-Gen. DINIS EFRAIME FRANCISCO NHANGUMBE.

Sindicato Nacional dos Trabalhadores dos Transportes Rodoviários e Assistência Técnica (SINTRAT): Avda Paulo Samuel Kankhomba 1568, 1° andar, 14, Maputo; tel. (1) 402390; Sec.-Gen. ALCANO HORÁCIO MULA.

Sindicato Nacional de Jornalistas (SNJ): Rua Gen. Pereira d'Eça 12, 1° andar, Maputo; tel. (1) 4998577; fax (1) 492031; f. 1978; Sec.-Gen. HILÁRIO M. E. MATUSSE.

Transport

The 'Beira Corridor', where rail and road links and a petroleum pipeline run from Manica, on the Zimbabwean border, to the Mozambican port of Beira, forms a vital outlet for the land-locked southern African countries, particularly Zimbabwe. Rail and road links also run from Ressano Garcia in South Africa to the port at Maputo, and from Malawi to the port of Nacala. Following the Acordo Geral de Paz (General Peace Agreement) in 1992, rehabilitation of the transport network began. In September 2000 the Nacala Corridor was officially launched; controlled by the Nacala Corridor Development Company, some US $900m. were expected to be invested in rehabilitating the transport and communications infrastructure, notably Nacala port and the railway line linking Mozambique and Malawi. Negotiations concerning the granting of similar concessions for the Maputo and Beira transport corridors, as well as for other principal railway lines, were proceeding with private contractors in 2000. In February 2000 much of the country's infrastructure in the southern and central provinces was devastated as the result of massive flooding. Railway lines, roads and bridges suffered considerable damage.

RAILWAYS

In 1999 the total length of track was 3,114 km. The railways are all state-owned. There are both internal routes and rail links between Mozambican ports and South Africa, Swaziland, Zimbabwe and Malawi. During the hostilities many lines and services were disrupted. Improvement work on most of the principal railway lines began in the early 1980s. In 1999 the World Bank approved a loan of US $100m. to help finance the reconstruction of the line linking the port of Beira with the coal-mining centre of Moatize; the total cost was estimated at some $300m. In 2000 it was announced that funding worth some $55m. was to be made available for the rehabilitation of the Limpopo railway line, which had been damaged by the floods earlier that year. The cost of repairing the damage to the railways caused by the floods was estimated at $7.3m.

Empresa Portos e Caminhos de Ferro de Moçambique (CFM-EP): Praça dos Trabalhadores, CP 2158, Maputo; tel. (1) 427173; fax (1) 427746; e-mail cfmnet@cfmnet.co.mz; internet www.cfmnet.co .mz; fmrly Empresa Nacional dos Portos e Caminhos de Ferro de Moçambique; privatized and restructured in 2002; Chair. RUI FONSECA; comprises four separate systems linking Mozambican ports with the country's hinterland, and with other southern African countries, including South Africa, Swaziland, Zimbabwe and Malawi:

CFM—Sul: Praça dos Trabalhadores, CP 2158, Maputo; tel. (1) 427173; fax (1) 427746; lines totalling 1,070 km linking Maputo with South Africa, Swaziland and Zimbabwe, as well as Inhambane–Inharrime and Xai–Xai systems; Exec. Dir CARLOS BAMBA NANGHOU; Dir of Railways FERNANDO MAÚSSE.

CFM—Norte: CP 16, Nampula; tel. (6) 212927; fax (6) 214320; lines totalling 872 km, including link between port of Nacala with Malawi; management concession awarded to Nacala Corridor Development Company (a consortium 67% owned by South African, Portuguese and US companies) in January 2000; Dir FILIPE NHUSSI; Dir of Railways MANUEL MANICA.

CFM—Zambézia: CP 73, Quelimane; tel. (4) 212502; fax (4) 213123; 145-km line linking Quelimane and Mocuba; Dir ORLANDO J. JAIME.

CFM—Centro: CP 472, Beira; tel. (3) 326997; fax (3) 325200; lines totalling 994 km linking Beira with Zimbabwe and Malawi, as well as link to Moatize (undergoing rehabilitation); Exec. Dir JOAQUIM VERÍSSIMO; Dir of Railways LUCAS MACHAVA.

ROADS

In 1999 there were an estimated 30,400 km of roads in Mozambique, of which 5,685 km were paved. In 1994 the Government announced a five-year road rehabilitation programme to reopen 11,000 km of roads closed during the hostilities, and to upgrade 3,000 km of paved roads and 13,000 km of secondary and tertiary roads. The programme, which was to cost an estimated US $24,000m., was to be financed mainly by international donors and the World Bank. In

1998 the Government announced a further programme, again financed by international donors, to be implemented from 1999. The programme aimed to increase the percentage of roads in 'good' or 'reasonable' condition from 39% to 70%. However, owing to the widespread destruction caused by the February 2000 flooding, much of this reconstruction work would have to be repeated.

Administraçao Nacional de Estradas (ANE): Avda de Moçambique 1225, CP 1294, Maputo; tel. (1) 475157; fax (1) 475290; e-mail pce.ane@teledata.mz; internet www.dnep.gov.mz; f. 1999 to replace the Direcção Nacional de Estradas e Pontes; implements government road policy through the Direcção de Estradas Nacionais (DEN) and the Direcção de Estradas Regionais (DER); Pres. Eng. CARLOS FRAGOSO; Dir (DEN) Eng. TIAGO MASSINGUE.

SHIPPING

The principal ports are Maputo, Beira, Nacala and Quelimane, handling an estimated 6.1m. metric tons of cargo in 1999. In mid-1999 plans were announced for the construction of a new deep-water port at Ponta Dobela, 70 km south of Maputo. The port, which was to form part of a special economic zone, was to receive a minimum investment of US $515m., and was expected eventually to handle 30m. tons of goods, principally minerals, per year. In January 2000 management of the port facilities at Nacala was awarded to a private consortium, the Nacala Corridor Development Company. In mid-2000 it was announced that the port of Maputo was to be managed by a British-led consortium, over a period of 15 years; their concession commenced in 2003. In early 2003 it was announced that the construction of the port at Ponta Dobela would begin within 18 months.

Empresa Portos e Caminhos de Ferro de Moçambique (CFM-EP): Praça dos Trabalhadores, CP 2158, Maputo; tel. (1) 427173; fax (1) 427746; e-mail cfmnet@cfmnet.co.mz; internet www.cfmnet.co.mz; fmrly Empresa Nacional dos Portos e Caminhos de Ferro de Moçambique; privatized and restructured in 2002; Port Dir CFM-Sul BOAVENTURA CHAMBAL; Port Dir CFM-Norte AGOSTINHO LANGA (Jr); Port Dir CFM-Centro CHINGUANE MABOTE.

Agência Nacional de Frete e Navegação (ANFRENA): Rua Consiglieri Pedroso 396, CP 492, Maputo; tel. (1) 427064; fax (1) 427822; Dir FERDINAND WILSON.

Empresa Moçambicana de Cargas, SARL (MOCARGO): Rua Consiglieri Pedroso 430, 1°–4° andares, CP 888, Maputo; tel. (1) 421440; fax (1) 302067; e-mail mocargo1@teledata.mz; internet www.mocargo.co.mz; f. 1982; shipping, chartering and road transport; Man. Dir MANUEL DE SOUSA AMARAL.

Manica Freight Services, SARL: Praça dos Trabalhadores 51, CP 557, Maputo; tel. (1) 426024; fax (1) 424595; e-mail achothia@manica.co.mz; international shipping agents; Man. Dir A. Y. CHOTHIA.

Maputo Port Development Company, SARL (MPDC): Avda 25 de Setembro 420, Edifício JAT, 5° andar, CP 2841, Maputo; tel. (1) 313920; fax (1) 313921; e-mail info@portmaputo.com; internet www.portmaputo.com; f. 2002; private-sector international consortium with concession (awarded 2003) to develop and run port of Maputo until 2018; CEO ALEC DON.

Mozline, SARL: Avda Karl Marx 478, 2° andar, Maputo; tel. (1) 303078; fax (1) 303073; e-mail mozline1@virconn.com; shipping and road freight services.

Navique, SARL: Avda Mártires de Inhaminga 4, CP 145, Maputo; tel. (1) 312706; fax (1) 426310; e-mail navique_adm@mail.garp.co.mz; Chair. J. A. CARVALHO; Man. Dir PEDRO VIRTUOSO.

CIVIL AVIATION

There are 16 airports, of which three are international airports.

Linhas Aéreas de Moçambique, SARL (LAM): Aeroporto Internacional de Maputo, CP 2060, Maputo; tel. (1) 465137; fax (1) 422936; e-mail flamingoclub@lam.co.mz; internet www.lam.co.mz; f. 1980; 80% state-owned; operates domestic services and international services to South Africa, Tanzania, Mayotte, Zimbabwe and Portugal; Chair. and Dir-Gen. JOSÉ RICARDO ZUZARTE VIEGAS.

Sociedade de Transportes Aéreos/Sociedade de Transporte e Trabalho Aéreo, SARL (STA/TTA): CP 665, Maputo; tel. (1) 742366; fax (1) 491763; e-mail dido@mail.tropical.co.mz; internet www.sta.co.mz; f. 1991; domestic airline and aircraft charter transport services; acquired Empresa Nacional de Transporte e Trabalho Aéreo in 1997; Chair. ROGÉRIO WALTER CARREIRA; Man. Dir JOSÉ CARVALHEIRA.

Tourism

Tourism, formerly a significant source of foreign exchange, ceased completely following independence, and was resumed on a limited scale in 1980. There were 1,000 visitors in 1981 (compared with 292,000 in 1972 and 69,000 in 1974). With the successful conduct of multi-party elections in 1994 and the prospect of continued peace, there was considerable scope for development of this sector. By mid-1998 some 138 tourism projects, involving investment totalling US $900m., had been approved. By the late 1990s tourism was the fastest growing sector of the Mozambique economy, and in 2000 it was announced that a comprehensive tourism development plan was to be devised, assisted by funding from the European Union. In 2002 there were 45 hotels in Mozambique, offering some 4,129 hotel beds, which represented an increase of 39% on 2000. The opening of the Great Limpopo Transfrontier Park in April 2002, with South Africa and Zimbabwe, was expected to attract additional tourists. Foreign tourist arrivals in 2001 were 483,700.

Fundo Nacional do Turismo: Avda 25 de Setembro 1203, CP 2758, Maputo; tel. (1) 307320; fax (1) 307324; e-mail futur@futur.org.mz; f. 1993; hotels and tourism; CEO ZACARIAS SUMBANA.

Sociedade do Desenvolvimento do Turismo do Indico (INTUR): Maputo; f. 2001; promotion of tourism in the northern Nacala Development Corridor.

MYANMAR

Introductory Survey

Location, Climate, Language, Religion, Flag, Capital

The Union of Myanmar (Myanma Naing-ngan—formerly Burma) lies in the north-west region of South-East Asia, between the Tibetan plateau and the Malay peninsula. The country is bordered by Bangladesh and India to the north-west, by the People's Republic of China and Laos to the north-east and by Thailand to the south-east. The climate is tropical, with an average temperature of 27°C (80°F) and monsoon rains from May to October. Average annual rainfall is between 2,500 mm and 5,000 mm in the coastal and mountainous regions of the north and east, but reaches a maximum of only 1,000 mm in the lowlands of the interior. Temperatures in Yangon (Rangoon) are generally between 18°C (65°F) and 36°C (97°F). The official language is Myanmar (Burmese), and there are also a number of tribal languages. About 87% of the population are Buddhists. There are animist, Muslim, Hindu and Christian minorities. The national flag (proportions 5 by 9) is red, with a blue canton, in the upper hoist, bearing two ears of rice within a cog-wheel and a ring of 14 five-pointed stars (one for each state), all in white. The capital is Yangon.

Recent History

Burma (now Myanmar) was annexed to British India during the 19th century, and became a separate British dependency, with a limited measure of self-government, in 1937. Japanese forces invaded and occupied the country in 1942, and Japan granted nominal independence under a Government of anti-British nationalists. The Burmese nationalists later turned against Japan and aided Allied forces to reoccupy the country in 1945. They formed a resistance movement, the Anti-Fascist People's Freedom League (AFPFL), led by Gen. Aung San, which became the main political force after the defeat of Japan. Aung San was assassinated in July 1947 and was succeeded by U Nu. On 4 January 1948 the Union of Burma became independent, outside the Commonwealth, with U Nu as the first Prime Minister.

During the first decade of independence Burma was a parliamentary democracy, and the Government successfully resisted revolts by communists and other insurgent groups. In 1958 the ruling AFPFL split into two wings, the 'Clean' AFPFL and the 'Stable' AFPFL, and U Nu invited the Army Chief of Staff, Gen. Ne Win, to head a caretaker Government. Elections to the Chamber of Deputies in February 1960 gave an overwhelming majority to U Nu, leading the 'Clean' AFPFL (which was renamed the Union Party in March), and he resumed office in April. Despite its popularity, however, the U Nu administration proved ineffective, and in March 1962 Gen. Ne Win intervened again, staging a coup to depose U Nu (who was subsequently detained until 1966). The new Revolutionary Council suspended the Constitution and instituted authoritarian control through the government-sponsored Burma Socialist Programme Party (BSPP). All other political parties were outlawed in March 1964.

During the next decade a more centralized system of government was created, in an attempt to win popular support and to nationalize important sectors of the economy. A new Constitution, aiming to transform Burma into a democratic socialist state, was approved in a national referendum in December 1973. The Constitution of the renamed Socialist Republic of the Union of Burma, which came into force in January 1974, confirmed the BSPP as the sole authorized political party, and provided for the establishment of new organs of state. Elections to a legislative People's Assembly took place in January 1974, and in March the Revolutionary Council was dissolved. U Ne Win (who, together with other senior army officers, had become a civilian in 1972) was elected President by the newly created State Council. Burma's economic problems increased, however, and in 1974 there were riots over food shortages and social injustices. Student demonstrations took place in 1976, as social problems increased. Following an attempted coup by members of the armed forces in July, the BSPP reviewed its economic policies, and in 1977 a new economic programme was adopted in an attempt to quell unrest.

An election in January 1978 gave U Ne Win a mandate to rule for a further four years, and in March he was re-elected Chairman of the State Council. In May 1980 a general amnesty was declared for political dissidents, including exiles (as a result of which U Nu, who had been living abroad since 1969, returned to Burma in July). Gen. San Yu, formerly the Army Chief of Staff, was elected Chairman of the State Council in November 1981; U Ne Win, however, remained Chairman of the BSPP. At the fifth Congress of the BSPP, in August 1985, U Ne Win was re-elected for a further four-year term as Chairman. Elections for a new People's Assembly were held in November.

In August 1987, owing to the country's increasing economic problems, an unprecedented extraordinary meeting, comprising the BSPP Central Committee, the organs of the State Council and other state bodies, was convened. U Ne Win proposed a review of the policies of the past 25 years, and acknowledged the need to correct any shortcomings. In September the announcement of the withdrawal from circulation of high-denomination banknotes, coupled with rice shortages following a poor harvest, provoked student riots (the first civil disturbances since 1976). Owing to continued economic deprivation, further student unrest in Rangoon (now Yangon) in March 1988 culminated in major protests, which were violently suppressed by riot police under the direct command of U Sein Lwin, the BSPP Joint General Secretary. Further demonstrations, to demand the release of rioters detained in March, started in June. The Government's response was again extremely brutal, and many demonstrators were killed. In July vain attempts were made to counter the growing unpopularity of the Government, including the removal from office of Maj.-Gen. Min Gaung, the Minister of Home and Religious Affairs, and U Thien Aung, the head of the People's Police Force in Rangoon. (The Prime Minister, also, was subsequently dismissed.) Finally, at an extraordinary meeting of the BSPP Congress in July, U Ne Win resigned as party Chairman and asked the Congress to approve the holding of a national referendum on the issue of a multi-party political system. The Congress rejected the referendum proposal and the resignation of four other senior members of the BSPP, including that of U Sein Lwin, but accepted the resignation of U San Yu, the BSPP Vice-Chairman.

The subsequent election of U Sein Lwin to the chairmanship of the BSPP by the party's Central Executive Committee, and his appointment as Chairman of the State Council and as state President, increased popular discontent and provoked further student-led riots. Martial law was imposed on Rangoon, and thousands of unarmed demonstrators were reportedly massacred by the armed forces throughout the country. In August 1988 students appealed for a general strike, and U Sein Lwin was forced to resign after only 17 days in office. He was replaced by the more moderate Dr Maung Maung, hitherto the Attorney-General, whose response to the continued rioting was conciliatory. Martial law was revoked; Brig.-Gen. Aung Gyi (formerly a close colleague of U Ne Win, now an outspoken critic of the regime), who had been detained under U Sein Lwin, was released; and permission was given for the formation of the All Burma Students' Union. Demonstrations continued, however, and by September students and Buddhist monks had assumed control of the municipal government of many towns. In that month U Nu requested foreign support for his formation of an 'alternative government'. The emerging opposition leaders, Aung Gyi, Aung San Suu Kyi (daughter of Gen. Aung San) and Gen. (retd) Tin Oo (a former Chief of Staff and Minister of Defence), then formed the National United Front for Democracy, which was subsequently renamed the League for Democracy and later the National League for Democracy (NLD).

At an emergency meeting of the BSPP Congress in September 1988 it was decided that free elections would be held within three months and that members of the armed forces, police and civil service could no longer be affiliated to a political party. Now distanced from the BSPP, the armed forces, led by Gen. (later Senior Gen.) Saw Maung, seized power on 18 September, ostensibly to maintain order until multi-party elections could be arranged. A State Law and Order Restoration Council (SLORC) was formed, all state organs (including the People's Assembly, the State Council and the Council of Ministers) were abolished, demonstrations were banned and a night-time curfew was imposed nation-wide. Despite these measures, opposition movements demonstrated in favour of an interim civilian government, and it was estimated that more than 1,000 demonstrators were killed in the first few days following the coup. The SLORC announced the formation of a nine-member Government, with Saw Maung as Minister of Defence and of Foreign Affairs and subsequently also Prime Minister. Although ostensibly in retirement, it was widely believed that U Ne Win retained a controlling influence over the new leaders. The new Government changed the official name of the country to the Union of Burma (as it had been before 1973). The law maintaining the BSPP as the sole party was abrogated, and new parties were encouraged to register for the forthcoming elections. The BSPP registered as the National Unity Party (NUP), with U Tha Kyaw, the former Minister of Transport, as its Chairman. In December 1988, owing to disagreements with Suu Kyi, Aung Gyi was expelled from the NLD after he had founded the Union National Democracy Party. Tin Oo was elected as the new NLD Chairman. U Nu returned to prominence as the leader of a new party, the League for Democracy and Peace (LDP), and also commanded the support of the new Democracy Party.

From October 1988 to January 1989 Suu Kyi campaigned in townships and rural areas across the nation, and elicited much popular support, despite martial law regulations banning public gatherings of five or more people. In March 1989 there were anti-Government demonstrations in many cities, in protest at the increasing harassment of Suu Kyi and the arrest of many NLD supporters and activists. In July Suu Kyi cancelled a rally to commemorate the anniversary of the assassination of her father, owing to the threat of government violence; two days later, both she and Tin Oo were placed under house arrest, accused of 'endangering the State'.

In May 1989 electoral legislation was ratified, providing for multi-party elections to be held on 27 May 1990, and permitting campaigning only in the three months prior to the election date. In June 1989 the SLORC changed the official name of the country to the Union of Myanmar (Myanma Naing-ngan), on the grounds that the previous title conveyed the impression that the population consisted solely of ethnic Burmans. The transliteration to the Roman alphabet of many other place-names was changed, to correspond more closely with pronunciation.

In December 1989 Tin Oo was sentenced by a military tribunal to three years' imprisonment, with hard labour, for his part in the anti-Government uprising in 1988. In the same month U Nu was disqualified from contesting the forthcoming general election, owing to his refusal to dissolve the 'alternative government' that he had proclaimed in September 1988. In January 1990 U Nu and 13 members of the 'alternative government' were placed under house arrest. Five members subsequently resigned and were released. Later in January, Suu Kyi was barred from contesting the election, owing to her 'entitlement to the privileges of a foreigner' (a reference to her marriage to a British citizen) and her alleged involvement with insurgents.

Martial law was revoked in eight townships in November 1989, and in a further 10 in February 1990. It was reported that during 1989 tens of thousands of residents had been forcibly evicted from densely populated areas in major cities, where anti-Government demonstrations had received much support, and resettled in rural areas. In January and April 1989 a prominent human rights organization, Amnesty International, published information regarding violations of human rights in Myanmar, including the torture and summary execution of dissident students. This was followed by criticism from the UN later in the year.

In May 1990 93 parties presented a total of 2,296 candidates to contest 492 seats at the general election for the new assembly; there were also 87 independent candidates. Despite previous efforts to weaken the influence of known leaders and to eliminate dissidents, the voting was reported to be free and orderly. The NLD received 59.9% of the total votes and won 396 of the 485 seats that were, in the event, contested; the NUP obtained 21.2% of the votes, but won only 10 seats. The NLD demanded the immediate opening of negotiations with the SLORC, and progress towards popular rule. However, the SLORC announced that the election had been intended to provide not a legislature but a Constituent Assembly, which was to draft a constitution establishing a 'strong government', and was to be under the direction of a national convention to be established by the SLORC. The resulting draft constitution would have to be endorsed by referendum, and subsequently approved by the SLORC. In July the SLORC announced Order 1/90, stating that the SLORC would continue as the *de facto* Government until a new constitution was drafted. Elected members of the NLD responded (independently of their leadership) with the 'Gandhi Hall Declaration', urging that an assembly of all elected representatives be convened by September.

In August 1990, at an anti-Government protest held in Mandalay to commemorate the killing of thousands of demonstrators in 1988, troops killed four protesters, including two Buddhist monks. In September the SLORC arrested six members of the NLD, including the acting Chairman, Kyi Maung, and acting Secretary-General, Chit Hlaing, on charges of passing state secrets to unauthorized persons. Kyi Maung was replaced as acting NLD Chairman by U Aung Shwe, a former ambassador to Australia and an original member of the NLD Central Executive Committee. Also in September NLD representatives discussed plans to declare a provisional government in Mandalay, without the support of the party's Central Executive Committee. Influential monks agreed to support the declaration, which was to be made in October, but the plan was abandoned after government troops surrounded monasteries. The SLORC subsequently ordered the dissolution of all Buddhist organizations involved in anti-Government activities (all except nine sects) and empowered military commanders to impose death sentences on rebellious monks. More than 50 senior members of the NLD were arrested, and members of all political parties were required to endorse Order 1/90: in acquiescing, the NLD effectively nullified its demand for an immediate transfer of power.

In December 1990 a group of candidates who had been elected to the Constituent Assembly fled to Manerplaw, on the Thai border, and announced a 'parallel government', the National Coalition Government of the Union of Burma (NCGUB), with the support of the Democratic Alliance of Burma (DAB), a broadly based organization uniting ethnic rebel forces with student dissidents and monks. The self-styled Prime Minister of the NCGUB was Sein Win, the leader of the Party for National Democracy (PND) and a cousin of Suu Kyi. The NLD leadership expelled members who had taken part in the formation of the 'parallel government', despite broad support for the move in the NLD. The SLORC annulled the PND's registration as a political party and, subsequently, the elected status of the eight members of the NCGUB. In February 1991 the SLORC annulled the registration of the LDP. Two other parties were similarly banned in early 1991. In April Gen. (later Senior Gen.) Than Shwe, the Vice-Chairman of the SLORC and the Deputy Chief of Staff of the armed forces, officially announced that the SLORC would not transfer power to the Constituent Assembly, as the political parties involved were 'subversive' and 'unfit to rule'. In response to continued pressure from the SLORC, the NLD effected a complete reorganization of the party's Central Executive Committee, replacing Suu Kyi as General Secretary with the previously unknown U Lwin, and Tin Oo with the former acting Chairman, U Aung Shwe.

In July 1991 the SLORC retroactively amended electoral legislation adopted in May 1989, extending the grounds on which representatives of the Assembly could be disqualified or debarred from contesting future elections to include convictions for breaches of law and order. More than 80 elected representatives had already died, been imprisoned or been forced into exile since the election in May 1990. In September 1991 the SLORC declared its intention to remain in charge of state administration for a further five to 10 years. In that month U Ohn Gyaw was appointed Minister for Foreign Affairs in place of Saw Maung, becoming the first civilian in the Cabinet.

In October 1991 Suu Kyi was awarded the Nobel Peace Prize. Sein Win attended the presentation of the award to Suu Kyi's family in Oslo, Norway, in December, gaining the Norwegian Government's *de facto* recognition of the NCGUB. In Myanmar students who staged demonstrations (the first since 1989) to coincide with the ceremony, protesting against Suu Kyi's continued detention and demanding progress towards democracy, were dispersed by security forces. Universities and colleges, which had reopened in May 1991, were closed, and thousands of teaching staff were dismissed or sent for re-education. It was subsequently announced that Suu Kyi had been expelled from the NLD. In January 1992 Tin Oo's expulsion from the NLD was announced in a broadcast.

Three additional members were appointed to the SLORC in January 1992, and the Cabinet was expanded to include seven new ministers, four of whom were civilians. The changes, together with a reorganization of senior ministers in February, were widely perceived to benefit the Chief of Military Intelligence, Maj.-Gen. (later Lt-Gen.) Khin Nyunt (First Secretary of the SLORC). Khin Nyunt was widely regarded as the most powerful member of the SLORC, owing to U Ne Win's continued patronage. Divisions within the ruling junta between Khin Nyunt and the more senior officers were becoming increasingly evident. In March Than Shwe replaced Saw Maung as Minister of Defence, and in April Saw Maung retired as Chairman of the SLORC and Prime Minister for reasons of ill health. Than Shwe was subsequently appointed to both these posts. The SLORC promptly ordered the release of several political prisoners, including U Nu, and announced that Suu Kyi could receive a visit from her family. Than Shwe indicated that he was prepared to meet Suu Kyi personally to discuss her future. In June the first meeting took place between members of the SLORC and opposition representatives from the remaining 10 legal parties, in preparation for the holding of a national convention to draft a new constitution.

In January 1993 the National Convention finally assembled, but was adjourned several times during the year, owing to the objections of the opposition members to SLORC demands for a leading role in government for the armed forces. The SLORC reacted to what it regarded as opposition intransigence by suspending any conciliatory gestures (which had included the revocation of two martial law decrees and amnesties for a total of 534 political prisoners), and many arrests were reported. Towards the end of the year the Chairman of the National Convention's Convening Committee, U Aung Toe (the Chief Justice), announced (seemingly without grounds) that a consensus existed in favour of the SLORC's demands, which comprised: the inclusion, in both the lower and upper chambers of a proposed parliament, of military personnel (to be appointed by the Commander-in-Chief of the Armed Forces); the election of the President by an electoral college; the independent self-administration of the armed forces; and the right of the Commander-in-Chief to exercise state power in an emergency (effectively granting legitimate status to a future coup).

In September 1993 an alternative mass movement to the NUP (which had lost credibility through its election defeat) was formed to establish a civilian front through which the armed forces could exercise control. The Union Solidarity and Development Association (USDA), the aims of which were indistinguishable from those of the SLORC, was not officially registered as a political party, thus enabling civil servants to join the organization, with the incentive of considerable privileges. In January 1994 large numbers of people were apparently coerced into joining USDA rallies to demonstrate support for the constitutional proposals presented by the SLORC.

In January 1994 the National Convention reconvened, and in April it was adjourned, having adopted guidelines for three significant chapters of the future Constitution. Accordingly, Myanmar was to be renamed the Republic of the Union of Myanmar, comprising seven states (associated with some of the country's minority ethnic groups) and seven divisions in central and southern Myanmar (largely representing the areas populated by the ethnic Bamars—Burmans). The Republic would be headed by an executive President, elected by the legislature for five years; proposals for the disqualification of any candidate with a foreign spouse or children would prevent Suu Kyi from entering any future presidential election. Reconvening in September, the Convention again stressed that the central role of the military (as 'permanent representatives of the people') be enshrined in the new Constitution. It was proposed that legislative power be shared between a bicameral Pyidaungsu Hluttaw (Union Parliament) and divisional and state assemblies, all of which were to include representatives of the military. The Pyidaungsu Hluttaw was to comprise the Pyithu Hluttaw and the Amyotha Hluttaw (House of Nationalities): the former would comprise 330 elected deputies and 110 members of the armed forces, and would be elected for five years. The latter would be constituted with equal numbers of representatives from the proposed seven regions and seven states of the Republic, as well as members of the military, and was to comprise a maximum of 224 deputies. A general election was provisionally scheduled for 2 September 1997 (although it was not actually held). The session was adjourned in April 1995.

Meanwhile, in July 1994 Khin Nyunt announced what appeared to be a major change of policy: that the SLORC was prepared to hold talks with Suu Kyi. In February a delegation led by a member of the US Congress had been granted permis-

sion to visit Suu Kyi, who had expressed her willingness to negotiate with the SLORC on all issues except her exile. In August a second US Congressman led a delegation to Yangon, meeting with Khin Nyunt. In September, following mediation by a senior Buddhist monk between Suu Kyi and leading members of the SLORC, Suu Kyi was permitted to leave her home for the first time to meet Than Shwe and Khin Nyunt. In October Suu Kyi held a second meeting with senior SLORC members. In November, however, a further US delegation was not permitted to visit Suu Kyi. It was reported, none the less, that she had met other detained members of the NLD, including Tin Oo. In January 1995 the SLORC announced that Suu Kyi would be freed only when the new Constitution had been completed; Suu Kyi simultaneously rejected suggestions that she might reach a compromise with the SLORC on the terms for her release. In February leading members of the SLORC held talks in Yangon with an envoy of the UN Secretary-General. In March the Government released 31 political prisoners, including Tin Oo and Kyi Maung.

In July 1995 Suu Kyi was unexpectedly granted an unconditional release from house arrest. The SLORC, which thus hoped to attract greater foreign investment, was in a powerful position: the armed forces were united; political dissent had been effectively suppressed; and cease-fire accords had been reached with nearly all the ethnic insurgent groups. On her release Suu Kyi made a conciliatory speech, urging negotiations with the SLORC and a spirit of compromise. Suu Kyi swiftly reconciled the early leaders of the NLD, including Kyi Maung and Tin Oo, with the new leadership which had compromised with the SLORC. Hundreds of supporters gathered daily to hear Suu Kyi speak outside her house in Yangon without being dispersed by security forces. Suu Kyi was reinstated as General Secretary of the NLD in October, in a reorganization of the party's executive committee; Tin Oo and Kyi Maung were named Vice-Chairmen. Aung Shwe, who had led the 'legal' NLD and represented the party at the National Convention, was retained as party Chairman. The NLD ignored the announcement by the SLORC's Election Commission that the appointments of Suu Kyi, Tin Oo and Kyi Maung were illegal under rules requiring the Commission's approval of leadership changes.

In November 1995 a report was published by the UN investigator into human rights in Myanmar, claiming that the SLORC was using forced labour for infrastructural and historical projects. The SLORC denied the allegations, insisting that donating one's labour was a Buddhist tradition in the country. The UN report also described complaints of summary executions and rape by the armed forces. In April 1996 a further UN report claimed that forced labour, torture and arbitrary executions were still widespread in Myanmar.

In November 1995 the National Convention reconvened. The NLD was becoming increasingly frustrated by the SLORC's relative success in marginalizing Suu Kyi through its failure to open talks with the NLD and its insistence that the National Convention was the proper forum for discussions. (Suu Kyi was, of course, not a member of the National Convention.) The NLD attended the opening session of the Convention, in the hope that the SLORC would respond positively to its requests to expand the Convention to make it truly representative. However, its proposals were ignored and the NLD withdrew from the Convention, denouncing it as illegitimate and undemocratic, and for the first time appealed for international support for its cause. The SLORC, which had already begun to imprison NLD supporters for petty crimes, reacted strongly to the NLD boycott, officially expelling the NLD from the Convention and threatening to 'annihilate' anyone threatening national interests. In December Suu Kyi appealed for the revival of proscribed political parties and the release of imprisoned pro-democracy activists.

During 1996 and 1997 NLD meetings and publications were prohibited, and arrests of its members were frequent. In May 1996 more than 260 members of the NLD (mostly delegates elected to the Constituent Assembly in 1990) were arrested prior to the opening of the party's first congress. The majority were detained for the duration of the congress, which only 18 NLD members were able to attend; at least nine of those arrested subsequently had charges brought against them. The congress, meanwhile, resolved to draft an alternative constitution. In June the SLORC intensified its action against the NLD with an order banning any organization that held illegal gatherings or obstructed the drafting of the new Constitution by the National Convention; members of a proscribed party could be liable to between five and 20 years' imprisonment. In September police erected road-blocks around Suu Kyi's house, and again detained NLD activists, in order to prevent the holding of a further congress. Suu Kyi's telephone line was disconnected, and she was unable to deliver her weekly speech for the first time since her release from house arrest. From October the road-block was resumed each week with the purpose of preventing access to Suu Kyi's speech. The SLORC recommenced talks with NLD officials later that month. However, relations quickly deteriorated following an attack on vehicles in which Suu Kyi and other NLD leaders were travelling.

In late October 1996 student action in Yangon, in protest against the detention and brutal treatment of fellow students, prompted further repression and numerous arrests (among those detained was Kyi Maung). This was followed in early December by the largest pro-democracy demonstration since 1988, involving more than 2,000 students. (The students also voiced educational, in addition to political, concerns.) The gathering was dispersed peacefully, although some 600 demonstrators were temporarily detained. Smaller student demonstrations continued sporadically until mid-December, when Suu Kyi (although she denied involvement) was briefly confined to her home, and tanks were deployed in Yangon; university establishments were closed indefinitely. At the end of December some 50 members of the Communist Party of Burma (CPB) and of the NLD were arrested in connection with the student protests. In late January 1997 14 people, including at least five NLD members, were convicted of involvement in the unrest and sentenced to seven years' imprisonment.

In early January 1997 Suu Kyi was allowed to deliver her weekly speech for the first time in three months. However, the SLORC imposed new restrictions on media access to Suu Kyi, and barricades remained outside her home. In March there were further arrests of NLD members across the country, together with an increased army presence in several towns. Also in March a series of attacks on Muslim targets by Buddhist monks took place across the country. These attacks were rumoured to have been organized by opponents within the regime of Myanmar's application to join the Association of South East Asian Nations (ASEAN, see p. 154), in an attempt to alienate Muslim-dominated members of the grouping. Schools were closed, but reopened in August, while universities (which had been shut in December 1996 for the third time since 1988) remained closed.

In early April 1997 a bomb attack at the home of the Second Secretary of the SLORC, Tin Oo, resulted in the death of his daughter. The Government attributed the bombing to anti-Government groups based in Japan; however, major opposition groups in exile denied involvement in the attack, which was denounced by the NLD. The attack was rumoured to be related to a power struggle between Khin Nyunt, who was increasingly regarded as a moderate, and the more conservative Commander-in-Chief of the Army and Vice-Chair of the SLORC, Gen. Maung Aye, who commanded the support of Tin Oo. The arrest and detention of NLD members increased during 1997, while government propaganda vilifying the opposition grew more frequent and Suu Kyi's freedom of movement and association remained restricted. In December the SLORC announced that Kyi Maung had resigned as Vice-Chairman of the NLD as a result of conflict between himself and Suu Kyi, a claim dismissed as false by the NLD. In July 1997, however, Khin Nyunt invited the NLD Chairman, Aung Shwe, to a meeting, which constituted the first high-level contact between the SLORC and the NLD since the release of Suu Kyi from house arrest in July 1995. A further meeting between the SLORC leadership and the NLD was due to take place in mid-September, but was cancelled by the opposition, who insisted that future discussions required the participation of Suu Kyi in her capacity as Secretary-General of the NLD. The SLORC granted permission for an NLD congress to be held in September.

On 15 November 1997 the ruling junta unexpectedly announced the dissolution of the SLORC and the creation of its immediate replacement, the State Peace and Development Council (SPDC). The 19-member SPDC comprised exclusively military personnel; younger regional military commanders were included (largely to prevent them from developing local power bases), whilst the four most senior members of the SLORC retained their positions at the head of the new junta: Than Shwe was appointed Chairman, Maung Aye Vice-Chairman, Khin Nyunt First Secretary and Tin Oo Second Secretary. A number of former members of the SLORC were ostensibly promoted to an 'Advisory Group', which was, however, subsequently abol-

ished; five members of this group, who had also held positions in the Cabinet, were placed under house arrest in December, pending investigations into allegations of corruption. The SPDC immediately implemented a reorganization of the Cabinet. The new 40-member Cabinet included 25 former ministers, but, in contrast to the SLORC (the members of which had virtually all held cabinet portfolios), only one member of the SPDC, Than Shwe, was appointed to serve concurrently as a cabinet minister. Among the more junior members of the Cabinet were an increased number of civilian appointees, largely selected from the USDA. The restructuring of the junta and the Cabinet appeared to benefit Khin Nyunt, as several supporters of Maung Aye were removed from power. In December the SPDC announced a further cabinet reorganization (which included the finance and national planning portfolios), and the SPDC announced the appointment of a new Chairman (the Minister of Hotels and Tourism, Maj.-Gen. Saw Lwin) and Vice-Chairmen of the National Convention Convening Commission; however, the Convention, which had adjourned in March 1996, remained in recess.

Harassment and persecution of members and leaders of the NLD and other opposition movements continued throughout 1998. In March 40 people were arrested on charges of complicity in a conspiracy allegedly led by the exiled All-Burma Students Democratic Front (ABSDF, an armed movement formed in 1988 by students within the DAB, which had officially renounced its armed struggle in 1997) to assassinate leaders of the military junta and initiate terrorist attacks on government offices and foreign embassies. The ABSDF, which rejected the allegations, was accused of complicity with the NLD. Six of the accused were sentenced to death at the end of April. However, the SPDC unexpectedly authorized an NLD party congress, attended by 400 delegates, at the end of May to celebrate the eighth anniversary of the general election. In June the NLD demanded that the SPDC reconvene the Pyithu Hluttaw, in accordance with the results of the 1990 election, by 21 August. Some 40 elected NLD representatives were detained at the end of June, and others were forced to sign pledges restricting their freedom of movement. In July the SPDC ordered NLD elected representatives to report to their local police station twice a day and confined them to their townships. During July and August Suu Kyi attempted to visit NLD members outside the city, in an effort to exert pressure on the SPDC to comply with the NLD's demands. On four separate occasions the opposition leader was prevented from continuing her journey by road-blocks set up by the ruling junta. On one such occasion in July Suu Kyi was forcibly returned to her home by security forces after a six-day protest in her car, following government refusals to comply with her demands for the release of detained opposition members and the commencement of substantive dialogue with the NLD. In a further incident in August, she was returned to her home by ambulance after spending 13 days in her car, prompting considerable international criticism of the SPDC regime, particularly from the US Government. During Suu Kyi's protest in August Khin Nyunt held a reportedly cordial meeting with the NLD Chairman, Aung Shwe.

Shortly before the NLD's prescribed deadline for convening the Pyithu Hluttaw, the SPDC published an official rejection of the NLD's demands. The NLD responded by declaring its intention unilaterally to convene a 'People's Parliament', which would include elected representatives of all the ethnic minority groups. On the day that Suu Kyi abandoned her protest at the road-block, student demonstrations took place in Yangon (for the first time since December 1996), in support of the NLD's demand for the convening of the legislature. In September thousands of students staged anti-Government demonstrations, which were dispersed by security forces. Arrests of opposition activists increased dramatically, and by early September 193 elected NLD members of the Pyithu Hluttaw and hundreds of party supporters had been detained. In the same month a 10-member Representative Committee, led by Suu Kyi and Aung Shwe, was established by the NLD to act on behalf of the 'People's Parliament' until a legislature could be convened under the 1990 election law. The Committee (which claimed a mandate based on the authorization of more than one-half of the representatives of the Pyithu Hluttaw elected in 1990, many of whom were in detention) asserted that all laws passed by the military junta over the previous 10 years had no legal authority, and also demanded the immediate and unconditional release of all political prisoners. Four parties representing Shan, Mon, Arakanese and Zomi ethnic groups expressed their support for the 'People's

Parliament', together with the ABSDF. In the same month 15 senior military officers were reportedly arrested for allegedly planning to meet with Suu Kyi, and a number of large pro-Government rallies were held in Yangon. The NLD condemned the alleged use of coercion, intimidation and threats by government military intelligence units to secure the involuntary resignations of vast numbers of NLD members and the closure of a number of regional party headquarters. Following the death in custody in October of a member of the NLD, detained by the SPDC since early the previous month, the NLD also formally condemned the junta's treatment of detained opposition party members in a letter to Than Shwe. (In August of the same year an elected representative of the NLD, Saw Win, had died in prison while serving an 11-year term of imprisonment, the third NLD member of the Pyithu Hluttaw to die in custody.) In October UN Assistant Secretary-General Alvaro de Soto met with SPDC leaders and also with Suu Kyi during a visit to Myanmar. He reportedly offered large-scale financial and humanitarian aid to the junta in exchange for the initiation of substantive dialogue with the NLD. During October and November about 300 opposition members were released by the Government; however, a further 500 were believed to remain in detention.

In March 1999, despite requests from several foreign Governments, the ruling junta refused to grant a visa to Suu Kyi's terminally ill husband, Michael Aris. The junta instead encouraged Suu Kyi to visit Aris in the United Kingdom; however, Suu Kyi declined to leave the country for fear that she would not be permitted to return. Following Aris's death later the same month, more than 1,000 supporters of Suu Kyi were permitted to attend a Buddhist ceremony held at Suu Kyi's home in Yangon marking her husband's demise.

In April 1999 the UN adopted a unanimous resolution deploring the escalation in the persecution of the democratic opposition in Myanmar. Nevertheless, the harassment and intimidation of NLD members continued, with the resignations from the party of nearly 300 members reported in July 1999; further resignations were reported in November and in January 2000. In December 1999 it was reported that an elected representative of the People's Assembly, U Maung Maung Myint, had been forced to resign by the ruling SPDC. The lack of political progress by the NLD in 1999 led to the formation of a breakaway faction of the party by a prominent party member, Than Tun, who was subsequently expelled from the NLD.

In August 1999 a series of protests was staged by supporters of the democratic opposition to mark the anniversary of the massacre of thousands of pro-democracy demonstrators by the military Government in 1988. In October Myanmar's Supreme Court issued a declaration rejecting a claim by the NLD that its activities had been 'continuously disrupted, prevented and destroyed' and that hundreds of its members had been illegally detained. In April 2000 Suu Kyi alleged that more than 40 youth members of the NLD had been arrested by the SPDC for their involvement in party activities. In a statement issued in May the NLD called upon the military Government to end the use of forced labour and to recognize the results of the 1990 election.

Opposition radio sources continued to give details of small-scale protests throughout 2000 and 2001. In mid-January 2001 farmers in Shan State protested over the Government's rice-purchasing policy, leading to an unknown number of arrests. A rare bomb explosion in May 2001 reportedly killed 12 people, and left eight others injured in a market in Mandalay. In the same month it was reported that religious riots in Toungoo, Pegu province, had led to the deaths of 24 Buddhist monks. The disturbances spread to other towns, prompting allegations that the SPDC had instigated the riots in an attempt to divert public attention from political and economic problems.

Aung San Suu Kyi also continued her persistent opposition to the SPDC. In August 2000 Suu Kyi and 14 NLD colleagues attempted to visit members of the party in Kunyangon, a town just outside Yangon. The group was stopped by a military roadblock, but refused to return home until allowed to pass. A nine-day stand-off then occurred, finally ending with Suu Kyi and the NLD members being forcibly returned to Yangon. Suu Kyi and eight others were kept under house arrest for the next two weeks. In early September the SPDC raided the NLD headquarters, and detained a number of other party leaders in their homes. Undeterred, the NLD announced that it was to draft a new constitution for the country, an act declared illegal in 1996 and punishable by 20 years' imprisonment. Later in the month Suu Kyi attempted to leave Yangon again, this time by train to

Mandalay, only to be told that all trains were full. The NLD leader was once again returned home and placed under house arrest, while NLD Vice-Chairman Tin Oo and eight other party workers were taken to a government 'guest house'. Pressure on the NLD increased in late October 2000, when a deadline for an eviction order for the party to vacate its premises expired. The landladies responsible for the eviction order had been incarcerated by the SPDC for allowing the NLD to use loudspeakers, but claimed that their decision to evict had not been influenced by external coercion.

Despite the sustained suppression of the opposition party and the prevention of protest, the SPDC's treatment of its political rivals became markedly more liberal from mid-2000. In July the SPDC reportedly allowed 60,000 university students to resume their education. The undergraduate universities, however, were relocated in the suburbs, in order to avoid demonstrations in the city centres that might draw in other civilians. Razali Ismail, a Malaysian diplomat newly appointed as the UN Secretary-General's Special Envoy to Myanmar, was allowed access to Suu Kyi during a four-day visit in October 2000, and in the same month James Mawdsley, a British human rights activist sentenced to 17 years' imprisonment in Myanmar in September 1999, was released (see below).

Conciliation between the SPDC and the NLD was confirmed in early January 2001, when it was announced that the two parties had been holding secret talks since October, the first high-level discussions between the opponents since 1994. Lt-Gen. Khin Nyunt met with Suu Kyi several times, although the details of the talks remained closely guarded. Some analysts feared that the resumption of discussions was merely a cynical ploy by the Government to attract foreign investment and curb economic sanctions, a view supported by the fact there was little initial evidence of progress.

In January 2001, in a further placatory gesture, the SPDC ordered the media to stop the regular acrimonious attacks on Suu Kyi and the NLD. In the same month the government-controlled Yangon division court dismissed a lawsuit brought by Suu Kyi's US-based brother, Aung San Oo, who claimed ownership of half of Suu Kyi's house. Although foreigners cannot buy or transfer property in Myanmar, San Oo had been granted an exemption from the Government in July 2000, and thus requested half the family property according to Myanma inheritance law. In October 2001, however, the court rejected Suu Kyi's application to have her brother's claim dismissed. The hearing was subsequently adjourned on several occasions and in December 2003 was postponed until February 2004. At the end of January 2001 the SPDC released NLD Vice-Chairman Tin Oo and 84 other party supporters, who had been detained since Suu Kyi's attempted train journey in September 2000. A few days later a delegation of the European Union (EU, see p. 208) was permitted to meet with Suu Kyi, as was Dr Paulo Sérgio Pinheiro, UN human rights envoy to Myanmar, in April 2001.

In February 2001 Lt-Gen. Tin Oo, the army chief of staff and, as the Council's Second Secretary, the SPDC's fourth most powerful member, was killed in a helicopter crash. While the accident was officially attributed to bad weather and mechanical failure, there were rumours of an assassination, as Lt-Gen. Tin Oo had survived two previous attempts on his life, in 1996 and 1997.

In June 2001, as discussions continued, the Government ordered the release of a number of NLD members from prison and permitted the reopening of the NLD headquarters and several branch offices, although those outside Yangon remained closed. In July Aye Win, an imprisoned cousin of Suu Kyi, was released, together with several other NLD detainees. However, in the same month Suu Kyi failed to attend Martyrs' Day ceremonies held in Yangon to commemorate the assassination of her father in 1947. Her non-attendance prompted speculation that talks with the Government were foundering, a rumour denied by the SPDC. In August the release of Aung Shwe, Chairman of the NLD, and of Vice-Chairman Tin Oo, was hailed as an indication of progress. Shortly afterwards Ismail held further discussions with Suu Kyi during a visit to Yangon and voiced cautious optimism that she might come to an agreement with the Government.

In November 2001 two senior army generals—Lt-Gen. Win Myint (widely regarded as the fourth most powerful individual in the country) and Deputy Prime Minister Tin Hla—were dismissed. While no official explanation was given, the dismissals were thought to be connected to the fact that the two men were under investigation for corruption. As both had expressed only muted support for the ongoing talks with Suu Kyi, there was also speculation that their replacement would be more conducive to the attainment of a political settlement. Two days later the SPDC announced that five government ministers were to retire. While two Deputy Prime Ministers, Rear Adm. Maung Maung Khin and Lt-Gen. Tin Tun, had been expected to step down, the departure of Win Sein, Minister of Culture, Aung San, Minister of Co-operatives, and Saw Tun, Minister of Immigration and Population, had not been foreseen. No official explanation was given for the changes. However, it was thought that their removal constituted an attempt to improve the Government's corrupt and anti-democratic image. In the same month Razali Ismail visited the country again. It was hoped that he would be able to revitalize the ongoing negotiations between the SPDC and Suu Kyi and accelerate the release of political prisoners, using the prospect of international aid as an incentive. Upon his departure, Ismail expressed satisfaction with the progress that had been made.

In December 2001 Nobel Prize laureates attending a gathering in Oslo issued the Government with a manifesto demanding the release of Suu Kyi and the remaining political prisoners. In response, the Government issued a statement stressing that both parties were working together to reach a satisfactory political settlement. In late January 2002 it was reported that Suu Kyi had met privately with Gen. Than Shwe for the first time since 1994, raising hopes that the two sides might be close to reaching a breakthrough. However, in February 2002 international pressure on the SPDC to release all remaining political prisoners (an estimated 1,500, according to Amnesty International) and begin a more substantive dialogue with the NLD increased, prompted by the release of a critical report by the US Government (see below). The Myanma Government responded by releasing five further detainees and expressing its confidence that a successful conclusion to the negotiation process was imminent.

In March 2002 the son-in-law of U Ne Win, Aye Zaw Win, and three of U Ne Win's grandsons were arrested on charges of plotting to overthrow the Government. It was alleged that they had intended to abduct three government leaders and force them to form a figurehead government under U Ne Win's influence. Four senior military officials—the Commander-in-Chief of the Air Force, Maj.-Gen. Myint Swe, the Chief of Police, Maj.-Gen. Soe Win, and two regional commanders, Brig.-Gen. Chit Than and Maj.-Gen. Aye Kwye—were dismissed and questioned in connection with the attempted coup. Ne Win and his daughter, Sandar Win, were placed under house arrest. Despite suspicions that the coup allegations were linked to internal conflicts within the military, owing to the insubstantial nature of the evidence gathered to support the charges, it was announced in April that those arrested would stand trial for high treason. In September, following their trial, U Ne Win's four relatives were convicted of the treason charges against them and sentenced to death. They entered appeals against the sentences. In December U Ne Win himself died while under house arrest.

In May 2002 Aung San Suu Kyi was finally released from house arrest. The SPDC stated that her release was unconditional and that it would not attempt to impose any restrictions upon her travel. Shortly afterwards Suu Kyi urged the immediate resumption of dialogue with the junta, which had ceased following her liberation. In June she travelled to Mandalay on her first political trip since she was freed; the journey passed without incident. In August Razali Ismail returned to the country with the intention of promoting further political dialogue between the NLD and the SPDC. Meanwhile, Suu Kyi challenged the SPDC to prove its commitment to the achievement of democracy in the country by ordering the swift and unconditional release of all political prisoners. In the following month a delegation from the EU also visited Myanmar and met with Suu Kyi. It failed, however, to secure a meeting with any members of the SPDC. In November the junta announced the release of 115 prisoners, the largest number to have been freed since negotiations began. However, the releases were dismissed by both the USA and human rights groups as inadequate. Razali Ismail returned to the country, but made little progress towards encouraging political reconciliation.

In early 2003 representatives from Amnesty International were permitted to enter Myanmar for the first time and to hold talks with Aung San Suu Kyi. Following the visit, the human rights organization condemned Myanmar's judicial system. Meanwhile, 12 political activists in the country were arrested on

suspicion of planning anti-Government activities. In February it was reported that Suu Kyi wanted economic sanctions to be maintained against the Myanma Government until it began a meaningful dialogue with the opposition. In the same month it was announced that Lt-Gen. Soe Win would assume the previously vacant post of Second Secretary of the SPDC. Meanwhile, the Minister of Health, Maj.-Gen. Ket Sein, and the Minister of Finance and Revenue, U Khin Maung Thein, were permitted to retire. They were replaced, respectively, by Dr Kyaw Myint and Maj.-Gen. Hla Tun. In the following month UN envoy Paulo Sérgio Pinheiro restated a UN demand that the junta release all remaining political prisoners, estimated to number 1,200, and enter into serious dialogue with the opposition. Later that month a bomb exploded in Yangon, killing one person, during celebrations being held to commemorate Armed Forces Day. An unexploded bomb was also discovered near the US embassy on the same day.

In April 2003, during a news conference, Aung San Suu Kyi issued a rare criticism of the SPDC for refusing to enter into any substantive dialogue with the opposition. In May 10 members of the NLD were imprisoned on charges that they had organized public protests and participated in clandestine activities. Later in the same month the political situation in Myanmar deteriorated further when violent confrontations occurred in the town of Ye-u, in the north of the country, between government supporters and opposition members travelling with an entourage carrying Aung San Suu Kyi. While the SPDC insisted that the violence had been provoked by the opposition, it was subsequently reported that the clashes had occurred when Suu Kyi and her supporters were ambushed and attacked by pro-Government forces. It was estimated that around 80 members of the entourage had died as a result. On the following day it was reported that Suu Kyi had been taken into 'protective custody' by the SPDC; meanwhile, the headquarters of the NLD, together with NLD offices across the country, were closed down, 17 other members of the NLD were also detained, and all universities under the control of the Ministry of Education were shut indefinitely. In June UN envoy Razali Ismail proceeded with a planned visit to Myanmar. Ismail was permitted to meet with Suu Kyi and confirmed that she had not sustained any injuries from her involvement in the recent violence. The junta's detention of Suu Kyi prompted widespread international criticism. At a meeting of ASEAN ministers of foreign affairs held later in that month the organization transgressed its traditional policy of non-interference in the affairs of other member states, calling for Suu Kyi to be freed and for Myanmar to make a peaceful transition to democratic practices. Later in June, following the failure of its appeal to the SPDC for the liberation of Suu Kyi, the country's largest aid donor, Japan, announced that it had suspended all economic aid. In July the Government announced that it had freed 91 of the NLD activists detained after the violence of May and permitted a delegation from the International Committee of the Red Cross (ICRC) to visit Suu Kyi; the delegates subsequently confirmed that she was in good health, contradicting reports from the US State Department, which claimed that she had gone on a hunger strike.

In July 2003 it was reported that three cabinet Ministers—Minister of Industry (No. 1) U Aung Thaung, Minister of Forestry Aung Phone and Minister of Agriculture and Irrigation Maj.-Gen. Nyunt Tin—had all been dismissed. In late August a major reorganization of the Government was announced, during which the former First Secretary of the SPDC, Gen. Khin Nyunt, replaced Field Marshal Than Shwe as Prime Minister. Than Shwe retained the defence portfolio, however. Lt-Gen. Soe Win became First Secretary and was replaced as Second Secretary by Lt-Gen. Thein Sein. Khin Nyunt subsequently announced that the Government intended to reconvene the National Convention, which had been in recess since 1996, in order to draw up a new constitution and move towards the holding of new elections. However, no schedule was announced for the proposed developments, leading to criticism that the announcement was merely an attempt to encourage the removal of international sanctions against the country and the resumption of aid.

In September 2003 it was announced that Aung San Suu Kyi had returned to her home and was being held under house arrest, having undergone major surgery in hospital. A further visit to Myanmar by Razali Ismail in the following month failed, however, to secure her release or to end the political deadlock. Paulo Sérgio Pinheiro returned to the country in late October. In December nine people were sentenced to death, having been convicted of high treason; they were amongst 12 people arrested in July for allegedly plotting to overthrow the ruling junta. In January 2004 the release of a further 151 members of the NLD held in connection with the violence of the previous May was announced and, in the following month, Vice-Chairman of the NLD Tin Oo was released into house arrest, having been imprisoned since May 2003. Also in January 2004, following a meeting with government officials, representatives from 25 ethnic groups and alliances rejected the proposed 'road map' to democracy outlined by Prime Minister Gen. Khin Nyunt in August 2003 and reiterated demands for the Government to begin talks with the opposition. However, following a visit to the country in March, Razali Ismail expressed confidence that the SPDC would adhere to the 'road map' and proclaimed his trip to have been a success.

After Burma gained independence in 1948, various groups conducted armed insurgency campaigns against government forces. The most effective of the ethnic-based insurgency groups was the Karen (Kayin) National Union (KNU), founded in 1948, which led a protracted campaign for the establishment of an independent state for the Karen ethnic group (restyled Kayin in the transliteration changes of 1989), partly through the activities of its military wing, the Karen (Kayin) National Liberation Army (KNLA). The KNU was a member of the National Democratic Front (NDF), an organization which at one time comprised 11 ethnic minority groups—including Kachin, Karenni (Kayinni), Mon, Shan, Pa-O, Palaung, Wa, Arakanese (Rakhine) and Lahu parties—formed in 1975 (by five groups, originally) with the aim of making Burma a federal union and opposing both the Government and, initially, the CPB. The CPB was one of the most well-organized insurgent movements, in military terms, and gained control of significant areas in northern Burma. By May 1986 the various minority groups in the NDF had agreed to relinquish their individual demands for autonomy, in favour of a unified demand for a federal system of government. At the same time, the CPB withdrew its demand for a 'one-party' government and entered into an alliance with the NDF. At the second NDF Congress in June 1987, Maj.-Gen. Bo Mya, the President of the KNU and Chief of Staff of the KNLA, was replaced as NDF President by Saw Maw Reh, a former Chairman of the Karenni (Kayinni) National Progressive Party (KNPP), and further leadership changes removed all KNU representatives from senior NDF positions. The new NDF leaders advocated the establishment of autonomous, ethnic-based states within a Burmese union.

The insurgent groups were sympathetic to anti-Government movements in the major cities. Continued attacks throughout 1988 engaged the government forces in the border areas, leaving fewer of them to impose order in the towns. In September the Karens announced plans to co-operate with protesting students and Buddhist monks to work towards the achievement of democracy. After the armed forces seized power, insurgents intensified operations, aided by at least 3,000 students whom the Karen rebels agreed to train and arm. In November 22 anti-Government groups, led by members of the NDF, formed the DAB. Bo Mya was elected President.

In April 1989 dissatisfaction with the leadership of the CPB led to a mutiny by Wa tribesmen, who constituted an estimated 80%–90% of the CPB's membership. Rebellious Wa soldiers captured the CPB headquarters, and the party's leaders were forced into exile in the People's Republic of China. The leaders of the mutiny subsequently accepted SLORC proposals for the former forces of the CPB army to become government-controlled militia forces in exchange for supplies of rice, financial support and development aid. The former CPB troops agreed to use their main forces against the 25,000-strong rebel separatist Mong Tai (Shan State) Army (formerly the Shan United Army), whose leader, Khun Sa, controlled much of the drug trade in the 'Golden Triangle', the world's major opium-producing area, where the borders of Myanmar, Laos and Thailand meet. The SLORC also approached members of the NDF, and was successful in securing agreements with the Shan State Progressive Party in September 1989, the Pa-O National Organization in March 1991 and the Palaung State Liberation Organization in May of that year. In July, at the third NDF Congress, these three movements were expelled, reducing the NDF's membership to eight organizations, and Nai Shwe Kyin was elected as the NDF's new President.

In December 1988, following a visit by the Prime Minister of Thailand, the SLORC granted licences to Thai business interests to exploit raw materials in Burma, in return for much-needed foreign exchange. Although there was no announcement

of any official Thai-Burmese agreement, subsequent offensives by government forces against rebel groups achieved unprecedented success, with troops frequently attacking insurgent bases from Thai territory. By December 1989 six KNU bases along the Thai border had been captured, and in January 1990 two more camps, harbouring a large number of student dissidents, were seized. In January 1990 the armed forces launched an offensive against Mon separatists. In February they succeeded in capturing Three Pagodas Pass, a principal 'black market' trade route between Thailand and Myanmar, and the headquarters of the New Mon State Party.

Intense fighting between government and rebel forces continued as the KNLA advanced into the lower central Ayeyarwady (Irrawaddy) Delta in late 1991. This potentially diversionary tactic failed to prevent a concerted attempt by government troops to seize control of the KNU and DAB headquarters, which was also the seat of the NCGUB. However, despite the use of sophisticated weaponry purchased from the People's Republic of China, government troops failed to capture the camp at Manerplaw. In March 1992 the Thai Government fulfilled prior threats of strong retaliation, forcing hundreds of Myanma troops out of entrenched positions taken up in order to attack the KNU headquarters from the rear. In April the SLORC officially suspended its offensive against the KNU, 'in the interests of national unity'. In October, however, government troops resumed hostilities, making several incursions into Thai territory. In December the Thai and Myanma Governments agreed to 'relocate' the Myanma armed forces, and in February 1993 they resolved to demarcate their common border.

In February and March 1993 the Kachin Independence Organization (KIO) attended peace talks with the Government in the Kachin state capital of Myitkyina. The Kachins were in a vulnerable position, since they were no longer able to obtain arms from the practically defunct CPB or through Thailand (as the Mong Tai Army controlled the territory between Kachin encampments and the Thai border). The SLORC was anxious to reach an accommodation with the Kachins, as the NCGUB would be severely weakened by the loss of their support (although a *de facto* national cease-fire had been in effect since October 1992). The KIO appeared to have signed a peace agreement in April but, owing to attempts by the Kachins to persuade other members of the DAB to enter discussions with the SLORC, the cease-fire was not announced until October. The agreement was ratified in Yangon in February 1994. The KIO was suspended from the DAB in October 1993 for negotiating separately with the SLORC, and the DAB reiterated its conditions for discussions with the SLORC in a series of open letters. Its stipulations included: the recognition of the DAB as a single negotiating body (the SLORC insisted on meeting each ethnic group separately); the location of the negotiating process in a neutral country; an immediate end to the forcible mass relocation of villagers; a new body to draft a constitution; and the release of all political detainees, beginning with Suu Kyi. Under Thai pressure, however, the DAB policy of negotiating as a front was unofficially abandoned. In February 2001 there were rumours of a coup within the KIO, as Chairman Lt-Gen. Zau Mai was replaced by his deputy, Maj.-Gen. Tu Jai. The rumours were swiftly denied, the reason for the replacement being given as Zau Nai's ill health.

In May 1994 the Karenni (Kayinni) National People's Liberation Front concluded a cease-fire agreement with the SLORC, reportedly the 11th insurgent group to do so. This was followed in July by the declaration of a cease-fire by the Kayan New Land Party, and in October by the declaration of a cease-fire by the Shan State Nationalities Liberation Organization. In December government forces launched a new offensive against the KNU, recapturing its headquarters at Manerplaw in January 1995 (and forcing many hundreds of KNU fighters across the border into Thailand). The virtual defeat of the KNU forces was attributed to their reportedly severe lack of ammunition and funds and also to the recent defection from the Christian-led KNU of a mainly Buddhist faction, which established itself as the Democratic Karen (Kayin) Buddhist Army (DKBA). The DKBA, which had comprised about one-tenth of the strength of the KNLA, allegedly supported the government forces in their offensive. In February 1995 the Myanma army captured the KNU's last stronghold, and in the following month Bo Mya resigned as the Commander-in-Chief of the KNLA (although he remained the leader of the KNU). In March the KNU declared a unilateral cease-fire, with the aim of initiating negotiations with the SLORC. Earlier in the month the KNPP reportedly became the

14th ethnic insurgent group to abandon its armed struggle against the SLORC. This agreement collapsed in June, however, as government troops entered areas designated in the accord to be under KNPP control. In August 5,000 troops were dispatched to suppress the KNPP rebellion. Clashes continued throughout the year, and in January 1996 government forces captured a major Kayinni stronghold. The KNPP continued fighting, however, with support from the ABSDF. In February 1996 talks between the KNU and the SLORC in Mawlamyine (Moulmein), calling for tripartite negotiations between the NLD, the NCGUB (which had re-elected Sein Win as its head in Sweden in July 1995) and the SLORC, were inconclusive.

Further talks between the SLORC and the KNU began in November 1996, but had collapsed by December. In January 1997 the DKBA, allegedly supported by government forces, attacked Kayin refugee camps in Thailand. The KNU claimed that requests in late January for further peace negotiations were rejected by the SLORC, which then initiated a new offensive against the KNU. Fighting between the KNU and government forces continued in early March, forcing several thousand Kayins across the border into Thailand. As a result of the forcible relocation of tens of thousands of Kayins away from KNU bases in Myanmar during 1997, further refugees fled to Thailand. The Thai armed forces denied collusion with the Myanma troops in the process of forced repatriations of Kayin refugees, who were believed to number more than 100,000 in mid-1997. In March 1998 the DKBA, supported by government troops, launched two further attacks on Kayin refugee camps in Thailand, prompting a retaliatory attack by the KNU on DKBA forces. In April 1999 the KNU issued a statement confirming the deaths of seven members of a group of 13 government officials whom they had abducted in February; the remaining six were said to have been released unharmed.

In January 2000 it was reported that 800–1,000 Kayins had fled across the border into Thailand, following clashes between government forces and the KNU. In the same month Gen. Bo Mya was succeeded as the leader of the KNU by the former Secretary-General of the organization, Saw Ba Thin. Following his appointment as leader, Ba Thin announced that, while the KNU intended to continue its struggle against the ruling SPDC, the movement was prepared to negotiate a political settlement with the military regime. It was subsequently reported by both government and independent sources that an initial but inconclusive round of talks between the KNU and the SPDC was held in February, followed by further discussions in March. However, in late 2000 the Government began to use 'scorched-earth' tactics to deprive the KNU of its support base, displacing up to 30,000 people in eastern Myanmar.

In January 2001 Johnny and Luther Htoo, teenage leaders of the Karen rebel group, God's Army, surrendered with 12 of their followers to the Thai authorities. While much smaller than the KNU or the KNLA, God's Army had gained international notoriety owing to the leadership of the twin boys, thought to be aged 13 or 14. Two of the 12 members who surrendered were believed to have been involved in a raid on a Thai village that had left six civilians dead in December 2000.

In April 2003 the KNU claimed responsibility for a series of explosions that had destroyed sections of a gas pipeline in Karen State over the previous two months, declaring that they had intended to draw the attention of the international community to the human rights abuses being perpetrated by government troops in the area. Several bombings along the border with Thailand in the following month were also attributed to the KNU. In December, however, Vice-Chairman of the KNU Bo Mya led a personal delegation to Yangon to explore the possibility of a potential cease-fire arrangement with the Government. In January 2004, having unified the KNU behind his initiative, Bo Mya and other KNU officials held talks with government representatives in Yangon. It was reported that the negotiations had resulted in the conclusion of an informal cease-fire arrangement between the two sides. Bo Mya had previously made any peace agreement conditional both on the release of Aung San Suu Kyi and other NLD detainees and on the Government's adherence to UN resolutions delineating a return to democracy for the country. It was hoped that a formal peace agreement would be concluded later in 2004, following a further planned meeting between the KNU and the Government.

Meanwhile, in December 1993 the SLORC initiated a major offensive against Khun Sa's Mong Tai Army encampments on the Thai border. During that month Khun Sa convened a Shan 'parliament' in his base of Homong, which was attended by

hundreds of delegates. This was followed, in May 1994, by Khun Sa's declaration of an independent Shan State, of which he declared himself 'President'. In the same month fighting intensified between government forces and the Mong Tai Army near the Thai border, with heavy losses reported on both sides. However, Khun Sa claimed that his army retained control of two-thirds of the Shan State. In July he was reported to have offered to end opium cultivation and to surrender to the government forces, in exchange for their withdrawal from the Shan State and a guarantee of Shan independence. In March 1995 government forces launched an intensive campaign, lasting several months, against the Mong Tai Army. In August a faction calling itself the Shan State National Army broke away from the Mong Tai Army, accusing Khun Sa of using Shan nationalism as a 'front' for drugs-trafficking. Khun Sa subsequently offered to relinquish areas under his control to an international force that could ensure the safety of the Shan whilst eradicating illicit drugs. Khun Sa's position was considerably weakened in September, as improving relations between Thailand and Myanmar led to a Thai pledge to close the common border, thus obstructing his supply routes, and cease-fires with neighbouring ethnic groups allowed the Government to deploy troops in hitherto inaccessible areas. Certain ethnic groups, notably the Wa, were also actively engaged in fighting the Mong Tai Army to gain control of the opium trade. In November Khun Sa announced his retirement from all political and military positions, citing his betrayal by the breakaway group. In January 1996 government troops entered Homong without resistance, and thousands of his former supporters surrendered. Although no formal agreement with the SLORC was announced, it was widely believed that Khun Sa had previously negotiated a settlement with the authorities since he was not detained and it was officially announced that he would not be extradited to the USA on drugs-trafficking charges. (Khun Sa was, moreover, later accorded the status of an honoured elder.) The Mong Tai Army was subsequently transformed into a militia volunteer unit under the command of the armed forces.

Between November 1996 and February 1997 there were reports of clashes between the Shan United Revolutionary Party (a faction of the Mong Tai Army that had not surrendered in January 1996) and government forces. In September 1997 the alliance between three of the major Shan groups who continued their resistance—including the Shan State National Army (SSNA), remnants of the MTA, and the Shan State Peace-keeping Council (SSPC) and its military wing, the Shan State Army (SSA)—was formalized, and the groups joined together in an enlarged SSA. In November it was reported that Shan separatist groups had launched a further offensive against government troops. In May 1999 it was reported that at least 300,000 Shan had been forced from their villages into resettlement camps by government troops. Clashes between SSA units and government forces were reported in December. In March 2000, following the group's announcement that it wished to seek a peaceful settlement with the ruling junta, the SSA issued a statement outlining cease-fire terms. It was later claimed by the SSA that these terms had been misinterpreted by the Government. In May several senior army officers died in an SSA ambush. In the following month more than 60 Shan and hill tribespeople, who had been forcibly relocated and had then attempted to return to their village, were reportedly killed by the Myanma military in a retaliatory attack. In similar incidents in the region in June, as many as 50 other villagers were believed to have been murdered. In 2001 the Government launched several offensives against SSA border camps, causing hundreds more Shan to flee the area. In September 2001 the leader of the SSA, Col Yodsuek, stated that the group would be willing to enter into peace talks with the SPDC.

In late 1996 Gen. Maung Aye ordered that the forces of the United Wa State Army (UWSA—who reached an accommodation with the SLORC in 1989) should withdraw from its principal base or surrender to the Government by the end of 1997. As the deadline approached, tension between the two sides increased until the UWSA was given permission to remain at the base for a further year. In January 2000 it was reported that the SPDC was to launch an operation to relocate 50,000 people from UWSA-controlled opium-growing areas with the alleged intention of eradicating the production of drugs in the areas by 2005. The relocation programme began to cause ethnic tension early in 2001, as the Shan complained that the Wa tribespeople were occupying land that they had previously owned. It was also claimed that the Wa were still growing opium, in spite of the fact that the scheme had been introduced supposedly to prevent heroin production. In February 2001 the office of the UN High Commissioner for Refugees (UNHCR) investigated reports that 300,000 Shan had fled over the border to Thailand as a result of the Wa influx.

In late 1989 the SLORC began resettling Bamar (Burman) Buddhists in the predominantly Muslim areas of Arakan (renamed Rakhine), displacing the local Rohingya Muslims. In April 1991 Rohingya refugees were forced over the border into Bangladesh, as a result of the brutal operations of the Myanma armed forces, including the destruction of villages, widespread killings and pillaging. The Rohingyas had been similarly persecuted in 1976–78, when more than 200,000 of them had sought refuge in Bangladesh. The Rohingyas had finally been repatriated, only to lose their citizenship following the introduction of new nationality legislation in 1982. In November 1991 the SLORC pledged to repatriate genuine Myanma citizens, but claimed that many of the refugees were illegal Bengali immigrants. In April 1992 the Myanma and Bangladeshi Governments signed an agreement providing for the repatriation of those Rohingya refugees in possession of official documentation. The repatriation programme was delayed, however, owing to the continuing flow of refugees to Bangladesh (reaching an estimated 270,000 by the end of June). The first Rohingya refugees were returned to Myanmar in September, without the supervision of UNHCR. Despite demonstrations by Rohingyas in Bangladesh against forced repatriation, refugees continued to be returned to Myanmar. The SLORC's agreement, in November 1993, to allow UNHCR access to repatriated Rohingyas was expected to accelerate the programme. In April 1994 guerrillas of the Rohingya Solidarity Organization carried out attacks in the Maungdaw area of Rakhine. By May 1995 more than 216,000 refugees had been repatriated. In July 1999, however, about 20,000 Rohingya refugees remained in camps in Bangladesh, despite the expiry of the official deadline for their repatriation in August 1997. In April 2000 the International Federation of Human Rights Leagues (FIDH) issued a report condemning the treatment of Rohingya Muslims by the Myanma Government, including forced labour, punitive taxes and extrajudicial killings. The FIDH claimed that the regime was attempting to force the exodus of Rohingyas from their native Rakhine and criticized UNHCR for its effective complicity with the Myanma regime in designating the more recent refugees as economic migrants. In February 2001 violence between Buddhist and Muslim communities in the state capital, Sittwe, was reported to have resulted in at least 12 deaths, prompting the Government to regulate further the movement of Rohingya and other Muslims in and out of Rakhine. In 2002 UNHCR continued to maintain a presence in the region.

The People's Republic of China restored diplomatic relations with Burma in 1978. From 1988, as Burma's international isolation deepened, China assumed an increasingly important role. It became Myanmar's principal aid donor, arms supplier and source of consumer goods, and delayed the passage of UN resolutions that were strongly critical of the SLORC's violations of human rights. In May 1997 an agreement was reached to establish a trade route through Myanmar to provide the Chinese province of Yunnan with access to the Indian Ocean. In the same year the Chinese Government signed a 30-year agreement with Myanmar that allowed for more than 200 Chinese fishing boats to operate in Myanma waters; the agreement was widely perceived as an indication of increasing Chinese influence in Myanmar. Furthermore, China announced the construction in Myanmar of two liquefied petroleum gas plants in October 2000 and also of a dry dock in February 2001. In December 2001 the Chinese President, Jiang Zemin, travelled to Myanmar, becoming the first Chinese Head of State to visit the country since 1985. Before his arrival the Government announced that it had ordered the release of more than 200 Chinese prisoners as a gesture of goodwill. Following successful discussions, the two Governments signed a series of bilateral agreements intended to enhance co-operative ties. It was reported that China had offered Myanmar US $100m. in aid and investment, although this was thought to be linked to Chinese demands that the ruling junta increase its efforts to eradicate the drug trade between the two countries.

Japan and the member states of ASEAN were anxious to halt Myanmar's excessive dependence on China for aid and trade. Myanmar, in its turn, applied to join ASEAN (which maintained a policy of 'constructive engagement' in relation to Myanmar) in an attempt to end its isolation, accelerate economic growth and gain protection from Western criticism of its internal affairs. In July 1994 Myanmar was invited to attend the annual meeting of ASEAN ministers responsible for foreign affairs, and in July 1995 it signed the organization's founding Treaty of Amity and Co-operation, a precursor to full membership. In July 1996 Myanmar was granted observer status, and in July 1997 the country was admitted as a full member of the organization. In May 1996 Myanmar joined the ASEAN Regional Forum (ARF, see p. 157) and in May 2000 the country hosted a high-level meeting of the economic ministers of the ASEAN member countries; the meeting, which was also attended by ministers from the People's Republic of China, Japan and the Republic of Korea, attracted strong criticism from the NLD. Myanmar enjoyed particularly cordial relations with Indonesia, and the military regime aspired to Indonesia's internationally accepted political system, in which the dominant role of the armed forces was enshrined in the Constitution. ASEAN links were strengthened by official visits from the Prime Minister of Cambodia, Hun Sen, in February 2000, and the Vietnamese Minister of Foreign Affairs, Nguyen Dy Nien, in October of the same year. In January 2001 Dr Mahathir Mohamad, Prime Minister of Malaysia and an integral figure in gaining entry for Myanmar into ASEAN, visited Yangon. Gen. Than Shwe and Gen. Khin Nyunt paid a reciprocal visit in September. Mahathir visited the country again in August 2002.

In the late 1990s bilateral relations between Myanmar and Thailand were rather less cordial than previously, with the Thai Government advocating a more limited 'flexible engagement' with Myanmar, in place of the ASEAN policy of 'constructive engagement' formerly endorsed by the country. Relations between the two countries were placed under some strain in late 1999 when a group of armed Myanma student activists, styled the Vigorous Burmese Student Warriors, seized control of the Myanma embassy in Bangkok in early October, demanding the release of all political prisoners in Myanmar and the opening of a dialogue between the military Goverment and the opposition. All 89 hostages were released by the activists within 24 hours, in exchange for the Thai Government's provision of helicopter transport to the Thai–Myanma border. The Thai Government's release of the perpetrators angered the ruling junta in Myanmar, and Myanmar closed its border with Thailand immediately after the incident. The border was re-opened to commerce in late November, although relations between the two countries remained strained. In January 2000 Thai troops shot dead 10 armed Myanma rebels who had taken control of a hospital in Ratchaburi, holding hundreds of people hostage. The rebels, who were reported by some sources to be linked to the Kayin insurgent group, God's Army, had issued several demands, including that the shelling of their base on the Thai–Myanma border by the Thai military be halted, that co-operation between the Thai and Myanma armies against the Kayins should cease, and that Kayin tribespeople be allowed to seek refuge in Thailand. Whilst the Thai Government denied reports that the perpetrators had been summarily executed after handing over their weapons, the brutal resolution of the incident was praised by the military Government in Myanmar.

There was renewed tension on the Thai–Myanma border in October 2000 when a Thai soldier was killed and two others were injured. It was unclear whether the clash was with Myanma troops or a faction allied to the Government. Tension was further heightened in November as 2,000 Myanma troops were deployed along the border, in preparation for an offensive against the KNU. In January 2001 it was reported that a Thai F-16 fighter aircraft had intruded into Myanma airspace, prompting the Government to announce the building of air defence systems along the border. Another border transgression occurred in February, when five Myanma soldiers were arrested by the Thai Border Patrol Police (BPP). The soldiers claimed that they were searching for food, whereas the BPP believed them to be gathering intelligence on Thai positions. On the previous day an offensive had been launched against the KNU, involving 300 Myanma troops, of whom five were killed. In mid-February there was a major incursion into Thai territory by some 200 Myanma troops, in pursuit of 100 SSA rebels. The troops clashed with Thai soldiers and occupied a hill that was within Thai territory for two days. At least two Thai villagers were killed, and officially 14 Myanma soldiers and two civilians also died. A cease-fire was signed, but this did not prevent Myanmar from ordering all SPDC troops on the border to be placed on full combat-ready status. By the end of February Thailand had detained 40 Myanma nationals for spying, according to Myanma figures, while the SPDC accused Thailand of providing support to the SSA.

In May 2001 Thai-Myanma relations deteriorated further when the Thai Government lodged a formal protest over an incident in which members of the DKBA had allegedly attacked a military unit situated in a Thai border village, causing the deaths of three civilians. A further protest was made several days later when the UWSA captured a hill believed to lie within Thai territory; the hill was later recaptured by Thai troops. In response, the Myanma Government demanded the withdrawal of Thai troops from 35 border outposts and claimed that the Thai army had launched air strikes into its territory, an accusation denied by the Thai authorities. The situation was further exacerbated by the publication of an article in a Myanma newspaper which Thailand claimed was insulting to its monarchy. In June Thai Prime Minister Thaksin Shinawatra arrived in Yangon for discussions which defused the tensions, although the two sides failed to reach any firm agreement as to how they would overcome the problems affecting their relations. In the following month the Thai Minister of Defence, Chavalit Yongchaiyudh, visited Myanmar and agreed to work with the SPDC to aid the forced repatriation of refugees on the Thai–Myanma border. In September Gen. Khin Nyunt made a three-day trip to Thailand, which was seen by many to constitute a starting point for a new era of improved bilateral relations. In January 2002 a joint Thai-Myanma commission (meeting for the first time since 1999) agreed to establish a task force to assist in the repatriation of illegal workers. In February the Thai Minister of Foreign Affairs, Surakiart Sathirathai, visited Yangon. During his stay both countries agreed to co-operate in controlling the cross-border drugs trade.

In mid-2002 relations with Thailand deteriorated sharply when fighting broke out on the border between government troops, allied with the UWSA, and the SSA. It was alleged that Thai troops had fired shells into the country, in the belief that the fighting had encroached upon Thai territory. In response, the Myanma Government accused Thailand of lending its support to the SSA. The joint border was closed shortly afterwards as tensions escalated. Border incursions continued as the bilateral relationship worsened. In August Surakiart Sathirathai met with leaders of the SPDC in an attempt to defuse the tensions; the border subsequently reopened in October. Relations continued to improve, owing in large part to the adaptation of a policy of 'soft engagement' by the Thai Government and, in early 2003, the two countries signed an unprecedented agreement pledging that future military exercises would be conducted at a suitable distance from the border.

In early 2004, in a reflection of the improved bilateral relationship, Myanmar announced that it was to award Thailand fishing concessions in its waters for one year. Fishing rights had been terminated in May 2001 following tensions on the joint border. A second 'Friendship Bridge' linking the two countries was also scheduled to open in April of that year.

In October 2002 the Australian Minister of Foreign Affairs, Alexander Downer, arrived in Myanmar; he was the most senior Australian politician to have visited the country for 20 years. During his stay he met with senior members of the SPDC and with Aung San Suu Kyi. However, following his departure Suu Kyi reportedly claimed that she would prefer Australia to lend its support to the international sanctions against the country rather than attempt to engage with its leaders.

Despite the killing of three Indian soldiers in a clash with Myanma troops in October 2000, relations between the two countries subsequently improved. Gen. Maung Aye paid a seven-day visit to India in November 2000, meeting both the country's President and Prime Minister. In mid-February 2001 India's Minister of External Affairs, Jaswant Singh, visited Myanmar, the first Indian cabinet minister to do so since the SLORC's assumption of power in 1988. While there, Singh officially opened the Tamu–Kalewa highway, a road built by India at a cost of US $22m. in order to increase bilateral trade with Myanmar. In January 2003 Minister of Foreign Affairs U Win Aung paid a visit to India, during which he met with the Prime Minister and several cabinet ministers. The two Governments agreed to hold regular consultations and to co-operate in counter-terrorism activities.

Following the release of Suu Kyi from house arrest in July 1995, Japan resumed substantial economic aid to Myanmar, which had been halted in 1988. In November 1999 the Japanese Prime Minister met with Senior Gen. Than Shwe during an ASEAN summit meeting in Manila; the meeting was the first

between the leader of a major world power and a senior member of the military Government since the junta's suppression of the democratic opposition in 1988. In April 2001 Japan accelerated its policy of engagement, promising a US $28m. aid programme intended to facilitate the upgrading of a hydroelectric power plant in Kayah (see Economic Affairs). The renewal of aid to the country was widely perceived to be a political gesture intended to reward the SPDC for its efforts to reach a settlement with the NLD. The international community criticized Japan's decision to resume aid as being premature in the light of Myanmar's failure to end forced labour and other human rights abuses in the country. In June 2003, following the junta's reimprisonment of Suu Kyi in May of that year, the Japanese Government suspended all economic aid to Myanmar. However, in early 2004 it was announced that Japan was to resume aid, having been satisfied that the release of some political prisoners by the SPDC constituted adequate progress towards democracy in the country.

In July 1996, as repression increased, Suu Kyi for the first time urged the imposition of international economic sanctions against Myanmar. From March 1997 the EU withdrew Myanmar's special trading status, in response to concerns over Myanmar's human rights record; later that year a meeting scheduled to take place in November between the EU and ASEAN was cancelled by the EU, owing to its objection to the representation of Myanmar at the talks. In early 1999 a further meeting between the EU and ASEAN, scheduled to be held in February, was postponed indefinitely as a result of continued disagreement between the two organizations regarding the proposed representation of Myanmar. However, an agreement was subsequently reached by the two sides to allow Myanmar to take a 'passive role' in the Joint Co-operation Committee meeting between the EU and ASEAN scheduled to take place in May. The SPDC became more open to the development of external relations when it allowed an EU delegation to visit Myanmar and hold talks with Suu Kyi in January 2001. Despite this, the EU extended its sanctions against Myanmar for a further six months in April 2001, owing to the human rights situation. However, in October the EU announced that it had decided to ease its sanctions. After Razali Ismail's fourth visit to Myanmar in November 2001, plans for a US $16m. HIV/AIDS prevention programme were mooted. Several countries, particularly Japan and the EU, indicated that they would be willing to support a carefully monitored international aid programme, and it was hoped that the prospect of the resumption of limited aid would encourage the Government to release more political prisoners. In January 2003 the Myanma Deputy Minister of Foreign Affairs, Khin Maung Win, was permitted to attend an EU-ASEAN summit meeting for the first time since Myanmar's suspension from the meetings in 1997. However, in April the EU elected to extend its sanctions against the country and to increase the list of SPDC officials subject to visa sanctions and 'freezing' of their assets. In early 2004 the EU remained under pressure further to expand economic sanctions against Myanmar following the imprisonment of Suu Kyi in May 2003.

In September 1999, meanwhile, a diplomatic dispute began between Myanmar and the United Kingdom after British consular staff were refused permission to visit two Britons in detention in Myanmar for their separate involvement in pro-democracy protest action. The British Government expressed its grave concern over their treatment. One of the two Britons was released in November. The second detainee, James Mawdsley, who had received a prison sentence of 17 years for entering the country illegally and carrying pro-democracy leaflets, was released in October 2000, following international pressure; he confirmed that he had been beaten heavily while in captivity.

In May 1997 the USA imposed trade sanctions in protest at persistent and large-scale repression by the SLORC. The sanctions prohibited further investment in Myanmar, but did not affect existing US interests in the country. In July 1997, at a ministerial meeting that followed the ASEAN conference, the US Secretary of State, Madeleine Albright, denounced Myanmar publicly for its poor human rights record and the country's lack of progress towards democracy. During 1998 the USA criticized the military junta in Myanmar for its treatment of Suu Kyi and also demanded the release of hundreds of political prisoners. In March 1999 Albright publicly criticized the regime for taking insufficient action to combat the production of and trade in narcotics within Myanmar. The USA showed its support for the SPDC-NLD talks with a visit by a senior State Department official to Suu Kyi in February 2001.

However, whilst welcoming the discussions, the US Government renewed its sanctions later in the year. In December pro-democracy activists in Myanmar accused the USA of neglecting their cause after a reappraisal of its foreign policy in the wake of the terrorist attacks on the country in September 2001 (see the chapter on the USA). They claimed that the US Government had moderated its criticism of the ruling military junta on the grounds that it suspected the international terrorist network, al-Qa'ida, had a presence in the country. In February 2002 a report issued by the US Government offered the prospect of an easing of sanctions, but only if the military junta released all remaining political prisoners and made further tangible progress towards democracy. However, following the detention of Aung San Suu Kyi in May 2003, in July the US President approved the Burmese Freedom and Democracy Act, already passed by Congress, banning all imports from Myanmar for three years and extending visa sanctions already imposed on SPDC officials.

In November 1998 the SPDC strongly denied claims made by the UN that the Myanma Government was responsible for the widespread abuse of human rights within the country. However, a report published in August by the International Labour Organization (ILO, see p. 86), following an investigation into the alleged use of forced labour and the suppression of trade unions in Myanmar, found the use of forced labour to be 'pervasive' throughout the whole country, and accused the military regime of using beatings, torture, rape and murder in the exaction of its forced labour policy, constituting a 'gross denial of human rights'. In June 1999 a resolution condemning Myanmar for its widespread use of forced labour was adopted by the member countries of the ILO, and the country was barred from participating in any ILO activities. (In the same month the ruling junta was accused by the human rights organization, Amnesty International, of perpetrating widespread abuses against ethnic minority groups.) Following the failure of the military Government to carry out the recommendations made by the ILO Commission of Inquiry in 1998 after the organization's initial investigation, in March 2000 the governing body of the ILO recommended that at its meeting in June the International Labour Conference take action to secure compliance by the ruling junta with the ILO's recommendations. In a statement issued in late March, the SPDC categorically rejected the governing body's decision and recommendations. Despite the Government's assurance in November 2000 that it would accept ILO monitors to verify the cessation of forced labour practices, the UN labour body voted to proceed with sanctions against Myanmar. This was the first time such action, the strongest available to the ILO, had been undertaken in the organization's 81-year history. The ILO subsequently requested its members to review their relations with Myanmar and to adopt sanctions. China, India, Malaysia and Russia voted against the action.

In September 2001 an ILO contingent arrived in Myanmar for a three-week visit intended to ascertain whether the military junta had honoured its promise to bring about the abolition of forced labour. In November the ILO issued a report concluding that, while some progress had been made, the practice was still endemic in many parts of the country. It recommended that a permanent ILO presence be established in Myanmar to monitor continued efforts to end forced labour in the region; discussions as to how this could be implemented headed the agenda during a further visit by the ILO in February 2002. The ILO delegation, however, was not permitted to see the NLD leader, Suu Kyi, during its visit and, upon departure, the head of the delegation expressed disappointment at the lack of co-operation it had received from the Myanma authorities. Despite this, in March the ILO agreed to establish a liaison office in the country and, in October, an ILO mission visited the country to assist further in the development of good labour practices. In early 2004, following a visit by an ILO envoy, the SPDC agreed to allow ILO representatives to work freely towards the elimination of forced labour practices in the country.

In October 1999 the UN Secretary-General's Special Envoy for Myanmar, Alvaro de Soto, arrived in the country to attempt, for the fifth time, to promote a dialogue between the military Government and the NLD; de Soto's efforts were, however, fruitless. In April 2000 de Soto was replaced as Special Envoy for Myanmar by a Malaysian diplomat, Razali Ismail, who subsequently arranged the secret dialogue between Suu Kyi and Lt-Gen. Khin Nyunt in October. In November the UN human rights envoy to Myanmar, Rajsoomer Lallah, resigned from his position, citing lack of financial and administrative assistance.

Lallah had previously produced a damning report of Myanmar's human rights situation, but had not been granted a visa throughout his four-year term. His successor, Dr Paulo Sérgio Pinheiro, was able to visit Myanmar in April 2001, within six months of taking office. He returned for a further visit in October, but was criticized by the NLD for his failure to spend enough time consulting with local communities. His visit had to be curtailed for reasons of ill health. In February 2002 Pinheiro visited the country for a third time and held further discussions with senior members of the SPDC and with Suu Kyi and other political prisoners. The Government released 11 political prisoners during his stay and, upon leaving, he declared his visit to have been a success. In October Pinheiro travelled to the country again; during his time there he investigated allegations, made by several human rights groups, that members of the Myanma armed forces routinely raped ethnic women along the border with Thailand. He also met with Suu Kyi. In March 2003 he paid a further visit to the country but curtailed his visit, having discovered a hidden microphone in a room where he was interviewing NLD prisoners. He later urged the SPDC to release all remaining political prisoners and enter into a serious dialogue with the opposition.

In May 1999 the ICRC, which had withdrawn from Myanmar in 1995 but reopened its office there in October 1998, regained permission from the ruling junta to visit a limited number of prisons in the country. Despite having been initially critical of the ICRC for reaching an agreement with the SPDC, Suu Kyi was reported subsequently to have expressed her support for the Committee's work with political prisoners. The ICRC sent a delegation to the country in July 2003, in order to ascertain that Suu Kyi was in good health following her recent imprisonment by the SPDC.

In July 2001 Minister of Foreign Affairs Win Aung travelled to Russia in order to finalize arrangements for the construction of Myanmar's first nuclear research reactor. In January 2002 the Government officially confirmed that it planned to build a reactor with Russian assistance.

Government

Following the military coup of September 1988, all state organs, including the People's Assembly, the State Council and the Council of Ministers, were abolished by the State Law and Order Restoration Council (SLORC), and the country was placed under martial law. Legislative elections took place in May 1990, but the SLORC subsequently announced that the opposition-dominated elected body was a Constituent Assembly, which was accorded no legislative power. During September 1992 a night curfew, imposed in 1988, and two martial law decrees, in force for three years, were revoked. A ban remained, however, on gatherings of more than five people. In early 1993 a National Convention, comprising members of the SLORC and representatives of the opposition parties, met to draft a new constitution; discussions continued until March 1996, when the National Convention was adjourned. In November 1997 the ruling military junta announced the dissolution of the SLORC and its replacement by the newly created State Peace and Development Council (SPDC). In August 2003 the SPDC announced its intention to reconvene the National Convention, which had remained in recess since 1996, in order that proceedings for the drafting of a new constitution could begin.

Defence

Myanmar maintains a policy of neutrality and has no external defence treaties. The armed forces are largely engaged in internal security duties. In August 2003 the armed services totalled about 488,000 men, of whom a reported 350,000 were in the army, 16,000 in the navy and 15,000 in the air force. Paramilitary forces included the People's Police Force of 72,000 men and the People's Militia of 35,000 men. In 2003 the defence budget was an estimated US $1,500m.

Economic Affairs

In 1986, according to estimates by the World Bank, Myanmar's gross national income (GNI), measured at average 1984–86 prices, was US $7,450m., equivalent to $200 per head. In 1990–2002, it was estimated, the population increased at an annual average rate of 1.6%. According to the Asian Development Bank (ADB), Myanmar's gross domestic product (GDP) increased, in real terms, by an annual average of 7.2% between 1990/91 and 2000/01 (years ending 31 March). Real GDP growth was officially declared to be 13.7% in 2000/01 and 11.1% in 2001/02.

However, according to the IMF, GDP increased by 6.2% in the former year.

According to the ADB, agriculture (including forestry and fishing) contributed an estimated 57.2% of GDP in 2001/02. The sector engaged an estimated 69.9% of the employed labour force in the previous year. Rice is the staple crop, and has traditionally been among Myanmar's principal export commodities. Exports of rice and rice products provided 21.6% of total export earnings in 1994/95; however, the proportion had declined to 4.4% by 2001/02. In 2003 the Government announced plans intended to liberalize the rice trade. However, in January 2004 it banned the export of rice for six months, a ban that resulted in significant overproduction and a consequent decline in domestic rice prices. In 2001/02 pulses and beans accounted for 11.1% of total exports. Other crops include sugar cane, groundnuts, maize, sesame seed, tobacco and rubber. Myanmar is one of the largest sources of illicit opium in the world, and it has been speculated that the Government is involved in its export. In 2003, according to a survey conducted by the UN Office on Drugs and Crime (see p. 41), Myanmar was the world's second biggest producer of opium, behind Afghanistan. However, ongoing government efforts to eradicate illicit poppy cultivation were achieving some success, reflected by an overall decline in opium production in 2003. The fishing sector is also important. Sales of teak and other hardwood provided 11.0% of total export revenue in 2001/02. (Teak is frequently felled illegally and smuggled across the border into Thailand.) Between 1990/91 and 2000/01, according to the ADB, the real GDP of the agricultural sector increased by an annual average of 5.8%. Annual agricultural GDP growth measured 11.5% in 1999/2000 and 11.0% in 2000/01.

Industry (including mining, manufacturing, construction and utilities) provided an estimated 10.5% of GDP in 2001/02, according to the ADB. The industrial sector engaged 12.2% of the employed labour force (excluding activities not adequately defined) in 1997/98. Between 1990/91 and 2000/01, according to the ADB, industrial GDP increased by an annual average of 10.7%. Industrial GDP growth measured 13.8% in 1999/2000 and 21.3% in 2000/01.

Mining and quarrying contributed an estimated 0.5% of GDP in 2001/02 and engaged 0.7% of the employed labour force in 1997/98. Production of crude petroleum decreased steadily from 1980, and from 1988 Myanmar was obliged to import petroleum. Significant onshore and offshore discoveries of natural gas and petroleum have resulted from exploration and production-sharing agreements with foreign companies, the first of which was signed in 1989. Other important minerals that are commercially exploited include tin, zinc, copper, tungsten, coal, lead, jade, gemstones, silver and gold; however, some of Myanmar's potentially lucrative mineral resources remain largely unexploited. According to the ADB, the GDP of the mining sector increased by an annual average of 18.3% between 1990/91 and 2000/01. Growth in the GDP of the mining sector measured 36.3% in 1999/2000 and 28.0% in 2000/01.

Manufacturing contributed an estimated 7.8% of GDP in 2001/02 and engaged 9.2% of the employed labour force in 1997/98. The most important branches are food and beverage processing, the production of industrial raw materials (cement, plywood and fertilizers), petroleum refining and textiles. The sector is adversely affected by shortages of electricity and the high price of machinery and spare parts. From mid-2003 a US ban on imports from Myanmar had a serious impact upon the textile sector; textiles and garments had previously constituted the majority of Myanmar's exports to the USA. The real GDP of the manufacturing sector increased, according to the ADB, at an average rate of 8.4% per year between 1990/91 and 2000/01. Manufacturing GDP rose by 14.5% in 1999/2000 and by 23.0% in 2000/01.

Energy is derived principally from natural gas, which accounted for 57.0% of electricity production in 2000; petroleum contributed 6.1% and hydroelectric power 36.9%. In January 2002 the Government announced that its third Five-Year Plan would give priority to the construction of three hydropower plants, in order to accelerate the development of the country's industrial sector. Imports of mineral fuels, lubricants, etc. accounted for 20.9% of total imports in 2001/02.

The services sector contributed 32.4% of GDP in 2001/02 and engaged 20.8% of the employed labour force in 1997/98. Tourism revenue increased substantially over the period 1992–95, and became the country's second largest source of foreign exchange in 1995/96. In 2001 tourist arrivals reached 204,862, while

revenue totalled approximately US $45m. in that year. Following the terrorist attack on the Indonesian island of Bali in October 2002 (see the chapter on Indonesia), the number of tourists visiting Myanmar increased substantially; it was believed that the country was perceived to be a safer destination than others in the region. According to the ADB, the GDP of the services sector increased by an average of 7.3% per year between 1990/91 and 2000/01. GDP growth in the sector measured 9.2% in 1999/2000 and 13.4% in 2000/01.

In 2001 Myanmar recorded a visible trade deficit of US $271.1m., and there was a deficit of $308.5m. on the current account of the balance of payments. In 2002 the principal sources of imports were the People's Republic of China (which supplied 21.8% of the total) and Singapore (20.1%); other major suppliers were Thailand, the Republic of Korea and Malaysia. The principal market for exports (31.7%) was Thailand; other significant purchasers were the USA (13.2%), India and the People's Republic of China. Illegal trade is widespread, and was estimated to be equivalent to 50% of official trade in 1995/96. The principal imports in 2001/02 were machinery and transport equipment, basic manufactures and mineral fuels and lubricants. The principal exports in that year were pulses and beans, teak and other hardwood and rice and rice products.

In the financial year ending 31 March 2000 there was a budgetary deficit of 1,580m. kyats, equivalent to 0.07% of GDP (according to the IMF). Myanmar's external debt at the end of 2001 totalled US $5,670m., of which $5,007m. was long-term public debt; in that year the cost of servicing external debt was equivalent to 3.1% of exports of goods and services. The annual rate of inflation averaged 11.9% in 1998–2002. Prices declined by 0.2% in 2000, but increased by 21.2% in 2001 and by 57.0% in 2002, according to the ADB. The number of registered unemployed persons in 1997/98 was equivalent to 2.5% of the labour force.

Myanmar is a member of the UN Economic and Social Commission for Asia and the Pacific (ESCAP, see p. 31), the Asian Development Bank (see p. 151) and the Colombo Plan (see p. 359), which promote economic development in the region. In July 1997 Myanmar acceded to the Association of South East Asian Nations (ASEAN, see p. 154). Myanmar was granted a 10-year period from 1 January 1998 to comply with the tariff reductions (to between 0% and 5%) required under the ASEAN Free Trade Area (AFTA), which was formally established on 1 January 2002.

Following the limited liberalization of Myanmar's centrally planned economy in 1988, the country began to attract foreign investment and to develop a small private sector. However, foreign investment was severely limited by international criticism of continued violations of human rights (culminating in the imposition of US sanctions in May 1997 and the decision of the European Union (EU) to revoke Myanmar's special trading privileges), inadequate infrastructure and widespread corruption. Consumer boycotts in the USA and Europe of companies investing in Myanmar led to the withdrawal from the country of several large investors. Myanmar was also affected by the regional economic crisis of 1997–98. The slow progress towards liberalization achieved since 1988 began to be reversed. Thus, from the late 1990s Myanmar was effectively sustained by a 'parallel' economy, mainly comprising unofficial border trade with the People's Republic of China, Thailand and India. The currency continued to depreciate sharply, and by September 2002 the kyat had declined to a low of 1,150 to the US dollar. The official exchange rate, meanwhile, remained at about six kyats to the dollar, having been fixed at the same level for nearly 40 years. In 2001 the seemingly more liberal stance shown by the SPDC began to mitigate international attitudes towards Myanmar, especially in Asia. In April Japan agreed to offer US $28m. in bilateral aid to Myanmar, for the purpose of the rehabilitation of a hydroelectric dam. In March 2001 the Government implemented its third Five-Year Plan. The previous plan had, according to the SPDC, achieved an average annual growth rate of 8.4%. The plan beginning in 2001 projected average annual GDP growth rates in excess of 8% until 2005/06. The main aims of the plan were: to promote the establishment of agro-based industries; to develop the power and energy sectors; to expand the agriculture, meat and fish sectors in order to meet local demand and provide a surplus for export; to establish forest reserves; to extend the health and education sectors; and to develop the rural areas. In November 2001 a report released by the ADB stressed that the Government needed to implement a wide range of reforms if Myanmar's prospects for growth were to improve. It warned that the junta's policy of funding its annual budget deficit through an expansion of credit from the country's central bank was unsustainable in the long term. In early 2003 the country's private banking sector experienced a crisis when the failure of several financial services groups to pay investors led to panic withdrawals from the country's 20 private banks. The Government was forced to intervene, imposing withdrawal limits and providing financial assistance to the banks that were most severely affected. In May 2003, following the rearrest of Suu Kyi, Myanmar's economic prospects deteriorated further. Japan, previously Myanmar's most important foreign donor, announced the suspension of economic aid, and the USA and the EU both strengthened their sanctions against the country, with the USA effectively banning all imports from Myanmar. The ongoing effect of the sanctions, combined with the junta's inconsistent agricultural policies and a dramatic increase in inflation, contributed to the continuing downturn in the economy in 2003. In March 2004 Japan announced that it intended to resume aid donations to the country, apparently owing to the release of several political prisoners earlier in the year. However, Myanmar's economic performance continued to depend in the long term upon an improvement in the country's political situation.

Education

Education is provided free of charge, where available, and is compulsory at primary level. Primary education begins at five years of age and lasts for five years. Primary enrolment was equivalent to 100% of children in the relevant age-group in 1995. Secondary education, beginning at 10 years of age, lasts for a further six years, comprising a first cycle of four years and a second of two years. In 1995 enrolment at secondary schools was equivalent to 32% of children in the relevant age-group. In 1994 total enrolment at tertiary level was equivalent to 5.4% of the relevant age-group (males 4.2%; females 6.7%). Emphasis is placed on vocational and technical training.

Current expenditure on education by the central Government in 2000/01 was 31,345m. kyats, representing 14.2% of total expenditure.

Public Holidays

2004: 3 January* (Kayin New Year), 4 January (Independence Day), 12 February (Union Day), 2 March (Peasants' Day, anniversary of the 1962 coup), 5 March* (Full Moon of Tabaung), 27 March (Armed Forces' Day), 13–16 April* (Maha Thingyan—Water Festival), 17 April* (Myanma New Year), 1 May (Workers' Day), 3 May* (Full Moon of Kason), 1 July* (Full Moon of Waso and beginning of Buddhist Lent), 19 July (Martyrs' Day), 28 October* (Full Moon of Thadingyut and end of Buddhist Lent), 12 November* (Deepavali), 26 November* (Tazaungdaing Festival), 6 December* (National Day), 25 December (Christmas Day).

2005: 4 January (Independence Day), 12 February (Union Day), 24 February* (Full Moon of Tabaung), 2 March (Peasants' Day, anniversary of the 1962 coup), 27 March (Armed Forces' Day), 13–16 April* (Maha Thingyan—Water Festival), 17 April* (Myanma New Year), 24 April* (Full Moon of Kason), 1 May (Workers' Day), 21 May* (Full Moon of Waso and beginning of Buddhist Lent), 19 July (Martyrs' Day), 12 October* (Full Moon of Thadingyut and end of Buddhist Lent), 1 November* (Deepavali), 14 November* (Tazaungdaing Festival), 6 December* (National Day), 23 December* (Kayin New Year), 25 December (Christmas Day).

* A number of holidays depend on lunar sightings.

Weights and Measures

The imperial system is in force.

Statistical Survey

Source (unless otherwise stated): Ministry of National Planning and Economic Development, 653–691 Merchant St, Yangon; tel. (1) 272009; fax (1) 282101.

Area and Population

AREA, POPULATION AND DENSITY

Area (sq km)	676,552*
Population (census results)	
31 March 1973	28,885,867
31 March 1983†	
Males	17,507,837
Females	17,798,352
Total	35,306,189
Population (UN estimates at mid-year)‡	
2000	47,544,000
2001	48,205,000
2002	48,852,000
Density (per sq km) at mid-2002	72.2

* 261,218 sq miles.
† Figures exclude adjustment for underenumeration. Also excluded are 7,716 Myanma citizens (5,704 males; 2,012 females) abroad.
‡ Source: UN, *World Population Prospects: The 2002 Revision.*

PRINCIPAL TOWNS
(population at census of 31 March 1983)

Yangon (Rangoon)	2,513,023	Pathein (Bassein)	144,096
Mandalay	532,949	Taunggyi	108,231
Mawlamyine (Moulmein)	219,961	Sittwe (Akyab)	107,621
Bago (Pegu)	150,528	Manywa	106,843

Source: UN, *Demographic Yearbook.*

Mid-2001 (UN estimate, incl. suburbs): Yangon 4,504,000 (Source: UN, *World Urbanization Prospects: The 2001 Revision*).

BIRTHS AND DEATHS
(UN estimates, annual averages)

	1985–90	1990–95	1995–2000
Birth rate (per 1,000)	31.3	29.9	26.5
Death rate (per 1,000)	13.3	12.3	11.5

Source: UN, *World Population Prospects: The 2002 Revision.*

Birth rate (2001): 23.8 per 1,000 (Source: UN, *Statistical Yearbook for Asia and the Pacific*).

Death rate (2001): 6.2 per 1,000 (Source: UN, *Statistical Yearbook for Asia and the Pacific*).

Expectation of life (WHO estimates, years at birth): 58.9 (males 56.2; females 61.8) in 2002 (Source: WHO, *World Health Report*).

EMPLOYMENT
(estimates, '000 persons aged 15 to 59 years)

	1995/96	1996/97	1997/98
Agriculture, hunting, forestry and fishing	11,848	11,960	12,093
Mining and quarrying	116	132	121
Manufacturing	1,481	1,573	1,666
Electricity, gas and water	19	21	26
Construction	354	378	400
Trade, restaurants and hotels	1,715	1,746	1,781
Transport, storage and communications	441	470	495
Community, social and personal services (excl. government)	563	577	597
Administration and other services	776	835	888
Activities not adequately defined	274	272	270
Total employed	17,587	17,964	18,359

Unemployed ('000 persons aged 18 years and over): 425.3 registered in 1998/99.

Source: mainly UN, *Statistical Yearbook for Asia and the Pacific.*

Health and Welfare

KEY INDICATORS

Total fertility rate (children per woman, 2002).	2.9
Under-5 mortality rate (per 1,000 live births, 2001)	109
HIV/AIDS (% of persons aged 15–49, 1999).	1.99
Physicians (per 1,000 head, 1999)	0.30
Hospital beds (per 1,000 head, 1999)	0.30
Health expenditure (2001): US $ per head (PPP)	26
Health expenditure (2001): % of GDP	2.1
Health expenditure (2001): public (% of total)	17.8
Access to water (% of persons, 2000).	68
Access to sanitation (% of persons, 2000)	46
Human Development Index (2001): ranking	131
Human Development Index (2001): value	0.549

For sources and definitions, see explanatory note on p. vi.

Agriculture

PRINCIPAL CROPS
('000 metric tons)

	2000	2001	2002
Wheat	94	96	100†
Rice (paddy)	21,324	21,914	22,780†
Maize	365	532	660†
Millet	169	159	160*
Potatoes	255	319	319*
Sweet potatoes	38	57	57*
Cassava	77	97	97*
Sugar cane	5,449	5,894	6,333*
Other sugar crops*	242	242	242
Dry beans	1,285	1,467	1,467*
Dry peas	28	100†	100*
Chick-peas	84	119	119*
Dry cow peas	77	152†	152*
Pigeon peas	189	300†	300*
Soybeans (Soya beans)	99	110	115†
Groundnuts (in shell)	634	731	700†
Sunflower seed	160	268	265†
Sesame seed	296	426	225†
Seed cotton	176	153	168†
Coconuts	225	275†	275†
Dry onions	476	593	593*
Garlic	67	82	82*
Other vegetables (incl. melons)*	2,800	2,850	2,850*
Plantains	354	400*	400*
Other fruits (excl. melons)*	955	965	965
Areca (Betel) nuts	39	51	51*
Tea (made)	19†	19†	19*
Pimento and allspice*	40	40	40
Tobacco (leaves)	47	48	48*
Jute	33	42	42*
Cotton (lint)	59	51	56†
Natural rubber	27	36	35*

* FAO estimate(s).
† Unofficial figure.

Source: FAO.

LIVESTOCK
('000 head, year ending September)

	2000	2001	2002
Horses*	120	120	120
Cattle	10,982	11,243	11,551
Buffaloes	2,441	2,502	2,552
Pigs	3,974	4,261	4,499
Sheep	390	403	432
Goats	1,392	1,439	1,542
Chickens	44,755	55,080	57,128
Ducks	6,173	6,000*	6,100*
Geese*	500	500	500

* FAO estimate(s).

Source: FAO.

LIVESTOCK PRODUCTS
('000 metric tons)

	2000	2001	2002
Beef and veal*	102.0	104.4	108.0
Buffalo meat*	20.4	20.9	22.1
Goat meat	7.0	7.3	7.8
Pig meat*	112.9	121.0	122.7
Poultry meat	198.8	220.3	256.6
Cows' milk	498.4	510.0	525.1
Buffaloes' milk	111.0	113.7	116.0
Goats' milk	7.3	7.5	8.1
Butter*	11.0	11.2	11.6
Cheese*	31.3	32.0	32.9
Hen eggs	77.5	85.9	101.7
Other poultry eggs	10.1	10.5	11.0
Cattle hides (fresh)*	21.5	22.0	22.0

* FAO estimates.

Source: FAO.

Forestry

ROUNDWOOD REMOVALS
('000 cubic metres, excl. bark)

	2000	2001	2002
Sawlogs, veneer logs and logs for sleepers	2,337	2,662	2,662*
Other industrial wood	1,275	1,300	2,877
Fuel wood	34,471	35,403	35,403*
Total	38,083	39,365	40,942

* FAO estimate.

Source: FAO.

SAWNWOOD PRODUCTION
('000 cubic metres, incl. railway sleepers)

	2000	2001	2002
Total (all broadleaved)	545	671	381

Source: FAO.

Fishing

('000 metric tons, live weight, year ending 31 March)

	1998/99	1999/2000	2000/01
Capture	919.4	1,069.7	1,166.9
Freshwater fishes	159.7	189.7	235.4
Marine fishes	731.7	849.0	900.5
Aquaculture	91.1	98.9	121.3
Roho labeo	86.2	93.9	115.8
Total catch	1,010.5	1,168.6	1,288.1

Source: FAO, *Yearbook of Fishery Statistics*.

Mining

(metric tons, unless otherwise indicated)

	2000	2001	2002*
Coal and lignite	52,811	41,736	57,000
Crude petroleum ('000 barrels) .	3,538	4,696	4,920
Natural gas (million cu m)† . .	8,477§	8,804	8,500
Copper ore‡	26,711	25,900	28,000
Lead ore*‡	1,200	900	500
Zinc ore‡	437	467	350
Tin concentrates‡	212	212	190
Chromium ore (gross weight)* . .	3,000	3,000	3,000
Tungsten concentrates‡ . . .	74	49	30
Silver ore (kilograms)‡ . . .	2,457	1,804	1,500
Gold ore (kilograms)‡§ . . .	250*	200*	200
Feldspar*§	12,000	10,000	10,000
Barite (Barytes)	30,370	31,015	18,000
Salt (unrefined, excl. brine)* . .	35,000	35,000	35,000
Gypsum (crude)	48,067	64,609	113,000
Rubies, sapphires and spinel ('000 metric carats)§	8,351	8,630	2,760
Jade	8,318	87	33

* Estimated production.
† Marketed production.
‡ Figures refer to the metal content of ores and concentrates (including mixed concentrates).
§ Twelve months beginning 1 April of year stated.

Source: US Geological Survey.

Industry

SELECTED PRODUCTS

('000 metric tons, unless otherwise indicated)

	1999	2000	2001
Raw sugar*	53	60	103
Refined sugar†	43	60	n.a.
Cigarettes (million)†	2,270	2,512	2,650
Cotton yarn†	4.8	5.7	5.5
Plywood ('000 cu m)	8	14	n.a.
Printing and writing paper . . .	16	17	20
Nitrogenous fertilizers‡	64	160	39
Petroleum refinery products ('000 barrels)§‖	5,605	5,536	5,286
Cement§	338,025	393,355	377,961
Tin—unwrought (metric tons)§ . .	149	212	212
Electric energy (million kWh, net)	4,558	5,028	n.a

Beer (hectolitres): 13,000 in 1994.

Woven cotton fabrics (million sq m): 16 in 1995.

* Data from FAO.
† Production by government-owned enterprises only.
‡ Production in terms of nitrogen during twelve months ending 30 June of stated year.
§ Twelve months beginning 1 April of year stated. Data from US Geological Survey.
‖ Figure includes gasoline, jet fuel, kerosene, diesel, distillate fuel oil and residual fuel oil.

Source (unless otherwise specified): UN, *Statistical Yearbook for Asia and the Pacific.*

Finance

CURRENCY AND EXCHANGE RATES

Monetary Units
100 pyas = 1 kyat.

Sterling, Dollar and Euro Equivalents (31 December 2003)
£1 sterling = 10.2189 kyats;
US $1 = 5.7259 kyats;
€1 = 7.2318 kyats;
1,000 kyats = £97.86 = $174.65 = €138.28.

Average Exchange Rate (kyats per US $)
2001   6.6841
2002   6.5734
2003   6.0764

Note: Since January 1975 the value of the kyat has been linked to the IMF's special drawing right (SDR). Since May 1977 the official exchange rate has been fixed at a mid-point of SDR 1 = 8.5085 kyats. On 1 June 1996 a new customs valuation exchange rate of US $1 = 100 kyats was introduced. In September 2001 the free market exchange rate was $1 = 450 kyats.

CENTRAL GOVERNMENT BUDGET

(million kyats, year ending 31 March)

Revenue*	1998/99	1999/2000	2000/01
Tax revenue	56,653	60,294	75,727
Taxes on income, profits and capital gains	20,515	21,169	26,140
Domestic taxes on goods and services	30,748	33,750	44,101
General sales, turnover or VAT .	22,720	24,576	32,961
Taxes on international trade and transactions	5,390	5,375	5,486
Other revenue	59,334	62,390	58,324
Entrepreneurial and property income	43,689	47,269	41,144
Administrative fees, nonindustrial and incidental sales	15,645	15,121	17,180
Capital revenue	79	211	257
Total	**116,066**	**122,895**	**134,308**

Expenditure†	1998/99	1999/2000	2000/01
Current expenditure	63,095	81,608	134,068
General public services, incl. public order	15,011	23,562	20,435
Defence	39,627	45,040	63,453
Education	9,572	12,132	31,345
Health	3,233	4,144	7,388
Social security and welfare . .	1,599	2,436	4,993
Recreational, cultural and religious affairs	2,114	2,013	2,668
Economic affairs and services .	41,015	46,641	66,132
Agriculture, forestry, fishing and hunting	17,918	19,479	38,447
Transportation and communication	22,161	26,279	25,917
Other current expenditure . .	11,588	17,332	24,475
Capital expenditure	60,969	71,889	87,187
Total	**124,064**	**153,497**	**221,255**

* Excluding grants received from abroad (million kyats): 524 in 1998/99; 221 in 1999/2000; 242 in 2000/01.
† Excluding lending minus repayments (million kyats): −528 in 1998/99; 63 in 1999/2000; −127 in 2000/01.

Source: IMF, *Government Finance Statistics Yearbook.*

INTERNATIONAL RESERVES

(US $ million at 31 December)

	2000	2001	2002
Gold*	10.6	10.2	11.0
IMF special drawing rights . .	0.1	0.6	0.1
Foreign exchange	222.8	399.9	469.9
Total	**233.5**	**410.7**	**481.0**

* Valued at SDR 35 per troy ounce.

Source: IMF, *International Financial Statistics.*

MONEY SUPPLY
(million kyats at 31 December)

	2000	2001	2002
Currency outside banks	344,728	494,521	718,633
Demand deposits at deposit money banks	119,746	206,349	290,520
Total money (incl. others) . .	464,968	701,153	1,009,471

Source: IMF, *International Financial Statistics.*

COST OF LIVING
(Consumer Price Index for Yangon; base: 1990 = 100)

	1997	1998	1999
Food (incl. beverages)	548.2	834.6	997.0
Fuel and light	457.3	590.2	632.3
Clothing (incl. footwear). . .	366.0	620.3	700.4
Rent	405.1	568.9	624.1
All items (incl. others) . . .	498.1	754.6	893.4

All items (base: 1990 = 100): 151.7 in 2000; 183.8 in 2001; 288.6 in 2002.
Source: ILO.

NATIONAL ACCOUNTS
(million kyats at current prices, year ending 31 March)
National Income and Product

	1996/97	1997/98	1998/99
Domestic factor incomes. . . .	773,940	1,087,997	1,534,089
Consumption of fixed capital . .	18,040	21,557	25,907
Gross domestic product (GDP) at factor cost	791,980	1,109,554	1,559,996
Indirect taxes, *less* subsidies . .	—	—	—
GDP in purchasers' values . .	791,980	1,109,554	1,559,996
Net factor income from abroad . .	−116	−69	−220
Gross national product . . .	791,864	1,109,485	1,559,776
Less Consumption of fixed capital	18,040	21,557	25,907
National income in market prices	773,824	1,087,928	1,533,869

Source: UN, *National Accounts Statistics.*

Expenditure on the Gross Domestic Product

	1997/98	1998/99	1999/2000
Final consumption expenditure .	987,513	1,419,709	1,906,136
Increase in stocks	−10,276	−7,604	48,325
Gross fixed capital formation . .	150,240	206,912	241,694
Total domestic expenditure. .	1,127,477	1,619,017	2,196,155
Exports of goods and services . .	6,290	7,700	9,394
Less Imports of goods and services	−14,258	−16,941	−15,248
GDP in purchasers' values . .	1,119,509	1,609,776	2,190,301
GDP at constant 1985/86 prices	75,123	79,460	88,134

Source: IMF, *International Financial Statistics.*

Gross Domestic Product by Economic Activity

	1999/2000	2000/01	2001/02
Agriculture, hunting, forestry and fishing	1,312,285	1,461,150	2,013,713
Mining and quarrying	10,842	15,032	16,119
Manufacturing	143,244	182,897	273,894
Electricity, gas and water . . .	2,558	3,444	3,125
Construction	40,425	46,044	76,668
Wholesale and retail trade . . .	524,403	613,686	855,864
Transport, storage and communications	105,669	153,371	188,776
Finance	2,215	2,641	3,231
Government services.	16,505	39,354	44,261
Other services	32,174	35,114	47,864
GDP in purchasers' values .	2,190,320	2,552,733	3,523,515

Source: Asian Development Bank, *Key Indicators of Developing Asian and Pacific Countries.*

BALANCE OF PAYMENTS
(US $ million)

	1999	2000	2001
Exports of goods f.o.b.	1,293.9	1,661.6	2,316.9
Imports of goods f.o.b.	−2,181.3	−2,165.4	−2,587.9
Trade balance	−887.3	−503.8	−271.1
Exports of services	512.2	477.9	423.6
Imports of services	−291.1	−328.1	−380.2
Balance on goods and services.	−666.3	−354.0	−227.7
Other income received . . .	51.6	35.5	35.9
Other income paid	−54.6	−168.8	−402.6
Balance on goods, services and income	−669.2	−487.3	−594.3
Current transfers received . . .	384.8	289.7	298.5
Current transfers paid	−0.3	−14.1	−12.8
Current balance	−284.7	−211.7	−308.5
Direct investment from abroad. .	255.6	258.3	210.3
Other investment liabilities . .	−4.4	−45.4	188.8
Net errors and omissions . . .	−12.4	−24.5	89.3
Overall balance	−45.9	−23.4	179.8

Source: IMF, *International Financial Statistics.*

External Trade

PRINCIPAL COMMODITIES*
(distribution by SITC, million kyats, year ending 31 March)

Imports c.i.f.	1999/2000	2000/01	2001/02
Food and live animals . . .	620	586	838
Mineral fuels, lubricants, etc. .	1,654	1,145	3,839
Animal and vegetable oils, fats and waxes	488	412	253
Chemicals and related products	1,871	1,924	1,787
Basic manufactures	4,125	4,401	4,548
Machinery and transport equipment.	4,868	3,754	5,110
Miscellaneous manufactured articles.	643	1,000	726
Total (incl. others)	16,265	15,073	18,378

Exports f.o.b.†	1999/2000	2000/01	2001/02
Food and live animals . . .	2,237	3,206	3,774
Dried beans, peas, etc. (shelled)	1,179	1,658	1,898
Crude materials (inedible) except fuels	1,819	1,401	2,750
Teak and other hardwood . . .	925	803	1,880
Basic manufactures	602	1,240	168
Miscellaneous manufactured articles.	176	1,570	104
Total (incl. others)	8,947	12,736	17,131

* Totals include, but distribution by commodities excludes, border trade, mainly with the People's Republic of China, Thailand and Bangladesh.
† Excluding re-exports.

Source: Asian Development Bank, *Key Indicators of Developing Asian and Pacific Countries.*

PRINCIPAL TRADING PARTNERS
(US $ million)

Imports	2000	2001	2002
China, People's Republic . . .	546.1	547.1	626.1
Germany	44.7	18.4	20.3
Hong Kong	97.9	70.1	74.8
India	52.9	58.4	63.3
Indonesia	71.2	70.9	64.4
Japan	215.6	205.3	131.8
Korea, Republic	318.3	255.3	277.0
Malaysia	254.2	216.7	217.4
Singapore	479.7	465.6	576.6
Thailand	554.7	390.5	355.9
Total (incl. others)	3,039.2	2,667.6	2,871.4

Exports	2000	2001	2002
China, People's Republic . . .	113.5	122.0	130.2
France	71.3	72.1	78.4
Germany	77.8	100.3	79.9
India	162.9	179.2	194.5
Japan	108.4	92.8	97.5
Malaysia	63.2	71.1	72.3
Singapore	99.8	102.1	97.3
Thailand	233.0	735.4	831.2
United Kingdom	67.3	87.4	87.8
USA	442.7	456.2	345.4
Total (incl. others)	1,995.5	2,644.0	2,622.0

Source: Asian Development Bank, *Key Indicators of Developing Asian and Pacific Countries.*

Transport

RAILWAYS
(traffic, million)

	1998	1999	2000
Passenger-kilometres . . .	3,948	4,112	4,451
Freight ton-kilometres . . .	988	1,043	1,222

Source: UN, *Statistical Yearbook.*

ROAD TRAFFIC
(registered motor vehicles at 31 March)

	1994	1995	1996
Passenger cars	119,126	131,953	151,934
Trucks	39,939	36,728	42,828
Buses	19,183	14,624	15,639
Motorcycles	71,929	82,591	85,821
Others	8,377	6,251	6,611
Total	258,554	272,147	302,833

Source: Department of Road Transport Administration.

Passenger cars: 177,900 in 1997; 177,600 in 1998; 171,100 in 1999; 173,900 in 2000 (Source: UN, *Statistical Yearbook*).

Commercial vehicles: 74,800 in 1997; 75,900 in 1998; 83,400 in 1999; 90,400 in 2000 (Source: UN, *Statistical Yearbook*).

INLAND WATERWAYS
(traffic by state-owned vessels)

	1993/94	1994/95*	1995/96†
Passengers carried ('000) . . .	36,003	26,582	24,491
Passenger-miles (million) . . .	617	531	544
Freight carried ('000 metric tons) .	3,172	3,194	3,158
Freight ton-miles (million) . . .	353	346	351

* Provisional.
† Estimates.

SHIPPING
Merchant Fleet
(registered at 31 December)

	2000	2001	2002
Number of vessels	123	124	124
Displacement (grt)	445,583	379,819	402,159

Source: Lloyd's Register-Fairplay, *World Fleet Statistics.*

International Sea-Borne Traffic
(state-owned vessels)

	1993/94	1994/95*	1995/96†
Passengers carried ('000) . . .	69	77	60
Passenger-miles (million) . . .	23	26	20
Freight carried ('000 metric tons) .	773	1,213	1,030
Freight ton-miles (million) . . .	2,655	2,765	2,807

* Provisional.
† Estimates.

CIVIL AVIATION
(traffic on scheduled services)

	1997	1998	1999
Kilometres flown (million) . . .	9	8	9
Passengers carried ('000) . . .	575	522	537
Passenger-km (million)	385	345	355
Total ton-km (million)	46	40	40

Source: UN, *Statistical Yearbook.*

Tourism

TOURIST ARRIVALS BY COUNTRY OF NATIONALITY

	1999	2000	2001
Australia	3,642	4,120	4,442
China, People's Republic . . .	12,148	14,336	16,788
France	13,594	13,313	12,461
Germany	9,039	9,920	11,450
India	5,083	5,605	5,572
Italy	6,925	6,852	6,618
Japan	25,319	21,930	20,118
Korea, Republic	5,885	7,423	7,581
Malaysia	7,583	9,938	11,296
Singapore	11,074	11,645	9,939
Taiwan	32,977	32,098	26,020
Thailand	19,392	19,070	17,123
United Kingdom	9,267	9,020	8,424
USA	10,270	12,669	13,524
Total (incl. others)	198,210	207,665	204,862

Source: World Tourism Organization, *Yearbook of Tourism Statistics.*

Tourism receipts (US $ million): 35 in 1999; 42 in 2000; 45 in 2001 (Source: World Bank).

Communications Media

	1999	2000	2001
Television receivers ('000 in use) .	323.3	344.3	n.a.
Telephones ('000 main lines in use)	249.1	266.2	295.2
Facsimile machines (number in use)	2,540	n.a.	n.a.
Mobile cellular telephones ('000 subscribers).	11.4	29.3	13.8
Personal computers ('000 in use) .	50	50	55
Internet users ('000)	0.5	1.0	10.0

Book production (1999): 227 titles.

Newspapers (1996): 5 dailies (average circulation 449,000).

Radio receivers (1999): 3,157,000 in use.

Sources: International Telecommunication Union; UNESCO, *Statistical Yearbook*; UN, *Statistical Yearbook*.

Education

(provisional, 1994/95)

	Institutions	Teachers	Students
Primary schools*	35,856	169,748	5,711,202
Middle schools	2,058	53,859	1,390,065
High schools	858	18,045	389,438
Vocational schools	86	1,847	21,343
Teacher training	17	615	4,031
Higher education	45	6,246	247,348
Universities	6	2,901	62,098

* Excluding 1,152 monastic primary schools with an enrolment of 45,360.

1997/98 (provisional): *Primary:* Institutions 35,877, Teachers 167,134, Students ('000) 5,145.4; *General Secondary:* Institutions 2,091, Teachers 56,955, Students ('000) 1,545.6; *Tertiary:* Institutions 923, Teachers 17,089, Students ('000) 385.3 (Source: UN, *Statistical Yearbook for Asia and the Pacific*).

Adult literacy rate (UNESCO estimates): 85.0% (males 89.1%; females 81.0%) in 2001 (Source: UN Development Programme, *Human Development Report*).

Directory

The Constitution

On 18 September 1988 a military junta, the State Law and Order Restoration Council (SLORC), assumed power and abolished all state organs created under the Constitution of 3 January 1974. The country was placed under martial law. The state organs were superseded by the SLORC at all levels with the Division, Township and Village State Law and Order Restoration Councils. The SLORC announced that a new constitution was to be drafted by the 485-member Constituent Assembly that was elected in May 1990. In early 1993 a National Convention, comprising members of the SLORC and representatives of opposition parties, met to draft a new constitution; however, the Convention was adjourned in March 1996 and remained in recess in early 2004. In November 1997 the SLORC was dissolved and replaced by the newly formed State Peace and Development Council (SPDC). In August 2003 the SPDC announced that it planned to reconvene the National Convention in 2004 in order that it could commence the drafting of a new constitution.

The Government

HEAD OF STATE

Chairman of the State Peace and Development Council: Field Marshal THAN SHWE (took office as Head of State 23 April 1992).

STATE PEACE AND DEVELOPMENT COUNCIL
(April 2004)

Chairman: Field Marshal THAN SHWE.

Vice-Chairman: Dep. Senior Gen. MAUNG AYE.

First Secretary: Lt-Gen. SOE WIN.

Second Secretary: Lt-Gen. THEIN SEIN.

Third Secretary: (vacant).

Other members: Rear-Adm. KYI MIN, Lt-Gen. KYAW THAN, Lt-Gen. AUNG HTWE, Lt-Gen. YE MYINT, Lt-Gen. KHIN MAUNG THAN, Maj.-Gen. KYAW WIN, Maj.-Gen. THURA SHWE MANN, Maj.-Gen. MYINT AUNG, Lt-Gen. MAUNG BO, Maj.-Gen. THIHA THURA TIN AUNG MYINT OO, Lt-Gen. TIN AYE.

CABINET
(April 2004)

Prime Minister: Gen. KHIN NYUNT.

Minister of Defence: Field Marshal THAN SHWE.

Minister of Military Affairs: Maj.-Gen. THIHA THURA TIN AUNG MYINT.

Minister of Agriculture and Irrigation: (vacant).

Minister of Industry (No. 1): (vacant).

Minister of Industry (No. 2): Maj.-Gen. SAW LWIN.

Minister of Foreign Affairs: U WIN AUNG.

Minister of National Planning and Economic Development: U SOE THA.

Minister of Transport: Maj.-Gen. HLA MYINT SWE.

Minister of Labour: U TIN WIN.

Minister of Culture: Maj.-Gen. KYI AUNG.

Minister of Co-operatives: Maj.-Gen. HTAY OO.

Minister of Rail Transportation: Maj.-Gen. AUNG MIN.

Minister of Energy: Brig.-Gen. LUN THI.

Minister of Education: U THAN AUNG.

Minister of Health: Dr KYAW MYINT.

Minister of Commerce: Brig.-Gen. PYI SONE.

Minister of Communications, Posts and Telegraphs and Minister of Hotels and Tourism: Brig.-Gen. THEIN ZAW.

Minister of Finance and Revenue: Maj.-Gen. HLA TUN.

Minister of Religious Affairs: Brig.-Gen. THURA MYINT MAUNG.

Minister of Construction: Maj.-Gen. SAW TUN.

Minister of Science and Technology: U THAUNG.

Minister of Immigration and Population and Minister of Social Welfare, Relief and Resettlement: Maj.-Gen. SEIN HTWA.

Minister of Information: Brig.-Gen. KYAW HSAN.

Minister of Progress of Border Areas, National Races and Development Affairs: Col THEIN NYUNT.

Minister of Electric Power: Maj.-Gen. TIN HTUT.

Minister of Sports: Brig.-Gen. THURA AYE MYINT.

Minister of Forestry: Brig.-Gen. THEIN AUNG.

Minister of Home Affairs: Col TIN HLAING.

Minister of Mines: Brig.-Gen. OHN MYINT.

Minister of Livestock and Fisheries: Brig.-Gen. MAUNG MAUNG THEIN.

Minister at the Office of the Prime Minister: U THAN SHWE, U KO LAY, Maj.-Gen. THEIN SHWE.

MINISTRIES

Office of the Chairman of the State Peace and Development Council: 15–16 Windermere Park, Yangon; tel. (1) 282445.

Prime Minister's Office: Minister's Office, Theinbyu St, Botahtaung Township, Yangon; tel. (1) 283742.

Ministry of Agriculture and Irrigation: Thiri Mingala Lane, Kaba Aye Pagoda Rd, Yangon; tel. (1) 665587; fax (1) 664493.

Ministry of Commerce: 228–240 Strand Rd, Yangon; tel. (1) 287034; fax (1) 280679; e-mail com@mptmail.net.mm; internet www .myanmar.com/Ministry/commerce.

Ministry of Communications, Posts and Telegraphs: 361 Pyay Rd, nr Hanthawaddy Circus, Sanchaung Township, Yangon; tel. (1) 515034; internet www.mcpt.gov.mm.

Ministry of Construction: 39 Nawaday St, Dagon Township, Yangon; tel. (1) 283938; fax (1) 289531.

Ministry of Co-operatives: 259–263 Bogyoke Aung San St, Yangon; tel. (1) 277096; fax (1) 287919.

Ministry of Culture: 131 Kaba Aye Pagoda Rd, Bahan Township, Yangon; tel. (1) 543235; fax (1) 283794; internet www.myanmar .com/Ministry/culture.

Ministry of Defence: Ahlanpya Phaya St, Yangon; tel. (1) 281611.

Ministry of Education: Theinbyu St, Botahtaung Township, Yangon; tel. (1) 285588; fax (1) 285480.

Ministry of Electric Power: 197–199 Lower Kyimyindaing Rd, Ahlone Township, Yangon; tel. (1) 229366; fax (1) 221006.

Ministry of Energy: 23 Pyay Rd, Yangon; tel. (1) 221060; fax (1) 222964; e-mail myanmoe@mptmail.net.mm; internet www.energy .gov.mm.

Ministry of Finance and Revenue: 26(A) Setmu Rd, Yankin Township, Yangon; tel. (1) 284763; internet www.myanmar.com/ Ministry/finance.

Ministry of Foreign Affairs: Pyay Rd, Dagon Township, Yangon; tel. (1) 222844; fax (1) 222950; e-mail mofa.aung@mptmail.net.mm; internet www.myanmar.com/Ministry/mofa.

Ministry of Forestry: Thirimingala Lane, Kaba Aye Pagoda Rd, Yangon; tel. (1) 289184; fax (1) 664459; internet www.myanmar .com/Ministry/Forest.

Ministry of Health: Theinbyu St, Botahtaung Township, Yangon; tel. (1) 277334; fax (1) 282834; internet www.myanmar.com/ Ministry/health.

Ministry of Home Affairs: cnr of Saya San St and No. 1 Industrial St, Yankin Township, Yangon; tel. (1) 549208; internet www .myanmar.com/Ministry/Moha.

Ministry of Hotels and Tourism: 77–91 Sule Pagoda Rd, Kyauk-tada Township, Yangon; tel. (1) 282705; fax (1) 287871; e-mail mtt .mht@mptmail.net.mm; internet www.myanmar.com/Ministry/ Hotel_Tour.

Ministry of Immigration and Population: cnr of Mahabandoola Rd and Theinbyu St, Botahtaung Township, Yangon; tel. (1) 249090; internet www.myanmar.com/Ministry/imm&popu.

Ministry of Industry (No. I): 192 Kaba Aye Pagoda Rd, Yangon; tel. (1) 566066; internet www.myanmar.com/Ministry/MOI-1.

Ministry of Industry (No. II): 56 Kaba Aye Pagoda Rd, Yankin Township, Yangon; tel. (1) 666134; fax (1) 666135; e-mail dmip@ mptmail.net.mm; internet www.myanmar.com/Ministry/moi2.

Ministry of Information: 365–367 Bo Sung Kyaw St, Yangon; tel. (1) 245631; fax (1) 289274.

Ministry of Labour: Theinbyu St, Botahtaung Township, Yangon; tel. (1) 278320; fax (1) 256185.

Ministry of Livestock and Fisheries: Theinbyu St, Botahtaung Township, Yangon; tel. (1) 280398; fax (1) 289711.

Ministry of Military Affairs: Yangon.

Ministry of Mines: 90 Kanbe Rd, Yankin Township, Yangon; tel. (1) 577316; fax (1) 577455; internet www.myanmar.com/Ministry/ Mines.

Ministry of National Planning and Economic Development: 653–691 Merchant St, Pabedan Township, Yangon; tel. (1) 241918; fax (1) 282101.

Ministry of Progress of Border Areas, National Races and Development Affairs: Minister's Office, Theinbyu St, Botahtaung Township, Yangon; tel. (1) 280032; fax (1) 285257.

Ministry of Rail Transportation: 88 Theinbyu St, Yangon; tel. (1) 292769.

Ministry of Religious Affairs: Kaba Aye Pagoda Precinct, Mayan-gone Township, Yangon; tel. (1) 665620; fax (1) 665728; internet www.myanmar.com/Ministry/religious.

Ministry of Science and Technology: 6 Kaba Aye Pagoda Rd, Yankin Township, Yangon; tel. (1) 667639; fax (1) 651026.

Ministry of Social Welfare, Relief and Resettlement: Theinbyu St, Botahtaung Township, Yangon; tel. (1) 665697; fax (1) 650002; e-mail social-wel-myan@mptmail.net.mm; internet www.myanmar .com/Ministry/social-welfare.

Ministry of Sports: Minister's Office, Theinbyu St, Botahtaung Township, Yangon; tel. (1) 553958.

Ministry of Transport: 363–421 Merchant St, Botahtaung Town-ship, Yangon; tel. (1) 296815; fax (1) 296824; internet www .myanmar.com/Ministry/Transport.

Legislature

CONSTITUENT ASSEMBLY

Following the military coup of 18 September 1988, the 489-member Pyithu Hluttaw (People's Assembly), together with all other state organs, was abolished. A general election was held on 27 May 1990. It was subsequently announced, however, that the new body was to serve as a constituent assembly, responsible for the drafting of a new constitution, and that it was to have no legislative power. The next legislative election was provisionally scheduled for September 1997, but did not take place.

General Election, 27 May 1990

Party	% of Votes	Seats
National League for Democracy	59.9	392
Shan Nationalities League for Democracy	1.7	23
Arakan (Rakhine) League for Democracy	1.2	11
National Unity Party	21.2	10
Mon National Democratic Front	1.0	5
National Democratic Party for Human Rights	0.9	4
Chin National League for Democracy	0.4	3
Kachin State National Congress for Democracy	0.1	3
Party for National Democracy	0.5	3
Union Pa-O National Organization	0.3	3
Zomi National Congress		2
Naga Hill Regional Progressive Party		2
Kayah State Nationalities League for Democracy		2
Ta-ang (Palaung) National League for Democracy		2
Democratic Organization for Kayan National Unity		2
Democracy Party		1
Graduates' and Old Students' Democratic Association		1
Patriotic Old Comrades' League	12.8	1
Shan State Kokang Democratic Party		1
Union Danu League for Democracy Party		1
Kamans National League for Democracy		1
Mara People's Party		1
Union Nationals Democracy Party		1
Mro (or) Khami National Solidarity Organization		1
Lahu National Development Party		1
United League of Democratic Parties		1
Karen (Kayin) State National Organization		1
Independents		6
Total	**100.0**	**485**

Political Organizations

A total of 93 parties contested the general election of May 1990. By October 1995 the ruling military junta had deregistered all except nine political parties:

Kokang Democracy and Unity Party: Yangon.

Mro (or) Khami National Solidarity Organization: f. 1988; Leader U SAN THA AUNG.

National League for Democracy (NLD): 97B West Shwegondine Rd, Bahan Township, Yangon; f. 1988; initially known as the National United Front for Democracy, and subsequently as the League for Democracy; present name adopted in Sept. 1988; central exec. cttee of 10 mems; Gen. Sec. Daw AUNG SAN SUU KYI; Chair. U AUNG SHWE; Vice-Chair. U TIN OO, U KYI MAUNG.

National Unity Party (NUP): 93C Windermere Rd, Kamayut, Yangon; tel. (1) 278180; f. 1962 as the Burma Socialist Programme Party; sole legal political party until Sept. 1988, when present name was adopted; 15-mem. Cen. Exec. Cttee and 280-mem. Cen. Cttee; Chair. U THA KYAW; Jt Gen. Secs U TUN YI, U THAN TIN.

Shan Nationalities League for Democracy: f. 1988; Leader KHUN HTUN OO.

Shan State Kokang Democratic Party: 140 40 St, Kyauktada; f. 1988; Leader U YANKYIN MAW.

Union Karen (Kayin) League: Saw Toe Lane, Yangon.

Union Pa-O National Organization: f. 1988; Leader U SAN HLA.

Wa National Development Party: Byuhar St, Yangon.

The following parties contested the general election of March 1990 but subsequently had their legal status annulled:

Anti-Fascist People's Freedom League: Bo Aung Kyaw St, Bahan Township, Yangon; f. 1988; assumed name of wartime resistance movement which became Myanmar's major political force after independence; Chair. Bo KYAW NYUNT; Gen. Sec. CHO CHO KYAW NYEIN.

Democracy Party: f. 1988; comprises supporters of fmr Prime Minister U NU; Chair. U THU WAI; Vice-Chair. U KHUN YE NAUNG.

Democratic Front for National Reconstruction: Yangon; f. 1988; left-wing; Leader Thakin CHIT MAUNG.

Lahu National Development Party: f. 1988; deregistered 1994; Leader U DANIEL AUNG.

League for Democracy and Peace: 10 Wingaba Rd, Bahan Township, Yangon; f. 1988; Gen. Sec. U THEIN SEIN.

Party for National Democracy: Yangon; f. 1988; Chair. Dr SEIN WIN.

Union National Democracy Party (UNDP): 2–4 Shin Saw Pu Rd, Sanchaung Township, Yangon; f. 1988 by Brig.-Gen. AUNG GYI (fmr Chair. of the National League for Democracy); Chair. U KYAW MYINT LAY.

United League of Democratic Parties: 875 Compound 21, Ledauntkan St, Sa-Hsa Ward, Thingangyun Township, Yangon; f. 1989.

United Nationalities League for Democracy: Yangon; an alliance of parties representing non-Bamar nationalities; won a combined total of 65 seats at the 1990 election.

Other deregistered parties included the Arakan (Rakhine) League for Democracy, the Mon National Democratic Front, the National Democratic Party for Human Rights, the Chin National League for Democracy, the Kachin State National Congress for Democracy, the Zomi National Congress, the Naga Hill Regional Progressive Party, the Kayah State Nationalities League for Democracy, the Ta-ang (Palaung) National League for Democracy, the Democratic Organization for Kayan National Unity, the Graduates' and Old Students' Democratic Association, the Patriotic Old Comrades' League, the Union Danu League for Democracy, the Kamans National League for Democracy, the Mara People's Party and the Karen (Kayin) State National Organization.

The following groups are, or have been, in armed conflict with the Government:

Chin National Army: Chin State.

Chin National Front: f. 1988; forces trained by Kachin Independence Army 1989–91; first party congress 1993; conference in March 1996; carried out an active bombing campaign in 1996–97, mainly in the Chin State; Pres. THOMAS TANG NO.

Communist Party of Burma (CPB): f. 1939; reorg. 1946; operated clandestinely after 1948; participated after 1986 in jt military operations with sections of the NDF; in 1989 internal dissent resulted in the rebellion of about 80% of CPB members, mostly Wa hill tribesmen and Kokang Chinese; the CPB's military efficacy was thus completely destroyed; Chair. of Cen. Cttee Thakin BA THEIN TIN (exiled).

Democratic Alliance of Burma (DAB): Manerplaw; f. 1988; formed by members of the NDF to incorporate dissident students, monks and expatriates; Pres. Maj.-Gen. Bo MYA; Gen. Sec. U TIN MAUNG WIN; Remaining organizations include:

All-Burma Student Democratic Front (ABSDF): Dagwin; f. 1988; in 1990 split into two factions, under U Moe Thi Zun and U Naing Aung; the two factions reunited in 1993; Leader U NAING AUNG; Sec.-Gen. AUNG THU NYEIN.

Karen (Kayin) National Union (KNU): f. 1948; in process of negotiating peace agreement with SPDC in 2004; Chair. SAW BA THIN; Vice-Chair. Maj.-Gen. Bo MYA; Sec.-Gen. MAHN SHA; Military wing: **Karen (Kayin) National Liberation Army (KNLA)**; c. 6,000 troops; Chief of Staff Gen. TAMALABAW.

Karenni (Kayinni) National Progressive Party: agreement with the SLORC signed in March 1995 but subsequently collapsed; resumed fighting in June 1996; Chair. Gen. AUNG THAN LAY; Military wing: **Karenni (Kayinni) Revolutionary Army**.

God's Army: breakaway faction of the KNU; Leaders JOHNNY HTOO, LUTHER HTOO (surrendered to the Thai authorities in Jan. 2001).

National Democratic Front (NDF): f. 1975; aims to establish a federal union based on national self-determination; largely defunct.

National Socialist Council of Nagaland: Sagaing Division; comprises various factions.

Shan State Army (SSA): enlarged in Sept. 1997 through formal alliance between the following:

Shan State National Army (SSNA): Shan State; f. 1995; breakaway group from Mong Tai Army (MTA); Shan separatists; 5,000–6,000 troops; Leaders KARN YORD, YEE.

Shan State Peace Council (SSPC): fmrly Shan State Progressive Party; Pres. HSO HTEN; Gen. Sec. KARN YORD; Gen. Sec. KARN YORD; cease-fire agreement signed in Sept. 1989, but broken by SSA elements following establishment of above alliance in Sept. 1997; Military wing: original **Shan State Army** (5,000 men); Leaders SAI NONG, KAI HPA, PANG HPA.

Other MTA remnants also participated in the alliance.

Vigorous Burmese Student Warriors: f. 1999.

Most of the following groups have signed cease-fire agreements, or reached other means of accommodation, with the ruling military junta (the date given in parentheses indicates the month in which agreement with the junta was concluded):

Democratic Karen (Kayin) Buddhist Organization: Manerplaw; breakaway group from the KNU; Military wing: **Democratic Karen (Kayin) Buddhist Army**.

Kachin Democratic Army: (Jan. 1991); fmrly the 4th Brigade of the Kachin Independence Army; Leader U ZAW MAING.

Kachin Independence Organization (KIO): (Oct. 1993); Chair. U LAMON TU JAI; Military wing: **Kachin Independence Army**.

Karen (Kayin) Solidarity Organization (KSO): f. 1997; fmrly All Karen Solidarity and Regeneration Front; breakaway group from the KNU; 21-mem. exec. cttee; advocates nation-wide cease-fire and the settlement of all national problems through negotiations; Pres. SAW W. P. NI; Sec.-Gen. MAHN AUNG HTAY.

Karenni (Kayinni) National People's Liberation Front: (May 1994); Leader U TUN KYAW.

Kayan National Guard: (Feb. 1992).

Kayan New Land Party: (July 1994); Leader U THAN SOE NAING.

Myanmar National Democracy Alliance: (March 1989).

National Democracy Alliance Army: (June 1989).

New Democratic Army: Kachin; (Dec. 1989).

New Mon State Party: (June 1995); Chair. (vacant); Military wing: **Mon National Liberation Army**.

Palaung State Liberation Organization: (April 1991); Military wing: **Paulung State Liberation Army**; 7,000–8,000 men.

Pa-O National Organization: (Feb. 1991); Chair. AUNG KHAM HTI; Military wing: **Pa-O National Army**.

Shan State Nationalities Liberation Organization: (Oct. 1994); Chair. U THA KALEI.

United Wa State Party: (May 1989); fmrly part of the Communist Party of Burma; Military wing: **United Wa State Army** (10,000–15,000 men); Leaders CHAO NGI LAI, PAO YU CHANG.

Since 1991 the National Coalition Government of the Union of Burma, constituted by representatives elected in the general election of 1990, has served as a government-in-exile:

National Coalition Government of the Union of Burma (NCGUB): Washington Office, 1319 F St NW, Suite 303, Washington, DC 20004, USA; tel. (202) 639-0639; fax (202) 639-0638; e-mail ncgub@ncgub.net; internet www.ncgub.net; Prime Minister Dr SEIN WIN.

Diplomatic Representation

EMBASSIES IN MYANMAR

Australia: 88 Strand Rd, Yangon; tel. (1) 251810; fax (1) 246159; Ambassador PAUL GRIGSON.

Bangladesh: 11B Thanlwin Rd, Yangon; tel. (1) 515275; fax (1) 515273; e-mail bdootygn@mptmail.mm; Ambassador A. B. MANJOOR RAHIM.

Brunei: 51 Golden Valley, Bahan, Yangon; tel. (1) 510422; fax (1) 512854; Ambassador Pehin Datu PEKERMA Dato' Paduka Haji HUSSIN BIN Haji SULAIMAN.

Cambodia: 34 Kaba Aye Pagoda Rd, Yangon; tel. (1) 546157; fax (1) 546156; e-mail recyangon@mptmail.net.mm; Ambassador HUL PHANY.

China, People's Republic: 1 Pyidaungsu Yeiktha Rd, Yangon; tel. (1) 221281; fax (1) 227019; e-mail chinaemb_mm@mfa.gov.cn; Ambassador Li Jinjun.

Egypt: 81 Pyidaungsu Yeiktha Rd, Yangon; tel. (1) 222886; fax (1) 222865; Ambassador Mohamed El Meneissy.

France: 102 Pyidaungsu Yeiktha Rd, POB 858, Yangon; tel. (1) 212523; fax (1) 212527; Ambassador Jean-Michel Lacombe.

Germany: 32 Nat Mauk St, POB 12, Yangon; tel. (1) 548951; fax (1) 548899; e-mail post@botschaftrangun.net.mm; Ambassador Dr Klaus Wild.

India: 545–547 Merchant St, POB 751, Yangon; tel. (1) 243972; fax (1) 254086; e-mail amb.indembygn@mptmail.net.mm; Ambassador Rajiv Kumar Bhatia.

Indonesia: 100 Pyidaungsu Yeiktha Rd, POB 1401, Yangon; tel. (1) 254465; fax (1) 254468; e-mail kbriygn@indosat.net.id; Ambassador Wyoso Projowarsito.

Israel: 15 Khabaung St, Hlaing Township, Yangon; tel. (1) 515115; fax (1) 515116; e-mail yangon@israel.org; Ambassador Yaakov Avrahami Meron.

Italy: 3 Inya Myaing Rd, Golden Valley, Yangon; tel. (1) 527100; fax (1) 514565; e-mail ambitaly@ambitaly.net.mm; internet www.embassyofitaly-yangon.org; Ambassador Raffaele Miniero.

Japan: 100 Natmauk Rd, Yangon; tel. (1) 549644; fax (1) 549643; e-mail embassyofjapan@mptmail.net.mm; Ambassador Yuji Miyamoto.

Korea, Republic: 97 University Ave, Yangon; tel. (1) 515190; fax (1) 513286; e-mail hankuk@koremby.net.mm; Ambassador Lee Kyung-woo.

Laos: A1 Diplomatic Quarters, Franser Rd, Yangon; tel. (1) 222482; fax (1) 227446; Ambassador Chanthavy Bodhisane.

Malaysia: 882 Diplomatic Quarters, Pyidaungsu Yeiktha Rd, Yangon; tel. (1) 220249; fax (1) 221840; e-mail mwyangon@mweb.com.na; Ambassador Dato' Cheah Sam Kip.

Nepal: 16 Natmauk Yeiktha Rd, POB 84, Tamwe, Yangon; tel. (1) 545880; fax (1) 549803; e-mail rnembygn@datseco.net.mm; Ambassador Dibya Dev Bhatta.

Pakistan: A4 Diplomatic Quarters, Pyay Rd, Dagon Township, Yangon; tel. (1) 222881; fax (1) 221147; e-mail parepygn@myanmar.com.mm; Ambassador Yousuf Shah.

Philippines: 50 Saya San Rd, Bahan Township, Yangon; tel. (1) 558149; fax (1) 558154; e-mail phyangon@mptmail.net.mm; Ambassador Phoebe Abaya Gomez.

Russia: 38 Sagawa Rd, Yangon; tel. (1) 241955; fax (1) 241953; e-mail rusinmyan@mptmail.net.mm; Ambassador Gleb A. Ivashentsov.

Serbia and Montenegro: 114A Inya Rd, POB 943, Yangon; tel. (1) 515282; fax (1) 504274; e-mail yuamb@yangon.net.mm; Chargé d'affaires a.i. Vladimir Stamenović.

Singapore: 238 Dhamazedi Rd, Bahan Township, Yangon; tel. (1) 559001; fax (1) 559002; e-mail singemb@seygn.com.mm; internet www.mfa.gov.sg/yangon/; Ambassador Simon Tensing de Cruz.

Sri Lanka: 34 Taw Win Rd, POB 1150, Yangon; tel. (1) 222812; fax (1) 221509; e-mail srilankaemb@mpt.net.mm; Ambassador D. M. M. Ranaraja.

Thailand: 73 Manawhari St, Dagon Township, Yangon; tel. (1) 224647; fax (1) 225929; e-mail thaiygn@mfa.go.th; Ambassador Suphot Dhirakaosal.

United Kingdom: 80 Strand Rd, POB 638, Yangon; tel. (1) 370863; fax (1) 289566; e-mail chancery.Rangoon@fco.gov.uk; Ambassador Vicky Bowman.

USA: 581 Merchant St, POB 521, Yangon; tel. (1) 379880; fax (1) 256018; e-mail info.rangoon@state.gov; internet rangoon.usembassy.gov; Chargé d'affaires Carmen Maria Martinez.

Viet Nam: 317–319 U Wisara Rd, Sanchaung Township, Yangon; tel. (1) 524285; fax (1) 524658; e-mail vnembmyr@bertech.net.mm; Ambassador Pham Quang Khon.

Judicial System

A new judicial structure was established in March 1974. Its highest organ, composed of members of the People's Assembly, was the Council of People's Justices, which functioned as the central Court of Justice. Below this Council were the state, divisional, township, ward and village tract courts formed with members of local People's Councils. These arrangements ceased to operate following the imposition of military rule in September 1988, when a Supreme Court with five members was appointed. A chief justice, an attorney-

general and a deputy attorney-general were also appointed. In March 2003 a deputy chief justice, four more justices and two further deputy attorney-generals were appointed.

Office of the Supreme Court

101 Pansodan St, Kyauktada Township, Yangon; tel. (1) 280751.

Chief Justice: U Aung Toe.

Attorney-General: Aye Maung.

Religion

Freedom of religious belief and practice is guaranteed. In 1992 an estimated 87.2% of the population were Buddhists, 5.6% Christians, 3.6% Muslims, 1.0% Hindus and 2.6% animists or adherents of other religions.

BUDDHISM

State Sangha Maha Nayaka Committee: c/o Dept of Promotion and Propagation of the Sasana, Kaba Aye Pagoda Precinct, Mayangone Township, Yangon; tel. (1) 660759.

CHRISTIANITY

Myanmar Naing-ngan Khrityan Athin-dawmyar Kaung-si (Myanmar Council of Churches): Myanmar Ecumenical Sharing Centre, 601 Pyay Rd, University PO, Yangon 11041; tel. (1) 533957; fax (1) 296848; f. 1974 to succeed the Burma Christian Council; 13 mem. churches; Pres. Rev. Saw Mar Gay Gyi; Gen. Sec. Rt Rev. Smith N. Za Thawng.

The Roman Catholic Church

Myanmar comprises three archdioceses and nine dioceses. At 31 December 2002 an estimated 1.1% of the total population were adherents.

Catholic Bishops' Conference of Myanmar

292 Pyi Rd, POB 1080, Sanchaung PO, Yangon 11111; tel. (1) 525868; fax (1) 527198; e-mail clspcbcm@mptmail.net.mm.

f. 1982; Pres. Most Rev. Charles Maung Bo (Archbishop of Yangon).

Archbishop of Mandalay: Most Rev. Paul Zingtung Grawng, Archbishop's House, 82nd and 25th St, Mandalay 05071; tel. (2) 36369.

Archbishop of Taunggyi: Most Rev. Matthias U Shwe, Archbishop's Office, Bayint Naung Rd, Taunggyi 06011; tel. (81) 21689; fax (81) 22164; e-mail matthias@myanmar.com.mm.

Archbishop of Yangon: Most Rev. Charles Maung Bo, Archbishop's House, 289 Theinbyu St, Botataung, Yangon; tel. (1) 246710.

The Anglican Communion

Anglicans are adherents of the Church of the Province of Myanmar, comprising six dioceses. The Province was formed in February 1970, and contained an estimated 45,000 adherents in 1985.

Archbishop of Myanmar and Bishop of Yangon: Most Rev. Samuel San Si Htay, Bishopscourt, 140 Pyidaungsu Yeiktha Rd, Dagon PO (11191), Yangon; tel. (1) 285379; fax (1) 251405.

Protestant Churches

Lutheran Bethlehem Church: 181–183 Theinbyu St, Mingala Taung Nyunt PO 11221, POB 773, Yangon; tel. (1) 246585; Pres. Rev. Jenson Rajan Andrews.

Myanmar Baptist Convention: 143 Minye Kyawswa Rd, POB 506, Yangon; tel. (1) 223231; fax (1) 221465; e-mail mbc<mbc@mptmail.net.mm; f. 1865 as Burma Baptist Missionary Convention; present name adopted 1954; 550,104 mems (1994); Pres. Rev. U Tha Din; Gen. Sec. Rev. Dr Simon Pau Khan En.

Myanmar Methodist Church: Methodist Headquarters, 22 Signal Pagoda Rd, Yangon; Bishop Zothan Mawia.

Presbyterian Church of Myanmar: Synod Office, Falam, Chin State; 22,000 mems; Rev. Sun Kanglo.

Other denominations active in Myanmar include the **Lisu Christian Church** and the **Salvation Army**.

The Press

DAILIES

Botahtaung (The Vanguard): 22–30 Strand Rd, Botahtaung PO, POB 539, Yangon; tel. (1) 274310; daily; Myanmar.

Guardian: 392–396 Merchant St, Botahtaung PO, POB 1522, Yangon; tel. (1) 270150; daily; English.

Kyehmon (The Mirror): 77 52nd St, Dazundaung PO, POB 819, Yangon; tel. (1) 282777; daily; Myanmar.

Myanmar Alin (New Light of Myanmar): 58 Komin Kochin Rd, Bahan PO, POB 21, Yangon; tel. (1) 250777; f. 1963; fmrly Loktha Pyithu Nezin (Working People's Daily); organ of the SPDC; morning; Myanmar; Chief Editor U Soe Myint; circ. 400,000.

New Light of Myanmar: 22–30 Strand Rd, Yangon; tel. (1) 297028; internet www.myanmar.com/nlm; f. 1963; fmrly Working People's Daily; organ of the SPDC; morning; English; Chief Editor U Kyaw Min; circ. 14,000.

PERIODICALS

A Hla Thit (New Beauty): 46 90th St, Yangon; tel. (1) 287106; international news.

Dana Business Magazine: 72 8th Street, Lanmadaw Township, Yangon; tel. and fax (1) 224010; e-mail dana@mptmail.net.mm; economic; Editor-in-Chief William Chen.

Do Kyaung Tha: Myawaddy Press, 184 32nd St, Yangon; tel. (1) 274655; f. 1965; monthly; Myanmar and English; circ. 17,000.

Gita Padetha: Yangon; journal of Myanma Music Council; circ. 10,000.

Guardian Magazine: 392/396 Merchant St, Botahtaung PO, POB 1522, Yangon; tel. (1) 296510; f. 1953; nationalized 1964; monthly; English; literary; circ. 11,600.

Kyee Pwar Yay (Prosperity): 296 Bo Sun Pat St, Yangon; tel. (1) 278100; economic; Editor-in-Chief U Myat Khine.

Moethaukpan (Aurora): Myawaddy Press, 184 32nd St, Yangon; tel. (1) 274655; f. 1980; monthly; Myanmar and English; circ. 27,500.

Myanma Dana (Myanmar's Economy): 210A, 36th St, Kyauktada PO, Yangon; tel. (1) 284660; economic; Editor-in-Chief U Thiha Saw.

Myanmar Morning Post: Yangon; f. 1998; weekly; Chinese; news; circ. 5,000.

Myanmar Times & Business Review: Level 1, 5 Signal Pagoda Rd, Dagon Township, Yangon; tel. (1) 242711; fax (1) 242669; e-mail myanmartimes@mptmail.net.mm; internet www.myanmar.com/myanmartimes; f. 2000; Editor-in-Chief Ross Dunkley.

Myawaddy Journal: Myawaddy Press, 184 32nd St, Yangon; tel. (1) 274655; f. 1989; fortnightly; news; circ. 8,700.

Myawaddy Magazine: Myawaddy Press, 184 32nd St, Yangon; tel. (1) 274655; f. 1952; monthly; literary magazine; circ. 4,200.

Ngwetaryi Magazine: Myawaddy Press, 184 32nd St, Yangon; tel. (1) 274655; f. 1961; monthly; cultural; circ. 3,400.

Pyinnya Lawka Journal: 529 Merchant St, Yangon; tel. (1) 283611; publ. by Sarpay Beikman Management Board; quarterly; circ. 18,000.

Shwe Thwe: 529 Merchant St, Yangon; tel. (1) 283611; weekly; bilingual children's journal; publ. by Sarpay Beikman Management Board; circ. 100,000.

Taw Win Journal (Royal Journal): 149 37th St, Yangon; news; Editor-in-Chief Soe Thein.

Teza: Myawaddy Press, 184 32nd St, Yangon; tel. (1) 274655; f. 1965; monthly; English and Myanmar; pictorial publication for children; circ. 29,500.

Thwe Thauk Magazine: Myawaddy Press, 185 48th St, Yangon; f. 1946; monthly; literary.

Ya Nant Thit (New Fragrance): 186 39th St, Yangon; tel. (1) 276799; international news; Editor-in-Chief U Chit Win Mg.

NEWS AGENCIES

Myanmar News Agency (MNA): 212 Theinbyu Rd, Botahtaung, Yangon; tel. (1) 270893; f. 1963; govt-controlled; Chief Editors U Zaw Min Thein (domestic section), U Kyaw Min (external section).

Foreign Bureaux

Agence France-Presse (AFP) (France): 12L Pyithu Lane, 7th Mile, Yangon; tel. (1) 661069; Correspondent U Khin Maung Thwin.

Agenzia Nazionale Stampa Associata (ANSA) (Italy): POB 270, Yangon; tel. (1) 290039; fax (1) 290804; Rep. (vacant).

Associated Press (AP) (USA): 283 U Wisara Rd, Sanchaung PO 11111, Yangon; tel. (1) 527014; Rep. Aye Aye Win.

Xinhua (New China) News Agency (People's Republic of China): 105 Leeds Rd, Yangon; tel. (1) 221400; Correspondent Zhang Yuhfei.

Reuters (UK) and **UPI** (USA) are also represented in Myanmar.

Publishers

Hanthawaddy Press: 157 Bo Aung Gyaw St, Yangon; f. 1889; textbooks, multilingual dictionaries; Man. Editor U Zaw Win.

Knowledge Publishing House: 130 Bo Gyoke Aung San St, Yegyaw, Yangon; art, education, religion, politics and social sciences.

Kyipwaye Press: 84th St, Letsaigan, Mandalay; tel. (2) 21003; arts, travel, religion, fiction and children's.

Myawaddy Press: 184 32nd St, Yangon; tel. (1) 285996; journals and magazines; CEO U Thein Sein.

Sarpay Beikman Management Board: 529 Merchant St, Yangon; tel. (1) 283611; f. 1947; encyclopaedias, literature, fine arts and general; also magazines and translations; Chair. Aung Htay.

Shumawa Press: 146 West Wing, Bogyoke Aung San Market, Yangon; mechanical engineering.

Shwepyidan: 12A Haiaban, Yegwaw Quarter, Yangon; politics, religion, law.

Smart and Mookerdum: 221 Sule Pagoda Rd, Yangon; arts, cookery, popular science.

Thu Dhama Wadi Press: 55–56 Maung Khine St, POB 419, Yangon; f. 1903; religious; Propr U Tin Htoo; Man. U Pan Maung.

Government Publishing House

Printing and Publishing Enterprise: 228 Theinbyu St, Yangon; tel. (1) 294645; Man. Dir U Myint Thein.

PUBLISHERS' ASSOCIATION

Myanma Publishers' Union: 146 Bogyoke Market, Yangon.

Broadcasting and Communications

TELECOMMUNICATIONS

Posts and Telecommunications Department: Block 68, Ayeyar Wun Rd, South Dagon Township, Yangon; tel. (1) 591388; fax (1) 591383; e-mail dg.ptd@mptmail.net.mm; internet www.mcpt.gov.mm/ptd/; Dir-Gen. of Posts and Telecommunications Dept U Kyi Than.

Myanma Posts and Telecommunications (MPT): 43 Bo Aung Gyaw St, Kyauktada Township, Yangon; tel. (1) 297722; fax (1) 251911; internet www.mpt.net.mm; Man. Dir Col Maung Maung Tin.

BROADCASTING

Radio

Myanma TV and Radio Department (MTRD): 426 Pyay Rd, Kamayut 11041, Yangon; POB 1432, Yangon 11181; tel. (1) 531850; fax (1) 530211; radio transmissions began in 1937; broadcasts in Bamar, Arakanese (Rakhine), Shan, Karen (Kayin), Kachin, Kayah, Chin, Mon and English; Dir-Gen. U Kyi Lwin; Dir of Radio Broadcasting U Ko Ko Htway.

In 1992 the National Coalition Government of the Union of Burma (NCGUB) began broadcasting daily to Myanmar from Norway under the name Democratic Voice of Burma (DVB). In 1995 it was believed that the DVB was being operated by Myanma student activists from the Norway-Burma Council, without any formal control by the NCGUB.

Television

Myanma TV and Radio Department (MTRD): 426 Pyay Rd, Yangon; tel. (1) 531850; fax (1) 530211; f. 1946; colour television transmissions began in 1980; Dir-Gen. U Khin Maung Htay; Dir of Television Broadcasting U Phone Myint.

TV Myawaddy: Hmawbi, Hmawbi Township, Yangon; tel. (1) 620270; f. 1995; military broadcasting station transmitting programmes via satellite.

Finance

(cap. = capital; res = reserves; dep. = deposits; m. = million; brs = branches; amounts in kyats)

BANKING

In July 1990 new banking legislation was promulgated, reorganizing the operations of the Central Bank, establishing a state-owned development institution, the Myanma Agricultural and Rural Development Bank, and providing for the formation of private-sector banks and the opening of branches of foreign banks.

Central Bank

Central Bank of Myanmar: 26A Settmu Rd, POB 184, Yankin Township, Yangon; tel. (1) 543511; fax (1) 543621; e-mail cbm.ygn@ mptmail-net.mm; f. 1968; bank of issue; cap. 350m., dep. 13,545m.; Gov. U KYAW KYAW MAUNG; 37 brs.

State Banks

Myanma Economic Bank (MEB): 1–19 Sule Pagoda Rd, Yangon; tel. (1) 289345; fax (1) 283679; provides domestic banking network throughout the country; Man. Dir U KYAW KYAW.

Myanma Foreign Trade Bank: 80–86 Maha Bandoola Garden St, POB 203, Kyauktada Township, Yangon; tel. (1) 284911; fax (1) 289585; e-mail mftb-hoygn@mptmail-net.mm; f. 1976; cap. 110m., res 483.9m., dep. 2,425.9m. (March 1999); handles all foreign exchange and international banking transactions; Chair. U KO KO GYI; Sec. U TIN MAUNG AYE.

Development Banks

Myanma Agricultural and Rural Development Bank (MARDB): 1–7 cnr of Latha St and Kanna Rd, Yangon; tel. (1) 226734; f. 1953 as State Agricultural Bank, reconstituted as above 1990; state-owned; cap. 60.0m., dep. 615.6m. (Sept. 1993); Man. Dir U CHIT SWE.

Myanma Investment and Commercial Bank (MICB): 170/176 Bo Aung Kyaw St, Botataung Township, Yangon; tel. (1) 250509; fax (1) 281775; e-mail micb.hoygn@mpt-mail.net.mm; f. 1989; state-owned; cap. 400m., res 786m., dep. 7,035m. (March 2000); Chair. and Man. Dir U MYA THAN; 2 brs.

Private Banks

In 2003 a crisis in Myanmar's private banking sector forced the closure of six of the country's 20 private banks. Following government intervention, three subsequently reopened in early 2004, having been cleared of committing banking irregularities.

Asia Wealth Bank: 638 cnr of Maha Bandoola St and 22nd St, Latha Township, Yangon; tel. (1) 243700; fax (1) 245456; e-mail customer@awb.com.mm; internet www.awb.com.mm; Chair. WIN MAUNG; Vice-Chair. AIK HTUN; 38 brs.

Asian Yangon Bank Ltd: 319/321 Maha Bandoola St, Botataung Township, Yangon; tel. (1) 245825; fax (1) 245865; f. 1994 as Asian Yangon International Bank Ltd; name changed as above in 2000.

Co-operative Bank Ltd: 334–336 Kanna Rd, Yangon; tel. (1) 272641; fax (1) 283063; Gen. Man. U NYUNT HLAING.

First Private Bank Ltd (FPB): 619–621 Merchant St, Pabedan Township, Yangon; tel. (1) 289929; fax (1) 242320; e-mail fpb.hq@ mptmail.net.mm; f. 1992 as the first publicly-subscribed bank; fmrly the Commercial and Development Bank Ltd; provides loans to private business and small-scale industrial sectors; cap. 765.35m. (March 2003); Chair. Dr SEIN MAUNG; 15 brs.

Innwa Bank Ltd: cnr 35th St and Merchant St, Yangon.

Kanbawza Bank Ltd: 615/1 Pyay Rd, Kamayut Township, Yangon; tel. (1) 538075; fax (1) 538069; e-mail kbz@mptmail.net.mm; Chair. U AUNG KO WIN; 22 brs.

Myanma Citizens Bank Ltd (MCB): 383 Maha Bandoola St, Kyauktada Township, Yangon; tel. (1) 273512; fax (1) 245932; f. 1991; Chair. U HLA TIN.

Myanma Oriental Bank Ltd: 166–168 Pansodan St, Kyauktada Township, Yangon; tel. (1) 246594; fax (1) 253217; e-mail mobl.ygn@ mptmail.net.mm; Chair. U MYAT KYAW; Man. Dir and CEO U WIN MYINT.

Myanma Universal Bank: 81 Theinbyu Rd, Yangon; tel. (1) 297339; fax (1) 245449; f. 1995.

Myanmar Industrial Development Bank Ltd: 26–42 Pansodan St, Kyauktada Township, Yangon; tel. (1) 249536; fax (1) 249529; f. 1996; cap. US $335m.

Myanmar May Flower Bank Ltd: 1B Yadanar Housing Project, 9 Mile Pyay Rd, Mayangone Township, Yangon; tel. (1) 666112; fax (1) 666110; e-mail mmb-hq@mptmail.net.mm; Chair. U KYAW WIN.

Myawaddy Bank Ltd: 24–26 Sule Pagoda Rd, Kyauktada Township, Yangon; tel. (1) 283665; fax (1) 250093; e-mail mwdbankygn@ mtpt400.stems.com; Gen. Mans U TUN KYI, U MYA MIN.

Prime Commercial Bank Ltd: 437 Pyay Rd, Kamayut Township, Yangon; tel. (1) 525990; fax (1) 522420; f. 1994; cap. 122.5m., dep. 358m.; Chair. Dr AUNG KHIN; Man. Dir U MAUNG MAUNG HAN; 2 brs.

Tun Foundation Bank Ltd: 165–167 Bo Aung Gyaw St, Yangon; tel. (1) 270710; Chair. U THEIN TUN.

Yadanabon Bank Ltd: 26th St, cnr of 84th and 85th Sts, Mandalay; tel. (2) 23577.

Yangon City Bank Ltd: 12–18 Sepin St, Kyauktada Township, Yangon; tel. (1) 289256; fax (1) 289231; f. 1993; auth. cap. 500m.; 100% owned by the Yangon City Development Committee; Chair. Col MYINT AUNG.

Yoma Bank Ltd: 1 Kungyan St, Mingala Taung Nyunt Township, Yangon; tel. (1) 242138; fax (1) 246548; Chair. SERGE PUN.

Foreign Banks

By November 2003 18 foreign banks had opened representative offices in Yangon.

STOCK EXCHANGE

Myanmar Securities Exchange Centre: 1st Floor, 21–25 Sule Pagoda Rd, Yangon; tel. (1) 283984; f. 1996; jt venture between Japan's Daiwa Institute of Research and Myanma Economic Bank; Man. Dir EIJI SUZUKI.

INSURANCE

At the end of November 2003 there were three representative offices of foreign insurance companies in Myanmar.

Myanma Insurance: 627–635 Merchant St, Yangon; tel. (1) 256244; fax (1) 283961; e-mail MYANSURE@mptmail.net.com; f. 1976; govt-controlled; Man. Dir Col THEW LWIN.

Trade and Industry

GOVERNMENT AGENCIES

Inspection and Agency Service: 383 Maha Bandoola St, Yangon; tel. (1) 276048; fax (1) 284823; works on behalf of state-owned enterprises to promote business with foreign companies; Man. Dir U OHN KHIN.

Myanmar Investment Commission: Ministry of National Planning and Economic Development, 653–691 Merchant St, Pabedan Township, Yangon; tel. (1) 241918; fax (1) 282101; Chair. U THAUNG; Vice-Chair. Maj.-Gen. TIN HTUT.

Union of Myanmar Economic Holdings: 72–74 Shwadagon Pagoda Rd, Yangon; tel. (1) 78905; f. 1990; public holding co; auth. cap. 10,000m. kyats; 40% of share capital subscribed by the Ministry of Defence and 60% by members of the armed forces.

CHAMBER OF COMMERCE

Chamber of Commerce and Industry: 504–506 Merchant St, Kyauktada Township, Yangon; tel. (1) 243151; fax (1) 248177; f. 1919; Gen. Sec. ZAW MIN WIN.

UTILITIES

Electricity

Myanma Electric Power Enterprise (MEPE): 197–199 Lower Kyimyindine Rd, Yangon; tel. (1) 220918; fax (1) 221006; e-mail mepe@mptmail.net.mm; Man. Dir U YAN NAING.

Water

Mandalay City Development Committee (Water and Sanitation Dept): cnr of 26th and 72nd Sts, Mandalay; tel. (2) 36173; f. 1992; Head of Water and Sanitation Dept U TUN KYI.

Yangon City Development Committee (Water and Sanitation Dept): City Hall, Yangon; tel. (1) 204052; fax (1) 246016; e-mail priycdc@mptmail.net.mm; internet www.yangoncity.com.mm; f. 1992; Head of Water and Sanitation Dept U ZAW WIN.

CO-OPERATIVES

In 1993/94 there were 22,800 co-operative societies, with a turnover of 23,603m. kyats. This was estimated to have increased to 24,760 societies, with a turnover of 20,927m. kyats, in 1994/95.

Central Co-operative Society (CCS) Council: 334/336 Strand Rd, Yangon; tel. (1) 274550; Chair. U THAN HLANG; Sec. U TIN LATT.

Co-operative Department: 259–263 Bogyoke Aung San Rd, Yangon; tel. (1) 277096; Dir-Gen. U MAUNG HTI.

WORKERS' AND PEASANTS' COUNCILS

Conditions of work are stipulated in the Workers' Rights and Responsibilities Law, enacted in 1964. Regional workers' councils ensure that government directives are complied with, and that targets are met on a regional basis. In January 1985 there were 293 workers' councils in towns, with more than 1.8m. members. They are co-ordinated by a central workers' organization in Yangon, formed in 1968 to replace trade union organizations which had been abolished in 1964. The Myanma Federation of Trade Unions operates in exile.

Peasants' Asiayone (Organization): Yangon; tel. (1) 82819; f. 1977; peasants' representative org.; Chair. Brig.-Gen. U THAN NYUNT; Sec. U SAN TUN.

Workers' Unity Organization: Central Organizing Committee, 61 Thein Byu St, Yangon; tel. (1) 284043; f. 1968; workers' representative org.; Chair. U OHN KYAW; Sec. U NYUNT THEIN.

Transport

All railways, domestic air services, passenger and freight road transport services and inland water facilities are owned and operated by state-controlled enterprises.

RAILWAYS

The railway network comprised 3,955 km of track in 1996/97, most of which was single track.

Myanma Railways: Bogyoke Aung San St, POB 118, Yangon; tel. (1) 280508; fax (1) 284220; f. 1877; govt-operated; Man. Dir U AUNG THEIN; Gen. Man. U THAUNG LWIN.

ROADS

In 1996 the total length of the road network in Myanmar was an estimated 28,200 km, of which an estimated 3,440 km were paved. In 2001/02 the total length of road accessible to motor vehicles was 28,598 km.

Road Transportation Department: 375 Bogyoke Aung San St, Yangon; tel. (1) 284426; fax (1) 289716; f. 1963; controls passenger and freight road transport; in 1993/94 operated 1,960 haulage trucks and 928 passenger buses; Man. Dir U OHN MYINT.

INLAND WATERWAYS

The principal artery of traffic is the River Ayeyarwady (Irrawaddy), which is navigable as far as Bhamo, about 1,450 km inland, while parts of the Thanlwin and Chindwinn rivers are also navigable.

Inland Water Transport: 50 Pansodan St, Yangon; tel. (1) 222399; fax (1) 286500; govt-owned; operates cargo and passenger services throughout Myanmar; 36m. passengers and 3.1m. tons of freight were carried in 1993/94; Man. Dir U KHIN MAUNG.

SHIPPING

Yangon is the chief port. Vessels with a displacement of up to 15,000 tons can be accommodated.

In 2002 the Myanma merchant fleet totalled 124 vessels, with a combined displacement of 402,159 grt.

Myanma Port Authority: 10 Pansodan St, POB 1, Yangon; tel. (1) 280094; fax (1) 295134; f. 1880; general port and harbour duties; Man. Dir U TIN OO; Gen. Man. U HLAING SOON.

Myanma Five Star Line: 132–136 Theinbyu Rd, POB 1221, Yangon; tel. (1) 295279; fax (1) 297669; e-mail mfsl.myr@mptmail .net.mm; f. 1959; cargo services to the Far East and Australia; Man. Dir U KHIN MAUNG KYI; Gen. Man. U KYAW ZAW; fleet of 26 coastal and ocean-going vessels.

CIVIL AVIATION

Mingaladon Airport, near Yangon, is equipped to international standards. The newly built Mandalay International Airport was inaugurated in September 2000. In 2002 plans for the construction of the country's third international airport, Hanthawaddy International Airport in Bago (Pegu), were finally approved; the airport was scheduled to become operational in 2007.

Department of Civil Aviation: Mingaladon Airport, Yangon; tel. (1) 665144; fax (1) 665124; e-mail dca.myanmar@mpt.mail.net.mm; Dir-Gen. U WIN MAUNG.

Air Mandalay: 146 Dhammazedi Rd, Bahan Township, Yangon; tel. (1) 525488; fax (1) 525937; e-mail info@airmandalay.com; internet www.airmandalay.com; f. 1994; Myanmar's first airline; jt venture between Air Mandalay Holding and Myanma Airways; operates domestic services and regional services to Chiang Mai and Phuket, Thailand, and Siem Reap, Cambodia; Chair. Dr TUN CHIN; Man. Dir ERIC KANG TIAN LYE; 242 employees.

Myanmar Airways (MA): 123 Sule Pagoda Rd, Yangon; tel. (1) 80710; fax (1) 255305; e-mail 8mpr@maiair.com.mm; internet www .maiair.com; f. 1993; govt-controlled; internal network operates services to 21 airports; Chief Operating Officer PRITHPAL SINGH.

Myanmar Airways International (MAI): 08–02 Sakura Tower, 339 Bogyoke Aung San Rd, Yangon; tel. (1) 255260; fax (1) 255305; e-mail 8mpr@maiair.com.mm; internet www.maiair.com; f. 1993; govt-owned; established by Myanmar Airways in jt venture with Highsonic Enterprises of Singapore to provide international services; operates services to Bangkok, Dhaka, Hong Kong, Kuala Lumpur and Singapore; Man. Dir GERARD DE VAZ.

United Myanmar Air: Summit Parkview Hotel, Yangon; f. 2003; jt venture between Myanmar Airways and Sunshine Strategic Investments Holdings of Hong Kong; international services to Bangkok, Hong Kong, Kuala Lumpur and Singapore; CEO EDWARD TAN.

Tourism

Yangon, Mandalay, Taunggyi and Pagan possess outstanding palaces, Buddhist temples and shrines. The number of foreign visitors to Myanmar declined severely following the suppression of the democracy movement in 1988. In the early 1990s, however, the Government actively promoted the revival of the tourism industry, and between 1995 and 1998 alone the number of hotel rooms almost doubled, reaching a total of nearly 14,000. In 2001 there were 204,862 foreign tourist arrivals (compared with only 5,000 in 1989). In 1999 revenue from tourism totalled an estimated US $35m.

Myanmar Hotels and Tourism Services: 77–91 Sule Pagoda Rd, Yangon 11141; tel. (1) 282013; fax (1) 254417; e-mail mtt.mht@ mptmail.net.mm; govt-controlled; manages all hotels, tourist offices, tourist department stores and duty-free shops; Man. Dir U KYI HTUN.

Myanmar Tourism Promotion Board: 5 Signal Pagoda Rd, Yangon; tel. (1) 243639; fax (1) 245001; e-mail mtpb@mptmail.net .mm; internet www.myanmar-tourism.com.

Myanmar Travels and Tours: 77–91 Sule Pagoda Rd, POB 559, Yangon 11141; tel. (1) 287993; fax (1) 254417; e-mail mtht@ mptmail.net.mm; govt tour operator and travel agent; handles all travel arrangements for groups and individuals; Gen. Man. U HTAY AUNG.

NAMIBIA

Introductory Survey

Location, Climate, Language, Religion, Flag, Capital

The Republic of Namibia (formerly known as South West Africa) lies in south-western Africa, with South Africa to the south and south-east, Botswana to the east and Angola to the north. The country has a long coastline on the Atlantic Ocean. The narrow Caprivi Strip, between Angola and Botswana in the north-east, extends Namibia to the Zambezi river, giving it a border with Zambia. The climate is generally hot, although coastal areas have relatively mild temperatures. Most of the country is subject to drought and unreliable rainfall. The average annual rainfall varies from about 50 mm (2 ins) on the coast to 550 mm (22 ins) in the north. The arid Namib Desert stretches along the west coast, while the easternmost area is part of the Kalahari Desert. The official language is English; however, most of the African ethnic groups have their own languages. At the 1991 census the most widely-spoken languages were Ovambo (used by 50.6% of the population), Nama (12.5%) and Kavango (9.7%). In addition, Afrikaans and German are widely used. About 90% of the population are Christians. The national flag (proportions 2 by 3) comprises a blue triangle in the upper hoist corner, bearing a yellow sun (a blue-bordered disc, surrounded by 12 triangular rays), separated from a green triangle in the lower fly corner by a white-bordered, broad red stripe. The capital is Windhoek.

Recent History

South West Africa became a German possession in 1884. The territory excluded the port of Walvis Bay and 12 small offshore islands, previously annexed by the United Kingdom and subsequently incorporated into South Africa. During the First World War South African forces occupied South West Africa in 1914, and in 1915 Germany surrendered the territory. In 1920 the League of Nations entrusted South Africa with a mandate to administer South West Africa. In 1925 South Africa granted a Constitution giving limited self-government to European (white) inhabitants only. No trusteeship agreement was concluded with the UN after the Second World War, and in 1946 the UN refused South Africa's request for permission to annex South West Africa. In 1949 the territory's European voters were granted representation in the South African Parliament. In 1950 the International Court of Justice (ICJ) issued a ruling that the area should remain under international mandate and that South Africa should submit it to UN control. South Africa refused to comply with this judgment. In October 1966 South Africa's security and apartheid laws were extended to South West Africa, retrospective to 1950.

Opposition within South West Africa to South African rule led to the establishment of two African nationalist organizations, the South West Africa People's Organisation (SWAPO—founded in 1957 as the Ovamboland People's Congress) and the South West African National Union (SWANU—formed in 1959). During 1966 SWAPO's military wing, the People's Liberation Army of Namibia (PLAN), launched an armed struggle for the liberation of the territory. PLAN operated from bases in Angola and Zambia, and was controlled by the external wing of SWAPO (led by Sam Nujoma—the organization's President from 1959). SWAPO also had a legal wing, which was tolerated in South West Africa.

South Africa was consistently criticized at the UN over its extension of apartheid to the territory. The UN General Assembly voted to terminate South Africa's mandate in October 1966, established a UN Council for South West Africa in May 1967, and changed the name of the territory to Namibia in June 1968. In 1971 the ICJ ruled that South Africa's presence was illegal. In 1973 the UN General Assembly recognized SWAPO as 'the authentic representative of the Namibian people', and appointed a UN Commissioner for Namibia to undertake 'executive and administrative tasks'.

In 1973 South Africa established a short-lived multiracial Advisory Council for the territory, but this was boycotted by SWAPO and most influential Africans. A multiracial constitutional conference on the territory's future, organized by the all-white South West Africa Legislative Assembly, was convened in Windhoek in September 1975, attended by representatives of the territory's 11 main ethnic groups. However, neither the UN nor the Organization of African Unity (OAU, now the African Union, see p. 137) recognized this so-called Turnhalle Conference, owing to its ethnic and non-democratic basis, and the legal wing of SWAPO refused to attend. In 1976 and 1977 proposals for procedures whereby Namibia was to achieve independence and formulate a constitution were made by the Turnhalle Conference, but rejected by SWAPO, the UN and the OAU. In September 1977 South Africa appointed an Administrator-General to govern the territory. In November the Turnhalle Conference was dissolved, and the Democratic Turnhalle Alliance (DTA), a coalition of conservative political groups representing the ethnic groups involved in the Turnhalle Conference, was formed.

In early 1978 talks were held between South Africa, SWAPO and a 'contact group' comprising Canada, France, the Federal Republic of Germany, the United Kingdom and the USA (at the time the five Western members of the UN Security Council). In March the contact group presented proposals for a Namibian settlement, including the holding of UN-supervised elections, a reduction in the numbers of South African troops in Namibia and the release of political prisoners. In September these proposals, conditionally accepted by both South Africa and SWAPO, were incorporated in UN Security Council Resolution 435. However, South Africa continued to implement its own internal solution for Namibia with an election for a Constituent Assembly in December. The election was contested by five parties, but boycotted notably by SWAPO. Of the 50 seats in the Assembly, 41 were won by the DTA. In May 1979 South Africa unilaterally established a legislative National Assembly, without executive powers, from the existing Constituent Assembly. In June, following the detention of about 40 of its activists, the legal wing of SWAPO closed its offices in Windhoek and dissolved its executive council.

All-party negotiations, held under UN auspices in Geneva, Switzerland, in January 1981, failed in their aim of arranging a cease-fire and eventual UN-supervised elections. Later in 1981 the contact group attempted to secure support for a three-phase independence plan. However, South Africa's insistence (supported by the USA) that any withdrawal of South African forces must be linked to the withdrawal of Cuban troops from Angola was rejected by Angola and the UN. Meanwhile, the Ministerial Council, formed in 1980 and chaired by Dirk Mudge (also Chairman of the DTA), assumed much of the Administrator-General's executive power in September 1981. However, the DTA was seriously weakened in early 1982 by the resignation of its President, Peter Kalangula, the leader of the only significant movement, other than SWAPO, supported by the Ovambo (Namibia's largest ethnic group). The Ministerial Council was dissolved in January 1983, when, after several months of disagreement with the South African Government regarding the future role of the DTA in the territory, Mudge resigned as Council Chairman. South Africa disbanded the National Assembly and resumed direct rule of Namibia, with Willem van Niekerk as Administrator-General.

The Multi-Party Conference (MPC) was established in November 1983, grouping, initially, seven internal political parties. Boycotted by SWAPO, it appeared to be promoted by South Africa as a means of settling the independence issue outside the framework of Resolution 435, and of reducing SWAPO's dominance in any future post-independence government for Namibia. None the less, South Africa continued to negotiate on the independence issue with SWAPO and Angola. In February 1984 South Africa and Angola agreed to a cease-fire on the Angola–Namibia border, and set up a joint commission to monitor the withdrawal of all South African troops from Angola. Angola undertook to ensure that neither Cuban nor SWAPO forces would move into the areas vacated by the South African troops. Nujoma pledged support for the agreement, but asserted that SWAPO would not abandon the armed conflict until there was a cease-fire in Namibia itself and until South Africa had agreed to UN-supervised elections. Discussions on the independence issue in mid-1984, involving van Niekerk, SWAPO and the MPC, ended inconclusively, as did negotiations in 1984–86 between the South African Government and the US Assistant Secretary of State for African Affairs.

In April 1985 the South African Government accepted a proposal by the MPC for a 'Transitional Government of National Unity' (TGNU) in Namibia. This was formally established in Windhoek in June, although the arrangement was condemned in advance by the contact group and was declared 'null and void' by the UN Secretary-General. The TGNU consisted of an executive Cabinet, drawn from a National Assembly of 62 members who were appointed from among the parties constituting the MPC. Its establishment was accompanied by the proclamation of a 'bill of rights', drafted by the MPC, which prohibited racial discrimination. A Constitutional Council was also established to prepare a constitution for an independent Namibia. The South African Government retained responsibility for foreign affairs, defence and internal security, and all legislation was to be subject to approval by the Administrator-General. Louis Pienaar replaced van Niekerk in this post in July.

In March 1986 South Africa stipulated a deadline of 1 August for the implementation of Resolution 435, on condition that all Cuban troops be withdrawn from Angola; this was, however, abandoned in June, on the grounds that no discernible preparation had been made to comply with this provision. In January 1987 SWAPO guerrillas resumed operations in white-owned farming areas for the first time since 1983. During 1987, following the liberalization of labour laws and the legalization of trade unions for black workers in 1986, the trade union movement became increasingly active. In mid-1987 the Constitutional Council published a draft document; however, South Africa indicated that it could not accept the lack of a guarantee of minority rights in the proposal. In March 1988 the Namibian Supreme Court declared the 'AG8' law of 1980 (providing for the election of 'second-tier' legislative assemblies and for the administration of education and health facilities on an ethnic, rather than a geographical, basis) to be in conflict with the 1985 'bill of rights'. In April 1988 President P. W. Botha of South Africa expressed impatience at the slow progress towards establishing a permanent constitution, and granted the Administrator-General powers to restrict newspapers that were deemed to promote 'subversion and terrorism', and also to organize ethnically-based local elections.

Both Angola and Cuba were reported in January 1988 to have accepted, in principle, the US demand for a complete withdrawal of Cuban troops from Angola, but they reiterated that this would be conditional on the cessation of South African support for the insurgent União Nacional para a Independência Total de Angola (UNITA). In July Angola, Cuba and South Africa reached agreement on 14 'essential principles' for a peaceful settlement, and in August it was agreed that the implementation of Resolution 435 would begin on 1 November. Also in August the Governments of South Africa, Cuba and Angola announced a cease-fire, to which SWAPO agreed, and South Africa undertook to withdraw all its forces from Angola. The November deadline was not met, owing to failure to agree on an exact schedule for the evacuation of Cuban troops from Angola. In December Angola, Cuba and South Africa signed a formal treaty designating 1 April 1989 as the implementation date for Resolution 435 and establishing a joint commission to monitor the treaty's implementation. (A further agreement was signed by Angola and Cuba, requiring the evacuation of all Cuban troops from Angola by July 1991.) A Constituent Assembly was to be elected in Namibia on 1 November 1989. South African forces in Namibia were to be confined to their bases, and their numbers reduced to 1,500 by July 1989; all South African troops were to have been withdrawn from Namibia one week after the November election. SWAPO forces were to be confined to bases in Angola in April, before being disarmed and repatriated. A multinational military observer force, the UN Transition Assistance Group (UNTAG), was to monitor the South African withdrawal, and civilian administrators and an international police force were to supervise the election. At the end of February the TGNU was formally disbanded, and on 1 March the National Assembly voted to dissolve itself: until independence the territory was governed by the Administrator-General, in consultation with a Special Representative of the UN Secretary-General, Martti Ahtisaari. Pienaar and Ahtisaari were to be jointly responsible for arranging the November election.

Implementation of Resolution 435 was disrupted by large-scale movements, from April 1989, of SWAPO guerrillas into Namibia from Angola, as a result of which the South African security forces, with the consent of the UN, suspended the cease-fire. About 280 SWAPO troops were reported to have been killed in the subsequent conflict. Following negotiations by the joint monitoring commission, conditions were arranged for an evacuation of the SWAPO forces to Angola, and in May the commission certified the cease-fire to be once more in force. In June most racially-discriminatory legislation was repealed, and an amnesty was granted to Namibian refugees and exiles: by late September nearly 42,000 people, including Nujoma, had returned to Namibia. Meanwhile, South Africa completed its troop reduction ahead of schedule.

Voting proceeded peacefully on 7–11 November 1989, with the participation of more than 95% of the electorate. The Constituent Assembly's 72 seats were contested by candidates from 10 political parties and alliances, and representatives of seven parties and fronts were elected. SWAPO received 57.3% of all votes cast and won 41 seats, while the DTA, with 28.6% of the votes, secured 21 seats. (In 1991 the South African Government admitted that it had contributed funds to the electoral campaigns of the DTA and several other political parties opposed to SWAPO.) Following the election, South Africa's remaining troops were evacuated from Namibia, while SWAPO's bases in Angola were decommissioned.

In February 1990 the Constituent Assembly adopted a draft Constitution, providing for a multi-party democracy based on universal adult suffrage. Later in the month the Constituent Assembly elected Nujoma as Namibia's first President. On 21 March Namibia finally achieved independence; the Constituent Assembly was redesignated the National Assembly, and Nujoma assumed executive power. A Cabinet, headed by the Constituent Assembly Chairman, Hage Geingob (a long-serving SWAPO activist), was also sworn in. In April British military advisers arrived in Namibia to assist in training the Namibian Defence Force (NDF), comprising former members of the demobilized PLAN and the disbanded South West Africa Territory Force.

In November 1991 the DTA, formerly a coalition of ethnically-based political groupings, voted to reconstitute itself as a single party, retaining Dirk Mudge as its Chairman. In the following month, at SWAPO's first Congress, Nujoma was re-elected as the party's President. SWAPO won control of nine of the country's 13 regional councils at elections in late 1992. An advisory National Council, comprising two members from each of the regional councils, was inaugurated as the second chamber of parliament in early 1993.

Following Namibia's independence, the port of Walvis Bay, its surrounding territory of 1,124 sq km and the 12 offshore Penguin Islands remained under South African jurisdiction. In September 1991 the Namibian and South African Governments agreed to administer the disputed territories jointly, pending a final settlement on sovereignty, and in August 1992 the two countries announced the forthcoming establishment of a joint administration authority. In August 1993, however, South Africa's multi-party constitutional negotiating committee instructed the Government to prepare legislation for the transfer of sovereignty over Walvis Bay to Namibia. Accordingly, negotiations between Namibia and South Africa resulted in bilateral agreements regarding the future of South African interests in the Walvis Bay area. Namibia formally took control of Walvis Bay and its islands from 1 March 1994. In August SWAPO won eight seats, and the DTA two, in Walvis Bay's first non-racial local elections.

Namibia's first post-independence presidential and legislative elections in December 1994 resulted in overwhelming victories for Nujoma and SWAPO. Nujoma was elected for a second term as President, securing 76.3% of the votes cast; his only challenger was the President of the DTA, Mishake Muyongo. (Although he remained DTA Chairman until 1995, Mudge had effectively retired from active politics.) SWAPO secured 53 of the elective seats in the National Assembly, with 73.9% of the valid votes cast. The DTA won 15 seats (with 20.8% of the votes), and the United Democratic Front (UDF) two. The remaining two seats were won by the Democratic Coalition of Namibia (an alliance of the National Patriotic Front and the German Union) and the Monitor Action Group. Although SWAPO now had a two-thirds' majority in the National Assembly, Nujoma gave assurances that no amendments would be made to the Constitution without prior approval by national referendum. Despite opposition claims of 'gross irregularities' in electoral procedures, international observers expressed satisfaction with the conduct of voting.

At the SWAPO Congress in May 1997 Nujoma was re-elected unopposed as party President. Among the resolutions endorsed by the Congress was a proposal that Nujoma should seek re-election for a third term as national President. It was agreed that the Constitution, which stipulates that a President may serve no more than two consecutive terms, could be exceptionally amended to allow Nujoma to seek a further mandate, since the incumbent had initially been appointed by the Constituent Assembly, and had only once been elected President on a popular mandate. The proposed third term for Nujoma was denounced by SWAPO's opponents as indicative of the regime's autocratic tendencies. In August 1998 a senior SWAPO official, Ben Ulenga, resigned as Namibia's High Commissioner to the United Kingdom, in protest at the proposed arrangement to allow Nujoma to seek a renewed mandate. Ulenga also opposed Namibia's military intervention in the Democratic Republic of the Congo (DRC, see below). In October the exceptional constitutional amendment was approved by the requisite two-thirds' majority in the National Assembly, having received the support of SWAPO's members; the amendment was similarly endorsed by the National Council in November. In March 1999 it was reported that Ulenga was to establish a new political party, the Congress of Democrats (CoD), with a view to contesting the presidential and legislative elections due later in the year.

Meanwhile, SWAPO secured control of 27 of the country's 45 local councils at elections in February 1998; the DTA took nine and the UDF three. Only about 40% of the electorate were reported to have voted, compared with more than 80% at local elections in 1992. Regional elections followed in December 1998, at which SWAPO won a majority in 11 of the 13 regional councils, thereby increasing its representation in the National Council to 22 seats. Turn-out by voters was, however, only about 30%.

In August 1998 the DTA's executive announced the suspension of Muyongo as party President, and dissociated the party from Muyongo's overt support for the secession of the Caprivi Strip—a narrow area of land extending in the north-east, between Angola and Botswana, as far as the Zambezi river (Namibia's border with Zambia). In November it emerged that Muyongo, leading the so-called Caprivi Liberation Movement (CLM), was among more than 100 people who, apparently armed, had crossed into Botswana in October, and who were now seeking asylum in that country. The Namibian Government stated that it had discovered plans for a secessionist rebellion, led by Muyongo and a chief of the Mafwe tribe, Boniface Mamili, in Caprivi. Representatives of the office of the UN High Commissioner for Refugees (UNHCR) subsequently advised the Botswana authorities that the secessionists' fears of persecution, should they be returned to Namibia, were 'plausible'. In subsequent weeks many more people crossed into Botswana, claiming to be fleeing harassment and persecution by the Namibian security forces: among those who left the country were many San/Bushmen, who were not believed to be associated with the secessionist movement. (In mid-2001 it was reported that many more San/Bushmen were considering leaving Namibia, again alleging harassment by the security forces.) During a visit to Botswana in March 1999 Nujoma reached an agreement with President Festus Mogae of that country, whereby the separatist leaders (whose extradition had hitherto been sought by Namibia in order that they could be tried on terrorist charges) would be accorded refugee status, on condition that they be resettled in a third country. Muyongo and Mamili were subsequently granted asylum in Denmark. The agreement also provided for the return to Namibia, under the auspices of UNHCR and without fear of prosecution or persecution, of the estimated 2,500 refugees who had crossed into Botswana since late 1998.

A period of apparent calm in the Caprivi region ended abruptly in early August 1999 with an armed attack by members of an organization styling itself the Caprivi Liberation Army (CLA), who targeted a military base at Mpacha airport and the police headquarters and offices of the Namibian Broadcasting Corporation in the regional capital, Katima Mulilo. At least eight members of the Namibian security forces and five CLA fighters were killed during the attack and its suppression. Nujoma responded by declaring a state of emergency in the region. While there was support within Namibia for the declaration, the CoD, as well as church leaders and human rights organizations, expressed concern at evidence of the ill-treatment of detainees. Several members of the Government were subsequently reported to have admitted that 'mistakes' were made in the aftermath of the attack; however, the army Chief of Staff, Maj.-Gen. Martin Shalli, maintained that the decisive response of the forces under his command had been justified. Visiting Katima Mulilo in late August, Nujoma announced an end to the state of emergency, although army and police reinforcements were to remain in Caprivi. Initially, 12 alleged rebels were remanded on charges of high treason, murder, public violence and illegal possession of firearms; the prosecution asserted that 17 known leaders of the CLA remained at large. Meanwhile, a further 47 suspects were charged with aiding and abetting the rebels. Repatriations of refugees from Botswana were halted following the attack on Katima Mulilo, although UNHCR expressed the hope that voluntary repatriations would resume as soon as the security situation in Caprivi was adequate to guarantee the safe return of refugees. In early 2000, however, following an escalation of instability in the region of the Namibia–Angola border, a further 400 Namibian nationals were reported to have fled to Botswana. In late 2001 officials from Botswana and Namibia held talks regarding the repatriation of about 500 Namibian refugees. In September of that year, in response to a request from the Namibian Government, the Gaborone Magistrates' Court in Botswana ordered the extradition of a group of suspected Caprivi separatists who were wanted to stand trial for high treason in connection with the attack on Katima Mulilo. The Namibian Government was also seeking to extradite Muyongo from Denmark to answer similar charges; the Danish Government stated that it was awaiting advice from UNHCR before making a decision. In October 2003, after numerous delays, the trial commenced of 121 Namibians charged with offences related to the attack on Katima Mulilo. In February 2004 the trial judge ruled that 13 of the defendants were 'irregularly before the court', as a result of a process of 'disguised extradition' whereby they had been removed from Zambia and Botswana, and ordered their release. The Government indicated that it would seek permission to appeal to the Supreme Court against this ruling. It was reported that the 13 defendants thus acquitted had been immediately rearrested on their release.

Meanwhile, presidential and legislative elections, which were held on 30 November and 1 December 1999, resulted in an overwhelming victory for Nujoma and SWAPO, with Ulenga and the CoD apparently winning support at the expense of the DTA. In the presidential election Nujoma was returned for a third (and final) term of office with 76.8% of the votes cast, while Ulenga took 10.5% and Katuutire Kaura (Muyongo's successor as President of the DTA) 9.6%. SWAPO won 55 of the elective seats in the National Assembly, with 76.1% of the votes cast (thus ensuring that it retained the two-thirds' majority required to amend the Constitution); the CoD and the DTA each won seven seats (taking, respectively, 9.9% and 9.5% of the total votes cast).

Geingob was reappointed Prime Minister in a reorganization of the Cabinet announced by Nujoma in March 2000. The functions of the Ministries of Foreign Affairs and of Information and Broadcasting were merged (under Theo-Ben Gurirab). A further cabinet reshuffle was effected in January 2001.

In March 2001 it emerged that the Government had banned its ministries and offices from advertising in *The Namibian*, claiming that the newspaper was too critical of government policies. Furthermore, in May Nujoma issued a directive ordering all government departments to cease purchasing *The Namibian*. In November Nujoma announced that he would not be standing for a fourth term as President on the expiry of his current mandate in 2004, which would have necessitated a constitutional amendment. In August 2002 Nujoma reorganized his Cabinet; Gurirab was appointed Prime Minister, replacing Geingob, who resigned from the Government, having declined the position of Minister of Regional and Local Government and Housing, which was accepted by Joel Kaapanda. It was reported that Nujoma considered Geingob a threat to his authority. Hidipo Hamutenya became Minister of Foreign Affairs, Information and Broadcasting. In May 2003, in a further reallocation of portfolios, Nangolo Mbumba was replaced as Minister of Finance by Saarah Kuugongelwa-Amadhila, while Mbumba became Minister of Information and Broadcasting.

In March 1993 UNITA alleged that members of the NDF had crossed the border into southern Angola to assist Angolan government forces in offensives against UNITA, and subsequently claimed that some 2,000 Cuban troops had landed at Namibia's southern port of Lüderitz, from where they had been transferred to Angola to assist government forces. The Namibian authorities denied any involvement in the Angolan conflict, however. In April it was disclosed that NDF troops had been dispatched to the border region to protect two hospitals that were said to be under threat of attack by UNITA, following repeated border incursions and the reported intimidation of Namibian citizens. A 550-km stretch of the Okavango river border was closed from September 1994, following the deaths of three Namibians in an attack attributed by the Namibian authorities to UNITA. In September 1995 the Namibian Government announced the formation of a border control unit to assist police and NDF troops deployed along the Okavango. In November the two countries' defence and security commission agreed new measures aimed at facilitating the work of border patrols. Namibia subsequently announced that the Government was to contribute 200 NDF troops to the UN peace-keeping mission in Angola.

Following the attack on Katima Mulilo by Caprivi separatists in August 1999, the Namibian Government alleged that UNITA was lending military and logistical support to the CLA. (Links were also reported with the separatist Barotse Patriotic Front in Zambia, and the Namibian authorities alleged that the CLA had received training on Zambian territory.) There was considerable speculation that not only was Caprivi an important supply route for UNITA, but also that the Angolan rebel movement was attempting to divert resources of the Namibian armed forces away from the conflict in the DRC (q.v.).

Tensions in the region of the Namibia–Angola border escalated from late 1999, after the two countries began joint patrols targeting UNITA, and the Namibian Government authorized the Angolan armed forces to launch attacks against UNITA from Namibian territory. In February 2000 it was announced that Nujoma and President José Eduardo dos Santos of Angola had agreed to implement measures to restore security in the border region; by June, when a curfew was imposed on the north-eastern border with Angola, more than 50 Namibians had been killed in cross-border raids by the Angolan rebels. Continuing conflict in southern Angola resulted in a large number of refugees entering Namibia (some 6,000 arrived from Angola between November 1999 and August 2000, although increased border security subsequently reduced the flow). In October Namibian security forces announced that 82 suspected UNITA 'soldiers and collaborators', arrested several months previously, would be deported without trial. However, the deportation order on these and 15 other detainees was ruled illegal in March 2001, and 78 remained in detention in Namibia; all were released and free to return to Angola in December 2002, although their repatriation was subsequently delayed by the Angolan authorities. In March 2001 President Nujoma ordered a further reinforcement of the Namibian military presence in Caprivi. In October UNITA rebels were reported to have destroyed an electricity substation in the Kavango region, and in November a group of unidentified gunmen killed four people in western Caprivi before escaping to Angola. In February 2002 five alleged UNITA and CLA guerrillas were arrested and killed by NDF troops in western Caprivi; the NDF claimed that they were responding to an attack on a civilian vehicle in the area.

In April 2002 the Namibian Government welcomed the signing of a formal cease-fire agreement by the Angolan Government and UNITA, some six weeks after the death of Jonas Savimbi, the UNITA leader. Some stability was restored in the Kavango and Caprivi regions in mid-2002, and in August a number of Angolan refugees were repatriated; the majority of them, estimated at around 20,000, were due to return home in mid-2003, under the auspices of UNHCR.

Following independence, Namibia became a member of the UN, the Commonwealth, the OAU and the Southern African Development Co-ordination Conference—now the Southern African Development Community (SADC, see p. 331). Despite expressed concerns at South African dominance of the regional economy, the Nujoma regime has forged close links with post-apartheid South Africa, and in 1994 SWAPO contributed funds to the electoral campaigns of the African National Congress of South Africa and the Pan-Africanist Congress. President Nelson Mandela visited Namibia in August of that year, and in December South Africa announced the cancellation of Namibia's pre-independence bilateral debt; South African property in Namibia was also to be transferred to the Namibian authorities. In February 1997 legislation providing for the cancellation of the debt (now amounting to N $1,200m.) was formally approved by the South African Parliament. Nujoma made his first state visit to South Africa in May 1996. In August 2001 the foreign minis-

ters of Namibia and South Africa held talks regarding their 400 km border; Namibia claimed its southern border extended to the middle of the Orange river, while South Africa claimed that its territory stretched to the northern bank. (When South Africa's borders were reassessed in 1994, following its first democratic elections, the Surveyors-General of both Namibia and South Africa had agreed to place the border in the middle of the river, but the agreement was never signed.) The confusion over the location of the border has led to differences over mineral and fishing rights in the river, as well as grazing rights on its islands.

In February 1995 it was announced that Namibia and Botswana were to refer a dispute regarding the demarcation of their joint border on the Chobe river (specifically, the issue of the sovereignty of the small, uninhabited island of Kasikili-Sedudu) for adjudication by the ICJ. The dispute was formally submitted to the Court in mid-1996. The ICJ ruled in December 1999 that the island formed part of the territory of Botswana; the judgment further ruled that nationals of (and vessels flying the flags of) Botswana and Namibia should enjoy equal treatment in the two channels around the island. Meanwhile, a joint initiative was announced in March of that year to counter smuggling and illegal border crossings between the two countries. In January 1998 the two countries' Joint Commission on Defence and Security held an emergency meeting, following allegations by Namibia that troops from Botswana had taken control of a further island in disputed border territory—Situngu Island in the Caprivi Strip. The Joint Commission agreed to expedite the establishment of a Joint Technical Commission for the demarcation of the border. Relations were complicated by the issue of Caprivi secessionism (see above). Situngu is claimed as Mafwe land; furthermore, Namibia's representative in discussions regarding the island, said to be a member of the secessionist movement, was reported to have fled to Angola. In 2003 Botswana and Namibia accepted the demarcation by a joint commission of their joint border along the Kwando, Linyanti and Chobe rivers.

From August 1998 Namibia, which was participating in regional efforts to resolve the conflict in the DRC, supported a Zimbabwean-led initiative by members of SADC (notably excluding South Africa) for military intervention in support of the regime of President Laurent-Désiré Kabila; as many as 2,000 Namibian troops were subsequently dispatched to the DRC, provoking vociferous criticism by opponents of Nujoma. Namibia's continuing military commitments in the DRC following the failure of the 1999 Lusaka accord (to which Namibia was a signatory), together with the need for additional army resources in north-east Namibia as a result of the Caprivi rebellion and the intensification of operations against UNITA (see above), necessitated the allocation of an additional N $173m. to defence in the supplementary budget for 1999/2000, announced in early 2000.

President Laurent-Désiré Kabila was assassinated in January 2001, and was succeeded by his son, Maj.-Gen. Joseph Kabila. Efforts to resolve the conflict in the DRC were accelerated, and in February proposals for the withdrawal of troops involved in the regional military intervention, including the estimated 2,000 Namibians, were approved by the participating countries, under the aegis of the UN Security Council. In March it was announced that Namibian forces would remain in the DRC until the specified date for withdrawal in May. All but an estimated 150 Namibian troops eventually withdrew from the DRC in September, although other foreign forces were still deployed in large numbers; at least 30 Namibian troops were reported to have been killed in three years of service. All Namibian troops had been withdrawn by the end of 2002. Meanwhile, the Namibian Government was criticized in February 2001, when it admitted, despite previous denials, that it owned a diamond mine in the DRC. The elder Kabila had granted the mine to a company controlled by the Namibian Government in 1999, allegedly in return for Namibian support in the conflict in the DRC.

Germany has been a major aid donor to Namibia since independence, and relations are generally close. In September 1995, none the less, during a visit by the German Chancellor, Helmut Kohl, some 300 members of the Herero ethnic group staged a demonstration outside the German embassy in Windhoek to demand compensation for suffering inflicted on the Herero under German rule. In June 1996 Nujoma made his first official visit to Germany. In March 1998 the German President, Dr Roman Herzog, made an official visit to Namibia, the first such visit by a German Head of State, and pledged his country's increased support for Namibia. In June 2001 the Herero filed a lawsuit in Washington, DC, USA, against three German companies (Deutsche Bank AG, Woermann Line and Terex Corporation), claiming US $2,000m. in reparation for the alleged exploitation and eventual extermination of some 65,000 Herero in 1904–07; a second lawsuit, for a further US $2,000m., was filed against the German Government in September. The case against Terex Corporation was subsequently withdrawn, after the company claimed that it was under different management at the time of the atrocities. In October 2003 it was reported that the Federal Court in Washington, DC, had ruled that it did not have jurisdiction over the Herero case, and that the Herero were consequently considering filing a lawsuit in New York. In January 2004, at a commemoration of the Herero uprising against German rule in 1904, the Government of Germany expressed its regret for the extermination of Herero, but declared itself unwilling to pay compensation to descendants of the victims.

Government

On 21 March 1990 Namibia became independent, and the Constitution took effect. Executive authority is held by the President, who is the Head of State. According to the Constitution, the President shall be directly elected by universal adult suffrage for a term of five years, and permitted to hold office for a maximum of two terms. (In late 1998 legislation was approved whereby the Constitution was to be exceptionally amended to allow the incumbent President to seek a third term of office.) Legislative power is vested in the National Assembly, comprising 72 members directly elected by universal adult suffrage and as many as six non-voting members nominated by the President. The National Assembly has a maximum term of five years. An advisory National Council, comprising two representatives from each of the country's 13 regional councils, elected for a six-year period, operates as the second chamber of parliament. Each region has its own Governor.

Defence

In August 2003 the Namibian Defence Force numbered an estimated 9,000 men; there was also a 200-strong coastguard, operating as part of the Ministry of Fisheries and Marine Resources, and a paramilitary force of 6,000. In January 2002 the Government announced that it was establishing a navy, to commence operations in 2005, and constructing a naval base at Walvis Bay, with assistance from the Brazilian Government, which was also to train Namibian naval officers. Projected budgetary expenditure on defence for 2003 was N $950m.

Economic Affairs

In 2002, according to estimates by the World Bank, Namibia's gross national income (GNI), measured at average 2000–02 prices, was US $3,253m., equivalent to US $1,780 per head (or $6,650 per head on an international purchasing-power parity basis). During 1990–2002, it was estimated, the population increased at an average annual rate of 2.4% per year, while gross domestic product (GDP) per head increased, in real terms, by an average of 1.9% per year. Overall GDP increased, in real terms, at an average annual rate of 4.3% in 1990–2002. Real GDP increased by 2.7% in 2001 and by 3.0% in 2002.

According to the Bank of Namibia, agriculture (including hunting, forestry and fishing) contributed 11.2% of GDP in 2002. About 39.7% of the labour force were employed in the sector in 2002. Namibia has potentially one of the richest fisheries in the world. Government revenue from sales of fishing concessions was projected at N $70m. in the financial year ending 31 March 1999, and exports of fish and fish products provided 28.5% of total export earnings in 1998. Legislation aimed at developing aquaculture was adopted in 2003, and a number of fish farms were established. The principal agricultural activity is beef production; the production of karakul sheepskins is also important. In addition, sealing and ostrich farming are practised on a commercial basis. The main subsistence crops are maize, millet and root crops, although Namibia remains highly dependent on imports of basic foods, especially in drought years. Plantations of seedless grapes were developed on the banks of the Orange river in the late 1990s, and projected growth in production was expected to make them the second largest agricultural export after beef. In 2002 the South African Government granted Namibia limited access to fish in its territorial waters. Agricultural GDP increased at an average annual rate of 4.1% in 1990–2002. Agricultural GDP decreased by 0.4% in 2001, but increased by 3.0% in 2002.

Industry (including mining, manufacturing, construction and power) contributed 30.4% of GDP in 2002, and engaged 15.0% of the employed labour force in 1991. During 1990–2002 industrial GDP increased by an average of 2.3% per year. Industrial GDP increased by 1.6% in 2001 and by 1.8% in 2002.

Mining and quarrying contributed 14.3% of GDP in 2002, and engaged 3.7% of the employed labour force in 1991. Namibia has rich deposits of many minerals, and is among the world's leading producers of gem diamonds (some 95% of diamonds mined in Namibia are of gem quality). Diamond-mining contributed 81.8% of the sector's GDP in 2001, and diamonds are the principal mineral export, accounting for an estimated 50.1% of export earnings in 2002; in 2000 Namibia produced 5% of world diamond output by value. The mining of offshore diamond deposits is of increasing importance, with offshore recoveries of gem-quality diamonds accounting for about 56% of the country's output in 1999. Some US $500,000m.-worth of diamonds were estimated to be lying on the continental shelf off the Namibian coast in 2001. A new Diamond Act, liberalizing exploration, came into force in 2000. Uranium is also an important mineral export. In addition, zinc, lead, gold, salt, fluorspar, marble and semi-precious stones are extracted, and there are also considerable deposits of hydrocarbons, lithium, manganese, tungsten, cadmium and vanadium. Namibia is also believed to have substantial reserves of coal, iron ore and platinum. Copper production, which ceased in 1998, following the liquidation of the Tsumeb Corporation, resumed at the former Tsumeb sites in September 2000. The Skorpion zinc mine and refinery near Rosh Pinah, opened in mid-2003 by Anglo American plc, was expected to contribute some 4% of GDP on reaching full production in the second half of 2004. Production of an estimated 150,000 metric tons of zinc per year was anticipated over a period of 15 years. In late 2001 development began on a mine and smelter complex for high-grade silicon metal at Omaruru. Mining GDP increased at an average annual rate of 2.7% in 1993–2001; the sector's GDP decreased by 1.7% in 2000 and by 6.1% in 2001.

Manufacturing contributed 10.7% of GDP in 2002, and engaged 5.8% of the employed labour force in 1991. The sector has hitherto remained underdeveloped, largely owing to Namibia's economic dependence on South Africa. The principal manufacturing activities are the processing of fish (which contributed 19.4% of manufacturing GDP in 2001) and minerals for export; brewing, meat processing and the production of chemicals are also significant. Namibia's first diamond-cutting and -polishing factory was inaugurated in 1998. Manufacturing GDP increased by an average of 2.6% per year in 1990–2002. Manufacturing GDP increased by 0.8% in 2001 and by 3.5% in 2002.

In 2000 97.6% of Namibia's electricity production was derived from hydroelectric power. There is a hydroelectric station at Ruacana, on the Cunene river at the border with Angola, and a second hydroelectric power station was planned at Divundu on the Okavango river; a project to construct a power station at Epupa remained stalled in 2004, following a disagreement between the Namibian and Angolan Governments over the most appropriate site. Sizeable offshore deposits of natural gas are also to be exploited commercially: a planned 750-MW power plant would supply the domestic market, and it is anticipated that a surplus will be produced for export to South Africa. Domestic electricity generation increased significantly in 2000, enabling the proportion of electrical energy imported to be reduced to 34.8% in that year. A power transmission line, linking the Namibian and South African electricity grids, was inaugurated in southern Namibia in 1999. Imports of mineral fuels and lubricants accounted for 5.9% of the value of total merchandise imports in 1997.

The services sector contributed 58.4% of GDP in 2002. Tourism is expanding rapidly, and has been the focus of a major privatization initiative. The acquisition of Walvis Bay in March 1994, and subsequent establishment there of a free-trade zone, was expected to enhance Namibia's status as an entrepôt for regional trade. By March 2004 it was estimated that the free-trade zone had attracted some N $80m. of direct foreign investment. The GDP of the services sector increased at an average annual rate of 4.4% in 1990–2002. Services GDP increased by 3.9% in 2001 and by 3.5% in 2002.

In 2002 Namibia recorded a visible trade deficit of US $178.9m., although there was a surplus of US $96.5m. on the current account of the balance of payments. South Africa is the dominant source of imports, providing 84.3% of the total in 1997. In 1993 the United Kingdom (34.4%) and South Africa (27.4%) were the principal markets for Namibian exports. The principal exports in 2002 were diamonds and other mineral products, food and live animals (notably fish and meat) and manufactured goods. The principal import groups in 1997 included food, live animals, beverages and tobacco; machinery and electrical goods; transport equipment; chemicals and chemical products; textiles, clothing and footwear; metals and metal products; and mineral fuels and lubricants.

In the financial year ending 31 March 2004 Namibia recorded an estimated overall budget deficit of N \$1,408.5m. In 1997 South Africa officially cancelled the external public debt inherited by Namibia at independence. Namibia's external debt was estimated at US \$716m. in 2003. The annual rate of inflation averaged 10.0% in 1990–2002; consumer prices increased by an average of 11.3% in 2002. Some 35% of the labour force were unemployed in 2001.

Namibia is a member of the Common Market for Eastern and Southern Africa (see p. 171), of the Southern African Development Community (see p. 331), and of the Southern African Customs Union (with Botswana, Lesotho, South Africa and Swaziland).

Despite a vulnerability to drought, Namibia's potential for economic prosperity is high, given its abundant mineral reserves and rich fisheries, as well as a well-developed infrastructure, all of which were enhanced by the acquisition, in 1994, of sovereignty over Walvis Bay and of important diamond-mining rights. However, Namibia's economic progress continues to be largely influenced by its dependence on South Africa. (The Namibian dollar, introduced in 1993, is at par with the rand.) Although the average level of income per head is among the highest in the region, there remain extreme disparities in the distribution of wealth; in 1994 land-reform legislation was enacted in an effort to redress this problem, but implementation has been very slow. In April 2001 the Government announced that it had allocated N \$100m. to acquire land for redistribution on a voluntary basis over a five-year period. At this time approximately 4,000 (mainly white-owned) farms occupied 52% of the total land area, while the Government had acquired only some 6% of the land required for resettlement. In October 2002 the Government announced that it was considering the seizure of white-owned farms for redistribution to the landless black population, and criticized white farmers for taking advantage of the voluntary basis for land redistribution by charging excessively high prices for their land. In March 2004 the Government estimated that it would cost more than US \$150m. over a five-year period to redistribute some 9m. ha of land among an estimated 240,000 applicants. At that time some 700 farms had already been transferred. Meanwhile, a rural exodus in recent years has resulted in high rates of urban unemployment and attendant social problems such as crime. The Nujoma Government's first National Development Plan, covering the period 1995–2000, aimed principally to reduce poverty and encourage sustainable economic growth (averaging 5% annually during the plan period) through policies of diversification, in an attempt to prevent potential over-dependence on the mining and fishing sectors. After a disappointing performance in 1998, the economy improved in 1999 and 2000. However, GDP growth slowed in 2001, to 2.7%, as a result of lower agricultural output, particularly in the fishing sector, before recovering slightly, to 3.0%, in 2002. The second National Development Plan, covering 2001–06, projected GDP growth of 4% per year over the period. In January 2002 it was reported that, with assistance from the Brazilian Government, Namibia planned to conduct a geological survey of the offshore continental shelf, with the intention of extending its exclusive economic zone from 200 to 350 nautical miles. In November 2001 Namibia became eligible to export certain products to the USA free from tariffs, under the African Growth and Opportunity Act (AGOA); it was estimated that 90% of products made in Namibia would qualify for duty-free access to the US market until 2008. In December 2002 and 2003 Namibia's eligibility for tariff preferences under AGOA was renewed. The continued expansion of the mining sector, notably at the Skorpion zinc mine and refinery, was expected to contribute significantly to increased real GDP growth in 2004 and 2005, which was forecast at 4.3% and 5.0%, respectively.

Education

Under the Constitution, education is compulsory between the ages of six and 16 years, or until primary education has been completed (whichever is the sooner). Primary education consists of seven grades, and secondary education of five. In 2000/01 total enrolment at primary and secondary schools was equivalent to 94% of the school-age population (males 92%; females 95%). Enrolment at primary schools included 82% of children in the relevant age-group (males 79%; females 84%), while the comparable ratio for secondary enrolment in that year was 38% (males 32%; females 44%). Higher education is provided by the University of Namibia, the Technicon of Namibia, a vocational college and four teacher-training colleges. In 1998/99 12,787 students were enrolled in tertiary education. Various schemes for informal adult education are also in operation in an effort to combat illiteracy. Budget forecasts for 1998/99 allocated N \$1,700.6m. (25.2% of total government expenditure) to education. Approximately 20% of total expenditure was allocated to education under the draft budget for 2001/02.

Public Holidays

2004: 1 January (New Year's Day), 21 March (Independence Day), 9–12 April (Easter), 1 May (Workers' Day), 4 May (Cassinga Day), 20 May (Ascension Day), 25 May (Africa Day, anniversary of the OAU's foundation), 26 August (Heroes' Day), 7 October (Day of Goodwill), 10 December (Human Rights Day), 25–26 December (Christmas).

2005: 1 January (New Year's Day), 21 March (Independence Day), 25–28 March (Easter), 1 May (Workers' Day), 4 May (Cassinga Day), 5 May (Ascension Day), 25 May (Africa Day, anniversary of the OAU's foundation), 26 August (Heroes' Day), 7 October (Day of Goodwill), 10 December (Human Rights Day), 25–26 December (Christmas).

Weights and Measures

The metric system is in use.

Statistical Survey

Area and Population

AREA, POPULATION AND DENSITY*

Area (sq km)	824,292†
Population (census results)	
21 October 1991	1,409,920
28 August 2001	
Males	936,718
Females	890,136
Total	1,826,854
Density (per sq km) at August 2001	2.2

* Including data for Walvis Bay, sovereignty over which was transferred from South Africa to Namibia with effect from March 1994. Walvis Bay has an area of 1,124 sq km (434 sq miles) and had a population of 22,999 in 1991.
† 318,261 sq miles.

ETHNIC GROUPS
(population, 1988 estimate)

Ovambo	623,000	Caprivian	47,000
Kavango	117,000	Bushmen	36,000
Damara	94,000	Baster	31,000
Herero	94,000	Tswana	7,000
White	80,000	Others	12,000
Nama	60,000	**Total**	1,252,000
Coloured	51,000		

PRINCIPAL TOWNS
(population at 1991 census)

Windhoek	147,056	Oshakati	21,603
Walvis Bay	22,999	Rehoboth	21,439

Source: Thomas Brinkhoff, *City Population* (internet www.citypopulation.de).

Mid-2001 (UN estimate, including suburbs): Windhoek (capital) 216,000 (Source: UN, *World Urbanization Prospects: The 2001 Revision*).

BIRTHS AND DEATHS
(UN estimates, annual averages)

	1985–90	1990–95	1995–2000
Birth rate (per 1,000)	41.2	40.9	38.0
Death rate (per 1,000) . . .	11.2	10.4	12.3

Source: UN, *World Population Prospects: The 2002 Revision*.

Expectation of life (WHO estimates, years at birth): 49.3 (males 48.1; females 50.5) in 2002 (Source: WHO, *World Health Report*).

ECONOMICALLY ACTIVE POPULATION
(persons aged 15 to 69 years, 2000 labour force survey)

	Males	Females	Total
Agriculture, hunting, and forestry.	69,782	56,677	126,459
Fishing	4,725	3,075	7,800
Mining and quarrying	3,154	713	3,868
Manufacturing	11,375	11,548	22,922
Electricity, gas and water . . .	3,709	484	4,193
Construction	20,740	1,048	21,788
Wholesale and retail trade, repair of motor vehicles, motorcycles and personal and household goods	17,220	21,683	38,902
Restaurants and hotels	3,006	4,671	7,677
Transport, storage and communications	12,243	2,065	14,308
Financial intermediation . .	2,489	2,444	4,933
Real estate, renting and business activities	17,880	21,437	39,318
Public administration and defence; compulsory social security . .	15,372	9,047	24,419
Education	11,742	18,797	30,538
Health and social work	2,993	10,143	13,135
Other community, social and personal services	24,324	21,965	46,289
Private households with employed persons	4,754	17,456	22,210
Extra-territorial organizations and bodies	155	172	327
Not classifiable by economic activity	1,166	1,599	2,765
Total employed	**226,828**	**205,021**	**431,849**
Unemployed	88,006	123,410	211,416
Total labour force	**314,834**	**328,431**	**643,265**

Source: ILO.

2002 (FAO estimates, '000 persons): Agriculture, etc. 311; Total labour force 783 (Source: FAO).

Health and Welfare

KEY INDICATORS

Total fertility rate (children per woman, 2002)	4.6
Under-5 mortality rate (per 1,000 live births, 2001) . . .	67
HIV/AIDS (% of persons aged 15–49, 2001)	22.50
Physicians (per 1,000 head, 1997)	0.30
Health expenditure (2001): US $ per head (PPP) . . .	330
Health expenditure (2001): % of GDP	6.7
Health expenditure (2001): public (% of total)	69.3
Access to water (% of persons, 2000)	77
Access to sanitation (% of persons, 2000)	41
Human Development Index (2001): ranking	124
Human Development Index (2001): value	0.627

For sources and definitions, see explanatory note on p. vi.

Agriculture

PRINCIPAL CROPS
('000 metric tons)

	2001	2002	2003
Wheat	6	7	8†
Maize	28	29†	33†
Millet	65	55*	51†
Sorghum	8	4†	5*
Roots and tubers*	270	270	270
Pulses*	9	9	9
Vegetables*	11	11	11
Fruit*	17	17	17

* FAO estimate(s).
† Unofficial figure.

Source: FAO.

LIVESTOCK
('000 head, year ending September)

	2001	2002	2003
Horses	53	53*	53*
Mules*	7	7	7
Asses	169	169*	169*
Cattle	2,509	2,509*	2,509*
Pigs	22	22*	22*
Sheep	2,370	2,370*	2,370*
Goats	1,769	1,769*	1,780*
Chickens*	2,600	2,600	2,600

* FAO estimate(s).

Source: FAO.

LIVESTOCK PRODUCTS
(FAO estimates, '000 metric tons)

	2001	2002	2003
Beef and veal	58	58	58
Mutton and lamb	7	7	7
Goat meat	4	4	4
Pig meat	1	1	1
Poultry meat	5	3	3
Other meat	5	4	4
Cows' milk	89	89	89
Hen eggs	2	2	2
Wool (greasy)	2	2	2
Cattle hides	6	6	6
Sheepskins	1	1	1
Goatskins	1	1	1

Source: FAO.

Forestry

Separate figures are not yet available. Data for Namibia are included in those for South Africa.

Fishing*

('000 metric tons, live weight)

	1999	2000	2001
Capture	533.4	532.5	490.8
Cape hakes (Stokvisse) . . .	166.6	162.8	173.5
Cape horse mackerel (Maasbanker)	322.1	344.3	309.4
Southern African pilchard . .	44.7	25.4	7.9
Aquaculture†	0.0	0.1	0.1
Total catch	**533.4**	**532.6**	**490.9**

* Figures include quantities caught by licensed foreign vessels in Namibian waters and processed in Lüderitz and Walvis Bay. The data exclude aquatic mammals (whales, seals, etc.). The number of South African fur seals caught was: 25,161 in 1999; 41,753 in 2000; 41,753 in 2001†.
† FAO estimate(s).

Source: FAO, *Yearbook of Fishery Statistics*.

Mining

(metric tons, unless otherwise indicated)

	1999	2000	2001
Copper ore*	—	5,620†	12,392
Lead concentrates*	9,885	11,114	13,025
Zinc concentrates*	35,140	39,126	31,803
Silver ore (kilograms)* . . .	9,670	9,287	12,679
Uranium oxide	3,171	3,201	2,640
Gold ore (kilograms)* . . .	2,005	2,417	2,851
Fluorspar (Fluorite)‡ . . .	71,011	66,128	81,245
Salt (unrefined)	503,479	576,000	523,000
Diamonds ('000 metric carats):			
gem†	1,633	1,552	1,490
industrial†	82	—	—

* Figures refer to the metal content of ores and concentrates.
† Estimated production.
‡ Figures (on a wet-weight basis) refer to acid-grade material.
Source: US Geological Survey.

Industry

SELECTED PRODUCTS
(metric tons)

	1999	2000	2001
Cement*	150,000	150,000	—
Unrefined copper (unwrought) . .	—	5,082	27,015

* Estimated production.
Source: US Geological Survey.

Finance

CURRENCY AND EXCHANGE RATES

Monetary Units
100 cents = 1 Namibian dollar (N $).

Sterling, US Dollar and Euro Equivalents (31 December 2003)
£1 sterling = N $11.8504;
US $1 = N $6.6400;
€1 = N $8.3863;
N $1,000 = £84.39 = US $150.60 = €119.24.

Average Exchange Rate (N $ per US $)
2001   8.60918
2002   10.54070
2003   7.56475

Note: The Namibian dollar was introduced in September 1993, replacing (at par) the South African rand. The rand remained legal tender in Namibia.

CENTRAL GOVERNMENT BUDGET
(N $ million, year ending 31 March)

Revenue*	2001/02	2002/03	2003/04†
Taxation	8,166.0	9,329.8	9,784.7
Taxes on income, profits and capital gains	3,285.6	4,442.3	3,758.0
Taxes on property	64.1	79.3	90.0
Domestic taxes on goods and services	2,107.4	2,135.7	2,821.0
Taxes on international trade and transactions	2,641.2	2,596.9	3,035.7
Other taxes	67.6	75.6	80.0
Non-tax revenue	757.1	1,121.1	994.9
Entrepreneurial and property income	463.4	703.2	663.4
Fines and forfeitures	18.2	19.6	20.0
Administrative fees and charges	254.0	382.3	275.7
Return on capital from lending and equity	21.4	15.9	35.8
Total	8,923.0	10,450.9	10,779.6

Expenditure	2001/02	2002/03	2003/04†
Current expenditure	8,674.7	9,503.0	10,367.2
Personnel expenditure . . .	4,325.5	4,708.9	5,201.2
Expenditure on goods and other services	1,977.3	1,993.6	2,027.3
Interest payments	602.7	907.6	877.4
Subsidies and other current transfers	1,769.2	1,892.8	2,261.3
Capital expenditure	1,627.7	1,895.7	1,876.8
Capital investment	1,267.0	1,158.7	1,364.1
Capital transfers	25.0	87.2	112.7
Total lending and equity participation	335.7	649.7	400.0
Total	10,302.4	11,398.7	12,244.0

* Excluding grants received from abroad (N $ million): 174.9 in 2001/02; 111.2 in 2002/03; 55.9 2003/04.
† Revised estimates.
Source: Bank of Namibia.

INTERNATIONAL RESERVES
(US $ million at 31 December)

	2001	2002	2003
IMF special drawing rights . . .	0.02	0.02	0.03
Reserve position in IMF	0.05	0.06	0.08
Foreign exchange	234.18	323.05	325.11
Total	234.25	323.13	325.22

Source: IMF, *International Financial Statistics*.

MONEY SUPPLY
(N $ million at 31 December)

	2001	2002	2003
Demand deposits at deposit money banks	5,805.2	6,152.4	7,266.8
Total money (incl. others) . . .	6,312.7	6,698.2	7,851.4

Source: IMF, *International Financial Statistics*.

COST OF LIVING
(Consumer Price Index for Windhoek; base: December 1992 = 100)

	2000	2001	2002
Food	172.0	191.7	229.2
Beverages and tobacco	267.0	290.3	314.0
Housing, fuel and power . . .	202.1	217.7	231.0
Clothing and footwear	183.9	196.1	208.8
All items (incl. others)	189.5	207.0	230.5

Source: Bank of Namibia, *Annual Report* (2002).

NATIONAL ACCOUNTS
(N $ million at current prices)
National Income and Product

	2000	2001	2002
Compensation of employees	9,340	10,304	11,115
Operating surplus	9,167	10,907	12,121
Domestic factor incomes	18,507	21,211	23,236
Consumption of fixed capital	3,103	3,559	4,003
Gross domestic product (GDP) at factor cost	21,610	24,770	27,239
Indirect taxes	2,995	3,109	3,920
Less Subsidies	610	663	552
GDP in purchasers' values	23,995	27,216	30,607
Factor income received from abroad	1,721	1,705	1,952
Less Factor income paid abroad	1,491	1,714	1,369
Gross national income	24,226	27,207	31,189
Less Consumption of fixed capital	3,103	3,559	4,003
National income in market prices	21,123	23,648	27,187
Other current transfers from abroad	3,272	3,323	3,549
Less Other current transfers paid abroad	262	312	308
National disposable income	24,133	26,659	30,428

Expenditure on the Gross Domestic Product

	1999	2000	2001
Government final consumption expenditure	6,262	6,819	7,562
Private final consumption expenditure	12,240	14,192	16,500
Increase in stocks	57	171	418
Gross fixed capital formation	4,760	4,460	6,039
Total domestic expenditure	23,319	25,641	30,518
Exports of goods and services	9,548	10,811	12,075
Less Imports of goods and services	11,773	12,119	14,785
Statistical discrepancy	−413	−338	−577
GDP in purchasers' values	20,681	23,995	27,231

Gross Domestic Product by Economic Activity

	2000	2001	2002
Agriculture, hunting, forestry and fishing	2,343	2,581	3,104
Mining and quarrying	2,610	3,663	3,945
Manufacturing	2,371	2,604	2,961
Electricity, gas and water	605	620	867
Construction	473	776	617
Trade, restaurants and hotels	3,085	3,481	4,074
Transport, storage and communications	1,383	1,532	1,885
Finance, insurance, real estate and business services	3,068	3,461	3,649
Government services	5,071	5,520	5,736
Other community, social and personal services	201	216	242
Other services	437	487	555
Sub-total	21,647	24,941	27,635
Less Financial services indirectly measured	273	330	349
GDP at basic prices	21,372	24,611	27,285
Taxes, less subsidies, on products	2,318	2,722	2,816
GDP in purchasers' values	23,690	27,333	30,101

Source: Bank of Namibia.

BALANCE OF PAYMENTS
(US $ million)

	2000	2001	2002
Exports of goods f.o.b.	1,312.8	1,147.0	1,071.6
Imports of goods f.o.b.	−1,430.0	−1,325.5	−1,250.5
Trade balance	−117.2	−178.5	−178.9
Exports of services	232.5	218.0	237.3
Imports of services	−332.0	−263.4	−234.8
Balance on goods and services	−216.7	−223.9	−176.4
Other income received	245.7	195.5	176.1
Other income paid	−246.5	−288.2	−148.1
Balance on goods, services and income	−217.5	−316.6	−148.4
Current transfers received	419.2	347.4	276.1
Current transfers paid	−37.9	−36.4	−31.2
Current balance	163.8	−5.5	96.5
Capital account (net)	112.6	95.8	107.5
Direct investment abroad	−1.7	12.5	4.7
Direct investment from abroad	118.9	36.1	51.2
Portfolio investment assets	−77.5	−180.2	−154.5
Portfolio investment liabilities	40.8	29.0	28.7
Other investment assets	−437.2	−378.4	−283.5
Other investment liabilities	133.6	66.8	18.3
Net errors and omissions	−156.4	−12.9	80.8
Overall balance	−103.3	−336.9	−50.2

Source: IMF, *International Financial Statistics*.

External Trade
PRINCIPAL COMMODITIES

Imports c.i.f. (US $ million)	1995	1996	1997
Food and live animals / Beverages and tobacco	332.2	348.7	404.0
Mineral fuels and lubricants	87.7	96.3	99.0
Chemicals and related products	170.1	186.5	188.2
Wood, paper and paper products (incl. furniture)	101.2	89.3	92.2
Textiles, clothing and footwear	117.4	125.6	126.3
Metals and metal products	127.4	122.3	126.3
Machinery (incl. electrical)	305.2	266.6	251.3
Transport equipment	275.2	274.2	246.1
Total (incl. others)	1,648.4	1,630.9	1,675.0

Source: IMF, *Namibia: Statistical Appendix* (February 1999).

Exports f.o.b. (N $ million)	2000	2001*	2002*
Food and live animals	1,372.8	1,399.9	1,632.8
Diamonds	4,245.4	4,506.5	5,603.9
Other mineral products	1,287.9	1,672.5	2,106.4
Manufactured products	1,562.7	1,612.3	1,630.1
Total (incl. others)	9,195.0	9,839.0	11,195.7

* Provisional figures.

Source: Bank of Namibia, *Annual Report* (2002).

PRINCIPAL TRADING PARTNERS

Imports c.i.f. (US $ million)	1995	1996	1997
Germany	29.7	23.7	33.3
Norway	16.2	3.4	2.9
Russia	13.4	9.5	17.3
South Africa	1,431.7	1,443.4	1,412.7
United Kingdom	25.5	15.8	7.2
USA	22.6	35.9	69.0
Zimbabwe	17.0	18.7	7.1
Total (incl. others)	1,648.6	1,630.9	1,675.0

Source: IMF, *Namibia: Statistical Appendix* (February 1999).

Exports f.o.b. (N $ million)	1993
Belgium	232
Côte d'Ivoire	70
France	87
Germany	140
Japan	411
South Africa	1,153
Spain	258
Switzerland	74
United Kingdom	1,450
USA	51
Total (incl. others)	4,213

Source: Bank of Namibia, Windhoek.

Transport

RAILWAYS

	1994/95	1995/96
Freight (million net ton-km)	1,077	1,082
Passengers carried ('000)	110	124

Source: TransNamib Ltd, Windhoek.

ROAD TRAFFIC
(motor vehicles in use at 31 December)

	1994*	1995*	1996
Passenger cars	61,269	62,500	74,875
Buses and coaches	5,098	5,200	10,175
Lorries and vans	60,041	61,300	59,352
Motorcycles and mopeds	1,450	1,480	1,520

Total vehicles in use (excluding road tractors, motorcycles and mopeds): 137,650 in 1997; 137,650 in 1998*; 123,568 in 1999*.

2000: Passenger cars 68,565; Buses and coaches 1,924; Lorries and vans 73,598; Road tractors 2,912; Motorcycles and mopeds 2,849.
* Estimates.

Source: International Road Federation, *World Road Statistics*.

SHIPPING
Merchant Fleet
(at 31 December)

	2000	2001	2002
Number of vessels	119	121	126
Displacement (gross registered tons)	63,142	65,822	69,488

Source: Lloyd's Register-Fairplay, *World Fleet Statistics*.

Sea-borne Freight Traffic
('000 freight tons*, year ending 30 August, unless otherwise indicated)

	1999/00†	2000/01	2001/02
Port of Lüderitz:			
goods loaded	93.6	143.3	171.2
goods unloaded	39.5	105.1	101.7
goods transhipped	14.1	10.0	4.6
Port of Walvis Bay:			
goods loaded	723.4	720.7	915.8
goods unloaded	1,460.3	1,452.1	1,225.1
goods transhipped	40.0	56.6	60.3

* One freight ton = 40 cu ft (1.133 cu metres) of cargo capacity.
† Year ending 30 September 2000.
Source: Namibian Ports Authority, Walvis Bay.

CIVIL AVIATION
(traffic on scheduled services)

	1997	1998	1999
Kilometres flown (million)	7	7	5
Passengers carried ('000)	183	200	165
Passenger-km (million)	882	614	528
Total ton-km (million)	116	57	47

Source: UN, *Statistical Yearbook*.

Tourism

FOREIGN TOURIST ARRIVALS*

Country of origin	1996	1997	1998
Angola	144,915	158,188	179,237
Botswana	16,011	17,695	21,269
Germany	50,899	54,952	61,560
South Africa	172,544	187,687	217,937
United Kingdom	11,562	12,555	15,909
Total (incl. others)	461,310	502,012	614,368

* Excluding same-day visitors: 63,752 in 1996; 69,162 in 1997.

2001: Angola: 237,691; Botswana: 29,699; Germany: 52,976; South Africa: 241,809; United Kingdom: 13,941; Total (incl. others) 670,497;.

Source: World Tourism Organization, *Yearbook of Tourism Statistics*.

Tourism receipts (US $ million): 293 in 1996; 333 in 1997; 288 in 1998 (Source: World Bank).

Communications Media

	1999	2000	2001
Television receivers ('000 in use)	65	67	n.a.
Telephones ('000 main lines in use)	108.2	110.2	117.4
Mobile cellular telephones ('000 subscribers)	30.0	82.0	100.0
Internet users ('000)	6.0	30.0	45.0

2002 ('000 subscribers): Mobile cellular telephones 150.

Source: International Telecommunication Union.

Radio receivers ('000 in use): 232 in 1997 (Source: UNESCO, *Statistical Yearbook*).

Daily newspapers (1997): 4; average circulation ('000 copies) 10 (Source: UNESCO, *Statistical Yearbook*).

Non-daily newspapers (1997): 5; average circulation ('000 copies) 9 (Source: UNESCO, *Statistical Yearbook*).

Education

(1998/99)

	Institutions	Teachers	Students Males	Students Females	Students Total
Primary	1,362	11,992	193,169	193,478	386,647
Secondary	n.a.	5,093	51,203	58,873	110,076
Tertiary	n.a.	619	6,537	6,250	12,787

Source: UNESCO, Institute for Statistics.

Adult literacy rate (UNESCO estimates): 82.7% (males 83.4%; females 81.9%) in 2001 (Source: UN Development Programme, *Human Development Report*).

Directory

The Constitution

The Constitution of the Republic of Namibia took effect at independence on 21 March 1990. Its principal provisions are summarized below:

THE REPUBLIC

The Republic of Namibia is a sovereign, secular, democratic and unitary State and the Constitution is the supreme law.

FUNDAMENTAL HUMAN RIGHTS AND FREEDOMS

The fundamental rights and freedoms of the individual are guaranteed regardless of sex, race, colour, ethnic origin, religion, creed or social or economic status. All citizens shall have the right to form and join political parties. The practice of racial discrimination shall be prohibited.

THE PRESIDENT

Executive power shall be vested in the President and the Cabinet. The President shall be the Head of State and of the Government and the Commander-in-Chief of the Defence Force. The President shall be directly elected by universal and equal adult suffrage, and must receive more than 50% of the votes cast. The term of office shall be five years; one person may not hold the office of President for more than two terms*.

THE CABINET

The Cabinet shall consist of the President, the Prime Minister and such other ministers as the President may appoint from members of the National Assembly. The President may also appoint a Deputy Prime Minister. The functions of the members of the Cabinet shall include directing the activities of ministries and government departments, initiating bills for submission to the National Assembly, formulating, explaining and assessing for the National Assembly the budget of the State and its economic development plans, formulating, explaining and analysing for the National Assembly Namibia's foreign policy and foreign trade policy and advising the President on the state of national defence.

THE NATIONAL ASSEMBLY

Legislative power shall be vested in the National Assembly, which shall be composed of 72 members elected by general, direct and secret ballots and not more than six non-voting members appointed by the President by virtue of their special expertise, status, skill or experience. Every National Assembly shall continue for a maximum period of five years, but it may be dissolved by the President before the expiry of its term.

THE NATIONAL COUNCIL

The National Council shall consist of two members from each region (elected by regional councils from among their members) and shall have a life of six years. The functions of the National Council shall include considering all bills passed by the National Assembly, investigating any subordinate legislation referred to it by the National Assembly for advice, and recommending legislation to the National Assembly on matters of regional concern.

OTHER PROVISIONS

Other provisions relate to the administration of justice (see under Judicial System), regional and local government, the public service commission, the security commission, the police, defence forces and prison service, finance, and the central bank and national planning commission. The repeal of, or amendments to, the Constitution require the approval of two-thirds of the members of the National Assembly and two-thirds of the members of the National Council; if the proposed repeal or amendment secures a majority of two-thirds of the members of the National Assembly, but not a majority of two-thirds of the members of the National Council, the President may make the proposals the subject of a national referendum, in which a two-thirds' majority is needed for approval of the legislation.

* In late 1998 the National Assembly and National Council approved legislation whereby the Constitution was to be exceptionally amended to allow the incumbent President to seek a third term of office.

The Government

HEAD OF STATE

President and Commander-in-Chief of the Defence Force: Dr SAMUEL DANIEL NUJOMA (took office 21 March 1990; elected by direct suffrage 7–8 December 1994; re-elected 30 November–1 December 1999).

THE CABINET
(April 2004)

President: Dr SAMUEL DANIEL NUJOMA.

Prime Minister: THEO-BEN GURIRAB.

Deputy Prime Minister: Rev. HENDRIK WITBOOI.

Minister of Home Affairs: JERRY EKANDJO.

Special Adviser for Security Affairs: PETER TSHEEHAMA.

Minister of Foreign Affairs: HIDIPO HAMUTENYA.

Minister of Information and Broadcasting: NANGOLO MBUMBA.

Minister of Basic Education, Sport and Culture: JOHN MUTORWA.

Minister of Higher Education, Vocational Training, Science and Technology and Sport: NAHAS ANGULA.

Minister of Mines and Energy: NICKY IYAMBO.

Minister of Justice: ALBERT KAWANA.

Attorney-General: PENDUKENI IVULA-ITHANA.

Minister of Trade and Industry: JESAYA NYAMU.

Minister of Agriculture, Water and Rural Development: HELMUT ANGULA.

Minister of Defence: ERIKKI NGHIMTINA.

Minister of Finance: SAARAH KUUGONGELWA-AMADHILA.

Minister of Health and Social Services: Dr LIBERTINA AMATHILA.

Minister of Labour: MARCO HAUSIKU.

Minister of Regional and Local Government and Housing: JOEL NATANGWE KAAPANDA.

Minister of Environment and Tourism: PHILEMON MALIMA.

Minister of Works, Transport and Communications: MOSES AMWEELO.

Minister of Lands, Resettlement and Rehabilitation: HIFIKEPUNYE POHAMBA.

Minister of Fisheries and Marine Resources: ABRAHAM IYAMBO.

Minister of Prisons and Correctional Services: ANDIMBA TOIVO YA TOIVO.

Minister of Women's Development and Child Welfare: NETUMBO NANDI-NDAITWAH.

Minister without Portfolio: NGARIKUTUKE TJIRIANGE.

MINISTRIES

Office of the President: State House, Robert Mugabe Ave, PMB 13339, Windhoek; tel. (61) 2707111; fax (61) 221780; e-mail angolo@op.gov.na; internet www.op.gov.na.

Office of the Prime Minister: Robert Mugabe Ave, PMB 13338, Windhoek; tel. (61) 2879111; fax (61) 230648; internet www.opm.gov.na.

Ministry of Agriculture, Water and Rural Development: cnr Robert Mugabe Ave and Peter Muller St, PMB 13184, Windhoek; tel. (61) 2087111; fax (61) 229961.

Ministry of Basic Education, Sport and Culture: Troskie House, Uhland St, PMB 13186, Windhoek; tel. (61) 2933111; fax (61) 224277.

Ministry of Defence: PMB 13307, Windhoek; tel. (61) 2049111; fax (61) 232518.

Ministry of Environment and Tourism: Swabou Bldg, Post St Mall, PMB 13346, Windhoek; tel. (61) 2842111; fax (61) 221930; e-mail tourism@iwwn.com.na; internet www.tourism.com.na.

Ministry of Finance: Fiscus Bldg, John Meinert St, PMB 13295, Windhoek; tel. (61) 2099111; fax (61) 230179.

Ministry of Fisheries and Marine Resources: Brendan Simbwaye Sq., PMB 13355, Windhoek; tel. (61) 2053911; fax (61) 233286; e-mail mfmr@mfmr.gov.na; internet www.mfmr.gov.na.

Ministry of Foreign Affairs: Govt Bldgs, Robert Mugabe Ave, PMB 13347, Windhoek; tel. (61) 2829111; fax (61) 223937; e-mail headquarters@mfa.gov.na; internet www.mfa.gov.na.

Ministry of Health and Social Services: Old State Hospital, Harvey St, PMB 13198, Windhoek; tel. (61) 2039111; fax (61) 227607.

Ministry of Higher Education, Vocational Training, Science and Technology and Sport: Government Office Park, Luther St, PMB 13391, Windhoek; tel. (61) 2706111; fax (61) 253672; e-mail svansyl@mhevst.gov.na.

Ministry of Home Affairs: Cohen Bldg, Kasino St, PMB 13200, Windhoek; tel. (61) 2922111; fax (61) 2922185.

Ministry of Information and Broadcasting: Windhoek.

Ministry of Justice: Justitia Bldg, Independence Ave, PMB 13248, Windhoek; tel. (61) 2805111; fax (61) 221615.

Ministry of Labour: 32 Mercedes St, Khomasdal, PMB 19005, Windhoek; tel. (61) 2066111; fax (61) 212323.

Ministry of Lands, Resettlement and Rehabilitation: Brendan Simbwaye Bldg, Goethe St, PMB 13343, Windhoek; tel. (61) 2852111; fax (61) 254240.

Ministry of Mines and Energy: 1st Aviation Rd, PMB 13297, Windhoek; tel. (61) 2848111; fax (61) 238643; e-mail info@mme.gov.na; internet www.mme.gov.na.

Ministry of Prisons and Correctional Services: Brendan Simbwaye Bldg, Goethe St, PMB 13323; tel. (61) 2846111; fax (61) 233879.

Ministry of Regional and Local Government and Housing: PMB 13289, Windhoek; tel. (61) 2975111; fax (61) 226049.

Ministry of Trade and Industry: Govt Bldgs, PMB 13340, Windhoek; tel. (61) 2837111; fax (61) 220148; internet www.mti.gov.na.

Ministry of Women's Development and Child Promotion: Windhoek.

Ministry of Works, Transport and Communications: PMB 13341, Windhoek; tel. (61) 2088111; fax (61) 228560.

President and Legislature

PRESIDENT

Presidential Election, 30 November–1 December 1999

Candidate	% of votes
Samuel Nujoma (SWAPO)	76.8
Ben Ulenga (CoD)	10.5
Katuutire Kaura (DTA)	9.6
Justus Garoeb (UDF)	3.0
Total	**100.0**

NATIONAL ASSEMBLY*

Speaker: Mosé Penaani Tjitendero.

General Election, 30 November–1 December 1999

Party	% of votes	Seats
South West Africa People's Organisation of Namibia (SWAPO)	76.1	55
Congress of Democrats (CoD)	9.9	7
Democratic Turnhalle Alliance of Namibia (DTA)	9.5	7
United Democratic Front (UDF)	2.9	2
Monitor Action Group (MAG)	0.7	1
Others	0.9	—
Total	**100.0**	**72**

* In addition to the 72 directly elected members, the President of the Republic is empowered to nominate as many as six non-voting members.

NATIONAL COUNCIL

Chairman: Kandindima (Kandy) Nehova.

The second chamber of parliament is the advisory National Council, comprising two representatives from each of the country's 13 Regional Councils, elected for a period of six years.

Political Organizations

Christian Democratic Action for Social Justice (CDA): Ondwangwa; f. 1982; supported by Ovambos and mems of fmr National Democratic Party; Leader Rev. Peter Kalangula.

Congress of Democrats (CoD): 8 Storch St, POB 40905, Windhoek; tel. (61) 256954; fax (61) 256980; internet cod.namweb.com.na; f. 1999; Leader Ben Ulenga; Sec.-Gen. Ignatius Shixwameni.

Democratic Coalition of Namibia (DCN): Windhoek; f. 1994 as coalition of the National Patriotic Front, the South West African National Union (withdrew from coalition in Nov. 1994) and the German Union; Leader Moses Katjiuongua.

Democratic Turnhalle Alliance of Namibia (DTA): POB 173, Windhoek; internet www.framework.co.za/dua/namibia/dta.html; f. 1977 as a coalition of ethnically-based political groupings; reorg. as a single party in 1991; Pres. Katuutire Kaura; Chair. Johan de Waal.

Federal Convention of Namibia (FCN): Windhoek; f. 1988; Leader Johannes Diergaardt; federalist; opposes unitary form of govt for Namibia; an alliance of ethnically-based parties, including:

  NUDO—Progressive Party Jo'Horongo: f. 1987; Pres. Mburumba Kerina.

  Rehoboth Bevryde Demokratiese Party Rehoboth Free Democratic Party or **Liberation Front (RBDP):** Leader Johannes Diergaardt; coalition of the **Rehoboth Bevrydingsparty** Leader Johannes Diergaardt and the **Rehoboth Democratic Party** Leader K. G. Freigang.

Monitor Action Group (MAG): POB 80808, Olympia, Windhoek; tel. (61) 252008; fax (61) 229242; e-mail monitor@cyberhost.com.na; f. 1991; fmrly National Party of South West Africa; Leader Kosie Pretorius.

Namibia Movement for Independent Candidate: Windhoek; f. 1997; Leader Justice Kawadenge.

Namibia National Democratic Party: Windhoek; Leader Paul Helmuth.

Namibia National Front: Windhoek; Leader Vekuii Rukoro.

National Democratic Party for Justice (NDPFJ): f. May 1995 as SWAPO for Justice by fmr mems of SWAPO; reorg. as a political party in Nov. 1996, when it claimed to have 3,000 mem; Pres. Nghiwete Ndjoba.

South West Africa People's Organisation of Namibia (SWAPO): Windhoek; f. 1957 as the Ovamboland People's Congress; renamed South West Africa People's Organisation in 1960; adopted present name in 1968; Pres. Dr Samuel Daniel Nujoma; Vice-Pres. Hifikepunye Pohamba; Sec.-Gen. Ngarikutuke Tjiriange.

South West African National Union (SWANU): Windhoek; f. 1959; Pres. Rihupisa Kandando.

United Democratic Front (UDF): POB 20037, Windhoek; tel. (61) 230683; fax (61) 237175; f. 1989 as a centrist coalition of eight parties; Nat. Chair. Eric Biwa; Pres. Justus Garoeb.

Workers' Revolutionary Party: Windhoek; f. 1989; Trotskyist; Leaders Werner Mamugwe, Hewat Beukes.

The **Caprivi Liberation Army (CLA)**, f. 1998 as the Caprivi Liberation Movement, seeks secession of the Caprivi Strip; conducts mil. operations from bases in Zambia and Angola; political wing operates from Denmark as the **Caprivi National Union**, led by Mishake Muyongo and Boniface Mamili.

Diplomatic Representation

EMBASSIES AND HIGH COMMISSIONS IN NAMIBIA

Algeria: 111a Gloudina St, Ludwigsdorf, POB 3079, Windhoek; tel. (61) 221507; fax (61) 236376; e-mail ambalg.wkh@iwwn.com.na; Chargé d'affaires a.i. A. I. Bengueuedda.

Angola: Angola House, 3 Dr Agostinho Neto St, Ausspannplatz, PMB 12020, Windhoek; tel. (61) 227535; fax (61) 221498; Ambassador Dr Garcia Pires.

Botswana: 101 Nelson Mandela Ave, POB 20359, Windhoek; tel. (61) 221942; fax (61) 221948; High Commissioner Tuelenyana Rosemary Ditlhabi-Oliphant.

Brazil: 52 Bismarck St, POB 24166, Windhoek; tel. (61) 237368; fax (61) 233389; e-mail orlando@iwwn.com.na; Ambassador Orlando Galvêas Oliveira.

China, People's Republic: 13 Wecka St, POB 22777, Windhoek; tel. (61) 222089; fax (61) 225544; e-mail chinaemb@iafrica.com.na; Ambassador Chen Laiyuan.

Congo, Republic: 9 Korner St, POB 22970, Windhoek; tel. (61) 257517; fax (61) 240796; Ambassador A. Kondho.

Cuba: 31 Omuramba Rd, Eros, POB 23866, Windhoek; tel. (61) 227072; fax (61) 231584; e-mail embacuba@iafrica.com.na; Ambassador Sergio González González.

Egypt: 10 Berg St, POB 11853, Windhoek; tel. (61) 221501; fax (61) 228856; Ambassador Hussein A. M. Wahby.

Finland: Sanlam Centre, 5th Floor, Independence Ave, POB 3649, Windhoek; tel. (61) 221355; fax (61) 221349; e-mail sanomat.win@formin.fi; internet www.finland.org.na; Ambassador Kirsti Lintonen.

France: 1 Goethe St, POB 20484, Windhoek; tel. (61) 2276700; fax (61) 276710; e-mail frambwdk@iafrica.na; internet www .ambafrance-na.org; Ambassador Philippe Perrier de la Bathie.

Germany: Sanlam Centre, 6th Floor, 154 Independence ave, POB 231, Windhoek; tel. (61) 273100; fax (61) 222981; e-mail info@german-embassy-windhoek.org; internet www .german-embassy-windhoek.org; Ambassador Harald N. Nestroy.

Ghana: 5 Nelson Mandela Ave, POB 24165, Windhoek; tel. (61) 221341; fax (61) 221343; High Commissioner H. Mills-Lutterodt.

India: 97 Nelson Mandela Ave, POB 1209, Windhoek; tel. (61) 226037; fax (61) 237320; e-mail hicomind@mweb.com.na; High Commissioner Yogendra Kumar.

Indonesia: 103 Nelson Mandela Ave, POB 20691, Windhoek; tel. (61) 221914; fax (61) 223811; Chargé d'affaires Theo Waymuri.

Kenya: Kenya House, 5th Floor, 134 Robert Mugabe Ave, POB 2889, Windhoek; tel. (61) 226836; fax (61) 221409; e-mail kenyanet@mweb.com.na; High Commissioner Binsai J. Chepsongol.

Libya: 69 Burg St, Luxury Hill, POB 124, Windhoek; tel. (61) 234454; fax (61) 234471; Chargé d'affaires a.i. H. O. Alshaoshi.

Malawi: 56 Bismarck St, POB 13254, Windhoek; tel. (61) 221391; fax (61) 227056; High Commissioner A. Mnthambala.

Malaysia: 10 Von Eckenbrecker St, POB 312, Windhoek; tel. (61) 259344; fax (61) 259343; e-mail malhicom@iwwn.com.na.

Mexico: Southern Life Tower, 3rd Floor, 39 Post St Mall, POB 13220, Windhoek; tel. (61) 229082; fax (61) 229180; e-mail embamexn@iway.na; Charge d'affaires a.i. José Luís García.

Netherlands: 2 Crohn St, PMB 564, Windhoek; tel. (61) 223733; fax (61) 223732; e-mail nlgovwin@namib.com.na.

Nigeria: 4 Omuramba Rd, Eros Park, POB 23547, Windhoek; tel. (61) 232103; fax (61) 221639; e-mail nignam@web.com.na; High Commissioner B. M. Hirse.

Portugal: 24 Robert Mugabe Ave, POB 443, Windhoek; tel. (61) 237928; fax (61) 237929; e-mail emport@mweb.com.na; Ambassador Maria do Carmo Allegro de Magalhães.

Russia: 4 Christian St, POB 3826, Windhoek; tel. (61) 228671; fax (61) 229061; e-mail rusembna@iafrica.com.na; Ambassador Vyacheslav D. Shumskii.

South Africa: RSA House, cnr Jan Jonker and Nelson Mandela Aves, POB 23100, Windhoek; tel. (61) 229765; fax (61) 224140; High Commissioner B. S. S. Mabizela.

Spain: 58 Bismarck St, POB 21811, Windhoek; tel. (61) 223066; fax (61) 223046; e-mail embespna@mail.mae.es; Ambassador Francisco Javier Pérez-Griffo y de Vides.

Sweden: Sanlam Centre, 9th Floor, POB 23087, Windhoek; tel. (61) 2859111; fax (61) 2859222; e-mail embassy.windhoek@sida.se; Chargé d'affaires Göran Hedebro.

United Kingdom: 116 Robert Mugabe Ave, POB 22202, Windhoek; tel. (61) 274800; fax (61) 228895; e-mail bhc@mweb.com.na; High Commissioner Alasdair MacDermott.

USA: 14 Lossen St, Ausspannplatz, PMB 12029, Windhoek 9000; tel. (61) 221601; fax (61) 229792; e-mail HealyKc2@state.gov; internet www.usembassy.namib.com; Ambassador Kevin J. McGuire.

Ukraine: Windhoek; Ambassador Ihor M. Turyanskiy.

Venezuela: Southern Life Tower, 3rd Floor, 39 Post St Mall, PMB 13353, Windhoek; tel. (61) 227905; fax (61) 227804; e-mail embaven@com.na; Chargé d'affaires Abraham Quintero.

Zambia: 22 Sam Nujoma Dr., cnr Mandume Ndemufayo Rd, POB 22882, Windhoek; tel. (61) 237610; fax (61) 228162; High Commissioner S. L. Mumbi.

Zimbabwe: cnr Independence Ave and Grimm St, POB 23056, Windhoek; tel. (61) 228134; fax (61) 226859; Ambassador Mary Sibusisiwe Mubi.

Judicial System

Judicial power is exercised by the Supreme Court, the High Court and a number of Magistrate and Lower Courts. The Constitution provides for the appointment of an Ombudsman.

Chief Justice: Simpson Mtambanengwe (acting).

Religion

It is estimated that about 90% of the population are Christians.

CHRISTIANITY

Council of Churches in Namibia: 8 Mont Blanc St, POB 41, Windhoek; tel. (61) 217621; fax (61) 62786; e-mail ccn.windhoek@iafrica.com.na; f. 1978; eight mem. churches; Pres. Bishop Hendrik Frederik; Gen. Sec. Nangula Kathindi.

The Anglican Communion

Namibia comprises a single diocese in the Church of the Province of Southern Africa. The Metropolitan of the Province is the Archbishop of Cape Town, South Africa.

Bishop of Namibia: Rt Rev. Nehemiah Shihala Hamupenbe, POB 57, Windhoek; tel. (61) 238920; fax (61) 225903; e-mail shihala@africaonline.com.na.

Dutch Reformed Church

Dutch Reformed Church in Namibia: 34 Feldstreet, POB 389, Windhoek; tel. (61) 225073; fax (61) 227287; e-mail ngkn@iway.na; internet www.ngkn.com.na; f. 1898; 23,724 mems in 43 congregations; Sec. Rev. Clem Marais.

Evangelical Lutheran

Evangelical Lutheran Church in Namibia (ELCIN): PMB 2018, Ondangwa; tel. (56) 24241; fax (56) 240472; e-mail elcinhq@ednweb.com.na; internet www.elca.org/dgm/country_packet/packets/namibia/elcin.html; Moderator Rev. Herman Oosthuisen; Presiding Bishop Apollos Kaulinge.

Evangelical Lutheran Church (Rhenish Mission Church): POB 5069, Windhoek; tel. (61) 224531; f. 1967; Pres. Bishop Hendrik Frederik.

German Evangelical-Lutheran Church in Namibia: POB 233, Windhoek; tel. (61) 224294; fax (61) 221470; e-mail delk@namibnet .com; 5,000 mems; Pres. Bishop Reinhard Keding.

Methodist

African Methodist Episcopal Church: Windhoek; tel. (61) 62757; Rev. B. G. Karuaera.

Methodist Church of Southern Africa: POB 143, Windhoek; tel. (61) 228921.

The Roman Catholic Church

Namibia comprises one archdiocese, one diocese and one apostolic vicariate. At 31 December 2002 an estimated 17.4% of the population were adherents of the Roman Catholic Church.

Bishops' Conference

Namibian Catholic Bishops' Conference, POB 11525, Windhoek; tel. (61) 224798; fax (61) 228126; e-mail ncbc@windhoek.org.na.

f. 1996; Pres. (vacant).

Archbishop of Windhoek: (vacant), POB 272, Windhoek 9000; tel. (61) 227595; fax (61) 229836; e-mail rcharch@iafrica.com.na.

Other Christian Churches

Among other denominations active in Namibia are the Evangelical Reformed Church in Africa, the Presbyterian Church of Southern Africa and the United Congregational Church of Southern Africa.

JUDAISM

Windhoek Hebrew Congregation: POB 563, Windhoek; tel. (61) 221990; fax (61) 226444; e-mail steinitz@nweb.com.na.

BAHÁ'Í FAITH

National Spiritual Assembly: POB 20372, Windhoek; tel. (61) 239634; e-mail don@iafrica.com.na; mems resident in 215 localities.

The Press

Abacus: POB 22791, Windhoek; tel. (61) 235596; fax (61) 236467; weekly; English; educational; circ. 31,000.

AgriForum: 114 Robert Mugabe Ave, PMB 13255, Windhoek; tel. (61) 237838; fax (61) 220193; e-mail richter@agrinamibia.com.na; monthly; Afrikaans, English; publ. by Namibia Agricultural Union; Editor RICHTER ERASMUS; circ. 5,000.

Allgemeine Zeitung: 49 Stübel St, POB 2127, Windhoek; tel. (61) 225822; fax (61) 220225; e-mail az-news@mweb.com.na; internet www.az-namibia.de; f. 1916; daily; German; Editor-in-Chief EBERHARD HOFFMANN; circ. 4,800 (Mon.–Wed.), 5,900 (Thur.–Fri.).

Aloe: POB 59, Windhoek; tel. (61) 2902056; fax (61) 2902006; monthly; English; edited by the Windhoek Municipality; Editor SIMON HOABEB; circ. 45,000.

Caprivi Vision: f. 2002; regional newspaper for Caprivi region; Editor RISCO LUMAMEZI.

CCN Information: Council of Churches in Namibia, POB 41, Windhoek; f. 1980; 11 a year.

Namib Times: Seventh St, POB 706, Walvis Bay; tel. (64) 205854; fax (64) 204813; 2 a week; Afrikaans, English, German and Portuguese; Editor PAUL VINCENT; circ. 4,300.

Namibia Brief: Independence Ave, POB 2123, Windhoek; tel. and fax (61) 251044; quarterly; English; Editor CATHY BLATT; circ. 7,500.

Namibia Business Journal: POB 9355, Windhoek; tel. (61) 228809; fax (61) 228009; Editor MILTON LOUW; circ. 4,000.

Namibia Economist: 7 Schuster St, POB 49, Windhoek 9000; tel. (61) 221925; fax (61) 220615; e-mail info@economist.com.na; internet www.economist.com.na; f. 1986; weekly; English; business; Editor EDGAR BRANDT; circ. 7,000.

Namibia Focus: Windhoek; tel. (61) 227182; fax (61) 220226; monthly; English; business; Editor JOHAN ENGELBRECHT; circ. 30,000.

Namibia Review: Turnhalle Bldg, Bahnhof St, PMB 13344, Windhoek; tel. (61) 222246; fax (61) 224937; e-mail nreview@mib.gov.na; govt-owned; monthly; Editor ELIZABETH KALAMBO-MULE; circ. 5,000.

Namibia Today: POB 24669, Windhoek; tel. (61) 229150; fax (61) 229150; 2 a week; Afrikaans, English, Oshiherero, Oshiwambo; publ. by SWAPO; Editor KAOMO-VIJINDA TJOMBE; circ. 5,000.

The Namibian: John Meinert St, POB 20783, Windhoek; tel. (61) 236970; fax (61) 233980; e-mail info@namibian.com.na; internet www.namibian.com.na; daily; English; Editor GWEN LISTER; circ. 11,000.

The Namibian Worker: POB 50034, Bachbrecht, Windhoek; tel. (61) 215037; fax (61) 215589; Afrikaans, English, Oshiwambo; publ. by National Union of Namibian Workers; Editor-in-Chief C. R. HAIKALI; circ. 1,000.

New Era: PMB 13364, Windhoek; tel. (61) 234924; fax (61) 235419; govt-owned; 2 a week; English; Editor RAJAH MUNAMAVA; circ. 10,000.

Republikein 2000: 11 Omuramba Rd, Eros, Windhoek; tel. (61) 2972000; fax (61) 2972025; e-mail alwyn@republikein.com.na; internet www.republikein.com.na; f. 1977; daily; Afrikaans, English and German; organ of DTA of Namibia; Editor GERT JACOBIE; circ. 12,000 (Mon.–Wed.), 15,000 (Thur.–Fri.).

Tempo: 49 Stuebel St, POB 1794, Windhoek; tel. (61) 225822; fax (61) 223110; f. 1992; weekly; English and German; Editor DES ERASMUS; circ. 11,000.

Visitor: POB 23000, Windhoek; tel. (61) 227182; fax (61) 220226; monthly; English; tourist information; Editor JOHAN ENGELBRECHT; circ. 10,000.

The Windhoek Advertiser: 49 Stuebel St, POB 3436, Windhoek; tel. (61) 230331; fax (61) 225863; e-mail advertsr@iwwn.com.na; f. 1919; daily; English; Editor DEON SCHLECHTER; circ. 5,000 (Mon.–Wed.), 7,000 (Thur.–Fri.).

Windhoek Observer: 49 Stuebel St, POB 2255, Windhoek; tel. (61) 221737; fax (61) 226098; f. 1978; weekly; English; Editor HANNES SMITH; circ. 14,000.

NEWS AGENCIES

Namibia Press Agency (Nampa): POB 61354, Windhoek; tel. (61) 221711; fax (61) 221713; e-mail admin@nampa.org; internet www.nampa.org; CEO N. HAMUNIME.

Foreign Bureaux

Informatsionnoye Telegrafnoye Agentstvo Rossii—Telegrafnoye Agentstvo Suverennykh Stran (ITAR—TASS) (Russia): POB 24821, Windhoek; tel. and fax (61) 232909; Correspondent PAVE MYLTSEV.

Inter Press Service (IPS) (Italy): POB 20783, Windhoek; tel. (61) 226645; Correspondent MARK VERBAAN.

South African Press Association (SAPA): POB 2032, Windhoek; tel. (61) 231565; fax (61) 220783; Representative CARMEN HONEY.

Xinhua (New China) News Agency (People's Republic of China): POB 22130, Windhoek; tel. (61) 226484; fax (61) 226484; Bureau Chief TENG WENYI.

Reuters (UK) is also represented in Namibia.

PRESS ASSOCIATIONS

Journalist Association of Namibia (JAN): Windhoek; tel. (61) 236970; fax (61) 248016; e-mail shirumbu@iafrica.com.na; f. 1992; Chair. DAVID LUSH.

Press Club Windhoek: POB 2032, Windhoek; tel. (61) 231565; fax (61) 220783; Chair. CARMEN HONEY.

Publishers

BAUM Publishers: POB 3436, Windhoek; tel. (61) 225411; fax (61) 224843; Publr NIC KRUGER.

Clarian Publishers: POB 5861, Windhoek; tel. (61) 251044; fax (61) 237251; Publr CATHY BLATT.

ELOC Printing Press: PMB 2013, Oniipa, Ondangwa; tel. and fax (6756) 40211; f. 1901; Rev. Dr KLEOPAS DUMENI.

Gamsberg McMillan Publishers (Pty) Ltd: POB 22830, Windhoek; tel. (61) 232165; fax (61) 233538; e-mail gmp@iafrica.com.na; internet www.macmillan-africa.com/contacts/namibia.htm; Man. Dir HERMAN VAN WYK.

Longman Namibia: POB 9251, Eros, Windhoek; tel. (61) 231124; fax (61) 224019; Publr LINDA BREDENKAMP.

National Archives of Namibia: Eugène Marais St, PMB 13250, Windhoek; tel. (61) 2935213; fax (61) 2935217; Man. J. KUTZNER.

New Namibia Books (Pty) Ltd: POB 21601, Windhoek; tel. (61) 221134; fax (61) 235279; Publr JANE KATJAVIVI.

Out of Africa Publishers: POB 21841, Windhoek; tel. (61) 221494; fax (61) 221720; e-mail books@mweb.com.na; Man. VIDA LOCHNER.

PUBLISHERS' ASSOCIATION

Association of Namibian Publishers: POB 21601, Windhoek; tel. (61) 235796; fax (61) 235279; f. 1991; Sec. PETER REINER.

Broadcasting and Communications

TELECOMMUNICATIONS

Telecom Namibia Ltd (Telecom): POB 297, Windhoek; tel. (61) 2019211; fax (61) 248723; internet www.telecom.na; f. 1992; state-owned; Chair. T. HAIMBILI; Man. Dir T. MBERIRUA.

Mobile Telecommunications Ltd (MTC): POB 23051, Windhoek; tel. (61) 249570; fax (61) 249571; f. 1994; cellular telecommunications co; Man. Dir B. GUVE.

Multicom: POB 80425, Windhoek; tel. (61) 264755; fax (61) 264756; f. 1994; Gen. Man. G. VAN WYK.

BROADCASTING

Radio

Namibian Broadcasting Corpn (NBC): POB 321, Windhoek; tel. (61) 2913111; fax (61) 216209; e-mail nbcho@iwwn.com.na; f. 1990; broadcasts on eight radio channels in 11 languages; Dir-Gen. Dr BEN MULONGENI.

Channel 7: POB 20500, Windhoek; tel. (61) 218969; fax (61) 215572; Man. NEAL VAN DEN BERGH.

Katutura Community Radio: POB 22355, Windhoek; tel. (61) 263768; fax (61) 262786; Dir FREDERICK GOWASEB.

Radio Antenna (Radio 99): POB 11849, Windhoek; tel. (61) 223634; fax (61) 230964; e-mail radio99@mweb.com.na; f. 1994; Man. Dir MARIO AITA.

Radio Energy (Radio 100): POB 11849, Windhoek; tel. (61) 224947; fax (61) 230964; Man. Dir MARIO AITA.

Television

Namibian Broadcasting Corpn (NBC): POB 321, Windhoek; tel. (61) 2913111; fax (61) 216209; e-mail nbcho@iwwn.com.na; internet www.nbc.com.na; f. 1990; operates national television channel; programmes in English; Dir-Gen. Dr Ben Mulongeni.

Multi-Choice Namibia: POB 1752, Windhoek; tel. (61) 222222; fax (61) 227605; commercial television channels; Gen. Man. Harry Aucamp.

Finance

(cap. = capital; res = reserves; dep. = deposits; m. = million; brs = branches; amounts in Namibian dollars)

BANKING

Central Bank

Bank of Namibia: 71 Robert Mugabe Ave, POB 2882, Windhoek; tel. (61) 2835111; fax (61) 2835228; e-mail general.inquiries@bon .com.na; internet www.bon.com.na; f. 1990; cap. 40.0m., res 1,048.7m., dep. 1,270.5m. (Dec. 2002); Gov. Tom K. Alweendo; Deputy Gov. P. Hartman.

Commercial Banks

Bank Windhoek Ltd: Bank Windhoek Bldg, 262 Independence Ave, POB 15, Windhoek; tel. (61) 2991122; fax (61) 2991620; e-mail info@bankwindhoek.com.na; internet www.bankwindhoek.com.na; f. 1982; cap. 4.7m., res 283.2m., dep. 2,939.0m. (March 2002); Chair. J. C. Brandt; Man. Dir J. J. Swanepoel; 22 brs.

City Savings and Investment Bank (CSIB): FGI House, 2nd Floor, Post St Mall, Windhoek; tel. (61) 221262; fax (61) 221555; e-mail csib@solarium.iwwn.com.na; total assets 2,493m. (Mar 2001); f. 1994; merged with South West Africa Building Society (Swabou) 2000; CEO M. A. Bashah; Chair. A. Mushimba.

Commercial Bank of Namibia Ltd: 12–20 Bülow St, POB 1, Windhoek; tel. (61) 2959111; fax (61) 2952046; e-mail service@ c-bank.com.na; internet www.c-bank.com.na; f. 1973; controlled by SND Investment Holdings Ltd; cap. 16.0m., res 16.4m., dep. 2,012.8m. (Dec. 2002); Chair. Michael J. Leeming; Man. Dir Stephanus du Plessis; 10 brs.

First National Bank of Namibia Ltd: 209/211 Independence Ave, POB 195, Windhoek; tel. (61) 2992222; fax (61) 2992125; e-mail info@fnbnamibia.com.na; internet www.fnbnamibia.com.na; f. 1986; cap. 1.0m., res 593.4m., total assets 3,270.1m. (June 2002); Chair. H. D. Voigts; Man. Dir S. H. Moir; 28 brs and 22 agencies.

Namibian Banking Corpn: Carl List Haus, Independence Ave, POB 370, Windhoek; tel. (61) 225946; fax (61) 223741; Chair. J. C. Westraat; Man. Dir P. P. Niehaus; 3 brs.

Standard Bank Namibia Ltd: Standard Bank Centre, Post St Mall, POB 3327, Windhoek; tel. (61) 2949111; fax (61) 2942240; e-mail info@standardbank.com.na; internet www.standardbank .com.na; f. 1915; controlled by Standard Bank Investment Corpn; cap. 1.7m., res 311.5m., dep. 3,984.2m. (Dec. 2002); Chair. L. S. Hangala; Man. Dir O. M. Tidbury; 19 brs and 17 agencies.

Agricultural Bank

Agricultural Bank of Namibia (Agribank): 10 Post St Mall, POB 13208, Windhoek; tel. (61) 2074200; fax (61) 2074289; e-mail agribank@iafrica.com.na; f. 1922; total assets 739.1m. (March 2001); Chair. Dr Franz Stellmacher.

Merchant Bank

UAL—Namibia: Windhoek; f. 1997; subsidiary of UAL Merchant Bank Ltd (South Africa); Man. Dir Steve Galloway.

STOCK EXCHANGE

Namibian Stock Exchange (NSX): Shop 8, Kaiserkrone Centre, Post St Mall, POB 2401, Windhoek; tel. (61) 227647; fax (61) 248531; e-mail heikon@nsx.com.na; internet www.nsx.com.na; f. 1992; Chair. Exec. Cttee P. Hango; Gen. Man. Heiko Niedermeier.

INSURANCE

Allianz Insurance Co of Namibia Ltd: POB 3244, Windhoek; tel. (61) 226897; fax (61) 231070; e-mail mbakoh@allianz.co.na; Man. Dir H. Mbako.

W. Biederlack & Co: Metje-Behnsen Bldg, 2nd Floor, Independence Ave, POB 365, Windhoek; tel. (61) 233177; fax (61) 233178; e-mail group@w-biederlack.com; f. 1990.

Commercial Union Insurance Ltd: Bülow St, POB 1599, Windhoek; tel. (61) 37137.

FGI Namibia Ltd: POB 2516, Windhoek; tel. (61) 225450; fax (61) 229195; f. 1993; short-term insurance; Man. Dir Peter Opperman.

Incorporated General Insurance Ltd: 10 Bülow St, POB 2516, Windhoek; tel. (61) 37453; fax (61) 35647.

Insurance Co of Namibia (INSCON): POB 2877, Windhoek; tel. (61) 275900; fax (61) 233808; e-mail rudi.jacobs@inscon.com.na; short-term insurance; Gen. Dir F. Otto.

Lifegro Assurance Ltd: Independence Ave, POB 23055, Windhoek; tel. (61) 33068.

Lumley Insurance Group: POB 1011, Windhoek 9000; tel. (61) 224471; fax (61) 234802; f. 1953; Chair. and Man. Dir Ingo Rix.

Metropolitan Life Ltd: Goethe St, POB 3785, Windhoek; tel. (61) 239140; fax (61) 248191; Chair. M. L. Smith; Man. Dir R. A. V. E. Fouche.

Mutual and Federal Insurance Co Ltd: Mutual and Federal Centre, 7th Floor, 227 Independence Ave, POB 151, Windhoek; tel. (61) 2077111; fax (61) 2077205; f. 1990; Gen. Man. R. I. Sanger.

Namibia National Insurance Co Ltd: Bülow St, POB 23053, Windhoek; tel. (61) 224539; fax (61) 238737; fmrly Federated Insurance Co Ltd.

Old Mutual Life Assurance Co. (Namibia) Ltd: Mutual Platz, 5th Floor, Post St Mall, POB 165, Windhoek; tel. (61) 2993999; fax (61) 223838; e-mail dkotze@oldmutual.com; internet www .oldmutual.com.na; Chair. J. S. Kirkpatrick.

Protea Assurance Co Ltd: Windhoek; tel. (61) 225891.

Sanlam Life Assurance Ltd: Bülow St, POB 317, Windhoek; tel. (61) 36680.

Santam Insurance Ltd: Independence Ave, POB 204, Windhoek; tel. (61) 238214; fax (61) 235225; Man. Dir C. J. Engelbrecht; Dep. Man. Dir H. Ochse.

Southern Life Assurance Ltd: Southern Tower, Post Street Mall, POB 637, Windhoek; tel. (61) 234056; fax (61) 231574; Man. Dir L. Lombaard.

Trade and Industry

GOVERNMENT AGENCIES

Karakul Board of Namibia—Swakara Fur Producers and Exporters: PMB 13300, Windhoek; tel. (61) 237750; fax (61) 236122; e-mail agrapels@agra.com.na; internet www.agra.com.na.

Meat Board of Namibia: POB 38, Windhoek; tel. (61) 33180; fax (61) 228310; f. 1935; Chair. John le Roux; Gen. Man. Paul Strydom.

Meat Corpn of Namibia (MEATCO NAMIBIA): POB 3881, Windhoek; tel. (61) 216810; fax (61) 217045; e-mail hoffice@meatco .com.na; internet www.meatco.com.na.

Namibian Agronomic Board: POB 5096, Windhoek; tel. (61) 224741; fax (61) 225371; e-mail christof@nammic.com.na; Man. C. Brock.

National Petroleum Corpn of Namibia (NAMCOR): Windhoek; Man. Dir Skerf Pottas.

DEVELOPMENT ORGANIZATIONS

Namibia Development Corpn: 11 Goethe St, PMB 13252, Windhoek; tel. (61) 2069111; fax (61) 247841; e-mail info@ndc.org.na; internet www.ndc.org.na; f. 1993; promotes foreign investment and provides concessionary loans and equity to new enterprises; manages agricultural projects; undertakes feasibility studies; Chair. P. T. Damaseb; Man. Dir I. I. Namaseb.

Namibia Investment Centre: Ministry of Trade and Industry, Brendan Simbwaye Sq., Block B, Goethe St, PMB 13340, Windhoek; tel. (61) 2837335; fax (61) 220278; e-mail nic@mti.gov.na; Exec. Dir D. Nuyoma.

National Housing Enterprise: POB 20192, Windhoek; tel. (61) 2927111; fax (61) 222301; f. 1983; provides low-cost housing; Chair. V. Rukoro; CEO K. R. M. Kavekotora.

CHAMBERS OF COMMERCE

Chamber of Mines of Namibia (CMIN): POB 2895, Windhoek; tel. (61) 237925; fax (61) 222638; e-mail chammin@mweb.com.na; f. 1979; Pres. André Neethling; Gen. Man. John Rogers; 65 mems (2003).

Namibia National Chamber of Commerce and Industry (NNCCI): POB 9355, Windhoek; tel. (61) 228809; fax (61) 228009; e-mail nnccihq@iwwn.com.na; internet www.ncci.org.na; f. 1990; Pres. Dr L. Hangala; CEO Sam Geiseb (acting).

Windhoek Chamber of Commerce and Industries: SWA Building Society Bldg, 3rd Floor, POB 191, Windhoek; tel. (61) 222000; fax (61) 233690; e-mail whkchamber@lianam.lia.net; f. 1920; Pres. H. SCHMIDT; Gen. Man. T. D. PARKHOUSE; 230 mems.

EMPLOYERS' ORGANIZATIONS

Construction Industries Federation of Namibia: 22 Stein St, Klein, POB 1479, Windhoek; tel. (61) 230028; fax (61) 224534; e-mail cif@namibnet.com; Pres. ERNST KEIBEL.

Electrical Contractors' Association: POB 3163, Windhoek; tel. (61) 37920; Pres. F. PFAFFENTHALER.

Motor Industries Federation of Namibia: POB 1503, Windhoek; tel. (61) 37970; fax (61) 237251.

Namibia Agricultural Union (NAU): PMB 13255, Windhoek; tel. (61) 237838; fax (61) 220193; e-mail nau@agrinamibia.com.na; Pres. J. M. DE WET.

Namibia Chamber of Printing: POB 363, Windhoek; tel. (61) 237905; fax (61) 222927; Sec. S. G. TIMM.

UTILITIES

Namibia Power Corpn (Pty) Ltd (NamPower): NamPower Centre, 15 Luther St, POB 2864, Windhoek; tel. (61) 2054111; fax (61) 232805; e-mail register@nampower.com.na; internet www.nampower.com.na; Chair. M. SHIKONGO; Man. Dir Dr LEAKE S. HANGALA.

Northern Electricity: POB 891, Tsumeb; tel. (67) 222243; fax (67) 222245; private electricity supply co; Man. Dir C. G. N. HUYSEN.

TRADE UNIONS

There are several union federations, and a number of independent unions.

Trade Union Federations

Confederation of Labour: POB 22060, Windhoek.

National Allied Unions (NANAU): Windhoek; f. 1987; an alliance of trade unions, representing c. 7,600 mems, incl. Namibia Wholesale and Retail Workers' Union (f. 1986; Gen. Sec. T. Ngaujake; 6,000 mems), and Namibia Women Support Cttee; Pres. HENOCH HANDURA.

Namibia Trade Union (NTU): Windhoek; f. 1985; represents 6,700 domestic, farm and metal workers; Pres. ALPHA KANGUEEHI; Sec.-Gen. BEAU TJISESETA.

Namibia Trade Union Council (NTUC): Windhoek; f. 1981; affiliates include Northern Builders' Asscn.

National Union of Namibian Workers (NUNW): POB 50034, Windhoek; tel. (61) 215037; fax (61) 215589; f. 1972; Pres. RISTO KAPENDA; Sec.-Gen. PETER NAHOLO (acting); 87,000 mems.

Affiliates include:

Mineworkers' Union of Namibia (MUN): f. 1986; Chair. ASSER KAPERE; Pres. EINO NTINDA (acting); Gen. Sec. JOSEPH K. HENGARI; 12,500 mems.

Namibia Food and Allied Workers' Union: f. 1986; Chair. MATHEUS LIBEREKI; Pres. DAVID NAMALENGA; Gen. Sec. MAGDALENA IPINGE (acting); 12,000 mems.

Namibia Metal and Allied Workers' Union: f. 1987; Chair. ANDRIES TEMBA; Gen. Sec. MOSES SHIKWA (acting); 5,500 mems.

Namibia Public Workers' Union: f. 1987; Chair. STEVEN IMMANUEL; Gen. Sec. PETER ILONGA; 11,000 mems.

Namibia Transport and Allied Workers' Union: f. 1988; Chair. TYLVES GIDEON; Gen. Sec. IMMANUEL KAVAA; 7,500 mems.

Other Unions

Association for Government Service Officials: Windhoek; f. 1981; Chair. ALLAN HATTLE; 9,000 mems.

Namibia Building Workers' Association: Windhoek; Sec. H. BOCK.

Public Service Union of Namibia: POB 21662, Windhoek; tel. (61) 213083; fax (61) 213047; f. 1981; Sec.-Gen. STEVE RUKORO.

Transport

RAILWAYS

The main line runs from Nakop, at the border with South Africa, via Keetmanshoop to Windhoek, Kranzberg, Grootfontein, Tsumeb, Swakopmund and Walvis Bay. There are three branch lines, from Windhoek to Gobabis, Otjiwarongo to Outjo and Keetmanshoop to Lüderitz. The total rail network covers 2,382 route-km. There are plans for a railway line connecting Namibia with Zambia, as part of a programme to improve transport links among the members of the Common Market for Eastern and Southern Africa; plans to extend the northern railway line by 248 km, from Tsuneb to Ondangwa, were announced in 2001.

TransNamib Holdings Ltd: TransNamib Bldg, cnr Independence Ave and Bahnhof St, PMB 13204, Windhoek; tel. (61) 2981111; fax (61) 227984; e-mail pubrelation@transnamib.com.na; internet www.transnamib.com.na; state-owned; Chair. OTTO HERINGEL; Man. Dir Dr PEINGONDJABI T. SHIPOH.

ROADS

In 2000 the road network comprised 66,467 km of roads, of which 4,470 km were main roads. A major road link from Walvis Bay to Jwaneng, northern Botswana, the Trans-Kalahari Highway, was completed in 1998, along with the Trans-Caprivi highway, linking Namibia with northern Botswana, Zambia and Zimbabwe. The Government is also upgrading and expanding the road network in northern Namibia.

SHIPPING

The ports of Walvis Bay and Lüderitz are linked to the main overseas shipping routes and handle almost one-half of Namibia's external trade. Walvis Bay is a hub port for the region, serving land-locked countries such as Botswana, Zambia and Zimbabwe.

Namibian Ports Authority (NAMPORT): 13th Road, POB 361, Walvis Bay; tel. (64) 2082201; fax (64) 2082320; e-mail jerome@namport.com.na; internet www.namport.com.na; f. 1994; Chair. DIRK H. CONRADIE; CEO WESSIE WESSELS.

Pan-Ocean Shipping Services Ltd: POB 2613, Walvis Bay; tel. (64) 203959; fax (64) 204199; e-mail kirovg@iafrica.com.na; f. 1995; Man. Dir JÜRGEN HEYNEMANN; Gen. Man. GEORGE KIROV.

CIVIL AVIATION

There are international airports at Windhoek and Walvis Bay, as well as a number of other airports throughout Namibia, and numerous landing strips.

Air Namibia: TransNamib Bldg, cnr Independence Ave and Bahnhof St, POB 731, Windhoek; tel. (61) 223019; fax (61) 221910; e-mail aguibeb@airnamibia.com.na; internet www.airnamibia.com.na; f. 1959 as Namib Air; state-owned; transfer to majority (70%) private ownership delayed in 2004; domestic flights and services to Southern Africa and Western Europe; Chair. VEKUII RUKORO; CEO GERNOT RIEDEL (acting).

Kalahari Express Airlines (KEA): POB 40179, Windhoek; tel. (61) 245665; fax (61) 245612; e-mail keaadmin@kalahariexpress.com.na; f. 1995; domestic and regional flights; Exec. Dir PEINGONDJABI SHIPOH.

Tourism

Namibia's principal tourist attractions are its game parks and nature reserves, and the development of 'eco-tourism' is being promoted. In the late 1990s tourism was one of the fastest growing sectors of the Namibian economy. Tourist arrivals in Namibia in 1998 totalled 614,168. In that year tourism receipts were US $288m.

Namibia Tourism: PMB 13346, Capital Bldg, Ground Floor, 272 Independence Ave, Windhoek; tel. (61) 2849111; fax (61) 284-2364; e-mail tourism@iwwn.com.na; internet www.iwwn.com.na/namtour.

NAURU

Introductory Survey

Location, Climate, Language, Religion, Flag, Capital

The Republic of Nauru is a small island in the central Pacific Ocean, lying about 40 km (25 miles) south of the Equator and about 4,000 km (2,500 miles) north-east of Sydney, Australia. Its nearest neighbour is Banaba (Ocean Island), in Kiribati, about 300 km (186 miles) to the east. The climate is tropical, with a westerly monsoon season from November to February. The average annual rainfall is about 2,060 mm (80 ins), but actual rainfall is extremely variable. Day temperatures vary between 24°C and 34°C (75°–93°F). Of the total population in 1983, 61.7% were Nauruans. Their language is Nauruan, but English is also widely understood. The majority of Nauruans are Christians, mostly adherents of the Nauruan Protestant Church. The national flag (proportions 1 by 2) is royal blue, divided by a narrow horizontal yellow stripe, with a 12-pointed white star at the lower hoist. The island state has no official capital, but the seat of the legislature and most government offices are in Yaren district.

Recent History

Nauru, inhabited by a predominantly Polynesian people, organized in 12 clans, was annexed by Germany in 1888. In 1914, shortly after the outbreak of the First World War, the island was captured by Australian forces. It continued to be administered by Australia under a League of Nations mandate (granted in 1920), which also named the United Kingdom and New Zealand as co-trustees. Between 1942 and 1945 Nauru was occupied by the Japanese, who deported 1,200 islanders to Truk (now Chuuk), Micronesia, where many died in bombing raids or from starvation. In 1947 the island was placed under UN Trusteeship, with Australia as the administering power on behalf of the Governments of Australia, New Zealand and the United Kingdom. The UN Trusteeship Council proposed in 1964 that the indigenous people of Nauru be resettled on Curtis Island, off the Queensland coast. This offer was made in anticipation of the progressive exhaustion of the island's phosphate deposits, and because of the environmental devastation resulting from the mining operations. However, the Nauruans elected to remain on the island. Between 1906 and 1968 41m. metric tons of phosphate were mined. Nauru was accorded a considerable measure of self-government in January 1966, with the establishment of Legislative and Executive Councils, and proceeded to independence on 31 January 1968 (exactly 22 years after the surviving Nauruans returned to the island from exile in Micronesia). In early 1998 Nauru announced its intention to seek UN membership and full Commonwealth membership (Nauru had hitherto been a 'special member' of the Commonwealth, not represented at meetings of Heads of Government). The decision was largely based on the islanders' desire to play a more prominent role in international policies relating to issues that affect them, most notably climate change (see below). Nauru became a full member of the Commonwealth in May 1999, and a member of the UN in September of that year.

The Head Chief of Nauru, Hammer DeRoburt, was elected President in May 1968 and re-elected in 1971 and 1973. Dissatisfaction with his increasingly personal rule led to the election of Bernard Dowiyogo (leader of the recently-established, informal Nauru Party) to the presidency in 1976. Dowiyogo was re-elected President after a general election in late 1977. However, DeRoburt's supporters adopted tactics of obstruction in Parliament, and in December 1977 Dowiyogo resigned, in response to Parliament's refusal to approve budgetary legislation; he was re-elected shortly afterwards, but was again forced to resign in April 1978, following the defeat of a legislative proposal concerning phosphate royalties. Lagumot Harris, another member of the Nauru Party, succeeded him, but resigned three weeks later when Parliament rejected a finance measure, and DeRoburt was again elected President. He was re-elected in December of that year, in December 1980 and in May and December 1983.

In September 1986 DeRoburt resigned, following the defeat of a government budget proposal; he was replaced as President by Kennan Adeang, who was elected in Parliament by nine votes to

DeRoburt's eight. However, after holding office for only 14 days, Adeang was defeated in a parliamentary vote of 'no confidence', and DeRoburt subsequently resumed the presidency. Following a general election in December Adeang was again narrowly elected President. However, he was subsequently ousted by another vote of 'no confidence', and DeRoburt was reinstated as President. The atmosphere of political uncertainty generated by the absence of a clear majority in Parliament led DeRoburt to dissolve Parliament in preparation for another general election in January 1987, at which the incumbent was re-elected to the presidency by 11 votes to six. In February Adeang announced the establishment of the Democratic Party of Nauru, essentially a revival of the Nauru Party. Eight members of Parliament subsequently joined the new party, which declared that its aim was to curtail the extension of presidential powers and to promote democracy. In August 1989 a parliamentary motion of 'no confidence' in DeRoburt (proposed by Adeang) was approved by 10 votes to five, and Kenas Aroi, a former Minister for Finance, was subsequently elected President. Aroi resigned in December, owing to ill health, and after a general election in the same month Bernard Dowiyogo was re-elected President, defeating DeRoburt by 10 votes to six. The next presidential election, held shortly after a general election in November 1992, resulted in victory for Dowiyogo, by 10 votes to seven, over Buraro Detudamo.

At a general election held in November 1995, when a total of 67 candidates contested the 18 parliamentary seats, all cabinet members were re-elected. A subsequent presidential election resulted in Lagumot Harris's defeat of the incumbent Dowiyogo by nine votes to eight. The resignation of the Chairman of Air Nauru, following allegations of misconduct, prompted Parliament to vote on a motion of 'no confidence' in the Government in November 1996. The motion was narrowly approved and Harris was replaced by Dowiyogo as President. Later that month, however, Dowiyogo's new Government was itself defeated in a parliamentary vote of 'no confidence', and Kennan Adeang was elected to the presidency. A widespread perception that the new Government lacked experience was thought to be a major factor prompting a further motion of 'no confidence' in December, at which Adeang was similarly removed from office. At a subsequent presidential contest Reuben Kun, a former Minister for Finance, defeated Adeang by 12 votes to five, on the understanding that his administration would organize a general election. An election duly took place on 8 February 1997, at which four new members were elected to Parliament, following an apparent agreement between the supporters of Harris and those of Dowiyogo to end the political manoeuvring that had resulted in several months of instability in Nauru. At the election to the presidency, on 13 February, Kinza Clodumar (nominated by Dowiyogo) defeated Harris by nine votes to eight.

In early 1998 five members of Parliament (including former President Lagumot Harris) were dismissed by Adeang, the Speaker, for refusing to apologize for personal remarks about him that had been published in an opposition newsletter. At the resultant by-elections, held in late February 1998, three of the five members were re-elected. A motion expressing 'no confidence' in the President was approved in June, and Dowiyogo was consequently elected to replace Clodumar. In a further vote of 'no confidence', in late April 1999 Dowiyogo was defeated by 10 votes to seven; his replacement was Rene Harris, previously Chairman of the Nauru Phosphate Corporation. Former President Lagumot Harris died in September 1999.

Following legislative elections held on 8 April 2000, Rene Harris was re-elected President, narrowly defeating Dowiyogo by nine votes to eight. Ludwig Scotty was elected Speaker of Parliament. However, Scotty and his deputy, Ross Cairn, subsequently resigned, stating only that they were unable to continue under the 'current political circumstances'. Harris therefore tendered his resignation and was replaced by Dowiyogo, whereupon Scotty and Cairn were re-elected to their posts in the legislature. Observers attributed the manoeuvring to shifting political allegiances within the legislature.

In early 2001, in another reversal to Dowiyogo's leadership, Anthony Audoa, the Minister for Home Affairs, Culture, Health and Women's Affairs, resigned and requested that Parliament be recalled. He claimed that Dowiyogo had squandered Nauru's wealth during his various tenures as President and that in promoting the island as a tax haven he had allowed Nauru to be used by Russian criminal gangs to 'launder' their illegal funds, prompting speculation that he intended to mount a challenge for the presidency.

In late March 2001 Dowiyogo was ousted from the presidency in a parliamentary vote of 'no confidence' while he was undergoing hospital treatment in Australia. The motion, which was passed by two votes, led to Rene Harris regaining the presidency. In October, however, Harris was flown to Australia for emergency medical treatment for a diabetes-related illness, during which time Remy Namaduk performed the role of acting President. Allegations that Nauru's 'offshore' financial centre was being used extensively by Russian criminal organizations for 'laundering' the proceeds of their illegal activities had led Dowiyogo to order a full review of the industry in March 1999. The Government subsequently stated that it intended to modernize legislation governing the island's financial sector. In early 2000 President Rene Harris announced that Nauru was to suspend its 'offshore' banking services and improve the accountability of existing banks on the island, as part of the Government's efforts to bring Nauru's financial services regulations into conformity with international standards. Dowiyogo similarly reaffirmed his commitment to reform the 'offshore' sector, following his election in April 2000. However, in February 2001 11 members of Nauru's 18-member legislature signed a petition requesting that Dowiyogo attend a special session of Parliament to answer questions relating to the island's alleged role in 'laundering' significant funds from Russian criminal organizations. The allegations originated in claims by Russia's central bank that some US $70,000m. of illegal funds had been processed in 'offshore' banks in Nauru. It was estimated that 400 such banks existed on the island in early 2001. The Government subsequently drew up an Anti-Money Laundering Act in August 2001, but the Paris-based Financial Action Task Force (FATF—established in 1989 on the recommendation of the Group of Seven (G-7) industrialized nations, see p. 363) found that the new laws contained several deficiencies and imposed sanctions in December. The Government announced revised anti-money-laundering legislation in the same month, and was considering legal action against the FATF in early 2002. Meanwhile, following Islamist attacks on New York and Washington, DC, on 11 September 2001, Nauru's financial system was subject to international scrutiny, amid suspicion that it might have been used as a conduit for the terrorists' funds.

On 8 January 2003 President Rene Harris was defeated in a motion of 'no confidence' by eight votes to three and was replaced by Bernard Dowiyogo. The vote followed a political crisis resulting from the defeat of the Government's budget proposals at the end of December 2002, as well as reports of increasing dissatisfaction with Harris's alleged economic mismanagement of the country. Nauru's deteriorating financial situation, in addition to the Government's decision to accept more than 1,000 asylum-seekers in return for aid from Australia, were believed to be major factors in the loss of confidence in Harris, which had led to the defection to the opposition of two cabinet ministers, two backbenchers and the Speaker in late 2002. However, Harris applied to the Supreme Court, and on 10 January 2003 an injunction was issued against Dowiyogo accepting the presidency. This decision had been based on the fact that only 11 of the 18 members of Parliament had attended the session when the vote took place, thus rendering it invalid; Harris and his Cabinet had staged a boycott of Parliament when the motion was to be proposed. Despite the injunction, Dowiyogo maintained his position and appointed a new Cabinet. Several days of confusion and political instability ensued. Finally, Harris was reinstated as President, following the intervention of Nauru's Melbourne-based Chief Justice. However, he resigned from the presidency the following day. In the resultant contest Dowiyogo defeated Kinza Clodumar by nine votes to eight to become the new President on 20 January. A lack of support for Dowiyogo within Parliament continued to create problems, however, amid appeals for an early election to resolve the impasse.

Meanwhile, a complete collapse of Nauru's telecommunications system in early January 2003 increased the problems experienced by the island. Nauru, thus, effectively became cut off from the rest of the world with external contact only possible when ships equipped with satellite telephones were calling. A speech by Dowiyogo claiming that Nauru was on the verge of bankruptcy, unable to pay its public servants or to send its sick citizens to Australia for treatment, and appealing to donor countries for emergency assistance, could not be transmitted for almost a month. Telecommunications services were restored in early March following a visit from a technician supplied by Australia's government aid agency, AusAID.

In early March 2003 Dowiyogo travelled to Washington, DC, at the request of the US Government, which had threatened to impose harsh economic sanctions on the island and to repossess Air Nauru's only aircraft, if Nauru did not discontinue its 'offshore' banking services. The administration of George W. Bush was reported to have been angered by the possibility that individuals with links to terrorist organizations might have used the island's financial services to 'launder' their funds; some 400 'offshore' banks were registered on the island in the early 2000s. Consequently, Dowiyogo agreed to sign executive orders not to renew any banking licences or to issue any further so-called 'investor passports'. Shortly after the meeting, however, Dowiyogo collapsed and, following emergency heart surgery, died on 9 March. Derog Gioura was appointed acting President and on 20 March was elected by nine parliamentary votes to seven. Legislation providing for the expiry of most 'offshore' banking licences within 30 days (and for the remainder within six months) was passed by Parliament in late March, in accordance with the agreement that Dowiyogo had signed in the USA. At the end of March acting President Derog Gioura himself suffered a heart attack and was flown to Australia for treatment.

A general election took place on 3 May 2003, at which six new members were elected to the legislature. However, the new Speaker resigned one day after his election, and with no further nominations for the position, Parliament was unable to proceed to a presidential election. The impasse was resolved when a Speaker was finally elected in late May and Ludwig Scotty won the subsequent presidential election, defeating Kinza Clodumar with 10 parliamentary votes to seven. Scotty, who named a new six-member Cabinet in June, stated his Government's intention to focus on 'prudent management and financial stability'. However, on 8 August Scotty was ousted from office by a 'no confidence' motion and replaced by Rene Harris, who became the fourth President of 2003. The reasons for Scotty's removal were not clear, although concerns had been expressed about his plans to close the recently opened embassies in Washington, DC, and Beijing, and there had been speculation that he intended to switch Nauru's diplomatic allegiance from the People's Republic of China back to Taiwan (see below).

In August 2003 workers at the Nauru Phosphate Corporation began a strike in support of demands for almost six months of unpaid salaries. Opposition politicians claimed that the dispute was an indication of more widespread dissatisfaction with corruption and mismanagement in the industry and within the Government.

In January 2004 President Rene Harris was flown to Australia amid rumours that he had suffered a physical collapse and was in a poor state of health. Officials declined to respond to queries surrounding the President, merely stating that Derog Gioura would be acting President in his absence. In the following month the Minister for Justice resigned, precipitating a vote of 'no confidence' in the President. The country faced a further political crisis when the motion received an equal number of votes in favour and against. Moreover, when Parliament was unable to agree on the election of a new Speaker, following the resignation of the incumbent in early April, the resulting impasse meant that Parliament could not be formally convened.

Following the annual review of the FATF in February 2004, it was decided that Nauru should remain on the group's list of non-co-operative countries and territories, owing to the island's failure to implement effective measures to combat the practice of international 'money-laundering'. As a result of continued US pressure, however, and on the same day as the FATF meeting, Nauru's Parliament approved a new law to address the problem of 'money-laundering', along with legislation to close down the country's offshore banks. In December 2003, meanwhile, following the island's commitment to improve transparency and to exchange information on tax matters with other countries, Nauru had been removed from a list of unco-operative tax havens, issued in April 2002 by the Organisation for Economic Co-operation and Development (OECD, see p. 295).

In September 2001 Nauru agreed to accept 310 of 460 predominantly Afghan asylum-seekers who were on board a Norwegian freighter, the *MV Tampa*, unable to disembark on Christmas Island as Australia refused to grant them entry into its territory (see the chapter on Christmas Island, see p. 604). The Australian Government agreed to fund the processing of the asylum-seekers and to pay an undisclosed sum to Nauru, which was to house the asylum-seekers for three months while their claims for asylum were assessed. Following the interception of several other boats carrying asylum-seekers in Australian waters later the same month, Nauru received a pledge of $20m. from the Australian Government for agreeing to host 800 asylum-seekers. In December 2001 Nauru signed an agreement with Australia's Minister for Foreign Affairs to accommodate a total of 1,200 at any one time, in return for a further $A10m. of aid, to be allocated to education, health and infrastructure programmes. During a brief visit to Australia in January 2002, the President of Nauru declared that the bilateral agreement should end as originally envisaged. However, local residents and owners of the land upon which the camps were located expressed concern over the delays in processing the asylum-seekers' claims. Processing was due to be completed by July 2002, and in May Australia offered monetary assistance to Afghan asylum-seekers as an incentive to return to their homeland. In June the President announced that he anticipated that all the asylum-seekers would have left Nauru within six months. However, in December some 700 people remained in the camps, despite the deportation of more than 100 Afghan asylum-seekers to Kabul. In the same month the President signed a new agreement with Australia's Minister for Foreign Affairs to extend the duration of the camps' operations and to accommodate up to 1,500 asylum-seekers.

In mid-2003 the Australian Government was accused of cruelty for detaining some 100 children in the camps on Nauru and for failing to reunite families held in separate camps for extended periods. The Nauruan Government was subject to further criticism when the visa of a Catholic priest and prominent human rights activist was withdrawn hours before he was due to visit refugees detained on the island. It was believed that Nauruan officials had been instructed to cancel the visa by the Australian Government. Concerns about the conditions at the camps and the welfare of the detainees increased during 2003, and in December some of those held began a hunger strike in order to attract attention to their situation. A reported 40 asylum-seekers particpated in the strike, some of whom stitched their lips together. The Nauruan Government's subsequent appeals for medical assistance from Australia to care for the hunger strikers, many of whom required hospital treatment during the following weeks, were refused. The emerging rift between the two countries intensified when Nauru's Minister of Finance, Kinza Clodumar, condemned remarks made by Australia's Minister for Immigration, Amanda Vanstone, who had said that the health of the hunger strikers was of no concern to Australia. Clodumar, who stated that his country's limited medical resources could not cope with a problem of this scale, accused Australia of failing to recognize its obligations in continuing to ignore the plight of the asylum-seekers on Nauru. The strike ended about one month after it had begun, and in mid-January 2004 the Australian Government sent a delegation to inspect medical facilities available to asylum-seekers on the island. The resultant report, however, which found services for those held in detention to be adequate, was widely regarded as flawed, as it had failed to examine any of the detainees and had been compiled solely by Australian government officials.

In February 1987 representatives of the British, Australian and New Zealand Governments signed documents effecting the official demise of the British Phosphate Commissioners, who from 1919 until 1970 had overseen the mining of Nauru's phosphate deposits. President DeRoburt subsequently expressed concern about the distribution of the Commissioners' accumulated assets, which were estimated to be worth $A55m. His proposal that part of this sum be spent on the rehabilitation of areas of the island that had been mined before independence was rejected by the three Governments involved. DeRoburt subsequently established a commission of inquiry to investigate proposals for rehabilitation. The commission proposed that the three Governments provide one-third ($A72m.) of the estimated rehabilitation costs. In 1989 Australia's refusal to contribute to the rehabilitation of former phosphate mining areas prompted Nauru to institute proceedings, claiming compensation from Australia for damage to its environment, at the International Court of Justice. However, in 1993, following negotiations between President Dowiyogo and the Australian Prime Minister, Paul Keating, a Compact of Settlement was signed, under which the Australian Government was to pay some $A107m. to Nauru. New Zealand and the United Kingdom subsequently agreed to contribute $12m. each towards the settlement. An investigation into methods for the rehabilitation of the damaged areas of the island included plans to use landfill to encourage the restoration of vegetation to the mined areas, and the re-establishment of many of the species of flora and fauna that had previously been abundant on the island. In mid-1995 a report commissioned by the Government published details of a rehabilitation programme extending over the next 20–25 years and costing $A230m. The success of the rehabilitation scheme, however, was dependent on the co-operation of landowners, some of whom were expected to continue to allow areas to be mined for residual ore once phosphate reserves had been exhausted. In mid-1997 Parliament approved the Nauru Rehabilitation Corporation (NRC) Act, providing for the establishment of a corporate body to manage the rehabilitation programme. The NRC held its inaugural meeting in May 1999. The rehabilitation programme (which was to be partly financed from the Compact of Settlement with Australia) was expected to transform the mined areas into sites suitable for agriculture, new housing and industrial units. The project, however, was hampered considerably by delays, and in early 2004 the chair of the NRC resigned, reportedly in frustration at problems regarding the implementation of a feasibility study into the mining of residual phosphate.

As a result of a strike by pilots of Air Nauru, begun in 1988, the Governments of Australia and New Zealand withdrew certification of the airline, concerned that it was not complying with safety standards. Air Nauru resumed operations in 1989, and diplomatic relations with Australia (which had been suspended in the previous year) were restored. In July 1998 the airline was transferred to the Australian aviation register in order to achieve improved surveillance and safety standards. In February 2001 Nauru's transport links with the rest of the world were severed when Air Nauru suspended all its operations, following a report by the Civil Aviation Safety Authority in Australia. The organization claimed that Air Nauru had failed to maintain an effective management structure, did not have sufficiently qualified staff and that the airport in Nauru did not meet regulatory requirements owing to frequent disruptions to electricity and communications services. The suspension was lifted in the following month. It was hoped that the installation of three new electricity generators in June would resolve some of the problems outlined in the report.

Nauru was persistently critical of France's use of the South Pacific region for nuclear-weapons testing, and was one of the most vociferous opponents of the French Government's decision in mid-1995 to resume its nuclear-testing programme. Diplomatic relations, suspended between the two countries in 1995, were formally resumed in early 1998.

In early 2001 Nauru voiced strong opposition to the US Government's plans to develop a missile defence system, in which missiles are deployed to shoot down other missiles in flight. Government officials in Nauru expressed fears that testing of the system in the region could result in missile debris landing on the Pacific islands.

The President of Nauru met the Cuban Minister of Foreign Affairs in November 2001 at a UN meeting, where they agreed to establish diplomatic relations between their two countries and discussed a proposed technical and economic co-operation agreement whereby Nauru would be provided with health experts from Cuba.

In 1989 a UN report on the 'greenhouse effect' (the heating of the earth's atmosphere and a resultant rise in sea-level) listed Nauru as one of the countries that might disappear beneath the sea in the 21st century, unless drastic action were taken. The Government of Nauru strongly criticized Australia's refusal, at the December 1997 Conference of the Parties to the Framework Convention on Climate Change (see UN Environment Programme, see p. 53), in Kyoto, Japan, to reduce its emission of pollutant gases known to contribute to the 'greenhouse effect'.

In August 2001 Nauru hosted the Pacific Islands Forum summit meeting, despite a problematic shortage of accommodation, caused by the presence of contingents of officials from Australia, refugee agencies, the UN and Eurest (the company subcontracted to operate Nauru's refugee camp). Fiji had been expected to perform this role, but its participation had been opposed owing to its failure to reinstate democratic rule following the coup of the previous year.

In July 2002 a political crisis emerged after President Rene Harris decided unilaterally to recognize the People's Republic of China, thus ending 22 years of diplomatic relations with Taiwan. Several cabinet ministers opposed the shift in policy, and the controversy increased after Harris immediately accepted US $60m. in aid and $77m. in debt annulment from the People's Republic of China. Following the switch in allegiance, Taiwan announced that it would take legal action to recover a loan of US $12.5m. which it had arranged to make available to Nauru.

In February 2003 two diplomatic missions were opened, in Washington, DC, and in Beijing, primarily to address US concerns over 'money-laundering' and international terrorism (fears regarding the latter increased when, in the same month, two members of al-Qa'ida were found to be travelling on Nauruan passports). However, in July President Scotty announced plans to close the missions, citing economic constraints and his belief that they were not serving their intended purpose. Representatives in China and the USA expressed surprise at the announcement and queried the President's motives, in particular his commitment to ending the lucrative sale of Nauruan passports.

In February 2004 Nauru announced the establishment of diplomatic relations with Iceland. The two countries cited their common reliance on the sea as a unifying factor between them.

Government

Legislative power is vested in the unicameral Parliament, with 18 members elected by universal adult suffrage for up to three years. Executive authority is vested in a Cabinet, which consists of the President of the Republic, elected by the Parliament, and ministers appointed by him. The Cabinet is collectively responsible to Parliament. Responsibilities for administration are divided between the Nauru Local Government Council and the Government. The Council, an elected body of nine members from the country's 14 districts, elects one of its members to be Head Chief.

Defence

Nauru has no defence forces: under an informal arrangement, Australia is responsible for the country's defence.

Economic Affairs

In 1999, according to UN estimates, Nauru's gross domestic product (GDP), measured at current prices, was US $34m., equivalent to $2,830 per head. In 1991–99, it was estimated, GDP decreased, in real terms, at an average annual rate of 5.9%. The population increased by an annual average of 2.0% per year in 1990–2000. The UN estimated that GDP declined, in real terms, by 7.3% in 1997, by 1.9% in 1998 and again by 1.9% in 1999. According to official estimates, Nauru's GDP grew by 0.8% in 2000. Real GDP growth of around 3% was predicted for 2001.

Agricultural activity comprises mainly the small-scale production of tropical fruit, vegetables and livestock, although the production of coffee and copra for export is increasingly significant. According to FAO, agriculture engaged some 20% of the economically active population in 2001. Coconuts are the principal crop. Bananas, pineapples and the screw-pine (*Pandanus*) are also cultivated as food crops, while the islanders keep pigs and chickens. However, almost all Nauru's requirements (including most of its drinking water) are imported. Increased exploitation of the island's marine resources was envisaged following the approval by Parliament of important fisheries legislation in 1997 and 1998. Funding for a new harbour for medium-sized vessels was secured from the Government of Japan in 1998, and in early 1999 the Marshall Islands Sea Patrol agreed to provide assistance in the surveillance of Nauru's exclusive economic zone. Revenue from fishing licence fees totalled $A8.5m. in 2000.

Until the early 1990s Nauru's economy was based on the mining of phosphate rock, which constituted four-fifths of the island's surface area. Phosphate extraction has been conducted largely by indentured labour, notably by I-Kiribati and Tuvaluan workers. Exports of phosphates declined to an average of 0.51m. tons annually in 1990–97 (compared with 1.58m. tons per year in the 1980s), mainly owing to the collapse of the Australian market. As a result of the Asian financial crisis, exports of phosphate declined by almost 18% in 1998 compared with the previous year. In 2001 phosphate exports were suspended in the second half of the year when a processing plant

was blockaded by landowners seeking additional compensation for the use of their land by the plant. Mining production, meanwhile, decreased by 7.9% in 2000. Primary deposits of phosphate are expected to be exhausted by 2005. Feasibility studies have been conducted into the mining of secondary and residual deposits, although this activity would be less profitable. An Australian engineering company was expected to undertake a detailed survey of the island's potential for secondary phosphate mining in early 2004. Revenue from phosphate sales has been invested in a long-term trust fund (the Nauru Phosphate Royalties Trust (NPRT), the assets of which totalled about US $900m. in 1992), in the development of shipping and aviation services, and in property purchases in Australia and elsewhere.

Energy is derived principally from imported petroleum. Output of electrical energy totalled 30m. kWh in 2000.

The country's trade balance deteriorated significantly in 2001. Although imports decreased by 16.3%%, exports declined by 61.5% compared with the previous year, resulting in a trade deficit of US $18.4m. The principal imports are food and live animals (which comprised 83.7% of total imports in 1993/94, while beverages accounted for a further 4.1%), machinery and transport equipment (2.8%) and non-metallic mineral manufactures (4.9%). Phosphates are the most important export, earning $A38.1m. in 1995; exports of crude fertilizers to Australia totalled $A8.5m. in 2001. The principal export markets in 2001 were New Zealand (which purchased 30.6% of the total), Australia (25.3%), Thailand (15.8%) and the Republic of Korea (12.3%).(The principal sources of imports were Australia (supplying 49.4%), the USA (16.9%) and Indonesia (7.9%).

The national budget for 1998/99 envisaged total revenue of $A38.7m. and expenditure of $A37.2m. (dramatically reduced from expenditure of $A61.8m. in the previous year). According to the Asian Development Bank (ADB), the budgetary deficit was projected at the equivalent of 6.1% of GDP in 1999/2000 and at 10.6% in 2000/01. A fiscal deficit of $A40m.–$A50m. was envisaged in 2001/02. Total public debt was equivalent to 60.8% of GDP in 2000, an apparent improvement on figures in previous years. In 2000 overseas development assistance was estimated at US $4.0m., of which $2.9m. was bilateral aid. Development assistance from Australia amounted to $A3.3m. in 1999/2000. Nauru's external debt was estimated at $A280m. in 2000. In that year the cost of debt-servicing was equivalent to an estimated 13% of total revenue from the exports of goods and services. Consumer prices increased by 4.0% in 1998, by 6.7% in 1999 and by 17.9% in 2000; the annual rate of inflation averaged 4.0% in 2001. The rate of unemployment among those aged 15–19 in the late 1990s was estimated by the ADB to be 33% of males and 52% of females.

Nauru is a member of the Pacific Community (see p. 323), of the Pacific Islands Forum (see p. 325) and of the UN Economic and Social Commission for Asia and the Pacific (ESCAP, see p. 31), all of which aim to promote regional development. Nauru is also a member of the Asian Development Bank (ADB, see p. 151).

After gaining independence in 1968, Nauru benefited from sole control of phosphate earnings and, as a result, its income per head was among the highest in the world. This, however, had serious repercussions for the country, which became excessively dependent on imported labour, imports of consumer goods and convenience foods, causing health and social problems. Another effect of phosphate mining was to render 80% of the island both uninhabitable and uncultivable, leading to chronic overcrowding. Nauru lost a significant amount from its Phosphate Royalties Trust during the 1990s through theft and fraud by accountants and other financial advisers. Measures to reform the financial sector, in response to allegations that Nauru's 'offshore' banking services were being abused for the purposes of 'money-laundering', were announced in early 2000. However, serious allegations of 'money-laundering' re-emerged in 2001, leading the Financial Action Task Force (FATF–see above) to impose counter-measures, prescribing increased monitoring, surveillance and transparency in financial transactions. Despite these measures, in March 2003 the US Government of George W. Bush obliged Nauru's President to sign papers effectively ending the island's 'offshore' banking industry or face severe economic sanctions. The country remained on the FATF list in 2004, following the organization's annual review in February. However, Nauru was removed from the OECD's's list of unco-operative tax havens in December 2003. Nauru received significant financial assistance in late 2001 in exchange for co-operating with Australia in its 'Pacific Solution' to the problem of asylum-seekers (see Recent History). By the end of 2001, in addition to meeting the costs of detaining the refugees in camps, the Australian Government had committed total aid exceeding $A30m. The aid was allocated to various programmes, including $A10m. towards fuel to power the island's electricity generators and $A3m. towards the purchase of new generators. Nauru's GDP declined throughout the 1990s, and in the early 2000s the economic outlook remained poor. It was unclear how the substantial budgetary deficit envisaged for 2001/02 would be fully financed; the Government had hitherto relied upon loans from official bilateral sources, overseas corporations or funds from the NPRT, the assets of which had been seriously depleted by 2001. The Bank of Nauru, meanwhile, another source of budgetary support and financing of phosphate royalty payments to landowners, was believed to have become practically insolvent. During 2001, furthermore, the repeated suspensions of Air Nauru's operations, owing to lack of funds, had led to serious disruptions in the provision of food, fuel and other essential supplies to the island. By early 2002 government payrolls and payments to several creditors had been severely delayed. In January 2003 President Dowiyogo broadcast an appeal for emergency aid, claiming that the island was on the verge of bankruptcy. A report published by the ADB in April stated that Nauru's economic situation was very serious and deteriorating. Furthermore, the report claimed that development assistance given to the country in the past had had little impact because of a lack of political commitment to change and a shortage of skills among the working population. In late 2003 the Australian Government announced that it was considering the possibility of offering Australian citizenship to Nauruans when revenue from the island's role as an immigration detention centre (which since 2001 had constituted Nauru's most important source of income) was no longer available. In April 2004 receivers acting on behalf of creditors in the USA seized Nauru's property portfolio, including five buildings in Sydney and Melbourne. The Nauruan Government had been given until early May to repay a debt of more than US $200m. to a US finance corporation.

Education

Education is compulsory for Nauruan children between six and 16 years of age. Primary education begins at the age of six and lasts for seven years. Secondary education, beginning at 13 years of age, lasts for up to four years. In 1995 there were four pre-primary schools, six primary schools and four secondary schools with a total of 138 teachers. In 1985 there were four vocational schools with four teachers. In 1984 Nauruans studying overseas at secondary and tertiary levels numbered 88. There is a university extension centre, linked with the University of the South Pacific in Suva, Fiji. An estimated 1% of the adult population were illiterate in 1993–95.

Public Holidays

2004: 1 January (New Year's Day), 31 January (Independence Day), 9–12 April (Easter), 17 May (Constitution Day), 26 October (Angam Day), 25–26 December (Christmas).

2005: 1 January (New Year's Day), 31 January (Independence Day), 25–28 March (Easter), 17 May (Constitution Day), 26 October (Angam Day), 25–26 December (Christmas).

Statistical Survey

Source (unless otherwise stated): General Statistician, Nauru Government Offices, Yaren.

AREA AND POPULATION

Area: 21.3 sq km (8.2 sq miles).

Population: 8,042 (Nauruan 4,964, Other Pacific Islanders 2,134, Asians 682, Caucasians—mainly Australians and New Zealanders—262) at census of 13 May 1983; 9,919 (5,079 males, 4,840 females) at census of 17 April 1992; 11,845 (official estimate) at mid-2000.

Density (mid-2000): 556 per sq km.

Principal Towns (population, 1992 census): Aiwo (capital) 600; Anetan 427; Anabar 320; Anibare 165. Source: Thomas Brinkhoff, *City Population* (internet www.citypopulation.de).

Births, Marriages and Deaths (1995): Registered live births 203 (birth rate 18.8 per 1,000); Registered marriages 57 (marriage rate 5.3 per 1,000); Registered deaths 49 (death rate 4.5 per 1,000).

Expectation of Life (WHO estimates, years at birth): 62.7 (males 59.7; females 66.5) in 2002. Source: WHO, *World Health Report*.

Economically Active Population (census of 30 June 1966): 2,473 (Administration 845, Phosphate mining 1,408, Other activities 220).

HEALTH AND WELFARE

Key Indicators

Total Fertility Rate (children per woman, 2002): 3.9.

Under-5 Mortality Rate (per 1,000 live births, 2001): 30.

Physicians (per 1,000 head, 1995): 1.57.

Health Expenditure (2001): US $ per head (PPP): 1,015.

Health Expenditure (2001): % of GDP: 7.5.

Health Expenditure (2001): public (% of total): 88.7.
For sources and definitions, see explanatory note on p. vi.

AGRICULTURE, ETC.

Principal Crop and Livestock (FAO estimates, 2002): Coconuts 1,600 metric tons; Pigs 2,800 head; Chickens 5,000 head. Source: FAO.

Fishing (FAO estimates, metric tons, live weight of capture, 2001): Total catch 400. Source: FAO, *Yearbook of Fishery Statistics*.

MINING

Phosphate Rock ('000 metric tons): 487 in 1998; 600 (estimate) in 1999; 500 (estimate) in 2000. The phosphoric acid content (in '000 metric tons) was: 185 in 1998; 230 (estimate) in 1999; 195 (estimate) in 2000. Source: US Geological Survey.

INDUSTRY

Electric Energy (million kWh): 32 in 1998; 33 in 1999; 33 in 2000. Source: *UN, Industrial Commodity Statistics Yearbook*.

FINANCE

Currency and Exchange Rates: Australian currency: 100 cents = 1 Australian dollar ($A). *Sterling, US Dollar and Euro Equivalents* (31 December 2003): £1 sterling = $A2.3796; US $1 = $A1.3333; €1 = $A1.6840; $A100 = £42.02 = US $75.00 = €59.38. *Average Exchange Rate* (US $ per Australian dollar): 1.9334 in 2001; 1.8406 in 2002; 1.5419 in 2003.

Budget (estimates, $A '000, year ending 30 June 1999): *Revenue:* 38,700; *Expenditure:* 37,200.

EXTERNAL TRADE

Principal Commodities ($A '000, year ending 30 June 1994): *Imports:* Food and live animals 38,420; Beverages 1,890; Non-metallic mineral manufactures 2,268; Non-electrical machinery 758; Transport equipment 534; Total (incl. others) 45,906. *Exports:* Total 45,111. *1995* ($A '000): Total exports 38,081.

Principal Trading Partners (US $ million, 2001): *Imports:* Australia 13.51; India 1.31; Indonesia 2.17; New Zealand 1.05; USA 4.62; Total (incl. others) 27.37. *Exports:* Australia 2.26; Japan 0.62; Republic of Korea 1.10; New Zealand 2.74; Thailand 1.41; Total (incl. others) 8.95. Source: UN, *Statistical Yearbook for Asia and the Pacific*.

TRANSPORT

Road Traffic (1989): 1,448 registered motor vehicles.

Shipping: *Merchant Fleet* (displacement, '000 grt at 31 December): 15 in 1991 (at 30 June); 5 in 1992; 1 in 1993. Source: Lloyd's Register of Shipping. *International Freight Traffic* (estimates, '000 metric tons, 1990): Goods loaded 1,650; Goods unloaded 59. Source: UN, *Monthly Bulletin of Statistics*.

Civil Aviation (traffic on scheduled services, 1999): Kilometres flown (million) 2; Passengers carried ('000) 143; Passenger-km (million) 254; Total ton-km (million) 25. Source: UN, *Statistical Yearbook.*

COMMUNICATIONS MEDIA

Radio Receivers (1997): 7,000 in use*.

Television Receivers (1997): 500 in use*.

Telephones (main lines, 2000): 1,800 in use†.

Mobile Cellular Telephones (2000): 1,200 subscribers†.

* Source: UNESCO, *Statistical Yearbook.*

† Source: International Telecommunication Union.

EDUCATION

Pre-primary (2002): 6 schools; 46 teachers; 634 pupils.

Primary (2002): 5 schools; 64 teachers; 1,566 pupils.

Secondary (2002): 4 schools; 40 teachers; 609 pupils.

Vocational (2001): 6 teachers; 38 students.
Source: Department of Education, Yaren, Nauru.
Nauruans studying at secondary and tertiary levels overseas in 2001 numbered 85.

Directory

The Constitution

The Constitution of the Republic of Nauru came into force at independence on 31 January 1968, having been adopted two days previously. It protects fundamental rights and freedoms, and vests executive authority in the Cabinet, which is responsible to a popularly elected Parliament. The President of the Republic is elected by Parliament from among its members. The Cabinet is composed of five or six members, including the President, who presides. There are 18 members of Parliament, including the Cabinet. Voting is compulsory for all Nauruans who are more than 20 years of age, except in certain specified instances.

The highest judicial organ is the Supreme Court and there is provision for the creation of subordinate courts with designated jurisdiction.

There is a Treasury Fund from which monies may be taken by Appropriation Acts.

A Public Service is provided for, with the person designated as the Chief Secretary being the Commissioner of the Public Service.

Special mention is given to the allocation of profits and royalties from the sale of phosphates.

The Government

HEAD OF STATE

President: RENE HARRIS (elected 8 August 2003).

CABINET
(April 2004)

President, Minister for Foreign Affairs, Minister of Civil Aviation, Minister of Home Affairs and Culture, Minister of Industry, Minister of Investments and Minister of Public Service: RENE HARRIS.

Minister of Economic Development, Minister of Education and Vocational Training, Minister of Telecommunications, Minister of Transportation and Minister assisting the President: BARON WACA.

Minister of Finance and Minister of Good Governance: KINZA CLODUMAR.

Minister of Health and Minister of Sports: KIERAN KEKE.

Minister of Justice and Minister of Marine Resources: (vacant).

Minister of Works, Planning and Housing Development: DOGABE JEREMIAH.

MINISTRIES

Office of the President: Yaren, Nauru.

Ministry of Education: Yaren, Nauru; tel. 444-3130; fax 444-3718.

Ministry of Health and Youth Affairs: Yaren, Nauru; tel. 444-3166; fax 444-3136.

Ministry of Finance: Aiwo, Nauru; tel. 444-3140; fax 555-4477.

Ministry of Justice: Yaren, Nauru; tel. 444-3160; fax 444-3108.

Ministry of Works and Community Services: Yaren, Nauru; tel. 444-3177; fax 444-3135.

Legislature

PARLIAMENT

Parliament comprises 18 members. The most recent general election took place on 3 May 2003.

Speaker: (vacant).

Political Organizations

Democratic Party of Nauru: c/o Parliament House, Yaren, Nauru; f. 1987; revival of Nauru Party (f. 1975); Leader KENNAN ADEANG.

Naoero Amo (Nauru First): c/o Parliament House, Yaren, Nauru; e-mail visionary@naoeroamo.com; internet www.naoeroamo.com; f. 2001; Co-Leaders DAVID ADEANG, KIERAN KEKE.

Diplomatic Representation

EMBASSY IN NAURU

China, People's Republic: Yaren; Ambassador XU SHIGUO.

Judicial System

The Chief Justice presides over the Supreme Court, which exercises original, appellate and advisory jurisdiction. The Resident Magistrate presides over the District Court, and he also acts as Coroner under the Inquests Act 1977. The Supreme Court is a court of record. The Family Court consists of three members, one being the Resident Magistrate as Chairman, and two other members drawn from a panel of Nauruans. The Chief Justice is Chairman of the Public Services Appeals Board and of the Police Appeals Board.

SUPREME COURT
tel. 444-3163; fax 444-3104.

Chief Justice: BARRY CONNELL (non-resident).

DISTRICT COURT

Resident Magistrate: G. N. SAKSENA.

FAMILY COURT

Chairman: G. N. SAKSENA.

Religion

Nauruans are predominantly Christians, adhering either to the Nauruan Protestant Church or to the Roman Catholic Church.

Nauruan Protestant Church: Head Office, Nauru; Moderator (vacant).

Roman Catholic Church: POB 16, Nauru; tel. and fax 444-3708; Nauru forms part of the diocese of Tarawa and Nauru, comprising Kiribati and Nauru. The Bishop resides on Tarawa Atoll, Kiribati.

The Press

Central Star News: Nauru; f. 1991; fortnightly.

Nasero Bulletin: Nauru; tel. 444-3847; fax 444-3153; e-mail bulletin@cenpac.net.nr; fortnightly; English; local and overseas news; Editor SEPE BATSIUA; circ. 500.

The Nauru Chronicle: Nauru; Editor RUBY DEDIYA.

Broadcasting and Communications

TELECOMMUNICATIONS

Nauru Telecommunications Service: Nauru; tel. 444-3324; fax 444-3111; Dir EDWARD W. R. H. DEYOUNG.

BROADCASTING

Radio

Nauru Broadcasting Service: Information and Broadcasting Services, Chief Secretary's Department, POB 77, Nauru; tel. 444-3133; fax 444-3153; e-mail ntvdirector@cenpac.net.nr; f. 1968; state-owned and non-commercial; expected to be corporatized in the late 1990s; broadcasts in the mornings in English and Nauruan; operates Radio Nauru; Station Man. RIN TSITSI; Man. Dir GARY TURNER.

Television

Nauru Television (NTV): Nauru; tel. 444-3133; fax 444-3153; e-mail ntvmanager@cenpac.net.nr; began operations in June 1991; govt-owned; broadcasts 24 hrs per day on 3 channels; most of the programmes are supplied by foreign television companies via satellite or on videotape; a weekly current affairs programme is produced locally; Man. MICHAEL DEKARUBE; Dir of Media GARY TURNER.

Finance

(cap. = capital; res = reserves; dep. = deposits; m. = million; amounts in Australian dollars unless otherwise stated)

BANKING

State Bank

Bank of Nauru: Civic Centre, POB 289, Nauru; tel. 444-3238; fax 444-3203; f. 1976; state-owned; cap. 12.0m., res 123.0m., dep. 141.0m. (Dec. 1994); Chair. MARCUS STEPHEN.

INSURANCE

Nauru Insurance Corporation: POB 82, Nauru; tel. 444-3346; fax 444-3731; f. 1974; sole licensed insurer and reinsurer in Nauru; Chair. NIMES EKWONA.

Trade and Industry

GOVERNMENT AGENCIES

Nauru Agency Corporation: POB 300, Aiwo, Nauru; tel. 555-4324; fax 444-3730; e-mail nrugrp@cenpac.net.nr; functions as a merchant bank to assist entrepreneurs in the registration of holding and trading corporations and the procurement of banking, trust and insurance licences; Chair. RENE HARRIS; Gen. Man. S. B. HULKAR.

Nauru Corporation: Civic Centre, Yaren, Nauru; f. 1925; operated by the Nauru Council; the major retailer in Nauru; Gen. Man. A. EPHRAIM.

Nauru Fisheries and Marine Resources Authority: POB 449, Nauru; tel. 444-3733; fax 444-3812; e-mail nfmra@cenpac.net.nr; f. 1997.

Nauru Phosphate Corporation: Aiwo, Nauru; tel. 444-3839; fax 444-2752; f. 1970; operates the phosphate industry and several public services of the Republic of Nauru (including provision of electricity and fresh water) on behalf of the Nauruan people; responsible for the mining and marketing of phosphate; Gen. Man. JOSEPH HIRAM; Chair. ALI AMWANO.

Nauru Phosphate Royalties Trust: Nauru; e-mail nprtnau@cenpac.net.nr; statutory corpn; invests phosphate royalties to achieve govt revenue; extensive international interests, incl. hotels and real estate; Sec. NIRAL FERNANDO.

Nauru Rehabilitation Corporation (NRC): Nauru; f. 1999; manages and devises programmes for the rehabilitation of those parts of the island damaged by the over-mining of phosphate; Chair. ALI AMWANO.

UTILITIES

Nauru Phosphate Corporation: Aiwo, Nauru; tel. 555-6481; fax 555-4111; operates generators for the provision of electricity and supplies the island's water; Chair. (vacant); Gen. Man. JOSEPH HIRAM.

Transport

RAILWAYS

There are 5.2 km of 0.9-m gauge railway serving the phosphate workings.

ROADS

A sealed road, 16 km long, circles the island, and another serves Buada District. There were 1,448 registered vehicles in 1989.

SHIPPING

As Nauru has no wharves, passenger and cargo handling are operated by barge. In late 1998 finance was secured from the Japanese Government for the construction of a harbour in Anibare district. Work on the project began in 1999.

Nauru Pacific: Government Bldg, Yaren, Nauru; tel. 444-3133; f. 1969; operates cargo charter services to ports in Australia, New Zealand, Asia, the Pacific and the west coast of the USA; Man. Dir (vacant).

CIVIL AVIATION

Air Nauru: Directorate of Civil Aviation, Government of Nauru Offices, POB 40, Yaren, Nauru; tel. 444-3274; fax 444-3705; e-mail write2us@airnauru.com.au; internet www.airnauru.com.au; f. 1970; corporatized in 1996 and moved to Australian aviation register in mid-1997; operates passenger and cargo services to Kiribati, Fiji, New Caledonia, Solomon Islands, Guam, Palau, the Philippines, the Federated States of Micronesia, Hawaii (USA), Australia and New Zealand; Chair. and CEO KEN McDONALD.

NEPAL

Introductory Survey

Location, Climate, Language, Religion, Flag, Capital

The Kingdom of Nepal is a land-locked Asian country in the Himalaya mountain range, with India to the east, south and west, and Tibet (the Xizang Autonomous Region), in the People's Republic of China, to the north. The climate varies sharply with altitude, from arctic on the higher peaks of the Himalaya mountains (where the air temperature is permanently below freezing point) to humid subtropical in the central valley of Kathmandu, which is warm and sunny in summer. Temperatures in Kathmandu, which is 1,337 m (4,386 ft) above sea-level, are generally between 2°C (35°F) and 30°C (86°F), with an annual average of 11°C (52°F). The rainy season is between June and October. Average annual rainfall varies from about 1,000 mm (40 ins) in western Nepal to about 2,500 mm (100 ins) in the east. The official language is Nepali, which was spoken by 48.6% of the population in 2001. Other languages include Maithir (12.3% in 2001) and Bhojpuri (7.5%). Some 80.6% of the population were Hindus in 2001, with 10.7% Buddhists and 4.2% Muslims. The national flag (proportions 4 by 3) is composed of two crimson pennants, each with a blue border. The upper section contains a white crescent moon (horns upwards and surmounted by a disc with eight rays) and the lower section a white sun in splendour. The capital is Kathmandu.

Recent History

Nepal is an hereditary monarchy, but for more than 100 years, until 1951, effective power was held by the Rana family, who created the post of hereditary Prime Minister. A popular revolution, led by the Nepali Congress Party (NCP), ousted the Ranas and restored King Tribhuvan to power. A limited constitutional monarchy was established in 1951. During most of the 1950s government was controlled by the monarchy, first under Tribhuvan and then, after his death in 1955, under his son, Mahendra. In February 1959 King Mahendra promulgated Nepal's first Constitution, providing for a bicameral parliament, including a popularly-elected lower house. Elections held later that month resulted in victory for the NCP, led by Bisweswor Prasad (B. P.) Koirala, who became Prime Minister. However, the King retained a certain degree of power, and persistent differences between the King and the Prime Minister led to a royal coup in December 1960: Nepal's first brief period of democracy was thus brought to an abrupt end. The King dismissed the Council of Ministers and dissolved Parliament. A royal decree of January 1961 banned political parties. King Mahendra accused the Koirala administration of corruption, and in December 1962 he introduced a new Constitution, reasserting absolute royal power and providing for a 'partyless' system of government, based on the Panchayat (village council), with a Prime Minister appointed by the King. This office was filled successively by Dr Tulsi Giri (1962–65), Surya Bahadur Thapa (1965–69) and Kirti Nidhi Bista (1969–70, 1971–73). King Mahendra himself was Prime Minister from April 1970 to April 1971. In January 1972 King Mahendra died and was succeeded by his son, Birendra. Nagendra Prasad Rijal became Prime Minister in July 1973, and held office until December 1975, when Dr Giri was reappointed. The new Government made major changes to the Constitution, which allowed for a widening of the franchise and more frequent elections to the Rashtriya Panchayat (National Assembly), but in no way were the King's powers eroded. In September 1977 Dr Giri resigned and was succeeded by Bista.

B. P. Koirala, the former Prime Minister and an advocate of parliamentary democracy, was acquitted of treason in February 1978. Returning from abroad a year later, he was placed under house arrest in April 1979, but then released, partly to appease students who had been demonstrating for reforms. National unrest grew and, after King Birendra announced in May that there would be a national referendum on whether to restore multi-party democracy, Bista resigned and was succeeded as Prime Minister by Thapa. In the referendum, held in May 1980, 54.8% of the voters supported the Panchayat system with reforms. As a result, the King formed a Constitutional Reforms Commission, and in December he issued a decree under which amendments to the Constitution were made, including the proviso that the appointment of the Prime Minister by the King would henceforth be on the recommendation of the Rashtriya Panchayat. In accordance with the new provisions, direct legislative elections were held in May 1981, the first of their kind since 1959, although still on a non-party basis. Thapa was re-elected by the Rashtriya Panchayat as Prime Minister in June 1981, and the King installed a new Council of Ministers (on the recommendation of the Prime Minister). An extensive ministerial reshuffle took place in October 1982, but this failed to stem increasing official corruption and economic mismanagement. In July 1983, for the first time in the 23-year history of the Panchayat system, the incumbent Prime Minister, Surya Bahadur Thapa, was ousted, and a new Council of Ministers was formed by a former Chairman of the Rashtriya Panchayat, Lokendra Bahadur Chand, who had successfully introduced a motion expressing 'no confidence' in Thapa.

In March 1985 the NCP held a convention in Kathmandu, and in May it embarked upon a campaign of civil disobedience, aimed at restoring a multi-party political system and parliamentary rule under a constitutional monarchy. In June there was a series of bomb explosions, resulting in loss of life. The explosions were apparently co-ordinated by two newly-formed anti-monarchist and anti-Government groups, the Janawadi Morcha (Democratic Front) and the Samyukta Mukti Bahini (United Liberation Torch-bearers). These bombings united an otherwise seriously divided legislature against the terrorists, and forced the predominantly moderate opposition to abandon the campaign of civil disobedience and to disclaim any responsibility for the explosions. In August the Rashtriya Panchayat approved a stringent anti-terrorist law, and more than 1,000 people were arrested in connection with the unrest.

In January 1986 the Government announced that a general election would be held in May. In March the King accepted the resignation of the Prime Minister and the Council of Ministers, and appointed an interim Government for the pre-election period, led by a former Prime Minister, Nagendra Prasad Rijal. About 64% of the electorate voted in the election, in spite of appeals by the NCP and the pro-China faction of the Communist Party of Nepal (CPN) (neither of which presented candidates) for a boycott of the polls. All the candidates in the election were nominally independents, but it was reported that among the 72 new entrants to the Rashtriya Panchayat (40 members retained their seats) were at least 16 members of the Marxist-Leninist faction of the CPN. In June the King nominated 25 additional members of the new Rashtriya Panchayat, and Marich Man Singh Shrestha (previously Chairman of the Rashtriya Panchayat) was elected unopposed by the Assembly as the new Prime Minister. A few days later, on the recommendation of the Prime Minister, the King appointed a new Council of Ministers. In late 1986, to counter the growing influence of the communist faction in the Rashtriya Panchayat, several senior figures (including Jog Meher Shrestha, a former government minister, and Chand) established a 'Democratic Panchayat Forum', which expressed full support for the non-party system.

Members of the NCP and the Marxist-Leninist faction of the CPN participated (as independents) in local elections in March–April 1987. The opposition achieved only limited success, and the NCP subsequently claimed that there had been extensive electoral fraud and intimidation of voters by supporters of the Panchayat system. NCP candidates, however, were elected to a number of important mayoral posts in Kathmandu and elsewhere.

In 1986–87 the Nepalese Government continued its policy of press censorship, in an effort to curb anti-Government criticism. In June 1987, in an apparent attempt to improve the image of the Panchayat system, the Government initiated an anti-corruption campaign, during the course of which several senior officials were arrested for drugs-trafficking and other offences. In December the Government announced plans to reorganize government ministries and departments, in an effort to make them more efficient. In early 1988 the Government continued its policy of suppressing opposition. In January the President of the

NCP was arrested, and in February more than 100 people, who were planning to demonstrate in support of the NCP mayor of Kathmandu (who had been suspended from office for his anti-Panchayat stance), were also detained. In March an extensive government reshuffle included the establishment of a new Ministry of Housing and Physical Planning. In October there was another major reorganization of the Council of Ministers.

In September 1989 the Government arrested more than 900 NCP supporters, in a seeming effort to prevent them from celebrating the anniversary of the birth of Nepal's first elected Prime Minister, B. P. Koirala (who died in 1982). During these celebrations the NCP demonstrated in protest against the failings of the country's non-party political system. In November the leaders of the NCP held a meeting in Kathmandu with members of several other left-wing and communist political groups, to discuss the proposed formation of a country-wide peaceful 'movement for the restoration of democracy'. At the meeting they stated that the aims of the movement would be the alleviation of Nepal's severe economic problems (including the trade dispute with India, see below), the restoration of full democracy, the transfer from absolute to constitutional monarchy, the immediate replacement of the Panchayat Government by an interim national government, the removal of the ban on political activities, and the introduction of a multi-party system. In January 1990 a co-ordination committee to conduct the Jana Andolan (People's Movement) was formed by the NCP and the newly-formed United Left Front (ULF, which was led by Sahana Pradhan and comprised six factions of the CPN and a labour group), despite the Government's efforts to pre-empt its inauguration by arresting hundreds of activists (including many students) and by banning, or heavily censoring, more newspapers. During the consequent violent confrontations between protesters and police that took place in February, it was officially estimated that 12 people were killed and hundreds more were arrested. Violent demonstrations, strikes and mass arrests continued throughout March. At the end of the month the Minister of Foreign Affairs, Shailendra Kumar Upadhayaya, resigned from his post, following differences with the Prime Minister regarding the Government's management of the crisis. A few days later there was an extensive government reshuffle, including the dismissal of nine ministers who allegedly opposed the Government's acts of repression against the pro-democracy movement. In an effort to end the political unrest, the King dismissed Shrestha's Government on 6 April and nominated a restricted four-member Council of Ministers, under the leadership of the more moderate Chand. King Birendra also offered to establish a body that would examine the possibility of altering the Constitution and to hold discussions with the opposition, and he promised to initiate an official inquiry into the 20 deaths that had occurred during demonstrations since February. Despite these concessions, the situation worsened later the same day. A temporary curfew was imposed on the capital, and many political agitators were arrested. The Government immediately initiated talks with the opposition, and on 8 April the King announced that the 30-year ban on political parties was to be ended, thus enabling the future holding of multi-party elections, and that a commission to study constitutional reform was to be established. At the same time, the Jana Andolan suspended its campaign of demonstrations. Many political activists continued to agitate, however, demanding the removal of the formal structure of the Panchayat system. A week later, the King accepted the resignation of Chand from his post as Prime Minister, dismissed the Council of Ministers and announced the dissolution of the Rashtriya Panchayat. King Birendra then invited the opposition alliance of the NCP and the ULF to form an interim government. On 19 April a new 11-member coalition Council of Ministers (including two ministers nominated by the King and two independents), under the premiership of the President of the NCP, Krishna Prasad (K. P.) Bhattarai, was sworn in. The new Prime Minister announced that a general election would be held, on a multi-party basis, within a year. The principal task of the interim Government was to prepare a new constitution in accordance with the spirit of multi-party democracy and constitutional monarchy. King Birendra stated that he was committed to transforming his role into that of a constitutional monarch, and, following further violent clashes in Kathmandu between anti-royalists and police, he ordered the army and the police to comply with the orders of the interim Government in order to facilitate a smooth transition to democracy.

In mid-May 1990 King Birendra announced a general amnesty for all religious and political prisoners. On 21 May he delegated the legislative powers of the dissolved Rashtriya Panchayat to the new Council of Ministers, so that the Council was empowered to enact, amend and repeal legislation in order to bring about the introduction of a multi-party democracy. At the end of the month the King formed a nine-member Constitutional Recommendation Commission, based on the suggestions of the Prime Minister, which, after consulting the various parties, was to prepare a draft constitution and present it to the King within three months. In July the death sentence was abolished and the laws restricting freedom of the press and freedom of association were repealed. In addition, the King suspended almost one-half of the articles in the Constitution to enable the interim Government to function smoothly. The draft of the new Constitution, which was published at the end of August, recommended the introduction of a constitutional monarchy; a democratic multi-party system and a bicameral legislature, composed of a 205-member House of Representatives (Pratinidhi Sabha) and a 60-member National Assembly (Rashtriya Sabha); the official guarantee of fundamental rights (including freedom of expression); an independent judiciary; and the placing of the army under the control of a three-member National Defence Council, headed by the Prime Minister. The draft Constitution recognized Hinduism as the country's dominant religion. It also, however, guaranteed freedom for religious minorities to practise their beliefs (although restrictions on proselytizing were to remain in force). Under the draft Constitution, the King would be allowed to declare a state of emergency on the advice of the Council of Ministers, but such declarations would have to be approved by the House of Representatives within three months. A crucial clause in the new Constitution required the King 'to obey and protect' the Constitution: under the old regime, the King was considered to be above the Constitution. The draft Constitution was approved by the Council of Ministers on 15 October and sent to the King for his endorsement. King Birendra, however, amended the draft in a final effort to retain sovereign authority and full emergency powers. This retrograde action provoked violent protests. The Council of Ministers rejected most of the proposed amendments in the royal counterdraft, but agreed to the King's proposal to establish a Council of State (Raj Parishad), with a standing committee headed by a royal appointee. The 15-member committee was to be composed of eight royal appointees and seven other members, including the Prime Minister, the Ministers of Defence and Foreign Affairs, the Chief Justice of the Supreme Court and the Chief of Army Staff. Bhattarai stressed, however, that the formation of this committee would not alter the democratic nature of the new Constitution, since it would not function as a parallel body to the Council of Ministers. He also emphasized that the King would only be permitted to act on judicial, executive and legislative matters on the advice of the Council of Ministers. The new Constitution was officially promulgated by the King on 9 November.

The communist movement in Nepal suffered a set-back in December 1990, when four of the seven constituent members of the ULF broke away from the front, citing their lack of representation in the interim coalition Council of Ministers. Sahana Pradhan stated, however, that the three remaining factions would continue to operate as the ULF. In January 1991 two major factions of the CPN (the Marxist and Marxist-Leninist factions) merged to form the CPN (Unified Marxist-Leninist—UML).

The process for the holding of a successful general election began with the registration of political parties and the delimitation of 205 constituencies. Of the 44 political parties registered by the election commission, however, only 20 actually participated in the general election, which was held on 12 May 1991. The NCP decided to contest the election alone and not on the basis of an electoral alignment with any of its former Jana Andolan partners. The communists interpreted the NCP's move as the result of an increased understanding between the palace and the NCP on the basis that both wanted to forestall the rise of communism in the country. Consequently, relations between the NCP and the UML became strained and competitive. The general election was not only peaceful, but was also characterized by a good turn-out (65.2% of the electorate). The NCP won a comfortable majority (110 of the 205 seats in the lower house), but it was soundly defeated by the UML in the eastern hill districts and in some parts of the Terai. In Kathmandu, supposedly an NCP stronghold, the party lost all of the seats but one. By winning 69 seats, the UML established itself as the second largest party in the House of Representatives, followed by the United People's Front (UPF), an amalgam of radical, Maoist groups, with nine seats. Two other communist organizations—the Nepal Workers' and Peasants' Party and a faction of the CPN—received two seats each, thus making a total communist tally in the House of Representatives of 82 seats. The Nepali Sadbhavana Party (NSP), which, despite the constitutional prohibition against regional-based parties, was a plains- or Terai-based party, obtained six seats, all of which were in the Terai. The Rashtriya Prajatantra Party (Chand) and the Rashtriya Prajatantra Party (Thapa), led by the former Prime Ministers of those names, fared badly in the election, winning only four seats—the latter one and the former three. All of the three independent candidates who won seats subsequently joined the NCP. Acting Prime Minister Bhattarai lost his seat in the capital, and was replaced in the premiership by Girija Prasad (G. P.) Koirala, the General Secretary of the NCP and brother of the late B. P. Koirala.

By the end of 1991 unity within the ruling NCP was threatened by growing internal dissent amongst its leadership, particularly between the senior leader, Ganesh Man Singh, and G. P. Koirala. In December the Prime Minister carried out a reshuffle of the Council of Ministers introducing more of his own supporters as new ministers. The Government suffered a further set-back in April 1992 when a *bandh* (general strike), organized by the communist and other opposition parties in Kathmandu in protest against price rises, water shortages and alleged government corruption, resulted in the deaths of at least seven demonstrators following violent clashes with the police. Despite the consequent imposition of curfews in the capital and in the neighbouring town of Lalitpur, the opposition staged a number of anti-Government protest marches and demonstrations during the following week. The success of a second general strike, which was held in early May, demonstrated the continuing strength of the radical left. It brought Kathmandu to a standstill and, unlike the earlier general strike, passed off without violent incidents. Despite the strikes and the rising cost of living, the NCP performed well in the local elections held throughout the country in May and June; of especial note was the party's strong showing in the Kathmandu valley where it had performed so badly in the 1991 general election. There were, however, widespread reports of corruption and malpractice.

Under the leadership of G. P. Koirala, the centrist NCP Government shifted to the right. The public image of the monarchy and leading members of the former Panchayat regime were rehabilitated with government support. No charges were brought against senior officials of the former administration for corruption or human rights violations. Replicating the patronage system of the Panchayat regime, the NCP rapidly began to dominate the public administration structure. The ruling party's persistent failure to democratize its internal bodies and the absence of open election to posts in the party leadership met with criticism both within and without the NCP.

In addition to opposition from the leadership of his own party, G. P. Koirala was faced with increasing criticism from the opposition parties themselves, which focused on an agreement drawn up by the Prime Minister in December 1991 granting India access to water from the Tanakpur barrage on the Mahakali River, the terms of which were only subsequently revealed to the Nepalese House of Representatives. Alleging that the agreement constituted a treaty affecting national sovereignty, and therefore requiring a two-thirds' majority in the House of Representatives, the opposition launched a campaign calling for the resignation of Koirala on the grounds of unconstitutional behaviour. An indeterminate Supreme Court ruling in December 1992 on Koirala's action only intensified the protest.

In January–February 1993 the national UML congress abandoned much of the party's Marxist dogma and tacitly acknowledged its commitment to working within a democratic multi-party system. However, the untimely deaths of the party's General Secretary, Madan Bhandari, and Politburo member Jiv Raj Ashrit, following a road accident in mid-May, threw the UML into disarray. The rejection by the UML of the findings of a government inquiry, which concluded that the deaths had been accidental, provoked nation-wide protests in support of demands for an independent inquiry into the so-called 'Dhasdunga Incident'. In late May Madhav Kumar Nepal was appointed as the new General Secretary of the UML.

In the mean time, the rehabilitation of officials of the former Panchayat regime continued. In January 1993 the King appointed senior figures of the old administration, including former Prime Ministers Chand and Shrestha, to the 121-member Council of State (Raj Parishad), in a move designed both to rehabilitate former Panchayat officials and to reassert his leadership role over them. In June the right-wing Rashtriya Prajatantra Party (RPP, formed in February 1992, following a merger of the Chand and Thapa factions) held its first national conference in Kathmandu, an event that would have been inconceivable three years previously, when its leaders were forced into hiding by the democracy movement.

In August 1993 the UML signed an agreement with the NCP, providing for the permanent withdrawal of the UML from anti-Government agitation in return for the ruling party's pledge to establish an independent commission to investigate the 'Dhasdunga Incident'. The UPF and other left-wing groups, however, continued their campaign of nation-wide general strikes and demonstrations demanding, amongst other things, the Prime Minister's resignation over the Tanakpur controversy and a curb on the NCP's increasing hold on power over public life. The Government was also criticized for its apparent inability to resolve the deteriorating economic situation, for its perceived subservience to India, and for its alleged involvement in corruption. Further serious rifts became apparent within the ruling NCP when the party's President, K. P. Bhattarai, lost a legislative by-election to the UML candidate in Kathmandu in February 1994; his defeat was widely attributed to G. P. Koirala's public opposition to his candidature. At the end of the month the Prime Minister rejected demands for his resignation made by supporters of Bhattarai in the NCP's Central Executive Committee. In March the Government survived a vote of 'no confidence' (by 113 votes to 81) presented to the House of Representatives by the UML. The opposition itself suffered from internal dissension in mid-1994 when both the UPF and the CPN (Unity Centre) split into competing factions, while the UML continued to be divided between radical and conservative camps. The crisis within the NCP culminated on 10 July when followers of Ganesh Man Singh withdrew their support for Koirala, who thereby lost his parliamentary majority. Consequently the Prime Minister offered his resignation, and on the following day the King dissolved the House of Representatives. Koirala was appointed as interim Prime Minister pending the holding of a general election, which was brought forward from mid-1996 to 15 November 1994. At the general election, which attracted a turn-out of 58%, the UML unexpectedly emerged as the single largest party, winning 88 of the 205 seats in the House of Representatives, while the NCP won 85 seats. At the end of the month the UML formed a minority Government under the premiership of its moderate Chairman, Man Mohan Adhikari. In late December the communist Government won a vote of confidence in the House of Representatives (as required by the Constitution for a new administration to continue in power).

On 11 June 1995 the NCP registered a parliamentary motion of 'no confidence' against the communist Government and, in conjunction with the RPP and the NSP, submitted a memorandum to King Birendra, staking their claim to form an alternative government. On the recommendation of the Prime Minister, who wished to avert the passage of the motion, the King dissolved the legislature on 13 June and announced that fresh elections were to be held on 23 November. Adhikari and his Council of Ministers were to function as a caretaker Government, pending the general election. In an apparent attempt to win popular support in the run-up to the election, Adhikari's interim administration substantially increased budgetary expenditure and implemented a number of welfare programmes. The opposition, angered by the communists' mode of electioneering, challenged the dissolution of the House of Representatives in the Supreme Court. In a controversial ruling, declared on 28 August, the Supreme Court decided that the dissolution of the lower house on the advice of a minority administration (when a majority coalition was ready to assume power) had, indeed, been unconstitutional. The House of Representatives was consequently reconvened and the election abandoned. The UML Government was defeated in a vote of 'no confidence' on 10 September, by 107 votes to 88. On 12 September a coalition Government, composed of members of the NCP, the RPP and the NSP, and headed by the NCP's parliamentary leader, Sher Bahadur Deuba, was formed.

In early March 1996 the Government introduced a number of security measures following a series of violent clashes between a group of Maoist activists and the police in western Nepal, which resulted in the deaths of at least 11 people (by the end of the year more than 100 people had been killed as a result of the insurgency). The left-wing extremists (many of whom were members of the underground Communist Party of Nepal—Maoist and the UPF) had launched a 'people's revolutionary war' in the hills of Nepal in February, demanding the abolition of the constitutional monarchy and the establishment of a republic. Later in March the Government survived a parliamentary motion of 'no confidence', tabled by the UML, by 106 votes to 90. In May G. P. Koirala was elected to replace Bhattarai as President of the NCP; for the first time since its foundation, the party elected its leader by ballot. The coalition Government was weakened by internal divisions and achieved little during 1996 (with the notable exception of the Mahakali Treaty, see below). In early December seven RPP members of the Council of Ministers resigned from their posts and the faction of the party led by Chand withdrew from the ruling coalition; the Government, however, which continued to enjoy the support of the RPP faction led by Thapa, narrowly survived a legislative vote of 'no confidence' (presented by the UML) later that month. In early January 1997 five of the former RPP ministers who had resigned from the Government in the previous month reversed their position and pledged their support for Deuba's administration; a few days later four of these politicians were reinstated in the Government as part of a ministerial reshuffle. The Government suffered a set-back at the end of the month when the UML, already the largest party in the House of Representatives, increased its strength from 87 to 90 deputies, following its success in three by-elections. Deuba's administration finally collapsed in early March when it lost a vote of confidence in the House of Representatives. Chand was appointed as the new Prime Minister (for the fourth time) at the head of a coalition Government composed of members of the RPP, the UML, the NSP and the Nepal Workers' and Peasants' Party. The new Government, however, seemed unstable from the outset, since the members of the Thapa faction of the RPP refused to support Prime Minister Chand and the ideological differences between the communists and the former pro-monarchists appeared insuperable. Although Chand held the premiership, the UML, as the largest component of the coalition, was responsible for more ministerial posts than the RPP. In May and June the communists replaced the NCP as the country's dominant force in local government, following resounding successes in local elections. These elections were marred, however, by violent clashes between supporters of the main political parties in which about 30 people were killed. In mid-June more than 10,000 NCP supporters demonstrated in Kathmandu in protest over alleged electoral irregularities on the part of the UML during the recent polls. During 1997 the UML suffered from factional infighting, with a major rift developing between Deputy Prime Minister Bam Dev Gautam and the General Secretary of the party, Madhav Kumar Nepal. This factionalism served to destabilize the coalition Government further. In August a strike organized by an alliance of left-wing groups (known as the National Democratic Front) in protest at the rise in the price of fuel and a proposed anti-terrorist law brought Kathmandu and surrounding towns to a standstill. In the following month an anti-defection bill, the aim of which was to prevent politicians from deserting their own party and thus to bring stability to Nepal's politics, was unanimously approved by the House of Representatives.

On 4 October 1997 the Government lost a parliamentary vote of 'no confidence' (by 107 votes to 94) tabled by the NCP. A few days later King Birendra appointed Thapa, the President of the RPP, to replace Chand as Prime Minister. A new coalition Government, comprising members of the RPP and the NSP, took office on the following day. On 9 October the new coalition administration won the requisite parliamentary vote of confidence (by 109 votes to two—the UML abstained). In December Prime Minister Thapa expanded the Council of Ministers in a reshuffle that introduced members of the NCP and a number of independents into the coalition. In January 1998 Nepal was once again faced with political upheaval when Thapa recommended to the King that he dissolve the House of Representatives and set a date for mid-term elections. The Prime Minister presented the petition for fresh polls following a decision by the UML and dissident members of the RPP (including Chand) to introduce a parliamentary vote of 'no confidence' against the Government. Uncertain as to how to act in this political impasse, the King referred the matter to the Supreme Court (the first time a Nepalese monarch had ever done so). In early February the Court advised King Birendra to convene a special session of the House of Representatives to discuss a 'no confidence' motion against Thapa's Government. Although the Supreme Court's

advice was not binding, the King called the parliamentary session. The 'no confidence' motion, which was presented on 20 February, was, however, defeated, by 103 votes to 100. Meanwhile, in mid-January Chand and nine other rebel deputies were expelled from the RPP; they immediately re-established a breakaway faction known as the RPP (Chand). In March the UML suffered a serious reverse when about one-half of the party's parliamentary deputies formed a breakaway faction entitled the Communist Party of Nepal (Marxist-Leninist) (ML). Bam Dev Gautam was unanimously elected as the new party's leader. The creation of the new party left the UML with 49 deputies, while the ML claimed the support of 40 deputies.

Under an agreement reached in October 1997 when Thapa assumed power, the Prime Minister was to transfer the leadership of the coalition Government to the NCP within an agreed time frame. By early April 1998, however, Thapa appeared reluctant to relinquish his post, and the NCP threatened to withdraw support for the Government unless the Prime Minister resigned immediately. Thapa tendered his resignation, and the President of the NCP, G. P. Koirala, was appointed Prime Minister in mid-April, taking office with only two other ministers. After obtaining a parliamentary vote of confidence, by 144 votes to four, the Prime Minister substantially expanded his Council of Ministers. Koirala stated that amongst the top priorities of the one-party minority Government would be the tackling of the Maoist insurgency (which had escalated in recent months). In August, in a seeming attempt to strengthen his own precarious administration and to encourage the UML's communist rivals, the Prime Minister invited the ML to join in alliance with the NCP and to form a coalition government. A new coalition administration was consequently established on 26 August (with the NCP retaining the most important ministries), giving Prime Minister Koirala an adequate parliamentary majority. Meanwhile, the 'people's war' waged by the Maoist activists in the hills of west Nepal gathered momentum. In May the Government launched a large-scale police operation in an effort to curb the guerrilla violence, and in July the Minister of Home Affairs claimed that a total of 257 people had died as a result of the Maoist uprising.

In December 1998 the ML withdrew from the coalition Government, alleging that its ruling partner, the NCP, had failed to implement a number of agreements drawn up between the two parties and other political groups in August. Prime Minister G. P. Koirala tendered his resignation, but was asked to head a new coalition Council of Ministers, which was to hold power in an acting capacity pending the holding of a general election. On the recommendation of the Prime Minister, the King appointed a new coalition administration, comprising members of the NCP, the UML and the NSP, and, for the first time in eight years, a nominee of the King, on 25 December. In mid-January 1999 the acting Government won a convincing vote of confidence in the House of Representatives, and on the following day the King dissolved the legislature in preparation for the forthcoming general election.

In late April 1999 the UML suffered a set-back when its veteran leader and former Prime Minister, Man Mohan Adhikari, died during the electoral campaign. In May the NCP won an outright majority in the general election (held over two rounds), securing 110 of the 205 seats in the lower house; the UML obtained 68 seats and the RPP (Thapa) took 11 seats, while the ML and the RPP (Chand) both failed to win a single seat. Voting was conducted relatively peacefully, according to government sources, despite threats by the Maoist insurgents to disrupt the electoral process. A new Council of Ministers, headed by the veteran NCP leader, K. P. Bhattarai, and composed solely of NCP members, was appointed at the end of the month. In late June the UML won all six seats in elections to the National Assembly, and in August Dr Mohammad Mohasin of the RPP was elected Chairman of the upper house.

In late November 1999, in an effort to resolve the Maoist insurgency, which, according to government sources, now affected (moderately to severely) 31 of Nepal's 75 districts and had led to the deaths of more than 1,000 people, the Prime Minister offered to grant the guerrillas an amnesty and various rehabilitation measures if they surrendered their arms and entered into negotiations with the Government. In response, the insurgents (who were estimated to number 5,000–6,000 and to have the support of about 8,000 sympathizers) stated that they were not prepared to enter into peace talks until arrest warrants issued against their leaders were withdrawn, official investigations were carried out into alleged extrajudicial killings of suspected militants by the police, and imprisoned activists were released. In an attempt to facilitate the peace process, the Government established a six-member high-level negotiation commission under the convenorship of former Prime Minister Sher Bahadur Deuba, which was charged with finding a solution to the Maoist situation that met with the approval of all political parties (including the insurgents themselves).

In mid-December 1999 the ruling NCP, despite a number of by-election victories, was once again beset by internecine strife when about 80 pro-Koirala legislators initiated an attempt to oust (by means of a petition) the Prime Minister from his position as the NCP's parliamentary party leader (which would automatically lead to his removal from the premiership). Koirala had initially been supportive of Bhattarai's premiership, but had since become a vociferous critic of his rival's administration, particularly with regard to the Government's perceived mismanagement of the Maoist crisis. In February 2000, on the recommendation of Prime Minister Bhattarai, the King carried out a minor reorganization of the Council of Ministers, including the appointment of Ram Chandra Poudel, a former Speaker of the lower house, as Deputy Prime Minister; the ministerial reshuffle was prompted by the earlier resignation of the Minister of Finance, Mahesh Acharya, following a disagreement with the Prime Minister over the appointment of the new Governor of the Central Bank. A few days after the government reorganization, the Minister of Education, Yog Prasad Upadhyaya, resigned in protest at the appointment of Poudel as Deputy Prime Minister. The political unrest culminated in the registration of a vote of 'no confidence' by 58 dissident NCP legislators against Prime Minister Bhattarai; this move led to the immediate resignation of 11 government ministers. The NCP's parliamentary party was scheduled to vote on the no-confidence motion in late February; however, following the attainment of a secret agreement between the Prime Minister and the NCP President, G. P. Koirala, including Bhattarai's reported assurance that he would stand down voluntarily within a fortnight, the proposal was withdrawn. A second motion of 'no confidence' in Bhattarai, who continued to hold the premiership amid rumours that he wished to hand over the post to a younger, 'second generation' leader, was registered by 69 predominantly pro-Koirala legislators in the NCP secretariat in mid-March. Under such pressure, Prime Minister Bhattarai pre-empted the holding of a no-confidence vote and tendered his resignation to the King. It was announced that G. P. Koirala was to be the new Prime Minister (for the fourth time), following his election as parliamentary party leader of the NCP (Koirala polled 69 votes, while his rival, Deuba, secured 43 votes); this election process replaced the party's traditional method of choosing a parliamentary leader through consensus. Koirala and a new Council of Ministers were sworn in by the King on 22 March, and vowed to continue the basic programmes and policies that the previous NCP Government had adopted. In mid-April, on the recommendation of the Council of Ministers, King Birendra reduced the number of ministries from 26 to 21. In May a Human Rights Commission was formed following accusations by various bodies that both the security forces and the Maoist guerrillas had committed human rights violations, including murder and torture.

In early April 2000 Prime Minister Koirala activated the National Defence Council, which, according to the Constitution, comprised the Prime Minister, the Minister of Defence and the Commander-in-Chief of the Royal Nepal Army, to resolve the Maoist crisis. In comparison to the inadequately-trained and poorly-armed police force, which had suffered numerous casualties, the army was much better equipped to deal with the insurgency, and Koirala expressed his wish to mobilize the armed forces in the ongoing fight against militant activity. The possibility of the deployment of the armed forces met with immediate criticism from various Nepalese human rights groups, which claimed that mobilization of the army would lead to an escalation in corruption. In the same month Deuba reportedly held preliminary talks with leaders of the UPF regarding the resolution of the Maoist uprising.

In June 2000 the CPN (Maoist) accepted the Government's invitation for dialogue; however, in August the party refused to enter negotiations, owing to the Government's failure to fulfil certain conditions. In mid-July the Government abolished bonded labour. In August the Minister for Water Resources, Khum Bahadur Khadka, was dismissed owing to his involvement in a campaign against the Prime Minister. Later that month the Government banned strikes in 'essential services',

including banks and telecommunications. In the mean time, strikes continued to take place intermittently throughout the year.

Nepal experienced floods from early August 2000, causing fatalities and damage to crops and, later, food shortages. At the end of the month the Maoist crisis worsened. During two Maoist attacks in Dolpa and Lamjung, 24 police officers were killed and 44 were injured. The Royal Nepal Army was criticized for failing to intervene to protect the police from insurgents. The Minister of Home Affairs, Govinda Raj Joshi, resigned after admitting his failure to 'maintain law and order in the country'. The Prime Minister responded to the confusion over the command and control structure of the army by giving Mahesh Acharya, the Minister of Finance, the additional portfolio of defence. G. P. Koirala had hitherto always retained this portfolio personally, but it had become clear that the Government and army needed an independent defence minister, clarification of the army's ambiguous role and the development of a procedure for mobilizing the army, absent from the 1991 Constitution. It was later decided that the Government would employ a dual approach: using the army, as well as encouraging negotiations in order to resolve the Maoist crisis. In the mean time, the RPP (Chand) merged with the RPP (Thapa); the Chand-led RPP was formally closed down in late 2000.

At the end of October 2000 the first direct unofficial negotiations began between the Government and the CPN (Maoist); however, they soon ended, and the violence resumed in early November. In the same month the high-level commission charged with finding a solution to the Maoist crisis (see above) produced a report advising the Government and Maoist insurgents to cease violence and participate in negotiations. The report also recommended that the Government improve and modernize its security forces. The UML leader, who had earlier held negotiations with the insurgents, ruled out any alliance with the Maoist group until it abandoned the use of force.

In January 2001 a no-confidence motion against Prime Minister Koirala, demanding that he be removed as leader of the party, was defeated. The motion, led by the former Prime Minister, Sher Bahadur Deuba, was brought about by Koirala's perceived failure to control both the Maoist insurgency and corruption. Shortly afterwards Deuba began a nation-wide campaign to remove the Prime Minister from the NCP leadership and announced his candidacy for the party presidency, to be determined in mid-January. Nevertheless, at the party's general convention, Koirala was re-elected NCP President.

In January 2001 the Minister for Tourism and Civil Aviation, Tarani Datta Chataut, resigned following a controversial agreement to lease an Austrian aircraft to the Royal Nepal Airlines Corporation. In early February leading opposition parties issued a memorandum to the Prime Minister, demanding his resignation over the aircraft deal and also the worsening security situation. Koirala strongly denied his involvement in the leasing of the Austrian aircraft. The King then approved a reorganization of the Council of Ministers, on the recommendation of Prime Minister Koirala. However, shortly after the new cabinet was announced, two ministers withdrew their names, criticizing Koirala for making decisions without consulting other senior leaders. Palten Gurung later reneged on his decision, but Khum Bahadur Khadka refused to join the Council of Ministers. In March the Prime Minister faced increasing opposition from within and outside his party. Further ministerial resignations followed. The opposition continued to disrupt parliamentary proceedings, and, as a result, the King prorogued the National Assembly and House of Representatives in early April. In early May the Minister of Water Resources, Baldev Sharma Majgaiya, resigned. At the end of the month the anti-corruption commission cleared the Prime Minister of involvement in the controversial aircraft agreement, but filed cases against 10 other people, including the former minister, Chataut. At the same time, Koirala was accused of accepting bribes in another aircraft deal. The opposition continued to demand his resignation and organized a nation-wide strike in protest against the Government's alleged misuse of power. Meanwhile, in the first half of 2001 several unsuccessful attempts were made by the Government and Maoist militants to embark upon a peace process.

On 1 June 2001 King Birendra, Queen Aishwarya and six other members of the royal family were shot dead; the heir to the throne, Crown Prince Dipendra, was gravely wounded. Another family member, Dhirendra Shah, died later in hospital. Initial reports suggested that Prince Dipendra had shot members of his family before shooting himself, following a dispute between himself and his mother, regarding his intentions to marry Devyani Rani (the daughter of a prominent Nepalese politician), of whom the Queen disapproved. Prince Gyanendra, the deceased King Birendra's brother, however, issued a statement claiming that the deaths were the result of an accidental discharge of an automatic weapon. Immediately after the incident Prince Dipendra was pronounced King, and Prince Gyanendra was appointed regent. On 4 June King Dipendra died and was succeeded by Prince Gyanendra. These events caused unrest in Kathmandu, and a curfew was imposed. In the mean time, rumours about the killings began to spread. Few believed the statement given by Gyanendra. Some suggested that Maoist insurgents were to blame; others claimed India was responsible. On 6 June three journalists of the daily newspaper, *Kantipur*, were arrested and charged with sedition for publishing an article written by a Maoist leader supporting a conspiracy theory that Gyanendra (who was not present at the incident) and his son Paras Shah, who was not harmed in the shooting, had planned the events. (The charges were withdrawn in mid-August.) Following his accession, King Gyanendra established a commission to investigate the killings. The commission, comprising the Chief Justice, K. P. Upadhyaya and the Speaker of the House of Representatives, T. Ranabhat, duly concluded that Dipendra had been responsible for the shootings and that at the time had been under the influence of drugs and alcohol. It was established that prior to the incident, he had telephoned his girlfriend, Devyani Rani, three times. He then changed into his military uniform, returned to the gathering and indiscriminately shot members of his family, before shooting himself. King Gyanendra bestowed the title of Queen on his wife, Princess Komal, but did not declare his son the Crown Prince until the end of October, owing to his unpopularity among the public, caused by his profligate behaviour.

In late June 2001 elections to 16 seats in the National Assembly took place. The UML won eight seats, bringing its total to 23 and rendering it the largest bloc in the chamber. In June–July Maoist leaders, taking advantage of the discontent in Nepal, intensified their activities. On 13 July the Deputy Prime Minister, Ram Chandra Poudel, resigned, owing to disagreements with the Prime Minister over policy towards the insurgency. Some few days later a senior Maoist leader declared that he would enter negotiations on the condition that the Prime Minister resigned. On 19 July Prime Minister Koirala resigned, citing his failure to curb the Maoist insurgency and longstanding corruption allegations. A few days later the NCP elected former premier Sher Bahadur Deuba as its new leader; King Gyanendra appointed Deuba as Prime Minister on the same day and a new Council of Ministers was sworn in on 26 July. Prime Minister Deuba retained a number of Koirala's cabinet members in an effort to ensure stability and initially kept many of the major portfolios for himself.

Immediately after his appointment Prime Minister Deuba persuaded the Maoist leaders to reciprocate his offer of a cease-fire and agree to enter dialogue. Prior to the negotiations, both sides took a series of confidence-building measures: the Maoist activists released 31 kidnapped police officers, and the Government set free over 30 Maoist leaders and published the names of 273 guerrillas still imprisoned. At the same time Parliament passed legislation to establish an Armed Police Force and to develop the co-ordination of regional development and security. The Government released a further 68 insurgents after the first two rounds of negotiations in August and September 2001. Despite the cease-fire, Maoist insurgents continued to carry out violent acts. During the peace talks tens of thousands of people held demonstrations against the fighting. The third round of negotiations, which took place in November, ended in failure, owing to the Maoists' continued demand for the dissolution of the Constitution, the establishment of an interim government, the election of a constituent assembly and, ultimately, a republic. The Government, in contrast, was prepared to offer a much less radical set of changes. Two days later the CPN (Maoist) leader Pushpa Kamal Dahal announced the end of the cease-fire. The Maoists established a parallel central government, the 'United People's Revolutionary Government', and resumed their violent campaign. The Maoists set up parallel governments in 40 of the country's 70 districts, and established direct rule in 22 districts in western Nepal. The violence escalated; on 26 November the King declared a state of emergency and authorized, for the first time, the deployment of the army to curb the insurgency. The King termed the Maoists as 'terrorists' and promulgated the Terrorist and Disruptive Activities Ordi-

nance 2001, which sanctioned a number of counter-terrorist measures, including the suspension of civil liberties and media restrictions. The number of people killed in the five-year 'people's war' had risen to more than 2,300 by the end of December. In mid-December Prime Minister Deuba declared that he would not resume negotiations with the Maoists until they surrendered their arms.

Meanwhile, in early September 2001 the Government implemented a radical land reform programme, which was designed to help poor, landless farmers. The programme was supported by the UML, but opposed by smaller parties. Major landowners who risked losing part of their land opposed the limit to the size of individual landholdings. In mid-August Deuba announced that discrimination against Dalits (or 'untouchables') would henceforth be illegal and pledged to pass legislation ending the caste system. A national commission for Dalit welfare and a National Women's Commission were also to be established. In mid-October the Government was reorganized and expanded.

In early January 2002 the Nepal Rastra Bank froze the bank accounts of individuals and organizations associated with Maoist militants. In mid-February Maoist insurgents launched their heaviest-ever offensive against government outposts. More than 150 people, mainly soldiers and police officers, were killed in the fighting. In response to the attacks, the army was instructed to use offensive as well as defensive measures to combat the insurgency. On 21 February the legislature voted to extend the state of emergency for three months. Although the opposition criticized the Government for its handling of the insurgency and for failing to react to warnings that major attacks were imminent, it voted for the extension after the Prime Minister agreed to establish social and economic development programmes in poor rural areas where Maoists were active, and ensured the fair use of the emergency powers. In order to mark the sixth anniversary of the Maoist insurgency and to protest against the state of emergency, the guerrillas organized a two-day nation-wide general strike.

In the mean time, in mid-February 2002 the UML and its breakaway faction, the ML, merged. The party was reunited ahead of local elections scheduled to take place in May. The merger of the more moderate communist parties was regarded largely as a move to counter the influence of the Maoist insurgents. In mid-March the Minister of Forest and Soil Conservation, Gopal Man Shrestha, resigned amid allegations of corruption. Shrestha refuted the allegations presented by his deputy, Surendra Hamal, who was also forced to resign after the UML disrupted parliamentary proceedings. Strikes occurred in March, severely affecting businesses and schools. Schools, as well as government buildings, infrastructure and army and police outposts, were attacked. The Human Rights Commission issued its first annual report in which it accused the Maoist insurgents of committing serious human rights abuses. The commission also criticized the Government for violating human rights. On 4 April the Government reduced the controversial restrictions it imposed on the media and political parties as part of the state of emergency. The violent campaign escalated in mid-April, leading to hundreds of fatalities. In May Deuba tabled a parliamentary motion proposing an extension of the six-month state of emergency (which was due to expire on 25 May), prompting strong opposition from within and outside his party. Members of the governing NCP, led by former premier G. P. Koirala, accused Deuba of not consulting them before recommending an extension and urged the Government to withdraw its parliamentary motion. The rift in the party led King Gyanendra to dissolve unexpectedly the House of Representatives on 22 May, on the recommendation of the Prime Minister. A general election was scheduled to take place on 13 November, and the incumbent Government was instructed to rule the country in the interim. Political leaders strongly condemned this decision. On 23 May Deuba was suspended from his party and three days later was expelled from the NCP for three years. In the mean time, three ministers, including the Minister of Finance, resigned in protest at the calling of early elections. In late May King Gyanendra extended by three months the state of emergency. Meanwhile, in early May the army launched a heavy attack against Maoist insurgents in Rolpa district, resulting in the deaths of, according to government sources, 548 guerrillas, three soldiers and one police officer. A series of counter-attacks and attacks ensued, leading to hundreds of fatalities; by the end of May some reports estimated that more than 4,000 people had been killed since the beginning of the insurgency. In mid-May Maoist activists set fire to Mahendra Sanskrit University, causing millions of rupees worth of damage; no one was killed in the incident. The attack on Nepal's only Sanskrit university was motivated by the Maoists' opposition to compulsory Sanskrit education at state-managed schools on the grounds that it promoted the interests of the Brahmin caste, while disregarding other castes. On 9 May the Maoist leader made an offer of a one-month cease-fire by e-mail to newspapers in Kathmandu; Deuba promptly rejected the proposal, repeating his request for the insurgents to renounce violence. International human rights organizations voiced concern over reports of human rights violations by the army. The editor of the pro-Maoist newspaper *Janadisha* was arrested by security forces in May; it was later reported that he died while in custody, allegedly under torture.

In mid-June 2002 the NCP officially split during a 'general convention' held by the Deuba faction. The Minister of Agriculture, Mahesh Acharya, resigned shortly afterwards, in response to the party crisis. Eventually, in mid-September the Election Commission recognized the faction led by G. P. Koirala as the official NCP; Deuba could either join Koirala or form a new party. Several days later Deuba's minority breakaway faction registered as a new political party, the Nepali Congress Party—Democratic (NCP—D). Meanwhile, in April the Nepal Sadbhavana Party split into two factions and in July two communist parties, the National People's Front and United People's Front, merged to form the People's Front Nepal. Also in July, interim Prime Minister Deuba was accused of acting unconstitutionally when he presented the 2002/03 budget as a royal decree, thereby undermining a 1995 Supreme Court ruling, which defined the way in which interim administrations could introduce budgets. In September the Minister of Physical Planning and Works resigned, owing to an ongoing official investigation into his property assets.

In the mean time, the state of emergency expired in late August 2002. As a result the Maoists intensified their violent campaign, leading to hundreds of fatalities in September. It was reported that by the end of September about 3,000 people had been killed since the collapse of peace negotiations in November 2001. In mid-September 2002 the Government rejected Pushpa Kamal Dahal's offer of a cease-fire, on the grounds that it lacked credibility. In response to protests by the Federation of Journalists over the alleged treatment of journalists in custody, in early September the Government issued a list of 16 journalists detained in Kathmandu under the anti-terrorism legislation.

In early October 2002 Deuba requested King Gyanendra to postpone the general election by one year, citing the deteriorating law and order situation. However, King Gyanendra dismissed the Prime Minister and the interim Council of Ministers for reportedly failing to organize the general election. The King assumed executive power and postponed indefinitely parliamentary elections scheduled for November. On 11 October King Gyanendra appointed a nine-member interim Government, headed by the former premier and monarchist Lok Bahadur Chand. Most of the members of the new cabinet were civil servants or professionals. The NCP, UML and legal experts condemned the dismissal of Deuba and his Government and the establishment of a new Council of Ministers as unconstitutional. Furthermore, the Maoist argument appeared to be strengthened by the King's act of 'feudal absolutism'. In mid-November the King disregarded demands by political parties to create a new government composed of their members, instead reorganizing and expanding the interim Council of Ministers to include a former UML member, businessmen and independents. Interim Prime Minister Chand relinquished 14 portfolios under the government changes. At the same time, amid continuing violence and disruption, the Deputy Prime Minister stated that the interim Government was prepared to enter negotiations with the CPN (Maoist) and would consider the latter's demand for an elected constituent assembly. In December the human rights organization Amnesty International issued a damning report on the human rights situation in Nepal since the collapse of peace talks in November 2001. The army and Armed Police Force were severely criticized for the reported 'unprecedented levels' of human rights abuses, including torture, arbitrary dentention and deaths in custody. In addition, the report accused Maoist insurgents of torturing and killing captives, taking hostages and recruiting children. The report claimed that nearly one-half of the 4,366 people who had died in the conflict since late 2001 were civilians, killed by both security forces and Maoists.

On 26 January 2003 suspected Maoist militants shot dead the chief of the Armed Police Force, Inspector-General Krishna Mohan Shrestha, in Kathmandu; his wife and bodyguard were

also killed. Three days later the CPN (Maoist) and Government announced an immediate cease-fire and agreed to resume peace negotiations after the Government agreed to declassify Maoist activists as terrorists, to withdraw rewards offered for the arrest of Maoist leaders and to cancel international police warrants issued for the guerrilla leaders. In February a series of informal talks took place; at the end of the month the Maoists presented two conditions for the resumption of formal negotiations: the release of Maoist prisoners and the army to return to the barracks. A 22-point code of conduct was signed by the chief government negotiator and Minister of Physical Planning and Construction, Narayan Singh Pun, and the Maoist leader, Baburam Bhattarai, in mid-March. According to the code, the Government would release prisoners gradually and give Maoists equal access to the state-controlled media; there was no mention of the army moving back to the barracks, however. Both sides also agreed formally to cease hostilities. The following day a Maoist negotiator declared that, while a communist republic continued to be the CPN (Maoist)'s goal, the militant group would comply with the public's decision on the future of the monarchy. In the mean time, Chand continued unsuccessfully to involve political parties in the peace process and therefore to form a broad-based negotiating team. The political parties and the Maoists questioned the interim Government's authority to negotiate with the Maoists. At the end of March Maoist negotiators began consultations with the NCP and UML on planned peace talks. In early April several hundred students participated in an anti-Government demonstration that was provoked by the shooting of a student leader by police during an earlier protest. Two days later the King dismissed the Ministers of Home Affairs, of Education and of Industry, Commerce and Supplies, supposedly to placate the protesters. The portfolios were shared between the Prime Minister and Deputy Prime Minister.

The interim Government and Maoist representatives commenced formal negotiations at the end of April 2003; it was reported that the CPN (Maoist) demanded the release of Maoist prisoners, participation in an interim government and the creation of a constituent assembly, but did not include the abolition of the monarchy in its agenda. At the second round of peace talks, which took place on 9 May, the Government agreed to release several Maoist detainees and to restrict army troops to within 5 km of their barracks. Both sides also achieved consensus on the composition of a committee to monitor the code of conduct guiding the cease-fire. The third round of negotiations, which eventually took place on 17–19 August, ended in impasse over the Maoists' demand for an elected assembly to draft a new constitution. Although the two sides agreed to meet again in a week's time, on 27 August the leader of the CPN (Maoist), Pushpa Kamal Dahal, ended the seven-month cease-fire and withdrew from the peace process. On the following day the Government reclassified the insurgents as 'terrorists' after violent activity resumed. Thousands of people marched in Kathmandu at the end of August to urge the Government and Maoist militants to resume peace talks. Meanwhile, on 25 August former premier Deuba survived an assassination attempt by suspected Maoist militants.

In the mean time, at the end of May 2003 Prime Minister Chand resigned in response to pressure from leaders of the major political parties. The parties (the NCP, UML, Nepal Workers' and Peasants' Party, Nepali Sadbhavan Party—Anandi Devi, and People's Front Nepal), with the support of students, had held demonstrations against the Chand Government and the King almost relentlessly. On 4 June the King appointed the monarchist and former premier Surya Bahadur Thapa as Prime Minister, rejecting the nomination by the five opposition parties of Madhav Kumar Nepal, the General Secretary of the UML. One week later the King appointed a new interim Council of Ministers, composed entirely of members of the monarchist RPP. Thapa had invited M. K. Nepal and Deuba to join the Government, but the leading politicians refused, maintaining that Thapa's appointment was unconstitutional. Opposition parties held a large demonstration in Kathmandu, demanding Thapa's resignation, the reinstatement of the legislature and the establishment of an all-party government. In late August Nepal's major political parties refused Thapa's appeal for co-operation, instead pledging to launch a new set of nationwide protests in support for the return of parliamentary democracy. On 1 September, however, the Government banned all demonstrations or public gatherings of five or more people in the Kathmandu valley, owing to fears of infiltration by Maoist guerrillas. None the less, over a week later more than 1,000 pro-democracy protesters, including former premier G. P. Koirala, were arrested for defying the ban and taking part in a demonstration.

The CPN (Maoist) fully resumed its violent campaign in September 2003. Bomb explosions, assassinations and violent clashes had led to the deaths of at least 200 people by the end of the month. In the same month the Maoists organized a three-day general strike, which severely affected businesses, transport services and schools throughout most of the country. In mid-September the police filed charges against 21 members of the CPN (Maoist), including Pushpa Kamal Dahal and Baburam Bhattarai, for the murder in January of the Inspector-General of the Armed Police Force and two others (see above). Violence continued throughout October. According to a report published at the end of the month by the Nepal human rights group the Informal Sector Service Centre (INSEC), more than 1,000 people had died in the violence since the collapse of the cease-fire. In mid-October Amnesty International claimed that at least 30 people had 'disappeared' during military operations since the resumption of violence. Meanwhile, Dahal had issued a statement declaring that the CPN (Maoist) would, henceforth, target US-supported organizations instead of infrastructure targets. In response, the US Administration announced at the end of the month that it had banned the CPN (Maoist), listing the group as a threat to national security (the USA was already providing the Nepalese army with military assistance for its campaign against the Maoist insurgents).

In mid-November 2003 it was reported that a high-ranking Nepalese army officer had died in the violence. At the end of the month the international police agency, Interpol, issued arrest warrants for 11 senior CPN (Maoist) officials, including Dahal and Baburam Bhattarai. The conflict appeared to escalate in December. In mid-December the Government announced that it would grant an amnesty to anyone who surrendered by mid-February 2004. This message was dismissed by Maoist leaders; however, in a statement issued in January, the CPN (Maoist) spokesman Krishna Bahadur Mahara declared that his organization would accept a constitutional monarchy on condition that the King resigned as Supreme Commander-in-Chief of the army and that he confronted some 250 members of the armed forces who were allegedly 'working against the state'. Mahara also declared that the Maoists were ready for dialogue provided that the King and political parties were prepared for 'change without additional bloodshed'. The Maoist leader Baburam Bhattarai, however, emphasized in an interview two days later that a people's republic remained the chief aim of the CPN (Maoist). In the same month the Maoists announced the formation of autonomous people's governments in 10 districts under their control. At the end of the month the CPN (Maoist) stated that it would give priority to development in these areas, and that representatives of the King and the USA were banned from operating in districts under Maoist influence. At the same time, the Nepalese army announced that 15 soldiers had been convicted of human rights violations and other criminal activities, and sentenced to up to six years' imprisonment; six other soldiers had been dismissed from the army for illegal activity committed during military operations against Maoist guerrillas. It was reported in mid-February that more than 555 Maoist militants had surrendered to security forces since the launch of the amnesty in December 2003; the deadline of the amnesty was extended to 12 April 2004. The violence increased, meanwhile. The Maoists held intermittent nation-wide general strikes, adversely affecting businesses and schools. The number of people killed in the eight-year 'people's war' had risen sharply to more than 9,130 by mid-March, of whom more than 1,500 had died since the collapse of the cease-fire in August 2003. It was also reported that more than 250 people had 'disappeared' since August.

Meanwhile, it was reported in mid-November 2003 that the central committee of the RPP had requested Prime Minister Thapa to resign for failing to form an all-party government following his appointment. Thapa, however, maintained the support of the King and, thus, was able to remain in his position. In mid-December the five main opposition parties organized another demonstration against the King. In January 2004 there were almost daily student-led pro-republic protests in Kathmandu. At the end of the month the opposition parties issued a joint statement offering formal support to the student movement. This action provided evidence that the NCP, a committed supporter of the constitutional monarchy, and the UML were

reconsidering their views towards the monarchy. In early February, as part of a two-week tour around the troubled mid-western region, King Gyanendra gave a public address in the city of Nepalganj. During the speech, the King appealed for an end to the insurgency and appeared to seek an active role in governing democracy. Opposition parties criticized the King, claiming that he was not committed to multi-party democracy and the constitutional monarchy, and pledged to intensify their protests against 'regression'. Prime Minister Thapa, meanwhile, announced that the interim Government was preparing to hold a general election soon. The opposition, however, maintained that the Thapa Government was illegitimate and should be replaced by an all-party government, which in turn would hold elections and enter a peace process with the Maoist militants. In March the leaders of the five main opposition parties announced that a constitutional monarchy had not been successful and that, henceforth, their movement would be directed at achieving the establishment of a republic; a debate on the relevance of the monarchy would be taken to the village level. Meanwhile, in early March King Gyanendra reorganized and expanded the Council of Ministers, appointing Dr Bhek Bahadur Thapa as the Minister of Foreign Affairs and Health and allocating Kamal Thapa, the incumbent Minister of Information and Communications, the additional portfolios of home affairs and local development. In early April the Minister of Forest and Soil Conservation, Culture, Tourism and Civil Aviation, and of Land Reform and Management, Sarbendra Nath Shukla, resigned following controversies over his statement in the Special Court in support of an RPP leader charged with corruption; Prime Minister Thapa was assigned his portfolios. In early May the Prime Minister tendered his resignation as a result of the continuing political *impasse*. The resignation prompted the collapse of the entire Government; King Gyanendra authorized Thapa to remain in office in an acting capacity pending the formation of a new administration.

In 1978 the old Trade and Transit Treaty between Nepal and India was replaced by two treaties (renewed in the mid-1980s), the one concerning bilateral trade between the two countries, the other allowing Nepal to develop trade with other countries via India. Relations with India deteriorated considerably in March 1989, however, when India decided not to renew the treaties, insisting that a common treaty covering both issues be negotiated. Nepal refused, however, stressing the importance of keeping the treaties separate, on the grounds that trade issues are negotiable, whereas the right of transit is a recognized basic right of land-locked countries. In response, India closed 13 of the 15 transit points through which most of Nepal's trade is conducted. Severe shortages of food and fuel ensued, and the prices of basic products increased significantly. It was widely believed that a major issue aggravating the dispute was Nepal's purchase of weapons (including anti-aircraft guns) from the People's Republic of China in 1988, which, according to India, violated the Treaty of Peace and Friendship concluded by India and Nepal in 1950. Diplomatic relations between Nepal and India remained strained throughout 1989, with trade at a virtual standstill. Following several rounds of senior-level talks, a joint communiqué was signed by the two countries in June 1990, restoring trade relations and reopening the transit points, and assuring mutual consultations on matters of security. A few days earlier, as an apparent gesture of goodwill to India, the Nepalese Government had told the Chinese Government to defer indefinitely the delivery of the final consignment of weapons destined for Nepal. The visit to Kathmandu by the Indian Prime Minister in February 1991 (the first official visit to Nepal by an Indian head of government since 1977), shortly after it was announced that the first free elections there were to be held in May, helped to reaffirm the traditionally amicable ties between the two countries. Separate trade and transit treaties (valid for five and seven years respectively) were signed during a visit by Prime Minister Koirala to India in December 1991; these treaties were both subsequently renewed on expiry. A major breakthrough in Indo-Nepalese relations was achieved in February 1996, when the Prime Ministers of the two countries formally signed a treaty in New Delhi regarding the shared utilization of the waters of the Mahakali River basin (for irrigation, general consumption and the production of hydroelectric power). The costs and benefits of the project, which involved the construction of a massive hydroelectric power plant, were to be divided between Nepal and India, although not, some critics claimed, to Nepal's benefit. Despite protests by left-wing opposition parties, the Mahakali Treaty was ratified by the House of

Representatives in September. During a visit to Nepal by the Indian Prime Minister in June 1997, the Mahakali Treaty was formally endorsed and India granted Nepal access to Bangladeshi ports through a new transit facility across Indian territory via the Karkavita-Phulbari road (this facility was extended and improved in 1998). Some tension in Indo-Nepalese relations, nevertheless, remained; this centred on border demarcation disputes and, in particular, on the Indian border police's use of territory that Nepal claims as its own in the far west of the country (namely the strategically-situated Kalapani junction between India, Nepal and China, which covers an area of about 35 sq km). In June 2000 the Nepalese Government announced that the border would be delineated by 2003. In early August 2000 Prime Minister Koirala paid a visit to India, around four years after the previous visit by a head of government. Koirala succeeded in improving Indo-Nepalese relations, which had been strained by the hijacking of an Indian Airlines aircraft from Kathmandu in December 1999. In June 2000 Indian Airlines' operations to Kathmandu were resumed, ending a five-month suspension. Although Nepal was keen to renegotiate the Treaty of Peace and Friendship concluded by Nepal and India in 1950, India agreed to discuss the treaty only at foreign secretary level; therefore, it was unlikely that a solution would be achieved in the immediate future. In late 2001 India supplied Nepal with two helicopters and arms to assist the neighbouring country in its struggle against the Maoist insurgency. India repeated its offer of financial assistance in early 2002. In March both countries extended for five years the 1996 bilateral trade treaty. The Nepalese and Indian Governments also held talks on the civil disorder problem in Nepal; India promised to provide the necessary support. From early 2003, however, the Indian Government became increasingly concerned about King Gyanendra's perceived disregard for democracy.

The People's Republic of China has contributed a considerable amount to the Nepalese economy, and the first meeting of a joint committee on economic co-operation took place in 1984. This committee met for a second time (and thenceforth annually) in Kathmandu in 1986, when China agreed to increase its imports from Nepal in order to minimize trade imbalances. Relations between Nepal and China improved further during the late 1980s and 1990s, as indicated by reciprocal visits made by high-ranking Nepalese and Chinese officials (notably, a state visit to Nepal was conducted by the Chinese President, Jiang Zemin, in 1996). In May 2001 the leaders of Nepal and China signed a six-point co-operation agreement to improve cross-border trade, increase road and aviation links and to promote tourism.

In 1985 it was agreed that Nepal's border with Tibet (the Xizang Autonomous Region) should be opened. Following the outbreak of ethnic violence in Tibet in 1989, however, the border between Nepal and Tibet was closed indefinitely. In 1991 the interim Government of Nepal cancelled a visit by the Dalai Lama, the Tibetan leader in exile, on 'technical grounds'. The cancellation followed Chinese protests made to the Nepalese Government against the proposed visit. The Nepalese authorities have been consistent in their commitment to the 'One China' policy and in their efforts to repatriate refugees fleeing from Tibet. In 1993 G. P. Koirala paid an informal visit to Tibet—the first visit to the region by a Nepalese Premier since the 1950s. In 1995, however, the Nepalese authorities banned a proposed peace march by Tibetans through Nepalese territory. During a visit to China by the Nepalese Minister of Foreign Affairs in August 2000, an agreement was reached to allow Nepal greater use of a new road in Tibet. Greater technological and economic co-operation was also achieved, therefore noticeably increasing bilateral trade. Nepal provoked strong criticism from the UN and Western governments in late May 2003, after it helped Chinese officials to deport 18 Tibetan refugees from Kathmandu to Tibet. Nepal's usual policy was to transfer Tibetan refugees to officials of the UN High Commissioner for Refugees. It was reported in late June that a further 19 Tibetans had been arrested in the western Nepalese district of Accham.

Ties with Bangladesh are also significant, particularly regarding the utilization of joint water resources. Large-scale migration from Bangladesh has resulted in a notable demographic transformation in Nepal, with the Muslim population increasing from around 4% of the total in the early 1990s to, unofficially, about 10% by the end of the decade. In January 2001 the Nepalese Minister of Foreign Affairs visited Bangladesh, where agreements on greater economic and transport co-operation were reached. In December 1982 Nepal and Pakistan strengthened their trade links by renewing a 1962 agreement,

and in 1983 they established a joint economic commission and a regular air link.

In late 1991 thousands of Bhutanese of Nepalese origin began to arrive at refugee camps in eastern Nepal, following the outbreak of political and ethnic unrest in Bhutan. By early 1996 nearly 100,000 refugees were living in eight camps in the districts of Jhapa and Morang. In the first half of 1993 talks were held between Bhutanese and Nepalese government officials regarding proposals to resolve the issues at stake. The Nepalese Government steadfastly refused to consider any solution that did not include the resettlement in Bhutan of all ethnic Nepalese refugees living in the camps. This proposal was rejected by the Bhutanese Government, which claimed that the majority of the camp population were not actually Bhutanese. The deadlock was apparently broken, however, when a joint statement was signed by the Ministers of Home Affairs of Bhutan and Nepal in July, which committed each side to establishing a 'high-level joint committee' to work towards a settlement (including the categorization of the refugees). In a notable shift in strategy, in January 1996 the Nepalese Government transferred the responsibility of handling the Bhutanese refugee problem from the Ministry of Home Affairs to the Ministry of Foreign Affairs. In April 1997 more than 10,000 Bhutanese refugees gathered at a mass demonstration in the eastern Nepalese town of Damak to call for UN intervention in the crisis. They also demanded that the Nepal Government either resolve the refugee problem or, failing that, 'internationalize' it. Nepal and Bhutan finally achieved a breakthrough at the 10th round of negotiations in December 2000. Both countries agreed that nationality would be verified on the basis of the head of the refugee family for those over 25 years of age. Refugees under 25 years of age would be verified on an individual basis. By the end of January 2001 a Joint Verification Team (JVT) had concluded the inspection of refugee camps; verification of 98,897 people claiming refugee status (including 13,000 minors born in the camp) began at the end of March, commencing with the Khudanabari camp. The Nepalese press criticized the JVT for being too slow: by early July the status of 4,128 individuals had been verified. In late 2001 the verification of individuals in the Khudanabari camp was completed. However, despite two further rounds of negotiations, the process reached a standstill in early 2002, with Bhutan reluctant to accept the individuals already verified, and both Governments undecided over the most suitable way to continue the verification process. In mid-March the refugees decided to send a petition to the King of Bhutan in order to draw the attention of the international community to their difficulties.

In January 2003 Bhutan hosted the 12th ministerial joint committee (MJC), at which the two Governments finally harmonized their positions on each of the four categories. The 14th MJC in May resolved all the remaining issues in order to finalize the categorization process. Details of the results of the verification process at Khudanabari were published on 18 June: 74 families (293 people) were in Category I (forcefully evicted Bhutanese people); 2,182 families (8,595 people) were in Category II (Bhutanese who had emigrated); 817 families (2,948 people) were in Category III (non-Bhutanese people); and 85 families (347 people) were in Category IV (Bhutanese who had committed criminal acts). Despite the new Nepalese Government from late May criticizing the agreements and several political parties in Nepal calling for the Nepalese Government to repudiate the deal, arrangements were being made to conduct the repatriation to Bhutan of most of the families in Category I by the end of 2003. The 15th MJC, held in Thimphu, Bhutan, in October, was hailed as very successful by the leader of Nepal's delegation. It was agreed at the meeting that the JVT would return to the Nepalese district of Jhapa in November to review the remaining appeals from people in the Khudunabari camp and then begin verification of the Sanischare camp. The committee also decided that Bhutan would be fully responsible for any Category I persons, while Category II people could apply for either Bhutanese or Nepalese citizenship, in accordance with the respective laws. Any appeals by people in Category III were to be resolved by the end of January 2004. However, on 23 December 2003 the Bhutanese members of the JVT, while explaining the remaining procedures to Sector A residents of the Khudanabari camp, were attacked by several thousand other camp members protesting against the terms and conditions of the agreement. The JVT members were withdrawn to Thimphu and it was expected that the repatriation of some of the Category I people would not be completed by mid-February 2004, as had been earlier planned. The attack, described by a Nepalese government spokesman as regrettable, was discussed by the two administrations at the South Asian Association for Regional Co-operation (SAARC, see p. 329) summit meeting in early January, and further talks were to be held by the Ministers of Foreign Affairs in an attempt to avoid a recurrence.

Nepal pursues a non-aligned foreign policy, and had diplomatic relations with 113 countries in early 2000. Nepal (with six other countries) is a founder member of SAARC, formally established in 1985; the Association's permanent secretariat was established in Kathmandu in 1987. Kathmandu hosted a SAARC summit meeting in January 2002, despite rising tension in the region.

Government

Under the provisions of the Constitution promulgated in November 1990, Nepal is a constitutional monarchy. The Constitution provides for a bicameral Parliament, comprising a 205-member House of Representatives (Pratinidhi Sabha) and a 60-member National Assembly (Rashtriya Sabha), as the supreme legislative body. The House of Representatives is elected for a five-year term, and members of the National Assembly hold office for a six-year term. Executive power is vested in the King and the Council of Ministers, which is answerable to the House of Representatives. The King appoints the leader of the party that commands a majority in the House of Representatives as Prime Minister, while other ministers are appointed, from among the members of Parliament, on the recommendation of the Prime Minister.

For the purposes of local administration, Nepal is divided into five development regions, 14 zones, 75 districts, 3,995 village development committees and 36 municipalities.

Defence

In August 2003 Nepal's total armed forces numbered 63,000 men. Military service is voluntary. An Armed Police Force was formed in 2001 to counteract the Maoist insurgency and numbered 7,000 in August 2003. The defence budget for 2002/03 was projected at NRs 7,228m.

Economic Affairs

In 2002, according to estimates by the World Bank, Nepal's gross national income (GNI), measured at average 2000–02 prices, was US $5,621m., equivalent to $230 per head (or $1,350 per head on an international purchasing-power parity basis). During 1990–2002, it was estimated, the population increased at an average annual rate of 2.4%, while gross domestic product (GDP) per head increased, in real terms, by an average of 2.1% per year. Overall GDP increased, in real terms, at an average annual rate of 4.5% in 1990–2002. Real GDP grew by 4.7% in 2001, but decreased by 0.5% in 2002.

Agriculture (including forestry and fishing) contributed an estimated 38.1% of GDP in the fiscal year ending 15 July 2002. The sector engaged 76.1% of the employed labour force in 1999. The principal crops are rice, maize, millet, wheat, sugar cane, potatoes and vegetables and melons. During 1990–2002 agricultural GDP increased by an average of 2.5% per year. The agricultural sector grew by 4.3% in 2001 and 1.7% in 2002.

Industry (comprising mining, manufacturing, construction and utilities) employed only 9.8% of the labour force in 1999, but provided an estimated 21.9% of GDP in 2001/02. About 60% of Nepal's industrial output comes from traditional cottage industries, and the remainder from modern industries. During 1990–2002 industrial GDP increased at an average annual rate of 6.8%. Industrial production grew by 8.7% in 2000, by 2.5% in 2001 and by 1% in 2002.

Mining employed only 0.08% of the labour force in 1999, and contributed an estimated 0.5% of GDP in 2001/02. Mica is mined east of Kathmandu, and there are also small deposits of lignite, copper, talc, limestone, cobalt and iron ore. Geophysical investigations have indicated that the Siwalik range and the Terai belt are potential prospective areas for petroleum.

Manufacturing contributed an estimated 8.4% of GDP in 2001/02, and employed about 5.8% of the labour force in 1999. Manufacturing GDP increased by an average annual rate of 8.0% in 1990–2002. Manufacturing production grew by 3.6% in 2001, but declined by 5.9% in 2002. The principal branches of the sector include textiles—particularly carpets and rugs, food products, wearing apparel and tobacco products. Traditional cottage industries include basket-making and the production of cotton fabrics and edible oils.

Energy is derived principally from traditional sources (particularly fuelwood). Imports of mineral fuel and lubricants (mainly for the transport sector), however, comprised an estimated 14.3% of the cost of total imports in 2001/02. In addition, Nepal's rivers are exploited for hydroelectric power (HEP) production, but in July 2002 it was estimated that only about 1% of the country's huge potential generating capacity (83m. kW) was being utilized. In January 2004 the 144,000-kW Kali Gandaki A HEP plant was officially inaugurated. The project, the country's largest, began generating electricity in 2002. Nepal was hoping to export excess electricity to India. Several other HEP projects were under construction in the early 2000s.

The services sector employed 14.0% of the labour force in 1999. The sector contributed an estimated 40.0% of GDP in 2001/02. The GDP of the services sector increased at an average annual rate of 5.9% in 1990–2002. By 1996 tourism had emerged as Nepal's major source of foreign exchange; in 1999/2000 revenue from tourism amounted to 12.9% of total foreign-exchange earnings. In 2000 the number of foreign visitors declined to 463,646, compared with 491,504 in the previous year, owing to the suspension of Indian Airlines flights in the first five months of the year, regular strikes and security fears. In 2001 the number of tourists declined again, to 361,247, owing to the massacre of most of the royal family in June, intermittent strikes and the escalating Maoist insurgency. The reduction in the number of foreign visitors was also due to regional tension and the attacks on the USA in September. The worsening domestic security situation caused tourist arrivals to decline by 28% in 2002.

In 2001 Nepal recorded a visible trade deficit of US $765.2m., and there was a deficit of $339.3m. on the current account of the balance of payments. In 2002 India was the principal source of imports (supplying 20.4% of the total) and the principal market for exports (47.0%). Other major trading partners were the People's Republic of China, the United Arab Emirates and the USA. The principal exports in 2001/02 were basic manufactures, manufactured goods and articles and garments. The principal imports were basic manufactures, machinery and transport equipment, and mineral fuels and lubricants.

In 2002 there was an estimated overall budget deficit of NRs 16,749m. (equivalent to 3.8% of GDP). Foreign aid plays a vital role in the Nepalese economy. Nepal's total external debt was US $2,700m. at the end of 2001, of which $2,643m. was long-term public debt. In that year the cost of debt-servicing was equivalent to 4.9% of receipts from exports of goods and services. The annual rate of inflation averaged 8.6% in 1990–2001. The national urban consumer-price index rose by 2.5% in 2000 and by 2.7% in 2001. According to official figures, inflation increased by 2.9% in 2002. According to the Asian Development Bank (ADB, see p. 151), in 1999/2000 47% of Nepali workers were underemployed, while urban unemployment, a major problem, particularly among educated youths, stood at 7%.

Nepal is a member of the UN Economic and Social Commission for Asia and the Pacific (ESCAP, see p. 31), the ADB, of the Colombo Plan (see p. 359) and of the South Asian Association for Regional Co-operation (SAARC, see p. 329), all of which seek to encourage regional economic development. Nepal's entry into the World Trade Organization (WTO, see p. 343) was approved in September 2003, and membership was expected to take effect in 2004.

With an inhospitable terrain, comprising isolated valleys and very high mountains, Nepal is among the least developed countries in the world. Successive administrations since 1991 have followed a policy of economic liberalization: many state enterprises have been privatized (although there have been numerous delays in the process), and there have been attempts to reduce the fiscal deficit, to increase revenue mobilization, to restructure and improve the financial sector, and to institute and operate open trade and investment policies. In February 1993, as part of a series of economic reforms introduced in an attempt to develop industry further and to increase exports to countries other than India, the Nepalese rupee was made fully convertible for current-account transactions. Nepal's Ninth Five-Year Plan (1997–2002) was launched in July 1997, with projected expenditure of US $7,170m. The main goal of the Plan was to eliminate poverty and reduce unemployment by focusing on the vital agricultural sector. However, unemployment increased, and the rate of growth achieved during the period reached only 3.6%, compared with the targeted 6%. Despite protests by the business sector, value-added tax (VAT) was fully implemented by the Government in August 1999. The high VAT threshold was lowered in the budget for 2000/01. For the first time in 19 years, Nepal's GDP registered a negative growth rate in 2001/02: the economy contracted by 0.5%, according to official figures, largely owing to negative growth rates in the non-agricultural sector. Tourism and foreign trade fared particularly poorly, owing to a worsening internal security situation, regional tension and the suicide attacks on the USA. Although the extension of the 1996 trade treaty with India was forecast to boost trade with India, the global economic slowdown adversely affected Nepal's export industry. However, the remittances of some 700,000 Nepalese working abroad provided a boost for the economy. A moderate recovery in 2002/03 was facilitated by the cease-fire agreement in January 2003. GDP growth rose to 2.4% in 2002/03, largely owing to a revival of the manufacturing sector, export trade and tourist industry. Preliminary estimates indicated that Nepal's exports and imports increased in that year by 3.3% and 15.2%, respectively. Tax collection also improved, and significant progress was made in the implementation of financial-sector reforms. The interim Government's 2003/04 budget (announced in July 2003) depended heavily on foreign aid to achieve the development expenditure target and projected an ambitious GDP growth rate of 4.5%. The collapse of the cease-fire in late August and the worsening political situation, however, made these targets unlikely to be met (although in February 2004 the ADB predicted that overall GDP growth would recover to about 4%). In the first half of the fiscal year remittances and tourism receipts grew; the trade deficit, however, widened owing to a higher growth of imports compared with exports. The price of major commodities (food and non-food) also increased in this period, resulting in a rise in inflation. In 2002 the interim Government launched the Tenth Five-Year Plan, which aimed for a 4.3%–6.2% growth rate during 2002–07. One of the objectives of the plan was to reduce the level of poverty to 30% from 42%. The 2003/04 development budget gave priority to projects in areas such as education, drinking water and roads. The budget also introduced the theme of public-private partnerships. In November 2003 the IMF approved a three-year US $72m. Poverty Reduction and Growth Facility for Nepal, in support of the country's povery reduction strategies. In order to attract further foreign investment, however, the restoration of law and order was essential: the precarious security situation continued to pose the greatest risk to economic growth and poverty reduction.

Education

Primary education, beginning at six years of age and lasting for five years, is officially compulsory and is provided free of charge in government schools. Secondary education, beginning at the age of 11, lasts for a further seven years, comprising a first cycle of three years (lower secondary), a second of two years (secondary) and a third of two years (higher secondary). In 2000/01 the total enrolment at primary and secondary schools was equivalent to an estimated 87% of the school-age population. Primary enrolment in that year was equivalent to 118% of children in the relevant age-group (boys 128%, girls 108%), while the comparable ratio for secondary enrolment was 51% (boys 58%, girls

43%). There are four state universities: the Tribhuvan University in Kathmandu, the Mahendra Sanskrit Viswavidyalaya in Beljhundi, Dang, the Purbanchal University and the Pokhara University. In addition, there is one private university in Banepa. Altogether, the universities had more than 120,000 students in 1999/2000. Projected expenditure on education by the central Government in the 2002/03 budget was NRs 14,286m. (16.6% of total spending). The Eighth Five-Year Plan (1992–97) included proposals to introduce free compulsory secondary education in phases over the next 10 years. By 2000 compulsory education had been implemented in only seven of Nepal's 75 districts.

Public Holidays

The public holidays observed in Nepal vary locally. The dates given below apply to Kathmandu.

2004: 11 January (National Unity Day), 26 January (Vasant Panchami—Advent of Spring Day), 30 January (Martyrs' Day), January/February (Lhosar, Tibetan New Year), 18 February (Maha Shivaratri—in honour of Lord Shiva), 19 February (Rashtriya Prajatantra Divas—National Democracy Day), 6 March (Phagu Purnima—Holi Festival Day), 30 March (Ram Nawami—Lord Ram's Birthday), 14 April (Navabarsha—New Year's Day), 20 April (Ghode Jatra—Horse Festival), 1 May (Labour Day), 4 May (Lord Gautam Buddha's Birthday), 7 July (King Gyanendra's Birthday), 30 August (Janai Purnima—Sacred Thread Ceremony), 6 September (Janmashtami—Lord Krishna's Birthday, and Children's Day), 17 September (Haratalika Teej—Women's Festival), 27 September (Indra Jatra—Festival of Rain God), September/October (Ghatasthapana), 22 October (Dasain—Durga Puja Festival, and Bhai Tika—Brothers' Day), 9 November (Constitution Day), 12 November (Diwali—Festival of Lights and, over three days, Laxmi Puja), 29 December (King Birendra's Birthday).

2005: 11 January (National Unity Day), 30 January (Martyrs' Day), 2 February (Lhosar, Tibetan New Year), 13 February (Vasant Panchami—Advent of Spring Day), 19 February (Rashtriya Prajatantra Divas—National Democracy Day), 8 March (Maha Shivaratri—in honour of Lord Shiva), 9 March (Ghode Jatra—Horse Festival), 25 March (Phagu Purnima—Holi Festival Day), 14 April (Navabarsha—New Year's Day), 18 April (Ram Nawami—Lord Ram's Birthday), 21 April (Lord Gautam Buddha's Birthday), 1 May (Labour Day), 7 July (King Gyanendra's Birthday), 19 August (Janai Purnima—Sacred Thread Ceremony), 21 August (Children's Day), 27 August (Janmashtami—Lord Krishna's Birthday), 6 September (Haratalika Teej—Women's Festival), September/October (Ghatasthapana), 12 October (Dasain—Durga Puja Festival), October (Bhai Tika—Brothers' Day), 1 November (Diwali—Festival of Lights and, over three days, Laxmi Puja), 8 November (Indra Jatra—Festival of Rain God), 9 November (Constitution Day), 29 December (King Birendra's Birthday).

Weights and Measures

The metric system has been officially adopted but traditional local and Indian systems of weights and measures are widely used.

Statistical Survey

Source (unless otherwise stated): National Planning Commission Secretariat, Singha Durbar, POB 1284, Kathmandu; tel. 4225879; fax 4226500; e-mail npcs@wlink.com.np; internet www.npc.gov.np.

Area and Population

AREA, POPULATION AND DENSITY

Area (sq km)	147,181*
Population (census results)	
22 June 1991	18,491,097
22 June 2001†‡	
Males	11,563,921
Females	11,587,502
Total	23,151,423

Population (official estimates at mid-year)§	
1999	22,367,048
2000	22,904,000
2001	23,593,000
Density (per sq km) at June 2001	157.3

* 56,827 sq miles.

† Population is *de jure*.

‡ Includes estimates for certain areas in 12 districts where the census could not be conducted, owing to violence and disruption.

§ Not adjusted to take account of the 2001 census results.

Capital: Kathmandu, population (for urban agglomeration) 1,081,845 at 2001 census.

PRINCIPAL TOWNS
(population at 2001 census)

Kathmandu	671,846	Mahendranagar	80,839
Biratnagar	166,674	Butawal	75,384
Lalitpur	162,991	Janakpur	74,192
Pokhara	156,312	Bhaktapur	72,543
Birgunj	112,484	Hetaunda	68,482
Dharan	95,332	Dhangadhi	67,447
Bharatpur	89,323		

BIRTHS AND DEATHS
(UN estimates, annual averages)

	1985–90	1990–95	1995–2000
Birth rate (per 1,000)	38.9	37.3	35.3
Death rate (per 1,000)	14.4	12.7	11.1

Source: UN, *World Population Prospects: The 2002 Revision.*

2001 (estimates): Birth rate 33.1 per 1,000; Death rate 9.6 per 1,000.

Expectation of life (WHO estimates, years at birth): 60.1 (males 59.9; females 60.2) in 2002 (Source: WHO, *World Health Report*).

ECONOMICALLY ACTIVE POPULATION
(1999 labour force survey)

Agriculture, hunting, forestry and fishing	7,203,000
Mining and quarrying	8,000
Manufacturing	552,000
Electricity, gas and water	26,000
Construction	344,000
Trade, restaurants and hotels	522,000
Transport, storage and communications	135,000
Financing, insurance, real estate and business service	51,000
Community, social and personal services	614,000
Activities not adequately defined	8,000
Total employed	9,463,000

Source: Central Bureau of Statistics.

Mid-2002 (estimates in '000): Agriculture, etc. 10,897; Total labour force 11,729 (Source: FAO).

Health and Welfare

KEY INDICATORS

Total fertility rate (children per woman, 2002)	4.3
Under-5 mortality rate (per 1,000 live births, 2001)	91
HIV/AIDS (% of persons aged 15–49, 2001)	0.49
Physicians (per 1,000 head, 1995)	0.04
Hospital beds (per 1,000 head, 1997)	0.17
Health expenditure (2001): US $ per head (PPP)	63
Health expenditure (2001): % of GDP	5.2
Health expenditure (2001): public (% of total)	29.7
Access to water (% of persons, 2000)	81
Access to sanitation (% of persons, 2000)	27
Human Development Index (2001): ranking	143
Human Development Index (2001): value	0.499

For sources and definitions, see explanatory note on p. vi.

Agriculture

PRINCIPAL CROPS
('000 metric tons)

	2000	2001	2002
Wheat	1,184	1,158	1,258
Rice (paddy)	4,216	4,165	4,133*
Barley	31	30	31
Maize	1,445	1,484	1,511
Millet	295	283	283
Potatoes	1,183	1,314	1,473
Other roots and tubers†	100	105	104
Sugar cane	2,103	2,212	2,248
Beans, dry	25	27	27†
Lentils	137	143	148
Other pulses	58	56	55†
Mustard seed	123	132	135
Vegetables and melons	1,500	1,669	1,723
Fruit (excl. melons)	549	590	586
Spices†	32	33	35
Jute and jute-like fibres	15	16	17
Tobacco (leaves)	4	4	4

* Unofficial figure.
† FAO estimate(s).

Source: FAO.

LIVESTOCK
('000 head, year ending September)

	2000	2001	2002
Cattle	7,023	6,983	6,979
Buffaloes	3,526	3,624	3,701
Pigs	878	913	934
Sheep	852	850	840
Goats	6,325	6,478	6,607
Chickens	18,620	19,790	21,370

Source: FAO.

LIVESTOCK PRODUCTS
('000 metric tons)

	2000	2001	2002
Beef and veal*	48.0	47.2	46.8
Buffalo meat	121.8	124.8	127.9
Mutton and lamb	2.9	2.9	2.8
Goat meat	36.9	37.8	38.6
Pig meat	14.6	15.2	15.6
Poultry meat	13.0	13.5	14.4
Cows' milk	337.5	342.7	352.1
Buffaloes' milk	759.6	781.4	806.7
Goats' milk*	60.5	63.0	64.0
Ghee*	19.3	19.7	20.3
Poultry eggs	23.4	25.7*	26.1*
Wool: greasy	0.6	0.6	0.6
Wool: scoured*	0.5	0.5	0.5

* FAO estimate(s).

Source: FAO.

Forestry

ROUNDWOOD REMOVALS
('000 cubic metres, excluding bark)

	2000	2001	2002
Sawlogs, veneer logs and logs for sleepers	1,260	1,260	1,260*
Fuel wood*	12,763	12,744	12,728
Total	14,023	14,004	13,988*

* FAO estimate(s).

Source: FAO.

SAWNWOOD PRODUCTION
('000 cubic metres, including railway sleepers)

	1999	2000	2001
Coniferous (softwood)*	20	20	20
Broadleaved (hardwood). . . .	610	610	610
Total	630	630	630

* FAO estimates.

2002: Production as in 2001 (FAO estimates).

Source: FAO.

Fishing

('000 metric tons, live weight)

	1999	2000	2001
Capture	12.8	16.7	16.7
Freshwater fishes	12.8	16.7	16.7
Aquaculture	13.0	15.0	16.6
Common carp	2.6	3.0	3.4
Bighead carp	2.0	2.3	2.5
Grass carp (White amur) . . .	0.7	0.8	0.9
Silver carp	3.9	4.5	5.0
Other cyprinids	3.8	4.4	4.8
Total catch	25.8	31.7	33.3

Source: FAO, *Yearbook of Fishery Statistics.*

Industry

SELECTED PRODUCTS
('000 metric tons unless otherwise indicated, year ending 15 July)

	1997/98	1998/99	1999/2000
Cement	276.5	190.6	248.0
Steel rods	125.3	106.6	144.9
Jute goods	51.4	49.3	49.7
Raw sugar	67.2	75.5	77.2
Tea	2.3	2.3	3.6
Vegetable ghee	28.9	87.0	91.3
Beer and liquor (million litres) . .	17.0	22.1	28.9
Soft drinks (million litres) . . .	24.0	29.1	n.a.
Paper	16.2	19.5	18.6
Cigarettes (million)	8,127	7,315	7,125
Cotton textiles (million sq metres)	3.2	3.3	26.3*
Synthetic textiles (million sq metres)	18.7	17.8	15.6*
Soap	39.1	47.7	73.7

* Million metres.

2000/01 ('000 metric tons): Cement 222.0; Steel rods 143.0; Jute goods 34.0; Raw sugar 78.0; Tea 8.0; Soap 5.5.

2001/02 ('000 metric tons): Cement 233.0; Steel rods 140.0; Jute goods 31.0; Raw sugar 82.0; Tea 8.7; Soap 55.0.

Sources: National Planning Commission Secretariat, Kathmandu, Asian Development Bank, *Key Indicators of Developing Asian and Pacific Countries,* and *Far Eastern Economic Review, Asia 2001 Yearbook.*

Finance

CURRENCY AND EXCHANGE RATES
Monetary Units
100 paisa (pice) = 1 Nepalese rupee (NR).

Sterling, Dollar and Euro Equivalents (31 December 2003)
£1 sterling = NRs 132.14;
US $1 = NRs 74.04;
€1 = NRs 93.51;
1,000 Nepalese rupees = £7.568 = $13.506 = €10.694.

Average Exchange Rate (rupees per US $)
2001   74.949
2002   77.877
2003   76.141

BUDGET
(NRs million, year ending 15 July)*

Revenue†	2000/01‡	2001/02§	2002/03‖
Taxation	38,865	40,397	45,928
Taxes on income, profits and capital gains	9,114	9,248	9,863
Taxes on property	616	929	1,101
Domestic taxes on goods and services	16,583	16,580	19,205
Taxes on international trade and transactions	12,552	13,641	15,760
Other revenue	7,971	8,199	9,675
Charges, fees, fines, etc. . .	1,931	1,879	2,556
Sales of goods and services . .	1,184	1,052	1,239
Dividends	2,336	2,676	2,885
Interest receipts	1,440	860	1,066
Total	46,837	48,596	55,603

Expenditure	2000/01‡	2001/02§	2002/03‖
Regular expenditure	37,079	44,079	49,104
General administration . . .	8,027	10,961	11,225
Defence	3,813	5,785	7,228
Social services	10,692	13,454	14,130
Education	8,226	10,413	10,968
Health	1,547	2,115	2,151
Economic services	2,533	2,965	3,260
Agriculture-related . . .	544	575	774
Infrastructure	924	1,055	1,132
Interest payments	4,698	5,720	8,006
Other purposes	7,315	5,194	5,255
Development expenditure . . .	35,009	30,210	37,132
Social services	12,873	11,108	16,860
Education	2,784	2,402	3,318
Health	1,972	1,702	2,748
Provision of drinking water . .	2,407	2,077	3,773
Economic services	22,136	19,102	20,273
Agriculture-related	6,624	5,716	5,413
Infrastructure	12,779	11,028	12,800
Total	72,087	74,289	86,236

* Figures refer to the regular and development budgets of the central Government.

† Excluding grants received (NRs million, estimates): 6,753 in 2000/01; 6,686 in 2001/02; 8,372 in 2002/03.

‡ Revised figures.

§ Estimates.

‖ Forecasts.

Source: IMF, *Nepal: Selected Issues and Statistical Appendix* (September 2002).

2003/04 (NRs million, forecast): *Revenue:* Total 62,227 (Grants 15,512). *Expenditure:* Regular 60,555; Development 41,845; Total 102,400.

Source: Federation of Nepalese Chambers of Commerce and Industry, Kathmandu.

INTERNATIONAL RESERVES
(US $ million at mid-December)

	2001	2002	2003
Gold*	6.5	6.5	6.5
IMF special drawing rights	0.1	—	0.8
Reserve position in IMF	7.2	7.8	8.6
Foreign exchange	1,030.4	1,009.8	1,191.6
Total	1,044.2	1,024.1	1,207.5

* Valued at US $42.5 per troy ounce.

Source: IMF, *International Financial Statistics*.

MONEY SUPPLY
(NRs million at mid-December)*

	2000	2001	2002
Currency outside banks	44,526	51,699	56,022
Private sector deposits with monetary authorities	3,160	3,570	2,350
Demand deposits at commercial banks	15,343	n.a.	n.a.
Total money	63,028	n.a.	n.a.

* Excluding Indian currency in circulation.

Source: IMF, *International Financial Statistics*.

COST OF LIVING
(National Consumer Price Index; base: 1990 = 100)

	1997	1998	1999
Food (incl. beverages)	198.9	229.5	247.1
Fuel and light	196.5	204.6	215.4
Clothing (excl. footwear)	187.7	200.3	211.5
Rent	227.2	237.8	242.0
All items (incl. others)	197.7	220.5	235.8

2000: Food 240.5; All items 241.4.

2001: Food 243.7; All items 248.0.

Source: ILO, *Yearbook of Labour Statistics*.

NATIONAL ACCOUNTS
(NRs million at current prices, year ending 15 July)

National Income and Product

	1995/96	1996/97	1997/98
Domestic factor incomes*	228,991	256,891	270,641
Consumption of fixed capital	4,465	5,670	7,182
Gross domestic product (GDP) at factor cost	233,456	262,561	277,823
Indirect taxes, *less* subsidies	15,457	17,952	18,724
GDP in purchasers' values	248,913	280,513	296,547
Factor income from abroad *Less* Factor income paid abroad	3,566	4,661	6,025
Gross national product (GNP)	252,479	285,174	302,572
Less Consumption of fixed capital	4,465	5,670	7,182
National income in market prices	248,014	279,504	295,390
Other current transfers from abroad (net)†	900	1,009	1,157
National disposable income	248,914	280,513	296,547

* Compensation of employees and the operating surplus of enterprises.
† Excluding official grants.

Source: UN, *National Accounts Statistics*.

Expenditure on the Gross Domestic Product

	1999/2000	2000/01	2001/02*
Government final consumption expenditure	34,579	40,973	45,387
Private final consumption expenditure	287,947	309,107	326,108
Increase in stocks	18,376	21,480	16,965
Gross fixed capital formation	73,314	78,017	84,165
Total domestic expenditure	414,216	449,577	472,625
Exports of goods and services	88,360	91,821	77,796
Less Imports of goods and services	123,055	131,403	123,143
GDP in purchasers' values	379,521	410,194†	428,033†
GDP at constant 1994/95 prices	277,751	291,139	293,595

* Provisional figures.
† Including adjustments.

Source: Central Bureau of Statistics, Kathmandu.

Gross Domestic Product by Economic Activity

	1999/2000	2000/01	2001/02*
Agriculture, forestry and fishing	144,644	149,040	156,384
Mining and quarrying	1,815	1,981	2,091
Manufacturing	33,550	35,566	34,616
Electricity, gas and water	5,942	6,989	9,339
Construction	37,373	39,571	43,984
Trade, restaurants and hotels	42,895	45,381	42,817
Transport, storage and communications	29,336	33,050	34,800
Finance and real estate	36,919	41,835	43,636
Community and social services	33,810	40,060	42,826
Sub-total	366,284	393,473	410,493
Less Imputed bank service charges	10,708	11,912	12,269
Indirect taxes, *less* subsidies	23,945	28,633	29,809
GDP in purchasers' values	379,521	410,194	428,033

* Provisional figures.

Source: Central Bureau of Statistics, Kathmandu.

BALANCE OF PAYMENTS
(US $ million)

	1999	2000	2001
Exports of goods f.o.b.	612.3	776.1	720.5
Imports of goods f.o.b.	−1,494.2	−1,590.1	−1,485.7
Trade balance	−881.9	−814.0	−765.2
Exports of services	655.1	505.9	413.3
Imports of services	−212.5	−199.9	−214.7
Balance on goods and services	−439.2	−508.0	−566.6
Other income received	55.8	72.2	70.3
Other income paid	−28.4	−35.2	−58.8
Balance on goods, services and income	−411.9	−471.0	−555.2
Current transfers received	182.3	189.0	240.2
Current transfers paid	−26.9	−16.7	−24.3
Current balance	−256.5	−298.7	−339.3
Other investment assets	48.2	128.6	11.2
Investment liabilities	−72.8	−52.6	−228.0
Net errors and omissions	58.3	145.7	256.5
Overall balance	−222.7	−77.0	−299.6

Source: IMF, *International Financial Statistics*.

OFFICIAL DEVELOPMENT ASSISTANCE
(US $ million)

	1998	1999	2000
Bilateral donors	218.8	212.3	234.7
Multilateral donors	189.4	138.8	155.1
Total	408.2	351.1	389.8
Grants	255.1	255.0	251.6
Loans	153.1	96.1	138.2
Per caput assistance (US $)	18.7	15.7	17.0

Source: UN, *Statistical Yearbook for Asia and the Pacific.*

External Trade

PRINCIPAL COMMODITIES
(NRs million, year ending 15 July)

Imports c.i.f.	1999/2000*	2000/01	2001/02
Food and live animals	10,839	5,994	7,054
Crude materials (inedible) except fuels	7,012	7,560	6,891
Mineral fuels and lubricants	9,098	11,269	15,231
Animal and vegetable oils and fats	4,446	5,589	7,888
Chemicals and pharmaceuticals	14,474	12,942	12,505
Basic manufactures	34,420	41,188	32,619
Machinery and transport equipment	20,548	23,028	18,835
Miscellaneous manufactured articles	6,683	7,210	4,799
Total (incl. others)	108,505	115,687	106,731

Exports f.o.b.	1999/2000*	2000/01	2001/02
Food and live animals	4,240	4,777	5,411
Animal and vegetable oils and fats	3,230	4,104	7,478
Chemicals and pharmaceuticals	3,933	4,042	3,229
Basic manufactures	15,839	18,909	17,337
Miscellaneous manufactured articles	21,509	22,651	12,616
Total (incl. others)	49,823	55,654	47,540

* Revised figures.

Exports of carpets (NRs million, year ending 15 July): 9,842 in 1999/2000; 8,592 in 2000/01; 6,210 in 2001/02.

Exports of garments (NRs million, year ending 15 July): 13,942 in 1999/2000; 13,125 in 2000/01; 7,825 in 2001/02.

Source: Asian Development Bank, *Key Indicators of Developing Asian and Pacific Countries.*

PRINCIPAL TRADING PARTNERS
(US $ million)

Imports	2000	2001	2002
China, People's Republic	216.8	163.4	146.1
Hong Kong	107.5	57.8	58.1
India	157.7	174.2	189.0
Japan	34.1	23.8	17.2
Kuwait	31.9	34.4	36.6
Saudi Arabia	37.8	40.8	43.3
Singapore	108.4	81.6	75.8
Thailand	31.9	33.0	24.1
United Arab Emirates	85.9	92.6	98.5
Total (incl. others)	1,058.2	915.4	925.0

Exports	2000	2001	2002
Bangladesh	3.6	3.8	3.6
France	14.2	7.8	6.5
Germany	87.3	65.4	43.3
India	216.8	238.5	258.8
Italy	8.4	8.3	7.8
Japan	25.7	10.3	5.9
Switzerland	11.6	5.1	5.2
United Kingdom	16.2	12.9	12.1
USA	220.2	198.2	150.6
Total (incl. others)	676.2	613.0	550.8

Source: Asian Development Bank, *Key Indicators of Developing Asian and Pacific Countries.*

Transport

ROAD TRAFFIC
(vehicles registered at 30 June)

	2000
Cars, jeeps and vans	53,073
Buses and minibuses	12,054
Trucks and tankers	20,011
Motorcycles	147,157
Tractors	20,469

CIVIL AVIATION
Royal Nepal Airlines Corporation
(traffic on scheduled services)

	1997	1998	1999
Kilometres flown (million)	11	11	9
Passengers carried ('000)	755	754	583
Passenger-km (million)	908	908	1,023
Total ton-km (million)	99	99	108

Source: UN, *Statistical Yearbook.*

Tourism

FOREIGN TOURIST ARRIVALS

Country of residence	1999	2000	2001
Australia	11,997	12,138	10,711
Bangladesh	10,003	9,365	8,108
France	23,942	24,028	20,788
Germany	25,990	25,907	21,809
India	140,672	96,995	63,722
Italy	12,656	11,384	8,503
Japan	38,566	40,841	28,554
Netherlands	16,872	15,878	13,049
Sri Lanka	12,413	16,628	9,874
United Kingdom	34,281	35,080	31,897
USA	38,681	39,377	31,440
Total (incl. others)	491,504	463,646	361,247

Tourism receipts (US $ million): 168 in 1999; 167 in 2000; 137 in 2001.

Source: World Tourism Organization, *Yearbook of Tourism Statistics.*

Visitor arrivals (by air only): 215,922 in 2002 (Source: Nepal Tourism Board, Kathmandu).

Communications Media

	1999	2000	2001
Television receivers ('000 in use) .	150	170	n.a.
Telephones ('000 main lines in use)	253.0	266.9	298.1
Facsimile machines (number in use)*	8,000	n.a.	n.a.
Mobile cellular telephones ('000 subscribers).	5.5	10.2	17.3
Personal computers ('000 in use)	60	70	80
Internet users ('000)	35.0	50.0	60.0
Daily newspapers (titles)* . . .	n.a.	189	n.a.
Non-daily newspapers (titles)* . .	n.a.	2,554	n.a.

1997: Radio receivers ('000 in use) 840.

2002: Telephones ('000 main lines in use) 327.7; Mobile cellular telephones ('000 subscribers) 21.9.

* Year ending 15 July.

Sources: UNESCO, *Statistical Yearbook*; International Telecommunication Union.

April 2001: Daily newspapers 193.

Education

(2001)

	Institutions	Teachers	Students
Primary	24,943	96,659	3,853,618
Lower Secondary.	7,340	26,678	1,058,448
Secondary.	4,113	18,846	449,296

Higher Secondary: 789 institutions in mid-2003.

Source: Ministry of Education and Sports, Kathmandu.

Adult literacy rate (UNESCO estimates): 42.9% (males 60.5%; females 25.2%) in 2001 (Source: UN Development Programme, *Human Development Report*).

Directory

The Constitution

The main provisions of the Constitution, which was promulgated by the King on 9 November 1990, are summarized below:

The preamble to the Constitution envisages the guarantee of the fundamental rights of every citizen and the protection of his liberty, the consolidation of parliamentary government, the constitutional monarchy and the multi-party system, and the provision of an independent judicial system. Sovereignty resides in the Nepalese people. The Constitution is the fundamental law of the land.

Nepal is a multi-ethnic, multi-lingual, democratic, independent, indivisible, sovereign, Hindu and constitutional monarchical kingdom. Nepali is recognized as the national and official language.

FUNDAMENTAL RIGHTS

Part Three of the Constitution provides for the fundamental rights of the citizen: all citizens are equal before the law; no discrimination is to be practised on the basis of religion, race, sex, caste, tribe or ideology; no person can be deprived of his liberty except in accordance with the law; capital punishment remains abolished; freedom of expression, freedom to assemble peaceably and without arms, freedom to form trade unions and associations, and freedom of movement are also guaranteed. Similarly, pre-censorship of publications is prohibited and, thus, the right to press and publications is ensured. In the sphere of criminal justice, the following rights are specified in the Constitution: no person is to be punished unless made punishable by law; no person may be tried more than once for the same offence; no one is compelled to testify against himself; no one is to be given punishment greater than that which the law at the time of the offence has prescribed; cruelty to detainees is prohibited; no person is to be detained without having first been informed about the grounds for such an action; and the detainee must appear before the judicial authorities within 24 hours of his arrest. In addition, provision has also been made to compensate any person who is wrongfully detained. A person's right to property is ensured, and the right to protect and promote one's own language, script and culture, as well as the right to education up to primary level in the child's mother tongue, have been safeguarded. Similarly, the right to practise religion and to manage and protect religious places and trusts has been granted to the country's various religious groups. The right to secrecy and inviolability of the person, residence, property, documents, letters and other information is also guaranteed.

GOVERNMENT AND LEGISLATURE

His Majesty the King is the symbol of Nepalese nationality and of the unity of the people of Nepal. The expenditures and the privileges relating to His Majesty and the royal family are determined by law. His Majesty's income and property are exempt from tax.

The executive powers of the country are vested in His Majesty and the Council of Ministers. The direction, supervision and conduct of the general administration of the Kingdom of Nepal are the responsibility of the Council of Ministers. All official duties undertaken by His Majesty, except those which are within his exclusive domain or which are performed on the recommendation of some other institutions or officials, are discharged only on the advice of, and with the consent of, the Council of Ministers. His Majesty appoints the leader of the party that commands a majority in the House of Representatives as Prime Minister, while other Ministers are appointed, from among the members of Parliament, on the recommendation of the Prime Minister. The Council of Ministers is answerable to the House of Representatives. In the event that no single party holds an outright majority in the House, the member who commands a working majority on the basis of the support of two or more parties shall be asked to form the Government. Should this also not be the case, His Majesty may ask a member of the party with the largest number of deputies to form the Government. In the event of these exceptional circumstances, the leader forming the Government must obtain a vote of confidence in the House within 30 days. If such confidence is lacking, His Majesty is to dissolve the House and to order a fresh election to be held within six months. The Parliament is bicameral, comprising the House of Representatives and the National Assembly. His Majesty, the House of Representatives and the National Assembly together form the Parliament of the country. The House of Representatives has 205 members, and all persons who have attained the age of 18 years are eligible to vote for candidates, on the basis of adult franchise. The National Assembly has 60 members, consisting of 10 nominees of His Majesty, 35 members, including three female members, elected by the House of Representatives, and 15 members elected by the electoral college, which includes the heads of the local committees of various development regions. The tenure of office of the members of the House of Representatives is five years, and that of the members of the National Assembly six years.

THE JUDICIARY

The judicial system has three tiers: the Supreme Court, the Appellate Courts and the District Courts. The Supreme Court is the principal Court and is also a Court of Record. The Supreme Court consists of a Chief Justice and 14 other Judges. The appointment of the Chief Justice is made on the recommendation of the Constitutional Council, while other Judges of the Supreme Court, the Appellate Courts and the District Courts are nominated on the recommendation of the Judicial Council. All Judges are appointed by His Majesty on such recommendations.

OTHER INSTITUTIONS

The Constitution also makes provisions for the establishment of a Council of State (Raj Parishad) and its standing committee, a Public Service Commission, Auditor General, Election Commission, Attorney-General, Abuse of Authority Investigation Commission, etc.

POLITICAL PARTIES

Political parties are required to register with the Election Commission, and, to be officially recognized, at least 5% of the candidates presented by a party must be female and the party should obtain at least 3% of the total votes cast at the election to the House of Representatives. It has been specifically provided that no law that bans, or imposes restrictions on, political parties may be enacted.

EMERGENCY PROVISIONS

If and when there is a grave emergency in the country, caused by threat to the sovereignty, indivisibility or security of the country (owing to war, foreign aggression, armed revolt or extreme economic depression), His Majesty may declare a state of emergency in the country. Such a declaration must obtain the approval of the House of Representatives within three months. During the period of emergency, fundamental rights, with the exception of the right of recourse to *habeas corpus*, may be suspended.

AMENDMENTS

The Constitution may be amended by a two-thirds majority in each House of Parliament. No changes, however, would be allowed to alter the spirit of the preamble.

DEFENCE

His Majesty is the Supreme Commander-in-Chief of the Royal Nepal Army. The Royal Nepal Army is administered and deployed by His Majesty on the recommendation of the National Defence Council. The Commander-in-Chief is appointed on the recommendation of the Prime Minister. The National Defence Council consists of the Prime Minister, as Chairman, the Minister of Defence and the Commander-in-Chief.

Official matters that involve, *inter alia*, the subjects of defence and strategic alliance, the boundaries of the Kingdom of Nepal, agreements on peace and friendship, and treaties concerning the utilization and distribution of natural resources, have to be approved by a two-thirds majority of the members of both Houses in a joint session of Parliament.

Note: The King invoked emergency powers in 2002, suspending scheduled parliamentary elections and taking on executive authority.

The Government

HEAD OF STATE

King: HM King GYANENDRA BIR BIKRAM SHAH DEV (succeeded to the throne 4 June 2001).

INTERIM COUNCIL OF MINISTERS
(May 2004)

Following the resignation of interim Prime Minister Surya Bahadur Thapa on 7 May 2004, King Gyanendra Bir Bikram Shah Dev entered negotiations with political leaders with a view to forming a new government. In the mean time, Thapa and the interim Council of Ministers were to remain in office in an acting capacity.

Prime Minister and Minister of Royal Palace Affairs, of Defence, of Industry, Commerce and Supplies, of Law, Justice and Parliamentary Affairs, of Agriculture and Co-operatives, of Population and the Environment, of Water Resources, of Land Reforms and Management, of Women, Children and Social Welfare, of Forest and Soil Conservation, of Science and Technology, of Labour and Transport Management and of General Administration: SURYA BAHADUR THAPA.

Minister of Foreign Affairs and of Health: Dr BHEK BAHADUR THAPA.

Minister of Home Affairs, of Local Development and of Information and Communications: KAMAL THAPA.

Minister of Finance: Dr PRAKASH CHANDRA LOHANI.

Minister of Education and Sports: HARI BAHADUR BASNET.

Minister of Physical Planning and Works: BUDDHI MAN TAMANG.

Minister of State for Women, Children and Social Welfare: RENU KUMARI YADAV.

MINISTRIES

Prime Minister's Office: Singha Durbar, Kathmandu; e-mail info@pmo.gov.np; internet www.pmo.gov.np.

Ministry of Agriculture and Co-operatives: Singha Durbar, Kathmandu; tel. 4225108; fax 4225825; e-mail moa@fert.mos.com .np; internet www.moac.gov.np.

Ministry of Culture, Tourism and Civil Aviation: Singha Durbar, Kathmandu; tel. 4225556; fax 4227758; e-mail motca@ntc .net.np; internet www.tourism.gov.np.

Ministry of Defence: Singha Durbar, Kathmandu; tel. 4228089; fax 4228204; e-mail info@rna.mil.np; internet www.rna.mil.np.

Ministry of Education and Sports: Keshar Mahal, Kantipath, Kathmandu; tel. 4411599; fax 4412460; internet www.moe.gov.np.

Ministry of Finance: Foreign Aid Co-ordination Division, POB 12845, Kathmandu; tel. 4259837; internet www.facd.gov.np.

Ministry of Foreign Affairs: Shital Niwas, Maharajganj, Kathmandu; tel. 4416011; fax 4416016; e-mail mofa@mos.com.np; internet www.mofa.gov.np.

Ministry of Forest and Soil Conservation: Singha Durbar, Kathmandu; tel. 4224892; fax 4223868; internet www.biodiv-nepal .gov.np.

Ministry of General Administration: Harihar Bhavan, Lalitpur; tel. 5525183; fax 5523358; e-mail moga@wlink.com.np; internet www.moga.gov.com.np.

Ministry of Health: Ramshah Path, Kathmandu; tel. 4262587; fax 4262543; e-mail info@moh.gov.np; internet www.moh.gov.np.

Ministry of Home Affairs: Singha Durbar, Kathmandu; tel. 4226996; fax 4227186; e-mail homehmg@wlink.com.np; internet www.moha.gov.np.

Ministry of Industry, Commerce and Supplies: Singha Durbar, Kathmandu; tel. 4251174; fax 4220319; internet www.moics.gov.np.

Ministry of Information and Communications: Singha Durbar, Kathmandu; tel. 4220150; fax 4221729; e-mail moichmg@ntc.net.np; internet www.moic.gov.np.

Ministry of Labour and Transport Management: Tridevi Marg, Kathmandu; tel. 419252; fax 419251; internet www.moltm.gov.np.

Ministry of Land Reform and Management: Singha Durbar, Kathmandu; tel. 4221660; fax 4220108.

Ministry of Law, Justice and Parliamentary Affairs: Singha Durbar, Kathmandu; tel. 4222847; fax 4243025; e-mail molaw@ wlink.com.np; internet www.moljpa.gov.np.

Ministry of Local Development: Sri Mahal, Pulchowk, Lalitpur; tel. 5521727; fax 5522045; e-mail info@mld.gov.np; internet www .mld.gov.np.

Ministry of Physical Planning and Works: Singha Durbar, Kathmandu; tel. 4228285; fax 412199.

Ministry of Population and the Environment: Singha Durbar, Kathmandu; tel. 4245367; fax 4242138; e-mail info@mope.gov.np; internet www.mope.gov.np.

Ministry of Science and Technology: Singha Durbar, Kathmandu; tel. 4244608; fax 4225474; e-mail most@most.gov.np; internet www.most.gov.np.

Ministry of Water Resources: Singha Durbar, Kathmandu; tel. 4227347.

Ministry of Women, Children and Social Welfare: Singha Durbar, Kathmandu; tel. 4240408; fax 4241516; e-mail mwcsw@ntc .net.np.

COUNCIL OF STATE

The Council of State (Raj Parishad) has a standing committee headed by a royal appointee. The 15-member committee is composed of eight royal appointees and seven other members, including the Prime Minister, the Ministers of Defence and Foreign Affairs, the Chief Justice of the Supreme Court and the Chief of Army Staff.

Chairman of Standing Committee: PARSHU NARAYAN CHAUDHURY.

Legislature

PARLIAMENT

Rashtriya Sabha
(National Assembly)

The Rashtriya Sabha has 60 members, consisting of 10 nominees of the King, 35 members (including three women) elected by the Pratinidhi Sabha (House of Representatives), and 15 members elected by the electoral college, which includes the heads of the local committees of various development regions. The tenure of office of the members of the Rashtriya Sabha is six years.

Chairman: RAMPRIT PASHWAN.

Pratinidhi Sabha
(House of Representatives)

The 205-member Pratinidhi Sabha is elected, on the basis of adult franchise, for five years.

Speaker: TARANATH RANABHAT.

Deputy Speaker: CHITRA LEKHA YADAV.
General Election, 3 and 17 May 1999

Party	Seats
Nepali Congress Party (NCP)	111
Communist Party of Nepal (Unified Marxist-Leninist—UML)	71
National Democratic Party (NDP)	11
Rashtriya Jana Morcha	5
Nepali Sadbhavana Party	5
Nepal Workers' and Peasants' Party	1
Samyukta Janmorcha Nepal	1
Total	**205**

Notes: Polling was deferred until 8 and 23 June 1999 in four constituencies, owing to the deaths of candidates. The Pratinidhi Sabha was dissolved on 22 May 2002. A general election, originally scheduled for 13 November, was postponed indefinitely on 4 October.

Political Organizations

According to the 1990 Constitution, political parties are required to register with the Election Commission, and, in order to be officially recognized, 5% of the candidates presented by a party must be female and the party should obtain at least 3% of the total votes cast in the election to the House of Representatives. The Constitution also specifies that no law may be adopted that bans, or imposes restrictions on, political parties.

Communist Party of Nepal (Maoist): f. 1990 as Communist Party of Nepal (Unity Centre) in 1990, renamed as above in 1995; underground political movement; orchestrates 'people's war' in hills of west Nepal (since 1996); advocates abolition of constitutional monarchy and establishment of people's republic; Leaders PUSHPA KAMAL DAHAL ('PRACHANDA'), Dr BABURAM BHATTARAI.

Communist Party of Nepal (Mashal): Kathmandu; Leader CHITRA BAHADUR.

Communist Party of Nepal (Unified Marxist-Leninist) (UML): Madan Nagar, Balkhu, POB 5471, Kathmandu; tel. 4278081; fax 4278084; e-mail uml@ntc.net.np; internet www.cpnuml.org; f. 1991 when two major factions of the Communist Party of Nepal (CPN; f. 1949; banned 1960; legalized 1990)—the Marxist and Marxist-Leninist factions—merged; the Communist Party of Nepal (Marxist-Leninist—ML) seceded in 1998 and rejoined the UML in 2002; the Communist Party of Nepal (Verma) merged with the UML in 2001; Gen. Sec. MADHAV KUMAR NEPAL.

Communist Party of Nepal (United): Dillibazar, POB 2737, Kathmandu; tel. 4430869; fax 4411642; Leader BISHNU B. MANANDHAR.

Green Nepal Party: Kalikasthan, POB 890, Kathmandu; tel. and fax 4438402; e-mail greennepal@htp.com.np; f. 1997; Pres. PUSP PRASAD LUINTEL.

Janawadi Morcha (Democratic Front): Indrachowk, Itumbahal, Kathmandu; tel. 4211033; Pres. RAM RAJYA PRASAD SINGH.

Nepal Praja Parishad: Battisputali, Kathmandu; tel. 4471616; f. 1936; banned 1961; legalized 1990; Pres. RAM HARI SHRESTHA; Gen. Secs Dr MEENA ACHARYA, MAHESWOR SHARMA.

Nepal Samata Party: Bishalnagar, Kathmandu; f. 2002; aims to promote and safeguard the democratic movement; Pres. Lt-Gen. NARAYAN SINGH PUN.

Nepal Workers' and Peasants' Party: Golmadhi Tole, 7-Bhaktapur, Kathmandu; tel. 4610974; fax 4613207; Chair. NARAYAN MAN BIJUKCHHE (ROHIT).

Nepali Congress Party (NCP): Bhansar Tole, Teku, Kathmandu; tel. 4227748; fax 4227747; e-mail ncparty@ntc.net.np; internet www.nepalicongress.org.np; f. 1947; banned 1960; legalized 1990; Pres. GIRIJA PRASAD KOIRALA; Gen. Sec. SUSHIL KOIRALA; 135,000 active members, 500,000 ordinary members.

Nepali Congress Party—Democratic (NCP—D): Kathmandu; f. 2002 as a breakaway faction of the NCP; Leader SHER BAHADUR DEUBA.

Nepali Janata Dal: Tripureshwor, Kathmandu; tel. 4212389; f. 1990; advocates the consolidation of the multi-party democratic system and supports the campaign against corruption; Leader KESHAR JUNG RAYAMAJHI.

Nepali National Congress: Lazimpat, Kathmandu; tel. 4411090; Pres. DILLI RAMAN REGMI.

Nepali Sadbhavana Party (NSP) (Nepal Goodwill Party): Shantinagar, New Baneshwor, Kathmandu; tel. 4488068; fax 4470797; f. 1990; promotes the rights of the Madhesiya community, who are of Indian origin and reside in the Terai; demands that the Government recognize Hindi as an official language, that constituencies in the Terai be allocated on the basis of population, and that the Government grant citizenship to those who settled in Nepal before April 1990; in 2003 the party split into two factions, one led by Babri Prasad Mandal, known as the Mandal Group, and the other led by Anandi Devi Singh, known as the Anandi Devi group.

People's Front Nepal: Kathmandu; f. 2002 following merger of National People's Front and United People's Front; Chair. AMIK SERCHAN; Vice-Chair. LILAMANI POKHAREL.

Rashtriya Janata Parishad (National People's Council): Dillibazar, Kathmandu; tel. 4415150; f. 1992; royalist; aims to defend democracy, nationalism and sovereignty; Pres. MAITRIKA PRASAD KOIRALA; Vice-Pres. KIRTI NIDHI BISTA.

Rashtriya Prajatantra Party (RPP) (National Democratic Party—NDP): Kamal Pokhari, Kathmandu; tel. 4437058; fax 4435173; internet rppnepal.org; right-wing; Chair. PASHUPATI SHUMSHERE J. B. RANA; Asst Gen. Sec. KHEM RAJ PANDIT.

Diplomatic Representation

EMBASSIES IN NEPAL

Australia: Suraj Niwas, Bansbari, POB 879, Kathmandu; tel. 4371678; fax 4371533; Ambassador K. GARDNER.

Bangladesh: Maharajgunj Ring Rd, POB 789, Kathmandu; tel. 4372843; fax 4373265; e-mail bdootktm@wlink.com.np; Chargé d'affaires a.i. GOLAM SARWAR.

China, People's Republic: Baluwatar, POB 4234, Kathmandu; tel. 4415383; fax 4411388; Ambassador SUN HEPING.

Denmark: Baluwatar, Lalita Niwas Rd, POB 6332, Kathmandu; tel. 4413010; fax 4411409; e-mail danemb@wlink.com.np; Chargé d'affaires GERT MEINECKE.

Egypt: Pulchowk, Lalitpur, POB 792, Kathmandu; tel. 4524844; fax 4522975; Ambassador ABD EL-HAMID MOHAMED TABAK.

Finland: Lazimpat, POB 2126, Kathmandu; tel. 4416636; fax 4416703; e-mail finembka@mos.com.np; internet www.south-asia.com/embassy-Finland; Chargé d'affaires a.i. ASKO LUUKKAINEN.

France: Lazimpat, POB 452, Kathmandu; tel. 4412332; fax 4418288; e-mail ambafr@mos.com.np; Ambassador CLAUDE ABROSINI.

Germany: Gyaneshwar, POB 226, Kathmandu; tel. 4412786; fax 4416899; e-mail gerembnp@mos.com.np; Ambassador RÜDIGER LEMP.

India: Lainchaur, POB 292, Kathmandu; tel. 4411940; fax 4413132; e-mail eipi@mos.com.np; internet www.south-asia.com/embassy-India; Ambassador KRISHNA V. RAJAN.

Israel: Bishramalaya House, Lazimpat, POB 371, Kathmandu; tel. 4411811; fax 4413920; e-mail israelem@mos.com.np; Ambassador AVRAHIM NIR.

Japan: Panipokhari, POB 264, Kathmandu; tel. 4426680; fax 4414101; Ambassador MITSUAKI KOJIMA.

Korea, Democratic People's Republic: Jhamsikhel, Lalitpur, Kathmandu; tel. 4521084; Ambassador JON SONG MYONG.

Korea, Republic: Himshail, Red Cross Marg, Tahachal, POB 1058, Kathmandu; tel. 4270172; fax 4272041; e-mail koreasamb@mos.com.np; Ambassador HWANG BOO-HONG.

Myanmar: Chakupath, Patan Gate, Lalitpur, POB 2437, Kathmandu; tel. 5524788; fax 5523402; e-mail emb@myanmar.wlink.com.np; Ambassador U MYINT SWE.

Norway: Surya Court, Pulchowk, Lalitpur, POB 20765, Kathmandu; tel. 5545307; fax 5545226; e-mail emb.kathmandu@mfa.no.

Pakistan: Panipokhari, POB 202, Kathmandu; tel. 4411421; Ambassador MUHAMMAD NASSER MIAN.

Russia: Baluwatar, POB 123, Kathmandu; tel. 4412155; fax 4416571; Ambassador VLADIMIR V. IVANOV.

Sri Lanka: Chundevi Rd, Maharajgunj, POB 8802, Kathmandu; tel. 4413623; fax 4418128; e-mail embassy@srilanka.info.com.np; Ambassador GRACE A. ASIWARHAM.

Thailand: Jyoti Kendra, Thapathali, POB 3333, Kathmandu; tel. 4213912; fax 4420408; Ambassador POWTHEP VANACHINDA.

United Kingdom: Lainchaur, POB 106, Kathmandu; tel. 4410583; fax 4411789; e-mail britemb@wlink.com.np; internet www.britain.gov.np; Ambassador KEITH BLOOMFIELD.

USA: Panipokhari, POB 295, Kathmandu; tel. 4411179; fax 4419963; Ambassador MICHAEL E. MALINOWSKI.

Judicial System

According to the 1990 Constitution, the judicial system is composed of three tiers: the Supreme Court (which is also a Court of Record), the Appellate Courts and the District Courts. The Supreme Court consists of a Chief Justice and up to 14 other judges. The Chief Justice, whose tenure of office is seven years, is appointed by the King on the recommendation of the Constitutional Council, while all other judges are appointed on the recommendation of the Judicial Council.

Chief Justice: GOVINDA BAHADUR SHRESTHA.

Attorney-General: SUSHIL KUMAR PANT.

Religion

At the 2001 census, an estimated 80.6% of the population professed Hinduism (the religion of the royal family), while 10.7% were Buddhists and 4.2% Muslims. The actual number of Muslims in the country was considered to be much higher, owing to immigration from Bangladesh. There were an estimated 101,976 Christians in Nepal in 2001.

BUDDHISM

All Nepal Bhikkhu Council: Vishwa Shanti Vihara (World Peace Temple), 465 Ekadantamarga, Minbhawan, New Baneshwar, POB 8973, Kathmandu; tel. 4482984; fax 4482250; e-mail vishwa@ntc.net .np; internet www.vishwavihara.org.

Nepal Buddhist Council: Nahtole, Lalitpur 20; tel. 534277; e-mail nepal_bp@hotmail.com; Contact MAHISWOR RAJ BAJRACHARYA.

CHRISTIANITY

Protestant Church

Presbyterian Church of the Kingdom of Nepal: POB 3237, Kathmandu; tel. and fax 4524450.

The Roman Catholic Church

The Church is represented in Nepal by a single apostolic prefecture. At December 2002 there were an estimated 6,681 adherents in the country.

Apostolic Prefecture: Church of the Assumption, Everest Postal Care P. Ltd, POB 8975 EPC-343, Kathmandu; tel. 5542802; fax 5521710; e-mail anath@wlink.com.np; f. 1983 as Catholic Mission; Prefect Apostolic Fr ANTHONY FRANCIS SHARMA.

The Press

PRINCIPAL DAILIES

The Commoner: Naradevi, POB 203, Kathmandu; tel. 4228236; f. 1956; English; Publr and Chief Editor GOPAL DASS SHRESTHA; circ. 7,000.

Daily News: Bhimsensthan, POB 171, Kathmandu; tel. 4279147; fax 4279544; e-mail manju-sakya@hotmail.com; f. 1983; Nepali and English; Chief Editor MANJU RATNA SAKYA; Publr SUBHA LAXMI SAKYA; circ. 20,000.

Dainik Nirnaya: Bhairawa; tel. 520117; Nepali; Editor P. K. BHAT-TACHAN.

Gorkhapatra: Dharma Path, POB 23, Kathmandu; tel. 4221478; fax 4222921; f. 1901; Nepali; govt-owned; Editor-in-Chief KRISHNA BHAKTA SHRESTHA; circ. 75,000.

The Himalayan Times: International Media Network Nepal (Pvt) Ltd, APCA House, Baidya Khana Rd, Anam Nagar, POB 11651, Kathmandu; e-mail editorial@thehimalayantimes.com; internet www.thehimalayantimes.com; English; Exec. Editor KUMAR PRASAD SAPKOTA.

Janadoot: Ga 2–549, Kamal Pokhari (in front of the Police Station), Kathmandu; tel. 4412501; f. 1970; Nepali; Editor GOVINDA BIYOGI; circ. 6,500.

Kantipur: Shantinagar, Naya Baneshwor, POB 8559, Kathmandu; tel. 4473798; fax 4470178; internet www.kantipuronline.com; Nepali; Chief Exec. HEM RAJ GYAWALI; Editor YUBARAJ GHIMIRE.

Kathmandu Post: Subidhnagar, Naya Baneshwor, POB 8559, Kathmandu; tel. 4480100; fax 4470178; e-mail kpost@kantipur.com .np; internet www.kantipuronline.com; f. 1993; English; Chief Editor SHYAM BAHADUR; Editor SUMAN PRADHAN; circ. 30,000.

Motherland: POB 1184, Kathmandu; English; Editor MANINDRA RAJ SHRESTHA; circ. 5,000.

Nepal Samacharpatra: Sagarmatha Press, Ramshah Path, Kathmandu; e-mail sadhana@mail.com.np; f. 1945; Nepali; Editor NARENDRA BILAS PANDEY; circ. 1,000.

Nepali Hindi Daily: Maitidevi Phant, Shantinagar 32, POB 49, Kathmandu; tel. 4436374; fax 4435931; e-mail das@ntc.net.np; f. 1954; evening; Hindi; Publr UMA KANT DAS; Chief Editor VIJOY KUMAR DAS; circ. 65,000.

Rising Nepal: Dharma Path, POB 1623, Kathmandu; tel. 4227493; fax 4224381; internet www.south-asia.com/news-ktmpost.html; f. 1965; English; Editor-in-Chief GYAN BAHADUR RAI (acting); circ. 20,000.

Samaj: National Printing Press, Dillibazar, Kathmandu; f. 1954; Nepali; Editor MANI RAJ UPADHYAYA; circ. 5,000.

Samaya: Kamal Press, Ramshah Path, Kathmandu; f. 1954; Nepali; Editor MANIK LALL SHRESTHA; circ. 18,000.

Swatantra Samachar: Kathmandu; tel. 4419285; f. 1957; Editor MADAN DEV SHARMA; circ. 2,000.

SELECTED PERIODICALS

Agricultural Credit: Agricultural Training and Research Institute, Agricultural Development Bank, Head Office, Ramshah Path, Panchayat Plaza, Kathmandu; tel. 4220756; fax 4225329; 2 a year; publ. by the Agricultural Development Bank; Chair. Dr NARAYAN N. KHATRI; Editor RUDRA PD DAHAL.

Arpan: Bhimsensthan, POB 285, Kathmandu; tel. 4244450; fax 4279544; e-mail manju-sakya@hotmail.com; f. 1964; weekly; Nepali; Publr and Chief Editor MANJU RATNA SAKYA; circ. 18,000.

Awake Weekly Chronicle: Kathmandu; English.

Commerce: Bhimsensthan, POB 171, Kathmandu; tel. 4279636; fax 4279544; e-mail manju-sakya@hotmail.com; f. 1971; monthly; English; Publr and Chief Editor MANJU RATNA SAKYA; Editor SUBHA LAXMI SAKYA; circ. 12,000.

Current: Gautam Marg, Kamalpokhari, Kathmandu; tel. 4419484; fax 4413554; e-mail kiran_gautam@hotmail.com; f. 1982; weekly; Nepali; Man. Editor KIRAN GAUTAM; Publr and Editor DEVENDRA GAUTAM; circ. 10,000.

Cyber Post: Kathmandu; fortnightly; computers, electronics.

Foreign Affairs Journal: 5/287 Lagon, Kathmandu; f. 1976; 3 a year; articles on Nepalese foreign relations and diary of main news events; Publr and Editor BHOLA BIKRUM RANA; circ. 5,000.

Himal, The South Asian Magazine: POB 7251, Kathmandu; tel. 4543333; fax 4521013; e-mail info@himalmag.com; internet www .himalmag.com; f. 1987; monthly; political, business, social and environmental issues throughout South Asia; Editor-in-Chief KANAK MANI DIXIT; Marketing Man. SUMAN SHAKYA.

The Independent: Shankher Deep Bldg, Khichhapokhari, POB 3543, Kathmandu; tel. 4249256; fax 4226293; e-mail independ@mos .com.np; internet www.nepalnews.com/independent.htm; f. 1991; weekly; English; Editor SUBARNA B. CHHETRI.

Janadharana (People's Opinion): Kathmandu; e-mail dharana@ nepalimail.com; internet www.nepalnews.com.np/dharana.htm; weekly; left-wing; Managing Editor SUBHASHANKAR KANDEL.

Janmabhumi: Janmabhumi Press, Tahachal, Kathmandu; tel. 4280979; e-mail sirishnp@hotmail.com; internet www.catmando .com; weekly; Nepali; Publr and Editor SHIRISH BALLABH PRADHAN.

Koseli: Kathmandu; weekly; Nepali.

Madhuparka: Dharma Path, POB 23, Kathmandu; tel. 4222278; f. 1986; monthly; Nepali; literary; Editor-in-Chief KRISHNA BHAKTA SHRESTHA; circ. 20,000.

Mulyankan: Kathmandu; monthly, left-wing; Editor SHYAM SHRESTHA.

Matribhoomi (Nepali Weekly): Ga 2-549, Kamal Pokhari (in front of the Police Station), Kathmandu; tel. 4412501; weekly; Nepali; Editor GOVINDA BIYOGI.

Nepal Chronicle: Maruhiti; weekly; English; Publr and Editor CHANDRA LAL JHA.

Nepal Overseas Trade Statistics: Trade Promotion Centre, Pulchowk, Lalitpur, POB 825, Kathmandu; tel. 4532642; fax 4525464; e-mail tpcnep@mos.com.np; internet www.tpcnepal.org.np; annual; English.

Nepal Trade Bulletin: Trade Promotion Centre, Pulchowk, Lalitpur, POB 825, Kathmandu; tel. 5532642; fax 5525464; e-mail tpcnep@mos.com.np; internet www.tpcnepal.org.np; 3 a year; English; Editor NABIN RAJ SHARMA.

Nepali Times: Himalmedia Pvt Ltd, POB 7251, Kathmandu; tel. 4543333; fax 4521013; e-mail editors@nepalitimes.com; internet www.nepalitimes.com; f. 1955; weekly; Nepali; Publr and Editor CHANDRA LAL JHA; circ. 9,000.

People's Review: Pipalbot, Dillibazar, POB 3052, Kathmandu; tel. 4417352; fax 4438797; e-mail preview@ntc.net.np; internet www.peoplesreview.com.np; weekly; English; Editor-in-Chief PUSHPA RAJ PRADHAN; circ. 15,000.

Rastrabani: Kathmandu; tel. 4410339; weekly; Nepali; Chief Editor HARI LAMSAL.

Sanibariya: Kathmandu; weekly.

Sanghu Weekly: Kathmandu; weekly; Editor GOPAL BUDHATHOKI.

Saptahik Weekly: Kathmandu; weekly; Nepali.

Spotlight: POB 7256, Kathmandu; tel. 4410772; e-mail spotlight@mos.com.np; f. 1991; weekly; English; Editor MADHAV KUMAR RIMAL.

Swatantra Manch Weekly: POB 49, Kathmandu; tel. 4436374; fax 4435931; e-mail das@ntc.net.np; f. 1985; weekly; Nepali; Publr and Chief Editor V. K. DAS; Circulation Man. D. K. DAS; circ. 30,000.

The Telegraph: Ghattekulo, Dillibazar, POB 4063, Kathmandu; tel. 4419370; e-mail tgw@ntc.net.np; weekly; English; Chief Editor NARENDRA P. UPADHYAYA.

Vashudha: Makhan, Kathmandu; monthly; English; social, political and economic affairs; Publr and Editor T. L. SHRESTHA.

NEWS AGENCIES

Rastriya Samachar Samiti (RSS): Prithivi Path, POB 220, Kathmandu; tel. 4227912; fax 4227698; f. 1962; state-operated; Gen. Man. MUKUNDA PARAJULI.

Foreign Bureaux

Agence France-Presse (AFP): Bhote Bahal-South, Hansa Marg, POB 402, Kathmandu; tel. 4253960; fax 4222998; e-mail afpresse@mos.com.np; Chief of Bureau KEDAR MAN SINGH.

Associated Press (AP) (USA): Thapathli Panchayan, POB 513, Kathmandu; tel. 4212767; Correspondent BINAYA GURACHARYA.

Deutsche Presse-Agentur (dpa) (Germany): KH 1-27 Tebahal Tole, POB 680, Kathmandu 44601; tel. 4224557; Correspondent K. C. SHYAM BAHADUR.

Inter Press Service (IPS) (Italy): c/o Nepal Press Institute, POB 4128, Kathmandu; tel. and fax 4228943; Correspondent DHRUBA ADHIKARY.

Kyodo News (Japan): 1773/32 Surya Bikram Gyawali Marg, Battisputali, Kathmandu; tel. 4470106; fax 4480571; e-mail acharyam@mos.com.np; Correspondent MADHAV ACHARYA.

Reuters (United Kingdom): POB 3341, Kathmandu; tel. 4372152; fax 4373814.

United Press International (UPI) (USA): POB 802, Kathmandu; tel. 4215684; Correspondent BHOLA BIKRAM RANA.

PRESS ASSOCIATIONS

Federation of Nepalese Journalists (FNJ): Baghbazar, Kathmandu; tel. 4247538; e-mail fnjnepal@mail.com.np; Pres. SURESH ACHARYA.

Nepal Journalists' Association (NJA): Maitighar, POB 285, Kathmandu; tel. 4262426; fax 4279544; e-mail manju-sakya@hotmail.com; 5,400 mems; Pres. MANJU RATNA SAKYA; Gen. Sec. NIRMAL KUMAR ARYAL.

Press Council: Sanchargram, Tilganga, Kathmandu, POB 3077, Kathmandu; tel. 4469799; fax 4469878; e-mail prescoun_mdf@wlink.com.np; internet www.presscouncil.org; f. 1970; Chair. KEDAR NATH ACHARYA; Admin. Officer BISHNU PRASAD SHARMA.

Publishers

Educational Enterprise (Pvt) Ltd: Mahankalsthan, POB 1124, Kathmandu; tel. 4223749; e-mail ishwarbshrestha@yahoo.com; educational and technical.

International Standards Books and Periodicals (Pvt) Ltd: Bhotahity Bazaar, Chowk Bhitra, POB 3000, Kathmandu 44601; tel. 4262815; fax 4264179; e-mail u2@ccsl.com.np; f. 1991; Chief Man. Dir YOGYNDRA LALL CHHIPA; Chief Exec. and Man. Dir GANESH LALL SINGH CHHIPA.

Lakoul Press: Palpa-Tansen, Kathmandu; educational and physical sciences.

Mahabir Singh Chiniya Main: Makhan Tola, Kathmandu.

Mandass Memorials Publications: Kathmandu; Man. BASANT RAJ TULADHAR.

Pilgrims Book House: Thamel, POB 3872, Kathmandu; tel. 4700942; fax 4700943; e-mail pilgrims@wlink.com.np; internet www.pilgrimsbooks.com; f. 1986; Asian studies, religion and travel; Propr PUSHPA TIWARI.

Pilgrims Publishing Nepal (Pvt) Ltd: Goldhunga, POB 21646, Kathmandu; tel. 4356764; e-mail johnsnepal@wlink.com.np; internet www.pilgrimsbooks.com; f. 2000; Exec. Dir JOHN SNYDER; Man. Dir BISHOW BHATTA.

Ratna Pustak Bhandar: Bhotahity Tole, POB 98, Kathmandu; tel. 4223026; fax 4248421; e-mail rpb@wlink.com.np; f. 1945; textbooks, general, non-fiction and fiction; Propr RATNA PRASAD SHRESTHA.

Royal Nepal Academy: Kamaladi, Kathmandu; tel. 4221241; fax 4221175; f. 1957; languages, literature, social sciences, art and philosophy; Dep. Admin. Chief T. D. BHANDARI.

Sajha Prakashan: Pulchowk, Lalitpur, POB 20259, Kathmandu; tel. 5521118; fax 5544236; e-mail amarkumal2002@hotmail.com; f. 1966; educational, literary and general; Chair. BISHNU PRASAD GHIMIRE; Gen. Man. NAVA RAJ KARKI.

Trans Asian Media Pvt Ltd: Thapathali Crossing, POB 5320, Kathmandu; tel. 4242895; fax 4223889; Man. Editor SHYAM GOENKA.

Government Publishing House

Department of Information: Ministry of Information and Communications, Singha Durbar, Kathmandu; tel. 4220150; fax 4221729.

Broadcasting and Communications

TELECOMMUNICATIONS

Nepal Telecommunications Authority: 768/12 Thir Bam Sadhak, POB 9754, Baluwatar, Kathmandu; tel. 4446001; fax 4446006; e-mail ntra@nta.gov.np; internet www.nta.gov.np; telecommunications regulatory body; Chair. SURESH KUMAR PUDASAINI.

Nepal Telecommunications Corpn: Bhadrakali Plaza, POB 11803; Kathmandu; tel. 4246034; fax 4222424; e-mail rkt@ntc.net.np; internet www.ntc.com.np; f. 1975; monopoly provider; scheduled for transfer to private sector; Man. Dir CHET PRASAD BHATTARAI.

United Telecom: Kathmandu; jt venture between Indian-owned Mahanagar Telephone Nigam Ltd (26.7%), Videsh Sanchar Nigam Ltd (26.7%) and Telecom Consultants India (26.7%) and Nepal Venture (Pvt) Ltd (20%).

BROADCASTING

Radio

Radio Nepal: Radio Broadcasting Service, HM Government of Nepal, Singha Durbar, POB 634, Kathmandu; tel. 4241923; fax 4221952; e-mail radio@engg.wlink.com.np; internet www.radionepal.org; f. 1951; broadcasts on short wave, medium wave and FM frequencies in 20 regional languages, incl. Nepali and English for 18 hours daily (incl. two hours of regional broadcasting in the morning and evening); short-wave station at Khumaltar and medium-wave stations at Bhainsepati, Pokhara, Surkhet, Dipayal, Bardibas and Dharan; FM stations at Kathmandu, Kanchanpur, Rupandehi, Chitwan, Makawanpur, Bara, Jumla and Mustang; Exec. Dir SHAILENDRA RAJ SHARMA.

Television

In 1986 Nepal's first television station began broadcasting within the Kathmandu valley.

Nepalese Television Corporation: Singha Durbar, POB 3826, Kathmandu; tel. 4228447; fax 4228312; broadcasts 32 hours a week; programmes in Nepali (50%), English (25%) and Hindi/Urdu (25%); regional stations at Pokhara, Biratnagar and Hetuada; Gen. Man. TAPA NATH SHUKLA; Dep. Gen. Man. (Technical) RAVINDRA S. RANA; Dep. Gen. Man. (Productions) DURGA NATH SHARMA.

Shangri-La Channel (Pvt) Ltd: Sangharsh Chamber, Gyaneshwor, POB 5852, Kathmandu; tel. 4415299; fax 4416333; Chief Exec. NEER SHAH.

Space-Time Network: Iceberg Bldg, 3rd Floor, Putali Sadak, Kathmandu; tel. 4419133; fax 4419504; f. 1994; satellite transmission service.

Finance

(auth. = authorized; cap. = capital; p.u. = paid up; m. = million; dep. = deposits; res = reserves; brs = branches; amounts in Nepalese rupees)

BANKING

Central Bank

Nepal Rastra Bank: Central Office, Baluwatar, POB 73, Kathmandu; tel. 4419804; fax 4414553; e-mail nrb@mos.com.np; internet www.nrb.org.np; f. 1956; bank of issue; 100% state-owned; cap. 10m., res 23,623.5m., dep. 19,241.2m. (July 2000); Gov. Dr TILAK RAWAL; 9 brs.

Domestic Commercial Banks

Kumari Bank Ltd: Putalisadak, POB 21128, Kathmandu; tel. 4232112; fax 4231960; e-mail kumaribank@info.com.np; f. 2001; auth. cap 1,000m. (April 2001); Chair. NOOR PRATAP RANA.

Nepal Bank Ltd: Nepal Bank Bldg, Dharmapath, New Rd, POB 36, Kathmandu; tel. 4221185; fax 4222383; e-mail arbnbl@wlink.com .np; f. 1937; 41% state-owned, 59% owned by Nepalese public; cap. 378m., res 489.6m., dep. 21,570.5m. (July 1997); CEO J. CRAIG MCALLISTER; 126 brs.

Nepal Industrial and Commercial Bank Ltd (NIC Bank): Kamaladi, Ganeshthan, POB 7367, Kathmandu; tel. 4222336; fax 4241865; e-mail kamaladi@nicbank.com.np; internet www.nicbank .com.np; f. 1998; privately owned; cap. US $6.68m., res $0.70m., dep. $42.06m. (March 2004); Chair. JAGDISH PRASAD AGRAWAL; CEO SASHIN JOSHI; 6 brs.

Rastriya Banijya Bank (National Commercial Bank): Singha Durbar Plaza, Kathmandu; tel. 4252595; fax 4252931; e-mail rbbcm@mail.com.np; f. 1966; 100% state-owned; cap. 1,172m., res 268m., dep. 33,329m. (July 1999); Chair. BASHDEV RAM JOSHI; 212 brs, 4 regional offices.

Joint-venture Banks

Bank of Kathmandu Ltd: Kamal Pokhari, POB 9044, Kathmandu; tel. 4414541; fax 4418990; e-mail info@bok.com.np; f. 1993; 55% owned by Nepalese public, 45% by local promoters; cap. 233.6m., res 41.6m., dep. 5,724.1m. (July 2001); Chair. B. R. SINGH.

Everest Bank Ltd: New Baneshwor, POB 13384, Kathmandu; tel. 4481017; fax 4482263; e-mail ebl@mos.com.np; internet www.ebl .com.np; f. 1994; 50% owned by directors, 20% by Punjab National Bank (India), 30% by the Nepalese public; cap. 235.5m., res 159.6m., dep. 4,482.1m. (Jan. 2002); Exec. Dir S. S. DABAS; 22 brs.

Himalayan Bank Ltd: Karmachari Sanchaya Kosh Bldg, Tridevi Marg, Thamel, POB 20590, Kathmandu; tel. 4227749; fax 4222800; e-mail hbl@hbl.com.np; internet www.hbl.com.np; f. 1993; 20% owned by Habib Bank Ltd (Pakistan); cap. 390m., res 261.7m., dep. 17,634.8m. (July 2001); Chair. HIMALAYA S. J. B. RANA; CEO PRITHIVI BAHADUR PANDEY; 8 brs.

Nabil Bank Ltd (Nabil): Nabil House, Kamaladi, POB 3729, Kathmandu; tel. 4429546; fax 4429548; e-mail nabil@nabilbank.com .np; internet www.nabilbankltd.com; f. 1984 as Nepal Arab Bank Ltd, name changed as above Jan. 2002; 50% owned by National Bank of Bangladesh, 30% by the Nepalese public and 20% by Nepalese government financial institutions; cap. 491.7m., res 654.8m., dep. 15,923.7m. (July 2002); Chair. SATYENDRA PYARA SHRESTHA; Vice-Chair. DAYARAM GOPAL AGRAWAL; 17 brs.

Nepal Bangladesh Bank Ltd: Bijulibazar, New Baneshwor, POB 9062, Kathmandu; tel. 4780770; fax 4780316; e-mail nbblho@nbbl .com.np; internet www.nbbl.com.np; f. 1994; 50% owned by International Finance Investment and Commerce Bank Ltd (Bangladesh), 20% by Nepalese promoters and 30% public issue; cap. 238.2m., res 211.2m., dep. 8,610.4m. (July 2001); Man. Dir GANESH PRASAD ADHIKARY; Chair. JEET BAHADUR SHRESTHA; 15 brs.

Nepal Credit and Commerce Bank Ltd: Bagh Bazar, POB 12559, Kathmandu; tel. 4246105; fax 4244610; f. as Nepal Bank of Ceylon, reconstituted as above in Sept. 2002 after Bank of Ceylon (Sri Lanka) sold its shares to NB Group (Nepal); Man. Dir NARENDRA BHATTARAI; 11 brs.

Nepal Investment Bank Ltd: Durbar Marg, POB 3412, Kathmandu; tel. 4228229; fax 4226349; e-mail info@nibl.com.np; internet www.nibl.com.np; f. 1986 as Nepal Indosuez Bank Ltd, name changed as above in June 2002; 50% owned by a consortium of Nepalese investors, 20% by general public, 15% by Rastriya Banijya Bank and 15% by Rastriya Beema Sansthan; cap. 295m., res 343m., dep. 7,923m. (July 2003); Chair. UDAY NEPALI SHRESTHA; Chief Exec. Dir PRITHIVI B. PANDE; 12 brs.

Nepal SBI Bank Ltd: Corporate Office, Hattisar, POB 6049, Kathmandu; tel. 4435516; fax 4435612; e-mail nsblco@mos.com.np; f. 1993; 50% owned by State Bank of India, 30% by Nepalese public, 15% by Employees' Provident Fund (Nepal) and 5% by Agricultural Development Bank (Nepal); Chair. B. P. ACHARYA; Man. Dir B. B. DAS.

Nepal Sri Lanka Merchant Bank Ltd: NSLMB Bldg, Kalamadi, POB 12248, Kathmandu; tel. 4440300; fax 4441034; e-mail nslmb@ info.com.np; Exec. Dir VED MAN SINGH MALLA.

Standard Chartered Bank Nepal Ltd: Grindlays Bhavan, Naya Baneshwor, POB 3990, Kathmandu; tel. 4246753; fax 4226762; f. 1986; 50% owned by Standard Chartered Grindlays (USA), 33% by Nepal Bank Ltd and 17% by the Nepalese public; cap. 340m., res 765m., dep. 16,520m. (July 2002); Chair. B. N. NEPAL; CEO RAJEEV KULKARNI; 8 brs.

Development Finance Organizations

Agricultural Development Bank: Ramshah Path, Kathmandu; tel. 4262885; fax 4262616; e-mail info@adbn.gov.np; internet www .adbn.gov.np; f. 1968; 93.6% state-owned, 2.1% owned by the Nepal Rastra Bank, and 4.3% by co-operatives and private individuals; specialized agricultural credit institution providing credit for agricultural development to co-operatives, individuals and asscns; receives deposits from individuals, co-operatives and other asscns to generate savings in the agricultural sector; acts as Government's implementing agency for small farmers' group development project, assisted by the Asian Development Bank and financed by the UN Development Programme; operational networks include 14 zonal offices, 37 brs, 92 sub-brs, 52 depots and 160 small farmers' development projects, 3 Zonal Training Centres, 2 Appropriate Technology Units; Chair. SHYAM PRASAD MAINALI.

Nepal Development Bank: Heritage Plaza, POB 11017, Kamaladi, Kathmandu; tel. 4245753.

Nepal Housing Development Finance Co Ltd: POB 5624, Kathmandu; tel. 4490259; fax 4493573; e-mail nhdfc@ntc.net.np; Chief Exec. INDRA PRASHAD KARMACHARYA.

Nepal Industrial Development Corporation (NIDC): NIDC Bldg, Durbar Marga, POB 10, Kathmandu; tel. 4228322; fax 4227428; e-mail nidc@wlink.com.np; f. 1959; state-owned; holds investments of 5,609.9m. in 1,125 industrial enterprises (2000/01); offers financial and technical assistance to private-sector industries; in 2000/01 approved a total of 9.41m. in loans and working capital, and disbursed 8.17m.; Gen. Man. UTTAM NARAYAN SHRESTHA.

STOCK EXCHANGE

Nepal Stock Exchange Ltd (NEPSE): Singha Durbar Plaza, POB 1550, Kathmandu; tel. 4250735; fax 4262538; e-mail nepse@stock .mos.com.np; internet www.nepalstock.com; f. 1976; reorg. 1984; converted in 1993 from Securities Exchange Centre Ltd to Nepal Stock Exchange Ltd; 96 listed cos, 120 scripts; Gen. Man. MUKUNDA NATH DHUNGEL; Man. (Admin. and Market Operations) M. P. SHARMA; Man. (Information, Planning and Development) P. BHATTARAI.

INSURANCE

Alliance Insurance Co Ltd: Durbar Marg, POB 10811, Kathmandu; tel. 4222836; fax 4241411; e-mail sk@aic.wlink.com.np.

Everest Insurance Co: Kantipath, POB 8857, Kathmandu; tel. 4243631; fax 4240083.

Himalayan General Insurance Co Ltd: Durbar Marg, POB 148, Kathmandu; tel. 4231581; fax 4223906; e-mail ktm@hgi.com.np; internet www.hgi.com.np; f. 1993; CEO MAHENDRA KRISHNA SHRESTHA.

National Insurance Co Ltd: Tripureswor, POB 376, Kathmandu; tel. 4250710; fax 4261289; e-mail natinsur@ccsl.com.np; Man. A. S. KOHLI.

National Life and General Insurance Co Ltd: Lazimpat, POB 4332, Kathmandu; tel. 4412625; fax 4416427; e-mail nlgi@mail.com .np; Chief Exec. S. K. SINGH; Pres. OM SINGH.

Neco Insurance Ltd: Hattisar, POB 12271, Kathmandu; tel. 4427354; fax 4418761.

Nepal Insurance Co Ltd: NIC Bldg, Kamaladi, POB 3623, Kathmandu; tel. 4221353; fax 4225446; e-mail nic@wlink.com.np.

The Oriental Insurance Co Ltd: Jyoti Bhavan, POB 165, Kathmandu; tel. 4221448; fax 4223419; e-mail oriental@wlink.com.np.

Premier Insurance Co (Nepal) Ltd: 1988 Ram Rukmani Sadan, Kamaladi Marg, POB 9183, Kathmandu; tel. 4417765; fax 4420554; e-mail premier@picl.com.np; internet www.premier-insurance.com .np; Man. Dir SURESH LAL SHRESTHA.

Rastriya Beema Sansthan (National Insurance Corpn): RBS Bldg, Ramshah Path, POB 527, Kathmandu; tel. 4213882; fax

4262610; e-mail beema@wlink.com.np; f. 1967; Gen. Man. BIR BIKRAM RAXAMAJHI.

Sagarmatha Insurance Co Ltd: Kathmandu Plaza, Block Y, Kamaladi, POB 12211, Kathmandu; tel. 4240896; fax 4247941; e-mail sagarmatha@insurance.wlink.com.np; Exec. Dir K. B. BASNYAT.

United Insurance Co (Nepal) Ltd: I. J. Plaza, Durbar Marg, POB 9075, Kathmandu; tel. 4246686; fax 4246687; e-mail uic@mail.com .np.

Trade and Industry

GOVERNMENT AGENCY

National Planning Commission (NPC): Singha Durbar, POB 1284, Kathmandu; tel. 4225879; fax 4226500; e-mail npcs@npcnepal .gov.np; internet npc.gov.np:8080; Vice-Chair. Dr NARAYAN KHADKA.

DEVELOPMENT ORGANIZATIONS

Agriculture Inputs Corporation: Teku, Kuleshwar, POB 195, Kathmandu; tel. 4279715; fax 4278790; f. 1966; govt-owned; sole supplier of inputs for agricultural development (procuring and distribution of chemical fertilizers, improved seeds, agricultural tools and plant protection material) at national level; operates seeds multiplication programme (paddy, wheat, maize and vegetable); seed processing plants at Dang, Hetauda, Itahari, Janakpur, Nepalgunj and Sidharthanagar; Chair. MOHANDEV PANT; Gen. Man. ARJUN KUMAR THAPA.

National Productivity and Economic Development Centre: Balaju, POB 1318, Kathmandu; tel. 4350566; fax 4350530; e-mail npedc@wlink.com.np; internet www.panasia.org.sg/nepalnet/npedc/ html; functions as secretariat of National Productivity Council; provides services for industrial promotion and productivity improvement through planning research, consultancy, training, seminars and information services; Gen. Man. BHARAT GYAWALI.

National Trading Ltd: Teku, POB 128, Kathmandu; tel. 4227683; fax 4225151; e-mail natreli@mos.com.np; f. 1962; govt-owned; imports and distributes construction materials and raw materials for industry; also machinery, vehicles and consumer goods; operates bonded warehouse, duty-free shop and related activities; brs in all major towns; Chair. SONAFI YADAV; Gen. Man. MADHAV JUNG RANA.

Nepal Foreign Trade Association: Bagmati Chamber, 1st Floor, Milan Marg, Teku, POB 541, Kathmandu; tel. 4223784; fax 4247159; e-mail nfta@mos.com.np; Pres. ASHOK KUMAR AGRAWAL; Vice-Pres. AKHIL K. CHAPAGAIN.

Nepal Resettlement Co: Pulchowk, Lalitpur; tel. 521397; f. 1963; govt-owned; engaged in resettling people from the densely populated hill country to the western Terai plain.

Nepal Tea Development Corporation: Bijulibazar, Kathmandu; tel. 4220422.

Trade Promotion Centre (TPC): Pulchowk, Lalitpur, POB 825, Kathmandu; tel. 5525348; fax 5525464; e-mail tpcnep@mos.com.np; internet www.tpcnepal.org.np; f. 1971 to encourage exports; govt-owned; Exec. Dir N. C. LAMICHHANE.

CHAMBERS OF COMMERCE

Federation of Nepalese Chambers of Commerce and Industry (FNCCI): FNCCI Bldg, Pachali Shahid Shukra FNCCI Milan Marg, Teku, POB 269, Kathmandu; tel. 4262061; fax 4261022; e-mail fncci@mos.com.np; internet www.fncci.org; f. 1965; comprises 86 District Municipality Chambers (DCCIs), 50 Commodity Associations, 424 leading industrial and commercial undertakings in both the public and private sector, and nine Bi-national Chambers; publishes annual statistical profile *Nepal and the World* and bi-annual directory of members; Pres. RAVI BHAKTA SHRESTHA; Dir-Gen. BADRI PRASAD OJHA.

Birganj Chamber of Commerce and Industries: Brita, Birganj-4; tel. 522290; fax 526049; e-mail bicci@atcnet.com.np; internet www .bicci.org.np; Pres. BABU LAL CHACHAN.

Lalitpur Chamber of Commerce and Industry: Mangal Bazar, Patan Durbar Sq., POB 26, Lalitpur; tel. 5521740; fax 5530331; e-mail lcci@mos.com.np; internet www.lcci.org.np; f. 1967; Exec. Sec. PRADHUMAN LAL SHRESTHA.

Nepal Chamber of Commerce: Chamber Bhavan, Kantipath, POB 198, Kathmandu; tel. 4230947; fax 4229998; e-mail chamber@ wlink.com.np; internet www.nepalchamber.com; f. 1952; non-profit organization promoting industrial and commercial development; 8,000 regd mems and 16,000 enrolled mems; Pres. RAJESH KAZI SHRESTHA; Sec.-Gen. SURESH KUMAR BASNET.

INDUSTRIAL AND TRADE ASSOCIATIONS

Association of Craft Producers: Ravi Bhavan, POB 3701, Kathmandu; tel. 4275108; fax 4272676; e-mail craftacp@mos.com.np; internet acp.org.np; f. 1984; local non-profit organization providing technical, marketing and management services for craft producers, manufacturer, exporter and retailer of handicraft goods; Programme Co-ordinator REVITA SHRESTHA.

Association of Forest-based Industries and Trade: Thapathali, POB 2798, Kathmandu; tel. 4216020.

Association of Nepalese Rice and Oil Industries: Ganabahal, POB 363, Kathmandu; tel. 4250001; fax 4249723; e-mail ktm@ golchha.com; Pres. PASHUPATI GIRI; Gen. Sec. HULASCHAND GOLCHHA.

Association of Pharmaceutical Producers of Nepal: 63/284, Chhetrapati, POB 4506, Kathmandu; tel. 4415330; fax 4436395; e-mail vaidya@vpharma.wlink.com.np.

Cargo Agents Association of Nepal: Thamel, POB 5355, Kathmandu; tel. 4419019.

Central Carpet Industries Association of Nepal: Bijulibazar, POB 2419, Kathmandu; tel. 4496108; fax 4475291; e-mail ccia@enet .com.np; internet www.nepalcarpet.org; Pres. A. G. SHERPA.

Computer Association of Nepal: 235/39 Dobidhara Marg, Kathmandu; tel. 4432700; fax 4434836; e-mail info@can.org.np; internet www.can.org.np; f. 1992; Pres. LOCHAN LAL AMATYA.

Footwear Manufacturers' Association of Nepal: Khichapokhari, POB 648, Kathmandu; tel. 4228131; fax 4416576.

Garment Association of Nepal: Shankhamul Rd, New Baneshwor, POB 21332, Kathmandu; tel. 4780691; fax 4780173; e-mail gan@ntc.net.np; internet www.ganasso.org; Pres. KIRAN P. SAAKHA.

Handicrafts Association of Nepal: Maitighar, POB 784, Kathmandu; tel. 4243015; fax 4222940; e-mail han@wlink.com.np; internet www.nepalhandicraft.com.np.

Nepal Association of Travel Agents: Gairidhara Rd, Goma Ganesh, Naxal, POB 362, Kathmandu; tel. 4419409; fax 4418684; e-mail nata@mail.com.np; internet www.nata.org.np; f. 1966; 240 mems.

Nepal Cottage and Small Industries Association: Teku, Kathmandu; tel. 4212876.

Nepal Forest Industries Association: Gyaneshwor, POB 1804, Kathmandu; tel. 4411865; fax 4413838; e-mail padmasri@ccsl.com .np.

Nepal Leather Industry and Trade Association: Baghbazar, POB 4991, Kathmandu; tel. 4410315.

Nepal Plastic Manufacturers' Association: Kupondol, Kathmandu; tel. 4211981.

Nepal Tea Planters' Association: Bhadrapur; tel. 520183.

Nepal Textile Industries Association: Kupondol, Lalitpur; tel. 5523693; Pres. MAHESH LAL PRADHAN.

Nepal Trans-Himalayan Trade Association: Kantipath, Kathmandu; tel. 4223764; Vice-Chair. NIL KANTHA CHAULAGAIN.

UTILITIES

Electricity

Butwal Power Co Ltd: POB 126, Kathmandu; tel. 4525732; fax 4527898; partially privatized in 2003.

Chilime Hydropower Co Ltd: Kathmandu; 51% owned by Nepal Electricity Authority; Dir DAMBER BAHADUR NEPALI.

Electricity Development Centre: Exhibition Rd, POB 2507, Kathmandu; tel. 4227262; fax 4227537; f. 1993; under Ministry of Water Resources; Dir-Gen. VIJAY SHANKER SHRESTHA.

Nepal Electricity Authority: Ratna Park, Kathmandu; tel. 4227725; fax 4227035; e-mail neamd@mos.com.np; internet www .nea.org.np; f. 1985 following merger; govt-owned; Man. Dir Dr J. L. KARMACHARYA.

Water

Nepal Water Supply Corpn: Tripureswor Marg, Kathmandu; tel. 4253656; fax 4223484; f. 1990; govt-owned; Exec. Chair. ARUN KUMAR RANJITKAR.

TRADE UNIONS

Trade unions were banned in Nepal in 1961, but were legalized again in 1990, following the success of the pro-democracy movement and the collapse of the Panchayat system.

Nepal Trade Union Congress (NTUC): POB 5507, Kathmandu; tel. 4527443; fax 4527469; e-mail ntuc@mos.com.np; internet www

.ntuc.org.np; f. 1947; 20 affiliated unions; affiliated to ICFTU; Sec.-Gen. LAXMAN PRASAD PANDEY.

Democratic Confederation of Nepalese Trade Unions (DECONT): POB 13440, Kathmandu; tel. and fax 4488486; internet www25.brinkster.com/decont; f. 1997; Chair. KHILANATH DAHAL.

General Federation of Nepalese Trade Unions (GEFONT): Man Mohan Labour Bldg, GEFONT Plaza, POB 10652, Kathmandu; tel. 4248072; fax 4248073; e-mail info@gefont.org; internet www.gefont.org; f. 1989; 16 affiliated unions; Chair. MUKUNDA NEUPANE.

Transport

Ministry of Labour and Transport Management: Tridevi Marg, Kathmandu; tel. 419252; fax 419251; internet www.moltm.gov.np; Sec. MUKTI PRASAD KAFLE.

Nepal Transport Corpn (Napal Yatayat Sansthan): Kathmandu; tel. 4222547; f. 1966; scheduled for transfer to private ownership; controls the operation of road transport facilities, railways, ropeway, trucks, trolley buses and container services; Gen. Man. A. B. SHRESTHA.

Interstate Multi-Modal Transport (Pvt) Ltd: Shiva Sabitri Sadan, 240 Red Cross Marg, Tahachal, Kalimati, Kathmandu; tel. 4271473; fax 4271570; e-mail rauniar@mos.com.np; internet www.rauniar.com; f. 1975; provides freight forwarding, customs clearance, warehousing and shipping services, transport consultancy; Gen. Man. ANAND S. RAUNIAR.

RAILWAYS

Janakpur Railway: Khajuri, Janakpur; tel. 52082; HQ Jayanagar, India; f. 1937; 53 km open, linking Jayanagar with Janakpur and Bijalpura; narrow gauge; 11 steam engines, 25 coaches and vans, and 20 wagons; Man. J. B. THAPA.

Nepal Government Railway: Birganj; f. 1927; 7 steam engines, 12 coaches and 82 wagons; Man. D. SINGH (acting).

ROADS

In mid-2001 there were 15,458 km of roads, of which 4,577 km were black-topped. Around Kathmandu there are short sections of roads suitable for motor vehicles, and there is a 28-km ring road round the valley. A 190-km mountain road, Tribhuwana Rajpath, links the capital with the Indian railhead at Raxaul. The Siddhartha Highway, constructed with Indian assistance, connects the Pokhara valley, in mid-west Nepal, with Sonauli, on the Indian border in Uttar Pradesh. The 114-km Arniko Highway, constructed with Chinese help, connects Kathmandu with Kodari, on the Chinese border. In the early 1990s the final section of the 1,030-km East–West Highway was under construction. A number of north–south roads were also being constructed to connect the district headquarters with the East–West Highway. In November 1999 the World Bank agreed to provide Nepal with a loan of US $54.5m. for the construction and maintenance of roads (particularly in the far west of the country).

A fleet of container trucks operates between Kolkata and Raxaul in India and other points in Nepal for transporting exports to, and imports from, third countries. Trolley buses provide a passenger service over the 13 km between Kathmandu and Bhaktapur.

ROPEWAY

A 42-km ropeway links Hetauda and Kathmandu and can carry 22 metric tons of freight per hour throughout the year. Food grains, construction goods and heavy goods on this route are transported by this ropeway.

CIVIL AVIATION

Tribhuvan International Airport is situated about 6 km from Kathmandu. In 2001 Nepal had an estimated 44 airports, five of which were tarred.

Royal Nepal Airlines Corporation (RNAC): RNAC Bldg, Kantipath, POB 401, Kathmandu 711000; tel. 4220757; fax 4225348; internet www.royalnepal.com; f. 1958; 100% state-owned (scheduled for transfer to private ownership); scheduled services to 37 domestic airfields and international scheduled flights to Europe, the Middle East and the Far East; Chair. BAL KRISHNA MAN SINGH; Gen. Man. MOHAN PRASAD KHANAL (acting).

The monopoly of the RNAC in domestic air services came to an end in 1992. By 1999 there were about 12 private airlines in Nepal serving internal routes.

Buddha Air: Jawalakhal, Lalitpur, POB 2167, Kathmandu; tel. 4521015; fax 4537726; e-mail buddhaair@wlink.com.np; internet www.buddhaair.com; f. 1997; domestic passenger services; Man. Dir BIRENDRA BASNET.

Gorkha Airlines: New Baneshwor, POB 9451, Kathmandu; tel. 4487033; fax 4471136; e-mail gorkha@mos.com.np; internet www.yomari.com/gorkha/; f. 1996; scheduled and charter passenger and cargo flights to domestic destinations; Exec. Chair. PRAJJWAAL SHRESTHA.

Lumbini Airways (Pvt) Ltd: Min Bhavan, POB 6215, Kathmandu; tel. 4482725; fax 4483380; e-mail lumbini@resv.wlink.com.np; f. 1996; scheduled passenger and cargo flights to domestic destinations; Man. Dir R. K. SAKYA.

Necon Air Ltd: Kalimatidole, Necon Hamlet, Airport Area, POB 10038, Kathmandu; tel. 4473860; fax 4471679; e-mail info@necon.mos.com.np; internet www.neconair.com; f. 1992; scheduled and charter flights to domestic destinations and to India; Chair. and Man. Dir NARAYAN SINGH PUN.

Tourism

Tourism is being developed through the construction of new tourist centres in the Kathmandu valley, Pokhara valley and Chitwan. Regular air services link Kathmandu with Pokhara and Chitwan. Major tourist attractions include Lumbini, the birthplace of Buddha, the lake city of Pokhara and the Himalaya mountain range, including Mt Everest, the world's highest peak. In 1989, in an effort to increase tourism, the Government abolished travel restrictions in 18 areas of north-western Nepal that had previously been inaccessible to foreigners. Following the restoration of parliamentary democracy in 1990, tourist arrivals in Nepal rose considerably. Further travel restrictions in the remote areas of the kingdom were abolished in 1991, and efforts have been made to attract foreign investment in the Nepalese tourism industry, but the insurgency in the west has hindered development in the early 2000s. Nepal received an estimated 463,646 tourists in 2000. The number of visitor arrivals declined to 361,237 in 2001. Tourism receipts rose from US $153m. in 1998 to $168m. in 1999 but declined in 2000 to $167m. and again in 2001 to $137m. Hotel bed capacity increased from 32,214 in 1999 to an estimated 36,163 in 2001. The Government granted access to a further 103 mountains, raising the total number of mountains open to climbers to 263, in an effort to promote tourism.

Nepal Tourism Board: Tourist Service Centre, Bhrikuti Mandap, Kathmandu; tel. 4256909; fax 4256910; e-mail info@ntb.wlink.com.np; internet www.welcomenepal.com; f. 1998.

Association of Tourism: Thamel, Kathmandu; tel. 4424740.

Hotel Association Nepal (HAN): Kamalpokhari, POB 2151, Kathmandu; tel. 4412705; fax 4424914; e-mail info@hotelassociation.org.np; internet www.hotelassociation.org.np; f. 1966; Pres. NARENDRA BAJRACHARYA.

Tourist Guide Association of Nepal: Durbar Marg, POB 4344, Kathmandu; tel. 4225102.

Trekking Agents Association of Nepal: Naxal, POB 3612, Kathmandu; tel. 4419245.

THE NETHERLANDS

Introductory Survey

Location, Climate, Language, Religion, Flag, Capital

The Kingdom of the Netherlands is situated in western Europe, bordered to the east by Germany and to the south by Belgium. Its northern and western shores face the North Sea. The climate is temperate: the average temperature in January is 0°C (32°F), and the summer average is 21°C (70°F). The national language is Dutch. There is a Frisian-speaking minority (numbering about 400,000). About one-third of the inhabitants are Roman Catholics and about one-quarter are Protestants, while most of the remainder do not profess any religion. The national flag (proportions 2 by 3) has three equal horizontal stripes, of red, white and blue. The capital is Amsterdam, but the seat of government is The Hague ('s-Gravenhage).

Recent History

The Netherlands was occupied by Germany during the Second World War. Following its liberation in 1945, the country chose to abandon its traditional policy of neutrality, subsequently becoming a member of Western European Union (WEU, see p. 337) and the North Atlantic Treaty Organization (NATO, see p. 289). The Treaty establishing the Benelux Economic Union (see p. 359) between the Netherlands, Belgium and Luxembourg was signed in 1958 and came into force in 1960. The Netherlands was a founder member of the European Community (EC—now European Union—EU, see p. 208). Indonesia, formerly the Netherlands East Indies, was granted independence in 1949, except for West New Guinea, which was transferred to Indonesia in 1963. In 1975 Suriname became independent, leaving the Netherlands Antilles as the only remaining Dutch dependency. Aruba, formerly part of the Netherlands Antilles, was granted separate status within the Kingdom of the Netherlands in 1986.

Queen Juliana, who had reigned since 1948, abdicated in favour of her eldest daughter, Beatrix, in April 1980, following the adoption in February of a constitutional amendment that allowed for the accession of the reigning monarch's eldest child, regardless of gender.

All post-war administrations have been formed by various coalitions between the several 'confessional' Catholic and Protestant and 'progressive' Socialist and Liberal parties. At a general election held in April 1971 the left made substantial gains. In July 1972 the Government was forced to resign after losing its working majority in the Second Chamber of the States-General (see Government, below). Another general election took place in November 1972, at which the 'confessional' parties suffered a major reverse, and in May 1973 a new Government was formed by a left-of-centre coalition under the leadership of Dr Johannes (Joop) den Uyl of the Labour Party (Partij van de Arbeid—PvdA). This administration modified the fiscal structure and guaranteed minimum wage levels for all adult workers.

The coalition collapsed in March 1977, following disagreement over land-reform legislation; a general election followed in May. Attempts to form a left-of-centre coalition between the PvdA, the Christian Democratic Appeal (Christen Democratisch Appèl—CDA)—an alliance of 'confessional' groupings, which united in 1980 to form a single party—and Democraten '66 were unsuccessful, and in December 1977 Andries van Agt (of the CDA) formed a centre-right coalition Government of the CDA and the right-wing People's Party for Freedom and Democracy (Volkspartij voor Vrijheid en Democratie—VVD). The new coalition was supported by only 77 of the 150 members of the Second Chamber and was notably weakened by ministerial disagreements on NATO policy and the extent of reductions in public expenditure. Nevertheless, the Government survived its full term in office. A general election was held in May 1981, and a centre-left coalition was formed in September, led by van Agt and comprising the CDA (the party with the largest representation in the Second Chamber), the PvdA and Democraten '66. The Council of Ministers resigned after only five weeks in office, owing to its failure to agree on economic strategy. In November the three-party coalition accepted a compromise economic programme, but deep divisions within the Government continued to delay effective action on the economy. The coalition collapsed

again in May 1982: all six PvdA ministers resigned when their ambitious job-creation plan was cut, after which van Agt led a minority interim Government of the CDA and Democraten '66.

Although at a general election held in September 1982 the PvdA secured the greatest number of seats in the Second Chamber (47), the election produced a significant swing to the right. Talks on the formation of a new administration continued until November, when a centre-right CDA-VVD coalition was established under the leadership of Rudolphus (Ruud) Lubbers, a former Minister of Economic Affairs, who had recently succeeded van Agt as Chairman of the CDA. The CDA-VVD coalition was returned to power at a general election in May 1986, with (as in 1982) the two parties winning 81 of the 150 seats in the Second Chamber. A loss of nine seats by the VVD was offset by a corresponding gain by the CDA, which, with 54 seats, became the party with the largest representation in the Second Chamber. The election did, none the less, produce a shift towards the centrist parties, with the PvdA and Democraten '66 (D66—as the party was restyled) both gaining seats at the expense of smaller radical groups. Following the election, Wim Kok, a former trade unionist, replaced Joop den Uyl as parliamentary leader of the PvdA. A new CDA-VVD coalition was formed in July.

In May 1989 the VVD caused the collapse of the Government by refusing to support Lubbers' proposals for the financing of a 20-year National Environment Policy (NEP), which was to involve a reduction in government spending in sectors such as defence and housing, an increase in taxes on motor fuels, and the abolition of tax concessions for commuters using private transport. A general election was called for September, at which the CDA again secured 54 seats in the Second Chamber, while the PvdA took 49 seats (three fewer than in 1986). The VVD lost five seats to rival parties. An alliance of left-wing organizations, GroenLinks, won six seats. In October 1989 negotiations between the CDA and the PvdA culminated in the formation of a centre-left coalition, again led by Lubbers. The coalition accord envisaged increased welfare provision, to be funded by a reduction in defence expenditure, as well as a programme of job-creation and reductions in certain categories of taxation. Wim Kok was appointed Deputy Prime Minister and Minister of Finance. In August 1990 the Government introduced an amended version of the NEP, designated the National Environment Policy Plus (NEPP), which was to be financed by both the Government and the industrial sector. The NEPP was to be implemented at a faster pace than its predecessor, and placed strong emphasis on energy conservation and improvements in waste disposal and recycling. Instead of abolishing the system of tax deductions for car commuters (an unpopular proposal under the NEP), the NEPP advocated limiting the standard tax allowance for motorists and increasing excise duties on fuel. Proposals by the CDA, in mid-1991, to limit government expenditure by reforming the extensive disability benefit programme of the national welfare system were a source of friction with the PvdA. However, the PvdA eventually agreed to a compromise whereby the number of years of entitlement to full disability payments was to be restricted. The Government's decision led to widespread protest actions in September of that year.

In November 1992 the Second Chamber ratified the Treaty on European Union, which had been signed by EC Heads of Government at Maastricht in December 1991; the First Chamber similarly approved the Treaty in December 1992.

The CDA lost its leading position in the Government at the May 1994 general election, winning only 34 seats in the Second Chamber. The PvdA, which had focused its election manifesto on unemployment and reductions in social welfare, became, with 37 seats, the party with the largest representation in the Chamber. Both the VVD and D66 improved upon their performances at the previous general election, securing 31 and 24 seats respectively. The remaining 24 seats were distributed among eight smaller parties and special issue groups, including two organizations representing the interests of the elderly. As the combined seats of the CDA and PvdA amounted to less than an absolute majority, negotiations on a three-party coalition agreement commenced between the PvdA, the VVD and D66. Progress was initially retarded by deeply-entrenched disagreement between the VVD and PvdA over the latter's reluctance to sanction severe reductions in social welfare spending. Following several concessions by the PvdA (including the proposed privatization of some social benefits), a PvdA-VVD-D66 coalition, with Wim Kok as Prime Minister, was eventually agreed in August. The CDA (now led by Enneüs Heerma, Lubbers having retired from domestic politics following the May election) was thus excluded from the Council of Ministers for the first time since 1917.

In April 1996 the Government agreed that its liberal policy on the personal consumption of recreational 'soft' drugs should be subject to stricter controls, in response to protests by France and other neighbouring states that drugs-trafficking from the Netherlands would be facilitated by the withdrawal of EU border controls under the Schengen agreement.

The PvdA won increased representation at the general election to the Second Chamber held on 6 May 1998, taking 45 seats (with 29.0% of the total votes cast). The VVD also polled well, securing 38 seats (with 24.7% of the votes), while the CDA's representation was further reduced, to 29 seats (18.4%). D66 performed poorly, winning only 14 seats (with 9.0% of the poll), having lost votes to GroenLinks and the Socialist Party (Socialistische Partij). None the less, the PvdA, VVD and D66 agreed to renew their coalition (it was considered that D66 would be useful as an intermediary in conflicts of policy between the two leading partners), and a new Government, headed by Wim Kok, was inaugurated in August.

In October 1992 a cargo aircraft belonging to El Al, the Israeli national carrier, crashed into a densely-populated suburb of Amsterdam, killing at least 43 people. Following persistent speculation as to the nature of the cargo aboard the flight, and the widely-held opinion that the official response to the disaster and subsequent concerns had been inadequate, a parliamentary committee was established in October 1998 to investigate the Government's response to the crash. The inquiry was ordered after the Israeli Government had confirmed reports published in a Dutch newspaper that the cargo had included depleted uranium (used as ballast) and chemical components of sarin nerve gas, although the Israelis denied that the aircraft had been carrying 'dangerous goods'. The inquiry investigated claims that residents and workers who had been in contact with the wreckage had suffered ill health since the disaster, as well as allegations that Dutch ministers had been aware of the nature of the cargo. As hearings proceeded, it emerged that aviation officials had known of the contents of the aircraft from the time of the accident, and evidence of a lack of liaison between the transport and health ministries focused particularly on the former minister responsible for transport, Annemarie Jorritsma-Lebbink (now Deputy Prime Minister and Minister of Economic Affairs), and Els Borst-Eilers (the Deputy Prime Minister and Minister of Welfare, Public Health and Sport). The committee's report, published in April 1999, found that there was a direct link between the accident and the high incidence of ill health around the site of the crash, and was severely critical of the failure of the Prime Minister to co-ordinate government action with respect to the disaster. El Al was accused of failing to co-operate with accident investigators. The report none the less concluded that there was no evidence of attempts by the Netherlands Government to conceal details of the flight's cargo.

At provincial council elections, held on 3 March 1999, the opposition CDA took the largest share of the votes cast; the VVD outperformed the PvdA, while considerable successes for Groen-Links were largely at the expense of D66. The outcome left the Government with only a slender majority in the First Chamber, which is elected by the Provincial Councils.

In mid-May 1999 the First Chamber rejected the Government's proposal to allow the use of referendums on policy issues, a key demand of D66, after the refusal of a prominent member of the VVD to support the measure. D66 subsequently announced that it could no longer work with the VVD, and withdrew from the ruling coalition, prompting the resignation of the Council of Ministers. However, following a series of talks between the three parties, chaired by a mediator appointed by Queen Beatrix, all sides agreed to accept compromise proposals on referendums which would not require· alterations to the Constitution, and in early June the Government formally withdrew its resignation. All ministers were reappointed, with the exception of the Minister of Agriculture, Nature Management and Fisheries, Haijo Apotheker, who resigned from his post,

claiming that he had not received the full support of his government colleagues for his plan to resolve legal difficulties over the proposed restructuring of the pig-farming industry. The Dutch press, however, suggested that Apotheker's resignation had in fact been provoked by public criticism of his ministry's failure to alert consumers to the risk to public health caused by the contamination of animal feed, produced in Belgium and supplied to the Netherlands, with the carcinogenic chemical dioxin (see the Recent History of Belgium). Laurens Jan Brinkhorst, a member of the outgoing European Parliament, subsequently replaced Apotheker. In January 2001 the three coalition parties reached a new agreement over the introduction of the use of referendums, subject to approval by the First Chamber. The new proposals were for a judicially non-binding referendum (i.e., the Government and the legislature would not, by law, have to act on the result of a referendum, although there would be consensus to respect the voters' will) and would not require a change to the Constitution.

In July 1999 the Government announced that it was to launch an investigation into the finances of the regional authorities after it emerged that the province of Zuid-Holland had made loans to listed companies amounting to 1,700m. guilders, more than one-and-a-half times its annual budget. The province's financial irregularities were revealed after the collapse of a Dutch company trading in Central and South America to whom the authorities had lent some 47.5m. guilders. The investigative commission, reporting its findings in October, criticized the Provincial Executive of Zuid-Holland for assuming banking functions in 1995. It stated that the decision to do so had been unauthorized and democratically inadmissible because it bypassed the Provincial Council. No adequate measures had been taken to minimize the risk involved and many rules and regulations had been transgressed.

In September 1999 anonymous allegations were made of widespread financial irregularities within Rotterdam City Council involving the Minister of Home Affairs, Dr Bram Peper, the former mayor of Rotterdam. The Council established a commission to investigate the city's financial activities, including the allegations made against Peper. In January 2000 two Dutch national newspapers reported that accountants had discovered dubious entries in the city's accounts amounting to some 100,000 guilders. Further allegations made by the press in March that Peper made use of an official car of greater value than the permitted ministerial allowance, thus transgressing the codes of ministerial conduct, and that he had withheld a report in the early 1990s criticizing his performance as mayor finally led to Peper's resignation from his government post. In its report the commission ruled that, although generally control of council expenditure was carried out lawfully and purposefully, a relatively high proportion of controls had been too lax and considerable levels of expenditure would not have met Rotterdam Council's own regulations. The commission, however, did not rule on the conduct of individual council members. In December 2000, moreover, the public prosecutor decided to drop all charges of misconduct against Peper.

In May 2000 an explosion at a fireworks depot in the middle of a residential estate in the eastern city of Enschede caused the deaths of at least 21 people and the destruction of nearly 400 homes. A commission was established to investigate public safety issues in the light of the explosion. A judicial inquiry was also held which resulted in the arrests of five police-officers and two local government officers on charges of accepting gifts of fireworks in exchange for neglecting to perform adequate safety controls of fireworks companies. The two directors of the fireworks company were also arrested on suspicion of breaching fireworks storage regulations. The commission, reporting at the end of February 2001, concluded that public authorities had not sufficiently prioritized public safety issues and that there had been inadequate supervision of the fireworks industry. The Ministries of Justice, Defence and Housing, Spatial Planning and the Environment and the Industrial Trade Supervisory Board attracted particular criticism for having failed in their duties.

In September 2000 protests by road hauliers over the high price of motor spirit (petrol), which included the blockade of the seat of government, The Hague, prompted the Council of Ministers to agree on a number of fiscal measures to help ease the pressure of high fuel prices, although the agreement did not include the reductions of taxes on fuel sought by the protesters. Also in September the First Chamber approved laws giving same-sex couples the same legal status as heterosexuals, including the right to marriage and adoption (the legislation came into effect in April 2001). Legal recognition of homosexual partnerships had been granted in 1998.

In February 2001 the Netherlands suffered an outbreak of foot and mouth disease affecting its livestock. The outbreak was concentrated primarily in the east of the country, although there were sporadic outbreaks in other regions. The Government pursued a policy of slaughter and disposal, with a cull of some 265,000 animals (although only 26 cases of the disease were actually identified), to contain the outbreak, despite the preference of a large number of farmers for vaccination. A protest by farmers in a village in the east of the country led to the arrest of some 13 people. By early May, however, the situation was considered to be under control. In July the Government announced the lifting of the remaining export restrictions that had been imposed at the outset of the epidemic.

During 1992–93 Parliament debated and approved legislation codifying a procedure for the practice of euthanasia in circumstances where it was repeatedly requested by an incurably ill patient. In April 2001 the First Chamber passed a bill legalizing euthanasia by 46 votes to 28, making the Netherlands the first country in the world to do so. (In November 2000 the Second Chamber had passed the bill by 104 votes to 40.) The practice was to be subject to strict criteria. The key conditions according to which life could lawfully be ended were that the patient was terminally ill and in unbearable pain with no prospect of improvement. Euthanasia became legal in April 2002.

In August 2001 Kok announced that he would not seek re-election for a further term in office at the general election, scheduled for May 2002. He also announced that he would step down as Party Leader of the PvdA and subsequently endorsed the appointment of Ad Melkert, the Parliamentary Leader of the party, as his successor. In September 2001 Jaap de Hoop Scheffer, the Parliamentary Leader of the CDA, resigned, claiming that he had inadequate support from senior party chiefs to lead a successful campaign in the approaching general election. He was replaced by Pieter (Peter) Balkenende the following month.

In October 2001 the Government approved a bill to allow cannabis to be prescribed as a painkiller in cases where conventional drugs had failed. (On 1 September 2003 the legislation was passed by Parliament, thereby making the Netherlands the first country in the world to provide medicinal cannabis on the national health service. The drug was to be produced by two authorized growers and rigorously controlled for quality.) In a further proposed liberalization of drug laws the Government requested that Parliament endorse its plan to give free heroin, in combination with methadone, to addicts deemed to be 'beyond help'. The proposal was announced in the light of research demonstrating that long-term heroin users were able to function better in society under the scheme.

In April 2002, following the publication of a report by the Netherlands Institute for War Documentation into the massacre of some 7,000 Bosnian Muslims by Bosnian Serb troops in Srebreniča (Bosnia and Herzegovina) in 1995, which blamed the Dutch Government, the Dutch military and the UN for their respective roles in failing to prevent the atrocity (the report claimed that the 100 lightly armed Dutch peace-keeping troops who had been stationed in the town at the time had been ill-trained and had no clear mandate), the entire Council of Ministers resigned. At the request of Queen Beatrix, the Government agreed to remain in office in a caretaker capacity pending the forthcoming general election, which was scheduled to be held on 15 May 2002. In addition, the Chief of Staff of the army, Gen. Ad van Baal, who had been the second-highest ranking officer in the army at the time of the massacre, also resigned.

Further investigations by a parliamentary commission, in November 2002, into the failure of the Dutch authorities to prevent the massacre at Srebreniča in 1995 revealed that the former Government had been aware of the likelihood of atrocities occurring in the UN camp. The former Minister of Development Co-operation in that administration, Jan Pronk, admitted that the possibility of such killings had in fact been discussed in a meeting of the Council of Ministers on 11 July 1995, the very day the mass murders had occurred. In January 2003 the parliamentary commission concluded that the Netherlands bore responsibility for the massacre, that the Government had failed adequately to plan the mission and that the Dutch army had suppressed details of its failures.

On 6 May 2002 the charismatic and controversial politician Pim Fortuyn was shot dead in Hilversum, in central Nether-

lands, just days before the holding of the general election, in which his newly established party, the populist and anti-immigration Lijst Pim Fortuyn (LPF), was expected to secure a substantial proportion of votes. Fortuyn had formed the movement following his dismissal in January as leader of the Leefbar Nederland (LN) party for his anti-immigration rhetoric. In late November 2002 Volkert van der Graaf, an animal-rights activist who had been arrested shortly after Pim Fortuyn's murder, confessed to killing the politician. At his trial, which began in late March 2003, van der Graaf claimed that he believed Fortuyn had presented a threat to vulnerable members of society. He was convicted in April and received a prison sentence of 18 years. Appeals were lodged by van der Graaf and by the prosecution, who demanded life imprisonment; in mid-July, however, the original sentence was upheld.

At the general election of 15 May 2002 the CDA won 43 of the 150 seats in the Second Chamber, with 27.9% of the valid votes cast. The LPF, aided by revulsion at Fortuyn's murder, took 26 seats (with 17.0% of the votes), the VVD won 24 seats (15.4%) and the PvdA, obtained 23 seats (15.1%). In the light of their electoral defeats, both the PvdA and the VVD changed their Parliamentary Leaders, to Jeltje van Nieuwenhoven and Gerrit Zalm, respectively.

Balkenende was inaugurated as Prime Minister on 21 July 2002, leading a coalition Government comprising the CDA, the LPF and the VVD. However, the same day, a Suriname-born LPF minister in the Ministry of Emancipation and Family Affairs, Philomena Bijhout, resigned when it was confirmed that she had been linked to a Surinamese militia group involved in political killings in the former Dutch colony in December 1982. The LPF suffered a further setback when allegations were made by a newspaper that their new leader, Mat Herben, had tried unfairly to influence the selection procedure for the LN's electoral candidates when Fortuyn was still leader and Herben a party member. Herben resigned at the end of July and was subsequently replaced by Harry Wijnschenk, a motor magazine publisher.

The new Government detailed policies to reform the health insurance and social security system and reduce the number of illegal immigrants to the Netherlands. In early October 2002 the Minister of Immigration and Integration opened a new college for the instruction of Muslim religious leaders, imams, in Dutch values and social conventions. The course was compulsory for new imams who faced deportation if they practised without passing the exam.

Meanwhile, the LPF was riven by factionalism and personal acrimony. In addition to the expulsion of two party members who objected to Wijnschenk's leadership style, in early October 2002 a feud developed between the Minister of Public Health, Welfare and Sport and Deputy Prime Minister, Dr Eduard Bomhoff, and the Minister of Economic Affairs, Herman Heinsbroek. Wijnschenk approached Heinsbroek regarding his possible appointment as the party's Parliamentary Leader. Heinsbroek subsequently articulated his ambition to assume the deputy premiership, resulting in a damaging dispute with the incumbent Deputy Prime Minister, Bomhoff. The party was unable to resolve the deep personal and political rivalry between the two ministers. Despite the subsequent resignations of Heinsbroek and Bomhoff from the Council of Ministers, the LPF's coalition partners refused to co-operate further with the party and the Government resigned on 16 October after just 87 days in power. Balkenende presided over a minority Government, comprising the CDA and the VVD, pending a general election, which was scheduled for January 2003. In December 2002 the VVD Minister of Defence, Benk Korthals, resigned after a parliamentary inquiry accused him of misleading the legislature over corruption in the construction industry.

In December 2002 four men appeared in court charged with having links to the militant Islamist al-Qa'ida organization, and with conspiring to attack the US embassy in Paris and a US military base in Belgium in 2001. However, the men—one Dutch national of Ethiopian origin, one French national and two Algerians—were acquitted at the end of the month when the court ruled that evidence against them had been improperly obtained by the police.

In the general election of 22 January 2003, in which 79.9% of the electorate participated, the CDA won 44 seats in the Second Chamber (securing 28.6% of total votes cast), while the PvdA increased its number of seats from 23 to 42 (27.3%) under its charismatic new leader, Wouter Bos. The LPF, again led by Mat Herben, following the resignation of Wijnschenk in late 2002, secured only eight seats, while the D66 obtained six. Although the popularity of the right-wing LPF had declined sharply, the electoral manifestos of the mainstream parties addressed the issues raised by the movement. Of these, immigration became a prominent subject of debate, the VVD echoing Fortuyn's statement that the Netherlands was already 'full'. In late January negotiations began regarding the formation of a coalition administration led by Balkenende. Disagreements between the CDA and the PvdA over Dutch support for an impending US-led military campaign to remove the regime of Saddam Hussain in Iraq hampered progress. In mid-March, in his capacity as Prime Minister of the interim administration, Balkenende announced that, while Dutch troops would not assist in the campaign, some units of the armed forces and weapons would be supplied to help defend Turkey, should the conflict escalate. The PvdA responded by proposing a motion that the Netherlands should not provide assistance for the military campaign, either in the form of personnel or of materials; the motion was defeated. Negotiations resumed in late March and, as the US-led coalition entered Iraq, both parties expressed their support for the military operation. In early April, however, talks collapsed following the failure of the two sides to agree on budgetary expenditure cuts to revive a stagnant economy. The following month the CDA negotiated the formation of a centre-right coalition with the VVD and the D66, thereby gaining a slender majority of six in the 150-seat Second Chamber. The coalition Government, under the renewed premiership of Balkenende, was formally sworn in by Queen Beatrix on 27 May. In late May the provincial councils elected a new First Chamber in which the CDA-VVD-D66 coalition also obtained a majority, securing 41 of the 75 seats. The new Council of Ministers largely resembled the caretaker administration formed in October 2002. The CDA held eight portfolios, the VVD six and the D66 held two. Two new Deputy Prime Ministers were appointed: Gerrit Zalm of the VVD, who was also assigned the post of Minister of Finance, and Thomas Carolus (Thom) de Graaf of the D66, who was also named as Minister of Government Reform and Kingdom Relations. One of the stated priorities of the incoming Government was a pledge to tackle the problems of illegal drugs and crime. The new administration proposed the extension of police powers to stop and search people and the introduction of compulsory identity cards for citizens from the age of 14 years.

Meanwhile, in March 2003 Princess Margarita lodged a criminal complaint against former Prime Minister Wim Kok and the Dutch secret service. The princess claimed that the Government had acted illegally in obtaining confidential documents and information relating to her husband (Edwin de Roy van Zuyderwijn, a commoner whom she had married in 2001) and herself, which were later released by her aunt, Queen Beatrix, to the public. Balkenende admitted that van Zuyderwijn had indeed been subject to background checks, but that these were routine for anyone marrying into the royal family. (In July it was reported that Princess Margarita and Zuyderwijn had separated.)

In April 2003 the Dutch important food export industry was adversely affected by an epidemic of avian influenza. By the end of the month more than 18m. chickens had been destroyed in a precautionary cull to prevent the epidemic from spreading to neighbouring countries. During the outbreak the Netherlands, one of the world's largest egg and poultry exporters, was estimated to have suffered losses of around €2m. a day.

In September 2003 the Government announced its intention to reform the Netherlands' generous social security system, which had been rendered increasingly expensive by the combination of a rapidly increasing ageing population and a decline in the workforce. The proposed reforms included the reduction of hospital budgets by 5%, the limitation of free dental care to those aged 18 years or under, and the introduction of charges for non-prescription drugs. The Government planned to increase the involvement of the private sector in health care, thereby transferring certain costs from the State to the individual. Under the proposed reforms, a non-refundable health insurance excess of €250 would be introduced in 2005, and in the following year the public and private health care systems would merge and a standard insurance scheme would be offered by the various private health insurance companies. In an effort to encourage more people to work (the rate of unemployment had risen from only 3% in 2001 to an estimated 7% in 2004), the Government planned to make the eligibility criteria for disability and unemployment benefits more stringent; in addition, incentives for early retirement were to be abandoned.

In December 2003 Rotterdam City Council adopted a highly controversial policy paper that aimed to restore the city's socio-economic balance by building expensive rather than affordable housing and by restricting the issue of residence permits to those who earned at least 20% more than the minimum wage and who spoke a good level of Dutch. A parliamentary report published the following month highlighted a perceived unwillingness to integrate on the part of some immigrants and judged that the tolerant multiculturalist policies practised over the previous 30 years had generally failed.

The number of asylum applications for those seeking residency in the Netherlands fell from 43,500 in 2000 to 10,000 in 2003. Nevertheless, the new coalition Government that assumed power in May 2003 introduced a number of stringent new policies regarding immigrants and asylum-seekers. In late January 2004 the Government announced that a maximum of only 22,000 immigrants from the 10 new EU member states (which were scheduled to join the EU on 1 May) would be permitted to settle in the Netherlands. This was termed a temporary control policy which aimed to prevent the destabilization of the employment market. In mid-February Parliament approved a bill that would permit the deportation of 26,000 failed asylum-seekers over the following three years. The legislation applied to asylum-seekers who had arrived in the Netherlands before 1 April 2001 and who had exhausted their appeals. It authorized the removal of their welfare benefits, and the provision of a repatriation payment and a free flight to their country of origin. The controversial law, which was condemned by human rights groups and considered too severe by the political left, was welcomed by certain sectors of society (particularly among those with low rates of pay) that felt threatened by the rising level of unemployment.

In early December 2003 Dr Bernard Rudolf Bot succeeded Jaap de Hoop Scheffer as Minister of Foreign Affairs when the latter was appointed Secretary-General of NATO.

Government

The Netherlands is a constitutional and hereditary monarchy. Legislative power is held by the bicameral States-General. The First Chamber has 75 members and is indirectly elected for four years by members of the 12 Provincial Councils. The Second Chamber comprises 150 members and is directly elected by universal adult suffrage for four years (subject to dissolution), on the basis of proportional representation. The Head of State has mainly formal prerogatives, and executive power is exercised by the Council of Ministers, which is led by the Prime Minister and is responsible to the States-General. The monarch appoints the Prime Minister and, on the latter's recommendation, other ministers. Each of the 12 provinces is administered by a directly-elected Provincial Council, a Provincial Executive and a Sovereign Commissioner, who is appointed by Royal Decree.

Defence

The Netherlands is a member of NATO (see p. 289). Conscription to the armed forces was ended in August 1996, and a gradual reduction in the number of military personnel is ongoing. The total strength of the armed forces at 1 August 2003 was 53,130: army 23,150, navy 12,130, air force 11,050 and Royal Military Constabulary 6,800. In August 1995 a joint Dutch-German army corps, numbering 28,000 men, was inaugurated, and in January 1996 the operational units of the Royal Netherlands Navy merged with the Belgian navy under the command of the Admiral of the Benelux. In the 2004 budget, defence was allocated €7,700m. In November 2000 the Netherlands committed 5,000 troops to a proposed joint European Union rapid reaction force, which was to be ready to be deployed by 2003.

Economic Affairs

In 2002, according to estimates by the World Bank, the Netherlands' gross national income (GNI), measured at average 2000–02 prices, was US $386,774.4m., equivalent to $23,960 per head (or $27,470 per head on an international purchasing-power parity basis). During 1990–2002, it was estimated, the population grew at an average annual rate of 0.6% per year, while gross domestic product (GDP) per head increased, in real terms, at an average annual rate of 1.9% in 1990–2002. Overall GDP increased, in real terms, at an average annual rate of 2.5% in 1990–2001; growth in 2001 was an estimated 6.7%, but fell to 3.6% in 2002.

Agriculture (including hunting, forestry and fishing) contributed 2.3% of GDP in 2000. Although only 3.1% of the employed labour force were engaged in the sector in 2002, the Netherlands is a net exporter of agricultural products: in 2003 exports of food and live animals provided 12.6% of total export earnings. The principal crops are potatoes, sugar beet, wheat and onions. The main agricultural activity is horticulture; market gardening is highly developed, and the production of cut flowers and bulbs has traditionally been a significant industry, although its contribution to export earnings has declined in recent years. Livestock farming is also an important activity. During 1990–2000 agricultural GDP increased, in real terms, at an average annual rate of 2.3%; following an increase of 3.3% in 2001, it fell by 0.6% in 2002.

Industry (including mining, manufacturing, construction and power) contributed an estimated 26.1% of GDP in 2002. About 20.0% of the employed labour force were engaged in the sector in 2002. Industrial GDP increased, in real terms, at an average annual rate of 1.7% in 1990–99; it rose by 5.5% in 2001 and by 0.8% in 2002.

Extractive activities provided 2.6% of GDP in 2002. In that year about 0.1% of the employed labour force were engaged in mining and quarrying. The principal mineral resource is natural gas. Total extraction in 2002 was an estimated 75,000m. cu m. Reserves of petroleum and salts are also exploited. The GDP of the mining sector declined, in real terms, at an average annual rate of 1.2% in 1995–99; it increased by 19.2% in 2001, but subsequently decreased by 10.0% in 2002.

Manufacturing contributed 16.1% of GDP in 2002. The sector accounted for 13.4% of the employed labour force in 2001. Measured by the value of output, the principal branches of manufacturing in 1999 were food products, beverages and tobacco (accounting for 22.4% of the total), electrical and optical equipment (9.8%) and basic chemicals and man-made fibres (9.8%). Several multinational companies are domiciled in the Netherlands. Manufacturing GDP increased at an average annual rate of 2.4% in 1995–99; it grew by an estimated 1.2% in 2001 and by an estimated 0.1% in 2002.

In 2000 natural gas provided 57.5% of total electricity production, coal 28.4%, petroleum 3.5%, nuclear energy 4.4% and hydroelectric power 0.2%. Imports of mineral fuels comprised 5.9% of the value of total imports in 2003; fuel exports accounted for 2.8% of total exports by value in that year. In recent years successive governments have sought to promote the utilization of 'renewable' energy resources.

The services sector contributed an estimated 71.6% of GDP in 2002, and engaged 73.4% of the employed labour force in 2001. Within the sector, financial services, tourism and transport are of considerable importance. The GDP of the services sector increased, in real terms, at an average annual rate of 3.1% in 1990–99; it rose by 4.1% in 1998 and by 3.8% in 1999.

In 2002 the Netherlands recorded a visible trade surplus of €26,995m. and there was a surplus of €9,457m. on the current account of the balance of payments. In 2003 the principal source of imports was Germany (contributing 20.0% of the total); other major suppliers were Belgium (11.3%), the USA (7.8%), the United Kingdom (7.2%) and France (5.5%). Germany was also the principal market for exports (accounting for 24.4% of the total); other major purchasers in 2003 were Belgium (11.9%), the United Kingdom (10.3%), France (10.0%) and Italy (6.0%). The principal exports in 2003 were office machines and automatic data-processing machines, petroleum, road vehicles and organic chemicals. The principal imports in that year were also office machines and automatic data-processing machines, followed by petroleum, road vehicles, and telecommunications and sound equipment.

In 2002 the Netherlands recorded an overall budgetary deficit of €6,902m., equivalent to 1.6% of GDP. In the same year government debt, according to IMF figures, was estimated to be equivalent to 51.0% of GDP. In 1990–2002 the annual rate of inflation averaged 2.7%. Consumer prices increased by 3.3% in 2002 and by 2.1% in 2003. The annual average rate of registered unemployment grew from 2.3% in 2002 to 3.4% in 2003.

The Netherlands is a founder member of the European Union (EU, see p. 208), of the Benelux Economic Union (see p. 359), of the Organisation for Economic Co-operation and Development (OECD, see p. 295) and of the European Bank for Reconstruction and Development (EBRD, see p. 203).

In the early 1990s the hitherto buoyant, export-led growth of the Dutch economy was undermined by a series of budget deficits, a high level of unemployment and fluctuations in international prices for natural gas. The administration of Wim Kok (1994–2002), pursuing a policy of economic consensus, which helped to limit industrial unrest, sought to reduce public expenditure, to restrain labour costs and to deregulate commercial activity, and shifted much of the burden of social-security contribution from the employer to the employee. This, together with the increasing importance of part-time work, contributed to a progressive reduction in the level of unemployment from 1992. Between 1995 and 2000 the Netherlands recorded annual rates of economic growth above the EU average. In 1999 the Netherlands recorded its first budgetary surplus (equivalent to about 1% of GDP) for some 25 years. However, the state of the economy deteriorated sharply between 2001 and 2003, recording average annual GDP growth of just 0.5%. Registered unemployment rose from 2.0% of the total labour force in 2001 to 3.4% in 2003. The global economic downturn was particularly severely felt in the Netherlands as a result of the country's dependence on trade. This was further exacerbated by a decline in competitiveness owing to a combination of decreasing industrial production and increasing labour costs. (Labour costs in the Netherlands had risen 10% more than those of competing countries between 1997 and 2003.) Between 2001 and 2003 government revenue also decreased, while expenditure continued to mount. This trend was provoked by a drop in investment spending, and by the increasing demands for state-funded health care, welfare benefits and pensions, all of which stemmed from rising levels of unemployment and demographic ageing. Balkenende's administration, which came to power in May 2002, proposed to stimulate the economy by enhancing competitiveness and commercial productivity. In order to achieve this, the Government pledged to simplify commuter travel regulations, to reduce administrative costs for businesses by one-quarter during its term in office, and to negotiate a two-year wage 'freeze' with the trade unions. The austerity budget announced in September 2003 for the following year proposed a €16,900m. reduction in government expenditure and a comprehensive reform of the health system. It aimed to encourage labour participation by restricting access to unemployment and disability benefits and by the planned abolition in 2005 of early retirement tax benefits. The Government maintained that these stringent measures were necessary in order to adhere to the EU Stability and Growth Pact (SGP). In October the trade unions agreed to a freeze in collectively agreed wages during 2004, with the possibility of a minimal pay increase in 2005, dependent on economic performance. In return, the Government agreed to postpone the abolition of early retirement tax relief until 2006. In 2004 unemployment was predicted to reach 7% and the planned budget deficit of 2.4% of GDP was based on an economic growth forecast of 1%. However, in February 2004 official sources forecast that, without increased revenue or spending cuts, the budget deficit would reach 3.3% of GDP in 2004, thus breaking the 3% ceiling laid down in the SGP.

Education

There are two types of school in the Netherlands: public schools, which are maintained by municipalities, and attended by about 35% of all school children; and private schools, which are, for the most part, denominational and are attended by almost 65% of the school-going population. Both types of school are fully subsidized by the State. Schools are administered by school boards, responsible to the local authorities or to the private organizations that operate them, thus providing teachers with considerable freedom. The Minister of Education, Culture and Science, advised by an education council, is responsible for educational legislation and its enforcement.

Full-time education is compulsory in the Netherlands from five to 16 years of age, and part-time education is compulsory for a further two years. Some 98% of four-year-old children also attend primary schools. Primary education lasts for eight years and is followed by various types of secondary education. Pre-university schools provide various six-year courses that prepare pupils for university education. General secondary education comprises senior and junior secondary schools, providing five- and four-year courses that prepare pupils for higher vocational institutes and senior secondary vocational education respectively. In all types there is latitude in the choice of subjects taken. In 2000/01 166,948 students were enrolled at the Netherlands' 13 universities, while some 311,000 students were enrolled at the 65 institutes of higher vocational education. In addition, 22,000 students were registered with the Open University at 1 January 2001/02. Education, culture and science were allocated

€25,700m. (equivalent to some 19.1% of total expenditure) by the central Government in the 2004 budget.

Public Holidays

2004: 1 January (New Year's Day), 9 April (Good Friday), 12 April (Easter Monday), 30 April (Queen's Day), 20 May (Ascension Day), 31 May (Whit Monday), 25–26 December (Christmas).

2005: 1 January (New Year's Day), 25 March (Good Friday), 28 March (Easter Monday), 30 April (Queen's Day), 5 May (Ascension Day), 16 May (Whit Monday), 25–26 December (Christmas).

Weights and Measures

The metric system is in force.

Statistical Survey

Source: Netherlands Central Bureau of Statistics, Prinses Beatrixlaan 428, POB 959, 2270 AZ Voorburg; tel. (70) 3373800; fax (70) 3877429; e-mail infoservice@cbs.nl; internet www.cbs.nl.

Area and Population

AREA, POPULATION AND DENSITY

Area (sq km)	
Land	33,873
Inland waters	3,479
Coastal water	4,175
Total	41,528*
Population (census results)†	
1 January 1991‡	15,010,445
1 January 2001‡	
Males	7,909,855
Females	8,077,220
Total	15,987,075
Population (official estimate at 1 January)†	
2002	16,105,285
2003	16,192,572
2004	16,254,933
Density (per sq km of land) at 1 January 2004	479.9§

* 16,034 sq miles.
† Population is *de jure*.
‡ Based on a compilation of continuous accounting and sample surveys.
§ Land area only.

PROVINCES

	Land area (sq km)*	Population (1 January 2003)†	Density (per sq km)
Groningen	2,340	572,997	245
Friesland	3,356	639,787	191
Drenthe	2,649	481,254	182
Overijssel	3,337	1,100,677	330
Flevoland	1,421	351,680	247
Gelderland	4,983	1,960,422	393
Utrecht	1,363	1,152,218	845
Noord-Holland	2,657	2,573,120	968
Zuid-Holland	2,867	3,439,982	1,200
Zeeland	1,805	378,348	210
Noord-Brabant	4,929	2,400,198	487
Limburg	2,164	1,141,889	528
Total	33,871	16,192,572	478

* Figures refer to area at 1 January 2000.
† Provisional.

PRINCIPAL TOWNS

(population of municipalities at 1 January 2003)*

Amsterdam (capital)†	735,562	Arnhem	141,528
Rotterdam	599,651	Zaanstad	139,464
's-Gravenhage (The Hague)†	463,826	's-Hertogenbosch	132,501
Utrecht	265,151	Amersfoort	131,221
Eindhoven	206,118	Haarlemmermeer	122,902
Tilburg	197,917	Maastricht	121,982
Groningen	177,172	Dordrecht	120,043
Almere	165,106	Leiden	117,689
Breda	164,397	Zoetermeer	112,594
Apeldoorn	156,198	Zwolle	109,955
Nijmegen	155,741	Emmen	108,198
Enschede	152,321	Ede	104,771
Haarlem	147,097		

* Provisional figures.
† Amsterdam is the capital, while The Hague is the seat of government.

BIRTHS, MARRIAGES AND DEATHS

	Live births*		Marriages		Deaths*	
	Number	Rate (per 1,000)	Number	Rate (per 1,000)	Number	Rate (per 1,000)
1996	189,521	12.2	85,140	5.5	137,561	8.9
1997	192,443	12.3	85,059	5.4	135,783	8.7
1998	199,408	12.7	86,956	5.5	137,482	8.8
1999	200,445	12.7	89,428	5.7	140,487	8.9
2000	206,619	13.0	88,074	5.5	140,527	8.8
2001	202,603	12.6	82,091	5.0	140,270	8.7
2002	202,083	12.5	85,808	5.3	142,355	8.8
2003	200,689	12.4	n.a.	n.a.	141,082	8.7

* Including residents outside the country if listed in a Netherlands population register.

Expectation of life (years at birth): 78.6 (males 76.0; females 81.1) in 2002 (Source: WHO, *World Health Report*).

IMMIGRATION AND EMIGRATION

Immigrants from	2000	2001	2002
Belgium	5,755	5,599	5,357
France	3,513	3,179	3,084
Germany	8,438	8,227	7,959
Turkey	5,794	6,355	6,496
United Kingdom	7,817	7,893	6,805
Europe (unspecified)	27,154	26,214	22,804
Aruba and Netherlands Antilles	13,090	10,916	8,425
Suriname	3,435	3,416	3,356
USA	5,872	5,697	5,679
America (unspecified)	5,251	5,524	5,393
Afghanistan	4,248	4,069	2,418
Iraq	4,037	2,815	1,278
Asia (unspecified)	16,863	19,100	18,055
Morocco	4,445	5,199	5,123
Africa (unspecified)	13,824	15,933	16,255
Oceania	2,131	2,312	2,079
Total (incl. others)	132,850	133,404	121,250

Emigrants to	2000	2001	2002
Belgium	8,006	8,588	9,270
France	3,154	3,163	3,431
Germany	7,654	9,013	10,822
Spain	2,867	2,846	3,150
Turkey	1,177	949	883
United Kingdom	6,141	6,448	6,050
Europe (unspecified)	9,189	9,057	9,092
Aruba and Netherlands Antilles	3,656	4,125	4,974
Suriname	772	776	972
USA	5,356	4,990	4,672
America (unspecified)	2,836	2,653	2,810
Asia	5,419	5,352	5,540
Africa	3,018	3,327	3,067
Australia	1,458	1,466	1,408
Oceania (unspecified)	497	564	587
Total (incl. others)	61,200	63,317	66,728

ECONOMICALLY ACTIVE POPULATION
(sample surveys, '000 persons aged 15 to 64 years)

	2000	2001	2002
Agriculture, hunting, forestry and fishing	259	236	246
Mining and quarrying	6	4	7
Manufacturing	1,107	1,094	1,077
Electricity, gas and water supply	35	34	38
Construction	469	508	487
Wholesale and retail trade	1,275	1,247	1,252
Hotels and restaurants	286	290	315
Transport, storage and communications	474	480	454
Financial intermediation	277	298	279
Real estate, renting and business activities	950	947	973
Public administration and defence	493	545	561
Education	466	483	518
Health and social work	1,074	1,140	1,169
Other community, social and personal service activities	362	353	367
Private households with employed persons	4	3	5
Extra-territorial organizations and bodies	2	2	1
Activities not adequately defined	254	261	277
Total employed	7,793	7,925	8,026

Unemployed ('000 persons aged 15–64): 188 in 2000; 146 in 2001; 170 in 2002.

Total labour force ('000 persons aged 15–64): 7,732 in 2000 (males 4,410; females 3,322); 7,860 in 2001 (males 4,454; females 3,406); 7,941 in 2002 (males 4,477; females 3,464).

Health and Welfare

KEY INDICATORS

Total fertility rate (children per woman, 2002)	1.7
Under-5 mortality rate (per 1,000 live births, 2001)	5
HIV/AIDS (% of persons aged 15–49, 2001)	0.21
Physicians (per 1,000 head, 2000)	3.2
Hospital beds (per 1,000 head, 2000)	10.8
Health expenditure (2001): US $ per head (PPP)	2,612
Health expenditure (2001): % of GDP	8.9
Health expenditure (2001): public (% of total)	63.3
Access to water (% of persons, 2000)	100
Access to sanitation (% of persons, 2000)	100
Human Development Index (2001): ranking	5
Human Development Index (2001): value	0.938

For sources and definitions, see explanatory note on p. vi.

Agriculture

PRINCIPAL CROPS
('000 metric tons)

	2000	2001	2002
Wheat	1,143	991	1,057
Barley	287	387	315
Maize†	162	150	158
Rye	29	17	17
Triticale (wheat-rye hybrid)	36	21	24
Potatoes	8,127	7,015	7,363
Sugar beet	6,727	5,947	6,250
Cabbages	288	266	240
Lettuce	72	65	70*
Spinach	49	35	40*
Tomatoes	520	550	580*
Cauliflower	54	43	40
Cucumbers and gherkins	410	425	410*
Aubergines (Eggplants)	37	31	35*
Chillies and green peppers	285	285	290*
Dry onions	821*	765	883
Leeks and other alliaceous vegetables	95	100	102*
Green beans*	45	45	40
Green peas†	82	77	75
Carrots	385	378	375
Mushrooms	263	270	280
Other vegetables*	160	170	170
Apples	461*	390	333†
Pears	203	78*	175†
Strawberries	52	50*	52*
Flax fibre and tow	31	25	25

* FAO estimate(s).
† Unofficial figure(s).

Source: FAO.

LIVESTOCK
('000 head, year ending September)

	2000	2001	2002*
Horses and ponies	118	121	122
Cattle	4,070	4,047	4,050
Chickens	104,015	100,334	98,000
Sheep	1,308	1,296	1,300
Goats	179	221	215
Pigs	13,118	13,037	13,000

* FAO estimates.

Source: FAO.

LIVESTOCK PRODUCTS
('000 metric tons)

	2000	2001	2002
Beef and veal	471	364	464*
Mutton and lamb	18	18	22†
Pig meat	1,623	1,433	1,420
Chicken meat	697	701	701*
Turkey meat	43	42†	42†
Cows' milk	11,155	11,291	10,842
Cheese	690	662	642
Butter	126	130	118
Hen eggs	668	662	653*
Cattle hides (fresh)†	48	48	48

* Unofficial figure.
† FAO estimate(s).

Source: FAO.

Forestry

ROUNDWOOD REMOVALS
('000 cubic metres, excl. bark)

	2000	2001	2002
Sawlogs, veneer logs and logs for sleepers	572	497	398
Pulpwood	197	148	189
Other industrial wood	110	84	116
Fuel wood	160	136	136*
Total	1,039	865	839*

* FAO estimate.

Source: FAO.

SAWNWOOD PRODUCTION
('000 cubic metres, incl. railway sleepers)

	2000	2001	2002
Coniferous (softwood)	247	168	149
Broadleaved (hardwood)	143	100	104
Total	390	268	253

Source: FAO.

Fishing

('000 metric tons, live weight)

	1999	2000	2001
Capture	514.6	495.8	518.2
European plaice	37.5	35.1	33.8
Blue whiting	32.9	43.1	63.6
Atlantic horse mackerel	84.9	67.0	84.0
Atlantic herring	78.7	75.2	66.4
Sardinellas	115.8	112.8	134.5
Atlantic mackerel	27.8	32.4	33.1
Common edible cockle	50.9	19.6	—
Aquaculture	108.8	75.3	52.1
Blue mussel	100.8	66.8	43.6
Total catch	623.4	571.1	570.2

Note: Figures exclude aquatic plants and aquatic mammals. Aquatic mammals are recorded by number rather than by weight. The number of whales and porpoises caught was: 2 in 2000.

Source: FAO, *Yearbook of Fishery Statistics*.

Mining

	2000	2001	2002
Crude petroleum ('000 barrels)	17,633	18,000*	18,000
Natural gas (million cu metres)†	69,180	74,232	75,000
Salt ('000 metric tons)*	5,000	5,000	5,000

* Estimated production.

† Figures refer to gross volume of production. Marketed output (in million cu metres) was: 68,157 in 2000; 73,296 in 2001; 74,000 in 2002.

Source: US Geological Survey.

Industry

SELECTED PRODUCTS
('000 metric tons, unless otherwise indicated)*

	1998	1999	2000
Sand and quartz	14,843	13,555	8,333
Gravel and crushed stone	6,345	6,943	7,283
Margarine	310	404	404
Raw sugar	n.a.	1,217	1,153
Refined sugar	825	1,120	1,061
Cocoa powder (metric tons)	183,000	186,425	200,249
Cocoa butter (metric tons)	179,000	177,584	180,302
Prepared animal feeds	15,381	15,132	14,203
Beer ('000 hectolitres)	23,040	23,799	24,956
Mineral waters ('000 hectolitres)	1,330	1,300	1,521
Soft drinks ('000 hectolitres)	15,670	15,489	17,243
Cigars (million)	2,015	2,195	2,215
Veneer sheets ('000 cubic metres)†	17	19	19
Mechanical wood pulp†	129	117	137
Newsprint†	349	376	415
Other printing and writing paper†	875	892	930
Other paper and paperboard†	1,956	1,844	1,854
Packing containers of paper or paper board	1,420	1,279	1,162
Soda ash	400	350	350
Synthetic dyestuffs	26,393	25,354	24,916
Nitrogenous fertilizers(a)†	1,548	1,081	1,109
Phosphate fertilizers(b)†	343	355	53
Synthetic rubber	184	162	116
Washing powders and detergents	424	454	397
Jet fuels	6,340	6,967	7,111
Kerosene	189	195	376
Motor spirit (petrol) and other light oils	14,913	13,190	14,263
Naphthas	9,646	9,122	11,303
Gas-diesel (distillate fuel) oil	21,251	21,682	21,994
Residual fuel oils	14,448	11,145	11,215
Lubricating oils	624	614	647
Petroleum bitumen (asphalt)	474	710	740
Liquefied petroleum gas	3,652	3,871	3,683
Coke	2,837	2,327	2,127
Coke-oven gas (terajoules)	24,098	19,766	18,875
Clay building bricks ('000 cu metres)	1,662	1,863	1,507
Cement‡	3,200	2,480	2,450
Pig-iron	5,562	5,307	4,969
Crude steel	6,377	6,075	5,667
Aluminium (unwrought):			
primary	264	286	300
secondary	102	88	119
Refined lead: secondary‡	13	20	22
Zinc (unwrought): primary	217	221	217
Merchant vessels launched ('000 grt)	194	44	48
Internal combustion engines ('000)	n.a.	16	16
Bicycles ('000)	1,019	1,022	1,155
Electricity (million kWh)	90,903	91,242	92,110

2001 ('000 metric tons, unless otherwise indicated): Veneer sheets ('000 cubic metres) 18†; Mechanical wood pulp 130†; Newsprint 399†; Other printing and writing paper 846†; Other paper and paperboard 1,929†; Soda ash 400; Nitrogenous fertilizers (a) 1,013; Phosphate fertilizers (b) 174†; Cement 3,400; Pig-iron 5,305; Crude steel 6,000; Bicycles ('000) 1,042.

2002 ('000 metric tons, unless otherwise indicated): Veneer sheets ('000 cubic metres) 11†; Mechanical wood pulp 132†; Newsprint 357†; Other printing and writing paper 890†; Other paper and paperboard 2,099†.

* Official figures refer to activity by establishments employing 20 or more persons. For manufactured goods, except for cement, petroleum, coal and basic metal products, such data relate to sales (rather than production) by the relevant establishments.

† Output during 12 months ending 30 June of the year stated. Figures are in terms of (a) nitrogen or (b) phosphoric acid.

‡ Data from US Geological Survey.

Sources: partly UN, *Industrial Commodity Statistics Yearbook* and *Monthly Bulletin of Statistics*; FAO, *Yearbook of Forest Products*; IRF, *World Road Statistics*.

Finance

CURRENCY AND EXCHANGE RATES

Monetary Units
100 cent = 1 euro (€).

Sterling and Dollar Equivalents (31 December 2003)
£1 sterling = 1.4131 euros;
US $1 = 0.7918 euros;
100 euros = £70.77 = $126.30.

Average Exchange Rate (euros per US $)
2001   1.1175
2002   1.0626
2002   0.8860

Note: The national currency was formerly the guilder. From the introduction of the euro, with the Netherlands' participation, on 1 January 1999, a fixed exchange rate of €1 = 2.20371 guilders was in operation. Euro notes and coins were introduced on 1 January 2002. The euro and local currency circulated alongside each other until 28 January, after which the euro became the sole legal tender.

BUDGET
(million euros)

Revenue	2002	2003	2004
Taxation	110,900	111,700	106,300
Wage and income taxes	28,300	27,500	26,100
Company tax	19,100	18,100	15,900
Dividend tax	3,700	3,800	3,300
Inheritance tax	1,700	1,600	1,400
Gambling tax	200	200	200
VAT	35,000	36,200	35,500
Motor vehicle taxes	9,300	10,100	9,800
Excise duties	8,000	8,500	9,200
Environmental taxes	3,600	4,000	3,200
Import duties	1,800	1,500	1,500
Consumer tax	200	200	200
Other revenue	18,700	17,600	17,400
Total	**129,600**	**129,300**	**123,700**

Expenditure	2002	2003	2004
Education, culture and science	23,100	24,800	25,700
Social security and employment	19,500	20,600	22,700
General public services	13,300	14,200	13,300
Housing and community amenities	11,900	12,600	11,900
Public health, welfare and sport	8,300	9,500	11,100
Foreign affairs and development co-operation	10,400	9,900	9,400
Transport and public works	8,000	8,700	8,200
Defence	7,000	7,300	7,700
Home affairs	4,500	4,900	5,000
Justice	4,800	4,600	5,000
Finance	3,400	3,700	3,800
Housing, planning regulation and environmental management	3,400	3,500	3,500
Agriculture, nature and food quality	2,100	2,100	1,900
Economic affairs	1,800	1,700	1,600
Other	4,200	4,700	3,600
Total	**125,700**	**132,800**	**134,400**

General budget (million euros): *Revenue* 96,730 in 1999 (current 91,977; capital 4,754); 106,728 in 2000 (current 99,112; capital 7,617); 114,909 in 2001 (current 110,110; capital 4,799). *Expenditure* 99,608 in 1999 (current 92,127; capital 7,481); 105,164 in 2000 (current 96,217; capital 8,946); 115,383 in 2001 (current 105,298; capital 10,085) (Source: IMF, *Government Finance Statistics Yearbook*).

INTERNATIONAL RESERVES
(US $ million at 31 December)*

	2000	2001	2002
Gold†	7,993	7,863	9,385
IMF special drawing rights	653	759	697
Reserve position in IMF	1,988	2,352	2,849
Foreign exchange	7,004	5,930	6,017
Total	**17,638**	**16,904**	**18,948**

* Excluding deposits made with the European Monetary Institute (now the European Central Bank).
† Valued at market prices.
Source: IMF, *International Financial Statistics*.

MONEY SUPPLY
(million euros at 31 December)

	2000	2001	2002
Currency issued	18,730	11,394	19,357*
Demand deposits at banking institutions	131,893	150,975	152,526

* Currency put into circulation by De Nederlandsche Bank was 17,465 million euros.
Source: IMF, *International Financial Statistics*.

COST OF LIVING
(Consumer Price Index; base: 2000 = 100)

	2001	2002	2003
Food	107.0	110.5	111.7
Rent, fuel and light	105.0	108.5	112.5
Clothing (incl. footwear)	101.8	105.0	101.8
Health	102.9	105.5	107.5
Transport	102.7	104.8	107.6
Communications	99.1	101.3	103.5
Recreation and culture	103.2	105.1	105.6
All items (incl. others)	104.2	107.6	109.9

NATIONAL ACCOUNTS

National Income and Product
(million euros at current prices)

	2000	2001*	2002*
Compensation of employees	205,691	220,304	231,856
Operating surplus	90,262	92,530	92,511
Domestic factor incomes	**295,953**	**312,834**	**324,367**
Consumption of fixed capital	61,216	65,886	69,580
Gross domestic product (GDP) at factor cost	357,169	378,720	393,947
Indirect taxes	52,432	57,888	58,820
Less Subsidies	7,310	7,481	8,118
GDP in purchasers' values	**402,291**	**429,127**	**444,649**
Factor income received from abroad (net)	1,712	−3,881	−9,148
Gross national product (GNP)	**404,003**	**425,246**	**435,501**
Less Consumption of fixed capital	61,216	65,886	69,580
National income in market prices	342,787	359,360	365,921
Other current transfers abroad (net)	−3,251	−3,686	−4,275
National disposable income	**339,536**	**355,674**	**361,646**

* Figures are provisional.

Expenditure on the Gross Domestic Product
(million euros at current prices)

	2000	2001*	2002*
Government final consumption expenditure	291,930	313,391	330,755
Private final consumption expenditure			
Increase in stocks	389	226	–977
Gross fixed capital formation.	88,955	93,003	92,155
Total domestic expenditure	381,274	406,620	421,933
Exports of goods and services	271,432	280,273	278,429
Less Imports of goods and services	250,415	257,766	255,713
GDP in purchasers' values	402,291	429,127	444,649
GDP at constant 1995 prices	363,086	367,499	368,392

* Figures are provisional.

Gross Domestic Product by Economic Activity
(million euros at current prices)

	2000	2001*	2002*
Agriculture, hunting, forestry and fishing	10,010	10,338	9,712
Mining and quarrying	10,035	11,959	10,759
Manufacturing	64,088	64,887	64,931
Electricity, gas and water supply	7,280	8,300	9,276
Construction	21,342	23,265	24,305
Wholesale and retail trade; repair of motor vehicles, motorcycles and personal household goods	49,279	51,055	53,061
Hotels and restaurants	7,215	7,621	8,047
Transport, storage and communications	25,936	27,083	28,058
Financial and business activities	100,851	107,577	112,254
Public administration and social security	23,888	25,662	27,334
Defence	3,595	3,788	3,932
Education	14,356	15,526	16,627
Health and social work	26,940	30,123	34,093
Other community, social and personal service activities	12,955	14,033	14,921
Private households with employed persons	1,496	1,626	1,762
Sub-total	379,266	402,843	419,072
Taxes *less* subsidies on imports	7,219	7,560	7,177
Imputed VAT	28,517	32,671	33,776
Consumption of imputed bank services	–12,711	–13,947	–15,376
GDP in purchasers' values	402,291	429,127	444,649

* Figures are provisional.

BALANCE OF PAYMENTS
(million euros)

	2000	2001	2002
Exports of goods f.o.b.	221,947	228,356	223,800
Imports of goods f.o.b.	–202,828	205,088	–196,805
Trade balance	19,120	23,268	26,995
Exports of services	53,624	57,205	57,424
Imports of services	–55,839	–60,021	–58,812
Balance on goods and services	–2,214	–2,816	–1,387
Other income received	47,320	45,974	37,215
Other income paid	–48,922	–49,871	–46,507
Balance on goods, services and income	15,304	16,555	16,316
Current transfers received	4,755	4,991	5,294
Current transfers paid	–11,546	–12,528	–12,152
Current balance	8,512	9,018	9,457
Capital account (net)	566	–3,571	–614
Direct investment abroad	–79,820	–54,215	–28,632
Direct investment from abroad	65,464	57,266	30,921
Portfolio investment assets	–70,047	–68,203	–70,536
Portfolio investment liabilities	60,543	83,376	51,434
Financial derivatives assets	89,676	97,673	75,045
Financial derivatives liabilities	–94,306	–104,209	–81,851
Other investment assets	–31,266	–75,761	–43,853
Other investment liabilities	50,249	58,726	64,171
Net errors and omissions	737	–513	–5,688
Overall balance	–308	413	147

Source: De Nederlandsche Bank.

OFFICIAL ASSISTANCE TO DEVELOPING COUNTRIES
(million euros)

	1999	2000	2001*
Total	3,549	4,081	4,251

* Provisional figure.

External Trade

PRINCIPAL COMMODITIES
(distribution by SITC, million euros)

Imports c.i.f.	2001	2002	2003
Food and live animals	18,249	17,672	17,940
Crude materials (inedible) except fuels	8,458	7,874	7,940
Mineral fuels, lubricants, etc.	22,164	20,686	21,178
Petroleum, petroleum products, etc.	17,612	16,626	17,088
Crude petroleum	12,245	10,699	10,846
Chemicals and related products	24,785	25,018	24,611
Organic chemicals	6,850	6,176	6,238
Basic manufactures	26,497	25,037	24,329
Machinery and transport equipment	85,163	77,590	77,073
Office machines and automatic data-processing equipment	25,962	22,809	23,789
Telecommunications and sound equipment	11,555	8,558	8,419
Other electrical machinery, apparatus, etc.	16,886	17,225	15,559
Road vehicles (incl. air-cushion vehicles) and parts (excl. tyres, engines, and electrical parts)	15,046	14,295	13,583
Passenger motor vehicles (excl. buses)	8,252	7,767	7,091
Miscellaneous manufactured articles	28,912	27,390	27,326
Total (incl. others)	218,340	205,575	204,494

Exports f.o.b.	2001	2002	2003
Food and live animals	29,280	29,339	29,391
Vegetables and fruit	7,633	7,866	8,006
Crude materials (inedible) except fuels	11,614	12,115	12,566
Mineral fuels, lubricants, etc.	22,224	19,004	19,234
Petroleum, petroleum products, etc.	14,398	12,144	12,145
Chemicals and related products	36,915	38,332	38,832
Organic chemicals	9,904	9,922	9,269
Plastics in primary form	7,613	7,565	7,608
Basic manufactures	23,999	23,474	23,668
Machinery and transport equipment	83,153	76,171	74,911
Office machines and automatic data-processing equipment	28,918	25,966	24,446
Automatic data-processing machines	18,734	16,091	15,056
Telecommunications and sound equipment	9,562	6,321	6,445
Other electrical machinery, apparatus, etc.	17,343	16,528	16,443
Thermionic tubes, transistors etc.	8,312	8,115	8,191
Road vehicles (incl. air-cushion vehicles) and parts (excl. tyres, engines, and electrical parts)	11,002	11,157	10,449
Miscellaneous manufactured articles	26,570	25,752	25,766
Total (incl. others)*	241,339	232,704	232,422

* Including victuals and stores supplied to foreign ships and aircraft.

PRINCIPAL TRADING PARTNERS
(million euros)

Imports c.i.f.	2001	2002	2003
Belgium	20,177.8	22,593.7	23,025.7
Brazil	2,569.1	2,180.1	2,298.0
China, People's Republic	8,844.6	8,929.5	10,434.4
Denmark	2,148.6	2,115.3	2,047.3
France	12,617.0	11,838.3	11,244.1
Germany	40,253.0	39,932.1	40,819.2
Hong Kong	1,449.9	1,249.6	1,209.1
Ireland	3,808.9	3,690.7	3,877.7
Italy	6,173.0	6,250.8	5,895.3
Japan	8,696.3	6,400.7	6,477.7
Korea, Republic	2,146.9	2,865.4	1,916.6
Malaysia	3,696.9	3,683.0	3,579.0
Norway	4,504.1	3,735.4	3,832.0
Russia	3,463.5	3,784.4	4,448.4
Saudi Arabia	2,321.5	1,568.5	2,008.3
Singapore	3,386.0	3,380.3	2,806.5
Spain	4,741.6	4,389.3	4,357.0
Sweden	4,379.4	4,070.4	4,047.8
Switzerland	2,379.0	2,391.0	2,557.5
Taiwan	4,703.9	3,508.5	4,294.3
United Kingdom	19,458.2	16,476.3	14,760.7
USA	21,524.8	18,248.5	15,960.1
Total (incl. others)	218,329.6	205,574.9	204,494.0

Exports f.o.b.	2001	2002	2003
Austria	3,829.0	3,343.4	3,597.6
Belgium	28,502.4	27,481.9	27,623.6
Denmark	3,430.0	3,390.1	3,264.2
France	24,944.1	23,399.4	23,224.7
Germany	61,696.9	56,465.5	56,633.2
Italy	15,076.0	14,275.3	13,889.5
Japan	2,522.3	2,363.7	2,135.4
Poland	2,587.3	2,765.3	2,660.5
Spain	8,474.1	8,249.1	8,642.8
Sweden	4,953.1	4,464.4	4,579.1
Switzerland	3,910.6	3,869.0	3,779.4
United Kingdom	26,884.3	25,525.5	23,880.2
USA	10,559.6	11,396.0	11,264.5
Total (incl. others)	241,339.0	232,703.7	232,421.6

Transport

RAILWAYS
(traffic)

	1996	1997	1998
Passenger-km (million)	14,131	14,485	14,879
Freight ton-km (million)	3,123	3,406	3,778

ROAD TRAFFIC
('000 motor vehicles in use at 1 August)

	1998	1999	2000
Passenger cars	5,931	6,120	6,343
Buses and coaches	11	11	11
Lorries and vans	648	710	779
Road tractors	49	53	57
Motorcycles	373	392	414
Mopeds	524	n.a.	n.a.

SHIPPING

Inland Waterways
(transport fleet at 1 January)

	1997	1998	1999
Number of vessels	5,067	5,003	4,577
Carrying capacity ('000 metric tons)	5,859	5,589	5,212

Inland Waterways
(freight traffic, million metric tons)

	1996	1997	1998
Internal transport: Commercial	61.2	75.7	79.3
Internal transport: Private	28.2	20.9	19.3
International transport	201.1	224.5	219.7

Merchant Fleet
(at 31 December)

	2000	2001	2002
Number of vessels	1,317	1,337	1,316
Displacement ('000 gross registered tons)	5,167.7	5,605.0	5,664.3

Source: Lloyd's Register-Fairplay, *World Fleet Statistics.*

Sea-borne Freight Traffic
('000 metric tons)

	1997	1998	1999
Goods loaded	88,667	85,137	92,000
Goods unloaded	312,864	319,684	305,000

CIVIL AVIATION*
(Netherlands scheduled air services—million)

	1994/95	1995/96	1996/97
Kilometres flown	259	283	304
Passenger-kilometres	41,767	45,531	50,350
Total ton-kilometres	7,362	8,108	8,630

* Figures refer to KLM operations only. Years from 1 April to 31 March.

Tourism

FOREIGN TOURIST ARRIVALS
('000)*

Country of origin	1999	2000	2001
Belgium	647	677	629
France	472	512	455
Germany	3,046	2,884	2,657
Italy	350	374	343
Spain	229	250	259
United Kingdom	1,726	1,838	1,939
Total (incl. others)	9,881	10,003	9,500

* Arrivals at all accommodation establishments.

Source: World Tourism Organization, *Yearbook of Tourism Statistics*.

Tourism receipts (US $ million): 6,996 in 1999; 7,217 in 2000; 6,722 in 2001 (Source: World Tourism Organization).

Communications Media

	2000	2001	2002
Television receivers ('000 in use)	8,600	n.a.	n.a.
Telephone ('000 main lines in use)	9,879	10,003	10,003
Mobile cellular telephones ('000 subscribers)	10,710	11,900	11,700
Personal computers ('000 in use)	6,300	6,900	6,900
Internet users ('000)	3,900	5,300	8,590

1996: Daily newspapers: number 38; average circulation ('000 copies) 4,753; Non-daily newspapers: number 63; average circulation ('000 copies) 590.

1997: Radio receivers ('000 in use) 15,300; Facsimile machines ('000 in use) 600.

Book production (1993): 34,067 titles, excluding pamphlets.

Sources: UNESCO, *Statistical Yearbook*; UN, *Statistical Yearbook*; International Telecommunication Union.

Education

(2000/01—Full-time)

	Institutions	Students ('000)
Primary	7,721	1,664.0
Secondary	834	894.2
Adult and vocational	62	446.9
Higher professional	56	306.6
University	12	164.7

Source: Ministry of Education, Culture and Science.

Directory

The Constitution

The Netherlands' first Constitution was adopted in 1814–15. The present Constitution, the first new one since 1848, came into force on 17 February 1983. Its main provisions are summarized below:

THE KINGDOM OF THE NETHERLANDS

The Kingdom of the Netherlands consists of territories in Europe (the Netherlands) and in the Caribbean (the Netherlands Antilles and Aruba). Under the Charter for the Kingdom of the Netherlands, signed by Queen Juliana in 1954, these territories constitute a single realm, ruled by the House of Orange-Nassau.

THE MONARCHY

The Netherlands is a constitutional monarchy with a parliamentary system of government. The Constitution regulates the royal succession and the regency in great detail. A successor to the Throne may be appointed by Act of Parliament if it appears that there will otherwise be no successor. The Bill for this purpose shall be discussed and decided upon in a joint session of the two Chambers of the States-General (Staten Generaal). The Sovereign is succeeded by his or her eldest child. The age of majority of the Sovereign is 18 years. Until the Sovereign has attained that age, the royal prerogative shall be exercised by a Regent.

ELECTORAL SYSTEM

The Parliament of the Netherlands is the Staten Generaal and is composed of two Chambers, a First and a Second Chamber. The Second Chamber, which is the more important politically, consists of 150 members, and is directly elected for four years on the basis of proportional representation. The First Chamber comprises 75 members and is elected by the (directly-elected) members of the Provincial Councils.

Nearly all Dutch nationals who have attained the age of 18 years are entitled to take part in the election for the Second Chamber. Those not entitled to vote are certain groups of non-resident nationals, mentally disordered and legally incompetent persons.

To be eligible for membership of the Staten Generaal, a person must be a Dutch national, must have attained the age of 18 years and must not have been disqualified from voting.

MINISTERIAL RESPONSIBILITY

The Ministers, led by the Prime Minister, are responsible to the Staten Generaal for all acts of government. This means, for example, that the power of the Government (Sovereign and Ministers) to dissolve one or both Chambers of the Staten Generaal is ultimately subject to the judgment of the Staten Generaal. The right to declare war and conclude treaties can, in principle, only be exercised subject to prior parliamentary approval. The Constitution contains provisions concerning the transferral of legislative, executive and judicial power to international institutions and on the legal supremacy of self-executing provisions of treaties.

The Prime Minister and the other Ministers are appointed and dismissed by Royal Decree. Ministries are established by Royal Decree.

A Council of Ministers is formed by a so-called 'formateur' (usually the future Prime Minister), who will have been assured of the support of a majority in the Second Chamber of the Staten Generaal.

A Minister may not be a member of the Staten Generaal. However, Ministers have the right to attend sittings of the Chambers and may take part in the deliberations. They must supply the Chambers, either orally or in writing, with any information requested, provided that this cannot be deemed to conflict with the interests of the State.

A statement of the policy that is to be pursued by the Government is given by the Sovereign every year on the third Tuesday in September before a joint session of the two Chambers of the Staten Generaal.

Acts of Parliament are passed jointly by the Government and the Staten Generaal. Bills, including the draft budget, must be introduced into the Second Chamber. The Second Chamber has the right to amend bills; the First Chamber can only accept or reject a bill. Revision of the Constitution requires two parliamentary readings of the bills that contain the proposed changes. In between the two readings, the Staten Generaal must be dissolved and elections held.

THE COUNCIL OF STATE

The Council of State is the Government's oldest and most important advisory body. It must be consulted on all bills and draft general administrative orders. The Council is also an important court for administrative disputes.

The Sovereign is President of the Council of State, but the day-to-day running of the Council is the responsibility of its Vice-President.

Its other members—usually former politicians, scholars, judges and business executives—are appointed for life.

LOCAL GOVERNMENT

The Netherlands is divided into 12 provinces. Provinces may be dissolved and established by Act of Parliament. The provincial administrative organs are the Provincial Council, the Provincial Executive and the Sovereign's Commissioner. The Provincial Council—directly elected, as is the Second Chamber, on the basis of proportional representation—forms the provincial equivalent of the Parliament. Each Provincial Council elects, from among its members, a Provincial Executive.

The Sovereign's Commissioner is appointed and dismissed by Royal Decree. Each Commissioner presides over both the Provincial Council and the Provincial Executive. The provincial administrative organs have the constitutionally guaranteed power to regulate and administer their own internal affairs. They may also be required by, or pursuant to, Act of Parliament to provide regulation and administration. At present there are 636 municipalities in the Netherlands. The municipal administrative organs are the Municipal Council (directly elected by the local inhabitants), the Municipal Executive (chosen by the Council from among its members) and the Burgomaster (appointed and dismissed by Royal Decree). The Burgomaster (Mayor) presides over both the Municipal Council and the Municipal Executive. The Municipal Council has the power to make local regulations.

The Government

HEAD OF STATE

Queen of the Netherlands: HM Queen BEATRIX WILHELMINA ARMGARD (succeeded to the throne 30 April 1980).

COUNCIL OF MINISTERS
(April 2004)

A coalition comprising the Christen-Democratisch Appèl (CDA, Christian Democratic Appeal), the Volkspartij voor Vrijheid en Democratie (VVD, People's Party for Freedom and Democracy) and the Democraten 66 (D66).

Prime Minister, Minister of General Affairs: Dr JAN PIETER (JAN PETER) BALKENENDE (CDA).

Deputy Prime Minister, Minister of Finance: GERRIT ZALM (VVD).

Deputy Prime Minister, Minister of Government Reform and Kingdom Relations: THOMAS CAROLUS (THOM) DE GRAAF (D66).

Minister of Foreign Affairs: Dr BERNARD RUDOLF (BEN) BOT (CDA).

Minister of the Interior and Kingdom Relations: JOHANNES WIJNANDUS (JOHAN) REMKES (VVD).

Minister of Defence: HENRICUS GREGORIUS JOZEPH (HENK) KAMP (VVD).

Minister of Economic Affairs: LAURENS JANS BRINKHORST (D66).

Minister of Immigration and Integration: MARIA CORNELIA FREDERIKA (RITA) VERDONK (VVD).

Minister of Justice: JAN PIET HEIN (PIET HEIN) DONNER (CDA).

Minister of Agriculture, Nature Management and Fisheries: Dr CORNELIS PIETER (CEES) VEERMAN (CDA).

Minister of Education, Culture and Science: MARIA JOSEPHINA ARNOLDINA VAN DER HOEVEN (CDA).

Minister of Social Affairs and Employment: AART JAN DE GEUS (CDA).

Minister of Public Health, Welfare and Sport: JOHANNES FRANCISCUS (HANS) HOOGERVORST (VVD).

Minister of Housing, Spatial Planning and the Environment: SYBILLA MARIA DEKKER (VVD).

Minister of Development Co-operation: ANNA MARIA AGNES (AGNES) VAN ARDENNE (CDA).

Minister of Transport, Public Works and Water Management: KARLA MARIA HENRIËTTE PEIJS (CDA).

Minister Plenipotentiary for the Netherlands Antilles: CAREL P. DE HASETH.

Minister Plenipotentiary for Aruba: ALICIA A. TROMP-YARZAGARAY.

There are, in addition, 10 Secretaries of State.

MINISTRIES

Office of the Prime Minister, Ministry of General Affairs: Binnenhof 20, POB 20001, 2500 EA The Hague; tel. (70) 3564100; fax (70) 3564683; internet www.minaz.nl.

Ministry of Agriculture, Nature Management and Fisheries: Bezuidenhoutseweg 73, POB 20401, 2500 EK The Hague; tel. (70) 3786868; fax (70) 3786100; internet www.minlnv.nl.

Ministry of Defence: Plein 4, POB 20701, 2500 ES The Hague; tel. (70) 3188188; fax (70) 3187888; e-mail defensie.voorlichting@co.dnet.mindef.nl; internet www.mindef.nl.

Ministry of Economic Affairs: Bezuidenhoutseweg 30, POB 20101, 2594 AV The Hague; tel. (70) 3081986; fax (70) 3474081; e-mail ezinfo@postbus51.nl; internet www.ez.nl.

Ministry of Education, Culture and Science: Europaweg 4, POB 25000, 2700 LZ Zoetermeer; tel. (79) 3232323; fax (79) 3232320; e-mail info@minocw.nl; internet www.minocw.nl.

Ministry of Finance: Korte Voorhout 7, POB 20201, 2500 EE The Hague; tel. (70) 3427540; fax (70) 3427900; internet www.minfin.nl.

Ministry of Foreign Affairs: Bezuidenhoutseweg 67, POB 20061, 2500 EB The Hague; tel. (70) 3486486; fax (70) 3484848; e-mail minbuza@buza.minbuza.nl; internet www.minbuza.nl.

Ministry of Housing, Spatial Planning and the Environment: Rijnstraat 8, POB 20951, 2500 EZ, The Hague; tel. (70) 3393939; internet www.minvrom.nl.

Ministry of Immigration and Integration: operates under Ministry of Justice (see below).

Ministry of the Interior and Kingdom Relations: Schedelhoekshaven 200, POB 20011, 2500 EA The Hague; tel. (70) 4266426; fax (70) 3639153; e-mail info@minbzk.nl; internet www.minbzk.nl.

Ministry of Justice: Schedelhoekshaven 100, POB 20301, 2500 EH The Hague; tel. (70) 3707911; fax (70) 3707900; e-mail voorlichting@minjus.nl; internet www.justitie.nl.

Ministry of Public Health, Welfare and Sport: Parnassusplein 5, POB 20350, 2500 EJ The Hague; tel. (70) 3407911; fax (70) 3407834; internet www.minvws.nl.

Ministry of Social Affairs and Employment: Anna van Hannoverstraat 4, POB 90801, 2509 LV The Hague; tel. (70) 3334444; fax (70) 3334033; internet www.szw.nl.

Ministry of Transport, Public Works and Water Management: Plesmanweg 1, POB 20901, 2500 EX The Hague; tel. (70) 3516171; fax (70) 3517895; internet www.minvenw.nl.

Office of the Minister Plenipotentiary for the Netherlands Antilles: Badhuisweg 173–175, POB 90706, 2509 LS The Hague; tel. (70) 3066111; fax (70) 3066110.

Office of the Minister Plenipotentiary for Aruba: R. J. Schimmelpenninncklaan 1, 2517 JN The Hague; tel. (70) 3566200; fax (70) 3451446; e-mail mail@arubahuis.nl; internet www.arubahuis.nl.

Legislature

STATEN GENERAAL
(States-General)

President of the First Chamber: YVONNE TIMMERMAN.

President of the Second Chamber: FRANS W. WEISGLAS.

First Chamber

Election, 25 May 2003

	Seats
Christen-Democratisch Appèl	23
Partij van de Arbeid	19
Volkspartij voor Vrijheid en Democratie	15
GroenLinks	5
Socialistische Partij	4
Democraten 66	3
Christen Unie	2
Staatkundig Gereformeerde Partij	2
Lijst Pim Fortuyn	1
Independent	1
Total	**75**

Second Chamber

General Election, 22 January 2003

	Votes	%	Seats
Christen-Democratisch Appèl	2,763,480	28.6	44
Partij van de Arbeid	2,631,363	27.3	42
Volkspartij voor Vrijheid en Democratie	1,728,707	17.9	28
Socialistische Partij	609,723	6.3	9
Lijst Pim Fortuyn	549,975	5.7	8
GroenLinks	493,802	5.1	8
Democraten 66	393,333	4.1	6
Christen Unie	240,694	2.1	3
Staatkundig Gereformeerde Partij	150,305	1.6	2
Total (incl. others)	**9,654,475**	**100.0**	**150**

Advisory Councils

Raad van State (Council of State): POB 20019, 2500 EA The Hague; tel. (70) 4264426; fax (70) 3651380; internet www.raadvanstate.nl; up to 28 mems nominated by the Sovereign; advises on legislation, constitutional issues, international treaties and all matters of national importance; Vice-Pres. H. D. TJEENK WILLINK.

Sociaal-Economische Raad (Social and Economic Council): Bezuidenhoutseweg 60, 2594 AW The Hague; POB 90405, 2509 LK The Hague; tel. (70) 3499499; fax (70) 3832535; e-mail ser.info@ser.nl; internet www.ser.nl; f. 1950; tripartite advisory body; to advise Govt on social and economic policy; monitors commodity and industrial boards; 33 mems, of which 11 belong to the Netherlands trade union federations, 11 belong to the employers' organizations, and 11 are independent experts in social and economic affairs appointed by the Crown; Pres. H. H. F. WIJFFELS.

Political Organizations

Centrumdemocraten (CD) (Centre Democrats): POB 84, 2501 CB The Hague; tel. (70) 3469264; internet www.xs4all.nl/centrumd/index.html; right-wing nationalist party; Chair. JOHANNES JANMAAT; Sec. W. B. SCHUURMAN; 1,500 mems.

Christen-Democratisch Appèl (CDA) (Christian Democratic Appeal): Dr Kuyperstraat 5, POB 30453, 2500 GL The Hague; tel. (70) 3424888; fax (70) 3643417; e-mail bureau@cda.nl; internet www.cda.nl; f. 1980 by merger of three 'confessional' parties; Chair. M. L. A. VAN RIJ; Parliamentary Leader JAN PIETER (JAN PETER) BALKENENDE; 80,000 mems.

Christen Unie (Christian Union): POB 439, 3800 AK Amersfoort; tel. (33) 4226969; fax (33) 4226968; e-mail bureau@christenunie.nl; internet www.christenunie.nl; f. 2000 by merger of two 'evangelical' parties, the Gereformeerd Politiek Verbond (Reformed Political Asscn) and the Reformatorische Politieke Federatie (Evangelical Political Federation); interdenominational, based on biblical precepts; Chair. M. VAN DAALEN; Parliamentary Leader A. ROUVOET; c. 25,000 mems (2004).

Democraten 66 (D66): Noordwal 10, 2513 EA The Hague; tel. (70) 3566066; fax (70) 3641917; e-mail landelijk.secretariaat@D66.nl; internet www.D66.nl; f. 1966; Chair. ARNOLD PECHTOLD; Leader BORIS DITTRICH; 12,500 mems.

Fryske Nasjonale Partij (FNP) (Frisian National Party): FNPhûs, Obrechtstrjitte 32, 8916 EN Ljouwert; tel. (58) 2131422; fax (58) 2131420; e-mail fnphus@globalxs.nl; internet www.fnp.nl; f. 1962; promotes federalism and greater regional autonomy; Leader JOHANNES KRAMER.

GroenLinks (The Green Left): POB 8008, 3503 RA Utrecht; tel. (30) 2399900; fax (30) 2300342; e-mail info@groenlinks.nl; internet www.groenlinks.nl; f. 1990 by merger of the Communistische Partij van Nederland, Evangelische Volkspartij, Pacifistisch Socialistische Partij and Politieke Partij Radikalen; Chair. HERMAN MEŸER; Parliamentary Leader FEMKE HALSEMA; 20,500 mems (Jan. 2004).

De Groenen (Green Party): POB 1251, 3500 BG Utrecht; tel. (40) 2043413; e-mail info@degroenen.nl; internet www.degroenen.nl; f. 1983; Chair. AART VAN ACQUOIJ; Sec. FRANK PLATE.

Leefbaar Nederland (LN) (Liveable Netherlands): POB 18581, 2502 The Hague; tel. 09001419; fax (35) 6721300; e-mail info@leefbaar.nl; internet www.leefbaar-nederland.nl.

Lijst Pim Fortuyn (LPF): Albert Plesmanweg 43 M, 3088 GB Rotterdam; tel. (10) 7507050; fax (10) 7507051; e-mail info@

lijst-pimfortuyn.nl; internet www.lijst-pimfortuyn.nl; f. 2002; right-wing, populist, anti-immigration; Leader MAT HERBEN.

Nieuwe Communistische Partij Nederland (NCPN) (New Communist Party of the Netherlands): Haarlemmerweg 177, 1051 LB Amsterdam; tel. (20) 6825019; fax (20) 6828276; e-mail manifest@wanadoo.nl; internet www.ncpn.nl; f. 1992.

Nieuwe Midden Partij (NMP) (New Centre Party): POB 285, 1250 AG Laren; tel. (30) 2729487; e-mail info@nmp.nl; internet www.sdnl.nl/nmp; f. 1970; campaigns on economic issues; Leader MARTIN DESSING.

Partij van de Arbeid (PvdA) (Labour Party): Herengracht 54, POB 1310, 1000 BH Amsterdam; tel. (20) 5512155; fax (20) 5512250; e-mail pvda@pvda.nl; internet www.pvda.nl; f. 1946 by merger of progressive and liberal organizations; democratic socialist; Chair. RUUD KOOLE; Party Leader AD MELKERT; Parliamentary Leader WOUTER BOS; 58,527 mems (August 2002).

Socialistiese Arbeiderspartij (SAP) (Socialist Workers' Party): Sint Jacobsstraat 16, 1012 NC Amsterdam; tel. (20) 6259272; fax (20) 6203774; e-mail redactie@grenzloos.nl; internet www.grenzeloos.org; f. 1974; Trotskyist.

Socialistische Partij (SP) (Socialist Party): Vijverhofstraat 65, 3032 SC Rotterdam; tel. (10) 2435555; fax (10) 2435566; e-mail sp@sp.nl; internet www.sp.nl; f. 1972; Leader JAN MARIJNISSEN; 43,538 mems (Jan. 2004).

Staatkundig Gereformeerde Partij (SGP) (Reformed Political Party): Laan van Meerdervoort 165, 2517 AZ The Hague; tel. (70) 3029060; fax (70) 3655959; e-mail partijbureau@sgp.nl; internet www.sgp.nl; f. 1918; Calvinist; female membership banned in 1996; Chair. Rev. A. VON HETEREN; Parliamentary Leader BAS J. VAN DER VLIES; Sec. P. A. ZEVENBERGEN; 25,600 mems (2003).

Verenigde Senioren Partij (VSP) (Union Party of the Elderly): POB 26, 3100 AA Schiedam; tel. and fax (10) 4262533; internet www.vsp2001.nl; Chair. J. P. M. BOS.

Volkspartij voor Vrijheid en Democratie (VVD) (People's Party for Freedom and Democracy—Netherlands Liberal Party): POB 30836, 2500 GV The Hague; tel. (70) 3613061; fax (70) 3608276; e-mail alg.sec@vvd.nl; internet www.vvd.nl; f. 1948; advocates free enterprise, individual freedom and responsibility, but its programme also supports social security and recommends the participation of workers in profits and management; Chair. BAS EENHOORN; Parliamentary Leader GERRIT ZALM; 48,000 mems.

Diplomatic Representation

EMBASSIES IN THE NETHERLANDS

Albania: Anna Paulownastraat 109 B, 2518 BD The Hague; tel. (70) 4272101; fax (70) 4272083; e-mail embalba@xs4all.nl; Ambassador QIRJAKO QIRKO.

Algeria: Van Stolklaan 1–3, 2585 JS The Hague; tel. (70) 3522954; fax (70) 3540222; Ambassador NOUREDDINE DJOUDI.

Argentina: Javastraat 20, 2585 AN The Hague; tel. (70) 3654836; fax (70) 3924900; e-mail fepbaj@mrecic.gov.ar; internet www.embassyargentina.nl; Ambassador JOSÉ MARÍA BERRO MADERO.

Australia: Carnegielaan 4, 2517 KH The Hague; tel. (70) 3108200; fax (70) 3107863; internet www.australian-embassy.nl; Ambassador STEPHEN BRADY.

Austria: van Alkemadelaan 342, 2597 AS The Hague; tel. (70) 3245470; fax (70) 3282066; e-mail den-haag-ob@bmaa.gv.at; Ambassador Dr ERWIN KUBESCH.

Bangladesh: Wassenaarseweg 39, 2596 CG The Hague; tel. (70) 3283722; fax (70) 3283524; e-mail amb.vanbangladesg@wanadoo.com; Ambassador LIAQUAT ALI CHOUDHURY.

Belarus: Anna Paulownastraat 34, 2518 BE The Hague; tel. (70) 3631566; fax (70) 3640555; Ambassador VLADIMIR GERASIMOVICH.

Belgium: Alexanderveld 97, 2585 DB The Hague; tel. (70) 3123456; fax (70) 3645579; e-mail thehague@diplobel.org; Ambassador LUC TOIRLINCK.

Bolivia: Nassaulaan 5, 2514 JS The Hague; tel. (70) 3616707; fax (70) 3620039; e-mail embolned@xs4all.nl; internet www.europanas.com/Bolivia-Pbajos-en.htm; Ambassador ESTHER ASHTON.

Bosnia and Herzegovina: Bezuidenhoutseweg 223, 2495 AL The Hague; tel. (70) 3588505; fax (70) 3584367; e-mail ba-emb-nl-hag@wanadoo.nl; internet www.xs4all.nl/~bih; Chargé d'affaires a.i. ZELJKO JERKIĆ.

Brazil: Mauritskade 19, 2514 HD The Hague; tel. (70) 3023959; fax (70) 3561273; e-mail basemb@dataweb.nl; Ambassador GILBERTO VERGNE SABOIA.

Bulgaria: Duinroosweg 9, 2597 KJ The Hague; tel. (70) 3503051; fax (70) 3584688; e-mail bulnedem@xs4all.nl; internet www .embassy-bulgaria.nl; Ambassador VALENTIN PORIAZOV.

Cameroon: Amaliastraat 14, 2514 JC The Hague; tel. (70) 3469715; fax (70) 3652979; internet www.cameroon-embassy.nl; Ambassador ISABELLE BASSONG.

Canada: Sophialaan 7, POB 30820, 2500 GV The Hague; tel. (70) 3111600; fax (70) 3111620; internet www.canada.nl; Ambassador SERGE APRIL.

Cape Verde: Burgemeester Patijnlaan 1930, 2585 CB The Hague; tel. (70) 3469623; fax (70) 3467702; e-mail embcuned@worldonline .nl; Ambassador JÚLIO VASCO DE SOUSA LOBO.

Chile: Mauritskade 51, 2514 HG The Hague; tel. (70) 3123640; fax (70) 3616227; e-mail echilenl@echile.nl; internet www.echile.nl; Ambassador CRISTIÁN DE JESÚS TOLOZA CASTILLO.

China, People's Republic: Adriaan Goekooplaan 7, 2517 JX The Hague; tel. (70) 3065061; fax (70) 3551651; Ambassador XUE HAN-QUIN.

Colombia: Groot Hertoginnelaan 14, 2517 EG The Hague; tel. (70) 3614545; fax (70) 3614636; Ambassador GUILLERMO FERNÁNDEZ DE SOTO.

Congo, Democratic Republic: Violenweg 2, 2597 KL The Hague; tel. (70) 3547904; fax (70) 3541373; Ambassador JACQUES MASANGU-A-MWANZA.

Costa Rica: Laan Copes van Cattenburg 46, 2585 GB The Hague; tel. (70) 3540780; fax (70) 3584754; e-mail embajada@embacrica .demon.nl; internet www.ambassade-costarica.nl; Ambassador EDGAR UGALDI ALVAREZ.

Croatia: Amaliastraat 16, 2514 JC The Hague; tel. (70) 3632942; fax (70) 3927823; e-mail croemb.haag@mvp.hr; Ambassador FRANE KRNIĆ.

Cuba: Scheveningseweg 9, 2517 KS The Hague; tel. (70) 3606061; fax (70) 3647586; e-mail embacuba@xs4all.nl; internet www .embacuba.nl; Ambassador ELIO EDUARDO RODRÍGUEZ PERDOMO.

Cyprus: Surinamestraat 15, 2585 GG The Hague; tel. (70) 3466499; fax (70) 3924024; e-mail cyprus@xs4all.nl; Ambassador IOANNA MALLIOTIS.

Czech Republic: Paleisstraat 4, 2514 JA The Hague; tel. (70) 3469712; fax (70) 3563349; e-mail hague@embassy.mzv.cz; internet www.mfa.cz/hague; Ambassador PETR KUBERNÁT.

Denmark: Koninginnegracht 30, 2514 AB The Hague; tel. (70) 3025959; fax (70) 3025950; e-mail info@danishembassy.nl; internet www.danishembassy.nl; Ambassador JOHN BERNHARD.

Ecuador: Koninginnegracht 84, 2514 AJ The Hague; tel. (70) 3463753; fax (70) 3658910; e-mail embecua@bart.nl; Ambassador (vacant).

Egypt: Badhuisweg 92, 2587 CL The Hague; tel. (70) 3542000; fax (70) 3543304; Ambassador MUHAMMAD NAGUIB.

Estonia: Parkstraat 15, 2514 JD The Hague; tel. (70) 3029050; fax (70) 3029057; e-mail embassy.haag@mfa.ee; Ambassador PRIIT PALLUM.

Finland: Groot Hertoginnelaan 16, 2517 EG The Hague; tel. (70) 3469754; fax (70) 3107174; Ambassador PEKKA SÄILÄ.

France: Smidsplein 1, 2514 BT The Hague; tel. (70) 3125800; fax (70) 3125824; e-mail info@ambafrance-nl.org; internet www .ambafrance-nl.org; Ambassador ANNE GAZEAU-SECRET.

Germany: Groot Hertoginnelaan 18–20, 2517 EG The Hague; tel. (70) 3420600; fax (70) 3651957; e-mail ambduits@euronet.nl; internet www.duitse-ambassade.nl; Ambassador Dr EDMUND DUCK-WITZ.

Ghana: Laan Copes van Cattenburch 70, 2585 GD The Hague; tel. (70) 3384384; fax (70) 3062800; e-mail info@ghanaembassy.nl; internet www.ghanaembassy.nl; Ambassador Dr GRACE AMPONSAH-ABABIO.

Greece: Amaliastraat 1, 2514 JC The Hague; tel. (70) 3638700; fax (70) 3563040; e-mail gr.emb.hague@dataweb.nl; Ambassador G. J. KAKLIKIS.

Holy See: Carnegielaan 5 (Apostolic Nunciature), 2517 KH The Hague; tel. (70) 3503363; fax (70) 3521461; Apostolic Nuncio Most Rev. FRANÇOIS BACQUÉ (Titular Archbishop of Gradisca).

Hungary: Hogeweg 14, 2585 JD The Hague; tel. (70) 3500404; fax (70) 3521749; e-mail hga@hungarianembassy.nl; internet www .hungarianembassy.nl; Ambassador TIBOR KISS.

India: Buitenrustweg 2, 2517 KD The Hague; tel. (70) 3469771; fax (70) 3617072; e-mail ambassador@indianembassy.nl; internet www .indianembassy.nl; Ambassador SHYAMALA B. COWSIK.

Indonesia: Tobias Asserlaan 8, 2517 KC The Hague; tel. (70) 3108100; fax (70) 3643331; internet www.indonesia.nl; Ambassador MUHAMMAD JUSUF.

Iran: Duinweg 20–22, 2585 JX The Hague; tel. (70) 3548483; fax (70) 3503224; e-mail consulate@iranianembassy.nl; internet www .iranianembassy.nl; Ambassador HOSSEIN PANAHI AZAR.

Iraq: Johan de Wittlaan 16, 2517 JR The Hague; tel. (70) 3469683; Chargé d'affaires a.i. BALKISS M. AL-MAHDAWY.

Ireland: Dr Kuyperstraat 9, 2514 BA The Hague; tel. (70) 3630993; fax (70) 3617604; e-mail info@irishembassy.nl; internet www .irishembassy.nl; Ambassador RICHARD TOWNSEND.

Israel: Buitenhof 47, 2513 AH The Hague; tel. (70) 3760500; fax (70) 3760555; e-mail ambassade@israel.nl; internet www.israel.nl; Ambassador EITAN MARGALIT.

Italy: Alexanderstraat 12, 2514 JL The Hague; tel. (70) 3021030; fax (70) 3614932; e-mail italemb@worldonline.nl; internet www.italy.nl; Ambassador MARIO BRANDO PENSA.

Japan: Tobias Asserlaan 2, 2517 KC The Hague; tel. (70) 3469544; fax (70) 3106341; Ambassador HIROHARU KOIKE.

Jordan: Badhuisweg 79, 2587 CD The Hague; tel. (70) 4167200; fax (70) 4167209; e-mail jordanembassy@wanadoo.nl; internet www .jordanembassy.nl; Ambassador MAZEN M. ARMOUTI.

Kenya: Nieuwe Parklaan 21, 2597 LA The Hague; tel. (70) 3504215; fax (70) 3553594; e-mail kenre@dataweb.nl; Ambassador LEONARD NJOGU NGAITHE.

Korea, Republic: Velengde Tolweg 8, 2517 JV The Hague; tel. (70) 3586076; fax (70) 3504712; Ambassador KEUN SEOP OHM.

Kuwait: Carnegielaan 9, 2517 KH The Hague; tel. (70) 3603813; fax (70) 3924588; internet www.kuwaitembassy.nl; Ambassador ALI KHALED J. AL-SABAH.

Latvia: Balistraat 88, 2585 XX The Hague; tel. (70) 3063934; fax (70) 3062858; e-mail embassy.netherlands@mfa.gov.nl; Ambassador BAIBA LAIZANE.

Lebanon: Frederikstraat 2, 2514 LK The Hague; tel. (70) 3658906; fax (70) 3620779; e-mail amb.lib@wanadoo.nl; Ambassador MICHEL EL-KHOURY.

Libya: 15 Parkweg, 2585 JH The Hague; tel. (70) 355886; fax (70) 3559075; Sec. of the People's Bureau HAMED ELHOUDERI.

Luxembourg: Nassaulaan 8, 2514 JS The Hague; tel. (70) 3647589; fax (70) 3462000; Ambassador JEAN GRAFF.

Macedonia, former Yugoslav republic: Laan van Meerdervoort 50c, 2517 AM The Hague; tel. (70) 4274464; fax (70) 4274469; e-mail repmak@wanadoo.nl; Ambassador MILIJANA DANEVSKA.

Malaysia: Rustenburgweg 2, 2517 KE The Hague; tel. (70) 3506506; fax (70) 3506536; e-mail malaysia@euronet.nl; Ambassador NOOR FARIDA BINTI MOHD ARIFFIN.

Mexico: Burgermeester Patijnlaan 1930, 2585 BC The Hague; tel. (70) 3602900; fax (70) 3560543; e-mail embamex@bart.nl; internet www.embamex-nl.com; Ambassador SANDRA FUENTES-BERAIN.

Morocco: Oranjestraat 9, 2514 JB The Hague; tel. (70) 3469617; fax (70) 3614503; Ambassador ALI EL MHAMDI.

New Zealand: Carnegielaan 10, 2517 KH The Hague; tel. (70) 3469324; fax (70) 3632983; e-mail nzemb@xs4all.nl; Ambassador DAVID PAYTON.

Nicaragua: Laan Copes van Cattenburch 84, 2585 GD The Hague; tel. (70) 3225063; fax (70) 3508331; Ambassador JOSÉ FRANCISCO ARGÜELLO GÓMEZ.

Nigeria: Wagenaarweg 5, 2597 LL The Hague; tel. (70) 3501703; fax (70) 3551110; e-mail nigembassy@nigerianembassy.nl; internet www.nigerianembassy.nl; Ambassador Dr OLATOKUNBO AYOKA AWO-LOWO-DOSUMU.

Norway: Lange Vijverberg 11, 2513 AC The Hague; tel. (70) 3117611; fax (70) 3659630; e-mail embhague@mfa.no; internet www .noorwegen.nl; Ambassador KÅRE BRYN.

Oman: Nieuwe Parklaan 9, LA The Hague; tel. (70) 3615800; fax (70) 3605364; Ambassador KHADIJA HASSAN SALMAN AL-LAWATI.

Pakistan: Amaliastraat 8, 2514 JC The Hague; tel. (70) 3648948; fax (70) 3106047; e-mail parepnl@planet.nl; internet www .embassyofpakistan.com; Ambassador MUSTAFA KAMAL KAZI.

Peru: Nassauplein 4, 2585 EA The Hague; tel. (70) 3653500; fax (70) 3651929; e-mail embperu@bart.nl; Ambassador JOSÉ ANTONIO ARRO-SPIDE DEL BUSTO.

Philippines: Laan Copes van Cattenburch 125, 2585 EZ The Hague; tel. (70) 3604820; fax (70) 3560030; e-mail ph@bart.nl; Ambassador ROMEO A. ARGUELLES.

Poland: Alexanderstraat 25, 2514 JM The Hague; tel. (70) 7990100; fax (70) 3602810; e-mail ambhaga@polamb.nl; internet www.polamb.nl; Ambassador Jan Michalowski.

Portugal: Bazarstraat 21, 2518 AG The Hague; tel. (70) 3630217; fax (70) 3615589; e-mail am.portugal@wxs.nl; Ambassador João Manuel Guerra Salgueiro.

Romania: Catsheuvel 55, 2517 KA The Hague; tel. (70) 3543796; fax (70) 3541587; e-mail sicrned@tip.nl; internet home.tiscali.nl/romanianembassy; Ambassador Iulian Buga.

Russia: Andries Bickerweg 2, 2517 JP The Hague; tel. (70) 3451300; fax (70) 3617960; e-mail ambrucon@ambru.nl; internet www.netherlands.mid.ru; Ambassador Kirll G. Gevorgian.

Saudi Arabia: Alexanderstraat 19, 2514 JM The Hague; tel. (70) 3614391; fax (70) 3630348; Ambassador Abdelmuhsen Mohammed S. al-Ballaa.

Serbia and Montenegro: Groot Hertoginnelaan 30, 2517 EG The Hague; tel. (70) 3632397; fax (70) 3602421; e-mail yuambanl@bart.nl; Ambassador Maja Mitrović.

Slovakia: Parkweg 1, 2585 JG The Hague; tel. (70) 4167777; fax (70) 4167783; e-mail embslow@bart.nl; internet www.hague.mfa.sk; Ambassador Ján Kuderjavý.

South Africa: Wassenaarseweg 40, 2596 CJ The Hague; tel. (70) 3924501; fax (70) 3460669; e-mail info@zuidafrika.nl; internet www.zuidafrika.nl; Ambassador Priscilla Jana.

Spain: Lange Voorhout 50, 2514 EG The Hague; tel. (70) 3024999; fax (70) 3617959; e-mail ambassade.spanje@worldonline.nl; internet www.claboral.nl/es/emba/Depen.htm; Ambassador Carlos Manuel de Benavides Salas.

Sri Lanka: Jacob de Graefflaan 2, 2517 JM The Hague; tel. (70) 3655910; fax (70) 3465596; e-mail nlslmesn@wanadoo.nl; internet www.srilankanembassynl.org; Ambassador Lokugamage Rupasena Karunatilaka.

Sudan: Laan Copes van Cattenburch 81, 2585 EW The Hague; tel. (70) 3605300; fax (70) 3617975; e-mail sudani@worldonline.nl; Ambassador Abuelgasim Abdelwahid Shiekh Idris.

Suriname: Alexander Gogelweg 2, 2517 JH The Hague; tel. (70) 3650844; fax (70) 3617445; Ambassador E. S. R. Amanh.

Sweden: J W Frisolaan 3, 2517, JS The Hague; tel. (70) 4120200; fax (70) 4120211; e-mail ambassaden.haag@foreign.ministry.se; internet www.swedenabroad.com/thehague; Ambassador Björn Ingvar Skala.

Switzerland: Lange Voorhout 42, 2514 EE The Hague; tel. (70) 3642831; fax (70) 3561238; e-mail vertretung@hay.rep.admin.ch; internet www.eda.admin.ch/denhaag; Ambassador Dr Wilhelm Schmid.

Thailand: Laan Copes van Cattenburch 123, 2585 EZ The Hague; tel. (70) 3450632; fax (70) 3451929; Ambassador Thana Duangratana.

Tunisia: Gentsestraat 98, 2587 HX The Hague; tel. (70) 3512251; fax (70) 3514323; Ambassador Emna Chtioui-Aouij.

Turkey: Jan Evertstraat 15, 2514 BS The Hague; tel. (70) 3604912; fax (70) 3617969; e-mail turkishembassy@euronet.nl; Ambassador Tacan Ildem.

Ukraine: Groot Hertoginnelaan 26, 2517 EG The Hague; fax (70) 3615565; e-mail embukr@wxs.nl; Ambassador Dymtro Markov.

United Kingdom: Lange Voorhout 10, 2514 ED The Hague; tel. (70) 4270427; fax (70) 4270345; internet www.britain.nl; Ambassador Sir Colin Budd.

USA: Lange Voorhout 102, 2514 EJ The Hague; tel. (70) 3109209; fax (70) 3614688; e-mail julier.moyes@state.gov; internet www.usemb.nl; Ambassador Clifford Sobel.

Uruguay: Mauritskade 33, 2514 HD The Hague; tel. (70) 3609815; fax (70) 3562826; e-mail uruholan@wxs.nl; internet www.europanas.com/Uruguay-PBajos.htm; Ambassador Dr Carlos Gianelli.

Venezuela: Nassaulaan 2, 2514 JS The Hague; tel. (70) 3651256; fax (70) 3656954; e-mail embvene@xs4all.nl; Ambassador Norman Rafael Pino de Lion.

Viet Nam: Nassauplein 12, 2585 EB The Hague; tel. (70) 3648917; fax (70) 3648656; Ambassador Dinh Thi Minh Huyen.

Yemen: Surinamestraat 9, 2585 GG The Hague; tel. (70) 3653936; fax (70) 3563312; Ambassador Abdulmalik A. Aleryani.

Judicial System

Justices and judges must have graduated in law at a Dutch university, and are nominated for life by the Crown. The justices of the Supreme Court are nominated from a list of three compiled by the Second Chamber of the States-General.

SUPREME COURT

De Hoge Raad der Nederlanden

Kazernestraat 52, POB 20303, 2500 EH The Hague; tel. (70) 3611311; fax (70) 3658700; internet www.rechtspraak.nl.

f. 1838; For appeals in cassation against decisions of courts of lower jurisdiction. As a court of first instance, the Supreme Court tries offences committed in their official capacity by members of the States-General and Ministers. Dealing with appeals in cassation a court is composed of five or, in more straightforward cases, of three justices (Raadsheren).

President of the Supreme Court: W. E. Haak.

Procurator-General: A. S. Hartkampe.

Secretary of the Court: Mrs E. Hardogs.

COURTS OF APPEAL

Gerechtshoven: Five courts: Amsterdam, Arnhem, 's-Hertogenbosch, Leeuwarden, The Hague. A court is composed of three judges (Raadsheren); appeal is from decisions of the District Courts of Justice. Fiscal Divisions (Belastingkamers) of the Courts of Appeal deal with appeals against decisions relating to the enforcement of the fiscal laws (administrative jurisdiction). The court of Arnhem has a Tenancy Division (Pachtkamer), composed of three judges and two assessors (a tenant and a landlord), and a Penitentiary Division (Penitentiaire Kamer), composed of three judges and two experts. The Tenancy Division hears appeals from decisions of all Canton Tenancy Divisions. The Penitentiary Division hears appeals against refusals of release on license, which is usually granted after two-thirds of a prison sentence longer than one year, unless there are special objections from the Minister of Justice. A Companies Division (Ondernemingskamer) is attached to the court at Amsterdam, consisting of three judges and two experts as assessors.

DISTRICT COURTS OF JUSTICE

Arrondissementsrechtbanken: There are 19 courts for important civil and penal cases and for appeals from decisions of the Canton Judges. A court is composed of three judges (Rechter); no jury; summary jurisdiction in civil cases by the President of the Court; simple penal cases, including economic offences, generally by a single judge (Politierechter). Offences committed by juveniles are (with certain exceptions) tried by a specialized judge (Kinderrechter), who is also competent to take certain legal steps when the upbringing of a juvenile is endangered. Economic offences, and in particular environmental offences, are also dealt with by a specialized judge sitting alone.

CANTON COURTS

Kantongerechten: There are 62 courts for civil and penal cases of minor importance. A court consists of a single judge, the Canton Judge (Kantonrechter). Each Canton Court has a Tenancy Division (Pachtkamer), presided over by the Canton Judge who is assisted by two assessors (a landlord and a tenant).

ADMINISTRATIVE COURTS

The administrative courts regulate relations between the authorities and citizens according to the provisions of the General Administrative Law Act. The majority of cases are heard by the Administrative Law Sections of the District Courts, while appeals are heard by the Administrative Law Division of the Council of State (Afdeling Bestuursrechtspraak van de Raad van State), which also acts as the court of sole and last instance in the majority of cases concerning education, the environment and spatial planning. In addition, cases relating to certain areas of administrative law are heard by the following bodies:

Centrale Raad van Beroep (Central Appeals Council): POB 16002, 3500 DA Utrecht; tel. (30) 2233000; hears appeals against decisions of the District Courts in matters concerning the public service and social security.

College van Beroep voor het Bedrijfsleven (Trade and Industry Appeals Tribunal): POB 20021, 2500 EA The Hague; tel. (70) 3813910; ; hears in first and last instance appeals against decisions enforcing socio-economic and agricultural legislation made by certain bodies, such as regulatory bodies and Chambers of Commerce, and by certain ministers.

Administration Law Section, Aliens Division, District Court of The Hague: court of sole and last instance in cases involving immigration; brs in Zwolle, Den Bosch, Amsterdam and Haarlem. The introduction of a limited right of further appeal is pending.

Tariefcommissie (Tariff Commission): court of sole and last instance for all customs and excise disputes.

Religion

About one-third of the population are Roman Catholics and about one-quarter are Protestants. In 1998 it was estimated that some 4.4% of the population were Muslim.

CHRISTIANITY

Raad van Kerken in Nederland (Council of Churches in the Netherlands): Kon. Wilhelminalaan 5, 3818 HN Amersfoort; tel. (33) 4633844; e-mail rvk@raadvankerken.nl; internet www .raadvankerken.nl; f. 1968; 13 mem. churches; Pres. Prof. Dr A. H. C. VAN EIJK; Gen. Sec. Drs H. J. BAKKER.

The Roman Catholic Church

The Netherlands comprises one archdiocese and six dioceses. At 31 December 2002 there were an estimated 4,973,612 adherents in the country.

Bishops' Conference

Nederlandse Bisschoppenconferentie, Biltstraat 121, POB 13049, 3507 LA Utrecht; tel. (30) 2334244; fax (30) 2332103; e-mail secrbk@ rkk.nl; internet www.omroep.nl/rkk.

f. 1986; Pres. Cardinal Dr ADRIANUS J. SIMONIS (Archbishop of Utrecht).

Archbishop of Utrecht: Cardinal Dr ADRIANUS J. SIMONIS, Aartsbisdom, Maliebaan 40, POB 14019, 3508 SB Utrecht; tel. (30) 2338030; fax (30) 2311962; e-mail secretariaat@aartsbisdom.nl; internet www.de-oase.nl.

Protestant Churches

Christelijke Gereformeerde Kerken in Nederland (Christian Reformed Churches in the Netherlands): Vijftien Morgen, POB 334, 3900 AH Veenendaal; tel. (318) 582350; e-mail lkb@cgk.nl; internet www.cgk.nl; f. 1834; Relations Dir Rev. J. G. H. VAN DER VINNE; c. 73,400 mems; 180 churches.

First Church of Christ, Scientist: c/o ACOP, Andries Bickerweg 1B, 2517 JP The Hague; tel. (70) 3208861; e-mail fccs.denhaag@ 12move.nl; churches at Amsterdam, Haarlem and The Hague.

Deutsche Evangelische Gemeinde (German Evangelical Church): Bleijenburg 3B, 2511 VC, The Hague; tel. (70) 3465727; fax (70) 3649165; e-mail wodo.blaffert@planet.nl; Leaders Pastor D. BLAFFERT, Pastor W. BLAFFERT.

Dutch Mennonites: Algemene Doopsgezinde Sociëteit, Singel 454, 1017 AW Amsterdam; tel. (20) 6230914; fax (20) 6278919; e-mail info@ads.nl; internet www.doopsgezind.nl; f. 1811; Pres. ANNE S. DE JONG; Sec.-Gen. H. W. STENVERS; 11,000 mems; 121 parishes.

Evangelische Broedergemeente (Hernhutters): Annastr. 5c, 3062 KA Rotterdam; tel. (10) 4049224; f. 1746; Pres. Pastor J. W. TL. RAPPARLIÉ; 3,000 mems in Holland; six parishes.

Hersteld Apostolische Zendingkerk (Restored Apostolic Missionary Church): Hogerbeetsstraat 32, 2242 TR Wassenaar; tel. (70) 5113995; fax (70) 5113995; e-mail s.de.jong.hazk@hazknederland .org; internet www.hazknederland.org; f. 1863; Pres. Apostle for the Netherlands H. F. RIJNDERS; Sec. J. L. M. STRAETEMANS; 500 mems; 10 parishes.

Remonstrantse Broederschap (Remonstrant Brotherhood): Nieuwe Gracht 27A, 3512 LC Utrecht; tel. (30) 2316970; fax (30) 2311055; e-mail info@remonstranten.org; internet www .remonstranten.org; f. 1619; Pres. Dr W. VAN DER BURG; Gen. Sec. M. A. BOSMAN-HUIZINGA; 10,000 mems; 46 parishes.

Samen op Weg-Kerken (Uniting Protestant Churches): Joseph Haydnlaan 2A, POB 8504, 3503 RM Utrecht; tel. (30) 8801415; fax (30) 8801445; e-mail info@sowkerken.nl; internet www.sowkerken .nl; comprises three churches that were scheduled to unite in May 2004.

Evangelisch-Lutherse Kerk (Evangelical Lutheran Church): Joseph Haydnlaan 2A, POB 8399, 3503 RJ Utrecht; tel. (30) 8801441; fax (30) 8801447; c. 15,000 mems; 55 parishes.

De Gereformeerde Kerken in Nederland (The Reformed Churches in the Netherlands): Joseph Haydnlaan 2A, POB 8399, 3503 RJ Utrecht; tel. (30) 8801441; fax (30) 8801447; e-mail ldc-synodesecretariaat@sowkerken.nl; f. 1892; Calvinist; has a General Synod which is elected every two years by the 13 Particular (district) Synods; 842 churches, 1,228 officiating ministers, 676,000 mems.

Nederlandse Hervormde Kerk (Netherlands Reformed Church): Joseph Haydnlaan 2A, POB 8399, 3503 RJ Utrecht; tel. (30) 8801441; fax (30) 8801447; e-mail LDC-synodesecretariaat@ sowkerken.nl; internet www.sowkerken.nl; was from 16th to 18th century the State Church. Its nine church provinces are subdivided into 75 districts, 144 fraternals and 1,316 parishes, under the jurisdiction of the General Synod; Sec.-Gen. Rev. Dr B. PLAISIER; 1.9m. mems.

Unie van Baptistengemeenten in Nederland (Union of Baptist Churches in The Netherlands): Biltseweg 10, 3735 MC Bosch en Duin; tel. (30) 2284457; fax (30) 2251798; e-mail unie-baptisten@ solcon.nl; f. 1881; Pres. J. DE BOER; Treasurer A. VAN DEN HOEF; 12,127 mems.

Other Christian Churches

Anglikaans Kerkgenootschap (Anglican Church): Riouwstraat 2, 2585 HA The Hague; tel. (70) 3555359; e-mail churchoffice@ stjohn-stphilip.org; internet www.stjohn-stphilip.org; f. 1698; British Chaplain Rev. MICHAEL SANDERS.

Katholiek Apostolische Gemeenten (Catholic Apostolic Church): 1e De Riemerstraat 3, 2513 CT The Hague; tel. (70) 3555018; f. 1867; seven parishes in the Netherlands and three in Belgium.

Oud-Katholieke Kerk van Nederland (Old Catholic Church): Kon. Wilhelminalaan 3, 3818 HN Amersfoort; tel. (33) 4620875; fax (33) 4630442; e-mail info@okkn.nl; internet www.okkn.nl; f. 1723 in the Netherlands with Jansenist influence; refuses to accept papal infallibility and other 'new' dogmas of the Roman Catholic Church; full communion with the Anglican Churches since 1931; Leader Archbishop of Utrecht Mgr J. A. O. L. VERCAMMEN (18 parishes); Bishop of Haarlem Mgr Dr J. L. WIRIX-SPEETJENS (11 parishes); Bishop of Deventer (vacant); 10,000 mems; also churches in Europe and USA.

Vrij-Katholieke Kerk (Liberal Catholic Church): Diedenweg 29, 6703 GS Wageningen; tel. (31) 7413679; e-mail frank.den.outer@ freeler.nl; internet www.lcc.cc; f. 1916; Bishop Rt Rev. F. R. DEN OUTER; 10 congregations; 2 bishops; 25 priests; 1,000 mems.

JUDAISM

Portugees-Israëlietisch Kerkgenootschap (Portuguese-Israelite Federation): mr Visserplein 3, 1011 RD Amsterdam; tel. (20) 6245351; fax (20) 6254680; e-mail pig-amsterdam@euronet.nl; Pres. R. S. CORTISSOS.

BAHÁ'Í FAITH

National Spiritual Assembly (Bahá'i Community of the Netherlands): Riouwstraat 27, 2585 GR The Hague; tel. (70) 3554017; fax (70) 3506161; e-mail nsa@bahai.nl; internet www.bahai.nl; f. 1962; mems resident in 190 locations (1998).

The Press

Newspapers first appeared in Amsterdam in the early seventeenth century and were soon established in other cities. The Constitution guarantees the freedom of the press.

PRINCIPAL DAILIES

Alkmaar

Dagblad Kennemerland: POB 2, 1800 AA Alkmaar; tel. (72) 5196196; fax (72) 5124152; HDC Media.

Dagblad voor West-Friesland: POB 2, 1800 AA Alkmaar; tel. (72) 5196196; fax (72) 5124152; HDC Media.

Enkhuizer Courant: POB 2, 1800 AA Alkmaar; tel. (72) 5196196; fax (72) 5124152.

Noordhollands Dagblad: POB 2, 1800 AA Alkmaar; tel. (72) 5196196; fax (72) 5124152; e-mail redactie@nhd.hdc.nl; internet www.nhd.nl; morning; Editor G. TEN DAM; circ. 150,000 (2002).

Alphen aan den Rijn

Rijn en Gouwe: POB 1, 2400 AA Alphen a/d Rijn; tel. (172) 487444; fax (172) 487478; f. 1871; morning; Editor L. M. HESKES; circ. 40,000 (2001).

Amersfoort

Amersfoortse Courant: POB 1262, 3800 BG Amersfoortse; tel. (33) 4647225; fax (33) 4647251; e-mail redacticac@un.wegener.nl; internet www.amersfoortecourant.nl; f. 1887; evening; Editor-in-Chief J. J. LODEWIJKS; circ. 35,000 (2002).

Veluws Dagblad: POB 500, NL–3990 DM Houten; tel. (34) 1413072; fax (34) 1415579; e-mail redactievd@un.wegener.nl; internet www.destentor.nl; morning; Editor-in-Chief G. SELLES; circ. 11,345 (2002).

Amsterdam

Het Financieele Dagblad (Financial Daily): 85–87 Weesperstraat, POB 216, 1000 AE Amsterdam; tel. (20) 5928711; fax (20) 5928700; e-mail webred@fd.nl; internet www.fd.nl; f. 1796; morning; Editor A. BAKKER; circ. 52,000.

Het Parool: Czaar Peterstraat 213, POB 433, 1000 AK Amsterdam; tel. (20) 5584444; fax (20) 5584351; e-mail redactie@parool.nl; internet www.parool.nl; f. 1940; evening; Dir F.C.R. CAMPAGNE; Editor ERIK VAN GRUIJTHUIJSEN; circ. 95,120.

De Telegraaf: POB 376, 1000 EB Amsterdam; tel. (20) 5859111; fax (20) 5858017; e-mail redactie@telegraaf.nl; internet www.telegraaf .nl; f. 1893; morning; Editors E. BOS, J. OLDE KALTER; circ. 800,000 (2002).

Trouw (Loyalty): POB 859, 1000 AW Amsterdam; tel. (20) 5629444; fax (20) 6681608; e-mail redactie@trouw.nl; f. 1943; morning; Editor F. VAN EXTER; circ. 130,000.

De Volkskrant (The People's Journal): POB 1002, 1000 BA Amsterdam; tel. (20) 5626222; fax (20) 5622448; e-mail promotie@ volkskrant.nl; internet www.volkskrant.nl; f. 1919; morning; Editor P. I. BROERTJES; circ. 372,100.

Apeldoorn

Apeldoornse Courant: POB 833, 7301 BB Apeldoorn; tel. (55) 5388388; fax (55) 5388200; e-mail rvbe@wegener.nl; internet www .apeldoornsecourant.nl; f. 1903; evening; Chief Editor GERT SELLES; circ. 150,000.

Arnhemse Courant: POB 99, 7300 AB Apeldoorn; tel. (55) 5388388; fax (55) 5388200; internet www.arnhemsecourant.nl; f. 1814; evening; Editor G. DIELESSEN; circ. 31,400.

Deventer Dagblad: Brink 91, 7411 BZ Deventer; tel. (57) 0686468; fax (57) 0686462; e-mail reddeveneterdagblad.nl; internet www .deventerdagblad.nl; f. 1869; Editor L. ENTHOVEN; circ. 34,849.

Het Gelders Dagblad: POB 99, 7300 AB Apeldoorn; tel. (55) 5388388; fax (55) 5388200; internet www.geldersdagblad.nl; f. 1903; evening; Editor Dr G. BIELDEREMAN.

Reformatorisch Dagblad: POB 670, 7300 AR Apeldoorn; tel. (55) 5390222; fax (55) 5412288; e-mail redactie@refdag.nl; internet www .refdag.nl; f. 1971; evening; Editor-in-Chief W. B. KRANENDONK; Man. Dir B. VISSER; circ. 59,000 (2003).

Assen

Drentse en Asser Courant: POB 36, 9400 AA Assen; tel. (592) 329500; fax (592) 314890; e-mail dgd.redactie@hazewinkel.nl; internet www.drentsecourant.nl; f. 1823; evening; Editor G. VOGE-LAAR.

Barneveld

Barneveldse Krant: Marconistraat 33, POB 67, 3770 AB Barne-veld; tel. (342) 494911; fax (342) 494240; e-mail e.v.d.brink@bdu.nl; internet www.barneveldsekrant.nl; f. 1871; evening; Editor J. VAN GINKEL; circ. 10,800.

Nederlands Dagblad: POB 111, 3770 AC Barneveld; tel. (342) 411711; fax (342) 411611; e-mail redactie@ud.nl; internet www.nd .nl; f. 1944; morning; Editors J. P. DE VRIES, P. A. BERGWERFF; circ. 34,000.

Breda

BN/De Stem (The Voice): POB 3229, 4800 MB Breda; tel. (76) 5312311; fax (76) 5312355; e-mail l.krijneni@uitg-zwn.nl; internet www.bndestem.nl; f. 1860; morning; Man. Dir A. A. M. VERREST; circ. 145,769.

Delft

Delftsche Courant: POB 18, 2600 AA Delft; tel. (70) 3190911; internet www.delftschecourant.nl; evening; circ. 11,151 (2001).

Deventer

Gelders-Overijsselse Courant: POB 18, 7400 AA Deventer; tel. (570) 648444; fax (570) 621324; evening.

Dordrecht

De Dordtenaar: POB 54, 3300 AB Dordrecht; tel. (78) 6324711; fax (78) 6324729; e-mail redactie@dordtenaar.nl; f. 1946; morning; Editor H. KERSTIENS; circ. 38,000.

Eindhoven

Eindhovens Dagblad: POB 534, 5600 AM Eindhoven; tel. (40) 2336336; fax (40) 2436954; e-mail redactie@eindhovensdagblad.nl; internet www.eindhovensdagblad.nl; Editor JOEP VAN DER HART; circ. 130,000 (2002).

Enschede

Dagblad Tubantia: POB 28, 7500 AA Enschede; tel. (53) 4842842; fax (53) 4842230; internet www.tctubantia.nl; f. 1872; evening; Editor G. DRIEHUIS; circ. 152,600 (incl. *De Twentsche Courant Tubantia* below).

De Twentsche Courant Tubantia: POB 28, 7500 AA Enschede; tel. (53) 4842842; fax (53) 4842230; f. 1844; circ. see Dagblad Tubantia above.

Groningen

Dagblad van het Nouden: POB 60, 9700 MC Groningen; tel. (50) 5844844; fax (50) 5844109; e-mail qijs.lensink@hazewinkel.nl; internet www.dvhn.nl; f. 1888; morning; Editors H. BLANKEN, P. SIJPERSME; circ. 180,000.

Haarlem

Haarlems Dagblad: POB 507, 2003 PA Haarlem; tel. (23) 5150150; fax (23) 5310296; e-mail redactie.hd@hdc.nl; internet www .haarlemsdagblad.nl; f. 1656; evening; Editor J. G. C. MAJOOR; circ. 51,520 (2002).

IJmuider Courant: POB 507, 2003 PA Haarlem; tel. (23) 5150150; fax (23) 5317337; internet www.ijmuidercourant.nl; evening.

The Hague

Haagsche Courant: POB 16050, 2500 AA The Hague; tel. (70) 3190922; fax (70) 3906447; e-mail redactie@haagschecourant.nl; internet www.haagschecourant.nl; evening; Editor J. P. TER HORST; circ. 105,000.

Nederlandse Staatscourant: Chr. Plantijnstraat 2, POB 20020, 2500 EA The Hague; tel. (70) 3789422; fax (70) 3855505; e-mail staatscourant@sdu.nl; internet www.sdu.nl/staatscourant/vandaag; f. 1814; morning; Editor A. M. DEN HAAN; circ. 14,600.

Heerlen

Limburgs Dagblad: POB 3100, 6401 DP Heerlen; tel. (45) 739911; fax (45) 5739264; internet www.limburgsdagblad.nl; f. 1918; morning; Editor HANS GOESSENS; circ. 75,000 (2002).

's-Hertogenbosch

Brabants Dagblad: POB 235, 5201 HB 's-Hertogenbosch; tel. (73) 157157; fax (73) 132229; internet www.brabantsdagblad.nl; f. 1771; morning; Editor T. VAN DER MEULEN; circ. 158,290 (2001).

Eindhovens Dagblad: POB 534, 5600 AM Eindhoven; tel. (40) 2336336; fax (40) 2436954; e-mail redactie@eindhovensdagblad.nl; internet www.eindhovensdagblad.nl; circ. 130,000 (2001).

Hilversum

De Gooi en Eemlander: Seinstraat 14, 1223 AE Hilversum; tel. (35) 6257911; fax (35) 6257246; e-mail redactie.nieuwsdienst@ge .hdc.nl; internet www.gooienemlander.nl; f. 1871; evening; Editor H. VAN ZENDEREN; circ. 45,000 (2002).

Leeuwarden

Friesch Dagblad: POB 412, 8901 BE Leeuwarden; tel. (58) 2987654; fax (58) 987540; e-mail fd@frieschdagblad.nl; f. 1903; evening; Editor L. KOOISTRA; circ. 22,000 (2001).

Leeuwarder Courant: POB 394, 8901 BD Leeuwarden; tel. (58) 2845845; fax (58) 2845409; e-mail redactie@leeuwardercourant.nl; internet www.leeuwardercourant.nl; f. 1752; evening; Editor R. MULDER; circ. 112,000.

Leiden

Leidsch Dagblad: POB 54, 2300 AB Leiden; tel. (71) 5356356; fax (71) 5321429; internet www.leidschdagblad.nl; f. 1860; evening; Editor J. G. C. MAJOOR; circ. 41,464 (2001).

Maastricht

Dagblad De Limburger: Postbus 1056, 6201 MK Maastricht; tel. (43) 3502000; fax (43) 3501879; e-mail nieuwsdienst@ld.mgl.nl; internet www.limburger.nl; f. 1845; morning; Editor FONS VEL-DERSEN; circ. 180,000.

Nijmegen

De Gelderlander: Voorstadslaan 2, POB 36, 6500 DA Nijmegen; tel. (24) 3650611; fax (24) 3650209; e-mail redactie@gelderlander.nl; internet www.gelderlander.nl; f. 1848; morning; Editor U. D. JONKER; circ. 164,300 (2001).

Purmurend

Nieuwe Noordhollandse Courant (NNC): POB 14, 1442 BZ Purmurend; tel. (299) 432071; fax (299) 430205.

Roosendaal

Brabants Nieuwsblad: POB 1052, 4700 BB Roosendaal; tel. (165) 578888; fax (165) 578149; f. 1862; morning; Editor G. BIELDERMAN; circ. 55,000.

Rotterdam

Algemeen Dagblad: Marten Meesweg 35, POB 8983, 3009 TC Rotterdam; tel. (10) 4066206; fax (10) 4066958; e-mail ad@ad.nl; internet www.ad.nl; f. 1946; morning; Editor O. GARSCHAGEN; circ. 380,000 (2001).

NRC Handelsblad BV: Marten Meesweg 35, POB 8987, 3009 TH Rotterdam; tel. (10) 4066111; fax (10) 4066967; e-mail nrc@nrc.nl; internet www.nrc.nl; f. 1970; evening; Editor F. E. JENSMA; circ. 262,000 (2003).

Rotterdams Dagblad: POB 1162, 3000 BD Rotterdam; tel. (10) 4004296; fax (10) 4128449; e-mail digitaal@luna.nl; internet www.rotterdamsdagblad.nl; f. 1991; evening; Editor F. ECKHARDT; circ. 102,222 (2001).

Utrecht

Utrechts Nieuwsblad: POB 500, 3990 DM Houten; tel. (30) 6399911; fax (30) 6399226; e-mail info@wumn.wegener.nl; internet www.utrechtsnieuwsblad.nl; f. 1993; evening; Chief Editor R. VAN ZANTEN; circ. 86,840 (2001).

Vlissingen

Provinciale Zeeuwse Courant: POB 18, 4380 AA Vlissingen; tel. (118) 484000; fax (118) 472404; internet www.pzc.nl; f. 1758; morning; Editor A. L. OOSTHOEK; circ. 61,495 (2001).

Zwolle

Zwolse Courant: POB 29, 8000 AA Zwolle; tel. (38) 4275275; fax (38) 4219453; e-mail zwolsecourant@wugo.wegener.nl; internet www.zwolsecourant.nl; f. 1790; morning; Editor H. BELTMAN; circ. 37,680.

SELECTED WEEKLIES

Adformatie: POB 75462, 1070 AL Amsterdam; tel. (20) 5733644; fax (20) 6793581; e-mail redactie@adformatie.nl; internet www.adformatie.nl; advertising, marketing and media; circ. 35,000.

Aktueel: POB 94210, 1090 GE Amsterdam; tel. (20) 5979600; fax (20) 5979682.

Avrobode: s'-Gravelandseweg 52, 1217 ET Hilversum; tel. (35) 6717911; fax (35) 717443; publ. by Algemene Omroepvereniging; radio and TV guide; circ. 791,986.

Boerderij: Hanzestraat 1, POB 4, 7000 BA Doetinchem; tel. (314) 349446; fax (314) 344397; e-mail boerderij@reedbusiness.nl; internet www.boerderij.nl; f. 1915; farming; Editor-in-Chief MARCEL HENST; circ. 65,000.

Donald Duck: Haaksbergsweg 75, 1101 BR Amsterdam; tel. (20) 4300300; fax (20) 4300315; f. 1952; children's interest; weekly; Publisher A. VAN DER AA; circ. 62,784.

Elsevier: POB 152, 1000 AD Amsterdam; tel. (20) 5159222; fax (20) 5159900; f. 1945; current affairs; Chief Editor H. J. SCHOO; circ. 135,000.

Fancy: POB 1610, 2130 JA Hoofddorp; tel. (23) 5565117; fax (23) 5565116; e-mail fancy@sanoma-uitgevers; internet www.fancy.nl; teenage girls interest; circ. 120,000.

HP/De Tijd (The Times): Amsterdam; tel. (20) 5734811; fax (20) 5734406; f. 1845 as daily; changed to weekly in 1974; Christian progressive; current affairs; Dir A. VISSER; circ. 37,580.

Libelle: POB 1742, 2130 JC Hoofddorp; tel. (23) 5564002; fax (23) 5564003; e-mail f.stuy@sanoma-uitgevers.nl; internet www.libelle.nl; f. 1934; women's interest; Editor-in-Chief FRANSKA STUY; circ. 587,754.

Margriet: POB 1640, 2130 JA Hoofddorp; tel. (23) 5564200; e-mail redactie@margriet.nl; internet www.margriet.nl; f. 1939; women's interest; Dir A. VISSER; circ. 499,868.

Mikro-Gids: Zeverijnstraat 6, 1216 GK Hilversum; tel. (35) 6726751; fax (35) 6726752; f. 1974; radio and TV guide; Dir C. ABBENHUIS; circ. 468,280.

NCRV-Gids: POB 25900, 1202 HW Hilversum; tel. (35) 6726801; fax (35) 6726863; f. 1966; publ. by Nederlandse Christelijke Radio Vereniging; radio and TV guide; Dir C. ABBENHUIS; circ. 419,363.

Nederlands Tijdschrift voor Geneeskunde (Dutch Journal of Medicine): POB 75971, 1070 AZ Amsterdam; tel. (20) 6620150; fax (20) 6735481; e-mail redacfie@ntvg.nl; internet ntvg.nl; f. 1856; Editors Prof. Dr J. VAN GIJN, Prof. Dr H. G. M. ROOIJMANS; Exec. Editors Dr W. HART, Prof. Dr A. J. P. M. OVERBEKE; circ. 30,000.

Nieuwe Revu: POB 1750, 2130 JD Hoofddorp; tel. (23) 5564321; fax (23) 5564290; e-mail revu@tijdschriften.vnu.com; internet www.nieuwerevu.nl; f. 1968; general interest; Editor-in-Chief JILDOU VAN DER BIJL; circ. 127,802.

Panorama: Ceylonpoort 5-25, 2037 AA Haarlem; tel. (23) 5304304; fax (23) 5361624; internet www.panorama.nl; f. 1913; general interest; Dir R. VAN VUURE; circ. 194,466.

Privé: POB 125, 1000 AC Amsterdam; tel. (20) 5853375; fax (20) 5854111; f. 1977; women's interest; Editors W. P. J. SMITT, H. VAN DER MEYDEN; circ. 490,000.

Story: POB 1760, 2130 JD Hoofddorp; tel. (23) 5564894; fax (23) 5564911; f. 1974; women's interest; Editor ANGELA HOOGEVEEN; circ. 272,700.

TeleVizier: Zeverijnstraat 6, POB 20002, 1202 AB Hilversum; tel. (35) 6726834; fax (35) 6726712; e-mail redactie.televizier@akn.nl; internet www.televizier.nl; publ. by Algemene Omroepvereniging; radio and TV guide; circ. 258,487.

Tina: Ceylonpoort 5-25, 2037 AA Haarlem; tel. (23) 5304304; fax (23) 5352554; f. 1967; teenage interest; circ. 112,191.

TrosKompas: POB 9430, 1090 GH Amsterdam; tel. (20) 5979580; fax (20) 5979507; f. 1966; radio and TV guide; Editor JOLANDE VOS.

TV Krant: POB 9430, 1090 GH Amsterdam; tel. (20) 5979580; fax (20) 5979507; f. 1990; radio and TV guide; Editor JOLANDE VOS.

Vara TV Magazine: POB 175, 1200 AD Hilversum; tel. (35) 6711445; fax (35) 6711429; e-mail tv.magazine@vara.nl; radio and TV guide; Editor DAAN DIJKSMAN; circ. 500,000.

Veronica: POB 22000, 1202 CA Hilversum; tel. (35) 6463333; fax (35) 6463300; e-mail michael.kroonbergs@veronica.nl; f. 1971; radio and TV guide; Editor M. KROONBERGS; circ. 1,250,000.

Viva: POB 1630, 2130 JA Hoofddorp; tel. (23) 5565165; fax (23) 5565200; e-mail redactie@viva.nl; internet www.viva.nl; women's interest; Dir HENK ROELOFS; circ. 149,461.

VNU: Ceylonpoort 5-25, 2037 AA Haarlem; POB 1, 2000 MA Haarlem; tel. (23) 5463463; fax (23) 5463912; e-mail vnupr@hq.vnu.com; circ. 174,250.

Voetbal International: POB 1050, 1000 BB Amsterdam; tel. (20) 5518711; fax (20) 6229141; f. 1965; football; Chief Editor C. VAN CUILENBORG; circ. 199,190.

VPRO-Gids: POB 11, 1200 JC Hilversum; tel. (35) 6712665; fax (35) 6712285; e-mail gids@vpro.nl; radio and TV guide; Dir H. VAN DALFSEN; circ. 254,000.

Vrij Nederland: POB 1254, 1000 BG Amsterdam; tel. (20) 5518711; fax (20) 6247476; e-mail redactie.vn@weekbladpers.nl; f. 1940; current affairs; Editor XANDRA SCHUTTE; circ. 80,000.

SELECTED PERIODICALS

Art, History and Literature

De Architect: POB 34, 2501 AG The Hague; tel. (70) 3045833; fax (70) 3045806; e-mail architect@wkths.nl; internet www.deArchitect.nl; Dir H. TILMAN; circ. 8,000.

Kunstbeeld: POB 318, 2280 AH Rijswijk; tel. (70) 3941007; fax (70) 3938382; monthly; art, esp. sculpture; Editor ROBERT ROOS; circ. 15,000 (2002).

Spiegel Historiael: Molukkenstraat 200, E5, 1098 TW Amsterdam; tel. (20) 6652759; fax (20) 6657831; e-mail s.h@inter.nl.net; f. 1966; monthly; history and archaeology; circ. 8,000.

Tableau Fine Arts Magazine: Capellalaan 65, 2132 JL Hoofddorp; tel. (23) 5565377; fax (23) 5565376; e-mail tableau@sanoma-uitgevers.nl; every 2 months; Editor RONALD KRAAYEVELD; circ. 17,000.

Tijdschrift voor Geschiedenis (Historical Review): Instituut voor Geschiedenis RUU, Kromme Nieuwe Gracht 66, 3512 HL Utrecht; tel. (30) 2537868; e-mail tvg@let.uu.nl; f. 1886; quarterly; Editor Dr KEES RIBBENS.

Economic and Business

Computable: POB 1905, 2003 BA Haarlem; tel. (23) 5463413; fax (23) 5465526; e-mail computable@bp.vnu.com; internet www .computable.nl; Dir E. HVEKSTRA; circ. 96,636.

Elektronica: POB 23, 7400 GA Deventer; tel. (570) 648699; fax (570) 610918; e-mail hdevries@kluwer.nl; internet elektronica .profpages.nl; f. 1953; 11 a year; electronics design; Editor HENK DE VRIES; circ. 7,000.

Intermediair: Ceylonpoort 5–25, 2037 AA Haarlem; tel. (23) 5463455; fax (23) 5465530; e-mail redactie@intermediair.nl; internet www.intermediair.nl; f. 1995; weekly; business recruitment; Editor KARIN VAN GILST; circ. 240,678.

Management Team: VNU Business Publications, POB 1907, 2003 BA Haarlem; tel. (318) 521422; fax (318) 523136; internet www.mt .nl; f. 1980; monthly; management; Editor M. TEN HOLTE; circ. 142,000 (2001).

PCM (Personal Computer Magazine): Ceylonpoort 5–25, 2037 AA Haarlem; tel. (23) 5463704; fax (23) 5465524; internet www.pcmweb .nl; f. 1982; monthly; computing; Editor-in-Chief FERDINAND SENNEMA; circ. 94,997.

Trade Channel: Holland Business Press BV, Sophiastraat 1, 2011 VT Haarlem; tel. (23) 5319022; fax (23) 5317974; e-mail pvroom@ tradechannel.com; internet www.tradechannel.com; f. 1945; monthly, 2 edns: Trade Channel Consumer Goods and Trade Channel Industrial & Technical Products; promote imports and exports; Editor HENK VAN CAPELLE; circ. 13,286 (consumer edn), 55,000 (technical edn).

Home, Fashion and General

Ariadne Women: Capellalaan 65, POB 1919, 2130 YM Hoofddorp; tel. (23) 5566770; fax (23) 5361624; f. 1946; monthly; home decoration; Editor MONIQUE WIEMEYER; circ. 169,198.

Het Beste uit Reader's Digest: POB 23330, 1100 DV Amsterdam; tel. (20) 56789111; fax (20) 6976422; e-mail hetbeste@readersdigest .nl; internet www.readersdigest.nl; f. 1957; monthly; general interest; Man. Dir OALA STEENKS; circ. 304,453.

Cosmopolitan: POB 1730, 2130 JC Hoofddorp; fax (23) 5565259; e-mail cosmopolitan@tijdschriften.vnu.com; internet www .uilenstein.nl/cosmo; f. 1982; monthly; women's interest; Editor M. SIFFELS; circ. 108,406.

Kijk: Ceylonpoort 5-25, 2037 AA Haarlem; tel. (20) 4300455; fax (20) 4300450; sports, science, technology and adventure; circ. 92,993.

Knipmode: POB Capellalaan 65, POB 1900, 2130 JL Hoofddorp; tel. (23) 5565006; fax (23) 5566771; internet www.knipmode.nl; monthly; fashion and needlework; Editor-in-Chief Y. ANNEVELD-DE WIT; Publr E. ARIËUS; circ. 124,000.

Nouveau: Ceylonpoort 5-25, 2037 AA Haarlem; tel. (23) 304304; fax (23) 350621; f. 1986; women's interest; Dir K. P. M. VAN DE PAS; circ. 134,669.

Opzij: POB 2748, 1000 CS Amsterdam; tel. (20) 5518525; fax (20) 6227265; e-mail opzij@redactie.weekbladpers.nl; internet www.opzij .nl; f. 1972; monthly; feminist themes; Editor CISCA DRESSELHUYS; circ. 80,000.

Ouders van Nu: POB 1762, 2130 JP Hoofddoorp; tel. (23) 5565066; fax (23) 5565095; e-mail ouders@tijdschriften.vnu.com; internet www.oudersvannu.nl; f. 1967; monthly; childcare; Editor K. KROON-STUIVER; circ. 156,720.

Playboy: POB 1662, 2130 JB Hoofddorp; tel. (23) 5463369; fax (23) 5463924; e-mail playboy@tidjschriften.vnu.com; internet www .playboy.nl; f. 1983; monthly; Editor PAUL KOOPAL; circ. 85,348.

TIP Culinair: POB 1632, 2130 JA Hoofddorp; tel. (23) 5565466; fax (23) 5565488; e-mail tipculinair@sanoma-uitgevers.nl; internet www.tipculinair.nl; f. 1977; monthly; cookery; Gen. Editor DOSIA BREWER; circ. 120,000.

VT-Wonen: Ceylonpoort 5-25, 2037 AA Haarlem; tel. (30) 822511; fax (30) 898388; f. 1964; monthly; home-owning and decorating, circ. 210,374.

Leisure Interests and Sport

Autokampioen: POB 93200, 2509 BA The Hague; tel. (70) 3146688; fax (70) 3146279; e-mail autokampioen@anwb.nl; f. 1908; publ. by Royal Dutch Touring Club (ANWB); motoring; fortnightly; Editor J. VROOMANS; circ. 70,000.

Grasduinen (Browsing): Postbus 23209, 1100 DT Amsterdam; tel. (20) 7510110; fax (20) 7510111; e-mail grasduinen@smm.nl; internet www.grasduinen.nl; monthly; leisure, healthy living, art; Editor LIEES LOOGMAN KANNEKENS; circ. 51,000.

Kampeer en Caravankampioen: POB 93200, 2509 BA The Hague; tel. (70) 3146691; fax (70) 3146692; f. 1941; monthly;

camping and caravanning; publ. by Royal Dutch Touring Club (ANWB); Editor F. VOORBERGEN; circ. 139,601.

Kampioen: POB 93200, 2509 BA The Hague; tel. (70) 3146285; fax (70) 3146983; e-mail kampioen@anwb.nl; internet www.anwb.nl; f. 1885; monthly; recreation and tourism; publ. by Royal Dutch Touring Club (ANWB); Editor E. LODEWYKS; circ. 3,700,000.

101 Woonideeën: POB 1702, 2130 JC Hoofddorp; tel. (23) 5564590; fax (23) 5564505; e-mail 101woonideeen@sanoma-uitgevers.nl; internet www.101woonideeen.nl; f. 1957; monthly; home ideas; Editor M. WIEMEYER; circ. 95,000.

Reizen Magazine: POB 93200, 2509 BA The Hague; tel. (70) 3146670; fax (70) 3147610; e-mail reizen@anwb.nl; internet www .reizen.nl; monthly; tourism, travel; publ. by Royal Dutch Touring Club (ANWB); Editor-in-Chief HARRI THEIRLYNCK; circ. 60,000.

Sport International: POB 225, 2800 AE Gouda; tel. (182) 599366; fax (182) 516650; internet www.si.nl; f. 1981; monthly; Editor J. LINSE; circ. 47,350.

Waterkampioen: POB 93557, 2509 BA The Hague; tel. (70) 3141470; fax (70) 3147356; e-mail waterkampioen@anwb.nl; internet www.anwbmedia.nl; f. 1927; fortnightly; water sports and yachting; publ. by Royal Dutch Touring Club (ANWB); Editor DICK WILLIAM HARINCK; circ. 54,000.

Scientific and Medical

Huisarts en Wetenschap: POB 3176, 3502 GD Utrecht; tel. (30) 2881700; fax (30) 2870668; monthly; medical; Editor Dr FRANS J. MEIJMAN; circ. 8,500.

Natuur & Techniek: Segment Special Interest Media, POB 75, 6190 AB Beek (L); tel. (46) 4389444; fax (46) 4370161; e-mail natutech@xs4all.nl; internet www.natutech.nl; f. 1932; monthly; Editor R. DOBBELAER; circ. 47,360.

Technische Revue: POB 4, 7000 BA Doetinchem; tel. (314) 349911; fax (314) 361522; internet www.ebi.nl; monthly; review of new products; Chief Editor M. L. MATSER; circ. 28,000.

Statistics

Statistisch Jaarboek van het Centraal Bureau voor de Statistiek (Statistical Year Book of the Netherlands): Prinses Beatrixlaan 428, POB 4000, 2270 JM Voorburg; tel. (70) 3373800; fax (70) 3877429; internet www.cbs.nl; f. 1899; also *Netherlands Official Statistics* (quarterly) and 300 other publs; Dir-Gen. Dr R. B. J. C. VAN NOORT.

NEWS AGENCY

Algemeen Nederlands Persbureau (ANP) (Netherlands News Agency): POB 1, 2501 AA The Hague; tel. (70) 4141414; fax (70) 4140560; e-mail redactie@anp.nl; f. 1934; official agency of the Netherlands Daily Press Asscn; Man. Dir P. F. E. TESSELAAR; Editor-in-Chief R. DE SPA.

Foreign Bureaux

Anadolu Agency: State de Colombes 56, 1098 VT Amsterdam; tel. (20) 6913714; e-mail amsterdam@anadoluajansi.com.tr.

Associated Press (AP) (USA): Keizersgracht 205, POB 1016, 1000 BA Amsterdam; tel. (20) 235057; Bureau Chief ABNER KATZMAN.

Deutsche Presse-Agentur (dpa) (Germany): Eisenhowerlaan 150, 2517 KP The Hague; tel. (70) 3584499; fax (70) 3521637; Correspondent EDGAR DENTER.

Dow Jones Newswires: POB 1016, 1000 BA Amsterdam; tel. (20) 6260770; fax (20) 6235616; Correspondent NEIL MOORHOUSE.

Informatsionnoye Telegrafnoye Agentstvo Rossii— Telegrafnoye Agentstvo Suverennykh Stran (ITAR—TASS) (Russia): J. van Oldenbarneveltlaan 96, 2582 NZ The Hague; tel. and fax (70) 3553876; f. 1945; Correspondent VALENTIN VOLKOV.

Reuters (UK): Drentestraat 11, 1083 HK Amsterdam; POB 74734, 1070 BS Amsterdam; tel. (20) 5045000; fax (20) 5045040; e-mail amsterdam.newsroom@news.reuters.com; internet www.reuters .com; Chief Correspondent EMMA THOMASSON.

Rossiyskoye Informatsionnoye Agentstvo—Novosti (RIA— Novosti) (Russia): Nieuwe Parklaan 15, 2597 LA, The Hague; tel. (70) 3586958; fax (70) 3512108; Dir A. POSKAKUKHIN.

Agence France-Presse (AFP), **Agenzia Nazionale Stampa Associata (ANSA)** (Italy), **Inter Press Service (IPS)** (Italy) and **UPI** (USA) are also represented in the Netherlands.

PRESS ORGANIZATIONS

Buitenlandse Persvereniging in Nederland (Foreign Press Asscn in the Netherlands): Oudezijds Voorburgwal 129, 1012 EP Amsterdam; tel. (20) 4221209; fax (20) 4212411; e-mail annettebirschel@euronet.nl; internet www.bpv-fpa.nl; f. 1925; Pres. ANNETTE BIRSCHEL; Sec. JANA SANCHEZ; 120 mems.

Centraal Bureau voor Courantenpubliciteit van de Nederlandse Dagbladpers (CEBUCO) (Central Advertising Bureau of the Netherlands Daily Press): Hoogoorddreef 5, POB 12040, 1100 AA Amsterdam; tel. (20) 4309100; fax (20) 4309129; e-mail info@cebuco.nl; internet www.cebuco.nl; f. 1935; Dir Dr M. J. KUIP.

De Nederlandse Nieuwsbladpers (NNP) (Organization of Local Newsmedia in the Netherlands): Drentsestraat 10, 3821 BP Amersfoort; tel. (33) 4481650; fax (33) 45481650; e-mail nnpnl@nnp.nl; internet www.nnp.nl; f. 1945; asscn of publrs of non-daily local newspapers and other local newsmedia; Pres. T. ROSKAM; Dir J. M. PEKELHARING; 52 mems.

Nederlandse Vereniging van Journalisten (Netherlands Union of Journalists): Joh. Vermeerstraat 22, POB 75997, 1070 AZ Amsterdam; tel. (20) 6766771; fax (20) 6624901; e-mail vereniging@nvj.nl; internet www.villamedia.nl; f. 1884; 9,500 mems.

Vereniging De Nederlandse Dagbladpers (NDP) (Dutch Asscn of Daily Newspaper Publrs): Amsterdam; tel. (20) 6763366; fax (20) 6766777; f. 1908; Chair. W. F. DE PAGTER; Gen. Sec. J. W. D. GAST; 34 mems.

Publishers

Uitgeverij Altamira BV: Blekersvaartweg 19A, Heemstede; tel. (23) 5286882; e-mail altamira@tip.nl; f. 1985; philosophy, psychology, New Age, health and spirituality.

Uitgeverij Ankh-Hermes BV: Smyrnastraat 5, POB 125, 7400 AC Deventer; tel. (570) 678900; fax (570) 624632; e-mail info@ankh-hermes.nl; internet www.ankh-hermes.nl; health, eastern and western religions, astrology, alternative medicine, psychology, esoterics; Dir A. STEENBERGEN; Publrs E. TEN SELDAM, A. KLUWER.

Anthos: Herengracht 435–437, 1017 BR Amsterdam; tel. (20) 5245411; fax (20) 4200422; literature, cultural history, biographies, history, politics; Dir. R. AMMERLAAN.

APA (Academic Publishers Associated): POB 806, 1000 AV Amsterdam; tel. (20) 6265544; fax (20) 5285298; e-mail info@apa-publishers.com; internet www.apa-publishers.com; f. 1966; subsidiaries: Holland University Press, Fontes Pers, Oriental Press, Philo Press, van Heusden, Hissink; new and reprint edns in the arts, humanities and science; Dir G. VAN HEUSDEN.

BV Uitgeverij De Arbeiderspers: Herengracht 370–372, POB 2877, 1000 CW Amsterdam; tel. (020) 5247500; fax (20) 6224937; e-mail info@arbeiderspers.nl; participant in Weekbladpers holdings group; general, fiction and non-fiction; Dir R. C. HAANS.

A. Asher & Co BV: Zeeweg 264, POB 258, 1970 AG Ijmuiden; tel. (255) 523839; fax (255) 510352; e-mail info@asherbooks.com; internet www.asherbooks.com; f. 1830; natural history; Dir M. J. ROOS.

Bert Bakker BV: Herengracht 406, 1017 BX Amsterdam; tel. (20) 6241934; fax (20) 6225461; e-mail pbo@pbo.nl; internet www.pbo.nl; f. 1893; Dutch and international literature, sociology, history, politics, science; Dir MAI SPIJKERS.

John Benjamins BV: Klaprozenweg 105, POB 36224, 1033 NN Amsterdam; tel. (20) 6304747; fax (20) 6739773; e-mail customer.services@benjamins.nl; internet www.benjamins.com; f. 1964; linguistics, philology, psychology, management and organization, art history; antiquarian scholarly periodicals; Man. Dirs J. L. BENJAMINS, Mrs C. L. BENJAMINS-SCHALEKAMP, SELINE BENJAMINS.

Uitgeverij De Bezige Bij BV: Van Miereveldstraat 1, POB 75184, 1070 AD Amsterdam; tel. (20) 3059810; fax (20) 3059824; e-mail info@debezigebij.nl; internet www.debezigebij.nl; f. 1945; Publr ROBBERT AMMERLAAN.

Erven J. Bijleveld: Janskerkhof 7, 3512 BK Utrecht, POB 1238, 3500 BE Utrecht; tel. (30) 2317008; fax (30) 2368675; e-mail bijleveld.publishers@wxs.nl; f. 1865; psychology, sociology, philosophy, religion and history; computer books (as Bijleveld Press); Mans J. B. BOMMELJÉ, L. S. BOMMELJÉ.

Boekencentrum Uitgevers: Goudstraat 50, POB 29, 2700 AA Zoetermeer; tel. (79) 3615481; fax (79) 3615489; e-mail info@boekencentrum.nl; internet www.boekencentrum.nl; bibles, books and magazines; Dir N. A. DE WAAL.

Bohn Stafleu Van Hoghum BV: Het Spoor 2, POB 246, 3990 GA Houten; tel. (30) 6385838; fax (30) 6383839; e-mail klantenservice@bsl.nl; internet www.bsl.nl; mem. of Wolters Kluwer NV holdings group; social sciences, humanities, medical, dental and nursing; Dir P. J. A. SNAKKERS.

Boom Uitgeverij BV: Prinsengracht 747–751, 1017 JX Amsterdam; tel. (20) 6226107; fax (20) 6253327; e-mail mail@virgeverijboom.nl; internet www.uitgeverijboom.nl; f. 1842; fmrly Boom Pers BV, Meppel; philosophy, educational and social sciences, environment, history; Man. Dir E. A. VAN INGEN.

Uitgeverij Bosch & Keuning: Dorpsstraat 74, POB 24, 3730 AA De Bilt; tel. (30) 2204014; fax (30) 2202667; f. 1925; general non-fiction; Publr CHRIS HERSCHDORFER.

Bosch & Keuning Uitgeversgroep: Ericastraat 1, POB 1, 3740 AA Baarn; tel. (35) 5482411; fax (35) 5422509; f. 1925; holdings group; Dir J. ATEMA.

Brill Academic Publishers: Plantijnstraat 2, POB 9000, 2300 PA Leiden; tel. (71) 5353500; fax (71) 5317532; e-mail cs@brill.nl; internet www.brill.nl; f. 1683; academic books and periodicals (mainly in English); classics, medieval, renaissance and oriental studies, comparative religion, biology; Pres. R. J. KASTELEYN.

A. W. Bruna Uitgevers BV: Kobaltweg 23–25, POB 40203, 3504 AA Utrecht; tel. (30) 2470411; fax (30) 2410018; e-mail helpdesk@awbruna.nl; internet www.awbruna.nl; f. 1868; general fiction and non-fiction; Dir J. A. A. BOEZEMAN.

Uitgeverij G. F. Callenbach BV: Ijsseldijk 31, POB 5018, 8260 GA Kampen; tel. (38) 3392507; fax (38) 3328912; e-mail lvessen@kok.nl; f. 1854; mem. of Bosch & Keuning Uitgeversgroep; Publr J. BIJL.

Uitgeverij Cantecleer BV: Julianalaan 11, POB 309, 3740 AM Baarn; tel. (35) 5486600; fax (35) 5486645; e-mail cancleer@worldonline.nl; f. 1948; mem. of Bosch & Keuning Uitgevers group; Man. Dir H. SCHWURMANS.

Elsevier NV: Van de Sande Bakhuyzenstraat 4, 1061 AG Amsterdam; POB 470, 1000 AL Amsterdam; tel. (20) 5159111; fax (20) 6832617; f. 1979 by merger; Dir-Gen. CRISPIN DAVIS; subholdings include some 60 subsidiaries in the Netherlands and abroad specializing in: reference works, handbooks, weekly magazines, newspapers, trade and technical publs, (postgraduate) scientific books and journals, audiovisual materials, further education study courses, databases; also includes.

> **Excerpta Medica Medical Communications:** Van de Sande Bakhuyzenstraat 4, 1061 AG Amsterdam; tel. (20) 5159222; fax (20) 6854171.

> **Elsevier Science BV (Academic Publishing Division):** Sara Burgerhartstraat 25, 1055 KV Amsterdam; POB 2400, 1000 CK Amsterdam; tel. (20) 4853911; fax (20) 4852457; incorporates the following divisions: life sciences, earth science, social sciences and economics, chemistry, engineering and technology, physics and materials sciences, computer sciences and mathematics.

Uitgeverij Van Gennep BV: Keizersgracht 524, 1017 EK Amsterdam; tel. (20) 6247033; fax (20) 6247035; e-mail vangennep@wxs.nl; history, social theory, political science, biographies, literature; Man. Publr CHRIS TEN KATE.

Uitgeverij J. H. Gottmer/H. J. W. Becht BV: Prof. van Vlotenweg 1A, POB 160, 2060 AD Bloemendaal; tel. (23) 5411190; fax (23) 5274404; e-mail post@gottmer.nl; internet www.gottmer.nl; f. 1937; fiction, non-fiction, children's books, religion, spirituality, travel guides; Dir C. G. A. VAN WIJK.

Gouda Quint BV: Willemsplein 2, POB 23, 7400 GA Arnhem; tel. (85) 454762; fax (85) 514509; f. 1735; mem. of Wolters Kluwer NV holdings group; law and taxation; Dir K. H. MULDER.

Uitgeverij Holland BV: Spaarne 110, 2011 CM Haarlem; tel. (23) 5323061; fax (23) 5342908; e-mail info@uitgeverijholland.nl; f. 1922; literature, reference, science, children's books; Dir R. VAN ULZEN.

Uitgeverij Hollandia BV: Eemdijk 124, POB 160, 2061 EB Bloemendaal; tel. (233) 5411190; fax (233) 5274404; e-mail tm@gottmer.nl; f. 1899; travel, yachting and nautical books; Dir TONNIS MUNTINGA.

Kluwer Academic Publishers BV: van Godewijckstraat 30, POB 989, 3300 AZ Dordrecht; tel. (78) 6576000; fax (78) 6576254; e-mail services@wkap.nl; internet www.wkap.nl; f. 1988; mem. of Wolters Kluwer NV holdings group; publrs of books and journals on, *inter alia*, philosophy, logic, mathematics, linguistics, sinology and oriental studies, social history, economics, econometrics, geophysics, space research, astronomy, chemistry, physics, energy, life and environmental sciences; Dir J. K. SMITH.

Uitgeversmaatschappij J. H. Kok BV: Ijsseldijk 31, POB 5019, 8260 GA Kampen; tel. (38) 3392555; fax (38) 3327331; e-mail algemeen@kok.nl; internet www.kok.nl; f. 1894; theology, belles-lettres, science, periodicals; mem. of Bosch & Keuning holdings group; nine subsidiaries; Dir B. A. ENDEDIJK.

> **Ten Have BV:** Ijsseldijk 31, POB 5018, 8260 GA Kampen; tel. (38) 3392510; fax (38) 3392518; e-mail pdboer@kok.nl; internet www.kok.nl; f. 1831; imprint of J. H. Kok Uitgeefmaatschappij; religious; Dir B. ENDEDIJK; Editor P. DE BOER.

Kosmos-Z&K Uitgevers: St Jacobsstraat 125, POB 14095, 3508 SC Utrecht; tel. (30) 2349211; fax (30) 2349247; mem. of Veen Uitgevers Groep; Man. Dir A. DE GROOT.

Lemniscaat BV: Vijverlaan 48, POB 4066, 3006 AB Rotterdam; tel. (10) 2062929; fax (10) 4141560; e-mail info@lemniscaat.nl; internet www.lemniscaat.nl; f. 1963; philosophy, psychology, care of the disabled and mentally handicapped, books for juveniles and young adults, picture books; Dir J. C. BOELE VAN HENSBROEK.

Uitgeverij Leopold/Elzenga BV: Singel 262, POB 3879, 1001 AR Amsterdam; tel. (20) 5511250; fax (20) 4204699; e-mail info@leopold.nl; internet www.leopold.nl; f. 1923; mem. Weekbladpers BV; children's books; Gen. Dir R. FRANCISSEN.

Uitgeverij Luitingh-Sijthoff BV: Leidsegracht 105 A, 1017ND Amsterdam; tel. (30) 205307340; fax (30) 20626251; e-mail info@luitingh-sijthoff.nl; Luitingh; f. 1946; Sijthoff; f. 1851; merged in 1989; mem. of Veen Bosch en Keuning Uitgevers publishing group; fiction and popular non-fiction; Man. Dir J. A. B. LEPPINK.

Malmberg BV: Leeghwaterlaan 16, POB 233, 5201 AE Den Bosch; tel. (73) 6288811; fax (73) 6210512; e-mail malmberg@malmberg.nl; internet www.malmberg.nl; f. 1885; educational; Dir J. M. EIJKENS.

J. M. Meulenhoff BV: Herengracht 505, POB 100, 1000 AC Amsterdam; tel. (20) 5533500; fax (20) 6258511; e-mail info@meulenhoff.nl; internet www.meulenhoff.nl; f. 1895; literature, historical, political, social/cultural, art, paperbacks and pocket books; Dir ANNETTE PORTEGIES.

Nienhuis Montessori International BV: Industriepark 14, POB 16, 7020 AA Zelhem; tel. (314) 627127; fax (314) 627128; f. 1800; holdings group; publrs and printers specializing in scientific books and periodicals; Dir A. J. NIENHUIS.

Uitgeverij Ploegsma BV: Keizersgracht 616, POB 19857, 1000 GW Amsterdam; tel. (20) 6262907; fax (20) 6242994; subsidiary: Uitgeverij De Brink; Dir M. BRINKMAN.

Uitgeverij De Prom BV: Pr. Marielaan 8, POB 1, 3740 AA Baarn; tel. (35) 5422141; fax (35) 5423855; f. 1981; mem. of Bosch & Keuning holdings group; literature and art books; Dir W. HAZEU.

Em. Querido's Uitgeverij BV: Singel 262, POB 3879, 1001 AR Amsterdam; tel. (20) 5511262; fax (20) 6391968; internet www.querido.nl; f. 1915; subsidiary: Uitgeverij Nijgh & van Ditmar; participant in 'Singel 262' holdings group; general fiction, history, children's books, translations from Latin and Greek texts; Dir ARY T. LANGBROEK.

Uitgeverij La Rivière & Voorhoeve Kampen: Stationsplein 62, POB 133, 3740 AC Baarn; tel. (35) 5418855; fax (35) 5413174; f. 1876; mem. of Kok holdings group; general non-fiction, children's books; Dirs B. A. ENDEDIJK, A. C. VAN DAM; Man. Editors K. VAN DER SCHEER, J. H. TIMMERMAN, N. HARMSEN.

Editions Rodopi BV: Tijnmuiden 7, 1046 AK Amsterdam; tel. (20) 6114821; fax (20) 4472979; e-mail orders-queries@rodopi.nl; internet www.rodopi.nl; f. 1966; Dir F. A. VAN DER ZEE.

Samsom BV: Prinses Margrietlaan 3, 2404 HA Alphen a/d Rijn; tel. (172) 466633; fax (172) 475933; e-mail heemskerk@samsom.nl; f. 1882; mem. of Wolters Kluwer NV holdings group; books and periodicals on business, social and marketing management, law, education, the environment; Dir A. M. HEEMSKERK.

SDU: Christoffel Plantijnstraat 2, POB 20025, 2500 EA The Hague; tel. (70) 3789911; fax (70) 3854321; e-mail sdu@sdu.nl; internet www.sdu.nl; Dirs S. VAN OOSTROM, B. JONGSMA.

BV Uitgeverijen 'Singel 262': Singel 262, POB 3879, 1001 AR Amsterdam; tel. (20) 5511262; fax (20) 6203509; holding group; Man. Dir P. F. M. DE JONG.

A. J. G. Strengholt Boeken, Anno 1928 BV: Hofstede Oud-Bussem, Flevolaan 41, POB 338, 1400 AH Bussum; tel. (35) 6958411; fax (35) 6946173; f. 1928; health, biography, music, current affairs, parapsychology; sports; cookery; Dir A. VAN POELGEEST.

Swets & Zeitlinger Publishers, BV: Heereweg 347B, POB 825, 2160 SZ Lisse; tel. (252) 435111; fax (252) 415888; e-mail orders@swets.nl; internet www.szp.swets.nl; f. 1901; subscription agent for periodicals worldwide; publr of books and journals; Dir P. RUSTENBURG.

Uitgeverij De Tijdstroom BV: Asschatterweg 44, 3831 JW Leusden; tel. (342) 450867; fax (342) 450365; e-mail tijdstroom@planet.nl; internet www.tijdstroom.nl; f. 1921; educational and professional publications on health and welfare, periodicals in these fields; Dir C. H. J. STAVENUITER.

Unieboek BV: Onderdoor 7, POB 97, 3990 DB Houten; tel. (30) 6377660; fax (30) 6377600; internet www.unieboek.nl; f. 1890; holdings group incorporating 10 publishing houses; general and juvenile literature, fiction, popular science, history, art, social, economics, religion, textbooks, etc.; Dir W. VAN GILS.

Uitgeverij L. J. Veen BV: Herengracht 481, 1017 BT Amsterdam; tel. (20) 5249800; fax (20) 6276851; f. 1887; literature, fiction, non-fiction; Man. Dir A. DE GROOT.

Veen Bosch en Keuning Uitgevers NV: Mariaplaaks 21C POB 8049, 3503 RA Utrecht; tel. (30) 2349211; fax (30) 2300145; e-mail algemeen@veenboschenkeuning.nl; publishing group; Dir A. DE GROOT.

VNU Business Publications BV: Ceylonpoort 5-25, POB 4020, 2031 EA Haarlem; tel. (23) 5463463; fax (23) 5463931; e-mail info@bp.vnu.com; internet www.vnubp.nl; trade and fashion, careers, IT, personal computer, management, training.

West Friesland BV: Slijksteeg 4, POB 2308, 1620 EH Hoorn; tel. (229) 248820; fax (229) 218944; f. 1943; novels, biographies, children's books, paperbacks, young adults; Man. Dir B. E. ENDEDIJK; Editor-in-Chief F. H. JONKERS.

Wolters Kluwer NV: Apollolaan 153, POB 75248; 1070 AE Amsterdam; tel. (20) 6070400; fax (20) 6070490; e-mail info@wolterskluwer.com; internet www.wolters-kluwer.com; international publishing group; Chair. Dr ROBERT PIETERSE (acting).

Wolters-Noordhoff BV: Damsport 157, POB 58, 9700 MB Groningen; tel. (50) 5226922; fax (50) 5277599; e-mail info@wolters.nl; f. 1836; educational and scientific books, educational software, geographical and historical atlases and maps; Dir Dr M. J. VAN DALEN.

PUBLISHERS' ASSOCIATIONS

Koninklijke Vereniging van het Boekenvak (KVB) (Royal Association for the Book Trade): Frederiksplein 1, POB 15007, 1001 MA Amsterdam; tel. (20) 6240212; fax (20) 6208871; e-mail info@kvb.nl; internet www.kvb.nl; f. 1815; Chair. A. NUIS; Exec. Dir CONNIE VERBERNE; 928 mems.

Nederlands Uitgeversverbond (NUV) (Dutch Publrs' Asscn): Atlas Kantorenpark, Gebouw Azië, Hoogoorddreef 5, POB 12040, 1100 AA Amsterdam Zuidoost; tel. (20) 4309150; fax (20) 4309179; e-mail info@nuv.nl; internet www.nuv.nl; Chair. Prof. H. J. L. VONHOFF; Dir J. BOMMER; 140 mems.

Broadcasting and Communications

TELECOMMUNICATIONS

Regulatory Authority

Onafhankelijke Post en Telecommunicatie Autoriteit (OPTA): Babylon Bldg, Tower B, Koningin Julianaplein 30, POB 90420, 2509 LK The Hague; tel. (70) 3153500; fax (70) 3153501; e-mail mail@opta.nl; internet www.opta.nl; f. 1997; supervises compliance with legislation, settles disputes, manages the telephone number database; Dir Dr H. C. BAKKER.

Service Providers

Ben: Rijswijkseweg 60, POB 16272, 2500 BG The Hague; tel. (6) 14095000; e-mail info@ben.nl; internet www.t-mobile.nl; 100% owned by Deutsche Telekom; mobile telephone operator.

Debitel/Cellway: POB 6700, 2130 LT Hoofddorp; internet www.debitel.nl.

Dutchtone: POB 95313, 2509 CH The Hague; tel. (70) 8899000; fax (70) 8898000; e-mail info@dutchtone.nl; 100% owned by Orange SA.

Enertel n.v.: K. P. van der Mandelelaan 130–144, POB 25226, 3001 HE Rotterdam; e-mail info@enertel.nl; internet www.enertel.nl; owned by Greenfield Capital Partners; CEO CEES MEEUWIS.

Koninklijke KPN NV: POB 30000, 2500 GA The Hague; tel. (70) 3434343; fax (70) 3436568; e-mail webmaster@kpn.com; internet www.kpn.com; privatized 1989; operates KPN Mobile; 31.5% state-owned; CEO ADRIANUS SCHEEPBOUWER.

KPN Broadcast: POB 850, 1200 AW Hilversum; tel. (30) 2386238; fax (30) 2386659; e-mail info@kpnbroadcast.nl; internet www.kpnbroadcast.com; provides internet services and analogue, digital and satellite broadcasting services.

Xantic: POB 30012, 2500 GA The Hague; tel. (70) 3434543; fax (70) 3434796; e-mail xantic@xantic.net; internet www.xantic.net; provides communications systems.

Libertel Netwerk: POB 1500, 6201 BM Maast; e-mail roaming@libertel.nl; internet www.libertel.nl; f. 1999; 70% owned by Vodafone/AirTouch; Chief Exec. JOHN DE WIT.

MCI WorldCom BV: Rembrandt Tower, Amstelplein 1, Amsterdam; tel. (20) 7112000; e-mail info@wcom.nl; internet www.wcom.nl; integrated voice, data and internet telecommunications products.

Talkline: POB 426, 3740 AK Baarn.

Telekabel NV: POB 8000, 6880 CA Velp.

Telfort BV: POB 23079, 1100 DN Amsterdam Zuid-Oost; tel. 0800-1771; internet www.telfort.com; owned by BT wireless, a subsidiary of British Telecom; Gen. Dir TON AAN DE STEGGE.

UPC Nederland NV: POB 80900, 1005 DA Amsterdam; tel. (20) 7755731; fax (20) 7756724; e-mail mediarelations@upc.nl; internet www.upc.nl; subsidiary of UGC Europe; holds cable monopoly in Amsterdam; internet, telephone, television and radio service provider.

BROADCASTING

Under the Netherlands public broadcasting system the two co-ordinating bodies work with the seven licensed broadcasters to provide a complete range of programmes.

Co-ordinating Bodies

Nederlandse Programma Stichting (NPS) (Dutch National Broadcasting Service): POB 29000, 1202 MA Hilversum; tel. (35) 6779333; fax (35) 6774517; e-mail publiek@nps.nl; internet www.nps.nl; Dir W. J. M. VAN BEUSEKOM.

Publieke Omroep (Netherlands Public Broadcasting): POB 26444, 1202 JJ Hilversum; tel. (35) 6779222; fax (35) 6772649; internet www.omroep.nl; f. 1969; co-ordination of Dutch national public broadcasting and news, sports and teletext programmes on five national public radio and three TV channels; fmrly Nederlandse Omroep Stichting; Chair. HARM BRUINS SLOT.

Broadcasting Associations

Algemene Omroepvereniging AVRO: 's-Gravelandseweg 80, POB 2, 1200 JA Hilversum; tel: (35) 6717911; fax (35) 6717439; e-mail info@avro.nl; internet www.avro.nl; f. 1923; independent; general broadcaster; 800,000 mems; Pres. M. SANDERS; Vice-Pres. P. SCHNABEL.

Evangelische Omroep (EO): Oude Amersfoortseweg 79, POB 21000, 1202 BA Hilversum; tel. (35) 6474747; fax (35) 6474727; e-mail eo@eo.nl; internet www.eo.nl; f. 1967; Protestant; Chair. A. VAN DER VEER; Man. Dirs A. P. DE BOER, A. G. KNEVEL, H. N. HAGOORT.

Katholieke Radio Omroep (KRO): 's-Gravelandseweg 80, POB 23000, 1202 EA Hilversum; tel. (35) 6713911; fax (35) 6713666; internet www.kro.nl; f. 1925; Catholic; 615,000 mems; Pres. F. C. H. SLANGEN; Dir A. C. G. VERLIND.

Nederlandse Christelijke Radio Vereniging (NCRV): Bergweg 30, POB 25000, 1202 HB Hilversum; tel. (35) 6719911; fax (35) 6719285; e-mail info@ncrv.nl; internet www.ncrv.nl; f. 1924; Protestant; more than 550,000 mems; Chair. F. BRINK; Gen. Man. H. J. HEMINK.

Omroepvereniging VARA: Sumatralaan 49, POB 175, 1200 AD Hilversum; tel. (35) 6711911; fax (35) 6711333; e-mail vara@vara.nl; internet www.vara.nl; f. 1925; social-democratic and progressive; 515,000 mems; Pres. V. M. M. KEUR.

Omroepvereniging VPRO: Media Park, Sumatralaan 49, POB 11, 1200 JC Hilversum; tel. (35) 6712911; fax (35) 6712220; e-mail info@vpro.nl; internet www.vpro.nl; f. 1926; progressive; 440,463 mems; Pres. S. PIERSMA; Gen. Dir P. SCHRURS; Dir of Radio A. J. HEERMA VAN VOSS; Dir of TV D. LUNENBORG.

TROS: Lage Naarderweg 45–47, POB 28450, 1202 LL Hilversum; tel. (35) 6715715; fax (35) 6715236; e-mail publiekservice@tros.nl; internet www.tros.nl; f. 1964; independent; general broadcaster; 573,664 mems; Chair. K. VAN DOODEWAERD.

Radio

There are five privately-owned national radio stations that are operated on a public-service basis, as well as 13 regional stations and about 330 local stations.

Television

Television programmes are transmitted on three public channels, each of which is allocated to a different combination of broadcasting associations and other organizations, and on the commercially-funded channels RTL4 and RTL5. Nearly all Dutch households are able to receive at least one satellite station.

SBS 6/NET5: Plantage Middenlaan 14, POB 18179, 1001 ZB Amsterdam; e-mail info@sbs6.nl; internet www.sbs6.nl; private broadcaster; Dir HARRY SLOAN.

United Pan-Europe Communications NV: POB 80900, 1005 DA Amsterdam; tel. (20) 7729729; fax (20) 7729988; e-mail service@upc.nl; internet www.upc.nl; cable broadcaster; Chair MICHAEL T. FRIES.

Overseas Broadcasting

BVN TV: Witte Kruislaan 55, POB 222, 1200 JG Hilversum; tel. (35) 6724333; fax (35) 6724343; e-mail bvn@rnw.nl; internet www.bvn.nl; f. 1998 by Radio Nederland Wereldomroep, VRT and Nederlandse Omroep Stichting (NOS); daily international transmissions of news and cultural programmes from public service broadcasters in Flanders and the Netherlands; Dir of Programmes P. LANDMAN.

Radio Nederland Wereldomroep (Radio Netherlands International): Witte Kruislaan 55, POB 222, 1200 JG Hilversum; tel. (35) 6724337; fax (35) 6724352; e-mail planning@rnw.nl; internet www.rnw.nl; f. 1947; public service broadcaster; daily transmissions in Dutch, English, Indonesian, Papiamento, Portuguese and Spanish; programme and transcription services for foreign radio and TV stations; Radio Nederland Training Centre (for students from developing countries); Pres. LODEWIJK W. D. BOUWENS.

Finance

(cap. = capital; res = reserves; dep. = deposits; m. = million; brs = branches; all values are given in euros, unless otherwise stated)

BANKING

Central Bank

De Nederlandsche Bank NV: Westeinde 1, POB 98, 1000 AB Amsterdam; tel. (20) 5249111; fax (20) 5242500; e-mail info@dnb.nl; internet www.dnb.nl; f. 1814; nationalized 1948; cap. 500m., res 12,651m., dep. 10,305m. (Dec. 2001); Pres. A. H. E. M. WELLINK; Exec Dirs H. J. BROUWER, A. SCHILDER, J. KONING, D. E. WITTEVEEN, J. PH. W. KNOPPER; 4 brs.

Principal Commercial Banks

ABN AMRO Bank NV: Gustav Mahlerlaan 10, POB 283, 1000 EA Amsterdam; tel. (20) 6289393; fax (20) 6287740; e-mail postbox@abnamro.com; internet www.abnamro.com; f. 1991 by merger of Algemene Bank Nederland NV and Amsterdam-Rotterdam Bank NV; cap. 1,704m., res 9,077m., dep. 456,554m. (Dec. 2002); Chair. RIJKMAN W. J. GROENINK; 915 brs nationally.

Bank Nederlandse Gemeenten NV: Koninginnegracht 2, POB 30305, 2500 GH The Hague; tel. (70) 3750750; fax (70) 3454743; e-mail info@bng.nl; internet www.bng.nl; f. 1914; 50% state-owned; cap. 139.0m., res 2,139.0m., dep. 61,133.0m. (Dec. 2001); Pres. P. P. VAN BESOUW.

Banque Artesia Nederland NV: Herengracht 539-543, POB 274, 1000 AG Amsterdam; tel. (20) 5204911; fax (20) 6247502; e-mail artesia@artesia.nl; internet www.artesia.nl; f. 1863; fmrly Banque Paribas Nederland; cap. 163.9m. guilders, res 180.5m. guilders, dep. 7,856.0m. guilders (Dec. 2000); Chair. M. LAUWERS; 10 brs.

C en E Bankiers NV: Herculesplein 5, 3584 AA Utrecht; tel. (30) 2560911; fax (30) 2540919; e-mail info@CenEbankiers.nl; internet www.CenEbankiers.nl; f. 1922; present name adopted 1998; owned by ING Bank NV; cap. 5.4m., res 200.1m., dep. 2,674.8m. (Dec. 2000); Chair. H. H. IDZERDA; Gen. Mans P. A. J. VERBAAS, A. A. RÖELL.

Commerzbank (Nederland) NV: Herengracht 571–579, POB 140, 1000 AC Amsterdam; tel. (20) 5574911; fax (20) 6272446; e-mail cbnl@commerzbank.com; f. 1973 as Europartners Bank (Nederland) NV; name changed as above 1984; cap. 40.9m., res 190.5m., dep. 3,776.6m. (Dec. 2001); Gen. Mans Dr R. H. WEDEL, G. W. LIEBCHEN.

Dexia Bank Nederland NV: Herengracht 182, POB 11363, 1001 GJ Amsterdam; tel. (20) 5571571; fax (20) 5571414; f. 2001; formed by Oct. 2001 merger of Bank Labouchere NV (f. 1990) and Kempen and Co NV, owned by Dexia banking group; dep. 5,398.1m., total assets 7,290.1m. (Dec. 2001); Chair. D. BRUNEEL; 1 br.

Fortis Bank (Nederland) NV: Blaak 555, POB 1045, 3000 BA Rotterdam; tel. (10) 2701010; fax (10) 4148391; e-mail info@fortis.com; internet www.fortis.com; f. 1999 by merger of VSB Bank and Generale Bank Nederland; Chair SJOERD VAN KEULEN.

Friesland Bank NV: Zuiderstraat 1, POB 397, 8901 BD Leeuwarden; tel. (58) 2994499; fax (58) 2994591; e-mail service@frieslandbank.nl; internet www.frieslandbank.nl; f. 1913 as Coöperatieve Zuivel-Bank; dep. 5,397.8m. euros, total assets 6,242.0m. guilders (Dec. 2001); Chair. Dr A. OFFRINGA; Gen. Mans T. BRANBERGEN, E. C. LEKKERKERKER; 33 brs.

Indonesische Overzeese Bank NV (Indover Bank): Stadhouderskade 84, POB 526, 1000 AM Amsterdam; tel. (20) 5700700; fax (20) 6626119; e-mail info@indover.com; internet www.indoverbank.com; f. 1965; cap. 48.0m., res 98.9m., dep. 698.7m. (Dec. 2002); Pres. MUHAMAD MUCHTAR; Chair. MUKHLIS RASYID; Exec. Vice-Pres. D. VAN LEEUWEN.

ING Bank NV (ING Barings): POB 1800, De Amsterdamse Poort, 1000 BV Amsterdam; tel. (20) 5415411; fax (20) 5415444; e-mail fi@ingbank.com; internet www.ingbank.com; f. 1991; dep. 386,087m., total assets 443,356m. (Dec. 2001); Chair. EWALD KIST; more than 400 brs.

Kas Bank NV: Spuistraat 172, POB 24001, 1000 DB Amsterdam; tel. (20) 5575911; fax (20) 5576100; e-mail info@kasbank.com; internet www.kasbank.com; f. 1806 by merger, name change as above in Jan. 2002; cap. 15.7m., res 161.1m., dep. 5,384.2m. (Dec. 2001); Man. Dir F. S. VON BALLUSECK.

F. van Lanschot Bankiers NV: Hooge Steenweg 29, POB 1021, 5200 HC 's-Hertogenbosch; tel. (73) 5483548; fax (73) 5483648; e-mail vanlanschot@vanlanschot.nl; internet www.vanlanschot.nl; f. 1737; dep. 9,217.2m., total assets 10,748,821m. (Dec. 2001); Chair. (vacant); 34 brs.

Mizuho Bank Nederland NV: Apollolaan 171, POB 7075, 1007 JB Amsterdam; tel. (20) 5734343; fax (20) 5734372; e-mail dkbedp@axxel.nl; f. 2000 by merger of Dai Ichi Kangyo Bank Europe NV and Fuji Bank Nederland NV; cap. 112.7m., res 13.4m., dep. 1,686.5m. (Dec. 2000); Man. Dir T. KONDO.

NIB Capital Bank NV: Carnegieplein 4, POB 380, 2501 BH The Hague; tel. (70) 3425425; fax (70) 3651071; e-mail thehague@nibcapital.com; internet www.nibcapital.com; f. 1945 as Herstelbank; cap. 1,362.0m., res. 651.0m., dep. 17,061.0m. (Dec. 2002); Chair. M. L. GEDOPT; 1 br.

Postbank NV: Haarlemmerweg 506, POB 21009, 1000 EX Amsterdam; tel. (20) 5846133; fax (20) 5846132; internet www.postbank.nl; f. 1985; retail bank operating through post offices; owned by ING Group NV.

Rabobank Nederland (Coöperatieve Centrale Raiffeisen-Boerenleenbank BA): Croeselaan 18, POB 17100, 3500 HG Utrecht; tel. (30) 2160000; fax (30) 2161973; e-mail rabocomm@rn.rabobank.nl; internet www.rabobank.nl; f. 1898; res 19,418.0m., dep. 319,257.0m., total assets 374,720.0m. (Dec. 2002); Chair. RIK VAN SLINGELANDT (acting); 1,727 brs.

SNS Bank NV: Croeselaan 1, 3503 BJ Utrecht; tel. (30) 2915100; fax (30) 2915300; e-mail info@snsbank.nl; internet www.sns.nl; f. 1971 as Bank der Bondsspaarbanken NV, name changed as above in 2002; cap. 340.0m., res 1,068.0m., dep. 33,208m. (Dec. 2002); Chair. M. W. J. HINSSEN; 200 brs.

Staal Bank NV: Lange Houtstraat 8, 2511 CW The Hague; tel. (70) 3101510; fax (70) 3650819; e-mail info@staalbankiers.nl; f. 1916 as Bankierskantoor Staal & Co NV; name changed as above 1998; dep. 3,992.5m., total assets 4,571.6m. (Dec. 2001); Chair. J. S. HESP; Man. Dirs H. W. TE BEST, P. F. C. GÖBEL.

Bankers' Association

Nederlandse Bankiersvereniging (Netherlands Bankers' Asscn): POB 3543, 1001 AH Amsterdam; tel. (20) 5502888; fax (20) 6239748; e-mail info@nvb.nl; internet www.nvb.nl; f. 1989; Chair. C. H. A. COLLEE; Dir H. G. M. BLOCKS.

STOCK EXCHANGES

A supervisory authority, the Netherlands Securities Board, commenced activities in 1989.

Euronext Amsterdam: Beursplein 5, 1012 JW Amsterdam; POB 19163, 1000 GD Amsterdam; tel. (20) 5505555; fax (20) 5504899; e-mail info@euronext.nl; internet www.aex.nl; f. 2001 by merger of Amsterdam Exchanges, Paris Bourse and Brussels Exchanges; unitary stock and options exchange; CEO GEORGE MÖLLER.

There are also financial futures, grain, citrus fruits and insurance bourses in the Netherlands; a 'spot' market for petroleum operates from Rotterdam.

INSURANCE COMPANIES

AEGON Nederland: Mariahoeveplein 50, POB 202, 2501 CE The Hague; tel. (70) 3443210; fax (70) 3475238; internet www.aegon.nl; f. 1983 by merger; life, accident, health, general and linked activities; Chair. JOHAN VAN DER WERF.

Delta Lloyd Verzekeringsgroep NV: Spaklerweg 4, POB 1000, 1000 BA Amsterdam; tel. (20) 5949111; fax (20) 937968; internet www.deltalloyd.nl; f. 1807; subsidiary of Commercial Union PLC (UK); Chair JACQUES VAN DIJK.

De Eerste Nederlandsche: POB 325, 1170 AH Badhoevedorp; tel. (20) 6143340; fax (20) 6696556; e-mail eerstenl@pobox.com; internet www.eerste.nl; all branches.

Fiducia BV: Ruysdaelplein 42, 2282 BJ Rijswijk; tel. (70) 4140404; fax (70) 4140405; e-mail fiducia@remax.nl; internet www.fiducia.nl; f. 1990.

Fortis ASR Verzekeringsgroep NV: Weena 70, POB 100, 3000 AC Rotterdam; tel. (10) 4017465; fax (10) 4125490; internet www.asr.nl; f. 2000 by merger of ASR Verzekeringsgroep NV (f. 1720) and AMEV Nederland NV (f. 1883); owned by the Fortis group; Chair. J. C. VAN EK.

Generali Verzekeringsgroep: Diemerhof 42, 1112 XN Diemen; tel. (20) 6604444; fax (20) 3983000; e-mail info@generali.nl; internet www.generali.nl; f. 1870; life and non-life.

ING Verzekeringen NV: Strawinskylaan 2631, 1077 ZZ Amsterdam; tel. (70) 5415411; fax (70) 5415423; internet www.ing.com; f. 1963; Chair. C. A. J. HERKSTRÖTER.

Nationale-Nederlanden Levensverzekering Maatschappij NV (Life Assurance): Weena 505, 3013 AL Rotterdam; tel. (10) 4449111; fax (10) 4449222; f. 1863; Chairs A. W. SLOOTWEG, G. M. A. M. VAN STAVEREN.

Nationale-Nederlanden Schadeverzekering Maatschappij NV (General Insurance): POB 90504, 2509 LM The Hague; tel. (70) 3418080; fax (70) 3416551; f. 1970; Chair. D. BRANDS.

RVS Levensverzekering NV: Weena 505, 3013 AL Rotterdam; tel. (10) 4012911; fax (10) 4012933; internet www.rvs.nl; f. 1838; mem. of Internationale-Nederlanden group; life; Chair. H. W. SMID.

Insurance Associations

Pensioen- en Verzekeringskamer (Chamber of Insurance and Pensions): POB 929, 7301 BD Apeldoorn; tel. (55) 3576677; fax (55) 3576565; e-mail info@pvk.nl; internet www.pvk.nl; f. 1923; Pres. D. E. WITTEVEEN.

Verbond van Verzekeraars (Asscn of Insurers): Bordewijklaan 2, POB 93450, 2509 AL The Hague; tel. (70) 3338500; fax (70) 338510; e-mail info@verzekeraars.nl; internet www.verzekeraars.nl; f. 1978; Chair. P. F. M. OVERMARS; Gen. Man. Prof. Dr E. J. FISCHER.

Trade and Industry

GOVERNMENT AGENCIES

Nederlands Centrum voor Handelsbevordering (NCH) (Netherlands Council for Trade Promotion): Bezuidenhoutseweg 181, POB 10, 2501 CA The Hague; tel. (70) 3441544; fax (70) 3853531; internet www.handelsbevordering.nl; Man. Dir H. G. VAN BUREN.

Netherlands Foreign Investment Agency: Bezuidenhoutseweg 16A, POB 20101, 2500 EC The Hague; tel. (70) 3798818; fax (70) 3796322; e-mail info@nfia.nl; internet www.nfia.nl; govt agency; facilitates foreign direct investment.

CHAMBERS OF COMMERCE

There are numerous Chambers of Commerce and Industry in the Netherlands. The most important are:

Kamer van Koophandel en Fabrieken voor Amsterdam (Chamber of Commerce and Industry for Amsterdam): De Ruyterkade 5, 1013 AA Amsterdam; POB 2852, 1000 CW Amsterdam; tel. (20) 5314000; fax (20) 5314799; e-mail post@amsterdam.kvk.nl; internet www.amsterdam.kvk.nl; f. 1811; Dir-Gen. Dr JACOB BEVAART.

Kamer van Koophandel Rotterdam (Chamber of Commerce for Rotterdam): Blaak 40, 3011 TA Rotterdam; POB 450, 3000 AL Rotterdam; tel. (10) 4027777; fax (10) 4145754; e-mail post@rotterdam.kvk.nl; internet www.rotterdam.kvk.nl; f. 1803; Pres. F. J. LAVOOIJ.

Kamer van Koophandel voor Haaglanden (The Hague Chamber of Commerce): Koningskade 30, 2596 AA The Hague; POB 29718, 2502 LS The Hague; tel. (70) 3287100; fax (70) 3240684; e-mail info@denhaag.kvk.nl; internet www.denhaag.kvk.nl; Pres. M. J. VAREKAMP; Sec.-Gen. Dr G. ZANDSTEEG.

EMPLOYERS' ORGANIZATIONS

LTO-Nederland (Netherlands Agricultural Organization): Prinsevinkenpark 19, 2585 HK The Hague; POB 29773, 2502 LT The Hague; tel. (70) 3382700; fax (70) 3382810; internet www.lto.nl; f. 1995; Chair. GERARD DOORNBOS; Sec.-Gen. DIRK DUIJZER; 65,000 mems.

Netherlands Elektronica- en Radiogenootschap: POB 39, 2260 AK Leidschendam; tel. (70) 3325112; fax (70) 3326477; internet www.nerg.nl; f. 1921; Pres. Prof. Dr W. C. VAN ETTEN; Sec. G. DE GROOT; 700 mems.

Nederlandsche Maatschappij voor Nijverheid en Handel (NMNH) (Netherlands Society for Industry and Trade): Jan van Nassaustraat 75, 2596 BP Den Haag; tel. (70) 3141940; fax (70)

3247515; e-mail info@nmnh.nl; internet www.nmnh.nl; f. 1777; Dir-Gen. GEERT VAN DER TANG; more than 7,000 mems.

Nederlandse Tuinbouwraad (NTR) (Netherlands Horticultural Council): POB 462, 2800 AL Gouda; tel. (71) 5659596; fax (71) 5659610; e-mail cmoerman@vgb.nl; f. 1908; Chair. Dr HEIN VAN ASPEREN ; Sec. J. W. A. GRIEP.

Vereniging VNO–NCW (Confederation of Netherlands Industry and Employers): Bezuidenhoutseweg 12, POB 93002, 2509 AA The Hague; tel. (70) 3490349; fax (70) 3490300; f. 1997 as merger of Verbond van Nederlandse Ondernemingen VNO and Nederlands Christelijk Werkgeversverbond; represents almost all sectors of the Dutch economy; Pres. JOHANNES C. BLANKERT; Dir-Gen. J. J. H. JACOBS; mems: 150 asscns representing more than 25,000 enterprises.

UTILITIES

Electricity

E.ON Benelux BV: POB 909, 2270 AX Voorburg; tel. (70) 3820028; fax (70) 3383901; e-mail info@eon-benelux.com; internet www.eon-benelux.com; f. 2000; replaced Electriciteitsbedrijf Zuid Holland (EZH) (f. 1941); supplies energy to large-volume customers and distributors.

ENECO: POB 96, 2900 AB Capelle a/d Ijssel; tel. (10) 4576979; fax (10) 4577784; internet www.eneco.nl.

Essent: POB 9501, 9703 LM Groningen; internet www.essent.nl; f. 1999 by merger of Edon Group and Pnem Mega Group; electricity and gas supply.

Nuon ENW: POB 40021, 6803 HA Arnhem; e-mail nuon@nuon.com; internet www.nuon.com; f. 1999; energy and water; Dir T. SWELHEIM.

Sep: POB 575, 6800 AN Arnhem; tel. (26) 3721111; fax (26) 4430858.

Tennet BV: Utrechtseweg 310, POB 718, 6812 AS Arnhem; tel. (26) 3731111; fax (26) 3731112; e-mail servicedesk@tennet.org; internet www.tennet.org; f. 1999; independent; Dutch Transmission System Operator; manages 220/380 kV national grid and supplies electricity to direct suppliers; Dir MEL KROON.

Gas

The last stage of the liberalization of the gas market in the Netherlands was scheduled to take place in January 2004 (postponed from January 2003). The functions of the wholesale and transport group, NV Nederlansdse Gasunie, were to be divided into a transport company, which would be state-owned, and a trading business, which would be shared equally by ExxonMobil and Shell.

ENECO: see above.

Essent: see above.

NV Nederlandse Gasunie: Concourslaan 17, POB 19, 9700 MA Groningen; tel. (50) 5219111; fax (50) 5211999; internet www.nvnederlandsegasunie.nl.

RWE Obragas NV: POB 300, 5700 AH Helmond; tel. (492) 594888; fax (492) 594990; internet www.rwegas.nl.

Water

Nuon: see above.

VEWIN: POB 1019, 2280 CA Rijswijk; tel. (70) 4144750; fax (70) 4144420; e-mail vewin@vewin.nl; internet www.vewin.nl.

TRADE UNIONS

Central Federations and affiliated unions are mainly organized on a religious, political or economic basis. The most important unions are those of the transport, metal, building and textile industries, the civil service and agriculture.

Central Federations

Christelijk Nationaal Vakverbond in Nederland (CNV) (Christian National Federation of Trade Unions): Ravellaan 1, POB 2475, 3500 GL Utrecht; tel. (30) 2913911; fax (30) 2946544; e-mail cnv@cnv.nl; internet www.cnv.nl; f. 1909; Pres. D. TERPSTRA; Gen. Sec. J. WESTERBEEK-HUITINK; 360,000 mems.

Eleven affiliated unions, of which the principal unions are:

CNV Bedrijvenbond (Industry, Food and Transport): Prins Bernhardweg 69, POB 327, 3990 GC Houten; tel. (30) 6348348; fax (30) 6348200; e-mail info@cnv.net; internet www.cnv.net.

CNV Dienstenbond (Service Industries, Media and Printing): Polarisave 175, POB 3135, 2130 KC Hoofddorp; tel. (23) 5651052; fax (23) 5650150; e-mail cnvdienstenbond@cnvdibo.nl; internet www.cnvdienstenbond.nl; f. 1894; Pres. D. SWAGERMAN; Sec. R. J. ROTSHUIZEN; 36,000 mems.

CNV Publieke Zaak (Public-Sector Union): Carnegielaan 1, POB 84500, 2508 AM The Hague; tel. (70) 4160600; fax (70) 4160690; e-mail denhaag@cnvpubliekezaak.nl; internet www.cnvpubliekezaak.nl; Pres. P. J. KOESLAG; Sec. K. KRUITHOF; 84,000 mems.

Hout- en Bouwbond CNV (Wood and Building): Oude Haven 1, 3984 KT Odijk; tel. (30) 6597711; fax (30) 6571101; e-mail info@hbbcnv.nl; internet www.hbbcnv.nl; f. 1900; Pres. D. VAN DE KAMP; Chair. A. A. VAN WIJNGAARDEN; 52,000 mems.

Onderwijsbond CNV (Education): Boerhaavelaan 5, POB 732, 2700 AS Zoetermeer; tel. (79) 3202020; fax (79) 3202195; e-mail algemeen@ocnv.nl; internet www.ocnv.nl.

Federatie Nederlandse Vakbeweging (FNV) (Netherlands Trade Union Confederation): POB 8456, 1005 AL Amsterdam; tel. (20) 5816300; fax (20) 6844541; e-mail persvoorlichting@vc.fnv.nl; internet www.fnv.nl; f. 1975 as confederation of the Netherlands Federation of Trade Unions (f. 1906) and the Netherlands Catholic Trade Union Federation (f. 1909); Pres. L. J. DE WAAL; Vice-Pres. C. E. ROOZEMOND; Gen. Sec. A. REGEER; 1,234,361 mems.

Seventeen affiliated unions, of which the principal are:

ABVAKABO FNV (Government Personnel, Civil Servants, Private Health Workers, Social Workers, Post and Telecom Workers, Public Utility Workers): Boerhaavelaan 1, POB 3010, 2700 KT Zoetermeer; tel. (79) 3536161; fax (79) 3521226; e-mail post@abvakabo.nl; internet www.abvakabo.nl; f. 1982; Pres. G. VAN HUYGEVOORT; Gen. Sec. P. GORTZAK; 360,000 mems.

Algemene Onderwijsbond (AOb) (Education): POB 2875, 3500 GW Utrecht; tel. (30) 2989898; fax (30) 29880; e-mail onderwijsbond@aob.nl; internet www.aob.nl; f. 1997 as merger between Algemene Bond van Onderwijspersoneel and NGL–Dordrecht; Pres. J. TICHELAAR; Gen. Sec. MARTIN KNOOP; 75,000 mems.

FNV Bondgenoten (Transport, Metal and Steel, Information Technology, Electrotechnical, Textiles, Financial Services, Retail, Wholesale, Foods, Agriculture): Varrolaan 100, POB 9208, 3506 GE Utrecht; tel. (30) 2738222; fax (30) 2738225; internet www.bondgenoten.fnv.nl; f. 1998 by merger; Pres. H. VAN DER KOLK; Sec. (vacant); 500,000 mems.

FNV Bouw (Building): Houttuinlaan 3, POB 520, 3440 AM Woerden; tel. (348) 575575; fax (348) 414970; e-mail info@fnvbouw.nl; internet www.fnvbouw.nl; f. 1917; Pres. D. VAN HAASTER; Int. Sec. BEN J. WILMS; 150,000 mems.

FNV KIEM (Printing and Allied Trades): J. Tooropstraat, POB 9354, 1006 AJ Amsterdam; tel. (20) 3553636; fax (20) 3553737; e-mail algemeen@fnv-kiem.nl; internet www.fnv.nl/kiem; Pres. R. VAN TILBORG; Gen. Sec. H. LEISINK; 55,000 mems.

Nederlandse Politiebond (Police): Boerhaavelaan 1, POB 393, 2700 AJ, Zoetermeer; tel. (79) 3536161; fax (79) 3521226; e-mail info@politiebond.nl; internet www.politiebond.nl; f. 1946; Pres. J. F. W. VAN DUIJN; Gen. Sec. FRANS VAN DER HEIDEN; 22,500 mems.

Consultative Organization

Stichting van de Arbeid (Labour Foundation): Bezuidenhoutseweg 60, 2594 AW The Hague; tel. (70) 3499577; fax (70) 3499796; internet www.stvda.nl; f. 1945; central organ of co-operation and consultation between employers and employees; 16 bd mems; Jt Pres J. H. SCHRAVEN, L. J. DE WAAL; Sec. Drs E. H. BROEKEMA.

Land Reclamation and Development

Without intensive land-protection schemes, nearly the whole of the north and west of the Netherlands (about one-half of the total area of the country) would be inundated by sea-water twice a day. A large part of the country (including a section of the former Zuiderzee, now the Ijsselmeer) has already been drained.

The Delta Plan, which was adopted in 1958 and provided for the construction of eight dams, a major canal, several locks and a system of dikes, aimed to shorten the southern coastline by 700 km and to protect the estuaries of Zeeland and Southern Holland. The final cost of the delta works project, which had originally been projected at 2,500m. guilders, totalled around 14,000m. guilders, as the result of a complex adaptation to ensure the preservation of the delta's ecological balance.

The Ministry of Transport, Public Works and Water Management is responsible for land reclamation and waterways.

Transport

RAILWAYS

About 70% of the Dutch railway network is electrified; the remaining track carries diesel electric and diesel stock. There were 2,808 km of state-operated railways in 1999, providing mainly passenger services. The infrastructure of the Dutch railway network remains wholly under public ownership. Until early 2002 the main railway operator, Nederlandse Spoorwegen (NS), was partially privatized, but, following a sharp deterioration in the quality of service, was taken back under government control. NS retains a majority of the passenger and freight rolling stock, and station premises, while there is a small number of additional, privately-owned network service providers. In 1999 the Government announced the construction of a high-speed line between Amsterdam and the Belgian border.

Lovers Rail: POB 2109, 1000 CC Amsterdam; tel. (20) 4212202; fax (20) 4210997; internet www.loversrail.nl; f. 1996; 70% owned by CGEA; operates regular services between Amsterdam and Haarlem, also seasonal trains between Amsterdam and Keukenhof.

Nederlandse Spoorwegen NV (NS): Antwoordnummer 4470, POB 2025, 3500 VE Utrecht; tel. (30) 2359111; fax (30) 2332458; internet www.ns.nl; f. 1937; partially privatized until early 2002, when the Government reasserted management control; operates most railway lines in the Netherlands; Man. Dir (vacant).

NS Stations: POB 2534, 3500 GM, Utrecht; tel. (30) 2352500; fax (30) 2311490; station management co; Dir Z. J. J. VAN WYCK.

NS Vastgoed: POB 2319, 3500 GH, Utrecht; tel. (30) 3004310; fax (30) 3004400; property management and property development co; Dir H. E. PORTHEINE.

NoordNed Personenvervoer BV: Stationsplein 4, POB 452, 8901 BG Leeuwarden; tel. (58) 2335646; fax (58) 2335636; e-mail t .degnua@noordned.com; internet www.noordned.com; f. 1999; operates train and bus services in North and South-West Friesland; operated by Arriva Nederland.

Railion Benelux NV: POB 2060, 3500 GB Utrecht; tel. (30) 2354004; fax (30) 2354334; e-mail info@railion.nl; internet www .railion.nl; international goods transport by rail.

ROADS

In 1999 there were 2,235 km of motorway, 6,650 km of main roads, 57,500 km of secondary roads and 59,400 km of other roads in the Netherlands. It was announced in 1988 that five tunnels were to be constructed under inland waterways in the 'western corridor' of the Netherlands, in an attempt to alleviate severe traffic congestion in that region. The construction of the first tunnel, under the river De Noord, was completed in 1993, and the construction of the second was under way in the mid-1990s. Cycling is a popular means of transport in the Netherlands, and in 1996 there were 19,100 km of cycle paths.

INLAND WATERWAYS

An extensive network of rivers and canals navigable for ships of 50 tons and over, totalling 5,046 km, has led to the outstanding development of Dutch inland shipping. About one-third of goods transported inside the Netherlands are carried on the canals and waterways. Dutch inland shipping has access to Germany and France along the Rhine and its branch rivers, and to France and Belgium along the Meuse and Scheldt (including the Rhine-Scheldt link). Ocean traffic reaches Rotterdam via the New Waterway, and the 21-km long North Sea Canal connects Amsterdam to the North Sea. Following severe river flooding in early 1995, the Government announced the inauguration of a five-year programme to improve and strengthen the Netherlands' river dikes defence system.

SHIPPING

The Netherlands is one of the world's leading shipping countries. At the end of 2002 the merchant fleet comprised 1,316 vessels, with a combined displacement of 5,666,430 gross registered tons. The Rotterdam complex, incorporating the Europoort for large oil tankers and bulk carriers, is the main EU port and the busiest port in the world, handling some 322m. metric tons of cargo in 2002.

Principal Companies

Amasus Chartering BV: Zijlvest 26, Farmsum, POB 250, 9930 Delfzijl; tel. (596) 610744; fax (596) 616551; e-mail chartering@ amasus.nl; internet www.rah-shipping.com; shipowners, managers and operators; Man. Dir S. VONK.

Hudig & Veder's Stoomvaart Maatschappij BV: Debussystraat 2, POB 1030, 3160 AE Rhoon; tel. (10) 5066600; fax (10) 5019684; f. 1882; charter services; liner service to Ireland; Man. Dir J. G. A. FONTEIN.

KNSM-Kroonburgh BV: Boompjes 40, POB 958, 3000 AZ Rotterdam; tel. (10) 4007222; fax (10) 4007221; e-mail knsm.rtm@wxs .nl; liner services from Rotterdam and Antwerp to southern Iberia and Morocco; owned by P&O/Nedlloyd Group; Gen. Man. S. SMULDERS.

Koninklijke Vopak NV: Westerlaan 10, POB 863, 3000 AW Rotterdam; tel. (10) 4002911; fax (10) 4139829; e-mail info@vopak.com; internet www.vopak.com; f. 1999; Chair. C. J. VAN DEN DRIEST.

Royal Nedlloyd NV: POB 487, 3000 AL Rotterdam; tel. (10) 4007111; fax (10) 4006460; internet www.nedlloyd.com; Chair. A.H. LAND.

Seatrade Groningen BV: Laan Corpus den Hoorn 200, POB 858, JS Groningen; tel. (50) 5215300; fax (50) 5215300; shipowners, managers and operators; Man. Dir J. A. N. WESTERBEEK.

Spliethoff's Bevrachtingskantoor BV: Radarweg 36, POB 409, 1000 AK Amsterdam; tel. (20) 4488400; fax (20) 4488500; shipowners, managers and operators; Man. P. J. M. G. HELDERMAN.

Stena Line: Stationsweg 10, POB 2, 3150 AA Hoek van Holland; tel. (174) 389333; fax (174) 389309; e-mail info@stenaline.nl; internet www.stenaline.com; operates daily (day and night) ferry services for accompanied private cars, commercial freight vehicles and trailers between Hoek van Holland and Harwich (UK); Man. Dir W. DE LANGE.

Van Uden Maritime BV: POB 1123, 3000 BC, Rotterdam; tel. (10) 2973100; fax (10) 4851044; e-mail group@van-uden.nl; internet www .van-uden.nl; f. 1848; agencies in Rotterdam, Antwerp, Amsterdam; liner operators; and representatives; international chartering; Man. D. P. F. DUTILH.

Vroon BV: Haven Westzijde 21, POB 28, 4510 AA Breskens; tel. (117) 384910; fax (117) 384218; shipowners, managers and operators; Chair. and Man. Dir P. W. VROON.

Wagenborg Shipping BV: Marktstraat 10, POB 14, 9930 AA Delfzijl; tel. (596) 636911; fax (596) 636250; internet www .wagenborg.com; shipowners, managers and operators; Man. Dirs Dr E. VUURSTEEN, Dr G. R. WAGENBORG.

Wijnne & Barends' Cargadoors- en Agentuurkantoren BV: POB 123, 9930 AC Delfzijl; tel. (596) 637777; fax (596) 637790; e-mail wyba@wijnne-barends.nl; internet www.wijnne-barends.nl; shipowners, managers and operators; cargo services and agents; Man. Dir D. P. MAKKINJE.

Shipping Associations

Federatie van Werknemers in de Zeevaart (Dutch Seafarers' Federation): Heemraadssingel 323, POB 25131, 3001 HC Rotterdam; tel. (10) 4771188; fax (10) 4773846; e-mail fwz.nl@wxs.nl.

Koninklijke Vereniging van Nederlandse Reders (KVNR) (Royal Assen of Netherlands' Shipowners): Wijnhaven 65B, POB 2442, 3000 CK Rotterdam; tel. (10) 4146001; fax (10) 2330081; e-mail kvnr@kvnr.nl; internet www.kvnr.nl; f. 1905; Chair. A. KORTELAND; Man. Dir P. A. TH. VAN AGTMAAL; 300 mems.

Vereniging Nederlandse Scheepsbouw Industrie (Netherlands Shipbuilding Industry Association): Boerhaavelaan 40, POB 138, 2700 AC Zoetermeer; tel. (79) 3531165; fax (79) 3531155; e-mail info@vnsi.nl; internet www.vnsi.nl; promotes Dutch shipbuilding on a national basis; Man. Dir R. J. SCHOUTEN; 95 mems.

CIVIL AVIATION

The main Dutch airport is at Schiphol, near Amsterdam. There are also international airports at Zestienhoven for Rotterdam, Beek for Maastricht and at Eelde for Groningen. Schiphol expanded rapidly during the late 1990s, from 25.3m. passengers in 1995 to 40.7m. in 2002. A fifth runway was opened in early 2003, while it was intended that the scheduled privatization of Schiphol would attract further investment in the airport's infrastructure.

Air Holland BV: Breguetlaan 67, POB 75116, 1117 ZR Schiphol; tel. (20) 3164444; fax (20) 3164445; e-mail info@airholland.nl; internet www.airholland.nl; f. 1991; passenger and cargo charter flights; entered administration in Nov. 1999; Man. Dir L. SAUWEN.

KLM (Koninklijke Luchtvaart Maatschappij NV) (Royal Dutch Airlines): Schiphol Airport, POB 7700, 1117 ZL Schiphol; head office: Amsterdamseweg 55, 1182 GP Amstelveen; tel. (20) 6499123; fax (20) 6488069; internet www.klm.com; f. 1919; world's oldest commercial airline; regular international air services; in 2003 KLM announced plans to merge with Air France; the merger would create Europe's largest airline; KLM shareholders would acquire an estimated 20% of Air France KLM but retain 51% of voting rights in the Dutch operating company; 14% state-owned; subsidiaries: KLM Cityhopper, KLM UK; Pres.-Dir and CEO LEO VAN WIJK; Gen. Sec. H. E. KUIPÉRI.

Martinair Holland NV: POB 7507, 1118 ZG Schiphol Airport; tel. (20) 6011222; fax (20) 6011303; internet www.martinair.com; f. 1958; 50% owned by Nedlloyd; world-wide passenger and cargo services; Pres. and CEO AMIE VERBERK.

Schreiner Airways: Diamantlaan 1, 2132 WV Hoofddorp; tel. (23) 5555525; fax (23) 5555520; e-mail management.saw@schreiner.nl; internet www.schreiner.nl; f. 1945; scheduled flights and leasing services; Man. Dir TJAPKO VAN WIJK.

Transavia Airlines: POB 7777, 1118 ZM Schiphol Airport; tel. (20) 6046555; fax (20) 6484637; f. 1966; scheduled and charter services to leisure destinations; 80% owned by KLM; Pres. PETER J. LEGRO.

Tulip Air: POB 12059, 3004 GB Rotterdam; e-mail info@tulipair.nl; internet www.tulipair.com; f. 1988; air taxi and passenger charter services; Man. Dir J. A. VAN DER MEER.

Tourism

The principal tourist attractions in the Netherlands are the cosmopolitan city of Amsterdam, which receives nearly one-half of all tourist visits, the old towns, the canals, the cultivated fields of spring flowers, the outlying islands, the art galleries and modern architecture. Some 9.5m. foreign tourists stayed in hotels and boarding houses in the Netherlands in 2001. Receipts from tourism totalled an estimated US $6,722m. in 2001.

Toerisme Recreatie Nederland (Netherlands Board of Tourism): Vlietweg 15, POB 458, 2260 MG Leidschendam; tel. (70) 3705705; fax (70) 3201654; e-mail info@holland.com; internet www.holland.com; f. 1968; Man. Dir F. J. VAN DRIEM.

Royal Dutch Touring Club ANWB: POB 93200, 2596 EC The Hague; tel. (70) 3147147; fax (70) 3146969; f. 1883; CEO GUIDO H. N. L. VAN WOERKOM; 55 brs in Europe; 4m. mems.

NETHERLANDS DEPENDENCIES

ARUBA

Introductory Survey

Location, Climate, Language, Religion, Flag, Capital

Aruba is one of the group of Benedenwindse Eilands or 'Leeward Islands', which it forms with part of the Netherlands Antilles (q.v.), and lies in the southern Caribbean Sea, 25 km north of Venezuela and 68 km west of the island of Curaçao (Netherlands Antilles). The climate is tropical, with an average annual temperature of 28°C (82°F), but is tempered by north-easterly winds. Rainfall is very low, averaging only about 425.5 mm (16.8 ins) annually. The official language is Dutch, but the dominant language is Papiamento (a mixture of Dutch, Spanish, English, Arawak Indian and several West African dialects). Spanish and English are also spoken. Most of the inhabitants profess Christianity and belong to the Roman Catholic Church, although a wide variety of other denominations are represented. The national flag (proportions 2 by 3) is blue, with two narrow yellow horizontal stripes in the lower section and a white-bordered four-pointed red star in the upper hoist. The capital is Oranjestad.

Recent History

The Caribbean island of Aruba was claimed for Spain in 1499, but was first colonized by the Dutch in 1636 and subsequently formed part of the Dutch possessions in the West Indies. Administered from Curaçao after 1845, in 1954 Aruba became a member of the autonomous federation of the Netherlands Antilles. The establishment in 1929 of a large petroleum refinery on the island, at San Nicolaas, led to the rapid expansion of the economy and a high standard of living for the islanders. However, many Arubans resented the administrative dominance of Curaçao, and what they regarded as the excessive demands made upon Aruban wealth and resources by the other five islands within the Netherlands Antilles. The island's principal political party, the Movimentu Electoral di Pueblo (MEP), campaigned, from its foundation in 1971 onwards, for Aruban independence and separation from the other islands. In a referendum held in Aruba in March 1977 82% of voters supported independence and withdrawal from the Antillean federation. The MEP used its position in the coalition Government of the Netherlands Antilles, formed in 1979, to press for concessions from the other islands towards early independence for Aruba. In 1981 (after the MEP had withdrawn from the Government of the Netherlands Antilles) a provisional agreement regarding Aruba's future was reached between the Dutch and Antillean Governments. Following further discussions, it was agreed in March 1983 that Aruba should receive separate status (*status aparte*), within the Kingdom of the Netherlands, from 1 January 1986, achieving full independence in 1996. The Dutch Government would remain responsible for defence and external relations until independence, while Aruba was to form a co-operative union with the Netherlands Antilles (the Antilles of the Five) in economic and monetary affairs.

At local elections in April 1983 the MEP increased its representation to 13 of the 21 seats in the Staten (parliament), and the leader of the MEP, Gilberto F. (Betico) Croes, remained as leader of the island Government. Austerity measures, introduced in an attempt to alleviate the adverse effects of the closure (announced in October 1984) of the San Nicolaas petroleum refinery, provoked a series of strikes and demonstrations by civil servants in protest at wage reductions and price rises. The MEP consequently lost popular support, and, following elections to the Staten in November 1985, the MEP was succeeded in government by a coalition of four opposition parties led by the Arubaanse Volkspartij (AVP). Aruba achieved separate status, as planned, on 1 January 1986, and Jan Hendrik Albert (Henny) Eman, leader of the AVP, became its first Prime Minister. Croes died in November 1986; he was succeeded as leader of the MEP by Nelson O. Oduber.

From 1988 Aruba began to enjoy an economic recovery, based on tourism. However, the MEP claimed that the benefits to the whole community were limited, and also criticized Eman's stated reservations about independence in 1996 and his refusal to negotiate with the Netherlands about transitional arrangements. At a general election in January 1989 the MEP came within 28 votes of securing an absolute majority in the Staten. The number of seats held by the MEP increased from eight to 10, and in February Oduber formed a Government in coalition with the Partido Patriótico Arubano (PPA) and the Accion Democratico Nacional (ADN). (Both these parties had been in the previous Government, and retained one seat each at the election.)

The MEP and the AVP each secured nine seats in the Staten at the January 1993 general election, while the three remaining seats were won by the ADN, the PPA and the Organisacion Liberal Arubano (OLA). Despite gaining fewer votes than the AVP, the MEP administration remained in office, renewing the coalition with the ADN and the PPA. In April 1994, however, Oduber announced the Government's resignation, following the withdrawal of the ADN and the PPA from the coalition. In May, following lengthy inter-party negotiations, it was agreed that a fresh general election would be held. Government functions were to be undertaken in the interim by the MEP. The general election was held on 29 July: the AVP secured 10 seats, while the MEP won nine seats and the OLA the remaining two. In late August Eman formed a Government in coalition with the OLA.

In March 1994 the Governments of Aruba, the Netherlands and the Netherlands Antilles convened in The Hague, the Netherlands, and decided to cancel plans for Aruba's transition to full independence, due to take place in 1996. The possibility of a transition to full independence at a later date was not excluded, but was not considered a priority, and would, moreover, require the approval of the Aruban people, by referendum, as well as the support of a two-thirds' majority in the Staten.

In September 1997 the Staten was dissolved after the OLA withdrew from the coalition. A general election was thus held on 12 December; this resulted in a political composition identical to that of the 1993 polls. Following protracted negotiations, the AVP and the OLA renewed their coalition in mid-1998, and a new Council of Ministers, headed by Eman, was appointed.

In October 2000 Air Aruba, the national carrier, suspended all operations after a Taiwanese lease company demanded the return of three aircraft following stalled payments amounting to US $9m. Subsequently, the US Federal Aviation Authority withdrew Air Aruba's landing rights and in November the carrier was declared bankrupt with the loss of 330 jobs.

In June 2001 the governing coalition collapsed, following the withdrawal of the OLA's support for the AVP's plan to privatize the Aruban Tourism Authority. As a result, the legislative elections that had been scheduled to be held in December were brought forward to 28 September. The MEP comfortably defeated the incumbent AVP in the elections, securing 52.4% of the votes cast and 12 seats in the Staten. The AVP legislative representation was reduced to six seats. The three remaining seats were shared between the PPA (two) and the OLA (one). The electoral turn-out among those eligible to vote was 86.5%. Oduber was once again appointed Prime Minister and a new single-party Government, with an unprecedented opportunity to pass legislation through the Staten, took office in November.

In August 2002 a US developer, Ralph Sanchez, won US $20.5m. in damages from the Aruban Government, to be paid over five years, at a court case in Miami, Florida (USA). Sanchez claimed that the previous Government of Henny Emman had, following environmental concerns, failed to honour a contract, signed in 2000, to build a motor-racing circuit on Aruba. In November the judge reduced the sum of damages to $19.1m. because of an accounting error by Sanchez's financial expert. None the less, the Government disputed the verdict and announced its intention to launch an appeal. In addition, the Aruban Government announced it was commencing a criminal investigation of Sanchez and would possibly seek his extradition.

Aruba's relations with the Antilles of the Five improved after 1986. In 1987 Aruba agreed to undertake economic co-operation, and in 1988 the three Dutch 'Leeward Islands' initiated a joint project for the development of tourism. Aruba's relations with the 'metropolitan' Netherlands were dominated at this time by the latter's pressure for more control to be exercised over the large amount of aid that it gave to Aruba, and by the issue of independence, in particular the future arrangements for the island's security: Aruba's strategic position, close to the South American mainland, and the possibility of its being used as a base for drugs-trafficking, were matters of particular concern. In September 1990 Aruba announced that it was to adopt the 1988 UN Convention on measures to combat trade in illegal drugs; a joint Dutch and Aruban team was formed to conduct investigations. In December 1996, however, the USA included Aruba on its list of major drugs-producing or transit countries. New legislation to facilitate the extradition of suspected drugs-traffickers and money-launderers took effect in October 1997. US naval and air force patrols began operating from a base in Aruba in May 1999 in an effort to counter the transport of illicit drugs. In 2001 the Caribbean Financial Action Task Force commended the Government on its efforts in combating money-laundering. Following Aruba's inclusion, in June 2000, on a list of so-called 'nonco-operative tax havens' drawn up by the Organisation for Economic Co-operation and Development (OECD, based in Paris, France), in 2001 the Government of Aruba pledged to reform the territory's financial sector in order to conform to OECD's guide-lines by 2005. In October the Minister of Justice, Rudy Croes, visited The Hague to discuss the issue of independence with the Dutch Government. Relations between Aruba and the Netherlands deteriorated, however, when the Dutch Government forced Aruba to introduce a more stringent policy on visa conditions. In November 2003 Aruba signed an agreement with the USA to exchange tax information in order to combat illegal financial activities, such as money-laundering, that are associated with international terrorism and drugs-trafficking.

After acquiring separate status, Aruba fostered relations with some of its Caribbean neighbours and with countries in Latin America. This included the development of ties with Venezuela, which had traditionally laid claim to the Dutch 'Leeward Islands', including Aruba.

Government

Aruba has separate status within the Kingdom of the Netherlands. Legislative power is held by the unicameral Staten (parliament) of 21 members, elected by universal adult suffrage for four years (subject to dissolution). Executive power in all domestic affairs is vested in the Council of Ministers (led by the Prime Minister), responsible to the Staten. The Governor, appointed by the Dutch Crown for a term of six years, represents the monarch of the Netherlands on Aruba and holds responsibility for external affairs and defence. The Governor is assisted by an advisory council.

Defence

The Netherlands is responsible for Aruba's defence and military service is compulsory. The Governor is Commander-in-Chief of the armed forces on the island. A Dutch naval contingent is stationed in Aruba, primarily to combat drugs-trafficking and organized crime. In May 1999 the USA began air force and navy patrols from a base on Aruba as part of efforts to prevent the transport of illegal drugs.

Economic Affairs

In 1997, according to the World Bank, Aruba's gross national income (GNI), measured at average 1995–97 prices, was estimated to be US $1,181m. During 1995–2002 the population increased at an average annual rate of 2.2% per year, while gross domestic product (GDP) per head increased, in real terms, by an average of 3.1% per year. Overall GDP increased, in real terms, at an average annual rate of 2.4% during 1995–2002. In 2002 real GDP decreased by 2.5%.

Owing to the poor quality of the soil and the prohibitive cost of desalinated water, the only significant agricultural activity is the cultivation of aloes (used in the manufacture of cosmetics and pharmaceuticals); aloe-based products are exported. Some livestock is raised, and there is a small fishing industry (although in the mid-1990s fishing production contributed only some 12.5% of Aruba's annual consumption of fish and fish products). In 2000 the agricultural sector engaged 0.6% of the employed labour force.

The industrial sector, and the island's economy, was formerly based on the refining and transhipment of imported petroleum and petroleum products. In the early 1980s this sector accounted for one-quarter of GDP and provided almost all Aruba's exports. The San Nicolaas petroleum refinery ceased operations in 1985; however, in 1990 the plant partially reopened, following renovation; following further construction and revision works, production reached an estimated 202,000 b/d in 1999, an increase of 26% on the previous year's total. Following a further US $250m. renovation in 2000, production increased to 280,000 b/d. However, in April 2001 the refinery closed temporarily following an explosion; as a result, output fell by some 42% in the final quarter of 2001, compared with the corresponding period in 2000. There is a large petroleum transhipment terminal on Aruba, and a small petrochemicals industry. An advanced-technology coker plant opened in 1995 to supply liquefied petroleum gas, largely for export to the USA. There are believed to be exploitable reserves of hydrocarbons within Aruban territory, and Aruba also has reserves of salt.

Light industry is limited to the production of beverages, building materials, paints and solvents, paper and plastic products, candles, detergents, disinfectants, soaps and aloe-based cosmetics. There is a 'free zone', and the ports of Oranjestad and Barcadera provide bunkering and repair facilities for ships. In 1996 the Ports of Aruba Masterplan was presented, proposing the relocation (over a 20-year period) of all cargo operations to Barcadera, leaving Oranjestad's port to accommodate commercial, recreation and resort activities. The construction sector, which grew steadily in the 1980s, declined in importance following a moratorium on the construction of new hotels in 1992. Industry (including mining, manufacturing, construction and power) engaged 16.4% of the employed labour force in 2000.

The service industries are Aruba's principal economic activity, employing 83.0% of the active labour force in 2000. Financial services are well established in Aruba, particularly the data-processing sector, an important service to US companies in particular. Aruba's principal source of income is tourism; the hotels and restaurants sector alone was estimated to provide 10.5% of Aruba's GDP in 2002. However, in 2001 there was a slight decrease in the number of visitor arrivals, attributed mainly to the global economic slowdown and to the effects on tourism of the terrorist attacks on the USA in September of that year. The number of stop-over visitors decreased by 4.3%, to 691,420 while the number of cruise-ship passengers contracted by 0.6%, to 487,296. In 2002 the overall number of visitor arrivals increased, by 3.9%; however, this disguised a further 7.1% decrease in the number of stop-over visitors, to 642,627. The number of cruise-ship passengers increased by 19.5%, to 582,195. Strong growth in the first two months of 2003 was undermined by the repercussions of the US-led military campaign in Iraq; as a result, an overall decline in the tourism sector was recorded in that year. The number of stop-over visitors decreased slightly, to 641,906, and the number of cruise-ship passengers fell by 6.8%, to 542,327. In 2002 receipts from tourism totalled US $903.3m.

Aruba is obliged to import most of its requirements, particularly machinery and electrical equipment, chemical products and foodstuffs; in 2002 the island recorded a visible trade deficit of A Fl. 965.4m., and there was a deficit on the current account of the balance of payments of A Fl. 514.6m. In 2002 the principal source of imports, excluding the petroleum sector and the 'free zone', was the USA (60.4% of the total); other major sources were the Netherlands, the Netherlands Antilles and Venezuela. The principal markets for exports in 2002 was also the USA (accounting for 40.4% of the total), followed by Venezuela, the Netherlands Antilles and the Netherlands.

In 2002 the budget deficit was A Fl. 27.8m. In 1994 the level of Dutch development assistance was approximately US $35.5m. In 1998 Aruba received $10.7m. in bilateral aid and $0.6m. in multilateral aid. At the end of 2001 total government debt was A Fl. 1,243.1m. (equivalent to 36.3% of GDP), of which 42.1% was owed to external creditors, primarily the Government of the Netherlands. The average annual rate of inflation was 3.0% in 1995–2003. Consumer prices increased by 4.2% in 2002 and by 2.2% in 2003. 6.9% of the labour force were unemployed in 2000.

As part of the Kingdom of the Netherlands, Aruba is classed as an Overseas Territory in association with the European Union (see p. 208). It forms a co-operative union with the

Antilles of the Five in monetary and economic affairs. Aruba also has observer status with the Caribbean Community and Common Market (CARICOM, see p. 164).

The closure of the San Nicolaas petroleum refinery in 1985 and Aruba's separation from the rest of the Netherlands Antilles in 1986 prompted the Aruban administration to institute a policy of retrenchment and austerity, except for investment in tourism development. By the beginning of the 1990s, however, the economy was performing strongly, stimulated by rapid growth in the construction and tourism sectors, and the reopening of the refinery in 1990. In 1992, following six consecutive years of rapid economic growth, during which period there was a threefold increase in hotel capacity, a moratorium was imposed on construction in the tourism industry, partly in recognition of the adverse environmental impact on the island and also to preserve the island's reputation as an exclusive holiday destination for the wealthy. Economic growth subsequently slowed to a more sustainable level during the remainder of the decade, with real GDP growth rates at an average of between 3%–4% annually. During the the past decade Aruba has maintained low levels of inflation and of unemployment, and in the early 21st century was considered to be one of the most prosperous islands in the Caribbean. Concern has, however, been expressed that Aruba's high public-sector wage bill and the generous nature of Aruba's social welfare system, combined with the island's ageing population, will threaten the future stability of public finance, which has already been hindered by a narrow taxation base and poor revenue collection. Reports in early 2002 claimed that Aruba's economic problems were worse than previously expected, with the repercussions of the terrorist attacks on the USA in September 2001 badly affecting the tourism and construction sectors, and real GDP duly declined by 0.7% in that year and by a further 2.5% in 2002. Despite this, in early 2003 the IMF predicted growth of 4% in 2003, owing to a sharp increase in private and public investment (including a series of government programmes worth some US $200m.), and a modest revival in tourism. However, following the negative effect on tourism of the US-led military campaign in Iraq from March 2003 and the weak performance of the Venezeulan economy, projected growth for the year was reduced to 1%.

Education

A Compulsory Education Act was introduced in 1999, to cover the four-to-16 age group. Kindergarten begins at four years of age. Primary education begins at six years of age and lasts for six years. Secondary education, beginning at the age of 12, lasts for up to six years. The main language of instruction is Dutch, but Papiamento (using a different spelling system from that of the Antilles of the Five) is used in kindergarten and primary education and in the lower levels of technical and vocational education. Papiamento is also being introduced onto the curriculum in all schools. In Aruba there are two institutes of higher education: the University of Aruba, comprising the School of Law and the School of Business Administration, which had 208 students in 1999/2000; and the Teachers' College, which had 180 students in 2000/01. There is also a community college. The majority of students, however, continue their studies abroad, generally in the Netherlands. The Government allocated a planned 12.6% of budget expenditure to education in 1999, equivalent to an estimated 3.4% of GDP.

Public Holidays

2004: 1 January (New Year's Day), 25 January (Gilberto F. (Betico) Croes' Birthday), 23 February (Lenten Carnival), 18 March (National Anthem and Flag Day), 9–11 April (Easter), 30 April (Queen's Day), 1 May (Labour Day), 20 May (Ascension Day), 25–26 December (Christmas).

2005: 1 January (New Year's Day), 25 January (Gilberto F. (Betico) Croes' Birthday), 14 March (Lenten Carnival), 18 March (National Anthem and Flag Day), 25–28 March (Easter), 30 April (Queen's Day), 1 May (Labour Day), 5 May (Ascension Day), 25–26 December (Christmas).

Weights and Measures

The metric system is in force.

Statistical Survey

Sources (unless otherwise stated): Department of Economic Affairs, Commerce and Industry (Direktie Economische Zaken, Handel en Industrie), Sun Plaza Bldg, L. G. Smith Blvd 160, Oranjestad; tel. 5821181; fax 5834494; e-mail deaci@setarnet.aw; internet www.arubaeconomicaffairs.com; Centrale Bank van Aruba, J. E. Irausquin Blvd 8, POB 18, Oranjestad; tel. 5822509; fax 5832251; e-mail cbaua@setarnet.aw; internet www.cbaruba .org.

AREA AND POPULATION

Area: 193 sq km (74.5 sq miles).

Population: 66,687 (males 32,821, females 33,866) at census of 6 October 1991; 93,333 (males 44,664; females 48,669) at mid-2002.

Density (mid-2002): 483.6 per sq km.

Principal Towns (population estimates, 2002): Oranjestad (capital) 20,700; Sant Nicolaas 17,400. Source: Stefan Helders, *World Gazetteer* (internet www.world-gazetteer.com).

Births and Deaths (2001): Registered live births 1,266 (birth rate 13.8 per 1,000); Registered deaths 477 (death rate 5.2 per 1,000).

Expectation of Life (years at birth): Males 70.0; Females 76.0 in 2000.

Economically Active Population (persons aged 15 years and over, 2000): Agriculture, hunting and forestry 251; Manufacturing electricity, gas and water 2,940; Construction 3,892; Wholesale and retail trade, repairs 7,112; Hotels and restaurants 7,651; Transport, storage and communications 2,905; Financial intermediation 1,485; Real estate, renting and business activities 3,722; Public administration, defence and social security 3,573; Education 1,431; Health and social work 1,986; Other community, social and personal services 2,776; Private households with employed persons 1,870; Other 324; Total employed 41,918; Unemployed 3,118; Total labour force 45,036.

HEALTH AND WELFARE

Under-5 Mortality Rate (per 1,000 live births, 1996): 4.1.

Physicians (per 1,000 head, 1999): 1.28.

Hospital Beds (per 1,000 head, 1995): 37.0.

Health Expenditure (% of GDP, 1998): 2.5.

Access to Water (% of persons, 1995): 100.

Access to Sanitation (% of persons, 1995): 100.
Source: partly Pan American Health Organization.
For definitions, see explanatory note on p. vi.

FISHING

Total catch (metric tons, live weight, 2001): 163 (Groupers 15, Snappers and jobfishes 45, Wahoo 60, Other marine fishes 43). Source: FAO, *Yearbook of Fishery Statistics*.

INDUSTRY

Electric Energy (million kWh, 2002): 824.6.

FINANCE

Currency and Exchange Rates: 100 cents = 1 Aruban gulden (guilder) or florin (A Fl.). *Sterling, Dollar and Euro Equivalents* (31 December 2003): £1 sterling = A Fl. 3.195; US $1 = A Fl. 1.790; €1 = A Fl. 2.261; A Fl. 100 = £31.30 = $55.87 = €44.23. Note: The Aruban florin was introduced in January 1986, replacing (at par) the Netherlands Antilles guilder or florin (NA Fl.). Since its introduction, the currency has had a fixed exchange rate of US $1 = A Fl. 1.79.

Budget (A Fl. million, 2002): *Revenue:* Tax revenue 610.0 (Taxes on income and profits 301.3, Taxes on commodities 213.5, Taxes on property 33.7, Taxes on services 47.1, Foreign exchange commission 14.4); Other current revenue 103.8; Total 713.8, excluding grants received (37.4). *Expenditure:* Wages 261.7; Employers' contributions 66.0; Wage subsidies 108.1; Goods and services 149.4; Interest payments 38.2; Investments 13.3; Other expenditure 179.8; Total 816.4.

International Reserves (US $ million at 31 December 2002): Gold 36.00; Foreign exchange 334.94; Total 370.94. Source: IMF, *International Financial Statistics*.

Money Supply (A Fl. million at 31 December 2002): Currency outside banks 127.84; Demand deposits at commercial banks 705.49; Total money (incl. others) 844.49. Source: IMF, *International Financial Statistics*.

Cost of Living (Consumer Price Index at December; base: September 2000 = 100): 103.4 in 2001; 107.7 in 2002; 110.1 in 2003.

Gross Domestic Product (A. Fl. million at current prices): 3,327 in 2000; 3,399 in 2001; 3,421 in 2002.

Expenditure on the Gross Domestic Product (A. Fl. million at current prices, 2002): Government final consumption expenditure 899; Private final consumption expenditure 1,800; Increase in stocks 32; Gross fixed capital formation 766; *Total domestic expenditure* 3,497; Exports of goods and services 2,370; *Less* Imports of goods and services 2,445; *GDP in purchasers' values* 3,421.

Balance of Payments (A Fl. million, 2002): Exports of goods f.o.b. 2,708.0; Imports of goods f.o.b. –3,673.4; *Trade balance* –965.4; Exports of services 1,883.7; Imports of services –1,114.3; *Balance on goods and services* –196.0; Other income received 60.4; Other income paid –259.2; *Balance on goods, services and income* –394.8; Current transfers received 62.9; Current transfers paid –182.7; *Current account balance* –514.6; Capital account (net) 36.9; Direct investment abroad –5.6; Direct investment from abroad 420.9; Portfolio investment assets 38.7; Portfolio investment liabilities 30.1; Other investment (net) 28.0; Net errors and omissions 4.7; *Overall balance* 39.0.

EXTERNAL TRADE

Principal Commodities (A Fl. million, 2002): *Imports c.i.f.:* Live animals and animal products 90.8; Food products 146.8; Chemical products 163.4; Base metals and articles thereof 102.1; Machinery and electrical equipment 249.6; Transport equipment 119.2; Total (incl. others) 1,361.6. *Exports f.o.b.:* Live animals and animal products 18.1; Machinery and electrical equipment 11.1; Transport equipment 3.2; Art objects and collectors' items 8.5; Total (incl. others) 62.3. Note: Figures exclude transactions of the petroleum sector and those of the Free Trade Zone of Aruba.

Principal Trading Partners (A Fl. million, 2002): *Imports c.i.f.:* Japan 35.5; Netherlands 172.5; Netherlands Antilles 44.7; USA 822.5; Venezuela 41.0; Total (incl. others) 1,361.6. *Exports f.o.b.:* Colombia 5.0; Netherlands 6.3; Netherlands Antilles 9.2; USA 25.2; Venezuela 12.4; Total (incl. others) 62.3. Note: Figures exclude transactions of the petroleum sector and those of the Free Trade Zone of Aruba.

TRANSPORT

Road Traffic (motor vehicles in use, December 2002): Passenger cars 42,802; Lorries 804; Buses 391; Taxis 398; Rental cars 3,324; Other cars 549; Motorcycles 960; Total 49,228.

Shipping (2001): *Arrivals:* Oil tankers 390; Cruise ships 298.

Civil Aviation: *Aircraft Movements:* 36,508 in 2000; 34,566 in 2001; 33,748 in 2002. *Passenger Arrivals:* 809,087 in 2000; 821,454 in 2001; 759,085 in 2002.

TOURISM

Tourist Arrivals: 1,178,716 (691,420 stop-over visitors, 487,296 cruise-ship passengers) in 2001; 1,224,822 (642,627 stop-over visitors, 582,195 cruise-ship passengers) in 2002; 1,184,233 (641,906 stop-over visitors, 542,327 cruise-ship passengers) in 2003.

Tourism Receipts: US $903.3m. in 2002.

COMMUNICATIONS MEDIA

Radio Receivers (1997): 50,000 in use.

Television Receivers (1997): 20,000 in use.

Telephones (2001): 37,132 main lines in use.

Facsimile Machines (1996): 3,600 in use.

Mobile Cellular Telephones (2001): 53,000 subscribers.

Internet Users (2001): 7,912.

Daily Newspapers (1996): 13 titles (estimated circulation 73,000 copies per issue).
Sources: mainly UNESCO, *Statistical Yearbook*; International Telecommunication Union and UN, *Statistical Yearbook*.

EDUCATION

Pre-primary (2000/01): 23 schools; 2,737 pupils; 105 teachers.

Primary (2000/01): 33 schools; 8,849 pupils; 415 teachers.

General Secondary (2000/01): 10 schools; 4,251 pupils; 242 teachers.

Technical-Vocational (2000/01): 2 schools; 3,237 pupils; 263 teachers.

Community College (1999/2000): 1 school; 1,187 pupils; 106 teachers.

University (1999/2000): 1 university; 208 students; 24 tutors.

Teacher Training (2000/01): 1 institution; 180 students; 25 teachers.

Special Education (2000/01): 4 schools; 272 pupils; 56 teachers.

Private, Non-aided (1999/2000): 4 schools; 553 pupils; 58 teachers.

International School (2000/01): 154 pupils; 25 teachers.

Adult Literacy Rate (official estimates, 2000): Males 97.6%; Females 97.1%.

Directory

The Constitution

On 1 January 1986 Aruba acquired separate status (*status aparte*) within the Kingdom of the Netherlands. The form of government is similar to that for the Netherlands Antilles, which is embodied in the Charter of the Kingdom of the Netherlands (operational from 20 December 1954). The Netherlands, the Netherlands Antilles (Antilles of the Five) and Aruba each enjoy full autonomy in domestic and internal affairs, and are united on a basis of equality for the protection of their common interests and the granting of mutual assistance. In economic and monetary affairs there is a co-operative union between Aruba and the Antilles of the Five, known as the 'Union of the Netherlands Antilles and Aruba'.

The Governor, who is appointed by the Dutch Crown for a term of six years, represents the monarch of the Netherlands in Aruba. The Government of Aruba appoints a minister plenipotentiary to represent it in the Government of the Kingdom. Whenever the Netherlands Council of Ministers is dealing with matters coming under the heading of joint affairs of the realm (in practice mainly foreign affairs and defence), the Council assumes the status of Council of Ministers of the Kingdom. In that event, Aruba's Minister Plenipotentiary takes part, with full voting powers, in the deliberations.

A legislative proposal regarding affairs of the realm and applying to Aruba as well as to the 'metropolitan' Netherlands is sent, simultaneously with its submission, to the Staten Generaal (the Netherlands parliament) and to the Staten (parliament) of Aruba. The latter body can report in writing to the Staten Generaal on the draft Kingdom Statute and designate one or more special delegates to attend the debates and furnish information in the meetings of the Chambers of the Staten Generaal. Before the final vote on a draft the Minister Plenipotentiary has the right to express an opinion on it. If he disapproves of the draft, and if in the Second Chamber a three-fifths' majority of the votes cast is not obtained, the discussions on the draft are suspended and further deliberations take place in the Council of Ministers of the Kingdom. When special delegates attend the meetings of the Chambers this right devolves upon the delegates of the parliamentary body designated for this purpose.

The Governor has executive power in external affairs, which he exercises in co-operation with the Council of Ministers. He is assisted by an advisory council which consists of at least five members appointed by him.

Executive power in internal affairs is vested in a nominated Council of Ministers, responsible to the Staten. The Aruban Staten consists of 21 members, who are elected by universal adult suffrage for four years (subject to dissolution), on the basis of proportional representation. Inhabitants have the right to vote if they have Dutch nationality and have reached 18 years of age. Voting is not compulsory.

The Government

HEAD OF STATE

Queen of the Netherlands: HM Queen BEATRIX.

Governor: OLINDO KOOLMAN (took office in 1992).

COUNCIL OF MINISTERS
(April 2004)

Prime Minister and Minister of General Affairs and Utilities: NELSON ORLANDO ODUBER.

Deputy Prime Minister and Minister of Social Affairs and Infrastructure: MARISOL J. TROMP.

Minister of Education: FREDIS J. REFUNJOL.

Minister of Finance and Economic Affairs: NILO J. J. SWAEN.

Minister of Justice: HYACINTHO RUDY CROES.

Minister of Public Health and the Environment: CANDELARIO A. S. D. (BOOSHI) WEVER.

Minister of Sports, Culture and Labour: TAI FOO RAMON LEE.

Minister of Tourism and Transportation: EDISON BRIESEN.

Minister Plenipotentiary and Member of the Council of Ministers of the Realm for Aruba in the Netherlands: ALICIA A. TROMP-YARZAGARAY.

Minister Plenipotentiary of the Realm for Aruba in Washington, DC (USA): HENRY BAARH.

MINISTRIES

Office of the Governor: Plaza Henny Eman 3, Oranjestad.

Office of the Prime Minister: Government Offices, L. G. Smith Blvd 76, Oranjestad; tel. 5880300; fax 5880024.

Ministry of Education: L. G. Smith Blvd 76, Oranjestad; tel. 5830937; fax 5828328.

Ministry of Finance and Economic Affairs: L. G. Smith Blvd 76, Oranjestad; tel. 5880269; fax 5880347; e-mail minfin.ecaffairs@setarnet.aw.

Ministry of General Affairs and Utilities: L. G. Smith Blvd 76, Oranjestad; tel. 5839022; fax 5838958.

Ministry of Justice: L. G. Smith Blvd 76, Oranjestad; tel. 5839131; fax 5825388.

Ministry of Public Health and the Environment: L. G. Smith Blvd 76, Oranjestad; tel. 5834966; fax 5835082.

Ministry of Social Affairs and Infrastructure: L. G. Smith Blvd 76, Oranjestad; tel. 5880700; fax 5880032; e-mail minszi@email.com; internet www.minszi.aw.

Ministry of Sports, Culture and Labour: L. G. Smith Blvd 76, Oranjestad; tel. 5839695; fax 5835985.

Ministry of Tourism and Transportation: L. G. Smith Blvd 76, Oranjestad; tel. 5839035; fax 5835084.

Office of the Minister Plenipotentiary for Aruba: R. J. Schimmelpenninckllaan 1, 2517 JN The Hague, Netherlands; tel. (70) 356-6200; fax (70) 345-1446.

Legislature

STATEN

President: FRANCISCO W. CROES, Staten, L. G. Smith Blvd 72, Oranjestad.

General Election, 28 September 2001

Party	% of votes	Seats
Movimentu Electoral di Pueblo	52.5	12
Arubaanse Volkspartij	26.6	6
Partido Patriótico Arubano	9.6	2
Organisacion Liberal Arubano	5.7	1
Others	5.6	—
Total	100.0	21

Political Organizations

Acción Democratico Nacional (ADN) (National Democratic Action): Oranjestad; f. 1985; Leader PEDRO CHARRO KELLY.

Aliansa Democratico Arubano (Aruban Democratic Alliance): Oranjestad; internet www.partidoaliansa.org; Leader ROBERT FREDERICK WEVER.

Arubaanse Volkspartij (AVP) (Aruba People's Party): Oranjestad; tel. 5833500; fax 5837870; f. 1942; advocates Aruba's separate status; Leader MICHIEL GODFRIED EMAN.

Conscientisacion y Liberacion Arubano (CLA) (Concentration for the Liberation of Aruba): Oranjestad; Leader MARIANO DUVERT BLUME.

Movimentu Electoral di Pueblo (MEP) (People's Electoral Movement): Santa Cruz 74D, Oranjestad; tel. 5854495; fax 5850768; e-mail mep@setarnet.aw; internet www.setarnet.aw/organisationpage/mep; f. 1971; socialist; 1,200 mems; Pres. and Leader NELSON ORLANDO ODUBER.

Organisacion Liberal Arubano (OLA) (Aruban Liberal Organization): Oranjestad; f. 1991; Leader GLENBERT FRANCOIS CROES.

Partido Patriótico Arubano (PPA) (Patriotic Party of Aruba): Oranjestad; internet www.visitaruba.com/ppa/jrpeterson; f. 1949; social democratic; opposed to complete independence for Aruba; Leader BENEDICT (BENNY) JOCELYN MONTGOMERY NISBETT.

Judicial System

Legal authority is exercised by the Court of First Instance. Appeals are heard by the Joint High Court of Justice of the Netherlands Antilles and Aruba.

Attorney-General of Aruba: THERESA D. CROES-FERNANDES PEDRA.

Courts of Justice: J. G. Emanstraat 51, Oranjestad.

Religion

Roman Catholics form the largest religious community, numbering more than 80% of the population. The Anglicans and the Methodist, Dutch Protestant and other Protestant churches have a total membership of about 6,500. There are approximately 130 Jews.

CHRISTIANITY

The Roman Catholic Church

Aruba forms part of the diocese of Willemstad, comprising the Netherlands Antilles and Aruba. The Bishop resides in Willemstad (Curaçao, Netherlands Antilles).

Roman Catholic Church: J. Yrausquin Plein 3, POB 702, Oranjestad; tel. 5821434; fax 5821409.

The Anglican Communion

Within the Church in the Province of the West Indies, Aruba forms part of the diocese of the North Eastern Caribbean and Aruba. The Bishop is resident in The Valley, Anguilla.

Anglican Church: Holy Cross, Weg Seroe Pretoe 31, Sint Nicolaas; tel. 5845142; fax 5843394.

Protestant Churches

Baptist Church: Aruba Baptist Mission, SBC, Paradera 98-C; tel. 5883893.

Church of Christ: Pastoor Hendrikstraat 107, Sint Nicolaas; tel. 5848172.

Dutch Protestant Church: Wilhelminastraat 1, Oranjestad; tel. 5821435.

Evangelical Church: C. Huygenstraat 17, POB 272, Oranjestad; tel. 5822058.

Faith Revival Center: Rooi Afo 10, Paradera; tel. 5831010.

Iglesia Evangelica Pentecostal: Asamblea di Dios, Reamurstraat 2, Oranjestad; tel. 5831940.

Jehovah's Witnesses: Guyabastraat 3, Oranjestad; tel. 5828963.

Methodist Church: Longfellowstraat, Oranjestad; tel. 5845243.

New Apostolic Church: Goletstraat SA, Oranjestad; tel. 5833762.

Pentacostal Apostolic Assembly: Bernhardstraat 185; tel. 5848710.

Seventh-day Adventist: Weststraat, Oranjestad; tel. 5845896.

JUDAISM

Beth Israel Synagogue: Adriaan Laclé Blvd, Oranjestad; tel. 5823272; fax 5823534.

BAHÁ'Í FAITH

Spiritual Assembly: Bucutiweg 19, Oranjestad; tel. 5823104.

The Press

DAILIES

Amigoe di Aruba: Patriastraat 13, POB 323, Oranjestad; tel. 5824333; fax 5822368; e-mail amigoearuba@setarnet.aw; internet amigoe.com; f. 1884; Dutch; Gen. Man. and Editor-in-Chief MICHAEL O. WILLEMSE; circ. 12,000 (in Aruba and Netherlands Antilles).

Aruba Today: Weststraat 22, Oranjestad; tel. 5827800; fax 5827093; e-mail today@bondia.com; Editor-in-Chief VANJA ODUBER.

Bon Dia Aruba: Weststraat 22, Oranjestad; tel. 5827800; fax 5827044; e-mail comment@bondia.com; internet www.bondia.com; Dir VICTOR WINKLAAR.

Diario: Engelandstraat 29, POB 577, Oranjestad; tel. 58826747; fax 58828551; e-mail diario@setanet.aw; internet www.diarioaruba.com; f. 1980; Papiamento; morning; Editor/Man. JOSSY M. MANSUR; circ. 15,000.

Extra: Dominicanessenstraat 17, Oranjestad; tel. 58834034; fax 5821639; Papiamento; Dir C. FRANKEN.

The News: Italiestraat 5, POB 300, Oranjestad; tel. 5824725; fax 5826125; f. 1951; English; Publr GERARDUS J. SCHOUTEN; Editor BEN BENNET; circ. 6,900.

Nobo: Dominicanessenstraat 17, Oranjestad; tel. 5834034; fax 5827272; Dir ADRIAAN ARENDS.

La Prensa: Bachstraat 6, POB 566 Oranjestad; tel. 5821199; fax 5828634; f. 1929; Papiamento; Editor THOMAS C. PIETERSZ.

NEWS AGENCIES

Algemeen Nederlands Persbureau (ANP) (The Netherlands): Caya G. F. (Betico) Croes 110, POB 323, Oranjestad; tel. 5824333; fax 5822368.

Aruba News Agencies: Bachstraat 6, Oranjestad; tel. 5821243.

Publishers

Aruba Experience Publications NV: L. G. Smith Blvd 58, Oranjestad; tel. 5834467.

Caribbean Publishing Co (CPC) Ltd: L. G. Smith Blvd 116, Oranjestad; tel. 5820485; fax 5820484.

De Wit Stores NV: L. G. Smith Blvd 110, POB 386, Oranjestad; tel. 5823500; fax 5821575; e-mail dewitstores@setarnet.aw; f. 1948; Man. Dir R. DE ZWART.

Gold Book Publishing: L. G. Smith Blvd 116, Oranjestad; tel. 5820485; fax 5820484.

Oranjestad Printing NV: Italiestraat 5, POB 300, Oranjestad; Man. Dir GERARDUS J. SCHOUTEN.

ProGraphics Inc: Italiestraat 5, POB 201, Oranjestad; tel. 5824550; fax 5822526; e-mail vadprinting@setarnet.aw; f. 2001; fmrly VAD Printers Inc.

Publicidad Aruba NV: Wilhelminastraat 101, Oranjestad; tel. 5825132.

Publicidad Exito Aruba SA: Domenicanessenstraat 17, POB 142, Oranjestad; tel. 5822020; fax 5824242; f. 1958.

Rozenstand Publishing Co: Cuquisastraat 1, Oranjestad; tel. 5824482.

Van Dorp Aruba NV: Caya G. F. (Betico) Croes 77, POB 596, Oranjestad; tel. 5823076; fax 5823573.

Broadcasting and Communications

TELECOMMUNICATIONS

Servicio di Telecomunicacion di Aruba (SETAR): Seroe Blanco z/n, POB 13, Oranjestad; tel. 5251576; fax 5836970; e-mail setar@setarnet.aw; internet www.setar.aw; f. 1986; Man. Dir PATRICIO NICOLAS.

BROADCASTING

Radio

Canal 90 FM Stereo: Van Leeuwenhoekstraat 26, Oranjestad; tel. 5824134.

Cristal Sound 1-01 7 FM: J. G. Emanstraat 124A, Oranjestad; tel. 5827726; fax 5820144.

Radio 1270: Bernardstraat 138, POB 28, Sint Nicolaas; tel. 5845602; fax 5827753; commercial station; programmes in Dutch, English, Spanish and Papiamento; Dir F. A. LEAUER; Station Man. J. A. C. ALDERS.

Radio Carina FM: Datustraat 10A, Oranjestad; tel. 5821450; fax 5831955; commercial station; programmes in Dutch, English, Spanish and Papiamento; Dir-Gen. ALBERT R. DIEFFENTHALER.

Radio Caruso Booy FM: G. M. De Bruynewijk 49, Savaneta; tel. 5847752; fax 5843351; commercial station; broadcasts for 24 hrs a day; programmes in Dutch, English, Spanish and Papiamento; Pres. HUBERT E. A. BOOY; Gen. Man. SIRA BOOY.

Radio Galactica FM: J. G. Emanstraat 120, Oranjestad; tel. 5820999; fax 5838999; f. 1990; Dir MODESTO J. ODUBER; Station Man. MAIKEL J. ODUBER.

Radio Kelkboom: Bloemond 14, POB 146, Oranjestad; tel. 5821899; fax 5834825; e-mail radiokelkboom@setarnet.aw; f. 1954; commercial radio station; programmes in Dutch, English, Spanish and Papiamento; Owners CARLOS A. KELKBOOM, E. A. M. KELKBOOM; Dir EMILE A. M. KELKBOOM.

Radio Victoria: Washington 23, POB 5291, Oranjestad; tel. 5873444; fax 5873444; e-mail radiovictoria@setarnet.aw; f. 1958; religious and cultural FM radio station owned by the Radio Victoria

Foundation; programmes in Dutch, English, Spanish and Papiamento; Pres. N. J. F. ARTS.

Voz di Aruba (Voice of Aruba): Van Leeuwenhoekstraat 26, POB 219, Oranjestad; tel. 5824134; commercial radio station; programmes in Dutch, English, Spanish and Papiamento; also operates Canal 90 on FM; Dir A. M. ARENDS, Jr.

Television

ABC Aruba Broadcasting Co NV: Royal Plaza Suite 223, POB 5040, Oranjestad; tel. 5838150; fax 5838110; e-mail 15atv@setarnet.aw.

Tele-Aruba NV: Pos Chiquito 1A, POB 392, Oranjestad; tel. 5857302; fax 5851683; e-mail telearuba@hotmail.com; internet www.telearuba.aw; f. 1963; formerly operated by Netherlands Antilles Television Co; commercial; govt-owned; Gen. Man. M. MARCHENA.

Finance

(cap. = capital; res = reserves; dep. = deposits; m. = million; brs = branches; amounts in Aruban florin)

BANKING

Central Bank

Centrale Bank van Aruba: J. E. Irausquin Blvd 8, POB 18, Oranjestad; tel. 5822509; fax 5832251; e-mail cbaua@setarnet.aw; internet www.cbaruba.org; f. 1986; cap. 10.0m., res 113.1m., dep. 398.9m. (Dec. 2002); Pres. ANTHONY R. CARAM; Exec. Dirs K. A. H. POLVLIET, J. R. FIGAROA-SEMELEER.

Commercial Banks

Aruba Bank NV: Caya G. F. (Betico) Croes 41, POB 192, Oranjestad; tel. 5821550; fax 5829152; e-mail abank@setarnet.aw; internet www.arubabank.com; f. 1925; cap. and res 21m., dep. 300m. (1996); Man. Dir and CEO ILDEFONS D'ANDELO SIMON; 7 brs.

Banco di Caribe NV: Vondellaan 31, Oranjestad; tel. 5832168; fax 5832422; e-mail bdcaua@setarnet; internet www.bancodicaribe.com; f. 1987; Gen. Man. E. A. DE KORT; 1 br.

Caribbean Mercantile Bank NV: Caya G. F. (Betico) Croes 53, POB 28, Oranjestad; tel. 5823118; fax 5824373; e-mail executive_office@cmbnv.com; internet www.cmbnv.com; f. 1963; cap. 4.0m., res 43.0m., dep. 714.9m. (Dec. 2001); Pres. L. CAPRILES; Man. Dir W. G. CARSON; 5 brs.

Interbank Aruba NV: Caya G. F. (Betico) Croes 38, POB 96, Oranjestad; tel. 5831080; fax 5824058; e-mail info@interbankaruba.com; internet www.interbankaruba.com; f. 1987; owned by Fundacion Cas pa Comunidad Arubano (FCCA) since 2001; Man. Dir IRVING A. DURAND; 3 brs.

RBTT Bank Aruba NV: Italiestraat 36, Sasakiweg, Oranjestad; tel. 5833221; fax 58821756; e-mail firstet@setarnet.aw; internet www.rbtt.co.tt; f. 2001; formerly First National Bank of Aruba NV (f. 1985 and acquired by Royal Bank of Trinidad and Tobago Ltd in 1998); total assets US $125.3m. (Dec. 2000); Chair. PETER J. JULY; Pres. EDWIN L. TROMP; 6 brs.

Investment Bank

Aruban Investment Bank NV: Wilhelminastraat 32–36, POB 1011, Oranjestad; tel. 5827327; fax 5827461; e-mail aib@setarnet.aw; internet www.arubainvestmentbank.com; f. 1987; Pres. P. C. M. VAN DER VOORT VAN ZIJP.

Mortgage Banks

Fundacion Cas pa Comunidad Arubano (FCCA): Sabana Blanco 66, Oranjestad; tel. 5823884; fax 5836272.

OHRA Hypotheek & Postspaarbank NK: L. G. Smith Blvd 60, Oranjestad; tel. 5839666; fax 5839498; e-mail info@ohrabank-aua.com.

'Offshore' Banks

Inarco International Bank NV: Punta Brabo z/n, Arulex Bldg, Oranjestad; tel. 5822138; fax 5832363.

Citibank NA: Punta Brabo z/n, Arulex Bldg, Oranjestad; tel. 5822138; fax 5832363.

INSURANCE

There were nine life insurance companies active in Aruba in December 2001.

Trade and Industry

DEVELOPMENT ORGANIZATION

Department of Economic Affairs, Commerce and Industry (Direktie Economische Zaken, Handel en Industrie): Sun Plaza Bldg, L. G. Smith Blvd 160, Oranjestad; tel. 5821181; fax 5834494; e-mail deaci@setarnet.aw; internet www.arubaeconomicaffairs.com; Dir HUMPHREY O. VAN TRIKT.

CHAMBER OF COMMERCE AND INDUSTRY

Aruba Chamber of Commerce and Industry: J. E. Irausquin Blvd 10, POB 140, Oranjestad; tel. 5821566; fax 5833962; e-mail auachamber@setarnet.aw; internet www.arubachamber.com; f. 1930; Pres. ALAN H. RILEY; Exec. Dir L. C. DE SOUZA.

TRADE ASSOCIATION

Aruba Trade and Industry Association: ATIA Bldg, Pedro Gallegostraat 6, POB 562, Oranjestad; tel. 5827593; fax 5833068; e-mail atiaruba@setarnet.aw; internet www.atiaruba.org; f. 1945; Pres. G. M. PETERSON.

UTILITIES

Electricity and Water

Utilities Aruba NV: govt-owned holding co.

Electriciteit-Maatschappij Aruba (ELMAR) NV: Wilhelmi-nastraat 110, Oranjestad; tel. 5823700; fax 5828991; e-mail elmar.aruba@setarnet.aw; internet www.elmararuba.com; independently-managed co, residing under Utilities Aruba NV; electricity distribution; Man. Dir ISMAEL W. F. WEVER.

Water en Energiebedrijf Aruba (WEB) NV: Balashi 76, POB 575, Oranjestad; tel. 5854600; fax 5857681; e-mail info@webaruba.com; internet www.webaruba.com; f. 1991; independently managed co, residing under Utilities Aruba NV; production and distribution of industrial and potable water, and electricity generation; Gen. Dir JOSÉ LACLÉ.

Gas

Aruba Gas Supply Company Ltd (ARUGAS): Barcadera z/n, Oranjestad; tel. 5851198; fax 5852187; e-mail arubagas@setarnet.aw.

BOC Gases Aruba: Balashi 21N, POB 190, Oranjestad; tel. 5852624; fax 5852823.

TRADE UNIONS

Federashon di Trahadonan Arubano (FTA) (Aruban Workers' Federation): Bernardstraat 23, Sint Nicolaas; tel. 5845448; fax 5845504; f. 1964; independent; affiliated to World Confederation of Labour; Sec.-Gen. ANSELMO PONTILIUS.

There are also several unions for government and semi-government workers and employees.

Transport

There are no railways, but Aruba has a network of all-weather roads.

Arubus NV: Sabana Blanco 67, Oranjestad; tel. 5827089; fax 5828633; state-owned company providing public transport services.

SHIPPING

The island's principal seaport is Oranjestad, whose harbour can accommodate ocean-going vessels. There are also ports at Barcadera and Sint Nicolaas.

Aruba Ports Authority NV: L. G. Smith Blvd 23, Oranjestad; tel. 5826633; fax 5832896; e-mail aruports@setarnet.aw; f. 1981; responsible for the administration of the ports of Oranjestad and Barcadera; Dir M. H. HENRÍQUEZ.

Coastal Aruba Refining Co NV: Seroe Colorado, POB 2150, Sint Nicholas; tel. 5894904; fax 5849087; f. 1989; petroleum refinery, responsible for the administration of the port of Sint Nicolas; Gen. Man. DAVID LAM.

Principal Shipping Companies

Beng Lian Shipping S. de R. L. A. V. V.: Dominicanessenstraat 22, Oranjestad.

Magna Shipping Co: Koningstraat 52, Oranjestad; tel. 5824349.

Rodoca Shipping and Trading SA: Parkietenbos 30, Barcadera Harbour; tel. 5850096; fax 5823371; fmrly Aruba Shipping and Chartering Co NV.

Windward Island Agencies: Heyligerweg, POB 66, Oranjestad.

CIVIL AVIATION

The Queen Beatrix International Airport, about 2.5 km from Oranjestad, is served by numerous airlines, linking the island with destinations in the Caribbean, Europe, the USA and Central and South America. In November 2000 the national carrier, Air Aruba, was declared bankrupt.

Avia Air: Queen Beatrix International Airport, Oranjestad; tel. 5834600; fax 5826355; f. 1987; domestic and regional services.

Tourism

Aruba's white sandy beaches, particularly along the southern coast, are an attraction for foreign visitors, and tourism is a major industry. The number of hotel rooms increased from 2,078 in 1986 to 6,831 in 2002. In 2003 most stop-over visitors came from the USA (72.4%), Venezuela (8.5%) and the Netherlands (5.7%). In 2003 641,906 stop-over visitors and 542,327 cruise-ship passengers visited Aruba. Receipts from tourism visitors totalled US $903.3m. in 2002.

Aruba Tourism Authority (ATA): L. G. Smith Blvd 172, Oranjestad; tel. 5823777; fax 5834702; e-mail ata.aruba@aruba.com; internet www.aruba.com; f. 1953; plans to make the state-controlled ATA operationally independent are pending; Man. Dir MYRNA JANSEN-FELICIANO.

Aruba Hotel and Tourism Association: L. G. Smith Blvd 174, POB 542, Oranjestad; tel. 5822607; fax 5824202; e-mail ahata@setarnet.aw; internet www.aruba.com; CEO HORACE HORD.

Cruise Tourism Authority—Aruba: POB 5254, Suite 227, Royal Plaza Mall, L. G. Smith Blvd 94, Oranjestad; tel. 5833648; fax 5835088; e-mail int1721@setarnet.aw; internet www.arubabycruise.com; Exec. Dir KATHLEEN ROJER.

THE NETHERLANDS ANTILLES

Introductory Survey

Location, Climate, Language, Religion, Flag, Capital

The Netherlands Antilles (Antilles of the Five) consists of two groups of islands in the Caribbean Sea, about 800 km (500 miles) apart. The main group, lying off the coast of Venezuela, consists of Bonaire and Curaçao which (together with Aruba, 68 km to the east of Curaçao) are known as the Benedenwindse Eilands or 'Leeward Islands'; to the north-east lie the small volcanic islands of St (Sint) Eustatius (also known as Statia), Saba and St (Sint) Maarten (the northern half of the last island being a dependency of the French overseas department of Guadeloupe),

known as the Bovenwindse Eilands or 'Windward Islands' (although actually in the Leeward group of the Lesser Antilles). The climate is tropical, moderated by the sea, with an average annual temperature of 27.5°C (81°F) and little rainfall. The official languages are Dutch and Papiamento (a mixture of Dutch, Spanish, Portuguese, English, Arawak Indian and several West African dialects), which is the dominant language of the 'Leeward Islands'. English is the official and principal language of the 'Windward Islands'. Spanish is also widely spoken. Almost all of the inhabitants profess Christianity: the people of the 'Leeward Islands' and Saba are predominantly Roman Catholics, while those of St Eustatius and St Maarten are predominantly Protestants. The state flag (proportions 2 by 3) is white, with a red vertical stripe in the centre, crossed by a horizontal blue stripe on which there are five white five-pointed stars (one for each of the main islands) arranged in an oval. The capital is Willemstad, on the island of Curaçao.

Recent History

The 'Leeward Islands', already settled by communities of Arawak Indians, were discovered by the Spanish in 1499 and were seized by the Dutch in the 1630s. Curaçao became prosperous in the late 17th and 18th centuries as an entrepôt for trade in the Caribbean. The Dutch settled the 'Windward Islands', once settled by Carib Indians, in the mid-17th century. After frequent changes in possession, the islands (including Aruba) were finally confirmed as Dutch territory in 1816. The two groups were administered as Curaçao and Dependencies between 1845 and 1948. Slavery was abolished in 1863, and the islands suffered from an economic decline until the establishment of petroleum refineries on Curaçao and Aruba, in 1918 and 1929, respectively. During the Second World War Queen Wilhelmina of the Netherlands promised independence, and in 1954 a Charter gave the federation of six islands full autonomy in domestic affairs, and declared it to be an integral part of the Kingdom of the Netherlands.

Divisions of political allegiance within the territory have been along island, rather than policy, lines, and a series of coalition Governments has frequently paralysed decision-making. In 1969 serious rioting and looting broke out in Willemstad after a demonstration by workers in the petroleum industry. Troops had to be sent from the Netherlands to quell the disturbances and to restore order. In February 1970 the socialist Government of Ciro Kroon resigned over the nomination of a new Governor, and in 1971 the Government of E. Petronia resigned over the rejection by the Staten (parliament) of new financial measures.

Following elections to the Staten in June 1977, a coalition Government was formed, with the leader of the Democratische Partij (DP), Silvio Rozendal, as Prime Minister. After a boycott of the session by the Movimentu Electoral di Pueblo (MEP) of Aruba and the Frente Obrero i Liberashon 30 di mei (FOL), the Staten was eventually convened by a Governor's decree in October. Rozendal resigned in April 1979, and elections were held in July. A coalition administration was formed by the Movimentu Antiyas Nobo (MAN), the MEP and the Unión Patriótico Bonairiano (UPB), with Dominico (Don) Martina, the leader of the MAN, as Prime Minister. The DP joined the coalition Government in December 1980.

In Aruba resentment of the administrative dominance of Curaçao resulted, in 1971, in the establishment of the pro-independence MEP. In 1981 a series of talks regarding Aruba's future began with the Netherlands Government. However, in September the MEP representatives in the Staten withdrew their support for the Government on the question of Aruba's rights to possible discoveries of petroleum off its coast. The Government's majority was restored by the inclusion of the DP—St Maarten (DP—StM) member for the 'Windward Islands' in the coalition, but a DP resignation in January 1982 precipitated a further crisis. A general election in June failed to resolve the situation, and it was not until October that agreement was reached on the formation by Martina of a new coalition, which excluded the MEP.

In March 1983 agreement was finally reached whereby Aruba would be given separate status (*status aparte*) within the Kingdom of the Netherlands from January 1986, with the prospect of full independence in 1996 (for further details, see Aruba, q.v.). Arguments persisted regarding the division of the Antilles' financial reserves, and over rights to explore for petroleum and other minerals. In June 1984 Martina's coalition Government resigned. A five-party coalition was eventually formed in September, with Maria Liberia-Peters of the conservative Partido Nashonal di Pueblo (PNP) as Prime Minister.

At a general election in November 1985 the PNP gained the largest number of seats in the Staten for the Antilles of the Five (six out of 22), but was unable to secure enough support from other parties to form a government. Martina once again became Prime Minister and formed a coalition Government. During 1986–87 the Government was forced to introduce a series of economic austerity measures, following Aruba's separation from the Netherlands Antilles and the decline of both the petroleum-refining industry and 'offshore' financial services. The Government resigned in March 1988, after losing the support of the DP—StM and the FOL. In May Liberia-Peters formed a coalition with all the parties represented in the Staten except for the MAN and the DP—Curaçao (DP—C).

In January 1989 Martina revealed that successive Curaçao administrations had diverted revenues from the 'offshore' financial sector into a fund that had not been declared to The Hague during negotiations for budgetary support. The Netherlands had recently exerted pressure for more control to be exercised over the large amount of aid that it provided for the Netherlands Antilles. By the early 1990s it appeared that, while the 'metropolitan' Government was unwilling to allow the complete disintegration of the federation, it was prepared to consider a less centralized system or the creation of two federations in the separate island groups.

At a general election in March 1990 the PNP increased the number of its seats (all on Curaçao) to seven, again making it the largest single party in the Staten, and, after some weeks of negotiations, Liberia-Peters assumed the leadership of a broadly-based coalition. In March 1992 the FOL and its partner at the 1990 election, the Social Independiente, withdrew from the Government. Liberia-Peters formed a new coalition with the DP—StM, the UPB and the DP—C. In September 1993 the DP—StM withdrew, although the Government maintained its majority in the Staten with the support of an independent deputy and subsequently that of the Windward Islands People's Movement (WIPM).

A referendum was conducted on Curaçao in November 1993 regarding its constitutional status; 73.6% of the electorate voted for a continuance of the island's status as a member of the Antillean federation. The option of separate status, favoured by the Government, received only 17.9% of the votes cast. As a result of this defeat, the WIPM and the UPB withdrew their support, thus leaving the Government without a majority in the Staten. Liberia-Peters resigned, and Alejandro Felippe Paula, a professor at the University of the Netherlands Antilles, subsequently agreed to head an interim Government. A general election took place in February 1994, at which a Curaçao-based party, the Partido Antía Restrukturá (PAR), led by Miguel A. Pourier, became the largest single party (with eight seats) in the Staten. Pourier assumed the leadership of a broadly-based coalition Government, which was inaugurated in March.

Referendums on status were conducted on St Maarten, St Eustatius, Saba and Bonaire in October 1994. On St Maarten 59.8% of the electorate voted to remain within the Antillean federation, while the option of autonomy within the Kingdom of the Netherlands received 32% of the vote. On St Eustatius 86.3% of voters opted for continued membership of the Antillean federation, while the equivalent vote on Saba was 90.6%. On Bonaire (where voting took place one week later) some 88% of voters favoured continued federation.

A general election was held on 30 January 1998, at which the PAR lost four of its eight seats in the Staten. The PNP retained its three seats, while a new party, the Partido Laboral Krusada Popular (PLKP), also took three seats. The loss of support for the PAR was attributed to the unpopularity of austerity measures imposed by the outgoing Government. Pourier failed in his attempts to form a new coalition, largely owing to the opposition of the PNP, the PLKP and the FOL (which together held eight of Curaçao's 14 seats) to the PAR's economic policies. A new coalition Government, with Susanne F. C. Camelia-Römer of the PNP as Prime Minister, was finally agreed in early May, only to collapse later in the month, when it was revealed that the designated Minister of Traffic, Transport and Communication, Nelson Monte, a member of the FOL, was under criminal investigation for alleged evasion of import duties. A new Government was sworn in on 1 June. The coalition comprised six parties, with the support of 13 of the 22 members of the Staten.

In late 1998 the Government adopted a National Recovery Plan, which aimed both to reduce the government's fiscal deficit and also to generate growth in the economy through the introduction of measures intended to stimulate investment. The Government proceeded to implement several of the measures designed to increase state revenues, which had been recommended by the National Plan Committee. However, the Government's subsequent attempts to reduce state expenditure proved to be highly controversial, and proposals to reduce the public sector work-force by some 2,400—principally through cuts in the civil service of the central Government and of the island Government of Curaçao—caused great tension between Camelia-Römer's PNP and its fellow Curaçao-based coalition partners, the PLKP and the FOL, which led, in October 1999, to the collapse of both the central Government and the island Government of Curaçao.

In November 1999 former Prime Minister Pourier formed a new broadly-based coalition Government, which had the support of 18 of the 22 members of the Staten. Concerns were, however, expressed that Pourier's Government would face the same problems as the previous administration in its attempt fully to implement the National Recovery Plan, and this was, to some extent, anticipated by Pourier's appointment of Camelia-Römer as Minister for the National Recovery Plan and Economic Affairs.

A referendum on the constitutional future of St Maarten took place on 23 June 2000. Only 4% of participants in St Maarten favoured maintaining the *status quo*. Some 69% favoured obtaining *status aparte* within the Kingdom of the Netherlands, 14% favoured complete independence and 12% preferred a restructuring of the Antilles of the Five. Although the Dutch Government indicated that it would not support a request by St Maarten to receive *status aparte*, it supported the establishment of a commission to explore the possibilities of St Maarten adopting *status aparte*. In January 2001 the Dutch Minister for the Commonwealth, Klaas de Vries, suggested that he would not exclude the possibility of a *status aparte* for St Maarten, as long as certain conditions were met. However, in February 2003 Johan Remkes, the new Dutch Minister of Home Affairs, said the Netherlands would not permit St Maarten to leave the federation. Despite this set-back, St Maarten had signed an agreement with the central Government in August 2002 that would permit the island's executive council to take out loans on its own initiative, without seeking permission from the central bank. Furthermore, in late 2002 the executive council proposed to the central bank that discussions should begin on a separate monetary system for St Maarten.

In December 2000 an agreement was reached with the Dutch Government on the compulsory acculturation of Antillean migrants to the Netherlands; Pourier had threatened to resign if his coalition partners opposed the accord. The high level of unemployment, particularly among the younger members of the Antillean community in the Netherlands, and the steady influx of new migrants in recent years had led the Dutch Government to propose that the Netherlands Antilles adopt legislation whereby those under 25 years of age would be granted permission to emigrate to the Netherlands only after attending acculturation classes designed to facilitate their integration into Dutch society.

The elections of 18 January 2002 were won by the FOL, led by Anthony Godett, which had campaigned against the stringent measures imposed by the IMF. The FOL won five seats in the 22-seat Staten (and 23.0% of the popular vote). Pourier's party, the PAR, won four legislative seats and 20.4% of the popular vote. The PNP won three seats (13.4% of the ballot), the PLKP, the DP—StM and the UPB each won two seats (12.1%, 5.5% and 3.6%, respectively), and the WIPM, the Democratische Partij—Statia (DP—StE), the Democratische Partij—Bonaire (DP—B) and the National Alliance (comprising the National Progressive Party and the St Maarten Patriotic Alliance) each gained one legislative seat. None the less, despite the party's victory, attempts by the FOL to form a coalition Government failed because of allegations of corruption and mismanagement of funds by party leaders. Eventually, in June 2002 a coalition Government that included representatives of the PAR, the PNP, the PLKP, the DP—StM, the UPD and the DP—StE took office, under the leadership of the new PAR leader, Etienne Ys, replacing Pourier's caretaker Government.

In January 2003 the Minister of Public and Social Development, Tilly Pikerie, resigned after an investigation was launched into allegations that she used a government car for personal, rather than work, purposes. Earlier in the month a member of Curaçao's Island Council, resigned amid allegations that he had accepted bribes from a Dutch-based construction company. Two other members of the Council resigned in December following similar allegations, which they denied. Later in January 2003 parliament approved new anti-corruption regulations for the National Audit Chamber, which monitors government spending.

Local elections in Curaçao in May 2003 were won by the FOL under the leadership of Anthony Godett, who had been detained by the police in April for alleged corrupt activities. The victory of Godett's party, known for its independent and assertive attitude towards the Netherlands and the IMF, was expected to impact negatively on the implementation of IMF measures and the island's political relationship with the Netherlands, which had improved under the PAR leadership. Later in the same month

Prime Minister Ys' cabinet resigned to allow the FOL to form a fresh governing coalition (comprised of the FOL, the PNP, the PLKP, the UPB, the DP—StE and the WIPM), based on new local political alliances. In late July Ben Komproe of the FOL was sworn in as Prime Minister on a temporary basis, as Godett could not be approved for the post while he faced corruption charges. On 11 August Mirna Luisa Godett, the sister of the FOL leader, was elected by the party to the post of Prime Minister, despite not being a member of the Staten. Komproe, meanwhile, was appointed Minister of Justice. Following the conviction in December of Anthony Godett (and 16 other party members, business leaders and officials) for fraud, embezzlement and corruption charges, in January 2004 the governing coalition almost lost control of the legislature when the WIPM and the UPB withdrew their support. The Government managed to retain its majority, however, when the DP—B and the National Alliance agreed in principle to join the coalition later in the same month. Although the National Alliance later reversed its decision, after other coalition members refused to appoint the Alliance's Leader, William Brewster, as Minister of Public Health and Social Development, the governing coalition retained a small majority of seats (12 out of 22). In February the Staten rejected a motion proposed by the opposition (and directed at Anthony Godett) that legislators found guilty of corruption be prevented from retaining their parliamentary seats.

Meanwhile, as anticipated, relations between the Netherlands Antilles and the Dutch Government worsened following the advent of the FOL-dominated Government. In August 2003 Mirna Luisa Godett announced that a delegation of Dutch MPs would not be officially received when they visited the territory. Furthermore, she vowed not to speak Dutch, only English. The Dutch Minister of Kingdom Relations responded by pledging to speak only Dutch, since neither the Netherlands Antilles nor the Netherlands were 'part of the British Empire'. Godett also announced plans to hold a referendum in 2004 on a proposal to replace the guilder with the US dollar as the territory's official currency. Her administration further alienated the Dutch Government by its support of a proposal to remove a body scanner at Curaçao's international airport, which had been installed in an attempt to combat the increasing drugs trade between Amsterdam and the Caribbean. Relations continued to worsen during the remainder of 2003, especially following a visit to the Netherlands Antilles in November by the Dutch State Secretary of Defence, Cees van der Knaap, who allegedly declared that there was little point in doing business with the Antillean adminstration, and with Godett in particular. In January 2004 Godett accused Dutch officials of spying on her Government after it emerged that local justice officials, including Dick Piar, the Attorney-General, had met two visiting Dutch ministers without her knowledge. Tension was further exacerbated by Godett's rejection of a Dutch proposal to ban known drugs-traffickers from Antillean airlines.

The Government lost its parliamentary majority on 5 April 2004 after four parties (the PNP, the PLKP, DP—B and the DP—StE) withdrew from the FOL-led coalition after failing to effect the resignation of the Minister of Justice, Ben Komproe. The coalition partners accused Komproe of allowing the FOL's main political donor, Nelson Monte, who was serving a custodial sentence for corruption, to stay in a luxury hospital rather than be jailed. After the Staten voted in favour of a 'no confidence' motion against the Government, the Prime Minister submitted her resignation on 6 April; Komproe, Richard Salas, the Minister of Transport and Communications, and Maurice Adriaens, the Minister Plenipotentiary and Member of the Council of Ministers of the Realm of the Netherlands Antilles, also resigned. Komproe's position had already been weakened by his failure to reverse the rising crime rate on Curaçao and by his brother's alleged involvement in fraud. His strongly worded criticism of the decision of Piar to meet privately with Dutch officials had also contributed to his unpopularity. In the wake of the resignations, the Governor, Fritz Goedgedrag, appointed an *informateur*, a working party charged with consulting the territory's political organizations over whether to reform the government with a new coalition or to hold fresh elections. The *informateur* was scheduled to submit its report to the Governor on 10 May, after which a *formateur*, dedicated to the task of forming a new government, would then be appointed. It was expected that a new regime would be in place by the end of May. Meanwhile, in April Anthony Godett was in the process of appealing against his conviction for corruption-related charges.

Government

The Governor of the Netherlands Antilles, appointed by the Dutch Crown for a term of six years, represents the monarch of the Netherlands in the territory, and has executive power over external affairs. The Governor is assisted by an advisory council. Executive power in internal affairs is vested in the Council of Ministers. The Council is responsible to the Staten (parliament), which has 22 members elected by universal adult suffrage for four years (subject to dissolution). The administration of each island is conducted by its own Island Council, Executive Council and Lieutenant-Governor.

Defence

Although defence is the responsibility of the Netherlands, compulsory military service is laid down in an Antilles Ordinance. The Governor is the Commander-in-Chief of the armed forces in the islands, and a Dutch contingent is stationed in Willemstad, Curaçao. The Netherlands also operates a Coast Guard Force (to combat organized crime and drugs-smuggling), based at St Maarten and Aruba. In May 1999 the US air force and navy began patrols from a base on Curaçao to combat the transport of illegal drugs.

Economic Affairs

In 1994 the gross national income (GNI) of the Netherlands Antilles, measured at current prices, was an estimated US $1,550m., equivalent to some $8,800 per head. In 1990–2002 the population increased by an average of 1.3% per year, while gross domestic product (GDP) increased, in real terms, by an average of 0.4% per year during 1990–95, and stood at some $2,682m. in 2002 (equivalent to $12,247 per head). Real GDP declined by 2.3% in 2001, but increased by 0.4% in 2002.

Agriculture, together with forestry, fishing and mining, contributed only 0.6% of GDP in 1997. Agriculture, forestry and fishing employed 1.1% of the working population on Curaçao in 2000. Some 8% of the total land area is cultivated. The chief products are aloes (Bonaire is a major exporter), sorghum, divi-divi, groundnuts, beans, fresh vegetables and tropical fruit. A bitter variety of orange is used in the production of Curaçao liqueur. There is also some fishing.

Industry (comprising manufacturing, construction, power and water) contributed 16.7% of GDP in 1997. Industry (including mining, manufacturing, power and construction) employed 18.0% of the working population on Curaçao in 2000.

The mining and quarrying sector employed only 0.3% of the working population on Curaçao in 2000. Apart from some phosphates on Curaçao (exploited until the mid-1980s), and some limestone and salt on Bonaire, the islands have no other significant mineral reserves. Aggregate is quarried on St Maarten and consumed primarily by the local construction industry.

Manufacturing contributed 5.7% of GDP in 1997, and employed 9.0% of the working population on Curaçao in 2000; activities include food-processing, production of Curaçao liqueur, and the manufacture of paint, paper, soap and cigarettes. Bonaire has a textile factory, and Curaçao's 'free zone' is of considerable importance in the economy, but the 'Windward Islands' have very few manufacturing activities. Petroleum-refining (using petroleum imported from Venezuela) is the islands' principal industrial activity, with the Curaçao refinery leased to the Venezuelan state petroleum company. Production capacity at the refinery was 116.8m. barrels per year in 2001, according to the US Geological Survey; however, industrial action in Venezuela led to the closure of the refinery during December 2002–March 2003, impacting heavily upon the islands' economy. In 2000 the Government sponsored a geologic review of offshore sediments that are located 5 km south-west of Saba; results indicated the potential of a resource of 500m. barrels of petroleum. Petroleum transhipment is also important, and ship repairs at the Curaçao dry dock make a significant contribution to the economy. In 1998 fuel imports comprised 54.4% of total merchandise imports.

The services sector contributed 82.7% of GDP in 1997, and engaged 81.0% of the employed labour force on Curaçao in 2000. The Netherlands Antilles is a major 'offshore' financial centre. In June 2000 the Netherlands Antilles was urged by the Organisation for Economic Co-operation and Development (OECD) to improve the accountability and transparency of its financial services; in response, the Government announced that it was to review its taxation legislation to comply more closely with OECD's standards. In April 2002 the Netherlands Antilles was removed from the list of those countries deemed to be unco-operative tax 'havens' after OECD favourably assessed the

Government's legislative amendments. In the same month an agreement was signed with the USA, pledging to share information on tax matters, with the aim of combating money-laundering and associated criminal activities. The financial and business services sector contributed 24.7% of GDP in 1997, and employed 14.4% of the Curaçao working population in 2000. Operational income from the offshore sector increased significantly in the early to mid-1990s, from NA Fl. 210.6m. in 1992 to NA Fl. 375.6m. in 1995. A major industry for all the islands (particularly St Maarten) is tourism, which is the largest employer after the public sector. In late 2001 and early 2002 the tourist industry suffered from the repercussions of the terrorist attacks on the USA in September 2001. However, the number of cruise-ship passenger arrivals rallied strongly in the second half of 2002 and, although the number of stop-over visitors declined, tourism receipts were reported to have increased by 7.6% in that year overall, compared with 2001. The outlook for 2003 was not so positive, however; the tourism sector was expected to contract as a result of the economic downturn in the USA and the repercussions of the US-led military campaign in Iraq. In addition to tourism, Curaçao, in particular, has sought to establish itself as a centre for regional trade, exploiting its excellent harbours. In 1998 a free-trade zone was established at the island's airport, which further enhanced Curaçao's entrepôt status.

In 2002 the Netherlands Antilles recorded a visible trade deficit (excluding most transactions in petroleum) of NA Fl. 1,026.8m., much of which was offset by revenue from services; there was a deficit of NA Fl. 32.3m. on the current account of the balance of payments. The petroleum industry dominates the trade figures of the Netherlands Antilles, particularly of the 'Leeward Islands'. In 1998 the principal source of imports (43.4%) was Venezuela (which provides crude petroleum), and the principal market for exports (15.3%) was the USA. The USA is an important trading partner for all the islands of the Netherlands Antilles, as are the Netherlands and other Caribbean countries. Petroleum is the principal commodity for both import and export, and accounted for 54.4% of imports and 86.0% of exports in 1998. The Netherlands Antilles also imports machinery and transport equipment, manufactured goods, and chemicals and related products, while it exports aloes, Curaçao liqueur and some light manufactures.

In 2002 the general Government (including island governments) recorded a budgetary deficit of NA Fl. 142.3m., which was equivalent to some 3.0% of GDP. In the same year the central Government recorded a deficit of NA Fl. 52.5m. on its budget. The administrations of the islands tend to operate with deficits. At the end of 2000 the combined public domestic debts of the central Government and the island Government of Curaçao were NA Fl. 3,236.2m. (67.4% of GDP). Total foreign debt stood at NA Fl. 559.8m. in 2000, owed chiefly to the Netherlands. The foreign debt in 2000 was estimated to be the equivalent of 12.7% of GDP. In 1998 the Netherlands Antilles received $125.7m. in bilateral aid and $3.4m. in multilateral aid. The average annual rate of inflation was 2.3% in 1995–2002. Consumer prices increased by an average of 15.8% in 2001 and by 0.4% in 2002. The rate of unemployment in the labour force was an estimated 14.2% for the Netherlands Antilles as a whole in 2002; 15.6% of the Curaçao work-force were unemployed in the same year. Figures from the 2001 census showed that the rate of unemployment in St Maarten stood at 12.2%, with the rate of youth unemployment at 24.1%.

The Netherlands Antilles, as part of the Kingdom of the Netherlands, has the status of an Overseas Territory in association with the European Union (see p. 208). In 1988 the Netherlands Antilles was accorded observer status by the Caribbean Community and Common Market (CARICOM, see p. 164).

The relative isolation of the individual islands has led to the development of semi-independent economies, and economic conditions vary considerably between them. Notwithstanding, the Netherlands Antilles experienced relatively strong economic growth in the 1980s and early 1990s, but the past decade witnessed a progressive weakening of the economy, leading to a prolonged recession, high unemployment and increasing rates of emigration. The direct causes of this decline were considered to be the decline in both the financial services and the petroleum-refining industries, combined with the damage to tourist infrastructure caused by Hurricanes Luis and Marilyn in September 1995. Under the terms of the structural adjustment programme (SAP), undertaken from 1996 in consultation with the IMF, which aimed to eliminate the fiscal deficit over a period of four years, the civil service was to be rationalized, public sector wages were to be frozen and pension arrangements reviewed, while new indirect taxes were to be introduced. Successive administrations, however, recorded only limited success in implementing the terms of the SAP and its successor, the National Recovery Plan, which was adopted in late 1998, in part owing to the great unpopularity of many of the measures to be undertaken. Following stringent measures announced by the Pourier Government in June 2001, the Dutch Government released NA Fl. 153m. (to be spent in 2002–06) to encourage sustained economic development and to support the Netherlands Antilles Government in improving the quality of its administration and education systems. The Netherlands was expected to approve the release of €125m. in additional funds in 2003, and the Dutch and Netherlands Antillean Governments agreed on a more prominent role for the Central Bank in the monitoring and implementation of the IMF targets. During rounds of the Article IV consultation visits in March 2003, an IMF team concluded that although the Netherlands Antilles is experiencing a period of 'fragile growth', there was a continued need for financial reforms and savings, especially in the health-care sector, government institutions and limited companies. In 2002 the long formation period of the new Government and the consequent lack of a government programme, coupled with the slowing world economy and weak international tourism market, damaged confidence, leading to only a slight increase in real GDP, according to central bank figures. Continued low-level growth was anticipated in 2003–05.

Education

Education was made compulsory in 1992. The islands' educational facilities are generally of a high standard. The education system is the same as that of the Netherlands. Dutch is used as the principal language of instruction in schools on the 'Leeward Islands', while English is used in schools on the 'Windward Islands'. Instruction in Papiamento (using a different spelling system from that adopted by Aruba) has been introduced in primary schools. Primary education begins at six years of age and lasts for six years. Secondary education lasts for a further five years. The University of the Netherlands Antilles, sited on Curaçao, had 671 students in 1996. In April 2002 the Netherlands Government made more than €12.7m. available for improvements to education provision in the Netherlands Antilles. In 1995 local government expenditure on education in the Antilles of the Five was NA Fl. 178.9m. (19.3% of total spending by the island governments).

Public Holidays

2004: 1 January (New Year's Day), 19 January (Bonaire only: Carnival Rest Day), 23 February (Curaçao and Bonaire only: Lenten Carnival), 29 March–1 April (Easter), 30 April (Queen's Day), 1 May (Labour Day), 8 May (St Maarten, Saba and St Eustatius only: Celebration of World War II Victory), 20 May (Ascension Day), 31 May (St Maarten, Saba and St Eustatius only: Whit Monday), 1 July (Emancipation Day), 2 July (Curaçao Day), 21 July (St Maarten, Saba and St Eustatius only: Schoelcher Day), 26 July (Carnival), 6 September (Bonaire Day), 21 October (Antillian Day), 1 November (St Maarten, Saba and St Eustatius only: All Saints' Day), 11 November (St Maarten Day), 16 November (St Eustatius Day), 6 December (Saba Day), 15 December (St Maarten, Saba and St Eustatius only: Kingdom Day), 25–26 December (Christmas).

2005: 1 January (New Year's Day), 19 January (Bonaire only: Carnival Rest Day), 14 March (Curaçao and Bonaire only: Lenten Carnival), 25–28 March (Easter), 30 April (Queen's Day), 1 May (Labour Day), 5 May (Liberation Day and Ascension Day), 8 May (St Maarten, Saba and St Eustatius only: Celebration of World War II Victory), 16 May (St Maarten, Saba and St Eustatius only: Whit Monday), 1 July (Emancipation Day), 2 July (Curaçao Day), 21 July (St Maarten, Saba and St Eustatius only: Schoelcher Day), 25 July (Carnival), 6 September (Bonaire Day), 21 October (Antillian Day), 1 November (St Maarten, Saba and St Eustatius only: All Saints' Day), 11 November (St Maarten Day), 16 November (St Eustatius Day), 6 December (Saba Day), 15 December (St Maarten, Saba and St Eustatius only: Kingdom Day), 25–26 December (Christmas).

Weights and Measures

The metric system is in force.

Statistical Survey

Sources (unless otherwise stated): Centraal Bureau voor de Statistiek, Fort Amsterdam, Willemstad, Curaçao; tel. (9) 61-1329; internet www.gov.an/cbs; Bank van de Nederlandse Antillen, Simon Bolivar Plein, Willemstad, Curaçao; tel. (9) 434-5500; fax (9) 461-5004; e-mail info@centralbank.an; internet www.centralbank.an.

AREA AND POPULATION

Area (sq km): Curaçao 444; Bonaire 288; St Maarten (Dutch sector) 34; St Eustatius 21; Saba 13; Total 800 (309 sq miles).

Population: 189,474 at census of 27 January 1992 (excluding adjustment for underenumeration, estimated at 3.2%); 175,653 (males 82,521, females 93,132) at census of 29 January 2001 (preliminary results); 219,000 (estimate) at mid-2002. *By Island* (estimate, 31 December 1996): Curaçao 152,700; Bonaire 14,169; St Maarten (Dutch sector) 36,231; St Eustatius 2,609; Saba 1,466. Source: partly UN, *World Population Prospects: The 2002 Revision.*

Density (per sq km, 31 December 1996): Curaçao 344; Bonaire 49; St Maarten (Dutch sector) 1,066; St Eustatius 124; Saba 113; Total 259; Total 273.8 at mid-2002.

Principal Town: Willemstad (capital), population (UN estimate, incl. suburbs): 125,000 at mid-2001. Source: UN, *World Urbanization Prospects: The 2001 Revision.*

Births, Marriages and Deaths (1999, excl. St Eustatius unless otherwise indicated): Registered live births 2,803; Birth rate 13.7 per 1,000; Registered marriages 1,418 (1996, incl. St Eustatius); Registered deaths 1,321; Death rate 6.4 per 1,000. Source: UN, *Population and Vital Statistics Report.*

Expectation of Life (UN estimates, years at birth): 75.5 (males 72.5; females 78.4) in 1995–2000. Source: UN, *World Population Prospects: The 2000 Revision.*

Economically Active Population (Curaçao only, '000 persons aged 15 years and over, 2000): Agriculture, forestry and fishing 0.56; Mining and quarrying 0.14; Manufacturing 4.68; Electricity, gas and water 0.91; Construction 3.69; Wholesale and retail trade, repairs 9.86; Hotels and restaurants 3.67; Transport, storage and communications 4.03; Financial intermediation 3.47; Real estate, renting and business activities 4.05; Public administration, defence and social security 4.99; Education 2.92; Health and social work 4.25; Other community, social and personal services 3.27; Private households with employed persons 1.70; Extra-territorial organizations and bodies 0.06; *Total employed* 52.24 (males 27.35, females 24.88); Unemployed 8.53 (males 3.72, females 4.81); *Total labour force* 60.77 (males 31.07, females 29.69). *Total employed* (Curaçao, Bonaire, St Maarten, St Eustatius, Saba): 71,308 in 2002 (Source: IMF, *Netherlands Antilles: Selected Issues and Statistical Appendix* (June 2003)).

HEALTH AND WELFARE

Under-5 Mortality Rate (per 1,000 live births, 2002): 14.2.

Physicians (per 1,000 head, 1999): 1.4.

Hospital Beds (per 1,000 head, 1996): 6.15.

Health Expenditure: % of GDP (1995): 4.5.
Source: Pan American Health Organization.
For definitions, see explanatory note on p. vi.

AGRICULTURE, ETC.

Livestock (FAO estimates, '000 head, year ending September 2002): Asses 3; Cattle 1; Pigs 2; Goats 13; Sheep 8; Poultry 135. Source: FAO.

Livestock Products (FAO estimates, metric tons, 2002): Pig meat 180; Poultry meat 300; Cows' milk 410 (FAO estimate); Hen eggs 510. Source: FAO.

Fishing (FAO estimates, metric tons, live weight, 2001): Capture 950 (Wahoo 230; Skipjack tuna 30; Blackfin tuna 45; Yellowfin tuna 130; Atlantic blue marlin 40); Aquaculture 5; *Total catch* 955. Source: FAO, *Yearbook of Fishery Statistics.*

MINING

Production ('000 metric tons, 2001, estimate): Salt 500. Source: US Geological Survey.

INDUSTRY

Production ('000 metric tons, unless otherwise indicated, 2000): Jet fuel 910; Kerosene 46*; Residual fuel oils 5,112; Lubricating oils 392*; Petroleum bitumen (asphalt) 1,022*; Liquefied petroleum gas 99; Motor spirit (petrol) 1,755*; Aviation gasoline 12*; Distillate fuel oils (gas oil) 2,525*; Sulphur (recovered) 30 (2001); Electric energy (million kWh) 1,120.
* UN estimate.
Sources: UN, *Industrial Commodity Statistics Yearbook* and US Geological Survey.

FINANCE

Currency and Exchange Rates: 100 cents = 1 Netherlands Antilles gulden (guilder) or florin (NA Fl.). *Sterling, Dollar and Euro Equivalents* (31 December 2003): £1 sterling = NA Fl. 3.195; US $1 = NA Fl. 1.790; €1 = NA Fl. 2.261; NA Fl. 100 = £31.30 = $55.87 = €44.23. *Exchange Rate:* In December 1971 the central bank's mid-point rate was fixed at US $1 = NA Fl. 1.80. In 1989 this was adjusted to $1 = NA Fl. 1.79. The US dollar also circulates on St Maarten.

Central Government Budget (NA Fl. million, 2002): *Revenue:* Tax revenue 533.6 (Taxes on property 17.8, Taxes on goods and services 382.4, Sales tax 250.3, Licences 16.3, Taxes on international trade and transactions 127.7, Other taxes 5.7); Non-tax and capital revenue 72.0; Total 616.5 (incl. grants received 10.9). *Expenditure:* Wages and salaries 208.3; Other goods and services 86.2; Interest payments 107.5; Subsidies to public companies 17.6; Current transfers 213.9; Capital expenditure (incl. transfers and net lending) 35.5; Total 669.0. *Total General Government Budget* (incl. island governments, NA Fl. million, 2002): *Revenue:* 1,243.4; *Expenditure:* 1,385.7. Source: IMF, *Netherlands Antilles: Selected Issues and Statistical Appendix* (June 2003).

International Reserves (US $ million at 31 December 2002): Gold (national valuation) 78; Foreign exchange 406; Total 484. Source: IMF, *International Financial Statistics*.

Money Supply (NA Fl. million at 31 December 2002): Currency outside banks 235.2; Demand deposits at commercial banks 1,064.9; Total (incl. others) 1,300.1. Source: IMF, *International Financial Statistics*.

Cost of Living (Consumer Price Index; base: 1995 = 100): All items 114.9 in 2000; 117.0 in 2001; 117.5 in 2002. Source: IMF, *International Financial Statistics*.

Gross Domestic Product (million NA Fl. at current prices, 1997): Agriculture, fishing, mining, etc. 28.7; Manufacturing 271.0; Electricity, gas and water 194.4; Construction 330.6; Wholesale and retail trade 926.4; Hotels and restaurants 163.2; Transport, storage and communications 500.1; Financial intermediation 538.7; Real estate, renting and business activities 634.4; Healthcare and social services 199.5; Other community, social and personal services 196.8; Services to households 26.9; Government services 748.1; *Sub-total* 4,758.8; *Less* Imputed bank service charge 221.7; *Gross domestic product* 4,537.1. Source: IMF, *Netherlands Antilles: Recent Developments, Selected Issues and Statistical Appendix* (May 2001).

Balance of Payments (US $ million, 2002): Exports of goods f.o.b. 575.5; Imports of goods f.o.b. –1,602.4; *Trade balance* –1,026.8; Exports of services 1,716.0; Imports of services –769.6; *Balance on goods and services* –80.4; Other income received 91.0; Other income paid –90.3; *Balance on goods, services and income* –79.7; Current transfers received 368.8; Current transfers paid –256.8; *Current balance* 32.3; Capital transfers (net) 27.7; Direct investment abroad –1.1; Direct investment from abroad 7.9; Portfolio investment assets –38.4; Portfolio investment liabilities 0.9; Other investment assets 0.2; Other investment liabilities 39.3; Net errors and omissions –9.1; *Overall balance* 59.5.

EXTERNAL TRADE

Principal Commodities (US $ million, 1998): *Imports c.i.f.:* Petroleum, petroleum products, etc. 1,103.4 (Crude petroleum 1,000.6); Machinery and transport equipment 178.3; Total (incl. others) 2,028.1. *Exports f.o.b.:* Petroleum, petroleum products, etc. 1,028.6; Basic manufactures 39.9; Total (incl. others) 1,195.9. Source: UN, *International Trade Statistics Yearbook*.

Principal Trading Partners (US $ million, 1998): *Imports c.i.f.:* Brazil 87.5; Ecuador 32.0; Germany 41.9; Iraq 127.9; Japan 24.2; Netherlands 153.1; USA 333.2; Venezuela 879.6; Total (incl. others) 2,028.1. *Exports f.o.b.:* Aruba 22.1; Bahamas 19.7; Belgium-Luxembourg 34.0; Canada 35.6; Colombia 17.3; Dominican Republic 42.8; El Salvador 20.2; France-Monaco 55.2; Germany 14.0; Guatemala 24.2; Guyana 32.8; Haiti 20.8; Honduras 40.0; Netherlands 66.5; Panama 64.4; Suriname 13.6; USA 183.4; Venezuela 163.6; Total (incl. others) 1,195.9. Source: UN, *International Trade Statistics Yearbook*.

TRANSPORT

Road Traffic (motor vehicles registered, 1996): Passenger cars 75,105, Lorries 17,031, Buses 722, Taxis 430, Other cars 2,842, Motorcycles 1,541, Total 97,671.

Shipping: *International Freight Traffic* (Curaçao, '000 metric tons, excl. petroleum, 1997): Goods loaded 215.2; Goods unloaded 516.7. *Merchant Fleet* (registered at 31 December 2002): Number of vessels 201; Total displacement 1,391,130 grt (Source: Lloyd's Register-Fairplay, *World Fleet Statistics*).

TOURISM

Tourist Arrivals: *Stop-overs:* 674,800 in 2000; 657,600 in 2001; 651,300 in 2002 (Source: IMF, *Netherlands Antilles: Recent Developments, Selected Issues and Statistical Appendix* (May 2001). *Cruiseship Passengers* (Bonaire, Curaçao and St Maarten only): 1,220,076 in 2000; 1,209,025 in 2001; 1,416,466 in 2002.

COMMUNICATIONS MEDIA

Radio Receivers (1997): 217,000 in use.

Television Receivers (1999): 71,000 in use.

Telephones (2000): 80,000 main lines in use.

Mobile Cellular Telephones (1998): 16,000 subscribers.

Internet Users (1999): 2,000.

Daily Newspapers (1996): 6 titles (estimated circulation 70,000 copies per issue).
Sources: UNESCO, *Statistical Yearbook*; UN, *Statistical Yearbook*; International Telecommunication Union.

EDUCATION

Pre-primary (1996): 77 schools; 7,720 pupils; 342 teachers.

Primary (1996): 85 schools; 24,286 pupils; 1,139 teachers.

Junior High (1996): 16 schools; 5,282 pupils; 261 teachers.

Senior High (1996): 5 schools; 3,141 pupils; 200 teachers.

Technical and Vocational (1996): 37 institutions; 8,875 pupils; 623 teachers.

Special Education (1996): 18 schools; 1,616 pupils; 204 teachers.

Teacher Training (1996): 1 institution; 217 students; 26 teachers.

University of the Netherlands Antilles (1996): 671 students; 92 teachers.

Adult Literacy Rate (UNESCO estimates): 96.5% (males 96.5%; females 96.5%) in 2000.

Directory

The Constitution

The form of government for the Netherlands Antilles is embodied in the Charter of the Kingdom of the Netherlands, which came into force on 20 December 1954. The Netherlands, the Netherlands Antilles and, since 1986, Aruba each enjoy full autonomy in domestic and internal affairs and are united on a basis of equality for the protection of their common interests and the granting of mutual assistance.

The monarch of the Netherlands is represented in the Netherlands Antilles by the Governor, who is appointed by the Dutch Crown for a term of six years. The central Government of the Netherlands Antilles appoints a Minister Plenipotentiary to represent the Antilles in the Government of the Kingdom. Whenever the Netherlands Council of Ministers is dealing with matters coming under the heading of joint affairs of the realm (in practice mainly foreign affairs and defence), the Council assumes the status of Council of Ministers of the Kingdom. In that event, the Minister Plenipotentiary appointed by the Government of the Netherlands Antilles takes part, with full voting powers, in the deliberations.

A legislative proposal regarding affairs of the realm and applying to the Netherlands Antilles as well as to the 'metropolitan' Netherlands is sent, simultaneously with its submission, to the Staten Generaal (the Netherlands parliament) and to the Staten (parliament) of the Netherlands Antilles. The latter body can report in writing to the Staten Generaal on the draft Kingdom Statute and designate one or more special delegates to attend the debates and furnish information in the meetings of the Chambers of the Staten Generaal. Before the final vote on a draft the Minister Plenipotentiary has the right to express an opinion on it. If he disapproves of the draft, and if in the Second Chamber a three-fifths' majority of the votes cast is not obtained, the discussions on the draft are suspended and further deliberations take place in the Council of Ministers of the Kingdom. When special delegates attend the meetings of the Chambers this right devolves upon the delegates of the parliamentary body designated for this purpose.

The Governor has executive power in external affairs, which he exercises in co-operation with the Council of Ministers. He is assisted by an advisory council, which consists of at least five members appointed by him.

Executive power in internal affairs is vested in the nominated Council of Ministers, responsible to the Staten. The Netherlands Antilles Staten consists of 22 members, who are elected by universal adult suffrage for four years (subject to dissolution). Each island forms an electoral district. Curaçao elects 14 members, Bonaire three members, St Maarten three members and Saba and St Eustatius one member each. In the islands where more than one member is elected, the election is by proportional representation. Inhabitants have the right to vote if they have Dutch nationality and have reached 18 years of age. Voting is not compulsory. Each island territory also elects its Island Council (Curaçao 21 members, Bonaire 9, St Maarten 7, St Eustatius and Saba 5), and its internal affairs are managed by an executive council, consisting of the Gezaghebber (Lieutenant-Governor) and a number of commissioners. The central Government of the Netherlands Antilles has the right to annul any local island decision which is in conflict with the public interest or the Constitution. Control of the police, communications, monetary affairs, health and education remain under the jurisdiction of the central Government.

On 1 January 1986 Aruba acquired separate status (*status aparte*) within the Kingdom of the Netherlands. However, in economic and monetary affairs there is a co-operative union between Aruba and the Antilles of the Five, known as the 'Union of the Netherlands Antilles and Aruba'.

The Government

HEAD OF STATE

Queen of the Netherlands: HM Queen BEATRIX.

Governor: Dr FRITZ M. DE LOS SANTOS GOEDGEDRAG.

COUNCIL OF MINISTERS
(April 2004*)

The Government comprised a five-party coalition of the Frente Obrero i Liberashon 30 di Mei (FOL), Partido Nashonal di Pueblo (PNP), Partido Laboral Krusado Popular (PLKP) the Democratische Partij—Bonaire (DP—B) and the Democratic Partij—Statia (DP—StE).

Prime Minister: MIRNA LUISA GODETT (FOL).

Minister for Economic Affairs and Labour: ERROL A. COVA (PLKP).

Minister of Finance: ERSILIA T. M. DE LANNOY (PNP).

Minister of Justice: BEN. KOMPROE (FOL).

Minister of Education, Culture, Youth and Sports: HERBERT DOMACASSE (DP—B).

Minister of Transport and Communications: RICHARD SALAS (FOL).

Minister of Public Health and Social Development: JOAN THEODORA BREWSTER (PNP).

Minister Plenipotentiary and Member of the Council of Ministers of the Realm of the Netherlands Antilles: MAURICE ADRIAENS (FOL).

Attorney-General of the Netherlands Antilles: DICK A. PIAR.

* On 6 April 2004 the Prime Minister, the Minister of Transport and Communications, the Minister of Justice and the Minister Plenipotentiary and Member of the Council of Ministers of the Realm of the Netherlands Antilles resigned after the FOL-led governing coalition collapsed. Following a consultation process led by the Office of the Governor, a new Government was expected to be in place by the end of May.

GEZAGHEBBERS
(Lieutenant-Governors)

Bonaire: RICHARD N. HART, Wilhelminaplein 1, Kralendijk, Bonaire; tel. (7) 175330; fax (7) 175100; e-mail gezag@bonairelive.com.

Curaçao: LISA DINDIAL, Centraal Bestuurskantoor, Concordiastraat 24, Willemstad, Curaçao; tel. (9) 461-2900.

Saba: ANTOINE J. M. SOLAGNIER, The Bottom, Saba; tel. (416) 3215; fax (416) 3274; e-mail antoine@solagnier.com.

St Eustatius: IRWIN E. TEMMER, Oranjestad, St Eustatius; tel. (3) 2213.

St Maarten: FRANKLYN E. RICHARDS, Central Administration, Secretariat, Clem Labega Sq., POB 1121, Philipsburg, St Maarten; tel. (54) 26085; fax (54) 24172; e-mail cabgov@sintmaarten.net; internet www.sintmaarten.net/gis.

MINISTRIES

Office of the Governor: Fort Amsterdam 2, Willemstad, Curaçao; tel. (9) 461-2000; fax (9) 461-1412; e-mail kabinet@kgna.an.

Ministry for Economic Affairs and Labour: Scharlooweg 106, Willemstad, Curaçao; tel. (9) 465-6236; fax (9) 465-6316; e-mail info.DEZ@ibm.net.

Ministry of Education, Culture, Youth and Sports: Boerhavestraat 16, Otrobanda, Willemstad, Curaçao; tel. (9) 462-4777; fax (9) 462-4471.

Ministry of Finance: Pietermaai 17, Willemstad, Curaçao; tel. (9) 432-8000; fax (9) 461-3339; e-mail g.d.dirfin@curinfo.an.

Ministry of Justice: Willhelminaplein, Willemstad, Curaçao; tel. (9) 463-0299; fax (9) 465-8083.

Ministry of Public Health and Social Development: Santa Rosaweg 122, Willemstad, Curaçao; tel. (9) 736-3530; fax (9) 736-3531; e-mail vornil@cura.net.

Ministry of Transport and Communications: Fort Amsterdam 17, Willemstad, Curaçao; tel. (9) 461-3988.

Office of the Minister Plenipotentiary of the Netherlands Antilles: Antillenhuis, Badhuisweg 173–175, 2597 JP The Hague, the Netherlands; tel. (70) 306-6111; fax (70) 306-6110.

Legislature

STATEN

Speaker: D. A. S. LUCIA (PNP).

General Election, 18 January 2002

Party	% of votes	Seats
Frente Obrero i Liberashon 30 di mei	23.0	5
Partido Antía Restrukturá	20.6	4
Partido Nashonal di Pueblo	13.4	3
Partido Laboral Krusado Popular	12.1	2
Unión Patriótico Bonairiano	3.6	2
Democratic Party—St Maarten	5.5	2
Democratische Partij—Bonaire	2.6	1
National Alliance*	4.8	1
Democratic Party—Statia	0.5	1
Windward Islands People's Movement	0.5	1
Total (incl. others)	100.0	22

*Comprising the St Maarten Patriotic Alliance and the National Progressive Party.

Political Organizations

Democratische Partij—Bonaire (DP—B) (Democratic Party—Bonaire): Kaya America 13A, POB 294, Kralendijk, Bonaire; tel. (7) 5923; fax (7) 7341; f. 1954; also known as Partido Democratico Boneriano; liberal; Leader JOPIE ABRAHAM.

Democratische Partij—Curaçao (DP—C) (Democratic Party—Curaçao): Neptunusweg 28, Willemstad, Curaçao; tel. (9) 75432; f. 1944; Leader RAYMOND BENTOERA.

Democratische Partij—Sint Maarten (DP—StM): Tamarind Tree Dr. 4, Union Rd, Cole Bay, St Maarten; tel. (5) 31166; fax (5) 24296; Leader SARAH WESCOTT-WILLIAMS.

Democratische Partij—Statia (DP—StE): Oranjestad, St Eustatius; Leader KENNETH VAN PUTTEN.

Frente Obrero i Liberashon 30 di mei (FOL) (Workers' Liberation Front of 30 May): Mayaguanaweg 16, Willemstad, Curaçao; tel. (9) 461-8105; internet www.fol.an; f. 1969; socialist; Leaders ANTHONY GODETT, RIGNALD LAK, EDITHA WRIGHT.

Movimentu Antiyas Nobo (MAN) (Movement for a New Antilles): Landhuis Morgenster, Willemstad, Curaçao; tel. (9) 468-4781; internet www.man.an; f. 1971; socialist; Leader DOMINICO (DON) F. MARTINA.

National Progressive Party: Willemstad, Curaçao; contested the 2002 elections as the National Alliance with the St Maarten Patriotic Alliance (q.v.).

Nos Patria (Our Fatherland): Willemstad, Curaçao; Leader CHIN BEHILIA.

Partido Antía Restrukturá (PAR) (Restructured Antilles Party): Fokkerweg 28, Willemstad, Curaçao; tel. (9) 465-2566; fax (9) 465-2622; e-mail par@partidopar.com; internet www.partidopar.com; f. 1993; social-Christian ideology; Leader ETIENNE YS.

Partido Kousa Akshan Sosial (KAS): Santa Rasaweg Naast 156, Willemstad, Curaçao; tel. (9) 747-2660; Leader BERNARD S. A. DEMEI.

Partido Laboral Krusado Popular (PLKP): Schouwburgweg 44, Willemstad, Curaçao; tel. (9) 737-0644; fax (9) 737-0831; internet www.cura.net/krusada; f. 1997; progressive; Leader ERROL A. COVA.

Partido Nashonal di Pueblo (PNP) (National People's Party): Winston Churchillweg 133, Willemstad, Curaçao; tel. (9) 869-6777; fax (9) 869-6688; internet www.pnp.an; f. 1948; also known as Nationale Volkspartij; Social Christian Party; Pres. MARIA LIBERIA-PETERS; Leader SUSANNE F. C. CAMELIA-RÖMER.

Partido Obrero di Bonaire (Bonaire Workers' Party): Kralendijk, Bonaire.

Partido Union den Reino Ulandés (PURU): Binnenweg 11, Willemstad, Curaçao; Leader FREDDY I. ANTERSUN.

People's Democratic Party (PDP): Philipsburg, St Maarten; tel. (5) 22696; Leader MILLICENT DE WEEVER.

People's Progressive Party: Philipsburg, St Maarten.

Saba Democratic Labour Movement (SDLM): Saba; tel. (4) 63311; fax (4) 63434; Leader STEVE HASSELL.

Saint Eustatius Alliance (SEA): Oranjestad, St Eustatius; Leader INGRID WHITFIELD.

Serious Alternative People's Party (SAPP): St Maarten; Leader JULIAN ROLLOCKS.

St Maarten Patriotic Alliance (SPA): Frontstraat 69, Philipsburg, St Maarten; tel. (5) 31064; fax (5) 31065; contested the 2002 elections as the National Alliance with the National Progressive Party (q.v.); Leader VANCE JAMES, Jr.

Social Independiente (SI): Willemstad, Curaçao; f. 1986 by fmr PNP mems in Curaçao; formed electoral alliance with FOL for 1990 election; Leader GEORGE HUECK.

Unión Patriótico Bonairiano (UPB) (Patriotic Union of Bonaire): Kaya Sabana 22, Kralendijk, Bonaire; tel. (7) 8906; fax (7) 5552; 2,134 mems; christian-democratic; Leader RAMONSITO T. BOOI; Sec.-Gen. C. V. WINKLAAR.

Windward Islands People's Movement (WIPM): Windwardside, POB 525, Saba; tel. (4) 2244; Chair. and Leader WILL JOHNSTON; Sec.-Gen. DAVE LEVENSTONE.

Judicial System

Legal authority is exercised by the Court of First Instance (which sits in all the islands) and in appeal by the Joint High Court of Justice of the Netherlands Antilles and Aruba. The members of the Joint High Court of Justice sit singly as judges in the Courts of First Instance. The Chief Justice of the Joint High Court of Justice, its members (a maximum of 30) and the Attorneys-General of the Netherlands Antilles and of Aruba are appointed for life by the Dutch monarch, after consultation with the Governments of the Netherlands Antilles and Aruba.

Joint High Court of Justice

Wilhelminaplein 4, Willemstad, Curaçao; tel. (9) 463-4111; fax (9) 461-8341.

Chief Justice of the Joint High Court: Dr L. A. J. DE LANNOY.

Attorney-General of the Netherlands Antilles: D. A. PIAR.

Secretary-Executive of the Joint High Court: Dr N. V. RIBEIRO.

Religion

CHRISTIANITY

Most of the population were Christian, the predominant denomination being Roman Catholicism. According to the 1992 census, Roman Catholics formed the largest single group on four of the five islands: 82% of the population of Bonaire, 81% on Curaçao, 65% on Saba and 41% on St Maarten. On St Eustatius the Methodists formed the largest single denomination (31%). Of the other denominations, the main ones were the Anglicans and the Dutch Reformed Church. There were also small communities of Jews, Muslims and Bahá'ís.

Curaçaose Raad van Kerken (Curaçao Council of Churches): Barenblaan 11, Willemstad, Curaçao; tel. (9) 737-3070; fax (9) 7362183; f. 1958; six member churches; Chair. IDA VISSER; Exec. Sec. PAUL VAN DER WAAL.

The Roman Catholic Church

The Netherlands Antilles and Aruba together form the diocese of Willemstad, suffragan to the archdiocese of Port of Spain (Trinidad and Tobago). At 31 December 2002 the diocese numbered an estimated 224,809 adherents (about 80% of the total population). The Bishop participates in the Antilles Episcopal Conference, currently based in Trinidad and Tobago.

Bishop of Willemstad: Rt Rev. LUIGI ANTONIO SECCO, Bisdom, Breedestraat 31, Otrobanda, Willemstad, Curaçao; tel. (9) 462-5857; fax (9) 462-7437; e-mail bisdomwstad@curinfo.an.

The Anglican Communion

Saba, St Eustatius and St Maarten form part of the diocese of the North Eastern Caribbean and Aruba, within the Church in the Province of the West Indies. The Bishop is resident in The Valley, Anguilla.

Other Churches

Iglesia Protestant Uni (United Protestant Church): Fortkerk, Fort Amsterdam, Willemstad, Curaçao; tel. (9) 461-1139; fax (9) 465-7481; f. 1825 by union of Dutch Reformed and Evangelical Lutheran Churches; Pres. D. J. LOPES; 3 congregations; 11,280 adherents.

Methodist Church: Oranjestad, St Eustatius.

Other denominations active in the islands include the Moravian, Apostolic Faith, Wesleyan Holiness and Norwegian Seamen's Churches, the Baptists, Calvinists, Jehovah's Witnesses, Evangelists, Seventh-day Adventists, the Church of Christ and the New Testament Church of God.

JUDAISM

Reconstructionist Shephardi Congregation Mikvé Israel-Emanuel: Hanchi di Snoa 29, POB 322, Willemstad, Curaçao; tel. (9) 461-1067; fax (9) 465-4141; e-mail board@snoa.com; internet www.snoa.com; f. 1732; on present site; about 350 mems.

Orthodox Ashkenazi Congregation Shaarei Tsedek: Leliweg 1A, Willemstad, Curaçao; tel. (9) 737-5738; 100 mems.

The Press

Algemeen Dagblad: Daphneweg 44, POB 725, Willemstad, Curaçao; tel. (9) 747-2200; fax (9) 747-2257; e-mail adcarib@cura.net; internet www.ad-caribbean.com; daily; Dutch; Editor NOUD KÖPER.

Amigoe: Kaya Fratumam di Skirpiri z/n, POB 577, Willemstad, Curaçao; tel. (9) 767-2000; fax (9) 767-4084; e-mail management@amigoe.com; internet www.amigoe.com; f. 1884; Christian; daily; evening; Dutch; Dir INGRID DE MAAIJER-HOLLANDER; Editor-in-Chief MICHAEL WILLEMSE; circ. 12,000.

Bala: Noord Zapateer nst 13, Willemstad, Curaçao; tel. (9) 467-1646; fax (9) 467-1041; daily; Papiamento.

Beurs- en Nieuwsberichten: A. M. Chumaceiro Blvd 5, POB 741, Willemstad, Curaçao; tel. (9) 465-4544; fax (9) 465-3411; f. 1935; daily; evening; Dutch; Editor L. SCHENK; circ. 8,000.

Bonaire Holiday: POB 569, Curaçao; tel. (9) 767-1403; fax (9) 767-2003; f. 1971; tourist guide; English; 3 a year; circ. 95,000.

Bonaire Reporter: Kaya Gob. Debrot 200-6, Bonaire; internet bonairereporter.com; English; weekly.

The Business Journal: Indjuweg 30A, Willemstad, Curaçao; tel. (9) 461-1367; fax (9) 461-1955; monthly; English.

Colors: Liberty Publications, Curaçao; tel. and fax (9) 869-6066; e-mail colors@curacao-online.net; internet www.curacao-online.net/colors; f. 1998; general interest magazine; 4 a year; Publr TIRZAH Z. B. LIBERT.

De Curaçaosche Courant: Frederikstraat 123, POB 15, Willemstad, Curaçao; tel. (9) 461-2766; fax (9) 462-6535; f. 1812; weekly; Dutch; Editor J. KORIDON.

Curaçao Holiday: POB 569, Curaçao; tel. (9) 767-1403; fax (9) 767-2003; f. 1960; tourist guide; English; 3 a year; circ. 300,000.

Daily Herald: Bush Rd 22, POB 828, Philipsburg, St Maarten; tel. (54) 25253; fax (54) 25913; e-mail editorial@thedailyherald.com; internet www.thedailyherald.com; daily; English.

Extra: W. I. Compagniestraat 41, Willemstad, Curaçao; tel. (9) 462-4595; fax (9) 462-7575; daily; morning; Papiamento; Man. R. YRAUSQUIN; Editor MIKE OEHLERS; circ. 20,000.

Newsletter of Curaçao Trade and Industry Association: Kaya Junior Salas 1, POB 49, Willemstad, Curaçao; tel. (9) 461-1210; fax (9) 461-5422; f. 1972; monthly; English and Dutch; economic and industrial paper.

Nobo: Scherpenheuvel w/n, POB 323, Willemstad, Curaçao; tel. (9) 467-3500; fax (9) 467-2783; daily; evening; Papiamento; Editor CARLOS DAANTJE; circ. 15,000.

Nos Isla: Refineria Isla (Curazao) SA, Emmastad, Curaçao; 2 a month; Papiamento; circ. 1,200.

La Prensa: W. I. Compagniestraat 41, Willemstad, Curaçao; tel. (9) 462-3850; fax (9) 462-5983; e-mail webmaster@laprensacur.com; internet www.laprensacur.com; f. 1929; daily; evening; Papiamento; Man. R. YRAUSQUIN; Editor SIGFRIED RIGAUD; circ. 10,750.

Saba Herald: The Level, Saba; tel. (4) 2244; f. 1968; monthly; news, local history; Editor WILL JOHNSON; circ. 500.

St Maarten Guardian: Vlaun Bldg, Pondfill, POB 1046, Philipsburg, St Maarten; tel. (5) 26022; fax (5) 26043; e-mail guardian@sintmaarten.net; f. 1989; daily; English; Man. Dir RICHARD F. GIBSON; Man. Editor JOSEPH DOMINIQUE; circ. 4,000.

St Maarten Holiday: POB 569, Curaçao; tel. (9) 767-1403; fax (9) 767-2003; f. 1968; tourist guide; English; 3 a year; circ. 175,000.

Teen Times: St Maarten; e-mail info@teentimes.com; internet www .teentimes.com; for teenagers by teenagers; sponsored by The Daily Herald; English; Editor-in-Chief MICHAEL GRANGER.

Ultimo Noticia: Frederikstraat 123, Willemstad, Curaçao; tel. (9) 462-3444; fax (9) 462-6535; daily; morning; Papiamento; Editor A. A. JONCKHEER.

La Unión: Rotaprint NV, Willemstad, Curaçao; weekly; Papiamento.

NEWS AGENCIES

Algemeen Nederlands Persbureau (ANP) (The Netherlands): Panoramaweg 5, POB 439, Willemstad, Curaçao; tel. (9) 461-2233; fax (9) 461-7431; Representative RONNIE RENS.

Associated Press (AP) (USA): Roodeweg 64, Willemstad, Curaçao; tel. (9) 462-6586; Representative ORLANDO CUALES.

Publishers

Curaçao Drukkerij en Uitgevers Maatschappij: Willemstad, Curaçao.

Ediciones Populares: W. I. Compagniestraat 41, Willemstad, Curaçao; f. 1929; Dir RONALD YRAUSQUIN.

Drukkerij Scherpenheuvel NV: Scherpenheuvel, POB 60, Willemstad, Curaçao; tel. (9) 467-1134.

Drukkerij de Stad NV: W. I. Compagniestraat 41, Willemstad, Curaçao; tel. (9) 462-3566; fax (9) 462-2175; e-mail kenrick@destad .an; f. 1929; Dir KENRICK A. YRAUSQUIN.

Holiday Publications: POB 569, Curaçao; tel. (9) 767-1403; fax (9) 767-2003.

Offsetdrukkerij Intergrafia NV: Essoweg 54, Willemstad, Curaçao; tel. (9) 464-3180.

Broadcasting and Communications

TELECOMMUNICATIONS

East Caribbean Cellular NV (ECC): 13 Richardson St, Philipsburg, St Maarten; tel. (54) 22100; fax (54) 25675; e-mail info@ eastcaribbeancellular.com; internet www.eastcaribbeancellular .com; f. 1989.

Servicio de Telekomunikashon (SETEL): F. D. Rooseveltweg 337, POB 3177, Willemstad, Curaçao; tel. (9) 833-1222; fax (9) 868-2596; e-mail setel@curinfo.an; internet www.curinfo.an; f. 1979; telecommunications equipment and network provider; state-owned, but expected to be privatized; Pres. ANGEL R. KOOK; Man. Dir JULIO CONSTANSIA; 400 employees.

Smitcoms NV: Dr A. C. Wathey Cruise & Cargo Facility, St Maarten; tel. (54) 29140; fax (54) 29141; e-mail matthews@ sintmaarten.net; internet smitcomsltd.com; f. 2000; international telephone network provider; Man. Dir CURTIS K. HAYNES.

St Maarten Telephone Co (TelEm): C. A. Cannegieter St 17, POB 160, Philipsburg, St Maarten; tel. (54) 22278; fax (54) 30101; e-mail lpeters@telem.an; internet www.sinmaarten.net; f. 1975; local landline and value-added services, also operates TelCell digital cellular service; 15,000 subscribers; Man. Dir CURTIS K. HAYNES.

United Telecom Services (UTS): Schouwburgweg 22, POB 103, Willemstad, Curaçao; tel. (9) 777-0101; fax (9) 777-1238; e-mail info@antele.com; f. 1908; fmrly called Antelecom NV; Chair. DAVID DICK; Man. Dir HENDRIK J. EIKELENBOOM.

BROADCASTING

Radio

Easy 97.9 FM: Arikokweg 19A, Willemstad, Curaçao; tel. (9) 462-3162; fax (9) 462-8712; e-mail radio@easyfm.com; internet www .easyfm.com; Dir KEVIN CARTHY.

Radio Caribe: Ledaweg 35, Brievengat, Willemstad, Curaçao; tel. (9) 736-9555; fax (9) 736-9569; f. 1955; commercial station; programmes in Dutch, English, Spanish and Papiamento; Dir-Gen. C. R. HEILLEGGER.

Radio Curom (Curaçaose Radio-Omroep Vereniging): Roodeweg 64, POB 2169, Willemstad, Curaçao; tel. (9) 462-6586; fax (9) 462-5796; f. 1933; broadcasts in Papiamento; Dir ORLANDO CUALES.

Radiodifusión Boneriana NV: Kaya Gobernador Debrot 2, Kralendijk, Bonaire; tel. (7) 8273; fax (7) 8220; e-mail vozdibon@ bonairenet.com; Owner FELICIANO DA SILVA PILOTO.

Voz di Bonaire (PJB2) (Voice of Bonaire): broadcasts in Papiamento, Spanish and Dutch.

Ritme FM (PJB4): broadcasts in Dutch.

Radio Exito: Wolkstraat 15, Willemstad, Curaçao; tel. (9) 462-5577; fax (9) 462-5580.

Radio Hoyer NV: Plasa Horacio Hoyer 21, Willemstad, Curaçao; tel. (9) 461-1678; fax (9) 461-6528; e-mail hoyer@cura.net; internet www.radiohoyer.com; f. 1954; commercial; two stations: Radio Hoyer I (mainly Papiamento, also Spanish) and II (mainly Dutch, also English) in Curaçao; Man. Dir HELEN HOYER.

Radio Korsou FM: Bataljonweg 7, POB 3250, Willemstad, Curaçao; tel. (9) 737-3012; fax (9) 737-2888; e-mail master@korsou.com; internet www.korsou.com; 24 hrs a day; programmes in Papiamento and Dutch; Gen. Man. ALAN H. EVERTSZ.

Laser 101 (101.1 FM): tel. (9) 737-7139; fax (9) 737-5215; e-mail master@laser101.com; internet www.laser101.fm; 24 hours a day; music; English and Papiamento; Gen. Man. ALAN H. EVERTSZ.

Radio Paradise: ITC Bldg, Piscadera Bay, POB 6103, Curaçao; tel. (9) 463-6103; fax (9) 463-6404; Man. Dir J. A. VISSER.

Radio Tropical: Willemstad, Curaçao; tel. (9) 652467; fax (9) 652470; Dir DWIGHT RUDOLPHINA.

Trans World Radio (TWR): Kaya Gouverneur N. Debrotweg 64, Kralendijk, Bonaire; tel. (717) 8800; fax (717) 8808; e-mail 800am@ twr.org; internet www.twr.org; religious, educational and cultural station; programmes to South, Central and North America, Caribbean in six languages; Pres. THOMAS J. LOWELL, Jr; Station Dir RICHARD FULLER.

Voice of St Maarten (PJD2 Radio): Plaza 21, Backstreet, POB 366, Philipsburg, St Maarten; tel. (5) 22580; fax (5) 24905; also operates PJD3 on FM (24 hrs); commercial; programmes in English; Gen. Man. DON R. HUGHES.

Voice of Saba (PJF1): The Bottom, POB 1, Saba; studio in St Maarten; tel. (5) 63213; also operates The Voice of Saba FM; Man. MAX W. NICHOLSON.

There is a relay station for Radio Nederland on Bonaire.

Television

Leeward Broadcasting Corporation—Television: Philipsburg, St Maarten; tel. (5) 23491; transmissions for approx. 10 hours daily.

Antilliaanse Televisie Mij NV (Antilles Television Co): Berg Arraret, POB 415, Willemstad, Curaçao; tel. (9) 461-1288; fax (9) 461-4138; f. 1960; operates Tele-Curaçao (formerly operated Tele-Aruba); commercial; govt-owned; also operates cable service, offering programmes from US satellite television and two Venezuelan channels; Dir JOSÉ M. CIJNTJE; Gen. Man. NORMAN K. RICHARDS.

Five television channels can be received on Curaçao, in total. Relay stations provide Bonaire with programmes from Curaçao, St Maarten with programmes from Puerto Rico, and Saba and St Eustatius with programmes from St Maarten and neighbouring islands. Curaçao has a publicly-owned cable television service, TDS.

Finance

(cap. = capital; res = reserves; dep. = deposits; m. = million;
brs = branches; amounts in Netherlands Antilles guilders unless
otherwise stated)

BANKING

Central Bank

Bank van de Nederlandse Antillen (Bank of the Netherlands Antilles): Simon Bolivar Plein 1, Willemstad, Curaçao; tel. (9) 434-5500; fax (9) 461-5004; e-mail info@centralbank.an; internet centralbank.an; f. 1828 as Curaçaosche Bank, name changed as above 1962; cap. 30.0m., res 111.4m., dep. 688.6m. (Dec. 2002); Chair. RALPH PALM; Pres. EMSLEY D. TROMP; 2 brs on St Maarten and Bonaire.

Commercial Banks

ABN AMRO Bank NV: Kaya Flamboyan 1, POB 3144, Willemstad, Curaçao; tel. (9) 763-8000; fax (9) 737-0620; f. 1964; Gen. Man. H. V. IGNACIO; 6 brs.

Antilles Banking Corpn (Curaçao) NV: Wilhelminaplein 14–16, POB 763, Willemstad, Curaçao; tel. (9) 461-2822; fax (9) 461-2820; f. 1989 as McLaughlin Bank NV; name changed as above in 1997; Pres. SHAFFIE WIHBY; 3 brs.

Antilles Banking Corpn (St Maarten) NV: Cannegieterstreet, POB 465, Philipsburg, St Maarten; tel. (5) 25908; fax (5) 25964; f. 1988; Man. Dirs F. BOWMAN, C. A. GREIGG-DUNCAN.

Banco di Caribe NV: Schottegatweg Oost 205, POB 3785, Willemstad, Curaçao; tel. (9) 432-3000; fax (9) 461-5220; e-mail info@bancodicaribe.com; internet www.bancodicaribe.com; f. 1973; dep. 721.3m. , total assets 784.7m. (Dec. 2002); Chair. P. H. DE JONGH; CEO E. DE KORT; Dir R. HENRIQUEZ; 3 brs.

Banco Mercantil CA (Banco Universal): Abraham de Veerstraat 1, POB 565, Willemstad, Curaçao; tel. (9) 461-8241; fax (9) 461-1824; f. 1988; Gen. Man. FRANK GIRIGORI.

Banco de Venezuela NV: POB 131, c/o Amicorp NV, Bronsweg 8A, Willemstad, Curaçao; tel. (9) 434-3500; fax (9) 434-3533; f. 1993; Man. Dirs H. P. F. VON AESCH, R. YANES, V.E. BORBERG.

Bank of Nova Scotia NV (Canada): Backstreet 64, POB 303, Philipsburg, St Maarten; tel. (5) 23317; fax (5) 22562; f. 1969; Man. ROBERT G. JUDD.

Barclays Bank plc (UK): 29 Front St, POB 941, Philipsburg, St Maarten; tel. (5) 23511; fax (5) 24531; f. 1959; Man. EDWARD ARMOGAN (offices in Saba and St Eustatius).

Chase Manhattan Bank NA (USA): Chase Financial Center, Vlaun Building, Cannegieter Road (Pondfill) and Mullet Bay Hotel, POB 921, Philipsburg, St Maarten; tel. (5) 23726; fax (5) 23692; f. 1971; Gen. Man. K. BUTLER.

CITCO Banking Corporation NV: Kaya Flamboyan 9, POB 707, Willemstad, Curaçao; tel. (9) 732-2322; fax (9) 732-2330; e-mail cbc@citco.com; f. 1980 as Curaçao Banking Corporation NV; Man. Dir and Gen. Man. R. F. IRAUSQUIN; Man. Dir A. A. HART.

Fortis Bank (Curaçao) NV: Berg Arrarat 1, POB 3889, Willemstad, Curaçao; tel. (9) 463-9300; fax (9) 461-3769; internet www .fortisbank.com; f. 1952 as Pierson, Heldring and Pierson (Curaçao) NV, became Meespierson (Curaçao) NV in 1993, name changed as above 2000; international banking/trust company; Man. Dir GREGORY ELIAS.

Giro Curaçao NV: Scharlooweg 35, Willemstad, Curaçao; tel. (9) 433-9999; fax (9) 461-7861; Gen. Dir L. C. BERGMAN; Financial Dir H. L. MARTHA.

ING Bank NV (Internationale Nederlanden Bank NV): Kaya W. F. G. (Jombi) Mensing 14, POB 3895, Willemstad, Curaçao; tel. (9) 732-7000; fax (9) 732-7502; f. 1989 as Nederlandse Middenstandsbank NV, name changed as above 1992; Gen. Man. MARK SCHNEIDERS.

Maduro & Curiel's Bank NV: Plaza Jojo Correa 2–4, POB 305, Willemstad, Curaçao; tel. (9) 466-1100; fax (9) 466-1130; e-mail info@mcb-bank.com; internet www.mcb-bank.com; f. 1916; as NV Maduro's Bank, 1931 merged with Curiel's Bank; affiliated with Bank of Nova Scotia NV, Toronto; cap. 50.0m., res 110.6m., dep. 2,828.5m. (Dec. 2002); Chair. N. D. HENRIQUEZ; Man. Dirs WILLIAM H. L. FABRO, RON GOMES CASSERES; 24 brs.

Orco Bank NV: Dr Henry Fergusonweg 10, POB 4928, Willemstad, Curaçao; tel. (9) 737-2000; fax (9) 737-6741; e-mail info@orcobank .com; internet www.orcobank.com; f. 1986; cap. 30.7m., res 27.5m., dep. 523.9m. (Dec. 1999); Chair. E. L. GARCIA; Man. Dir I. D. SIMON.

Rabobank Curaçao NV: Zeelandia Office Park, Kaya W. F. G. (Jombi), Mensing 14, POB 3876, Willemstad, Curaçao; tel. (9) 465-2011; fax (9) 465-2066; internet www.rabobank.com; f. 1978; cap. US $53.0m., res US $–19.2m., dep. US $3,632.0m. (Dec. 2002); Chair. S. SCHAT; Gen. Man. J. S. KLEP.

SFT Bank NV: Schottegatweg Oost 44, POB 707, Willemstad, Curaçao; tel. (9) 732-2900; fax (9) 732-2902.

Windward Islands Bank Ltd: Clem Labega Square 7, POB 220, Philipsburg, St Maarten; tel. (5) 22313; fax (5) 24761; affiliated to Maduro and Curiel's Bank NV; f. 1960; cap. and res 3.6m., dep. 53.6m. (Dec. 1984). Man. Dirs VICTOR P. HENRÍQUEZ, W. G. H. STRIJBOSCH.

'Offshore' Banks
(without permission to operate locally)

ABN AMRO Bank Asset Management (Curaçao) NV: Kaya Flamboyan 1, POB 3144, Willemstad, Curaçao; tel. (9) 736-6755; fax (9) 736-9246; f. 1976; Man. D. M. VROEGINDEWEY.

Abu Dhabi International Bank NV: Kaya W. F. G. (Jombi), Mensing 36, POB 3141, Willemstad, Curaçao; tel. (9) 461-1299; fax (9) 461-5392; internet www.adibwash.com; f. 1981; cap. US $20.0m., res $30.4m., dep. $329.3m. (Dec. 2001); Pres. QAMBAR AL MULLA; Man. Dir NAGY S. KOLTA.

Banco Caracas NV: Kaya W. F. G. (Jombi) Mensing 36, POB 3141, Willemstad, Curaçao; tel. (9) 461-1299; fax (9) 461-5392; f. 1984; Pres. GEORGE L. REEVES.

Banco Consolidado NV: Handelskrade 12, POB 3141, Willemstad, Curaçao; tel. (9) 461-3423; f. 1978.

Banco Latino NV: De Ruyterkade 61, POB 785, Willemstad, Curaçao; tel. (9) 461-2987; fax (9) 461-6163; f. 1978; cap. US $25.0m., res $12.3m., dep. $450.8m. (Nov. 1992); Chair. Dr GUSTAVO GÓMEZ LÓPEZ; Pres. FOLCO FALCHI.

Banco Provincial Overseas NV: Santa Rosaweg 51–55, POB 5312, Willemstad, Curaçao; tel. (9) 737-6011; fax (9) 737-6346; Man. E. SUARES.

Banque Artesia Curaçao NV: Castorweg 22–24, POB 155, Willemstad, Curaçao; tel. (9) 461-8061; fax (9) 461-5151; f. 1976 as Banque Paribas Curaçao NV; name changed as above 1998.

Caribbean American Bank NV: POB 6087, TM1 10, WTC Bldg, Piscadera Bay, Willemstad, Curaçao; tel. (9) 463-6380; fax (9) 463-6556; Man. Dir Dr MARCO TULIO HENRÍQUEZ.

F. Van Lanschot Bankiers (Curaçao) NV: Schottegatweg Oost 32, POB 4799, Willemstad, Curaçao; tel. (9) 737-1011; fax (9) 737-1086; f. 1962; Man. A. VAN GEEST.

First Curaçao International Bank NV: Office Park Zeelandia, Kaya W. F. G. (Jombi) Mensing 18, POB 299, Willemstad, Curaçao; tel. (9) 737-2100; fax (9) 737-2018; f. 1973; cap. and res US $55m., dep. $244m. (1988); Pres. and CEO J. CH. DEUSS; Man. M. NEUMAN-ROUIRA.

Toronto Dominion (Curaçao) NV: c/o SCRIBA NV, Polarisweg 31–33, POB 703, Willemstad, Curaçao; tel. (9) 461-3199; fax (9) 461-1099; f. 1981; Man. E. L. GOULDING.

Union Bancaire Privée (TDB): J. B. Gorsiraweg 14, POB 3889, Willemstad, Curaçao; tel. (9) 463-9300; fax (9) 461-4129.

Other offshore banks in the Netherlands Antilles include American Express Overseas Credit Corporation NV, Banco Aliado NV, Banco del Orinoco NV, Banco Mercantil Venezolano NV, Banco Principal NV, Banco Provincial International NV, Banunion NV, CFM Bank NV, Citco Banking Corporation NV, Compagnie Bancaire des Antilles NV, Deutche Bank Finance NV, Ebna Bank NV, Exprinter International Bank NV, Integra Bank NV, Lavoro Bank Overseas NV, Lombard-Atlantic Bank NV, Middenbank (Curaçao) NV, Netherlands Caribbean Bank NV, Noro Bank NV, Premier Bank International NV.

Development Banks

Ontwikkelingsbank van de Nederlandse Antillen NV: Schottegatweg Oost 3C, POB 267, Willemstad, Curaçao; tel. (9) 747-3000; fax (9) 747-3320; e-mail obna@curinfo.an; f. 1981.

Stichting Korporashon pa Desaroyo di Korsou (KORPDEKO): Breedestraat 29C, POB 656, Willemstad, Curaçao; tel. (9) 461-6699; fax (9) 461-3013.

Other Banks

Postspaarbank van de Nederlandse Antillen: Waaigatplein 7, Willemstad, Curaçao; tel. (9) 461-1126; fax (9) 461-7561; f. 1905; post office savings' bank; Chair. H. J. J. VICTORIA; cap. 21m.; 20 brs.

Spaar- en Beleenbank van Curaçao NV: MCB Salinja Bldg, Schottegatweg Oost 130, Willemstad, Curaçao; tel. (9) 466-1585; fax (9) 466-1590.

There are also several mortgage banks and credit unions.

Banking Associations

Association of International Bankers in the Netherlands Antilles: Chumaceiro Blvd 3, POB 220, Curaçao; tel. (9) 461-5367; fax (9) 461-5369; e-mail info@ibna.an; internet www.ibna.an; Pres. PETER BLESS.

Bonaire Bankers' Association: POB 288, Kralendijk, Bonaire.

Curaçao Bankers' Association (CBA): A. M. Chumaceiro Blvd 3, Willemstad, Curaçao; tel. (9) 465-2486; fax (9) 465-2476; e-mail shaffie.wihby@mcb-bank.com; Pres. SHAFFIE WIHBY; Sec. ANDY VRUTAAL.

Federashon di Kooperativanan di Spar i Kredito Antiyano (Fekoskan): Curaçaostraat 50, Willemstad, Curaçao; tel. (9) 462-3676; fax (9) 462-4995; e-mail fekoskan@attglobal.net.

International Bankers' Association in the Netherlands Antilles: Scharlooweg 55, Willemstad, Curaçao.

The Windward Islands Bankers' Association: Clem Labega Square, Philipsburg, St Maarten; tel. (5) 22313; fax (5) 24761.

INSURANCE

Amersfoortse Antillen NV: Kaya W. F. G. Mensing 19, Willemstad, Curaçao; tel. (9) 461-6399; fax 461-6709.

Aseguro di Kooperativa Antiyano (ASKA) NV: Scharlooweg 15, Willemstad, Curaçao; tel. (9) 461-7765; fax (9) 461-5991; accident and health, motor vehicle, property.

Ennia Caribe Schaden NV: J. B. Gorsiraweg 6, POB 581, Willemstad, Curaçao; tel. (9) 434-3800; fax (9) 434-3873; f. 1948; general; life insurance as Ennia Caribe Leven NV; Pres. DONALD BAKHUIS; Man. Dir ALBARTUS WILLEMSEN.

ING Fatum: Cas Coraweg 2, Willemstad, Curaçao; tel. (9) 777-7777; fax (9) 461-2023; f. 1904; property insurance.

MCB Group Insurance NV: MCB Bldg Scharloo, Scharloo, Willemstad, Curaçao; tel. (9) 466-1370; fax (9) 466-1327.

Netherlands Antilles and Aruba Assurance Company (NA&A) NV: Pietermaai 135, Willemstad, Curaçao; tel. (9) 465-7146; fax (9) 461-6269; accident and health, motor vehicle, property.

Seguros Antilliano NV: S. b. N. Doormanweg/Reigerweg 5, Willemstad, Curaçao; tel. (9) 736-6877; fax 736-5794; general.

A number of foreign companies also have offices in Curaçao, mainly British, Canadian, Dutch and US firms.

Insurance Association

Insurance Association of the Netherlands Antilles (NAVV): c/o Ing Fatum, POB 3002, Cas Coraweg 2, Willemstad, Curaçao; tel. (9) 777-7777; fax (9) 736-9658; Pres. R. C. MARTINA-JOE.

Trade and Industry

DEVELOPMENT ORGANIZATIONS

Curaçao Industrial and International Trade Development Company NV (CURINDE): Emancipatie Blvd 7, Landhuis Koninsplein, Curaçao; tel. (9) 737-6000; fax (9) 737-1336; e-mail curinde@attglobal.net; internet curinde.com; f. 1980; state-owned; manages the harbor free zone, the airport free zone and the industrial zone; Man. Dir E. R. SMEULDERS.

Foreign Investment Agency Curaçao (FIAC): Scharlooweg 174, Curaçao; tel. (9) 465-7044; fax (9) 461-5788; e-mail fiac@curinfo.an.

World Trade Center Curaçao: POB 6005, Piscadera Bay, Curaçao; tel. (9) 463-6100; fax (9) 462-4408; e-mail wtccur@attglobal.net; Man. Dir HUGO DE FRANÇA.

CHAMBERS OF COMMERCE

Bonaire Chamber of Commerce and Industry: Princess Mariestraat, POB 52, Kralendijk, Bonaire; tel. (7) 5595; fax (7) 8995.

Curaçao Chamber of Commerce and Industry: Kaya Junior Salas 1, POB 10, Willemstad, Curaçao; tel. (9) 461-3918; fax (9) 461-5652; e-mail businessinfo@curacao-chamber.an; internet www.curacao-chamber.an; f. 1884; Chair. HERMAN BEHR; Exec. Dir PAUL R. J. COMENENCIA.

St Maarten Chamber of Commerce and Industry: C. A. Cannegieterstraat 11, POB 454, Philipsburg, St Maarten; tel. (54) 23590; fax (54) 23512; e-mail coci@sintmaarten.net; f. 1979; Exec. Dir J. M. ARRINDELL VAN WINDT.

INDUSTRIAL AND TRADE ASSOCIATIONS

Association of Industrialists of the Netherlands Antilles (ASINA): Kaya Junior Salas 1, Willemstad, Curaçao; tel. (9) 461-2353; fax (9) 465-8040; Pres. R. M. LUCIA.

Bonaire Trade and Industry Asscn (Vereniging Bedrijfsleven Bonaire): POB 371, Kralendijk, Bonaire.

Curaçao Exporters' Asscn: World Trade Center Curaçao, POB 6049, Piscadera Bay, Curaçao; tel. (9) 463-6151; fax (9) 463-6451; e-mail cea@curacao-inc.an; f. 1903; Business Dir MURIEL M. LARMONIE.

CIFA (Curaçao International Financial Services Asscn): Chumaceiro Blvd 3, POB 220, Curaçao; tel. (9) 461-5371; fax (9) 461-5378; e-mail info@cifa.an; internet www.cifa.an; Pres. GREGORY E. ELIAS.

Curaçao Trade and Industry Asscn (Vereniging Bedrijfsleven Curaçao—VBC): Kaya Junior Salas 1, POB 49, Willemstad, Curaçao; tel. (9) 461-1210; fax (9) 461-5652; Pres. DEANNA CHEMALY; Exec. Dir R. P. J. LIEUW.

UTILITIES

Electricity and Water

Aqualectra Production NV (KAE): Rector Zwijsenstraat 1, POB 2097, Curaçao; tel. (9) 433-2200; fax (9) 462-6685; e-mail mgmt@aqualectra.com; internet www.aqualectra.com.

GEBE NV: Pond Fill, W. J. A. Nisbeth Rd, POB 123, St Maarten; tel. (5) 22213; fax 24810; f. 1961; Man. Dir J. A. LAMBERT.

Water & Energiebedrijf Bonaire (WEB) NV: Carlos Nicolaas 3, Kralendijk; tel. (7) 8244.

TRADE UNIONS

Algemene Bond van Overheidspersoneel (ABVO) (General Union of Civil Servants): POB 3604, Willemstad, Curaçao; tel. (9) 76097; f. 1936; Pres. F. S. BRITTO; Sec. S. J. HEERENVEEN; 5,000 mems.

Algemene Federatie van Bonaireaanse Werknemers (AFBW): Kralendijk, Bonaire.

Central General di Trahado di Corsow (CGTC) (General Headquarters for Workers of Curaçao): POB 2078, Willemstad, Curaçao; tel. (9) 462-3995; fax (9) 462-7700; f. 1949; Sec.-Gen. OSCAR I. SEMEREL.

Curaçaosche Federatie van Werknemers (Curaçao Federation of Workers): Schouwburgweg 44, Willemstad, Curaçao; tel. (9) 76300; f. 1964; Pres. WILFRED SPENCER; Sec.-Gen. RONCHI ISENIA; 204 affiliated unions; about 2,000 mems.

Federashon Bonaireana di Trabou (FEDEBON): Kaya Krabè 6, Nikiboko, POB 324, Bonaire; tel. and fax (7) 8845; Pres. GEROLD BERNABELA.

Petroleum Workers' Federation of Curaçao: Willemstad, Curaçao; tel. (9) 737-0255; fax (9) 737-5250; affiliated to Int. Petroleum and Chemical Workers' Fed.; f. 1955; Pres. R. G. GIJSBERTHA; approx. 1,500 mems.

Sentral di Sindikatonan di Korsou (SSK) (Confederation of Curaçao Trade Unions): Schouwburgweg 44, POB 3036, Willemstad; tel. (9) 737-0794; 6,000 mems.

Sindikato di Trahado den Edukashon na Korsou (SITEK) (Curaçao Schoolteachers' Trade Union): Landhuis Stenen Koraal, Willemstad, Curaçao; tel. (9) 4682902; fax (9) 4690552; 1,234 mems.

Windward Islands' Federation of Labour (WIFOL): Pond Fill, Long Wall Rd, POB 1097, St Maarten; tel. (54) 22797; fax (54) 26631; e-mail wifol@sintmaarten.net; Pres. THEOPHILUS THOMPSON.

Transport

RAILWAYS

There are no railways.

ROADS

All the islands have a good system of all-weather roads. There were 590 km of roads in 1992, of which 300 km were paved.

SHIPPING

Curaçao is an important centre for the refining and transhipment of Venezuelan and Middle Eastern petroleum. Willemstad is served by the Schottegat harbour, set in a wide bay with a long channel and deep water. Facilities for handling containerized traffic at Willemstad were inaugurated in 1984. A Mega Cruise Facility, with capacity for the largest cruise ships, has been constructed on the Otrobanda side of St Anna Bay. Ports at Bullen Bay and Caracas Bay also serve Curaçao. St Maarten is one of the Caribbean's leading ports for visits by cruise ships and in January 2001 new pier facilities were opened which could accommodate up to four cruise ships and add more cargo space. Each of the other islands has a good harbour, except for Saba which has one inlet, equipped with a large pier. In May 2002 the Netherlands provided NA Fl. 9.6m. for the repair of Saba's port, which sustained severe hurricane damage in 1999. Many foreign shipping lines call at ports in the Netherlands Antilles.

Curaçao Ports Authority: Werf de Wilde, POB 3266, Willemstad, Curaçao; tel. (9) 461-4422; fax (9) 461-3907; e-mail cpamanag@cura.net; internet curports.com; Man. Dir RICHARD LOPEZ-RAMIREZ.

Curaçao Shipping Association: Kaya Flamboyan 11, Willemstad, Curaçao; tel. (9) 737-0600; fax (9) 737-3875; Pres. K. PONSEN.

St Maarten Ports Authorities: St Maarten; tel. (5) 22472.

Principal Shipping Companies

Caribbean Cargo Services NV: Jan Thiel w/n, POB 442, Willemstad, Curaçao; tel. (9) 467-2588.

Curaçao Dry-dock Co Inc: POB 3012, Curaçao; tel. (9) 733-0000; fax (9) 736-5580; e-mail marketing@cdmnv.com; internet www.cdmnv.com; f. 1958; Man. Dir MARIO RAYMOND EVERTSZ.

Curaçao Ports Authority (CPA) NV: Werf de Wilde z/n, POB 689, Curaçao; tel. (9) 434-5999; fax (9) 461-3907; e-mail cpamanag@cura.net; internet www.curports.com; Man. Dir RICHARD LOPEZ-RAMIREZ.

Curaçao Ports Services Inc NV (CPS): Curaçao Container Terminal, POB 170, Curaçao; tel. (9) 461-5079; fax (9) 461-6536; e-mail cps@ibm.net; Man. Dir KAREL JAN O. ASTER.

Dammers & van der Heide, Shipping and Trading (Antilles) Inc: Kaya Flamboyan 11, POB 3018, Willemstad, Curaçao; tel. (9) 737-0600; fax (9) 737-3875; e-mail general@dammers-curacao.com; Man. Dir J. J. PONSEN.

Gomez Transport NV: Zeelandia, Willemstad, Curaçao; tel. (9) 461-5260; fax (9) 461-3358; e-mail gomez-shipping@ibm.net; Man. FERNANDO DA COSTA GOMEZ.

Hal Antillen NV: De Ruyterkade 63, POB 812, Curaçao.

Intermodal Container Services NV: Fokkerweg 30, Willemstad, POB 3747, Curaçao; tel. (9) 461-3330; fax (9) 461-3432; Mans A. R. BEAUJON, N. N. HARMS.

Kroonvlag Curaçao NV: Maduro Plaza, POB 231, Curaçao; tel. (9) 737-6900; fax (9) 737-1266; e-mail hekro@cura.net.

Lagendijk Maritime Services: POB 3481, Curaçao; tel. (9) 465-5766; fax (9) 465-5998; e-mail ims@ibm.net.

S. E. L. Maduro & Sons (Curaçao) Inc: Maduro Plaza, POB 3304, Willemstad, Curaçao; tel. (9) 733-1501; fax (9) 733-1506; e-mail hmeijer@madurosons.com; Man. Dir. H. MEIJER; Vice Pres. R. CORSEN.

St Maarten Port Services: POB 270, Philipsburg, St Maarten; tel. (5) 22304.

Anthony Veder & Co NV: Zeelandia, POB 3677, Curaçao; tel. (9) 461-4700; fax (9) 461-2576; e-mail anveder@ibm.net; Man. Dir JOOP VAN VLIET.

CIVIL AVIATION

There are international airports at Curaçao (Dr Albert Plesman, or Hato, 12 km (7.5 miles) from Willemstad), Bonaire (Flamingo Field) and St Maarten (Princess Juliana, 16 km (10 miles) from Philipsburg); and airfields for inter-island flights at St Eustatius and Saba. In 1998 a free trade zone was inaugurated at the international airport on Curaçao. A US $90m. project to expand Princess Juliana Airport was expected to commence in early 2003. Financing was

secured for the construction of new passenger terminal building at Dr Albert Plesman Airport in September 2003.

Dutch Caribbean Airlines (DCA): Hato International Airport, Curaçao; tel. (9) 733-8888; fax (9) 733-8300; e-mail anlm03@ibm.net; internet www.flydca.com; f. 1964 as Antilliaanse Luchtvaart Maatschappij (ALM—Antillean Airlines) to assume responsibilities of the Caribbean division of KLM (the Netherlands), changed name as above in 2002; majority govt-owned since 1969 and privatization pending in 2004; internal services between Bonaire, Curaçao and St Maarten; external services to destinations in North and South America and within the Caribbean; Pres. and CEO Ir MARIO R. EVERTSZ.

Windward Islands Airways International (WIA—Winair) NV: Princess Juliana Airport, POB 2088, Philipsburg, St Maarten; tel. (5) 452568; fax (5) 454229; e-mail info@fly-winair.com; internet www.fly-winair.com; f. 1961; govt-owned since 1974; scheduled and charter flights throughout north-eastern Caribbean; Man. Dir JOHN STRUGNELL.

Tourism

Tourism is a major industry on all the islands. The principal attractions for tourists are the white, sandy beaches, marine wildlife and diving facilities. There are marine parks in the waters around Curaçao, Bonaire and Saba. The numerous historic sites are of interest to visitors. The largest number of tourists visit St Maarten, Curaçao and Bonaire. In 2002 stop-over visitors totalled some 651,300 (of whom 58.5% were on St Maarten). In 2002 1,416,466 cruise-ship passengers visited St Maarten, Curaçao and Bonaire (of whom 74.5% were on St Maarten). The destruction caused on St Maarten by Hurricanes Luis and Marilyn in September 1995 caused a drastic decrease in tourism arrivals to the Netherlands Antilles in 1995, compared to the previous year, while there was a concomitant fall in tourism earnings of 12.1%. The sector recovered in the remainder of the decade; however, stop-over tourism has declined in recent years.

Bonaire Tourism Corporation: Kaya Grandi 2, Kralendijk, Bonaire; tel. (7) 8322; fax (7) 8408; e-mail info@tourismbonaire.com; internet www.infobonaire.com; Dir E. BEUKENBOOM.

Curaçao Tourism Development Bureau (CTDB): Pietermaai 19, POB 3266, Willemstad, Curaçao; tel. (9) 461-6000; fax (9) 461-2305; e-mail info@ctbd.net; internet www.curacao-tourism.com; f. 1989; Dir JAMES HEPPLE.

Saba Tourist Office: Windwardside, POB 527, Saba; tel. (4) 162231; fax (4) 162350; e-mail iluvsaba@unspoiledqueen.com; internet www.sabatourism.com; Dir GLENN C. HOLM.

St Eustatius Tourist Office: Fort Oranje Straat z/n, Oranjestad, St Eustatius; tel. (3) 182433; fax (3) 182433; e-mail euxtour@goldenrock.net; internet www.statiatourism.com; Dir ALIDA FRANCIS.

St Maarten Tourist Bureau: Vineyard Office Park, W. G. Buncamper Rd 33, Philipsburg, St Maarten; tel. (5) 22337; fax (5) 22734; internet www.st-maarten.com; Dir CORNELIUS DE WEEVER.

HOTEL ASSOCIATIONS

Bonaire Hotel and Tourism Association: Kralendijk, Bonaire; Man. Dir HUGO GERHARTS.

Curaçao Hospitality and Tourism Association (CHATA): POB 6115, Kurason Komèrsio, Curaçao; tel. (9) 465-1005; fax (9) 465-1052; e-mail information@chata.org; internet www.chata.org; Pres. ROLF SPRECHER.

St Maarten Hospitality and Trade Association: W. J. A. Nisbeth Rd 33A, POB 486, Philipsburg, St Maarten; tel. (542) 0108; fax (542) 0107; e-mail info@shta.com; internet www.shta.com.

NEW ZEALAND

Introductory Survey

Location, Climate, Language, Religion, Flag, Capital

The Dominion of New Zealand lies in the South Pacific Ocean, about 1,750 km (1,100 miles) south-east of Australia. It consists of North Island and South Island, separated by the narrow Cook Strait, and several smaller islands, including Stewart Island (or Rakiura) in the south. The climate is temperate and moist, with an average temperature of 12°C (52°F), except in the far north, where higher temperatures are reached. The official language is English, but the indigenous Maori inhabitants (an estimated 14.1% of the total population at the census of March 2001) also use their own language. At the 2001 census, 15.7% of respondents professed adherence to the Anglican Church, 13.0% being Roman Catholics and 11.5% Presbyterians. The national flag (proportions 1 by 2) is dark blue, with a representation of the United Kingdom flag as a canton in the upper hoist. In the fly are four five-pointed red stars, edged in white, in the form of the Southern Cross constellation. The capital is Wellington, on North Island.

Recent History

New Zealand is a former British colony. It became a dominion, under the British Crown, in 1907 and achieved full independence by the Statute of Westminster, adopted by the British Parliament in 1931 and accepted by New Zealand in 1947.

In 1962 Western Samoa (now Samoa, q.v.), formerly administered by New Zealand, achieved independence, and in 1965 the Cook Islands attained full internal self-government, but retained many links, including common citizenship, with New Zealand. In October 1974 Niue, one of New Zealand's island territories, obtained similar status 'in free association with New Zealand'. New Zealand retains two Dependent Territories, Ross Dependency and Tokelau (for details of New Zealand's Dependent and Associated Territories, see p. 3133).

In December 1972 the first Labour Government for more than 12 years came to power, under the leadership of Norman Kirk, after a succession of New Zealand National Party administrations. The New Zealand Labour Party took office at a time when the economy was thriving, mainly as a result of a sharp increase in international prices for agricultural commodities. However, this prosperity was accompanied by inflation. Higher domestic demand and the international energy crisis of 1973–74 led to a rapid rise in imports, a reduction in exchange reserves and a severe balance-of-payments problem. The Labour Government's foreign policy was more independent than that of its predecessors. It phased out New Zealand's military commitments under the South-East Asia Treaty Organization and established diplomatic relations with the People's Republic of China.

Norman Kirk died in August 1974, and Wallace Rowling, hitherto Minister of Finance, became Prime Minister in September. The economic recession worsened, and in November 1975 a general election resulted in victory for the National Party, which won 55 of the 87 seats in the House of Representatives, while the Labour Party took the remaining 32 seats. The new Government, under Robert (later Sir Robert) Muldoon, who had led the National Party since July 1974, introduced austere economic policies, and in 1976 reduced the annual intake of migrants from 30,000 to 5,000, while conducting a campaign against illegal immigrants.

New Zealand continued to suffer a very low rate of economic growth and increasing unemployment. Popular dissatisfaction with Muldoon's sometimes controversial leadership was reflected at the general election in November 1978. The National Party retained power, with 50 of the 92 seats in the enlarged House of Representatives, but its share of the total vote fell from 47.2% in 1975 to 39.8%. Labour won more votes (40.4% of the total) but fewer seats (41). The Social Credit Party received 17.1% of the total votes, compared with only 7.4% in 1975, but obtained only one seat. In the November 1981 election Muldoon's majority was further reduced. The National Party won 47 of the 92 seats in the House, while Labour, which again received more votes, won 43 seats and Social Credit (despite obtaining 20.6% of votes cast) only two.

In February 1984 Muldoon's Government antagonized New Zealand's trade unions by effecting legislation to ban 'closed shop' agreements with employers, thus giving employees the right to choose whether or not to join a trade union. Further legislation was used in June to compel striking construction workers to return to work. In the same month, faced with dissent within his own party, Muldoon called an early general election for July. The Labour Party obtained 43% of the total votes and secured 56 of the 95 seats in an enlarged House of Representatives, while the National Party, with 36% of the votes, took 37 seats: it was thought that the National Party had lost considerable support to the newly-formed New Zealand Party, a right-wing party which won 12.3% of the votes (but no seats) after campaigning for a minimum of government intervention in the economy. David Lange (the leader of the Labour Party since February 1983) became Prime Minister. James McLay, who had been deputy leader of the National Party since March 1984, defeated Muldoon in an election for the leadership of the party in November 1984, but he was replaced as party leader by his deputy, James (Jim) Bolger, in March 1986.

The Labour Government introduced controversial deregulatory measures to improve the country's economic situation. The initial success of these measures, together with widespread popular support for the Government's anti-nuclear policy (see below), contributed to a second victory for the Labour Party in a general election in August 1987. Of the 97 seats in the enlarged House of Representatives, the Labour Party secured 58, and the National Party 39. (The Democratic Party lost both the seats that its predecessor, the Social Credit Party, had won at the 1984 election.) Of the votes cast, the Labour Party received 47.4%, and the National Party 42.8%.

In 1987 Lange's Government initiated a controversial policy of 'privatization' of state-owned enterprises. In November 1988 policy disagreements prompted Lange to dismiss the minister responsible for the privatization programme, Richard Prebble. Lange was accused by cabinet colleagues of acting without consultation, and in December Roger (later Sir Roger) Douglas, the Minister of Finance, declared that he would not serve another term under Lange. Douglas was promptly dismissed from office, and later that month unsuccessfully challenged Lange for the leadership of the Labour Party. In May 1989 the formation of the New Labour Party (led by a former president of the Labour Party, Jim Anderton) was announced: the party aimed to appeal to disillusioned Labour supporters. In early August Douglas was elected by Labour MPs to a vacant cabinet post, thus prompting Lange to resign. Shortly afterwards, Geoffrey Palmer, hitherto the deputy leader of the Labour Party, was elected the Labour Party's parliamentary leader and Prime Minister.

In January 1990 Palmer undertook a wide-ranging government reshuffle. The return of Richard Prebble to the Cabinet, in his former post as Minister for State-Owned Enterprises, provoked considerable anger within the Labour Party. The Government also aroused hostility by its introduction of a substantial fee for tertiary-level students. The continued sale of state assets, especially that of the telecommunications company, Telecom, was also unpopular (although a portion of the proceeds from the Telecom sales was to be invested in education and health). On 4 September 1990, less than eight weeks before the next general election, Palmer resigned as Prime Minister. Public opinion polls had indicated that Labour, under his leadership, had lost support to the National Party, and members of the Cabinet had consequently urged him to resign. Michael Moore, the Minister of External Relations and Trade (who had also contested the August 1989 leadership election), replaced Palmer as Prime Minister and Labour Party leader. Moore promised to act promptly to avert the enormous budget deficit forecast for 1991/92 and, two weeks later, he secured an agreement with the country's trade union leaders regarding restricted pay settlements. In October 1990, none the less, the National Party won 47.8% of the votes at the general election, taking 67 of the 97 seats in the House of Representatives. The Labour Party, with 35.1% of the votes, won 29 seats, while the NewLabour Party retained its sole seat, obtaining 5.2% of the votes. Jim Bolger, as leader of the National Party, thus became Prime Minister at the head of a Government that promised to continue Labour's strict budgetary and monetary controls. The sale of state assets would also continue.

In November 1990 the new Government's first economic proposals were outlined. They included the repeal of legislation on equal pay for women, and envisaged reductions in public spending, particularly in the field of social welfare. In December the Government announced measures that entailed proposed reductions in unemployment benefit, family benefits, and in medical and sickness payments, and prepared for the introduction of a system whereby users of medical and educational services (hitherto provided free of charge) would be required to pay, according to a means test. These measures were received with anger by social and church groups. Protest marches took place in April 1991, and plans for a 'freeze' in the levels of old-age pensions prompted groups representing the elderly unsuccessfully to petition the British monarch (through the Governor-General) to dismiss the Government. Two National Party members of the House of Representatives resigned from the party in August, in protest against the proposals, and the Minister of Maori Affairs, Winston Peters (who had openly criticized the Government's economic strategy), was dismissed in October. In November Sir Robert Muldoon announced that he would resign from the legislature in early 1992, in protest against the Government's economic policies. Earlier in the month criticism had prompted the Government to withdraw its stringent means-testing measures for the allocation of state pensions, but the overall level of payments remained lower than previously.

In December 1991 a coalition was formed by minor parties as a challenge to the two main parties. The grouping, known as the Alliance, consisted of the NewLabour Party, the New Zealand Democratic Party, the Green Party of Aotearoa—New Zealand and Mana Motuhake. In its first electoral test (the by-election in February 1992 that had been precipitated by Muldoon's resignation) the Alliance campaigned for the provision of education and health care free of charge and the return to the public sector of 'privatized' state assets. The National Party retained the seat in the by-election, but with a greatly reduced majority. The Alliance secured 38% of the votes, only 5% less than the National Party.

In September 1992 a preliminary referendum on proposed electoral reform was held. The electorate voted overwhelmingly in favour of the abolition of the 'first-past-the-post' system and for its replacement by a form of proportional representation; of the four alternatives offered, the mixed member proportional (MMP) system (similar to that used in Germany) received the greatest support. A second, binding referendum was to be arranged to coincide with the next general election, scheduled for late 1993. The new rules were to be implemented at the 1996 election.

In March 1993, in an attempt to improve the National Party's chances of re-election, a minor reorganization of the Government was carried out. Changes included the replacement of Simon Upton, Minister of Health responsible for the implementation of unpopular hospital reforms, by Bill Birch, a close associate of Bolger. The highly controversial charges for hospital beds were abolished by the new Minister. In the same month the outspoken Winston Peters, who had continued to embarrass the Government, resigned from his parliamentary seat in order to stand for re-election as an independent candidate. The by-election in April resulted in an overwhelming victory for Peters, the major political parties having declined to present candidates. In July Peters established New Zealand First, and announced that the party would contest all 99 seats at the forthcoming general election.

At the election, held on 6 November 1993, the National Party, which had campaigned mainly on the Government's record of economic recovery, was narrowly returned to office, receiving 35.2% of the total votes cast and securing 50 seats in the House of Representatives. The Labour Party, with 34.7% of the votes, won 45 seats, the Alliance two and New Zealand First two. At the concurrent, second referendum on electoral reform, 54% of voters favoured the adoption of the MMP system. A new Government was appointed in late November. Changes included the replacement of Ruth Richardson as Minister of Finance by Bill Birch, the latter being succeeded as Minister of Health by Jenny Shipley. Michael Moore, the parliamentary leader of the Labour Party, was replaced by Helen Clark, the former Deputy Prime Minister and Minister of Health. In August 1994 the Govern-

ment narrowly retained its majority at a by-election brought about by the unexpected resignation of Ruth Richardson from the House of Representatives.

In October 1994 a former cabinet minister, Peter Dunne, resigned from the Labour Party, following differences over the party's policy on taxation, and declared his intention to remain in the House of Representatives as an independent member. He subsequently established a new party, Future New Zealand. The traditional two-party system was further challenged in early 1995, when support for ACT New Zealand, co-founded by Sir Roger Douglas (reformist Minister of Finance in 1984–88) who had recently announced his return to politics, began to increase rapidly. In June 1995, however, the position of the ruling party was strengthened by the formation of United New Zealand by seven members of the House of Representatives (four National, two Labour and the leader of Future New Zealand, Peter Dunne). The new grouping pledged its support for the Government on issues of confidence. In February, for the first time since the early 1930s, a formal coalition Government was established when the National Party formed an official alliance with United New Zealand. In the ensuing government reorganization, Peter Dunne joined the Cabinet as Minister of Revenue and Internal Affairs. In April 1996, defections from the two major parties and realignments having continued, a National member of the House of Representatives left the ruling coalition to join New Zealand First, thus becoming the ninth member of the National Party to depart since the 1993 election. As a result, the number of parliamentary seats held by the National Party was reduced to 41. In March, meanwhile, Sir Michael Hardie Boys replaced Dame Catherine Tizard as Governor-General.

The first general election under the MMP system was held on 12 October 1996. No party achieved an outright majority. The National Party, with 34.1% of the votes, won 44 of the 120 seats in the expanded House of Representatives, the Labour Party (28.3%) secured 37 seats and New Zealand First (13.1%) garnered 17 seats, while the Alliance won 13 seats, ACT New Zealand eight and United New Zealand one. A notable development was the increase in the number of Maori MPs from six to 15, a figure almost equivalent to the proportion of Maori (the country's aboriginal inhabitants) in the population as a whole. Although the election result initially appeared to favour the formation of a centre-left coalition under the leadership of Helen Clark, complex negotiations finally led to the establishment in December of an alliance between the National Party and New Zealand First, led by Winston Peters.

Jim Bolger thus continued as Prime Minister. Winston Peters was appointed Deputy Prime Minister and Treasurer, the latter newly-created post carrying responsibility for the drafting of the country's budget. Although Peters had previously discounted the possibility of a reconciliation and of entering into a coalition with the National Party, he had unexpectedly altered his stance in exchange for concessions on economic policy. These concessions included the deferment of proposed reductions in income tax, to enable increased expenditure in areas such as health and education. The incoming Cabinet incorporated a total of five members of New Zealand First. Don McKinnon of the National Party retained the foreign affairs portfolio, and Bill Birch continued to hold nominal responsibility for finance.

In September 1997 proposals for the introduction of a compulsory retirement savings scheme were overwhelmingly rejected by the electorate in a referendum. The holding of the referendum had been a condition of New Zealand First's participation in the ruling coalition, but the Prime Minister had also actively supported the proposed pension reforms. In the following month thousands of protesters took to the streets to demand the resignation of the Government, the latter's policies on health and education having drawn particular criticism.

In November 1997, following a leadership challenge from Jenny Shipley, a cabinet minister whose portfolios now included transport and women's affairs, the Prime Minister announced his intention to resign. Jenny Shipley was thus sworn in as New Zealand's first woman Prime Minister in December, reiterating the National Party's commitment to a continuation of the partnership with New Zealand First. In the ensuing government reorganization, most supporters of Jim Bolger retained their portfolios but were downgraded. Winston Peters continued as Deputy Prime Minister, while other members of New Zealand First also remained in the Cabinet. Wyatt Creech was appointed deputy leader of the National Party, in place of Don McKinnon, who retained the foreign affairs portfolio.

In November 1997, meanwhile, following the Alliance's rejection of a Greens' proposal to establish a coalition arrangement, the Green Party of Aotearoa decided that at the next general election it would stand as a separate political party but would remain a member of the Alliance until that time. In January 1998 the Liberal Party announced that it was to be dissolved and merge with the Alliance.

In May 1998 the outcome of a parliamentary by-election to fill the seat vacated by Jim Bolger confirmed the electorate's growing disillusionment with the coalition Government. Although the seat was retained by the National Party, its majority was decimated. The candidate of ACT New Zealand unexpectedly received more votes than his counterpart from the Labour Party. In July Tau Henare, the Minister of Maori Affairs, was removed as deputy leader of New Zealand First, upon the publication of a government report that emphasized the adverse effects on the Maori population of the various economic reforms implemented since 1987. In August 1998, following an acrimonious dispute regarding the sale of the Government's stake in Wellington airport, the Prime Minister dismissed Winston Peters from the post of Deputy Prime Minister and Treasurer. The dissolution of the coalition Government was then announced. Rejecting demands for an early general election, Jenny Shipley reallocated many cabinet portfolios. Wyatt Creech was appointed Deputy Prime Minister, while Bill Birch became Treasurer. Although Tau Henare (who in late 1998 founded a new party, Mauri Pacific) was the only former New Zealand First minister to retain his post within the Cabinet, three other erstwhile members of the National Party's former coalition partner remained as ministers outside the Cabinet. Despite the defection of Winston Peters to the opposition, the Prime Minister was able to secure the support of eight of the 16 New Zealand First representatives in the legislature, and in September she survived a vote of confidence in the House. In the same month, in an attempt to raise public concern over the social effects of government policy, in particular the plight of low-income families, the Anglican Church initiated an ecumenical 'Hikoi of Hope', in which protesters from both ends of the country marched to Wellington and converged upon the House of Representatives.

In December 1998 the minority Government's position was further weakened by the unexpected resignation of a supporting independent (and former New Zealand First) MP, following the administration's decision to proceed with its acquisition of 28 F-16 fighter aircraft from the USA. (The contract to lease the aircraft, however, was cancelled in March 2000 by the new Labour Government.) The Prime Minister was placed under further pressure in early 1999, when it was alleged that the Minister of Tourism, Murray McCully, had acted inappropriately with regard to the handling of a major contract for the advertising business of the New Zealand Tourism Board. In February, as the Prime Minister became personally implicated in the affair and as opposition MPs accused her of deliberately misleading the legislature over her association with the head of the advertising agency in question, the Government won a motion of 'no confidence' by 61 votes to 59. Claiming that the ruling party had intended to exploit its links with the agency during the next general election campaign, the Labour Party demanded an inquiry into the Government's alleged payments to departing members of the New Zealand Tourism Board and into the Board's expenditure on overseas promotions. In March the $NZ53m. marketing contract with the agency was terminated. Murray McCully relinquished the tourism portfolio in April.

During the course of 1999 the Government was also embarrassed by the award of a series of controversial severance payments to senior officers of the fire service, the work and income support services and other public bodies, in addition to the settlements reached with executives of the Tourism Board. In November, only three days before the forthcoming general election, the Prime Minister dismissed the Minister of Immigration, an independent Maori MP, following his offer of residency rights to a group of Chinese immigrants in return for substantial investment in Maori schemes.

At the election, conducted on 27 November 1999, the opposition Labour Party won the largest share of votes cast. A recount of votes in one constituency, where the Green Party candidate then unexpectedly took the seat from the incumbent National MP, combined with the incorporation of 'special votes' (which included those cast by New Zealanders overseas), led to a substantial modification of the initial results. Having secured

38.7% of the votes cast, the Labour Party was finally allocated 49 of the 120 seats in the House of Representatives, while the National Party, which had won 30.5% of the votes, received 39 seats. The Alliance was allocated 10 seats and ACT New Zealand nine seats. Under the recently-introduced system of proportional representation, the Green Party's victory in the one constituency automatically entitled the movement to a further six seats in the legislature. New Zealand First's representation declined to five seats; the party's leader, Winston Peters, only narrowly retained his seat. United New Zealand took the one remaining seat. Having previously discounted any co-operation with the Green Party, the Labour Party was thus obliged to seek the support not only of the Alliance but also of the seven Green MPs.

The leader of the Labour Party, Helen Clark (who had served as Deputy Prime Minister in 1989–90), thus became Prime Minister. The minority Government, which incorporated several members of the Alliance, took office in December 1999. Jim Anderton, the leader of the Alliance, was appointed Deputy Prime Minister, Minister for Economic Development and Minister for Industry and Regional Development. The treasury and finance portfolios were assigned to Dr Michael Cullen, while Phil Goff became Minister of Foreign Affairs and Trade and also assumed responsibility for the justice portfolio.

In a non-binding, citizen-initiated referendum held on the same day as the general election, a majority of voters favoured a reduction in the number of members of the House of Representatives from 120 to 99; voters also favoured a reform of the criminal justice system, including the placing of greater emphasis on the needs of victims of crime.

One of the new Government's stated priorities was the 'Closing the Gaps' initiative, which aimed to address the socio-economic disparities between the Maori and non-Maori communities, particularly in health, housing, education, income and the incidence of crime. Among its first actions were the repeal of the Employment Contracts Act, the restoration of the state monopoly in the provision of accident compensation and the cancellation of the contract to lease 28 F-16 fighter aircraft from the USA. The new Government was strongly criticized by opposition politicians and accused of racism, following its decision in mid-2000 to sell a 25% share of a lucrative radiowaves company (which auctions high frequency radio positions to telecommunications companies) to a Maori trust under its 'Closing the Gaps' policy.

In June 2000 the Prime Minister was obliged to dismiss the Minister of Maori Affairs, Dover Samuels, following allegations of sexual misconduct. Moreover, the administration suffered further controversy in February 2001 when two cabinet ministers, Marian Hobbs and Phillida Bunkle, resigned amid speculation that they had abused the system of parliamentary allowances. All three, however, were subsequently cleared of the allegations, and in late March Hobbs and Samuels were reinstated to government positions in a minor reshuffle. On 4 April 2001 Dame Silvia Cartwright (New Zealand's first female High Court Judge) took office as Governor-General. Her appointment represented a significant achievement for women in New Zealand public life, and created an unprecedented situation in which the five most important public roles in the country (those of Prime Minister, Leader of the Opposition, Attorney-General, Chief Justice and Governor-General) were all occupied by women.

The Minister of Defence, Mark Burton, rejected demands for his dismissal in August 2001, following the publication of a report critical of the tendering process that had resulted in the purchase of 105 US Lav-3 armoured vehicles costing $NZ652m., which had been described as unsuitable for the peace-keeping, rather than combat, duties for which they were intended.

In October 2001 Jenny Shipley, the leader of the opposition National Party, resigned and was replaced by Bill English, a former Minister of Health. The incoming leader renamed the party the New National Party. In December Jim Anderton was placed under considerable pressure from left-wing members of the Alliance to withdraw his support for the Government's military involvement in Afghanistan, following the Prime Minister's confirmation that New Zealand Hercules transport aircraft had landed in Afghanistan, to assist in the US-led military campaign there (see the chapter on Afghanistan). In early April 2002, after months of wrangling, the Alliance split. Anderton and six other members of the party agreed to form a breakaway party, later named the Progressive Coalition party, but continued to support the ruling coalition. The seven members of the legislature were expelled from the Alliance in late April. At the same time Laila Harré, Minister of Women's Affairs, Youth Affairs and Statistics, succeeded Anderton as leader of the Alliance and confirmed her support for the Government until the next legislative elections. In June the Prime Minister announced that the next general election was to be held earlier than planned, in late July, largely owing to the collapse of the Alliance, and a dispute between the Labour Party and the Greens over the Government's decision not to renew a moratorium banning the commercial release of genetically modified organisms (which expired in October 2003).

In April 2002, following extensive consultations, the Government announced the proposed replacement of the monarch's Privy Council (based in London, United Kingdom) as New Zealand's court of final appeal by an independent Supreme Court, consisting of five judges headed by the Chief Justice. The requisite legislation was passed in October 2003; the new court was expected to begin functioning in July 2004. In mid-June 2002 the House of Representatives endorsed strict new legislation to combat the illegal trafficking of people.

Some 77% of the registered voters participated in the general election, which took place on 27 July 2002. The Labour Party won 41% of the party votes, thereby securing a second term in office. The party, failed, however, to secure an overall majority in the House of Representatives, winning 52 of the 120 seats. New Zealand First received 10% of the vote (13 seats); ACT New Zealand 7% (nine seats); the Greens 7% (nine seats) and United Future New Zealand 7% (eight seats). The Progressive Coalition won 1.7% of the party votes and secured two seats, while the Alliance failed to secure any parliamentary representation. The National Party performed badly at the election, winning only 21% of the party votes; its representation declined by 12 seats to 27. Clark, unable to reach an agreement with the Greens on the issue of genetically modified organisms, formed a minority coalition Government with the Progressive Coalition. The Labour Party leader secured the support of United Future New Zealand. In early May 2003 Mark Gosche, the Minister of Corrections, of Housing and of Pacific Island Affairs and for Racing, resigned. The Prime Minister carried out a government reorganization one week later.

In June 2003 Clark announced that the Government intended to draw up new legislation to ensure that the country's coastline and seabed were owned by the Crown, following a ruling by the Court of Appeal that Maori tribes could pursue their own claims to ownership of the Malborough Sands foreshore and seabed in South Island. Maori attacked the Government's 'draconian' and 'colonialist' actions. In late June the House of Representatives approved the Prostitution Reform Bill, which decriminalized prostitution and provided a legal framework for the sex industry. In October the legislature voted overwhelmingly in favour of the Anti-Terrorism Act, which extended the powers of the police force. The act, an extension of the 2002 Terrorism Suppression Act, created new offences including: improperly dealing with nuclear and radioactive materials; causing the infection of animals; contaminating products, such as food and water; and harbouring a terrorist. The Green Party opposed the legislation, claiming that the law would infringe upon civil liberties.

In February 2004 the Minister of Commerce and of Immigration, Lianne Dalziel, was forced to resign after it transpired that she had lied over the disclosure to the media of a document relating to the deportation of a Sri Lankan youth. The Prime Minister ordered an inquiry into the obtaining by Dalziel of a confidential legal document and into officials' involvement in its subsequent circulation. A cabinet reshuffle was subsequently effected: among the changes, the Minister of Transport, of Corrections, of Communications and for Information Technology, Paul Swain, was assigned the immigration portfolio in place of his responsibilities for transport. Meanwhile, in the same month the new leader of the opposition National Party, Don Brash, a former governor of the central bank, announced that if he won power he would discontinue all forms of positive discrimination for Maori, considering the 'special privileges' to be unnecessary and divisive. Brash also pledged to abolish the parliamentary seats reserved for Maori and to repeal 'divisive, race-based' legislation. Clark accused Brash of creating disharmony by breaking the national consensus on dealing with Maori affairs; nevertheless, two days later she promised a review of state assistance for Maori, agreeing that policies should be based on need and not on any perceived privilege. In the February government reorganization, Clark also created the post of Co-ordinating Minister for Race Relations after opinion polls showed a decline in support for her administration over its policies towards the Maori. The portfolio was assigned to the Minister of Education, of State Services, and for Sport and Recreation, Trevor Mallard; he was given the immediate responsibility of conducting a full review of government policy.

During 1987, meanwhile, there were protests by the Maori concerning their cultural and economic rights and, in particular, their claims to land in accordance with the Treaty of Waitangi, concluded in 1840 by the British Government and Maori leaders, whereby sovereignty had been ceded to the United Kingdom in return for the Maori people's retention of hunting and fishing grounds. In November 1987 a ruling by the Waitangi Tribunal, reconvened in 1975 to consider retrospectively the claims of Maori land rights activists, recommended the restoration of an Auckland harbour headland to the Maori people. By 1994 about 75% of the country was subject to land claims by Maori groups. In December of that year the Government offered the sum of $NZ1,000m., payable over a 10-year period from September 1992, in full and final settlement of outstanding claims for compensation. The condition that all future land claims be renounced, however, was rejected by most Maori groups. In the same month an historic agreement between the Government and the Tainui people of Waikato provided for the return of land confiscated in 1863 and for the deposit over a period of five years of $NZ65m. in a land acquisition trust.

In February 1995 the Waitangi Day celebrations were disrupted by Maori protesters, as a result of which the annual ceremony to commemorate the signing of the 1840 Treaty, attended by the Prime Minister and the Governor-General, had to be abandoned. In May the Prime Minister and the Queen of the Tainui people signed an agreement relating to a full and final settlement, valued at $NZ170m., of land grievances dating back to 1863. Increasing ethnic tension, however, was demonstrated by the destruction in September 1995 of an old school building by Maori protesters involved in a land dispute and by the burning down in October of an historic church, known as the 'Maori Cathedral', at Otaki, in an apparent retaliatory arson attack by white extremists. In November, in a significant ceremony in Wellington, Queen Elizabeth II gave her personal assent to the legislation ending the Tainui grievances when she signed the Waikato Raupatu Claims Settlement Act, which implemented the $NZ170m. agreement, including the return of 15,780 ha of land, and which incorporated an apology from the Crown for the loss of lives and for the confiscation of property. A final settlement payment of $NZ13m. was made to the Tainui tribe in late 2000. In October 1996, as more modest agreements continued to be reached, the Government announced a $NZ170m. provisional settlement with the South Island's Ngai Tahu (one of New Zealand's smallest Maori tribes) regarding the group's long-standing claim for compensation. In early 1997 Maori leaders, pursuing a claim first lodged by tribal advocates in 1991, embarked upon a lawsuit aimed at the official alteration of New Zealand's name to Aotearoa ('Land of the Long White Cloud').

In July 1997 a Maori tribe that had been driven off its land in the 1840s lodged a claim to the site of the Parliament building in Wellington. The Ngati Tama also presented claims to other areas of the capital, while declaring their willingness to negotiate. At a ceremony in Wellington in September 1997, following six years of negotiations, the Government and the Ngai Tahu reached a formal agreement, subject to approval by the tribe's members, regarding the compensation of $NZ170m. The Government's offer also included the right to name mountains and rivers, often in combination with the English equivalents, and incorporated a full apology from the Crown. In November, the tribal beneficiaries having voted overwhelmingly in favour of the arrangements, the historic deed of full and final settlement was signed by the Prime Minister and representatives of the Ngai Tahu. In March 1998 the Ngai Tahu Claims Settlement Bill was duly submitted to the House of Representatives, where it received approval six months later. In July, exercising for the first time its power of compulsory recommendation, the Waitangi Tribunal ordered the Government to return to the Ngati Turangitukua land (now valued at $NZ6.1m.) which had been confiscated from its Maori owners more than 30 years previously to permit the construction of housing for workers engaged on an electric power project in the central North Island. In early 2000 a joint land claim was lodged by five Maori tribes of the central North Island. With the forestry claim alone worth an estimated $NZ588m., the application was potentially the largest ever submitted to the Waitangi Tribunal. In March 2001 the Ngati Ruanui became the first Taranaki tribe to conclude a deed of settlement with the Government, amounting to $NZ41m. In early 2003 the Ngati Awa voted in favour of a treaty settlement with the Government, which included an apology from the Crown, the return of 64 ha of land and $NZ42m.

In response to Maori grievances over fishing rights, the Government introduced, in 1988, a Maori Fisheries Bill, under the provisions of which 2.5% of current fishing quotas were to be restored to the Maori people annually for the following 19 years. However, Maori activists alleged that the proposed legislation was racially discriminatory, since it stipulated that no other Maori fishing claim would be considered by the Waitangi Tribunal until the 19 years had elapsed. The bill was also condemned by some white New Zealanders, as, if implemented as proposed, it would guarantee the Maori people about 50% of the country's entire fishing rights by the year 2008. In August 1992, finding that the Government had failed to honour its obligations under the Treaty of 1840, the Waitangi Tribunal recommended that ownership of most of the fisheries of South Island be transferred to the Ngai Tahu. In November 1992, in the hope of reaching a permanent settlement, the Government advanced the sum of $NZ150m. to a Maori consortium to enable the latter's purchase of a 50% stake in the country's biggest inshore fishing company. In early 1996 the Treaty of Waitangi Fisheries Commission, established to resolve the issue of the allocation among Maori of resources valued at $NZ200m., had yet to deliver its recommendations. In April the Court of Appeal declared that, despite having no coastline, urban Maori constituted an *iwi* (tribe) and were therefore directly entitled to a share of these fishery assets. The case was subsequently referred to the Privy Council in London. Its decision, announced in January 1997, overruled the Court of Appeal's definition of an *iwi*. In mid-1998 the Waitangi Tribunal ruled that urban Maori without blood ties should be accorded similar negotiating rights to those of traditional *iwi*. The historic decision thus acknowledged urban Maori trusts as modern tribes. In August, however, a High Court judge ruled in favour of traditional Maori tribes, effectively declaring that urban Maori groups had no claim to fishery assets. In October 1999, furthermore, the urban Maori claim was rejected by the Court of Appeal.

In April 1997 urban Maori were outraged at a proposal by the Treaty of Waitangi Fisheries Commission to allocate up to $NZ300m. of fishery assets on a tribal basis, rather than according to *iwi* size as the populous northern tribes demanded. The Ngai Tahu and other *iwi*, meanwhile, argued that the length of coastline and traditional fishing grounds should determine the allocation of assets. In early 1998, following an incident in late 1997 when a fishing boat reportedly landed several metric tons of snapper without commercial quota rights, it was announced that new regulations were to govern the management of 'customary' fishing by *tangata whenua* (people of the land), whereby Maori are permitted to take an unlimited amount of seafood provided that it is not for pecuniary gain.

From 1984 the Lange Government's pledge to ban from New Zealand's ports all vessels believed to be carrying nuclear weapons or powered by nuclear energy caused considerable strain in the country's relations with Australia and the USA, its partners in the ANZUS military pact (see p. 368). The ban was duly imposed in February 1985. In July 1986 the US Government announced its intention to devise new, bilateral defence arrangements with Australia, and in August the USA's military obligations to New Zealand under the ANZUS Treaty were formally suspended. In February 1987 the US Government announced its decision not to renew a 1982 memorandum of understanding (due to be renegotiated in June of that year), whereby New Zealand was able to purchase military equipment from the USA at favourable prices. The Lange Government subsequently defined a new defence strategy, based on increased self-reliance for the country's military forces. In June 1987 legislation banning nuclear-armed ships was formally enacted by the House of Representatives, despite strong opposition from the National Party. In September 1989 New Zealand agreed the terms for a joint venture with Australia to build as many as 12 naval frigates to patrol the South Pacific. The decision proved to be very contentious because of the high costs and because of allegations that the Government was succumbing to political pressure from Australia to return to the ANZUS alliance and abandon its independent anti-nuclear stance. In March 1990 the opposition National Party announced

its support for the anti-nuclear policy, a position that it retained after its election to office in October.

Following the US Government's decision, in September 1991, to remove nuclear weapons from surface naval vessels, Bolger announced that his administration would reconsider the law banning visits from nuclear-armed and nuclear-propelled warships. The review would focus on the nuclear propulsion ban, which was seen as the obstacle to a renegotiated alliance with Australia and the USA. In July 1992 the USA announced that its warships no longer carried tactical nuclear weapons. In December the report commissioned by the Prime Minister was released. The committee of scientists concluded that the dangers of permitting nuclear-powered vessels to enter New Zealand waters were minimal. Despite these findings, no immediate change to the anti-nuclear legislation was envisaged. In February 1994 the Prime Minister welcomed the US decision to resume senior-level contacts with New Zealand, suspended since 1985. As relations continued to improve, in December 1994 the USA announced that nuclear-armed warships would not be dispatched to New Zealand, thus acknowledging the latter's ban. In early 1995 the Prime Minister was warmly received in Washington, DC, by President Bill Clinton. In August 1998, during a visit by the US Secretary of State, the Prime Minister of New Zealand strongly reiterated her country's long-standing ban on visits by nuclear-armed or nuclear-powered vessels. Following his attendance at the summit meeting of the Asia-Pacific Economic Co-operation (APEC) forum held in Auckland in September 1999, President Clinton announced the end of the 14-year ban on New Zealand's participation in military exercises with the USA, in preparation for the dispatch of a multinational peace-keeping force to East Timor (now Timor-Leste—q.v.), of which New Zealand troops were to form part.

Meanwhile, New Zealand's trading relations with the USA were strained during 1999 by the latter's imposition of tariffs on imports of New Zealand lamb. However, in December 2000 the World Trade Organization (WTO, see p. 343) ruled in favour of New Zealand's case against the tariffs, and upheld the decision when the USA appealed against the ruling. The Prime Minister visited the USA in March 2002 for a series of meetings with the US President, Secretary of State and other senior officials, raising hopes among members of New Zealand's business community that a free-trade agreement between the two nations could be achieved, despite New Zealand's adherence to its anti-nuclear policy.

The Government quickly expressed support for the USA following the suicide attacks of 11 September 2001 and offered to share intelligence in the effort to combat terrorism. In October the administration provided troops from the Special Air Service (SAS) for the US-led military campaign against the al-Qa'ida (Base) organization, held principally responsible for the attacks, and its Taliban hosts in Afghanistan. US policy in the 'war on terror', however, was a source of concern in New Zealand. In 2003, in the build-up to the US-led military campaign to remove the regime of Saddam Hussain in Iraq, the Government stated that it would favour action in Iraq only through the UN, a stance that was popularly supported in New Zealand. Relations with the US Administration were affected as a result. This was unlikely to help New Zealand's attempts to achieve a free-trade agreement between the two nations. In May Prime Minister Clark warned the USA and the United Kingdom that by invading Iraq without the endorsement of a UN resolution, they had set a dangerous precedent, and that they might later regret unleashing the 'law of the jungle', particularly as China was set to become a dominant world power. New Zealand, however, decided to provide humanitarian support for Iraq and sent a team of army engineers and defence force staff to assist in the rehabilitation of the country once the UN authorized reconstruction efforts following the ousting of Saddam Hussain. The Government had already sent forces to Afghanistan to assist in the reconstruction there and in March 2004 agreed to send SAS troops back to the South Asian country to take part in the search for senior al-Qa'ida leaders.

In July 1985 the *Rainbow Warrior*, the flagship of the anti-nuclear environmentalist group, Greenpeace (which was to have led a flotilla to Mururoa Atoll, in French Polynesia, to protest against France's testing of nuclear weapons in the South Pacific), was blown up and sunk in Auckland Harbour. One member of the crew was killed as a result of the explosion. Two agents of the French secret service were tried for manslaughter in November and sentenced to 10 years' imprisonment, initially in Auckland. The French Government made repeated requests for the release or repatriation of the agents, and in July 1986 the two Governments eventually reached an agreement, whereby the agents were to be transferred to detention on Hao Atoll, in French Polynesia, for three years. The French Government made a formal apology for its part in the sabotage operation, and paid the New Zealand Government $NZ7m. in compensation. By May 1988, however, both the agents had been taken back to France, ostensibly for medical reasons. When neither agent was returned to the atoll, Lange referred the matter to the UN in October: in May 1990 an arbitration panel ruled that France's repatriation of the agents constituted a substantial violation of the 1986 agreement, but it announced that the agents would not be required to return to Hao Atoll. France agreed to pay an initial US $2m. into a joint fund intended to foster close and friendly relations between the two countries. In April 1991 the French Prime Minister, Michel Rocard, visited New Zealand and again apologized for the sinking of the *Rainbow Warrior*, while reiterating that French testing of nuclear weapons in the Pacific was to continue. However, relations between the two countries deteriorated in July, following the French Government's announcement that it had conferred an honour for distinguished service on one of the two agents responsible for the sabotage of the *Rainbow Warrior*. The issue re-emerged in November, when a third French agent, also suspected of involvement in the 1985 incident, was arrested, at New Zealand's instigation, in Switzerland. In December 1991, however, the New Zealand Government decided against seeking the man's extradition, on the grounds that the case was now considered to be closed. France announced the suspension of its nuclear testing in the South Pacific in April 1992. In May 1993 the first French warship to visit New Zealand since 1985 entered Auckland Harbour. (Similarly, in June 1995 the first British warship to visit New Zealand for 12 years arrived in Wellington.)

In June 1995 President Chirac's announcement that France was to resume its nuclear-testing programme in the South Pacific aroused international condemnation. New Zealand suspended military relations with France, and the New Zealand ambassador to Paris was recalled. In August, in response to public pressure, the New Zealand Government dispatched a naval research vessel to the test area. The first in the new series of tests was carried out in early September. Later in the month the International Court of Justice ruled that it could not reopen New Zealand's case against France, brought in 1973. France's continuation of its testing programme, in defiance of world opinion, was a major issue at the Commonwealth heads of government meeting held in Auckland in November 1995. New Zealand's relations with the United Kingdom were strained by the British Prime Minister's apparent support for France's position; upon his arrival in Auckland, thousands of anti-nuclear demonstrators took to the streets to express their outrage. In March 1996 (the French tests having been concluded) France, the United Kingdom and the USA finally acceded to the South Pacific Nuclear-Free Zone Treaty (Treaty of Rarotonga—Pacific Islands Forum, see p. 325), thus opening the way to improved relations with New Zealand and other Pacific nations. In October 1997, following a two-day official visit to Paris by the New Zealand Prime Minister, the resumption of normal relations with France was declared.

In August 1996 the Prime Minister refused to comment on the disclosure that New Zealand had supplied to the United Kingdom secret intelligence information on Japan and on countries in the South Pacific region. The apparent existence of close links with the US security services, as part of an international espionage network, aroused much controversy in New Zealand. In the same month, during a visit to South Africa, the Prime Minister acknowledged that the Government's decision to permit the controversial Springbok Rugby Tour of New Zealand in 1981 (prior to the abandonment of the apartheid system) had been a mistake.

Although New Zealand's trade with the People's Republic of China is of increasing significance, relations have been strained by the issue of China's nuclear-testing programme. Relations were further strained in September 1996 when the Dalai Lama, the exiled spiritual leader of Tibet, paid a four-day visit to New Zealand, where he was welcomed by the Prime Minister. In September 1997, however, the New Zealand Deputy Prime Minister expressed support for China's bid to join the WTO. In November 1998 New Zealand's decision to accord Taiwanese government officials similar privileges to those granted to representatives of the People's Republic provoked serious concern in China. During a visit to China in July 1999, however, the Prime Minister of New Zealand reaffirmed her country's support for the 'one China' policy. An official visit to China by the Prime Minister in April 2001 was intended to improve New Zealand's trading position with the country, prior to its accession to the WTO. A senior Chinese official, on a diplomatic tour of the Asia-Pacific region, met with New Zealand's Deputy Prime Minister in April 2002, when New Zealand reconfirmed its 'one China' policy.

New Zealand remained committed to its aim of the global elimination of all nuclear weapons, and in November 1996 was a co-sponsor of a UN resolution, overwhelmingly adopted by the General Assembly, to promote the establishment of a nuclear-weapons-free southern hemisphere. In December the Deputy Prime Minister of New Zealand announced that the Government was to finance a lawsuit against the United Kingdom that was being prepared by former servicemen (and veterans' widows) who had long campaigned for compensation for their exposure to the effects of British hydrogen bomb tests conducted in the South Pacific region in the late 1950s. In January 1997 New Zealand lodged a strong protest with the Japanese Government regarding the proposed route of a ship transporting nuclear waste to Japan from France. In March 1998 the New Zealand Prime Minister travelled to Japan, the first official visit by the country's head of government for 22 years. Relations with Japan, however, continued to be strained by a fishing dispute relating to Japan's perceived failure to conserve stocks of southern bluefin tuna, as agreed in a treaty of 1993, of which Australia was also a signatory. (In July 1998, following a protest to Japan's ambassador in Wellington, New Zealand closed its ports to all Japanese tuna-fishing vessels.) In August 1999 an international tribunal ruled in favour of New Zealand and Australia. In early 2000, the Labour Party's commitment to the protection of the environment having been reaffirmed, the new Government of New Zealand became embroiled in a further dispute relating to Japan, this time relating to the latter's controversial whaling programme. The Prime Minister, Helen Clark, announced her intention to raise the issue with Japan on an official visit to that country in April 2001, and expressed her Government's desire to pursue proposals for a southern seas whale sanctuary through the International Whaling Commission (see p. 352). In December 2000 New Zealand reiterated its opposition to nuclear waste shipments in response to the news that a shipment of high-level waste had left the United Kingdom for Japan, warning that the vessel must not enter New Zealand's exclusive economic zone. In October of that year New Zealand had ratified the Waigani Convention (signed by all South Pacific Forum members in 1995, except Marshall Islands and Tuvalu), which bans the export of hazardous and radioactive waste to the Pacific Islands.

Meanwhile, New Zealand continued to play an active role in Pacific island affairs. In 1997, in the quest for peace in Papua New Guinea, it participated in a peace-keeping force on the secessionist island of Bougainville. New Zealand hosted discussions between the Papua New Guinea Government and representatives of the secessionist movement, and in January 1998 a permanent ceasefire agreement was signed in Christchurch. The agreement was successfully implemented at the end of April. New Zealand strongly condemned the coup in Fiji in May 2000, which led to the overthrow of the Indian-led, elected Government of the country and prompted outbreaks of racially-motivated violence throughout the islands. New Zealand's Minister of Foreign Affairs and Trade, Phil Goff, led a Commonwealth delegation, together with his Australian counterpart, to negotiate with the ethnic militias involved in a coup in Solomon Islands in June 2000. The New Zealand naval frigate, *Te Kaha*, was dispatched to the islands to serve as a venue for peace talks, and the country pledged to contribute to a group of international peace-keepers following the signing of a ceasefire agreement in October. In mid-2003 New Zealand troops joined forces from Australia and several Pacific Islands to provide a peace-keeping force in Solomon Islands.

In September 2001 relations with Australia were strained by the failure of Ansett, the Melbourne-based airline. Ansett's owner, Air New Zealand, had been unable to find a purchaser for the loss-making company, which was therefore placed in receivership. In Melbourne irate Ansett staff blockaded an aircraft upon which the New Zealand Prime Minister was due to travel, and the Australian media demanded a boycott of New Zealand products. Nevertheless, in the same month the New Zealand Government helped Australia to resolve an international crisis, when it agreed to accept up to 150 of the refugees stranded aboard the Norwegian vessel, the *MV Tampa* (see the chapter on Christmas Island). Despite international pressure, neither Australia nor Indonesia (where they had embarked) were willing to accept the asylum-seekers for the duration of the processing of their claims. The Indonesian President, meanwhile, had paid an historic official visit to New Zealand in June 2001. In December, as the former Indonesian province of East Timor proceeded towards full independence, New Zealand announced that, at the request of the UN transitional administration, its 660 peace-keeping troops, would remain in the territory until November 2002.

Following lengthy negotiations, New Zealand established diplomatic relations at ambassadorial level with the Democratic People's Republic of Korea in March 2001.

As part of her golden jubilee tour of the Commonwealth, Queen Elizabeth II visited New Zealand in February 2002. Having previously stated that New Zealand's eventual transition to a republic was inevitable, the Prime Minister attracted some criticism for her absence from the country on the day of the Queen's arrival. In response to the international condemnation of the conduct of Zimbabwe's presidential election of March 2002, which subsequently led to that country's suspension from the Commonwealth, New Zealand followed the European Union, Canada and the USA in imposing a travel ban on senior members of the Zimbabwe Government in April. New Zealand also announced a ban on sales of armaments to Zimbabwe and that any New Zealand-based assets and investments found to belong to the Zimbabwean President or his associates would be 'frozen'.

Government

Executive power is vested in the British monarch, as Head of State, and is exercisable by an appointed representative, the Governor-General, who must be guided by the advice of the Executive Council (Cabinet), led by the Prime Minister. (In March 1994 the Prime Minister indicated that New Zealand might become a republic.) Legislative power is vested in the unicameral House of Representatives, elected for three years by universal adult suffrage. A system of mixed member proportional representation was introduced at the election of October 1996, when the legislature was expanded to 120 seats: 65 electorate members, including five seats reserved for Maori, and 55 being chosen from party lists (adjusted to 67, six and 53, respectively, at the 1999 election). The Governor-General appoints the Prime Minister and, on the latter's recommendation, other Ministers. The Cabinet is responsible to the House.

Defence

The ANZUS Security Treaty (see p. 368) was signed by New Zealand in 1951. New Zealand also participates in the Five-Power Defence Arrangements with Australia, Malaysia, Singapore and the United Kingdom. The total strength of active forces in August 2003 was 8,610: army 4,430, navy 1,980, air force 2,200. Reserves totalled 10,800. The defence budget for 2002/03 was estimated at $NZ1,202m.

Economic Affairs

In 2002, according to estimates by the World Bank, New Zealand's gross national income (GNI), measured at average 2000–02 prices, was US $53,054.8m., equivalent to US $13,710 per head (or $20,020 per head on an international purchasing-power parity basis). During 1990–2002, it was estimated, the population increased at an average annual rate of 1.0%, while gross domestic product (GDP) per head increased, in real terms, by an average of 1.9% per year. Overall GDP increased, in real terms, at an average annual rate of 2.9% in 1990–2002. According to official figures, growth was an estimated 4.4% in 2002.

Agriculture (including hunting, fishing, forestry and mining) contributed 8.1% of GDP (in constant prices) in the year ending March 2002. About 8.8% of the employed labour force were engaged in the sector (excluding mining) in 2002. The principal crops are barley, wheat and maize. Fruit (particularly kiwi fruit, apples and pears) and vegetables are also cultivated. New Zealand is a major producer of wool. In the year ending March 2003 exports of wool were worth $NZ953m. Meat and dairy products are important, contributing 14.0% and 16.8% of export earnings, respectively, in 2002. The forestry industry showed strong expansion in the early 1990s. In 2002 exports of cork and wood totalled $NZ1,878.3m. (equivalent to 6.1% of total export earnings). The fisheries sector is of increasing significance, exports in 2002 being worth $NZ1,483.8m. (equivalent to 4.8% of total export earnings). Between 1989/90 and 1999/2000 agricul-

tural GDP (including hunting, fishing, forestry and mining) increased by an average of 4.0% per year. Compared with the previous year, agricultural GDP increased by 3.3% in 2000/01.

Industry (including mining, manufacturing, construction and utilities) engaged 22.7% of the employed labour force in 2002. The industrial sector (excluding mining) provided 22.6% of GDP (at constant prices) in the year ending March 2002. Between 1989/90 and 1999/2000 industrial GDP (excluding mining) increased at an average annual rate of 1.2%. Industrial GDP increased by 0.6% in 2000/01, compared with the previous year.

Mining contributed only 1.2% of GDP in the year ending March 2001, and employed 0.2% of the working population in 2002. New Zealand has substantial coal reserves; petroleum, natural gas, iron, gold and silica are also exploited. A considerable amount of natural gas is used to produce synthetic petrol. In April 2002 Crown Minerals announced that approximately 50,000 sq km of the offshore Canterbury Basin were to be tendered out to oil exploration companies in 2003, pending a study of the petroleum source rock potential of the basin.

Manufacturing contributed an estimated 16.2% of GDP (at constant prices) in the year ending March 2002. The sector engaged 15.5% of the employed labour force in 2002. The principal branches of manufacturing are food products, printing and publishing, wood and paper products, chemicals, metals and metal products, machinery and transport equipment. Between 1989/90 and 1999/2000 manufacturing GDP increased by an average of 1.5% per year. Manufacturing GDP expanded by 2.5% in 2000/01, compared with the previous year.

Energy is derived mainly from domestic supplies of natural gas, petroleum and coal. Hydroelectric power supplied about 63.1% of total energy output in 2000. Imports of petroleum and its products comprised 9.3% of the total value of merchandise imports in 2002.

The services sector provided 69.3% of GDP (in constant prices) in 2001/02. This sector engaged 68.5% of the employed labour force in 2002. In the year ending March 1988 tourism became the single largest source of foreign exchange. Receipts (excluding international air fares) totalled $NZ6,141m. in 2002. Visitor arrivals reached 2.1m. in 2003. Between 1989/90 and 1999/2000 the GDP of the services sector increased at an average annual rate of 2.8%. Compared with the previous year, it expanded by 3.4% in 2000/01.

In 2002 New Zealand recorded a visible trade surplus of US $502m., but there was a deficit of US $2,269m. on the current account of the balance of payments. In 2002 the principal sources of imports were Australia (23.0%), the USA (13.7%) and Japan (11.7%), which were also the principal markets for exports in that year (Australia 20.0%, the USA 15.3% and Japan 11.5%). The United Kingdom, other members of the European Union and Asian countries are also important trading partners. The principal exports in 2002 were meat, dairy products, vegetables and fruit, fish, cork and wood, and machinery. The principal imports were road vehicles and other machinery and transport equipment, manufactured articles, basic manufactures and chemicals.

In the year ending June 2003 an estimated budgetary surplus of $NZ2,505m. was recorded, equivalent to 2.0% of GDP. In March 2003 New Zealand's external debt stood at $NZ132,396m., of which $NZ17,701m. was official government debt. The average rate of unemployment decreased from 7.5% of the labour force in 1998 to 5.2% in 2002. Annual inflation averaged 1.9% in 1990–2002. Consumer prices increased by 2.7% in 2002 and by 1.8% in 2003.

New Zealand is a member of the Organisation for Economic Co-operation and Development (see p. 295), Asia-Pacific Economic Co-operation (APEC, see p. 147), the Pacific Community (see p. 323), the Pacific Islands Forum (see p. 325) and of the Cairns Group (see p. 408). New Zealand is also a member of the Colombo Plan (see p. 359) and the UN Economic and Social Commission for Asia and the Pacific (ESCAP, see p. 31). In 1982 New Zealand signed an agreement for a 'closer economic relationship' (CER) with Australia, aiming to eliminate trade barriers between the two countries by 1995. These were, in fact, eliminated in July 1990.

Upon taking office in late 1999, the minority Labour Government embarked upon a programme of reforms in the health, education and housing sectors. In addition, some $NZ175m. was allocated for projects aimed at the Maori population. These proposals were to be financed by an increase in income tax on those earning more than $NZ60,000 annually. The new Government also planned to curb the programme of transferring state assets to the private sector. Having been sold to private interests in 1989, Air New Zealand was returned to state ownership in late 2001, following heavy financial losses. In October, in an arrangement costing $NZ885m., the Government announced that it was purchasing an 83% stake in the airline, the continued operations of which remained vital to the country's tourism industry. The bid by the Australian airline company, Qantas Airways Ltd, to buy a 22.5% stake in Air New Zealand was rejected by competition regulators in New Zealand and Australia in April 2003. Although in the short term tourist arrivals were affected by the terrorist attacks on the USA in September 2001, the consequences were less serious than originally feared, as New Zealand was regarded as a relatively safe destination. New Zealand was comparatively well placed to withstand the repercussions of the overall deceleration of the global economy in 2001, and in 2002 an increase in tourism earnings (in the year ending September 2002 tourism earnings expanded by 13.2%) and continued growth in agriculture resulted in strong real GDP growth of around 4.4%. Economic growth decelerated in 2003, to an estimated 2.9%. Export receipts decreased, owing to the rise in value of the New Zealand dollar against the US dollar, resulting in a trade deficit. The rise in international commodity prices from mid-2003, however, partially offset the increase in the currency's value. Furthermore, despite the negative impact of the decline in net immigration on housing demand, house-building permits continued to increase and the construction industry maintained its strong performance. The tourism sector improved, despite the strength of the New Zealand dollar and the outbreak in Asia of Severe Acute Respiratory Syndrome, and this, in turn, helped to boost employment rates. A budget surplus in 2002/03 was also achieved, for the 10th successive year. GDP growth was expected to reach 2.9% in 2004.

Education

State education is free and, for children between six and 16 years of age, compulsory. Primary education lasts from five to 11 years of age, after which children transfer to secondary schools until a maximum age of 18. As a proportion of children in the relevant age-groups, the enrolment ratios in 1997 were 100% in primary schools and 90% in secondary schools. In July 2003 a total of 456,782 students were enrolled in primary schools and 257,586 in secondary schools. In addition, 44,782 pupils attended composite schools, providing both primary and secondary education. There are eight universities, as well as 20 polytechnics, offering education at the post-secondary level. Changes introduced in 1991 obliged most students to pay part of their fees: parental income is tested to determine the level of allowances. Budgetary expenditure on education by the central Government in the financial year ending 30 June 2003 was estimated at $NZ7,576m., representing 18.1% of total spending.

Public Holidays

2004: 1–2 January (New Year), 6 February (Waitangi Day, anniversary of 1840 treaty), 9–12 April (Easter), 25 April (ANZAC Day, anniversary of 1915 landing at Gallipoli), 7 June (Queen's Official Birthday), 25 October (Labour Day), 25 December (Christmas Day), 26 December (Boxing Day).

2005: 1–2 January (New Year), 6 February (Waitangi Day, anniversary of 1840 treaty), 25–28 March (Easter), 25 April (ANZAC Day, anniversary of 1915 landing at Gallipoli), 6 June (Queen's Official Birthday), 24 October (Labour Day), 25 December (Christmas Day), 26 December (Boxing Day).

In addition to these national holidays, each region celebrates an anniversary day.

Weights and Measures

The metric system is in force.

Statistical Survey

Source (unless otherwise stated): Statistics New Zealand, Aorangi House, 85 Molesworth St, POB 2922, Wellington 1; tel. (4) 495-4600; fax (4) 472-9135; e-mail info@stats.govt.nz; internet www.stats.govt.nz.

Area and Population

AREA, POPULATION AND DENSITY

Area (sq km)	270,534*
Population (census results)†	
5 March 1996	3,618,303
6 March 2001	
Males	1,823,004
Females	1,914,273
Total	3,737,277
Population (official estimates at mid-year)	
2001	3,880,500
2002	3,939,100
2003	4,009,200
Density (per sq km) at mid-2003	14.8

* 104,454 sq miles.

† Figures refer to the population usually resident. The total population (including foreign visitors) was: 3,681,546 in 1996; 3,820,749 in 2001.

ADMINISTRATIVE REGIONS
(census of March 2001)

	Area (sq km)	Population	Density (per sq km)
North Island			
Northland	13,296	140,133	10.5
Auckland	5,048	1,158,891	229.6
Waikato	26,170	357,726	13.7
Bay of Plenty	11,428	239,412	21.0
Gisborne	8,355	43,974	5.3
Hawke's Bay Region	13,764	142,947	10.4
Taranaki	7,227	102,858	14.2
Manawatu-Wanganui	22,687	220,089	9.7
Wellington	8,056	423,765	52.6
Total North Island	**116,031**	**2,829,798**	**24.4**
South Island			
Tasman	14,538	41,352	2.8
Nelson	444	41,568	93.6
Marlborough	12,493	39,558	3.2
West Coast	23,351	30,303	1.3
Canterbury	45,845	481,431	10.5
Otago	31,476	181,542	5.8
Southland	25,392	91,005	3.6
Total South Island	**153,540**	**906,753**	**5.9**
Area outside regions	963	726	0.8
Total	**270,534**	**3,737,277**	**13.8**

PRINCIPAL CENTRES OF POPULATION
(population at census of 6 March 2001)

Auckland	1,074,507	Palmerston North	72,681
Wellington (capital)	339,747	Hastings	58,139
Christchurch	334,107	Napier	54,534
Hamilton	166,128	Nelson	53,685
Dunedin	107,088	Rotorua	52,608
Tauranga	95,694		

BIRTHS, MARRIAGES AND DEATHS

	Live births* Number	Rate (per '000)	Marriages† Number	Rate (per '000)	Deaths* Number	Rate (per '000)
1995	57,671	15.8	20,452	5.6	27,813	7.6
1996	57,280	15.4	20,453	5.5	28,255	7.6
1997	57,604	15.3	19,953	5.3	27,471	7.3
1998	57,251	15.1	20,135	5.3	26,206	6.9
1999	57,053	15.0	21,085	5.5	28,117	7.4
2000	56,605	14.7	20,655	5.4	26,660	7.0
2001	55,799	14.5	19,972	5.1	27,825	7.0
2002	54,021	13.7	20,690	5.3	28,065	7.1

* Data for births and deaths are tabulated by year of registration rather than by year of occurrence.

† Based on the resident population concept, replacing the previous *de facto* concept.

Expectation of life (WHO estimates, years at birth): 78.9 (males 76.6; females 81.2) in 2002 (Source: WHO, *World Health Report*).

IMMIGRATION AND EMIGRATION
(year ending 30 June)

	2000/01	2001/02	2002/03
Long-term immigrants*	69,489	92,663	97,250
Long-term emigrants†	78,755	59,848	54,733

* Figures refer to persons intending to remain in New Zealand for 12 months or more, and New Zealand citizens returning after an absence of 12 months or more.

† Figures refer to New Zealand citizens intending to remain abroad for 12 months or more, and overseas migrants departing after a stay of 12 months or more.

ECONOMICALLY ACTIVE POPULATION
('000 persons aged 15 years and over, excl. armed forces)

	2000	2001	2002
Agriculture, hunting, forestry	150.1	161.5	161.3
Fishing	4.1	3.9	3.6
Mining and quarrying	3.8	3.5	3.7
Manufacturing	281.5	289.1	290.8
Electricity, gas and water	8.5	10.1	9.8
Construction	118.4	112.1	120.7
Wholesale and retail trade; repair of motor vehicles, motorcycles and personal and household goods	311.1	314.1	316.8
Restaurants and hotels	92.9	94.5	106.9
Transport, storage and communications	110.9	112.4	113.3
Financial intermediation	55.4	52.2	53.7
Real estate, renting and business activities	175.5	180.7	190.2
Public administration and defence; compulsory social security	91.3	93.4	84.5
Education	129.7	137.3	146.7
Health and social work	142.4	158.0	172.8
Other community, social and personal service activities	86.2	88.7	92.2
Private households with employed persons	8.6	7.3	6.6
Extra-territorial organizations and bodies	0.9	0.9	1.0
Activities not adequately defined	7.9	4.0	2.2
Total employed	1,779.0	1,823.4	1,876.8

— continued	2000	2001	2002
Unemployed	113.4	102.3	102.5
Total labour force	1,892.4	1,925.7	1,979.3
Males	1,036.1	1,050.1	1,079.7
Females	856.3	875.6	899.6

Source: ILO, *Yearbook of Labour Statistics*.

Health and Welfare

KEY INDICATORS

Total fertility rate (children per woman, 2002)	2.0
Under-5 mortality rate (per 1,000 live births, 2001)	6
HIV/AIDS (% of persons aged 15–49, 2001)	0.06
Physicians (per 1,000 head, 2000)	2.2
Hospital beds (per 1,000 head, 1998)	6.2
Health expenditure (2001): US $ per head (PPP)	1,724
Health expenditure (2001): % of GDP	8.3
Health expenditure (2001): public (% of total)	76.8
Human Development Index (2001): ranking	20
Human Development Index (2001): value	0.917

For sources and definitions, see explanatory note on p. vi.

Agriculture

PRINCIPAL CROPS
('000 metric tons)

	2000	2001	2002
Wheat	326	364	355
Barley	302	296	406
Maize	181	177	157
Oats	35	36	27
Potatoes	500	500	500
Dry peas	64	39	25
Cabbages	36	32	32
Lettuce	37	37	37
Tomatoes	87	87	87
Cauliflower	56	56	56
Pumpkins, squash and gourds	155	155*	155*
Green onions and shallots	240	245*	240*
Green peas	60	60	45
Carrots	77	77	77
Green corn	101	101*	98*
Other vegetables (excl. watermelons)*	153	153	152
Grapes	80	71	119
Apples	620	485	537
Pears	42	33	38
Kiwi fruit	262	271	241
Other fruits (excl. canteloupes and other melons)	103	96	104

* FAO estimate(s).

Source: FAO.

LIVESTOCK
('000 head at 30 June)

	2000	2001	2002
Cattle	9,015	9,281	9,633
Sheep	42,260	40,033	39,546
Goats	183	183	183
Pigs	369	354	341
Horses	73*	77	76
Chickens	13,000	13,000	13,000
Ducks*	180	170	180
Geese*	65	65	68
Turkeys*	60	70	70

* FAO estimate(s).

Source: FAO.